Contemporary Business Law and the Legal Environment

PRINCIPLES AND CASES

Contemporary Business Law and the Legal Environment

PRINCIPLES AND CASES

J. DAVID REITZEL, M.S., J.D.
Professor of Business Law
California State University, Fresno

GORDON B. SEVERANCE, J.D., Ph.D
Professor of Business Law
LeTourneau University

MICHAEL J. GARRISON, J.D.
Associate Professor of Business Law
North Dakota State University

RALPH D. DAVIS, M.B.A., J.D.
Adjunct Lecturer
Illinois Institute of Technology

FIFTH EDITION

THE HOEBER SERIES

McGRAW-HILL, INC.

New York   St. Louis   San Francisco   Auckland   Bogotá   Caracas
Lisbon   London   Madrid   Mexico City   Milan   Montreal   New Delhi
San Juan   Singapore   Sydney   Tokyo   Toronto

CONTEMPORARY BUSINESS LAW AND THE LEGAL ENVIRONMENT
Principles and Cases

Copyright © 1994 by McGraw-Hill, Inc. All rights reserved. Previously published under the title of *Contemporary Business Law: Principles and Cases.* Copyright © 1990, 1986, 1982, 1980 by McGraw-Hill, Inc. All rights reserved. Printed in the United States of America. Except as permitted under the United States Copyright Act of 1976, no part of this publication may be reproduced or distributed in any form or by any means, or stored in a data base or retrieval system, without the prior written permission of the publisher.

This book is printed on acid-free paper.

2 3 4 5 6 7 8 9 0 DOW DOW 9 0 9 8 7 6

ISBN 0-07-051912-9

This book was set in Goudy Old Style by The Clarinda Company.
The editor was Kenneth A. MacLeod;
the designer was Joan Greenfield;
the production supervisor was Richard A. Ausburn.
Project supervision was done by The Total Book.
R. R. Donnelley & Sons Company was printer and binder.

Library of Congress Cataloging-in-Publication Data

Contemporary business law and the legal environment: principles and cases / J. David Reitzel . . . [et al.].—5th ed.
    p.   cm.
  Rev. ed. of: Contemporary business law. 4th ed. c1990.
  "The Hoeber series."
  Includes bibliographical references and index.
  ISBN 0-07-051912-9
    1. Commercial law—United States—Cases.   I. Reitzel, J. David.
II. Hoeber, Ralph Carl Louis.   III. Contemporary business law.   IV. Title: Hoeber series.
KF888.C6   1994
346.73'07—dc20
[347.3067]   93-37330

PREFACE

In the Fifth Edition of Contemporary Business Law, we have pursued a single goal—to produce the most readable, stimulating, business-focused law text available for business undergraduates. To accomplish the task, we reorganized the book, added five new chapters, virtually replaced the content of five others, lightened the prose throughout, and interspersed a host of critical thinking, business planning, and informational boxes. The result is an open, inviting textbook designed for maximum student comprehension and covering the full range of business law and legal environment topics usually encountered in multipurpose business schools.

New Content and Special Features of the Fifth Edition

Five new chapters give *Contemporary Business Law* an expanded legal environment content and a sharper focus on key business law topics:

- Chapter 3: Business and the Constitution
- Chapter 47: Accountants' Liability
- Chapter 49: Consumer Law
- Chapter 50: Computer Law
- Chapter 51: Law and the Environment

Five other chapters were completely rewritten to make vital background material more accessible or to enhance substantive coverage:

- Chapter 1: Introductory Fundamentals: Law and Legal Reasoning
- Chapter 4: Administrative Agencies and the Regulatory Process
- Chapter 5: Law and Business Ethics
- Chapter 22: Sales Warranties and Products Liability
- Chapter 54: Business Law in a Global Economy

Many additional legal developments and enhanced coverages appear in the fifth edition. Among them are

- Interesting new cases throughout
- The 1990 amendments to UCC Articles 3 and 4
- The Limited Liability Company statutes
- Commercial speech
- Competitive torts
- Intellectual property
- Products liability
- Electronic funds transfer
- UCC Articles 2A, Leases, and 4A, Funds Transfers (brief treatments where appropriate)

Perhaps even more significant from a general learning perspective are the legal reasoning, ethics, critical thinking, and informational elements appearing throughout the book. These include the unique Chapter 1 tracing the process of judicial decision-making, the Ethics in Practice sections—ten in all—located at the end of each part, and an abundance of boxes strategically placed within chapters.

Each Ethics in Practice section features a set of three to six ethics problems drawn largely from the news media and relevant to the law topics presented in the part. When used (as background) with Chapter 5 (Law and Business Ethics), these sections provide a substantial ethics component for any course in which *Contemporary Business Law* may be used. Occasional boxes entitled A Question of Ethics give students further opportunity to analyze and respond to ethical concerns.

As a group, the boxes serve two main purposes. Many provide supplemental information. For example, in Chapter 1, boxes contain provocative supplemental essays. In the contracts chapters, boxes are used to present sales-law counterparts of common law contract rules without overburdening the text. In the commercial paper chapters, 1990 amendments to Articles 3 and 4 are discussed largely in boxes, since fewer than half the states have adopted them. Other informational boxes describe trends in the law, case developments, and an occasional legal curiosity.

Boxes of another type raise questions for students to answer as they progress through a chapter. Headings include:

Test Your Knowledge
You Be the Judge
A Question of Ethics
———and Business Planning
Point to Consider

These critical thinking boxes serve diverse purposes. Occasionally, a box raises a preliminary question as a matter of orientation or introduction. Most permit students to pause and reflect on what they are reading—by encouraging them to check their mastery of textual material or consider its ethical or practical implications.

Finally, *Contemporary Business Law* has its usual complement of line drawings, tables, cases, end-of-chapter review questions and case problems, chapter summaries, glossary, and index—all of which facilitate the use of the book.

Organization and Appendixes

In keeping with its sleeker aspect, *Contemporary Business Law* has the ten parts listed below and appendices containing the United States Constitution, the Uniform Commercial Code, the Uniform Partnership Act, the Uniform Limited Partnership Act, and the Model Business Corporation Act.

Part One: Law, Ethics, and the Legal System
Part Two: Tort and Criminal Law
Part Three: Contracts
Part Four: Sales of Goods; Products Liability
Part Five: Property and Estates
Part Six: Debtor-Creditor Relationships
Part Seven: Commercial Paper
Part Eight: Agency
Part Nine: Business organizations
Part Ten: Government Regulation; Computer Law; International Business Law

Supplemental Materials

Four supplements have been designed for use with *Contemporary Business Law*.

The *Study Guide*, by James Highsmith, California State University, Fresno, provides general study help, including aid for reading and briefing cases; chapter review objectives and outlines; and independent study questions and case problems, with answers.

The *Instructor's Manual*, by the text authors and Ida Jones, California State University, Fresno, features teaching notes; case briefs and comments; solutions to the case problems, commentary on the in-text Ethics in Practice sections; transparency masters; and factors to consider or solutions for every in-text critical thinking box. A computerized version of the *Instructor's Manual* is also available.

The *Test Bank*, by Ida Jones and Victoria Armstrong, San Joaquin Delta Community College, provides over 2400 test items in a chapter-by-chapter format that can be used easily with or without a computer. For adopters who use computers, McGraw-Hill will provide, on request, a computerized version of the *Test Bank*.

The *CPA Exam Study Guide*, by text author Michael Garrison, contains an abundance of study material for the law part of the CPA exam. Designed for use with *Contemporary Business Law* and employing key concept outlines and prior CPA exam questions, the *CPA Exam Study Guide* provides a solid and efficient basis for CPA exam preparation.

Acknowledgments

This edition marks the retirement of Nathan J. Roberts, a gifted writer and esteemed colleague who, after careers as Brigadier General of the Army and Professor of Law at Loyola Law School, Los Angeles, contributed immeasurably to the first four editions.

In preparing the fifth edition, we were aided greatly by the following reviewers: Robert B. Bennett, Jr., Butler University; Richard Coffinberger, George Mason University; Edward F. Coyne, San Jose City College;

Mary Jane Dundas, Arizona State University; Frank Forbes, University of Nebraska–Omaha; Edward I. Gac, University of Colorado; Andrea Giampetro–Meyer, Loyola College; Hubert D. Glover, Clemson University; Tom Goldman, Bucks Community College; Dale Arrison Grossman, Cornell University; Marsha E. Hass, College of Charleston; Janine Hiller, Virginia Polytechnic State University; E. Clayton Hipp, Wake Forest University; Donald W. Ireland, University of Minnesota–Duluth; Lucy Katz, Fairfield University; S. Jay Sklar, Temple University; and Narciso Tenorio, Mankato State University.

Professor Ralph Davis gratefully acknowledges the contributions of Dena Economou (of the Chicago law firm Tressler, Soderstrom, Maloney & Priess, Chicago) and Carla Michelotti, Senior Vice President, Assoc, General Counsel, Leo Burnett Company, Inc., Chicago.

J. DAVID REITZEL
GORDON B. SEVERANCE
MICHAEL J. GARRISON
RALPH D. DAVIS

CONTENTS

About the Authors xxv
Table of Cases xxvii

PART ONE
LAW, ETHICS, AND THE LEGAL SYSTEM

Chapter 1
Introductory Fundamentals: Law and Legal Reasoning 3

Law—Impossible to Define in So Many Words 3

Law—Dynamic and Prospective 4

Business Law—A New and Different Way of Reasoning 9
Legal Reasoning—Case Reasoning and Statutory Interpretation 9
Legal Philosophies 15

New Concepts, Words, and Meanings 18
Common Law and Equity 19
Public Law and Private Law 20
Criminal Law and Civil Law 20
Substantive and Procedural Law 21

All States Except Louisiana 21

Summary 21

Review Questions 22

Chapter 2
The Legal System: Courts, Civil Procedure, and Alternative Dispute Resolution 23

Sources and Rank of Law in the United States 23
Constitutional Sources of Law 23
Legislative Sources of Law 25
Judicial Decisions as a Source of Law 25
Rank of Laws in the United States 29

Civil Procedure 30
Procedures Prior to Trial 31
Trial of Cases 34
Appeals 36

The Court System 37
Function of the Courts 37
Jurisdiction of the Courts 38
Federal Court System 39
State Court System 40

Alternative Dispute Resolution 42
Negotiation 42
Arbitration 42
Mediation 43
Mini-Trials 43

Summary 43

Review Questions 44

Chapter 3
Business and the Constitution 45

The Historical Development of the Constitution 46
The Framing of the Constitution and the Bill of Rights 46
The Civil War Amendments 47
The Rise of Federal Power and the Fall of Economic Liberties 47
The Modern Protection of Personal Freedoms and Minority Rights 48

Federal and State Power to Control Economic Activity 48
The States and the Police Power 48
Federal Power and the Commerce Clause 50

The Relationship between Federal and State Law 51
Dual Business Regulation 51
Federal Supremacy and Preemption 51
State Regulation of Interstate Business Activities 52

Economic Freedoms under the Constitution 54
Business Property and Operations 55
Freedom of Contract 61

Advertising and Promotion of Goods and Services 62

Constitutional Protection for Business Political Participation 64
The First Amendment and Corporate Political Freedom 64
Lobbying and Issue Advertising 64
Corporate Campaign Spending 65

Summary 66

Review Questions 67

Case Problems 67

Chapter 4
Administrative Agencies and the Regulatory Process 69

Scope and Function of Administrative Law 71
Meaning of Administrative Law, Administrative Agency, and Administrative Process 71
Legislative Delegation of Powers to Agencies 71
Constitutionality of Legislative Delegation of Power to Agencies 72
Rulemaking and Other Agency Functions 72
Quasi-Executive Functions 78

Judicial Review 80
Nonreviewable Matters 81
Reviewable Agency Decisions 81
Evidentiary Standards That Restrict Agency Factfinding 82
Standing, Exhaustion, and Ripeness Doctrines 82

Managerial Considerations and Political Influences 83
Business Monitoring of Administrative Agencies 83
Judicial Deference to Agency Interpretation of Statutes 84
Political Influences 86
Jurisdictional Overlap 88

Summary 89

Review Questions 89

Case Problems 90

Chapter 5
Law and Business Ethics 92

This Book's Approach to Business Ethics 93
What Is Business Ethics? 93
Ethics Terminology 93
Role of Rights, Utility, and Justice 94
Law and Ethics—A Brief Comparison 95

Why Study Business Ethics? 96
Ethical Standards as Part of the Law 96
Ethics as a Factor in Business Decision Making 97
Ethics as a Way to Judge Law 98

Theories of Ethics 99
Consequence-Based Ethics—Utilitarianism as an Example 99
Duty-Based Ethics—Kant's Categorical Imperative as an Example 99

Practicing Business Ethics 100
Nature of Moral Reasoning 100
Applying Ethical Theories 101

The Case of the Breaching Homeowner 102
Moral Dilemmas: The Problem of Conflicting Values and Roles 103

Institutional Ethics: Corporate Social Responsibility 104

Professional and Corporate Codes of Ethics 106

Review Questions 107

Ethics in Practice for Part One 108

PART TWO
TORT AND CRIMINAL LAW

Chapter 6
Nature of Torts; Intentional Torts 113

Nature of Torts 114
Meaning of Torts 114
Crimes Distinguished from Torts 114
Classes of Torts 115

Intentional Harm to the Person 115
Battery; Assault 115
False Imprisonment 116
Defamation 117
Invasion of Privacy 122
Infliction of Mental Distress 124
Misuse of Legal Process 127

Intentional Harm to Property 127
Trespass to Real Property 128
Nuisance 128

Trespass to Personal Property 129
Conversion 129

Fraud 129
False Representation or Concealment of Material Fact 130
Concealment and the Duty of Disclosure 130
Knowledge of Falsity; Intent to Induce Action 131
Justifiable Reliance 131
Resulting Injury 131

Summary 133

Review Questions 133

Case Problems 134

Chapter 7
Negligence and Liability without Fault 136

Negligence 136
Nature of Negligence 136
Elements of Negligence 136
Duty of Care 136
The Standard of Care 137
Breach of Duty 140
Proof of Negligence 140
Negligent Misrepresentation 143
Causation 143
Damages 146
Defenses to Negligence 146

Liability without Fault 150
Strict Products Liability 150
Abnormally Dangerous Activities 153
Liability for Injuries by Animals 154

Summary 155

Review Questions 155

Case Problems 156

Chapter 8
Competitive Torts and Intellectual Property 158

Competitive Torts 158

Wrongful Entry into Business 159

Interference with Business Relations 159

Defamation and Disparagement 164

Unfair Trade Practices 165

Intellectual Property 168
Trademarks 168
Copyrights 172
Patents 176
Trade Secrets 178

Summary 178

Review Questions 180

Case Problems 180

Chapter 9
Criminal Law and Business 182

Criminal Law Principles 182
Nature of Criminal Law 182
Classification of Crimes 183
Elements of a Crime 183
Defenses to Criminal Liability 186

Criminal Procedure and the Constitutional Rights of the Accused 188
Nature of Criminal Procedure 188
Investigation 188
Arrest 191
First Appearance 191
Information or Indictment 191
Pretrial Procedure 191
Trial 191
Criminal Sentences 192
Appeal 192

White-Collar Crimes 192
What Are White-Collar Crimes? 192
Corporate Criminal Liability 193
Bribery 194
Offenses in Violation of Public Health and Safety Laws 195
Criminal Fraud 197
Securities Laws Violations 197
Antitrust Offenses 198
RICO 198
Larceny and Embezzlement by Employees 198

Summary 199

Review Questions 199

Case Problems 199

Ethics in Practice 201

PART THREE
CONTRACTS

Chapter 10
Introduction to the Law of Contracts 205

Nature of Contracts; Importance of Contract Law 206
Meaning of Contract 206
Requirements for a Contract 206
Significance of Contracts and Contract Law 207

Development of Contract Law 207
Classical View of Contract Law 208
Contemporary View of Contract Law 208

Classification of Contracts 211
Express and Implied Contracts 211
Unilateral and Bilateral Contracts 211
Executory and Executed Contracts 212
Enforceable, Unenforceable, Voidable, and "Void" Contracts 212
Formal and Informal Contracts 212

Doctrines Related to Contract Law 213
Quasi Contract 213

Promissory Estoppel 216

Presentation of Contract Law in This Book 217

Summary 217

Review Questions 218

Case Problems 218

Chapter 11
The Agreement: Offer and Acceptance 220

Nature of an Offer 220
Offer Distinguished from Nonoffer 220
Language of Commitment 221
Rewards, Price Quotes, Auctions, and Bids 222
Serious Proposal 223
Definite and Complete Terms 224

Termination of Offers 228
Termination by Lapse of Time 228
Termination by Revocation 228
Termination by Rejection or Counteroffer 230
Termination by Death or Incapacity of Offeror or Offeree 232
Termination by Loss of Subject Matter or Supervening Illegality 232

Acceptance 232
Acceptance of Offer for Unilateral Contract 233
Acceptance of Offer for Bilateral Contract 234

Summary 238

Review Questions 239

Case Problems 239

Chapter 12
Consideration 242

The Requirement of Consideration 243
Meaning of Consideration 243
Illusory Promise; Requirements Contract 247
Adequacy of Consideration; Sham or Nominal Consideration 248

Problems Relating to Consideration 249
Performance of Existing Legal Duty 249
Composition Agreement 255
Forbearance to Sue on a Claim 255

Promises Enforceable without Regard to Consideration 257
Promises to Perform Prior Legal Duty 258
Promises Enforceable Because of Promissory Estoppel 258
Charitable Subscriptions 259

Summary 259

Review Questions 260

Case Problems 260

Chapter 13
Minor's Right to Disaffirm; Other Grounds for Avoidance 262

Avoidance on Ground of Incapacity 262
Contractual Capacity of Minors 263
Contractual Capacity of Other Persons 268

Avoidance on Ground of Defective Assent 269
Duress 269
Undue Influence 270
Misrepresentation 273
Mistake 274

Avoidance on Ground of Unconscionability 277

Avoidance under Consumer Protection Laws 278

Summary 279

Review Questions   279
Case Problems   280

Chapter 14
Illegal Agreements   282

Illegal Agreements in General   282
Nature and General Effect of Illegal Agreements   282
Agreements Illegal by Constitution or Statute   283
Agreements Judicially Declared Contrary to Public Policy   284

Common Types of Illegal Agreements   287
Agreements Not to Compete   288
Agreements Involving Usury   291
Agreements in Violation of Sunday-Closing Statutes   292
Agreements in Violation of Licensing Statutes   293
Confession of Judgment Clauses in Promissory Notes   295
Agreements Involving Interference with Governmental Processes   295

Effect of Illegality   298
The General Rule   298
Exceptions to the General Rule   298
Effect of Partial Illegality   298
Effect of Knowledge of Intended Illegal Use   299

Summary   299

Review Questions   299

Case Problems   300

Chapter 15
A Writing as a Requirement; the Parol Evidence Rule   302

Writing Requirements under the Statute of Frauds   302
Classes of Contracts Covered by the Statute   303
Requirements Regarding the Writing   311
Alternatives to the Writing   312
Modification or Rescission of Contracts Covered by the Statute   316

Effect of Adopting a Writing: Parol Evidence Rule   316
How the Parol Evidence Rule Works   316
Where the Parol Evidence Rule Does Not Apply   317

Summary   318

Review Questions   318

Case Problems   319

Chapter 16
Rights and Duties of Third Persons   321

Third-Person Beneficiary Contracts   321
Meaning of Third-Person Beneficiary   321
Reason for Recognizing Rights of Beneficiaries   322
Vesting of Beneficiary's Rights   324
Promisor's Defenses against the Beneficiary   325

Assignment of Contract Rights   325
Meaning and Nature of Assignment   325
Assignments Which Are Not Legally Effective   328
Successive (Dual) Assignments   331
Warranties of the Assignor   332

Delegation of Contract Duties   332
Meaning of Delegation   332
Delegable and Nondelegable Duties   334
Assignment of "The Contract"   336
Liability of the Delegatee   336

Summary   337

Review Questions   337

Case Problems   338

Chapter 17
Performance, Breach, and Discharge of Contracts; Remedies for Breach of Contract   340

Performance, Breach, and Discharge of Contracts   340
Meaning of Performance, Breach, and Discharge   340
Role of Conditions in Defining and Discharging Duty of Performance   342
Discharge by Performance   343
Other Bases for Discharge   345

Remedies for Breach of Contract; Quasi-Contractual Remedy   349
Remedies for Breach of Contract   349
Quasi-Contractual Remedy   359

Summary   359

Review Questions   359

Case Problems   360

Ethics in Practice   362

PART FOUR
SALES OF GOODS; PRODUCTS LIABILITY

Chapter 18
Introduction to the Law of Sales; the Sales Contract 367

Purposes, Key Concepts, and Coverage of Article 2 368
Purposes of the Law of Sales 368
Key Concepts of the Law of Sales 369
Transactions Covered by Article 2 375

The Sales Contract 378
Formation of the Sales Contract 378
Interpretation of the Sales Contract 383
Form of the Sales Contract—UCC Statute of Frauds 386
Alteration of the Sales Contract 386

Summary 387

Review Questions 387

Case Problems 388

Chapter 19
Delivery and Storage of Goods; Documents of Title 390

Delivery and Storage of Goods 390
Delivery of Goods 390
Storage in Warehouses 394

Documents of Title 397
Kinds of Documents 397
Principle of Negotiability 398
Bailee's Obligations and Liabilities under Document 404
Conflicting Claims to the Goods 407

Summary 407

Review Questions 407

Case Problems 408

Chapter 20
Transfer of Title and Risk of Loss; Title of Good Faith Purchasers 410

Transfer of Title and Risk of Loss 410
Transfer of Title 410
Transfer of Risk of Loss 411

Title of Good Faith Purchasers 417
Where Seller Had Voidable Title 417
Where Goods Were Entrusted to Merchant Seller 417

Summary 419

Review Questions 419

Case Problems 420

Chapter 21
Performance of the Sales Contract; Remedies for Breach of Contract 422

Performance of the Sales Contract 422
Performance: General Concepts 422
Seller's Obligation to Deliver 424
Buyer's Obligation to Accept and Pay 425
Excuse for Nonperformance or Substitute Performance 430

Remedies for Breach of Contract 433
What Constitutes a Breach of Contract 433
Remedies of Seller and Buyer 434
Agreements Concerning Remedies; Limitation of Remedies 440

Summary 442

Review Questions 442

Case Problems 443

Chapter 22
Sales Warranties and Products Liability 445

Contract as a Basis of Products Liability 447
UCC Warranties of Title 448
UCC Warranties of Quality 448
Cumulation and Conflict of Warranties 454
Third-Party Beneficiaries of UCC Quality Warranties 454
Limits on Usefulness of UCC Quality Warranties 458

Tort as a Basis for Products Liability 458
Negligence as a Basis of Product Liability 459
Strict Liability as a Basis of Products Liability 460
Misrepresentation as a Basis of Product Liability 467

Summary 468

Review Questions 469

Case Problems 469

Ethics in Practice 471

PART FIVE
PROPERTY AND ESTATES

Chapter 23
Nature and Importance of Property; Personal Property and Bailments 475

Nature and Importance of Property 475
Meaning of Property 475
Title and Other Property Rights 475
Classes of Property 476
Legal Protection of Private Property 477
Rationale for Protecting Private Property 477
Legal Restrictions on Private Property 480

Personal Property 480
Acquisition by Purchase 480
Acquisition by Creation 480
Acquisition by Gift 480
Acquisition by Taking Possession 483
Acquisition by Accession 486
Acquisition by Confusion 486

Bailments 486
Meaning of Bailment 487
Classes of Bailments 487
Creation of Bailments 487
Rights and Duties of the Bailor and the Bailee 490

Summary 497

Review Questions 497

Case Problems 497

Chapter 24
Real Property: Nature, Acquisition, Ownership, and Control 499

Physical Elements of Real Property 499
Airspace 499
Crops and Timber 500
Minerals 500
Oil and Gas 500
Water 500

Fixtures 501
Tests for a Fixture 501

Acquisition of Ownership of Real Property 504
Purchase 504
Gift 506
Will or Descent 506
Adverse Possession 506
Transfer by Deed 509

Types of Ownership of Real Property 512
Sole Ownership 512
Common Law Cotenancies 512
Marital Tenancies 513
Partnership Property 515
Condominiums and Cooperatives 515

Public and Private Controls on the Use of Real Property 515
Zoning and Government Land Use Controls 516
Government's Power of Eminent Domain 517
Nuisances and Common Law Restrictions on Land Use 519
Restrictive Covenants 520

Summary 520

Review Questions 521

Case Problems 521

Chapter 25
Interests in Real Property 523

Freehold Estates in Real Property 523
Fee Simple Estates 523
Life Estates 524

The Landlord-Tenant Relationship 525
The Leasehold Estate 525
Nature and Requirements of a Lease 525
Types of Leases 526
Rights and Duties of Landlord and Tenant 526
Transfer of Interests under a Lease 530
Termination of Leases 532

Easements 533
Meaning of Easement 533
Methods of Creating Easements 533
Use and Maintenance of Easements 535

Liens on Real Property 537
Meaning and Classification of Liens 537
Mortgages and Voluntary Liens on Real Property 537
Involuntary Liens on Real Property 543

Summary 544

Review Questions 544

Case Problems 545

Chapter 26
Estates, Wills, and Trusts 547

Intestate Succession 548
Order of Intestate Succession 548
Succession in Special Situations 549

Wills 550
What Is a Will? 550
Why Make a Will? 550
The Testator 550
Formal Requirements of a Will 553
Limitations of Disposition by Will 556

Revocation and Modification of Wills 557
Codicils to Wills 557
Revocation by Act of Testator 558
Revocation by Operation of Law 559

Probate 559
Proving the Will 559
The Personal Representative 560
Rights and Duties of the Personal Representative 560
Claims against Estates 561
Distribution of Assets 561

Trusts 562
Types of Trusts 562
Creation and Requirements of Trusts 564
Duties of the Trustee 565
Allocation of Principal and Income 567
Termination of Trusts 567

Summary 568

Review Questions 568

Case Problems 568

Chapter 27
Insurance 570

The Nature of Insurance 570
The Principle of Pooling Risk 570
Reinsurance 571
Insurance Terminology 571

The Insurance Contract 573

Contract of Adhesion 574
When Is the Contract Formed? 574
Assignability of Insurance Contracts 576
Insurance Pricing and Dividends 577

Duties, Defenses, and Rights of Insurers and Others 578
Duties of the Insurer 578
Duties of Insured 582
Defense of Insurer 582

Personal Risks: Life and Health Insurance 585
Life Insurance 585
Health Insurance 586

Property Risks; Property and Liability Insurance 587
Property Insurance 587
Liability Insurance 587
Subrogation and Coinsurance 588

Regulation of the Insurance Business 590
Federal Regulation 590
State Regulation 591

Roles of Insurance Agents and Brokers 591
Traditional Functions of Agents and Brokers 591
Agents and Brokers as Financial Advisers 592

Summary 592

Review Questions 593

Case Problems 593

Ethics in Practice 595

PART SIX
DEBTOR-CREDITOR RELATIONSHIPS

Chapter 28
Purpose and Types of Secured Transactions; Suretyship 599

Nature and Types of Secured Transactions 600
Nature of a Secured Transaction 600
Types of Secured Transactions 600

Suretyship 606
Nature, Creation, and Kinds of Suretyship 606
Liability, Defenses, and Discharge of Surety 609
Rights of Surety and Cosurety 614

Summary 616

Review Questions 616
Case Problems 617

Chapter 29
Secured Transactions in Personal Property 619

Purpose and Coverage of UCC Article 9 619
Purpose of Article 9 619
Coverage of Article 9 621

Acquiring and Perfecting a Security Interest 622
Attachment of a Security Interest 622
Perfection of a Security Interest 623

Priorities among Conflicting Interests 629
Priorities among Conflicting Security Interests in the Same Collateral 629
Priority between a Security Interest and the Interest of a Third-Person Purchaser 634
Priority of Mechanics' Liens 635
Priorities of Security Interests in Fixtures 635
Priorities of Security Interests in Accessions and Commingled Goods 635

Default and Foreclosure 636
Meaning of Default 636
Rights and Duties of Secured Party upon Debtor's Default 636

Summary 639
Review Questions 639
Case Problems 639

Chapter 30
Bankruptcy 642

Creditors' Rights and Debtor Relief under State Law 642
Joe's Financial Failure 642
How Joe May Settle His Unpaid Debts under State Law 644
Composition and Extension Agreements 644
Assignments for the Benefit of Creditors 644

Federal Bankruptcy Law and Administration 645
The Bankruptcy Code 645
Role of State Law 645
Kinds of Bankruptcy Proceedings 645

Liquidation (Straight or Ordinary Bankruptcy) 645
Commencement of Straight Bankruptcy 646
The Automatic Stay 646
Functions of Trustee and Judge 647
The Bankruptcy Estate 647
Trustee's Power to Collect and Liquidate the Estate 647
Trustee's Status as Lien Creditor and Bona Fide Purchaser 648
Avoidance of Fraudulent Transfers 649
Voidable Preferences 652
The Debtor's Exemptions 654
Claims of Creditors 655
Priority of Claims 655
Discharge 656
Nondischargeable Debts 658
Reaffirmation 659

Business Reorganizations 659
Debtor in Possession 660
Role of Creditors' Committee 660
Plan of Reorganization 660
Acceptance and Confirmation of the Plan 661

Repayment Plans for Debtors with Regular Income 662
The Chapter 13 Plan 663
Confirmation of the Plan 663
Discharge 664

Summary 664
Review Questions 664
Case Problems 664
Ethics in Practice 666

PART SEVEN
COMMERCIAL PAPER

Chapter 31
Nature of Commercial Paper; Negotiable Form 671

Types and Nature of Commercial Paper 672
Types of Commercial Paper 672
Negotiable Character of Commercial Paper— An Overview 676

Dual Nature of Commercial Paper 678
Some Business Uses of Commercial Paper 679

Negotiable Form 680
Minimum Language Required for Negotiable Form 680
Language That Destroys Negotiability 683
Language and Omissions Not Affecting Negotiability 686
Rules for Interpreting Common Ambiguities 688

Summary 689

Review Questions 689

Case Problems 689

Chapter 32
Personal and Real Defenses; Negotiation of Commercial Paper 691

Personal and Real Defenses 691
Personal Defenses 692
Real Defenses 694

Negotiation of Commercial Paper 697
Issue of an Instrument 698
Negotiation of an Instrument 698

Summary 709

Review Questions 710

Case Problems 710

Chapter 33
Holder-in-Due-Course Status; FTC Limits 712

Holder-in-Due-Course Status 712
Requirements for Holder-in-Due-Course Status 712
Payee as Holder in Due Course 719
Rights of Transferees; Shelter Provision 721

FTC limits 725
Reasons for the FTC Limits 725
The FTC Rule 725

Summary 726

Review Questions 727

Case Problems 727

Chapter 34
Liability of the Parties; Discharge 730

Contractual Liability of the Parties 730
Liability of Primary Parties 731
Liability of Secondary Parties 731
Liability of Accommodation Parties 736
Signatures by Agents and Forgers 736
Effect of Indorsement by Imposter or Dishonest Agent 737

Discharge from Contractual Liability 740
Common Methods of Discharge 740
Effect of Discharge on Holder in Due Course 743

Warranty Liability 743
Transfer Warranties 744
Presentment Warranties 745

Summary 747

Review Questions 747

Case Problems 748

Chapter 35
Checks; Relationship between Bank and Customer; Electronic Funds Transfers 750

Checks 750
Special Nature of Checks 750
Certified Checks 752

Relationship between Bank and Customer 752
Contract between Bank and Customer 752
Nature of Bank-Customer Relationship 755
Check Collection Process 755
When Bank May Charge Customer's Account 758
Bank's Liability for Wrongful Dishonor 759
Stop-Payment Order 761
Customer's Duty to Report Unauthorized Signature or Alteration 762
Final Payment Rule 766
Effect of Customer's Death or Incompetence 767
Bank's Liability for Conversion 767

Electronic Funds Transfers 767
Consumer EFT Applicatons 767
Commercial EFT Applications—Interbank Transfers and Article 4A 769

Summary 769

Review Questions 770

Case Problems   770

Ethics in Practice   772

PART EIGHT
AGENCY

Chapter 36
Nature of Agency Relationships   777

Agency Relationships   778
Principal and Agent   778
Employer and Employee   778
Principal and Independent Contractor   779

Establishing an Agency   783
The Principal-Agent Relationship   783
Capacity of Principal and Agent   783
Kinds of Agents   783
The Principal and Agent Agreement   784

Power of Agent to Bind Principal in Contract   785
Agent's Actual Authority; Agent's Apparent Authority   786
Ratification of Agent's Acts   789
Agent's Authority by Operation of Law   792

Contractual Rights and Obligations of Principal, Agent, and Third Party   792
Disclosed Principal   793
Partially Disclosed Principal   795
Undisclosed Principal   795

Summary   798

Review Questions   798

Case Problems   799

Chapter 37
Agency and Tort Liability   800

Liability for Torts Resulting in Physical Injury   800
Agent Independent Contractor's Torts Causing Physical Injury   801
Employees' Torts Causing Physical Injury   801
Application of Respondeat Superior   802
Can an Agent's Willful Tort outside Scope of Employment Be Ratified?   816

Liability for Torts Not Resulting in Physical Injury   818
Basis of Principal's Liability   818
Remedies of Principal against Agent   820

Summary   821

Review Questions   821

Case Problems   822

Chapter 38
Agents' and Principals' Duties to Each Other; Termination of Agency   824

Duties Agents Owe to Principals   824
Duty to Perform Work with Care and Skill   825
Duty of Obedience to Principal's Instructions   825
Duty to Perform Services Personally   827
Duty to Communicate Pertinent Information   827
Duty to Keep and Render Accounts   829
Fiduciary Duty of Loyalty   829

Obligations of Principals to Agents   834
Duty to Compensate Agent   834
Duty to Keep and Render Accounts   835
Duty to Provide Means to Accomplish the Work   835
Duty to Continue Employment of Agent; Wrongful Discharge   836
Duty to Provide a Safe Workplace   840
Duty to Compensate Agent for Injuries   840

Remedies of Principals and Agents for Breach of Obligations   840

Termination of Agency   841
Methods of Termination   841
Notice to Third Parties of Termination   843

Summary   844

Review Questions   844

Case Problems   845

Ethics in Practice   847

PART NINE
BUSINESS ORGANIZATIONS

Chapter 39
Introduction to Business Organizations; Formation of Partnerships; Rights and Duties of Partners   851

Introduction to Business Organizations   851
Five Common Forms of Business Organization   851

Forming a Partnership; Rights and Duties of Partners   853
Is a Partnership an Entity or an Aggregate?   853
What Is a Partnership?   854
Establishing the Partnership Agreement   857
Who May Be a Partner?   857

Partnership Property   861
Partner's Interest in the Partnership   861
Partner's Rights in Specific Partnership Property   862

Rights and Duties of Partners   863
Rights of Partners among Themselves   863
Duties of Partners   867

Power of Partners to Obligate Partnership and Copartners   870
Power to Obligate by Contract   870
Power to Obligate by Statement against Interest   870
Power to Obligate by Notice or Knowledge   870
Power to Obligate by Tortious Act   871

Summary   873

Review Questions   873

Case Problems   874

Chapter 40
Termination of Partnerships   876

Dissolution of Partnerships   876
Dissolution Not in Violation of Partnership Agreement   877

Dissolution in Violation of Partnership Agreement   881
Dissolution by Operation of Law   883

Dissolution by Court Decree   884

Winding Up Partnerships   885
Who Conducts the Winding Up? Compensation   885

The Winding-Up Process   887
Limitation on Partners' Powers during Winding Up   887
Settlement of Partnership Accounts   888
Partners' Fiduciary Responsibilities during Winding Up   890

Continuation of Partnership Business without Winding Up   892
Continuation after Wrongful Withdrawal or Expulsion of Partner   892
Continuation after Retirement or Death of a Partner   893
Creditors' Rights against Continuing Partners   895
Creditors' Rights against Departed Partners   895

Summary   896

Review Questions   897

Case Problems   897

Chapter 41
Limited Partnerships and Limited Liability Companies   899

Limited Partnerships   900
Nature and Development of Limited Partnerships   900
Formation of Limited Partnerships   901
General Partners   907
Limited Partners   910
Winding Up and Termination of Limited Partnerships   917

Limited Liability Companies   917
What Is a Limited Liability Company?   918
What Are the Tax Advantages of a Limited Liability Company?   918
Qualifying an LLC to Be Taxed as a Partnership   918
LLCs—A Viable Hybrid   919

Summary   919

Review Questions   920

Case Problems   920

Chapter 42
Nature and Formation of Corporations   922

What Is a Corporation?   922

Development of Modern Corporation Law   922

State Incorporation Laws   923
Federal Laws Affecting Corporations   923

Nature of Modern Corporations   924
Characteristics of Corporations   924
Kinds of Corporations   925

Formation of Corporations   930
Preincorporation Activities   930
Creating the Corporation   933
The Organizational Meeting: Agenda and Bylaws   935

Liability of Corporate Members   937
De Jure Corporation   937
De Facto Corporation   938
Corporation by Estoppel   939
Liability of Members of Firm Improperly Labeled a Corporation   939
Disregarding Corporateness—Piercing the Corporate Veil   940

Termination of Corporations   944

Summary   945

Review Questions   946

Case Problems   946

Chapter 43
Financing Corporations   948

Debt Financing; Bonds   948
Short-Term Financing   948
Long-Term Bond Financing   949

Equity Financing—Stocks   949
Nature of Shares of Stock   949
Issuance of Shares   951
Classes of Shares   954

Thin Corporations   956

Transfer of Securities   959
Indorsements Required   959
Lost or Stolen Certificates   961
Restrictions on Transfer   961

Dividends and Other Corporate Distributions   962
Dividend Distributions   962
Other Corporate Distributions   967

Summary   968

Review Questions   969

Case Problems   970

Chapter 44
Management of Corporations   972

The Corporate Entity: Powers and Liabilities   972
Sources of Corporate Powers   972
Ultra Vires Acts   973

Corporation Directors and Officers   977
Directors   977
Officers   979
Duties Owed by Directors and Officers   980
Protection against Takeover   988

Unique Management Problems of Close Corporations   989
Management Problems of Close Corporations Analyzed   989
Some Solutions to Close-Corporation Problems   992

Summary   994

Review Questions   994

Case Problems   995

Chapter 45
Shareholders' Powers, Rights, and Liabilities   997

Powers of Shareholders   997
Election and Removal of Directors   997
Amendment of Articles   998
Acquisitions by Merger or Consolidation   998
Sale of All Assets of a Corporation   999
Appraisal Rights of Dissenting Shareholders   1000
Corporate Dissolution   1002

Shareholders' Meetings   1004
Annual and Special Meetings   1004
Notice of Meetings; Waiver of Notice   1004
Proxy Voting   1005
Quorum and Voting Requirements   1006
Voting Eligibility   1006
Election of Directors; Cumulative Voting   1006

Shareholders' Rights   1007
Preemptive Rights   1007
Right to Examine Corporate Books   1008
Rights of Action   1010

Shareholders' Liabilities   1012
Liability for Unpaid Subscriptions   1013
Liability for True Value of Shares   1013

Liability for Unlawful Dividends and
  Distributions   1013
Liability of Controlling Shareholders   1013

Summary   1015

Review Questions   1016

Case Problems   1016

Chapter 46
Securities Regulation: Protecting Investors   1018

State Securities Regulation   1018

Federal Securities Regulation   1018

Definition of a Security   1019

The 1933 Act: Regulating New Issues of Securities   1023
Registration Requirements   1023
Disclosure and Integrated Registration   1025
Offer and Sale of Securities   1025
Exemptions   1025
Enforcement of the 1933 Act   1029

The Securities Exchange Act of 1934   1031
Reporting Requirements under the 1934 Act   1031
Antifraud Section 10(b) and Rule 10b-5; Insider
  Trading   1032
Short-Swing Insider Trading and Reporting;
  Section 16(b)   1036
Proxy Statements   1037
Corporate Takeovers   1039
Enforcement of the 1934 Act   1042

Summary   1042

Review Questions   1043

Case Problems   1043

Chapter 47
Accountants' Liability   1045

The Accountant-Client Relationship   1046
Nature of Accounting Services   1046
The Contract between Accountant and Client   1048
Duty of Confidentiality   1048

Common Law Liability of Accountants   1052
Contract Liability and Breach of Fiduciary
  Duty   1052
Liability for Fraud   1052
Liability for Professional Negligence   1053
Liability to Third Parties   1055

Federal Statutory Liability of Accountants   1059
Liability under the Securities Act of 1933   1059
Liability under the Securities Exchange Act of
  1934   1060
RICO   1063

Criminal and Administrative Liability   1064
State Law   1064
Federal Law   1064

Summary   1065

Review Questions   1066

Case Problems   1066

Ethics in Practice for Part Nine   1069

PART TEN
GOVERNMENT REGULATION; COMPUTER LAW; INTERNATIONAL BUSINESS LAW

Chapter 48
Law of Labor and Employment   1073

Labor-Management Relations   1075
The National Labor Relations Act   1075
The Taft-Hartley Act   1077
The Landrum-Griffin Act   1078

Equal Employment Opportunity   1087
Title VII   1087
Other Sources of Employment Discrimination
  Law   1095

Wage and Hour Laws   1097

Workers' Compensation   1098
Coverage; AOE and COE   1098
Amount of Compensation   1098
Exclusions   1098
Funding   1099

Occupational Safety and Health   1099

Summary   1099

Review Questions   1100

Case Problems   1100

Chapter 49
Consumer Law 1102

State Law 1103
Common Law 1103
Statutes 1104

Federal Law and Regulation 1107
Product Warranty—Magnuson-Moss Warranty Act 1107
Product Integrity 1108
Credit 1109
Unfair and Deceptive Practices 1112
Consumer Information and Privacy 1116

Summary 1119

Review Questions 1119

Case Problems 1120

Chapter 50
Computer Law 1121

Property Rights in Computer Technology 1122
Copyrights of Computer Technology 1122
Patents on Computer Technology 1125
Computer Trade Secrets 1125

Computer Transactions 1127
Governing Law—Sales or Contract Law? 1127
Formation and Terms of the Computer Transaction 1130
Warranty Liability 1134

Computer Tort Liability 1135
Negligence and Computer Malpractice 1135
Strict Liability and Fraud 1137

Computer Crimes 1137
Kinds of Computer Crime 1138
Laws Applicable to Computer Crimes 1139

Computers and Privacy 1140
Access to Private Information 1140
E-Mail and Computer Communications 1141
Computer Telemarketing 1141
Computer Monitoring 1141

Summary 1142

Review Questions 1142

Case Problems 1143

Chapter 51
Law and the Environment 1145

The Traditional Approach 1146
Intentional Interference with Property or Person 1147
Nuisance 1148
Negligence 1149
Strict Liability 1149

Environmental Statutes and Regulation 1151
State and Local Environmental Control 1152
Federal Environmental Laws and Regulation 1152

Summary 1161

Review Questions 1162

Case Problems 1162

Chapter 52
Introduction to Antitrust Law; the Sherman Act 1164

Development of Antitrust Law 1164
The Rise of Trusts in the United States 1164
Enactment of Laws to Promote Competition 1165

The Sherman Antitrust Act 1165
Purpose and Scope of the Act 1165
Enforcement of the Act 1166
Court Interpretation of Section 1 1169
Proving Monopolization under Section 2 1181
General Intent to Monopolize 1182

Summary 1185

Review Questions 1186

Case Problems 1186

Chapter 53
The Clayton, Robinson-Patman, and Federal Trade Commission Acts 1188

The Clayton Act 1188
Purpose and Scope of the Clayton Act 1188
Section 2—Price Discrimination 1188
Defenses to Liability under the Act 1190
Exclusive Dealing 1191
Tying Arrangements 1192
Corporate Mergers—Section 7 1193
Private Enforcement of the Clayton Act 1200

The Federal Trade Commission Act 1202

National Cooperative Research Act—Joint Ventures with Competitors 1202
Joint Ventures and JRDVs; National Cooperative Research Act 1202

Antitrust Exemptions and Extraterritoriality 1202
Express Exemptions 1203
Implied Exemptions 1204
Extraterritoriality of Antitrust Laws 1207

Summary 1209

Review Questions 1210

Case Problems 1210

Chapter 54
Business Law in a Global Economy 1213

The Nature of International Business Transactions 1213
Can Robles Market His Tortilla Technology on a Global Basis? 1213
Emerging Global Competition 1214
Free Trade or Economic Nationalism? 1214

Nature and Sources of International Law 1214
Sources of Public International Law 1215
Sources of Private International Law—Conflict of Laws 1217

The International Contract 1220
Content 1220
Choice-of-Law, Choice-of-Forum Clauses 1220
Convention on Contracts for the International Sale of Goods 1221
Commercial Arbitration Clauses 1221

Alternative Ways of Doing Business Abroad 1223
Direct Sales 1223
Distributorships and Licensing Arrangements 1225
Joint Ventures 1225

Transnational Business Corporations 1226

Sovereign Regulation of International Trade 1226
Why a Country Regulates International Trade 1226
Regulation of Imports—Protectionism or Consumerism? 1226
Regulation of Exports—Licensing and Other Controls 1229
Regulation of Money across International Borders 1229
Extraterritoriality of Sovereign Business Regulations 1231
Foreign Government Takeovers of Foreign Investments 1231
Judicial Limits on Extraterritorial Business Regulation 1232

Summary 1234

Review Questions 1234

Case Problems 1235

Ethics in Practice 1236

APPENDIXES

1 United States Constitution 1239
2 Uniform Commercial Code (1978), with 1987 and 1990 Amendments 1249
3 Uniform Partnership Act 1356
4 Uniform Limited Partnership Act (1976), with 1985 Amendments 1367
5 Revised Model Business Corporation Act (1984), as Amended 1374

Glossary 1381
Index I-1

ABOUT THE AUTHORS

J. DAVID REITZEL is Professor of Business Law, California State University, Fresno. Before that, he was Professor and Chairman of the Department of Business Law at The American College, Bryn Mawr, Pennsylvania, and Professor of Business Law at St. Cloud State University in Minnesota. Professor Reitzel holds a J.D. degree from Indiana University and B.S. and M.S. degrees from Purdue University. Admitted to the Indiana and federal bars in 1969, Professor Reitzel has served as Editor-in-Chief of the American Business Law Journal and has written numerous articles and papers, many dealing with business law education. In 1992, he received the Ralph C. Hoeber award for "Critical Thinking and the Business Law Curriculum," an article appearing in the *Journal of Legal Studies Education*.

GORDON B. SEVERANCE is Professor of Business Law, LeTourneau University, Emeritus Professor of Law, California State University, Los Angeles, and Emeritus Professor of Business Law, University of Nevada, where he also served as Acting Dean of the College of Business Administration. Professor Severance has taught at Occidental College, California State University at San Diego, and the University of Southern California. A magna cum laude graduate of Stanford University, where he also received an M.A. degree, Professor Severance holds a J.D. and Ph.D. (economics) from the University of Southern California. A member of Phi Beta Kappa, Professor Severance is a past president of the Pacific Southwest Business Law Association. He is president and director of an international import-export corporation and has authored numerous articles in the area of international business law. In 1990 Professor Severance, as a Fulbright Scholar, taught international business at the Makerere University School of Law in Uganda, where he was also an advisor to the government's constitutional revision committee.

MICHAEL J. GARRISON is Associate Professor of Business Law in the College of Business Administration at North Dakota State University, where he has also served as the Associate Dean and the Coordinator of Accounting. He received his J.D. degree from the University of North Dakota School of Law, graduating first in his class. A member of the Order of the Coif, he has authored journal articles and conference proceedings and is a staff editor for the *American Business Law Journal* and the *Midwest Law Review*. In 1988, he received the Ralph C. Hoeber Award and the Articles Editor Award for the best major article in Volume 25 of the *American Business Law Journal*. In 1990 he was again so honored for his article in Volume 27. He has served as the President of the Midwest Academy of Legal Studies in Business and on the President's Advisory Committee of the Academy of Legal Studies in Business. He recently received the Teacher of the Year Award in the College of Business Administration at NDSU.

RALPH D. DAVIS is a marketing and advertising consultant in Chicago and an adjunct faculty member at Illinois Institute of Technology, Stuart School of Business, where he formerly served as Lecturer in Marketing and Law and as Director of the school's JD/MBA and Executive MBA programs. Davis holds a J.D. degree from Northwestern University and an A.B. and an M.B.A. from the University of Chicago. A member of the Illinois Bar, Davis is a frequent writer on business, legal, ethical, and social issues. He received two awards from the American Business Law Association (now the Academy of Legal Studies in Business): the Holmes/Cardozo Award in 1988 for the outstanding paper of the year and Best Article in *The American Business Law Journal* in 1990. In 1991, Davis's book, *False Teeth to a Chicken: Products, Advertising & You*, was released in softcover by International Publishing Corporation. Before joining the academic community, Davis was an advertising executive at Leo Burnett, U.S.A.

TABLE OF CASES

A & B Freight Line, Inc. v. Ryan 591
Adams v. Zayre Corp. 117
American Machinery Movers, Inc. v. Continental Container Service, Inc. 492
American Sate Bank v. Northwest South Dakota Production Credit Assoc. 720
Anderson v. Service Merchandise Co. 141
Apple Computer, Inc. v. Microsoft Corporation 1122
Arco v. USA Petroleum 1201
Austin v. Michigan Chamber of Commerce 65
Auto Workers v. Johnson Controls 1092

In re Estate of Baker 552
Bank of New York v. Amoco Oil Co. 402
Bankwest, N.A. v. Williams 960
Barnett Bank v. Regency Highland Condominium Assoc. 685
Basic Incorporated v. Levinson 1040
Bass v. Bass 855
Bergh v. Mills 871
Board of Education v. Pico 7
Boich Mining Company v. NLRB 1086
Bradley v. American Smelting and Refining Co. 1150
Broadview Apartments Co. v. Baughman 489
Brookfield Associates v. Estate of Bacon 877
Buenger v. Varco Pruden 412
Butterfield Lumber, Inc. v. Peterson Mortgage Co. 603

Caleb & Co. v. E.I. Du Pont de Nemours & Co. 965

Calvin Klein Ltd. v. Trylon Trucking Corp. 393
Carson v. Davidson 945
Castille v. Folck 835
Catalano, Inc. v. Target Sales, Inc. 1171
Centaur Partners v. National Intergroup, Inc. 936
Chaplin v. Sanders 508
Chemical Waste Management, Inc. v. Hunt 53
Chevron v. Natural Resources Defense Council, Inc. 84
Clearwater v. State Farm Mutual Auto. Insurance Co. 579
Cleveland Board of Education v. Loudermill 77
Contemporary Mission, Inc. v. Famous Music Corp. 333
Continental Ill. Nat'l Bank v. Allen 905
Continental TV, Inc. v. GTE Sylvania, Inc. 1174
Cripe v. Atlantic First National Bank of Daytona Beach 271
Crookham & Vessels, Inc. v. Larry Moyer Trucking, Inc. 251
Crown Controls, Inc. v. Smiley 797

Darlage v. Crane 885
DeBaun v. First Western Bank & Trust Co. 1014
Derico v. Duncan 293
Diversified Graphics, Ltd. v. Ernst & Whinney 1136
Dixie Pipe Sales, Inc. v. Perry 993
Dodge v. Ford Motor Co. 963
Doliner v. Brown 4

Doe v. Dominion Bank of Washington   528
Dohanyos v. Prudential Insurance Co.   575

Eastman Kodak Company v. Image Technical Services, Inc.   1184
Edgewater Motels, Inc. v. A. J. Gatzke   813
Eklund v. Vincent Brass & Aluminum Co.   310
Erickson v. Monarch Industries, Inc.   817
Escott v. BarChris Construction Corp.   1029

Fabry Partnership v. Silver Queen Limited Partnership   903
In re Estate of Harry Feir   558
Feist Publications, Inc., v. Rural Telephone Service Company, Inc.   174
Field Lumber Co. v. Petty   254
Finalco, Inc. v. Roosevelt   723
First Nat. Bank & Trust v. Scherr   864
First Nat'l Maintenance Corp. v. NLRB   1082
First Nat'l State Bank of New Jersey v. Commonwealth Federal Savings & Loan Assoc.   253
Ford v. Venard   502
Friedman v. New Westbury Village Associates   860
FTC v. Indiana Federation of Dentists   1178
FTC v. PPG Industries, Inc.   1196
FTC v. Superior Court Trial Lawyers Assoc.   1177
FTC v. Ticor Title Ins. Co.   1206

Gateway Potato Sales v. G.B. Investment Co.   913
Gelder Medical Group v. Webber   880
Gering v. Smith Company   828
Gilbride v. Dover Nissan, Inc.   373
Glanzer v. St. Joseph Indian School   942
Graybar Electric Co. v. Sawyer   305

Green v. Geer   132
Green v. United States   807

Hapney v. Central Garage, Inc.   289
Harik v. Harik   734
Harmon v. Chrysler Corporation   1105
Henderson v. Professional Coatings Corp.   811
Hendricks & Associates, Inc. v. Daewoo Corporation   439
Hindman v. Salt Pond Associates   882
Homewood Investment Co. v. Moses   610
Hooper v. Yoder   890
Hustler Magazine v. Jerry Falwell   125

Investors Savings & Loan Association v. Ganz   540
Island Air, Inc. v. LaBar   162

Jason's Foods, Inc. v. Peter Eckrich & Sons, Inc.   414
J. Bar H., Inc. v. Johnson   986
Julian v. Christopher   531

Kashfi v. Philbro-Salomon, Inc.   296
Kelly v. Central Bank and Trust Co. of Denver   703
Kemp v. Budget Rent-A- Car Systems, Inc.   495
Kirk v. Kirk's Auto Electric, Inc.   953
Koval v. Peoples   341
In re Kraft, Inc.   1114

L. A. Gear, Inc. v. Thom McAn Shoe Company   177
Lancaster v. Greer   329
LaFleur v. C. C. Pierce Co.   275
Larsen Leasing, Inc. v. Thiele, Inc.   436
Lechmere, Inc. v. NLRB   1076

Lessley v. Hardage   226
Levy v. Leavitt   866
Lewis v. The Equitable Life Assurance Society   119
Locke v. Arabi Grain & Elevator Company, Inc.   418
Lojek v. Pedler   627
Lovering v. Seabrook Island Property Owners   974
Lucas v. South Carolina Coastal Council   56

M & M Transport, Co. v. Schuster   347
Macke Co. v. Pizza of Gaithersburg, Inc.   335
Maduff Corporation v. Deloitte, Haskins & Sells   1054
Malachowski v. Bank One, Indianapolis   566
Marine Midland Bank-Central v. Cote   637
Marsh v. Gentry   867
Master Distributors, Inc. v. Pako Corporation   171
Masters, Mates & Pilots v. Brown   1079
In re Mazzola   657
Mauch v. Manufacturers Sales & Service, Inc.   151
McCain v. Phoenix Resources, Inc.   912
McIntyre v. Balentine   148
McLain v. Real Estate Board of New Orleans   1168
Medford Irrigation District v. Western Bank   764
Mellon Bank v. Donegal Mutual Ins. Co.   693
Mellon Bank v. Metro Communications, Inc.   650
Mennonite Deaconess Home & Hospital, Inc. v. Gates Engineering Co.   450
Mitsubishi Motors v. Soler Chrysler-Plymouth   1222
Moore v. City of East Cleveland   13
Moore v. The Regents of the University of California   478
Moxley v. Laramie Builders, Inc.   505

Mustang Transp. Co. v. Ryder Truck Lines, Inc.   804

Nationwide Mutual Insurance Co. v. Darden   781
NBD-Sandusky Bank v. Ritter   632
NLRB v. Exchange Parts Co.   1080
Neilson Business Equipment Center, Inc., v. Monteleone   1128
New York v. Burger   189
Northwestern Bank v. Neal   684

Oak Park Currency Exchange, Inc. v. Maropoulos   746
Olin Corporation v. FTC   1197

Palmer v. BRG of Georgia   1173
Panhandle Eastern Pipe Line Company v. Smith   231
Paramount Communications v. Time, Inc.   981
Parkhill v. Nusor   715
Peters v. Morse   307
Pfluger v. Colquitt   793
Pierce v. Plogger   256
Polo Fashions, Inc. v. Craftex, Inc.   167
Powers v. Hastings   314
PPG Industries, Inc. v. United States   1228
Progressive Casualty Ins. Co. v. Ehrhardt   790
Prudential-Bache Securities, Inc. v. Citibank   738
Pusateri v. E.F. Hutton & Co.   819

Quechee Lakes Rental Corp. v. Boggess   825

Raritan River Steel Co. v. Cherry, Bekaert & Holland   1057
Ratner v. Central Nat'l Bank of Miami   931
Ray v. Flower Hospital   485

In re Estate of Reiman   555
Republic Insurance Company v. Hires   580
Reves v. Ernst & Young   1021
Rivas v. District International Trucks   461
Roy v. Stephen Pontiac-Cadillac, Inc.   431
Rudolph v. Arthur Andersen & Co.   1061
Rutherford v. Darwin   707

Samuel M. Feinberg Testamentary Trust v. Carter   1011
Save Our Community v. U.S. Environmental Protection Agency   1155
In re Trust Estate of Schaefer   894
Schwartz v. Marien   1008
Szajna v. General Motors Corporation   456
Shearson Lehman Hutton, Inc. v. Tucker   976
Sierra Pacific Industries, Inc. v. Carter   831
Soldau v. Organon, Inc.   236
Stahl v. Metropolitan Dade County   145
Stanek v. National Bank of Detroit   753
Star Chevrolet Co. v. Green   265
Step-Saver Data Systems, Inc. v. The Software Link, Inc.   1133
Stringer v. Car Data Systems, Inc.   1000
Swiftships, Inc. v. Burdin   214
Swire Pacific Holdings, Inc. v. Morgan and Taylor Holding Co.   428
Systems Design and Management Information, Inc. v. Kansas City Post Office Employees Credit Union   376

Tanzi v. Fiberglass Swimming Pools, Inc.   958
Texas Trading & Milling Corp. v. Federal Republic of Nigeria   1232
Tri-Circle, Inc. v. Brugger Corp.   788
Tunkl v. Regents of the University of California   285
Twin City Bank v. Isaacs   759

Union Bank v. Wolas   653
In re Union Carbide Corporation Gas Plant Disaster   1218
Union Carbide Corp. v. Oscar Mayer Foods Corp.   384
United Blood Services v. Quintana   138
United Elec. Contractors, Inc. v. Prog. Builders, Inc.   941
United States v. Amtreco, Inc.   1159
United States v. Park   195
United States v. United States Gypsum Co.   184

Vanna White v. Samsung Electronics America, Inc.   123
Vastine v. Bank of Dallas   613
Veale v. Rose   869
Vick v. H.S.I. Management, Inc.   323
In re Villa Maria, Inc.   1003
Virginia Bankshares, Inc. v. Sandberg   1037

Wade v. Jobe   356
Wagenheim v. Alexander Grant & Co.   1050
Wallace v. Milliken & Co.   837
In re Estate of Weinsaft   245
Western Mining Corp. v. Standard Terminals, Inc.   395
Western States Minerals Corp. v. Jones   838
Wilensky v. Blalock   879
Wilkes v. Springside Nursing Home, Inc.   991
Wilson v. Steele   695
Wright v. Horse Creek Ranches   536
Wrights Beauty College v. Bostic   1009
Wyler v. Feuer   908

Yee v. City of Escondido   518

Zlotoff v. Tucker   351

Contemporary Business Law and the Legal Environment

PRINCIPLES AND CASES

PART ONE

Law, Ethics, and the Legal System

CHAPTER 1
Introductory Fundamentals: Law and Legal Reasoning

CHAPTER 2
The Legal System: Courts, Civil Procedure, and Alternative Dispute Resolution

CHAPTER 3
Business and the Constitution

CHAPTER 4
Administrative Agencies and Regulatory Process

CHAPTER 5
Law and Business Ethics

Ethics in Practice

CHAPTER 1

Introductory Fundamentals: Law and Legal Reasoning

At the outset of your study of business law you may be harboring thoughts that the subject is narrow and confined to business things. However, if you were to trace your own activities in a given day and then examine how law touches those activities, you just might be astounded. The mattress you sleep on, the toothpaste you use, your morning coffee, orange juice, and breakfast cereal all are examples of products whose safety and goodness are subject to regulation. The content of your morning newspaper, even the advertising, is protected by the First Amendment of the U.S. Constitution. The television and radio stations you tune into are all subject to Federal Communications Commission regulation. The car or bus you take to school is subject to a myriad of laws—licensing, exhaust emission testing, and insurance requirements, for example. If you walk to school, the sidewalk under your feet is likely to have been constructed according to municipal codes, and that same sidewalk's existence may have been made possible by an easement on someone's private property. Whether you think about it or not, your very presence in a business law class itself is a result of your school's performing a legally enforceable contract with you. At any given moment of the day or night, there is a swirl of common law duties all around you—and around everybody else, including businesses.

In fact, in our consumer-oriented society it is difficult to isolate parts of our lives that are untouched by business enterprise in some way. And law touches every aspect of business life. Consequently, while "business law" may sound confined to the law affecting business enterprises, it actually concerns laws that affect you both directly and indirectly at every moment of every day.

We will begin by exploring just what law is.

LAW—IMPOSSIBLE TO DEFINE IN SO MANY WORDS

The word "law" has many meanings, and this word is used variously in different fields. For example, physical science has its law of gravity, and the social science of economics has the law of supply and demand. These examples of "laws" have fairly precise definitions, so precise that they can be expressed by mathematical formulas and numerical graphs.

The same precision is not possible in **jurisprudence**—the scientific study of law. Over the years, legal scholars have offered dozens of definitions of law, but none of them is universally accepted as absolutely definitive. This difficulty in defining law stems from its being an ever changing abstraction. From one culture to another, and even within the same culture, the abstract idea of what law is varies and changes over time.

We get close to the essence of what law is, however, when we view law as a dynamic and evolving system of social control. Law is not a long list of "dos and don'ts." Law is neither our shared morals nor our shared ethics, though both morals and ethics can be found in law. For this reason, it is possible for something to be legal, yet immoral—or moral, yet illegal. As an example, Moslems may think it immoral for a Moslem woman to wear a bikini on a California beach, but the act certainly is not illegal in California. Similarly, a Southeast-Asian immigrant living in Texas may consider it moral to drown himself and his children upon being disgraced by the infidelity of his spouse, but this immigrant's actions are certainly illegal in Texas. In the first case in this book, you will see an example of the relationship of ethics to law—a case in which behavior that you might consider unethical was held legal.

Even though we—as many others before us—cannot fully define the word "law," throughout this book the word "law" will generally refer to the *social results* of an *evolutionary lawmaking process* whereby a *government develops a system of rules and regulations, enforceable by penalties, to control the conduct of its people*. "Business law" refers to those parts of the law most closely connected with business activities.

LAW—DYNAMIC AND PROSPECTIVE

In our legal system, judges perform the crucial task of determining just what the law is as it pertains to disputes before them and then applying that law. This task is extraordinarily difficult today because judges cannot simply make decisions and impose them on the people as a tyrant might. Judges must explain the reasons for their decisions. Judging is also difficult because inherent in every case there is some kind of dispute. This means that day in and day out judges hear only cases in which both parties believe they are on the correct side of the law.

The judge's task is further complicated by the fact that law is *dynamic*, changing according to the cases which come up. No two cases are exactly alike. Newer cases on a particular topic may contain new elements that force judges to rethink and modify an old rule. Thus, in deciding a slightly more complex new case, the judge may develop and apply a *revision* of the old rule. This new rule will stand until a subsequent case is sufficiently different to require further adjustment, or until future judges believe that the policy justifications for the rule are no longer valid.

Law is also *prospective*—forward-looking—because its aim is to help society avoid such disputes in the future and to assist in decision making in future cases. This prospective aspect of law also makes decision making difficult for judges—because, in addition to deciding who wins the present case, they must also consider how their decision will affect the future behavior of people.

To get a firsthand feel for how law is dynamic and prospective, assume that you are the judge in this first case, *Doliner v. Brown*. Do not worry that you do not know about the law yet. This case is, at bottom, about "fairness," the basic notions about which you should already have.

CASE 1.1 **Doliner v. Brown** • 21 Mass. App. 692, 489 N.E. 1036 (1986)

FACTS Doliner was in the process of negotiating with the owners of an apartment house. He was considering purchasing the property and converting the apartments into condominiums. Without obtaining promises of confidentiality, Doliner discussed details of his plans to buy the apartment house with Green and Bendetsen, to secure financing from them. After that meeting, Green and Bendetsen

| CASE 1.1 Continued | met with Brown to persuade Brown to participate in the financing. At about the same time, the owners of the apartment building and Doliner agreed upon a purchase price. However, because Doliner's ability to finance the purchase was still in question, Doliner and the building owners did not complete a sales contract. Brown, instead of participating in Doliner's financing of the purchase, took the opportunity for himself and bought the property. Doliner sued Brown for engaging in an "unfair method of competition" and in an "unfair or deceptive act or practice" prohibited by a Massachusetts statute. |

How would you decide this case if you were the judge? Would you conclude that since Doliner did not have a signed sales contract as the law requires, anyone, including Brown, could buy the apartment house? Or would you instead consider what business would be like if the law permitted everyone to act like Brown? If Doliner was wronged by Brown, should the law step in? Or should the law reinforce the idea that people like Doliner should be more careful in their business dealings? However, if you decide in favor of Brown, aren't you supporting a law which, by requiring a written contract, encourages people to distrust one another? Also, if Brown wins this case, are the law and the courts rewarding people who behave like Brown? On the other hand, if Doliner wins the case, is not the law acting to protect people from their own carelessness? Why should the law protect people who can protect themselves simply by being careful?

Now see what the judges had to say about this case. Before reading their decision, you should be aware that Brown won in the trial court, that Doliner appealed, and that the following opinions are from the higher-level appellate court. Though courts and court systems will be discussed in a later chapter, here you should be aware that the higher-level appellate court that decided this case was comprised of three judges. Below, Judge Kaplan states the view held by the majority of the court, and Judge Brown states how he disagrees with the majority.

| CASE 1.1 Continued

OPINION | KAPLAN, J. . . . As one of the actors in this story put it, Brown "scooped" Doliner. . . . [However], a competitor may "interfere" with another's contractual expectancy by picking the deal off for himself, if, in advancing his own interest, he refrains from employing wrongful means. [The court found that Brown did not commit any wrongful acts such as fraud or deceit.]

The remedy of businessman against businessman [in the statute] may be invoked against an "unfair method of competition," or an "unfair or deceptive act or practice." . . . As to ["unfair method of competition"], Brown was not engaged in any practice considered abusive of, or injurious to competition such as . . . theft of trade secrets. . . . As to ["unfair or deceptive act or practice"], . . . it is recognized that the language is broad enough to take in some reprehensible acts committed in business contexts that elude conventional definitions and categories. The courts are not invited by the statute to punish every departure from "the punctilio of an honor the most sensitive," but they may enforce standards of behavior measurably higher than [deliberate breach of faith and |

**CASE 1.1
Continued**

trust]. They need not necessarily endorse a pattern of behavior because it happens to be current in the market place. . . . The situations have to be sized up one by one. In our view, the present case is outside [the statute] unless we are prepared to say that the statute enacts a rule . . . by which a party is to be barred from competing for a business advantage because he is made aware that another has been exerting himself to the same end. That would be an extravagant rule of law.

JUDGMENT

Affirmed.

DISSENT

BROWN, J. . . . I only wish that the law would aid the needy as assiduously as it does the greedy. Brown did more than sabotage Doliner's contractual expectancy; he "pick[ed] the deal off for himself."

In the real estate game, one never commits fully until the "numbers" have been canvassed fully. Here, the numbers were very clearly set out by Green and Bendetsen during their visit with Brown. . . . No sooner had the two messengers departed than [Brown] rushed to the phone, putting in motion his plan to "scoop" the entire deal. If that is not wrong, . . . then perhaps there is something amiss in the common law and in our statutory scheme.

Fundamental principles of decency and fairness, resplendent in other areas of common law, ought to be recognized here. I disapprove of the view which condones conduct as reprehensible as that exhibited by [Brown] . Ethics and morality do have a place in our economic system. . . .

. . . In this case, I would characterize the totality of [Brown's] conduct as having been infused with a high enough "level of rascality," not only to have raised the plaintiff's eyebrow, but also to have permitted him to recover under the statute.

[The statute] has established in general, for businesses as well as for consumers, a path of conduct higher than that trod by the crowd in the past. It troubles me to see such a substantial deviation from that path.

Notice how the judges struggled to arrive at and support their opinions on what the law should be. Notice too that while neither judge made reference to the future, both expressed concern over the rules which would guide people's future actions.

And notice how this case shows that the law is dynamic: The judges were affecting the law by more tightly figuring out than before what a law meant and how to apply it. The case changed the law a little, if only to make the law just a little clearer. You also can see from this case that law is forward-looking: The judges' opinions revealed their concern with the rule of law and its future effect on society.

The dynamic aspect of law can seem frustrating to the business law student. Sometimes as you read cases later in this book in which a trial court decides one way and a higher court decides the opposite way, you may wonder how one can know the correct answer to a question of law when the judges themselves disagree with one another. After all, judges are experts and students are not. Such seeming frustration, however, is actually a signal that you are at the gateway to the excitement and challenge of legal studies. When you encounter overturned cases and judicial disagreement, you are being invited to enter the fray as well—to use your powers of reason and your judgment. Additionally, judicial decisions are often more than reason, judgment, and application of law—they involve matters of discretion and value judgment, matters in which you too can participate as an onlooker in the process.

The following case presents you with an opportunity to jump in and think how a decision should have come out. The case shows you not only how judges sitting on both high and low courts disagree with one another but also that law possesses dynamic qualities.

CASE 1.2	**Board of Education v. Pico** • 457 U.S. 853, 102 S. Ct. 2799 (1982)
FACTS	While attending a conference supported by a politically conservative association (Parents of New York United), several members of the Island Trees Board of Education acquired lists of books characterized by the association as "objectionable" and "improper . . . for school students." The Board of Education later determined that eleven books on those lists (books such as *Slaughterhouse Five*, by Kurt Vonnegut, Jr., *The Naked Ape*, by Desmond Morris, *A Hero Ain't Nothin' But a Sandwich*, by Alice Childress, and *Soul on Ice*, by Eldridge Cleaver) were in its school libraries. Having characterized the books as "anti-American, anti-Christian, anti-Semitic, and just plain filthy," the Board decided to remove nine of those eleven books from the library, and to make one book, *Black Boy*, by Richard Wright, available only with parental approval. One book, *Laughing Boy*, by Oliver LaFarge, was later returned to the library. Some students sued the Board of Education seeking injunctive relief to stop the Board from carrying out the book removal, arguing that the Board's decision violated their free speech right to receive information as protected under the First Amendment of the U.S. Constitution.
RESULT AT TRIAL COURT	The District Court granted a summary judgment, a ruling that no trial is necessary, in favor of the Board of Education, stating that First Amendment rights were not violated and that the Board of Education's orders "restricted access only to certain books which [the Board] believed to be . . . vulgar."
RESULT ON APPEAL TO THE SECOND CIRCUIT	By a 2-to-1 majority, the federal Appeals Court for the Second Circuit reversed the decision of the trial court. This majority concluded that the Board of Education had not offered enough justification for its action to remove the books. One member of the majority saw the case as "turning on the contested factual issue of whether [the decision of the Board to remove the books] was motivated by a justifiable desire to remove books containing vulgarities and sexual explicitness, or rather by an impermissible desire to suppress ideas."
RESULT ON APPEAL TO THE U.S. SUPREME COURT	The high court upheld the Second Circuit Court's reversal, but rendered no opinion. Though a majority of justices supported the circuit court's ruling against the Board of Education, there was no Supreme Court majority as to the *reasons* for reversing the lower court. A plurality of justices (Brennan, Marshall, Stevens, and, in part, Blackmun) joined in one opinion, stating: "We are therefore in full agreement with [the Board of Education] that local school boards must be permitted 'to establish and

CASE 1.2 Continued

apply their curriculum in such a way as to transmit community values.' . . . At the same time, however, we have necessarily recognized that the discretion of [school boards] must be exercised in a manner that comports with the transcendent imperatives of the First Amendment. . . .[I]n sum, students do not 'shed their rights to freedom of speech or expression at the schoolhouse gate. . . . [T]he right to receive ideas is a necessary predicate to the *recipient's* meaningful exercise of his own rights of speech, press, and political freedom. . . . [W]e hold that local school boards may not remove books from the school library shelves simply because they dislike the ideas contained in those books and seek by their removal to 'prescribe what shall be orthodox in politics, nationalism, religion, or other matters of opinion.'"

Justice White concurred in the judgment (i.e., agreed that the lower court's decision should be reversed), but did not agree with the plurality's reasoning. According to Justice White, "[This] Court seems compelled to go further and issue a dissertation on the extent to which the First Amendment limits the discretion of the school board to remove books from the school library. I see no necessity for doing so at this point."

The four remaining Justices (Burger, Chief Justice, and Powell, Rehnquist, and O'Connor) dissented, stating: "The First Amendment . . . must deal with new problems in a changing world. . . . Were [the plurality's decision] to become law, this Court would come perilously close to becoming a 'super censor' of school board library decisions. . . . No amount of 'limiting' language could rein in the sweeping 'right' the plurality would create. . . . In essence, the plurality's view transforms the availability of the 'optional' reading into a 'right' to have this 'optional' reading maintained at the demand of teenagers. . . . According to the plurality, the evil to be avoided is the 'official suppression of ideas.' It does not follow that the decision to *remove* a book is less [of an] 'official suppression' than the decision not to acquire a book desired by someone. Similarly, a decision to eliminate certain material from the curriculum, history, for example, would carry an equal—probably greater—prospect of 'official suppression.' Would the decision be subject to our review?"

In this case, notice that the Supreme Court justices were split 4-1-4. Four of them agreed on both the judgment and the reasons for the judgment. One justice agreed with the judgment, but disagreed with the first four as to reasons. The remaining four justices disagreed with the first four on both the judgment and the reasons. Consequently, all that can be said from this case by itself is that only the judgment carries agreement from a majority (4 plus 1) of nine justices.

The *Pico* case was an extraordinarily difficult one to decide, and because the Supreme Court justices could not agree, the situation leaves lower courts with unclear guidance on how to decide future, similar cases. This lack of clarity, however, does not mean that law and court decisions are matters of mere whim. Clarity may evolve in later cases. All the while, courts must grapple with tough issues about which reasonable people can disagree, and those courts are forced to make judgments. As in the *Pico* case, the coherent reasoning behind those judgments may be put off until a later case emerges which allows the Supreme Court to revisit the issues. Additionally, the practice of a court to delay hammering out its disagreements among justices has an efficiency dimension. Without such a practice, the U.S. Supreme Court would decide far fewer cases and hence deny others access to this high court in favor of just a few tough cases.

BUSINESS LAW—A NEW AND DIFFERENT WAY OF REASONING

In law, as in most serious studies, the basic aims are first to understand and then to predict. If law were just a large collection of fixed social rules, we would merely have to look them up and mechanically apply them. However, remember that law is ever changing and forward-looking. Accordingly, your study of business law is aimed in part at helping you deal with the evolution of law and to anticipate—to predict—how questions of law may be decided in the future. The late U.S. Chief Justice Oliver Wendell Holmes, Jr., asserted that law is what the courts *will* do, not what they have done.

So, at this early point of your adventure into business law studies, you should equip yourself with tools of legal reasoning that will help you predict what the courts will do, and hence what the law will be.

Legal Reasoning—Case Reasoning and Statutory Interpretation

Legal reasoning is an unusual kind of reasoning—so unusual that nearly four centuries ago, England's Chief Justice Edward Coke had a heated dispute with King James I on whether the king himself could make court judgments. James I asserted that law was based on reason, and that he could reason as well as a judge. At the risk of his neck, Coke argued that although the king was a very smart fellow, he didn't know the laws of England and, moreover, the king had only the ability to apply "natural" reason. Coke contended that legal cases "are not to be decided by natural Reason but by the artificial Reason and Judgment of Law. . . ."[1] In the end, Coke kept his neck and head, and the notion of "artificial" reasoning lives on with us in legal reasoning today.

To get to the basics of legal reasoning and its built-in artificiality, one first has to accept the false assumption that "law is a system of known rules applied by a judge[.]"[2] For a variety of reasons, however, the rules cannot really be known. Here, we will discuss two of those reasons.

First is the inadequacy of language—the inescapable imprecision and ambiguity in words and sentences. Whether the words of law are created by a legislature such as the U.S. Congress or a city council or by judges in their case opinions or by any other lawmaker, they are subject to interpretation in any next future case in which a judge has to figure out just what those words mean.

Second, some law is new or at least has never been written down before. For example, in 1991 the "reasonable woman" standard in sexual harassment cases was first stated. Throughout the history of American and British common law, judges had used the "reasonable man" standard whenever "reasonableness" was in question. Now, in sexual harassment cases, and perhaps in other types of cases in the future, conduct considered "reasonable" to a man might not be considered "reasonable" to a woman—hence, the new "reasonable woman" standard. Although this standard is new, it carries the force of law in some 1991 cases as if it had always been there. Judges invented it because a new type of case could not be resolved without it.

Once you get beyond the make-believe that legal rules are fixed and unchangeable, and can recognize that legal rules develop over time to meet changing conditions, then legal reasoning loses much of its mystery. To understand legal reasoning, one basically has to recognize that legal reasoning is done case by case and employs a rudimentary three-step process.

Step 1. The current case is compared with at least one previous similar case.

Step 2. The previous case or cases are analyzed for the rules found in them, and those rules are restated and perhaps adapted a bit to meet new conditions.

Step 3. The rules, as previously stated in earlier cases or as revised, are then applied to the current case.

---

[1] For an account of the dispute between James I and Edward Coke, see Catherine Drinker Bowen, THE LION AND THE THRONE (1957), pp. 291–306.

[2] This quote and the following discussion are adapted from Edward H. Levy, AN INTRODUCTION TO LEGAL REASONING (1949), pp. 1–7.

> **BOX 1.1**
>
> ### Points to Consider
>
> Some of the persons sitting on the U.S. Supreme Court when *Pico* was decided are no longer on the Court. If a similar case were to come before the U.S. Supreme Court today, would you predict a similar outcome? Would you feel more comfortable in your prediction if you knew how the new justices think about such issues? Are there more things you would want to know before making a prediction?
>
> One useful technique in legal analysis is to look at how the U.S. Supreme Court itself views a particular case. Since the time that *Board of Education v. Pico* was decided, Supreme Court justices and the majority of the Court have referred several times to the *Pico* case in supporting their opinions for other decisions. As they do, the meaning of *Pico* gets clearer; the case itself and the law evolve. Here is a sampling—in chronological order—of what *Pico* has been taken to stand for.
>
> - Recognition that "the First Amendment rights of speech and association extend also to high school students." *Bender v. Williamsport Area School District*, 475 U.S. 534, 556, 106 S. Ct. 1326, 1339 (1986) (from Justice Powell's dissenting opinion).
> - A split case in which "all Members of the Court, otherwise sharply divided, acknowledged that the school board has the authority to remove books that are vulgar." *Bethel School District v. Fraser*, 478 U.S. 675, 684, 106 S. Ct. 3159, 3165 (1986) (from majority opinion).
> - Recognition that "the discretion of the States and local school boards in matters of education must be exercised in a manner that comports with the transcendent imperatives of the First Amendment." *Edwards v. Aguillard*, 482 U.S. 578, 583, 107 S. Ct. 2573, 2577 (1987) (majority opinion).
> - Acknowledgment "that public schools are vitally important 'in the preparation of individuals for participation as citizens,' and as vehicles for 'inculcating fundamental values necessary to the maintenance of a democratic political system.'" *Westside Community Schools v. Mergens*, 496 U.S. 226, 265, 110 S. Ct. 2356, ____ (1990) ∎

This three-step process gives effect to the concept of **stare decisis**—the legal concept that similar cases should be treated similarly. Notice that the concept is not that like cases should be treated alike. Because every legal case is different, there is no such thing as a case that is exactly like another. However, the three-step process of *stare decisis* does provide society with some great measure of predictability. The more similar a new case is to an earlier one, the more likely the outcomes will be similar and the new outcome predictable.

This rudimentary three-step process is at the core of what is called **case reasoning.** However, the underlying simplicity of case reasoning can cause difficulty. Given the vast body of existing case law, each side of a dispute usually can find cases that are factually similar to the dispute at hand and whose outcomes are favorable to its own side. To influence the judge and win the case, each side of the dispute will attempt to show that the other side's supporting cases are not really similar to the case being litigated; that is, case reasoning entails "distinguishing" previous cases. As in seeking out cases for their similarity, demonstrating that a case is dissimilar to the current dispute involves analyzing the facts and conditions of the previous case.

Moore v. City of East Cleveland, which appears later in this chapter, shows how judges look to previous cases, decide whether those cases apply, and then use other reasoning as well to arrive at a conclusion of law.

However, case reasoning is not all that is involved in legal reasoning. What happens when a judge has to decide a case involving a topic

> **BOX 1.2**
>
> ## New Law Evolves—The Example of the "Reasonable Woman" Standard
>
> The "reasonable man" standard, used for centuries in the British and American common law and in the interpretation of statutes containing the word "reasonable," now has a new wrinkle.
>
> Within four days of each other in early 1991, two decisions involving complaints of workplace sexual harassment* abandoned application of the "reasonable man standard," one that looks supposedly at the conduct of a reasonable person, and applied a "reasonable woman" standard for the first time.
>
> This new standard offers legal recognition that "conduct that many men consider unobjectionable may offend many women"† and be a significant contributing factor in making a "hostile environment" in the workplace. These new cases analyzed sexual harassment from the victim's perspective and acknowledged that some activities that could be viewed reasonable to a man (such as off-color joke telling and compliments on physical attributes) might not be so "reasonable" to a woman.
>
> Feminist critics of the law argue that many of the abstract rules and principles in the law are gender-biased in favor of males, and applauded the creation of the "reasonable woman" standard.
>
> Thorny issues, however, are likely to emerge in judicial application of the "reasonable woman" standard to other laws involving sexual harassment. For example, in April of 1992 a House committee of the Illinois legislature rejected a bill that would have amended that state's Human Rights Act to include a "reasonable woman" standard in sexual harassment cases. The committee chose to maintain the law's current language, which calls for a "reasonable person" standard. Does this mean that a judge in a future case involving this Illinois law cannot apply a "reasonable woman" standard because Illinois legislators specifically rejected it?
>
> Another thorny issue is likely to emerge as well. The rationale behind the "reasonable woman" standard rests on the general view that men find various kinds of conduct (such as jokes and appraisal of body parts) as less objectionable than women do. Does this mean that men will have tougher standards to meet in order to assert workplace sexual harassment against them? After all, women possess the capacity to be sexually harassing as well. Would this mean that women can tell off-color jokes to men without its contributing to a hostile work environment, but men cannot do the same with women? When a court looks at sexual harassment from the victim's perspective, is it fair to apply different standards depending upon gender?
>
> *Robinson v. Jacksonville Shipyards, Inc.*, 760 F. Supp. 1486 (1991), and *Ellison v. Brady*, 924 F.2d 872 (9th Cir. 1991). Though *Robinson* was decided first, *Ellison* is considered the leading case.
>
> †*Ellison v. Brady*, 924 F.2d 872, 878 (9th Cir. 1991).

the courts have never ruled on before, or must apply a statute that the courts have never applied before? This kind of case is called a **case of first impression.** Judges are not permitted simply to make up new law on a whim. They have to develop a rational basis for their decisions. For judge-made law on new topics, the reasoning resembles the three-step process involved in the application of *stare decisis*. What is different is that in making new law, the judges look at and analyze related areas of law, social customs, traditions, and social policies, and then arrive at a conclusion. When you read the case *Moore v. City of East Cleveland*, you will see how the judges found "law" in American traditions and history regarding the sanctity of the family.

This leaves the final basic element of legal reasoning—**statutory interpretation.** Before judges decide how to apply a statute, they must first decide what the statute means. Like case reasoning, statutory interpretation is simple to describe but can become complex in a real case. At its core, statutory interpretation addresses the question: What does this law mean?

As an example of the apparent simplicity but actual complexity of interpreting a statute, let's say that a dormitory rule states "No overnight guests." This seems fairly clear. However, you don't have to stretch your imagination very far to see that this rule requires interpretation. Suppose that you are on the dormitory disciplinary board. How do you apply the rule to a situation in which a friend visits a person in the dorm and the two people chat from 10 p.m. to 5:30 a.m. just before daybreak, when the visitor goes home to go to bed? Somehow, you will have to define what "overnight" means. Or a dorm resident and a student from a nearby dormitory work on a class project all night in the dorm lounge after the library has closed. How do you apply the rule, or do you apply it at all? The answer depends upon how you define "guest."

Judges have five basic tools for interpreting statutes. In the dormitory example, you used the first tool when you considered what the words "No overnight guests" meant in plain language. This first tool is called the **plain meaning rule.** When judges use it, they give the words of the statute their ordinary meaning and do not look for hidden or unusual meanings. For many kinds of statutes, the plain meaning rule is enough. For example, a city ordinance which states "No Smoking in Municipal Buildings" probably does not require much analysis beyond its plain meaning—what the words reveal to ordinary, reasonable people.

The second tool of statutory interpretation is to view a statute in light of its **legislative history.** Looking into the legislative history behind a rule helps a person resolve ambiguities. In our dormitory example involving the two students in an all-night study session, you might analyze what was behind the making of the rule to determine the meaning of "guest." To do so, you might use a source such as the minutes of the dormitory council that made the rules. Those minutes might reveal one of two things. First, if the council discussed the rule's language, there might exist in the record some clarification about who is considered a "guest." Second, even if the minutes don't discuss the wording of the rule, there still might be indications of what purpose the rule is supposed to accomplish. If, for example, you found that the purpose of the rule was to promote an educational atmosphere in the dorm, you might conclude that a person not from the dorm but working on a school project is not a "guest."

So it is with analyzing legislative history in law. Instead of dormitory minutes, the sources of the history behind the law include previous but rejected drafts of bills, congressional committee hearings, legislative debates, joint committee reports on conflicting versions of a bill, and other related but defeated legislative bills—anything official that aids in understanding a specific statute. Moreover, as with the all-night dormitory example, the history can be employed two ways: first to determine the **intent** of the rule and second to determine the **purpose** of the rule. This is not double-speak; these words (intent and purpose) do not mean the same thing. To analyze legislative *intent* is to determine what ideas the lawmaking body intended its words to communicate. To analyze legislative *purpose* is to ferret out what overall purposes, goals, or aims the legislation is to serve. Say, for example, an ordinance prohibits "vehicles" in public parks. A child's tricycle is certainly a "vehicle" within the plain meaning of the word. But did the City Council intend for the police to arrest kids riding trikes in the park? Surely this was not the council's *intent*. A look to the *purpose* behind the ordinance would likely reveal that the rule was to promote pedestrian safety and tranquillity in public parks, and hence, as the legislative purpose shows, a tricycle is not a "vehicle" within the meaning of the ordinance. In the case *Moore v. City of East Cleveland*, which follows this section, you will see how a court defines "family."

The third tool of statutory interpretation is **previous interpretations** made by courts in earlier decisions. This tool is basically like case reasoning discussed earlier. So that similar cases are decided similarly, previous interpretation serves as a tool not only to understand the meaning of a statute but also to promote stability and predictability of the law. The fact that a previous interpretation exists, however, does not necessarily mean that the court must follow it. For example, a higher appellate court is not bound to follow an interpretation from a lower court. Chapter 2, which discusses the courts, will address the relationships of courts with one another.

The fourth tool is **public policy.** Not to be confused with the legislative *purpose* of a specific statute, public policy is a general concept which encompasses widely acknowledged notions on what is good for society. While public policy is a useful tool for judges, it is equally useful for you to understand law better by appreciating the underlying policy rationale. For example, a longstanding public policy is that our society should provide equal employment opportunity to everyone, regardless of race, creed, national origin, gender, and age. Imagine, however, that the actress Madonna tries out for the part of Martin Luther King, Jr., in a movie-length docudrama, and the producer refuses to consider her because of her gender, age, and race. If Madonna subsequently sues, a court would be forced to look into whether Madonna's situation falls within the law's exceptions and whether such exceptions are consistent with public policy. In this make-believe example, a court would likely find that the public policy discouraging discrimination would lead to bizarre, socially undesirable results if applied to this particular employment situation.

The final tool is a body of **principles of interpretation.** These principles are fairly technical and are largely beyond the scope of this book. An example of one such principle, however, is the so-called constructive "and." Suppose a statute says, "Nudity or obscene conduct is prohibited on state-owned beaches." In applying this statute to conduct occurring on the beach, a court would interpret (construe) the word "or" to mean "and." Thus, "or" takes on the law-imposed (constructive) meaning of "and." Why are such verbal contortions necessary? If the word "or" were construed only to prohibit either nudity or obscene conduct, then presumably a person would not be violating the law by doing both prohibited acts at once. To prevent this probably unintended result, the courts simply read "or" as meaning "and."

Many of the elements of legal reasoning are present in the following case. When you read it, look in particular for the court's case reasoning and how the court treats and distinguishes previous statutory interpretations, employs *stare decisis,* looks to the statutory purpose and goals, and then considers an overriding public policy—the sanctity of the family—all to arrive at a single judgment of law.

CASE 1.3   Moore v. City of East Cleveland • 431 U.S. 494, 97 S. Ct. 1932(1977)

FACTS   Mrs. Inez Moore lived in public housing in East Cleveland along with her son, Dale Moore, Sr., and her two grandsons, Dale Moore, Jr. and John Moore. John Moore was not Dale Moore's son; he was his nephew who took residence in Mrs. Moore's apartment after his mother died.

The City of East Cleveland filed criminal charges against Mrs. Moore for keeping an "illegal occupant" (John Moore) in her apartment after Mrs. Moore received notice of violation and failed to remove her grandson from the premises.

At trial court, Mrs. Moore's lawyer filed a motion to dismiss the charges against her on the grounds that the city's ordinance which classified her grandson as an "illegal occupant" was unconstitutional. The trial court overruled her motion, and she was subsequently convicted and sentenced to five days in jail and a $25 fine. The Ohio Court of Appeals affirmed the trial court's judgment.

CASE 1.3 Continued	The Ohio Supreme Court denied review of the case. Five years later the U.S. Supreme Court heard this case on appeal.
OPINION	Justices POWELL, BRENNAN, MARSHALL and BLACKMUN. . . . The city [of East Cleveland] argues that our decision in *Village of Belle Terre v. Borass* [a case which upheld an ordinance forbidding illegal occupants] requires us to sustain the ordinance attacked here. . . . But one overriding factor sets this case apart from *Belle Terre*. The ordinance there affected only *unrelated* individuals. It expressly allowed all who were related by "blood, adoption, or marriage" to live together. . . . East Cleveland, in contrast, has chosen to regulate the occupancy of its housing by slicing deeply into the family itself. This is no mere incidental result of the ordinance. On its face it selects certain categories of relatives who may live together and declares that others may not. In particular, it makes a crime of a grandmother's choice to live with her grandson in circumstances like those presented here. A host of cases, tracing their lineage to *Meyer v. Nebraska* (1923) and *Pierce v. Society of Sisters* (1925), have consistently acknowledged a "private realm of family life which the state cannot enter." Of course, the family is not beyond regulation. But when the government intrudes on choices concerning family living arrangements, this Court must examine carefully the importance of the governmental interests advanced and the extent to which they are served by the challenged regulation. When thus examined, [the East Cleveland] ordinance cannot survive. The city seeks to justify it as a means of preventing overcrowding, minimizing traffic and parking congestion, and avoiding an undue burden on . . . the school system. Although these are legitimate goals, the ordinance before us serves them marginally, at best. For example, . . . [t]he ordinance would permit a grandmother to live with a single dependent son and children, even if his school-age children number a dozen, yet it forces Mrs. Moore to find another dwelling for her grandson John. . . . We need not labor the point. [East Cleveland's] ordinance has but a tenuous relation to alleviation of the conditions mentioned by the city. The city would distinguish the cases [we rely here upon]. [The city] points out that none of [the cases] "gives grandmothers any fundamental rights with respect to grandsons," and suggests that any constitutional right to live together as a family extends only to the nuclear family—essentially a couple and its dependent children. Our decisions establish that the Constitution protects the sanctity of the family precisely because the institution of the family is deeply rooted in this Nation's history and tradition. It is through the family that we inculcate and pass down many of our most cherished values, moral and cultural. Ours is by no means a tradition limited to respect for the bonds uniting the members of the nuclear family. The tradition of uncles, aunts, cousins and especially grandparents sharing a household along with parents and children has roots equally venerable and equally deserving of constitutional recognition. . . . Even if conditions of modern society have brought about a decline in extended family households, they have not erased the accumulated wisdom of civilization,

> **CASE 1.3 Continued**
>
> gained over the centuries and honored throughout our history, that supports a larger conception of the family. . . . Especially in times of adversity, such as the death of a spouse or economic need, the broader family has tended to come together for mutual sustenance and to maintain or rebuild a secure home life.
>
> [T]he Constitution prevents East Cleveland from standardizing its children—and its adults—by forcing all to live in certain narrowly defined family patterns.
>
> **JUDGMENT** Reversed.

Legal Philosophies

There is still more to legal reasoning than the application of the reasoning tools we have discussed so far. In American law today there are several schools of legal philosophy, all operating at once and shaping the direction of developments and trends in law. Since one of the basic purposes of studying law is to enhance your ability to predict what the law will be and how judges will decide cases, we now discuss five of the most influential schools of legal philosophy plus one emerging school of legal philosophy which may be influential in the future.

The Legal Positivist School. The name of the legal positivist school derives from what is called "positive law," defined as commands of a sovereign. In the United States, commands (or rules) of a sovereign come principally, but not exclusively, from executive orders, legislation, court opinions, and administrative bodies. Legal positivism has been the most dominant philosophy for the last two centuries. What distinguishes this school from others is that its proponents believe that the legal is completely separate from the moral. Perhaps you have heard the anecdote about the exasperated loser in a court case who exclaimed to the judge, "Your honor! Is there no justice in this court?" To which the judge replied, "If you came here for justice, you came to the wrong place." Behind this anecdote is legal positivist philosophy—"Law is law, whether it is just or not."

The Natural Law School. The name of this school comes from what is known as "natural law," defined as law derived from nature, encompassing both secular and nonsecular concepts of nature. The chief distinguishing characteristic of the natural law school is the underlying view that *law is discovered*—from nature or from divine sources. As you can discern, this legal philosophy recognizes a moral component in law. You can easily find natural law underpinnings in the founding of the United States and in the U.S. Constitution. For example, the Declaration of Independence begins with "We hold these truths to be self-evident, that all Men are created equal, that they are endowed by their Creator with certain unalienable Rights, that among these are Life, Liberty, and the Pursuit of Happiness. . . ." Notice that man's "unalienable Rights" were said to come from a divine source. In the U.S. Constitution, the source of "property" rights is the natural law notion that a person's labor when combined with natural resources (e.g., land) creates property which the state is obliged to protect. In contemporary society, we see natural law notions having substantial influence, as in the ongoing pro-life vs. pro-choice struggles in the courts and in the legislatures. Also, during the 1991 confirmation hearings of then Supreme Court Justice-designate Clarence Thomas, U.S. senators inquired extensively on his adherence to natural law philosophy.

The Legal Realist School. The legal realist school of legal philosophy is perhaps the most difficult to describe briefly because the label "legal realist" covers a broad range of almost contradictory philosophies. What the legal realists appear to share is a belief that previous schools of jurisprudence had scarcely any basis in "reality," hence the name "legal realism" for the school of jurisprudence that would change all that. The legal realists also appear to agree that law, as expressed in court opinions, does not come from logic. Some of the legal realists focus on what courts and officials actually do rather than upon what the law says—looking at past legal cases and their outcomes to serve as data to assist prediction on how future cases will come out but that past legal cases do not dictate future outcomes. Yet other legal realists assert that all kinds of extraneous psychological and physical influences (including what a judge ate for breakfast) go into a judicial decision.

While the legal realism movement died out in the 1930s, its influence is pervasively present today. The drafting of the Uniform Commercial Code, which you will study later in this course, was overseen by a noted legal realist, Karl Llewellyn, who coincidentally preferred to call legal realism a movement, not a school.

The Chicago School. Arguably an offshoot of the legal realists by virtue of its attention to what courts and officials actually do, the Chicago school applies the social science of economics to the study of law. As its name suggests, the originating work of this school of legal philosophy grew out of interdisciplinary studies in law and economics studies at the University of Chicago. What distinguishes this school from others is that it attempts to explain and to predict law in economic terms. The Chicago school has had considerable recent influence, particularly in securities law, antitrust law, and employment law. Critics of the Chicago school charge that the school's emphasis on economic efficiency is, at best, descriptive and explanatory of law but is not normative (that is, what the law *should* be).

Sociological Jurisprudence and the Historical School. This category of legal philosophy overlaps with legal realism. In fact, some of the sociological jurisprudents are also labeled as legal realists, Roscoe Pound and Karl Llewellyn being among the most notable. What distinguishes this category from others and gives the category its name is its view that sources of law are derived from such things as customs and traditions and that law can be explained by social conditions and history. Though this category of jurisprudence has been more influential in Europe, its influence can also be seen in the United States. Recall from earlier in this chapter that in the case *Moore v. City of East Cleveland*, the court opinion relied heavily upon sociological considerations such as the American traditions and customs of extended families' living together especially in times of adversity. The influence of this school is also seen in the Uniform Commercial Code, which you will study in later chapters devoted to sales.

The Critical Legal Studies School. Also known as CRITS, this school gets its name because of its critical analysis of law. Rejecting the proposition that law is objective and neutral, this school challenges the underpinnings not only of law but also of legal education. Generally speaking, this group sees law as a deceptive social mechanism for the preservation of power of those who have it and that law and law training, in themselves, are sources of social conditioning which act to perpetuate the values and interests of existing power groups. While today many observers see the CRITS at the fringe of jurisprudence, the CRITS have considerable presence in some elite law schools, notably Harvard, and their influence may grow as they and their students assume positions of prominence and authority.

Following is an essay by Professor David E. Van Zandt of Northwestern University, School of Law about what goes into a judge's decision. Notice that the four-century-old argument about legal reasoning between James I and Chief Justice Coke still lingers. The author appears to take James I's side of the reasoning argument. You "judge" for yourself.

How Do Judges Think?*

How do judges think? My short answer is: just like everybody else. While that answer may seem obvious, legal scholars have expended much effort on the question. The question is important because the results of judges' thinking—judicial decisions—can change people's lives. . . .

Given the importance of the questions and the amount of attention it has received, one might think that judges' reasoning processes have received careful empirical analysis. Unfortunately, that is not so. While there have been good studies of the decision making of that other important decision maker—the jury—similar empirical studies of how judges reach their decisions are few. The main reason is access: judges are busy public officials.

So, it is not surprising that most studies of judicial reasoning have been based only on the judge's written decisions or on the author's own experience as a judge's law clerk or, in some cases, as a judge. The studies must piece together the picture of judicial reasoning using a good deal of imagination.

These efforts have led to four distinct models of judicial reasoning. . . .

The first model, the "legal science" or the "legal formalist" model asserts that a judge reasons like an idealized scientist. When faced with a decision, a judge first reviews all the prior cases similar to the case at hand. From the results of those cases and the reasoning in the written decisions, he or she works out a general principle from which each of the results in those cases can be derived. The general principle is then applied to the facts of the case at hand. A good written decision is an accurate, if truncated, description of the process of reasoning.

This model of reasoning is called legal science because the judge (or legal scholar) treats prior written decisions as the empirical evidence that he or she manipulates to yield general principles. . . . The judge is merely a good scientist who discovers the principle contained in the cases, not the creator of it. The term "science" is used here in a very old-fashioned way. The science is normative and moral. . . .

The second model, pressed by the pragmatists and legal realists . . . , stands this aspect of the legal science approach on its head. It suggests that a judge surveys all the facts . . . and decides which party should win. This decision is attributed variously to the political philosophy, psychology, social or economic class, or even the breakfast menu of the judge. In one famous account written by a sitting judge, the decision was said to be the product of a "hunch." Having reached that decision, the judge then writes an opinion to defend the result. The written opinion may or may not reflect the true reasons for the decision. It does, however, follow the convention of asserting that the result follows from some general legal rule accepted by most people. But the actual decision precedes this defense and is not affected by it. . . .

A more recent model, called "analogical reasoning," is a product of the legal process school which flourished in the 1950s and 1960s. It is probably the model that most lawyers would identify as most descriptive of good legal reasoning, no doubt in part because their law teachers and casebooks were heavily influenced

Continued

(and former Attorney General) Edward Levi: "[Legal reasoning is] reasoning from case to case." The judge first finds a prior case that has factual similarities to the case at hand. He then identifies the rule of law inherent in the first case. That rule is then modified to apply to the case at hand. The crux of the method is establishing and defending factual analogies between cases....

In a popular, current model of judicial reasoning that seems to meld both the realist and the analogical approach, some legal scholars have appealed to the idea of "practical reason" as a model for judicial reasoning. Leaning on Aristotle's distinction between theoretical and practical reason, this view suggests that a judge must evaluate a case in its context. The judge must both sympathetically understand the opposing litigants' positions and evaluate them with detachment. A good decision is one that balances the particulars of a case with more abstract principles....

All of these models may seem somewhat mysterious to the layperson. That is because they all assert that judges employ a method of reasoning different from what ordinary people seem to use. While law schools would be delighted if that were so, we should prefer a more parsimonious explanation.

My own view is that the reasoning processes that judges employ are no different from those we all use everyday. Our goal in reasoning about practical problems is to produce useful information in the most cost-effective way to assist us in achieving our desires. We rarely "reinvent the wheel" through systematic investigation and analysis; instead we rely on our stock of knowledge, that collection of moral and empirical information about the world that we have developed from our past experiences....

Judges are no different. They are under great pressures to make decisions quickly; they do not have the luxury of systematic analysis that most of the models ... suggest. Instead, judges resort to their own stock of knowledge.... When faced with a case, they tend to base their decisions on the knowledge which they share with the rest of us—unless there are good reasons to dig further or to rethink an issue. A reason why judges would follow the ruling in a prior case is that, absent other good reasons, they have no reason to rethink a result that other judges have reached in the past....

As we all know, common sense works well in some cases, but fails miserably in others. Because judges' reasoning is simply human reason applied in the legal sphere, we should not expect it to have a higher success rate.*

*Reprinted with permission of Professor David E. Van Zandt, Northwestern University, School of Law. This article appeared in January 1992 in *Perspectives on the Professions*, a publication of the Center for the Study of Ethics in the Professions, Illinois Institute of Technology, Chicago.

NEW CONCEPTS, WORDS, AND MEANINGS

Though the days of lawyers and judges using obscure Latin and Greek terms are far behind us, the language of law still carries terms that can befuddle the ordinary person.

By the time you reach the end of this book, you will have encountered Latin phrases such as *res ipsa loquitur* and *respondeat superior*, which remain in the legal vocabulary. You will also encounter English terms such as "promissory estoppel" and "assignee," which don't easily roll off the tongue. Moreover, such common-sounding words as "tort," "tenancy," and "consideration" have legal meanings somewhat or greatly different from their commonplace day-to-day meanings. But don't panic. These legal terms are attached to important legal concepts, and should be fairly easy to remember.

At this point, you might be harboring a question—that is, "Why not just use plain English?" Our response to you is that we will indeed use plain English—along with the legal terms. However, you will likely discover that legal language is actually a handy and speedy shorthand to capture concepts that would otherwise require many more words to describe. In this section, we are going to introduce a few basic terms and their accompanying concepts that you will need for the remainder of the course.

Common Law and Equity

To appreciate the terms **common law** and **equity,** we have to go back in history almost a thousand years. After the Norman invasion of England in 1066, William the Conqueror and his successors moved rapidly to unite the country under one rule. Under William, the King's Court developed into a system of separate royal courts spread throughout England. In this system, the important court decisions were written down in a format that lives in the law today. Like the cases you have already seen in this chapter, these ancient case opinions set out the key facts, the issues of law, the decision, and its rationale.

At first the judges' rulings on a particular topic differed from court to court. Eventually, however, the judges began harmonizing their opinions with those of other judges to achieve the degree of uniformity needed for a national law. Indeed, as the cases accumulated, they became a body of law accepted throughout England, common to everyone—hence, the term *common law.* The legal principles in these cases were not orders from the king, nor were they statutes imposed by a legislature. The common law evolved case by case and was made by judges.

However, there was a problem with the common law. As individual court decisions amassed, they more finely defined various legal principles. Those legal principles, in turn, became increasingly rigid in their application to specific cases. The resulting inflexible application of legal principles began to produce unfair and unjust outcomes, causing the people to be dissatisfied with the royal courts. Moreover, the common law remedies (the relief the courts could order) were limited to the recovery of land, personal property, and money damages.

The rigidity of the common law system and the inadequacy of its remedies led to the development of a supplemental court of *equity* whose origins date back to 1270. In response to the dissatisfaction of the people, the king turned their complaints over to a high church official called the chancellor. Where appropriate, the chancellor fashioned so-called extraordinary remedies for special cases that the common law system was not handling well. Eventually, the chancellor's case-by-case approach became formalized and evolved into a separate court of chancery under a special judge called a "chancellor in equity." This special judge and, later, justices of the chancery court could ignore the rigid, unfair common law rules. As would be expected of officials who derived their authority from the church, they could and did apply their own "discretion," their "sense of justice" and "conscience" to the cases before them to produce a fair result. These "courts of equity" developed remedies beyond recovery of property or damages. For example, by means of the **injunction,** they ordered people to refrain from doing harmful acts to others; by means of the equitable remedy of **specific performance,** they required people to actually perform their contracts instead of forcing the other person to sue for inadequate money damages. These and other "extraordinary" remedies are an important part of the modern law.

Before the founding of the United States, the British colonists brought the *common law* and *equity* with them and employed the British system in colonial courts. Later, the U.S. Constitution, adopted in 1787, recognized both common law and equity in Article III. Today, common law and equity are the foundations of our state law.

In the old days, common law courts and courts of equity (chancery courts) were completely separate. Today, lawsuits in common law and in equity are heard in the same court and are decided by the same judge. Yet the philosophic distinction between common law and equity remains very much alive, as you will understand later in this course, particularly when you study contracts.

Today, whether one sues another on the basis of the common law or in equity depends chiefly upon the remedy sought. If the person suing seeks money damages or recovery of land or other property, the judge will apply the common law. If the person suing seeks an "extraordinary" remedy such as an injunction or the specific performance of a contract, the case will be heard in equity. If both types of remedies are pursued, the case will be heard in both the common law and equity, and in the United States the case will be heard in the same court by the same judge.

Public Law and Private Law

Immediately, you are probably struck with the question: Isn't all law public law? In the sense that law is available to everyone, all law is indeed public. However, to lawyers public law and private law are two quite different things.

Public law deals with the organization of government and with its relation to the people. This category of law includes **constitutional law** (law which sets out the plan and method by which government conducts the public's business), **administrative law** (law controlling the regulatory activities of government agencies like the Federal Trade Commission, and law created by such agencies), and **criminal law** (law relating to offenses against the state). Each of these three subcategories of public law has an entire chapter devoted to it later in this book.

Private law deals with the legal relationships among private persons and organizations. Of the many subcategories of private law, four are basic and important in the study of business law:

1 The *law of contracts*. This area of law is concerned with the rights and duties arising out of promises which the law will recognize and will enforce.

2 The *law of property*. Fundamental to the allocation of resources in our society, this area of law deals with ownership, possession, use, and disposition not only of tangible things like clothing and machinery but also of intangible things like inventions, software, and writings. The law of sales, secured transactions, and commercial paper (e.g., personal checks) is a blend of contract law and property law.

3 The *law of torts*. Developed in the common law, the law of torts is very broad and encompasses the noncontractual obligations that members of society have not to harm each other. Tort law requires persons who have committed a private wrong (other than a breach of contract) to compensate the injured party for that wrong.

4 The *law of business relations*. This area of law includes the law of agency, partnerships, and corporations. It deals with the legal relationships among members of business organizations and with the rights and duties of third parties affected by agency, partnership, or corporate relationships.

Criminal Law and Civil Law

Criminal law defines offenses against the state (i.e., the general public) and prescribes punishments for those offenses. Most crimes—such as theft and murder—are defined by legislation. However, some criminal law statutes merely refer to a crime by its common law name and leave the courts to apply a common law definition to the offense. In a criminal law case, the government (state or federal) is the **plaintiff** (the term for a person initiating a lawsuit). The one charged with a criminal offense is the **defendant** (the person being sued).

In the United States, **civil law** refers to the law relating to private rights and remedies (common law and equity) sought by plaintiffs against a person who has committed a private wrong (a tort or a breach of contract).

Substantive and Procedural Law

Substantive law is concerned with the recognition of rights, duties, privileges, and immunities. The laws of contracts, property, torts, and business relations are examples. **Procedural law,** in contrast, specifies any formal steps to be followed in enforcing the rights granted by substantive law.

ALL STATES EXCEPT LOUISIANA

In several chapters of this book, you will see the State of Louisiana being singled out as the solitary exception to what is generally true regarding law in most states in the United States. Louisiana is an exception because the fundamental legal scheme in Louisiana has its roots in a system very different from that of the other states.

Louisiana was settled by the French. Unlike the British, the French did not have a tradition of common law and equity. Instead, they brought with them their *civil law system,* derived from that of the ancient Romans. A civil law system is based on a written legal code instead of an accumulation of judge-made common law. In a civil law system, a judge's main task is to apply this preexisting written law to cases as they arise, and *not* to make law as the English common law judges did. Under a civil law system, there is no application of the concept of *stare decisis*. Instead, judges apply general principles found in the civil code to a particular case in question.[3]

Because much of the state law in Louisiana is fundamentally different from that of the other 49 states, the Louisiana exception must be pointed out. However, constitutional law and other federal law apply in all states, including Louisiana, and Louisiana's *criminal* law is based on the English common law. Also, Louisiana has adopted much of the Uniform Commercial Code, which all other states have adopted in its entirety. In Chapter 2, sources of law—both state and federal—will be discussed in greater detail.

SUMMARY

Because society in the United States has become so consumer-oriented, it is difficult to find an aspect of our lives which the subject of business law does not touch in some way.

The definition of "law," and correspondingly "business law," is elusive in its particulars. In general, however, law consists of the social results of an evolutionary lawmaking process whereby the government develops a system of rules and regulations. "Business law" is the law connected with business activities.

Law is ever changing and forward-looking. As society changes over time, so do society's laws. If this were not so, the dead hand of the past would govern aspects of our lives which could not have been anticipated when old laws were made. When creating a rule of law, courts and legislatures attempt to anticipate future difficulties. Consequently, law is also forward-looking. While morals and ethics may be found in law, law is not itself an accumulation of moral guidelines and ethical norms. It is indeed possible for something to be legal that to some is immoral or unethical—or, conversely, moral or ethical, yet illegal.

One reason for studying business law is to learn to predict what the law will be. Since law is ever changing, the tools you acquire in a course of business law will help you understand legal dynamics so that you can better shape your own conduct and the conduct of businesses you will be associated with. Your understanding of what is behind the law and what courts use as rationale for their decisions enhances your ability to predict.

To comprehend judicial decisions, one must understand not only the rudiments of legal reasoning but also the various and competing legal philosophies that lawyers, judges, and even legislators use. The three-step process of case reasoning, which employs the notion of *stare decisis* (that is, that similar cases should be treated similarly), is one of the key forms of legal reasoning.

---

[3] Recall that in the United States "civil law" means something entirely different: It means the (judge-made) common law applying to private wrongs like torts and breaches of contract.

Understanding legal reasoning also requires that one understand the basic tools used to interpret statutes. Those tools include looking for the plain meaning of a statute and investigating the statute's legislative history.

REVIEW QUESTIONS

1. How does this chapter define law? Why is law difficult to define?

2. Explain why the task of being a judge of a legal case is difficult.

3. What are the basic steps of case-by-case reasoning? What is the relevance of the concept of *stare decisis* in these steps?

4. When a judge interprets a statute, what interpretative tools does the judge have at his or her disposal? Explain each one.

5. What is meant when a case is said to be "distinguished" from another? Why is it important for cases to be distinguished?

6. What are the most prominent and influential legal philosophies today? Explain each one. How can it help to know legal philosophies in a business law course?

7. What is meant by "common law" and "equity"? What is distinctive about "equity" in comparison with "common law"?

8. What is the difference between "public law" and "private law"? Give examples and explain. How is this distinction different from the one between "criminal law" and "civil law"? Additionally, what is the difference between "civil law" (as used in comparison with criminal law) and "civil law" (as used to describe a legal system)?

9. Is it possible for an act to be unethical but legal? Is it possible for an act to be illegal and moral simultaneously? Explain your answer.

10. Explain the difference between the "intent" of a legal rule and the "purpose" of a legal rule.

11. What is public policy? What role does public policy play in judicial decisions? Is it possible for an act to be in technical violation of a law, yet be in accordance with public policy? If such an act is possible, must judges in their decisions follow the letter of the law or must they follow public policy?

12. If a majority of judges sitting on a court agree on a judgment in a case but disagree on the reasons for it, what may be concluded from their decision? If a similar case were to arise in the future, what assessments of the predictability of its outcome would you make? What if the judges were unanimous in the judgment but in disagreement about the reasons for the judgment? Would future cases be more or less predictable? If the judges were unanimous in both the judgment and the rationale, would the outcome in the next future case be more or less predictable?

CHAPTER 2

The Legal System: Courts, Civil Procedure, and Alternative Dispute Resolution

This chapter is exceedingly important for you. Here, we explore the workings of the legal system to see generally how judges apply law to resolve legal disputes. To do this, we first look into the sources of law and how laws operate in relation to one another. Then, in the second and third sections of this chapter, we deal with legal procedure and the court system. Here you will encounter basic concepts and terms central to the process of deciding cases: "summary judgment," "directed verdict," "demurrer," "appellee," and a host of others that appear and reappear in cases throughout the book. Last, since traditional litigation can be expensive and time-consuming, we look into "alternative dispute resolution," a term applied to less formal dispute resolution practices gaining ever greater acceptance as a substitute for litigation.

SOURCES AND RANK OF LAW IN THE UNITED STATES

In the United States, the law must accommodate the diverse and often opposing needs and desires of a huge population. The complex legal structure required for such a task is rooted in our constitutional system of government.

The U.S. Constitution recognizes two levels of government—federal and state. Consequently, we have fifty-two major governmental entities[1] capable of making law. Through a process of delegation, thousands of smaller governmental entities and subdivisions (U.S. possessions and territories, cities, counties, towns, etc.) have the power to make law. Within each major governmental entity (state and federal), law comes from judicial, legislative, and administrative sources.

Constitutional Sources of Law

The Constitution allocates governmental power in two principal ways: (1) between the federal and the state governments and (2) among the three branches of the federal government. This fact so affects business activity that Chapter 3 is devoted entirely to the relationship between business and the Constitution. As a basis for understanding the legal system in general, however, a brief overview of constitutional processes appears here.

Federal-State Allocation of Powers. The *federal* government has **express powers**—those enumerated (expressed) in the Constitution. Among the most important are the power to levy and

---

[1] The fifty U.S. states, Washington, D.C., and the federal government.

collect taxes, to regulate interstate commerce, to provide for the general welfare, to enact a bankruptcy law, and to establish a patent and copyright system.

The federal government also has **implied powers** that are not specifically named in the Constitution but that are necessary and proper for carrying out the enumerated powers. The federal government has, for example, the implied power to incorporate a national bank as a means of carrying out its express powers to impose and collect taxes, to borrow money, to regulate commerce, and to raise and support armies. The express powers and their accompanying implied powers give the federal government a broad basis for regulating human affairs, including those relating to business.

The Constitution reserves the remaining powers for the states and the people.[2] The powers of a state include its **police power**—that is, the power of the state, through its legislature, to limit the personal freedom and property rights of persons for the protection of the public safety, health, and morals and for the promotion of the public convenience and general prosperity. State laws against crime, residential zoning ordinances, and the regulation of the manufacture and sale of intoxicating beverages are examples of the exercise by a state of its police power.

There is no police power expressly conferred on the federal government. However, in the exercise of its commerce and other powers, Congress indirectly exercises control over many of the social and economic problems that the states may attack directly under their police power. The federal antitrust laws, the Civil Rights Act of 1964 prohibiting racial discrimination in interstate commerce, and a variety of federal statutes pertaining to industrial safety are examples of congressional use of the commerce power to control problems that the states often address directly.

Powers of the federal government frequently overlap those of the states. Consequently, conflicts between state and federal law arise. How such conflicts are resolved is discussed later in this chapter.

Distribution of Powers within the Federal Government. The federal Constitution distributes federal powers among three branches of government—the legislative, the judicial, and the executive. Each branch of the federal government thus has an area of primary responsibility. Congress has the power to make laws authorized by the Constitution. The federal judiciary has the power to decide cases and controversies. The President of the United States has executive powers and duties. The President is the Commander in Chief of the armed forces, has the power to make treaties (subject to the concurrence of the Senate), and is required to "take Care that the Laws be faithfully executed."

The distribution of powers among the three branches of government is known as the **separation of powers,** and it serves two main purposes:

1 It enables each branch of government to exercise its constitutional prerogatives without undue interference by the other branches.
2 It prevents the excessive accumulation and unchecked use of power by a would-be dictator.

However, the separation of powers is not absolute. For efficiency of governmental operation, considerable overlapping of functions is necessary. Although the courts have been granted the power to decide cases and controversies, officers who hold hearings for administrative agencies also decide controversies, and in so doing they carry out a "quasi-judicial" function. The power to make law is vested in Congress, but the courts frequently decide cases by applying common law principles to topics for which there is no statutory law. To the extent that such decisions are legal precedents, the courts thus make law. In reality the federal government is one of separation and overlap of powers. Most state

---

[2]The Tenth Amendment states: "The powers not delegated to the United States by the Constitution, nor prohibited by it to the States, are reserved to the States respectively, or to the people."

constitutions follow the model of the federal Constitution with regard to separation and overlap of powers.

As a further protection against the excessive accumulation of power, the powers of a branch of government are limited by powers possessed by one or both of the other branches. For instance, the Supreme Court has the power to declare legislation and executive exercises of power unconstitutional. Subject to the approval of the Senate, the President fills vacancies in the Supreme Court, and the President may veto legislation. Congress may enact laws affecting the structure of the federal court system and the activities of the President; and by a process of **impeachment** (accusation), trial, and conviction, Congress may remove the President, the Vice President, and other civil officers of the United States (including members of the judiciary) from office for committing high crimes and misdemeanors. Similar checks and balances are found in the state governments, most of which pattern their constitutions after the federal Constitution.

Legislative Sources of Law

The word **legislation** is ordinarily used to refer to statutes passed by Congress and by state legislatures. But the legislative power of the United States and the various states may be exercised in more than one way. The phrase **enacted law** is usually used to designate the exercise of the legislative power in its broadest sense. Enacted law can be said to include the following classes of law:

1. Federal and state constitutions
2. Federal and state statutes (acts)
3. Federal treaties
4. Executive orders and proclamations issued by the President of the United States or by state governors when authorized by statute
5. Administrative rules and regulations when authorized by statute, which have the force and effect of law
6. Ordinances of the subdivisions of the states, such as cities and towns

Judicial Decisions as a Source of Law

Judicial decisions are a twofold source of law: (1) Courts, through their decisions, interpret and test the validity and application of enacted laws in the light of constitutional provisions and the intent of the Congress, legislature, local government, or agency that formulated them. (2) In areas not covered by legislation, courts apply the common law, expand it with decisions that apply to new situations, and, if necessary, develop new common law principles. Thus, courts sometimes *make* law.

Judicial Interpretation and Construction of Statutes. As you may recall from Chapter 1, **interpretation** of a statute is the process of discovering and explaining the meaning of any unclear language. **Construction** of a statute is the process of discovering and explaining the legal effect which the statute is to have. Construing a statute may involve interpreting unclear language, but it mainly involves such tasks as determining the purpose or policy of the statute, deciding how the provisions of a complex statute are related, and deciding to what specific people or things the statute applies. "Interpretation" and "construction," though fundamentally different in function, are often used loosely in judicial opinions to refer to either the meaning or the application of a statute or to some combination of the two.

Determination of Constitutionality. Sometimes a statute is alleged to be not only unclear but also unconstitutional. Accordingly, the first task of a court often is to determine whether the statute conforms to the requirements of the relevant constitution, state or federal. How courts go about that task is discussed in Chapter 3.

Role of Stare Decisis in Judicial Decision Making. In Chapter 1, the concept of **stare decisis**—that similar cases be treated similarly—was introduced. Here, we take the concept one step further and look at its role in judicial decision making.

In the United States, the rule of *stare decisis* applies in the following way: If a decision was rendered by a higher court of the state in which a case is being tried (or by the Supreme Court of the United States), and that decision can be applied to the case presently before the lower court, then the higher court's decision is binding upon the lower court and must be followed. However, if the decision came from the highest court of another state, it may be taken into consideration by the judge but need not be followed. Thus, courts in different states sometimes express different views as to the principles of law involved and, on occasion, as to their application. This creates a "majority rule" reflecting the view of the courts in a majority of the states and, correspondingly, a minority rule.

There is a twofold difficulty in applying the doctrine of *stare decisis*. First, attorneys for the plaintiff or defendant can usually find *conflicting precedents* to support the positions of their respective clients. For example, while rowing a boat in Utah, Aquaman negligently injures Buoyant, who is swimming nearby. Buoyant obtains a $100,000 personal injury judgment against Aquaman. Aquaman's only asset is an automobile insurance policy paying up to $100,000 to any victim of Aquaman's negligence "occurring while Aquaman is operating a *vehicle*." Buoyant sues the insurance carrier for the $100,000, alleging Aquaman's negligence *while operating a vehicle*. No Utah cases define "vehicle." But the insurance carrier's attorney finds several out-of-state cases holding that "vehicle" does *not* include a boat, while Buoyant's attorney finds a case holding that it does. There is an obvious conflict among the precedents, and the court must resolve it.

At this point in our example, the second difficulty in applying *stare decisis* arises: Courts are not bound to follow a case in which the key facts differ significantly from those in the case under consideration. Where two cases are sufficiently different from each other factually, the one is said to be "distinguishable" from the other. So, by arguing that the other side's precedents are distinguishable from *Aquaman v. Buoyant*, each attorney here will try to persuade the court not to follow the precedent that is against the client's interest. For example, if victim Buoyant's precedent involved a motorboat, the insurance company lawyer will argue that it does not apply to the present case because Buoyant was struck by a rowboat. Buoyant's lawyer will make a similar effort to discredit the insurance company's precedents, by arguing that they, too, involved motorboats and so are inapplicable to the present case. On what basis, then, will the judge decide the case?

In deciding the case, the judge will determine (1) which cases argued by counsel have key facts substantially like those of the case before the court and are therefore sound precedents, and (2) which of the out-of-state cases, if any, state a desirable rule of law for Utah to adopt and follow—which, that is, embody sound policy concerning the handling of injuries caused by negligent rowboaters in Utah. In this example, the judge is called upon to decide a **case of first impression** in Utah, that is, a case which raises a question of law that has not previously been decided in that state.

Conflicts between lines of case precedent, and differences in the underlying facts, create uncertainty about the outcome of a lawsuit. Lawyers almost always differ with their rivals about how precedents should apply to the facts in their clients' case, and opposing attorneys usually argue their positions skillfully. Consequently, in cases where both sides have sound policy arguments, it may be difficult to predict which line of precedent the court will apply to the case at hand. Indeed, in cases of first impression, courts often develop rules of their own, rejecting out-of-state law as ill-reasoned, reflective of poor policy, or otherwise inadequate. Similar uncertainty exists when there is a split of case law authority in the court's own state and the court must choose which line of precedent to follow.

In deciding a particular case, appellate courts generally follow their earlier case precedents. However, they will not hesitate to reverse a long-standing decision if warranted by changed economic and social circumstances. When the rule of law of an earlier case is reversed by a later decision, a new case precedent has been established which is then followed by the lower courts in resolving subsequent suits involving the same principle of law.

Modern Role of Equity in Judicial Decisions.

As noted in Chapter 1, the English developed courts of equity to supplement the inadequate courts of law. In most American states today, "law" and "equity" are merged into a single court system, and legal and equitable principles are administered by the same judge. So, despite our tendency to refer to courts of equity and law as separate, in reality, they are physically unified. It is their *functions* that remain separate and distinguishable.

The primary focus of modern equity courts is on "balancing the equities" between the parties, largely by relying upon equitable maxims and the court's sense of justice as a guide to judicial decision making. An equity court wields broader powers than does a court of law. The judge sitting as a "court of conscience" (equity court) is less restricted by case precedents than he or she would be as a court of law. The equity judge also has wide discretion in making decisions, and only if it is clearly abused will a decision be reversed on appeal. Unlike the judgment of a court of law which is usually for money damages, the equity judge's decision, called a **decree,** may reserve for many years jurisdiction to resolve future issues that may arise between the parties. For example, in a divorce case (a proceeding in equity), the divorce decree often retains jurisdiction over the parties to modify the amount of monthly alimony initially ordered by the court.

In recent years equity courts have significantly expanded their role as an instrument of social reform. For example, in an appeal from an equity court's decree in *Brown v. Board of Education,*[3] the U.S. Supreme Court held that separate educational facilities for blacks and whites are inherently unequal. The trial court retained jurisdiction to administer a far-reaching school busing program.

Differences between actions at law and actions in equity. Because of the growing importance of equity courts in our judicial system, it is essential that businesspeople understand the basic differences between law and equity. The major differences between suits at law and in equity are set out in Table 2.1. The three most important differences are:

1 In an action at law the plaintiff generally is seeking only a money judgment for damages. In an action in equity the main relief sought is some equitable remedy, though often the plaintiff also seeks money for damages accumulated to date. The equitable remedy sought may be a **decree** declaring a status (such as a decree declaring the rights and duties of the parties to a business contract or one adjudging a person bankrupt), or an **order** prohibiting the defendant from engaging in an act or commanding the defendant to perform an act.

Today, to persuade a judge in a court of law to hear a case as an equity matter, a plaintiff must show: (1) that the remedy in an action at law is inadequate, and (b) that the plaintiff has acted reasonably or fairly in dealing with the defendant, or at least is not a wrongdoer. The remedy at law (a money judgment) might be inadequate because the plaintiff needs the thing the defendant promised but failed to deliver, or because of the defendant's continuing wrong. For example, if a defendant commits trespass by wrongfully using a landowner's private road each day, a money judgment for damages up to the date of the trial would not compensate the plaintiff for damages arising from such wrongful use in the future.

2 Law and equity differ with respect to the method of determining facts at the time of trial. The Constitution guarantees a jury trial in most actions at law, whereas in equity there is no jury trial: The equity judge decides the facts.

3 Finally, law and equity differ in the method of enforcing a judgment. To enforce a judgment at law, the person to whom a judgment was awarded must undertake a second legal process, called **execution.** Execution of a judgment at law is the process of procuring a writ of execution from the clerk of the court and having the sheriff seize the defendant's property and sell it to satisfy the judgment. In contrast, decrees in equity are enforceable directly against the respondent (defendant) by means of a **con-**

---

[3]347 U.S. 483 (1954).

Table 2.1 Major Differences between a Suit at Law and a Suit in Equity

	Action at Law	Action in Equity
Nature of relief sought by plaintiff	A money judgment for damages to compensate plaintiff for the loss sustained.	A decree of an equity judge: (a) ordering defendant to do or not do an act (injunction), or (b) declaring a status (e.g., decree of divorce, bankruptcy, or quieting title to real estate).
Time within which suit must be filed	Plaintiff must file suit within the time period fixed by the state statute of limitations.	Plaintiff must file within a reasonable time after the event which gave rise to the cause of action (doctrine of laches).
Jurisdiction of the court	Plaintiff must show injury from defendant's conduct arising out of facts containing all of the elements of a legal cause of action (e.g., negligence, fraud, trespass).	Plaintiff must show: (a) the law remedy is inadequate for any one of the following reasons: (1) There is a continuing wrong by defendant; (2) the law remedy would require a multiplicity of law suits; (3) if plaintiff obtained judgment in a suit at law, it could not be collected because of the insolvency of the defendant; (4) difficulty of measuring damages in money terms; *and* (b) great and irreparable injury to property will result if equitable relief is not granted (e.g., a tenant wrongfully cutting down the landlord's forest).
Method of finding facts at trial	Plaintiff (or defendant) has the right to request a trial by jury; if no request, trial is by the judge.	The equity judge finds the facts as well as rules upon issues of law. (Some states permit an *advisory* jury to recommend findings of fact to the equity judge.)
Method of enforcing judgment or decree	Levy of execution; the sheriff seizes money of defendant or sells defendant's property to satisfy the judgment.	Contempt-of-court proceedings may be initiated by plaintiff against a defendant who disobeys an equity decree, and defendant can be fined or sentenced to a jail term, or both.

tempt-of-court proceeding. A respondent who refuses to obey a decree in equity can be sent to jail or fined until he or she obeys the decree or shows a willingness to obey.

Equitable remedies. The most familiar equitable remedies are the injunction, specific performance of a contract, rescission of a contract, an accounting for profits, and the imposition of a constructive trust. Specific performance, rescission, and other remedies applicable to contracts are discussed later in this book. Two equitable remedies—injunction and specific performance—need special mention here.

An **injunction** is a judicial order to perform an act **(mandatory injunction)** or, more commonly, an order to refrain from performing an act which threatens irreparable harm **(prohibitory injunction).** Temporary and permanent injunctions may be issued in many situations: for example, in labor disputes; in situations involving a **nuisance** (a use of property in such a way as to harass, annoy, or harm neighbors); and in situations involving violations of civil rights.

Specific performance will be ordered where (money) damages are inadequate to compensate the nondefaulting party to a contract for the failure of the defaulting party to perform or to deliver the specific thing promised. Damages are inadequate, for example, where the thing to be delivered is unique. A work of art is considered unique, and its purchaser will usually be granted specific performance where the seller can deliver it but refuses to do so. However, a court will not order the specific performance of a contract for personal services even though those services are unique, as this would in effect impose involuntary servitude. Courts of equity also will not make orders whose enforcement is impractical; for example, many large-scale construction contracts would be impractical to enforce specifically.

Administrative Sources of Law in the United States. Day-to-day operations of government rest largely in the hands of administrative agencies such as the Internal Revenue Service, the Federal Trade Commission, and the National Labor Relations Board. The regulations of an administrative agency, when published in a government publication called the *Federal Register,* have the force and effect of law. Chapter 4 discusses administrative law, emphasizing the authority of administrative agencies to regulate the conduct, scope, and size of business organizations.

Rank of Laws in the United States

Rank of enacted laws in order of authority. Our legal system would be unworkable if law were not ranked in some order of authority. The federal Constitution heads all enacted laws in authority.[4] Next below it are the statutes and treaties of the United States. U.S. statutes and treaties are of equal rank. When federal- and state-enacted law covers the same subject matter, the federal law prevails. When only state law is involved, the state constitution ranks highest, followed by state statutes. Below the statutes come the ordinances of the state's subdivisions.

Constitutional federal statutes which carry out some federal power take precedence over conflicting state statutes. However, much nonconflicting state law can coexist. For example, the federal Bankruptcy Code expressly looks to state law for the regulation of certain aspects of bankruptcy. Where federal statutes are silent as to the role of state law, nonconflicting state regulation is valid except in three situations: (1) where national uniformity of federal regulation is required, (2) where the federal government has "preempted" (taken exclusive control of) the field, and (3) where the state statute does not usurp federal authority but otherwise violates the Constitution.

Rank of common law in relation to enacted law. In terms of substantive coverage, the common law ranks below all classes of enacted law. Since the Constitution makes the legislature the main lawmaking body, a rule of common law will be applied only where there is no valid enacted law. However, the fact that the common law ranks below enacted law should not lead us to minimize the role of the courts. They have the exclusive responsibility for developing the common law, and they have the ultimate responsibility for determining the constitutionality and the meaning of enacted law. Moreover, when courts interpret constitutions and statutes, their interpretations affect the content of the enacted law.

---

[4]Article 6 of the U.S. Constitution provides a framework for ranking enacted law: "This Constitution, and the Laws of the United States which shall be made in Pursuance thereof; and all Treaties made, or which shall be made, under the Authority of the United States, shall be the supreme Law of the Land; and the Judges in every State shall be bound thereby, any Thing in the Constitution or Laws of any State to the contrary notwithstanding."

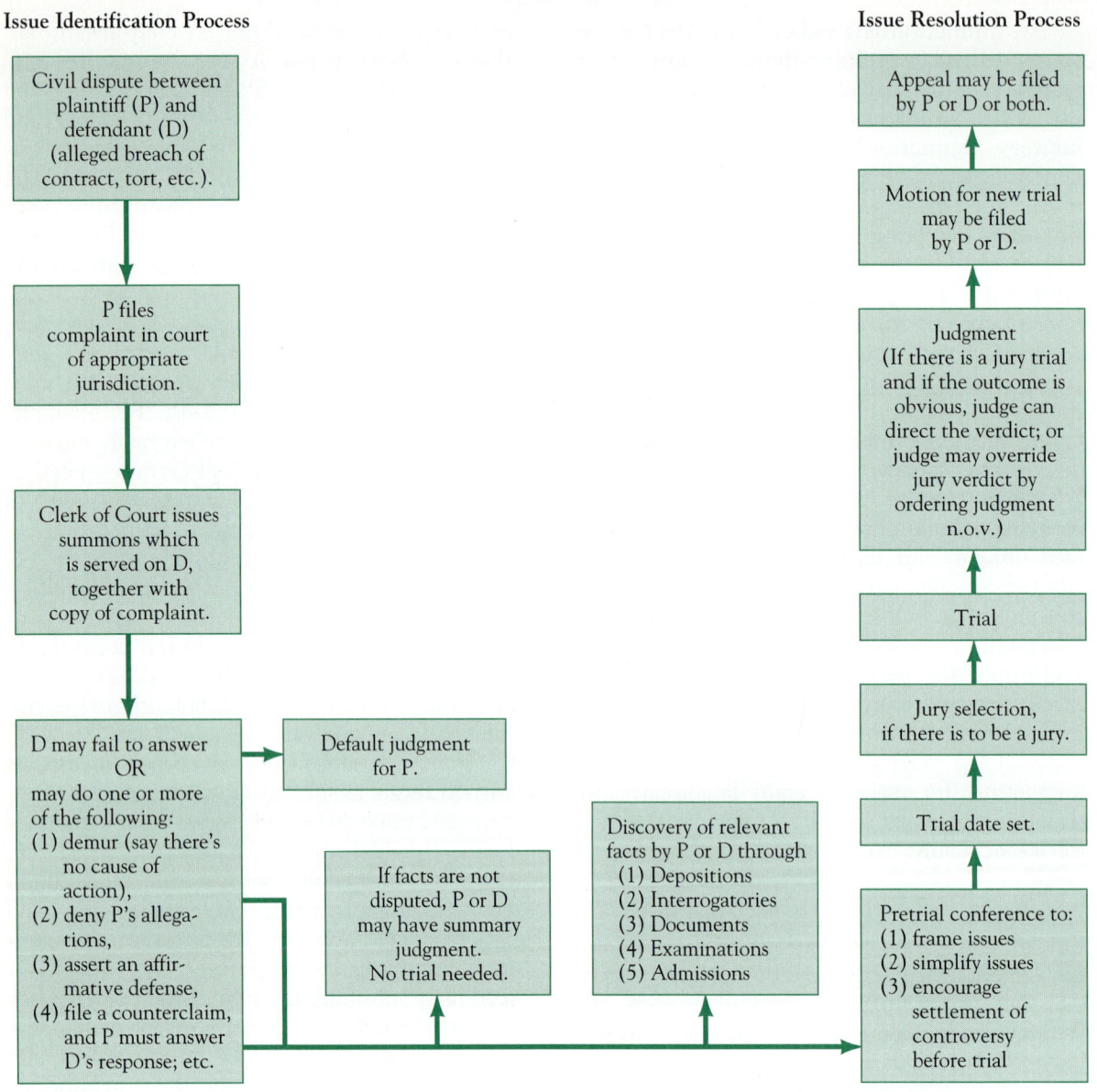

Figure 2.1 Flow of civil litigation.

Rank of administrative rules. In addition to the great number of federal and state statutes, there are the rules and regulations of federal, state, and local administrative agencies. These rules and regulations have the force and effect of law, and they rank ahead of common law decisions in approximately the way that federal and state statutes do.

CIVIL PROCEDURE

When disputes between individuals or business firms cannot be resolved amicably, litigation often results. This part of the chapter discusses the steps in the trial of cases, from beginning to end. Knowledge of these steps, shown in Figure 2.1, and of the terms used in litigation will be useful in understanding the cases presented in the following chapters. Often, an appeal to a higher court is based on a defect alleged to exist in one or more steps in the trial of a case.

Procedures Prior to Trial

Pleadings. Pleadings are the initial written statements presented to the trial court by each party to a civil suit. The function of pleadings is to reduce the controversy to its essential issues.

Summons and complaint. The party who initiates a civil lawsuit is the **plaintiff.** The party being sued is called the **defendant.** The plaintiff initiates a lawsuit by filing with the court a statement variously called a *complaint, petition,* or *declaration.*[5] The complaint must contain a statement of the facts constituting the cause of action, in ordinary and concise language, and a demand for the relief which the plaintiff claims. For example, the plaintiff may state, "On January 1, the defendant drove his automobile in a negligent manner and collided with the plaintiff, causing great bodily injury." The plaintiff would then request damages in a certain amount, such as $100,000. This request, called the *prayer,* varies according to the nature of the action. For example, a plaintiff may pray that a tenant who has not paid rent be ordered to vacate the plaintiff's apartment.

The plaintiff brings the defendant under the jurisdiction of the court by serving the defendant with a copy of the complaint and a document called a *summons.* A summons is, in effect, an order of the court directing the defendant to appear in court within a certain time period, usually 30 days. In the summons the defendant is advised that if no action is taken within the 30 days, the plaintiff may take a judgment against the defendant by default. In a **default judgment,** the plaintiff receives what he or she asked for in the prayer (e.g., damages or equity remedy) without further court proceedings. Ordinarily, "serving" a copy of the summons and complaint (called *service of process*) is accomplished by handing the papers to the defendant in person. This may be done by a professional process server or a court official such as a sheriff or a marshall. However, when the defendant cannot be found, provisions in most states allow for **substituted service.** Such service may be accomplished by mailing or by advertising in a newspaper.

Demurrer. After receiving the copy of the summons and complaint, the defendant must file with the court a **responsive pleading** within the required time in order to avoid a default judgment. There are several pleadings that a defendant may file. The defendant may challenge the court's jurisdiction or the legal sufficiency of the plaintiff's complaint by means of a document called a "demurrer," or in some states a "motion to dismiss." A demurrer to a complaint challenging its legal sufficiency says in effect: "Even if the facts alleged in the complaint are assumed to be true, still the complaint does not state a cause of action against the defendant." For example, Greasemonkey alleges in a complaint that Junkheap brought a car to Greasemonkey which Greasemonkey could not repair, thereby injuring Greasemonkey's reputation as an auto repairer. For this injury to reputation, Greasemonkey seeks $10,000 in damages. Junkheap would likely file a demurrer to the complaint, alleging that the complaint, while stating true facts, fails to state a legal cause of action and should be dismissed. In short, Junkheap's demurrer asserts that even if Greasemonkey's facts are absolutely true, Greasemonkey has no basis in law upon which to sue because Junkheap has committed no legal wrong.

A demurrer raises an issue of law which the court must then decide. If the court *sustains* the demurrer, the judge is ruling that the plaintiff has failed to state a recognized cause of action. The plaintiff ordinarily is then given time to file an amended complaint. If the plaintiff fails to file an amended complaint, a judgment of dismissal will be filed. If the court *overrules* the demurrer, the judge is ruling that the plaintiff has stated a recognized cause of action—that is, has alleged a wrong which, if proved, entitles the plaintiff to a remedy. The defendant is then given time to file a further pleading. If the de-

---

[5]The requirements for a complaint vary from state to state. States such as Indiana and California, however, have requirements that are typical of those states which have modernized their civil procedure rules. In this chapter, we will use as models the more modern procedure rules.

fendant fails to do so, a default judgment will be entered for the plaintiff. Whether the demurrer is sustained or overruled, the losing party has a right to appeal the court's ruling. Many cases in this textbook involve an appeal from a demurrer or a motion to dismiss. On appeal the question is: Did the trial court correctly decide the issue of whether the plaintiff stated a recognized cause of action?

Answer and counterclaim. The defendant in a civil lawsuit most commonly chooses to file another type of responsive pleading called an **answer.** An answer may contain a **general denial,** that is, the defendant denies everything contained in the complaint, or a **specific denial,** that is, the defendant denies the truth of one or more of the essential allegations of the complaint and admits the truth of the other allegations.

An answer may contain one or more affirmative defenses. An **affirmative defense** is an allegation of some new matter as a bar to plaintiff's recovery. An affirmative defense asserts basically, "Yes I did what the plaintiff alleges, but there is a legally supportable reason why I did it." For example, Hapless alleges in a complaint that defendant Deadbeat failed to repay a $1,000 loan. If the debt was indeed outstanding but Deadbeat has received a bankruptcy discharge from all debts, Deadbeat may file an answer admitting the debt, but alleging bankruptcy as an affirmative defense. Other examples of affirmative defenses are statute of limitations and statute of frauds. These and many other defenses are presented in various chapters later in this book.

In most states the defendant may assert a counterclaim as a part of the answer. A **counterclaim** asserts that the defendant has a claim against the plaintiff. The defendant's claim need not be related to the plaintiff's cause of action stated in the original complaint. For example, Chump sues Shifty, alleging breach of a contract. Shifty may file a counterclaim alleging that Chump made defamatory statements about Shifty which, in turn, caused Shifty to suffer damages.

A counterclaim is the *defendant's* complaint, and the defendant becomes a plaintiff for the matter alleged in the counterclaim. Accordingly, the original plaintiff must file an answer, called a **reply,** or risk dismissal of the plaintiff's own complaint. In the above example, the court would be presented with two suits: Chump suing Shifty for breach of contract; and Shifty suing Chump for defamation.

Summary Judgment. At various points during the pleading stage of litigation, either party to the lawsuit may make a motion for a **summary judgment.** The summary judgment procedure is designed to dispose of suits in which there is no genuine issue of fact for a judge or jury to decide. The judge conducts an informal hearing to review the pleadings. The parties may file affidavits (sworn statements) of witnesses who would be called by the parties to testify if a trial were held. If the pleadings and affidavits reveal no material issue of fact, the judge makes a ruling that no trial is necessary and enters a judgment for the plaintiff or defendant. Like the demurrer, the summary judgment procedure helps to avoid the expense of unnecessary trials. If a judge grants a motion for summary judgment, the losing party may appeal to a higher court.

Discovery. At one time there was a feeling in the legal profession that a lawsuit should be a battle of wits, with each side guarding its case jealously and making the adversary's trial preparations as difficult and onerous as possible. Often the parties did not know until the day of trial what witnesses the other party would call to testify. To minimize the element of surprise, to improve and speed up the trial of cases, and to encourage settlements before trial, all states today allow and encourage the parties to learn, before trial, as much as possible about the adversary's case. There are five major devices for discovery of facts before trial:

Depositions
Interrogatories
Inspection of documents and property
Physical and mental examinations
Request for admissions

Depositions. A **deposition** is a statement under oath made at a hearing held out of court and after due notice to the other side. Ordinarily, each party will request permission to take the deposition of the other party and the party's key witnesses. A hearing is arranged typically at the office of one party's attorney, but such a hearing could be held at any reasonable location. A court reporter records the questions and answers and prepares a written transcript for the witness to sign. In recent years, a growing number of courts have encouraged the use of videotaped depositions. The need for a written transcript is eliminated; and if the videotape is presented at trial, the judge or jury can view the witness and better evaluate the person's credibility. Courts, however, do not uniformly accept videotaped depositions at trial. Many prohibit them.

Depositions serve various purposes: to discover what testimony to expect at the trial; to obtain testimony while it is fresh in the mind of the witness; to impeach (discredit) a person's testimony at the trial by showing that the testimony varies from the deposition; and to preserve testimony where there is danger that it may be unavailable at the trial. For example, a deposition may be desirable if a witness is elderly, has a serious illness, or is likely not to be available for the trial. Often, attorneys will take the deposition of an expert witness, such as a doctor or engineer, and use the deposition at the trial in place of actual testimony. Expert witnesses receive large fees for testifying at trials, and their schedules are often such that it may be difficult to secure their attendance at the trial.

Interrogatories. **Interrogatories** are written questions addressed by one party in a case to the other party to elicit information that can be used as a basis for further questions at a deposition hearing or at the trial of the case. An interrogatory may be used, for example, to demand a list of the other party's witnesses.

Interrogatories are relatively inexpensive and can be served informally (usually by mail) and answered without the necessity of the presence of a court reporter or opposing attorney. Ordinarily, the answers must be given in writing, under penalty of perjury. As with depositions, the answers can be used for impeachment (testing the truth of testimony with evidence) purposes at a trial.

Inspection of documents and property. Either party to a case may secure a court order permitting the party or an agent to inspect, copy, or photograph documents or tangible things in the possession or control of another. For example, in a case where the plaintiff alleges personal injury the defendant may wish to inspect medical or hospital records pertaining to the injury.

Physical and mental examinations. When the physical or mental condition of a party is in controversy, the court may issue an order requiring the party to submit to an examination by a physician. In many lawsuits both parties will request an examination by physicians. Often, the doctors' opinions as to a party's condition are at odds with one another, and the judge or jury must then weigh the credibility of each physician.

Request for admissions. Either party may serve upon the other party (usually by mail) a request to admit the genuineness of some document or the truth of some assertion described or set forth in the request. Failure to deny in writing and under oath the genuineness of the document or the truth of the assertion constitutes an admission of its genuineness or truth. The admission relieves the requesting party of the burden of producing proof on that point at the trial.

In general, the information sought by discovery must be relevant to the subject matter of the lawsuit. For example, in most cases it would be improper to ask in a deposition hearing or in an interrogatory for a party or witness to disclose one's social security number. But it is not required that the information sought be used in evidence at a trial or that the information be admissible evidence. Thus, a plaintiff is entitled to discover the existence and scope of the defendant's insurance coverage, although such information is usually not admissible as evidence in a trial.

Pretrial Conference. In most states the courts require a pretrial conference in civil suits. A **pretrial conference** is a meeting of the judge and attorneys, and sometimes the parties, held usually two or three weeks before trial. The conference serves two purposes. One purpose is to shorten the time of trial by refining or narrowing the issues, clarifying the pleadings through amendments, and placing a limitation on the number of witnesses and exhibits. The second purpose of the pretrial conference is to encourage an out-of-court settlement. At the end of the conference, if no settlement has been reached, the judge sets a date for the trial.

Trial of Cases

Before the trial date, the plaintiff and defendant must decide whether the trial will be by judge or by jury. In some suits no jury is allowed, as in suits for equity relief. In other suits either party may request a jury but is not required to do so (i.e., they may *waive* a jury). If either side requests a jury, a deposit of jury fees ordinarily must be made in advance of the trial date. On the day of a jury trial, the first step is for the parties to select a jury. The remaining steps in a trial are substantially the same whether or not a jury is used.

Opening Statements of Counsel. Ordinarily, the next step in a civil trial with a jury consists of opening statements by attorneys for the plaintiff and for the defendant. The purpose of the opening statements is to outline the general nature of the case and to indicate the kinds of evidence to be offered, so that the judge or jurors may understand the significance of each item of evidence as it is introduced.

Presentation of Evidence. The plaintiff proceeds next to introduce evidence to prove the allegations of the complaint. The word "evidence" is used in different senses. As used here, evidence means anything presented at the trial for the purpose of inducing belief in the truth or falsity of some contention. The two chief methods of inducing belief are the testimony of witnesses and physical evidence such as X rays, fingerprints, or a damaged bicycle. *Testimony* is secured by calling a witness, swearing the person in, and asking the person questions.

Degree of proof required. There is an important difference in the degree of proof required to win a civil lawsuit and the degree of proof required to win a criminal case. Most of us are familiar with the statement that in order to convict a defendant of a criminal offense, the prosecutor must prove the facts "beyond a reasonable doubt." In other words, if the judge or jury is not overwhelmingly convinced of the defendant's guilt, the defendant must be acquitted. In a civil lawsuit the plaintiff must prove his or her case "by a preponderance of the evidence." This ordinarily means that the plaintiff's evidence simply must be more credible than the defendant's evidence. Thus, the standard of proof is lower in civil cases and easier to achieve. This explains in part why a defendant may be acquitted of a crime (say, assault and battery) and yet be liable to a plaintiff in a civil suit based on the same set of circumstances.

Types and rules of evidence. The primary method of proving facts in a civil lawsuit is to present the testimony of witnesses. When a witness is put on the stand, the person is first examined by the attorney who called the person as a witness. This is called **direct examination** and is followed by a **cross-examination** conducted by the attorney for the other side. Ordinarily, the purpose of cross-examination is to show the witness's lack of credibility by, for example, casting doubt on his or her powers of observation. The attorney may try to impeach the witness by showing that the witness's answers on the stand differ from those given in a deposition or interrogatories. The cross-examination may be followed by a **redirect examination,** in order to give the witness an opportunity to explain or modify answers given on cross-examination. The trial judge has discretion to allow the examination to proceed to a re-cross-examination, or even beyond.

In addition to presenting witnesses' testimony to prove facts, it may be necessary to present physical evidence. Physical evidence may consist of objects or documents which have been verified as authentic. Items of physical evidence are called **exhibits** and are tagged with a number for future reference (e.g., "Plaintiff's 1"). The rules of evidence governing the introduction of exhibits and the testimony of witnesses are numerous and technical. These rules may be the basis for a party to "object" to a question of a witness or to the introduction of physical evidence, the judge then either *sustaining* or *overruling* the objection. Many of the rules are designed to protect a jury of laypersons from irrelevant and prejudicial material.

Motions at close of evidence. After the plaintiff has called all witnesses for the plaintiff's side and has introduced all physical evidence desired, the plaintiff "rests." At this point the defendant may make a **motion for nonsuit** (in some states called a **motion to dismiss**). By such a motion the defendant contends that the plaintiff has failed to prove his or her case, as outlined in the complaint and opening statements. If the judge agrees, a judgment of nonsuit is entered in favor of the defendant. If the judge does not agree, the motion will be denied, and the defendant proceeds to introduce evidence to contradict the plaintiff's evidence. The defendant calls witnesses and introduces physical evidence in the same manner as the plaintiff did.

When there is a trial by jury, either party, or both, may make a **motion for directed verdict** at the close of defendant's evidence. By such a motion a party contends that the facts proved are so clear that reasonable people could not differ as to the outcome of the case. If the judge directs a verdict for a party, the judge thereby takes the case away from the jury and then enters a judgment for the party who made the motion. If neither party moves for a directed verdict, the judge may on his or her own motion order a directed verdict.

Closing Arguments of Counsel. After all evidence is presented, the attorneys for each party are allowed to make final or closing arguments. These usually take place before the judge's charge to the jury. In the final argument, each attorney will review the evidence produced by his or her side and emphasize its adequacy and credibility, discuss the evidence produced by the other side to show its inadequacy and lack of credibility, and indicate the conclusions of fact that may reasonably be drawn from the evidence.

Charge to the Jury. When there is a trial by jury, the judge instructs the jurors after closing arguments by both attorneys as to the law to be applied in their deliberations. Normally the judge instructs the jury that its duty is to determine the facts of the case; to accept the law as stated by the judge; and, by applying the law so stated to the facts so determined, to reach a decision for the plaintiff or the defendant. These instructions are a guide to assist the jury in reaching a verdict. For example, the judge may say, "Negligence means the failure to exercise reasonable care to prevent harm to others. If you find that the defendant drove his car so unreasonably fast in a residential area as to cause injury, you must find the defendant has committed the tort of negligence." Attorneys may, and often do, submit to the judge written instructions which they request the judge to include in the charge to the jury. The refusal to include a requested instruction or to give the instruction in the wording requested is often the basis of an appeal to a higher court.

Verdict of the Jury. After receiving the judge's instructions, the jury retires to the jury room to consider the evidence and reach a verdict. In federal courts and in many state courts the jury verdict must be unanimous. Some states, such as California, authorize a verdict in a civil action to be reached by vote of three-fourths of the jurors. When the jury has reached its verdict, it returns to the courtroom and in the presence of the judge (and usually in the presence of the parties and their attorneys) announces its verdict.

The type of verdict just considered—that is, a verdict for plaintiff or defendant reached by applying the law as stated by the judge to the facts as found by the jury—is called a **general verdict.** If a general verdict is given for the defendant, the jurors' functions terminate; if the verdict is for the plaintiff in a civil action for damages, the jury must fix the amount of damages to which the plaintiff is entitled.

Another type of verdict is a **special verdict.** Such a verdict generally consists of answers to specific questions asked by the judge without any attempt to reach a decision for either party. The judge then decides the case by applying the law to the facts as given in the special verdict.

Judgment; Motions after Trial. The last step in the trial of a case is the judgment. A **judg-**

ment is the decision of the court. The judge might simply state that the defendant is liable to plaintiff for $100,000. Often, after the judgment in a jury trial is entered in the court records, the losing party will make a motion for **judgment notwithstanding the verdict,** also called a judgment *non obstante veredicto* (n.o.v.). The judge will grant the motion and enter judgment for the losing party only if there is no substantial evidence to support the decision of the jury. In some states the judge on his or her own motion may reject the jury verdict and enter a judgment for the other party. The party whose verdict is overturned usually will appeal to a higher court.

After the judgment is entered, a *motion for a new trial* may be made by either party. There are several grounds upon which to make a motion for a new trial. If the plaintiff has won the case, the defendant may move for a new trial on the grounds that the judge committed prejudicial error in the conduct of the trial or that the damages assessed are excessive. For example, the defendant may claim that the judge improperly refused to allow the defendant to introduce important evidence at the trial. A party may be granted a new trial if the other party, or the party's attorney, was guilty of prejudicial misconduct during the trial. However, a party is not entitled to a new trial if the party's own attorney was negligent or incompetent. A new trial may be granted where the losing party shows new evidence was discovered after the trial. However, the party must prove that the evidence is significant and could not have been obtained before trial by due diligence. The plaintiff, although the winner, may move for a new trial on the ground that the damages awarded are insufficient under the evidence.

If a motion for a new trial is granted by the judge, the case is again put on the trial calendar. If the motion is denied, the moving party may appeal. In certain instances, the judge may order a denial of a new trial if the plaintiff consents to a reduction in the amount of the judgment (called a **remittitur**). Or the judge may order a new trial unless the defendant consents to an increase in the amount of the judgment (called an **additur**).

Appeals

After the entry of judgment, the party who feels dissatisfied by the outcome may file an appeal. Normally the loser appeals; sometimes the winner appeals (e.g., the plaintiff may allege that the damages awarded were inadequate under the evidence); occasionally both parties appeal. The party who files an appeal is called the **appellant.** The other party is called the **appellee,** or the **respondent.**

In the cases you will be reading in the following chapters the appellant's name usually appears first (e.g., *Jekyll v. Hyde*). The order of the names probably will not be the same as appears in the trial court, and this may cause some confusion. Suppose, for example, that Hyde sued Jekyll in the superior court. The case would be entitled *Hyde v. Jekyll*. Hyde would be the plaintiff and Jekyll the defendant. If Hyde won the case and Jekyll appealed, the appeal case would usually be retitled *Jekyll v. Hyde*.

Review of the Case. The appellate court does not retry the case. No new evidence is allowed, and there is no jury. The appellate court reviews the case as conducted in the trial court to see if any error of law or of conduct was committed. Usually the appellate court limits review to such questions as: Did the trial judge properly exclude or admit evidence, follow proper procedure, or state or apply the law accurately? If the trial judge committed error, was the error serious enough to warrant reversal of the judge's decision?

Sometimes an appellate court conducts a limited review of the facts found by the trial court. Such a review is necessary in deciding whether a summary judgment or a judgment n.o.v. was warranted. It should be noted, however, that an appellate court will not overturn a trial court's ruling unless the ruling is in serious disharmony with the evidence. The trial judge and jury, having the witnesses physically present, are in a better position than an appellate court to evaluate the credibility of witnesses. The appellate court therefore does not reweigh the evidence. The appellate court reviews the complete record of the trial of the case and listens to oral arguments by the attorneys for both parties, who also submit written "briefs" to support their arguments.

Decision and Opinion. After consideration of the record and the arguments made, the appellate court announces its decision (judgment) in writing. This decision is ordinarily accompanied by a written opinion in which the court explains the basis or reasons for its decision. If the appellate justices do not agree unanimously, a dissenting opinion may be written. Some cases presented in this text contain a majority opinion or "holding" of the case, followed by a dissenting or "minority" opinion.

The decision by an appellate court ordinarily takes one of three forms: (1) If the appellate court finds that no error of law has occurred, it will **affirm** the judgment of the trial court. (2) If prejudicial error is found, the appellate court may **reverse** or **modify** that judgment. (3) When the evidence does not clearly justify a decision for one party or the other, the appellate court may *reverse* and *remand* the judgment of the trial court. To **remand** the case means that the appellate court directs the trial judge to hold a new trial or to take other action regarding the case.

The opinions of the highest appellate courts of each state are published in two places: (1) in the official state reports and (2) in a series of books called *The National Reporter System,* where opinions are grouped by geographic areas of the United States. For example, turn to page 4 where the first case in this book appears. The letters and numbers under the case name are called the *citation*. The citation "21 Mass. App. 692, 489 N.E.2d 1036 (1986)" means the full text of the case is printed in volume 21 of the *Massachusetts Appeals Court Report* beginning at page 692, and is also printed in volume 489 of the *Northeastern (Second) Reporter* beginning at page 1036. The numbers in parentheses signify the year of the decision, 1986.

THE COURT SYSTEM

In most states the same court system handles both criminal and civil cases. To distinguish between criminal matters and civil, first realize that *crimes* are offenses against the state as the sovereign authority. Since such offenses are against the entire society, against *the public,* it is the state (i.e., government) that brings suit, not the victim of the crime, and it is the states' attorneys who prosecute in criminal cases, not private attorneys. Other functions and procedures unique to criminal law are discussed in Chapter 9, but as this book deals with commercial law, the discussion of the court system and procedure that follows will focus upon civil law matters.

Function of Courts

The word "court" has various meanings. At times it is synonymous with "judge," as when a judge tells an attorney to address his or her remarks "to the court and not to the opposing counsel." At other times it indicates the place where a judicial tribunal functions, as in the statement that *trials* must take place "in court," whereas *orders* may be signed "in chambers" (the judge's office). Usually, however, **court** means a tribunal established by the state or federal government for the administration of justice.

The main function of a court is to decide controversies between parties in a lawsuit—the **litigation,** a term which comes to us from Latin roots meaning *to dispute*. The parties in dispute are called **litigants,** and the court's decision is called a **judgment.** Since the court's main function is to resolve disputes, it ordinarily will not answer hypothetical questions; it will not advise, for example, what a person's rights would be under a *proposed* contract. But, if there is a real dispute to be decided, the courts may *declare the rights* of parties to a controversy even though no actual wrong has occurred. These judgments, called **declaratory judgments,** in which rights are declared without ordering the parties to do anything, are useful because they permit rights to be determined (as under existing leases, contracts, wills of deceased persons, statutes, etc.) before harmful action has been taken. Several cases presented in later chapters involve requests for declaratory judgments.

Jurisdiction of Courts

The word "jurisdiction" is used in different senses, but for our purpose **jurisdiction** means *the authority or power of a court to hear and decide controversies*. In order to process a case, a court must have two kinds of jurisdiction:

- Jurisdiction over the subject matter (type of case)
- Jurisdiction over the property or over the litigants

Jurisdiction over the subject matter in a case depends on the hierarchy within the court system, and on limitations set within states and for federal districts. A court may have jurisdiction to hear breach-of-contract cases, for example, but be limited to suits in which no more than $10,000 is claimed for damages. Another court can hear divorce cases but not hear challenges to ordinances or statutes.

Jurisdiction over property (called **in rem jurisdiction**) is limited generally to a defined geographic area. Generally, a state court will have authority to handle cases involving lands lying within the state but not over lands beyond its borders.

Jurisdiction over the parties (called **personal jurisdiction**) is necessary when a party seeks to impose personal liability on another, such as an action for an injunction or for damages, or for alimony or child support. If both parties reside in the same community, the suit will be decided by the local courts. But a jurisdictional dispute can arise if one party's permanent home (called **domicile**) is in another state.

Two concepts—*implied consent* and *minimum contacts*—help a court decide if it has jurisdiction over persons domiciled elsewhere. An example is a business based in Michigan that regularly transports goods to Ohio, Indiana, and Illinois; it has at least minimum contact in each of those states and can come under their courts' jurisdiction. Another example involves nonresident motorists. Most states have a statute under which an out-of-state driver is said to impliedly consent to the jurisdiction of the local courts over any lawsuit arising from use of the highways. Such a driver can be held liable in these "foreign" (not home) states and be called to court there.

Because the United States Constitution established a dual system of government, two sets of courts—federal and state—have also been established. Where only one court has the authority to hear and decide a case, the court is said to have **exclusive jurisdiction.** Where two or more courts have authority, they have **concurrent jurisdiction** over the case. In some classes of cases the jurisdiction of the federal courts is exclusive; in other cases, federal and state courts have concurrent jurisdiction.

Exclusive Federal Jurisdiction. The U.S. Congress has given the federal courts exclusive jurisdiction over certain classes of cases where the subject of dispute is a federal statute or regulation. For example, cases involving antitrust laws, bankruptcy, patents, trademarks, copyrights, and suits to review decisions by federal administrative agencies may be brought only in federal courts.

While cases within the exclusive jurisdiction of the federal courts often are complex and involve millions of dollars, Congress has specified no minimum amount for such cases; thus, a suit under the federal Internal Revenue Code to obtain a refund of tax must be filed in a federal court even though the amount sought is only a few dollars.

Concurrent Jurisdiction. The most common type of case involving concurrent jurisdiction is one where the parties to the lawsuit are citizens of different states or nations (referred to as **diversity of citizenship**). Under present law the federal courts have jurisdiction in diversity-of-citizenship cases only when the matter in controversy exceeds the sum or value of $50,000. Let us suppose that Slick, a resident of New York, wishes to sue Chowder, a resident of Maryland, for breach of contract and seeks $80,000 in damages. If Chowder is subject to the jurisdiction of courts in New York (based on implied consent, minimum contacts, etc.), Slick may sue in either a federal court or in the state court of New York. If Chowder is not subject to the jurisdiction of courts in New York, Slick

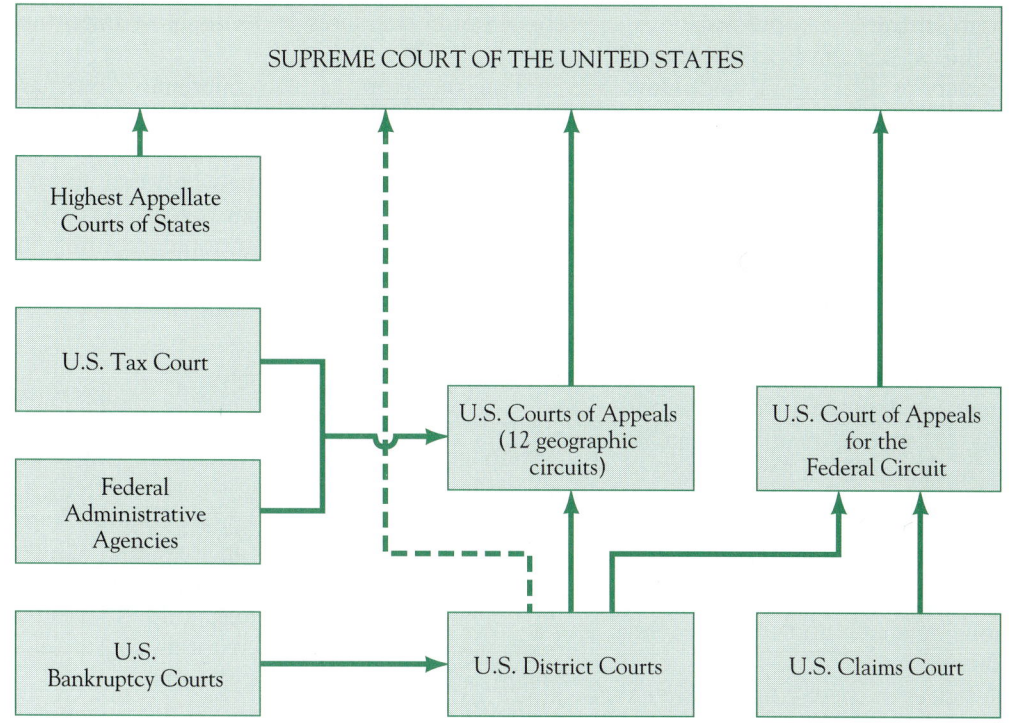

Figure 2.2 The federal court system.

may sue in either a federal or a state court in Maryland.

Exclusive State Jurisdiction. State courts have exclusive jurisdiction over certain obvious classes of cases such as divorce, child custody, and probate of wills of deceased persons. In addition, the most common types of civil lawsuits for damages, such as those resulting from automobile collisions, ordinarily involve parties living in the same state and come under the exclusive jurisdiction of state courts. When the parties to a lawsuit not involving federal law both reside in the same state or in different states but the sum involved is $50,000 or less, the state courts have exclusive jurisdiction. Thus, in the example above, if both Slick and Chowder reside in New York, the state court would have exclusive jurisdiction over the case regardless of the amount of damages asked. Or, if they resided in different states but Slick's damages were less than $50,000, Slick would have no choice but to sue Chowder in a state court.

Federal Court System

The U.S. Constitution provides that the "judicial power of the United States shall be vested in one Supreme Court, and in such inferior [lower] courts as the Congress may from time to time ordain and establish."[6] At present the federal court system consists of district courts, courts of appeals, the Supreme Court, and various special courts. Figure 2.2 illustrates the federal court system.

The President of the United States, with the advice and consent of the Senate, appoints judges who serve on federal courts for the period of their good behavior—meaning a lifetime appointment unless impeached.

District Courts. The district courts are the trial courts of the federal judicial system. Ordinarily, a litigant begins a federal lawsuit in a U.S. district court. There is one such court for each fed-

[6]U.S. Constitution, Art. III, Sec. 1, par. 1.

eral judicial district. In the less populous states, a district covers the whole state; in the more populous states, such as California and New York, there are several federal districts.

Depending upon the volume of cases filed, the court may consist of one, two, or more judges. Most cases are tried before a single judge; a few types of cases are tried before a panel of three judges.

Courts of Appeals. If a litigant is dissatisfied with the judgment rendered by the district court, the party may file an appeal with a higher court. The courts of appeals hear all appeals from district courts except for a few classes of cases where appeals may be taken directly to the Supreme Court. They also review orders of federal administrative agencies, such as the Consumer Product Safety Commission, the Environmental Protection Agency, and the Federal Trade Commission.

Originally the judges of these courts traveled a circuit and the courts were called *circuit courts of appeals*. There are at present twelve geographic circuits serving the fifty states. A panel of three judges hears appeals. The court of appeals does not retry a case which has been tried in a district court. Instead, the judges review a stenographic record of the trial to determine if an error of law was made in the trial. For example, a litigant may file an appeal alleging that the district court judge improperly denied a motion or gave the jury an erroneous instruction.

The Supreme Court. The chief function of the Supreme Court is its appellate function. Most of the cases it reviews come from the courts of appeals, although a few come from other federal courts and even from the highest state courts. Even though the highest appellate courts of the states are not part of the federal court system per se, they may have their decisions appealed to the Supreme Court when the issue in the case involves a federal question. Accordingly, these courts are included in Figure 2.2.

A litigant is not entitled as a matter of right to be heard in the U.S. Supreme Court. This is true even if a case involves a federal question. The Supreme Court has discretion to choose only the cases it deems most important to hear.

The members of the Supreme Court are called "justices." The Constitution is silent about the size of the Supreme Court, and the number of justices has varied between six and ten. It is now, and for many years has been, nine. There is no constitutional requirement that a person be a judge, or even a lawyer, to be appointed to the Supreme Court.

Special Courts. From time to time Congress has created special courts for limited purposes or for certain geographic areas. The more important special courts, with their jurisdictions briefly indicated, are as follows: (1) U.S. Claims Court: to hear nontort claims against the United States; (2) U.S. Tax Court: to hear cases involving collection of federal taxes; and (3) miscellaneous courts, including territorial courts (e.g., Guam) and the U.S. military courts.

In 1982 Congress established the U.S. Court of Appeals for the Federal Circuit. This court is based in Washington, D.C. Its functions are to review decisions of the U.S. district courts involving customs and patents and to review decisions of the U.S. Claims Court.

State Court Systems

The court systems of the states vary in details but are alike in fundamentals. Every state has a series of local trial courts of original jurisdiction and a court of appeals. The dissimilarities consist primarily in the variety of local courts, in the number of levels of appellate courts, and in the titles given to some of the courts. Figure 2.3 illustrates a typical state court system.

Judges of state courts are selected in various ways. In many states judges are elected by the citizens. In some states the governor appoints all judges. In a few states, there is a combination of appointment and election in which judges are appointed for their first term and then if a judge desires to continue in office after the expiration of the appointive term, the judge must stand for election. Often no other candidate's name appears on the ballot; the only decision the voters

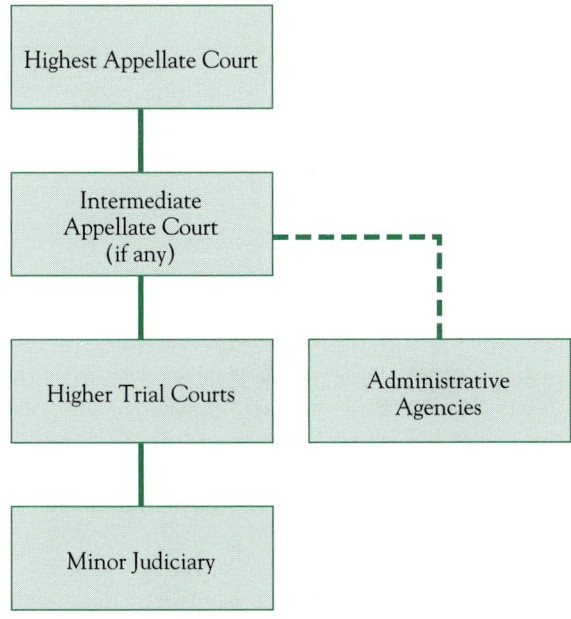

Figure 2.3 A typical state court system.

make is whether the incumbent shall be returned to office.

Trial Courts. In most states trial courts are divided into two groups—the minor judiciary and the higher trial courts.

The minor judiciary. Traditionally, officers called "justices of the peace" handle legal cases of minor nature. A justice of the peace is not required to be, and usually is not, a legally trained person. Typically, this minor judicial officer is elected by citizens in the local community. In many states the lowest trial court is called a city court, police court, or municipal court. The jurisdiction of such courts is limited.

Most states have created a special tribunal called "small claims court." This court has very limited jurisdiction; the usual maximum in damages that a party in a civil action may ask for is $1,500 to $2,000, though an emerging trend is for states to increase these maximums. There are several benefits to filing a suit in small claims court: (1) There is very little cost to the parties; (2) a hearing is held to resolve the dispute very soon after suit is filed; and (3) the trial is held in an informal manner. In some states litigants may not be represented by lawyers. The major disadvantage of a small claims suit is the limited right to appeal.

Higher trial courts. In every state there is a court of general and original jurisdiction for each county. It may be called the district court, the superior court, or the circuit court. In New York, this level of court is called "supreme court"; in Ohio, it is called "court of common pleas." In California, the jurisdiction of superior courts over civil suits is limited to cases involving an amount in controversy exceeding $25,000.

In some states, and especially in the more populous counties of some states, the courts of *general jurisdiction* are supplemented by one or more courts of *special jurisdiction*. The most commonly found courts of special jurisdiction are criminal courts, equity courts, and probate courts.

Appellate Courts. In most states the highest appellate court is called the supreme court. In New York, however, the highest appellate court is called the "court of appeals." Members of this high-level court are usually called *justices*. The number of justices serving in the highest state court varies; usually the number is either five or seven. In most states the governor appoints all supreme court justices, although in a few states such as Illinois they are elected by the citizens.

Many states have an appellate court intermediate between the trial courts and the state supreme court. A dissatisfied litigant may appeal from the trial court to the court of appeals, alleging an error of law was made by the trial judge. In Texas there are two intermediate appellate courts: the court of criminal appeals and the court of civil appeals.

As in the federal court system, appeals are heard by a panel of three justices. No new evidence is allowed; the court simply reviews the trial procedure and evidence from the stenographic record of the trial. A litigant who is dissatisfied with the decision of a court of appeals may appeal to the state supreme court. In some states appeal to the state supreme court is allowed as a matter of right. In others, such as California, an appeal to the supreme court is largely a matter of privilege, and the practice is for the court to grant the privilege only in the most important cases.

ALTERNATIVE DISPUTE RESOLUTION

The courts in many states are crowded with cases, and there is a long wait for litigants to get to trial. In some urban settings such as Chicago's Cook County, the time to get to trial in civil cases can be seven to nine years. Moreover, the costs of civil litigation sometimes are staggering. Attorney's fees, cost of depositions, and fees of expert witnesses are but a few of the items each party to a suit must pay for. Additionally, legal disputes often cause a disruption to what were good, long-standing business relationships before the disputes arose. Today, a growing trend is for the parties to a dispute to attempt to avoid litigation by means of alternative dispute resolution.

The key approaches to alternative dispute resolution are (1) negotiation, (2) arbitration, (3) mediation, and (4) mini-trials. The important features of these alternative approaches are summarized here.

Negotiation

The plain meaning of **negotiation** explains much of what it is. Simply, the parties to a dispute talk out their problems. While any form of communication (telephone, mail, etc.) can be used in negotiation, the most common form is face-to-face, in-person negotiation between attorneys from both sides, sometimes involving the parties directly.

Negotiation is the most common way to dispute resolution, even when a formal lawsuit has been filed. In fact, the vast majority of civil lawsuits are resolved this way. When you hear of a case being "settled out of court," it is the process of negotiation that helped the settlement occur.

In negotiation, there are few procedural rules imposed, except by agreement of the parties themselves, who set the level of formality of the negotiation meetings. Sometimes, however, state or federal statutes impose certain procedural rules in negotiation, such as in labor dispute negotiations.

Arbitration

Arbitration is a nonjudicial method of resolving civil disputes. Rather than file a lawsuit, the disputing parties agree to let a neutral third party decide who is right and who is wrong. The parties select an arbitrator or sometimes a panel of three arbitrators. The arbitrator may be a retired judge or a person who is skilled in an area that is the subject of dispute. For example, if two parties have a disagreement involving the performance of a construction contract, they may choose a licensed contractor as an arbitrator. An arbitrator's decision, called an **award,** is binding on the parties and is subject to only a limited judicial review. Usually a party must show an illegal award, fraud, or gross mistake in order to obtain a judicial review. Absent such showing, the arbitrator's award has the force and effect of a judgment at law.

The features of arbitration which can make it a desirable way to resolve disputes are (1) it is usually less formal than a trial; (2) the rules of evidence are greatly relaxed; and (3) it is more cost- and time-efficient than going to trial. Arbitration is not a perfect alternative to a court trial, and has features which can discourage some disputing parties from using this approach. Such features are (1) no right to a jury; (2) admissibility of hearsay evidence; and (3) generally lower legal competence of arbitrators.

In rare instances and as a means of alleviating increasing court congestion, arbitration may be imposed by law (state or federal legislation) and is called **compulsory arbitration.** It is usually limited to public-interest emergency disputes between public employees—such as police officers, fire fighters, or teachers—and their employers. Compulsory *judicial arbitration* statutes provide that cases where the plaintiff is asking for damages under a certain amount, usually $20,000 to $25,000, shall be decided by arbitrators who usually are attorneys and who apply the same rules of evidence that are used in a judicial trial. A party who is not satisfied with the arbitrator's award may appeal and demand a judicial trial.

Although compulsory judicial arbitration is new and the right to appeal is liberal, the results thus far appear positive. In most states arbitration has significantly reduced the number of cases awaiting judicial trial.

Mediation

Mediation, an informal process, involves a third party—a mediator—to expedite the process of reaching a satisfactory resolution to a dispute. The third party in no way acts as a decider. Rather, the mediator aids in clarifying the issues to both sides and acts to open communication and understanding between the parties.

If mediation is successful, the outcome is a settlement agreement as if the parties had negotiated without the aid of a third party. In mediation, there are no awards, no rules of evidence, no mandatory binding outcome.

Mini-Trials

As the name suggests, **mini-trials** are little trials. However, instead of evidence being presented to a judge or a jury, the cases of the disputing parties are presented to the parties themselves.

Most commonly, mini-trials are used for disputes between companies in which the top executives are often not aware of the details of the dispute. Accordingly, what makes mini-trials work—when they do—is that company executives from both sides who have the full authority to settle a dispute are presented shortened cases and arguments by the attorneys from the opposing sides.

Then, without their attorneys, the executives meet with each other for the purpose of negotiating an outcome. As a *Wall Street Journal* article[7] put it, "After hearing arguments from both sides, these executives are able to appreciate, usually for the first time, the merits and downsides of their case. It is this balanced perspective that leads to speedy, economical settlements."

Legal disputes, moreover, are often destructive of business relationships. Mini-trials represent a way not only of avoiding destruction of relationships but also providing the parties with a way to find their own agreement, itself a positive influence to business relationship building.

SUMMARY

At the most basic level, any legal system involves two components—the law and the forum in which to apply the law.

In the United States, laws come from several sources—federal, state, and local—and by different entities such as legislatures, administrative agencies, courts, and executive arms of government.

The U.S. Constitution provides a framework on how all the various laws operate in relation to one another. Moreover, the Constitution allocates governmental power as between federal and state government and as between the three branches of the federal government.

Civil procedure is a system of rules on how disputing parties in noncriminal litigation present and resolve their controversy before a civil court. This system of rules covers the whole process from the initial filing of a complaint to start a lawsuit to the rules surrounding how to handle judgments and appeals after a trial has occurred.

The federal court system is comprised of several courts. District courts are the initial trial courts of the federal system. Depending upon the nature and location of the dispute, there are several intermediate appellate courts in the federal system. The highest court is the U.S. Supreme Court.

Though state court systems vary from state to state, the lowest court is typically from the minor judiciary—such as small claims court. The highest state court is typically a state supreme court. Depending upon the state, there are one or more intermediate appellate courts

---

[7]J.F. Henry, "Business Is Enough of a Trial: Why Go to Court?" *The Wall Street Journal,* July 24, 1989, at A14.

between the lowest courts and the supreme court.

Because civil litigation is often expensive and lengthy, alternative forms of dispute resolution have gained greater prominence in the United States. These forms of alternative dispute resolution are negotiation, arbitration, mediation, and mini-trials.

REVIEW QUESTIONS

1. (a) What are the sources of law in the United States? (b) What method or means is used by each of the sources to express the law?

2. (a) What are the chief differences between actions at law and actions in equity? (b) Describe or define the following equitable remedies: injunction and specific performance.

3. (a) What is the main function of a court? (b) What is the purpose of a declaratory judgment? (c) Explain how an action for declaratory judgment is consistent with a court's main function.

4. (a) What is the general meaning of jurisdiction? (b) Describe and give an illustration of jurisdiction over the subject matter. (c) Define personal jurisdiction and explain when it is required.

5. (a) Give two examples of classes of cases over which the federal courts have exclusive jurisdiction. (b) What is required for a federal court to have jurisdiction over a case involving citizens of different states? (c) To what extent do the *state* courts have jurisdiction over cases involving citizens of different states?

6. (a) List the items a defendant may include in an answer. (b) What is a counterclaim? (c) What happens if a plaintiff fails to answer a counterclaim? (d) Why do you think states allow, or even encourage, counterclaims?

7. (a) What is the purpose of a summary judgment? (b) Describe a circumstance for which a judge will grant a motion for summary judgment?

8. (a) What is the purpose of discovery devices? (b) Explain the purpose and use of "deposition," "interrogatory," and "request for admission of facts."

9. (a) Briefly describe the difference between opening and closing arguments in a trial. (b) Explain the difference between the degree of proof required to win a civil lawsuit and the degree of proof required for a conviction in a criminal case. (c) What is a motion for nonsuit? (d) What is a motion for directed verdict?

10. (a) What are the various forms of alternative dispute resolution? (b) Compare and contrast their features. (c) Which type of alternative dispute resolution appears to be less injurious to business relationships? Why? (d) Why do you think a party might wish to have a trial by jury rather than an arbitration proceeding?

CHAPTER 3

Business and the Constitution

The U.S. Constitution is simultaneously the legal foundation of our representative democracy, the supreme law of the nation, and the primary source of government power to regulate business and economic activity. The Constitution establishes the internal organization of the federal government. It divides power between the state and federal levels of government, and it distributes power among the branches of the federal government.

The Constitution also defines the relationship between the citizen and the state (i.e., the government, whether state or federal). The Constitution is founded on the principles of majority rule and citizen control of the government. Yet it limits the extent to which the majority may interfere with the rights of the individual. The Bill of Rights (the first ten amendments to the Constitution) and other guarantees of individual liberty in the Constitution create "zones of freedom" into which the government may not unduly intrude. Thus, our Constitution preserves a democratic system of government while at the same time limiting the state's power over individuals in certain important spheres of personal activity.

This chapter approaches the study of the Constitution from a business perspective while emphasizing fundamental principles of constitutional law. The first part reviews the development of the Constitution, which through formal amendments and interpretations by the Supreme Court, has changed significantly since the states adopted it in 1789. The second part focuses on the power of the government (state and federal) to control economic activity, while the third part discusses the relationship between federal and state power. Given the prevalence of government regulation of business, it is important to understand the government's power to control the economy, and the extent to which the states and the federal government may regulate business activities.

The fourth part discusses the constitutional rights of business. It explores the economic freedoms guaranteed by the Constitution, particularly the protection provided business property and operations, freedom of contract, and commercial advertising. The fifth part is devoted to the political rights of business firms—among them the constitutional right to engage in business lobbying, corporate-issue advertising, campaign spending, and other political activities that enable business to play an active role in the formation of public policy.

THE HISTORICAL DEVELOPMENT OF THE CONSTITUTION

The Framing of the Constitution and the Bill of Rights

During the Revolutionary War, the states in 1778 formed a loose union—a new nation-state—under the Articles of Confederation. This fragile confederation of semiautonomous states held together during the war, the rebellion against England providing the states with a common national purpose. In the years after the war, however, it became quite apparent that the Articles of Confederation were inadequate as a basis for a national government. The power of Congress under the Articles of Confederation was severely limited in several ways. A two-thirds vote of the thirteen states was required for any government action, the national government had no power to enforce the laws it passed, and the government had little power to raise revenues to fund its operations. As a result, the national government could not cope with the dire financial situation facing the nation in the postwar period.

The states for their part added to the problems caused by the weak national government. Under the Articles of Confederation, the states retained the power to regulate economic activities and they exercised this power for the benefit of in-state merchants. Economic protectionism was the order of the day with each state passing laws restricting the free movement of goods and commerce among the states. The destructive trade wars waged by the states stifled the economic vitality of the nation. The impact of protectionism and the impotency of the national government under the Articles led to popular dissatisfaction with the system and to calls for a new national order.

In 1787, a Constitutional Convention met in Philadelphia and developed a new constitution. The constitution they created was a uniquely political instrument, representing a compromise between the large and small states, and between the advocates of a strong national government and the defenders of states' rights. The new constitution corrected the primary flaws in the Articles of Confederation. It created a strong national government with the power to manage its financial affairs and enforce its laws. However, it also preserved state power by limiting the national government to the exercise of specific, enumerated powers. Powers not expressly granted to the federal government under the U.S. Constitution were retained by the states. Similarly, the Constitution eliminated the serious problem of state economic protectionism by conferring on the federal government the power to regulate interstate and international commerce. Consequently, the power of the states to impede the interstate movement of goods was effectively eliminated.

The public and many of the framers of the Constitution were concerned about the creation of a strong central government and the potential for the abuse of power by the national government. Given the historical experience with British rule, and the government oppression in Europe that led many of our forebears to come to the New World, this concern with concentrated power was understandable. In part, the division of power between the states and the national government served to reduce this danger by creating a federal government of limited powers and preserving state power. But the Constitution also incorporated a system whereby the federal government's power would be dispersed among the three branches of government at the national level, ensuring that no one person or group would have control of the national government. Under this concept of **separation of powers,** the Constitution assigned a key function of government to each of the three branches. Article I granted to Congress the power to make law; Article II gave the President the power to administer and enforce the law; and Article III conferred upon the Supreme Court the power to interpret the law and to decide cases and controversies.

To further reduce the danger of concentrated power, the Constitution also contains a system of **checks and balances** under which each branch of government has some power over another branch within its constitutionally created sphere of authority. For example, although Congress has the primary power to make laws, both the President and the Supreme Court have a role in the legislative process. The veto power allows the President to reject laws passed by Congress and thus to play an active part in the creation of law. Similarly, the Supreme Court's power of judicial review permits the Court to overturn laws that violate the Constitution. In short, because of the separation of powers and the system of checks among the branches, government action by any one branch requires the cooperation of the other branches. Thus, ours is truly a government of shared power with no element having dominant political control.

One glaring omission in the Constitution was the lack of any express guarantee of religious, political, and economic freedoms. Many of the framers of the Constitution believed that such an express statement of individual freedoms was unnecessary, either because the Constitution implicitly guaranteed fundamental rights or because the state constitutions adequately protected personal freedom. The general public, however, wary of the abuses of government power prior to the Revolution, demanded a Bill of Rights. The first Congress of the United States under the newly ratified Constitution drafted the Bill of Rights—consisting of the first ten amendments—which was ratified by 1791. Ironically, the Bill of Rights, once thought superfluous by a number of the framers, is today the single most important protection for individual liberties in the Constitution.

The Civil War Amendments

The Constitution has been amended seventeen times since the adoption of the Bill of Rights. Amendments guarantee the right of women and blacks to vote, allow for the imposition of an income tax, and limit the number of terms a President may serve. Perhaps the most important amendment to the Constitution was the Fourteenth, which was ratified in 1868. The Fourteenth Amendment was a direct consequence of the Civil War, the war that brought an end to slavery, a system that is now constitutionally prohibited under the Thirteenth Amendment. Prior to the Civil War, the Constitution contained few limitations on the power of the states to restrict individual liberties. The Bill of Rights protected the people only from the federal government and therefore provided no restraint on the states.

The equal protection and due process clauses of the Fourteenth Amendment, however, placed significant limits on the states. The equal protection clause, designed to protect the newly freed slaves from discriminatory treatment, mandates equal treatment under state law. State laws that discriminate on a suspect basis (e.g., race) or with regard to fundamental rights (e.g., the right to vote) are generally unconstitutional. The due process clause similarly protects the people from state laws that deprive an individual of "life, liberty, or property." Through a process called **selective incorporation,** the Supreme Court has held that "life, liberty, or property" includes most of the fundamental freedoms contained in the Bill of Rights. Thus, individual liberties, such as the freedoms of speech, press, and religion guaranteed under the First Amendment from infringement by the federal government, are now also protected from state infringement under the due process clause of the Fourteenth Amendment. The Fourteenth Amendment has, therefore, become the primary constitutional limitation on the states.

The Rise of Federal Power and the Fall of Economic Liberties

The industrial revolution that followed the Civil War transformed the national economy from a small-merchant, agrarian-based system to one dominated by large manufacturing entities. Although the industrial age provided substantial economic benefits through mass production techniques and advanced technologies, the period also saw the "dark side" of capitalism: the exploitation of child labor, the suppression of unions, and the rise of the trusts (monopolies that dominated large sectors of the economy). In line with the free market orientation of the economic and social scientists of the day, the Supreme Court of the 1800s interpreted the Constitution to protect the capitalist system from legislative attempts at reform, generally relying on the due process clause of the Fourteenth Amendment to strike down government interference with freedom of contract and the right to do business. As a result of the judicial interpretation of due process, many laws enacted to ameliorate the most serious abuses in the economy were held unconstitutional, including child labor restrictions and minimum wage requirements.

The industrial revolution also created an integrated economy dominated by national, not local, markets. Because effective regulation of such a national economy could not be accomplished by the states, the federal government began to impose regulations on interstate business activities. Beginning with the creation of the Interstate Commerce Commission in 1887, and with it the regulation of the railroads, the federal government became increasingly involved in the regulation of business. The Supreme Court of the 1800s, however, viewed the power of the federal government as a limited one. Business activities such as mining, manufacturing, and agriculture, for example, were considered "local" or "intrastate" and thus beyond the reach of the federal government's power to regulate interstate commerce.

This restrictive interpretation of federal government power, and the strong protection of economic liberties under the Constitution, continued until the depression in the 1930s. In 1937, the Supreme Court abandoned its narrow construction of the commerce clause in a case involving a federal law regulating labor-management relations. The Supreme Court held that the federal government can regulate intrastate business activities (e.g., the manufacturing and production of goods) when the local activities have an *effect* on interstate commerce. This change in constitutional interpretation greatly expanded the power of Congress to regulate the economy. The Court also adopted a passive judicial approach to laws regulating economic rights after 1937. Rather than act as a "superlegislature" to pass on the wisdom of social and economic legislation (by holding that such laws lack "due process"), the Supreme Court has left the legislatures free to make policy choices regarding economic freedoms. In fact, since 1937 the Supreme Court has consistently upheld laws that restrict property rights and freedom of contract. Thus, a major development of modern constitutional history is the expansion of federal legislative power under the commerce clause and the retreat of the Supreme Court from its strong protection of economic liberties.

The Modern Protection of Personal Freedoms and Minority Rights

Despite the deferential approach of the Supreme Court to social and economic regulations, the Court has remained active in the protection of personal freedoms and the rights of minorities. Because certain personal freedoms (e.g., of speech and press) are so essential to the proper functioning of the political process, the Court has carefully guarded these **preferred freedoms** from infringement by officials in power, thus ensuring the fairness and openness of the democratic system. The Supreme Court has also confronted a related problem concerning minority rights. Because the democratic process is founded upon the principle of majority rule, it does not provide an adequate check on laws oppressive to minority groups. The Court has been careful, therefore, to protect the constitutional rights of racial, ethnic, religious, and political minorities. Thus, although the Supreme Court now leaves business and economic regulation largely to the legislature, the Court vigorously protects personal freedoms and minority rights against undue legislative infringement.

FEDERAL AND STATE POWER TO CONTROL ECONOMIC ACTIVITY

The States and the Police Power

Our Constitution creates a unique system of **federalism** under which government power is divided between the states and the federal government. The theory of the Constitution is that the states retained all power not granted to the federal government. So, for example, the states surrendered to the federal government the power to regulate interstate commerce to enable the federal government to control commercial activity among the states. At the same time,

BOX 3.1
Developments in the Law
The Twenty-seventh Amendment?

In 1789, the first Congress under the Constitution proposed twelve amendments, ten of which were ratified and became known as the Bill of Rights. One of the amendments, proposed by James Madison, provided as follows:

No law, varying the compensation for the services of the Senators and Representatives, shall take effect, until an election of Representatives shall have intervened.

This compensation amendment failed to secure the necessary three fourths of the states required for ratification under Article V of the Constitution, it being rejected by five states and ratified by only six.

Constitutional scholars and historians generally considered the amendment to be a dead letter. However, in 1982 Gregory Watson, a student at the University of Texas, wrote a paper for a government course in which he argued that the compensation amendment was still viable because Congress had not set a time limit for ratification of the amendment. He received a "C" for the course, but his interest in the topic led him to start a crusade to secure adoption of the compensation amendment. As a result of his efforts, thirty-two more states ratified the amendment between 1984 and 1992, Michigan becoming the thirty-eighth state on May 7, 1992. In an act of political courage, both the House and Senate voted to approve the amendment.

But was the amendment properly ratified? Can an amendment proposed in 1789, which failed to achieve the necessary number of states for ratification, lie dormant for 200 years and be ratified in 1992? Article V of the Constitution is silent on the time within which an amendment must be ratified. Some commentators have argued that a proposed amendment must be ratified within some reasonable time to ensure that it represents a political consensus of the people at the time it was proposed. Others, like Gregory Watson, contend that unless Congress restricts the time period for an amendment to be ratified, it is open indefinitely.

If the amendment was properly ratified, what is its effect? Relying on the amendment, twenty-seven members of Congress and others challenged the constitutionality of the Ethics Reform Act of 1989 which provides automatic cost-of-living adjustments (COLAs) for congressional salaries. A federal district court in *Boehner v. Anderson,* 809 F. Supp. 138 (D. D.C. 1992) rejected the challenge, reasoning that the COLAs under the 1989 law did not take effect until after the intervening congressional election in 1990. Thus, the law complied with the letter of the Twenty-seventh Amendment. The court in *Boehner* rejected the argument that the Twenty-seventh Amendment requires Congress to enact a new law for every pay raise.

What do you think about the Twenty-seventh Amendment? Did the ratification comply with the Constitution? Does the amendment prohibit Congress from enacting a law providing for automatic annual pay increases?

however, the states retained the power to regulate intrastate commercial activity. The Tenth Amendment to the Constitution expressly guarantees this division of political power. It provides that "[t]he power not delegated to the United States by the Constitution, nor prohibited by it to the States, are reserved to the States respectively, or to the people."

The residual power retained by the states is referred to as the **police power**—the inherent power of the states to regulate for the public health, safety, welfare, and morals. This police power is the foundation upon which the states have actively regulated business activity. Health and safety laws, consumer protection statutes, the licensing of professionals, and workers' compensation laws are some of the vast array of state legislation affecting economic activity. Under the broad scope of the police power, the states have the authority to regulate the use and enjoyment of property, the terms and conditions of business contracts, and the manner in which business operates in the marketplace.

Federal Power and the Commerce Clause

In contrast, the framers of the Constitution created a federal government of delegated powers. Congress has no power to legislate in a particular sphere—economic or social—unless it can identify a particular grant of authority in the Constitution that empowers it to act. Unlike the states, which have the inherent power to legislate under the police power, the federal government was established as a government of **enumerated powers.**

Nevertheless, within the framework of enumerated powers, the framers gave the federal government broad fiscal and regulatory authority. Article I, Section 8, of the Constitution details the extensive legislative authority of Congress. Among the powers granted to Congress are the power to raise and spend money, to declare war and provide for the national defense, to establish a system of federal courts inferior to the Supreme Court, and to define crimes against the nation. In terms of economic regulation, the federal government has the power to coin money, to establish a system for copyright and patent protection, to create a bankruptcy system, and to set up a post office. The taxing and spending powers are also important tools which Congress can use to control and stimulate economic activity. Congress has the power to raise money, by borrowing "on the credit of the United States" or through the imposition of "Taxes, Duties, Imposts and Excises," and to spend money for "the common Defense and general Welfare."

Congress also has **implied powers,** powers not expressly delegated to it under the Constitution. In the landmark case of McCullough v. Maryland,[1] the Supreme Court held that Congress had the power to establish a national bank even though no such power was expressly contained in Article I, Section 8. The Court reasoned that the creation of a national bank was a legitimate legislative *means* of implementing Congress' power to regulate commerce, to raise money, and to provide for the national defense. Thus, under the implied powers doctrine, Congress is free to adopt any legislative program to carry out its express powers under the Constitution.

Although the doctrine of implied powers greatly enlarged the regulatory authority of Congress, the primary source of federal power to control the economic life of the nation is the **commerce clause.** The commerce clause provides that "Congress shall have power . . . to regulate commerce with foreign nations, among the several states, and with the Indian tribes." Under the modern interpretation of the clause, Congress can regulate any activity (social or economic) when that activity has an effect on interstate commerce.

The best example of the breadth of federal power is the case of *Wickard v. Filburn.*[2] The constitutional issue in *Wickard* was whether Congress had the power under the commerce clause to regulate wheat grown and consumed on the farm. Under the Agriculture Adjustment Act of 1938, Congress established a system of acreage allotments for individual farmers to control the production of wheat. Roscoe Filburn, a small farmer in Ohio, having been allotted 11.1 acres, grew wheat on 23 acres and used part of his harvest for his family. He challenged the law, claiming that it exceeded the power of Congress under the commerce clause. The Supreme Court rejected Filburn's contention that Congress had no power to control that part of a farmer's production of wheat that was consumed on the farm. The Court reasoned that since the price for wheat in the marketplace is a product of aggregate consumer demand, and since a farmer who grows his own wheat will have less need (and thus less demand) for wheat from the mar-

---

[1] 17 U.S. (4 Wheat.) 316 (1819).
[2] 317 U.S. 111 (1942).

ketplace, the market price for wheat will be affected by home consumption. Although Roscoe Filburn's effect on the marketplace was minimal, the Court further reasoned that if all farmers grew and consumed wheat in violation of the production quotas, the effect on the market price would be significant.

The standard adopted in *Wickard* is called the **cumulative effect** test. Because this standard allows Congress to regulate business whenever the combined activities of all regulated businesses have an effect on interstate commerce, the commerce clause power is very broad. Moreover, the Supreme Court will generally defer to a congressional judgment that an activity has an effect on interstate commerce. For example, the Court recently upheld a federal law regulating surface coal mining operations, accepting congressional findings that strip mining had an effect on interstate commerce. The Court declared that federal regulation under the commerce clause is valid as long as Congress has a conceivable basis for its conclusion that the regulated activity has an effect on interstate commerce.

THE RELATIONSHIP BETWEEN FEDERAL AND STATE LAW

Dual Business Regulation

The Constitution allows both levels of government to simultaneously regulate a particular business or industry practice, and dual regulation by the state and federal governments is common in our federal system. The regulation of securities (e.g., stocks and bonds) sold to the public provides an illustrative example. The issuance (initial sale) of new securities to the public is governed by a federal law, the Securities Act of 1933. The Act requires an issuer (the company selling the security) to file a registration statement with the Securities and Exchange Commission prior to any sale, unless the security or the sale is exempt. The registration statement, along with a prospectus given to investors, contains detailed information about the securities and the financial condition of the issuer. It is designed to provide investors with material information upon which they can make their investment decision. The issuer must also comply with the securities laws of the states in which the security will be sold. Some states have a registration requirement similar to federal law. Others require the issuer to "qualify" the security (establish the soundness of the investment). In either event, the issuer must comply with the requirements of both state and federal law.

Federal Supremacy and Preemption

Despite the prevalence of business regulation at both the state and federal levels, the Constitution grants to Congress sole authority over certain matters. For example, the states are prohibited from coining money, entering into treaties, and taxing imports or exports (without the consent of Congress). Moreover, even where the state and federal governments have dual authority, Congress may elect to exercise exclusive regulatory control, since under the **supremacy clause** of the Constitution, federal law is superior to state law. Thus, as long as Congress is acting within its constitutional powers (including the commerce clause), it may choose to be the sole regulator—for example, to provide uniform national regulation.

When Congress exercises exclusive regulatory control, we refer to this as **preemption. Express preemption** occurs when a federal law or regulation contains a provision that limits state authority over a given regulatory sphere. For example, the Airline Deregulation Act of 1978 provides that "no State . . . shall enact or enforce any law . . . relating to rates, routes, or services of any air carrier. . . ." The Supreme Court held in *Morales v. Trans World Airlines, Inc.*[3] that this provision preempted state laws prohibiting deceptive fare advertising.

Implied preemption, on the other hand, occurs when the federal law or regulation does not contain a preemption provision, but federal law is so extensive as to leave no room for state regulation or state law conflicts with federal law.

[3]112 S. Ct. 2031 (1992).

For example, if it is impossible to comply with both federal and state law, the state law is impliedly preempted. When such a conflict exists, the courts presume that Congress intended federal law to control over state law.

To resolve an issue of implied preemption, the courts must determine the underlying reason or purpose for the federal law and the effect that compliance with state law will have on federal objectives. When compliance with state law frustrates the purposes of federal law, it is preempted. For example, Burbank, California, passed an ordinance prohibiting jet airplanes from taking off from the city airport between 11 p.m. and 7 a.m. The Supreme Court held that the ordinance was preempted by the Federal Aviation Act because it interfered with the Federal Aviation Administration's ability to control air traffic flow and thereby insure the safety of the public, important objectives of the federal law.

State Regulation of Interstate Business Activities

As was noted earlier, the commerce clause was designed to prevent state economic protectionism. The commerce clause still serves this purpose by imposing a constitutional limit on state power to regulate interstate commerce. However, the commerce clause does not bar all state regulation. Many state laws have a permitted incidental effect on the interstate marketplace. The commerce clause prohibits two types of state laws: (1) laws that **unfairly discriminate** against interstate commerce, and (2) neutral (nondiscriminatory) laws that place an **undue burden** on interstate commerce.

Unfair Discrimination against Interstate Commerce. Barriers to free trade can take many forms, but the most common are laws restricting out-of-state businesses from entering local markets. State legislators naturally respond to political pressure by passing laws that protect local interests at the expense of out-of-state firms; but discriminatory laws of this type are almost always declared unconstitutional by the Supreme Court. State laws that discriminate against interstate commerce or that favor in-state economic groups over their out-of-state competitors are presumed invalid unless the state can show (1) that the discrimination serves state interests unrelated to economic protectionism, and (2) that these purposes cannot be served by some nondiscriminatory regulation.

For example, a Florida law prohibited out-of-state financial institutions (banks and bank holding companies) from owning in-state investment advisory services. Florida contended that the law served two purposes: (1) it protected Floridians from fraudulent practices, and (2) it prevented economic concentration in its finance market. The Supreme Court struck down the law, noting that there was no showing that out-of-state financial institutions were more prone than local ones to fraudulent or monopolistic practices. The Court also noted that the state had many regulatory alternatives at its disposal to deal with fraud and monopoly power. The state was, therefore, unable to establish any justification for treating out-of-state companies differently from in-state businesses or to show why its interests could not be served by a less discriminatory measure.

In Case 3.1, the Court grapples with the issue of the constitutionality of a state tax on the importation of out-of-state hazardous waste. As you read the case, you should be aware that the Supreme Court had previously ruled that waste is an article of commerce.

CASE 3.1 Chemical Waste Management, Inc. v. Hunt • 112 S. Ct. 2009 (1992)

FACTS Alabama is one of only sixteen states that have commercial hazardous waste landfills. The nation's largest facility is located in Emelle, Alabama, and is owned and operated by Chemical Waste Management, Inc. The wastes and substances being landfilled at the Emelle facility include substances that are inherently dangerous to human health and safety and to the environment, such as toxic wastes which contain poisonous and cancer-causing chemicals. Since its opening in 1977, increasing amounts of out-of-state hazardous wastes were shipped to the Emelle facility. From 1985 through 1989, the tonnage of hazardous waste received per year doubled, and up to 90 percent of the waste was shipped in from other states. In response, Alabama passed a law imposing a fee of $25.60 per ton on hazardous waste disposed of at a commercial landfill and an additional disposal fee of $72 per ton on hazardous wastes generated outside the state. Chemical Waste Management filed suit in state court seeking to enjoin enforcement of the Act. The trial court declared the additional fee to be in violation of the commerce clause, the Alabama Supreme Court reversed, and the Supreme Court granted certiorari.

OPINION WHITE, J. . . . No State may attempt to isolate itself from a problem common to the several States by raising barriers to the free flow of interstate trade. . . .

The Act's additional fee facially discriminates against hazardous waste generated in States other than Alabama, and the Act overall has plainly discouraged the full operation of [the] Emelle facility. . . .

The State, however, argues that the additional fee imposed on out-of-state hazardous waste serves legitimate local purposes related to its citizens' health and safety. Because the additional fee discriminates both on its face and in practical effect, the burden falls on the State "to justify it both in terms of the local benefits flowing from the statute and the unavailability of nondiscriminatory alternatives adequate to preserve the local interests at stake." . . .

The [State's interests] may all be legitimate. . . . But . . . [a]s found by the Trial Court, ". . . there is absolutely no evidence before this Court that waste generated outside Alabama is more dangerous than waste generated in Alabama. . . ." The burden is on the State to show that "the discrimination is demonstrably justified by a valid factor unrelated to economic protectionism" . . . and it has not carried this burden.

Ultimately, the State's concern focuses on the volume of the waste entering the Emelle facility. Less discriminatory alternatives, however, are available to alleviate this concern, not the least of which are a generally applicable per-ton additional fee on all hazardous waste disposed of within Alabama . . . or a per-mile tax on all vehicles transporting hazardous waste across Alabama roads . . . or an evenhanded cap on the total tonnage landfilled at Emelle . . . which would curtail volume from all sources. . . .

. . . [The] record establishes that the hazardous waste at issue in this case is the same regardless of its point of origin. . . . [A]dequate means other than overt discrimination meet Alabama's concerns. . . .

> **CASE 3.1
> Continued**
>
> **JUDGMENT** The decision of the Alabama Supreme Court is reversed and the cause remanded. . . .
>
> **DISSENT** REHNQUIST, C.J. . . . [T]he Court continues to err by its failure to recognize that waste—in this case admittedly hazardous waste—presents risk to the public health and environment that a State may legitimately wish to avoid, and that the State may pursue such an objective by means less Draconian than an outright ban. Under force of this Court's precedent, though, it increasingly appears that the only avenue by which a State may avoid the importation of hazardous wastes is to ban such waste disposal altogether, regardless of the waste's source of origin. . . . The Court . . . refuses to acknowledge that a safe and attractive environment is the commodity really at issue in cases such as this. . . . The result is that the Court today gets it exactly backward when it suggests that Alabama is attempting to "isolate itself from a problem common to the several States." . . . To the contrary, it is the 34 States that have no hazardous waste facility whatsoever, not to mention the remaining 15 states with facilities all smaller than Emelle, that have isolated themselves. . . .

Undue Burden on Interstate Commerce. Nondiscriminatory (neutral) state laws that impose burdens on interstate commerce are subject to a different constitutional analysis. In contrast to discriminatory laws that are per se unconstitutional, neutral laws are constitutional unless they impose an undue burden on interstate commerce. To determine when the burden is undue, the Supreme Court looks at two factors: (1) the extent to which the law will serve legitimate interests in public health, welfare, or safety, and (2) the nature of the burden imposed on the free flow of goods in interstate commerce. For example, the Supreme Court struck down an Iowa statute generally prohibiting 65-foot double-trailer trucks on its roads. The law, designed to promote traffic safety, imposed a substantial burden on interstate commerce. To comply with the law, which was different from the laws of all other states in the West and Midwest, trucking firms had to use shorter trucks, separate the double-trailers at the border, or reroute their shipments through adjoining states. Since the record indicated that the double-trailers were as safe as 55-foot trailers, and thus the state's interest in safety was not furthered by the law, the Court concluded that it imposed an undue burden on interstate commerce.

ECONOMIC FREEDOMS UNDER THE CONSTITUTION

As was noted earlier, the Constitution limits the government's authority to control certain personal, social, and political activities. Because the Constitution also protects economic freedoms, it creates an area of conflict between the economic rights of business and the government's power to protect the public health, safety, and welfare. To what extent can the government control business activities for the benefit of employees or consumers, for example, without depriving businesses of their constitutional rights?

This section concentrates on the economic freedoms under the Constitution by focusing on the power of the government to regulate important activities of a business firm. Before we address these economic freedoms, however, some preliminary observations are in order about the nature of constitutional rights in general.

First, people and businesses have a host of constitutional rights that are generally unrelated to most commercial transactions and business enterprises. For example, the Constitution contains an implicit guarantee of privacy which protects certain intimate decisions concerning marriage and procreation from government control. This right of privacy obviously has little or no application to the typical business corporation, unless, for example, the business is engaged in the sale of contraceptives. This chapter, however, emphasizes those constitutional guarantees which are of more general application to business.

Second, when we speak of constitutional rights, we are referring to limitations on what the *government* (not private persons) can do. The Constitution protects businesses (indeed, *all* persons) from governmental interference. (The law of property, torts, and contracts protects businesses from private interference.) For a business to claim a violation of constitutional rights, therefore, there must be **state action**—i.e., a restriction on freedom imposed by the government, be it federal, state, county, or municipal.

Third, laws restricting the exercise of constitutional rights may be valid if the government demonstrates the need for a restriction. The burden imposed on the government will vary depending upon the importance of the constitutional right in question. To judge whether the government has met its burden, the Supreme Court has developed "tests" of constitutionality that fall into three major categories: **strict scrutiny, intermediate scrutiny,** and **minimum scrutiny.**

The Court employs strict scrutiny, for example, when a law interferes with fundamental personal and political rights, such as the right to vote. To satisfy strict scrutiny—the most demanding constitutional standard—the government must establish that the government restriction is the most limited means of furthering a "compelling state interest" (an interest of paramount societal concern such as the elimination of racial discrimination). In contrast, minimum scrutiny is frequently employed to judge the constitutionality of laws restricting property rights and freedom of contract. A law satisfies minimum scrutiny when it is rationally related to a "conceivable state interest." Under this **rational basis** test, the government must show

only that the law is a reasonable way of achieving some legitimate (not necessarily important or compelling) public purpose. Under intermediate scrutiny, the government must show that the government restriction is a limited way of furthering an "important" or "substantial" government interest. For example, the Court uses a form of intermediate scrutiny to judge laws banning truthful commercial advertising. Finally, the Court sometimes employs a **balancing** test rather than applying any distinct level of judicial scrutiny. Under a balancing analysis, the Court weighs (balances) the importance of the government interest against the severity of the restriction on individual liberty to determine whether the law is constitutional.

Business Property and Operations

Because business operates to earn a profit in the marketplace, the most important rights of business from a strictly economic perspective are the constitutional protection of property and the freedom accorded business operations. These economic freedoms include the right to use and enjoy property, the right to enter the marketplace, and the freedom to structure and organize the firm and its processes. Government regulation of property and business operations has taken many forms, from laws requiring a license to practice a trade, profession, or business, to direct controls on the use of property. There are three primary constitutional limitations on government regulation of property and business operations: the limitation on government "takings" of property, the requirement that any deprivation of property or liberty comport with "due process of law," and the guarantee of equal treatment under the law.

Takings of Property.
The government can take (seize) private property for public projects such as roads, bridges, and dams. However, this **power of eminent domain** is limited by the Constitution. Under the **taking clause** of the Fifth Amendment and the due process clause of the Fourteenth Amendment, the government, whether federal, state, or local, can take private property only for a public purpose and must pay the owner a "just compensation."

When the government exercises its power of eminent domain and "condemns" private property, there is no doubt that a "taking" has occurred. But the Supreme Court has never limited the concept of a taking to direct seizures of ownership. A taking occurs also when government restrictions on the *use* of property are so burdensome that its economic value is lost. A law that destroys the value of property without actually taking ownership is sometimes called a **regulatory taking.**

Determining when a regulation results in a taking is a difficult constitutional judgment. Most land use controls such as zoning of property and environmental restrictions are a legitimate and beneficial exercise of legislative power. Yet they may significantly restrict the physical use of the regulated property and thus diminish its value. The Supreme Court has generally upheld government restrictions that prevent the most profitable use of property, as long as the owner can make some beneficial use of it. For example, a New York City landmark preservation law prevented the owner of the Grand Central Terminal from building an office complex above the station, depriving the owner of several million dollars of rental revenue per year. Noting that the owner could still use the property as a railroad terminal and realize a reasonable return on the investment, the Supreme Court held that no taking had occurred and that the law was valid.

In contrast, the Supreme Court is likely to find a taking when the government regulation amounts to a physical occupation of property rather than a mere restriction on its use. In *Nollan v. California Coastal Commission*,[4] the Court held that the state of California could not, as a condition for a building permit, require an owner of property on the ocean to give the public the right to cross the owner's beach. Such a regulation was considered to be nothing more than the taking of an important property right (the right to the exclusive possession of the land), and could not be imposed without compensation to the owner.

In Case 3.2, the Supreme Court addresses the issue of the government's power to prohibit a particular use of land to protect the public from serious environmental harm. If such a prohibition deprives the owner of all beneficial use of the property, has a taking occurred?

[4] 483 U.S. 825 (1987).

CASE 3.2 **Lucas v. South Carolina Coastal Council • 112 S. Ct. 2886 (1992)**

FACTS   In 1986, Davis H. Lucas paid $975,000 for two residential lots on the Isle of Palms, a barrier island situated eastward of the City of Charleston in South Carolina, on which he intended to build single-family homes. In 1988, however, the South Carolina Legislature enacted the Beachfront Management Act to protect the beach/dune system along the South Carolina coast from erosion. The legislature found that development too close to the beach/dune system "jeopardized the stability of the beach/dune system, accelerated erosion, and endangered adjacent property." Under the Act construction of occupiable improvements was flatly prohibited seaward of the "baseline" connecting the landward-most "points of erosion . . . during the past forty years." The South Carolina Coastal Council fixed the baseline landward of Lucas's parcels which had the effect of barring him from erecting any permanent habitable structures on his two parcels. A state trial court found that the Act's permanent ban on construction "deprived Lucas of any reasonable economic use of the lots . . . and rendered them valueless." It thus concluded that the properties had been "taken" by operation of the Act, and it ordered the South Carolina Coastal Council to pay "just compensation" in

**CASE 3.2
Continued**

the amount of $1,232,387.50. The Supreme Court of South Carolina reversed and the U.S. Supreme Court granted certiorari.

OPINION

SCALIA, J. . . . [We] recognized in [*Pennsylvania Coal Co. v. Mahon*] . . . that, "while property may be regulated to a certain extent, if regulation goes too far it will be recognized as a taking."

Nevertheless, our decision in *Mahon* offered little insight into when, and under what circumstances, a given regulation would be seen as going "too far" for purposes of the Fifth Amendment. In 70-odd years of succeeding "regulatory takings" jurisprudence, we have generally eschewed any "set formula" . . . preferring to engage in . . . essentially ad hoc, factual inquiries." We have, however, described at least two discrete categories of regulatory action as compensable without case-specific inquiry into the public interest advanced in support of the restraint. The first encompasses regulations that compel the property owner to suffer a physical "invasion" of his property. . . .

The second situation in which we have found categorical treatment appropriate is where regulation denies all economically beneficial or productive use of land. . . .

We have never set forth the justification for this rule. Perhaps it is simply . . . that total deprivation of beneficial use is, from the landowner's point of view, the equivalent of a physical appropriation. . . .

On the other side of the balance, affirmatively supporting a compensation requirement, is the fact that regulations that leave the owner of the land without economically beneficial or productive options for its use—typically, as here, by requiring land to be left substantially in its natural state—carry with them a heightened risk that private property is being pressed into some form of public service under the guise of mitigating serious public harm. . . .

We think, in short, that there are good reasons for our . . . belief that when the owner of real property has been called upon to sacrifice all economically beneficial uses in the name of the common good . . . he has suffered a taking. . . .

Where the State seeks to sustain regulation that deprives land of all economically beneficial use, we think it may resist compensation only if [it] shows that the proscribed use interests were not part of his title to begin with. . . . It seems to us that the property owner necessarily expects the uses of his property to be restricted, from time to time, by various measures newly enacted by the State. . . . And in the case of personal property, by reason of the State's traditionally high degree of control over commercial dealings, he ought to be aware of the possibility that new regulation might even render his property economically worthless. . . . In the case of land, however, we think the notion . . . that title is somehow held subject to the "implied limitation" that the State may subsequently eliminate all economically valuable use is inconsistent with the historical compact recorded in the Takings Clause. . . .

It seems unlikely that common-law principles would have prevented the erection of any habitable or productive improvements on petitioner's land. . . . The question, however, is one of state law to be dealt with on remand. We emphasize that to win its case South Carolina must . . . identify background principles of nuisance and property law that prohibit the uses [Lucas] now intends in

CASE 3.2 Continued

the circumstances in which the property is presently found. Only on this showing can the State fairly claim that, in proscribing all such beneficial uses, the Beachfront Management Act is taking nothing.

JUDGMENT

The judgment is reversed and the case remanded. . . .

DISSENT

BLACKMUN, J. . . . The South Carolina Supreme Court found that the Beachfront Management Act did not take petitioner's property without compensation. The decision rested on [the] premise . . . that the State has the power to prevent any use of property it finds to be harmful to its citizens. . . .

If this state legislature is correct that the prohibition on building in front of the setback line prevents serious harm, then, under this Court's prior cases, the Act is constitutional. "Long ago it was recognized that all property in this country is held under the implied obligation that the owner's use of it shall not be injurious to the community, and the Takings Clause did not transform that principle to one that requires compensation whenever the State asserts its power to enforce it." . . . The Court consistently has upheld regulations imposed to arrest a significant threat to the common welfare, whatever their economic effect on the owner. . . .

Petitioner never challenged the legislature's findings that a building ban was necessary to protect property and life. . . . Nothing in the record undermines the General Assembly's assessment that prohibitions on building in front of the setback line are necessary to protect people and property from storms, high tides, and beach erosion. Because that legislative determination cannot be disregarded in the absence of such evidence . . . and because its determination of harm to life and property from building is sufficient to prohibit that use under this Court's cases, the South Carolina Supreme Court correctly found no taking.

Due Process of Law. The Fifth and the Fourteenth Amendments prohibit the federal government and the state governments respectively from depriving a person of "life, liberty, or property, without due process of law." **Due process** (fair government conduct when restricting basic rights) has both a substantive and procedural component.

Substantive due process. **Substantive due process** has to do with the *content* of a law or regulation—with the rights it confers or the duties it imposes. A law lacks substantive due process if it is arbitrary, wholly unreasonable, or irrelevant to legislative policy. A law barring blond-haired people from the teaching profession would lack substantive due process (and violate other constitutional provisions as well), since hair color is not rationally related to teaching competence. In contrast, a law requiring building contractors to demonstrate technical competence before being licensed is related to the government interest in protecting the public welfare, and so does not deprive the burdened contractors of substantive due process.

Prior to 1937, the Supreme Court used substantive due process to invalidate many laws that restricted economic freedoms, applying a form of strict scrutiny in the area of business rights. In the modern era, the Supreme Court has taken quite a different approach. It now uses a rational basis standard to resolve issues of substantive due process. Under this standard, a law offends substantive due process only when it is wholly unrelated to any conceivable state interest. In applying this test, the Court generally defers to the judgment of the legislature as to the need for government regulation, thus giving the legislature wide latitude to exercise its powers.

Procedural due process. **Procedural due process** is concerned with the steps or process that the government follows when depriving a person of constitutionally protected rights. The government must follow procedures that are fair to individuals whose rights will be affected. A procedural due process case involves two key questions. First, did the government deprive an individual of a property or liberty right? If not, due process steps are not required. Second, if the government did restrict a protected interest, what procedural steps were required to ensure fair treatment of the individual?

The threshold issue is whether the government has deprived one of a constitutional right to property or liberty. **Property** includes any common law right to the possession, use, or enjoyment of tangible or intangible assets. Absolute ownership (title) is not essential; property includes lesser interests as well, such as a tenant's right to possess and use an apartment under a lease. Property also encompasses government entitlements, such as a business license, even though they amount to privileges provided by the state. **Liberty** consists of a range of protected interests beyond freedom from bodily restraint, including the right to pursue a lawful profession, trade, or business. Thus, government action restricting an individual's right to do business, for example, based on a judgment as to the individual's competency, education, or moral fitness must satisfy due process standards.

Notice and a hearing—the basic features of due process—are essential in any case to ensure fair treatment of the individual. Notice informs a person of the action contemplated by the government. A hearing provides the person with an opportunity to contest the government action. The precise procedural steps—the type of hearing and notice—required under the due process clause will vary, however, depending upon a number of factors. In determining "what process is due," the Supreme Court employs a balancing test in which it considers the property or liberty interests affected by the government action, the countervailing government or private interests served by the government action, the risk of error in the procedures employed, and the cost and value of employing additional procedures.

For example, in *Connecticut v. Doehr*,[5] the Court struck down a Connecticut statute that allowed the plaintiff (the person bringing a civil lawsuit) to "attach" (seize) the real estate of the defendant (the person being sued), without prior notice and a hearing and before a trial on the merits. The Supreme Court concluded that such a prejudgment attachment was a significant infringement of the defendant's property rights and that without a hearing or trial, the risk of error was substantial. The Court considered the plaintiff's countervailing interest—ensuring the availability of assets to pay if the suit was successful—minimal, since there was no allegation that the defendant would transfer or conceal his property before trial.

As *Connecticut v. Doehr* demonstrates, the government must provide individuals a hearing *before* any government deprivation of property. Only under limited circumstances has the Court allowed government seizures without a prior hearing (called **summary administrative actions**). For example, to protect the public health, the Court has allowed summary seizures of unwholesome food and mislabeled products. Recently, the Supreme Court upheld a federal law authorizing the Secretary of the Interior to order a mine owner immediately to stop mining operations to prevent imminent environmental damage. The Court noted, however, that only an emergency can justify summary administrative action; and even in emergencies, procedural due process requires a prompt postseizure hearing.

Equal protection. Legislation frequently classifies businesses differently and subjects the classes to different rules and regulations. The result is discriminatory treatment under the law. The major constitutional impediment to such unequal treatment is the **equal protection clause** of the Fourteenth Amendment, which provides that no *state* shall "deny to any person . . . the equal protection of the laws." The

---

[5] 111 S. Ct. 2105 (1991).

> **BOX 3.2**
>
> ### Developments in the Law: Punitive Damages and Due Process
>
> In a civil lawsuit, the jury may sometimes award punitive damages to the prevailing party, a sum of money in addition to the amount necessary to compensate him or her (compensatory damages). Punitive damages are designed to punish the wrongdoer and to deter others from committing similar wrongs. The amount is generally left to the discretion of the jury, which is supposed to consider the wrongfulness of the conduct and the need to deter others in its determination.
>
> With increasing frequency, juries have awarded huge punitive damage awards in recent years. For example, in 1993, a Georgia jury awarded over $100 million in punitive damages to the parents of a child who died in an allegedly defective General Motors truck. Such awards have been criticized by businesses and others who contend that punitive damage awards are unpredictable, are the product of jury prejudices, and represent a form of unfair wealth redistribution. The critics have been successful in convincing many state legislatures to limit the amount of punitive damages a jury may award.
>
> The opponents have also attacked the constitutionality of punitive damages, claiming a violation of substantive and procedural due process. The Supreme Court addressed this issue in *Pacific Mutual Life Insurance Co. v. Haslip*, 111 S. Ct. 1032 (1991). In *Haslip*, a jury awarded the plaintiff, who was defrauded by an insurance agent, $200,000 in compensatory and $840,000 in punitive damages. The Court upheld the award noting that the jury was properly instructed on the basis for punitive damages under Alabama law and that both the trial judge and the Alabama Supreme Court provided a substantive review of the jury's award to ensure that the amount was not excessive.
>
> The *Haslip* Court suggested that a 4 to 1 ratio between punitive and compensatory damages was "close to the line" of constitutional permissibility. In *TXO Production Corp. v. Alliance Resources Corp.*, ____ U.S. ____, 1993 U.S. Lexis 4403 (1993), the Court recently upheld a West Virginia jury award of $19,000 in compensatory and $10 million in punitive damages against TXO Production Corp. TXO, a company whose net worth was estimated to be between $2.2 and $2.5 billion, brought a frivolous lawsuit against Alliance Resources in an attempt to force Alliance to agree to a reduction in TXO's royalty payments under an oil and gas lease. The Court indicated that although the actual damages to Alliance were small, the potential damages were in the millions of dollars. The award was not considered excessive in light of the potential harm to Alliance, TXO's bad faith, and TXO's wealth. Under what circumstances should an award of punitive damages be considered a violation of due process? ■

Supreme Court has held that the due process clause of the Fifth Amendment also forbids unjustifiable *federal* discrimination.

Discriminatory statutes are subject to different tests of constitutionality depending upon the basis for and the rights affected by the discrimination. Laws discriminating on the basis of a **suspect** criterion such as race or national origin, or that burden **fundamental rights** such as the right to vote, are subject to strict scrutiny. This standard requires the government to demonstrate a compelling need for the discrimination, a heavy constitutional burden that few laws will satisfy. For example, in *City of Richmond v. J. A. Croson Co.*,[6] the Supreme Court recently invalidated a minority business set-aside law that required businesses having contracts with the city to subcontract (set aside) 30 percent of the work to minority-owned enterprises. The Court held the law unconstitutional because the city failed to prove past discrimination in the Richmond construction industry.

[6]109 S. Ct. 706 (1989).

Similarly, legislative classifications based on a **quasi-suspect** criterion such as sex or illegitimacy are subject to intermediate scrutiny. Laws discriminating against women, for example, must bear a "close and substantial relationship to important government interests." In contrast, the Supreme Court takes a more lenient approach to **social or economic legislation** (laws that burden nonfundamental rights such as the right to property and that do not discriminate on a suspect or quasi-suspect basis). The Court requires that such laws satisfy the rational basis standard applied in substantive due process inquiries. Since most business regulation will fall into the category of economic legislation, the government has great latitude to discriminate among similarly situated businesses. For example, the Court upheld a 1977 Minnesota law banning the sale of milk in nonreturnable plastic containers, but allowing the sale in nonreturnable paperboard containers. The Court held that Minnesota might have made a policy choice to proceed one step at a time in protecting the environment, dealing with plastic first and leaving paperboard for the future. Thus, in matters of economic regulation, the government may discriminate among businesses if there is at least some conceivable reason for its actions.

Freedom of Contract

Freedom to contract is vital to a market economy. Contracts enable people to arrange a variety of legally enforceable exchanges, such as those for goods and services. The government's protection of contract rights also gives stability to commercial arrangements, allowing businesses to plan and structure their economic decisions.

The Constitution protects freedom of contract in two important ways. First, the right to contract receives a limited due process protection. Second, the contract clause restricts government "impairments" of contracts.

Liberty of Contract. The right to contract is considered a "liberty" interest under the due process clauses. Consequently, freedom of contract has been subject to the varying standards of due process protection discussed earlier in this chapter. Before 1937, the Supreme Court struck down many laws that interfered with liberty of contract, such as those protecting workers, setting prices, or otherwise controlling contract terms. Illustrative of this period is the 1905 case, *Lochner v. New York*.[7] In it, a New York law setting a maximum of 60 hours per week for bakery employees was held to be an unconstitutional infringement on the liberty of contract. Since 1937, however, the Court has applied the rational basis test not only to property cases, but to liberty of contract cases as well. Because a regulation need serve only some conceivable government interest to be constitutional, the government has the same broad leeway to regulate the content of private contracts that it has to regulate other economic freedoms.

Impairments of Contract. Before the Constitution was adopted, the early state legislatures enacted various forms of "debtor relief" laws in response to political pressure from the financially distressed populace. These laws allowed debtors to escape or delay the repayment of lawful debts. To prevent the states from impairing the rights of creditors, and to protect other legitimate contractual expectations, the framers of the Constitution added the **contract clause:** "No State shall . . . pass any . . . Law impairing the Obligation of Contracts." The Supreme Court has held that the requirements of due process impose a similar limitation on the federal government.

In an early contract clause case, the Supreme Court held that there is no **impairment** of contract when a law merely regulates *future* contracts—i.e., those entered into *after* the passage of the law. The contracting parties are presumed to know any law that is in effect when a contract is made. Therefore, the parties accept as part of the contract the conditions imposed by existing law, and no impairment of contract rights can occur when a law operates prospectively. This interpretation allows the government to regulate future contracts without violating the contract clause.

[7]198 U.S. 45.

A contract impairment occurs only when the law changes or modifies the rights or duties of parties under existing contracts. The absolute language of the contract clause seems to invalidate any impairment of contract rights, but the Supreme Court has employed a balancing test to laws impairing contracts. The Court weighs two factors when it decides a question of contract impairment: (1) the severity of the impairment, and (2) the importance of the government interest. If a law significantly changes the parties' reasonable expectations under a contract, the government must establish that the law is a reasonable means of furthering a "significant and legitimate purpose" (i.e., correcting a societywide problem). For example, the Court upheld a state law setting the price of natural gas even though it impaired a contract between an energy company and a utility by lowering the price the utility would pay. Not only did the Court believe that the parties could have reasonably expected government price controls, since the energy industry has traditionally been regulated, but the Court found that any impairment was justified by the government interest in protecting consumers from escalating gas prices and in stabilizing the marketplace. Thus, because the law imposed no substantial impairment and served significant public purposes, it was constitutional under the contract clause.

Advertising and Promotion of Goods and Services

Advertising, the primary means used by business to market its products, may be essential for business success. It is also important to consumers. By providing them with information, advertising aids intelligent choices in the marketplace and reduces the costs associated with searching for goods. Society may also benefit because commercial advertising stimulates competition in the marketplace. Despite the obvious benefits of commercial advertising, it has frequently been restricted by the states, particularly in certain professions. The major constitutional protection for commercial advertising is the free speech guarantee of the First Amendment.

Commercial Advertising. In the landmark 1976 case of *Virginia Board of Pharmacy v. Virginia Citizens Consumer Council*,[8] the Court declared that **commercial speech** (commercial advertising and other forms of speech proposing a commercial transaction) was protected under the First Amendment. In that case, a consumer group, the Virginia Citizens Consumer Council, challenged a Virginia statute prohibiting pharmacists from advertising prices for prescription drugs. The Court held that the law violated the First Amendment. The Court reasoned that consumers and society have an interest in the free flow of commercial information. It rejected the paternalistic idea that the government should be able to "protect" consumers from the consequences of their own free choices by shielding them from truthful product information.

Although commercial speech is protected by the First Amendment, it does not receive the same protection that political and ideological expression enjoys. Commercial speech is protected because it provides useful information to consumers, not because it plays an important role in the public debate on political and social issues. Consequently, unlike political expression, which is protected even if the ideas expressed are "false" or "dangerous," commercial advertising that is untruthful or deceptive is not protected. The government, for example, can prohibit false advertising and deceptive trade practices.

What the Supreme Court has generally found unconstitutional are laws prohibiting truthful product or service advertisements. The Court has struck down laws banning advertising by lawyers, by sellers of real estate, by manufacturers of contraceptives, and by state-regulated utilities. To test the constitutionality of commercial speech restrictions, the Court employs intermediate scrutiny. Any restriction of truthful, nonmisleading advertising must directly serve a substantial government interest and be narrowly tailored to serve that interest. Few laws restricting truthful advertising have satisfied this demanding standard. For example, the Supreme

---

[8] 425 U.S. 784.

Court invalidated a Cincinnati ordinance prohibiting the dissemination of commercial publications (but allowing the dissemination of newspapers) in newsracks on public property. The law prohibited 62 commercial newsracks, but left 1,500–2,000 newspaper newsracks on the public sidewalks. The Court conceded that Cincinnati had a legitimate interest in safety and the attractive appearance of its streets and sidewalks. However, given the marginal benefit from the limited, selective ban on newsracks, and the city's failure to regulate the size, number, or appearance of all newsracks, it concluded that the city failed to demonstrate that the discriminatory ban was narrowly tailored to further the government's interests.

Despite the strong constitutional protection for truthful commercial advertising, the Supreme Court has allowed the government to restrict the promotion of harmful or socially undesirable products. For example, the Court upheld a law restricting truthful advertising by gambling casinos. The Court reasoned that since the government could wholly prohibit gambling, it could also take the less intrusive step of allowing gambling but restricting its promotion. The Court further suggested that the government could restrict the advertising of other harmful products and services such as cigarettes, alcohol, and prostitution.

Personal Selling. Commercial information can be communicated in a number of ways, including door-to-door sales and telemarketing. Although the Supreme Court has held that personal selling and promotion are forms of commercial speech protected by the First Amendment, it has also recognized the detrimental aspects of personal commercial solicitations, including the potential for consumer deception and invasion of privacy. The constitutionality of laws prohibiting or restricting personal solicitations will depend upon whether the government can show that the solicitations are harmful and that the restriction is necessary to protect consumers. So, for example, the Court has held that the state may prohibit attorneys from personally soliciting clients for personal gain because lawyers, who are trained as

---

BOX 3.3

Point to Consider: Autodialers and the First Amendment

Can the government ban the use of autodialers—computers that automatically dial telephone numbers and leave prerecorded messages? To protect consumers from the annoyance of computer-generated calls, Congress passed the Telephone Consumer Protection Act of 1991. The law prohibits businesses from making computer-generated calls to residential telephones without the prior express consent of the party called. Forty states also have restricted the use of autodialers.

Small businesspersons, like Kathryn and Ronald Moser of Lucky Leprechaun Co., a chimney-sweeping business in Keizer, Oregon, claim the federal law violates their First Amendment rights. They successfully challenged an Oregon law prohibiting the commercial use of autodialers in *Moser v. Frohnmayer*, 845 P.2d 1284 (1993). The Oregon Supreme Court held the law unconstitutional under the free speech clause of the Oregon Constitution. They also formed the National Association of Telecomputer Operators, an organization of small businesses using autodialers, and challenged the constitutionality of the Telephone Consumer Protection Act. A federal district court has issued a preliminary injunction enjoining the enforcement of the federal law pending the outcome of their lawsuit. In the meantime, the U.S. Supreme Court let stand the decision of the Minnesota Supreme Court in *State of Minnesota v. Casino Marketing Group, Inc.*, 491 N.W.2d 882 (1992), upholding a Minnesota law prohibiting the commercial use of autodialers without the consent of the telephone subscriber.

How should the court resolve the First Amendment challenge to the Telephone Consumer Protection Act? Are computer-generated, prerecorded messages more or less intrusive than other forms of telemarketing? Should the government restrict businesses from making any uninvited telephone solicitations? Would such a law be constitutional? ■

advocates, can unfairly persuade vulnerable persons to hire them. By contrast, the Court recently struck down a Florida law prohibiting certified public accountants from personally soliciting clients, holding that Florida did not prove that the ban on solicitation was necessary to protect consumers or to prevent unethical practices by CPAs. The Court reasoned that CPAs are trained to be objective and independent, not to be advocates, and that their clients, typically businesspeople, are far less susceptible to manipulation than an accident victim solicited by an attorney.

CONSTITUTIONAL PROTECTION FOR BUSINESS POLITICAL PARTICIPATION

Though protective of economic freedoms important to business, the Constitution does not significantly reduce the federal or state power to control business activities. The primary restraint on government regulation of economic activity is *political*, not constitutional. If people believe that economic regulation is unnecessary or unreasonable, the resulting political pressure from the affected groups will encourage legislators and Congress to curb any excesses (e.g., the modern push for deregulation of the airlines). Because the political process is so important, the political rights of business are discussed in this section.

The First Amendment and Corporate Political Freedom

The primary constitutional basis for citizen participation in the political process is the First Amendment. By protecting political expression, political association, and political action (campaign spending, lobbying, petitioning), the First Amendment guarantees the freedom to participate in the formation of public policy. Laws regulating political freedoms are subject to strict scrutiny, and thus the government's power to restrict political rights is very limited.

The extent to which the First Amendment protects the political activities of business corporations is a controversial issue of constitutional policy. Some commentators believe that a business corporation, as an artificial person created by state law, is not entitled to participate in politics. They view corporate political involvement as dangerous because of the financial resources at the disposal of most major corporations and because of the dependence of modern politicians on money for their campaigns. The Supreme Court addressed this issue in *First National Bank of Boston v. Bellotti*,[9] a case involving a Massachusetts law prohibiting business corporations from spending money to express their views in certain ballot-issue elections. The Supreme Court held that corporate political speech was protected under the First Amendment because society has an interest in hearing all sides of a political debate, including corporate opinions on matters of public importance. Subjecting the law to strict scrutiny, the Court declared it unconstitutional because Massachusetts failed to show that corporate spending would harm the democratic process.

Lobbying and Issue Advertising

Lobbying, perhaps the most common way in which businesses participate in politics, is protected by the First Amendment. The right to petition the government protects business lobbying even when it is designed to restrain competition. Recently, business firms have engaged in **issue advertising**, the dissemination of corporate political statements in the form of paid advertisements in the print media. Mobil Oil Company, for example, has waged an extensive campaign with issue advertisements expressing the company's position on the national budget deficit, economic protectionism, and taxes. Utility companies have also used a form of direct-mail issue advertising, sending political materials with their customer billings. The government cannot restrict such direct political advocacy. When the New York Public Service Commission prohibited utilities from inserting commentary on "contro-

[9] 435 U.S. 765 (1978).

versial issues of public policy" in their billing envelopes, the Supreme Court declared the order unconstitutional. The Court reasoned that corporations have a First Amendment right to express their opinions on any political issue, regardless of how controversial.

Corporate Campaign Spending

In the *Bellotti* case discussed earlier, the Supreme Court held that the state could not prohibit a business corporation from spending money in a referendum or initiative election. The Court, however, was not faced with a question of corporate spending in support of or in opposition to a candidate for office. Corporate campaign spending in a candidate election is restricted under a federal law that allows corporations to spend monies on federal candidate campaigns only through a political action fund financed by the voluntary contributions of managers and shareholders. In Case 3.3, the Supreme Court addresses the constitutionality of a state law similar to the federal statute.

CASE 3.3 **Austin v. Michigan Chamber of Commerce** • 494 U.S. 652 (1990)

FACTS Michigan law prohibits corporations (other than media corporations) from making campaign expenditures in support of or in opposition to candidates for state office. However, the law allows corporations to establish a separate campaign fund made up of voluntary contributions from persons associated with the corporation to engage in campaign spending in a candidate election.

The Michigan Chamber of Commerce, a nonprofit corporation whose members are primarily business corporations, established such a political fund. The Chamber wanted, however, to use its treasury funds to pay for a newspaper advertisement endorsing a state legislative candidate in violation of the law. The Chamber brought a lawsuit to have the law declared unconstitutional. The federal district court found the law constitutional, the Sixth Circuit Court of Appeals reversed, and the state appealed to the Supreme Court.

OPINION MARSHALL, J. . . . The State contends that the unique legal and economic characteristics of corporations necessitate some regulation of their political expenditures to avoid corruption or the appearance of corruption. . . . State law grants corporations special advantages—such as limited liability, perpetual life, and favorable treatment of the accumulation and distribution of assets—that enhance their ability to attract capital and to deploy their resources in ways that maximize the return on their shareholders' investments. These state-created advantages . . . permit them to use "resources amassed in the economic marketplace" to obtain "an unfair advantage in the political marketplace." . . .

Michigan's regulation aims at a [particular] type of corruption in the political arena: the corrosive and distorting effects of immense aggregations of wealth that are accumulated with the help of the corporate form and that have little or no correlation to the public's support for the corporation's political ideas. . . . [T]he unique state-conferred corporate structure that facilitates the amassing of large treasuries warrants the limit on independent expenditures. . . . [T]he state has articulated a sufficiently compelling rationale to support its restriction on independent expenditures by corporations. . . .

**CASE 3.3
Continued**

The Chamber contends that even if the [law] is constitutional with respect to for-profit corporations, it nonetheless cannot be applied to a nonprofit ideological corporation like a chamber of commerce. . . . [M]ore than three-quarters of the Chamber's members are business corporations. . . . Because the Chamber accepts money from for-profit corporations, it . . . does not possess the features [of an ideological corporation] that would compel the State to exempt it from [the law]. . . .

Similarly, we find that the Act's exemption of media corporations . . . does not render the statute unconstitutional. . . . [M]edia corporations differ significantly from other corporations because their resources are devoted to the collection of information and its dissemination to the public. . . . The media exception ensures that the Act does not hinder or prevent the institutional press from reporting on and publishing editorials about newsworthy events. . . . [T]he press' unique societal role . . . does provide a compelling reason for the State to exempt media corporations. . . .

JUDGMENT We therefore reverse the decision of the Court of Appeals.

DISSENT SCALIA, J. . . . "Attention all citizens. To assure the fairness of elections by preventing disproportionate expression of views of any single powerful group, your Government has decided that the following associations of persons shall be prohibited from speaking or writing in support of any candidate: _____" In permitting Michigan to make private corporations the first object of this Orwellian announcement, the Court today endorses the principle that too much speech is an evil that the democratic majority can proscribe. I dissent because that principle is contrary to our case law and incompatible with the absolutely central truth of the First Amendment: that government cannot be trusted to assure through censorship the "fairness" of political debate.

SUMMARY

Responding to the problems of a weak national government under the Articles of Confederation, the framers of the Constitution created a new federalism. Under the Constitution, a strong central government was formed. The enumerated powers of Congress under Article I, Section 8, of the Constitution, including the taxing and spending powers, give the federal government broad regulatory authority. The primary source of federal power to control the economy is the commerce clause. Under the modern cumulative effect principle, Congress can regulate local business activities whenever the activities of all similarly situated businesses will have an effect on interstate commerce.

Similarly, the states have extensive power to regulate business under their inherent police power. But state power is limited by federal power in several respects. First, the federal government has exclusive regulatory authority over certain subjects. Second, the supremacy clause of the Constitution allows federal law to preempt state law. Third, the commerce clause invalidates state laws that discriminate against or impose an undue burden on interstate commerce.

Businesses enjoy some significant constitutional protections for their activities. Business property is protected from government takings of property. A taking can occur when the government exercises its power of eminent domain or when a government regulation deprives the owner of the value of his or her property. Business contracts are protected from government impairments under the contract clause. The Constitution also protects business property and liberty interests under the due process and equal protection clauses. Procedural due process generally requires that individuals be afforded notice and a hearing before their rights are infringed. Under the rational basis test for substantive due process or equal protection challenges, however, the legislature has wide latitude to restrict business activities and to discriminate among similarly situated businesses.

Truthful commercial advertising receives substantial protection under the First Amendment. Commercial speech can be restricted, however, if it is false or misleading or promotes harmful products. The Court has also given expansive protection for corporate political speech, business lobbying, and issue advertising under the First Amendment.

REVIEW QUESTIONS

1. How did the Constitution correct the major flaws in the Articles of Confederation?

2. Explain the importance of the Civil War amendments.

3. Define the police power of the states.

4. How is government power allocated between the federal government and the states under the Constitution?

5. Explain the scope of federal regulatory power under the commerce clause.

6. Explain the difference between express and implied preemption.

7. What is a regulatory taking? What factors do the courts consider in determining whether a law constitutes a taking?

8. Why is commercial advertising protected under the First Amendment? What arguments could be made to support the position that commercial advertising should not be protected speech?

9. Should the government limit corporate campaign spending? Explain.

CASE PROBLEMS

1. Congress passed the National Trail System Act Amendments of 1983, the so-called Rails-to-Trails Act, which authorizes the Interstate Commerce Commission to approve the transfer of railroad right-of-ways to state and local governments and private groups for use as recreational trails. Rather than abandon a railroad line, a railroad can enter into an agreement under which the government unit or private group assumes financial and managerial responsibility for the railroad right-of-way. The interim use for recreational purposes preserves the right-of-way for possible future railroad use. The railroads, however, do not generally own the land under their lines, and this property would generally "revert" (return) to the landowner upon an abandonment of the line. But under the Act, lines converted to recreational trails are not considered abandoned and therefore the property does not revert to the landowner.

J. Paul Preseault owns land in Vermont over which a railroad had a right-of-way. The right-of-way was transferred to the city of Burlington for interim use as a public trail under a rails-to-trails agreement approved by the ICC. Preseault challenges the Act, claiming that Congress did not have the power to enact the law under the commerce clause. The ICC argues that the Act served two legitimate government purposes: (1) the preservation of railroad right-of-ways for future reactivation (rail banking), and (2) the establishment of recreational use of trails on an interim basis. How will the courts analyze the commerce clause issue? If creating recreational trails was the sole purpose of the Act, would the law be a valid exercise of the commerce clause? Is there another constitutional basis upon which a challenge to the law can be made? What is the likely result of that challenge?

2. The Pennsylvania Subsidence Act generally prohibits mining that causes subsidence damage (damage caused by the lowering of strata over a coal mine because of the extraction of underground coal) to public buildings, cemeteries, and private homes. To implement the law, the Pennsylvania Department of Environmental Resources (DER) requires that a certain percentage of coal underneath protected areas be left in the ground. Between 1966 and 1982, coal companies have had to leave 27 million tons of coal in place, approximately 2 percent of the coal in thirteen affected mines. The Keystone Coal Association, an association of coal companies, challenges the law, claiming that it violates the taking clause by depriving the owners of their right to extract all the coal from their mines. What factors will the courts consider in determining the taking issue? What is the likely outcome of the case?

3. Under a federal law, the Fair Labor Standards Act, covered employers are required to pay a minimum wage of $4.25/hour to most employees. However, the Act allows employers to pay $3.35/hour to workers who are under 20 years old and engaged in on-the-job training. Alfred Thompkins, age 19, was employed by General Fabricators and paid the subminimum training wage. Older workers under the company's on-the-job training program are being paid at the higher wage rate under the Act. Thompkins brings a lawsuit claiming that the law violates his right to equal treatment under the Fifth Amendment. What test will the courts use to determine the constitutionality of the law? Is the law constitutional? Why? How would the constitutional standards change if the subminimum wage was limited to young male workers? Explain.

4. A Maine law prohibits any person from importing live bait fish, including golden shiners, into the state. Robert J. Taylor, the owner of a bait business in Maine, imported 158,000 golden shiners. When Taylor was prosecuted for violating the importation ban, he challenged the constitutionality of the law under the commerce clause. At the hearing on the constitutional question, the state of Maine submitted evidence indicating that out-of-state golden shiners have parasites not common to indigenous golden shiners and that shipments of live baitfish could accidentally contain harmful nonnative species. Introduction of the parasites and nonnative species, the state argued, would endanger the pristine aquatic ecology of Maine. Moreover, the state's experts testified that there was no feasible method of inspecting and removing the parasites and nonnative fish from shipments into the state. No other state imposes a blanket ban on the importation of bait fish. Who are the direct beneficiaries of the Maine law? Is the law constitutional? Why?

5. For many years, Pacific Gas & Electric Company, a state-regulated utility, sent a newsletter called *Progress* to its customers in its billing envelopes. *Progress* contained information on energy conservation, discussions of public issues, and political opinion and commentary. Under an order of the California Public Utilities Commission, a group of citizens representing rate payers (utility customers) in utility proceedings, called Toward Utility Rate Normalization (TURN), was granted access to the billing envelopes of Pacific Gas to communicate with rate payers. The Commission allowed TURN to use the "extra space" in the envelopes four times a year to raise funds to participate in rate-setting proceedings. Pacific Gas contested the order, asserting that its First Amendment rights were violated because it was being forced to disseminate the viewpoints of TURN with which it disagreed. What arguments could be made to support the constitutionality of the Commission's order? What test of constitutionality will the courts employ to resolve the First Amendment issue? In your opinion, does the order violate the First Amendment rights of the corporation? Explain.

CHAPTER 4

Administrative Agencies and the Regulatory Process

In the twentieth century, the United States has emerged as a commercial society comprising giant corporations, powerful labor unions, huge white-collar service organizations, and uncountable numbers of entrepreneurs and small businesses serving a spectrum of needs for consumers, government, and other businesses. At the same time, a vast government has developed to accommodate the needs of a huge and expanding population.

Despite the benefits of commerce, however, we face serious social and economic problems. Many stem directly from our industrialization and commercial development: unemployment, labor strife, inadequate retirement income, costly and inefficient health care, pollution of the environment, and increasingly scarce resources. Others, such as racial and sexual discrimination, have cultural and ethnic origins. Government programs and functions require increasing amounts of routine processing. Some of our problems are temporary; most persist over time.

Early in this century, lawmakers recognized that government could not address issues of such magnitude by the traditional method of enacting laws that were enforceable only in the courts. Instead, state and federal legislatures increasingly delegated to the executive branch and to "independent" administrative agencies the duty to handle routine matters and the right to exercise problem-solving discretion. The agencies were to do these things by (1) making rules having the force of law and (2) conducting triallike hearings to adjudicate disputes over application of those rules.

Most people never go before a court of law. But every day their lives are affected by the decisions of state and federal administrative agencies. These agencies seek to promote the public good or to prevent public harm by enforcing rules against unfair competition, unsafe automobiles, unsanitary food and meat, industrial accidents, unhealthy working conditions, employer discrimination against unions, dangerous nuclear waste disposal—and more. Likewise, businesses, whether large multinational corporations or sole proprietorships, are much more likely to face administrative regulation than to be involved in litigation.

Regulation of business operates at all levels of government—federal, state, county, parish, township, city, and village. Regulation of business can occur even at the city ward or precinct level—as where a special board governing a historic district issues rules on permissible architecture, demolition, or restoration of buildings, or even the size, makeup, and color of signs identifying business establishments in the area.

While this chapter mostly addresses federal administrative agencies and processes and their impact on business, you should keep in mind that states and localities have administrative counterparts for many federal agencies. Table 4.1 presents a list of federal agencies that a hypothetical company is likely to have to deal with. The list would be much longer if state agencies were included.

Within the last hundred years, the alphabet soup of regulatory bodies has become a plain fact of modern life, widely accepted despite earlier constitutional battles surrounding the emergence of agencies in the 1930s. There is no longer, for example, a serious claim that an agency violates the separation-of-powers doctrine by simultaneously having legislative, executive, and judicial functions. Today, while constitutional issues periodically emerge from the conduct of agencies, it is unlikely that any will

Table 4.1   Federal Agencies Affecting an Individual Business

Gardner Company, a hypothetical corporation, is a publicly held food processing company doing business in two states. Listed below are some of the federal administrative agencies that affect Gardner Company's business activities:

- Securities and Exchange Commission (SEC), governing the trading and issue of company stock and proper financial reporting.
- Food and Drug Administration (FDA), governing the quality of food products, packaging, product labeling, and plant inspection.
- United States Department of Agriculture (USDA), governing the quality, packaging, labeling, and inspection of meat and poultry products.
- Internal Revenue Service (IRS), responsible for collecting company taxes and employee withholding taxes.
- Social Security Administration, in tandem with the IRS, responsible for collecting employer and employee social security contributions.
- National Labor Relations Board (NLRB), governing labor contract disputes and overseeing employee elections on union representation.
- Equal Employment Opportunity Commission (EEOC), with rules prohibiting discrimination and sexual harassment in the workplace and requiring periodic compliance reporting.
- Veterans Administration (VA), with rules encouraging the hiring of U.S. military veterans.
- Occupational Safety and Health Administration (OSHA), governing workplace health and safety.
- Federal Trade Commission (FTC), governing advertising and marketing practices and competitive activities between companies.
- Environmental Protection Agency (EPA), established to oversee activities such as waste removal and prevent pollution of the environment.
- U.S. Customs Service, governing the import of raw and finished products.
- Patent and Trademark Office, with rules for protecting the company's trademarks.

Depending upon the specific activities of the hypothetical Gardner Company, more federal agencies, such as the Immigration and Naturalization Service, could affect its business. In total, there are roughly sixty independent administrative agencies and several hundred more organized under the Executive Office of the President, so many that the government produces the hefty *United States Government Manual* to list them all.

shake either the existence or the essence of the nation's administrative machinery.

So, this chapter emphasizes modern administrative agencies, law, and process. The chapter discusses the major features of administrative process, some current constitutional disputes involving agencies, and a number of practical considerations of interest to businesspeople. Of central importance throughout is the broad discretion many agencies bring to bear on social and economic problems.

SCOPE AND FUNCTION OF ADMINISTRATIVE LAW

Meaning of Administrative Law, Administrative Agency, and Administrative Process

Administrative law is any law concerning the powers and procedures of administrative agencies, including the rules under which agencies create regulations, and the rules that permit a party aggrieved by an agency decision to petition for judicial review by a court. Administrative law is found in constitutions, statutes, and court decisions, as well as in agency decisions, rules, and regulations.

Administrative agency means any public officer, board, bureau, authority, or commission—other than legislatures and courts—having power to determine public rights and obligations by making rules and rendering decisions. The term refers equally to agencies organized within a department of government (e.g., the Patent and Trademark Office in the executive branch's Department of Commerce) and those organized separately from any such department (e.g., the Federal Trade Commission). An agency is said to be **independent** if the President lacks power to discharge its head without cause.

Administrative process in this chapter means the procedure through which administrative agencies carry on their work.

Legislative Delegation of Powers to Agencies

State and federal administrative agencies are created by an **enabling statute.** Typically, a federal enabling statute establishes a board or commission with a chairperson and four to six members, defines the subject matter jurisdiction of the agency, and delegates to it three kinds of powers:

1 A broad quasi-legislative rulemaking power
2 A quasi-judicial power to adjudicate whether an individual or business has violated statutory law or agency rules
3 A quasi-executive power to perform such functions as licensing, investigating and prosecuting violations, and advising the public by interpreting agency rules to parties affected by them

Why are agency powers called "quasi"? The answer stems from a concern that conferring legislative, judicial, and executive powers upon a single agency would interfere with the separation of powers so vital to our form of government. In holding that agencies may legitimately exercise multiple powers, the courts have concluded that agencies do not possess legislative and judicial power, but only "quasi-legislative" and "quasi-judicial" power. "Quasi" means "similar to but not the same as." Like legislatures and courts, agencies may make rules and decide disputes, *but only* within the narrow jurisdiction delegated to them—hence, an agency's powers are not the same as those of a legislature or a court.

For example, a state legislature may delegate to its Industrial Accident Commission power to make rules concerning workers' compensation and to adjudicate whether a particular worker is entitled to benefits. However, although the commission's rules *resemble* legislation and its hearings *resemble* court trials, these activities are so narrow in scope that the agency cannot be said to be using the **plenary** (broad) **power** characteristic of the legislative, executive, and judicial branches of government. Moreover, as the courts have frequently noted, checks and balances built into the administrative agency structure provide safeguards against abuse of power. Unlike the legislature, which is independent of the other branches of government, an agency is at all times under the control of the legislature, which can always limit an agency's

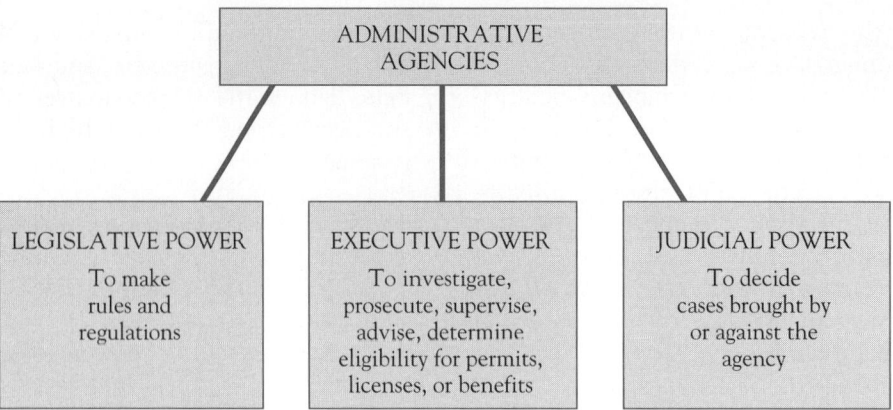

Figure 4.1 Powers of administrative agencies.

activities by cutting its budget appropriations, by passing laws further restricting its activity, or by abolishing it altogether. Similarly, court review of agency hearings and orders—called **judicial review**—provides an independent check by the judiciary on the abuse of the power of agencies, which technically operate under the executive branch of government. The Supreme Court has held that this judicial check is sufficient to meet the traditional requirement that the powers of the three branches of government should be separate.

In carrying out their various functions, agencies exercise a considerable discretion. The scope of an administrative agency's discretion to make and enforce rules is determined by the express or implied powers delegated to the agency by the enabling statute. Although an agency cannot legally exercise any power or discretion in excess of that which has been constitutionally delegated to it by the legislature, courts today tend to interpret delegations of authority broadly. (See Figure 4.1.)

Constitutionality of Legislative Delegation of Power to Agencies

Early in this century, utility companies adversely affected by rate regulations imposed by public utility commissions questioned their regulatory authority as an unconstitutional delegation of legislative power. In ruling on these challenges, courts developed the **primary standard** doctrine. Under it, a delegation of rulemaking power to an agency is not unconstitutional if the legislature establishes primary standards or guidelines to govern and limit the agency's exercise of power. Such a standard helps the courts, when reviewing the enabling statute, to decide whether the agency's power is sufficiently limited.

The rationale for the primary standard, and for the use of agencies in general, is that delegation of some power to agencies is "necessary in order that the exercise of legislative power does not become a futility."[1] From this fundamental idea come two basic principles of administrative law: (1) Congress may enact legislation to become operative upon the happening of some event or state of facts and may leave to others (agencies) the responsibility of determining when the event or state of facts occurs. (2) Congress may declare a policy or determine a standard, and may empower some officer or agency to fill in the details needed for implementation.

Rulemaking and Other Agency Functions

Rulemaking is a fundamental agency task in day-to-day agency operations, and agencies have different approaches to carrying it out. Conse-

---

[1] *Sunshine Anthracite Coal Co. v. Adkins*, 310 U.S. 381, 398 (1940).

quently, we need to explore two basic models of administrative agency rulemaking—the legislative model and the adjudicative model—and also consider the executive functions of agencies.

Some laws apply generally to administrative agencies. As a threshold matter, we will discuss those general laws first.

Laws Affecting How Administrative Agencies Function. Several important laws place limits on agency operations. For example, to minimize unwarranted government secrecy, the Freedom of Information Act (FOIA) requires that, under certain conditions, agency information must be made available to the public upon request. The Government-in-the-Sunshine Act requires various agencies to open certain types of meetings to public observation. The Federal Privacy Act (FPA) restricts agencies from disclosing personal records of individuals without their consent. The two laws most affecting daily operations, however, are the Administrative Procedure Act (APA) and the Federal Register Act.

Administrative Procedure Act (APA). In the 1930s many of the agencies created to administer economic recovery and reform tended to expand power and to act arbitrarily. Also, there often was public confusion about procedure, because each agency developed its own system for making rules and for enforcing them in adjudication hearings. To establish more uniform agency procedures for rulemaking and adjudications, and to minimize agency misuse of power, Congress in 1946 enacted the Administrative Procedure Act (APA). The APA also set out specific grounds for judicial review—that is, for appeal to the courts by any party adversely affected by agency action.

In recent years, Congress has tended not to rely on the APA, but instead to specify in detail (in enabling statutes) the procedures that the agency must follow in rulemaking and adjudications, tailoring such procedures to meet the needs of the particular agency. For example, in creating the Occupational Safety and Health Administration, it was recognized that OSHA would be establishing a wide range of safety rules on an industry-by-industry basis. Consequently, in the enabling statute, Congress provided for "informal notice-and-comment rulemaking," a speedy procedure that would simplify OSHA's task of drafting hundreds of regulations as quickly as possible. Generally, however, if an enabling statute is silent concerning rulemaking, adjudication, and judicial review procedures, then the provisions of the APA are applicable.

The specific provisions of the APA that are most useful in this chapter appear in two later subsections: The Legislative Model and The Adjudicative Model.

Federal Register Act. Enacted in 1935, the Federal Register Act created the Federal Register system, which publishes three important references: (1) the United States Government Manual, (2) the Federal Register, and (3) the Code of Federal Regulations (CFR). The Manual lists the address of each federal agency and its regional offices. The Federal Register provides notice in a single source of agencies' official acts. Published each business day, it gives notice of an agency's public rulemaking hearings, for example. In addition, the Federal Register publishes both proposed rules and adopted rules. The APA provides that most agency rules (also referred to in this chapter as "regulations") cannot be enforced until they have been published in the Register. Section 553(b) of the APA provides that such publication is constructive notice that makes a rule binding on all persons affected by it, regardless of whether they have actual knowledge of it.

When a federal agency has adopted and published a final rule in the *Federal Register,* it is republished in the *Code of Federal Regulations* (CFR) and appears in the same section as all other current regulations for that agency. Thus, if the Federal Trade Commission (FTC), for example, adopted a new regulation within the last few days, one would likely find it in the *Federal Register,* along with any new regulations that other agencies might have adopted. However, to have access to all current regulations of the FTC, one would ordinarily turn to the section of the *Code of Federal Regulations* devoted to that agency.

Models of Agency Rulemaking. Rules (or regulations) issued by administrative agencies are created along the lines of two distinct models or some combination of these two models: the legislature and the court.

Administrative agencies possess both quasi-legislative and quasi-judicial powers, and these two powers provide the basis for the models of agency rulemaking.

The legislative model. As a legislature creates statutes for general application, administrative agencies create rules and regulations intended to apply generally—and to everyone at the same time. In this way, administrative agencies operate like legislatures because they produce prospective rules that forward the objectives of legislation in which Congress delegated them specific rulemaking powers. Hence, administrative agencies are acting in Congress' place.

When agencies make rules, however, they must follow defined procedures. Unless Congress designates procedures to the contrary, an agency's rulemaking activities are governed by the Administrative Procedure Act (APA), which was briefly discussed earlier.

Section 553 of the APA outlines the procedures an agency must follow when engaging in legislative-type rulemaking. Key features of this statute which govern rulemaking procedures are:

1 *Notice.* An agency must publish proposed rules in the *Federal Register* unless all persons affected by the proposed rule have been notified in person or have been otherwise given actual notice of the proposed rules. Formal notice must contain the following:
   - Statement of time, place, and nature of public rulemaking proceedings
   - Reference to the legal authority under which the rule is proposed
   - Terms of the proposed rule or a description of the subjects or issues involved
2 *Opportunity for the public to participate in rulemaking.* An agency must give interested persons the opportunity to participate. Such opportunity can take the form of public submission of written data, views, or arguments for or against the proposed rule. An agency can—but is not required to—give an opportunity for oral presentation of arguments.
3 *Concise general statement of final rule.* After an agency has considered the relevant matters presented to it, the agency must make a concise statement of the rule along with a statement of its basis and purpose.
4 *Fair timing.* An agency must either publish or give service (personal notice) of a final rule not less than 30 days before its effective date.
5 *Right to petition.* An agency must give interested persons the right to petition for the issuance, amendment, or repeal of a rule.

Some federal agencies, such as the Federal Trade Commission (FTC) and the Food and Drug Administration (FDA), rely heavily on the legislative model for rulemaking. For example, the FDA conducted hearings at many locations around the country on the subject of what information should be printed on food labels. Over a 2-year period, the FDA actively encouraged involvement not only of the affected businesses, but also of consumers and other interested groups. The resultant record of the hearings and submitted data and opinion to the FDA is measured in the thousands of pages.

The adjudicative model. The adjudicative model gets its name because new rules are created on a case-by-case basis. These rules, like court-made rules, apply first to the individuals involved in a dispute and then later apply generally to the public.

Derived from their quasi-judicial powers, agencies function like courts. Instead of judgments, they issue **orders.** Such orders have the force of law upon those involved in the dispute before the agency. These orders, moreover, also function as rules for others who were not involved in the adjudication—something like how the concept of *stare decisis* (i.e., that similar cases be treated similarly) is applied by courts in decisions involving statutory interpretation and common law decisions.

An agency which uses the adjudicative model for rulemaking, however, cannot rely exclusively upon its quasi-judicial powers. Generally, to use the adjudicative model for rulemaking, an agency begins by issuing very broad rules as in the legislative model. The agency then proceeds on a case-by-case basis issuing orders which, in turn, function indirectly as rules.

Not all formal adjudications result in orders that become rules. Some types of formal adjudications, such as for the issuance/renewal of a broadcasting license by the Federal Communications Commission (FCC), never result in rules, whereas most adjudication before the National Labor Relations Board (NLRB) modify existing rules or create new ones.

The APA has specified procedures for formal adjudication, discussion of which follows.

Formal Adjudications. Formal adjudications are often referred to as "trial-type" or "evidentiary" hearings. They are required by the APA only when a statute calls for adjudication "on the record after opportunity for an agency hearing." This kind of adjudication constitutes only a small proportion of total adjudications, the remainder being informal. However, statutes increasingly are commanding agencies to conduct formal adjudications.

1 *Notice*. Procedural due process spelled out in the APA gives a respondent the right to timely notice of agency charges as well as the time of the hearing. Such notice is given when an agency issues and serves a respondent with a complaint setting forth its factual contentions. If the outcome of an adjudication will affect other parties, such as competitors, an agency may notify interested parties and provide them with an opportunity to participate in the hearing. Upon a showing of good cause, an interested party who has a vital interest in the outcome of the adjudication may be permitted to intervene in the case as a respondent. In licensing cases, if there are two applicants where the rules permit only one license to be granted, a **comparative hearing** must be held in which both applicants have an opportunity to demonstrate the strength of their claims and the weaknesses of the competing application.

2 *Discovery*. In court, litigants have the right to pretrial discovery by means of depositions or written interrogatories (questions) which enable them to know the evidence of the adverse party well ahead of trial. However, in agency adjudications discovery rights are extremely limited. The APA confers no discovery privileges upon a respondent, but under the FOIA, a respondent has access to relevant, unprivileged information contained in agency files.

3 *Trial: presenting evidence and cross-examination*. A formal adjudication case is tried before an administrative law judge (ALJ), who conducts an evidentiary hearing similar to a federal nonjury trial. When authorized to do so by a statute, such as the National Labor Relations Act, the ALJ may issue subpoenas requiring witnesses to appear and testify. Otherwise, Section 556(d) of the APA sharply limits the right to a full hearing, since the agency can require that all or part of the evidence be submitted in written form. Under this procedure, witnesses' verified written statements are submitted to the opposite party, who then is given time to reply with written rebuttal statements. The APA also gives agencies wide discretion to limit cross-examination. Since cross-examination is used to test a witness's memory, bias, logic, accuracy, expertise, and perception, prohibiting or restricting cross-examination may seriously affect the quality of an agency decision. Regardless of the method used to admit evidence, agency prosecutors must ordinarily prove their case by a "preponderance of the evidence."

4 *Admissibility of Evidence*. Administrative treatment of the rules of evidence further illustrates the agency approach to procedural due process. In an administrative hearing, there is no jury—an administrative law judge makes the findings of fact. Because parties to an administrative hearing often cannot afford an attorney and the rules of evidence are too complex for laypeople to understand and apply, administrative agencies almost universally admit evidence that would not be admissible in a court of law. For example, courts refuse to admit certain kinds of "hearsay" evidence (statements made by a witness on the authority of another, and not from personal knowledge or observation). The reason for excluding hearsay evidence is that the maker of the statement is not available

in court for cross-examination to test his or her credibility. Therefore, exclusion of hearsay testimony is traditionally viewed as necessary to avoid the danger that a jury will base its findings of fact upon unreliable evidence. However, it is now well settled by reviewing courts that hearsay evidence is admissible in administrative hearings. This is justified because the trier of fact is an ALJ who, as a trained lawyer, has the expertise to recognize hearsay and to give it little or no weight. Moreover, the courts will set aside an agency determination on appeal unless there is direct testimony to support its findings.

5 *Separation of functions.* Just as the Constitution requires separation of *powers* among the legislative, executive, and judicial branches of government, an administrative agency must draw a clear line between its *quasi-executive* power to investigate and prosecute violations of agency rules, and its *quasi-judicial* responsibility to conduct adjudication hearings. This distinction between these activities is called *separation of functions*.

6 *Decision and appeal.* At the conclusion of the hearing, the ALJ prepares findings of fact and conclusions of law, and makes an *initial* decision, which becomes final unless the agency or commission modifies it. In contrast, a *recommended* decision *must* be acted upon by the agency before it becomes final.

Informal Agency Adjudications. The vast majority of administrative adjudications involve informal action in which only minimal statutory safeguards protect the rights of the individual. Because the APA makes no provision for informal adjudications, agencies lack a uniform procedure for making decisions. The Freedom of Information Act and Privacy Act guarantee the right to notice of the rules, orders, or policy statements that the agency will use against an individual as well as access to agency documents needed to support a claim or defense. However, the most significant protection for the individual respondent is the Fifth Amendment restraint on the federal government that no person shall be "deprived of life, liberty, or property, without due process of law." State administrative agencies are restricted by a similar provision in the Fourteenth Amendment. The U.S. Supreme Court has interpreted this phrase to include the right to *procedural fairness*—that is, reasonable notice that an individual's rights are about to be affected by agency action, and an opportunity to be heard before final action is taken.

In recent years, two troubling questions have arisen: (1) At what stage of informal proceedings is a respondent entitled to a hearing? (2) Where the enabling statute fails to specify informal adjudication procedures, what type of hearing should be provided? The U.S. Supreme Court has ruled on these questions, but the decision spelling out what due process requires for one agency is often not applicable to another. Two cases in which the Court considered the claim that the Social Security Administration had not observed procedural due process will illustrate. In *Goldberg v. Kelly* (1970), the Supreme Court held that termination of welfare benefits without first holding an evidentiary hearing was a denial of procedural due process. The decision emphasized that since Goldberg's livelihood was at stake, a hearing before cutting off his benefits was justified. Six years later in *Mathews v. Eldridge* (1976), again involving termination of social security benefits without a hearing, the Supreme Court held that procedural due process was *not* violated.

For informal agency adjudications, a continual nagging question is "What process is due?"—a full evidentiary hearing or something more informal. The following case provides a more recent example on how thorny this question remains. Though this case involves an individual, you should keep in mind that the question of "What process is due?" similarly applies to businesses as well.

CASE 4.1   Cleveland Board of Education v. Loudermill • 470 U.S. 532 (1984)

FACTS

In 1979, the Cleveland Board of Education hired James Loudermill as a security guard. On his job application, Loudermill stated that he had never been convicted of a felony. Eleven months later, as part of a routine examination of his employment records, the Board discovered that in fact Loudermill had been convicted of grand larceny in 1968. By a letter dated November 3, 1980, the business manager of the Board informed Loudermill that he had been dismissed because of his dishonesty in filling out the employment application. Loudermill was not given an opportunity to respond to the charge or to challenge his dismissal. On November 13, the Board adopted a resolution officially approving his discharge.

Under Ohio law, Loudermill was a "classified civil servant." Such employees can be terminated only for cause, and may obtain administrative review if discharged. Pursuant to this law, Loudermill filed an appeal with the Cleveland Civil Service Commission on November 12, 1980. The Commission appointed a referee, who held a hearing on January 29, 1981. Loudermill argued that he thought his larceny conviction was a misdemeanor, and not a felony, and hence he did not lie on his application. Though the referee recommended Loudermill's reinstatement, the Commission heard arguments on July 20, 1981, and announced that it would uphold his dismissal.

Loudermill brought his case before the federal district court, alleging that the Ohio law pertaining to termination of civil servants was unconstitutional because it did not allow an employee an opportunity to respond to charges prior to dismissal. The district court dismissed the case for failure to state a claim on which relief could be granted. On appeal, however, the court found that Loudermill had been deprived of due process. The Cleveland Board of Education petitioned the Supreme Court for certiorari, and Loudermill cross-petitioned for review of rulings adverse to him.

OPINION

WHITE, J. . . . [Loudermill's] federal constitutional claim depends on [his] having had a property right in continued employment. If [he] did, the State could not deprive [him] of this property without due process.

Property rights are not created by the Constitution, "they are created and their dimensions are defined by existing rules or understandings that stem from an independent source such as state law. . . ." [Loudermill was a] "classified civil service employee[s], entitled to retain [his] position "during good behavior and efficient service," who could not be dismissed "except . . . for . . . [cause]." The statute plainly supports the conclusion, reached by [the lower court], that the respondent possessed property rights in continued employment.

[However, in a 1974 federal employee case], the plurality [of this court] reasoned that where the legislation conferring a substantive right also sets out the procedural mechanism for enforcing that right, the two cannot be separated:

. . . "[Where] the grant of a substantive right is inextricably intertwined with the limitations on the procedures which are to be employed in determining that right, a litigant . . . must take the bitter with the sweet."

In light of . . . holdings [after the 1974 case], it is [now] settled that the "bit-

**CASE 4.1
Continued**

ter with the sweet" approach misconceives the constitutional guarantee. If a clearer holding is needed, we provide it today. The point is straightforward: the Due Process Clause provides that certain substantive rights—life, liberty, and property—cannot be deprived except pursuant to constitutionally adequate procedures. The categories of substance and procedure are distinct. . . . "Property" cannot be defined by the procedures provided for its deprivation any more than can life or liberty. The right to due process "is conferred, not by legislative grace, but by constitutional guarantee. While the legislature may elect not to confer a property interest in [public] employment, it may not constitutionally authorize the deprivation of such an interest, once conferred, without appropriate procedural safeguards."

In short, once it is determined that the Due Process Clause applies, "the question remains what process is due."

. . . An essential principle of due process is that a deprivation of life, liberty, or property "be preceded by notice and opportunity for hearing appropriate to the nature of the case." We have described "the root requirement" of the Due Process Clause as being "that an individual be given an opportunity for a hearing before he is deprived of any significant property interest." This principle requires "some kind of a hearing" prior to the discharge of an employee who has a constitutionally protected property interest in his employment. . . .

. . . We have pointed out that "[the] formality and procedural requisites for [a] hearing can vary, depending upon the importance of the interests involved and the nature of the subsequent proceedings." In general, "something less" than a full evidentiary hearing is sufficient prior to adverse administrative action. . . .

In only one case, *Goldberg v. Kelly*, has the Court required a full adversarial evidentiary hearing prior to adverse governmental action. . . . [T]hat case presented significantly different considerations than are present in [the present case involving] public employment. . . .

The essential requirements of due process, and all that [Loudermill] seeks or that the Court of Appeals required, are notice and an opportunity to respond. The opportunity to present reasons, either in person or in writing, why proposed action should not be taken is a fundamental due process requirement. The tenured public employee is entitled to oral or written notice of the charges against him, an explanation of the employer's evidence, and an opportunity to present his side of the story. To require more than this prior to termination would intrude to an unwarranted extent on the government's interest in quickly removing an unsatisfactory employee.

JUDGMENT   Affirmed and remanded for further proceedings.

Quasi-Executive Functions

The major executive functions of agencies are:

1 Issuing licenses and permits and determining eligibility of applicants for governmental benefits such as welfare payments
2 Investigating violations of statutes or administrative rules
3 Prosecuting such violations
4 Supervising industry activities such as banks
5 Advising the legislature of agency activities as well as giving advice to individuals or

businesses concerning how they are affected by agency rules and how to comply with them

Most agencies perform all these functions but in varying degrees. For example, the National Labor Relations Board spends much of its time prosecuting unfair labor practices, whereas the Securities and Exchange Commission concentrates a large part of its time on granting permits to corporations to issue and sell new securities. State licensing boards direct most of their efforts to testing applicants and issuing licenses to doctors, accountants, building contractors, drivers, and other persons.

Agency Investigations, Searches, and Inspections. Agencies investigate individual and corporate members of a regulated industry to obtain "legislative facts" (e.g., statistical data) needed for rulemaking and to obtain evidence necessary to prosecute violations of statutes or agency rules. The extent of an agency's power to compel disclosure of information depends upon the legislative delegation to the agency. For example, Congress has granted power to the FTC to inspect records of businesses, issue subpoenas, and "report orders" and "civil investigative demands" requiring businesses to submit information. Such inquiries, however, must be for a lawful purpose, must be relevant to the agency's mission, and must not seek information that is privileged because of the Fifth Amendment's guarantee against self-incrimination. Indeed, the most significant limitations on agencies' investigative powers are the constitutional prohibitions of the Fifth Amendment against compelling testimony involving self-incrimination, and the Fourth Amendment against unreasonable searches. These liberties have been vigorously guarded by the Supreme Court in recent years.

A warrant is not necessary, however, if the owner of property consents to a search, or in case of emergencies such as putting out a fire. The Supreme Court has held that warrantless searches are permissible in certain businesses that are subject to licensing and intensive regulation such as selling retail liquor or firearms.

Prosecuting Violations. Millions of applications, claims, or tax returns are filed each year with agencies such as the Veterans Administration, the Social Security Administration, and the Internal Revenue Service. If an agency decides to take adverse action, it serves a formal complaint upon an individual or business. This commences an adjudication proceeding involving a trial-type hearing under the APA. However, the APA requires agencies to provide an opportunity for settlement, so most agencies have established rules governing settlement negotiation procedures. Since agency prosecutors have almost unlimited discretion to settle cases, most disputes are resolved through informal compromises. Often a respondent is asked to sign a **consent order,** which reflects the terms of a compromise settling the dispute but which generally does not constitute an admission of violation of a statute or agency rule.

Many agencies have statutory power to take extraordinary action in emergency situations involving public health or safety. For example, the Consumer Product Safety Commission can remove a dangerous product from the market, the Federal Deposit Insurance Corporation can take over an "unsafe and unsound" bank, the Food and Drug Administration can seize property such as contaminated food, the Securities and Exchange Commission can suspend trading of a company's stock in the securities market, and the Federal Aviation Administration can suspend an airline pilot's license *before* an adjudication hearing is commenced. Statutes prescribe safeguards against the abuse of such power by requiring prior court approval of the action proposed by some agencies, or by providing that the agency must conduct a trial-type hearing immediately after the emergency action is taken.

Some agencies, such as the Federal Trade Commission and the National Labor Relations Board have statutory power to issue **cease-and-desist orders** prohibiting unlawful activity. In addition, many statutes provide for the imposition of civil penalties or fines each day such an order is disobeyed. Alternatively, in more serious cases, many agencies can apply directly to a federal court for an injunction restraining conduct that endangers the public health, safety, or economic interests.

In addition to civil fines and penalties, many regulatory statutes provide for criminal sanctions against violators. For example, a person who willfully files fraudulent financial statements with the SEC can be prosecuted for a felony under the criminal provisions of the Securities Act, or can be sued in a civil action. If an agency decides to pursue criminal liability, the matter is referred to the Department of Justice for prosecution in the courts, since agencies are not equipped to provide the jury trials that criminal defendants have a right to demand.

Because of the expense and delay of criminal trials, most agencies prefer to pursue civil penalties.

Supervising and Advising. Where pervasive regulation is required, some agencies devote most of their time to informal supervision. For example, the Federal Home Loan Bank has a large staff of examiners that conducts regular audits of the nation's savings and loan associations. Administrators license new associations and branches, issue rules setting reserve requirements, and require periodic reports. Formal proceedings are rarely used, as most of the agency's business is conducted by informal conferences.

Most agencies expend considerable time in giving advice to individuals and businesses. For example, the IRS has hundreds of employees who answer the public's questions concerning taxes. Formal advice may be given in the form of (1) a "no-action" letter indicating an agency will not prosecute a borderline violation, (2) a "private letter ruling" on a tax matter, or (3) a "declaratory order" under APA Sec. 554(e), permitting the agency to terminate a controversy or remove uncertainty about the issues. APA Sec. 554(e) also gives assurance that such order is binding on the agency. Agencies also educate the public on new rules and warn consumers about dangerous products. Threat of adverse publicity is sometimes used to induce a violator to comply with agency rules. However, the trend is for agencies to adopt internal rules that restrict comment to the media on pending cases, or that require advance notification to the business affected, so that it can prepare a response.

JUDICIAL REVIEW

The great power that has been delegated to administrative agencies can be abused. Some agencies have expanded their power beyond appropriate limits. Others, under time pressure to process thousands of decisions, have adopted procedural shortcuts that have denied due process of law to individuals and businesses. These shortcuts have steadily chipped away at the right to have reasonable discovery and cross-examination, to subpoena witnesses and present oral testimony, or to exclude hearsay evidence. Informal rulemaking has even failed in many cases to guarantee a hearing before adverse action is taken.

During the last half-century, many forces have developed to retard or limit agency abuse of power. Newspaper and television media can quickly expose agency misdeeds to public view, often triggering action by elected representatives in the legislature. Legislatures, in turn, have an impressive array of weapons at their disposal for curbing agency abuse. They can enact laws limiting the powers of an agency, or even abolish it. They can signal an agency to institute reforms by drastically limiting its budgetary appropriations, or by conducting investigative hearings to expose agency irregularities. Individual legislators are generally very effective with "casework"—that is, assisting constituents by means of friendly but authoritative direct contact with agencies. When an agency receives a letter with a "Member of Congress" tag, it is often given priority attention. In addition, agency leadership is appointed by the President with the "advice and consent" of the Senate—a further source of legislative influence on agencies.

Notwithstanding the techniques legislators use to limit agency power, the most important continuing restraint against abuse by the administrative bureaucracy is judicial review of agency actions. While media publicity or legislative investigations may eventually change unfair policies or rules, judicial review usually offers the only opportunity for immediate relief to a private party who has been mistreated by an agency.

Judicial review is the process by which the legality of agency action is scrutinized by state or federal courts. This section will discuss (1) the scope of judicial review, (2) how agency decisions come before an appellate court for review, and (3) the standards and principles that reviewing courts apply in ruling on the legality of agency actions.

The purpose of judicial review is to make sure that the administrative process works as it is supposed to. This means, basically, that a court must allow an agency to exercise the discretion the legislature gave it, while preventing the agency from exceeding its powers. However, a reviewing court may not, in the name of judicial review, simply substitute its own judgment for an agency decision it doesn't like. As one circuit court has said:

Judicial review must operate to ensure that the administrative process itself will confine and control the exercise of discretion. Courts should require administrative officers to articulate the standards and principles that govern their discretionary decisions in as much detail as possible. Rules and regulations should be freely formulated by administrators, and revised when necessary. Discretionary decisions should more often be supported with findings of fact and reasoned opinions. When administrators provide a framework for principled decision making, the result will be to diminish the importance of judicial review by enhancing the integrity of the administrative process, and to improve the quality of judicial review in those cases where judicial review is sought.[2]

The power of courts to review administrative action has developed from three sources: statutes, the Constitution, and judicial decisions. Our discussion begins with the types of cases in which court review is prohibited.

Nonreviewable Matters

Some laws specifically deny the power of judicial review. For example, one statute provides that

[2]*Environmental Defense Fund, Inc. v. Ruckelshaus*, 439 F.2d 584 (D.C. Cir. 1971).

the decisions of the Administrator of Veterans' Affairs on *any* question of law or fact regarding benefits for veterans and their dependents or survivors is not reviewable "by any court of the United States."[3] In a case involving exposure of military personnel to the chemical Agent Orange, the court interpreted this statute, and ruled that the administrator's alleged failure to provide adequate medical treatment to servicemen exposed to Agent Orange in Vietnam was not subject to judicial review. This court reasoned that Congress' denying judicial review was a legitimate means of preventing "second guessing" by the courts.[4]

Under the Administrative Procedures Act (APA), judicial review of federal agency decisions is prohibited when such review is precluded by statute.

Reviewable Agency Decisions

Section 706 of the APA provides that the reviewing court shall decide all relevant questions of law, interpret constitutional and statutory provisions, and determine the meaning or applicability of the terms of an agency action. The reviewing court shall:

1 Compel agency action unlawfully withheld or unreasonably delayed and
2 Hold unlawful and set aside agency action, findings, and conclusions found to be
  - arbitrary, capricious, an abuse of discretion or otherwise not in accordance with law . . .
  - contrary to constitutional right, power, privilege or immunity
  - in excess of statutory jurisdiction . . .
  - without observance of procedure required by law
  - unsupported by substantial evidence . . .

In a few limited situations, federal district courts can review agency actions. Since these are trial courts, testimony and additional evidence can be received to supplement incomplete or inadequate agency findings of fact.

[3]39 U.S.C.A. Sec. 211(a).
[4]*Agent Orange Product Liability Litigation*, 818 F.2d 194 (2d Cir. 1987).

The federal Hobbs Act grants judicial review in the U.S. courts of appeal from all *final* administrative orders. The term **final administrative order** includes decisions in formal and informal rulemaking as well as adjudications. However, because courts of appeal are not equipped to conduct trials or to receive testimony, and must rely on the evidence developed at the agency rulemaking or adjudicatory hearing, rarely is a de novo review—an entire new trial on the issues of fact—permitted. The appellate courts will simply apply one of the various tests discussed in the next section to determine if the agency findings of fact are properly supported by the evidence. Since most agency records on appeal satisfy the evidentiary test that is used, agency findings of fact are seldom set aside by the reviewing court. However, reviewing courts have full jurisdiction to rule on issues of law, including matters of statutory or constitutional interpretation.

Evidentiary Standards That Restrict Agency Factfinding

The APA provisions for judicial review, discussed in the preceding section, contain two different tests of the adequacy of agency factfinding. Under either standard, the courts will usually accept an agency determination of facts.

First, the "substantial evidence" test is used in "on the record" *formal* rulemaking or adjudication. It requires that the reviewing court should set aside agency action which is unsupported by substantial evidence from the record as a whole. This means that there must be enough evidence in the record that a reasonable person could reach the same conclusion as the agency.

The second and more lenient standard is the "arbitrary and capricious" test, which applies to *informal* rulemaking or adjudications. It requires only that the informal agency rule or decision have some rational factual basis. The Supreme Court has said that the arbitrary-capricious standard requires a reviewing court to determine that (1) after considering *all the relevant factors*, (2) the agency did not make a "clear error of judgment."[5] In applying the test, courts are not allowed to substitute their judgment for that of the agency so long as there is a factual basis for the ruling and a rational link between the facts and the informal rule or decision.

The practice of the courts in deferring to an agency's interpretation of facts—particularly in matters involving technical expertise—is called "agency deference." Courts will also grant considerable deference to an agency's interpretation of its own enabling statute.

Standing, Exhaustion, and Ripeness Doctrines

Other standards and principles are applied by courts of appeal when reviewing agency actions. These include the standing, exhaustion, and ripeness doctrines.

Standing. Article III, Section 2, of the Constitution extends the judicial power of the courts only to "cases" and "controversies"—that is, actual, existing disputes in which the adversaries are genuinely opposed to each other. Thus, under APA Sec. 706 only a party "adversely affected or aggrieved by agency action" has the right (standing) to obtain judicial review. The Supreme Court has held that to have standing, the complainant must show (1) that he or she is aggrieved in fact, that is, has suffered substantial direct—not remote—injury as the result of agency action, and (2) that the interest an aggrieved party seeks to protect is within the range of interests that are arguably protected by the Constitution, statute, or regulation.

Exhaustion and Ripeness. Even though an injury is sufficiently direct to give a complainant standing to obtain judicial review, the *exhaustion* doctrine permits the court to dismiss the appeal where it appears that a party has not first exhausted all available administrative remedies. The underlying reason for the doctrine is that

---

[5]*Citizens to Preserve Overton Park, Inc. v. Volpe*, 401 U.S. 402 (1971).

since most agencies have internal procedures for reconsideration and appeal of an adverse decision, they should be given an opportunity to apply their expertise to correct their own errors before review in the courts. When an enabling statute specifically requires exhaustion, courts have no choice but to apply the doctrine. However, in exceptional cases, courts may not require exhaustion of administrative remedies if the complainant can show that following such procedure would cause irreparable damage.

The *ripeness* doctrine holds that until an agency makes a final decision and develops an adjudication or rulemaking record sufficient to enable a court to comprehend the nature of the problem, the case is not "ripe" for review. By avoiding premature judicial review, the doctrine prevents courts from entangling themselves in abstract disagreements over administrative policies and protects agencies from judicial interference until administrative decisions have been finalized. For example, an appeal to a court challenging a *proposed* agency rule that has not been *finally* adopted would not be "ripe" for review.

MANAGERIAL CONSIDERATIONS AND POLITICAL INFLUENCES

The subjects of administrative agencies, administrative law, and administrative process are riddled with complications. Not only are administrative agencies the most numerous lawmaking bodies—measured in the hundreds at the federal level—but also the quantity of rules governing a wide array of activities is vast. The U.S. Internal Revenue Code, with its accompanying rules and regulations, is said to be, by itself, the largest and most complex body of law ever created. Moreover, some aspects of administrative law are highly technical. The topics of informal rulemaking and hybrid rulemaking, for example, are for that reason beyond the scope of this chapter.

This chapter provides a broad framework for understanding administrative agencies and their processes. That purpose continues in this section, which is devoted to practical concerns involving administrative agencies. It suggests useful perspectives that should help businesspeople cope with the vastness of administrative agency activity.

Business Monitoring of Administrative Agencies

Recall from earlier in the chapter that all proposed and final rules created by federal agencies are required to be published in the *Federal Register*. Moreover, final rules are also to be published in the Code of Federal Regulations (CFR). The entire body of law relevant to federal regulation is found in publications and documents from four sources: (1) the United States Code (USC), which contains all federal law emanating from Congress and signed by the President, and includes all statutes which either enable an agency to act or provide agencies with substantive law to interpret and enforce; (2) the *Federal Register*, discussed above; (3) the *Code of Federal Regulations*, also discussed above; and (4) court decisions and interpretations, found in the federal case reporting system.

These publications are generally available in law libraries or in libraries in the federal depository system.

It is common for large companies to maintain their own libraries of the above material and to have a staff whose sole responsibility is to monitor the agency activity relevant to their businesses and to report that activity to management. A slight change in a single agency rule can have substantial effect on a company's operations and profitability, and accordingly it is a wise practice for managers to keep abreast of new developments. Additionally, knowledge of upcoming rulemaking hearings, for example, is important so that representatives of the company or of industry groups can participate in those hearings and provide data, opinion, or arguments for or against a proposed rule.

But what are small businesses and entrepreneurs to do? Such businesses lack the resources to maintain libraries and staffs—even to hire lawyers extensively—for keeping track of what agencies are doing. Moreover, there are thousands of small businesses located in parts of the country where the nearest law library or federal depository library is a considerable distance away. After all, administrative agency activity is just as important to their businesses as it is to large companies, the difference being merely scale.

Though not an official part of the administrative agency process, trade and industry associations help smaller enterprises in two essential ways. First, associations perform functions for small businesses that staffs provide in large companies. They inform association members of various agency activities and provide advice and guidance on how to deal with the developments. They alert members when their participation in agency hearings and other matters would be most useful and influential. Second, associations operate as surrogates for their members. When it is impractical for association members to devote their individual resources to participation in either formal or informal rule-making proceedings, associations can represent the members' interests. This activity is otherwise known as lobbying.

Judicial Deference to Agency Interpretation of Statutes

In areas of law other than administrative law, courts assert that they ultimately are the ones to interpret the meaning of statutes. Administrative agencies, however, have a different status regarding statutory interpretation, because courts defer to an agency's interpretation of law unless the interpretation is arbitrary, capricious, or clearly contrary to the statute in question.

From a practical standpoint, this means that a challenge to an agency's interpretation of a statute will fail if the agency's interpretation is within a reasonably permissible range. The agency's construction of a statutory ambiguity, for instance, need not be the best one or the only one. A reviewing court might disagree with how an agency construed a particular law, but the disagreement most likely will not even be stated in the reviewing court's opinion because the important question for the reviewing court is whether the meaning an agency has attached to a law is within permissible bounds.

The following case, *Chevron v. Natural Resources Defense Council, Inc.*, is the leading case on the subject of judicial deference.

CASE 4.2 — Chevron v. Natural Resources Defense Council, Inc.
• 467 U.S. 837 (1984)

FACTS

In 1981, the Environmental Protection Agency (EPA) promulgated rules pursuant to the Clean Air Act Amendments of 1977. Congress enacted the Clean Air Act Amendments to impose requirements applicable to States that had not achieved national air quality standards. These States were termed "nonattainment" States which were required by the new amendments to establish a permit program regulating "new or modified major stationary sources" of air pollution.

The new rules allowed a State to adopt a plantwide definition of the term "stationary source" of air pollution. Generally, a permit may not be issued for a new or modified stationary source of pollution unless several stringent conditions are met. However, under the definition in the new rules, an existing plant that contains several pollution-emitting devices may install or modify one piece of equipment without meeting the permit conditions if the alteration will not increase the total emissions from the plant.

In effect, the new rules allowed States to treat all the pollution-emitting devices within a plant or industrial grouping as though they were encased in a

CHAPTER 4: ADMINISTRATIVE AGENCIES AND THE REGULATORY PROCESS • 85

CASE 4.2 Continued

"bubble," and allowed States not to force stringent conditions on each new or modified pollution-emitting device.

The Natural Resources Council and others filed a petition in the U.S. Court of Appeals (D.C. Circuit) for a review of the new rules issued by the EPA. The Court of Appeals set aside the regulations.

Chevron, U.S.A., Inc., and others intervened to argue on behalf of the EPA and appealed this case to the U.S. Supreme Court.

OPINION

STEVENS, J. . . . The question presented by [this case] is whether EPA's decision to allow States to treat all of the pollution-emitting devices within the same industrial grouping as though they were encased within a single "bubble" is based on a reasonable construction of the statutory term "stationary source." . . .

The [appeals] court observed that the relevant part of the amended Clean Air Act "does not explicitly define what Congress envisioned as a 'stationary source,['] to which the permit program . . . should apply," and further stated that the precise issue was not "squarely addressed in the legislative history." In light of the [appeals court's] conclusion that the legislative history bearing on the question was "at best contradictory," it reasoned that "the purposes of the non-attainment program should guide our decision here." . . . Since the purpose of the permit program—its "raison d'etre," in the court's view—was to improve air quality, the [appeals] court held that the bubble concept was inapplicable. . . . It therefore set aside the regulations . . . as contrary to law. . . . We now reverse.

. . . When a court reviews an agency's construction of the statute which it administers, it is confronted with two questions. First, always, is the question whether Congress has directly spoken to the precise question at issue. If the intent of Congress is clear, that is the end of the matter; for the court, as well as the agency, must give effect to the unambiguously expressed intent of Congress. If, however, the court determines Congress has not directly addressed the precise question at issue, the court does not simply impose its own construction on the statute, as would be necessary in the absence of an administrative interpretation. Rather, if the statute is silent or ambiguous with respect to the specific issue, the question for the court is whether the agency's answer is based on a permissible construction of the statute.

"The power of an administrative agency to administer a congressionally created . . . program necessarily requires the formulation of policy and the making of rules to fill any gap left, implicitly or explicitly, by Congress." If Congress has explicitly left a gap for the agency to fill, there is an express delegation of authority to the agency to elucidate a specific provision of the statute by regulation. Such legislative regulations are given controlling weight unless they are arbitrary, capricious, or manifestly contrary to the statute. Sometimes the legislative delegation to an agency . . . is implicit rather than explicit. In such a case, a court may not substitute its own construction of a statutory provision for a reasonable interpretation made by the administrator of an agency.

We have long recognized that considerable weight should be accorded to an executive department's construction of a statutory scheme it is entrusted to administer, and the principle of deference to administrative interpretations "has

CASE 4.2 Continued	been consistently followed by this Court whenever decision as to the meaning or reach of a statute has involved reconciling conflicting policies, and a full understanding of the force of the statutory policy in the given situation has depended upon more than ordinary knowledge respecting the matters subjected to agency regulations. . . . In light of these well-settled principles it is clear that the Court of Appeals misconceived the nature of its role in reviewing the regulations at issue . . . and [we] conclude that the EPA's use of [the "bubble"] concept here is a reasonable policy choice for the agency to make.
JUDGMENT	Reversed.

Political Influences

The various political influences upon the operation of administrative agencies are as fluid and complex as politics in U.S. society as a whole—with all the nuances, tenuous balances of interests, conflicts, and odd alliances that can be found in politics in general.

The fact that politics plays a role in the course of agency activities can be better appreciated when one looks at how the power of administrative agencies is kept in check. Specifically, the three branches of government (judicial, legislative, and executive) provide checks over agency power, and two of the three branches are inherently and inescapably political—Congress and the President. Table 4.2 provides a summary of the checks on agency power by the three branches of federal government.

Here we will discuss the three most visible aspects of administrative agencies that are subject to political influence—appointments, funding, and pressure groups.

Appointments. Key personnel in federal administrative agencies are appointed by the President, and confirmed by the "advice and consent" of the Senate. Such personnel include (1) Cabinet members, such as the Secretary of Agriculture and the Secretary of Labor, who head the executive departments over those named areas; (2) commissioners of independent agencies, such as the Federal Communications Commission (FCC) and the Federal Trade Commission (FTC); and (3) directors and other high posts in dependent executive agencies, such as the Federal Bureau of Investigation (FBI) and the Central Intelligence Agency (CIA).

Not only are the appointments themselves subject to the winds of politics, but the policy preferences of the appointees are in the political crucible. For example, under President Carter's administration, various appointees were more interventionist in their enforcement of agency rules. Perhaps the most notable was President Carter's FTC chairman, Michael Pertschuk, who came under fire for being too zealous. In sharp contrast, the administrations of Presidents Reagan and Bush preferred a "hands off" policy as to regulation of business, and key appointees were selected, in part, because they espoused a similar policy preference. The "hands off" policy, accordingly, became apparent in administrative agencies, particularly when the agencies exercised their discretion on enforcement decisions. For example, during the terms of Presidents Reagan and Bush, enforcement in antitrust areas (by the FTC and Department of Justice) and enforcement on workplace safety (OSHA) diminished considerably even though the regulations on the books changed little. Today, President Clinton appears to be taking a more "hands on" approach, particularly with the health care industry.

For some agencies, the political and partisan aspects of appointments have been officially recognized in law. For example, law specifies that five commissioners serve on the Federal Trade Commission (FTC), but that no more than three of those commissioners be from the politi-

Table 4.2 Checks on the Power of Federal Administrative Agencies

Legislative Checks

- Power to create, expand, limit, and eliminate agencies through enactment of law
- Oversight and investigation—usually performed by congressional committees or subcommittees
- Power of the purse—to review and determine agency budgets
- Appointment confirmation or denial—by the Senate
- Ongoing influence by powerful individual members of Congress or groups of members—e.g., by threat of new legislation or by threat of nonapproval of budgets and so forth

Executive Checks

- Power to appoint key personnel, subject to Senate confirmation
- Power to remove key personnel from executive (dependent) agencies (top appointees in independent agencies serve for specified terms)
  Power to review and to recommend agency budgets—via the Office of Management and Budget (OMB)
- Power to issue executive orders affecting dependent agencies—e.g., President Bush's order for a moratorium on new regulations going into effect in 1992
- Ongoing influence through use of threat to exercise of above powers

Judicial Checks

- Power to review agency rules or conduct
- Power to issue injunctions and orders—upon a showing of possible irreparable harm if agency acts or fails to act

---

cal party of the President. Consequently, if a commissioner from a party different from the President's were to resign or to serve out the term, the President might have to appoint a new commissioner from outside the President's political party to maintain the partisan/political balance in key roles in the agency.

Funding. The extent to which an agency can execute what has been delegated to it by law depends upon the resources allocated to it. While the U.S. Constitution specifies that Congress holds the ultimate power over the spending of government funds, as a practical matter others in government have substantial influence over funding decisions for administrative agencies.

Outside of Congress, the most powerful source of influence over funding is the Office of Management and Budget (OMB), itself a dependent agency under the President. Generally staffed with highly qualified professionals, the OMB serves as advisor to the President, who is responsible for budget recommendations to Congress. As advisor, the OMB deals not only with budgetary and financial matters, but also with issues involving the management of administrative agencies.

It is common for lobbyists, business analysts, journalists, and others to monitor OMB activities and recommendations, because what is happening in the OMB is likely to be the best guide on how future policies will be carried out. The amount of funds recommended to be allocated reflects the administration's priorities and policies. The importance of a particular agency in carrying out the executive branch's policies can be measured in the adequacy or inadequacy of funding.

From a businessperson's standpoint, funding is perhaps one of the best measures for assessing how much effect a particular agency might have on one's business. For example, the business press periodically carries news stories which report the enforcement budget of the Internal

Revenue Service (IRS) and its effect on the probabilities of whether returns of taxpayers from various income brackets will be subject to review or audit.

Pressure Groups. Because hundreds of administrative agencies are "dependent" and hence under the close control of the executive branch, their conduct—and even some of their regulations—can be changed with a stroke of the President's pen. With such power in a single office, it is not surprising that interest groups often focus lobbying activity on the White House.

During President Bush's administration, for example, a pressure-group tug-of-war with research scientists, biomedical companies, research universities, and others against pro-life pressure groups resulted in the President's issuing an executive order forbidding the use of fetal tissue in government funded research overseen by the National Institutes of Health (NIH). With President Clinton in office, the balance of influence among these groups shifted, resulting in an executive order which essentially repealed the previous executive order involving fetal-tissue research.

Pressure-group influence upon independent agencies can also be seen. In the late 1970s, the Federal Trade Commission (FTC) became much more aggressive in its rulemaking and enforcement activity, a posture which FTC critics characterized as overly pro-consumer. Business groups, bar associations, groups representing the media, advertisers, insurance companies, and others first attempted to use their influence in the rulemaking proceedings, but did not succeed. Following those efforts, the same groups instead directed their influence to Congress, resulting in legislation which stripped the FTC of its power to make rules governing specific areas. Moreover, Congress used its power over FTC funding to force the agency's conduct to be within Congress' wishes. However, even this was not accomplished without a political showdown. The FTC, of course, lost, but not without Congress suggesting that it was serious about cutting off FTC funds. The agency actually went unfunded for a day, after which suitable compromises were quickly reached.

Jurisdictional Overlap

Duplicative or contradictory rules imposed by different agencies can frustrate businesses in their efforts to comply with the law, and can drive up their costs. Consider, for example, a retailer specializing in equipment for outdoor sports. The hunting equipment department is regulated by several agencies, both local and federal. Complying with the requirements of one is not sufficient to satisfy another. Sales of 12-gauge shotguns, for instance, are regulated by the Bureau of Alcohol, Tobacco, and Firearms (BATF), which requires sellers to keep a record of gun purchasers' names and the serial numbers of the firearms. Though the Federal Bureau of Investigation (FBI) does not regulate the sale of firearms, this agency can demand reporting and retrieval of records from the retailer. It is not enough for the retailer to respond that the BATF has the records; this retailer must respond to the FBI's specific request for information—duplicate reporting of essentially the same information. Additionally, state and local counterparts of the Bureau of Alcohol, Tobacco, and Firearms may have similar, but not quite the same, reporting requirements. Jurisdictional overlap such as this obviously can be quite costly and frustrating to businesses, whatever their size.

Greater difficulties arise from jurisdictional overlap than merely duplication of enterprise effort. Sometimes, full compliance with one agency can put a business in jeopardy of noncompliance with rules of another agency. A former commissioner of the Food and Drug Administration (FDA) has labeled this possibility as the interagency jurisdictional "squeeze play."[6]

Events from the mid-1980s provide an example. The Federal Trade Commission has primary jurisdiction over, among other things, advertising such as a package blurb which states "new and improved." The Food and Drug Administration's jurisdiction over food labeling includes not only food package labels but also advertising, which the FDA considers secondary label-

---

[6]Hutt, "Government Regulation of Health Claims in Food Labeling and Advertising," 41 *Food Drug Cosm. L.J.* 3, 25 (1986).

ing. Under direction from Congress,[7] the Federal Trade Commission (FTC), which has primary jurisdiction over advertising and sales practices, embarked on a program to encourage food manufacturers to include more health and nutrition information in advertising and on labels. Following this encouragement, a cereal manufacturer, Kellogg's, with assistance from the National Cancer Institute (NCI), began an advertising and on-label "health awareness" campaign which advised consumers that a high-fiber diet was associated with low incidence of certain types of cancer. However, because Kellogg's "health awareness" campaign made disease-prevention claims, it risked FDA sanction and product seizure. By FDA regulation, a product which claims the cure, mitigation, or prevention of disease is considered a drug, and since Kellogg's cereal had not been approved as a drug, the FDA could take action on the basis that the cereal was a misbranded drug, and could remove the product from retail shelves. Kellogg's found itself in the middle of an interagency jurisdictional "squeeze play," and the matter was resolved not with agency adjudication or court review, but by a political showdown with the FTC, NCI, and PHS (Public Health Service) facing off against the FDA. The FDA, exercising its discretion, decided not to enforce against Kellogg's. A similar, but not as dramatic, political resolution of issues surrounding health information on food labels occurred in late 1992 between the FDA and the U.S. Department of Agriculture (USDA), and the matter was resolved politically by the President.

SUMMARY

Administrative law concerns the powers and procedures of administrative agencies, public entities other than legislatures and courts, having power to determine private rights through making rules and rendering decisions.

[7]National Consumer Health Information and Health Promotion Act, Pub. L. No. 94-317, 90 Stat. 695 (1976); Public Health Service Act (amendments), Pub. L. No. 95-622, Section 262, 92 Stat. 3412, 3435 (1978); Health Promotion and Disease Prevention Amendments of 1984, Pub. L. No. 98-551, 98 Stat. 2815 (1984).

Administrative agencies are created by acts of federal, state, or local legislatures, and they may have three kinds of powers delegated to them: quasi-legislative power, quasi-judicial power, and executive power.

At the federal level, the procedures of administrative agencies are limited by the Administrative Procedure Act (APA) unless the enabling statute of an agency specifies differently. The goal of the APA is to provide fairness in agency rulemaking and judicial behavior by imposing a standard set of procedures upon agencies.

Two prototypes of agency rulemaking exist—the legislative model and the adjudicative model. Agencies employ either of these models or some combination of both, in addition to their quasi-judicial powers and executive powers.

Agency rules and decisions may be challenged in the courts through a process known as judicial review. By law, however, some agency matters may not be reviewed by courts. Moreover, when a challenge is against an agency's interpretation of a statute, courts generally defer to the agency interpretation unless it is arbitrary, capricious, or contrary to the stated policies of the legislature.

Politics necessarily plays a role in administrative agencies. The legislative and executive branches of the federal government—both highly political branches of government—control between them agency funding and appointments of personnel.

REVIEW QUESTIONS

1. **(a)** What powers may a legislature delegate to an administrative agency? **(b)** Explain each of those powers.

2. Explain the courts' reasoning for their holding that a delegation of powers to an administrative agency does not violate the separation-of-powers doctrine.

3. **(a)** What are the two basic models of agency rulemaking? **(b)** Describe the differences between those two models. **(c)** What features of the Administrative Procedure Act (APA) affect how the basic models of rulemaking function? **(d)** List those features.

4. What are the key differences between formal adjudication and informal adjudication?

5. What is the substantial evidence rule and what is its purpose?

6. List and explain the major quasi-executive functions of an administrative agency.

7. (a) Are all agency rules and decisions subject to judicial review? **(b)** Explain your answer in detail.

8. (a) What is required to establish "standing" for a court to review an administrative decision? **(b)** Define the doctrine of exhaustion as it pertains to judicial review. **(c)** What is the ripeness doctrine and why is it useful for reviewing courts?

9. (a) What does the concept of judicial deference apply to? **(b)** What importance does this concept have to a challenger of an agency's interpretation of a statute?

10. Explain how administrative agencies are politically influenced and how such influence can come about.

11. (a) What checks on the power of administrative agencies do the three branches of government possess? **(b)** Do some branches have more checks on such power? **(c)** Explain your answer.

12. Is it possible for different administrative agencies to regulate similar activities? Explain your answer.

CASE PROBLEMS

1. Cure-It Pharmaceutical Company developed a lotion to be used for reducing the pain from sunburn. The lotion's active ingredient, a topical anesthetic, was the same as the one used by a competitor's product, which was the leading brand. The advertising for Cure-It's lotion claimed that the lotion was effective in eliminating or reducing sunburn pain. Before the advertising was exposed to the public, the president of Cure-It conferred with scientists in the company's laboratories and with technical people outside the company. They all agreed that the active ingredient was indeed an effective topical pain reducer or eliminator. However, Cure-It did not perform any tests of its own until after the product was on the market. Those tests confirmed what Cure-It's scientists and others had said—namely, that the product worked as claimed.

After Cure-It had introduced its product to the marketplace with advertising, the Federal Trade Commission requested substantiation for Cure-It's advertising claims. An FTC rule requires that before a specific product claim may be advertised, the advertiser must establish that the claim be substantiated. The FTC sanctioned Cure-It because the claim was not substantiated by product tests until after the product and the advertising were in the market. Cure-It appealed the FTC ruling in federal court, arguing that the advertising for the lotion was true and that the FTC's "prior substantiation" rule should not apply in this case, in light of the president's conferral with specialists and the competing product with the same ingredient making similar claims in its advertising.

How should the reviewing court decide this case?

2. Professor Brilliant of Premier State University received formal notice that he was to be laid off indefinitely from his position for budgetary reasons. Professor Brilliant had taught for 15 years at Premier State and had secured tenure. Also, all employees of the state university system, of which Premier State was a part, are considered "civil servants" whose employment is governed by the state's Civil Servant Commission, which was created by the state's Civil Servant Act. That act, and the rules promulgated by the Civil Servant Commission, specify that employees are entitled to formal notice and a hearing before termination. Professor Brilliant, however, believed that his tenured status and his academic contract precluded the possibility of his being laid off or terminated for any reason other than just cause (misconduct, malfeasance, and so forth). So, instead of participating in the termination hearings, Professor Brilliant sued Premier State University in state district court, arguing breach of contract. In court, Premier State moved that the case be dismissed. How should the court decide? What should be the basis for this decision?

3. The National Economic Commission (NEC) scheduled meetings in 1989 in order to get expert testimony on national economic issues and to have discussions with experts. The NEC and the administrator of the General Services Administration (GSA) wanted these meetings to be closed. Because the issues to be discussed involved possible national budget cuts and possible new taxes, plus expert forecasts on possible outcomes, the closed meetings were intended to allow participants to speak freely. Additionally, the NEC did not want to arouse the unwarranted fears and speculation that a frank open meeting on sensitive economic issues might prompt. The concern was that such fear and speculation could adversely affect the activity on securities exchanges and other national markets. Public-interest groups, newspapers, and other press organizations objected to the closed meetings and sued in federal district court, seeking an injunction against the closed meetings. How should the federal district court decide? Why?

4. Goldman, an Orthodox Jew and an ordained rabbi, was an officer in the Air Force serving as a clinical psychologist. He wore a yarmulke (skullcap) while on duty indoors. Military rules specify acceptable headgear for military personnel on military installations. Goldman's yarmulke was not within the rules. After warnings that he would be subject to court-martial if he continued to wear the yarmulke, Goldman sued the Secretary of Defense, claiming that the regulation abridged his First Amendment right to free exercise of religion. Goldman won his case in federal district court, but the U.S. Court of Appeals reversed, holding that the military's interest in uniformity justified strict enforcement of its regulations. The U.S. Supreme Court also ruled in favor of the military. What aspect of administrative law played an important role in this case? Why is this First Amendment case also an administrative law case?

CHAPTER 5

Law and Business Ethics

Law has multiple functions: minimizing disorder, encouraging cooperative relations, and protecting an amazing variety of interests from encroachment by others. As far-reaching and varied as law is, however, it is only one strand in the regulatory fabric. Other institutions—family, church, school, social clubs, and scientific, literary, and professional societies—pursue in their own ways many of the ends that law does.

Often, people look to law for an indication of what behavior is moral. Law provides some answers, at least in the sense of penalizing destructive and encouraging productive behavior. But much law is noncommittal about morals. Knowing that a vast population holds legitimately conflicting opinions about almost anything, many lawmakers try to remain neutral. Indeed, it is widely accepted in our pluralistic society that law should leave people reasonably free to exercise their own discretion, and should regulate only where needed to assure the rights and safety of others. Thus, while law closely regulates areas fundamental to the public welfare, people generally must rely on their own senses of values or ethics—derived largely from nonlaw institutions—as a guide to what is right in their daily affairs.

In business this is especially so. Almost every business decision or relationship has ethical implications: what products to make; what methods to use; what markets to pursue; what price to charge; how to act toward suppliers, customers, competitors, employers, employees, coworkers, inspectors, and the community where one's business resides. Law establishes outer limits of propriety; within those limits businesspeople are free to make their own decisions.

Discovering what the law requires is relatively easy, since legal requirements take the form of published rules (legislation, administrative regulations, court cases, or executive orders) that must be followed in the situations specified by the government. Discovering what ethics requires can be more difficult. Whether as owner, manager, or employee, we all face choices that involve conflicting ethical or moral values. Often, we must develop ethical rules or guidelines for ourselves. The problem is how to steer an ethical course given the complexity of business, the diversity of ethical or moral values that people bring to the workplace, and the conflicting but often equally persuasive considerations one faces as a business decision maker.

Understanding the nature of ethical dilemmas and how to resolve them can improve business efficiency and make business more satisfying to all concerned. Consequently, university courses devoted exclusively to business ethics are gaining prominence. But there is a good reason for also studying business ethics *as part of a business law course*. Like law, ethics is a controlling and facilitating force. Each—law and ethics—operates in its own sphere, with its own methods. Yet law and ethics overlap and interact with each other, and ethics provides a yardstick for measuring the quality of law. To understand law fully, then, we need to understand its links with ethics.

THIS BOOK'S APPROACH TO BUSINESS ETHICS

This chapter is not, and cannot be, a substitute for a course in business ethics. Ethics is much too complex to be covered adequately in so brief a space. This book can, however, introduce you to the complementary roles that ethics and law play in business decision making. And it can help you develop an approach to resolving business-related ethical dilemmas, especially those for which law provides no clear guidelines. In the process, you will see more clearly where law ends and ethics begins, and the strengths and weaknesses of each as a regulator of conduct.

This book has two major ethics components. The first one is this chapter. It could be entitled "Ethics in a Nutshell," because it provides a brief overview of ethics—nature, concepts, terminology—and discusses the meaning of business ethics. The other component is the Ethics in Practice problems found at the end of each part of this book. Most of the problems summarize incidents reported in the news media or reported by students to the authors. The problems provide practice in analyzing and resolving ethical dilemmas at the personal and corporate levels of business operations. They can be resolved by applying ethical principles discussed in or suggested by this chapter.

Students who already have a background in business ethics can reinforce their understanding of law and ethics by reviewing here the ethical principles previously learned and applying them to the business situations presented in the Ethics in Practice sections. Students lacking such a background will—through this chapter, the Ethics in Practice problems, and the occasional references to ethics found in the law chapters—receive a practical introduction to business ethics.

WHAT IS BUSINESS ETHICS?

Ethics, a branch of philosophy, examines fundamental questions about what is good and bad in a society, and about the nature of moral duty and obligation. Is profit making moral? If not always, under what circumstances? What does it mean to be honest? If honesty is preferable to dishonesty, why? What makes a moral duty binding? We might assume that profit making is moral, and that every person has a moral duty, not just a legal one, to be honest. The "proof" for such assumptions (or lack of it) is found in the rigorous analysis, argumentation, and reasoning typical of courses in ethical theory, a topic well beyond the scope of this book.

The evaluation of specific business practices is another matter entirely. On a day-to-day basis, business is a stream of transactions, activities, and relationships. It can be a source of satisfaction or a source of anxiety to the participants and to the public. If business activity is worrisome to those affected by it, they need a method for analyzing the situation to see what the trouble is. Often, they will need to know whether a practice or transaction is right, not just whether it is legal. Therefore, throughout this book applied ethics and its subset, business ethics, have relevance.

Ethics Terminology

Applied ethics, a branch of the discipline called ethics, involves moral standards and values that guide one's daily conduct.[1] A **value** is an opinion about the worth of a thing or a state of affairs. In this country, many people cherish the idea of free enterprise; that is, they hold it as a value.

---

[1]This discussion of ethics is based on Manuel G. Velasquez, BUSINESS ETHICS (1988) and Rogene A. Bucholz, FUNDAMENTAL CONCEPTS AND PROBLEMS IN BUSINESS ETHICS (1989).

A **moral standard** is a criterion or measure of right behavior. Moral standards include moral norms and moral principles. **Moral norms** are specific standards of conduct indicating what constitutes acceptable behavior by members of a group. Because we prize freedom of speech in our democratic society, shouting down or physically attacking a speaker with whom we disagree is widely considered unacceptable. Yet we are allowed to rebut the speaker's views even to the point of discourtesy, as long as we await our turn to be heard. Thus, moral norms prohibit, allow, or require certain specific actions. **Moral principles** are more general standards of conduct. They are used to evaluate not only the behavior of individuals but also the adequacy of institutions and social policies, including those pertaining to business.

Business ethics "concentrates on how moral standards apply . . . to business policies, institutions, and behavior."[2] Business ethics takes a variety of forms: the **personal ethics** of individuals involved in business activities; the concept of **corporate social responsibility** (discussed later in this chapter); and **codes of professional conduct** applicable to doctors, lawyers, accountants, insurance agents, engineers, and similar groups.

Questions of business ethics arise at three levels of decision making: *individual, organizational,* and *systemwide.*[3] Examples are, respectively, a manager's use of personal judgment to resolve daily business problems where law or company policy is not clear; a corporation's developing a company code of ethics or a company policy on hiring and firing; and a legislature's deciding whether private property rights should be curtailed for the benefit of the public.

Role of Rights, Utility, and Justice

Moral principles concern such things as rights, utility, and justice, qualities that are especially prominent in business ethics. The word **right** suggests that individuals are entitled to protection of certain freedoms and interests. Rights may be legal (created and enforced by law) or moral (available as a matter of conscience or ethical judgment). A minimum wage law gives employees a legal right to a specified hourly rate of pay; but because of their contributions to profitability, minimum wage employees may have a moral right to a higher, "living" wage.

The moral principle of **utility** concerns net social benefits produced by institutions, social policies, and the behavior of individuals. Typically, questions of utility are resolved by applying a sort of cost-benefit analysis. Should a smelly meat-packing plant that makes life miserable for hundreds of neighboring residents be forced to relocate at great expense? Is it acceptable to spend billions on space exploration while many peoples of the earth suffer from disease and famine? Should a drug manufacturer adopt an expensive sampling system that will increase the detection of defective drugs by only 1 percent?

Justice implies fairness of treatment, giving people what they deserve. In law, justice means that a person has received a benefit or a penalty provided by law, in a proceeding that was impartial and fair. In ethics, justice implies equitable treatment generally, without regard to whether it is required by law. For justice to exist, like cases must be treated alike. This means that people who are equals in relevant ways must receive equal treatment.

In law and ethics, three kinds of justice are prominent. **Retributive justice,** dealing with the punishment of wrongdoers, is a goal of the criminal law and the tort doctrine of punitive damages. **Compensatory justice,** concerning reimbursement for monetary losses caused by others, is a goal of contract and tort law. Topics relating to these types of justice are discussed elsewhere in this book.

The third type, **distributive justice,** concerns how equitably benefits and burdens are distributed among members of society. As philosopher John Rawls has noted, we face a conflict: Generally, we recognize that social cooperation makes possible a better life for all of us than any would have if each were to live solely

---

[2] Velasquez, op. cit., p. 18.
[3] Buchholz, op. cit., pp. 31–32 (citing Kenneth E. Goodpaster).

by his or her own efforts. Yet each person has a self-interest in how the benefits produced by cooperation should be distributed, each preferring a larger to a lesser share.[4]

The conflict—between self-interest and social cooperation—produces countless questions: Should childless people have to pay the taxes that support the schools? Should medical care be available only to those who can pay for it? Should factories be allowed to dump pollutants into the rivers and thereby transfer disposal costs to the taxpayers instead of the customers who bought the products? Should corporate executives receive 500 times the pay of the average production worker? One of the major concerns of ethics, and of Professor Rawls's work in particular, is developing a general theory of distributive justice for resolving the conflict.

Rawls's theory has two fundamental principles:

First: each person is to have an equal right to the most extensive basic liberty compatible with a similar liberty for others. Second: social and economic inequalities are to be arranged so that they are both (a) reasonably expected to be to everyone's advantage, and (b) attached to positions and offices open to all.[5]

Moreover, the hypothetical person who is to make the actual distribution of benefits and burdens must act from behind a "veil of ignorance," not knowing his or her own abilities or station in life, and thus not being in a position to act selfishly or against the interests of others.[6]

We can easily reject arbitrarily imposed inequalities such as those resulting from race or gender discrimination. But others occur naturally. For example, people born with special skills or talents tend to be paid substantially more than people of lesser ability. Since such inequalities were not caused by anybody's wrongdoing, should they just be accepted as natural and inevitable, as libertarian philosophers recommend? Or should government or the private sector intercede to spread the wealth more evenly?

Achieving distributive justice is very difficult, in part because there are so many criteria for assigning benefits and burdens. Suppose you own a company. Five jobs become available, and 700 people apply. Should you give the jobs to the five most needy applicants, the five most skilled, or the five who would expend the most effort? Need is a suitable criterion for dispensing medical care or welfare benefits, but it may not be useful for selecting production workers. Willingness to work hard is not a sufficient hiring criterion if the applicant cannot acquire the needed skills. Skill is worth little if the applicant is lazy.

Given our competitive free enterprise system and your self-interest in profits, you probably would give the jobs to applicants who would make the greatest contribution to your business. The ethical challenge would be to select employees of reasonable skill and dedication without resorting to irrelevant factors. Justice implies that two crane operators of equal skill, dedication, and experience should receive the same consideration for your job opening even though one is a man and the other a woman. If applicants are substantially unequal in qualifications, however, justice implies that the less qualified should not receive the job.

Law and Ethics—A Brief Comparison

If you are new to the study of ethics, you may find it helpful to start comparing ethics and law. Some points of similarity and difference were mentioned earlier. Here are a few more.

In terms of creation and enforcement, ethics differs considerably from law. Law is created by the government, and its prohibitions are enforced through the threat of fines, imprisonment, and other penalties imposed by government. In contrast, ethical standards are created by an appeal to reason, and enforced by personal and cultural factors largely apart from the government: one's upbringing, the church, the esteem of friends and colleagues, the pressure of the market. The penalty for a breach of ethics is social in nature. It may consist of no more than a reprimand or a temporary loss of respect. A se-

---

[4] John Rawls, A THEORY OF JUSTICE (1971), p. 4.
[5] Rawls, op. cit., p. 60.
[6] Ibid., p. 12.

rious breach of ethics could cost the offender a job or a valued family, personal, or business relationship or status. The *law* does not compel one to observe ethical standards. The compulsion, if any, is psychological, social, or economic: Few people are so hard-hearted that the opinions of others do not matter. Even the occasional callous professional may heed ethical standards sufficiently to avoid losing the economic benefit of the license to practice.

Both legal and ethical standards require people to control their self-interests. The law prohibits a variety of conflicts of interests—situations in which a trusted person uses his or her position to profit improperly from the trusting person. In ethics, the duty to control self-interest is much broader. While the weight to be given to self-interest varies greatly among schools of ethical thought, the general idea is this: If one is to be fair or to do justice, one cannot unreasonably favor oneself at the expense of others. The moral obligation to control self-interest is closely related to another feature of moral conduct—impartiality. In ethics, as in law, decision makers are expected to treat all *like* interests equally, and not to give greater weight to one's own interests or to those of friends.

Law and ethics differ in another important way. Law can be changed by a vote of the lawmakers. Ethical standards cannot be changed by a vote. They derive their validity from the adequacy of the reasons given to justify them. Until those reasons change, the ethical standards remain in force.

WHY STUDY BUSINESS ETHICS?

We return now to a question suggested earlier in the chapter: Why should ethics be part of a business law course? Three key reasons come to mind:

1 Law adopts many ethical standards and thus removes them from the realm of voluntary conduct. To understand their legal obligations, businesspeople need to understand the underlying ethical values.

2 A sense of personal and corporate ethics supplements the law as a guide to right business conduct. An understanding of ethics and moral reasoning can be invaluable for testing the rationality and fairness of business decision making.

3 A study of ethics, values, and policy provides a basis for judging the quality of law and for seeking change.

Ethical Standards as Part of the Law

Ethical standards appear in a variety of legal contexts, some old and some new. The U.S. Constitution forbids the taking of life, liberty, or property without due process of law. Due process requires that rules of law have at least a rational purpose and that litigation and other procedures be fair and fairly administered. Thus, in protecting fundamental values, the Constitution embodies our general preference for honesty and fair play. Often viewed as mainly a limit on *governmental* intrusion into private affairs, due process can apply to private misconduct as well. For example, in limiting the traditional right of employers to fire employees "at will," many courts today require employers to demonstrate a valid reason for terminating employment, and some courts require employers to use an impartial hearing in arriving at the decision.

The honesty and fair play ethic, a moral standard, underlies much of the law discussed in this book. The Uniform Commercial Code (UCC) requires the parties to a wide range of commercial transactions to act in "good faith," which the UCC defines in part as "honesty in fact." The UCC forbids a party to a sales contract to engage in "unconscionable" practices, defined broadly to include any sales practice that oppresses or unfairly surprises the other party. Corporate insiders cannot legally trade in the securities of their own companies unless they first disclose to the other party any "material inside information" they have that affects the transaction. Because home solicitation sales often involve high-pressure sales tactics, laws give many consumers a "cooling-off" period within which to reconsider a credit purchase of goods or services. Lawmakers may emphasize honesty and fairness mainly to promote economic values such as stability and efficiency in the marketplace. More likely, they recognize moral values as the bedrock upon which economic values lie.

To understand the law and to judge its quality, one needs to consider the moral values it promotes. However, it is not always clear what ethical standards, if any, the law incorporates. Box 5.1 asks you to consider the possibilities for five well-known bodies of law.

> **BOX 5.1**
> **Ethical Values Underlying Law**
>
> What ethical values, if any, do you think might underlie the following laws?
>
> - Laws prohibiting misleading advertising
> - Laws limiting automobile emissions
> - Laws requiring restaurants and hotels to serve all persons regardless of race or color
> - Laws providing financial assistance to poor families with dependent children
> - Laws prohibiting firms from monopolizing the market

Ethics as a Factor in Business Decision Making

Business decision making is a process of making choices in pursuit of a firm's business objectives. These choices, often made in the context of day-to-day problem solving, have technical, legal, and social dimensions.

Business operations cover a wide range of activities—product development, marketing, distribution, financing, labor and customer relations, and the like. To deal with them adequately, a manager must be able to apply different kinds of knowledge to problems as they arise. A manager deals with the technical aspects of business problems by applying relevant business theory. Handling the legal aspects involves applications of business law. Managing the *social* aspects requires attention to ethical or moral standards.

Ethical standards fit into the decision-making picture in at least two ways. First, if accepted and practiced by most people, they produce a suitable environment for transacting business and resolving business problems. Cooperation, fair dealing, and respect for the needs, desires, and freedoms of others promote commercial harmony and satisfaction. They also imply an approach to business that is both ethical and practical: the willingness of individuals to restrain their own self-interests to advance the mutual best interests of everyone. Second, ethical standards permit people to evaluate specific business practices for their moral or social quality, and to discard or correct the destructive ones. In this role, ethics guides the multitude of business decisions that law and statements of corporate policy do not cover.

Ethical standards may be difficult to apply, because they involve value judgments almost exclusively. A value judgment is a matter of opinion, often producing no clearly "right" solution. Consequently, ethical principles may seem so apart from the concrete, authoritative world of business theory and law that managers ignore or fail to recognize them. Yet ethical concerns often are the deciding factor in evaluating a business plan. Suppose that Goodheart Distributors is debating whether to market cigarettes to older minors. Although cigarette advertising on television has been banned, developing an effective marketing strategy without TV ads is technically feasible. Sales of cigarettes to older minors are legal in most states and are profitable. But a belief that cigarettes are addictive and harmful to people's health might raise ethical concerns about the propriety of marketing them to minors, especially by a company such as Goodheart, which takes pride in selling only wholesome products.

The expectations of those affected by business also help define the role of ethics in business decision making. Customers expect courteous treatment and fair value for their money. Communities expect businesses to keep the physical environment reasonably clean and to pay their fair share of taxes in exchange for the community services they receive. Businesses expect fair treatment from government and support from the local communities. Employees look to business for self-fulfillment. Whatever their specific jobs, people usually take pride in doing them well, in contributing to a worthy effort, and, of course, in receiving appropriate monetary rewards. Sleazy or unethical business practices by the company or co-workers—or by outsiders such as suppliers and community leaders—diminish the feeling of self-worth, harm morale, and may damage the business itself. To avoid such consequences, managers need to be alert to discrepancies between the company's ethical environment and the reasonable expectations of all concerned.

Ethics as a Way to Judge Law

Business students take law courses to learn how to detect potential legal problems, consult effectively with legal counsel, and comply with basic legal requirements. But learning to *evaluate* the law may be the most valuable outcome of law study. In day-to-day operations, the ability to evaluate enhances one's ability to detect, consult, and comply. In the longer term, businesspeople may wish to participate in lawmaking. Intelligent participation, whether as a voter, lobbyist, or legislator, requires the ability to evaluate existing and proposed law and the processes by which it is made.

How can one judge the quality of law? A first step is to determine the reasoning behind it—that is, to discover its purpose, rationale, or underlying **policy** (a course of action chosen from among alternatives to guide people's conduct). Then one must decide whether the purpose is worthy and whether the law, as designed, will be effective for carrying it out. For example, Congress might consider raising taxes to reduce family and corporate incomes, hoping thereby to reduce inflation. A decision to tax for that reason is a policy judgment. The wisdom of the policy and the effectiveness of the resulting law are matters for debate and evaluation.

To evaluate a law, a person may have to weigh conflicting social, economic, and ethical factors. Suppose, for example, that a statute grants liquor wholesalers the exclusive right to distribute beer statewide, with each major brand being assigned to a different distributor. Is the law good or bad?[7] Exclusive distribution rights could produce higher profits in the marketing of popular brands. Higher profits could benefit shareholders and employees, and even the general public through business expansion and increased tax revenues. But since distributors might now fix prices at arbitrarily high levels, the law could be challenged as anticompetitive and anticonsumer. On safety, health, or moral grounds, however, the law might be thought beneficial because it could price beer out of the reach of poor overindulgers. Some would question whether the fate of any overindulger, rich or poor, is the proper concern of government as long as the purchase is legal; or whether poor but responsible users should have their choices limited by economic manipulation.

Sorting through competing considerations such as these reveals the various impacts a law

---

BOX 5.2

Legal/Political Decisions and the Value of Human Life

Highway designers have done studies on the relationship between highway speed limits and the incidence of injury and death. Their findings: Basically, the higher the speed limit, the higher the rates of death and injury. But supporters of higher speed limits often argue on the basis of economics—a higher speed limit means less time in transit, correspondingly lower labor costs, and so forth.

If you were a legislator trying to devise the optimum speed limit law, what factors would you consider and how would you weigh them? Would the following additional factors be relevant? Are there others?

- Decreased fuel consumption efficiency at higher speeds, and increased road damage
- Who causes traffic accidents on the open highways, and who gets injured
- To whom you are responsible as a legislator

---

[7]This example and the related commentary are adapted from J. David Reitzel, "Critical Thinking and the Business Law Curriculum," 9 *J. Legal Stud. Educ.* 471, 495 (1991).

has on the public. It might also reveal the legislature's rationale for its ordering of policy priorities, the role of special-interest groups in policy formulation, the abuses that sometimes occur, corrective measures that can be taken, and political and social forces that can overwhelm the best of policy intentions.

THEORIES OF ETHICS

How can a person use ethics to understand and evaluate laws and business decisions? A first step is to consider some basic approaches to making moral judgments.[8]

Two approaches are prominent in business ethics. *Teleological* theories of ethics emphasize the consequences of conduct. Under utilitarianism, one of many teleological approaches, the best course of action is that which produces the most good or the most net benefits for society. *Deontological* theories, illustrated by Kant's "categorical imperative," emphasize the moral quality of the conduct itself: If an action does not conform to certain moral criteria, it is wrong even if doing it might occasionally produce net benefits for society.

Consequence-Based Ethics— Utilitarianism as an Example

Utilitarians judge conduct by the amount of good it produces. Lying is generally considered bad because it defeats the victim's reasonable expectations and creates an atmosphere of distrust. Yet a lie can produce more good than bad—for example, where a woman with a dangerous heart condition is told for her own protection that her severely injured child received only minor injuries. If the good consequences (protecting the mother) outweigh the bad (creating an atmosphere of distrust), utilitarians might find this lie morally acceptable. However, its utility cannot be determined merely by considering its consequences to the actor or the people acted upon. An act is morally correct only if it leads to the greatest possible good (or the least possible bad) for *everyone* affected by it. Moreover, an act is not necessarily correct just because its benefits outweigh its costs. It must be judged by comparing it with *all available alternative* actions. The alternative that produces the maximum net benefit is the morally correct one.

The aim of utilitarianism, then, is to promote human welfare by minimizing harm, by maximizing benefits, or by doing both. Accomplishing that goal involves the following steps: (1) determining what alternative actions are available in a specific situation, (2) estimating the costs and benefits (economic and social) that a given act would produce for everyone affected by it, and (3) choosing the alternative that produces the most total good or the least total bad.

BOX 5.3

Point to Consider

How do we measure "the good" to determine whether an act or rule is ethical under utilitarian theory? Does the weighing of benefits and costs depend upon one's personal value system? Consider the beer distribution statute discussed in the preceding section, and the speed limit problem.

Duty-Based Ethics—Kant's Categorical Imperative as an Example

By evaluating actions solely in terms of the total good produced, utilitarian theory poses a major difficulty. It ignores the moral quality of conduct and provides no method for distributing benefits among members of society. Utilitarians might approve of murdering a cruel manager if doing so would produce a net benefit for the population affected by the murder—the actor, the manager, workers harmed by the manager's conduct, the families of all concerned, and so on. Or, because cheap vegetables greatly benefit the general population, utilitarians might approve of paying migrant farm workers only a subsistence wage. Yet murder is an obvious violation of fundamental human rights, and paying farm work-

---

[8]This discussion is based on Buchholz, op. cit., Chs. 3 and 4; and Velasquez, op. cit., Ch. 2.

ers too little for the great good they do results in an unjust distribution of society's benefits.

Duty-based (deontological) theories of ethics focus on the moral quality of conduct itself. One has a duty to take the action that is inherently right, moral, or fair, *regardless* of its immediate consequences. Since, like utilitarians, deontologists hope for the betterment of society, they clearly expect moral conduct to produce good results generally. But they do not evaluate conduct on the basis of how much pleasure or good a specific action produces. If an act is moral, it is correct even though it might produce pain. Conversely, if an act is immoral it cannot be correct even if it produces a surplus of benefits.

In duty-based ethics, what makes an act moral or immoral? According to the German philosopher Immanuel Kant (1724–1804),[9] people act morally by doing willingly what reason demands, and there are basic principles of reason that rational (thinking) beings possess in common. Certain moral commands, called **categorical imperatives,** are binding on us (imperative) because they are logically justified by reason. They are "categorical" because the duties they create have no exceptions.

The categorical imperative requires that people treat one another as *free persons equal to everyone else*. To conform to the requirements of the categorical imperative—to be moral—conduct must meet two criteria:

1 An action must be *universalizable* and *reversible*. That is, its rationale must be consistently applicable to everyone, and one must be willing to have that reasoning applied even against oneself.
2 The actor must treat others as *ends in themselves*, and not merely as a means to an end. That is, one must respect the right of others freely to pursue their own legitimate interests, and not simply exploit others without regard to their needs and concerns.

Deceptive advertising, a form of lying, is immoral under both of these criteria. First, rational beings could not accept deception as a universal practice. If everyone lied, no one could know who is speaking the truth, and advertising would be useless. Reversibility is missing too, since a deceptive advertiser would not like to be victimized by someone else's deceptive ad. Second, by using deception to gain an unwarranted personal advantage, the advertiser shows disrespect for the worth of others and compromises their right to act freely in their own best interests.

In contrast, honoring a fairly bargained contract regardless of the consequences is moral. Rational people would find the practice universally acceptable, because it allows people to rely on contract promises and thus gives effect to their reasonable expectations. Reversibility exists, because honoring a contract is the kind of conduct that one prefers from others. Moreover, by honoring a contract promise, its maker respects others as equals and helps them pursue their own legitimate interests.

PRACTICING BUSINESS ETHICS

How does one put ethics theory to practical use? One might begin by considering the nature of moral reasoning and some applications of the ethical theories just discussed.

Nature of Moral Reasoning

Stages of Moral Development. According to psychologist Lawrence Kohlberg, the ability to make moral judgments develops in several stages. As people mature in their moral reasoning, they see that personal values differ and that what is moral is a matter of opinion.[10] They begin to tolerate other people's values and to accept democratic processes as a way of resolving value conflicts. The most mature moral thinkers accept **universal ethical principles** as the basis for morality. These principles are not inflexible moral rules imposed by a higher authority. Rather, they are self-chosen principles that re-

---

[9] Kant's philosophy has a vigorous life today in its own right, but also as a basis for modern philosophical thought. For example, John Rawls acknowledges Kantian theory as a basis for his own theory of distributive justice. Rawls, op. cit., Preface.

[10] Reitzel, op. cit., p. 482 (citing R. Bybee and R. Sund).

quire one to evaluate moral dilemmas thoughtfully, in terms of justice, the reciprocity and equality of human rights, and respect for the dignity of human beings as individual persons. Being based on reason, they are principles that any rational person can find acceptable. Utilitarianism and Kant's categorical imperative are examples of reason-based universal ethical principles.

The Process of Moral Reasoning. But how does moral reasoning actually work? Moral reasoning is a process of evaluating conduct by applying a moral standard to it and deciding whether the conduct is right or wrong. The process has three steps:

1. Clearly identifying or expressing the moral standard that one intends to apply.
2. Examining the conduct in question for evidence that it conforms to or violates the moral standard.
3. Making a moral judgment that the conduct is right or wrong.

Suppose the Construction Contractors Association has been discriminating against women when hiring crane operators. Of fifty crane operator positions filled in the city last year, only three (6 percent) of those hired were women. Yet the pool of qualified applicants was 30 percent women. The Civil Rights Act forbids this type of gender discrimination, but the association members do not believe that the Civil Rights Act applies to their situation, and perhaps it does not. However, even if the Act does not apply, *you* think the discrimination is wrong, and as executive secretary of the association, you want to persuade its members to change their minds. Your moral reasoning would be as follows:

> MORAL STANDARD: It is wrong to deny women their preferred livelihood by discriminating against them in hiring.
> EVIDENCE: The city's pool of crane operator applicants, all equally qualified, reliable, and willing to work, is 30 percent women. Yet only 6 percent of last year's positions were filled by women. The qualified women who were not hired as crane operators have found only much lower-paying jobs or remain unemployed.
> MORAL JUDGMENT: The city's construction firms have unjustly discriminated against female crane operators.

How do you know that your moral reasoning is sound? One way to decide is to check whether there is internal or external justification for the moral position you took.[11]

Internal justification concerns (1) logical consistency between a moral judgment and its basis in ethical theory and (2) the soundness of the evidence supporting the judgment. Utilitarians could find gender-based employment discrimination a societal evil because it arbitrarily excludes its victims from their preferred livelihood, robs them of self-esteem, or reduces their family income—causing far more harm than good. Kantians could find the practice objectionable for lack of universalizability, reversibility, and respect for the right of others freely to pursue their own legitimate interests. The employment statistics reveal a gender-based discrimination by the city's construction firms, and there is evidence of economic deprivation. Sociological and psychological studies might be needed to verify the other harms alleged.

Suppose that some contractors still doubt that gender-based employment discrimination is unjust. An appeal to **external justifications** might be convincing. They include the *use of reason* (logical argumentation); *social contract theory* (the idea that to minimize friction, rational people would agree to live by certain principles); *cultural justification* (the view that a judgment is sound if it is consistent with deeply held cultural values); and *procedural justification* (the view that a moral standard is sound if it was developed carefully, clearly, impartially, and rationally).

Applying Ethical Theories

Sometimes a more formal application of ethical theory will be helpful. How would you resolve

---

[11]Buchholz, op. cit., Ch. 5.

the following hypothetical case under, first, the utilitarian theory, and then in terms of Kant's categorical imperative?

THE CASE OF THE BREACHING HOMEOWNER

Mary hires Paul to remodel her bathroom for $5,000. Paul is to begin the work in 2 weeks, and in preparation draws up detailed plans for some of the installations. On the weekend before Paul is to begin the job, Mary learns that Pamela will do the same work for $100 less. When Paul arrives to begin the remodeling, Mary tells him that she has hired Pamela for the job. Paul protests, pointing out that his bid for the job was low and he will profit little from it, he has spent considerable time preparing for the job, he bought some supplies needed for the work, and he will have to lay off the employee who was to help him. Mary says she is willing to pay any damages that Paul can prove in court.

Recall that the *utilitarian approach* involves three steps: (1) determining what alternative actions or rules are available in a specific situation, (2) estimating the economic and social costs and benefits that an act or rule produces for everyone affected by it, and (3) choosing the alternative that produces the most total good or the least total bad.

Here, contradictory contract rules may be involved.

1 Paul may believe that "breaching a contract is morally unacceptable and is forbidden."
2 Mary may believe that "it is morally acceptable to breach a contract if the breaching party is willing to pay the damages that result."

Under **rule utilitarianism,** a rule is morally correct if the total utility produced by everyone's following it is greater than the good produced by following an alternative rule.

If everyone follows Paul's rule forbidding contract breaches, every contracting party will receive the agreed-to performance, and losses to third persons such as employees will be minimized. The cost of litigation will be zero because all contracts would be performed, and the general public will have confidence in contractual promises. However, Paul's rule requires the performance of bad bargains as well as good ones, and of contracts that later become unprofitable because of unexpected conditions such as the rising cost of materials. Even Paul would be unable to minimize such losses by simply withdrawing early from an unprofitable contract and paying damages.

Mary's rule has the benefit of increasing her social and economic flexibility. The rule allows her to fire Paul and employ a woman plumber, a member of a group that may have been underemployed or discriminated against in the past. If Paul finds a lawsuit too costly to pursue, Mary will save $100. On the costs side, by following her rule Mary will defeat Paul's reasonable expectation of employment, deprive his employee of a job, and by refusing to perform perhaps cause others to doubt Paul's competence or character. Her rule also will contribute to uncertainty in the marketplace, since one could no longer have full confidence in contract promises.

What weights would you assign these harms and benefits? Are there others on either side? Would Mary's paying damages compensate Paul for all losses? On balance, which is the better rule—Paul's or Mary's?

How does Mary's breach of contract fare under *Kant's categorical imperative?* Recall that for conduct to be moral under Kantian theory, (1) it must be universalizable and reversible and (2) the actor must treat others as ends in themselves and not merely as a means to an end.

It would be difficult to find Mary's conduct universalizable or reversible. Her breaching a fairly bargained contract would not be acceptable in principle, because such conduct would undermine people's confidence in contract promises and defeat their reasonable expectations of performance. Nor would Mary find the practice acceptable in principle if she were the victim.

Mary's conduct has failed the first test of the categorical imperative, but not necessarily the second. If Mary had hired Paul intending to fire him upon finding someone else to work for less, she certainly would be using Paul only as a means to an end. However, if Mary felt strongly about women's employment rights, and learned after employing Paul that Pamela was a plumber, Mary's hiring and then firing Paul would not necessarily have involved a selfish or exploitative intent. Moreover, by recognizing Paul's right to damages, Mary reveals some respect for Paul's interests and concerns. A truly callous exploiter would deprive him of even his obvious legal rights.

If Paul had induced Mary into the contract by improper means such as fraud, her refusal to perform would be legally and morally justified. Paul did not engage in such conduct, and the contract was fairly bargained. But what if Paul later proved difficult to work with or was rude to Mary's children? Would her refusal to honor the contract be morally acceptable? Recall that a duty having the status of a categorical imperative is not subject to any exceptions whatever. One must carry it out despite discomfort. If Paul's work were sound and his personal deficiencies were within reasonable limits, Mary probably would be morally required to honor the contract.

Moral Dilemmas: The Problem of Conflicting Values and Roles

One might expect strong personal values to be a sure guide to ethical business conduct. But values differ from person to person, and one's own values may be in conflict or may change. Because different values take us down different ethical paths, we often experience moral confusion or uncertainty.

How can people deal with the uncertainty arising from conflicting values? The following strategy might help: (1) understand the sources, content, and variable nature of values; (2) establish priorities when values collide; and (3) if possible, take action to resolve the resulting ethical dilemma.

Personal values have many origins. We acquire values through personal experience. We adopt values held by others—parents, teachers, friends, social clubs, political parties, employers, churches, the military. And we make value judgments about every conceivable subject: the worth of sports, human life, power steering, illegal drugs, whales, rock music, the free enterprise system.

More often than we might suspect, values change over time. Edward L. Bernays, the public relations pioneer, reportedly encouraged American women to smoke in public and helped a bacon producer convince Americans that heavy breakfasts are better than light ones. Millions of Americans enthusiastically embraced both positions. Today, knowledge of lung cancer and cholesterol has caused many to question the wisdom of these practices. When first introduced, child labor laws, the minimum wage, and the recognition of labor unions were fiercely resisted by large segments of the business community. Today, most businesspeople accept them as reasonable and normal.

Where values differ, conflict arises. Suppose you believe that human life should be protected at all costs. Then you discover that your employer, a car manufacturer, plans to resist modifying a defective gas tank design on the assumption that wrongful death damages will be less than the cost of modifications. Your employer's maximizing profits by endangering the lives of

---

BOX 5.4

A Question of Risk

It is well known that product designers face many trade-offs. Cost versus safety is only one. What if a manufacturer could make an absolutely safe automobile, though at a cost that most people could not afford? Should public policy, via wrongful death cases and other tort sanctions, encourage safer cars and thus effectively allow only wealthier persons to own them? What factors or values—what priorities—should be considered?

What if you want a less expensive car and are willing to forgo some safety features to get it? Would it be unethical for a car manufacturer to satisfy your wants, even if the designers knew in advance that the less expensive version would unavoidably cause some injury and death? Does your knowledge of the safety situation have any bearing on the quality of the company's ethics?

customers conflicts directly with your belief in the sanctity of life. What should you do?

You might protest to upper management, secretly inform the news media of the company's plan, quit your job, or simply remain silent. Your decision would depend on a host of factors: how strongly you feel about protecting the lives of strangers, how you think management would react to your protest, how badly you need the job, how you feel about the act of "whistleblowing," and how your future prospects would be affected should you be fired for taking a stand. To arrive at a decision, you would have to balance your conflicting roles—as a faithful employee, as a citizen with an ethical duty to the public, and perhaps as a person with family responsibilities.

INSTITUTIONAL ETHICS: CORPORATE SOCIAL RESPONSIBILITY

One might wonder why the car manufacturer in the preceding discussion would refuse to modify the defective gas tanks and thus consciously endanger lives simply to maximize profits. Aren't corporations, like individuals, expected to act in socially responsible ways—to act ethically? Such a corporate duty has long been recognized. However, the specific conduct this duty requires of managers is still being debated.

In the eighteenth century, the public's economic welfare was thought to depend on competition among individuals acting in their own self-interests, free to use private property as they saw fit. Since the conduct of individuals would be open to public scrutiny, the business excesses of individuals would be controlled by the "invisible hand" of market forces.

Today, this ideology still appeals to many. They believe that allowing corporations to pursue their own self-interests will produce the maximum benefit for society; that the corporation has a purely economic function; and that the main obligation of corporate management is to maximize profits for the shareholders. As economist Milton Friedman put it, "[T]here is one and only one social responsibility of business—to use its resources and engage in activities designed to increase its profits so long as it stays within the rules of the game, which is to say, engages in open and free competition without deception or fraud."[12]

In Friedman's view, the function of the corporate manager

is to conduct the business in accordance with [the owners'] desires, which generally will be to make as much money as possible while conforming to the basic rules of the society, both those embodied in law and those embodied in ethical custom. . . . [T]he manager is the agent of the individuals who own the corporation . . . and his primary responsibility is to them.[13]

But many other commentators and business leaders believe that corporations and their managers have broader responsibilities. As corporations have grown over the years, they have had great impact, for good and for ill, on the users of their products and services worldwide, and on the economic, social, and physical lives of the communities in which their plants and offices are located. Long ago, many believe, large corporations ceased being just economic institutions under shareholders' control and became socioeconomic institutions tightly controlled by management. These facts and the size of modern corporations put them well beyond the influence of the "invisible hand."

To restrain the negative forces that modern corporations have the power to generate, new ethical norms have arisen, contributing to a body of ethical thought called *corporate social responsibility*. "The essence of the corporate social responsibility concept is the notion that business organizations have societal obligations that transcend economic functions of producing and distributing scarce goods and services and generating a satisfactory level of profits for their shareholders."[14] Proponents of corporate social responsibility argue that corporations are more

---

[12]Milton Friedman, CAPITALISM AND FREEDOM (1962), p. 133.

[13]Friedman, "The Social Responsibility of Business Is to Increase Its Profits," *New York Times Magazine,* Sept. 13, 1970, p. 33.

[14]Edwin M. Epstein, "The Corporate Social Policy Process and the Process of Corporate Governance," 25 *American Business Law Journal* 361, 373 (1987).

than just privately owned economic entities—they are also citizens with rights and duties, and social actors whose conduct can affect millions of people. Consequently, managers have responsibilities, not only to shareholders but also to other stakeholders such as employees, consumers, and the communities where the corporation operates. Corporate managers, then, are not only *agents of shareholders*; they are in a sense also *agents of society*. As such, they should do more than lawfully generate profits. They should spend corporate time and money on social concerns such as environmental pollution, unemployment arising from plant relocation, industrial hazards to employee health, and improvement of the quality of life in the host communities.

> **BOX 5.5**
>
> ### Another Way to View It
>
> The social consequences of corporate activities could also be seen as economic costs, known as **externalities.** What if public policy makers could identify and assess these externalities more accurately? It might be possible, then, to make companies pay these costs and pass them on to the ultimate consumer. But *should* lawmakers do this if the result would be to drive some companies out of business? ∎

Within recent decades, many ethical norms, such as those condemning the pollution of the environment, racial discrimination in employment, and unwarranted threats to employee safety and health, have been incorporated into statutory law or administrative regulation and have become legal norms as well. Other concerns, such as improving the quality of life in the host community, remain largely if not exclusively a matter of moral obligation. One key question is the extent to which a nonlegal ethical concern must be business-related to fall within a firm's corporate social responsibility.

How has corporate America responded to these new thoughts about corporate social responsibility? A few firms resist them vigorously. Some do only what is required by law or try to negotiate minimum compliance. But many more accept the idea of corporate social responsibility (often seen as a desirable alternative to governmental regulation) and actively implement it. Recently, the term "corporate social *responsiveness*" has been used to describe the implementation process—a process of strategic management by which a corporation may "anticipate and respond to rapidly changing and escalating social expectations" in its decision making.[15] The emphasis is on *how*, not whether, the corporation should address the concerns of the broader society. Socially responsive management (1) selects appropriate ethical standards, (2) evaluates competing claims for societal improvement, and (3) allocates personnel and funds to those projects with the highest priority. Social auditing and accounting, the development of corporate codes of ethics, the adoption of industrywide ethical standards, and an ongoing involvement with the community are characteristics of corporate social responsiveness.

> **BOX 5.6**
>
> ### Point to Consider
>
> You are the CEO of Clothescorp, a manufacturer of men's and women's clothing. The board of directors is evaluating a proposal to relocate the firm from its present small-town location in a southern state to a foreign country that has a very low wage scale for the kinds of workers you will need. Despite the costs of the move, it eventually will be quite profitable to Clothescorp. Will the move be a socially responsible act? Consider its impact on:
>
> - The present production workers
> - The southern community where they work
> - The Clothescorp shareholders
> - The foreign workers and their country
> - U.S. consumers
>
> Are there other stakeholders whose interests should be considered? ∎

[15]Ibid., p. 375.

PROFESSIONAL AND CORPORATE CODES OF ETHICS

To become a member of a profession, one must meet special educational and licensing requirements for the occupation involved. In addition, most professions have a code of ethics that applies to members. By one count, the number of professional codes is 338 and growing.[16] Doctors, lawyers, and CPAs have them, but, obviously, so do many other professional groups: engineers, journalists, real estate agents, financial analysts, tax advisors, nurses, public administrators, architects.

Professional codes of ethics state the norms that should govern professional behavior. These norms vary among professions, since different professions serve people in different ways. Within a given profession the ethical norms may differ from country to country. And sometimes the norms change over time. For example, the 1912 code for electrical engineers stated, "Technical discussions and criticisms of engineering subjects should not be conducted in the public press, but before engineering societies or through technical publications." The 1979 successor code requires members, in protecting the safety, health, and welfare of the public, to "speak out against abuses in these areas affecting the public interest."[17]

A professional code of ethics may be *aspirational* only, in that it states ideals that professionals should strive for. The Hippocratic oath of the medical profession is aspirational. Or a code may be *regulatory*, in that it imposes rules of conduct and enforces them with sanctions such as public reprimands or the suspension or loss of the license to practice. Many codes are a combination of these two types. The lawyers' elaborate Model Rules of Professional Conduct (1982) is largely regulatory.

Professional codes serve a variety of purposes. First, by forbidding conflicts of interests and other misconduct, they provide professional groups with a basis for disciplining wayward members. Second, because the courts honor codes that are fair and reasonable, they provide a degree of self-regulation and professional autonomy, and a measure of protection against improper demands of clients. At the same time, such codes benefit clients by providing professional accountability that otherwise might not exist. Finally, they inspire public confidence by revealing the characteristic values and functions of specific professions. For example, a certified public accountant's audit of a firm is supposed to provide reliable financial information to outsiders such as lenders and investors. The professional association's code of ethics emphasizes the CPA's duty to remain independent and objective when conducting an audit, even though the company being audited hired the CPA.

Professional ethics represents a bridge between law and ethics. Although the codes emphasize the "ought-to's" of professional business activity, there often is a degree of formal enforcement characteristic of law and not usually associated with other business ethics.

Much of what has been said about professional ethics applies also to corporate codes of ethics. In recent years, literally thousands of corporations have developed such codes. They typically state ideals that the corporation hopes to attain in its relationship with the public and, often, with its employees, customers, and suppliers. In addition, the codes may impose standards of employee conduct. These standards commonly govern relationships among employees and between employees and third persons such as suppliers and customers. They may state the general obligations that firm and employee owe to each other and to the public, specify preferred ways of resolving conflicts, and even forbid specific misconduct such as sexual harassment or the taking of kickbacks from suppliers. Corporate codes of ethics often appear in employee handbooks. Failure of employees to comply with the rules may result in dismissal or other sanctions. Thus, like professional codes, corporate codes of ethics may be regulatory or aspirational or both. If developed through consensus, as ethical standards by na-

---

[16] Michael Davis, "The Ethics Boom: What and Why," 34 *The Centennial Review* 163, 168 (1990).

[17] Davis, op. cit., p. 182, fn. 7.

ture must be to be effective, they will be a useful and moderating force in labor-management relations.

REVIEW QUESTIONS

This springboard chapter is meant to help you size up and resolve problems of business ethics, starting with those in the Ethics in Practice sections of this book. To that end, you might want to consider the following questions. They are *not* the kinds of review questions typical of the other chapters. The questions here ask you (1) to do some independent thinking on topics only alluded to in the chapter and (2) to concentrate your thoughts about the nature of ethics and its role in business decision making.

1. In general, problem solving involves at least the following overlapping steps: (a) recognizing or defining the problem; (b) analyzing the situation to determine what factors, interests, or concerns are involved; (c) weighing those concerns and deciding which should have priority; and (d) resolving the problem or proposing a solution. Is this general problem-solving methodology consistent with the methods suggested in the chapter for resolving ethical dilemmas?

2. In resolving problems of business ethics, what values would you expect to encounter? Those in the list below? Any others? What priority would you give them? How will you handle conflicting values?

> An honest day's work for an honest day's pay
> Freedom of individual expression and development
> Loyalty to one's employer, employee, friend, spouse
> Democratic decision making
> Efficiency and cost containment
> Cooperation for mutual benefit
> Harmony with the environment
> Corporate social responsibility

3. People have multiple roles in life—citizen, spouse, parent, friend, church member, employee, and so on. Often these roles are in conflict. How might such conflicts affect your resolution of ethical problems you encounter? For example, if you had to decide which of two equally qualified subordinates to promote, would it matter that one is your close friend or relative? What if your boss orders you to do something at work that is legal but contrary to the teachings of your church. How will you proceed?

ETHICS IN PRACTICE

As Chapter 5 indicates, law alone is not a sufficient basis for business decision making, because almost every business problem has social or ethical dimensions that law cannot or should not address. So we look beyond the law for guidance, especially to ethical standards derived from personal experience, business custom and usage, or society at large.

To resolve business problems effectively, we must be able to recognize ethical dilemmas when they appear, analyze them, and apply ethical standards of behavior, including any that may be imbedded in law. But ethical standards often conflict, so we also need to establish priorities among standards when dealing with ethical concerns. Sometimes the law itself is the problem. It may seem so inadequate or wrongheaded as a rule of conduct that we want to evaluate and challenge it. When we do so, ethics and policy questions mix.

To emphasize the relationships between law and ethics in business decision making, this book provides the following:

- Chapter 5, entitled "Law and Business Ethics," an overview of business ethics and the process of resolving ethical problems
- Within the law chapters, occasional boxes entitled "A Question of Ethics"
- At the end of each part, a set of Ethics in Practice problems relating to the law covered in the part.

Most of the Ethics in Practice problems in this book are based on events reported in the news media. A few come directly from the experiences of students and others. Usually the problems do not involve a violation of law. Occasionally, however, the ethical quality of law comes into question through a recently decided court case or a proposed or enacted statute.

Each problem emphasizes business ethics, corporate social responsibility, or professional ethics. *Business ethics* focuses mainly on day-to-day business activities, especially on the way in which individuals deal with others within or outside the firm. *Corporate social responsibility* is more concerned with the extent to which a business firm should pursue social objectives beyond profit making. *Professional ethics* indicates how a properly functioning professional—doctor, lawyer, accountant, stockbroker, and so on—should act toward others, especially when rendering professional services, dealing with other professionals, or helping formulate public policy relating to the profession.

Addressing ethical problems can be a daunting task, since ethical decision making requires us to sort through a host of subtle, often conflicting considerations and make value judgments without the benefit of clear-cut rules. As a point of departure for resolving ethical problems, questions like the following might be helpful:

1. If a violation of law is involved, what weight should be given to the violation? It's against the law to steal, but would stealing food from a supermarket to save a starving child's life be as serious an ethical violation as stealing food from a starving person to add to the thief's ample supply?
2. What interests are in conflict? Resolving an ethical problem requires one first to identify what the dispute is about, and this can be done in terms of the "interest" that each disputing party has—i.e., the concern or desire that each one has.

3   What level of self-interest is involved? We expect and encourage people to act in their own self-interest, as long as they do so reasonably and productively. But self-interest often blinds people to the interests of others and leads to overreaching. At what point does the pursuit of self-interest become unethical?

4   Whose standards or norms of conduct apply in this situation? Yours? Mine? Those of the church, union, lodge, or corporation? An ideal developed by a great philosopher? When norms of conduct are in conflict, how do we choose which to apply? What priorities should they receive?

5   In applying a rule or a norm of conduct, what weights and priorities should conflicting interests receive? Between your self-interest and mine, which should prevail? Should one's self-interest prevail over that of the community, employer, government? Does the *kind* of interest matter—life vs. property, freedom vs. property, animal life vs. human life? Must one interest always win out over another, or can conflicting interests be accommodated?

6   Would an ethical approach such as utilitarianism, Kant's categorical imperative, Rawls's veil of ignorance, or libertarianism provide an acceptable basis for weighing, balancing, or prioritizing?

PROBLEMS IN ETHICS

1. Drugco, a 1,000-store chain of pharmacies operating in several states, loses about $20 million to shoplifters each year. To combat shoplifting, Drugco has instituted a new policy: Instead of routinely prosecuting alleged shoplifters under the criminal statutes, local Drugco stores may allow suspected shoplifters to buy their way out of trouble by paying the store $200. The procedure is as follows: When shoplifters are caught, the store manager is to have them arrested if they seem like professional criminals. However, if they seem to be amateur, casual shoplifters, the manager may let them go after verifying their names and addresses. In about a week, the freed suspects receive letters demanding payment of the $200. If they refuse to pay, Drugco sues them in small claims court for civil damages. Most persons accused of shoplifting have been paying up. **(a)** Given your understanding of "due process of law," is there anything about the new policy that makes you feel uncomfortable? **(b)** Suppose you are interviewing for a job as a Drugco manager and are asked your opinion of the new policy. Would your status as an applicant affect your evaluation? How? **(c)** If you are uncomfortable with the new policy, would you feel better knowing that it has the approval of authorities in twenty-six states? Why?

2. Downtown merchants in Sonoma asked the city manager to do something to make more parking spaces available for shoppers. The city manager responded by hiring Ron, a new "meter man," and providing him with a new motorized cart. Ron tripled the average number of parking tickets—from 200 to 600 per month. Although virtually all the tickets were justified, the city clerk's office has been flooded with complaints. "I thought it was pretty Scroogey," complained Lydia, cited and fined $20 during the Christmas season for parking slightly into a red zone during a shopping trip. "It doesn't encourage you to come back for fear you're going to get zapped." Merchants now fear that strict enforcement of parking regulations will scare away customers. The police lieutenant has instructed Ron to be more lenient—for example, by ticketing only cars parked halfway into an adjoining space. Should parking law enforcement policy be so easily influenced by downtown merchants and the volume of citizen complaints?

3. In a 1991 study, sociologist Penelope Canan and law professor George Pring examined 228 lawsuits in which people were sued for large sums after protesting a variety of business and governmental actions. For example, when a New York homeowner carried a picket sign to protest a developer's plans to cut down woods for a new subdivision near her house, the developer brought a $6.5 million libel suit against her in a civil court. In California, a developer filed a similar suit for $40 million against three homeowner groups and some private citizens after they successfully campaigned for a ballot measure calling for a moratorium on land development. The average claim for damages was $9 million, and the average case lasted for about 3 years. Most cases were dismissed for lack of a meritorious claim. Called SLAPP suits (for Strategic Lawsuits Against Public Participation), they allegedly are designed to discourage people from challenging private ventures that need a license or public permit, or from publicly criticizing public servants or alleged polluters. But, said a building industry lobbyist, "So-called citizen activists know they can shut a project down" by forcing unwarranted public hearings and permit appeals and thus impairing the developer's ability to get financing. Moreover, "Groups bent on stopping development . . . wrap themselves in the flag of environmentalism when what they really want to do is keep low income [people] and people of color out of their neighborhoods." Is it ethical for developers to sue people for protesting the projects in question?

4. Tax examiners at one IRS regional center were told to ignore certain mistakes that would result in refunds to 112,000 taxpayers, most of them elderly. The refunds would average about $19 per taxpayer. An IRS spokesperson said the refunds were so small that it would be "burdensome" to ask taxpayers to dig through their records. Suppose the IRS has no legal duty to inform taxpayers of their mistakes. Is there a moral duty?

5. A California legislator introduced a bill that would bar a doctor from referring a patient to a lab or a health care facility in which the doctor has an ownership interest. What ethical problem does the proposed legislation address?

6. Irene recently was appointed president of her company with authority to implement a pension plan. She immediately hired her husband Dennis as vice president and asked him to develop a pension plan for all employees. The plan he developed complies with the law, but the production workers believe the plan treats them unfairly while unduly favoring upper management. Irene agrees with the production workers, but knows that if she rejects the plan, Dennis will be embarrassed and angry and their marriage will be in jeopardy. However, if she accepts the plan, the production workers' morale and output will decline. Did Irene create an ethical problem by hiring Dennis?

PART TWO

Tort and Criminal Law

CHAPTER 6
Nature of Torts; Intentional Torts

CHAPTER 7
Negligence and Liability without Fault

CHAPTER 8
Competitive Torts and Intellectual Property

CHAPTER 9
Criminal Law and Business

Ethics in Practice

CHAPTER 6

Nature of Torts; Intentional Torts

When is a manufacturer responsible for the harm caused by its defective products? Under what circumstances is a doctor, lawyer, or accountant liable for malpractice? Can a customer who slips and falls in a store obtain damages from the owner? To answer these questions, we look to the law of **torts,** the body of law designed to give people redress for civil wrongs other than a breach of contract. Tort law determines when and why a person must pay compensation for the injuries he or she inflicts on others.

In developing the rules of torts, the courts engage in a delicate balancing between one individual's freedom of action and another's interest in property or person. To determine whether an individual is responsible for injuries to person or property, the law primarily focuses on the culpability of the actor or wrongdoer. Rarely do the courts hold a person liable for harm without some showing of **fault.** Thus, if I intentionally strike my neighbor, I will have to pay for his or her injuries. From a moral and economic perspective, I should have to compensate him or her because the injuries were caused by my deliberate act. Similarly, if I carelessly push my lawn mower over my neighbor's foot, I will have to pay for his or her injuries. Liability would be based on my fault in failing to exercise reasonable care.

Although we have developed a system of tort liability that is primarily based on fault, the courts also take into consideration other factors in determining when a person must compensate others. The courts also consider which party is in the best position to prevent or insure against the loss and the relative economic position of the parties. For example, in most states a manufacturer can be liable without fault for injuries caused by its defective products. Lawmakers impose this "strict liability" because manufacturers are in a better position than customers to prevent product defects, customers rely on manufacturers to supply safe products, and the economic losses caused by defective products should be borne by those who profit from their sale. Thus, modern lawmakers consider a range of policy concerns, including the fault of the actor in causing the injuries, in determining whether to impose tort liability.

This part of the book examines three important areas of tort law and criminal law. Intentional torts are discussed in this chapter. Negligence and liability without fault are reviewed in Chapter 7. Competitive torts involving economic rights and business interests are discussed in Chapter 8. Chapter 9 examines criminal law and business.

NATURE OF TORTS
Meaning of Torts

A **tort** is "a civil wrong other than breach of contract, for which the court will provide a remedy in the form of an action for damages."[1] The person who commits a tort, called the **tortfeasor,** must compensate the victim for damages to the victim's person (e.g., physical or emotional injuries), property (e.g., damages to buildings or machinery), or economic interests (e.g., interference with contract rights).

Every tort has certain recognized *elements,* facts that must be proved by the injured party to recover damages. For example, to establish the tort of negligence (discussed further in Chapter 7), the plaintiff must prove four elements:

- The defendant had a duty to exercise due care.
- He or she breached that duty (failed to live up to the standard of care).
- The victim suffered injuries.
- The injuries were caused by the tortfeasor's acts.

The law also has developed certain **defenses**—i.e., reasons or circumstances that will justify or excuse the commission of what otherwise would be a tort. For example, a person has a privilege or right to use force against another in self-defense. This privilege allows an individual to repel a physical attack as long as he or she uses *reasonable* force. In a suit by the injured attacker, the self-defense privilege, if established at trial by the defense, will prevent any tort recovery. Our study of torts will focus on the elements of torts as well as the defenses.

Tort liability is a matter of policy for each state to decide. State courts and legislatures recognize new torts from time to time, apply existing torts definitions to new fact situations, and abolish old torts as social conditions change. For example, invasion of privacy was not generally recognized as a tort before the 1930s, but is so recognized today. Its development reflects a change in our society from an agrarian social system to a highly industrialized, urban society in which privacy interests are endangered. In contrast, recognized torts will be abandoned if they become outmoded. For example, the courts have generally abolished the tort of breach of promise to marry because it is inconsistent with modern social customs. Thus, the law of torts, like all areas of the law, is an evolutionary body of rules and principles.

Crimes Distinguished from Torts

A given act may constitute both a crime and a tort. For example, the act of holding a person hostage is both the crime of "kidnapping" and the tort of "false imprisonment." In such a case the government can prosecute the perpetrator for a criminal offense. In the criminal case, the victim is only a state's witness. At the same time, the victim can sue the perpetrator for damages in a separate civil lawsuit.

A crime is different from a tort, and the functions of the criminal and tort systems are different. A **crime** is an offense against the sovereign authority—i.e., an offense against the state. As a public wrong, a crime is prosecuted by the local, state, or federal government; and the sanction for its commission is punishment by fine, imprisonment, or death. The purpose of the criminal system is to protect society by punishing (and possibly rehabilitating) the wrongdoer, and thereby deterring others (and the perpetrator) from committing similar wrongs.

In contrast, a tort is a wrong against another individual—an unreasonable interference with private rights—for which the injured party can sue for damages. The civil suit is commenced by the victim, and the sanction imposed for the commission of a tort is an award of money damages. Although tort law is also concerned with preventing others from committing wrongs, the primary purpose of the tort system is to compensate the innocent victim for his or her losses, not to punish the wrongdoer.

---

[1] PROSSER AND KEETON ON THE LAW OF TORTS (5th ed. 1984), p. 2.

Classes of Torts

Torts are classified as intentional torts, negligence, or liability without fault.

Intentional Torts. An intentional tort is one in which the tortfeasor acts with **intent.** Intent in tort law does not necessarily mean an evil or malicious motive or purpose, nor does it require an intent to harm or injure the victim. Intent is tortious if the perpetrator acted with the purpose of interfering with the rights of another or acted in such a way that an interference with those rights was substantially certain to follow from his or her actions. As a practical joke, Michelle pulls a chair from under John as he is sitting down, causing him to fall to the floor. Michelle would have the intent necessary for a tort, because either she intended John to fall or she knew or should have known that his fall was substantially certain to follow from her actions.

Intentional torts are considered the most serious torts because of the purposeful action of the tortfeasor. So the legal consequences of committing an intentional tort may be more severe than for an unintentional tort. The victim of *any* tort can sue for **compensatory damages**—to cover medical bills, lost wages, mental distress, and other actual costs. But **punitive damages** ordinarily are awarded only if the defendant's conduct was willful, malicious, fraudulent, or particularly oppressive. They are imposed to punish the defendant and to deter others from such extreme misconduct.

Negligence and Liability without Fault. A person who causes injury to another without intending to do so can be liable for the tort of negligence, or can be held liable in tort even though not at fault. **Negligence** is the broadest area of tort liability. It is based upon a person's failure to exercise due care for the protection of others. In a negligence case, the tortfeasor is held liable because he or she failed to exercise reasonable care. The operator of an automobile who drives carelessly and causes an accident with a pedestrian is guilty of negligence. Liability without fault, called **strict liability,** is limited to a class of cases in which neither intent nor negligence is necessary to hold a person liable for losses to others. Alice's pet tiger bites Wu Ling, her neighbor. Alice is responsible even if she took extraordinary steps to prevent any injuries to her friends. Because of the inherent risk of harm in keeping a wild animal for a pet, keepers of wild animals do so at their peril and are liable without fault.

INTENTIONAL HARM TO THE PERSON

The intentional torts involving harm to the person include assault, battery, false imprisonment, infliction of mental distress, defamation, invasion of privacy, malicious prosecution, wrongful use of civil proceedings, and abuse of process. They are designed to protect a host of personal interests—physical and emotional well-being, peace of mind, liberty and freedom of movement, reputation, and privacy and solitude—from unlawful invasion by others.

Battery; Assault

Battery is the intentional, harmful, or offensive touching of another person without consent or legal justification. The tort occurs when the intentional contact is either physically harmful or personally offensive. An employer's nonconsensual sexual contact with an employee can constitute a battery as well as a form of sexual discrimination (i.e., sexual harassment). Moreover, the contact need not be to the plaintiff's body but extends to the plaintiff's "person." Intentionally knocking a cane from the hand of a blind man, removing a person's hat without permission, or grabbing a plate out of someone's hand are batteries. The degree of harm or offense suffered by a victim is relevant in the determination of the damages awarded in a lawsuit.

> **BOX 6.1**
> **A Question of Policy**
>
> Why do the courts, in developing the tort of battery, define "person" broadly to include one's clothing, things one is carrying, and so on? ∎

Assault occurs when one intentionally causes another to be in apprehension of an immediate battery. To establish apprehension, a plaintiff must prove that the defendant threatened to use force and had the apparent present ability to carry out this threat. Ann makes an oral threat to shoot Kenji while pointing a pistol at him that he believes is loaded. Ann is liable for the tort of assault even though she knows the pistol is unloaded. An assault can also take the form of an attempted battery that fails. If Raoul shoots a pistol at Andrea and the bullet misses her, no battery has occurred. But Andrea was likely fearful of an immediate battery, and Raoul is therefore guilty of an assault. What if Andrea was asleep and for some reason did not hear the gunshot and wake up? No assault has been committed because she was not apprehensive of an imminent battery and there was no interference with her peace of mind, the interest protected by the law against assault.

In an action for assault or battery, two major defenses are available to the defendant: **consent** and **privilege.** The plaintiff's consent may be expressed by words or implied from conduct. Consent is implied, for example, in athletic contests such as boxing, football, and baseball, where the participants are assumed to consent to the physical contact normally associated with the sport.

Whether consent is express or implied, the tort of battery may occur if a party exceeds the consent given. Abel consents to have Dr. Barr perform an operation on his nose. While Abel is unconscious and under an anesthetic, Dr. Barr decides that Abel would look better if his eyelids were also altered, and she performs this procedure too. Dr. Barr may be held liable for the tort of battery (even if Abel looks better).

An assault or battery may be excused if such conduct was "privileged." The most common privilege asserted is self-defense, which allows one to use reasonable force to prevent personal harm. The privilege applies where the defendant is in actual danger of harm and also where there is no danger but the defendant reasonably believes there is. The privilege is limited to the use of force which reasonably appears to be necessary to protect against the threatened injury.

The privilege of using reasonable force extends to defense of a third person who is in immediate danger of attack. Deadly force, force designed to cause death or serious bodily harm, may be used only when the defendant has reason to believe he or she is threatened with death or serious physical harm.

The privilege of using reasonable force may also extend to the protection of property where there is danger of immediate damage or wrongful appropriation. Ordinarily, there is no privilege to use deadly force in protection of property. A landowner is privileged to install a spiked wall or fence to prevent trespassers, but may be liable in tort if a thief is injured or killed as a result of the landowner's setting a spring gun or keeping a vicious watchdog at large.

False Imprisonment

False imprisonment is the intentional confinement of another without consent or legal justification. Confinement means that a person is restricted to a limited area and lacks knowledge of a reasonable means of escape. A wrongdoer can confine another by (1) a physical restraint on a person's movement, (2) a threat of force to that person or to a member of his or her immediate family, (3) a threat of force or force directed against a person's property, or (4) a refusal to release a person from confinement when there is a duty to do so.

Allegations of false imprisonment frequently occur when a retail merchant detains a customer suspected of shoplifting. If an action is filed against a merchant for false imprisonment, the merchant may be able to assert the **shopkeeper's privilege.** In virtually every state, a merchant has a statutory right to detain customers suspected of theft. In order to qualify for the privilege, however, the merchant must prove that he or she had **probable cause**—reasonable grounds to believe the plaintiff committed a crime (shoplifting, petty theft). Even with probable cause, the merchant may be liable if the customer is detained for an unreasonable length of time or in an unreasonable manner.

The defendant in a false imprisonment action may also avoid liability by proving the plaintiff consented to restriction of his or her movement. For example, if a store customer, after being accused of committing a crime, voluntarily accompanies the merchant to a store office to clear up the matter, the merchant has not committed false imprisonment.

The following case illustrates a typical lawsuit between a department store and a customer suspected of shoplifting.

CASE 6.1 **Adams v. Zayre Corp.** • 499 N.E.2d 678 (Ill. App. 1986)

FACTS

Mary Adams entered the Zayre store with her daughter and son. Terry Jo Buckner, the store's security manager, testified that she observed Mary pick up a pink radio, walk across two aisles, and put it into her purse. She picked up some underwear and then went to the domestics department, where she selected two blankets.

Mary then went with her daughter to the checkout lanes and paid cash for the underwear and blankets. Terry, still watching Mary, checked the domestics department to see if Mary left the radio there; then Terry and three security personnel confronted Mary after she left the store.

Terry testified that nobody touched Mary and that she willingly returned to the store. Mary testified that she was held by the arm until she returned through the entrance of the store, where she was released and escorted into the security room.

In the security room the Zayre employees searched Mary's purse and her daughter's purse and found nothing. After about 15 minutes a man came in with Mary's blankets and sales receipt. He gave her the receipt and stated that the pink radio was not in the blankets. Mary asked to leave but the employees ignored her request. They were writing up a report and told her she would have to wait until they were done processing. After another 15 minutes a man came in and told her she could leave. She asked to leave through a back door because people in the store had looked at her and laughed when she was brought in.

Mary sued Zayre for false imprisonment and after a trial received a judgment for $2,500 compensatory damages and $30,000 punitive damages. Zayre appealed.

OPINION

STROUSE, J. . . . False imprisonment consists of the unlawful restraint, against a person's will, of that individual's personal liberty or freedom of locomotion. . . . Defendant [Zayre] is, however, afforded protection by sections 16A-5 and 16A-6 of the Criminal Code. [The statute empowers a merchant who has reasonable grounds to believe that a person has committed retail theft to detain such person in a reasonable manner for a reasonable length of time.]

A review of the record reveals . . . a case of false imprisonment. [Adams] testified that the security guard grabbed her by the arm after she exited the store. A minor struggle ensued, after which she was forcibly led back into the store and ushered to a security area. Four witnesses testified that she was under their forcible control.

> **CASE 6.1**
> **Continued**
>
> . . . The record reflects that the jury could have found defendant's actions to be unreasonable—both in manner of execution and time of detention. "The use of unnecessary force on suspected shoplifters by store personnel, as well as rudeness and harassment of the suspects, have been factors upon which the courts have determined either that the manner of detention was not reasonable as intended by the statute or that a finding to that effect was supportable." . . . There was also corroborated testimony that defendant detained plaintiff for one-half hour—15 minutes of which was after they had concluded their search and investigation and determined that there were no grounds to continue holding the plaintiff. Further, based on the disputed testimony, the jury could have found that no reasonable grounds existed for holding the plaintiff. . . .
>
> We last address defendant's contention that punitive damages are inappropriate. Punitive damages are permitted where an arrest is effected recklessly, oppressively, insultingly or willfully, with a design to oppress and injure. . . . The manner of plaintiff's apprehension has already been described. This apprehension was conducted in violation of the store's own guidelines as to the manner in which a suspect is observed and detained. These guidelines provide that a store security officer making an arrest must have continual and unbroken surveillance of a subject after the alleged taking, up to the actual apprehension of the subject.
>
> . . . Here, the jury found a factual basis for the punitive award and we cannot say that the jury's award of punitive damages was against the manifest weight of the evidence.
>
> **JUDGMENT** Affirmed.

Defamation

Defamation is the publication of a false statement that attacks a person's reputation. Defamation includes two torts—libel and slander. **Libel** is defamation committed in writing or in some other permanent form such as a television or radio broadcast. It may take the form of newspaper articles, verses, pictures, signs, motion pictures, cartoons, and caricatures. Libel may also involve conduct conveying a defamatory message, such as hanging a person in effigy or a bank dishonoring a customer's valid check. **Slander** is defamation committed by means of oral communication. The defamatory matter is expressed in spoken words and may be communicated person to person.

Defamatory Statement. The essence of defamation is harm to a person's good name or reputation in the community. Consequently, in order to constitute slander or libel, the statement must be defamatory—i.e., it must be of a nature to reflect upon the defamed person's character or to disgrace him or her. For example, it is defamatory to say falsely that a person is a drunk, a liar, or incompetent at his or her job. The courts have awarded damages to one accused of being a member of the Communist party, to one accused of refusing to pay his just debts, and to a kosher meat dealer accused of selling bacon. Defamation does require a statement of fact. Thus, no tort is committed if one voices a derogatory "opinion" about another or engages in name calling, such as making an insulting reference to another's ancestry or profession, where it is clear that the defendant is not objectively asserting a fact.

Publication. Because a person's reputation is based on the esteem and respect to which that person is held by others in the community, to hold a defendant liable in an action for defamation, the plaintiff must prove that the false statement was "published"—that is, communicated to someone other than the plaintiff. The publication need not be to a large group; communication of a defamatory statement to a single person is generally enough. For example, delivery of a message to a telegraph company for transmission is a publication to the employee receiving it.

A statement communicated only to the plaintiff, however, is not defamation because it cannot have an effect on the plaintiff's reputation in the community. And as a general rule, the plaintiff cannot repeat the statement to others and then sue the originator of the statement for defamation. However, a minority of states recognize an exception to this rule and allow a defamation suit under the doctrine of compelled self-publication. This doctrine is discussed in Case 6.2.

CASE 6.2 **Lewis v. The Equitable Life Assurance Society**
• 389 N.W.2d 876 (Minn.1986)

FACTS The Equitable Life Assurance Society of the United States employed Carole Lewis, Mary Smith, Michelle Rafferty, and Suzanne Loizeaux as dental claim approvers in its St. Paul office. In 1980, they were sent to Pittsburgh to assist the company's office there. Prior to their trip, the women, who had never traveled on company business before, were not given any written instructions on travel expenses nor were they told that expense reports would have to be filed. Each received a $1,400 travel advance, which, having no instruction to the contrary, they spent in full.

When they returned to St. Paul, each received a personal letter of commendation for their job performance while in Pittsburgh. They were also informed for the first time that they would have to submit expense reports. They prepared reports detailing their expenditures while in Pittsburgh, but were told on several occasions to change the reports. The company wanted them to lower their expense figures to recoup $200 from each employee. When they refused to alter the reports, they were fired for "gross insubordination."

The company neither published nor stated to any prospective employer that the plaintiffs had been terminated for gross insubordination. But when the women interviewed for new jobs, prospective employers asked them to disclose their reason for leaving the company, and each indicated that she had been terminated for "gross insubordination" and attempted to explain the situation. Only one plaintiff found employment while being completely forthright with a prospective employer. All of them suffered emotional and financial hardship as a result of being discharged by the company, including a loss of severance pay.

The women sued Equitable for defamation. A jury awarded each of the plaintiffs $75,000 in compensatory and $150,000 in punitive damages. The Minnesota Court of Appeals affirmed and the defendant appealed to the Minnesota Supreme Court.

OPINION AMDAHL, C.J. . . . In order for a statement to be considered defamatory, it

**CASE 6.2
Continued**

must be communicated to someone other than the plaintiff, it must be false, and it must tend to harm the plaintiff's reputation and to lower him or her in the estimation of the community. . . . Generally, there is no publication where a defendant communicates a statement directly to a plaintiff, who then communicates it to a third person. . . . The question raised is whether a defendant can ever be held liable for defamation when the statement in question was published to a third person only by the plaintiff. . . .

. . . Courts that have considered the question . . . have recognized a narrow exception to the general rule that communication of a defamatory statement to a third person by the person defamed is not actionable. . . . These courts have recognized that if a defamed person was in some way compelled to communicate the defamatory statement to a third person, and if it was foreseeable to the defendant that the defamed person would be so compelled, then the defendant could be held liable for the defamation. . . .

The trend of modern authority persuades us that Minnesota law should recognize the doctrine of compelled self-publication. . . . The concept of compelled self-publication does no more than hold the originator of the defamatory statement liable for damages caused by the statement where the originator knows, or should know, of circumstances whereby the defamed person has no reasonable means of avoiding publication of the statement or avoiding the resulting damages. . . . In such circumstances, the damages are fairly viewed as the direct result of the originator's actions. . . .

In the present action, the record indicates that plaintiffs were compelled to repeat the allegedly defamatory statement to prospective employers and that the company knew plaintiffs would be so compelled. . . .

We . . . reverse the award of punitive damages. . . . We are concerned that the availability of punitive damages may tend to encourage publication of defamatory statements [by] the plaintiff. . . . [and] deter employer communication of the reason for discharge. . . . When an employer's reputation and its liability for potentially large money damage are at stake . . . the employer may refuse to state a reason when discharging an employee. . . . [S]uch a result would not serve the interests of the public.

[W]e hold that punitive damages are not available in defamation actions based upon compelled self-publication. . . .

Damage to Reputation. Although the plaintiff must suffer injury to reputation, the law of defamation allows the jury to presume damages in cases of libel and in cases of **slander per se.** For example, slander per se occurs when the defamatory statement affects the plaintiff in his or her business, trade, or profession. Calling a salesperson dishonest or a liar would be slanderous per se. Other types of slander per se involve assertions that the plaintiff has a loathsome disease, has engaged in sexual misconduct, or has committed a crime of "moral turpitude." In these cases, the jury is allowed to assess damages without proof of any actual reputational injury to the plaintiff.

Truth. In most states truth is a complete defense to a defamation action. For example, suppose Charles maliciously and in an attempt to embarrass Andrea makes the statement "Andrea is a thief." If Andrea is in fact a convicted embezzler, she could not recover damages from

Charles for defamation. In certain circumstances, she may have a cause of action against Charles for the tort of invasion of privacy. That tort is discussed in the next section.

Privilege. A second defense to defamation is privilege—absolute, qualified, or constitutional. Privileges are based upon the idea that the defendant should be allowed to make statements in order to further some interest of social importance without the fear of a defamation suit. In some instances the interest is deemed to be of such great importance that the defendant is given complete or absolute immunity regardless of motive or the reasonableness of conduct.

Absolute privilege protects the following:

- Statements made in a civil or criminal action or quasi-judicial proceeding by the parties, witnesses, lawyers, judges, and jurors, as long as the statements are relevant or pertinent to an issue in the proceeding
- Statements made by federal and state legislators performing their duties and by witnesses in legislative and quasi-legislative hearings
- Statements made by superior officers of the executive departments and branches of the federal and state governments in the exercise of their duties (in some states the privilege extends to lower-level state officers and local government officials)

A **qualified** or **conditional privilege** is available to a defendant when an individual in good faith publishes information in furtherance of his or her own legitimate interests or the interests of others. Conditional privileges are recognized on public policy grounds and are designed to encourage the free flow of information in society. For example, communications between a past employer and a prospective employer of the plaintiff are subject to a conditional privilege. Because the communication is made to protect the legitimate interests of the prospective employer, it is subject to a conditional privilege. Other recognized interests include one's own financial interest or credit standing. Communication between a credit bureau and a bank regarding a borrower's credit history are conditionally privileged. The defense of qualified privilege also protects communications among persons with a common interest, such as partners, corporate officers, and members of professional associations.

A conditional privilege is not absolute, however. To avoid liability, the defendant must prove that the defamatory statement was published not only for a proper purpose but also in good faith and in a reasonable manner. If a defendant abuses his or her qualified privilege, the plaintiff may hold the defendant liable in an action for defamation. For example, the qualified privilege is lost if the defendant communicates defamatory matter to a person who has no legitimate interest in it. Suppose that an employer discharges an employee and later is requested by a prospective employer to give a letter of reference. If, in the letter the employer states falsely that the employee was incompetent, the defendant may assert the defense of qualified privilege. But, if the former employer publishes the letter in a newspaper, any qualified privilege is lost.

The qualified privilege also may be lost if the defendant acts with **common law malice,** either express or implied. **Express malice** means the defendant acted from spite or ill will, not from a legitimate desire to further a recognized interest. **Implied malice** means the defendant acted recklessly—i.e., he or she had no reasonable grounds for believing the statement.

A **qualified constitutional privilege** exists to publish defamatory statements about a public figure or public official. In *New York Times v. Sullivan*,[2] the Supreme Court held that the First Amendment protects false, defamatory statements about public officials. The Court recognized that one inevitable by-product of a free, democratic society is unfair and potentially defamatory criticism of public officials and their performance in office.

To protect uninhibited debate on matters of public importance, a defendant who publishes a false defamatory statement about a public official or a public figure may not be held liable unless the defendant acted with "actual malice." **Actual malice** in this context means that the

---

[2] 376 U.S. 254 (1964).

defendant knew the statement was false or showed a reckless disregard for the truth by making the statement.

The constitutional privilege applies if the person defamed is a public official or a public figure.[3] **Public officials** include those high-ranking government officers, whether executive, legislative, or judicial, who control the conduct of government. No complete definition has yet been given, but it is clear that not all public employees are public officials. Police officers and public teachers, however, are held to be public officials.

Public figures include two groups of people: (1) persons who have achieved fame and notoriety, such as sports figures and well-known entertainers, and (2) persons who voluntarily thrust or inject themselves into the forefront of public controversy in order to influence the outcome of issues, such as consumer advocates and environmentalists. Prominent individuals and celebrities have greater access to the mass media than do private persons and thus can counteract the effects of defamation. Also, those public figures who are involved in public controversies must expect to be the object of public discussion.

Unlike public officials and public figures, private persons need not prove actual malice in a defamation suit. In general, private persons must prove only that the defendant was negligent in publishing the defamatory statement. However, when the defamatory statement involves a matter of public interest, a private person must establish actual malice in order to recover presumed and punitive damages.

Invasion of Privacy

The tort of invasion of privacy protects individuals from four separate wrongs:

1. **Appropriation**—the use of a person's name or likeness without consent for business purposes. A typical example is using a sports figure's photograph without consent to promote the sale of a product.

2. **Intrusion**—an unreasonable intrusion into a person's seclusion or private affairs. Examples

---

BOX 6.2

Defamation Law and Business Planning

To recover damages for termination of employment, discharged workers are relying increasingly on the law of defamation. It is estimated that defamation actions against employers constitute one third of all the defamation lawsuits that ultimately go to trial. An employer can face substantial damage awards in such actions. For example, a jury in Texas recently awarded a 41-year employee of Procter & Gamble Co. 15.6 million dollars in damages after the company fired him for allegedly stealing a company telephone and posted notice of the theft on 11 company bulletin boards.

What can a business do to avoid or minimize the risk of a defamation suit by a discharged employee? Since most of this litigation stems from employee references, some companies are adopting a no-comment policy, providing prospective employers with no information on the reason for an employee's termination. A survey by the *Chicago Tribune* found that 75% of companies provide only the name, date, and position in response to requests for references. Arbitration clauses in employment contracts may be an alternative approach. Having employment discharge disputes resolved by arbitration may reduce litigation costs, minimize negative publicity, and diminish the potential for a staggering damage award. Employers should also exercise caution in discharging employees, conduct thorough and objective investigations of any employee wrongdoing, and exercise discretion in making statements about the reasons for an employee's dismissal.

What other steps should employers take to avoid defamation lawsuits? In the above case involving Procter & Gamble, what should the company have done to reduce the risk of a defamation suit by the discharged employee?

---

[3] The Supreme Court extended the constitutional privilege to defamatory statements about public figures in *Curtis Pub. Co. v. Butts*, 388 U.S. 130 (1967).

include illegal entry of one's home, illegal wiretapping, and unauthorized investigation of one's bank account.

3. **Public disclosure of private facts**—the publishing of private information about a person which is offensive and objectionable. An example is publishing the history and the present identity of a reformed criminal.

4. **False light**—the publishing of a highly objectionable statement that is false or conveys a false impression about a person. An example is improperly using a photograph of an honest taxi driver in connection with a magazine article on cheating taxi drivers. When the information published is false and defamatory, the injured person may have an additional cause of action for defamation.

Several defenses are available to a defendant in an action for invasion of privacy. Consent, express or implied, is one. Privilege—absolute, conditional, or constitutional—is another. For example, a news reporter is allowed to publish information of public interest about a public figure. In a suit for false light or public disclosure of private facts, a public person must prove actual malice. A person who is not a public figure but who becomes involved in a matter of public interest suffers a similar loss of privacy. For example, a victim of or a witness to a crime has no cause of action if he or she is identified in the news media and his or her personal or family background is exposed to public view. The courts permit this invasion of a person's privacy because there is a legitimate public interest in newsworthy events.

In Case 6.3, the court discusses the first type of invasion of privacy: commercial appropriation of a person's identity. This is also called the "right of publicity."

CASE 6.3

Vanna White v. Samsung Electronics America, Inc.
• F.2d (9th Cir. 1992)[1992 U.S. App. Lexis 19253]

FACTS

Vanna White is the hostess of *Wheel of Fortune,* one of the most popular game shows in television history. An estimated 40 million people watch the program daily. Capitalizing on the fame which her participation in the show has bestowed on her, White markets her identity to various advertisers.

David Deutsch Associates, Inc., prepared a series of advertisements for Samsung Electronics America, Inc., Each of the advertisements depicted a current item from popular culture and a Samsung electronic product in the twenty-first century. The ads suggested that the Samsung product would still be in use at that time. One of the ads for Samsung videocassette recorders depicted a robot dressed in a wig, gown, and jewelry which Deutsch consciously selected to resemble Vanna White's hair and dress. The robot was posed next to a game board (instantly recognizable as the *Wheel of Fortune* game show set), in a stance for which White is famous. The caption of the ad read: "Longest running game show. 2012 A.D."

Unlike other celebrities used in the campaign, Vanna White neither consented to the ads nor was paid. She sued Samsung and Deutsch in federal district court under the right of publicity. The district court granted summary judgment against White, finding that neither her name nor her likeness was appropriated by the defendants. She appealed.

OPINION

GOODWIN, J. . . . [T]he right of publicity is not limited to the appropriation of name or likeness. . . .

**CASE 6.3
Continued**

In [*Midler v. Ford Motor Co.*], this court held that, even though the defendants had not used [Bette] Midler's name or likeness, Midler had stated a claim for violation of her . . . right of publicity because "the defendants . . . for their own profit in selling their product did appropriate part of her identity" by using a Midler sound-alike.

In *Carson v. Here's Johnny Portable Toilets, Inc.*, the defendant had marketed portable toilets under the brand name "Here's Johnny"—Johnny Carson's signature "Tonight Show" introduction—without Carson's permission. . . . [T]he sixth circuit found . . . that the right was implicated because the defendant had appropriated Carson's identity by using . . . the phrase "Here's Johnny."

These cases teach not only that the common law right of publicity reaches means of appropriation other than name or likeness, but that the specific means of appropriation are relevant only for determining whether the defendant has in fact appropriated the plaintiff's identity. . . .

Viewed separately, the individual aspects of the advertisement in the present case say very little. Viewed together, they leave little doubt about the celebrity the ad is meant to depict. . . . Indeed, defendants themselves referred to their ad as the "Vanna White" ad. We are not surprised.

Television and other media create marketable celebrity identity value. Considerable energy and ingenuity are expended by those who have achieved celebrity value to exploit it for profit. The law protects the celebrity's sole right to exploit this value whether the celebrity has achieved her fame out of rare ability, dumb luck, or a combination thereof. We decline Samsung and Deutsch's invitation to permit the evisceration of the common law right of publicity through means as facile as those in this case. . . .

JUDGMENT   Affirmed in part, reversed in part, and remanded.

Infliction of Mental Distress

Infliction of mental distress (also called **outrage**) is the intentional or reckless infliction of severe mental suffering by means of extreme or outrageous conduct. Although the courts have always awarded damages for the emotional distress caused by other torts (e.g., assault and battery), the common law was reluctant to recognize an independent tort for the intentional infliction of mental distress. The common law courts were skeptical of claims for emotional injury and were concerned that emotional damage claims could be too easily fabricated. Today, although the courts recognize outrage as a separate tort, the elements of the tort reflect its common law history. The courts have limited the scope of the tort by requiring two important elements: outrageous conduct by the tortfeasor and severe emotional injury to the victim.

Generally, extreme and outrageous misconduct means conduct exceeding all bounds of human decency. For example, a person was held liable for falsely telling a woman that her husband was seriously injured and in a hospital, causing the woman to suffer emotional trauma and physical injury. In contrast, the common indignities we suffer on a daily basis—abusive language and obscene gestures—are not generally considered extreme enough to constitute outrage.

Outrage can occur in a commercial setting. Collection agencies and creditors have been held liable to debtors for outrageous high-pressure tactics.[4] For example, a veterinarian was held liable for outrage when he threatened to kill his customer's dog unless she paid the bill for his services. Communications between employer and employee, particularly in the context of a discharge, can give rise to an outrage claim. In one case, a manager of a restaurant who suspected embezzlement by one of his waitresses announced to the employees that he would start firing them alphabetically until the wrongdoer came forward. The court held that such conduct, if established at trial, was sufficiently outrageous to allow the plaintiff, who was innocent of any wrongdoing, to recover for intentional infliction of mental distress.

What is outrageous may also depend upon the context of the communication and the particular plaintiff or defendant. Children, for example, may be more susceptible to emotional harm, and conduct may be outrageous when directed to a child but not outrageous if directed to an adult. Similarly, certain businesses may be liable for obscene or abusive language directed at their customers. Innkeepers (operators of motels or hotels), common carriers (railroads, bus lines, airlines, etc.), and public utilities (telephone companies, power companies, etc.) have been held liable to patrons for language of employees that is profane, indecent, or grossly insulting to people of ordinary sensibilities.

In most states the plaintiff need not suffer physical illness in order to recover damages for the tort of infliction of mental distress but the defendant cannot recover for mere hurt feelings. Generally, the defendant must suffer severe emotional trauma or distress.

In Case 6.4, the Supreme Court holds that there is a First Amendment privilege to make outrageous comments about a public figure.

---

[4]Debt collectors may also be liable for abusive practices under the Fair Debt Collection Practices Act, discussed in Chapter 49.

CASE 6.4 Hustler Magazine v. Jerry Falwell • 485 U.S. 46 (U.S. 1988)

FACTS Jerry Falwell is a nationally known minister and commentator on politics and public affairs. He is host of a nationally syndicated television show and was the founder and president of a political organization formally known as the Moral Majority. He is also the founder of Liberty University in Lynchburg, Virginia, and is the author of several books and publications.

The November 1983 issue of *Hustler* magazine featured a "parody" of an advertisement for Campari Liqueur entitled "Jerry Falwell talks about his first time." This parody was modeled after actual Campari ads that included interviews with various celebrities about their "first times." At the end of each interview, it was clear that this meant the first time the celebrity tasted Campari Liqueur. The *Hustler* magazine piece copied the form and layout of these Campari ads, and chose Jerry Falwell as their featured celebrity person. In the alleged "interview" with him, he stated that his "first time" was during a drunken incestuous rendezvous with his mother in an outhouse. Small print at the bottom of the page contained a disclaimer that read, "Ad parody—not to be taken seriously."

Jerry Falwell sued Hustler Magazine, Inc., Larry C. Flynt, and Flynt Distributing Co. for libel and intentional infliction of emotional distress. The jury rejected his libel claim, specifically finding that the ad parody could not "reasonably be understood as describing actual facts about [Falwell] or actual events in which [he] participated." The jury ruled for Falwell on the intentional infliction of

CASE 6.4
Continued

emotional distress claim, however, and awarded him $100,000 in compensatory damages, as well as $50,000 in punitive damages from each of the defendants. The U.S. Court of Appeals for the Fourth Circuit affirmed the judgment and the defendants appealed to the Supreme Court.

OPINION

REHNQUIST, C.J. . . . This case presents us with a novel question involving First Amendment limitations upon a State's authority to protect its citizens from the intentional infliction of emotional distress. We must decide whether a public figure may recover damages for emotional harm caused by the publication of an ad parody offensive to him, and doubtless gross and repugnant in the eyes of most. . . .

The sort of robust political debate encouraged by the First Amendment is bound to produce speech that is critical of those who hold public office or those public figures who are "intimately involved in the resolution of important public questions or, by reason of their fame, shape events in areas of concern to society at large." . . .

Of course, this does not mean that any speech about a public figure is immune from sanction in the form of damages. Since *New York Times Co. v. Sullivan* . . . we have consistently ruled that a public figure may hold a speaker liable for the damage to reputation caused by publication of a defamatory falsehood, but only if the statement was made "with knowledge that it was false or with reckless disregard of whether it was false or not." . . .

[Falwell] argues, however, that a different standard should apply in this case because here the State seeks to prevent not reputational damage, but the severe emotional distress suffered by the person who is the subject of an offensive publication. . . . In [his] view, so long as the utterance was intended to inflict emotional distress, was outrageous, and did in fact inflict serious emotional distress, it is of no constitutional import whether the statement was a fact or an opinion, or whether it was true or false. . . .

While such a bad motive may be deemed controlling for purposes of tort liability in other areas of the law, we think the First Amendment prohibits such a result in the area of public debate about public figures. . . .

Were we to hold otherwise, there can be little doubt that political cartoonists and satirists would be subjected to damages awards without any showing that their work falsely defamed its subject. . . .

Despite their sometimes caustic nature, from the early cartoon portraying George Washington as an ass down to the present day, graphic depictions and satirical cartoons have played a prominent role in public and political debate. . . .

[Falwell] contends, however, that the caricature in question here was so "outrageous" as to distinguish it from more traditional political cartoons. . . . "Outrageousness" in the area of political and social discourse has an inherent subjectiveness about it which would allow a jury to impose liability on the basis of the jurors' tastes or views, or perhaps on the basis of their dislike of a particular expression. . . .

We conclude that public figures and public officials may not recover for the tort of intentional infliction of emotional distress by reason of publications such

> **CASE 6.4 Continued**
>
> as the one here at issue without showing in addition that the publication contains a false statement of fact which was made with "actual malice." . . .
>
> **JUDGMENT**
>
> The judgment of the Court of Appeals is accordingly reversed.

Misuse of Legal Process

To protect people from unjustifiable litigation, the courts recognize three torts involving misuse of legal process: malicious prosecution, wrongful use of civil proceedings, and abuse of process. The wrongful filing of civil suits or criminal charges can cause substantial damages to the defendant in terms of litigation expenses, negative publicity, and even false imprisonment. Society has a strong interest in compensating victims for the misuse of the legal system and in preventing the use of the courts for improper purposes. On the other hand, society has an equally strong interest in encouraging the proper use of the civil and criminal justice system. Therefore, a person who initiates civil or criminal proceedings against another is given a large degree of freedom to make mistakes without being liable for a tort, thus reflecting a social policy that encourages use of the courts for resolution of legitimate disputes and for bringing criminals to justice.

Malicious Prosecution. Malicious prosecution is the initiation of a meritless criminal prosecution against another for an improper purpose. The plaintiff—the person improperly prosecuted—must prove three elements: (1) the criminal prosecution terminated in his or her favor; (2) there was no probable cause to prosecute the plaintiff; and (3) the instigator acted maliciously in bringing the criminal charges. "Malice" in this context means that the instigator's primary purpose in bringing the criminal proceedings was something other than bringing an offender to justice.

Wrongful Use of Civil Proceedings. The majority of states today recognize as a tort the wrongful initiation of a civil suit. To establish the **wrongful use of civil proceedings,** the courts generally require the same three elements to be present as in malicious prosecution—termination of the civil suit in favor of the person sued, lack of probable cause to sue, and malice. The plaintiff must also prove that he or she suffered actual harm, such as the expenses incurred in defending the civil action or a loss of business. A "nuisance" suit initiated in an attempt to secure a settlement is one example of the wrongful use of civil proceedings.

Abuse of Process. Abuse of process is the use of legal process for an ulterior or illegitimate purpose—e.g., some purpose other than the recovery of damages in a civil suit. Unlike malicious prosecution or wrongful use of civil proceedings, there is no requirement that the prior action terminate in favor of the defendant or that there be an absence of probable cause. It is the improper motivation of the person instigating the suit that forms the basis of the tort. For example, a business that commences a civil suit in an attempt to harm the reputation of a competitor and drive away its customers, not to recover damages, commits an abuse of process.

Table 6.1 summarizes the intentional torts involving harm to the person.

INTENTIONAL HARM TO PROPERTY

Property as used in this discussion refers to things people own, such as land, furniture, and accounts receivable. The phrase "harm to property" means physical damage (i.e., injury) to the property or wrongful interference with the use or possession of property.

Table 6.1 Concept Summary: Intentional Harm to the Person

Tort	Nature of Harm
Battery	Harmful or offensive contact
Assault	Fear of imminent battery
False imprisonment	Restriction on freedom of movement
Defamation (libel, slander)	Damage to reputation
Invasion of privacy	
Appropriation	Commercial appropriation of identity
Intrusion	Invasion into seclusion or private affairs
Public disclosure of private facts	Objectionable publicity about private life
False light	Offensive publicity that conveys false impression about person
Infliction of mental distress (outrage)	Emotional injury
Misuse of legal procedure (malicious prosecution, wrongful use of civil proceedings, abuse of process)	Cost of unjustified litigation, annoyance, inconvenience, loss of liberty, harm to reputation

Trespass to Real Property

The tort of **trespass to real property** occurs when a person intentionally, and without consent or legal justification, enters upon another's real property or causes an object or a third person to enter the property. **Real property** includes the land and all things imbedded in it or firmly attached to it, such as minerals, trees, fences, and buildings. Thus, one may be held liable in tort for walking across another's lawn, cutting down a neighbor's tree, or painting someone's barn without permission. A mistaken belief that the land belongs to the defendant, or that he or she has consent, is not a defense.

Real property customarily includes the airspace above the surface of the land and materials below the surface. Thus, a person may be liable for trespass by causing an object to enter the airspace of another without permission. For example, if Arnold has a large tree planted on his land the branches of which extend over the boundary line of his property into the airspace above the land of his neighbor, Bella, Arnold may be liable to Bella in damages for trespass.

Nuisance

A **private nuisance** is an unreasonable interference with the use and enjoyment of another's real property. (A **public nuisance,** by contrast, is an unreasonable interference with the rights of a substantial portion of the community.) For example, excessive noise, dust, smoke, noxious gases or smells, or vibrations that substantially annoy or disturb another property owner's rights may be a private nuisance. To determine whether a particular interference is a nuisance, the courts consider such factors as the seriousness of the harm to the plaintiff, the character of the land, and the social importance of the defendant's conduct. Thus, a continuous emission of toxic fumes from a dump in a residential neighborhood may be a nuisance while periodic smoke from a neighbor's fireplace may not be. By imposing liability for a nuisance only when the interference is unreasonable, nuisance law attempts to strike a balance between the rights of one landowner to use his or her property as he or she sees fit and the rights of another property owner to the beneficial enjoyment of his or her property.

Trespass to Personal Property

The tort of **trespass to personal property** (sometimes called **trespass to chattels**) is the intentional damage to or interference with another's personal property without consent or legal justification. **Personal property** as used here means movable or portable things, such as appliances or furniture. The tort of trespass to personal property usually involves temporary use of an item or slight harm to the item. Thus, a person who takes another's car for a joyride commits a trespass. The plaintiff's damages ordinarily would be the value of loss of use of the property and any drop in value of the item caused by the defendant.

Conversion

Conversion is the wrongful exercise of control over another's personal property. The essential difference between conversion and trespass to personal property is the degree of harm caused by the defendant. Conversion requires more than mere damage to property; the defendant (converter) must appropriate or use another's property in a manner that is inconsistent with the person's ownership. The following illustrates acts that give rise to a cause of action for conversion:

- Wrongfully taking possession of another's property for an indefinite period, as by stealing
- Improperly selling or transferring possession of one person's property to another person, as by delivering goods to the wrong person
- Wrongfully retaining another's property, as by a repair shop refusing to return goods until an exorbitant repair bill is paid
- Destroying another's property or substantially altering it so as to make it unusable, as by killing or maiming someone's animal

A converter will be liable in damages even though he or she acts in good faith or under a mistake of law or fact. A car dealer that wrongfully repossesses an automobile commits a conversion even if the dealer believed it had a right to take the car. In an action for conversion the plaintiff need not prove the defendant had an evil state of mind or an improper purpose in interfering with possession of the plaintiff's property. Thus, an innocent purchaser of stolen property may be liable for the tort of conversion. However, if one innocently receives lost or stolen property merely for purposes of storage or transportation, the courts would not hold the warehouser or the carrier liable. In such a case the defendant is not asserting ownership of the goods.

In an action for conversion, the owner recovers the full value of the property at the time of conversion and, upon payment of the judgment, the converter becomes the owner of the property. Thus, an action for the tort of conversion is appropriate only when the defendant has so seriously damaged or interfered with the plaintiff's possession as to justify a forced sale of the article. Rather than sue for the value of the property, an owner may want the property returned. Possession may be recovered by filing a lawsuit and, without waiting for trial of the case, securing a court order called a "writ of replevin." In some states the procedure is called "claim and delivery." The plaintiff must post a bond to protect any legitimate interests of the defendant.

Table 6.2 summarizes the intentional property torts.

FRAUD

Fraud is discussed separately because of its importance to business law. Fraud, the intentional deception of another, is a tort for which the victim can recover damages and a defense to the enforcement of a contract. When fraud occurs in a contractual setting, the victim has the option to sue for damages or cancel the contract. The effects of fraud and misrepresentation on commercial transactions are discussed in connection with the law of contracts in Chapter 13. Here fraud is examined as a tort giving rise to damages for personal or economic harm.

To recover in an action for the tort of fraud, sometimes called **deceit,** the plaintiff must prove the following elements:

- A false representation of material fact
- Knowledge that the representation was false
- Intent to induce another to act
- Justifiable reliance on the representation
- Injury resulting from such reliance

Table 6.2 Concept Summary: Intentional Harm to Property

Tort	Nature of Harm
Trespass to real property	Invasion of right to exclusive possession of real property
Nuisance	Interference with use and enjoyment of real property
Trespass to personal property	Damage to or interference with personal property
Conversion	Appropriation of personal property

The first three elements focus on the defrauder, the last two on the victim.

False Representation or Concealment of Material Fact

The essence of fraud is deceit by one person which generally takes the form of a misrepresentation of fact. A person can misrepresent facts by oral or written statements or by conduct. Turning back the odometer of a car is a misrepresentation by conduct.

For an act to constitute fraud, there must be a misrepresentation of a **material** fact. A fact is something that exists now or in the past; material facts are those that would affect the person's decision in a particular transaction. For example, a statement by the seller of a retail store concerning the profits of the business is a representation of past or present facts which would be material to a buyer's decision to purchase the business.

Fraud does not generally include a false statement of opinion, of value, or of law. Sellers of goods often make a statement such as "This is the best television on the market" or "My house is worth $100,000." The law treats such "sales talk" or "puffing" as the seller's opinion only, not a statement of fact. Future expectations are also not considered statements of fact. Thus, a prediction—such as "This business will be profitable"—is not a statement of fact.

However, a person may be held liable for misstatements of opinion, value, or law where it is reasonable for the other party to rely on the statements. One such situation is where one of the parties is an expert or claims to have special knowledge or competence in a particular field. Thus, the opinion of a real estate broker as to the value of land or the opinion of an attorney upon a point of law will be considered a statement of fact. A person also commits fraud by making a statement of future expectations that is inconsistent with present or past facts. A seller of an automobile who represents that it will get 20 miles per gallon commits fraud if he or she knows that the car never got over 10 miles per gallon.

Concealment and the Duty of Disclosure.

Fraud can also take the form of a concealment of material facts. Concealment occurs when a person takes active steps to hide information or facts from the other party. This is to be contrasted with the failure to volunteer information to the other party. Historically, silence, or a failure to disclose facts of which one has knowledge, was not considered fraudulent. In negotiating a contract, the law did not generally require one party to fully disclose information to the other party. Today, however, a growing number of exceptions to this general rule reflect increasing concern for the consumer's right to full and accurate information and for ethical behavior in the marketplace.

The exceptions create a *duty of disclosure* under certain circumstances. For example, one party is not permitted to tell a half-truth during the negotiation process. Similarly, the law imposes a duty to disclose facts when a person makes statements that are true or believed to be true when made, but the person later acquires information that renders the prior statements false. James offers to sell his business to Kara. He tells her that the firm is solvent, relying on the unaudited books of the company. If James later receives an audit report from his accountant indicating that the business is insolvent, he would be under a duty to disclose that fact to Kara to correct the misimpression created by his prior statement.

In recent years many states have also imposed a duty of disclosure in sales transactions where one party has knowledge of *latent* or hidden defects in the property for sale. For example, suppose that in a real estate transaction the seller's house has a major structural defect in the foundation and the seller knows about it. If the buyer is not aware of the condition because it is not visible or apparent during his or her inspection of the house, the seller would commit fraud if the house is sold without disclosing this condition to the buyer. However, a party is not required to disclose facts that are obvious or that could be discovered by reasonable inspection.

BOX 6.3 **A Question of Ethics**

Is it ethical for a party negotiating a contract to remain silent and fail to fully disclose to the other party all information he or she may have that is material to the contract? ∎

Knowledge of Falsity and Intent to Induce Action

To establish fraud, the plaintiff must prove that the defrauder knew that his or her representations were false and intended to induce another to act upon it. Knowledge of falsity is sometimes referred to as scienter. Scienter exists when a person makes a statement knowing that it is false or not believing that it is true or in reckless disregard as to whether it is true or false. Thus, a person who represents something as being true of his or her own knowledge but who is in fact completely ignorant of the subject is reckless and is treated in the law as knowingly making a false statement.

Justifiable Reliance

Simply put, justifiable reliance means that the plaintiff relied on (acted because of) the defendant's misrepresentation in making his or her decision, and that the reliance was reasonable. It is not necessary to prove that the defendant's misrepresentation was the sole reason for plaintiff's decision. It is sufficient for the plaintiff to prove that the misrepresentation was a substantial factor in influencing his or her decision. Thus, there may be justifiable reliance where a plaintiff's decision to buy or sell an article was based on information obtained from several sources, including the defendant's false representation.

Resulting Injury

The defrauded party must establish that his or her reliance on the misrepresentations of the defendant caused personal harm or economic losses. In the typical fraud case the plaintiff has been induced to purchase property or services. Because of the misrepresentations, the property or services are not worth the goods, money, or services exchanged for them, resulting in economic loss to the plaintiff. The plaintiff can recover damages, called **direct damages**,[5] for this economic loss. In appropriate cases the plaintiff may also be entitled to **special or consequential damages**—indirect losses caused by the fraud that are foreseeable, such as the cost of renting a car when a defective automobile breaks down. Punitive damages are also recoverable when the fraud is willful, malicious, or particularly oppressive.

In Case 6.5 the court discusses a fraud claim in connection with the concealment of a latent defect in a house put up for sale.

---

[5]Two methods are used to measure direct damages for the tort of fraud: the majority *benefit-of-bargain* rule and the minority *out-of-pocket* rule. Under the majority rule, the successful plaintiff recovers the difference between the actual value of the property or service received and the value the plaintiff would have had if the property had been as represented. Under the minority rule, the plaintiff recovers only the difference between the actual value and the price paid for the property.

CASE 6.5   Green v. Geer • 720 P.2d 656 (Kan. 1986)

FACTS

In 1982, Ernest and Phyllis Green purchased the home of Paul and Susan Doleshals. Don Geer was the real estate agent for the Doleshals in the sale. Prior to the sale, the Greens advised John Barnes, a salesman for Geer, they would not buy a house unless it had a dry basement. When they viewed the Doleshal house, there was a puddle of water in the basement. The Doleshals and Barnes represented to the Greens that the water problem was caused by settling of the basement window wells and advised them that the problem could be solved by terracing the yard so the water would drain away from the windows. A clause was inserted in the real estate contract that called for the terracing of the front yard by the Doleshals.

Within a few days of the Greens' moving into the house, the basement water problems reappeared in spite of the reterracing of the lawn. The water came from the seam between the floor wall and from a crack in the floor.

The Greens sued the Doleshals and Geer for fraud. Evidence presented at trial established a major problem with water leaking into the Greens' basement; moreover, the Doleshals knew the problem was not simply leaking window wells, yet they failed to reveal the gravity of the problem to their agent or to the Greens. The trial court found for the Greens and awarded them judgment in the amount of $4,835 for basement repair and loss of stored goods. The Doleshals and Geer appealed.

OPINION

HERD, J. . . . We have held that when a vendor or lessor has knowledge of a defect in property which is not within the fair and reasonable reach of the vendee or lessee and which he could not discover by the exercise of reasonable diligence, the silence and failure of the vendor or lessor to disclose the defect in the property constitute actionable fraudulent concealment. . . . In order for silence regarding a defect to constitute fraud, the seller must have knowledge of a material defect that is not within the fair and reasonable reach of the buyer and which is not discoverable by reasonable diligence. . . .

The Doleshals argue that their actions could not constitute fraudulent concealment because they did not have knowledge of a material defect. Sufficient evidence exists to support the trial court's conclusion that the Doleshals knew the actual cause of the basement condition. . . .

The Doleshals contend that even if a material defect existed, it was discoverable by reasonable diligence and the Greens failed to exercise such diligence. The Greens, when viewing the Doleshal house prior to sale, observed a 6 foot by 12 foot puddle of water on the basement floor. They were quickly informed by Barnes that the source of the water was a leaking window well and Mr. Doleshal would take care of the problem by reterracing the front yard. . . . The Greens had no reason to disbelieve [the] statements concerning the source of the water problem. Nor did they have reason to doubt the statements of Mr. Doleshal, a builder and carpenter experienced in home construction. Under these circumstances, it cannot be said that the Greens failed to exercise reasonable diligence to ascertain the existence of material defects. . . .

CASE 6.5 Continued

Geer [the real estate agent] argues there was no basis for holding him liable for the damages sustained by the Greens. . . .

[T]he evidence [does not] support a finding that Geer fraudulently misrepresented the source of the problem to the Greens. If an agent makes false representations on behalf of his principal honestly believing them to be true, the mental element of fraud is lacking and he is not guilty of fraud and is not liable for such, although the principal may have known that such representations were false.

The statements made by Barnes [Geer's salesman] regarding the source of the basement water problem proved to be false. However, in making the statements, Barnes was simply passing on information from the Doleshals. Therefore, Barnes' representations did not amount to fraud and thus there was no basis for holding Geer liable for the damages sustained by the Greens.

JUDGMENT The judgment is affirmed in part and reversed in part.

SUMMARY

Tort liability is based on conduct which is socially unreasonable. Important in determining what is unreasonable is the balance between an injured person's claim to protection and the defendant's claim to freedom of action. Various kinds of civil wrongs are recognized as torts in contemporary law. They are classified according to the nature of the wrongdoer's conduct as intentional torts, negligence, or liability without fault.

The major intentional torts involving harm to the person are battery, assault, false imprisonment, defamation (libel and slander), invasion of privacy, infliction of mental distress (outrage), malicious prosecution, wrongful use of civil proceedings, and abuse of process. Battery is the only one of these torts in which bodily contact is essential. The remaining torts generally involve interference with the other person's freedom of movement, peace of mind, or privacy, or injury to the person's reputation. A plaintiff can recover compensatory damages to cover medical bills, lost wages, and mental distress. If the defendant was willful, malicious, or particularly oppressive, the plaintiff may also recover punitive damages. In a tort action, the defendant may avoid liability by proving one or more defenses, such as consent or privilege.

Truth is an absolute defense to an action for defamation but is no defense to an action for infliction of mental distress or invasion of privacy. Absolute and conditional privileges are also defenses to a libel or slander suit. The constitutional privilege under the First Amendment provides a defense to the defendant in an action for defamation, public disclosure of private facts, false light invasion of privacy, and outrage brought by a public official or public figure.

The major intentional torts involving harm to property are trespass to real property, nuisance, trespass to personal property, and conversion. In an action for trespass, the plaintiff is compensated for the harm to property or for loss of possession. In an action for conversion, the owner recovers the full value of his or her personal property or secures the return of the property.

Fraud is an important tort that frequently arises in connection with business transactions in which money or property is exchanged. The tort of fraud involves an intentional misrepresentation or concealment of a material fact justifiably relied on by another to his or her injury.

REVIEW QUESTIONS

1. Explain the differences between a crime and a tort.

2. Define the torts of battery and assault.

3. Why is it important for a businessperson to have some knowledge of the tort of false imprisonment?

4. Do you think the courts should adopt the doctrine of compelled self-publication?

5. Explain conditional privilege and how it may be lost.

6. List and give examples of the four main forms of invasion of privacy.

7. Should the law require extreme and outrageous conduct for the tort of infliction of mental distress? Explain. If not, what should the law require?

8. Why does the law require malice for the torts of malicious prosecution and wrongful use of civil proceedings?

9. Explain the differences between the torts of trespass to personal property and conversion.

10. What policy reasons justify the traditional rule that a party to a contract is not under a duty to disclose to the other party material facts of which he has knowledge?

CASE PROBLEMS

1. Mrs. Rice, while in the Super X Drugstore, placed makeup, lipstick, and cologne in a Rose's Department Store sack. At the checkout counter, Mrs. Rice did not remove the items from the sack or offer to pay for them. As she was preparing to leave the store, Mrs. Rice was stopped and escorted to the employees' lounge. According to witnesses she admitted taking the three items, but Mrs. Rice testified that she thought she had paid for the three items and in any event had no intent to steal. The store manager called the police, and Mrs. Rice was taken to the police station, where she was arrested. She was detained at the drugstore for 25 to 30 minutes. The trip to the police station took some 5 to 8 minutes, and she was served with an arrest warrant some 5 to 15 minutes later. Mrs. Rice filed suit for false imprisonment and the jury returned a verdict in her favor, awarding her $75,000 as compensatory damages and $75,000 as punitive damages. Should this verdict be upheld?

2. Burke was the executive director of the New Brunswick Parking Authority. In June 1976 Burke's young daughter, who worked for the authority as a parking attendant, confessed to having stolen two bank bags containing her shift's receipts for two days. The city director of finances engaged Rosenthal and Attinger, accountants, to conduct a detailed audit of the authority. They had been the city's accountants for many years and made annual audits for the authority. Their special audit itemized ten specific "weaknesses and deficiencies in internal control" of the authority and made ten recommendations for correcting them. At least some of the alleged weaknesses were false. For example, an alleged failure to deposit cash receipts daily was in fact due to the bank's failure to record deposits after banking hours.

The authority's board of commissioners removed Burke from office. The resolution charged him with "negligent operation of the Parking Authority, which borders on misappropriation or misuse of the property of the authority and . . . serious inefficiency in the discharge of his duties" for failing to follow the recommendations in the special audit. The resolution referred to "serious accounting and financial problems . . . uncovered by the Accounting Firm of Rosenthal and Attinger. . . ." Burke was reinstated to his job with back pay after a lawsuit. Then, Burke sued the three commissioners and the accountants for defamation (libel). What privileges can the accountants and the commissioners raise in their defense? What will Burke have to prove to overcome the privileges? Who will likely win the lawsuit?

3. Martinez was a junior high school student. The *Democrat-Herald*, a newspaper, published a story discussing drug use in the local junior high school. Included were several photographs of what were called "apparent drug transactions" between junior high school students. Martinez was one of the students in the photographs. She sued for invasion of privacy alleging that (a) the defendant used her photograph without consent for commercial benefit and (b) the publicity put her in a false light. At trial, the court allowed evidence to be introduced that Martinez was a user of marijuana. Evidence also was introduced showing that the newspaper's circulation had been decreasing and that it had laid off several employees. The story about drugs appeared in the "People" section of the newspaper rather than in the "hard news" section. Should the newspaper be liable for either of the two types of invasion of privacy alleged?

4. In October 1984 Francis Heneghan brought his 1973 Cadillac to Cap-A-Radiator shop to have his radiator repaired. He told Jim Peister, manager of the shop, that his radiator was leaking and asked how much it would cost to repair. Peister told him $59.95. No written estimate was prepared and no inspection of the radiator was made. Later that morning Peister telephoned Heneghan's wife and told her that upon inspection the radiator should be replaced, not repaired, at a cost of approximately $200. Mrs. Heneghan called Peister back and advised him that Mr. Heneghan did not want the radiator replaced or repaired. Peister then told her that there would be a $25 service charge for checking out the radiator and removing it. When Heneghan returned to the shop to pick up his car Peister said that the radiator was not reinstalled and that Heneghan would have to pay $25 to have it reinstalled. Heneghan left and the vehicle remained on the premises. In January 1985 the shop told Heneghan to pick up his car or he would be liable for storage charges. Heneghan sued for conversion. Should he recover?

5 Barbara retained Ian, an attorney, to represent her in a proceeding to increase spousal support and child support granted her in a divorce. On two occasions she and Ian had sexual intercourse with each other. Before they did so, Barbara told Ian that she would not engage in sexual relations with him if there was any likelihood of her becoming pregnant. Ian told her not to worry, saying, "I can't possibly get anyone pregnant." She understood this to mean that he was sterile by nature or as the result of a vasectomy. As a result of sexual intercourse with Ian, Barbara became pregnant. The pregnancy was tubal, and in order to save her life, Barbara had her fallopian tube removed and was rendered sterile. Does Barbara have a cause of action against Ian for one or more torts?

6. Reed purchased a house from Kong. Although they were aware of its history, neither Kong nor his real estate agents told Reed that a woman and her four children were murdered in the house 10 years earlier. Kong and the agent represented that the premises were in good condition and fit for an "elderly lady" living alone. After Reed moved in, neighbors informed her that no one was interested in purchasing the house because of the stigma. Reed paid $76,000, but the house was worth only $65,000 because of its past. Do these facts satisfy all the elements required for the tort of fraud?

CHAPTER 7

Negligence and Liability without Fault

Most people do not intentionally inflict harm on others. However, one may unintentionally harm the person or property of another and become liable in tort for damages. The two major areas of liability for the unintentional infliction of harm are negligence and liability without fault. The first part of this chapter discusses negligence. The last part is devoted to several areas of liability without fault.

NEGLIGENCE

Nature of Negligence

Negligence is the failure to exercise due care when there is a foreseeable risk of harm to others. The tort of negligence may be illustrated by the following comparison. A person who intentionally drives a car into a pedestrian is liable for a battery. One who carelessly drives a car at an excessive rate of speed and cannot stop it in time to avoid a collision with a pedestrian commits negligence.

Elements of Negligence

To establish negligence, a plaintiff must prove four elements:

- **Duty**—the defendant owed a duty to exercise care for the protection of the plaintiff.
- **Breach of duty**—the defendant failed to exercise due care, i.e., breached the duty owed to the plaintiff.
- **Causation**—the defendant's breach of duty was the actual and proximate cause of the plaintiff's damages.
- **Damages**—the plaintiff suffered actual loss or damage.

Duty of Care

The first element of negligence, the duty of care, means that the defendant has a legal duty to protect the plaintiff against harm. In general, the common law imposes a duty of care whenever a person's conduct creates a foreseeable risk of harm to others. For example, if I cut down a large tree in my backyard, it may fall on my neighbor's house. Because my actions create a risk of property damage or personal injuries, I am under a duty to exercise due care for the protection of my neighbor. By contrast, a farmer who cuts down a tree would not have a duty to exercise due care for the protection of a neighbor who lives several miles away, because the farmer's cutting down the tree does not create a foreseeable risk of harm to the neighbor's person or property.

The duty of care can arise by statute, by contract, or by custom within a business or industry. Laws regulating how we drive our automobiles create a duty to exercise due care by following the rules of the road. A contract to perform services creates a duty to exercise due care in the performance of the work. For example, an accountant or lawyer is under a duty to exercise professional care and judgment in giving tax advice to a client.

The existence and nature of the duty of care may depend upon the relationship between the plaintiff and defendant. Thus, an owner of land is under a duty to maintain his or her property in a safe condition for the protection of **business invitees**—actual or potential customers or clients—who enter the property. In contrast, the landowner is generally not under a duty to protect trespassers from dangerous conditions on the property. Absent special circumstances, the landowner is not liable to a trespasser for injuries caused by the landowner's failure to maintain his or her property in a safe condition. Similarly, the common law recognizes no duty to come to the aid of another in peril. An Olympic swimmer standing on the side of a pool is not under a legal duty to save a drowning child. However, a lifeguard is under such a duty because of the obligations he or she agreed to perform, and if the child is drowning because of the conduct of another, the person who caused the danger is under a duty of rescue.

The Standard of Care

The judge or jury in a lawsuit for negligence must determine if the defendant breached the duty of care he or she owed to the plaintiff by failing to exercise the standard or level of care required of the defendant. Ordinarily, the defendant will be held to the "reasonable prudent person" standard — the same level of care that a hypothetical reasonable person would exercise under similar circumstances. In other cases, the defendant will be held to a higher professional standard of care.

The Reasonable Prudent Person Standard.
Negligence is often described as the failure to do

> **BOX 7.1**
> ### Trends in the Law: Duty to Protect Another from Criminal Harm
>
> You own a large, multilevel parking ramp in a downtown metropolitan area. A customer is attacked and raped as she enters her car parked in the lot. The customer sues you for negligence in failing to take reasonable security measures to protect her from criminal harm. Are you liable? Do you owe a duty to protect your customers from criminal assaults by third persons?
>
> The common law generally recognizes no duty to protect another from the criminal acts of third persons. Increasingly, however, courts are recognizing exceptions to this general rule. For example, motel operators are under a duty to take reasonable security measures to protect their guests when they are aware of past criminal acts of violence at the motel. A landlord may be under a similar duty to protect its tenants. The courts have also imposed a duty on business owners to protect business invitees from foreseeable criminal acts on the premises, such as robberies and criminal assaults.
>
> Whether a duty to protect another from criminal acts of third persons will be recognized depends upon two factors: the relationship between the parties and the foreseeability of the criminal harm. In the parking lot case, if criminal assaults are foreseeable (e.g., prior assaults have occurred in the area or on the premises), you may be under a duty to exercise reasonable care for the protection of your customers. If so, your liability will ultimately depend on whether you breached that duty by failing to exercise due care.
>
> What social policies justify the imposition of a duty to protect another from criminal harm? Under what circumstances should the law require such a duty? ■

what the ordinary prudent person would do under the same or similar circumstances. The ordinary prudent person conducts himself or herself with due care and in a reasonable manner. The standard is an *objective* one—i.e., the law does not consider a defendant's age, intelligence, experience, or judgment. The same reasonable prudent person standard is generally required of all of us. However, when evaluating the defendant's behavior, courts make allowances if the defendant is handicapped with blindness, deafness, or other physical disability. Also, in judging the conduct of a child, the judge or jury determines what is reasonable to expect from children of like age, intelligence, and experience to the defendant. Only when a child engages in an adult activity, like driving a car or flying a plane, does the law impose the adult reasonable person standard on a child.

The Professional Standard of Care. A professional or a person who possesses or claims to possess superior knowledge or skill is held to a higher standard of conduct than the ordinary prudent person. Physicians, dentists, attorneys, accountants, and other professionals have specialized skill, training, and education. In a lawsuit for professional negligence, the professional must exercise the judgment and skill followed by members of the profession in good standing in the same or a similar community. A failure to live up to the standard of care constitutes professional negligence, sometimes called **malpractice.**

The following case addresses the question of whether a blood bank is under an ordinary or professional standard of care in screening its blood donors for the AIDS virus.

CASE 7.1   **United Blood Services v. Quintana** • 827 P.2d 509 (Colo. 1992)

FACTS   United Blood Services (UBS), a nonprofit blood bank, operates blood centers throughout the western United States, procures whole blood from volunteer donors, processes the blood, and supplies it to hospitals. In April 1983, UBS received a donation of blood that was tainted with the AIDS virus. It knew that the donor of the blood pursued a "gay lifestyle."

Plaintiff Mrs. Quintana suffered a gunshot wound and was taken to a hospital, where she received the tainted blood when she underwent emergency surgery. One year after the surgery, Mrs. Quintana tested positive for the AIDS virus and was later diagnosed as suffering from AIDS.

Mrs. Quintana and her husband sued UBS for negligence, claiming that UBS failed to properly screen the blood donor for potential infection with the AIDS virus. The trial court refused to allow the Quintanas' expert witness, Dr. Marcus Conant—a dermatologist who had extensive experience in AIDS research and treatment—to testify concerning the standard of care applicable to UBS's blood banking operations. It was his opinion that in 1983 the national blood banks knew that the AIDS virus was transmissible in blood and that one of the highest-risk groups for AIDS was homosexual males. He further believed that blood banks ignored the warnings and advice of AIDS experts and were negligent in not implementing more stringent screening and testing procedures for blood donors.

The trial court ruled that because Dr. Conant was not directly practicing in the blood banking industry, he could not testify concerning the appropriate screening and testing procedures of the blood banking community. The jury returned a verdict in favor of UBS, the court of appeals reversed, and the Colorado

**CASE 7.1
Continued**

Supreme Court granted review to consider the applicable standard of care and the admissibility of plaintiff's expert testimony.

OPINION

QUINN, J. . . . A cause of action in tort arises out of a violation of a legal duty imposed upon an actor to avoid causing harm to others. . . .

Legal duty is defined in terms of a standard of care. . . . For those practicing a profession involving specialized knowledge or skill, reasonable care requires the actor to possess the standard minimum of special knowledge and ability, and to exercise reasonable care in a manner consistent with the knowledge and ability possessed by members of the profession in good standing. . . .

While a defendant practicing a profession is entitled to be judged by a standard of care applicable to the professional school to which the defendant belongs . . . that standard is not always conclusive proof of due care. . . . If the standard adopted by a practicing profession were to be deemed conclusive proof of due care, the profession itself would be permitted to set the measure of its own legal liability, even though that measure might be far below a level of care readily attainable through the adoption of practices and procedures substantially more effective in protecting others against harm than the self-decreed standard of the profession. . . . In a professional negligence case, therefore, a plaintiff should be permitted to present expert opinion testimony that the standard of care adopted by the school or practice to which the defendant adheres is unreasonably deficient by not incorporating readily available practices and procedures substantially more protective against the harm caused to the plaintiff than the standard of care adopted by the defendant's school or practice. . . .

We turn now to whether, as the court of appeals concluded, UBS's conduct should be measured by the general negligence standard of ordinary reasonable care or whether, as the trial court ruled, UBS's conduct should be measured by a professional standard of care applicable to the blood banking community to which UBS belongs.

Because [Colorado law] expressly categorizes the acquisition, preparation, and transfer of human blood or its components for medical transfusion as "the performance of a medical service," the statutory scheme clearly contemplates that a blood bank's conduct in procuring or processing blood is to be measured by a professional standard of care. . . . The acquisition and preparation of human blood for use in medical transfusion and the safeguarding of donated blood against contamination require the exercise of medical and scientific expertise by health care professionals in both the donor screening and the blood testing stages of the process. Any alleged negligence of a blood bank in performing those operations can occur only by reason of the action or inaction of its officers and employees functioning as health care professionals. We thus hold that UBS's conduct in acquiring and testing the blood subsequently used in treating Mrs. Quintana must be judged by a professional standard of care. . . .

[T]he trial court, after having correctly ruled that a professional standard of care applied to UBS's conduct, erroneously applied that standard. . . . The trial court's [excluding evidence] of the blood banking community's [deficient] screening and testing procedures [permits] the blood banking community to establish

CASE 7.1 Continued	its own standard of legal liability despite . . . evidence . . . that the blood banking community had adopted unreasonably deficient practices and procedures in place of substantially more protective and readily available safeguards. We hold, therefore, that the trial court's exclusion of the Quintana's proffered expert opinion evidence was error.
JUDGMENT	We accordingly affirm the judgment of the court of appeals and . . . return the case to the district court for a new trial. . . .

Breach of Duty

Having established a duty to exercise care for the protection of the plaintiff, the plaintiff must then prove that the defendant failed to live up to the required standard of care. The judge or jury compares the conduct of the defendant with the presumed conduct of the ordinary prudent person under the same or similar circumstances. If the defendant's conduct does not measure up to the model standard of conduct, the defendant has breached the duty of care.

In applying the reasonable person standard, the law considers the circumstances and context of the defendant's behavior. Determining whether the defendant's conduct was unreasonable requires a balancing of factors. The defendant's conduct is judged by (1) the severity of damage that might occur and (2) the probability that such damage will occur, compared with (3) the expense or inconvenience in taking precautions. The defendant is considered negligent if his or her conduct is such that factors (1) and (2) are greater than factor (3). For example, storing gasoline near an open fireplace in a house is unreasonable conduct and thus negligent. The risk of probable injury if the gasoline is ignited is great because gasoline is highly flammable and an explosion is likely to cause serious personal injuries or property damage. The risk outweighs the cost or inconvenience in taking precautions such as storing the gasoline away from the fire.

Proof of Negligence

Two procedural aids may help the plaintiff to establish a breach of the standard of care: the doctrine of negligence per se and the doctrine of *res ipsa loquitur*.

Negligence Per Se. Per se means "of itself" or "by itself." The doctrine of negligence per se permits the plaintiff to use the defendant's violation of a statute as proof that the defendant committed the tort of negligence. A criminal or regulatory statute or an administrative regulation may establish a standard of behavior for the community. Thus, if a defendant violates it, his or her conduct automatically constitutes failure to live up to the standard of the ordinary prudent person and therefore is negligence—"per se."

Negligence per se applies only if the plaintiff is within the class of individuals intended to be protected by the statute and if the harm suffered is of the kind which the statute is intended to prevent. Negligence per se is often utilized in a lawsuit resulting from an automobile accident. Suppose the plaintiff is injured when the defendant runs a red light and crashes into plaintiff's car. Traffic control statutes are enacted to protect users of highways and public streets from the risk of automobile accidents and the resulting harm to person or property. The plaintiff is within the class of persons to be protected by the traffic signal statute and suffers the kind of harm intended to be prevented. Thus, the doctrine of negligence per se would apply to the case.

The majority of states treat the defendant's unexcused violation of a statute as conclusive proof of negligent conduct. Thus, in a lawsuit the plaintiff need not submit further evidence to prove the first two elements of a cause of action for negligence. However, to recover damages, the plaintiff must of course prove the other elements of a cause of action for negligence: damages and causation. Other states treat a violation of a statute as mere evidence of negligence that is not binding on the jury.

Res Ipsa Loquitur. Negligent conduct can be proved by **direct** or **circumstantial** evidence. Direct evidence is evidence that directly proves the defendant's negligence, while circumstantial evidence is evidence from which the jury or court may infer negligent conduct. Testimony from a witness who saw the defendant speeding or carelessly driving his or her car is an example of direct evidence. On the other hand, testimony from a witness who heard a crash and then saw the defendant's car up against a telephone pole is circumstantial evidence of negligent driving. From the accident and other circumstances, the jury may conclude (infer) that the driver was being negligent. When circumstantial evidence of negligence is strong, such that a reasonable juror could conclude that an accident was more likely than not the defendant's fault, it is sufficient to prove negligence.

Occasionally, the only evidence of the defendant's failure to exercise due care is the injury to the plaintiff. Although the law does not generally presume negligence from the mere occurrence of an accident, under the doctrine of **res ipsa loquitur,** a Latin phrase meaning "the thing speaks for itself," the judge or jury is allowed to infer negligence from the circumstantial evidence surrounding the plaintiff's injury. To utilize *res ipsa loquitur,* however, the plaintiff must prove three things:

- The event which caused the plaintiff's injury is of a kind that ordinarily does not occur in the absence of someone's negligence.
- The accident was caused by an instrumentality within the exclusive control of the defendant at the time of the injury.
- The plaintiff did not contribute to his or her injuries.

Suppose that a patient undergoes heart surgery in a hospital and receives a serious burn to his leg during the operation. The hospital and its employees have no explanation for the burn. In his negligence action against the hospital, the patient may rely on the doctrine of *res ipsa loquitur* to prove negligence: Burns to an area of the body other than the area of surgery do not normally occur in the absence of someone's negligence; the hospital and its employees are presumably in exclusive control of the operating room; and the patient did not contribute to the injury. Under *res ipsa loquitur,* an inference of negligence would arise. Note that the doctrine does not guarantee that the patient will prevail in the lawsuit. The hospital may introduce evidence to contradict the inference of negligence or to prove a defense. It is only in the absence of evidence to the contrary that *res ipsa loquitur* would likely result in a verdict for the plaintiff.

The doctrine has been applied to a wide variety of situations. Some examples are a falling elevator, the explosion of a boiler, an unexplained plane crash, a barrel falling out of a window, and a sponge left in a patient following surgery. Case 7.2 illustrates the application of *res ipsa loquitur* to an injury occurring on a business premises.

CASE 7.2	**Anderson v. Service Merchandise Company** • 485 N.W.2d 170 (Neb. 1992)
FACTS	In June of 1986, Kathy Anderson was standing in the checkout line of Service Merchandise's retail store when an overhead light fixture fell and struck her on the back of the neck, head, and shoulder, resulting in personal injuries and medical expenses. Service Merchandise had a contract with Sylvania Lighting Services Corporation to maintain the lighting system by changing the "ballasts" and "sockets" on a periodic basis. Sylvania had performed work in May and Septem-

**CASE 7.2
Continued**

ber of 1985 and had done a lighting inspection in May of 1986. Notwithstanding the service contract, Service Merchandise employees regularly changed lights in the system when they burned out.

Anderson sued Service Merchandise and Sylvania, relying on the doctrine of *res ipsa loquitur*. The trial court granted summary judgment for the defendants on the ground that neither was in exclusive control of the light fixture. Anderson appealed.

OPINION

SHANAHAN, J. . . . As expressed in *Widga v. Sandell* . . . concerning the doctrine and elements of res ipsa loquitur: When an instrumentality under the exclusive control and management of the alleged wrongdoer produces an occurrence which would not, in the ordinary course of things, come to pass in the absence of the negligence of the one having such management and control, the occurrence itself, in the absence of explanation by the alleged wrongdoer, affords evidence that the occurrence arose as a result of the alleged wrongdoer's negligence. . . .

**ANDERSON'S
RES IPSA CASE**

"In the ordinary course of things," part of a light fixture attached to a building's ceiling does not, in the absence of negligence, fall and injure an invitee. Thus, . . . in Anderson's case the focal point is "exclusive control." . . .

Sylvania

What constituted Sylvania's "inspection" of the system in May 1986 . . . is undisclosed. Therefore, Sylvania's last . . . physical contact with the lighting system was in September 1985. . . . Thus, there was a hiatus of approximately 9 months between Sylvania's last physical work . . . and the light fixture's falling on Anderson. . . . [T]he record before us shows that Sylvania actually worked on the system a total of only 12 hours over 3 days during the 15-month period before Anderson's accident. . . . Thus, Sylvania's control . . . is so attenuated and lacking in continuity that [it] is nonexistent. . . . Without res ipsa loquitur, Anderson presented no evidence of Sylvania's negligence; therefore, the district court properly granted summary judgment to Sylvania. . . .

Service Merchandise

Service Merchandise contends that it lacked exclusive control because [it] contracted with Sylvania for periodic inspection and service of the store's overhead lighting fixtures. . . .

As a business possessor of real estate, Service Merchandise has a duty to exercise reasonable care to keep the premises safe for its business invitees. . . . [Its] duty to use reasonable care . . . is a nondelegable one. . . . [A] business possessor . . . cannot shift the duty of reasonable care to an agent or independent contractor employed to maintain all or part of the premises. . . . Therefore, even assuming that Sylvania was negligent and that Sylvania's negligence was the proximate cause of Anderson's injuries, "exclusive control" for the purposes of res ipsa loquitur remained with Service Merchandise. . . .

> **CASE 7.2**
> **Continued**
>
> To summarize, Service Merchandise was in "exclusive control" of the premises for purposes of res ipsa loquitur because [it] possessed, and, therefore, controlled the site of the accident and had a nondelegable duty to exercise reasonable care for the protection of Anderson, a business invitee. . . . Since Anderson has established all the elements of res ipsa loquitur . . . the district court erred by granting summary judgment to Service Merchandise.
>
> **JUDGMENT** Affirmed in part, and in part reversed and remanded. . . .

Negligent Misrepresentation

A person may negligently make a false statement of fact by failing to exercise due care to determine the truth. This **negligent misrepresentation** involves the same elements as fraud, except that the plaintiff need not prove scienter or knowledge of falsity. Liability is limited to persons in the business of supplying advice or information for the guidance of others, such as accountants, attorneys, insurance agents, and real estate brokers.[1] They are liable to their clients if they negligently misrepresent facts upon which their clients justifiably rely to their detriment. So, for example, an attorney who falsely informs a client that a seller has good title to land without conducting a reasonable examination of the land title records is liable for resulting loss if the client relies on the advice in buying the property.

Causation

To hold the defendant liable, the plaintiff must prove that the defendant's negligence was the cause of the injury. Sometimes the cause is obvious, as where the defendant carelessly drives a car and hits the plaintiff. But at other times, determining the cause of an injury is more difficult. For example, suppose a tenant is mugged upon entering his or her apartment. Is the landlord's failure to maintain adequate security the cause of the tenant's injuries? Or is the cause of the tenant's injuries the criminal act of the person committing the assault? To hold the landlord liable under these circumstances, the plaintiff must prove that the landlord's failure to exercise reasonable care for the protection of the tenant was both the actual and proximate cause of the tenant's injury.

Actual Cause. The concept of **causation** requires a cause-and-effect relationship between the plaintiff's injury and the defendant's negligent conduct: The negligent conduct must be the **actual cause** (sometimes called **cause in fact**) of the plaintiff's injury. A plaintiff establishes actual cause by proving that the injury would not have occurred without ("but for") the negligence of the defendant. Under this **"but for" test,** actual cause is proved if we can say "but for the defendant's conduct the plaintiff would not have been injured." If the plaintiff's injury would have occurred without the defendant's negligence, the negligence is not the actual cause of the injury. Dan drives his car knowing that it has defective brakes. A child suddenly darts directly in front of the car, and Dan's car strikes and injures the child. If Dan would have hit the child even if the car had good brakes, his negligence is not the actual cause of the child's injury.

In negligence cases, there can be **concurring causes**—two or more that happen at the same time. When there are concurring causes, a de-

---

[1] A person who enters into a contract relying on the negligent misrepresentations of the other party may also be able to rescind (cancel) the contract. This right of rescission exists even if the party misrepresenting the facts is not in the business of supplying advice to others. See the discussion of misrepresentation in Chapter 13.

fendant is liable if his or her negligence was a **substantial factor** in the plaintiff's injury. Rita and Mary simultaneously drive loud motorcycles at high rates of speed so close to a man with a heart condition that he suffers a heart attack. He may hold both Rita and Mary liable. Neither cyclist can escape liability by arguing that the harm would have occurred without her negligence (i.e., that the harm would have happened anyway). Each defendant is liable if her negligent conduct was a material or substantial factor in causing the injury.

Proximate Cause. In addition to showing that the defendant's negligence was an actual cause of the plaintiff's injury, the plaintiff must also prove that the negligence was a **proximate cause.** The purpose of the proximate cause requirement is to relieve the defendant of responsibility for losses that were remote or unforeseeable. While our ethical standards require responsibility for conduct—and liability for negligence—we also hold that legal responsibility should end when consequences cannot reasonably be anticipated. Suppose a rental agency negligently furnishes a car with smooth tires to a surgeon, not knowing he is driving to a rural town to perform minor surgery. A tire blows out and the doctor cannot operate. The patient's arm becomes infected and later has to be amputated. Under the "but for" test, the rental agency's negligence is an actual cause of the patient's loss. But for the bad tires, there would have been no blowout, no infection, and no amputation. Many courts would hold, however, that the agency's negligence was not a proximate cause of the patient's loss, because the amputation was not a reasonably foreseeable consequence of the agency's conduct.

The defendant is liable, however, where it is only the *extent* of the plaintiff's injury that is not reasonably foreseeable. Kim negligently "rear-ends" Judy's car in a minor collision, but because of Judy's heart condition, the shock of the accident causes her death. Since some injury to Judy was reasonably foreseeable, Kim is liable for Judy's death. As often has been said, a defendant "takes his victim as he finds him."

Intervening or Superseding Cause. Intervening cause is another factor that limits the extent of a defendant's liability for negligence. An **intervening cause** is one that occurs *after* the defendant's negligence and alters the consequences. Ordinarily, the defendant remains liable if the intervening cause of plaintiff's injury was reasonably foreseeable. Ali suffers a shattered leg in an automobile accident caused by Robert's negligence. Ali undergoes emergency surgery at the hospital, but because of the doctor's negligence, he suffers permanent impairment to his leg. The doctor's malpractice is an intervening cause. However, most courts would conclude that Robert could reasonably foresee the doctor's negligence, and thus Robert is liable for the full extent of Ali's injuries.

Suppose, however, that the doctor operating on Ali intentionally injected him with a lethal poison, causing his death. Is Robert liable for the intervening battery committed by the doctor? Probably not. Such an unforeseeable intervening cause is called a **superseding cause.** If a superseding cause occurs, the defendant will not be held liable because the defendant's negligence is not considered a proximate cause of plaintiff's injury.

Nevertheless, although intentional torts and crimes of others will frequently be considered superseding causes, a person may be liable for losses resulting from the criminal acts of others. Consider the example of the tenant who is mugged while entering his or her apartment. The courts have held that a landlord is liable for failing to protect against, or warn a tenant of, possible harm from criminal assault when the landlord knew of past similar incidents in the neighborhood and could reasonably foresee a future occurrence. In such circumstances, the assault is an intervening but not a superseding cause of the tenant's injuries.

The following case illustrates the causation element in a negligence case.

CASE 7.3	**Stahl v. Metropolitan Dade County** • 438 So.2d 14 (Fla. App. 1983)
FACTS	Andrew Stahl, a 13-year-old boy, was riding his bicycle to school on a bicycle path built by Metropolitan Dade County on the north side of S.W. 128 Street. Children regularly used the path, and this was known to Dade County. The path, built in 1971, was made of asphalt and was about 5 feet wide. It had never received maintenance and was very bumpy in places where tree roots had grown underneath. Seeking to avoid one such area, Andrew rode off the path onto a parallel grassy area which had trees growing in it, and into the adjoining street. He was immediately struck and killed by an oncoming car. Andrew would have struck a tree had he not headed into the street. Andrew's father sued Dade County, alleging negligence in the maintenance of the bicycle path. Dade County was granted summary judgment on the grounds that its negligence was not the proximate cause of the accident. Plaintiff (the father) appealed.
OPINION	HUBBART, J. . . . In the instant case, all agree that for summary judgment purposes the first two elements of the plaintiff's negligence (wrongful death) action are shown on this record, . . . It is solely the third element of "proximate cause" which is in dispute in this case. . . . The Florida courts, in accord with most other jurisdictions, have historically followed the so-called "but for" causation-in-fact test, that is, ". . . there must be such a natural, direct, and continuous sequence between the negligence act (or omission) and the (plaintiff's) injury that it can reasonably be said that *but for* the (negligent) act (or omission) the injury would not have occurred." . . . Florida courts, in accord with courts throughout the country, have for good reason been most reluctant to attach tort liability for results which, although caused-in-fact by the defendant's negligent act or omission, seem to the judicial mind highly unusual, extraordinary, bizarre, or, stated differently, seem beyond the scope of any fair assessment of the danger created by the defendant's negligence. . . . The test most often employed by the courts is the so-called "foreseeability" test. . . . Plainly, the "foreseeability" test finds a particularly consistent application in that large group of cases where, as claimed here, a plaintiff's injury is caused-in-fact by the defendant's negligence and, in addition thereto, by other "intervening causes" independent of said negligence. . . . If an intervening cause is foreseeable the original negligent actor may still be held liable. . . . Plainly, the defendant Dade County's negligence in failing to properly maintain the bicycle path in question at the point where Andrew Stahl, the plaintiff's decedent, departed from the path was a cause-in-fact of the said decedent's death. Utilizing the "but for" test of actual causation, it is clear that "but for" the defendant's negligence herein, Andrew would not have been forced off the bicycle path, would not have been propelled onto an adjoining grassy area where menacing trees were located, would not have driven onto the adjoining street to avoid hitting the said trees, and would not have been struck and killed by an oncoming car. "But for" the defendant's negligence in the maintenance of the bicy-

**CASE 7.3
Continued**

cle path, this tragic sequence of events would never have occurred. At the very least, a genuine issue of material fact is presented making a summary judgment inappropriate here. . . .

Given, then, a proper showing of causation-in-fact in this case, we move on to determine whether the car/bicycle collision herein was a reasonably foreseeable consequence of the defendant's alleged negligent maintenance of the bicycle path herein. . . .

We think that a reasonable jury on these facts could find that the negligent maintenance of the bicycle path would likely force a young bicyclist such as Andrew Stahl off the path to avoid a spill, across an adjoining grassy area and onto the street where he might be hit by a car. Stated differently, we do not, as a matter of law, see this as a highly unusual, extraordinary or bizarre occurrence flowing from the negligent omission herein.

From our common experience, we know that a bicyclist has a certain momentum as he travels along a bicycle path. Upon discovery of a hazardous condition on the path he, very likely, may be forced to detour off the path onto whatever adjoins the path without being able to stop. Where, as here, the adjoining strip is a grassy area approximately five feet in width with menacing trees growing therein, he may very well be forced to drive into the adjoining street to avoid hitting the trees and is likely thereafter to be hit and killed by an oncoming car. True, the child's action in this case in driving into the street and the oncoming car's action in striking the child represent intervening causes-in-fact of the child's death in this case. Neither of these causes, however, can be said to be unforeseeable as a matter of law because plainly they could be reasonably expected from the defendant's initial negligence herein. At any rate, we think this is a question of fact for the jury on this record and was not a proper basis for entering a summary judgment. . . .

JUDGMENT Reversed and remanded.

Damages

The harm suffered as a consequence of another's negligence may be physical (personal injuries) or economic (financial loss or property damage). In a personal injury case, for example, the plaintiff may recover damages for lost wages, permanent disabilities, and pain and suffering.

The courts have been reluctant to award damages where the plaintiff's injury is limited solely to mental distress. As with the tort of outrage, the major objection to recovery for negligent infliction of emotional distress is the danger of fictitious claims. Because of the judicial skepticism of mental distress injuries, most states permit the plaintiff to recover damages for negligently inflicted emotional distress only if the defendant's act caused immediate physical consequences to the plaintiff, such as a nervous disorder, or caused mental distress followed by physical consequences. For example, a pregnant woman who suffers mental distress from a defendant's negligence may recover damages if the distress results in a later miscarriage.

Defenses to Negligence

At common law, there were two major defenses to the tort of negligence: contributory negligence and assumption of the risk. Today most states have abandoned the contributory negli-

> **BOX 7.2**
>
> **A Question of Policy: Emotional Harm to Bystanders**
>
> Dixie Whetham had just given birth to her daughter, Tami Lynn. A hospital employee carried the child to Dixie's hospital bed. In the presence of her mother, the employee dropped Tami Lynn, and the infant struck her head upon the tiled floor, sustaining a fracture to her skull. Dixie suffered severe emotional shock and sued the hospital. Can a bystander like Dixie recover for emotional distress caused by witnessing the negligent injury of another?
>
> The courts have had great difficulty in resolving this issue. In most states, a bystander cannot recover unless he or she was threatened by the negligent act. Since Dixie was not personally in danger, she will lose under that rule. In a few states recovery has been permitted when four elements are present: (1) the injury inflicted on the third person is serious and of a nature to cause mental distress to the bystander; (2) the shock results in physical harm to the bystander; (3) the bystander is a close relative to the person injured; and (4) the bystander is present at the time of the injury to the third person or suffers the shock almost immediately after the accident. Dixie will likely win in one of these jurisdictions.
>
> Which is the better rule from a policy perspective? ■

gence defense and have adopted a system of comparative negligence under which damages are apportioned according to the relative fault of the parties.

Contributory Negligence. **Contributory negligence** (sometimes called "contributory fault") is a failure by the plaintiff to exercise due care for his or her own safety, a failure that becomes a contributing cause of the plaintiff's own injury.

At common law, contributory negligence was a complete bar to plaintiff's recovery—a negligent defendant was not liable to the plaintiff if plaintiff was in any way contributorily at fault. Legal scholars and courts have severely criticized the doctrine as unfair, because under it a plaintiff who is slightly negligent may not recover any damages from a defendant who is greatly negligent. Despite the criticism, a small number of states still recognize the defense.

In contributory negligence states, the courts have developed exceptions and modifications to eliminate some of the harsh consequences of the rule. The most important limitation is the **last clear chance** doctrine. Under this rule, a negligent plaintiff can recover damages from the defendant if the defendant had an opportunity to avoid the accident by exercising reasonable care but failed to do so. Thus, a pedestrian who carelessly walks across a street can hold a negligent driver liable if the defendant had the last clear chance to avoid the accident.

Comparative Negligence. The dissatisfaction of the courts with the absolute defense of contributory negligence led to the adoption of **comparative negligence.** Today the great majority of states have adopted comparative negligence systems in various forms either by court decision or by statute. Comparative negligence requires the judge or jury to determine the relative fault of the parties and apportion damages between the plaintiff and the defendant according to the fault of each. Thus, if the defendant is found to be 75 percent at fault and the plaintiff is found to be 25 percent at fault, the plaintiff will recover only 75 percent of his or her monetary damages. If the plaintiff sustained $10,000 worth of injuries, the jury would award the plaintiff $7,500.

The states have adopted two different forms of comparative negligence: pure and modified comparative negligence. A *minority* of states follow a **pure comparative negligence** rule. Under this rule, if the jury determines that the plaintiff is 99 percent at fault, he or she can still recover 1 percent of his or her damages, that portion caused by the defendant's negligence.

Most states reject the pure form because it allows a recovery by a plaintiff who was more at fault than the defendant. Instead, the majority have adopted a **modified comparative negligence** system which does not allow a recovery by a plaintiff whose negligence is greater than the defendant's. Where the plaintiff and defendant are equally (50 percent and 50 percent) at fault, the states using the modified defense differ as to the plaintiff's recovery of damages. In most states, the plaintiff recovers 50 percent of his or her damages; in other states the plaintiff receives nothing.

In Case 7.4, the Tennessee Supreme Court abandons the contributory negligence defense in favor of a modified comparative negligence system.

CASE 7.4 **McIntyre v. Balentine** • 833 S.W.2d 52 (Tenn. 1992)

FACTS In the early morning darkness of November 2, 1986, Harry Douglas McIntyre and Clifford Balentine were involved in a motor vehicle accident near Savannah, Tennessee, resulting in severe injuries to McIntyre. As Balentine was traveling south on Highway 69, McIntyre entered the highway (also traveling south) from a truck stop parking lot, and shortly after McIntyre's pickup truck was struck by Balentine's Peterbilt tractor.

McIntyre sued Balentine and his employer for negligence. Testimony at trial suggested that Balentine was speeding. The defendants raised contributory negligence as a defense, contending that McIntyre was operating his vehicle while intoxicated. Although both men had consumed alcohol the evening of the accident, McIntyre's blood alcohol level was measured at .17 percent by weight, in excess of the legal limit.

The jury returned a verdict in favor of the defendants and McIntyre appealed. The court of appeals affirmed, but the Supreme Court of Tennessee granted plaintiff's application for permission to appeal in order to decide whether to adopt a system of comparative fault in Tennessee.

OPINION DROWOTA, J. . . . The common law contributory negligence doctrine has traditionally been traced to Lord Ellenborough's opinion in *Butterfield v. Forrester*, 11 East 50, 103 Eng. Rep. 926 (1809). There, plaintiff, "riding as fast as his horse would go," was injured after running into an obstruction defendant had placed in the road. Stating as the rule that "one person being in fault will not dispense with another's using ordinary care," plaintiff was denied recovery on the basis that he did not use ordinary care to avoid the obstruction. . . . The contributory negligence bar was soon brought to America as part of the common law, and proceeded to spread throughout the states. . . .

In Tennessee . . . we have continued to follow the general rule that a plaintiff's contributory negligence completely bars recovery. . . . Equally entrenched in Tennessee jurisprudence are exceptions to the general all-or-nothing rule: contributory negligence does not absolutely bar recovery where defendant's conduct was intentional . . . where defendant's conduct was "grossly" negligent . . . where defendant had the "last clear chance" with which, through the exercise of ordinary care, to avoid plaintiff's injury . . . or where plaintiff's negligence may be classified as "remote." . . .

Between 1920 and 1969, a few states began utilizing the principles of comparative fault in all tort litigation. . . . [T]hen, between 1969 and 1984, comparative fault replaced contributory negligence in 37 additional states. . . . In 1991,

> **CASE 7.4**
> **Continued**
>
> South Carolina became the 45th state to adopt comparative fault . . . leaving Alabama, Maryland, North Carolina, Virginia, and Tennessee as the only remaining common law contributory negligence jurisdictions. . . .
>
> We conclude that it is time to abandon the outmoded and unjust common law doctrine of contributory negligence and adopt in its place a system of comparative fault. Justice simply will not permit our continued adherence to a rule that, in the face of a judicial determination that others bear primary responsibility, nevertheless completely denies injured litigants recompense for their damages.
>
> We recognize that this action could be taken by our General Assembly. However, legislative inaction has never prevented judicial abolition of obsolete common law doctrines, especially those such as contributory negligence, conceived in the judicial womb. . . .
>
> Two basic forms of comparative fault are utilized by 45 of our sister jurisdictions, these variants being commonly referred to as either "pure" or "modified." In the "pure" form, a plaintiff's damages are reduced in proportion to the percentage negligence attributed to him; for example, a plaintiff responsible for 90 percent of the negligence that caused his injuries nevertheless may recover 10 percent of his damages. In the "modified" form, plaintiffs recover as in pure jurisdictions, but only if the plaintiff's negligence either (1) does not exceed ("50 percent" jurisdictions) or (2) is less than ("49 percent" jurisdictions) the defendant's negligence.
>
> Although we conclude that the all-or-nothing rule of contributory negligence must be replaced, we nevertheless decline to abandon totally our fault-based tort system. We do not agree that a party should necessarily be able to recover in tort even though he may be 80, 90, or 95 percent at fault. We therefore reject the pure form of comparative fault.
>
> We recognize that modified comparative fault systems have been criticized as merely shifting the arbitrary contributory negligence bar to a new ground. . . . However, we feel the "49 percent rule" ameliorates the harshness of the common law rule while remaining compatible with a fault-based tort system. We therefore hold that so long as a plaintiff's negligence remains less than the defendant's negligence the plaintiff may recover; in such a case, plaintiff's damages are to be reduced in proportion to the percentage of the total negligence attributable to the plaintiff.
>
> **JUDGMENT** The judgment of the Court of Appeals is reversed . . . and the case is remanded to the trial court for a new trial. . . .

Assumption of Risk. Assumption of risk is the voluntary undertaking of a known risk by the plaintiff. Assumption of risk may be express or implied. Express assumption of risk generally results from a contract or written release in which the risk was made clear to the plaintiff. For example, an operator of a "bungee jumping" crane may require users to sign an agreement in advance waiving any claims against the operator for negligence.

Implied assumption of risk requires that the plaintiff have knowledge of a particular risk and voluntarily proceed to encounter it. A spectator at a baseball game is injured by a flying baseball and sues the stadium, alleging that the owner failed to provide a protective screen for spectators. The stadium owner has the defense that upon entering the stadium the plaintiff assumed the known risk of being hit by a ball, and that all spectators at a baseball game impliedly

> **BOX 7.3**
> ### You Be the Judge
> Assume that you are on the jury in the new trial of *McIntyre v. Balentine*. How would you resolve the question of comparative fault? What percentage of fault would you attribute to McIntyre and what percentage of fault would you attribute to Balentine? Would your decision be influenced by the fact that McIntyre will recover nothing if his negligence is greater than 49 percent? ∎

> **BOX 7.4**
> ### Vicarious Tort Liability and Business Planning
> One of the costs of doing business is the expense associated with the tort liability system. Businesses are subject to **vicarious tort liability**—liability for the torts committed by their employees within the scope of their employment.[3] So, for example, if the driver of your delivery van, while making a delivery, drives negligently and runs over a person in the street, you will usually be held liable for the pedestrian's injuries.
>
> How does a business plan for this potential liability? Securing an adequate amount of liability insurance is perhaps the best means of ensuring that monies are available to pay for civil damage awards. But what steps can businesses take to reduce the risk of civil liability? ∎
>
> [3] Chapter 37 contains a detailed discussion of the liability of an employer for the torts of its employees.

consent to the ordinary risks of harm associated with the game.

In determining whether the plaintiff assumed the risk of the defendant's negligence, the judge or jury applies a subjective test, and does not require the plaintiff to measure up to the "ordinary prudent person" standard of care. That is, the court considers the particular plaintiff's age, experience, and knowledge, since these are important factors affecting the person's ability to understand and consent to the danger involved in the particular situation.

The effect of the comparative negligence rule on the defense of assumption of risk varies greatly among the states.[2] In some states express assumption of risk remains as a complete defense, but implied assumption of risk is treated as a form of comparative negligence, and the plaintiff's damages are reduced. In a few states assumption of risk, whether express or implied, is retained as an absolute defense.

LIABILITY WITHOUT FAULT

The remainder of this chapter is devoted to a discussion of liability without fault, sometimes called **strict** (or absolute) **liability.** As the term implies, there are situations where a person may be held liable for injuring another even though the person has no intent to injure anyone and, in fact, acts with the utmost care to prevent harm to others. Although the conduct of the one causing injury is blameless, the law allocates the risk of loss to the defendant for reasons of social policy. For example, the law imposes strict liability on a manufacturer of a defective product to protect consumers and to require product sellers to bear the social costs of products they produce. There are three major areas of liability without fault: strict products liability, liability for injuries from abnormally dangerous activities, and liability for injuries by animals.

Strict Products Liability

The law of products liability is complex and is particularly important to manufacturers and other businesses that sell or lease goods. Chapter 22 discusses the history and development of the law and presents various contemporary theories of liability. This section is devoted to one theory: strict products liability.

[2] A similar split exists with respect to the effect of the adoption of comparative negligence on the "last clear chance" doctrine. Many comparative negligence states have held that the doctrine has been abolished; other comparative negligence states still recognize the doctrine.

The overwhelming majority of states have adopted the rule imposing liability without fault for defective products contained in Section 402A of the *Restatement (Second) of the Law of Torts*, which provides as follows:

One who sells a defective product that is unreasonably dangerous is liable to the ultimate user or consumer if the seller is engaged in the business of selling such a product and the product reaches the user or consumer without substantial changes in the condition in which it is sold.

A major reason for adopting this rule of liability without fault is social policy. The courts have repeatedly stated that the risk of injury from defective products should be borne by the manufacturer or seller, who can insure against losses and distribute the cost to the public as an expense of doing business.

Under this rule, the plaintiff must prove that the product is **unreasonably dangerous.** The plaintiff need not prove that the seller was negligent, and, in fact, the seller may be liable even though he or she exercised all possible care to prevent harm to others. A product is unreasonably dangerous if it is dangerous beyond the contemplation of the ordinary consumer or user—i.e., it does not meet the reasonable expectations of the ordinary consumer as to its safety. The plaintiff can establish this by showing a defective design (e.g., a machine press without an adequate guard to prevent injuries to workers), a manufacturing defect (a quality control breakdown in the production process), or a labeling defect (improper warnings or instructions).

All business sellers in the chain of distribution of a product, including the maker of a defective component part, the manufacturer of the product, the wholesaler, and the retailer, are liable for the plaintiff's injuries. Courts recently have extended strict liability to commercial lessors, businesses engaged in the leasing of products. Thus, an automobile or equipment rental business is liable without fault for injuries caused by a defect in the goods leased. The courts have also allowed persons other than users and purchasers (such as family members, guests, or mere bystanders) to recover damages for injury resulting from a defective product when in their view the injury was foreseeable. However, the plaintiff can recover only for physical injury or property damage caused by the dangerous product, not economic losses (e.g., lost sales or profits caused by defective equipment).

Assumption of risk and unforeseeable misuse of the product are defenses in a strict products liability lawsuit. The defendant may assert that the plaintiff made an abnormal use of the product which the defendant could not reasonably foresee, such as using a glass bottle to hammer a nail. Similarly, a plaintiff who has knowledge of a dangerous defect but continues to use the product may be guilty of assumption of risk. States generally do not allow the defense of contributory negligence. Thus, the plaintiff's careless use of the product or failure to inspect the product for defects is generally not a defense. However, some states apply comparative negligence rules to strict products liability actions.

In Case 7.5 the court discusses strict products liability and the possible defenses to liability.

CASE 7.5	**Mauch v. Manufacturers Sales & Service, Inc.** • 345 N.W.2d 338 (N.D. 1984)
FACTS	Kathleen Mauch was injured while using a "Mr. Big Tow" nylon rope, manufactured by the defendant, Manufacturers Sales & Service, Inc., to pull apart one tractor with another on the Mauchs' farm. She was driving the pulling tractor when the hook attached to the other tractor broke. The nylon rope instantly recoiled toward Kathleen's tractor, hurling the broken hook which was still

**CASE 7.5
Continued**

attached to it through the tractor cab window. The hook struck Kathleen, injuring her seriously.

She sued Manufacturers on theories of negligence and strict products liability. The Mauchs asserted that Manufacturers negligently breached a duty to warn Kathleen that nylon rope when stretched and then released may recoil with tremendous force. The Mauchs also asserted that the nylon rope, because it was sold without an adequate warning of its dangerous recoil propensities, was in an unreasonably dangerous condition. Manufacturers asserted as a defense at the trial that Kathleen's injuries were proximately caused by her own negligent use of the tow rope. In support of that assertion, it introduced evidence that the hook broke and recoiled toward Kathleen's tractor cab because she had attached the rope to the tractor being pulled by placing the hook into a hole located on the drawbar instead of properly inserting the hook into a clevis and drawpin arrangement.

The trial court refused to instruct the jury on strict liability, and the case was submitted solely on the negligence theory. The jury found that the proximate cause of Kathleen's injuries was 50 percent attributable to Manufacturers' negligence and 50 percent attributable to Kathleen's negligence. The district court entered a judgment of no recovery under the North Dakota comparative negligence statute. Mauch appealed.

OPINION

VANDEWALLE, J. . . . The district court instructed the jury on the Mauchs' negligence theory but refused to instruct on their strict-liability theory on the ground that, in a failure-to-warn case such as this, the two theories are indistinguishable and instructing on both would serve only to confuse the jury. On appeal, the Mauchs assert that the district court erred in refusing to instruct the jury on their strict-liability theory. We agree.

Although the authorities disagree over this issue, we believe that recovery sought under a negligent failure-to-warn theory and recovery sought under a products-liability theory of marketing a product which is defective and unreasonably dangerous because it is not accompanied by adequate warnings are two separate and distinct theories of recovery. . . .

This court, in *Olson v. A.W. Chesterton Company* . . . recognized that under Restatement (Second) Torts, Section 402A, one who manufactures or sells a product has a duty to warn of dangers inherent in its intended use and also to warn of dangers involved in a use which can be reasonably anticipated. Thus a manufacturer or seller can be held liable under a products-liability theory for selling a product, which, although meeting every requirement for its designed utility and although properly manufactured, is marketed without adequate warnings to make the product free from unreasonable danger to the user. . . .

If the jurors had been given a products-liability instruction, they might have found that the "Mr. Big Tow" nylon rope was not accompanied by adequate warnings regarding its recoil propensities and was therefore in a defective and unreasonably dangerous condition to the user or consumer.

Manufacturers asserts that the district court's failure to give a products-liability instruction does not require a reversal of the judgment because the jury found that Kathleen's contributory negligence was 50 percent . . . [and] the Mauchs

**CASE 7.5
Continued**

would not be entitled to recover any damages under either a negligence or a products-liability theory. To resolve this issue it is necessary for us to discuss the defenses that are available in a products-liability action, and in that context, to determine whether or not a plaintiff's negligence is a defense. . . .

There is disagreement among the courts as to whether or not the plaintiff's negligence, in the sense of a failure to exercise ordinary care for one's own safety, constitutes a defense in a products-liability action. . . .

. . . The focus of a products-liability action is on whether or not the product is defective and unreasonably dangerous, and thus the reasonableness of the plaintiff's conduct under negligence concepts is not relevant to this action. The defenses which we have previously recognized . . . of assumption of risk and unforeseeable misuse are, in our opinion, adequate to protect a seller or manufacturer from unjust liability in a case of this type.

. . . We conclude that a plaintiff's ordinary contributory negligence . . . is not a defense in a products-liability action. . . . [I]n view of the Legislature's acceptance of comparative-negligence principles . . . and in following a course which we believe is most fair and just to all parties, we hold that where an unreasonably dangerous defect of a product and the plaintiff's assumption of risk or unforeseeable misuse of the product are concurring proximate causes of the injury suffered, the trier of fact must compare those concurring causes to determine the respective percentages by which each contributed. . . . We further hold that the comparison of causation under a products-liability claim should be on a pure comparative-causation basis. . . . Thus the plaintiff's misuse of the product will reduce the recovery by the percentage of damage attributable to the misuse. . . .

To summarize, we recognize the defense of assumption of risk—the seller has a reduced liability to one who is aware that a product is defective and unreasonably dangerous, has a reasonable opportunity to choose whether or not to expose himself to the danger, and voluntarily proceeds to use the product. We also recognize the defense of unforeseeable misuse—the seller's liability is reduced where the plaintiff misuses the product in a manner for which the seller could not be expected to anticipate or provide in the manufacture or sale of the product and where the misuse is a proximate cause of the damages sustained.

JUDGMENT The . . . judgment is reversed and the case is remanded for a new trial on the Mauchs' products-liability cause of action.

Abnormally Dangerous Activities

As a general rule, one is liable without fault for injuring the person or property of another by an **abnormally dangerous activity.** In determining whether a particular activity is abnormally dangerous, the *Restatement (Second) of Torts* Section 520 identifies the following factors:

- The existence of a high degree of risk of some harm to the person, land, or chattels of another
- The likelihood that the harm resulting from it will be great
- The inability to eliminate the risk by the exercise of reasonable care
- The extent to which the activity is not a matter of common usage
- The inappropriateness of the activity to the place where it is carried on
- The extent to which the value of the activity to the community is outweighed by its dangerous attributes

Typical examples of abnormally dangerous activities are blasting in a residential neighborhood, crop dusting near livestock, storing quantities of explosives in the heart of a city, and drilling an oil well in a populated area. Such highly dangerous activities are inappropriate or unusual for that particular place and generally cannot be conducted without injury to persons or property regardless of the level of care taken by the defendant.

On the other hand, the courts have held that the following are not abnormally dangerous: storing gasoline in a service station, maintaining an ordinary fire in a factory, and stocking a small quantity of dynamite for sale in a hardware store. A person who engages in these activities is not liable without fault for injuring another but may be liable for the tort of negligence if the person fails to exercise due care. An activity may be abnormally dangerous at one point in time, but lose that character because of advances in technology or changes in common usage. For example, in the early decades of the twentieth century, flying an airplane was considered an abnormally dangerous activity, and aircraft operators were held strictly liable for harm to others. In most states today, because of the safety of modern airplanes, the owner or operator of an airplane is held liable only when negligence is proved.

The defendant may assert the defense of assumption of risk and prove that the plaintiff voluntarily exposed his or her person or property to the risk from the abnormally dangerous activity. Also, statutes ordinarily immunize persons and firms from liability for laying gas or electric lines in public streets or doing blasting for the state, provided they are not guilty of negligence. In general, however, the plaintiff's contributory fault is not a defense.

Liability for Injuries by Animals

Liability for the damages caused by a person's animals depends upon a number of factors, but an important one is whether the animal is wild or domesticated. The owner is strictly liable for injuries inflicted by a wild animal, an animal that is dangerous by its nature and incapable of being domesticated. Such animals include lions, tigers, bears, elephants, and wolves. As a general rule, liability is absolute even though the animal has been raised as a pet and has shown no outward signs of being dangerous.

A different common law rule pertains to domestic animals and domesticated wild animals that normally are not likely to injure people. The owner is liable for injuries inflicted only if the owner knows, or has reason to know, of a dangerous propensity in the particular animal. Domestic animals include dogs, cats, sheep, horses, and cows. Some courts have held that

---

BOX 7.5

Developments in the Law: Tort Reform

Is there an insurance crisis because of excessive jury awards in tort lawsuits? Does the tort liability system detrimentally affect the competitiveness of American business? Are doctors engaged in expensive defensive medicine to avoid malpractice actions? Are we becoming an overly litigious society with too many lawyers?

Some commentators, professionals, and politicians argue that the tort liability system is out of control and needs to be reformed. Lawyers and consumer advocates argue that the system provides civil justice to innocent victims and protects consumers from harmful products and negligent professionals. Our society is engaged in a spirited public debate about the tort system and its future.

The movement to reform the tort system has resulted in significant changes by state legislatures in the liability system crafted by the courts. Almost all states have adopted some form of "tort reform" measures. These laws take many forms but frequently they impose a cap on damages in tort cases, limit the recovery of punitive damages and recovery for noneconomic losses (e.g., pain and suffering), limit the liability exposure of professionals, and impose sanctions for frivolous suits.

Should the tort liability system be reformed in other ways? If so, how would you change the system?

deer and monkeys are wild animals capable of being domesticated. In many states the legislatures have enacted special statutes which hold an owner strictly liable for injuries from a dog, regardless of the owner's knowledge or prior warning.

In most states, the owner of an animal that is likely to roam and injure the person or property of another is liable without fault for damages inflicted when the animal enters upon another's land. Such animals include cattle, horses, sheep, hogs, turkeys, chickens, and most wild animals, since their natural tendency is to escape.

In an action for injuries inflicted by an animal, the defendant may assert assumption of risk as a defense. If the plaintiff voluntarily exposed himself or herself to a known risk, such as teasing a pet leopard, the owner is not liable. To avoid liability for a vicious watchdog, a landowner must post *adequate warnings* of the dog's presence. A "Beware of Dog" sign may not be adequate to warn someone that the dog is vicious and not just a dog that barks at people. In most states the defendant is not allowed to assert contributory negligence as a defense, but comparative negligence is applied in some states.

SUMMARY

Negligence is the failure to exercise due care when there is a foreseeable risk of harm to others. In order to recover damages in a lawsuit for negligence, the plaintiff must prove four elements: (1) the defendant owed a duty of care to the plaintiff; (2) the defendant failed to exercise due care; (3) the defendant's negligence was the cause of the plaintiff's injury; and (4) the plaintiff suffered actual loss or damage. A duty of care arises when one should foresee that his or her conduct will create an unreasonable risk of harm to others. Whether the defendant has exercised due care is determined by comparing the defendant's behavior to the applicable standard of care. The defendant will be held liable if his or her conduct fails to comply with the reasonable person standard or a higher level of care imposed on professionals. Two major procedural doctrines assist the plaintiff in proving that the defendant was negligent. Negligence per se permits use of the defendant's unexcused violation of a criminal statute to establish negligence. *Res ipsa loquitur* is used when there is no direct evidence of the defendant's negligence but there is circumstantial evidence from which an inference of negligence can be drawn.

The plaintiff must also prove that he or she suffered damages and that the defendant's negligent conduct caused his or her injuries. Causation means that the defendant's negligence was an actual and proximate cause of the plaintiff's injury. Actual cause is determined by applying the "but for" test or the substantial factor test for concurring causes. Proximate cause is a limitation on the defendant's liability based on foreseeability.

In a few states, contributory negligence is a defense in a lawsuit for negligence. Comparative negligence, in either the pure or the modified form, is provided in the great majority of states and has largely replaced contributory negligence. Assumption of risk, either express or implied, is another defense.

There are three major areas of liability without fault or strict liability: liability for injuries by animals, liability for injuries from abnormally dangerous activities, and strict products liability. In a strict liability lawsuit a business seller is liable for the personal injuries or property damage caused by its defective products. The defendant may assert the defense of assumption of risk and unforeseeable misuse in a products liability action.

REVIEW QUESTIONS

1. List the four elements of a cause of action for negligence.

2. How is the duty of care related to the concept of foreseeability?

3. Explain the reasonable prudent person standard.

4. Why is it necessary for the plaintiff to have expert testimony in a professional negligence suit?

5. Explain the doctrines of negligence per se and *res ipsa loquitur*.

6. How is liability for negligent misrepresentation different from liability for fraud?

7. Explain the purpose of proximate cause.

8. Explain the difference between contributory negligence and assumption of risk.

9. From a policy perspective, which of the various forms of comparative negligence is the best? Why?

10. Explain the social policies behind strict products liability and liability for abnormally dangerous activities.

CASE PROBLEMS

1. In 1985, Jane Doe purchased a house from Lindner Construction in a "planned unit development." There were several unsolved problems with the house at closing, and so the realtor put them on a "punch list" of items to be corrected. The realtor retained a key to Jane Doe's unit after the closing to allow workers access to the unit to correct these problems. A short time after Jane moved into the house, the problems were rectified, but the realtor retained a key to her unit. The key was kept in a box in an unlocked closet in the office of the development. The office was kept locked at night, but other persons had access to the office during the day. One of those individuals was Samuel Carpenter, who was hired by Lindner Construction as an independent contractor to perform wallpapering and painting. Carpenter had problems with alcohol, including three DUI convictions. When he was working in the office, Carpenter took one of the keys to the office several months before October of 1986. On October 9, 1986, Carpenter entered the office using the stolen key and took the pass key for Jane Doe's house. He and his cousin entered Doe's house and raped her. Jane Doe sued Lindner Construction and the realtor for negligence in the handling of the pass key and employment of Carpenter. Who will likely win the case? Why?

2. Julie Bowen went to the office of attorney David Arnold to discuss dissolution of her 11-year marriage to Ronald Bowen. Arnold explained dissolution procedures generally and discussed discovery devices available. About 2 months later Julie returned to Arnold's office with her husband, who was not represented by a lawyer. Ronald presented a written settlement proposal which gave Julie 12 percent of his 91.8 percent ownership in his landscaping business, Prairie Restorations. Ronald valued the business at $60,000. Julie received other assets in return for relinquishing her interest in the business. Arnold told her that in a contested proceeding she could receive anywhere from 0 to 50 percent of the value of her husband's interest in the business. He also told her that he did not have enough information to verify Ronald's valuation and that an independent appraisal could be performed. Julie said that she trusted her husband's valuation and declined to order an appraisal. Ronald offered to make his financial records available but Arnold did not ask to see them. Following court approval of the settlement and dissolution, Julie remarried. She later filed a legal malpractice action against Arnold, alleging that he was negligent in not conducting discovery and not informing himself and Julie completely and accurately of the financial assets of the couple. Julie's expert witness testified that the value of Prairie Restorations at the time of settlement was $103,447. Arnold's expert witness testified it was worth $48,740. **(a)** What standard of care should be used by the judge or jury to determine liability? **(b)** Who do you think should win the lawsuit?

3. Terri Ann Saucier was in the Winn-Dixie food store walking toward checkout counter number 8 when she slipped on a milk puddle. She lost her balance and fell to the floor, injuring her lower back. Witnesses testified that a few small milk puddles of 2 or 3 inches in diameter pooled in the aisles near the checkout counter. No one saw the milk before the accident and the exact length of time that the milk remained on the floor could not be determined. Winn-Dixie testified that the entire store was swept and mopped each morning before opening. Cleaning during the day was performed on an "as needed" basis. There were no periodic inspections for spills or other hazards, but all thirty-five employees were instructed to be on the lookout for dangerous conditions. Saucier sued Winn-Dixie for negligence and received a jury verdict of $20,000. Should this award be upheld?

4. Avis left a rental car unattended in the parking lot at the Miami International Airport with the key in the ignition, the door open, and the car lights flashing. The car was subsequently stolen. The thief operated the car negligently and collided with a car driven by Charlie Vining, severely injuring him. The area around the airport had the highest incidence of auto theft in Dade County. Avis had vehicles stolen in the past. Vining sued Avis for negligence. The trial court dismissed the complaint, stating that even if Avis were negligent it was not liable because the criminal act of stealing the car broke the chain of causation. Is Avis's negligence the proximate cause of Vining's injuries?

5. Moughon was driving her car to the repair shop. As she came around a curve, the car went up over the right curb and out of control, and then came back into the street and across the center line into the left lane, where it collided with Wolf's car. Wolf sued Moughon, alleging negligence per se in failing to keep her vehicle on the right side of the road in violation of a Texas statute. Moughon claimed unavoidable accident and testified that she had her brakes repaired 2 days before and that when she drove the car home the vehicle would pull to the right each time she applied the brakes. Who should win the lawsuit?

6. Koos produced grass seed on 55 acres of land. After the seed was harvested, Koos and a crew equipped with mobile water trucks burned the field by setting fire to dry straw. They first plowed a protective strip around the perimeter. While the field was being burned, Roth's adjoining field caught fire, causing $8,000 of damage. No one saw how the fire on Roth's property started, but witnesses stated that probably a whirlwind carried burning material from Koos's field. Roth sued, and Koos defended that he should not be liable for an unintentional and nonnegligent injury to Roth's property. Who should win the lawsuit?

7. On October 28, 1981, John Hinman, a mail carrier, noticed a large dog barking at him from across the street. Suddenly, another dog owned by Reid Alter came running toward Hinman "flying through the air." The dog "ran" past Hinman without touching him, but it caused Hinman to spin around, and he suffered a back injury from the encounter. A witness likened the scene from the cartoon Blondie and Dagwood. Hinman sued Alter under a statute imposing strict liability on the owner of an attacking dog that read as follows:

If a dog, without provocation, attacks or injures any person who is acting peaceably in any place where the person may lawfully be, the owner of the dog is liable in damages to the person so attacked or injured.

Should the owner be liable to Hinman for his injuries? Explain.

CHAPTER 8

Competitive Torts and Intellectual Property

The American concept of free enterprise is woven into the fabric of our economic life. By inspiring innovation and efficiency, competition enhances our standard of living and strengthens our economy. But competition also invites unethical or illegal practices which could, unless restrained, stifle lawful business and harm the general public. In this chapter we consider a basic restraint—the law of **competitive torts**, which forbids wrongful interferences with commercial or business rights.[1]

This chapter also considers the protection of intellectual property such as trade secrets, patents, copyrights, and trademarks. Intellectual property is an important asset because it gives the owner a competitive advantage in the marketplace. The wrongful appropriation of another's intellectual property is a competitive tort.

COMPETITIVE TORTS

In our free enterprise economy, a businessperson or firm is not liable for economic harm to competitors caused by legitimate price and product competition. The law of competitive torts provides a remedy only when the business methods or practices are "unfair" or "improper." What is unfair depends upon society's judgment as to the propriety of particular business practices, a judgment that will change over time as society's ethical and social norms evolve.

In balancing the conflicting interests of competitors in the marketplace, however, the law provides adequate room for aggressive competition. Thus, manufacturers and other sellers can lawfully compete by improving their products, promoting their sale, and building customer satisfaction and brand loyalty. On the other hand, courts routinely provide a remedy when a business engages in fraudulent marketing as by adopting a product name so similar to one already used by a competitor that a purchaser cannot easily distinguish between the products of the two companies. Thus, the manufacturer of "M & M" candies has a legal remedy if a competitor markets a similarly packaged candy under the name "M & N." Such deceptive marketing of goods harms not only the manufacturer, but also consumers who are misled as to the maker of the candy. Society has a substantial interest in preventing such harmful practices and thereby maintaining free and fair competition in the marketplace.

---

[1] Government regulation of the marketplace under the antitrust laws, laws that are also designed to ensure fair competition, are discussed in Chapters 52 and 53. Laws protecting consumers from unfair marketplace practices are discussed in Chapter 49.

Competitive torts fall within the broader term "unfair competition," a topic too extensive for one chapter. So, excluded from our discussion are such obviously improper acts as harassing a competitor's customers, blocking the ingress or egress of a competitor's delivery trucks, and paying a competitor's employees to commit sabotage. This section focuses instead on four broad categories of competitive torts:

- Wrongful entry into business
- Interference with business relations
- Defamation and disparagement
- Unfair trade practices

Wrongful Entry into Business

It is a cardinal principle of American free society that, in general, a person may engage in any business he or she chooses and may compete with other businesses for customers. Unless a new enterprise stoops to improper business practices, it is not required to account for the losses it inflicts on a competitor because of the new enterprise's products. However, statutes and the common law restrict the right to engage in a particular business, trade, or profession. For example, under the common law, a person cannot engage in a business solely to drive someone out of business or inflict harm on another. The seminal case is *Tuttle v. Buck*,[2] a case in which the plaintiff, a barber, sued a wealthy banker who allegedly opened a competing barbershop for the sole purpose of ruining the plaintiff's business and driving him out of town. The Minnesota Supreme Court held that the complaint stated a legitimate basis for suit—i.e., that the defendant's actions in maliciously entering the trade constituted a tort for which the plaintiff could recover damages. Thus, when a person enters a particular trade or business not for economic reasons, but rather to inflict harm on another, this constitutes a tort—i.e., the wrongful entry into business.

Statutes, too, may limit entry into a business or profession. For example, governmental units often grant exclusive franchises to individuals or firms, such as the right to operate a railroad line or broadcasting station. Any attempt by another person to invade such an exclusive right is subject to a restraining order and a fine, and possibly to a judgment for damages.

Similarly, state statutes may restrict entry into a business or a profession by requiring applicants to meet specific qualifications or be approved by an examining board. For example, proof of qualification is required before someone can practice medicine or law, or become a real estate broker, security salesman, or electrical contractor. Ordinarily, it is the state's responsibility to take corrective action against a person who does business without the requisite license. However, many courts permit a licensed member of a profession to bring an action on behalf of the entire protected group to restrain a person who wrongfully attempts to enter the field.

Interference with Business Relations

People use *contracts* to establish their understandings when they make a business deal. If you offer to buy my stereo for $400 and I say yes, we have a contract. You and I are the "parties" to the contract. It gives each of us an expectation of the promised performance. Under the law of contracts and sales (discussed in Chapters 10–22), if either of us fails to perform ("breaches" the contract), the other has a right to sue for the resulting damages. The right of one party to sue the other for breach is called an "action in contract."

This action in contract—this dispute between the immediate contracting parties—is *not* the subject of this chapter. Rather, the focus here is on interference *by outsiders* with the contractual relationship between you and me, either during the process of our *making* the contract or during the process of *performing* it after it is made. The right to make a contract and to have it performed is necessary to the orderly conduct of business affairs, so much so, in fact, that the law provides tort protection against outsiders who improperly interfere with other people's contracts.

Intentional Interference with a Prospective Economic Advantage. The tort of **intentional interference with a prospective economic**

[2] 119 N.W. 946 (1909).

advantage is committed when a person intentionally and improperly causes another not to enter into a contract with a third party—i.e., interferes with the *making* of a contract. The tort imposes liability for intentional interference if the parties *were actually* negotiating for a contract, or even before negotiations if there was a potential economic or business relationship between the parties.

The interference must be intentional and "improper"—i.e., without legal justification or privilege. An improper interference occurs when (1) the methods used are not within the privilege of fair competition, as is illustrated in Case 8.1, or (2) the purpose or motive is malicious or improper. As was said by the court in *Herron v. State Farm Mutual Ins. Co.*, "Whether an intentional interference by a third party is justifiable depends upon a balancing of the importance, social and private, of the objective advanced by the interference against the importance of the interest interfered with, *considering all circumstances* including the nature of the actor's conduct and the relationship between the parties."[3]

If an inducement not to engage in a contract serves a legitimate end and no improper means is used (e.g., the interference was neither unjustified nor illegal), the action is said to be justifiable or privileged, and there is no tort. Competition carried on in an *acceptable manner* between businesses may cause one of them not to receive an expected contract with a third person. Under that circumstance, the interference with the making of the contract is simply a common instance of a *privileged interference*. Thus, a manufacturer may with impunity offer a better price discount to induce a retailer to buy its merchandise rather than the products of a competitor. The competitor who loses business as a result cannot successfully complain that this was an improper interference with an economic advantage.

Refusals to deal. What of the situation where a person seeks to purchase from someone who simply refuses to sell? Such an occurrence, although technically not an interference with the

---

[3] 56 Cal. 2d 202, 206 (1961).

> **BOX 8.1**
>
> ### Law in Practice
>
> In 1979, George and Jermine Wing built a house on property they owned near Story, Wyoming. They put the property up for sale and placed a "For Sale" sign in the front yard. In April of 1980, Mr. and Mrs. Charles Thomson made an offer to buy the house, but the sale was not completed when the Thomsons were unable to sell their home. Several months later, the Thomsons raised enough money to buy the property and prepared a purchase agreement. Before signing the agreement, they traveled to the property to inspect it. During the inspection, they were approached by the neighbors, Paul and Carolyn Martin. The Martins told the Thomsons that they intended to put up a steel building next to the property; that the property flooded; that the septic system was not approved; and that the property was not accessible during the winter. The steel building was constructed, but the other information was not accurate. As a result of the Martins' statements, however, the Thomsons made no offer to buy the property.
>
> The Wings sued the Martins for intentional interference with an economic advantage. What will be the likely outcome? Would the result be different if the information about the property was true?

making of a contract, is so closely akin to it that its brief consideration is appropriate here. Although as a general rule, an individual is free to choose whether to sell or not to sell his or her products, this freedom is sometimes curtailed. A statute, such as the Civil Rights Act of 1964, or a public utility franchise, may require that a company serve the public without discrimination. Also, if a refusal to sell is for the purpose of creating an illegal monopoly, the refusal is improper. Moreover, although an individual acting alone may be privileged to refuse to deal with another, under certain circumstances the refusal is tortious because it is part of a concerted effort with others (a conspiracy). Thus, firms Ace Tire

Co., Bill's Tire Co., and Carolina Tire Co., acting *independently of one another*, legally may refuse to deal with the Southern Tire Co.; but if the three firms enter into an agreement not to deal with Southern in order to force it out of business or to force it into a price combine, the refusal to deal constitutes a business tort.

Intentional Interference with a Contract. An outsider's interfering with the performance of a contract already in existence constitutes the tort of **intentional interference with a contract.** Any intentional and improper interference which prevents performance of a contract between others makes performance more expensive or burdensome, or otherwise causes a breach of contract, entitling an injured plaintiff to damages.

Inducing a breach of contract is the most common form of the tort of intentional interference with a contract. An individual who intentionally induces a breach of contract is liable if the following conditions are present:

- A contract existed.
- The individual knew of the existence of the contract and intended to bring about its breach.
- The individual's conduct caused a breach of contract.
- The breach was the proximate result of the plaintiff's damages.
- The individual's conduct was "improper" (not privileged or justified).

An example is the attempted takeover of Getty Oil Company by Pennzoil Company during the 1980s. In 1984, Pennzoil offered to buy Getty, and Getty's board of directors accepted the offer. Representatives of both companies shook hands and toasted the agreement with champagne. However, before their agreement was signed, Texaco, Inc., offered Getty a higher price. Getty's directors accepted Texaco's offer and did not follow through with the Pennzoil agreement. Pennzoil sued Texaco for improper interference with its contract with Getty. In 1986, a Texas jury found that Getty and Pennzoil had entered into a contract and that Texaco, with knowledge of the contract, had intentionally caused its breach. The jury awarded Pennzoil $10.53 billion against Texaco, $7.53 billion in compensatory and $3 billion in punitive damages. The court of appeals upheld the judgment but reduced the punitive damages by $2 billion and the Texas Supreme Court held there was no reversible error. Texaco subsequently paid Pennzoil $3 billion in settlement of the judgment.

The courts do not require that the outsider cause a *breach* of an enforceable contract to be liable for the tort of interference with a contract. Even if a contract provides that it is terminable at the will (i.e., at the election) of the parties to it, a third person is not privileged, without justification, intentionally to induce a termination of the contract. The law is designed to prevent the wrongful *interference* with the contractual relationship between two parties, regardless of the type of contract that they have entered into.

The discussion of the requirement of "improper" interference and the factors used to determine whether there was legal justification or privilege with respect to interfering with an economic advantage are generally applicable to the tort of interference with a contract. However, although bona fide competition furnishes a legal justification for interfering with the *creation* of a contract, it does *not* furnish legal justification for inducing *breach* of a contract. The following case makes clear that the right to compete does not give license to improperly interfere with another's business relationships.

CASE 8.1 Island Air, Inc. v. LaBar • 566 P.2d 972 (Wash. App. 1977)

FACTS Island Air., Inc., operated an air service between the Anacortes Airport and the San Juan Islands in Puget Sound, transporting parcels for United Parcel Service, Inc. Its contract with UPS was terminable after 60 days' notice by either party.

Les LaBar told officers of Island Air that he was interested in purchasing the airline if he could have financial information upon which to determine Island Air's value. Island Air furnished the information, including detailed information about the airline's income from the UPS contract, with the understanding that the matters revealed were confidential; that the information would be used only to estimate Island Air's value to determine a fair purchase price; and that the information would not be used by LaBar for the purpose of competing with Island Air. LaBar used the confidential information to submit an offer to UPS to carry its parcels to the islands on more favorable terms than under Island Air's contract. When UPS canceled its contract with Island Air and entered into a new contract with LaBar, Island Air sued LaBar, claiming, among other things, that LaBar had tortiously interfered in plaintiff's business relationship with UPS. The trial court held for Island Air and LaBar appealed.

OPINION CALLOW, J. . . . Did [LaBar] tortiously interfere with the business relationship between Island Air and United Parcel Service or were the actions . . . justified as permissible competition?

[LaBar asserts] that his actions were justified because (1) the contract between [Island Air] and UPS was terminable at will; (2) UPS did not breach the contract . . . but terminated it according to its terms; [and] (3) public policy encourages and promotes competitive contract bidding. . . . We do not agree.

The fact that the contract was terminable on 60 days' written notice, and that UPS's termination . . . was in accordance with these terms, is not dispositive. Liability for the unjustifiable interference in another's commercial relations is not dependent on the existence of an enforceable contract . . . [nor does it] depend upon whether a contractual relationship was breached. . . . Further, the fact that a party's terminable at will contract is ended in accordance with its terms does not defeat the party's claim for damages caused by an unjustifiable interference. . . .

[LaBar] maintains that his conduct was purely competitive, and argues that his status as a competitor grants him an unfettered hand in the marketplace. We disagree.

We support the principles of free competition, but a claim of competition *alone* does not justify interference by a stranger to a contract. . . .

Whether or not a course of conduct will be deemed to be improper in an interference situation depends upon the facts of each case. . . . Here, the means employed by the defendant to gain a competitive advantage involved the acquisition and use of confidential information for a competitive purpose in violation of an [agreement] not to compete. Substantial evidence was presented . . . that this information was not available in the marketplace, and would not have been provided . . . had not [LaBar] agreed to use it solely for the purpose of evaluating the potential purchase of Island Air. . . . We concur in the characterization

CASE 8.1 **Continued**	of [LaBar's] acts as "improper," and adopt the reasoning expressed in *Wear-Ever Aluminum, Inc. v. Townecraft Indus. Inc.* . . . as follows: "The role of the court is to raise the standard of business morality and care, not judicially to sanction tortious activities. Higher standards benefit and protect both the innocent members of an industry and the general public. . . ."
JUDGMENT	The judgment is affirmed.

Boycotts. A seeming exception to the rule that the law looks with disfavor upon inducing a breach of contract exists when the act involves peaceful persuasion and the objective sought to be accomplished results in benefit to the public. Assume, for example, that a labor union in furtherance of a strike pickets an employer's plant. Not wanting to cross the union's picket line, Jin's Trucking Company breaches its contract with the plant. Although the union had induced that contract breach, it will not be liable in tort because it is generally recognized that the public interest in improved working conditions transcends the right of a contracting party not to have a contract interfered with by a stranger to it. However, a labor union can be restrained and even held liable in damages if its action violates the law against unfair labor practices such as engaging in a secondary boycott. A **secondary boycott** is strike activity—a form of illegal business coercion—directed at suppliers or customers of one's employer instead of solely (and legally) against the employer with whom one has a labor dispute.

Interference with Employer-Employee Relations. Interfering with employer-employee relations is an aspect of the broader competitive tort of interference with business relations. A staff of trained employees is a most important element of any successful business organization, requiring time and money to develop. If a trained employee is induced to leave a company in order to work for a competitor, the new employer may reap a considerable economic advantage. Not only will the new employer be saved the expense of training the employee but it may also "inherit" some of the other company's manufacturing processes and customers and perhaps learn something of its trade secrets. A contract of employment, therefore, represents a valuable property right. To protect that property interest, and to prevent a competitor from utilizing the trade secrets learned by an employee, employers often require employees to sign an **agreement not to compete.** Agreements not to compete in an employment contract, discussed in detail in Chapter 14, are generally enforceable, and, therefore, a business can sue a former employee who breaches the agreement by going to work for a competitor.

A business may also be able to sue a competitor that lures away an employee and thereby interferes with an existing employment contract. Inducing an employee to change employment may be a wrongful interference whether the initial employment relationship was established in writing or orally and whether the initial employment was for a specified term or at will. However, the courts give considerable weight to the economic right of an employee to pursue a higher-paying job, and courts are reluctant to hold an employer liable for interference simply because he or she hires an employee of a competitor.

The right of an employee to change jobs is not, however, a license to an employer to entice an employee away from working for a competitor for an improper purpose. If Brick Company hires the manager of Aspen Corporation, a competitor, to secure valuable trade secrets, then the pirating away of the employee is *malicious*. Under such circumstances, the new employer, Brick Company, wrongfully interfered with the preexisting employer-employee relationship and committed the tort of intentional interference with a contract.

Defamation and Disparagement

Any business is entitled to compete with other firms free from attacks on its reputation and the products it sells. This part of the chapter deals with competitive torts involving (1) defamation of a business firm's reputation and (2) disparagement of its property.

Defamation of Business Reputation. When a derogatory statement impugns the reputation of a businessperson or firm, such as a corporation or a partnership, a suit can be brought for **defamation,** a tort whose elements were discussed in Chapter 6. Defamation of a business occurs when an unprivileged statement adversely affects the credit rating of a businessperson or firm or otherwise attacks the honesty or character of the business. For example, if a credit bureau, in response to a request from one of its members, sends a report erroneously indicating that a company is in bankruptcy, this constitutes defamation.

In a case of business defamation, the defendant has all the defenses which may be used in a suit involving personal defamation. Therefore, truth and the defenses of absolute or qualified privilege may be asserted. Thus, in the above example, the credit bureau may claim a qualified privilege to provide information to its members. As you recall, a qualified privilege exists when information is being communicated in good faith for a legitimate business purpose. If the credit bureau acted in good faith, believing that the company was in bankruptcy, and published it only to the firm that requested the credit report, it will establish a qualified privilege. If, however, it circulates the derogatory report indiscriminately, or knowing that the information was false, the defense of privilege would not be established.

Disparagement of Business Property. A distinct tort which is related to defamation is **disparagement,** or what is sometimes called "injurious falsehood." Whereas defamation damages a firm's interest in its reputation, disparagement damages a business's interest in the economic value of its products and property. The tort of disparagement includes the common law torts of slander of title and slander of quality (usually called trade libel).

Slander of title. This tort involves the unprivileged publication of untrue matter which casts doubt upon, or denies, the validity of another's title or interest in any kind of property and the publication causes financial loss. Slander of title involves actions such as wrongfully filing for record a mortgage or claim of lien upon the property; wrongfully asserting that a third person has some interest in the property; wrongfully stating that the owner of the property cannot legally deliver its possession to another; or, in bad faith, claiming that use of a competitor's product will result in a patent infringement suit.

Slander of quality. Slander of quality, or trade libel, is the unprivileged publication of false matter which indicates that another's property lacks the *characteristics* its vendor claims for it or which indicates that the property is unfit for the purposes for which it is being sold or leased. This tort is akin to slander of title, but here the financial loss is caused by belittling the *quality* of another's property, rather than the *title* to it. Slander of title always involves a statement of fact, but trade libel may be either a false statement of fact or a dishonest expression of opinion made in such circumstances that the vendibility of the property will probably be diminished.

It is possible for a single improper publication to constitute both a trade libel and a defamation. Such a situation would exist, for instance, when the statement not only disparages the quality of an article but also reflects upon the honesty of the owner or storekeeper who offers it for sale. But the two torts are different. Disparagement requires the plaintiff to prove a false, injurious statement, while defamation places the burden of proving truth on the defendant as a defense to liability. Also, the courts generally require the plaintiff in a disparagement case to prove *special damages,* economic losses caused by the disparaging statements. In some cases of defamation, the jury is allowed to presume damages to reputation caused by a plaintiff's derogatory statements.

Defenses against Disparagement of Property. Just as privilege is a defense in actions for defamation, it is a defense in actions for disparagement of property. For example, a qualified privilege exists when the publication is made in a reasonable manner or, as many courts say, without malice, and to satisfy a purpose which the law recognizes as justifiable. For example, in a dispute over the title to an automobile, if one of the parties claims title to the vehicle honestly believing it to be his or hers, a qualified privilege can be asserted in a slander of title suit. Another example of a qualified privilege are statements touting a seller's products that may implicitly attack the quality of a competitor's products. Although a seller may exaggerate the benefits of his or her merchandise, even to claiming that it is "the world's best" (known as "puffing"), no *untruthful direct attack* may be made on another's wares. Thus, the Emerald Soap Co. may advertise that its soap washes clothes brighter and cleaner than any other soap even though that statement impliedly disparages the soap manufactured by other companies. However, Emerald is not privileged untruthfully to say, "Our soap washes clothes brighter and cleaner than X's because their soap does not dissolve in water."

Unfair Trade Practices

Unfair trade practices encompass all interferences with the right of a business to enjoy its goodwill and other trade advantages it possesses. Unfair trade practices take many forms. Among them are fraudulent marketing and wrongfully imitating a company's product design or packaging. A person injured by an unfair trade practice has a number of remedies. He or she can sue under the common law of unfair competition or seek a civil remedy under state or federal unfair trade practices statutes.

The Common Law of Unfair Competition— Palming Off. The term **palming off** refers primarily to falsifying the source or maker of a product or service. By misrepresenting the maker of a product, a business can "pass off" inferior goods to a purchaser. For example, suppose a store displays the sign "Arrow Shirts" above a stack of shirts on a counter in such a way as to indicate that all the shirts in the pile are Arrow brand, but actually only one or two are Arrow shirts and the rest are an inferior brand. If a purchaser buys one of the inferior shirts believing it to be an Arrow brand, the store has engaged in unfair competition. By palming off the shirts, the store harms the consumer, who overpays for an inferior product, and Arrow, which loses sales—and reputation if

---

BOX 8.2

Point to Consider

During a drought in 1981, sales of bottled water increased in Milltown, New Jersey. The local newspaper, owned by the Sentinel Publishing Company, published several articles written by Kathleen Dzielak about the water shortage and the bottled water industry. Dzielak tried to learn the source of the spring water sold by Dairy Stores, Inc., which was bottled by Krauszer's Dairy, Inc., but Krauszer's declined to provide the information. She took a bottle of the water to several laboratories for testing, one of which reported the presence of chlorine. The paper ran a story under the headline, "Spring water/Independent lab analysis casts doubt on content." The article quoted the director of the Paterson Clinical Laboratory as stating, "I can't see how it could possibly be spring water unless the spring source was contaminated and chlorine was added at the source." Krauszer's contended that chlorine was not added to the water and that the water came from springs. It sued the *Sentinel*, Dzielak, and the laboratory for defamation.

Is this lawsuit for defamation or disparagement? Should the law recognize a First Amendment privilege, as with defamation, for disparaging statements by the media about a company's products? If so, should a First Amendment privilege extend to nonmedia persons, such as the testing lab in the above case or to consumer testing agencies like Consumers Union, the publisher of *Consumer Reports*?

consumers erroneously associate the inferior shirts with the company.

Another method of "palming off" is for a competitor to imitate the name, physical appearance, or packaging of a product. By imitating the form or style of another's product or its distinctive wrapping, a competitor may be able to pass off its goods to unsuspecting consumers. But, in order to retain the public benefit which free competition offers, the law allows considerable latitude to business concerns to copy the styles and designs of their competitors as long as no consumer deception occurs. Unless a product or its design is protected under a patent or a copyright, competitors are generally free to imitate the physical appearance of the product. Although the copying and sale of a product may economically harm the maker, the courts generally will neither restrain nor cause the imitator to respond in damages as long as the imitator (1) does not resort to unfair methods in securing the copy (e.g., stealing the trade secret for a product) or (2) does not make the imitation so similar to the original that the public would be misled as to the source of the article.

Assume that the Beacon Company makes a very popular flashlight, the "Apollo," that is not patented. The Nite-Light Company copies Beacon's design and sells an identical flashlight at a lower price. Nite-Lite uses its own brand name, "Right-Lite," on the package and product. Nite-Lite's imitation is probably lawful because consumers are not being misled as to the maker of the product. Had Nite-Lite adopted a similar brand name (e.g., the "Apolla") or imitated the packaging or other attributes of the product in a way to cause consumer confusion as to source, "palming off" may have occurred.

State Unfair Competition Laws and the Lanham Act. To protect consumers and competitors from unfair trade practices, many states have adopted **unfair competition laws** which prohibit unfair and deceptive marketing, promotional, and sales practices, including false or deceptive advertising. An example is the Uniform Deceptive Trade Practices Act, which has been adopted by twelve states. The Act provides a civil remedy in the form of *injunctive relief* and an award of costs and attorney's fees to competitors injured by false advertising and other deceptive practices. Other states allow civil *damage suits* by competitors and consumers injured by deceptive or unfair trade practices. The North Carolina law, discussed in Case 8.2, like statutes in several states, provides a treble (triple) damage remedy for unfair trade practices.

At the federal level, competitors injured by false advertising or unfair trade practices can bring civil actions under Section 43(a) of the **Lanham Act.** The Act, which also provides trademark protection, has become a broad, national unfair competition law. It provides a civil remedy for a firm injured by a competitor's false advertising or "palming off" of goods—up to three times the amount of actual damages proved.

BOX 8.3

The Lanham Act Section 43(a)

Any person who, on or in connection with any goods or services, or any container for goods, uses in commerce any word, term, name, symbol, or device, or any combination thereof, or any false designation of origin, false or misleading description of fact, or false or misleading representation of fact, which—

(1) is likely to cause confusion, or to cause mistake, or to deceive as to the affiliation, connection, or association of such person with another person, or as to the origin, sponsorship, or approval of his or her goods, services, or commercial activities by another person, or

(2) in commercial advertising or promotion, misrepresents the nature, characteristics, qualities, or geographic origin of his or her or another person's goods, services, or commercial activities

—shall be liable in a civil action by any person who believes that he or she is or is likely to be damaged by such act.

A business injured by the false advertising of a competitor has a remedy under Section 43(a). Traditionally, a person could bring a false advertising suit under the Lanham Act only when a firm falsely represented its own products. False statements about a competitor's products were not covered by the law. However, as amended, the Act now imposes civil liability on any person who uses any false or misleading representation of fact about "his or her or another person's" goods, services, or commercial activities. Also, in enforcing the Act civilly, the courts usually limited injured competitors to an injunction. Increasingly, however, the courts have awarded substantial money damages to firms injured by false advertising campaigns by competitors. For example, U-Haul International, the truck rental company, recovered $40 million from Jartran, a competitor, as damages in connection with a false price-advertising campaign by Jartran. The trial court found actual damages of $20 million and doubled the judgment amount.

Section 43(a) also provides a remedy for trade dress infringement. **Trade dress** refers to the combination of design elements that make up the total image of a business and the overall appearance of its products or services. It includes such features as the size, shape, color, and texture of a product. A competitor which imitates a firm's trade dress in such a way that the two products are confusingly similar may be liable for infringement. So, for example, in *Two Pesos, Inc. v. Taco Cabana, Inc.*,[4] the Supreme Court upheld a jury's conclusion that Taco Cabana had infringed the trade dress of Two Pesos, a Mexican restaurant chain, by intentionally copying the interior design and layout of the chain's restaurants.

Case 8.2 illustrates a suit for unfair competition under state law. It also addresses the difficult issue of computing damages for unfair trade practices.

[4]112 S. Ct. 2753 (1992).

CASE 8.2	**Polo Fashions, Inc. v. Craftex, Inc.** • 816 F.2d 145 (4th Cir. 1987)
FACTS	Polo Fashions, Inc., the plaintiff, is a well-known distributor of clothing for men and women designed by Ralph Lauren. The company uses the trade names POLO and RALPH LAUREN. Either name appears on labels affixed at the back of the neck of each garment. Plaintiff also embroiders on the breast of its knitted sport shirts a fanciful representation of a polo player mounted on a horse. Defendant, Craftex, Inc., manufactures knitted sport shirts. During 1982 and 1983 the company manufactured and the defendants sold 1,388 dozen knitted sport shirts bearing an embroidered emblem substantially identical to the plaintiff's polo player symbol. Craftex attached inside the back of the neck of each shirt a label bearing the words Knight of Armor. Plaintiff filed action against the defendants alleging, among other causes of action, common law trademark infringement and unfair competition. The district court found that the defendants made a profit of $14,837.72 in the manufacture and sale of the sport shirts and that the plaintiff had suffered damages in that amount. The court then tripled the damages under North Carolina's Unfair Trade Practices Act and the defendants appealed.
OPINION	HAYNSWORTH, CIR. J. . . . The North Carolina common law of unfair competition in the context of trademarks and trade names is similar to the federal law of trademark infringement. Unfair acts of a defendant are actionable when they damage a plaintiff's legitimate business. . . . Such damages are suffered when a rival adopts for his own goods a sign or symbol in an apparent imitation

**CASE 8.2
Continued**

of another's that would likely mislead prospective purchasers and the public as to the identity of the goods. . . . Such damage was suffered by the plaintiff in this case when the defendants placed on the market demonstrably inferior goods bearing the polo player symbol.

The North Carolina unfair trade practices statute prohibits unfair methods of competition and unfair or deceptive acts or practices. . . . As used in the statute, the words "unfair methods of competition" have not been precisely defined by the North Carolina courts, although it has been suggested that they encompass any conduct that a court of equity would consider unfair. . . . A practice is unfair if it is unethical or unscrupulous, and it is deceptive if it has a tendency to deceive. . . .

The defendants contend, however, that there is no likelihood of confusion because of a label affixed inside the back of the neck of each shirt bearing the words Knight of Armor. The plaintiffs never used such a mark as Knight of Armor, but even the most sophisticated purchaser, seeing the polo player symbol on the front of the shirt, might suppose the plaintiff had adopted another trademark in addition to POLO, RALPH LAUREN and POLO BY RALPH LAUREN. Moreover, in the after sale context, one seeing the shirt being worn by its owner would not see the label on the back of the neck. Seeing the polo player symbol, it is likely that the observer would identify the shirt with the plaintiff, and the plaintiff's reputation would suffer damage if the shirt appeared to be of poor quality. . . .

On the facts of this case we think that the likelihood of confusion was so unassailably established as to warrant the district court's entry of summary judgment for the plaintiff as to liability. . . .

It cannot be said that the defendants' infringement caused the plaintiff to lose the sales of the number of shirts sold by the defendants. Nor can it be said that the plaintiff lost sales equivalent to the total dollar sales of the shirts by the defendants. The retail price of plaintiff's shirts was several times the retail price at which the defendants' goods were sold. It is more than likely that some buyers of the defendants' shirts would not have been willing to pay the higher price necessary to purchase one of the plaintiff's shirts. That the plaintiff's sales were adversely affected, however, can hardly be denied . . . plaintiff's damages should be limited to the defendants' profits, and that is what was done. The district court properly . . . trebled that amount under the North Carolina statute. . . .

JUDGMENT Affirmed.

INTELLECTUAL PROPERTY

The intellectual property of a business is generally understood to mean its trademarks, trade names, patents, copyrights, and trade secrets. The misappropriation of a firm's intellectual property is a type of unfair competition and a competitive tort. Why intellectual property is so protected can be seen from the following discussion of trademarks, copyrights, patents, and trade secrets.

Trademarks

Trademarks—any word, symbol, device, or design adopted and placed on an article offered for

Table 8.1 Concept Summary: Competitive Torts

Tort	Nature of Tort
Wrongful entry into business	Malicious or illegal entry into business or profession
Intentional interference with prospective economic advantage	Wrongful interference by an outsider with a person's right to enter into a contract with a third party
Intentional interference with a contract	Wrongful interference by an outsider with a person's right to performance under a contract
Defamation	Unprivileged statement attacking the honesty or character of a person
Disparagement	Unprivileged statement attacking a person's title to property or the quality of his or her goods and services
Palming off	Misrepresentation of the source or producer of a product to pass off inferior goods to consumers
False advertising (Lanham Act)	False or misleading statement of fact in commercial advertising or promotion that misrepresents the person's or another person's goods or services
Trade dress infringement (Lanham Act)	Imitation of the overall appearance of a person's products or services that is likely to confuse consumers as to source

sale, or on its container, to identify its source—are governed by the common law and the Lanham Act, the federal trademark registration statute. Trademarks are an integral part of a firm's strategy to differentiate its products and services from other competitors and to establish consumer brand loyalty. A trademark belongs to the firm that first adopts and uses it. Its owner is protected from **infringement,** use by someone else without permission.

Registration. Trademark registration under the Lanham Act is optional. If a trademark is not registered, the owner has a property right known as a **common law trademark.** A common law trademark is protected from infringement, under both state law and Section 43(a) of the Lanham Act. But in order for the trademark owner to receive maximum protection, the mark must be registered. Registration of a trademark under the Lanham Act extends its geographical reach nationally, furnishes proof of the date its use began, and provides the owner with statutory remedies for infringement that supplement those of the common law. It is "prima facie evidence" (presumptive evidence) of the registrant's exclusive right to use the mark in commerce which becomes "incontestable" 5 years after registration and continuous use by the owner. Incontestability means that the registrant's exclusive right to use the mark cannot generally be challenged by others.

To register, a person using a trademark or having a legitimate intent to use a mark in the future files an application with the Patent and Trademark Office. It is examined by the office, published, and unless a timely objection is filed, a certificate is issued. It is effective for 10 years and may be renewed for an unlimited number of additional 10 year periods.

Types of Marks. The Lanham Act provides for the registration of service marks, certification marks, and collective marks. **Service marks** are marks that identify a service (rather than a product) of a firm such as "Holiday Inn," "Century 21" (realtors), and "Lucky" (grocery stores). A **certification mark** indicates that the goods meet the quality standards of the mark's owner (e.g., "UL" for Underwriters Laboratories' safety standards for consumer products) or the geographic origin of the goods ("Roquefort" for sheep milk's cheese cured in the caves of Roquefort, France). A **collective mark** is a mark that is adopted by an organization to identify the product or services of its members (e.g., the collective service mark "PGA" of the Professional Golfers Association). A **trade name,** the organizational name for a business, such as International Business Machines or Kellogg Company, cannot be registered under the Lanham Act.[5] A business is protected from infringement of its trade name under the law of unfair competition.

Requirement of Distinctiveness. Not every word or name that a company uses to identify its products can be protected as a trademark. A mark must be **distinctive** in order to be protected. Place or personal names, or words normally descriptive of an article or of its use generally, may not be trademarked, as such words should be available to anyone. Thus, a **descriptive** term, describing a characteristic or ingredient of an article (e.g., "After Tan Lotion"), cannot be trademarked unless it has acquired a secondary meaning. In contrast, a **suggestive** term ("Coppertone" for suntanning lotion) suggests rather than describes a quality or characteristic of a product and can be trademarked. Similarly, an **arbitrary or fanciful** term (e.g., "Q-Tips" and "Kodak"), one that bears no relationship to the product, is inherently distinctive and can be trademarked.

Secondary Meaning. Although general words of description, geographic references, and surnames ordinarily are not "distinctive," such words can be trademarked if they have acquired a secondary meaning. A **secondary meaning** exists when a mark has been used for such a long time, or in connection with a particular producer in the trade, that in the minds of the consuming public the product is associated with that particular producer. In that event, the name has acquired a secondary meaning, and use of the name by another company would deceive the consuming public. For example, "Philadelphia Cream Cheese" and "McDonald's" have acquired a secondary meaning, because consumers associate the cream cheese product and the fast-food restaurant with a particular business. The Supreme Court has said with respect to Coca-Cola:

The name means a single thing coming from a single source, and well known to the community. . . . In other words, "Coca-Cola" probably means to most persons the plaintiff's familiar product to be had everywhere rather than a compound of particular substances. . . . [It] has acquired a secondary significance and has indicated the plaintiff's product alone.[6]

In that case, it was found that unfair competition resulted when Koke Co. used a name so similar to Coca-Cola that it would probably deceive purchasers and cause them to buy its soft drink believing it to be the "real thing."

In the case that follows, the court considers whether a particular shade of color can be trademarked if it has acquired a secondary meaning.

---

[5]A trade name can also serve as a trademark or service mark (e.g., Xerox).

[6]*Coca-Cola Co. v. Koke Co. of America*, 254 U.S. 143, 146 (1920).

CASE 8.3	**Master Distributors, Inc. v. Pako Corporation** • 986 F.2d 219 (8th Cir. 1993)
FACTS	Master Distributors, Inc. (MDI), manufactures and sells "Blue Max," a splicing tape which is used to attach undeveloped film to a leader card for photoprocessing through a minilab machine that develops the film and prints the photographs. Although leader splicing tape was traditionally black, it can be created in any color, and MDI dyed its tape blue. Blue Max is well known and enjoys a reputation as the industry standard. Both distributors and customers often order it by asking for "the blue tape" or simply for "blue." Pakor, Inc., a photographic supplies distributor, was one of MDI's distributors. When Pakor began manufacturing and selling its own brand of blue leader splicing tape, "Pakor Blue," MDI brought a lawsuit alleging, among other claims, an infringement of its common law trademark in the color blue. The trial court granted Pakor's motion for partial summary judgment dismissing MDI's claim to a trademark in the blue color of its tape. MDI appealed.
OPINION	GIBSON, J. . . . The United States Supreme Court has never expressly denied the possibility that color can be protected as a trademark. . . . In 1985, the Federal Circuit allowed Owens-Corning to register the color pink as a trademark for fibrous glass insulation. . . . [T]he court . . . concluded that color met the [Lanham] Act's definition of "trademark," and was not specifically excluded from protection. . . . [I]n the only other decision to squarely face this issue . . . the manufacturer of a sugar substitute product that was packaged in a blue, single-serving packet brought suit to enjoin another manufacturer from packaging its sugar substitute in a blue, single-serving packet. The district court [held] that color alone could not be protected [and] the Seventh Circuit affirmed. . . . We are not persuaded by the three traditional arguments against [trademark] protection [of color]—the color depletion theory, shade confusion, and the functionality doctrine. . . . Proponents of the color depletion theory assert that there are only a few possible colors a manufacturer can choose for a product, and allowing one manufacturer to monopolize a color "in all of its shades" will inhibit competition. We agree that allowing a manufacturer to monopolize red "in all of its shades" would deplete the color choices available to other market participants. Allowing a manufacturer who has met all the normal requirements for obtaining trademark protection to protect a specific shade of color, however, is another matter. . . . [A] manufacturer's mere use of a certain color will not automatically grant it proprietary rights—the manufacturer must establish all the normal requirements for trademark protection, including secondary meaning. Until secondary meaning has been established in every distinguishable shade of color and in no color at all, a highly improbable situation, there will always be an option to a new market entrant. Although protecting particular shades of color may result in some shade confusion problems, we agree that "deciding likelihood of confusion among color shades . . . is no more difficult or subtle than deciding likelihood of confusion

CASE 8.3 Continued

where word marks are involved." Triers of fact must often answer close and difficult questions, and the traditional likelihood of confusion standard should be applied to distinguish similar colors, as it is when similar slogans, symbols, numbers, or words are compared. . . . The final traditional argument—the functionality doctrine—provides that if color is essential to the utility of a product or is the natural color of the product, then no party may acquire exclusive trademark rights in that feature or color. The majority in Owens-Corning recognized that, "as with utilitarian features in general, when the color applied to goods serves a primarily utilitarian purpose, it is not subject to protection as a trademark." The functionality doctrine, therefore, is not inconsistent with protection of some color trademarks. . . .

Therefore . . . if MDI can establish all the normal trademark requirements in the blue color of its Blue Max leader splicing tape, that shade may be protected against infringement.

JUDGMENT Reversed and remanded for further proceedings.

Generic Terms. A **generic** term, one that refers to the type or class of product, cannot be registered as a trademark. So, the term "chocolate fudge" or "personal computer" cannot be trademarked. Sometimes a trademark is so commonly used to refer to a class of product that it *becomes* a generic designation for that type of article, and thus loses its distinctiveness and its trademark quality. Since the trademark no longer solely identifies a *particular* source or brand but describes the article in general, it may be used by anyone to describe the article, provided, of course, there is no attempt to palm off the new product as the original. For example, "Aspirin" was once a brand name. Today it is a generic term that any manufacturer may use to describe a pain reliever derived from salicylic acid. Similarly, the terms "thermos," "cellophane," and "toll house cookies," originally trademarks, have now become generic terms. A court has ruled, however, that "Coke" has not become a generic name applicable to all cola drinks.

Trademark Infringement. Trademark infringement occurs when there is an *intentional or unintentional* use of a trademark that is so similar to a previously established trademark of another firm that it is likely to confuse prospective purchasers as to the source of the product. In determining the likelihood of confusion, the courts look at a number of relevant factors including:

- The strength of the trademark
- The similarity between plaintiff's and defendant's marks
- The competitive closeness of their products
- The intent of the alleged infringer to pass off goods as those of the trademark holder
- The sophistication of consumers of the goods and evidence of any actual consumer confusion

The trademark owner can bring a civil suit for an injunction to stop the infringement. The trademark holder can also sue to recover the profits that the defendant derived from the infringement and up to three times the plaintiff's actual damages. Criminal sanctions may also be imposed.

Copyrights

Article I, Section 8, clause 8, of the Constitution provides that "Congress shall have the power to . . . promote the progress of sciences and useful arts, by securing for limited times to authors and inventors the exclusive right to their respective writings and discoveries." Pursuant to this grant

> **BOX 8.4**
> **Trademarks and Business Planning**
>
> What actions can a business take to ensure that its trademark does not become generic? A firm should develop a comprehensive strategy to prevent its trademark from becoming the next thermos or cellophane. Internally, a firm must educate its employees and marketers on the proper use of the company's trademark. For example, employees should be advised to use the trademark as an adjective, not as a noun (e.g., Vaseline petroleum jelly, not Vaseline) in communications and advertisements. Externally, the firm must monitor the use of its trademark by others—the media, consumers, and competitors—and take appropriate action against any infringement. The Coca-Cola Company has been very successful in its efforts to prevent its "Coke" and "Coca-Cola" trademarks from becoming generic terms. The company maintains a Trade Research Department that investigates restaurants and other businesses. Department employees will order a "Coke" at an establishment to see if the business will provide a substitute cola. If after testing a drink, the company determines that it is not Coke, it can sue for infringement. It is estimated that the company brings 30–35 of these infringement suits per year.
>
> Educating the general public on the proper use of a company's trademark may also be useful. Xerox, for example, has waged an expensive advertising campaign to persuade consumers to properly use its Xerox trademark as an adjective (Xerox copiers) and not as a verb (to xerox instead of to copy) or as a noun (xeroxes instead of copies). Whatever strategy is developed, a business should be diligent in its efforts to protect its trademarks and fully document the measures it has taken. ∎

of authority, Congress has enacted copyright laws over time, expanding the scope of copyright protection as technology changed. The present law, the Copyright Act of 1976, as amended, was also a product of international conventions on copyright protection. The law incorporates the requirements of a multilateral copyright treaty, the 1886 Berne Convention for the Protection of Literary and Artistic Works, which the United States joined on March 1, 1989.

Nature of Copyrights. Copyright law protects "original works of authorship fixed in any tangible medium of expression, now known or later developed, from which they can be perceived, reproduced, or otherwise communicated, either directly or with the aid of a machine or device." It covers books, movies, plays, musical compositions, and works of art. Computer programs are protected (see discussion in Chapter 50), and Congress recently extended protection to architectural designs.

The copyright gives the author the exclusive right to the work, its distribution or production, including any derivative works. A copyright for work created after January 1, 1978, lasts for the life of the author plus 50 years after the author's death. A **work made for hire,** a work produced by an employee for an employer or produced within the scope of his or her employment, lasts for 75 years from the date of first publication. The employer owns the copyright on a work made for hire.

To be copyrighted, a work must show certain minimum levels of *creativity* and *originality*. Copyright protection will not be granted for an abstract idea, nor can facts be copyrighted. Only the author's manner of expressing an idea or compiling the facts can be copyrighted. Case 8.4 discusses the rationale for the distinction between expression and facts.

| CASE 8.4 | **Feist Publications, Inc. v. Rural Telephone Service Company, Inc.**
•111 S. Ct. 1282 (1991) |
|---|---|

FACTS Rural Telephone Service Company is a certified public utility that provides telephone service to several communities in northwest Kansas. Rural publishes a typical telephone directory, consisting of white and yellow pages. Feist Publications, Inc., is a publishing company that specializes in areawide telephone directories. Unlike a typical directory, Feist's directories cover a much larger geographical range, reducing the need to call directory assistance or consult multiple directories.

To obtain white pages listings for its areawide directory, Feist approached each of the eleven telephone companies operating in northwest Kansas and offered to pay for the right to use its white pages listings. Of the eleven telephone companies, only Rural refused to license its listings to Feist. Unable to license Rural's white pages listings, Feist used them without Rural's consent.

Rural sued for copyright infringement, the district court granted summary judgment to Rural, and the Court of Appeals for the Tenth Circuit affirmed. The Supreme Court granted certiorari.

OPINION O'CONNOR, J. . . . This case concerns the interaction of two well-established propositions. The first is that facts are not copyrightable; the other, that compilations of facts generally are. . . .

There is an undeniable tension between these two propositions. Many compilations consist of nothing but raw data—i.e., wholly factual information not accompanied by any original written expression. On what basis may one claim a copyright in such a work? . . .

The key to resolving the tension lies in understanding why facts are not copyrightable. . . . To qualify for copyright protection, a work must be original to the author. Original, as the term is used in copyright, means only that the work was independently created by the author (as opposed to copied from other works), and that it possesses at least some minimal degree of creativity. To be sure, the requisite level of creativity is extremely low; even a slight amount will suffice. . . . Originality does not signify novelty; a work may be original even though it closely resembles other works so long as the similarity is fortuitous, not the result of copying. . . .

It is this bedrock principle of copyright that mandates the law's seemingly disparate treatment of facts and factual compilations. . . . [F]acts do not owe their origin to an act of authorship. The distinction is one between creation and discovery: the first person to find and report a particular fact has not created the fact; he or she has merely discovered its existence. . . .

Factual compilations, on the other hand, may possess the requisite originality. The compilation author typically chooses which facts to include, in what order to place them, and how to arrange the collected data. . . . These choices as to selection and arrangement, so long as they are made independently by the compiler and entail a minimal degree of creativity, are sufficiently original. . . .

This protection is subject to an important limitation. . . . [C]opyright protection may extend only to those components of a work that are original to the

**CASE 8.4
Continued**

author. . . . Others may copy the underlying facts from the publication, but not the precise words used to present them. . . .

It may seem unfair that much of the fruit of the compiler's labor may be used by others without compensation. . . . [But] the primary objective of copyright is not to reward the labor of authors, but "to promote the Progress of Science and useful Arts." To this end, copyright assures authors the right to their original expression, but encourages others to build freely upon the ideas and information conveyed by a work. This principle, known as the idea/expression or fact/expression dichotomy, applies to all works of authorship. . . . [Allowing the copying of facts] is neither unfair nor unfortunate. It is the means by which copyright advances the progress of science and art. . . .

The question . . . is whether Rural selected, coordinated, or arranged these uncopyrightable facts in an original way. . . . Rural simply takes the data provided by its subscribers and lists it alphabetically by surname. The end product is a garden-variety white pages directory, devoid of even the slightest trace of creativity. . . .

We conclude that the names, towns, and telephone numbers copied by Feist were not original to Rural and therefore were not protected by the copyright in Rural's combined white and yellow pages directory. . . .

JUDGMENT   Reversed.

Copyright Notice and Registration. For works created prior to March 1, 1989, a copyright notice was required in order to receive legal protection. This was accomplished by placing upon all publicly distributed copies of the work the word copyright, or a symbol such as ©, or an abbreviation meaning copyright; the year of first publication; and the name of the owner or an abbreviation. Under the Berne Convention and the Copyright Act, notice is no longer required. An author should, however, still include a copyright notice on his or her work. An infringer cannot rely on the defense of innocent infringement if the work has a copyright notice.

Registration of a copyright is accomplished by filing a registration form, paying a small filing fee, and depositing copies of the work with the Copyright Office in the Library of Congress. It is not necessary to register to secure copyright protection, although it is advantageous to do so. Registration is generally a prerequisite to an infringement suit and is necessary to recover attorney's fees and statutory damages.

Copyright Infringement. An infringement of a copyright occurs when a person copies the work or creates a later work that is *substantially similar* to the copyrighted work. The Copyright Act provides substantial remedies for infringement. The court may issue an injunction and order the impounding and subsequent destruction of all infringing copies made in violation of the copyright owner's exclusive rights. The owner can recover actual damages (i.e., lost profits, injury to reputation, and loss of business) and, in the court's discretion, attorney's fees. In lieu of actual damages, the owner can recover statutory damages, an amount set by the court between $200 and $100,000. A person who willfully infringes a copyright may also be subject to fine and imprisonment.

Fair Use. The Copyright Act permits a person, without the owner's consent, to copy excerpts from a copyrighted work if the copying is within the bounds of **fair use.** The rationale for the fair use doctrine is that certain uses of a copyrighted work are so important to the advancement of knowledge and the arts that they override the copyright owner's interest in the exclusive right to his work. For example, the courts often consider copying for educational, historic, or scientific purposes within fair use. Publishing excerpts from a book for purposes of scholarly criticism or news reporting, for example, is a form of fair use. The Copyright Act sets forth four factors to be considered in determining whether a use is fair:

- The purpose and character of the use, including whether the use is for commercial purposes
- The nature of the copyrighted work
- The substantiality of the portion of the work copied
- The effect on the value of and the potential market for the work

Commercial use of copyrighted material, particularly when the use has a significant impact on the market for the work, will not generally be considered fair use. For example, Kinko's was held liable for infringement when it copied excerpts from copyrighted books and combined them into course "packets" that were sold to college students. In contrast, the Supreme Court held that the personal, noncommercial use of video recording machines to record a broadcast for viewing at a later time (so-called home time-shifting) was a fair use. Noncommercial uses will not usually be considered unfair unless the copyright owner can establish that the use is harmful or adversely affects the potential market for the work.

Patents

The Constitution authorizes, and Congress has enacted, patent laws which give to inventors for an extended period of years the exclusive right to market their "brain children." By giving the inventor a monopoly for a period of years, patent law encourages the expenditure of time, energy, and resources for research, innovation, and the development of new technology. At the same time, it seeks to advance scientific knowledge.

Nature of Patents. A patent may be issued for a process (e.g., a way to bond cloth); a machine (an innovative sewing machine); a manufacture (a new toy); a composition of matter (a new plastic); a plant (a novel hybrid rose); or an ornamental design for an article of manufacture (a unique shoe design).[7] A normal patent lasts 17 years. A design patent lasts only 14 years. At the end of the patent period, the invention becomes part of the public domain. Any competitor can then copy and market the patented article.

Patentability. The requirements of patentability are more demanding than the standards for copyright protection. The invention or discovery must be **useful, novel,** and **nonobvious** (not an obvious variation of some article already known or in existence). To acquire a patent, the creator must file, within one year of the public use or publication of the invention, an application with the Patent and Trademark Office. The Patent Office determines whether the patent meets the criteria for patentability. The patent holder gives notice to the public that the article is patented by placing on it the word "Patent" (or "Pat.") and the patent number.

Patent Infringement. Patent infringement occurs when a person, without the consent of the patent owner, makes, uses, or sells a patented article within the United States during the term of the patent. In the event of a patent infringement, the patent holder may bring suit to enjoin the infringement and to recover damages. Such suits are notoriously involved and costly. Since the patent holder may be required to prove the validity of his or her patent as well as the fact of infringement, the litigation may place in jeopardy the very valuable property right that a patent represents. Therefore, not infrequently, a patent holder, instead of resorting to a lawsuit, sells to the infringer a license to use the patented product or design.

Case 8.5 is a suit for the infringement of a design patent. This decision of the Court of Appeals for the Federal Circuit is particularly important because that appellate court has exclusive jurisdiction over all appeals of patent decisions by the federal district courts.

---

[7]Under the Semiconductor Chip Protection Act of 1984, the creator of "mask work," the primary device used in the manufacture of a semiconductor chip, is given the exclusive right for 10 years to reproduce and distribute the mask or chip.

CASE 8.5 L.A. Gear, Inc. v. Thom McAn Shoe Company
• 988 F.2d 1117 (Fed. Cir. 1993)

FACTS

In 1987 L.A. Gear designed a line of women's and girls' athletic shoes identified as L.A. Gear's "Hot Shots" shoes. U.S. Design Patent No. 299,081 was granted on December 27, 1988.

L.A. Gear concentrated over 70 percent of its advertising expenditures on these shoes, at a cost of over $5 million in 1988. This line of shoes was a commercial success, with 4 million pairs sold by February of 1989.

Melville Corporation sells shoes in discount stores, through its divisions Thom McAn and Meldisco. In 1988, Melville, observing the success of L.A. Gear's Hot Shots design, decided to copy it, and designers used the L.A. Gear shoes as models for the Melville imitations. L.A. Gear sued Melville and its divisions and the court enjoined further infringement of L.A. Gear's design patent. Melville appealed.

OPINION

NEWMAN, J. . . . Melville raised defenses of patent invalidity and non-infringement, on the following premises:

Functionality

Melville . . . argues . . . that the design of the '081 patent is "functional" and that the patent is therefore invalid. . . .

A design patent is directed to the appearance of the article. . . . [T]he design . . . is deemed to be functional when the appearance of the claimed design is "dictated by" the use or purpose of the article. . . . If the particular design is essential to the use of the article, it cannot be the subject of a design patent.

Melville argues that each element comprising the '081 design has a utilitarian purpose. . . . That elements of the '081 design, such as the delta wing or the side mesh, also provide support for the foot does not mean that the specific design of each element . . . is dictated by primarily functional considerations. . . . The district court remarked on the existence of a myriad of athletic shoe designs in which each of the functions identified by Melville as performed by the '081 design elements was achieved in a way other than by the design of the '081 patent. When there are several ways to achieve the function of an article of manufacture, the design of the article is more likely to serve a primarily ornamental purpose. . . .

Obviousness

A patented design must meet the substantive criteria of patentability, including non-obviousness. . . .

In applying the law . . . obviousness . . . is reviewed from the viewpoint of a designer of ordinary skill or capability in the field to which the design pertains. . . . [A] holding of obviousness requires that there be some teaching or suggestion whereby it would have been obvious to a designer of ordinary skill to make the particular selection and combination made by the patents. . . .

The district court found that all of the elements of the design of the '081 patent were known, but that these particular elements had not previously

> **CASE 8.5 Continued**
>
> been combined in a single shoe design. . . . [It] concluded that there was no teaching or suggestion in the prior art of the appearance of the claimed design as a visual whole. We discern no error in this conclusion. . . .
>
> **Infringement**
>
> Design patent infringement requires a showing that the accused design is substantially the same as the claimed design. . . .
>
> Design patent infringement relates solely to the patented design, and does not require proof of unfair competition . . . or allow avoidance of infringement by labeling. . . . Although Melville argues specific differences in features . . . the district court . . . recognized that the novelty resided in the overall appearance of the combination. . . .
>
> **JUDGMENT** Affirmed.

Trade Secrets

State trade secret law provides an alternative to federal copyright and patent protection for intellectual property. The Uniform Trade Secrets Act, prepared by the National Conference of Commissioners on Uniform State Laws, has been adopted by twenty states. In states that have not adopted it, trade secret protection is governed by the common law.

Nature of Trade Secrets. A **trade secret** is any process, formula, device, or information that is kept secret by a firm and gives it a competitive advantage in the marketplace. Examples of trade secrets are an engineering process, a method of utilizing a tool, a computer program, a quality control procedure, a customer attitude study, and a delivery route. Like a patent, trade secret law often protects an invention or technological innovation of a business firm. But the scope of trade secret law is broader than patent law. A firm can have a trade secret in information, such as a customer list, that cannot be patented. Moreover, to be protected, a trade secret need not be novel or nonobvious. Trade secrets are protected as long as a business firm takes reasonable steps to prevent the public disclosure of the information and the information gives the firm some economic advantage. And, as long as such reasonable steps are maintained, the duration of a trade secret, unlike the limited time period for a patent, is potentially indefinite.

Misappropriation. The wrongful appropriation of trade secrets is a competitive tort for which the owner has a civil remedy. A willful misappropriation of trade secrets may also be a crime. When a competitor gains the knowledge of a business's trade secret dishonestly, as through industrial espionage or commercial bribery, through the abuse of a confidence, or through the disclosure of the trade secret by a former employee of the business, a misappropriation has taken place.

However, just as a firm is privileged as a normal incident of competition to copy the physical characteristics of a product, a firm is allowed to copy another's business methods and processes provided the information making such imitation possible comes into the copier's possession legitimately. Proper means of acquiring trade secrets include "reverse engineering," the process of breaking down an article to learn how it works, and independent development. Thus, unlike a patent, which provides the owner with the exclusive right to make, use, and transfer his or her invention, a trade secret can be copied by a competitor if there is no wrongful acquisition of the "secret" to a product or process.

SUMMARY

While competition is inherent in the business world, our free enterprise economy does not justify conduct which is contrary to acceptable commercial standards. Business practices which violate such standards are competitive torts. Competitive torts may be grouped into the following four broad categories: wrongful entry into business; interference with business relations; defamation and disparagement; and unfair trade practices.

Wrongful entry into business occurs when a business is established for a malicious purpose. Interference with business relations consists of the related torts of interference with a prospective economic advantage and interference with a contract. An unprivileged dissemination of statements attacking the honesty or creditworthiness of a business constitutes the tort of defamation; where the statements casts doubt upon the validity of title to or the qualities of a business firm's property or products, it constitutes the tort of disparagement.

Engaging in unfair trade practices may consist of "palming off" a product for that of another manufacturer or false advertising. The Lanham Act and state statutes supplement the common law of unfair competition by providing civil remedies for false advertising and trade dress infringement.

Intellectual property developed by a business is protected from infringement or misappropriation by competitors. Trademarks are words or symbols that exclusively identify a seller's products. Original and creative works are protected under copyright law. Patent law protects novel, useful, and nonobvious inventions by granting the creator a limited monopoly on the patented article. A firm's property right in secret business information and processes is also protected under state trade secret law.

Table 8.2 Concept Summary: Intellectual Property

	Nature of Property	Requirements for Protection	Duration
Trademark	Word, symbol, device, or design that identifies the maker or source of product or service, including service marks, collective marks, and certification marks	Adoption and use of mark by producer Inherently distinctive mark or mark that has secondary meaning Registration optional but advisable	Registration effective for 10-year, renewable terms
Copyright	Original works of authorship Includes books, movies, musical compositions, works of art, computer programs, architectural designs	Minimum level of originality and creativity Registration optional but advisable	Life of the author plus 50 years Work made for hire lasts for 75 years from date of first publication
Patent	Invention of a process, manufacture, plant, composition, or an ornamental product design	Novel, useful, and nonobvious Registration required	Normal patent—17 years Design patent—14 years
Trade secrets	Process, formula, device, method, or information	Has economic value Reasonable steps to maintain secrecy No registration	As long as it remains secret

REVIEW QUESTIONS

1. Explain the differences between the tort of interference with a prospective economic advantage and interference with a contract.

2. Why should a person be liable for inducing a breach of contract when the contract provides that it may be terminated by either party at will?

3. What is meant by an "improper" interference in the torts of intentional interference with an economic advantage and intentional interference with a contract?

4. What is slander of title? How is it different from trade libel?

5. Distinguish between defamation and disparagement.

6. How should the courts calculate damages in a false advertising suit by an injured competitor?

7. Distinguish among a trademark, a service mark, and a trade name.

8. Should the law provide a very broad or narrow scope for the fair use of copyrighted materials? Explain the conflicting policies involved in your position.

9. Explain the differences between protecting a new innovative process under patent and trade secret law.

10. Since a patent stifles competition, what is the public policy justification for granting a patent?

CASE PROBLEMS

1. AM International had a written contract with DP Service for the latter to exclusively distribute AM's products to wholesalers for a stated period of time. AM wanted to modify that agreement to permit it also to sell its own products to wholesalers. DP refused and before the contract came to an end, AM breached it. DP brought suit against AM for the tort of intentional interference with its prospective economic advantage under the contract. Did AM commit the alleged tort? Explain.

2. Avtec Industries, Inc., installed and serviced video and audio systems and rendered engineering and maintenance service for such companies as AT&T and Georgia Power Company. It had an agreement with defendant Sony, which required Avtec, at its own expense, "to have at least one of its technically oriented personnel, with an electronic background, trained at a service school designated by" Sony. Serge Caleca, who was highly qualified, was hired by Avtec to work as a technician in its service department. Caleca was given on-the-job training by Avtec and was also sent to the Sony service school. While at the school, Caleca expressed an interest in working for Sony. A job came open and Caleca applied for the position. In September he left Avtec and started to work for defendant Sony. Avtec sued Sony, charging that as a result of its dealership agreement, it maliciously interfered with Avtec's contractual relationship with Caleca by hiring him away. Who will likely win the suit? Why?

3. Meister Brau, Inc., secured a trademark on labels containing the name LITE beer. It later sold its interest in the LITE trademark to Miller Brewing Company. Miller used the term LITE on labels for a beer lower in calories than Miller's regular beer. Miller spent considerable money advertising the beer. Soon other brewers, including G. Heileman Brewing Company, marketed reduced-calorie beers labeled or described as "light." Miller filed a trademark infringement action against G. Heileman. G. Heileman claimed that the mark was a common descriptive term and the trademark was, therefore, invalid. Who should prevail? Explain.

4. Henry Perky in 1895 secured a patent on a pillow-shaped biscuit cereal made of baked whole wheat which was called, in the patent, "shredded wheat." Perky was associated with the Natural Food Company. The name of that company was, in 1908, changed to the Shredded Wheat Company. In 1930 its business and goodwill were acquired by the National Biscuit Company, the plaintiff. Perky's patent would have expired in 1909, but in 1908 the patent was declared invalid because at least as early as 1894 shredded wheat had been manufactured although not patented. Registration of the name "Shredded Wheat" as a trademark was refused because those words described an article of food which had been produced and sold for more than 10 years. However, the National Biscuit Company continued to make and sell its shredded wheat.

The Kellogg Company, the defendant, since 1927 made and sold a shredded wheat breakfast food under the name "Kellogg's Shredded Whole Wheat Biscuit." Its product is also in pillow shape, although each biscuit is about two-thirds the size of those produced by the National Biscuit Company. In 1932 National Biscuit Company sued the Kellogg Company for unfair competition. The U.S. Supreme Court dismissed the bill of complaint. However, two of the justices in a dissenting opinion stated, "[T]he Kellogg Company is fraudulently seeking to appropriate to itself the benefits of the goodwill" created by the National Biscuit Company.

Do you agree with the majority or with the opinion of the dissenting justices? What is the basis for your conclusion?

5. Klamath Lumber Co., the plaintiff, manufactures and sells at wholesale load binders (equipment used in handling logs and cut lumber). Klamath had expended much time and energy to secure creditworthy customers. Clarence Miller was employed as Klamath's shop manager and his wife, Hilda, worked in its office. While still employed there, the Millers, the defendants, secretly began the construction of a drill press similar to one used by Klamath.

They later quit their jobs with Klamath and manufactured binders similar to those made by Klamath. The Millers created a customer list based almost entirely upon the names Hilda remembered were Klamath's customers. Klamath brought suit to enjoin the Millers from soliciting Klamath's customers. The Millers responded that they had not copied Klamath's customer list but had merely relied on their memories to assist them in developing their own list of potential customers and that all those names could be found in business directories. Should the court grant the injunction? Why or why not?

CHAPTER 9

Criminal Law and Business

Why is a chapter on criminal law included in a business law text? After all, business law is based on the principles of *civil* law. The answer is that, unfortunately, we must recognize that some criminal activities are so closely linked with the conduct of business that they have become known as **business crimes,** or **white-collar crimes.** Such crimes add about 15 percent to the price of all goods and services sold in the United States. They cost the public more than do the crimes of larceny, robbery, burglary, and auto theft combined.

To understand the scope of business crime, it is first necessary to understand what criminal law is and how the justice system operates. This chapter, therefore, begins by explaining the nature of criminal law, the essential elements of a crime, and the defenses to criminal liability. It then discusses criminal procedure, noting key differences between criminal prosecutions and civil suits, and the constitutional rights of defendants in the criminal process. Against that background, the chapter discusses individual business crimes.

CRIMINAL LAW PRINCIPLES
Nature of Criminal Law

A **crime** is the commission of an act, or a failure to act (an omission), which the law forbids and for which the law imposes a penalty. A crime is a *public* offense committed against the government, state or federal. As an offense against society, it is punishable in a criminal proceeding brought by the state or federal government. Today, almost all crimes are statutory. State criminal codes and the U.S. Criminal Code define what actions constitute offenses against states and the United States, respectively.

Most acts recognized as crimes today have been outlawed since ancient times. But as technology, social standards, and ethics change over time, our views of what offends society also change. In colonial America, a person could be charged with practicing witchcraft and, if found guilty, burned at the stake. Today, there is no such offense and no such punishment. Before the invention of the airplane, it was impossible to commit the offense of hijacking a plane; until the appearance of credit cards, an offense based upon their misuse was unknown. Today, hijacking an airplane is a federal offense and all jurisdictions have crimes outlawing credit card theft and fraud. Thus, criminal law is never static. Society weighs the schemes people devise to enrich themselves. If some are found sufficiently harmful, the state legislature or Congress enacts new criminal statutes to outlaw them.

Legal scholars generally identify four underlying purposes served by the punishment of convicted criminals in our criminal justice system:

- Specific and general deterrence
- Societal protection
- Retribution
- Rehabilitation

Deterrence refers to the desired effect that criminal sanctions have on the individual punished and on others in society. Specific deterrence means that we punish a criminal wrongdoer to discourage (deter) him or her from committing crimes in the future. General deterrence means that punishment of a wrongdoer deters others in society from committing criminal acts. Societal protection, the second purpose, is served by the incapacitation of a criminal who is sentenced to prison and thereby removed from society. Retribution means that society imposes a punishment as a form of public revenge. Because the victim of a crime is prohibited from exacting an "eye for an eye," a criminal sanction is imposed to satisfy both individual and public needs for vengeance. Finally, rehabilitation is one of the major cornerstones of the modern criminal system. Alternative sentencing approaches, such as community service and addiction treatment, are designed to change behavior so that individuals convicted of crimes will become productive members of society.

Classification of Crimes

Crimes may be classified in a number of ways. One form of classification is by kind of wrong or injury: (1) crimes against the person, such as murder, rape, manslaughter, battery, and assault; (2) crimes against property, such as arson, larceny, and embezzlement; and (3) crimes against the government, such as treason, making a false official statement, and violating election laws.

The most important classification is based on the seriousness of the crime and degree of permissible punishment. Thus classified, a crime is either a felony or a misdemeanor.[1]

---

[1] Treason, a betraying or breach of allegiance to the government, is a constitutional crime and is usually not included within the common categories of criminal acts.

Felonies, the most serious crimes, are generally defined as crimes punishable by imprisonment in a state prison (rather than in a county jail) for more than 1 year. A person convicted of a felony may also be fined. In jurisdictions which authorize the death sentence, certain felonies (called **capital offenses**) are punishable by execution.

A **misdemeanor** is a lesser crime. A misdemeanor such as shoplifting is generally punishable by fine and possibly by imprisonment for no more than 1 year in an institution other than a state prison.

A misdemeanor should not be confused with an **infraction.** An infraction is a minor wrong and in most states is not considered to be a criminal offense. Infractions involve such departures from community standards as minor traffic offenses and parking violations. Punishment is normally a fine or the withdrawal of a privilege such as the right to drive a motor vehicle, or, in many jurisdictions, the optional requirement that the offender attend a course of instruction in a traffic school in lieu of a fine.

Elements of a Crime

A crime generally consists of two essential elements: an act or a failure to act and criminal intent.

The Act. To commit an offense, an act must take place which the law forbids or there must be the failure to do something which the law requires. For example, a person who steals another's property commits an act which the law forbids; a person who meets the minimum filing requirements yet fails to file an income tax return omits to do something the law requires.

The mere *intention* to commit a crime, unaccompanied by any act in furtherance of that intention, is not a crime. Likewise, an act that is only *preparatory* to the commission of an unlawful act is generally not a crime. However, criminal liability is imposed for the inchoate (uncompleted) crimes of **attempt** and **conspiracy.** An attempt requires two elements: an intent to commit a crime and a substantial step, beyond mere preparation, toward the commission of that crime. A conspiracy involves two or more persons who (1) enter into an agreement (the conspiracy) to commit a crime and (2) who take some action in furtherance of the conspiracy. The act requirement for a conspiracy need not be a substantial step and it can be mere preparation for the crime.

Criminal Intent. For an act or omission to be criminal, it must have been committed with an evil purpose or with a blameworthy or person-endangering state of mind called **mens rea** or **criminal intent.** Such an intent is identified in statutes by words such as "knowingly," "wrongfully," "corruptly," "willfully," "fraudulently," "intentionally," "maliciously," "feloniously," and "wantonly." Criminal intent is almost always proved by circumstantial evidence. The jury may infer intent from the act committed on the premise that people are presumed to intend the natural consequences of their voluntary acts. Thus, if Barry took a hand tool owned by his employer, Stark Co., and pawned it, the jury, in Barry's trial for larceny, may presume that he intended to deprive Stark Co. of its property permanently, a necessary ingredient of the crime of larceny.

Some crimes require a mental state other than criminal intent. Statutes may prohibit conduct that is done recklessly or negligently. Different homicide offenses illustrate this point. Murder requires that a person cause the death of another with a specific intent to kill. In contrast, involuntary manslaughter requires only reckless conduct causing the death of another. Because of the difference in culpability, the penalty imposed for murder is more severe than that for involuntary manslaughter.

Strict Liability Crimes. Some crimes require no criminal intent or mental state. The mere commission of the prohibited act is sufficient without any showing of intent, knowledge, recklessness, or negligence. Most of these crimes, however, are **regulatory offenses**—white-collar crimes that are designed to control the activities of business for the public health, safety, or welfare. For example, the penal provisions of the federal Food, Drug, and Cosmetic Act, illustrated by Case 9.3, and of the truth-in-lending laws (discussed in Chapter 49) are examples.

Crimes under state motor vehicle laws are frequently strict liability offenses. Driving under the influence (DUI) of alcohol or any other drug does not require an intent to drive in an intoxicated condition or knowledge that one is intoxicated. Another offense of this class involves the sale of intoxicating liquor to minors. In many states, as a matter of public policy, it is a criminal offense to sell liquor to minors even if the seller did not know that the purchaser was a minor. However, not all regulatory offenses are strict liability crimes. As the case that follows demonstrates, the courts will not lightly presume that a criminal offense does not require a guilty mental state.

CASE 9.1	United States v. United States Gypsum Co. • 438 U.S. 422 (1978)
FACTS	United States Gypsum Co. and several other major gypsum board manufacturers were charged with violations of §1 of the Sherman Antitrust Act for engaging in a conspiracy to fix the price of gypsum board. Gypsum board or wallboard is the primary component of interior walls and ceilings in residential and commercial construction. The wallboard industry was highly concentrated, with the eight largest companies accounting for some 94 percent of national sales. The focus of the government's price-fixing case at trial was interseller price verification—that is, the practice allegedly followed by the gypsum board manufacturers of telephoning a competing producer to determine the price currently being offered on gypsum board to a specific customer. The government contended that these price exchanges were part of an agreement among the defendants

**CASE 9.1
Continued**

to fix the price of wallboard and had the effect of stabilizing prices and policing agreed-upon price increases.

The trial court's instruction to the jury on the issue of criminal intent read as follows: "The law presumes that a person intends the necessary and natural consequences of his acts. Therefore, if the effect of the exchanges of pricing information was to raise, fix, maintain, and stabilize prices, then the parties to them are presumed, as a matter of law, to have intended that result." The jury returned guilty verdicts against each of the defendants, but the Court of Appeals for the Third Circuit reversed the convictions. The Supreme Court granted certiorari.

OPINION

BURGER, C.J. . . . We hold that a defendant's state of mind or intent is an element of a criminal antitrust offense which must be established by evidence . . . and cannot be taken from the trier of fact through reliance on a legal presumption of wrongful intent from proof of an effect on prices. . . . We are unwilling to construe the Sherman Act as mandating a regime of strict-liability criminal offenses.

We start with the familiar proposition that " [the] existence of a mens rea is the rule of, rather than the exception to, the principles of Anglo-American criminal jurisprudence." . . . [I]ntent generally remains an indispensable element of a criminal offense. This is as true in a sophisticated criminal antitrust case as in one involving any other criminal offense. . . .

While strict-liability offenses are not unknown to the criminal law and do not invariably offend constitutional requirements the limited circumstances in which Congress has created and this Court has recognized such offenses attest to their generally disfavored status. Certainly far more than the simple omission of the appropriate phrase from the statutory definition is necessary to justify dispensing with an intent requirement. In the context of the Sherman Act, this generally inhospitable attitude to non-mens rea offenses is reinforced by an array of considerations arguing against treating antitrust violations as strict-liability crimes.

The Sherman Act, unlike most traditional criminal statutes, does not, in clear and categorical terms, precisely identify the conduct which it proscribes. Both civil remedies and criminal sanctions are authorized with regard to the same generalized definitions of the conduct proscribed—restraints of trade or commerce and illegal monopolization—without reference to or mention of intent or state of mind. . . .

[T]he behavior proscribed by the Act is often difficult to distinguish from . . . economically justifiable business conduct. Indeed, the type of conduct charged in the indictment in this case—the exchange of price information among competitors—is illustrative in this regard. The imposition of criminal liability . . . for engaging in such conduct which only after the fact is determined to violate the statute because of anticompetitive effects, without inquiring into the intent with which it was undertaken, holds out the distinct possibility of overdeterrence; salutary and procompetitive conduct . . . might be shunned by businessmen who chose to be excessively cautious in the face of uncertainty regarding possible exposure to criminal punishment. . . . The criminal sanctions would be used, not to punish conscious and calculated wrongdoing at odds with statutory proscriptions, but instead simply to regulate business practices regardless of the intent with which they were undertaken.

> **CASE 9.1
> Continued**
>
> For these reasons, we conclude that the criminal offenses defined by the Sherman Act should be construed as including intent as an element.
>
> **JUDGMENT**
>
> Accordingly, the judgment of the Court of Appeals is Affirmed.

Vicarious Criminal Liability. Can one be convicted of a crime on the basis of another person's actions—i.e., **vicarious criminal liability?** In general, the answer is no. Criminal liability is personal, and an individual is punished for his or her own blameworthy acts, not the acts of others. But there are exceptions. For example, a person who procures the commission of a crime may be held criminally responsible for that crime. The person's conduct in hiring the criminal is just as blameworthy as that of the individual who actually committed the crime.

But what about a person who is innocent of any wrongdoing? Employers are sometimes held criminally responsible for the wrongful conduct of their employees even though they did not know about, authorize, direct, or participate in the crime. Most of these crimes are regulatory offenses. So, for example, it may be a crime to sell "short weight" and a business whose employees sell short-weight goods even without the owner's knowledge or consent is guilty of an offense. The purpose of vicarious criminal liability is to ensure that businesses exercise a high degree of care in hiring individuals and exercise sufficient control over their employees to assure compliance with applicable laws. Although vicarious liability is imposed in many jurisdictions, some states limit the punishment to a fine, refusing to allow imposition of jail or imprisonment for innocent, regulatory offenses.

Defenses to Criminal Liability

An individual charged with a crime may have a legal justification for the crime (e.g., self-defense and defense of property) or lack the necessary capacity to commit a crime (e.g., insanity, minority, and intoxication). This section discusses some of the most important defenses to criminal liability. You should be aware, however, that other defenses are recognized and may be asserted in a particular case, including such defenses as entrapment, alibi, and the statute of limitations.

Defense of Person and Property. A person is permitted to use force in self-defense and in de-

> **BOX 9.1**
>
> **Point to Consider**
>
> Melvin Davis was the president of Kwickie Food Stores, a chain of approximately 100 convenience food stores, and held a retail wine license for a Kwickie Store in Peachtree City, Georgia. On Sunday August 16, 1981, Jim Renew, an employee of the store, sold wine to a minor. Davis had no knowledge of and did not authorize this sale. Davis was convicted of selling alcoholic beverages to a minor under a law providing: "The licensee is responsible for the conduct or actions of his employees while in his employment." He was fined $200 and given a 60-day suspended jail sentence.
>
> Davis argues on appeal that the imposition of vicarious liability for actions of his employee—which were taken without his knowledge, consent, or authorization and which are not the result of negligence attributable to him—violates substantive due process. Do you agree? How would you balance the interests of the public in controlling the sale of alcohol to minors with the individual's interest in being free of the consequences of a criminal conviction? How do you think the appellate court will rule on this issue? Why?

fending others. The law generally requires that the individual or another be faced with an imminent threat of force or violence, and that he or she use only that force which is reasonable to use in self-defense or to aid the person threatened. The defense-of-person defense does not allow the individual attacked to use excessive force or to subject the attacker to force once the attack has been repulsed. In addition, significant limitations are recognized when an individual uses deadly force—force designed to cause death or grievous bodily injury. Deadly force is permissible only when the individual is threatened with immediate death or serious bodily harm.

Defense of property is also a defense to criminal liability. Force is permissible only when it is reasonably necessary to defend one's property from loss, theft, or damage. As with defense of person, the defense is limited to reasonable force. Deadly force is generally not permissible to protect property other than in defense of an individual's home. The states have different rules as to when deadly force can be used in the home. In some states it is limited to self-defense situations; in others it can be used to stop a person from committing a felony in the home. If the owner is not present in the home, deadly force will generally not be authorized. So, for example, property owners have been convicted for injuries to others caused by spring guns and other deadly traps, even when the person injured was a trespasser or burglar.

Insanity and Diminished Capacity. Although insanity is a controversial defense, it is of limited importance because defendants rarely raise the defense, and when it is raised, it is not usually successful. Under the standard for criminal insanity, called the M'Naghten Rule or the *right and wrong test*, an individual is criminally insane only if that person was so mentally unsound because of mental disease, defect, or illness (1) as not to know what he or she was doing, or (2) if, knowing what he or she was doing, nonetheless did not know that the act was wrong. Moreover, the defendant who is found to be criminally insane is subject to civil commitment and generally will be confined to a mental institution.[2]

Some jurisdictions recognize the related defense of *diminished mental capacity*. In those states, an accused may claim that he or she, although not insane at the time of the alleged offense, was not capable, because of mental illness, of forming, in his or her mind, the intent necessary to be guilty of the crime charged. For example, for a person to be convicted of murder there must be proof that the homicide was intended. If diminished capacity is established, the accused may be found guilty, not of murder, but only of a lesser offense such as manslaughter for which intent is not an element.

Intoxication. Intoxication as a defense depends upon whether the intoxication was voluntary or involuntary. Voluntary intoxication is generally not a defense, although voluntary intoxication may be used to show that the individual did not have the necessary criminal intent. As with diminished capacity, this may result in a conviction for a lesser crime. By contrast, involuntary intoxication is a defense to any crime if the intoxication rendered the perpetrator criminally insane. Involuntary intoxication can occur when a person mistakenly consumes a drug or intoxicant or when medically prescribed drugs have an adverse effect on a person.

Minority. To protect people from having to bear the stigma of a criminal conviction for a youthful caper, all states have now adopted some form of juvenile or youthful offender law. A youthful offender (the age depending on the state) who is accused of a criminal act normally is not charged with the commission of a specific crime but only with being a juvenile delinquent. If the charge is proved, the youth may be held in a juvenile detention center for a limited period of

---

[2]The Comprehensive Crime Control Act of 1984, an extensive revision of the U.S. Criminal Code, has also made the defense more difficult to establish by providing that a person who, in the federal courts, defends on the ground of insanity at the time of the offense has the burden to prove his or her insanity.

time and is usually treated as a person requiring help and guidance rather than punishment.

> **BOX 9.2**
>
> ### Developments in the Law: Battered Woman Syndrome
>
> Jane Doe lived in constant fear of her life. Her husband, John, was physically and psychologically abusive to her. During their 2-year marriage, she was assaulted 23 times. John would become intoxicated, threaten to kill her, and beat Jane's head against the wall, floor, doors, or the car. She was taken to the emergency room with neck injuries and broken bones on three occasions. Despite the abuse, Jane tried to get help for him, and John frequently assured her that he loved her and that he would change. But, finally, after a drunken assault one night, Jane shot and killed him as he was lying on the couch.
>
> She was charged with murder and raised self-defense, offering expert testimony on *battered woman syndrome*, the characteristics of a woman living in an abusive relationship. Thirty-two states allow the admission of expert testimony on battered woman syndrome. Courts have allowed such testimony to show that it is normal for abused women to remain in the relationship, rather than escape, and that battered women live in a state of apprehension and fear of violence and death. Obviously, such testimony is essential to show whether use of deadly force is justified, particularly where the threat of death is imminent. ■

CRIMINAL PROCEDURE AND THE CONSTITUTIONAL RIGHTS OF THE ACCUSED

Nature of Criminal Procedure

Criminal procedure refers to the various steps involved in bringing to trial (prosecuting) a person accused of crime. These procedures differ from the civil procedures discussed in Chapter 2 for enforcing contract rights or collecting tort damages. One reason for the differences is the extensive protections accorded criminal defendants by the U.S. Constitution. We will look at criminal procedure and the rights of the accused by exploring the stages in a criminal case. The specific steps differ somewhat among states and between the federal and state systems. Figure 9.1 outlines the typical stages in a felony prosecution.

Investigation

The first stage of a felony prosecution involves the detection or observation of crimes by the police or private citizens. Prior to a defendant's arrest, the government may investigate the facts. This may include searching the defendant's person or property and seizing evidence.

If the government searches a person's home, property, or anything else in which he or she has

Figure 9.1 Stages in a felony case.

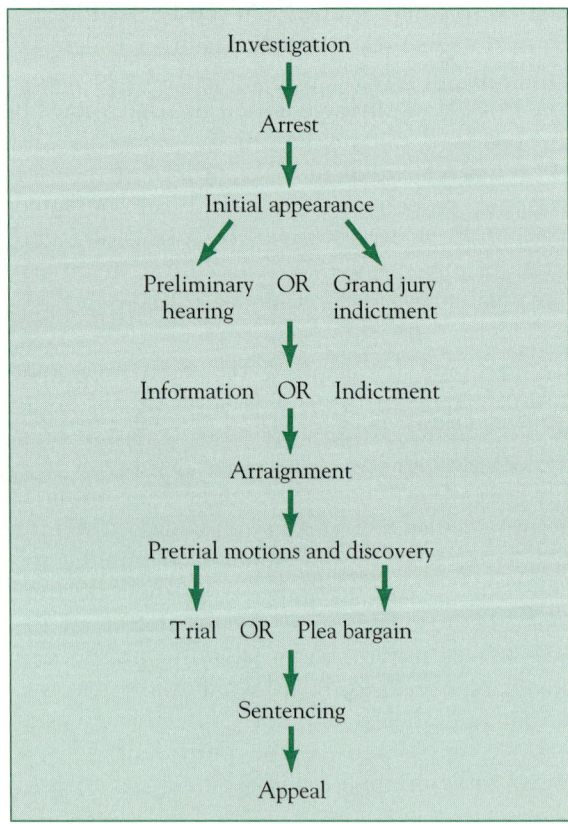

a reasonable expectation of privacy, it must comply with the Fourth Amendment, which forbids unreasonable searches and seizures. A violation of the Fourth Amendment usually results in the suppression in court of all evidence derived from the search or seizure. This **exclusionary rule** was developed by the Supreme Court to deter police illegality.

Not all searches and seizures are unreasonable. Generally, the police must obtain a warrant in order for a search or seizure to be constitutional. The police secure a warrant by providing a judge with "probable cause" for the search. **Probable cause** is a reasonable factual basis for the government to believe that the place to be searched contains relevant evidence of a crime. Warrantless searches are considered unreasonable unless the search or seizure falls within one of the exceptions to the warrant requirement. For example, under the "automobile" exception, the warrantless search of an automobile is lawful when the police have probable cause. Exceptions to the warrant requirement have also been recognized for border searches, "hot pursuit" situations, searches of persons under arrest, and seizures of evidence in "plain view" of a police officer.

Frequently, representatives of government agencies, such as health and safety officials and building code inspectors, will conduct an inspection of a business and its property. Although such an inspection is considered a search requiring a warrant, warrants for administrative inspections can be issued without the usual showing of probable cause. When the regulatory law authorizes the administrative search, the courts will generally issue a warrant if the government can show some administrative need for the inspection.

No warrant will be necessary if an administrative inspection falls within one of the exceptions to the warrant requirement. For example, by *consenting* to an inspection, a business owner has waived any expectation of privacy. The Supreme Court has created another exception for "closely regulated" industries, businesses that are so extensively controlled by the government for the protection of the public that they give up any expectation of privacy. Examples include the alcohol, firearms, and mining industries. In Case 9.2, the Court discusses whether a junkyard is a closely regulated business and, if so, what is required for a warrantless search.

CASE 9.2 New York v. Burger • 482 U.S. 691 (1987)

FACTS Joseph Burger, the owner of a junkyard in Brooklyn, New York, was engaged in the business of dismantling automobiles and selling their parts. On November 17, 1982, five New York City police officers came to his junkyard and asked to see his license and his "police book"—the record of the automobiles and vehicle parts in his possession. When Burger replied that he had neither a license nor a police book, the officers conducted an inspection of the premises pursuant to §415-a5 of the New York Vehicle and Traffic Laws. The officers determined that Burger was in possession of stolen vehicles and parts and arrested him. He was charged with possession of stolen property. He moved to suppress the evidence obtained as a result of the inspection, but the trial court denied the motion and the Appellate Division affirmed. The New York Court of Appeals, however, reversed, holding that §415-a5 violated the Fourth Amendment's prohibition of unreasonable searches and seizures. The U.S. Supreme Court granted certiorari.

OPINION BLACKMUN, J. . . . This case presents the question whether the warrantless search of an automobile junkyard, conducted pursuant to a statute authorizing

**CASE 9.2
Continued**

such a search, falls within the exception to the warrant requirement for administrative inspections of pervasively regulated industries. . . .

The Court long has recognized that the Fourth Amendment's prohibition on unreasonable searches and seizures is applicable to commercial premises, as well as to private homes. . . . An expectation of privacy in commercial premises, however, is different from, and indeed less than, a similar expectation in an individual's home. This expectation is particularly attenuated in commercial property employed in "closely regulated" industries. . . . "Certain industries have such a history of government oversight that no reasonable expectation of privacy could exist for a proprietor over the stock of such an enterprise."

[A] warrantless inspection . . . in the context of a pervasively regulated business, will be deemed to be reasonable only so long as three criteria are met. First, there must be a "substantial" government interest [served by] the inspection. . . . Second, the warrantless inspections must be "necessary to further [the] regulatory scheme." . . . Finally, "the statute's inspection program, in terms of the certainty and regularity of its application [must] provid[e] a constitutionally adequate substitute for a warrant." In other words, the regulatory statute must perform the two basic functions of a warrant: it must advise the owner of the commercial premises that the search is being made pursuant to the law and has a properly defined scope, and it must limit the discretion of the inspection officers. . . .

Searches made pursuant to §415-a5, in our view, clearly fall within this established exception to the warrant requirement for administrative inspections in "closely regulated" businesses. [T]he nature of the regulatory statute reveals that the operation of a junkyard, part of which is devoted to vehicle dismantling, is a "closely regulated" business in the State of New York. The provisions regulating the activity of vehicle dismantling are extensive. An operator cannot engage in this industry without first obtaining a license, which means that he must meet the registration requirements and must pay a fee. . . . [T]he operator must maintain a police book regarding the acquisition and disposition of motor vehicles and vehicle parts, and make such records and inventory available for inspection by the police or any agent of the Department of Motor Vehicles. The operator also must display his registration number prominently at his place of business, on business documentation, and on vehicles and parts that pass through his business.

The New York regulatory scheme satisfies the three criteria necessary to make reasonable warrantless inspections pursuant to §415-a5. First, the State has a substantial interest in regulating the vehicle-dismantling and automobile-junkyard industry because motor vehicle theft has increased in the State and because the problem of theft is associated with this industry. . . . Second, regulation of the vehicle-dismantling industry reasonably serves the State's substantial interest in eradicating automobile theft. . . . Third, §415-a5 provides a "constitutionally adequate substitute for a warrant." The statute informs the operator of a vehicle-dismantling business that inspections will be made on a regular basis. Section 415-a5 also sets forth the scope of the inspection and, accordingly, places the operator on notice as to how to comply with the statute. In addition, it notifies the operator as to who is authorized to conduct an inspection.

JUDGMENT

Accordingly, the judgment of the New York Court of Appeals is reversed. . . .

Arrest

An **arrest,** normally made by a police officer as the first formal step in a criminal prosecution, is the act of taking a person into custody for the commission of a crime. In general, misdemeanor arrests cannot be made without a warrant unless the offense was committed in the officer's presence. In contrast, a warrantless felony arrest based on probable cause is lawful whether or not the crime was committed in the presence of the officer. The Fourth Amendment requires that any arrest be based on probable cause and that the manner of the arrest comply with search and seizure rules. Thus, an officer cannot enter a house to make a felony arrest unless the officer has a warrant or there is an exception, such as "hot pursuit" of a fleeing, dangerous felon.

In the landmark case of *Miranda v. State of Arizona,*[3] the Court held that an arrested person must not be questioned by the police unless first warned of his or her right to remain silent, to be represented by an attorney, and to have the attorney present during questioning. The basis of the Miranda Rule is the Fifth Amendment privilege against self-incrimination. If the "Miranda warnings" are not given to an accused who is interrogated by the police after being taken into custody, any statement (such as a confession) the accused makes to the police (and any other evidence derived from the confession) may not be used in evidence against that individual at trial.

First Appearance

After an arrest, the defendant will appear before the court at a first appearance. In both misdemeanor and felony cases, the defendant will be advised of his or her rights and the criminal charges. In misdemeanor cases, the defendant will also enter a plea of guilty or not guilty to the charges. If the defendant pleads not guilty or enters no plea, the case will be set on for trial. Ordinarily, in felonies no plea is entered until the arraignment. The court will also set *bail* at the first appearance.

[3]384 U.S. 436 (1966).

Information or Indictment

An accused is formally charged with the commission of an offense by a document called an **information** filed by the prosecuting (district) attorney. In a felony case, the information is usually filed after a **preliminary hearing**, held to determine whether there is probable cause to have a trial of the defendant. However, a felony may be charged (and in some states is required to be) by an **indictment** issued by a grand jury. A grand jury determines whether probable cause exists to charge the defendant. If the grand jury indicts the defendant, the accused must go to trial. Once an information or indictment is filed in a felony case, the accused appears at an **arraignment** and enters a plea to the charge.

Pretrial Procedure

If the defendant pleads not guilty, the case is scheduled for trial. Prior to trial, the defendant and the government may seek discovery or make various motions (requests) to the court. Discovery in a criminal case is less extensive than in a civil case. However, in many states the parties will disclose their trial witnesses, the defense will give notice of certain defenses (e.g., insanity and alibi), and the government will disclose its police and investigatory reports to the defense. The defense can move to suppress evidence, alleging violations of the Fourth Amendment, for example, or for a **change of venue,** a request to change the place of trial because of pretrial publicity.

By agreement with the prosecuting attorney, the accused may plead guilty to a lesser offense than that charged, in exchange for receiving a lesser punishment than might otherwise have been imposed. This is called a **plea bargain.**

Trial

The Sixth Amendment guarantees an accused the right to a trial by a jury selected from a fair cross section of the community. At trial, the defendant has extensive constitutional rights. Among them are the right to counsel, the right to be confronted by the witnesses for the prosecution, the right to compel witnesses to be present at the trial, and the Fifth Amendment right not to testify. From the evidence presented at trial, the jury in a criminal case must determine *beyond a reasonable doubt* that the accused is guilty.

Criminal Sentences

In most states, the trial judge exercises a great deal of discretion in determining the sentence he or she believes is appropriate to the offense and to the convicted individual.[4] Although mandatory minimum sentences may be required by statute for some crimes, most criminal codes merely set the maximum sentences which may be imposed. Generally, the trial judge may order a jail sentence suspended in whole or in part and place conditions upon the suspension of the sentence, such as drug or alcohol rehabilitation.

Appeal

Like a defendant in a civil case, a criminal defendant may appeal *from* a conviction. In contrast, the prosecution cannot appeal a verdict of not guilty following a trial because the double jeopardy clause of the Fifth Amendment prohibits a retrial of a criminal defendant by the same court on the same charge.

WHITE-COLLAR CRIMES

What Are White-Collar Crimes?

The term "white-collar crime" was first used to characterize a crime committed by a person of respectability in the course of his or her occupation—someone who, figuratively, went to work wearing a white collar. However, that concept has since been broadened. In current criminal

---

[4]In federal court, the court's discretion is limited. Defendants are sentenced according to the federal sentencing guidelines, which establish a narrow sentencing range based on the severity of the offense, criminal history of the defendant, and certain mitigating or aggravating circumstances. The court can depart from the guidelines only in unusual situations, and either the government or the defendant may appeal a departure.

> **BOX 9.3**
>
> **Point to Consider:
> Sentences for White-Collar Criminals**
>
> Traditionally, white-collar crimes were viewed as nonviolent property crimes for which jail sentences were rarely imposed. Increasingly, however, courts have been giving white-collar criminals jail time. And a recent federal law requires jail time for white-collar "kingpins." The Financial Crime Kingpin Statute applies to any person who "organizes, manages, or supervises a continuing financial crimes enterprise" and receives $5 million from that enterprise in any year. Enacted in 1990 in the wake of the savings and loan scandal, the law mandates a $10 million fine and a minimum jail sentence of 10 years (life imprisonment may be imposed). The first person convicted under the law was Roy Harris, who was charged with defrauding five banks out of more than $150 million.
>
> What social policies are furthered by sentencing white-collar criminals to jail? In the case of Roy Harris, is a 10-year jail term for a first-time offense too extreme? How should the law deal with the sentencing of white-collar criminals?

---

justice usage, the focus of the meaning of white-collar crime has shifted to the nature of the crime instead of to the persons or occupations involved. White-collar crimes cover a wide range of specific crimes, all of which are nonviolent and are committed for financial gain. They often involve some sort of fraud, guile, misrepresentation, or evasion of statutory directions designed for the protection of the public.

Thus, a white-collar crime will frequently be committed by the managers or employees of a business firm. A misrepresentation of a corporation's financial statements to its stockholders; an unlawful manipulation of a publicly traded stock; false advertising; bribery of a public official; the sale of adulterated foods; and illegal political contributions are all examples. Businesses are also the *victims* of white-collar crimes. For instance, the unauthorized invasion of a company computer to secure stored secret data, the embezzlement or pilferage of money or supplies by an employee, the theft of securities by a broker, and a fraudulent insurance claim are white-collar crimes.

We will consider such disparate offenses as bribery, violations of public health and safety laws, consumer frauds, violations of securities and antitrust laws, and larceny and embezzlement by an employee. But before we examine specific crimes, we need to address the question of corporate criminal liability.

Corporate Criminal Liability

White-collar crimes are often committed by businesses operating as corporations. The issue of corporate criminal liability is a complex one because the corporation is an *artificial* legal entity created by law, not a natural person. Traditional notions of criminal law, such as criminal intent, are not easily applied to corporate criminal behavior. Moreover, corporate criminal liability is always vicarious, based on the actions of the natural persons who manage and run the business.

At common law, a corporation could not be guilty of a crime because it lacked the capacity to form the necessary criminal intent. But with the advent of strict liability crimes, regulatory offenses that were designed to control business behavior to protect the public health and safety, the law began to recognize corporate criminal responsibility. Today, a corporation can be convicted of any crime. Liability is generally based on the actions of the persons in control of the business. So, for example, the corporation is liable for the criminal acts authorized or directed by the board of directors, the president, or high-level officers of the corporation. A corporation may also be liable for the criminal acts of lower-level managerial persons. In many states, the courts require three elements to hold a corporation criminally responsible for the acts of its lower-level agents:

- The corporate agent must have the authority to act for the corporation and be acting within the scope of his or her business responsibilities.
- The agent must act, at least in part, to further the corporation's business interests.
- The criminal acts must be authorized, tolerated, or ratified (accepted after the fact) by corporate management. Some jurisdictions do not require this last element.

To illustrate, suppose the used car manager of an automobile dealership corporation engages in a scheme of defrauding consumers by turning back the odometer settings on used cars. If corporate management knows about the practice and allows it to continue, the corporation will be criminally liable for the fraud. The manager had the authority to handle used car sales, the scheme benefited the dealership, and management tolerated the criminal fraud. Note that in cases of corporate crime, both the corporation and the agents committing the crime are guilty of the offense.

BOX 9.4

Developments in the Law: The California Corporate Criminal Liability Act

In 1990, California passed the California Corporate Criminal Liability Act, a law that may become a model for other states. It requires corporations and managers to disclose to the appropriate regulatory agency and to warn employees of a "serious concealed danger" in a product or at the workplace. Corporate violators are subject to fines of $1 million and managers may be sentenced up to 3 years in jail. The tough law has been called the "be a manager, go to jail" act by its critics.

The first prosecution under the act was precipitated by the death of a worker who was killed when his hand was caught on a machine stacking salt bags at a Cargill, Inc., plant. The company entered a no-contest plea to the charge. California prosecutors are presently investigating whether Dow Corning, Inc., violated the law by failing to disclose dangers in their silicone-gel implants.

Bribery

Bribery is the illicit giving or promising to give something of value to another to induce that individual to take some desired action. Bribery may be (1) of a public official, (2) of a businessperson (commercial bribery), or (3) of a foreign official.

An offer of a gift or a favor is a bribe if it is accompanied by a corrupt intent. If such an intent is present, the guise under which the offer or payment is made is immaterial. It may be, for instance, a donation to a police ball or to a political party. The bribe offer may be anything the receiver considers to be of value, such as money, clothing, a price advantage, inside information which might lead to financial gain, free travel, or sexual favors.

Bribery of Public Officials. Bribery of public officials is the effort to influence a public servant to handle an official matter in a way that serves a private interest. Such a private interest may be, for example, to thwart official interference with an illegal activity, to secure a building permit or business license, to defeat or effect passage of a statute or ordinance, or to forestall prosecution of a criminal act.

Illustrative of the bribery of public officials is a March 1984 case. There, in exchange for bribes, employees of the Philadelphia-based Defense Industrial Supply Center of the Department of Defense gave the defendants, Standard Air Parts and its president, confidential pricing information on bids made by the defendants' competitors for the sale of articles to the government. Having improperly received this information, Standard Air Parts was able to bid at prices which resulted in that company being awarded more than $2.3 million worth of defense contracts. The president of Standard and the company itself were charged with and found guilty of, among other offenses, ten counts of bribing public officials. The president was sentenced to 4 years in prison and fined $208,000. Standard Air Parts was fined an additional $159,000.

Commercial Bribery. Commercial bribery is the bribery of an employee or agent of a business to influence the conduct of the employer's business. Commercial bribes may be made to secure business, to cover up inferior products or services, to gain inside information concerning competing bids, to secure preferential treatment above competitors, or to acquire proprietary information. An example is a business that offers to pay an employee of a competing company to commit acts of industrial espionage such as turning over his or her employer's pricing schedules, customer lists, or secret manufacturing processes. Similarly, a wholesaler who bribes a liquor store manager not to carry a competitor's product or to give that wholesaler preferred shelf space commits commercial bribery.

A *kickback* is a common form of commercial bribery. For example, Doe, a buyer for a large retail chain store, bought for his company a quantity of blue jeans from producer X, paying $9.75

BOX 9.5

Law in Practice

N.J. Gendron Lumber Co. instituted a sales promotion program it called the "Acapulco Adventure." The promotion included form letters to each of its business customers inviting them to cocktails and dinner at which Gendron would introduce its "Great Escape" plan and literature inviting Gendron's customers to go to "fabulous Acapulco." For a given volume of purchases the customers would win a free trip to "frolic in the sun." Edmund Michalski, the plant manager of defendant, Great Northern Homes, Inc., received the promotional literature and he made purchases for his employer from Gendron.

Gendron sued Great Northern when Great Northern failed to pay for the purchases. Great Northern claimed that Gendron had wrongfully induced Michalski, its employee, to buy from Gendron for Great Northern's account—that is, that Gendron had committed the crime of commercial bribery. Did Gendron commit commercial bribery? Explain.

per pair. The next year, Doe made a private arrangement that X would charge the store $9 per pair and would pay Doe, "under the table," 25 cents for each pair delivered.

Commercial bribery is not recognized as a crime in all states, and there is no general federal law proscribing commercial bribery. However, the Sherman Antitrust Act, the Clayton Act, and the Robinson-Patman Act (see Chapters 52 and 53) may apply in particular situations. Commercial bribery is also a "predicate act" under RICO, which is discussed in a later part of this section.

Bribery of Foreign Officials. Bribes, kickbacks, and other forms of gratuitous payment to foreign officials are sometimes made to obtain new business, to avert expropriation or nationalization of property, or to avoid the expulsion of an individual by a foreign government. Although bribes may be a way of life in some countries, bribery of government officials is contrary to the law of practically every country. Because of the widespread bribery of foreign officials by U.S. businesses, brought to light during the Watergate investigations, Congress enacted the Foreign Corrupt Practices Act in 1977. The Act makes it illegal for a businessperson to give anything of value to any foreign government official to influence official action. Severe penalties may be imposed for violation of the Act.

Offenses in Violation of Public Health and Safety Laws

The federal Food, Drug, and Cosmetic Act is one of many laws enacted to protect the public health and environment. It established the Food and Drug Administration, authorizing it to publish regulations setting standards for the quality of the foods we eat and for the effectiveness of the drugs we buy. Violations of the Act and FDA regulations are strict liability offenses. A first conviction is a misdemeanor, but if the offender is again convicted of any violation of the Act, or if there was an intent to defraud or mislead, the crime is a felony.

Case 9.3, an illustrative prosecution under the federal Food, Drug, and Cosmetic Act, is also a leading case on the liability of corporate officers for corporate crimes.

CASE 9.3   **United States v. Park** • 421 U.S. 658 (1975)

FACTS   John Park was the president of Acme Markets, Inc., a large national food chain. In 1971, the FDA found unsanitary conditions at Acme's Baltimore warehouse. The FDA advised Park by letter of the unsanitary conditions. A second inspection in 1972 found that the conditions had improved, but there was still rodent infestation and rodent-contaminated foods. Acme and Park were charged with a violation of §301 of the Food, Drug, and Cosmetic Act for storing the "adulterated" food. Acme pleaded guilty, but Park did not. At Park's trial, he testified that as chief executive officer of the company, he was responsible for the entire operation of the business, including the storage of foods. He delegated responsibility to other subordinates, however, and in particular had conferred with a firm attorney who had informed him that the Baltimore division vice president would be taking corrective action regarding the "adulterated" food. The trial court instructed the jury that in order to convict Park, "he need not have personally participated in the situation," but he must have had "a position of authority and responsibility in the situation out of which the charges arose." The court of appeals reversed, holding that although the offense did not require criminal intent, proof of "wrongful action" on the part of Park was an essential element. The Supreme Court granted certiorari.

**Case 9.3
Continued**

OPINION

BURGER, J. . . . . In [*United States v. Dotterweich*] this court looked to the purposes of the [Food, Drug, and Cosmetic] Act and noted that they "touch phases of the lives and health of people which, in the circumstances of modern industrialism, are largely beyond self-protection." It is observed that the Act is of "a now familiar type" which "dispenses with the conventional requirement for criminal conduct—awareness of some wrongdoing. In the interest of the larger good it puts the burden of acting at hazard upon a person otherwise innocent but standing in responsible relation to a public danger."

. . . [T]he principle [has] been recognized that a corporate agent, through whose act, default, or omission the corporation committed a crime, was himself guilty individually of that crime. The principle [has] been applied . . . not only to those corporate agents who themselves committed the criminal act, but also to those who by virtue of their managerial positions or other similar relation to the actor could be deemed responsible for its commission.

In the latter class of cases, the liability of managerial officers did not depend on their knowledge of, or personal participation in, the act made criminal by the statute. Rather, where the statute under which they were prosecuted dispensed with "consciousness of wrongdoing," an omission or failure to act was deemed a sufficient basis for a responsible corporate agent's liability. It was enough in such cases that, by virtue of the relationship he bore to the corporation, the agent had the power to prevent the act complained of.

Thus *Dotterweich* and the cases which have followed reveal that in providing sanctions which reach and touch the individuals who execute the corporate mission—and this is by no means necessarily confined to a single corporate agent or employee—the Act imposes not only a positive duty to seek out and remedy violations when they occur, but also, and primarily, a duty to implement measures that will insure that violations will not occur. The requirements of foresight and vigilance imposed on responsible corporate agents are beyond question demanding, and perhaps onerous, but they are no more stringent than the public has a right to expect of those who voluntarily assume positions of authority in business enterprises whose services and products affect the health and well-being of the public that supports them. . . .

We cannot agree . . . that the Government had the burden of establishing "wrongful action" [by Park]. . . . [T]he Government establishe[d] [its] case when it introduce[d] evidence . . . that the defendant had, by reason of his position in the corporation, responsibility or authority either to prevent . . . , or promptly to correct, the violation complained of, and that he failed to do so. . . .

We conclude that . . . the charge [to the jury] . . . contained an adequate statement of the law. . . .

JUDGMENT

Reversed.

Criminal Fraud

Fraudulent actions affecting business fall into two categories: (1) business fraud and (2) consumer fraud.

Business Fraud. Business fraud occurs when an individual defrauds a business firm of its money or property by deception or misrepresentation. For example, through various schemes, several individuals established MasterCard and Visa accounts in banks by representing themselves as legitimate businesses. They then defrauded the banks by submitting for payment phony customer credit card purchases. Depending upon the circumstances, persons committing business fraud may be prosecuted for any number of state and federal crimes, including theft by deception or false pretenses, mail or wire fraud, embezzlement or misappropriation of money or property, and forgery.

Consumer Fraud. Consumers are often victimized by the fraudulent acts of "con artists" and dishonest merchants. Increasingly, lawmakers have passed statutes designed to protect the public from suppliers of goods and services who may take unfair advantage of their customers. Consumer law, discussed at length in Chapter 49, provides for criminal penalties in certain cases of consumer fraud. The following are typical examples of consumer fraud:

- *Appliance service rip-offs.* A customer is charged an amount in excess of the amount agreed beforehand for the repair of an appliance, but is forced to pay it in order to gain return of the appliance.
- *Automobile sales and repair frauds.* A commercial garage makes unnecessary repairs to a customer's vehicle, or the customer is billed for work that was not actually performed.
- *Home improvement frauds.* A contractor is paid for remodeling a house, but fails to pay the companies that supplied the materials. When the suppliers file liens against the property, the homeowner is forced to pay the suppliers to discharge their liens, thereby in effect paying twice for the materials.
- *Merchandising fraud.* In addition to such obvious fraud as false or deceptive advertising, merchants sometimes take advantage of customers by selling used goods as new merchandise, by improperly setting gasoline pumps, and by "palming off" articles of inferior quality as the goods of a reputable, well-known manufacturer.

Securities Laws Violations

The laws and regulations governing the issuance and trading of corporate securities are discussed at length in Chapter 46. However, at this point it is important to recognize that the issuance, sale, and purchase of securities (stocks and bonds) furnish a fertile field for white-collar crimes. Examples of securities offenses are fraudulent schemes for the sale of worthless stocks or bonds and the unlawful use of "inside information" to secure a profit in the securities markets. Carlos, a company director, knows that a medicine his firm manufactures is about to be withdrawn from the market because it produces harmful side effects. Knowing that the price of his company's stock will fall when news of the withdrawal is released, Carlos sells his own stock in the company. Such a stock sale, based upon "inside information," is illegal.

One of the most sensational securities fraud cases was the recent prosecution of Michael Milken. Milken was in charge of the junk bond division for Drexel Burnham Lambert, Inc., the Wall Street investment banking firm. After a 3-year government investigation and a 98-count indictment, Milken entered into a plea agreement in 1990 under which he pled guilty to six felonies, including securities fraud and other crimes. He was sentenced to 10 years in prison, fined $200 million, and paid $400 million into a restitution fund for his victims.

Milken admitted to defrauding investors, cheating clients of Drexel by falsely reporting the price at which their securities had been sold, and to conspiracy with Ivan Boesky, a well-known corporate takeover entrepreneur, to conceal Mr. Boesky's securities holdings. Previously, the Securities and Exchange Commission imposed a $100 million civil penalty upon Ivan

Boesky, and he was also sentenced by a federal court to a jail term of 3 years.

Antitrust Offenses

Congress has enacted various laws to prevent businesses from engaging in any activity considered to be in restraint of trade. Among these *antitrust laws* (the subject of Chapters 52 and 53) are the Sherman Antitrust Act and the Clayton Act as amended by the Robinson-Patman Act of 1936 (see Case 9.1). Antitrust offenses are classic examples of white-collar crimes. Such laws are designed to prevent business concerns from, among other improper activities, fixing prices in agreement with their competitors or engaging in corporate mergers that would restrict free competition.

Price-fixing agreements among competitors and bid-rigging schemes are examples of violations of the antitrust laws that the federal government prosecutes. Penalties for violating the antitrust laws may be severe. Fines may be levied not only upon the firms involved but also upon the individual wrongdoers, such as company managers, and jail sentences may also be imposed.

RICO

The Racketeer Influenced and Corrupt Organizations Act (RICO) was passed by Congress out of concern with the infiltration of legitimate businesses by organized crime. RICO makes it a crime for any person

- To use monies derived from a "pattern of racketeering activity" to secure an interest in an "enterprise" (individual, partnership, corporation, or other legal entity) that is engaged in interstate business or whose activities affect interstate commerce
- To acquire an interest in such an interstate business through a "pattern of racketeering activity"
- To conduct or participate in, as an employee or associate of an enterprise, a "pattern of racketeering activity"
- To conspire to violate any of the above prohibitions

The key to RICO is the requirement of a "pattern of racketeering activity." Racketeering consists of a violation of certain state and federal crimes, including murder, kidnapping, gambling, robbery, and extortion. To be guilty of a "pattern of racketeering activity," a person must commit at least two acts of racketeering (called "predicate acts") within a 10-year period. Two unrelated predicate acts are not sufficient. The Supreme Court recently held that the violations must be "related" and "continuous"—i.e., either a series of related violations over a substantial period of time or present violations coupled with the threat of future racketeering activity.[5] Criminal violators of RICO are subject to a fine of $20,000 per violation and a maximum jail sentence of 20 years. Also, proceeds of the illegal enterprise are subject to forfeiture.

Although a violation of the Act is a criminal offense, RICO provides a civil remedy under which a person injured by a violation can sue for treble damages (three times the actual damages), costs, and attorney's fees. Both legitimate and illegitimate business enterprises can be sued under the broad scope of the "pattern of racketeering activity" concept. Among the "predicate acts" of racketeering activity are wire fraud, mail fraud, securities fraud, and bribery. A legitimate commercial enterprise faces potential liability under the Act if the plaintiff can connect it with one or more of these white-collar crimes. Moreover, the Supreme Court has held that a criminal conviction under RICO is not necessary for bringing a civil lawsuit. Because of the broad scope of RICO, and the treble damage remedy that encourages civil RICO suits against legitimate businesses, the Act has been severely criticized by business interests. Attempts to persuade Congress to reform the Act, however, have been unsuccessful.

Larceny and Embezzlement by Employees

Any consideration of white-collar crime must recognize that a business may also be the *victim*.

---

[5]*H.J. Inc. v. Northwestern Bell Telephone Co.*, 492 U.S. 229 (1989).

Larceny and embezzlement of an employer's property, by computer and other means, are all too common. *Larceny* is the wrongful taking of the property of another with the intent permanently to deprive the owner of its possession. *Embezzlement* is the wrongful withholding of the property of another by someone to whom that property has been entrusted.

In many firms theft (larceny) or embezzlement by employees of cash, tools, spare parts, office supplies, and other materials are very real problems. Most of these activities are carried on by people with no criminal records. Detection is difficult, and criminal prosecution—when it is undertaken—furnishes but slight deterrence to others. Yet the losses from this type of white-collar crime are greater than all the nationwide robbery and burglary losses combined. Such business crimes have a great impact on the economy of the country, since commercial enterprises include as a part of their overhead the losses they suffer from white-collar crimes—and thus these losses are ultimately charged to the consumer.

SUMMARY

A crime is an unlawful act punishable by the state. Any offense which is punishable by imprisonment for more than 1 year or by the imposition of a death sentence is a felony. All lesser offenses are misdemeanors.

A crime involves two elements: an act and criminal intent. Some crimes, strict liability offenses, require no criminal mental state. Criminal liability is personal; however, the law may impose vicarious criminal liability for some regulatory offenses. A person charged with a crime can raise a defense. Recognized defenses include defense of person, defense of property, insanity, intoxication, and minority.

Criminal procedure refers to the various steps involved in prosecuting someone accused of having committed a crime. The Constitution provides significant rights to the accused in the criminal process.

Business crime, or white-collar crime, refers to a nonviolent criminal act related to business. Among such crimes are bribery; federal Food, Drug, and Cosmetic Act violations; securities law violations; antitrust offenses; criminal fraud; RICO violations; and larceny and embezzlement by employees.

REVIEW QUESTIONS

1. What are the purposes of the criminal justice system?

2. What is a strict liability crime? How is it different from vicarious criminal liability?

3. What is the exclusionary rule?

4. Explain the exception to the warrant requirement for "closely regulated" businesses.

5. What is the difference between an indictment and an information?

6. Explain the difference between discovery in a criminal case and discovery in a civil case.

7. Why is it important for businesspeople to have an understanding of white-collar crimes?

8. Under what circumstances should business corporations be criminally liable for the acts of lower-level managerial employees?

9. Why is commercial bribery a crime in many jurisdictions?

10. Should Congress change RICO? How?

CASE PROBLEMS

1. Otto's girlfriend, Susan, refused to see him any more. Otto learned that, since breaking up with him, Susan was dating Felix, who shared an apartment with Otto. Otto bought a package of Rough-on-Rats, a rat poison which is also fatal to humans if ingested, intending to put some in Felix's breakfast coffee at his first opportunity. However, before the opportunity arose, Felix saw the Rough-on-Rats, and he asked Otto what it was for. Otto replied, "I'll tell you. You stole my girl, and I'm going to kill you." What offense did Otto commit?

2. Richard Brush, a minor, illegally entered Carmine Falco's home through a side bathroom window. Falco's home had been burglarized the day before and on several previous occasions. As Brush opened the bathroom door, he was killed by a rifle positioned on a chair in the living room. Falco was not home at the time. He was charged with manslaughter, convicted, and sentenced to 2 years' probation. Was Falco guilty of manslaughter? Explain.

3. Sixty undergraduate students from the State University of New York at Alfred held a dinner dance at Penn Valley Resorts, Inc. Penn Valley's president arranged for the dinner, including an open bar. William Frazier, a 20-year-old student, became intoxicated and was killed in a car accident driving home from the dinner. The president personally served Frazier and did so after Frazier was visibly intoxicated. The corporation was convicted of manslaughter. On appeal, the corporation claimed that it could not be convicted because the board of directors did not authorize or condone the acts of the president. Should the conviction be reversed? Explain.

4. Minnesota customers of Northwestern Bell Telephone Co. (Bell) filed a civil RICO class action against Bell, some of its officers, and members of the Minnesota Public Utilities Commission (MPUC), the state regulatory agency responsible for setting telephone rates. The lawsuit alleged that between 1980 and 1986, Bell and its officers gave five bribes to members of the MPUC, causing it to approve unreasonable and excessive telephone rates. This conduct was said to constitute a "pattern of racketeering activity." Are the allegations of the complaint sufficient to state a cause of action under RICO? Explain.

5. The Grand View Department Store advertises Levi jeans at half the price for which other stores are selling them. The only Levi jeans the store has are small children's sizes. When a customer comes into Grand View to purchase a pair of Levis for herself, she is told that the only Levi jeans the store has for sale are the children's small size, but that the store has a full range of Calvin Klein jeans. These jeans are not on sale, and though they are more costly, their price is fair and is no greater than the price of Calvin Klein jeans in other stores. Competitors of Grand View claim that the store's advertising is false or misleading and that the store should be prosecuted for consumer fraud. Are the competitors correct? Explain.

ETHICS IN PRACTICE

Crimes and intentional torts are inherently unethical, since the conduct in question is intentional, often malicious, and against the interests of the immediate victims and society. But violations such as negligence and regulatory crimes are unintentional and therefore not as morally blameworthy as intentional misconduct. Sometimes justifications are offered for misconduct, as where a person commits a wrong to prevent what is perceived as a greater wrong. These justifications may or may not be sufficient to relieve one of moral responsibility. Often we encounter conduct that does not violate criminal or tort law, but is ethically suspect. We then must decide whether the conduct crosses the line between acceptable and unacceptable and, if it does, what to do about it. The problems that follow illustrate a number of these possibilities and concerns.

PROBLEMS IN ETHICS

1. As reported in *Time* (March 18, 1991) a new heart drug called TPA "hit the market in 1987 in a blinding flash of pitchmen, promotion and public relations hoo-ha." Ten times as expensive as streptokinase, a competing older drug, TPA was touted as clearly superior to the competition. Though many U.S. doctors became skeptical of these claims as they used the product, the majority "bought the pitch, and the new drug became the favored method of breaking up clots in heart-attack victims," in part, perhaps, because several studies had showed that TPA worked more quickly to open blocked arteries. Then an international team of researchers found TPA to be no better at saving lives than streptokinase, and that TPA may have carried "a slightly greater risk of causing strokes." (Later, in 1993, an international study showed a "narrow but definable advantage for TPA" when administered with heparin, a drug that prevents the blood from clotting.)

Why, despite the doubtful advantages and the price difference—about $2,500 per treatment for TPA v. $220 a dose for streptokinase—did U.S. doctors so widely prescribe TPA? The *Time* article suggested some reasons: (1) Cost is still not a primary concern of U.S. doctors, though it seems to be in Canada and Europe, where streptokinase plus ordinary aspirin remains the standard anticlotting therapy. (2) Pervasive fear of malpractice suits pressure U.S. doctors to use the latest techniques. (3) TPA's manufacturer, Genentech, launched an aggressive promotional campaign, "relentlessly promoting its product not just to doctors and patients but to researchers as well."

Though citing the campaign as "the biggest reason" for TDA's wide acceptance, the article did not describe Genentech's specific promotional practices in marketing TPA. It did, however, describe some promotional practices of other drug companies, for example:

- *Frequent prescriber plan.* Wyeth-Ayerst Laboratories gave doctors 1,000 points on American Airlines' frequent-flyer program for each patient they put on the hypertension drug Inderal LA.
- *Profitable research.* As part of a "study," Roche paid doctors $1,200 if they prescribed the antibiotic Rocephin for 20 hospital patients.
- *Big-shot program.* In return for purchasing vaccines, Connaught Labs awarded points redeemable for VCRs, personal computers, and TVs.

(a) Is it ethical for drug companies to use such promotional practices? **(b)** Is it ethical for doctors to respond to them by prescribing the products? **(c)** Should the promotional practices of drug companies be regulated by the Food and Drug Administration?

2. Janice, an assistant chief in a fire department district, told prosecutors that two fire chiefs ordered her to falsify salary records to obtain a greatly inflated pension for one of them—a $98,000 pension based on an ending salary of $90,000. Five years earlier, Janice had worked up the final salary figure for another former chief, who is now receiving a $72,000-a-year pension though his ending salary was only $55,000. The pension recipients face criminal charges. Janice could also face prosecution for her participation. However, as she told reporters, she felt at the time that her chief approached her for assistance that she had better do what her bosses said or she could be fired. "The fire service is para-military. My whole career I've followed directions. I am used to being a confidential employee." Assume that Janice's cooperation in the fraudulent activities is criminal. Has she given a justification that would relieve her from moral responsibility for her acts?

3. Jonesco, a construction company, builds houses. A couple of days before completing one project, Jonesco instructed the power company to disconnect temporary power poles, and told the subcontractors they would need portable generators to finish the work. Later, Susan, the owner of a nearby house, learned that instead of using a portable generator, one subcontractor entered her garage while she was at work and plugged his power tools into her garage outlets. Outraged, Susan called the police, the state contractors' license board, and the power company. All agreed that the subcontractor had made an illegal entry and had stolen electricity, and that she had a good claim against him and Jonesco. Upon being advised that the district attorney probably would not be interested in pursuing the matter as a criminal case, Susan decided not to bring criminal charges. Instead, Susan asked Jonesco to pay her September power bill as reparation for the subcontractor's illegal conduct. Jonesco apologized to Susan, told the subcontractors "Don't do this again," and offered her $10 for the electricity, the actual cost of which Jonesco estimated at about 46 cents. Susan rejected the offer and sued Jonesco in small claims court for $93—the amount of her September power bill plus 1 day's lost wages. **(a)** Is there any ethical justification for the subcontractor's conduct? **(b)** Did Jonesco act ethically in offering Susan $10? To answer, would you need to know whether Jonesco had been involved in similar incidents in the past? **(c)** Did Susan act ethically in demanding $93? Would it be helpful to consider the kinds of harm that Susan suffered? Are other factors relevant?

PART THREE

Contracts

CHAPTER 10
Introduction to the Law of Contracts

CHAPTER 11
The Agreement: Offer and Acceptance

CHAPTER 12
Consideration

CHAPTER 13
Minor's Right to Disaffirm; Other Grounds for Avoidance

CHAPTER 14
Illegal Agreements

CHAPTER 15
A Writing as a Requirement; The Parol Evidence Rule

CHAPTER 16
Rights and Duties of Third Persons

CHAPTER 17
Performance, Breach, and Discharge of Contracts; Remedies for Breach of Contract

Ethics in Practice

CHAPTER 10

Introduction to the Law of Contracts

In every society, from the primitive to the modern, people have always needed food, clothing, shelter, and other essentials. What people could not make or grow, they sought from others. As societies developed beyond the subsistence stage, individuals acquired luxuries and began to engage in cooperative efforts—defense agreements, irrigation systems, public roads, private housing, banking, entertainment, the arts, and so on.

Such endeavors involve fundamental processes of exchange in which people must rely on the promises of others. So, all societies have customs, rituals, and social sanctions aimed at promise enforcement. The traditional native American Cheyenne Indian society had no formal law. Yet the Cheyenne had a rich set of rituals and customs which guided reciprocal (give-and-take) behavior. Though the Cheyenne had no courts, a Cheyenne who departed from the customary methods of reciprocity would receive some sort of social punishment from the community.[1]

In modern America, social customs and rituals operate similarly to those of the ancient Cheyenne. For example, a family might have a custom of rotating the annual family reunion among adult family members. Absent legally required formalities covered in this and subsequent chapters, a court of law is unlikely to order an unwilling member to host the family event. Yet social pressures from the family may enforce appropriate reciprocal behavior regarding the reunion.

Informal social pressures serve reasonably well as a basis for promise enforcement within families and within relatively small, homogeneous societies. In a large, pluralistic society such as ours, however, social sanctions are not enough. We deal often with strangers, in impersonal markets. In our culturally diverse society, and in international markets, people with different value systems disagree, sometimes dramatically, about which promises should be enforced, and how.

To overcome such difficulties, most countries long ago adopted law as a principal means of promise enforcement. In the United States, the **law of contracts** provides a set of social rules for private exchanges. This law recognizes most private agreements as contracts and enforces them either by requiring their performance or, more commonly, by awarding damages for their breach.

Contract law can be confusing. Some of the functions it once served have been discarded.

---

[1] Karl N. Llewellyn and E. Adamson Hoebel, THE CHEYENNE WAY (1961), Chs. 3, 9, and 10.

Others remain in force today. To indicate the general nature and purposes of modern contract law, this chapter sketches some of its historical development, outlines its modern-day content and terminology, and introduces some legal doctrines that supplement it. First, though, the chapter takes up the meaning of contract.

NATURE OF CONTRACTS; IMPORTANCE OF CONTRACT LAW

Meaning of Contract

A **contract** may be defined simply as a promise or set of promises that the courts will enforce. A contract may also be defined as a legally enforceable agreement. This agreement often consists of an exchange of promises between two persons, called "parties," who hope to strike a bargain that is acceptable to each party. In exchange for Ann's promise to pay Ben $2,000, Ben promises to paint Ann's house. Under either of the above definitions, the transaction is a contract.

Since promises are a vital part of contracting, it is helpful to consider the legal meaning of promise and its contractual function. A **promise** is "a manifestation [showing] of intention to act or to refrain from acting in a specified way, so made as to justify a promisee in understanding that a commitment has been made."[2] The party who makes a promise is called the **promisor**. The one to whom the promise is made is called the **promisee**. The "commitment" is the promisor's pledge or assurance that he or she will perform in the way specified, and it ordinarily is made to induce the promisee into a contract. Because the ability to rely on commitments is essential for planning and carrying out business activities, the law protects promisees' expectations of performance by enforcing contractual and certain other kinds of promises.

A promise may be communicated by language or by nonverbal conduct. When communicating in language, a promisor need not use the word "promise." Expressions such as "I will pay" and "I'll give you $10 for it" are promises to pay.

Often, promises are inferred from nonverbal conduct. For example, at an auction, a promise to pay may be inferred from the bidder's act of raising a hand or a card. This is so regardless of any secret intention of the bidder not to pay. Contracting parties such as a seller at an auction usually can rely on external (objective) manifestations of intention and are not bound by internal (subjective) intentions that contradict the outward manifestations.

Requirements for a Contract

The usual goal of contracting parties is an exchange of values: money for goods or for real estate, goods for services, and so on. There may be a period of negotiation or bargaining during which the parties "dicker" back and forth to establish the price and other terms. The resulting contract will call for one party to render a performance (or to make a promise to perform) in exchange for the other party's return performance or promise.

A contract for an exchange of values usually must meet the following requirements:

1 *Agreement*. **Agreement** is defined as a manifestation of mutual assent ordinarily arrived at by a process of offer and acceptance (which may or may not involve bargaining over terms). Ann asks Ben to paint her house for $2,000. Ann is the **offeror** (the person making an offer) and Ben is the **offeree** (the person receiving the offer). A contract forms, or "arises," when the offeree (Ben) indicates agreement to, or "accepts," the offer.

2 *Consideration*. The promises must be supported by **consideration.** Ann's promise to pay money is consideration for Ben's promise to paint her house. His promise to paint the house is consideration for her promise to pay money. (Thus, usually, each contracting party is both a promisor and a promisee.)

---

[2]*Restatement (Second) Contracts*, Sec. 2(1).

3. *Capacity.* The parties involved must have **capacity** (mental or legal ability) to contract.
4. *Lawful Purpose (Legal Object).* The agreement must serve a **purpose** that is **permitted by law.** For example, an agreement to buy heroin for recreational use or for resale would not be a contract because the agreement has an illegal purpose.

For certain types of contracts, there is another requirement: a writing or a legally acceptable substitute. Each of these requirements is discussed further in the following chapters.

Significance of Contracts and Contract Law

Contract law is a body of rules governing the formation, performance, and enforcement of contracts. Its major purpose is to protect the reasonable expectations of individuals, businesses, and governments that contracts will be binding on and enforceable by the parties. Because contracts are enforceable, private parties can make personal and business plans of immense variety, confident of receiving the bargained-for exchange or a court-ordered equivalent (usually a money payment called "damages"). The large-scale, long-term business planning necessary for a modern industrial society would be difficult to achieve without the legal enforceability of contracts.

As a part of business studies, contract law is tremendously significant because it underlies or is related to all major areas of law affecting business. Chapters 10 to 17 deal mostly with the "common law" of contracts—i.e., the modern American version of its forerunner, the English common law of contracts. Common law contract principles appear throughout the law governing employment, labor-management relations, partnerships, corporations, antitrust and merger problems, secured transactions such as mortgages, insurance, and the landlord-tenant relationship. The law of contracts has been adapted to serve special needs. For example, we have a special body of contract law governing the sale of goods—Article 2 of the Uniform Commercial Code (UCC). An even more specialized body of contract law—Article 3 of the UCC—applies to commercial paper: the checks, notes, drafts, and certificates of deposit used in financial transactions. Even the law of bankruptcy requires attention to contract principles, since the courts must decide which of the troubled debtor's contracts are to be enforced and which are not. A study of the concepts, principles, and technical vocabulary of contract law will aid immensely in understanding most other business law.

DEVELOPMENT OF CONTRACT LAW

Like law in general, the law of contracts has changed over the centuries in response to changes in social conditions, needs of the population, and philosophies of government. The development of American contract law during the eighteenth, nineteenth, and twentieth centuries presents a striking example of how law evolves to meet new needs.[3]

As late as the eighteenth century, contract law in America reflected a frontier culture of small towns, farmers, and small traders, and an attitude, established in medieval times, that a thing had a fair or a "just" price that would change little over time. One role of this early contract law, especially as applied by the courts of equity, was to assure fairness of exchanges between individuals. So, if a contracting party was overcharged, the court would look into the equivalency of the exchange (adequacy of the consideration), at least to the extent of refusing to enforce a grossly unequal bargain. Thus, the courts of this period acted as monitors of contracts and awarded damages in accordance with a fair price standard that was independent of the agreement of the parties.

---

[3]The discussion of the development and nature of contract law is based largely on M. Horwitz, THE TRANSFORMATION OF AMERICAN LAW (1977), L. Friedman, CONTRACT LAW IN AMERICA (1965), R. Pound, THE SPIRIT OF THE COMMON LAW (1921), and C. Fried, CONTRACT AS PROMISE (1981).

Classical View of Contract Law

Market Economy, Laissez-faire, and Freedom of Contract. As a part of the industrial revolution, the first large commodities markets appeared in this country early in the nineteenth century. With them came great changes in contract law and philosophy that caused the nineteenth century to be known as the "classical period" of contract. Influenced by Adam Smith's "invisible hand" (the laissez-faire economic theory that market forces determine value) and the fact that market values fluctuate, legal writers and judges rejected the eighteenth-century idea of a fixed just price. Instead, value was now thought to rest on a host of variable, subjective factors which a court was in no position to evaluate—for example, supply and demand, the relative value of other investments, and, above all, the individual needs and preferences of the bargaining parties. Consequently, price and other terms of a contract could be properly determined only by the agreement of a willing buyer and seller, each acting in his or her own self-interest in a free market with a minimum of governmental interference.

During the nineteenth century, then, contract law came to reflect the following premises:

1. Contracting parties should have a broad freedom to contract as they like—to make economic decisions subject only to a few limitations imposed by law for the prevention of fraud, the protection of minors, and so on.
2. Parties dealing "at arm's length" (as wary strangers) are presumed equal in bargaining power and thus capable of protecting themselves from being taken advantage of: **caveat emptor** ("Let the buyer beware").
3. Contracts should be enforced because the parties, being creatures of free will, intend the consequences of their actions: promisees' reliance on the promised performances.
4. Since value is subjective (personal to the contracting parties), only the contracting parties are competent to judge whether the things exchanged are equivalent. Therefore, the bargain struck by the parties will not be overturned merely for inadequacy of consideration; indeed, harsh bargains are to be expected in a market economy and ordinarily will be enforced.
5. However, although the heart of contracting is the "meeting of the minds" (agreement) of the contracting parties, the interpretation and construction of a contract (determining what the parties meant) is a question of law for the court to decide. Thus, the court has the power to conform the parties' meaning to external rules of law with which their actual intent might otherwise conflict.

Role of Nineteenth-Century Contract Law. In the eighteenth century, contracts served mainly to transfer ownership of an existing thing for an equivalent value. But in the emerging market economy of the nineteenth century, people began using contracts to assure themselves of a *future* performance for an agreed future consideration—to reduce the risk of loss in an impersonal, fluctuating market. The function of contract became that of ensuring an expected future return, even if the bargain turned out badly for the other party. It was no longer the function of courts to assure equivalence of exchange. Their function was now to enforce the legitimate agreements of contracting parties, and most agreements were considered legitimate even if one party could demonstrate that he or she had received the worst of the bargain. Contract rules based on the face-to-face dealings of the eighteenth century were on the way out. Replacing them were the uniform, consistent, abstract rules thought necessary for protecting expectations in the impersonal national markets of the nineteenth century.

Contemporary View of Contract Law

Though many nineteenth-century contract principles apply today, twentieth-century contract law and contract-related doctrines reveal a substantial movement away from previous contract philosophy and practice.

Viewed broadly, the modern contract law of most states consists of three major, interrelated elements. They are:

1. *The common law of contracts,* a body of state law applying to contracts such as those for real estate and services.
2. *The Uniform Commercial Code* (UCC), another body of state law which applies to contracts more likely to be involved in interstate commerce—e.g., contracts for sales of goods. To foster efficient distribution of goods, many UCC contract rules differ substantially from their common law counterparts.
3. *Government regulation,* state and federal statutes and administrative rules affecting contracts.

> **BOX 10.1**
> **A Question of Ethics**
>
> Some people argue that breaching a contract is not a moral violation, because the non-breaching party has a cause of action for compensatory damages which, in theory, make the plaintiff "whole." Under this view, a contract is merely an economic accommodation between strangers. A breach, especially for the purely economic reason of securing a better price, is consistent with the idea of an impersonal free market in which values, including harms flowing from a breach of contract, can and should be reduced to money terms.
>
> Do you subscribe to this view? If not, what moral responsibility should a contracting party have for the logical consequences of breach? Should not ethical businesspeople recognize the "ripple" effect of their breaches and avoid those that are without substantial justification? ∎

Uniform Commercial Code. Mass production and the development of national markets caused buyers and sellers of goods to do business across state lines. However, the law applying to contracts for the sale of goods (like the common law applying to other contracts) varied considerably from state to state. To facilitate interstate commerce in goods, legal scholars drafted a number of "uniform acts" for the individual state legislatures to adopt so that all states would be operating under the same commercial law. The Uniform Sales Act, adopted between 1907 and 1941 in thirty-six states and the District of Columbia,[4] introduced substantial uniformity into the law of sales. Eventually, the Uniform Commercial Code replaced the Uniform Sales Act and other uniform acts on related topics. The Code, now in effect in all states except Louisiana, has nine articles on topics of commercial law.[5] Article 2 governs sales of goods.

As noted in the sales chapters of this book, Article 2 provides flexible rules of contracting well suited to the vast numbers of fast-paced sales transactions occurring daily. Unlike the cumbersome common law rules governing real estate and services contracts, Article 2 emphasizes ease of contract formation; judicial discretion in contract enforcement (but in light of actual business practices); ethical business conduct and fair dealing, especially by merchants; and, for breach of contract, practical remedies that permit business to continue with a minimum of interruption.

In every state, most people will contract for services or real estate, and also for goods. Consequently, the residents of all states (except perhaps Louisiana, where the common law of contracts was never adopted) will encounter two rather different bodies of contract law governing bargained-for exchanges: the common law of contracts and Article 2. Yet these bodies of law are closely related. For example, where Article 2 does not provide a rule to cover a sales contract situation, the common law contract rules apply.

Restatement (Second) of the Law of Contracts. Early in this century, the American Law Institute (ALI), a group of legal scholars and practitioners, saw a need for more uniformity in the common law than then existed. The ALI published a number of works, called *Restatements*, on major law topics such as contracts, torts, and

---

[4]Robert J. Nordstrom, HANDBOOK OF THE LAW OF SALES (1970), p. 4.

[5]Louisiana, being of French background, adopted Roman civil law in its French form as the basis of its legal system. Consequently, Louisiana has a civil code somewhat like the UCC. Although Louisiana has not adopted the UCC as such, its legislature has adopted in substance Articles 1, 3, 4, 5, 7, 8, and 9.

agency. Having examined thousands of often conflicting court cases, the ALI presented (in the form of written rules, examples, and commentary) its best estimate of the common law for each topic, stating the majority positions of the courts and a number of significant minority positions. Often criticized as creating an illusion of legal certainty when in fact law constantly grows and adjusts to social forces, the *Restatements* nevertheless have been persuasive to judges as they decide cases.

The *Restatement of the Law of Contracts*, published in 1932, reflected the nineteenth-century ideal for a law of contracts—precise, abstract, impersonal rules aimed at allocating risk in huge, impersonal markets. Nearly 50 years later, the ALI published the *Restatement (Second) of the Law of Contracts*. It reflects modern developments in and attitudes toward contract law. In particular, it adopts, for application to all contracts, many flexible, discretionary UCC rules formerly limited to sales of goods.

A *Restatement*, unlike a uniform act enacted into law by a legislature, is not an official statement of law. The rules and principles of a restatement are merely guidelines for the courts. However, over time, significant portions of the *Restatements* have become law in many states by a process of judicial incorporation. Some parts of *Restatement (Second)* have been adopted by many courts in the United States, while other parts have been ignored. As the provisions of *Restatement (Second)* are incorporated into the common law of contracts, there will be a narrowing of the differences between it and the law of sales, and a modernization of the common law.

Government Regulation Affecting Contracts.

From early times, the government has placed limits on what people may do to one another through contract. The eighteenth-century court's limiting a seller to a "just price" is one example of judicial intervention into private agreements to protect a weaker party. Even in the nineteenth century when the parties' decision as to value was supposed to remain undisturbed, judges would intervene indirectly to remedy extreme cases of exploitation—for example, by interpreting vague contract language against the exploiter. As discussed later in the section entitled "Contracts of Adhesion," modern courts have been considerably more active in coming to the aid of weaker parties.

Legislatures also have a fairly long history of regulating contractual relations. In 1921, Dean Roscoe Pound, in *The Spirit of the Common Law*, made note of "statutes requiring payment of wages in cash, statutes regulating conditions of labor, and legislation with respect to non-living wage, minimum wage, and the like." Today, state and federal regulation of employment contracts is pervasive, and other legislative and administrative agency limitations on freedom of contract abound. The UCC imposes an obligation of good faith on all parties to Code transactions, gives the parties a right to avoid (cancel) "unconscionable" (oppressively unfair) contracts or contract clauses, and imposes warranties (guarantees of quality) in the sale of goods if the seller does not take care to exclude them. In most states, legislatures or administrative agencies regulate, on behalf of customers, the terms of contracts for insurance, water and electricity, and the like. And there is a large and growing amount of federal regulation of private contracts, often in the form of disclosure statutes protecting consumers, such as the Truth-in-Lending Act, the Real Estate Settlement Procedures Act, and the Fair Credit Billing Act, to be discussed in later chapters.

Contracts of Adhesion.

A traditional assumption underlying contract law is that each party, in negotiating a contract, has sufficient bargaining power to prevent the other from taking undue advantage. In many instances, this assumption holds true. Large corporations, for example, usually can fend for themselves when dealing with one another, as can most people who negotiate the purchase of a used car from a neighbor. Often, however, one party, usually a borrower or a buyer dealing with a large firm, has no meaningful choice with regard to some or all of the contract terms. They are imposed by the stronger party against the weaker party's wishes, usually by means of a standard-form contract. Rather than permit the form to be varied, the firm or industry imposing it simply refuses to deal with anyone who will not accept its terms. A contract thus imposed is called a **contract of adhesion.** Most contracts for consumer goods, insurance, mortgages, consumer credit, automobiles, and a host of other goods and services are contracts of adhesion.

Standard-form contracts serve legitimate functions in our economy and usually are enforced despite a weaker party's lack of consent to imposed terms. Many businesses could not function on a large scale if the terms of each transaction had to be negotiated individually. Transaction costs for sellers of inexpensive goods and services could become prohibitive. The insurance industry, which must be able to calculate and limit risk, would be unable to do so if insurance contracts varied with each customer. Yet, people upon whom terms can be imposed can be unfairly exploited. Despite the presumption that all contracting parties are equals, even nineteenth-century courts took steps to remedy the worst abuses of superior bargaining power. Twentieth-century courts, legislatures, and administrative agencies have recognized the misuse of standard-form contracts as a major problem and have developed a variety of ways to combat it. They include:

- Interpreting the contract in favor of the weaker party.
- Finding that the stronger party did not give consideration.
- Requiring disclosure of key information.
- Regulating content, as in insurance and utilities contracts.
- Applying the concept of unconscionability, discussed earlier.[6]

CLASSIFICATION OF CONTRACTS

The study of contract law often involves reference to particular kinds of contracts. The following paragraphs describe some common types of contracts and some of their characteristics. A given contract may fit into more than one category.

Express and Implied Contracts

An **express contract** is one in which the terms of the contract are stated in words. An **implied contract** (sometimes called an "implied-in-fact" contract) is one in which the terms of the contract are wholly or partly inferred from conduct or from surrounding circumstances. When Jane, on passing a market where she has an account, picks up a bag of oranges marked $1.09, holds up the bag, and waits until the clerk nods, the promise to pay $1.09 (and, in fact, the whole contract) is implied by the conduct of the parties. In legal effect there is no difference between an express contract and an implied contract. They differ merely in the manner in which assent is manifested.

Unilateral and Bilateral Contracts

In a **unilateral contract,** one party makes a promise in exchange for the other party's performing an act. Ann tells Ben, "Mow my lawn and I'll pay you $10." This is an offer for a unilateral contract because Ann (the promisor) expects Ben (the promisee) to accept her offer by performing the requested act (mowing). In contrast, a **bilateral contract** is one in which both parties make promises. Ann says to Ben, "I'll pay you $10 to mow my lawn. Will you mow it Friday for that price?" Ann has made an offer for a bilateral contract because Ben is to indicate his acceptance by making a verbal response that either states or implies a promise to mow the yard on Friday ("Yes," or "Yes, I'll mow your lawn on Friday for $10").

In a bilateral contract between Ann and Ben, a contract arises as soon as Ben communicates his acceptance to Ann. Consequently, as soon as Ben accepts the offer, he is obligated to mow the yard on Friday, and Ann is obligated to pay him $10 upon his completing the job. In the unilateral contract situation, however, a contract does not arise until Ben at least begins his performance. Consequently, unilateral contracts tend to arise later than bilateral contracts, and

---

[6]David W. Slawson., "Standard Form Contracts and Democratic Control of Lawmaking Power," 84 *Harvard Law Review* 529 (1971).

there is more time for the offeror (Ann) to revoke (cancel) the offer.

Under older rules pertaining to unilateral contracts (still observed in some states), there was no contract until the offeree *completed* the performance. So, in those days the offeree (Ben) risked having the offer canceled after beginning the performance, but before completing it. Since partial performance was not sufficient to create a contract, the offeree was not entitled to the contract price. However, as explained later in this chapter, the offeree (Ben) was entitled to the reasonable value of his part performance, under the doctrine of "quasi contract" (often called *quantum meruit*).

Executory and Executed Contracts

An **executory contract** is one that is yet to be performed. Ann says to Ben, "I'll pay you $10 to mow my lawn. Will you mow it tomorrow?" and Ben says "Yes." Ann and Ben have entered into an executory bilateral contract. It is executory because neither party to it has yet performed.

An **executed contract** is one that has been performed. If Ben mows the lawn and Ann pays him $10, the contract is fully executed. If Ben mows the lawn but Ann fails to pay, the contract is *partially executed*. It could also be said to be *partially executory*, since Ben has performed but Ann has not.

Enforceable, Unenforceable, Voidable, and "Void" Contracts

An **enforceable contract** is one for the breach of which the law gives a remedy. The usual remedy is a judgment for monetary damages. In appropriate circumstances (discussed in Chapter 17), the equitable remedy of specific performance is available.

An **unenforceable contract** is one meeting the basic requirements of mutual assent, consideration, legal object, and parties with capacity to contract, but which the law will not enforce because of a failure to comply with some other legal requirement. For example, contracts for the sale of land must be in writing to be enforceable. An oral contract for the sale of land ordinarily is unenforceable.

A **voidable contract** is one which a party may either enforce or get out of (avoid) as that person chooses. For example, a person who was induced to enter a contract by the other party's fraud may avoid (cancel) the contract, or may enforce it and have damages for any loss caused by the fraud.

A **"void" contract,** if there can be such a thing, is nothing more than an attempt at contracting that never produced a contract because some essential contractual element (mutual assent, consideration, legal object, or capacity of the parties) was missing. A person who has been declared insane by a court lacks contractual capacity. That person's alleged contract is void.

Formal and Informal Contracts

A **formal contract** is one to which the law gives special effect because of the formalities or the special language used in creating it. At common law, a written promise (e.g., to make a gift) to which the promisor's seal (e.g., a wax emblem) was attached was enforceable because the sealed document complied with the formalities prescribed by law, and not because there was any consideration given for the promise. In most states, the legal effect of a seal has been abolished. Today, the most common formal contracts are **negotiable instruments** (commercial paper) such as checks. To create a negotiable instrument, a person must use a particular form or style of language. A negotiable instrument has legal characteristics that differ from those of ordinary contracts. How negotiable instruments differ from ordinary contracts is discussed in Chapters 31 to 35.

Informal contracts are those for which the law does not require a particular set of formalities or special language. The parties may use any style of language they please, as long as the usual requirements for a contract (mutual assent, consideration, and so on) are met. The contract may be oral, or it may even be inferred from the parties' conduct, in the absence of a statute requiring a writing. If the parties use language to create an informal contract, it can be as elaborate or as sketchy as they desire. A phone call or a quick exchange of letters or telegrams may be sufficient to create a contract. Often, however, an informal contract is very carefully planned, as where a manufacturer's law department spends months developing a detailed standard-form contract for dealers to use. Sometimes called "simple" contracts, informal contracts may in fact be very complicated.

DOCTRINES RELATED TO CONTRACT LAW

Two important doctrines—quasi contract and promissory estoppel—supplement modern contract law. Centuries old, quasi contract provides a damage remedy to prevent *unjust enrichment* where a person conferred a benefit on someone else, but that other person had made no promise to pay or for some other reason had no contractual obligation to pay.

In promissory estoppel cases there is always a promise, but (as in quasi contract) the transaction either did not develop into a contract or fell short of an enforceable contract. Promissory estoppel provides for the enforcement of promises (where classical contract rules would not), to the extent of the promisee's *justifiable reliance* on the promise. Largely a twentieth-century development, it is perhaps the most significant advance in contract law since the nineteenth-century movement away from the just-price doctrine. Indeed, some writers believe that promissory estoppel may be replacing contract as a basis for promise enforcement.[7]

Quasi Contract

Sometimes people deliver goods, improve real estate, or render services to others without benefit of an enforceable contract. They might have delivered goods by mistake to the wrong person or improved the wrong real estate. They might

[7] E.g., G. Gilmore, "The Death of Contract" (1974), though in 1981 Professor Gilmore himself reportedly found contract law "not only alive and well but bursting at the seams." E. Allan Farnsworth, "Developments in Contract Law During the 1980's: The Top Ten," 41 *Case W. Reserve* 203, 222 n. 116 (1990).

have thought there was a contract when in fact none arose. Or the contract that they did negotiate might have turned out to be unenforceable. These people are not entitled to a *contract* price, because their attempt to contract, if any, failed. But they might be entitled to an *alternative* remedy (an amount in lieu of contract damages) under the doctrine of quasi contract.

Quasi contracts (sometimes called implied-in-law contracts) are not contracts at all; they are obligations imposed by law *to prevent unjust enrichment* of one person at another's expense. The obligation is created by law, not by mutual assent, and in fact often is imposed contrary to one's wishes.

To recover damages in a lawsuit based on quasi contract, the plaintiff ordinarily must prove three things: (1) The plaintiff conferred a benefit on the defendant; (2) the plaintiff reasonably expected to be paid for the benefit, or at least did not intend it as a gift; and (3) allowing the defendant to retain the benefit without paying for it would unjustly enrich the plaintiff.

The amount of damages in quasi contract is the *reasonable value* of services rendered or property delivered, and *not* some contract price that might have been agreed to. The expression *quantum meruit* (meaning "as much as he deserves") often is used in quasi-contract cases to describe this reasonable value.

The following situations illustrate the nature of quasi contract and its relationship to contract law:

- Before leaving for work, Art writes the following note to Betty and leaves it in her mailbox: "I'll pay you $20 to mow my lawn this afternoon." After Betty has mowed half the lawn, Art returns home and refuses to let her complete the job. Since the law of Betty's state requires that she complete the mowing in order to accept Art's offer for a unilateral contract, no contract arose, and Betty has no cause of action for the contract price of $20. However, under the principle of *quantum meruit*, she is entitled to the reasonable value of her services. Ordinarily, "reasonable value" is the rate customarily charged in the community. If the customary rate for mowing lawns the size of Art's is $30, Betty should receive $15 for the half she mowed.

- Al agrees orally to sell his house to Bob for $50,000 plus 10 percent annual interest. Bob is to pay $400 per month until the purchase price is paid, and Al is then to transfer ownership to Bob by means of a document called a "deed." Bob moves into the house, and during the next 3 years makes major repairs. Seeing the improvements, Al cancels the oral contract and brings suit to evict Bob. Since oral contracts for the sale of real estate are not enforceable in Al's state, Al wins the eviction suit and moves back into the house. Bob had no contract with Al for the repairs, but under the law of quasi contract is entitled to their reasonable value.
- Ann, a physician, discovers Ben unconscious by a roadside and renders emergency medical services. Ben dies without regaining consciousness, and Ann files a claim against Ben's estate for payment for her services. Ann had no contract with Ben because, being unconscious, he lacked capacity to contract and also was incapable of the assent necessary for a contract. Nevertheless, Ann has a quasi-contract remedy for the reasonable value of her services.

Sometimes the courts deny quasi-contract recovery even though the defendant received a benefit. For example, the court will deny recovery if the plaintiff did not reasonably expect to be paid. A physician who treats a member of his or her immediate family ordinarily would not be allowed quasi-contract recovery for services rendered. Nor would an "officious intermeddler" be allowed a quasi-contract recovery. An intermeddler is a person who intrudes into other people's business affairs or tries to force benefits upon another. Ann leaves her car at a service station for an oil change. When she returns, Ben, the service station operator, demands payment not only for the oil change but also for a tune-up he gave the car without Ann's consent. Ben, an intermeddler, has neither a contract for the tune-up nor a right to a quasi-contract recovery. In contrast, a physician coming to the aid of an unconscious person in an emergency is not considered an intermeddler. Most courts reason that it is simply good public policy to assure physicians of reasonable payment as an inducement to aid helpless victims with whom contracting may be impossible.

The following case illustrates the nature of quasi contract.

> **BOX 10.2**
>
> **Point to Consider**
>
> To succeed in a quasi-contract case, a plaintiff ordinarily must show that the other party was unjustly enriched by the plaintiff's action. In each of the three illustrations above, what did the other party receive that, if it were kept without payment, would result in his or her unjust enrichment?

CASE 10.1 Swiftships, Inc. v. Burdin • 338 So. 2d 1193 (La. App. 1976)

FACTS Defendant Burdin, owner of a 40-foot cabin cruiser, wanted to replace the boat's two-part canopy with a one-piece, all-aluminum canopy. He contracted with plaintiff Swiftships, Inc., to do the work for $3,435 and paid Swiftships a $700 deposit. The contract specified "Bond 185 Excursion Edging" on the new canopy. This kind of edging consisted of a slotted round molding which fits over the edges of the aluminum plate to cover the rough edges. It was easy to install, since it could be bent around the edge of the canopy by hand and fastened by tack welding.

**CASE 10.1
Continued**

During the construction of the canopy, Burdin decided that the Bond 185 edging was not massive enough. He instructed Swiftships to install a different and larger edging. Swiftships did so. The new edging had to be fabricated by Swiftships and required a solid weld all around the canopy. When the work was completed, Swiftships submitted a bill for $8,146. Burdin refused to pay, contending that the contract price was $3,435. Swiftships sued Burdin for $7,446 (the billed amount minus the $700 deposit).

The trial court held that there was no contract for the higher amount (apparently because the parties had not agreed on price), but that plaintiff was entitled to recover damages on the basis of *quantum meruit*. The trial court awarded plaintiff $6,137, disallowing amounts billed as "overtime pay," since Burdin had not imposed a time limit for completing the work. Contending that "the amount claimed by plaintiff exceeded the enrichment received by the defendant and should have been reduced," defendant Burdin appealed.

OPINION

HOOD, J. . . . Quantum meruit is an equitable doctrine, based on the concept that no one who benefits by the labor and materials of another should be unjustly enriched thereby. Under those circumstances, the law implies a promise to pay a reasonable amount for the labor and materials furnished, even in the absence of a specific contract therefor. . . .

The amount which [a plaintiff] can recover on quantum meruit, however, is subject to a double limitation: (1) Plaintiff cannot recover more than the actual value of the materials and labor furnished for defendant, including a fair profit; and (2) plaintiff cannot recover more than the amount defendant was enriched by his furnishing of labor and materials. . . .

The evidence . . . shows that the actual value of the labor and materials furnished by plaintiff . . . was $8,146, as shown in the itemized statement. . . . There, in fact, is no evidence in the record tending to show that any of the charges listed in that statement are excessive. . . .

[T]he burden of proof rests on defendant, and not the plaintiff, to prove that the sum claimed by plaintiff exceeds the amount by which he was enriched. In this case, defendant has failed to show that the amount of labor and materials furnished by plaintiff exceeded the enhanced value of the boat, and defendant thus is not entitled to have plaintiff's claim reduced.

Defendant contends . . . that the charges pertaining to the edgings "should certainly not be over one hundred percent of the [original contract amount]. We agree that the charges made by plaintiff for the edging on the canopy seem high. The trial judge also felt that "the figures exceed the enrichment received by the defendant," although there was no evidence as the amount of the enrichment, and partly for that reason he reduced the award by the amount of overtime wages charged by plaintiff. We have reviewed the evidence, and we cannot say that the trial judge erred in the award which was made to plaintiff. . . .

JUDGMENT

The judgment appealed from is affirmed. . . .

PROMISSORY ESTOPPEL

Under traditional contract law, one's promise is enforceable only when a contract arises, usually after a process of offer and acceptance establishing an exchange of consideration. But often the classical rules of contract formation are not compatible with reasonable business practices, and people rely on promises only to learn later that no enforceable contract arose. In such a situation, a court might apply the doctrine of **promissory estoppel** to enforce a promise that would be unenforceable under the traditional rules of contracting.[8] Thus, promissory estoppel fills a gap in contract law.

To say that a promisor is "estopped" means only that the promisor is prevented by law from avoiding liability for harm caused by his or her promise.

Promissory estoppel is based on the promisee's detrimental (injurious) reliance on the promise. *Reliance* means that the promisee did something (or failed to do something) because of the promise. Suppose your plane leaves for a foreign country in 15 minutes, you have forgotten to renew the insurance on your house, and a friend promises to renew the insurance for you. The friend fails to do so, and your house is destroyed by fire. By not renewing the insurance yourself, you have relied on your friend's promise. Your reliance is *detrimental* because you suffered a loss as a result of the broken promise.

Section 90 of both *Restatements* sets forth three elements, or requirements, of promissory estoppel:

1. There must be a promise that the promisor should reasonably expect to induce action or forbearance (intentional nonaction) on the part of the promisee.
2. The promise must induce the action or forbearance. That is, the promisee must act in justifiable reliance on the promise to his or her detriment. Under *Restatement (Second)*, promisee reliance is *not* required for charitable subscriptions.
3. The situation must be such that injustice can be avoided only by enforcement of the promise.

The doctrine of promissory estoppel originated as a basis for enforcing gift promises within the family (e.g., a promise to give land), charitable promises, and so on. Today it is a basis for enforcing commercial promises as well—for example, where the promisee justifiably relied on a contract offer but was prevented from accepting it, or on a contract that arose but never became enforceable. Pedro orally contracts to employ Tomas for 2 years. Relying on Pedro's oral promise, Tomas moves his family across the country, buys a house on credit, reports for work, and performs well. Two months later, Pedro fires Tomas and hires Gloria, Pedro's new sister-in-law. Under contract law, the agreement between Pedro and Tomas is not enforceable because it was not in writing. In many states, however, Tomas would be entitled to damages resulting from his detrimental reliance on Pedro's promise. The damages would include at least the cost of moving and any money lost on the purchase of the house. Depending on the court's view of what "justifiable reliance" means, Tomas might also be entitled to damages for breach of the employment contract.

Promissory estoppel has been applied even more broadly—for example, to promises made during the course of negotiations preliminary to a contract offer. In *Hoffman v. Red Owl Stores, Inc.*,[9] Hoffman sold his grocery store and bakery business, moved his family to another town, and purchased a building lot in reliance on Red Owl's repeated assurances that Hoffman would receive a supermarket franchise. He had bought the grocery store to gain experience in the grocery business. In preparing himself to operate the franchise, he incurred a variety of losses and expenses. When the supermarket deal did not materialize, Hoffman brought suit. No contract had arisen, because Red Owl's representations

---

[8] Promissory estoppel is used in three main situations: (1) where an offer was made but not accepted, as discussed in Chapter 11; (2) where the person to whom the promise was made gave no consideration; and (3) where an oral contract was not enforceable for lack of a writing required by law, as discussed in Chapter 15.

[9] 133 N.W.2d 267 (Wis. 1965).

were too indefinite to constitute a contractual offer. The court held, however, that Hoffman had a cause of action based on promissory estoppel. By promising a franchise and encouraging Hoffman's preparations, Red Owl should have expected the action that Hoffman took. By following Red Owl's suggestions for gaining business experience, selling the bakery at a loss, losing his down payment on the lot, and incurring moving and rental expenses, Hoffman justifiably relied to his detriment on Red Owl's promise. Red Owl was held liable to Hoffman for the resulting losses and expenditures.

> **BOX 10.3**
>
> ### You Be the Judge
>
> Phil invited Maria (not their real names) to the senior prom. Especially for the occasion, Maria bought a gown and a new pair of shoes. Shortly before the prom, Phil broke their date and invited someone else. Maria demanded that he pay for the gown and shoes. He refused, and she sued him for the amount she had paid. Assume that Phil would have no contractual liability. Could he be liable to Maria under the doctrine of promissory estoppel?
>
> Suppose the situation were reversed: Phil rented a tuxedo and a limousine and paid for nonrefundable pre-prom dinner tickets, only to have Maria break the date at the last minute to attend with someone else. Would Maria be liable to Phil? ■

PRESENTATION OF CONTRACT LAW IN THIS BOOK

Chapters 11 to 17 deal mainly with common law principles governing contracts in general. Contract formation, the nature of consideration, writing requirements, grounds for avoiding contracts, the assignment of contract rights to third persons, and remedies for breach of contract are among the topics that apply to informal contracts of all kinds, including those for real estate, services, insurance, suretyship, and sales of goods. Since the UCC has affected the common law of contracts, Chapters 11 to 17 highlight relevant Code rules and concepts, usually by discussing them in **boxes** located within the text. Chapters 18 to 22 concentrate on sales of goods, emphasizing the unique qualities of sales transactions and the substantial differences between the law of sales and the common law of contracts. Of course, the study of general contract principles also requires attention to promissory estoppel and quasi contract.

Many kinds of contracts—those concerning insurance, suretyship, employment, and the extension of credit, for example—are discussed in separate chapters throughout the book. Since such law topics present special questions of public policy, an important focus of those chapters is government regulation affecting the content of the contracts involved. Chapters 11 to 17 also illustrate how legislation affects contracts, and in those chapters there is considerable discussion of judicial limits on freedom of contract.

Finally, presented elsewhere in the book are some highly specialized adaptations of contract law such as the law of negotiable instruments (the most prevalent kind of formal contract), documents of title, and corporate securities. Understanding the concept of negotiability, for example, first requires an understanding of the law of assignments, a key topic presented in the general discussion of contract law.

SUMMARY

A contract is a promise or an agreement that a court will enforce. Contract law governs the formation, performance, and enforcement of contracts. Its major purpose is to protect reasonable expectations that contracts will be binding on and enforceable by the parties.

The law of contracts has changed over the centuries in response to changes in social conditions. In the eighteenth century, its main goal was to transfer ownership of an existing thing and to assure fairness of exchanges between individuals. The nineteenth-century goal was to protect expectations of future performance in impersonal national markets.

In most states, twentieth-century contract law consists of three interrelated elements: the common law of contracts; Article 2 of the UCC, applying to sales of goods; and government regulation affecting contracts. Modern contract law continues many nineteenth-century principles, but there is more emphasis on flexibility of contracting, judicial discretion in contract enforcement, fair dealing, and practical remedies aimed at continuing business without interruption. There is also considerably more government regulation of contracting and a greater interest by the courts in coming to the aid of weaker parties who, for example, may be exploited by contracts of adhesion. Although such contracts ordinarily are enforced, twentieth-century courts, legislatures, and administrative agencies have developed a variety of ways to combat their misuse.

Contracts are classified in a variety of ways: as express or implied; unilateral or bilateral; executory or executed; enforceable, unenforceable, voidable, or "void"; and formal or informal.

Two important doctrines—quasi contract and promissory estoppel—supplement modern contract law. Quasi contract provides a damage remedy (reasonable value of a benefit conferred) to prevent unjust enrichment where a person conferred the benefit in the absence of a contract. Promissory estoppel, a most significant development in twentieth-century contract law, provides promise enforcement where classical rules of contract formation do not, on the basis of the promisee's justifiable reliance on the promise.

REVIEW QUESTIONS

1. (a) What is the meaning of "contract"? (b) Explain the meaning of "promise" as used in the law of contracts. (c) What function do promises serve in contracting?

2. (a) Is bargaining an essential element of a contract? (b) What are the usual requirements for the creation of a contract for an exchange of values?

3. What is the major purpose of contract law?

4. (a) In general, how has contract law changed over the centuries? (b) What are the main features of nineteenth-century contract law? (c) Have these features been abandoned by twentieth-century contract law?

5. (a) In most states, what constitutes twentieth-century contract law? (b) In what ways, if any, has twentieth-century contract law departed from that of the nineteenth century? (c) What have the Uniform Commercial Code and the *Restatement (Second) of Contracts* contributed to present-day contract law?

6. Give five examples of how the government regulates contracting.

7. (a) Is every standard form contract a contract of adhesion? (b) Are contracts of adhesion enforceable?

8. (a) How is the doctrine of quasi contract related to the law of contract? Consider the underlying purpose of quasi contracts and the statement "quasi contracts are not contracts at all." (b) Give examples of situations where quasi-contract principles would apply and where they would *not* apply. (c) To what amount of damages is a winning plaintiff entitled in a quasi-contract case?

9. (a) How is promissory estoppel related to the traditional law of contracts? (b) What circumstances must exist for the application of promissory estoppel? (c) To what amount of damages is a winning plaintiff entitled in a promissory estoppel case?

CASE PROBLEMS

1. Lillith and her husband Frazer bought a house on credit. To get their loan from Fourth Bank, they were required to sign a complex standard-form contract. It had a preprinted clause saying, "Payments are due on the first day of each month. If a payment is not made on or before the tenth day of the month, Bank shall charge a LATE FEE amounting to 5 percent of the payment due that month." Both Lillith and Frazer objected to the clause, but signed the loan contract anyway. At Christmas of the following year, Bank failed to deliver the customary payment notice. Lillith and Frazer forgot to make their January payment by the 10th, but made it on January 24. Bank sent them a bill for the late fee. Are they contractually obligated to pay it?

2. On September 1, Seller and Buyer sign a written agreement which states that on September 20 Seller is to deliver 5 kilograms of a certain substance to Buyer, and that Buyer is to pay the specified price on or before October 10. Seller delivers the substance as promised. It is October 5, and Buyer has not yet paid for it. Is the contract: **(a)** Express or implied? **(b)** Unilateral or bilateral? **(c)** Executory or executed? **(d)** Formal or informal? **(e)** Enforceable or "void"?

3. Builder, Inc., wants to build a local schoolhouse, and plans to bid on the job (make an offer to the school district). In preparing its own bid, Builder takes bids from a number of subcontractors for various parts of the work—concrete floors, roofing, plumbing, and so on. Gymco bids for the gymnasium floor work, promising to do it for $100,000. Gymco's bid is the lowest for the floor work. Builder uses Gymco's figures in preparing Builder's bid, which the school district later accepts. Elated that it now has the contract, Builder phones Gymco to accept its $100,000 offer to do the flooring. Before Builder can accept, however, Gymco says, "I'm canceling my offer to do the floor for $100,000. The price is now $120,000." Builder hires another flooring contractor for $107,000 and sues Gymco for the $7,000 difference between Gymco's bid price and the other contractor's price. Does Builder have a legal basis for its suit against Gymco?

CHAPTER 11

The Agreement: Offer and Acceptance

The circumstances leading to a contract vary enormously. Two neighbors negotiate the sale of a used car over their back fence; an international corporation takes a year to sell its billion-dollar subsidiary; a small firm deals repeatedly with a large corporation or the government. The parties may be equal in bargaining power. More often, they are decidedly unequal.

As the reported litigation reveals, making a contract can be a troublesome process. The complexity of some transactions impedes agreement. The sheer size of some corporations and government can make it difficult to know with whom one is dealing. One may want out of a transaction that the other party wants to enforce. Often, people simply do not understand the basic rules of contract formation and make errors. Knowledge of the rules does not guarantee a trouble-free contracting process, but it can provide a basis for avoiding certain kinds of difficulties and for resolving others more efficiently.

Ordinarily, we reach contractual agreement by a process of offer and acceptance in which one person, the **offeror,** makes an offer to another person, the **offeree.** An **offer** is a communication—a proposal for an exchange of values—that creates a power of acceptance in the offeree. If the offeree **accepts** the offer ("exercises" the power of acceptance), a contract results, and both parties are bound by its terms.

However, either party can terminate an offer before it is accepted. For example, the offeror might revoke (withdraw or cancel) the offer. Or the offeree might reject it, make a counteroffer, or remain silent and allow the offer to expire. An offer can also be terminated "by operation of law," as where the offeree dies or the subject matter of the offer is destroyed. Once an offer terminates, the offeree no longer has a power of acceptance. Any attempt to accept a terminated offer is ineffective, and no contract arises.

This chapter examines the law of offer and acceptance. The chapter discusses, first, the nature of an offer and what is required to create one and, second, the circumstances under which offers are terminated. Third is a discussion of acceptance: how an offeree accepts an offer and when the acceptance is legally effective.

NATURE OF AN OFFER
Offer Distinguished from Nonoffer

An **offer** is a statement or other communication by which the offeror gives the offeree a **power of acceptance**—the legal ability to accept (agree to) the offer and thereby to create a contract. But how can one tell an offer from a communication that is not an offer? An offer normally does three things:

1. It indicates the *exchange of "consideration"* (the "this for that") that the offeror has in mind.
2. It identifies an *offeree* (a person or group who is to have the power of acceptance).
3. It reveals a *commitment* by the offeror to deal with the offeree.

Since each party to a contract expects to benefit from it, an offeror must give something to get something, and so will propose an exchange of **consideration** (legal value that each party expects to receive). Consequently, the offer usually: (1) expresses or implies a promise by the offeror to do or refrain from doing some stated thing, and (2) requests from the offeree a return act or promise of performance. Since an offer by definition confers a power of acceptance on a specific person (or class of persons) called an "offeree," it necessarily indicates who is to be the offeree, i.e., who is to have the power of acceptance. Ann's statement, "I'll sell my horse Thunder for $5,000" reveals an exchange that Ann finds acceptable, but it is not an offer. Ann's statement made to Ben, "I'll sell Thunder *to you* for $5,000," is an offer because Ann, in addition to indicating the exchange she wants, has identified Ben as the offeree. And, by *promising* to sell Thunder to Ben, Ann has committed herself to dealing with him. So, while nonoffers may propose an exchange that the proposer finds acceptable, only offers *commit* the proposer to a contract with an *offeree*.

Where negotiating parties exchange communications over a period of time, it may be necessary to analyze each communication, or several communications together, to determine whether the qualities needed for an offer are present and, if they are, when the offer arose.

Language of Commitment

To determine whether a person has made the commitment required for an offer, one may need to distinguish language of commitment from statements of intention, negotiatory statements, and invitations to submit offers. Ann says to Bob, "I am going to sell my camera for $100," and Bob replies, "I'll take it; here's the $100." There is no contract; a reasonable observer would conclude that Ann's statement was not an offer (i.e., was not a promise to sell the camera to Bob). It was only a statement of her *intention* to deal in the future with a person as yet unidentified; it did not reveal the present commitment to deal with Bob needed for an offer.

> **BOX 11.1**
>
> ### Test Your Knowledge
>
> In the situation just described, however, *Bob* has made an offer to Ann. How so? Consider whether the three qualities normally present in an offer are present here. ■

Statements leading up to an offer are called *negotiatory statements*. People use negotiatory statements for a variety of reasons—to sound out the other party before making an offer, to maneuver him or her into making the first statement about price, or to invite bids (offers). Thus, a person does not make an offer by saying, "My car is worth $3,000" or "I should get at least $3,000 for my car."

As usually worded, circulars, catalogs, and newspaper advertisements are not offers, but are mere *invitations* to submit offers. Consider the following newspaper advertisement: "FOR SALE—1989 Ford truck for only $9,000. Cash or trade." This ad can be understood to say, "I will sell my 1989 Ford truck for $9,000 or will trade it for another vehicle." The ad describes an exchange acceptable to the advertiser, and it makes a promise to sell. However, it is not an offer because it does not identify an offeree and thus makes no commitment to sell to any particular person. The ad is merely an invitation to interested persons to make an offer to the advertiser. Similarly, an L.L. Bean mail-order catalog is an invitation to make an offer by ordering merchandise. Offerees receive strategic benefits from their offeree status: (1) They can reject offers if the amount ordered exceeds the quantity of goods available for sale. (2) They can reject the offers of customers whose creditworthiness is in doubt.

> **BOX 11.2**
> ### Government Regulation of Contracts
>
> Despite the offeree status of most advertisers, government regulation limits the right of many sellers to reject offers. For example, merchants who refuse to sell goods at advertised prices may be in violation of state or federal laws prohibiting false or deceptive advertising, unfair trade practices, and the like. Many such laws require a seller to stock a sufficient supply of advertised goods to meet a reasonably expectable demand for them or to give "rain checks" if the supply runs out. And sellers covered by the Civil Rights Act of 1964 may not reject offers merely on the basis of race, color, religion, sex, or national origin. However, these laws do not change the fact that, ordinarily, an advertiser merely invites offers and may reject them for legitimate reasons. ■

> **BOX 11.3**
> ### You Be the Judge
>
> In 1956, the Great Minneapolis Surplus Store placed the following advertisement in a Minneapolis newspaper:
>
> Saturday 9 a.m.
> 2 Brand New Pastel
> Mink 3-Skin Scarfs
> Selling for $89.50
> Out they go
> Saturday. Each. . . . $1.00
> 1 Black Lapin Stole
> Beautiful,
> worth $139.50. . . . $1.00
> First Come
> First Served
>
> At 9:00 a.m. on the appointed day, Lefkowitz was first in line at the store, presented a dollar, and demanded the Lapin stole. The store refused to deal with him. Was Lefkowitz entitled to the Lapin stole? ■

Incidentally, the use of the word "offer" in an ad is not sufficient in itself to make the ad an offer. All ads are "offers" in the nonlegal sense of announcing the availability of something for sale. But a *contractual* offer creates a power of acceptance in an offeree. To constitute that kind of offer, an ad must go beyond a mere announcement of availability and make a commitment to sell to whoever is identified as an offeree. That person could be a specific individual ("Tom Jones"), a member of a limited class of people ("the first ten customers who respond to this ad"), or anyone in an unlimited class of people ("the public"). Is the ad in Box 11.3 an offer?

Rewards, Price Quotes, Auctions, and Bids

Often it is not clear whether a particular proposal was an offer or merely an invitation or other preliminary negotiation. When deciding such issues, the courts will consider not only the language used but also the surrounding circumstances. Ordinarily, a communication addressed to a group or to the public at large is less likely to be held an offer than is one addressed to an individual. However, **notices of reward** (normally addressed to the public at large and not a specific person) are held to be offers. The notice may contain a promise to pay money (e.g., "$100 for safe return of my dog Charlie"), but lack an express commitment to pay it to a particular person. Yet a court can usually infer from the surrounding circumstances the offeror's commitment to pay the money to the person who responds to the offer by providing the requested item or information.

Usually, a statement on a price tag in a store is considered to be a **price quote** and not an offer. The reasons that newspaper advertisements usually are not offers apply equally here. Thus, "For Sale, $29.95" usually means no more than a willingness to consider an offer to buy at $29.95. The customer who wishes to purchase the item and tenders $29.95 to the store is the offeror.

The question of who is the offeror and who is the offeree is significant in **auctions** of goods, land, or other property. Auctions may be either **with reserve** or **without reserve.** These terms indicate whether the auctioneer (who acts on behalf of the seller) has reserved (retained) the privilege of withdrawing the property from sale during the bidding process. In an auction *with reserve* the auctioneer is the offeree and has the power of acceptance. As offeree, he or she may reject all bids. In an auction *without reserve* the auctioneer is much like an offeror, with the bidders competing to determine who will win the power of acceptance. After the auctioneer calls for bids in an auction without reserve, the property cannot be withdrawn unless no bid is made within a reasonable time. In either type of auction (with or without reserve), a bidder may withdraw his or her bid until the auctioneer announces the completion of the sale by the fall of the hammer or in some other customary way.

Unless an auction is expressly advertised to be without reserve, it is *with* reserve. An auction with reserve tends to produce a fair market value because the seller, as offeree, may reject all bids and await a more favorable market. In contrast, an auction without reserve tends to produce lower prices because the seller, being the offeror, has no power to reject low bids. However, the auction without reserve may be useful for moving property quickly. Section 2-328 of the Uniform Commercial Code codifies the common law of auctions and applies it to sales of goods.

Building contractors and others commonly seek **competitive bids** (offers) from subcontractors when developing their own bids for a project. For example, a general contractor might invite bids from several roofing subcontractors, expecting to accept the lowest responsible bid. Ordinarily, the advertisement or letter of invitation is not itself an offer, since such communications usually make no commitment to deal with any particular bidder. Yet, like any other ad, an invitation to bid *can* be an offer, as where it says, "This contract will be awarded to the lowest responsible bidder." As noted later in this chapter, bidders may revoke their bids at any time before acceptance, unless prevented from doing so by the doctrine of promissory estoppel.

> **BOX 11.4**
> **Government Regulation of Contracts**
>
> Most contracting with the government—federal, state, or local—is regulated by statute. Statutes commonly specify how bids are to be made, limit a bidder's right to withdraw a bid, and impose special requirements such as a performance bond (a type of insurance protecting the government against defective performance). So, a *government's* ad promising "This contract will be awarded to the lowest responsible bidder" may *not* be an offer, since the bidder may have to qualify in additional ways.
>
> To protect the public from being overcharged, statutes ordinarily require that contracts be awarded to the lowest responsible bidder. In many federal defense contracts, however, there is no such requirement. The national safety, so the argument goes, should not be jeopardized by the imposition of price limitations on contracts of such vital concern. ■

Serious Proposal

To constitute an offer, a proposal must be made with serious intent, or appear to be so made. The offeror's subjective intent is not important; the test is whether an ordinary reasonable observer would consider the offeror's proposal to be serious. Bette attends an auction and bids $500 for an antique clock. It is irrelevant that she thinks to herself that she does not have $500 and that she secretly hopes someone else will make a higher bid and relieve her of her foolish commitment. The auctioneer is justified in treating Bette's bid as a serious proposal, that is, as an offer.

Statements obviously or apparently made in jest, or under the stress of great excitement, or as bravado or bluff are not offers. The classic case involving the stress of great excitement is *Higgins v. Lessig*.[1] An old harness worth about

[1] 149 Ill. App. 459 (1893).

$15 had presumably been stolen. When defendant Lessig discovered the loss, he became "much excited" and using "rough language and epithets" said he would give $100 to any person who found out who the thief was. Plaintiff, who had been present when Lessig made the statement, furnished the information and sought to recover the reward. The trial court found for the plaintiff. However, the appellate court reversed the judgment on the ground that the defendant's language was not to be regarded as a serious proposal but "as the extravagant exclamation of an excited man."

Definite and Complete Terms

Courts are reluctant to "make a contract for the parties," and often have stated that to be enforceable, a contract must contain reasonably definite and complete terms. The essential terms usually include the names of the parties, the subject matter involved (description, quantity), the price, and the time and place for performance. Sometimes the offer contains all the essential terms. If the offer lacks needed terms, but requires the offeree to specify them in the acceptance, the offer and acceptance together may meet the requirement of reasonable definiteness.

The case of *Minneapolis & St. Louis Railway v. Columbus Rolling Mill*[2] illustrates an offer requiring definite terms in the acceptance. Defendant Rolling Mill offered by letter to sell plaintiff 2,000 to 5,000 tons of iron rails at a specified price. In its decision, the court said: "This offer would authorize the plaintiff to take at his election any number of tons not less than two thousand nor more than five thousand, on the terms specified." If the plaintiff had elected to take, say, 3,000 tons, there would have been a contract, although considered alone the offer was not reasonably definite as to quantity.

An offer need be only *reasonably* definite. Promises of performance to be rendered "immediately" or "at once" or "as soon as possible" have been held to meet this requirement. Similarly, quantities and prices have been held reasonably definite even though qualified by such expressions as "about" or "more or less" or "approximately." But a proposal to pay "a fair share of my profits" was held to be conjectural and thus not reasonably definite.

Often business conditions make it difficult or impossible for a seller or buyer to specify an exact quantity of goods. Instead, Fred may offer to sell to Grace all the oranges to be grown on Fred's citrus ranch during the next season; or Carlo may offer to buy from Sara all the paint he will need for the next 2 years in the operation of his automobile body shop. Upon acceptance, the first type of offer becomes an "output" contract; the second becomes a "requirements" contract. Although both could be considered indefinite as to quantity, the courts enforce them.

BOX 11.5

NOTE: Throughout the contracts chapters you will find a number of boxes like this one, devoted to UCC rules pertaining to the sale of goods. This is for your convenience, since some contracts courses cover only the common law of contracts, while others include some coverage of sales law. In this book, see Chapters 18–22 for more on sales law.

Output and Requirements Contracts in Sales of Goods

Section 2-306 of the UCC continues the common law policy of enforcing output, requirements, and other exclusive dealing contracts, and requires the parties to act in good faith when establishing the amount of *goods* to be delivered. A seller may not force an unreasonably large output on the buyer; and a buyer may not demand an unreasonably large delivery under a requirements contract. What is reasonable is to be determined in light of any stated estimate contained in the contract. If there is no such estimate, the amount may be measured by prior dealings between the parties or by what is normal in the trade or industry in comparable circumstances. Thus, the law provides needed contract flexibility while protecting the parties from surprisingly large variations in outputs and requirements.

---

[2]119 U.S. 149 (1866).

BOX 11.6
Contract Formation in Sales of Goods

Article 2 of the UCC departs sharply from the common law approach to contract formation and the implication of missing terms. Traditionally, the common law has required a rather precise process of offer and acceptance for a contract to arise—reflecting, perhaps, a preference for negotiating each deal carefully and deliberately as is appropriate in real estate transactions. In contrast, contracts for the sale of *goods* are made with a minimum of formality by businesspeople in a hurry, often across state lines. To promote business efficiency, Section 2-204 permits a contract for the sale of goods to "be made in any manner sufficient to show agreement, including conduct by both parties which recognizes the existence of a contract . . . even though the moment of its making is undetermined." Moreover, nearly every term of a sales contract can be implied, including price, "if the parties have intended to make a contract and there is a reasonably certain basis for giving an appropriate remedy." Indeed Article 2 makes elaborate use of "gap-fillers" (Code-imposed terms on topics the parties failed to address).

Suppose Sam delivers 300 gallons of heating oil to Betty without stating a price, and she uses it. Though there might have been no specifically identifiable moment of agreement, Sam and Betty's conduct reveals their intention to make a contract. But they left the price term "open." Where no price is stated, UCC Section 2-305 imposes "a reasonable price at the time for delivery." What is reasonable can be determined in a variety of ways. Mass-produced items such as household appliances, lumber, or oil have market prices that probably will be taken as reasonable. For unique goods such as art objects or custom clothing whose market price is uncertain, a court might use an expert's appraisal to establish a reasonable price.

If a material (major) term has been omitted, a proposal may not be reasonably definite and complete. Some material terms, however, may be *implied* by the offer. For example, if a contract fails to state the time for performance, the courts usually will hold that the offer implied a reasonable time.

Whether material terms such as price will be implied depends greatly on the subject matter of the contract. Because land is such a valuable and limited resource and often is the major asset of its owner, the common law traditionally has required a high degree of definiteness in contracts for its sale. Accordingly, if an offer for real estate fails to state a price, the courts will not infer one and will hold that the offer is too indefinite to enforce. Even a slight vagueness in stating the price of land has been sufficient for some courts to refuse to "make a contract for the parties." As noted in Box 11.6, however, courts are much more willing to imply terms in contracts for the sale of goods.

Contracts for services are governed by the common law. If the price has been left open, the courts will more readily infer a reasonable price than if the subject of the contract were real estate. Generally, however, the courts are not so liberal in supplying a price for services as they would be in a sale of goods, unless they have adopted the *Restatement (Second)* provisions on open terms (similar to those of UCC Article 2).

The following case discusses the rule that the terms of an offer must be reasonably definite and complete.

CASE 11.1 Lessley v. Hardage • 727 P.2d 440 (Kan. 1986)

FACTS Samuel Hardage employed Dean Lessley as executive vice president of Hardage's real estate development business. The parties agreed that Lessley would receive an annual salary of $55,000, life and health insurance, and a company car. In addition, Hardage had a "golden handcuffs" plan by which key employees would share in company projects. Hardage promised that 10 percent of each project would be set aside for key employees. This would then be distributed to the key employees based upon a determination by Mr. Hardage of the percentage that each person would receive. This percentage was to be based upon the quantity and quality of each employee's work. After Lessley had been employed about 20 months, Hardage increased the "golden handcuffs" plan to the lesser of 25 percent of the total project or 50 percent of Hardage's interest in the project. Soon thereafter, a dispute arose concerning the plan, and Lessley was fired. He filed suit for breach of contract and received judgment for $161,800, representing amounts due under the "golden handcuffs" plan. Hardage appealed, contending that the oral contract was not sufficiently definite and certain to create an obligation to pay bonuses.

OPINION MILLER, J. . . . The general rule for evaluating the sufficiency of the definiteness of contractual terms is stated in *Hays v. Underwood, Administrator* . . . :

> [I]n order for an agreement to be binding it must be sufficiently definite as to its terms and requirements as to enable a court to determine what acts are to be performed and when performance is complete. The court must be able to fix definitely the legal liability of the party. We have adhered to this general rule. . . .

Again, however, the courts generally have so far deviated from the general rule and set up so many exceptions that it is an exceptional case where the rule can be followed as a complete guide to the determination of the sufficiency and the definiteness of the terms of a contract.

The courts will so construe an instrument as to carry the intentions of the parties into effect where possible. . . . The law will favor upholding a contract against a claim of uncertainty where one of the parties has performed his part of the contract. A contract may contain imperfections or be lacking in detail but it will not be held void for uncertainty if the court, under the recognized rules of construction, can ascertain the terms and conditions by which the parties intended to be bound. . . .

In the past, this court has required only reasonable certainty in contracts. In *Richards Aircraft Sales, Inc. v. Vaughn* . . . we said: "[A]bsolute certainty is not required—only reasonable certainty is necessary."

The basic issue in this case is whether the reservation of discretion by Hardage renders the contract so indefinite as to be unenforceable. . . . There is authority on both sides of this issue, and no Kansas case is directly on point.

In *Borden v. Skinner Chuck Co.* . . . the court determined that a statement in a booklet issued by the employer that bonuses were customarily paid and were entirely within the discretion of the Board of Directors did not constitute a direct and enforceable offer to pay a bonus. In contrast, Hardage promised the

**CASE 11.1
Continued**

plaintiff that 10% (later 25% or 50%) of equity or cash would be set aside from each venture for key employees. While the exact amount of each employee's share was to be determined later, there was a definite promise to give a particular group of employees a fixed share of the cash or equity. . . . The case most similar to the case at hand is *Hilgenberg v. Iowa Beef Packers*. . . . *Hilgenberg* involved a bonus of indefinite amount—it was to be a percentage of the employee's salary, but no employee was told of the precise percentage. However, the employer had allocated, though not segregated, $14,175 for the payment of bonuses. The jury found that the bonus in *Hilgenberg* was supported by consideration, and it found that the plaintiffs were entitled to the money set aside by the employer. The court apportioned the amount set aside among the employees.

. . . Lessley argues, correctly, that the mere existence of a discretionary duty does not render a contract unenforceable. Typically, a good faith obligation is implied to limit the exercise of discretion. . . .

The essential term claimed to be lacking in the employment agreement before us is the amount of the cash Lessley would receive. Hardage led employees to believe that they would be compensated in a manner commensurate with the work they did on each project—the quantity and quality of their work. This does not appear to us to be an immeasurable, indefinite compensation scheme. Hardage agreed to place a fixed percentage, readily ascertainable, aside, the same to be divided among key personnel. Once the total sum due the employees was fixed, the allocation of that amount among the key employees would seem here, as in *Hilgenberg*, a matter which a court or jury, upon proper evidence, may determine.

The trial court relied on *Heckard v. Park* . . . in denying Hardage's motion for summary judgment. In [the syllabus] of that opinion, we said:

> The law implies that contractual provisions requiring the exercise of judgment or discretion will be honestly exercised and faithfully performed.

Lessley had fully performed the work required of him by the contract. We hold that the oral contract between Lessley and Hardage, as established by the evidence and found by the jury, was sufficiently definite and certain to create an obligation on the part of the employer to pay percentages of retained equity interest and cash to the key employees. We further hold that, while the precise amount of the cash award to which plaintiff is entitled was not fixed in the contract, it is easily determinable, and in this instance was properly determined by the jury upon the basis of the evidence before it. The obligation of honest judgment implied in contracts where the exercise of judgment or discretion is involved cannot be used as a shield to prevent recovery by the plaintiff in this action. We do not regard the precise amount to which plaintiff is entitled to be an essential term of the agreement, where the amount can readily be determined by the jury.

JUDGMENT   . . . [A]ffirmed.

Communication to Offeree. An offer creates a power of acceptance when the offeror communicates it to the person or persons for whom it was intended. Ordinarily, the offeror makes the offer in person to the offeree; by telephone, letter, telegram, or FAX; or through the offeror's agent. Communication is completed when the offeree or the offeree's agent receives the offer.

> **BOX 11.7**
> **Point to Consider**
>
> For an offer to be communicated, must the offeree actually read and understand it? Or should the courts consider an offer communicated if it reaches the home or business address of the offeree? As a matter of policy, what meaning of "communicated" should the courts adopt?

TERMINATION OF OFFERS

Several things can happen in the period following communication of an offer. Sometimes the offeree accepts it immediately and a contract arises, as where the parties negotiate face to face or by phone. When they negotiate by mail, the offeree may take time to consider the offer, or may simply put off responding. If the offeree wants to accept, delay can cause problems. For example, the offeror might revoke the offer or say that it expired before the offeree accepted.

When an offer terminates, the offeree's power of acceptance ends. An offer may be terminated in either of two main ways: (1) by an act of one of the parties or (2) by operation of law. Terminations by an act of a party include those caused by lapse of time (offeree's failure to accept before the offer expires), revocation by the offeror, and rejection or counteroffer by the offeree. Terminations by operation of law include those caused by death of the offeror or offeree, loss of the subject matter, and supervening illegality.

Termination by Lapse of Time

The offeree might wait too long to accept an offer—until the lapse of the time specified by the offeror for acceptance, or until an unreasonably long time has passed.

Specified Time Limitation. An offer may be worded to terminate on a specified date: "This offer will remain open until 5 p.m., October 10." Difficulty arises when a time limitation is ambiguous. Suppose Cora mails a letter giving Gloria "10 days to accept or reject this offer." Did Cora intend the 10-day period to begin when the letter was sent or when it was received? Most courts hold that the time begins on the day the offeree receives the letter.

Implied Time Limitation. Where an offeror does not specify a time limitation, the offer remains open for a reasonable time. What is reasonable depends on the circumstances surrounding the transaction. An offer to buy or sell perishable goods such as eggs terminates sooner than an offer involving durable goods. An offer to sell a used bicycle on a crowded campus where demand is high terminates sooner than an offer to sell where demand is low. An offer for a commodity with a volatile price terminates sooner than an offer for a price-stable commodity such as sand. And an offer terminates sooner rather than later if the offeror communicates a sense of urgency by using a fast medium of communication such as a FAX message.

> **BOX 11.8**
> **Test Your Knowledge**
>
> An offeree's saying "I accept" after an offer has expired fails as an acceptance. But the words might be a counteroffer. How so? What qualities typical of an offer are present?

Termination by Revocation

Ordinarily, an offeror can **revoke** (withdraw) an offer any time before acceptance despite promising not to do so. If the offeror states, "This offer will remain open until May 10," the offeror may revoke the offer on May 5. By revoking, the offeror may be acting unethically but has not violated the law.

The offeror's power of revocation raises two major concerns: What limits are there on the power, and what specific acts are required for revocation?

Limits on Power of Revocation—Irrevocable Offers. Offerees often must prepare for or begin performance before accepting the offer. If it is revoked unexpectedly, the offeree may suffer hardship. To protect offerees, courts and legislatures have imposed limits on offerors' ability to revoke their offers.

1. *Options.* One limit is the irrevocability resulting from an **option contract.** Ann says to Ben, "I'll sell you my horse Thunder for $5,000, and for $5 you have 30 days to decide." Ben pays the $5. For $5, Ben has purchased 30 days during which to consider Ann's offer. Under this contract ($5 for 30 days' time), Ben has the "option," or choice, of either accepting or rejecting Ann's offer to sell Thunder for $5,000. In essence, Ben has made a contract whose object is to make Ann's offer (to sell Thunder) irrevocable for 30 days.
2. *Some offers for unilateral contracts.* Under traditional contract rules, an offer for a unilateral contract is not accepted (and no contract arises) until the offeree completes the requested act. Where the act takes time to perform and the offeror revokes the offer before the act is completed, the offeree faces difficulty. In *some* unilateral contract situations (discussed later, in the section on acceptance of unilateral contract offers), the courts treat the offeree's *beginning* of performance as an act sufficient to create an *option contract* that gives the offeree a right to continue performance.
3. *Merchant's "firm offer" in sale of goods.* Some offers are made irrevocable by statute—for example, many bids made to government agencies and, under Section 2-205 of the UCC, "firm offers" of merchants. A **firm offer** is a written and signed offer of a merchant to buy or sell goods, where the writing gives assurance that the offer will be held open. Such an offer is not revocable within the time-period provisions of Section 2-205, even though the offeror was not paid to keep the offer open.

As illustrated in the accompanying box, the courts use **promissory estoppel** to make some offers irrevocable.

> **BOX 11.9**
> **Promissory Estoppel to the Rescue**
>
> Ben, a building contractor, wants to construct the new City Parking Garage. Before he can prepare his bid (offer) on the project, he must first collect price information from many subcontractors, each of whom may compete with others for various parts of the work—concrete, electrical, plumbing, elevators. Al submits the lowest bid of $500,000 for the electrical work, and Ben incorporates it into his own offer to City. City accepts Ben's bid, thus obligating him to build the garage for the price he promised. But before Ben can accept Al's bid, Al revokes it and raises the price to $600,000. Since there is no contract between Al and Ben for the $500,000 price, Al has no obligation under traditional contract rules to perform as promised. However, Ben *relied* on Al's promise to do the work for $500,000, and under the doctrine of promissory estoppel Ben can enforce that promise. Ben's reliance is *justifiable* because, as Al surely had reason to know, there is no other practical way for building contractors to operate than by relying on unaccepted bids. Ben relied to his *detriment* by committing himself to a contract with City on the basis of Al's original bid. To protect general contractors in situations like this, courts often hold that promissory estoppel makes subcontractors' bids irrevocable.

What Constitutes Revocation. Ordinarily, one revokes an offer by notifying the offeree that it has been withdrawn. No special wording is required, and the notice may be given in any way that informs the offeree of the revocation. In most states, a revocation is effective when the offeree receives it.[3]

Notice of revocation need not come directly from the offeror, however. John offers to sell his car to Wally and gives Wally 5 days to decide. On the third day John sells the car to Sara and she informs Wally of the sale. Since Wally has received reliable information that John took action inconsistent with a contract with Wally, the offer to Wally is terminated.

A revocation can occur even though the offeree does not know of the offeror's change of mind. Where an offer has been made to the public generally, as in an offer to pay a reward, the offeror may withdraw the offer by giving public notice of revocation. If the offeror gives the same amount of publicity to the revocation that the offer received, revocation is effective even against a person who knew of the offer but not of the revocation.

> **BOX 11.10**
> **Test Your Knowledge**
>
> Fidel, an orange grower, places an ad in the city newspaper offering to pay $5,000 to the first person who invents an electronic fruit fly repellant. The next day he changes his mind and broadcasts on local radio several spot announcements revoking his offer. Within a week, Carlos, who knew of the offer but not the revocation, delivers an electronic fruit fly repellant to Fidel. Is his revocation effective? ■

Termination by Rejection or Counteroffer

An offeree **rejects** an offer by communicating an intention not to accept it. Rejection terminates the offer unless the offeror (1) has indicated a contrary intention or (2) has been paid to keep the offer open for a fixed period that has not yet expired, as in an option contract.

A rejection may be express, or implied by words or conduct. For example, the offeree may reject by saying, "Your offer is not acceptable," or by tearing a written offer to pieces and throwing them into a wastebasket in the presence of the offeror.

Usually, a rejection is not effective until the offeror receives it. In the meantime, the offeree still has the power of acceptance (unless the offer has already been terminated in some way other than rejection). Ben receives an offer from Ann and mails her a letter of rejection. Ben then changes his mind about rejecting. He could telephone Ann and accept the offer before she receives the letter of rejection.

A **counteroffer** is an offer made by the *offeree* to the offeror relating to the same matter as the original offer but differing from it in one or more particulars. Arnold offers to sell his car to Barbara for $1,500 and she replies, "I will give you $1,000 for the car." Barbara has made a counteroffer. Although Barbara's counteroffer impliedly rejects and therefore terminates Arnold's original offer, it differs from an outright rejection: Negotiations between the parties are still alive. Arnold now may accept the counteroffer, reject it outright, or make a counter-counteroffer to Barbara. Figure 11.1 illustrates two things: (1) the legal effect of a counteroffer on the offeror's power of acceptance (P/A), and (2) the options available to an offeror (A) who receives a counteroffer from the offeree (B).

Not all counteroffers impliedly reject the original offer. For example, in response to Arnold's offer to sell his car to Barbara for $1,500, Barbara says, "I am considering your offer, but I will buy immediately if you will take $1,000." Barbara has made a counteroffer, but

Figure 11.1 Counteroffer—offeror's options.

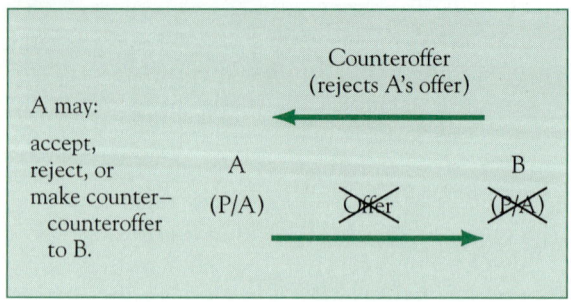

---

[3] By statute in California and a few other states, a written revocation becomes effective when posted or put into the course of transmission by any reasonable mode.

she obviously has not rejected Arnold's original offer.

Rejections and counteroffers should be distinguished from mere requests for information. Ann offers to sell her house to Ben for $80,000. Ben says, "I am considering your offer, although I think the price is too high. Would you be willing to reduce it to $75,000?" Ben's response is not a rejection of Ann's offer; on the contrary, it tells her that her offer is still being considered. Neither is Ben's response a counteroffer. He has merely inquired about a price reduction and has not substituted an offer of his own for Ann's.

A statement that seems to be an acceptance may really be only a counteroffer. Arnold offers to sell his car to Barbara for $1,500 in one cash payment, and Barbara says, "I accept your offer of $1,500 if you'll let me pay in three equal monthly installments." By departing from the payment terms of Arnold's offer, Barbara has made a counteroffer (sometimes called a **conditional acceptance**) and has impliedly rejected the offer. To constitute an acceptance, the offeree's response must exactly match (be a "mirror image" of) the offer, and not include an additional or different term.

An acceptance is *un*conditional, however, if the offeree states a condition merely expressing a term implied in the offer. Thus, an acceptance can be unconditional despite the offeree's requiring a certificate of title from the offeror or specifying that payment will be made within a reasonable time.

The following case involves the problem of an offeree's adding words to the offeror's proposal and illustrates the "grumbling assent."

CASE 11.2   Panhandle Eastern Pipe Line Company v. Smith
- 637 P.2d 1020 (Wyo. 1981)

FACTS   Panhandle Eastern Pipe Line Company fired its employee, Nowlin Smith, Jr. After discussions with Smith's union representative, Panhandle sent a letter to Smith offering to withdraw the discharge if he would agree to certain terms and conditions. Smith signed the letter under the typewritten words, "Understood, Agreed To and Accepted," added some handwritten notations, and again signed his name. Panhandle claimed that Smith made a counteroffer by adding terms and conditions to the offer, and the company refused to rehire him. The notation added by Smith was a request to see his personnel file at the company and to contest any mistakes he found there. Smith sued for breach of contract and received a judgment of $40,000. Panhandle appealed.

OPINION   BROWN, J. . . . The law of contract formation dictates that one who modifies an offer has usually rejected the offer and made a counteroffer, and that no contract exists unless the original offeror accepts the counteroffer. . . . An offer must be accepted unconditionally; but there is, as always, an exception to the rule. An acceptance is still effective if the addition only asks for something that would be implied from the offer and is therefore immaterial. . . . A Panhandle supervisor, Mr. Smith, and a company machinist, who was also a union representative, all testified that all Panhandle employees had the right to see their personnel files. Panhandle's offer to withdraw its discharge and eventually reinstate Mr. Smith carried with it the implication that he would be able to see his personnel record when he was once again an active employee.

Besides reserving the right to see his personnel file, Mr. Smith wrote that his personnel file contained mistakes, and that he was having financial problems,

CASE 11.2 Continued	apparently as a result of the company's actions. Williston has described the kind of acceptance Mr. Smith made as one showing "an abundance of caution," and Corbin has called it a "grumbling acceptance," which in this case it certainly appeared to be. The acceptance was unenthusiastic to be sure, but it was an acceptance nevertheless. Mr. Smith signed his name under the words "Understood, Agreed To and Accepted." He wrote that he agreed to the terms and conditions. . . . His "grumbling acceptance" should stand. . . .
JUDGMENT	The district court had jurisdiction to hear the dispute and correctly decided that a contract did exist and had been breached. Its damage award was supported by sufficient evidence. We therefore affirm.

Termination by Death or Incapacity of Offeror or Offeree

The death or incapacity of the offeree, and usually that of the offeror, terminates an offer by operation of law.

Incapacity is a lack of legal or physical ability to contract, usually resulting from a disability such as mental illness, narcotics addiction, or extreme intoxication. For the offer to be terminated, there must previously have been an adjudication of incapacity, or the disability must be so serious that the affected person does not understand the nature and consequences of the transaction. People under lesser disabilities may have capacity to make or to receive offers. However, as discussed in Chapter 13, any resulting contract may be voidable by the person with the disability.

The death of the offer*ee* terminates the offer because only an offeree has a power of acceptance and the offeree's death makes acceptance impossible.

The death of the offer*or* also terminates the offer[4]—unless it has been made irrevocable for a period extending beyond the offeror's death. In general, *contracts,* including option contracts, are binding on the estates of deceased parties. Ben pays Ann $10 for 30 days in which to consider her offer to sell him Blackacre. She dies on the third day. Under the option contract between Ben and Ann, the offer to sell Blackacre is still open despite Ann's death. (Of course, if Ann's offer had been for her personal services, such as surveying Blackacre and drawing up plans for a housing development, her death makes her performance impossible and discharges the option contract.) Even ordinary offers could remain binding on a deceased offeror's estate if the circumstances required for promissory estoppel exist.

Termination by Loss of Subject Matter or Supervening Illegality

The loss or destruction of the subject matter of a proposed contract terminates the offer. Thus, if the offer concerns the purchase of a drilling rig that is destroyed before the offer is accepted, the offer is terminated.

If a proposed contract or performance becomes illegal after an offer has been made but before it is accepted, the offer is terminated by "supervening illegality." Eric offers to sell a ton of salmon to Row's Cannery. Before Cannery can accept the offer, the state legislature enacts a law, effective immediately, prohibiting further sales of salmon for the current year. The statute makes Eric's proposed performance illegal and terminates the offer.

ACCEPTANCE

Acceptance is the offeree's manifestation of assent to the terms of the offer. Under the com-

---

[4]In most states, the offeror's death terminates the offer at once, but in some states the offer is not terminated until the offeree knows of the offeror's death. John D. Calamari and Joseph M. Perillo, THE LAW OF CONTRACTS (1987), p. 94.

mon law rules of contract formation, the acceptance must exactly match (be a mirror image of) the offer, and not include different or additional terms. Al's offer says, "I'll sell my farm Redacre to you for $300,000." Betty's letter of reply says, "I accept your offer. Any dispute arising from this transaction is to be settled by arbitration." Because she introduced a new term, Betty has not accepted Al's offer, but has instead made a counteroffer. This traditional mirror-image rule is still widely applied to contracts for real estate or services. However, the rule is inconsistent with modern business practices in the sale of *goods*. For those transactions the mirror-image rule has been replaced by the more efficient UCC Article 2 rule discussed in Box 11.11 which follows.

Acceptance of Offer for Unilateral Contract

An offer to enter into a unilateral contract requests from the offeree an *act* of performance in exchange for the offeror's promise. Usually the act takes time to perform.

Where performance takes time, the offeror's revoking the offer poses a special problem for the offeree. Under traditional contract rules, no acceptance of a unilateral contract offer occurs (and no contract arises) until the offeree fully performs the requested act. Clyde writes to Debbie, "If you'll paint my apartment while I'm away tomorrow, I'll pay you $500. Key is under the mat; paint is in the hall." If Clyde can revoke his offer when Debbie has painted half the

---

BOX 11.11

Battle of the Forms—Counteroffers in Sales Contracts

Each day millions of contracts for goods arise from an exchange of preprinted forms, one prepared by the buyer's lawyer and the other by the seller's. Each lawyer drafts the form to give his or her client the most advantage. Because the interests of buyers and sellers conflict, their forms are unlikely to match exactly. Consequently, if the common law mirror-image rule applied to a sale of goods, an offeree-seller could not be sure of a contract until the offeror-buyer actually performed by, for example, accepting goods that the offeree sent. But one purpose of a contract is to assure the offeree at the earliest possible moment that the offeror will be bound if the offeree accepts. If the offeror may escape contractual liability just because the offeree's form departs from the terms of the offer, the offeree faces uncertainty as to whether a contract exists.

To reduce uncertainty in the formation of *sales* contracts, Section 2-207 of the UCC provides that the offeree's expression of acceptance "operates as an acceptance even though it states terms additional to or different from those offered." Ann offers to buy a printing press from Ben for $50,000. Ann's order form says nothing about how a dispute between her and Ben will be resolved if the printing press is defective. She assumes she will have the normal right to go to court. But Ben's acceptance form says, "Disputes relating to this transaction shall be resolved by arbitration." Although Ben's acceptance does not mirror Ann's offer, a contract arises because the two forms agree on enough terms for a sales contract. Under the Code, the arbitration clause is merely a proposal for an addition to the contract contemplated by Ann. Because the arbitration clause is considered a "material" departure from Ann's offer, the clause will not be binding on her unless she actually agrees to it.

Can Ben make a counteroffer to Ann? Yes, but he must *express* it. That is, he must say something like "I'll sell you the printing press for that price, but only if you agree to arbitrate any dispute that may arise from this sale." Whether a contract arises between Ann and Ben depends now on whether Ann accepts Ben's counteroffer.

apartment, Debbie will have no right to the contract price and will have to rely on a suit in quasi contract for the reasonable value of her incomplete performance. For the protection of offerees such as Debbie, the courts have developed three main approaches to the unilateral contract revocation problem:

1. If (as here) the offer permits Debbie to accept *only* by *doing* the work, her *beginning* it is sufficient to create an option contract. By beginning, she acquires a legal right to continue the job or not, as she chooses, for having never promised a performance, she never became obligated to render one. To *accept* the offer and earn the contract price, however, Debbie must perform completely and must do so within the time stated in the offer, or if none is stated, within a reasonable time. If she chooses not to complete the performance, she may be entitled to a quasi-contract recovery for the reasonable value of her part performance. (This is essentially the rule of Section 45 in both *Restatements*.)

2. If the offer is worded so that Debbie may accept either by *doing* the work or by *promising* to do it, her beginning it is an *immediate* acceptance *and an implied promise* to complete the work. Clyde leaves Debbie a note: "I'll pay you $500 to paint my apartment tomorrow. You can accept this offer by phone before 9:00 tonight; otherwise just go ahead and do the work tomorrow while I'm away." Debbie accepts by beginning the work the next morning. Both she and Clyde are bound by the contract. Clyde is liable for payment if Debbie makes a timely performance, and Debbie is liable for breach of contract if she fails to perform as requested. (This is essentially the rule of Section 62 of *Restatement (Second)* and Section 2-206 of the UCC.)

3. Clyde may be prevented by the doctrine of promissory estoppel (Section 90 of both *Restatements*) from revoking his offer after Debbie begins performance. As Clyde could foresee, Debbie relied to her detriment on his promise.

To be entitled to the contract price rather than a quasi-contract remedy, Debbie must paint the entire apartment. However, the courts allow for minor imperfections in performance. If Debbie fails to paint a small portion of the house, she nevertheless has "substantially performed" the requested act and is entitled to the contract price minus the cost to Clyde of having another painter finish the job. This *doctrine of substantial performance* is discussed in Chapter 17 and applies to unilateral and bilateral contracts alike.

Acceptance of Offer for Bilateral Contract

An offeree accepts an offer for a bilateral contract by communicating the requested return promise to the offeror. Usually such offers require the return promise to be expressed in words. Sometimes, however, the return promise can be manifested by the performance of some act, such as the nod of a head. In certain limited situations, acceptance of a bilateral offer takes place even though the offeree remains silent and does nothing.

Acceptance by Words Expressing Assent. No particular words are required to accept an offer for a bilateral contract. The offeree may say "I accept your offer" or "OK," or use any other words indicating unequivocal acceptance. An ambiguous expression such as "Your order will receive our prompt and careful attention" casts doubt on whether the offeree accepted.

Communication of acceptance. To communicate an acceptance, the offeree must inform the offeror of it. There is no communication if the offeree merely says "I accept" in a vacant room or to his or her own agent, or writes "I accept" on an offer letter without delivering it to the offeror. However, "communicate" does not necessarily require that the offeror actually receive the offeree's message of acceptance. The offeree's reasonable *attempt* to communicate the message—for example, by mailing a letter—may be sufficient.

Medium of acceptance; when and where acceptance becomes effective. Usually, offerors say nothing about how acceptance is to be communicated, so a court may have to decide whether an attempt to accept was effective. Jarvis mails an offer to Harriet, saying nothing about medium of acceptance. Harriet mails a letter of acceptance. Is her acceptance effective when she mails (dispatches) it or when Jarvis receives it? The answer depends on whether the offeree has complied with the "deposited acceptance rule."

Under the **deposited acceptance** ("mailbox") **rule,** an acceptance is effective (i.e., a contract arises) at the *time of dispatch* if the offeree uses an *authorized medium* of acceptance while the offer is still open. The deposited acceptance rule places the risk of a lost or delayed acceptance on the offeror. This risk allocation contributes to commercial efficiency in two ways: (1) Upon properly dispatching an acceptance, offerees have the protection of a contract and can immediately make commitments to others. (2) Offerors are in a better position than offerees to detect lost or delayed mail, mainly because offerors know when offers were sent and when to expect a response.

What media are authorized? Where the offeror requires the offeree to use a particular medium of acceptance, only the required medium is authorized. An attempt to accept by a different medium is ineffective, even if the offeror receives the message while the offer is still open. Steel Corporation mails an offer to construct a warehouse. It says, "You must accept this offer by United Express overnight letter." The offeree may not accept by any other medium. A telegram saying "I accept your offer" is ineffective as an acceptance but is instead a counteroffer.

Where the offeror says nothing about the medium of acceptance, the offeree is impliedly authorized (by law) to accept by *any reasonable medium*. Such an acceptance is effective upon dispatch. A medium of acceptance may be reasonable if, for example, it is the one used by the offeror, it is customary in similar transactions, or its speed and reliability match the urgency of the transaction.

If the offeree uses an *unreasonable* medium, a contract arises when the offeror *receives* the message (if the offer is still open). By telegram, Harry offers to sell Greenacre to Stella, stating that he must sell quickly because he is leaving the country soon. Instead of replying by telegram, FAX, or phone, Stella accepts by mail, a considerably slower medium of communication. Given the urgency suggested by Harry's conduct, Stella's using the mail may be unreasonable. If so, there is no acceptance when she mails the letter. But a contract will result when Harry receives the acceptance if the offer is still open then. This traditional rule applies also to sales of goods.[5]

BOX 11.12

Point of Law: The Problem of the Wrong ZIP Code

By telegram, Francine offers to sell you a carload of tomatoes, and asks you to "respond by return mail." The address she gives is correct, but in your haste to respond, you use a wrong ZIP code. Under traditional contract rules, your misdirected acceptance would be effective only upon *receipt*, even though you used an authorized medium. UCC Section 1-201(38) changes the misdirected acceptance rule for *sales of goods*, by making your acceptance effective upon *dispatch* if it reaches the offeror by the time a properly sent message would have arrived. Your misdirected letter might well be timely, if postal employees read the whole address and not merely the erroneous ZIP code.

For real estate and other nonsales contracts, *Restatement (Second)*, Section 67, also departs from the traditional rule, by making authorized but misdirected acceptances effective upon dispatch if receipt is timely. ∎

Offers requiring a particular medium of acceptance serve legitimate purposes, but tend to make contract formation inefficient—for exam-

---

[5]*Restatement (Second)*, Section 67, departs from this traditional rule. Section 67 makes acceptance by an unreasonable medium effective *upon dispatch* if the offeror receives it by the time that a message sent by a reasonable medium would have arrived. However, despite a *Restatement (Second)* note to the contrary, UCC Section 1-201(38) does *not* do the same thing for a sale of goods. That section deals with improperly addressed (misdirected) acceptances, not with acceptance by an unreasonable medium. Calamari and Perillo, op. cit., p. 116.

ple, a requirement that the offeree use a letter when a FAX message would do. Therefore, unless the offeror's language clearly and unmistakably requires a particular medium, the courts interpret offerors' statements as "suggestive." Where the offeror has merely *suggested* the use of a particular medium ("We await your acceptance letter"), the offeree may use any reasonable medium.

The following case illustrates the operation of the deposited acceptance rule.

CASE 11.3   Soldau v. Organon, Inc. • 860 F.2d 355 (9th Cir. 1988)

FACTS   Defendant Organon, Inc., fired plaintiff John Soldau. By letter, Organon offered him double the usual severance pay in exchange for his signing a release of all claims against Organon. Soldau signed and dated the letter, which stated the terms of the release, and deposited it in a mailbox outside a post office. Upon returning home, he found a check from Organon for the increased severance pay. He immediately returned to the post office, persuaded a postal employee to open the mailbox, and retrieved the release. After cashing the check, he sued Organon, alleging violations of state and federal age discrimination law. From a judgment for Organon, Soldau appealed.

OPINION   PER CURIAM: . . . The district court [held that] "the release was deemed fully communicated to Organon, and a binding contract was formed, at the time the plaintiff deposited the executed release in the mailbox. The fact that plaintiff retrieved the release from the mailbox is of no consequence under California . . . law."

The district court was clearly correct. . . . Soldau does not argue to the contrary. Instead, he contends that the formation and validity of the release are governed by federal law, and [it] would not have been effective unless and until it had been received by Organon. . . . Under federal as well as California law, [however,] Soldau's acceptance was effective when it was mailed.

The so-called "mailbox" or "effective when mailed" rule was adopted by the Supreme Court prior to *Erie R.R. Co. v. Tompkins*, [a 1938 case]. We could not change the rule, and there is no reason to believe the Supreme Court would be inclined to do so. It is almost universally accepted in the common law world. It is enshrined in the *Restatement (Second) of Contracts* §63(a), and endorsed by the major contract treatises.

. . . Commentators [have pointed] to the long history of the rule; its importance in creating certainty for contracting parties; [and] its essential soundness, on balance, as a means of allocating the risk during the period between the making of the offer and the communication of the acceptance . . . to the offeror. . . .

JUDGMENT   Since Soldau's contractual obligation to release Organon in return for . . . the enhanced severance payment arose when Soldau deposited his acceptance in the post office mailbox, his subsequent withdrawal of the acceptance was ineffectual.

Affirmed.

> **BOX 11.13**
>
> ### A Problem of Timing
>
> Timing is critical in contract formation. Did the offeree revoke the offer before the offeror accepted it? If so, there is no contract.
>
> The diagram below shows an exchange of letters between A, the offeror, and B, the offeree. The offer was sent on May 1 and received on May 5. The revocation was sent on May 3 and received on May 6. The acceptance was sent on May 6 and received on May 9. Do A and B have a contract? Would the question be easier to answer if B had used an *un*reasonable medium of acceptance such as a carrier pigeon?
>
>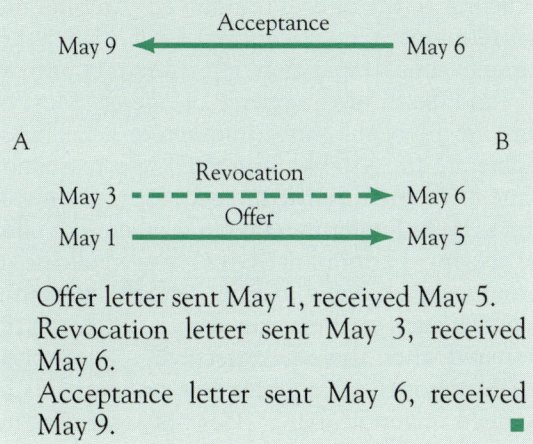
>
> Offer letter sent May 1, received May 5.
> Revocation letter sent May 3, received May 6.
> Acceptance letter sent May 6, received May 9. ■

Effect of acceptance plus rejection. The deposited acceptance rule—that an acceptance by any reasonable medium becomes effective on proper dispatch—does *not* apply where a notice of rejection precedes the notice of acceptance. The reason is that the rejection notice might be the first to reach the offeror, and the offeror should be entitled to act on it immediately—for example, by selling perishable goods quickly to another buyer. For the offeror's protection, an acceptance dispatched *after* a rejection has been sent is not effective until received. Thus, when a rejection precedes an acceptance, the first one to reach the offeror is the effective one.

What happens if the offeree sends the *acceptance* first, and then a rejection? Here, the courts apply the general rule that the acceptance is effective when properly dispatched. However, if the notice of rejection reaches the offeror first, and the offeror changes his or her position in reliance on it, the offeree is estopped (barred) from enforcing the contract.

Acceptance by Act Indicating Assent. Some offers for a bilateral contract can be accepted by an act which *implies* a promise. A nod of the head, the raising of a hand, and the fall of an auctioneer's hammer are common examples. Similarly, taking possession of something or exercising dominion over it may constitute acceptance. Curtis, a contractor, has a pile of lumber stored on a vacant lot. Curtis tells Donna to "take a look at the lumber. If it's worth $80 to you, haul it away." Donna hauls it away. Her taking possession of the lumber is an acceptance of the offer and an implied promise to pay the $80.

Acceptance by Silence. The mere silence of an offeree in response to an offer does not constitute acceptance. Al says to Ben, "I'll sell you Blackacre for $200,000. If I don't hear from you by May 1, I shall assume that you accept my offer." Ben remains silent. There is no acceptance. Ben might not have heard the offer, or might have heard it but simply chose to ignore it. The law does not permit Al to force a contract on Ben without better evidence of his intention to contract.

However, if the offeree's silence is accompanied by other circumstances from which assent reasonably can be inferred, silence *can* constitute acceptance. Two examples follow:

1. An offeree can accept by silently taking the benefit of offered services with reasonable opportunity to reject them, and with reason to know that the offeror expects payment. Ann offers to give Ben's child ten lessons in computer programming on Ben's home computer, for $12 per lesson. Ben says nothing. The next day Ann begins the instruction. Though present, Ben does not object. Ben is bound to pay for the lessons.

2. Silence operates as an acceptance where, because of previous dealings or customary trade practice, it is reasonable for an offeree to notify a customer of the offeree's intention not to accept. Office Supply Co. sends out a salesperson to solicit orders (offers) for office supplies "subject to acceptance by the home office." If Office Supply's practice has been invariably to fill the customer's orders or to give prompt notice of its inability to fill a particular order, its silence will be treated as an acceptance.

> **BOX 11.14**
> **Government Regulation of Contracts**
>
> In the past, people received unordered merchandise in the mail, together with a letter seeking payment and stating, "If we do not hear from you in five days, we shall assume that you have accepted our offer." To avoid the trouble and expense of returning the goods, or perhaps not knowing how, many offerees used the merchandise or discarded it. Many courts held that a contract resulted from such actions, reasoning that keeping the goods implied acceptance of the seller's offer. To prevent unscrupulous merchants from flooding consumers with unwanted goods and harassing them with repeated billings and threats of lawsuits, the federal and state legislatures enacted a variety of consumer protection statutes. For example, under the Postal Reorganization Act of 1970, a person who receives unordered merchandise by mail may treat it as a gift, and so has no liability for payment. A Federal Trade Commission rule serves a similar purpose. It makes it an unfair trade practice for a commercial seller to send unordered merchandise.

SUMMARY

The kind of contract used to arrange exchanges between the parties is based on an agreement—a manifestation of mutual assent reached through offer and acceptance.

An offer confers a power of acceptance on an offeree and thus the ability to accept the offer and make a contract. An offer normally indicates the exchange that the offeror has in mind, identifies the offeree (the person with the power of acceptance), and reveals a commitment by the offeror to deal with the offeree. To be an offer, a proposal must contain language of commitment (express or implied); be made with serious intent; be sufficiently definite and complete in its terms as to reveal the parties' bargain; and be communicated to the offeree. In general, offers involving real estate must be more detailed than offers involving services and goods.

A power of acceptance may be exercised any time before the offer is terminated. An offer may be terminated in a variety of ways, including lapse of time, revocation, rejection or counteroffer, and death of the offeror or offeree. Most offers are revocable any time before acceptance. Some are irrevocable for a fixed or a reasonable time if (1) they are the subject of an option contract (including unilateral offers where the offeree begins performance), (2) the doctrine of promissory estoppel applies, or (3) a statute makes a class of offers irrevocable. Offers are terminated when the offeror receives a rejection or a counteroffer. A counteroffer ordinarily is an implied rejection, but it does not terminate negotiations.

Acceptance is the offeree's manifestation of assent to the terms of the offer. Under the common law, the acceptance must be a mirror image of the offer, or a counteroffer results. The mirror-image rule applies to contracts such as those for real estate or services. But in the sale of goods it has been replaced by a UCC rule under which a contract usually arises even though the acceptance departed from the terms of the offer.

To accept a unilateral offer, the offeree must perform the requested act. However, where the requested act takes time to perform, the offeree's beginning the performance is sufficient to create an option contract that enables the offeree to continue the performance and accept the offer. Where the offeree may accept an offer by either performing or promising to perform, the beginning of performance is an acceptance binding both offeror and offeree.

An offeree ordinarily uses words to accept an offer for a bilateral contract; sometimes the words are inferred from an act such as nodding at an auction. The acceptance must be communicated to the offeror, but "communication" does not necessarily require that the offeror receive the offeree's message. Under the deposited acceptance rule, dispatching an acceptance by a medium invited by the offeror creates a contract. Where the parties are silent about the medium of acceptance, the offeree's dispatching an acceptance via any reasonable medium creates a contract. If the medium is unreasonable, a contract forms when the offeror receives the acceptance if the offer is still open.

Mere silence in response to an offer does not constitute acceptance. However, if the offeree's silence is accompanied by circumstances from which assent reasonably can be inferred, silence can constitute acceptance. Consumer protection statutes permit consumers to treat merchandise as a gift when merchants mail it unsolicited in the expectation that the consumer will use and feel compelled to pay for it.

REVIEW QUESTIONS

1. Alice says to Bob, "I'll sell my horse Rascal for $1,000." Has she made an offer?

2. Ordinarily, catalogs are considered merely invitations to make offers, with the sellers being offerees. What benefits do sellers receive from this offeree status?

3. In terms of offeror-offeree status, what difference does it make whether an auction is "with reserve" or "without reserve"? What difference does it make economically?

4. (a) Why would a person use a requirements contract or an output contract? (b) Is there any limit on the amount of goods that can be demanded from the seller under a requirements contract?

5. (a) "All material terms must be expressed for a proposal to be sufficiently definite to be an offer, but minor terms may be implied." Is this statement true? (b) Regarding contract formation and the implication of missing terms, how does the policy of Article 2 of the UCC differ from that of the common law?

6. Amy offers to sell her car to Becky. Becky says, "I accept your offer on condition that you supply the title papers for the car." Is there a contract?

7. Under what circumstances will the death of the offeror *not* terminate the offer?

8. Why does Article 2 of the UCC make the mirror-image rule inapplicable to contracts for the sale of goods?

9. (a) Explain how the deposited acceptance rule works. (b) Under this rule, who bears the risk of a lost communication? Why does that person bear the risk?

10. If an offeree uses an unreasonable medium of acceptance, can there be an acceptance? If so, when and where?

CASE PROBLEMS

1. Oliver and Southworth had several discussions about the sale of Oliver's land. On June 17 Oliver sent the following letter to Southworth, with copies to three other neighbors: "Enclosed please find the information about the ranch sales that I had discussed with you previously. These prices are the market value according to the records of the Grant County Assessor. Please contact me if there are any questions." The enclosed note stated, "Selling approximately 2.933 acres in Grant County in T. 165 S., R. 31 E., W.M. near Seneca, Oregon, at the assessed market value of: Land $306,409. Improvements $18,010. Total $324,419. Terms available—29 percent down—balance over 5 years at 8 percent interest. Negotiate sale date for December 1, 1976 or January 1, 1977." Southworth immediately responded with a letter stating, "I accept your offer." Oliver denied that he had made an offer, claiming that his letter was only a starting point for further negotiation with the four interested parties. Was there a contract between Oliver and Southworth?

2. In preparing a bid for the construction of a school, Hagerman Construction Corporation sought bids for athletic lockers. Lyon Metal Products offered to supply the lockers for $16,824. Lyon's bid was the lowest of four received by Hagerman, so Hagerman used it in computing its own bid. On February 12 Hagerman learned that it was the lowest bidder on the school project, as did Lyon 3 or 4 days later. On March 1 Hagerman sent Lyon a letter of intent stating that a formal contract would be sent about June 10. Lyon did not respond to this letter. On June 5, Hagerman sent a formal contract, but Lyon never received it because it was incorrectly addressed. On September 6, Lyon withdrew its bid and submitted a new price of $28,750. Hagerman obtained the lockers from another supplier for $24,787 and sued Lyon for damages. The trial court awarded Hagerman $7,963, and Lyon appealed, contending that it had never made a contract with Hagerman. Should the judgment for Hagerman be affirmed?

3. Phyllis Chaplin sued Consolidated Edison Company of New York, Inc. (Con Ed), alleging that the company discriminated against epileptics in violation of federal law. In August 1981, Con Ed's attorney, Sheila Rosenrauch, sent a settlement proposal to Chaplin's attorney, James C. Francis IV. Francis replied that Chaplin had "a series of objections to the proposed settlement." Rosenrauch then stated in a letter of September 16 that Con Ed was still willing to settle on the terms stated, but "if this agreement is not satisfactory to your client in its present form, then I must withdraw all offers of settlement." Francis wrote on September 17 that he could not convince his client to accept the terms. Shortly thereafter a U.S. circuit court of appeals decided a separate case in which it held that the federal law did not create a private cause of action for epileptics. On September 30, Francis wrote to Rosenrauch and said Chaplin had had "a change of heart" and decided to accept the offer. Rosenrauch replied by telephone that the settlement was no longer acceptable. Was there mutual assent (offer and acceptance) here?

4. Bertha Ruther hired John Thor to sell a farm she owned. On April 12, Pribil made a written offer to buy the farm for $68,000. Ruther signed an acceptance on the same day and handed a copy of the agreement to Thor for delivery to Pribil. Thor returned to his office and had his secretary send a letter to Pribil with a copy of the agreement enclosed. The letter was postmarked "April 15, 1976 p.m." Pribil received it on April 16. However, at 11:42 a.m. on April 15, Ruther had phoned Thor, saying she was going to "terminate the contract." Immediately after receiving the call, Thor phoned Pribil and told him that Ruther was not going to sell the farm. Pribil sued for breach of contract. Holding that there was a contract, the trial court ruled in favor of Pribil. Was the trial court correct?

5. Vincent Benya submitted a written offer to buy 5,243 acres of timberland from S&T Paper Co. The purchase price was $605,000, with a deposit of $5,000, an additional $146,000 at closing, and the balance to be paid in annual payments over 10 years with interest at 9 percent. Seller was to give buyer a warranty deed at closing, 60 days from date of agreement. S&T's attorney inserted several items into the letter: deposit of $10,000, an additional $141,000 at closing, the balance to be paid in quarterly payments with interest at 10 percent, and seller to give buyer a special warranty deed. A lawsuit resulted between the parties, and the trial court concluded that the changes made by S&T to Benya's offer were minor and did not constitute a counteroffer, since the purchase price, closing date, and cash required were substantially the same. The court held there was a binding contract between the parties. Was the judgment of the trial court correct?

6. Crouch sent a letter to Purex inquiring about buying a building and its contents. Crouch received a letter from Purex signed by Frank Knox giving a price of $500. Crouch then sent a letter to Knox which read: "I guess we will buy the building for the amount you quoted, $500. I am sending you a personal check for this amount. . . ." The check was made out to Frank Knox and stated on its face that it was "for Silica building and equipment in and about that building." Knox endorsed the check to Purex, and Purex deposited it. Shortly thereafter, Knox sent Crouch a telegram stating that the check was deposited by mistake and Purex would issue a check to him. Purex then sent a letter to Crouch, enclosing a $500 check and stating that it could not accept Crouch's offer because the building and machinery had been sold to someone else prior to receipt of Crouch's check and letter. Crouch filed suit against Purex for breach of contract. Who should win?

CHAPTER 12

Consideration

For centuries, the courts have recognized the need to enforce promises. If people could not rely on the promises of strangers, doing business would be unreasonably difficult. Yet the courts have never enforced *all* promises. Purely social promises (e.g., to love someone or to attend a party in one's honor) and most promises to make a gift are not enforceable. What distinguishes enforceable promises from unenforceable ones?

To be enforceable under the early common law, a promise had to be in writing, and the writing had to bear the seal or insignia of the promisor. The writing then had to be delivered to the promisee or to the promisee's agent. Completing these steps was evidence to a largely illiterate population that the promisor took the transaction seriously and intended to be bound. Even a promise to make a gift was enforceable if sealed and delivered.

The sealed promise was an early type of **formal contract,** one enforceable simply because the promisor had complied with formalities prescribed by law, and without regard to whether the promisor had received something in exchange for the promise. As literacy and the ability to make a signature increased, the ceremonial role of the seal diminished. Today, the UCC makes seals inoperative in sales of goods. A number of states have made seals inoperative for all contracts, and other states have reduced their legal effect. However, although the sealed promise is of little importance in today's contract law, other kinds of formal contracts—negotiable instruments, letters of credit, and so on—are widely used. A promisor's use of legally required formalities, then, is one basis for enforcing promises.

But as trade and commerce developed in England, people needed a broader range of promise enforcement. The largely rural population of that era conducted most of its business orally and had little use for time-consuming contract formalities. By the early fourteenth century, courts were enforcing some kinds of unsealed promises and were seeking some basis—some underlying idea or theory—for determining which unsealed (informal) promises should be enforceable. The courts now recognize three alternative bases for the enforcement of **informal promises:**

- Consideration
- Promissory estoppel
- Statutes and case law imposing liability where consideration or the justifiable reliance needed for promissory estoppel is lacking[1]

[1] John E. Murray, Jr., Murray on Contracts (1974), p. 125.

In the twentieth century, promissory estoppel has become a significant basis for promise enforcement. Yet consideration remains the most common basis for enforcing informal promises. The first two parts of this chapter discuss consideration. The third part discusses promissory estoppel and other bases for promise enforcement.

THE REQUIREMENT OF CONSIDERATION

The need to enforce bargained-for exchanges led courts to develop the requirement of consideration. A person usually performed an act, or promised to do so, because some other person promised a return performance such as a payment of money. Each person's promise was made "in consideration of" (because of and in exchange for) the other person's promise, and each promise created an expectation of performance. To protect those expectations, the courts long ago began to enforce informal promises that had been induced by consideration.

Meaning of Consideration

Consideration is the thing or legal right that one gives up to induce another person to part with something—the *price* that one pays. Homer wants June's antique Jaguar car. To induce June to part with it, Homer might offer her money, or his 1955 Ford Thunderbird, or his promise to release her from a debt that she owes him. Any of these things would be consideration for June's promise to sell the car to Homer.

For a thing to be consideration (i.e., for it to be sufficient as a basis for a contract), it must meet two requirements: (1) it must be bargained for and (2) giving it up must be a legal detriment to the person who gave it.[2]

Bargained-for Exchange; Reciprocal Inducements. To be consideration for a promise, a performance or a return promise must be *bargained* *for*. A thing is bargained for if it is sought by the promisor (and is given by the promisee) in exchange for the promise.[3] Ann says to Ben, "I'll pay you $20 to mow my lawn," and Ben responds by mowing Ann's lawn. Ann (the offeror-promisor) promised to pay Ben $20 in exchange for his services; and Ben mowed the lawn as a result of and in exchange for Ann's promise of payment. The prospect of Ben's mowing the lawn *induced* Ann to promise him the payment, and her promise of payment induced Ben to mow the lawn. This is the **reciprocal bargaining relationship** required for Ben's act to be consideration for Ann's promise to pay. Since Ann received consideration for her promise, it is enforceable.

In contrast, suppose Al says to his daughter Bea, "I am going to buy a new car next month. I promise to give you my old car at that time." Here, because Al seeks nothing in return for his promise, there is no bargained-for exchange. Al has merely promised to make a gift to Bea. Since Al has received no consideration for his promise, it is unenforceable.

Legal Detriment. Not only must consideration be bargained for, it must be a *giving up* of something. Accordingly, the courts usually define consideration in terms of a legal detriment to the promisee. A promisee gives consideration by suffering a legal detriment in response to the promisor's promise.

To suffer a **legal detriment,** the promisee must *give up a legal right*. This means that, in exchange for the promisor's promise, the promisee must (1) do (or promise to do) something that he or she is not legally required to do or (2) refrain from doing (or promise to refrain from doing) what she or he is legally permitted to do.[4] Ann says to Ben, "I'll pay you $20 to mow my lawn." Ben mows the lawn. In doing so, he suffers a legal detriment by performing an act that he was not legally obligated to perform. That is, he gives up his legal right to use his time for other purposes and thus, by suffering a legal detriment, gives Ann consideration for her

---

[2]Often, consideration is defined as "either legal detriment to the promisee or legal benefit to the promisor." John D. Calamari and Joseph M. Perillo, THE LAW OF CONTRACTS (1987), p. 188.

[3]*Restatement (Second) of the Law of Contracts*, Section 71.

[4]Calamari and Perillo, op. cit., p. 187.

promise to pay $20. As in the bargained-for exchange discussed earlier, there must be a cause-and-effect relationship between the promise and the detriment. This means essentially that the promise must *induce* the detriment, and that each must be given in exchange for the other.

> **BOX 12.1**
>
> ### Consideration and Out-of-Court Settlements
>
> Ann negligently damages Ben's car, giving him a right to sue her for the loss. Neither Ann nor Ben has insurance covering this kind of loss. To avoid a lawsuit, Ann tells Ben, "I'll pay you $3,000 to cover the damage if you promise not to sue me," and Ben accepts her offer. Both believe that $3,000 is a reasonable estimate of the damage. By agreeing not to sue Ann, Ben gives up a legal right, suffers a legal detriment, and thus gives Ann a consideration that makes enforceable her promise to pay $3,000. Likewise, Ann's promise is a legal detriment to her which, having induced Ben's promise not to sue, is a consideration that makes Ben's promise enforceable.
>
> The transaction just described is an *out-of-court settlement*. Such settlements are favored by the law because they resolve disputes without burdening the court system. ∎

When a promisee suffers a legal detriment, the promisor gains a corresponding legal benefit.[5] In the out-of-court settlement discussed in Box 12.1, Ben suffered a legal detriment by agreeing to refrain from suing Ann. Ann received a corresponding legal benefit: a right, upon paying $3,000, not to be sued by Ben.

There is an important distinction between *legal* and *actual* benefits and detriments. Most people enter into contracts expecting to gain something of real value. Since they ordinarily expect an actual, economic benefit for whatever they must give up in exchange, they naturally think in terms of actual benefits and detriments—money for services, money for real estate, and so on.

But for consideration to exist (and for a promise to be enforceable), the promisee need suffer only a *legal* detriment. The often-cited case of *Hamer v. Sidway*[6] illustrates the point. There, an uncle promised to pay his nephew $5,000 if he would, among other things, "refrain from . . . using tobacco" until he was 21. The nephew refrained. The uncle did not pay, and died. The nephew transferred his claim against the uncle's estate to Hamer, who sued the uncle's estate for the $5,000. The court held that by forbearing to use tobacco, the nephew had suffered a *legal detriment.* Consequently, there was consideration for the uncle's promise to pay $5,000, even though abstaining probably was an *actual* physical *benefit* to the nephew. (Furthermore, when the uncle obtained the performance for which he had bargained, he received a legal benefit—a restriction of the nephew's freedom of action—even though the nephew's performance did not benefit the uncle economically.)

By defining consideration in terms of legal rather than actual benefits and detriments, courts accomplish two things. First, in ordinary circumstances, the courts thereby leave the problem of economic valuation to the parties to the contract. Second, the courts provide an abstract guideline that is applicable to an immense variety of contractual exchanges.

Most of the preceding examples involve *unilateral* contracts, in which there is only one promisor and one promisee. In a *bilateral* contract, both parties make promises and each party is both a promisor and a promisee.

For a typical *bilateral* contract to arise, each party must give consideration for the other party's promise—that is, each party must suffer a legal detriment. Amy says to Bob, "I'll sell you my car for $900, delivery and payment to be made in 2 weeks. Is that satisfactory to you?" Bob says, "Yes, I'll pay you the $900 upon delivery." Amy has suffered a legal detriment by promising to deliver the car to Bob and thus

---

[5] Ibid., p. 188.

[6] 121 N.Y. 538 (1891).

giving up her right to do something else with it. Similarly, Bob has suffered a legal detriment by giving up his right to use his $900 in some other way. The parties have created an executory bilateral contract. As it happens, Amy and Bob will receive actual benefits and suffer actual detriments if they perform their contractual obligations in 2 weeks, but this fact is irrelevant to the existence of consideration. Because each party suffered a *legal* detriment, the consideration necessary for a contract exists immediately upon the exchange of promises, and the failure of either party to perform later as promised (or even a present *threat* not to perform later) entitles the other party to a remedy (e.g., damages) for breach of contract. Figure 12.1 shows the movement of consideration in a typical executory bilateral contract.

The following case discusses the meaning of consideration.

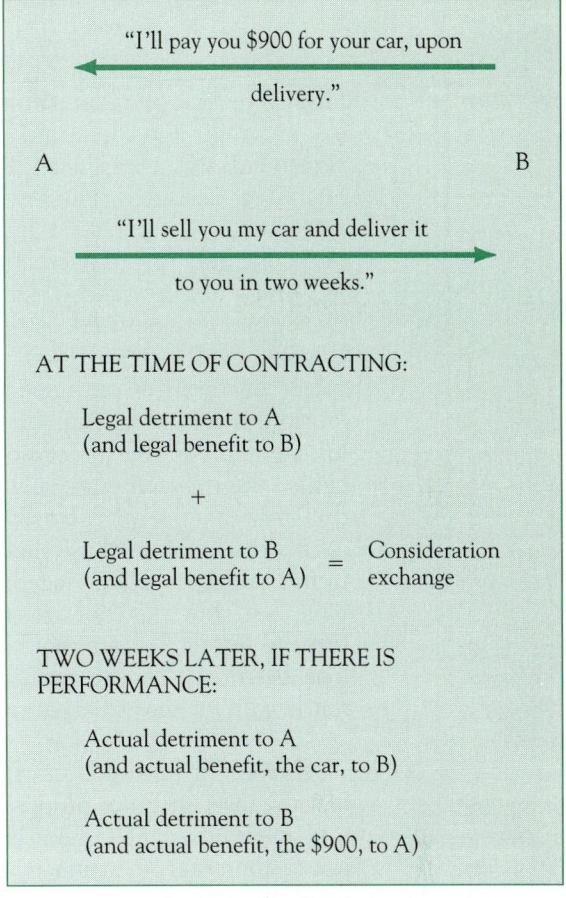

Figure 12.1 Consideration in bilateral contract.

CASE 12.1	**In re Estate of Weinsaft** • 647 S.W.2d 179 (Mo. App. 1983)
FACTS	In 1972, Thomas L. Weinsaft signed a written agreement with his son, Nicholas L. Weinsaft. Thomas agreed that during his lifetime he would not transfer any interest in his 765 shares of stock of Crand Manufacturing Company unless he first gave Nicholas an opportunity to purchase it. Upon Thomas's death, Nicholas was to have the "option and right to purchase all of the . . . stock" from Thomas's estate. The agreement recited that it was entered into "in consideration of $10.00 and other good and valuable consideration, including the inducement of Second Party [Nicholas] to remain the chief executive officer of said company." Thomas died in 1980. Nicholas gave notice that he intended to buy the stock, but one of the beneficiaries under Thomas's will objected, contending that Nicholas had given no consideration for Thomas's promises. Alleging that there was a binding contract, Nicholas brought suit to compel the estate to transfer the shares to him. The trial court granted judgment to Nicholas, and the beneficiary (here called "Intervenor") appealed.

> **CASE 12.1**
> **Continued**
>
> **OPINION**
>
> PREWITT, J. . . . Plaintiff as the one relying on the agreement had the burden [of proving] consideration. . . . However, that burden was met when the agreement was introduced in evidence and no evidence established that the recitals of consideration were erroneous. The recitation of consideration in an agreement . . . creates a presumption that the recitals are true, which presumption continues unless overcome by evidence to the contrary. . . .
>
> Intervenor contends that the recitation of consideration was insufficient because the agreement "does not specify to whom the $10.00 and other good and valuable consideration flows" and the ambiguities in such a document should be resolved against the optionee [plaintiff Nicholas]. We see no merit in this contention. It is obvious that the consideration recited was to the decedent [Thomas] for the grant of the options contained in the agreement. If the consideration included the inducement of plaintiff to remain as chief executive officer as it stated, then that and the other considerations could . . . flow [only] to the decedent.
>
> Plaintiff remained as chief executive officer, and this was sufficient consideration. Plaintiff was not legally obligated to work for the corporation and could have left, but did not do so. Consideration sufficient to support a contract may be either a detriment to the promisee or a benefit to the promisor. . . . The detriment to the promisee may consist of his doing anything . . . he is not [legally] bound to do or refraining from doing anything he has the right to do. . . .
>
> Intervenor [also contends] that the contract is void because it purports to effect the disposition of property at death without complying with the statutory requirements for a will. That contention also must be denied. The agreement was not testamentary because it was a contract made and in force during the decedent's lifetime. . . .
>
> **JUDGMENT**
>
> . . . [A]ffirmed.

Movement of Consideration. The consideration (i.e., performance or return promise) demanded by a promisor usually moves from the promisee to the promisor. But the promisor can require that consideration be given to someone else. Ann promises to pay Bob $200 if he delivers a guitar to her son Tom. Bob delivers the guitar to Tom. Bob's act of delivery is consideration for Ann's promise even though Bob made no promise to Ann and did not deliver the guitar to her.

Because the contract between Ann and Bob is intended to benefit Tom, it is called a **third-person beneficiary contract.** Such contracts (discussed further in Chapter 16) may be unilateral, as above, but often are bilateral. In a bilateral third-person beneficiary contract, the movement of consideration is different from that just described for a unilateral contract. Ann says to Bob, a guitar dealer, "I'll pay you $200 for this guitar if you'll promise to deliver it to my son Tom." Bob says, "OK, I'll deliver it to him." Bob's promise, made to Ann, is consideration for her promise to pay the $200. Here Ann immediately receives a legal benefit (Bob's promise to deliver the guitar to Tom), while Tom later receives an actual benefit, the guitar. Figure 12.2 illustrates the movement of consideration in a bilateral, third-person beneficiary contract.

Consideration Distinguished from Motives. Consideration should not be confused with the motive for giving it. "Love and affection" may

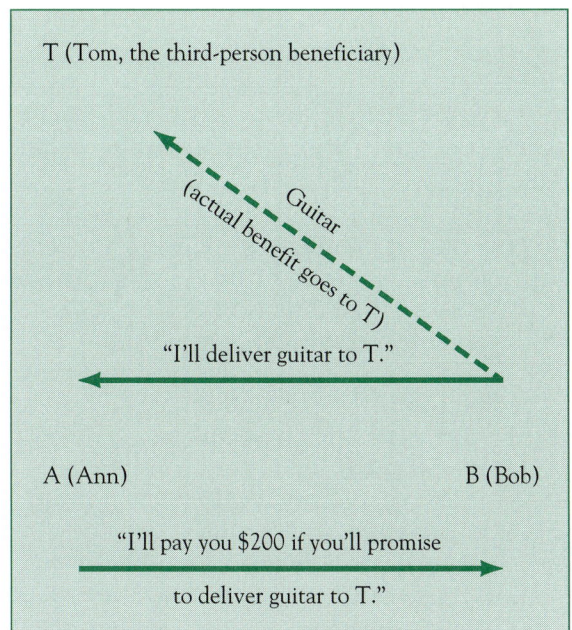

Figure 12.2 Movement of consideration in bilateral third-person beneficiary contract.

be compelling motives for making a promise, but they do not reveal an act of bargaining. Alicia writes to her daughter, "In consideration of my love and affection, I promise to send you $1,000 on your twenty-first birthday." Alicia bargained for nothing in exchange for her promise, which, being unsupported by consideration, is only a promise to make a gift.

In the case of *Hamer v. Sidway*, discussed earlier, the uncle made his promise to pay the nephew $5,000 in exchange for the nephew's giving up tobacco and other vices. The uncle's promise might have been motivated by a desire to protect or to improve his nephew's health, by a desire to impose his moral code on the nephew, or even by a desire to torment the nephew, hoping he would be too weak-willed to "kick the habit." Whatever a promisor's motive, the promise is enforceable if the promisee gives consideration, as the nephew did by avoiding the vices.

"Past Consideration"—No Consideration.

Consideration is something given in exchange for a promise and to induce it. Accordingly, anything that occurred *before* a promise was made cannot be consideration. A father says to his son, "I am so happy you stayed in college and received your degree. In consideration of that fact, I promise to pay you $1,000 at the end of next month." Undoubtedly the father has a *motive* for his promise—his pride in his son's accomplishment. However, the promise is unenforceable because the son's graduation was not something bargained for or induced by the promise. The fact that a past event cannot be something bargained for has given rise to the statement "Past consideration is no consideration." Though sometimes used by judges, the expression "past consideration" is self-contradictory; that which occurred before the promise cannot be consideration at all.

Illusory Promise; Requirements Contract

Sometimes a statement seems to be a promise but does not obligate the "promisor" to any performance whatever. Such statements are called **illusory promises.** Sam says to Bess, "I'll deliver to you at $3.25 per bushel whatever corn you order within the next 30 days, up to 5,000 bushels." Bess responds by saying, "I'll buy at that price as many bushels as I shall order from you within that period." Although Bess seems to have made a promise, in fact she has not committed herself to purchase any corn. Her promise is illusory, is not a legal detriment to her, and is not consideration for Sam's promise.

In contrast, if Bess had promised to buy as many bushels (not to exceed 5,000) as she would *need in her business*, the promise would not be illusory. The arrangement is called a **requirements contract,** and Bess's business needs provide an objective standard for determining some minimum amount of purchase. Because requirements contracts are useful and because the amount to be purchased does not depend solely on the whim of the buyer, courts routinely enforce them. Similarly, an **output contract** (one obliging the buyer to purchase the seller's whole production) is enforceable even though the size of the output cannot presently be known.

If a promisor has an unrestricted right to cancel an agreement—for example, to cancel it without notice—the promise is illusory and cannot be consideration for the other party's promise or performance. But if the right to cancel is restricted in any way, courts ordinarily will hold that the promise is not illusory. Sometimes a right to cancel is conditioned on (is not to occur until) the happening of some event such as a strike or a war. Or the promisor is required to give 30 days' notice of cancellation. In such instances, the promise is not illusory because the promisor is obligated to perform for some minimum amount of time.

> **BOX 12.2**
> ### Exclusive Dealing Contracts Under the UCC
>
> As noted in the previous chapter, the UCC presumes the validity of **requirements, output,** and other **exclusive dealing** contracts for *goods*, despite some older case law holding that such contracts are illusory.
>
> Manufacturers often use exclusive dealings contracts to give distributors the exclusive right to distribute the manufacturer's goods in a given territory. But such a contract might have a clause allowing the manufacturer to terminate the contract at any time. Or the contract might not require the distributor to accept any minimum amount of goods for resale. Is the contract therefore illusory? No. UCC Section 2-306 requires the seller to use its best efforts to supply goods and the buyer to use its best efforts to promote their sale. Thus, both buyer and seller have Code-imposed minimum obligations.

Adequacy of Consideration; Sham or Nominal Consideration

Orville owns an old painting and agrees to sell it to Martin for $450. Then Orville learns that the painting is worth $800 and refuses to deliver it to Martin, alleging that the consideration Martin gave was inadequate. Does Orville have a valid basis for getting out of the contract?

Probably not. Ordinarily, any legal detriment, no matter how economically inadequate, constitutes consideration. If the courts were to substitute their ideas of relative values for those expressed by the parties in their agreements, endless litigation, delay, and uncertainty would result. Moreover, today's courts, like those of the nineteenth century, are reluctant to interfere with freedom of contract by relieving an adult party of a bad bargain. Mistaken judgments about value are likely in competitive markets, may be offset by gains in other transactions, and often are reasonably relied on by the other party. Accordingly, the economic decisions of contracting parties usually are binding even though one of them may suffer loss.

Nevertheless, gross inadequacy of consideration may be evidence that only a gift was intended, or it may be relevant in resolving other contract issues. Ann persuades Ben to pay her $10,000 for $3 worth of foreign currency. The gross disparity between what Ben gave and what he received may be circumstantial evidence of Ann's fraud, duress, overreaching, or undue influence, or of Ben's mistake or incapacity. These problems are discussed further in Chapter 13.

Often agreements state that a promise was made "in consideration of $1," even though the $1 was neither bargained for by the promisor nor paid by the promisee. The pretended payment is called **sham** or **nominal** consideration and usually is not acceptable as consideration. Alicia, intending to give her new car to her son Mike, promises to deliver it to him later in the month "in consideration of $1." Alicia may have used this language in the mistaken belief that the law requires it for a gift, or because she wanted to disguise the gift as a sale. Whatever her reasoning, the "consideration" is a pretense, and in most states Alicia's promise is not enforceable. In contrast, suppose Alicia owes a large unpaid balance on the purchase price, and promises to deliver the car to Mike "in consideration of $1 and Mike's assuming my car debt." Even if the $1 was only a matter of form, his promise to assume Alicia's debt, being a legal detriment to him and given in exchange for Alicia's promise to deliver the car, is a consideration that makes her promise enforceable.

PROBLEMS RELATING TO CONSIDERATION

The courts must deal with a variety of problems relating to consideration. Many arise during the performance of a contract. For example, a buyer of goods that are rapidly falling in value might persuade the seller to accept a lower price than the buyer originally agreed to. A builder might run into unanticipated difficulties and pressure the client into paying more than the contract requires. The creditors of a troubled debtor might agree to accept less than originally owed. Are such promises enforceable? To decide, the courts may have to determine whether consideration is present and, if it is not, whether the promise should be enforced anyway.

Performance of Existing Legal Duty

At common law, performing or promising to perform an act that one was already legally obligated to perform was not consideration for another person's promise. Still widely followed, this **preexisting duty rule** applies (1) where the existing duty is imposed by statute or by the common law and (2) where a person is already under a contractual obligation to render a specified performance but later demands more for it (or insists on doing less than originally promised).

Existing Statutory or Common Law Duty. Performing an act already required by law is not consideration. Ann and Ben, the county sheriff, see Tom steal Ann's car. Ann says to Ben, "I'll pay you $100 to arrest that man." Ben does so and demands the $100. Ann's promise is not enforceable because Ben, as sheriff, already had a duty to arrest Tom. In making the arrest, Ben suffered no new legal detriment and conferred no new legal benefit on Ann, who as a citizen was already entitled to have Ben perform his duty. Similarly, a promise to pay a witness to tell the truth in court is not enforceable. Witnesses are already required by law to tell the truth, and doing so cannot be a new legal detriment to them. Moreover, since no one has a right to commit a tort or a crime, Joe's promise not to smash Bob's computer is not consideration for Bob's promise to pay Joe $50.

Existing Contractual Duty. Like statutes and the common law, a contract establishes legal duties that are binding on the parties. Sometimes, however, the parties agree to modify the contract so that one party's obligation increases while the other party's duty remains the same. Does a promise to pay or do more for the *same return consideration* bind the promisor? The question is troublesome to the courts.

Under the preexisting duty rule, if the promisor receives no consideration for the new promise, the court is not supposed to enforce it. Indeed, for the modification of contracts covered by the common law, most courts *do* require consideration for the new promise. Yet many one-sided modifications of existing contractual obligations are quite reasonable even if the promisor did not receive consideration for the new promise. Where the benefiting promisee is acting fairly, some courts will enforce the new promise even though the existence of consideration may be doubtful. In a few states, modifications made because of circumstances unforeseen by the parties, and modifications upon which the other party has reasonably relied, are enforceable even though consideration clearly is lacking.

Understanding how the courts handle the preexisting duty problem as it relates to modified contracts requires, first, an understanding of two basic contract situations:

1 In April, Amy hires Bill to work for her as marketing director for a 1-year term at $500 per week, the term to begin in July. In June, Amy and Bill agree to modify the contract so that Bill will receive $550 per week for the same work. Under the preexisting duty rule, Amy's promise to pay the additional $50 is unenforceable. Having already contracted to work as marketing director for $500 per week, Bill suffered no new legal detriment for Amy's promise to pay the extra $50, conferred no new legal benefit on Amy, and therefore gave no consideration for Amy's promise.

2. Amy hires Bill as marketing director at $500 per week for a 1-year term beginning in July. In May, Bill receives an offer from another company, and Amy and Bill agree in writing to cancel (rescind) the April contract, each saying in effect, "I'll free you from your obligation under the April contract if you'll free me from mine." Because each party's promise is bargained for and given in exchange for the other's promise, both Amy and Bill receive consideration and the rescission agreement is a binding contract canceling the April contract. Bill suffered the requisite legal detriment by giving up his right to receive $500 per week from Amy; Amy suffered a legal detriment by giving up her right to Bill's services as marketing director. Since neither Amy nor Bill has any further duty under the April employment contract, both are free to contract with whom they please. So, if in June Amy rehires Bill as marketing director at $600 per week for a 1-year term, Bill owes no preexisting contractual duty to Amy that could prevent enforcement of her promise to pay $600.

Situation 1 above is relatively uncontroversial; that is, most courts would find Amy's promise to pay the extra $50 unenforceable for lack of consideration. Situation 2 is likewise uncontroversial; most courts would find the contract of rescission sufficient to cancel the original contract and prepare the way for an enforceable later contract between the same parties.

However, many contract modification cases fall between these clear extremes. Ann hires Bob to build an asphalt road along one side of Ann's farm for a stated sum; after partial performance, Bob discovers he will lose money on the job and threatens to quit unless Ann agrees to pay more. To persuade Bob to continue, Ann promises to pay him an additional $3,000, and Bob completes the work. Is Ann's promise enforceable?

The answer may depend on the reason for Bob's underestimating the cost of the road. If Bob was negligent in preparing his bid—or if he intentionally underbid to get the job, expecting to raise the price later—nearly all courts would hold that Bob was under a preexisting duty to build the road for the price originally agreed to and so gave no consideration for Ann's promise to pay more. Application of the preexisting duty rule is common in circumstances such as these, to prevent contractors from extorting a higher price when they themselves caused or should have anticipated the loss.

Suppose, however, that Bob would lose money because of some **unforeseeable circumstance** such as an earthquake of unusual severity that destroyed part of the work, and Ann agreed to pay more than the original contract price to get Bob to continue. Some courts would enforce Ann's agreement to pay more, reasoning that the extra work, being unforeseeable, was not a part of the original bargain, and Bob's doing it was consideration for Ann's promise of extra payment.

The courts differ on how unforeseeable the circumstance must be for the extra work to be new consideration. Some courts require a high degree of unforeseeability, ruling that labor disputes, most increases in the cost of materials, and most bad weather are foreseeable. A few courts accept a lesser degree of unforeseeability as sufficient, as long as the person seeking the extra payment was not negligent. Case 12.2 involves a contractor-promisee who encounters difficulties that he did not foresee. But were they *foreseeable?*

CASE 12.2   Crookham & Vessels, Inc. v. Larry Moyer Trucking, Inc.
• 699 S.W.2d 414 (Ark. App. 1985)

FACTS

Crookham & Vessels, Inc. was the general contractor on a project to build an extension of a railroad. Crookham subcontracted with Larry Moyer Trucking, Inc., which was to do the excavation and dirt work according to plans and specifications. Moyer started work and soon encountered a problem in constructing ditches. Water would not drain out of the ditches because the culverts through which they were to drain were clogged off the jobsite. This caused the ditches to collapse, requiring Moyer to redig the ditches repeatedly. Moyer threatened to quit work unless he received extra pay for redigging the ditches. Crookham agreed, but later refused to pay. Moyer filed suit and received a verdict for $3,998.39 due on the contract and $12,095 for "extra ditching." Crookham appealed.

OPINION

COOPER, J. . . . Under Arkansas law, there must be additional consideration when the parties to a contract enter into an additional contract. . . .

> Mere performance of an existing contract or a part thereof, is of itself no consideration for a new promise to the party performing. . . . If, without legal justification, one party to a contract breaks it, or threatens to break it, and to induce performance on his part the adversary party promises to pay more than was provided for by the original contract, there is in principle no consideration for such promise, as the party who threatens to break the contract does, when he finally performs it, no more than he was bound in law to do.

> Here, the contract admittedly required the appellee [Moyer] to dig the ditches so that he met the specifications at the time the project was approved, and it is undisputed that that is what the appellee did. Where the work performed is covered under the terms of the contract, as here, there can be no recovery for it as extra work. . . . Here, . . . the appellee had the duty to acquaint himself before bidding with the conditions, nature, and extent of the work to be performed, and the condition of the culverts in question could have been taken into account. In Arkansas, it is settled that "[i]nconvenience or the cost of compliance with the contract or other like thing cannot excuse a party from the performance of an absolute and unqualified undertaking to do that which is possible and lawful." . . . *Accord, Baton Rouge,* 304 F.Supp. at 585 ("Where one agrees to do, for a fixed sum, a thing possible to be performed, he will not be excused or become entitled to additional compensation because unforeseen difficulties are encountered"). Here the appellee did no more than was required by its contract; the unforeseen clogged culverts merely made it more difficult. The appellant has received no additional consideration for its alleged promise to pay extra, having gotten no more than it bargained for in the first place. Therefore, the jury verdict in the amount of $12,095.00 for the "extra ditching" must be overturned.

JUDGMENT

There has been no appeal of the award of $3,998.39 for costs under the contract. . . . Therefore, we can, and do, modify the judgment by deleting the jury's award and affirming the award of $3,998.39 for contract costs and the prejudgment interest thereon.

Part payment of a liquidated claim. One variation of the preexisting duty rule involves part payment of a liquidated claim. A debt (or claim) is said to be **liquidated** when there is no dispute about its existence or amount. Al agrees to repair Bev's bulldozer for $350, makes the repairs, and sends her a bill for that amount. Bev's debt is "liquidated" because Bev and Al have agreed on the price. If Bev (the debtor) can later persuade Al (the creditor) to accept part payment of the liquidated debt as payment in full, is Al's promise to do so binding?

Part payment of a liquidated debt, made when it is due or past due, is not consideration for the creditor's promise to accept the part payment as payment in full. Suppose Bev insists that Al's $350 charge is too high, and he agrees to accept $250 as payment in full but later sues Bev for an additional $100. Al will prevail. Bev's original agreement to pay $350 created a liquidated debt. Thus, Bev has a preexisting duty to pay $350, and, having suffered no new legal detriment for Al's promise to accept $250, gave no consideration for that promise.

The part payment rule operates satisfactorily where the creditor's charge is reasonable and especially where, in addition, the debtor is trying to take unfair advantage of the creditor. However, the rule has been criticized as tending to defeat the legitimate expectations of debtors who *in good faith* persuade creditors to reduce what may have been an exorbitant price. Consequently, the courts have been "astute to find consideration" if the debtor has done anything at all in connection with the payment that he or she was not originally obliged to do.[7] For example, suppose Bev is insolvent and is considering voluntary bankruptcy. If, in exchange for Al's promise to accept $250 in full satisfaction of the debt, she agrees not to declare bankruptcy, Al's promise is enforceable. This new agreement (if actually carried out) is an **accord and satisfaction** of Al's original claim against Bev. Their new agreement is the "accord," and its performance is the "satisfaction." The consideration needed for an accord and satisfaction can occur in many other ways—for example, where Bev (acting in good faith) pays Al $250 and, in addition, gives him a potato, or pays at a place other than that required by the contract, or pays before the due date of the original debt.

The courts are not the only protectors of debtors who have negotiated a lower payment in good faith. The undesirable consequences of the part payment rule to debtors have caused some state legislatures to modify or abolish it. For example, in California, New York, and Pennsylvania, a debtor may enforce a creditor's *written* release of a balance owed even though the debtor gave no new consideration.

> **BOX 12.3**
>
> **Sales of Goods—Where Consideration Is Not Required**
>
> Similarly, under UCC Section 2-209(1), written (and some oral) agreements modifying sales contracts need no consideration to be binding. The *Daily Informer*, a regional newspaper, agrees to buy its next year's requirements of newsprint paper from Pulpco at a specified price per ton. Later, the *Informer* agrees to a price increase of $12 per ton for the life of the contract. Under the UCC, the *Informer*'s promise to pay more is binding even though Pulpco gave no new consideration for it. (However, as noted in Chapter 18, the *Informer*'s promise would *not* be binding if Pulpco acted in bad faith by imposing the price increase without good reason.)
>
> Also, as noted in the previous chapter, a merchant's *firm offer* needs no consideration to be binding on the merchant.

Settlement of an unliquidated claim; payment-in-full checks. The part payment rule does not apply if the debt is *un*liquidated. A claim is **unliquidated** when there is an honest dispute about the existence of an indebtedness or, more commonly, about its amount. Al repairs Bev's bulldozer, saying nothing about the price, and he later sends her a bill for $350. Protesting that the bill is unreasonably high, Bev offers $250 as payment in full. Al reluctantly agrees to accept the $250 as payment in full, does so, and later

---
[7]Murray, op. cit., Sec. 86.

sues Bev for an additional $100. Al's promise to accept $250 is binding on him. Why?

Because there was no agreement on price at the time of contracting, Bev's debt was unliquidated. Since Al performed the repairs, though, a court probably would hold that a reasonable price for his services was implied. But by accepting the $250 that Bev offered, Al reached an *accord* with her—an agreement on price that replaces the reasonable price that a court would have inferred. By giving up their respective rights to have a court decide what is reasonable, each gave consideration for the other's promise: Al for Bev's promise to pay $250, and Bev for Al's promise to accept it as payment in full. Bev's paying the $250 was a satisfaction of the accord.

The result would be the same if (with no prior agreement on price) Bev had sent Al a check for $250 marked "Payment in full of bulldozer repair bill," and Al cashed the check. Because Al knew or had reason to know the terms of Bev's payment offer, his cashing the check is an acceptance that creates an accord. There is an accord even if Al crosses out the notation before cashing the check and later sues Bev for an additional $100. Obviously, Al has not in fact agreed to accept $250 as final payment; but largely to resolve disputes efficiently, the vast majority of courts treat check cashing in these circumstances as conclusive evidence of the creditor's agreement to the terms offered. If Al wanted to pursue the $350, he should have returned Bev's payment-in-full check and brought suit for $350. He would, of course, run the risk that the court would find something less than $350 to be a reasonable payment for his services. Box 12.4 describes the treatment of payment-in-full checks in sales of goods.

What happens when a debtor owes an account that is partly liquidated and partly in dispute, and he or she offers a check made out for the liquidated amount but marked "payment in full" of the whole account? May the creditor cash the check and later collect the unliquidated portion of the debt? Some courts hold that the creditor may collect the balance of the claim. They reason that the debt is liquidated as to the amount admittedly due, the debtor has a preexisting duty to pay it, and doing so therefore is not consideration for the creditor's promise (implied from cashing the check) to release the debtor from the balance of the claim. *M*ost courts hold that the creditor *cannot* collect the unpaid balance. They reason that if any part of the claim is in dispute, the entire debt is unliquidated, and a payment offered and accepted as payment in full is a binding accord and satisfaction.

The case that follows involves an account that is partly liquidated and partly unliquidated. The debtor offers as full payment of the whole account an amount substantially less than the amount he admitted was due.

> **BOX 12.4**
> **Payment-in-Full Checks in Sales of Goods**
>
> Can a person who receives a check marked "payment in full" nullify the effect of that language by adding a statement such as "This check is cashed under protest," and thus reserve a right to collect the balance allegedly owed? At least for the sale of goods, Section 1-207 of the UCC seems to permit such action, and the New York courts have so held. The states of Delaware, Florida, Massachusetts, and New Hampshire may be in agreement with the New York position. The courts of *most* states, however, hold that Section 1-207 does *not* replace the accord and satisfaction rule applying to payment-in-full checks. See Calamari and Perillo, op. cit., Sec. 4-11. The 1990 amendments to the UCC make clear that Section 1-207 is not meant to apply to payment-in-full checks. ∎

CASE 12.3 Field Lumber Co. v. Petty • 512 P.2d 764 (Wash. App. 1973)

FACTS

Petty, a general contractor, made numerous purchases from Field Lumber Co. Field's ledger statement showed a balance of $1,752.21 in October 1970. Petty acknowledged a balance of $1,091.96 but disputed the difference of $660.25, which represented an allegedly unauthorized $292.60 purchase by an employee and a 1-percent-per-month finance charge. In early October 1970, Petty mailed a check for $500 to Field Lumber Co. with a letter clearly stating that the check must be accepted in full settlement of the claim or returned. The letter also stated that the funds had been borrowed. In response, Field Lumber Co. notified Petty by telephone that it would require full payment, but cashed the $500 check.

Field sued to recover $1,252.21. The trial court held that cashing the check under the described circumstances discharged Petty from any further liability on the account. Field appealed.

OPINION

FARRIS, J. . . . We reverse. We recognize the general rule that where a sum due is unliquidated or disputed and a remittance of an amount less than that claimed is sent to the creditor with a statement explaining that it is in full satisfaction of the claim, the acceptance of such a remittance by the creditor constitutes an accord and satisfaction.

However, this rule is not applicable where a portion of the alleged debt in excess of the amount paid is acknowledged and not in dispute. In such a case a debtor cannot unilaterally tender a lesser sum than that which it is agreed is due and owing and rely upon the retention of that sum as full settlement of the debt unless there is some additional consideration given therefor. An accord and satisfaction is founded on contract, and a consideration therefor is as necessary as for any other contract.

The recognition of a debt in a fixed amount and in excess of the $500 which was tendered under the circumstances here precludes the finding of an accord and satisfaction unless there is proof of new consideration. It has long been the rule in this state that payment of an amount admitted to be due can furnish no consideration for an accord and satisfaction of the entire claim.

Here we cannot find a scintilla of evidence indicating that any new consideration was given. Petty did not borrow the sum after agreeing with Field . . . that he would do so if it would be accepted as full settlement. He borrowed the money of his own volition and then simply mailed the check with a letter after efforts had been made and were continuing to be made to recover the full amount. To find an accord and satisfaction here where a definite portion of the alleged debt was acknowledged to be due and owing and therefore liquidated and undisputed would place a creditor at a disadvantage in accepting partial payments from a reluctant debtor, since by doing so he would be jeopardizing his right to receive the balance, even though in law that balance was in fact due him. It is true that courts look with favor on compromise, but this means genuine compromise, arrived at through mutual agreement.

> **CASE 12.3 Continued**
>
> The payment of $500 here was a payment on account; whether the disputed sum of $660.25 is due and owing is a proper subject for litigation. The cause is remanded for determination of the question of the balance due on account.
>
> **JUDGMENT** Reversed and remanded.

Composition Agreement

A **composition agreement** is an arrangement between a debtor and two or more creditors whereby the debtor, who is unable to pay the full amount owed, agrees to pay a smaller sum to each of the creditors, and they agree to accept their pro rata portions in *full* satisfaction of their claims. Don owes $6,000 to Al, $4,000 to Betty, and $2,000 to Carla. Unable to pay the whole amount because of business losses, Don offers his creditors a composition agreement under which each creditor is to receive 50 percent of his or her claim. If the creditors agree to cancel the balances owed, a composition results. In most states, Don will be discharged from his obligation to each of the participating creditors upon making the part payment he promised.

Sometimes the creditor tries to cancel the composition and collect the amount originally owed, arguing that the debtor gave no consideration for the creditor's promise to accept the smaller amount as full payment of the original, liquidated debt. The courts have found consideration in a variety of ways, some logical and some not. Some courts say, logically, that the legal detriment required to support the creditor's promise is the debtor's giving up his or her legal right to declare bankruptcy and thus have all the debts canceled in their entirety. Other courts say that a composition is really an agreement among creditors, with the debtor being a third-person beneficiary of their contract. Under it, each creditor incurs a legal detriment by giving up the right to force payment of the amount originally due, in exchange for the other creditors' promises to accept less as full payment.

Some courts do not attempt to justify enforcement of composition agreements on the basis of consideration. Instead, they base their decisions on the ground of public policy, reasoning that composition agreements settle a group of claims expeditiously at a minimum of expense to the parties, and that such out-of-court settlements lessen the ever increasing volume of litigation.

A composition agreement applies only to the creditors who are parties to it. If Betty had refused to enter into the agreement discussed above, she would not have shared in the distribution of Don's assets; but neither would she be precluded from later attempting to collect the full $4,000 Don owed her.

Forbearance to Sue on a Claim

Everyone has a right to litigate a valid claim. Giving up the right to do so is a legal detriment which, if bargained for, constitutes consideration. While driving their cars, Amy and Bob collide in an intersection. They are unsure who was at fault. However, thinking that Bob was more at fault than she was, Amy promises not to sue Bob if he agrees to pay her $2,500 (a reasonable estimate of her damages). Bob agrees but later refuses to make payment, and Amy sues him for breach of contract. Bob argues that his promise is unenforceable because Amy gave no consideration for it. Because Amy had a right to sue Bob for damages, she suffered a legal detriment when she promised not to sue him, and therefore gave consideration for his promise to pay the $2,500.

A person may believe that he or she has a valid claim (whether in tort or for breach of contract), when in fact it is invalid. Can a forbearance to sue be consideration if the forbearing person's claim turns out to be invalid? Because the courts favor out-of-court settlements, the answer usually is yes, so long as (1) the claim involves *uncertainty as to the facts or the law* or (2) the promisor had a *good faith belief* at the time of contracting that the claim was valid. Al honestly believes that Bev has breached her contract with him, and he promises not to sue her if she will pay him $500. Although unconvinced that she breached it, Bev pays. Al's forbearance to sue is consideration for Bev's payment. This result seems sound because Al's belief in his claim is honest, Bev was uncertain, and out-of-court settlements ease the burden on the courts. Moreover, Bev could have refused to pay, thus forcing Al to decide whether it would be cost-effective to sue her.

In contrast, suppose that Al, knowing he has no contract with Bev, agrees not to sue her for its breach. Bev, erroneously thinking that she had contracted with Al (because she signed forty-three contracts last month), agrees to pay him $500. In agreeing not to assert a clearly unfounded claim, Al gives up nothing, incurs no legal detriment, and so gives no consideration for anything that might have been given in exchange for the alleged "forbearance."

Case 12.4 involves a person who forbore to sue, by agreeing not to rescind (cancel) a contract.

CASE 12.4 Pierce v. Plogger • 286 S.E.2d 207 (Va. 1982)

FACTS Harold Pierce contracted to buy a house from Marshall Plogger for $63,000. Before the closing date, Pierce discovered that the basement leaked badly and the air-conditioning system did not work properly. Pierce refused to close until Plogger signed a written warranty covering the leaking basement and the malfunctioning air conditioner. According to Pierce, his agreeing to close also depended on Plogger's making a 1-year oral warranty covering unknown defects in the entire house. Plogger corrected the air-conditioning system and contracted with Acme Weatherproofing Company to stop the leakage in the basement. The leakage continued.

Within 3 months after closing, Pierce detected movement in one of the foundation walls against which dirt had been piled to level the front yard. An architect hired by Pierce reported that the wall was defective and might collapse unless repaired. When Plogger refused to make the repairs, Pierce had the work done for $3,385 and brought suit for breach of warranty. Plogger denied giving Pierce an oral warranty and claimed that Pierce knew of the crack in the basement wall but never complained. From a district court judgment for Pierce, Plogger appealed to the circuit (trial) court. In the circuit court, the trial judge entered judgment for Plogger upon a jury verdict in Plogger's favor. Pierce appealed.

OPINION THOMPSON, J. . . . The evidence reveals that, before contracting with Plogger, Pierce inspected the basement during a dry period. After signing the contract but before closing, he discovered a cracked basement wall and a severe leakage. Plogger agreed, but failed, to correct the defects before closing. On condition that Plogger give the express oral and written warranties, Pierce agreed to close and not pursue his remedy in rescission. Pierce's agreement to forego suit constitutes valuable consideration for the warranties.

In *Hooff v. Paine* . . . we said: "The law is well settled that forbearance . . .

**CASE 12.4
Continued**

to prosecute a well-founded or doubtful claim is a sufficient consideration for a contract. On the other hand, the forbearance to prosecute an invalid, worthless or unfounded claim is not a consideration recognized by the law as valuable." We reaffirmed our prior comments on consideration in *Dulany Foods, Inc. v. Ayers* . . . where we said:

> Concerning adequacy [existence?] of consideration, it was held in *Brewer v. Bank of Danville* . . . : "Consideration is, in effect the price bargained [and] paid for a promise. It may be in the form of a benefit to the party promising or a detriment to the party to whom the promise is made. It matters not to what extent the promisor is benefited or how little the promisee may give for the promise. A very slight advantage to the one party or a trifling inconvenience to the other is generally held sufficient to support the promise."

Even if Pierce's right to rescind is doubtful, we hold that as a matter of law the forbearance of Pierce to pursue legal action prior to settlement was a sufficient consideration for the written warranty. . . . [W]e hold that [whether the alleged oral warranty was given is] a factual issue [that] should be resolved; . . . we [also] hold, under the evidence in this record, [that] the written warranty was supported by valuable consideration. . . .

JUDGMENT Reversed and remanded.

PROMISES ENFORCEABLE WITHOUT REGARD TO CONSIDERATION

Many legal scholars find the concept of consideration elusive and the search for it sometimes forced and arbitrary.

The case of *Wright & Seaton, Inc. v. Prescott*[8] illustrates the point. There Prescott had promised not to engage in postemployment competition with his employer, Wright & Seaton, for 3 years. Two weeks before the expiration of the 1-year employment contract, Prescott quit his job and began working for Wright & Seaton's competitor. Prescott contended that his promise not to compete was unenforceable for lack of consideration because Wright & Seaton's offer of employment was illusory. It was illusory, Prescott said, because Wright & Seaton could terminate his employment at any time, with or without cause, upon giving Prescott written notice. The court held that even though Wright & Seaton had a very broad right to terminate Prescott's employment,

the promise of employment was not illusory. By agreeing to give Prescott written notice of termination, Wright & Seaton had incurred a legal detriment which, though small, was consideration for Prescott's promise not to work for a competitor for 3 years.

Despite the triviality of the consideration in this case, the result seems sound because Wright & Seaton was performing its side of the bargain, while Prescott appears unreasonable in canceling the agreement late in the term of employment to avoid the noncompetition clause. But what if the *employer* had been the unreasonable one, intending, for example, to employ Prescott for a short time, fire him, and then invoke the 3-year noncompetition clause? If the court mechanically applied the rule that "any detriment, no matter how small, constitutes consideration," injustice would result because the employer would be allowed to use a technical application of the consideration doctrine to impose hardship on the employee. Yet, if to avoid this injustice the court held that the requirement of written notice is *not* consideration, the resulting rule would be inconsistent with what had been decided before.

[8]420 So. 2d 623 (Fla. App. 1982).

In fact, as many commentators have noted, the courts often have manipulated the doctrine of consideration to avoid injustice, thus creating confusion and inconsistency in the law. Whether a consideration requirement is needed at all has been questioned. Some commentators have urged that it be abandoned, and that contracting parties be required merely to indicate a "deliberate and serious intent" to make a contract. Most courts and legislatures, however, adhere to the traditional approach of creating exceptions to the consideration requirement. Some promises that are enforceable without consideration, such as modifications of sales contracts, have already been mentioned. The remainder of this chapter discusses other major exceptions to the consideration requirement.

Promises to Perform Prior Legal Duty

In most states, where a contractual duty has been terminated by operation of law, a subsequent promise to perform the terminated duty may be enforceable even if the promisor receives nothing for the new promise. Examples include a promise made (1) following bar of the original duty by the statute of limitations and (2) following a debtor's discharge in bankruptcy.

Promise Following Bar by Statute of Limitations. All states have statutes of limitations prescribing time limits within which legal action must be started. A person who fails to bring his or her lawsuit within the time prescribed by the statute loses the right to do so. That is, the suit is "barred" by the statute. Carmen contracts to pay David $500, Carmen breaches the contract, and David fails to sue her within the time allowed by the statute of limitations. Carmen's contractual duty is discharged (extinguished), and David can never compel Carmen to pay the discharged debt.

Suppose, however, that Carmen later promises to pay David the discharged amount. Since David ordinarily will not have given any consideration for Carmen's promise, is her promise to pay the barred debt enforceable? In most states, a debtor's written promise to pay a barred debt is enforceable without consideration. Moreover, in the absence of a writing, many courts treat a part payment by the debtor as an implied promise to pay the barred debt if the payment is voluntary and if the circumstances reveal an intention to pay the unpaid balance. Some judges say that the debt, together with "moral obligation," is sufficient "consideration" to support the new promise to pay. Other courts make clear that they are enforcing the new promise as an exception to the requirement of consideration, because they feel it is good public policy to do so.

Promise Following Discharge in Bankruptcy. Under federal bankruptcy law, a troubled debtor may receive a discharge in bankruptcy from his or her debts, and a financial "fresh start." Before 1978, debtors often "reaffirmed" one or more of the discharged debts and found themselves still obligated to pay even though they received no consideration for the new promise. Believing that many financial institutions were unfairly pressuring unwitting debtors into reaffirming their discharged debts and endangering their fresh start, the drafters of the 1978 Bankruptcy Code sharply limited the ability of debtors to make reaffirmation agreements. Today, no reaffirmation agreement is enforceable unless it (1) was made before the discharge was granted and (2) it complies with numerous Code-imposed rules designed to inform and protect the debtor. These rules are discussed in Chapter 30 under Discharge Hearing; Reaffirmation; Protection of Discharge. If a reaffirmation agreement complies with them, it is enforceable even though the debtor receives no consideration for the new promise to pay.

Promises Enforceable Because of Promissory Estoppel

Promissory estoppel is an alternative to the doctrine of consideration as a basis for enforcing promises. As discussed and illustrated in Chapters 10 and 11, a promisor is "estopped" (prevented by law) from avoiding liability for the consequences of his or her promise if three circumstances exist:

1 There is a promise that the promisor should reasonably expect to induce action on the part of the promisee.
2 The promise induces such action—i.e., the promisee justifiably relies on the promise to his or her detriment. Under *Restatement (Second)*, promisee reliance is *not* required for charitable subscriptions.
3 Injustice can be avoided only by enforcement of the promise.

Charitable Subscriptions

A **charitable subscription** is a promise to make a gift to a charity. "Charitable" refers not merely to institutions founded for the purpose of aiding people in unfortunate circumstances, but also to institutions such as churches, schools, colleges, libraries, museums, and hospitals. A "subscription" is usually a signed promise by each of several persons to contribute a sum of money specified on a subscription form. Are such gift promises enforceable?

Charitable subscriptions have been widely enforced in the United States, in keeping with the general feeling that private philanthropy serves an important function in our society. Some courts have purported to find consideration for charitable subscriptions in the exchange of promises among subscribers; other courts have found it in the implied promise of the charity to use the funds in ways indicated by the subscription agreement. The difficulty with such enforcement rationales is that the typical charitable giver does not have a bargaining intent, but intends only to make a gift. Consequently, modern courts tend to explain enforcement of such subscriptions on the basis of promissory estoppel instead of traditional consideration theory. However, because many charities could not show the detrimental reliance required by promissory estoppel, some courts have held that reliance is not required for the enforcement of charitable subscriptions. This is the position of Section 90 of *Restatement (Second)*.

SUMMARY

The courts enforce many types of promises. Formal contracts are enforceable because the promisor used legally required formalities. Informal promises may be enforced on the basis of consideration, promissory estoppel, or statutes and case law imposing liability for reasons of policy, where consideration or the circumstances required for promissory estoppel are lacking.

Consideration may be defined as a legal detriment to the promisee, bargained for by the promisor. A legal detriment is the promisee's giving up a legal right. For the detriment to be consideration, it must be induced by the promise and given in exchange for it. By defining consideration in terms of legal rather than actual benefits and detriments, the courts leave economic valuation to the contracting parties.

"Past consideration" is not consideration because the promise, having been made after the happening of the act for which it was given, did not induce the act. An illusory promise is not consideration because the promisor makes no enforceable commitment. Ordinarily, the courts will not look into the adequacy of consideration, except, for example, where inadequacy may be evidence of fraud or of intent to make a gift. Although consideration can have small economic value, sham or nominal consideration will not make a promise enforceable.

The performance of a preexisting statutory or common law duty is not consideration for a promise. Nor is the performance of a preexisting contractual duty consideration for a promise to pay or to do more than was originally agreed to. But if an existing contract is rescinded by mutual agreement, the parties are free to contract as they like.

Part payment of a liquidated claim is not consideration for the creditor's promise to accept the payment as payment in full. However, if the debtor makes a lesser payment and, in addition, does something he or she was not originally obligated to do, the creditor's promise to accept less is enforceable as an accord and satisfaction. Similarly, a creditor's cashing a check offered as payment in full of an *unliquidated* debt is an accord and satisfaction. A composition agreement is enforceable even though the agreement involves liquidated debts. A promise to forbear from suing another person is a legal detriment if the one forbearing had a valid claim, a doubtful claim, or an honest belief that his or her claim was valid.

Some promises are enforceable despite a lack of consideration—for example, modifications of sales contracts, a written promise to pay a debt that has been barred by a statute of limitations, and some bankruptcy reaffirmation agreements. Under the doctrine of promissory estoppel, a promise not supported by consideration may be enforceable if the promisee justifiably relied on the promise to his or her detriment.

REVIEW QUESTIONS

1. (a) Briefly explain or describe four bases of promise enforcement used in our legal system. (b) As a basis of promise enforcement, how does consideration differ from promissory estoppel?

2. Is an out-of-court settlement a contract? Explain in terms of bargain and legal detriment.

3. Al insures his life for $100,000, naming his wife Tina as beneficiary. Diagram the movement of consideration.

4. Benita repairs the roof of her father's house. Pleased with her work, the father says, "Next week I'm going to pay you $300 for that job." Is the father's promise enforceable? Why or why not?

5. John agrees to sell his car to Hector for $2,000. The car has a market value of $4,000. Contending that the consideration is inadequate, John refuses to go through with the deal, and Hector sues John for breach of contract. (a) On these facts, will the court consider adequacy of consideration? (b) Under what circumstances, if any, would a court consider adequacy of the consideration?

6. Judge Sharp refuses to rule on Sue's case unless she agrees to pay him $100. Sue agrees, the judge rules, and Sue later refuses to pay the $100. Is Sue's promise enforceable?

7. Under what circumstances will a promise to accept part payment of a liquidated debt be binding on a creditor? Give examples.

8. Illustrate "accord and satisfaction" as it applies to (a) a liquidated debt and (b) an unliquidated debt.

9. Some courts hold that composition agreements lack consideration, but enforce them anyway. Why?

10. A promise to pay a debt barred by the statute of limitations lacks consideration. Under what circumstances will such a promise be enforced?

CASE PROBLEMS

1. Osborne was chairman of the board of Locke Steel Chain Co. He entered into a retirement agreement with Locke whereby the company would pay him $15,000 a year for life. Osborne was to hold himself available for consultation and advice with the company and not to compete with the company in its domestic or foreign markets. The company paid Osborne for 3 years and then, after trying to reduce the payments, repudiated the contract. Locke claimed the consideration given by Osborne was inadequate to justify payment of $15,000 a year for life. Is this a sufficient reason to justify Locke's repudiation of the contract?

2. Argeros contracted with Pennsylvania to paint all metal surfaces on five bridges. The contract described bridge No. 4 as including an "open type steel beam bridge flooring." The weight of the bridge was shown as "approximately 180 tons." Argeros looked at the bridge prior to submitting his bid but did not calculate its dimensions. While painting bridge No. 4, he determined that it weighed 260 tons and requested extra compensation. The Pennsylvania Deputy Chief Engineer instructed Argeros to complete the work, which he did. Argeros then filed a claim for $6,900 for painting the surfaces represented by the additional tonnage. Argeros asserted that the engineer's instruction was an oral modification of the contract and that he performed extra work pursuant to the oral modification of the original contract. Should his claim be allowed?

3. In 1976 Ramona and Lee dissolved their marriage, and Ramona was granted $200 per month as a single sum for the support of two minor children. By 1981 Lee was behind $7,800 in payments. Ramona offered to settle the back child support for $4,500 and to amend the decree of divorce to provide for $100 per month after February 1, 1981. Lee agreed to pay $1,000 in cash and to give Ramona his note for $3,500 in full satisfaction of back child support. Ramona accepted the proposal and Lee, in reliance on the agreement, borrowed a substantial sum of money to meet business obligations. Ramona then secured a court order to attach $7,800 of the loan proceeds. Lee filed suit for the return of the funds, claiming there was an accord, which satisfied his obligation of back child support. Was there an accord?

4. Fred was driving an automobile owned by his employer when it was hit by a pickup truck insured by Aetna. Fred suffered personal injuries and filed a claim against Aetna. A claims adjuster contacted Fred and offered a settlement. She said that Aetna would pay him $184.25 for medical bills and $200 for his injuries. Aetna sent a check for $384.25, on the front of which was written in block letters "CLAIM SETTLEMENT." Fred endorsed the check on the back and wrote underneath "NOT A RELEASE OF ANY CLAIMS," and deposited the check. Fred sued Aetna for damages for his personal injuries. Aetna defended that there was an accord and satisfaction. Who should win?

5. Mary Veilleux agreed to purchase a residence from Merrill Lynch Relocation Management, Inc., for $126,000. Before the closing of the sale, Veilleux discovered the house had a leaky basement, and she said that she did not want to go through with the purchase. The settlement date was imminent. After negotiations, Veilleux agreed to sign the settlement papers in return for Merrill Lynch's promise to repair the basement. After the sale closed, work was done on the basement but it did not stop the leak. Veilleux then had the work done by a company known to her. Merrill Lynch refused to pay for the work, and Veilleux filed suit. The trial court held that there was no consideration for the promise to repair and gave judgment for Merrill Lynch. Was the trial court correct?

6. Benjamin Ravelo was a police officer with the Honolulu Police Department. He was accepted for a position with the County of Hawaii Police Department. A letter from the county stated that he would be sworn in as a police recruit on January 2, 1979. After receiving the letter, he resigned from the Honolulu Police Department, and his wife, Marlene, resigned from her job. They made plans to move from Honolulu to Hilo and to remove their children from private school. On December 20, 1978, Benjamin was informed by the county that he was not going to be hired after all. Mr. and Mrs. Ravelo tried to but could not get their jobs back. They both sued the county for breach of contract. Under the civil service law Benjamin would have been only a probationary employee whose employment was terminable without cause at any time during his probationary period. Holding that the county's promise of employment was illusory, and without considering whether promissory estoppel applied to the case, the trial court dismissed the Ravelos' complaint. Was the trial court correct in doing so?

CHAPTER 13

Minor's Right to Disaffirm; Other Grounds for Avoidance

Courts usually enforce contracts without regard to whether a party made a good or a bad bargain. Even a contract of adhesion normally will be enforced, as long as the party with the superior bargaining power does not exercise it in an oppressive way.

Yet, where circumstances warrant, the courts permit people to avoid (cancel) their contracts. For example, insane persons may avoid their contracts, as may minors and the victims of duress, undue influence, fraud, mistake, and unconscionability.

A person can exercise the **power of avoidance** in a variety of ways. One might simply return unwanted goods and demand one's money back, or in some other way make clear to the other party that the contract has ended. This is called **rescinding** or **disaffirming** the contract. Or, if the other party brings suit to enforce the contract, the party wishing to avoid (disaffirm) it need only plead his or her right of avoidance as an affirmative defense. Or one may go to court and seek the **equitable remedy of rescission**. To rescind a contract in this formal way, one ordinarily must (1) act promptly and fairly, (2) return or offer to return anything received from the other party, and (3) demand the return of whatever the other party received.

This chapter deals with four major bases for avoiding an agreement: (1) lack of (or limited) contractual capacity, (2) a defect in the assent required for a bargained-for exchange, (3) unconscionability, and (4) consumer protection statutes granting consumers a right of avoidance.

AVOIDANCE ON GROUND OF INCAPACITY

Capacity is the ability or power to do something. A person has *contractual capacity* if he or she (1) can understand the nature and consequences of making a contract, (2) can physically manifest assent to a bargain, and (3) is permitted by law to make the contract in question. A person who lacks or suffers an impairment of these abilities is under a **disability,** and so has a total or partial **incapacity** (lack of capacity). Most people have **full** contractual capacity; that is, they are mentally and physically able to contract for anything the law permits. A few (e.g., some insane persons) have no capacity to contract. Between these extremes are persons having **limited** contractual power. Minors, for example, are presumed to have a disability common to youth—immaturity and inexperience that make them vulnerable to exploitation.

So, although minors generally are permitted to make contracts, the law protects minors from their disability by allowing them to avoid most of their contracts. In a few states minors cannot make certain kinds of contracts—for example, in California, a contract involving land.

When a person sues to enforce a contract, the court presumes that both parties possessed full contractual capacity when the contract was made. To overcome this presumption, the disaffirming party must demonstrate that at the time of contracting, his or her contractual capacity was impaired. The following discussion deals first with the contractual capacity of minors, and then with that of mentally incompetent persons and persons temporarily under the influence of alcohol or other drugs.

Contractual Capacity of Minors

For centuries, the law has permitted minors (called "infants" at common law) to avoid or "disaffirm" most of their contracts. The reasons include:

- Minors need protection from their immaturity, inexperience, and tendency to buy impulsively.
- Minors are especially likely to be the victims of unscrupulous adults.
- Young minors may not understand the nature and consequences of their contracts.

The policy of protecting minors is very strong. To further that policy, the law gives minors a right to enforce contracts against adults *or* to disaffirm such contracts without having to show misconduct by the adult. However, because of the one-sidedness of the right to disaffirm, some people may refuse to contract with minors, who therefore may be unable to acquire essential goods and services. To encourage businesses to supply such "necessaries," the law requires minors to pay for them.

Some people think that minors may be receiving too much protection at the expense of adults who treat minors fairly. Because of TV and advances in education, minors may be more sophisticated than they once were and thus more likely to take advantage of unsuspecting adults. In part to protect the legitimate interests of adults, the law of most states imposes limits on the right of minors to disaffirm contracts. The more common ones are discussed later in this chapter.

Period of Minority. The age at which minority ends for the purpose of contracting does not necessarily correspond with the age or ages that a state sets for other purposes. State law may set one age at which a person has the capacity to make a will, another age for acquiring a driver's license, and still another for legally purchasing liquor. In the vast majority of states, the age of majority for most *contract* purposes has been lowered from 21 (the traditional common law age of majority) to 18. In most states married minors retain their right of disaffirmance.

Some minors want to transact business, but find that adults are reluctant to deal with them because of their power of disaffirmance. To aid such minors, a number of states permit their **judicial emancipation.** This is a procedure in which a minor seeks to give up the right of disaffirmance. A court investigates the facts. If the judge finds that removal of disabilities serves the best interests of the minor and that the minor can handle his or her own business affairs, the judge will sign an order of emancipation. The order lets the minor contract like an adult—that is, without a right to disaffirm on the ground of minority. Thus, adults are encouraged to deal with minors.

In the so-called **parental emancipation,** parents surrender their right to the care, custody, and earnings of their minor child and renounce their parental duties. Parental emancipation occurs, for example, where the minor is working and the parents consent to the minor's leaving home and establishing a separate residence. Parental emancipation has *no effect* on the contractual capacity of the minor; the minor still may disaffirm his or her contracts.

Disaffirmance of Minors' Voidable Contracts. The right of a minor to disaffirm a contract is absolute. This means that a minor needs no reason to disaffirm and may do so regardless of his or her personal experience, education, or sophistication. Thus, a minor nearly 18 and well-versed in the law of minors' rights has the same right to disaffirm as does a child of 10.

Most courts hold that the power of disaffirmance is personal to the minor. This means that during the minor's lifetime, only the minor may exercise the power, and upon the minor's death only the minor's heirs or a personal representative may exercise it. An adult party to a contract with a minor has no similar power of disaffirmance; the adult is bound to the contract unless the minor disaffirms it. Where both parties to a contract are minors, each may disaffirm.

> **BOX 13.1**
>
> ### Point to Consider
>
> Although the vast majority of courts hold that a minor's right of disaffirmance is personal to the minor, a *few* decisions have permitted the minor's parent or guardian to disaffirm the minor's contract, even over the minor's objections. What are the arguments for and against allowing parents and guardians to disaffirm minors' contracts? ■

A minor may disaffirm (avoid) a contract in any way that makes clear his or her unwillingness to be bound by it. The disaffirmance may be oral or written, and may be accomplished with or without a lawsuit. If the other party sues to enforce the contract, the minor may disaffirm by pleading minority as a defense. Or the minor may disaffirm by filing a suit to set aside the transaction. More commonly, a minor will disaffirm by, for example, simply returning unwanted goods and demanding the return of the price paid.

Whatever the method of disaffirmance, the minor generally must (1) disaffirm during minority or within a reasonable time after attaining majority, (2) demand the return of any consideration (e.g., money or goods) transferred to the other party, and (3) return or offer to return any consideration received if it is still in the minor's possession. What constitutes a reasonable time after attaining majority varies according to the circumstances. Mel, a minor, buys an expensive racing bicycle, uses it every day, and soon after his eighteenth birthday decides to disaffirm the contract. Mel will have relatively little time to disaffirm. His frequent use of the bicycle reduces its value. Allowing Mel to continue using it a long time after reaching majority and then to disaffirm the contract would be unjust to the seller. In contrast, if Mel had never used the bicycle, or if he had used it infrequently, the court might allow him a longer time after reaching majority to disaffirm. Upon disaffirmance, a minor is entitled to the return of any property still in the hands of the other contracting party (or to its value if it cannot be returned).

> **BOX 13.2**
>
> ### UCC Limit on Minors' Rights
>
> Under UCC Section 2-403(1), a minor may *not* recover *goods* from an innocent ("good faith") *third-person* purchaser. Mary, a minor, sells her car to Alice, an adult. If Mary disaffirms the contract while Alice still has the car, Mary is entitled to have the car back from Alice. But suppose Alice sells and delivers the car to Tom before Mary disaffirms the contract with Alice. If Tom had no notice of Mary's minority, he is entitled to keep the car, and Mary's only recourse is against Alice for its value. Some states have enacted statutes extending this Code principle to contracts other than those for the sale of goods. ■

Upon disaffirmance, the minor must return whatever was received if he or she still has it. However, the courts disagree about what a minor should be required to pay if the property is lost, destroyed, or damaged. Under the *majority* rule, the minor need return only what he or she still possesses no matter what the extent of the loss. One rationale is that the immaturity leading minors into improvident contracts may cause them to be careless in handling the property later, and minors should be fully protected from that immaturity. Under the *minority* rule, a minor can disaffirm a contract, but must pay for benefits received or at least account for depreciation. Under either rule, if the minor has sold or exchanged property purchased from the adult and still has the proceeds (e.g., money), the minor must transfer the proceeds to the adult. Case 13.1 discusses the requirements for disaffirmance and applies the majority rule.

CASE 13.1   Star Chevrolet Co. v. Green • 473 So. 2d 157 (Miss. 1985)

FACTS   Kevin Green was 16 years old on August 14, 1981, when he purchased a 1979 Camaro for $4,642.50 from Star Chevrolet. In November 1981, after the car blew a head gasket and became inoperable, Kevin informed Star Chevrolet that he was disaffirming the contract. He demanded the return of the purchase price and offered to return the Camaro, but Star Chevrolet would not accept it unless it was restored to its original condition.

In January 1982, Kevin brought suit for the purchase price. The car sat for 4 or 5 months until Kevin finally replaced the head gasket himself and drove the car. In June 1982, the Camaro was heavily damaged in an accident, after which the car had a salvage value of $1,500. Kevin was credited with the salvage value in an insurance settlement, the proceeds of which he used to buy another car. Later Kevin received a judgment for the purchase price of the car, and Star Chevrolet appealed.

OPINION   SULLIVAN, J. . . . Upon disaffirmance of a minor's contract, he is required to return the consideration received by him if he still has such consideration in his possession, or if it is within his powers to do so. . . . This requirement can be complied with not only by an actual return of the consideration but also by a tender or offer to return it. . . .

From the time Kevin disaffirmed the contract in November, 1981, until suit was filed, Star Chevrolet refused to fully refund the purchase price unless the Camaro's blown head gasket was repaired. This position was erroneous. . . . Kevin's duty to tender the vehicle was not contingent upon its restoration to [its] condition at the time of sale. . . . We [also reject the contention] that Kevin's tender was inadequate because he failed to engage a wrecker to transport the vehicle . . . , when it appears that to do so would have been a vain or useless thing, since [Star Chevrolet] would not have [made] the full refund to which [Kevin] was entitled under law. Accordingly, we hold that the complaint for rescission, including [a copy of] the . . . letter of disaffirmance, sufficiently alleged an offer of tender. . . .

. . . [T]he right of a minor to disaffirm his contract is based upon sound public policy to protect the minor from his own improvidence and the overreaching of adults. . . . It is the policy of the law to discourage adults from contracting with minors, and the adult cannot complain if, as a consequence of his violation of this rule of conduct, he is injured by the minor's exercise of the right of disaffirmance, since this injury might have been avoided if the adult had declined to enter into the contract. . . . The general rule is that upon disaffirmance of a minor's contract, he is required to return the consideration only if it is still in his possession. The minor who disaffirms a contract is not obliged to return the

**CASE 13.1
Continued**

consideration received by him or its equivalent where during his minority he has wasted, squandered, destroyed, used, or otherwise disposed of the consideration. . . .

Finally, depreciation in the value of the vehicle due to the minor's misuse or neglect, short of [an] intentional or grossly negligent act amounting to an independent tort, is not allowable by way of recoupment. In other words, the minor is not liable for damages [resulting from] the very improvidence and indiscretion of infancy against which the law seeks to protect him. . . .

Turning to the facts of this case, the minor clearly had the consideration, i.e., the vehicle, in his possession when he first notified appellant of the disaffirmance of the contract. Had appellant [Star Chevrolet] offered the minor, as the law required, a full refund of his purchase price, the minor clearly would have been required to return the vehicle. . . . Instead, the appellant did not, and while suit was pending the minor repaired the vehicle and began to use it. There is no hint in the record that the accident which destroyed the vehicle was the result of any deliberate design on the minor's part to fraudulently deprive appellant of that which would have placed him in status quo. For aught that appears in the record, the accident was caused by [ordinary] carelessness and improvidence [of the minor]. Disaffirmance at this point would have required the appellant to refund the full purchase price and the appellee, in turn, to return the damaged Camaro, since the law does not condition a minor's right to disaffirm a contract upon placing the other party in status quo, but . . . requires [only] the return of whatever consideration remains in the minor's hands. . . .

. . . We are urged to offset the minor's recovery by the $1,500 salvage value of the [Camaro] on the ground that the minor had the duty to tender this consideration to appellant in order to receive a refund of the full purchase price.

We are persuaded that the appellant's contention is sound. . . . Accordingly, the damages assessed against Star Chevrolet Company are reduced from $4,642.50 to $3,142.50.

JUDGMENT   Affirmed as modified.

Effect of Misrepresentation of Age. Most courts hold that a minor who has intentionally misrepresented his or her age to induce a contract *can* avoid the contract. However, the courts differ on whether the minor is liable in tort for that misrepresentation. Minors are liable for their torts generally, and most courts hold that a minor is liable for the tort of deceit (fraud). This majority view reflects a belief that the law should not protect minors from their intentional wrongdoing. A minority of courts hold that minors should *not* be held liable in deceit, because such liability enables adults to enforce indirectly contracts that the law permits minors to avoid. The minority view is based on the idea that lying about one's age is a folly of youth from which minors should be protected.

Ratification of Minor's Voidable Contracts. **Ratification** of a minor's contract is a showing, upon reaching adulthood, of an intention to honor a contract entered into during minority. A minor cannot ratify a contract until he or she becomes of age. Any purported ratification during minority is ineffective.

A ratification may be expressed in words or implied from conduct. Unless a statute provides otherwise, an *express ratification* may be made orally. Any wording suffices as long as it indicates an intention to be bound. An adult's making a definite promise to perform a contract entered into while a minor is one way to express such an intention.

In an *implied ratification*, the intention to be bound is inferred from the person's conduct. A month before reaching her majority, Brenda buys some diving gear on credit. A week after reaching her majority, she sells the gear. Her exercising ownership rights by selling the gear is inconsistent with an intent to disaffirm the contract; rather, Brenda reveals an intent to ratify it. Continuing as an adult to use or pay for property purchased during minority is another way to ratify a contract. A simple failure to disaffirm within a reasonable time after attaining majority also results in a ratification.

Liability of Minors for Necessaries. A minor's right to avoid contracts entirely is limited to those for luxuries. The situation is different for necessities (called "necessaries" at common law).

Ordinarily, a minor's parents or guardian will provide the minor with food, clothing, and other necessities of life. But if no one else provides them, the minor can contract for them and later disaffirm the contract in accordance with the general rule regarding minors' contracts. However, the minor will be liable *in quasi contract* to the provider of the necessaries, for their *reasonable value*. The law places this liability on minors mainly for their protection. If minors could avoid all obligation to pay, they might have difficulty in securing necessaries.

The quasi-contractual liability of minors for necessaries is their reasonable value only, and not the amount the disaffirmed contract would have imposed. Mary, a minor, signs a contract to lease an apartment for 1 year at $500 per month. Her contractual liability is $6,000. After 3 months, Mary disaffirms the contract and vacates the apartment without having paid any rent. By disaffirming, Mary avoids the duty to pay for the apartment for 12 months, and she is no longer bound to the $500 monthly rate specified in the lease contract. She is liable instead for the reasonable value of the 3 months' housing she actually received. That amount might be more or less than the rental amount stated in the lease. If a court decides that $300 per month is reasonable, Mary's former landlord is entitled to $900.

What things are necessaries? The answer depends on the minor's personal and family circumstances, including the minor's *station in life*. Clothing of high fashion may be necessary for a wealthy minor destined for a public life, but not for a minor of poorer or more private circumstances. Another factor is whether the minor was *emancipated* at the time he or she made the contract. More household furnishings would be considered necessaries for an emancipated minor living alone than for an unemancipated minor living at home where the things are provided. For a married emancipated minor, the range of necessaries would be even broader.

Courts have held that food, clothing, shelter, medical services, tools of a trade, and some degree of education are necessaries. Other goods and services have been so characterized by some courts. Examples are a reasonable fee for legal services for the enforcement of a tort claim and a reasonable fee paid to an employment agency for assistance in finding a job for a married minor.

Contracts That Minors Cannot Disaffirm. For a variety of reasons, statutes and court decisions prohibit minors from avoiding certain contracts for luxuries—that is, nonnecessaries.

Some state statutes prohibit a minor from disaffirming a contract that has been approved by a court. Examples are a contract employing a minor as an entertainer, and a contract settling a minor's tort claim for injuries suffered in an automobile accident. Other state and federal statutes denying minors the right to disaffirm apply directly to specific kinds of contracts—for example, those for student loans, bank accounts, insurance, and military enlistments. And where a guardian sells a minor's property under court order as prescribed by statute, the minor cannot disaffirm the sale.

The courts, too, have limited the minor's right of disaffirmance. For example, minors generally cannot disaffirm their bail bond contracts, because permitting avoidance "would be contrary to sound public policy." Courts also deny the right to disaffirm where, by contracting, the minor promised to do only what the law would require of the minor anyway. For example, a minor father who contracted to support his illegitimate child was not permitted to disaffirm, because in making the contract he promised to do only what the law already required.

> **BOX 13.3**
> **Avoidance of Minor's Contracts—General Rules**
>
> | | |
> |---|---|
> | Who can avoid? | Usually, only the minor |
> | How? | By any act indicating an intent not to be bound by the contract |
> | When? | During minority and for a reasonable time after reaching age of majority |
> | What must minor return to adult? | Any remaining consideration |
> | What must adult return to minor? | Any money or property paid or its value |

Contractual Capacity of Other Persons

Mentally Incompetent Persons. Ordinarily, a mentally incompetent person's contract is voidable, just as a minor's contract is voidable, and for the same reason—to protect persons unable to protect themselves against imposition. In protecting the mentally incompetent, however, the law also tries to protect the justifiable expectations of the other contracting party.

Mental incompetence takes many forms. Among them are mental illness or insanity, serious deficiencies in intelligence, and mental disability from old age, accidents, or disease. Mental incompetence may be mild or severe.

Test of mental incompetence. What degree of mental impairment is required for a person's contract to be voidable? The general test is: Did the person have, at the time of contracting, sufficient mental capacity to understand the nature and consequences of the transaction—was he or she capable of making a rational decision? If not, the contract is voidable. However, a victim of mental illness may have **lucid intervals,** i.e., may from time to time regain the ability to understand his or her business affairs. A contract made during such an interval is binding on both parties.

Effect of mental incompetence. The courts consider a number of factors when deciding what effect mental incompetence should have on the impaired person's agreements. Two key ones are: (1) Was the transaction executory or executed? (2) Before the transaction occurred, had a court declared the impaired person mentally incompetent and appointed a guardian?

A person might be mentally incompetent without appearing so and without having been declared so by a court. Such a person's *executory* contract is avoidable, either by the impaired person upon regaining mental capacity or by that person's later appointed legal representative—even if the other party did not know of the mental incapacity. If the contract was *executed,* however, and the other party had no reason to know of the mental incompetence, the contract is *binding* on the mentally incompetent person if under the circumstances avoidance would be unjust to the other party. Avoidance would be unjust, for example, where the other party was unaware of the impairment, the impaired person was treated fairly, and the other party would suffer unrecoverable losses as a result of the avoidance.

Sometimes a court declares a person to be mentally incompetent and appoints a guardian (or conservator) to handle his or her affairs. After the adjudication of incompetence, only the guardian can make contracts for the incompetent, and any agreements made by the incompetent person after the adjudication are *void,* not voidable. This is significant where the incompetent party's property finds its way into the hands of a third person. A court declares Mel mentally incompetent and appoints a guardian for him. Later Mel sells his car to Brad for a tenth of its value. Then Brad sells the car to Cora for its full value and leaves the country.

Cora knew nothing of the transaction between Mel and Brad. However, since Mel's agreement was void, Brad did not receive ownership of the car, and neither did Cora. Mel is entitled to the car; Cora's only recourse is against Brad.

Like minors, mentally incompetent persons are liable in quasi contract for the reasonable value of necessaries.

Persons under the Influence of Alcohol or Other Drugs. In most respects, the law treats the contracts of persons impaired by alcohol or other drugs the same way it treats the contracts of mentally incompetent persons. For example, where a guardian or conservator has been appointed to handle the affairs of a drug abuser or chronic alcoholic, any transaction the impaired person later enters is *void*.

Where there is no guardian, an intoxicated person's contract is *voidable* if at the time of contracting he or she is too impaired to understand the nature and consequences of the transaction. However, intoxication is generally viewed as self-induced, and the courts tend to be skeptical about claims of resulting incapacity. Yet, where a person has some understanding despite intoxication (and thus *has* contractual capacity), the tendency is to grant relief if the other party induced the intoxication or took unfair advantage of the intoxicated party's condition.

AVOIDANCE ON GROUND OF DEFECTIVE ASSENT

Bargained-for exchange requires real agreement—genuine assent—between contracting parties. But a person might have been lied to about the quality of merchandise, or wrongfully forced into a ruinous contract, or wrongfully persuaded to act contrary to his or her best interests. Or the parties may have been mistaken about critical facts. In all these instances, assent is defective. To protect individuals (and, indirectly, to protect the integrity of the market) the law permits contracting parties to avoid their contracts on a variety of grounds involving defective assent. They include duress, undue influence, fraud, misrepresentation, and mistake.

Duress

Duress is a wrongful threat, by words or conduct, that overcomes the free will of the person threatened. Many courts today view duress as a wrongful threat that induces assent on the part of a victim who has *no reasonable alternative* but to do what the threatening party demands, such as signing a contract very unfavorable to the victim. Typically, the threatening party gains money or property to which he or she is not entitled. The resulting contract is voidable by the victim.

The traditional elements of duress are (1) a wrongful threat and (2) fear that overcomes the victim's free will.

Wrongful Threat. Much business conduct involves express or implied threats that are not wrongful. Threatening to deal with someone else if a supplier will not give one a better price is the essence of healthy competition, and in the absence of extraordinary circumstances certainly is not wrongful. Nor is it wrongful to threaten a civil lawsuit in a good faith effort to settle a dispute out of court. But many kinds of threats are wrongful and can lead to duress. They include threats to the person, threats to property, and threats to one's business or means of earning a living.

The following threats to the *person* may lead to duress:

1. A threat to injure the person being threatened; his or her spouse, child, or other relative; or any other person such as an employee, if the threat actually induces the threatened person's assent.
2. A threat of criminal prosecution to force someone to make a contract.

Ann discovers that Ben, her employee, stole goods from her, and threatens him with criminal proceedings unless he agrees to pay her $3,000, the value of the goods. Fearing he will be sent to prison, Ben agrees. He is under duress and may rescind the contract. The harsh sanctions of the criminal law are intended to promote the safety of the public, and Ann is misusing them to force settlement of a private dispute. By agreeing to suppress prosecution if Ben will pay, and thus interfering with the state's ability to challenge criminal conduct, Ann acts contrary to the public good. Indeed, by concealing Ben's felony, Ann herself commits a crime called **misprision of felony**. Instead of using the criminal law for what it was not intended, Ann is expected to pursue her *civil* claim against Ben for the value of the stolen goods (or to *threaten* to pursue it to force Ben to settle out of court).

> **BOX 13.4**
> ### Common Sense to the Rescue
> But is it realistic to expect Ann in the heat of anger to carefully phrase her request for repayment in terms of a civil action? Probably not. So, a number of states have statutes or case law permitting employers and other victims of theft to demand payment for stolen goods without themselves being subject to a charge of extortion. Similar laws permit recipients of bad checks to threaten "bad check" prosecutions to force civil collection.

Threats to *property* include threats to damage, destroy, or wrongfully seize or withhold real or personal property. Sam, a supplier calling on Ron at his retail store, threatens to smash Ron's uninsured plate glass window with a brick unless Ron signs a contract for goods. To save the glass, Ron may have no reasonable alternative to signing. Preventing Sam's action may not be possible or may pose an unacceptable risk to Ron; and the police may be too far away to help. Ron's contract is voidable for duress even if he needed the goods and the price was fair. Another example: Lenders take mortgages on real estate to secure repayment of a loan for which the real estate is "collateral." Where the debtor fails to pay what is owed, the lender's threat to foreclose the mortgage is coercive, but rightful. The threat would be wrongful, however, if the lender made it to force a payment that the lender knows is excessive.

Threats to *a person's business* or means of earning a livelihood may result in a type of duress commonly called **economic duress** or **business compulsion.** To avoid a contract on the basis of economic duress, one ordinarily must prove irreparable injury to his or her business or livelihood if the defendant were to carry out the wrongful threat. Largecorp falsely alleges patent infringement and threatens to "tie you up in court for the rest of your life" unless Mario transfers to Largecorp a novel invention that Mario developed. A court would find economic duress because Largecorp is attempting to gain something to which it is not entitled, and Mario faces financial ruin if forced to defend against the false charge.

> **BOX 13.5**
> ### Trends in the Law
> In a growing number of cases, courts hold that a threatened act need not necessarily be *unlawful* to be *wrongful* in the sense required for a showing of duress. Horace, an at-will employee, owns shares in the employer corporation. Ordinarily, an employer may fire an at-will employee without cause. However, if the employer threatens to fire Horace unless he sells the shares back to the corporation, and the threat overcomes Horace's will, the sale is voidable for duress. The threat constitutes an abuse of the employer's rights. For a discussion of the trend, see Calamari & Perillo, *The Law of Contracts* (1987), p. 340.

Overcoming of Free Will. To constitute duress, a threat must produce fear sufficient to overcome a party's free will. In most states, this means the actual will of the threatened person. Courts consider a party's age, mental capacity, and other relevant circumstances. Since the law protects the unusually timid, the threatened individual need not be as brave as the "ordinary reasonable person." Box 13.6 raises a question of duress.

Undue Influence

Undue influence occurs when one party overcomes the free will of the other party by *unfair*

> **BOX 13.6**
>
> **You Be the Judge**
>
> Three painters filed mechanics' liens against an apartment house owned by Harry Friedman. Claiming they had not been paid for work performed at the apartments, the painters hired attorney Paul Mancino to file suit to foreclose their liens. At the time, Friedman was trying to obtain a bank loan, which required that the liens against the apartment house be removed. To settle the dispute with the painters, Friedman paid them through Mancino, and they in return signed releases of their claims against the property. Later, Friedman learned that the mechanics' liens had not been released as agreed and contacted Mancino. Mancino said that the painters had not paid $350 in legal fees they owed him, and that unless Friedman paid the $350 he (Mancino) would not file the releases. Friedman signed a promissory note payable to Mancino for $350 plus interest. Mancino filed the releases, but Friedman, alleging that he had signed the note under duress, refused to pay it when it came due. Mancino filed suit to enforce the note. Assume that Mancino's refusal to file the liens was not illegal, but that it was a breach of professional ethics applicable to lawyers. Was Mancino's conduct wrongful in the sense required for a holding of duress? ■

persuasion. Sometimes the result of the unfair persuasion is a contract unusually favorable to the unfair persuader. But often the persuader's objective is a gift from the other party, or a provision in that person's will that favors the persuader over the other party's family members.

Unfair persuasion is most likely to occur in either of the following situations:

1. A person is under the domination of another person.
2. There is such a relationship of trust and confidence (called a "fiduciary relationship") between two persons that one of them is justified in assuming that his or her best interests will be protected by the other.

In the first category, a person may be under the *domination of another person* because of mental weakness, ignorance, lack of experience, old age, poor health, physical handicap, emotional strain, or financial distress.

The second category embraces relationships of trust and confidence, called **fiduciary relationships,** such as parent and child, guardian and ward, husband and wife, physician and patient, attorney and client, and pastor and parishioner. If a confidential relationship existed when a transaction benefiting the trusted person was entered into, the burden of proof is on that person to prove the transaction was not procured by undue influence. Thus, for example, if an attorney prepares a will for a client in which the attorney is to receive a large sum of money in preference to the client's legal heirs, a court would require the attorney to prove that she or he did not exercise undue influence over the client.

In the following case the court discussed the defense of undue influence.

CASE 13.2	**Cripe v. Atlantic First National Bank of Daytona Beach** • 422 So. 2d 820 (Fla. 1982)
FACTS	Carrie Hare owned several apartment buildings in Daytona Beach. Joe and Sereata Cripe were her tenants for 7½ months each year. In 1966 Mrs. Hare, then 80 years old, asked Joe to help her manage her rental business. The rental income was placed in joint accounts so that Joe could sign checks both for business expenses and for her personal expenses. In return for their services, the Cripes

**CASE 13.2
Continued**

were given free rent and utilities year-round and, upon Mrs. Hare's death, Joe would receive the balances in the joint bank accounts. In 1969 the state condemned (took) part of Mrs. Hare's property to widen a highway, and she received $31,000. At Joe's suggestion, Mrs. Hare deposited the money in the joint names of herself and Joe.

Mrs. Hare died in 1976. She left three joint accounts containing $12,700, $10,900, and $32,000, respectively. Joe obtained the funds as survivor. As representative of her estate, Atlantic First National Bank of Daytona Beach sued to recover the funds, alleging that Joe had obtained them by undue influence. The trial court held for the defendants Cripe. Bank appealed. The district court reversed the trial court's decision. The Cripes then appealed to the Florida Supreme Court.

OPINION

BOYD, J. . . . [T]here is a presumption of undue influence when the stronger party gains a financial benefit from the weaker, and [the] burden is on the stronger party to rebut the presumption.

. . . [T]he agreement between Mrs. Hare and the Cripes, pertaining to the management of her properties and the supervision of her personal care in exchange for the remaining balances in the accounts maintained for meeting her business and personal expenses, must be considered separately from the transaction by which Mr. Cripe obtained permission to deposit the condemnation proceeds into a joint account. On appeal, the district court should have [considered] the two transactions separately.

The evidence showed that the Cripes began to manage Mrs. Hare's apartment business and to supervise her personal care in 1966. There was no evidence . . . that at the time this arrangement began . . . there was a confidential relationship between them. . . . Therefore, with regard to the agreement for management services and personal care in exchange for an apartment and the remaining balances on the death of Mrs. Hare, the district court erred in holding that a presumption of undue influence was raised. . . . [T]here was sufficient evidence for the trial court to conclude that the plaintiff bank was entitled to no relief with regard to the account balances that derived from the arrangement. . . .

With regard to the $32,000 certificate of deposit derived from the condemnation award, however, the considerations are different. By the time Mrs. Hare obtained the condemnation settlement award in 1969, a close and dependent relationship had developed between herself and Joe Cripe. [Evidence showed] that after he had been managing her affairs for some time, she became dependent upon him for financial services and advice and that she placed her trust in him. A confidential relationship had developed. From that point forward, Joe Cripe was prohibited from using his position of trust and confidence for acquisition of personal gain or to acquire property without full, fair and adequate consideration. The condemnation proceeds were deposited in a joint account because Mr. Cripe asked Mrs. Hare to do so. Since there was a confidential relationship and active procurement of a financial benefit, a presumption of undue influence arose. . . .

In an attempt to [rebut this presumption], Mr. Cripe explained that Mrs. Hare agreed to deposit the money in a joint account because he had handled the

CASE 13.2 Continued	condemnation transaction and knew more about it than she did. There was no evidence, however, that Mr. Cripe provided anything more than routine administrative services in connection with the compensation award, services which he was already obligated to perform as Mrs. Hare's property manager. In return for some relatively insignificant paperwork, the Cripes received a sum of money out of all proportion to the services provided. Petitioners argue that there was insufficient proof of active procurement with regard to the deposit of the condemnation proceeds into a joint account. There was evidence, however, that Mrs. Hare's mental condition had deteriorated and she had become totally dependent on the Cripes. Where there is such inequality of mental strength, active procurement can be shown by evidence, as there was here, of a request or suggestion by the dominant party. Therefore with regard to the condemnation funds, the district court was correct in finding undue influence from the evidence. . . .
JUDGMENT	The decision of the district court of appeal [pertaining] to the two joint accounts . . . containing $12,700 and $10,900 respectively was in error and should be quashed. That portion of the district court's decision [pertaining] to the $32,000 certificate of deposit . . . was correct and should be approved. Accordingly, the decision of the district court is quashed in part and approved in part.

Misrepresentation

A **misrepresentation** is an untrue statement of fact. It may be innocent or fraudulent. A misrepresentation is **innocent** if the person who made it does not know the statement is false. If the person knows the statement is false and intends to deceive or mislead someone with it, the statement is **fraudulent.** Whether innocent or fraudulent, a misrepresentation that induces a person into a contract may give that party a right to rescind (avoid) it, or to use the misrepresentation as an affirmative defense if the misrepresenter tries to enforce the contract.

Intentional Misrepresentation (Fraud). Sometimes, however, where the misrepresentation is fraudulent, the defrauded person prefers to sue in *tort* for fraud damages. Alice, an art dealer, owns a forged painting. Knowing it is worth only $100, Alice tells Betty, a less experienced art dealer, that it is authentic. Betty knows that the painting, if authentic, is worth $10,000 in the retail art market. Consequently, she pays Alice's asking price of $5,000. Under the UCC loss-of-bargain rule for fraud damages (applicable to sales of goods), Betty is entitled to $9,900 to compensate her for the loss of her expected bargain.[1] If Alice's fraud was especially malicious or oppressive, Betty may also be entitled to punitive damages.

As noted in Chapter 6, to hold a defendant liable for the *tort* of fraud, the plaintiff must prove the following:

- Defendant's misrepresentation of a *material* fact
- Defendant's fraudulent conduct (i.e., knowledge that the representation was false and intent to induce the plaintiff to act)
- Plaintiff's justifiable reliance on the misrepresentation
- Resulting injury (loss) to the plaintiff

[1] UCC Section 2-721. Under this **loss-of-bargain rule** (also in effect in a majority of states for *nonsales* transactions), Betty is entitled to the difference between the value of the forged painting ($100) and the value the painting would have had if it had been authentic as represented ($10,000). If Alice had defrauded Betty in a *nonsales* transaction— e.g., a sale of real estate—Betty might have been subject to the minority **out-of-pocket rule** for fraud damages. Under that rule, she could recover from Alice only the difference between the value of the thing received ($100) and the amount paid ($5,000).

Much less is required to *rescind a contract* on the basis of fraud or to establish fraud as a *defense* in a breach-of-contract action. To rescind or defend, the victim ordinarily need not show materiality or harm—only reliance on a fraudulent misrepresentation of fact.[2] The less demanding proof requirements for rescission or defense make sense because the victim seeks only to be returned to the position he or she was in before the contract was made, and is not seeking compensation for a lost bargain or punitive damages. Suppose Betty bought the forged painting as discussed above but there is no established retail market value for it. She might be better off rescinding the contract (returning the painting and receiving her money back) than trying to prove a market value for authentic paintings where such values are in doubt. Moreover, since Betty can rescind without proving that Alice's fraud is material, Alice cannot profit from her wrongdoing.

Innocent Misrepresentation.

In nearly all states, innocent misrepresentation is not a tort. Therefore, a party who contracts in reliance on an innocent misrepresentation ordinarily is limited to rescinding the contract or to raising misrepresentation as a defense to enforcement. However, to be of legal consequence, an innocent misrepresentation must be of a *material* fact, whereas materiality usually is not an essential aspect of a rescission action based on fraud.

Mistake

Mistake is a belief that is not in accord with the facts.[3] Mistake as used in contract law means an erroneous belief that is not induced by the fraud or misrepresentation of the other contracting party. Some frequently recurring kinds of mistakes are:

- Mistake in connection with words used
- Mutual mistake of fact
- Unilateral mistake of fact
- Mistake of law

Mistake in Connection with Words Used.

Modern law usually takes an objective approach toward expressions of assent. If John, who owns a Ford and a Dodge, means to offer his Ford for sale but mistakenly says, "I'll sell you my Dodge for $495," and Bill replies in good faith, "I accept your offer," there is a contract for the sale of the Dodge. "In good faith" means that Bill must not know or have reason to think that John misspoke. If John's Dodge was reasonably worth $1,500, Bill's acceptance may be ineffective. An offeree is not allowed to "snap up" an offer that is too good to be true.

Sometimes an offer contains a **latent** (not yet obvious) **ambiguity.** In the above illustration there was only one possible meaning of "my Dodge." Suppose, however, that John owned two Dodges—a 1930 model and a 1970 model. If John thought that he was selling the 1930 Dodge and Bill thought he was buying the 1970 Dodge, there is no contract. Only if both parties actually intended the same subject matter could there be a contract.

In the preceding illustration, a court will not decide which Dodge the parties intended. Because of their error, there simply was no agreement to enforce. However, the courts will correct transcription errors where the parties clearly have agreed on the subject matter. Paula orally agrees to sell "Lot 6 of the Blackacre Tract" to Don. When Paula's secretary prepares the written contract, he mistakenly describes the land as "Lot 9 of the Blackacre Tract." In this situation either party may seek the remedy of reformation. **Reformation** means that a court will order that the written document be corrected to conform to the terms of the oral agreement.

Mutual Mistake of Fact.

While making a contract, both parties may mistakenly assume the existence of a vital fact. Upon discovering their false assumption, either may rescind the contract or use the mistake as a defense to the other's lawsuit.

---

[2]*Restatement, Contracts*, Section 476; *Restatement (Second) Contracts*, Section 164. Apparently following purely tort cases, a number of courts have denied contract rescission unless the fraud was material. However, the presence of fraud in the contracting process raises some policy considerations that put into question the materiality requirement. Calamari & Perillo, op. cit., p. 359.

[3]*Restatement (Second) Contracts*, Section 151.

To free the parties from liability, the mutual mistake must concern a fact that is basic to their bargain (e.g., identity, quality, or quantity of the subject matter), and cannot be merely a matter of opinion. Nadja buys a violin. Both she and the seller believe it is a genuine Stradivarius. Later she learns it is an imitation worth a fraction of the sale price. Nadja may rescind the contract on the ground of mutual mistake of fact.

No rescission would be allowed, however, if both parties had expressed their ignorance about violins and simply guessed this one to be genuine. Where there is **conscious uncertainty** about a key fact, both parties assume the risk of being wrong, and the price paid probably reflects that risk. Similarly, a *mistake of opinion, value, or judgment* is not a basis for avoiding a contract. Ed sells his horse because he believes it is too slow to race competitively. Ed may not rescind if the horse later does race successfully and its value rises.

Case 13.3 involves a mutual mistake of fact.

CASE 13.3 **LaFleur v. C.C. Pierce Co.** • 496 N.E.2d 827 (Mass. 1986)

FACTS Plaintiff Michael LaFleur was injured at work in January 1975 when a forklift blade fell on his right foot. He returned to work within 2 weeks but continued to experience pain. His injury was diagnosed as a sprain of his great right toe. He was offered a desk job, but was discharged in May 1976 for failure to report for work.

In August 1976, LaFleur filed a claim with the Industrial Accident Board and agreed to a lump-sum settlement of $4,000. The agreement stated that the lump sum was in lieu of "all weekly payments now or in the future due me under the Workmen's Compensation Act, for all injuries" received from the accident, and "this is a complete and final settlement of my claim and . . . I will not be able to reopen my claim or seek further benefits because of this injury." LaFleur continued to experience pain. In January 1977 he was diagnosed as having arterial occlusive (Buerger's) disease. Because of the disease, he eventually had both of his legs amputated above the knees.

LaFleur filed a complaint against his former employer and its insurer, requesting that the lump-sum settlement be rescinded on the ground of mutual mistake, and that the case be recommitted to the Industrial Accident Board. From a judgment for defendants, LaFleur appealed.

OPINION HENNESSEY, C.J. The issue presented by this case is whether a settlement agreement may be set aside on the ground of mutual mistake where the parties were unaware at the time of entering the agreement that the injured person had suffered a serious and unknown injury. . . .

. . . Dr. Edward D. Frank, an assistant professor of surgery at Harvard Medical School . . . concluded that LaFleur's arterial occlusive disease existed at the time of the accident, but had not been diagnosed "because the disease is rare and difficult to detect." Dr. Frank further attested that the forklift accident had injured LaFleur's arterial system and had aggravated the preexisting arterial disease. The injury to the arterial system was "completely separate, and distinct in nature" from the sprained toe which was diagnosed after the accident. Finally, Dr. Frank attested that the forklift accident was causally related to the amputation of

CASE 13.3 Continued

LaFleur's legs. . . . [N]one of the parties knew at the time the settlement was executed that LaFleur was afflicted with Buerger's disease, or that the forklift accident had aggravated this condition. . . .

The legal principles underlying the doctrine of mutual mistake are well established. Where there has been a mistake between the parties as to the subject matter of a contract, there has been no "meeting of the minds," and the contract is voidable at the election of the party adversely affected. . . . The mistake must be shared by both parties, and must relate to an essential element of the agreement. . . . The mistake must involve a fact capable of ascertainment at the time the contract was entered into, and not a mere expectation or opinion about future events. . . . A contract will not be rescinded for mutual mistake where one party was aware at the time the contract was signed that he had limited knowledge as to essential facts, but nonetheless assumed the risk that circumstances would prove to be other than as expected. . . .

In *Tewksbury v. Fellsway Laundry, Inc.,* . . . we declined to set aside a release for personal injuries on the ground of mutual mistake. . . . We held that . . . to invalidate a release [for] mutual mistake, the mistake must relate to a past or present fact material to the contract and not to an opinion respecting future conditions. . . . Because the plaintiff's osteomyelitis developed after the accident and execution of the release . . . any misapprehension by the parties related to a future condition and not to a fact capable of ascertainment at the time of contract.

. . . In this case, however, we are dealing with a separate condition which existed and yet was unknown to the parties at the time of contract. Although this presents a question of first impression in this Commonwealth, the great weight of authority in other jurisdictions supports the view that a release of claims for personal injuries may be avoided on the ground of mutual mistake if the parties at the time of signing the agreement were mistaken as to the *existence* of an injury as opposed to the unknown *consequences* of known injuries. . . .

Our analysis of the doctrine of mutual mistake leads us to adopt the "unknown injury" rule followed by most other jurisdictions. . . . By application of the "unknown injury" rule, it is clear that there is a genuine factual issue presented on the record which precludes summary judgment for the defendants. . . .

JUDGMENT The judgment is reversed, and the case is remanded to the Superior Court for trial. . . . If LaFleur prevails on his claim of mutual mistake and the settlement agreement is rescinded, he will be entitled to have his case remanded to the Industrial Accident Board. *So ordered.*

Unilateral Mistake of Fact. Under a traditional rule, if a party to a contract assents on the basis of his or her own mistake, the mistake is not a ground for relief unless the other party knows or has reason to know of it. Bob, a bidder for a subcontract on a construction project, makes a computational error so that his bid is materially less than it otherwise would have been. George, the general contractor, accepts the offer, and Bob later wants to rescind the contract. Under the traditional rule, whether Bob may do so depends on whether his error was obvious to George ("palpable"). If the bid was so low that George should have realized an error had been made, he will not be allowed to "snap up" Bob's offer. Otherwise, Bob is bound, even though he might suffer a loss.

When would Bob's error be sufficiently obvious to George that Bob could have rescission? Suppose that George received several bids around $750,000, his own estimates show that the lowest profitable bid is likely to be $700,000, and Bob's bid is $500,000. Under the "palpable error" test, George is on notice of Bob's error, and Bob may rescind. However, a substantial disparity among bids does not, by itself, necessarily put the offeree on notice that the lowest one was in error. It is not uncommon for intended, profitable bids to vary dramatically in size, especially those for smaller home repair contracts. The critical factor here is that George had information from his own sources about what the minimum profitable bid should be.

The rule regarding palpable mistake does not apply to errors in judgment, value, or opinion. If Roger offers to sell his car for $500 and Sally accepts, knowing that the car is a classic worth $5,000 and that Roger is unaware of this fact, there is a contract and Roger may not rescind.

Today, courts sometimes grant rescission on the basis of one's own mistake of fact (or allow one to use unilateral mistake as a defense) even though the other party had no reason to know of the mistake. However, relief is available only under the following conditions:

1 The mistake must be material.
2 The mistake must be of grave consequence to the mistaken party.
3 Usually the mistake must not be caused by the mistaken party's gross negligence.
4 Giving relief to the mistaken party must not seriously harm the other party.
5 The mistaken party must promptly notify the other party of the mistake.

Mistake of Law. Mistake of law means ignorance of law, or a wrong conclusion as to the effect of law upon a known set of facts. Under older law, a contracting party ordinarily would be denied relief for a mistake of law unaccompanied by a mistake of fact. This approach produced many harsh results. Modern courts recognize that statutes and case law often are so complex, contradictory, or poorly stated that even skilled lawyers have difficulty interpreting them. Today, in many states relief for mistake of law is treated like relief for mistake of fact. That is, relief is granted if the mistake of law is either (1) mutual or (2) unilateral but obvious to the other party.

AVOIDANCE ON GROUND OF UNCONSCIONABILITY

Lawmakers have long been concerned with protecting weak, often uneducated contracting parties from overreaching by unscrupulous, stronger ones. The law of fraud serves this policy. Yet many misleading and exploitive business practices fall short of established wrongs such as fraud, duress, and undue influence. High-pressure selling of shoddy goods while depriving the buyer of meaningful remedies by use of fine-print clauses is an example. Out of long-standing legal efforts to combat such practices has emerged the concept of **unconscionability** which appears in UCC Sections 2-302 and 208 of *Restatement (Second)*.

Unconscionability is yet another basis for rescinding a contract or for defending against its enforcement. If a contract is unconscionable, a court may refuse to enforce it in its entirety. If some term of a contract is unconscionable, the court may enforce the remainder of the contract without the unconscionable term, or it may limit the application of the unconscionable term in such a way as to avoid any unconscionable result.

Because it can take so many forms, unconscionability has no rigid definition. Instead, the courts apply guidelines such as **oppression** and **unfair surprise** on a case-by-case basis. Any contract or term that oppresses or unfairly surprises a contracting party may be unenforceable even though the practice involved does not constitute fraud or some other traditional variety of illegal conduct.

Over the years, the courts have identified many practices that may be unconscionable. These practices have been classified as either **procedural** or **substantive** unconscionability. The resulting buildup of case law provides specific guidance for the courts as they decide what new practices and variations of old ones should be declared unconscionable.

Procedural unconscionability has to do with an unfair or deceptive process of contract formation. Procedural unconscionability may occur, for example, where a seller uses high-pressure salesmanship or, by means of a clause in fine print placed near the end of a complex contract, seeks secretly to deprive a semiliterate buyer of rights which buyers normally would not wish to give up if the topic were discussed.

Substantive unconscionability has more to do with unreasonably harsh terms of a contract than with a deceptive process of contract formation. An excessively high price might be held unconscionable, as in *Jones v. Star Credit Corp.*[4] There, the plaintiffs, who were welfare recipients, agreed, after a visit from a salesman representing Your Shop At Home Service, Inc., to pay $900 for a home freezer unit with a maximum retail value of $300. With the addition of credit charges, credit life insurance, credit property insurance, and sales tax, the purchase price totaled $1,234.80. After paying $619.88, the plaintiffs sought to avoid the agreement. The defendant claimed that with various added credit charges, the plaintiffs still owed $819.81. Holding that the agreement was unconscionable, the court noted the exorbitant price, the high credit charges, the fact that the plaintiffs' very limited financial resources were known to the sellers at the time of the sale, and the consequent probability that the sellers knowingly took advantage of the plaintiffs.

Substantive unconscionability also occurs where a seller-creditor in an installment sale of goods or services unduly restricts the buyer-debtor's remedies for breach of contract or unduly expands the creditor's own remedial rights. In *Williams v. Walker-Thomas Furniture Co.,*[5] the buyer, a welfare mother with seven children and a monthly income of $218, purchased items of furniture from the seller on credit over a period of 5 years. The contract of sale contained a provision giving the seller a security interest in all the items of furniture until the account was fully paid, instead of the more usual security interest in only the items not yet paid for. The buyer missed payments on the last item, a stereo set costing $514.95. Although she had previously made payments of more than $1,400 on a total debt of $1,800, so that the balance due was less than the purchase price of the stereo, the seller sought to repossess all the furniture. The appellate court held, in effect, that the trial court could find the contract unconscionable if the circumstances surrounding the sale involved oppression and unfair surprise. These elements would be present if, for example, the buyer had no meaningful choice as to the terms of the contract and if it contained terms unreasonably favorable to the seller; if the buyer had no reasonable opportunity to understand the terms; or if important terms were hidden by the use of fine print and deceptive sales practices.

The case just discussed had elements of both procedural and substantive unconscionability. This is typical of unconscionability cases. And, in general, the less meaningful the choice of terms to the buyer (i.e., the greater the oppression or unfair surprise), the less it matters that the term might appear fair in normal contract situations.

AVOIDANCE UNDER CONSUMER PROTECTION LAWS

We have in this country a wide variety of federal and state "consumer protection" laws. The legislation is intended to protect people from deceptive advertising, hidden charges for loans, inaccurate credit reports, unfair billing practices, undue loss as the result of lost or stolen credit cards, and a host of other evils that befall consumers in their day-to-day transactions. Some of the legislation requires disclosure of interest rates, finance charges, and other contractual terms. A few consumer protection statutes are designed to combat high-pressure sales tactics and unfair business practices. They do this in part by giving consumers a "cooling off" period within which to reconsider certain transactions and to rescind them if they wish. Consumer protection laws are discussed further in Chapter 49.

---

[4]298 N.Y.S.2d 264 (N.Y. Sup. Ct. 1969).
[5]350 F.2d 445 (D.C. Cir. 1965).

SUMMARY

The law allows people to avoid contracts for such reasons as minority, mental incompetence, duress, fraud, and unconscionability. A person may exercise the power of avoidance by rescinding the contract or by pleading the right of avoidance as a defense to contract enforcement.

The law protects minors from imprudent contracts while also protecting the legitimate interests of adult parties. A minor may disaffirm a contract while still a minor or within a reasonable time thereafter, by demanding the return of the consideration given and returning whatever was received if he or she still has it. However, minors have a quasi-contractual liability for necessaries and in various states are not permitted to disaffirm certain types of contracts.

Mentally incompetent persons have a similar power of avoidance. A person is considered mentally incompetent if unable at the time of contracting to understand the nature and consequences of the transaction. Where a mentally impaired person's contract is executed, it is not avoidable if the other person had no reason to know of the incompetence and avoidance would be unjust to the other party. If a court declares a person mentally incompetent and appoints a guardian, any later contract attempt by the incompetent person usually is void. Regarding avoidance, intoxicated persons are treated much like mentally incompetent persons.

People also may avoid contracts on the basis of defective assent caused by duress, undue influence, misrepresentation, or mistake. Duress is the use of a wrongful threat to coerce a person into a contract. Undue influence is the use of unfair persuasion to gain advantage over another person, as where a fiduciary takes advantage of a client to gain control of the client's property. Misrepresentation, whether innocent or fraudulent, gives the victim a right to rescind the contract or a defense to enforcement. To rescind on the basis of fraud, the victim is not required to show that the fraud was material or that it caused injury. For a person to rescind on the basis of innocent misrepresentation, however, the misrepresentation must be material.

Various types of mistakes may give a contracting party a basis for rescission. They include mutual and unilateral mistakes of fact. In unilateral mistake, the mistaken party is the one seeking relief. Under the older "palpable error" test, the mistaken party is held to the contract unless the error was obvious to the other party. Today there may be relief for unilateral mistakes that are not obvious to the other party.

Contracts may be avoided, in total or in part, for unconscionability, a concept developed to combat misleading and exploitive business practices falling short of traditional wrongs such as fraud. State and federal consumer protection laws give consumers a right to avoid certain of their contracts.

REVIEW QUESTIONS

1. (a) For what reasons does the law permit people to avoid their contracts? **(b)** How might a person exercise the power of avoidance?

2. What effect does judicial emancipation have on a minor's power of avoidance? What effect does parental emancipation have?

3. From summer earnings, Carleton, age 14, buys a used car. His mother returns the car to the seller and demands Carleton's money back. Has Carleton's contract been disaffirmed?

4. Rita, age 16, buys an expensive racing bike on credit, uses it for the summer, and disaffirms the contract so she can pay for school clothing in the fall. Must Rita pay for the use of the bike?

5. With regard to minors' contracts, explain the meaning and legal effect of ratification.

6. (a) Is a minor liable for the retail price of necessaries? **(b)** Is an automobile a necessary?

7. What difference does it make that a mentally incompetent person's contract was executed rather than executory?

8. Rachel shoplifts an expensive dress she cannot afford. The store owner threatens to send her to jail unless she promises to pay. She promises. Can she later rescind her promise on the ground of duress?

9. In the preceding problem, has the store owner exercised undue influence?

10. (a) What must a person prove to rescind a contract on the basis of fraud? (b) How does this differ from what he or she would have to prove to win a suit for the tort of fraud?

11. Myra finds a pretty rock in her field. A local jeweler notices it and offers her $5 for it. Myra accepts, only to learn later that the rock is sapphire worth $10,000. May Myra rescind the contract?

12. (a) What makes a contract unconscionable? (b) Can a contract containing an unconscionable clause be enforceable?

CASE PROBLEMS

1. Steven Kiefer bought a Willys station wagon from Fred. At the time of sale Kiefer was 20 years old, married, and the father of one child. The age of majority was 21. Kiefer had difficulty with the car and returned it. He demanded return of the purchase price since he was a minor at the time of sale. Fred refused a refund, alleging (1) that Kiefer was emancipated and therefore was liable on the contract, and (2) that Kiefer had misrepresented his age by stating he was over 21 at the time of sale. If Fred can prove these allegations, is either one sufficient to deny Kiefer the right to disaffirm?

2. Vassyl Lonchyna was a minor when he signed a contract enlisting in the U.S. Air Force. At the time, Lonchyna was a college student and wanted to become a medical doctor. The contract specified that the Air Force would provide him with undergraduate and graduate education, and in return Lonchyna would serve on active duty in the Air Force for a specified number of years. At age 21 Lonchyna accepted a commission in the Air Force as a second lieutenant. Later he accepted promotion to first lieutenant. Three times he applied to the Air Force for "educational delays" deferring the start of his active duty commitment. Then Lonchyna filed suit to avoid the enlistment contract on the ground that he was a minor at the time he signed. Should the court grant Lonchyna's request for avoidance?

3. In November 1960, Logan Corporation agreed to buy two businesses owned by Litten. Logan promised to pay Litten's creditors, to employ Litten for 1 year at a stipulated salary, and to give Litten an option to buy 5,000 shares of Logan's stock. Litten transferred the businesses to Logan, but Logan refused to pay Litten's creditors in full. In January 1961, the creditors threatened Litten with bankruptcy. On January 9, Logan presented to Litten a new agreement which contained no stock option and no employment clause. Logan said the creditors would not be paid unless Litten signed the agreement. Litten signed the agreement and later filed suit to avoid the 1961 agreement and to enforce the terms of the November 1960 agreement. Should the court set aside the 1961 agreement?

4. Gary and Sara married in 1957 and had four children. In 1970 Gary was hospitalized for 8 weeks for mental problems, and in 1972 and early 1974 received drug therapy for paranoid schizophrenia. In December 1974, Gary suffered a recurrence and was committed to the state hospital. The hospital allowed him to work during the day at his job as a design engineer and return for treatment at night. While Gary was hospitalized, Sara filed for divorce. Both parties signed a separation agreement on February 20, 1975, in the office of Sara's attorney. Gary did not want the divorce and did not read the agreement. He was on extensive medication throughout February, and on February 20 received three drugs which adversely affected his reasoning powers. According to Sara, the parties negotiated $750 per month for child support and together reviewed the entire agreement. Gary denied setting the $750 monthly figure and stated that Sara originally asked for $1,100 out of his $1,300 net monthly income. Under the agreement, land inherited by Gary would be sold and the proceeds used to pay off the marital debts, with the balance to be divided equally. Other terms were onerous to Gary. He sued to rescind the agreement. How should the court rule?

5. Indiana residents Dale and Janice Shoup planned to build a retirement home in Florida. To finance it, they sought a short-term loan from Central National Bank of Greencastle (CNB). Explaining that Dale was retiring, they proposed to mortgage their Greencastle house, sell it as soon as possible, and pay off the loan with the proceeds. CNB agreed to this and prepared a note and mortgage papers for the Shoups to sign. The documents specified a 20-year loan at 10 percent annual interest and included a due-on-sale clause and a prepayment penalty clause. Neither clause was pointed out to or discussed with the Shoups before they signed the documents. The Shoups' attempt to sell their house failed after they moved to Florida. Over a year later they sold the house to the Fishers on an installment contract. A few days after the contract was recorded, an officer of CNB called Mrs. Shoup, advising her that the sale triggered the due-on-sale clause and that the debt would have to be paid immediately or refinanced at a higher rate of interest—13.5 percent for 3 years and 12 percent for the next 3. The Shoups did not respond to this proposal, and CNB brought suit to foreclose its mortgage. Alleging fraud, the Shoups filed a counterclaim. Who should prevail?

6. Amos Cobaugh was playing in the East End Open Golf Tournament. At the ninth tee he found a new Chevrolet Beretta and signs stating, "HOLE-IN-ONE Wins this 1988 Chevrolet Beretta GT Courtesy of KLICK-LEWIS . . . in Palmyra." Cobaugh aced the ninth hole and claimed his prize. Alleging mistake, Klick-Lewis refused to deliver. It had offered the car as a prize for a charity tournament two days earlier, and had failed to remove the car and sign prior to Cobaugh's hole-in-one. Cobaugh sued to compel delivery of the car. Who should prevail?

CHAPTER 14

Illegal Agreements

Society would be at risk if people could enforce agreements that violate the law. So we have a rule that to be a *contract*, an agreement must have a lawful purpose. But this apparently simple rule can be of uncertain application. For one thing, it is not always clear that an agreed act breaks the law. Consider the agreements in the accompanying box. Which, if any, should be illegal?

BOX 14.1
Agreements
- For $10,000, to sell one's baby to a stranger.
- For 10,000, to bear a child for an infertile couple.
- For payment of delivery expenses, a mother's releasing her baby for adoption.

The first part of this chapter examines the nature and general effect of illegal agreements; the second part, illegal agreements common in business. Then the chapter discusses situations where the courts aid a party to an illegal agreement despite the general rule to the contrary.

ILLEGAL AGREEMENTS IN GENERAL

Nature and General Effect of Illegal Agreements

Meaning and Effect of Illegality. An agreement is illegal if it is made or performed in violation of law, whether criminal or civil. "Law" includes constitutions, statutes, rules, and regulations of an administrative agency, and principles or policies of the common law. Generally, the courts will not enforce illegal agreements or in any other way give aid to either party, but there are significant exceptions to this rule.[1]

Some agreements are so obviously contrary to law that they are unenforceable in their entirety—for example, Jane and Joe's agreement to rob a bank. More often, contracts contain parts (called **clauses, provisions,** or **terms**) that are illegal, as where Joe agrees to sell a car to Jane on credit but at a higher rate of interest

---

[1] Many illegal agreements are held to be "void," but most are held merely to be unenforceable, and some are enforced despite the general rule to the contrary. The treatment of illegal agreements varies so greatly because the factors that make an act illegal vary, thus producing different degrees of illegality. Arthur L. Corbin, CORBIN ON CONTRACTS (one-volume edition 1952), Sec. 1374.

than permitted by law. Depending on how the illegal part affects the whole contract, a court may refuse to enforce the contract, may strike out the illegal part and enforce what remains, or may limit the application of the illegal part to achieve legality and prevent serious injustice.

Significance of "Public Policy." When deciding whether agreements are legal, a court often must decide whether they violate **public policy**—that is, whether they threaten the public good or endanger the community. Agreements that threaten the public good are "against public policy" and may be held illegal. The three private trash-hauling firms operating in Metropolis agree to divide the market so that each can collect garbage in a certain geographic area free from the competition of the others. Each firm now has its own monopoly and can charge excessive rates that must be paid by residents and businesses or their customers, to the injury of the whole community. Statutes and court decisions forbid such agreements because they violate that element of public policy which approves of free competition.

Constitutions, statutes, and administrative rules and regulations are declarations of public policy. In the absence of legislation, courts, too, may define public policy if called upon to determine whether an agreement is sufficiently threatening to the public to be declared illegal. Box 14.2 illustrates the variable nature of public policy.

Agreements Illegal by Constitution or Statute

An agreement may be illegal because it violates a statute. Violation may be evident because the statute states that the agreement is "illegal," "unlawful," "void," or "against public policy." But many statutes do not express the legislative intent to make an agreement illegal. So a court will have to determine the implied intent by *construing* the statute, i.e., deciding what its purpose is, what evils it seems intended to prevent, and thus whether it was meant to apply to the agreement in question. In *National Labor Rela-*

> **BOX 14.2**
> **Ethics, Values, and Public Policy**
>
> Every determination of public policy involves a value judgment—a balancing of competing interests, including the public interest. Such judgments may vary from state to state and change over time. For example, in *Marvin v. Marvin*, 557 P.2d 106 (Cal. 1976), the California Supreme Court held for the first time that an agreement between an unmarried man and woman regarding property acquired while they lived together may be enforceable. Traditionally, such an agreement has been held against public policy and unenforceable, since to enforce it might encourage people to live out of wedlock. As the court's change of position indicates, notions of what constitutes sound public policy are affected by changes in what the public and the lawmakers consider ethical, moral, or tolerable. ∎

---

tions Board v. Bratten Pontiac Corp.,[2] for example, Bratten induced its employees to agree not to unionize, by offering them new benefits while they were considering whether to join the union. A provision of the National Labor Relations Act makes it an **unfair labor practice** for an employer to interfere with the employees' right to join a union. Although the Act does not list the giving of benefits as a type of interference, the court held that Bratten's doing so while the union election was pending constituted an interference that made the agreement between Bratten and the employees unlawful and unenforceable.

Constitutions, too, often make agreements illegal. For example, it used to be a common practice for sellers of real estate to include in their sales contracts a clause (called a **restrictive covenant**) prohibiting occupancy by or sale to people of minority races. Although the U.S. Constitution does not expressly forbid such clauses, the Supreme Court held in *Shelley v.*

[2] 406 F.2d 349 (4th Cir. 1969).

Kraemer[3] that enforcement of such a clause by a state court or other state officer is a denial of the equal protection of the laws required by the Fourteenth Amendment. Consequently, racially discriminatory restrictive covenants are unenforceable in any state. Similarly, in a 1981 case,[4] the court granted a declaratory judgment to a construction company, holding that it need not comply with a New Jersey statute requiring it to hire citizens of New Jersey before hiring persons from out of state. Requiring the firm to favor New Jersey citizens in employment contracts would violate the privileges and immunities clause of the Constitution and make the contracts illegal.

> **BOX 14.3**
> **Government Regulation of Contracts**
>
> The Civil Rights Act, the Equal Pay Act, the Age Discrimination in Employment Act, and the Equal Credit Opportunity Act (all federal legislation) prohibit a wide variety of discrimination on the basis of race, color, religion, sex, national origin, and age. Although aimed mainly at employers and others who practice illegal discrimination directly against individuals, these acts would also be violated by agreements between, for example, a corporation and a labor union to practice the prohibited forms of discrimination. ■

Attitudes about public policy vary from state to state and change over time. This can be seen in two cases involving statutes prohibiting gambling agreements. In *Williams v. Weber Mesa Ditch Extension Co.*,[5] Williams purchased a $5 raffle ticket and was notified that he had won the prize, a 40-acre tract of land. Soon afterward, the defendant, a nonprofit corporation, nullified the raffle and held a new drawing because of the late arrival of tickets that had been delayed in the mails. Williams did not win the new drawing and brought suit to specifically enforce the first one. The supreme court of Wyoming held that the raffle was a gambling contract within the meaning of Wyoming's civil statute making gaming transactions "utterly void and of no effect." This case represents the traditional, still rather widely held view of lawmakers that gambling is so harmful to the public welfare that gaming contracts are not to be enforced.

Over the years, however, many state legislatures have decided that some forms of gambling such as lotteries and pari-mutuel betting on horse or dog races provide recreational and revenue-raising benefits that justify making them legal. With this change in attitude have come not only legalized gambling, but also changes in related law. Gambling on credit has long been viewed as detrimental to the public good, leading as it may to excessive losses, borrowing from loan sharks, and impoverishment. In *Gottlob v. Lopez*,[6] Lopez, while gambling in the Tropicana Casino in Atlantic City, borrowed $5,500 from Gottlob to continue gambling. Lopez did not repay the loan, and Gottlob brought suit. In holding that the gambling debt was enforceable, the court stated, "The 1976 constitutional amendment [authorizing casino gambling in Atlantic City] and the enactment of the Casino Control Act altered our public policy regarding enforcement of gambling debts incurred while wagering in a licensed casino." Before 1976, all New Jersey gambling debts were "utterly void and of no effect." The Casino Control Act now regulates the extension of credit to gamblers by licensed casino operators such as Tropicana, but it is silent about loans from nonlicensees such as Gottlob. Nevertheless, the court held that all loans contracted to facilitate legalized gambling are enforceable, even those made by unregulated persons like Gottlob.

Agreements Judicially Declared Contrary to Public Policy

The courts themselves can declare agreements void as against public policy, even though no

---

[3] 68 S. Ct. 836 (1948).
[4] *Neshaminy Constructors, Inc. v. Krause*, 437 A.2d 733 (N.J. Super. Ct. Ch. Div. 1981).
[5] 572 P.2d 412 (Wyo. 1977).
[6] 501 A.2d 176 (N.J. Super. Ct. App. Div. 1985).

statute forbids them. Some agreements are so threatening to the public welfare that virtually all agreements of the class would be held to violate public policy. Agreements to commit a crime or a tort are an example. Other kinds of agreements, such as contracts of adhesion and exculpatory clauses, are not necessarily harmful and will be denied enforcement only if misused.

Contracts of Adhesion. A **contract of adhesion** (often, a "standard-form" contract) involves so great a disparity of bargaining power that the weaker party has no choice but to accept the terms imposed by the stronger party or forgo the transaction. As noted in Chapter 10, contracts of adhesion serve legitimate functions in our economy and usually are enforced. Yet, because of the great disparity of bargaining power that characterizes contracts of adhesion, people upon whom they are imposed are vulnerable to exploitation. In the absence of bargaining power, what is their protection?

One protection is the sense of fairness and responsibility possessed by most businesspeople. Another protection might be a vigorous competition among sellers. Sometimes the terms of a contract are monitored by an administrative agency for the benefit of individual consumers. The insurance commissions of most states, for example, require that insurance companies include in their policies certain clauses protecting the interests of those who purchase insurance coverage. And, whether motivated by ethical considerations or merely by the pressures of competition, many businesses choose not to exercise their superior bargaining power in oppressive ways. If ethical and competitive protections fail, the courts and legislatures may intervene. The courts have invalidated contracts or clauses in a variety of ways—for example, by holding that an adhesive contract or clause is contrary to public policy.

Exculpatory Clauses. **Exculpatory clauses** are contractual provisions whose aim is to exempt a contracting party from the payment of damages for his or her own misconduct. Such clauses frequently are held contrary to public policy.

Ordinarily, the courts will not enforce an exculpatory clause that relieves a contracting party of responsibility for his or her own criminal conduct, intentional torts, or "gross" negligence. In such instances, freedom of contract gives way to the public's need for protection against contractual arrangements which, by protecting wrongdoers, tend to induce a lack of regard for the safety or rights of others. A clause that exempts a person from liability for his or her own "simple" (ordinary) negligence might or might not be upheld. If the clause is freely consented to by parties of substantially equal bargaining power, the court ordinarily will uphold it as an appropriate way to shift risk of loss. In contrast, if the clause is a part of a *contract of adhesion* so that the weaker party has no choice but to bear the consequences of the other party's simple negligence, the clause might be invalidated.

In Case 14.1, the California Supreme Court applied a state statute to a contract of adhesion containing an exculpatory clause. This leading case is noteworthy for its discussion of the circumstances under which such clauses will be held invalid.

CASE 14.1   Tunkl v. Regents of University of California • 383 P.2d 441 (Cal. 1963)

FACTS   The University of California at Los Angeles Medical Center admitted Hugo Tunkl as a patient. Tunkl, in great pain, under sedation, and probably unable to read, signed a document containing the following clause:

> RELEASE: The hospital is a nonprofit, charitable institution. In consideration of the hospital and allied services to be rendered and the rates charged therefor, the patient . . . hereby releases The Regents of the University of California and the hospital

**CASE 14.1
Continued**

from any and all liability for the negligent or wrongful acts or omissions of its employees, if the hospital has used due care in selecting its employees.

Alleging that personal injuries resulted from the negligence of two physicians employed by the Medical Center, Tunkl sued the Regents for damages. Mr. Tunkl died after suit was brought, and Mrs. Tunkl was substituted as plaintiff. She stipulated that the hospital had selected its employees with due care. The trial court entered judgment for the Regents, and plaintiff appealed.

OPINION

TOBRINER, J. This case concerns the validity of a release from liability for future negligence imposed as a condition for admission to a charitable research hospital. . . . [W]e have concluded that an agreement between a hospital and an entering patient affects the public interest and that, in consequence, the exculpatory provision included within it must be invalid under Civil Code section 1668. . . . [Section 1668] states: "All contracts which have for their object, directly or indirectly, to exempt anyone from responsibility for his own fraud, or willful injury to the person or property of another, or violation of law, whether willful or negligent, are against the policy of the law."

[The California] courts' interpretations of [section 1668] have been diverse. . . . The court in *England v. Lyon Fireproof Storage Co.* . . . categorically states, "The court correctly instructed the jury that—'The defendant cannot limit its liability against its own negligence by contract, and any contract to that effect would be void.'" . . . The recent case of *Mills v. Ruppert* . . . , however, apparently limits "[N]egligent . . . violation of law" exclusively to statutory law. Other cases hold that the statute prohibits the exculpation of gross negligence only; still another case states that the section forbids exemption from active as contrasted with passive negligence. . . .

In one respect, [however,] the decisions are uniform. [They] have consistently held that the exculpatory provision may stand only if it does not involve "the public interest." . . .

If, then, [an] exculpatory clause which affects the public interest cannot stand, we must ascertain those factors or characteristics which constitute the public interest. . . . [T]he courts have revealed a rough outline of that type of transaction in which exculpatory provisions will be held invalid. . . . [T]he attempted but invalid exemption involves a transaction which exhibits some or all of the following characteristics. It concerns a business of a type generally thought suitable for public regulation. The party seeking exculpation is engaged in performing a service of great importance to the public, which is often a matter of practical necessity for some members of the public. The party holds himself out as willing to perform this service for any member of the public who seeks it, or at least for any member coming within certain established standards. As a result of the essential nature of the service, in the economic setting of the transaction, the party invoking exculpation possesses a decisive advantage of bargaining strength against any member of the public who seeks his services. In exercising a superior bargaining power the party confronts the public with a standardized adhesion contract of exculpation, and makes no provision whereby a purchaser may pay additional reasonable fees and obtain protection against negligence. Finally, as a result of the transaction, the person or property of the purchaser is

**CASE 14.1
Continued**

placed under the control of the seller, subject to the risk of carelessness by the seller or his agents. . . .

While obviously no public policy opposes private, voluntary transactions in which one party, for a consideration, agrees to shoulder a risk which the law would otherwise have placed upon the other party, the above circumstances pose a different situation. In this situation the releasing party does not really acquiesce voluntarily in the contractual shifting of the risk. . . . Since the service is one which each member of the public . . . may find essential to him, he faces, despite his economic inability to do so, the prospect of a compulsory assumption of the risk of another's negligence. The public policy of this state has been, in substance, to posit the risk of negligence upon the actor; in instances in which this policy has been abandoned, it has generally been to allow or require that the risk shift to another party better or equally able to bear it, not to shift the risk to the weak bargainer.

In light of the decisions, we think that the hospital-patient contract clearly falls within the category of agreements affecting the public interest. To meet that test, the agreement need only fulfill some of the characteristics above outlined; here, the relationship fulfills all of them. Thus the contract of exculpation involves an institution suitable for, and a subject of, public regulation. . . . That the services of the hospital to those members of the public who are in special need of the particular skill of its staff and facilities constitute a practical and crucial necessity is hardly open to question.

The hospital, likewise, holds itself out as willing to perform its services for those members of the public who qualify for its research and training facilities. While it is true that the hospital is selective as to the patients it will accept, such selectivity does not negate its public aspect or the public interest in it. . . .

In insisting that the patient accept the provision of waiver in the contract, the hospital certainly exercises a decisive advantage in bargaining. The would-be patient is in no position to reject the proffered agreement, to bargain with the hospital, or in lieu of agreement to find another hospital. . . . [We must] conclude that the instant agreement manifested the characteristics of the so-called adhesion contract. Finally, when the patient signed the contract, he completely placed himself in the control of the hospital; he subjected himself to the risk of its carelessness.

[The court then rejected the defendants' arguments in support of their exculpatory clause. The court also pointed out that although the clause was invalid, the plaintiff must prove negligence on the part of the physicians.]

JUDGMENT   The judgment is reversed.

COMMON TYPES OF ILLEGAL AGREEMENTS

As traditionally understood, **illegality** refers to conduct that violates the law each time it occurs, regardless of the circumstances. Joe hires Anna to steal Omar's property. The transaction and all others like it lack the legality required for a contract to arise. Joe and Anna have not created a contract. They have merely made an agreement that is **void,** i.e., that creates no legal rights whatever.

In contrast, a contract or a clause might violate the law in some circumstances but not in others. For example, a clause prohibiting competition might be wrongful or not, depending on the circumstances surrounding the contract. It cannot be said that the act of prohibiting competition is inherently evil, because the law sometimes permits it. Nevertheless, when done under forbidden circumstances, the act is wrongful and is illegal to the extent, at least, of denying enforceability to the noncompetition clause. The following pages discuss a few representative types of agreements that might or might not be illegal, depending on the circumstances.

Agreements Not to Compete

Types of Agreements Not to Compete. Much of our law is aimed at preserving free trade and an active competition among sellers so that the public will have an abundance of goods and services without being forced to pay unreasonably high prices. In general, price fixing, monopolistic combinations of firms in restraint of trade, and other types of agreements not to compete are against public policy. Controlling large-scale restraints on trade is the purpose of the Sherman Act, the Clayton Act, and other antitrust law discussed in Chapters 52 and 53.

However, some agreements not to compete are beneficial and even necessary for businesses to operate efficiently. Two important examples are:

- An agreement by the seller of a business not to compete with the buyer
- An agreement by an employee not to compete with the employer after the termination of the employment

Because these agreements would prohibit a person from engaging in his or her livelihood, the courts are reluctant to enforce them except for compelling reasons. For what reasons and to what extent may such agreements be enforced?

Agreement by seller of a business. Where the owner of a business sells it as a "going concern," the buyer rightfully expects to receive all of the business assets, including the continued patronage of the seller's customers (their **goodwill**), free from the seller's interference until the buyer has had a reasonable opportunity to establish his or her own business reputation. To protect goodwill, the buyer might require the seller to sign a covenant (promise) not to compete with the buyer. The courts will enforce such a covenant if it is reasonable. Usually a restraint is reasonable if it is so limited in duration and in territory covered as to protect only the goodwill purchased. A covenant by the seller of a small store with a neighborhood trade not to compete for 6 months anywhere within the city might be unduly burdensome to the seller and unenforceable. A covenant by the seller of a firm doing a statewide business not to compete for a year anywhere in the state might be reasonable.

Agreement by employee. Often employees must sign employment contracts containing covenants not to compete with the employer upon termination of the employment. A covenant may forbid setting up a business in competition with the former employer, working for a competitor, or revealing the former employer's trade secrets. Even in the absence of a covenant, an employee has no right to reveal the employer's trade secrets, and so a covenant prohibiting such conduct will be enforced.

An employee's agreement not to *compete* with the former employer, however, may or may not be enforceable. Enforcing such a covenant may seriously hamper the employee in his or her efforts to earn a living, or it may deprive the public of the benefit that could result from competition between the employer and the former employee. To be enforceable, an employee's covenant not to compete must be reasonable in duration and territory covered, *and* it must be reasonably necessary to protect a legitimate business interest of the employer. To determine whether a particular covenant is reasonable, a court must consider the degree of hardship it imposes on the employee, the harm to the public resulting from the reduced competition, and the employer's interests that might be at risk—customer lists, secret processes, and so on.

Divisibility of Agreements Not to Compete.

Suppose that Bob, the buyer of a small delicatessen store whose business extends for a twelve-block radius, requires Sue, the seller, to agree not to compete within a radius of 20 miles. Immediately after the sale, Sue announces that within the next few days she will open a new delicatessen three blocks from her former location. Bob seeks an injunction restraining Sue from opening the store. Most courts would agree that Bob has demanded an unreasonably broad restriction on Sue's right to conduct a business. But they would also agree that Sue threatens to interfere unreasonably with the goodwill Bob thought he had purchased. Whom should the courts protect?

Some courts refuse to enforce overly broad restrictions, and thus would deny Bob injunctive relief. They refuse enforcement to encourage buyers to be cautious and to draft clauses that will be reasonable. In these jurisdictions, buyers who draft overly broad clauses do so at the risk of losing all protection. Other courts would hold that because a twelve-block limitation would have been reasonable, the restrictive agreement is enforceable at least to that extent. In granting the buyer injunctive relief, these courts treat overly broad agreements as "divisible," or "severable" (partially enforceable), especially where the overbreadth seems inadvertent or where the reasonableness of the restriction was difficult to estimate. A similar problem arises—and a similar split of authority occurs—where an agreement not to compete specifies a time limit greater than necessary to protect the purchaser.

The case that follows involves a franchise agreement. The validity of its covenant not to compete is governed by principles similar to those just discussed.

CASE 14.2 **Hapney v. Central Garage, Inc.** • 579 So. 2d 127 (Fla. App. 1991)

FACTS Defendant David Hapney worked in various auto repair shops where he learned to install and repair auto and truck air-conditioning systems. In 1988 he went to work for plaintiff Gulfcoast. He signed an agreement not to compete with Gulfcoast for 3 years "on the west coast of Florida from Crystal River to Naples or inland 100 miles" upon termination of employment. Gulfcoast taught Hapney to install cruise controls and cellular telephones in automobiles. He had no significant contacts with Gulfcoast's customers, and he acquired no trade secrets or confidential business information of Gulfcoast. In 1989, Hapney quit his job and began working for a direct competitor of Gulfcoast. Gulfcoast brought an action to enforce the covenant not to compete. The trial court issued a temporary injunction against Hapney, and Hapney appealed.

OPINION PATTERSON, J. . . . Under the common law of England, a contract restricting a person's right to pursue his trade or occupation was deemed void as against public policy. Medieval concepts that a person could not pursue a trade in which he had not been apprenticed made the rule necessary, because prohibiting a person from working under the supervision of one other than his original employer would leave the person in involuntary servitude or unable to provide for himself and his dependants. . . .

With the passage of time, the ancient rules of apprenticeship were abandoned, and it became recognized that in special circumstances limited restraints of competition were both necessary and proper to protect an employer's proprietary rights. . . . Thus evolved the distinction between contracts prohibiting competition per se, which were prima facie invalid . . . and contracts protecting

**CASE 14.2
Continued**

an employer from unfair competition from a former employee who had obtained trade secrets, or other confidential information, or special relationships with customers during the course of his employment. . . . These basic concepts are embraced in the law of our state. . . .

In 1953 the legislature enacted [a statute] which acknowledged the common law principle that contracts in restraint of trade are void. The statute provides an exception which [states] that an employee "may agree with his employer, to refrain from carrying on or engaging in a similar business and from soliciting old customers of such employer." . . .

The statute is silent on the issue of whether for such contracts to be valid they must relate to the protection of a proprietary interest of the employer. Thus, we must determine if such requirement is to be implied in the statute or whether the legislature has intended to authorize contracts which prohibit competition per se. No Florida decision addresses this precise question. . . .

Our review of the [law] of our sister states which permit employee noncompetition agreements reveals an overwhelming majority requiring, at a minimum, that such contracts be reasonably related to the protection of a "legitimate business interest" or "protectible interest" of the employer. The rule, generally stated, is that an employer may not enforce a post-employment restriction on a former employee simply to eliminate competition per se; the employer must establish its legitimate business interest to be protected. . . .

The Supreme Court of Tennessee expressed the rule as follows:

> Any competition by a former employee may well injure the business of the employer. An employer, however, cannot by contract restrain ordinary competition. In order for an employer to be entitled to protection, there must be special facts present over and above ordinary competition. These special facts must be such that without the covenant not to compete the employee would gain an unfair advantage in future competition with the employer. . . .

. . . [T]he general rule stated above is an integral part of our law [and] is implied in [the Florida statute]. . . .

. . . [W]e now [consider] what may constitute [a protectible interest of the employer]. Generally, three such interests are recognized: (1) trade secrets and confidential business lists, records, and information, (2) customer goodwill, and (3) to a limited degree, extraordinary or specialized training provided by the employer. . . .

"Extraordinary" is that which goes beyond what is usual, regular, common, or customary in the [employee's] industry. . . . The rationale is that if an employer dedicates time and money to the extraordinary training and education of an employee, whereby the employee attains a unique skill . . . then it is unfair to permit that employee to use [the skill] to the benefit of a competitor when the employee has contracted not to do so. The precise degree of training or education which rises to the level of a protectible interest will vary from industry to industry and is a factual determination to be made by the trial court. Needless to say, skills which may be acquired by following the directions in the box or learned by a person of ordinary education by reading a manual do not meet the test. . . .

. . .[T]he trial court found that Hapney "received significant training in the installation of cruise controls and cellular telephones in autos" during his em-

**CASE 14.2
Continued**

ployment by Gulfcoast. . . . In view of our determination that such training must be extraordinary, it may appear remote that Hapney's training can rise to the level of a protectible interest. Nevertheless, we cannot totally foreclose Gulfcoast from pursuing the issue because it was not specifically addressed by the trial court. . . .

We hold (1) a covenant not to compete which prohibits competition per se violates public policy and is void; (2) [to be valid,] a covenant not to compete [must protect a legitimate business interest of the employer]; (3) it is the employer's burden to plead and prove the underlying protectible interest; (4) trade secrets, customer lists, and the right to prevent direct solicitation of existing customers are, per se, [protectible interest]; (5) other business interests, such as . . . extraordinary training or education may constitute protectible interests depending upon the proof adduced. . . .

JUDGMENT

. . . Gulfcoast has failed to plead or prove a legitimate business interest to be protected as the foundation of Hapney's covenant not to compete. The temporary injunction is therefore vacated with leave to Gulfcoast to serve amended pleadings if it so elects. Reversed and remanded.

BOX 14.4

You Be the Judge

A state statute makes void any contract that forbids a person from being employed in a lawful profession, trade, or business. However, the statute provides for an exception: A buyer of a business may enforce a noncompetition clause against the seller if the clause is reasonable in time and in geographic coverage, and if it protects a legitimate interest of the buyer.

Argos hires Angela to work for him as vice president in charge of marketing. As part of the employment contract, Argos grants Angela an insubstantial interest in his business, on condition that she will sell the interest back to Argos and enter a noncompetition agreement when her employment ends. Assume that the agreement is properly limited in duration and geographic coverage. Is it enforceable against Angela? ■

Agreements Involving Usury

Meaning and Effect of Usury. To discourage the charging of exorbitant interest, almost every state has a statute specifying the highest rate of interest that may be charged for a loan of money. **Usury** is the charging of any rate of interest in excess of that permitted by law.

Statutes usually specify a maximum rate of interest of general application for "normal" loans and a series of higher maximum rates for other kinds of loans, for example, loans by pawnbrokers and small loan companies. Typically these latter kinds of loans involve small amounts of money and relatively high costs of collection. The bookkeeping expenses attending such loans, together with the doubtful creditworthiness of many of the borrowers, warrant higher maximum interest rates.

The states differ in their treatment of usurious agreements. In some states usurious agreements are void, and the overreaching lender forfeits interest *and* principal. In other states a usurious agreement is voidable, but only as to the amount of interest in excess of the amount permitted by law. In still other states the agreement is voidable as to the usurious amount, and the injured party may recover a penalty of double or triple the usurious amount.

Effect of Usury Limits on Availability of Credit. Statutes imposed usury limits long before the need for massive amounts of credit developed. When the need developed, the market price of business and consumer credit was forced up, well beyond the limits imposed by the usury statutes, and lenders diverted their funds to more lucrative markets.

To encourage lenders to provide businesses with an adequate supply of credit, the laws of many states now exempt loans to corporations from the limits imposed by the usury statutes. Other state laws encourage the extension of consumer credit by exempting certain types of consumer loans and lenders from the coverage of the usury statutes—for example, consumer real estate loans, car loans, and installment loans made by banks and credit unions.

The courts, too, have recognized the need for more consumer credit and in a number of ways have contributed to its availability. Chief among these contributions was the development of the **time-price doctrine.** When a person makes immediate payment for goods at a store, he or she is charged a "cash" price, which supposedly represents the lowest price at which the seller is willing to do business. If the buyer is permitted to purchase the goods on a credit (e.g., installment payment) basis, the seller runs a higher risk of nonpayment. To compensate for the added risk, the seller may charge a higher price (called the time price) for the goods. Under the time-price doctrine (in those states that still impose it), the sale of goods on credit is not a loan, and the difference between the cash price and the time price is not considered interest. This is so even though the difference is commonly expressed in terms of a percentage of the cash price. Thus, credit sales of goods are sometimes held not to be subject to the usury statutes.

Reform of Consumer Credit Extension and Usury Law. Legislatures typically have imposed flat limits on the rates of interest which can legally be charged, and they have left to the courts the task of deciding which methods of interest calculation violate the statutes. Some methods of calculating or expressing interest disguise the actual rate of interest being charged and were originally devised to circumvent the statutory limits on interest. Some of these methods are still in use. They tend to confuse borrowers and to make comparison shopping for credit difficult.

Within recent years there have been significant attempts to reform the law relating to credit extension and usury. The federal Truth-in-Lending Act[7] and the Uniform Consumer Credit Code (UCCC)[8] impose disclosure requirements on the lenders to whom the laws apply. Under both laws, lenders must disclose to borrowers the true cost of credit in terms they can understand: in terms of an **annual percentage rate** (APR) as that rate is defined in the applicable law. The UCCC is more than a disclosure statute. It also provides maximum rates of interest which can legally be charged, prohibits false and misleading credit advertising, and imposes other restrictions on lenders. Both the UCCC (in the states that have adopted it) and the Truth-in-Lending Act apply to all extensions of consumer credit: bank loans, credit sales of goods, and other forms of consumer credit.

Agreements in Violation of Sunday-Closing Statutes

Many states have statutes prohibiting or regulating certain kinds of Sunday transactions. Such statutes are commonly referred to as Sunday-closing laws, or **blue laws,** and in colonial times were intended to encourage the practice of religion. Today, the First Amendment and the Fourteenth Amendment of the U.S. Constitution forbid laws "respecting an establishment of religion, or prohibiting the free exercise thereof."

Nevertheless, Sunday-closing legislation will be upheld if its purpose is rational and nonreligious and if the legislation does not violate the due process or equal protection guarantees of the state or federal constitutions. Sunday-closing laws will be upheld, for example, where they have an economic justification or where they

---

[7]Officially known as Title I, Consumer Credit Protection Act, 15 U.S.C. Secs. 1601–1665, 1671–1677 (1976).

[8]As of April 1993, adopted by Colorado, Guam, Idaho, Indiana, Iowa, Kansas, Maine, Oklahoma, South Carolina, Utah, Wisconsin, and Wyoming.

are merely an exercise of a state's police power to provide a day of rest, amusement, and family togetherness. In some states, Sunday-closing laws are generally enforced; in others, they are generally ignored.

Agreements in Violation of Licensing Statutes

All states have statutes requiring a person to obtain a license, certificate, or diploma before carrying on certain occupations. Licenses are required of professionals such as doctors, lawyers, and public accountants; of skilled workers such as electricians, plumbers, contractors, and beauticians; and of businesspeople such as pawnbrokers, liquor dealers, and restaurant operators.

Usually, licensing statutes provide that any person who engages in a designated occupation or business without obtaining the required license is subject to a fine. However, most licensing statutes do not state whether an unlicensed person may enforce his or her contracts with customers or clients.

To decide this question, courts look to the character of the statute. Some licensing statutes are **regulatory,** designed to protect the public against unprincipled and unqualified persons. Other licensing statutes are **revenue-raising** measures that impose a license simply to collect a tax. If a statute is regulatory, unlicensed persons ordinarily cannot recover payment for services rendered or for goods delivered. Licensing statutes applying to building contractors usually are regulatory in nature. A building contractor who does not have the required license normally is not allowed to recover compensation for services performed in constructing improvements on someone's land. By denying compensation to violators of regulatory licensing statutes, the courts encourage unlicensed practitioners to withhold services until they have acquired minimum qualifications thought necessary for the safety of the public.

In contrast, city or county business licensing ordinances ordinarily are revenue-raising measures. A business that fails to acquire the required license may be fined by the taxing authority but may still enforce contracts and recover compensation for services rendered.

Whether a statute is regulatory or revenue-raising is only one of the tests that courts apply when deciding whether to award violators compensation for their services. Others are: Did the unlicensed person perform the contract well? Did the performance endanger public safety, health, or morals? Would denial of recovery cause a substantial loss to the unlicensed person and an undeserved windfall to the other party?

In the following opinion, the Alabama Supreme Court was asked to interpret an Alabama consumer loan statute so that a U.S. district court could apply it in a federal case.

CASE 14.3	Derico v. Duncan • 410 So. 2d 27 (Ala. 1982)
FACTS	Doing business as Federal Building Service, defendant Thomas R. Duncan contracted with plaintiff Mattie Derico to repair and re-side her house. Duncan charged her $6,381 for the work and, to secure payment of the home-repair debt, asked her for a first mortgage on her home. To get the mortgage, Duncan advanced her the $7,619 she needed to pay off the existing first mortgage, which carried an 8 percent annual interest rate. The $14,000 consumer debt that she now owed Duncan was financed at 12.78 percent annual interest, for a total of $27,439.20 in principal and interest. In a 4-month period, Duncan had made approximately 20 such loan agreements with homeowners. However, he had not acquired the license required by law "to engage in the business of making consumer loans."

CASE 14.3 Continued

Seeking to rescind the loan agreement, Derico sued Duncan in a federal district court. To decide the case, the federal court had to apply the Alabama Consumer Finance statute (the "Mini-Code"). The Mini-Code requires those engaged in the business of making consumer loans to first obtain a license, and it provides criminal sanctions for willful violations. However, because the Mini-Code had not yet been authoritatively interpreted, the federal district court asked the Alabama Supreme Court to answer the following question: "Does [Duncan's] failure, which was not willful, to obtain a license according to Section 5-19-22 [of the Mini-Code] affect [Derico's] obligation under the loan contract . . . and if so, to what extent?"

Duncan admitted his failure to obtain the required license, but contended that the exclusive statutory remedy for violating the Mini-Code was a fine or imprisonment, neither of which applied to him because his failure was not willful.

OPINION

JONES, J. . . . Plaintiff, however, reasons that § 5-19-22 is a "regulatory statute" and, therefore, that Defendant's violation of that statute renders the loan agreement between the parties null and void.

. . . [W]ere we to accept Defendant's reasoning, he would avoid any and all penalty for his unlawful conduct. . . . We hold that established Alabama law mandates our rejection of Defendant's contention.

[Since the 1918 case of *Bowdoin v. Alabama*], contracts made in violation of regulatory statutes enacted for the protection of the public have been rendered null and [void]. . . .

In turning to the statute now before us, we observe that the tenor of the Mini-Code . . . is one of consumer (public) protection. [The court then discussed 13 features of the Mini-Code, including its establishing a Consumer Protection Council; the buyer's right to cancel a home solicitation sale; creditors' liabilities for making excessive finance charges; the requirement that creditors engaging in the consumer loan business obtain a license; and the administrator's authority to investigate licensees, revoke licenses, and take other legal action against licensees.]

We can see [only] one purpose for the legislature's painstaking delineation of these requirements: the protection of the public when dealing with those who make consumer loans through the strict regulation and supervision of the creditors themselves. Section 5-19-22 is clearly regulatory in nature and not, as defendant would have us hold, merely revenue-producing. . . .

Having found, then, that the aim of both the . . . Mini-Code and § 5-19-22 is the protection of the consumer . . . we must concomitantly hold that [the criminal sanctions section] is not the exclusive source of remedies for violations of the [Mini-Code]. Indeed, as we have always held to be the law in Alabama, whenever regulation and protection are the goal of a statute, contracts [that violate it] are null, void, and unenforceable. . . .

In this context, then, we . . . hold that contracts made in violation of the requirements of the Mini-Code are null, void, and unenforceable as a matter of public policy. Further, we hold that [defendant's failure to obtain the required license] was in direct violation of § 5-19-23(a).

> **CASE 14.3**
> **Continued**
>
> **JUDGMENT** Therefore, that portion of plaintiff's indebtedness represented by the loan (as distinguished from the debt on the contract to repair) is void, including both the principal and the interest. [And] the interest charges on the voided loan cannot be added to the construction debt so as to render those charges usurious. CERTIFIED QUESTION ANSWERED. All the Justices concur.

Confession of Judgment Clauses in Promissory Notes

A person who borrows money or buys a house, car, or business on credit promises to repay the borrowed amount, and usually must sign a **promissory note** for that amount plus interest. Most note forms contain a number of clauses that specify the rights and duties of creditor and debtor. One often included is the **confession-of-judgment** clause. It is so named because, by agreeing to it, the debtor gives written permission for the creditor's attorney to go to court and "confess judgment" against the debtor for the full amount of the debt upon the debtor's failure, justified or not, to make payments as they fall due. A note containing such a clause is a **cognovit note.** If a creditor can enforce a cognovit note, the debtor is not entitled to notice of the court action, cannot raise any defenses to payment that he or she might have, and cannot appeal the judgment.

Lucia buys a flower shop from Carl and signs a cognovit note for the purchase price to be paid in monthly installments. Later, learning that Carl fraudulently overstated the accounts receivable, she withholds the next monthly payment to force Carl to lower the purchase price to reflect the true value of the business. Carl can immediately go to court and confess judgment against Lucia. Since she cannot raise her defense of fraud and cannot appeal the judgment, she is left in the uncomfortable position of having to bring an independent lawsuit to resolve the problem. In the meantime, Carl is free to execute the judgment.

Because of the misuses to which cognovit notes can be put, most states severely limit their enforcement. Many statutes declare the confession-of-judgment clause void regardless of the kind of credit transaction. Others prohibit the use of such clauses in consumer credit transactions. Still others limit their enforceability—for example, by allowing the debtor to raise certain defenses to payment despite clause language to the contrary. Only a few states permit the unrestricted use of cognovit notes, usually on the ground that they encourage the extension of credit by making debt collection easier and most creditors will not abuse them.

Agreements Involving Interference with Governmental Processes

An agreement that interferes with the orderly processes of government—federal, state, or local—is against public policy. The interference might consist of corrupting a public official (legislative, executive, or judicial) or misleading the official's judgment. The forbidden agreements commonly interfere with the legislative process or the judicial process.

Interference with the legislative process sometimes occurs through lobbying. Everyone has the right to try, by presenting facts and arguments in an open and aboveboard manner, to persuade legislators to vote for or against proposed legislation. But no one has a right to persuade public officials by bribery, threats, or other improper means. An agreement with a public official that he or she will take action in exchange for an improper inducement is illegal, and unenforceable, regardless of whether the aim is to influence the passage of a law, the content of an administrative rule or regulation, or the government's awarding a contract. Also illegal is an agreement with one's agent that he or she will procure official action by improper means.

The most common form of **interfering with the judicial process** is the bribery of a witness, juror, or judge. Bribery takes many forms: money or an interest in a business in exchange for favorable action; or even, where a judge is up for reelection, a promise to swing votes in the judge's favor for deciding a case a certain way.

An illegal interference might be indirect, as where a party to a lawsuit agrees to pay a witness a fee greater than permitted by statute. The agreement is illegal (at least where the witness is in the jurisdiction and subject to subpoena) because the payment may predispose the witness to favor the paying party rather than to speak the truth. Witness-fee statutes commonly exempt expert witnesses from the fee limitation. An agreement to pay an expert any reasonable compensation is legal, provided the agreement does not make payment contingent on the outcome of the case.

The ban against agreements interfering with the judicial process applies to criminal as well as to civil proceedings. Dan steals money from his employer and Dan's father agrees to repay the amount if the employer will not press charges against Dan. The agreement is contrary to public policy as an interference with the enforcement of the criminal law. The father's promise to pay is unenforceable, and so is the employer's promise not to press charges.

Case 14.4 involves an interference with the governmental contracting processes of a foreign country—an act of "influence peddling" contrary to the public policy of both that country and the United States.

> **BOX 14.5**
>
> **Point to Consider**
>
> Is it sound public policy to exempt expert witnesses from the fee limitation imposed on ordinary witnesses? Consider whether expert witnesses are less inclined than ordinary witnesses to slant their testimony in favor of the paying party.

CASE 14.4   **Kashfi v. Philbro-Salomon, Inc.** • 628 F.Supp. 727 (S.D.N.Y. 1986)

FACTS   Plaintiff A. M. Kashfi signed a written agreement with Lazar Beresiner, who allegedly was acting on behalf of defendant Philbro-Saloman, Inc., and its English subsidiary, Derby & Co., to arrange an oil barter agreement between Philbro and the Iranian government. The oil was to be sold and the proceeds used by the Iranian government to buy American-made military aircraft. According to Kashfi, an Iranian citizen residing in California, he set up a series of meetings between key Iranian officials and Philbro, a Delaware trading corporation that deals in oil, metals, and other commodities. Kashfi contends that in June 1976, the Shah of Iran approved the oil barter transaction, that the agreement resulted in the sale of $2.4 billion worth of Iranian oil, and that Philbro owes him $24 million, the 1 percent fee provided for in the written agreement. Kashfi brought suit for that amount. Philbro, denying that the oil barter transaction was ever executed, moved for summary judgment.

OPINION   TENNEY, D.J. . . . [Philbro] argues that the summary judgment should be granted . . . because the agreement is illegal under Iranian law and therefore is unenforceable. The Court agrees.

Summary judgment is . . . appropriate in this case because the contract sued on contravenes Iranian law and is therefore unenforceable. . . . A party to an illegal contract cannot ask a court of law to help him enforce that contract. Re-

**CASE 14.4
Continued**

lief is denied to such a plaintiff, not because the court favors the defendant, but rather because the court will not aid a party whose claim arises out of his own immoral or illegal act. . . .

The legality of a contract is ordinarily determined in accordance with the law of the place where the contract is performed. . . . In the case at bar, it is undisputed that performance was rendered in Iran. Iranian law, therefore, is controlling. . . .

In the case at bar, the Court concludes that the contract is unenforceable because it violates Iran's penal statute—the Law for the Punishment of the Use of Influence Contrary to Justice and Legal Provisions . . . (the "Influence Law"). Articles One and Two of the Influence Law essentially prohibit an individual from being paid to exercise his good standing or influence with a public official. . . . Essentially, the plaintiff is seeking to be paid for having used his personal and political contacts for the defendant's benefit, which is precisely the type of conduct that is prohibited by the Iranian Influence Law.

The plaintiff himself admits that he is seeking compensation for exercising his influence. In his amended complaint, the plaintiff states that Beresiner wanted him to "use his contacts and influence in Iran to obtain meetings with . . . key cabinet members and the Shah of Iran himself, in order to present defendant's proposals." . . . In this . . . Statement, the plaintiff declares that he was an intimate friend of Alam, the Minister of the Imperial Court, and admits . . . that Alam facilitated business for him with the government of Iran based on the personal relationship between the plaintiff and Alam. . . .

The . . . agreement . . . also contravenes the public policy of the United States. Exercising personal or political influence with government officials in order to obtain a government contract is expressly prohibited by [the federal Procurement Statute]. . . .

Obviously the . . . agreement in the instant case is not invalidated by the federal Procurement Statute, since the United States government was not involved. However[,] . . . [t]he Iranian Influence law is similar to the federal Procurement Statute, and . . . it appears that the objectives of both laws are the same. The purpose of the Procurement Statute is threefold: (1) to prevent the use of improper influence in connection with securing government contracts; (2) to eliminate arrangements which encourage inequitable and exorbitant fees that bear no reasonable relationship to the services rendered; and (3) to prevent contracts being awarded on a basis other than merit. . . . These objectives can also be ascribed to the Iranian Influence Law. In order to enforce the [agreement] in this case, the Court would essentially have to disregard these objectives.

[Court's footnote: "It is interesting to note . . . that the plaintiff is seeking . . . a fee which . . . appears to bear little relationship to the value of the services actually performed. Moreover, the plaintiff stated . . . that Alam facilitated business for him based on their friendship, [a practice] which essentially undermines the policy of awarding a contract based on merit rather than personal contacts."]

JUDGMENT

Thus, for the reasons set forth above, the Court concludes that the . . . agreement is unenforceable.

EFFECT OF ILLEGALITY

The General Rule

Ordinarily, the courts will aid neither party to an illegal agreement. If the agreement is completely executory, neither party can compel performance or have damages from the other. If the agreement is completely executed, neither party can rescind it. Moreover, where one party has performed and the other has not, the party who performed cannot recover the performance or its value, and cannot compel the other party to perform. So one wrongdoer may be unjustly enriched at the expense of the other.

Exceptions to the General Rule

A rigid application of the general rule would defeat other policies of the law and produce injustice. To prevent this, the courts recognize a number of exceptions to the rule.

Parties Not Equally at Fault. Where the parties to an illegal agreement are not equally at fault (not **in pari delicto**), the party who was less at fault will be allowed to recover any performance rendered or its value.

Courts commonly apply this principle where one was induced to enter into an illegal agreement by the fraud, duress, or undue influence of another. Ann, heavily in debt, fears that her creditors will seize all her property. Working on her fears, Ben, her lawyer, induces Ann to turn her property over to him, promising to return it when her financial troubles are over. Ben refuses to return the property, and Ann sues. Although she transferred the property to cheat her creditors, the courts will allow Ann to recover her property. Refusal to do so would reward the more blameworthy of the parties to the illegal agreement.

Withdrawal from Illegal Agreement. Where the illegal part of an illegal agreement has not yet been performed, the other party can withdraw from the transaction and recover any performance or its value. The performing party is said to have a **locus poenitentiae**—a place or opportunity for repentance.

An application of the repentance doctrine is a bettor's withdrawal from a wager in a state where bets are illegal. Suppose that each party to a wager deposits money with a stakeholder who has agreed to pay the winner of the bet. By depositing money, each party has partially performed the agreement. However, performance of the illegal part of the agreement does not occur until the money is paid to the winner. At any time before payment, either party may withdraw from the bet by giving notice of repudiation to the stakeholder. If the stakeholder ignores the notice and pays the wager, the stakeholder is liable to the party who attempted to withdraw.

Party Protected by Statute. Some statutes protect people by making a particular type of agreement illegal. For example, many statutes require corporations to disclose financial information about the company before selling its securities (stocks and bonds). To do this, a corporation must "register" new securities with federal or state authorities. When a member of the protected class—here, potential purchasers—agrees to buy unregistered securities, that person is usually entitled to some kind of relief despite the illegality of the transaction. If the statute does not specify a remedy, the court will grant an appropriate one—for example, rescission of the agreement should the purchaser want to cancel the deal. If the court refused to aid either party, the purchasers for whose benefit the statute was enacted would be unable to get their money back and would be deprived of the protection the legislature intended.

Effect of Partial Illegality

Some agreements are only partly illegal. The general rule is that the illegal part taints the whole agreement and makes it void. However, where the agreement is **divisible,** i.e., where the legal part of the agreement can be separated from the illegal part, most courts will enforce the legal part. Some agreements are clearly divisible—for example, an agreement to sell several articles at a designated price for each article. Even if one of the articles cannot legally be sold, the agreement could be enforced as to the other articles. However, if the agreement called for the sale of those same articles for one lump sum, the agreement would be indivisible and void.

Effect of Knowledge of Intended Illegal Use

Sometimes a person agrees to supply property or services, not knowing that the other party will use the thing for an unlawful purpose. The supplier can enforce the agreement, but the other party cannot. Ann agrees to rent a dock to Ben. Unknown to her, he intends to use it for smuggling goods into the country. If Ben finds another dock better suited for his purposes and refuses to pay the rent, Ann can recover damages for breach of contract; but if Ann changes her mind about renting the dock to Ben, he cannot enforce the agreement. A person seeking to accomplish an unlawful purpose may not enforce such a "facilitating contract"—that is, a contract made to enable him or her to accomplish the unlawful purpose.

SUMMARY

An agreement is illegal if it is made or performed in violation of a constitution, statute, or other declaration of public policy. An agreement contravenes public policy if it tends to harm the public.

Contracts of adhesion and exculpatory clauses may or may not contravene public policy, depending on the circumstances. Courts are reluctant to enforce agreements not to compete except for compelling reasons, but many such restraints are enforceable if properly limited. For example, an agreement by the seller of a business not to compete with the buyer usually is enforceable if it is so limited in duration and territory covered as to protect only the interest purchased. In contrast, a restriction that unreasonably deprives a person of the opportunity to engage in gainful employment will not be enforced.

Many other kinds of agreements are illegal. Among them are agreements to pay a usurious rate of interest and agreements involving interference with governmental processes. Many states prohibit the use of confession-of-judgment clauses in promissory notes.

Some classes of agreements present special problems. The law of usury must protect borrowers from overreaching lenders without unduly limiting the supply of consumer credit. A Sunday-closing law is unconstitutional if its purpose is to establish or prevent the free exercise of religion, but it may be constitutional if it has an economic or other nonreligious basis.

Ordinarily, the courts will aid neither party to an illegal agreement. However, this rule is subject to many exceptions that give effect to various policies of the law. For example, where an agreement is illegal, the party who was less at fault may be allowed to recover any performance rendered or its value. Similarly, a party protected by a statute may have a remedy despite the illegality of the transaction.

REVIEW QUESTIONS

1. In 1992, New York became the eighteenth state to ban surrogate parenting for profit. A year or two earlier, a French Supreme Court ruling banned such contracts in France. Suppose a surrogate parenting contract is challenged in a state that has not addressed the issue. Who could resolve the issue, and what public policy factors should be considered?

2. (a) Is a contract of adhesion void as against public policy? (b) Is a clause that exempts a contracting party from the payment of damages for her or his own negligence enforceable?

3. Even though there might be a justification for enforcing an agreement not to compete, the agreement will not be enforced unless the restraint it imposes is reasonable. Under what general circumstances will the restraint be held reasonable?

4. How do the Truth-in-Lending Act and the Uniform Consumer Credit Code affect agreements for the extension of credit?

5. Suppose a person is required to obtain a license before rendering services. Under what circumstances will a person who fails to obtain the required license be denied compensation for services rendered? Why?

6. Why do most states either declare confession-of-judgment clauses in promissory notes void or limit their enforceability?

7. An agreement involving interference with governmental processes is unenforceable. Give an example.

8. Give an example of a policy of the law justifying an exception to the general rule that a court will not aid either party to an illegal agreement.

CASE PROBLEMS

1. Rupert's Oil Service made numerous deliveries of fuel oil to two properties owned by Reginald Leslie. State law required fuel oil to be delivered through a meter which "shall print the gallonage reading of the meter before and after delivery is made and each ticket shall be locked in the meter between readings so as to prevent fraud." A violation of the proof-of-delivery requirement was a criminal offense, but the statute did not say whether sellers could collect for unmetered deliveries. About $6,500 worth of Leslie's delivery tickets were metered as required by law; about $5,000 worth were not. Leslie paid about $7,750 on the account, and Rupert's sued for the unpaid amount allegedly owed. Leslie contended that he should not have to pay for the unmetered deliveries. Must Leslie pay?

2. Kambiz Noghrey married Farima Human. At the hotel just before the wedding ceremony, Mr. Noghrey signed the following premarital agreement: "I, Kambiz Noghrey, agree to settle on Farima Human, the house . . . in Sunnyvale . . . and $500,000 or one-half of my assets, whichever is greater, in the event of a divorce." Seven and one-half months later, Farima filed for divorce. At trial, Farima testified that she signed the document because it is hard for an Iranian woman to remarry after a divorce. There was conflicting testimony about whether Kambiz had been coerced by the bride's parents into signing the agreement. The trial court held that the antenuptial agreement was valid. Contending that the agreement was void as against public policy, Kambiz appealed. Did the agreement violate public policy?

3. Edward Kellums worked for Roger Robert and was fired. When later applying for work with National Furniture, Kellums signed the following release: "I authorize investigation of all statements contained herein and the references listed above to give you any and all information concerning my previous employment and any pertinent information they may have, personal or otherwise, and release all parties from all liability for any damage that may result from furnishing same to you." When contacted by National, Robert made several statements about Kellums which, if not true, would clearly have been slanderous. Alleging that the statements were false, Kellums sued Robert for slander. The trial court entered a summary judgment for Robert, apparently on the ground that the release Kellum signed barred his claim. Did the release bar Kellums' claim?

4. Maura Wiscomb was seriously injured in a collision between the motorcycle she was operating and an automobile driven by her husband. She sued him in negligence. He turned the matter over to his insurance company (Mutual), which provided liability and uninsured motorist coverage for both Wiscomb vehicles. Seeking a declaratory judgment, Mutual denied liability, citing a family or household exclusion clause contained in the insurance policy: "Exclusions: This policy does not apply . . . (1) to bodily injury to the insured or any member of the family of the insured residing in the same household as the insured." The Financial Responsibility Act of the state of Washington requires drivers to demonstrate financial responsibility by filing a certificate of insurance, posting a bond, or depositing $60,000 worth of securities with the state. Few, if any, Washington insurance companies offered policies without the exclusion clause. The trial court held that Mutual was not liable. The court of appeals reversed, holding the clause void as against public policy. Mutual appealed to the Washington Supreme Court. Should the clause be enforced?

5. Wilcom operated a "drag strip" where, for a fee, persons could engage in automobile timing and acceleration runs. Winterstein entered a race but was required to sign a document purporting to release Wilcom from liability for any injuries Winterstein might suffer while racing. Near the end of his run, his car hit a 100-pound cylinder head lying on the track. Winterstein sustained permanent injuries. The cylinder head was not visible to him when he commenced the race, but it was visible to Wilcom's employees who were stationed in a tower to watch for any hazards on the track. Alleging that Wilcom's employees were negligent and that the release was unenforceable, Winterstein sued Wilcom for damages. Was Winterstein entitled to damages?

6. Robins & Weill, Inc., an insurance agency engaged in the general insurance business, employed Mason and Hill to sell commercial insurance and to service the accounts. Both men signed employment contracts containing a covenant not to compete with Robins & Weill in the general insurance business for 3 years in Guilford County, where Robins & Weill did business. Several years later, Mason and Hill opened their own general insurance business, competing with Robins & Weill in Guilford County. Upon leaving Robins & Weill, Hill took with him a copy of its customer list. To enforce the covenant not to compete, Robins & Weill sought an injunction against Mason and Hill. The trial court granted a preliminary injunction against Mason and Hill. They appealed, and the court of appeals upheld the injunction to the extent that it prevented defendants from selling commercial property and casualty insurance, but stayed it to the extent that it forbade defendants from selling other lines of general insurance. Should the court of appeals have upheld the preliminary injunction in its entirety?

7. Columbia Construction Co. hired Rapp Contracting Co. to install a water system in a townhouse complex being built for Highpoint Townhouses, Inc. Rapp completed the work and filed a mechanic's lien on the townhouse property. Highpoint did not pay, and Rapp sued to enforce the lien. Highpoint contended that the contract, and therefore the mechanic's lien, was unenforceable under a statute making it "unlawful for any person to engage in the work of plumbing . . . in the District of Columbia unless he is licensed [as] or is an employee of a licensed master plumber." The statute also provided that plumbing done by an unlicensed employee of a licensed master plumber "shall be done under the immediate personal supervision of the licensed man." Rapp admitted lacking a master plumber's license, but argued that Columbia had contracted with Federline, a master plumber, to acquire the permit required to tap into District water mains. According to Rapp, "we [did the installation] under their permit," but "I had no contact with the master plumber at all on the job, with regards to that permit." However, Rapp did do the work under the scrutiny of a District of Columbia inspector. The trial court ordered enforcement of the lien, and Highpoint appealed. Was the trial court correct in enforcing the lien?

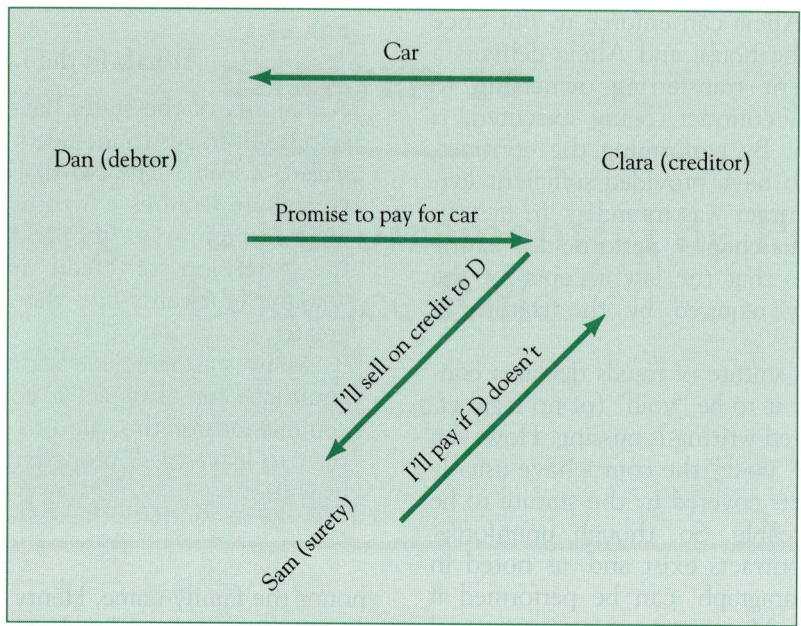

Figure 15.1 Suretyship relationship.

have to pay even if Dan refuses to do so for no good reason. The writing requirement protects people (family or friends) who may be under social pressure to take on heavy obligations without considering the risks, and usually without receiving payment. But the writing requirement applies also to commercial suretyship transactions. An oral promise by a fidelity (bonding) company given to an employer to make good any embezzlement of company funds by an employee is not enforceable, nor (usually) is the oral promise of the president of a corporation to pay a supplier if the corporation doesn't.

Frequently, though, people promise to pay someone else's debt because they will themselves receive a substantial benefit. Because such promises are beneficial to the people making them, the courts have created an exception to the suretyship provision of the statute, called the **main-purpose** or **leading-object** rule: When the surety's main purpose is to obtain some personal pecuniary or business advantage, the promise is "not within" (is not covered by) the statute, and the surety's promise is therefore enforceable even though oral. Dan contracts to build a house for Sue, who has already contracted to resell it. Dan then contracts to buy the building materials from Cora, but gets into financial trouble and fails to pay for some of the materials furnished. Cora refuses to deliver any more materials until she receives payment for those already delivered. Sue, fearing that a delay may cause her to default on her contract to sell the house, orally promises to pay Cora for any materials furnished if Dan does not pay for them. Sue's oral promise is enforceable because her main purpose in making it was to get the house built on schedule for her own benefit.

Case 15.1 illustrates the application of the main-purpose rule to a major investor in a corporation.

CASE 15.1   Graybar Electric Co. v. Sawyer • 485 A.2d 1384 (Me. 1985)

FACTS   For several years, Pine Tree Electric Co., an electrical contractor, bought equipment and supplies on credit from Graybar Electric Co. (plaintiff). When Pine Tree failed to pay its bills on time, Graybar cut off its credit. An owner of Pine Tree sought financial help from an employee who approached Sawyer, his father-in-law, about financing his contribution. Sawyer (defendant) invested $100,000 in the company himself and later lent Pine Tree an additional $300,000.

After investing, Sawyer required Pine Tree to hire a comptroller. In a reorganization of the company, Sawyer became the sole preferred stockholder with all the voting power and elected himself vice president. In July 1980, Sawyer met with Graybar representatives, and Graybar reopened Pine Tree's credit account. When Pine Tree made no payment on its account in August and September, Graybar placed a hold on Pine Tree's pending orders, including a $30,000 telephone switch that Pine Tree was to install in Lewiston for the New England Telephone Company. At a second meeting called to straighten out the credit problem, Sawyer allegedly told Graybar representatives that if Pine Tree did not pay its account, he would arrange to have it paid. Graybar again reopened Pine Tree's line of credit and delivered the telephone switch to Pine Tree. Pine Tree never paid for it and went into bankruptcy. Contending that Sawyer had orally promised to pay the Pine Tree account if Pine Tree did not, Graybar sued Sawyer for the price of the switch. From a judgment for Graybar, Sawyer appealed.

OPINION   McKUSICK, C. J. . . . [The Maine Statute of Frauds] provides that "no action shall be maintained in any of the following cases: . . . to charge any person upon special promise to answer for the debt, default, or misdoings of another . . . unless the promise, contract or agreement . . . is in writing and signed by the party to be charged therewith." This traditional component of the Statute of Frauds has, however, long been subject to an exception in a case where the promisor's main purpose in making his [oral] promise is to secure some benefit for himself. . . .

[R]ecent formulations of the rule [are based on] the idea that the promise, though collateral, is enforceable because the promisor does not need the protection against his own generous impulses afforded by the Statute of Frauds. *Restatement (Second) of Contracts* § 116 (1981). Where a surety's main objective is to serve his own pecuniary or business advantage, the gratuitous element of the suretyship is eliminated, the likelihood of disproportion in the values exchanged is reduced, and the context of commercial dealings provides evidentiary safeguards. . . .

Both the common law rule and the *Restatement* formulation focus on whether the evidence adduced at trial justifies the conclusion that the promisor's main purpose was to advance his own interests. The benefit that a promisor must expect to receive under the main purpose rule in order to be held to his [oral] promise must be substantial, immediate, and pecuniary, though it may flow to the promisor through benefit to the principal obligor. . . . The jury instruction in the present case gave a thoroughly adequate statement of the law on the main purpose rule. . . .

CASE 15.1 Continued

The evidence before the jury amply supports its finding . . . that Sawyer intended by his promise to procure an immediate and substantial benefit flowing directly to himself. Sawyer had outstanding loans to Pine Tree of almost $300,000. He admitted in testimony that he needed to keep the business going in order to be paid back. The activities he undertook to get the business back on its feet financially were extensive. He followed [up on] his initial loan of $100,000 by lending Pine Tree further large sums of money with the obvious purpose of keeping jobs going. He structured the loan transactions to give himself, as the sole voting stockholder, all of the authority formerly held by the board of directors. He reserved to himself the control of Pine Tree's borrowing. He guaranteed letters of credit necessary for Pine Tree to obtain two other jobs. . . . He received interest on his loans to Pine Tree through the fall and winter of 1980 and the spring of 1981. He also received $18,000 . . . in partial repayment of the principal amount of the loans. He testified at length about his desire to increase Pine Tree's profitability so that he could be paid back. . . . In view of the necessity of maintaining the flow of supplies to Pine Tree in order to keep the business going, and the necessity of its staying in business if Sawyer was to be repaid, the jury could reasonably find that Sawyer's oral promise, given to avoid serious difficulties for Pine Tree, was intended to confer on him a direct and substantial benefit. . . .

The facts of the present case resemble closely those of the cited Maine cases and are well within the purview of the rule as contemplated in the *Restatement*. In the *Maine Candy* case, for example, the promisor gave an oral promise of payment of past debts to keep the business going so that he could recover his own investment. . . . Comparison of the present case with those authorities demonstrates that it falls within the accepted ambit of the main-purpose doctrine. . . .

JUDGMENT Judgment affirmed.

Contract upon Consideration of Marriage. The marriage provision in the statute of frauds applies to contracts or promises "in consideration of marriage." Usually the bargain involves a promise to give money or property in exchange for a marriage or a promise of marriage. Such bargains, known as property settlements, often are used as estate-planning devices by people with established families who wish, upon remarriage, to protect the interests of existing heirs. But prenuptial agreements and other property settlements are not enforceable unless in writing. Phil tells Miriam, "If you will marry me, I'll transfer to you my 5,000 shares of IBM stock." Phil's promise must be in writing to be enforceable. The same is true where Phil's father promises to give Miriam a house if she will marry Phil.

The marriage provision does not apply to mutual promises to marry. As stated in *Withers v. Richardson*, an 1844 Kentucky case, "It would be imputing to the legislature too great an absurdity to suppose that they had enacted that all our courtships, to be valid, must be in writing." Thus, in many states an exchange of oral promises to marry can create an enforceable contract. But sometimes people have falsely alleged the existence of such a contract in an attempt to extort payments of money or to embarrass a former lover, and there have been sensational "breach-of-promise" trials. To curb such abuses, some states have statutes providing that the breach of a promise to marry (in a situation involving merely mutual promises to marry) does not give rise to a cause of action.

Contract for Sale of Goods. Article 2 of the Uniform Commercial Code governs the sale of goods. Article 2 has its own statute of frauds, UCC § 2-201. Under that section, a contract for the sale of goods for a price of $500 or more is not enforceable unless the party against whom enforcement is sought has signed "some writing sufficient to indicate that a contract for sale has been made between the parties." This basic rule has a number of exceptions that are discussed in Chapter 18. For example, under the circumstances spelled out in § 2-201, a contract between merchants for goods worth more than $500 may be enforceable even though oral. Reasons for such exceptions are discussed later in this chapter.

Contract for Sale of Interest in Land. Under the statute of frauds, a contract for the sale of an interest in land must be in writing to be enforceable. Such interests (discussed in Chapter 25) include contracts to sell or buy land; leases of land (unless the lease is within a statutory exception for short-term leases); real estate mortgages; and express easements (e.g., a right-of-way over land, granted by the owner to a utility company or to an adjoining landowner).

Statutes in most states exempt short-term leases from the land contract provisions of the statute of frauds. A lease is usually called "short term" if it is for a term of a year or less. In most states an oral lease for a 1-year term is enforceable without regard to when the term is to begin.

Contracts for the sale of *oil, gas, or other minerals* still in the ground at the time of contracting are contracts for the sale of goods (and are subject to the UCC statute of frauds) if the seller (landowner) is to "sever" the mineral from the land. If the buyer is to enter the seller's land and do the severing or extracting, the contract is one "affecting land" (is similar to a lease) and must conform to any statute-of-frauds provision pertaining to the sale of an interest in land. However, *growing crops* or other things attached to realty and capable of severance without material harm to the land are defined in the UCC as *goods,* regardless of whether the buyer or the seller is to do the severing. Thus, contracts for growing crops and for buildings or equipment to be salvaged are subject to the UCC statute of frauds and its $500 rule.

The writing required to evidence a contract for the sale of land should not be confused with the writing (called a **deed**) commonly used for actually transferring ownership and having the transfer recorded in the public land records. A deed is a document signed by a **grantor** conveying (transferring) an interest in realty, and may be used to make either a sale or a gift to the **grantee.** The writing required by the statute of frauds merely evidences an intention to contract. Usually it is not adequate as evidence of a transfer of ownership.

Case 15.2 discusses an important question: Whether granting plaintiff's claim in *quantum meruit* would inappropriately circumvent the land contract provision of the statute of frauds.

CASE 15.2   **Peters v. Morse** • 466 N.Y.S.2d 506 (App. Div. 1983)

FACTS   Peters, a licensed practical nurse, began caring for Lyle and Harriet Nelson, an elderly couple, on October 10, 1976. She visited the Nelson home each day to attend to their medical needs and to do normal household chores. After Mrs. Nelson died in July 1977, Peters continued to perform the same services for Mr. Nelson until his death on August 31, 1979. During his final illness, Peters moved into the Nelson residence to provide continuous care for him. Peters was never paid for her services but relied upon the Nelsons' repeated oral promises that

**CASE 15.2
Continued**

they would convey their farm to her upon their deaths. In a will, executed just before his death, Lyle Nelson left Peters nothing. She then brought suit against the executor of Mr. Nelson's estate, seeking recovery in *quantum meruit* for the reasonable value of her services and, in a second cause of action, enforcement of an oral agreement by the Nelsons to devise (will) the farm to her. The trial court dismissed the complaint in its entirety, holding that the contract cause of action was barred by a statute-of-frauds provision requiring a contract to make testamentary disposition to be in writing. The court refused to allow the *quantum meruit* claim on the ground that allowing it would also violate the statute of frauds. Peters appealed.

OPINION

KANE, J.P. . . . During appellate argument, plaintiff conceded that the contract cause of action had been properly dismissed, leaving for resolution only the *quantum meruit* ruling.

The fact that an express contract is unenforceable because of its failure to comply with the Statute of Frauds does not mean that quasi-contractual recovery for the reasonable value of services rendered is, therefore, necessarily unavailable. . . . Indeed, the right to recover [in quasi contract] has long been recognized in the specific circumstances presented, namely, when there has been an oral contract to make a bequest, and there is nothing in either [the statute of frauds or a cited case] which alters this durable rule. Special Term's fear of undermining the requirement that a contract to make a testamentary disposition be in writing is unfounded because the recovery afforded persons like plaintiff is limited to the reasonable value of services they performed; the consideration which would have been forthcoming had the terms of the oral agreement been enforced is irrelevant unless it can be helpful in determining the reasonable value of the services provided. That this distinction is real is evidenced by the fact that plaintiff can receive only the value of her services and not the property promised by decedents.

[In the Dombrowski case], *quantum meruit* was inappropriate because of the intimate relationship between the plaintiff and decedent, the compensation the plaintiff received from decedent during the latter's lifetime, and the complete absence of proof of the reasonable value of the plaintiff's services. In contrast, plaintiff in the instant case performed important services which are well documented; her relationship with the Nelsons was not one which would suggest that she aided them without expectation of pay, and she presented a bill for her services during Mr. Nelson's lifetime. . . .

JUDGMENT

. . . [J]udgment modified . . . by reversing the dismissal of plaintiff's first cause of action for the reasonable value of her services. . . .

Contract Not Performable within a Year. Long-term contracts (those not to be performed within a year of their making) must be in writing to be enforced. However, because courts prefer to enforce oral contracts that serve a useful social purpose, they have tended to interpret the class of long-term contracts narrowly and, consequently, to enforce a variety of oral contracts that seem long term but commonly are held to be short term.

To accomplish this, most courts interpret "*not to be performed within a year*" as "*cannot* be performed within a year." If performance of the contract could conceivably occur within 1 year, the contract is not covered by the statute and need not be evidenced by a writing. Annette contracts to support Ben for the rest of his life. Since the contract could conceivably be performed within a year because Ben might die at any time, the contract is enforceable even though oral. In contrast, a contract to support Ben for the next 4 years could not possibly be performed in less than a year, and it is not enforceable unless evidenced by a writing.

Oral contracts may be *terminable* at any time for a variety of reasons such as the death or the bankruptcy of one of the parties, even though performance would require more than a year. In deciding whether such a contract is long term or short term, most courts look at what is required for *performance*. Bart orally agrees to work for Simon for a term of 2 years, and each has a right to terminate the contract upon giving 30 days' notice. A termination within a year is possible, but not a performance, which requires 2 years. Under the majority view, the contract is long term and must be in writing to be enforced.

The critical 1-year period begins to run at the time of the *making* of the contract. But the time at which the law considers a contract to be made can differ from the time the contracting parties might have had in mind. On December 31, Art orally agrees to work for Beth for "a year," with work beginning the next day and ending the following December 31. Actually, the year's work will end a few hours *more* than a year from the making of the contract, so technically the contract should be in writing to be enforced. However, most courts apply the rule that the law disregards fractions of a day. Thus, through a legal fiction (here, a judicial pretense that the contract was made on January 1 and therefore will be performed *within* a year), the contract is considered short term and enforceable though oral.

Suppose, instead, that Art and Beth's oral contract is for a term of 9 months, that it is signed on January 1, and that performance is to begin on June 1 of the same year. This is a *long-term* contract (for which a writing is required), because performance cannot be completed until a year and 3 months after the January 1 making of the contract. (Recall, however, that an oral *lease* for a year *is* enforceable in most states even if the term of the lease is to begin sometime after the lease agreement was made.)

"Performed within a year" means fully performed within the year. Consequently, if either party to a contract promises a performance that cannot be fully completed within a year, all the promises in the contract are within the statute and must be evidenced by a writing. "But unlike other provisions of the Statute, the one-year provision does not apply to a contract which is performed on one side at the time [the contract] is made."[2] Thus, if Ben borrows $15,000 from Annette, and Ben orally promises to repay the loan in three semiannual payments of $5,000 each, Annette can enforce the contract against Ben, because by making the loan Annette completely performed her part of the bargain when the contract was made.

Where one of the parties to an oral long-term contract later completes his or her performance, the statute does not prevent enforcement of the other party's promise.[3] Most courts hold that full performance by the one party makes the contract enforceable against the other.

Case 15.3 involves an oral employment contract. The court goes beyond the statute-of-frauds issue to discuss the nature and varieties of "permanent" employment contracts, a subject of much confusion and concern.

[2]*Restatement (Second) of the Law of Contracts* (1981), Sec. 130, comment *d*.
[3]Ibid., Sec. 130(2).

| CASE 15.3 | **Eklund v. Vincent Brass & Aluminum Co.**
● 351 N.W.2d 371 (Minn. App. 1984) |

FACTS In 1977, Paul Vincent, president of defendant Vincent Brass & Aluminum Co., hired Clyde Eklund (plaintiff) as vice president of sales on the understanding that the position was permanent, as long as Eklund performed satisfactorily. The employment agreement was oral. In accepting Vincent's offer, Eklund, then a 47-year-old general sales manager for U.S. Steel Supply Corp., gave up a 26-year career with that company.

According to Mr. Vincent, Eklund understood his job, worked very hard, and developed sales and administrative programs that increased sales. Eklund received pay raises and bonuses. In 1980, Vincent retired, recommending Eklund, Mike White, and Norman Smith as potential successors. Smith was chosen to succeed Vincent as vice president and general manager of Vincent Brass.

Smith soon fired Eklund without warning or explanation, and a few months later fired White. Sales decreased after Eklund's termination. Eklund immediately sought comparable employment, but in 1983 accepted a job at less than two-thirds of his compensation at Vincent Brass. Eklund sued Vincent Brass for wrongful termination of the oral employment agreement. The trial court dismissed Eklund's claim for breach of contract, holding that (1) there was no written contract complying with the statute of frauds, and (2) an employment contract of indefinite duration is terminable at will. Eklund appealed.

OPINION FOLEY, J. . . . [The Minnesota statute of frauds states]: "No action shall be maintained, in either of the following cases, upon any agreement, unless such agreement, or some note or memorandum thereof, expressing the consideration, is in writing, and subscribed by the party charged therewith: (1) Every agreement that by its terms is not to be performed within one year [from] the making thereof. . . ."

"The test is simply whether the contract by its terms is capable of full performance within a year, not whether such occurrence is likely." . . .

The trial court [erroneously] relied on *Roaderick v. Lull Engineering* . . . in holding that Eklund's alleged contract for permanent employment until retirement was not enforceable because it could not be performed within one year. . . . In *Roaderick*, the employee's alleged oral contract called for a *minimum* of two years' employment. [Therefore the contract] literally could not be performed in less than one year . . . [and its enforcement] was barred by the statute of frauds.

In [*Bussard v. College of St. Thomas*, however,] the employee's alleged oral contract for permanent employment had no minimum term but was to last so long as the employee wished. This contract could be fully performed within a year[;] therefore the court held: "The statute of frauds is clearly not an impediment to plaintiff's proof of an oral agreement. A contract of permanent employment is 'performable within a year' because of the possibility of death within a year. Numerous cases . . . so hold." . . .

Here, Eklund's alleged contract for permanent employment until retirement, so long as he performed satisfactorily, could have been fully performed within one year under any of the following circumstances: (1) Eklund's death, (2) Eklund['s voluntary departure], or (3) Eklund['s failure] to perform satisfactorily.

**CASE 15.3
Continued**

The trial court erred in granting Vincent Brass summary judgment on the basis that the statute of frauds barred proof of Eklund's oral contract of employment.

The trial court [also] held that even if Eklund could prove a contract for permanent employment, such an indefinite contract is terminable at the will of either party under the rule of *Skagerberg v. Blandin Paper Co.*, . . . and *Cederstrand v. Lutheran Brotherhood*. . . .

Although generally an assertion of a permanent employment contract is interpreted as employment at-will, all the evidence must be evaluated, including the intentions of the parties, to determine whether the contract was in fact indefinite as to duration [i.e., for "permanent" employment].

If a jury determines [that] the parties intended an indefinite contract, Eklund may still overcome the presumption that his contract is terminable at-will. The "at-will rule" . . . is only a rule of construction—not one of substantive law. *Pine River State Bank v. Mettille*. . . . The Minnesota Supreme Court explains: ". . . The cases which reason that the at-will rule takes precedence over even explicit job termination restraints, simply because the contract is of indefinite duration, misapply the at-will rule. . . ."

In *Cederstrand*, the Minnesota Supreme Court recognized that an employee may prove he was to be "dismissed only for cause by proving a contract to that effect." . . .

[In *Pine River*, the court stated], ". . . The [parties may agree] that the employment will not be terminable by the employer except pursuant to their agreement, even though no consideration other than services to be performed is expected by the employer or promised by the employee." . . .

The trial court erred in granting Vincent Brass summary judgment on this claim for breach of contract. Eklund produced evidence which indicates his alleged contract may be enforceable despite the general presumption that an alleged permanent employment contract is not enforceable. At trial Eklund should be given an opportunity to prove [that his contract] included a job security provision, limiting his dismissal to unsatisfactory performance.

JUDGMENT Affirmed in part, reversed in part and remanded.

Requirements Regarding the Writing

The primary purpose of a statute of frauds is to require reliable evidence that an alleged contract was indeed entered into. To accomplish this purpose, the English statute relied mainly on a requirement that "the agreement . . . or some memorandum or note thereof, shall be in writing, and signed by the person to be charged" with breach of contract. Most states have adopted the same or similar wording. Certain questions arise regarding the statutory requirements:

1 What content must the memorandum have?
2 What form may it take?
3 What is a "signature," who must do the signing, and where may the signature be placed?
4 When may the memorandum be made and signed?

Content. To be sufficient evidence of a contract, the memorandum ordinarily must:

- Identify with reasonable certainty the subject matter of the contract and the parties to it

- Sufficiently indicate that a contract with respect to that subject matter has been made between the parties
- State with reasonable certainty the essential terms of the unperformed promises in the contract

The subject matter and the parties do not have to be identified with precision—only with reasonable certainty. For example, a memorandum describing the subject matter of a contract as "my lot on the corner of Grant Street and Fourth Avenue in the County of X, State of Y" is sufficiently definite if the seller owns only one of the four lots on the intersection of Grant Street and Fourth Avenue. Similarly, a party may be identified by name or initials, even though there may be other persons with the same name or initials. Where there is no dispute as to the parties, a person may be sufficiently identified as a party to the contract by simply possessing a memorandum signed by the other party.

Form. No particular form is required for the memorandum. It may be in the form of a letter, a receipt, an order blank, an invoice, a check, an entry in an account book, or an entry in a diary. It may consist of several writings if one of the writings is signed and the writings in the circumstances clearly indicate that they all relate to the same transaction.

Signature. The signature may consist of any symbol made or adopted with an intention to authenticate the writing as that of the signer—name, initials, rubber stamp, and so on. Most statutes of frauds state that the memorandum must be "signed by the party to be charged," meaning the party to be charged with breach of contract in any subsequent legal proceeding. Signatures need not appear at any particular place on the memorandum unless the statute provides otherwise.

Time. The memorandum does not have to be created at the time of contracting. Some courts consider it timely if it is made and signed before suit is instituted. Others permit it to be made or signed any time before or after contract formation.

> **BOX 15.2**
>
> ### You Be the Judge
>
> According to witnesses, Alfred Doran, the operator of a newspaper stand, orally agreed to sell his interest in it to R. Shaeffer, Jr., for $1,000, with the transfer to take place on September 1, 1977. In early August, Mr. Doran committed suicide, leaving the following note:
>
> > Relative to newsstand R. Shaeffer Jr. was to buy same for $1,000 it is a steal at price but he is great boy and deserves it carry this out. . . . (Signed) Al.
>
> Alleging a violation of the statute of frauds, the administrator of the Doran estate refused to transfer the newsstand to Shaeffer. Under the New York statute of frauds, the contract involved here had to be in writing to be enforced. Was the suicide note sufficient for enforcing the contract?

Alternatives to the Writing

Sometimes a person knows about the statute-of-frauds writing requirement, but enters into an oral agreement intending later to use his or her own lack of compliance with the statute as a means of avoiding contractual liability. For example, Melissa might orally contract to sell her house on credit, intending to collect a few monthly payments before using the lack of a writing as an excuse for repudiating the contract. Thus, the statute itself can be used as an instrument of fraud against persons ignorant of the writing requirement or too lacking in bargaining power to compel a writing. More frequently, neither contracting party knows of the requirement, or the parties find compliance with it inconvenient. To prevent the injustice that can arise from refusal to enforce an oral contract covered by the statute of frauds, the legislatures and the courts have developed substitutes for the normally required writing.

Legislatively Developed Alternatives. Under the Uniform Commercial Code, a writing is only one of several ways to evidence a contract for the sale of goods. Other ways include part performance of an oral sales contract, admitting in court to an oral sales contract, and failure by a nonsigning merchant to respond to certain kinds of written communications. Often, these alternative kinds of evidence are just as reliable as a writing would be in revealing contractual intent. UCC § 2-201, the statute of frauds applicable to sales of goods, is discussed further in Chapter 18.

BOX 15.3

Modern Technology and the Statute of Frauds

Sometimes statutory language is broad enough to encompass modern alternatives to the traditional writing. One court held that a tape recording of an oral agreement for the sale of corporate securities (e.g., stocks and bonds) complied with the writing requirement of UCC § 8-319, the applicable statute of frauds. Noting that under the UCC the term "writing" includes "printing, typewriting, or any other intentional reduction to tangible form," the court held that the tape recording, agreed to by both parties, was a reduction of the oral contract to tangible form. There was no need for a signature here, the court added, because the identity of the oral contractors had been clearly established by other means. The purpose of the statute of frauds—preventing fraud and perjury by use of evidence more reliable than the unassisted memory of witnesses—had been accomplished by an alternative to the usual writing. *Ellis Canning Co. v. Bernstein,* 348 F. Supp. 1212 (D. Colo. 1972). ∎

Judicially Developed Alternatives. Two judicially developed doctrines—**equitable estoppel** and **promissory estoppel**—provide ways of preventing injustice from the misuse of the writing requirement.

Equitable estoppel. Courts have long held that if one party to a contract has misrepresented (or has concealed) a material fact and the other party has relied on the misrepresentation to his or her detriment, the party who made the misrepresentation is "estopped" (prohibited) from denying the asserted fact.[4] Chuck tells Alice, "I have signed a memorandum of our oral agreement and have just mailed it to you," when in fact he has not done so. If Alice substantially changes her position in reliance on Chuck's statement and later sues him for breach of the oral contract, he probably will be estopped from setting up the defense of the statute of frauds.

Promissory estoppel. Within recent years, promissory estoppel has been widely used to enforce oral contracts that otherwise would be unenforceable for failure to comply with the statute of frauds.[5] For promissory estoppel to be used this way, its usual elements must be present—a promise, justifiable reliance by the promisee, harm, and so on. But courts are reluctant to substitute promissory estoppel for the statute-of-frauds requirement unless the situation really "cries out" for that action. So enforcement of the oral contract must be necessary to avoid injustice. In evaluating the degree of injustice, the courts consider several factors. A key one is the extent to which the promisee's conduct reveals that a contract was actually made. However, the courts in a shrinking minority of states refuse to substitute promissory estoppel for the required writing, on the ground that to do so would undermine the statute of frauds.

A forerunner of promissory estoppel, the judicial **doctrine of part performance,** is applied mainly to oral land contracts. Courts of equity

---

[4]John E. Murray, Murray on Contracts (1974), Sec. 333. See also Cal. Civ. Code, Sec. 163: "Where a contract which is required to be in writing is prevented from being put into writing by the fraud of a party thereto, any other party who is by such fraud led to believe that it is in writing, and acts upon such belief to his prejudice, may enforce it against the fraudulent party."

[5]John D. Calamari and Joseph M. Perillo, The Law of Contracts (1987), Sec. 19-48. *Restatement (Second) Contracts,* Sec. 139. Note that this section applies to *contracts* that violate the statute of frauds, as well as to promises not supported by consideration.

have long held that an oral contract for the sale of land will be specifically enforced when the contract has been partly performed *if* the purchaser takes action which is "unequivocally referable to the oral agreement" (makes clear that a *sale* of land was intended) and has reasonably relied on the agreement to his or her substantial detriment. As is discussed in Case 15.4, for an oral land contract to be enforceable, possession of the land must be transferred to the purchaser *and*, usually, either of the following must occur: (1) payment of all or a substantial portion of the purchase price or (2) the making of valuable improvements upon the land by the purchaser.[6]

[6]*Restatement (Second), Contracts*, Sec. 129.

CASE 15.4   **Powers v. Hastings** • 612 P.2d 371 (Wash. 1980)

FACTS   Plaintiffs Dorothy and Clarence Powers wanted to buy a farm owned by defendants Robert and Hazel Hastings. When they could not secure financing, the Hastingses orally agreed to lease them the farm for 3 years with an option to purchase any time before July 1, 1976. To make the property operable as a dairy farm, the Powerses repaired and improved it. They also moved their dairy herd onto the farm and increased its size from 75 to 95 cows. Milk prices dropped. The Powerses stopped making payments in October 1974 and attempted but failed to obtain financing to buy the property. The Hastingses denied the option's existence, disputed the terms of sale, evicted the Powerses, and sold the farm to a third party in March 1975. The Powerses sued the Hastingses for breach of contract and obtained a jury verdict for $40,000. The judge set aside the verdict and dismissed the complaint. The Powerses appealed. The court of appeals reversed the trial court, and the Hastingses appealed.

OPINION   WRIGHT, J. . . . The trial judge [found the lease-option agreement] unenforceable under the statute of frauds. He further concluded there was not any part performance to take the agreement outside the statute because (1) the payment of rentals and the possession point unmistakably to the lease rather than the option, and (2) the improvements do not unequivocally . . . point to the option.

. . . As [one] ground for reversal, the [court of appeals] concluded there was substantial evidence before the jury of part performance, including the Powerses' possession, substantial improvements and payments "far in excess of a reasonable monthly rental value for the farm." . . .

. . . [S]ubstantial evidence of the terms, character and existence of the agreement, and of part performance supports the jury's verdict and makes judgment notwithstanding that verdict erroneous. . . .

An affidavit signed by Robert Hastings and admitted into evidence (1) acknowledges he entered an agreement with Clarence Powers providing that the farm would be leased for 3 years, beginning July 1, 1973, with an option to purchase exercisable any time before July 1, 1976; (2) specifies payment amounts ($1,000 per month for the first year and $1,500 per month for the next two years), the purchase price ($185,000) and the amount of the monthly installment payments (at least $1,300 "or something close to that"); [and] (3) states the Powerses assumed the property taxes and insurance premiums beginning July 1, 1973. Hastings repeatedly confirmed these terms while testifying [as did] Hazel

CASE 15.4 Continued

Hastings and Clarence and Dorothy Powers. In addition, Clarence Powers and Robert and Hazel Hastings testified that the interest rate on the deferred balance would fluctuate with the Land Bank rate. . . .

The evidence leaves no doubt as to the relationship intended by the parties in their oral agreement. . . . [T]he parties here clearly contemplated an option in the Powerses to purchase the Hastings farm. . . .

The elements involved in determining if there is sufficient part performance to "remove" an oral contract for the sale or lease of real property from the operation of the statute of frauds are: (1) delivery and assumption of actual and exclusive possession; (2) payment or tender of consideration; and (3) the making of permanent, substantial and valuable improvements, referable to the contract. . . . [A]ll three elements appear to be present in the instant case. . . .

First, the Powerses unquestionably had actual, exclusive possession of the farm pursuant to the agreement. Furthermore, $1,000 per month was paid during the first year of the lease and the payments increased to $1,500 per month July 1, 1974. One $1,500 [payment] and one $800 partial payment were made before monthly payments ceased. There is evidence [that] these payments were consideration for the option: [Clarence Powers so testified. In the second year the annual return to Hastings] would total $18,000 or nearly 10 per cent of the agreed purchase price. That return was on a farm that needed substantial repairs and required a dairy herd. Moreover, the payments substantially exceeded the $750 payments the Hastingses were making on the property to the Land Bank. The parties agreed the Powerses would pay taxes and insurance and they actually made three insurance payments. The jury could have concluded rightly that these "rent" and insurance payments indicated an optionee's interest.

Finally, the Powerses made substantial improvements, expending more than $5,000, excluding their own considerable labor, on improvements worth $14,520. . . . One acquaintance of the Powerses worked 3 months on the projects and other labor was necessary, as well. Although some of the improvements were required by the milk inspector, many were initiated by the Powerses.

Robert Hastings twice admitted . . . that had the buildings, milking parlor and shed been in as good shape when they entered into the lease-option as they were after the repairs, the owners initially would have asked $220,000 for the farm instead of the $185,000 they unquestionably agreed on with the Powerses. Furthermore, the farm sold for $225,000. There clearly was sufficient evidence to show [that] these improvements were permanent, substantial and valuable. . . .

. . . [P]etitioners state the payments here do not point to existence of an option agreement, but instead are attributable to the rental agreement. . . . [H]owever, the . . . payments were made pursuant to a single lease-option agreement. . . . Moreover, the substantial rate of return during the second year of the agreement—when considered in light of the farm's [poor] condition and the Powers' obligation to furnish the dairy herd—supports the jury's apparent conclusion [that] the Powerses were paying for more than a bare lease. . . .

Although the strongest case for part performance is presented where all three part performance elements—possession, payments and improvements—are present, this court repeatedly has found sufficient part performance where two ele-

CASE 15.4 Continued	ments exist. . . . At least two elements are present in the instant case as well, including substantial and valuable improvements. . . .
JUDGMENT	Because there is sufficient evidence to persuade a fair-minded person of the existence, character and terms of the contract and of part performance, the purpose of the statute of frauds—prevention of fraud arising from uncertainty inherent in oral contracts—would not be served by its application in the instant case. For the reasons stated, the judgment of the Court of Appeals, which reversed the trial court's judgment, is affirmed. The cause is remanded and the trial court is instructed to enter judgment based upon the verdict, with interest, in favor of the Powerses.

Modification or Rescission of Contracts Covered by the Statute

Modification of Contract. If a contract is modified by a subsequent agreement and the contract as modified is within the statute of frauds, the requirements of the statute must be satisfied. Wilma orally contracts to employ Jennifer for a term of 6 months beginning the first of the next month. On the first of that month, on the recommendation of Jennifer's former employer, Wilma agrees to employ Jennifer for 18 months. The oral agreement as modified exceeds 1 year and must be in writing to be enforceable.

Rescission of Contract. Suppose the parties to an executory contract (such as a written employment contract for a term exceeding 1 year) wish to rescind (cancel) it orally. Usually they may do so. This is true, also, of executory contracts for the sale of land. However, where land has been *transferred* by an effective deed, an agreement to rescind the transaction is a contract for the transfer of an interest in land and is required by the statute of frauds to be in writing to be enforced.

EFFECT OF ADOPTING A WRITING: PAROL EVIDENCE RULE

Often people make preliminary agreements or promises in negotiating a contract and later sign a writing called an **integration** that supposedly represents their final agreement on terms. What happens if a party alleges that one of these prior statements (called **parol evidence**), and not what was said in the integration, truly states the parties' agreement?

Consider Lars's offer to sell his dairy farm to Rachel for $500,000. She thinks the price is too high, so in a series of notes and phone calls, Lars agrees to "throw in the seed corn, hay, and tractor in the big barn." Thinking she will receive these additional items, Rachel asks Lars to draw up the contract. His attorney drafts a five-page contract detailing the transaction, its financing, and other terms commonly included in a sale of real estate. Without reading the contract, Rachel signs it, only to discover later that it says nothing about the seed corn, hay, or tractor, which Lars now refuses to deliver. In a lawsuit for breach of contract, will Rachel be entitled to these items, or has the written contract superseded the prior agreements?

How the Parol Evidence Rule Works

The **parol evidence rule** prohibits a court from considering evidence of *prior or contemporaneous* agreements that conflict with a writing that the parties intend as the "final embodiment of their agreement."[7] The general idea behind the rule is to promote certainty and security of transactions by giving binding effect to a final writing in-

---

[7]Calamari and Perillo, op. cit., p. 135.

tended to be a *complete and exclusive* statement of the agreement. Called a **complete integration,** such a writing supersedes earlier, tentative, often oral agreements that the parties ordinarily intend to abandon, and it supposedly minimizes perjury. Rachel's parol evidence (Lars's notes and phone calls) directly contradicts their final writing. If it is a complete integration, the parol evidence rule prevents Rachel's evidence from being considered for determining the terms of the contract—whether to contradict or supplement the integration—unless some exception to the rule applies.

How can one tell whether a document is an integration? Sometimes the document has a **merger** or **integration clause** stating that the writing is a complete expression of the parties' agreement. Ordinarily, the courts give effect to merger clauses. However, if a merger clause is a term of adhesion, or if the writing is obviously incomplete, the court may set aside the clause and admit parol evidence. Where there is no merger clause, the court will examine the writing to see if it appears complete. If it contains the terms usually found in contracts that are considered to be complete, the court will treat the writing as an integration in the absence of contrary evidence.

Where the Parol Evidence Rule Does Not Apply

Even though the parol evidence rule does not permit a completely integrated agreement to be contradicted or supplemented by prior agreements, it has *no application* to agreements entered into *subsequent* to the writing. Thus, where an integrated contract is modified or rescinded by a subsequent oral or written agreement, there is no violation of the parol evidence rule.

Also, there are many exceptions to the parol evidence rule. It serves to exclude evidence of prior negotiations only where there is a direct conflict between an *unambiguous* integration and the information sought to be presented to the court. For many purposes, parol evidence of prior negotiations is freely admissible—for example, to clear up an ambiguity in the integration or to resolve an allegation of fraud. Although the parol evidence rule forbids Rachel's parol evidence, it may be admissible under the fraud exception to establish the true contract terms—if she can demonstrate by reasonable proof that fraud may have occurred. Parol evidence is admissible for other purposes: for example, to determine whether an agreement was illegal or lacked consideration or whether a writing constitutes a full or only a partial integration.

A **partially integrated agreement** states something less than the totality of the parties' understanding, but as to the portion covered, the writing is complete. Under the parol evidence rule, an unambiguous partial integration may not be contradicted but *may be supplemented* by evidence of prior negotiations or agreements, oral or written. And, as in complete integrations, parol evidence will be admitted to resolve ambiguities and to resolve other questions such as the presence of fraud.

> **BOX 15.4**
>
> ### Test Your Knowledge
>
> You want to buy a sports car and spend several days negotiating the purchase. You request a red car, but there is only a yellow one on the lot. The salesperson says, "If you'll take the yellow one, we'll throw in an air conditioner free." You agree, and the salesperson prepares a detailed contract for you to sign. Pressed for time, you sign later that day without reading the contract. After taking delivery of the car, you read the contract and discover that the seller charged you for the air conditioner. The seller refuses to adjust the purchase price, and you sue, alleging breach of the promise to supply an air conditioner free. Will you win the lawsuit? Will the judge even allow you to present your evidence of the salesperson's promise? Consider the application of the **parol evidence rule**—the timing of the salesperson's promise, whether the contract was an integration (total or partial), and whether some exception to the parol evidence rule might apply.

SUMMARY

The statute of frauds applies to classes of contracts thought to affect such important interests of contracting parties that writings should be required as evidence of contractual intent. Except where a statute of frauds or some other special statute requires a writing for the formation or enforcement of a contract, an oral contract is as enforceable as a written one.

The classes of contracts commonly covered by a state statute of frauds are a contract of an executor or administrator to answer for duty of the decedent; a contract to answer for the debt or default of another; a contract made upon consideration of marriage; a contract for the sale of goods for a price of $500 or more; a contract for the sale of an interest in land; and a contract not performable within 1 year.

The primary purpose of a statute of frauds is to require reliable evidence that an alleged contract was indeed entered into. To accomplish this purpose, the statute requires that an agreement covered by the statute, or some memorandum or note thereof, shall be in writing and signed by the person to be charged with breach of contract in any subsequent legal proceeding.

The statute of frauds can itself be used as an instrument of fraud or oppression against persons ignorant of the writing requirement or too lacking in bargaining power to compel a writing. To prevent injustice which can arise from misuse of the writing requirement, the courts apply the doctrines of equitable estoppel, promissory estoppel, and part performance in the enforcement of some oral contracts. Under some statutes of frauds, such as the one applicable to sales of goods, a writing is only one of the several ways to evidence a contract. Other ways include part performance and admitting to a contract in court. If a contract is modified and the contract, as modified, is within the statute of frauds, the modified contract must conform to the requirements of the statute.

A statute of frauds indicates what evidence is required for enforceability of a contract. The parol evidence rule indicates what evidence a court will consider in determining the content of a contract. The parol evidence rule does not, in litigation, permit admission of evidence of an oral or written agreement made prior to an integrated agreement if the prior agreement conflicts with the terms of the integration.

REVIEW QUESTIONS

1. What is the purpose of a statute of frauds?

2. (a) Why is a promise of an executor to pay the debt of the decedent out of the executor's own funds covered by the statute of frauds? **(b)** Under what circumstance would such a promise be enforceable?

3. A surety's promise to pay the debt, default, or miscarriage of another must be evidenced by a writing to be enforceable. **(a)** Illustrate a contract of suretyship. **(b)** Explain the operation and significance of the main-purpose rule.

4. (a) To what kinds of contracts involving marriage as consideration does the statute of frauds apply? **(b)** To what kinds of such contracts does the statute not apply? Why?

5. (a) Explain to which of the following contracts the land contract provision of the statute of frauds applies: purchase of land, lease of land, mortgage, contract for sale of oil, contract for sale of growing crops. **(b)** Distinguish between a deed and the writing required by the statute of frauds for a land contract.

6. (a) How do the courts distinguish between contracts which are performable within a year and those which are not? **(b)** What is the significance of the distinction? **(c)** A makes an oral contract to support B for the rest of B's life. Under the statute of frauds, is the oral contract enforceable? Explain.

7. What kind of writing will satisfy the statute of frauds?

8. (a) How can the statute of frauds be used as an "instrument of fraud or oppression"? **(b)** Illustrate how *legislatures* have attempted to prevent the injustice which can arise from the misuse of the statute-of-frauds writing requirement. **(c)** Describe two ways in which the *courts* have attempted to prevent the injustice arising from the misuse of the statute-of-frauds writing requirement. **(d)** Under what circumstances might a court enforce an oral land contract?

9. Are oral modifications and rescissions of contracts covered by the statute of frauds? Explain.

10. (a) What is the purpose of the parol evidence rule? **(b)** Illustrate its operation.

CASE PROBLEMS

1. Holmdel Heights Construction Co. was developing some land for home building. Sugarman owned 18 percent of Holmdel's stock and, as its attorney, was owed $14,000 for legal services. Holmdel hired Schoor Associates to do engineering and planning work for the development, but failed to pay Schoor as agreed. Schoor ceased working. To secure additional financing, Holmdel needed more engineering work done at once. At a conference on financing, Sugarman orally agreed to pay all of Holmdel's outstanding and future bills, in the event of Holmdel's default, if Schoor would continue the engineering work. Schoor continued the work but received no further payment. Because Holmdel was insolvent, Schoor Associates sued Sugarman for the amounts due them. He contended that his promise was unenforceable under the statute of frauds. The trial court rendered judgment for Schoor, the appellate court reversed the judgment, and Schoor appealed. Should Sugarman be held liable on his oral promise to pay for the engineering work?

2. The Bank and Trust Company of Old York Road (Bank) held a mortgage on real estate owned by Eastgate Enterprises. Bank foreclosed the mortgage and, as permitted by statute, charged Eastgate for costs and attorney's fees. To obtain a release of the mortgage, Eastgate paid costs and fees totaling $9,455.36. Eastgate then brought suit to recover that amount from Bank, alleging that Bank had breached an oral agreement not to foreclose the mortgage. The trial court dismissed Eastgate's complaint on the ground that the oral agreement was unenforceable under the Pennsylvania statute of frauds. Eastgate appealed. Was the oral agreement enforceable?

3. In 1954, Allstate Insurance Co. orally agreed to employ Gilliland until his retirement age of 62, as long as he substantially complied with Allstate's lawful instructions. Allstate was to notify him if he was not fulfilling his duties so that he could correct any deficiencies. Gilliland soon began participating in profit sharing, pension, and savings plans and continued his participation until Allstate terminated his employment in 1972 without good cause or prior notice. As a result of the termination, Gilliland lost profits and earnings and the amount that would have accumulated in the pension fund had he remained employed until retirement. Gilliland sued Allstate for breach of the oral contract. From a judgment for Allstate, Gilliland appealed, alleging that the statute of frauds did not bar enforcement of the contract. Would enforcement of the oral contract violate the statute of frauds?

4. McMahan owned a 10-acre lot (the Bluff Road property) which he used as a source of fill dirt and gravel in the construction of an interstate highway. McMahan needed additional fill dirt, and Koch, McMahan's project manager, attempted to acquire it from Wegehoft's land located adjacent to the Bluff Road property. Wegehoft agreed to sell fill dirt to McMahan, but only if McMahan would sell Wegehoft the Bluff Road property. Koch drafted, and he and Wegehoft signed, a handwritten note containing the following provision: "F. McMahan Const. Co. will give Wegehoft the option to buy approximately $8\frac{1}{2}$ acres located at 4404 Bluff Road for the price of $5,000. . . ." Koch said he would have an official contract prepared. Wegehoft never received such a contract. During the next 3 years, Wegehoft made repeated inquiries of Koch about a deed to the Bluff Road property. McMahan denied that there was an agreement for the sale of the property, and Wegehoft brought suit for specific performance. At trial, McMahan challenged the sufficiency of the memorandum to satisfy the statute of frauds. Was the memorandum sufficient?

5. Mr. Sylvia owned some mortgaged real estate. He was in default on mortgage payments, and to avoid foreclosure of the mortgage, he agreed orally to sell the property to Weale. Weale secured a bank commitment to finance the purchase, paid an attorney $150 for examining the title and doing other legal work relating to the property, and spent $2,860 for a survey of the land. In the meantime, Cole learned of the proposed sale, visited the property, and saw the survey work. He then offered to purchase the land, and he and Sylvia signed a contract of sale. Weale and Cole brought separate actions against Sylvia for specific performance. In a single hearing, the trial court granted specific performance to Weale and ordered Cole to file a release of his recorded written purchase agreement. Cole appealed. Was Weale entitled to specific performance?

6. The Kiefers owned 274 acres of land, approximately 70 acres of which was farmable. Francis Gegg farmed the 70 acres as a tenant on a "cash-rent" basis. He also cared for the rest of the property, maintaining the gravel road, cleaning out the creek bed, clearing brush and weeds, and improving the land's drainage system. Kiefer was pleased with his tenant's work and over the years told him, "Now, Franco, you take care of this land because some day it will be your own." After his wife's death in January 1979, Kiefer's health deteriorated. During Kiefer's illness, he and Gegg discussed the sale of the farm, apparently agreeing on a price of $45,000. In March or April, Gegg visited a local banker to arrange a $45,000 loan to buy the farm. On April 15, Gegg asked Kiefer whether he was ready to sell his property. Kiefer said yes, indicated that he "had turned everything over" to his nephew William, and asked if his nephew had brought the deed to Gegg. The nephew had not done so. On May 1, Kiefer died without a will and had made no plans with his nephew to transfer the land to Gegg. Gegg brought suit for specific performance of the oral contract. Should the court order specific performance?

7. Arlo Essex was a successful service station operator. In 1968, Skelly Oil Co. sought him out as a lease operator for a Skelly station then under construction. During negotiations Essex expressed concern about a clause in the proposed lease giving either party the option to cancel it on 30 days' notice. The Skelly representatives assured Essex that the language in the lease was merely a formality and that if Essex ran a good operation, he could remain in the location until he decided to retire. Essex then agreed to terminate his existing lease of an Apco station and to sign the Skelly lease. In 1973, Skelly canceled the lease and converted the station into a self-service operation called Surfco. Alleging fraud, Essex sued Skelly. One Skelly representative said he and others were instructed in Skelly training sessions to overcome prospective lessees' resistance to the cancellation clause by assuring them that the clause would not be used to terminate a lease except for unsatisfactory performance by the lessee. Essex won a jury verdict for actual and punitive damages. The trial court entered a judgment n.o.v. for Skelly, apparently on the ground that the written lease should prevail over the parol evidence concerning fraudulent misrepresentations. Essex appealed. Should the jury verdict for Essex be reinstated?

CHAPTER 16

Rights and Duties of Third Persons

People use contracts in different ways to accomplish a variety of business purposes. Often, only two parties are involved, as when Al promises to work for Beth for an agreed wage, or Alicia promises to sell a new car to Gordon for a specified price. Frequently, however, contracts involve more than two persons. Al promises to make semiannual payments to Lifeco Insurance Co. in exchange for Lifeco's promise to pay $50,000 to Tina at Al's death. Tina is a **third-person beneficiary** of the contract between Al and Lifeco. Or Alicia sells a car to Gordon on credit, intending to sell to Creditcorp for immediate cash Gordon's promise to make future payments for the car. Alicia's sale of Gordon's promise is an **assignment** to Creditcorp of her contract rights against Gordon.

This chapter focuses on contracts involving third persons. The first part of the chapter deals with third-person beneficiary contracts. The second and third parts deal with the assignment of contract rights and the delegation of contract duties.

THIRD-PERSON BENEFICIARY CONTRACTS

Under the English common law, a person could not sue for breach of a contract unless he or she was one of the contracting parties—i.e., was "in privity of contract" with the person being sued. A mere contract beneficiary was considered an outsider to the contracting process and had no enforceable rights.[1] Today, for reasons discussed later in this chapter, all states recognize the right of third-person beneficiaries to sue for breach of contracts made for their benefit.

Meaning of Third-Person Beneficiary

To be a third-person beneficiary of a contract (i.e., to have a right to enforce a contract made by others), one must be *intended by the contracting parties* to receive the performance that was the subject of their bargain. Figure 16.1 represents a third-person beneficiary contract. In it, Alice is the **promisor** (the person promising the performance that the third person is to receive), Ben is the **promisee** (the other contracting party), and Tina is the **third-person beneficiary** who is to receive Alice's performance.

Intended beneficiary is modern terminology, used in many states to describe any beneficiary

---

[1] John E. Murray, Jr., MURRAY ON CONTRACTS (1974), Secs. 276 and 277.

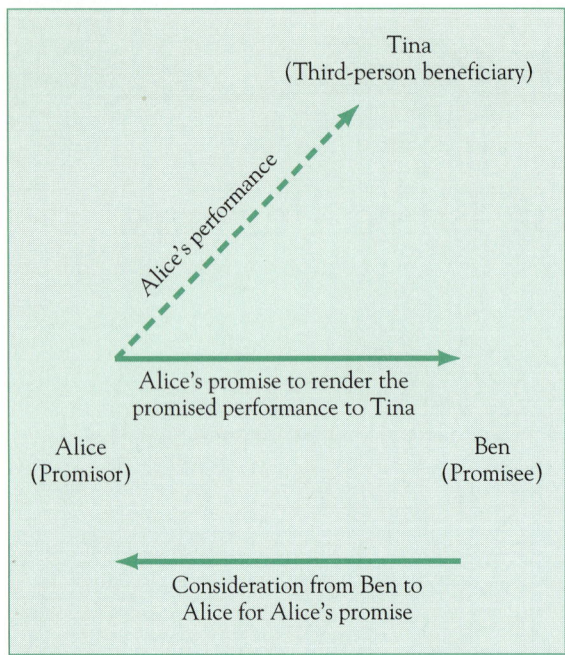

Figure 16.1 Third-person beneficiary contract.

Mortgage is the third-person creditor beneficiary of the assumption contract between Ann and Bill.

Most states allow any intended beneficiary to sue the promisor directly for breach of contract, because the beneficiary was meant to have rights under the contract.[2] In contrast, a contract may benefit people who have no connection with it and whom the contracting parties had no intention of benefiting. Ben hires Ann to tear down a dilapidated tenement house he owns and to replace it with a beautiful apartment building. The contract, if carried out, may well enhance the value of all properties in the neighborhood, and their owners may benefit from Ann's promised performance. But at best those owners are **incidental beneficiaries.** As such they have no rights under the contract if it is performed, and no right to sue Ben or Ann if either breaches it. Incidental beneficiaries are *not* included within the meaning of "third-person beneficiary."

To enforce a contract, intended beneficiaries do not have to be identified by name, nor do their identities have to be known at the time of contracting. It is sufficient that the beneficiary can be identified at the time performance is due. Oilcorp contracts with the state to provide emergency roadside service to travelers on a freeway as a part of its duties under its exclusive service station franchise. A traveler injured because of Oilcorp's failure to provide emergency service is an intended beneficiary and has a cause of action for Oilcorp's breach of contract. Similarly, if Lifeco Insurance contracts with Bob to pay $100,000 at his death to his "children" or to his "estate," the description of the intended beneficiaries is sufficient.

who has a right to enforce the contract. However, a substantial number of states use older terminology. In those states there are two types of intended third-person beneficiaries—donee and creditor.

Benita insures her life for $50,000 with Lifeco Insurance, and names her husband Tim as the beneficiary of the policy. He is a **donee beneficiary** because Benita's purpose is to confer a gift upon him at her death. Suppose, however, that Benita buys an expensive car on credit, insures her life for the amount of the unpaid purchase price, and makes Tom, the car dealer, the beneficiary. Tom is a **creditor beneficiary** because Benita's purpose in naming Tom as beneficiary is to fulfill a legal obligation that she owes him—the duty to pay for the car.

Likewise, the so-called **assumption contracts** involve creditor beneficiaries. Ann agrees to buy from Bill a house that he has been buying on credit. Town Mortgage Co. (Bill's lender) holds a mortgage on the house, and as part of the purchase price Ann agrees to assume (promises to pay) Bill's remaining mortgage debt. Town

Reason for Recognizing Rights of Beneficiaries

One reason for allowing a donee beneficiary to enforce the contract is that often only the beneficiary can do so effectively. Benita names Tim as the beneficiary of her $50,000 Lifeco policy

---

[2] A few states may still limit suit to either donee or creditor beneficiaries, but this is increasingly unlikely.

> **BOX 16.1**
>
> **Test Your Knowledge**
>
> Horace hired Frederick, an attorney-at-law, to prepare Horace's will. Horace carefully specified which property Miriam, his only surviving relative, was to receive and which was to go to a charity. Horace died soon afterward. Because of serious errors Frederick made in writing the will, Miriam received $150,000 less than Horace had intended. Miriam now wants to sue Frederick for breach of contract. Does she have a legal basis for doing so? ∎

and dies 5 years later. Lifeco refuses to pay. Tim is the most logical person to bring suit. If Tim could not enforce the insurance contract and Benita's estate failed to do so, Benita's purpose would be defeated. Even the life insurance industry prefers that beneficiaries have enforcement rights, since life insurance policies would be unmarketable if surviving beneficiaries could not enforce them.

Also, allowing a beneficiary to sue the promisor directly avoids unnecessary litigation. Benita dies and Lifeco Insurance refuses to pay Tom (her creditor beneficiary) the amount still owed for Benita's new car. Tom contracted with Benita and has a right to collect the unpaid purchase price from her estate if Lifeco Insurance refuses to pay. However, because it is inefficient to require Tom to sue Benita's estate and to require her estate in turn to sue Lifeco, Tom can sue Lifeco directly.

Case 16.1 involves an intended third-person beneficiary, and an allegation of negligence that breached the contract.

CASE 16.1   **Vick v. H.S.I. Management, Inc.** • 507 So. 2d 433 (Ala. 1987)

FACTS   Plaintiff Karen Vick, a tenant of defendant Haversham Townhouse (managed by defendant H.S.I. Management), was injured in a fall down some steps in a dark pathway. A handrail near the steps was broken or missing. Three sources of light existed on the premises: a dusk-to-dawn light, floodlights, and porch lights for the individual residents. None of these lights was working at the time of the accident, nor had they been working for several weeks previously. Defendant Alabama Power Co. (APCo) was under contract with Haversham to maintain the dusk-to-dawn light. Alleging that the defendants negligently maintained the premises and breached their contractual obligation to maintain the premises in a safe and adequately lighted condition, Vick filed suit. From a summary judgment for the defendants, Vick appealed. The court held that the summary judgment in favor of Haversham and H.S.I. Management should not have been granted. The court then discussed APCo's summary judgment.

OPINION   SHORES, J. . . . We also hold that it was error to grant summary judgment in favor of APCo. It is undisputed that prior to July 2, 1984, the date of Vick's accident, APCo had contracted with Haversham to install and maintain outdoor lights on the premises of Haversham apartments. Obviously, the contract was for the benefit of the tenants at Haversham apartments.

In *Harris v. Board of Water & Sewer Commissioners* . . . , the plaintiff was an owner of a restaurant and motel which were destroyed by fire. When the firemen arrived on the scene, they found that the fire hydrants were dry. As a result, the motel and restaurant were totally destroyed. The Board of Water and Sewer

**CASE 16.1
Continued**

Commissioners . . . had a contract [to provide water]. As part of its contractual obligation. . . , the Board was to provide fire hydrants and to maintain an adequate [water supply].

In *Harris*, the trial court granted the Board's motion to dismiss Harris's complaint alleging breach of contract and negligent maintenance. This Court reversed the order of dismissal entered by the trial court. . . . [W]e cited *MacPherson v. Buick Motor Co.*, . . . which set forth the following well-known principle of tort law:

> [W]here one party to a contract assumes a duty to another party to that contract, and it is foreseeable that injury to a third party—not a party to the contract—may occur upon a breach of that duty, the promissor owes that duty to all those within the foreseeable area of risk. . . .

Like those in *Harris*, the facts of the present case fall within that rule. APCo contracted with Haversham to provide outdoor lighting. It is foreseeable that without the outdoor lights, a third party, such as Vick, could be injured while attempting to use the common grounds on the premises. See also, *Harvard v. Palmer & Baker Engineers, Inc.*, . . . where this Court recognized an action against an engineering corporation for the wrongful death of a motorist in a tunnel where it was alleged that the corporation negligently performed an investigation of the tunnel pursuant to a contract with the City of Mobile.

In *Williams v. Jackson* . . . the Court of Civil Appeals held:

> [O]ne who undertakes to perform a contract may be determined to owe a duty to others not privy to the contract to perform his obligations under the contract without negligent injury to such others. Such duty may arise from the foreseeability that such others may be injured by negligent performance, or duty may arise from the knowledge that others are relying upon a proper performance. . . .

Applying the above principles of law, we hold that it was error to grant APCo summary judgment. . . . We hold that the evidence . . . presents genuine issues of material fact which Vick is entitled to have submitted [to a jury].

JUDGMENT

We, therefore, reverse the judgment and remand this case for further proceedings. . . .

Vesting of Beneficiary's Rights

A beneficiary has no cause of action against the promisor for breach of the beneficial promise unless the beneficiary's rights have **vested** (become established). Vesting can occur at a variety of times, depending on the circumstances. Most life insurance policies have a standard-form clause permitting the insured party (the promisee) to change the beneficiary at any time. Under such insurance policies, the beneficiary's rights to the face amount of the policy ordinarily do not vest until the death of the insured person. In contrast, if an insurance policy does *not* provide for a change of beneficiary, or *prohibits* such a change, the beneficiary's rights vest when the beneficiary is named—usually when the insurance contract is made. In other situations—especially where a promisor has a right to revoke the beneficial promise—the beneficiary's rights may vest when he or she brings suit on the contract or materially changes his or her position in justifiable reliance on the promise.

Promisor's Defenses against the Beneficiary

Whether a beneficiary may enforce the beneficial promise also depends on the enforceability of the contract between the promisor and the promisee. The promisor may assert against the beneficiary any defense that the promisor could have asserted against the promisee if the promisee had sought to enforce the contract—fraud, mistake, absence of mutual assent or consideration, illegality, violation of the statute of frauds, lack of capacity, and the like. Beth hires Grace, a minor, to give guitar lessons to Bess's son Juan. If Grace refuses to carry out her part of the bargain and Juan sues Grace for breach of contract, Grace may assert her defense of infancy.

ASSIGNMENT OF CONTRACT RIGHTS

Meaning and Nature of Assignment

Beth agrees to install an electronic security system in Al's office building for $40,000, payment to be made when she finishes the work 3 months from now. Beth has Al's written promise of future payment, but she needs immediate cash to pay her employees. She can get it by selling Al's promise to Cora for, say, $37,000 so that Cora can collect the $40,000 from Al later. Or perhaps Beth does not need cash, but just wants Cora to have Al's promise as a birthday gift. Whether Beth's purpose is to obtain cash or to make a gift, she accomplishes it by transferring ("assigning") to Cora Al's promise to pay.

Meaning of Assignment. An **assignment** is the *present transfer* of an existing right (often, a contract right) by its owner (Beth) to someone else (Cora). Beth, the person doing the transferring, is the **assignor.** Since the assigned right may consist of a promise made to the assignor, Beth may also be called the **promisee, obligee** (person to whom an obligation is owed), or **creditor.**[3] Cora, the person to whom the right (here, Al's promise to pay) is assigned, is the **assignee.** In a sale or gift of a right, the assignor transfers ownership of it; consequently, when a right is assigned, the assignor's (Beth's) interest in the obligor's (Al's) performance ends, and the assignee (Cora) becomes the person entitled to Al's performance.

Figure 16.2 illustrates an assignment of a contract right. Beth sells goods or services to Al on credit. Al (the obligor) promises to pay Beth in the future, perhaps by making installment payments. Beth now has a contract right against Al, but no cash. To raise immediate cash, Beth assigns to Cora Al's promise to pay. In exchange for the assigned promise, Cora (the assignee) gives money (or other consideration) to Beth. Thus, in Figure 16.2, the assignee is a purchaser of the assigned right. If Beth had *given* Cora the assigned right, there would of course be no arrow representing movement of consideration from Cora to Beth.

Requirements for Assignment. Ordinarily, an assignment may be made in any form. Any act or statement, written or oral, indicating an intention to make a present transfer of a right usually is sufficient. However, the assignment of some kinds of rights poses special problems that require statutory regulation. For example, wages often are the last asset that a struggling debtor may have available. Where assignments of wages are permitted, statutes commonly require a writing as evidence of a wage assignment.

Since a right may be assigned as a gift, an assignor's receiving consideration for a right obviously is not required for an assignment to be effective. But under the law of gifts, a gift is not effective until the property involved is delivered. So the courts do not regard a *gift assignment* as having been made until the assignee-donee acquires a substantial measure of control over the property. If the property being assigned is a contract right represented by a document such as a bank savings account book, the gift assignment may be accomplished by, for example, the assignor's delivering the document to the assignee or the assignee's agent.

Effect of Notice of Assignment. Until the obligor (Al) receives *notice* of the assignment,

---

[3] Al is the **promisor, obligor** (person who owes an obligation), or **debtor.**

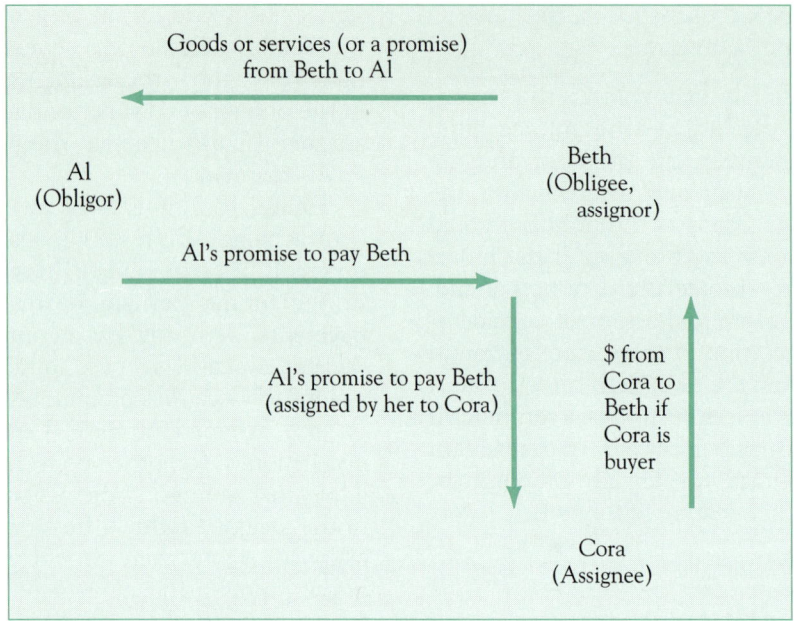

Figure 16.2 Assignment of contract rights.

he owes no duty to the assignee (Cora). Until then, Al's only duty is to the assignor-obligee (Beth). When notified of the assignment, however, Al must render performance to Cora and not to Beth unless Beth has been authorized to receive payment for Cora. Commercial assignees often do authorize assignors to collect assigned customer accounts on behalf of the assignees. But an obligor without notice of assignment cannot be required to pay twice.

Legal Position of the Assignee. How does assignee Cora determine that $37,000 is an appropriate amount to pay for Al's promise to pay Beth $40,000 in 3 months for an electronic security system? Cora will consider a number of factors when negotiating the price—for example, whether an alternative investment would be more profitable, and whether she faces a substantial risk of noncollection. Assessing the amount of risk requires Cora to consider what rights she acquires if she buys Al's promise, and what collection problems she might face if, for example, Beth's work is not satisfactory to Al.

An assignee "stands in the shoes" of the assignor. This statement means two things:

1 The assignee (Cora) acquires the *rights that the assignor (Beth) had* at the time of the assignment. They include the right to the obligor's (Al's) performance and any related right that Beth might have had, such as any priority of payment that the law gives her over Al's other creditors if Al becomes insolvent. However, Cora does not get any rights beyond those possessed by Beth.

2 The assignee takes the assigned rights *subject to defenses* of the obligor. Al may assert against Cora any defense that he could have asserted against Beth (illegality of the contract, failure of the consideration that Beth was supposed to give for Al's promise, fraud by Beth, Al's infancy, and so on). Al may also assert any defense arising after the assignment was made but *before he received notice* of the assignment. Examples are: (a) Al paid Beth before receiving notice of the assignment. (b) Beth has released Al from any further obligation. (c) Beth and Al have re-

scinded or modified their contract so that Al now owes nothing or owes a smaller amount. Because Cora cannot enforce Al's promise if he has a good defense to payment, she faces a substantial risk of noncollection. Accordingly, she will tend to pay less for the assigned right than if she could take it free from Al's defenses.

Suppose Beth defrauded Al by substituting a cheap security system for the expensive one she billed him for. Al has a cause of action against Beth for fraud damages, including punitive damages. Does he also have one against Cora for fraud when Beth assigns her rights to Cora? The answer is no. The assignee's "standing in the shoes" of the assignor means only that Cora acquires the rights of the assignor, and faces the same defenses that Al could have raised against Beth had there been no assignment. Al can use Beth's fraud as a *defense* against Cora if she sues him for the amount he promised. But under the common law rules of assignment, Al has no cause of action against Cora for fraud, since she did not commit fraud.

Effect of Waiver-of-Defenses Clause. To reduce an assignee's risk of noncollection, and consequently to make assigned rights more valuable, assignors or assignees often insert **waiver-of-defenses** clauses into the contract forms to be signed by obligors such as Al. Under such a clause, Al "agrees" not to assert against an assignee (Cora) any claim or defense that Al may have against the assignor (Beth). If enforceable, the waiver-of-defenses clause would require Al to pay Cora despite a defective performance or other misconduct by Beth. For any redress, Al would have to seek out Beth, who might be insolvent, uncooperative, or unavailable for suit.

Case law is in a state of disagreement on the enforceability of waiver-of-defenses clauses. Some jurisdictions enforce them because they enhance the value of assigned rights. The value of such rights increases as the risk of noncollection decreases. Other jurisdictions refuse to enforce such clauses because they often surprise buyers and leave them without effective remedies for defective performances.

BOX 16.2

Government Regulation of Contracts— A Question of Policy

Contrary to the common law rules of assignment just discussed, some consumer protection statutes *do* make assignees liable for misdeeds of assignors. The South Carolina Consumer Protection Act subjects assignees of consumer credit sale contracts to any claim that the obligor has against the assignor. Thus, if assignor Beth defrauded obligor Al, he could bring a fraud action against the assignee Cora, as if Cora had personally committed the fraud. *Rosemond v. Campbell*, 343 S.E.2d 641 (S.C. App. 1986).

Assume that the assignee is a bank that knew nothing of the assignor's fraud. Is it good public policy for the South Carolina statute to make the assignee bank liable for the assignor's fraud? What are the pros and cons of this consumer protection practice? ■

BOX 16.3

Government Regulation of Contracts

Waiver-of-defenses clauses are made void or are given only limited enforceability by a variety of state and federal laws. For example, a rule of the Federal Trade Commission renders invalid waiver-of-defenses clauses in *consumer credit* transactions. 16 *Code of Federal Regulations* 433 (amended and effective April 14, 1977). As to transactions not involving consumer credit, waiver-of-defenses clauses remain enforceable in some states.

Article 9, Section 9-206(1), of the UCC makes a waiver-of-defenses clause enforceable as to some defenses, but not as to others. Thus, with regard to assertability of defenses, Article 9 treats a contract with a waiver-of-defenses clause much like a negotiable instrument. The law of negotiable instruments is discussed in Chapters 31 to 35. ■

Assignments Which Are Not Legally Effective

The law allows most types of contract rights to be assigned. However, to protect the obligor (Al), the law does not recognize an assignment of a contract right where Beth's transferring it would materially change Al's duty; materially increase the burden or risk imposed upon him by his contract; or materially impair his chance of obtaining a return performance. Furthermore, there can be no effective assignment of contract rights where the assignment is forbidden by statute or is otherwise against public policy, or where assignment is validly precluded by contract. Some of these situations are illustrated in the following paragraphs.

Assignments Materially Varying the Obligor's Duty or Risk. The most obvious material change in an obligor's duty is a substantial variation in the nature or quantity of performance to be rendered. Suppose Al contracts with Beth to paint her portrait, and she attempts to assign her rights under the contract to Carl. Painting Carl's portrait is not the same as painting Beth's portrait. If assignment were permitted, the nature of Al's performance would be changed. The assignment is not effective unless Al consents to it. Or suppose that Alco, a small oil producer, contracts to furnish Bencorp all the oil it needs for its business, and that Bencorp sells the business and attempts to assign to the purchaser Alco's promise to supply oil to Bencorp. If the purchaser's needs for oil are materially greater than Bencorp's, the assignment will not be effective unless Alco consents to it, because of the unexpected burden Alco would otherwise face.

Some rights are of such a nature that their transfer causes no substantial change in the obligor's (Al's) performance. A common example is the right of a creditor (Beth) to a payment of money for her completed performance. All that remains is for Al to pay, and under the law it can make no difference to him who receives the money—Beth or her assignee. Therefore, a creditor ordinarily may assign the right to an earned money payment without the consent of the obligor.

However, an assignor may not unilaterally increase the obligor's risk. Suppose that Beth's house is insured by Allfire, a fire insurance company, and that Beth sells the house to Carl and assigns the fire insurance policy to him. The assignment is ineffective unless Allfire consents. Presumably one of the risk factors that insurance companies consider when setting their rates is the safety record of the insured person. Allowing insured persons to assign a policy without the consent of the insurer could result in increasing the insurer's risks and in impairing the insurer's ability to insure effectively.

Assignments Impairing Obligor's Return Performance. Nor may an assignment materially reduce the obligor's chances of obtaining the expected return performance. Al contracts with Beth, a famous race car driver, to manage her car-leasing business for 10 percent of the net profits. The business is well known because of Beth's racing success. Then she sells her business to Carl, who intends to rename it, and assigns to him her rights to Al's services as manager. The assignment is ineffective without Al's consent, since he may be deprived of the special benefit he expected from Beth's racing reputation. Even in ordinary employment contracts, the employer may not assign the right to the employee's services without his or her consent. All such contracts are considered so personal in nature that any assignment would impose a material change on the employee.

In Case 16.2, a credit buyer of real estate wants to assign his rights to another person. Can he substitute another buyer for himself without the seller's consent?

CASE 16.2 Lancaster v. Greer • 572 S.W.2d 787 (Tex. Civ. App. 1978)

FACTS Plaintiff Greer entered into an earnest money contract with Bates, agreeing to sell him 467 acres of land on credit. Bates, who planned to develop the land and resell parts of it from time to time, placed the required $2,000 earnest money in escrow. As part of the deal, Bates was to begin construction of an access road to the property.

Substantial development problems arose, and Bates decided to abandon the contract and forfeit the $2,000. He arranged for the money to be transferred to Greer, and without Greer's knowledge assigned to defendant Lancaster all rights Bates may have had in the contract. About a month later, Greer negotiated a resale of the property, only to discover on the day set for closing that Lancaster had earlier that day recorded the purported assignment in the county land records. Alleging that the recorded assignment document was void and constituted a "cloud" on his title to the land, Greer brought suit against Lancaster. Holding that the contract between Greer and Bates was nonassignable, the trial court entered a summary judgment in favor of Greer. Lancaster appealed.

OPINION MOORE, J. . . . On appeal Lancaster [argues that] the sales contract in question is assignable as a matter of law. In reply, Greer argues that the contract was not assignable because it involved the extension of credit to Bates. The sole . . . issue to be determined is whether the contract is assignable.

Paragraph 1 of the . . . contract between Greer and Bates contains a description of the land in question as well as the method by which payment for the land shall be [made]. . . .

Paragraph 2 of the contract allows the purchaser to sell any or all of the said tracts of land and provides for the release of the vendor's lien and deed of trust lien affecting such tract provided $600 per acre is paid to the seller's escrow agent. Paragraph 2 provides in pertinent part:

> It is further agreed that the above described deed shall contain a provision to the effect that the Buyer will be permitted to sell tracts of any size, and the Seller will execute a release of the vendor's lien and deed of trust lien affecting such tract provided that the sum of $600.00 per acre in the tract to be released shall be deposited with the . . . escrow agent. The money . . . shall be used for the purpose of meeting the principal and interest payments. . . .

Nowhere does the contract authorize assignment, nor does the contract prohibit assignment. The present action turns on the question of the assignability of the earnest money contract. The general rule is that all contracts are assignable. . . . However, there are some well-recognized exceptions to the rule. One exception is that rights arising out of a contract which involve[s] an extension of credit between the parties to the contract are not assignable. . . . It has been held that contracts for the sale of real estate which provide for credit from the seller are not assignable. . . .

The rationale underlying the exception to the general rule is that credit contracts by their very nature involve a relationship between the seller and the buyer of personal confidence and trust, such that the seller must have intended

CASE 16.2 Continued

the rights conferred by the contract to be exercised only by him in whom he actually confided. . . . Whenever the contracting parties have relied on the skill, character or credit of each other, the law will not permit one of the parties to substitute for himself another person in whom the opposite party may not repose an equal trust or confidence. . . .

As the essential nature of the earnest money contract is one extending credit, a relationship of personal trust and confidence was intended and created between Greer and Bates such that the law will not permit in the absence of Greer's consent the substitution of another part for Bates. It is undisputed that Greer did not consent to the assignment. This relationship of personal trust is not only borne out in paragraphs 1 and 2 of the contract but also in paragraph 4. The seller places reliance not only on the buyer's financial ability but also on their personal relationship of trust and confidence by obligating the buyer to commence the construction of an access road to the property in question. . . .

JUDGMENT We hold that the earnest money contract is not assignable in whole or part as a matter of law since it involves an extension of credit by the seller to the purchaser, and because of the personal confidence and trust involved in building an access road. . . . It follows that the instrument assigning the contract from Bates to Lancaster is null and void. . . . The judgment of the trial court is affirmed.

Assignments Forbidden by Statute or Public Policy. Federal and state statutes prohibit or regulate the assignment of certain types of claims. For example, a federal statute makes assignment of a claim against the federal government void except where the claim has already been allowed and a Treasury warrant for payment has been issued. This statute tends to minimize litigation against the government. Most states have statutes prohibiting the assignment of future wages or regulating in amount and method the assignment of future or earned wages, veterans compensation, old age and disability payments, and the like. These statutes ease pressures on debtors to spend their incomes far in advance of receipt.

In the absence of a regulatory statute, the courts will invalidate assignments that are against public policy. Suppose Betty is injured by Alicia's negligence but does not want to sue because the loss was small and she and Alicia are good friends. May Betty assign her cause of action against Alicia to Christine? Most courts would hold the assignment void. Christine's trading in other people's lawsuits is against public policy because it interferes with the tendency of many potential litigants to settle their claims out of court, or tends to stir up disputes and ill will where injured persons would not have thought to sue at all. However, if Betty herself brings suit and wins a judgment against Alicia, Betty *can* assign the judgment to Christine. Because the judgment has reduced Betty's unliquidated tort claim to a liquidated claim for money damages, it is now assignable like any other money debt.

Assignment Prohibited by Contract. Contracts often contain a "nonassignability" clause forbidding the obligee (Beth in Figure 16.2) from assigning his or her rights. In deciding whether to enforce the clause, the courts consider the principle of freedom of contract (which supports enforcement) and the policy of free alienation (transfer) of property (which justifies invalidating the clause).

Generally, nonassignability clauses are enforceable, since the obligor (Al in Figure 16.2) usually has a substantial interest to protect. But sometimes Al's need to prevent assignment is small, whereas Beth's need to assign is great.

Then the policy of free alienation may prevail. Most courts will not enforce clauses prohibiting Beth's assignment of money claims that have been earned by performance—for example, the assignment of amounts owed to her for a house she recently painted or a claim under an insurance policy after loss has occurred. And in most states clauses prohibiting the assignment of rights under contracts for the purchase of real estate are against public policy. Suppose Art agrees to sell Becky his house in exchange for monthly payments for the next 10 years, and a contract clause says she cannot resell the house. Three years later, Becky sells the house to Connie and moves to another state. Most courts would uphold Becky's assignment of her rights to Connie, since, as discussed later in this chapter, Becky remains liable to Art for the unpaid debt, and Becky's need to assign is great. Note that the risk factors here differ from those in Case 16.2. There, Bates abandoned his contract with Greer before any performance—forfeiting the $2,000 as damages for his breach, effectively removing himself from any further liability, and putting Greer in a precarious economic position.

> **BOX 16.4**
> **Nonassignability Clauses and the UCC**
>
> Like most courts, the Uniform Commercial Code invalidates nonassignability clauses that impose unreasonable restraints on the alienation of property. For example, UCC § 2-210(2) permits a *seller of goods* to assign his or her right to damages for the buyer's breach of the whole contract, or any right to payment resulting from the seller's full performance, despite an agreement to the contrary. A similar provision in UCC Article 9 applies to *assignments of accounts receivable*. It makes "ineffective" any contract term prohibiting a creditor from assigning the account debtor's obligation to pay, even where the creditor has not yet fully performed. Ann hires Beth to install $3,000 worth of plumbing in Ann's house. Payment is due 60 days after Beth completes the work, and the contract states that she is not to assign her rights under the contract. Before beginning work, she assigns the account to Carl for $2,700. The assignment is valid. ∎

Successive (Dual) Assignments

Sometimes, through mistake, negligence, or fraud, a person assigns the same right to two or more assignees. Which assignee has priority? In the United States, there are three different views about who should win.[4]

The **New York rule** is that as between successive assignees of the same right, the first in time has priority. The reasoning is that when an effective assignment is made, the assignor has no further rights that could be subject to a second assignment.

The New York rule is subject to some exceptions. For example, a subsequent assignee prevails where the prior assignee negligently failed to take possession of documents evidencing the assignment and thus enabled the assignor to transfer the documents to a second assignee. Also, where the first assignment is revocable or voidable, as where a gift has been promised but not delivered, the second assignment reveals the assignor's intent to revoke or avoid the first assignment, and the second assignee wins.

The **English rule** is that the assignee who first notifies the obligor of the assignment has priority, if that assignee is without notice of a prior assignment and has given value (i.e., is a good faith purchaser). This rule encourages assignees to give prompt notice to obligors so that they can answer inquiries about who owns the claim and thus help prevent fraud.

Both *Restatements* adopt the **Massachusetts rule.** Under this rule, the first assignee prevails unless a subsequent one (who must be a good faith purchaser) does one of four things: (1) obtains payment from the obligor, (2) recovers a judgment against the obligor, (3) obtains the obligor's promise to pay the subsequent assignee, or (4) receives delivery of a tangible token such as a bank passbook or a promissory note that must be surrendered to the obligor.

---

[4]John D. Calamari and Joseph M. Perillo, THE LAW OF CONTRACTS (1987), Secs. 18–21.

These common law rules have been developed by the courts for settling disputes between assignees of the same *contract right*. Similar concepts are evident in the host of statutes that impose recording or filing requirements for protecting other types of property from the claims of others. Recording and filing statutes are discussed in the parts of this book dealing with property and secured transactions.

Warranties of the Assignor

Suppose that an assignee (Cora) tries to collect payment from the obligor (Al) but is met with a valid defense. What recourse has Cora against the assignor (Beth)? Where Beth makes an assignment *for value (consideration)*, she makes three **implied warranties** (guarantees imposed by law upon her even without her knowledge):

1 The right assigned actually exists.
2 It is subject to no limitations or defenses other than those stated or apparent to Cora at the time of assignment.
3 Beth will do nothing to defeat or impair the value of the assignment to Cora.

An assignment of a supposed but nonexisting claim is a breach of the first warranty listed above. Assignment of a claim that is subject to Al's defense of fraud is a breach of the second warranty. Beth's unauthorized collection of the debt from Al is a breach of the third warranty.

Assignors do *not* impliedly warrant that the obligor is solvent or will perform. If Cora is unwilling to assume the risk of Al's insolvency or nonperformance, she should require Beth to make an *express* warranty of these things. Where Beth receives consideration for such a warranty, she will be liable to Cora if Al fails to perform.

Must assignors make implied warranties? No. The parties (assignor and assignee) may agree that there is no warranty, express or implied. If the parties are silent about warranties, however, the assignor makes the three implied warranties previously discussed.

DELEGATION OF CONTRACT DUTIES

Al contracts with Beth, agreeing to pay her $25,000 for a swimming pool to be built in his backyard. In setting up the contract, Al conferred on Beth a contract right to $25,000. But in exchange for Al's promise, Beth made a return promise to Al that created in her a *duty of performance*—to provide a swimming pool. Depending on the terms of the contract, Beth might perform her duty in any of several ways. She might, for example, build the pool herself, perhaps with the assistance of employees. Or she might do part of the job and subcontract other parts such as the electrical and concrete work. Or she might have an understanding with Al that she will not personally build the pool; instead, she will find someone else (Carl) to build it. To carry out the transaction, Beth will **delegate** to Carl her duty to build the pool and at the same time (for, say, $1,000) **assign** to Carl her rights against Al. Thus, for a $1,000 payment, Carl ends up with the duty to build the pool and the right to $25,000 from Al.

Meaning of Delegation

When a person assigns a right, the assignee receives ownership of it, and the assignor's interest in it ceases. But a contracting party who undertakes a *duty* is not allowed to put it aside casually. He or she is expected to perform the duty or to be responsible for its performance. Because assignment implies an absence of any further interest in or concern about the thing assigned, duties may not be assigned. Duties may only be delegated. **Delegation** means no more than that a person under a duty of performance (Beth) authorizes another person (Carl) to render the required performance. The person who delegates the duty is often called the **delegator,** and the person to whom the duty is delegated is called the **delegatee.**

Figure 16.3 illustrates an assignment of a contract right and a delegation of the assignor's duty of performance. Note that Figure 16.3 is a modification of Figure 16.2 and that *for the purposes of delegation,* Beth is the obligor (person

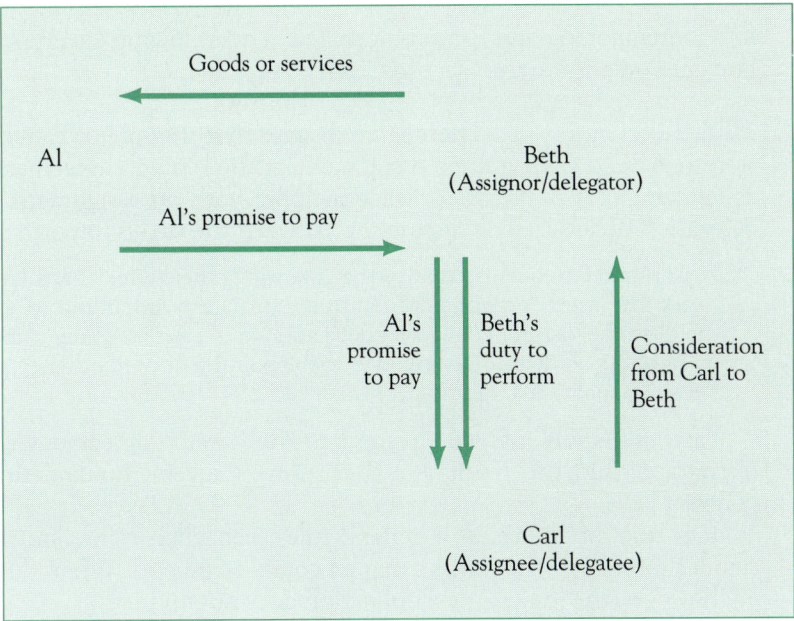

Figure 16.3 Assignment of rights and delegation of duties.

owing the delegated duty to Al) and Al is the obligee.

The delegator (Beth) remains liable to the contract obligee (Al) for any failure of the delegatee (Carl) to perform. Beth will be released from liability to Al only if Al consents to the release. (An arrangement totally releasing the delegator from liability is called a **novation.**)

Case 16.3 illustrates the continuing liability of the delegator of a contractual duty.

CASE 16.3	**Contemporary Mission, Inc. v. Famous Music Corp.** • 557 F.2d 918 (2d Cir. 1977)
FACTS	Contemporary Mission, Inc. (Contemporary), a group of Roman Catholic priests who write, produce, and publish musical compositions and recordings, owned all the rights to a rock opera entitled *Virgin*. In 1972, Contemporary entered a contract with Famous Music Corporation (Famous) in which Famous agreed to manufacture, promote, and sell records made from the master-tape recording of *Virgin*. Tony Martell, the president of Famous, had successfully distributed the rock operas *Tommy* and *Jesus Christ Superstar*. The following year, Contemporary entered another contract with Famous for the distribution of recordings of musical compositions other than *Virgin*. This contract was called the Crunch Agreement. In 1974, Famous's record division was sold to ABC-Dunhill Record Corporation (ABC Records). Contemporary was told that it would have to look to ABC Records for performance of the contracts. ABC Records refused to perform the contracts, and Contemporary sought to hold Famous liable for breach of contract. The trial court rendered judgment

**CASE 16.3
Continued**

for Contemporary, and Famous appealed. The following excerpts from the appellate opinion pertain only to the Crunch Agreement.

OPINION

MESKILL, Cir. J. . . . There is no dispute that the sale of Famous's record division to ABC constituted an assignment of the Crunch agreement to ABC. The assignment of a bilateral contract includes both an assignment of rights and a delegation of duties. The distinction between the two is important.

> Perhaps more frequently than is the case with other terms of art, lawyers seem prone to use the word "assignment" inartfully, frequently intending to encompass within the term the distinct concept of delegation. . . . An assignment involves the transfer of rights. A delegation involves the appointment of another to perform one's duties. J. Calamari & J. Perillo, Contracts sec. 254 (1970).

Famous's arguments with respect to the Crunch agreement ignore this basic distinction, and the result is a distortion of several fundamental principles of contract law.

It is true, of course, as a general rule, that when rights are assigned, the assignor's interest in the rights assigned comes to an end. When duties are delegated, however, the [delegator's] obligation does not end.

> One who owes money or is bound to any performance whatever cannot by any act of his own, or by any act in agreement with any other person, except his creditor, divest himself of the duty and substitute the duty of another. . . . This is sufficiently obvious when attention is called to it, for otherwise obligors would find an easy practical way of escaping their obligations. 3 Williston on Contracts sec. 411 (3d ed. 1960).

This is not to say that one may not delegate his obligations. In fact, most obligations can be delegated—as long as performance by the [delegatee] will not vary materially from performance by the [delegator]. The act of delegation, however, does not relieve the [delegator] of the ultimate responsibility to see that the obligation is performed. If the [delegatee] fails to perform, the [delegator] remains liable. . . .

JUDGMENT

The judgment of the district court is affirmed in all respects except as to its ruling with regard to lost royalties, and the case is remanded to the district court for further proceedings in accordance with this opinion.

Delegable and Nondelegable Duties

Beth contracts to build a swimming pool for Al, but Al and Beth say nothing about delegation. May Beth delegate her duty to Carl without Al's consent? The answer depends on whether the duty is delegable or nondelegable.

Unless a clause in the contract forbids delegation, Beth ordinarily may delegate her duty of performance over the objections of the obligee (Al) where Carl's substitute performance would be substantially the equivalent of Beth's performance. Duties that normally may be delegated without Al's consent include the duty to:

- Pay money
- Deliver standard merchandise
- Manufacture ordinary goods
- Build according to a set of plans and specifications

In contrast, a duty is nondelegable if its performance requires special skill or the personal attention of the would-be delegator. Duties which Beth may *not* delegate without Al's consent include the duty to:

- Support a relative
- Provide professional services (e.g., architectural services such as designing a swimming pool and supervising its construction)
- Farm "on shares" (tenant shares output of farm with landlord)
- Represent another as an exclusive sales agent
- Manufacture a special class of high-quality goods
- Render personal services to an employer

For the protection of obligees such as Al, the courts enforce contract clauses which forbid the delegation of duties, even where a duty would otherwise be delegable. Some delegations are forbidden by law, usually because the performance, if delegated, would vary materially from that contracted for.

Case 16.4 involves an attempted delegation over the objections of the obligee.

CASE 16.4   Macke Co. v. Pizza of Gaithersburg, Inc. • 270 A.2d 645 (Md. 1970)

FACTS   The defendant Pizza Shops, retail outlets under common ownership, contracted with Virginia Coffee Services, Inc. (Virginia), to have cold-drink vending machines installed in each of their six locations. The machines were owned and serviced by Virginia.

In 1967, The Macke Company (Macke) purchased the assets of Virginia, and Virginia assigned the six vending machine contracts to Macke. The Pizza Shops attempted to terminate the contracts, and Macke brought suit against each of the shops for breach of contract. The court rendered judgment for the defendants, and Macke appealed.

OPINION   SINGLEY, J. . . . In the absence of a contrary provision—and there was none here—rights and duties under an executory bilateral contract may be assigned and delegated, subject to the exception that duties under a contract to provide personal services may never be delegated, nor [may] rights be assigned, under a contract where *delectus personae* ["choice of the person"] was an ingredient of the bargain. *Crane Ice Cream Co. v. Terminal Freezing & Heating Co.* . . . held that the right of an individual to purchase ice under a contract which by its terms reflected a knowledge of the individual's needs and reliance on his credit and responsibility could not be assigned to the corporation which purchased his business. [In another case] our predecessors held that an advertising agency could not delegate its duties under a contract which had been entered into by an advertiser who had relied on the agency's skill, judgment and taste.

The six machines were placed on the appellees' premises under a printed "Agreement-Contract." . . . We cannot regard the agreements as contracts for personal services. They were either a license or concession granted Virginia by the appellees, or a lease of a portion of the appellees' premises, with Virginia agreeing to pay a percentage of gross sales as a license or concession fee or as rent, and were assignable by Virginia unless they imposed on Virginia duties of a personal or unique character which could not be delegated.

The appellees earnestly argue that they had dealt with Macke before and had chosen Virginia because they preferred the way it conducted its business. Specifi-

CASE 16.4 Continued

cally, they say that service was more personalized, since the president of Virginia kept the machines in working order, that commissions were paid in cash, and that Virginia permitted them to keep keys to the machines so that minor adjustments could be made when needed. Even if we assume all this to be true, the agreements with Virginia were silent as to the details of the working arrangements and contained only a provision requiring Virginia to "install . . . the above listed equipment and . . . maintain the equipment in good operating order and stocked with merchandise."

We think the Supreme Court of California put the problem of personal service in proper focus a century ago when it upheld the assignment of a contract to grade a San Francisco street:

> All painters do not paint portraits like Sir Joshua Reynolds, nor landscapes like Claude Lorraine, nor do all writers write dramas like Shakespeare or fiction like Dickens. Rare genius and extraordinary skill are not transferable, and contracts for their employment are therefore personal, and cannot be assigned. But rare genius and extraordinary skill are not indispensable to the workmanlike digging down of a sand hill or the filling up of a depression to a given level, or the construction of brick sewers with manholes and covers, and contracts for such work are not personal, and may be assigned. . . .
>
> . . . [T]he difference between the service the Pizza shops happened to be getting from Virginia and what they expected to get from Macke did not mount up to such a material change in the performance of obligations under the agreements as would justify the appellees' refusal to recognize the assignment. . . . Modern authorities . . . hold that, absent provision to the contrary, a duty may be delegated, . . . and that the promisee cannot rescind, if the quality of the performance remains materially the same. . . .

JUDGMENT Judgment reversed. . . .

Assignment of "The Contract"

Sometimes a nonassignability clause prohibits the assignment of "this contract." Did the parties intend to prohibit the assignment of rights or to prohibit the delegation of duties or to prohibit both? The common law rule is that such ambiguous language bars only the delegation of the assignor's duty of performance, and *not* the assignment of rights. This rule has been adopted by Section 2-210(3) of the UCC and is consistent with the policy that rights should be more freely transferrable than duties.

The phrase "the contract" or "this contract" is similarly ambiguous when used to *make* an assignment. Beth writes on the back of her contract with Al, "For value received, I assign this contract to Carl—(Signed) Beth," and hands it to Carl. Does Beth's language accomplish both an assignment of rights and a delegation of duties? As to contracts on subjects covered by the common law of contracts (real estate, services, etc.), the courts disagree. Some courts hold that Beth has only assigned her rights; others hold that she has both assigned her rights and delegated her duties. For the sale of goods, however, the UCC provides that language like Beth's accomplishes both an assignment of rights and a delegation of duties.

Liability of the Delegatee

Carl, the delegatee, might promise to perform Beth's duty as a favor to her, for nothing. Because he has received no consideration for his promise, he has no contractual obligation to Beth and is not liable to either Beth or Al for failure to perform the delegated duty.

But where as a part of the deal Carl also receives an assignment of Beth's rights, he has received the required consideration and is liable to Beth for breach of his promise to perform her duty. Is he also liable to Al, Beth's obligee? If Beth's contract with Al was a sale of goods, the UCC applies. Under its provisions, Carl is liable to Al for failure to supply the goods. If the Code does not apply (as in a sale of real estate or services), Carl is still liable to Al in all but a few states, because Carl's promise to perform Beth's duty is part of a third-person beneficiary contract, enforceable by intended beneficiaries like Al.

SUMMARY

Noncontracting third persons may acquire contract rights in either of two ways—by being an intended third-person beneficiary or by the process of assignment.

The law allows any intended beneficiary (donee or creditor) to sue the promisor directly for breach of contract if the beneficiary's rights have vested. However, the promisor may assert against the beneficiary any defense that the promisor could have asserted against the promisee.

An assignment is the transfer of a right by its owner to a third person. The assignee acquires whatever the assignor had, and takes the assigned right subject to any defense that the obligor could have asserted against the assignor. A right is assignable unless its transfer would materially vary the duty of the obligor, increase the obligor's risk under the contract, or impair the obligor's chances of obtaining return performance; or unless assignment of the right is forbidden by law or by a valid nonassignability clause. A person who assigns the same right two or more times raises the question of who has priority. Under one rule, the first assignee in time prevails. Under another, the assignee who first notifies the debtor of the assignment wins.

An assignor for value impliedly warrants that the right assigned actually exists, that it is subject to no limitations or defenses other than those stated or apparent at the time of the assignment, and that the assignor will do nothing to defeat or impair the value of the assignment.

Duties cannot be assigned, but can be delegated unless the delegatee's performance will differ materially from the delegator's, or unless delegation is forbidden by law or by the contract. Delegation of a duty does not relieve the delegator from his or her duty of performance unless the obligee expressly releases the delegator from the duty.

A valid prohibition of the assignment of "the contract" bars only the delegation of duties. Under the UCC and some case law, the assignment of "this contract" accomplishes both an assignment of rights and a delegation of duties. A delegatee who receives consideration for promising to perform a delegated duty is liable to the delegator, and usually to the obligee, for failing to perform the duty.

REVIEW QUESTIONS

1. (a) Must a person be specifically named as a third-person beneficiary to be one? Explain. **(b)** Why are third-person beneficiaries allowed to enforce the beneficial promises?

2. (a) When does a beneficiary acquire a cause of action for breach of a beneficial promise? **(b)** What defenses may the promisor assert against the suing beneficiary?

3. (a) Why do people assign their contract rights? **(b)** Define "assignment" and distinguish it from the creation of rights in a third-person beneficiary.

4. What is the legal position of the person to whom contract rights have been assigned?

5. What are **(a)** the purpose and **(b)** the legal standing of waiver-of-defenses clauses?

6. Give three examples of assignments that would not be legally effective.

7. What two policies might a court consider when deciding whether to enforce a "nonassignability clause"?

8. (a) Distinguish the New York rule pertaining to successive assignments of the same contract right from the English rule. (b) Which rule is the more sound?

9. (a) Illustrate how the three warranties of the assignor can be breached. (b) How might an assignee be protected against the risk of the debtor-obligor's insolvency?

10. (a) Why might a businessperson delegate a contractual duty? (b) In terms of legal effect, what is the difference between an assignment of rights and a delegation of duties? (c) Under what circumstances may a delegator be released from liability to the person entitled to the delegator's performance?

11. (a) Where the parties to a contract say nothing about the delegation of duties, under what circumstances may the duties be delegated? (b) How will a court treat a contract clause that forbids delegation?

12. Under what circumstances will a delegatee be liable on his or her promise to perform the delegated duty?

CASE PROBLEMS

1. Hidbrader had a franchise from Fiat Distributors, Inc. (FDI), to sell Fiat automobiles. In 1976, Hidbrader notified FDI that he intended to terminate the franchise agreement and go out of business. He had on hand eighteen unsold Fiats—four 1976 models and fourteen 1975 models. The franchise agreement gave FDI the option, at termination, to repurchase any Fiats that "FDI shall in its sole discretion select," at the price Hidbrader had paid. To induce a local bank to finance Hidbrader's Fiat dealership, FDI had signed the following agreement with the bank: "We (FDI) will repurchase in case of termination of this franchise by either party, not more than thirty new and unused . . . Fiats." Rather than repurchase the eighteen cars, FDI insisted that Hidbrader stay in business and sell them. He did so, and lost money on each car. Later, in litigation relating to the franchise termination, Hidbrader alleged that FDI had breached its contractual obligation to repurchase the eighteen cars at his cost, and so had caused him loss. Did FDI have an obligation to repurchase the eighteen Fiats?

2. Security Savings & Loan Association (Security) held a mortgage on the home of the Knickelbeins. According to them, their payments included monthly amounts to cover a homeowners' insurance policy to be procured by Security on their behalf, but because of Security's failure to make the premium payment, the insurance was terminated in 1971. In 1974, Mr. Schell was attacked by a dog owned by the Knickelbeins. Mr. Schell died, and Mrs. Schell sued Security for damages, alleging that she was a third-person beneficiary of the mortgage contract between the Knickelbeins and Security and so had a right to sue Security for its failure to provide insurance coverage. Security contended that she was not a third-person beneficiary. From a decision for Mrs. Schell, Security appealed. Should the trial court's decision be upheld?

3. Shapiro, the president of a lumber and supply corporation, obtained a loan on its behalf. As security for the loan, the corporation assigned to the bank the corporation's rights under construction contracts it was to perform. The corporation experienced financial difficulty, and Shapiro applied the proceeds of the contracts to other corporate debts. Upon failure of the corporation to repay the loan, the bank sued the corporation for the conversion of funds to which the bank was entitled. (Conversion is defined as an unauthorized exercise of the right of ownership over personal property belonging to another, to the exclusion of the owner's rights.) Did the corporation convert the bank's funds?

4. The Equitable Life Assurance Society, owner of the Decatur North Professional Building, hired Builders Glass to recaulk the exterior of the building. The contract stated that "all work done by [Builders] will hold a 10-year guarantee." About a year later, Equitable sold the building to Decatur North Associates, which soon discovered leakage problems that it attributed to Builders' deficient recaulking job. Later, Equitable assigned its recaulking agreement with

Builders to Decatur North, including the 10-year guarantee. Decatur North then sued Builders Glass for breach of the guarantee. Builders contended that the guarantee was not assignable. Was it?

5. DeMatteo, the general contractor on a highway construction project, hired Dirt Movers, Inc., to supply gravel and dirt for the project. Dirt Movers was paid about $209,000 for materials delivered between June and December 1979. As agreed, DeMatteo withheld nearly $11,000 in "retainages," to be paid later upon Dirt Mover's satisfactory performance and a determination by the Department of Public Works (DPW) of the actual quantity of material delivered. In December, Dirt Movers assigned its retainages to Graves Equipment, Inc. The project was shut down for the winter. When it was resumed in the spring, Dirt Movers failed to deliver materials, and DeMatteo purchased them elsewhere at an increased cost of about $19,000. Then assignee Graves sought payment of the retainage amount from DeMatteo. Must DeMatteo pay?

6. In 1968, Eastern Woodworking Co. bought eleven lots from Chimney Hill Corporation, a housing development consisting of over 900 lots and a large area of "common land" containing recreational facilities, roads, and a water system. A document filed in the public records stated that an annual charge would be imposed against each lot in Chimney Hill for the right to use the common lands and related facilities. The money was to be paid to Chimney Hill or its "successors" or "assigns." However, Eastern's purchase agreement stated, "There will be one annual charge . . . until one or more of the lots have been improved." In 1975, Chimney Hill conveyed the common land to the Chimney Hill Owners' Association, Inc., and assigned to the Association the right to collect the annual charge. The Association billed Eastern for the annual charge for each of the eleven lots. Arguing that none of its lots had yet been improved, Eastern paid only one assessment, and the Association brought suit for the additional amount allegedly owed. Must Eastern pay the charges for an additional ten lots?

7. Smith sold a taxicab company to Wrehe. Wrehe made a partial payment but still owed Smith $15,000 under the contract. With Smith's consent, Wrehe then assigned "the contract" to a corporation. The assignee-corporation made some payments but soon defaulted, and Smith sued Wrehe for the balance due under the contract. Wrehe contended that only the assignee was liable to Smith. Was Wrehe liable to Smith?

CHAPTER 17

Performance, Breach, and Discharge of Contracts; Remedies for Breach of Contract

Most contracting parties expect to give and receive the promised performances. But the circumstances surrounding a contract may change from what the parties originally planned. The agreed performance may have become impossible, the parties might disagree about the kind or degree of performance required by the contract, or the contract may have been superseded by a later one. In such situations a court may have to decide whether a contract has been **discharged** (i.e., performed or in some other way terminated). If a contract obligation has not been discharged, a failure or refusal to perform it is a **breach** of the contract for which the aggrieved (offended) party may have a **remedy** such as damages, rescission, or specific performance.

The first part of this chapter discusses the performance, breach, and discharge of contractual obligations. The second part discusses (1) remedies that are available for breach of a contractual obligation that has not been discharged, and (2) the quasi-contractual remedy that may be available in the absence of an enforceable contract.

PERFORMANCE, BREACH, AND DISCHARGE OF CONTRACTS

Meaning of Performance, Breach, and Discharge

Performance is the carrying out of the obligations imposed by a contract. Al agrees to sell his car to Ben for $800, delivery and payment to be made 30 days from now. Al performs by delivering the car at the time promised; Ben performs by paying then.

"The contract" means the parties' agreement as supplemented or limited by law. Because a major goal of contract law is to foster performance, the law will supply many missing terms. Al and Ben forgot to specify the place for delivery. Under the Uniform Commercial Code (the law applying to sales of goods), the place for delivery is Al's business or residence. If the agreement contains an illegal term such as a usurious interest rate or an unconscionable clause, the courts will not enforce that term even though the parties might have agreed to it, but will limit enforcement to the remaining provisions if they are sufficient to constitute a contract.

Breach is any failure of a party to perform a duty imposed by the contract. Failure to perform constitutes a breach even though the aggrieved party might have suffered no harm as a result of it. A refusal *now* to perform an obligation scheduled for *future* performance is called an **anticipatory repudiation** or **anticipatory breach** of the contract.

Discharge is the termination of a contractual obligation. Performance is the usual method of discharge. Discharge may occur also where, for example, the parties to a contract agree to cancel it or the agreed performance has become illegal or impossible to carry out.

Case 17.1 discusses how a statute becomes a part of "the contract."

CASE 17.1   Koval v. Peoples • 431 A.2d 1284 (Del. Super. 1981)

FACTS   Defendant Peoples agreed to construct a house for the Kovals [plaintiffs]. The contract provided that Peoples would provide a well. He delivered a house and a well, but the Kovals claimed that the water was polluted and unfit for domestic use. Alleging breach of contract, the Kovals sued for damages, including the cost of installing a water purifier system. Peoples filed a motion for summary judgment.

OPINION   TAYLOR, J. . . . [I]t is undisputed that [defendant] did provide a well which produced water. The issue is whether [his] contractual obligation required him to provide a well whose water would comply with the water quality requirement of the building and plumbing codes adopted by New Castle County and the drinking water standards found in the regulations of the State Board of Health.

In the law of contracts, it is a recognized principle that existing laws form a part of a contract. This principle was stated by this court in *Trader v. Jester* . . . in the following language:

> The rule is well established that the laws in force at the time and place of making the contract enter into and form a part of it as if they had been expressly referred to, or incorporated in, its terms. The obligation of the contract is measured by the standard of the laws existing at the time of the making of the contract.

This principle applies equally to municipal ordinances. Courts in various states have held that contracts for performance of work are controlled by governmental regulations relating to the manner in which the work may be performed or the quality of the work, in the absence of express contract provision to the contrary. . . .

Courts have used different approaches in reaching the result that government regulations have an effect on contractual obligations and rights. In some cases the court has presumed that the parties intended to incorporate existing laws. Some courts have merely stated the proposition that in the absence of contrary provisions in the contract, existing laws are an obligation of the contract with the same effect as if expressly set forth in the contract. Other courts have held that existing law is an implied term of every contract. [Still others] have held

CASE 17.1 Continued

that in the sale of a new house there is an implied warranty that the builder-vendor has complied with the building code. . . .

The significance of the above cited decisions is their unanimity that a statute or ordinance which purports to impose a requirement or a restriction on a [contract's] subject matter . . . will be given effect in the application and enforcement of the contract unless the contract by clear language removes the contractual undertakings from the effect of the law or ordinance. . . .

In this State, statutes and codes . . . designed to protect the health . . . of the public establish a standard governing construction, equipping or use of facilities or property. . . . I conclude that compliance with applicable laws and regulations is a requirement and condition of building contracts for work to be performed in this State unless the contract expressly provides for a different measure of performance. . . .

. . . [T]he building and plumbing codes applicable to New Castle County . . . require dwelling houses to be supplied with potable water. I conclude that a well provided under a contract for the construction of a dwelling house must meet the water requirements for the dwelling house as those requirements have been established by law. . . . Here there is no contract language showing that the parties intended the contractual obligation to depart from the requirements of the law. . . . I conclude that the water quality standards found in the State Board of Health regulations determine the requirements for potable water as that term is used in the Codes adopted by New Castle County.

JUDGMENT

. . . I find sufficient evidence that the well water did not meet the standards of the regulations to withstand defendant's motion for summary judgment. . . . [T]he motion is denied.

Role of Conditions in Defining and Discharging Duty of Performance

A party to a contract might **condition** his or her performance on the occurrence or nonoccurrence of some fact or event. If the condition does not occur, then the party for whose benefit it was made is discharged from performance. Kyle, a resident of Minnesota, agrees to work at Linda's dairy in Nebraska on condition that he can find a place to live near the dairy at least 1 week before his employment is to begin. Kyle's duty to work for Linda in Nebraska will not become effective unless the condition is met or is waived by Kyle. If he cannot find living quarters within the agreed time, there has been a failure of the condition and he is discharged from his obligation. Or suppose that Buildo Corp. agrees to dig a tunnel to be completed within 18 months. The contract may include the condition that any time lost because of labor disputes will not be counted against the 18 months and the completion date will be extended accordingly. As these examples indicate, contractual conditions contribute to flexibility of contracting. They also help to establish the circumstances under which a contractual duty may be discharged.[1]

Express (actual) **conditions**—those *stated* by the parties *or implied-in-fact from their conduct*—must be literally complied with for the obliged party to be entitled to the return performance. The statement, "You are required to present a

---

[1]Traditionally, conditions have been classified, in terms of time of occurrence, as conditions "precedent," "subsequent," or "concurrent." These classifications have been challenged as unsound, and the *Restatement (Second) of the Law Contracts* has abandoned some of that terminology. John E. Murray, MURRAY ON CONTRACTS (1974), Sec. 141.

written breakdown of costs before you will be paid for your work," is an express condition. To be entitled to payment, you must comply literally with the condition. An oral breakdown of costs will not do (unless, of course, the other party waives the writing).

Constructive conditions—those *imposed by law* instead of by the parties' agreement—need to be only substantially complied with for the obliged party to be entitled to the return performance. Harlan agrees to pave Felicia's driveway and remove the debris for $900. They say nothing about time of payment. It is a constructive condition that Harlan must complete the paving and remove the debris before he will be entitled to payment, but a "substantially" complete (as opposed to a literally complete) performance will do. So if Harlan inadvertently misses a few shovelfuls of debris, he will still be entitled to payment (minus whatever Felicia must pay someone else to finish the job).

Discharge by Performance

A party to a contract discharges contractual obligations by performing them within the time established by the contract. If the contract does not specify a time for performance, it is due within a reasonable time after the contract is made. Sometimes, however, a party (1) offers a performance that is refused, (2) performs but fails to do so exactly as the contract requires, or (3) states in advance that he or she will not perform when the time for performance arrives. What are the rights of the aggrieved party?

Effect of Tender of Performance. A person who makes a **tender** (an offer) **of performance** may be discharged from the obligation to perform—if, for example, the other party unjustifiably withholds the cooperation necessary for the tendering person to do the work. Al contracts with Beth to repair the roof of her house "in a good and workmanlike manner," i.e., according to the standard practices of the roofing industry in that locality. But Beth does not approve of the way Al is preparing to do the work and tells him that he "absolutely may not put a ladder against the house." Al says he will do the work in a way recognized by the trade as proper but that he cannot get onto the roof without using a ladder. Beth refuses to let him proceed. Beth's withholding her cooperation in response to Al's tender discharges him from any further duty of performance and entitles him to an appropriate remedy—for example, to damages for lost profits.

Effect of Defective Performance (Breach) on Discharge. What kind of breach of contract by one party will discharge the other party from his or her duty to perform? Often discussed under the label of "doctrine of substantial performance," the problem can also be considered in terms of whether the breach of contract is material or nonmaterial.

A **material breach** is so serious that the nonbreaching party may be deprived of the benefit expected from the breaching party's performance. A material breach discharges the nonbreaching party from any duty to perform. In contrast, a **nonmaterial breach** does not deprive the nonbreaching party of the benefit of the bargain, and does not discharge that party, though the breach may cause inconvenience, annoyance, or extra expense for which the nonbreaching party may have damages. Ann contracts to build a house for Ben. She pours the foundation, but does nothing further and leaves town. Ann has committed a material breach of the contract and Ben is discharged from his duty to pay her for the house. In contrast, if Ann builds a house according to plans and specifications, except that she installs cheap doorknobs instead of the expensive ones called for by the contract, Ann has *substantially performed*. She has breached the contract, but the breach is nonmaterial. Ben is not discharged from his duty to pay Ann for the house, but because of Ann's nonmaterial breach, Ben may subtract from the contract price his cost of securing and installing the specified hardware.

So a party to whom a contractual duty is owed has a remedy for *any* breach of that duty, whether the breach is material or not. The availability of remedies for any breach tends to discourage people from treating their contractual commitments lightly. However, a nonmaterial breach *does not discharge* the other party. If it did, one could escape a contractual obligation on the basis of the other party's trivial deficiency. This would upset the legitimate expectations of substantially performing parties that they will be paid.

What breaches are material? The contracting parties can decide, though often the courts must do so.

Breaches made material by contract terms. By using express conditions, the parties may require strict compliance with the terms of the contract. In doing so, they have made the expressed terms material. Consider, for example, a contract for the sale of land. Usually it specifies the day for "closing"—that is, the day upon which the transaction is to be formally completed. Ordinarily, the seller's failure to convey the land on that day, or the buyer's failure to pay then, is *not* a material breach of the contract. A party's minor delay serves only to *postpone* and not discharge the other party's duty of performance. The aggrieved party does, of course, have a remedy for any loss caused by the delay.

However, the parties to the contract can make the closing date material by agreeing that "time is of the essence." This phrase means that the failure of a party to perform on the closing date is material and shall discharge the other party. For the closing date to be made so important, however, the courts ordinarily require an actual agreement (whether express or implied-in-fact) that time is to be of the essence. The mere presence of a preprinted time-of-the-essence clause in the contract is not, by itself, sufficient to show that agreement. The parties can make other topics material. Examples are the use of certain materials or methods of manufacture, specific inspections or tests, or a special way of crating and shipping.

Breaches made material by court decisions. Where the parties have said nothing about materiality and the courts must decide, the courts consider a variety of factors. Among them are whether the breach was willful, the degree of hardship experienced by the aggrieved party, and the amount of performance that has been rendered as compared to the amount yet to be completed. Normally, a court will find the following kinds of breach, among others, to be material: unreasonable delay in performance, delivery of seriously defective goods or the wrong goods, failure to deliver any goods, inability to deliver clear title to land, or substantial failure to render services bargained for.

> **BOX 17.1**
>
> ### You Be the Judge
>
> Design & Corrosion Engineering, Inc. (D&C), contracted to fill in potholes and sweep and overlay with asphalt Piggly Wiggly's grocery store parking lot for $24,512. The layer of asphalt was to be 1½ inches thick over an area of 5,478 square yards. When the work was completed, Piggly Wiggly refused to pay, alleging that the work was totally unsatisfactory because of loose gravel, big rocks coming up in the parking lot, areas around light poles that had not been compacted, loose joints and rough spots on the parking lot, and an average asphalt depth of only 1.36 inches. D&C's employee in charge of the work cited an industrywide "rule of thumb" that less than 500 tons of asphalt is sufficient to cover the area to a depth of 1½ inches. But, he said, he applied 528.54 tons, some of which was diverted from sound areas of the parking lot at Piggly Wiggly's request and placed on a back access road. D&C has sued for the contract price. At the time of trial the parking lot had been in use 7 days a week for about 8 months, with no evidence that Piggly Wiggly had any remedial work done. Who should prevail? ■

Effect of Anticipatory Breach. Where a party makes a material *anticipatory* breach (e.g., states that he or she will not perform when the time for performance arrives), the aggrieved party is not required to wait for the now unlikely performance. Instead, almost all courts allow the aggrieved party to suspend his or her own performance and either (1) sue immediately for breach of contract, (2) await a change of mind by the breaching party, or (3) take other steps such as finding a substitute for the performance

> **BOX 17.2**
> **Substantial Performance in Sales of Goods**
>
> In **sales of goods,** the doctrine of substantial performance does not apply. Instead, Article 2 imposes the "perfect tender rule." It permits a buyer to reject goods for even small defects—*substantial* performance by the seller is not enough. The rule is meant to prevent sellers from taking advantage of distant buyers by "palming off" slightly defective or nonconforming goods. But, since buyers could take unfair advantage of the perfect tender rule, it has a number of exceptions for the protection of sellers. The perfect tender rule is discussed in Chapter 21.

promised by the breaching party. If the aggrieved party seeks a substitute for the promised performance, he or she is discharged from liability to the breaching party and is entitled to damages for any higher costs encountered in acquiring the substitute performance. However, if the breaching party *retracts* the repudiation before the aggrieved party acts in response to it, the majority common law rule is that there is no breach of contract. For sales of goods, a UCC rule says that the repudiating party's retraction reinstates the repudiating party's rights under the contract.

Other Bases for Discharge

The kinds of discharge discussed so far result from performance, a failure to perform, or the occurrence or nonoccurrence of a circumstance specified in a condition. But there are other bases for discharging a contracting party.

Discharge by Subsequent Agreement. The parties to a contract may wish to end it without performing, or, intending to perform, may wish to alter the performance obligations in some way. Subsequent agreements of the parties are useful for such purposes. The following paragraphs describe some common types of subsequent agreements and the extent to which they discharge the obligations imposed by the original contracts.

Mutual rescission. In general, **rescission** means cancellation of a transaction. A *mutual rescission* is the voluntary act of putting an end to an executory bilateral contract by means of an agreement to do so. Mike, a young professional athlete enjoying unexpected success, becomes more valuable to his employer. As a preliminary to negotiating a new personal services contract, Mike and his employer agree to rescind the old one. The agreement of rescission is itself a new contract, agreed to without going to court, in which each party discharges the other by surrendering the rights that were established by the old personal services contract. The mutual surrender of rights constitutes the consideration necessary for, and the performance of, the contract of rescission that clears the way for the new personal services contract.

Accord and satisfaction; substitute contract. Instead of rescinding the original contract, the parties to it may wish to substitute a new set of performance obligations for those imposed by the original contract. So they may resort to an **accord and satisfaction** or to the very similar **substitute contract.** Where the new agreement is not made until after the maturity or breach of the original contract, the new agreement is called an accord and the performance of it is called a satisfaction. Where the new agreement is made before the maturity or breach of the original agreement, the new agreement is usually called a substitute contract. An accord and satisfaction or a substitute contract discharges the original contract if the parties to the new agreement so intended.

Novation. A **novation** is used to accomplish the substitution of *parties* to a contract, with or without a change in the performance obligations. Ben has a contract with Ann, but he is unable to perform it. Then Ann agrees with Ben and Carol that (1) for the payment promised to Ben, Carol will perform Ben's duties under the original contract, and (2) Ben will be freed from any further liability to Ann. The resulting contract is a novation under which Ben is discharged from his duties under the original contract.

Release; contract not to sue. In its broad sense, a **release** is any discharge from liability. The release of a contractual obligation usually is accomplished by means of a writing. In some states a written release is effective without consideration, if sealed and delivered. In other states a release is invalid unless supported by consideration. Where one party to a contract promises never to sue the other for breaching it, the promise, if supported by consideration, constitutes a **contract not to sue** and discharges the other party.

Discharge by Impossibility, Frustration, or Impracticability.
Sometimes the circumstances surrounding a contract change so drastically that the contract originally contemplated (1) cannot be performed, (2) is no longer of value to the obligee (party to whom performance is owed), or (3) can be performed only with great hardship or loss to the obligor. So the party adversely affected might seek a discharge on the ground of impossibility of performance, frustration of purpose, or impracticability of performance.

Impossibility of performance occurs where a promised performance literally is no longer possible (or never was possible). Performance is impossible where, for example, Ann hires Ben to manage her business but he dies or becomes incapacitated before his performance is due or completed. Or impossibility may result from destruction of an object or a source of supply expressly required for performance, as where Ann sells her 1961 Corvette to John for a July delivery but the car is destroyed in May. Sometimes a performance is declared illegal after the contract was made. Although the act contracted for may still be physically possible, the performance may be declared "impossible" because performance would be against the law.

In situations involving **frustration of purpose,** performance is possible and legal despite the changed circumstances. But the performance is no longer of value to the party who once sought it. Art has an apartment that commands an excellent view of the Rose Bowl parade. He agrees to rent the apartment to Beth for the day of the parade so she can view it in comfort. An earthquake causes the parade to be cancelled. Beth's purpose in leasing the apartment is frustrated. Unless the contract expressly imposed the risk of cancellation on Beth, she may be discharged from the rental contract.

Where a contract involves **impracticability** of performance, the performance is possible and legal, but it has become so extremely burdensome due to circumstances unforeseeable (or reasonably unforeseen) at the time of contracting that a court will not enforce the contract. A mere increase in costs will not make a performance impracticable. Rather, the unexpected circumstance must have so altered the essential nature of the performance that the obligated party faces catastrophic loss far beyond any that might normally have been expected. For $1,000,000, Acme agrees to build a dam for City. If the project costs an extra $100,000 to complete because Acme's engineers failed to detect ordinarily detectable geological formations, Acme will have to bear the extra cost even if the company sustains a loss on the contract. Because the geological formations were reasonably foreseeable, Acme's performance will not be held impracticable. In contrast, suppose an earthquake of record intensity opens a deep crack in the dam site that will cost $10,000,000 to fill before the dam can be constructed. Here the cost increase is so great that, given the unforeseeability of the earthquake, a court is likely to hold performance of the contract impracticable.

As Case 17.2 illustrates, the courts are reluctant to discharge a contract on the ground of impracticability or frustration of purpose, even though the obligor might lose money in performing it. While obligors often face heavy competition, small margins of profit, and a variety of uncertainties of performance, obligees rely on agreed prices when seeking financing or setting up other contracts. So, in the absence of a contrary agreement, the obligor generally is considered to have assumed the ordinary risks and difficulties of the contract.

CASE 17.2	**M&M Transport. Co. v. Schuster** • 13 B.R. 861 (S.D.N.Y. 1981)
FACTS	Plaintiff M&M Transportation Co. (M&M), in the business of intra- and interstate transport, was the owner of operating rights granted by the Interstate Commerce Commission. The long-standing practice of the ICC was to restrict entry into the trucking industry by stringently limiting the opportunity of a motor carrier to obtain operating rights from the ICC. Rather, a transport company ordinarily would have to purchase operating rights from a company that already owned them.

M&M became financially troubled, and in a 1977 bankruptcy sale sold its operating rights to defendant Schuster for $650,000. Schuster made several payments on the purchase price. In 1980, Congress enacted the Motor Carriers Act. The Act "deregulated" the trucking industry, making entry into the trucking industry easy, and substantially lessening the value of Schuster's once-exclusive rights. Alleging that deregulation frustrated his purpose in buying the rights, Schuster refused to pay M&M the balance of nearly $300,000 due under the contract. M&M brought suit and moved for a summary judgment in its favor. |
| **OPINION** | ROY BABITT, Bankruptcy Judge. . . . There is no dispute that these defendants were represented at the sales by knowledgeable businessmen, all cognizant of the risks involved and mindful of the industry. A policy of deregulation was considered by the national legislature as far back as 1971. . . . That [the rights sold by M&M] were at all times subject to regulation by the ICC or by the legislature cannot be questioned. . . .

Under the principle of commercial frustration, a party responsible for an otherwise lawful contractual obligation is discharged from performance, where that performance, although possible, is rendered undesirable or oppressive because of supervening events. . . . This principle is an offshoot of the twentieth century's rejection of a judicial hands-off policy towards contracts. It reflects increased judicial involvement in private contracts. It is an affirmation of the reality that there are situations where society's needs are best served by *not* enforcing the performance of senseless contracts. . . . Essentially, the principle of commercial frustration affords a means by which courts allocate risk in order to decide who is to bear the burden of any event not provided for by the parties' agreement. . . . The basic test is whether the parties contracted on a basic assumption that a particular contingency would not occur. . . .

With these guiding principles in mind, the court now turns to the law of New York, the governing law as the parties agreed. New York, to a large extent, follows the principle of commercial frustration, as outlined in the Restatement (Second) of Contracts § 285. . . .

The Restatement breaks this rule down into three inquiries: (1) The purpose that is frustrated must have been a principal purpose of that party in making the contract. Here, there is no doubt that the defendants determined their bids and entered into these contracts in order to take advantage of the restrictive regulatory structure which made it virtually impossible for others to obtain operating rights from the ICC. . . . (2) The frustration must be substantial. This element |

CASE 17.2 Continued

is to ensure that the defense of commercial frustration will not be accepted in cases where performance has become merely less profitable. . . . [T]he change achieved by the 1980 law substantially lessened the value of the rights purchased. . . . [But the] lessened profitability occasioned by the 1980 statute is no different [from] a change in fashion and the impact of such change on the profits of the purchaser of . . . mini or maxi dresses.

The final element, (3), is that the non-occurrence of the frustrating event must have been a basic assumption on which the contract was made. This makes the foreseeability of the event a factor in the determination. . . . A careful reading of the record . . . discloses that [this factor] is fatal to defendants' defense. . . . Here, the defendants made their agreements knowing full well that the value of the rights they bought depended on an unchanged regulatory structure, but one that always was and remained subject to change. . . .

Although defendants argue against the foreseeability of deregulation, the facts belie the premise. [Schuster's] affidavit . . . says:

> In June 1977, and for years previously thereto, the undersigned [was] aware that there had been discussions in Congress about the possibility of some changes in the Interstate Commerce Act, but these discussions had never materialized into any concrete proposal with any realistic prospect of adoption by Congress, and many of the proposals given the most serious consideration did not contemplate the substantial elimination of the limited entry into the marketplace which had always been incident to ICC operating rights.

This affidavit demonstrates ample knowledge of the possibility of deregulation. That defendants chose to disbelieve or to dismiss the possibility as a serious threat was a personal assessment. That defendants bid as they did with knowledge of a potential deregulation was a matter of their business judgment. For all that appears their bids might have been pitched not only to the possibility of diminished profits but to the judgment that their expectations would measure up to their investment even if deregulation, in fact, were to come. . . . [T]hese defendants could have insisted that if deregulation were to come within a set period, the sales would be nullified. They chose not to [do so]. . . .

Here, the only frustration is the defendants, in that known risks they assumed have turned out to their disadvantage. . . . Commercial frustration is no defense where no unusual or unforeseeable event prevented performance and where provision could readily have been made for what actually occurred.

JUDGMENT . . . [P]laintiff is entitled to the grant of summary judgment. . . .

Discharge by Operation of Law. Sometimes contractual obligations are discharged by law, regardless of the will of the parties. Illustrations include discharges by bankruptcy or the "running" of the statute of limitations. A *discharge in bankruptcy* is granted by a court and releases the debtor from the contractual obligations covered by the discharge. (However, many debts are not dischargeable in bankruptcy—alimony, back taxes, and so on—and to be effective, the discharge must be pleaded as a defense to an action on a contract covered by it.) The *"running" of the statute of limitations* (expiration of the time permitted for bringing suit) also bars enforcement of a contract.

REMEDIES FOR BREACH OF CONTRACT; QUASI-CONTRACTUAL REMEDY

Contracts can be breached in many ways, and the resulting harms can vary tremendously. To protect aggrieved parties in these various circumstances, the law provides a number of remedies, each meant to protect some interest of the aggrieved party. The remedies usually sought are damages (the traditional common law—or "legal"—remedy discussed in Chapter 1), and rescission and specific performance ("equitable" remedies). The remainder of this chapter discusses the interests protected by contract remedies, some common kinds of contractual damages, three equitable remedies relating to contracts, and the quasi-contractual remedy that may be available where there is no enforceable contract.

Remedies for Breach of Contract

Interests Protected by Contract Remedies. Legal and equitable remedies for breach of contract protect three interests of the nonbreaching party: the expectation interest, the reliance interest, and the restitution interest.

The **expectation interest** is the gain or profit that one expects from the contract. The expectation interest usually is protected by an award of damages equaling the value of the expected performance. You agree to pay $500 for a used car, the seller refuses to deliver, and you have to pay $700 for a comparable model. Your expectation interest translates into $200 in damages, the amount needed from the breaching seller for you to fulfill your expectation of obtaining that particular kind of car. Where the legal remedy of damages is inadequate to accomplish that result, the equitable remedy of specific performance may be available to the aggrieved party. You agreed to pay $500 for a unique bottle for your collection, but the seller refuses to deliver. Money damages won't be adequate to give effect to your contract expectation, so a court will instead order the seller to perform the contract by delivering the bottle.

The **reliance interest** is the interest of the nonbreaching party in recovering costs of preparing for the hoped-for performance. The seller might have altered machinery or contracted for supplies to fill a special order for the buyer. The buyer might have made preparations to store, sell, or use goods that the seller promised to deliver. In either situation the nonbreaching party may have suffered a monetary loss that is recoverable from the breaching party as reliance damages.

The **restitution interest** is the interest of the nonbreaching party in recovering a benefit (amounting to less than full performance) that he or she conferred on the other party. A buyer might have made a partial payment for land promised but not conveyed. A seller might have made a partial delivery for which payment was promised but not made.

A party seeking restitution may wish to recover property delivered or, instead, to recover its value. A return of the property itself is called **specific restitution;** a payment of the *value* of a benefit conferred is called **substitutionary restitution;** a return of property together with compensation for a decrease in its value is called **mixed restitution.**[2] Substitutionary restitution is necessary where the benefit cannot be returned—for example, where services were rendered or goods were consumed. Mixed restitution is useful where the property to be restored has been damaged or has depreciated.

The "Legal" Remedy—Damages. A court awards **damages** by ordering a payment of money that compensates a plaintiff for harm caused by the defendant's breach of the contract—i.e., that puts the aggrieved party in the same economic position he or she would have been in had the contract been performed. To do this, a damage award must protect all three interests if they were violated—not only the expectation interest, but the reliance and restitution interests as well.

A judgment for damages (the traditional remedy "at law") is the sole remedy where a pay-

---

[2] Dan B. Dobbs, HANDBOOK ON THE LAW OF REMEDIES (1973), Sec. 4.4.

ment of money is an adequate substitute for the performance promised by the breaching party. Ben contracts to sell 5,000 tons of #1 wheat to Carl, the price of wheat then rises 5 percent above the contract price, and Ben breaches the contract by selling all his wheat to Sue. If #1 wheat is readily available from other sources, Carl's only remedy is a judgment for damages in an amount sufficient to cover the higher cost of substitute wheat and any extra expenses required to procure it.

Kinds of damages. A breach of contract can cause many kinds of loss to the aggrieved party, or no loss at all. Consequently, the courts award damages of various kinds, depending on the degree or kind of harm suffered by the aggrieved party. They include:

1. **Compensatory damages.** An award of money that will repay the injured party for loss caused by the breach of contract. Compensatory damages may be **general** or **special** (consequential).
2. **Nominal damages.** An insignificant sum awarded to the aggrieved party where there is a breach of contract but no real injury, or where there is a real injury but the plaintiff's evidence fails to show the amount. An award of nominal damages entitles the aggrieved party to recover court costs (but, usually, not attorney's fees).
3. **Punitive (exemplary) damages.** An amount awarded to punish or make an example of the defendant for malicious or fraudulent conduct. Punitive damages are above and beyond any compensatory damages that might be awarded. Since most contract breaches are not considered malicious even if intentional, punitive damages for breach of contract are rare.

Compensatory damages, whether general or special, are usually the major concern in a breach-of-contract suit. **General damages** are those that the law presumes to have resulted directly from the wrong complained of, without regard to any special circumstances of the plaintiff. Sue, a dealer in construction equipment, agrees to sell a tractor to Ben, a building contractor, for $50,000 and to deliver it on March 1. In breach of the contract, Sue fails to deliver the tractor, and Ben must buy that kind of tractor from Sam for $55,000, the market price on March 1. Ben has suffered $5,000 in general damages. General contract damages usually consist of the difference between the contract price and the market price at the time performance is due. If the market price is lower at that time, Ben suffers no general damages (but may receive nominal damages).

Special (consequential) damages result from special circumstances about which the parties knew or had reason to know at the time of contracting. Special damages are independent of general damages. At the time of contracting, Ben tells Sue that he needs the tractor by March 1 so he can avoid a $10,000 penalty for breaching a construction contract with Cora. Sue promises but fails to deliver the tractor by that date. Ben buys a replacement tractor for the same price, but is not able to buy it in time to avoid the penalty. Ben has suffered $10,000 in special damages, the amount of the penalty that he had to pay Cora. If Ben had to pay a higher price for the replacement tractor, he would have suffered both general and special damages.

What if *Ben* had been the breaching party in these situations? Sue, the seller, would have remedies that protect her expectation and other interests.

Liquidated damages clauses. A contract may contain a clause stipulating an amount of damages to be paid for breach of contract. Or the clause might provide a formula for calculating damages in the event of breach. Often used in construction contracts, contracts for supplying goods, and fixed-term employment contracts such **liquidated damages clauses** take the place of a judicial determination of damages and are enforceable if limited to compensating the injured party for loss.

Liquidated damages clauses are *not* enforceable, however, if they are **penal** in nature—that is, if they merely penalize the breaching party, without regard to actual damages, for committing the breach. A liquidated damages provision that awards to the injured party an amount disproportionate to the actual damages sustained, or likely to have been sustained, will not be enforced.

Case 17.3 illustrates the position of most courts, that liquidated damages clauses are enforceable where two conditions exist at the time of contracting:

1. It appears to the parties that the harm flowing from the breach will be difficult to estimate accurately.
2. There is a reasonable relation between the damages agreed on and those expected to occur in the event of breach.

CASE 17.3

Zlotoff v. Tucker • 201 Cal. Rptr. 692 (Cal. App. 1984)

FACTS Plaintiff Zlotoff owned two adjoining vacant lots and, in the same block, a skating rink and an adjoining parking lot next to E. R. Cota's office building. For several years Cota, his employees, and visitors used Zlotoff's parking lot without permission, angering Zlotoff. In 1977, Zlotoff listed his vacant lots for sale. Defendant Tucker offered to buy them. During negotiations, Zlotoff told Tucker of his anger toward Cota over misuse of the parking lot and said he did not want Cota to become owner of the vacant lots. Zlotoff asked Tucker if he was related to Cota. Tucker said no. Tucker was in fact Cota's nephew.

Zlotoff then sold the lots to Tucker under a written contract of sale that expressed Zlotoff's reluctance to sell to Cota, that forbade Tucker to do so directly or indirectly, and that contained a clause requiring Tucker to pay $20,000 plus attorney's fees, costs, and interest in the event that Cota became owner of the lots, through Tucker, within 10 years of the sale to Tucker. Less than a year later Cota became owner of the lots in a transaction involving Tucker. Zlotoff sued Tucker for breach of contract and fraud. The trial court awarded Zlotoff $20,000 plus attorney's fees and interest, and $2,500 in punitive damages for Tucker's fraud. Tucker appealed.

OPINION GERALD BROWN, Presiding Judge . . . [Under § 1671 of the California Civil Code], "The parties to a contract may agree therein upon an amount which shall be presumed to be the amount of damages sustained by a breach therefor, when, from the nature of the case, it would be impracticable or extremely difficult to fix the actual damage."

At the time Zlotoff sold Tucker the vacant lots it was reasonably foreseeable, given Zlotoff's anger toward Cota, [that] Zlotoff would suffer mental and emotional damages if Tucker breached the agreement by [conveying] the property to Cota. Zlotoff testified: "It was very difficult evaluating my pain and suffering and the inconvenience and discomfort I had with Cota all of these years." Under these circumstances the court properly found [that] such damages were difficult to ascertain when the parties entered into their agreement. Further, on this record the court could properly find [that] the $20,000 liquidated damages clause resulted from the parties' reasonable efforts to ascertain what damages Zlotoff would suffer if Tucker resold the vacant lots to Cota. Before accepting Tucker's offer, Zlotoff told Tucker about his feelings toward Cota and his desire [that] Cota not become owner of the vacant lots. . . . Zlotoff also told Tucker [that] $20,000 was the difference between the listing price and a price he had earlier

**CASE 17.3
Continued**

quoted to Cota. Further, Tucker signed the $20,000 liquidated damages clause only after Zlotoff agreed to Tucker's requested modifications limiting the period of Tucker's liability for reselling the property to Cota. . . .

Tucker contends the court should not have enforced the parties' liquidated damages agreement because such agreement improperly restricted his right to dispose of the vacant lots Zlotoff sold him. . . . However, section 711 prohibits only unreasonable restraints on alienation. . . . [The trial] court said: ". . . I'm inclined to think that this restraint was a reasonable one, and I'm so finding for the reason that the feelings of Mr. Zlotoff which have been termed by the defense a vendetta were ones that a reasonable person can have, where his property is interfered with, trespassed upon and so forth, and where attempts to [resolve the dispute] by amicable discussions have been fruitless." Under the circumstances here the court properly found the limited restrictive clause was reasonable. . . . Any restraint on alienation under the parties' agreement . . . was minimal. . . . [T]he parties' agreement affected reconveyance only as to two specifically named persons and limited any restriction to the earlier of 10 years or the date Zlotoff sold the nearby skating rink. The court properly enforced the . . . agreement. . . .

Tucker contends the court erroneously awarded Zlotoff punitive damages for breach of contract. However, Tucker misconstrues the court's findings. Zlotoff pleaded [a cause of action for fraud]. . . . After trial the court found Zlotoff proved his allegations of . . . fraud. The court properly awarded Zlotoff punitive damages under section 3294 after specifically finding Tucker committed "rather gross fraud."

JUDGMENT   The judgment is affirmed.

"Equitable" Remedies. Often, a payment of money damages is not an adequate remedy for a breach of contract. Where the legal remedy is inadequate, the aggrieved party may be entitled to an equitable remedy: reformation, rescission, or specific performance of the contract.

Sometimes, through mistake or fraud, a written contract does not express the actual agreement of the parties. For example, Art Gallery agrees to pay Maria $5,000 for her painting but the written contract shows the price to be $500. Maria may bring a suit in equity for the **reformation** (correction) of the contract so that it will express the true agreement of the parties.

Sometimes a person has a valid reason for rescinding (canceling) a contract—fraud, mistake, duress, and the like—but is uncertain about his or her legal right to do so (or is unable to do so) without the aid of a court. The court-ordered equitable remedy of **rescission** is available. When seeking rescission, the plaintiff petitions the court to order cancellation of the contract and to restore what the plaintiff has parted with. Since the plaintiff must "do equity to receive equity," the plaintiff ordinarily must make or offer restitution (a return) of anything the plaintiff received from the defendant under the contract.

A plaintiff might be denied rescission even though the remedy at law is inadequate. Suppose that Anne, in negotiating the sale of her drugstore to Bill, fraudulently overstates the assets of the business by 20 percent. Bill learns of the fraud 2 weeks after taking possession of the store but continues to operate it for a year while the volume of business declines to almost zero due to his mismanagement. Bill then brings suit in equity to rescind the contract, expecting to return the now worthless drugstore to Anne and to receive from her the amount he paid for it. Bill will be denied the remedy of rescission. Under the equitable doctrine of **laches** (which forbids unreasonable delay in asserting one's rights), and under the principle that Bill must "do equity to receive equity," he must seek rescission (and make a good faith attempt to return the business) within a reasonable time after learning of Anne's fraud. It would be unreasonable to permit Bill, who learned of the fraud early, to ruin the business over the course of a year and then to return to Anne the worthless remains. Despite being denied the equitable remedy of rescission, however, Bill may pursue his legal remedy of damages if the time specified in the applicable statute of limitations has not expired.

Specific performance is available where the remedy at law (damages) is inadequate to compensate for loss caused by a failure to perform a contractual duty. Art contracts with Roberto for a painting, but Roberto changes his mind and refuses to deliver it. Art must have the artwork itself to enjoy its special qualities. Roberto can be compelled by a court of equity specifically to perform the contract by delivering the painting to Art. Similarly, a contract for the purchase of land, or of some interest in it, is specifically enforceable, since each parcel of real estate is considered under Anglo-American law to have unique physical features or some special commercial value such as a good location that cannot be adequately compensated for by a payment of money.

Sometimes, though, a court will withhold specific performance even though the remedy at law is inadequate and will instead limit the plaintiff to his or her remedy at law. The courts prefer not to impose offensive personal relationships on contracting parties. So a court will not compel the specific performance of a contract for personal services—entertaining, landscaping, hairstyling, sales management, and dentistry being examples. Nor will the court specifically enforce a contract to marry or, usually, a contract to enter into a partnership.

Courts also refuse to grant specific performance where judicial supervision of the performance is impractical or beyond the ability of the court. Some partnership agreements that do not impose an offensive personal relationship would nevertheless be impractical for the court to enforce specifically, as would some contracts to arbitrate and some construction or repair contracts. Large-scale construction contracts would be especially difficult to enforce specifically, and injured parties to such contracts often are left to their remedy at law.

Case 17.4 discusses what is necessary for a plaintiff to qualify for the remedy of specific performance.

CASE 17.4	**First Nat'l State Bank of New Jersey v. Commonwealth Federal Savings & Loan Assoc.** • 610 F.2d 164 (3d Cir. 1979)
FACTS	Mathema Developers began construction of the Glen Oaks Shopping Mall. As in most real estate developments, financing was to take place in two stages: (1) a short-term construction loan from a commercial bank and (2) a long-term "permanent" loan from a savings institution or an insurance company. Defendant Commonwealth Federal Savings & Loan Association made Mathema a commitment for $3,500,000 in permanent financing. A short time later, plaintiff First National Bank of New Jersey made Mathema a $3,600,000 construction loan. In making the loan, First National relied on Commonwealth's earlier consent to Mathema's assigning to First National the long-term loan commitment made by Commonwealth. After First National disbursed the construction funds, it sought a closing of the long-term financing Commonwealth had promised. By this time,

**CASE 17.4
Continued**

the shopping mall was in grave economic difficulties, and Commonwealth refused to make the loan. When the builder was unable to keep up its loan payments, First National foreclosed its construction mortgage, began operating the mall at a loss, and sued Commonwealth for specific performance of the commitment. The federal district court ordered specific performance. Commonwealth appealed, alleging that specific performance should not be granted to enforce mortgage loan agreements.

OPINION

ADAMS, Cir. J. . . . We come now to what appears to be the most provocative issue on this appeal, namely whether the decree of specific performance was proper. Under New Jersey law, the "right to the equitable remedy of specific performance turns upon the existence of an adequate remedy at law; and the adequacy of the legal remedy of compensation depends upon the facts . . . of the particular case." . . . Generally, the remedy at law is said to be inadequate in two situations: (1) where damages would be insufficient because the subject matter of the contract is of such a special nature that it resists translation into [money]; or (2) where "damages are impracticable" because "it is impossible to arrive at a legal measure of damages at all, or at least with any sufficient degree of certainty." . . .

Traditionally, courts have been reluctant to grant specific performance of agreements to lend or borrow money, inasmuch as money is intrinsically fungible. The more recent cases, however, and especially those involving construction loans, have shown a greater recognition that specific performance may be justified in exceptional circumstances. . . .

The district judge . . . found that New Jersey law supported the principle that a contract for the financing of a shopping center is unique, in the sense that the term has been used in cases granting specific performance, because the subject matter itself is "unavailable in similar form." Further, he ascertained that the damages suffered by First National were not susceptible to accurate calculation and that "an award of damages would fail to make plaintiff whole."

In so holding, the trial judge placed principal reliance on *Selective Builders, Inc. v. Hudson City Savings Bank* . . . , a case from a New Jersey trial court. . . . [Selective Builders, Inc., sought specific performance . . . against Hudson City Savings Bank, which had issued a permanent mortgage loan commitment on an apartment complex. . . . The [court] ordered specific performance of the loan. . . . Damages at law were held inadequate because (1) it would be difficult to calculate damages, (2) a damage award would not make plaintiff whole, and (3) the rights of third parties would be prejudiced if only damages were awarded. . . . [court's footnote].]

Commonwealth attempts to distinguish *Selective Builders* . . . because the developer there had tried without success to secure other mortgage financing, while there is no evidence here that First National made any such effort. But the court in *Selective Builders* quoted approvingly from a decision . . . that emphasized the futility of seeking alternative mortgage financing for an obviously failed project: "The would-be permanent mortgage lender must contemplate that if, at the last minute, it cancels its commitment such action would be disastrous to the borrower; that in such event obtaining a new permanent mortgage loan would be

> **CASE 17.4**
> **Continued**
>
> well-nigh impossible [because] whatever brought about the cancellation would [surely] prevent another lender from entering the fray. . . ." We . . . reject Commonwealth's assertion that specific performance was improper because First National should have attempted to mitigate its damages by obtaining substitute performance at a higher interest rate.
>
> [Since the estimated value of the shopping mall varied from a low of $1,070,000 to a high of $3,500,000], there is ample evidence in the record to support the district court's conclusion that accurate calculation of damages was impracticable in this case.
>
> As between the construction lender and the permanent lender, it does not appear unreasonable to place the risk of the success or failure of a real estate venture on the latter. Real estate developments generally are riskier than other business investments, and therefore mortgage rates are significantly higher than interest rates on most other loans. If the permanent lender can escape its commitment when a project seems to have failed, that party will have achieved a significant shifting of risks without a corresponding shift in the returns on successful ventures. A permanent lender's primary security on such a venture is the capitalized value of the project, and so it is the permanent lender, not the construction lender, that has the responsibility and presumably the expertise to analyze the business risks. It is therefore appropriate to place the risk of the project's nonviability on the permanent lender. . . .
>
> **JUDGMENT** The judgment of the district court will be affirmed.

Limits on Damage Remedies. A plaintiff's right to recover damages for breach of contract is limited. The principal limits on the recovery of damages are reflected (1) in rules concerning certainty and foreseeability of damages and (2) in the requirement that a plaintiff minimize (mitigate) his or her damages where reasonably possible.

Certainty of damages; foreseeability of special damages. A plaintiff must prove the amount of loss with reasonable *certainty*. In a suit for damages, the amount of loss may be determined by reference to market values. Where there is no established market, the amount of loss may be determined by other means such as an appraisal.

The recovery of special (consequential) damages is subject to additional limits, mainly because special damages represent losses due to special or unusual circumstances surrounding the breach of contract. Juanita plans to manufacture machines and to sell them to thousands of customers. Her supplier's delivering defective parts could cause Juanita extensive damages. Should Mark, her supplier, be liable not only for general damages but also for special damages such as Juanita's lost profits or amounts paid to injured customers? Whether Juanita will be allowed to recover damages for all her losses is determined in part by rules governing foreseeability of special damages.[3]

The main policy of the law of damages is to make the plaintiff "whole"—that is, to protect his or her expectation and reliance interests. Limiting this policy is the somewhat conflicting policy of protecting the defendant from unexpected and potentially ruinous awards of special damages, even though all the damages claimed actually flowed from the defendant's breach. To place a reasonable limit on "remote" damages, American courts have followed *Hadley v. Baxen-*

---

[3] The discussion that follows is based mainly on Dobbs, op. cit., Sec. 12.3.

dale, a famous English case decided in 1854.[4] Under principles developed from that case, the courts have refused to award special damages unless at the time of contracting they were "foreseen by" or were "within the contemplation of" the parties to the contract.

Some older courts would not hold a defendant liable for special damages unless the defendant had actually agreed to pay them. Today, most courts hold that special damages can be within the parties' contemplation in the absence of any such agreement. It is sufficient that the breaching defendant had at the time of contracting *reason to know* of potential special damages. Article 2 of the UCC (governing sales of goods) has adopted this position. So, if Mark, Juanita's supplier, knows that the parts are to be used in a manufacturing process, Mark has reason to know that defective parts may cause a variety of production and resale losses. Thus, Mark can foresee the special damages.

[4]156 English Reports 145.

Mitigation of damages. A plaintiff may not recover damages for losses he or she could reasonably have avoided. This general rule of damages applies to breaches of contract. Suppose Ann is wrongfully discharged in breach of her 2-year employment contract. She has a damage remedy for that breach, but her recovery of damages may be reduced by amounts she could reasonably have earned by taking other suitable employment. A manufacturer that continues to manufacture goods after the buyer repudiates the contract may not be allowed the expenses of the continued manufacture as damages unless the continuation is a commercially reasonable attempt to avoid loss. These examples illustrate the **rule of avoidable consequences.** The rule is not meant to defeat legitimate claims for damages. Rather, in applying it, the courts intend to disallow damage claims only where (and to the extent that) a very modest effort by the plaintiff would have reduced the plaintiff's loss.

Case 17.5, a landlord-tenant dispute, involves many of the topics covered in this chapter.

CASE 17.5	**Wade v. Jobe** • 818 P.2d 1006 (Utah 1991)
FACTS	In June 1988, defendant Lynda Jobe rented a house from plaintiff Clyde Wade and moved in with her three young children. She soon discovered numerous defects in the house and within a few days had no hot water. The water heater had been extinguished by accumulated sewage, which also produced a foul odor throughout the house. Jobe notified Wade, who several times pumped the sewage from the basement onto the sidewalk and relit the water heater. These and other problems persisted from July through October 1988. In November, Jobe notified Wade that she would withhold rent until the sewage problem was solved permanently. The situation did not improve, and in December the City Inspection Division declared the premises unsafe for human occupancy owing to the lack of a sewer connection and other problems. Jobe moved out, and Wade sued for $770 in unpaid rent. Jobe filed a counterclaim, seeking an offset against rent owed because of the uninhabitable condition of the premises. Holding that Utah law did not recognize an implied warranty of habitability for residential rental premises, the trial court granted judgment to Wade, and Jobe appealed.
OPINION	DURHAM, J. . . . At common law, the leasing of real property was viewed primarily as a conveyance of land for a term. . . . At a time when the typical lease was for agricultural purposes, it was assumed that the land, rather than any im-

**CASE 17.5
Continued**

provements, was the most important part of the leasehold. . . . Under the rule of caveat emptor, a tenant had a duty to inspect the premises to determine their safety and suitability for the purposes for which they were leased. . . . Moreover, absent deceit or fraud on the part of the landlord or an express warranty to the contrary, the landlord had no duty to make repairs during the course of the tenancy. . . .

Unlike tenants in feudal England, most modern tenants bargain for the use of structures on the land rather than the land itself. . . . Modern tenants, like consumers of goods, . . . frequently have no choice but to rely on the landlord to provide a habitable dwelling. . . . Where they exist, housing shortages, standardized leases, and racial and class discrimination place today's tenants . . . in a poor position to bargain effectively for express warranties and covenants [promises] requiring landlords to lease and maintain safe and sanitary housing. . . .

[Under the UCC,] implied warranties are designed to protect ordinary consumers who do not have the knowledge, capacity, or opportunity to ensure that goods which they are buying are in safe condition. . . . [For residential leases] the implied warranty of habitability [has been adopted in over forty states and the District of Columbia] to protect the tenant as the party in the less advantageous bargaining position. The residential landlord warrants that the leased premises are habitable at the outset of the lease term and will remain so during the course of the tenancy. . . . Consistent with prevailing trends in consumer law . . . we reject the rule of caveat emptor and recognize the common law implied warranty of habitability in residential leases.

. . . To guide the trial court in determining whether there is a breach of the warranty of habitability, we describe some general standards that the landlord is required to satisfy. [T]he warranty . . . does not require the landlord to maintain the premises in perfect condition at all times, nor does it preclude minor housing code violations or other defects. Moreover, the landlord will not be liable for defects caused by the tenant. . . . Further, the landlord must have a reasonable time to repair material defects before a breach can be established.

As a general rule, the warranty of habitability requires that the landlord maintain "bare living requirements" . . . and that the premises are fit for human occupation. . . . Failure to supply heat or hot water, for example, breaches the warranty. A breach is not shown, however, by evidence of minor deficiencies such as the malfunction of venetian blinds, minor water leaks or wall cracks, or a need for paint. . . .

[We remand] this case to the trial court to determine whether the landlord has breached the implied warranty of habitability as defined in this opinion. If the trial court finds a breach of the warranty of habitability, it must then determine damages.

. . . Under the prevailing contemporary view of the residential lease as a contractual transaction, . . . the tenant's obligation to pay rent is conditioned upon the landlord's fulfilling his part of the bargain. . . .

Once the landlord has breached his duty to provide habitable conditions, there are at least two ways the tenant can treat the duty to pay rent. The tenant may continue to pay rent to the landlord or withhold the rent. If the tenant continues to pay full rent to the landlord during the period of uninhabitability, the

**CASE 17.5
Continued**

tenant can bring an affirmative action to establish the breach and receive a reimbursement for excess rents paid. Rent withholding, on the other hand, deprives the landlord of the rent due during the default, thereby motivating the landlord to repair the premises. . . .

In general, courts have applied contract remedies when a breach of the warranty of habitability has been shown. One available remedy, therefore, is damages. Special damages may be recovered when, as a foreseeable result of the landlord's breach, the tenant suffers personal injury, property damage, relocation expenses, or other similar injuries. . . . General damages recoverable in the form of rent abatement [reduction] or reimbursement to the tenant are more difficult to calculate.

Several different measures for determining the amount of rent abatement to which a tenant is entitled have been used by the courts. The first of these is the fair rental value of the premises as warranted less their fair rental value in the unrepaired condition. . . . Another measure is the contract rent less the fair rental value of the premises in the unrepaired condition. Methodological difficulties inherent in both of these measures, combined with the practical difficulties of producing evidence on fair market value, however, limit the efficacy of those measures for dealing with residential leases. For this reason, a number of courts have adopted what is called the "percentage diminution" (or percentage reduction in use) approach which places more discretion with the trier of fact.

Under the percentage diminution approach, the tenant's recovery reflects the percentage by which the tenant's use and enjoyment of the premises has been reduced by the uninhabitable conditions. . . . In applying this approach, the trial court must carefully review the materiality of the particular defects and the length of time such defects have existed. . . .

. . . [W]e think that the percentage diminution approach has a practical advantage in that it will generally obviate the need for expert testimony and reduce the cost and complexity of enforcing the warranty of habitability. . . .

JUDGMENT

The decision of the trial court . . . regarding the implied warranty of habitability . . . is reversed. We remand this case to the trial court to determine whether the landlord breached the implied warranty of habitability as defined in this opinion. If the trial court determines that he was not in breach, the landlord will be entitled to payment for all the past due rent. If the trial court determines that his breach of the warranty of habitability totally excused the tenant's rent obligation (i.e., rendered the premises virtually uninhabitable), the landlord's action to recover rent due will fail. If the trial court determines that the landlord's breach partially excused the tenant's rent obligation, the tenant will be entitled to a percentage rent abatement for the period during which the house was uninhabitable.

Quasi-Contractual Remedy

Suppose the following situations:

- Dr. X notices an unconscious stranger lying on a roadside and renders emergency medical services. The stranger dies without regaining consciousness.
- X makes improvements on a house under an oral purchase agreement that is not enforceable as a contract because of failure of the parties to comply with the statute of frauds.
- X transports her children to school because the school board refuses to perform its statutory duty to do so.

None of these situations involves a contract. Yet in each one X has conferred a benefit on someone. To prevent the "unjust enrichment" of the person benefited (or in the first situation perhaps to encourage the rendering of emergency services), the law provides a restitutionary remedy called **quasi contract.** Under the law of quasi contract, the plaintiff may recover the thing conferred if it is specifically restorable. Otherwise, the plaintiff may recover the reasonable value of the property or services conferred.

A quasi-contractual remedy is available only where there is no enforceable contract. Mercedes has partly performed services called for by her contract with Rafael and has rightfully rescinded it on the ground that full performance has become impossible. The contract no longer exists and cannot be the basis for Mercedes' recovery of damages. However, she may be entitled to recover in quasi contract the value of her services. In quasi contract the measure of her damages is the reasonable value (ordinarily the market value) of her services and *not* the price established by the now-ineffective contract.

SUMMARY

The duties of contracting parties are determined by their contract. A party discharges his or her duty by performance or, sometimes, by tendering the required performance.

A material breach of contract by one party may discharge the other, either immediately or when the material failure to perform cannot be cured. In addition to discharge by performance, by failure of a condition, and by material breach, there are other kinds of discharge. They include discharge by subsequent agreement; by impossibility, frustration, or impracticability; and by operation of law.

Remedies for breach of contract protect three interests of the nonbreaching party. The expectation interest is the interest that a party has in receiving the benefit of the bargain. The reliance interest is the interest of a party in recovering costs incurred in preparing for the hoped-for performance. The restitution interest is the interest of a party in recovering his or her partial performance.

Money damages, the remedy at law, is the preferred remedy. Where the remedy at law is inadequate, the equitable remedy of reformation, rescission, or specific performance may be available. Liquidated damages clauses may be enforced if they are not penal.

A plaintiff must prove damages with reasonable certainty. The principal limits on the recovery of damages are reflected in rules concerning certainty of damages and foreseeability of special damages. A plaintiff may not recover damages for losses which the plaintiff could reasonably have avoided. For many situations where there is no enforceable contract, there is a quasi-contractual remedy, provided by the law to prevent unjust enrichment.

REVIEW QUESTIONS

1. Describe the relationship among performance, breach, and discharge.

2. Illustrate how the use of a condition may help establish the circumstances under which a contractual duty will be discharged.

3. (a) How may a party to a contract discharge his or her duty of performance? **(b)** Why are remedies available for nonmaterial breaches of contract? **(c)** What is the legal effect of a material breach? When will this effect occur?

4. (a) Must a mutual rescission involve a return of partial performances to be effective? **(b)** How does an accord and satisfaction differ from a novation?

5. How does discharge by impossibility differ from discharge by frustration? From discharge by impracticability? In your answer illustrate each kind of discharge.

6. Juanita signs a contract providing that she will pay $3,000 if she fails to render the services required of her by the contract. Under what circumstances might this provision be enforceable?

7. (a) Does being denied an equitable remedy affect the availability of the legal remedy of damages? **(b)** In what situations, and for what reasons, might a court refuse to order specific performance even though the remedy at law is inadequate?

8. Distinguish between general and special damages.

9. List three kinds of restitution and describe a typical use for each.

10. With regard to special damages, what is the purpose of the "foreseeability" requirement?

11. Explain the meaning and operation of the rule of avoidable consequences.

12. What is the relationship between quasi-contractual and contractual remedies?

CASE PROBLEMS

1. Mahacek operated a trucking company. When his truck developed major engine problems, he took it to International Harvester Co. (IH) for repair. IH gave Mahacek a detailed price quotation of $4,469.58 for the repairs. When the repairs were completed, IH said the charges exceeded $6,900, and demanded payment in cash. In negotiations with IH, Mahacek made three offers—to pay $4,469.58 by charging it to his account, to pay $6,900 by charging it to his account, and to pay $4,469.58 in cash. Mahacek did not have the cash, but his brother had agreed to lend it to him. IH refused all three offers and retained the truck, claiming a common law artisan's (mechanic's) lien in it to secure payment. IH brought suit for its charges, and Mahacek counterclaimed for damages for wrongful detention of the truck. A jury awarded Mahacek $16,500. IH was granted a judgment notwithstanding the jury's verdict on the ground that Mahacek had failed to discharge the artisan's lien. Assume that IH had agreed to repair the truck for $4,469.58. Was any one of Mahacek's offers sufficient to discharge the lien and thus to make IH's retention of the truck wrongful?

2. The Warrens hired Denison to construct a house on their property. The contract price was $73,400. After the Warrens took possession of the house, a dispute arose over the quality of construction. Because of the dispute the Warrens withheld the balance of $48,000 due under the contract and brought suit for a declaratory judgment. In their suit they sought a discharge from their remaining obligations under the contract, alleging that Denison had failed to perform his obligations. The jury found that when the Warrens took possession of the house it was fit for the ordinary purposes for which houses are used. The jury also found that $2,000 in repairs would be required to correct defective work. Did Denison's defective performance discharge the Warrens from their remaining obligations under the contract?

3. Oxford Funding Corp. agreed to purchase real estate from James H. Northrup, Inc., and made a down payment on the purchase price. Northrup was to deliver the property together with rental permits required under the Town Code. On the day before the date set for closing, Oxford canceled the transaction and demanded that Northrup return the down payment. Although the permits were easily obtainable, Northrup had not yet acquired them. Oxford contended that the lack of the permits constituted a title defect that justified the cancellation, and brought suit to recover the down payment from Northrup. Northrup argued that Oxford's cancellation was an anticipatory repudiation of the contract that entitled Northrup to keep the down payment. Who should prevail?

4. For several years, Lovorn was a sales representative for Iron Wood Products Corp. Then a dispute developed between them over the amount of commissions that Iron Wood owed Lovorn. After considerable correspondence between the parties, Iron Wood tendered to Lovorn a check for $7,707.87. On its reverse side the check read, "Endorsement constitutes acceptance of final payment in full and without recourse for the period ending December 27, 1975." Lovorn endorsed the check, cashed it, and sued Iron Wood for commissions allegedly still unpaid. Iron Wood contended that Lovorn's cashing the check constituted an accord and satisfaction of the dispute over commissions. Did the parties reach an accord and satisfaction?

5. D.H.M. Industries (plaintiff) leased a 500,000-square-foot warehouse to Central Port Warehouses, Inc. (defendant), for a 20-year term at a total rental of $10.5 million. Defendant paid plaintiff a security deposit of $126,525 (about 2 months' rent). The lease provided that if the lease was terminated, plaintiff had the right to retain the security deposit and to collect damages from the defendant. Defendant wrongfully refused to take possession of the premises, thus breaching and terminating the lease. In plaintiff's suit for damages the defendant sought the return of the security deposit, alleging that the lease provision relating to the security deposit imposed a penalty. The trial court held that the amount of the security deposit had been agreed upon as liquidated damages. Was the trial court in error?

6. Dupre, a rice farmer familiar with internal combustion engines, hired Tri-Parish Flying Service to repair an irrigation pump engine that was using oil excessively. Tri-Parish installed new piston rings and said the excessive oil consumption would cease after the rings sealed. The condition persisted, and Dupre made numerous complaints. Tri-Parish assured Dupre that he could continue to use the engine until Tri-Parish could take it back to the shop for a check after the irrigation season. Before the end of the season the engine threw a rod and was a total loss. Dupre sued for damages for loss of the engine and for partial loss of his rice crop. The trial court held that Dupre was not entitled to damages because, by continuing to use the malfunctioning engine, he had failed to mitigate his damages. Dupre appealed. In a companion suit Tri-Parish sought payment for the repairs. **(a)** Did Dupre violate his duty to mitigate damages? **(b)** If not, to what damages was Dupre entitled? **(c)** Was Tri-Parish entitled to payment for the repairs?

ETHICS IN PRACTICE

Every society needs to allocate goods, labor, and other resources among the population. In classic economic theory, the ideal method is a voluntary allocation resulting from millions of contracts bargained for in an impersonal market. But this theory also says that a person need not perform a contract that has become unprofitable. The breacher is required only to compensate the aggrieved party for resulting loss. Thus, traditionally the law of contract remedies has not distinguished malicious breaches from other breaches, nor awarded punitive damages for breach of contract, nor granted specific performance where compensation in money is an adequate substitute for the promised performance. Indeed, a person may find it advantageous to breach a contract whenever he or she will have a net gain after compensating the aggrieved party. Under classical economic theory, breaching a contract to avoid loss to oneself is not unethical, as long as the aggrieved party receives compensation for loss.

However, as the drafters of *Restatement (Second)* have said:

> This traditional response is not without its shortcomings. Its focus on the pecuniary aspect of breach fails to take account of notions of the sanctity of contract and the resulting moral obligations to honor one's promises. The analysis of breach of contract in purely economic terms assumes an ability to measure value with a certainty that is not often possible in the judicial process. The analysis also ignores the "transaction costs" inherent in the bargaining process and in the resolution of disputes, a defect that is especially significant where the amount in controversy is small.[1]

So what human and social values other than money should one consider when contemplating a breach of contract? Nonmonetary harms to the other party? The effect on future relation-

[1]*Restatement (Second)*, Chapter 16, Introductory Note.

ships? The ripple effect of harms that reach beyond the immediate parties? Costs that actually are not recoverable despite the law's ideal of "making the plaintiff whole"?

Breach is not the only ethical concern relating to contracts. The mere act of seeking or entering a contract could be ethically suspect even though entirely legal. Contracts to sell illicit drugs are illegal; contracts to market tobacco or alcohol ordinarily are not, despite the adverse effects of such products on users' health. Thus we have some fundamental questions: Given the general utility of contracting, what ethical limits are there on its *uses* or subject matter? If the subject matter is ethically acceptable, can the same be said about the *techniques* by which people are induced into a contract? When, if ever, should the government step in to regulate? Obviously, these contract questions touch other areas such as consumer protection and torts, discussed elsewhere in this book.

PROBLEMS IN ETHICS

1. Lancelot, an optometrist, gives eye examinations and owns the lens and frames dispensary that forms a part of his office area. Lancelot examines a patient, finds no significant change from the previous lens prescription, and finds the patient's present lenses and frames to be in excellent condition. During the examination, Lancelot explains in elaborate detail, and several times, that the patient's insurance covers the cost of the examination, new lenses, and up to $60 for new frames. As Lancelot knows, the patient was aware of the coverage, but emphasizes that "if you don't use it, you lose it." Is there an ethical problem here?

2. Marvin placed a newspaper ad reading: "Government jobs in your area." The ad listed salaries ranging from $9,000 to $16,000 and gave a telephone number but no address. Bob called the number and was asked to give his Visa charge account number for a catalog that would explain details. The charge for the catalog was $29.95. Bob assumed that the catalog would list and explain specific jobs with specific salaries at specific locations. However, Bob received a brochure that merely listed names, addresses, and telephone numbers of government employment offices. Bob could have gotten the same material from the U.S. Government Printing Office at no charge. The brochure offered a refund if the purchaser was dissatisfied, but it gave no return address. Assume that Marvin has not violated the law. Has he, however, committed a breach of ethics by selling what was available to buyers free? Would your answer be different if Marvin had charged only $3?

3. You are an airport clerk for a car rental company. Car rental companies, yours included, sell insurance policies, called "collision damage waivers," as an option in the rental contracts. The waivers provide minimal coverage at great cost per dollar of coverage, are highly profitable for rental companies, and can increase daily rental fees by as much as 48 percent. When quoting rental fees over the phone, the companies do not include the damage waiver cost, but encourage customers to buy the coverage when they arrive to rent a car. Your company and many others do not mention to customers that about 60 percent of personal auto insurance policies and a number of credit cards already provide coverage equivalent to or better than that of the collision damage waivers. Should you inform customers of the potential duplication of coverage?

4. Mary hires Paul to remodel her bathroom for $5,000. Paul is to begin the work in 2 weeks, and in preparation draws up detailed plans for some of the installations. On the weekend before Paul is to begin the job, Mary learns that Pamela will do the same work for $100 less. When Paul arrives to begin the remodeling, Mary tells him that she has hired Pamela for the job. Paul protests, pointing out that his bid for the job was very low, that he has spent considerable time preparing for the job, that he will profit very little from it, and that he needs the work to keep his assistant employed. Mary says she is willing to pay any damages that Paul can prove in court. **(a)** Is Mary's conduct consistent with her rights and obligations under the law? **(b)** If her conduct is consistent with legal norms, is it ethical? Upon what factors do you base your response? Does it matter, for example, that Pamela is a woman? **(c)** Would your response in (b) above differ if Paul's assistant were a mentally retarded person with little chance of alternative employment?

5. Light & Power Co. (Lightco) plans to dam a stream and build a hydroelectric generating station there. The land needed for the project is worth about $250 per acre. Lightco instructs Fred, its employee, to dress up as a farmer, tell the present landowners that he wants to buy their land for a tree farm, and acquire it as cheaply as possible without revealing that he works for Lightco. Having been taught that it is a sin to tell a lie, Fred is uncomfortable with his assignment. However, he wants to move up in the Lightco organization. Knowing that other Lightco employees have been transferred or demoted for refusing similar assignments, Fred does as he is told. He pays some sellers $300 per acre, but is able to buy similar land of several elderly people for $100 per acre. Later, Fred unexpectedly receives a bonus of $50 for each acre of land bought for less than $150. He feels very guilty about the bonus. **(a)** Is Lightco's approach to acquiring the land legal? Ethical? **(b)** Is it legal for Fred to have paid the elderly people only $100 per acre when he paid others $300 per acre for similar land? Is it right for him to have done so? **(c)** What norms might be in conflict to cause Fred's feeling of discomfort with his assignment? **(d)** What should Fred do with the bonus? Does it matter that Fred's wife is seriously ill and will require expensive hospital treatment?

6. Dr. Smith, a general medical practitioner, receives free samples of drugs from a variety of drug companies. As part of her treatment of patients, she dispenses the drugs and bills the patients for them, charging about 10 percent less than the patients would have to pay at the local drugstore. **(a)** In terms of general contract law, is Dr. Smith's conduct legal? Assume that there is no special statute or professional regulation forbidding doctors from selling free samples. **(b)** Is Dr. Smith's conduct ethical? If not, would it be all right for her to give the free samples to patients without charge? **(c)** Suppose you are Dr. Smith's office manager and she instructs you to seek out large supplies of unused free samples from other doctors so that she can give all her patients free drugs. Would this be an ethical thing for her to do? **(d)** Suppose Dr. Smith instructs you to seek out unused free samples for her to sell to patients for 50 percent of the drugstore price. How would you feel about doing so? Why?

PART FOUR

Sale of Goods; Products Liability

CHAPTER 18
Introduction to the Law of Sales; The Sales Contract

CHAPTER 19
Delivery and Storage of Goods; Documents of Title

CHAPTER 20
Transfer of Title and Risk of Loss;
Title of Good Faith Purchasers

CHAPTER 21
Performance of the Sales Contract;
Remedies for Breach of Contract

CHAPTER 22
Sales Warranties and Products Liability

Ethics in Practice

CHAPTER 18

Introduction to the Law of Sales; The Sales Contract

Despite the enormous rise of the U.S. service economy, the United States remains the single largest market for goods. Consumers, producers, suppliers, wholesalers, distributors, and many others engage in transactions for goods of immense variety. The average modern supermarket, for example, carries between 15,000 and 20,000 different products, stocked mostly in case quantities or larger. Thousands of producers make those products, and thousands more suppliers provide raw and fabricated materials to them. Compound these thousands of producers and suppliers with a gigantic national web of resellers, distributors, and wholesalers, and you can begin to appreciate the vast number of participants and billions of transactions in goods that occur in order to make the modern phenomenon of the supermarket possible. Moreover, the supermarket accounts for merely a fraction of the national total of transactions in goods.

Today, even medium-sized businesses use purchase order forms and acceptance forms daily by the ream. Each one of those forms has the binding force of law variously behind it. It is common for large producers to engage in transactions with ongoing suppliers without humans actually bargaining with one another—computers linked between them initiate, send, and confirm orders. These lightning-fast links are also variously binding, all according to law.

The common law of contracts is poorly suited for such fast-paced business. If the common law of contracts were to govern trading, commerce would slow down to a crawl. Approximately three centuries ago, long before our speedy communications and high-tech time, merchants deemed the land-oriented common law of contracts as too cumbersome for the needs of traders. So they developed their own commercial law, based on the customs of merchants. Originally, these merchants enforced this new body of law, not through the standing court system, but in their own various trade organizations. International and unifying in character, this "law merchant," as it came to be known, was fairly well adapted to fast-moving transactions in goods.

In England, as commerce began to replace agriculture as the main enterprise, the law of sales emerged from the law merchant as one of the many distinct bodies of commercial law, and judges began to incorporate the law merchant (and the law of sales) into the common law. Eventually, the law of sales was put into statutory form in England by the enactment of the Sales of Goods Act in 1893. This statutory law provided the basis in the United States of the

Uniform Sales Act, which was superseded by Article 2 of the Uniform Commercial Code (UCC).

Today, when you consider the great number and complexity of transactions in goods, you might conclude that Article 2 of the Uniform Commercial Code is a remarkably straightforward and small set of fairly flexible laws. Though the law of sales under Article 2 is a variation of the common law of contracts discussed in earlier chapters of this book, some Article 2 rules differ greatly from their common law counterparts. A key difference you should always keep in mind is that the common law applies to contracts for real estate, personal services, and so on. The contract rules in Article 2, however, apply only to contracts involving *goods*—office equipment, cars, boats, clothing, food, and similar things.

Furthermore, a business deal may involve a number of Code[1] transactions, not just the law of sales. Suppose you sell office equipment at retail and need to purchase 100 floor lamps from a manufacturer. Article 2 governs the formation and performance of the sales contract. But if the lamps are delivered by a common carrier such as a railroad or a trucking company, ownership may be transferred to you by means of an Article 7 document of title called a "bill of lading." You might pay for the lamps with a check (governed by Article 3) that will be cashed by the seller in accordance with the banking rules of Article 4. Or, if you arrange a credit rather than a cash purchase, the seller probably will reserve an Article 9 "security interest" in the lamps so that the seller can repossess them in the event that you fail to pay for them. If you arrange a credit from a foreign manufacturer, the seller might require you to provide an Article 5 "letter of credit." Subsequent chapters of this book discuss not only the law of sales but also documents of title, secured transactions, letters of credit and checks, and other commercial paper used in payment and in financing.

The first part of this chapter deals with Article 2—its purposes, key concepts, and coverage. The second part deals with the sales contract itself.

---

[1] The Uniform Commercial Code is often referred to—in whole or in part—as the Code.

PURPOSES, KEY CONCEPTS, AND COVERAGE OF ARTICLE 2

Purposes of the Law of Sales

Before the development of the UCC, the law governing commercial transactions varied considerably from state to state. The differences in law hampered interstate commerce because a national or regional seller of goods, by conforming to the laws of one state, could run afoul of the laws in another.

To facilitate a national trade in goods, the Code drafters simplified and modernized the law of commercial transactions; encouraged the expansion of commercial practices through custom, usage, and the agreements of contracting parties; and tried to make the law among the various jurisdictions uniform.

Today, the law governing commercial transactions remains state law. But as the law's title suggests, the Uniform Commercial Code promoted uniformity. The Code has been adopted among the states to such an extent that considerable consistency has been achieved among all but one of the states—Louisiana. However, all states adopting the Code have a right to amend this law as they see fit.

Accordingly, though a single statement of the UCC appears in Appendix 2, do not mislead yourself into believing that this statement of law applies word for word in all states. Also, do not despair just because there exist state-to-state variations. Particularly today, when individual states actively encourage economic development within their borders, it is in their interest to facilitate the smooth flow of national and international business through their states so that they can attract new enterprise and participate in the vital economy around them. Part of the way for states to attract national and international business within their borders is to avoid having laws that discourage commerce. The UCC provides a legal template for states to adopt and follow, and generally, states have not strayed substantially from the basic provisions of the Code.

A key area of emphasis in Article 2 of the

UCC is on the actual performance of sales contracts. Raw materials, equipment, and supplies must arrive on a schedule that permits a manufacturer to meet commitments to buyers who, in turn, may have made commitments to other buyers. For the distribution process to operate efficiently, each person in it must be able to rely on the performance of others, with little time to engage in an elaborate contracting process. As noted later in this chapter, Article 2 reduces the opportunities for a contracting party to delay his or her promised performance or to escape contractual obligations without good reason.

A basic policy thread runs throughout the Code. The policy is to encourage sound basic business practices and *ethical* business conduct. As you proceed through this chapter and later chapters on the law of sales, you will likely see that the Code does not divorce the ethical from the practical. Perhaps a better example than any other body of statutory law, the UCC is a legal and practical application of general business ethics—emphasizing not only what is right and fair, but also what works and is sensible. The discussion on "good faith," which follows, provides one such example of how practicality and ethics go hand in hand in the Code.

Key Concepts of the Law of Sales

Good Faith. All persons who engage in transactions covered by the Code must use good faith in performing their contracts and in enforcing obligations owed to them.

There are two meanings of "good faith" that apply to sales transactions. The first meaning is "honesty in fact" (actual honesty even though the person might have been careless) in the conduct or transaction concerned [1-201].[2] This meaning applies to *all* persons subject to the Code. The second meaning, which applies to *merchants* (the next key concept to be discussed), is "honesty in fact" *and* the "observance of reasonable commercial standards of fair dealing in the trade" [2-103].

Thus, merchants and nonmerchants alike must be honest in their dealings, but merchants must be especially careful not to take unfair advantage of those with whom they deal or to cause them loss. For example, sometimes a merchant-buyer has the right to reject delivered goods. If the seller has no agent or place of business where the rejection occurs, the merchant-buyer meets the obligation of good faith by disposing of the rejected goods in accordance with reasonable instructions of the seller or, *in the absence of instructions,* by selling *perishable* goods for the seller's account [2-603(1)]. A merchant-buyer who leaves rejected tomatoes on a loading dock to rot may be honest in fact but the merchant-buyer would not be observing reasonable commercial standards of fair dealing with regard to the distant seller and therefore would not be acting in good faith.

Merchant. Article 2 applies to *sales transactions* without regard to whether the parties to the sales contract are merchants or nonmerchants. However, merchants are subject to special rules of Article 2. Some of these rules expedite sales by replacing common law rules that might impede the formation or performance of sales contracts. Others make clear the rights or duties of a merchant in transactions with other merchants or with nonmerchants. Table 18.1 shows the purposes of some key Article 2 sections which apply to merchants.

In one sense, **merchant** means a person who deals in goods of the kind involved in the transaction [2-104]. This kind of merchant is the professional trader or dealer in goods so familiar to us in our day-to-day transactions, and is referred to later in this chapter as "dealer-merchant."

But the meaning of merchant under Article 2 is not limited to dealers in goods. The word also applies to persons who, though not personally dealing in goods in the manner of professional traders, nevertheless by their occupa-

---

[2] The hyphenated numbers in brackets refer to sections of the Uniform Commercial Code reprinted in Appendix 2. The number 1-201 means "Article 1, Section 201" and is commonly read as "Section 1-201."

> **BOX 18.1**
>
> ### Uniform Commercial Code—The Statutory Scheme of Things
>
> The whole text of the UCC can, at first, seem very intimidating to the uninitiated. Once you get the scheme behind its structure, you need not be intimidated at all.
>
> In Appendix 2, you will find the first nine articles of the Uniform Commercial Code. Eight of these articles contain specific legal codes governing an array of commercial transactions. One of the articles, Article 1, applies to every one of the subsequent articles.
>
> Here's an easy way of thinking how the Code works. If, for example, you are referring to Article 2, which governs transactions in the sale of goods, keep in mind that both Article 2 *and* Article 1 apply. Similarly, reference to Article 9 also requires reference to Article 1. The statutory scheme is that Article 1 provides *general* provisions and definitions. However, more specific provisions on the same concept are sometimes required as the Code gets more specific in Articles 2 and beyond. For example, "good faith" is defined in Article 1 as "honesty in fact in the conduct or transaction concerned." Another definition of good faith appears in Article 2 and applies more specifically to merchants, and this definition is: "honesty in fact and the observance of reasonable commercial standards of fair dealing in the trade."
>
> Notice that the two definitions do not contradict each other. Rather, the Article 2 definition is a narrower one. So the way to understand and apply these two definitions is to use them together with the following result—everyone doing a transaction in the sales of goods is held to an Article 1 standard ("honesty in fact") but merchants are held to a higher and narrower Article 2 standard (both "honesty in fact" and "observance of reasonable commercial standards of fair dealing").
>
> Consequently, when you see in this and later chapters reference to Article 1 in a discussion of Article 2 provisions, don't let it confuse you. By design, Article 1 is a part of each and every subsequent article of the Code.
>
> Below is how the Code, as it appears in Appendix 2, is organized:
>
> Article 1: *General Provisions*, applying to the whole Code.
>
> Article 2: *Sales*, governing transactions in the sales of goods.
>
> Article 3: *Commercial Paper*, governing the negotiability of instruments such as checks, certificates of deposits, notes, and so forth.
>
> Article 4: *Bank Deposits and Collections*, governing the duties and liability of banks in the handling of customer accounts, CDs, and the like.
>
> Article 5: *Letters of Credit*, dealing with the rules and concepts of letters of credit, whether issued by banks or others.
>
> Article 6: *Bulk Transfers*, governing the transfer in bulk of an enterprise or its inventory that is not in its ordinary course of business.
>
> Article 7: *Warehouse Receipts, Bills of Lading, and Other Documents of Title*, applying to consignment, bailment, storage, and other such arrangements.
>
> Article 8: *Investment Securities*, applying to the issue, transfer, and registration of various kinds of securities.
>
> Article 9: *Secured Transactions; Sales of Accounts and Chattel Paper*, applying to security interests created by contracts in goods. ■

tions are expected to have the knowledge or skill peculiar to the business practices or goods involved. An insurance company that buys office equipment and supplies, for example, is a merchant as to the ordinary business practices—such as ordering and taking delivery of goods—that ought to be familiar to any person in business. Merchant also includes even those persons or organizations that *employ* someone to conduct business activities. Thus, a college

Table 18.1 Some UCC Article 2 Sections Having Special Application to Merchants

Section	Topic	Purpose of Section
2-103(1)(b)	Good Faith	To provide a higher and more objective test of good faith for the merchant than for the nonmerchant
2-201(2)	Statute of Frauds	To reduce compliance requirements between merchants; thus, to expedite contract formation
2-205	Firm Offer	To protect offeree's expectation that certain offers by merchants will remain open without consideration
2-207(2)	Counteroffer	To expedite contract formation between merchants by reducing right to invoke common law counteroffer rules
2-209(2)	Modification of Contract	To force evidence (nonmerchant's signature) that nonmerchant agreed to modification of the contract
2-509(3)	Risk of Loss	To impose risk of loss upon merchant, in certain circumstances, until buyer receives the goods

or university can be classified as a merchant if it has a regular purchasing department or business personnel who are familiar with business practices [2-104, comment 3].

Dealer-merchants are subject to sales rules that do not apply to other merchants. For example, only dealer-merchants make certain warranties (guarantees) concerning the quality of the goods they sell. These and other warranties are discussed in Chapter 22. In contrast, *all* merchants are subject to those rules of Article 2 designed to make the contracting process more efficient and fair. And all merchants are subject to higher standards of commercial conduct than those that apply to nonmerchants, as you saw in the preceding discussion on good faith.

Identification (of Goods) to the Contract. The parties to a sale may need to know precisely when the sale occurred, the earliest moment at which the buyer may insure undelivered goods against loss, or what rights the buyer has to demand the delivery of particular goods. The answers to such questions may depend in part on whether goods have been "identified" (i.e., designated) as the subject of a *particular* contract of sale.

The parties may make an "explicit" (clearly stated) agreement as to when the goods will be identified to the contract [2-501]. In the absence of an explicit agreement, Article 2 provides the rules. Where the contract is for the sale of goods "already existing and identified" (e.g., particular goods owned or possessed by the seller), identification *to the contract between the seller and the buyer* occurs as soon as the contract is made. If the contract is for crops or for the unborn young of animals, identification occurs when the crops are planted or when the animals are conceived. If the contract is for the sale of "future goods" other than crops or animals (e.g., goods yet to be manufactured or acquired by a supplier for a retailer), identification occurs when the goods are shipped, marked, or otherwise designated as the goods to which the contract refers.

An important consequence of identifying goods to a contract is that the buyer immediately obtains a limited right called "special property" and an "insurable interest"[3] in the goods even though the buyer might not yet be the owner.

For example, suppose that Alpha Department Store orders 1,000 video cameras from Zeta Electronics. Zeta Electronics then manufactures 2,000 video cameras and marks 1,000 of them as the ones to be shipped to Alpha Department Store. Alpha does not yet own or have title to this equipment. However, because the 1,000 video cameras have been identified to the contract, Alpha has a Code-created "special property" in the equipment and therefore may insure them against loss, if Alpha pays for them in advance or makes contracts for their resale before receiving them. Furthermore, if Zeta becomes insolvent before delivering the video cameras, Alpha is entitled to those in which it has a special property interest *and* for which it has made arrangements for payment. Alpha is thus protected from the claims of Zeta's creditors.

Other Key Concepts. Some Code concepts—unconscionability, course of performance, course of dealing, and usage of trade—are of ethical and practical significance. All but one of these concepts—unconscionability—are discussed later in this chapter under the general heading of The Sales Contract.

---

[3] An *insurable interest* is a financial stake in property or in someone's life that will justify the person who has that stake in insuring the property or life against loss. If there never was an insurable interest, a contract of insurance is not enforceable against the insurance company.

Here, we will explore unconscionability as it is treated by the Code and the courts. Earlier in Chapter 13 in discussions on fraud, misrepresentation and duress, you encountered how a party to a contract may avoid or cancel the contract because of wrongdoing by the other party. While the UCC also makes such grounds for avoidance available to the parties of a sales contract, it goes farther than classic contract common law and allows contract avoidance on the basis of unconscionability. Over the years, the courts had difficulty combating many harmful business practices that fell short of fraud and other established wrongs. As a result, the courts developed the concept of **unconscionability,** specifically recognized as an additional ground for sales contract avoidance.

The precise definition of Article 2 unconscionability, however, is left to the courts to work out on a case-by-case basis. Generally speaking, a contract or a contractual clause is unconscionable if it is so one-sided as to "oppress" or "unfairly surprise" the party upon whom it is imposed. An unconscionable contract or clause is unenforceable even though the practice involved does not constitute fraud or the like. A court may refuse to enforce any unconscionable term and enforce the remainder of the contract, or may so limit the application of an unconscionable term as to avoid an unconscionable result [2-302].

The courts have identified a number of practices, in specific circumstances, that may be—but also might not be in other circumstances—unconscionable. Suppose that a seller, by means of a clause in fine print placed in the middle of a complicated form, seeks secretly to deprive the buyer of a right that the buyer normally would not agree to give up if the topic were discussed, such as a warranty that the goods are fit for ordinary purposes. Such a clause could be found to be unconscionable. High-pressure selling may be a form of unconscionability, as are other tricky or deceptive business practices. Moreover, an excessively high price could also be held unconscionable. But remember, unconscionability depends upon the circumstances.

For example, suppose a furniture seller, by means of a clause in an installment-sale contract, retains for as long as the buyer's account is not fully paid a security interest in all items sold to the buyer over a period of years. Then the seller seeks to repossess a whole houseful of furniture because a semiliterate buyer missed a payment on a small item. If the value of the furniture to be repossessed greatly exceeds the amount of the unpaid debt, or the buyer did not understand the unusual consequences of missing a payment (that is, losing all the furniture purchased from this seller), the clause that provides for repossession is likely to be held unconscionable. In contrast, a similar clause in a sales agreement between two large corporations that have legal departments or sophisticated purchasing agents is likely to be enforceable. This different outcome is likely because it is presumed that these large corporations have both the business experience and better bargaining positions with regard to the contract terms, and are likely to understand those terms and assess the risks.

The following case addresses questions of good faith and unconscionability.

CASE 18.1 Gilbride v. Dover Nissan, Inc.
• No. 87C-MR-20 slip op. (Del. Super. Ct. 1989)

FACTS In January 1986, Marie Gilbride, 82 years old at the time of the transaction, purchased a 1986 Nissan Pulsar from Dover Nissan, Inc., for $15,382, of which she paid $9,882 in cash and received $5,500 as a trade-in allowance for her previous car. Between 1981 and the time of her death (1987), Gilbride had bought six new cars. She liked owning and driving a new car.

In the last 8 years of Gilbride's life, her physical and mental condition deteriorated, and she developed certain "bizarre eccentricities," the most noticeable being her appearance. She regularly wore oversized T-shirts, mismatched shoes and socks, and advertising buttons of all types. Often, she was seen on the boardwalk at Rehoboth Beach, Delaware, pushing a shopping cart and rummaging through trash cans. In addition, she "exuded an overpowering and ever-present odor of urine about her." Her apartment, where she kept more than 25 cats, was disheveled and haphazardly clean.

Gilbride's accountant, who had prepared her taxes for 10 years, reported that she had no concept of times or dates, never knew how much money was in her accounts, claimed that she had "lost" her Internal Revenue Service 1099 Forms for the previous year, and had written at least one bad check to the IRS. Her accountant was concerned about her check writing, and even whether she mailed her tax returns. Her accountant had the opinion that Gilbride showed "limited capacity" to anyone who dealt with her.

Gilbride, however, was reported as kind and good-natured. She lived alone, cooked, cleaned, and drove her car as she saw fit. She was never institutionalized, never adjudicated an incompetent, and never had a guardian to see over her affairs.

After Gilbride died, the executor of her estate sued Dover Nissan on behalf of her estate.

OPINION STEELE, J. . . . The complaint alleges that [Dover Nissan] took unfair advantage of Gilbride since, at the time of contracting, Gilbride was incompetent. In addition, it is alleged that [Dover Nissan] violated the good-faith requirement

**CASE 18.1
Continued**

of [UCC Article 1-203] and the unconscionable contract provision of [UCC Article 2-302].

. . . I find Gilbride's appearance and other documented eccentricities not to be a true indication of her competence. The real evidence before this court is the fact that she lived alone and took complete care of herself. . . . She was independent in every sense of the word. Probably the most telling fact is that Gilbride purchased new automobiles regularly. . . . I find no basis to conclude that she was so obvious[ly] incompetent that [Dover Nissan] was on notice that she lacked capacity to enter into the sales transaction in question.

[As to the] issue of good-faith dealing . . . , [UCC 1-203] provides: Every contract or duty within this sub-title imposes an obligation of good faith in its performance or enforcement.

"Good faith" is defined . . . as "honesty in fact in the conduct or transaction concerned." I must agree with [Dover Nissan] that [the executor of the estate] presented no evidence showing that [Dover Nissan] acted dishonestly in dealing with Gilbride. . . . [T]he salesman who sold the vehicle to Gilbride reviewed the transaction with her and felt that she understood it. . . . [The] sales manager also reviewed the details with her. The only evidence from which one could even remotely infer overreaching was the sale price [which was] $2,500 to $3,000 higher than [a similar model] three months later. [S]o many variables affect the purchase price, [such as] value of trade-in, the options chosen, the customer's ability to negotiate, and even the time of year. . . . Simply because one customer bargains for and received a "better" deal than another does not mean that the dealer acted dishonestly in a transaction less favorable to a customer.

[As to the] issue of unconscionability, [UCC 2-302(1)] provides in pertinent part: If a court, as a matter of law, finds the contract or any clause of the contract to have been unconscionable at the time that it was made, the court may refuse to enforce the contract, . . . or it may so limit the application of any unconscionable clause as to avoid any unconscionable result.

The test for unconscionability is that "a contract is unconscionable if it is 'such as no man in his senses and not under delusion would make on the one hand and no honest or fair man would accept on the other.'" "It is generally held that the unconscionability test involves the question of whether the provision amounts to the taking of unfair advantage by one party over the other."

[The evidence does not support] that Dover Nissan took unfair advantage. [There is no claim] that the automobile failed to operate properly, was defective or could not meet the expectations of the purchaser. [The main argument the executor of Gilbride's estate makes] is that Gilbride purchased more car and at a greater price than she needed or was warranted.

The price disparity . . . does not shock the Court's conscience in light of the many variables which are a part of a sales transaction. Plaintiff's claim that the contract was unconscionable is without merit.

JUDGMENT

In favor of the defendant, Dover Nissan, Inc.

Transactions Covered by Article 2

Unless the context otherwise requires, Article 2 applies to *transactions* in goods [2-102]. By their express terms, many sections of Article 2 apply only to contracts for the sale of goods, and not to other kinds of transactions such as gifts or leases of goods. However, the drafters of the Code intended to encourage the application of certain Code principles directly or "by analogy" to a wider range of transactions than just sales. For example, buyers injured by defective goods often have the benefit of an Article 2 warranty. In many states, the courts imply a similar non-Code warranty in a *lease* of goods because similar policy justifies the warranty. The courts of some states apply Article 2 warranty provisions directly to nonsales transactions such as leases and bailments of goods.

Here, we will focus on Article 2 transactions. Article 2 applies especially to the **sale of goods.** A sale is the passing of title to goods from the seller to the buyer, in return for a consideration called the price [2-106]. The price can be made payable in money, goods, or realty, or *in some other way* [2-304]. Thus, a legally binding *promise* to pay—whether with money, goods, realty, or otherwise—is another way of paying the price. As to the meaning of **title,** suppose you buy a used car and agree to make twelve monthly payments. The seller probably will retain a "security interest" (often called "title") so that the seller can repossess the car if you fail to make the payments. Yet, at the time of the sale, *you* receive basic ownership rights in the car—the right to use, enjoy, and sell it—subject only to your seller's right to be paid. These basic ownership rights constitute the kind of title referred to in the definition of "sale." In a **contract to sell** goods, the seller agrees to transfer title to the buyer at some future time. This kind of sales contract is used, for example, where the seller does not yet own existing goods or where the goods have not yet been produced.

Article 2 applies only to transactions in **goods.** In general, *goods* refer to things that are movable at the time they are identified to the contract for sale [2-105]. Although the primary focus of Article 2 is upon movable things, goods include the unborn young of animals, growing crops or other things attached to realty and capable of severance with material harm to it, timber to be cut, and minerals (including gas and oil) to be removed from realty by the seller [2-105(1); 2-107]. Goods also include money *if* the money is a commodity. Thus, coin collections are considered goods. "Goods" do *not* include real estate, personal services, or intangible personal property such as corporate securities, patent rights, and bank accounts. Sales of such nongoods are subject to the common law of contracts, which often differs from the law of sales. Computer software, as will be discussed later in Case 18.2, is treated under the Code by some states as "goods," while in other states it is not.

Article 2 does not apply to any transaction that is intended to operate *only* as a security transaction, even though goods may be involved. *Pledges* and *chattel mortgages* (discussed in Chapter 29) are intended to operate only as security transactions. However, a *conditional sales*

BOX 18.2

A Trend in the Law, UCC Article 2A

A growing number of states, in order to better apply the law of sales to transactions in leases, have adopted Article 2A of the UCC.* This article applies specifically to *leases of goods,* and covers a wide variety of transactions ranging from a consumer's rental of a car or small tool to long-term commercial leases of aircraft or industrial equipment. Article 2A does *not* apply to a lease intended as a secured transaction; security "leases" (security interests "disguised as leases") are covered by Article 9 of the Code.

In content, Article 2A closely resembles Article 2, and its basic features are nearly the same. However, there are differences, and as relevant, the major differences will be discussed in this and later chapters.

In many states Article 2 will continue to apply directly or indirectly to leases of goods until those states adopt Article 2A.

*At least 25 states, with legislation pending in others.

contract is meant to effect a sale of goods while creating a security interest for the seller, who retains the security interest until the goods are paid for. Article 2 governs the sale aspects of a conditional sales contract, and Article 9 governs the security aspects.

The courts do not agree on how to treat transactions involving a combination of goods and services. Consider how an automobile "tune-up" transaction should be treated. When a mechanic replaces parts and adjusts the engine, is it a sale of goods or a sale of services? The distinction is very important, particularly if the parts are defective and cause injury. If the transaction is classified as a sale of *goods*, an Article 2 warranty—assuring that the goods are not defective—often is available as the basis of a lawsuit. If the transaction is classified as a sale of *services*, the common law of contracts—often containing no implied warranties against defects—applies.

Many courts settle the "goods versus services" matter by deciding whether the sale is *predominantly* for goods or services. Thus, if the amount or value of the goods is relatively insignificant in the transaction, these courts will hold that it is a sale of services, outside of the Code. However, the relative amount or value of the goods is not the only factor that courts may consider in mixed transactions. A court may place more importance on the question of who should bear the loss resulting from the use of defective goods. A transfusion of contaminated blood, for example, usually is treated as an aspect of medical services and thus as not subject to sales warranties. Courts and legislatures adopting this position believe that persons who provide essential medical services should be held liable only for negligence or intentional misconduct. In contrast, the courts of some states hold that medical supplies other than blood are goods, and that Article 2 warranties should apply.

The following case decides whether the sale of software is a transaction in goods to be governed by the Code.

CASE 18.2 **Systems Design and Management Information, Inc. v. Kansas City Post Office Employees Credit Union**
• 788 P.2d 878 (Kan. App. 1990)

FACTS Systems Design and Management Information, Inc. (SDMI), develops computer software programs for credit unions, and had an ongoing relationship with the Kansas City Post Office Employees Credit Union (Credit Union) since 1984. At roughly the time the Credit Union planned to merge with a similar Telephone Employees Credit Union, SDMI and a computer company worked together to attempt to get the new account created by the merger.

In November 1986, SDMI held a demonstration of new software, called Generic System, which worked on the computer company's hardware. As a result of this demonstration, the Credit Union decided to buy SDMI's Generic System.

Immediately, major problems with the system became apparent—inability to run the payroll, inability to generate certain daily reports, nonfunctioning printers and terminals, and inability to perform all the normal operations during regular working hours. Though SDMI and Credit Union attempted to rectify the problems and solved many of them, problems with account balances and the like continued to plague the system, albeit less than before.

In April 1987, Credit Union quit using the Generic System software without giving notice to SDMI. SDMI, in turn, sued Credit Union to recover the outstanding indebtedness on the software. The trial court entered judgment in favor of Credit Union. SDMI appealed.

CASE 18.2
Continued

OPINION

WAHL, J. . . . SDMI argues the Uniform Commercial Code should have governed the trial of this case because computer software is "goods" under the U.C.C. We agree.

"Goods" is defined in Article 2 of the U.C.C. as "all things (including special manufactured goods) which are movable at the time of identification to the contract for sale other than the money in which the price is to be paid, investment securities (article 8) and things in action." [2-105(1)]

. . . According to [1-102(2)], the purpose and policy of the U.C.C. is: "(a) to simplify, clarify and modernize the law governing commercial transactions; (b) to permit the continued expansion of commercial practices through custom, usage and agreement of the parties; [and] (c) to make uniform the law among the various jurisdictions."

We must determine whether the . . . agreement between SDMI and Credit Union was for goods or services. The test when dealing with a mixed contract is "not whether they [goods or services] are mixed, but, granting that they are mixed, whether their predominant factor, their thrust, their purpose reasonably stated, is the rendition of service, with goods incidentally involved . . . or is a transaction of sale, with labor incidentally involved."

Contracts for a data processing service's skill, . . . and contracts for analysis, collection, storage, and reporting of data . . . have been held not to fall under the U.C.C. as sales of goods. In the present case [involving SDMI], there is general agreement that SDMI is not a service bureau, [and such holdings do not apply].

Another line of cases involves contracts for the sale of custom software designed specifically for the customer's needs. [In one of these cases], the court found the sales aspect of the transaction to be predominant while employee training, repair services, and system upgrading were all incidental. . . . The court did say, due to the variance in software based upon the needs of the customer, it would engage in a case-by-case analysis on this issue. [In a separate case], the court found software was not goods. This case involved custom-designed accounting software and the court reasoned the contract was for the program producer's "knowledge, skill, and ability," and the product on which the program was transmitted was incidental to the contract.

The cases in which we find the closest analogy to the case before us involve the sale of both computer hardware and software as a system. [Though a computer company worked with SDMI on the proposal], the case before us involves only the software, not the hardware.

[In one of these closely analogous cases], the court said, "Although the ideas or concepts involved in the custom-designed software remained [the producer's] intellectual property, [the buyer of the software] was purchasing the product of these concepts." [In another analogous case], the court ruled sale of computer hardware and software as a package, termed a turn-key system, was goods and the consulting services . . . with the sale were ancillary to the contract."

> **CASE 18.2 Continued**
>
> Prior to entering into an agreement, . . . Credit Union attended a demonstration [of it at SDMI]. Therefore, we conclude the software was movable at the time of identification to the contract, satisfying the requirement of the definition of goods. . . . SDMI remains the owner of the accounting program as intellectual property. Credit Union purchased only a reproduction or the result of the programmer's skill.
>
> We hold this software to be goods and subject to the provisions of the U.C.C.
>
> **JUDGMENT** Reversed and remanded, in part, for further proceedings; affirmed, in part [on other issues].

THE SALES CONTRACT

Unless otherwise displaced by particular provisions of the UCC, the rules of law that apply to contracts generally apply as well to contracts for the sale of goods [1-103]. So a contract for the sale of goods must meet the usual requirements for the *formation* of a contract: mutual assent (offer and acceptance), an exchange of consideration, parties having legal capacity to contract, and a legal objective (purpose). Contracts for the sale of goods are also subject to many general legal principles relating to the *form* and *interpretation* of contracts. However, the UCC modifies most of these aspects of general contract law to adjust them to sales transactions and contemporary business needs.

Formation of the Sales Contract

Article 2 Standard for Contract Formation. People create sales contracts in a wide variety of ways. Some spell out the terms of the contract in great detail, as in the purchase of a new car. Others say very little or nothing, as in the purchase of goods at a supermarket. On occasion, what is said or done is so vague and sketchy that no contract arises. Consequently, the courts are sometimes faced with the question of what minimum conduct is required to create a sales contract.

As you discovered in previous chapters on the common law of contracts, courts look at various kinds of conduct—both verbal and physical—to determine whether an agreement existed and, if so, the intent of the parties. The UCC provides courts with more flexibility than the common law in making such a determination. Specifically, under Article 2, a contract for the sale of goods may be made *in any manner* sufficient to show agreement, including conduct by both parties which acknowledges the existence of a contract [2-204(1)]. The contract may arise even though the exact moment at which agreement arose cannot be determined [2-204(2)]. Furthermore, even though one or more terms are left open, there can still be a contract for sale if the parties have intended to make a contract and there is a reasonably certain basis for a court to give an appropriate remedy for breach of the contract [2-204(3)].

Acts Required for Contract Formation. Article 2 specifies some minimum acts of contracting required of the buyer and the seller. First, before there can be a sales contract, the *parties* to it must be identified. Suppose that you have recently opened a bakery and need some flour. You phone a local supplier and say, without identifying yourself, "Please send some wheat flour right away." The supplier's employee says, "OK." As of this moment there is no contract because you and the supplier have not said enough to enable a court to give an appropriate remedy to either of you if called upon to do so. The supplier does not even know with whom it is dealing.

Suppose now that you identify yourself so that the supplier can make a delivery. There still is no contract because you have not said how much flour you want. To have an enforceable sales contract you ordinarily must specify the *quantity* of the goods you seek.[4] Must you specify the *kind* of wheat flour as well? Though a statement of kind would be helpful, it is not always necessary for a contract to arise. Particularly, if you have had prior transactions with this supplier, the supplier might know from past experience with you what you mean by "wheat flour." As to *price*, the Code provides that the parties can make a contract even though the price is not specified. Where the parties intend to make a contract but state no price, the price is a "reasonable" price as of the time set for delivery [2-305]. A reasonable price might be the current market price if there is one. Thus, as a practical matter, no sales contract is likely to arise unless the *parties* to it and the *quantity* of goods have been spelled out somehow. The other term essential for a contract to exist, the *price*, may be supplied by law.

Where the parties to a contract fail to state a term such as price or time or place of delivery, the term is said to have been left *open*. Costs of production might not be known at the time of the sale, the market price might fluctuate, or the parties might simply have forgotten to state a price or some other term.

Intending for the Code to be flexible and adaptable to various commercial needs, the drafters of Article 2 recognized that it is normal and necessary for businesspeople to contract with a minimum of detail, often on the basis of a phone call. By permitting open terms, and by providing rules of law to "fill the gaps" left by the open terms, the Code accomplishes two things. First, it enables the parties to contract quickly where price or other information is not immediately available. Second, it fosters performance of agreements that under nonsales law might have been considered too indefinite to enforce.

Offer under Article 2.
Some of the common law rules governing contract offers in *nonsales* transactions are unsuitable for sales of goods.

Under the Code, these rules regarding offers have been replaced. Discussion of two of the most important of these rules follows.

Firm offer. Under the common law of contracts, a person who has promised to hold an offer open for a fixed time is not required to honor that promise unless the person making the promise has received consideration for it. The Code rule operates differently. If a *merchant* states in a *signed writing* that the offer to buy or sell goods will be held open, this statement cannot be revoked merely for lack of consideration [2-205]. The promise to hold the offer open is binding for the time stated or, if no time is stated, for a reasonable time not to exceed 3 months. Thus, merchants who make firm offers cannot upset the reasonable expectations of offerees.

Offer seeking prompt or current shipment of goods. The rule is stated in 2-206(1)(b), but the following example should help make it clearer. Suppose a retail fish dealer needs a supply of cod to replenish store stock immediately and places this order: "Ship me 50 cases of fresh frozen cod at once." This is an offer for a unilateral contract because the dealer expects the cod seller to accept the offer by performing the act requested by the dealer. Under common law rules, such an offer can be accepted *only* by the seller-offeree's performing the requested act—here, a shipment made at once. An attempt by the offeree to accept by, for example, phoning or telegraphing an immediate *promise* to ship promptly would be ineffective, and the offeror would be free to revoke the offer. The ability to revoke gives the offeror the opportunity to "play the market," often to the surprise and injury of the shipper, who is in fact making a prompt shipment just a few minutes or hours after the promise was sent. To prevent this kind of injurious surprise, Article 2 provides that an offeree may accept an offer for prompt or current shipment by making *either* a prompt shipment or a prompt promise to ship, unless the offeror has made it very clear that the offer can be accepted only by a prompt shipment [2-206].

Acceptance under Article 2.
Though some UCC rules on the acceptance of offers resemble common law rules, the UCC departs from those

---

[4]Except, for example, in a "requirements" contract. An agreement to buy "all the wheat flour I shall need in my business next year" is a requirements contract whose quantity term has been left open to be filled in later as the buyer's needs dictate.

> **BOX 18.3**
>
> ### Point to Consider
>
> Since Article 2 does not govern the sale of services, are there situations in which the UCC rules governing "offers seeking prompt or current shipment of goods" might be the best rules for courts to use to govern transactions in services?
>
> For example, could an unfair surprise situation arise in the hiring of migrant farm workers? Suppose a farmer were to announce on radio, "I need workers now and am paying $10 per hour." When migrant workers arrive, the farm owner offers only to pay the minimum possible because more workers than needed showed up. In such a situation, is the farm owner "playing" the labor market with the migrant workers? Does the service that migrant farm workers provide resemble a commodity in goods more than a personal service?
>
> Could a similar injury from a revoked offer similarly affect some professionals such as accountants? If compliance audits, for example, more resemble commodities than a unique service, should a similar rule apply to offers seeking prompt or current performance of professional services? ∎

rules that unreasonably obstruct the formation of sales contracts.

Authorized medium of acceptance. The mechanics of accepting an offer under Article 2 may be summarized as follows:

1 The acceptance is effective at the point of dispatch if the offeree has used an *authorized medium* of acceptance.

2 Where the offeror stipulates that a particular medium of acceptance must be used, only the stipulated medium is authorized. For example, Beta offers to sell goods to Gamma, stating, "This offer may be accepted only by a letter addressed to me at my place of business." Gamma immediately mails a letter of acceptance to Beta's business address. The acceptance is effective and a contract arises when Gamma mails the letter. If Gamma uses a medium other than the one Beta stipulated, there is no acceptance. However, Gamma's use of a different medium does not necessarily destroy Gamma's power of acceptance, because unless otherwise indicated by the offeror (Beta), an offer is open for a reasonable time. Gamma therefore may have time remaining to use the required medium of acceptance, but runs the risk that Beta will revoke the offer or that the offer may terminate before Gamma exercises power of acceptance.

Under Article 2, the offeror will not be held to have required a particular medium of acceptance unless the requirement has been "unambiguously indicated" to the offeree [2-206(1)]. So a court may hold that the words "Please respond by letter" do not make the letter the sole permitted medium of acceptance, but instead indicate that an acceptance by another medium may be effective, at least when received.

3 Where an offeror says nothing regarding the medium of acceptance, the offer may be accepted in any manner and by any medium reasonable under the circumstances [2-206]. Some courts applying the common law have ruled that offerors impliedly authorize only those acceptance media that are at least as fast as the medium used to make the offer. The Code position is that a slower medium may in some circumstances be reasonable and therefore effective upon dispatch.

Another appropriate method of acceptance, under certain circumstances, is to start performance on the sales contract. For example, Buyer telegraphs Seller in a distant state to begin manufacturing and shipping goods immediately. Buyer, however, faces some uncertainty if Seller begins performance but does not inform Buyer of the fact. To reduce this uncertainty, Article 2 requires Seller to give Buyer notice within a reasonable time that performance has begun. If Seller does not give the notice, Buyer may treat the offer as having expired before acceptance [2-206(2)]. Thus, Buyer will be free to acquire the goods from another source without liability to Seller even though Seller may have in fact begun performance.

Article 2 counteroffer rules. Under the common law, most states require that the offeree respond exactly to the terms of the offer. Referred to as the "mirror-image rule," this common law rule does not acknowledge that a contract arises if an offeree departs from the terms of an offer in even a small way. Such a departure, under the common law, is seen as an offer rejection and a counteroffer.

The mirror-image rule, however, is inconsistent with modern business practices in the sales of goods. Each day millions of contracts for goods are arranged by an exchange of preprinted forms—one prepared by the legal counsel of the buyer, another prepared by the legal counsel of the seller. Both counsels are hired to serve the interests of their clients and will draft the form in a way that gives their separate clients the most advantage. Consequently, the forms are unlikely to match, and a mirror-image agreement is unlikely to be accomplished. If governed by the common law, parties to a transaction involving these different forms would be very uncertain whether they have an enforceable binding agreement.

To reduce delay and harmful surprise in the formation of sales contracts, the drafters of Article 2 abandoned the mirror-image rule. The offeree, however, is still permitted under the Code to make a counteroffer by *stating* one's intentions not to be bound to a contract unless the offeror assents to whatever additional or different terms the offeree has introduced [2-207(1)].

For example, suppose that Sigma Company offers to sell Delta Company a computer for $50,000, and Delta responds with the statement, "We accept your offer, but only on the condition that you agree to arbitrate any dispute arising out of this sale instead of going to court." Delta has made a counteroffer, and there is no contract unless Sigma accepts it.

But if Delta makes a timely statement of acceptance that introduces different or additional terms and does so without *expressly* conditioning the acceptance on Sigma's assent to the new terms, they are to be treated by the court as mere proposals for addition to the contract [2-207(2)]. Now suppose further that Sigma made its offer to Delta on its preprinted sales form that said nothing about arbitration, and Delta responded with its own preprinted form that contained on its reverse side a clause stating "Disputes relating to this transaction shall be resolved by arbitration." Although Delta's form contains an arbitration clause, Delta has not used language expressly requiring Sigma's assent to the clause. So, since the offer and acceptance forms reveal agreement as to enough terms for a contract (computer for $50,000 and identification of the parties to the sale), a contract arises despite the fact that the acceptance does not mirror the offer. Courts sometimes have difficulty sorting out various terms of agreement when buyers and sellers exchange complicated forms, and the problem is called "the battle of the forms."

Article 2 provides a set of general rules to govern whether proposed new terms may become part of the sales contract. Those rules are summarized as follows:

1. If the new term is a major departure from or addition to the offer, the new term will not become a part of the contract unless the offeror actually consents to the major new term. The essential concern is whether the new term "materially alters" the offer, and the question of what is material is left to a court to decide. Two examples of what courts have held to be a new term that materially alters the offer are (a) an offeree-buyer's substituting a lower price than the one offered, no matter how slight the price change; and (b) the offeree's addition of an arbitration clause.

2. *Between merchants,* a *minor* new term—such as an insignificant variation as to method or time of delivery—*will* become a part of the contract *unless* the merchant-offeror does one of two things to prevent the minor term from being included: (a) When first making the offer, the merchant-offeror *expressly limits* the offeree's acceptance to the terms of the offer. Or (b) having failed to so limit the offer, the merchant-offeror later gives the offeree *notice* of the offeror's objection to the minor new term and does so within a *reasonable time* after the term has been communicated to the offeror.

In summary of Article 2 rules on counteroffers and new proposed terms, a sales contract arises if the parties agree on the basic terms necessary for a contract; and no major alterations may be imposed on any offeror with that person's consent. Also, a minor new term may not be imposed on a *nonmerchant-offeror* without the nonmerchant's consent. However, a merchant-offeror must take action to prevent a merchant-offeree's proposed minor term from becoming part of the sales contract.

Figure 18.1 illustrates the UCC treatment of the offeree's additional terms.

Sometimes the writings of buyer and seller are so much in conflict that no contract results from the exchange of writings. Yet, because the seller shipped goods and the buyer accepted and paid for them, a contract of some sort arose. In the event of a dispute between buyer and seller about the quality of the goods, the price, or other matters, what are the terms of the contract? A court will determine what the parties actually contracted for and will use whatever writings or other conduct or terms are supplied by the UCC [2-207(3)].

Later in this chapter, Case 18.3 provides an example of a court resolving a "battle of the forms" dispute.

Shipment of nonconforming goods as an acceptance. Sometimes a seller fills an order by shipping goods that differ from what was ordered—perhaps by accident, perhaps on purpose. If the nonconforming shipment was intentional, the seller's action may have been in bad faith on the hope that the buyer will not notice the substitution. However, the seller could have been acting in good faith by intentionally sending nonconforming goods. For example, the seller might have known that the buyer needed the goods immediately and, lacking the exact goods ordered, shipped similar goods as an accommodation to the buyer.

Suppose that Tailor, a blouse manufacturer, orders for prompt shipment 1,000 bolts of white silk cloth from Mill Company, which ships 1,000 bolts of white nylon cloth instead. At common law, a judge would have held that Mill Company has not accepted Tailor's offer and therefore cannot be liable for breach of contract. Under Article 2, if Mill Company ships the nylon *without giving notice* that the goods are nonconforming, the shipment *is* an acceptance and—at the same time—a breach of contract. The purpose of this rule is to discourage sellers from negligently filling orders or deceiving buyers. However, where Mill Company gives Tailor *timely notice* that the goods are nonconforming, the shipment is *not* an acceptance, and Mill Company will not be liable for breach of contract. This notice is especially important and practical if Tailor receives mail at its business office but the goods are delivered to employees elsewhere. If Tailor has notice that the cloth is nylon but uses it anyway, there is a contract. If Tailor decides not to use the goods, Tailor may ship them back at Mill Company's expense. Notice that this rule also encourages sellers to accommodate buyers who may need substitute goods for maintaining production schedules, and to act reasonably in doing so.

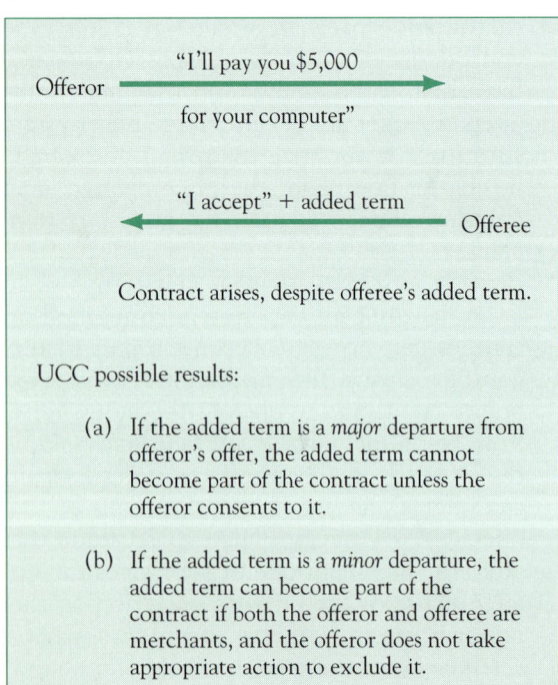

Figure 18.1 UCC treatment of offeree's added term.

Offeror → "I'll pay you $5,000 for your computer"

Offeree ← "I accept" + added term

Contract arises, despite offeree's added term.

UCC possible results:

(a) If the added term is a *major* departure from offeror's offer, the added term cannot become part of the contract unless the offeror consents to it.

(b) If the added term is a *minor* departure, the added term can become part of the contract if both the offeror and offeree are merchants, and the offeror does not take appropriate action to exclude it.

Interpretation of the Sales Contract

Where a sales agreement is so sketchy or poorly worded that its terms are in doubt, a court may have to interpret it. **Interpretation** is a process by which a judge decides what legal obligations each party to the agreement undertook and whether the agreement amounts to an enforceable contract. A part of the judge's task might be to determine *which* of the parties' written and oral statements are included in the contract, and *what meaning* the parties' words should have. Contractual interpretation is largely beyond the scope of this book. However, businesspeople can benefit from knowing generally how the Code and the courts approach the problem of interpretation.

Meaning of "Contract."
Since interpretation may be viewed as a judicial search for a contract, the meaning of "contract" becomes important. Under the Code, **contract** means the total legal obligation that results from the parties' agreement, as that agreement is affected by the Code and by any other applicable rules of law [1-201(11)]. **Agreement** means the bargain of the parties in fact, as found in their language or by implication from other circumstances, such as course of performance, course of dealing, and usage of trade [1-201(3)]. Since a sales contract includes obligations imposed by the Code and by other law, the parties must at least act in good faith and avoid unconscionable conduct. The Code and other law also fill in certain terms left open by the parties. Thus, a "sales contract" consists of the agreement of the parties as that agreement is limited and supplemented by law.

The Parol Evidence Rule.
Often the parties to a sales contract make a variety of written and oral statements in the process of negotiating the terms of the contract, and then they sign a writing called an "integration" that supposedly represents their final decision as to the terms of the contract.

But what happens if one of the parties alleges that one of these prior statements, called "parol evidence," and not the term that appears in the integration, truly states the parties' agreement? A court will apply the Article 2 **parol evidence rule**, which specifies that terms in a "writing intended by the parties as the final expression of their agreement with respect to such terms" are not to be contradicted by evidence of any prior agreement or by evidence of a contemporaneous oral agreement [2-202]. The same is true of terms agreed to by the parties in confirmatory memoranda agreeing on the term in dispute. However, agreed-to terms may be explained or supplemented by course of dealing, by usage of trade, or by course of performance. Agreed-to terms may also be explained or supplemented by evidence of consistent additional terms, unless the judge finds that the parties intended the writing to be not only a "final" but also a "complete and exclusive" statement of terms.

In summary, then, a court ordinarily will not admit into evidence any parol statement that directly contradicts an unambiguous term in an integration. The unambiguous term, and not the contradictory earlier statement, will be taken by the court as an accurate statement of the parties' agreement. But parol evidence *is* admissible to clear up vague or ambiguous language, to settle allegations of fraud, to supply missing terms where the final writing was not intended to be complete and exclusive, and so on. A court sorts through the many conflicting statements that the parties might make and arrives at the selection of words that the court will hold to be the language of the contract.

Course of Performance, Course of Dealing, Usage of Trade.
After deciding what statements are to be considered part of the contract, the court may have to determine the meaning of unclear language. The meaning intended by the parties is to be determined by their language and conduct, read and interpreted in light of commercial practices and other relevant circumstances [1-205, comment 1].

To aid interpretation, the Code gives special prominence to "course of performance," "course of dealing," and "usage of trade." **Course of performance** refers to how a particular transaction is carried out. There can be no course of performance unless there are repeated occasions for performance, such as several deliveries of coal to be made under a single contract of sale. Suppose that a contract for the delivery of coal says nothing about how large each delivery shall be. The buyer's acceptance of a series of small deliveries could establish a course of performance that would bind the buyer as to the next delivery [2-208(1)].

Course of dealing refers to a series of transactions, not just the performance on one transaction. A course of dealing—a pattern of prior contracts—can establish a background for the interpretation of the immediate transaction [1-205(1)]. Suppose that for each of five previous winters a buyer of home heating oil has always paid the delivery person in cash. The seller's acceptance of this practice sets a course of dealing upon which the buyer may rely until notified differently, even if the driver absconds with the cash.

A **usage of trade** is any practice or method of dealing that is so regularly observed in a place, vocation, or trade that a party to a sales contract is justified in expecting that the practice will be observed in this contract too [1-205(2)]. It is usage of trade in the seed corn business that sellers of seed corn make no guarantees of yield. A buyer who knew nothing of this usage of trade could be nevertheless bound by it.

Case 18.3, which follows, provides an example of how a court interpreted a sales contract and also involves a "battle of the forms" problem.

CASE 18.3

Union Carbide Corp. v. Oscar Mayer Foods Corp.
- 947 F.2d 1333 (7th Cir. 1991)

FACTS

Union Carbide sold plastic casings that Oscar Mayer uses in manufacturing sausages. In 1980, the prices in Union Carbide's invoices to Oscar Mayer included two 1 percent sales taxes imposed by the city of Chicago. Another supplier of sausage casings to Oscar Mayer began charging a price 1 percent below Union Carbide's, by accepting orders at a location outside of Chicago. When Oscar Mayer informed Union Carbide of this, Union Carbide instructed its customers to likewise send orders to an address outside of Chicago in order to avoid the taxes. Thus, Union Carbide had met and beat the other supplier's discount by lowering its price 2 percent.

Eight years later the Illinois tax authorities decided that the two sales taxes were due notwithstanding the change of address. They assessed $88,000 in back taxes and $55,000 in interest on Union Carbide who paid the amount, and brought suit against Oscar Mayer to recover the amount of back taxes, claiming that Oscar Mayer had agreed to indemnify Union Carbide for all sales tax liability. The company based its claim on the following provision printed on the back of Union Carbide's invoices:

> In addition to the purchase price, Buyer shall pay Seller the amount of all governmental taxes . . . that Seller may be required to pay with respect to the production, sale or transportation of any materials delivered hereunder.

The trial court granted summary judgment in favor of Oscar Mayer. Union Carbide appealed.

OPINION

POSNER, J. . . . We think that Union Carbide has misread the contract and this is

**CASE 18.3
Continued**

clear enough to be determined without a trial. . . . We also agree with the . . . [trial] judge that if read as an indemnity clause the quoted provision is a material alteration in the parties' contract and is therefore unenforceable against Oscar Mayer because not agreed to. . . . [The] "mirror image" rule was widely believed to take insufficient account of the incorrigible fallibility of human beings engaged in commercial . . . dealings, and is changed by the [UCC], which allows an acceptance to make a contract even if it adds terms to the offer. Moreover, if it is a contract between "merchants" (in the sense of "pros" . . . as Union Carbide and Oscar Mayer are), the additional terms become part of the contract. But not any additional terms; only those to which the offeror would be unlikely to object because they fill out the contract in an expectable fashion, and hence do not alter it materially. If a term added by the offeree in his acceptance works a material alteration of the offer, the acceptance is still effective, but the term is not: that is, the contract is enforceable minus the term the offeree tried to add.

An alteration is material if consent to it cannot be presumed. . . . What is expectable, hence unsurprising, is okay; what is unexpected, hence surprising, is not. Not infrequently the test is said to be "surprise or hardship."

This is not the end of the analysis, however. Like most doctrines of contract law, the doctrine of material alteration is an aid to interpretation rather than an ironclad rule. . . . [C]onsent can be inferred from other things besides the unsurprising character of the new term: even from silence, in the face of a course of dealings that makes it reasonable for the other party to infer consent from a failure to object.

To summarize, a term inserted by the offeree is ineffectual (1) if the offer expressly limits acceptance to the terms of the offer, or (2) if the new term (a) makes a material alteration, in the sense that consent to it cannot be presumed, and (b) there is no showing that the offeror in fact consented to the alteration—whether (i) expressly, or (ii) by silence against the background of a course of dealings.

Oscar Mayer [does not] deny that it was contractually obligated [to pay sales taxes]. . . . If the sales tax rates had risen, Oscar Mayer would have had to pay the higher rates. What difference does it make, asks Union Carbide, if the increase took the form of an assessment of back taxes? It makes a big difference, amounting to a material alteration to which Oscar Mayer did not consent either explicitly or implicitly. If a tax increase showed up on an invoice, Oscar Mayer would have to pay but might then decide to cease buying casings from Union Carbide. . . . To assume responsibility for taxes shown on an individual invoice is quite different from assuming an open-ended, indeed incalculable, liability for back taxes. . . . [T]his is not a case where consent can realistically be inferred from Oscar Mayer's silence in the face of a succession of acceptances (Union Carbide's invoices) containing the new term.

There was no breach of contract.

JUDGMENT Affirmed.

Form of the Sales Contract—UCC Statute of Frauds

The parties to a sales contract are not required to use any particular form of contract. As long as they provide the minimum amount of information required for a contract to arise, they may say as little or as much as they like about its terms, in whatever language or sequence of clauses they prefer. Yet some rules of law do affect the form of some sales contracts. The Article 2 **statute of frauds** requires that specified kinds of sales contracts be evidenced by a *writing* or by some *legally acceptable substitute*.

The purpose of the statute of frauds is to require clear evidence—beyond mere oral statements of the parties—that a contract actually arose. This evidence is especially important where one person insists, but the other person denies, that a contract arose. As discussed in Chapter 15, statute-of-frauds requirements apply only to sales contracts involving a price of $500 or more. Some states, however, specify a different amount. Under Article 2A, a writing is required if rental payments total $1,000 or more.

Under the basic Article 2 rule, such a contract is not enforceable unless the party against whom enforcement is sought has signed some writing sufficient to indicate that a contract for sale has been made between the parties. Article 2 does *not* require that all the terms of the contract be stated. The writing is sufficient if it is signed by the party to be charged with breach of contract, specifies a quantity of goods, and indicates that the parties intended to enter into a contract [2-201]. The quantity need not be accurately stated, but the contract is not enforceable for more than the quantity stated in the writing.

Two classes of sales transactions are enforceable even though the party against whom enforcement is sought has signed nothing. Both classes of transactions involve situation where one party would be subjected to unfair surprise if the other party were permitted to cancel an agreement merely because the canceling party has signed nothing.

The first class consists of contracts "between merchants" in which a writing exists but has not been signed by the person against whom enforcement is sought. Suppose that a merchant, Retailer, telephones an offer to dealer, Office Supply, to buy a particular cash register for $1,000; that Office Supply replies over the phone, "I accept your offer"; and that Office Supply immediately sends Retailer a written confirmation of the contract. Three weeks later, Retailer, pointing out that no signed agreement exists, denies that the oral contract binds it. The statute of frauds is satisfied *without* Retailer's signature if the following things happen: (1) Within a reasonable time after the oral transaction, Retailer receives a writing confirming the contract and the writing is sufficiently detailed to be enforceable against the sender, Office Supply. (2) Retailer has reason to know the contents of the writing. And (3) Retailer does not give written notice of its objection to the contents of the writing within 10 days after receiving it.

In the second class of sales transactions there usually is no writing, but there may be convincing alternative evidence that the parties made a contract. If a party *admits in court* that a contract for sale was made, the oral contract can be enforced as to the quantity of goods admitted. If an oral contract has been *partially performed,* it is enforceable as to the goods for which the seller accepted payment, or as to goods that the buyer received and accepted. Oral contracts for goods to be *specially manufactured* for the buyer may also be enforceable—if the manufacturer has begun to make or procure them before notice of repudiation by the buyer and the goods are not suitable for sale in the ordinary course of the seller's business.

Alteration of the Sales Contract

After forming a sales contract, the parties may wish to modify it. They may want to change the time or place of delivery, specifications in the goods ordered, warranty obligations, or even the price. Under the general law of contracts, such modifications may not be enforceable unless both parties receive new consideration. Yet it is common practice for honest people to agree to, and to rely on, modifications that are not supported by consideration. Under Article 2, an agreement modifying a sales contract needs no consideration to be binding [2-209].

But sometimes a party to a sale forces a modification on the other party by, for example, threatening to withhold delivery of essential goods unless the purchaser "agrees" to pay more. Article 2 provides protections against such misconduct. One protection is the UCC requirement that any party to a Code transaction must act in good faith. In applying the good faith rule, a court may require the person seeking a modification to prove that there is a real need for it—for example, that the higher price to which the buyer agreed is justified by an actual increase in the price of raw materials. Another protection is the fact that the statute of frauds must be satisfied if the contract, as modified, will be for a price of $500 or more. Thus there will be evidence that the other party actually agreed to the modification.

There is a third protection. The parties to a signed agreement may require in their agreement that any modification or cancellation of the contract must be evidenced by a signed writing for the change to be enforceable, a "no oral modifications" clause. However, when such a clause is supplied by a merchant to a nonmerchant, the clause will not be binding on the nonmerchant unless the nonmerchant signs it separately.

What happens when the parties fail to provide a required writing and agree to an oral modification anyway? If one party *materially changes his or her position in reliance* on the oral modification, the other party has *waived* the protection of the required writing. For example, suppose that Contractor orders 10 tons of flagstone from Quarry for delivery in 10 days, and their contract requires any modification to be in writing. Three days after contracting, Contractor calls Quarry to postpone delivery for another 15 days because of a construction slowdown. Quarry agrees to the postponement. Quarry, knowing that it will receive more flagstone before the 15-day postponement elapses, sells its entire inventory to a third party. If Contractor then wants delivery on the original date, it cannot insist on it. Contractor waived its right to cancel the oral agreement because Quarry *relied* on the oral agreement.

SUMMARY

The general purpose of the UCC is to simplify, unify, and modernize the law of commercial transactions. The Code encourages sound business practices, ethical business conduct, and performance of sales contracts. Merchants generally have greater duties than do nonmerchants, and all parties to Code transactions must use good faith in carrying them out.

Article 2 applies to sales of goods and to contracts to sell goods at a future time. In general, *goods* means all things that are movable at the time of identification to the contract. Article 2 does not apply to transactions other than goods.

Article 2 is more flexible than the common law in the rules governing the formation of sales contracts. A sales contract may be made in any manner sufficient to show agreement. Article 2's version of the statute of frauds and its rules governing contract changes also are more flexible and reflect the fast-paced needs of business.

A good example of how law and ethics can go hand in hand, the Code has several ethical concepts embedded into its underlying policies; among them are good faith and fair dealing. Ethics and practicality also are intertwined in the Code's recognition of the concepts of course of performance, course of dealing, and usage of trade.

REVIEW QUESTIONS

1. A sale of goods may involve other UCC transactions too. Explain or illustrate.

2. Why is it necessary to have a body of sales law apart from the general law of contracts?

3. A basic policy of the UCC is to encourage sound and ethical business practices. Explain how the following Code concepts contribute to carrying out that policy: **(a)** merchant, **(b)** good faith, and **(c)** identification of goods to the contract.

4. **(a)** To what transactions does Article 2 apply? **(b)** How might a court treat a contract involving a mixture of goods and services?

5. Explain whether the following statement is true: "Before there can be a sales contract, the parties, the price, and the quantity of goods must be identified."

6. How and why does Article 2 depart from common law rules with regard to an offer for a unilateral contract? A firm offer?

7. (a) What is the effect of using a medium of acceptance that has been authorized by the offeror? (b) How does an offeree know what medium of acceptance has been authorized?

8. How and why does Article 2 depart from common law rules with regard to (a) counteroffers and (b) a shipment of nonconforming goods as an acceptance?

9. Explain generally how a court will interpret a sales contract whose terms are in doubt.

10. In what main way does unconscionability differ from other, more traditional, grounds for avoiding a sales contract?

11. (a) How may the Article 2 statute of frauds be satisfied? (b) If a writing is used, what must the writing contain?

12. An agreement modifying a sales contract needs no consideration to be binding. How, then, may a buyer be protected if the seller forces the buyer to agree to a higher price by threatening to withhold delivery of essential goods?

CASE PROBLEMS

1. Alwinseal ordered goods from PPG for $65,000. PPG shipped them and sent Alwinseal an acknowledgment of the offer. PPG also sent a price list indicating a higher price than Alwinseal had offered to pay. PPG billed Alwinseal for $72,977.04, in accordance with PPG's new price list. Alwinseal paid the bill, claimed it had been overcharged by $7,977.04, and brought suit for the return of that amount. Was Alwinseal entitled to the amount it claimed?

2. Schmerdlapp, who runs a concession stand on the Atlantic City boardwalk, discovered near the end of business on a hot summer day that he was almost out of paper cones, which he uses to dispense "Snow Cones." He called Donohue Supply, his regular supplier, and ordered ten cases of #35 paper cones, saying that he needed them "immediately." The phone clerk replied, "You'll have them by start of business tomorrow." Later, the owner of Donohue Supply discovered that they were out of #35 paper cones, and instructed an employee to pack and ship #30 cones instead. (a) Under what circumstances would Schmerdlapp be bound to a contract for goods he did not order? (b) Under what circumstances would Schmerdlapp not be bound? (c) Would it make a difference if Donohue Supply had sent, and Schmerdlapp accepted, a similar substitute on previous occasions?

3. Just Born, Inc., a candy manufacturer, purchased gelatin from Stein & Co. Just Born telephoned its orders and followed up with written purchase orders specifying terms such as price, quantity, and description of goods. Stein responded by sending Just Born a "Sales Acknowledgment Agreement" and shipping the gelatin to Just Born's plant. Stein & Co.'s agreement form contained an "arbitration clause" requiring any dispute to be settled by arbitration rather than in court. The gelatin was unfit for its intended use, and Just Born brought suit for damages. Stein & Co. insisted that the dispute be submitted to arbitration. Was Just Born bound by the arbitration clause?

4. Michel, Inc., made seven oral agreements to purchase yarn from Anabasis Trade, Inc. In each of the seven transactions, Anabasis (seller) sent Michel a written confirmation containing an arbitration clause. Michel signed and returned the first confirmation. Michel knew that the form contained the arbitration clause but never objected to it. Michel did not object to the inclusion of a 30-day rather than a 60-day credit term contained in the second and third confirmations, and these terms were changed to suit Michel. Later, Michel discovered that the yarn did not conform to the contract specifications. Anabasis insisted that the dispute be submitted to arbitration. Michel brought an action to stay (stop) arbitration proceedings. The trial court

held that the arbitration clause did not become part of the contract unless both parties explicitly agreed to it. Was the trial court correct?

5. Hoping to be admitted to the practice of law, Jaiswal, a certified public accountant, purchased over $1,400 worth of legal textbooks from Matthew Bender & Co. The invoices contained the names and addresses of buyer and seller, the date, the payment terms, descriptions and prices of the books, and a clause which entitled the purchaser to return the merchandise within 30 days for a full refund. Jaiswal was admitted to the bar, but several months after the sale refused to pay for the books, claiming they had been sold on approval and that the salesperson had assured him that he could return them if he decided they were not useful. Bender sued for the price of the books. Was Jaiswal liable for payment?

6. Sebasty, a farmer, made an oral agreement to sell 14,000 bushels of wheat to Perschke Hay and Grain for $3.40 per bushel. Perschke immediately sent Sebasty a written confirmation of the agreement, which Sebasty received. Under the agreement, Perschke was to pick up the wheat about 6 months later. In the meantime, the price of wheat rose, and when the time for performance arrived, Sebasty refused to provide the wheat. Alleging breach of contract, Perschke sued Sebasty for more than $14,000 in damages. Sebasty contended that the oral agreement was not enforceable because it did not comply with the statute of frauds. Part of Sebasty's defense rested on his allegation that he was not a merchant. **(a)** On what statute-of-frauds rule was plaintiff Perschke relying? **(b)** For the purpose of that rule, was Sebasty a merchant?

CHAPTER 19

Delivery and Storage of Goods; Documents of Title

Making a contract of sale is only the first step in what can be a complicated process of getting goods from seller to buyer. Often, goods are put on a carrier for transport or in a warehouse for storage, their movement from buyer to seller being controlled by the use of documents of title. The goods may be lost or damaged in transit, and different people may claim ownership of the same goods. Under what circumstances is a carrier or a warehouse liable for lost or damaged goods? Who is entitled to the goods where ownership is disputed? These questions are the focus of this chapter.

DELIVERY AND STORAGE OF GOODS

Delivery of Goods

Delivery by Common and Private Carriers. The Uniform Commercial Code recognizes that sellers of goods often, if not usually, perform on their contracts by having an intermediary actually deliver the goods. Such an intermediary is a **carrier**—an individual or a business firm engaged in transporting passengers or goods for hire.

A carriage contract for the transport of goods is a **bailment** in which the bailor (the owner or another shipper) places the goods in the custody of the bailee (the carrier) for the purpose of safe transport to a person or a firm authorized by the shipper to receive them. Carriers of property include railroads, barge and ship lines, airlines, trucking companies, pipeline companies that transport oil or natural gas, and express companies whose business is the speedy delivery of small packages of goods or money.

A carrier has claim against goods in its possession for any unpaid transportation and related charges [7-307]. This legal claim is called a **lien.** The carrier may enforce a lien by selling the amount of the goods necessary to pay its legitimate charges [7-308]. A carrier loses its lien on any goods that it voluntarily delivers or unjustifiably refuses to deliver.

Carriers are classified into two types: common and private. A **common carrier** offers its services to the public and must carry for all who apply, as long as there is room and no legal excuse for refusing to render the service. An express company, which by definition hauls only small packages, would have a legal excuse for refusing to haul passengers.

A common carrier has extensive liability for damage to or loss of goods being transported. Like any other bailee, a common carrier is liable for loss caused by its negligence and intentional

> **BOX 19.1**
>
> ### A Few Words on Bailments
>
> A **bailment** is the legal relationship that results where one person (the bailor) transfers possession of personal property to another person (the bailee) under such circumstances that the bailee is under a duty to return the item to the bailor or to dispose of it as directed by the bailor.
>
> Bailment relationships arise in more legal settings than in just the sale of goods. For example, a bailment relationship is created when you are required to check your bookbag at the campus bookstore, or when you check your coat at a restaurant. Consequently, bailments can be governed not only by the UCC but also by state law, most usually common law.
>
> Depending upon the party most at benefit from a bailment relationship, there are varying duties of care imposed upon bailees. These duties and other aspects of bailments are covered in Chapter 23. ■

torts such as *conversion* of the bailor's goods.[1] But in most states common carriers also are liable for loss due to causes beyond the carrier's control, such as fires, wrecks, theft, and violent mobs. The English courts began imposing this broader "insurer's" liability in the 1500s because common carriers or their employees could easily steal the goods, sell them, and pretend that the goods had been lost. Today the common carrier's liability as an insurer is based on additional factors: the total value of the goods being shipped, the vast distances involved, and the difficulty a seller would have in proving a carrier's negligence or fraud.

There are limits to the liability of a common carrier, however. A common carrier is not liable, for example, for losses caused solely by an "act of God" such as a tornado or an earthquake, an act or fault of the party hiring the carrier, or the dangerous or perishable nature of the goods themselves. Furthermore, unless forbidden by law to do so, a common carrier may limit the amount of damages recoverable by a bailor where the carrier's rates are dependent on value and the bailor is given an opportunity to declare a higher value (probably for payment of a higher rate) [7-309]. The right to limit damages applies to the carrier's liability as an *insurer* (i.e., for loss from causes beyond the carrier's control) and to its liability for its own *negligence*. But a common carrier may *not* totally exempt itself from these liabilities, and it is not permitted even to limit its liability for *converting* the bailor's goods to its own use. Any other rule would reward wrongdoing by allowing the converter to keep the difference between the actual value of the converted property and any limited amount stated in the contract of carriage.

Table 19.1 summarizes the liabilities of a common carrier.

Private carriers, including "contract" carriers, ordinarily are used to meet the special needs of shippers who find access to a common carrier lacking or its service unsatisfactory. An isolated rancher might hire a private carrier to haul cattle to market or to a loading yard to await the arrival of a common carrier. A manufacturer or a wholesaler might use a private carrier for deliveries to remote regions or to local areas not served by common carriers.

Private carriers differ considerably from common carriers. Private carriers do not hold themselves out as ready to serve the public generally and are not required to do so. Rather, they carry goods only for those persons with whom the carriers choose to contract. Unlike common carriers, private carriers are *not* liable as insurers of the goods. They are liable only as bailees, for loss caused by (1) their own negligence, including that of their employees and other agents, and (2) their intentional misconduct, and that of their employees/agents, such as conversion of the goods. Thus, a private carrier would be liable for theft committed by its employees but would not be liable for thefts committed by

---

[1] Conversion is the act of taking or using someone else's personal property as one's own, without legal justification. Recall from Chapter 9, a thief is a converter. So is a carrier or other bailee that delivers goods to the wrong person, uses the bailed goods as the bailee's own, or wrongfully refuses to release the goods to the bailor or to release them in accordance with the bailor's instructions.

Table 19.1 Liabilities of a Common Carrier

Common carrier IS LIABLE for loss caused by:
   Intentional torts by the carrier, its employees, or its other agents.
      Example: An employee's willful damage to goods or conversion of goods to the employee's or carrier's own use.
   Negligence by the carrier, its employees, or its other agents.
      Example: The carrier's failure to exert the appropriate level of care over shipped goods resulting in damage or loss.

Common carrier IS LIABLE as *insurer* for losses beyond its control.
      Example: Losses caused by fires, wrecks, theft, or violent mobs.

BUT

Common carrier MAY LIMIT its insurer's and negligence liability if:
   1 Shipping rates depend on value of the goods, *and*
   2 The party hiring the carrier is allowed to declare higher value

Common carrier is NOT LIABLE for loss caused by:
   1 Act of God
   2 Act or fault of the party hiring the carrier
   3 Dangerous or perishable nature of the goods

Table 19.2 Liability of a Private Carrier

Private carrier IS LIABLE for loss caused by:
   Intentional torts by the carrier, its employees or other agents
   Negligence by the carrier, its employees or other agents

BUT

Private carrier usually MAY ENTIRELY EXCLUDE liability for its own ordinary negligence

Private carrier IS NOT LIABLE
   1 As insurer, or
   2 For loss caused by an act of God, and the like

---

strangers unless the carrier or its employees failed to use ordinary care to prevent the thefts. Private carriers are freer than common carriers to exclude liability for negligence. Private carriers usually may enforce contract clauses that exempt them from liability for ordinary negligence, but usually they may not enforce clauses that purport to exempt them from liability for *gross* negligence or for intentional misconduct.

Table 19.2 summarizes the liability of a private carrier.

Although a common or private carrier may be liable for loss of goods in its custody, sometimes the carrier is not liable. So, in a transaction in goods, either the buyer or the seller who has contracted the carrier must absorb the loss. The UCC provides "risk-of-loss rules," discussed in the next chapter, that determine who—the buyer or the seller—must absorb the loss or, if a carrier is liable, who must seek compensation from the carrier. UCC risk-of-loss rules apply also to "noncarrier" and "pickup" deliveries.

Noncarrier and Pickup Deliveries. Especially in the retail sale of bulky goods such as furniture, sellers commonly deliver the goods to the buyers by means of the sellers' own delivery vehicles. This kind of delivery is called a "noncarrier delivery" because the seller does not use a common or a private carrier. Sellers of many other kinds of goods—such as dairy products, fuels for home or commercial use, soft drinks, baked goods, and small hand tools—make noncarrier deliveries to customers for resale or for the customers' own use.

Many buyers use their own vehicles to pick up the goods at the seller's premises. For example, a building contractor might have a fleet of trucks for pickup of gravel, lumber, and other building materials. Customers of local supermarkets and department stores ordinarily pick up the goods at the store rather than having the store make a noncarrier delivery. In the sale of automobiles, for example, the customer may visit the seller's premises several times to work out the terms of the sale and then return a few days later to pick up the automobile after it has been prepared by the seller for use.

The following case deals with limits of liability of a common carrier when the carrier admits to gross negligence.

CASE 19.1   Calvin Klein Ltd. v. Trylon Trucking Corp. • 892 F.2d 191 (2d Cir. 1989)

FACTS   Trylon is a New Jersey trucking firm in the business of transporting goods from New York City's airports to its customers' facilities. Calvin Klein Ltd. (Klein), a clothing company and a customer of Trylon's for at least 3 years, had used Trylon for hundreds of shipments. In those deliveries, Klein would contact Trylon to pick up the shipment from the airport for delivery to Klein's facility. After completing the carriage, Trylon would forward an invoice to Klein which contained a limitation-of-liability provision as follows:

> In consideration of the rate charged, the shipper agrees that the carrier shall not be liable for more than $50.00 on any shipment accepted for delivery to one consignee unless a greater value is declared, in writing, upon receipt at the time of shipment and charge for such greater value paid, or agreed to be paid, by the shipper.

On March 27, 1986, a shipment of 2,833 blouses from Hong Kong arrived at JFK Airport, and Klein arranged for Trylon to deliver them to Klein. On April 2, Trylon dispatched a driver for the shipment, a driver who then stole Trylon's truck and its contents. The shipment was never recovered. Klein sent a letter to Trylon to recover full value of the lost blouses, $150,000. In absence of a response from Trylon, Klein sued to recover the loss. The trial court held in favor of Klein. Trylon appealed.

Though the parties agreed that Trylon is liable to Klein for the loss of the shipment and that Trylon was grossly negligent in the hiring and supervision of the driver and that Klein was aware of the $50 limitation on liability, the parties left at issue whether the limitation-of-liability clause was valid and enforceable when the carrier admits to being grossly negligent.

OPINION   MINER, J. . . . [This] appeal presents a novel issue under New York law: whether a limitation of liability agreement between shipper and a carrier is enforceable when the shipment is lost as a result of the carrier's gross negligence.

Trylon . . . argues that the limitation [of liability] is enforceable despite its conceded gross negligence. [Klein] contends that . . . no agreement existed between the parties as to a liability limit. . . . Alternatively, [Klein] points to two different public policy reasons why the limitation provision . . . is unenforceable. First, Trylon's gross negligence resulted in the loss, and public policy prohibits the enforcement of an exculpatory provision which attempts to relieve the contracting party of liability under such circumstances. Second, the $50 limit was unreasonably low and therefore unenforceable. We address those contentions.

A common carrier . . . is strictly liable for the loss of goods in its custody. . . . Even in the case of loss from theft by third parties, liability may be imposed upon a negligent common carrier.

A shipper and a common carrier may contract to limit the carrier's liability in cases of loss to an amount agreed to by the parties, so long as the language of the limitation is clear, the shipper is aware of the terms of the limitation, and the shipper can change the terms by indicating the true value of the goods being

**CASE 19.1
Continued**

shipped. . . . The limitation of liability provision involved here clearly provides that, at the time of delivery, the shipper may increase the limitation by written notice . . . and by payment of a commensurately higher fee.

[Klein] and Trylon were business entities with an on-going commercial relationship involving numerous carriages. . . . Here, each carriage was under the same terms and conditions as the last, including a limitation of Trylon's liability. This is not a case in which the shipper was dealing with the common carrier for the first time or contracting under new or changed terms. [Klein] was aware of the terms and was free to adjust the limitation upon a written declaration of the value of a given shipment, but failed to do so with the shipment at issue here. Since Klein failed to adjust the limitation, the limitation applies here, and no public policy that dictates otherwise can be identified.

[Klein] . . . argues that the limitation is so low as to be void. . . . [The] amount is immaterial because [Klein] had the opportunity to negotiate the amount of coverage by declaring the value of the shipment . . . , and we find all of [Klein's] arguments to the unreasonableness of the limitation to be without merit.

JUDGMENT

Reversed and remanded to the district court with instructions to enter judgment against Trylon in the sum of $50.

**BOX 19.2
A Question of Law to Consider**

In the case *Calvin Klein Ltd. v. Trylon Trucking Corp.*, Judge Miner emphasized that Klein and Trylon had an ongoing relationship involving hundreds of shipments. This fact was important to the outcome of the case.

What if, however, the incident of the stolen shipment had occurred in the very first transaction between Klein and Trylon? Would this make a difference in the outcome? What if, unknown to Klein, Trylon had had a pattern of lost or stolen shipments resulting from its gross negligence? Would the outcome be different?

What if the carrier, knowing that its liability was limited, purposely performed on its delivery contracts less carefully, and this point could be proved? Would this fact make a difference? Would the good faith provision in UCC Article 1 have any relevance? ■

Storage in Warehouses

Often an owner of goods must store them in a warehouse until they are sold. A **warehouse** is a building or other enclosed area used to hold goods temporarily or for an indefinite time. When a person stores goods at a warehouse, a bailment relationship is created. The owner or other depositor of the goods is the bailor. The **warehouser,** a person or firm engaged in the business of receiving and storing goods for hire, is the bailee.

A warehouse may be public or private. A **public warehouse** holds itself out as willing to store goods for any member of the public who seeks and pays for the storage service. Grain elevators buy grain from farmers willing to sell, but they also store grain for any farmer who wishes to wait for a higher price. Because they store for anyone seeking that service, grain elevators are public warehouses. In contrast, a **private warehouse** stores goods only for those persons with whom it chooses to contract.

A public warehouse is subject to more governmental regulation than is a private warehouse. Aside from this difference, the distinction between a public and a private warehouse is not very significant, since neither kind is liable as an insurer of stored goods unless by special agreement or under an occasional state statute imposing such liability on a public warehouse. Rather, public and private warehouses usually are liable only *as bailees* for loss of or damage to the goods during storage—that is, for loss due to their negligence and their intentional misconduct in caring for the goods.

Like carriers, warehouses may limit their liability for negligence during storage. As noted in Case 19.2, this liability may be limited in the contract of storage to a specific amount per item, subject to the bailor's right to increase the valuation. If the bailor declares a higher value, the warehouse has a right to charge a higher rate for storage [7-204]. Like a carrier, a warehouse has a possessory lien on the goods for storage charges [7-209].

CASE 19.2   **Western Mining Corp. v. Standard Terminals, Inc.**
- 577 F. Supp. 847 (D.C. Pa. 1984)

FACTS   Western Mining, a seller of nickel products in North and South America, stored large quantities of nickel briquettes used in steelmaking at defendant Standard Terminals' warehouse facility in Arnold, Pennsylvania. The nickel came to the United States from Australia aboard ships in sealed containers delivered from the port of entry to the warehouse by common carrier. Standard Terminals (Warehouse) would store the nickel, advise Western Mining of the amount received, and issue warehouse receipts. Upon sale of the nickel, Western Mining would notify Warehouse of the amount and destination of the nickel to be delivered. Warehouse would then remove the nickel from storage, load it onto the carriers' vehicles, and prepare bills of lading and other shipping documents. Western Mining and Warehouse kept separate running paper inventories of the nickel and verified their records by physical inventories twice a year.

Twice in 1982 amounts of nickel totaling 8 metric tons valued at about $50,000 were discovered to be missing from the warehouse. Bailor and bailee reviewed their records separately to determine if there was a bookkeeping error. The parties' accounts were in agreement and did not explain why the nickel was missing. Warehouse admitted the nickel was missing but denied any specific factual knowledge of what happened to it. A clause in the warehouse receipts issued to Western Mining reads as follows:

> Limit of Bailee's liability [for] damage or loss is $200 a net ton. Should Bailor desire that side limit be increased, the storage rate shall be increased by three cents per month for each additional $100. Nothing herein contained shall preclude Bailor from taking out such insurance protection against fire or any other casualty as it may deem advisable.

Alleging that Warehouse had converted the missing nickel, Western Mining brought suit for its value.

OPINION   MENCER, D.J. . . . This civil action for damages presents a number of some-

**CASE 19.2
Continued**

what unsettled questions of law in the . . . area of bailments with warehousemen. . . .

Under Pennsylvania law, a bailment for the mutual benefit of the bailor and the bailee requires the bailee to exercise reasonable and ordinary care. When a bailment is shown to exist, the bailor makes out a prima facie case against his bailee for hire for recovery of the value of the unreturned bailed goods by showing his delivery of the goods to the bailee and the latter's failure to redeliver them upon the bailor's demand. . . . Western Mining, the bailor, urges the extension of this rebuttable presumption of negligence to cover conversion of the bailed goods. The United States Court of Appeals for the Third Circuit had defined the Pennsylvania common law tort of conversion as ". . . an act of willful interference with the dominion or control over a chattel, done without lawful justification, by which any person entitled to the chattel is deprived of its use and possession." . . . The plaintiff urges our adoption of the reasoning of [a New York court which] . . . found that, where there was proof of delivery to a bailee and of a subsequent failure to return bailed goods coupled with the bailee's failure to adequately explain such failure, a presumption of conversion on the part of the bailee was appropriate.

The distinction between negligence on the part of a bailee as opposed to conversion . . . where, as here, the goods for all practical purposes no longer exist may seem inconsequential at first blush. The importance, however, relates to the measure of damages available to the bailor. The Uniform Commercial Code Section 7-204(2) . . . provides that a warehouseman's liability in the case of loss or damage may be contractually limited. Such a limitation is ineffective when the warehouseman converts the bailed goods "to his own use." Unless there is adequate justification [for our presuming conversion on the part of the defendant], any recovery to which the plaintiff is entitled will be limited to $200 per ton.

[Some courts have cited the above New York case with favor.] There is, however, case law which expressly rejects [it]. [A federal district court] found that conversion under Indiana law . . . requires some affirmative wrongful act and, because the bailor failed to introduce "'direct evidence of any positive wrongful act,'" granted summary judgment in favor of the bailee. . . . Pennsylvania, like Indiana, requires a willful interference with the dominion or control of a chattel in order to establish conversion. . . . There is no evidence in the record of any "positive wrongful act" by the bailee in its handling of Western Mining's nickel[;] therefore, a presumption of conversion by the bailee is inappropriate and we will not charge Standard Terminals with liability for the full value of the missing nickel on that basis.

Western Mining next argues, in effect, that even assuming no conversion by Standard Terminals[,] the actions of Standard Terminals were so egregious as to constitute gross negligence [and that] a finding of gross negligence is sufficient to defeat the applicability of any liability limitation. . . . [W]e find as a matter of law that the events surrounding the disappearance of the plaintiff's nickel do not constitute gross negligence on the part of Standard Terminals.

The result of our ruling is that, because of the delivery of nickel to Standard Terminals by Western Mining, Western Mining's demand of return of the nickel

CASE 19.2 Continued	and Standard Terminal's failure to return the bailed nickel, the loss of the nickel may be presumed to be as a result of Standard Terminals' negligence.
JUDGMENT	Standard Terminals held liable to Western Mining in the amount of $200 per metric ton as contracted for in the warehouse receipts covering the bailment agreement.

DOCUMENTS OF TITLE

Documents of title are an important part of the paperwork necessary for getting goods from sellers to buyers. A **document of title** is any writing that in the *regular course of business or financing* is treated by the courts as adequate proof that the person in possession of it is entitled to receive and sell or otherwise dispose of the document and the goods it covers [1-201(15)]. To be a document of title, the writing must indicate that it is issued by or addressed to a bailee, such as a carrier or a warehouseman, and must purport to cover identified goods in the bailee's possession.

A document of title serves three practical functions. First, it is a receipt: a written acknowledgment given by a bailee that the depositor or shipper left the specified goods with the bailee for storage or shipment. Second, it is a contract between the bailor and the bailee for the storage or the transport of the goods. Third, it is *evidence of title to (ownership of) the goods*.

Kinds of Documents

The two principal documents of title are the warehouse receipt and the bill of lading. A **warehouse receipt** is a writing issued by a warehouser to the person or firm that deposits the goods at the warehouse for storage. The depositor is the bailor; the warehouser is the bailee.

A **bill of lading** is a writing, issued by a carrier, evidencing the carrier's receipt of goods for shipment. The person delivering the goods to the carrier for shipment is the shipper and also the bailor; the carrier is the bailee. The shipper-bailor's act of delivering goods to a carrier for transport is called a **consignment.** The shipper

(bailor) is the **consignor.** The person to whom the carrier is to deliver the goods at their destination is the consignee. Suppose Alpha Company delivers goods to XYZ Railroad in Atlanta for transport to Kappa Corporation in Denver. Alpha is the shipper, the bailor, and the consignor; the railroad is the carrier and the bailee; and Kappa is the **consignee.**

A **through bill** of lading is one issued by a carrier (to the shipper-bailor) for the transport of goods over the carrier's own lines for a certain distance and then over connecting lines to the destination. A through bill would be used, for example, where a railroad in the consignor's city does not go to the consignee's city but a connecting railroad does. A carrier that issues a through bill is liable not only for its own breach of the carriage contract, but also for any breach of the contract by the connecting carrier such as failure to deliver the goods to the proper person. The connecting carrier must honor the terms of the through bill even though the connecting carrier did not issue it [7-302].[2]

Where a seller ships goods by truck or air and then mails the bill of lading to the buyer, the goods often arrive at their destination before the bill of lading does. This is inconvenient for buyers who need the goods right away and for carriers who have little storage space at the point of destination. So, the seller may use a **destination bill** of lading. A destination bill is

[2]Article 7 of the UCC governs documents of title where the goods are shipped within a state. Where goods are transported in interstate or foreign commerce, federal law applies. For example, the federal Bills of Lading Act applies to interstate shipments of goods by a common carrier. Although state law (Article 7) differs in some ways from the federal law governing documents of title, there is little difference as to the general principles discussed in this chapter.

issued *at the destination* by the carrier or its agent so that the buyer (consignee) may take possession of the goods immediately upon their arrival. Suppose that Sigma, a Los Angeles seller, delivers goods to an airline for shipment to Beta, a New York buyer, and instructs the airline to issue the "airbill" (bill of lading) *in New York* to a bank named by Sigma. The airline may issue the airbill to the New York bank even before the goods reach New York. In accordance with Sigma's advance instructions, the bank collects payment from Beta and hands the airbill over to Beta, which then can immediately use the airbill to get the goods from the airline rather than having to wait for the airbill to arrive in the mail while the goods remain in storage.

Principle of Negotiability

Documents of title may be either negotiable or nonnegotiable in form. The distinction can be of great importance to persons who use or are affected by such documents.

Negotiable Form: Its Effect on Who Is Entitled to the Goods. For a warehouse receipt or a bill of lading to be in *negotiable* form, the document must contain "order" or "bearer" language. That is, the document must *state* that the goods are to be delivered to the *bearer* of the document or to the *order* of a person named in the document to receive the goods. A document reading "Deliver five desks to bearer" or "Deliver five desks to McGraw-Hill or order" is in negotiable form.

The form of a document, negotiable versus nonnegotiable, tells us *who* is entitled to have the goods from the bailee. A bailee who issues a negotiable document of title must deliver the goods described in the document to any "holder" who surrenders it to the bailee. A **holder** is any person, even a stranger to the bailee, who seems to be rightfully in possession of a negotiable document (one containing the required order or bearer language). Suppose that Sigma Company, intending to sell certain goods when a buyer can be found, delivers the goods to Walt's Warehouse for storage. At Sigma's request, Walt makes the warehouse receipt out to "Sigma Company or [Sigma Company's] order" and issues it to Sigma. The receipt is negotiable in form, and Sigma is its holder. When Sigma finds a buyer (Beta Corporation), Sigma needs merely to "indorse"[3] the receipt (sign it on the back or in some other appropriate place, much as one would indorse a check) and deliver the receipt to Beta. Beta is now the holder and as such has the right, upon surrendering the document to Walt's Warehouse, to have the goods.

In contrast, a document that *lacks* order or bearer language is *nonnegotiable* in form. A bailee who issues a nonnegotiable document must deliver the goods only to the person specifically named in the document to receive them, or in accordance with that person's written instructions. Suppose that Sigma in the preceding paragraph had instructed Walt to make the receipt out to Sigma only ("to Sigma Company" without other language such as "to the order of"). The receipt would be nonnegotiable in form. Such a receipt obligates Walt to deliver the goods to Sigma and to no one else unless Sigma gives Walt a contrary delivery instruction in writing. Sigma might do this by means of a separate document called a "delivery order," or by writing on the warehouse receipt itself a statement of assignment ("Sigma Company hereby assigns all rights under this document to Beta Corp.") and delivering the receipt to Beta (the assignee).

Legal Rights Acquired by a Transferee of the Document. Whether a document of title is negotiable or nonnegotiable helps determine *what rights to the goods* a buyer (or other transferee) of the document acquires from the seller (or other transferor). The purchaser of a *non*negotiable document is merely an assignee and as such receives only the rights that the seller had. Suppose Theta Boutique delivers an antique desk to Walt's Warehouse, which issues to Theta a nonnegotiable warehouse receipt (one made out "to

---

[3]The verb "indorse" as spelled here is used consistently in the text of the UCC. In this chapter and all others covering UCC topics, the word "indorse" will be used instead of the more standard "endorse."

Theta Boutique"). Then Sigma Company somehow fraudulently induces Theta to assign the receipt to Sigma. Sigma sells the document (and, of course, the desk it represents) to Beta Corporation, an antiques dealer who knows nothing of Sigma's fraud. Beta presents the document to Walt's and receives possession of the desk. Later, Theta demands the desk from Beta. Beta is merely Sigma's assignee and, as such, has only the rights that Sigma had. When Sigma committed fraud, it became liable to Theta for the return of the desk or for its value. Beta, Sigma's assignee, is in no better position than Sigma was, and Theta has a right to recover the desk or its value from Beta. If Theta chooses to hold Beta liable, it will have to get the value of the desk from Sigma, absorb the loss, or pass it on to others such as an insurance company. In Figure 19.1, Beta receives a nonnegotiable warehouse receipt from Sigma, but because of Sigma's fraud it is not entitled to the desk.

In contrast, a good faith purchaser of a *negotiable* document may, in proper circumstances, take the document (and the goods) *free from* many defenses or claims of others to the goods. Suppose that Theta in the preceding paragraph had received a warehouse receipt made out to "Theta Boutique or order" and that because of Sigma's fraud Theta indorsed and delivered the receipt to Sigma, which then sold it to Beta. Knowing nothing of Sigma's fraud, Beta is a "holder to whom the document has been duly negotiated" (Article 7's version of a good faith purchaser); as such Beta takes the document

Figure 19.1 Nonnegotiable warehouse receipt.

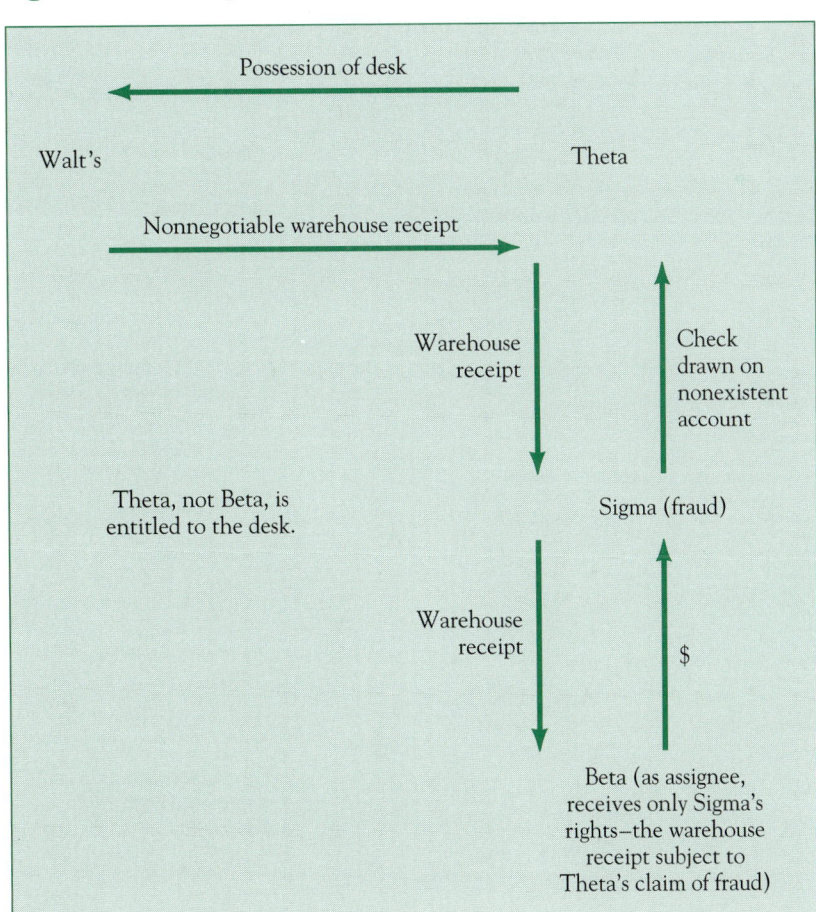

and the goods *free from* Theta's claim of fraud. Theta may recover the value of the goods from *Sigma* (the defrauder), but Beta (the good faith purchaser) keeps the goods and is not liable to Theta for its value. In this way, the law frees good faith purchasers from a variety of risks, and parties like Theta that are in a better position to protect themselves must pursue the wrongdoer, absorb any loss, or pass it on to others. The protection of good faith purchasers, widely known in the business community, works to increase the market value of goods whose ownership or other interest are exchanged by documents. The reason for the higher market value is that the risk of loss to good faith purchasers is diminished.

In Figure 19.2, Beta has received a *negotiable* warehouse receipt and therefore is entitled to the antique desk free from Theta's defense of fraud.

Good faith purchaser protection exists *only* where the transferee of the document takes it by a "due negotiation." For there to be a *due negotiation*, five requirements must be met [7-501]:

1 The document must be *negotiable* in form—issued "to bearer" or "to [Sigma Company, for example] or order."

2 The negotiable document must be in the possession of a *holder*. A holder is a person in possession of a bearer document, a person in posses-

Figure 19.2 Negotiable warehouse receipt.

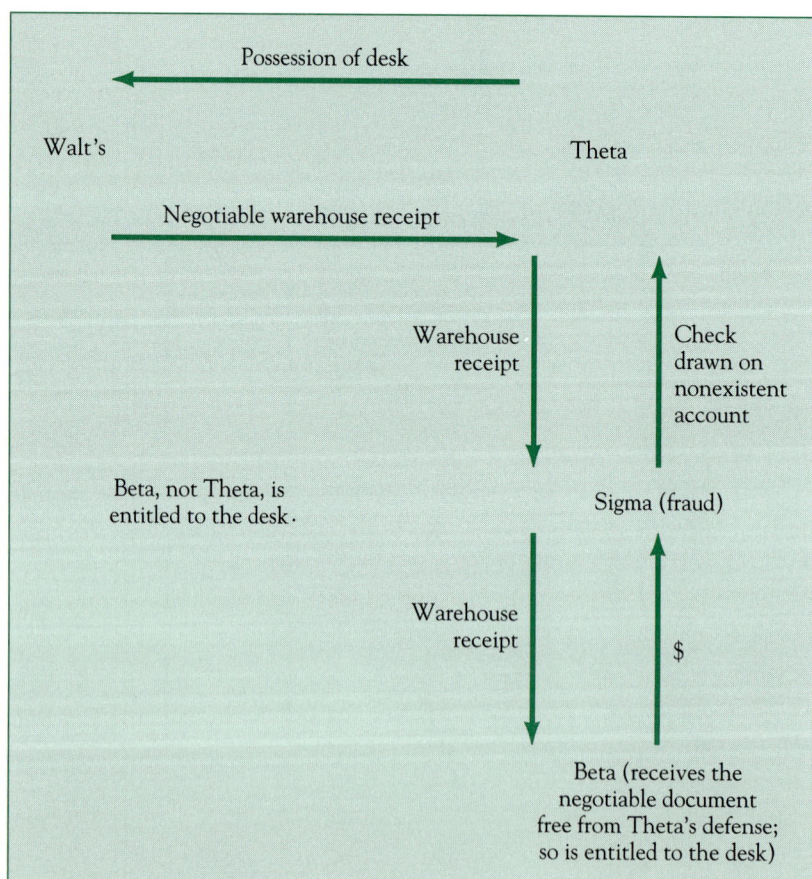

sion of an order document issued to that person, or a person in possession of an order document issued to someone else and properly indorsed to the possessor. A document issued "to Sigma Company or order" and merely signed on the back by Sigma is indorsed "in blank." By indorsing "in blank," Sigma converts the order document into a *bearer* document. A *finder* or a *thief* of a bearer document is a *holder* and has the power to transfer it, because the finder or thief appears to be rightfully in possession of the lost or stolen document. If Sigma indorses an order document by writing "Deliver to Beta, (signed) Sigma," the indorsement is "special," and Beta must also indorse before another person can be a holder.

3 The holder must give *value* for the negotiable document. That means that the holder must *purchase* it. Under Article 7, "value" means any consideration sufficient to support a simple contract. This includes a binding promise to be performed in the future. Thus, executory (not yet performed) as well as executed (performed) promises constitute "value" under Article 7.

4 The holder must purchase the document *in good faith* and must be *without notice of any defense or claim* of another person to it. Thieves (or finders) of bearer documents can be holders, but they cannot be in good faith (honest) because they know that they are claiming someone else's property. Furthermore, a thief is on notice of the true owner's claim to the document. However, if a thief is a holder and sells the document to an innocent person, that person can be a good faith holder who is without notice of the true owner's claim of ownership.

5 The negotiable document must be *negotiated* (transferred by delivery if it is a bearer document, or by delivery and indorsement if it is an order document) *in the regular course of business or financing* and not, for example, by someone who does not reasonably appear to be in the business of trading in goods. Suppose that a postal employee finds a bearer document made out for "fifty boxcars of processed uranium" and sells the document to a metals dealer who knows that a mail carrier sold him the document. It is not reasonable for the dealer to believe that the postal employee is the owner of the document. The dealer will likely be denied the benefits of a due negotiation by anyone (such as the true owner of the uranium) who can prove that the negotiation by the mail carrier was outside the regular course of the metals-trading business.

In summary, there are essentially two benefits of a due negotiation. First, the good faith purchaser receives from the *seller* of the document (a) title to (ownership of) the document and, consequently, the right to sell or to otherwise dispose of it, and (b) title to the goods themselves—both free from many defenses or claims of other persons—for example, from a previous owner's defense that the seller acquired the document by means of fraud [7-502]. Second, the good faith purchaser receives, as a result of due negotiation, the direct obligation of the *issuer* (the warehouse or the carrier) to hold or deliver the goods according to the terms of the document.

When a dispute arises on whether "due negotiation" has occurred and whether a purchaser was without notice of any defense or claim, the dispute might not be resolved by operation of law. Rather, the dispute requires a jury's or judge's finding of fact, as the following case illustrates.

CASE 19.3	**The Bank of New York v. Amoco Oil Company**
	• No. 90 Civ. 1617 (JFK) slip. op. (S.D.N.Y. 1991)

FACTS

Beginning in 1982, Amoco used platinum as a catalyst in oil refining. In order to satisfy short-term needs, Amoco sometimes leased platinum from precious metal trading firms, one such firm being Drexel Burnam Lambert Trading Corporation (Drexel).

At the start of a platinum lease, Amoco issued a document called a holding certificate to the trading company which originally was held by the trading firm. This document stated that Amoco held the platinum for the account of the trading firm and that the platinum that Amoco was holding was "encumbered." At the end of a lease, the trading firm returned the certificate to Amoco, and Amoco was instructed what to do with the platinum.

At the request of one of the trading companies Amoco did business with, Amoco began to issue certificates "for the account or order of" the trading firms and stating that Amoco was holding the platinum "unencumbered" or "free of all liens and encumbrances." Soon following, trading companies including Drexel began to transfer the holding certificates, indorsing them over to a bank.

Drexel often borrowed money from the plaintiff, Bank of New York, on an overnight basis. In March 1989, the Bank began accepting precious metal "holding certificates" as collateral. In December 1989, Drexel sent three Amoco holding certificates to the Bank as collateral, and then defaulted on the loan.

Bank of New York then demanded that Amoco deliver the platinum to the Bank's account in return for the Bank's surrender of the holding certificate. Amoco refused, apparently because of its assertion of rights to possess the platinum through the end of the lease.

The Bank then found a buyer of Amoco's holding certificates who would purchase them only if the Bank obtained a commitment of delivery and if Amoco issued new holding certificates that were free from indorsements. Amoco again refused, but later agreed to deliver 22,230 troy ounces of a specified grade of platinum to the Bank and that the Bank would limit its claim for damages to $550,000.

Following this, the market for platinum plummeted, and Bank of New York claimed it was actually damaged in the amount of $1,138,176 and sued Amoco in federal district court.

Both Amoco and Bank of New York moved for summary judgment in their separate favors.

OPINION

KEENAN, D.J. . . . Under U.C.C. 7-502, a holder to whom a negotiable document of title has been duly negotiated acquires not only absolute title to the documents and goods but also the right to have the goods delivered by the possessor of the goods free of any defense or claim. Accordingly, the outcome of this case turns upon the answers to three questions:

1. Were the holding certificates documents of title covered by U.C.C. Article 7?
2. If the holding certificates were documents of title, were they negotiable?

**CASE 19.3
Continued**

3. If the holding certificates were negotiable, did [Drexel] duly negotiate the documents to the Bank?

Because the resolution of the first question set forth above requires resolution of a disputed question of material fact, summary judgment for either side would be inappropriate.

U.C.C. 1-201(15) defines a "document of title" as a bill of lading, dock warrant, warehouse receipt or order for the delivery of goods, and also any other document which in the regular course of business or financing is treated as adequately evidencing that the person in possession of it is entitled to receive, hold and dispose of the document and the goods it covers. To be a document of title a document must purport to be issued by or addressed to a bailee and purport to cover goods in the bailee's possession which are either identified or a fungible portion of an identified mass.

The Bank contends that the holding certificates fit within the last sentence of 1-201(15) because . . . banks "routinely and in the regular course of financing accepted holding certificates from . . . [trading firms] as collateral for loans." Amoco contends that the proof offered by the Bank . . . is insufficient to support a summary judgment. The Court agrees. The practices of banks in accepting holding certificates as collateral involve factual [not legal] disputes that must be resolved at trial.

The third question set forth above gives rise to additional factual disputes that can be resolved only at trial. According to U.C.C. 7-501(4), a title document is duly negotiated if it is "negotiated in the manner stated in this section to a holder who purchases it in good faith without notice of any defense against it or claim to it on the part of any person and for value, unless it is established that the negotiation is not in the regular course of business or financing or involves receiving the document in settlement or payment of a money obligation."

The important contested element . . . is whether the Bank took the certificates with notice that Amoco had a leasehold claim to the platinum. [Both plaintiff and defendant offer conflicting evidence.]

Because there remains a factual dispute involving the Bank's knowledge of Amoco's interest in the platinum, summary judgment for either side would be inappropriate.

JUDGMENT   Both motions for summary judgment denied.

Typical Uses of Negotiable and Nonnegotiable Documents. A businessperson needs to know how negotiable and nonnegotiable documents actually work in the physical distribution of goods in order to be able to choose between the two kinds on the basis of his or her own business needs. Suppose that Kappa, a wholesale seller of groceries, purchases 5,000 cases of canned sardines for resale to supermarkets in Kappa's city. Having no storage facilities of her own, Kappa deposits the sardines at Walt's Warehouse and is issued a nonnegotiable warehouse receipt (one made out "to Kappa"). As a matter of routine record keeping, Walt retains a copy of the receipt so that his employees will know that the goods are to be delivered to Kappa and to no one else. If Kappa instructs Walt to deliver the sardines to Kappa, Walt will do so *without* requiring Kappa to surrender the warehouse receipt. To prove that he has delivered the sar-

> **BOX 19.3**
> **A Question of Law to Consider**
>
> Would the outcome of the case *The Bank of New York v. Amoco Oil Company* have been different if the bank had admitted knowledge of Amoco's lease of platinum from Drexel at the time that the bank accepted the "holding certificates" as collateral?
>
> With this additional "fact," would it be appropriate for a judge to grant summary judgment? If yes, in whose favor? Why? ∎

dines to the person entitled to them (here, Kappa), all Walt needs to do is to have Kappa (or an agent of Kappa) "sign" for the goods when Kappa receives them. Kappa's signature together with Walt's copy of the warehouse receipt is proof of a proper delivery.

But Kappa does not want Walt to deliver the goods to it. Rather, Kappa wants to *control* their delivery to the supermarkets for which the sardines are intended. Suppose Zeta's Supermarket orders ten cases of sardines from Kappa. Kappa will prepare a "delivery order" instructing Walt to release ten cases of sardines to Zeta. Zeta will pay Kappa for the sardines, take the delivery order to Walt, and receive ten cases of sardines. Walt will require Zeta to surrender the delivery order and sign for the ten cases so that Walt will have evidence that Kappa gave the instruction and that Walt made a proper delivery. Kappa still has the nonnegotiable warehouse receipt and the ability, therefore, to control the delivery of the other 4,990 cases of sardines. Note, incidentally, that a delivery order is itself a document of title, and that Kappa, not Walt, is its issuer. A delivery order is an example of a document of title that is "addressed to" a bailee.

Suppose instead that Kappa had been issued a *negotiable* warehouse receipt (one made out "to bearer" or "to the order of Kappa"). Kappa could accomplish a delivery of the ten cases to Zeta by means of the negotiable warehouse receipt, but the delivery process would be awkward and slower. The reason is that Kappa must *surrender* a negotiable document of title to Walt in order to receive the goods or to have Zeta receive them. Even though Kappa wants only a partial delivery of the 5,000 cases (here, ten cases), Kappa still must actually deliver the document to Walt so that he can write on it that ten cases have been delivered. Thus, if Kappa should later sell the negotiable document, a holder to whom it is duly negotiated will be on notice that he or she is entitled only to 4,990 cases. Negotiable documents are very suitable for transferring goods as a single unit to one buyer, but they are inefficient for making partial deliveries to many different buyers.

Bailee's Obligations and Liabilities under Document

Regardless of whether a document of title is negotiable or nonnegotiable, the bailee (the warehouse or the carrier) issuing it has certain obligations and liabilities. However, some of these obligations and liabilities do vary according to whether the document is negotiable or nonnegotiable.

Warehouser's Obligation to Keep Goods Separate; Fungible Goods Exception.

Ordinarily a bailee has a duty to return to the bailor the specific thing bailed or to dispose of it as the bailor instructs. Since many warehouses are large and very crowded, goods can easily be misplaced, and the warehouser might be unable to make a prompt delivery. To make locating the goods easier and delivery more certain, the law requires that a warehouser keep separate from all other goods those covered by a particular warehouse receipt, unless the receipt provides otherwise [7-207].

There is an important exception for **fungible** goods. Goods are *fungible* if one unit (a bushel of grain, a barrel of oil, etc.) is, by nature or by usage of trade, the equivalent of any other unit of that size. Fungible commodities such as oil of a particular grade often are purchased from many sellers and stored and transported in bulk. Because it would be impractical for a warehouse to keep each lot of fungible goods separate, fungible goods may be commingled (mixed or stored in one mass). A mass of commingled fungible goods—e.g., a mass of wheat or corn in a grain elevator—is owned in common by all the persons who contributed to the mass or who have acquired a share in it. The warehouser—e.g., the owner of a grain elevator—is liable to each owner of the mass for that person's share. Recall from Case 19.3, *The Bank of New York v. Amoco*, that the documents of title involved in that case were for platinum. Since Amoco used the platinum in oil refining, it is very unlikely that the same platinum under the document was the same platinum delivered back. In that case, platinum was a fungible good.

Obligation to Deliver to "Person Entitled under Document"; Excuse for Nondelivery. Unless excused by law, a warehouser or a carrier must deliver the goods to the person entitled to them by the terms of the document, and not to someone else [7-403]. Under a *negotiable* document, the "entitled person" is the *holder*. Suppose Lightfoot delivers goods he owns to Cautious Carriers; that Cautious Carriers issues a negotiable bill of lading to Lightfoot; and that Lightfoot intends to travel to a particular destination and pick up the goods when they arrive there. The negotiable bill will be made out "to bearer" or "to Lightfoot or order," as Lightfoot chooses. In either event, Lightfoot is the holder as long as he possesses the bill of lading, and Cautious Carriers must deliver the goods to him if he surrenders the bill and satisfies the bailee's lien (pays the shipping charges owed to the carrier).

Suppose the bill is made out "to bearer" and Lightfoot sells the goods to Omni and delivers the bill to him. Omni is now the holder because he is in possession of a bearer document, and he is entitled to the goods.

May a finder or a thief of a bearer document be entitled to the goods? Suppose Lightfoot, from the previous example, loses the bearer document, Cheatham (a dishonest person) finds it. Before Lightfoot can notify Cautious Carriers of the loss, Cheatham takes the document to the carrier and asks for the goods. Cheatham is the holder because he is in possession of a bearer document, and he appears to be entitled to the goods. If Cautious Carriers *in good faith* delivers the goods to Cheatham, Cautious Carriers cannot be held liable to Lightfoot [7-404]. Cautious Carriers is in good faith if, as here, the carrier lacks notice that Cheatham is not the true owner of the document. Cheatham's taking delivery will, of course, be wrongful as to Lightfoot, and Lightfoot will have a cause of action against Cheatham for damages or for the goods themselves.

Who is the holder of an *order* document of title? The answer depends on how the order document is indorsed. Suppose Lightfoot's bill of lading is made out "to Lightfoot or order." Then Lightfoot sells the goods to Omni, indorses the bill "in blank" (i.e., merely signs Lightfoot's name on the back of the bill without naming anyone as indorsee), and delivers the bill to Omni. Omni is the holder because he is in possession of a properly indorsed "order bill" of lading, and he is entitled to the goods.

Since Lightfoot's in-blank indorsement converts the order bill of lading into a *bearer* document, any finder or thief will be a holder. By making a "special" indorsement such as "Deliver to Omni, (signed) Lightfoot," Lightfoot can preserve the order character of the document and thereby make sure that only Omni will be the holder. Because Lightfoot has identified Omni in the indorsement as the person to have the document, only Omni can be its holder, and only Omni is entitled to the goods. Now Omni must indorse the bill before anyone else can become the holder.

Under a *nonnegotiable* document (one issued "to Lightfoot") the "person entitled under the document" is the person named in the bill to receive the goods *or* is someone to whom that person has issued a delivery order. Suppose Cautious Carriers issues Lightfoot a bill of lading made out "to Lightfoot." Lightfoot is the only person entitled to the goods. However, Lightfoot can issue to Omni a delivery order (or assign the bill) and thereby instruct Cautious Carriers to make a full or partial delivery to Omni. Omni thus becomes the person entitled to the goods.

In a number of situations the bailee is *excused* for failing to deliver the goods to the person entitled to them by the terms of the document, regardless of whether the document is negotiable or nonnegotiable. Four excuses are illustrated in the following paragraphs:

1 *Delivery of the goods to a person with "paramount title"*—i.e., with superior ownership rights. For example, Scuzz steals goods from Hapless; delivers them to Walt, the warehouseman, who issues Scuzz a negotiable warehouse receipt; and sells the goods to Blameless, indorsing and delivering the document to Blameless. In the meantime Hapless, the true owner, learns where the goods are and talks Walt into releasing the goods to Hapless. Then Blameless, a holder to whom the document was duly negotiated, presents it to Walt, who refuses to deliver any goods to her. Although Blameless is the person entitled *under the document* to receive the goods, Walt has no delivery obligation to Blameless because Walt has delivered the goods to Hapless, who, because he is the true owner, has paramount title. The result would be the same if Walt, not knowing the situation, had by blind chance delivered the goods to Hapless.

2 *Damage to or loss of the goods for which the bailee is not liable.* A tornado destroys a freight train and all the goods in it. The carrier is not liable because the loss was due to "an act of God," a source of loss beyond even a carrier's liability as an insurer.

3 *A valid limitation of the bailee's liability.* Cautious Carriers, a common carrier, imposes a liability limit of $7 per pound for cloth it transports. Without declaring a higher value, Sumptuous Materials Corp. ships cloth containing gold thread. The cloth, worth $50 per pound, is ruined owing to the negligence of Cautious Carriers' employees. The carrier's liability is $7 per pound.

4 *Rival claims to the goods.* Where two or more persons claim the same goods, the bailee is excused from delivery until the bailee has had a reasonable time to determine which of the rival claims is valid, or to bring a legal action to require the claimants to seek a court determination of their rights.

Liability for Bailee's Nonreceipt or Misdescription of Goods. Suppose that through mistake or fraud a warehouse (or a carrier) issues Seagull a document of title without ever receiving the goods from her, or that it issues a document that misdescribes the goods, as where the document says, "5,000 pounds of lobster" but the warehouse (bailee) actually received 5,000 pounds of low-grade shark meat fit only for pet food. Then Seagull sells the document to Beach, a good faith purchaser, who knows nothing of the warehouse's nonreceipt or misdescription. The warehouse is liable to Beach for any loss caused by the nonreceipt or misdescription [7-203; 7-301]. Good faith purchasers are protected in these circumstances *without regard* to whether the document is negotiable or nonnegotiable. However, if the document *conspicuously* and *truthfully* indicates that the issuer *does not know* whether the goods were received or whether they conform to the description, the issuer is *not* liable to Beach. If the document says, for example, "contents, condition, and quality unknown," "this package said to contain," or "shipper's weight, load, and count," Beach is on notice of the nonreceipt or misdescription and should have looked into the situation before buying the document. Thus, the law protects warehousers and carriers who honestly do not know what was received and who give clear notice of that fact.

Liability Where Document Is Lost or Missing. Beta purchases a properly issued document of title, but then it is lost, stolen, or destroyed. At Beta's request, a court may order the bailee to deliver the goods to Beta or to issue her a substitute document. The bailee may comply with the court's order without liability to anyone who might later present the missing document to the bailee and demand the goods [7-601]. If the missing document was negotiable, it might have been in bearer form when lost or stolen. To protect an innocent *purchaser* of a missing negotiable document, Beta must "post security" (e.g., purchase a type of insurance) to indemnify anyone who suffers loss as a result of buying the missing document. If the document was nonnegotiable, the court is permitted but not required to order Beta to post security.

Conflicting Claims to the Goods

Occasionally, a consignee, transferee, or even holder to whom a document has been duly negotiated is not entitled to receive the goods and must seek a legal remedy from the transferor or someone else, or absorb the loss. Two examples follow.

Unauthorized Bailment. Even good faith purchasers acquire no rights to goods that have been bailed with a carrier or a warehouse totally without the authority of the true owner [7-503]. Suppose Scuzz steals goods from Hapless, stores them at Walt's Warehouse, and duly negotiates the warehouse receipt to Blameless. Because a thief acquires no ownership rights in the stolen goods, Hapless has "paramount title" and is entitled to the goods even if they have been delivered to Blameless.

Change of Shipping Instructions under Nonnegotiable Bill of Lading. Unless the bill of lading states otherwise, a carrier may, upon receiving proper instructions, deliver the goods to a person or a destination *other than* that stated in the bill [7-303]. For example, a consignor on a nonnegotiable bill of lading is entitled to change the shipping instructions. Suppose Stamper contracts to sell a printing press to Beacon, delivers it to Cautious Carriers, and has the nonnegotiable bill made out "to Beacon." Then Stamper, in breach of his contract with Beacon, sells the press to Xanadu and instructs Cautious Carriers to deliver the press to Xanadu instead of to Beacon. Xanadu, if a buyer of the press in the ordinary course of business (i.e., if a good faith purchaser), is entitled to the press, and Beacon is left to pursue Stamper for a remedy.

SUMMARY

Goods may be transported by common or private carrier. A common carrier serves the public generally and has extensive liability for loss of or damage to the goods. A private carrier may choose with whom to contract and is liable as a bailee only, and not as an insurer.

Often goods are stored in a public or private warehouse. Warehouses are liable as bailees for loss of or damage to the goods during storage.

Documents of title are used to control the movement of goods from sellers to buyers. A document of title is a receipt, a contract of storage or carriage, and evidence of title to the goods. The two major kinds are the warehouse receipt and the bill of lading. Each may be negotiable or nonnegotiable.

Negotiable documents differ from nonnegotiable ones in two main respects: what person is entitled to the goods, and what rights are acquired by a transferee of the document. The transferee of a nonnegotiable document is an assignee and receives only the rights that the transferor had. A holder of a negotiable document can receive more rights than the transferor had, but only if the document has been "duly negotiated" to the holder.

A bailee has obligations and liabilities under a document of title, whether negotiable or nonnegotiable. For example, the bailee is required to deliver the goods described in the document, unless it contains a proper disclaimer of liability for misdescription of the goods. Sometimes the bailee's obligations are excused, as where the bailee delivered the goods to a person with paramount title.

REVIEW QUESTIONS

1. How does the liability of a common carrier differ from that of a private carrier for loss of or damage to the goods?

2. To what extent, if any, may a carrier limit its liability for loss of the goods?

3. What liability does a warehouser have for loss of the goods?

4. (a) Define a document of title. **(b)** What are its functions? **(c)** Explain the difference between a through bill of lading and a destination bill.

5. (a) What language would you use to create a

negotiable document of title? A nonnegotiable document? **(b)** What are the two main differences in legal effect between a negotiable and a nonnegotiable document of title?

6. (a) What is required for a "due negotiation" of a document of title? **(b)** Explain whether a person who finds or steals a document of title can be its holder. **(c)** Explain whether a person who buys a stolen document can be a person to whom a document has been duly negotiated.

7. (a) What are the benefits of a due negotiation? **(b)** Under what circumstances would a nonnegotiable warehouse receipt be preferable to a negotiable one?

8. (a) Suppose a carrier releases goods to a person who has stolen the bill of lading. Is the carrier liable to the true owner of the document? Explain. **(b)** An earthquake breaks valuable antique bowls stored in a warehouse. Is the warehouser liable to the bailor? Why or why not?

CASE PROBLEMS

1. Mitchell stored her household furnishings with All American Van & Storage Co. (Storage). Under the written contract of storage, Mitchell was to pay all storage charges on a monthly basis. Also, Storage could exercise its warehouser's lien by selling Mitchell's goods if the storage charges remained unpaid for 3 months and if, in the opinion of Storage, such action would be necessary to protect its accrued charges. Over the next 8 months Mitchell failed to pay any of the charges. Her unpaid bill totaled $804.30. On October 20, Storage notified her that her goods would be sold on November 7 if she did not pay the charges by October 31. Despite her claim that she was soon to receive a substantial sum of money from the Social Security Administration—a claim substantiated by two attorneys—Storage sold the goods on November 7 for $925.50, an amount insufficient to cover the debt plus costs of sale. Three weeks later Mitchell received a Social Security disability payment of $5,500. Alleging that Storage had breached a duty of good faith by refusing to delay the sale, Mitchell brought suit for damages. The trial court entered summary judgment for Storage, and Mitchell appealed, contending she should have been allowed to go to trial on the question of good faith. Should Mitchell have been allowed to go to trial?

2. Sanfisket, Inc., stored 2,500 pounds of frozen shrimp with Atlantic Cold Storage Corp. Atlantic issued Sanfisket a nonnegotiable warehouse receipt containing a clause limiting Atlantic's liability to 50 cents per pound. Six months later Sanfisket demanded delivery, but Atlantic was unable to locate the shrimp. Alleging conversion, Sanfisket sued Atlantic for $8,000, the market value of the lost shrimp. The trial court held that the evidence permitted a finding of negligence but not conversion, and awarded Sanfisket $1,250, the limit of Atlantic's liability under the warehouse receipt. Sanfisket appealed. The appellate court upheld the trial court on the question of conversion. However, Sanfisket contended that it had not been notified of the clause of limitation, that the clause was not conspicuous, and therefore that Atlantic should be held fully liable for its negligence. Should the clause be enforced under Section 7-204(2) of the UCC?

3. En route to Florida, Kinloch and his wife stopped in Mobile, Alabama. While there, Kinloch stored personal property with Teague Brothers Transfer & Storage Co. He received a warehouse receipt from Teague, signed it as bailor of the goods, was listed on the receipt as owner of the goods, and paid the storage fee. A month later Kinloch and his wife separated. Then Mrs. Kinloch took the warehouse receipt to Mobile and requested and received the goods. When Kinloch later demanded delivery, Teague was unable to comply, and Kinloch sued Teague for the value of the goods. Teague contended that its good faith and the wife's possession of the warehouse receipt excused Teague for liability for misdelivery. Was Teague liable to Kinloch for the value of the goods?

4. Crawford sold two carloads of bulk fertilizer to Cunningham, who paid by check. Crawford delivered the fertilizer to M-K-T Railroad and received two nonnegotiable bills of lading. Cunningham promptly resold the fertilizer to Clock. A few days later Cunningham's bank returned Cunningham's check to Crawford for lack of sufficient funds to cover it. The fertilizer was still in transit. Crawford certified to the railroad that he was the true owner of the fertilizer and reconsigned it to another customer. Having already paid Cunningham for the fertilizer, Clock sued the Railroad and Crawford. Is the railroad liable to Clock? Is Crawford?

5. Mrs. Smiley and her husband contracted with Allied Van Lines for transfer and storage of household goods. They were given a bill of lading. Soon following, the Smileys initiated divorce proceedings. Mrs. Smiley notified Allied Van Lines to hold the household goods and not to deliver them. After this notice had been given to Allied, the carrier delivered the household goods to Mrs. Smiley's husband. Mrs. Smiley died, and the executor of her estate brought an action against Allied to recover damages for misdelivery of the goods. How should the court decide? On what basis?

6. Armour & Co. (Armour) hired a common carrier, Rush Delivery Service (Rush), to transport and deliver a shipment of meat from the Penn Central rail yards to four separate buyers. When Rush attempted to deliver to the first buyer, the buyer told Rush that the delivery was after the time it accepted delivery. Rush's driver called in for instructions on what to do, and Armour instructed him to deliver the meat the next day, and was further told that Rush could leave its delivery truck in one of Armour's nearby lots. After locking the truck, Rush's driver left the truck in Armour's lot and took the keys with him. The next morning Rush's driver discovered that the truck was missing. Armour sued Rush for the value of the lost shipment. What issues would the court determine as most important? How should the court decide on those issues? What additional information, if any, would a court need to assist its decision?

CHAPTER 20

Transfer of Title and Risk of Loss; Title of Good Faith Purchasers

Chapter 19 focused on the physical movement of goods from seller to buyer, on the liability of carriers and warehouses for loss, and on how documents of title are used in the delivery process. This chapter focuses on the contractual relationship between the buyer and the seller and on the rights of third persons to whom the buyer may sell the goods. Here, three questions are of particular concern: (1) When does title to (ownership of) the goods pass from the original seller to the buyer? (2) When does the risk that the goods will be lost or damaged in transit pass from the original seller to the buyer? (3) Where goods are resold by the buyer to a third-person purchaser, under what circumstances does the third person take the goods free from the claims of another such as the original seller?

TRANSFER OF TITLE AND RISK OF LOSS

Transfer of Title

Accountants use the concept of title (ownership) as the basis for determining entries in the books of their clients. Consequently, the UCC Article 2 title passage rules are of special significance to accountants whose clients deal in goods. On rare occasions, the parties to a sales contract will themselves want to know precisely when title to the goods passes from seller to buyer. Suppose that a state taxes goods and other personal property owned by its citizens. A citizen of such a state is not required to pay the tax until he or she actually owns the goods—until title passes. The exact time that a buyer receives title is governed by general rules of title passage contained in Article 2 of the UCC and discussed in the following paragraphs.

When Title Passes from Seller to Buyer. Subject to two limitations, the parties to a sales contract may agree when and how title is to be transferred ("pass") from the seller to the buyer. Their agreement should be explicit—clearly stated. The limitations to their agreement are:

1 The seller cannot pass title until the goods have been *identified to the contract*. That is, for title to pass, the goods must exist and must be designated as the ones intended for the particular buyer.

2 Any reservation of title by a seller who is extending credit to the buyer is to be considered as nothing more than the reservation of a "security interest" [2-401]. The unpaid seller's keeping such an interest does not prevent the passage to the buyer of basic rights of ownership commonly associated with the word "title."

Where seller and buyer do not state when title is to pass, rules stated in Article 2 apply. Under those rules, if delivery is to be made *by moving the goods*, title passes when and where the seller completes performance with reference to the *physical delivery* of the goods, even though a document of title is to be delivered at a different time and place [2-401]. So, if you order a sofa from a department store and the seller agrees to make a noncarrier delivery to you at your house, you get title to the sofa when the store completes the promised delivery.

But suppose you order a sofa from a manufacturer located in another state. Now the sofa will have to be delivered by a carrier; and the time at which the manufacturer "completes performance with reference to physical delivery" depends on whether you and the seller created a "shipment" or a "destination" contract. If, regarding delivery, the seller agreed merely to see to it that the sofa would be shipped, the seller has entered into a **shipment contract,** and title passes to you when the seller puts the sofa into the custody of the carrier. If, however, the seller specifically agreed to be responsible for actually getting the goods to the destination, the seller has entered into a **destination contract,** and title passes to you when the sofa actually arrives at the destination.

If delivery is to be made *without moving the goods*, other rules apply. Suppose you buy a sofa that the seller has stored in a warehouse in your city, and the seller is to make delivery by means of a document of title (warehouse receipt or delivery order). Title passes when and where the seller delivers the document to you. If no documents are to be delivered, title to identified goods passes at the time and place of contracting, as where you go to a department store, make a contract to purchase a sofa for cash or on credit, and take it home in your own vehicle.

When Title Revests in Seller. Normally a buyer has the right to inspect the goods and to decide whether to accept or reject them. If, as in a shipment contract, the buyer receives title before seeing the goods and later rejects them, title goes back to ("revests in") the seller regardless of whether the rejection was rightful or wrongful. Once the buyer accepts the goods, however, title will revest in the seller only if the buyer justifiably revokes acceptance—for example, after discovering a hidden defect. These revesting rules are intended to make clear who owns the goods when there is a dispute about their quality.

Transfer of Risk of Loss

Sometimes goods are lost, damaged, or destroyed without the fault of either the buyer or the seller. Yet one or the other will have to absorb the loss or try to collect from the person responsible for the loss, usually a carrier, warehouser, or insurer. The parties to a sales contract may decide for themselves which one is to bear the risk of loss or how it will be shared. Where the parties remain silent as to risk, Article 2 assigns it by means of practical rules that tend to place the risk of loss upon the party (seller or buyer) who is likely to have actual control of the goods, who is likely to insure them as they move through the delivery process, or who is likely to be better able to prevent loss. Risk of loss is *never* assigned on the basis of who had title when the loss occurred, since a person can acquire title (legal ownership) long before learning of danger to the goods or acquiring sufficient control of them to take preventive measures.

The following rules apply where the parties to the sales contract are silent as to risk of loss. Some of the rules apply to situations involving a breach of contract; others apply to situations involving no breach.

Risk of Loss Where There Is No Breach of Contract. These rules apply to situations involving goods shipped by carrier, goods held by a bailee, "pickup" and noncarrier delivery of goods, and goods subject to a right of the buyer to return them to the seller.

When goods are to be delivered by *carrier*, the assignment of risk depends on whether the parties have entered into a shipment or a destination contract. In a *shipment* contract, the risk of loss passes from the seller to the buyer when the seller properly delivers the goods to the carrier. In a *destination* contract, the risk passes to the buyer when the goods are presented at the stated destination in such a way as to enable the buyer to take delivery from the carrier [2-509(1)].

In commercial practice, the shipment contract, with its early risk-shifting feature, is considered the normal kind of contract for arranging a carrier delivery. A contract is a *shipment* contract where the buyer and seller agree merely that the goods are to be shipped, without stating that the seller is to be responsible for a safe delivery. For example, Best-Lube telephones Sigma Supply with the following order: "Please send five barrels of oil by express." Sigma puts the barrels in the custody of a carrier. Best-Lube and Sigma have created a shipment contract because their words and actions have fallen short of putting the responsibility for a safe delivery on Sigma. Sigma is justified in feeling no further responsibility for the oil because, having put it in the custody of the carrier, Sigma no longer controls it; Sigma's insurance probably no longer covers it; Sigma might already have received payment; *and* there is no indication from Best-Lube that it expects Sigma rather than the carrier to guarantee the oil's safe arrival.

For the less usual *destination* contract to arise—the kind that imposes risk of loss on the seller for the entire trip—the contract must contain specific language requiring the seller to remain responsible for the goods until they actually reach the buyer. If in the previous example, a destination contract would have arisen if Best-Lube had stated: "Please send five barrels of oil by express. Best-Lube will pay for them only upon their safe arrival."

Seller and buyer can specify a shipment or a destination contract in another way, by using standard shipping terms or instructions whose risk-of-loss consequences have been spelled out by Article 2. A St. Paul book manufacturer promises to ship to a New York buyer 300 books "FOB [free on board] St. Paul." Use of this expression creates a shipment contract, and the risk of loss shifts to the New York buyer when the seller puts the books into the possession of the carrier at St. Paul [2-319]. In contrast, a promise by the St. Paul seller to deliver books "FOB New York" would create a destination contract under which "the seller must at his own expense and risk transport the goods to that place and there tender delivery of them." Similarly, "FAS [free alongside a vessel at] the port of shipment" creates a shipment contract; and "FAS the port of destination" creates a destination contract.

The term "CIF" means that the price includes in a lump sum the *cost* of goods and the *insurance* and *freight* to the named destination. The term "C&F," or "CF," means that the price includes the *cost* of the goods and the *freight* charges to the named destination. Despite the word "destination," these terms create a *shipment* contract [2-320]. If a New York buyer says to a St. Paul seller, "Ship 300 books CIF New York," the buyer in effect appoints the seller as an agent for the purchase of insurance and the payment of freight. By performing the CIF delivery obligations, the seller shifts the risk of loss to the buyer upon delivery of the goods to a carrier.

CASE 20.1	Robert L. Buenger v. Varco Pruden • 713 P.2d 771 (Wyo. 1986)
FACTS	Robert Buenger, doing business under the name of Buenger Construction Company, contracted with Varco Pruden for the purchase of buildings to be erected at Buenger's jobsite in Gillette, Wyoming. Documents between Buenger and Pruden provided for F.O.B.–destination or F.O.B.–jobsite. Though invoices stated: "JOBS ARE TO BE SHIPPED FREIGHT PREPAID," freight charges were collected from Buenger at delivery. The bill of lading form from Varco to Buenger contained a notation, "PLEASE BILL

CASE 20.1 Continued	FREIGHT CHARGES TO: Varco Pruden" with a further blank space included as "Prepaid." Buenger sought credits from Pruden for the delivery charges, and a dispute arose between the parties on who was to pay them. The trial court held in favor of Pruden. Buenger appealed.
OPINION	URBIGKIT, J. . . . We consider the effect of F.O.B.–destination on the seller's responsibility for freight costs, and reverse the trial-court decision charging the buyer. The trial court . . . by opinion letter stated: [Buenger] . . . asserts that he is entitled to several credits. He points to the contract provision which states the buildings are to be delivered "FOB jobsite" as supporting his claim to a credit for freight charges paid by him. Under the [UCC], FOB destination does not mean that the seller is agreeing to pay for freight costs, but merely that the seller is accepting the risk to the goods during shipment. We find [UCC 2-319] to be determinative in a contrary fashion to the trial-court decision: (a) Unless otherwise agreed the term F.O.B. (which means 'free on board') at a named placed, even though used only in connection with the stated price, is a delivery term under which: (i) When the term is F.O.B. the place of shipment, the seller must at that place ship the goods in the manner provided in this article [2-504] and bear the expense and risk of putting them into the possession of the carrier; or (ii) When the term is F.O.B. the place of destination, the seller must at his own expense and risk transport the goods to that place and there tender delivery of them in the manner provided in this article [2-503]. In the terminology of the industry, the differentiation is between a destination or shipment contract. The agreement of the parties controlled by the designation used and this case is clearly a destination agreement whereby freight charges remain with the seller. Under the purchase documents, the seller, Varco Pruden, owed costs for freight to Gillette for the buildings, and amounts paid by Buenger to secure freight release upon delivery are chargeable by offset and counterclaim.
JUDGMENT	Reversed and remanded.

When goods are held by a *bailee* (a warehouse or a carrier) to be delivered *without being moved*, the risk of their loss may be passed from seller to buyer in any of three ways:

1 Risk of loss passes from the seller when the buyer receives a *negotiable* document of title covering the goods.

2 Where the buyer receives a *nonnegotiable* document of title, risk of loss does not pass to the buyer immediately. A buyer who receives a nonnegotiable document is only an assignee and so takes the goods subject to the rights of others who, for example, might claim the goods as collateral for a loan to the seller. To protect the buyer from claims of third persons, the Code leaves the risk of loss with the seller until the bailee receives notice of the buyer's right to the

goods—or until the buyer has had a reasonable time after receiving the document to give the bailee that notice. Upon the bailee's receiving the notice (or upon the passage of the reasonable time), the risk of loss passes from the seller to the buyer. However, the buyer takes the goods *free from* all rival claims to them. Even so, a bailee who knows of a rival claim before receiving notice of the buyer's rights might refuse to honor the document. The bailee's refusal "defeats the [seller's] tender" of the document and thus makes the seller liable to the buyer.

3 Sometimes goods to be sold are stored with a bailee who does not issue a document of title, as where a boat is docked at a marina or a dog is housed in a kennel. Where there is no document of title, risk of loss passes from seller to buyer when the bailee is informed of *and acknowledges* the buyer's right to the goods [2-509(2)].

In *pickup* and *noncarrier deliveries*, the time that risk of loss shifts from seller to buyer depends on whether the seller is a *merchant* or a *nonmerchant*. Suppose that Bob, by telephone, buys a sofa from Sue. The parties are silent about risk of loss, but Sue says, "You may pick up the sofa any morning during the next 3 days." On the morning of the second day, Bob arrives to pick up the sofa only to learn that it was destroyed by fire the preceding night.

If Sue is a *merchant,* the risk is upon Sue, since the risk of loss does not pass from a merchant seller to the buyer until the buyer's *actual receipt* of the goods [2-509(3)]. This rule applies even though the buyer has made full payment and has been notified that the goods are at his or her disposal. The rule also applies where Sue is to make a noncarrier delivery to the buyer's premises. The reason for the rule is that a merchant is likely to have insurance coverage on goods as long as they remain in his or her possession, whereas the buyer is not likely to have insurance on goods not yet possessed.

If Sue is a *nonmerchant* seller, the risk is on Bob. Risk of loss passes from a nonmerchant seller to the buyer upon the seller's *tender* (offer) of delivery. The seller makes a tender of delivery by notifying the buyer that the goods are available to the buyer [2-503(1)]. Thus, where Sue is a nonmerchant, the risk of loss may pass to Bob *before* Bob actually receives the goods.

CASE 20.2

Jason's Foods, Inc. v. Peter Eckrich & Sons, Inc.
• No. 83 C 2896 (N.D.Ill. 1984)

FACTS Jason's Foods, Inc. (Jason's), and Peter Eckrich & Sons, Inc. (Eckrich), entered into a contract on December 20, 1982 for the sale of 38,000 pounds of ribs. Eckrich sent Jason's a purchase order requesting that the ribs be shipped by means of transfer of storage at a storage warehouse ("warehouse"). Eckrich further requested that Jason's "advise" Eckrich of the date on which the transfer would take place. Jason's sent Eckrich a notice confirming that the ribs would be transferred between January 10 and 14, 1983, at the warehouse.

The shipment of the ribs was made on January 13, 1983 by means of transfer in storage. Upon receiving the order to transfer in storage, the warehouse's representative began processing the nonnegotiable documents, but did not send the nonnegotiable warehouse receipts to Eckrich until January 17, 1983. On that day, a fire occurred in the warehouse, and the ribs were destroyed. The nonnegotiable warehouse receipts did not arrive at Eckrich until January 24, 1983. No oral or written communication from the warehouse was received by Eckrich until after the fire.

**CASE 20.1
Continued**

Jason's brought suit against Eckrich to recover the amount of the contract. Both parties moved for motions of summary judgment.

OPINION

PLUNKETT, D.J. . . . This case is about ribs. Lots of ribs. Thirty-eight thousand pounds of ribs. Thirty-eight thousand pounds of ribs which were barbecued, but not in the normal manner.

Presently before the court are the parties' cross-motions for summary judgment. For the reasons set forth below, Eckrich's motion is granted and Jason's motion is denied.

The only issue presented is that of determining upon which party the risk of loss of the ribs rested on the day that the fire destroyed them. . . . [N]o material factual dispute exists [between the parties] with respect to that issue, and thus that summary judgment is appropriate.

While the parties are free to decide contractually who must bear the risk of loss in a given situation [2-509(4)], the Uniform Commercial Code . . . provides a statutory scheme for resolving risk of loss problems in the event that the parties fail to do so. Neither party alleges that an express agreement allocating the risk of loss was made in this case, and therefore, resort to the relevant sections of the U.C.C. is necessary.

Since neither party breached its contractual obligations, [2-509] of the U.C.C. applies. [It provides]:

> (2) where the goods are held by a bailee to be delivered without being moved, the risk of loss passes to the buyer
>
> > (a) on his receipt of a negotiable document of title covering the goods; or
> >
> > (b) on acknowledgement by the bailee of the buyer's right to possession of the goods; or
> >
> > (c) after his receipt of a non-negotiable document of title or other written direction to deliver, as provided in subsection (4)(b) of Section 2-503.
>
> (3) In any case not within subsection (1) or (2), the risk of loss passes to the buyer on his receipt of the goods if the seller is a merchant; otherwise the risk passes to the buyer on tender of delivery.

At the time of performance, when the sale was consummated, the ribs were in the possession of the bailee. Delivery took place without moving the goods. For this reason, we find that subsection (2) of . . . 2-509 is applicable. . . . Moreover, subsection (2)(b) is the only applicable part of [Section] 2-509.

The U.C.C.'s risk of loss provisions are based on the principle that the party who is in the best position to insure against loss should bear the risk of loss. Given this policy, shifting the risk from the seller to the buyer upon receipt of notice to the seller that the transfer has been made makes little sense. While the seller may no longer have control of the goods, the buyer does not have control either. The more logical approach is to shift the risk of loss to the buyer only upon notice to the buyer that he now has control of the goods. Since the bailee gave no acknowledgement to Eckrich before the fire destroyed the ribs, the risk of loss did not pass to Eckrich.

Jason's . . . contends that Eckrich had actual knowledge of the transfer in

CASE 20.2 Continued	storage because Eckrich had in its possession the confirming notice stating that the transfer would be made between January 10 and January 14. Such notice, however, was at best an estimate of when the transfer would take place. The fact that a four day period was given for a process that takes minutes to complete indicates that Jason's did not know precisely when the ribs would be in the warehouse or when the transfer would take place. As such Eckrich cannot be charged with actual knowledge of what Jason's itself did not know with precision. Furthermore, Jason's and the bailee actually knew when the transfer did take place, and Eckrich did not. Placing the risk of loss on the party who knew least well the particulars of the transfer would be extremely unfair.
JUDGMENT	Eckrich's motion for summary judgment granted; Jason's motion for summary judgment denied.

Some sales contracts give the buyer the *right to return the goods to the seller* even though they conform to the contract. There are two kinds of such sales. A seller may find the first kind, the "sale on approval," useful in breaking down the sales resistance of reluctant consumers. Or, a seller who wants to induce a merchant to stock a new product might resort to the second kind, the "sale or return."

A contract that grants a right to return conforming goods might not make clear which of the two kinds of sales was intended. The distinction is necessary for assigning risk of loss. If goods are delivered primarily for the buyer's use, the transaction is a **sale on approval,** and the risk of loss rests on the seller until the buyer accepts—and approves—the goods [2-327]. If the goods are delivered primarily for resale, the transaction is a **sale or return,** and the risk passes from seller to buyer in accordance with the rules that apply to the particular delivery situation involved. Thus, where goods are shipped by carrier, the risk of loss passes from the seller to the buyer either at the point of shipment or at the point of destination, depending on the kind of shipping terms used by the parties. If the buyer returns goods in accordance with the sale-or-return provision of the contract, the return is at the buyer's risk and expense.

Risk of Loss Where There Is Breach of Contract. The risk of loss usually falls totally or partially on the party who breaches a sales contract. Suppose a *seller* breaches by delivering defective goods. The risk of their loss remains on the seller until: (1) The *seller corrects* (cures) the defects. For example, this could be accomplished by replacing the goods. Or, (2) the *buyer accepts* the goods in spite of their defects [2-510]. However, where the buyer accepts goods, later learns of hidden defects, and then rightfully revokes the acceptance because of the defects, the buyer may *to the extent of any deficiency in his or her effective insurance coverage* treat the risk of loss as having rested on the seller from the beginning.

If the *buyer* breaches the contract before the risk of loss has shifted to the buyer, the seller sometimes may, to the extent of any deficiency in his or her effective insurance coverage, treat the risk of loss as resting on the buyer for a commercially reasonable time before the risk normally would have shifted. Suppose Bigdeal Department Stores orders 500 radios from Sonics Corporation for delivery by carrier at the end of 15 days, and Sonics immediately *identifies* the 500 radios to be shipped to Bigdeal. Ten days later Bigdeal breaches the contract by canceling the order. Later on the day of the breach, the 500 radios are destroyed by fire, and just before the fire Sonics' insurance expired. The risk of loss ordinarily would not pass to Bigdeal until Sonics puts the goods into the custody of the carrier for shipment to Bigdeal. This has not occurred yet. However, because Sonics *identified the goods to the contract* before Bigdeal breached it, and because Sonics had no insurance at the time of loss, the risk of loss is on Bigdeal, and Bigdeal must pay for the radios in full. This is a much greater liability than the contract damages Bigdeal would have had to pay if the radios had not been destroyed.

TITLE OF GOOD FAITH PURCHASERS

The law protects good faith purchasers of property, including good faith purchasers of goods. A person who buys *stolen* property acquires no rights in it because the thief had none. The true owner may recover the stolen property or its value from the purchaser, who, by claiming it as the purchaser's own, has committed the tort of conversion. But in many other circumstances the purchaser acquires ownership of property despite claims of prior owners.

To be entitled to take goods free from claims of aggrieved prior owners, a person must (1) be a "purchaser," (2) receive the goods in good faith, and (3) give value for the goods [2-403]. **Good faith** means honesty in fact in the transaction. If the purchaser is a merchant, good faith requires, in addition, conformance to reasonable commercial standards of fair dealing in the trade. In the law of sales, as in the law governing documents of title, a person gives **value** by giving any consideration sufficient to support a simple contract. Value, therefore, could consist of an executory (unperformed) promise.

The requirement that the protected person be a "purchaser" can be a source of confusion. In its ordinary sense "purchaser" means a person who buys something, and buying implies the giving of value. But the UCC adopts a broader, technical meaning of "purchaser." Under the UCC, a **purchaser** is a person who takes property by sale, negotiation, mortgage, *gift*, or any other voluntary transaction creating an interest in property. Thus, someone who receives a gift is a "purchaser" but is not a purchaser "for value"; consequently he or she may lose the property to an aggrieved prior owner.

In two basic situations, illustrated below, a good faith purchaser *for value* takes the goods free from the claims of prior owners: (1) where the seller acquired a "voidable" title from a prior owner, and (2) where a merchant seller had no title but sold goods that were "entrusted" to him or her.

Where Seller Had Voidable Title

Suppose that Scuzz, a dealer in new and used garden equipment, fraudulently induced Hapless to sell and deliver to Scuzz a garden tractor at a ridiculously low price. Hapless intentionally transferred the tractor to Scuzz, but because of Scuzz's fraud, Scuzz received only a voidable title. Consequently, Hapless has a right to rescind (avoid, cancel) the contract and to get the tractor back from Scuzz. However, if Scuzz had sold the tractor to a good faith purchaser for value, Hapless's only recourse would be a lawsuit against Scuzz for damages, and the purchaser would be entitled to the tractor itself, free from Hapless's claim of fraud [2-403]. Thus, Scuzz, a person with *voidable* title, can confer on a good faith purchaser for value a better title than Scuzz had.

Where Goods Were Entrusted to Merchant Seller

Suppose Scuzz's father lent his own tractor to Scuzz, and without his knowledge Scuzz sold it to Blameless, one of Scuzz's customers. Scuzz's father has "entrusted" his tractor to Scuzz, a merchant. Any entrusting of goods to a merchant *who deals in goods of that kind* gives the merchant power to transfer all rights *of the entruster* to a "buyer in the ordinary course of business" [2-403]. Such a buyer is similar to a good faith purchaser for value and receives the same kind of protection. Here Blameless may keep the tractor even though Scuzz had no title at all but only possession resulting from the entrustment. Thus, the law puts the risk of an unauthorized sale on the entruster, who is in a better position than the innocent purchaser to prevent loss. (Note that if Scuzz's father had stolen the entrusted tractor, he would have had no rights in it, and Blameless could lose the tractor to the true owner.)

Protection of good faith purchasers is found in many branches of the law besides the law of sales. For example, under Article 3 of the UCC, holders in due course are similar to good faith purchasers. Specifically, holders in due course take negotiable notes and checks free from many defenses of issuers. Similar treatment is accorded good faith purchasers of negotiable securities (Article 8); many retail purchasers of goods subject to security interests (Article 9); and holders of "duly negotiated" documents of title (Article 7). Market values are enhanced, and commerce is benefited, if the good faith purchaser's perception of risk is minimized. Reducing that perception of risk requires prior owners to take more care in their transactions, track down wrongdoers, or sometimes absorb loss.

The following case deals with an issue of entrustment under the UCC.

CASE 20.3 Locke v. Arabi Grain & Elevator Company, Inc.
• 399 S.E.2d 705 (Ga. App. 1990)

FACTS Bobby Locke (Locke), CEO and principal stockholder of Leeco Farm Center, Inc., also doing business under the name Worthco Farm Center (Worthco), hired a Mr. Hobby (Hobby) as Worthco's manager. During Hobby's tenure at Worthco—from February 1986 through March 1987—Hobby had sold corn stored with Worthco to Arabi Grain & Elevator Company (Arabi) and pocketed the proceeds. There was evidence that Hobby and members of his family had previously done business with Arabi, and that Arabi did not know that Hobby was employed by Worthco.

Locke brought a suit against Arabi in trover and conversion (wrongful taking of ownership of found goods or wrongful interference with the goods of another). The trial court granted summary judgment in favor of Arabi. Locke appealed.

OPINION DEEN, J. . . . [Locke] based his case on trover and conversion. Were this a simple trover case, the outcome in favor of Locke would have been abundantly clear; however, the "entrusting statutes" of the Uniform Commercial Code [2-403(2) & (3)] call for a different result.

[Persuasive authority] addresses "entrusting" as follows: "An entrusting of property, defined by [2-403(3) of the UCC] as any acquiescence by the owner of the goods in the retention of those goods by another, may result in the owner's loss of title to the property if the entrustee is a merchant who deals in similar goods. Under [2-403(2)], a merchant who deals in goods of the same kind as those entrusted is empowered to convey the same title as that held by the entrustor to a buyer in the ordinary course of business. While this provision protects buyers who may be unaware of the risk that the property is owned by another person, it limits the original owner's remedy to seeking recovery for the value of the goods from the merchant."

[In a federal case applying Nebraska law], the court . . . determined that when a grain elevator owner supplied soybeans to the owner of a receiving elevator through the person whose status as a merchant was in dispute, an entrustment occurred within the meaning of [2-403(2)]. The elevator owner shipped soybeans to the receiving elevator, the trucker [for the seller] represented that the beans belonged to him; consequently he, rather than the grain elevator, re-

CASE 20.3
Continued

ceived payment. The receiving elevator contended that the elevator owner should bear the loss because it entrusted the beans to the trucker as a merchant, who was empowered by [2-403] to transfer ownership. . . . [T]he court noted that the elevator owner was aware that the trucker occasionally bought and sold grain, and that personnel at the receiving elevator had prior dealings with the trucker acting as a seller of grain. The court stated that occasional merchandising, known to the entruster, satisfied the requirements of [2-403(2)], and therefore concluded that the trucker was empowered to transfer the elevator operator's rights to the receiving elevator in the ordinary course of business.

Judge Marshall [formerly Georgia's Chief Justice] . . . summarized [entrusting] in [a 1975 case]: "The general thrust of the cases involving 'entrusting' of goods to a dealer is aimed at the protection of the purchaser, where the latter acts in 'good faith' and the owner takes the risk by placing or leaving his chattel with a merchant of his own choosing who could convert or otherwise misdeal it. . . . The Georgia courts have . . . protected the good faith purchaser in the 'entrusting' situations, both under the UCC . . . and the old sales law."

This court has continued to apply the statutory language in the same manner as in [the above cases]: "The language of [UCC 2-403(2) & (3)] is quite clear: actual entrustment to the merchant or dealer, gives the power to transfer 'all rights of the entruster' to a buyer in the ordinary course of business."

JUDGMENT Affirmed.

SUMMARY

Sometimes a party to a sales contract needs to know when title to the goods passes from seller to buyer. If delivery is to be made by moving the goods, title passes when and where the seller completes the physical delivery of the goods. If delivery is to be made without moving the goods, title passes when and where the seller delivers a document of title or, if no document is involved, at the time of contracting.

Where goods are lost or damaged, someone must bear the loss. The person who bears the risk of loss must either absorb it, perhaps through insurance coverage, or take the initiative to collect from the person actually responsible for the loss, such as a negligent carrier.

Risk of loss is never assigned on the basis of who had title at the time of loss. Rather, rules of Article 2 assign the loss to either the buyer or the seller, mainly on the basis of who is in the better position to control or to insure the goods. The risk-of-loss rules apply to situations involving goods shipped by carrier, goods held by a bailee, pickup and noncarrier deliveries, and goods subject to a right of the buyer to return them to the seller. Some of the rules apply where there is a breach of the sales contract; others apply to situations involving no breach.

A good faith purchaser for value may take goods free from the claims of prior owners. Such a purchaser gets no rights in stolen goods, but he or she does acquire ownership where the seller had voidable title. Where the purchaser bought goods in the ordinary course of business from a merchant dealer to whom they had been entrusted, the purchaser acquires whatever rights the entruster had.

REVIEW QUESTIONS

1. If you contract to buy goods, when do you receive title (ownership)? Why might you need to know?

2. (a) What is the basis upon which the law assigns the risk that goods will be lost or damaged during delivery? (b) Does risk of loss pass from seller to buyer when the buyer receives title? Explain or illustrate.

3. (a) When does risk of loss pass under a shipment contract? When does it pass under a destination contract? **(b)** How do you know whether a contract is a shipment or a destination contract?

4. When does risk of loss pass where the goods are to be delivered without being moved?

5. When does risk of loss pass in a pickup or a noncarrier delivery? Why then?

6. When does risk of loss pass under contracts that give a buyer a right to return the goods?

7. What effect does breach of contract have on passage of risk of loss?

8. In the expression "good faith purchaser for value," why are the words "for value" necessary?

9. Illustrate the two basic situations in which a good faith purchaser for value takes the goods free from the claims of prior owners.

CASE PROBLEMS

1. Dana Debs, Inc., a dress and suit manufacturer in New York City, received a written order from Lady Rose Stores, Inc., of Westbury, Long Island, for the purchase of 288 garments. The order was on Lady Rose's printed form, and it advised Dana Debs to "ship via Stuart, 453 W. 57th St., New York City." Stuart Express Co., Inc., picked up the shipment. Later Stuart wrote Dana Debs that the entire shipment had been lost and that Stuart's limit of liability was $1 per garment, as indicated in the bill of lading. Dana Debs, the seller, then informed Lady Rose Stores of the loss and presented a bill for $1,756.80, the amount of the loss. Lady Rose contended that a destination contract had been created, and that risk of loss therefore could not pass to Lady Rose until Stuart tendered delivery at the destination. Was this a destination contract?

2. Silver ordered custom furniture from Wycombe for delivery to Silver's home. Wycombe informed Silver in writing that the furniture was ready for shipment. Silver paid for it, telling Wycombe to ship one room of furniture but to hold the other until instructed further. Before Wycombe received further instructions, the remaining furniture was destroyed by fire. Wycombe was not at fault. Silver's insurance company paid Silver for the loss and sought reimbursement from Wycombe. Wycombe refused to pay, contending that Silver's instruction to hold the furniture created a bailment, that Wycombe's notice to Silver constituted an acknowledgment of Silver's right to the goods, and that Wycombe had thereby shifted the risk of loss to Silver. Was the insurance company entitled to reimbursement from Wycombe?

3. Mrs. Conway purchased a necklace from Larsen Jewelers on a "layaway plan" under which the seller sets aside the item in question until the full purchase price is paid. Conway paid a total of $265 on the purchase price of $450. Then a burglar broke into the store and stole the necklace from a locked safe. As between Conway and Larsen, who must bear the loss?

4. Klein, a wholesale jeweler, and Lopardo, a retail jeweler, had a long-standing business relationship. Klein would deliver jewels to Lopardo, who would sell them to retail customers and pay Klein the agreed price. If unable to sell the jewels, Lopardo would return them to Klein. Approximately 10 days after Lopardo received two diamonds, they were stolen from his jewelry store. Who should bear the loss?

5. Chyrchel purchased three mobile homes from Southland Mobile Home Corp. The price included installation of facilities. A service crew employed by Southland was to install a new gas range in one of the trailers, hook up electrical and gas lines, and complete similar work. During the installation, Chyrchel smelled gas and asked the crew to check for leaks. A few days later, before the installations were completed, an explosion and fire damaged the trailer and made it uninhabitable. Southland refused to refund the purchase price or to replace the trailer. Alleging breach of contract, Chyrchel sued Southland for damages. Southland defended on the basis that the sale was complete before the fire and that the risk of loss therefore had passed to the buyer. Had the risk of loss passed to Chyrchel?

6. Marcus agreed to buy a Mainship boat from Corrigan's Yacht Yard & Marine Sales, Inc., and delivered his Silverton boat to Corrigan's in part payment, but without delivering the certificate of registration. Later, Corrigan's contracted to sell the Silverton boat to Heiselman. When Corrigan's failed to deliver Marcus's new boat on the date promised, Marcus rescinded the contract and retrieved the Silverton boat from Corrigan's. Heiselman sued Marcus in conversion for damages. Marcus contended that he never lost title to the Silverton boat because title was to transfer only upon receipt of and as payment for the new boat. Was Heiselman entitled to damages?

CHAPTER 21

Performance of the Sales Contract; Remedies for Breach of Contract

Many disputes between the parties to a sales contract concern the question of performance. Has the seller delivered what was promised? Has the buyer made the agreed payment? If either has failed to live up to the terms of the agreement, what remedy is available to the other? The first part of this chapter discusses the performance obligations of seller and buyer. The second part discusses their remedies for breach of the sales contract.

PERFORMANCE OF THE SALES CONTRACT

The physical acts required for the performance of a particular sales contract vary according to the kind of delivery process to which the parties agreed—delivery by carrier, seller's noncarrier delivery, buyer's picking the goods up at the seller's place of business, or delivery of a document of title without moving the goods. Yet the legal principles governing performance are the same for all methods of delivery. Consider, for example, the steps normally taken in carrying out a sale involving a delivery by carrier:

1. Beta (the buyer) orders a desk from Sigma.
2. Sigma identifies the desk to the contract—for example, marks it "for Beta."
3. Sigma begins physical delivery by putting the desk in the custody of the carrier. How this is done is discussed later in the chapter.
4. The desk arrives, and Beta *inspects* it.
5. If the desk has obvious defects, Beta *rejects* it.
6. Upon Beta's rejection, Sigma attempts to *cure* (correct) the defects. If cure is timely, Beta must *accept* the desk or be liable for breach of contract.
7. If the desk arrives undamaged, Beta accepts it.
8. Where Beta accepts the desk and later discovers hidden defects, Beta *revokes* the *acceptance* and returns the desk to Sigma.
9. If there is no basis for rejecting the desk, Beta *pays* the price, less any proper deductions for minor damage or shortages such as a missing drawer pull.

Although the precise steps required for physical delivery vary from one method to another, the acts of inspection, rejection, and cure are common to all types of delivery. Figure 21.1 shows the usual sequence of events that may occur during an attempt to perform a sales contract.

Performance: General Concepts

Obligations of the Parties. Sellers and buyers "perform" by meeting the obligations that they

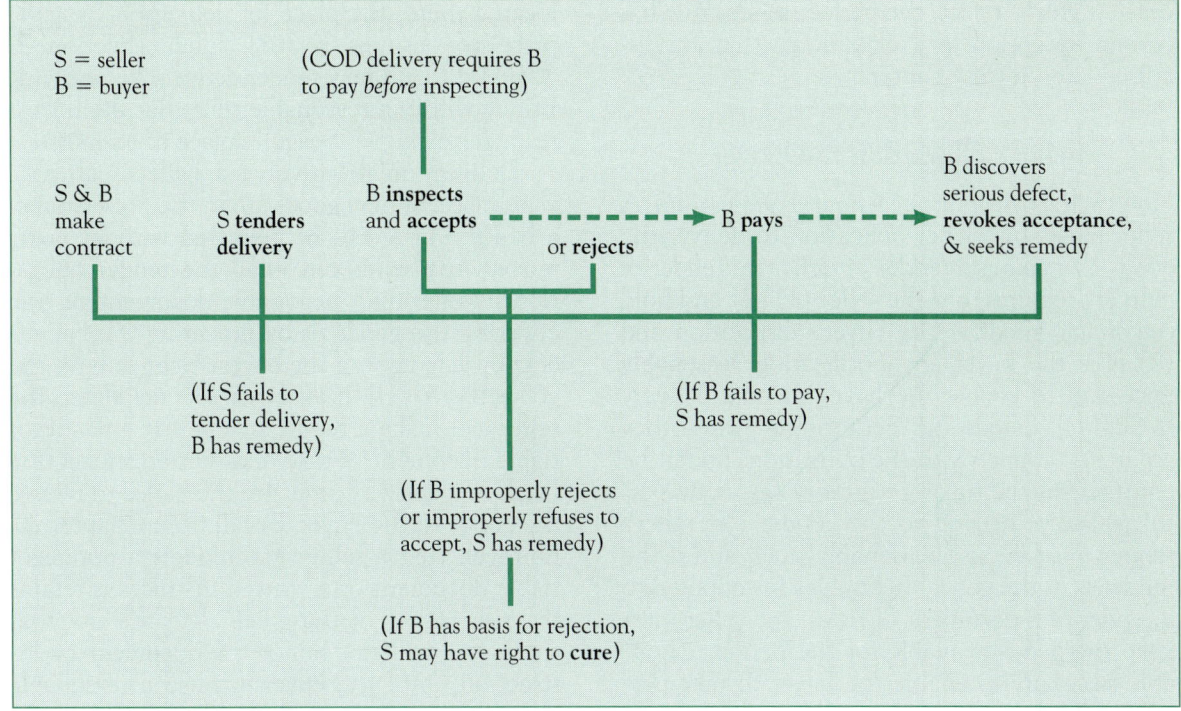

Figure 21.1 Performance of sales contract.

undertake by entering into a contract. In a sale of goods, the general obligation of the *seller* is to transfer ownership of the goods and to deliver them as required by the contract. Under UCC Article 2, the obligation of the *buyer* is to accept the goods and to pay for them as required by the contract [2-301]. The agreement of the parties, as supplemented or as limited by law, constitutes "the contract" by which the performance obligations of the parties are to be measured.

Meaning of "Tender." Sellers and buyers meet their performance obligations by making a "tender" of performance. A **tender** is an offer of performance by one party that, if unjustifiably refused, places the other party in default and permits the tendering party to have remedies for breach of contract. For example, Bodybuilder orders barbells from Strongstuff to be delivered to Bodybuilder's house on Tuesday. Late Monday night Bodybuilder decides to cancel the contract. Early Tuesday morning, Strongstuff's truck arrives at Bodybuilder's house with the barbells in good condition. Strongstuff has made a tender of delivery. If Bodybuilder refuses to accept the barbells, Bodybuilder will be in breach of the contract.

The Perfect Tender Rule. If the goods or the seller's tender of delivery fails *in any respect* to conform to the contract, the buyer may reject the goods (or the tender) [2-601]. This rule, called the **perfect tender rule,** protects the buyer from having to track down missing documents; from having to accept faulty documents, such as a warehouse receipt that lacks a necessary indorsement; or from having to argue with the seller about the sufficiency of an incomplete performance, such as a truckload of cotton that is missing one bale. The protection provided by this rule is especially important to buyers who are geographically distant from sellers. However, to prevent buyers from taking undue advantage of the right to reject, the perfect tender rule has certain exceptions or "relaxations" that are discussed later in this chapter.

Seller's Obligation to Deliver

How Seller Meets the Delivery Obligation. A seller meets his or her obligation to deliver the goods by making a tender of delivery. Tender of delivery requires that the seller (1) put and hold *conforming* goods at the buyer's disposition and (2) give the buyer any notification reasonably necessary to enable the buyer to take delivery [2-503(1)]. Goods are "conforming" when they are in accordance with the obligations under the contract, including any warranty (assurance) as to quality of or title to the goods. The seller's tender must be at a reasonable hour, and if the tender is of the goods themselves (as opposed to a tender of a document of title), the seller must keep the goods available for the period reasonably necessary to enable the buyer to take possession. Unless otherwise agreed, the buyer must furnish facilities reasonably suited to the receipt of the goods.

Tender Requirements for Common Types of Delivery. The specific acts required for an effective tender of delivery vary according to the kind of delivery agreed to by the parties to the sales contract or imposed by the UCC where the parties were silent as to delivery. Once the kind of delivery has been established, the specific acts required for an effective tender can be determined by applying the Code sections on tender. The following paragraphs discuss the tender requirements of some common types of delivery.

Delivery involving no carrier. Often delivery occurs at the seller's place of business. Suppose, for example, that Briney signs a contract to buy from Seagull Company a particular motorboat from Seagull's stock of boats, that the motorboat is to be specially equipped from Seagull's stock of accessories, and that the contract says nothing about the time and place of delivery. Seagull must make delivery within a reasonable time [2-309]. Since Seagull is a dealer who has a place of business, and since the boat and accessories are located there, the place for delivery is Seagull's place of business [2-308]. Under Section 2-503(1), Seagull may tender delivery by notifying Briney within a reasonable time that the boat is ready for pickup at Seagull's place of business.

Delivery might involve a bailee such as a warehouse. Where goods are in the possession of a bailee and are to be delivered without being moved, the seller can fulfill the tender obligation by offering a negotiable document of title covering the goods or by procuring the bailee's acknowledgment of the buyer's right to have the goods [2-503(4)]. *If the buyer does not object,* the seller can make a tender by offering a *nonnegotiable* document of title or a written instruction (such as a delivery order) to the bailee to release the goods to the buyer. Recall from Chapter 20, however, that a seller who tenders a nonnegotiable document or a written instruction retains the risk of loss of the goods, and the risk that the bailee will not honor the document or instruction, until the buyer has had a reasonable time to present it to the bailee. Furthermore, the bailee's refusal to honor the nonnegotiable document or written instruction *defeats* the seller's tender—that is, the bailee's refusal means that the seller has made no effective tender. All documents required for making a tender must be in correct form.

Delivery involving a carrier. Unless displaced by a contrary agreement, rules of Article 2 govern tender in common types of deliveries involving a carrier. Under a *shipment* contract (defined in Chapter 20), the seller fulfills his or her tender obligation by completing four steps: (1) putting conforming goods in the possession of a carrier, (2) making a reasonable contract for their transportation, (3) obtaining and promptly delivering or tendering in due form any document necessary to enable the buyer to obtain possession of the goods, and (4) promptly notifying the buyer of the shipment [2-504]. The costs of shipping will be included in the price of the goods, or the buyer will pay the shipping charges separately.

Except for installment contracts, the perfect tender rule permits the buyer to reject nonconforming goods even for minor defects; and the seller's failing to provide a required document is always a basis for the buyer to reject a tender of delivery. Also, if the seller fails to notify the buyer of the shipment or fails to make a proper contract for the transportation of the goods, the buyer may reject the goods—*but only if the seller's failure causes the buyer a material delay or loss* [2-504]. These rules relating to shipment contracts thus place upon the seller the responsibility for arranging suitable transportation, but relax the perfect tender rule to protect the seller from harmless error in making the arrangements.

Suppose BiLow, a Michigan grocer, orders 500 crates of grapefruit from Sitrus, a Florida grapefruit seller. Sitrus properly ships conforming grapefruit by rail to BiLow, but Sitrus forgets to notify BiLow of the shipment. When the grapefruit arrives, the stationmaster immediately notifies BiLow of its arrival. BiLow suffers no harm from Sitrus's failure to notify him of the shipment and cannot reject the grapefruit. Table 21.1 lists relaxations of the perfect tender rule.

Under a *destination* contract, the seller fulfills the tender obligation by completing three steps: (1) putting and holding conforming goods *at destination* for the buyer's disposition, (2) giving the buyer any notification reasonably necessary to enable the buyer to take delivery, and (3) tendering any required documents in correct form [2-503(3)].

Seller's Cure of Improper Delivery. A seller may have a right to "cure" an improper tender or an improper delivery. Suppose Slashprice sells a power saw to Birchtree, who requires delivery on or before June 1. Slashprice delivers the saw on May 25, but Birchtree rejects it because some parts are missing. Slashprice may give notice of its intention to cure the nonconforming delivery and when *within the time set by the contract for performance* may make a conforming delivery [2-503]. Even where Slashprice has taken back the nonconforming goods and refunded the purchase price, Slashprice may effect cure if it can do so before the time for performance expires. The time for performance is the time stated in the contract—here, June 1. If no time was stated, the time for performance is a reasonable time.

Sometimes, to reduce the harmful effects of the buyer's surprise rejection of the goods, the UCC gives to the seller the right to cure a defective tender *after* the time set for performance. Where a buyer rejects a nonconforming tender that the seller had *reasonable grounds to believe would be acceptable* with or without money allowance, the seller may, upon notifying the buyer "seasonably" (in a timely manner), have a *further* reasonable time to substitute a conforming tender. For example, suppose Bender orders Brand X galvanized pipe from SupplyCo for delivery at noon on November 1. At the appointed hour SupplyCo delivers Brand Y pipe of the same kind and quality for the same price. If Bender rejects the Brand Y pipe, and if SupplyCo reasonably believed that the delivery of Brand Y pipe would be acceptable, SupplyCo is entitled to a further reasonable time to cure the nonconformity.

Buyer's Obligation to Accept and to Pay

Where the seller has properly tendered conforming goods, the buyer is obliged to accept them and to pay the price. However, the buyer's obligations are conditioned on a right to inspect the goods. Where a tender of delivery does not conform to the contract, the buyer may have a right to reject the goods or to revoke any acceptance—and to recover any payment—that the buyer might have made.

Meaning and Effect of Buyer's Acceptance. **Acceptance** of goods means that the buyer, in accordance with the contract, takes as his or her

---

Table 21.1   Relaxations of Perfect Tender Rule

A perfect tender is NOT required where:
1. The contract so provides.
2. Seller fails to notify seller of shipment or fails to make a proper transportation contract, but **no material delay or loss to buyer** results.
3. Seller has **time remaining** under contract **to cure** defects.
4. In an installment contract, **nonconformity** of goods is **minor**.

own the goods that the seller has appropriated (set aside) for the contract. The buyer may accept by words, action, or silence when it is time for the buyer to speak. Acceptance may occur in a variety of ways—for example, by the buyer's telling the seller that the goods are conforming or that the buyer will take or retain them in spite of their nonconformity; by the buyer's failure to make an effective rejection; or by the buyer's doing some act inconsistent with the seller's ownership, such as reselling the goods or incorporating building materials into a building [2-606]. If the buyer's act is wrongful, acceptance does not occur (and the buyer commits the tort of conversion) unless the wrongful act is ratified by the seller.

The legal effect of acceptance is that the buyer becomes obligated to pay the contract price [2-607]. Moreover, a buyer who has accepted a defective tender is *barred from any remedy*, including a remedy for breach of warranty, unless the seller is *notified* of the defect within a reasonable time after it has been or should have been discovered. Notice is required so that the seller may take steps to cure a defective performance or, where defective goods are alleged to have caused harm, so that the seller may adequately prepare for negotiation or defense of a lawsuit. What constitutes "reasonable" notice depends on the facts of the case. An injured consumer who is unaware of the requirement to notify the seller may be allowed more time to give notice than a merchant would be.

Buyer's Right to Inspect the Goods. The buyer may make a reasonable inspection of the goods to see whether they conform to the contract. Usually, the right to inspect may be exercised before payment or acceptance. Accordingly, when the seller is required or authorized to send the goods to the buyer, the buyer may take custody of the goods for the purpose of inspection without being considered to have accepted the goods. With rare exceptions, no agreement by the parties can displace the right of inspection [2-513, comment 1].

Even though the right to inspect usually may be exercised before payment, the buyer can be required by contract to pay first and inspect later. For example, unless otherwise agreed, CIF ("cost of goods, insurance, and freight"), COD ("collect on delivery"), cash against documents, and similar contract clauses require payment *before* inspection. Upon inspection after payment, the buyer may, of course, reject nonconforming goods and have appropriate remedies such as damages. And even where the contract requires the buyer to make payment before inspection, the buyer may withhold payment if the nonconformity is obvious without inspection [2-512]. The buyer is not required, for example, to pay for goods that obviously are not the goods ordered.

Sometimes a CIF contract contains a clause providing for payment *on or after arrival* of the goods. The presence of such a clause gives the buyer the right to "such preliminary inspection as is feasible" *before* making payment [2-321(3)]. The clause merely postpones the time for payment. It does not, by itself, change the risk-of-loss consequences of a CIF contract. If the goods do not arrive, payment is due to the seller when the goods should have arrived.

Buyer's Options on Improper Delivery. Within limits imposed by the Code, a buyer may *reject* an improper tender or an improper delivery of goods. In some situations the buyer may *revoke acceptance* of defective goods.

Rejection of goods. In general, a buyer may reject goods that do not conform to the contract. Specifically, the buyer may "(a) reject the whole; or (b) accept the whole; or (c) accept any commercial unit or units and reject the rest" [2-601]. A **commercial unit** is an amount of goods that in business practice is treated as a single whole for purposes of sale, and whose division would materially impair its value or character (e.g., a machine, a bale of cotton, a carload of wheat).

The rejection must be made within a reasonable time after delivery or tender of the goods, and the buyer *must seasonably* (in a timely manner) *notify* the seller of the rejection [2-602]. In addition, the buyer must specify the defects upon which the buyer bases the rejection, if those defects are ascertainable by inspection [2-605]. The requirement that defects be specified is for the protection of the seller's right to cure any curable defects. A buyer who merely rejects a delivery without stating any real objections to it may be acting in commercial bad faith, seeking only to get out of a deal which has become unprofitable. Such conduct is not permitted. A buyer's failure to reject in accordance with Code rules *results in acceptance* and liability for payment.

The buyer's right of rejection is limited by important Code rules regarding installment contracts. An **installment contract** is one that requires or authorizes the delivery of goods in separate lots which are to be separately accepted. The buyer may reject a nonconforming installment (delivery of goods) *only if* the nonconformity *substantially impairs* the value of that installment *and cannot be cured* [2-612]. Suppose, for example, that Bench, a skilled furniture maker, uses 1,000 board-feet of high-quality walnut lumber each week. To meet production needs Bench orders 10,000 board-feet to be delivered in ten weekly installments of 1,000 board-feet each at 8 a.m. sharp each Monday. Sawmill, the seller, delivers the first three installments, but the fourth lot, delivered at 7 a.m. Monday, is so knotty that Bench cannot use it. Bench may reject the fourth installment because the nonconformity substantially impairs its value. The rejection is effective unless Sawmill can make a substitute delivery of conforming lumber by 8 a.m.

The installment-contract restriction on a buyer's right to reject goods is a second exception to the perfect tender rule. The purpose of the exception is to prevent a buyer from, for example, seizing on a trivial defect as an excuse to reject goods that are, in fact, substantially what was ordered. In a shipment contract, the goods ordinarily will be at the buyer's place of business when rejected. The seller might be hundreds of miles away. If the seller had to prove that the goods and their tender were perfect, considerable expense could be involved, and the buyer would be in a position to threaten rejection to force a lower price. To protect the *seller,* the Code therefore prohibits the buyer from rejecting the goods unless the defect substantially impairs the value of the installment and cannot be cured. To protect the *buyer,* the Code permits the buyer to have damages for any defect, no matter how trivial.

Where one or more installments are so defective that they substantially impair the value of the *whole contract* (and cannot be cured), the buyer may cancel the contract and have other remedies such as damages. However, if the buyer accepts a nonconforming installment without seasonably notifying the seller of cancellation, or brings suit as to past installments only, or demands performance of future installments, the buyer *loses* the right to cancel the breached contract and, in effect, reinstates it.

An installment contract *may* require accurate conformity in quality as a condition to the seller's right to the buyer's acceptance, *but only if there is a real need* for such conformity. To be enforceable, a provision requiring accurate conformity in quality must have some basis in reason and must avoid imposing hardship by surprise. For example, a requirement of strictly accurate conformity might be enforceable in a purchase of surgeon's tools or delicate parts for a space shuttle, but not in a purchase of waste logs to be processed into chipboard.

Revocation of acceptance. Suppose that you accept goods that are defective. In two principal situations, you may have a right to revoke your acceptance of goods whose nonconformity *substantially impairs* their value to you [2-608]: (1) You may revoke where you knew of the substantial nonconformity but accepted the goods on the reasonable assumption that the defect would be cured and it has not been seasonably cured. (2) You may revoke where, *not knowing* of the substantial nonconformity, you *reasonably* accepted because of (a) the difficulty of discovering the substantial nonconformity before acceptance, or (b) the seller's assurances (express or implied) that the goods had no defects. You may revoke as to the entire lot of goods accepted or as to any subdivision of the lot that constitutes a commercial unit. Revocation of acceptance must occur within a reasonable time after you discover or should have discovered the substantial nonconformity. You may *not* revoke if the goods have undergone substantial change for reasons *other than* their own defects, such as your failure to store them properly. Nor may you revoke your acceptance where you knew of the defects at the time of acceptance but had no reason to assume that the defects would be cured, as where an obviously damaged camera is sold "as is."

As noted in Table 21.2, although a person may *reject* goods for even a trivial defect (where the perfect tender rule applies), one cannot *revoke acceptance* unless the defect in the goods is substantial. One reason is that rejection occurs when the goods are still new, or at least unused by the rejecting buyer, while revocation occurs after the buyer has taken possession of the goods and in all likelihood has used them. It would be unfair to sellers to allow buyers easily to revoke acceptance of depreciated goods.

Table 21.2 Rejection v. Revocation of Acceptance

Rejection:	Available to buyer to *any* defect, no matter how minor, unless perfect tender does not apply.
Revocation of Acceptance:	Available to buyer only if nonconformity is *substantial*.

Case 21.1, which follows, addresses issues of acceptance, rejection, revocation of acceptance, and seasonability.

CASE 21.1 Swire Pacific Holdings, Inc. v. Morgan and Taylor Holding Co.
• No. 90-3121 slip op. (S.D.N.J. 1990)

FACTS Between May 3, 1990 and May 31, 1990, Swire Pacific Holdings, Inc., doing business under the name of Swire Magnetics Company (Swire), furnished to Morgan and Taylor Holding Co., doing business under the name of New Age Video (New Age), a large quantity of videotapes for the agreed price of $235,407.05. New Age, however, allegedly paid only $5,000 for the tapes. New Age then sold the videotapes to a number of other buyers.

In July 1990 Swire and New Age entered into agreements in an attempt to devise a payment schedule. At that time, New Age did not mention defectiveness of the videotapes during the negotiations.

Swire brought suit against New Age to collect payment from New Age. New Age, however, in its defense stated that it had been receiving defective returns from its retail customers since August 1990.

Swire moved for summary judgment.

OPINION WOLIN, D.J. . . . To prevail in this motion, plaintiff must establish its right to recover the price of goods accepted under the Uniform Commercial Code [2-709]. [It] provides that:

> (1) When the buyer fails to pay the price as it becomes due the seller may recover, together with any incidental damages . . . the price . . . of goods accepted.

Under [UCC 2-606] (What Constitutes Acceptance of Goods), goods are accepted when the buyer:

> (b) fails to make an effective rejection [2-602(1)], but such acceptance does not occur until the buyer has had a reasonable opportunity to inspect them; or (c) does any act inconsistent with the seller's ownership.

Thus, Swire has the burden of demonstrating that New Age has accepted all of the goods within the meaning of [the above subsections of UCC 2-606].

**CASE 21.1
Continued**

[T]he circumstances under which goods [may] be rightfully rejected is governed by [UCC 2-602] . . . which states that:

> (1) Rejection of goods must be within a reasonable time after their delivery or tender. It is ineffective unless the buyer seasonably notifies the seller.

In the present case, it appears that Swire was not notified that New Age allegedly received defective goods until . . . September 14, 1990 [after New Age was sued to collect payment].

The outcome of [Swire's] motion for summary judgment depends upon whether, as a matter of law, [New Age's] notice was unseasonable. . . . [A Pennsylvania case, tried on the merits with similar facts], indicates that a rightful rejection is plausible in circumstances like those [in this case]. Therefore, [Swire] has not shown that, as a matter of law, [New Age] did not make an effective rejection of the allegedly defective goods. . . .

[Swire] further contends that by reselling the tapes . . . , New Age committed "an act inconsistent with the seller's ownership" and thus accepted the goods under [UCC 2-606(1)(c)]. However, Comment 4 to [UCC 2-606] adds: the provisions [of UCC 2-606(1)(c)] are subject to the sections dealing with rejection by the buyer which permit the buyer to take certain actions with respect to the goods . . . without effecting an acceptance of those goods.

Because there is a genuine issue as to whether New Age rightfully rejected the goods under [UCC 2-602], it cannot be said as a matter of law, New Age accepted the goods under [UCC 2-606(1)(c)].

. . . [UCC 2-608] provides an alternative remedy for the buyer of defective goods by allowing him to revoke his acceptance where he has already accepted the goods. . . . [It] provides in relevant part[:]

> (1) the buyer may revoke his acceptance of a lot or commercial unit whose nonconformity substantially impairs its value to him if he has accepted it . . . (b) without discovery of such non-conformity if his acceptance was reasonably induced either by the difficulty of discovery before acceptance. . . . (2) Revocation of acceptance must occur with a reasonable time after the buyer discovers or should have discovered the ground for it. . . . It is not effective until the buyer notifies the seller of it.

New Age's notification of the alleged defects in the tapes may have served as a partial revocation of acceptance. As such, the Court cannot find as a matter of law that New Age did not revoke its acceptance in regard to the allegedly defective tapes.

[Swire] contends that New Age's allegations of having received defective tapes are "sham" and intended only to delay payment. However, . . . the Advisory Committee [on civil procedure] states:

> Where an issue as to a material fact cannot be resolved without observation of witnesses in order to evaluate their credibility, summary judgment is inappropriate.

Thus, [Swire's] argument concerning [the "sham"] is inappropriate at this stage in the proceedings.

JUDGMENT Motion for summary judgment denied.

Buyer's Obligation to Pay for Goods Accepted. A buyer meets the obligation to pay the price by making payment in accordance with the contract. If the parties have not stated how payment is to be made, the buyer may pay in any customary manner, unless the seller demands payment in legal tender (money) and gives any extension of time reasonably necessary to procure it [2-511]. This rule protects the buyer from a surprise demand for cash. For the protection of sellers who accept checks, however, a buyer's payment by check is only a conditional payment and is defeated by refusal of the bank upon which the check was drawn to pay it.

If the parties have not stated the time and the place for payment, either of the following rules applies: (1) payment is due at the time and place at which the buyer is to receive the goods; or (2) where delivery is to be made by means of documents of title, payment is due at the time and place at which the buyer is to receive the documents, regardless of where the goods are to be received. Both of these rules are subject to any right of the buyer to inspect the goods before payment.

If the goods are lost in transit, and if the risk of loss has shifted to the buyer, the buyer is obligated to make payment at the time and place at which he or she was to receive the goods. Suppose that a foreign seller ships goods to a New York buyer under a CIF contract and the goods are lost at sea. A CIF contract places the risk of loss on the buyer when the seller properly puts the goods in the custody of the carrier. Because the buyer acquires the risk of loss when the carrier receives the goods, the buyer must pay for them despite their nonarrival and must rely on the insurance provided for in the CIF contract.

Where the parties have agreed to an extension of credit, the credit term governs the time, place, and manner of payment to the extent that the credit term discusses these matters.

Excuse for Nonperformance or Substitute Performance

If the performance of a contractual obligation becomes more burdensome than the obligated party anticipated, that party might ask to be excused from performance. In general, the parties to a contract are excused from their performance obligations when performance has been rendered impossible or unreasonably burdensome by circumstances beyond the contemplation of the parties at the time of contracting.

Excuse for Nonperformance. Article 2 adopts "commercial impracticability" as the main basis for excusing nonperformance of obligations under a sales contract. The article also provides rules that apply where an agreed method of payment or delivery fails and a substitute method is sought by the aggrieved (injured) party.

Commercial impracticability. Unless the seller has assumed a greater obligation, the seller is excused for delay in delivery or for nondelivery of goods *if* performance has been made *impracticable* by a certain type of unexpected occurrence [2-615]. The seller is excused if the agreed performance has been made impracticable because of an applicable foreign or domestic governmental regulation or order. Suppose that a manufacturer agrees to make and sell sophisticated electronics equipment to a buyer in a foreign country. If the foreign buyer's government later unexpectedly forbids the importation of such equipment, the manufacturer is excused from performance.

The drafters of Article 2 explain the meaning of *commercial impracticability* as follows:

Increased cost alone does not excuse performance unless the rise in cost is due to some unforeseen contingency which alters the essential nature of the performance. Neither is a rise or a collapse in the market in itself a justification, for that is exactly the type of business risk which business contracts made at fixed prices are intended to cover. But a severe shortage of raw materials or of supplies due to a contingency such as war, embargo, local crop failure, unforeseen shutdown of major sources of supply, or the like, which either causes a marked increase in cost or altogether prevents the seller from securing supplies necessary to his performance, is within the contemplation of this section [2-615, comment 4].

Where commercial impracticability only *partially* impairs the seller's capacity to perform, the seller must *allocate* production and deliveries among his or her customers in a fair and reasonable manner. Regardless of the degree of impairment, the seller will *not* be excused from performance unless he or she seasonably notifies the buyer that there will be a delay or nondelivery. If there is a partial impairment, the seller must also inform the buyer of any production or delivery quota to which the buyer is entitled.

In response to the seller's notice of a material delay or an allocation of goods, the buyer may, by written notification to the seller, elect to do one of the following: (1) terminate (and thereby discharge) any unperformed portion of the contract or (2) modify the contract by agreeing to take the available quota [2-616]. The buyer may terminate the whole of an installment contract if the seller's deficiency *substantially impairs* the value of the whole contract. Where a seller is excused from performance because of unforeseen circumstances, the buyer is also excused, despite any agreement to the contrary.

Case 21.2 illustrates the general reluctance of the courts to discharge a contracting party on the basis of commercial impracticability unless the unexpected circumstance is truly unforeseeable and the loss so great as to lie beyond the reasonable expectations of the parties.

CASE 21.2 **Raymond Roy v. Stephen Pontiac-Cadillac, Inc.**
• 543 A.2d 775 (Conn. App. 1988)

FACTS On November 7, 1985, Raymond Roy (Roy) agreed to purchase a three-quarter-ton GMC truck with a 350 V-8 engine, standard four-speed transmission, AM radio, painted step-bumper, power steering, and C-Bar from Stephen Pontiac-Cadillac, Inc. (Stephen). The truck was not in stock and had to be ordered from the manufacturer.

On December 5, 1985, the manufacturer notified Stephen that the vehicle ordered was not available because it required a "heavy duty package," which would have increased the cost charged by the manufacturer.

Stephen notified Roy of the problem and offered Roy various options, all of which Roy rejected. Roy notified Stephen that he considered Stephen to have repudiated the contract.

The following month, Roy purchased a three-quarter-ton Chevrolet truck with a 350 V-8 engine from a different dealership. This truck was equipped with the "heavy duty package." Roy also paid more for this truck than he had agreed to pay Stephen for the GMC truck.

Roy sued Stephen, among other things, for breach of contract. The trial court concluded that Stephen's performance under the contract was excused by virtue of the doctrine of impossibility of performance. Roy appealed.

OPINION BORDEN, J. . . . A modern statement of the impossibility doctrine appears in a leading case. . . . "It is now recognized that '[a] thing is impossible in legal contemplation when it is not practicable; and a thing is impracticable when it can only be done at an excessive and unreasonable cost.' The doctrine ultimately represents the ever-shifting line, drawn by courts hopefully responsive to commercial practices and mores, at which the community's interest in having contracts enforced according to their terms is outweighed by the commercial senselessness of requiring performance. When the issue is raised, the court is asked to construct a condition of performance based on changed circumstances, a process

**CASE 21.2
Continued**

which involves at least three reasonably definable steps. First, a contingency—something unexpected—must have occurred. Second, the risk of the unexpected occurrence must not have been allocated either by agreement or by custom. Finally, occurrence of the contingency must have rendered performance commercially impracticable."

The transactions in this case involved the sale of goods. It is therefore controlled by the UCC. [UCC 2-615] . . . provides in relevant part: "Except so far as a seller may have assumed a greater obligation . . . nondelivery in whole or in part by a seller . . . has been made impracticable by the occurrence of a contingency the non-occurrence of which was a basic assumption on which the contract was made. . . ."

Section 2-615 . . . codifies the modern approach to the common law doctrine which is variously termed "impossibility," "impracticability," or "frustration of purpose."

The cases and commentary suggest that "[t]he applicability of the defense of commercial impracticability [under 2-615] turns largely on foreseeability. The relevant inquiry is whether the risk of the occurrence . . . was so unusual or unforeseen and the consequences . . . so severe that to require performance is to grant the buyer an advantage he did not bargain for in the contract. . . .

These rules apply whether the contingency occurs after the agreement was made—so called "supervening impossibility"—or the contingency exists at the time of the agreement—so called "existing impossibility."

This case presents a situation of existing impossibility. This was not a case where the manufacturer changed its product line or product specifications after the dealer agreed to deliver a vehicle using then current product information.

The question, then, is whether [Stephen] had "reason to know the facts that made performance impossible." . . . Under . . . circumstances of undisputed testimony by [Stephen's] agent, [Stephen] had reason to know and should have known that GMC would not build the truck . . . without certain heavy duty equipment. Because [Stephen] was in a position to know that performance would require additional cost, it must be held, as a matter of law, [that Stephen] . . . "assumed a greater obligation" to perform the contract, and was not entitled to be excused from performing that obligation pursuant to [UCC] 2-615.

JUDGMENT   Reversed and remanded.

Casualty to identified goods. Sometimes a contract is for a sale of a specific item or a lot of goods that is destroyed or damaged before the buyer actually receives the goods. Suppose Slashprice Discounters has a dozen Brand X refrigerators of a discontinued model on display. Eleven are green and one is yellow, and no others of that model are available to Slashprice. Bungalow, the buyer, makes clear that he needs the yellow refrigerator because it fits the color scheme of his kitchen. Bungalow buys the yellow refrigerator, but before Slashprice can deliver it, it is destroyed by fire. Is Slashprice liable to Bungalow for failure to deliver the yellow refrigerator?

The answer is "no." Where the contract requires for its performance specific goods that were identified when the contract was made, and the goods suffer casualty (damage) without fault of either party *before* the risk of loss passes to the buyer, then if the loss is *total*, the contract is *avoided*—that is, neither seller nor buyer has any enforceable rights under the contract. If the loss is partial, the buyer may nevertheless demand inspection and at the buyer's option either treat the contract as avoided or accept the goods with due allowance from the contract price, but without any other right against the seller [2-613]. Here, since Slashprice is a merchant, the risk of loss does not pass to Bungalow until he actually receives the goods. Because the loss of the yellow refrigerator is total, Slashprice has no obligation to tender the refrigerator, and Bungalow has no obligation to pay for it. In contrast, if Bungalow had purchased *a* refrigerator of the discontinued model (instead of specifying the yellow one), Slashprice would be obliged to tender a Brand X refrigerator and Bungalow would be obliged to accept it and to make payment. However, if Slashprice's entire stock of the discontinued model had been destroyed, Slashprice would be excused from performance on the ground of impracticability.

Excuse for Substitute Performance. Sometimes the parties to a sales contract agree to a particular method of delivery or of payment. What happens if the *agreed method of delivery* fails—for example, if an agreed type of carrier becomes unavailable without the fault of either party? The parties are required to use a commercially reasonable substitute carrier if one is available [2-614]. If there is no commercially reasonable substitute for the agreed method of delivery, both parties may be excused from their performance obligations on the ground of impracticability.

Where the *agreed means or manner of payment* fails because of domestic or foreign governmental regulation, the seller is required to make delivery only if the buyer provides a payment that is commercially a substantial equivalent. Suppose Swelter Company contracts to sell refrigerators to a foreign buyer, and the buyer's government devalues its currency to one-tenth the value it had at the time of contracting. Swelter is entitled to a payment substantially equivalent to the payment agreed upon and may refuse delivery if the substantial equivalent is not forthcoming. Where the buyer has already taken delivery of the goods, payment in accordance with the regulation discharges the buyer's obligation unless the regulation is discriminatory, oppressive, or predatory.

REMEDIES FOR BREACH OF CONTRACT

A seller of goods expects to receive the price, and the buyer expects to receive goods that conform to the contract. If one party does not perform his or her contractual obligations, the other party may suffer inconvenience, monetary loss, or even a serious disruption of business. To minimize the difficulties that can result from a breach of a sales contract, Article 2 provides a number of remedies for the seller and the buyer. These remedies are available upon a breach or a threatened breach of the performance obligations discussed earlier in this chapter—the obligation of the seller to transfer and to deliver the goods and the obligation of the buyer to accept and to pay for them. The remainder of this chapter discusses the meaning of "breach of contract," the remedies of seller and buyer for breach of contract, and the extent to which the parties may limit remedies by means of the contract.

What Constitutes Breach of Contract

Failure of one party—upon tender of performance by the other party—to perform obligations imposed by the sales contract including any warranty obligations constitutes a breach of the contract. For example, the seller might deliver the wrong kind of goods, unmerchantable or stolen goods, fewer goods than specified in the contract, or no goods at all. Or the seller might deliver the goods later than required by the contract, perhaps too late for the buyer to use them. The buyer might default, thereby breaching the contract, by refusing to accept goods that conform to the contract or by refusing to pay all or part of the price. It should be noted, however, that unless the person entitled to performance *first tenders* his or her own performance, the other person's failure to perform is *not* a breach. Thus, the law of sales requires a positive indication from the person seeking a remedy for breach that that person had a real desire for performance and is not now merely seeking to enforce a contract that both parties had abandoned.

Often, the parties to a sales contract agree that their performances will be carried out at some future time, as where an auto dealer sells a car to a consumer, to be delivered and paid for 3 months from the date of the contract. But before the time scheduled for delivery, the buyer or the seller may express to the other party an intention not to go through with the contract. This refusal in advance to perform the contract is called a **repudiation** (or an *anticipatory breach*) of the contract. Such a repudiation gives the other party "reasonable grounds for insecurity," and the aggrieved (wronged) party has a right to "adequate assurance of due performance" [2-609].

The wrongdoer's failure to provide adequate assurance where such an assurance is warranted is also a repudiation of the contract. Upon a repudiation that will *substantially* impair the value of the contract to the aggrieved party, that party may suspend his or her own performance. Then the aggrieved party may await performance for a commercially reasonable time or take the remedial steps, such as canceling the contract [2-610]. However, the repudiating party (the wrongdoer) is free to retract the repudiation until the aggrieved party cancels the contract, materially changes his or her position, or otherwise indicates that he or she considers the repudiation final [2-611].

Suppose, for example, that Bigspread has ordered 500 cabinets to be built by SigmaCo and installed in Bigspread's apartment complex before June 1, but on May 1 SigmaCo's manufacturing plant and many of the cabinets that have been built are seriously damaged by fire. Bigspread has reason to doubt whether SigmaCo can perform as promised, and Bigspread is entitled, upon making written demand, to an assurance of SigmaCo's due performance. If SigmaCo cannot make such an assurance—for example, by providing reasonable evidence of ability to perform despite the fire—Bigspread may treat the contract as breached and get cabinets elsewhere. Similarly, SigmaCo might have agreed to extend credit to Bigspread only to learn soon afterward that Bigspread has failed to pay other creditors. Bigspread's ability to produce reasonable evidence of creditworthiness and to give valid reasons for failing to pay the other creditors might constitute an adequate assurance of due performance to SigmaCo. The defaulting party has a reasonable time, not to exceed 30 days, to give the assurance.

Remedies of Seller and Buyer

The purpose of the UCC remedies for breach of contract is to put the aggrieved party in as good a position as that party would have been had the contract been fully performed [1-106]. More specifically, the remedies discussed in this chapter are intended to protect three main interests of seller and buyer: the expectation, the reliance, and the restitution interests. The **expectation interest** is the gain that the nondefaulting party expected to make had the defaulting party performed. The **reliance interest** is the interest of the nondefaulting party in recovering costs incurred in preparing for the hoped-for performance. For instance, the seller might have altered machinery solely to fill a special order for the buyer. The buyer might have made special arrangements to accommodate or sell goods that the seller promised but failed to deliver. The **restitution interest** is the interest of the nondefaulting party in recovering a benefit which that party conferred on the other party. The buyer might have made a prepayment on the price of the goods; the seller might have made a partial delivery.

Remedies of the Seller. Remedies are available to a seller where the buyer has breached the contract. The buyer breaches by (1) wrongfully rejecting the goods, (2) wrongfully revoking acceptance of the goods, (3) failing to make a payment due on or before delivery, or (4) repudiating as to all or part of the contract [2-703]. With respect to the goods affected by the breach, the seller may do one or more of the following.

1 The seller may *withhold delivery of the goods* where, for example, the buyer repudiates the contract or fails to make a payment due on or before delivery. Furthermore, where the seller learns before the buyer receives the goods that the buyer is *insolvent,* the seller may refuse to make delivery except for cash and, as noted in the next paragraph, may stop delivery of goods already on their way to the buyer [2-702].

2 The seller may *stop delivery of goods in the possession of a carrier or other bailee* [2-705]. If the reason for stoppage is the buyer's *insolvency,* the seller may stop the delivery, regardless of its size. But where the reason for stoppage is the seller's *insecurity* or something else not involving insolvency of the buyer, the right to stop delivery is limited to carload, truckload, planeload, or larger shipments. The reason for this limitation is to minimize the burden on carriers that would result if sellers were permitted to stop delivery of any shipment, no matter how small. A seller making a small shipment to a solvent buyer of doubtful credit can avoid loss by shipping COD. Moreover, where stoppage occurs for insecurity, the seller is merely suspending performance and awaiting the buyer's assurance of due performance. If the buyer makes the assurance, the seller is not entitled to resell or divert the goods.

3 As a preliminary to the remedy of resale or to an action for the price of the goods, the seller may *identify conforming goods to the contract.* If the goods are unfinished, the seller may either "complete the manufacture and wholly identify the goods to the contract, or cease manufacture and resell for scrap or salvage value, or proceed in any other reasonable manner" [2-704].

4 The seller may *resell the goods and recover damages* [2-706]. The resale must be made in good faith and in a commercially reasonable manner. Where the resale price is lower than the contract price, "the seller may recover the difference between the resale price and the contract price, together with any incidental damages . . . but less expenses saved in consequence of the buyer's breach." *Incidental damages* include, but are not limited to, any commercially reasonable expenses incurred in stopping delivery, transport, and caring for the goods after the buyer's breach, and returning or reselling the goods [2-710].

5 The seller may *recover damages for nonacceptance or repudiation by the buyer.* The usual measure of damages is "the difference between the market price at the time and place for tender and the unpaid contract price, together with any incidental damages . . . but less expenses saved in consequence of the buyer's breach" [2-708(1)]. Suppose that Blacktop contracts to buy a large car from Snazzy Auto for $20,000. Shortly before the time scheduled for delivery, a severe oil shortage develops. Blacktop, thinking that the large car will use more gasoline than might be obtainable, cancels the contract. Because of the oil shortage, and despite Snazzy Auto's best efforts, Snazzy can resell the car for only $10,000. Snazzy is entitled to $10,000 damages (the difference between the market price and the unpaid contract price), together with any incidental damages (such as interest or storage charges that accumulate while Snazzy attempts to find another buyer), but less any expenses that Snazzy saved because of Blacktop's breach (such as labor costs saved because the second buyer declined the undercoating and decorative painting ordered by Blacktop). Since the demand for large cars is weak, this measure of damages will "make the seller whole"—that is, will put the seller in as good a position as Blacktop's performance would have done.

6 When the buyer fails to pay the price as it becomes due, the seller may *recover the price of the goods.* This remedy is limited to **(a)** situations where the buyer has accepted the goods; **(b)** most situations where conforming goods have been lost or damaged after the risk of their loss has passed to the buyer; and **(c)** situations where goods identified to the contract cannot be resold at a reasonable price—for example, where furniture designed in compliance with a customer's specifications is so ugly that it can be sold only as scrap [2-709].

7 To the extent justified by the buyer's breach, the seller may *cancel the contract.*

8 In a *few* situations the seller has a right to *reclaim delivered goods.* For example, the seller may reclaim the goods from the buyer where the contract requires payment on delivery, the goods were delivered, payment was demanded, and the buyer paid by a check that "bounced" [2-507]. However, the seller may *not* reclaim the goods where the buyer has already transferred them to a good faith purchaser for value.

The seller has a right of reclamation in another situation: Where the seller makes a credit sale and discovers that the buyer was insolvent when the goods were delivered, the seller may reclaim them from the buyer (but not from the buyer's good faith purchaser for value) *if* the seller makes written demand within 10 days after the buyer receives the goods [2-702].

The following case deals with the remedy of reselling goods and recovering damages.

CASE 21.3   **Larsen Leasing, Inc. v. Thiele, Inc.** • 749 F. Supp. 821 (W.D. Mich. 1990)

FACTS

Thiele, Inc. (Thiele), manufactured ten trailers which were sold to VenKal Truck Equipment and Service, who sold the trailers to Larsen Leasing, Inc. (Larsen). Larsen, in turn, leased the trailers to S.M.E. Leasing, Inc.

In 1984, S.M.E. began to experience defect problems with the ten trailers, and refused to make lease payments. Larsen repossessed eight of the trailers, and notified all parties that the trailers could be inspected. Later, Larsen also notified that the trailers could not be put into use without complete rebuilding and that Larsen had sought buyers. In that notice it identified that Max Larsen, Inc., a company specializing in sale and repair of heavy vehicles and a sister corporation to Larsen Leasing, Inc., had offered $6,000 each (or $48,000 total) for the eight trailers. After receiving no response from the other parties, Larsen sold the trailers to Max Larsen, Inc., which eight days later sold them to Freuhauf Corporation for a total of $56,000.

Larsen sued Thiele to recover the price of the trailers, but submitted the $48,000 sales figure as representing the sales proceeds. Thiele, learning of the sister corporation's sale of the trailers for $56,000, urged that $56,000 should be the figure used in determining the sales proceeds and sought an $8,000 refund from Larsen.

OPINION

SCOVILLE, U.S. Magistrate . . . The sole issue in dispute is whether the sale of the eight trailers from Larsen Leasing, Inc. to Max Larsen, Inc. was "made in good faith and in a commercially reasonable manner" in accordance with U.C.C. [Section] 2-706. Thiele, in essence, contends that the sale was not commercially reasonable because of the relationship between [the sister corporations], the immediate sale to Freuhauf, and the resulting profit made by Max Larsen, Inc.

There is a dearth of reported case law addressing the question of the commercial reasonableness of a U.C.C. [Section] 2-706 sale to a related corporation for purposes of mitigating losses. One point is clear: A private sale under [UCC] 2-706 to an affiliated corporation is not per se commercially unreasonable. The question, therefore, is whether the sale in this particular case was commercially

**CASE 21.3
Continued**

reasonable in light of all relevant facts. . . . In addressing this question, the pivotal issue . . . concerns allocation of the burden of proof.

When a seller avails himself of the remedy of resale under Article II, he bears the burden of showing that the sale was made in good faith and in a commercially reasonable manner. The seller is in the best position to know what affirmative steps were taken to ensure that any sale was conducted in good faith and in a commercially reasonable manner. . . . Accordingly, the court concludes that Larsen Leasing bears the burden of showing that the sale to Max Larsen, Inc. [met the UCC's burden]. Larsen Leasing has not carried its burden.

The . . . facts reveal that on November 25, 1985, Max Larsen, the principal operator of Larsen Leasing, was informed that he could dispose of the trailers "by public auction or some other commercially reasonable sale." The recitation of facts then jumps six months to May 27, 1986, when counsel for Larsen Leasing informed the other parties that "Larsen Leasing, Inc. has sought out buyers. The best offer is Max Larsen, Inc. . . ." The factual record contains no details concerning attempts by Larsen Leasing to contact other buyers, or any other possible prices for the trailers. This is a fatal deficiency in the record, as the court has no facts upon which to gauge the reasonableness of the sale. The record merely reveals that Larsen Leasing, Inc., run by Max Larsen, did not find a buyer for over six months; yet Max Larsen, Inc., run by the same person, found a buyer in eight days. Simply stated, the absence of any evidence . . . prevents this court from concluding that the sale to Max Larsen, Inc. was commercially reasonable.

Larsen Leasing . . . argues that Thiele should not be heard to cry foul, because Thiele could have bought the trailers for $48,000 and then resold them for a profit. This argument avoids the issue. The burden was not on Thiele to insure that Larsen Leasing's sale was reasonable.

JUDGMENT Find in favor of Thiele, Inc. in the amount of $8,000 plus accrued interest and its costs to be taxed.

Remedies of the Buyer. Remedies are available to a buyer where the seller has breached the contract. The seller breaches (1) by failing to make delivery or (2) by repudiating part or all of the contract. The seller is also in breach where (3) the buyer rightfully rejects the seller's tender or (4) the buyer justifiably revokes acceptance [2-711]. With respect to the goods affected by the seller's breach (including breach of a warranty), the buyer may do one or more of the following:

1 To the extent justified by the seller's breach, the buyer may *cancel the contract.*

2 The buyer may *recover so much of the price as has been paid* and, as explained later, *may have damages.*

3 The buyer may *"cover" and have damages as to all the goods affected,* whether or not the seller has identified them to the contract. The buyer **covers** by making or arranging in good faith a substitution of goods (from another source) for those due from the seller. The buyer may also recover from the seller, as damages, the difference between the cost of cover and the contract price, "together with any incidental or consequential damages . . . but less expenses saved in consequence of the seller's breach" [2-712]. *Incidental damages* resulting from the seller's breach include, for example, expenses reasonably incurred in inspecting, receiving, transporting, or caring for goods rightfully rejected, and expenses reasonably incurred in effecting cover. *Consequential damages* resulting

from the seller's breach include "(a) any loss resulting from general or particular requirements and needs of which the seller at the time of contracting had reason to know and which could not reasonably be prevented by cover or otherwise; and (b) injury to person or property proximately resulting from any breach of warranty" [2-715].

4 The buyer may *recover damages for nondelivery* [2-713]. The measure of damages for nondelivery or for repudiation by the seller is the difference between the market price at the time when the buyer learned of the breach, and the contract price, together with any incidental and consequential damages, less expenses saved as a result of the seller's breach. This remedy applies only when and to the extent that the buyer has not covered.

5 Where an *insolvent* seller identifies goods to the contract but fails to deliver them or repudiates the contract, the buyer may *obtain the identified goods* from the insolvent seller [2-502].

6 The buyer may *obtain specific performance*. "Specific performance may be decreed where the goods are unique or in other proper circumstances" [2-716]. According to the drafters of the Code, "Specific performance is no longer limited to goods which are already specific or ascertained at the time of contracting. The test of uniqueness under this section must be made in terms of the total situation which characterizes the contract." Output and requirements contracts involving a particular source or market present the typical commercial specific performance situation. However, "uniqueness is not the sole basis of the remedy under this section, for the relief may also be granted 'in other proper circumstances,' and inability to cover is strong evidence of 'other proper circumstances'" [2-716, comment 2].

7 In a few situations the buyer may have a *right of replevin* [2-716]. **Replevin** is an action taken to acquire identified goods that the seller has wrongfully withheld from the buyer. Replevin is available (a) where the buyer is unable to effect cover after reasonable effort; (b) where the circumstances reasonably indicate such an effort will be useless; or (c) where the seller has shipped the goods and has kept a security interest in them, and the buyer has made or tendered satisfaction of the security interest. Replevin and specific performance are similar in that the buyer seeks the goods themselves. But replevin is available only where the goods are identified to the contract, while specific performance is available as to unidentified goods.

A buyer may have other remedies in addition to those listed above. For example, upon rightful rejection or justifiable revocation of acceptance, the buyer has a security interest in goods in his or her control for any payments the buyer has made on their price, and for expenses of handling and resale [2-711]. A buyer who has accepted goods and given *timely* notice of defects may recover damages for loss due to any nonconformity of tender [2-714]. Recall that a buyer who has accepted a defective tender is *barred from any remedy*, including a remedy for breach of warranty, unless the buyer *notifies* the seller of the defect within a reasonable time after it has been or should have been discovered.

Finally, upon giving proper notice to the seller, the buyer may "deduct all or any part of the damages resulting from any breach of the contract from any part of the price still due under the same contract" [2-717].

CASE 21.4	**Hendricks & Associates, Inc. v. Daewoo Corporation** • 923 F.2d 209 (1st Cir. 1991)
FACTS	Champion Products, Inc. (Champion), a wholesaler of sporting apparel, provided Hendricks with design specifications for a new line of sportswear (Stripe Collection) which Champion planned to market. Hendricks & Associates, Inc. (Hendricks), an import agent, selected Daewoo Corporation (Daewoo), a Korean concern, to manufacture the Stripe Collection. Champion and Hendricks had a long-standing, ongoing business relationship involving other product lines. There were no direct contractual relations, however, between Daewoo and Champion. Champion placed purchase orders with Hendricks, and Hendricks, in turn, placed purchase orders with Daewoo. The Hendricks purchase orders required Daewoo to deliver the Stripe Collection goods directly to Champion in three shipments. The first shipment had serious quality defects, as did the second shipment. Champion, after inspection, also determined that the third shipment was unacceptable. However, Hendricks and Daewoo had received full payment from Champion. Hendricks brought suit against Daewoo for $213,486.61 in consequential damages, the total amount of what Champion had paid, and for $150,000 in consequential damages for anticipated future profits allegedly lost by Hendricks as a consequence of Champion's termination of the business relationship between Champion and Hendricks. The trial jury awarded Hendricks $275,000 in consequential damages in connection with Champion's payments and an additional $375,000 in consequential damages for Hendricks' loss of future profits. The court then denied Daewoo's motion for a judgment *n.o.v.* and denied a motion for a new trial on the condition that Hendricks remit excess damages on the $275,000 award. The $375,000 award was permitted to stand. Daewoo appealed.
OPINION	CYR, J. . . . The fundamental principle of law upon which damages for breach of contract are assessed is that the injured party shall be placed in the same position he would have been in, if the contract had been performed, so far as loss can be ascertained to have followed as a natural consequence and to have been with the contemplation of the parties as reasonable men as a probable result of the breach. . . . These common law principles comport with the letter and spirit of UCC Section 2-715(2) . . . [which] adopts the rule that a seller is liable for all consequential damages of which he had reason to know in advance, but requires the buyer to mitigate damages. . . . [The Uniform Commercial Code] permits an award of consequential damages for prospective profits lost as "the natural, primary, and probable consequence of the breach," . . . unless 1) the loss was not "such as in the common course of events reasonably might have been expected, at the time the contract was made, to ensue from a breach," (citation omitted) or, 2) the extent of the loss has not been evidenced with a fair degree of certainty. In the idiom of the Uniform Commercial Code, prospective profits are recov-

**CASE 21.4
Continued**

erable as consequential damages insofar as their loss was caused by a breach which deprived the nonbreaching party of "general and particular requirements and needs" of which the breaching party, "at the time of contracting, had reason to know." . . . The requirement of "foreseeability" speaks to what is "reasonably contemplated by the parties. . . ."

There was substantial evidence from which a rational jury could have found that Daewoo had reason to know, when it entered into the Stripe Collection contracts, that there had been a continuous business relationship between Hendricks and Champion dating back to 1983, and that a reasonably prudent seller in Daewoo's position should have realized that it was probable that yet further deliveries of defective garments to Champion would have a severely detrimental effect on the Hendricks-Champion business relationship, even resulting in its outright termination and consequent loss of future Champion contracts.

We can . . . conclude that no loss of prospective profits in an amount even approaching the $375,000 consequential damages award was proven in the manner required by . . . law. . . . When "damages are sought[,] they must be proved and not left . . . to speculation."

On the basis of Hendricks's own evidence, . . . the . . . projection, at most, might expect $45,000 in profits from Champion. . . .

The jury could have found, without impermissible resort to surmise and speculation, that Hendricks was entitled to recover no more than $45,000 for loss of prospective profits as a consequence of Daewoo's breach. Accordingly, the judgment award of consequential damages for loss of prospective profits is affirmed, conditioned on a remittitur [reduction] of damages in excess of $45,000.

JUDGMENT Affirmed and remanded for further proceedings consistent herewith.

Agreements Concerning Remedies; Limitation of Remedies

Under the UCC, reasonable agreements that modify or limit Code remedies will be given effect. Thus, seller and buyer may tailor their remedies to fit their special situation, as long as neither party takes undue advantage of the other.

Agreements Concerning Remedies. Like the general law of contracts, the UCC permits the parties to specify in the contract an amount of money (called **liquidated damages**) that a defaulting party must pay for breaching the contract. A liquidated damages clause is enforceable only if the amount is reasonable in light of (1) the anticipated or actual harm caused by the breach, (2) the difficulty of proving loss, and (3) the impracticality of obtaining an adequate remedy without the clause [2-718]. A term fixing an unreasonably large amount as liquidated damages is void as a penalty. Similarly, a clause fixing an unreasonably small amount would probably be unenforceable because it would be considered unconscionable.

Suppose that Bumpercrop, a rice farmer, is contracting to buy a large irrigation pump from Agri-Equip Dealers. If the pump fails and the crop is damaged, Bumpercrop might have difficulty proving the exact extent of the loss, since no one can predict with certainty how many bushels of rice would have been produced if the pump had not failed. But Bumpercrop might be able to negotiate a liquidated damages clause stating that Agri-Equip will pay a certain amount per acre if the pump fails and causes damage to the crop. If the amount stated in the clause is a reasonable estimate of the anticipated loss, the clause will be enforceable. The amount will be reasonable if, for example, it is based on Bumpercrop's past rice production and if the clause gives Agri-Equip credit for any part of the crop that can be salvaged.

Suppose that Bumpercrop makes a down payment on the pump and the contract states that Agri-Equip may keep the down payment as liquidated damages if Bumpercrop breaches the contract. Then Agri-Equip delivers a conforming pump and Bumpercrop wrongfully rejects it. Whether Agri-Equip may enforce the liquidated damages clause depends on whether the amount of the down payment is a reasonable estimate of Agri-Equip's loss. Agri-Equip is entitled to compensation for loss, but is not permitted to penalize Bumpercrop by enforcing a forfeiture clause. If the down payment is very small compared to the loss, Agri-Equip may keep it and have further damages [2-718]. If the down payment is substantially larger than the loss, Agri-Equip will have to make a partial refund.

Suppose now that Bumpercrop makes a down payment but the contract says nothing about liquidated damages or how the down payment will be treated if Bumpercrop breaches the contract. Then Agri-Equip delivers a conforming pump and Bumpercrop wrongfully rejects it. Under a rule of the UCC, Agri-Equip may, *without having to prove damages,* keep some or all of Bumpercrop's down payment. Agri-Equip may keep 20 percent of the total value of the contract up to a maximum of $500. However, Agri-Equip must return to Bumpercrop any excess unless Agri-Equip can prove that the damages resulting from Bumpercrop's breach exceeded the amount of down payment Agri-Equip is entitled to keep [2-718]. Let's say that Bumpercrop contracted to pay $5,000 for the pump, and made a $1,000 down payment. Upon Bumpercrop's breach, Agri-Equip resold the pump for $5,000. Agri-Equip may keep $500 of Bumpercrop's down payment, but must return the other $500.

Note that the UCC itself, not a clause in the contract, permits the aggrieved seller to keep the money, perhaps because the seller may have minor losses and costs of resale that are difficult to calculate.

BOX 21.1

How Can a Limitation Clause "Fail of Its Essential Purpose"?

The UCC was intended to be both fair and flexible. The drafters acknowledged that they could not put into the Code all the dimensions of transactions. Consequently, many aspects of the UCC are not defined with hard precision. Clauses of limitation of remedies which fail of their essential purposes provide one such example. Courts, when facing an issue of remedy limitation, have to determine its application depending upon the unique circumstances of the case.

Here is one example. In *Wilson Trading Corp. v. David Ferguson, Ltd.,** Wilson contracted to sell yarn to Ferguson. A clause provided that no claims would be allowed for defects discovered after weaving, knitting, or processing. Ferguson knitted a shipment of yarn into sweaters, washed them, and discovered that the color of the yarn had "shaded," meaning that the yarn color varied from piece to piece and within pieces. This "shading" made the sweaters unmarketable. Ferguson gave Wilson prompt notice of the defect, which, Ferguson alleged, could not reasonably be discovered in the normal manufacturing process until after knitting and washing. The court held that if Ferguson could establish its factual allegations at trial, the clause of limitation would have "failed its 'essential purpose'" and would have deprived the buyer of the value of the bargain. Consequently, the clause would have to "give way to the general Code rule that a buyer has a reasonable time to notify the seller of breach of contract after he discovers or should have discovered the defect." ∎

*244 N.E.2d 685 (N.Y. 1968).

Limitation of Remedies. The remedies provided by Article 2 may be limited—or supplemented—by agreement of the parties. For example, the contract between Bumpercrop and the seller of the irrigation pump might have limited the seller's liability to the replacement of defective parts. However, if the limitation is unconscionable, it will not be enforced. In transactions involving *consumer* goods, the limitation of consequential damages for *personal* injury is presumed to be unconscionable [2-719]. In other transactions the limitation of damages is not *presumed* to be unconscionable, but the aggrieved person may prove that the limitation was in fact unconscionable.

Sometimes a clause of limitation appears to be fair and reasonable, but because of the circumstances that actually arose, it "fails of its essential purpose" so that the buyer is left without a remedy. In such a situation the limitation is ineffective and the general remedy provisions of the Code apply.

Also, to the extent described in Chapter 49, the Magnuson-Moss Warranty Act prohibits the exclusion of implied warranties where a supplier of a "consumer product" has made a full warranty. However, a *conspicuous* exclusion or limitation of *consequential damages* will be enforced if it appears on the face of the consumer product warranty.

SUMMARY

The obligation of the seller is to transfer and deliver the goods, and that of the buyer is to accept and pay for them. The seller meets the delivery obligation by making a tender of delivery. Tender requires that the seller put and hold conforming goods at the buyer's disposition and give the buyer any notice reasonably necessary to enable the buyer to take delivery.

Within limits imposed by the Code, such as the one pertaining to installment contracts, the buyer may reject a tender that fails in any respect to conform to the contract. The seller has a right to "cure" an improper tender before, and sometimes after, the time for performance has expired.

The buyer's obligation to accept and to pay is conditioned on the buyer's right to inspect the goods. Upon acceptance, the buyer is obligated to pay the contract price. In two main situations, the buyer may revoke acceptance of nonconforming goods. Unless otherwise agreed, the buyer may pay in any customary way. The seller may require payment in money but must give any extension of time reasonably necessary for the buyer to procure such a payment.

The parties may be excused from their performance obligations if the agreed performance has been made commercially impracticable by an unforeseen occurrence that alters the essential nature of the performance. Where an agreed method of payment or delivery fails, the aggrieved party may be entitled to a substitute performance.

A party to a sales contract is entitled to a remedy if the other party is in breach of the contract. The purpose of the UCC remedies is to put the aggrieved party in as good a position as the other party's full performance would have done. An aggrieved seller may, for example, withhold delivery of the goods, stop delivery of goods in the possession of a carrier, or have an action for the price; an aggrieved buyer may cancel the contract, "cover" and have damages as to the goods affected by the seller's breach, or have other remedies.

The remedies of Article 2 may be limited or supplemented by agreement of the parties to the contract. An unconscionable limitation of remedies will not be enforced. Where a supplier of a consumer product makes a full warranty, the Warranty Act requires that an exclusion or limitation of consequential damages appear conspicuously on the face of the warranty.

REVIEW QUESTIONS

1. (a) In general, how does a seller fulfill the seller's tender obligation? **(b)** What specific acts are required for a seller to fulfill the tender obligation in a shipment contract?

2. In what kinds of situations may a seller "cure" an improper tender or delivery?

3. (a) What constitutes acceptance of goods? **(b)** What is the legal effect of acceptance?

4. (a) How is the buyer's right to inspect the goods related to the buyer's obligation to accept the goods? (b) How does a COD clause in a sales contract affect the buyer's right to inspect the goods?

5. (a) In general, under what circumstances may a buyer reject the seller's tender of delivery? (b) With regard to an installment contract, under what circumstances may a buyer reject an installment? Cancel the whole contract?

6. In what two main situations may a buyer revoke acceptance of goods?

7. Explain the meaning and legal effect of commercial impracticability as an excuse for nonperformance.

8. (a) Illustrate how a sales contract can be breached by the seller and by the buyer. (b) With regard to default, explain the significance of "reasonable grounds for insecurity." (c) What is "repudiation"? (d) Under what circumstances may an aggrieved party have a remedy for repudiation?

9. (a) Under what circumstances may a seller recover the price of goods when the buyer fails to make payment? (b) Describe three other remedies of the seller.

10. (a) Explain the meaning and significance of "cover" as a buyer's remedy. (b) Describe three other remedies of the buyer.

11. (a) Under what circumstances will a liquidated damages clause be enforceable? (b) May a seller keep a defaulting buyer's down payment? Explain.

12. To what extent may a sales contract limit the remedies provided by Article 2?

CASE PROBLEMS

1. The Linscotts bought a double-width mobile home to be delivered and set up on a rural lot. Delivery and setup were completed in February, and the Linscotts moved in. They immediately encountered problems: The windows and storm windows were defective; the roof leaked; and the insulation was so inadequate that the furnace ran constantly without sufficiently warming the living areas. When spring arrived, the factory representative made some repairs. When summer arrived, he offered to install fiberglass insulation. The Linscotts refused to allow him to reinsulate unless he used foam core insulation. This request was refused, and Smith, the seller, made no further effort to repair the home. In the fall and winter other troubles developed. Copper water pipes froze and burst, electrical service went out, a hot water heater burned out, kitchen cabinets came apart, the floor cracked, and an oven malfunctioned. The Linscotts sued Smith for damages. The trial court held that the Linscotts were not entitled to damages because they had improperly prevented Smith from curing the defects. The Linscotts appealed. Was the trial court in error?

2. Oberg bought a new Chevrolet from Phillips and soon discovered numerous defects in engine performance, body, steering, paint, and accessories. During the first 3 months of Oberg's ownership, the car was in the seller's shop for 30 whole days and parts of 12 to 15 more days. After an unsuccessful repair session near the end of the first 2 months, Oberg gave Phillips a specific amount of time to repair the car. Phillips did not comply. Oberg then, in writing, revoked his acceptance of the car, and sued Phillips for breach of contract. Phillips contended that all the defects were trivial and that Oberg therefore had no basis for revoking his acceptance. Did Oberg have a legal basis for revoking?

3. Automated Controls, Inc. (ACI), agreed to design, manufacture, and sell to MIC Enterprises, Inc. (MIC), a system of solid-state electronic control boxes for use on center-pivot "Blu-Max" irrigation machinery made by RVC, Inc., and distributed by MIC. ACI was to deliver six control boxes and a timer by January 1976 for field testing. By February 16, 1976, ACI could deliver only one box. But, as ACI knew, timing was critical to MIC in coordinating the manufacture and the marketing of the Blu-Max machines. Consequently, MIC placed an order for a quantity of the untested control devices to be delivered in twelve monthly installments. ACI delivered some, and MIC paid for them. However, after several attempts, ACI could not make the control boxes work, and in June 1976 MIC canceled the contract. ACI sued MIC for breach of contract. Was MIC within its rights in canceling the contract?

4. Weller agreed to manufacture ice scrapers and snow brushes, place Talon's name on them, and ship them directly to Talon's customers. Under the agreement, Weller extended $47,000 credit to Talon. After checking Talon's credit record, Weller's president tried to locate Talon's president, but Weller's numerous phone calls were never returned. Weller became concerned about payment and demanded from Talon assurances of performance. Failing to receive them, Weller suspended shipments to Talon's customers for about 10 days. During this time Weller and Talon amended their agreement to give Talon more time to pay. Shipments resumed. Talon's debt increased to about $74,000. Weller sued for the amount owed. Talon argued that the amended agreement was not binding because Talon signed it under duress as a result of Weller's wrongful suspension of shipments. Weller contended that the suspension was rightful because Weller had reasonable grounds for insecurity. Was Weller's suspension of shipments to Talon's customers wrongful?

5. CIS, a computer broker, agreed to deliver a satisfactory computer to the Huntington Beach Union High School District, and to do so by the end of July. CIS was unable to make delivery. Because the offers of other bidders expired on July 12, School District had to rebid the contract and to pay a price almost $60,000 higher than CIS's contract price. School District sued CIS for $60,000 in general damages plus almost $10,000 in consequential damages. The trial court awarded School District the $10,000 in consequential damages, but it awarded only $12,000 in general damages on the ground that the second-lowest bid in the original bidding exceeded CIS's by only that much. School District appealed. Should the trial court's award of damages be upheld?

6. Begley was injured in an accident when the brakes on his Jeep failed. In 1976 Begley sued Reliable Motor Co. (the dealer) and American Motors Corp. (the manufacturer) for damages, alleging defects in the braking system and breach of warranty. Two years and five months later Reliable and AMC in turn sued the manufacturer of the brakes (Bendix Corp.) and the manufacturer of the brake fluid (Wagner Electric Corp.) for breach of warranty. Bendix and Wagner had no previous notice of Begley's suit. Bendix and Wagner denied liability, alleging unreasonable delay on the part of Reliable and AMC in giving notice of the breach of warranty. Should Bendix and Wagner be held liable to Reliable and AMC?

7. Rita Donohue purchased two refrigerators, one for use in her home and the other for use in her business. On the face of each sales contract was the following clause in large type: "IF THIS REFRIGERATOR IS DEFECTIVE, SELLER'S LIABILITY SHALL BE LIMITED TO THE REPLACEMENT OF DEFECTIVE PARTS OR A REFUND OF THE PURCHASE PRICE AS THE SELLER ELECTS." The motors of both refrigerators were defective and shorted out, causing fires. The fire in Donohue's home damaged the kitchen and injured her. The fire at Donohue's place of business destroyed an expensive copier and injured an employee. The seller agreed to refund the purchase price, but it refused to pay any other damages. Donohue sued the seller for all damages caused by the defective refrigerators. How should the case be decided as to **(a)** the refrigerator in Donohue's home and **(b)** the refrigerator in Donohue's place of business?

CHAPTER 22

Sales Warranties and Products Liability

Of the billions of products sold worldwide each day, a small but significant number are defective. Some defects are the fault of negligent manufacturers or of retailers that negligently prepare goods for sale. But often manufacturers are not at fault. Because individual inspection of mass-produced goods is not feasible, defects may escape detection despite excellent quality control efforts. Occasionally a product is so new and complex that its defects are not readily apparent to the seller or the buyer.

Whatever the degree of fault on the part of sellers, defective products exact a heavy toll of economic loss and personal injury. How this loss should be distributed is of great concern to sellers, injured persons, insurance companies, and foreign and domestic governments. It is also the subject of a collection of legal rules called *products liability law*. That law defines the obligation of sellers to compensate buyers, users, and even bystanders for loss or injuries caused by defective products.

Products liability losses are of two basic kinds: direct and indirect (consequential). *Direct loss* consists of the decreased value of the goods themselves as a result of a defect. This kind of loss is compensated for by an award of *direct* or *general damages*—for example, the cost of replacing or repairing the defective goods. *Indirect losses* are those caused by defective goods, in addition to the decreased value of the goods themselves—for example, personal injuries, damage to the property of others, or business interruption caused by the defective product. This kind of loss is compensated for by an award of *consequential damages*. An illustration follows.

Bloom, a commercial vegetable gardener, purchases a new garden tractor from SupplyCo for $3,000 cash. Because of a manufacturing defect, the engine explodes without warning the second time Bloom uses the tractor, injuring Bloom and a neighbor passing by on the sidewalk, and causing a fire that destroys the tractor and the neighbor's house. As indicated in Chapter 21, Bloom may revoke his acceptance of the tractor and recover the purchase price from SupplyCo. If SupplyCo is solvent, Bloom is thus protected from the loss of the tractor itself. But what if SupplyCo is insolvent? May Bloom recover the value of the tractor from the manufacturer? Perhaps more important to Bloom and his neighbor, whom, if anyone, may they hold liable for the consequential losses—the personal injuries to themselves and the loss of the neighbor's house? These losses are substantial and may be far beyond SupplyCo's ability to pay. Under the modern law of products liability, both SupplyCo *and* the manufacturer (among others) might be liable for the losses.

Products liability law is a good example of how law evolves in response to changing social conditions. Centuries ago, goods produced for sale were relatively simple products, and buyers usually purchased them directly from the makers. Buyers were expected to examine the goods and to judge for themselves whether the goods were free from defects and fit for the buyers' purposes—caveat emptor: "Let the buyer beware." Under the law of that era, a person injured by a defective product could not maintain an action for damages unless he or she was "in privity of contract" (had a direct contractual relationship) with the seller, and then only if the seller had expressly guaranteed the quality of the goods. If purchases were made directly from the maker, as was usual, the buyer would be in privity of contract with the maker. If the buyer purchased an article from someone other than the maker, the buyer had no right of action against the manufacturer.

Then, during the mid-1700s came the industrial revolution. Machinery and power tools replaced hand tools. Large-scale industrial production led to mass advertising and to complicated systems for distributing huge amounts of goods. Increasingly, goods were distributed in packaged form by "middlemen" who knew little about their quality. Products became vastly more complicated and dangerous. No longer could purchasers easily inspect the goods and judge for themselves the merits of what they had bought. A seller's representations of claims whether by advertising or other means of communication could became dangerous because purchasers of unfamiliar products were no longer able to question the manufacturer personally or to recognize false statements if made. As industry developed, the doctrine of caveat emptor and the privity requirement made less and less sense.

Despite increased danger to the public from defective products, the courts were slow to discard the privity-of-contract requirement. In keeping with the laissez-faire philosophy of the nineteenth century, the courts were reluctant to impose liability on a seller with whom an injured person had not contracted. Moreover, there was strong sentiment among the courts and legislatures for protecting industry from liabilities that might impede its growth. As the use of middlemen increased, the privity requirement became a substantial barrier to the recovery of damages by injured consumers. Their contracts normally would be with retailers, not with manufacturers, and without privity of contract there could be no recovery of damages from the manufacturers who had produced the defective goods. In Figure 22.1, B (buyer) is in privity of contract with R (retailer), but not with W (wholesaler) or M (manufacturer).

In the early 1900s, the courts began slowly to discard the privity-of-contract requirement. During recent decades, court decisions and legislation (especially the Uniform Commercial Code) have made dramatic changes in the law with respect to who should bear the cost of injury resulting from the use of defective products. The law has developed a number of theories of products liability that shift the burden of loss from the injured buyer, user, or bystander to the manufacturer, wholesaler, or retailer; and the privity requirement has been virtually aban-

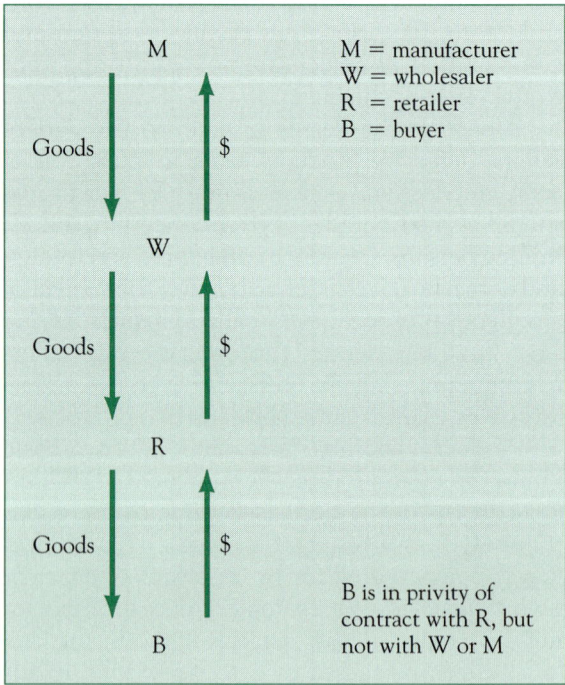

Figure 22.1   Privity of contract.

doned. The most common causes of action available to the injured person have their basis in two general areas of law—in contract and in tort. From these two general areas, there are several legal theories upon which to base a suit. In contract, two types of legal action based on warranty theories might be available to an injured plaintiff: breach of express product warranties and breach of implied warranties. In tort, the bases of legal action are basically three: negligence, strict liability, and misrepresentation. Frequently, an injured plaintiff makes claims based on all possible theories in the same complaint. If one cause of action does not fit the situation, the plaintiff might succeed with another.

While this chapter appears in the Sales portion of this text, products liability law is a subject area involving much more than what is contained in the Uniform Commercial Code. This chapter will start with UCC warranty provisions as a basis for products liability, and then will turn to tort concepts of liability for injurious products.

CONTRACT AS A BASIS OF PRODUCTS LIABILITY

In contract law, most situations in which liability is found for defective products revolve variously around warranties. And much of the law of warranty is found in Article 2 of the UCC and in the federal Magnuson-Moss Warranty Act, which governs consumer goods (see Chapter 49). Here, because they are most pertinent to products liability, the important warranty provisions of Article 2 will be explored.

Recall that Article 2 applies specifically to the "sales of goods," but UCC warranty provisions have been applied "by analogy" to some transactions other than sales, such as leases of goods. The warranty provisions of Article 2A apply directly to leases of goods and are nearly identical to those of Article 2, but also recall that Article 2A, which governs leases, has been adopted by only twelve states. Consequently, whether applied directly or by "analogy," the warranty provisions of Article 2 are an important collection of rules in products liability.

Originally, the term "warranty" meant a promise or an agreement by the seller that (1) the thing sold had a certain level of quality or (2) the seller had title to the thing and could confer ownership upon the buyer. Today, under the UCC, warranties created by the seller's promises (or *other* "affirmations" of fact) are called **express warranties.** Article 2 of the UCC recognizes express warranties of title and express warranties of quality.

After the industrial revolution, courts began to impose warranty obligations upon the seller where, for example, the seller was *silent* about whether he or she intended to make a warranty. Warranties that are imposed by law are called **implied warranties.** Under Article 2, a seller can be subject to implied warranties of quality (1) where the seller says nothing about warranties, or (2) where the seller attempts to exclude implied warranties but fails to use properly the methods of exclusion required by the Code. Implied warranties are *in addition* to any express warranty that the seller might have made. Article 2 also imposes a warranty of title on most sellers who are silent about what ownership rights the buyer is to receive; but for the reason stated later in this chapter, this nonverbal title warranty is not classified as an implied warranty.

The main function of a warranty is to establish the characteristics of a thing (the kind of ownership or the level of quality) to which the purchaser or another person is entitled as a result of the existence of the warranty. In a sale of goods, a warranty may be the only practical source of remedy for loss due to a defect in the title to or the quality of the goods. A plaintiff is entitled to damages upon proof that (1) a warranty was made (or imposed by law), (2) the product does not conform to the standard of title or of quality established by the warranty, and (3) the plaintiff suffered harm as a result of the breach of the warranty.

In the following discussion of UCC title and quality warranties, special attention is given to how warranties are made; what kind of ownership or level of quality is established by a warranty; how a seller may exclude warranties; and who, besides the buyer, is protected if a warranty is made.

UCC Warranties of Title

Nature and Scope of Title Warranties. If a seller says to a buyer, "I own these goods free and clear," the seller has made an express warranty of title [2-313]. But usually the parties to a sale are silent as to title. If the parties are silent, the Code imposes upon the seller a warranty that (1) the title conveyed shall be good and its transfer rightful and (2) the goods shall be delivered free from any security interest or other lien of which the buyer at the time of contracting has no actual knowledge [2-312].

Sometimes goods are manufactured and sold in violation of trademark or patent rights. To protect the buyer, the Code imposes upon a *merchant-seller regularly dealing in goods of the kind* a warranty that the goods do not infringe upon the trademark or patent of any third person. However, if a buyer furnishes specifications for goods to be assembled, prepared, or manufactured by the seller, the buyer is responsible for avoiding infringement, unless the buyer and the seller have agreed to the contrary.

Exclusion or Modification of Title Warranties. Sometimes goods are sold "as is" or "with all faults." Section 2-316(3) permits sellers to disclaim "all implied warranties" by the use of such expressions. Are these expressions sufficient to exclude the nonverbal warranty of good title, rightful transfer, and freedom from liens? The answer is no. A person who buys something "as is" may be willing to take his or her chances as to the quality of the thing, but the buyer still expects to become the owner. To protect the buyer from an unexpected exclusion of the nonverbal warranty of title, Article 2 *limits the meaning of implied warranty to "implied warranty of quality."*

The nonverbal warranty of good title may be excluded or modified *only* by specific language or by circumstances that give the buyer reason to know that the seller does not have or claim ownership [2-312]. The "specific language" requirement could be met by the seller's statement that the seller does not warrant title, or that the seller warrants title only to a limited extent. However, the buyer is expected to recognize the fact that in certain circumstances sellers do not warrant title. For example, sales by sheriffs, executors, and foreclosing lienors are so out of the ordinary commercial course that their peculiar character is immediately apparent to the buyer. No warranty obligation is imposed upon such a seller.

UCC Warranties of Quality

A warranty of quality establishes a level of quality to which goods must conform if the seller is to avoid liability for breach of warranty. The level of quality established by an express warranty is determined by the seller's statements or other representations. The level of quality established by an implied warranty is measured by the concept of "merchantability" or of "fitness for a particular purpose."

The Code permits a seller to disclaim all implied warranties or, if the seller wishes, to substitute for an implied warranty a less burdensome express warranty. Yet the nature of the marketing process, certain features of the Code, the Magnuson-Moss Warranty Act, and the growing tendency of courts to resolve warranty doubts in favor of consumers limit the opportunities for a seller to escape warranty liability altogether.

Express Warranties of Quality. A seller may refrain from making express warranties, but express warranties can arise in ways that the seller might not anticipate. Under Section 2-313, *any affirmation of fact or promise made by the seller to the buyer which relates to the goods and becomes part of the basis of the bargain* creates an express warranty. Any seller who advertises goods is subject to having the advertising claims construed as factual, and some courts have held that a retail seller has adopted the statements made by the manufacturer, even though the retailer personally has said nothing concerning the goods.

Furthermore, under the Code an express warranty can arise without the use of words. *Any description of the goods*, including drawings and sketches, or *any sample or model* "which is made part of the basis of the bargain" creates an express warranty that the goods will conform to the description, sample, or model [2-313]. As long as businesspeople make normal use of advertising, models, samples, and diagrams, express warranties are likely to be made.

An express warranty must rest on some statement or other affirmation of *fact*, not on mere opinion or "sales puffing" of the seller. Despite the strong movement away from caveat emptor, the buyer is expected to detect and discount such nonfactual sales talk as "this is the finest stereo on the market." Statements made by sellers may range from those that are clearly opinion to those that are clearly fact. In the middle are statements that a court may have to interpret as either fact or opinion. The background against which a statement is made becomes important in interpreting it. Thus, a former garage mechanic who sold a used car to a nurse was held to have made an express warranty when he stated, "This is a car I can recommend. . . . It is in A-1 shape."[1]

Under the Code's "basis of the bargain" test, postsale talk may, and often does, create an express warranty. Even though an affirmation is made after a contract has been entered into, the affirmation may create expectations that the product will do what the seller promised. For instance, a person who buys a packaged product and later reads descriptive information contained within the carton may be led to make a use of the product that he or she would not have made if the seller had remained silent. The statement should be regarded as an indicator of quality level and as an aspect of the bargain. Moreover, under the "basis of the bargain" test, assurances given when the goods are delivered and advertisements that are read after the sale could create express warranties.

Implied Warranties of Quality. Unless warranties are properly excluded, the Code imposes an implied warranty of merchantability, or an implied warranty of fitness for a particular purpose, or both. The warranties differ with regard to who makes them, how they are made, what quality level is established by each, and how they may be excluded.

Implied warranty of merchantability. A warranty that the goods shall be merchantable (fit for their *ordinary* purposes) is implied in a contract for their sale if the seller is a *merchant* with respect to goods of that kind [2-314]. A seller is a merchant if he or she deals in goods of the kind sold or gives the appearance of having knowledge of the goods. Normally, a person making an isolated sale of goods is not a merchant and therefore is not subject to the implied warranty of merchantability. However, the nonmerchant seller of goods is required by the good faith provision of the Code to disclose any material hidden defects of which he or she has knowledge.

To be merchantable, goods must meet the minimum standards of merchantability set by the Code. Fungible goods must be of fair, average quality within the description. All goods must pass without objection in the trade under the contract description; be fit for the ordinary purposes for which such goods are used; run of even kind, quality, and quantity within each unit and among all units; be adequately contained, packaged, and labeled as the sales agreement may require; and conform to the promises or affirmations of fact made on the container or label, if any [2-314(2)].

Other attributes of merchantability may arise by usage of trade or through the development of case law. Goods usually are not "fit" for their ordinary purposes unless they can be used safely. The degree of safety required for a product to be considered merchantable is developed in the case law. Some courts hold that goods may be fit for their ordinary purposes even though a few persons suffer allergic reactions or other isolated injuries not common to ordinary people. The warranty of merchantability is not breached unless the goods fall below the required level of quality.

Implied warranty of fitness for a particular purpose. A warranty of fitness for a particular (special) purpose is implied where, at the time of contracting, three circumstances exist: (1) the seller has reason to know any particular purpose for which the goods are required, (2) the seller has reason to know that the buyer is relying on the seller's skill or judgment to select or furnish suitable goods, and (3) the buyer actually relies

---

[1]*Wat Henry Pontiac Co. v. Bradley*, 210 P.2d 348 (Okla. 1949).

on the seller's skill or judgment [2-315]. Suppose that Pinnacle, a budding sportsperson, tells the owner of a sporting goods store that Pinnacle will soon go on a mountain-climbing expedition for the first time and needs some good climbing shoes. The owner says nothing but produces a pair of climbing shoes that Pinnacle quickly examines and buys. The seller has made an implied warranty of fitness for a particular purpose. The seller knows the particular purpose for which Pinnacle needs the shoes. Since the seller knows that Pinnacle is a novice climber, the seller also has reason to know that Pinnacle is relying on the seller to supply shoes that are suitable for that purpose. (The fitness warranty would be express if the store owner had said, "These shoes are just what you are looking for.") The situation would be different if the owner had sold climbing shoes to "Cleats" Morton, a professional mountain climber with whom the seller had dealt many times before and who had always made his own choice of shoes, usually disregarding the seller's advice. The seller would have no reason to believe that Cleats relied on the seller's judgment. Therefore, an element necessary for an implied warranty of fitness to arise would be missing. Merchants and nonmerchants alike can be subject to an implied warranty of fitness.

An increasing number of judges hold that advertising can contribute to the existence of an implied warranty of fitness. A seller who advertises his or her product expects, in part, to persuade buyers that the product is suitable for a certain purpose or purposes. A warranty could be implied even though the seller never meets the buyer.

Under an implied warranty of fitness, the goods are defective if not fit for the particular purpose for which they were furnished. But how is the minimum level of fitness for a particular purpose to be defined? Is a lotion unfit if one user out of millions is allergic to ordinarily safe ingredients? The difficult question, as yet unresolved, is how much harm is tolerable, given the general utility of a product. Most courts hold that a product is fit if it is safe for use by "normal" people. This approach works well enough when the number of unusually sensitive users is very small and their injuries are slight. If injury is widespread or severe, the court could find a breach of the warranty of fitness, find the seller negligent (e.g., for failure to provide conspicuous warnings), or impose strict liability in tort, which will be discussed later in this chapter. The problem of defining the minimum level of quality exists also with regard to the warranty of merchantability.

Case 22.1 discusses whether express and implied warranties were present in a contract to replace a roof.

CASE 22.1

Mennonite Deaconess Home & Hospital, Inc. v. Gates Engineering Co.
• 363 N.W.2d 155 (Neb. 1985)

FACTS The Beatrice Community Hospital (hospital), owned by Mennonite Deaconess Home and Hospital, Inc. (plaintiff), discovered leaks in the roof over the geriatrics wing. After unsuccessful attempts to repair the roof, the hospital decided to replace it. One option was to replace it with a flat, layered roof of the type originally installed. Another option, the one chosen by the hospital, was a one-ply roofing system consisting of a rubberlike material attached to the outside perimeter of the building and rubber sheeting laid loose across the roof, sealed at the overlaps, and weighted down with rock ballast.

Hospital authorities met with Leonard Russell, an agent of Gates Engineering Co. (defendant), which manufactured a single-ply roofing system, and David Nece, president of Armstrong Construction Co., which was to install it. Russell said, "I came along with Mr. Nece to show and explain the Gates single-ply sys-

CASE 22.1 Continued

tem." Russell also provided brochures describing the roofing system. One read in part, "WARRANTY PROVISIONS: Gates Engineering provides single source responsibility for roofing and flashing with each roofing system. Whether roofing new construction or re-roofing on existing structure, each GACOFLEX system requires consideration and approval by Gates' technical staff and installation by a registered system roofing contractor. Under these conditions a 10-year roof warranty is available." Gates's prior approval was required for a contractor to be a registered System I roofing contractor. A second brochure stated in part, "Each installation is carefully considered and approved by Gates's technical staff and installed by a Registered System I Roofing Contractor."

The hospital contracted with Armstrong and Gates for installation of the Gates roofing system and a 10-year warranty. Then representatives of all three inspected some roof projections and an expansion joint about which the hospital was concerned. The hospital was assured that the Gates system would handle the problem.

During installation, a field representative of Gates was present on the job for about two-thirds of the time. Later, Gates refused to issue the warranty because of numerous errors that Armstrong made in installing the roof. Soon after the Gates inspection, the roof began leaking. Gates and Armstrong refused to make repairs, and the hospital eventually replaced the entire roof with a system from another company. The hospital learned about a year after the installation of the Gates system that Armstrong had never been registered by Gates and had never installed a one-ply roof before. The hospital sued Gates for breach of express and implied warranties of the Gates roofing system. From a jury verdict for the hospital, Gates appealed.

OPINION

KRIVOSHA, C.J. . . . [We first] turn to the question of whether the transaction upon which suit was brought was a "sale of goods" within the meaning of the Uniform Commercial Code or, rather, was a contract for the rendering of "services." If the transaction was really a contract for services and not a sale of goods, the provisions of [Article 2 of the Code] do not apply. . . . [T]he U.C.C. applies where the principal purpose of the contract is the sale of goods, even though in order for the goods to be utilized, some installation is required. . . .

We believe that an examination of the contract, the brochures, and the evidence adduced at trial [make clear] that this contract had as its predominant factor the roofing material manufactured by Gates and only incidentally involved installation by a contractor approved by Gates. The evidence establishes that the hospital was not simply purchasing a new roof of any type or description. Quite to the contrary, . . . the hospital determined, after careful consideration, to use the one-ply system specifically manufactured and supplied by Gates. The contract specifically identified the type of roof to be installed and further identified it in such a manner that nothing other than the Gates material could be used. It is clear to us that what was being purchased here was a completed roof of the type manufactured by Gates, though installed by others approved by Gates. . . . [T]he provisions of the [U.C.C.] apply. . . .

Gates agrees that an express warranty may be created in an advertising brochure, but argues that before such warranty may arise, the language in the

**CASE 22.1
Continued**

brochure must evidence a clear intent to create the warranty. Gates then argues that because it was merely selling the roofing material, exclusive of installation, and that because the parties agree that the failure of the roof was the result of poor installation and not defective material, there is insufficient evidence in the record to sustain the verdict of the jury. We believe . . . [that] Gates simply misconstrues the nature of the transaction. The hospital was not contracting for the purchase and installation of any [common] roof. It was, in fact, purchasing a "roofing system," designed, manufactured, and supplied by Gates and installed by persons approved by Gates under its supervision. . . .

. . . Gates attempted to explain away the language of the brochures by maintaining that the statements contained in [them] were the things that an architect or contractor was responsible to perform if a good job was to be accomplished and if the warranty was to be issued. The evidence simply does not support that view. . . .

The evidence [revealed] that statements made by the Gates representative at the initial meeting were intended to be relied upon by the hospital. One of those statements was that before Armstrong would be permitted to install the roof, it would have to be a registered System I applicator. . . . [Another was that] the roof would be installed by a registered System I roofing contractor . . . in a manner conducive to good workmanship. . . . Further, the hospital was assured that someone from Gates would be on the roof during installation. Obviously, the point of having a representative of Gates on the roof during installation was . . . to ensure that the material was installed correctly. Yet, notwithstanding the presence of that representative, the record discloses that the installation was defective. . . . All of these statements constituted affirmations of fact or promises which constituted express warranties, breached by Gates. . . . We [now] turn to the question of whether there was a breach of [the] implied warranties . . . of merchantability [and] fitness [provided for in the Code]. . . .

. . . Gates argues that . . . the material itself was not defective and, in fact, the damage which resulted was caused by the defective installation and not by the condition of the goods. . . . [However, the] hospital was not purchasing raw material. It was purchasing a roofing system which was partially dependent upon proper installation. . . .

To establish a breach of [the] implied warranty of merchantability, there must be proof that there was a deviation from the standard of merchantability at the time of sale and that such deviation caused the plaintiff's injury. . . . In order for the goods to be merchantable under [Section] 2-314, they must be at least such as are fit for the ordinary purposes for which such goods are used. . . . The record is without dispute that Gates was to provide the hospital with a one-ply System I roof which would not leak when installed. That, they did not do. This, then, was evidence of a breach of [the warranty of merchantability].

The conditions under which a breach of [the] implied warranty of fitness exist[s] are also present in this case. . . . [T]o recover for a breach of an implied warranty of fitness, the purchaser must prove that (1) the seller had reason to know of the buyer's particular purpose, (2) the seller had reason to know that the buyer was relying on the seller's skill or judgment to furnish the appropriate goods, and (3) the buyer . . . relied upon the seller's skill or judgment. . . .

CASE 22.1 Continued	Once again, we believe that the evidence was sufficient to permit a jury to find . . . the necessary elements. Certainly, the jury could find that Gates had reason to know of the hospital's particular purpose for the roof. Likewise, the jury could find that Gates had reason to know that the hospital was relying on Gates' skill or judgment to furnish the appropriately installed roof. Indeed, the hospital told Gates it was. And, finally, the jury could . . . find that the hospital relied upon Gates' skill or judgment. It was only after the hospital was contacted by the representatives of Gates and assured of the quality of the roof that it purchased the Gates roof rather than another one-ply roof.
JUDGMENT	Affirmed.

Exclusion or Modification of Quality Warranties. Once made, an *express warranty* is difficult to disclaim. Section 2-316(1) states a general principle that words or conduct creating an express warranty, and words or conduct negating warranty, shall be construed wherever reasonable as consistent with each other, but that "negation or limitation is inoperative to the extent that such construction is unreasonable." Suppose that Slick, a used car dealer, makes an express oral warranty in the sale of a used car to Hapless. If the contract that Hapless signs contains a disclaimer of "all warranties, express or implied," the disclaimer will be unenforceable. Slick has taken the trouble to make an express warranty that is calculated to capture Hapless's attention. To give effect to Slick's disclaimer of his own express warranty would be an unreasonable action.

What if Slick makes an express oral warranty but the contract disclaims all warranties and further states that the writing is the final and exclusive expression of the agreement? Will the parol evidence rule of Section 2-202 prevent proof of the oral warranty? It might, but Hapless might be able to demonstrate that Hapless did not agree that the writing should be considered final and exclusive. Under Section 2-202, the parties must agree. Litigation of the agreement issue is difficult because at its heart is the credibility of Hapless and Slick on a question of fact. The same is true about the question of whether Slick actually made the express warranty.

Implied warranties of quality may be excluded in either of two ways: (1) by the buyer's examining the goods or refusing to examine them or (2) by the use of appropriate exclusionary language. If the buyer examines the goods (or a sample or model) before entering the contract, there is no implied warranty with regard to obvious defects. Nor is there an implied warranty as to obvious defects if the seller demands that the buyer examine the goods but the buyer refuses. Making goods available for inspection does not constitute a demand. The seller must make clear that the buyer is assuming the risk of defects which the examination ought to reveal. Exclusion by examination applies only to obvious defects, not to hidden ones; it also applies only to implied warranties, not to express warranties on which the buyer clearly indicates that he or she is relying.

Except in certain situations governed by the Magnuson-Moss Warranty Act, a seller who wishes to disclaim implied warranties by using exclusionary language may do so by using an expression like "as is," "with all faults," or other language that, in common understanding, calls the buyer's attention to the exclusion of warranties and makes plain that there is no implied warranty [2-316(3)(a)]. Implied warranties may also be excluded by complying with the provisions of Section 2-316(2). Under that subsection, an *implied warranty of merchantability* may be excluded orally or by a writing, but the exclusionary language must mention "merchantability." If the disclaimer is written, the language of disclaimer must be conspicuous. Under the same subsection, an *implied warranty of fitness* can be excluded only by a conspicuous writing, but the exclusionary language may be general. A conspicuous general statement, such as "There are no warranties which extend beyond the description on the face hereof," is sufficient to exclude an implied warranty of fitness.

Strict compliance with the warranty exclusion provisions of the Code is not always sufficient to exclude an implied warranty. Some courts have held that certain attempts at exclusion are against public policy. In the pre-Code case of *Henningsen v. Bloomfield Motors*, 161 A.2d 69 (N.J. 1960), all automobile manufacturers doing business in New Jersey had adopted the same printed disclaimer of implied warranties and had substituted a "parts only" express warranty. Automobile buyers could not negotiate with the manufacturers for a more extensive warranty. The Supreme Court of New Jersey held that under these circumstances, an attempt by Bloomfield Motors to disclaim an implied warranty of merchantability was against public policy and was therefore invalid.

Cumulation and Conflict of Warranties

In a sale of goods, a number of warranties may exist at the same time. For example, a *merchant-seller* can be subject to a warranty of title, a warranty against infringement of a patent or a trademark, an implied warranty of merchantability, and an implied warranty of fitness for a particular purpose. In addition, any number of express warranties can be created, including express warranties of merchantability and fitness. To the extent that these express and implied warranties are consistent with one another, the buyer receives an accumulation of express and implied assurances. If a warranty of any kind is excluded, the seller remains subject to all other warranties that were made or imposed but that were not excluded.

Where there is a *conflict* of warranties, the intention of the parties to the sales contract determines which one is dominant. Section 2-317 states three tentative rules of construction for the guidance of the court: (1) exact or technical specifications displace an inconsistent sample or model or general language of description; (2) a sample from an existing bulk displaces inconsistent general language of description; and (3) express warranties displace inconsistent implied warranties other than an implied warranty of fitness for a particular purpose.

Suppose that a building contractor is interested in a new type of high-strength building block. The contractor inspects a sample, reads the results of a laboratory test conducted by the manufacturer, and purchases from the manufacturer a large quantity of the blocks. The blocks conform in strength to the sample but not to the laboratory test results supplied to the buyer as a part of the sales promotion. Which warranty prevails—the one arising from the sample or the one arising from the test results? Under rule (1) in the preceding paragraph, the contractor is entitled to blocks that conform in strength to the specifications stated in the laboratory report.

Third-Party Beneficiaries of UCC Quality Warranties

Sometimes a defective product causes loss to someone other than the purchaser. The seller might admit to making a warranty but may argue that the warranty should run only to the purchaser and not to others such as bystanders who might have been injured. Section 2-318 of the UCC gives certain "beneficiaries" the benefit of the same warranty or warranties that the buyer received in the contract of sale. Figure 22.2 shows the chain of distribution from manufacturer (M) to buyer (B), and it illustrates a spectrum of people who, in addition to the buyer, might be entitled to the seller's warranty.

There are three alternative versions of Section 2-318: Alternatives A, B, and C. Although they have a common purpose (to give beneficiaries the same warranty that the buyer received), they differ greatly as to who may be a beneficiary and as to the kinds of injury for which a beneficiary may receive a remedy.

Recall the situation described at the beginning of this chapter. A defective garden tractor engine exploded, injuring Bloom (the buyer) and his neighbor and causing a fire that destroyed the tractor and the neighbor's house. Suppose that neither the manufacturer nor the

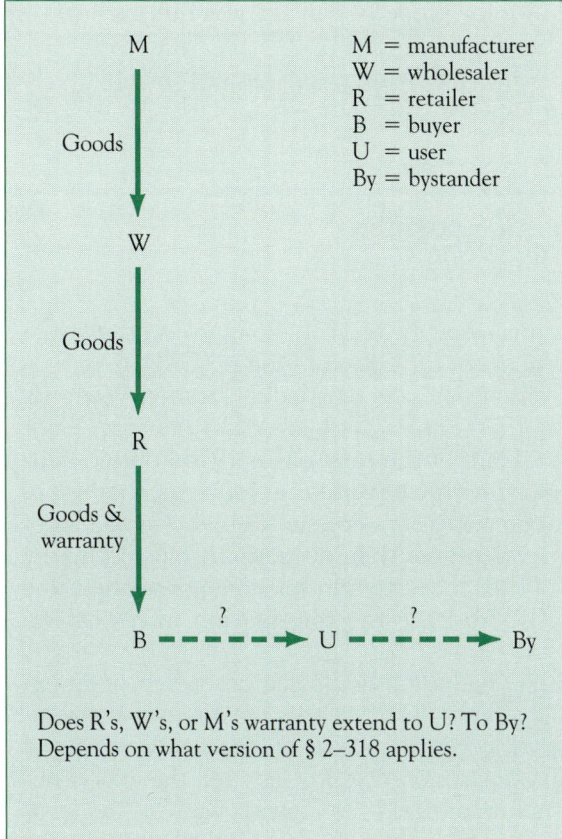

Figure 22.2 Third-party beneficiaries of buyer's warranty.

retail seller excluded the implied warranty of merchantability. To whom, besides Bloom, does the warranty of each seller run? The answer depends on which version of Section 2-318 is in effect in the state whose law applies to the situation. Most states (over thirty) have adopted Alternative A or some version of it. Some states have adopted Alternative B or C or some variation. California has not enacted the section, relying instead on other consumer law.

Alternative A provides:

A seller's warranty whether express or implied extends to any natural person who is in the family or household of his buyer or who is a guest in his home if it is reasonable to expect that such person may use, consume or be affected by the goods and who is injured in person by breach of the warranty.

This alternative is the most restrictive of the three. It permits recovery of damages only for personal injuries, not for injury to property. Bystanders, nonfamily members, and guests in automobiles are unprotected, unless the court is willing to include them in the protected class of beneficiaries by some process of interpretation. Bloom's neighbor is not within the protected class. Moreover, if the language of Alternative A were applied literally (as the courts of a couple of states have done), even an injured member of Bloom's family would be limited to a cause of action against the retail seller. The reason is that Alternative A extends the seller's warranty only to the beneficiaries of "his [the seller's] buyer." Since a manufacturer's immediate buyer ordinarily is a wholesaler, the manufacturer's warranty apparently would extend only to the beneficiaries of the wholesaler and not to beneficiaries of a consumer who buys from a retailer. However, a comment to Section 2-318 states that the section is neutral on the question of which sellers should be liable, and the courts of most states give a consumer-buyer's beneficiaries a cause of action against at least retailers and manufacturers.

Alternative B broadens the class of beneficiaries to whom a seller's warranty applies. The warranty "extends to any natural person [human being as opposed to a corporation] who may reasonably be expected to use, consume, or be affected by the goods and who is injured in person by breach of the warranty." Bloom's neighbor could reasonably be expected to "be affected" by an exploding engine. Under Alternative B the neighbor would be entitled to damages for personal injuries but not for loss of the house.

Alternative C is a variation of Alternative B. It differs from Alternative B in two ways: (1) Alternative C extends a seller's warranty to "any person" (not merely to a "natural" person) who may reasonably be expected to use, consume, or be affected by the goods; and (2) Alternative C permits a beneficiary to recover damages for injury to property as well as for injury to the person, unless the seller excludes or limits liability for injury to property. With regard to personal injury, a seller may not exclude or limit the operation of Alternative C. Under Alternative C, Bloom's neighbor is entitled to damages for personal injuries and for the loss of the house if liability for property damage was not excluded by the sellers.

The following case addresses the application of UCC 2-318.

CASE 22.2 **John L. Szajna v. General Motors Corporation**
• 115 Ill.2d 294, 503 N.E.2d 760 (Ill. 1986)

FACTS In August 1976, John Szajna (Szajna) bought a 1976 Pontiac Ventura from Seltzer Pontiac in Chicago. Seltzer, as agent for General Motors (GM), gave Szajna a folder which contained two warranties: one entitled a "Limited Warranty on 1976 Car" and another entitled "1976 Pontiac Passenger Car Emission Control System." It was alleged that thousands of the cars sold as 1976 Pontiac Venturas, including Szajna's, were equipped with Chevette transmissions; that use of the Chevette transmissions in Pontiac Venturas necessitates higher amounts of repairs and that they have shorter service lives than do transmissions ordinarily used in Pontiac Venturas; that use of the Chevette transmission lessens the value of the car; and that Szajna paid $375 to have the transmission in his car replaced.

Szajna sued GM on several counts, including one based on breach of an express warranty. For this count Szajna alleged, "Through its brochures, parts catalogues and repair manuals, as well as through the release of automobile news and information from its public relations department," [GM] "advised the expert observers, testers and reporters of the nature of the '1976 Pontiac Ventura' model as including the transmission designed for that size of car." No information was given to the public or the experts that some of the 1976 Pontiac Venturas were equipped with Chevette transmissions.

The trial court granted GM's motion to strike and dismiss Szajna's complaint. Szajna filed a motion to reconsider the complaint, which was also denied. The appellate court affirmed. The Illinois Supreme Court granted Szajna's petition for leave to appeal.

OPINION RYAN, J. . . . We must keep in mind that the law recognizes two kinds of privity which have been designated by the writers [experts and scholars] on the subject as horizontal and vertical. Horizontal privity is not, in reality, a state of privity but rather one of nonprivity. Their term refers to those who are not in the distributive chain of a product but who, nonetheless, use the product and retain a relationship with the purchaser, such as a member of the purchaser's family. Vertical privity refers to the relationship between those who are in the distributive chain. We are concerned here with vertical privity. The UCC does not directly address vertical privity. Section 2-318 of the UCC provides:

> A seller's warranty whether express or implied extends to any natural person who is in the family or household of his buyer or who is a guest in his home if it is reasonable to expect that such person may use, consume or be affected by the goods and who is injured in person by breach of the warranty. A seller may not exclude or limit the operation of this Section.

**CASE 22.2
Continued**

This section was adopted in this State in 1961 . . . , and is now referred to as alternative A.

The UCC comment says that this section is not intended to enlarge or restrict developing case law on whether the seller's warranties to his buyer who resells extend to other persons in the distributive chain.

In 1966, the UCC added alternative B, which extends the seller's warranty to any person who may reasonably be expected to use the goods and who is injured in person by a breach of the warranty. Thus, alternative B broadens the class of those to whom the seller's warranties apply from those listed in alternative A. Also added in 1966 was alternative C, which is the same as alternative B except the warranties extend to any person who may reasonably be expected to use the goods and who is injured by the breach of the warranty. Thus, alternative C does not require that the user be injured in person. Neither alternative B nor C has been adopted in Illinois. Therefore, in Illinois section 2-318 extends the warranty and is concerned only with horizontal privity. . . .

The UCC comment on alternative A . . . professes neutrality insofar as vertical privity and developing case law. . . . However, the remainder of the UCC speaks in terms of contractual relationship. . . . The professed neutrality of this section should not be viewed as an invitation to the courts to abolish the privity requirement but should be considered as an acknowledgment by the drafters that the law of implied warranty had developed along nonprivity lines in certain jurisdictions and could possibly develop further. . . .

Although section 2-318 may be neutral on the vertical-privity issue, the remainder of the UCC clearly recognizes the "consensual elements of commerce." The Kansas Supreme Court . . . stated: "An across-the-board extension of implied warranties to non-privity manufacturers or sellers, without regard to the nature of either the involved product or the type of damage sought, would spawn numerous problems in the operation of Article 2. . . ."

. . . [W]e have previously stated . . . our preference for applying contract law in . . . cases [such as this one]. We stated: "[A]pplication of the rules of warranty prevent a manufacturer from being held liable for damages of unknown and limited scope." We further stated: "We believe it is preferable to relegate the consumer to the comprehensive scheme of remedies fashioned by the UCC, rather than requiring the consuming public to pay more for their products so that the manufacturer can insure against the possibility that some of his products will not meet the business needs of some of his customers." . . .

We think it unnecessary to indulge in . . . judicial legislation . . . and the further judicial legislation necessary to reconcile nonprivity to the UCC requirements. We view judicial intervention unnecessary in view of the legislative concern expressed by certain enactments [federal warranty law] in this field. . . . We therefore decline to abolish the privity requirement in implied-warranty economic-loss cases.

JUDGMENT

Affirmed. Reversed and remanded on other grounds.

Limits on Usefulness of UCC Quality Warranties

Like other bases of products liability, warranty may be of little or no value to some persons injured by defective products. The UCC does not require a seller to make an express warranty, and the Code permits the seller to exclude warranties imposed by law. Indeed, in transactions covered by the Code it is common practice for a seller to exclude implied warranties entirely and to substitute a much narrower express warranty, one limited, for example, to the replacement of defective parts. Even where there is an implied warranty, the amount of damages recoverable may be sharply limited by the sales contract. In contrast, contractual disclaimers or limitations of strict tort liability or liability for gross negligence or for intentional torts ordinarily are not enforceable. Recall also that in many states an injured third party who is not a member of the buyer's family or a guest in the buyer's home has no warranty cause of action against the seller. And where a warranty cause of action exists, the plaintiff may be held to have assumed the risk of injury where the plaintiff knew of the defect and the risk was obvious.

Injured persons may face another problem when suing for breach of warranty: the UCC statute of limitations. A statute of limitations imposes a fixed maximum time within which a person must bring suit, so that plaintiffs are encouraged to bring their suits promptly, while evidence is still fresh and available. The UCC provides a rather generous amount of time for bringing suit—4 years, and more in some situations. However, the time for suing may be reduced to as little as 1 year by the original agreement of the parties. Moreover, the period, whatever its length, begins to run when the sales contract is breached—by, for example, the seller's breaching a warranty. With one exception, breach of warranty occurs when the goods are *tendered to the buyer* (offered for delivery), "regardless of the aggrieved party's lack of knowledge of the breach" [2-725(2)].[2] Goods such as Bloom's garden tractor may have hidden defects that do not become apparent until after the limitation period has expired. In such a situation, injured persons would be barred from any warranty remedy. In contrast, the limitations period that applies to a cause of action in *negligence* or *strict liability in tort* (usually 1 or 2 years) begins to run when the injury-causing condition *was or should have been discovered,* or when the injury occurred. In tort, then, the period for suing may extend indefinitely, because the time that the defect reveals itself, not the time that the product was tendered for delivery, usually marks the beginning of the period permitted for bringing suit. (For the protection of sellers, a few states specify that a suit in strict liability in tort must be brought within 6 to 12 years after the product was sold, regardless of whether the defect has been discovered by that time.)

TORT AS A BASIS FOR PRODUCTS LIABILITY

The tort basis for products liability has given rise to some of the most complex litigation in the history of law. Not only are matters of evidence complex, such as in the famous asbestos and DES cases, but the tort law itself is complicated and given to many permutations of application. Moreover, the variations of law from state to state can be substantial. It is, of course, beyond the scope of this book to explore the state-to-state differences of tort law in products liability—and the associated complexity.

Recall from Chapters 6 through 8 that tort law derives from the common law—that case by case, rules of law are applied and modified; even altogether new laws are created by this process. Tort law is state law as well. Consequently, a rule of law in one state does not apply in another state unless its courts adopt the particular rule. Additionally, some states have codified the tort rules as they apply to products liability. While such codification makes statutory products liability law, the source of the law remains

---

[2]The exception is that where a warranty "explicitly extends" to the future performance of the goods (e.g., the seller warrants the goods for 2 years), the UCC limitations period (1 to 4 years) does not commence until the time during the 2 years that the defect was or should have been discovered.

the common law and the major features of the rules retain the significant contours of the common law.

There are three basic theories in tort for the imposition of products liability—negligence, strict liability, and misrepresentation. Discussion of them now follows.

Negligence as a Basis of Products Liability

Elements of Negligence. A defendant is liable in negligence if the plaintiff proves four traditional elements of negligence:

1. A duty of care on the part of the defendant. The duty arises where the defendant should foresee a risk of harm to others from the defendant's conduct.
2. A failure of the defendant to exercise due care—that is, a failure to act reasonably in light of the foreseeable risk of harm to others.
3. A reasonably close causal connection between the failure to exercise due care and the resulting injury.
4. Actual loss to the plaintiff. In negligence and other products liability cases, the defendant is usually a manufacturer, a distributor, or some other supplier of goods.

The courts have developed a number of tests for determining when a duty of care arises. A manufacturer producing "inherently dangerous" goods, such as explosives or poisons, has a duty to foresee possible dangers of various kinds and to take reasonable measures to prevent harm. Under a long-standing and influential court decision,[3] a duty of care arises where a thing, if negligently made, may reasonably be expected to cause injury. Under other decisions, a duty of care arises if the goods are to be directly consumed, if the manufacturer can anticipate danger from the normal use of a product, or if the manufacturer can anticipate danger from the use that actually occurred. Under the latter two tests, a manufacturer of a caustic drain cleaner could be liable for failing to explain how to use the cleaning material safely, or for failing to provide a safety cap for the protection of children playing with the drain cleaner's package. Retailers and other suppliers of goods have duties of care that correspond with the degree of danger they should foresee in their capacities as retailers or other suppliers.

Negligent conduct takes a variety of forms. Liability has been found for negligent design of a product; for negligent inspection or assembly of parts; for negligent inspection of a finished product; for negligent testing of a product before, during, or after production; and for negligent packaging. Other typical forms of negligence are failure to give adequate instructions for the use of a product, failure to warn of known dangers, and representations made negligently as to the effectiveness of a product.

Limited Usefulness of Negligence in Suits by Injured Plaintiffs. From the injured plaintiff's point of view, negligence as a theory of products liability may be useless in some situations. The plaintiff must prove that the defendant acted negligently. For example, from the earlier example of injury from a defective product, how could Bloom prove that the defect in the garden tractor was the fault of the manufacturer? Acquiring proof of negligent design or of a negligent manufacturing process may require examination of the defendant's manufacturing facilities and processes. The defendant may be reluctant to provide the necessary information, and compelling the provision of such information, or otherwise acquiring it, if possible at all, can be costly. Moreover, when there are many participants in the channels of distribution and sales, the difficulty of establishing proof of negligent handling, preparation, and so forth can be overwhelming, if not impossible.

Sometimes the required causal connection between a particular defendant and the plaintiff's injury cannot be proved. Establishing that a soft drink bottle exploded and injured a shopper does not constitute proof that any act of the bottle manufacturer caused the bottle to explode. The injury-causing condition might have occurred while the bottle was in the cus-

---

[3]*MacPherson v. Buick Motor Co.*, 111 N.E. 1050 (N.Y. 1916).

tody of the wholesaler or the retailer, perhaps an intermediate shipper. In a proper case, the doctrine of *res ipsa loquitur* ("the thing speaks for itself") may place upon a defendant the burden of proving that he or she was *not* negligent. However, the doctrine is not universally available. Where it is available, the plaintiff must show (1) that the thing causing injury was in the defendant's exclusive control at the time of the alleged negligent act and (2) that the accident was one that ordinarily does not happen in the absence of negligence. Suppose an airliner crashes on a clear, calm day. A court might be persuaded to apply the doctrine of *res ipsa loquitur* on the theory that the plane and its maintenance were in the exclusive control of the airline, and that commercial airline crashes normally do not occur in the absence of negligence by airline employees. If *res ipsa loquitur* applies, the defendant is presumed negligent and must carry the burden of proving it was not negligent.

Plaintiffs in negligence cases face another difficulty. They must deal with a variety of defenses commonly raised by defendants. These include contributory negligence, comparative negligence, and assumption of the risk. *Contributory negligence* occurs where the plaintiff's own negligence in using the product contributes to his or her own injury, as where the instructions for using caustic drain cleaner are vague, but contrary to instructions that are given, the plaintiff causes an explosion by using five times the recommended amount in hot water. In its strictest applications, contributory negligence bars the plaintiff from any recovery of damages. Under the doctrine of *comparative negligence*, the plaintiff's own negligence is taken into account in determining how much damages the plaintiff may recover; the award to the plaintiff is reduced in proportion to the percentage of harm that is attributable to her or his negligence. Under the doctrine of *assumption of risk*, a plaintiff who knowingly and voluntarily confronts an obvious danger ordinarily may not recover damages for any resulting injury. Using a new but obviously frayed rope for mountain climbing in a nonemergency situation would constitute assumption of risk.

To avoid the defenses and the difficulties of proof that may be involved in a negligence suit, the law now permits a plaintiff to base products liability on tort theories other than negligence—most notably, strict liability.

Strict Liability as a Basis of Products Liability

If negligence cannot be proved and the seller has made no warranty, an injured plaintiff may wish to—and commonly does—rely on strict liability as a basis for recovering damages.

Nature and Scope of Strict Liability. Courts use the expression **strict liability** in two senses. In one sense, strict liability means a liability that flows from a breach of a warranty of quality. In another sense, the sense in which the expression is used in this chapter, strict liability means a liability imposed by tort law. Strict liability in tort is imposed when a defective or unreasonably dangerous product has caused injury or when injury results from a justifiable reliance on a material misrepresentation of the quality of a product. The liability is called "strict" because the plaintiff need not prove fault (negligence or fraud) on the part of the defendant. The liability is "in tort" because the existence of the liability does not depend on the existence of a warranty. Strict liability in tort usually cannot be disclaimed. The ability of sellers to disclaim or otherwise to avoid warranty liability for serious loss explains in large measure the rapid development of strict liability in tort as a basis for lawsuits.

Strict liability in tort has had its greatest growth since the 1960s, when state courts rapidly adopted Section 402A of the *Restatement (Second) of the Law of Torts* (1965). Today, more than 80 percent of the states have incorporated some version of Section 402A into their common law. Section 402A of *Restatement (Second), Torts* is as follows:

One who sells any product in a defective condition unreasonably dangerous to the user or consumer or to his property is subject to liability for physical harm thereby caused to the ultimate user or consumer, or to his property, if (a) the seller is engaged in the business of selling such a product, and (b) it is expected to and does reach the user or consumer without substantial change in the condition in which it is sold.

This rule applies even though the seller has exercised all possible care in preparing and selling the product and even though the user or consumer has not bought the product from the seller.

While the wording of Section 402A seems clear and straightforward, the application of this rule has required states to make further clarifications. As the rule is plainly stated, it would appear to make sellers and manufacturers the absolute insurers of anyone who would use their products, but states have generally avoided such a reading of Section 402A. In this chapter, it would be impossible to discuss all of the various difficulties courts have had with applying Section 402A. However, one of the most important aspects of application of the rule is the determination of what constitutes "unreasonably dangerous."

The overwhelming majority of states use what is called **risk-utility balancing** in some form or another. Simply put, risk-utility balancing assesses the usefulness of a product against the level of danger and risk in using the product in order to arrive upon a conclusion on whether a product is "unreasonably dangerous." If the danger or risk of a product outweighs its usefulness, then the product is unreasonably dangerous. For example, gasoline is well known for its dangerous qualities; it is also a useful, if not necessary, product in our modern society and economy. Merely because gasoline is highly flammable and is harmful if swallowed, these qualities alone do not subject the maker/distributor/seller of gasoline liable for whatever injury gasoline causes to the product's users. Rather, it is only if the risks of gasoline outweigh the utility of the product that liability could be found.

Case 22.3 provides an example how a court uses risk-utility balancing in applying Section 402A of *Restatement (Second), Torts*.

CASE 22.3   **Jose R. Rivas v. District International Trucks**
- C.A. No. 85-3411, slip op. (D.C. 1989)

FACTS   On May 28, 1984, Jose Rivas (Rivas) was injured while assisting a fellow employee of Action Trucking and Trash Removal (Action Trucking) in unloading trash from a garbage truck at a dump site in Virginia. Rivas was cleaning out metal debris in the hopper of the truck's trash compactor when the other employee, unaware that Rivas was physically inside the hopper, began lowering the compactor's packing plate by activating its control lever. Because Rivas was facing away from the packing plate, he did not realize that it was descending upon him until it started to grow dim inside the hopper. At that point, Rivas started to climb out of the hopper, but tried to retrieve one last piece of metal with the left part of his body when his left foot became caught between the packing plate and the sill of the hopper. Rivas suffered serious injury to his foot.

Rivas filed a products liability suit against District International Trucks, Inc. (District International), the company which sold the garbage truck to Action Trucking. This suit was also filed against Wilbar Truck Equipment (Wilbar), which supplied the Load-Master trash compactor; City Tank Corporation (City Tank), a subsidiary of Hagan Industries, Inc. (Hagan), and the sales arm of Old Dominion Manufacturing Co. (Old Dominion), also a subsidiary of Hagan, which manufactured the trash compactor; and Loadmaster Corporation and Hackney Industries (Loadmaster/Hackney), which sold the Load-Master trash compactor to Wilbar.

CASE 22.3 Continued

District International, Wilbar, and Loadmaster/Hackney filed motions for summary judgment against Rivas's claims.

OPINION

ATTRIDGE, U.S. Magistrate . . . Summary judgment is proper when, after review of the entire record, it is clear to the Court that there exists no genuine issue of material fact and that the moving party is entitled to judgment as a matter of law. . . .

It is not in dispute that [Rivas's] suit seeks redress of damages realized as a result of an allegedly defective trash compactor; there are no allegations of a faulty cab or chassis. Specifically, Rivas alleges: (1) the trash compactor should have had a guard gate which would have prevented him from putting his foot in the compactor; (2) the packing plate should have been designed to stop if the operator removed his hand from the control lever, or the packing plate should have operated in two steps, requiring reactivation before completing its packing cycle; and (3) the compactor should have had an alarm that continuously sounded when the compacting mechanism was in operation. He also alleges that adequate warnings were not displayed in the compactor. . . .

Elements of a Strict Liability Claim

Unfortunately, the law of strict liability in the District of Columbia is a product of court interpretation of a number of different cases; there is no one case that clearly sets out the "necessary elements of a D.C. strict liability claim." . . . [F]ollowing the traditional approach when there is no District of Columbia law on point, [we] look . . . to Maryland for guidance. . . .

In Maryland, a plaintiff may bring a cause of action in strict liability as is outlined in Restatement (Second) of Torts §402A. Section 402A provides, in pertinent part, one who:

> sells any product in a defective condition unreasonably dangerous to the user or consumer . . . is subject to liability for physical harm thereby caused to the ultimate user . . . if (a) the seller is engaged in the business of selling such a product, and (b) it is expected to and does reach the user without substantial change in the condition in which it is sold.
>
> . . . This rule applies even though the seller has exercised reasonable care and the user or consumer does not have any contractual relationship with the seller.

In applying this section to the facts in this case, both District International and Wilbar are "sellers" of the compactor. Wilbar, engaged in the business of selling compactors, sold this particular compactor to District International. District International, engaged in the business of selling garbage trucks, then sold the compactor, as part of the completed truck, to Action Trucking. In its original motion, District International claims that it merely supplied the compactor as a service to Action Trucking and that it derived no profit from that sale because it charged Action Trucking the same amount it paid to Wilbar. [District International], therefore, asserts that it cannot be considered a "seller" for strict liability purposes. . . . This Court finds this argument meritless for even if District International did not realize a profit on the compactor, it certainly derived a profit from the sale of the entire truck. . . . [T]herefore, that but for the compactor,

**CASE 22.3
Continued**

District International would not have sold the cab and chassis to Action Trucking. . . . The fact that [District International] did not make a profit on that particular aspect of the sale is irrelevant.

Having found that Wilbar and District International are "sellers" of the compactor, it is now necessary to determine whether [Rivas] has established that the compactor was defective and unreasonably dangerous because it lacked certain safety features. This Circuit, again following Maryland law, has applied the risk/utility balancing test. . . . Under this test, the plaintiff must show "that the magnitude of the danger from the product outweighed the costs of avoiding the danger—including, for example, any new dangers created and any reduction in the benefits of the product caused by the safer design." "[E]vidence of a design alternative, by itself, is not sufficient to impose liability. . . ."

. . . [Rivas] . . . submitted affidavits by his [expert] witnesses in which they state, upon the basis of their expertise in mechanical engineering and safety and upon their review of the record, that the compactor was unreasonably dangerous and unsafe as designed, and that any of the safety features enumerated in [Rivas's] . . . statement [of evidence], are relatively inexpensive to install and create little or no impact on the effectiveness of the compactor. . . . [The Court refers to their affidavits in evidence that state a similar conclusion]. . . . These affidavits . . . are sufficient . . . to make at least a prima facie showing of the elements set out in [Maryland case law], i.e., the magnitude of the risk in the compactor as designed outweighed the inexpensive costs of any of the design alternatives and that these alternatives would not have affected the utility of the compactor.

The defendants move to strike the affidavits on the ground that they contain unsupported factual conclusions. . . . [T]he Court finds that the affidavits satisfy the "knowledge" requirement of [the federal rules of evidence]; therefore, it would be improper to strike them.

. . . [Rivas] not only has established the essential elements to pursue a strict liability claim against defendants, . . . but has also set forth genuine issues of material facts which must be resolved at trial.

Misuse of Product

Lastly, the defendants argue that because [Rivas's] actions, in getting inside the hopper of the compactor and trying to retrieve one last piece of metal after he was aware that the packing plate was descending, were so reckless and unreasonable that they constitute misuse of the compactor, which results in a bar to his strict liability claim.

The Court agrees with the defendants that if a product is used for a purpose or in a manner that is not reasonably foreseeable, such misuse bars a claim of defective or unreasonable design of the product. There are factual questions on this foreseeability issue that make it impossible for this Court to find as a matter of law the [Rivas's] actions resulting in misuse of the product.

Conclusion

. . . [T]he Court finds that [Rivas] has not stated a cause of action against Hackney and Loadmaster Corporation [because they were not "sellers" within

CASE 22.3 Continued	the meaning of Section 402A]; therefore, they should be dismissed from this action. It further finds that the law in the District of Columbia on strict liability, as it has been developed by both District of Columbia and Maryland Courts, controls plaintiff's strict liability claim, and that plaintiff has set forth the necessary elements which would allow a jury to find those defendants liable under that claim and has set forth genuine issues of material facts which must be resolved at trial.
JUDGMENT	Motion for summary judgment denied.

Reasons for Imposing Strict Liability; Procedural Benefits. The reasons most commonly offered for imposing strict liability include the following:

1. Users of complex or packaged goods are usually in no position to examine the goods at the time of purchase. Since much advertising is calculated to convince the public that goods may be used safely, users of defective goods are especially vulnerable to injury. So, when a defective product causes injury, the loss should be shifted from the individual to the manufacturer.
2. Manufacturers are in the best position to distribute loss due to defective products as a cost of doing business, either by raising prices or by procuring insurance.
3. Imposing strict liability will exert pressure on manufacturers to police their operations more carefully and to make fewer defective products. Also, some courts impose strict liability on everyone in the distribution chain so that the injured plaintiff will have a better chance of recovering damages. The manufacturer may be beyond the reach of the plaintiff but may be liable to a middleman who has been required to pay damages to the plaintiff.

Strict tort liability provides injured plaintiffs with procedural advantages similar to those of an action in warranty. The plaintiff may prevail essentially by proving (1) that the doctrine applies to the plaintiff's situation, (2) that the product had a defect when it left the defendant's hands and was unreasonably dangerous to the plaintiff, and (3) that harm to the plaintiff resulted. Ordinarily, contributory negligence of the plaintiff is not a defense to a suit based on strict liability in tort. However, there are defenses available for defendants in strict liability suits. Three of the most common follow.

Defenses in Strict Liability. Consistent with the view that strict liability in tort is not a rule which imposes the obligation for product makers and sellers to be the absolute insurers of their products, defenses exist for product makers and sellers to avoid liability (or to reduce the amount of damages) under the appropriate circumstances.

Obviousness of hazard. The title of this defense is self-explanatory. If the hazard presented by a product is obvious and a plaintiff is injured by that hazard, the defendant can raise the obviousness defense. For example, an obvious characteristic of a knife is that it has a sharp edge. This obvious characteristic basically puts the user of a knife on notice to use the product with caution. Accordingly, if Gourmet is injured by cutlery made by Steeledge merely because of a sharp edge on one of Steeledge's knives, Steeledge (or whoever sold such knives) would have the defense of obviousness of hazard available in the event of a legal action in products liability. However, the defense would not be available if Gourmet were injured by the sharp blade because the knife's handle broke while Gourmet was using the knife in a reasonable manner. In this latter situation, the cause of the

BOX 22.1
How Is a Pet Tiger Like an Unreasonably Dangerous Product?

The quick answer to this question is that if you are injured by either someone's pet tiger or an unreasonably dangerous product, your suit for damages in most states would likely be based on strict liability in tort.

Imagine that your next-door neighbor nurtured a tiger cub to maturity and kept it in a fenced lot. Imagine further that your neighbor devoted great care and training to the animal so that it was accustomed to being around humans and was not only docile but lovable, so docile that the tiger was the playmate of your neighbor's 4-year-old daughter. Now suppose that you wanted to be ornery and decided to excite and taunt the tiger from the other side of the fence and that you succeeded in getting the animal so worked up so as to jump the fence and attack you, causing injury.

Who pays?

Plain notions of fairness might suggest that the person who taunted the animal should suffer the injury without any compensation from the tiger owner.

Before you answer the "Who pays?" question, however, you should understand that if the pet had been a regular dog, the above scenario would likely result in your having no basis upon which to sue successfully—in fact, the dog owner might have a suit against you if the dog was hurt as well. Perhaps, too, the dog owner could sue under other tort notions, such as trespass.

Simply because the animal was a tiger (or any other wild animal or other acknowledged dangerous creature), the owner pays. It scarcely matters that you taunted and teased the animal. It also doesn't matter what level of precaution your neighbor exerted to avoid injury by the tiger. Merely by having the animal, the owner of the tiger takes all responsibility for injury it causes—no matter who is really at fault.

Why should this be so? After all, dogs are temperamental too and account for many more bite injuries to humans than tigers do.

Law acknowledges the practical aspects of life. Dogs have been pets and companions of humans for longer than history has been recorded. Except for perhaps the militant dog hater, most people would find it hard to imagine a society without dogs. They are a part of human life—just like other kinds of common pets.

Tigers do not enjoy the same status. It is the very unusual person who attempts to have this wild animal as a domestic pet. While our law may allow someone to have a pet tiger, societal conventions and our law discourage such conduct. In short, as a society we don't want people to have pet tigers, but we have not gone so far generally as to ban someone from owning one. In other words, if you engage in conduct which society doesn't like, you pay.

In a fashion, this rationale is just like risk-utility balancing to determine whether a product is unreasonably dangerous. As a society, the risk of having tigers around outweighs its utility. Conversely, the utility of having dogs around outweighs the risk of injury they pose. The former imposes strict liability when injury occurs; the latter merely involves negligence with the dog owner not paying if the owner can show that the appropriate level of precaution (care/duty) was not breached.

And so it is with products. For example, a baseball bat can be a dangerous thing indeed, but try to imagine our life without it. A firearm, too, is an exceedingly dangerous product, but generally speaking it only becomes unreasonably dangerous when the firearm malfunctions.

Like pet dogs and pet tigers, our society has deemed that a properly functioning firearm is more like a dog. It is capable of causing injury but its utility outweighs its risks. A malfunctioning firearm, however, is more like a tiger—with society deeming its inherent risks outweighing its benefits.

> **BOX 22.1**
> **Continued**
>
> And the balance that society strikes can change. As an example, recently some municipalities have outlawed the owning of pitbull dogs. In those municipalities, an owner of a pitbull that injures someone is likely to face, not only criminal sanctions, but also a civil suit based on strict liability in tort. In those municipalities, society has stated that the risk of pitbull ownership outweighs its utility.
>
> Several decades ago, an automobile was considered to be an unreasonably dangerous contraption, dangerous like a pet tiger. Today, though cars can be very dangerous when misused, they are simply a part of our lives, more like a domesticated dog—unless they are manufactured or designed poorly, in which case, they are again like a pet tiger. ∎

injury was not the sharp blade but rather a defective handle whose hazards were not obvious.

Product misuse. This defense can arise when a product is used for purposes it was not intended to perform, and a plaintiff is injured as a result of this unintended use. Suppose that Vanity reasons that since a hemorrhoidal ointment shrinks tissue, it would be good for eliminating facial wrinkles and bags under the eyes, and that Vanity then uses the ointment to attempt to look younger.[4] If because of face and eye injuries Vanity sues the ointment maker or seller, the defendants would be able to raise the defense of product misuse, particularly if the product's instructions were clear as to its proper use and location of application.

Assumption of risk. Of the three defenses in strict liability, this defense is the least available. Some states have barred the defense under a similar rationale which makes contributory negligence unavailable as a defense. In the assumption-of-risk defense, the defendant has the burden to show that the plaintiff voluntarily and unreasonably used the product in face of a danger known to the plaintiff. Such a defense is difficult to mount, because the defendant has to establish that the plaintiff had knowledge of the hazard. For this defense, it is not necessary that the hazard be obvious—only that the plaintiff knew of it and acted unreasonably, hence assuming the risk of danger.

Moreover, it is possible to raise this defense even though the product was actually defective and caused the injury. However, in such a circumstance, the assumption-of-risk defense could work to reduce damages, perhaps not eliminate them altogether. Suppose that Gardener noticed that his lawn mower was spewing gasoline and oil while it was in operation and decided not only to continue operating the lawn mower but also to light his cigar, thereby causing a fire which injured Gardener. If Gardener then sued the lawn-mower manufacturer, the manufacturer might be able to raise the assumption-of-risk defense and reduce the damages, even if there were no dispute on the defectiveness of the lawn mower itself. Keep in mind, however, that the manufacturer would have to establish that Gardener proceeded with knowledge of the hazards and the inherent risk.

Limits on Usefulness of Strict Liability to Injured Plaintiffs. Strict liability, like the other bases of products liability, is not universally available to injured plaintiffs. The courts in a small minority of states have refused to adopt the doctrine of strict tort liability. Some of these courts have stated that the decision to adopt strict liability is for the legislature. The courts of some other states will not impose that doctrine if the plaintiff has suffered only property damage. These courts reserve strict liability for situations involving serious personal injury, prefer-

---
[4]This example is based on a true report. See "Closet Cosmetic," *Newsweek*, July 14, 1975, p. 56. The article reports that people with wrinkles were buying up hemorrhoidal ointment to use as a cosmetic despite manufacturer discouragement of such use.

ring to let most products liability matters be governed by warranty law and negligence.

> **BOX 22.2**
>
> ### Point to Consider
>
> How should the law handle a situation in which a product, when used properly, will cause certain injury but still remain a useful product? Vaccines are a good example. The vast majority of persons using a vaccine will be better off because they will now be immune from a serious disease. However, the maker of the vaccine knows that, say, ten out of a million users will die as a result of being inoculated. Who should pay?
>
> There are less exotic products than vaccines that face a similar problem. Peanut butter and other products containing peanut by-products can cause suffering and death to persons who are severely allergic to peanuts.
>
> There is probably little dispute that the utility of peanut butter or vaccines outweighs their risks. Yet people are injured and killed by these products.
>
> Most states acknowledge, as law, a comment provided by the drafters of Section 402A, *Restatement (Second), Torts*. Headed by the title "Unavoidably Unsafe Products," comment "k" of the *Restatement* states:
>
> > There are some products which, in the present state of human knowledge, are quite incapable of being made safe for their intended and ordinary use. These are especially common in the field of drugs. . . . Such a product, properly prepared, and accompanied by proper directions and warning, is not defective, nor is it *unreasonably* dangerous. . . . The seller of such products, . . . with the qualification that they are properly prepared and marketed, and proper warning is given, where the situation calls for it, is not to be held to strict liability for unfortunate consequences attending their use, merely because he has undertaken to supply the public with an apparently useful and desirable product, attended with a known but apparently reasonable risk.

Misrepresentation as a Basis of Products Liability

While there are notions of misrepresentation in warranty theories of products liability, those notions are based in contract law. In this section, the various tort notions of misrepresentation will be discussed. What distinguishes misrepresentation as a tort from similar notions in warranty is that the basis of the legal theory is not on the breach of a contract (of which a warranty, whether express or implied, is a part). Rather, in tort a legal action against a product maker or seller is based upon an independent "wrong" of some sort.

Misrepresentation can arise from many sorts of communication, including expressive conduct and silence. Commonly—as with warranties—sellers' communication and conduct, the content of advertising and promotional materials, instructions and warnings, packaging, and the like can all be sources of information upon which a legal action in misrepresentation can be based *if* the information is misleading and the user of the product justifiably relied upon the information.

Intentional Misrepresentation. This basis for products liability is perhaps the easiest to understand because it requires intentional wrongdoing. Specifically, the legal elements behind intentional misrepresentation are essentially the same as fraud, covered in Chapter 6. As noted in that chapter, an action in fraud requires a false representation with the intention of inducing another to rely upon that representation. If reliance upon the false representation is justified and the reliance causes injury, then the party making the false representation is liable. Suppose that Scuzz makes infants' toys, one of which is a stuffed bear whose eyes are fastened with sharp pins which Scuzz knows could harm infants if swallowed. The packaging for the stuffed bear carries a safety blurb stating, "Child tested. Absolutely safe." In actuality, no tests were conducted. Hapless buys one of Scuzz's stuffed bears, because of the safety blurb on the packaging, and Hapless's infant is later injured from swallowing one of the bear's eyes. Scuzz could be found liable because all of the elements of intentional misrepresentation were present. However, if Hapless had purchased the stuffed bear for Hapless's stuffed bear collection, not ever to be given to an infant, and Hapless later somehow trips over the stuffed bear and is injured, Scuzz would not be liable because Hapless never relied upon Scuzz's child safety claim, no matter how false it was.

Negligent Misrepresentation.
Liability based on the elements of negligence (duty, breach of duty, actual injury, breach of duty as the cause of injury), discussed earlier in this chapter, does not require that a false representation be intentional. This basis provides a way to impose liability for mistakes in the representation of products in advertising, labeling, and so forth which cause injury and which stem from lack of due care.

The problem with actions in negligent misrepresentation, as generally with actions in negligence in products liability, is the problem of proving the existence of a duty, the breacher of that duty, and whether the breach actually caused a plaintiff injury. In modern society, with a maze of sellers, distributors, and others making representations on the attributes of products, it can become difficult, if not impossible, to determine liability on the basis of the elements of negligence.

Increasingly, courts have relied on "faultless" bases of liability for misrepresentation and have adopted a strict liability rule, which follows.

Strict Liability for Misrepresentation.
Created to grapple with contemporary methods of advertising, sales promotion, and other avenues of commercial communication, Section 402B of *Restatement (Second), Torts* imposes a version of strict liability for misrepresentation. This section states:

> One engaged in the business of selling chattels who, by advertising, labels, or otherwise, makes to the public a misrepresentation of a material fact concerning the character or quality of a chattel sold by him is subject to liability for physical harm to a consumer of the chattel caused by justifiable reliance upon the misrepresentation, even though (a) it is not made fraudulently or negligently, and (b) the consumer has not bought the chattel from or entered into any contractual relation with the seller.

Notice that the key elements of the rule of Section 402B are (1) the existence of a misrepresentation (2) justifiable reliance, and (3) injury caused by the reliance. Section 402B applies exclusively to physical (not economic) injury and does not require any contractual (sales) relationship between the user and the person making the misrepresentation. Section 402B, however, has not been as widely adopted by courts as has Section 402A, discussed earlier in this chapter.

SUMMARY

Products liability law is in actuality an integrated accumulation of law comprised mostly of two broad branches of law—contract and tort. Accordingly, a person injured by a defective product has two broad bases upon which to sue—in contract and in tort. The contract basis for a products liability suit revolves around warranties. Though a products liability suit in tort may have many different kinds of causes of action, most suits fall under three theories in tort: negligence, strict liability, and misrepresentation.

Article 2 of the UCC provides for various warranties. These may be express or implied. A number of warranties may exist at the same time, and some (such as a warranty of quality) extend to third parties.

The distinguishing characteristics of the three theories of liability in tort are as follows: In negligence, the elements of duty, breach, injury, and direct cause must be present. In strict liability, there must exist an unreasonably dangerous product which causes injury—even though no one is at fault for the injury and even though the manufacturer may have exerted great care. In misrepresentation, whether on purpose or not, there must be a false or misleading statement upon which the injured party reasonably relied.

REVIEW QUESTIONS

1. Why has the privity-of-contract requirement been largely abandoned in products liability cases?

2. Why might the law of negligence be of limited usefulness to injured plaintiffs? Illustrate.

3. What must a plaintiff prove to obtain damages for loss due to a breach of warranty?

4. (a) What ownership attributes may a buyer be assured of under a warranty of title? **(b)** How may nonverbal title warranties be excluded?

5. (a) How may an express warranty of quality be made? **(b)** What would be the best way to avoid the liability that can result from an express warranty? **(c)** Is this method of avoiding liability compatible with normal business practices? Why?

6. Compare the implied warranty of merchantability with the implied warranty of fitness for a particular purpose with regard to **(a)** method of creation, **(b)** quality level assured, and **(c)** method of exclusion.

7. Suppose a seller orally states, "I do not warrant these goods." What warranties, if any, exist? What warranties, if any, cannot be excluded by law?

8. Compare Alternatives A, B, and C of Section 2-318 of *Restatement (Second), Torts* with regard to the class of people protected and the kind of injury protected against.

9. Why might the law of warranty be of limited usefulness to an injured plaintiff? Illustrate.

10. (a) What are the two main situations in which strict liability may be imposed? **(b)** For injured plaintiffs, what are the procedural benefits of strict liability in tort? **(c)** Why might strict tort liability be of limited usefulness to injured persons?

11. How is strict liability, as expressed in Section 402A of *Restatement (Second), Torts*, different from that in Section 402B? Explain. Give examples.

12. What is "risk-utility balancing" in products liability law and under what situations is it used?

CASE PROBLEMS

1. In 1980, Connie Daniell attempted to commit suicide by locking herself inside the trunk of a 1973 Ford LTD automobile. Because the trunk latch did not have an internal release or opening mechanism, Daniell remained in the trunk for about 9 days. Later, Daniell sued Ford Motor Company for damages, alleging psychological and physical injuries resulting from a defect in the design of the trunk latch. Is Daniell entitled to damages? In your answer discuss all three of the products liability theories applicable to her case: **(a)** negligence, **(b)** warranty, and **(c)** strict liability in tort.

2. Tiderman bought a new mobile home manufactured by Fleetwood Homes. Shortly after occupying it, she experienced severe eye and throat irritation. Her allergist diagnosed her as suffering from asthma caused by exposure to formaldehyde fumes emitted from particle board in the mobile home. She moved out, but continued to suffer severe asthma attacks. Alleging breach of the warranty of merchantability, she sued Fleetwood for rescission of the contract and for damages for her personal injuries. At trial, expert testimony indicated that 20 to 25 percent of the population is allergic or potentially sensitive to substances such as formaldehyde. Fleetwood's defense experts diagnosed Tiderman as having a genetic predisposition to asthma. From a $566,500 jury award to Tiderman, Fleetwood appealed. Whether the trial court's decision should be upheld depended on whether there was a breach of the warranty of merchantability. Was the warranty breached?

3. Troy asked Swan Island Sheet Metal Works to manufacture a stainless steel crab cooker. The cooker was to be modeled after one that Troy already owned, and it was to use a gas burner. Bader, president of Swan Island, lacked knowledge of gas burners and so informed Troy, who agreed that Bader should seek expert advice on the design of the burner. Bader did so, and delivered the cooker. The burner never worked properly, and Troy ruined 1,200 pounds of crab while attempting to use the cooker. Troy refused to pay for the cooker and sought damages arising from an alleged breach of the implied warranty of fitness for a particular purpose. The trial court awarded Troy $2,950 in damages. Swan Island appealed, arguing that since both Bader and Troy admitted ignorance of the design of gas burners, Troy could not have relied on Swan Island's expertise. Should the trial court's decision be reversed?

4. Mobley purchased a new car from Century Dodge and later discovered that the car had been involved in an accident. The contract of sale described the car as "new" and contained a disclaimer of all warranties, express or implied. Mobley sued Century Dodge for damages, alleging breach of an express warranty. Century Dodge contended that it had disclaimed any express warranty. Was Century Dodge's disclaimer effective to exclude an express warranty that the car was new?

5. Phillips purchased a horsewalker from Allen. A horsewalker is a device turned by an electric motor to exercise horses. The top is like an umbrella on a pole. Horses are attached to the arms of the umbrella, which then is rotated in a circle at varying speeds. Upon delivery of the device, Phillips asked to see it work. Allen installed a temporary extension cord, cautioning Phillips that a permanent, grounded electrical connection was needed to prevent electrical shocks and injury. A few days later Phillips attached four horses to the walker by means of steel chains. After the walker had been in operation for a while, one of the horses was killed by an electric shock and the other three were injured. Alleging breach of the warranties of merchantability and fitness for a particular purpose, Phillips sued Allen for damages. The trial court held that Allen was not liable to Phillips, and Phillips appealed. Should the verdict of the trial court be upheld?

6. Two teenagers, Nancy Moran and Randy Williams, while at a party in a friend's home, noticed that a lit Christmas candle at the event was not scented. Using a bottle of Fabergé perfume belonging to the host, they attempted to scent the lit candle. Because the perfume contained more than 82 percent alcohol, its flash point was 73° F. When the perfume was applied to the candle, a flame burst forth, burning Moran's neck and breasts. The perfume's label carried no warning of the hazard. What legal action or actions could Moran bring against the perfume's manufacturer? What defenses might be available to the manufacturer?

7. Bullock, Inc., manufactured a deep-fat fryer. Hoping to convince Bennigan's Restaurant to buy it, Bullock placed the fryer in Bennigan's kitchen on a trial basis. Thorpe, an employee of Bennigan's, was burned by boiling oil from the fryer and sued Bullock for damages. A state statute imposes strict liability on manufacturers of defective products "sold as new." Assume that the fryer was defective. Should Bullock be subjected to a lawsuit based on strict liability in tort?

ETHICS IN PRACTICE

It is difficult to think of a law that does not represent a value judgment on the part of the lawmakers. Even in setting speed limits, lawmakers must decide what conduct is appropriate (i.e., safe, efficient) and what is not. Some law promotes the values of special-interest groups to the detriment of the public welfare. Most law reflects values that are consistent with the common good.

The law of sales is an example of business law that reflects explicit value judgments of its drafters. In Article 2 (and, in fact, the whole Uniform Commercial Code), the drafters' basic concern is for efficiency of business transactions, itself a worthy economic goal. But as the comments to Code sections reveal, the drafters formulated many Code rules with the express purpose of fostering honesty and fair dealing—qualities that aid business efficiency but which most people would recognize as traditionally moral or ethical in tone. Problem 1 below focuses on values underlying rules of sales law. The remaining problems deal with the marketing of goods.

PROBLEMS IN ETHICS

1. Explain how each of the following rules of sales law promotes honesty and fair dealing: **(a)** the rule concerning accommodation shipments; **(b)** the rule that an offeree's expression of acceptance acts as an acceptance even though it states terms additional to or different from those stated in the offer, and the additional terms are construed as proposals for addition to the contract; **(c)** the rule concerning unconscionable contracts.

2. A 1991 newspaper article notes that "the makers of StarKist tuna fish, Knorr soup, Brim coffee and other familiar brands have quietly reduced their product's weight or volume—without changing the container's size or price to reflect the reduction." Examples:

- StarKist reduced its 6 1/2-ounce can of tuna to 6 1/8 ounces and shortened the can by 1/16 inch, but kept the price the same.
- Knorr repackaged its leek soup and recipe mix. The old, small box contained enough dry mix for four 8-ounce servings. The new, bigger box contains enough for only three 8-ounce servings.
- General Foods puffed up its Brim coffee beans so that 11.5 ounces now fill the can that used to hold 12 ounces.
- Lipton instant lemon-flavored tea was lightened from 4 ounces to 3.7 ounces without changing the container's size.

Though net weights are listed on the packaging, government and consumer groups say that these unadvertised changes are deceiving consumers. Manufacturers defend their moves, saying that consumers requested the shrunken contents or that technological developments enable the same number of servings despite weight reductions. How would you assess the ethical quality of these pricing practices?

3. "Scentco" is a manufacturer of perfumes that it distributes in only the most exclusive stores. Scentco perfumes sell at retail for $75 to $185 per ounce, depending on the scent. Using a chromatograph in a process of "reverse engineering," Jane is able to develop a very close approximation of the secret formulas of Scentco, and begins production under her "Smellco" label. Jane markets her line of perfumes in discount stores, drugstores, and groceries throughout the country for a retail price of $7.50 per ounce. Cost of production, packaging, and distribution is about $2 per ounce; Jane's price to her retailers is $4 per ounce. Jane uses the same ingredients that Scentco uses, and she pays the same amount for them that Scentco does. In her advertising, Jane constantly challenges users of her perfumes to try to distinguish them from their Scentco counterparts, and she provides Scentco and Smellco samples so that prospective customers may try. Most people cannot tell the difference between Scentco perfumes and the "clones" that Jane produces. Scentco and others in the perfume industry are very angry with Jane and her Smellco operation, but they have not been able to prove that she has violated the law. **(a)** Is Jane's conduct ethical? What about the way she acquired her perfume formulas? What about her marketing strategy and advertising technique? **(b)** Is Scentco acting ethically in the way it markets and prices its perfumes?

4. You are an electrical engineer working for a manufacturer of videocassette recorders (VCRs). The VCRs are among the cheapest on the market, selling at retail for $139. They break down early and often, and they carry a 30-day limited warranty. The average repair bill is $85. You know that by upgrading a few parts at the cost of $8 per unit, you can triple the life of the machine and make it the most reliable, though still one of the least expensive, VCRs on the market. Your supervisor, however, wants you to continue building the VCR cheaply so that the company's repair subsidiary will have more repair business or buyers will purchase a replacement more often. Most people who purchase the VCR have annual incomes of less than $15,000. **(a)** Is the company acting legally in refusing to upgrade the VCR? Is it acting ethically? **(b)** Suppose you decide that the company is acting unethically. (1) What should you do to remedy the situation? Discuss the matter with top management? Secretly place an anonymous telephone call to a national consumer magazine to alert its testing staff to the problem? Take no action? (2) Would the fact that you are scheduled for a "performance review" in 3 weeks affect your decision?

5. Old Joe, the smooth, fun-loving cartoon character depicted in Camel cigarette ads, has existed for only 4 years, and 1991 news article reported, "but he's as easily recognized by 6-year-olds as the immortal Mickey Mouse." According to the article, one study published in a special issue of the *Journal of the American Medical Association* asked 229 children ages 3 to 6 to match 22 advertising logos with pictures of the products they represent. The conclusion: "Very young children see, understand and remember advertising. Given the serious health consequences of smoking, the exposure of children to environmental tobacco advertising may represent an important health risk. . . ." In another study, Old Joe was recognized by 98 percent of high school students but by only 67 percent of adults. Yet R. J. Reynolds, the maker of Camel cigarettes, says Old Joe exists solely to persuade adult smokers to switch to Camel. The tobacco industry in general claims that it targets only adults who smoke, not children, and has funded efforts to discourage children and teenagers from smoking. What are the ethics of the Old Joe promotion?

PART FIVE

Property and Estates

CHAPTER 23
Nature and Importance of Property;
Personal Property and Bailments

CHAPTER 24
Real Property: Nature, Acquisition, Ownership, and Control

CHAPTER 25
Interests in Real Property

CHAPTER 26
Estates, Wills, and Trusts

CHAPTER 27
Insurance

Ethics in Practice

CHAPTER 23

Nature and Importance of Property; Personal Property and Bailments

Property law governs the ownership of *things* and the rights associated with ownership. "Things" includes not only land, buildings, and other **real property,** but also a huge variety of **personal property** such as automobiles, money, raw materials, factory equipment, trademarks, stocks and bonds, patents, franchises, and the "goodwill" of a business—anything, in short, that the law recognizes as capable of being owned.

Property law also governs the rights of persons who may have an interest in the property. So, for example, property law controls the relationship between landlord and tenant, and between mortgagor and mortgagee. It also establishes the limits of a property owner's freedom to use his or her property. The law imposes significant restrictions on the rights of property owners to protect other persons who may be harmed by the owner's use of property. As in other areas of the law, in determining the limits of a property owner's rights, the courts and lawmakers strive to balance the interests of the owner against the interests of other persons.

This chapter deals with the general nature and importance of property, especially private property, and with the law of personal property, particularly bailments. The next two chapters are devoted to real property.

NATURE AND IMPORTANCE OF PROPERTY

Meaning of Property

The word "property" is used in two different senses. In one sense, property refers to things owned, such as land, automobiles, and shares of stock in a corporation. We ordinarily think of property in this sense. In its legal sense, **property** refers to legally protected rights to use, possess, enjoy, and dispose of a thing. Land and other physical objects can exist where there is no law (e.g., rocks on the moon), but property rights can exist only where there is law to define and enforce them. Moreover, by protecting people in the exercise of property rights, the law contributes to the value of things. Land, automobiles, and other things would not be valuable (could not be exchanged in the marketplace) were it not for the owners' legally protected rights to use them freely, to sell them, or to give them to someone of their choice.

Title and Other Property Rights

The most extensive property right recognized by the law is ownership, generally referred to as

title. The title owner has the exclusive[1] right to use and possess, derive income from, and transfer by gift, sale, or will an object of property. The owner has a *bundle of rights*—a collection of legal interests, each of which may usually be transferred. The owner of property frequently transfers various property rights ("sticks out of the bundle") to others such as tenants, bailees, and creditors. For example, suppose that James leases his house to Susan for a year. Susan, as the tenant, has the exclusive right to possess, use, and enjoy the house as a residence for the lease period. The landlord, James, has temporarily given up one of the "sticks" in the bundle of rights (possession), but retains all other property rights to the house, including the right to enjoy the house by receiving rental payments, the future right to possess and use the house, and the ultimate power to dispose of the property by sale or other transfer. The **lease** of real property between Susan and James creates a landlord-tenant relationship. The parallel relationship in personal property law, where an owner leases personal property or transfers mere possession of personal property to another for a period of time, is called a **bailment.** Bailments are discussed in the last part of this chapter; the landlord-tenant relationship is explored in Chapter 25.

Because property rights have value in the marketplace, owners also use their property to secure credit from banks and other creditors. In exchange for a loan of money or the extension of credit, the owner may, in addition to a promise to repay the loan, transfer a property right to the creditor known as a **lien.** A lien is the creditor's interest in the owner's property that ensures the repayment of the debt. In the event the owner fails to repay the debt, the lienholder (the creditor) has the right to take and sell (foreclose on) the property. In this way, the property acts as security, minimizing the risk to the creditor of a debtor's default and thereby facilitating the extension of credit in society. A **mortgage** on real property (e.g., a building or a house) and a **security interest** in personal property (e.g., equipment and inventory) are two examples of liens. We examine mortgages and other liens on real estate in Chapter 25, and security interests in Chapter 29.

Classes of Property

Property may be classified as tangible or intangible, real or personal, and public or private. Because the law governing property rights differs depending upon the type of property, the distinction between these classes of property is important. For example, an owner must sign a formal instrument of conveyance, a **deed,** to transfer title to land or real estate. Such a deed is not necessary in the ordinary transfer of personal property, such as a book, clothing, or other goods. Similarly, state taxes imposed on property will be different for tangible and intangible property as well as for real and personal property.

Tangible and Intangible Property. Tangible property consists of things that have a physical existence, such as books, clothing, buildings, and land. Intangible property consists of things that do not exist in physical form but that have economic value, such as patents, copyrights, accounts receivable, and shares of stock.

To understand the concept of intangible property we need to observe an important distinction. We know, for instance, that a stock certificate is tangible personal property because it has a physical existence and can have value in and of itself as a collector's item. But the reason that an ordinary stock certificate has value in the commercial world is that the certificate *represents* an *intangible* property right—the right of ownership in a corporate entity. If the stock certificate is lost or destroyed (and the corporation still exists), the certificate can be replaced without the owner's loss of any rights in the corporation. The owner of a missing certificate remains a shareholder because the certificate is simply *evidence of ownership* and is not the corporate property itself.

Real and Personal Property. Real property consists of land, airspace above the land, and all things embedded in the land or firmly attached to it, such as minerals, trees, fences, and build-

---

[1] "Exclusive" does not mean unlimited. Restrictions on the use of private property are discussed in Chapter 24.

ings. Personal property is all property that is not real property and thus includes tangible things that are movable ("goods," "chattels") and intangible things that have economic value. Figure 23.1 diagrams the distinction between real and personal property.

It is possible for items to be changed in their classification from real to personal and from personal to real. For example, a tree is real property until it is severed from the land—either by a person cutting it down or by an act of nature, such as wind or flood. When the tree is severed it becomes movable and is reclassified as personal property. The reverse of this situation occurs when personal property becomes attached to the land. If the tree is cut into lumber, and a building contractor uses the lumber to build a house, the lumber is thereby converted to real property.

Public and Private Property. All property, whether tangible or intangible, real or personal, can be characterized as public or private. The essential difference is in designating who has the right to use, possess, enjoy, and dispose of the particular thing. Private property is that held by an individual or a business entity primarily for personal or corporate benefit. Public property is that held by a governmental unit or agency, whether federal, state, or local. To illustrate: A national monument, a state park, a county courthouse, and a city library are classified as public property because a governmental body owns them. By contrast, most buildings, houses, automobiles, and other things are private property; that is, a private individual or a corporation owns them.

Legal Protection of Private Property

As we have seen, the concept of property embodies the idea of a bundle of rights that are legally protected. Interference with an individual's right to use, possess, or transfer a thing is a violation of the person's property rights for which the law will provide a remedy. As discussed in Chapters 6, 7, and 8, the law of torts protects property from interference by others. For example, if someone intentionally enters your land without consent or carelessly damages your property, you may recover damages in a suit for trespass or negligence.

Private property is also protected against interference by the government. As noted in Chapter 3, the U.S. Constitution provides in the Fifth and Fourteenth Amendments that neither the federal nor any state government shall deprive a person of life, liberty, or *property* without due process of law. These provisions do not prevent the government from regulating a person's property, but they do require the government to observe due process. The Constitution further provides that the government cannot take private property for public use without paying the owner just compensation. The government's power to take property under the right of **eminent domain** and the government's power to regulate property under its police power are discussed in Chapter 24.

Rationale for Protecting Private Property

The primary reason advanced for legal protection of private property is that society benefits when resources are developed, not left to lie fallow. A free enterprise "market" economy such as

Figure 23.1 Circle of property.

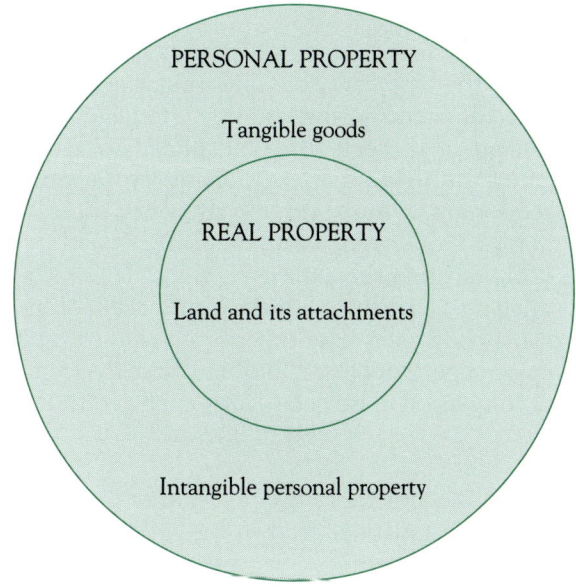

ours places high value on private property and on individual initiative as a major basis of production. In furtherance of these values, our law of property protects the individual's creations and acquisitions by giving him or her an exclusive right of ownership. Of course, there are limitations on development, such as zoning laws, that have been imposed for the protection of others. But, to the extent that we desire application of human knowledge and energy to natural resources, a choice of incentives to promote effective development is involved. The incentive to create, produce, and exchange is greatly increased when society gives protection to the owner of private property and permits the owner to retain the benefits of his or her labor. This rationale applies not only to utilization of physical objects but also to the area of intangibles. The law of patents and copyrights developed from the notion that intellectual effort that results in a valuable invention or creation should be protected from appropriation. This view is the proper response from a society that benefits from such creativity.

In Case 23.1, the court addresses the issue whether a patient owns the cells taken from his or her body during medical procedures. Such cells can be extremely valuable in medical research and biotechnology. Note how the court attempts to strike a balance between the rights of the patient and the interests of society in the advancement of medicine and science. Did it strike the proper balance?

CASE 23.1

Moore v. The Regents of the University of California
• 793 P.2d 479 (Cal. 1990)

FACTS

John Moore was treated for hairy-cell leukemia at the UCLA Medical Center by Dr. David Golde. Dr. Golde learned that Moore's blood contained substances which were valuable in commercial research. In October of 1976, Moore's spleen was removed at the recommendation of Dr. Golde, who, prior to the operation made arrangements to take portions of Moore's spleen to a separate research unit. He did not inform Moore of his plans to conduct this research nor request his permission. Moore returned to the UCLA Medical Center several times between November 1976 and September 1983 and during these visits Dr. Golde withdrew additional samples of blood.

In 1979, Dr. Golde established a cell line from Moore's T-lymphocytes (a type of white blood cell), and the Regents of the University of California, the owners of the UCLA Medical Center, acquired a patent on the cell line. He negotiated agreements for commercial development of the cell line, and under an agreement with Genetics Institute, acquired the rights to 75,000 shares of Genetics stock. Genetics Institute also agreed to pay him and the Regents at least $330,000 over 3 years.

Moore sued the Regents and Dr. Golde and others for using his cells in medical research without his consent, alleging a breach of fiduciary duty (lack of informed consent) and conversion of his body cells. The superior court dismissed the entire complaint, and the court of appeals reversed, holding that the complaint did state a cause of action for conversion. The defendants appealed to the California Supreme Court.

OPINION

PANELLI, J. . . . Moore . . . attempts to characterize the invasion of his rights as a conversion. . . . He theorizes that he continued to own his cells following

CASE 23.1 Continued

their removal from his body, at least for the purpose of directing their use, and that he never consented to their use in potentially lucrative medical research. . . .

To establish a conversion, plaintiff must establish an actual interference with his ownership or right of possession. . . . Since Moore clearly did not expect to retain possession of his cells following their removal, to sue for their conversion he must have retained an ownership interest in them. But there are several reasons to doubt that he did retain any such interest. First, no reported judicial decision supports Moore's claim, either directly or by close analogy. Second, California statutory law drastically limits any continuing interest of a patient in excised cells. . . . Pursuant to Health and Safety Code section 7054.4 . . . recognizable anatomical parts, [and] human tissues, . . . shall be disposed of by interment, incineration, or any other method [approved by] the state. . . . By restricting how the excised cells may be used . . . the statute eliminates so many of the rights ordinarily attached to property that one cannot simply assume that what is left amounts to "property." . . .

While we do not purport to hold that excised cells can never be property for any purpose whatsoever, the novelty of Moore's claim demands express consideration of the policies to be served by extending liability. . . .

Of the relevant policy considerations, two are of overriding importance. The first is protection of a competent patient's right to make autonomous medical decisions. . . . This policy weighs in favor of providing a remedy to patients when physicians act with undisclosed motives that may affect their professional judgment. The second important policy consideration is that we not threaten with disabling civil liability innocent parties who are engaged in socially useful activities, such as researchers who have no reason to believe that their use of a particular cell sample is, or may be, against a donor's wishes.

Research on human cells plays a critical role in medical research. This is so because researchers are increasingly able to isolate naturally occurring, medically useful biological substances and to produce useful quantities of such substances through genetic engineering. These efforts are beginning to bear fruit. Products developed through biotechnology that have already been approved for marketing in this country include treatments and tests for leukemia, cancer, diabetes, dwarfism, hepatitis-B, kidney transplant rejection, emphysema, osteoporosis, ulcers, anemia, infertility, and gynecological tumors, to name but a few. . . .

[T]here is no pressing need to impose a judicially created rule of [conversion] liability, since enforcement of physicians' disclosure obligations will protect patients against the very type of harm with which Moore was threatened. So long as a physician discloses research and economic interests that may affect his judgment, the patient is protected from conflicts of interest. Aware of any conflicts, the patient can make an informed decision to consent to treatment, or to withhold consent and look elsewhere for medical assistance.

JUDGMENT

[W]e hold that the allegations of Moore's third amended complaint state a cause of action for breach of fiduciary duty or lack of informed consent, but not conversion.

DISSENT

MOSK, J. . . . The concepts of property and ownership in our law are extremely broad. . . .

> **CASE 23.1**
> **Continued**
>
> Being broad, the concept of property is also abstract: rather than referring directly to a material object such as a parcel of land or the tractor that cultivates it, the concept of property is often said to refer to a "bundle of rights" that may be exercised with respect to that object. . . .
>
> In [many] instances, [a] limitation or prohibition diminishes the bundle of rights that would otherwise attach to the property, yet what remains is still deemed in law to be a protectible property interest. . . .
>
> The same rule applies to Moore's interest in his own body tissue: even if we assume that section 7054.4 limited the use and disposition of his excised tissue in the manner claimed by the majority, Moore nevertheless retained valuable rights in that tissue. Above all, at the time of its excision he at least had the right to do with his own tissue whatever the defendants did with it: i.e., he could have contracted with researchers and pharmaceutical companies to develop and exploit the vast commercial potential of his tissue and its products. . . . As noted above, the majority cite no case holding that an individual's right to develop and exploit the commercial potential of his own tissue is not a right of sufficient worth or dignity to be deemed a protectible property interest. In the absence of such authority—or of legislation to the same effect—the right falls within the traditionally broad concept of property in our law.

Legal Restrictions on Private Property

The freedom to use and enjoy private property is not without limits. The law restricts the use of property to protect the rights of others. Health, safety, and environmental laws restrict the use of business and personal property for the benefit of workers, consumers, and the general public. Motor vehicle laws, restricting the freedom of drivers, are designed to protect other motorists, pedestrians, and others who could be injured by the unlawful use of an automobile. Zoning ordinances and building codes restrict the rights of landowners for the benefit of tenants, other landowners, and communities.

The common law also restrains owners of property from using it in ways that harm others. A landowner is liable in damages to a person who is injured on or near the property through an intentional or negligent act, and in some instances, even if the owner is without fault. For example, a merchant may be liable in damages to a customer who slips and falls on a wet floor, and the lessor of a defective piece of equipment may be liable without fault to the lessee injured by it. Chapter 24 discusses legal restrictions placed on owners of real property.

PERSONAL PROPERTY

The most important aspects of the law of personal property involve the ownership and possession of such property. This section of the chapter deals with the various ways in which people acquire rights to personal property.

Acquisition by Purchase

Probably the most common method of acquiring ownership of personal property is by purchase from an owner. Sales of personal property are governed by the common law of contracts, or by specialized bodies of contract law, or both. For example, consumers and businesses purchase goods daily in the marketplace from a variety of sellers. Sales of goods are governed by Article 2 of the Uniform Commercial Code as supplemented by the common law of contracts.

Acquisition by Creation

Particularly important to business is acquiring property through creative activity. A person may acquire property rights by creating a song, a book, an invention, computer software, or an innovative manufacturing process. The creator may be protected under a copyright, patent, or trademark or under the law of trade secrets. Such products of the mind, generally referred to as **intellectual property,** are discussed in Chapter 8.

Acquisition by Gift

Another way to become owner of personal property is to receive it as a gift. A gift is a voluntary transfer of property without consideration. The person making the gift is the **donor;** the person receiving it is the **donee.**

Gifts may be classified as testamentary, inter vivos, or causa mortis. **Testamentary gifts** are those intended to take place at the death of the donor and ordinarily must be made by means of a will. Wills are discussed in Chapter 26. A gift **inter vivos** is one made between living persons; that is, the transfer takes place and the donor receives full ownership rights during the lifetime of the donor and donee. A gift **causa mortis** is a transfer (of personal property only) by a donor in the belief that he or she will die as a result of existing illness or injury, or from an imminent peril such as a sinking ship.

An inter vivos gift is a present transfer of property to the donee. As such, it is generally *irrevocable* by the donor—the donor cannot cancel the gift or take back the property. On the other hand, a gift causa mortis is revocable by the donor because it is made in contemplation of death and probably under emotional stress. Moreover, if the donor recovers from the illness or injury or escapes the peril, the gift is automatically revoked. Similarly, if the donee dies before the donor, this also revokes the gift causa mortis.

Three elements are required for gifts inter vivos and causa mortis:

- Donative intent
- Actual or constructive delivery of the property
- Acceptance of the gift by the donee

Donative Intent. To make a gift, the donor must intend for the donee to have the thing without paying for it—i.e., without giving consideration. Statements such as "Take it, it's

> **BOX 23.1**
> **Point to Consider: Who Owns an Idea?**
> Joyce McDonald thought she did. Under a suggestion plan of her employer, Oranco Enterprises, a steel fabricator, an employee who develops a suggestion to improve productivity is eligible for a bonus. Joyce had an idea to reduce the waste in the manufacturing process at her plant. But before she could submit the suggestion to her supervisor, a co-worker, Robert Welk, with whom she had discussed her suggestion in confidence, submitted it to Oranco management. The suggestion was later adopted by Oranco and Robert was given a $12,000 bonus.
>
> Joyce sued Robert for misappropriating her property—i.e., the idea she came up with. Will she prevail? Was it ethical for Robert to use her idea to win the bonus? What can a person do to protect "ideas" from appropriation by others?

yours" and "I want you to have this" are clear indications of the requisite donative intent. Where there is no clear indication of intent and a lawsuit results, the court must determine the donor's intent on the basis of whatever evidence is available.

The donor also must intend to make a *present* transfer of his or her rights in the thing if there is to be a gift. Suppose that John says to Mary, "I'll give you this horse at the end of the fifth race tomorrow." Since John did not intend a present transfer of ownership, there is no gift. Such a "future" gift is an unenforceable promise to make a gift. For the gift to be effective now, John must transfer ownership to Mary now.

Gifts, however, can be conditional such that the gift will be revoked in the event of some future event. For example, numerous courts have held that an engagement ring or other gift given in contemplation of marriage is made upon an implied condition that it is to be returned if the donee breaks the engagement without legal justification. If the *donor* unjustifiably breaks the engagement, however, the donee ordinarily may keep the gift.

Actual or Constructive Delivery. No gift occurs if the donor does not give up complete control and possession of the object. For example, if one person says to another, "I want you to have my watch," but continues to wear the watch, no gift is made. The requirement of delivery is usually met by physically handing the object to the donee and thereby giving up control and possession of it.

In some situations it is impractical to make physical delivery of an item, and the law allows a **constructive** (sometimes called **symbolic**) delivery. Giving the donee a key to a locker may, under some circumstances, be recognized as a delivery of the contents. Dan says, "I want you to have the jewelry in my locker," and gives Joan the only key. There is a delivery of the jewelry because Dan has given Joan, the donee, exclusive dominion and control over the jewelry.

Since physical delivery of *intangible* property is impossible, delivery of a symbol will be sufficient to constitute delivery of the underlying interest. For instance, delivery of a savings account passbook is usually sufficient to pass ownership of the account to a donee. Frequently, the donor will execute a written conveyance of an object—i.e., a letter or a document transferring ownership to the donee. The delivery of such a document is as effective in transferring ownership as is physical delivery of the object. For example, the gift of an automobile or a boat is usually accomplished by the donor's signing and delivering the certificate of ownership to the donee. Ownership of securities, accounts receivable, and other intangibles is often transferred by means of a written form of assignment.

In order to constitute a gift, delivery of an item need not necessarily be to the donee. Occasionally, a donor will turn over an item to a third person with instructions to deliver it to the donee or to hold it for the benefit of the donee. The question may then arise: Has the donor made a present transfer of his or her rights? The answer will depend upon the relationship of the third person to the donor.

Where the third person is an agent for the donor (e.g., the donor's employee), there is no present transfer of rights. An agent owes a duty to follow the instructions of his or her principal or employer. Thus, a donor who delivers an object to his or her agent could have a change of mind at any time and get the object back. Where the donor delivers an item to an agent of the *donee*, the donor does not retain control, and there is an effective delivery to the donee.

Acceptance. A person cannot be forced to accept something that he or she does not want. Some examples of items a person might not wish to accept as a gift are an automobile with an unpaid purchase price in excess of its current value, stock in a corporation on the verge of bankruptcy, and defective goods that require extensive repairs to be usable. To determine whether there has been an acceptance, the courts will look at the words and conduct of the donee as well as the nature of the property (whether beneficial or not). If the donee's con-

---

BOX 23.2

Law in Practice

Billie Jean McCune leased a safe deposit box at a bank. On December 12, 1978, her father, W. G. Brown, Sr., placed in the box $250,000 worth of gold Krugerrands and Mexican pesos. Brown was involved in a divorce proceeding with his wife and transferred the gold to his daughter in an attempt to defeat his wife's rights to the property. Brown claimed that his daughter understood that the gold was to be transferred back to him some time after the divorce. He retained keys to the safe deposit box which contained other items that belonged to him, including his will. McCune later claimed that Brown made an unconditional gift to her. Brown sued McCune to restrain her from removing the coins from the box.

Was there the necessary donative intent for a valid inter vivos gift? How should the law deal with "fraudulent" transfers—i.e., gifts and other transfers of property that are made to defraud creditors or defeat the rights of others? ■

duct indicates the donee's ownership of the property, the court may infer an intent to accept. For example, riding a bicycle received as a birthday present is an act of ownership. Since in most instances a gift will result in a benefit to the donee, in the absence of contrary evidence, the courts ordinarily will *presume* acceptance by the donee when there is an effective delivery.

Acquisition by Taking Possession

A person may acquire ownership of a movable object that is not owned by anyone by taking possession of it. *Possession* in its literal sense means control or power over an object. Taking possession of a movable object in today's world is rarely sufficient to establish ownership of the object. In an urban, industrial society, few objects are not owned by someone, but one of the primary methods recognized historically was taking possession of something in its natural state.

Wildlife. Many early court cases involve the acquisition of ownership of wild animals, fish, and bees. Such acquisition often was necessary for survival in a frontier society. At times, more than one person claimed ownership of an animal. Obviously, some rule governing ownership rights in wild animals was required. The rule that emerged was that ownership of a wild animal was obtained by taking the animal into possession (as by trapping or netting). This rule is still part of our contemporary common law.

Today, a person's survival is seldom at stake, and there are many conservation laws protecting endangered species of animals and birds from capture. All states have established seasons for hunting and fishing, and there is a prerequisite license. Failure to comply with state or local laws usually is a criminal offense. Only within the legal limits outlined by the appropriate governmental unit can a person acquire ownership of wild animals today.

Abandoned Property. A contemporary application of the acquisition-by-possession principle may occur today in regard to abandoned chattels. If an owner intentionally gives up possession of

---

BOX 23.3

Gifts and Financial Planning

Gifts may be an integral part of a person's financial planning. For example, under the Uniform Transfers to Minors Act (UFTA), an adult, usually a parent or grandparent, can make a gift of property to a minor child by transferring property to an adult "custodian." A parent can act as the custodian and invest the money or property for the college education of the child or for other purposes. This has some tax advantages because some or all of the income from the property will be taxed to the child at the child's income tax rate, which is generally lower than the parent's rate. Under the federal income tax code, before a child reaches 14, up to $1,200 in unearned income (e.g., dividends and interest income) is taxed at the child's rate (up to $600 is not taxable). After a child reaches 14, all the unearned income is taxed at the child's rate.

Gifts may also be part of an individual's estate plan—i.e., a plan for the disposition of his or her property (the "estate") upon death. The federal and state estate and inheritance taxes are important considerations in the development of an estate plan because any estate or inheritance tax will obviously reduce the value of the property that will ultimately pass to the decedent's heirs. The most significant tax is the federal government's estate and gift tax, which is a tax on the value of a person's estate at death, subject to certain deductions and credits. The estate also includes the value of gifts made during a person's lifetime. Although this prevents a person from simply giving away his or her property to avoid the estate tax, a person is permitted to give away $10,000 per year per donee free of any gift tax liability. Thus, an individual with a large estate can use yearly gifts to reduce the value of the estate at the time of his or her death and thereby minimize federal estate tax liability.

property, with the intent to relinquish ownership permanently, the item is **abandoned.** Ownership of an abandoned item may be acquired by taking possession of it with intent to exclude others. For example, if someone finds a broken watch lying in a trash barrel, the person may acquire ownership of it by picking it up and exercising control over it to the exclusion of others.

The finder must proceed cautiously, however, and first establish that the article has truly been abandoned, rather than lost. A person's intent in giving up possession of property is not always obvious. Courts usually consider three factors in determining the intent of the owner in relinquishing possession: (1) the location of the item, (2) the value of the item, and (3) the utility of the item. Trash barrels, public dumps, and roadside areas are all repositories for abandoned items. If an item is found in trash bin, and the item is unusable without the expenditure of a large sum of money for repair, it is probable that the owner chose to relinquish possession and ownership permanently. However, if an item of great value is found in any such place, the item has probably been lost by the owner without any intent to abandon it.

Lost Property. A different rule of law applies to lost, as distinguished from abandoned, property. If the owner unconsciously or unintentionally gives up possession of the chattel, without any intention of relinquishing ownership, the item is **lost.** For example, coins that fall through a hole in a person's pocket are not abandoned, but lost. One does not become the owner of lost property by taking possession of it. The finder does acquire, however, superior rights to the property against all persons except the rightful owner. Suppose Alice's dog wanders away from home and Ben finds and takes care of it. As a finder of lost property, Ben acquires a legally protected right of possession against everyone except Alice, the owner. However, since the dog was not abandoned, Ben does not become the owner.

In many states today the finder of a lost article can acquire full ownership of the item by complying with a lost property statute. Usually, the statute requires the finder to turn the property over to local authorities while the county clerk advertises the loss. When a specified time has elapsed after the required steps have been taken, and if the true owner has not claimed the property, ownership passes to the finder.

Mislaid Property. Another distinction that is important in determining property rights is whether an item is lost or mislaid. An item is lost when the disappearance is a result of something other than the owner's conscious conduct. By contrast, an item is **mislaid** if the owner intentionally places it somewhere and forgets to pick it up again. If you go to class, put down your textbook on the chair next to you, and leave at the end of class forgetting to take the book, the book is considered mislaid, not lost.

If an item was mislaid, the owner of the premises where the item was found, not the finder, is entitled to take possession. A customer places his or her sunglasses down on a store counter as he or she is paying for merchandise and then leaves without them. The proprietor of the store has a right of possession superior to that of a second customer who discovers the glasses. The rationale is that the owner logically can be expected to return to the premises as soon as he or she remembers where the item was left. In Case 23.2, the court discusses the difference between lost and mislaid property.

CASE 23.2   Ray v. Flower Hospital • 439 N.E.2d 942 (Ohio App. 1981)

FACTS Karen Ray was employed as a receptionist by Flower Hospital. At the information desk where she worked there was a drawer for keeping lost and found property. On the night of June 15, 1979, between 7:30 p.m. and 8:30 p.m., Karen noticed a soft-shell eyeglass case on the top of the information desk. Upon inspection, it was discovered to contain four diamond rings, a topaz pin, gold earrings, a diamond necklace, gold cuff links, and a gold coin. The property was placed in the hospital's safe, and the local police were notified. The newspaper lost and found column was checked for 30 days, but no one came forth to claim the jewelry. On December 13, 1979, Karen filed suit against Flower Hospital for declaratory judgment and return of the property to her. Flower Hospital argued that the eyeglass case, having been found on top of the information desk of the hospital, should be deemed to be mislaid property. The trial court granted Karen's motion for summary judgment, declaring the property to be lost and Karen to be the owner of the property. Flower Hospital appealed.

OPINION CONNORS, J. . . . 1 Ohio Jurisprudence 3d 23, Abandoned Property, Section 13, defines "mislaid property" as follows: ". . . property which the owner voluntarily and intentionally *laid down* in a place where he could again resort to it, which location the owner then forgot. . . . "

In contrast, "lost property" is defined as follows: ". . . property which the owner has involuntarily parted with through neglect, carelessness, or inadvertence, that is, property which the owner has unwittingly suffered to pass out of his possession and the whereabouts of which he has no knowledge. . . . Articles which are *accidentally dropped* in any public place, public thoroughfare, or street, are lost in the legal sense."

The substance then, of this court's analysis, must be a determination of whether the property in question is legally "lost" or legally "mislaid." . . .

It is uncontroverted that the eyeglass case containing the jewels was found lying on the top of the information desk, not on the floor of the hospital in front of the information desk. Further, it cannot be presumed that the property was lost or abandoned from the mere passage of time, although this is another fact or circumstance to be taken into consideration in the particular case. . . . [T]he six months that elapsed . . . from the time of discovery until the time that the appellee [Karen Ray] filed suit to ascertain the ownership of the property, did not create a presumption that the goods were either lost or mislaid.

The location in which the property was found . . . however, does aid this court in its labeling the goods as lost or mislaid property. The jewels were secreted away in a soft-shell eyeglass case. They were not found strewn across the floor whereby anyone walking into the hospital could view them. Further, the eyeglass case containing the jewels in this case was laid down on the top of the information desk by someone, presumably the owner, or someone seeking their return to the true owner by turning the case in to the "lost and found" desk, and was not dropped by inadvertence, negligence or carelessness as would be the case of lost property. From all of the facts and circumstances of this particular case, this court

> **CASE 23.2 Continued**
>
> finds that the property was mislaid, and, as such, should remain in the possession of the hospital.
>
> As was stated by the Supreme Court of Texas in the case of *Schley v. Couch*, . . . :
>
>> Mislaid property is presumed to be left in custody of owner or occupant of premises upon which it is found and he is generally entitled to possession of such property as against all except the owner thereof.
>
> Therefore, . . . it was error for the trial court to award title to mislaid property to the appellee [Ray].
>
> **JUDGMENT** Reversed.

Acquisition by Accession

Often a person's property is improved or added to by the labor and materials of another person, as where Ann's Auto Shop gives Raoul's car a tune-up at his request. Under the legal concept of **accession** (addition, augmentation), Raoul becomes the owner of whatever new value Ann's efforts produced. That is, he is entitled to any parts that Ann installed and to any new value to the car that resulted from her adjusting it during the tune-up. Raoul has, of course, an obligation to pay for the tune-up.

Suppose, however, that Tom steals Raoul's car, repaints it, and adds a radar detector. Later Tom is apprehended, the car is returned to Raoul, and Tom demands payment for the paint job and the radar detector. Under the law of accession, Raoul is entitled to anything that Tom added that cannot be removed without damage to the car. Since removing the paint would damage the car, Raoul acquires ownership of the paint job by accession and has no obligation to pay for it. However, because the radar unit can be removed without damage to the car, Tom is entitled to the radar detector or to its value. The policy of the law of accession, where the improver added value wrongfully, is to protect the innocent owner from loss, but not to punish the wrongdoer.

Acquisition by Confusion

Sometimes goods belonging to different persons are so commingled or intermixed that the owners cannot identify their particular goods. The intermixing, called **confusion,** usually is rightful, as where several owners voluntarily permit the confusion of grain of a particular grade for storage at a grain elevator. Each owner remains owner of his or her proportionate share of the entire mass. But sometimes confusion is wrongful. Tim, the owner of an unmeasured quantity of salad oil, steals an unknown quantity of Mary's salad oil and mixes it with his own. Since it is impossible to determine the quantity of Mary's oil, ownership of the whole mass passes to her by confusion. As the innocent party, she has no obligation to pay Tim for his oil. Tim, however, has the right to try to prove how much he owns, though as a thief he may find it difficult to persuade a court that the amount he claims is accurate.

BAILMENTS

Bailments involve the transfer of personal property to a person who acquires only a possessory interest in the property (does not become the owner). Bailments are a common commercial transaction. The leasing of automobiles and equipment, the storage and shipment of goods, and the repair of property are some examples. Bailments also occur outside of the commercial arena. For example, suppose you allow your roommate to use your car to run an errand. Although you do not charge a rental fee, the relationship is a bailment, and your friend is a bailee. If the car is damaged or stolen while in his or her possession, the law of bailments determines your roommate's liability for the loss.

Meaning of Bailment

A bailment is the legal relationship resulting from the transfer of possession of personal property from one person (called the **bailor**) to another person (called the **bailee**) with the understanding that the bailee will return the item to the bailor or dispose of it as directed by the bailor. Two points should be emphasized concerning this definition: (1) A bailment involves the transfer of possession only, without the transfer of ownership; where possession and ownership are both transferred, the transfer constitutes either a sale or a gift; and (2) because the bailee does not acquire title to the property, he or she is under a duty to return the property to the bailor or dispose of it according to the terms of the bailment agreement.

The voluntary transfer of possession of property referred to in the definition above implies an agreement between the parties. Thus, where goods come into a person's possession without the person's knowledge, he or she is not a bailee of the goods. For example, if a person agrees to store an "empty trunk" for a neighbor, the person is not a bailee of an overcoat that the neighbor neglected to remove from the trunk. However, the law sometimes imposes the duties of a bailee upon a person who comes into possession of another's property without an agreement with the owner. This is referred to as a **constructive bailment.** For example, the finder of lost property is a constructive bailee and has a duty to return the property to the rightful owner.

Classes of Bailments

Bailments may be classified as **mutual-benefit bailments** (sometimes called "bailments for hire") or **gratuitous bailments.** A mutual-benefit bailment is one in which each party receives some benefit. In a commercial bailment, where the bailee pays a price to have possession or use of the property, the relationship is a mutual-benefit bailment. On the other hand, a gratuitous bailment is one in which one of the parties receives a benefit in regard to the bailed article without being obligated to pay for the benefit. Gratuitous bailments can be for the **sole benefit of the bailor** (e.g., the gratuitous storage of the bailee's property), or for the **sole benefit of the bailee** (e.g., the gratuitous loan of the bailor's property).

A **special bailment** is one in which the bailee is an innkeeper (a hotel, a motel, etc.), a common carrier of goods (a railroad, an airline, etc.), or a warehouse. Special bailments are extensively regulated by the state and federal governments. In addition, warehousers and carriers issue documents of title in connection with the storage and shipment of goods. Documents of title and the liabilities of warehousers and carriers are discussed in Chapter 19. Table 23.1 summarizes the different types of bailments.

Creation of Bailments

A bailment is a simple relation, and its creation usually requires no particular formalities. The relation may exist even though there is no contract or written agreement between the bailor and the bailee. However, a lease of goods for which the total payments are more than $1,000 generally must be in writing to be enforceable under Article 2A of the Uniform Commercial Code.

The bailee must take possession of the property to create a bailment. In the ordinary bailment setting, such as a rental or storage of property, a transfer of possession clearly occurs when the bailee physically takes the property. But the issue of whether possession has transferred may arise in a number of cases where the alleged bailee claims that there was no transfer of possession to him or her. For example, suppose that you go to a restaurant tonight and hang your jacket in a coatroom. Does this constitute a bailment of the coat to the restaurant?

This particular issue occurs frequently in cases involving parking lots. Depending upon the circumstances, a parking lot can be a bailment of the automobile to the parking lot or a "lease" or "license" of space (real property) to the car owner. The distinction between the two

Table 23.1 Classification of Bailments

Type of Bailment	Example
Mutual-benefit bailments	
Leasing property	Consumer rents a car from Acme Rent-A-Car
	Business rents computer for office from computer supplier
Receiving possession to perform work on property	Owner leaves watch with jewelry store to be repaired
Gratuitous bailments	
Sole benefit of bailee	Owner loans chain saw to neighbor without charge
Sole benefit of bailor	Neighbor allows owner to store owner's automobile in neighbor's garage without charge
	Friend transports owner's furniture to owner's new apartment without charge
Special bailments	
Innkeepers	Hotel guest leaves valuables in hotel safe
Warehousers	Owner stores piano in commercial warehouse
Common carriers	Seller hires railroad or trucking company to transport goods to buyer

---

BOX 23.4

Developments in the Law: Leases of Personal Property and Article 2A of the Uniform Commercial Code

Leasing of personal property, particularly automobiles, computers, and equipment, has become a common method for consumers and businesses to acquire property. The growth of the commercial leasing business has also resulted in the development of a new article to the Uniform Commercial Code. In 1987, the National Conference of Commissioners on Uniform State Laws, the American Law Institute, and the Editorial Board of the Uniform Commercial Code approved Article 2A on leases. To date, 30 jurisdictions have adopted Article 2A and several states have adopting legislation pending. Moreover, many state courts in states that have not adopted Article 2A have applied Article 2 of the Code governing sale of goods to leases of personal property. In most states, therefore, bailments involving the lease of personal property will be governed by the Uniform Commercial Code.

Article 2A applies to any **lease,** defined as a "transfer of the right to possession and use of goods for a term in return for consideration." It does not apply to a lease that is intended to be a security interest or a conditional sale. This distinction between a "true lease" and a "security lease" is discussed in Chapter 29. Article 2A governs the formation, construction, and performance of leases as well as remedies for breach. It also has special rules for **finance leases.** A finance lease involves three parties. The lessor is usually a bank, financial institution, or other entity that does not manufacture, sell, or select the leased goods. The lessee selects the goods, and the lessor acquires the goods from a third-party supplier and then leases them to the lessee. Ordinarily, in a finance lease, the lessor does not assume any responsibility regarding the quality of the leased goods.

relations is important if the owner's car is stolen or damaged while in the parking lot. A bailee of goods assumes certain duties toward the goods, particularly the duty to exercise reasonable care for the protection of the property. These duties are discussed in the next section. One who merely leases a parking space to the car owner does not assume the duties of a bailee.

Since a bailment requires a transfer of possession, the test to be applied is whether the owner has given up control over the vehicle. For example, if a person drives a car into a self-service parking lot, parks the car, locks it, and takes the keys, a license of space, not a bailment, is created. The driver has not relinquished control over the car. On the other hand, if a person drives to a restaurant where an attendant parks the car, takes the key, and gives the owner a claim check, a bailment is created. The driver has given up control; possession has been transferred to the restaurant. Note that a transfer of possession is all that is required; it is not essential that the keys be surrendered. As the next case demonstrates, resolution of this issue depends upon the degree of control exercised by the parking lot over the automobile.

CASE 23.3 **Broadview Apartments Co. v. Baughman**
- 350 A.2d 707 (Md. App. 1976)

FACTS Glenn H. Baughman was a tenant in the Broadview Apartments located in northwest Baltimore. He paid Broadview $15 a month to park his car in the Broadview Garage. The garage was beneath the apartment building and was an enclosed two-level garage, one level in the basement and one on the ground (lobby) floor. Each level had a separate entrance and exit. There was no attendant at the lobby level, but there was one on the basement level. There was a security guard on duty 24 hours a day, and each tenant had a key to the garage door.

On the night of November 23, 1966, appellee parked his car in his assigned spot on the lobby level, locked the car, and took the keys with him. When he returned the next day, his car was gone. It was never recovered. Baughman filed suit for the loss of his automobile. The trial court held that Broadview was a bailee of the car and, as such, was liable for the value of the missing car. Broadview appealed.

OPINION MELVIN, J. . . . A bailment is "the relation created through the transfer of the possession of goods or chattels, by a person called the bailor to a person called the bailee, without a transfer of ownership, for the accomplishment of a certain purpose, whereupon the goods or chattels are to be dealt with according to the instructions of the bailor." . . .

Once the bailment relationship is proven[,] certain responsibilities flow from the relationship. The bailee in accepting possession of the bailed property assumes the duty of exercising reasonable care in protecting it. . . .

Where "a demand and an unexplained refusal to [return bailed property] are proven, a prima facie case of negligence is made out. . . . [The bailor] must prove the delivery, the bailment and the failure to return; thereupon, it is incumbent upon the bailee to explain that failure. . . . "If no bailment is shown, and the owner of the property is a mere licensee or lessee of the storage space, then in order to recover against the defendant garage owner the plaintiff would have

CASE 23.3 Continued

to prove specific acts of negligence on the part of the defendant. . . . Absent a bailor-bailee relationship, the plaintiff would not have the benefit of any . . . presumption of negligence that arises from a mere showing of non-return of his property if that relationship existed. . . .

The courts have uniformly found a delivery of possession to the parking lot operators, and therefore a contract for bailment, where the keys are surrendered with the car or where the car is parked by an attendant. . . . Some other factors which have been considered to be important are: (1) whether there are attendants at the entrances and exits of the lots, (2) whether the car owner receives a claim check that must be surrendered before he can take his car, (3) whether the parking lot is enclosed, and (4) whether the parking lot operator expressly assumes responsibility for the car. No single factor has been viewed as determinative of the issue. The law has probably been best stated in *Osborne v. Cline*, . . . where the New York Court of Appeals stated that

> Whether a person simply hires a place to put his car (licensor-licensee relationship) or whether he has turned its possession over to the care and custody of another (bailee-bailor relationship) depends on the place, the conditions and the nature of the transaction.

In the instant case we think the evidence is legally insufficient to establish that a bailor-bailee relationship existed. Appellee merely rented a parking space monthly: he parked his own car, locked the car and took the keys with him. There was no testimony that Broadview had a set of keys for the car or had any right or authority to move or exercise any control over the car. The parking garage was laid out in such a manner that it was possible for appellee to park his car without any attendant even being aware of his presence in the garage. Appellee entered into the monthly lease arrangement with full knowledge of how the garage operated. He was not required to check his car in or out, and there was no evidence whatsoever that control of the car was ever turned over to the operators of the garage, or that they ever accepted delivery or control. Nor was there any evidence that Broadview expressly contracted or asserted that the car would be safe from theft while in the garage. . . . The mere fact that he paid a monthly rent for an enclosed parking space . . . does not, standing alone, raise an inference of a bailment contract. . . .

JUDGMENT [R]eversed.

Rights and Duties of the Bailor and the Bailee

When a bailment relationship exists, the law imposes certain duties on the parties and gives them certain rights. For example, the bailee who leases property has the right to possess and use the property during the term of the lease. Along with these rights, the bailee assumes a duty to exercise reasonable care to protect the leased property from loss or damage and to return the property to the bailor at the end of the lease term. The rights and duties imposed by the law of bailments may be supplemented or modified by any written or oral agreement between the parties. For example, a bailee is not an insurer of the bailed property's safety; he or she is responsible for loss or damage to the bailed property only if the loss or damage was caused by his or her fault. However, the bailment agreement may require the bailee to insure the property or assume liability for any damage or loss. Therefore, to determine the rights and duties of the parties to a bailment, we must apply the law of bailments and the terms of the bailment agreement.

Bailee's Right to Possess the Bailed Property.
During the time that a bailment relation exists, the bailee has a right to the exclusive possession of the bailed property. The bailee has a cause of action for conversion or trespass against any person who wrongfully interferes with his or her right to possession.[2] Moreover, the bailee's right of possession is protected even against the bailor. Suppose that Andrews rents a fishing boat to Finkelman for a week, and 2 days later Andrews, without cause, repossesses the boat from him. Finkelman has a cause of action against Andrews because the bailee's present right to possession is superior to the bailor's rights to the property.

Bailee's Right to Use the Bailed Property.
Where the purpose of a bailment is the use of the bailed article or where the bailment agreement allows some use of the property by the bailee (e.g., a test drive of a car by a repair shop), the bailee has the right to use the article in an authorized manner. For example, if George borrows his neighbor's drill and wood bit, he may use them to drill holes in wood. If George drills a hole in wood and breaks the bit, he is liable for the damage only if he failed to exercise the appropriate degree of care. On the other hand, if the bailee uses the bailed property in an unauthorized way, the bailee is strictly liable for any damage to the property during the bailee's improper use. Charles boards his horse at a stable, and Deena, who works there, rides the horse in a parade without his permission. The horse is injured when it falls in a hole in the street caused by the negligence of the town. Charles can hold Deena responsible even if the horse was injured without any fault on her part. Moreover, unauthorized use of bailed property can be so significant that it constitutes a conversion, allowing the owner of the property to recover the market value of the property from the bailee.

Bailee's Duty to Exercise Care.
Every bailee owes to the bailor some degree of care for the protection of the bailed article. Under modern law, that standard is the degree of care that a reasonable person would exercise under all the circumstances of the case.[3] In determining the care required under this standard, the courts will consider, among other factors, the value of the bailed article (jewelry, work of art); the nature of the article (whether easily portable or not, whether easily damaged or not); the facilities available to the bailee for taking care of the bailed article; the experience of the bailee (whether a professional bailee or not); and the kind of community (metropolitan city or isolated rural town).

The degree of care will also vary depending upon the type of bailment. In gratuitous bailments, the degree of care is different from the typical mutual-benefit bailment where the bailee is under a duty of reasonable care. In a bailment for the sole benefit of the bailee, where the bailee uses the property of the bailor for free, the bailee is under a high standard of care. The bailee must exercise extraordinary care for the property and is liable for any slight fault. In contrast, in a bailment for the sole benefit of the bailor, where the bailee takes possession of bailor's property (for storage or shipment, for example) without any charge to the bailor, the bailee is under a minimal standard of care. The bailee is liable only if he or she was grossly negligent.

If the bailee fails to exercise the appropriate degree of care, and as a proximate cause the bailed goods are damaged, lost, stolen, or destroyed, the bailee is liable to the bailor. The bailee is not, however, an insurer of the goods unless the agreement so provides. In the absence of fault, the bailee is not liable for loss of or damage to the property. For example, if an unexpected hurricane occurs, destroying property in the possession of the bailee, the bailee cannot

---

[2] See the discussion of the torts of conversion and trespass in Chapter 6.

[3] Many of the principles discussed in this section are discussed more fully in Chapter 7. See also Chapter 19 regarding duties of care by warehousers and carriers.

be held liable. Suppose, however, that a hurricane warning is announced. The bailee must now take reasonable precautions to protect the bailed property against this foreseeable, known risk—for example, by boarding up doors and plate-glass windows. If the bailee does not do so and the goods are damaged, the bailee may be held liable for negligence.

Presumption of Negligence. In the event the bailor sues the bailee because goods were lost or damaged while in the bailee's possession, most courts would say that the bailee is *presumed* to be negligent and that the burden rests on the bailee to prove the precise cause of the loss or damage *and* to prove that he or she acted in a reasonable and prudent manner. For example, suppose someone leaves furniture in storage at a warehouse and thereafter a piece is stolen. The presumption is that the storage company was negligent in failing to prevent the theft and is liable. However, if the company can prove that the warehouse was secure and that a security guard patrolled regularly (e.g., monitoring with closed-circuit television), a court might properly conclude that the company had exercised the degree of care expected from a reasonable person and therefore was not liable to the bailor.

The burden is placed on the bailee to show the exercise of due care and the precise cause of the bailor's loss because the bailee is in possession of the facts concerning the disappearance or damage to the property while in the bailee's exclusive possession. Since it may be difficult for a bailor to obtain from the bailee or the bailee's employees the information needed to establish negligence, and because there are may be no independent witnesses to testify how a bailed article was lost or damaged, the law assists the bailor by establishing a presumption that the bailee was negligent. Case 23.4 discusses this presumption.

CASE 23.4	**American Machinery Movers, Inc. v. Continental Container Service, Inc.** • 436 So.2d 1289 (La. App. 1983)
FACTS	Continental Container Service, Inc., leased a 10-year-old diesel forklift from American Machinery Movers, Inc. About a month later, the forklift's engine failed. American sent a mechanic, Gerald Thomas, to the Continental yard, and he discovered that a piston had penetrated the side of the engine block, leaving a rather large hole in the motor. Thomas noted there was insufficient oil on the dipstick. He told American that in his opinion the damage to the engine was caused by operating the diesel without the required amount of oil. American filed suit for the full cost of repairs, $7,579. Continental defended that the machine failed simply because of age, and that it had maintained the forklift properly throughout the lease (a bailment). The trial court held for Continental. American appealed.
OPINION	AUGUSTINE, J. . . . [W]hen damage occurs to the leased object while in the possession of the lessee [bailee], it is *presumed* that the damage has resulted from the lessee's negligence, and it is therefore his burden to exonerate himself from liability by proving his freedom from fault. . . . The reason for the presumption is that, having been in possession of the leased object, the lessee is more able than the lessor [bailor] to explain the cause of damage or loss. . . . The immediate issue is whether the lessee, Continental, discharged its burden to prove that the damage to the diesel forklift was not caused by its negligence.

**CASE 23.4
Continued**

As previously stated, Continental defended this action on the ground that the forklift was ten years old and failed simply because of its age. To prove this fact, the defendant offered the testimony of Mr. William Little, Continental's president, who testified that the average life expectancy of a machine such as American's is, at most, five years. . . . [W]e do not consider the foregoing evidence to be sufficient to carry the defendant lessee's burden of proof. First, Mr. Little's testimony concerning the work-life of a machine such as American's was based upon the performance of similar forklifts in Continental's yard, where forklifts are in constant, heavy toil over the course of a forty-hour week. But according to Mr. Dennis Scandurro, American's vice-president, the forklift in question was never subjected to such a rigorous work schedule. . . .

Moreover, even assuming that Little's testimony allows the inference that American's forklift had a life expectancy of only a *few* more years than those in Continental's yard, and therefore, that American's diesel had lived *beyond* its expected work-life, that fact merely warrants a finding that old age fatigue was among the many possible causes of breakdown. But having undertaken the burden to prove a specific cause of failure, it is not enough for defendant to prove the mere possibility of that cause. . . . [C]onsidering the fact sought to be proved—the cause of a diesel engine's failure—is a rather technical one, we do not think it should suffice for "proof" to say merely that the machine was ten years old and had a life expectancy of five years. Such evidence, utterly lacking in specificity, completely fails to educate us as to how or why the diesel might have been damaged. Accordingly, we hold that the defendant has failed to dispel the presumption that the damage to American's forklift was caused by Continental's negligence.

With respect to the plaintiff's specific allegation that Continental was negligent in not maintaining a proper level of oil in the diesel, and that this negligence caused the engine to fail, the defendant responds that it had maintained the forklift properly. . . . Th[e] testimony [did not] establish that the forklift was properly maintained. . . . Continental's policy with regard to its own machines . . . required inspection of oil and water levels every *two* days. But in testimony and in briefs to this Court, Continental admits that this policy was not followed with respect to the leased forklift. . . .

American, on the other hand, has affirmatively established that which it was under no burden to prove: first, that Continental did not maintain the machine with the frequency required by its own policy, and second, that at the time the engine failed, the oil was well below the required level. Finally, American's mechanic testified that the engine failed *because* of low oil, and . . . his ultimate conclusion was not only reasonable, but also unrefuted.

JUDGMENT

Accordingly, the judgment of the district court is reversed, and there is judgment herein in favor of American Machinery Movers, Inc. and against Continental Services, Inc. . . .

Limitation of Bailee's Liability. In some situations the liability of the bailee may be limited or even eliminated by agreement of the parties. Parking lots, repair shops, checkrooms, and film processors frequently post signs or give their customers receipts or tickets that disclaim all liability or specify a maximum amount of liability for damage to the bailor's property. Are such limitations of liability legally effective?

Enforceability of such limitations is primarily governed by contract law and specifically the rules regarding communication of offers. If the disclaimer is effectively communicated to the bailor, and the bailor gives possession of the goods to the bailee, the bailor implicitly accepts the limitation of liability. In contract law, a message is communicated if the recipient either knows or reasonably *should* know the information it contains. For instance, if a sign is posted with letters large enough for the ordinary person to see upon entering the establishment, the usual bailor may be chargeable with *notice* of the terms posted. Ordinarily, however, the bailor will not be chargeable with notice of terms contained in small print on the back of a ticket stub. Thus, in order to be effective, the bailee must bring the limitation of liability to the attention of the bailor. If the disclaimer is properly communicated, the bailee's liability for negligence will be limited to the maximum amount agreed to by the parties, not the actual loss to the bailor. Most states will hold a bailee liable for the actual loss only if the loss is caused by the *gross negligence* or *intentional* actions of the bailee, the limitation of liability being ineffective to excuse the bailee from liability for intentional or reckless conduct. (See the discussion of exculpatory clauses in Chapter 14.)

Bailee's Duty to Return the Property. In a bailment relation the bailee must return the bailed property at the termination of the bailment or dispose of it as directed by the bailor. If the parties have agreed to a specified time period for the bailment, the right to possession of the item automatically reverts to the bailor at the expiration of the period (as, for example, renting an automobile for 1 week). If the relation is a bailment at will (i.e., no term is specified), the bailor can request return of the goods at any time. In either situation, the bailee must promptly return the goods; if the bailee refuses to return the bailed property or delivers the property to someone other than a person designated by the bailor (a misdelivery), the bailee is liable to the bailor for conversion.

The bailee can lawfully refuse to return the property to the bailor under certain circumstances. A bailee who performs services such as repairs is entitled to compensation for the work performed. If the bailor refuses to pay for the services, the bailee often has a legal right to retain possession of property until the charges are paid, a privilege called a **possessory lien.** And if the bailor continues to refuse to pay the charges for a specified period of time, statutory procedures in most states authorize the bailee to sell the bailed property at public auction to satisfy the unpaid bill. For examples, see the discussion of liens on personal property in Chapter 28.

Bailor's Right to Compensation. In a mutual-benefit bailment where the bailee leases the bailed goods, the bailee is obligated to compensate the bailor for that use. For example, a person who rents a trailer to haul goods must pay the bailor for the use of the trailer under the terms of the rental agreement. Generally, the lessee's duty to pay rent is dependent upon performance of the contract by the lessor. However, under Article 2A' of the Uniform Commercial Code, a lessee under a commercial finance lease (not a consumer lease) must pay the lessor regardless of the condition of the leased goods or any breach by the lessor. A finance lease is one in which the lessor does not select or manufacture the leased goods and does not, therefore, make any warranties as to their quality. This part of Article 2A is called the "hell or high water" provision because it requires the lessee to pay the lessor "come hell or high water." Note that a lessor may also insert a "hell or high water" clause in other nonfinance commercial lease agreements. Article 2A takes no position on the enforceability of such lease clauses, leaving that issue to be determined by other principles of law.

> **BOX 23.5**
>
> ### Point to Consider
>
> Is a "hell or high water" clause in a commercial lease in which the lessor supplies the leased goods unconscionable? What legitimate purposes does such a clause serve? What arguments could be made in support of and against the contention that such clauses are grossly unfair to the lessee? ∎

Bailor's Duty to Protect Bailee from Harm.

Bailors are under a duty to warn bailees of any known defects in the bailed property. Such a duty is imposed even when the bailment is for the sole benefit of the bailee. For instance, if a person loans a power mower to a neighbor knowing that the mower has a loose belt, the owner must inform the neighbor of the defect. If the bailor has knowledge of a defect and fails to disclose it to the bailee, he or she is negligent and liable for any harm to the bailee caused by the defect.

In a mutual-benefit bailment, the bailor is also obligated to make an inspection of the article to discover any defects prior to relinquishing possession to the bailee. For example, a car rental agency must inspect a vehicle before it delivers the car to the customer-bailee. If the rental agency fails to make a reasonable inspection that would have disclosed a defect in the car, the agency is liable for an injury that later occurs as a result of that defect.

Many states now have extended the law of product liability (discussed in Chapter 22) and hold commercial bailors liable without fault for injuries caused by a defect in goods leased. Under Article 2A, express and implied warranties may be created by a lease of property,[4] and many courts in jurisdictions not adopting Article 2A hold commercial lessors to the sales warranties under Article 2. Thus, for example, a lessee injured by a defective item can sue the lessor for breach of the implied warranty of merchantability if the leased good was not fit for ordinary use. Also, many courts impose strict products liability on commercial lessors of property. Case 23.5 addresses the rationale for imposing strict liability on commercial lessors and the type of defects for which a bailor will be held liable without fault.

---

[4]The lessor under a finance lease does not make any implied warranties regarding the condition of the leased property. The lessee can, however, sue the supplier of the goods for breach of warranty. Article 2A gives the lessee the benefit of any warranty made by the supplier to the lessor.

CASE 23.5 Kemp v. Budget Rent-A-Car Systems, Inc. • 453 N.W.2d 872 (Wis. 1990)

FACTS On January 29, 1985, Mary Kemp rented a 1984 Ford Tempo GL from Budget Rent-A-Car in Milwaukee, Wisconsin. She picked up her two sisters at Kenosha, and they drove to West Virginia to attend their brother's funeral. On the way back, Kemp's sister was driving on a wet interstate in Ohio when the three women heard a loud noise that sounded like a tire blowout. Kemp's sister applied the brakes, lost control of the car, and struck a bridge abutment. Kemp sued Budget for personal injuries sustained in the accident. She claimed that the noise before the accident was the right front tie rod breaking and that Budget was strictly liable for the lease of the defective vehicle. The trial court dismissed the products liability claim on the basis that Budget was not a seller or manufacturer of the automobile. Kemp appealed and the court of appeals certified the appeal to the Supreme Court of Wisconsin.

OPINION CECI, J. . . . The first issue before this court is whether a commercial lessor may

**CASE 23.5
Continued**

be held strictly liable in tort for damages resulting from the lease of a defective and unreasonably dangerous product. . . .

We are mindful of the rapid growth of the commercial leasing industry in recent years. We . . . are persuaded that the policy considerations which justify the imposition of strict liability on sellers and manufacturers apply to those who are engaged in the business of leasing products to the consuming public.

Like manufacturers and sellers, persons in the business of leasing continually introduce potentially dangerous instrumentalities into the stream of commerce. A commercial lessor is in a far better position than the lessee to distribute the cost of compensating product-related injuries by purchasing liability insurance and by adjusting the rent paid for the leased product to reflect this cost. In addition, the commercial lessor has the . . . facilities and the technical competence . . . to prevent the circulation of defective products by assuring that his or her products are constantly maintained. . . .

In fact . . . the policy considerations . . . arguably apply with greater force in the case of commercial lessors. The nature of the leasing industry is such that leased products are introduced and reintroduced into the consumer market with each new lease and are, therefore, put to more sustained use than are products owned by the user. The lessee has less opportunity than a buyer to select [a] product . . . and to inspect a product for defects. . . . Thus, the lessee is forced to rely to a greater extent than a buyer on the lessor's technical skill . . . and on his or her implied assurance that a product will be safe during the term of the lease. . . .

Budget argues that a commercial lessor leases used products and, therefore, should be subject to liability to the same extent as a seller of used products. [In] *Burrows v. Follett & Leach, Inc.* . . . this court concluded that a seller of used products was subject to strict liability for manufacturing and design defects but not . . . for defects arising after a product left the manufacturer. . . .

Defects in a used product typically arise before the product reaches the [used product] seller. . . . The used product seller is rarely familiar with the prior history of the product. . . . Further, the used goods market generally operates on the understanding that the seller makes no particular assurance as to quality. . . .

However[,] . . . [t]he commercial lessor is familiar with the characteristics and prior history of the products he or she leases and is in a position to discover and correct defects . . . by means of routine inspection, servicing, and repair. Further, by placing products on the market, the commercial lessor impliedly represents that those products will be fit for use. . . .

Accordingly, we hold that a commercial lessor may be held strictly liable . . . [for] defects which arise after the product leaves the manufacturer's control. . . .

JUDGMENT Reversed and . . . remanded. . . .

SUMMARY

Property means any right to use, possess, enjoy, and dispose of something that can be owned. The main classes of property are tangible and intangible, real and personal, public and private.

A person or firm can acquire ownership of personal property in various ways—for example, by purchase, by creation, or by gift. The elements of a valid gift are donative intent, delivery, and acceptance by the donee. Other methods of acquiring rights to property include accession, confusion, and possession. Thus, to acquire ownership in an abandoned chattel or wild animals, a person must take possession of it—i.e., must exercise control over it. However, the finder of lost or mislaid property does not automatically acquire ownership rights. The finder of lost property can acquire title to the property by complying with local statutes.

A bailment results from the transfer of possession, but not ownership, of personal property from the bailor to the bailee. There are two major classes of bailments: (1) gratuitous bailments, where only one party receives a benefit from the bailment relationship, and (2) mutual-benefit bailments, where each party receives a benefit from the bailment relationship.

Both parties to a bailment relationship have certain rights and duties. The bailee has the right to possession of the bailed article and, when appropriate, the right to use of the bailed article. The bailee has the duty to exercise reasonable care in the custody of the article, and to return it to the bailor or to someone designated by the bailor. The bailor must exercise due care to protect the bailee from defects in the bailed item; and in commercial situations involving a lease of property, the bailor is entitled to compensation from the bailee.

REVIEW QUESTIONS

1. Define the legal concept of property.

2. Are contract rights considered property? Explain.

3. How is private property protected under the law from interference by individuals and from interference by the government?

4. Under what circumstances should private property rights be sacrificed for the general public good?

5. Give examples of legal restrictions that the law places on the use, possession, and disposition of private property.

6. Why does the law require actual or constructive delivery for a gift to be effective?

7. Distinguish between lost and abandoned property; lost and mislaid property.

8. What is a bailment? How does it differ from a sale or a gift?

9. What factors do the courts consider in determining whether a parking lot is a bailment of a car or a lease of space for that car?

10. What can a business do to protect itself from liability for damages to property it leases from others?

CASE PROBLEMS

1. Equitable Trust Company purchased from Auxton Computer Enterprises a $20,000 computer program for tracking project performance. It also purchased from Pace Applied Technology two computer accounting systems for $15,000. All the programs were existing, prepackaged software of general application, known as "canned" programs, rather than programs specifically designed for Equitable. The Maryland Comptroller of the Treasury assessed a sales tax against Equitable based upon the prices paid for the computer programs under a statute that imposes a tax on "any tangible personal property." The comptroller contends that this is a sale of tangible property—i.e., the disks upon which the programs have been coded. Equitable contends that it is a nontaxable sale of intangible personal property—i.e., the program "knowledge" or "information" transferred to it. Is the property tangible or intangible? Why?

2. Bernice, a safe deposit box subscriber at the Old Orchard Bank, found $6,325 in currency on the seat of a chair in an examination booth in the safe deposit vault. The chair was partially under a table. Bernice turned the money over to the bank. The bank wrote to everyone who had been in the safe deposit vault area on the day of, or on the day preceding, the discovery. No one reported the loss of currency, and the money remained unclaimed for a year. The vault area was separated from a lobby by a gate, and entry was restricted to bank employees and customers. Under an Illinois statute, if any person finds lost money, the county clerk advertises for 3 weeks. If the owner does not appear within 1 year after the advertisement, ownership of the money passes to the finder. The advertisement was made, and 1 year elapsed. Is Bernice entitled to the $6,325?

3. Gullia landed his private airplane at Palm Beach International Airport and taxied it to Butler Aviation. He locked the plane and kept the key. The key opened the door locks and baggage compartments, but no key was necessary to operate the aircraft. The plane was logged on Butler's daily arrival sheet, and a Butler employee towed the plane to a parking area and tied it down. There was a fence around the airport perimeter. Butler controlled its area by stationing a security guard at its access gate and a dispatcher at a service counter at the other entrance. An employee checked nightly to see which aircraft were in the parking area. A week after Gullia's arrival an unknown person entered Butler's lot, paid the parking and refueling charges, and absconded with the plane. Did a bailment relationship exist between Gullia and Butler?

4. Carr purchased Kodak Ektachrome-X 135 slide film and during August 1970 vacationed in Europe with his family. Carr took a great many photographs, and upon his return to the United States, took eighteen rolls of exposed film to Hoosier Photo Supplies to be developed. He was given a receipt for each roll. Hoosier sent the film to Eastman Kodak Company for processing. Only fourteen rolls were returned to Hoosier. Carr sued Hoosier and Kodak for $10,000 damages. Kodak defends that its film is distributed in boxes printed with the following: "READ THIS NOTICE. This film will be replaced if . . . lost by us or any subsidiary company even though by negligence or other fault. Except for such replacement, the sale, processing, or other handling of this film for any purpose is without other warranty of liability." The receipt given to Carr by Hoosier contained similar language printed on the back side, limiting liability to replacement of film. At the trial it was established that Carr did not read either the notice on the packages of film he bought or the notice on the receipts. Should Carr recover damages from Kodak or Hoosier? Explain. Would your answer be different if Carr was an attorney and an amateur photographer who knew from experience that there was a limitation of liability printed on the boxes and on the receipts?

5. Mitchell was building a backyard fence, and a neighbor suggested he rent a post hole digger. At Burke Rental Center he rented a digger that was equipped with a slip, or centrifugal clutch, engineered to cause the auger to stop turning when it encountered an obstruction. The auger would resume operation when no longer in contact with the obstruction. Mitchell was unaware of this feature, and Burke's employees did not explain the operation of the slip to him. Mitchell took the machine home and, after a minute or two of operation, the auger and pulleys quit running. He reached down to check the V-belt on the machine and it started running again. Mitchell's hand was sucked into it and was severely injured. There was no guard on the V-belt to prevent a user from coming in contact with the hazard. What arguments could Mitchell advance to impose liability on Burke?

CHAPTER 24

Real Property: Nature, Acquisition, Ownership, and Control

For obvious reasons, real property is the most important form of property. Most food comes from the land, as do the raw materials used in the production of almost everything: goods of infinite variety, housing, factories, public buildings, military equipment, dams and highways, electrical generators, transmission lines, earth satellites, ships at sea—the list is endless. Key to our survival, land is a major source of wealth and power. Its use and control are vital to every individual, business, and government. Because of its fundamental importance, land has been the subject of countless wars and private disputes.

A major concern of early Anglo-American law was the development of a law of real property to govern ownership of land and its transfer, taxation, and succession at death. Today's law emphasizes, in addition, responsible *use* of land in the context of a hugely expanding population. Anyone who contemplates the acquisition of real property should understand the various methods of acquiring ownership, the types of ownership available, and the rights and duties involved in owning real property.

The first two parts of this chapter are devoted to a discussion of the physical elements customarily included in the term "real property" and the subject of "fixtures." The last three parts of the chapter are devoted to the acquisition, ownership, and control of real property.

PHYSICAL ELEMENTS OF REAL PROPERTY

The term "real property" customarily includes the surface of the land, things attached to the land, the airspace above the land, and materials below the surface. The surface includes things found in nature, such as water and soil, and things added by human effort, such as buildings and crops. Below the surface are found such things as minerals, oil, and gas. The law pertaining to each of these elements is complex and too extensive to be covered in a business law text. However, certain fundamental rules and principles are presented to give a basic understanding of this area of law.

Airspace

The owner of real property has the right to the airspace above the surface of his or her land. An ancient rule of common law was that ownership extended to the "periphery of the universe." There was little need to question this rule prior to the invention of the airplane. Today, airspace is treated as an economic resource that should be available for public use, and the landowner's rights have been restricted. The general rule is that the landowner owns that portion of the airspace above the land that the owner can use in connection with the beneficial and convenient enjoyment of the land surface.

Ownership of airspace can be transferred with or without the transfer of the land surface. The transfer usually occurs automatically in connection with transfer of the land surface. However, the separate transfer of airspace is a growing phenomenon in the United States. Such transfer occurs, for example, when a person buys into a high-rise condominium. In effect, the purchaser buys a cube of airspace in the building. Some of the legal aspects of condominiums are discussed later in this chapter.

Crops and Timber

Items that grow on the land, such as trees, shrubs, corn, and potatoes, are considered to be part of the real property. Thus, when real property is transferred by a landowner, any trees and growing crops automatically pass to the transferee, unless the owner specifically reserves rights in them. Ownership of growing trees and crops may be transferred separately from a transfer of the land. Harvested crops and felled trees are classed as personal property and do not automatically pass to the transferee of the land.

Minerals

All materials below the surface of an owner's land are part of the real property. Minerals, such as gold, silver, and copper, can be of great commercial value. The landowner can transfer ownership of the subsurface separately or as part of a transfer of the real property. Separate ownership of the subsurface normally includes the right to enter upon the surface of the land to remove minerals. The prudent landowner will not transfer ownership of the subsurface without having given due consideration to how much the transfer would restrict use of the surface of the land. In cases involving conflict between owners of the surface and owners of the subsurface, courts ordinarily hold that the subsurface owner's right of entry may not be restricted unless it is shown that the surface will be irreparably harmed.

Oil and Gas

Oil and gas occupy a unique position in the law because they are substances that flow from one place to another. The law regarding ownership of these physical elements differs in the various states. In most of the major oil-producing states, the landowner does not own any particular oil and gas below the land surface. The owner simply has the exclusive **right to drill** for oil and gas on his or her land and, if some is discovered, to extract it. The landowner may extract oil and gas from an underground pool, even if the boundaries of the pool extend under neighboring land. There are comprehensive state and federal laws restricting the amount of oil and gas that may be extracted. When the likelihood of an oil or a gas field exists, the usual practice in most states is for a group of landowners to grant the right to drill to one individual or firm, by means of leases. The typical lease provides that in the event oil or gas is found and is extracted by the driller, the payment that the landlord (or landlords) receives is a royalty based on the amount of oil or gas removed. For example, a common arrangement in oil leases is that the landowner (or landowners) receives the market value at the well of one-eighth of all oil extracted.

Water

Water on or below the surface of the land is real property. However, if the water is "severed" from the land and put in a container, its classification is changed to personal property. In arid parts of the western United States, local water agencies purchase water as they would purchase any commodity. The water is then transported by truck, pipeline, or canal and sold to farmers, ranchers, and consumers who may live hundreds of miles from the source of the water.

Water is a precious resource. The public policy of the federal and state governments is to preserve and protect that resource. Accordingly, statutes and court decisions restrict the water rights of landowners. In most states a landowner does not have the right to dig a well and take water from under the land in unlimited quantity. The owner may draw only the amount of water that he or she can reasonably and beneficially use. Likewise, a person who owns a parcel of land bordering on a stream or river has the right (called **riparian right**) to take reasonable quantities of water from the stream or river, but she or he cannot dam up the stream or dig a channel and divert the entire water flow onto his or her land. Downstream owners also have riparian rights, and these rights cannot be unreasonably interfered with by an owner upstream.

There are many disputes over the appropriation, use, pricing, contamination, and discharge of ground and surface water. These disputes involve competing classes of water users (e.g., ranchers, industries, consumers), environmental protection groups, and city, county, state, and national governments.

FIXTURES

A fixture is personal property that is permanently attached to real property such that it becomes part of the realty. For example, a building contractor who uses materials such as cement, lumber, and pipe to construct a house converts these goods into real property. Disputes over whether property has become a fixture occur in a number of different settings. For example, a landlord may object to a tenant removing property attached to the apartment (e.g., shelves, mirrors), claiming that the attached property has become a fixture. Similarly, a buyer of a house may object to the seller removing carpeting and appliances, arguing that these items of property are fixtures and therefore part of the house. If the parties have an agreement regarding ownership of the property in dispute, that agreement will be controlling. However, in the absence of such an agreement, the law of fixtures determines ownership of the property attached to the real estate.

Tests for a Fixture

To determine whether an item of personal property has become a fixture (and thus is to be

> **BOX 24.1**
> **Developments in the Law: Solar Rights**
>
> Who owns the sunlight? Can one landowner obstruct the light coming across his or her property and thereby diminish the efficiency of solar panels on a neighbor's property? The English common law recognized a doctrine called "ancient lights," under which a landowner who received sunlight across an adjoining property for a specified period of time acquired a right to continue that unobstructed access. American courts, disinclined to impose legal impediments to land development, did not recognize a common law right of access to light.
>
> With the energy crisis, however, and the movement to alternative sources of energy, particularly solar energy, the law has changed. State and local governments in most states have passed various forms of solar access legislation, including laws governing the creation of solar easements (the grant of a solar right of access) and local regulation of solar rights through the zoning and planning processes. New Mexico and Wyoming have passed Solar Rights Acts which declare that the right to use solar energy is a property right. And in *Prah v. Maretti*, 321 N.W.2d 182 (Wis. 1982), the Wisconsin Supreme Court recognized a common law right to prevent obstructions of light under a nuisance theory. Thus, the law of real property has evolved over time to meet the changing technological environment.

treated as real property), the courts apply several criteria. The three factors that are most important are (1) the degree of attachment (annexation) of the personal property to the realty, (2) the degree to which the personal property is adapted to the use of the realty, and (3) the probable intent of the annexor (the person making the attachment). These three factors are not always given equal weight by the courts; the relative importance of each factor depends on the individual circumstances.

Degree of Attachment. When an item is attached to realty in such a manner that removing the item would cause injury to it or to the realty to which it is attached, the courts consider such attachment strong evidence that the item is intended to be a fixture. One can reasonably infer that items attached by cement or by plaster were intended to remain permanently. Most heating and air conditioning systems are installed in buildings in such a way that to remove them would cause great injury, and therefore they usually are held to be fixtures.

The fact that an item is easily removable without injury to it or to the real property suggests that the affixing party intended for the item to remain personal property. However, ease of removal is not conclusive in determining whether an item was intended to be a fixture.

Adaptability to Use. An item of personal property that is beneficial or necessary to the ordinary use of the real property to which the item is attached is likely to be held a fixture, even though the item may be easily removable. For example, doors, windows, and hot-water heaters are usually removable without injury, but courts normally hold such items to be fixtures. These items are necessary to the ordinary use of real property, and the courts infer that the affixing party must have intended the items to be permanently part of the real property. Items that are custom-made for the particular premises, such as wall-to-wall carpeting and built-in kitchen appliances, are also normally held to be fixtures.

The courts seldom hold an item to be a fixture if it is not beneficial or necessary to the ordinary use of the real property. For example, a large pipe organ installed in a home was held to be personal property because it was a musical instrument and not a necessary part of a residence.

Intent of the Annexor. The courts also consider the probable (not actual) intent of the annexor (the person making the attachment). The presumed intent is based on a reasonable person standard: Would a reasonable person making the attachment intend to make a permanent improvement to the realty or a temporary attachment? To answer the question of the annexor's intent, the law primarily looks at that person's interest in the property. For example, owners of real property generally intend to permanently improve it when they make beneficial attachments to it. So, if Caleb puts a new built-in dishwasher in his kitchen, the courts will generally presume that he intended to make a permanent improvement to the house. The intent factor would suggest that the dishwasher is a fixture.

On the other hand, a tenant seldom intends to make a gift of personal property to the landlord by making a permanent improvement to the realty. Because a tenant's interest in the property is limited, the courts will presume that attachments to the premises are intended to be temporary. The presumption is particularly applicable to commercial buildings and business tenants. Business tenants will often attach shelves, counters, and other property to the leased property. These attachments are usually considered **trade fixtures** and are removable by the tenant at the end of the lease term.

In the following case the court applied the fixture tests to a common factual situation—that of placing a mobile home on a parcel of land.

CASE 24.1	Ford v. Venard • 340 N.W.2d 270 (Iowa 1983)
FACTS	In 1973 Norman Van Sickle moved a double-wide mobile home to a plot of land owned by Luelia Jedlicka. Van Sickle had a foundation poured, removed the mobile home's hitches and wheels, and had it set on the foundation by crane. He believed that the house became part of Jedlicka's real estate when it was set down. After 1973 Van Sickle welded the home into a single unit, put a roof over

**CASE 24.1
Continued**

the entire building, and joined the exterior together with siding. There was no way the house could be disassembled without tearing it apart and no way it could be moved as one unit except by a house mover.

In 1977 Henry Edsel Ford bought the land from Jedlicka. The contract included all "attached fixtures" as part of the real estate included in the sale. William Venard had a judgment against Van Sickle, and in 1982 he attempted to enforce it by attaching and forcing an execution sale of the mobile home. Ford sued Venard, claiming that he, not Van Sickle, owned the home. From a judgment for Venard, Ford appealed.

OPINION

HARRIS, J. . . . The first question is whether the mobile home was a fixture included under the terms of the land contract between Jedlicka and Ford. We think it plainly was. Under our common law rule personal property becomes a fixture when:

1. It is actually annexed to the realty, or to something appurtenant thereto;
2. It is put to the same use as the realty with which it is connected; and
3. The party making the annexation intends to make a permanent accession to the freehold.

See *Cornell College v. Crain*. . . . The intention of the party annexing the improvement is the "paramount factor" in determining whether the improvement is a fixture. "Physical attachment of the structure to the soil or to an appurtenance thereto is not essential to make the structure a part of the realty." On the other hand, a building which cannot be removed without destruction of a substantial part of its value becomes "almost unavoidably an integral part of the real estate. . . ."

Venard argues that Van Sickle's home does not pass the *Cornell College* test. He argues the home was not physically annexed to the realty and that Van Sickle never intended, for purposes outside the present lawsuit, for his home to be permanently attached to the freehold.

Ford maintains, on the other hand, that Van Sickle's home passes the *Cornell College* test. He relies on the facts that the home's tongues and wheels have been removed; it was set on a foundation and girders; it has been extensively remodeled into a single unit; and its removal would be expensive and damaging. He points out that the home was used as a homestead, which is the use for which the realty had been appropriated. . . .

We have found buildings to be fixtures in a number of cases. See *Cornell College* . . . (granary, corn crib and hog house, although built on removable skids); . . . [w]e found buildings were not fixtures in *Durband v. Noble* . . . (machine and feed sheds placed upon posts and "blocked up").

We are convinced the home became attached to the land. It could not be removed from its present location except in the sense that any permanent home could be. We hold that it has become an integral part of the real estate. . . .

JUDGMENT

Affirmed.

ACQUISITION OF OWNERSHIP OF REAL PROPERTY

There are various methods of acquiring ownership of real property. In some situations an individual (or a business firm) participates actively in a transaction to acquire ownership, as where a person contracts to purchase property. In other situations an individual acquires ownership without active participation, as where a person inherits property.

Purchase

The most common method of acquiring real property is by purchase, a transaction that is more complicated than a purchase of goods. A seller of real property will often employ the services of a real estate broker in order to locate a buyer for the property. The seller will enter into a contract with the broker called a **listing agreement,** under which the broker earns a commission if a ready, financially able, and willing buyer is located during the listing period. The broker acts as an agent for the seller, not the buyer, in the negotiation of the transaction and owes a strict fiduciary duty of loyalty to the seller.

Once a buyer is located, the parties will negotiate concerning the terms of the sale. If the parties reach an agreement, they will enter into a written contract of sale. Under the statute of frauds, an agreement for the purchase of real estate is not enforceable unless it is in writing. The written purchase agreement does not transfer title to the buyer of the property. Transfer of title occurs at the **closing** of the sale, when a deed is delivered to the buyer.

Prior to closing, the buyer will often arrange financing, typically through a mortgage transaction. Mortgages are discussed in Chapter 25. Also, the buyer will want to ensure that the seller has good (called **marketable**) title to the property free of any defects such as mortgages, liens, or breaks in the chain of title from the original owner. Two methods are used to ensure that the seller has clear title: **title examination** and **title insurance.** Title examination involves the buyer hiring an attorney to examine the title to the property, either the records on file in the local recording office or a property **abstract** (a compilation of relevant recorded documents relating to the real estate), and to give the buyer an opinion on marketable title. An alternative to the attorney's *title opinion* is title insurance. The buyer can purchase a policy of title insurance which protects the purchaser from any recorded title defects, subject to any exceptions contained in the policy.

When the deed is delivered at the closing, title to the real estate passes to the buyer. At common law, the buyer purchased the property without any guarantee or warranty of quality. Recently, however, most state courts have held that a builder-vendor (a person who constructs a house and sells the house and land to a buyer) gives an implied warranty of quality, known as the **implied warranty of habitability or fitness.** This implied warranty gives the buyer the right to sue the builder-vendor for damages if the home is not constructed in a reasonably skillful or workmanlike manner or is not suited for its intended use. In the case that follows, the court discusses whether this warranty of habitability is created by a builder of a home who is not a seller and whether the warranty should be extended to protect subsequent purchasers of the home.

CASE 24.2   Moxley v. Laramie Builders, Inc. • 600 P.2d 733 (Wyo. 1979)

FACTS   Laramie Builders, Inc., constructed a home for Oliver B. Wickham and his wife. On April 15, 1977, Merle and Della Moxley purchased this home from the Wickhams as well as the land upon which it was located. They moved into the home and gradually became aware that the electrical wiring on the premises was defective and dangerous. The Moxleys sued Laramie Builders, claiming that the wiring was planned, designed, and installed in an unlawful, careless, and negligent manner by unlicensed electricians when Laramie built the home in September 1975. The Moxleys also alleged that it was necessary to have the house rewired at a cost of $3,892, plus $20 for a state safety inspection. The Moxleys amended their complaint to include a claim for breach of the implied warranty of fitness and habitability. The trial judge dismissed the complaint and the Moxleys appealed.

OPINION   RADER, C.J. . . . There are [several issues]: 1. Should the implied warranty of habitability . . . be extended to a contractor, who is not a builder-vendor? We will answer, "yes." 2. Should the second or other subsequent purchaser of a home be accorded the benefits of the implied warranty of habitability . . . ? We will answer, "yes." . . .

We can see no difference between a builder or contractor who undertakes construction of a home and a builder-developer. To the buyer of a home the same considerations are present, no matter whether a builder constructs a residence on the land of the owner or whether the builder constructs a habitation on land he is developing and [sells] the residential structures as part of a package including the land. It is the structure and all its intricate components and related facilities that are the subject matter of the implied warranty. Those who hold themselves out as builders must be just as accountable for the workmanship that goes into a home . . . as are builder-developers.

Electric wiring enclosed within the framework of the home or covered by fixtures is expected to last and remain safe beyond the period of little more than two years disclosed by the timetable set out in the complaint. Absent some explanation to justify a different conclusion, it can be expected that at the end of such a short period, a home reaches a subsequent buyer without substantial change from the condition it was in at the time it was built, delivered to and possession taken by the first owner. . . . It is true that there is a point in time beyond which the implied warranty will have expired based on a standard of reasonableness. . . . However, we can only conclude that that point is not exceeded under the facts here presented.

There is a paucity of precedent on the liability of a builder to a second buyer or owner. However, *Barnes v. Mac Brown & Co., Inc.*, 1976, 264 Ind. 227, 342 N.E.2d 619, furnishes a reasonably workable rule. A builder's implied warranty of fitness for habitation runs not only in favor of the first owner but extends also to subsequent purchasers. However, this implied warranty is limited to latent defects which are not discoverable by the subsequent purchasers by reasonable inspection and which become manifest only after the purchase. . . .

The purpose of a warranty is to protect innocent purchasers and hold builders accountable for their work. With that object in mind, any reasoning which would

> **CASE 24.2**
> **Continued**
>
> arbitrarily interpose a first buyer as an obstruction to someone equally as deserving of recovery is incomprehensible. Let us assume for example a person contracts construction of a home and, a month after occupying, is transferred to another locality and must sell. Or let us look at the family which contracts construction, occupies the home and the head of the household dies a year later and the residence must, for economic reasons, be sold. . . . No reason has been presented to us whereby the original owner should have the benefits of an implied warranty or a recovery on a negligence theory and the next owner should not simply because there has been a transfer. Such intervening sales, standing by themselves, should not . . . effect an end to an implied warranty. . . . The builder always has available the defense that the defects are not attributable to him. . . .
>
> In conclusion . . . [a] home builder's implied warranty of fitness for habitation extends to subsequent purchasers for a reasonable length of time and is limited to latent defects which become manifest after the purchase. . . .
>
> **JUDGMENT** Reversed and remanded.

Gift

Another common method of acquiring ownership of real property is by gift. The three elements required to establish a valid gift of personal property are discussed in Chapter 23. Similar elements (intent to make a gift, delivery to the donee, and acceptance by the donee) are required to establish a gift of real property. Since physical delivery of real property is impractical, the requirement of delivery is usually met by the owner's signing a deed and handing the deed to the donee or to an agent of the donee with intent to relinquish all dominion and control over the property.

Dedication of real property is a gift by the owner to a governmental unit or agency on the condition that the property be used for a designated public purpose. The designated purpose might be for a park, street, beach, or historical landmark. The gift can occur during the donor's life or upon his or her death. There is typically a statutory procedure to be followed. The owner makes a formal offer to give certain real property to a city, state, or federal governmental unit or agency, indicating the use or uses to which the property may be put and any other conditions the unit or agency must meet. If the appropriate governmental officials decide to accept the gift on the conditions stated, a statute or an ordinance is formally passed, and the owner transfers the property to the governmental unit or agency. Thereafter, the government is responsible for the maintenance and operation of the facility.

In certain situations, a **common law dedication** can occur. If an owner of real property makes an offer, express or implied, to give ownership to the public, and if there is evidence of acceptance by the public, a dedication may take place without formal action. For example, if an owner freely allows the public to do such things as drive across the land, park cars on it, or have picnics on the land, a court may find that a common law dedication has occurred.

Will or Descent

An individual or a firm may acquire ownership of real property when someone dies. The owner of real property may have made a will, leaving the property to a named person or firm. If the owner dies without having made a will, the owner's real property passes to his or her heirs in accordance with the law of the state where the real property is located (see Chapter 26).

Adverse Possession

Occasionally, an individual or a firm acquires ownership of real property by adverse possession, an involuntary transfer of ownership without the consent of the owner. Suppose, for example, that Gerard moves into an abandoned cabin located on Lillian's land. He plants a garden and farms 2 acres, all without Lillian's permission. If Gerard claims ownership of the land and occupies it for a specified period of years, he will acquire ownership of the land unless, within the period specified by the statute of limitations, Lillian takes legal action to protect her title. The rationale for allowing such an involuntary transfer of ownership is that historically the law favored productive use of land over nonuse. If the owner of land did not use it, or at least care enough to visit it, for a prolonged period of time and a trespasser made some visible use of the land, the law rewarded the trespasser with title to the property. Since the result is harsh—transferring ownership against the owner's wishes—the requirements are strict, and few cases reach the courts. Most often, the types of controversies handled by the courts involve mistaken boundary lines or land that is occupied under an invalid deed.

To acquire ownership of real property by adverse possession, the claimant must take possession of the property and must prove that the occupation of the property was:

- Open and notorious
- Exclusive and hostile to the owner
- Under claim of right or color of title
- Continuous for the period required by state law (statutory periods range from 5 to 30 years)

In some states the claimant must also pay all property taxes levied against the property during the statutory period.

Open and notorious occupation means that the adverse possessor must actually use the real property in such a manner as to make his or her presence known. For example, constructing a building, enclosing land with a fence, or growing a crop would be a visible sign of occupancy. Whether the owner observes the activities of the adverse possessor is immaterial. The law simply requires occupancy of such a nature that any reasonable person who cared to look would know that the occupant claimed some interest in the property.

To establish hostile occupancy, the adverse possessor must be a trespasser, rather than a tenant or someone in possession with the permission of the owner. Exclusive possession means that the adverse possessor and the owner cannot be in joint possession of the property. If the owner or others possess the property at the same time, the claim of adverse possession will fail because the occupancy has not been exclusive.

In most states, the adverse possessor must take possession of the real property either under claim of right or under color of title. Claim of right usually means the claimant knows that he or she is a trespasser committing a wrongful act but intends to establish ownership of the real property against all others. Color of title means the adverse possessor has some written document (usually a deed) or judicial decree that appears to transfer ownership but that is legally defective.

There are certain situations in which an adverse possessor cannot acquire ownership of real property. For example, an adverse possessor usually cannot acquire ownership of real property held by a governmental agency for public use. Thus, ownership of land in a wilderness area held by the government cannot be acquired by an adverse possessor who meets all the requirements listed above.

In the following case the court discusses several of the elements required to establish title by adverse possession.

CASE 24.3   Chaplin v. Sanders • 676 P.2d 431 (Wash. 1984)

FACTS In 1957 or 1958, Mr. and Mrs. Hibbard cleared a parcel of land they owned of woods and overgrowth and set up a trailer park. To the east of the Hibbards' parcel was an undeveloped parcel of land owned by Mr. McMurray. There was no obvious boundary between the two parcels, and Mr. Hibbard cleared his land on the east up to a deep drainage ditch on McMurray's parcel. He then installed between the ditch and his property a paved road which encroached some 20 feet onto McMurray's land. After 1958 the area between the road and the drainage ditch was used by trailer park residents for parking, storage, garbage removal, and picnicking. Grass was mowed up to the ditch, and flowers were planted in the area.

In 1960 McMurray had a survey conducted and discovered the true boundary. He informed the Hibbards that their driveway encroached upon his land. In 1962 the Hibbards sold their land and trailer park to Mr. and Mrs. Gilbert. In the sale contract it was acknowledged that the blacktop road used by the trailer park encroached on the adjoining property. In 1976 the Gilberts sold the property to Mr. and Mrs. Sanders, who were given actual notice of the contract provision.

In May 1978, the Chaplins purchased the McMurray parcel of land. They filed suit against the Sanders to quiet title to the area used in connection with the trailer park. The trial court found that the Sanders and the prior owners had satisfied each element of adverse possession with regard to the road and its 3-foot shoulder but had not satisfied the open and notorious requirement with regard to the property between the roadway and the ditch. On appeal, the court of appeals held that, because the Sanders and their predecessors had received actual notice of McMurray's ownership, the requirement of hostility had not been satisfied for either parcel. The Sanders appealed to the Washington Supreme Court.

OPINION UTTER, J. . . . In order to establish a claim of adverse possession, the possession must be: (1) exclusive, (2) actual and uninterrupted, (3) open and notorious and (4) hostile and under a claim of right made in good faith. . . . The period throughout which these elements must concurrently exist is 10 years. . . .

The doctrine of adverse possession was formulated at law for the purpose of, among others, assuring maximum utilization of land, encouraging the rejection of stale claims, and, most importantly, quieting titles. [T]he doctrine . . . was originally intended to protect both those who knowingly appropriated the land of others and those who honestly entered and held possession in full belief that the land was their own. Thus, when the original purpose of the adverse possession doctrine is considered, it becomes apparent that the claimant's motive in possessing the land is irrelevant. . . . The "hostility/claim of right" element of adverse possession requires only that the claimant treat the land as his own as against the world throughout the statutory period. . . . His subjective belief regarding his true interest in the land and his intent to dispossess or not dispossess another is irrelevant to this determination. . . .

In the present case, due to the contract language manifesting Hibbard and Gilbert's recognition of McMurray's superior title, the [appeals] court determined that their possession was not hostile to McMurray's interest. Under our

**CASE 24.3
Continued**

holding today the contractual provision is no longer relevant. What is relevant is the objective character of Hibbard's possession and that of his successors in interest. . . .

The trial court found the character of possession to have been hostile for at least a 10-year period. We agree. The Sanders and their predecessors used and maintained the property as though it was their own for over the statutory period. This was sufficient to satisfy the element of hostility.

The Sanders also appeal from the trial court's finding that Parcel B [the property between the roadway and the ditch] was not possessed in an open and notorious manner.

[T]he requirement of open and notorious is satisfied if the title holder has actual notice of the adverse use throughout the statutory period. This is consistent with the purpose of the requirement, which is to ensure that the user makes such use of the land that any reasonable person would assume he is the owner. . . .

Here the trial court found that McMurray knew of the Hibbards' encroachment in 1960. He was aware of these encroachments until he sold to the Chaplins in 1978. . . . Mrs. Hibbard testified at trial that she and her husband consistently maintained and mowed Parcel B. It would have been so maintained in 1960 when Mr. McMurray informed the Hibbards that their road was encroaching on his land. We are compelled to conclude, from this evidence, that McMurray was aware of the Hibbards' use of the strip abutting the roadway. This conclusion is all the more compelling when the disparate condition of McMurray's undeveloped, overgrown property and the cleared, mowed and maintained strip of land separating the roadway and McMurray's land is considered. . . .

. . . The residents of the trailer park mowed the grass in Parcel B and put the parcel to various uses: guest parking, garbage disposal, gardening and picnicking. Some residents used portions of Parcel B as their backyard. The trial court concluded that the contrast between the fully developed parcel west of the drainage ditch and the overgrown, undeveloped parcel east of the drainage ditch was insufficient to put the owners of the eastern parcel on notice of the Sanders' claim of ownership. We disagree.

JUDGMENT

Accordingly, the case is reversed and remanded with directions to quiet title to the disputed property in the Sanders.

Transfer by Deed

Regardless of whether an owner of real property decides to sell it or to give it away, the actual transfer of ownership is accomplished by means of a document called a **deed.** The person transferring ownership (title) is the **grantor;** the person receiving it is the **grantee.** The legal requirements for a valid transfer of ownership by deed are:

- A competent grantor.
- A grantee identified in the deed.
- Words of conveyance in the deed.
- Sufficient legal description of the property.
- Proper execution of the deed by the grantor.
- Delivery and acceptance of the deed.[1]

---

[1]States may have other requirements for a valid deed or for a deed to be recorded. For example, most states require that a deed be acknowledged (signed before a public officer such as a notary public) for it to be recorded.

Types of Deeds. Various types of deeds are used in the United States to transfer ownership of real property. The more common types are the warranty deed, the grant deed, and the quitclaim deed.

In most midwestern and eastern states, the **warranty deed** is the type commonly used for transferring ownership of real property. Warranty deeds are classified as general or special. Figure 24.1 is a sample general warranty deed. In a **general warranty deed,** the grantor *expressly* warrants to the grantee that he or she has title to the property and that ownership is transferred free from *all* defects or encumbrances (liens, leases, easements), regardless of when they arose. Thus, if Cal gives Billy a general warranty deed, and there is an unpaid mortgage recorded before Cal acquired the property, Billy can sue Cal for any damages caused by the lack of clear title. In a **special warranty deed,** the grantor warrants against only those defects or claims arising *after* he or she acquired title. The special warranty deed is used mainly by trustees or by executors of deceased persons' estates who must transfer real property as part of their fiduciary duties. In the prior example, had Cal given Billy a special warranty deed, Billy would have no right to sue Cal, because the defect arose before Cal acquired the property. Note that any deed can provide that the grantee takes the property subject to certain mortgages or encumbrances. The grantor's warranty of title does not apply to any exceptions specified in the deed. (See Figure 24.1.)

A **grant deed** transfers the grantor's ownership to the grantee but gives the grantee less protection than a general warranty deed if, later on, a defect is discovered in the grantor's title. In many states a statute imposes upon the grantor implied covenants (promises) that (1) the grantor has not transferred the same real property or any interest in it to another grantee and (2) the grantor has not encumbered the property. For example, if Carla deeds land to James and later, using a grant deed, sells Sally the same real estate, Sally would have a cause of action against Carla for breach of the first implied covenant. However, a grant deed does not protect the grantee against all defects. Suppose that before Carla acquired the property, it was subject to a right-of-way (easement) entitling a neighbor to use a 10-foot-wide strip of the land as a driveway. Carla's grant deed gives Sally no cause of action against Carla, because Carla did not grant the easement to the neighbor and so did not breach an implied covenant.

A **quitclaim deed** transfers to the grantee whatever interest, if any, that the grantor may have in the property, but gives the grantee no protection from defects in the seller's title. The deed simply transfers any interest that the grantor has, and if it is later determined that the grantor had no interest in the property, the grantee will have no recourse under the deed against the grantor. However, the grantee may have a cause of action on other grounds such as fraud. Quitclaim deeds are used when a grantor wants to transfer property but is unsure of whether he or she actually has any interest in the property. For example, if Julian and Ralph both have a deed to property from the same grantor, and Julian wants to convey the property to Karen, who has agreed to take the property knowing that there is a dispute concerning ownership, Julian could use a quitclaim deed to transfer his interest to Karen without giving any warranty that he has any title to it.

Recording of Deeds. Ordinarily, no recording is necessary for the grantor's ownership to pass to the grantee. However, all states have a system of recording real estate documents that protect the grantee from third parties who claim an interest in the property. The recording statutes differ among the states, but essentially the statutes allow a public record to be made of all deeds and other documents affecting real property. An individual or business firm can "record" a deed by filing it at the office of a designated local government official, usually called a county "recorder" or "registrar." Recording a deed is considered sufficient notice to potential subsequent grantees, and other persons interested in the real property, that ownership has passed to the grantee.

The recording statutes also establish priority rules when more than one person has acquired a deed or other interest (e.g., a mortgage) to the

DATE: June 21, 19 93

STATE DEED TAX DUE: $ 20.00

(reserved for recording data)

FOR VALUABLE CONSIDERATION, John S. Olson and Lena A. Olson, husband and wife, GRANTOR (S),

HEREBY CONVEY (S) AND WARRANT (S) TO Robert A. Hanson and Helen R. Hanson, husband and wife, GRANTEES AS JOINT TENANTS WITH RIGHT OF SURVIVORSHIP, real property in Clay, County, Minnesota described as follows:

Lot 2, Block 3, Pleasant Home Addition to the city of Blackduck, County of Clay, State of Minnesota according to the plat of record recorded in Book 4 of Plats, page 88, of the County of Clay.

together with all hereditaments and appurtenances belonging thereto, subject to the following exceptions:

Restrictions under a Notice of Restrictions and Conditions recorded in Book 1502 of Deeds, pages 212-214, of the County of Clay.

Lena A. Olson
John S. Olson

State of Minnesota)
County of Clay) ss.

The foregoing instument was acknowledged before me this 21st day of June, 199 3, by John S. Olson and Lena A. Olson, GRANTORS.

Notarial Stamp or Seal

Claire L. Andersen
Person taking acknowledgement

This instument was drafted by:

Andrew Knox, Esq.

1221 Loon Drive

Blackduck, MN 56560

Figure 24.1 Sample general warranty deed.

same property. A grantee or mortgagee should always record his deed or mortgage immediately after delivery so as to put other persons on notice of the transfer. If a grantee delays in recording, another person may purchase the property and claim title to it. In such cases, the state's recording law will determine which grantee has priority.

The states have adopted three types of priority systems: **notice, notice-race,** and **race** statutes. Under a notice statute, a subsequent purchaser for value who had no notice or knowledge of a prior deed has priority over the first grantee. So, suppose Martin acquires a deed to Greenacre and does not record the deed. Then Harriette acquires a deed to Greenacre without any knowledge of the prior, unrecorded deed to Martin. Harriette will have superior title to Greenacre under a notice system. Even if she records her deed after Martin records his, she will have priority because at the time she got her deed, the deed to Martin was not recorded.

In contrast, under a notice-race statute, a subsequent purchaser for value who had no notice or knowledge of a prior deed will have priority *only* if the later deed is recorded first. In the prior example, Harriette will have title only if she also records her deed before Martin records his deed. Finally, in a race statute, a subsequent purchaser with knowledge of a prior, unrecorded deed who nevertheless accepts a second deed to the property has priority if he or she records first. This system, which results in "a race to the registry," is followed in very few states because it allows a purchaser who has knowledge of fraud by the grantor (in giving two deeds to the same property) to have priority rights to the property. Only innocent purchasers are protected under a notice or notice-race system. The states split about evenly in utilizing these two systems.

TYPES OF OWNERSHIP OF REAL PROPERTY

Various types of ownership of real property (and personal property) are possible, but no state recognizes all of them. When given a choice, an individual (or a firm) must decide which of the available types of ownership will best serve the person's needs or legal position.

Sole Ownership

The simplest form of ownership is ownership by one individual, corporation, or governmental unit or agency. Where ownership is acquired by purchase or by gift, the grantee will be named in the deed. The deed may describe an individual grantee as "a married woman" or "a single man" or "a Delaware corporation," but such descriptive language does not affect the individual nature of sole ownership.

Common Law Cotenancies

Several types of *co*-ownership are available to people who wish to own property together or who want to confer co-ownership upon others. The most prevalent forms of co-ownership are the **tenancy in common** and the **joint tenancy with right of survivorship.** Although these common law cotenancies have different attributes, they share certain features. The co-owners—**tenants in common** in a tenancy in common and **joint tenants** in a joint tenancy—have an undivided interest in the property and an equal right to use and possess the property. Rather than own specific parcels of the property, each of the co-owners has a fractional ownership of each portion of the property—of every rock, building, or tree. Consequently, no co-owner can claim the best land and force the others to take the worst. Nor can a co-owner sell the property without the consent of the other cotenants; a co-owner can sell only his or her fractional interest in the property. Property held under a joint tenancy or tenancy in common is also subject to voluntary or court-imposed *partition*. Partition is a process of physically dividing the realty up between the cotenants so that each may have sole ownership of his or her share. Both joint tenants and tenants in common have a right to seek a judicial partition of the property if disputes arise between the co-owners.

Creation. To establish a tenancy in common or a joint tenancy, the deed to the grantees should clearly indicate that the property is passing to the grantees in one form of ownership or the other. For example, if Benson and Moreno acquire property and want to hold it in a tenancy in common, a deed should say that the property is being transferred "to Benson and Moreno as tenants in common." To create a joint tenancy, the deed from the grantor typically would say, "to Benson and Moreno as joint tenants with right of survivorship."

What happens if the deed is ambiguous or unclear as to what type of co-ownership is being created? For example, what if the deed read only "to Benson and Moreno"? In most states, a conveyance to two or more persons will be *presumed* to create a tenancy in common (and not a joint tenancy) in the absence of an express indication otherwise. The presumption of tenancy in common also applies when individuals acquire co-ownership by will or by descent. Charles dies, leaving land "to my children, Dora and Elliot, jointly." Dora and Elliot acquire ownership of the land as tenants in common.

Tenancy in Common. In a tenancy in common, two or more individuals or firms acquire ownership of the same property and become cotenants. Each cotenant acquires an undivided fractional interest in the property and, as owner, can sell that interest, give it away, or leave it to someone by will. The person acquiring the cotenant's interest in the property becomes a cotenant. The fractional interests of tenants in common often are equal, but are not required to be. Thus, one of two cotenants could own an undivided two-thirds interest in a parcel while the other owns one-third. A major feature of tenancy in common is that when a cotenant dies, that person's interest goes to his or her heirs, and not to surviving cotenants.

Joint Tenancy. Joint tenancy is available in most states and often is selected by (or conferred upon) two or more purchasers who are closely related. In a joint tenancy, each cotenant owns an *equal* undivided interest in the entire parcel of real property, and is considered also to be the owner of the whole parcel. Ann and Ben own Blackacre as joint tenants. Each one owns an undivided one-half interest in Blackacre (which he or she can sell or give away during his or her lifetime), and each also owns the whole of Blackacre from the moment that the two of them became joint tenants, subject to the rights of the other person.

A major feature of joint tenancy is its so-called right of **survivorship.** Unlike a cotenant's interest in a tenancy in common, a joint tenant's interest does not pass to his or her heirs upon death. If one of two joint tenants dies, his or her undivided fractional interest immediately ceases, and the survivor becomes the sole owner. If one of three joint tenants dies, that person's undivided one-third interest ceases, and the two survivors now have undivided one-half interests as joint tenants.

When a joint tenant transfers his or her interest to another, the joint tenancy is said to be "severed" and becomes fully or partially a tenancy in common, depending on the number of joint tenants. Suppose Ann and Ben are joint tenants. Ann sells her one-half interest to Tom. Tom and Ben are now tenants in common. Thus, upon the death of Tom or Ben, either person's interest passes to his or her heirs, and not to the other cotenant. Suppose now that Ann, Ben, and Carl are joint tenants and Ann sells her one-third interest to Tom. He is a tenant in common as to Ben and Carl, but Ben and Carl continue to be joint tenants as to each other. If Ben dies, his one-third interest will be acquired by Carl, who will now own a two-thirds interest in the property in a tenancy in common with Tom.

Marital Tenancies

There are two joint ownership forms that can exist only between spouses: tenancy by the entirety and community property.

Tenancy by the Entirety. Some states have a type of co-ownership called **tenancy by the entirety,** which can exist only between husband and wife. Under English common law, husband and wife were viewed as one person. Consequently, when land was conveyed to them as co-

Table 24.1 Comparison of Tenancy in Common and Joint Tenancy

	Tenancy in Common	Joint Tenancy
Creation	Conveyance to grantees as "tenants in common," ambiguous language presumed to be tenancy in common	Conveyance to grantees as "joint tenancy with right of survivorship"
Cotenant's interest in property	Each tenant in common owns undivided interest, may be unequal	Each joint tenant owns equal undivided interest
Rights and remedies of cotenants	Tenants in common have equal right to possess and use property, right to transfer interest in property, partition remedy	Joint tenants have equal right to possess and use property, right to transfer interest in property, partition remedy
Effect of a transfer of cotenant's interest	Transfer has no effect on tenancy in common	Transfer severs joint tenancy, becomes tenancy in common, fully or partially
Effect of cotenant's death	Interest passes to cotenant's heirs	Interest passes to other joint tenant(s) by right of survivorship

owners, they received only a single ownership interest, an "entirety," which they owned together. If one tenant by the entirety died, the survivor became the sole owner of the whole, as in a joint tenancy. But because a married couple was viewed as one person incapable of having individual shares, neither one had an undivided one-half interest. Thus, neither husband nor wife could transfer a fractional interest (because neither person owned one). Nor could either of them transfer the whole without the consent of the other; they could transfer the whole property only by acting jointly. However, under common law an absolute divorce converted the tenancy by the entirety into a tenancy in common. In many states, the tenancy by the entirety has been abolished.

Community Property. Community property is a type of ownership found in only nine states in the United States.[2] Historically, the area within eight of these states was owned by France and Spain, both of which had adopted the civil law system of community property. The system was continued in the states later created out of this area. The ninth state, Wisconsin, adopted a form of community property in 1986, by enacting the Uniform Marital Property Act. Each of the nine states has developed its own laws regarding community property, and the subject is too extensive to be covered in a business law text. However, a few general observations can be made.

Community property is usually defined in such a way as to include property acquired by a husband or wife during the marriage, except property acquired by gift, by will, or by de-

[2] Arizona, California, Idaho, Louisiana, Nevada, New Mexico, Texas, Washington, and Wisconsin.

scent. This type of ownership is similar to both joint tenancy and tenancy in common in that each person (spouse) owns an undivided interest in a parcel of property. As with joint tenancy, the interests in community property are always equal. As with tenancy in common, either spouse may make a deed or a will disposing of his or her one-half interest in community property. If a spouse dies without a will, his or her community interest generally will pass under state statutes to the surviving spouse.

Any property owned by a spouse on the date of marriage and any property received by him or her thereafter by gift or inheritance is the *separate property* of that spouse. Separate property may be converted to community property by agreement of the spouses.

Partnership Property

Often, two or more persons conducting business together form a partnership, which acquires property (land, equipment, etc.) that the partners use in the business to produce income. Each partner has an undivided interest (a **tenancy in partnership**) in this so-called **specific partnership property.** At the death of a partner, his or her interest in the partnership itself (actually, the monetary value of that interest) passes to his or her heirs. However, the deceased partner's ownership interest in the specific partnership property automatically "passes" to the surviving partner or partners. Thus, although surviving partners must account to the deceased partner's heirs for the value of his or her share of the partnership itself, the heirs cannot disrupt the surviving partners' business by taking machinery or other assets that are needed for operating the business. Tenancy in partnership is discussed in detail in Chapter 39.

Condominiums and Cooperatives

In recent years, there has been a tremendous increase in the number of condominiums in the United States. A **condominium** type of ownership is utilized most often for residential purposes, but its use is rapidly expanding to office buildings and commercial property. Briefly stated, condominium ownership involves separate ownership of a unit in a multiunit building, combined with an interest in the common areas and the land. For example, if a grantee acquires ownership of a unit in a high-rise building, the grantee becomes the sole owner of that unit. In effect, the person owns a cube of airspace. Along with the ownership of that unit, the grantee acquires an undivided interest as tenant in common in the ground on which the building stands and in the "common areas" within the building, such as elevators, stairways, hallways, and recreation areas. In some planned communities, a condominium development may consist of a "campus" of buildings. In such developments, the common areas may include a clubhouse, swimming pool, golf course, and other recreational facilities.

The word "cooperative" has several senses. As used here, **cooperative** refers to a corporation that is organized for the sole purpose of owning and managing a multiunit building(s), such as an apartment house or an office building, and that sells shares of stock in the corporation. A purchase of shares of stock carries with it the right to occupy a unit (an apartment or office) in the building. Thus, the shareholder, unlike the purchaser of a condominium unit, does not own the particular unit of the building he or she occupies; all the units are owned by the cooperative. In legal effect, a unit in a condominium is real property, whereas a shareholder in a cooperative owns personal property.

PUBLIC AND PRIVATE CONTROLS ON THE USE OF REAL PROPERTY

Ordinarily, an owner of real property has the exclusive right to use the land in any way he or she chooses. This includes the use of the subsurface and the airspace above the surface. The owner is free to grow crops; to build a house, building, or other structure on the land; and to conduct business activities on the property, including mining, agriculture, and manufacturing. The owner's rights are not, however, unlimited. Both public restrictions, in the form of government regulations of land use, and private restrictions, in the form of common law duties and restrictive covenants, limit the landowner's use of the real property.

Zoning and Government Land Use Controls

The federal, state, and local governments impose an array of controls on a landowner's use of his or her property. For example, extensive environmental regulations, discussed in Chapter 51, have been created to protect the air, water, and land for the benefit of the public. An important regulatory area is local land use control, or zoning.

Zoning—The Basic Framework. Under their broad police power, the states can regulate land use for the protection of the public health, safety, morals, and welfare. Under zoning enabling acts, the states have delegated much of their authority over land use to political subdivisions, municipalities and other local governmental bodies. Pursuant to this grant of authority, city and county governments have enacted zoning ordinances to regulate land use.

The primary method of land use control is dividing a community into districts or zones and limiting the uses to which land can be put within those districts. So, for example, a community may designate a zone R-1 limited to single-family dwelling units. Apartment buildings, duplexes, and commercial uses would be prohibited within that zone. Other areas of the community might be zoned for other residential, agricultural, commercial, and industrial purposes. In this way, zoning preserves residential neighborhoods, protects property values, and prevents haphazard development of communities.

Zoning ordinances may also regulate the height, size, and appearance of buildings; the size of yards and open spaces; signs and billboards; and the amount of off-street parking. Zoning ordinances are supplemented by building and safety codes that regulate the construction, repair, or alteration of buildings and that control unsanitary and unsafe conditions on private property.

Nonconforming Uses and Variances. By restricting the use of property within a particular area, a zoning ordinance may create a hardship to particular landowners whose lots may not be suited to the designated use because of their size, characteristics, or particular location. And some uses of property that predate the passage of the zoning ordinance (e.g., a grocery store in a residential neighborhood), called **nonconforming uses,** cannot be lawfully prohibited without paying the owner just compensation. How do the zoning laws handle these problems?

To protect the rights of landowners, zoning laws allow nonconforming uses to continue. However, zoning ordinances generally provide for the termination of nonconforming uses under certain circumstances, such as the destruction of the property or the owner's abandonment of the nonconforming use. Additionally, the owner will usually not be allowed to expand or change the nonconforming use. Finally, some municipalities may set a period of time (called a "useful life") for the owner to recapture his investment in the property, after which the use must be discontinued.

A landowner whose present use of property is conforming but who wants to use his or her property in a way that is prohibited by the zoning ordinances must seek special permission from the local administrative body, often called a board of adjustment. After notice to affected landowners and a hearing, a **variance** can be granted if the owner establishes that the zoning application to his or her property creates an economic hardship—that is, the owner cannot get a reasonable return on the land under the zoning restriction. If the proposed use of the property will not significantly alter the overall character of the district, the board of adjustment has the discretion to grant a variance. A landowner can also seek to have an entire district rezoned to permit particular uses, but the courts will usually invalidate **spot zoning,** a change in the zoning for one or several lots within a district.

> **BOX 24.2**
> **Zoning and Business Planning**
>
> A business involved in the development of property for residential or commercial uses must be familiar with the local planning process and zoning regulations. Many communities have adopted master plans, through a planning commission, for the future development of the city or town. The master city plan will lay out the general location of streets, parks, public buildings, and open spaces. A developer who wants to subdivide a tract of land must submit a **subdivision master plan** to the local planning commission for approval. The plan must be consistent with any master plan and provide, among other things, for the proper arrangement of streets, adequate water, and sewers for the development, and open spaces for parks and other purposes. The developer cannot sell any lots, without securing the approval of the master subdivision plan, and he or she is usually subject to civil penalties for violating the law.
>
> Developers should also be familiar with modern innovations in zoning laws that provide flexibility in land development. Many communities now provide for **planned unit developments (PUDs).** A PUD is a large tract of land within a community that has been developed for a mixture of structures and uses. A PUD may have apartments and single-family houses as well as some commercial buildings. By clustering various uses and by creating a multiuse area, the developer may be able to provide a unique neighborhood environment with large open spaces. The PUD plan must be submitted to the planning commission, and its approval requires a public hearing and may be conditioned on the developer meeting certain standards. ∎

Government's Power of Eminent Domain

The state and federal governments also have the ultimate power of **eminent domain**—i.e., the authority to take private property for public use without the owner's consent. This right is limited by the Fifth and Fourteenth Amendments to the U.S. Constitution, which require (1) that the property be taken only for a public purpose and (2) that its owner be paid a just compensation. The legal procedure by which the power of eminent domain is exercised is called **condemnation.**

Before private property can be taken without the owner's consent, the acquiring agency must establish that the taking is for a public use. Early court cases recognized certain obvious public uses, such as streets, highways, military installations, public buildings, and reservoirs. The concept of public use has been steadily broadened over the years, and today courts rarely hold any contemplated use by a governmental unit or agency to be improper. Public use now includes urban renewal projects, automobile parking facilities, rapid-transit lines, and public recreational and entertainment facilities.

The right of eminent domain may be exercised not only by a governmental unit but also by a private corporation entrusted with performance of a public service. For example, public utility corporations supplying gas, electricity, and telephone service can condemn property for utility lines and poles. In such instances, the corporation acts under delegation of power from the state or federal legislature.

Not all the government's interferences with private property are takings (condemnations). For example, although zoning and environmental laws may substantially reduce the value of some realty, the regulation is not a taking as long as the owner can put the property to some beneficial use. See the discussion of regulatory takings in Chapter 3 (and Case 3.2).

In Case 24.4, the U.S. Supreme Court discusses whether a rent control law constitutes a taking of the owner's property. Rent control laws, which were originally developed during World Wars I and II as emergency measures, have become increasingly common in urban communities since the 1970s. The laws establish a ceiling on the amount a landlord can charge by pegging the rent to a particular time and allowing increases in rent only under specified conditions. Landlords have argued that the laws "physically take" their property because they "force" the landlord to allow tenants to remain on the premises at below-market rental rates. In the case that follows, the Court addresses that contention in the context of a local mobile home rent control ordinance and a state law protecting mobile home tenants.

CASE 24.4 **Yee v. City of Escondido** • 112 S. Ct. 1522 (1992)

FACTS In 1978, California passed the Mobilehome Residency Law, which limits the bases upon which a mobile home owner can be evicted from a mobile home park and bars owners of mobile home parks from requiring the removal of a mobile home upon sale. Eviction is permitted for nonpayment of rent, violation of law, and the park owner's desire to change the use of the property. When a mobile home is sold, the park owner cannot charge a transfer fee; nor can the owner refuse to rent if a new mobile home owner is financially able to pay. The law does not impose rent controls, but in 1988, the voters of Escondido approved a mobile home rent control ordinance that set rents at their 1986 levels and allowed increases only with the approval of the city council. John and Irene Yee, the owners of the Friendly Hills and Sunset Terrace mobile home parks in Escondido, brought suit, claiming that the rent control ordinance was an unconstitutional taking of property because it allowed park tenants the right to permanently occupy their real estate. The trial court dismissed the Yees' complaint, the California Court of Appeals affirmed, the California Supreme Court denied review, and the U.S. Supreme Court granted certiorari.

OPINION O'CONNOR, J. . . . Most of our [Takings Clause] cases . . . fall within two distinct classes. Where the government authorizes a physical occupation of property (or actually takes title), the Takings Clause generally requires compensation. But where the government merely regulates the use of property, compensation is required only if considerations such as the purpose of the regulation or the extent to which it deprives the owner of the economic use of the property suggest that the regulation has unfairly singled out the property owner to bear a burden that should be borne by the public as a whole. The first category of cases requires courts to apply a clear rule; the second necessarily entails complex factual assessments of the purposes and economic effects of government actions. . . .

[The Yees] do not claim that the ordinary rent control statutes regulating housing throughout the country violate the Takings Clause. Instead, their argument is predicated on the unusual economic relationship between park owners and mobile home owners. Park owners may no longer set rents or decide who their tenants will be. As a result, . . . any reduction in the rent for a mobile home pad causes a corresponding increase in the value of a mobile home, because the mobile home owner now owns . . . the right to occupy a pad at a rent below the value that would be set by the free market. Because . . . the park owner cannot evict a mobile home owner or easily convert the property to other uses, the argument goes, the mobile home owner is effectively a perpetual tenant of the park. . . . And . . . the mobile home owner can receive a premium from the purchaser corresponding to this increase in value. . . . As a result, [the Yees]

**CASE 24.4
Continued**

conclude, the rent control ordinance has transferred a discrete interest in land—the right to occupy the land indefinitely at a sub-market rent—from the park owner to the mobile home owner. . . .

This argument, while perhaps within the scope of our regulatory takings cases, cannot be squared easily with our cases on physical takings. The government effects a physical taking only where it requires the landowner to submit to the physical occupation of his land.

But the Escondido . . . ordinance . . . authorizes no such thing. [The Yees] voluntarily rented their land to mobile home owners. [N]either the City nor the State compels [them] to continue doing so. To the contrary, the Mobilehome Residency Law provides that a park owner who wishes to change the use of his land may evict his tenants. . . . Put bluntly, no government has required any physical invasion of [the Yees'] property.

[T]he state and local laws at issue here merely regulate . . . the relationship between landlord and tenant. This Court has consistently affirmed that States have broad power to regulate housing conditions in general and the landlord-tenant relationship in particular without paying compensation for all economic injuries that such regulation entails. When a landowner decides to rent his land to tenants, the government may place ceilings on . . . rents . . . or require the landowner to accept tenants he does not like without automatically having to pay compensation. . . .

The Escondido rent control ordinance . . . does not authorize an unwanted physical occupation of [the Yees'] property. It is a regulation of [the] use of their property. . . .

In this court, the Yees attempt to challenge the ordinance as a regulatory taking. [This claim is not] properly before us. . . . [It] is not fairly included in the question on which we granted certiorari.

JUDGMENT Affirmed.

Nuisances and Common Law Restrictions on Land Use

The common law restricts the rights of landowners for the protection of others. Landowners are under a duty not to create a **nuisance**—an unreasonable and substantial interference with the use and enjoyment of an owner's property. Nuisance law applies to noise, smoke, smells, and other offensive, unsanitary, or dangerous conditions (e.g., garbage dumps) that unreasonably interfere with the comfortable enjoyment of life or property. For example, the following have been held to be nuisances under the particular circumstances involved: a rock quarry, a drop-forging shop, a dilapidated wooden building, a slaughterhouse, an airport, the emission of smoke or odors, and the obstruction of a street or river. In determining whether a particular condition is an "unreasonable" and "substantial" interference so as to constitute a nuisance, the courts consider a range of factors, including the social utility of the disturbing activity, the nature of the locality, and the seriousness of the harm to the plaintiff. There is no set formula and each case turns on its own particular facts.

Another duty of the property owner is not to **encroach** on a neighbor's property. For example, an owner must not allow the roof of his or her house or the limbs of a tree to overhang into a neighbor's airspace. A property owner is also under a duty to exercise due care in the use and maintenance of the person's property in order to prevent injury to others on the property. Traditionally, the law distinguished between **invitees, licensees,** and **trespassers.** A landowner was under a duty to maintain his or her property in a safe condition for the benefit of invitees (e.g., business customers). In contrast, the owner owed a duty only to warn licensees (social guests and others on the property with the landowner's consent) of dangerous conditions on the property. And in terms of trespassers, the landowner was generally under no duty to maintain the premises or warn them of dangerous conditions. The landowner could be held liable only for intentional harm to trespassers. Some states have abandoned the common law rules in favor of a rule that requires the landowner to exercise reasonable care for others on the property. A person's status as a licensee or invitee is one of the circumstances considered in determining whether the owner exercised due care.

BOX 24.3

Point to Consider:
Is a Windmill a Nuisance?

Joseph Chaiken constructed a 60-foot-high windmill at his residence in Brigantine, New Jersey, a seaside community, to save on electric bills and to conserve energy. The windmill, located a short distance from Joel Rose's house, constantly produced noise that disturbed Rose and his family, causing stress-related symptoms, including nervousness and loss of sleep. It also interfered with the family's enjoyment of their house, making it difficult to read a book or watch television. The Rose family sued Chaiken to stop the noise, claiming the windmill was a nuisance. Who should prevail in court? Why? What arguments would you make to the court if you represented Chaiken? The Rose family? ■

Restrictive Covenants

In some situations, restrictions on land use are imposed on the owner of real property by deed or by contract. For example, when an individual acquires ownership of a parcel in a subdivision tract (including condominiums and cooperatives), the purchaser may be bound to certain restrictions on the use of the property. These **restrictive covenants** are set forth in the deed executed by the subdivider and are imposed for the protection of all present and future owners in the subdivision tract. Thus, each owner might be required to maintain his or her premises in a neat and safe condition at all times. Types of construction, the size of structures, and architectural design within the tract are often controlled under the deed restrictions. Entire communities have been planned and developed using deed restrictions as a form of private zoning.

SUMMARY

The term "real property" customarily includes the surface of the land, things attached to the land, airspace above the land, and materials below the surface. Ownership of any of these physical elements of real property can be transferred separately.

A fixture is an article which was once personal property but which has been attached to real property with the intent that it become a permanent part of the realty. In resolving fixture questions, the courts look at three factors: (1) the degree of attachment, (2) the adaptability of the item to the use of the real property, and (3) the presumed intent of the annexor.

Individuals and business firms can acquire ownership of real property in several ways. The most common ways are by purchase and by gift. In each instance, the transfer of ownership is accomplished by means of a warranty, grant, or quitclaim deed from the grantor to the grantee. The recording of a deed is not essential to the transfer of ownership from a grantor to a grantee; nevertheless, the deed should be recorded to protect the grantee from claims by third persons who may later acquire an interest in the property.

Various types of ownership of real property are possible, including tenancy in common and joint tenancy. The right of survivorship exists in a joint tenancy but not in a tenancy in common. Other forms of joint ownership are tenancy by the entirety, community property, tenancy in partnership, condominiums, and cooperatives.

Ordinarily, an owner of real property has the exclusive right to use, possess, enjoy, and dispose of the land, airspace, and subsurface. These rights are limited by duties to others imposed by common law, by governmental regulation under the police power, and by takings under the government's power of eminent domain. In addition, many duties are assumed by purchasers of real property as part of a contract of purchase in a subdivision tract.

REVIEW QUESTIONS

1. Explain how the law of riparian rights balances the rights of landowners to water.

2. Why is it important for a businessperson to understand the law of fixtures?

3. Explain the steps in the typical sale of real estate.

4. What are the methods of ensuring marketable title to real property?

5. What suggestions could you make to a landowner to help prevent loss of ownership to an adverse possessor?

6. What are the essential differences among the following: quitclaim deed, grant deed, warranty deed?

7. From a policy standpoint, which is the better recording system, the notice or notice-race system?

8. What options are available to a joint tenant who wants to terminate the joint tenancy?

9. Should rent control laws be declared unconstitutional as regulatory takings? Explain.

10. Discuss the reasons a developer might want to impose deed restrictions in a subdivision.

CASE PROBLEMS

1. In 1935, the United States acquired title to 121 acres of land for watershed protection and forestry purposes. The deed contained the following: "[Grantor reserves] all minerals in, upon, or under the above-described real estate, together with the right to prospect for and remove said minerals. . . ." In 1980, Downstate Stone Company acquired the right to all minerals from the heirs of the parties that had reserved the mineral rights in 1935. The lands were composed principally of limestone, which lay both on the surface and under topsoil. The lands were acquired under the Forestry Act and were administered by the Department of Agriculture as national forest lands. Downstate filed suit to determine if it was entitled to quarry limestone under the mineral reservation. Downstate admitted that limestone quarrying would require almost complete surface destruction; would level and remove the face of a 900-foot forested hill; and would leave a large open quarry area where there had been rocks, trees, and soil. Should the court permit Downstate to remove limestone under the 1935 mineral reservation?

2. Wilmington Water Corp. furnished water for commercial and residential uses. It maintained various pipes, mains, and storage tanks used in its water distribution system throughout New Castle County. The county imposed a property tax on the items, contending they were taxable as real property. Wilmington contended the items were personal property and not taxable. The storage tanks were steel and stood on metal legs bolted to concrete foundations. Other tanks rested on the ground by force of gravity. Thus, Wilmington argued that the items were easily removable. The structures were large and could be removed only with great difficulty. At least one tank had been removed after a useful life of 30 years. The county argued that removability was not important in this case because the items were to be used indefinitely or until the end of their useful life, since removal would affect the water supply. Should the items be taxed as real property?

3. The City of Oakland filed a lawsuit to acquire by eminent domain the Oakland Raiders professional football team, a franchise member of the National Football League. The Raiders argued (1) that the law of eminent domain does not permit the taking of intangible property (a football franchise) and (2) that the taking contemplated by Oakland could not be for any "public use" within the city's authority. Is either of these arguments valid?

4. Mike Zamiska executed a deed conveying title to certain land to himself and his son, George, "as joint tenants and as in common with the right of survivorship." Upon Mike's death, George claimed title to the land as surviving joint tenant. Other heirs of Mike claimed that the deed created only a tenancy in common and thus George was limited to ownership of an undivided one-half interest. Did Mike create a joint tenancy or a tenancy in common?

5. Mr. and Mrs. Herring acquired title to a parcel of land as joint tenants with the right of survivorship. Mrs. Herring executed a deed conveying to Clarence Carroll, her son by a previous marriage, all "her right, title, and interest" in the parcel of land. Upon her death, Mr. Herring claimed title to the land by right of survivorship. **(a)** Is his claim correct? **(b)** Would your answer be the same if Mr. and Mrs. Herring were tenants by the entireties?

6. The city of Scottsdale rezoned the area in and around the McDowell Mountains into the Hillside Conservation Area and the Hillside Development Area. No new development was permitted on land within the conservation area. Joyce Corrigan owned 4,800 undeveloped acres, 80 percent of which lay within the no-development line. The McDowell Mountains were unique, being the only hilly or mountainous terrain within the Scottsdale city limits. The primary purpose of the zoning ordinance was to preserve the mountains in their natural state for the benefit of all residents of the city. Corrigan filed suit, claiming the ordinance was unconstitutional because (1) it was an invalid exercise of the police power and (2) enforcement of the ordinance would amount to a "taking" of private property without compensation (i.e., a disguised exercise of eminent domain). Evidence showed that development in the mountains could result in unsightly scarring. Evidence also showed that under the Hillside Ordinance the land in the conservation area would have no monetary value, whereas without the ordinance the land would be worth from $1,250 to $4,500 per acre. Should the ordinance be declared unconstitutional?

CHAPTER 25

Interests in Real Property

A finite resource, land is much in demand for productive, residential, and public purposes. Ownership gives a person maximum control over the use of land, but ownership is not always possible or even economically advisable. So instead of buying it outright, many people, even the largest corporations, rent (lease) real property from its owners for a host of purposes, residential and commercial. Owners and nonowners alike often seek rights-of-way over (easements in) land owned by others, and taxation of realty provides state and local governments with vast amounts of revenue for public purposes. Consequently, the subject of interests in real property is important to almost everyone in contemporary society.

Three types of interests in real property are of special significance—estates, easements, and liens. Estates (ownership interests) in real property range from those conferring full ownership to those conferring considerably less than full ownership, such as a tenancy under a lease. Easements and liens are both nonownership interests in real property. An easement generally is a right to use the real property for some purpose, such as a driveway or right-of-way easement. A lien is the interest of a creditor in the real property of the owner-debtor that ensures repayment of the debt. The most common real estate lien is a mortgage.

The first two parts of this chapter deal with the nature of the different types of estates: freehold estates and leasehold estates (the landlord-tenant relationship). The last two parts of the chapter are devoted to easements and liens.

FREEHOLD ESTATES IN REAL PROPERTY

There are two classes of ownership interests in real property: freehold estates and leasehold estates. **Freehold estates** include those in which the duration of enjoyment is potentially infinite and those in which duration is measured by the life of a person. **Leasehold estates** include those in which the enjoyment is for a specified period of time and those in which the enjoyment is for an unspecified period not intended to be infinite.

Freehold estates may be divided into two major classes: **fee simple estates** and **life estates.** There are other types of fee estates, but they are more appropriately covered by a course in real estate law.

Fee Simple Estates

The estate that owners usually acquire in real property is the fee simple estate. A person owning property in fee simple has the fullest type of ownership—the largest "bundle of rights" possible under the law. The owner has the exclusive right to possess and enjoy the property, sell it, give it away, lease it to another, or borrow against it. Upon the death of the owner, a fee simple estate passes to the beneficiary or beneficiaries designated in the owner's will or to the decedent's heirs if there is no will. There are no technical words required to transfer a fee simple estate from a grantor to a grantee. In most states any properly executed deed is presumed to pass a fee simple estate, in the absence of specific words indicating that a lesser estate is intended.

Life Estates

A **life estate** is an estate for the life of a person. For example, a deed to "Alice for life" creates an estate that will automatically end when Alice dies. A deed to "Alice for the life of Ben" creates an estate that will end when Ben dies. In this latter example, if Alice dies before Ben, the unexpired portion of the life estate passes to Alice's heirs or to the beneficiaries under her will. During the existence of a life estate, the **life tenant** has a great many rights. The life tenant can use, possess, and enjoy the property; sell his or her interest; give it to a donee; borrow against it; or lease it to someone and collect the rents. However, any lease given by a life tenant cannot continue beyond the duration of the life estate. For example, if Alice, a life tenant, leases the property to Don for 10 years, there is no certainty that Don will be able to remain in possession for the full 10 years. If Alice dies and the life estate ends before the 10-year lease expires, Don must vacate the property.

Although a life tenant has many rights, he or she also has certain duties and obligations. The life tenant must keep all improvements on the property in good repair and must not use or treat the property in such a way as substantially to diminish its value. Any such abuse of the property is called **waste.** Specific examples of waste are permitting the house or fences to fall into disrepair and removing timber, earth, or minerals unnecessarily. Normally, the life tenant must pay the annual taxes assessed against the property and pay interest on any mortgage or other encumbrance on the property. The reason the law imposes these duties on the life tenant is to protect the value of the property for the person who will take possession at the termination of the life estate.

> **BOX 25.1**
>
> **Point to Consider:
> What Is a Life Estate Worth?**
>
> A life tenant can sell the life estate if he or she can find a willing buyer, but a purchaser can acquire the property only for the uncertain period of that life estate. If you were buying a life estate, how would you go about determining the price you would be willing to pay?

Future Interests. When a grantor transfers a life estate or a lease, someone will succeed to the use and possession of the property upon termination of that estate. Because that person's right to use, possess, and enjoy a parcel of property is to begin at some future time, he or she has a **future interest.** Although the right to possession and use of the property are delayed, a future interest is a property right that the owner can transfer and that will pass upon death to his or her heirs or beneficiaries. The law recognizes two major types of future interests: reversions and remainders.

Reversions. When the owner of real property transfers a life estate or leases the property, but retains the future right to the property, he or she has a **reversion.** For example, if Paula makes a deed conveying certain property to Ben "for his life" and makes no mention of who shall have possession and enjoyment when Ben dies, the general rule of law is that full possession and enjoyment will revert to the grantor, Paula, or to her heirs or beneficiaries should she predecease Ben. When a life estate or lease terminates, the owner of the reversion, called the **reversioner,** will have a fee simple estate.

Remainders. A **remainder** is an estate where possession and enjoyment of realty are to occur in the future, but the person who is to receive possession and enjoyment is someone other than the grantor or the grantor's heirs. For example, if Paula transfers certain real property to Ben "for his life, then to Anita," Anita acquires a remainder. Should Anita predecease Ben, her remainder interest will pass to her heirs or beneficiaries.

THE LANDLORD-TENANT RELATIONSHIP

Modern landlord-tenant law has changed significantly, and there has been a clear shift in the attitude of the courts and the legislatures toward the rights of tenants of residential property. At common law, the courts emphasized the "property" aspects of leases, viewing the lease as a conveyance of property to the tenant who took the leasehold premises in an "as is" condition. The doctrine of caveat emptor (buyer beware) as applied to the tenant clearly favored the landlord, particularly in disputes over the condition of the leased premises. Modern landlord-tenant law emphasizes the "contractual" aspects of leases, consistent with the reasonable expectations of the typical residential or commercial tenant. In a residential lease today, the tenant is concerned more with the quality of the residential unit and the services relating to the apartment—heat, light, electricity, plumbing, and security—than with the land itself. To protect the tenant's legitimate contractual expectations, the courts have abolished many of the common law doctrines. As you examine landlord-tenant law, keep in mind the historical development of the law and the modern trend to protect the contract rights of the parties under the lease.

The Leasehold Estate

As previously noted, a leasehold estate is an estate in real property having a duration of a specified period of time or an unspecified period not intended to be infinite. The holder of a leasehold estate (called a **tenant** or **lessee**) is given the exclusive right to possess and use certain premises during the leasehold period, or term. The owner of the property (called a **landlord** or

> **BOX 25.2**
>
> **Developments in the Law: The Uniform Residential Landlord and Tenant Act**
>
> In response to the significant changes in landlord-tenant law, and the lack of uniformity caused by differences in landlord-tenant law among the states, the National Conference of Commissioners on Uniform State Laws proposed a Uniform Residential Landlord and Tenant Act in 1972. The URLTA has been adopted, with modifications, in fifteen states. The act attempts to modernize landlord-tenant law by incorporating many of the doctrines that the courts and legislatures have fashioned to protect tenants. For example, the URLTA has provisions restricting the amount of security deposits, imposing a duty on the landlord to maintain the leased property in a habitable state, and providing remedies for a tenant when a landlord fails to repair the property. ■

lessor) retains a reversion. He or she has all the other rights of a full owner and will normally regain the right to possess and use the premises at the end of the term. **Premises** is a word used frequently in creating leaseholds and may mean land or a building or part of a building with or without the land.

Nature and Requirements of a Lease

The agreement between a landlord and a tenant is called a **lease.** A lease is both a contract setting forth the reciprocal rights and duties of the landlord and tenant concerning the use and possession of certain property and a conveyance of an estate in real property from one person to another. Although most people think of a lease as a written document, this is not always the case. In most jurisdictions, only leases for longer than 1 year have to be in writing. Even when the law does not require a lease to be in writing, sound business policy necessitates a written lease.

Types of Leases

There are two important types of leases: fixed-term tenancies and periodic tenancies.

Tenancies for a Fixed Term. The most common type of leasehold estate is the **tenancy for a fixed term,** often referred to as an **estate for years,** even though the duration of the tenancy may be for a single year or for a term shorter than a year. Most commercial leases are fixed-term tenancies. The lessor and lessee can agree upon a term of any length, unless a statute provides otherwise. Most states have a statute specifying maximum terms for certain kinds of leases. For example, in California the maximum term for leases on agricultural land is 51 years; for oil and gas lands, 99 years; for town and city lots, 99 years.[1] A lease for a term in excess of a statutory maximum is usually held to be invalid.

Periodic Tenancies. A **periodic tenancy** is an estate in real property that is created for a specified period of time and will continue for successive periods of the same length until the tenancy is terminated. The period may be month to month, year to year, or any term the parties agree upon. Frequently, a periodic tenancy arises by inference from the conduct of the parties. Suppose, for example, that a landlord agreed to rent certain premises to a tenant, and that no specified term was agreed upon, but that the tenant agreed to pay rent monthly. In the event of litigation, a court would normally hold that a month-to-month tenancy had been created. A periodic tenancy continues until one of the parties gives notice of termination or the parties mutually agree to end the lease.

Rights and Duties of Landlord and Tenant

Importance of the Lease. The relationship between landlord and tenant is primarily governed by the terms of the lease. Written leases will contain provisions concerning the rights and duties of the landlord and tenant. Customary terms in residential leases include provisions that the tenant is to pay all electric and gas bills accruing against the apartment during the term of the lease; that the tenant is not to sublet the apartment or assign the lease without the written consent of the landlord; that the tenant will deliver the premises at the expiration of the term in as good order and repair as when received, natural wear and tear excepted; and that the landlord or an agent shall have the right to enter the premises at any reasonable hour to examine them and to make repairs. Leases of commercial and industrial properties, involving long terms and properties of great value, usually contain more detailed provisions concerning rights and duties than do leases of residential properties.

Landlord's Right to Rent. The most fundamental right of the landlord is the right to receive the rental payments provided for in the lease. If the tenant defaults in the payment, the landlord has a cause of action for the unpaid rent. If the tenant unlawfully remains in possession of the premises, the law provides a remedy, called a **forcible** or **unlawful detainer** action, by which the landlord regains possession. Because a landlord cannot physically evict the tenant, the forcible detainer remedy is a speedy, summary legal proceeding.

The landlord also has the right to increase the rent under certain circumstances. In a periodic tenancy—a month-to-month tenancy, for example—the law generally allows the landlord to increase the rent by giving the tenant notice in advance of the increase (often 30 days). In a fixed-term tenancy, the landlord's right to increase the rent during the period of the lease is dependent upon the lease terms. Many commercial leases have rent **escalation** clauses allowing the landlord to increase the rent, for example, in the event of higher real estate taxes or rising energy costs. In the absence of such a clause in the lease, the landlord has no right to raise the rent. The landlord's power to increase the rent may also be restricted by **rent control** laws, which are discussed in Chapter 24.

---

[1] Calif. Civ. Code, Secs. 717, 718, and 718f.

At common law, when leased realty was destroyed or damaged by fire or other cause, the tenant bore the risk of loss and so had to continue paying the rent. This rule made sense then because most leases were of land for agricultural purposes, and the tenant could continue to use the land. Today, tenants commonly lease buildings for residential and commercial purposes, and destruction of the building would deprive the tenant of the benefit of the lease. Consequently, the statutes of most states reverse the common law rule, at least for commercial or residential leases. Under these statutes, where residential or commercial buildings are rendered unfit for occupancy or destroyed without the fault of either party, the tenant is relieved from the duty to pay rent.

Tenant's Right to Possession. The most fundamental right of the tenant is to have the exclusive possession and quiet enjoyment of the premises for the agreed term, free from interference by the landlord. The landlord's unlawfully evicting the tenant would deprive the tenant of the quiet enjoyment of the premises. Eviction can be actual (a physical removal of the tenant from the property) or constructive. A **constructive eviction** occurs where the landlord's acts or omissions deprive the tenant of the beneficial use of the property. For example, Tom leases an apartment from Lena for a year. Lena agrees to provide heat during the winter. She fails to do so, and the apartment becomes uninhabitable. Lena has constructively evicted Tom. Tom has a right to vacate the apartment without paying any more rent.

Landlord's Duty to Maintain the Premises. A major issue in many landlord-tenant disputes is the condition of the premises and the landlord's failure to maintain the property. At common law, the landlord was under no duty to maintain the premises or make needed repairs. There were some limited exceptions. For example, a landlord was under a duty to maintain common areas of an apartment building (e.g., stairs, sidewalks, and courtyards). And a landlord could agree to make certain repairs in the lease and thereby assume some obligation to maintain the leased premises. However, even if the landlord assumed a duty of repair, the common law treated that obligation and the tenant's obligation to pay rent as independent duties. Thus, if a landlord refused to make agreed-upon repairs, the tenant was still obligated to pay rent. The tenant's only remedy was a lawsuit against the landlord for damages.

Such rules may have been appropriate for an agrarian society in which the leases were primarily agricultural and the tenants had the limited skills necessary to make needed repairs. But most courts have considered these rules anachronistic in a modern industrial society in which residential tenants are purchasing a bundle of services from a landlord. Many courts now hold that the lessor impliedly warrants (guarantees) the habitability of a dwelling, reversing the common law rule. Under this **implied warranty of habitability,** the landlord must maintain the premises in a habitable condition throughout the term of the lease. Moreover, if the landlord fails to maintain the premises in a habitable state, the tenant can refuse to pay rent (and remain in possession) because the duty to pay rent is considered to be dependent upon the landlord's duty to maintain the property. The warranty applies only to residential leases; most courts have refused to extend the warranty to commercial leases. The warranty of habitability and the remedies available to a residential tenant for breach of the implied warranty are discussed in *Wade v. Jobe,* Case 17.5 in Chapter 17.

The implied warranty of habitability is a creation of the courts, a common law development. The state legislatures, in response to demands of tenant groups, have also enacted statutes requiring the landlord of a building intended for residency to keep it in habitable condition, except for waste or dilapidation caused by the tenant. Generally such statutes define "habitable" to include at least adequate plumbing, water supply, heating, and sanitation. These statutes often provide that if the landlord fails to make necessary repairs, the tenant may withhold rent or make the needed repairs and deduct the cost from the rent.

Landlord's Liability for Injuries to the Tenant. At common law, the landlord was generally not liable to the tenant for injuries caused by a defective condition on the premises. There were several exceptions. Landlords were under a duty to exercise reasonable care in maintaining common areas and in making repairs that they had assumed under the lease. Landlords could be held liable in cases where the premises were leased for use by the public. In terms of dangerous conditions on the premises, landlords were also liable if they *knew* of a "latent" (hidden) defect at the beginning of the tenancy and did not warn the tenant or concealed it. But the landlord was not under a general duty to maintain the property in a safe condition.

Modern law has expanded the liability of landlords for injuries to tenants. Many courts hold that a tenant can sue under the implied warranty of habitability and recover if the landlord failed to correct a dangerous condition of which he or she had notice. Other courts have abandoned the common law rule in favor of a rule that holds landlords liable if they fail to exercise reasonable care under the circumstances.

The leading case is *Sargent v. Ross*[2] in which the court held that a landlord could be liable for negligence in the case of a tenant's 4-year-old child who fell to her death on an outdoor stairway that was too steep and had an inadequate railing. And one state court, in a case in which a tenant lacerated his arm when he slipped and fell against a shower door made of untempered glass, has held landlords strictly liable for dangerous conditions. Although many states have rejected a rule of strict liability in favor of a rule of negligence, we can expect an expansion of landlords' liability to tenants for defective conditions on the leased premises in the future.

The courts have also moved away from the common law rule that landlords are not under a duty to protect tenants from criminal harm. Many courts now hold that landlords owe a duty to exercise reasonable care for the protection of tenants from foreseeable criminal acts of others. Case 25.1 discusses the application of that duty in the context of a commercial lease and the requirement that the criminal harm to the tenant be reasonably foreseeable for the landlord to be liable.

[2] 308 A.2d 528 (N.H. 1973).

CASE 25.1 Doe v. Dominion Bank of Washington • 963 F.2d 1552 (D.C. Cir. 1992)

FACTS In 1988 and 1989, Jane Doe (fictitious name) worked as a secretary for Fiscal Planning Services, Inc., a financial consulting firm, in an office building at 1430 K Street, N.W., in downtown Washington, D.C. Dominion Bank leased the office to Fiscal Planning. In 1989, the bank was in the process of selling the building, and by May of 1989, five of the building's thirteen floors were vacant. On May 24, 1989, Jane Doe came to work and made coffee. She then entered an elevator on the eleventh floor intending to go downstairs to get some tea at a nearby shop. She was dragged out of the elevator by a man who entered the elevator from the vacant ninth floor. The man then raped and robbed her in a vacant office. An investigation revealed that the elevators had not been programmed to bypass the vacant floors and that unlocked doors allowed access to those floors from a stairwell.

Doe sued Dominion Bank in federal district court claiming that the bank was negligent in failing to maintain reasonable security measures to protect her from foreseeable criminal assaults. At trial, she presented evidence that the bank was aware of thefts and burglaries from offices in the building, drug use and sexual activity in a building bathroom, and tenant complaints of threatening intruders.

**CASE 25.1
Continued**

After she presented her case, the trial court granted a directed verdict for the bank, finding that the rape was not reasonably foreseeable, citing Doe's failure to present evidence that the building was located in a high-crime area or to prove that assaults had occurred in the vicinity of the building prior to the incident. She appealed.

OPINION GINSBURG, C. J. . . .

Duty of a Commercial Landlord

As a general rule, a private person does not have a duty to protect another from a criminal attack by a third person. This court in *Kline,* however, . . . declared it the duty of residential landlords to exercise reasonable care to protect tenants from foreseeable criminal conduct in common areas of the leased premises. . . .

The Bank attempts to distinguish *Kline,* arguing that the case turned on the warranty of habitability . . . which [does] not apply in the commercial setting. . . . The [*Kline* court] did not rely on . . . an implied warranty rationale. . . .

"[T]he controlling reason for imposing a tort duty in *Kline* was that the apartment tenant would find it impossible to provide the security in common areas." The inability of an individual tenant to control the security of common hallways, elevators, stairwells, and lobbies does not depend on whether the building is commercial or residential. . . .

In sum, the D.C. landlord-tenant premises liability tort cases offer no principled ground on which to disallow the claim in question in a commercial setting while recognizing that the claim could be advanced were the building residential. . . .

Foreseeability

It is axiomatic that under a negligence regime, one has a duty to guard against only foreseeable risks. D.C. law imposes a heightened standard of foreseeability on plaintiffs seeking to hold a landlord liable for injuries resulting from a criminal act. . . . "This heightened showing . . . can be met . . . by a combination of factors which give the defendants an awareness of the danger of a particular criminal act."

[T]he condition of the premises is a critical factor in assessing the foreseeability of criminal harm. . . . The district court, however, . . . excluded from the foreseeability calculus Doe's evidence of the unsecured condition of vacant common areas at 1430 K Street. . . . Under D.C. precedent, if the condition of the premises is [a fact] the landlord knew or should have known . . . then the condition is relevant to a determination whether crime was foreseeable. . . .

The district court's emphasis on Doe's failure to prove that 1430 K Street was located in a high crime neighborhood reflects a similar rigidity. . . . No D.C. case . . . has established crime statistics, or testimony as to reputation of an area for criminal activity, as . . essential . . to a finding of foreseeability. There was ample evidence here that the Bank had incessant notice of criminal activity. . . . The proof in fact suggested that the office building itself was "high crime" prone. . . .

> **CASE 25.1 Continued**
>
> Doe presented evidence sufficient to allow the jury to decide whether the bank was on notice of the danger to tenants from assaultive criminal conduct by intruders at 1430 K Street. This included: deficient building security—unsecured vacant floors and offices, freely accessible via unlocked stairwells and unprogrammed elevators; criminal and unauthorized conduct within the building, including a burglary . . . and tenant complaints of threatening and aggressive intruders appearing in the building in the month preceding the rape. . . .
>
> **JUDGMENT** Reversed and remanded for trial.

Transfer of Interests under a Lease

Transfer by Landlord. The landlord can transfer his or her reversion to another. If the landlord dies, his interest passes to his or her heirs or beneficiaries. In any case where the landlord's interest in the property is transferred, the transferee becomes the landlord and is bound by the terms of the lease.

Transfer by Tenant. Unless the lease prohibits or limits the right to do so, the tenant may transfer all or part of the leasehold estate to another. There are two types of transfers of a tenant's interest under a lease: an assignment and a sublease. In an **assignment,** the tenant (assignor) transfers his or her total unexpired interest under the lease to a new tenant (the assignee), who acquires all rights of the former tenant and assumes the duty to pay rent. If the new tenant fails to pay rent, the landlord can hold him or her personally responsible. In addition, unless expressly released from liability for the rent, the former tenant (assignor) remains liable for any rent that the new tenant fails to pay.

In a **sublease,** the tenant transfers only a part of his or her interest to a subtenant and retains a reversionary interest. Suppose Chip leases an apartment off campus for 1 year from Donald and returns home for 3 months in the summer. He sublets the apartment to Dale for those 3 months. Dale becomes Chip's tenant. Unlike an assignment, however, Dale as a sublessee is obligated only to his sublessor, Chip, and has no personal obligation to pay Donald. Chip, on the other hand, remains the tenant of Donald, and is liable to him for the payment of rent. When Dale's sublease expires, Chip's reversionary interest takes effect, and Chip regains possession of the apartment for the balance of his 1-year term.

Restrictions on Transfer. The lease may contain a provision that either prohibits the tenant from transferring his or her interest or requires the landlord's consent to any transfer. Such a provision is strictly construed against the landlord because it restricts the ownership rights of the tenant. For example, if Terry's lease prohibits any "assignment of the lease," this will be construed strictly to mean only an assignment, not a sublease of the premises.

Rather than wholly prohibiting an assignment, the lease may contain a clause requiring the consent of the landlord to any transfer of the tenant's interest. Some clauses further provide that the landlord will not "unreasonably" withhold consent. Suppose a tenant finds a responsible substitute tenant who is financially able to pay rent and requests the consent of the landlord to an assignment. Can the landlord refuse to consent to the transfer? Unless the clause restricts the landlord's discretion, the traditional rule is that the landlord can, without justification, refuse to consent to a transfer. As the next case demonstrates, however, a minority of states hold that a landlord cannot arbitrarily withhold consent to a transfer.

CASE 25.2   Julian v. Christopher • 575 A.2d 735 (Md. 1990)

FACTS [T]he tenants, Douglas Julian and William J. Gilleland III, purchased a tavern and restaurant business, as well as rented the business premises from landlord, Guy D. Christopher. The lease stated in clause 10 that the premises, consisting of both the tavern and an upstairs apartment, could not be assigned or sublet "without the prior written consent of the landlord." Sometime after taking occupancy, the tenants requested Christopher's written permission to sublease the upstairs apartment. Christopher made no inquiry about the proposed sublessee, but wrote to the tenants that he would not agree to a sublease unless the tenants paid additional rent in the amount of $150 per month. When the tenants permitted the sublessee to move in, Christopher filed an action requesting repossession of the building. The trial court and the Circuit Court for Baltimore City found in his favor, and the tenants appealed to the Maryland Court of Appeals.

OPINION CHASANOW, J. . . . In 1961, this Court decided the case of *Jacobs v. Klawans* . . . and held that when a lease contained a "silent consent" clause prohibiting a tenant from subletting or assigning without the consent of the landlord, landlords had a right to withhold their consent to a subletting or assignment even though the withholding of consent was arbitrary and unreasonable.

Since *Klawans*, the trend has been in the opposite direction. "The modern trend is to impose a standard of reasonableness on the landlord in withholding consent to a sublease unless the lease expressly states otherwise." . . .

In a "silent consent" clause requiring a landlord's consent to assign or sublease, there is no standard governing the landlord's decision. Courts must insert a standard. The choice is usually between 1) requiring the landlord to act reasonably when withholding consent, or 2) permitting the landlord to act arbitrarily and capriciously in withholding consent. . . .

There are two public policy reasons why the law enunciated in *Klawans* should now be changed. The first is the public policy against restraints on alienation [power to transfer property]. The second is the public policy which implies a covenant of good faith and fair dealing in every contract.

. . . Restraints on alienation are permitted in leases, but are looked upon with disfavor and are strictly construed. . . . If a clause in a lease is susceptible of two interpretations, public policy favors the interpretation least restrictive of the right to alienate freely. Interpreting a "silent consent" clause so that it only prohibits subleases or assignments when a landlord's refusal to consent is reasonable, would be the interpretation imposing the least restraint on alienation and most in accord with public policy.

Since the *Klawans* decision, this Court has recognized that in a lease, as well as in other contracts, "there exists an implied covenant that each of the parties thereto will act in good faith and deal fairly with the others." . . . When the lease gives the landlord the right to exercise discretion, the discretion should be exercised in good faith, and in accordance with fair dealing; if the lease does not spell out any standard for withholding consent, then the implied covenant of good faith and fair dealing should imply a reasonableness standard.

> **CASE 25.2**
> **Continued**
>
> In the instant case, we need not expound at length on what constitutes a reasonable refusal to consent to an assignment or sublease. We should, however, point out that obvious examples of reasonable objections could include the financial irresponsibility or instability of the transferee, or the unsuitability or incompatibility of the intended use of the property by the transferee. . . . Where, as alleged in this case, the refusal to consent was solely for the purpose of securing a rent increase, such refusal would be unreasonable unless the new subtenant would necessitate additional expenditures by, or increased economic risk to, the landlord.
>
> **JUDGMENT** [R]eversed . . . and case remanded. . . .

Termination of Leases

Fixed-Term Tenancies. A fixed-term tenancy ends at the expiration of the term of the lease, unless there is an extension by the parties. Prior to the end of the term, neither party has the power to terminate the lease without cause. For example, a landlord would have just cause to terminate the lease if the tenant failed to pay rent or used the premises for illegal activities. At the termination of the lease, the tenant must vacate the premises. When a tenant holds over—remains in possession after the expiration of a tenancy for a fixed term without the landlord's consent—a **tenancy at sufferance** is created. In most states the landlord can institute an unlawful detainer action to evict the tenant at sufferance without first giving notice of termination of the tenancy. The tenant is liable for the reasonable rental value of the premises for the period that the tenant remains in possession after expiration of the fixed term. If the landlord accepts rent from a holdover tenant, a court very likely will hold that a periodic tenancy was created by the conduct of the parties. A landlord should therefore consider carefully the legal consequences before accepting rent from a tenant at sufferance.

What happens if a tenant vacates the premises before the end of the lease term? At common law, an abandonment by the tenant which was accepted by the landlord could constitute a **surrender and acceptance** (a form of mutual rescission) of the lease and would discharge the tenant from any further obligation to pay rent. In fact, if the landlord took possession of the premises and attempted to rerent it to recover his or her losses, this was frequently viewed as an implied acceptance of the tenant's surrender. Modern commercial leases frequently provide, however, that the tenant will continue to be liable for the unpaid rent for the term of the lease if he or she abandons the premises or is evicted for nonpayment of rent. In such cases, the landlord is under an obligation to take reasonable steps to relet the property in an attempt to mitigate (minimize) his or her losses. The tenant is liable only for the amount of unpaid rent less the amount the landlord received (or could have received) by reletting the premises.

Periodic Tenancies. A periodic tenancy continues indefinitely until the parties agree to terminate the tenancy or one of the parties gives notice of termination. Requirements regarding the method and time of notice vary among the states. A common requirement is that the notice must be given in writing for the same amount of time as the period of tenancy. Under such a statute, 30 days' notice would be sufficient to terminate a month-to-month tenancy.

Generally, either party can terminate the tenancy without cause. Because the landlord need not have any reason for the notice of termination, the power to terminate can be abused. This has caused significant problems for residential tenants, particularly those who seek to correct problems with dilapidated and uninhabitable premises. If a tenant reports building or health code violations to the local authorities in an attempt to force the landlord to repair the property or bring it up to code, can a landlord retaliate and terminate the tenancy by giving notice? Many courts have held that such a **retaliatory eviction** is not lawful.

In order to establish retaliatory eviction, the tenant must prove the following:

- The tenant's grievance was bona fide, reasonable, and serious in nature and had a foundation in fact.
- The tenant did not create the condition complained of.
- The grievance existed at the time the landlord commenced eviction proceedings.
- The overriding reason the landlord sought eviction was to retaliate against the tenant for exercising his or her rights.

EASEMENTS

Meaning of Easement

An **easement** may be defined as the right to use, or to prevent the use of, the real property of another in a specific manner.[3] For example, Archie grants to George, an adjoining landowner, the permanent right to drive his car over a designated portion of his land in order to get to and from the nearest public street. George has a right-of-way easement. His land is called the **dominant** tenement or parcel. Archie's land, the land that is subject to the burden of the easement, is called the **servient** tenement or parcel.

The above easement is an **easement appurtenant** because the easement benefits George's land and is considered one of the rights of the landowner. The easement is said to "run with the land" because the benefit of the easement will pass with any sale of the dominant parcel (the burden of the easement also passes with any sale of the servient parcel). If George sells his land to Michael, Michael acquires the right-of-way easement. In contrast, utility easements, under which a public utility has the right to run power lines across a landowner's property, are considered **easements in gross** because they are not created for the benefit of a particular tract of land.

An easement is an interest in real property, but it is not an estate in real property. The owner of an easement does not own the servient tenement but merely has the right to use it, or to prevent the use of it, in a certain way. An easement is similar to a **license.** Like the owner of an easement, a **licensee** has the right to use another's real estate for some purpose. But in contrast to an easement, which is an interest in the land, a license is usually a *personal* and *revocable* privilege granted by the landowner. Typical examples of licenses are a theater ticket, the rental of a parking lot space, and permission to hunt or fish on another's land.

Methods of Creating Easements

Creation by Express Grant or Reservation. The most common method of creating an easement is by deed, as discussed in Chapter 24. The owner of real property executes a deed that transfers to the grantee a limited right to use the property of the grantor. In some instances, a grantor transfers ownership of the property to another but expressly reserves an easement in the deed. For example, Agnes, the owner of a 10-acre parcel of land, executes a deed transferring to Robert the fee simple ownership in 5 acres but expressly reserves the right to use a 12-foot strip as a roadway for access to the land retained by her.

Creation by Implied Grant or Reservation. In some situations, an easement may be created by implied grant or reservation. For example, Andrew owns 100 acres of land on which he constructs an irrigation system with an open ditch running from the north portion to the south portion. After several years he transfers ownership of the south portion to Donna without making any mention of an easement. Under these circumstances a court very likely would infer that the parties must have intended Donna

---

[3] An easement that prevents a landowner from using his or her property in a given way is called a **restrictive covenant,** which is discussed in connection with land use controls in Chapter 24.

to have an easement in Andrew's land for irrigation purposes. Such an easement is known as an easement by implied grant. In a similar manner, if Andrew had sold the *north* portion of the land to Donna without mention of any easement, a court would be warranted in holding that Andrew has an irrigation easement by implied reservation. The following conditions must exist before an easement by implied grant or reservation will be recognized:

- The owner of real property must have transferred a portion of it to another person.
- At the time of the transfer, there must have been a long, obvious use of one portion of the property.
- The easement must be reasonably necessary to the beneficial use of the other portion of the property (the dominant tenement).

Creation by Necessity. In rare situations an easement may be created by necessity. Where an owner of real property transfers to a grantee a portion of the owner's property so that the grantee is left without a means of access, the parcel is said to be *landlocked*. Upon application to a court, the grantee may be given an easement for access to his or her parcel over the retained portion of the grantor's property. Such an easement must be absolutely necessary for the grantee, and not just convenient or desirable. Thus, a grantee who has access to a parcel of land but complains that the only way to get to the parcel is by way of a steep, narrow, winding road cannot expect a court to give an easement by necessity over a flatter portion of the grantor's retained property. If a grantor transfers ownership of real property and retains a portion that is inadvertently landlocked, the grantor is entitled to an easement by necessity over the transferred property.

Creation by Prescription. An easement by prescription arises from a person's use of real property contrary to the wishes of the owner. In most states, one who claims such an easement must show use of another's property that is open and notorious, hostile to the owner (i.e., the user must be a trespasser), and continuous for the period specified in the state statute of limitations.

The requirements are very similar to those for adverse possession, discussed in Chapter 24. The difference is that adverse *possession* results in the acquisition of ownership, while adverse *use* results in the acquisition of a prescriptive easement. Mary and Tom are neighbors. Almost daily for many years Mary has walked across a corner of Tom's property, eventually making a visible pathway. Tom objected many times during those years but took no legal action to prevent her use of his property, and he did not physically interrupt her use. Mary has acquired a prescriptive easement (if the statutory period of time has elapsed) and now has a legal right to continue walking across Tom's property. In some states, a landowner can prevent the creation of a prescriptive easement by posting signs stating, in effect, "Right to pass is by permission, and subject to control, of owner." Such language makes an otherwise adverse use permissive.

Creation by Dedication. Chapter 24 defines dedication as a method by which a governmental unit or agency may acquire ownership of real property. The process of dedication may also be used to create an easement. For example, an owner of land may offer a roadway easement to the local city government. If the city council passes an ordinance accepting the offer, the city acquires an easement by statutory dedication. The owner of the servient tenement retains the right to use the airspace above the roadway and the subsurface below the roadway as part of the fee simple estate.

In recent years, the creation of easements by common law dedication has been asserted in lawsuits between environmental groups and owners of recreational land. Some courts have found that common law dedications have occurred when the evidence showed that the landowners freely allowed the public to camp, picnic, or walk across their property. In some states the property owner can avoid such claims of dedication by posting an appropriate sign in plain sight.

Table 25.1 Concept Summary: Creation of Easements

Type of Easement	How Easement Created
Express grant or reservation	Deed conveying an easement to the grantee or reserving an easement for the grantor
Implied grant or reservation	Conveyance of one part of a tract of land
	A long, obvious use of one part of land for the benefit of the other part existed prior to conveyance
	That use is reasonably necessary for the benefit of the part transferred (implied grant) or the part retained (implied reservation)
Necessity	Conveyance of one part of a tract of land
	Part conveyed or part retained is landlocked, that is, without any means of access
Prescription	Open and notorious, hostile, and continuous use of another's land for a statutory period of time
Dedication	Owner offers to give a right to use the owner's land for public purposes to a government entity
	The entity accepts the offer

Use and Maintenance of Easements

The owner of an easement may exercise the right to use, or prevent the use of, the servient tenement according to the purpose of the easement and the circumstances surrounding its creation. Where an easement is created by *express grant*, a properly drawn deed will indicate the specific purpose of the easement, such as use of the land for a roadway, or for installation of power poles. Similarly, where an easement is created by *implied grant* or by *prescription*, there has been an obvious, open use that determines the extent of the easement owner's right to use the servient tenement. He or she will be able to use the property in the same manner as it was used previously.

The owner of an easement has the right and the duty to maintain and repair installations connected with the easement. For example, an easement owner may grade and pave the surface designated in a roadway easement. Or, if the easement is for utility purposes, the easement owner may enter the servient property to repair and replace water lines or sewer pipes as needed. The owner of the servient tenement may do as he or she wishes with the property as long as there is no unreasonable interference with the use, enjoyment, and maintenance of the easement created.

The following case involves an attempt by the easement owner to expand the usage of the easement.

CASE 25.3   Wright v. Horse Creek Ranches • 697 P.2d 384 (Colo. 1985)

FACTS   Geyer Ranch, an 830-acre cattle ranch, lies to the east of three large parcels known as the Buchheim Ranch, the Bull Ranch, and the Cockcroft Ranch. These four ranches were accessible from a county road by means of a private dirt road which traversed the Cockcroft, Bull, and Buchheim ranches before reaching the Geyer Ranch. The road was rocky, unsuitable for passenger cars, and passable only 6 months out of the year. For more than 20 years, the landowners had used the dirt road for access to their ranches.

In August of 1978 Horse Creek Ranches purchased the Geyer Ranch for the purpose of subdividing it into smaller parcels of no less than 40 acres each, to be sold as recreational residential property. On July 3 and 4, 1979 Horse Creek substantially widened the dirt road, removed rocks, trees, and brush, and flattened the roadbed. Richard Wright, owner of Buchheim Ranch, filed suit against Horse Creek to prohibit the allegedly unauthorized use of the access road. The trial court found that there was a trend in the area toward subdividing large ranches into smaller agricultural and recreational tracts, that Horse Creek's predecessors had established a prescriptive easement over Wright's ranch, and that Horse Creek's use to service owners of 40-acre tracts was reasonably foreseeable and not an unreasonable burden on the servient tenement. Wright appealed. The court of appeals affirmed, and Wright appealed to the Colorado Supreme Court.

OPINION   KIRSHBAUM, J. . . . Because the range of permissible uses of any particular easement is in the first instance defined by the circumstances surrounding the creation of that easement, precise delineation of the means by which a particular easement is acquired is critical to any determination of the extent to which the owner of the dominant estate is entitled to burden the servient estate. Our initial inquiry, therefore, must focus upon the nature of the easement Horse Creek owns.

. . .[T]he trial court concluded that the easement owned by Geyer had been obtained by prescription. . . . [The landowners] understood—that between 1957 and 1978 all of them had acquired easements by prescription over so much of the other properties as was necessary to obtain access to their properties. . . .

The conclusion that Horse Creek acquired an easement established by prescription, rather than one created by grant, is critical to the selection of the test to be applied to Wright's claim of unauthorized use of the easement. . . . Section 477 of the *Restatement of Property* offers the following principle as a reasonable standard for determining the extent of easements established by prescription: "The extent of an easement created by prescription is fixed by the use through which it was created." . . . [T]he beneficiary of an easement established by prescription will be permitted to vary the use of the easement to a reasonable extent. . . . [S]ection 479 of the *Restatement of Property* . . . states as follows

> In ascertaining whether a particular use is permissible under an easement appurtenant created by prescription there must be considered . . . the needs which result from a normal evolution in the use of the dominant tenement and the extent to which the satisfaction of those needs increases the burden on the servient tenement. . . .

CASE 25.3 Continued

Both the trial court and the majority of the Court of Appeals focused their attention almost exclusively on the "normal evolution" standard of section 479. . . .

The use to which the private road was put during the relevant prescriptive period was described by Bob J. Cockcroft and by Darrel Geyer as use primarily for ranching purposes, and occasional traffic by hunters, loggers and water commissioners. When asked if the road had ever been used "for access to any residence or home on the Geyer property," Cockcroft answered "[d]efinitely not." . . .

The evidence is unchallenged that from 1958 to 1978, the road was not used for residential purposes. . . .

The use to which Horse Creek seeks to put the easement includes use for recreational residential purposes. This represents a change in kind of use. It is a change which by necessity will subject the servient estate to increased burdens. Both Cockcroft and Wright testified that any increased traffic on the road would impede their ranching operations, and their testimony was not contradicted.

The change in the dominant estate, of course, is the change from a single, large agricultural enterprise to a recreational development area consisting of several smaller tracts owned by several individuals. The physical character of the easement has been substantially altered from a ten-foot wide primitive road to a passageway which now is twenty-one feet wide and accommodates two vehicles simultaneously. The purpose of the new use has changed from permitting infrequent access for ranching needs to encouraging frequent use by owners and their guests for recreational residence purposes. . . . Considering all of these factors, rather than focusing exclusively on the fact that subdivision of ranch properties was an inevitable phenomenon, we conclude that the trial court erred in enlarging the permissible use of the prescriptive easement acquired by Horse Creek to include recreational residence purposes. . . .

JUDGMENT The judgment is . . . reversed.

LIENS ON REAL PROPERTY

Meaning and Classification of Liens

In general, a **lien** is a claim or charge on property as security for the payment of a debt or for the performance of some other obligation. In one sense, a lien is a contingent claim held by a creditor. If the obligation is satisfied, there will be no interference with the debtor's right to use, possess, and enjoy his or her property. On the other hand, if the obligation is not satisfied, the lienholder may take steps (called "foreclosure") to sell the property and to apply proceeds from the sale to the debt.

There are two main classes of liens on real property: **voluntary liens,** which are created with the property owner's consent (e.g., mortgages), and **involuntary liens,** which are created without the property owner's consent (e.g., mechanic's liens). Only the most important voluntary and involuntary liens are discussed in the following sections.

Mortgages and Voluntary Liens on Real Property

Nature and Requirements of a Mortgage. A **mortgage,** the most common type of voluntary lien on real property, is an interest in real property given to secure the performance of some debt or obligation. The two parties to a mortgage are called the **mortgagor** (the borrower or debtor) and the **mortgagee** (the lender or creditor). Under the statute of frauds, a mortgage must be evidenced by a writing. There is no requirement that a mortgage instrument be recorded in order to create a lien on the property mortgaged. However, the mortgagee should have the instrument recorded at the local county recorder's office as a protection against a claim of any subsequent purchaser or any subsequent mortgagee or other lienholder. The priority rules (notice, notice-race, and race statutes) discussed in Chapter 24 apply to mortgages as well as deeds.

The mortgage device is used in connection with many different kinds of credit transactions. Usually, the device is used for either of two purposes:

1. The mortgage is used by a property owner as a means of borrowing a substantial sum of money for some personal or business reason. The property owner borrows from a lender, signs a promissory note, and executes a mortgage on his or her home or business property to secure the repayment of the money borrowed.
2. The mortgage is often the indispensable means of financing the purchase of real property. The person who desires to purchase the property has sufficient cash for a down payment but not enough to pay the balance of the purchase price. The buyer borrows the money from a lender and executes a mortgage to the lender. The financing is called a **purchase money mortgage.**

Mortgage Substitutes. In terms of financing a purchase of real estate or creating a credit transaction secured by real estate, there are at least two alternatives to a mortgage: a deed of trust and an installment sale of land under a contract for deed.

Trust deeds. About half the states recognize the **trust deed** as an acceptable security instrument in real estate transactions. To the creditor, a trust deed has several significant advantages over the mortgage, particularly in terms of foreclosure, and in some states the trust deed has virtually replaced the real property mortgage. States that refuse to recognize the trust deed on real property base the refusal on the ground that in the event of foreclosure debtors should have the procedural advantages connected with mortgages.

A trust deed is a document by which a debtor transfers the title to real property to a disinterested person (called a **trustee**) to be held in trust as security for the performance of an obligation, usually the payment of a debt. While there are only two parties to a mortgage, there are three parties to a trust deed: the **trustor** (the debtor), the **beneficiary** (the creditor), and the trustee. Although the trustee holds title to the real property, it is a bare legal title, not a true ownership interest. In legal effect, the trust deed is considered to be merely a lien on the real property. If the trustor meets his or her obligations, there will be no interference with the use and possession of the property. When the obligation is satisfied, the trustee will execute the necessary documents to reconvey title to the trustor. The trustee is typically given the power to sell the property if the debtor defaults, and to apply proceeds from the sale to the debt.

Since mortgages and trust deeds perform a similar function, they necessarily have many features in common. Most of the following discussion concerning mortgages is applicable to trust deeds as well. The major difference between a mortgage and a trust deed relates to foreclosure, as will be discussed later in the chapter.

Contract for deed. The **contract for deed** is an installment sale of land that performs the same function as a purchase money mortgage. In a contract for deed, the seller finances the sale and retains "legal" title to the property until all installment payments are made by the purchaser. The purchaser is considered the "equitable" owner of the property, is entitled to the use and possession of the property during the term of the contract, and is entitled to a deed to the property upon completion of the installment payments.

Contracts for deed are different from the typical mortgage in two respects. First, mortgages have traditionally been long-term financing arrangements, with the monthly payments being amortized over the term of the mortgage. For example, under a 20- or 30-year mortgage, the borrower-mortgagor will make equal monthly payments for the entire period of the loan, at which time the debt will be paid. On the other hand, contracts for deed tend to be short term financing arrangements that call for a substantial "balloon" payment at the end of the term of the contract. For example, Sally purchases a building for $100,000, with $10,000 down and the balance under a 5-year contract for deed. Her monthly payments will not pay off the entire amount in 5 years, so Sally will have to come up with the entire unpaid balance at the end of the contract period. Sally will probably have to secure traditional mortgage financing to pay off the balloon amount. Note that these observations are mere generalizations; some mortgages will have balloon payments and some contracts for deed will be long-term financing arrangements.

Second, contracts for deed are subject to forfeiture or cancellation if the purchaser defaults, a remedy that is different from the ordinary foreclosure of a mortgage. Rather than conduct a foreclosure sale upon default, the seller simply cancels the contract for deed and the purchaser forfeits all rights in the property. Many states limit the seller's right to cancel by requiring notice to the purchaser and a period of time within which the purchaser can cure the default and reinstate the contract.

Rights and Duties of the Mortgagor and Mortgagee. The *mortgagor* of real property ordinarily owns a fee simple estate and retains the right to use, possess, and dispose of the property. The mortgagor can lease the premises to another and collect rent. He or she can borrow further sums of money from other creditors and give subsequent mortgages to them. The typical mortgage instrument contains a list of duties specified by the mortgagee to be performed by the mortgagor. Some of the duties customarily included are to repay money borrowed; to keep the premises in good repair; to refrain from committing waste; to pay annual real property taxes; to pay any prior mortgage that may be on the property; to maintain adequate fire insurance on improvements; and not to transfer ownership without approval of the mortgagee.

The mortgagee has the right to performance of all the mortgagor's duties. Under the typical mortgage instrument the mortgagee has several duties. The mortgagee has a duty to lend money in accordance with the agreement of the parties. When the mortgagor pays back the loan, the mortgagee owes a duty to execute appropriate documents to remove the lien from the mortgagor's property. In the event foreclosure becomes necessary, the mortgagee owes a duty to act fairly and to follow the statutory procedure of the state. A mortgagee can transfer the mortgage to a third person and assign to such person the right to collect the debt that is secured by the mortgage. Upon the mortgagee's death, the mortgage passes to his or her heirs or beneficiaries. The transferee would be obligated to perform the mortgagee's duties mentioned above.

The following case involves violation of a duty imposed on the mortgagor by a mortgagee.

BOX 25.3

A Question of Ethics

During the 1970s, homes were often sold under contracts for deed because the high rates of interest on mortgage loans made purchasers unable to qualify for traditional financing. In many cases, a purchaser, who made a significant down payment as well as the monthly payments for the entire contract period, was unable to make the balloon payment because interest rates remained high. Many purchasers, unable to secure mortgage financing, forfeited their rights under their contracts and lost all their equity in the property. When a contract for deed is canceled, the seller reacquires all rights to the real estate and retains all monies paid under the contract. Given the circumstances, is it ethical for a seller to keep all monies paid by the purchaser under a contract for deed? ■

CASE 25.4 — Investors Savings & Loan Association v. Ganz
• 416 A.2d 918 (N.J. Super. Ct. 1980)

FACTS Mr. and Mrs. Ganz borrowed $50,000 from Investors Savings & Loan Association to finance the purchase of a home. The loan was secured by a mortgage in favor of Investors. In the mortgage loan application the Ganzs stated they would occupy the property. The mortgage contained the following condition:

> And it is further agreed that, if the mortgaged premises are not used as the primary place of residence and are not occupied by the Mortgagor during the term of the mortgage loan, then and in such event, the aforesaid principal sum with accrued interest shall, at the option of the Mortgagee, become due and payable immediately. . . .

In October 1979 Investors learned that tenants were renting the premises. It demanded that the balance due on the mortgage be paid in full. The Ganzs did not make this payment, and the premises continued to be tenant-occupied. Investors brought suit to foreclose the mortgage. The Ganzs filed an answer alleging that the acceleration clause and mortgage requirement that the Ganzs reside in the mortgaged premises were unconscionable and inequitable and created a forfeiture, and thus were of no force and effect. Investors moved for an order granting summary judgment.

OPINION KENTZ, J. . . . Where an acceleration clause is express and certain in its terms, such a clause requiring the payment of the entire balance due on the mortgage upon default in the performance of any covenant or condition of the mortgage is held to be a legitimate contractual obligation for credit on condition and not a penalty or forfeiture clause. . . .

The only remaining issue is whether the enforcement of the acceleration clause because of the violation of the owner occupancy requirement would be unconscionable or inequitable. This question appears to be one of first impression in this state.

[The Ganzs] contend that before such a clause can be enforced there must be shown some jeopardy or threat to the [mortgagee's] security and that [Investors] has demonstrated none. [They] argue that unlike cases in which the mortgagor has defaulted on payments due or in which the identity of the mortgagor changes, [they] remain responsible for the payments and are ready, willing and able to pay. Thus, they maintain that there is no jeopardy to plaintiff's security in the mortgage by virtue of the fact that they are not living in the premises.

[Investors] states by affidavit that historically the purpose of a savings and loan association has been to assist persons in acquiring a home in which to reside and that this has always been plaintiff's policy. . . . [It] contends that from its experience nonoccupying owners tend to restrict and minimize property maintenance and upkeep in order to enhance their financial return. [Investors] argues that such conduct leads to an unreasonable depreciation of the property and jeopardizes the security on which the loan was made. In order to prevent this result, the owner occupancy provision is made a condition of the loan. . . .

> **CASE 25.4 Continued**
>
> When a contract is clear and unambiguous a court is bound to enforce its terms as they are written and the court may not make a better contract for either of the parties. A court has no right to rewrite the contract by substituting new or different provisions from those clearly expressed in the contract. . . .
>
> In applying the foregoing to the facts of this case, I do not find that the owner occupancy requirement is unconscionable or inequitable. Given plaintiff's purpose to promote home ownership, its policy of not making loans except for that reason, . . . it cannot be said that its requirement of owner occupancy as a condition for the granting of a mortgage loan is unjust. [The Ganzs] were fully aware of this condition when they freely and voluntarily entered into the mortgage transaction. Furthermore, [Investors'] fear that the lack of owner occupancy might jeopardize its security is not unreasonable.
>
> **JUDGMENT**
>
> Since defendants have defaulted, plaintiff has the right to accelerate the due date of the unpaid balance of the debt and to require payment thereof. Such payment having not been made as demanded, summary judgment of foreclosure is appropriate.

Transfer of Mortgaged Property. The mortgagor generally retains the right to transfer the mortgaged property in the absence of any restriction in the mortgage. When a mortgagor sells the property, the purchaser can *assume* an existing mortgage or purchase the property *subject to* an existing mortgage. Whether a purchaser assumes a mortgage or purchases the property subject to a mortgage affects the purchaser's liability for the mortgage debt and the rights of the mortgagee against the purchaser.

Assumption of the mortgage. A purchaser who assumes an existing mortgage agrees to personally pay the mortgage debt. The creditor-mortgagee is a third-party beneficiary of the assumption contract and is entitled to hold the purchaser personally liable for the unpaid mortgage debt. Suppose Al purchases a house from Kim, assumes an existing $40,000 mortgage debt to First Fidelity Bank, and later defaults. Al is liable to First Fidelity for any deficiency after the foreclosure sale (the amount the debt exceeds the sale proceeds). Kim is also liable to First Fidelity for the deficiency because the transfer of the property to Al did not discharge Kim's obligation to First Fidelity (unless, of course, First Fidelity released her from the mortgage debt).

Purchasing subject to the mortgage. The purchaser or other transferee who acquires real estate but does not assume an existing mortgage takes the property "subject to" that mortgage. Because a transfer of real estate will not discharge an existing mortgage, a mortgage remains a lien on the real property after a sale. Thus, the purchaser's rights are subject to the rights of the mortgagee, who can foreclose if the mortgage debt is not paid. However, the purchaser is not personally liable for the debt when he or she buys subject to a mortgage. In the event of foreclosure, the purchaser is not liable for any deficiency; the mortgagee can hold only the seller-mortgagor liable for that deficiency.

> **BOX 25.4**
> **Mortgages and Business Planning**
>
> Whether the purchaser assumes an existing mortgage or purchases subject to an existing mortgage, the seller continues to have potential liability under the mortgage even after a sale of the real estate. What can a seller do to terminate his or her liability to the mortgagee when the property is sold?

Restrictions on transfer. The mortgage may contain a **due-on-sale** clause limiting the ability of the mortgagor to sell the mortgaged property. Due-on-sale clauses, which are generally enforceable, provide that the entire amount of the mortgage debt is due in the event of a sale of the property by the mortgagor. This allows the mortgagee-lender to call for the payment of the total mortgage debt upon a sale of the property. A purchaser will, therefore, need to secure the consent of the mortgagee to assume a mortgage or purchase subject to it. Due-on-sale clauses favor banks, savings and loans, and other real estate lenders. If the interest rate on the mortgage to be assumed is not favorable to the lender under present market conditions, the lender will be able to call in the mortgage and force the purchaser to refinance at a higher rate of interest.

Foreclosure of the Mortgage. If the mortgagor fails to make the monthly or periodic payments or otherwise fails to perform any of his or her duties under the mortgage, the mortgagee can demand that the mortgagor pay the entire amount of the mortgage debt. Most mortgage notes contain an **acceleration clause** that permits (but does not require) the mortgagee to accelerate the mortgage debt when there is a default. If the debt is not paid, the mortgagee has the right to foreclose—that is, to have the real property sold and apply the proceeds from the sale to the debt.

There are two major types of foreclosures: judicial foreclosures and power-of-sale foreclosures. A **judicial foreclosure** requires the mortgagee to commence a civil lawsuit to foreclose. If the mortgagee prevails, the property is sold under a judgment of foreclosure issued by the court. The sheriff or other officer of the court conducts a public sale of the property by auction and the proceeds are used to pay the mortgage debt. Judicial foreclosure is the primary method of foreclosure, and in some states the exclusive method. Other states permit the **power-of-sale foreclosure.** This type of foreclosure is conducted under a clause in the mortgage that gives the mortgagee the power to sell the property. Unlike a judicial foreclosure, the mortgagee does not have to file a lawsuit and secure a court order to sell the property. After notice to the mortgagor, the sale is conducted by a sheriff or other third party. This type of foreclosure is the method used to foreclose a trust deed.

Mortgagor's right of redemption. At any time prior to the foreclosure sale of the property, the mortgagor has a common law right of redemption (called the **equity of redemption**). In order to redeem, the mortgagor must usually pay the entire amount of the mortgage debt plus the costs associated with the foreclosure. If the mortgagor redeems, he or she prevents the foreclosure sale and is entitled to be restored to the property. Once the foreclosure sale has been conducted, the mortgagor's common law right of redemption ends. To protect mortgagors from the forfeiture of a foreclosure sale, many states also provide a statutory right of redemption after a foreclosure sale takes place—that is, a right for a limited time (e.g., 6 months to 1 year) to repurchase the property by payment of the foreclosure sale price to the high bidder. In many states, the mortgagor remains in possession of the property and continues to derive income from the property during the statutory period of redemption. Note that other persons with an interest in the property generally have a right of redemption, including purchasers from the mortgagor and junior mortgagees.

Sale proceeds and deficiencies. Unless the mortgagor exercises the right of redemption, the mortgaged property will be sold at a public sale to the high bidder. The sale proceeds will be applied first to pay off the mortgage debt and the costs of the sale. If there is any surplus after the mortgagee is paid, any "junior" mortgagees will be paid in the order of the priority of their mortgages. The mortgagor will be entitled to any remaining surplus.

In many foreclosure sales, the proceeds will be insufficient to pay the mortgage debt, resulting in a deficiency. Unless prohibited or restricted by law, the mortgagee is entitled to a deficiency judgment against the mortgagor. The mortgageer will have to try to collect that judgment, like any other judgment, from the nonexempt property of the debtor. Some states place significant restrictions on the creditor's right to secure a deficiency judgment, and others prohibit deficiency judgments in certain cases. For example, some jurisdictions prohibit it where the foreclosure was by power of sale, and others prohibit it where the mortgage is a purchase money mortgage.

Effect of sale. The purchaser at a foreclosure sale acquires the property free and clear of the foreclosed mortgage and any junior mortgages. Senior mortgages—i.e., mortgages that are superior to the foreclosed mortgage—are not discharged by the foreclosure sale. Thus, if there is a "first" mortgage on the property and the "second" mortgage is foreclosed, the purchaser acquires title to the property subject to the first mortgage.

Foreclosure of a Trust Deed. Under the terms of the typical trust deed the trustee is given the power to sell the property upon default by the debtor-trustor and to apply proceeds from the sale to the debt. The nonjudicial power-of-sale foreclosure by the trustee has certain advantages for the creditor. It avoids the delay involved in getting a court order for a sale and avoids the expenses of litigation, and in some states it allows the trustor no right of redemption after the sale.

To foreclose by power of sale, the trustee simply notifies all interested persons (the debtor, other lienholders) that the trustor has defaulted. After a short period of time allowed for reinstatement of the trust deed, the trustee advertises and conducts an auction sale. If the trustor has no right of redemption, the purchaser can immediately take possession, make improvements, lease, or even sell the property.

Involuntary Liens on Real Property

Several liens on real property can be created without the consent or approval of the owner. The statutes relating to such liens are complex and vary widely among the states. The general aspects of the more important involuntary liens are discussed below.

Mechanic's Liens. Contractors, subcontractors, and others who perform services or supply materials in the improvement of someone's real property are entitled to a **mechanic's lien** on the property improved. Nearly every state has a mechanic's lien statute, as discussed in detail in Chapter 28.

Attachment Liens. A **writ of attachment** enables an unsecured creditor to have the sheriff seize and hold the defendant's property pending the outcome of a lawsuit against the debtor. To "seize" real property, the sheriff records the writ of attachment in the county recorder's office. Once the writ is recorded, an **attachment lien** is created against the property. If the creditor obtains a judgment in the civil action, the plaintiff can have the property sold by foreclosure.[4]

Judgment Liens. A party to a civil lawsuit who secures a judgment awarding him or her money, called the **judgment creditor,** can record the judgment in the county or counties in which the **judgment debtor** (the losing party) owns real property. Once it is recorded, the judgment becomes a lien on any real property owned by the judgment debtor in the county. A **judgment lien** remains a lien on the property until the judgment is paid or is rendered inoperative by the expiration of the statutory period. In several states a judgment is valid for a period of 10 years, and in some states it may be renewed for one or more statutory periods.

Execution Liens. To collect a judgment, a judgment creditor can have the court issue a **writ of execution.** The writ orders the sheriff to seize and sell the judgment debtor's nonexempt property (property the law allows to be taken by creditors) to pay off the judgment debt. The

---

[4]The U.S. Supreme Court has severely restricted the creditor's right to a prejudgment attachment because attachment interferes with the debtor's constitutional right to use and dispose of his or her property *prior* to a court trial. *Connecticut v. Doehr,* 111 S.Ct. 2105 (1991) (discussed in Chapter 3); *Sniadach v. Family Fin. Corp.,* 395 U.S. 337 (1969).

sheriff usually records a notice of execution in the county where the judgment debtor's real property is located. Recording the notice creates an **execution lien** on the described parcels of property. The sheriff sets a time and place for foreclosure sale of the specific parcels, advertises, and conducts the sale in the same manner as that of a mortgage foreclosure sale. Some state statutes provide for a redemption period following the sale.

Tax Liens. A tax lien is a lien created by a governmental unit or agency to enforce collection of a tax. The most common tax lien in the United States is the property tax lien, which is an *automatic* lien (no recording is necessary) against the taxpayer's real property to secure the payment of real property taxes. If the taxes are not paid within the statutory time period, the government publishes a notice of sale in the paper and conducts an auction sale. There is typically no redemption period after sale, and the high bidder receives a tax deed immediately.

When the federal government or a state or local governmental taxing agency is attempting to collect an unpaid income tax, employment tax, sales tax, or other nonproperty tax, the governmental agency is usually required to record some type of delinquency notice in the county recorder's office to create a lien. In order to sell the taxpayer's real property, the taxing agency generally must follow a procedure similar to that for foreclosing a mortgage. Often the taxpayer is given a redemption period after sale to recover his or her property.

SUMMARY

There are three main types of interests in real property: estates, easements, and liens. An estate in real property is an ownership interest. Estates are either freeholds or leaseholds. The major freehold estates are fee simple estates and life estates. Leasehold estates are those in which a tenant acquires the right to exclusive possession of certain premises for a limited period of time. The two important types of leases are tenancies for a fixed term and periodic tenancies.

An easement is the right to use, or to prevent the use of, the real property of another in a specific manner. Easements may be created by express or implied grant or reservation, by necessity, by prescription, and by dedication.

A lien is a claim or charge on property as security for an obligation. If the owner of the property does not satisfy his or her obligation to the creditor, the creditor can take steps to foreclose the lien. Foreclosure usually involves a sale of the property at auction and the use of proceeds to satisfy the creditor's claim. Two major voluntary liens are the mortgage and the trust deed. The major involuntary liens on real property are mechanic's liens, attachment liens, judgment liens, execution liens, and tax liens.

REVIEW QUESTIONS

1. What is the essential difference between a freehold estate and a leasehold estate?

2. What is a future interest? Give an example of how a future interest might be created.

3. Should the implied warranty of habitability be applied to a commercial lease?

4. Explain the differences between an assignment and a sublease.

5. From the perspective of a business tenant, what are the advantages and disadvantages of entering into a fixed-term lease as opposed to a periodic tenancy?

6. What is an easement? How does it differ from a license?

7. If you were about to purchase a parcel of real property, what steps could you take to determine whether an easement had been created by any of the five methods of creating an easement?

8. What is the importance of a mortgage or deed of trust in a real estate transaction?

9. Explain the foreclosure process, including the rights of the mortgagor and the mortgagee in that process.

10. Explain the differences between an attachment lien, a judgment lien, and an execution lien.

CASE PROBLEMS

1. Leonard and Lillian Banaszak entered into a prenuptial agreement which provided that upon Leonard's death Lillian would receive a life estate in their homestead. Leonard's children were to have the remainder interest, and Lillian was obligated to maintain the property and pay the real estate taxes for the duration of the life estate. Leonard was ill. Before he and Lillian made the prenuptial agreement, his guardian (one of his children) mortgaged the property to secure a loan for the payment of Leonard's medical expenses. After Leonard died, Lillian refused to pay the interest on the mortgage. Leonard's children filed suit to require Lillian to pay the interest and, as part of her duty of maintenance, to pay for insurance covering possible loss or damage to the homestead. Does Lillian, as a life tenant, have to pay the interest on the mortgage and insurance for the property?

2. Dr. Davidow entered into a 5-year lease agreement with Inwood for medical office space. The lease required Dr. Davidow to pay Inwood $793.26 per month as rent. The lease also required Inwood to provide air conditioning, electricity, hot water, janitor and maintenance services, light fixtures, and security services. Shortly after moving into the office space, Dr. Davidow began experiencing problems with the building. The air conditioning did not work properly, often causing temperatures inside the office to rise above 85°F. The roof leaked whenever it rained, resulting in stained tiles and rotting, mildewed carpet. Pests and rodents often infested the office. The hallways remained dark because hallway lights went unreplaced for months. Cleaning and maintenance were not provided. The parking lot was constantly filled with trash. Hot water was not available. Several burglaries and various acts of vandalism occurred. Dr. Davidow finally moved out of the premises and discontinued rent payments approximately 14 months before the lease expired. Inwood sued Dr. Davidow for the unpaid rent and the case eventually reached the Texas Supreme Court, which addressed the issue of whether the implied warranty of habitability should be applied to commercial leases. How should the court rule on this issue? What policy reasons could be offered to support and to oppose the extension of the warranty to commercial leases?

3. A landlord, Toms Point Apartments, sought to evict a month-to-month tenant, Goudzward. The tenant raised the affirmative defense of retaliatory eviction. She alleged that she complained to the Attorney General's Office regarding the failure of the landlord to pay interest on rent security deposits and that she appeared at a hearing concerning the dismissal of the landlord's custodian. Goudzward claimed that the landlord retaliated for these acts by attempting to evict her. At the time the landlord commenced eviction proceedings, the tenants had collected the interest due them and the problem with the custodian had been resolved. Are these allegations sufficient to sustain the defense of retaliatory eviction?

4. Elizabeth Star Ayres and Clara Louise Quillen owned a tract of land in Sussex County, Delaware, known as "Bluff Point." Bluff Point is surrounded on three sides by Rehoboth Bay and on the fourth side by land owned by Irvin C. Walker. The two tracts of land were originally owned by Edward Goslee, who in 1878 transferred title to Bluff Point to his brother, Salathiel Goslee. Since at least 1928, a narrow dirt road across the land now owned by Walker has been the only means of access to Bluff Point. However, no deed was recorded evidencing the grant of a right-of-way easement to the owners of Bluff Point. The tracts remained in the Goslee family until Walker acquired his tract in 1986. After Walker purchased the tract, he attempted to prevent Ayres and Quillen from using the dirt road to get to Bluff Point. Ayres and Quillen brought suit claiming the right to an implied easement or an easement by necessity. Walker argued that the court should not recognize any easement across his land in part because there was access to Bluff Point by water. Ayres and Quillen argued that access by water was not feasible because the surrounding waters were very shallow. Should the court recognize an implied easement? An easement by necessity? How should the court handle the argument that there is access by water? Explain.

5. Norton borrowed $82,000 from Tucker Federal Savings and Loan Association and secured the debt with a mortgage on land in DeKalb County. The mortgage contained the following due-on-sale clause: "Should the title to the property become vested in any person or entity other than the mortgagor, the unpaid balance of the note shall become due and payable, at the option of the holder." Norton signed an installment contract agreeing to sell the land to Randall, and the contract was recorded. Under the contract Norton agreed to deliver a warranty deed upon either Randall's payment of the purchase price in full or Tucker Federal's approving Randall's assumption of the mortgage. The contract further provided that "no fee simple title passes upon execution of this agreement." The Randalls took possession of the property. Tucker Federal sued, claiming the due-on-sale clause was activated by the land sale contract. Did Norton violate the terms of the mortgage?

CHAPTER 26

Estates, Wills, and Trusts

A well-known radio talk show personality has said that to make a will is "an act of love" and that not to make a will is "an act of contempt." This chapter will, among other things, explain the meaning of this cryptic but very true statement.

When you die, what happens to the business you owned and operated? Who is entitled to the shares of stock and other property you accumulated during your years of successful business life? What arrangements can you make in your lifetime to direct the disposal after your death of those assets, called your **estate?**

Estate planning is the process of developing a plan for the future distribution of your property. One essential component of any estate plan is a will. By establishing a will, you can direct the distribution of your estate after your death. Without a will, your property will be distributed according to state law. As part of your will or during your lifetime, you can also establish a trust to achieve your estate planning objectives. A trust for the benefit of your family or others can provide productive and professional management of your property and resources for the benefit of your children and other dependents. A fundamental understanding of the law of wills and trusts is important both for personal and business reasons.

The law of wills and trusts is generally state law, because there are no federal inheritance laws other than taxing statutes. With our English common law background, our inheritance laws are similar from state to state (except for Louisiana, which has a civil law background). In a move toward achieving still greater uniformity among the states, the National Conference of Commissioners on Uniform State Laws has prepared, and submitted to the states for adoption, the Uniform Probate Code (UPC). Because of its increasing popularity, reference is made throughout this chapter to the UPC.

This chapter first considers the distribution of an estate of a person who dies without a will: the law of **intestate succession.** Next is a discussion of how a will is made, changed, or revoked and a summary of the process, called **probate,** by which the distribution of the estate of any deceased person (a decedent) is actually accomplished. Lastly, we consider how a legal device called a **trust** may add flexibility to a will and may even permit a decedent, after death, to control or limit the use of his or her estate by the individuals who inherited it.

INTESTATE SUCCESSION

Order of Intestate Succession

If a person dies without a will, he or she is said to die **intestate** and the **law of intestate succession** will determine the distribution of his or her estate. State intestacy laws are designed to assure that an intestate's estate will pass primarily to his or her surviving spouse (wife or husband) and surviving issue—that is, lineal descendants (children, grandchildren, great grandchildren). Under the UPC an intestate estate, after all debts have been paid, passes to eligible heirs in the order shown in Table 26.1.

Representation, referred to in Table 26.1, means that when a person who would have inherited from an intestate has died before the intestate and that individual leaves issue (children, grandchildren, and so on), such issue share equally the inheritance their parent would have received.

Intestate descent and distribution can best be understood by analyzing two hypothetical situations. For the first, assume that David dies intestate. His estate, after all debts and taxes have been paid, is valued at $350,000. David is survived by his wife and three children as well as by his mother, a sister, and a brother (see Figure 26.1).

Applying the UPC to this state of facts, since David is survived by his widow and more than one child, the widow receives $50,000 plus

Table 26.1 UPC Order of Inheritance of Intestate Estate

Eligible Person	Entitlement
Surviving spouse	
If no surviving issue or parent of decedent	Entire estate
If also surviving issue of decedent	$50,000 and one-half of balance of estate
If also surviving parent of decedent but no surviving issue	$50,000 and one-half of balance of estate
Surviving children or issue	
If no surviving spouse of decedent	Entire estate in equal shares by representation
If also a surviving spouse of decedent	One-half of estate after spouse's $50,000
Surviving parent or parents of decedent	
If also a surviving spouse	One-half of estate after spouse's $50,000
If no surviving spouse	Entire estate in equal shares
Surviving brothers or sisters or their issue	
If no surviving spouse, issue, or parents	Entire estate in equal shares by representation
Surviving grandparents or their issue	
If no surviving spouse, issue, parents, brothers, or sisters	Entire estate in equal shares by representation
None of the above	Entire estate escheats (becomes the property of) the state

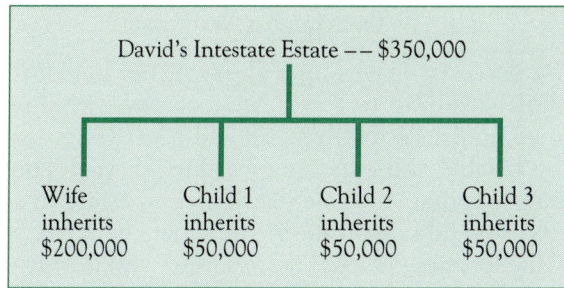

Figure 26.1 Distribution of estate to spouse and children.

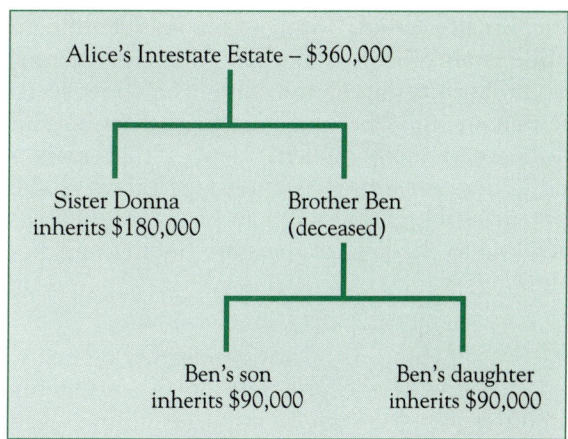

Figure 26.2 Distribution of intestate estate to immediate family.

one-half of the remainder of the estate, totaling $200,000, and the children equally divide the balance of the estate. David's mother, sister, and brother receive nothing because heirs in more preferred positions inherit the entire estate.

As another example, assume that Alice dies intestate, leaving no spouse or children. Alice is survived by her sister, Donna, who is married to Richard. She is also survived by a nephew and a niece, the children of her brother, Ben, who died some years ago. Ben's widow, Betty, is still living. Alice's estate of $360,000 will be distributed as shown in Figure 26.2.

As Alice is survived by no closer kin than her sister and the children of her deceased brother, Alice's estate is divided in half between them. The sister, Donna, inherits $180,000 and the brother's children, by right of representation of their father, Ben, inherit the remaining $180,000, dividing the sum equally between them, regardless of their ages. If Ben had been alive when Alice died, he would have inherited one-half her estate and his children would have inherited nothing. Although the sister's husband, Richard, and the borther's widow, Betty, were both alive when Alice died, they do not inherit from Alice because, not being her blood relatives, they are not in the inheritance chain.

Two of the more important differences between the UPC and the common law schemes for the distribution of intestate estates:

1 Under the common law there is no preference of $50,000 to the surviving spouse. (See Table 26.1.)

2 Under the common law, when no spouse, child, or immediate family survive the decedent, the estate is divided among the closest blood relatives of the decedent even though those relatives may be so far removed that they did not share the same grandparents with the intestate. Such a distant heir has been labeled a "laughing heir." Under the UPC, the property **escheats** (passes) to the state government under such circumstances.

Succession in Special Situations

Certain individuals to whom the regular order of distribution of intestate estates does not apply are (1) an adopted child, (2) an illegitimate child, (3) a child who has received a substantial gift from an intestate parent in the parent's lifetime, and (4) an individual who becomes ineligible to inherit.

Adopted Child. Generally, an adopted child is in effect transplanted into the adopting family and out of the natural family. The adopted child acquires all the rights of a natural child of the adoptive parents and is entirely cut off from any right to inherit from a natural parent who dies intestate.

Illegitimate Child. In all states an illegitimate child is an heir of its mother. Although there is no uniformity among the states as to how an illegitimate child becomes the heir of its natural father, the more modern view is that such a child inherits from its intestate father if the parent-child relationship can be established according to the laws of the state having jurisdiction.

Advancements (Gifts) to Children. Practically all states apply the **principle of advancements** in intestate distribution. In determining each child's share of an intestate's estate, a probate court takes into account any substantial gifts (advancements) previously given by the parent to any of his or her children. In this way the total benefits the children receive are equalized. In some states, and under the UPC, for a gift to be considered an advancement against an inheritance there must be some written evidence that it was so intended.

Ineligible Heir. Under the UPC, an individual who "intentionally and feloniously killed" (the ingredients of murder) the decedent is ineligible to inherit from the victim. Accordingly, if someone normally eligible to inherit has been convicted not of *murder* of the decedent but of some lesser homicide (such as manslaughter), where there is no intent to kill, he or she may still be eligible to inherit.

WILLS

What Is a Will?

A will is a person's instructions for the disposition of his or her property after death. The creator of the will is called the **testator** (a male) or **testatrix** (a female).[1] The will usually names a **personal representative** (sometimes called an **executor** or **executrix**) to administer the estate and may also appoint a guardian for minor children.

---

[1] For simplicity, the chapter will hereafter refer to the creator of a will as the testator.

Why Make a Will?

If a decedent leaves no will, his or her heirs inherit according to state intestacy laws, as outlined above. Why, then, should a person go to the trouble and expense of making a will? The answer is that the state distributes an estate in a cold and uncompromising manner, whereas a will expresses personal desires as to who is to inherit the property and how it is to be divided among the beneficiaries. The state gives no consideration to the needs of those who inherit or to whether the decedent and the heirs were on friendly terms. Moreover, no provision is made by the state for gifts to a church, to charity, or to close friends. A will is the means whereby the owner of property may make the ultimate demonstration of affection, compassion, and gratitude. Through a will a person may direct and *control* how his or her property and business interests will be disposed of. A will also makes possible the settlement of an estate, particularly one of appreciable size, with a minimum of delay and expense to those left behind. Thus, meaning is given to the cryptic sentence that opened this chapter.

The Testator

To be valid, the law requires that the maker of the will meet certain requirements. The testator must have, when executing the will, (1) the requisite mental capacity (called **testamentary capacity**) and (2) the intent to make a will (called **testamentary intent**). If either of these requirements is absent, the purported will is void and the decedent died intestate.

Testamentary Capacity. Testamentary capacity has two elements: (1) the testator must have attained statutory age (usually 18 years) before the will is executed (signed) and (2) at the time of its execution the testator must have had the mental capacity required by law.

Age. Pursuant to the above rule, if you made a will when you were 16 years old it is *not* a valid will. Nor does it become valid when you reach the statutory age. In order to have a valid will you must, after reaching statutory age, execute (sign) a new will (or reexecute your old will) in the manner required by the law of the state in which you live.

Mental capacity. Different courts apply different tests to determine whether or not a testator had the mental capacity to make a will. It can be said generally that you possessed the mental capacity to make a valid will if, at the time it was executed: (1) you knew you were signing a will, (2) you had the *capacity* to know the "natural objects of your bounty" (your spouse, children, and others who would be your natural beneficiaries) and the nature and extent of your property, and (3) you were able to make an orderly disposition of it. A perfect memory is not an element of mental capacity. It is not necessary that you know who all your relatives are, nor must you remember all your property, its location, or its value.

Soundness of mind sufficient to make a will is not the same as soundness of mind and mental capacity required to enter into a contract. Ordinarily, less mental capacity is required to make a valid will than to conduct regular business affairs. A testator need not be of above-average intelligence and, in fact, may have a very low IQ; may be very sick or very old; or may even be under a guardianship and still be legally competent to make a valid will.

Testamentary Intent. Testamentary intent is a necessary element of every will. It is present if the words of a will make clear that the instrument is intended to dispose of the signer's property effective *upon his or her death.* Although a will makes a gratuitous transfer of property, a transfer by will is not the same as an ordinary gift. To illustrate the difference, assume that Alice hands her ring to Marcy saying, "Here is my pearl ring. Take it; I'm giving it to you." Alice has made a gift to Marcy, who now owns the ring. But if Alice includes in her will a provision stating, "I give my pearl ring to Marcy," this is not a gift at the present time but only the expression of an intention of what shall be done with the ring after Alice dies. Until that time (because a will does not become effective until the testator's death), Alice remains owner of the ring. At any time before her death Alice may change her mind and sell the ring, give it to anyone she chooses, or change her will and leave the ring to someone other than Marcy.

Fraud; undue influence. If a bequest in a will is made as a result of fraud, duress, or undue influence on the testator by another, or if the testator is mistaken as to the nature of the instrument he or she is signing, the will does not reflect the true intentions of the testator and testamentary intent is absent. The conditions which establish fraud, duress, and undue influence, discussed in contract formation, are equally applicable in the execution of a will.

Undue influence is the most common circumstance affecting the testamentary intent of the maker of a will. The question of whether undue influence was exercised arises most frequently when the person alleged to have so acted occupied a confidential relationship to the testator. Someone in a confidential relationship to a testator might be, for example, a close family member, friend, housekeeper, guardian, attorney, doctor, nurse, pastor, or financial advisor. If someone in such a close relationship is a beneficiary under a will, the probate court may *presume* that undue influence was exercised. In that event the person in the confidential position has the burden to prove that he or she did not, in fact, exert undue influence if that issue arises during the probate proceedings.

In the following case, an individual who was in a confidential relationship to a testator was presumed to have exerted undue influence.

CASE 26.1 Estate of Baker • 182 Cal. Rptr. 550 (Cal. App. 1982)

FACTS

Dorothy Baker, an elderly woman, was told by her longtime friend Alta Potter that she (Alta) was in contact with the spirits of Dorothy's stepmother, Mary, and with a cousin, both of whom had died. Dorothy believed that Alta, a stockbroker, was a true psychic and medium. Dorothy's subsequent conduct, guided by the messages from her mother and cousin as communicated to her by Alta, was so bizarre (for example, she was prevailed upon to kill her pet cats) that Dorothy was alienated from her relatives and friends. In addition, she terminated her relationship with her own stockbroker and turned over her securities account to Alta.

At Dorothy's request, Alta recommended a lawyer to prepare Dorothy's will. The will was executed in 1977 in the lawyer's office but Alta was not present. In the will, Dorothy made small gifts to members of her immediate family but left the bulk of her estate to Alta, who was also named as executrix, and to Alta's grandson.

Alta told Dorothy that she (Dorothy) had to take a trip to Peru or her mother and cousin would be "earthbound" and Alta might not be able to communicate with them again. Dorothy hesitated about going because she was then 81 years of age, had had several heart attacks, and had been warned by her doctor against going to high altitudes. However, Alta insisted and Dorothy and Alta went to Peru, where Dorothy had another coronary attack. When she returned home she was hospitalized and died the following month.

Alta offered the will for probate. Clarence, Dorothy's brother, opposed probate of the clauses in the will in favor of Alta and Alta's grandson. Clarence alleged that Dorothy executed the will under the undue influence of Alta, who stood in a confidential relationship to her. (Other issues raised by Clarence are not here discussed.) The lower court granted Clarence's petition and Alta appealed.

OPINION

LILLIE, J. . . . Undue influence consists of conduct which subjugates the will of the testator to the will of another and causes the testator to make a disposition of his property contrary to and different from that which he would have done had he been permitted to follow his own inclination or judgment. A presumption of undue influence arises when there is a concurrence of the following elements: (1) the existence of a confidential or fiduciary relationship between the testator and the person alleged to have exerted the undue influence; (2) active participation by such person in the preparation or execution of the will; and (3) undue benefit to such person or another person under the will thus procured.

. . . The evidence establishes the existence of the first element. . . . "Confidential and fiduciary relations are, in law, synonymous, and may be said to exist whenever trust and confidence is reposed by one person in the integrity and fidelity of another." . . . Nor can it be denied that Alta . . . unduly profited under Dorothy's will. . . . Dorothy believed Alta to be a true psychic and medium. . . . Alta thus obtained total control of Dorothy's mind.

Activity on the part of the proponent in procuring execution of the will may be established by inference, that is, by circumstantial evidence. . . . In deter-

> **CASE 26.1 Continued**
>
> mining whether undue influence was exerted by the proponent upon the testator in the execution of his will, the jury is not limited to the actual time the will was executed, but may consider facts bearing upon undue influence both before and after execution so long as they tend to show such influence when the will was executed. . . . Nor need the one using the undue influence be present in person at the time of the execution of the document if the influence is present to constrain the party from exercising his free will.
>
> **JUDGMENT** The judgment is affirmed.

Mistake. If a person signs an instrument not knowing that it is a will, there is no testamentary intent and the purported will is void. A different rule is applied, however, where a testator knowingly makes a will and, on the basis of a mistaken belief, makes or omits to make a bequest. Such a mistake does *not* invalidate a will. For instance, suppose that Cecile heard erroneously that her friend Henry, who lived in a distant city and to whom Cecile intended to make a bequest, had died. As a result, Cecile made no provision in her will for Henry. If after Cecile's death Henry should claim to be entitled to receive the gift Cecile had assured him would be his, the court will *not* change the provisions of the will to *create* a gift for Henry. The reason is obvious: to do so would amount to the court rewriting the testator's will. Such a court action would invite no end of litigation over the validity of bequests, and the distribution of estates would be needlessly delayed. However, if Charlie had falsely told Cecile that Henry died in order that he (Charlie) would replace Henry in Cecile's will, then Charlie obtained his bequest through fraud. Henry, in an equity proceeding against Charlie, can have the court order Charlie to give up the amount of the bequest to Henry because Cecile left it to Charlie through Charlie's fraud.

Formal Requirements of a Will

A will is usually a formal written instrument. The law requires formality in large part because a will becomes operative in the future and upon the death of the testator. Consequently, the maker of the will is not available to testify concerning his or her wishes and the court must be able to rely on a written instrument. A will that meets the formal requirements of the law is called a **formal will.** Formal wills must be in writing, signed, and witnessed. Some states require, in addition, that such wills be dated and published. In the law of wills, "to publish" means to tell the witnesses that the paper being signed before them is a will. Some states and the UPC also recognize **holographic wills,** a will in the handwriting of the testator that is not witnessed. A few states also authorize oral wills, called **nuncupative wills.** Nuncupative wills are effective to transfer personal property only and are usually restricted to soldiers or sailors under combat conditions.

Figure 26.3 is a sample of a very short will. Note that despite its brevity it revokes all prior wills; it disposes of all the testator's property; in paragraph 4c it directs a "pour-over" to a trust (discussed later); and it appoints an executrix. It satisfies the formal requirements of a will that we will now consider.

Writing. While a formal will must be in writing, neither the kind of material upon which the writing appears nor the method of the writing is important. It may be handwritten, typed, printed, engraved, painted, or otherwise recorded on any kind of material.

By a process called "incorporation by reference," the overwhelming majority of states permit a testator to make the contents of another document, even if not actually among the papers constituting his or her will, a part of a valid will.

LAST WILL AND TESTAMENT

I, John Doe, a resident of the City of Miami, State of Florida, do declare this to be my last Will and Testament.

1. I revoke all previous Wills and Codicils heretofore made by me at any time.

2. I am married and the name of my wife is Jane Doe. All references in this Will to my wife are to her. I have never been previously married.

3. I have one child, Grace Doe, the issue of my marriage to my wife Jane. I have never had any other children.

4. I give, devise and bequeath all of my property, real, personal, and mixed, wherever situated as follows:

   a. I give One Thousand Dollars to the American Cancer Society, to be used by it for research purposes.

   b. I give One Thousand Dollars to my alma mater, The University of Florida, Gainesville, Florida, to be added to its general scholarship fund.

   c. I direct my executrix to transfer out of any money or property within my estate, One Hundred Thousand Dollars to the trustee of the Grace Doe Trust, established by me prior to the execution of this Will, for the benefit of my daughter Grace, to be added to and administered as a part of that trust.

   d. I give all the rest and residue of my property to my wife, Jane Doe, in fee simple. However, if she does not survive me then I give all of such property to the said Grace Doe Trust, to be administered as a part of that trust estate. And if my daughter, Grace Doe, does not survive both me and my wife, then I give all of said property to the American Cancer Society.

5. I nominate and appoint my wife, Jane Doe, as the executrix of this Will, to serve without bond. However, if she should predecease me or for any reason fails to qualify or declines to act as executrix, then I nominate and appoint Abner Archer, my attorney, as the executor of this Will, to serve with bond.

I subscribe my name to this Will this the first day of April 1985 in the City of Miami, County of Dade, in the State of Florida, in the presence of Mary Smith, Alfred T. Jones, and John P. Green, attesting witnesses, who subscribe their names hereto at my request and in my presence.

_____ *John Doe* _____

ATTESTATION CLAUSE

On this the 1st day of April, 1985, John Doe, known to us to be the person whose signature appears at the end of this Will, declared to us the undersigned, that the foregoing instrument, consisting of two pages of paper, including the page on which we have signed as witnesses, was his Will. He then signed the Will in our presence and at his request, in his presence and in the presence of each other, we now sign our names as witnesses.

Mary Smith _____ residing at *12 Main Street, Miami, Fla.*

Alfred T. Jones _____ residing at *44 Hope Road, Miami, Florida*

John P. Green _____ residing at *6 Seacoast Rd. Miami Fla.*

Figure 26.3 Form of a short will.

Although state rules for incorporation by reference may vary, it is generally required that the document must be in existence when the will is executed, the testator must intend the incorporation, and there must be appropriate reference within the will for the document to be incorporated. From the following case, however, it should be evident that the provisions of a will cannot be expanded by oral instructions of the testator.

CASE 26.2   **In the Matter of the Estate of Reiman** • 450 N.E.2d 928 (Ill. App. 1983)

FACTS   Paul Reiman executed in proper form a one-page will containing five paragraphs. Paragraph 1 directed the executor to pay all the testator's debts and the expenses of the administration of the estate. Paragraphs 2 and 3 made bequests of $10,000 each to Paul's mother and his sister. Paragraph 4 directed the executor to distribute the testator's remaining property "in accordance with the verbal guidelines given by me." Paragraph 5 nominates the executor. The heirs asked the court to strike out paragraph 4 as an improper testamentary direction. The court granted the heirs' motion and ordered the estate, except for the two $10,000 bequests, to be distributed according to the intestacy laws, as there was no residual clause in the will disposing of any property remaining in the estate after all gifts described in the will were made. The executor appealed.

OPINION   TRAPP, J. . . . No argument has been made by the executor that the direction to him to distribute in accordance with the testator's verbal guidelines as provided in paragraph 4 is a valid testamentary disposition. No such argument could, in fact, be made since it is fundamental that any disposition by way of verbal guidelines is prohibited by [law]. . . .

. . . [A] bequest or devise . . . which is the subject of the testator's future directions, or directions which may be at any time changed after execution of the will, are void unless the directions are in writing and attested in conformity with the statute on wills. . . .

Decedent's attempt to create an oral plan of testamentary devise by requesting the executor to follow "verbal guidelines" must fail. . . .

[T]his court has no choice but to declare [paragraph 4 void]. . . . As unfortunate as that result may be, it only underscores the necessity that a testator employ a knowledgeable scrivener to carry out his wishes.

JUDGMENT   Affirmed.

Signature of Testator. A formal will must be signed by the testator in a manner that complies with state requirements. In most states, the law does not specify the particular place on a will where the testator's signature should be affixed. In some states, however, a will must be signed at the end to assure that no pages purporting to be part of the will are later added.

Under conditions established by state law, a testator may sign with a mark, such as "X," or the testator's name may be written as his or her signature by someone else at the testator's request and in the testator's presence. In this way an illiterate or paralyzed person may execute a valid will.

Generally, there is no requirement that a formal will be dated. However, if a testator executes several wills which contain contradictory provisions and none bears a date, the court would have great difficulty determining which was the most recent and therefore the effective will. To avoid what could be drawn-out and expensive litigation, any will should be dated when it is executed.

Witnesses. A formal will must be witnessed in the manner required by the state where the will is to be effective. If it is not properly witnessed the testator died intestate. A majority of the states (and the UPC) require two witnesses to the execution of a will but a few states require three witnesses. There is no requirement that a formal will be notarized, and if a will is not properly witnessed a notarization does not make it legally effective.[2]

Any person who, at the time of signing as a witness, is competent to be a witness in court may sign as a witness to a will. The witnesses must observe the testator sign the will or, in most states, if the will was signed outside the presence of the witnesses, the testator may show them the document and signature and acknowledge that it is his or her signature.

The UPC does not require the witnesses to sign in the testator's presence or in the presence of each other. Many states, however, do impose these requirements to achieve a legal execution of a will. In some states, and it is the better practice, the witnesses write their addresses as well as their signatures so that they can be located if needed to testify at the probate of the will. The contents of the will are not divulged to the witnesses.

Under the UPC, a witness need not be disinterested—that is, the witness can be one of the beneficiaries under the will. If named as a beneficiary, the witness may inherit according to the will's terms. However, many states take a more restrictive attitude in order to reduce the possibility of fraud, duress, or undue influence in the execution of wills. Following the common law rule, a witness who is a beneficiary under the will can inherit no more than he or she would have received had the testator died intestate.

Holographic Wills. Most states and the UPC recognize the validity of a handwritten, unwitnessed will called a holographic will. In many states, to be legally effective a holographic will must be *entirely* in the testator's own handwriting. However, in some states and under the UPC, only the *material parts* of such a will need be in the testator's handwriting. In either event, it must be signed by the testator and, in some states, also dated. A holographic will need not be witnessed, but if it is witnessed the validity of the will is not thereby effected.

BOX 26.1

Law in Practice

Brenda Reed videotaped her "will" and left the videocassette tape in her safe deposit box. She died without a written will. Does the videocassette recording satisfy the requirements for a valid will?

Limitations on Disposition by Will

It is generally said that a competent testator may make any disposition by will that he or she chooses. However, the law makes exceptions to this rule for the protection of a surviving spouse and children. In some states the law also imposes limitations upon the gifts that interested witnesses may receive under a will.

Protection of Surviving Spouse. All states have laws which are aimed at preserving to a surviving wife or husband some portion of the estate of his or her deceased spouse. Such laws prevent one spouse from totally disinheriting the other spouse. At common law a spouse was protected under the common law rights of **dower** or **curtesy.** Today, a few states still apply the common law right of dower, which entitles a surviving wife to a life interest, free from her husband's debts, in one-third of the *real property* her husband owned at any time during their marriage,

---

[2]Many wills are notarized to satisfy the requirements of a "self-proved" will. See the discussion of "self-proved" wills in the Proving the Will section of this chapter.

and in which she did not, during the marriage, join in a deed conveying it to someone else. In those states, a surviving husband has a similar right called curtesy.

Because estates today frequently consist of both real and personal property, the common law rights of dower and curtesy do not sufficiently protect a surviving spouse. Therefore, most states and the UPC have done away with dower and have substituted the right of a surviving spouse to elect to receive, instead of the inheritance provided by the decedent's will, a statutory **elective** or **forced share** of the deceased spouse's estate. The elective share is computed under rather complex rules established by the UPC. A surviving spouse who elects to take such a share is said to "take against the will."

The nine community property states—Arizona, California, Idaho, Louisiana, Nevada, New Mexico, Texas, Washington, and Wisconsin—protect the interests of a surviving spouse by providing that all property, real and personal, acquired *during* the marriage through the efforts of *either* spouse, and the income from such property, is *community property* owned by *both* the husband and the wife. All other property owned by either spouse is *separate property*. Thus, money and property owned by Margaret before her marriage to Jim is Margaret's separate property; and property Jim inherited from his parents after his marriage to Margaret is Jim's separate property.

A testator in a community property state may by will leave his or her *separate* property to anyone he or she chooses, but there are limitations upon the disposal of *community* property. So if Jim after marrying Margaret starts a business with money he has earned since the date of that marriage, the business is owned by *both* Jim and Margaret. Jim may, by will, dispose of his half of the business to anyone he pleases. However, he cannot dispose of the other half because that half belongs to Margaret. At Jim's death she does not inherit her half from Jim because she already owns it by virtue of community property law. If Jim dies without leaving a valid will, his half of the business and his share of any other community assets also belong to Margaret, his widow, who then owns all their community property.

Protection of Surviving Children. A parent may, if he or she so chooses, completely disinherit a child. Instead of providing for a child by will, the parent may make gifts to more distant relatives, friends, charities, or even strangers. However, for the disinheritance of a child to be legally effective it must be evident *in the will* that the testator *intentionally* gave the child nothing. Such an intention can be expressed by mentioning the child by name anywhere in the will and making no gift or only a nominal gift to that child, or it may be by a statement specifically disinheriting the child.

Generally, if it is *not* evident in the will that the parent intentionally omitted his or her child, regardless of the child's age, the child is said to be **pretermitted.** A pretermitted child inherits as though its parent died intestate. The will otherwise remains effective for all other beneficiaries. Note that in the sample will (Figure 26.3), all the decedent's children are mentioned by name. This eliminates any potential pretermission problem.

REVOCATION AND MODIFICATION OF WILLS

A will is without legal effect until the testator dies. Until then, he or she may at any time revoke (cancel) the will or modify it. A change in a will can be accomplished by the testator executing a **codicil.** A will can be revoked either (1) by the intentional act of the testator or (2) by operation of law.

Codicils to Wills

Assume that Agatha executed a valid will on March 15, 1980. Later, she decides to add to the will a gift to her niece, Cathy, who was born after the will was written. Must Agatha write a new will? She may if she wishes, but it is not necessary. Instead, she may add an amendment, modification, or addition to her will, called a "codicil." The codicil must be in the form required in that state for a valid will. A formal or a holographic will (in a state where holographic wills are recognized) may have one or more formal or holographic codicils. Agatha's codicil might read something like this:

September 24, 1987. This is a codicil to my will executed by me on March 15, 1980. Paragraph 6(h) of that will is amended by adding, "I give $2,500 to my niece, Cathy."   [signed] Agatha B. Doe

[witnessed] Jan Roe
Larry Poe

Revocation by Act of Testator

A will may be revoked by a testator either (1) by a physical act to the document or (2) by executing a later will.

Revocation by Physical Act. To revoke a will by physical act, the testator must, *with the intent to revoke,* do something physical to the will which the state says constitutes a revocation, such as burning, tearing, or obliterating it (making it unreadable), or drawing lines through the signature. Most states permit the *partial revocation* of a will by a physical act directed to the part the testator wants to revoke. No witnesses are required for the physical revocation (or partial revocation) of either a formal or a holographic will. State statutes establish conditions under which a physical act of revocation may be accomplished by another person under the testator's direction.

Revocation by Later Instrument. A testator may also revoke a will be executing a later will which either expressly or by implication revokes the earlier one.

Revocation by express words. To remove any doubt as to the testator's intentions, a will usually contains a statement such as this: "This will revokes all wills and codicils heretofore made by me at any time." A subsequent formal will may revoke a holograph and a subsequent holograph may revoke a formal will.

As is shown by the next case, the revoking words must be a part of a later will or codicil.

CASE 26.3   **In re Estate of Harry Feir** • 701 P.2d 3 (Ariz. App. 1985)

FACTS   In 1979 the decedent, Harry Feir, then a resident of New Jersey, executed a will prepared for him at his request by attorney Kantor. On December 8, 1980, Feir sent a typewritten letter to the attorney in these words: "Please be advised that I am VOIDING my will which you prepared for me on November 10, 1979. Thank you. Cordially yours, Harry Feir." The letter was signed before a notary public. In 1981 Feir moved to Arizona, where he died in 1983. The original will and a copy of the typewritten letter of December 8, 1980, were found in the decedent's safe deposit box.

Feir's sister, the appellee, made application for intestacy proceedings of the decedent's estate. Kantor, as executor, the appellant, opposed that application and filed petition for the probate of Feir's will. A judgment was entered in favor of Feir's sister and Kantor appealed.

OPINION   HATHAWAY, J. . . . Appellant contends that the letter did not revoke the will. He argues that the court's ruling overlooks the similar statutory provisions of both New Jersey and Arizona [that read as follows]:

> Revocation by writing or by act. A will or any part thereof is revoked by either: (1) A subsequent will which revokes the prior will or part expressly or by inconsistency. (2) Being burned, torn, canceled, obliterated or destroyed, with the intent and for the

> **CASE 26.3**
> **Continued**
>
> purpose of revoking it. . . . This section is similar to § 2-507 of the Uniform Probate Code. . . . The official comment to [that] section explains that "revocation of a will may be by either a subsequent will or *an act done to the document.*" It is uncontested that the letter was not a subsequent will. It obviously does not comply with the statutory requirements for a will.
>
> . . . The letter did not call for nor accomplish any act performed to the document. Although that letter may have expressed the testator's intent to revoke the will, the omission of effecting a cancellation of the document is crucial and will not be overlooked. . . . A will must be revoked in the manner prescribed by statute. . . . The intent to revoke must be accompanied by an act which appears on the purported will. . . .
>
> **JUDGMENT**   The judgment of the trial court is reversed. . . .

Revocation by Implication. A later will which is *entirely inconsistent* with an earlier one revokes the earlier instrument by implication even though no specific words of revocation appear in the later will. An example of two entirely inconsistent wills might be this: Peter's will names Arlene, Bess, and Carl as the sole beneficiaries; Peter's later will names three entirely different people as the sole beneficiaries. The earlier will is revoked by implication. If the second will had made Arlene, Eve, and Fred the sole beneficiaries (i.e., one of the original beneficiaries plus two other new ones), the two wills would not have been *entirely* inconsistent. Both wills would be read together, possibly resulting in Arlene receiving two gifts—one under each will—a result which the testator really did not intend. The use of appropriate language could so easily have obviated the problem.

Revocation by Operation of Law

Under the UPC that part of a will which benefits a spouse is automatically, by operation of law, revoked when the parties are divorced or when their marriage is annulled. Unless the testator made a new will in favor of the divorced spouse, his or her property is disposed of as though the divorced spouse had predeceased the testator. As a mere separation of the parties is not a divorce, a separation does not revoke a will by operation of law. However, if the separation is accompanied by a complete property settlement, this constitutes a renunciation by the affected spouse of all benefits under a prior will. In some states which have not adopted the UPC, even a divorce with a property settlement does not cause a revocation of a will unless, in the settlement, the spouse expressly gives up the right to inherit by will.

PROBATE

Probate is the legal procedure for the administration and disposition of a decedent's estate. During probate, a personal representative is appointed; will contests are tried in court; the decedent's assets are marshaled (gathered); the decedent's estate is inventoried; his or her taxes, other debts, and the costs of administration are discharged; and the remainder of the estate is distributed to the intestate heirs or to the beneficiaries under the will if the decedent died with a will.

Proving the Will

The first step in a formal probate proceeding is the admission of the will to probate. Persons offering the will must establish that the will was properly executed by the testator. If, however, the will is **self-proved,** there is no need to prove its execution under the UPC. In a self-proved will, the testator must attest to it before a notary public or officer authorized to administer oaths, and there must be attached to the will an affidavit signed by the testator and two witnesses stating, in substance, that the testator was 18 or more years of age; that he or she voluntarily signed the will in the presence of the witnesses; and that the testator appeared to be of sound mind and was not acting under any undue influence.

Any person who has a direct interest in the estate and who would be economically benefited if the will were set aside may contest its admission to probate. Contest may be based on any claim against the will's validity, such as that it was not properly executed or that the decedent was subject to undue influence. The issues raised are usually tried before a jury and the ordinary rules of evidence are applied.

The Personal Representative

The probate court appoints a **personal representative** to handle the administration of the decedent's estate. In some states, the personal representative is called an **administrator** or **administratrix** (if the decedent died without a will) or an **executor** or **executrix** (if the decedent died with a will). The court generally appoints the person named in the will to be the personal representative unless that person is deceased, disqualified, or incompetent. A personal representative can be (and frequently is) a family member or friend who is a beneficiary under the will.

The personal representative has responsibility for the liquidation and distribution of the estate. He or she is responsible for the following: (1) publishing notice to estate creditors of the need to file their claims within the time allowed by law; (2) giving required notices to heirs or beneficiaries; (3) taking possession of, inventorying, and preserving the decedent's property; (4) paying taxes and allowable claims of creditors against the estate; and (5) distributing the remainder, if any, to the heirs or beneficiaries. In the performance of these functions, the personal representative has significant freedom under the UPC to perform or refuse performance of decedent's contracts, manage and dispose of assets, make repairs, insure property, compromise claims, and employ necessary assistants.

Rights and Duties of the Personal Representative. A personal representative is entitled to a reasonable compensation for the services rendered for the estate. In some states compensation is upon a scale fixed by statute according to the size of the estate; in other states compensation is fixed by the court; and in still others, following the UPC, it may be determined by the personal representative himself or herself.

Because the personal representative is holding and administering the estate property for the benefit of others, he or she is a fiduciary and owes a strict duty of loyalty to the estate. The personal representative is expected to show more than ordinary candor, consideration, and honesty in dealings on behalf of the decedent's estate. The representative is required to act in the best interests of the estate and exercise the same care in managing the estate's affairs as a prudent person would employ in managing his or her own affairs. Taking personal advantage of the business he or she conducts or profiting from the management of the estate is a breach of the personal representative's fiduciary duty. For example, a personal representative cannot purchase property from the estate because of the inherent conflict of interest in such a transaction.

The personal representative is liable to the estate for any improper gains or profits derived from the property of the estate. The personal representative may also be liable to the heirs or beneficiaries of the estate for any losses they suffer because of his or her mismanagement, breach of duty, or bad faith actions. To protect the estate from improper actions of the personal representative, the law requires the personal representative to file a bond with the court. In most jurisdictions, however, this requirement is waived where a will contains a provision stating that the personal representative need not file a bond.

Claims against Estates

A major purpose of probate administration is to protect the decedent's creditors and to settle all valid claims against the estate. **Nonclaim statutes** prescribe the time (usually 4 months from the publication of notice to creditors) and manner in which claims against an estate must be filed. If a claim is not filed within the prescribed time, then payment is forever barred. The personal representative receives and considers the claims that are filed and pays those determined to be valid. State statutes establish the order in which claims against an estate are paid. Costs of administration, funeral expenses, taxes, and reasonable and necessary costs of the decedent's last illness generally take priority over other claims.

Distribution of Assets

After the costs of administration and all valid claims have been settled, the personal representative distributes the remaining money and property to the heirs or beneficiaries, either under the will or according to the law of intestate succession. There are several possible problem areas which can arise in the distribution of the estate: (1) ambiguity or mistake in the words of a will, (2) insufficient assets in the estate to satisfy all the specified gifts, (3) a predeceased beneficiary, and (4) specific property not available for distribution.

Ambiguity or Mistake in Will. If more than one meaning can be given to a provision of a will, that provision is *ambiguous*. An example of ambiguity is a will which states, "I give my niece Sarah $100" and the testator has two nieces named Sarah—one Sarah Smith and the other Sarah Jones. Which Sarah inherits the $100? The court, after taking evidence to ascertain the testator's true intent, decides which of the nieces inherits the $100.

In another will there may be a *mistake* in the description of the beneficiary or of the property covered by a devise (gift of real property). For example, Leo's will makes a gift of "my house at 684 Oxford Lane" but, in fact, the address of the house is 184 Oxford Avenue. Again, the court takes evidence to determine which house Leo owned and thereby meant in his will.

Insufficient Assets in Estate. It sometimes happens that the assets in an estate are insufficient, after all the estate taxes and debts are paid, to complete all the gifts described in the will. The question then arises: Which gifts must be reduced or go unsatisfied? Courts settle the question by ordering the executor to **abate** (reduce or not pay) bequests in the following order: residual bequests abate first; general bequests abate next; and specific bequests abate last. Demonstrative bequests have characteristics of both general and specific bequests and, as such, abate with them. The following illustrations should make clear the characteristics of each of these classes of gifts and abatement. A provision of a will states:

1 "I give my gold watch to Alfred P. Jones." This is a **specific bequest** (gift of personal property) because it refers to a certain specified object. A **specific devise** is a gift of real property.
2 "I give $500 to my sister Dorothy." This is a **general bequest** of any $500 that can be found in the estate either in cash or through the sale of real or personal property not otherwise the subject of a gift.
3 "I give my sister Beatrice $500 payable from the money Tom Brown owes me, but if he does not pay his debt, then the $500 is payable from my general estate." A gift worded in this manner is called a **demonstrative bequest.** If it cannot be satisfied out of the particular source designated, it is treated as a general bequest.
4 "I give my good friend Joe Green all the rest and residue of my estate." This is called a **residual** devise or bequest. Joe is entitled to whatever remains in the estate after all specific, demonstrative, and general gifts have been paid.

As a general rule, all gifts within a class abate proportionately and the entire class abates before abatement applies to the next succeeding class.

Predeceased Beneficiary. If a beneficiary predeceases the testator or renounces a gift, the gift *lapses*—that is, it is of no effect—and the designated property or money may be applied to satisfy other gifts. If there are no unsatisfied gifts, it becomes part of the residual estate. Under two circumstances, however, there is no lapse: (1) where the will makes an alternative disposition of the property, such as a gift "to my cousin Arthur, if he is living and, if not, then to my cousin Joe," and (2) where an **antilapse statute** applies. The UPC antilapse clause provides, in effect, that when a gift is made to a blood relative who had the same grandparent as the testator and that relative predeceased the testator, survived by issue, the gift does not lapse but the issue of the deceased relative inherit it by right of representation. The antilapse statutes of many states are broader than the UPC version and apply to the issue of the nearest blood relatives of the testator even though they may not have had common grandparents.

Property Not Available for Distribution. If property called for in a *specific* gift is not in the estate, the gift is of no effect. This is called an **ademption by extinction.** Thus, if a will makes a gift to Louis of "my Chrysler car," and the car was destroyed in an accident that caused the testator's death, in most states Louis will not inherit the car because it doesn't exist. Although the majority of courts mechanically apply ademption by extinction, a growing number apply the testator's intentions to the facts and do not impose ademption by extinction if the property described in the will can be followed into some other form of property. For example, in some states, Louis would be entitled to any insurance settlement on the car.

TRUSTS

A trust is a flexible legal device that is instrumental in estate planning. A trust comes into being when a **maker** (also called **settlor** or **trustor**) conveys property to another person or entity, called a **trustee,** who holds legal title for the benefit of a third party, the **beneficiary.**

A trust makes it possible for someone to convey property to a trustee who will manage the property. The income earned by investing the trust funds as well as the trust principal itself can be devoted to specific purposes or objectives of the maker. For example, parents of minor children often establish a trust in their wills for the care and education of their children in the event of their death. In this way, a trust, like the will in which it is incorporated, serves as an important tool in the overall plan for the future disposition of the parents' estate. Figure 26.5 is an example of a simple trust.

BOX 26.2

Developments in the Law: The Living Will

The **living will** is a legal response to the medical and ethical dilemma caused by advances in medical technology that allow physicians to artificially maintain a patient's life. Recognizing that patients have a fundamental right to make medical decisions, particularly those that entail the prolonging of life, and that a patient's ability to make such decisions can be frustrated by the patient's incapacity to express his or her wishes at the time of treatment, most states have passed living will statutes. The living will is a declaration of the person's wishes concerning life-prolonging treatment, and whether those medical procedures should be withheld or withdrawn in the event of a terminal condition. Figure 26.4 is a sample of a living will. Many states also allow a person to create a **durable power of attorney for health care** under which a person appoints an "agent" (e.g., a family member) to make medical treatment and services decisions for him or her if the person becomes incapacitated.

Types of Trusts

Trusts can be classified as inter vivos or testamentary, private or charitable, and express or implied.

Inter Vivos and Testamentary Trusts. A trust that comes into being during the trustor's lifetime is called a **living,** or **inter vivos,** trust. The National Bank trust illustrated in Figure 26.5 is a simplified example of a living trust. A **testamentary** trust is a part of a will and, like the will of which it is a part, does not become effective

> ### DECLARATION
>
> This declaration is made this _____ day of _____ (month, year). I, _____, being of sound mind, willfully and voluntarily make known my desires that my moment of death shall not be artificially postponed.
>
> If at any time I should have an incurable and irreversible injury, disease, or illness judged to be a terminal condition by my attending physician who has personally examined me and has determined that my death is imminent except for death-delaying procedures, I direct that such procedures which would only prolong the dying process be withheld or withdrawn, and that I be permitted to die naturally with only the administration of medication or sustenance, or the performance of any medical procedure deemed necessary by my attending physician to provide me with comfort and care.
>
> In the absence of my ability to give directions regarding the use of such death-delaying procedures, it is my intention that this declaration shall be honored by my family and physician as the final expression of my legal right to refuse medical or surgical treatment and accept the consequences from such refusal.
>
> Signed _____
>
> City, County, and State of Residence _____
> (attestation of witnesses omitted)

Figure 26.4 Form of living will.

until the death of the testator; until that time it may be revoked or modified by the testator-trustor. When the testator-trustor dies, the assets he or she has designated in the will are transferred by the personal representative of the testator to the trustee and the testamentary trust comes into being.

Rather than establish a testamentary trust, a will can direct the personal representative to transfer assets from the estate into an existing inter vivos trust. Such a direction in a will is called a **pour-over provision,** meaning that assets are poured over from the estate into the trust. The sample will in Figure 26.3 contains a pour-over provision.

Private and Charitable Trusts. A **private** trust is normally established for the care, health, maintenance, support, and education of some particular person or group of people, including the trustor. It need not be so limited, however, and may be for any purpose not contrary to public policy. A **charitable** trust is solely devoted to a purpose which serves or benefits the general public—such as a trust to promote religion,

Figure 26.5 Form of a simple trust.

> I, (the maker) by these presents convey to NATIONAL BANK (the trustee) $300,000 (the trust fund) to invest such funds and to pay annually the income earned thereon to my husband, William, during his lifetime. Upon the death of my husband, the trust principal and any undistributed income shall be paid to my daughter, Anna.
>
> [The trustee's powers and obligations are set out.]
>
> Signed this the 4th day of March, 1988, at Boise, Idaho.
>
> June Alexander _____

education, health, or the arts, or to help the poor. The rules for the establishment and administration of charitable trusts are more liberal than those pertaining to private trusts. For example, a charitable trust can continue to exist indefinitely; the duration of a private trust is limited by law. In addition, a court of equity, applying what is called the **cy pres doctrine,** may devote the charitable trust to another, generally similar charitable purpose when it is impossible or impracticable to carry out the original purpose for which the trust was established. No like rule is applicable to a private trust, which ends when the purposes for which it was established have been accomplished or can no longer be attained.

Express and Implied Trusts. An **express** trust is one created expressly by the words or conduct of the maker. An **implied** trust is one imposed by law even though no express trust has been created by the maker. The law implies a trust to avoid some injustice or fraud or to carry out the true intent of the owner of the property. A **resulting** trust, one imposed to conform to the true intent of the maker, frequently exists when the requirements for a valid trust are not met. For example, if Alice, who is incompetent, transfers property to Ben, as trustee, no valid inter vivos trust is created. Ben holds the property in a resulting trust and is under an obligation to reconvey the property to Alice or her guardian. A **constructive** trust is imposed to remedy some wrongdoing or fraud. Suppose a corporate officer steals a business opportunity of the corporation for personal gain. When an officer commits such a wrong, the law will impose a constructive trust under which the officer will hold any property he or she improperly acquired as a trustee for the benefit of the corporation.

Spendthrift Trusts. Most states allow the establishment of **spendthrift** trusts, which are set up primarily to protect individuals who are unable to manage their own finances. In such a trust, the trustor directs that the beneficiary has no rights whatever in the trust property or to its income until the beneficiary actually receives it.

Therefore, if a creditor secures a judgment against the beneficiary, the creditor is unable to levy execution against the debtor-beneficiary's interest *in the trust fund,* since the beneficiary has not yet received it. Moreover, the beneficiary is unable to squander the trust assets by selling his or her future rights to trust property or income. Prior to a disbursement from the trust, any assignment of the beneficiary's interest is legally ineffective.

Creation and Requirements of Trusts

No particular formalities are necessary to establish an express trust. A trust involving personal property may be created orally or by the conduct of the maker. However, a trust involving real property must be in writing to satisfy the statute of frauds. A testamentary trust must also be in writing and satisfy the other requirements of the law relating to wills.

The requirements of a valid trust are as follows:

- The maker must have legal capacity.
- The trust property (called the res or corpus) must consist of presently existing real or personal property (not a mere future expectancy).
- The maker must make a present transfer of the property to the trust.
- A beneficiary or beneficiaries must be designated.

As a conveyance of property, a trust does not require consideration. It can be established for any lawful purpose, and therefore the beneficiary can be a person or a charity. The failure to name a trustee, or the trustee's refusal to serve, is not fatal to the trust. But the trustee and the beneficiary cannot be one and the same person or entity. No trust is created if Agnes transfers property to Sam, as trustee, and names Sam as the sole beneficiary. The trust fails because there is said to be a **merger** of legal and equitable title (Sam owns both). If on the other hand, Sam and Patrick are named cobeneficiaries, there is no merger and the trust is valid.

> **BOX 26.3**
>
> ## Trusts and Financial Planning
>
> Trusts are an essential tool for estate planning. For example, testamentary trusts can be used to minimize federal estate and gift tax liability. The estate tax law provides an unlimited marital deduction, which allows a person to give his or her spouse an unlimited dollar amount of property without tax liability, and a unified credit, the effect of which is to allow individuals to pass $600,000 free of estate tax. A trust may be used to take advantage of both tax deductions. A person with a large estate could transfer $600,000 to a "family trust," with income to the surviving spouse and the remainder to his or her children. As a transfer to a trust, this would not become part of the surviving spouse's estate (nor qualify for the unlimited marital deduction), but it would qualify for the unified credit. The remainder of the estate could go to the spouse, thereby taking advantage of the marital deduction. This has the effect of eliminating any estate tax on the deceased spouse's estate and reducing the estate of the surviving spouse (and the estate tax) while at the same time preserving the estate income for the survivor's benefit. When the surviving spouse dies, his or her estate can take advantage of the unified credit to preserve as much of the estate as possible for the benefit of the children or other heirs.
>
> An inter vivos trust is often used to avoid costs of probate. A living trust whose provisions continue to be effective after the death of its maker drastically lessens both the time and the cost of probate. There is normally a reduction in probate costs because the estate of the maker of the trust was reduced by the value of the property transferred to the trust during the testator's lifetime. Therefore, there is less property in the maker's estate subject to probate administration and costs.
>
> A recent development is the use of trusts by elderly persons who want to take advantage of government entitlement programs without dissipating their estate. Some government programs, such as Medicaid, deny benefits to persons who have sufficient property to pay for the benefits. To avoid having to dispose of personal wealth to secure the benefits, some elderly persons have transferred their property to irrevocable trusts (naming themselves as beneficiaries for life) and then sought benefits under government programs. Whether this transfer is effective will depend upon the government program and the terms of the trust. ■

Duties of the Trustee

A trustee, whether serving with or without compensation, is a fiduciary and owes extensive obligations to the beneficiaries of the trust. Among the most important of those obligations is the duty of absolute loyalty. The trustee must administer the trust in accordance with its terms, and must avoid any conflict of interest. For example, it is improper for the trustee to purchase trust property unless the trust instrument authorizes it or the trustee obtains court approval. If a trustee makes a private gain through breach of trust, he or she must turn over those profits to the estate.

The trustee must manage the trust property in a careful and prudent manner. A trustee is required to use reasonable care and skill to keep the trust estate productive and may make only such investments with trust funds as a prudent person would make in the disposition of his or her own funds, taking into consideration the probable income and the probable safety of the principal. This is known as the **prudent investor rule.** Under this standard, highly speculative investments are generally prohibited, and the trustee generally must diversify the trust assets to minimize financial risk to the trust. The next case discusses the prudent investor standard in connection with the trustee's obligation to diversify the trust's investments.

CASE 26.4	**Malachowski v. Bank One, Indianapolis** • 590 N.E.2d 559 (Ind. 1992)
FACTS	Bank One is the trustee of an irrevocable inter vivos trust created by Harry S. Noel in 1935. Income from the trust was to be paid to Noel's wife during her lifetime. Upon her death, income was to be paid in equal shares to the settlor's three children—Harry J. Noel, Barbara L. (Noel) Seawell, and Carol A. (Noel) Failey—or to their surviving issue.

When the Trust was created, its only asset was life insurance policies payable on the death of the settlor. The settlor died in 1943, and proceeds from the life insurance policies held by the Trust were lent to the estate. That loan was repaid in 1947 with 1,564 shares of Eli Lilly stock valued at $35,000. From that time until 1972, the corpus of the Trust consisted entirely of Lilly stock. In 1972, Bank One began selling Lilly stock to diversify the trust holdings over the objections of some of the settlor's children. At the time diversification began, the value of the Lilly stock and trust corpus held by the Trust was $2,400,000. Sales of the stock continued intermittently for 8 years until December 1985. The beneficiaries assert that the value of the corpus in 1985, if no Lilly stock had been sold, would have been approximately $360,000 greater than it was under Bank One's management.

In February 1988, the beneficiaries filed an action against Bank One seeking various forms of relief, including the restoration of Lilly stock sold by Bank One to the Trust. Bank One moved for summary judgment, and the trial court found that the sale of Lilly stock did not violate the terms of the Trust or constitute any breach of trust. The beneficiaries appealed. |
| **OPINION** | KRAHALIK, J. . . . The Beneficiaries' claim for breach of trust is premised on the argument that Bank One wrongfully sold the Lilly stock. Bank One responds that it sold the Lilly stock to comply with the "prudent investor" rule and, having complied with the rule, it cannot be subject to liability for breach of trust.

The "prudent investor" rule has been made applicable by statute in Indiana and provides in part:

> In acquiring, investing, reinvesting, exchanging, retaining, selling and managing property for any trust heretofore or hereafter created, the trustee thereof shall exercise the judgment and care under the circumstances then prevailing which men of prudence, discretion, and intelligence exercise in the management of their own affairs, not in regard to speculation, but in regard to the permanent disposition of their funds, considering the probable income as well as the probable safety of their capital. Ind. Code § 30-4-3-3(c)

Bank One asserts that absent an explicit direction in the trust instrument, a trustee is not required to maintain all of the assets of the trust in a single equity security. Bank One also suggests that absent such explicit direction, the prudent investor rule mandates diversification under the circumstances here.

Applying the prudent investor rule requires consideration of the particular factual circumstances in an individual case. As the *Restatement, Second, of Trusts* § 228, page 541 states: "Except as otherwise provided by the terms of the trust, the trustee is under a duty to the beneficiary to distribute the risk of loss by a rea- |

**CASE 26.4
Continued**

sonable diversification of investments unless under the circumstances it is prudent not to do so." . . . We do not agree with Bank One that as a matter of law diversification is positively required under the prudent investor rule.

The Beneficiaries present several circumstances that raise questions concerning the propriety of diversification. First, they claim that Bank One's motive for selling the Lilly stock was a self-serving attempt to increase the fees chargeable to the Trust and to use cash from the sale of the Lilly stock for investment in Bank One's common trust funds. . . .

In addition, the Beneficiaries point to Bank One's insistence that all beneficiaries sign an indemnity agreement before Bank One would consider not undertaking the diversification program. The effect of the indemnity agreement was to hold Bank One harmless for not diversifying the stock. . . .

The Beneficiaries also claim that by diversifying the Trust, Bank One failed to preserve Trust assets . . . because the sales of stock resulted in sizeable capital gains tax levied on the Trust corpus. Evidence showed that Bank One was aware of the significant reduction in the Trust corpus that would occur because of the 30% federal income tax imposed as a result of the sale of the stock. . . .

We conclude that the foregoing points raised by the Beneficiaries are sufficient to establish genuine issues of material fact precluding summary judgment for Bank One. Of course, we are unable to predict whether the Beneficiaries ultimately will be successful in establishing their claim against Bank One, but we conclude that our rules of procedure require that they have an opportunity to attempt to do so.

JUDGMENT Reversed and remanded.

Allocation of Principal and Income

The trustee is under a duty to properly allocate receipts and expenses between income and principal. For example, the simple trust (Figure 26.5) provides for the payment of trust income to the maker's husband (income beneficiary) for life and the distribution of the principal to the daughter (remainder beneficiary) when the husband dies. The trustee will have to credit receipts and charge expenditures to either income or principal to determine the income payable to the husband on a yearly basis. In the absence of directions in the trust instrument, the allocation is determined by the Uniform Principal and Income Act, which has been adopted in most states. Generally, ordinary receipts, such as rent, interest income, and cash dividends, will be allocated to income while extraordinary receipts, such as gains on the sale of principal and stock dividends, will be credited to principal. Similarly, ordinary expenses, such as repairs and regular taxes, will be charged to income while extraordinary expenses, such as capital improvements and taxes on the sale of principal, will be allocated to principal.

Termination of Trusts

An inter vivos trust can be terminated by the maker only if he or she retains a power of revocation in the trust instrument. One type of revocable trust is a *Totten* trust, which is a deposit of money in a bank account that is payable to a beneficiary upon the death of the depositor. The trust instrument may also specify the time when the trust terminates. Before that time, a trust for a specific purpose terminates when that purpose is accomplished or when that purpose is frustrated. For example, a trust for the college education of a child would be accomplished when the child graduates or frustrated if the child dies. Finally, a trust can be terminated by the voluntary agreement of the beneficiaries if the objectives of the trust are not thereby thwarted. A spendthrift trust, for example, cannot be terminated by the beneficiaries, because such a termination would defeat the purpose of the trust.

SUMMARY

A decedent's property may pass under the law of intestate succession or under the provisions of a properly executed will. To make a valid will, a testator must have both testamentary capacity and testamentary intent. If a person, in making a will, is subject to the fraud, duress, or undue influence of another, the maker is not expressing his or her testamentary intent and the will (or the portion thereof affected) is void.

A formal will must be in writing, signed, and witnessed by the number of witnesses (usually two) required by that state. A holographic will (not authorized in all states) must be entirely or in its material parts in the testator's own handwriting, signed and, in most states, dated. A holographic will need not be witnessed. A testator may amend a will by a codicil and may revoke it by physical destruction or by a later will which specifically revokes the earlier one or is entirely inconsistent with it.

Both testate and intestate estates are administered by a personal representative in a proceeding called probate. The personal representative takes charge of and inventories the assets of the estate, gives notice to creditors to file claims, pays valid claims filed within the period established by law, and then distributes the remaining assets among the beneficiaries.

A trust is a fiduciary relationship wherein the maker of the trust conveys property to a trustee who holds legal title of the property for the benefit of another (the beneficiary). The trustee may make only such investments with trust funds as a prudent person would make in the disposition of his or her own funds. A trust can add great flexibility to a will and is a major tool in estate planning.

REVIEW QUESTIONS

1. In a state that has adopted the UPC, if one spouse dies without having made a will, leaving a mother, a surviving spouse, and two children, who inherits the decedent's estate and in what shares?

2. What are the formal requirements of a will? What purpose do those requirements serve?

3. Explain the difference between testamentary capacity and testamentary intent.

4. Comment upon this statement: "If a person has the capacity to enter into a contract, he or she has the capacity to make a will."

5. Is it correct to say that in most states a person who has a large estate, consisting of both real and personal property, must make a formal will rather than a holographic will? Explain.

6. How can a person revoke a prior will? Amend it?

7. Distinguish among and give examples of residual, general, and specific gifts.

8. Explain the duties and liabilities of the personal representative.

9. Explain how trusts and wills are used for estate planning.

10. Why is an executor, an administrator, or a trustee subject to fiduciary duties in the performance of his or her obligations?

CASE PROBLEMS

1. Charles suspected that his wife, Nora, was having an affair with Fred. Charles warned Fred to stay away from his house. One evening, Charles saw his wife come into the house with Fred. Charles pointed a loaded shotgun at Fred. In the struggle that followed, the gun was discharged and Nora was killed. Charles was found guilty of manslaughter. Nora left no will. The probate court held that because he had intentionally brought about the armed confrontation resulting in Nora's death, Charles could not inherit from her. Do you think an appellate court would reverse the probate court's decision? Why or why not?

2. In 1975 a conservator was appointed over Hazel's person and estate. It had been alleged that, because of senile dementia, Hazel was unable to care for herself both financially and personally. She was not eating properly and was unclean and incontinent; her home was unkempt and filthy; she seemed "kind of dreamy"; she had lent large sums of money to friends without taking any notes or promises to repay; and she was easily confused and occasionally forgot dates, the time of the year, and what she was eating. Sometimes Hazel appeared extremely senile and at other times she seemed more normal and better oriented. In 1976 Hazel, then 89 years old, executed her formal will. The two witnesses to it testified she was mentally competent and knew that she was signing her will. Others testified that in the 1975–1977 period she was alert and able to carry on a coherent conversation. Hazel died in 1981. When her will was offered in probate, her competence to execute the will was questioned. How should the question be answered? Give the reasons for your response.

3. At age 17 Susan made a holographic will dividing the estate she inherited from her grandmother in equal shares among the charity Recording for the Blind, her parents, and her sister. Susan became a well-known novelist. She died at 35 years of age, having never married or changed her will. Susan's parents, her sister, and the charity all survived her. How will Susan's estate be distributed?

4. Elizabeth Hall was terminally ill in the hospital. A will was written according to her directions and brought to her to be signed. She executed the will before the proper number of witnesses. Two days after she died, it was discovered that the papers she signed were only pages 1, 2, 3, and 5 of a purported 5-page will. The lawyer who prepared the will produced the missing page 4. That page set out the duties of the executor. All the provisions disposing of her estate happened to be contained in the four pages that were before Mrs. Hall when she signed the will. What pages should be admitted to probate as Mrs. Hall's will? Why?

5. Jerry and Lela were married in North Dakota in 1970. Later that year Jerry executed a will, one article of which provided, "I give, devise, and bequeath to my wife, Lela Margaret Knudsen, all my estate both real and personal." In 1982 Jerry and Lela were divorced. In 1983 Jerry married Susan. He neglected to revoke or modify his 1970 will. Susan now asks your advice: Would she be entitled to any of Jerry's estate in the event of his death, or would it all go to Lela? North Dakota has adopted the Uniform Probate Code. What would your answer be? Explain.

6. Kirk was the owner of a motorcycle shop. He died intestate, survived by his wife, Emma, and by his two children from a former marriage. Emma was appointed administrator of Kirk's estate, which was then worth about $50,000. As required by law, she furnished a bond guaranteeing proper performance as administrator. Believing that she had inherited the business, Emma took over and ran it. She had no business experience, and by the end of a year it was practically worthless. Emma ceased to pay rent on the business premises, locked the door, and left a few motorcycles in the building. In all that time Emma did nothing to administer her deceased husband's estate. A year later Kirk's children petitioned the court to appoint a new administrator. Should a new administrator be appointed even though there are no apparent assets in the estate? What should be done?

CHAPTER 27

Insurance

We all risk business or personal loss from fire, theft, natural disasters, illness, injury, collision, or other catastrophe. Systematic effort to avoid such loss is called **risk management.** Risk managers limit economic loss in three ways:

1. **Risk control** prevents loss, for example, through installation of smoke alarms.
2. **Risk transfer** distributes risk among members of a group who share the financial burden of the loss. Risk transfer—the most common form of risk management—occurs whenever business transfers a particular risk to an insurance company.
3. **Self-insurance** is a plan to absorb losses, usually adopted by companies large enough to fund such plans by establishing special loss accounts.

THE NATURE OF INSURANCE

Insurance is a two-party contract (an **insurance policy**). In it, an insurance company (the **insurer**) agrees that in exchange for a payment (the **premium**) it will compensate another party (the **insured**) for a future loss from a specified harmful event. The transfer of the risk from the insured to the insurer ordinarily occurs when the insurance contract arises. If there is a loss covered by the policy, the insurer pays the insured in accordance with its terms. The payment to cover such loss is called **indemnity.**

The Principle of Pooling Risk

In all types of insurance, businesspeople transfer risk to professional risk takers—the insurance companies. Insurers are willing to accept risk because they know they can depend upon a principle that underlies all insurance—**pooling of risk.** The concept is simple. The insurer distributes the risk among a large group of persons who are similarly situated (the pool) so that *total* losses of the pool can be accurately estimated. Members of the insured class in the pool pay premiums based upon these estimated total losses. Thus, in pooling of risk, the insured trades off a certain but moderate loss—the premium payment—for an uncertain but possibly devastating loss. For example, suppose you are a good driver and want collision insurance for your car. The insurance company classifies you into a pool of 5,000 good drivers like yourself. By using statistical data, the insurer can estimate accurately the annual total cost of accidents of all the members in your pool, and charges you a premium equal to your pro rata share of that cost. Pooling of risk is simply spreading risk among members of a pool.

Reinsurance

Reinsurance is another important way of spreading risk, but with **reinsurance,** two or more insurance companies are *pooling the risk of having to pay an excessive number of claims*. Suppose Alpha Casualty's entire business consists of policies it has written insuring 10,000 Florida homes against hurricane loss. If all these homes are destroyed by a hurricane, Alpha Casualty will go bankrupt. But if Alpha enters into contracts with nine **reinsurance** firms, with each firm assuming the risk of loss of 1,000 homes, Alpha and the other nine companies are pooling the risk of having to indemnify homeowners whose residences are destroyed by a hurricane. The losses in Florida from hurricane Andrew in 1992 soared into billions, but because of reinsurance, no major casualty insurer became insolvent. **Reinsurance,** then, is *a contractual arrangement in which an insurance company transfers (cedes) a part of the group risk it has assumed to another insurance organization, a reinsurer*. The reinsurer agrees to reimburse the ceding company for part of the liability on its own policies. Just as an insurer is paid a premium by an individual, the reinsurer is paid by the ceding company to assume a risk too great for it to bear alone.

Insurance Terminology

Although insurance law is a branch of contract law, centuries of use have given special meanings to many contract terms found in insurance agreements. The meanings of several key terms are discussed next.

Meaning of the Insured. There are two basic meanings of "the insured"—one in property and liability insurance and the other in life insurance. In *property and liability* insurance, the insured is any person who is protected by a policy from risk of loss. For example, if Abe purchases automobile insurance covering liability for personal injuries resulting from negligent operation of his car, the policy will protect Abe as well as other licensed drivers to whom he might occasionally lend the car. Under the policy, all such persons are "insureds" and have a right to reimbursement from the insurer for amounts they are obliged to pay in settlement of claims from injured third parties.

In *life* insurance, the insured is the person whose life is the subject of the insurance contract. The death benefit specified in the policy will be paid to someone *other than the insured*—directly to a named third person called the **beneficiary.** In life insurance, as in other kinds of insurance, the insured will often not be a party to the insurance contract. For example, if Alice insures the life of her business partner, Brady, and names herself as beneficiary, Alice and the insurance company are the contracting parties; Brady is the "insured" ("the person whose life is the subject of the policy"); Alice is beneficiary and "policyowner."

Although life insurance policies often involve four parties—the insurer, the owner, the insured, and the beneficiary—in most cases the owner and the insured are the same person. For example, if Amy, a widow, wishes to provide funds for the education of her son, Ted, she may take out an "endowment" life insurance policy insuring her life, with premiums sufficiently high to build a cash surrender value of $50,000 over the next 15 years. Amy may name Ted as *beneficiary*, but she is the *insured*, and she is also the *owner*. If Amy dies tomorrow, she has created, overnight, a college fund for Ted. If she lives until Ted is college age, she can, as owner, cash the policy and use the funds for Ted's education.

Meaning of "Indemnity Principle." With the exception of life insurance, most insurance contracts are **indemnity contracts**—that is, the insurer promises to reimburse (indemnify) the insured for some loss. The **principle of indemnity** is based on the idea that insurance is designed to distribute losses, not to generate profits for the insured. Therefore, when there is a casualty, *an insured person should be limited to reimbursement (indemnity) for loss actually suffered*. Suppose that

Pam has identical medical insurance policies with two different insurers, that each policy will reimburse up to $5,000 in hospital expenses in the event that she becomes ill and requires a hospital stay. Assume also that each policy has a **coordination-of-benefits clause** (which permits an insurer to pay only a portion of a loss that is also covered by other insurance). Pam may collect only the amount of her loss ($5,000) and, under the coordination-of-benefits clause, *only a proportion* of her loss from each of the companies with which she has a policy. Because she has policies with two companies, she will collect $2,500 from each one. Since neither is liable for the whole loss, each company will refund to Pam an appropriate proportion of the premiums she paid. Coordination of benefits is consistent with the principle of indemnity: Pam is reimbursed for her loss but she is not permitted to make a profit. Not all insurance policies have coordination-of-benefits clauses, however. Some insurers believe that such clauses impede sales of insurance and create disputes between insurers that delay settlement of claims.

The principle of indemnity, in effect, says: "You shouldn't get something for nothing." It underlies many legal rules governing interpretation and enforcement of insurance contracts, such as the rule prohibiting use of insurance contracts as gambling devices. The application of such rules helps minimize costs of insurance by reducing a person's opportunities to make a net gain from the insurance system. The indemnity principle is applied mostly to property, liability, and health insurance.

Meaning of "Insurable Interest." A person who procures insurance must have an **insurable interest**—that is, a benefit to be realized from the continued existence of the property or person insured. Three reasons underlie this rule:

1. The principle of indemnity requires that an insured be reimbursed for an actual loss only; for example if you insure your neighbor's house and it burns down, you have not suffered an actual loss.
2. If the insured does not have a financial stake in the subject of the insurance, courts treat the contract as an illegal (and therefore unenforceable) wagering agreement. For example, one who insures the life of a total stranger for $1 million is simply gambling that early death will return a big profit from a small investment.
3. The insurable interest requirement minimizes **moral hazard**—the risk that the insured will carelessly or intentionally act to increase the amount or frequency of loss. Such acts include a tendency toward murder, fraud, arson, accidents, exaggeration of claims, or bad health habits.

Often, insurers deny life and property insurance claims because there never was an insurable interest.

Property. You have an insurable interest in personal or real property if you have a financial stake in it—that is, if you would suffer monetary loss should it be destroyed. For example, you have an insurable interest in your car but not in your neighbor's car. The owner who has legal title as well as persons holding title in a representative capacity, such as executors, guardians, and trustees (including a trustee in bankruptcy), all have an insurable interest. However, it is not necessary to hold legal title to property to have an insurable interest: *Any* property interest is insurable to the extent of the value of that interest.

There are many examples: a bank holding a mortgage to secure a home loan, the holder of a mechanic's lien or a judgment lien against land, any creditor such as a car dealer with a security interest in personal property, even an innocent purchaser of stolen property or a bailee of personal property—all have an insurable interest. When does the purchaser of real estate have an insurable interest? To avoid undue hardship on buyers, many states have adopted the Uniform Vendor and Purchaser Risk Act. It provides that risk of loss passes when the buyer acquires either possession or legal title, or both. A few other states have adopted the same rule through court decisions. The safest precaution for buyer and seller is to specify in their contract exactly when risk of loss passes so that the buyer can arrange for insurance to take effect at that moment.

Under UCC rules covering contracts for the sale of goods, a buyer obtains an insurable interest in the goods when they are *identified to the contract* (marked as the subject of a particular contract of sale), even though the buyer does not yet own or have possession of the goods. In property and liability insurance, the insurable interest need exist only *at the time of the loss*—a rule which permits contracting for insurance before acquiring property.

Life. Ordinarily, a person has an insurable interest in his or her own life, but to obtain valid insurance on the life of another, the person procuring the insurance must have an insurable interest—a financial stake—in the other's life. This requirement is met where there is a close family relationship, as where a person seeks insurance on the life of a spouse or minor child to cover the expenses resulting from that person's untimely death. Where an adult seeks insurance on a parent's life, however, or where a person seeks insurance on the life of a sister, uncle, niece, or other such relative, courts tend to require a showing of something more than the family relationship itself before holding that there is an insurable interest. Courts differ, however, as to whether an *existing* financial interest must be shown in such instances. Often much less will do. Thus, an aunt who supported her niece from infancy was held to have an insurable interest in her life, based on the expectation that the aunt might eventually receive a return benefit from the niece. If there is no family relationship, an *actual* financial interest is required. A creditor has an insurable interest in the life of the debtor, and a business entity has an insurable interest in the life of a key employee.

An insurer's denial of liability on a policy because of lack of an insurable interest should not be confused with denial of liability due to the insured's illegal conduct. Life policies excuse the insurer from paying the proceeds to the estate of a beneficiary who commits suicide, or to a husband-beneficiary who kills his wife to get the policy proceeds. Fire policies deny payment to persons who burn down their houses. In all these examples the policy owner has an insurable interest, but because of illegal conduct, policy terms deny payment of the proceeds to the principal beneficiary, and instead award them to alternate beneficiaries.

In life insurance, the insurable interest *must exist only when the policy is taken out*. This rule upholding the validity of a policy, even where the insurable interest ceases, permits a divorced wife-beneficiary to recover life insurance proceeds upon the death of her former husband. At the time of taking out **"keyperson" life insurance** on an executive, a company clearly has an insurable interest—that is, a stake in the continuation of the life of a key person who is valuable to the firm. Courts uniformly hold that even when this insurable interest ceases—for example, when the executive retires—the firm can still collect the policy proceeds upon the death of the executive. Moreover, a surviving spouse is not entitled to question whether the employer has an insurable interest—only the insurer can raise that issue. Table 27.1 defines some key terms related to insurance.

THE INSURANCE CONTRACT

An insurance policy is a contract subject to the general principles of contract law discussed in Chapters 10 to 17. Many policies are standard printed forms developed by the insurance industry or, in some cases, prescribed by state law. In addition, state statutes commonly require an

Table 27.1 Key Insurance Terms

The insured: In life insurance, the person whose life is insured. In property and liability insurance, the persons who are "covered."

Principle of indemnity: A rule that requires reimbursement only for the loss actually suffered.

Coordination-of-benefits clause: A rule permitting an insurer to pay only a portion of a loss also covered by other insurance.

Insurable interest: A rule requiring that persons obtaining insurance must have a stake in the continued existence of the person or property insured.

Moral hazard: The risk that the insured will negligently or intentionally cause a loss.

Casualty insurance: Insurance against loss due to unforeseen accident or event, e.g., fire, flood, or collision.

insurer to include certain provisions in its contract. Courts will read such mandated clauses into the policy, even if they don't appear in it.

Contract of Adhesion

In a contract of adhesion, the purchaser has little or no power to negotiate price or other terms. Most insurance contracts are of this type. Essentially the seller hands the buyer a complex standard-form contract on a "take it or leave it" basis. The buyer seldom reads or understands it, relying instead on statements of the seller.

Contracts of adhesion have legitimate uses, however. With an insurance contract, for example, if all terms of coverage had to be bargained individually, transaction costs would be prohibitive, limits of an insurer's liability would be uncertain, and losses would be impossible to predict. Nevertheless, unscrupulous insurers have often used contracts of adhesion to exploit the unwary customer. To curb abuse of standard-form agreements while preserving their advantages, state laws and agencies control the content of insurance contracts, and courts construe ambiguous policy terms strictly against the insurer which drafted them and in favor of the insured.

When Is the Contract Formed?

The insurer's liability under an insurance policy usually arises when the contract is formed, and it can greatly exceed amounts paid in premiums. Therefore, both the insurer and the insured have a keen interest in how offer-and-acceptance rules are applied to determine the precise moment that the contract becomes effective.[1] Most insurance originates with an **application,** often a part of the contract, that contains factual statements such as the insured's driving record or medical history. Ordinarily, insurance policies are sold by a representative of the insurer, called an **agent.** The agent's authority to contract on behalf of the insurer varies with the kind of insurance involved. For example, a property and liability insurer can always free itself from unacceptable risks by immediately canceling the policy. Therefore, it gives its agents broad authority to enter into binding contracts without consulting the company in advance. The agent often issues a temporary oral or written acceptance termed a **binder.** A property or liability applicant thereby acquires immediate coverage subject to possible cancellation.

In contrast, the right of life insurance companies to cancel life policies is sharply limited by law. Before issuing policies, life insurers thoroughly investigate whether applicants are in good health, have an insurable interest, or present problems of moral hazard. To provide time for investigation and to protect its right to decide whether to grant coverage, the life insurer often restricts its agents' authority to accept offers. However, the rules of offer and acceptance apply to four situations, each of which can result in the formation of a life insurance contract.

1 A person fills out an application for insurance but does not pay the first premium. At this point the applicant has addressed to the insurer an **invitation to make an offer.** The company, as an **offeror,** then makes an offer by presenting a policy for acceptance. The applicant, by paying the first premium, *has accepted the offer.*

2 The person pays the first premium upon completing application. The *applicant is the offeror.* The insurer delivers the policy to the applicant or to the insurer's agent for unconditional delivery to the applicant. The *insurer, by making delivery, has accepted the applicant's offer.* Many state courts follow the "constructive delivery" rule, illustrated in Case 27.1 below. It holds that when the insurer turns the policy over to its agent for unconditional delivery to the applicant, the policy is deemed to have been delivered even though the applicant never received it.

3 A person applies for insurance and pays the first premium. The *applicant is the offeror.* The agent immediately gives the applicant a **condi-**

---

[1] In most health and disability insurance, and in some life insurance sold to older people, even though the contract has been formed, the insurer may not be obligated to pay benefits if a "probationary" period has been specified during which benefits are limited or excluded.

tional receipt which states that the insurance is effective immediately (or on a certain date) *if* the applicant is found to be insurable. The *insurer has accepted the applicant's offer*. If the applicant is not insurable, there is no insurance coverage and the premium will be refunded. If the applicant proves to be insurable, coverage occurs at the time stated in the conditional receipt.

4 The insurance company gives its agent authority to make temporary binding contracts. The *agent accepts applicant's offer by issuing a* **binding receipt** or a temporary insurance policy which covers the applicant while the company decides whether to grant permanent coverage. The temporary coverage stops when the company issues a policy, or notifies the applicant that coverage is denied.

CASE 27.1 **Dohanyos v. Prudential Insurance Co.** • 952 F.2d 947 (6th Cir. 1992)

FACTS On April 25, 1990, Aaron Dohanyos (Aaron) signed a Prudential life insurance application. It provided that premiums would be "paid from money deducted out of my paycheck." The application also stated that the policy was subject to *acceptance* by Prudential and would be dated July 1. Further, *"no payment can be accepted by Prudential until after that date. I understand that no coverage will be provided until Prudential delivers my policy and receives the full initial monthly premium."* On June 28, Prudential, apparently unaware of the payroll deduction system arranged by its Detroit manager with Aaron's employer, sent Aaron a letter asking for direct payment of the premium for the month of July "by July 19," and also stating "POLICY DATE, July 1, 1990."

At about the same time, Prudential mailed from its home office to its Detroit office several of the employee policies, including Aaron's. The manager did not return from vacation until July 3. When he went to Aaron's employer to deliver the policy, he was told that Aaron had died in an accident on July 2. After Aaron's death, but prior to the July 19 deadline that Prudential had set for the first premium payment, Aaron's employer remitted a premium deducted from Aaron's paycheck. In addition, Mr. and Mrs. Dohanyos, Aaron's parents, had sent a check for the July premium. Prudential returned both of these items. The Dohanyos, as beneficiaries, claimed the face amount of the policy, $53,571. Prudential denied liability, and filed suit. The trial court entered judgment for Mr. and Mrs. Dohanyos, and Prudential appealed.

OPINION BROWN, J. . . . Michigan law recognizes constructive delivery which applies when a policy is mailed to an agent solely for the purpose of delivery, even if the policy is never delivered. . . . It is clear . . . Prudential manifested inconsistent intentions. The application and acknowledgment clearly require delivery to Aaron. The June 28 notice to Aaron, requiring payment of July's premium by July 19, however, is inconsistent with Prudential's intentions to enforce the delivery requirement. That notice indicated that Aaron would be covered for July if he paid the premium by July 19. And as the facts of this case demonstrate, the failure of Prudential's agent to arrange prompt delivery of the policy, as his letter to Aaron promised, is inexcusable. We conclude, therefore, that Prudential is estopped from relying upon the delivery requirement to defeat liability.

**CASE 27.1
Continued**

Prudential next asserts that Aaron never accepted the policy and that he was free to reject it. Therefore, it contends that no contract was ever formed. . . . The district court concluded that Prudential's conduct alone prevented the fulfillment of the acceptance requirement, and Prudential should not now be made the beneficiary of its own failure which deprived Aaron of the opportunity to fulfill the acceptance requirement. The district court's determination is correct. . . .

Prudential asserts that the failure to pay the first full month's premium while Aaron was alive, by the express terms of the policy, precluded coverage. It claims that the two attempts to pay the premium after Aaron's death were ineffective. Finally, it claims that, for the following two reasons, it did not waive or modify the payment requirement: (1) the June 28 notice requiring payment by July 19 could not modify the contract because there was no mutual consent to any modification; and (2) regardless of any modification or waiver of the due date for the first premium, the June 28 notice did not alter the requirement that the premium be paid while the insured was alive.

Michigan law recognizes waiver. . . . The insurer, for whose benefit the forfeiture provision (for failure to pay premiums on time) was made, has the unqualified right to waive it which need not be in writing but may be inferred from its acts. . . . The facts strongly support the conclusion that Prudential waived the prior-payment requirements. . . . Because it indicated its intent to collect for a full month's coverage even if payment were not received until well into the month, and because it indicated that it would accept payment if made by July 19, 1990, we conclude that Prudential waived any provisions requiring that payment of the premium precede the commencement of coverage or that the insured pay the premium while he remained alive.

JUDGMENT The trial court's judgment for Dohanyos is affirmed.

Assignability of Insurance Contracts

People have many reasons for attempting to assign their insurance policies. They might wish to sell or give away a policy of insurance on their life, or might wish to use the policy as collateral security for a loan. The assignability of an insurance policy depends on whether its terms restrict assignment, and upon the kind of insurance. Some kinds are assignable without restriction, some require the prior consent of the insurance company, and some are not assignable.

Property and Casualty. It is important to distinguish between an assignment of the *proceeds* of a casualty policy and an assignment of the *casualty policy itself*. A casualty policy is one that reimburses the insured person for loss resulting from mishaps, such as auto collision, fire, and natural disasters. Generally, an assignment of casualty policy *proceeds* can be made without restrictions, since only the transfer of the right to collect money is involved. For example, Amy, an elderly widow, decides that if her house burns down, she will live with her daughter, Beth, and that she wants to assign to Beth the proceeds of her fire policy. Before or after a fire, Amy can assign policy proceeds by separate agreement with Beth, or by attaching to the policy a form assigning the proceeds to Beth. Amy (not Beth) continues to be both the *insured* and the owner of the property. But suppose Amy wants to transfer title to her home to Beth, and also to *assign the casualty policy* to Beth.

As a general rule, contracts of property, casualty, and liability insurance are *not* assignable without the consent of the insurer. The reason for the rule is that a casualty insurer agrees to insure only after careful appraisal of *personal character traits* of the insured, such as accident-proneness, honesty, and past record. Suppose in the above illustration that Amy has a lifelong good safety record, while Beth has negligently caused four fires. If Amy is not required to first obtain consent of the insurer, the latter would be burdened with a higher risk than it had bargained for. Therefore, to aid insurers in screening out unacceptable risk, the law treats most property and liability insurance as a *personal* contract that is not assignable without the consent of the insurer.

Life Insurance. There are far fewer restrictions on assignment of life insurance than is the case with property and liability insurance. However, assignability of life insurance varies with the circumstances. *After the insured's death,* a life policy is a mere promise by the insurer to pay money and as such is freely assignable. The validity of a policyowner's assignment of a life policy *during the lifetime of the insured* depends upon the terms of the policy. Some life policies forbid assignment by the owner, and courts tend to give effect to such prohibitions during the insured's lifetime. But most policies do not prohibit assignment. Ordinarily a person who has such a policy on his or her own life may assign it. The property rights that are transferred consist mainly of (1) any cash value that might accumulate before the death of the insured and (2) the face amount of the policy (called the **death benefit**) that will be available upon the death of the insured.

If an insurance policy names a beneficiary to receive the death benefit, the assignee's right to the cash value may conflict with the rights of the beneficiary. The assignee often wants to cash out the policy; but the beneficiary wants to keep the policy in force until the time the death benefit is paid, and may even be willing to borrow against the loan value of the policy in order to keep up the premium payments. If the policy provides that the designation of beneficiary is *irrevocable*, the rights of the beneficiary prevail over those of the assignee. Where the beneficiary designation is *revocable*, courts in most states hold that the assignee's rights are superior to those of a revocable beneficiary. This majority rule, by protecting the assignee, makes it easier for the policyowner to use the policy as collateral for loans.

Insurance Pricing and Dividends

In fixing premium charges, an insurer must estimate its financial outlays, which include (1) overhead costs of maintaining staff and offices, (2) costs of paying beneficiaries upon death of the insured (this outlay must wait until the company has accumulated data about actual losses), and (3) a reasonable cash dividend that will be paid to the insurer corporation's stockholders. Against these estimated outlays, the insurer offsets *income* received—from the company's investments in real estate, government bonds, and other securities—a figure which also is not known in advance. If premiums collected from all the insureds significantly exceed actual outlays, the company may "adjust" the premium downward and pay the policyowner a **dividend.** Although a dividend is normally understood to be a share of corporate profits paid to stockholders, an insurance "dividend" is simply a refund of part of the price initially charged for the insurance. Federal tax law does not treat a policy dividend as income, but as a *nontaxable refund of an overcharge.*

The situation is slightly different in the case of a **mutual insurance company,** which has no stockholders but, in theory, is operated for the benefit of the policyowners. In considering whether to pay a *policyowner dividend,* a mutual company does not have to concern itself with setting aside a reasonable cash dividend to stockholders, since none exist. Whenever a mutual insurer declares a dividend, it is pro-rated to the policyowners in proportion to the insurance that they carry. The dividend may be paid to a policyowner in cash, or credited against annual premiums, so that each year the insured pays a lower amount than is called for in the policy contract. The fact that any profits not retained in a mutual insurance company can be credited pro rata to reduce the premium charges of policyowners accounts in part for the popularity of mutual life and casualty insurers.

DUTIES, DEFENSES, AND RIGHTS OF INSURERS AND OTHERS

Over several centuries, case law and statutes have spelled out the rights and duties of the insurer, the insured, and certain others. This evolutionary process has largely involved adapting contract law to the special needs of insurance transactions.

Duties of the Insurer

An insurer has a **duty to make prompt payment** of valid claims. Many state statutes provide special remedies to persons aggrieved by insurers that unjustifiably refuse to pay, or make late payment of, valid claims. These statutes typically require insurers to pay a cash penalty and claimant attorney's fees.

Liability insurers also have a **duty to defend** suits against insureds and, where circumstances warrant, a **duty to settle claims out of court.** Such claims fall into two broad categories that frequently arise in the business world: (1) **third-party claims** and (2) **first-party claims.** Two recent and important state supreme court decisions—illustrated below in Cases 27.2 and 27.3—explain clearly the *different standard of care that the law requires of insurers in third- and first-party cases*.

Case law in the last half-century has developed two new causes of action against the insurer in such cases. First, the courts have held that in every insurance contract there is an *implied covenant of good faith and fair dealing* between the carrier and the insured that neither will do anything to injure the right of the other to receive the benefits of the agreement. This implied *contractual* obligation requires the insurer to settle in an appropriate case even though the policy does not expressly impose that duty. Second, court decisions have declared that an insured also has a cause of action based upon the same elements, *in tort, for breach of the implied covenant*. This duty not to exercise *bad faith* arises from an insurance carrier's fiduciary duty as a supplier of services that affect the public interest. Most state statutes permit the jury in tort cases to award *punitive damages* whenever defendants *intentionally* engage in "bad faith," "malicious," "outrageous," or "oppressive" conduct that inflicts emotional distress on the plaintiff. Often, these statutes also authorize judges to award attorney's fees to the victims—an exception to the general rule that each party must bear its own attorney's fees. As we will see below, successful bad faith suits against insurers arising from first-party claims have resulted in punitive damage awards of millions of dollars.

Third-Party Claims. The insurer has a duty to investigate and settle, or litigate and defend, the claim of a third party against the insured. If the injured third party's claim is doubtful, the insurer is not required to settle out of court. On the other hand, the insurer's duty to settle claims out of court increases when (1) the probable judgment on a third-party claim greatly exceeds policy limits, (2) the validity of the claim is not in serious doubt, and (3) the claimant is willing to accept the policy maximum and to release the insured from liability for the excess. Many state statutes as well as court decisions provide that where the insured has requested the insurer to settle a third-party claim for policy limits but the insurer ignores the request, goes to trial resulting in judgment against the insured for in excess of policy limits, the insurer must pay not only the policy limits but the excess as well. This principle and the reasons underlying it are explained in the following case. Particularly important is the judge's clear distinction between first- and third-party bad faith claims.

CASE 27.2   Clearwater v. State Farm Mutual Auto. Insurance Co.
• 792 P.2d 719 (Ariz. 1990)

FACTS   In 1980 Edward Francis negligently drove his car into a motorcycle, killing its rider, Alfred Clearwater. His parents filed a wrongful death suit against Francis (defendant), who was insured by State Farm Mutual with liability coverage of $50,000. Before trial, State Farm refused three offers of settlement within policy limits, but never told Francis, the insured, about the offers.

A trial by jury resulted in a judgment of $125,000 against Francis. State Farm paid the $50,000 policy limits to the Clearwaters, leaving defendant Francis still facing liability for the unpaid judgment balance of $75,000. As is common in such cases, Francis assigned any and all of his bad faith claims against State Farm to the Clearwaters in return for their agreement not to execute judgment for the remaining $75,000 against him personally. As assignees of Francis, the Clearwaters then sued State Farm, and obtained a jury verdict for $75,000, the amount by which the wrongful death judgment exceeded Francis's policy limits. The court granted the Clearwaters an additional $25,237.75 for their attorney's fees, and entered judgment for $100,237.75 against State Farm. It appealed, claiming trial court error in refusing the following jury instruction: "An insurance company may challenge claims which are fairly debatable and is not guilty of bad faith in so doing."

OPINION   CORCORAN, J. . . . In every insurance policy there is a duty imposed by law of good faith and fair dealing. This obligation requires an insurance company . . . to deal in good faith and fairly with its insured in handling a claim against its insured . . . [and] to give equal consideration to the interests of its insured as it gives its own interests. . . .

The tort [of bad faith refusal to settle] arises from a breach of the duty of good faith and fair dealing implicit in all contracts. Bad faith actions against insurers are generally classified as either first- or third-party claims. These classifications are based on the type of insurance coverage provided by the policy in question. First-party coverage arises when the insurer contracts to pay benefits directly to the insured. Examples of first-party coverage include health and accident, life, disability, homeowner's, fire, title, and property damage insurance. In contrast, third-party coverage arises when the insurer contracts to indemnify the insurer against liability to third parties. The type of claim is not determined by the identity of the party bringing the bad faith action against the insurer. For example, a third-party action might be brought by the insured in the event that he is subjected to excess liability by reason of the insurer's bad faith refusal to settle. In that event, the standards applicable to third-party claims would govern the action, although it was brought by the insured, rather than a third-party assignee.

. . . Factors to be considered by the trier of fact in a third-party bad faith claim [are] : (1) the strength of the injured claimant's case on the issues of liability and damages; (2) attempts by the insurer to induce the insured to contribute to a settlement; (3) failure of the insurer to properly investigate the circumstances so as to ascertain the evidence against the insured; (4) the insurer's rejection of advice of its own attorney or agent; (5) failure of the insurer to inform

| CASE 27.2 Continued | the insured of a compromise offer; (6) the amount of financial risk to which each party is exposed in the event of a refusal to settle; (7) the fault of the insured in inducing the insurer's rejection of the compromise offer by misleading it as to the facts; and (8) any other factors tending to establish or negate bad faith on the part of the insurer. . . .

Thus, an insurer owes its insured the same duty of good faith and fair dealing in both first- and third-party actions. The standard for determining whether the insurer has breached its duty, however, is different in the two types of cases because of the different relationships and duties that exist between the parties. In third-party actions, the insurer exclusively controls settlement and the insured bears a disproportionate share of the risk if the insurer fails to accept a reasonable settlement offer within policy limits. The insured faces personal liability for an award exceeding policy limits, while the insurer's potential liability remains constant at policy limits. Therefore, although the "fairly debatable" standard sufficiently protects both parties' interests in first-party actions, . . . for third-party . . . analysis the instruction gives undue weight to a single factor. . . . We find no error in the trial court's refusal to give State Farm's requested "fairly debatable" instruction in this third-party action. |
|---|---|
| **JUDGMENT** | . . . In a third-party bad faith claim based on an insurer's refusal to accept a settlement offer within the policy limits, a "fairly debatable" instruction is improper. . . . [Judgment affirmed.] |

First-Party Claims. The *Clearwater* opinion distinguishes clearly between first- and third-party claims. Case 27.3 illustrates a *first-party* bad faith claim by the insured against his own insurance carrier. Unlike *Clearwater*, however, the insurer's bad faith in dealing with the insured involved such "conscious wrongdoing" that the plaintiff asked for *punitive* damages. This means that in addition to consequential damages to compensate him for his actual loss, he asked the jury to tack on a further sum to punish the insurance company for wrongdoing and to "teach it a lesson." The jury obliged, awarding $22.5 million in punitive damages because of its bad faith in handling a $13,000 damage claim!

CASE 27.3	**Republic Insurance Company v. Hires** • 810 P.2d 790 (Nev. 1991)
FACTS	Jack Hires (plaintiff) returned from a trip to find that vandals had burglarized and looted his home. He notified Republic Insurance Company (defendant), who had insured him under a homeowner's policy with a "replacement cost" endorsement. Republic sent their insurance adjuster to investigate the loss. He told Hires to buy new furniture and throw out the old. Hires heeded this advice, buying new furniture mostly on credit. Two weeks later, Republic told Hires they would not reimburse the cost of his new furniture ($2,242) but would allow only $400, their estimated cost of reupholstering the damaged furniture. When Hires estimated it would cost $580 to replace bedroom furniture, Republic said it

CASE 27.3
Continued

would allow $300. After bargaining Hires down on the replacement cost of each item, Republic then said it would pay only 65 percent of the total. Their excuse for this 35 percent across-the-board reduction was that Hires "lacked documentation." At the trial, one of Republic's claims adjusters testified that it was Republic's policy to begin negotiating at a reduced figure, so the policyholder would have the burden of arguing for a higher sum.

Republic also sent investigators into the neighborhood to develop evidence that Hires's family might have participated in the burglary. Hires testified that his close relationship with his neighbors changed after the investigation. Republic also encouraged the police to investigate the possibility that someone in the family was party to the crime. Republic's refusal to reimburse for the furniture Hires bought on credit created financial problems which finally led to a divorce. Five months after the burglary, Republic agreed to pay Hires $7,238—which was $5,800 under his demand. Hires accepted, reserving the right to contest the amount paid. He then sued Republic for the torts of bad faith, breach of contract, misrepresentation, and invasion of privacy. The jury returned a verdict of $410,000 in compensatory damages and $22.5 million in punitive damages. Republic appealed.

OPINION

YOUNG, J. . . . [The Nevada statute] authorizes an award of punitive damages where the defendant has been guilty of oppression, fraud or malice. . . . We conclude the evidence indicates Republic was guilty of oppressive conduct. . . . Evidence showed that the net worth of Republic was approximately $172 million. We conclude that $22.5 million is a larger sum than is necessary in this case to serve as a deterrent. . . . In this case any punitive damage award in excess of $5 million would be unreasonable and disproportionate to the behavior of Republic.

SPRINGER, J. (Separate concurring opinion) . . . Republic was guilty of "conscious wrongdoing" and "malicious intent"; but what aggravates the wrongdoing in this case is the massive oppression engaged in by Republic and Republic's focus on defeating the legitimate claims of its low income, relatively powerless clientele. . . . There is evidence to support the conclusion that this oppressive policy was employed in over one million claims per year. The amount "shaved" off . . . Hires' legitimate claim was around $5,800. If, for example, only a trifling $100 were shaved from each of a million claims each year, we would have a staggering fraud on the company's policy-holders of $100 million per year. This kind of fraud, this kind of oppression is indeed deserving of punishment.

JUDGMENT

The judgment of the trial court is affirmed in all respects except for the award of punitive damages. The judgment for punitive damages is reduced from $22.5 million to $5 million.

> **BOX 27.1**
> ### A Question of Ethics
>
> A Georgia jury recently awarded $105 million to a plaintiff in a products liability suit against General Motors. Typically 40 percent of the recovery would go to the victim who suffered personal injuries, and the remaining 60 percent to lawyers, investigators, doctors, expert witnesses, and court costs. But now the state of Georgia anxiously awaits the verdict to be upheld on appeal. Why? Its new law, following similar statutes in six other states, requires 75 percent of all punitive damage awards to be paid into the state treasury. Assuming the firm will pass the $105 million bill on to the firm's insurers, should premiums paid by business for products liability insurance be required to support state government?
>
> Some constitutional lawyers don't think so, arguing that the "takings" clause of the Fifth Amendment prohibits confiscation of private property for public use without just compensation. But on March 29, 1993, the U.S. Supreme Court, without comment, left intact a Florida law that allows the state to claim 60 percent of punitive damage awards. Why do states in growing numbers restrict punitive damage awards? What social policy issues are involved? ■

Duties of the Insured

In applying for insurance, the insured has a **duty to disclose material information**—that is, any facts which would influence the insurer's decision to refuse insurance or charge a higher premium because of a higher risk. In addition, insureds as well as other claimants have a **duty to present claims promptly** to the insurer. Policies typically require that claims and proof of loss be presented within a stated number of days after the event. If such policy provisions are *reasonable*, courts will enforce them because of the general benefit to the insured public that flows from prompt investigation and settlement of claim. A claimant who fails to present a timely claim or proof of loss will lose the insurance benefit unless there is an excuse for the delay.

The insured's **duty of assistance and cooperation** rises most frequently where insurance company lawyers are defending a suit against the insured. Typically, the plaintiff is suing for injuries caused by the insured's auto negligence. The insured's duty, usually imposed by the terms of the insurance contract, includes the obligation to notify the insurer promptly if suit is filed against the insured, attend hearings and trials, give evidence, help obtain the attendance of witnesses, refrain from interfering with legitimate defense and settlement efforts, and provide any other reasonable cooperation relative to trial of the case.

Defenses of Insurer

An insurer can avoid paying a claim on an insurance contract by raising any of the defenses that are available in a suit on an ordinary contract. Thus, if the policy was obtained by fraud (false representations of material facts or concealment of such facts) or if there is a breach of warranty, the insurer can defeat liability. The insurer can also use these same defenses to rescind the insurance contract.

In one way or another, all these defenses become available because the policyowner conceals the truth or furnishes false information to the insurance company. Yet accurate information is the insurer's stock-in-trade. To evaluate the risk, to decide whether to insure, and to determine the amount of the premium, the insurer must have solid facts about such matters as the insured's medical history, age, health, and driving record, as well as the cost, age, size, and condition of the insured's property. The insurance carrier obtains the data from the insured's signed application, which contains factual representations and warranties.

Concealment. An insurance applicant's intentional failure to disclose a *material* fact constitutes concealment and is a good defense if the insurer granted coverage while unaware of the concealed fact. Examples are a driver's failure to reveal convictions for drunk driving when applying for auto liability insurance and a homeowner's failure to reveal storage of large amounts of gasoline in the basement when applying for fire insurance.[2] Generally, an insurer can rescind the policy contract for *intentional* concealment, but not for *innocent* failure to disclose.

Misrepresentation (Fraud). In insurance law, a *representation* is an oral or a written statement of fact made by an insurance applicant to induce the insurer to extend coverage. When such a statement is false, it is a **misrepresentation** (also called a **false or fraudulent representation**). If the insurer *relies* upon it in issuing a policy, it is ground for rescinding (avoiding) the policy, *but only if the insurer meets its burden of proving that the misrepresentation is material* (relevant) to the transaction. An applicant for life insurance who states that she is in perfect health when in fact she has recently received hospital treatment for a severe heart attack has made a material misrepresentation. If the insurance company relied on the misrepresentation in issuing a policy, the company may rescind (avoid) the contract. If the insurer learned the true state of the applicant's health *before* issuing the policy, the insurer obviously has not *relied* on the misrepresentation and cannot rescind. But where there was no investigation, or where the insurer investigated but did not learn the truth, the insurer usually will be held to have relied on the applicant's misrepresentation. Most courts hold that the fraud defense is good even if the misrepresentation was *unintentional*.

Frequently, an insured who has been truthful in connection with the issuance of a policy, will falsify facts to induce the insurer to pay more than a claim is worth or to pay a wholly fraudulent claim. At such times, the insurer must go on the offensive and sue to recover damages for the tort of fraud and deceit and, in many cases, even file criminal charges for grand theft or insurance fraud.

Breach of Warranty. A **warranty** in an insurance policy is a written statement, description, or promise by an insurance applicant which guarantees the insurer that certain facts are literally true, and often promises that they will continue to be true while the policy is in effect. Warranties differ from representations in two important ways:

1 They are written into the policy and are an integral part of the contract, whereas most representations are either oral or in the *insurance application* but not in the policy.
2 They are *presumed to be material* (relevant), and if there is not strict compliance with warranties, the insurer can avoid the policy.

At common law, breach of a warranty was a complete defense for the insurer, regardless of the materiality of the breach. For example, suppose homeowner Max "warrants that no gasoline is or will be stored on the premises," yet he still has a half-gallon of gasoline in his basement workshop. At common law, even though the gas did not increase the damage of an upstairs fire, Max might find that his breach of warranty was sufficient ground for the insurer to avoid the policy and escape liability.

In the past, many insurers took advantage of this common law treatment of warranties by drafting complex warranty clauses that often deprived insureds of the coverage they reasonably expected. To remedy this harshness, courts began interpreting policies so as to restrict warranties and require that warranty terms appear conspicuously in the policy, together with a warning that failure to comply strictly with such terms could result in cancellation. Today, many state statutes provide that breach of a warranty is a ground for avoiding the policy only if the breach is *material*—that is, if it contributes significantly to the loss. Under such statutes, Max in the above illustration would be able to recover for his upstairs fire damage by proving that the gasoline in the basement was *irrelevant and not material* to the loss. Even without such statutes, courts frequently construe warranties as representations, thereby forcing the insurer to prove *materiality*. Statutes in most states declare warranty law largely inapplicable to *life insur-*

---

[2]If the insurer's application form specifically addressed such questions to the applicant, a false answer would constitute misrepresentation.

ance, so that life insurers no longer use breach of warranty as a defense against payment of claims.

Incontestability. Most life and some health insurance policies contain a clause stating that the policy is **incontestable** after the passage of 1 or 2 years. Incontestability means that the insurer may not avoid the policy for concealment, breach of warranty, or misrepresentation. Most states have laws requiring the inclusion of **incontestability clauses** in life insurance policies. Such statutes were enacted in part to counter the harshness of the common law doctrine of insurance warranties. Incontestability clauses are commonly used in life insurance policies, even where not required by law, because such protection enhances marketability.

Rights Contrary to Policy Provisions. Insurers, insureds, and other claimants may have rights that are not mentioned in their policies, or that are inconsistent with the policy provisions. For example, state laws may have been enacted to nullify provisions in an insurance policy, or to require the policy to contain provisions that have not been inserted in its pages. The insured has the benefit of such laws even though the policy does not reflect them.

Rights of claimants. To remedy the harshness of the common law of insurance, courts began developing interpretive techniques as a means of controlling abuse and overreaching by the insurers. For instance, instead of interpreting a description of insured property as a warranty (to which the property had to conform *exactly* to remain covered by the insurance), courts came to treat a description as merely an identification of the covered property, with no warranty significance. Thus, today a 1991 car might be inaccurately described as a 1992 model and yet be covered.

Courts today use many legal doctrines—such as waiver, election, and estoppel—to recognize rights that are inconsistent with policy language. A **waiver** is a voluntary relinquishment of a known right. An insurer might, for example, pay a claim even though the insured failed to notify the insurer of the loss within the time stated in the policy. If the insurer later seeks to retrieve the payment, a court is likely to say it *waived* its right to timely notice.

Election is a doctrine under which an insurer, by taking one course of action, is held to have disqualified itself from taking another course of action. For example, failure to pay a policy premium on time normally results in termination (lapse) of insurance coverage. However, some courts hold that an insurer, by accepting late payment, has *elected* to continue the policy in force; therefore the company is liable for any covered claim arising during what would have been the lapse period. In applying the doctrines of waiver and election, courts recognize two broader principles of law: (1) an insurer will be denied any unconscionable advantage in an insurance transaction, and (2) the reasonable expectations of policyowners will be honored.

Like election, **estoppel** is a doctrine that prevents an insurer from taking a later position that is inconsistent with an earlier statement upon which the insured has relied. Case 27.1, above, illustrates how courts apply the doctrines of waiver and estoppel. Sometimes the doctrine of estoppel is used to impose liability on a company that is not an insurer and permit a claimant to recover from it as if it were an insurer. Suppose Alan, as owner of an independent insurance brokerage business, tells Ben he will renew his automobile collision insurance before it expires next week, but fails to do so. Ben wrecks his car. No insurance company is liable to indemnify Ben, because Alan failed to renew Ben's policy with an insurer. However, Alan is liable to make good Ben's loss to the same extent as the coverage in the policy that Alan allowed to expire. Because Alan made a promise which Ben relied upon to his injury, Alan is *estopped* to deny that he is liable as an insurer.

Rights of insurers. Although defenses such as concealment and misrepresentation are not expressly mentioned in an insurance policy, they are nevertheless available to an insurer. In addition, the insurer may pursue the contract remedy of **reformation** by asking an equity court to *reform* the agreement to correct an error made in the preparation of the policy, or one arising from a mutual mistake about some matter such as the age of the insured.

PERSONAL RISKS: LIFE AND HEALTH INSURANCE

Life and health insurance policies protect against risks such as premature death, disability, unemployment, and outliving one's financial resources. In a family context, insurance can reimburse medical expenses, replace income lost from disability, and, at death, cover costs of last illness, burial, debts, taxes, and similar expenses. Insurance can also provide funds to meet special needs such as financing an education or paying off a home mortgage. Businesses can insure the lives of key personnel whose untimely death would cause financial hardship. Firms also use insurance as collateral for loans to finance the business, or to fund surviving partners' purchase of a deceased partner's interest from the heirs.

Life Insurance

Types of Life Insurance. There are four basic classes of contracts sold by life insurance companies: **term life, whole-life, endowment life,** and **annuity.** The first three classes enable a person to accumulate a fund for use or for investment and are associated in varying degrees with the risk of premature death. The phrase "life insurance" usually means term, whole-life, or endowment insurance—or one of the many combinations or variants of these three basic types. The fourth class of contract, the **annuity,** is a device for systematically *using up* an existing fund. An annuity, by providing periodic income, protects against the risk of outliving one's financial resources and is similar in principle to a life insurance *settlement option,* discussed below.

Term life insurance is a contract that furnishes life insurance for a fixed period ("term of years," commonly 1 or 5), with annual premiums that remain the same throughout the term. The policy's face value is payable only if death occurs during the term. Nothing is paid if the insured survives beyond the term. However, most term insurance policies include an option to renew for another term without requiring a favorable medical examination or other proof of insurability. Of course, the premium is increased at each renewal because the insurer pays more benefits as the insured's age increases and more insured persons die. Buyers of term insurance receive insurance protection only, usually with no buildup of cash values. The premium for term insurance is relatively low because it does not provide coverage past a given age, usually 65 or 70. **Convertible insurance** is a term policy that includes an option to convert it to "permanent" insurance without evidence of insurability.

Whole-life insurance (also called **straight, ordinary,** or **lifetime** insurance) is a contract of **permanent insurance** in the sense that the insured may pay premiums continuously, thus keeping the policy in effect for life. Even if the insured eventually quits paying premiums, there is a buildup of cash value that can be converted to paid-up insurance for a lesser amount. Paying for whole-life insurance is almost always done by means of **level-premium payments.** In the early years of the policy, the premium is far more than is needed to pay claims from the insured group. The excess amount is invested by the insurer and the proceeds are retained in a **legal reserve fund**—the source of **cash surrender values** that whole-life policies accumulate. The legal reserve fund will be sufficient to pay the increasingly frequent claims that arise in the later years. Thus, a whole-life policy is basically insurance with a forced-savings feature that finances, in advance, long-term insurance benefits for both policyowners and beneficiaries.

One of the many varieties of whole-life policies is the **limited-payment life policy,** in which premium payments are made for a limited number of years—20, for example—at which time the policy is fully paid up. Because of the cash-value feature, whole-life policies can be used as collateral for loans. Or, where the policyowner wishes to quit paying premiums before the policy is fully paid up, the cash value can be applied in a variety of ways to preserve a lesser degree of insurance coverage.

In an **endowment insurance** contract, the insured pays premiums for a stated number of years (the *endowment period*) and at the end of that time *receives the face amount of the policy.* If the insured dies before that time, the face amount is paid to a beneficiary, as with other life insurance. In effect, an endowment policy consists of a large savings fund resulting from accumulation and investment of a portion of the premium, plus term insurance whose face amount decreases as the endowment policy savings fund increases. In event of early death, term or even whole-life insurance provides larger insurance proceeds per premium dollar than endowment insurance.

Settlement Options. A life insurance policy **matures** when the insured dies or when the insured survives the time period of an endowment policy. At maturity, the face amount of the policy is available to the beneficiary or other person entitled to it. Such a person can choose the method of receiving payment from a number of **settlement options,** including a right to (1) receive a lump-sum settlement in cash; (2) leave the proceeds (principal) with the company, to receive the interest in periodic payments, and to withdraw principal from time to time or to specify how the principal is to be used up; (3) have the principal together with interest paid in equal installments over a fixed number of years; (4) receive payments of a stated amount until principal and interest are exhausted; and (5) have a variety of life income options, as with an annuity.

Health Insurance

Health insurance protects mainly against risk of temporary and permanent disability resulting from injury or illness. The term *health insurance* includes two major kinds of protection: (1) **dis-**

Table 27.2 Types of Health Insurance

Type of Health Insurance	Coverage
Disability income	Provides insured with periodic payments to substitute for income lost due to disability or sickness.
Medical expense	
Individual	Provides indemnity for hospital, physician, surgical, and nursing expenses; typically excludes risks too great to cover (e.g. military service, preexisting disabilities).
Major medical	Provides for extraordinary physician and hospital costs for catastrophic illnesses (e.g., cancer).
Group medical	"Master contract" between insurer and employer covers all employees (the group) regardless of insurability; cost paid by employer or employees, or shared by both.
Medicare	Medical expense reimbursement insurance for persons 65 or older; most of cost met by Social Security Administration. Medicaid is a similar, state-financed program for the poor.
Workers' compensation	State laws require employers to carry insurance covering medical expenses for work-related injuries or illness plus a lump-sum award for permanent disability.
"Rider" coverage	A supplemental agreement attached to an auto policy providing medical benefits when insured or others are injured in an auto accident; sometimes life policies have health riders.

ability income insurance and (2) **medical expense insurance.** These and various subclasses of medical expense are defined in Table 27.2. There is an endless variety of health insurance policies. Even some auto insurance furnishes medical and hospital benefits. Overlapping coverage is one reason health insurance costs are high.

Health insurance policies typically exclude excessively high risks. For example, the duration of an illness such as AIDS may be so unpredictable that there is no rational way to estimate premiums. Often, insurers exclude preexisting ailments from coverage in order to limit adverse selection—that is, the greater-than-normal tendency of one who is a poor risk to seek insurance. The main reason insurers exclude suicide and self-inflicted injuries, for example, is to limit adverse selection. Most health insurers also exclude coverage if the insured has workers' compensation.

PROPERTY RISKS; PROPERTY AND LIABILITY INSURANCE

Property Insurance

Nature of Property Insurance. Property insurance indemnifies a person who has an insurable interest in physical property (real or personal) for its loss or for the loss of its income-producing ability. Property insurance protects against loss from certain "perils." A **peril** is a cause of loss such as fire, flood, theft, or vandalism. Property insurance may be provided by means of either a specified-perils or an all-risk (all-perils) contract. In a **specified-perils contract,** the insurer will indemnify only losses resulting from the particular peril specified. A farmer's insurance against hail damage to crops is an example. In an **all-risk contract,** the insurer indemnifies the insured for loss resulting from any peril except those specifically excluded by the contract. A homeowner's **personal property floater** is an all-risk contract because it compensates covered losses even though the contract did not specify the particular peril. All-risk contracts are useful where the nature of the peril is difficult to predict.

The policy's terms limit the risk undertaken by a property insurer. Many policies impose a **deductible,** and all policies contain clauses of exclusion. A deductible is an amount of loss, specified in the policy, that the *insured* must absorb before the excess is paid by the insurer. Deductible amounts, common in automobile and homeowners' insurance, minimize insurance costs by eliminating small claims that are often subject to moral hazard. Exclusion clauses (e.g., damage from acts of war) confine the insured risk to manageable proportions.

A property loss may be *direct* or *indirect*. A **direct loss** is one resulting from physical damage to the property—for example, collision damage to a taxi. But loss of income as a *consequence* of the loss of use of the taxi is an **indirect loss.** Rental cost of a car to replace the cab during repairs is also an **indirect loss.**

Types of Property Insurance. A representative list of the kinds of property insurance available for protection against personal or business losses appears in Table 27.3. Most or all coverages are available on a single-peril, multiple-peril "package," or all-risk basis. Some coverages are limited to direct losses, most encompass indirect losses, and a few (such as business interruption insurance) protect primarily against indirect losses.

Liability Insurance

Nature of Liability Insurance. Liability insurance protects only against *tort* liability. Although it does *not* cover liability for breach of contract, it does cover tort liability *assumed* by contract. For example, if Ari rents a car and agrees to assume liability for damage to the car caused by his negligence, he can obtain insurance to cover the tort liability he agreed to assume. The sources and types of tort liability fall into several somewhat overlapping categories. They include:

1 Liability for one's own torts. Examples include negligent driving, professional malpractice, false imprisonment of a suspected shoplifter, libel, and slander.

Table 27.3 Types of Property Insurance

Type of Property Insurance	Coverage
Fire	Indemnifies losses resulting from accidental fire to insured buildings, contents, ships in port, and so on. Loss from a "friendly" fire is not covered—for example, valuables accidentally tossed into a furnace. But if a friendly fire escapes or becomes uncontrolled, a few courts hold it has become hostile and the loss is covered.
Crime	Pays for losses caused by the criminal acts of others, such as burglary. For example, banks carry insurance to indemnify losses from robbery.
Inland marine	Originally provided protection for goods transported other than by ocean. Today, it is used to cover a variety of transportation and nontransportation losses, whether or not incurred on waterways. Unlike other property insurance, generally, inland marine insurance is assignable by seller to buyer. This exception to the general rule is made to facilitate commercial shipping.
Accounts receivable	Protects against an inability to collect an account because of damage to records that prove the existence of the account.
Business interruption	Protects against losses due to inability of a business to operate because of fire, flood, or other hazards.
Automobile collision	Covers loss to the insured vehicle from its collision with another object. A separate rider is necessary to cover bodily injury or liability arising from collision, and to cover noncollision losses.

2. Liability of an employer for torts committed by employees in the course of their employment, including many intentional torts.
3. Liability for loss resulting from defective products, whether based on negligence, breach of warranty, or tort strict liability.
4. Liability resulting from ownership of property. Examples are liability to business invitees, residence guests, and some types of trespassers for losses owing to negligent maintenance of business or home, and strict liability arising from ownership of hazardous property such as a reservoir.

Types of Liability Insurance. Most of the tort exposures listed above may be insured against, although insurers commonly exclude from coverage some intentional torts committed by the insured—for example, assault and battery. Representative types of liability coverage appear in Table 27.4.

Subrogation and Coinsurance

Two concepts have special significance in property and liability insurance. The first, **subrogation,** refers to an insurance company's right to

Table 27.4 **Types of Liability Insurance**

Type of Liability Insurance	Coverage
Employers' liability	One type provides coverage for workers' compensation claims. Another protects the employer against claims of persons other than employees (e.g., business invitees).
Errors and omissions	Protects the insured from liability to a customer resulting from the insured's error or oversight. An insurance salesperson, for example, might forget to include a requested coverage.
Malpractice	Protects professionals such as doctors, lawyers, and accountants from liability for negligence in the practice of their professions.
Fidelity (guaranty)	Protects against loss due to embezzlement and other dishonesty of employees and other persons in positions of trust.
Automobile liability	Protects a motor vehicle operator or owner from liability to third persons as a result of the operation of the vehicle. About half the states have some form of "no fault" auto insurance law under which claims for personal injury (and in some states, for property damage) must be made against claimant's own insurance company, regardless of who was at fault. The aim of such laws is to reduce the cost of auto insurance by reducing litigation expense, but many "no fault" laws are ineffective for this purpose because the right to litigate to establish fault has been preserved even for small claims.
Homeowner's liability	Protects a homeowner from damage claims of invitees and others.

be substituted as a claimant against a person responsible for loss. The concept applies mainly to liability insurance. To illustrate, suppose Jack negligently hits Jill's car, causing $1,000 damage. Jill's casualty collision insurer pays the $1,000 repair bill on Jill's car. Jill's insurer is *subrogated* to Jill's right to sue or otherwise hold Jack responsible for the tort of negligence.

The second concept, **coinsurance,** applies to the insuring of commercial property.[3] A coinsurance clause is used by property insurers to prevent customers who underinsure commercial property from taking "unfair" advantage of a common method of setting rates for property insurance. Property rates are fixed at a certain amount per $1,000 of coverage on the preliminary assumption that all customers will carry their full share of the group risk by insuring their property for substantially full value. But if Brown and Smith own identical office buildings worth $100,000 each, and Brown insures hers for $20,000 while Smith insures his for $100,000, Smith pays a total premium that is five times larger than Brown's. This difference in premiums would be "fair" if large and small claims were in the equal balance implied by the

---

[3]Coinsurance has other meanings that are beyond the scope of this discussion. One applies to reinsurance and another to health insurance. Thus although two different health insurers' policies cover the same hospitalization costs, such "coinsurance" will still only permit the insured to collect no more than 100% of such cost.

flat premium rate per $1,000 of coverage. In fact, however, there are more small claims than large ones, because there are more partial than total losses. If all claims were paid in full, the group that pays less in premiums by underinsuring would receive proportionately more in claims "payout" than would the group that insures for full value. Rather than reduce the premium rate when a person insures for full or nearly full value, the insurer uses the coinsurance clause to reduce claims payouts to the group that underinsures. Coinsurance is fair because it assures rough equality of payout per premium dollar to all groups of insureds. However, it is a trap for unwary underinsureds who expect their losses to be fully covered.

How does a coinsurance clause work? It provides that if the owner's property is insured for at least a given percentage of its value (usually 80 percent), any loss will be paid in full up to the face amount of the policy. But if the property is insured for less than the required percentage, the owner must bear part of the loss and will recover from the insurer only the amount indicated by a specified formula. In the preceding paragraph, Brown insured her $100,000 office building for only $20,000. Suppose she sustains a fire loss of $20,000. She will recover only $5,000 from the insurer, according to one common formula developed for recovery:

Recovery

$$= \text{Actual loss} \times \frac{\text{Face amount of insurance}}{80\% \text{ of actual cash value of property}}$$

$$= \$20,000 \times \$20,000 / \$80,000$$

$$= \$20,000 \times 25\%$$
$$= \$5,000$$

Suppose now that Smith insures his $100,000 office building for $80,000. The coinsurance requirement is met. If Smith sustains a $20,000 fire loss, it will be paid in full. However, if the value of the building increases and there is no corresponding increase in the amount of insurance, Smith will not be in compliance with the coinsurance requirement and will have to bear part of the loss. *Residential* fire insurance often includes a **replacement cost clause** whose purpose is similar to that of a coinsurance clause.

REGULATION OF THE INSURANCE BUSINESS

Insurers' abuses are legion: the use of confusing contracts to exploit ignorance of the insuring public, unconscionable conduct in settling claims (illustrated in Case 27.3), overaggressive marketing—these factors combined with the quasi-monopolistic status of insurers make the insurance industry a prime target for government regulation. Courts try to strike a fair balance between insureds and insurers by denying any unconscionable advantage to insurers and by honoring the reasonable expectations of insureds and their beneficiaries. But the judiciary is only one aspect of federal and state insurance regulation.

Federal Regulation

In 1944, the Supreme Court held that an insurance company that conducts business across state lines is engaged in interstate commerce and is therefore subject to the regulatory power of the federal government, including the Sherman Antitrust Act[4] Prior to that decision, insurance regulation had largely been left to the states. After the decision, Congress enacted the McCarran-Ferguson Act to clarify the applicability of antitrust law to insurers.

Under the McCarran Act, regulation and taxation of insurance is left mainly to the states. However, the McCarran Act only partially exempts the insurance industry from antitrust laws. Those laws (Sherman, Clayton, and Federal Trade Commission Acts) apply to the *business of insurance to the extent that it is not regulated by state law*. Where states fail to regulate harmful practices in the **"business of insurance"** (i.e., the relation between insurers and policyholders), federal law applies. Since the McCarran Act

---

[4]*United States v. South-Eastern Underwriters Association*, 322 U.S. 533.

exempts only the "business of insurance," federal antitrust law applies to any aspect of an insurer's business that lies outside the relation between the company and its policyholders (assuming there is "commerce" jurisdiction, as discussed in Chapter 52). For example, antitrust applies to an insurer that conspires with a glass franchisor to fix the price of automobile replacement glass.

State Regulation

State law controls the incorporation, licensing, supervision, and liquidation of insurance companies. In most states, the insurance industry is regulated by an administrative agency called an **insurance commission.** Two of its important goals are to ensure (1) financial soundness of insurers by regulating their investments, capitalization, and reserves, and (2) reasonable and fair treatment to policyholders, insureds, and beneficiaries by requiring agents and brokers to be licensed and policies to contain protective measures (e.g., a nonforfeiture clause in a cash-value life policy). Commissions also prohibit harsh clauses such as those calling for suits against insurers to be commenced within a time period shorter than that required by the statute of limitations.

ROLES OF INSURANCE AGENTS AND BROKERS

Traditional Function of Agents and Brokers

Under the law of agency, an **agent** is a person who makes contracts on behalf of another person, the **principal,** and is subject to the principal's instructions and control. An **insurance agent** represents an insurance company (the principal) in negotiating and forming a contract for the sale of insurance to a customer. An **insurance broker** ordinarily does not represent a company but, rather, places an order for insurance on behalf of the *buyer* and is therefore the *buyer's* agent. However, as noted in Case 27.4 below, sometimes the broker is the agent of the *seller* and sometimes the agent of *both buyer and seller*. The rights and duties of principals, agents, and third persons are discussed in Part Eight of this volume.

CASE 27.4   A&B Freight Line, Inc. v. Ryan • 576 N.E.2d 563 (Ill. App. 1991)

FACTS   A&B Freight Line (plaintiff) sued West Bend Mutual Insurance (Mutual) and Ray Ryan, claiming that Ryan, an independent broker, placed insurance for plaintiff with Mutual, and overbilled A&B Freight $451,425.14 for insurance which Mutual had issued. Before operating his own insurance brokerage business, Ryan was employed as sales manager for Mutual, whose president was Ryan's brother-in-law. In the period when the overbilling occurred, Ryan had broker's authority from Mutual to bind it to a policy with an insured party, to bill and collect premiums, and to sign and deliver endorsements. Although Ryan could have written insurance on other companies, most of his business was with Mutual. Ryan told an employee of A&B Freight that he was an "employee" of West Bend Mutual. When A&B Freight accused Ryan of excessive charges, he confessed to overbilling. The trial court ruled that Ryan, as broker, was A&B Freight's agent, and granted summary judgment for the insurance company. A&B Freight appealed.

OPINION   REINHARD, J. The question of whether an insurance broker is an agent for the insured, the insurer, or both is generally a question of fact. . . . Independent in-

CASE 27.4 Continued

surance agents possess a certain duality which allows them to act as both agents and brokers. Although earlier case law drew a distinction between insurance agents and insurance brokers, a person's conduct and not title determines the relationship between the independent insurance agent, the insured and the insurer. Under certain circumstances, an independent agent may be an agent of both the insured and the insurer. . . . [There are] four factors to consider in determining whether an independent insurance agent was acting as the agent of the insured or insurer: (1) who first set the agent in motion; (2) who controlled the agent's action; (3) who paid the agent; and (4) whose interests the agent was attempting to protect.

. . . Applying the four factors to the facts surrounding the overbilling shows that Ryan was not solely plaintiff's agent at the time of the transactions at issue. First, Mutual Insurance set Ryan in motion by allowing him to bill and collect premiums . . . and to issue and deliver those policies to A&B Freight. Second, because Mutual authorized Ryan to bill and collect premiums, it controlled Ryan's actions. If Mutual did not authorize Ryan to bill and collect its premiums, A&B Freight would have paid its premiums directly to Mutual. Third, Mutual paid Ryan a commission for the premiums Ryan sold, although this factor is not given much weight. Fourth, although Mutual correctly argues that Ryan was protecting his own interests by overbilling plaintiff, Ryan was protecting Mutual's interest while billing and collecting the premiums for Mutual because he was ensuring that Mutual was compensated for the cost.

Mutual may be liable to A&B Freight if Ryan was an agent apparently acting within his authority while placed in a position by Mutual which enabled Ryan to overbill plaintiff. It is inconsequential whether the agent acted according to his instructions if he was acting within the scope of his apparent authority. . . .

JUDGMENT The judgment in favor of West Bend Mutual is reversed.

Agents and Brokers as Financial Advisors

The recent trend for agents selling insurance to also assume the role of *financial advisor* raises special problems. Agents selling insurance usually deal at arm's length with the buyer and can use emotional appeals or a variety of other promotional practices. Unlike sellers, financial advisors are often **fiduciaries** who are bound to a stricter standard of professional conduct. Clients, often uninformed about technical matters, defer to the judgment of the advisor, who can easily harm them through negligence, incompetence, or unfair advantage. When an insurance agent gives planning advice and also sells the financial product that is recommended for putting the plan into effect, there is a conflict of interest which should be fully disclosed to the client. Courts deal sternly with agent-advisors who are found to have such conflicts of interest and to have engaged in overreaching in the sale of insurance.

SUMMARY

Insurance is contractually transferring risk from insured to insurer, which spreads the risk by means of pooling and reinsurance. Since insurance is a system for distributing loss, insureds are limited by the principle of indemnity to loss actually suffered. A corollary rule requires an insurable interest—the insured must have a financial stake in property or in someone's life or health.

Contract law governs insurance policies and

the interpretation of contracts of adhesion. Courts construe ambiguous contracts against an insurer and in favor of the insured. An insurer has a duty to pay valid claims promptly. Liability insurers usually owe a duty to defend the insured in a lawsuit. Insurers are liable in tort for oppression or bad faith in dealing with insureds in first- and third-party cases. Insureds must present claims promptly and cooperate in lawsuits. Within limits, the insurer may invoke the defenses of concealment, breach of warranty, and misrepresentation.

Life and health insurance protect against risks of premature death, disability, and outliving one's financial resources. Term, whole-life, and endowment insurance help one accumulate a fund, whereas an annuity contract is used to liquidate an existing fund. Health insurance pays disability income and medical expenses.

Property insurance protects against loss of physical property or its income-producing ability. Liability insurance protects against tort liability. Subrogation—a right of substitution as claimant against a person responsible for loss—applies mainly to liability insurance. Coinsurance avoids disproportionate benefits being awarded to those who underinsure their property.

Insurance is subject to federal and state regulation that aims to ensure financial soundness of insurers and fair treatment of policyholders, insureds, and beneficiaries. An insurance agent sells insurance for an insurer. A broker can act as agent for both insured and insurer, but usually acts for the insured. An agent who acts as financial advisor may risk liability as a fiduciary.

REVIEW QUESTIONS

1. How are **(a)** pooling and **(b)** reinsurance used to distribute risk?

2. How are coordination of benefits and the principle of indemnity related?

3. When are there insurable interests in **(a)** property? **(b)** life?

4. How do court rulings on contracts of adhesion affect insurance?

5. (a) What legal duties are owed by an insurer? **(b)** What are the legal duties of the insured? **(c)** What are the legal consequences of an insurer's bad faith?

6. (a) What is the significance of treating statements in a life insurance application as representations and not as warranties? **(b)** What is the significance of incontestability?

7. Explain the meaning of **(a)** a "level" premium, **(b)** specified-perils property insurance, and **(c)** all-risk property insurance.

8. (a) Explain the kinds of liability insurance and the exclusions from each. **(b)** Explain the purpose of subrogation. **(c)** Explain the purpose of coinsurance.

9. What risks are faced by an insurance agent who also serves as financial advisor? Why?

CASE PROBLEMS

1. Ryan and Tickle decided to go into business together and operate Ryan Funeral Home, Inc. The firm's 477 shares of stock were distributed among twelve shareholders. Tickle bought 25 of the 50 shares that Ryan owned, and the two men had a 5-year option to buy the remaining stock from the other shareholders. Ryan and Tickle also purchased the Mullen Funeral Home, arranging to finance the unpaid balance over a period of 5 to 6 years. In 1972, to provide a fund by which the survivor could acquire ownership in the funeral homes, they purchased insurance on their joint lives. In early 1973, Ryan learned he had cancer. He died in 1975. Tickle collected the insurance policy proceeds and bought the outstanding interests in the two funeral homes. Ryan's widow claimed that Tickle did not have an insurable interest in Ryan's life and sued to recover the insurance proceeds for Ryan's estate. Did she have standing to sue? Was she entitled to the insurance proceeds?

2. Butler, unaware that an Austin-Healy was stolen, bought it for $3,500. Two years after the purchase, police returned the car to its lawful owner. Butler filed an insurance claim for the value of the car. The insurer claimed lack of insurable interest and refused to pay Butler for the loss, offering instead to refund the $56 premium that he had paid for the insurance. Did Butler have an insurable interest in the stolen car?

3. Eric sued on a claim against Allstate Insurance Co. The claim arose from a hit-and-run accident in which Eric's wife was killed while riding in an automobile owned by her and driven by Eric. An Allstate auto insurance policy covering the car contained an uninsured motorist clause which provided that Eric, as policyholder, could recover from Allstate for bodily injury caused by a hit-and-run driver. The New York uninsured motorist statute was enacted to recompense innocent victims of motor vehicle accidents for loss or injury inflicted by hit-and-run drivers. However, many fraudulent claims are filed in hit-and-run accidents because they are "easy to claim and difficult to disprove." To deter fictitious claims, the New York legislature imposed a requirement that the claimant have "physical contact" with the motor vehicle of the hit-and-run driver. The fatal injury occurred while Eric was westbound on a freeway when an unidentified eastbound car lost a wheel which jumped the median and crashed into the windshield of Eric's car, killing his wife. The eastbound driver put on his spare wheel and left without identifying himself. Allstate denied liability because there was no "physical contact" between Eric's car and the unidentified vehicle. Is Allstate liable on the policy?

4. Mr. and Mrs. Travis applied for a loan at Hancock Bank. The bank submitted a document intended to inform the Travises of the availability of life and disability insurance which, upon death, would pay off the mortgage, or in event of disability would provide income sufficient to pay the mortgage each month. By signing the form, Travis requested the bank to obtain the insurance, but through negligence of its clerk, the bank failed to do so. Two years later, Travis was injured in an accident and became totally disabled. Travis sued the bank and claimed that it should make monthly disability payments. The bank contended that Travis could not properly put it in the position of being a disability insurer merely by signing his name on a loan form next to a space which stated: "I want life and disability insurance." The bank further argued that it had not quoted Travis any terms, conditions, or premium for insurance coverage; no disability premium was ever paid or collected, no insurance application was submitted by Travis to any insurer, and no disability policy was issued. Is the bank liable as an insurer?

5. Briggs's outboard motorboat was insured by Nationwide Insurance Co. against any accident involving the use of the boat. While operating the boat, Briggs struck a big wave, jouncing his passenger. She complained of back pain and Briggs took her to an emergency hospital, where she was X-rayed, given Tylenol, and dismissed. Briggs told her to contact him if she had any medical bills or further problems. Two years later the passenger's attorney sent Briggs a letter threatening suit for personal injuries. Briggs turned it over to his insurer, which denied liability on the ground that Briggs had failed to give notice of the claim "as soon as possible" as stated in his policy. Briggs sued the insurer, asking the court to declare that the insurer had improperly disclaimed liability and to order the insurer to defend him. Should the insurer be ordered to defend Briggs?

6. Schultze Biscuit Co. used several large gas ovens to bake crackers. The ovens operated continually at 450°F. At the end of a working shift, an oven was accidentally left on with no product on the conveyer belt running through the oven. As a result, the temperature rose to 1,600°, causing damage to the oven in the sum of $150,000. When the insurer denied Schultze's claim for loss on the ground that the fire was "friendly," Schultze filed suit for the loss. Should Schultze prevail?

ETHICS IN PRACTICE

The law governing property, estates, wills, trusts, and insurance is extensive. But here, as in other areas of business activity, people's interests collide in ways often not anticipated or covered by law. Thus, ethical considerations may be as important as legal ones in deciding what course of action to take in a given situation.

Insurance, especially, is a very sensitive industry ethically. Customers pay billions of dollars annually for various kinds of insurance coverage and expect insurance companies to invest the proceeds properly and to pay claims quickly and fairly. Because insurance companies are in the business to make a profit, the interests of insurers obviously conflict with those of their customers and claimants: Payouts reduce profits. Thus, there is pressure on insurance companies to market aggressively and to limit payouts whenever possible. Moreover, salespeople receive much larger commissions for some kinds of insurance than for other kinds, and to increase earnings they may act contrary to the interests of their customers. Then there are the customers and claimants who file false claims against the insurers. Money, it is said, "is the root of all evil," and insurance companies which handle so much of it, are at the center of temptation. State insurance commissions and the civil and criminal law help control abuses. Yet many insurance and property situations present ethical as well as legal questions. Illustrations follow.

PROBLEMS IN ETHICS

1. In 1991, the California Supreme Court ruled 5 to 2 that an apartment owner had the right to bar tenants whose income was less than three times the rent charged, despite the tenants' claim that they could afford the rent. The would-be tenants argued that the owner's rental policy arbitrarily discriminated against the poor and disproportionately affected women, violating a California statute forbidding discrimination by businesses against customers. In rejecting these arguments, the court approved the owner's pricing policy as legal. Is it ethical?

2. Charles recently moved into the house next door to John. One weekend, when Charles and his family are away, John sees a new-model power lawn mower in Charles' backyard and wants to see how it works. If he likes it, he intends to buy one for a $100 discount at a 1-day sale that will end before Charles is likely to return. John knows that if he borrows the machine without Charles' permission, he will be committing a trespass. However, although he has not met Charles, John doubts that Charles would sue him for using the mower. Other than the violation of trespass law, are there ethical factors that John should consider?

3. You manage an apartment building. The owner, Leo, leases a unit to Sam and Sue on a month-to-month basis. Either he or the tenant can terminate the lease upon 30 days' notice. Sam and Sue have always paid their rent on time, are quiet, hardworking, and pleasant to all the neighbors, and attend church regularly. Recently, however, Leo has learned that Sam and Sue are not married. Leo's religion teaches that living out of wedlock is a mortal sin. Leo wants you to help him decide whether to terminate the lease. **(a)** What factors should you ask Leo to consider? **(b)** Will your personal belief about the propriety of living out of wedlock affect your advice? **(c)** Would it matter that five of Sam and Sue's immediate neighbors consider Sam and Sue's living arrangements scandalous and unacceptable?

4. A number of insurance companies contributed substantial sums of money to Mothers

Against Drunk Driving (MADD). The leaders of the California chapter endorsed voters' initiatives aimed at reforming California insurance law and reducing auto insurance premiums. Despite vigorous opposition by the insurance companies, the voters adopted one of the initiatives. Soon after the election, and allegedly at the insistence of the insurance companies, the national MADD directors fired the California MADD officials for endorsing the initiatives. (a) Was it ethical for the national MADD directors to fire the California officials? (b) If the insurance companies forced the firings, was their conduct ethical?

5. In his concurring opinion in *Republic Insurance Co. v. Hires*, (Case 27.3), Judge Springer raised an important ethical question:

Republic is a large subsidiary company with assets of about $172 million. If this were a personal, not a corporate, defendant one might not be concerned with a punishment that took [millions] from a rich and powerful person who preyed upon the weak and was guilty of an unjust and cruel abuse of power. In a case like this, however, it is to some degree the innocent . . . stockholders who suffer loss for the evil doings of corporate management.

Some commentators argue that this kind of punitive damage award punishes the innocent shareholder and does not have a deterrent effect on the corporate managers who actually committed the wrongful acts. They argue that [the value of the shareholders' stock is reduced], while the wages and salaries of the employees and officers of the corporation would remain untouched.

Opponents of the "innocent shareholder" theory state that loss or decline in value of an investment is a risk that investors must assume. They argue that the shareholder should not be allowed to enjoy "ill-gotten" gains. In addition they state that punitive damages cutting into the shareholders' pocketbooks will encourage the shareholders to exercise closer control over corporate operations.

How *should* punitive damages be assessed in dealing with corporate officials who engage in wrongdoing?

6. While vacationing with his friends Benny and Tammy, James fell off a cliff and was severely injured. James had no medical insurance, but Benny did through his employer. On the way to the hospital, Benny switched IDs so James could use Benny's insurance. James' medical care cost $49,000. Eventually, Benny, Tammy, and James were convicted of fraud for participating in the scheme. Was the friends' conduct an ethical violation, or only a legal one?

PART SIX

Debtor-Creditor Relationships

CHAPTER 28
Purpose and Types of Secured Transactions; Suretyship

CHAPTER 29
Secured Transactions in Personal Property

CHAPTER 30
Bankruptcy

Ethics in Practice

CHAPTER 28

Purpose and Types of Secured Transactions; Suretyship

Consumers and businesspeople borrow billions of dollars each year for all sorts of personal and business purposes: purchasing a car or home, financing an education, paying for a vacation trip or hospital stay, developing a business, or buying a corporation. To meet the heavy and varied demand for credit, lenders extend (grant) it in a variety of ways. If you want to buy a car but do not have the cash, you might get a loan from a bank. Or you might persuade the seller to accept monthly payments until the price is paid. Many credit purchases involve the use of a credit card. Often people will simply deliver goods or render services and bill you later.

But the extension of credit involves a risk that the debtor will **default:** fail to repay a loan or fail to pay for property or services bought on credit. To reduce the risk of default, a creditor may demand, or the law may provide, some sort of **security**—some backup source of payment that will be available to the creditor if the debtor fails to pay.

This chapter discusses the kinds of security arrangements commonly used in business, with major emphasis on the secured transaction. As used here, **secured transaction** means any contract between a creditor and a debtor that provides the creditor with a backup source of payment should the debtor break his or her promise to pay. Secured transactions are of two basic types: (1) those in which the creditor's backup source of payment is real or personal property (called **collateral security,** or simply **collateral**) and (2) those in which the creditor's security is the promise of some third person (a **surety**) to pay the debt. The surety's promise is given or imposed by law in addition to the debtor's promise to pay.

Some forms of security, such as the mechanic's lien discussed in the first part of this chapter, are not contractual. Rather, they are imposed by law in favor of certain creditors and therefore may exist without the knowledge of the debtor or the creditor.

The first part of this chapter surveys the kinds of security devices commonly associated with credit extension, noting only briefly those that are discussed more fully in other parts of this book. The second part focuses on suretyship, an important but sometimes overlooked type of secured transaction commonly encountered in business.[1]

---

[1] Public financing by the biggest borrower of all, the government, is beyond the scope of this book. Debt collection practices, unconscionability in credit card sales, and other consumer topics are discussed elsewhere in this book, especially in Chapter 30 (bankruptcy) and Chapter 49 (consumer law).

NATURE AND TYPES OF SECURED TRANSACTIONS

Nature of a Secured Transaction

How a secured transaction works can be seen by comparing an unsecured transaction with a secured one.

An unsecured creditor (one who extends credit without receiving any security) faces the maximum risk of nonpayment. Carl sells goods to Donna solely on the basis of her promise to pay later. An unsecured creditor, Carl has no right to repossess the goods if Donna fails to pay. Instead, to enforce his right to payment, Carl will have to sue Donna and obtain a judgment against her. If Donna refuses to honor the judgment, Carl will have to seek execution of it. To do this, Carl must get a writ of execution from the court. The writ orders the sheriff or other proper officer to seize and sell any of the debtor's property located within the jurisdiction of the court and to apply the proceeds of the sale to the debt. Carl's obtaining judgment will be of little value if Donna has no assets, leaves the jurisdiction, or is discharged from her debts in a bankruptcy proceeding. Carl could **garnishee** (lay legal claim to) Donna's wages, but garnishment laws limit the percentage of wages he may take, and Donna might be unemployed or earn little.

Carl would substantially reduce his risk of nonpayment by insisting on a *secured* transaction. Suppose the sales contract states that if Donna fails to make timely payment, Carl will have the right to repossess and sell the goods he sold her. Carl has reserved for himself a **security interest** in the goods and has become a secured creditor. Upon Donna's default, Carl will have a claim against Donna's general assets, and may have first rights, as against Donna's other creditors, to the goods he sold her. What Carl must do to have first rights to the goods is discussed in Chapter 29.

The main purpose of a secured transaction is to protect the creditor. Under modern security law, a defaulting debtor may lose the collateral and remains personally liable for any deficiency if the collateral is not valuable enough to cover the debt. But the law requires that the debtor be treated fairly too. If the collateral is worth more than the amount of the debt, the debtor is entitled to surplus proceeds realized upon the sale or other disposition of the collateral.

Types of Secured Transactions

Secured transactions can be classified in terms of the source of the backup payment that is available to the creditor upon the debtor's default. So there are (1) secured transactions in real estate, (2) secured transactions in personal property, and (3) suretyship transactions.

Where property is the collateral, the creditor acquires a **lien** (charge or claim) against the property. Some liens are imposed by law. Others are created by contract. Security devices can therefore also be classified in terms of how they arise—by law or by contract.

Liens Imposed by Law on Personal Property.

Often a person (the bailor) hires someone (the bailee) to repair, ship, or store the bailor's personal property. Under court decisions or statutes, the bailee has a **possessory lien** on the property for the amount the bailor agreed to pay for the service or, in the absence of a stated price, for the bailee's reasonable charges. The lien exists only as long as the bailee keeps possession of the property. If the bailee voluntarily gives the thing back to the bailor without receiving payment, the lien is lost and the bailee becomes an unsecured creditor. Donna delivers her antique clock to Carl for him to clean and repair, agreeing to pay him $50 for the work. Carl performs as agreed, but Donna refuses to pay the bill. Carl has a lien on the clock for $50, as long as he keeps the clock in his possession. Many state statutes permit Carl to enforce his lien by selling the clock in the manner prescribed by the statute—usually by giving Donna notice of the sale and advertising it. If no such enforcement provision exists, Carl may have to **foreclose** his lien. To foreclose, Carl must get a judgment against Donna for the amount owed and have the clock sold at a judicial sale. See Box 28.1.

Possessory liens on personal property are classified as specific or general. A **specific lien**

> **BOX 28.1**
>
> ### Does Carl Have a Possessory Lien?
>
> 1. Donna, having refused to pay for the repair work, sneaks into Carl's shop after hours and takes the clock. Because Carl did not voluntarily give up possession, he still has his lien. The result would be the same if Donna had by fraud or duress induced Carl to give up possession of the clock.
> 2. Carl, having agreed to clean and repair the clock for $50, presents Donna with a bill for $200 when she arrives to pick the clock up. Donna "tenders" (offers) the $50 she agreed to pay, but Carl insists on $200. Carl's lien is terminated, his possession is now wrongful, and he is liable to Donna for conversion of her property.
> 3. Donna calls Carl to her house to repair a grandfather clock. He repairs it there and later sends Donna a bill that is reasonable in amount. Donna refuses to pay Carl's reasonable charges. Since Carl never acquired possession of the clock, he has no lien on it and is therefore an unsecured creditor.

entitles the creditor to retain possession of the property as security for only the one debt involved in the immediate transaction. A **general lien** entitles the creditor to keep the property until the debtor has paid all debts owed to the creditor as a result of their general course of business. Carl repaired Donna's watch last week and delivered it to her, but she has not yet paid the $40 they agreed to. Now she tenders (offers) the $50 she agreed to pay for today's clock repair, but Carl wants to keep the clock until she also pays for the watch repair. Unless Carl and Donna agreed otherwise, Carl's lien on the clock is specific and therefore is not effective as to the earlier debt. Donna's tender of the $50 terminates the specific lien, and she is entitled to possession of the clock. As to the $40 for the watch repair, Carl is an unsecured creditor. If Carl's lien against the clock had been general, Carl would have been entitled to hold the clock until Donna also paid for the watch repair.

But general liens are available only to a few groups of businesspeople. Attorneys-at-law, bankers, and factors (selling agents to whom principals entrust goods for sale in the regular course of business), and sometimes a few others such as accountants, are granted general liens by law. Under a general lien, an attorney, for example, could hold a client's papers or other property that comes into the attorney's possession until all amounts owed the attorney are paid, even if the amounts are for a variety of separate debts. In contrast, most bailees have only a specific possessory lien. Bailees include repairpeople and other artisans, common carriers, innkeepers, warehousers, finders of property for the return of which a specific reward is offered, landlords who hold the property of defaulting tenants, and agisters (bailees who take possession of cattle for the purpose of feeding them).

Liens Imposed by Law on Real Estate. Like personal property, real estate can be subjected to a variety of liens. A landowner who is a losing defendant in a lawsuit may have his or her property subjected to a **judgment lien** in favor of the winning plaintiff. Land is also subject to a **tax lien** in favor of the state or other governmental unit for unpaid taxes. The **mechanic's lien** is imposed in favor of a person who *under a contract* has performed labor or furnished materials for the improvement of real estate. Like judgment and tax liens, a mechanic's lien is involuntary because it is imposed on the debtor by law rather than being contracted for. It provides the mechanic with a backup source of payment (the improved real estate) should the mechanic not receive payment from the person with whom he or she contracted (usually, the landowner or the landowner's general contractor).

The term "mechanic" is broader than it sounds. The statutes of most states grant a mechanic's lien to anyone who, under contract, furnishes labor, services, or materials for the improvement of land. Thus, carpenters, electricians, landscapers, concrete workers, brick masons, lessors of equipment, general contractors, subcontractors, surveyors, suppliers such as lum-

RECORDING REQUESTED BY

WHEN RECORDED MAIL TO

NAME
STREET ADDRESS
CITY
STATE
ZIP

(SPACE ABOVE THIS LINE FOR RECORDER'S USE)

MECHANIC'S LIEN
(Claim of Lien)

The undersigned, ______________________________ , referred to
(Full name of person or firm claiming mechanic's lien)

in this Claim of Lien as the Claimant, claims a mechanic's lien for the labor, services, equipment and/or materials described below, furnished for a work of improvement upon that certain real property located in the County of ______________________, State of California, and described as follows: ______________________________
(Description of property where the work and/or materials were furnished
Although the street address is sufficient, it is advisable to give both the street address and the legal description.)

____

After deducting all just credits and offsets, the sum of $______________________, together with interest thereon at the rate of
(Amount of claim due and unpaid)

______________________ percent per annum from ______________________, 19____, is due Claimant
(See note on reverse side) (Date when amount of claim became due)

for the following labor, services, equipment and/or materials furnished by Claimant: ______________________________
(General description of the work and/or materials furnished)

____

The name of the person or company by whom Claimant was employed, or to whom Claimant furnished the labor, services, equipment and/or materials is

____
(Usually name of person or firm who ordered from, or contracted with Claimant for the work and/or materials)

The name(s) and address(es) of the owner(s) or reputed owner(s) of the real property is/are: ______________________________

____
(This information can be obtained from the County Assessor's office where the real property is located)

SEE REVERSE SIDE FOR ADDITIONAL INSTRUCTIONS

Name of Claimant ______________________________
(See instructions on reverse side for proper signing)

By: ______________________________
(Signature of Claimant or authorized agent and title)

VERIFICATION

I, the undersigned, declare: I am the ______________________ of ______________________, the Claimant
(Title) (Name of Claimant)

named in the foregoing claim of mechanic's lien; I am authorized to make this verification for the Claimant; I have read the foregoing claim of mechanic's lien and know the contents thereof, and the same is true of my own knowledge.

I declare under penalty of perjury under the laws of the State of California that the foregoing is true and correct.

______________________, 19____ ______________________________
(Date of signature) (Signature of the individual who verifies that the contents of the claim of mechanic's lien are true)

WOLCOTTS FORM 1024—MECHANIC'S LIEN (Claim of Lien)—Rev 5-82
(price class 3)

1982 WOLCOTTS, INC

Figure 28.1 "Claim of lien" form (reprinted by permission of Wolcotts Legal Forms, Inc.).

beryards (often called "materialmen"), and many others fall within the meaning of mechanic. Ordinarily, labor and services must be performed, and materials must be delivered *and incorporated into the improvement,* before the mechanic, artisan, or supplier has a right to a lien against the property.

The procedure for obtaining and enforcing a mechanic's lien is governed by statute and varies from state to state. In general, however, the mechanic must give written notice (e.g., by certified mail) to affected persons (such as landowner, general contractor, or construction lender) that the mechanic has furnished labor, services, or materials for the improvement of the land. Then, after the mechanic completes the work, he or she must record a **claim of lien** (illustrated in Figure 28.1) in the courthouse of the county in which the improved land is located. The lien must be recorded within the time specified by the statute—say, 60 or 90 days after the work or contract has been completed. Upon complying with the statutory requirements, the mechanic has a lien against the property for the amount of the debt. Failure to comply means only that the mechanic is an unsecured creditor; the debt is still enforceable against the person who contracted for it.

Ordinarily, a mechanic has only a limited time to bring suit to enforce his or her lien—90 days after its creation, for example, or a longer time if the mechanic has extended credit. The time for enforcement is relatively short so that the landowner's title (ownership) will not be "clouded" (impaired) by the lien for an unreasonably long time. Mechanics' liens are enforced by a process of foreclosure. To foreclose, the mechanic must get a judgment for the amount due and a judicial order for the sale of the property.

The following case discusses the validity of a mechanic's lien against the *proceeds* of liened property that has been sold by a competing creditor.

CASE 28.1	**Butterfield Lumber, Inc. v. Peterson Mortgage Co.** • 815 P.2d 1330 (Utah App. 1991)
FACTS	On January 9, 1987, plaintiff Butterfield Lumber, Inc., began supplying materials to a job site for the construction of a building. Later that day, Peterson Mortgage recorded a trust deed (similar to a mortgage) on the property, to secure a construction loan that Peterson had made to the property owner. Butterfield supplied materials until April 10. On June 18, Butterfield recorded a notice with the county recorder's office that Butterfield claimed a mechanic's lien on the property. The property owner failed to pay for the materials supplied by Butterfield, and also defaulted on the loan from Peterson Mortgage. Butterfield brought suit to foreclose its mechanic's lien, naming Peterson Mortgage as a defendant. Upon receiving notice of Butterfield's suit, Peterson Mortgage sold the property at a trust deed sale to its president, Leon Peterson, who then sold the property to Peter Wright-Clark. Wright-Clark had no notice of Butterfield's mechanic's lien foreclosure suit because Butterfield had failed to file a *lis pendens* (notice of pending litigation). From a judgment for Butterfield, to be paid by Peterson Mortgage out of the proceeds from its sale of the property, Peterson appealed.
OPINION	GREENWOOD, J. [Peterson Mortgage argues] that Butterfield's mechanic's lien attached only to the . . . real property, and not to the proceeds of [the] sale of the property. . . .

**CASE 28.1
Continued**

The parties agree that Butterfield's . . . lien, because it relates back to the time when materials were first supplied to the property, had priority over Peterson Mortgage's [earlier recorded] trust deed. . . . [They] also agree that Butterfield's action to foreclose the mechanic's lien was timely commenced and that because Peterson Mortgage and Leon Peterson had actual knowledge of the foreclosure action, the lien was valid against their interests in the property. Finally, the parties agree that because no lis pendens was ever filed and because Wright-Clark, the ultimate purchaser of the property, had no actual notice of the lien foreclosure, Butterfield's mechanics' lien was void as against Wright-Clark's title to the property. . . .

The disagreement here is over the effect of Butterfield's failure to record a lis pendens upon its action to foreclose its lien against Peterson Mortgage. Peterson Mortgage argues that once the property was sold to Wright-Clark, who had no notice—either actual or by virtue of a recorded lis pendens—of the pending mechanic's lien foreclosure, Butterfield's lien vanished altogether. Peterson Mortgage claims support for this argument from a single sentence in [the Utah] mechanics' lien law. Section 38-1-3 reads . . . :

> Contractors, subcontractors, and all persons performing any services or furnishing or renting any materials or equipment used in the construction, alteration, or improvement of any building or structure or improvement to any premises in any manner . . . shall have a lien upon the property . . . for the value of the service rendered, labor performed, or materials or equipment furnished or rented. . . . *This lien shall attach only to such interest as the owner may have in the property.*

According to Peterson Mortgage, the final sentence of section 38-1-3 means that once it sold the . . . property, and thus no longer had an ownership interest in it, it held nothing to which Butterfield's lien could attach. Section 38-1-3 has never been so expansively construed, however, and to do so under the facts of this case would defeat the purpose of the mechanics' lien law.

The language in question has long been understood to mean simply that the owner of real property, within the meaning of the mechanics' lien law, can cause only his or her particular ownership interest, or bundle of property rights, to be burdened by a mechanics' lien. Where the [one] who directs property improvement is, for example, a lessee who [does so] without the authority of the lessor, only the leasehold interest is burdened by the resulting mechanics' lien; the lessor's interest is not affected. . . . The interpretation of the final sentence of section 38-1-3 urged by Peterson Mortgage would . . . defeat the purpose of the mechanics' lien law.

"The purpose of the Utah mechanics' lien law is to provide protection to those who enhance the value of a property by supplying labor or materials." . . . To effect that purpose, the law is to be construed broadly.

It is true, as pointed out by Peterson Mortgage, that . . . to obtain the protection afforded by the mechanics' lien law, the lien claimant must [pursue] the foreclosure action as required by section 38-1-11, and therefore Butterfield had no lien on the property once Wright-Clark purchased it. Section 38-1-11 thereby limits the protection afforded [improvers of] property so as to not affect one who purchases the property without notice of actions to foreclose a lien. This

CASE 28.1 Continued

limitation protects the interests of those who, like Wright-Clark, purchase property without actual knowledge of a pending lien foreclosure action. . . .

However, the section 38-1-11 protection . . . does not extend to those who acquire ownership *with* such notice. By the terms of section 38-1-11, the lien remains in effect "as to persons who have been made parties to the [foreclosure] action and persons having actual knowledge of the commencement of the action. . . ." Here, because Butterfield properly named and served Peterson Mortgage as a party to the lien foreclosure, it met the statutory requirements for preserving its lien against Peterson Mortgage's interest in the property in question.

By insisting that section 38-1-3 limits attachment of a mechanics' lien only to real property, Peterson Mortgage is seeking to create a loophole whereby in failing to protect its lien against possible third party purchasers without notice, a lienholder also loses the lien against an owner who is a notified party to an action to foreclose the lien. [According to Peterson Mortgage, all] such an owner needs to do is to sell the subject property to a third party without notice of the lien foreclosure, prior to the time the lien foreclosure is adjudicated, and the lien vanishes. We do not believe that the mechanics' lien law is intended to facilitate such a disappearing act with respect to lien rights against a party with notice of a lien foreclosure action. Such an interpretation would undermine the protection of laborers and materialmen that the law seeks to provide.

Courts in other jurisdictions have held that when a valid lien attaches to property and the owner of the property then disposes of it so as to extinguish the lien on the property itself, the lien attaches to the proceeds received by the owner. . . . The common underlying feature in the cases granting a lien on the proceeds from the disposal of liened property is an element of wrongfulness in the owner's disposal of the property. . . . This element is present here as well, in that Peterson Mortgage attempted to defeat Butterfield's judicial foreclosure of its mechanics' lien by instituting the speedier nonjudicial trust deed foreclosure and then causing the property to be sold to Wright-Clark, who was shielded from the lien. Additionally, we presume that the materials provided by Butterfield enhanced the property's value and thus the price paid by Wright-Clark. As a result, Peterson Mortgage received a benefit from its sale of those materials, as part of the property, to Wright-Clark.

JUDGMENT Therefore, we hold that . . . where the holder of a valid mechanics' lien has timely begun judicial lien foreclosure proceedings, and a party holding a property interest that is subject to the lien, aware of the pending foreclosure, disposes of the property to one who takes it free of the lien, the lien attaches to the proceeds gained from the sale. Accordingly, . . . the judgment of the trial court is affirmed.

Liens Created by Contract. Most significant commercially are those contractual arrangements giving lenders and sellers a security interest in real or personal property. Few people have enough cash to buy real estate outright. In fact, it may be unwise to do so, since a cash purchase of real estate—houses, land, or commercial properties—would divert financial resources that could be better applied to other consumer purchases or to other aspects of a business operation such as product development or the purchase of equipment. Three security devices are commonly used to finance the purchase of real estate—the **mortgage,** the **trust deed,** and the **land contract.** These security devices are discussed in Chapter 25.

Vast amounts of consumer and business credit are secured by an interest in personal property such as consumer goods, accounts receivable, negotiable instruments, inventory, and equipment. Secured transactions in personal property are so important commercially that they are the subject of Article 9 of the Uniform Commercial Code. Chapter 29 is devoted to secured transactions in personal property.

> **BOX 28.2**
>
> **You Be the Judge**
>
> Ruth, a licensed contractor, did construction work as a subcontractor on a new wing of a house that she thought was owned by Harmon. In fact, the owner lived in another state, and Harmon was a tenant who was adding the rooms without the owner's knowledge. Ruth properly gave Harmon notice of her improvements to the real estate, and she properly recorded a claim of lien. No lender was involved. Then, 30 days after recording the claim of lien, Ruth learned that Harmon had paid the general contractor in full. The general contractor, however, has not paid Ruth and shows no signs of doing so. What are Ruth's rights?

SURETYSHIP

In suretyship, a creditor's security is the promise of some third person, often a corporation, to pay the amount of loss if the obligated person fails to pay or to perform as promised. Suretyship is very important commercially, especially in transactions where property is unavailable or cannot easily be used as collateral. For example, in a highway construction project, the failure of a construction company to complete its assignment could cost its employer huge sums, far beyond the value of any property the company might own. Therefore, a construction company participating in public works projects ordinarily must provide a **performance bond,** a surety company's agreement to cover the employer's losses if the construction company fails to complete the project. Similarly, hay dealers, bank tellers, and countless others dealing with the public are required by their employers or by law to be "bonded."

Nature, Creation, and Kinds of Suretyship

Nature of Suretyship. As the preceding examples indicate, a **surety** is a person who, by contract or by operation of law, is liable for the debt, default, or miscarriage of another. To start up a small retail business, Dan seeks a loan from a bank. But the bank refuses to make the loan unless Dan finds a creditworthy person to cosign the promissory note that Dan will give to the bank in exchange for the loan. Dan's wealthy cousin Sara is willing to cosign the note even though she will have no interest in Dan's business. The note reads in part, "We, or either or us, agree to pay $10,000 to First Bank or its order one year from the date of this note. (Signed) Daniel Debtor and Sara Smith." Sara is a *surety* because, by cosigning the note, she contracted to be responsible for someone else's (Dan's) debt. In this particular kind of suretyship (cosigning a note), Dan's creditor may hold Sara liable on the note without first seeking payment from Dan. However, as between Dan and Sara, *Dan* is the person with ultimate liability and thus is the **principal debtor.** So if Sara is required to pay First Bank, Dan is liable to Sara.

In Figure 28.2, First Bank is the **creditor** (C), also known as the obligee. Dan is the **principal debtor** (D), also known as the obligor. Sara is the principal debtor's **surety** (S) and is also First Bank's debtor.

Note that in Figure 28.2, two contracts are involved: (1) the main contract between the principal debtor and the creditor, and (2) the "collateral" (backup) contract between the surety and the creditor.

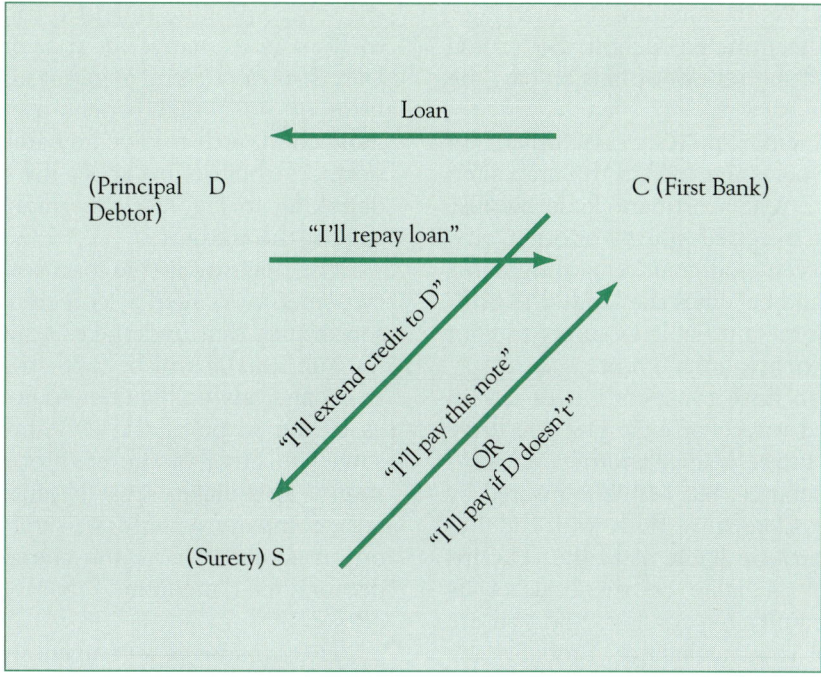

Figure 28.2 Parties to a suretyship transaction.

> **BOX 28.3**
> **Test Your Knowledge**
> Dan and Sara want to open a retail store. They borrow money from a bank and cosign the note. Is Sara a surety for Dan? ∎

A surety may be liable for the principal's **debt** (usually understood to mean an obligation to pay money). But a surety can be liable, too, for the principal's **default** (failure to perform a nonmoney obligation), as where Sara promises to make good any loss resulting from Dan's failure to perform his contract to deliver coal; or for the principal's **miscarriage** (tort or crime), as where Sara agrees to make good to Dan's employer any losses resulting from Dan's embezzlement or other mishandling of the employer's funds.

Creation of Suretyship. Usually suretyship is created by **express contract,** at the request of the creditor or the principal debtor.

But suretyship can arise without the knowledge of the parties, by **operation of law.** Recall from Chapter 16 what happens when a person assigns his or her rights under a contract and also delegates the duties he or she is required by the contract to perform. The delegator (until now, the principal debtor) remains responsible as a surety for the performance of those duties in the event that the delegatee (the new principal debtor) fails to perform, unless the obligee (person to whom the duty is owed) releases the delegator.

Suppose you want to sell your mortgaged house to Dora before you have paid off the debt. She agrees to pay $90,000 for the house, but you still owe Second Bank $70,000. Dora pays you $20,000 and "assumes" the mortgage. Since you have delegated to Dora your duty to pay Second Bank the $70,000, you are a surety for that amount unless and until the bank releases you from liability. Your suretyship liability arises even though the bank might not know that Dora has assumed the mortgage and even though you might not realize that you are still liable to the bank. Upon assuming the mortgage, Dora becomes the principal debtor. So, if you must pay because she refuses or fails to pay, she is liable to you.

The same principle applies to assignments of leases. Suppose you assign to Dan the unexpired portion of your 2-year apartment lease because your employer transferred you to another city. Although Dan receives all your remaining rights under the lease and becomes the landlord's principal debtor, you remain liable as surety to your former landlord for any unpaid rent.

Suretyship can arise by operation of law in other unexpected ways. For example, you drive negligently and injure Millie, another motorist. You have no insurance, but Millie is insured by Town Insurance Company. Both you and her insurance company are liable to Millie. The insurance company is liable on the basis of its contract to indemnify her for loss, and you are liable because of your negligence. Probably the insurance company will pay Millie immediately and seek payment from you, since you are ultimately liable. Under the law you are the principal debtor and the insurance company is, in this instance, a surety. As such the insurance company has, like any other surety, a right of **reimbursement** against you, the principal debtor.

Kinds of Suretyships.
The precise obligation that a surety has will be determined in part by the kind of suretyship that the surety undertook.

Gratuitous v. compensated suretyship. Some sureties are paid for their services and some are not. Those who are not paid are called **gratuitous, voluntary,** or **accommodation sureties** because their main purpose in undertaking the surety obligation is to help out a relative or friend and not to profit personally. However, gratuitous (accommodation) sureties *are* in fact contracting parties and are bound by their promises.

Suppose, for example, that your friend Dan makes an installment purchase of a car, and you cosign his note as surety without being paid to do so. You have made a binding contractual commitment to the seller. The consideration necessary for the suretyship contract to arise is the seller's promise (made to you) to sell the car to Dan, in exchange for your promise to pay if Dan does not. Since a gratuitous surety receives little or no actual benefit from the contract, most courts will resolve any ambiguities, vagueness, or other doubts about the scope of the undertaking in favor of the gratuitous surety and against the creditor.

The opposite is true for a **compensated surety,** sometimes called a "corporate" surety. A person or firm that undertakes a surety's obligation for hire usually will be held strictly to the contract, and any ambiguities, vagueness, or doubts as to the scope of the undertaking will be resolved in favor of the creditor and against the surety. This makes sense because, like an insurance company, a corporate surety estimates risks on an actuarial basis and charges the principal debtor a fee ("premium") that reflects the degree of risk.

The promise of a compensated surety to pay if the principal debtor does not is often called a bond. There are many types of **surety bonds,** among them the following:

1 **Bail, appearance,** or **appeal bond**—various surety bonds associated with criminal or civil legal proceedings. A *bail* or *appearance bond* is the surety's promise to pay a specified sum to the court in the event that the criminal defendant covered by the bond fails to show up for legal proceedings. An *appeal bond* is a surety's promise to cover the costs of appeal in a civil case.
2 **Bid bond**—a surety bond used in connection with public construction projects to protect the public agency (creditor) from loss if the bidder (principal debtor) withdraws the bid or, upon winning the right to the contract, refuses to enter into it.
3 **Performance bond**—a surety bond guaranteeing, for example, that a contractor will complete a construction contract or pay for labor and materials.
4 **Fidelity bond**—a surety bond protecting an employer against loss due to embezzlement, larceny, or gross negligence by an employee.
5 **Fiduciary bond**—a surety bond required by a

court to be provided by a trustee, executor, guardian, or other fiduciary to ensure proper performance of his or her duties.

6 **License** or **permit bond**—a suretyship bond required by state law before the state will issue a license or permit. The bond guarantees payment to an obligee for loss or damage resulting from operations of the licensee or permit holder.

Unconditional v. conditional suretyship. Surety relationships can also be classified according to the nature of the surety's promise or undertaking. In a traditional suretyship arrangement (e.g., the cosigning of a promissory note), the surety-cosigner makes an **unconditional promise** to pay and, like the principal debtor, is immediately liable to the creditor when the note is due. There is no requirement that the creditor first seek payment from the principal debtor. In another kind of unconditional suretyship called an **absolute guaranty,** the surety promises to pay or to perform upon the default of the principal debtor. Here, the surety has no liability until the principal debtor defaults, but if the debtor defaults, the surety is immediately liable. In a **conditional guaranty,** however, the creditor must do more than merely show that the principal debtor is in default. To hold the surety liable, the creditor must first make a reasonable attempt to exhaust the creditor's remedies against the debtor—for example, by suing the principal debtor and having the judgment returned unsatisfied.

Cosuretyship. Sometimes two or more sureties will bind themselves on behalf of a single principal debtor as **cosureties.** Cosureties must share the burden of the principal debtor's default, because although each has contracted to pay the full debt, a court would have no basis for imposing the whole loss on one while freeing the others.

Suppose Dan borrows $100,000 from Carla, and Sylvia cosigns the note at Dan's request. At the same time, at Carla's request, Sam (in writing) guarantees Dan's debt. Sylvia and Sam are cosureties. If Dan defaults, Sylvia and Sam must share the loss equally, unless they have agreed to share it in some different proportion. So, if Dan defaults and Carla compels Sylvia to pay the $100,000, Sylvia is entitled to a $50,000 payment, called **contribution,** from Sam. Similarly, two or more accommodation signers of a note ordinarily are cosureties, and any one of them who pays more than his or her share is entitled to contribution.

Liability, Defenses, and Discharge of Surety

Liability of Surety. The liability that a surety faces upon the default of the principal debtor is determined by (1) the contract between the creditor and the principal debtor, (2) the contract between the creditor and the surety, and (3) other factors such as whether the surety has the benefit of any defenses when called upon to pay.

Usually the surety is responsible for precisely the performance, or any unperformed part of it, that the principal debtor promised the creditor in the debtor-creditor contract—for example, to pay $10,000 plus 12 percent interest on July 17, or to deliver 50 tons of coal at the rate of 1 ton per week. Where the buyer of mortgaged real estate assumes the seller's mortgage, the seller (a surety by operation of law) is liable to the creditor for the amount of the assumed debt that remains unpaid. However, the contract between the surety and the creditor can *limit* the surety's liability, as where the surety promises, "If Dan defaults on his $10,000 obligation to you, I will pay $5,000."

Exactly *when* does a surety become liable to the creditor? The answer depends on whether the surety has primary or secondary liability. Under the law governing promissory notes, the maker (the debtor) and any cosigner (a surety signing as a co-maker), have made unconditional promises to pay. Thus, each one has **primary liability.** This means that the creditor has the right, when the note comes due (or upon the debtor's default), immediately to sue the surety without first seeking payment from the debtor. In contrast, where a surety says something like "I will pay Dan's debt if it is uncollectible," as in a conditional guaranty, the surety has **secondary liability.** Secondary liability is conditional. That is, some event such as uncollectibility must happen before the surety must pay. In the example just given, the surety has no liability until the creditor demonstrates that the debt is uncollectible. The creditor ordinarily will do this by getting a judgment against the debtor, attempting to collect on it, and having the judgment returned unsatisfied.

The next case addresses the problem that exists where the surety's maximum liability is less than the debt owed, and numerous creditors contend for the limited amount.

CASE 28.2 **Homewood Investment Co. v. Moses** • 608 P.2d 503 (Nev. 1980)

FACTS Home Lumber and Supply Co. furnished over $16,000 worth of materials to Homewood Investment Co. Homewood never paid, Home Lumber sued for the amount owed, and judgment was entered for Home Lumber against Homewood and others, including United Pacific Insurance Co., which had undertaken a $5,000 contractor's bond as surety for Homewood Investment. United appealed from the judgment, alleging that since there were several other unpaid suppliers, Home Lumber was entitled to only a portion of the $5,000 bond amount.

OPINION BATJER, J. . . . [W]e agree with United that Home Lumber is not entitled to the full amount of the surety bond. . . . United correctly asserts that Home Lumber is entitled to only a pro rata share of the $5,000 surety bond. [A Nevada statute] states that "[e]ach bond or deposit . . . shall be in favor of the State of Nevada for the benefit of any person who: . . . [a]s a supplier or materialman furnished materials or equipment for the construction contract." Subdivision 5 of that provision states that "[c]laims, other than labor claims, against a bond or deposit shall have equal priority . . . and if the bond or deposit is insufficient to pay all such claims in full, they shall be paid pro rata." There is evidence in the record that other claims against United have been asserted.

JUDGMENT Therefore, the case is remanded to the trial court for a determination of Home Lumber's pro rata share of the bond. . . .

Defenses and Discharge of Surety. The liability of a surety has limits, especially in circumstances involving misconduct of others. Often a surety can successfully raise a defense to his or her alleged liability and be discharged (freed) from it. Three kinds of defenses may be available: (1) the surety's own contractual defenses, (2) some of the contractual defenses available to the principal debtor, and (3) special suretyship defenses that usually arise after the surety undertakes the obligation.

Surety's own contractual defenses. A person has no suretyship liability if no contract arose or if, where one did arise, the surety exercises a right to avoid it. No contract arose if, for example, the person alleged to be a surety lacked capacity to contract or received no consideration for his or her promise. (Recall that even a so-called gratuitous surety receives consideration.) If a contract arose, the surety may avoid it where, for example, the creditor used fraud to procure the surety's promise. First Bank seeks a fidelity bond to protect it from any loss arising from embezzlement of customers' funds by the bank's employees. First Bank knows but does not reveal to the surety that three of the bank's employees have been convicted of embezzlement. First Bank's fraud in concealing or knowingly failing to reveal material information gives the surety a ground for avoiding the contract.

Sometimes a surety may assert the statute of frauds as a defense. A surety's agreement to answer for the debt, default, or miscarriage of another person is not enforceable unless it is in writing. Suppose Delbert is building himself a house on his own lot and is purchasing materials from Lumber Supply. Halfway through, Delbert fails to pay for some materials, and Lumber Supply refuses to deliver any more until Delbert persuades some creditworthy person to guarantee payment. At Delbert's request, Susan promises Lumber Supply on the phone that "If Del does not pay for materials when they are delivered, I will." Lumber Supply makes further deliveries, Del does not pay, and when called upon for payment Susan refuses. Her oral promise is not enforceable. However, if Susan's **main purpose** or **leading object** in making the promise had been to benefit *herself*, her oral promise would have been enforceable. Suppose Del, as a general contractor, is building the house for Susan on her lot. Here, Susan's main purpose in promising to pay Del's debt is to get her house built. Her oral promise to pay Del's debt is enforceable.

Principal debtor's contractual defenses. With some very important exceptions, the surety may assert against the creditor the defenses that the principal debtor could have asserted had there been only the contract between debtor and creditor. These defenses usually arise out of situations involving wrongdoing or default by the creditor. Suppose the creditor fraudulently induces the principal debtor into the contract of indebtedness. Most courts hold that a surety who did not know of the fraud when agreeing to be a surety may assert the principal debtor's fraud defense. (Some courts hold that the surety may not do so unless the principal debtor first repudiates the contract because of the fraud or duress.) Similarly, if the principal debtor received no consideration (e.g., the creditor did not make the promised loan or deliver the promised materials), the surety may assert that defense of the debtor and escape liability to the creditor.

In some situations the principal debtor has a defense that is unavailable to the surety. Suppose Sam cosigns a note so that his minor daughter Dora can buy a car. Dora wrecks the car and, as permitted under state law protecting minors, rescinds the contract. Sam does *not* have the benefit of Dora's defense of infancy. The fact that Dora might rescind and cause loss to the creditor-seller was the main reason for the creditor to require a surety in the first place, and Sam should have understood this when he became surety. In a few other situations the surety is not protected by the debtor's defenses. Ordinarily the surety will be liable to the creditor despite the debtor's defense of insanity, bankruptcy, lack of corporate capacity to undertake the debt in question, or (where the debtor is a public agency) the debtor's assertion of sovereign immunity. Again, these are the kinds of risks that surety and creditor probably contemplated as the main reason for the suretyship.

Special suretyship defenses. The purpose of **special suretyship defenses** is to protect the surety where acts of others increase the surety's risk or reduce the likelihood that the surety can recover the amount that will have to be paid on behalf of the principal debtor. The existence of a special suretyship defense in a particular instance, or the extent of it, depends on a number of factors: (*a*) Did the surety consent to the change that affects the surety's liability? If so, the surety remains liable. (*b*) Was the harm (e.g., an increased chance that the surety will have to pay) "material"? If not, a compensated surety remains liable. The more common special suretyship defenses are discussed in the following paragraphs.

1 *Performance of the principal debtor's duty.* If the principal debtor, the surety, or some third person performs the debtor's duty, not only the debtor but also the surety is discharged from any further liability.

2 *Release of the debtor by the creditor.* Where the creditor releases the debtor from the debtor's duty, the surety is also discharged. A **release** is a legally binding contract to give up a right that the releasing person has against the person to be released.

3 *Tender (offer) of performance*. The surety is discharged where the principal debtor or the surety makes a proper **tender of performance** which the creditor wrongfully refuses. However, the principal debtor is *not* discharged, because he or she has received the benefit of the contract with the creditor and should have to perform by, for example, repaying a loan. But in fairness to the debtor who made the tender, the creditor's wrongful refusal of tender immediately stops the running of interest.

4 *Surrender or impairment of collateral*. Sometimes a creditor has the benefit of a surety's obligation but also receives real or personal property from the debtor to secure the debt. The surety has a right to the benefit of the collateral. Therefore, where the creditor knows of the surety's obligation, the surety is discharged to the extent of any loss caused by the creditor's giving up the collateral or mishandling it in such a way as to reduce its value. Suppose Sarah becomes a surety where Clara lends $5,000 to Dale, who pledges (temporarily transfers possession of) 100 shares of his stock to Clara as additional security. The stock is worth $2,000. Then, before Dale's debt is due and without Sarah's consent, Clara returns the stock to Dale. Sarah is discharged as to $2,000 but remains liable as a surety for $3,000.

5 *Alteration of principal debtor's duty*. A surety is entitled to rely on the original terms of the contract between the principal debtor and the creditor. If those terms are changed without the consent of the surety in a way that increases the surety's risk, an uncompensated (accommodation) surety will be completely discharged. However, a compensated surety will be discharged only if the increase in the surety's risk is material. If the risk increases, but not materially, the compensated surety is not discharged but the surety's obligation is reduced by the amount of loss resulting from the change in the contract between the debtor and the creditor. No surety is discharged where the unconsented-to modification can only benefit the surety. The accompanying box illustrates the impact of minor and material alterations on accommodation and compensated sureties.

> **BOX 28.4**
>
> **Impact of Alterations on Accommodation and Compensated Sureties**
>
> 1 Don leases a building from Carmen for a period of 2 years at a monthly rental of $500, and Sam agrees to pay the rent if Don does not. Then Don and Carmen agree to reduce the rent to $450 per month. Sam is not discharged even if he is an uncompensated surety, since the change in Don and Carmen's contract can only benefit Sam. Sam would be liable, of course, only for the lesser amount.
> 2 Instead of changing the monthly rental, Don and Carmen agree to extend the 2-year term by 1 hour. If Sam is an uncompensated surety, he is discharged because there is an increase, though a small one, in his potential liability for the rent. If Sam is a *compensated* surety, he will not be discharged as to the 2-year term unless the court holds that the 1-hour extension is material—a highly unlikely holding.
> 3 Don fails to pay the last 2 months' rent and also fails to pay the rent for the extra hour. If Sam is a compensated surety, he is liable for the last 2 months' rent, but not for the hour's rent resulting from the minor modification.

Another type of alteration occurs where debtor and creditor make a legally binding agreement to extend the time for payment of the debt. Such an agreement immediately and completely discharges an uncompensated surety who did not consent to it. However, a *compensated* unconsenting surety is discharged only to the extent that he or she is harmed by the extension. Dora borrows $5,000 from Calvin, Dora signs a promissory note to repay the amount plus 10 percent annual interest at the end of 6 months, and Sally guarantees Dora's note. Without Sally's consent Dora and Calvin then enter into a binding contract to extend the time of payment for 3 more months. If Sally is an uncompensated surety, she is immediately and completely discharged from liability.

Table 28.1 Examples of Surety's Defenses to Payment

S's Defenses to Surety-Creditor Contract	S's Defenses Derived from Debtor-Creditor Contract	Special Suretyship Defenses
S's lack of capacity	C's fraud against D	Performance of D's duty
No consideration to S	C's duress	C's release of D
C's fraud against S	No consideration from C	S's tender of performance
	But not, usually, D's infancy D's insanity D's bankruptcy D's other lack of capacity	Increase of gratuitous S's duty
		Material increase of compensated S's duty
		C's surrender or impairment of collateral

S = surety, D = debtor, C = creditor.

If Sally is a compensated surety, she is discharged only to the extent that she is harmed by the extension. Sally would be harmed if called upon to pay the additional 3 months' interest that Calvin and Dora agreed to without Sally's consent. Moreover, if Dora became insolvent during the 3-month extension, Sally (even if she were a compensated surety) would also be discharged from liability to Calvin for the principal amount, because Sally agreed to bear the risk of Dora's insolvency for only 6 months, not 9.

Ordinarily, a legally binding agreement between debtor and creditor to increase the interest rate on a debt discharges an unconsenting surety. An agreement to *lower* the interest rate does not discharge the surety, who remains liable for the lowered amount.

Table 28.1 summarizes the defenses of the surety. Case 28.3 discusses one of those defenses.

CASE 28.3 **Vastine v. Bank of Dallas** • 808 S.W.2d 463 (Tex. 1991)

FACTS Advanced Communications, Inc. (ACI), signed promissory notes to finance the construction of townhouses. ACI defaulted on a note personally guaranteed by defendant William Vastine. Bank of Dallas, ACI's creditor, foreclosed on the property that secured payment of the note, but the property was not valuable enough to cover the debt. Bank then sued Vastine for the $411,000 deficiency. The trial court granted Bank a summary judgment, Vastine appealed, and the court of appeals affirmed the trial court's decision. Vastine appealed to the Supreme Court of Texas.

OPINION PER CURIAM . . . Vastine contends that he is not liable under the guaranty because the terms of the loan agreement between the Bank and ACI were materially altered or deviated from without his consent. Specifically, Vastine alleges that the Bank allowed ACI and its shareholders to deviate from the loan agree-

CASE 28.3 Continued

ment by: 1) exceeding building specifications with construction of expensive extras, 2) misappropriating lumber for shareholders' personal use, [and] 3) constructing more than six townhouses at one time. . . . [W]e hold that Vastine has raised a material issue of fact regarding . . . his suretyship defense.

Texas courts apply the rule of strictissimi juris in interpreting guaranty agreements, to refrain from extending the guarantor's obligation by implication beyond the written terms of the agreement. . . . It is well settled in Texas that a guarantor may rely and insist upon the terms and conditions of the guaranty being strictly followed, and if the creditor and principal debtor vary in any material degree from the terms of their contract, then a new contract has been formed and the guarantor is not bound to it. . . . The guaranty agreement signed by Vastine does not provide that the creditor and principal debtor may alter the contract without Vastine's consent; thus we cannot imply that Vastine has waived his suretyship defense of material alteration.

Guarantors and sureties are bound only by the precise terms of [their contracts] and are not obligated to watch over the contracting parties to see that performance conforms to the terms of the contract. . . . In [Old Colony Insurance Company v. City of Quitman], this Court held that sureties are released from liability when there is a material alteration in, and deviation from, the terms of the contract without the surety's consent and to its prejudice. The same rule that applies to sureties applies to guarantors. . . .

Vastine alleged in the trial court that deviations from the underlying loan agreement were made without his consent and that the deviations prejudiced him by increasing the risk of nonperformance and by substituting a new contract that he had not guaranteed. The summary judgment proof supports Vastine's allegations. [Court's footnote: The . . . proof consists of . . . testimony showing that: 1) from the beginning of construction more than six townhouses were built at a time, 2) the bank approved $72,000 in expensive extras such as swimming pools and spiral staircases not included in the plans and specifications, and 3) lumber materials were misappropriated during construction.] Thus, he has shown that a material issue of fact exists [regarding] his suretyship defense of material alteration of contract.

JUDGMENT The judgment of the court of appeals directly conflicts with [relevant case law]. Therefore . . . this court grants application for writ of error, reverses the court of appeals, and remands to the trial court for trial on its merits.

Rights of Surety and Cosurety

Upon the default of the principal debtor, the surety becomes obligated to perform—for example, to pay the creditor—if there are no defenses the surety can assert. If required to perform, the surety has certain rights against the principal debtor. The surety may be entitled to exoneration, reimbursement, or subrogation, or to some combination of these. If there are cosureties, the surety who pays may be entitled, in addition, to "contribution" from the others.

Rights of Surety. **Exoneration** is the right of a surety to have a court of equity compel a capable but reluctant principal debtor to pay. The rationale for exoneration is that the surety should not have to suffer the inconvenience and expense of having to pay out of the surety's own assets and then sue the principal debtor when the debtor has sufficient resources. The surety might choose exoneration rather than a suit for reimbursement where, for example, the surety's assets are real estate whose liquidation to pay the debt would cause undue hardship to the surety.

Upon the default of the principal debtor, the surety might simply pay the creditor and then sue the debtor for **reimbursement** (repayment). In general, a surety who has an obligation to perform for the debtor is entitled to be reimbursed by the debtor, but only after the surety actually pays the debt.

Often the duty of reimbursement exists even though the principal debtor did not consent to the suretyship—for example, where the debtor is unjustly enriched by the surety's performance. The unconsenting debtor will be unjustly enriched where the debtor is bound to perform, has not performed, and has no defense. Dan signs a note for $5,000 payable to Clara, for the purchase of an antique rug. At Clara's request but without Dan's knowledge, Shirley guarantees Dan's note. Before Dan can insure the rug, a thief steals it from him. The note falls due, Dan cannot pay, and Clara receives payment from Shirley. Despite the theft, Dan still has a duty to pay Clara the $5,000. Shirley, by making payment for Dan upon his default, has enriched him by discharging his duty to Clara, and Shirley is entitled to reimbursement even though Dan did not consent to the suretyship.

Sometimes, however, the principal debtor has no duty to reimburse the surety. For example, if the debtor has a defense that is good against the creditor and the surety pays, the surety (having no legal compulsion to pay) is a mere volunteer and is not entitled to reimbursement. Cora fraudulently induces Dan to sign a note for $10,000. Then, without Dan's knowledge Sue guarantees his note. The note falls due, Dan does not pay, and Cora receives payment from Sue, who knew nothing of Cora's fraud. Sue is not entitled to reimbursement from Dan because he, as a result of his fraud defense, was under no obligation to pay and therefore could not have been enriched by Sue's payment. Her payment to Cora was simply unnecessary and cannot be charged to Dan. However, Sue may be able to recover her payment from Cora on the ground of Cora's unjust enrichment.

In a number of other situations the surety is not entitled to reimbursement from the principal debtor. For example, if the debtor has received a discharge in bankruptcy as to the creditor's claim, the discharge also bars the surety's claim for reimbursement. If the debtor were required to pay the surety despite the discharge in bankruptcy, the discharge would not protect the debtor as intended by the drafters of the bankruptcy law. Similarly, for the protection of persons who lack capacity to contract, a surety may not have reimbursement from a debtor whose obligation is void or has been avoided because of the debtor's lack of capacity.

A surety who satisfies the principal debtor's duty to the creditor acquires a right of **subrogation**—a right to be substituted for the creditor, or to take over the creditor's rights, as against the principal debtor. The creditor might hold stock or other property as collateral security for the debt. The surety, as subrogee, is entitled to the collateral. Or the creditor might have obtained a judgment against the debtor and received payment of the judgment amount from the surety instead of having to take collection action. The surety, as subrogee, is entitled to stand in the shoes of the creditor and enforce the judgment against the debtor.

Rights of Cosurety. A cosurety who performs the principal debtor's duty is entitled to **contribution** from the other cosureties. Dan defaults on his obligation to pay Candice $300,000 and there are three cosureties. If there was no agreement among the three as to how much each would be liable for upon Dan's default, the three must share the loss equally. If Simon, the first cosurety, is required to make full payment to Candice, Simon is entitled to a $100,000 contribution from each of the other two cosureties.

Suppose there are two cosureties. Simon agrees to be liable for $200,000 of Dan's debt, while Sheila agrees to be liable for $100,000. Then Dan pays $150,000 and defaults as to the other $150,000. Simon and Sheila must contribute in accordance with the proportion established by their agreements. Simon is responsible for two-thirds of the loss and Sheila for one-third. If Sheila must pay Candice the whole $150,000, Simon must contribute $100,000.

Suppose Dan owes Cora $60,000, and Sid, Sue, and Saul are equal cosureties. Dan is in default, and Cora releases Sid from liability. Sue and Saul are thereby discharged from liability as to the share of loss Sid would have had to absorb. Cora is entitled only to $40,000—$20,000 from Sue and $20,000 from Saul.

Like sureties, cosureties have rights of subrogation and exoneration. Cosureties are entitled to be subrogated to collateral held by the creditor, in proportion to the amount of their individual liabilities.

BOX 28.5
Suretyship and Business Planning

1. You are hiring a general contractor to construct the central headquarters for your well-drilling business. What risks concerning the contractor's performance do you face? What kind of security should you seek from the contractor?
2. Archer will be the electrical subcontractor on the construction job just described. What risks concerning the project does she face? What security is available to her?
3. Fidelity Corp. has been asked to provide security for this project. It wants to participate but is concerned about the amount of risk involved. How might Fidelity Corp. alleviate its concern?

SUMMARY

The purpose of a secured transaction is to reduce the creditor's risk of nonpayment. Some security devices give the creditor a lien on real or personal property as the backup source of payment. The lien may be imposed by law or it may be created by contract. In suretyship, the source of backup payment is the surety's promise to pay if the debtor does not.

The law imposes mechanics' and other types of liens on personal and real property in favor of persons who repair, store, improve, or otherwise render services in connection with the property. Liens created by contract include secured transactions in personal property, secured transactions in real estate such as mortgages and land contracts, and contracts of suretyship. Contractual security devices are used to secure repayment of a loan or the purchase price of property or services.

A surety is responsible for the debt, default, or miscarriage of the principal debtor. The surety is liable for precisely the performance, or any unperformed part of it, that the debtor promised the creditor—unless the surety agreed to be liable only for a lesser amount, or unless the surety has a defense to payment. The surety may have the benefit of the surety's own contractual defenses, some contractual defenses that are available to the debtor, and special suretyship defenses such as an alteration of the debtor's obligation not consented to by the surety. If the surety is called on to perform, the surety may be entitled to exoneration, reimbursement, or subrogation. A cosurety who pays more than his or her share of the debt may be entitled also to contribution from the other cosureties.

REVIEW QUESTIONS

1. What practical advantage is there to being a secured creditor rather than an unsecured one?

2. (a) Under what circumstances will a bailee of personal property be entitled to enforce a possessory lien? **(b)** How does a specific possessory lien differ from a general one?

3. Under what circumstances may a person enforce a mechanic's lien against real property?

4. How does a land contract function as a security device?

5. Illustrate how suretyship can arise by operation of law.

6. How does a gratuitous surety differ from a compensated one? Is there any difference in legal liability? Explain.

7. What is a cosurety?

8. In defense to a claim that a surety is liable to the creditor, the surety may assert the surety's own contractual defenses. Give an illustration of such a defense.

9. A surety may assert some of the principal debtor's defenses but not all of them. Which ones may the surety *not* have the benefit of? Why?

10. Explain the purpose and give two illustrations of special suretyship defenses.

11. What is exoneration, and where is it likely to be sought?

12. (a) Under what circumstances may a surety have reimbursement from the debtor? *Not* have reimbursement? (b) Illustrate subrogation and contribution.

CASE PROBLEMS

1. Smith had a house built by a contractor. The task of furnishing hardwood flooring and laying it in the building was subcontracted to a third person who purchased the flooring from Johnson. The subcontractor did not install it properly, and the Smiths' architect ordered it removed and other flooring laid in its place. Upon failure of the subcontractor to pay for the flooring, Johnson brought suit to foreclose a mechanic's lien he had acquired on the Smiths' house to secure payment. Smith contended that because the flooring ultimately was not used in his house, Johnson was not entitled to a lien on the house. Did Johnson have a valid lien?

2. Just before the beginning of the irrigation season Larry brings three portable irrigation pumps to Carl for cleaning and repair. Carl completes the work and presents Larry with a bill for $150, the reasonable value of Carl's services. Larry is short on cash and needs the pumps right away. Carl releases two of them to Larry but holds the third one as security for payment of his bill. Larry contends that by releasing the first two pumps, Carl has lost his possessory lien on the third one as well. Does Carl have a lien on the third pump? Explain.

3. Deborah Lalonde bought a new Chevrolet from Domingues Motors on credit. Domingues retained a security interest in the car and required additional security. Deborah's father, John A. Lalonde, signed a guaranty agreement. Domingues assigned Deborah's promissory note, the chattel mortgage, and the surety agreement "with recourse" to General Motors Acceptance Corporation (GMAC). About a year later Deborah filed for a discharge in bankruptcy, leaving over $9,000 of the debt unpaid. The trustee in bankruptcy sold Deborah's interest in the car to GMAC in full satisfaction of its claim against the debtor's estate. Since GMAC had recourse against Domingues, GMAC sold the car back to Domingues, which in turn sold it at private sale for $5,200. Domingues then sued John Lalonde, on the basis of his guaranty agreement, for the amount of the debt remaining unpaid. In defense, Lalonde alleged that Deborah's discharge in bankruptcy also discharged him as surety. He also raised as a defense a state statute requiring a mortgage creditor who provokes a sale of the mortgaged property to first have the property appraised. Is either of these defenses good?

4. Lloyd Corporation leased restaurant premises to Karafume Tempura, Ltd. O'Connor, a shareholder, director, and corporate secretary of the lessee, received thirty-five additional shares for signing a document guaranteeing payment of the rent. The lease provided that "no typical American food will be offered for sale in or from [the restaurant] at any time during the life of this lease." The restaurant's business was poor; Lloyd later agreed, through a modification of the lease, to permit the restaurant to serve American food in addition to Japanese-style food. O'Connor knew of the change. Eventually, the restaurant failed, and Lloyd sought unpaid rent from O'Connor. O'Connor refused to pay, contending that he was a gratuitous surety, that the change in the lease increased his risk, and that he had not consented to the change. Should O'Connor be held liable for the rent?

5. Venkataraman was one of five partners whose related corporation manufactured frozen pizza. The partners agreed to contribute additional capital and to guarantee loans for the corporation as needed. The partnership agreement required adjustment of a partner's share to reflect unequal contributions of capital. While the partners had equal shares in the partnership, they guaranteed a loan and eventually were called on to pay $80,950. Then all the partners except Venkataraman contributed substantial additional sums to the partnership. Later, when Venkataraman's ownership share had dropped to 2.4 percent, the partners guaranteed a second loan of $62,000 and were called on to pay it, too. Venkataraman's partners argued that each partner was liable for 20 percent of the $142,950. Venkataraman argued that he was liable for only 0.7 percent ($1,000.65), the amount that matched his ownership interest in 1989, when the partners paid the guaranty amount due. Whose position is correct—Venkataraman's or his partners'?

CHAPTER 29

Secured Transactions in Personal Property

As noted in the previous chapter, creditors often insist on a backup source of payment (collateral) to which they can resort if a debtor fails to pay. Personal property—consumer goods, accounts receivable, inventory, equipment, and so on—is the collateral for vast amounts of consumer and business credit. Because secured transactions in personal property are so important commercially, they are governed by a special body of law—Article 9 of the Uniform Commercial Code.

This chapter discusses issues of interest to creditors and debtors alike:

- How, under Article 9, may a seller or a lender acquire a security interest in personal property and make the interest enforceable against the claims of rival creditors?
- Who is entitled to the collateral (who has **priority**) when rival creditors claim it upon the debtor's default?
- What rights does a secured party have to dispose of the collateral if the debtor fails to pay? What are the debtor's rights?

PURPOSE AND COVERAGE OF UCC ARTICLE 9

Purpose of Article 9

An Article 9 secured transaction is a contract between a creditor and a debtor. The nature of such contracts and how Article 9 operates to enforce them can be better understood by a brief look at pre-Code security devices involving personal property.

Long ago when demand for credit was relatively small, the **pledge** was the main security device involving personal property. To obtain a loan, the debtor (pledgor) gave possession of the collateral to the creditor (pledgee). Today, one might pledge a stereo set to a pawnbroker or 100 shares of stock to a bank as collateral for a loan. The pledgee possesses the collateral until the loan is repaid. If the loan is not repaid when due, the pledgee can sell the collateral to cover the debt.

From the viewpoint of creditors, the pledge has some distinct advantages. First, the creditor in possession can easily safeguard the collateral and dispose of it upon the debtor's default. Second, since the debtor lacks possession, other creditors are not likely to rely on that item of collateral and overestimate the debtor's wealth when deciding whether to make their own loans. Thus, the total amount of loans tends to correspond with the value of available collateral.

However, a creditor's possessing the collateral deprives the debtor of its use. This was a considerable problem during the industrial revolution, because manufacturers, for example, needed to use equipment for production while paying for it. This need forced the invention of secured transactions that allowed debtors to do just that—to use collateral while repaying a loan it secured, or while paying for the collateral itself.

But how were creditors to be properly protected? If the collateral were in the hands of the debtor, it might depreciate or be damaged. Or other creditors might make loans without knowing of an earlier lender's claim to the collateral. This difficulty was overcome with the **public-notice filing system.** By filing a paper in the public records in the county courthouse, a creditor could give notice to rival creditors of his or her interest in collateral possessed by the debtor. Today, creditors routinely file financing statements in county or state offices to give notice of their interests in collateral, and they often check those same public records to determine whether proposed collateral is free from the claims of others.

Many pre-Code, nonpledge secured transactions are in common use today. Suppose, for example, that Paul owns a printing press and needs a loan for his printing business. To secure the loan, he may give Laura Lender a **chattel mortgage,** a document giving her a property interest in the press (the chattel) until Paul repays the loan. To warn potential rival creditors of her interest in the press, Laura will file a copy of the chattel mortgage in the proper county or state office. In the meantime, Paul has possession of the press and substantial ownership rights that he has not transferred to Laura. Upon repaying the loan, Paul regains full ownership of the press. If Paul does not repay, Laura can exercise her interest in the collateral by having it sold to cover the debt. The **conditional sale contract** is similar to the chattel mortgage. Under it, a buyer receives and uses goods as owner, but the seller-creditor retains a property interest in them until the buyer-debtor makes the payments.

In both the chattel mortgage and the conditional sale contract, the creditor's property interest often is called "title." **Title,** however, has two legal meanings that can be confusing. In the law of property, title usually means full ownership—the right to possess, use, enjoy, and dispose of a thing by selling it, giving it away, or destroying it. But in the law of secured transactions, the "title" that a creditor holds to secure payment of a debt is only a *security* interest, not full ownership. Like any other security interest, the creditor's "title" gives the creditor a *limited* right to control or dispose of (e.g., sell) the collateral—a right that can be exercised only upon the debtor's default, and then only as to the amount of the debt still owed.

The pre-Code law of secured transactions had many shortcomings that made credit extension expensive and risky. Article 9 helped correct these problems in four main ways:

1. By substituting the single term **security interest** for the variety of expressions used in the past to describe the property right that the creditor holds as security. A UCC security interest is "an interest in personal property or fixtures which secures payment or performance of an obligation." In a pledge, possession of the debtor's property by the creditor is the UCC security interest. In a chattel mortgage or a conditional sale contract, the "title" that the creditor retains is the security interest.
2. By substituting a simplified public-notice filing system for the confusing and expensive pre-Code jumble of different files, records, and indexes for each type of security device.
3. By replacing older, widely varying priority schemes with a single **system of priorities** for resolving disputes between rival creditors who claim the same collateral.
4. By making a **commercially reasonable disposition** the basis for liquidating collateral (converting it into cash) after default.

Table 29.1 Interests of Debtor and Creditor in Collateral

Security Device	Debtor's Interest	Creditor's Security Interest
Pledge	Title (basic ownership rights)	Possession
Chattel mortgage	Possession and other ownership rights	"Title" (the limited UCC variety)
Conditional sale contract	Possession and other ownership rights	"Title" (the limited UCC variety)

Table 29.1 illustrates the interests held by debtor and creditor in three common types of secured transactions.

Coverage of Article 9

Except for certain classes of excluded transactions,[1] Article 9 applies to:

1. Any transaction (regardless of its form) that is intended to create a security interest in *personal property* or *fixtures*. (Fixtures are goods that have been annexed to real estate and are considered a part of it.)
2. Any *sale* of accounts or chattel paper.

Personal property includes goods and any intangible personal property customarily used as commercial security—stocks, goodwill, trademarks, accounts receivable, rights to refunds, and the like.

Why does Article 9 (dealing mostly with personal property) apply to security interests in fixtures (treated as real estate)? The answer is that the real estate laws of the states vary greatly as to creditors' rights. If the security aspects of fixture transactions were governed by real estate law, fixture creditors who sell nationally would have to keep track of a bewildering array of rules. Article 9 reduces creditors' uncertainty by providing a single set of rules that govern their rights both before and after the fixture is annexed to the real estate.

Why does Article 9, which applies mainly to *credit* transactions, apply also to *sales* of accounts and chattel paper? The answer requires a look at the nature of chattel paper and accounts and how their owners typically use them to raise money.

Chattel paper is a writing evidencing (1) a debtor's obligation to pay for goods bought on credit and (2) the seller's security interest in those goods. You buy a home freezer from West Store on credit, signing a promissory note for the purchase price and a conditional sale contract giving West a security interest in the freezer. Together these two documents constitute chattel paper. An **account** (often called an "account receivable") is any right to payment for goods or services that is *not* evidenced by an instrument (e.g., a promissory note) or chattel paper. A charge account at West Store is an example. If you buy a camera at West's and simply "charge it," West is an unsecured creditor as to the resulting account.

The chattel paper (or the account) is a property right owned by West that it can either sell outright or pledge as collateral for a loan. The problem is that these transactions—the sale and the pledge—look deceptively similar, since in both West would hand over possession of the chattel paper and receive money. Consequently, third persons such as West's potential new

---

[1] Twelve kinds of transactions are excluded from UCC Article 9 coverage [9-104]. For example, assignments of wages as security for debts are excluded because, the Code drafters thought, such assignments present important social problems whose solution should be a matter of local regulation. The use of life insurance as collateral and the creation and enforcement of mechanics' liens are excluded because they are covered by non-Code law.

Table 29.2 Secured Transactions Key Terms

Chattel paper: Document or documents evidencing (1) buyer-debtor's obligation to pay for goods and (2) seller-creditor's security interest in them.

Account: Any right to payment (for goods or services) not evidenced by an instrument or chattel paper. An account receivable.

Security interest: Any interest in personal property or fixtures that secures payment or performance of an obligation. An example is possession in a pledge or "title" in a chattel mortgage.

Security lease: Lease intended for security. It is so intended where the lessee has the right, for a nominal or no additional consideration, to become owner of the property when the lease expires.

---

lenders may be unable to tell whether West still owns the paper. To give those third persons a way to determine who owns it, Article 9 requires a *buyer* of West's chattel paper (or accounts) to inform the public of the purchase—for example, by filing a financing statement in the appropriate public records.

Article 9 also applies to transactions usually not thought of as secured transactions, *if* their purpose is to secure payment of an obligation. For example, to protect themselves from the claims of buyers' creditors, sellers often disguise sales of goods as "leases." In a **true lease** covered by UCC Article 2A (e.g., lease of a computer), the lessor retains title (ownership) and grants possession and usage rights to the lessee. The lessor intends to remain the owner. In a **security "lease"** covered by Article 9, however, the intention of the "lessor" is not to remain the owner, but to sell the goods and reserve a right to retrieve them if payment is not made. Since the "lease" is intended to secure payment of an obligation, the seller must follow the rules of Article 9 to prevail over other creditors of the buyer-"lessee."

How can one tell a security "lease" from a true lease? A lease is one intended for *security* if the parties agree that at the expiration of the lease the lessee shall become the owner of the property for no additional consideration or for only a nominal (insignificant) consideration [1-201(37)].

Table 29.2 lists some key terms relating to secured transactions.

ACQUIRING AND PERFECTING A SECURITY INTEREST

How does a creditor **(secured party)** acquire a security interest and make it effective against others? The creditor does so by (1) contracting for it with the debtor and (2) taking whatever additional steps the law requires to make the resulting security interest good against third persons. Article 9 speaks in terms of attachment and perfection. **Attachment** is the process of creating (agreeing to) a security interest and making it enforceable against the *debtor*. Without a security agreement, there can be no security interest in the property claimed as collateral. **Perfection** is the process of making the security interest enforceable against *third persons* who may try to claim the collateral for themselves. Often, creditors perfect their security interests by filing a financing statement in the public records as notice to rivals, but there are other methods.

Attachment of a Security Interest

Attachment Events. A security interest does not "attach" (arise), and therefore is not enforceable against the debtor, unless four **attachment events** occur:

1. The debtor and the creditor must make a **security agreement**—that is, must agree that a security interest is to be created [9-203].
2. The creditor must possess the collateral *or* the debtor must sign a security agreement that "reasonably identifies" the collateral [9-203; 9-110].
3. The secured party must give value. Otherwise there will be no debtor's obligation to be secured. The secured party usually gives value by making a loan, by selling goods on credit, or by making a binding commitment to extend credit.
4. The debtor must have rights in the collateral. Under the terms of the security agreement,

some or all of the debtor's rights are held by the secured party as the security interest.

The attachment events may occur in any order. Attachment cannot occur earlier than the completion of the last event, but the parties to the security agreement can postpone the time of attachment.

> **BOX 29.1**
>
> **You Be the Judge**
>
> Dr. X, a dentist, fitted Elvin with a set of false teeth. Despite many attempts by Dr. X to collect the $865 fee for the dentures, Elvin never paid. When Elvin returned to the dentist's office to have the dentures adjusted, Dr. X's assistant removed them, but, under Dr. X's instructions, refused to return them until Elvin paid the amount due. Elvin sued Dr. X for damages, alleging that Dr. X had wrongfully taken the teeth. Should Elvin win the lawsuit? Consider what is required for Dr. X to have a legal right to repossess the teeth. ∎

Attachment Involving After-Acquired Property Clauses and Future Advances Provisions. Creditors commonly include an **after-acquired property clause** in commercial secured transactions.[2] For example, a bank lends you $25,000 to expand your business and takes a security interest in all your business assets and in "any business assets [you] may hereafter acquire." By using such a clause, the bank obtains a security interest in both your present and your future assets, and is not limited to the specific assets you had on hand at the creation of the secured transaction. The after-acquired property is subject to the security interest as soon as you acquire rights in the property. Such a security interest is called a **floating lien.** The floating lien is especially useful in inventory and accounts receivable financing because only one security agreement is needed to create a security interest in a shifting mass of collateral.

The Code also permits the use of a **future advances** provision in the security agreement, so that the collateral put up by the debtor can secure future loans. Thus, without having to enter into a new security agreement for each new loan, the creditor safely and automatically gives value each time he or she extends new credit. Future advances provisions are especially useful where a creditor has agreed to make a large loan but the debtor needs the money only a bit at a time.

Table 29.3 lists some key terms relating to attachment.

> **BOX 29.2**
>
> **Contents of a Security Agreement**
>
> In addition to a description of the collateral, a security agreement usually includes the following:
>
> - Statement that the creditor has a security interest in the described collateral
> - Description of the loan or other value given by the creditor
> - Debtor's promise to maintain the collateral in good condition
> - Debtor's promise to insure the collateral
> - Debtor's promise not to sell the collateral to someone else or otherwise impair the creditor's security without the creditor's prior written consent
> - Statement that the debtor must provide additional collateral if the original collateral declines in value
> - List of events that constitute "default": debtor's failure to repay the debt or any installment, death of the debtor, failure of the debtor's business, and so on
> - Debtor's promise to deliver the collateral to the creditor upon debtor's default in paying the debt
> - Statement of creditor's right to repossess the collateral upon debtor's default ∎

Perfection of a Security Interest

Making a security agreement usually is not sufficient, by itself, to protect the secured party fully. For the secured party to receive maximum pro-

---

[2] Section 9-204 sharply limits the use of such clauses when the collateral is consumer goods.

> **Table 29.3 Key Terms Relating to Attachment**
>
> **Attachment:** Process by which debtor and creditor create a security interest and make it enforceable as between themselves. Involves four **attachment events.**
>
> **Security agreement:** An agreement between debtor and creditor that creates or provides for a security interest.
>
> **Secured party:** A creditor who receives a security interest.
>
> **After-acquired property clause:** A clause in a security agreement granting the creditor a security interest in any property the debtor now owns or may later acquire.
>
> **Floating lien:** A security interest, created by an after-acquired property clause, in a changing mass of collateral.
>
> **Future advances provision:** A clause in a security agreement permitting the collateral to secure future loans.

tection from rivals who might claim the collateral, the security interest must also be *perfected*. Ordinarily, these rivals will be:

- Other creditors of the debtor (as where several different banks might have lent the debtor money to begin a business)
- A buyer of the collateral from the debtor (as where the debtor sells encumbered inventory to customers)
- A mechanic or other artisan who has repaired or improved the collateral

Timely perfection of a security interest gives the secured party **priority** (first claim to the collateral) over most, but not all, of these competing claimants.

Methods of Perfection. Perfection may be accomplished in three ways: (1) automatically at the completion of the attachment events, (2) by the secured party's taking possession of the collateral, or (3) by the filing of a financing statement in the public records. Table 29.5 indicates which types of perfection may or must be used for particular types of collateral. A general discussion of perfection follows. A few specialized perfection rules are introduced later, in the section on priorities.

Perfection by attachment only. Article 9 grants the status of perfection to a few security interests, at least temporarily, even though nothing more than attachment has occurred. For example, credit sales of **consumer goods** are so numerous that requiring sellers to file a financing statement for each sale (or to retain possession of the goods until they are paid for) would impose an unreasonable burden on sellers and buyers. Therefore, under Article 9, a seller automatically and permanently perfects a **purchase-money security interest (PMSI)** in most consumer goods merely by completing the attachment events and thus has priority over rival creditors.[3]

Motor vehicles and fixtures often are consumer goods, but attachment-only perfection usually is *not* available for them. Filing a financing statement (or compliance with a certificate of title statute) is required to perfect a security interest in a motor vehicle that must be registered; and in many states boats, trailers, and mobile homes also are subject to such a requirement [9-302]. Moreover, in many states, filing financing statements on motor vehicles and the like must be done in a special *place*—in the records of title to motor vehicles, not in the usual personal property records (discussed later). A fixture filing (also discussed later) is required for perfecting a security interest in a fixture.

Perfection by secured party's having possession. For most types of collateral, a security interest is

---

[3] A purchase-money security interest is one taken or retained by a seller of the collateral—or, sometimes, one taken by a bank or other lender—to secure all or part of the purchase price [9-107].

perfected if the secured party possesses the collateral or if a third-person bailee possesses it on behalf of the secured party. The pledge (discussed earlier) and field warehousing involve perfection by possession. In **field warehousing,** inventory used as collateral is segregated in a fenced-off area of the borrower's—for example, a manufacturer's—premises and placed under the control of an independent warehouser who acts on behalf of the lender. As the debtor sells the inventory being used as collateral, the field warehouser releases the needed amounts and makes sure that the creditor-lender receives payment from the proceeds of the sale.

Usually possession is an alternative to filing, but for some collateral, possession is the required perfection method. For instance, because the public expects the possessor of money to own it, a security interest in money can be perfected only by the secured party's taking possession [9-304]. A similar rule applies to instruments (writings) such as checks.

Perfection by filing a financing statement. Security interests in most kinds of property may be perfected by filing a **financing statement** in the public records. The financing statement gives notice to the public that the secured party claims a security interest in the collateral. Public-notice filing allows debtors such as purchasers of business equipment to use the collateral while paying for it. Filing has other advantages: (1) sellers give notice of their security interests quickly and easily by filing in only one or two places, and (2) persons planning to buy expensive goods or to accept them as collateral for a loan can easily check the public records to determine whether the goods are encumbered. For some classes of collateral, such as accounts and general intangibles, filing is the required method of perfection because the property cannot be physically possessed by the secured party.

To be legally effective as a notice to the secured party's rival creditors, a financing statement must include at least the following information:

- The signature of the debtor
- The names and addresses of the debtor and the secured party
- A description of the item (such as "one Buick auto, serial #17") *or* a statement of the type of collateral (such as "all of the men's clothing at Holiday Clothiers, 44 State Street, Your City")

Where the collateral is closely identified with a particular parcel of land (e.g., crops, timber, minerals, fixtures), the financing statement must also contain a description of the land concerned [9-402(1)]. Figure 29.1 illustrates a typical financing statement form.

The amount of information required in the financing statement has been kept to a minimum because the reason for filing it is merely to give notice that the secured party may have a security interest in the collateral described. Potential rivals of the secured party, being able to see the financing statement in the public records, are expected to make further inquiry to determine the exact state of affairs between the secured party and the debtor.

The financing statement is not to be confused with the security agreement. A security agreement creates the security interest. It is part of the attachment process and does not, by itself, make the security interest enforceable against anyone other than the debtor. In contrast, the financing statement, when filed in the public records as part of the perfection process, gives third persons notice of the secured party's claim to the collateral. However, if a security agreement is in writing, contains the minimum information required for a financing statement, and is signed by the debtor, the security agreement itself may serve as a financing statement (i.e., may be filed), as may a *signed copy* of the security agreement.

The proper place to file a financing statement can be determined only by reference to the relevant state's version of Section 9-401. A state's filing system may be "central" (e.g., one main office located in the state capital) or "local" (e.g., offices located in each township or county). Usually the filing system is some combination of central and local files. Thus, users of the filing system who normally need to acquire credit information on a statewide basis can do so efficiently, while credit information about purely

Figure 29.1 Financing statement form.

Table 29.4 Key Terms Relating to Perfection

Financing statement: A brief notice, intended to be filed in the public records, of the secured party's claim to the collateral described in the statement.

Perfection: The process by which the secured party makes a security interest enforceable against rivals such as debtor's other creditors. Ordinarily accomplished by creditor's filing a financing statement or taking possession of the collateral. In some situations, Article 9 grants an attachment-only perfection status.

Purchase-money security interest: A security interest held by a seller of goods (or, sometimes, by a bank or other lender) to secure the purchase price.

Fixture filing: A financing statement covering goods that are or will be fixtures. Document must describe the fixture and the real estate involved and must state that the document is to be filed in the real estate records.

---

local businesses can normally be found in the county or township where the debtor resides or, sometimes, where the goods are located. (As noted earlier, many states require that financing statements covering motor vehicles and the like be filed in special records maintained for motor vehicles, and not in the usual personal property records.)

If goods are or are to become fixtures, a **fixture filing** is required, and the proper filing place is the office where a mortgage on the real estate concerned would be filed or recorded. The fixture filing must describe the fixture, must describe the real estate to which the fixture is to be annexed, and must say that the fixture filing document is to be filed in the real estate records.

Table 29.4 lists some key terms relating to perfection.

Case 29.1 discusses what constitutes a security agreement, and whether a failure to perfect a security interest affects the validity of the interest as between debtor and creditor.

CASE 29.1 **Lojek v. Pedler** • 42 UCC Rep. 1448 (Ohio 1986)

FACTS Lojek (plaintiff) owned several corporations that were in financial difficulty. To salvage them, Lojek and Pedler set up a plan of reorganization. During the financial dealings, Lojek agreed to lend Pedler $300,000, with which Pedler was to buy 3,000 shares of stock in a corporation formed to carry out the reorganization. Under the terms of a "Trust Agreement" signed by Lojek and Pedler, Pedler would pledge the shares as collateral for the amount he owed Lojek, and Rondy would hold the shares until the debt was repaid. The Agreement also provided that:

> In the event of the death of [Pedler] prior to the delivery of said shares to TRUSTEE [Rondy], then said stock certificates shall be immediately the property of [Lojek], in full satisfaction of said note.

Lojek paid Pedler $300,000 and Pedler received the stock, but Pedler died before delivering the shares to Rondy. Lojek demanded the stock from Pedler's estate (defendant). The executor refused Lojek's demand. Lojek brought suit, seeking a declaratory judgment to determine ownership of the shares. From a

> **CASE 29.1 Continued**
>
> judgment for Lojek, Pedler's estate appealed. The court of appeals reversed the judgment of the trial court, and Lojek appealed.
>
> **OPINION** BROWN, J. . . . The court of appeals held that, rather than creating a trust, "the parties intended to pledge the shares to secure Pedler's debt to Lojek." We agree. We also agree that "[s]ince the shares were never delivered either to Lojek or to Rondy as Lojek's agent, the security interest was not perfected pursuant to [§ 9-304]. However, the court of appeals erred in its conclusion that Lojek lost all rights granted by the Agreement because of his failure to perfect his security interest. . . .
>
> [Sec. 9-105(1)(l)] defines "security agreement" as "an agreement which creates or provides for a security interest." The Agreement in this case refers to Lojek's security interest as a "present assignment" of the stock "pursuant to a pledge of said stock" as collateral for Lojek's loan to Pedler. Thus, the Agreement in this case clearly meets that statutory definition. Further, the security interest attached to the collateral as provided by [§ 9-203]: (1) the debtor signed a security agreement which contained a description of the collateral (the Agreement); (2) value was given (Lojek's transfer of $300,000 to Pedler); and (3) Pedler, the debtor, had rights in the collateral. . . .
>
> The parties agree that Lojek failed to perfect his security interest in the stock according to the terms of [§ 9-304]. To so perfect his security interest, either Lojek or Rondy on Lojek's behalf would have had to take physical possession of the shares. By the terms of the Agreement, the parties intended that Pedler would deliver physical possession of the shares to Rondy who would act as Lojek's agent for purposes of perfection. However, ". . . a security agreement is effective according to its terms between the parties, . . ." [§ 9-201]. Therefore, as between Lojek and Pedler (and, by extension, Pedler's estate), . . . the terms of the Agreement governed Lojek's rights in the collateral.
>
> The Agreement contemplated the very situation which eventually occurred: "In the event of the death of . . . [Pedler] prior to the delivery of said shares to . . . [Rondy], then said stock certificates shall be immediately the property of . . . [Lojek], in full satisfaction of the note." Thus, for purposes of the Agreement, Pedler's death became a default-like event which triggered Lojek's legal right to take immediate possession of the collateral. . . .
>
> **JUDGMENT** Accordingly, we hereby reverse the judgment of the court of appeals, and enter final judgment in favor of plaintiff Lojek. . . .

Grace Periods. Frequently, practical business needs require that a secured party have extra time, called a **grace period,** to file or otherwise perfect a security interest. Article 9 provides such grace periods by giving some secured parties the benefit of a temporary attachment-only perfection status.

Suppose First Bank has a field warehousing arrangement with Martha Manufacturer and Martha receives an order for warehoused goods to be specially processed by her and shipped immediately to the buyer. Normally, a secured party who perfects by taking possession of the collateral (or, like First Bank, has a field warehouser do so) *loses* perfected status by giving possession of the collateral to the debtor. However, where, as here, collateral must be released to the debtor for storage, further processing, shipping, or similar routine business purposes, the secured party's security interest *remains* perfected for up to 21 days without filing [9-304(5)]. This rule causes the least disruption of ordinary business activities, minimizes filing fees for the secured party, and eases the burden of paperwork for the filing system. If the secured party needs a longer period of perfection, he or she must, before the 21 days expires, either file a financing statement or take possession of the collateral.

Likewise, a security interest in the **proceeds** of a debtor's disposition of collateral remains perfected for a short time. Suppose Sue sells Dora a lathe on credit and files a financing statement. If Dora sells the lathe to Terri, Sue's security interest in the lathe *continues for 10 days* in any identifiable cash or noncash proceeds of Dora's sale [9-306]. After that time Sue's security interest becomes "unperfected" unless Sue, within the 10 days, makes a special filing with respect to the proceeds or takes possession of them.

Sellers often retain purchase-money security interests (PMSIs) in **fixtures** or **collateral other than inventory** (e.g., business equipment such as a copier). Such sellers have 10 days after the fixture is annexed or the equipment is delivered to the debtor to perfect their PMSIs by filing a financing statement [9-313(4); 9-312(4)]. In the meantime their PMSIs are perfected by attachment only. Thus, suppliers may safely make early delivery and do the paperwork later.

Table 29.5 summarizes the methods of perfecting security interests.

PRIORITIES AMONG CONFLICTING INTERESTS

Sometimes collateral is not valuable enough to satisfy the claims of all creditors who have a security interest in it. Dan wants to open a hardware store. To finance the business, he gets a $50,000 start-up loan in January from First Bank. Dan's security agreement with First Bank has an after-acquired property clause granting First Bank a security interest in "all business assets that Dan presently owns and in any that he may hereafter acquire." In February Dan gets $20,000 additional start-up financing from Second Bank. Dan's security agreement with Second Bank also has an after-acquired property clause. In March, Dan buys a $3,000 computerized cash register on credit from Computocash, and $10,000 worth of inventory on credit from Hardware Suppliers. Then, in late March, Dan's business fails. First Bank immediately claims all Dan's business assets, which now consist of the unpaid-for cash register, the $10,000 worth of inventory bought on credit from Hardware Suppliers, and $5,000 worth of shelving and other business equipment. Second Bank claims the same assets; Computocash claims the cash register; and Hardware Suppliers claims the inventory that it sold to Dan on credit. Who gets the collateral?

The priorities provisions of Article 9 settle the dispute. Most conflicts over the collateral fall into one of the five categories discussed below.

Priorities among Conflicting Security Interests in the Same Collateral

Where two or more secured parties claim the same collateral, which one will prevail depends on a number of factors. Two are of special importance:

1 The *nature of the conflicting security interests*. Is one a purchase-money security interest (PMSI), or are all of them of the same kind?
2 If one of the conflicting security interests is a PMSI, *what kind of collateral* is involved?

Priorities among Security Interests: General Rule. The general Code rule is that (1) conflicting security interests rank according to priority in time of filing or other perfection, and (2) if the conflicting security interests are unperfected, the first to attach has priority [9-312(5)]. Ron owns an antique chest worth $5,000. Then he gets a $5,000 loan from Cora, who plans to take possession of the chest next week as security for the loan. In the meantime Ron gets an-

Table 29.5 Methods of Perfecting Security Interests

Type of Collateral	Where Defined	Perfection Method	Where Indicated
Account (receivable) Example: A buys goods or services, promising to pay later. The promise is an account if not evidenced by an instrument or chattel paper.	9-106	Filing required, but casual or isolated assignments need not be filed. See Section 9-104(f) for assignments not subject to rules of Article 9.	9-302(1)(e), (g)
Chattel paper Example: A buys goods from B and signs a promissory note and security agreement. The note and agreement constitute chattel paper.	9-105(1)(b)	Filing or possession by secured party.	9-304(1); 9-305
Document (of title) Examples: warehouse receipts, bills of lading, dock warrants. May be negotiable or nonnegotiable.	1-201(15), (45) 7-201(2) 9-105(1)(f)	Filing or possession for negotiable documents; 21-day perfection status is available. For nonnegotiable documents, other rules apply.	9-304(1) 9-304(5) 9-304(4), (5)
Instrument Examples: checks, drafts, notes, whether or not negotiable; investment securities (stocks and bonds).	9-105(1)(i)	Possession only, except where temporary perfection status is granted.	9-304(1), (4), (5)
General intangibles Examples: patents, copyrights, liquor licenses in some states.	9-106	Filing only.	9-302(1)
Goods	9-105(1)(h)	In general, filing or possession; 21-day perfection status is available.	9-302(1)(a); 9-305 9-304(5)
Consumer goods	9-109(1)	Usually attachment is sufficient for purchase money security interests in consumer goods. Filing or compliance with a certificate of title statute is required for motor vehicles, boats, trailers, and the like. For other security interests in consumer goods, general rules apply.	9-302(1)(d) 9-302(3) 9-302(4); 9-305
Equipment	9-109(2)	Filing, usually.	9-302(1)(a); 9-305
Farm products	9-109(3)	Filing.	By implication from 9-109(3)
Inventory	9-109(4)	Filing, usually.	9-302(1)(a)

other $5,000 loan from First Bank, which takes and files a security interest in the chest before Cora takes possession of it. Since First Bank perfected its security interest first, First Bank is entitled to the chest upon Ron's default. If Cora and First Bank both fail to perfect their security interests, Cora will prevail because her interest attached first.

Priority of Purchase-Money Security Interests. The after-acquired property clause so often put into security agreements by commercial lenders can cause serious difficulty for suppliers who sell goods to debtors on credit. Third Bank makes a start-up loan to New Corp., includes an after-acquired property clause in the security agreement, and files a financing statement. Then Northside Business Machines sells New Corp. a cash register on credit and retains a purchase-money security interest (PMSI). According to Third Bank's security agreement, the cash register, being after-acquired property, would now be subject to Third Bank's security interest. To protect suppliers and thus to encourage them to extend credit, Article 9 gives priority to the supplier's PMSI *if it is properly perfected.* If Northside does not comply exactly with the PMSI perfection requirements (discussed later), Third Bank has priority.

Recall that a PMSI arises where a *seller* of goods retains a security interest in them to secure their purchase price. But others than sellers can also have a PMSI. Second Bank lends you money for new office furniture and files a financing statement covering the furniture you bought. Though Second Bank is not the seller, it has a PMSI in the furniture because Bank advanced you the purchase price [9-107]. Note, however, that Bank would *not* have a PMSI (and would not have the resulting priority over other creditors) if you had used the loaned money for some other purpose such as buying a sports car. A *nonseller* who advances money to enable the debtor to purchase the collateral gets a purchase-money security interest only "if such value is in fact so used."

Special rules for perfecting PMSIs are found throughout Article 9. These rules—of major importance in commercial financing—vary according to whether the PMSI is in consumer goods, inventory, collateral other than inventory, or fixtures:

1 **Consumer goods.** The PMSI is perfected (and the credit seller gets priority over the buyer's other creditors) as soon as the PMSI *attaches*.
2 **Collateral other than inventory.** An example is equipment for a retail store or a machine for a factory. The PMSI must be perfected by filing no later than 10 days after the debtor *receives possession* of the collateral (20 days in some states).
3 **Inventory.** The purchase-money secured party (supplier or lender) must do *two* things *before* the debtor receives possession of the inventory: One, the secured party must perfect the PMSI by filing a financing statement, and two, the secured party must give written notice to record holders of conflicting security interests in the inventory (such as a bank with an after-acquired property clause) that the purchase-money secured party "expects to acquire a purchase-money security interest in inventory of the debtor" [9-312(3)].

Suppose Fifth Bank, under the future-advances provision of a filed loan agreement, grants Doris loans for the purchase of inventory. If Doris is fraudulent or careless, she might keep the money she borrowed from the bank for inventory and purchase the inventory on credit, granting to her inventory seller a PMSI in the inventory. The requirement that the seller give advance notice to Fifth Bank enables it to police Doris's inventory-purchasing activities and thus to avoid possible loss. And the seller, by complying with the Code requirements, gets protection from previously filed security interests and will therefore be more willing to extend credit.

4 **Fixtures.** The requirements for perfecting a PMSI in a fixture are discussed later under Priorities of Security Interests in Fixtures.

Case 29.2 discusses whether a PMSI in business equipment has priority over a bank's earlier perfected security interest.

CASE 29.2 NBD-Sandusky Bank v. Ritter • 471 N.W.2d 340 (Mich. 1991)

FACTS To secure a farm loan, Sam and Emily Ritter gave plaintiff NBD-Sandusky Bank (NBD) a security interest in their farm equipment. The security agreement contained an after-acquired property clause covering any farm equipment the Ritters might purchase in the future. NBD filed a financing statement on May 30, 1985.

On July 23, 1985, Mr. Ritter took delivery of a used John Deere Model 6600 Diesel Combine and other equipment bought on credit from Laethem Farm Service Company, to be financed by John Deere. On July 31, Ritter signed a loan contract and security agreement giving John Deere a security interest in the equipment. He also signed a financing statement. The contract stated that he was applying to John Deere for the loan, and would repay the amount "if this Loan Contract is accepted by Lender." Later that day, Laethem took an immediate credit on its account with John Deere for the portion of the purchase price that John Deere was to finance. Laethem then mailed the documents to John Deere. On August 7, John Deere filed the financing statement. On August 15, a representative of John Deere signed the loan contract and security agreement.

Later, the Ritters defaulted on their obligations to NBD. NBD sued the Ritters, Laethem, and John Deere, alleging that NBD's perfected security interest in the equipment had priority over all competing claims. From a judgment for NBD, John Deere appealed. The court of appeals affirmed the trial court's decision, and John Deere appealed to the Michigan Supreme Court.

OPINION BOYLE, J. . . . This is a priority dispute between two commercial lenders, each holding a perfected security interest in the same collateral. Appellant John Deere claims priority as a purchase money lender, and NBD claims priority under its "after-acquired property" clause. . . .

. . . John Deere's security interest falls within the statutory definition of a purchase money security interest since it was "taken by a person who by making advances or incurring an obligation gives value to enable the debtor to acquire rights in or the use of collateral if such value is in fact so used." . . .

[Section 9-312(5)] provides:

> A purchase money security interest in collateral other than inventory has priority over a conflicting security interest in the same collateral or its proceeds if the purchase money security interest is perfected at the time the debtor receives possession of the collateral or within 20 days thereafter.

Thus, the central issue here is whether John Deere complied with the Uniform Commercial Code's requirements so as to allow it to enjoy special priority status over competing claimants. The code focuses on two critical dates: when the debtor received possession of the collateral and when John Deere's purchase money security interest was perfected. . . .

It is uncontested that Mr. Ritter received physical possession of the farm equipment on July 23, 1985. Thus, we turn to the date John Deere perfected its purchase money security interest in the subject equipment. [For John Deere to have priority,] the security interest [must have "attached" and John Deere must have taken] all the applicable steps for "perfection" [by August 12]. The se-

**CASE 29.2
Continued**

quence of events is not determinative. [Section 9-303(1)] specifically provides [that] "if [perfection] steps . . . are taken before the security interest attaches, [the security interest] is perfected at the time when it attaches."

John Deere [took the required perfection steps] by filing [its] financing statement . . . on August 7, 1985. . . . The filing was made fifteen days after the debtor took physical possession of the collateral. [But since the filing may have preceded attachment, we must] further narrow our inquiry to the date John Deere's purchase money security interest attached. [Did it attach before the 20 days expired?]

. . . In this case, John Deere (the secured party) did not have possession of the collateral. Therefore, [for its security interest to "attach,"] John Deere was required to: (1) enter into a "security agreement" with the debtor, (2) reduce the agreement to a writing signed by the debtor and containing a description of the collateral, and (3) give value, and the debtor was required to (4) have rights in the collateral. . . . As soon as all these events took place, attachment occurred. . . .

The Court of Appeals focused on the language of the parties' loan contract and security agreement and held that the "agreement" and "value" elements of "attachment" were not satisfied until August 15, 1985, the date the document was [signed by John Deere]. In reaching its conclusion, the Court rejected John Deere's argument that the loan contract . . . was accepted [earlier] by performance, finding that the claim was unsupported by the evidence presented at trial. . . .

John Deere does not dispute that the loan contract and security agreement was conditioned upon [John Deere's] acceptance. It argues, however, that the document did not specify the method of acceptance and that [John Deere] accepted by performance earlier than the August 15, 1985, signature date. It argues that the Court of Appeals erred when it stated this claim was not supported by the evidence presented at trial. We agree.

[Section 9-105(1)(1)] defines a security agreement as: "an agreement which creates or provides for a security interest." . . . "'Agreement' means the bargain of the parties in fact as found in their language or by implication from other circumstances including course of dealing . . . or course of performance. . . ."

We have considered the parties' written security agreement and the course of performance and course of dealing testimony presented at trial, and find the parties' "bargain in fact" was that John Deere could accept [the loan application] by performance and that it did so earlier than the August 15 . . . signature date on the loan contract and security agreement.

First, we underscore that the loan contract . . . does not specify . . . that it may . . . be accepted [only] by John Deere's signature on the document. Second, we find convincing the uncontroverted testimony presented at trial . . . that it is John Deere's practice to accept a security agreement [before] the financing statement is filed. John Deere filed its financing statement on August 7. . . . Thus, we conclude that John Deere . . . "accepted" the loan contract and security agreement and satisfied the "agreement" element of attachment as of August 7. . . .

The record also indicates that on July 31, 1985, John Deere authorized Laethem to take an immediate credit on its account with John Deere. This is ad-

**CASE 29.2
Continued**

ditional evidence of John Deere's acceptance of the agreement by performance. It is also . . . evidence that John Deere "gave value." . . . [A] party gives "value" when it gives "a binding commitment to extend credit" or it gives "any consideration sufficient to support a simple contract." . . . Thus, we agree with Judge MacKenzie's conclusion in her dissenting opinion in the Court of Appeals that

> . . . immediately after Ritter signed the contract . . . Laethem received a . . . credit from John Deere and thus received its money. . . . [T]his transaction constitutes the giving of value by John Deere. . . .

The language of the relevant provisions of the Uniform Commercial Code . . . compels the conclusion that John Deere gave value on July 31 . . . and accepted the loan contract and security agreement at least by August 7. . . . Thus the "value" and "agreement" elements necessary for attachment were satisfied by August 7, 1985. Consequently, John Deere's purchase money security interest both attached and was perfected by that date.

JUDGMENT

Since John Deere perfected its purchase money security interest within twenty days from the date the debtor received the collateral, . . . its purchase money security interest should be given priority over all competing claims. We reverse the decision of the Court of Appeals and remand the case to the trial court for entry of judgment in favor of John Deere.

BOX 29.3

Article 9 and Business Planning

You have just opened your new company, Office Sales, Inc., and plan to sell bookcases, storage cabinets, and office equipment to customers throughout the state. Credit sales will account for about 50 percent of your business. To protect yourself from the claims of your customers' other creditors, you expect to retain a security interest in most of the items sold on credit. What forms and procedures will be involved? Consider the following typical credit transactions:

- Delivery of 15 desks to Desk Sales, Inc., which will resell them to businesses in the greater metropolitan area
- A specially designed floor-to-ceiling bookcase to be installed in the home of a newly licensed CPA
- An expensive color copier sold to Desktop Publishing for use in its business

Priority between a Security Interest and the Interest of a Third-Person Purchaser

Sometimes the conflict is between the secured party and a purchaser of the collateral from the debtor. A **buyer in ordinary course of business** (one who in good faith buys goods from a dealer) takes the goods *free of* a security interest created by the seller in favor of the seller's creditor. This is true even though the security interest is perfected and even though the buyer knows of its existence [9-307(1)]. This rule applies primarily where a dealer has granted to his or her lender a security interest in inventory and then makes sales from the inventory. The rule is intended to encourage buyers to pay full market value by minimizing their fear of loss at the hands of unseen creditors. To be protected, however, a buyer must act in good faith. If the buyer knows that the seller is *violating* the terms of the security agreement, the buyer lacks good faith and takes the goods subject to the security interest of the seller's creditor. Most good faith purchasers of other collateral such as chattel paper and negotiable instruments receive similar protection.

A dealer in **consumer goods** faces a serious problem when a consumer purchases the goods on credit and resells them to another consumer before paying for them. Camera Shop sells an expensive camera on credit to Joan for her personal use, Joan sells the camera to her neighbor Fred before making any payments, and Joan immediately spends the money and is now insolvent. If Camera Shop has retained a PMSI in the camera and has perfected the interest by *attachment only*, Camera Shop prevails over Joan's other creditors if she still has the camera—but the PMSI provides *no* protection against Fred. Fred may keep the camera if he bought it "without knowledge of the security interest, for value and for his own personal, family or household purposes" [9-307(2)]. However, if Camera Shop had perfected the PMSI *by filing* before Joan resold the camera to Fred, Camera Shop would be protected from a claim of ownership by Fred or any other subsequent purchaser. Whether a seller of expensive consumer goods should rely on attachment-only perfection or should instead undertake the extra expense of a filing is, of course, a matter of business judgment.

Priority of Mechanics' Liens

Sometimes goods subject to a security interest are sent out for repairs or improvements. What if the repairperson remains unpaid? Will his or her mechanic's lien have priority over the security interest? Section 9-310 gives priority to *common law* possessory liens for materials or services furnished with respect to goods subject to a security interest, even though the security interest was perfected earlier. Section 9-310 gives similar priority to *statutory* possessory liens *unless* the statute granting the lien expressly subordinates it to a prior security interest.

Priorities of Security Interests in Fixtures

Article 9 governs the priority of security interests in fixtures, but leaves the definition of "fixture" largely up to non-Code real estate law. However, "no security interest exists under the Article in ordinary building materials incorporated into an improvement on land" [9-313(2)]. The rights of materials sellers are governed by local real estate mechanic's lien laws.

The fixture priority rules are best understood by examining the conflicts they are meant to resolve. The usual conflict is between purchase-money fixture financers and real estate financers. The following paragraphs illustrate two major fixture priority conflicts.

1 Oscar owns an office building that needs a new furnace. Frank sells Oscar a furnace on credit, reserves a PMSI in it, and installs the furnace. But Oscar's building is subject to a recorded real estate mortgage in favor of Rachel. For Frank's PMSI in the furnace to prevail over Rachel's earlier recorded mortgage on the real estate, Frank must perfect his PMSI by a fixture filing within 10 days after the furnace is annexed [9-313(4)(a)].

2 Frank reserves a PMSI in a furnace to be installed in a *new* house that Oscar is having built, and Rachel is the construction financer. Rachel's **construction mortgage** will prevail over Frank's PMSI in the furnace if Rachel takes two steps: (1) She must record (file) the construction mortgage before the furnace is installed as a fixture, and (2) she must be sure that the furnace is installed (annexed) before the house itself is completed [9-313(6)]. By observing the required sequence of events—recording the construction mortgage, annexing the fixture, and completing the building—construction financers who may have advanced money for major appliances as well as for the basic building can protect themselves from a surprise PMSI held by a fixture seller.

Priorities of Security Interests in Accessions and Commingled Goods

Accessions are goods that are installed in or affixed to other goods. Orville owns a delivery truck, its engine burns out, and Orville's mechanic installs a replacement engine. The engine is an accession. The following priority rules apply to accessions.

1 To prevail over earlier perfected security interests in the whole thing (Orville's truck), the accession financer must be sure that the security interest in the accession (Orville's replacement engine) *attaches before* the accession is installed [9-314]. Orville gives Thrifty Loan a security interest in the truck to secure a loan, and Thrifty files a financing statement. Then the engine burns out, Orville buys a replacement engine from Sam on credit, and Sam acquires a PMSI before installing the engine. Since Sam's PMSI attached before the engine was installed, the PMSI in the engine prevails over Thrifty's earlier perfected security interest in the truck.

2 To prevail over subsequent purchasers and lenders, the accession financer must *perfect* the security interest in the accession (or the holder of the subsequent interest must know of the accession financer's interest) *before* the subsequent interest arises (attaches). Thrifty makes the loan and takes its security interest in the truck *after* Orville replaces the engine. Unless Thrifty knows of the accession financer's (Sam's) claim before extending credit, Thrifty will believe that the new engine is part of its collateral. Therefore, to prevail over Thrifty, Sam must have *perfected* his PMSI in the engine (or Thrifty must have known of it) *before* Thrifty's interest arose.

Commingled goods are those that are combined with others to form a single mass or product. For example, flour, sugar, and eggs may be commingled into cake mix. Where goods subject to a perfected security interest are commingled so that the identity of the commingled goods is lost in the mass, the security interest continues in the mass or product [9-315]. Where several such security interests continue in the mass, each of the various secured parties is entitled to a pro rata share of the mass. Egbert, Wheatley, and Sugarman sell eggs, flour, and sugar to Cake Mix Corp. and perfect their security interests. Then Cake Mix commingles the goods into a batch of cake mix. If Cake Mix fails to pay the suppliers, they have equal priority as to the mass, and each is entitled to share the batch of cake mix to the extent of his or her contribution to the mass.

DEFAULT AND FORECLOSURE
Meaning of Default

In general, a **default** is a failure to perform a legal duty. In secured transactions, nonpayment by the debtor is the most common default. The security agreement may identify additional ones such as the debtor's unauthorized sale of collateral, the debtor's failure to insure the collateral, the debtor's failure to furnish additional collateral if the value of the original collateral declines, the debtor's insolvency or bankruptcy, and loss or destruction of the collateral.

Rights and Duties of Secured Party upon Debtor's Default

When the debtor is in default, the secured party may enforce the security interest by taking possession of the collateral and (1) under certain circumstances *keeping* it in satisfaction of the debt or (2) *disposing* of the collateral in some commercially reasonable way, as by sale [9-501]. The secured party may also use any judicial procedure available under non-Code law (e.g., state foreclosure laws).

Acquiring Control of the Collateral. If the secured party does not already possess the collateral, he or she will need to acquire control of it. This can be done in a variety of ways. To collect accounts, the secured party may notify the debtor's customer to make payment directly to the secured party [9-502]. As to collateral in possession of the debtor, the secured party has two basic options. Unless otherwise agreed, the secured party may simply take possession of the collateral after default, if he or she can do so without breach of the peace [9-503]. Or the secured party may go to court to acquire possession (and *must* do so where a breach of the peace is threatened). In lieu of removing heavy equipment, the secured party may render it unusable (e.g., by removing a control device) and dispose of (e.g., sell) it on the debtor's premises.

What constitutes a **breach of the peace?** Ordinarily, an objection by the debtor or a custodian of the property to an attempted repossession involves a breach of the peace, since physical violence is a possible outcome. Breaking into the debtor's premises to get the collateral or posing as a police officer is also forbidden. But removing the collateral from a public street, a parking lot, or even the open parts of the debtor's premises is permitted, if done without objection by the debtor or a third party. As suggested by Case 29.3, mere lack of consent is not necessarily a peace-threatening objection.

CASE 29.3   Marine Midland Bank-Central v. Cote • 351 So. 2d 750 (Fla. App. 1977)

FACTS Marine Midland Bank had a purchase-money security interest in a car sold to Cote. Cote was in default, and Altes or his employee, acting on behalf of the bank, entered Cote's private property early one morning and removed the car from the open carport. Cote sued Altes and the bank for trespass and was awarded $2,500 in compensatory and $2,500 in punitive damages. Altes and the bank appealed.

OPINION SMITH, J. . . . [Florida decisions] approved repossessions in similar situations. But appellees [the Cotes] argue those cases involved security agreements which explicitly authorized the creditor to enter upon the debtor's premises to repossess the security. Here the security agreement stated only that

. . . when the Buyer is in default under this Contract . . . the Holder shall have all the rights and remedies of a secured party when a debtor is in default under a security agreement as provided under the Uniform Commercial Code, [appellees] hereby . . . agreeing that such rights and remedies include the Holder's right to take possession and dispose of the vehicle after default. . . .

We must decide whether the secured party's right to repossess collateral provided by the Florida UCC in § 9-503 includes a right to enter upon private property [in the absence of a contract provision specifically permitting entry].

In Northside Motors . . . the Supreme Court held [that] § 9-503 "is no more than a codification . . . of a common law right and a contract right recognized long [ago] and creates no new right." The Restatement (2d) of Torts, § 183 states that at common law:

(1) Except as otherwise agreed, a conditional vendor or lessor of a thing who is entitled to immediate possession thereof . . . is privileged, at a reasonable time and in a reasonable manner, to enter land in possession of the vendee or lessee, for the purpose of taking possession of the thing and removing it from the land.

Our Supreme Court recognized this privilege in Percifield v. State. . . . Courts in other jurisdictions have held a secured creditor privileged, under the UCC or the common law, to peacefully enter on the debtor's land when the security agreement authorizes repossession but does not specifically authorize entry. . . . While many of the cases approving entry by a creditor have involved a contract clause specifically authorizing entry, we have not found or been directed to any case holding a creditor liable because a security agreement lacked such a clause. Cases holding creditors liable for trespass or conversion have involved entry in to a dwelling, removal of collateral from an enclosed and secured garage, or some fraud or other misconduct by the creditor. . . .

> **CASE 29.3 Continued**
>
> We hold that, absent a contrary agreement, when a security agreement provides [that] the secured party has on default the rights and remedies provided by the UCC, the right of repossession stated by § 9-503 implies, just as it did at common law, a limited privilege to enter on the debtor's land. The privilege may be exercised only "without breach of the peace." . . .
>
> We do not undertake to define the limits of the privileged entry accorded a creditor under § 9-503. We hold simply that, unless the parties otherwise agree, when a vehicle is covered by a valid security agreement providing the creditor has a right to repossess the vehicle upon default, repossession of the vehicle from the debtor's unenclosed carport without threat or use of force is not trespass, regardless of whether the security agreement specifically authorizes entry upon the debtor's premises.
>
> **JUDGMENT** [The judgments are reversed.]

Disposing of the Collateral. After obtaining the collateral, the secured party will want to keep or dispose of it. The secured party's keeping it in satisfaction of the debt is called **strict foreclosure** and is appropriate where the value of the collateral is equal to or less than the amount of the debt. However, strict foreclosure is permitted only where the secured party gives written notice of intention to keep the collateral and the debtor does not object in writing [9-505(2)]. If the debtor makes timely objection to strict foreclosure, the secured party *must dispose* of the collateral. Disposal is required also where the collateral is *consumer goods* and the debtor has paid 60 percent of the purchase price or loan [9-505(1)].

The secured party may dispose of collateral in any **commercially reasonable** way, whether by sale, lease, or otherwise [9-504]. A foreclosure sale may be public or private, as long as it is commercially reasonable. In any sale or other disposition, the secured party receives the amount of proceeds necessary to cover the debt and foreclosure expenses. Any surplus goes to the debtor. However, the debtor remains liable for any deficiency unless otherwise agreed, or unless the secured party is denied a **deficiency judgment** for misconduct.

What misconduct could result in the secured party's being denied a deficiency judgment? Examples include:

- Violating a state statute requiring that repossessed goods be appraised before sale
- Destroying the goods during repossession
- Failing to give the debtor prior notice of the disposition of the collateral

In some states, making a commercially unreasonable disposition of collateral precludes the secured party from a deficiency judgment "as a matter of law"—that is, automatically, for violating the Article 9 disposition rules. However, Article 9 itself takes a different approach favored by many courts and legal commentators: The creditor who makes a commercially unreasonable disposition of collateral *is* entitled to a deficiency, but the debtor has a remedy under § 9-507 for any loss caused by a commercially unreasonable disposition. To collect a deficiency under this approach, the secured party ordinarily must prove that the fair market value of the collateral was less than the amount still owed.

Largely to protect the debtor, Article 9 imposes disposition rules that cannot be changed by the security agreement. For instance, the secured party must exercise reasonable care to preserve collateral in his or her possession, and the debtor has a right to **redeem** (buy back) repossessed collateral before it is disposed of. After default, however, the debtor may waive some of these rights.

Prior dealings between the debtor and the secured party may affect the secured party's right to repossess and dispose of the collateral. Suppose Dom is late with some of his payments and Candace accepts them without protest. Candace's conduct could cause Dom reasonably to believe that delay in making a future payment will not result in seizure of the collateral. Many courts will deny Candace the right to repossess the collateral unless, after permitting late payments, she notifies Dom that late payments will no longer be tolerated.

SUMMARY

To make credit extension easier and safer, Article 9 substituted the term "security interest" for the variety of pre-Code descriptive terms, developed a simplified public-notice filing system, established a system of priorities for the states to use in common, and set up a uniform method of liquidating collateral after default.

A secured party receives maximum protection if the security interest is attached and perfected. Attachment is the process of creating a security interest and making it enforceable against the debtor. Perfection is the process of making the security interest enforceable against others than the debtor. Perfection sometimes occurs upon completion of the attachment events, but more commonly occurs by the secured party's taking possession of the collateral or filing a financing statement.

A perfected purchase-money security interest (PMSI) usually prevails over earlier perfected security interests. In most other conflict situations, the first to perfect or, if there is no perfection, the first to attach prevails. Similar priority rules apply to fixtures.

Upon the debtor's default, the secured party has liberal repossession and disposition rights. However, the debtor is entitled to a commercially reasonable disposition of the collateral. The debtor is entitled also to any surplus realized from disposition of the collateral, but remains personally liable for any deficiency unless freed from that liability by the secured party's misconduct.

REVIEW QUESTIONS

1. **(a)** Why are security interests in fixtures covered by Article 9 rather than by real estate law? **(b)** Why does Article 9 cover sales of accounts and chattel paper?

2. **(a)** What is the Code definition of "security interest"? **(b)** Distinguish between a true lease and a "lease" that creates a security interest.

3. What must be done for a security interest to attach?

4. **(a)** What is a floating lien? **(b)** What is the purpose of an after-acquired property clause? Of a future-advances provision?

5. Explain the legal consequence of perfecting a security interest.

6. **(a)** Why is a PMSI given priority? **(b)** How may a PMSI in inventory be perfected? Why is the procedure relatively complex?

7. Naming the usual participants, illustrate each of the following: **(a)** conflicting security interests in the same collateral, and **(b)** conflicting security interests in a fixture.

8. What is the meaning of default?

9. How may the secured party repossess collateral upon the debtor's default?

10. Is a sale required for a disposition of collateral to be commercially reasonable? Explain.

CASE PROBLEMS

1. Doing business as Towanda Aviation Service, Simons received a loan from Citizens and Northern Bank (Bank) and gave Bank a security interest in his Piper Navajo airplane hangered at Towanda. Bank filed a financing statement. Reuter personally guaranteed the loan. When Towanda encountered financial difficulties, Simons and Bank sold the plane to cover Simons's debt, but the proceeds of the sale were insufficient. Claiming that he and a bank officer had agreed that he was to have a security interest in the plane, Reuter sued Bank for violating his rights as a secured party by failing properly to notify him of the repossession and sale of the airplane. Did Reuter have a security interest in the plane?

2. Monc's Consolidated Produce, Inc., lent money and strawberry plants to Cooperative La Paz, a group of strawberry growers. Cooperative signed a "Sales and Marketing Agreement" giving Monc's the exclusive right to market Cooperative's strawberries. The agreement also stated, "In order to secure all of Grower's obligations . . . Grower hereby gives to Shipper [Monc's] a security interest in all crops growing or to be grown on the above-described property . . . and the proceeds thereof, and agrees to sign a [financing] statement and any other documents needed to perfect Shipper's security interest." Monc's assigned its business to New West Fruit Corp., which learned that Cooperative was marketing the strawberry crop through New West's competitor, Coastal Berry Corp. Advising Coastal Berry of its contract with Cooperative, New West demanded that Coastal pay New West the amounts owed by Cooperative or allow New West to market the crop. Coastal denied any liability on the ground that New West had no valid security agreement with Cooperative, since the agreement did not specifically refer to advances of money or plants. Did New West have an enforceable security agreement?

3. S&J Holding Corp. was in the business of operating video games. In S&J's bankruptcy proceeding, June, Inc., one of S&J's creditors, claimed not only S&J's video and vending machines but also the cash revenues generated by them. June's perfected security agreement covered "all of the assets of Shazamm Enterprises, Inc., including all equipment, inventory, accounts receivable, contract rights, intangibles, video games, cigarette machines, coin changers, and any and all other personal property or assets owned and used by the debtor in its business wherever located as well as any and all personal property herein-after acquired. Products of collateral are covered." Did June have a valid, perfected security interest in the cash?

4. Fowler, doing business as White Oak Lawn & Garden Center, borrowed $25,000 from White Oak State Bank, which, on December 5, 1975, perfected its security interest in Fowler's inventory, equipment, accounts receivable, and life insurance. Fowler sold the Center to Winslow, who had borrowed $51,500 from the same bank and granted it a security interest in the Center inventory. Winslow paid off Fowler's $25,000 debt to Bank. On December 22, 1977, Bank marked Fowler's note "paid." In the meantime Winslow borrowed $20,000 from Barr and signed a security agreement covering Center inventory. On December 27, the Barrs filed their financing statement. On December 28, Bank filed its financing statement. In 1978 Winslow defaulted on the notes to Bank and Barr. Bank repossessed and sold the inventory without notifying Barr of the foreclosure. Later, alleging that he was entitled to the inventory and that Bank had wrongfully disposed of it, Barr sued Bank for damages. Was Barr entitled to the collateral?

5. Valway, a restaurant owner doing business as Ricardo's, gave Burlington Savings Bank a security interest in "all equipment and machinery . . . now owned or hereafter acquired" as collateral for a loan. Bank's financing statement, filed on June 8, 1981, described the debtor as "Richard M. Valway d/b/a [doing business as] Ricardo's." In August 1981, Valway purchased restaurant equipment on credit from Greg Restaurant Equipment & Supplies. As Bank knew, Greg retained a purchase-money security interest in the equipment. Greg's financing statement, filed 2 days later, listed the debtor as "Ricardo's." Valway defaulted on his debt to Greg, and Greg sued to repossess the equipment. Bank opposed Greg's suit, alleging that Greg's filing was defective and did not give Greg's PMSI priority over Bank's earlier perfected security interest. From a judgment for Greg, Bank appealed. Was Greg's filing sufficient to give Greg's PMSI priority?

6. Ray's Tires Co. bought a quantity of Goodyear tires on credit advanced by American Petrofina Marketing, Inc. (American), which took a security interest in the tires. Weiner guaranteed the Ray's Tires obligation. Ray's Tires defaulted. American repossessed the tires and sold them by private sale. The sale produced a deficiency of nearly $134,000. American then sought a deficiency judgment against Weiner, the guarantor. Holding that American had not disposed of the collateral in a commercially reasonable manner, the trial court denied American a deficiency judgment. American appealed. The appellate court held that a commercially unreasonable disposition of collateral does not, by itself, preclude a creditor from receiving a deficiency judgment. Was the appellate court correct?

CHAPTER 30

Bankruptcy

For most people, bankruptcy is a most unpleasant fact of life. A person with a bankruptcy discharge on his or her credit record may have difficulty obtaining new credit. If a bankrupt business must close down, employees lose their jobs and may lose back wages and pension benefits. Creditors may be unable to collect unpaid debts. Tax authorities lose a source of revenue and may be unable to collect unpaid taxes. Customers must look elsewhere for goods and services, suppliers lose a customer, and proprietors and shareholders may lose all or most of their investment.

Yet bankruptcy does have its positive aspects. Freed by their bankruptcy discharges from impossible burdens of debt accumulated for reasons beyond their control, individuals may once again be good credit risks and productive citizens. Bankruptcy law also preserves employment by providing opportunities for a troubled business to stay in operation while it regains its financial health. And bankruptcy law reduces the potential for wasteful conflict among creditors by providing for an orderly and fair distribution of the debtor's remaining assets in the event of a liquidation proceeding.

This chapter begins by discussing agreements between an insolvent debtor and his or her creditors under state insolvency law, an alternative to bankruptcy. Because of the limitations of state insolvency law, most financially distressed persons resort to federal bankruptcy law. The next part of the chapter discusses the nature and purpose of bankruptcy law. The remaining sections focus on the three major kinds of bankruptcy proceedings: liquidations, business reorganizations, and repayment plans for debtors with regular income.

CREDITORS' RIGHTS AND DEBTOR RELIEF UNDER STATE LAW

State insolvency law and bankruptcy law can best be understood by examining briefly how financial difficulty can develop and how the rights of creditors and the needs of debtors may collide. Consider, for example, the history of Joe's financial failure.

Joe's Financial Failure

Upon his graduation from State University, Joe set up a retail art supply store. Having no funds of his own, he borrowed $100,000 from First Bank as a start-up loan for renting a store building and purchasing equipment and inventory. First Bank took a security interest in all his inventory, equipment, and accounts receivable. Joe also purchased a copier, a cash register, and a computer on credit from Brenda's Business Machines for $20,000 under a purchase-money secured transaction. He bought $5,000 worth of art supplies on credit from Arts Unlimited and opened his store.

The business was a success. Joe bought a $100,000 home, which he financed with a $90,000 mortgage from Third Bank at 15 percent annual interest. He later undertook an expansion of his business with two new stores. He rented one of the buildings and purchased the other for $200,000, borrowing $120,000 from Second Bank for the purchase and giving the bank a mortgage on the property. The expansion was also financed with the profits from the first store and an unsecured $40,000 loan from his uncle. Joe leased a company car (a new Mercedes-Benz) for 5 years and $50,000 in payments, and purchased a delivery van for $30,000 in cash from Downtown Motors.

By now, Joe had fifteen employees. Things were going well until the economy was hit by a widespread recession. Many businesses in Joe's city laid off their employees, and schools cut back on their art programs. Joe's art supply sales dwindled. Accounts receivable became uncollectible. Within months, Joe fell behind in his payments. Joe's creditors—secured and unsecured—wanted immediate payment, but Joe could not pay. To make matters worse, the delivery van broke down because of a defect in the engine. Fearing financial ruin, Joe "sold" his second home, a lake cabin, to his brother for much less than its market value. He used a false financial statement to secure an unsecured $20,000 loan from Third Bank in an attempt to keep the business afloat. He also gave his uncle $40,000 in full payment of the prior unsecured loan.

The business continued to struggle; Joe couldn't even pay his employees. He then sought advice from his attorney and accountant, Carla.

Carla pointed out several things to Joe about his financial difficulties.

1 Joe's plight was caused in part by his own mismanagement of his financial affairs and by a too-rapid business expansion. But there were other causes more or less beyond his control—for instance, the economic recession and the willingness of some lenders to extend credit without adequately checking Joe's ability to repay.

2 Nevertheless, almost all of Joe's creditors have valid claims against Joe for payment. Other than Downtown Motors and the defective delivery van, none had committed fraud or other wrongdoing when extending credit to Joe, and all were entitled to payment in full. Moreover, the transfer of the lake property might be considered a "fraudulent conveyance" that the creditors could set aside, and Joe's use of a false financial statement to get a loan from Third Bank could be considered fraud.

3 However, despite their valid claims, Joe's creditors are limited by law in what they may do by way of debt collection activities. No creditor, secured or unsecured, may take debt collection action that violates the debtor's rights under the law. For example, creditors who engage in overly vigorous collection activity risk liability to the debtor for defamation, invasion of privacy, outrage, or other torts discussed in Chapters 6 and 7. The Fair Debt Collection Practices Act and other limitations exist on debt collection activity (discussed in Chapter 49).

4 If Joe is or remains in default, his secured creditors can peacefully repossess and sell the equipment, inventory, and accounts to satisfy the secured debts; banks having mortgages on his real estate can foreclose and have the real estate put up for sale. Joe's unsecured creditors—employees, trade creditors, landlords, and others—must bring suit, receive a judgment for the amount owed, and then attempt to collect by having Joe's nonexempt and unencumbered property, if any, seized and sold under an execution. Joe has certain **exemptions**—property the unsecured creditors cannot seize under state law, including his house (homestead exemption), clothing, and specific personal property.

5 Joe has a variety of options, including attempting to work out his debts with his creditors under state law or filing for liquidation or reorganization of his business under federal bankruptcy law.

How Joe May Settle His Unpaid Debts under State Law

Joe's creditors might be willing to forgo the cumbersome, costly, and sometimes futile process of debt collection and to consider alternative ways of receiving payment. Even Joe's secured creditors may face losses because the value of their collateral is less than the debts owed. And if Joe elects to file for bankruptcy, the creditors may face additional delays and further losses. One alternative to bankruptcy is a **private workout.** Workouts are agreements between a debtor and one or more creditors to satisfy his or her debts in whole or in part. A workout may involve a partial forgiveness of debt, a relinquishment of collateral to secured creditors in full satisfaction of certain debts, a restructuring of loan terms (e.g., an extension of time for or a reduction in amount of payments), or an infusion of new capital into a struggling business by third-party investors or existing creditors. A workout may also take the form of a composition or extension agreement or an assignment for the benefit of creditors.

Composition and Extension Agreements

Composition and extension agreements are contracts between a debtor and some or all of his or her creditors, by means of which a debtor and creditors agree to substitute a less burdensome obligation for the debts originally undertaken. In a **composition** agreement, the debtor agrees to pay the creditors some fraction (e.g., 20 percent) of the amount the debtor owes, in full settlement of the creditors' claims. Usually each creditor will receive the same percentage that all other creditors receive, in what is called a pro rata (equal percentage) distribution. However, the agreement may provide that some creditors—for example, those owed small amounts—will receive 100 percent of their claims. In an **extension** agreement, the debtor agrees to pay the full amount of all debts (with or without interest), but the creditors agree to allow the debtor to pay over a greater time (often 1 to 3 years) than originally agreed. The major drawback of a composition or extension agreement is that it is not binding on nonconsenting creditors, who may pursue the usual collection process and execute against the debtor's unencumbered assets even though such action prevents the debtor from carrying out the agreement.

Assignments for the Benefit of Creditors

A troubled debtor might choose to transfer property to a trustee for the benefit of his or her creditors. An **assignment for the benefit of creditors** (also called a **general assignment**) is a voluntary transfer by the debtor of all his or her available property to a person (the assignee or trustee) named by the debtor. The trustee's role is to (1) receive the debtor's property, (2) liquidate it (convert it into cash), and (3) distribute the cash to creditors in exchange for their promises to release the debtor from further liability. Under the terms of the assignment, each creditor may receive a pro rata (equal percentage) distribution, or some creditors may receive a larger proportion of their claims than other creditors receive. Once a general assignment is made, no unsecured creditor may execute on or otherwise obtain rights to the assigned property, but is instead limited to whatever distribution the assignment document provides. However, creditors who did not assent to the assignment are not bound by its terms; consequently, the debtor's future earnings will be subject to the claims of unpaid nonconsenting creditors. Furthermore, as noted later in this chapter, a creditor who is unhappy with a general assignment may be able to upset it by commencing federal bankruptcy proceedings against the debtor.

Instead of using procedures available under state law for resolving financial difficulty—or in the event those procedures fail—a debtor (or his or her creditors) might seek the aid of federal bankruptcy law, which is discussed in the next part of the chapter.

FEDERAL BANKRUPTCY LAW AND ADMINISTRATION

Federal bankruptcy law has two main purposes: (1) to provide a fair and evenhanded basis for distributing a debtor's available assets among creditors, and (2) to free the debtor from impossible burdens of debt and thus provide a "fresh start" so that the debtor may more quickly return to productive business activities. One aspect of the fresh-start policy is the practice of allowing some firms to stay in business while they attempt to recover their financial health. Permitting financially distressed firms, especially large ones, to reorganize and stay in business tends to minimize the disruption of employment and maintain the flow of goods and services to the public. The nature of federal bankruptcy law and how its purposes are carried out are the subjects of the paragraphs that follow.

The Bankruptcy Code

The U.S. Constitution gives Congress the power to regulate bankruptcies; and over the years since 1800, five different federal bankruptcy statutes have been in effect. The most recent one is the Bankruptcy Reform Act of 1978, referred to in this chapter as the Bankruptcy Code. The Bankruptcy Code[1] (as amended in 1984 and 1986), together with interpretive court decisions (and procedural bankruptcy rules and standards published by the U.S. Supreme Court), constitutes our national bankruptcy law.

Role of State Law

Under the supremacy clause of the Constitution, Congress probably could preempt (displace) all state insolvency law, but it has chosen not to do so. The Bankruptcy Code looks to state law for the resolution of a number of bankruptcy issues. Usually, the state law of property and of contracts will be followed for the purpose of determining, for example, what property the debtor owns. By express provision of the Code, state law may govern what property of the debtor (residence, tools, clothing, and so on) is exempt from the claims of creditors. Thus, state law supplements the Bankruptcy Code in the resolution of bankruptcy issues.

Kinds of Bankruptcy Proceedings

A Chapter 7 bankruptcy, known as a **straight** or **ordinary** bankruptcy, involves the liquidation of the debtor's nonexempt business and personal assets to pay his or her creditors and the discharge of the debtor from most of his or her debts. Chapter 11 entails a reorganization of the debtor's financial structure with the expectation that the business debtor will come out of bankruptcy and be able to continue in business as a viable concern. A Chapter 13 bankruptcy results in a 3- to 5-year plan for the adjustment of an individual's debts that calls for the individual to use his or her future income to pay off a certain part of the debts, after which the debtor receives a discharge. Liquidations, business reorganizations, and Chapter 13 plans are discussed in the next sections of the chapter.[2]

LIQUIDATION—STRAIGHT OR ORDINARY BANKRUPTCY

The purpose of a Chapter 7 liquidation proceeding is to convert the debtor's nonexempt assets into cash, to distribute it as dictated by the scheme of distribution provided in the Bankruptcy Code, and to grant the honest debtor a discharge from most of the remaining debts. Joe or his creditors could file a Chapter 7 petition,

---

[1] 11 USC, Sec. 101 et seq. Citations to the United States Code are to titles and their sections; thus, here, Title 11, Sec. 101 of the USC. In this chapter, only the section numbers are given, in brackets: e.g., [101], which means "Section 101 of the Bankruptcy Code."

[2] Railroads may be reorganized or liquidated under Chapter 11 of the Bankruptcy Code, but they are not otherwise eligible for bankruptcy. Municipal corporations are not liquidated, but may seek "adjustment" of their debts under Chapter 9 of the Code if state law authorizes them to do so. Stockbrokers and commodity brokers may be liquidated under Subchapters III and IV of Chapter 7. Railroad reorganizations, the adjustment of municipal debt, and the liquidation of stock and commodity brokers are beyond the scope of this book.

which would ultimately result in the liquidation of Joe's business and a discharge of most of his debts.

Commencement of Straight Bankruptcy

A Chapter 7 proceeding usually begins with the filing of a **voluntary petition** by the debtor. The filing constitutes an **order for relief**—a court order that the debtor is entitled to bankruptcy relief. Any "person" except a railroad, insurance company, bank, savings and loan association, or credit union[3] may file a voluntary petition to liquidate under Chapter 7 [109(b)]. *Person* includes individuals, partnerships, and corporations, but not governmental units [101(35)]. A husband and wife also can file a joint petition. Although a person must be a debtor to file bankruptcy, he or she need not be insolvent.[4]

Any person who qualifies for a voluntary liquidation, except a farmer[5] or charitable corporation, may be subject instead to an *involuntary* liquidation proceeding [303]. In an involuntary case, the order for relief is not automatic. The court holds a hearing to determine whether the conditions for an involuntary bankruptcy are present and if so, the court issues an order for relief. If not, the petition is dismissed. The requirements for a person to be declared an involuntary bankrupt are as follows:

- The petitioning creditor or creditors must have claims totaling at least $5,000 in unsecured debts.
- Where the number of creditors is twelve or more, three of them must join in the involuntary petition; otherwise, only one petitioning creditor is required.
- The alleged debtor must have given the creditor or creditors a **ground for relief:** either "the debtor is generally not paying such debtor's debts as such debts become due" (called an **equity insolvency** standard) or the debtor has, within 120 days of the filing of the involuntary petition, made a general assignment for the benefit of creditors [303(h)].

These requirements serve several purposes. They provide specific, numerical guidance to the court and thus facilitate the administration of bankruptcy law. The equity insolvency standard identifies the level of financial ill health at which creditors may seek protection against the wishes of the debtor. And they serve, in part, to protect the debtor from unfounded, trivial, or harassing claims. The debtor is protected if the allegations for an involuntary petition are not proved. The court may grant court costs to the debtor; and, if a trustee was appointed and took possession of the debtor's property, the court may award damages to the debtor. A bad faith petitioner may be liable for both compensatory and punitive damages even though no trustee was appointed [303(i)].

The Automatic Stay

The filing of the petition results in an **automatic stay** (suspension) of most other legal action and nonjudicial collection activity affecting the debtor's estate (property), until the bankruptcy case is over or until the bankruptcy court lifts (terminates) the stay. The automatic stay prevents creditors from taking any action to collect their debts from the debtor, and thus enables the trustee to preserve and administer the estate without undue interference. Thus, once Joe files a voluntary petition, his creditors cannot sue him or continue any suit, repossess or foreclose on collateral, enforce any judgment, or take any steps, judicial or nonjudicial, to collect on the debts. A creditor who violates the automatic stay is subject to punishment for contempt of court. A creditor who wants to proceed with

---

[3] Such businesses are regulated by federal or state administrative agencies, which are thought better equipped than the courts to handle their financial failure.

[4] The court does have the power, however, to dismiss a bankruptcy petition if the court determines that granting relief would be a **substantial abuse** of the bankruptcy process.

[5] A *farmer* is a person (individual, partnership, or corporation) who derived more than 80 percent of his or her gross income in the taxable year prior to bankruptcy from a farming operation owned or operated by that person [101(19)].

some collection action, such as a foreclosure sale, during the pendency of a bankruptcy must make a motion to the court to lift the stay and establish some justification for lifting the stay. Note that some nonbankruptcy actions, such as criminal actions against the debtor, are excluded from the operation of the automatic stay.

Functions of Trustee and Judge

Bankruptcy is not merely a judicial proceeding. It also involves the administration of the debtor's **estate** (i.e., the debtor's property) for the benefit of the debtor and the creditors. Two officials have major responsibility for administering the estate: the trustee in bankruptcy and the bankruptcy judge.

The **trustee in bankruptcy** is responsible for collecting, liquidating, and distributing the debtor's estate. These tasks require the trustee to inspect the property and business of the debtor, to decide whether to adopt or reject executory (yet to be performed) contracts and leases, to operate the business of the debtor under certain circumstances, and to perform a variety of routine tasks relating to the administrative process.

The **bankruptcy judge** has the usual judicial function of deciding any disputes that may arise during the bankruptcy process. Ordinarily the dispute will be between the trustee and a person affected by some act of the trustee in collecting and distributing the debtor's estate. The judge also has a number of administrative duties, such as appointing trustees and supervising their activities in the administration of debtors' estates.

The Bankruptcy Estate

The debtor's **estate** consists of a broad range of property interests either owned by the debtor as of the commencement of the bankruptcy case or recoverable for the estate by the trustee from someone other than the debtor [541]. Included in the estate are the following:

1 All legal and equitable interests of the debtor in property as of the commencement of the bankruptcy case, *except (a)* certain powers over property exercisable by the debtor solely for the benefit of others and *(b)* the debtor's beneficial interest under a trust when that interest cannot be transferred under nonbankruptcy law, such as the debtor's rights under a spendthrift trust.[6]

2 All interests of the debtor and the debtor's spouse in community property *if* the community property is under the sole, equal, or joint management or control of the debtor.

3 Any interest in property held by persons other than the debtor and recoverable by the trustee for the debtor's estate under various provisions of the Bankruptcy Code. The powers of the trustee to recover property for the estate, discussed later in this chapter, include the power to recover fraudulent conveyances and preferences.

4 Property that the debtor becomes entitled to within 180 days after the date of the filing of the petition under a divorce decree or a property settlement with the debtor's spouse, as an inheritance, or under a life insurance policy or death benefit plan. Other property acquired by the debtor after the filing of the bankruptcy is *not* included in the bankruptcy estate.

5 The income and other proceeds from property of the estate, and any interest or property that the estate acquires after the commencement of the case. Earnings from services performed by an *individual* debtor after the commencement of the case are *not* included in the debtor's estate.

Trustee's Power to Collect and Liquidate the Estate

The trustee must collect and liquidate the debtor's estate. This can involve considerable litigation concerning the recovery of property that belongs to the debtor's estate. The trustee is aided by the **turnover** provisions of the Code requiring holders of property to which the

---

[6] As discussed in Chapter 26, a spendthrift trust is one in which the beneficiary has no property right to the trust until trust income or property is distributed to him or her. Creditors may not seize trust funds until the beneficiary receives them. The Bankruptcy Code makes spendthrift trust provisions that are enforceable under state law effective also against the trustee in bankruptcy.

> **BOX 30.1**
>
> **Developments in the Law: ERISA Pension Plans and the Estate**
>
> The Employee Retirement Income Security Act of 1974 (ERISA) regulates private employer's pension plans. Qualified pension plans under the Act—such as Keough plans—must contain an "antialienation" provision under which an employee's plan benefits cannot be transferred or assigned. The Bankruptcy Code provides as follows: "A restriction on the transfer of a beneficial interest of the debtor in a trust that is enforceable under applicable nonbankruptcy law is enforceable in a case under this title." This provision excludes from the estate the debtor's rights under a spendthrift trust.
>
> In *Patterson v. Shumate*, 112 S. Ct. 2242 (1992), the U.S. Supreme Court held that a debtor's interest under an employee pension plan meeting the requirements of ERISA was also excluded from the bankruptcy estate. The Court rejected the argument that the bankruptcy exclusion was limited to trusts under state law, such as spendthrift trusts, where the debtor's ownership rights are restricted. It held that Joseph Shumate's interest under his employer's plan, valued at $250,000, was not part of his bankruptcy estate.
>
> What policy reasons justify the inclusion or exclusion of employee pension plans from the estate? ∎

debtor's estate is entitled, including property subject to a security interest and exempt property, to deliver it to the trustee [542; 543].

To administer the debtor's estate properly, the trustee has significant powers under the Code. The trustee has the (*a*) power to use, sell, or lease property and to borrow money, (*b*) power to assume or reject executory contracts and unexpired leases, and (*c*) power to assert defenses on behalf of the debtor.

Power to Use, Sell, or Lease Property. Often the trustee needs to use, sell, or lease property (of the debtor's estate) that is subject to the claims of persons such as secured creditors, or to borrow money in a manner that might threaten existing security or other interests. For example, it may be necessary for Joe's trustee to use encumbered (mortgaged) property, such as business equipment, to keep the business operation going. The trustee may use, sell, or lease encumbered (mortgaged) property, but only if the security interest or lien is adequately protected [363(e)]. Encumbered property may not be sold free and clear of the encumbrance unless, for example, the holder of the security interest consents or the price received for the property is greater than the value of the interest [363(f)].

Power to Assume or Reject Debtor's Contracts. Subject to court approval, the trustee may assume, reject, or assign executory contracts and unexpired leases of the debtor [365(a)]. For example, this power would enable Joe's trustee to reject burdensome transactions, such as the lease of the company automobile, and to transfer or sell any contract that is assignable under state law, such as Joe's lease of a store building (presuming the lease is assignable). Note that the trustee's rejection of a binding contract constitutes a breach of it and gives the aggrieved party a claim as an unsecured creditor against the debtor's estate.

Power to Assert Debtor's Defenses. To preserve the debtor's estate, the trustee may need to avoid contracts made by the debtor. To that end, the trustee may assert any personal defense or basis for suit that the debtor could have used against the other contracting party—such as duress, undue influence, fraud, or the statute of limitations [558]. Joe's trustee may be able to cancel the purchase of the defective delivery van, for example, asserting the defense of breach of warranty or fraud, and recover the purchase price paid for the benefit of the estate.

Trustee's Status as Lien Creditor and Bona Fide Purchaser

A **lien creditor** is a person whose debt or claim is secured by a lien on particular property. As a lien creditor, the trustee in bankruptcy will prevail over unperfected secured creditors. Recall that Joe purchased a copier, cash register, and computer from Brenda's Business Machines (BBM). BBM retained a purchase-money security interest (PMSI) in the equipment. As discussed in Chapter 29, to perfect a PMSI in the goods, and to have priority over perfected secured creditors, BBM must file a financing statement within 10 days after Joe received possession of the goods. If BBM failed to do so and Joe files for bankruptcy, the bankruptcy trustee will have the same priority as a lien creditor and will prevail over BBM. BBM will be left with a claim as an unsecured creditor for the price of the goods.

The trustee also has the status of a hypothetical **bona fide purchaser** of real property from the debtor [544(a)(3)]. Thus, the trustee may acquire the debtor's real estate free from whatever competing claims a real bona fide purchaser would have taken the property free from. Recall that Second Bank loaned Joe the money to purchase a store building. If Second Bank failed to record the mortgage, Joe's bankruptcy trustee would have the same rights as an innocent purchaser of that property. An innocent purchaser would acquire the property free of the unrecorded mortgage. Thus, Joe's trustee will acquire the property for the estate free of the mortgage. Again, Second Bank would lose its status as a secured creditor in the bankruptcy, but would have a claim as an unsecured creditor.

Avoidance of Fraudulent Transfers

The trustee has the power to avoid fraudulent transfers and recover the property for the estate. Such transfers are wrongful and avoidable because they deprive the debtor's estate of assets to which it is entitled, or because they undermine a fundamental bankruptcy policy—equality of distribution among creditors.

The trustee may avoid any **fraudulent transfer** of the debtor's property made within 1 year before the filing of the petition in bankruptcy [548].[7] Recall that Joe transferred title to his lake home to his brother for less than market value. This transfer may be a fraudulent transfer that the trustee can set aside.

Fraud may be either actual or constructive. The fraud is **actual** if the transfer or obligation involved an intent to hinder, delay, or defraud creditors. The fraud is **constructive** (involving no specific intention to defraud) if the debtor received less than a reasonably equivalent value for the transfer or obligation *and* (1) the debtor was insolvent or became insolvent as a result of the transaction or (2) the debtor was engaged in business, or was about to engage in a business or transaction, for which any property remaining with the debtor was an unreasonably small capital, or (3) the debtor intended to incur, or believed that the debtor would incur, debts that would be beyond the debtor's ability to pay as the debts matured. If Joe was insolvent (or rendered insolvent) at the time of the transfer, and the trustee can establish that Joe received less than a reasonably equivalent value for the lake home, then the transfer of the lake home may be set aside and the property recovered for the estate.

To constitute a fraudulent conveyance, the debtor need not *voluntarily* transfer property to escape his or her debts. The courts have held, for example, that a foreclosure sale where the sale price is less than the fair market value of the property can be a fraudulent conveyance. Another current issue is the extent to which a leveraged buyout of a corporation, a common practice during the acquisition and merger boom in the 1980s, can be set aside as a fraudulent conveyance. Case 30.1 addresses that issue.

---

[7]The trustee may also avoid any fraudulent obligation incurred by the debtor within the 1-year period, such as the debtor's contract to pay someone for services, performance of which the debtor at the time of contracting intends not to require.

CASE 30.1	**Mellon Bank v. Metro Communications, Inc.** • 945 F.2d 635 (5th Cir. 1991)
FACTS	Metro Communications was in the business of radio and television sports syndication. It would acquire broadcast rights for sporting events, sell the rights to broadcasters, and sell the advertising for the events. In April of 1984, Metro was acquired by Total Communications, Inc. (TCI), in a leveraged buyout. TCI was a subsidiary of Total Communication Systems, which was a subsidiary of Mass Communication and Management, Ltd. (MCM), companies that produced television programs of college athletic events. To finance the purchase, TCI borrowed $1.85 million from Mellon Bank which it used to purchase the stock of the company. The loan to TCI, a shell company, was guaranteed by Metro, TCS, and MCM. In addition to the guarantees, Metro conveyed to Mellon Bank a security interest in virtually all its property. This security agreement also covered a $2.3 million line of credit and a $2.25 million letter of credit extended to Metro by Mellon Bank. The letter of credit was used to purchase the broadcast rights for the PAC-10 football games. After the PAC-10 sued Metro and TCS for breach of contract, Metro filed a Chapter 11 reorganization petition in March of 1985. In an adversary hearing to determine the validity of Mellon Bank's security interest, the Unsecured Creditor's Committee claimed that the leveraged buyout of Metro was a fraudulent conveyance. The bankruptcy court held that Metro's guaranty and grant of a security interest was a fraudulent conveyance, and the district court affirmed. Mellon Bank appealed.

OPINION	ROSENN, J. . . . The present law of fraudulent conveyances has ancient roots. Section 548 is derived from the Statute of 13 Elizabeth passed by Parliament in 1571. The statute was aimed at a practice by which overburdened debtors placed their assets in friendly hands [and] [a]fter the creditors had abandoned the effort to recover their claims, the debtor would obtain a reconveyance of the property. . . . Such transactions operated as a fraud against the debtor's creditors because the debtor's estate was depleted without exchanging property of similar value. . . .
	    At first glance, it is difficult to reconcile the original purpose of the fraudulent conveyance laws with what has become a common, arms-length transaction—the leveraged buyout, or in business parlance, the LBO. . . . Nonetheless, a thorough understanding of the typical LBO transaction reveals that there is a potential for abuse of the debtor's creditors, particularly those who are unsecured. . . .
	    A leveraged buyout refers to the acquisition of a company (target corporation) in which a substantial portion of the purchase price paid for the stock . . . is borrowed and where the loan is secured by the target corporation's assets. . . .
	    TCI's acquisition of the target Metro followed the typical pattern: Mellon extended a loan of 1.85 million dollars to TCI for the purchase of Metro; Metro guaranteed the loan and secured it with its assets, thus significantly adding to its debt structure. . . .
	    The effect of the LBO is that a corporation's shareholders are replaced by secured creditors. . . . The level of risk facing the newly structured corporation rises significantly due to the increased debt to equity ratio. This added risk is

**CASE 30.1
Continued**

borne primarily by the unsecured creditors, those who will most likely not be paid in . . . bankruptcy. The lender . . . is at risk only to the extent that the loan is under-collateralized. . . .

The selling shareholders . . . are cashed out. . . . The new purchaser also benefits . . . by achieving ownership of the corporation. The lender is attracted by the higher interest rates and fees usually associated with LBOs. The target corporation, however, receives no direct benefit to offset the greater risk of now operating as a highly leveraged corporation. . . .

[T]he statutory language [of section 548] provides no exception for the leveraged buyout. . . . Section 548 . . . is broad enough to encompass a leveraged buyout transaction that falls within its terms. We therefore turn to the analysis of the particular requirements of section 548. . . .

Reasonably Equivalent Value

Because Metro did not receive the proceeds of the acquisition loan, it did not receive any direct benefits from extending the guaranty and security interest. . . . However, in evaluating whether reasonably equivalent value has been given . . . indirect benefits may also be evaluated. . . .

The bankruptcy court rejected Mellon's argument that one of the indirect benefits that Metro received . . . was the ability to borrow working capital from Mellon. The court reasoned that the 2.3 million dollar credit line . . . amounted to a liability because "all the debtor received was the opportunity to incur an additional $2.3 million of debt." The court concluded that because of accruing interest, Metro received "substantially less than a reasonably equivalent value. . . ." This analysis is flawed. The ability to borrow money has considerable value in the commercial world. . . .

The bankruptcy court also did not account for the value created by the LBO itself. . . . Through the LBO, Metro established a permanent relationship with a production company. . . . The complementary nature of the two corporations' businesses would appear to create a stronger and more profitable combination. What was unpredicted, however, was the Supreme Court's decision . . . holding that certain NCAA restrictions imposed on the broadcasting of college football games . . . violated antitrust laws [which] had the result of increasing competition and severely decreasing revenues from advertising. . . .

The value, however, of the synergy . . . and the value of obtaining credit are difficult to quantify . . . without the aid of expert witnesses. Regrettably, no such testimony was forthcoming in this case.

The value of the consideration received must be compared to the value given. . . . However, the court ignored the value of guarantees made by TCS and MCM [i]n valuing the cost of Metro's guaranty. . . . Thus, the value of the guaranty, 1.85 million dollars, must be reduced to the extent contribution was available. . . .

No evidence, however, has been offered regarding the value of these rights. . . . The [Unsecured Creditor's] Committee introduced no evidence to support its burden of showing that Metro received less than reasonably equivalent value. . . .

> **CASE 30.1**
> **Continued**
>
> **Insolvency or Undercapitalization**
> Under Section 548 . . . the Committee must also prove that the debtor was [insolvent or rendered insolvent as a result of the transfer]. . . . When we examine the balance sheet . . . we find . . . that the Mellon loans did not render Metro insolvent, even without considering the guarantees of TCS and MCM. . . .
>
> **JUDGMENT** Reversed and remanded.

Voidable Preferences

The trustee may also avoid preferential payments or transfers (preferences) to creditors. A transaction is a **preference** (and is therefore avoidable by the trustee) if the transfer (voluntary or involuntary) was made:

- To or for the benefit of a creditor
- On account of an **antecedent** or past debt (a debt owed before the debtor made the transfer)
- On or within 90 days before the filing of the bankruptcy petition
- When the debtor was insolvent (debtor is presumed insolvent during the 90-day period preceding the filing)
- In an amount such that the creditor received more than the creditor would have received in a Chapter 7 liquidation [547]

The trustee has additional powers to avoid preferences made to **insiders** (i.e., the debtor's relatives, partners, directors, officers, controlling shareholders). Preferences made to insiders within 1 year before bankruptcy are avoidable under the rule stated in the preceding paragraph.

In Joe's case, he paid back his uncle the full amount due under the prior unsecured loan. This is the typical preference in which a debtor faced with bankruptcy voluntarily pays a favorite creditor or supplier in full and leaves other creditors to share whatever remains. Note that Joe's uncle would be considered an insider, extending the preference period to 1 year prior to the filing of the petition.

Preferences can occur in other ways. Sometimes a creditor pressures a debtor into paying or seizes the property of the debtor through an execution or garnishment procedure. Also, the preference can take the form of a security interest given just before bankruptcy for an unsecured debt incurred much earlier and originally intended to be unsecured.

Limits on Avoidance Powers. Since the trustee's main function is to protect the interests of general (unsecured) creditors, the trustee's power to avoid preferences is subject to certain exceptions. Some transactions that appear to be preferences are not, and therefore they are not avoidable by the trustee. Suppose a supplier delivered goods to Joe 30 days before his bankruptcy and received full payment in cash. Because there is no past debt, this is not a preference. The Code considers this a **contemporaneous exchange for new value** [547(c)(1)].

The Code also has some exceptions to the preference rule. For example, the trustee cannot avoid a preferential payment up to $600 by a consumer debtor (one whose primary debts are consumer debts) [547(c)(7)]. Also excepted is a preferential payment by a business debtor of a debt incurred in the ordinary course of the debtor and creditor's business or financial affairs where the payment was made in the ordinary course of business according to ordinary business terms [547(c)(2)]. In Case 30.2, the Supreme Court analyzes the application of this exception to payments made on a long-term debt.

CASE 30.2	**Union Bank v. Wolas** • 112 S. Ct. 527 (1991)
FACTS	On December 17, 1986, ZZZZ Best Co., Inc., borrowed $7 million from Union Bank. On July 8, 1987, the debtor filed a voluntary petition under Chapter 7 of the Bankruptcy Code. During the preceding 90-day period, the debtor had made two interest payments totaling approximately $100,000 and had paid a loan commitment fee of about $2,500 to the Bank. The trustee of the debtor's estate filed a complaint against the Bank to recover those payments, claiming they were preferences. The Bankruptcy Court found that the loans had been made "in the ordinary course of business or financial affairs," and that both interest payments as well as the payment of the loan commitment fee had been made according to ordinary business terms and in the ordinary course of business. The Bankruptcy Court concluded that the payments were not avoidable preferences, and the district court affirmed. The Court of Appeals reversed, holding that the ordinary course of business exception was not available to long-term creditors. The Supreme Court granted certiorari.
OPINION	STEVENS, J. . . . We shall discuss the history and policy of §547 after examining its text. In subsection (b), Congress broadly authorized bankruptcy trustees to [avoid preferences] if five conditions are satisfied and unless one of seven exceptions defined in subsection (c) is applicable. . . . In this case, it is undisputed that all five of the foregoing conditions were satisfied and that the interest and loan commitment fee payments were voidable preferences unless excepted by subsection (c)(2). . . .
That subsection provides:
"The trustee may not avoid under this section a transfer—. . . . (2) to the extent that such transfer was—(A) in payment of a debt incurred by the debtor in the ordinary course of business or financial affairs of the debtor and the transferee; (B) made in the ordinary course of business or financial affairs of the debtor and the transferee; and (C) made according to ordinary business terms."
Instead of focusing on the term of the debt for which the transfer was made, subsection (c)(2) focuses on whether the debt was incurred, and payment made, in the "ordinary course of business or financial affairs" of the debtor and transferee. Thus, the text provides no support for [the trustee's] contention that §547(c)(2)'s coverage is limited to short-term debt. . . .
The Bank and the trustee agree that §547 is intended to serve two basic policies that are fairly described in the House Committee Report. The Committee explained:
A preference is a transfer that enables a creditor to receive payment of a greater percentage of his claim against the debtor than he would have received if the transfer had not been made and he had participated in the distribution of the assets of the bankrupt estate. The purpose of the preference section is twofold. First, by permitting the trustee to avoid prebankruptcy transfers that occur within a short period before bankruptcy, creditors are discouraged from racing to the courthouse to dismember the debtor during his slide into bankruptcy. The protection thus afforded the debtor often enables him to work his way out of a difficult financial situation through cooperation with all of his creditors. Second, and more important, the preference provi-

> **CASE 30.2 Continued**
>
> sions facilitate the prime bankruptcy policy of equality of distribution among creditors of the debtor. Any creditor that received a greater payment than others of his class is required to disgorge so that all may share equally. . . .
>
> As this comment demonstrates, the two policies are not entirely independent. On the one hand, any exception for a payment on account of an antecedent debt tends to favor the payee over other creditors and therefore may conflict with the policy of equal treatment. On the other hand, the ordinary course of business exception may benefit all creditors by deterring the "race to the courthouse" and enabling the struggling debtor to continue operating its business.
>
> [The trustee] places primary emphasis . . . on the interest in equal distribution.
>
> But the statutory text—which makes no distinction between short-term debt and long-term debt—precludes an analysis that divorces the policy of favoring equal distribution from the policy of discouraging creditors from racing to the courthouse to dismember the debtor. Thus . . . we must recognize that [the exception for long-term creditors] does further the policy of deterring the race to the courthouse. Whether Congress has wisely balanced the sometimes conflicting policies underlying §547 is not a question that we are authorized to decide.
>
> **JUDGMENT** The judgment of the Court of Appeals is reversed.

The Debtor's Exemptions

As a part of the fresh-start policy, the Bankruptcy Code permits an *individual* debtor to exempt certain property from the debtor's estate—i.e., to have it free from the claims of creditors. The Bankruptcy Code gives an individual debtor a choice between two exemption systems—state and federal—unless, as is permitted by the Code, the debtor's state has denied its citizens the right to elect the federal exemptions. States that choose to do this are said to have "opted out" of the federal exemption scheme. Well over thirty states have opted out, limiting their citizens to whatever exemptions the state laws provide.

Some states limit exemptions to no more than about $5,000 worth of property. In other states the exemptible amount can exceed $100,000. Under California law, for example, an individual debtor may exempt up to $45,000 equity in a residence and have many other exemptions. The dollar value of the federal list lies between these extremes. The federal exemptions include $7,500 equity in a residence; $1,200 equity in one motor vehicle; $4,000 in ordinary household furnishings and personal apparel, no single item to exceed $200 in value; $500 in family jewelry; $400 in any property (including cash), plus any unused portion of the residential equity exemption to a maximum of $3,750; $750 in books and tools of the debtor's trade; any unmatured life insurance contract owned by the debtor (other than a credit life insurance contract); up to $4,000 cash surrender or loan value of an unmatured life insurance contract on the life of and owned by the debtor; alimony and child support; certain rights in pension or profit-sharing plans; and awards from personal injury causes of action [522]. Many of the "opt out" states grant exemptions in a similarly broad range of property interests, but usually in smaller amounts.

In Joe's bankruptcy, the exemptions he can claim and whether he has a choice of exemptions will depend upon state law. In any event, he will want to take advantage of the most extensive exemption provisions allowed by law. In addition, he may want to engage in some prebankruptcy planning of his exemptions. For example, he can shift money or property that is not exempt into an exempt asset that he can retain after bankruptcy. Such prebankruptcy transfers are generally lawful, although creditors may attack them as fraudulent conveyances. If the debtor shifts all of his or her assets into exempt property leaving nothing for creditors, or makes last-minute transfers of property on the eve of a bankruptcy filing, the court is likely to consider it a fraudulent transfer. This issue is a difficult one because it involves a conflict of the dual policies of bankruptcy law—fairness to creditors and the fresh-start objective.

> **BOX 30.2**
>
> ### You Be the Judge
>
> Kenneth and Lucille Hanson, who farmed in South Dakota, had financial difficulties in the 1980s that caused them to file a Chapter 7 bankruptcy. Prior to filing, the Hansons appraised and sold some nonexempt property. They sold a car, two vans, and a motor home to their son, Robert, for $27,115, the property's appraised value. They also sold household goods and furnishings to Kenneth's brother for the appraised value of $7,300. With the proceeds, the Hansons acquired life insurance policies with cash surrender values of approximately $20,000 and prepaid $11,000 on their home mortgage. The life insurance policies and the homestead were exempt under South Dakota law. The Hansons' major creditor objected to these exemptions, claiming that the transfers were fraudulent conveyances.
>
> How should this issue be resolved? Why? Would it make a difference if possession of some of the transferred property was retained by the Hansons? Why? ∎

Claims of Creditors

A claim is defined broadly under the Code as "any right to payment, whether or not such right is reduced to judgment, liquidated, unliquidated, fixed, contingent, matured, disputed, undisputed, legal, equitable, secured or unsecured" [101(4)]. Three kinds of creditors have claims on the debtor's estate: secured creditors, unsecured creditors called **priority** creditors, and other unsecured creditors called **general** creditors. The rights of the various kinds of creditors depend on rules governing proof of claim, allowability of claims, and priority of payments.

Proof of Claim. The distribution process begins with the filing of a document called a **proof of claim.** Only unsecured creditors are required to file proofs of claim, but a secured creditor whose claim exceeds the value of the collateral is an unsecured creditor as to the amount of the deficiency, and a proof of claim is required for the recovery of the deficiency. A proof of claim must be filed within 6 months after the first meeting of creditors.

Allowability of Claims. Only **allowed** claims are eligible for payment out of the debtor's estate, and then, of course, allowed claims will be paid only to the extent that funds are available. Unless a proof of claim is timely filed, a claim cannot be allowed even though the claim is otherwise valid. Upon the filing of a proof of claim the claim is "deemed allowed" unless an interested party such as a creditor or the trustee objects to the allowance of the claim. If there is an objection, the bankruptcy court must determine the legitimacy and amount of the claim. For example, where the debtor has a defense to an alleged debt (e.g., fraud or failure of consideration), a claim for payment of the debt will not be allowed.

Priority of Claims

Secured Creditors. Secured creditors have property rights (security interests) that the trustee does not acquire. Only the debtor's "equity" in the collateral is included in the debtor's estate. The trustee does, however, receive the collateral itself for purposes of administration. The trustee may (and frequently does) abandon the collateral to the secured creditor if the debtor has no equity. The trustee can sell the collateral if the secured creditor is oversecured (value of collateral exceeds the debt). The proceeds of the sale will be used to pay the secured party, and any excess will become part of the estate for the benefit of other creditors. Thus, secured claims are paid in full if the collateral is sufficient to cover the secured debt. If not, the secured creditor has an unsecured claim for the amount of the debt less the value of the collateral.

Priority Creditors. Next in line are the **priority creditors,** so called because the Code gives them priority of payment over the claims of the general creditors. The principle of pro rata (equal percentage) distribution is applied throughout the Code's general scheme of distribution. So, if funds are sufficient, the "first priority" claims are paid in full, and any excess is applied to the "second priority" claims. This process is repeated until the money runs out or all unsecured creditors are paid. Where funds are not sufficient to pay a class of claims in full, each claimant of that class receives the same percentage of his or her claim that the other claimants of that class receive (e.g., 10 percent). Seven classes of priority claims receive pro rata payments in the following order [507]:

1. Claims for administrative expenses and expenses incurred in preserving and collecting the debtor's estate.
2. Claims of **gap creditors**—trade creditors who extended unsecured credit to the debtor in the ordinary course of business after the filing of an involuntary petition but before the appointment of a trustee. Priority status for such claims tends to forestall the cutting off of goods, services, and operating credit at the slightest hint of financial difficulty, and therefore to give the debtor an early opportunity to escape bankruptcy.
3. Claims of the debtor's employees for up to $2,000 each in wages earned within 90 days preceding bankruptcy or preceding the cessation of the debtor's business, whichever occurs first.
4. Claims for contributions to employee benefit plans for services within 180 days of the filing, up to $2,000 times the number of employees covered by the plan.
5. Claims of grain producers and fishermen for up to $2,000 each for grain or fish deposited with the debtor but not paid for or returned.
6. Claims of consumers for the return of up to $900 each in prebankruptcy deposits paid to the debtor for the purchase or rental of property not delivered or for services not rendered, where the property or services were for personal, family, or household use.
7. Claims for federal, state, and local taxes.

General Creditors. Finally, if any funds remain, the *general* creditors and a few other claimants receive a share of the debtor's estate [726].

In Joe's case, there are several secured creditors who will be paid in whole or in part from the proceeds of any sale of the collateral or who will receive the collateral if it is abandoned by the trustee. Once these secured claims are handled, there will be few if any assets available to pay the unsecured creditors. This is very typical in bankruptcy. If monies are available, there will be at least two priority creditors: Administrative expenses such as accountant's fees and expenses incurred in the operation of the business will be paid first, and then the employees, who have a priority claim for wages up to $2,000 earned within 90 days of the bankruptcy filing, will be paid. Any remaining monies would be paid to the trade creditors and other general creditors.

Discharge

Debtors under Chapter 7 may receive a discharge from most debts that remain unpaid after the distribution of the debtor's estate. However, only individuals are entitled to a discharge under Chapter 7. The law does not allow partnerships and corporations to receive a discharge. This eliminates the possibility of trading in bankrupt corporations and partnerships for tax purposes. Most debtors are eligible for a discharge under Chapter 7 only once every 6 years.

Denial of Discharge. A discharge in bankruptcy is intended for *honest* debtors. Certain kinds of debtor misconduct will result in the debtor's being denied a discharge altogether. The grounds for denying discharge altogether include the debtor's fraudulently transferring or concealing property (within 1 year before filing a bankruptcy petition) with intent to hinder, delay, or defraud a creditor or an officer of the estate; unjustifiably concealing or destroying business records or failing to keep adequate business records; making a false oath, a fraudulent account, or a false claim in connection with the bankruptcy case; failing to explain satisfactorily any loss of assets or deficiency of assets to meet the debtor's liabilities; and refusing to obey lawful orders of the court [727]. Case 30.3 illustrates a variety of such misconduct.

CASE 30.3 **In re Mazzola** • 4 B.R. 179 (D. Mass. 1980)

FACTS Dennis and Anne Mazzola filed a joint petition under Chapter 7 of the Bankruptcy Code on October 15, 1979. At the time of filing, Dennis Mazzola was the sole stockholder of the Dennis M. Construction Co., Inc., and was engaged in home construction. Just before the bankruptcy was filed, Wayne and Gayle LaVangie had been involved in bitter litigation with the Mazzolas over a claim of faulty home construction. In August of 1979, the LaVangies obtained an attachment on two parcels of property owned by the Mazzolas. In early September of 1979, the Mazzolas were able to get a dissolution of the attachment, sold the properties speedily, deposited the $14,000 received from the sale in the checking account of Dennis M. Construction Co., Inc., and used the proceeds to pay the corporation's creditors. The Mazzolas then filed a petition in bankruptcy on October 15, 1979. The LaVangies requested that the Mazzolas be denied a discharge, alleging that the Mazzolas made false oaths on their petition and transferred and concealed property within 1 year preceding the filing of the petition. The testimony adduced at trial revealed several false answers in the debtors' schedules and statement of affairs.

OPINION LAVIEN, B.J. . . . The purpose of section 727(a)(4)(A) [barring a discharge if the debtor knowingly and fraudulently, in or in connection with the case, made a false oath or account] is to ensure that dependable information is supplied for those interested in the administration of the bankruptcy estate on which they can rely without the need for the trustee or other interested parties to dig out the true facts in examinations or investigations. The trustee and creditors are entitled to [know] what property has passed through the bankrupt's hands during a period prior to his bankruptcy. A false statement in the schedules or statement of affairs due to mere mistake or inadvertence is insufficient for the denial of a discharge; fraudulent intent is necessary to bar a discharge. A reckless disregard of both the serious nature of the information sought and the necessary attention to detail and accuracy in answering may rise to the level of fraudulent intent necessary to bar a discharge. . . .

There is no question in the present case that the schedule and statement of affairs filed by the debtors contained numerous false statements. . . . The determinative issue with regard to the ultimate granting or denial of discharge is whether those false statements were knowingly and fraudulently [made]. . . .

After hearing and observing Mr. Mazzola at trial, the court finds the explanations offered by Mr. Mazzola for the false statements in the documents not credi-

**CASE 30.3
Continued**

ble. The present facts do not reflect mere mistake or inadvertence but rather are indicative at the very least of such a cavalier and reckless disregard for truthfulness as to cause the court to find fraudulent intent. The court finds Mr. Mazzola's explanation for the false answer to question 12b on the statement of affairs to be particularly disturbing. Question 12b clearly asks the debtors whether they have transferred any real or tangible personal property during the year immediately preceding the filing of the petition. . . . The debtors answered "No" to the question. Mr. Mazzola stated at trial, under oath, that he interpreted the question to ask if he currently owned any property. The court cannot accept this explanation as credible. Mr. Mazzola is not an unintelligent individual inexperienced in real estate transactions as is evidenced by the fact that for many years he made his living building homes and buying and selling real estate. . . . The question is entitled, in bold face, "Transfers of property." . . . In fact, the entire page of the statement of affairs asks questions *only* about transfers. . . .

None of this even attempts to explain why the transfer of the $14,000 from the sale of these properties to the corporation was not mentioned in the answer. Likewise, the explanations of the other false statements fall short of being credible. Mr. Mazzola claimed he failed to disclose the sole ownership of the corporation's stock because he believed it to have no value and that he failed to list the attachment because he considered it to be illegal and because it was dissolved approximately two weeks after it was granted. Individually any one of these explanations might appear plausible in the abstract, but when combined with the fact of the existence of the bitterly contested state court proceedings, the speed of the conveyances when the attachment was dissolved, the immediate transfer of the sale proceeds to the corporation which was not a party to the lawsuit, the subsequent abandonment of the state court proceeding, and the almost simultaneous filing [in bankruptcy] coupled with the blatantly false answers, there is simply too much self-serving "misunderstanding" and "mistake."

. . . I find that the statements were made with a calculated disregard for the importance of documents which were signed under penalty of perjury and on which a determination on the request for a discharge would be made. This reckless disregard for the truth is the equivalent of the fraudulent intent necessary to bar a discharge. . . .

JUDGMENT It is hereby ordered that . . . Dennis Joseph Mazzola and Anne Teresa Mazzola be denied discharges in bankruptcy. . . .

Nondischargeable Debts

Although an individual debtor may receive a discharge, certain debts are not covered by it and therefore remain binding on the debtor [523]. **Nondischargeable** debts include the following:

1 Debts for certain taxes—e.g., where the debtor made a fraudulent tax return or a willful attempt at evasion of taxes. (In general, tax debts more than 1 to 3 years old, depending on the kind of tax, *are* discharged in the absence of fraud, late filing, and the like.)

2 Debts contracted on the basis of the debtor's false pretenses, false representations, or actual fraud. A materially false written financial statement can be the basis for denying discharge of the debt for which it was given

(but not for denying a discharge altogether) where the debtor issued the statement with *intent to deceive* and the creditor *reasonably relied* on it.

3 *Presumed* nondischargeable are (a) consumer debts of $500 or more owed to a single creditor for luxury goods or services, incurred on or within 40 days before the order for relief, and (b) cash advances aggregating more than $1,000 that are extensions of consumer credit under an open-end credit plan, obtained by an individual debtor on or within 20 days before the order for relief. The purpose of the presumption is to discourage the practice of "loading up" on luxury items in anticipation of bankruptcy and later claiming them as exempt property.
4 Debts not scheduled by the debtor or others in time to permit a creditor without notice of the case to make a timely filing of a proof of claim.
5 Debts resulting from the debtor's embezzlement, larceny, or violation of a fiduciary duty.
6 Debts arising from alimony, maintenance, or child support awards.
7 Debts arising from the debtor's willful and malicious injury of another entity or willful and malicious injury to or conversion of an entity's property.
8 Debts arising from certain educational loans made, funded, or guaranteed by a governmental unit.
9 Governmental fines and penalties, except, for example, those relating to dischargeable taxes.
10 Debts arising from the debtor's liability for operating a motor vehicle while legally intoxicated.

In Joe's case, his student loans will usually be nondischargeable. Also, the loan from Third Bank, obtained under a false financial statement, may be nondischargeable if Joe acted with an intent to deceive and Third Bank reasonably relied on the statement. The reasonable reliance element requires the creditor to investigate the accuracy of the financial information provided by the debtor, if, for example, the creditor has no prior knowledge of the debtor or has information that the statement is inconsistent with the debtor's actual financial condition. Also, it is possible that the court will deny Joe a discharge on the basis of the fraudulent transfer of his lake property prior to filing for bankruptcy.

Reaffirmation

A debtor may want to **reaffirm** (agree to pay) a discharged debt. A consumer-debtor, for example, may want to redeem an automobile that would otherwise be repossessed.[8] To protect debtors from being pressured to reaffirm, reaffirmation agreements enforceable under state law must also conform to the following requirements:

1 The agreement must be made before the discharge is granted.
2 The agreement must clearly and conspicuously advise the debtor that he or she may rescind it any time before discharge or within 60 days after the agreement is filed with the court, whichever is later.
3 The agreement must be filed with the court, together with an affidavit by the debtor's attorney that the agreement represents the debtor's informed and voluntary consent and does not impose undue hardship on the debtor or the debtor's dependents.
4 The court must have held the discharge hearing and warned the debtor of the consequences of reaffirmation [524(c),(d)].

BUSINESS REORGANIZATIONS

A Chapter 11 reorganization is designed to allow a financially troubled firm to stay in business while it undergoes a process of financial rehabilitation. Reorganization is essentially a process of negotiation in which the debtor firm and its creditors develop a plan for the restruc-

---

[8]The debtor may redeem exempt property that is subject to a security interest by paying to the secured creditor the amount of the allowed secured claim [722]. The right to redeem applies to tangible personal property intended primarily for personal, family, or household use.

turing of the firm's debts to ensure the continuation of the business. Most of the rules of bankruptcy law that apply to Chapter 7 liquidations apply also to Chapter 11 reorganizations, including the persons eligible for bankruptcy,[9] the voluntary or involuntary filing of petitions, the trustee's powers, and the property of the estate. We will examine topics of special significance to reorganization cases.

In Joe's case, rather than liquidate his business under Chapter 7, he may attempt a Chapter 11 reorganization. However, there are certain drawbacks to Chapter 11. A reorganization is a complex and expensive proceeding. Most Chapter 11 reorganizations are not successful, resulting in the ultimate liquidation of the business. This is particularly the case with small businesses. Thus, filing Chapter 11 may simply delay the inevitable. It will, however, allow Joe to stay in business for some time and to try to formulate a plan for the future.

Debtor in Possession

One of the major advantages of Chapter 11 over Chapter 7 for a business debtor (like Joe) is that the debtor continues to operate the business as a **debtor in possession** (often referred to as the **DIP**). The bankruptcy judge can appoint a trustee only if requested to do so by a "party in interest" (e.g., a creditor or a shareholder or a committee of such persons) "for cause"—that is, because of dishonesty or incompetence of the debtor or, where the debtor is a corporation, because of dishonesty or incompetence of its management [1104]. The automatic stay freezes any actions by creditors to sue the debtor or collect on claims, thus giving the debtor time to develop a plan. While the plan of reorganization is being developed and put into effect, the DIP (or trustee) continues the business and tries to reduce business losses by selling unprofitable divisions of the company, reducing the work force,

closing plants or stores where necessary, or rejecting or renegotiating burdensome contracts. The DIP has most of the powers, rights, and duties of a trustee [1107(a)].

Role of Creditors' Committee

As soon as practicable after the court enters an order for relief under Chapter 11, the court must appoint a committee of unsecured creditors to recommend a plan for reorganizing the debtor. Ordinarily, the committee will consist of the seven largest unsecured creditors willing to serve. The principal tasks of the committee are to investigate the financial affairs of the debtor; to determine whether the business should continue to be operated; to determine whether to request the appointment of a trustee to displace the debtor in possession; and to consult with the debtor or trustee in the administration of the case [1103].

Plan of Reorganization

The key to a successful Chapter 11 is the **plan of reorganization.** The plan of reorganization determines how much creditors will be paid, whether owners such as shareholders will retain any interest in the company, and in what form the business will continue. The plan can separate claimants into classes and provide for different treatment among the classes. So, for example, Joe's plan could divide his unsecured creditors into employees, trade creditors, and others; and subdivide his secured creditors into categories. In this way, it may be easier to get the plan accepted by creditors and confirmed by the court. Note that the debtor has the exclusive right to submit a plan within 120 days of the bankruptcy filing, after which time creditors may also submit a plan. A debtor who fails to submit a plan may face a plan proposed by creditors calling for the liquidation of the debtor's business (called a **liquidating plan**). To prevent that, debtors can seek (and are often granted) an extension of the exclusivity period, a common practice that creditor interests have claimed is unfair and leads to unnecessary delay in Chapter 11 cases.

---

[9]The Supreme Court held in *Toibb v. Radloff,* 111 S. Ct. 2197 (1991) that an individual not engaged in business is eligible for Chapter 11. Nevertheless, most Chapter 11 cases are filed by business debtors.

> **BOX 30.3**
>
> ## A Question of Policy: Collective Bargaining Agreements and Chapter 11
>
> Some business firms have attempted to use Chapter 11 as a means to terminate their collective bargaining agreements with their unions. In 1984, Continental Airlines canceled its union contract with the Air Line Pilots Association in an effort to lower salaries and bring the company back to profitability. The bankruptcy court upheld the trustee's rejection of the union contract, despite the union's contention that the rejection was an unwarranted interference with collective bargaining rights protected by the National Labor Relations Act.
>
> The conflict between bankruptcy and collective bargaining policy had been governed by varying judicial standards. Some courts held that the trustee could reject a collective bargaining agreement only if it was so burdensome to the debtor that rejection was necessary for the reorganization to be successful. But in *NLRB v. Bildisco & Bildisco*, 104 S. Ct. 1188 (1984), the Supreme Court held that (1) the trustee does not commit an unfair labor practice by unilaterally modifying or terminating a collective bargaining agreement before the bankruptcy court rules on the propriety of rejection, and (2) the trustee's rejection of a union contract is permissible on a showing merely that the contract burdens the debtor's estate and the equities balance in favor of rejection.
>
> After the *Bildisco* decision, Congress, in the 1984 amendments to the Bankruptcy Code, imposed an intermediate standard. Now the trustee may not reject a collective bargaining agreement until after a court hearing and ruling on the propriety of the rejection. In the meantime, the trustee must make a proposal to union representatives as to what modifications of employee benefits are necessary to accomplish a reorganization that is fair to all affected parties. Then, in its ruling, the bankruptcy court may approve rejection of the union contract *only if* the court finds that (1) the trustee has made a proper proposal and has provided the union with information necessary to evaluate it, (2) the union has, without good cause, refused to accept the proposal, and (3) the balance of the equities clearly favors rejection of the contract [1113]. Some debtors have been able to meet this standard, but the amendments make it more difficult to reject collective bargaining agreements.
>
> What policy considerations justify the special treatment for collective bargaining agreements under the Bankruptcy Code? Should such agreements be given greater or lesser protection under the law? Why?

Acceptance and Confirmation of the Plan

To become effective, the plan ordinarily must be **accepted** (consented to) by a certain percentage of persons whose rights as creditors or owners have been impaired. The claim of a creditor or interest of an owner is **impaired** where the plan alters the legal, equitable, or contractual rights of its holder; where the plan fails to cure a preorganization default by the debtor; or where the plan provides for payment of less than the full amount or value of a claim or interest [1124]. A plan must also be **confirmed** by the bankruptcy court.

Acceptance of the Plan. A class of *creditors* has accepted the plan when holders of a simple majority in number and two-thirds in dollar amount of allowed claims approve the plan. A class of *ownership interests* has accepted the plan when holders of two-thirds in dollar amount of allowed interests approve the plan [1126].

The court has the power to force a plan on a nonconsenting class of creditors or interests under the **cram-down** provision of the Code if the plan treats the impaired class in a manner that is "fair and equitable" [1129(b)]. For the plan to be fair and equitable to a class of secured creditors, secured creditors usually must retain their liens and receive payments over time that equal the present market value of the collateral. On the other hand, a class of unsecured creditors can be forced to accept a plan if they receive a pro rata share of their claims and junior classes of claims or interests (e.g., shareholders) receive nothing (known as the **absolute priority** rule). This absolute priority rule also applies to a class of nonconsenting interests (e.g., a class of shareholders) who can be forced to accept less than the present value of their interest if junior interests receive nothing.

Confirmation of the Plan. A plan must be approved (confirmed) by the bankruptcy court. Among other criteria for confirmation, the plan must be submitted in good faith, priority payments must be paid in full, and the plan must be feasible—that is, it must not result in an immediate need for a reorganization or liquidation of the business. Confirmation makes the plan binding on creditors, shareholders, and other parties to the bankruptcy. The business comes out of bankruptcy with a discharge of all debts except, for example, nondischargeable debts of individual debtors [1141(d)]. After the plan is confirmed, the rights of creditors and shareholders are determined by the terms of the plan.

Repayment Plans for Debtors with Regular Income

Chapter 13 of the Code permits an *individual* debtor to develop a repayment plan and, upon completion of payments under the plan, to receive a discharge from most remaining debts [1328]. Chapter 13 is available on a voluntary basis only (creditors cannot file an involuntary petition against the debtor [303(a)]) to any individual (except a stockbroker or a commodity broker) who has regular income, unsecured debts of less than $100,000, and secured debts of less than $350,000. The debts must be owing and unpaid at the time of the debtor's application for relief. Chapter 13 may be particularly appealing to overburdened consumer debtors who are given a broader discharge of debts than under Chapter 7. It is also beneficial to unsecured creditors of a consumer debtor who often

---

BOX 30.4
Bankruptcy and Business Planning

Businesses should be aware of the ease with which individuals can (and do) file for bankruptcy and plan accordingly. The number of individual and business bankruptcies has skyrocketed in recent years. In 1981, for example, 360,000 bankruptcies were filed. By 1992, the number had jumped to 977,000. Most of these cases were consumer bankruptcies, although 71,000 were business filings. The big losers in bankruptcy are unsecured creditors, who usually receive little or nothing from the bankruptcy estate. Extending credit to individuals and businesses, particularly unsecured credit, thus presents a significant risk to any business. Businesses can reduce some of the risks associated with bankruptcy by exercising caution in extending credit and, if possible, requiring debtors to provide collateral.

Businesses should also be aware of the increasing use of Chapter 11 bankruptcy by business firms as a strategic tool. Some major American corporations filed for bankruptcy reorganization during the 1980s and '90s, including Texaco, Macy's, Continental Airlines, Johns-Manville Corporation, Drexel Burnham Lambert, Greyhound, and A. H. Robins Co. Often the firm was not insolvent, but the company filed for bankruptcy to reduce its liabilities or escape burdensome obligations. For example, Texaco filed a Chapter 11 after Pennzoil recovered a $10.3 billion judgment against Texaco for Texaco's wrongful interference with Pennzoil's agreement to buy Getty Oil. In its reorganization plan, Texaco was able to reduce its liability down to $3 billion. Similarly, Johns-Manville filed for bankruptcy in 1982 to stop a wave of asbestos-related lawsuits and to develop a plan for its mass tort liability. A. H. Robins faced similar mass tort exposure over its intrauterine device, the Dalkon Shield, when it filed under Chapter 11. Other firms have filed to avoid their union contracts and to reduce tax and other government liabilities.

receive more than they would receive in a straight bankruptcy. Chapter 13 is available to sole proprietors (not to corporations or partnerships) if the firm's liabilities do not exceed the Chapter 13 limits. Usually, however, Chapter 13 cases (sometimes called **wage earner plans**) are filed by consumer debtors.

The Chapter 13 Plan

Rather than liquidate the debtor's assets, Chapter 13 calls for the debtor to formulate a plan under which he or she will submit his or her future income to a trustee for the repayment (in whole or in part) or his or her debts. After the repayment plan is completed, the debtor is discharged from any remaining part of the debts. Typically, the debtor will propose either a composition or an extension plan. Payments under a plan (whether composition or extension) must be completed within 3 years after the court confirms the plan, or within 5 years if the court permits [1322]. Regardless of the kind of plan, the debtor must give the trustee control of the debtor's future income [1322], the trustee makes payments of claims [1326], and the debtor has the benefit of injunctive relief against creditors while the plan is being carried out.

Confirmation of the Plan

For a plan to be confirmed, it must be submitted in good faith and the debtor must be able to make the contemplated payments. Unsecured creditors must receive at least what they would receive in a Chapter 7 liquidation. In addition, if the trustee or a holder of an allowed unsecured claim objects to confirmation of the plan, the court cannot confirm it unless (1) the claim is to be paid in full or (2) all the debtor's disposable income for three years will be applied to payments under the plan [1325(b)]. This in effect creates a "best efforts" standard for confirmation of the plan.

Priority claims must be paid in full (so long as funds are available), unless particular priority claimants agree otherwise [1322(a)(2)]. The plan may unilaterally modify the rights of most other claimants (secured and unsecured), so long as all claims in a class receive the same treatment. However, for the plan to be binding on a nonconsenting secured creditor, either (1) a secured creditor must retain his or her lien and receive an amount equal to the value of the collateral or (2) the debtor must surrender the collateral to the secured creditor [1325(a)(5)].

BOX 30.5

Developments in the Law: Chapter 12—Family Farm Reorganizations

In 1986, Congress added Chapter 12 to the Bankruptcy Code. The chapter provides for reorganization plans for "family farmers." To be eligible as a family farmer, the debtor must (1) be engaged in farming operations (50 percent of gross income must come from farming) and (2) have debts not exceeding $1.5 million, of which at least 80 percent arise out of the farming operation. Under Chapter 12, the farm debtor remains in possession of the farm and continues to operate it as a debtor in possession. The family farmer must submit a plan of reorganization within 90 days of the filing of the petition. The farm reorganization plan can restructure the farmer's debts, and as in Chapter 13, the future income of the farm debtor will be submitted to a trustee under a 3- to 5-year plan. The court can confirm the plan if it is submitted in good faith and is feasible, if unsecured creditors are paid as much as they would get in Chapter 7, and if secured creditors retain their liens and are paid the value of their allowed claims. Debts owed to secured parties, particularly mortgages on the farmer's land and security interests on equipment, may be reduced to the fair market value of the collateral. Because Chapter 12 was designed to assist farmers faced with the farm crisis of the 1980s, it will expire on October 1, 1993, unless Congress acts to extend the law. In March of 1993, the House of Representatives passed legislation extending the "sunset" date for Chapter 12 to October 1, 1998. This legislation is expected to pass the Senate and be signed into law by the President.

Discharge

After the completion of all payments under the plan, the debtor receives a discharge. Under the "super discharge" in Chapter 13, all debts are discharged except alimony, child support, or spousal maintenance, most student loans, and long-term debts (e.g., a 30-year mortgage). A debtor who does not make all the payments under the plan because of circumstances beyond his or her control receives a discharge but is limited to the less extensive discharge provided by Chapter 7. Under Chapter 7, a debtor is entitled to a bankruptcy only once every 6 years, but the 6-year bar does not apply to a Chapter 13 debtor, who pays 70 percent of the unsecured claims under a repayment plan that was proposed by the debtor in good faith and that represents the debtor's best efforts [727(a)(9)]. The liberal rules relating to discharge in a Chapter 13 case have resulted in the creation of so-called Chapter 20 bankruptcies, in which a debtor files a Chapter 7 to discharge most of his or her debts and then follows that with a Chapter 13 repayment plan to handle any debts that survive the Chapter 7 discharge, such as debts incurred by fraud.

SUMMARY

Under state insolvency law, an insolvent debtor may make an arrangement with unpaid creditors for full or partial payment of the debts. Or the insolvent debtor or his or her creditors may be entitled to the benefits of federal bankruptcy law. Federal bankruptcy law has two main purposes: (1) to provide for a fair treatment of competing creditors and (2) to give overburdened debtors a fresh start in business.

A Chapter 7 bankruptcy is a liquidation proceeding in which the debtor's nonexempt assets are converted into cash, the monies are distributed in accordance with the scheme of distribution provided by the Bankruptcy Code, and the debtor is granted a discharge from most of the remaining debts. A debtor comes out of bankruptcy with certain exempt property, but he or she will still have to pay nondischargeable debts, such as alimony. Business firms often file under Chapter 11 in an attempt to reorganize their financial structure and stay in business. Chapter 13 permits individual debtors to develop a repayment plan and, upon completion of payments under the plan, to receive a discharge from most remaining debts.

REVIEW QUESTIONS

1. How may an insolvent debtor settle his or her debts under state law?

2. To a debtor, what are the main advantages of federal bankruptcy law as opposed to state insolvency law?

3. How does a Chapter 7 bankruptcy further the underlying purposes of bankruptcy law?

4. How are the duties of the trustee different in a Chapter 7 compared to a Chapter 13 case?

5. Why would an unsecured, general creditor want to file an involuntary petition in bankruptcy? What risks are associated with such a filing?

6. What two broad classes of property become part of the debtor's estate?

7. What is a fraudulent transfer? Give an example.

8. List two grounds for denial of a discharge.

9. Explain the significance of the "debtor in possession" under a Chapter 11 business reorganization proceeding.

10. What are the advantages of a Chapter 13 repayment plan for business debtors?

CASE PROBLEMS

1. Mona Olson inherited a one-third interest in 160 acres of unirrigated farmland from her grandmother. The will was admitted to probate on January 9, 1981. On January 21, Mona contracted to sell her interest in the real estate to her daughter Tammy for $5,000. On March 2, Tammy received a warranty deed to the property and made the final payment. On May 26, 1981, Mona and her husband filed a petition in bankruptcy. The trustee claimed that this property, as an inheritance of the debtor, was part of the estate. Is the trustee correct? On what other grounds could the trustee try to recover the property for the estate?

2. Bago Corporation, a manufacturer of industrial packaging, experienced financial difficulty as the result of a strike by its employees and eventually went into bankruptcy. Sixty days prior to bankruptcy, Bago purchased a load of packaging materials from Bagging Suppliers, Inc., paying with a company check. Bago delivered the load upon receipt of the check, but the check bounced. Ten days later, Bago paid Bagging Suppliers cash for the materials. The trustee sought to avoid the payment as a preference. Was the payment of Bagging Suppliers a preference? Explain.

3. Louis S. St. Laurent was the developer of Topsider Resort, a condominium located in the Florida Keys. First Federal had a mortgage on the resort property. St. Laurent sold time-share intervals, promising to convey the interests free and clear of any mortgage. Rather than pay off the mortgage, St. Laurent converted the purchase monies to his own use. The purchasers sued St. Laurent for fraud and a jury awarded them $48,705.22 in compensatory and $50,000 in punitive damages. St. Laurent filed for Chapter 7 bankruptcy and he claimed that the punitive damage award was dischargeable. The Bankruptcy Code provides that "any debt . . . for money, property or services . . . to the extent obtained by . . . false pretenses, a false representation, or actual fraud" is nondischargeable. St. Laurent argued that the term "debt" and the language "to the extent obtained by . . . fraud" encompassed only the damages caused by the fraud, not a punitive damage award. How should that issue be resolved? Why?

4. In the liquidation of Blotto, Inc., the following creditors filed timely proofs of claim: **(a)** three employees who had not been paid their wages of $1,000 each for 1 month preceding Blotto's bankruptcy; **(b)** 100 customers of Blotto, each of whom, prior to Blotto's bankruptcy, had paid Blotto a $50 unsecured deposit on pen and pencil sets that Blotto never delivered; **(c)** Second Bank, to which Blotto owed $8,000 secured by a valid, perfected security interest in collateral worth $4,000; **(d)** various administrative officials, lawyers, and accountants whose claims for services totaled $5,000. The trustee realized $14,500 upon liquidation of the debtor's estate. How much of its claim does each creditor or class of creditors receive?

5. Sadiron Corp. was undergoing a Chapter 11 reorganization. The debtor proposed a plan that called for all classes of creditors to receive 50 percent of their claims. There was one class of bonds (secured by the total assets of the corporation) and one class of debentures (unsecured debt). Most of the bondholders objected to the plan, and the requisite majority could not be persuaded to vote for it. May the plan be confirmed without the consent of the bondholders?

6. Curtis Johnson gave a mortgage on his farm to Home State Bank to secure promissory notes for $470,000. When Johnson defaulted on the notes, Home State started foreclosure proceedings. Johnson filed a Chapter 7 bankruptcy and was granted a discharge of his indebtedness to Home State Bank. After bankruptcy, the bank proceeded with a foreclosure, and a state court granted a foreclosure judgment for $200,000. Before the foreclosure sale, Johnson filed a Chapter 13 petition and proposed a plan to pay off the $200,000 in four installments and a final balloon payment. Home State argued that the debt had been discharged in bankruptcy and, therefore, the bank did not have a "claim" against the Johnson estate subject to repayment under a Chapter 13 plan. How should this issue be resolved? Why?

ETHICS IN PRACTICE

When a debtor fails to repay a loan, the ethical character of applicable law becomes most evident. Formerly, the law of debtor-creditor relations heavily favored the creditor by permitting harsh loan terms and collection practices. The law has evolved from this creditor-oriented laissez-faire approach to a modern emphasis on fair dealing between the parties. Yet, despite extensive state and federal regulation of debtor-creditor relations, the law does not reach all lending and borrowing practices that may be ethically suspect. Consider the ethical implications of the following problems.

PROBLEMS IN ETHICS

1. Bigbank wants to expand its highly lucrative credit card business. Mary Jones is in charge of the project. She proposes the use of "preauthorized" credit extension. It works this way: Bigbank will buy customer lists from a number of credit bureaus; will identify the people who are making minimum payments on credit cards they already own; and, without requiring a credit check of individuals, will send them unsolicited Bigbank credit cards carrying a $5,000 line of credit. The alternative, which Mary does not favor, is the use of "prescreened" credit extension, in which each candidate must first apply for a Bigbank card and then pass a credit check (paid for by Bigbank) that will reveal whether the applicant's income is sufficient to support Bigbank's additional line of credit. Mary knows that preauthorized credit will produce more defaults than will prescreened credit, but she believes that the savings on credit checks will more than make up for the defaults. **(a)** Smith, a member of Bigbank's board of directors and a recovering "spendaholic," is concerned about preauthorized credit and hires you, an outside consultant, to evaluate the ethics of the practice. What ethical problems, if any, do you see? **(b)** Would your report on the practice differ if you worked for Mary Jones and *she* was the one who asked you to evaluate it? **(c)** Would the content of your report to Mary Jones, your supervisor, be affected by your knowledge that she very much favors the extension of preauthorized credit?

2. *Timemag,* a weekly newsmagazine, mails renewal solicitations 6 months before current subscriptions expire. A customer who checks the "bill me" box soon receives a bill for the next year's subscription. If the customer does not pay promptly, he or she may receive the following communications: a "Payment Due" notice, a "Payment Overdue" notice that threatens to surrender the account for collection action, and a letter from a collection agency informing the recipient of his or her rights as a debtor and demanding a response before the "matter becomes any more delinquent." All this usually occurs while the old subscription has several months yet to run. **(a)** Why would *Timemag* engage in such a billing practice? **(b)** Is this billing practice ethical? **(c)** *Timemag* says it usually sends the customer eight bills and then reviews the situation before turning the account over to a collection agency. Is this practice more acceptable ethically than the other one? Why? **(d)** Evaluate the ethics of the following billing practice: Subscribers receive renewal notices that look like bills; subscribers who ignore them receive follow-up "overdue" notices that sometimes threaten collection agency action; if a subscriber ignores the second notice, the sender merely quits sending magazines when the subscription expires.

3. Mike and Sara Smith own a house in Oklahoma. They move to Virginia and buy a new house there. Because of the depressed housing market in Oklahoma, they cannot sell the old house for enough to cover the mortgage debt on it, nor can they rent it. When the bank approved the loan on the old house, it was worth much more than the amount of the debt, and no one foresaw the economic downturn that depressed the Oklahoma housing market. Now the mortgage payments on the two houses are a serious financial burden to the Smiths. They are considering just "walking away" from the Oklahoma house and letting the bank have it, hoping that the bank will absorb any loss. They know that it is difficult for banks to collect deficiency judgments from out-of-state debtors. They also know that while some lenders always pursue defaulting debtors for deficiencies, other lenders don't because pursuing the matter could be costly and might alienate prospective customers. The Smiths seek your advice on the ethics of their "walk away" plan. How would you respond if you were **(a)** a banker? **(b)** a CPA? **(c)** a lawyer? **(d)** a member of the clergy?

4. For decades, Asbesco manufactured insulation material containing asbestos fibers. Then, over 30 years ago, medical evidence indicated that the inhalation of asbestos fibers causes lung cancer. Thousands of workers and others who came into contact with insulation made by Asbesco developed lung cancer and related diseases. Many sued Asbesco for damages, alleging that their health problems resulted from their contact with Asbesco products. Although Asbesco is a very profitable corporation, its lawyers and accountants fear that liability resulting from present and future lawsuits will eventually drive Asbesco into bankruptcy. To protect against that possibility, company lawyers recommend that Asbesco immediately file for protection under Chapter 11 of the Bankruptcy Code. Under a Chapter 11 reorganization plan, Asbesco can sharply limit its liability to winners of products liability lawsuits and thus stay in business. Many of those suing are former employees of Asbesco whose efforts made Asbesco wealthy. Assume that it is legal for Asbesco to receive Chapter 11 protection. **(a)** Is it ethical for Asbesco to use Chapter 11 this way? **(b)** Does it matter that Asbesco has long known of the medical evidence linking asbestos fibers to lung disease?

PART SEVEN

Commercial Paper

CHAPTER 31
Nature of Commercial Paper; Negotiable Form

CHAPTER 32
Personal and Real Defenses;
Negotiation of Commercial Paper

CHAPTER 33
Holder-in-Due-Course Status; FTC Limits

CHAPTER 34
Liability of the Parties; Discharge

CHAPTER 35
Checks; Relationship between Bank and Customer;
Electronic Funds Transfers

Ethics in Practice

CHAPTER 31

Nature of Commercial Paper; Negotiable Form

Businesspeople use a variety of commercial documents designed for specific business purposes. They include:

- Warehouse receipts, bills of lading, and other documents of title used to distribute goods
- Mortgages, trust deeds, security agreements, and financing statements, used to provide security for loans
- Corporate securities such as stocks and bonds, sold to raise funds for business activities and bought as investments

We turn now to a class of commercial documents familiar to almost everyone: the checks, promissory notes, and other **commercial paper** (also called **negotiable instruments**) widely used as a *substitute for money* or as a *means of extending credit*.

Commercial paper law centers on a fact that at first may seem strange: A person who puts a negotiable instrument into circulation ("issues" a check or a note) may have to pay the stated amount even though he or she was cheated in the original transaction. John tricks Marcia into buying defective goods from him and cashes her check at a drugstore. If the store qualifies as a "holder in due course," as it probably does, it is entitled to payment from Marcia despite her trouble with John. This chapter discusses why this is so and, in overview, how it happens.

The chapter then takes up a key topic of negotiable instruments law: the language ("form") required for an instrument to be negotiable and thus to produce this seemingly odd result. Subsequent chapters deal in more depth with other topics introduced here—what defenses issuers such as Marcia may assert against strangers to the original transaction, how commercial paper is negotiated (transferred), what is required for a person to be a holder in due course, the liabilities indorsers may have, and so on. The final chapter of the series deals specifically with checks, the relationship between a bank and its checking account customers, and electronic funds transfer (including interbank transfers governed by Article 4A of the Uniform Commercial Code).

UCC Articles 3 and 4 govern commercial paper. A number of states have adopted the 1990 amendments of these articles.[1] Significant 1990 changes will be noted throughout the commercial paper chapters, usually in "boxes" headed Revised Article 3 (or 4).

[1] As of March 1993, Arkansas, California, Connecticut, Florida, Hawaii, Illinois, Kansas, Louisiana, Minnesota, Mississippi, Missouri, Montana, Nebraska, New Mexico, North Dakota, Oklahoma, Pennsylvania, Virginia, and Wyoming.

TYPES AND NATURE OF COMMERCIAL PAPER

Centuries ago merchants began to devise ways of paying for property and services without having to carry large sums of money. The **bill of exchange** (today called a **draft**) was used in Europe for that purpose as early as the fourteenth century. With the growth of banking, a special kind of draft called a **check** came into wide use. Today most business transactions are settled by check. Checks and other drafts serve as a temporary, safe, and efficient substitute for money. Another kind of commercial paper, the **promissory note,** is used primarily for extending credit.

A promissory note is the written promise of a person (a borrower or buyer) to pay a sum of money to another person (a lender or seller) at some future date.

Types of Commercial Paper

Although all commercial paper may be classified as either a note (promise) or a draft (order), Article 3 lists four varieties of commercial paper: notes (often called promissory notes), certificates of deposit, drafts, and checks [3-104].[2] A

---
[2] The bracketed numbers refer to the 1972 version of the UCC still used in many states.

Figure 31.1 Promissory note.

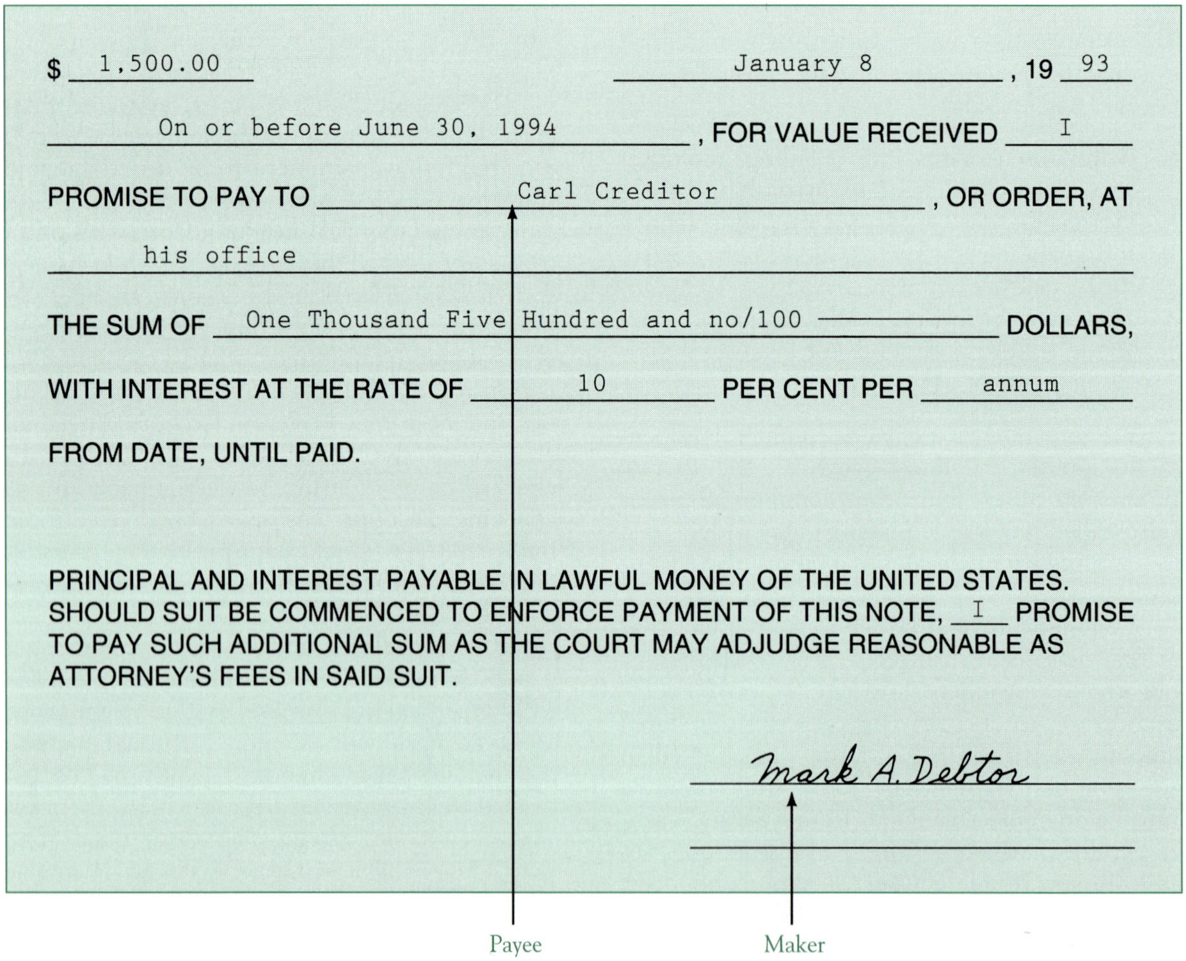

| $ 1,500.00 | January 8, 19 93 |

On or before June 30, 1994, FOR VALUE RECEIVED I PROMISE TO PAY TO Carl Creditor, OR ORDER, AT his office

THE SUM OF One Thousand Five Hundred and no/100 ———— DOLLARS,

WITH INTEREST AT THE RATE OF 10 PER CENT PER annum FROM DATE, UNTIL PAID.

PRINCIPAL AND INTEREST PAYABLE IN LAWFUL MONEY OF THE UNITED STATES. SHOULD SUIT BE COMMENCED TO ENFORCE PAYMENT OF THIS NOTE, I PROMISE TO PAY SUCH ADDITIONAL SUM AS THE COURT MAY ADJUDGE REASONABLE AS ATTORNEY'S FEES IN SAID SUIT.

Mark A. Debtor

Payee ↑ (Carl Creditor)   Maker ↑ (Mark A. Debtor)

certificate of deposit is a specialized type of note. A check is a specialized type of draft.

Promissory Notes. Notes are the simplest kind of commercial paper because they involve only two parties. A **note** is a writing in which one party (the **maker**) promises to pay a sum of money to another party (the **payee**). A note may be either a *demand* note (i.e., payable on demand of the payee or some other possessor called a **holder**) or a *time* note (payable at a definite time after it is issued). A note may or may not bear interest, depending on the agreement of the parties. The principal and any interest may be payable in installments (e.g., a specified amount per month), or principal and interest may be due all at once in a single payment. Figure 31.1 shows a simple form of a "single payment" time note.

Certificates of Deposit. A **certificate of deposit** (CD) is an acknowledgment by a *bank* of receipt of money with an engagement (promise) by the bank to repay it, plus interest. The bank (broadly defined to include savings and loan associations and other business organizations legally empowered to engage in the banking business) is the maker. The payee, ordinarily an individual or a business firm, deposits money with the maker and receives the CD which, because of the interest, may be attractive as an investment. There are two classes of CDs: **demand certificates** (payable on demand of the payee or another holder) and **time certificates** (often referred to as TCDs because they are payable at a definite time after they are issued). Figure 31.2 illustrates a TCD.

Drafts. Drafts involve three parties. A **draft** is an order (command) by one person (the **drawer**) directed to another person (the **drawee**) to pay a sum of money to a third person (the **payee**). The drawee can be any person or organization willing or obliged to obey the order. Tony's Pizza Parlor owes Anna $500 for a new oven she delivered, and Anna owes Cora $500. When Cora demands payment, Anna might not have the cash. Instead, Anna might "draw" (write out) a draft on Tony's Pizza Parlor for $500, name Cora as payee, and give the draft to Cora as payment (if this is agreeable to Cora). Cora may now present the draft to Tony's Pizza (the drawee) for payment, and if Tony's Pizza "honors" (pays) it, two debts are settled at one time. A draft may be made out to the payee in a variety of ways—e.g., to "bearer" or to the

Figure 31.2 Time certificate of deposit (by permission of Security Pacific National Bank).

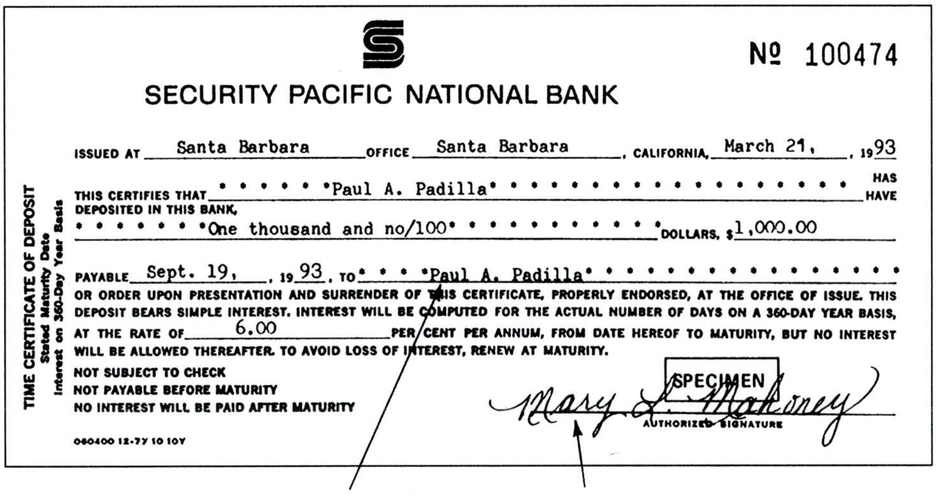
Nº 100474

SECURITY PACIFIC NATIONAL BANK

ISSUED AT Santa Barbara OFFICE Santa Barbara, CALIFORNIA, March 21, 1993

THIS CERTIFIES THAT * * * * * *Paul A. Padilla* * * * * * * * * * * * * * * * * * * HAS/HAVE DEPOSITED IN THIS BANK,

* * * * * * * *One thousand and no/100* * * * * * * * * * DOLLARS, $1,000.00

PAYABLE Sept. 19, 1993, TO * * * *Paul A. Padilla* * * * * * * * * * * * * * * OR ORDER UPON PRESENTATION AND SURRENDER OF THIS CERTIFICATE, PROPERLY ENDORSED, AT THE OFFICE OF ISSUE. THIS DEPOSIT BEARS SIMPLE INTEREST. INTEREST WILL BE COMPUTED FOR THE ACTUAL NUMBER OF DAYS ON A 360-DAY YEAR BASIS, AT THE RATE OF 6.00 PER CENT PER ANNUM, FROM DATE HEREOF TO MATURITY, BUT NO INTEREST WILL BE ALLOWED THEREAFTER. TO AVOID LOSS OF INTEREST, RENEW AT MATURITY.

NOT SUBJECT TO CHECK
NOT PAYABLE BEFORE MATURITY
NO INTEREST WILL BE PAID AFTER MATURITY

SPECIMEN
Mary L. Mahoney
AUTHORIZED SIGNATURE

TIME CERTIFICATE OF DEPOSIT
Stated Maturity Date
Interest on 360-Day Year Basis

060400 12-77 10 10Y

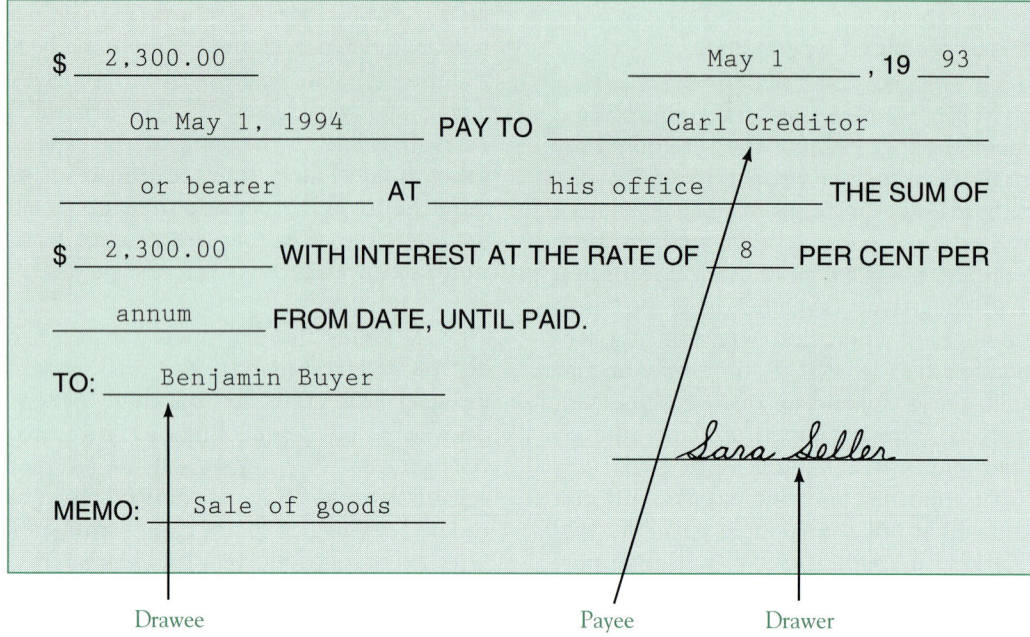

Figure 31.3 Draft.

order of a named third person such as Cora, the Internal Revenue Service, First Church, or even the drawer herself. An interest-bearing draft is illustrated in Figure 31.3.

Drafts are either demand drafts or time drafts. A **demand draft** is payable any time after issue, literally on demand of the payee or other holder made to the drawee. Statements such as "On demand pay . . . ," "At sight pay . . . ," and simply "Pay to . . ." are sufficient to indicate a demand draft.

A **time draft** is one payable at a specified time after issue. The time might be indicated merely by writing the date of issue on the draft and then filling in another blank with the future date on which payment is to be made, as in the draft illustrated in Figure 31.3. Or the time draft might say instead, "Sixty days after date pay. . . ." A draft reading "Sixty days after *sight* [by the drawee] pay . . ." is a time draft, but it requires **acceptance** by the drawee to fix the maturity date of the instrument. A drawee accepts by writing "Accepted" across the face of the draft and adding the date and the drawee's signature. Thus, the **acceptor** (drawee) engages (promises) to pay the draft when it falls due.

From the time a draft is drawn, the drawee is customarily referred to as a "party" to it. However, a drawee is not truly a party (a person who has contractual liability for the face amount) unless he or she *accepts* the draft—i.e., by signature agrees to pay it. Until then the drawee has no obligation to pay the draft [3-401]. Anna issues a time draft to Cora, payable 60 days after date. Anna is the only signer and therefore the only person liable to Cora for the face amount in the event that Tony's Pizza, the drawee, refuses to accept it. If Tony's Pizza accepts the draft, Tony's Pizza also becomes personally liable to Cora (or to a subsequent holder), and Cora has two sources of payment instead of one. If she decides to sell the draft now instead of waiting 60 days to collect it herself, the acceptor's signature increases the draft's value by reducing the purchaser's risk of noncollection.

Checks. A **check** is a draft (order) drawn on a bank and payable on demand [3-104(2)(b)].

The drawer is a customer who has an account at a drawee bank. The payee may be any individual, firm, or organization named on the face of the check whom the drawer wishes to receive payment. Typically, checks are made out on printed forms having blank spaces for the date of the check, the payee's name, the amount to be paid, and the drawer's signature, as in Figure 31.4. Checks are especially useful because they enable the drawer to make distributions from a single fund (the drawer's bank account) for paying debts and making gifts and purchases. And, because the checks issued by the drawer eventually "clear" the bank collection process and are returned to the drawer's bank and then to the drawer, the drawer has a record of expenditures.

When a bank draws a check on itself, the instrument is called a **cashier's check**. A check drawn by one bank on its account in another bank is called a **bank draft** or a **bank check**—or, under the 1990 revisions of Article 3, a **teller's check**. Some **money orders** are drawn on a bank and payable on demand. These money orders are classified as checks under the 1990 revisions.

A **traveler's check** is a three-party instrument purchased from a bank or other firm and carried instead of cash by travelers. The traveler is the drawer who, for purposes of identification, must sign the traveler's check twice—once when the seller issues it and a second time when the traveler cashes it. The bank or other issuing firm is the drawee. When the drawee is a nonbanking firm such as American Express, the so-called traveler's check is not a check at all, but is a draft subject to the Code rules relating to drafts.

Although frequently issued as gifts, checks usually are issued as part of an **underlying contract**—e.g., as payment for goods or services. Thus, there usually are two contracts: the check and the underlying transaction. Ann buys a typewriter from Typeshop and issues a check in payment. The check is one kind of *formal* contract (discussed in Chapter 10), and Ann, as a signer, is liable for the face amount to the payee (Typeshop) or to some other holder such as a business where Typeshop might have cashed Ann's check. Ann is also a party to the underlying *informal* contract (discussed in Chapter 10) between herself and Typeshop for the sale of the typewriter. Ann will be liable in damages to Typeshop if she breaches the underlying contract by, for example, stopping payment of the check without good reason.

Ordinarily, a check operates as only a **conditional** (not yet final) **payment** of the underlying obligation. The check does not become a final payment until honored (paid) by the bank on which it was drawn. Until the check is honored, its issuer remains liable on the underlying transaction. However, the seller's taking a check as conditional payment *postpones* the seller's right to sue on the underlying obligation [3-

Figure 31.4 Check (by permission of Security National Bank).

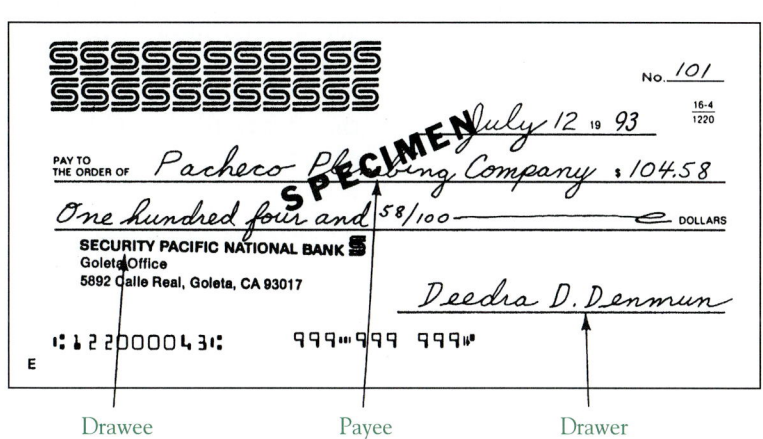

Drawee   Payee   Drawer

802(1)(b)]. If the drawee bank dishonors the check, as where the drawer has insufficient funds or orders the bank to stop payment, the right of the seller to sue on the underlying obligation is "revived." Thus, where Ann pays by check and the drawee bank dishonors it, Ann is in breach of the underlying contract, and Typeshop now may sue Ann for damages.

Negotiable Character of Commercial Paper—An Overview

Understanding the negotiable character of commercial paper requires an overview of some basic commercial paper concepts and practices, with a more detailed examination being reserved for later parts of this chapter and for subsequent chapters. Three terms are of special significance in the law of commercial paper: (1) negotiable form, (2) holder in due course, and (3) personal and real defenses.

Meaning of Negotiable Form. To say that an instrument (a note or draft) is **negotiable** or "negotiable in form" means simply that the writer of the instrument has used the language required by law for creating a negotiable instrument. Precisely what this language is and why it must be used is discussed later in this chapter. It is sufficient, for now, to know that a note or draft is either negotiable or nonnegotiable, depending on its *wording*; and that in certain situations, soon to be illustrated, a negotiable instrument can confer *greater rights* on its buyer than a nonnegotiable instrument can. Why a negotiable instrument confers greater rights requires a brief look at the meaning of "holder in due course" and "personal and real defenses."

Meaning of Holder in Due Course. Negotiable instruments are useful primarily because innocent third persons, if they qualify as holders in due course, ordinarily may collect the amount specified in the instrument even though the drawer or maker has a valid reason not to pay the payee. Sal takes his car to Roger for repair. Roger fraudulently overstates the repairs that are needed. Sal gives Roger a check as payment, and Roger cashes it at Tina's Supermarket, which knows nothing of the transaction between Sal and Roger. Tina's is a **holder in due course** of the check. To be a holder in due course, one must take a negotiable instrument *for value, in good faith,* and *without notice of defenses* such as Sal's. The personal characteristics required for holder-in-due-course status are discussed in Chapter 33.

Meaning of Personal and Real Defenses. However, whether a holder in due course takes a negotiable instrument free from a defense depends, also, on the *kind* of defense it is: personal or real. A holder in due course takes a negotiable instrument free from personal defenses but subject to real defenses. A **personal defense** is one involving wrongdoing or some other circumstance that the law says must remain a private matter between the immediate parties to a negotiable instrument (e.g., between the drawer of a check and the payee) instead of becoming a source of loss to a (third-person) holder in due course. Roger's fraud gives Sal a personal defense, which Sal cannot use against a holder in due course. In contrast, a **real defense** involves wrongdoing or some other circumstance so serious that the (real) defense is good against even a holder in due course. The bankruptcy of the maker or the drawer is a real defense. Personal and real defenses are discussed further in Chapter 32.

Significance of It All: Cashing a Check; Buying a Note. Commercial paper is useful to the business community because holders in due course (and most of their transferees) can purchase it in relative safety, confident that it will usually be collectable despite disputes between the parties to the underlying transaction. Two examples follow.

1 Sal, defrauded by Roger, stops payment on his check before Roger cashes it at Tina's supermarket. Sal's bank dishonors (refuses to pay) the check, and Tina's immediately takes it to Sal for payment. Sal's personal defense to payment (Roger's fraud) would be good against *Roger*, the payee, if Roger had kept the check and had himself sought payment from Sal after the bank

dishonored the check. *Tina's,* however, to whom Roger negotiated the check, is a holder in due course because Tina's paid for the check by cashing it and knew nothing of Roger's fraud when doing so. Therefore, Tina's took the check free from Sal's personal defense. Accordingly, Sal must pay Tina's the amount of the check and seek from Roger, the defrauding payee, any reimbursement (repayment) that might be due. The *legal* significance of holder-in-due-course status here is that Tina's takes the check free from Sal's personal defenses. One *practical* significance is that Tina's Supermarket, being free from personal defenses, will be more willing to cash checks for strangers than it would be if it had to absorb all losses.

> **BOX 31.1**
>
> ### Test Your Knowledge
>
> Rhonda had a carpet installed in her house. After completing the work, the installer stopped at Rhonda's place of business for payment. She paid with a check. Upon arriving home from work, however, Rhonda discovered that the carpet had been improperly installed and was not the color she had chosen. She immediately stopped payment on the check. A day later, the installer cashed Rhonda's check at a check-cashing business in the downtown area. When Rhonda's bank dishonored (refused to pay) the check, the manager of the check-cashing service sought payment from Rhonda. Must she pay? In arriving at your answer, what main things will you need to consider? ∎

2 You buy a car from Joe. Joe expressly warrants that the car is in perfect running condition. Lacking cash, you pay for the car with your single-payment negotiable promissory note for $4,000 plus 10 percent annual interest. The note is due 1 year from now. You will have to pay a total of $4,400 in principal and interest. Joe, the payee, could hold the note for a year and collect the $4,400 from you; but he needs cash now, so he immediately discounts (sells) the note to Brenda, a buyer of commercial paper, for $4,000. Thus, Joe has the $4,000 he needs now, and Brenda has a chance to make a profit by collecting the $4,400 in principal and interest from you when the note comes due.

A few days after these transactions, fire destroys your car because of a serious defect in its electrical system. The presence of the defect is a breach of Joe's warranty. You try to locate Joe, but learn that he has left town permanently for parts unknown. At the end of the year, Brenda presents the note to you for payment. You refuse to pay because Joe's breach of warranty made the car worthless. Unfortunately for you, the breach of warranty is a personal defense. Because Brenda became a holder in due course when she bought your note, she took it free from your personal defenses and is entitled to payment. You, the maker of the negotiable note, will have to absorb the loss if you cannot find Joe and make him pay.

As the preceding examples show, a negotiable instrument can confer upon a holder in due course more than the usual contract rights, since unlike a transferee (assignee) of an ordinary contract, a holder in due course of a negotiable instrument is free from personal defenses when attempting to collect payment. If an instrument is not negotiable in form (or is not transferred properly—is not "negotiated" as described in Chapter 32), its purchaser is merely an **assignee** and therefore takes the instrument subject to all defenses, personal and real. Indeed, the purchaser of a nonnegotiable instrument (an ordinary, "simple," or "informal" contract) can *never* be a holder in due course but is always a mere assignee, subject to all defenses. The law of assignments is discussed in Chapter 16.

A major practical significance of negotiability in the discounting of notes is that a holder in due course, being free from personal defenses of the maker, will tend to pay more for the note than if the purchaser were merely an assignee. Brenda in example 2 probably would have paid Joe much less for your note if it had not been in negotiable form, because as an assignee she would be subject to *all* your defenses, personal and real, and therefore would face a much greater risk of noncollection.

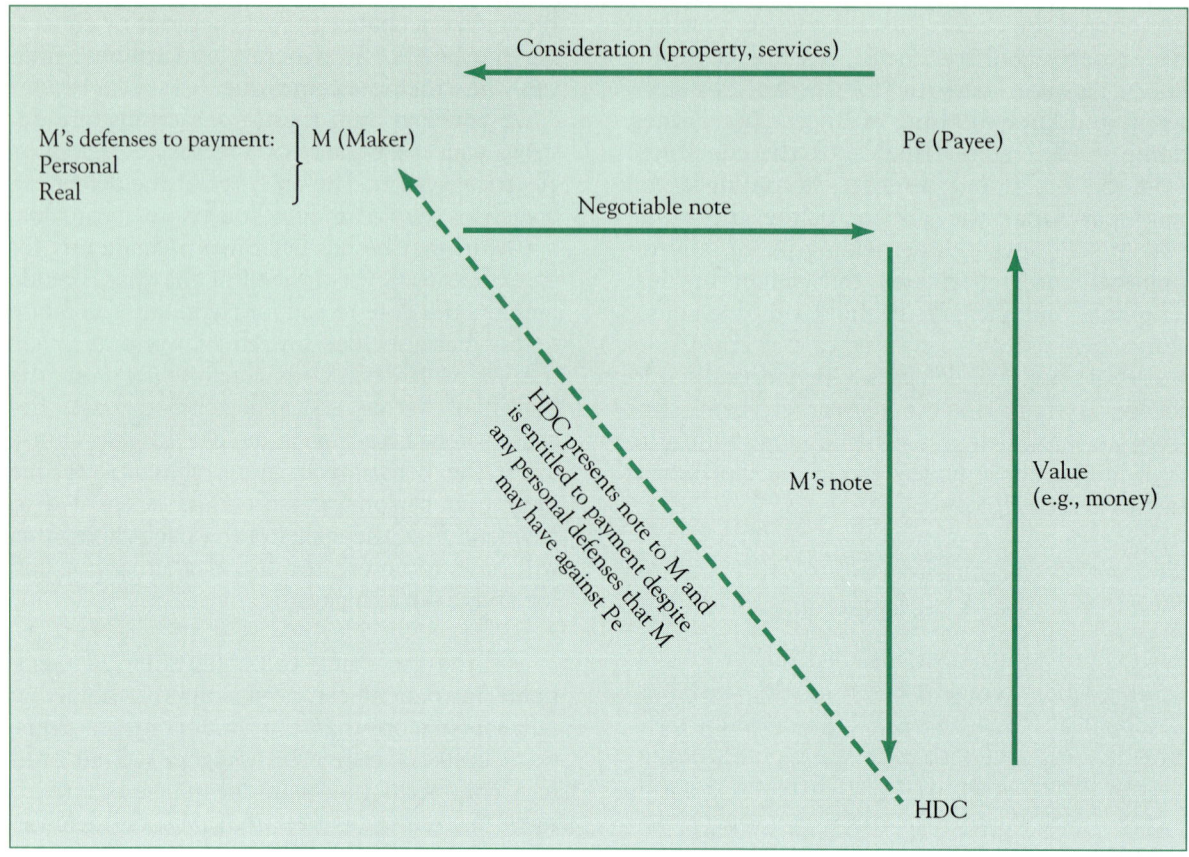

Figure 31.5 Legal significance of negotiability.

Figure 31.5 shows a typical sequence of events in which (1) the maker and the payee enter into an underlying contract, (2) the payee sells the negotiable note to a holder in due course (HDC), and (3) HDC presents the note to the maker for payment. If the maker has a personal defense, HDC is nevertheless entitled to payment from the maker. If the maker has a real defense, HDC is not entitled to payment from the maker; however, as noted in Chapters 34 and 35, HDC may be able to go back to the payee for payment.

Some people wrongly believe that a *nonnegotiable* instrument may not be transferred from one person to another. However, the fact that an instrument is negotiable has relatively little to do with its *transferability*. True, a negotiable instrument is easy to transfer because, as the next chapter reveals, the mechanics of a "negotiation" (the special kind of transfer applicable to a negotiable instrument) are simple. But under the law of assignments, many ordinary contract rights are freely transferable, especially the right to a money payment. The main difference between a negotiable document and a nonnegotiable document lies in the *number of defenses* a good faith purchaser must face when seeking payment. A holder in due course of a negotiable instrument faces fewer defenses to payment than does an assignee of a nonnegotiable instrument.

Dual Nature of Commercial Paper

Commercial paper is, simultaneously, a contract and a type of property. Commercial paper is a contract because Article 3 imposes on *any signer* an **engagement** (promise) to pay the face amount, regardless of whether the signer knew that he or she was making such a promise. People who indorse (sign) their payroll checks when cashing them probably do not realize that, by indorsing, they have *contracted* to pay the face amount if the drawer (employer) does not; but indeed they have so contracted—because Article 3 says so [3-413; 3-414].

Commercial paper is also a type of property that can be bought and sold. Recall from Chapter 29 that chattel paper, which consists of a promissory note and a security agreement, can itself be sold or pledged so that the business generating it can raise money before the note comes due. Also, many corporations issue commercial paper, in the form of promissory notes, for short-term financing. A person who buys such paper from the corporation may, in turn, sell it like any other property. Since commercial paper is property, it is subject to some rules of property law. For example, delivery of a negotiable instrument is required for conveying ownership of it to a donee (receiver of a gift) or to a buyer. And, as in the sale of goods, the law imposes warranties that may be available to a purchaser if the paper turns out to be defective in some respect. Warranties as they relate to commercial paper are discussed in Chapter 34.

Some Business Uses of Commercial Paper

Businesspeople use commercial paper in numerous ways. For example, a person or a firm usually buys a CD as an investment, to collect the interest. While holding the CD, however, one might pledge it as collateral for a loan, or might simply sell it to raise immediate cash for some personal or business purpose. The bank that issues a CD does so, of course, to attract funds to lend to its customers.

Often, the creation of commercial paper is only one step in a complex transaction involving many other documents. The following paragraphs describe some common business uses of notes and drafts and the role of negotiable instruments in complicated transactions.

Uses of Notes. Promissory notes are used mainly as evidence of indebtedness in loan transactions and in credit sales of property or services. Typically, a borrower signs a note that bears interest on the principal amount. The principal and interest may be due in one lump sum at a fixed future time (or on demand), or principal and interest may be payable in installments, often equal monthly installments. Sometimes the maker agrees to pay the interest in installments and to make a final "balloon" (large) payment consisting of not only the final installment of interest but also repayment of the principal. Frequently, lenders extend unsecured credit, solely on the basis of the borrower's personal note.

Usually, however, lenders insist that some third person cosign the note as *surety* (discussed in Chapter 28), or that the note be secured by real estate or other property that the lender may sell if the borrower fails to repay the loan. Widely used in financing the sale of goods is the **conditional sale contract.** It consists essentially of a promissory note signed by the buyer as maker, together with a security agreement giving the seller the right to repossess and sell the goods upon the buyer's default. Usually the notes are interest-bearing installment notes.

Uses of Drafts. Businesses use drafts most often in financing the sale of goods. Drafts are especially useful for this purpose when buyer and seller are strangers, are located some distance from each other, and make use of a reliable intermediary to handle the transaction.

Sally Seller is in Boston, Bob Buyer is in San Francisco, and Seller has agreed to extend 60 days' credit to Buyer for the purchase of a machine to be used in Buyer's business. This transaction will require the use of a 60-day time draft. When Seller ships the machine, she obtains a bill of lading from the carrier. She then draws a time draft reading, "To: Bob Buyer. Sixty days after sight pay to the order of Sally Seller $8,200." This amount covers the price of the machine plus shipping costs. Seller attaches the bill of lading, an invoice (itemized account of the goods), a security agreement, and a financing statement to the draft and takes it to her bank in Boston. The Boston bank forwards the draft with the attached documents to its correspondent bank in San Francisco. The San Francisco bank notifies Bob Buyer that the draft has arrived. He accepts the draft and signs the security agreement and the financing statement. The bank then delivers the bill of lading to Buyer so he can claim the machine when it arrives. The bank arranges to have the financing statement filed and, depending on Sally Seller's instructions, may hold the time draft for collection at the end of the 60 days, sell the draft to a buyer of commercial paper, or send it to Sally. Time drafts drawn by sellers on buyers and accepted by the buyers are called **trade acceptances,** and they can be sold or pledged as collateral for a loan.

NEGOTIABLE FORM

No purchaser of a note or a draft can be a holder in due course unless the instrument is in negotiable form. If the instrument lacks negotiable form, even an innocent purchaser will be merely an assignee, subject to all defenses of the maker or drawer.

The UCC sets forth eight requirements, all of which must be met for a note or draft to be in negotiable form. The instrument must:

1. Be in *writing*
2. Be *signed by the maker or drawer*
3. Contain a *promise or order* to pay that is
4. *Unconditional* in character
5. Be *payable in money*
6. Be made out for a *sum certain*
7. Be *payable* either *on demand* or *at a definite time* after its issue
8. Be *payable to the order of the payee* or *to bearer* [3-104]

If any one of these eight requirements is not met, the instrument is not in negotiable form, and all transferees are assignees only. As noted below, two of these requirements have been modified by the 1990 amendments.

Some types of commercial paper, such as checks, are extremely simple and easy to use. Other types, such as notes, can be quite complicated and lengthy because of the many protective clauses that a lender or seller will demand as a condition to making the loan or selling on credit. Sometimes the added language destroys negotiability, and sometimes a preprinted draft or note form is altered in such a way as to destroy negotiability. Thus we have two questions: (1) What minimum language is required for the creation of negotiable form? (2) Once a negotiable form is created, what clauses or language may be added to the instrument without destroying negotiability?

Minimum Language Required for Negotiable Form

The minimum language required for an instrument to be negotiable varies somewhat according to whether the instrument is a demand or a time instrument; however, some wording is common to all commercial paper.

Unconditional Promise or Order to Pay. To be negotiable, an instrument must contain language that clearly reveals the issuer's intention to make payment or to have a drawee pay. So, if the instrument is a note, it must contain the **maker's promise** to pay (e.g., "I promise to pay"; "I undertake to pay"). If the instrument is a draft, it must contain the **drawer's order** (command or instruction) to the drawee that the drawee is to pay (e.g., "Pay . . ."; "Pay to . . ."). A mere acknowledgment of debt ("IOU $50") is not a promise, because there is no expression of the debtor's intention to pay the amount owed. The intention to pay must be expressed. Likewise, language such as "I wish you would pay" is not an order to pay but is merely an authorization or a request.

The promise or order must be clear and definite; but for the instrument to be negotiable, and thus to circulate most freely or to bring the highest possible price, the promise or order must also be **unconditional** (without reservations; absolute). John's language, "I promise to pay Eva or order $100 if I receive from her one used typewriter by 5:00 p.m. Friday," is conditional (and the note in which the language appears is nonnegotiable) because John has made his obligation to pay $100 depend on Eva's delivering the typewriter. If Eva puts the note into circulation, every potential purchaser will have to investigate the underlying transaction to determine whether Eva delivered the typewriter. This burden of investigation is inconsistent with a major aim of commercial paper law: to remove as many doubts as possible about the collectability of drafts and notes. The requirement that the promise or order be unconditional is discussed further in the part of this chapter entitled Language That Destroys Negotiability.

Order or Bearer Language ("Language of Negotiability").

To be negotiable, an instrument must contain language expressing the issuer's intention that the instrument circulate freely. This **language of negotiability** can be either order language or bearer language, depending on the wishes of the parties. By using **order** language (e.g., "Pay *to the order of* Juan Jimenez" in a draft or "I promise to pay *to the order of* Juan Jimenez" in a note), the drawer or maker expresses a willingness for the payee to specify who will have the right to collect payment. By using **bearer** language (e.g., "Pay *bearer*" in a draft or "I promise to pay *bearer*" in a note), the drawer or maker expresses a willingness to pay anyone who is in possession of the instrument. The presence of bearer or order language assures any **transferee** (person who receives the instrument from the payee or other holder) that the issuer is willing to pay even a stranger.

In contrast, language such as "Pay Juan Jimenez" lacks the required order or bearer language and creates a nonnegotiable instrument. While a nonnegotiable instrument is collectable under the law of assignments (if there are no real or personal defenses), not only the payee but also every transferee is subject to any defense, including any personal defense, that the maker or drawer has. So, if a drawer strikes out the words "to the order of" on a preprinted check form, the drawer creates a nonnegotiable check. In doing so, the drawer preserves all personal defenses, but also increases purchasers' risk of noncollection and thus may have reduced the willingness of strangers to cash the check or to pay the full face amount for it.

BOX 31.2

Revised Article 3

Under the 1990 amendments, striking out the words "to the order of" does *not* deprive a *check* of negotiability. This new rule applies only to checks, however. Striking out preprinted language of negotiability from noncheck draft or note forms still makes those instruments nonnegotiable. ■

Wording Indicating That the Instrument Is for a "Sum Certain" Payable in Money.

To be negotiable, an instrument must be payable in money. An instrument is **payable in money** if it gives the payee the right to have payment in the currency of any domestic or foreign government (dollars, marks, rubles, pesos, etc.). So an instrument payable in wheat or corn cannot be negotiable. However, if the payee is given the option of demanding wheat or money, the instrument is payable in money. If the drawer or maker has the option of providing wheat or money, the instrument is not payable in money. The payment-in-money requirement enables a purchaser of the instrument to determine easily how much to pay for it, since calculations are made in some commonly accepted medium of exchange.

The requirement of a **sum certain** serves a similar purpose. If the sum is certain, a purchaser can determine quickly how much the maker or drawer owes, and therefore how much the purchaser should pay for the instrument. The sum is certain if the purchaser (or the payee) can, at the time set for payment, determine from the instrument itself without reference to any outside source the amount then payable. Sue signs a note reading, "I promise to pay the bearer of this note, on demand, $500 plus 10 percent annual interest," and delivers the note to Joe, who discounts it to Ann. Since Sue cannot predict when Ann will demand payment, Sue has no way of knowing how much interest she will owe Ann. Despite this, the sum is certain because Ann, the purchaser, will be able to compute exactly how much Sue, the maker, owes at the moment that Ann decides to demand payment. A provision in a note imposing a charge for late payment does not make the sum uncertain. Neither does a provision requiring the maker to pay attorney's fees for a collection suit upon the maker's default [3-106], or a higher rate of interest after default than before.

> **BOX 31.3**
>
> Some courts have held notes providing for variable interest rates nonnegotiable in form, on the ground that the sum is uncertain. Other courts have held such notes negotiable. To make clear that variable interest rates may be used without destroying negotiability, the 1990 amendments drop the "sum certain" language. Instead, to be negotiable, an instrument must specify **"a fixed amount of money with or without interest or other charges described in the promise or order."** ■

Signature of Maker or Drawer. The signature of the maker or drawer is required for the obvious reason that payees and other holders must be able to prove whose legal commitment the instrument represents. A **signature** is any symbol used or adopted by a party (e.g., a maker or drawer) with the present intention to authenticate the writing [1-201(39)]. So a signature can be handwritten or typed, or it can be made by an agent for the agent's principal, or it can consist of a trade name, an assumed name, a mark such as "X," or even a thumbprint.

The signature of a drawer or maker may appear in the body of the instrument. However, it normally appears at the end of the document. It is possible for the signature of the drawer or maker to appear on the reverse side of the instrument, but since such a placement is usually reserved for indorsements, it should be avoided for makers' and drawers' signatures because doubts could arise about who issued the instrument.

Language Making the Instrument Payable on Demand or at a Definite Time [3-109]. To be negotiable, an instrument must be **payable on demand** or at a **definite time** so that a purchaser can determine with ease and certainty two things: (1) when the purchaser will have a right to payment and (2) how much the drawer or maker will owe if the instrument bears interest. However, whether a *date* is required for negotiability depends on the other (nondate) language of the instrument, since definiteness can be provided in a variety of ways. Some time instruments do need a date for negotiability, as where the instrument reads, "Sixty days after date pay. . . ." No date is required, though, for a time instrument reading, "Sixty days after *sight* pay" or "I promise to pay 60 days after *demand*." In these instances, payment is at a definite time because the payee or other holder knows from the wording exactly when payment is due.

Demand instruments, including checks, need no date to be considered payable at a definite time. The payee or other holder of a demand instrument knows when he or she will demand payment and thus can compute with precision how much the drawer or maker will owe if the instrument bears interest. The blank for the date in a check form is used by the drawer to record the date that the drawer issued the check; the blank is not used to set a date for payment, since the payee or other holder can demand payment of the check for a substantial time after the date of issue. Usually, where no date for payment is stated, the instrument is a demand instrument, as where it reads, "I promise to pay . . . $100" [3-108].

Where payment is linked to an event that is uncertain as to time of occurrence, the instrument is not negotiable, and it does not become negotiable even though the event has occurred [3-109]. For example, a note reading "Payable 30 days after the death of my Uncle Abner" is nonnegotiable because the time of Uncle Abner's death is uncertain.

> **BOX 31.4**
>
> **Test Your Knowledge**
>
> On August 1, 1993, Mike Maker bought a used bulldozer on credit from Honest Abe's Bulldozer Sales, for use in Mike's construction business. Relying on Abe's statement that the machine was in excellent oper-

> **BOX 31.4 continued**
>
> tion, Mike signed a promissory note for the $60,000 purchase price. In fact, as Abe knew at the time of contracting, the machine was inoperable and nearly worthless. Abe has refused to remove it from Mike's premises. In the meantime, Abe sold the note to Happy Valley Bank, which now seeks payment from Mike. If the note is negotiable in form, Bank is a holder in due course and Mike will have to pay Bank the stated amount. If the note is not negotiable, Mike can assert his defense of fraud and will have no obligation to pay. Is the note negotiable?
>
> ### Promissory Note
>
> I, Mike Maker, promise to pay Honest Abe's Bulldozer Sales the principal sum of Sixty Thousand Dollars ($60,000.00) plus 12.7 percent annual interest, or, at Abe's option, five thousand(5,000) shares of common stock in Mike's Construction Company. Payment of this note is to be made upon Maker's completing the Green Earth Dam now under construction by Mike's Construction Company and scheduled for completion August 1, 1994. If Maker defaults in payment, Maker shall pay reasonable costs of collection and attorney's fees.
>
> (signed) Mike Maker ∎

Language That Destroys Negotiability

A note reading "On demand I promise to pay the bearer the sum of 50 dollars" is negotiable in form if signed by the maker. It contains an unconditional promise to pay and language of negotiability (the word "bearer"), and it states a sum certain that is payable on demand. Often, however, such instruments contain additional language. The additional language might have no effect on the negotiability of the instrument, or it might deprive the instrument of negotiability. For example, additional language that renders the sum uncertain or the time of payment indefinite deprives the instrument of negotiability and limits its purchaser to the rights of an assignee. Likewise, although they are perfectly legal, words that condition the promise of the drawer or maker destroy negotiability because they may create doubts in the mind of a purchaser about the collectability of the instrument. Or they may require a time-consuming investigation by the purchaser of the circumstances surrounding the transaction between the maker and the payee. Some common situations involving additional language are discussed next.

Express Conditions. If a promise or order is **expressly conditioned** on the happening or nonhappening of an event, the instrument is nonnegotiable. For example, a promise to pay "if the typewriter is delivered before June 4" expressly conditions the promise to pay on the delivery of a typewriter. An instrument containing such a promise is nonnegotiable. The promise or order must be to pay regardless of what happens, not just on the occurrence of one event.

Words Referring to Another Agreement. The terms of the promise or the order are to be determined solely by what is expressed on the instrument. If the instrument states that it is "subject to" or "governed by" another agreement, the promise or order is conditional. A note reads, "Subject to the terms and provisions of chattel mortgage #17 on file in the Amos County courthouse, I promise to pay bearer the sum of $1,000." This note is nonnegotiable because the holder must look to another document to learn the scope of the maker's promise. Placing such a burden on holders is contrary to the idea of free circulation and efficient collection. So the mere fact of subjecting the promise or order to the contents of an outside document destroys negotiability, regardless of what the outside document says.

People, however, often make a notation on the face of a negotiable instrument for record-keeping purposes. If a check, draft, or promissory note merely *refers* to an underlying transaction without making payment depend on the maker's or drawer's satisfaction with the underlying transaction, the reference does not make the order or promise conditional. Thus, a promise is not made conditional, and negotiability is not destroyed, by the statement, "This note is given for the purchase of goods as per contract of June 4, 19xx." Nor is a check rendered nonnegotiable by the notation, "For one red sofa."

Case 31.1 discusses whether assigning a nonnegotiable conditional sales contract together with a negotiable note destroys the negotiability of the note.

CASE 31.1 **Northwestern Bank v. Neal** • 248 S.E.2d 585 (S.C. 1978)

FACTS Defendant Neal purchased a boiler from Thomas Equipment & Supply Co. on credit, signing a conditional sales contract and a promissory note for $8,714.72. Thomas immediately assigned the documents for value to plaintiff Northwestern Bank. Alleging that the boiler was defective, Neal refused to pay the balance due on the note. Bank brought suit against Neal for the unpaid balance. From a judgment for Neal, Bank appealed.

OPINION NESS, J. . . . [T]he trial court ruled as a matter of law that the note and conditional sales contract merged and therefore were nonnegotiable, and [that] the bank was not a holder in due course. . . . The jury received the case on the [theory] that the appellant bank stood in the shoes of the original seller, Thomas, and was subject to any defenses that might be asserted against the seller. This was clear error. A suit by a holder in due course was improperly converted into a suit on a sales contract with the quality of the merchandise being [made] an issue. . . . [Section 3-104 of the UCC] provides:

> (1) Any writing to be a negotiable instrument . . . must (a) be signed by the maker or drawer; and (b) contain an unconditional promise or order to pay a sum certain in money . . .; and (c) be payable on demand or at a definite time; and (d) be payable to order or to bearer.

The instant note clearly meets the above requisites of negotiability. The trial court held that . . . the note merged with the conditional sales contract and could not be negotiable because [the contract] required certain conditions. While it is true that the conditional sales contract may not have been a negotiable instrument because it failed to meet the [unconditional language] requirement of [§ 3-104(1)(b)], that does not render the promissory note nonnegotiable.

We reject the single contract theory embraced by the trial court. The Bank of Commerce case, relied on by the lower court, is inapplicable because it involved a conditional sales contract with an attached note; here, the contract and the note were two separate documents. [Under § 3-119(2)], "A separate agreement does not affect the negotiability of an instrument."

We conclude that the trial court erred in holding that the two documents integrated into one writing. . . . The official comment to [§ 3-119(2)] illustrates the trial court's error in adopting the single contract theory:

> Subsection (2) rejects decisions which have carried the rule that contemporaneous writings must be read together to the length of holding that a clause in a mortgage affecting a note destroyed the negotiability of the note. The negotiability of an instrument is always to be determined by what appears on the face of the instrument alone,

CASE 31.1 Continued	and if it is negotiable in itself a purchaser without notice of a separate writing is in no way affected by it. If the instrument itself states that it is subject to or governed by any other agreement, it is not negotiable under this Article; but if it merely refers to a separate agreement or states that it arises out of such an agreement, it is negotiable. [Although] the appellant bank [possessed] a negotiable instrument, the question remains whether the bank is a holder in due course. . . . The bank paid value in good faith for the note on the day it was executed. It is undisputed that the assignment preceded any notice [to the bank about the quality of] the merchandise sold. Accordingly, the bank qualifies as a holder in due course.
JUDGMENT	The trial court erred in concluding that the note was nonnegotiable, and that the buyer's claims could be asserted against the bank. The very essence of a holder in due course is that he takes free of [the maker's personal] defenses against the seller. Reversed.

Words Limiting Source of Payment. For an instrument to be negotiable, the maker or drawer must subject his or her *general credit* (total wealth) to liability for payment, as opposed to limiting payment to some fraction of his or her assets. This requirement is consistent with the idea of giving a holder maximum assurance of collectability. A note reading "I promise to pay to the order of First Bank $3,000 out of this year's wheat crop" is nonnegotiable because the source of payment is a particular fund rather than the total assets of the maker. In contrast, an instrument reading "Pay $100 to the order of Paul Payee and charge the merchandise account" is negotiable. The instruction to charge the merchandise account is merely a bookkeeping instruction. The drawer has not expressed an intention to make the merchandise account the sole source of payment. If the drawer had said, "Pay *only out of* the merchandise account," the order would be conditional and the draft would be nonnegotiable.

There are two exceptions to the rule that for an instrument to be negotiable, payment cannot be limited to a particular fund. First, short-term instruments issued by a government, or by a governmental agency or unit, are *not* rendered nonnegotiable merely by the fact that payment is limited to a particular fund or to the proceeds of particular taxes or other sources of revenue [3-105]. Second, an instrument issued by a partnership or an unincorporated association limiting payment to "the entire assets" of the association is not rendered nonnegotiable, despite the fact that the limitation is intended to protect the partners or members from their usual personal liability. The general credit of the association is still available for payment.

In Case 31.2, the court decides whether payment of a note has been limited to a particular fund.

CASE 31.2	**Barnett Bank v. Regency Highland Condominium Assoc.** • 38 UCC Rep. 1289 (Fla. App. 1984)
FACTS	Defendant Regency Highlands Condominium Association (Condo) borrowed money from the condominium developer, Regency Highlands Associates, to pay for improvements that benefited Condo. Condo's promissory note stated, "Pay-

CASE 31.2 Continued

ment to be made as Capital Contributions are received from each apartment closing." The developer then sought a loan of its own and assigned Condo's note to plaintiff Barnett Bank as collateral. When the developer defaulted on its loan, Bank sought payment of Condo's note. Condo refused to pay, alleging that the developer had obtained the note from Condo by "fraud and trickery." Bank brought suit to enforce the note. From a judgment for Condo, Bank appealed.

OPINION

Downey, J. . . . [T]he trial court found that . . . the collateral note was not negotiable because it was conditional on its face. . . . The issue . . . is whether the statement on the note that "Payment to be made as Capital Contributions are received from each apartment closing" [makes the promise to pay conditional]. If it [does], the note is nonnegotiable and subject to any defenses the maker may have against the payee. . . .

. . . [F]or an instrument to be negotiable it must contain an unconditional promise to pay a sum certain in money. . . . However, an otherwise unconditional promise to pay is not made conditional by the fact that the instrument "indicates a particular account to be debited or any other fund or source from which reimbursement is expected. . . ." § 3-105(1)(f). The law favors negotiability and is reluctant to adopt rules that burden transferability of negotiable paper. . . . The terms of the instrument itself determine negotiability. . . . Furthermore, the Uniform Commercial Code comment to § 3-105 makes it clear that the conditional character of a promise to pay is not determined by matters [outside] the instrument, but by the instrument itself. [The comment] states: "So far as negotiability is affected, the conditional character of the promise or order is to be determined by what is expressed in the instrument itself. . . . In addition, § 3-105(2)(b) suggests that in order for a promise to be conditional, the restrictive language must be express because that section provides: "(2) A promise or order is not unconditional if the instrument . . . (b) states that it is to be paid only out of a particular fund or source. . . ." In our view, the legend appearing on the face of the . . . note does not make the promise to pay conditional, since the legend contains no words explicitly limiting payment to a particular fund or source. . . .

[The court then held that Bank was a holder in due course and so took the note free from Condo's defenses.]

JUDGMENT

Reversed and remanded. . . .

Table 31.1 gives examples of language that does and does not destroy negotiability.

Language and Omissions Not Affecting Negotiability

If a promise or order is unconditional, if the sum is certain, and if the time of payment is definite, an instrument that has the minimum required language of negotiability may be negotiable despite the presence of certain additional language. Sometimes the added language *does* in fact affect time of payment or other qualities pertaining to negotiability, but it is so beneficial that the UCC permits it and provides that it does not destroy negotiability. Other added language may or may not destroy negotiability. Some notable illustrations follow.

Table 31.1 Commercial Paper Language

Destroying Negotiability	Not Destroying Negotiability
Pay to the order of Typeshop $700 *if I receive from Typeshop one Magic X Typewriter before June 1, 19xx.*	Pay to the order of Typeshop $700. *(For one Magic X Typewriter.)*
This note is *subject to* the terms of contract 117, dated June 4, 19xx.	This note is given for the purchase of goods *as per* contract of June 4, 19xx.
Pay $500 to the order of Jones *only out of* the merchandise account.	Pay $500 to the order of Jones, *and charge* the merchandise account.

Acceleration Clauses. Often the parties to a negotiable instrument provide for acceleration (early payment) of the instrument. The maker of a note might want to pay it early to save on interest charges. The note might therefore read, "I promise to pay $1,000 to First Bank or order, together with 12 percent annual interest, on or before May 1, 19xx." The "on or before" language is an **acceleration clause** favoring the maker. Because the *maker* may choose when to pay the note, the time of payment could be considered indefinite from the viewpoint of the holder. However, the acceleration clause is so beneficial to the maker, and it causes the holder so little difficulty, that under the UCC its presence does not destroy negotiability [3-109].

The payee or other holder might also have the benefit of an acceleration clause, as where a holder is permitted to require early payment "if I deem myself insecure" (i.e., "if I come to doubt the ability of the maker or drawer to pay") or the instrument provides that it "shall become immediately due and payable upon any default in payment of interest or principal." The presence of such a clause does not affect negotiability. However, a holder who exercises an option to accelerate because of the holder's insecurity (fear of nonpayment) must have a good faith belief that the prospect of payment is impaired [1-208].

Confession-of-Judgment Clauses. Sometimes an instrument contains a clause that authorizes the holder to have an attorney "confess judgment" (enter a judgment in court) against the maker or drawer if the instrument is not paid when due, even though failure to pay may be justified. The judgment cuts off every defense that the maker may have, and it also cuts off the maker's right to appeal the judgment. **Confession-of-judgment clauses** are so harsh that in most states they are void. However, the presence of such a clause in a negotiable instrument does *not* destroy negotiability *if* the clause can be exercised only after the maker's default [3-112]. If the clause can be exercised at *any* time, its presence *does* destroy negotiability.

Other Language and Omissions. Like many of the clauses just discussed, the following terms (provisions) do not affect the negotiability of an instrument:

1. A statement that collateral has been given as security and that in case of default the collateral may be sold.
2. A promise to maintain or protect collateral or to give additional collateral. For example, a note may state that it is secured by a deposit of securities having a current market value of $4,800 and that on written demand from the holder, the maker agrees to deposit such additional collateral satisfactory to the holder as may be necessary to maintain the value of the collateral at $4,800. Normally, upon the maker's failure to provide the additional collateral, the holder is authorized to sell the collateral previously deposited and

apply the proceeds of the sale to the debt owed.

3. A term purporting to waive the benefit of any law for the advantage or protection of the obligor, as, for example, a maker's waiver of a homestead exemption. (A homestead is the land and buildings occupied by the owner as a home and in most states is at least partially exempted from seizure or sale for debts.)

4. A term in a draft that provides that by indorsing or cashing the draft the payee acknowledges full satisfaction of an obligation owed to the payee by the drawer.

Antedating or *postdating* has no effect on the negotiability of an instrument [3-114(1)]. However, these practices may affect the time of payment if the instrument is payable on demand or at a fixed period after date. Thus, if a demand instrument is issued May 20 but is dated June 1, payment cannot be demanded until June 1, and if an instrument that is payable "30 days after date" is issued on May 20 but is dated June 1, it is not payable until 30 days after the stated date (June 1).

Certain *omissions* do not affect negotiability. Commercial paper sometimes contains a reference to the consideration for which the instrument was given. Though useful as a record of the transaction, such a reference is not required for negotiability. Nor is the maker or drawer required to state the place where the instrument is drawn or payable.

It is customary and advisable for a maker or drawer to date a negotiable instrument. However, many instruments meet all the requirements for negotiability, including that of being payable on demand or at a definite time, even though undated. An ordinary check, for example, is a demand instrument which can be cashed immediately upon being issued. Since a date of issue is not required for establishing the time that payment is due, a date is not required for the check to be negotiable in form. The date line on a blank check has been provided for the convenience of the drawer in maintaining his or her records.

Rules for Interpreting Common Ambiguities

Like any other contract, a negotiable instrument may be so poorly worded that it requires interpretation. The UCC states a number of rules of interpretation that the courts are to apply [3-118]. These rules include the following:

1. Where there is doubt whether the instrument is a draft or a note, the holder may treat it as either.

2. Where handwritten terms differ from typewritten or printed terms, the handwritten terms control (prevail). Where typewritten terms differ from printed terms, the typewritten terms control.

3. Where the sum payable is expressed in words and also in figures, and the two expressions of amount differ, the sum payable is the one expressed in words. However, if the words are ambiguous, the sum payable is the one expressed in figures. (*Note:* A discrepancy between words and figures does *not*, by itself, render the sum uncertain.)

4. Where a provision for interest does not specify the rate of interest, the rate is the "judgment" rate at the place of payment. (A "judgment rate" is a rate of interest established by a state statute to be applied by the courts to judgments for damages where interest is an element of the damage award. The UCC adopts this rate for convenience and certainty.) If the instrument is dated, the interest will run from the date of the instrument; if it is undated, the interest will run from the date the instrument was issued.

BOX 31.5

Commercial Paper Law and Business Planning

You want to make a sizable loan to a business acquaintance, who has asked you to draft the note and include whatever provisions you feel are necessary. You have heard of the clauses listed below. Which ones, if any

BOX 31.5 continued

should you have your lawyer put into the note for your benefit?

1. An acceleration clause containing the language "on or before"
2. An acceleration clause containing the language "If I deem myself insecure"
3. A confession-of-judgment clause exercisable after the maker's default
4. A confession-of-judgment clause exercisable at any time
5. A clause requiring the maker to pay all costs of collection and attorney's fees resulting from the maker's default
6. A clause imposing an 8 percent interest rate, but raising it to 12 percent for any period after the maker's default that the note remains unpaid

SUMMARY

Commercial paper serves as a substitute for money and as a means of extending credit because a holder in due course, unlike the purchaser of an ordinary contract, takes commercial paper free from personal defenses of makers and drawers and other parties to it. Commercial paper is both a formal contract that imposes liability on any signer for the face amount and a type of property that can be bought and sold. Whether in the form of a three-party draft or a two-party note, commercial paper has a variety of business uses.

For a person to have the favored status of a holder in due course, commercial paper must be negotiable in form. An instrument will be negotiable if the maker or drawer uses certain minimum language prescribed by the UCC and avoids using additional language that renders the promise or order conditional or otherwise destroys negotiability. A number of contractual provisions in an instrument have no effect on its negotiability. Likewise, many omissions and the practice of antedating or postdating have no effect on negotiability.

REVIEW QUESTIONS

1. What are the two main functions of commercial paper?

2. What is the main function of a note?

3. How does a promissory note differ from a certificate of deposit?

4. (a) What is the basic function or use of a draft? (b) How does a demand draft differ from a time draft? (c) What is the meaning of "drawee"? Of "acceptor"?

5. (a) What is the main use or practical value of checks? (b) What is the relationship between a check and an "underlying transaction"? (c) Explain or illustrate the meaning of the statement, "A check operates as only a conditional payment of the underlying obligation." (d) Explain whether a traveler's check is a check or a draft.

6. A negotiable instrument can confer upon a holder in due course more than the usual contract rights. Using the expressions "negotiable form," "holder in due course," and "personal and real defenses," explain or illustrate how this is so.

7. A negotiable instrument is, simultaneously, a contract and a type of property. Explain.

8. Explain how a draft may be used, together with other documents, in financing the sale of goods.

9. What minimum language is required for an instrument to be in negotiable form? Is a date required? Explain.

10. (a) Give two illustrations of language that will destroy negotiability. (b) Give two illustrations of language that does not affect negotiability.

CASE PROBLEMS

1. Herb bought, on credit, a large-screen television set for use in the lobby of his motel. In payment he gave Mary, the seller, a negotiable promissory note for $3,000. She negotiated it to

First Finance Corp., a holder in due course. When the note came due, First Finance sought payment from Herb, but he refused to pay on the ground that Mary had lied to him about the performance characteristics of the TV set and that it had never worked satisfactorily. Assume that Mary had lied as Herb said and that the TV set was worthless. Is First Finance entitled to payment from Herb? Why or why not?

2. Bailey invested in California Dreamstreet, a joint venture that funded a cattle-breeding operation. His note read in part as follows: "DR. WILLIAM H. BAILEY . . . hereby promises to pay to the order to CALIFORNIA DREAMSTREET . . . the sum of Three Hundred Twenty Nine Thousand Eight Hundred ($329,800.00) Dollars. . . ." California Dreamstreet negotiated the note to a bank, which sought payment from Bailey. Asserting defenses to collection arising from alleged misconduct by California Dreamstreet, Bailey refused to pay. The bank contended, however, that it was a holder in due course and therefore was entitled to payment despite Bailey's defenses. Bailey argued that the bank was not a holder in due course because the language "pay to the order *to* California Dreamstreet" deprived the note of negotiable form. Was the note negotiable?

3. Shortly before her death, Ruby Eubanks received the following document from Mechanics Bank: "April 6, 1973. Mrs. Ruby Eubanks has deposited in this Bank $14,000 payable to the order of herself or Doyle Thomas in current funds 12 months after date on the return of this certificate properly endorsed with interest at 5 percent, per annum. (Signed) Mechanics Bank." The document was in her possession when she died. Both Doyle Thomas and the administratrix of her estate claimed the $14,000. If the document represented an ordinary bank deposit, Doyle Thomas would be entitled to the money under state banking law, which grants ownership of a joint bank account to the survivor. However, if the document was a negotiable certificate of deposit, it was Mrs. Eubanks' property at her death and became an asset of her estate. Was the document negotiable and thus an asset of Mrs. Eubanks' estate?

4. Ezekiel Freed bought a limited partnership interest in Earthquake Command System organized by Menlo Research Corporation. He paid for it with his promissory note for $40,000 plus 9 percent annual interest, due on September 21, 1988, payable to the order of Menlo or bearer. The note stated, "Said note is secured by and subject to the provisions of the partnership debt assumption agreement [PDAA] . . . which is incorporated herein." The PDAA listed several circumstances that would have to occur before payment of the note would be required, and it provided that the agreement was not assignable without Freed's written consent. Then Growth Equities Corp. (GEC) lent Menlo $700,000, taking as security a package of Menlo's limited partner investor promissory notes, including Freed's. Later, Menlo petitioned for bankruptcy, and GEC sought to collect on Freed's note. Freed contended that he had not given written consent to Menlo's assignment of the PDAA, and that this and other defenses to payment should be allowed because the note was nonnegotiable. Was Freed's note nonnegotiable?

5. A contractor's note, properly dated and signed, read: "I promise to pay to the order of Paul Payee within the next 60 days the sum of five thousand dollars ($5,000) from the jobs now under construction." Is the note a negotiable instrument? Which of the eight requirements may be in doubt?

6. Hank borrowed $50,000 from Jane so that he could establish his own hardware store. Jane required that Hank sign a promissory note for $50,000 payable to her order in ten annual installments plus 12 percent annual interest on the unpaid balance. The note stated, "This note shall immediately become due and payable with accrued interest whenever holder deems himself or herself insecure." Is this note negotiable? Which of the eight requirements may be in doubt?

CHAPTER 32

Personal and Real Defenses; Negotiation of Commercial Paper

As noted in the preceding chapter, a holder in due course has a favored status in the law. Unlike an ordinary holder or other assignee, a holder in due course takes commercial paper free from (1) rival claims of ownership and (2) personal defenses of issuers and other parties.

For a person to be a holder in due course, three circumstances must exist. He or she must:

1. Receive an instrument that is negotiable in form
2. Take the instrument by a method of transfer called **negotiation**
3. Have the special qualities required by law for holder-in-due-course status (be a good faith purchaser)

However, once the rights of a holder in due course have been established, they can be assigned to (and enforced by) persons who lack some of the qualities of a holder in due course.

This chapter deals with personal and real defenses, and then with the process of negotiation. The next chapter discusses the personal qualities required for holder-in-due-course status and how a person may acquire the rights of a holder in due course without personally being one.

PERSONAL AND REAL DEFENSES

People usually issue commercial paper as payment for property or services received from the payee, or as evidence of a loan made by the payee to the maker. Sometimes disputes arise about the quality or sufficiency of the payee's performance. Even where the payee has performed well, the issuer (maker or drawer) may nevertheless have a legal right, because of some other circumstance such as the issuer's minority, to cancel the underlying contract. Thus, an issuer may have one or more **defenses** against having to pay the payee. But the payee might have transferred the instrument to a holder in due course, who, having paid for it, naturally wants to collect. Whether the issuer must pay the holder in due course depends on whether the issuer's defense is personal or real. A holder in due course takes a negotiable instrument free from personal defenses but subject to real defenses of all parties (signers).

Although the following discussion emphasizes the defenses of makers and drawers, any party to a negotiable instrument (maker, drawer, acceptor, or indorser) can have a real or personal defense to payment. Moreover, some conditions such as insanity and wrongful acts such as fraud or duress can be either a personal or a real defense, depending on circumstances noted later. The "rival claims" of ownership from which holders in due course are protected often arise when an instrument is stolen or obtained by fraud. Such claims are illustrated in the part of this chapter dealing with negotiation of commercial paper.

Personal Defenses

A **personal defense** is one that the law says must remain a private matter between the immediate parties to a negotiable instrument (e.g., between issuer and payee) instead of causing loss to a holder in due course. So, where an issuer has only a personal defense, the issuer must pay any holder in due course and then initiate legal action against the payee for breach of the underlying contract, seek from the payee a voluntary repayment, or absorb the loss.

The personal defenses include the following:

1. The payee's fraud, misrepresentation, duress, or undue influence in inducing the maker or drawer into the underlying transaction.
2. Mistake of the kinds that would justify the maker or drawer in rescinding (canceling) the underlying contract.
3. Breach of warranty, especially in sales of goods.
4. Failure of performance (also called "failure of consideration") such as the inability or refusal to deliver property.
5. Nondelivery of the instrument.
6. Unauthorized completion of a signed instrument.

Many of these personal defenses are discussed elsewhere in this book. Some, however, need special mention here.

Fraud: There are two kinds of fraud: *fraud in the inducement* (always a personal defense), and *fraud in the execution* of the instrument (which can be a real defense under the circumstances described later in this chapter).

Fraud in the inducement gets its name from the fact that the payee induces (lures) the maker or drawer into voluntarily signing a negotiable instrument on the basis of the payee's lie about the underlying transaction. Sue fraudulently represents herself to John as a member of First Church seeking contributions for the church's missionary work. In fact, she does not belong to the church, and it has no missionary program. Not knowing this, John makes out a $100 check to Sue, who tells John she will indorse (sign) it over to the church. Instead, she cashes the check at a local supermarket and disappears with the money. The supermarket, a holder in due course, is entitled to payment from John free from his defense of fraud in the inducement.

A key factor in John's liability is that he knew he was signing a check, signed it voluntarily, and put it into circulation. His negligence (failing to investigate Sue's representations and issuing the check to Sue instead of to First Church) was great. Thus, John was in a better position than the supermarket to detect the fraud and prevent loss. But some fraud in the inducement is so skillfully committed that it is undetectable; therefore, its victims are blameless. Nevertheless, it is at least arguable that even blameless victims are in a better position than the holder in due course to prevent loss. This possibility of self-protection, together with the policy of enhancing the marketability of commercial paper, is the basis for the rule that all forms of fraud in the inducement, detectable or not, constitute merely a personal defense.

Nondelivery of the instrument: On June 20, Dora makes out a payroll check to her employee Paul, intending to deliver it to him on July 5. Before then, Paul takes the check without Dora's knowledge and indorses it to Harry, a holder in due course. When Dora discovers that the check is missing, she stops payment on it. Then Harry presents it to the drawee bank for payment. The bank refuses to pay, and Harry sues Dora, who denies liability to Harry because she never delivered the check to Paul. If Paul himself had tried to cash the check at the bank, Dora's defense of nondelivery would be good. However, since **nondelivery** of a signed instrument is a *personal* defense, it is not good against Harry, a holder in due course. Similarly, the defenses of **conditional delivery** ("This check is not good until you finish the job") and **delivery for a special purpose** ("I'm making this check out to you for you to deposit in my daughter's account") are personal defenses, good as between the parties but not good against a holder in due course.

Unauthorized completion of a signed instrument: May signs a check naming Paul as payee but leaves the amount blank, instructing Paul to fill in the amount later for an amount not to exceed $100. He fills in the amount for $500 and negotiates the check to Harry, a holder in due course. Harry is entitled to $500 from May, free from her personal defense that Paul lacked authority to complete the check for $500. By signing the check and permitting Paul to fill in the amount, May has created a trap for holders in due course and therefore should absorb any loss.

Case 32.1 discusses whether the fraud involved constitutes a real or a personal defense.

CASE 32.1 **Mellon Bank v. Donegal Mutual Ins. Co.**
• 29 UCC Rep. 912 (Pa. Ct. C.P. 1980)

FACTS   McConnell made an insurance claim against a person insured by Donegal Insurance Co. To settle the claim, Donegal issued McConnell a check for over $3,700, drawn on Farmer's First Bank. McConnell cashed the check at Mellon Bank, where he had an account, and received the proceeds in cash. Mellon Bank presented the check to Farmer's First Bank for payment, but Farmer's refused to honor the check because Donegal Insurance Co. had ordered Farmer's to stop payment, alleging that McConnell's insurance claim was fraudulent. Not being able to collect from the drawee because of the stop order, Mellon Bank sued Donegal, the drawer, for payment.

OPINION   DOYLE, J. . . . [P]laintiff's motion for summary judgment [is] before us for disposition.
   Defendant [Donegal] asserts that the deceit allegedly practiced by McConnell on defendant infects the instrument itself, viz.: it is a fraud and a "real" . . . defense available against anyone who asserts a claim on the instrument. Defendant's argument is based on a defense set forth in [§3-305(2)(b) of the UCC]. The . . . comment to the cited section states: "If under [local] law the effect of the . . . illegality is to make the obligation entirely null and void, the defense may be asserted against a holder in due course. Otherwise it is cut off." Defendant is bound by its pleadings and the defense which is *pleaded*, viz.: "fraudulent insurance claim." [Such a claim] is not the species of fraud in *esse contractus*, which renders an *instrument* void—it is only a deceit, a misrepresentation which induced the drawer to draw and deliver the instrument to malefactor McConnell. It is not a "real" defense available against a holder in due course. . . .
   We find that there is no substantial issue of fact regarding plaintiff's status as a holder in due course. . . . We find that plaintiff is a holder in due course. We find that the defenses raised by defendant are not "real" defenses. [Although defendant drawer must pay plaintiff, defendant] may recover from [payee] McConnell in a trespass action for deceit or may waive the tort and sue *in assumpsit*.

JUDGMENT   Ergo, we must . . . grant plaintiff's motion for summary judgment. . . .

Real Defenses

As noted in the previous chapter, **real defenses** involve circumstances of such serious consequences to makers, drawers, and other signers of commercial paper that the policy of protecting holders in due course must yield to the need to protect signers. Unlike a personal defense, a real defense is good against any person, even a holder in due course. Article 3 identifies a number of real defenses [3-305].

Infancy (minority): Infancy is a defense against a holder in due course "to the extent that it is a defense to a simple contract [the underlying transaction]" under non-Code law [3-305(2)(b)]. Recall from Chapter 13 that state law varies on the kinds of contracts a minor may rescind (cancel) and what the minor must do to be entitled to rescind. If state law permits a minor to rescind a contract, minority (infancy) is a real defense as to any negotiable instrument the minor gave in payment.

Mel, a minor, buys a camera (a luxury) and issues to Camera Shop a check for $500 in payment. Mel damages the camera, rescinds the contract, and places a stop-payment order on the check. Then Camera Shop negotiates the check to Harriet, a holder in due course. She presents it to Mel's bank, is refused payment, and sues Mel for payment. The law of Mel's state permits minors to rescind their contracts for luxuries merely by returning them even though damaged. Because state law permits Mel to rescind the underlying transaction, Mel has, under the UCC, a real defense to payment of the check. By denying payment to the holder in due course, the UCC supports the local policy of protecting minors who elect to rescind the underlying contract. (As indicated in Chapter 34, however, Harriet may be able to compel Camera Shop to make good her loss, on the ground that Camera Shop breached a transfer warranty. Thus, as the law intended, Camera Shop ultimately would bear the risk of dealing with minors.)

Incapacity other than minority; duress; illegality: The defense of "other **incapacity** [than minority]" refers to incapacities such as insanity, drunkenness, and lack of corporate capacity to do business. They and defenses such as duress are described in Chapter 13. The defense of **illegality,** discussed in Chapter 14, occurs most often where a maker or drawer issues an instrument to pay a gambling debt in violation of a law prohibiting gambling or has signed a note carrying an interest rate that exceeds the rate permitted by the usury laws. All the defenses just mentioned *may be real or personal, depending on state law.*

State law often distinguishes between instances of relatively minor wrongdoing that render an obligation merely **voidable** (rescindable at the option of an affected party) and those instances of serious misconduct that render the obligation **void** (of no legal effect whatever). The defenses of illegality, duress, and nonminority incapacity are *real* defenses *only if* state law "renders the obligation of the party a nullity" (*void*).

Duress provides an example. Forcing a person to sign a negotiable instrument at the point of a gun is in all states the kind of duress that renders the transaction void. The act of signing, though apparently creating a contractual obligation on the part of the issuer, created no obligation at all because of the duress, and the issuer has a *real* defense. In many states, however, forcing a person to sign a negotiable instrument under threat to prosecute the issuer's son for theft is a less serious form of duress that makes the issuer's obligation under the instrument merely voidable. Thus, the issuer has only a *personal* defense: one good against the wrongdoing payee should that person seek payment, but not good against a holder in due course.

Fraud in the execution: Fraud in the execution (signing) occurs where a payee persuades a person to sign a negotiable instrument by misrepresenting it as some other kind of document, or by indicating that the paper being signed is a negotiable instrument but misrepresenting its contents. Sometimes called "fraud in the essence" or "fraud in the factum," fraud in the execution may be either a real or a personal defense, depending on the circumstances surrounding the signing.

Fraud in the execution is a real defense if the payee or another wrongdoer "has induced the party to sign the instrument with neither knowledge nor reasonable opportunity to obtain knowledge of its character or essential terms" [3-305(2)(c)]. A trusted and faithful ex-employee of a blind person asks the former employer to sign a "letter of reference" that is in reality a check for $1,000 made out to the ex-employee. Probably the ex-employee's fraud is a real defense, good against even a holder in due course to whom the defrauder might negotiate the check. Only a court, however, can say with authority whether the blind drawer's defense is real or merely personal. If the drawer had reason to suspect wrongdoing by the ex-employee and had an opportunity to investigate but failed to do so, the defense is only a personal one even though the fraud concerned the nature of the document or its essential (important) terms.

Bankruptcy: One purpose of federal bankruptcy law is to provide a hopelessly overburdened debtor with a "fresh start," by means of a formal release from debt called a **discharge in bankruptcy.** To give effect to the federal policy of debtor relief (and to the similar policy of state insolvency laws), Article 3 makes a debtor's discharge in insolvency proceedings (state or federal) a real defense, good against even a holder in due course of a negotiable instrument issued by the debtor [3-305(2)(d)].

Unauthorized signature; material alteration: Unauthorized signature includes both a forgery and a signature made by an agent exceeding his or her actual *or apparent* authority. The defense is good even against a holder in due course, unless the alleged signer ratified the signature (approved it as his or her own after the signing) or is precluded (prevented) by law from denying it. Drew Candle Company employs Anna as a bookkeeper. Ordinarily a bookkeeper has no authority to write checks for his or her employer, but Anna *is* authorized to draw checks on Drew's bank account provided they are cosigned by the controller. Anna draws a check payable to her friend Pablo without securing the signature of the controller. Even if the check is negotiated to a holder in due course, Drew Company may assert the defense of unauthorized signature. However, Drew Company may be precluded from denying Anna's authority if it is careless in handling its checks—for example, if they are not kept in a secure place under proper supervision.

A **material alteration** (an unauthorized, significant change in the working of a negotiable instrument) may be a partial real defense or no defense at all. It is no defense where the issuer assented (agreed) to the alteration or contributed to its making through negligence or other fault. For example, if the payee raises the amount of an instrument while the issuer looks on, a holder in due course may collect the increased amount. Where the issuer did not assent and was not at fault, that person has a real defense good against a holder in due course, but only to the extent of the alteration, since "a subsequent holder in due course may in all cases enforce the instrument according to its original tenor" [3-407]. Donna draws a check for $200 payable to Pam. If Pam, without Donna's knowledge or negligence, raises the amount of the check to $1,200 and negotiates it to a holder in due course, Donna may be held liable only for the original amount, $200.

The following case discusses whether a holder in due course should be denied payment because a building contractor lacked a license to do business.

CASE 32.2   Wilson v. Steele • 259 Cal. Rptr. 851 (Cal. App. 1989)

FACTS   Millie C. Wilson owned an apartment building worth about $120,000 and lived there with her daughter, Naomi Williams. In 1979, Wilson granted Williams a general power of attorney to act on Wilson's behalf. In 1983, Williams contracted with Michael Jackson & Associates, an unlicensed contractor, to remodel the building for $28,047. Williams obtained a $31,053 construction loan from

**CASE 32.2
Continued**

Broadway Federal Savings and Loan Association and executed a promissory note and first deed of trust on the property in favor of Broadway Federal. The escrow company paid $28,047 to Michael Jackson & Associates and $3,006 to Williams. The remodeling work, however, remained largely uncompleted.

Then Williams borrowed $11,064 from Home Budget Improvement Service, a company owned by Jackson, and signed a promissory note secured by a second trust deed on her mother's property. Ronald and Ken Steele wanted to buy the Home Budget note. Jackson assigned the note to the Steeles for $7,000.

Millie Wilson died in 1985. Another daughter, Frances Wilson, was appointed administrator of her mother's estate. Wilson sued Williams, Michael Jackson & Associates, Home Budget, and the Steeles to cancel the Home Budget note. In the meantime, Williams and Jackson had disappeared. The matter proceeded to trial only as to the Steeles. Holding that they were holders in due course of the Home Budget note, the trial court granted judgment to the Steeles. Wilson appealed.

OPINION

KLEIN, J. . . . Wilson contends: (1) Home Budget's unlicensed status gives rise to an illegality defense which may be asserted against the Steeles. . . .

The Steeles submit the judgment is supported by the evidence, as Wilson failed to show the promissory note and second trust deed were in any way connected to the construction on the property, and they paid value and were without notice. . . .

Business and Professions Code section 7031 provides in relevant part:

> No person engaged in the business or acting in the capacity of a contractor, may bring or maintain any action in any court of this state for the collection of compensation for the performance of any act or contract for which a license is required by this chapter without alleging and proving that he was a duly licensed contractor at all times during the performance of such act or contract. . . .

The severe sanction of the statute prevents enforcement of an illegal contract and protects the public from the perils incident to contracting with incompetent or untrustworthy contractors. . . .

"[W]hen the object of the statute or ordinance in requiring a license for the privilege of carrying on a certain business is to prevent improper persons from engaging in that particular business, or is for the purpose of regulating it for the protection of the public . . . the imposition of the penalty amounts to a prohibition against doing the business without a license and a contract made by an unlicensed person in violation of the statute or ordinance is void." *Wood v. Krepps* (1914). . . .

The question becomes whether a contractor's unlicensed status is a defense which may be asserted against a holder in due course. . . .

California Uniform Commercial Code section 3305 provides: "To the extent that a holder is a holder in due course he takes the instrument free from . . . (2) All defenses of any party to the instrument with whom the holder has not dealt except [(b) such] incapacity, or duress, or illegality of the transaction, as renders the obligation of the party a *nullity*. . . ." (Italics added.)

[A comment to] section 3305 explains that if, under the local law, the effect

CASE 32.2
Continued

of an illegality is to render the obligation entirely null and void, such defense may be asserted against a holder in due course. . . .

The Steeles . . . resist the illegality defense on the ground there is no evidence the $11,064 note and second trust deed were for additional construction on the property. They urge this transaction was unrelated to any remodeling work and merely represented a cash loan from Home Budget to Williams, making the licensing defect irrelevant.

There was conflicting evidence on the issue of the purpose of the second loan. . . .

The trial court's statement of decision did not make a finding as to the purpose of the . . . loan. The trial court concluded the Steeles were holders in due course because they [gave value], were not parties to any of the Jackson activities, and entered into an arm's length, good faith transaction to purchase the [note]. However, [finding that] the Steeles were holders in due course does not dispose of the licensing/illegality defense. . . .

Here, the trial court failed to reach the essential remaining issue of whether, notwithstanding the Steeles' status as holders in due course, the illegality defense applied. For us to resolve the issue would be a usurpation of the trial court's function. Accordingly, the judgment must be reversed and the matter remanded for the trial court to make a finding as to the purpose of the . . . loan. If [it was] for construction, the licensing/illegality defense will bar the Steeles from enforcing the [note], irrespective of their status as holders in due course. However, if the trial court finds a cash loan to Williams, Home Budget's unlicensed status will be unavailing to Wilson.

JUDGMENT The judgment is reversed and the matter remanded for further proceedings consistent with this opinion. Wilson to recover costs on appeal.

BOX 32.1

Test Your Knowledge

Martin went to Paula's Discount Appliances to buy a new Ritecolor TV set, Model 7A, that Paula had advertised at $299, tax included. When Martin arrived at the store, Paula falsely told him that she had no more Model 7A sets in stock, but that she would sell him a more expensive Model 9A for the advertised price of $299. In fact, the Model 9A was a used set that she had repossessed the day before, worth approximately $100. Martin accepted her offer and issued her a check for $299. Paula negotiated the check to her employee Hal as payment for his past week's work. Hal skillfully raised the amount of the check to $399 and cashed it at Sally's Supermarket. In the meantime, Martin learned the truth about the TV set and stopped payment on the check. Martin's bank refused to pay the stopped check, and Sally sought payment from Martin. What defenses to payment does Martin have? Are any good against Sally? ■

NEGOTIATION OF COMMERCIAL PAPER

Issue and negotiation are parts of the process of putting commercial paper into circulation. Ordinarily the maker or drawer will issue the paper to a payee. The payee may keep the instrument and later collect payment, or may instead negotiate the instrument to a third person. The third person becomes a holder if all requirements for a negotiation are met, and can be a holder in due course by meeting, in addition, the requirements for holder-in-due-course status.

Issue of an Instrument

Issue means the *first delivery* of an instrument by its maker or drawer to another person, usually the payee, with the intention of granting the payee rights in the instrument [3-102]. Upon issue, the payee is a holder of the instrument. By making out a check and mailing it to the gas company, you become its issuer. The gas company becomes a holder when it receives (possesses) the check.

With respect to negotiable instruments, **delivery** means a voluntary transfer of possession [1-201(14)]. Where Dora makes out a check to Paul, and Paul picks it up from Dora's desk without authority while Dora is out of her office, there is no delivery. Neither is there a delivery if Dora merely hands the check to her own agent with instructions to take the instrument to Paul. Delivery does not take place until Dora or her agent gives control of the instrument to Paul or his agent.

An instrument can be issued even though the signer leaves lines blank for someone else to fill in [3-115]. Dora draws a check naming Paul as payee, leaves the lines for the amount blank, and gives the check to Paul with instructions to "fill in the amount I owe you." Because Dora signed the check and delivered it to Paul, it is issued even though it is incomplete. Issuing incomplete instruments is dangerous, since they could be filled out for more than the authorized amount and negotiated to a holder in due course, but the practice is convenient and relatively frequent. However, an incomplete instrument cannot be enforced until completed.

Negotiation of an Instrument

Negotiation can occur in a variety of ways, depending on the kind of paper involved (bearer or order) and the wishes or needs of the parties. A surprising variety of people have the power, though not always the right, to negotiate commercial paper. Where commercial paper is negotiated by indorsement, the indorser has several types of indorsements from which to choose. These topics relating to negotiation are discussed in the following paragraphs.

Meaning and Methods of Negotiation. Negotiation is the transfer of a negotiable (properly worded) instrument in such a way that the transferee becomes a holder [3-202]. (There can never be a negotiation unless the document is in negotiable form.) Ordinarily, a **holder** is a person in possession of bearer paper or in possession of order paper that has been (1) issued to him or her or (2) transferred to him or her properly indorsed (signed by the transferor). Thus, there are two methods of negotiation: (1) If the instrument is payable to bearer, it is negotiated by delivery alone. (2) If an instrument is payable to order ("Pay to the order of Joe Jones"), the holder (payee Jones) negotiates it by delivery together with any necessary indorsement (here, Jones' signature).

The term **order paper** refers not only to an instrument made out to the order of a named payee but also to an instrument that is indorsed by a holder such as the payee to a named transferee. Paul Payee indorses his payroll check (signs it on the back) as follows: "Pay John Jozinski, (signed) Paul Payee." The check, which was order paper when issued to Paul, continues to be order paper because Paul, the transferor, named John as the transferee. Now, for John to negotiate the check to someone else, John too must indorse it.

What happens if the holder of order paper, wanting to negotiate it, delivers it but forgets to add his or her indorsement? In that event, there has been a mere transfer of the instrument, not a negotiation. The transfer constitutes an assignment of the transferor's rights. Until the indorsement is supplied, the transferee is merely an assignee and is subject not only to real defenses but also to any personal defenses learned of before the indorsement is supplied. However, a **transferee for value** (i.e., a purchaser) is better off than an ordinary assignee. A transferee for value has "the specifically enforceable right to have (may have a court compel) the unqualified indorsement of the transferor" [3-201], and thus may become a holder in due course when the indorsement is supplied (if the transferee has the other qualities necessary for holder-in-due-course status).

Sometimes a payee presents an order instrument to his or her bank for deposit but forgets to make the necessary indorsement. The depositary bank may supply the missing indorsement and immediately credit the customer's account, unless the instrument contains such language as "payee's indorsement required." If the instrument contains such language, the bank must await the payee's actual indorsement [4-205].

Who May Negotiate an Instrument. Any holder of commercial paper or a person acting on the holder's behalf can negotiate it and thereby enable a properly qualified transferee to become a holder in due course. With one exception discussed in Chapter 34, a person who lacks holder status cannot negotiate commercial paper. A transfer by a nonholder ordinarily is merely an assignment of whatever rights the nonholder may have.

If a transferor is a holder, however, that person has the power to negotiate the instrument even though the negotiation may be wrongful. This is because "holder" is defined broadly enough to include any person who is or appears to be the rightful owner of the instrument, as far as a prospective purchaser can tell from what is written on the face and on the back of the instrument. Any possessor of paper made payable "to bearer" is a holder and can negotiate it, even though the possessor has stolen or found it. Order paper (such as a check made out to a named payee) that has been indorsed by the payee's merely signing it on the back (making an "in blank" indorsement) is another form of bearer paper. Anyone who possesses it, even a finder or a thief, is a holder and can negotiate it [3-301].

Recall that lack of delivery is a personal defense of the drawer, maker, or acceptor that is not good against a holder in due course. As illustrated below, the same principle operates to deprive payees and others in the chain of transfer of the personal defense of nondelivery when a holder in due course seeks payment from one of them. However, where a negotiation was wrongful, the wronged party has a cause of action against the transferor who committed the wrong. Some illustrations of rightful and wrongful negotiations follow.

1 Dora draws a check payable "to bearer" and delivers it to Paul. Paul, the payee, is a holder because he is in possession of bearer paper. Paul is the rightful owner and may negotiate the check. Paul's transferee will be a holder in due course if the transferee has the required qualities.

2 Dora draws a check payable "to bearer" and delivers it to Paul. Paul is a holder. Then Paul loses the check and Alfredo finds it. Alfredo is a holder because he is in possession of bearer paper. Alfredo has the *power* to negotiate the check and does so, even though Paul is the true owner and Alfredo's negotiation is wrongful as to Paul. Alfredo's transferee, Hanna, a holder in due course, takes the check free from Paul's personal defense of nondelivery (and Paul's claim of ownership). Paul's only recourse is against Alfredo for the tort of conversion.

3 Dora draws a check payable "to the order of Paul" and delivers it to him. Paul is a holder because he possesses an instrument drawn to his order. Then Paul indorses the check by writing his name on the back (thereby converting the check to *bearer* paper) and lays the check on his desk, intending to take it to the bank the next day. That night Tom sneaks into Paul's apartment and steals the indorsed check. Although Tom is a thief, he is a holder because he possesses properly indorsed order paper (which, because of the in-blank indorsement, is now bearer paper). As far as a prospective purchaser can tell from what is written on the check (Paul's name in the "payee" blank and Paul's name on the back as indorser), Tom is the rightful owner. Tom negotiates the stolen check to Hanna, a holder in due course, who takes it free from Paul's personal defense of nondelivery and claim of ownership. Paul's only recourse is against Tom, for the tort of conversion.

Legal Requirements for Indorsement. An **indorsement** is a signature, ordinarily found on the back of commercial paper and usually made by a payee or other transferor to show the indorser's intention to transfer ownership of the instrument. Like other signers (makers, drawers, acceptors), most indorsers can be liable contractually for the face amount of the instrument. Often, the payee *must* indorse to negotiate the instrument, as where a check is made out to a named payee. Where an instrument is made out "to bearer," an indorsement is not required by law as a part of the negotiation process. However, the *transferee* might insist on an indorsement simply out of habit or because the transferee knows that most indorsers, as signers, have potential liability for payment. The contractual liability of indorsers is discussed in Chapter 34.

To be effective, an indorsement must be written by or on behalf of the holder, since the holder is the proper person to transfer the instrument [3-202(2)]. An **unauthorized signature,** whether by a forger or by an agent exceeding his or her actual or apparent authority, is wholly inoperative as that of the purported indorser [3-404]. A person who takes an instrument indorsed by an agent runs considerable risk unless there is assurance that the agent has the requisite authority. An unauthorized indorsement provides the purported indorser (and the maker, drawer, or acceptor from whom payment is sought) with a *real* defense to payment—one that is good even against a holder in due course.

An instrument payable to the order of Al, Bob, *and* Cora is payable to them as a group and may be negotiated only by the indorsements of all of them. An instrument payable to the order of Al, Bob, *or* Cora is payable to any one of them and therefore requires the indorsement of only one [3-116].

Often, negotiable instruments are made payable to a named person with additional words describing the payee as an agent, an officer of a corporation or social club, or a fiduciary. For example, a check might be made out to the order of "Jane Doe, Attorney for Rachel Roe"; "Carlos Cash, Treasurer of the Country Club"; or "Fritz Fine, Trustee of the Smithers Trust." In all such instances, the agent, officer, or fiduciary may indorse the check by signing his or her name alone [3-117]. The descriptive words make clear that the agent, officer, or fiduciary is named as payee only for convenience in cashing the check for the person for whom it was intended.

When an instrument is made payable to a person under a trade name (e.g., a check made payable to the order of "Tony's Pizza"), the holder may indorse by using the trade name, by using his or her own name, or by using both [3-203]. A person paying the instrument (e.g., a maker or a drawee) or giving value for it (e.g., the payee's transferee) may require indorsement in both names. The same rules apply where the payee's name is misspelled. That is, the payee may indorse with either spelling or both spellings; a transferee for value may require the payee to indorse by using both spellings.

Where an instrument is payable to the order of a corporation, the name of the corporation should appear in the indorsement. Under case law interpreting the UCC, however, an indorsement such as "John Doe, Secretary-Treasurer" is legally sufficient as the indorsement of the corporation.

> **BOX 32.2**
>
> **You Be the Judge**
>
> Hiland Homes issued computer-generated checks to the order of "John Builder/Plywood City" in payment for construction work and materials. John indorsed the checks and cashed them at First Bank, the drawee. Plywood City did not indorse the checks and received none of the money. Alleging that First Bank erred in paying the checks without requiring Plywood City's indorsement, Hiland Homes sued First Bank for the amount of the checks. Is First Bank liable to Hiland Homes? ■

Types and Uses of Indorsements. The indorsements used to negotiate commercial paper can be described by the application of three sets of terms. An indorsement is either "in blank" or "special"; it is also either "unqualified" or "qualified"; it is also either "nonrestrictive" or "restrictive."

In-blank or special indorsement. An **indorsement in blank** is so called because it does not specify who the transferee is to be. The indorser merely signs his or her name. Darlene issues a check to the order of John Doe, and John signs it on the back, as in Figure 32.1. The check is indorsed "in blank." By using this type of indorsement, John has converted *order* paper to *bearer* paper. So the check can now be further negotiated by delivery alone [3-204].

Mailing a check indorsed in blank is risky, because any *possessor* of bearer paper, even a finder or a thief, can negotiate it [3-301]. A thief steals John's indorsed check from the mails and negotiates it to a holder in due course. John is deprived of all rights in the instrument, since a holder in due course takes it free from all rival claims of ownership [3-305(1)]. John's only recourse is to track down the thief.

John could protect himself from loss by using a special indorsement. A **special indorsement** names the person who is to receive ownership of the instrument. In Figure 32.2, the words "Pay Jane Doe, (signed) John Doe" is a special indorsement. Its legal effect is to continue the "order" character of the check. Thus, Jane's indorsement is required for further negotiation of the check. If it is lost or stolen before Jane indorses it, neither she nor John has much cause for worry. By his special indorsement John instructed others to pay Jane. They must follow John's instruction as to whom to pay. If the drawee bank, for example, disregards that instruction by paying a forger, the *drawee* must absorb the loss and attempt to track down the person to whom payment was made. (Note that a thief who steals the check and *forges* Jane's indorsement is *not* a holder and cannot negotiate the check [3-404]. The thief's transferee is merely an assignee who acquires no rights in the instrument because the thief had none.)

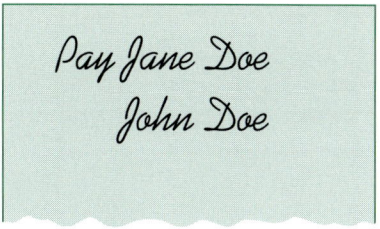

Figure 32.2

Although words of negotiability must appear on the *face* of an instrument to make it negotiable in form, their presence in or absence from an *indorsement* has no effect on the negotiability of the instrument. Indorsements simply give evidence of proper transfer and create potential liability on the part of indorsers; they neither create nor destroy negotiability of the instrument itself, no matter how they are worded.

Where an instrument is bearer paper on its face and carries no indorsement, the holder can protect against loss by using a special indorsement to convert the instrument into order paper. Jane draws a check payable to bearer and delivers it to Ann. Ann can protect herself against loss or theft by immediately naming herself as the indorsee in a special indorsement: "Pay Ann Bearer, (signed) Ann Bearer," as in Figure 32.3

A holder may convert a blank indorsement into a special indorsement by writing appropriate words above the signature of the indorser. Rachel receives the instrument shown in Figure

Figure 32.1

Figure 32.3

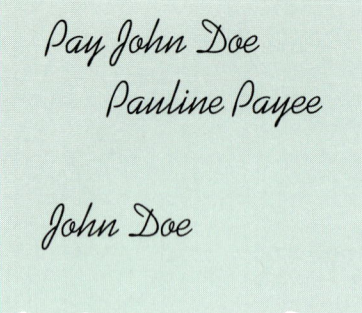

Figure 32.4

32.4. It is payable to bearer because the last indorsement, that of John Doe, is in blank. Figure 32.5 shows how Rachel can convert the blank indorsement shown in Figure 32.4 into a special indorsement to acquire the protection of order paper.

Unqualified or qualified indorsement. An indorser of a negotiable instrument may become liable for its face amount if the party who is supposed to pay fails or refuses to do so. This indorser's liability is a problem for anyone, such as an insurance agent or the treasurer of an organization, who is named as payee but really is collecting money for someone else. To negotiate the instrument, the agent must indorse it. To escape liability for the face amount if the instrument is not paid, the indorser must make a **qualified indorsement.**

Figure 32.5

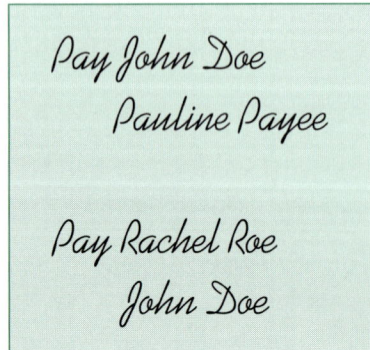

Pay Jane Doe,
John Doe,
without recourse

Figure 32.6

In Figure 32.6, John Doe qualifies his indorsement by using the words "without recourse." Unless the indorser uses "without recourse" or words of similar meaning, the indorsement is *unqualified* and the indorser has the usual liability for the face amount [3-414]. Using a qualified indorsement is a recommended practice for people who collect money for others. However, an indorser who routinely uses qualified indorsements on his or her own paper (paychecks and so on) may undermine its marketability by suggesting the existence of more risk than there is.

Nonrestrictive or restrictive indorsement. A **restrictive indorsement** specifies a particular use to which the indorsed instrument is to be put, or in some other way limits how the indorsee may deal with the instrument [3-205]. If no restriction or limitation is stated in the indorsement, it is nonrestrictive. Most restrictive indorsements are enforceable, but some are not [3-206]. The following paragraphs illustrate the various kinds of restrictive indorsements.

1 *Indorsements purporting to prohibit further transfer of an instrument.* John Doe, a payee, indorses his paycheck as follows: "Pay Jane Doe only, and no one else. Further transfer is hereby prohibited, (signed) John Doe." This restrictive indorsement is *unenforceable.* Commercial paper cannot serve its function as a substitute for money if indorsers can prevent further negotiation. Jane and subsequent transferees may negotiate the check despite John's limitation.

2 *Indorsement for deposit or collection.* Indorsements for deposit or collection are the most common types of restrictive indorsement. Figure 32.7 illustrates how John Doe could safely indorse a check that he must entrust to another for deposit.

Having indorsed his check "for deposit only," John delivers it to Ann, his bookkeeper, and tells her to deposit it in his bank account. How is John protected? Any transferee—such as a bank or a supermarket where Ann goes to cash the check—must pay or apply "consistently with the indorsement" any value given for the instrument [3-206(3)]. To the extent that Ann's transferee sees to it that the funds are deposited in John's account, the transferee becomes a holder for value and, probably, a holder in due course. However, if Ann's transferee does not obey the instruction given in the restrictive indorsement, the transferee is liable to the indorser for any loss resulting from the failure to heed the restriction.

Suppose Ann takes the check to Doe's bank, but instead of following Doe's instructions, she has the bank apply the proceeds of the check to a debt that *she* owes the bank. Ann is acting wrongfully, and so is the bank. In ignoring Doe's restrictive indorsement, the bank has failed to apply payment consistently with the indorsement, is not a holder for value, and cannot become a holder in due course of the check. Moreover, the bank has converted Doe's property and is liable to Doe for the amount of the check. The same would be true if the bank had disregarded other words signifying a purpose of deposit or collection, such as "For collection" or "Pay any bank."

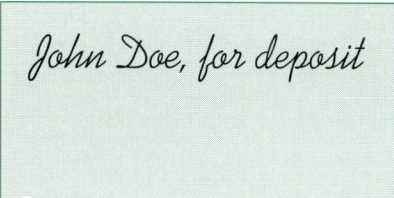

Figure 32.7

Any nonbank transferee is required to observe Doe's restrictive indorsement, but not all banks within the banking system are required to do so [3-206(3)]. The bank where Ann deposited the check is a **depositary bank.** Depositary banks must obey restrictive indorsements (if they are enforceable). But other banks could be involved. If the check was drawn on a bank in another state, the depositary bank would have to forward the check to the out-of-state bank (called the **payor bank**) for collection, perhaps through one or more **intermediary banks.** Because intermediary and payor banks must handle checks in bulk, it is impractical for them to determine whether all restrictive indorsements have been heeded. Therefore, intermediary and payor banks are permitted to ignore all restrictive indorsements except those of their immediate transferors and those of persons presenting instruments for payment.

In Case 32.3, the court discusses the legal effect of a variety of indorsements used by an alleged defrauder.

CASE 32.3	**Kelly v. Central Bank and Trust Co. of Denver** • 794 P.2d 1037 (Colo. App. 1989)
FACTS	Kelly and several hundred other plaintiffs in this class action lawsuit invested in a Cayman Islands entity, Tradecom, Ltd., a business involved in precious metals arbitrage. Their investments, in the form of cashier's checks, were payable to the order of Tradecom and delivered to Arvey Drown, Tradecom's purported agent. Drown indorsed these checks and deposited them in a checking account at Central Bank and Trust Co. of Denver. Later, he withdrew the money from the ac-

CASE 32.3 Continued

count and absconded with the funds.

There were 934 checks worth over $11,000,000. Most were indorsed: "Tradecom Limited For deposit only 072 575."

One check, for $57,000, was deposited under an indorsement by Central Bank's officer: "For deposit only 072 575 Tradecom by Mark E. Thomson Commercial Loan officer."

Others, totaling $576,850, were indorsed: "For deposit only 072 575."

Tradecom had no accounts at Central Bank. Account #072 575 was, instead, that of Equity Trading Corporation, a company owned and managed by Drown, the purported agent of Tradecom.

After losing most of their investments in Tradecom, plaintiffs sued Central Bank. They alleged that the check indorsements by Drown were unauthorized and ineffective; and that, over the course of 13 months, the Bank negligently or recklessly permitted Drown improperly to divert the checks, payable to Tradecom, into Equity Trading's checking account. From a summary judgment for Central Bank, Plaintiffs appealed.

OPINION

TURSI, J. . . . Plaintiffs first argue that summary judgment was inappropriate for Central Bank [on the issue of Drown's authority to cash checks for Tradecom].

[After reviewing the evidence, the appellate court agreed with the trial court that there was no significant doubt as to Drown's authority to act on behalf of Tradecom.]

Because there was no triable issue of fact concerning Drown's agency and authority to indorse and deposit the cashier's checks, and because proof of a forged or unauthorized indorsement is a necessary predicate to Central Bank's liability, plaintiffs could not prevail as to the 11 million dollars of checks that contained an indorsement which included the "Tradecom Limited" name. . . . Consequently, with respect to these checks indorsed with Tradecom's name, we conclude that the trial court properly granted summary judgment for Central Bank. . . .

The trial court erred, however, in granting Central Bank summary judgment on the $57,000 check indorsed by Central Bank's commercial loan officer.

[F]or Central Bank to . . . become a holder under this indorsement, and thus [to obtain] title, Central Bank would have . . . to have been authorized to provide Tradecom's indorsement under [§4-205(1)]. This, however, was impossible since Tradecom was not Central Bank's "customer." See In re Sun Belt Electrical Constructors, Inc. . . . (Bank not authorized to supply non-depositor third party payee's indorsement). Consequently, this indorsement is unauthorized as a matter of law, and summary judgment should not have been ordered for Central Bank on this check.

Plaintiffs also contend that the trial court erred in granting summary judgment for Central Bank on the remaining $519,850 of cashier's checks lacking any signature and merely indorsed "For deposit only 072 575." We agree. . . .

The term "indorsement" is generally understood to mean the indorser's writing of his or her signature on the instrument. . . . A check simply inscribed "For deposit only" to an account other than payee's account and without the payee's signature is not an effective "indorsement." . . .

If the instrument is order paper and the depository bank does not, or cannot,

**CASE 32.3
Continued**

supply the missing indorsement of its customer, the absence of an indorsement can be fatal to negotiation and transfer of title. . . . One such situation [occurs] when the depository bank's customer and the payee are not the same person. In [such a] case, the depository bank is unauthorized to, and cannot, supply the missing indorsement of the payee since the payee is not the bank's "customer" under [§4-205]. In this situation, the depository bank does not become a holder of the checks and does not obtain good title to them. . . .

In this case, it was undisputed that Drown, or someone in his employ, deposited $519,850 worth of cashier's checks at Central Bank bearing the simple inscription "For deposit only 072 575." These checks, which bore no signature indorsement of the payee, Tradecom, or anyone else, were paid and credited to account 072 575. This was not an account of Tradecom, which was not a customer of Central Bank. Under these circumstances, Central Bank was not a holder of these checks by negotiation. It obtained no title to these checks. It is, consequently, subject to conversion liability under [§3-419(1)(c)] for making payment on the equivalent of a forged indorsement.

Central Bank argues that it should not be liable to plaintiffs for conversion since (1) the inscription "For deposit only 072 575" constitutes a restrictive indorsement with which its employees complied. . . . We reject [this argument]. . . . Section [3-205] . . . does not declare that the words of restriction, "for deposit," constitute an "indorsement." Instead, [such words are] but a written direction which are inadequate, without a signature, to negotiate an instrument and transfer title of order paper. . . .

[Finally, as to the total loss claimed, plaintiffs contend that] the trial court erred in granting Central Bank summary judgment . . . alleging [that the Bank recklessly aided] Drown in his scheme to defraud. We agree. [Under a non-Code statute one who recklessly assists securities fraud has the same liability as the defrauder.]

Our review of the record . . . indicates there were sufficient facts, doubts, and inferences, to preclude summary judgment.

In the normal course of business, it is unusual for a corporate payee of checks to indorse them in blank and deliver them to third persons in the absence of an appropriate reason and pursuant to appropriate corporate authorization. Customarily, such reason and authorization are stated in the form of a corporate resolution which is submitted to the bank. . . .

Central Bank's own internal policy for accepting business deposits seemed to require as much. Tellers are instructed to examine appropriate resolutions on file to see if other account names may be on the account. Such inquiry, however, did not happen here since uncontradicted evidence indicates that Central Bank did not have any Tradecom resolutions or authorizations in its files. . . .

In light of these facts, the large number of checks, the large dollar amounts, and the fact that Central Bank's officers do not recall ever seeing a power of attorney or other authorization making Drown the agent of Tradecom, we conclude that a reasonable inference could be drawn that Central Bank's handling of deposits recklessly gave substantial assistance to Drown in his purported scheme to defraud. . . .

JUDGMENT [As to Drown's authority,] the judgment is affirmed. The judgment is otherwise reversed [and the case is remanded for further proceedings].

3 *Conditional indorsement.* Occasionally, a holder of an instrument will indorse it over to a merchant as payment for goods or services on the condition that the merchant-indorsee deliver the goods or render the services before receiving payment. Jane Doe, the payee of a check, indorses it "Pay to Able Computers provided they deliver a computer to me as per contract dated June 4." This is a conditional indorsement because of Jane's expressed intention that Able will not collect payment unless Jane receives the computer. As is true of an indorsement for deposit or collection, transferees must make payment consistently with the indorsement. So, when Able presents the check to the drawee bank, that bank must determine whether Able delivered the computer to Jane. If the bank ignores the condition—i.e., makes payment to Able even though Jane received no computer—Jane may compel the bank to pay her the amount of the check even though the bank has already paid Able.

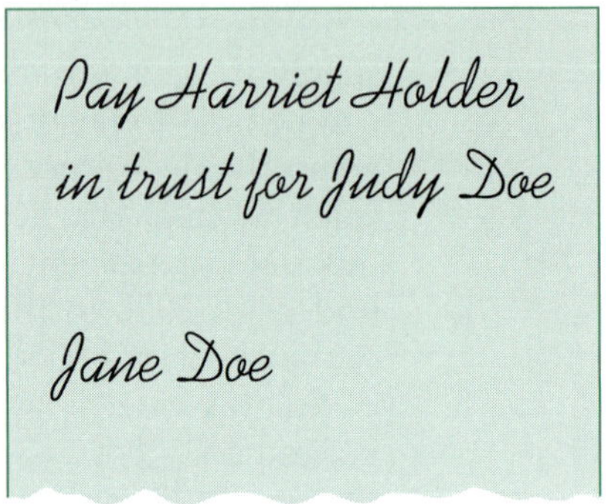

> *Pay Harriet Holder*
> *in trust for Judy Doe*
>
> *Jane Doe*

Figure 32.8

> **BOX 32.3**
>
> **Revised Article 3**
>
> The 1990 revisions make a conditional indorsement *ineffective* as to parties other than the indorser and indorsee. Subsequent holders for value and payors may simply ignore conditional indorsements. Thus, in the example of Jane and Able, the drawee bank has no duty to inquire about the delivery of the computer and must pay Able the amount of the check. ∎

4 *Trust indorsement.* Sometimes an indorser wants the indorsee to hold or to manage the proceeds of an instrument for the benefit of the indorser or someone else. As shown in Figure 32.8, Jane Doe, the payee of a note for $10,000, indorses it to Harriet for the benefit of Jane's daughter, Judy.

In acting for the benefit of Judy, Harriet might sell the note and use its proceeds for Judy's benefit. Or Harriet might breach the trust by selling the note and using the proceeds for herself. To qualify as a holder in due course, the *first taker* of the note from Harriet must be sure that Harriet applies the proceeds consistently with the indorsement [3-206(4)]. If Harriet transfers the note to Sam in payment of a debt that Harriet owes Sam, there are two bad results for Sam. First, he is not a holder in due course (and takes the note subject to any defenses the maker may have) because he knows that Harriet is applying the note to her own debt instead of collecting the amount for the benefit of Judy. Second, even if the note is collectable, Sam is liable to the trust for the

> **BOX 32.4**
>
> **Test Your Knowledge**
>
> How should you indorse the following checks?
>
> 1 You must deposit your paycheck today, but a doctor's appointment prevents you from getting to the bank. An acquaintance volunteers to deposit the check for you.
> 2 As treasurer of the Flyers' Club, you receive a check intended for the club but made out to you personally for $17,000.
> 3 You are the payee of a $50 check, and you want to give it to your friend Joan for her birthday. ∎

amount of the note because he disregarded the trust indorsement.

But Sam's *transferee* can be a holder in due course even though the transferee makes payment to Sam personally and not for the benefit of Judy. Fiduciaries such as Harriet often have broad powers to sell assets of the trust for management purposes, and this fact is well known in business circles. Sam sells the note to Sara. Although *Sam* is liable to the trust for the proceeds of the sale (since he is the first taker from Harriet and knows she received his payment for her personal use), Sara is not prevented from being a holder in due course just because she knows Sam bought the note from a fiduciary. Such sales usually are legitimate. However, if Sara knows at the time she buys the note that its sale to Sam was in *violation* of Harriet's fiduciary duties, Sara cannot be a holder in due course.

How should you indorse the checks described in Box 32.4?

Case 32.4 illustrates the consequences of a depositary bank's failure to observe a restrictive indorsement.

CASE 32.4 Rutherford v. Darwin • 29 UCC Rep. 899 (N.M. App. 1980)

FACTS Darwin was a general partner of two partnerships: Rancho Village Partners (Village) and The Settlement, Ltd. (Settlement). Darwin had full authority to manage the funds of both partnerships with his signature alone. In 1977 he made a "draw" against a construction loan made by a bank to Village, receiving the $300,000 amount in the form of a money order made out to Village as payee. Darwin indorsed it, "Deposit to the account of Rancho Village Partners, Ltd." Then he took it to First National Bank in Albuquerque (FNBIA), where both Village and Settlement had accounts, and had the amount deposited in Settlement's account despite the indorsement, which directed otherwise. Within 2 weeks of the deposit, Darwin wrongfully took most of the $300,000 for his own use. The other Village partners sued FNBIA for the embezzled amount and won a summary judgment. FNBIA appealed.

OPINION ANDREWS, J. . . . The words "Deposit to the account of Rancho Village Partnership, Ltd." clearly constitute a restrictive indorsement under [§3-205 of the UCC]. Section 3-206 imposes upon FNBIA the duty to pay consistently with the restrictive indorsement, and this duty gives rise to liability for the bank if it fails to do so. . . .

FNBIA contends that Darwin "waived" the restrictive indorsement, and thus released it from its duty to pay as directed by the indorsement. We conclude, however, that New Mexico does not recognize any doctrine of the waiver of restrictive indorsements, and thus we cannot accept FNBIA's theory.

[S]everal cases decided in other jurisdictions under the Uniform Negotiable Instruments Law (NIL) suggest that the doctrine [of waiver] was once generally recognized. . . . We are aware of no case decided since the Uniform Commercial Code [superseded] the NIL as the law governing negotiable instruments which has recognized the doctrine, and thus the dispositive issue is whether the doctrine survives as part of the common law under the UCC.

**CASE 32.4
Continued**

The NIL was silent on the key issue of this case; both the bank's duty to pay as directed by a restrictive indorsement and the waiver exception to that rule were matters of common law under the NIL. With the adoption of the UCC, the rule as to the duty of the bank was codified in §3-206.

Courts have frequently given effect to common law limitations and exceptions to newly codified common law rules. For example, many jurisdictions have held that a murderer may not take from the estate of his victim even where the general law of descent and distribution of the jurisdiction has been codified without the inclusion of that sensible and time honored common law limitation. However, the general rule is that:

> general and comprehensive legislation, prescribing minutely a course of conduct to be pursued and the parties and things affected, and specifically describing limitations and exceptions, is indicative of a legislative intent that the statute should totally supersede and replace the common law dealing with the subject matter. 2A Sutherland, Statutory Construction §50.05. . . .

We hold that the codification of the law of restrictive indorsements contained in the UCC is sufficiently comprehensive and detailed to exclude common law exceptions which are not mentioned. Section 3-206 . . . sets forth with particularity when and by whom restrictive indorsements must be observed; it must be inferred that if the legislature had intended that restrictive indorsements would become ineffective for some other reason, such a direction would have been included in this section or elsewhere in the UCC. . . .

FNBIA further argues [that] the indorser of an instrument should be allowed to waive the indorsement by analogy to §3-208, which states that one who reacquires an instrument may cancel [mark out] any indorsement which is not necessary to his title. . . . The section is not applicable because the instrument was not reacquired and because Darwin did not strike [cancel] the restrictive indorsement.

This second distinction is particularly important. The presence of an uncancelled restrictive indorsement on a negotiable instrument creates the legitimate expectation [in subsequent holders] that it was negotiated in accordance with the restriction, and thus it would, at least in some cases, tend to conceal embezzlement or misappropriation to allow such indorsements to be waived without being physically struck from the instrument. . . .

The circumstances of the transaction cry out for attention on the part of the bank. We hold, as a matter of law, that the bank had a duty to refuse to deposit the money to the account of The Settlement. The money order was restrictively indorsed to the account of an entity entirely different from that named on the accompanying deposit slip. The trial court observed that, particularly in light of the sum involved, the bank had an obligation to be sure that the money went into the proper account.

We adopt the reasoning of the New York Court of Appeals:

> The presence of a restriction imposes upon the depository bank an obligation not to accept that item other than in accord with the restriction. By disregarding the restriction, it not only subjects itself to liability for any losses resulting from its actions, but it also passes up what may well be the best opportunity to prevent the fraud. The

CASE 32.4 Continued	presentation of a check in violation of a restrictive indorsement is an obvious warning sign, and the depository bank is required to investigate the situation rather than blindly accept the check. . . .
JUDGMENT	. . . The decision of the trial court is affirmed. . . . [Dissenting opinion omitted.]

Right to Rescind an Indorsement. Sometimes a person negotiates an instrument in circumstances giving that person a right to rescind (cancel) the negotiation and to get the instrument back from the transferee [3-207]. Examples are:

1 A negotiation by a minor or other person having a right to rescind for lack of capacity. Dora, an adult, makes a check out to Paul, a minor. Paul cashes the check at a supermarket or indorses it over to a friend as a gift. *As long as the check remains in the possession of Paul's immediate transferee* (supermarket or friend), Paul may rescind the negotiation and get the instrument back from the transferee.
2 A negotiation obtained by fraud, duress, or mistake. The wronged person may rescind the negotiation and retrieve the instrument from the immediate transferee.
3 A negotiation made by a trustee in breach of a fiduciary duty owed to the beneficiary of the trust. The beneficiary (or his or her legal guardian or other legal representative) may rescind the negotiation and retrieve the instrument from the immediate transferee.

However, although the transferor has a right to *rescind* the negotiation as to the immediate transferee, the negotiation *is effective* to transfer title to (ownership of) the instrument to the transferee [3-207(1)], and the transferee, even if a wrongdoer, has the power to negotiate the check further. So, if the instrument reaches the hands of a holder in due course *before* the aggrieved person (Paul in example 1 above) exercises the right to rescind, the aggrieved person *loses* the right to rescind the negotiation. Being thus freed from most claims and defenses of transferors, holders in due course are encouraged to accept and to pay maximum value for commercial paper.

Paula, a minor, indorses her paycheck to Tom. Before Paula can rescind the negotiation on the ground of minority, Tom cashes the check at Ferndale Auto Supply, which knows nothing of the transaction between Paula and Tom. Paula has lost the right to rescind the negotiation; Ferndale, a holder in due course, may keep the check and enforce it against Dora, the drawer. Paula is limited to a cause of action for damages against Tom.

Note that minority (infancy) is a complete (real) defense to payment where the minor is *the maker or drawer* of an instrument; but (for the protection of holders in due course) minority is, in effect, only a personal defense where a minor is *negotiating* an instrument issued by a person of full capacity. Yet even a holder in due course cannot hold a minor *contractually* liable on his or her indorsement; so minority remains in some respects a real defense even in the process of negotiating instruments.

SUMMARY

Most personal defenses, which are not good against a holder in due course, arise out of disputes about the quality or sufficiency of the payee's performance of an underlying transaction with the maker or drawer. The personal defenses include fraud in the inducement, breach of warranty in a sale of goods, nondelivery of the instrument, and unauthorized completion of a signed instrument. Real defenses, which are good even against a holder in due course, include infancy to the extent that it is a defense to a simple contract, serious forms of duress and illegality, fraud in the execution of the instrument, and unauthorized signature and material alteration.

Any holder of commercial paper can negotiate it and thereby enable a properly qualified transferee to become a holder in due course. Bearer paper is negotiated by delivery; order paper, by delivery plus any necessary indorsement. Depending on the needs of the parties, indorsements may be in blank or special, unqualified or qualified, and nonrestrictive or restrictive. A transferor of commercial paper may have a right to rescind the negotiation, including any indorsement, but if the paper first gets into the hands of a holder in due course, the transferor cannot have the instrument itself back.

REVIEW QUESTIONS

1. What is the difference between a personal defense and a real defense? Illustrate each kind.

2. Who can have a personal or a real defense?

3. Is minority a personal or a real defense? Explain.

4. Is duress a personal or a real defense? Explain.

5. How could a negotiable instrument be put into circulation without being delivered by the maker or drawer to the payee?

6. (a) How may negotiation of a bearer instrument be accomplished? How may negotiation of an order instrument be accomplished? **(b)** What is the legal significance of negotiation? (For the answer, see Who May Negotiate an Instrument in this chapter.)

7. Suppose a person buys a negotiable order instrument but the transferor forgets to indorse it. What is the legal position of the buyer?

8. Illustrate how a person can have the power, but not the right, to negotiate commercial paper.

9. For what purpose is each of the following indorsements used: **(a)** special, **(b)** qualified, and **(c)** restrictive?

10. Explain whether all banks are required to heed an indorsement for deposit or for collection.

11. What might be the economic consequence of a person's always using qualified or conditional indorsements when indorsing checks or notes?

12. Often a person who negotiates commercial paper has a legal ground for rescinding the negotiation. If such a ground exists, may the wronged person retrieve the negotiated instrument? Explain.

CASE PROBLEMS

1. Paul fraudulently induced Mary to issue him a note reading: "July 2, 19xx. Sixty days after date I promise to pay Paul the sum of seven hundred dollars ($700.00), together with interest at the rate of 8 percent per annum. Value received. (Signed) Mary." The day after Paul received the note, he indorsed and sold it to Albert, who took it without notice of the fraud. Is Albert subject to Mary's defense of fraud?

2. Litton Systems (Litton) and Royal were divisions of Litton Industries. Litton decided to purchase photocopiers for its branch offices. Royal's salesman, Buquicchio, persuaded Litton Systems to lease copiers from Regent Leasing Corp. Unknown to Litton and Royal, Regent paid "service fees" to Buquicchio for "pushing" leases instead of sales. To finance the purchase of the copiers to be leased to Litton, Regent assigned the Litton leases to two banks for value. The leases contained waiver-of-defenses clauses intended to free assignees from any claims that Litton might have against Regent. Under the UCC, such leases have the effect of a negotiable instrument. Litton failed to make the payments due under the leases, and the banks brought suit. Litton denied liability, alleging that Regent's bribery of Buquicchio made the leases with Regent void, giving Litton a good defense even against holders in due course. From a judgment for the banks, Litton appealed. Did Litton have a good defense to payment?

3. To cover gambling losses incurred during private "freeze out" games of 21, Sandler drew checks in favor of Hutchings. Hutchings negotiated the checks to Nevada National Bank and received payment. When Nevada National presented the checks to the drawee bank for payment, that bank refused to honor them. Nevada National then sued Sandler for the unpaid amounts. Although gambling is legal in Nevada, a Nevada statute provides that all "notes drawn for the purpose of reimbursing or repaying any money knowingly lent or advanced for gaming are 'utterly void, frustrate, and of none effect.'" Sandler alleged that the statute gave him a good defense against payment. Was Nevada National, a holder in due course, entitled to payment from Sandler?

4. Kenneth Walcott's monthly mortgage payment was $610.59. He alleged that to cover his November 1985 payment, he mailed his paycheck plus a money order to Midatlantic Mortgage Co. He said that he wrote his name and mortgage number on, and affixed the Midatlantic mailing sticker to, the back of the check. Upon being notified that he was late with the November payment, Walcott learned that his check had been cashed by Bilko Check Cashing Corp. and deposited in Bilko's account with Manufacturers Hanover Trust (Bank). The check eventually was cleared through Citibank and charged to the account of the drawer, New York City Transit Authority. Alleging that a thief had stolen his paycheck and that Bank had wrongfully credited it to Bilko's account, Walcott sued Bank and Bilko for the amount of the check. A copy of the check showed Walcott's indorsement and the mortgage number, but there was no sign of the sticker. Should Walcott receive judgment for the amount of the check?

5. The Silver Slipper Gambling Hall and Saloon issued a payroll check to an employee, Mrs. Reggie Bluiett. She indorsed the check in blank and left it on a dresser in her home. The following day, she discovered that the check was missing. On that day, Freddie Watkins purchased two tires from Western Auto and paid for them with Mrs. Bluiett's payroll check, receiving the tires and a balance of about $112 in cash. Later, Watkins was charged with having obtained money under false pretenses from Western Auto. An essential element of the offense is that the person from whom the money is obtained must suffer injury or damage. Watkins was convicted of the charge and appealed. Should the conviction be upheld?

6. On May 16, 1969, the Bank of Hollywood Hills of Hollywood Hills, Florida, issued a cashier's check for $2,000 payable to "Richard and Grace Grimaldi." Four days later Richard indorsed the check "Grace Grimaldi by Richard Grimaldi" and presented it to a teller of the Beach National Bank located at Fort Meyers, Florida, where the Grimaldis had a joint account. The teller cashed the check and paid the full amount to Richard. On May 20 the cashier's check routinely arrived at the Bank of Hollywood Hills for payment. That bank refused to honor the check. Was it justified in refusing to honor the check? Explain.

CHAPTER 33

Holder-in-Due-Course Status; FTC Limits

A holder takes a negotiable instrument free from personal defenses and rival claims of ownership in either of two ways. One way is simply to possess the personal qualities required for holder-in-due-course status. The other is to receive the rights of a holder in due course by assignment under the **shelter provision** of the Uniform Commercial Code. However, in certain consumer credit transactions, a rule of the Federal Trade Commission prevents anyone from being a holder in due course. The first part of this chapter deals with the personal qualities needed to be a holder in due course. It also notes how a person may acquire the rights of a holder in due course without personally being one. The second part discusses the FTC limits on the availability of holder-in-due-course status.

HOLDER-IN-DUE-COURSE STATUS

Requirements for Holder-in-Due-Course Status

A **holder** (a possessor of bearer paper or of properly indorsed order paper) may become a **holder in due course** by doing three things: (1) giving value for the instrument, (2) taking it in good faith, and (3) taking it without notice of (a) defenses to payment, (b) rival claims of ownership, or (c) the fact (if true) that the instrument is overdue when received or has been dishonored [3-302(1)].

Giving Value. To qualify as a holder in due course, the holder must give value for the instrument. So, if the payee of a negotiable instrument indorses and delivers it to a transferee as a gift, the transferee is not a holder in due course.

The meaning of value in the law of commercial paper differs sharply from its meaning in the law of sales and secured transactions. In sales and secured transactions, value means any consideration, including an executory (unperformed) promise, sufficient to support a simple (informal) contract. In the law of commercial paper, **value** means *performed* consideration [3-303(a)]. Maria issues a negotiable note to Paula, and Paula transfers it to Hal in exchange for his promise to paint Maria's house *next week*. Hal has given consideration for the note (has "bought" it), but Hal has not yet given the required value for it because his promise has not yet been performed. When Hal does the painting, he will be a holder for value. If at that time he possesses the other qualities necessary for holder-in-due-course status, he will then be a holder in due course.

Suppose Maria's note has a principal (face) amount of $2,000 and Paula agrees to sell it to Hal in exchange for $1,000 to be paid when Hal receives the note, plus a used car to be delivered next week. Upon payment of the $1,000, Hal is a holder for value (and perhaps a holder in due course) to the extent of the *performed* consideration ($1,000). Hal will become a holder for value as to the rest of the note upon delivery of the used car.

As indicated in the preceding illustrations, value can take the form of money, services, goods, or other property such as real estate. But value takes other forms as well. Some common business examples follow.

1 A *bank's permitting a customer to withdraw money before a deposited item clears*. When a customer of a bank deposits an **item** (a check or some other negotiable instrument) for collection, the bank credits the customer's account with the amount of the item. Ordinarily the customer has no right to draw against the item until it "clears" (e.g., is collected by the bank). The bank's act of crediting the customer's account is, in effect, only a promise to give value—when the item clears. However, if the bank permits the depositor to draw against the item before it is collected, the bank gives value (and becomes a holder for value of the deposited item) to the extent to which the bank permits a precollection withdrawal of money [4-208(1)(a)].

Where a customer deposits a number of checks over time and makes withdrawals before the deposited checks clear, when are the proceeds of a particular check withdrawn? The UCC requires the application of the **first in, first out rule**. Marti opens a checking account on May 1 by depositing a check of $400; deposits similar checks on May 2 and on May 3; and withdraws $400 on May 5 and $400 on May 6. Under the first in, first out rule, the bank has given value on the check deposited May 1 at the time of the first withdrawal (May 5) and on the check deposited May 2 at the time of the second withdrawal (May 6) [4-208(2)]. Where a customer deposits an item and does not make a withdrawal, the bank is automatically a holder for value when the customer acquires a *right* to withdraw the amount of the item—i.e., when the item is collected or otherwise clears [4-208(1)(b)].

2 *Paying for commercial paper with a negotiable instrument*. A holder takes an instrument for value by giving, in return, an entirely different negotiable instrument. John sells Mary his certificate of deposit. Mary pays for it with a check. Mary is a holder for value.

3 *Making a loan and receiving a negotiable instrument as security*. Paul, the payee of a $5,000 note, wants to borrow $2,000 from Harriet. They agree that if Paul will indorse and deliver the note to Harriet for her to hold as security for the loan, Harriet will lend him the $2,000. The parties carry out the agreement. Harriet has given value for the note (to the extent of $2,000) by making the loan.

Often a buyer of commercial paper pays the face amount of the instrument as value. If you cash your payroll check at a supermarket, you ordinarily will receive the face amount because the check is a demand instrument that the supermarket can immediately convert into cash. But to give value, a buyer of commercial paper need not necessarily pay the face amount. The seller of a *time* instrument (such as a time draft or a note payable at a future date) wants cash now for an instrument that cannot be collected until later. Because the purchaser expects a profit and faces a risk of noncollection, the seller ordinarily will have to accept a **discounted** (reduced) amount for the instrument—i.e., something less than its total **yield** (face amount plus any interest). By paying a discounted amount, the purchaser of a time note can profit by selling it or by personally collecting the total yield when the note comes due.

For example, Maria issues a note for $100 plus 15 percent annual interest to Pearl, payable 1 year from date. Then Pearl immediately sells the note to Hal for $95. Here the total yield is $115. Hal's payment of $95 will give him a profit of 21 percent. However, he must wait a year to collect and must take the chance that Maria will refuse or be unable to pay. In the meantime, any inflation will erode his profit. All courts are likely to hold that Hal has given value. If he otherwise qualifies as a holder in due course (e.g., takes Maria's note without notice of her personal defenses), he is entitled to collect $115 from Maria when the note comes due, unless she has a real defense.

What minimum amount must Hal pay before a court will hold that he has given value for Maria's note? The main object of commercial paper law is to induce a holder in due course to pay *market value* for the instrument. Theoretically, the discounting process by which a buyer of commercial paper determines how much to pay for a negotiable instrument involves an assessment by the buyer of the risk factors pertaining to the instrument being purchased. Therefore, the amount paid would constitute market value only if the payment were reasonably related to the amount of risk associated with the negotiable instrument. Hal pays only $20 for Maria's note. If Maria seldom pays her debts, Hal's paying $20 for her note could be a realistic assessment of risk, and Hal would be a holder in due course entitled to collect the $115 from Maria when the note comes due. But if Maria has a good credit rating, Hal's $20 payment for a note yielding $115 would not constitute full market value. Hal would be a holder in due course as to $20 and only an assignee as to the rest.

However, many courts are reluctant to analyze the risk factors and decide whether full market value was given. Rather than rule that Hal's $20 payment did not constitute full value, courts often will consider instead whether Hal acted in good faith in making such a small payment.

Acting in Good Faith. To be a holder in due course, the holder must act in **good faith** when purchasing commercial paper. Under pre-1990 commercial paper law, "honesty in fact" is all that is required for a person to be in good faith [1-201(19)]. A holder will be considered dishonest (and lacking good faith) only if he or she (1) has *actual knowledge* of wrongdoing or defects concerning the paper, or (2) *consciously ignores* suspicious circumstances. The test of good faith that applies to commercial paper is "subjective." This means that a court will look at the actual experience, intelligence, and judgment of each individual when deciding whether that individual has acted honestly. An inexperienced person of low intelligence may be held to have acted in good faith in circumstances that should have aroused suspicion in a professional buyer of commercial paper.

> **BOX 33.1**
>
> ### Revised Article 3
>
> The 1990 amendments replace the subjective good faith standard with the objective "merchant's rule" of good faith found in other parts of the Code. In states adopting these amendments, good faith now means "honesty in fact and the observance of reasonable commercial standards of fair dealing." Thus, the so-called "white heart, empty head" test of good faith for holders in due course seems on the way out.

Because good faith is a matter of individual honesty, it cannot be described fully. However, the following illustrations suggest the general nature of good faith.

1   Maria issues a check for $800 to Paul. Paul negotiates it for $50 to Hal, a person of normal intelligence and experience. *Hal* lacks good faith even though he knows of no actual wrongdoing or defect concerning the check. Hal should wonder why Paul, the payee, would accept $50 for a check that Paul could cash for $800 merely by presenting it to the drawee bank.

2   Paul Payee procures a payroll check from Maria, his employer, by fraudulently overstating the number of hours he worked during the pay period. Maria instructs her bank to stop payment. Paul negotiates the check to his own bank in another town. Paul's bank knows nothing of the stop order and pays him the face amount without making inquiry of the drawee bank. Paul's *bank* is acting in good faith despite its failure to inquire. If Paul's bank were required

to inquire about stop orders in each of its thousands of daily transactions, there would be intolerable delays in processing checks and other commercial paper. Paul's bank is permitted to assume that a person who negotiates an instrument is acting honestly, unless the bank has knowledge of additional facts that should arouse its suspicions.

3   Paul's Roofing does repair work on apartment buildings, receives promissory notes from its customers, and discounts the notes to Paul's Finance Co., a financial subsidiary of Paul's Roofing. Paul is president of both companies. Paul's Roofing consistently defrauds its customers and does shoddy work, but Paul's Finance Co. denies knowledge of these practices and insists it is a holder in due course of the notes. In deciding whether *Paul's Finance Co.* has the good faith necessary for holder-in-due-course status, a court will consider the extent of the finance company's knowledge of the transactions that gave rise to the notes, as well as the closeness of the relationship between the finance company and the payee (Paul's Roofing) from which it purchased the paper. A finance company that is controlled by (or that controls) the payee or that buys great numbers of instruments from the payee at unusually large discounts is likely to be aware of questionable trade practices of the payee. Failure to investigate obviously suspicious circumstances can amount to bad faith.

Having No Notice of Defects. To be a holder in due course, a good faith holder for value must also take the instrument **without notice** (1) that it is overdue, (2) that it has been dishonored, or (3) that there is a defense to payment or a rival claim of ownership [3-302].

In contrast to the pre-1990 subjective test of good faith, the Code test for notice is objective and remains so under the 1990 amendments. Under the UCC, a person has notice of a fact when he or she has *actual knowledge* of it; receives *a notice such as a letter* in time to take action or avoid loss (even though the letter remains unread); or from all the facts and circumstances known to him or her at the time in question has *reason to know* that the fact exists [1-201(25)]. For a person subjectively to lack good faith, mental awareness of wrongdoing or suspicious circumstances is required. But to be *on notice* of a difficulty surrounding commercial paper, a person need only possess relevant information, whether or not that person has actual mental awareness of the difficulty.

The following case discusses constructive notice (reason to know) of a maker's defenses.

CASE 33.1   **Parkhill v. Nusor** • 123 Bankr. 55 (Bankr. 9th Cir. 1991)

FACTS   Irene Nusor fell behind in mortgage payments on her home and responded to Best Financial Consultants' advertisements offering attractive refinancing opportunities.

At a McDonald's restaurant, Best representatives promised to refinance her debt of about $98,000, pay off the two existing creditors, and provide Nusor with an additional $5,000 in spending money. For this, Nusor would pay Best a fee of $4,000. She signed a fee agreement and a blank form entitled "Installment Note." The note was filled in later by Best representatives, for $14,986.61 payable in full in 60 days (on December 23, 1987) at an annual interest rate of 18 percent. At a second meeting Nusor signed a deed of trust as security for the promissory note.

Best made only a single payment of $5,997.25 to one of Nusor's creditors, Zenith Home Loan. Best never refinanced Nusor's home or fulfilled its other promises. On December 2, Best assigned the note and deed of trust to Robin

CASE 33.1 Continued

Parkhill for $13,812.19. She bought the note without actual knowledge of Best's misrepresentations to Nusor.

In June 1988, Nusor filed a Chapter 13 petition in bankruptcy. Parkhill filed a claim against the debtor's estate, alleging that she was a secured creditor. Nusor sued under the Bankruptcy Code to avoid Parkhill's deed of trust. The trial court granted Nusor summary judgment, holding that the Installment Note was not a negotiable instrument, and that Nusor's defenses of fraud, misrepresentation, and failure of consideration were good against Parkhill. The court voided the deed of trust, allowing Parkhill only a general, unsecured claim of $5,997.25. Parkhill appealed.

OPINION

VOLINN, B.J. . . . We affirm the judgment below in most respects but on different grounds, and we reverse in part.

There are [two] principal issues on this appeal . . . : (a) Whether the Installment Note is a negotiable instrument, [and] (b) whether Parkhill is a holder in due course. . . .

[W]e disagree with the trial court's ruling that the Installment Note was not a negotiable instrument.

The trial court found that the Installment Note has two principal defects: (1) It does not contain the name of a maker, and (2) its "form" is not "adequate." First, with respect to the note's identification of the maker, the statute requires only that the note "be signed by the maker." There is no dispute that Nusor's signature appears at the bottom of the note. The fact that Nusor is [unclearly] described as "a married woman, as her sole and separate property" . . . does not destroy the note's negotiability.

Second, the court does not explain why it found the note's form inadequate. Apparently, it accepted Nusor's argument . . . that the note omits the requisite unconditional promise or order by a maker because there is a punctuation mark (a period) after the identification of Nusor and before the promise to pay. The note's first line reads: "in installments and at the times hereinafter stated, for value received I the undersigned, Irene Vazquez-Nusor, a married woman as her sole & separate property." The second line begins "promises to pay to Best Financial Consultants. . . ." Nusor argues that since the name of the maker is not identified at the beginning of the second line, which begins with the verb "promises," the note fails to meet the requirements of [§ 3-104].

[A Code comment states] that courts should find against negotiability . . . where there is not at least a "clear equivalent" for the language required by the statute. In this case, however, we find that the Installment [Note's language] satisfies this "clear equivalence" test. The inadvertent placement of the period does not undermine the note's negotiability. . . .

Whether Parkhill is a holder in due course turns on Parkhill's satisfying the requirements of [§ 3-302]. Nusor argues that Parkhill fails to meet this standard because . . . the note's clumsy draftsmanship and its exceptional rate of return . . . gave Parkhill at least constructive notice of Nusor's defenses. Nusor states that these "irregularities . . . would certainly cause a reasonably prudent person to question the note's validity and thereby be placed on notice." We agree and hold that Parkhill was not a holder in due course. . . .

CASE 33.1 Continued

[UCC § 3-304(1)] sets forth the conditions under which "irregularities" in the instrument puts the holder on notice:

(1) The purchaser has notice of a claim or defense if (a) the instrument is so incomplete, bears such visible evidence of forgery or alteration, *or is otherwise so irregular* as to call into question its validity, terms or ownership. . . . (Emphasis added).

The term "notice" is further defined in § 1201(25)(c), which provides that one has notice of a fact when "from all the facts and circumstances known to him at the time in question he or she has *reason to know* that it exists." (Emphasis added). . . .

In this case, Parkhill did not seek interest income in the usual manner. She answered a newspaper advertisement. Presumably, after communicating with Best, she calculated the rate of return. The content of the Installment Note . . . clearly indicated that this was an unusual type of commercial transaction. For the discounted price of $13,812.19, Parkhill was assigned a note designed to provide her in 21 days . . . the face value of the Installment Note ($14,986.61) plus 18 percent per annum interest. . . . Thus, Parkhill's total anticipated return was $1,624.02. This amount represents the equivalent of an annual interest rate of over 203 percent, a return far in excess of the reasonable expectations of any investor who in good faith seeks a favorable rate of return. In addition, we find it significant that Parkhill made no inquiry about the note's origins notwithstanding its manifestly unusual terms. See Stewart v. Thornton . . . (holder in due course protection "cannot be used to shield one who simply refuses to investigate when the facts known to him suggest an irregularity concerning the commercial paper he purchases.")

The imprecise form of the Installment Note, combined with its exorbitant rate of return, were sufficient to divest Parkhill of holder in due course status and to subject her to Nusor's defenses. . . . See Salter v. Vanotti . . . (where notice was imputed to a purchaser who made no effort to inquire as to possible defenses notwithstanding a 40% discount . . . and a contract provision giving the maker of the note the right to rescind the agreement).

JUDGMENT Accordingly, we hold that Parkhill is not a holder in due course and is therefore subject to Nusor's defenses of fraud in the inducement and failure of consideration. . . . However, [since the failure of consideration was not total,] we do not agree with the trial court's determination that the deed of trust, originally conveyed to Best and subsequently assigned to Parkhill, should also be nullified. . . . Parkhill should be allowed a secured, rather than an unsecured, claim [for $5,977.25, the amount that Best paid Zenith Home Loan.]

Notice that instrument is overdue [3-304(3)]. A negotiable instrument is **overdue** when the day of its maturity has passed and the instrument remains unpaid. An overdue instrument carries an increased risk of nonpayment. A person who takes an instrument with notice that it is overdue falls short of the innocence required of holders in due course.

Whether a person has notice that an instrument is overdue depends greatly on whether the instrument is a time or a demand instrument, or on the terms (contents) of the instru-

> **BOX 33.2**
>
> **Test Your Knowledge**
>
> Morton bought an out-of-state residential lot on credit from Peter. Morton signed a promissory note for the $27,000 purchase price plus 13 percent annual interest, payable in equal monthly installments over the 5-year term of the note. Because Morton could not visit the site, he relied on Peter's statement that the lot was "an A-1 building site in a growing suburban area." In fact, as Peter knew, the lot consisted of swampland near a garbage dump with a growing population of mosquitoes, rats, and other vermin.
>
> A month after making the purchase, Morton learned the truth about the lot. Unable to locate Peter, and knowing that Peter often sold notes to members of his family, Morton mailed to each one a letter explaining the situation. Hector, Peter's brother, received a copy of the letter but tossed it aside without reading it. Three days later, Peter sold Morton's note to Hector, who knew nothing about the lot and who from early childhood had deeply trusted Peter—naively, many of the family thought. Whether Hector can collect on the note depends on whether he is a holder in due course. Is he? Consider the qualities of good faith and notice of defenses. ∎

ment. The following illustrations involve *time* instruments.

1 In January, Maria issues Paula a note for $1,000. The note states that it is payable on May 1. On May 20 Paula sells the note to Hal for $900. Hal can read and is mentally alert. Because the due date (May 1) appears on the note, and because Hal should know he is buying it on May 20, Hal is on notice that the instrument is overdue and should wonder why Paula is selling the note to him instead of collecting the amount from Maria. Hal is not a holder in due course.

2 In January, Maria issues Paula a note for $1,000. The note states that it is payable on May 1. It contains an acceleration clause which Paula may exercise "if Paula deems herself insecure." On April 3, Paula learns that Maria might not be able to pay the note on May 1. Feeling insecure, Paula exercises the clause (requires Maria to pay the $1,000 early, on April 3); but after paying the note, Maria leaves it in Paula's possession. On April 16, Paula sells the note to Hal. If Hal knows or has reason to know that acceleration has occurred, he has notice that the instrument is overdue [3-304]. If he is without such notice, he can be a holder in due course entitled to Maria's payment even though Maria has already paid the note.

The purchaser of a *demand* instrument such as a check or a demand note has notice that it is overdue (and cannot be a holder in due course) if at the time of purchase the purchaser has reason to know that *demand has already been made*, or that the purchaser is taking the instrument *more than a reasonable time after its issue*. For *checks* drawn and payable within the United States and its territories, this reasonable time is *presumed* to be 30 days [3-304(3)(c)]. So, if Mary issues Paula a check on June 1, and Paula negotiates it to Hal on July 5, Hal has taken an overdue instrument and cannot be a holder in due course—unless he can "rebut" the presumption (prove that a longer time than 30 days was reasonable, given the circumstances in which he found himself).

Notice that instrument has been dishonored. **Dishonor** is (1) a refusal by the maker of a note or the drawee of a draft to *pay* the instrument when it is due, or (2) a drawee's refusal to *accept* a *time* draft [3-307; 3-501, comment 3]. A holder who purchases an instrument with notice that it has been dishonored is taking risks beyond those normally associated with the taking of commercial paper, and does not deserve the special status enjoyed by a holder in due course. A holder could receive notice of dishonor by means of the letters NSF (nonsufficient funds) stamped on the face of a check, or by information about dishonor received from some other source.

Notice of a defense or a rival claim. A holder who takes an instrument with notice of a defense to payment or of a rival claim of ownership cannot be a holder in due course. Examples follow.

1 Maria issues a check to Paula in payment for defective goods that Paula delivered to Maria. Hal, Paula's employee, knows of the defects. Paula later negotiates Maria's check to Hal in lieu of his regular paycheck. Hal is on notice of Maria's defense (failure of consideration or breach of warranty) and cannot be a holder in due course.

2 Paul indorses his paycheck in blank and places it on the dashboard of his car. On the way to the bank the check blows out the window. Hal sees the check land on the ground and sees Fay Finder pick it up. Soon Fay negotiates the check to Hal. Hal is on notice of Paul's claim of ownership and cannot be a holder in due course.

A person can be on notice of a maker's or a drawer's defenses even though he or she is not aware of any particular wrongdoing by the payee. A purchaser cannot be a holder in due course if the instrument is *incomplete,* if the instrument is *irregular* on its face, or if there are *other defects*. Examples of these sources of notice follow.

1 Maria signs and issues a check to Paul, but she leaves the line for the amount blank. As Paul knows, she intended to fill the check out for $100. Paul so informs Hal and, without filling out the amount, negotiates the check to Hal for $100. Because Hal is the taker of an incomplete instrument, he is automatically on notice of any defenses Maria might have (e.g., failure of consideration or Paul's fraud), even though he has no knowledge of any particular defense [3-304(1)(a)].

2 Suppose that Hal, in the preceding illustration, fills in the amount of $100 in Lisa's presence and negotiates the check to her for $100. Lisa has taken a completed instrument. Her knowledge that an incomplete instrument has been completed does *not*, by itself, charge her with notice of a defense or claim. She must also have notice that the completion was *improper* [3-304(4)(d)].

3 Maria issues a note to Paul for $100. Paul crudely alters the amount to read $1,000. The alteration is so obvious that it can be readily detected. This is an example of "irregular" paper. Because of the obvious irregularity, a purchaser is on notice of wrongdoing and cannot be a holder in due course. An instrument stamped "NSF" or "Payment stopped" also is irregular.

4 Paula is trustee for Judy. Maria issues a check for $1,000 "to the order of Paula for the benefit of Judy." Paula owes Hal a $1,000 payment on Paula's car and negotiates the check to Hal in payment of Paula's personal debt. Because the check reads "for the benefit of Judy," Hal is on notice that Paula has negotiated it in breach of her fiduciary duty. This is one of those "other defects," notice of which prevents Hal from being a holder in due course [3-304(2)].

Payee as Holder in Due Course

A payee ordinarily is not a holder in due course. To be a holder in due course, the holder must, for example, take the instrument without notice of any defense. Where there is a defense, the payee will usually know of it, since normally the payee deals directly with the maker or drawer. Thus, if Paul fraudulently induces Dora to draw a check payable to his order, Paul, the payee, knows of the fraud.

Under some circumstances, however, a payee can be a holder in due course [3-302(2)]. A payee will not necessarily have notice of a defense where the payee and the maker or drawer deal with each other through an intermediary. Don draws a check payable to Paymore Drugstore, leaves the amount blank, and instructs his agent, Arnold, to buy some merchandise and fill the check out for the amount of the purchase. Instead, Arnold fills the check out for more than the amount authorized, and Paymore takes it for value, in good faith, and without notice of Arnold's lack of authority. Paymore, the payee, is a holder in due course.

Case 33.2 discusses the effect of taking a year-old check on the alleged holder-in-due-course status of a transferee who was also a payee.

CASE 33.2

American State Bank v. Northwest South Dakota Production Credit Assoc. • 404 N.W.2d 517 (S.D. 1987)

FACTS Fort Pierre Livestock Auction, Inc. (Auction, plaintiff), sold cattle for Gene Hunt. In payment, Auction issued check 19074 for $31,730.23, made out to Hunt and two other payees, one of which was Hunt's creditor, the Northwest South Dakota Production Credit Association (PCA, defendant). Then Auction discovered that it had miscounted the cattle, and issued check 19331 for $36,343.95 to the same payees as a replacement for check 19074. Thinking it had successfully stopped payment on the replaced check, Auction did not ask Hunt to return it. The drawee, American State Bank, denied receiving the stop-payment order.

A year later, on October 26, 1984, a PCA representative met with Hunt to arrange repayment of a delinquent loan. Hunt delivered checks 19074 and 19331 to PCA in exchange for the forgiveness of his remaining debt. PCA did not know that one check replaced the other or that Auction had tried to stop payment on check 19074. PCA's agent telephoned Auction's manager and told him "a couple of old [Hunt] checks were going to be deposited."

Both checks cleared through Auction's account with American State Bank. Upon discovering that the bank had debited its account for both checks, Auction informed PCA that one check was meant to replace the other and demanded repayment for check 19074. Alleging it was a holder in due course, PCA refused Auction's demand. Auction sued PCA to recover the amount of the check. The trial court held that Auction had the defense of lack of consideration because check 19331 replaced check 19074, but it also ruled that PCA was a holder in due course and therefore took check 19074 free from that defense. Auction appealed.

OPINION KONENKAMP, Circuit J. . . . To be [a holder in due course], a party must take the instrument for value, in good faith, and without notice that it is overdue, or dishonored, or of any defense against or claim to it by any person. . . . The fact that PCA was a payee does not [in itself] disqualify [PCA as a holder in due course. However, *as payee*, PCA never became a holder in due course because PCA never received possession of the check and therefore never became a holder]. If a party fails to qualify as [a holder in due course], then . . . he takes the instrument subject to:

> *(a)* All valid claims to it on the part of any person; and *(b)* All defenses of any party which would be available in an action on a simple contract; and *(c)* The defenses of want or failure of consideration, nonperformance of any condition precedent, nondelivery, or delivery for a special purpose. . . .

[In the October 26, 1984, transaction,] PCA took check 19074 for value and in good faith, but knew it was a year old; therefore, the only issue is whether PCA had notice [that] check 19074 was overdue. Under [§3-304(3) of the UCC]:

> The purchaser has notice that an instrument is overdue if he has reason to know . . . *(c)* That he is taking a demand instrument after demand has been made or more than

**CASE 33.2
Continued**

a reasonable length of time after its issue. *A reasonable time for a check drawn and payable within the states and territories of the United States and District of Columbia is presumed to be thirty days.* . . .

This presumption is rebuttable . . . and we can envision instances where a delay of more than thirty days may be legitimate in the ordinary course of commerce, but PCA offered no justification for a year's delay. At the trial, PCA's representative testified he obtained the year-old check when Hunt simply pulled it out of his briefcase and handed it to him.

PCA concedes that it knew the check was a year old, but argues its telephone call to [Auction] warning of its imminent deposit of old Hunt checks along with [Auction's] apparent acquiescence overcomes the [presumption] that check 19074 was overdue. . . .

[However, when] PCA's agent called [Auction,] he made no mention of the check numbers, their amounts, or dates; and [Auction's] manager made no comment which would lead the agent to believe the checks were not overdue, but only acknowledged the agent's intention to deposit them.

PCA's warning to [Auction] that it was about to deposit Hunt's "old checks" was insufficient to negate what was plainly visible on the check's face: a year-old date. Since it had notice that check 19074 was overdue, PCA was not a holder in due course. The trial court's finding to the contrary was clearly erroneous.

JUDGMENT Reversed. . . .

Rights of Transferees; Shelter Provision

The transfer of an instrument "vests in the transferee such rights as the holder has therein" [3-201(1)]. This rule states the general rule applying to assignments, that an assignee gets whatever rights the assignor had. Maria buys from Paul three carts for use in her business and pays for them with a demand note made out to the order of Paul. Paul delivers two carts, which Maria uses, but he never delivers the third cart. In the meantime, Paul has negotiated the note to his daughter Harriet as a gift. Although Maria has the defense of nondelivery as to the one cart, Paul is entitled to payment for the two carts he delivered. Harriet, who has not given value for the note, takes it subject to Maria's defense of nondelivery. But since Paul's transfer of the note vests in Harriet the rights that Paul had, Harriet is entitled to collect on the note to the extent justified by Paul's partial performance.

The same principle applies to the rights acquired by a holder in due course. When a holder in due course negotiates commercial paper, the transferee ordinarily acquires the *rights* of a holder in due course even if the transferee personally cannot qualify as one. Hal, a holder in due course of a note, negotiates it to Arnold as a gift. Since Arnold did not give value, he is not a holder in due course. But, as assignee of Hal's rights, Arnold acquires whatever rights Hal had—in this case, Hal's right as a holder in due course to have payment free from personal defenses and rival claims of ownership. Arnold is a holder "through" a holder in due course.

Section 3-201 of the UCC, the so-called **shelter provision,** gives holders through a holder in due course the same freedom from claims and defenses that a holder in due course enjoys. The policy behind it is to provide the holder in due course a free market for the paper. Providing a free market is accomplished by allowing holders who may be mere assignees to collect payment free from claims and per-

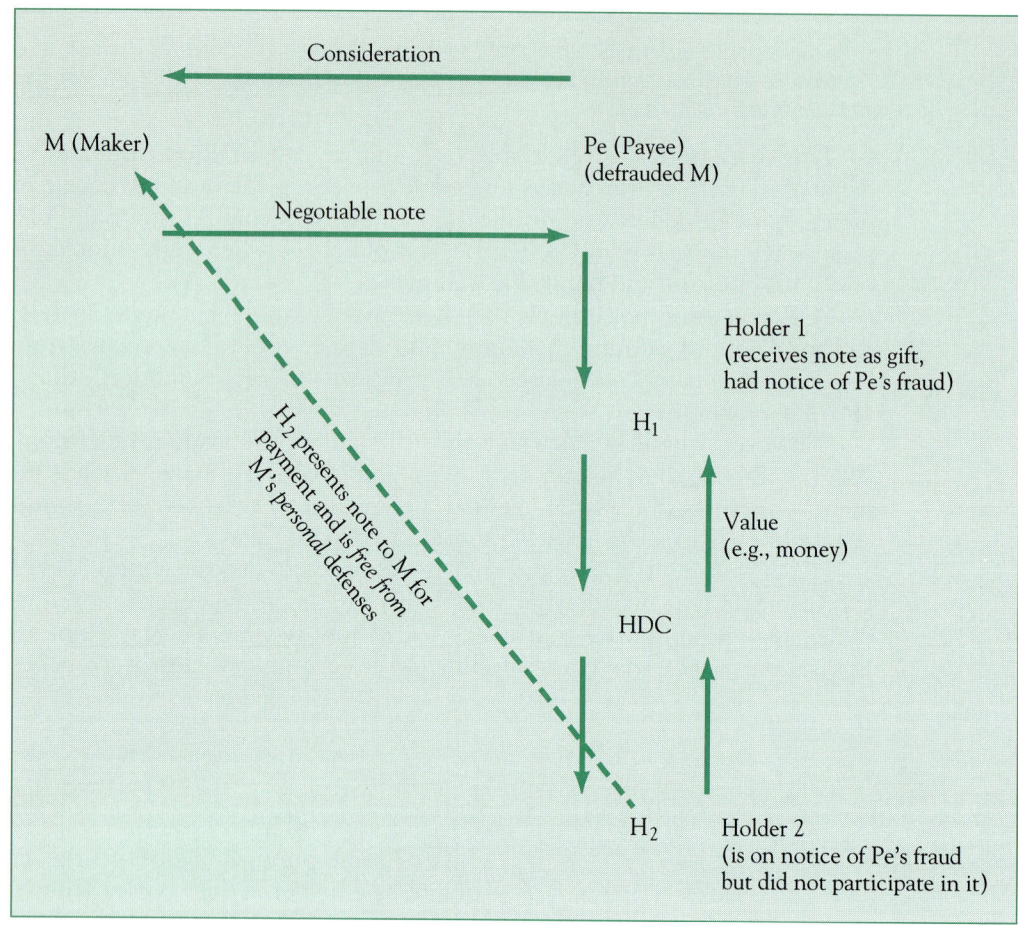

Figure 33.1 Shelter provision.

sonal defenses, since those assignees will thus be inclined to pay full value to the holder in due course. Figure 33.1 represents a series of negotiations (in the figure, from Pe to H_1; from H_1 to HDC; and from HDC to H_2) in which H_2, though not personally a holder in due course, takes M's note from HDC *free from* M's personal defenses.

However, *some* transferees of a holder in due course are *disqualified* from receiving holder-in-due-course rights. A transferee who has been a *party to* (a participant in rather than merely on notice of) any fraud or illegality affecting the instrument, or who as a *prior* holder had notice of a defense or claim, cannot improve his or her position by taking from a later holder in due course. Attempts by prior holders to improve their positions by selling paper to a holder in due course and then receiving it back will be of no avail. In Figure 33.2, H_1 was not a holder in due course when he or she received M's note from Pe. H_1 is prohibited from improving his or her position by selling the note to HDC and buying it back. Consequently, H_1 takes the note *subject to* M's personal defenses.

Case 33.3 illustrates the operation of the shelter provision.

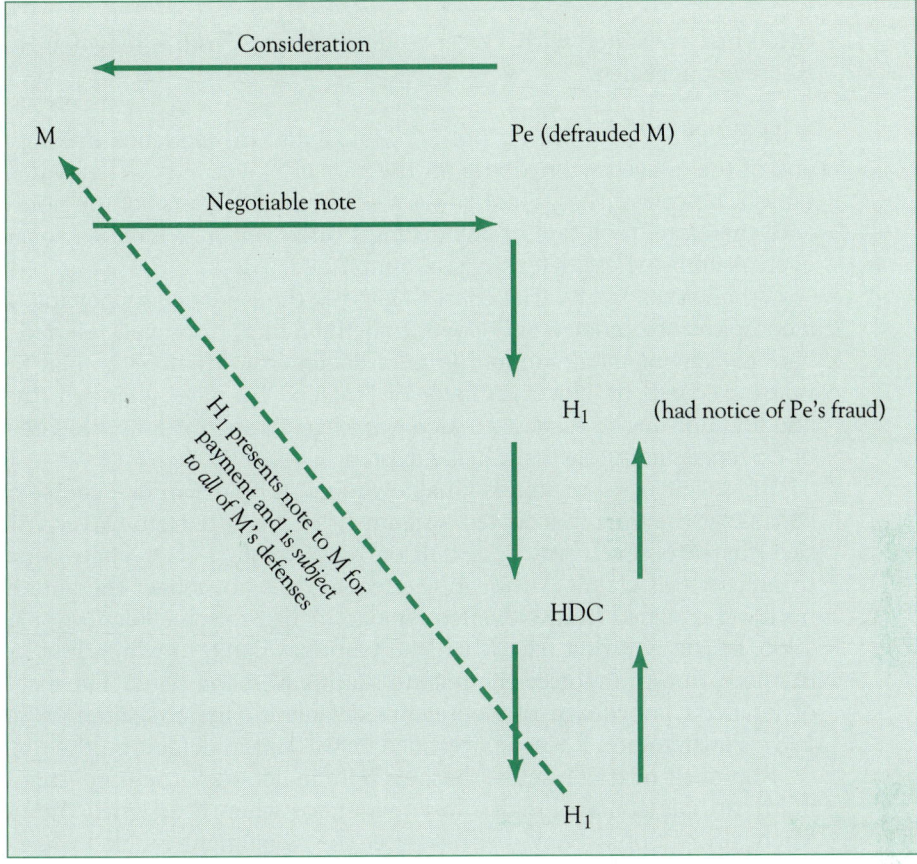

Figure 33.2 Shelter provision—a variation.

CASE 33.3 **Finalco, Inc. v. Roosevelt** • 3 Cal. Rptr. 2d 865 (Cal. App. 1991)

FACTS Dover Asset Group, Inc., sold interests in computer equipment owned by Dover and leased to Finalco, marketing them as a tax shelter. Roosevelt purchased two "units," paying approximately $8,000 in cash and executing a promissory note for the balance. Dover assigned the note to Finalco sometime before June 1986. Finalco negotiated it to Michigan National Bank, which in turn indorsed it to Marine Midland Bank. Later, Finalco reacquired the note.

Roosevelt did not expect to make payments on the note, because they were to be covered by Finalco's lease payments to Dover. This turned out to be true for 1986. However, by January 1987 the note was in default, and Finalco demanded payment. Roosevelt made some payments in 1987 and 1988. In October 1988, Finalco filed suit for the unpaid balance. In defense to the suit, Roosevelt alleged that Dover had violated federal and state securities laws and RICO (the Racketeer Influenced and Corrupt Organizations Act). Roosevelt also alleged that Fi-

CASE 33.3 Continued

nalco had conspired with Dover to defraud him. From a judgment for Finalco, Roosevelt appealed.

OPINION

JOHNSON, J. . . . We do not . . . find sufficient evidence linking Finalco to any of the alleged wrongdoing on the part of Dover. . . . The evidence did establish, however, [that] Finalco was a holder in due course of the note sued upon and, therefore, took free of any defenses Roosevelt may have had against Dover even assuming those defenses were established. . . .

When asked by the trial court to identify the evidence supporting his claim of a conspiracy by Finalco and Dover to defraud him, Roosevelt referred to the private placement memorandum [a sales document], Finalco's annual reports, and notes executed by Dover in favor of Finalco. We have reviewed this evidence and find nothing to suggest Finalco was aware of any tortious scheme on the part of Dover, assuming such a scheme existed. . . .

Roosevelt [also] contends Finalco was not a holder in due course of the note because at the time it accepted assignment of the note from Dover, it was on notice [that] Roosevelt was in default on his payments. . . . There is no evidence to support this claim. Although the record does not reflect the date Roosevelt's note was assigned from Dover to Finalco, it had to have been prior to June 25, 1986, because on that date Michigan National Bank, to whom Finalco indorsed the note, in turn indorsed the note to Marine Midland Bank. The first indication of Finalco's knowledge of Roosevelt's default is Finalco's letter of January 21, 1987. Furthermore, Roosevelt testified he was not in default on the note in 1986.

Roosevelt next contends [that] even if Finalco took the note from Dover as a holder in due course, Finalco lost that status when it assigned the note to the Michigan National Bank, because after the assignment Finalco was no longer a holder. . . . Furthermore, [Roosevelt alleges,] when Finalco subsequently reacquired Roosevelt's note several months before trial, it did not take as a holder in due course because by then Finalco clearly knew Roosevelt was in default. . . .

Roosevelt's argument ignores [UCC §3-201(1)], which provides, "Transfer of an instrument vests in the transferee such rights as the transferor has therein. . . ."

[The policy of this "shelter" provision is] "to assure the holder in due course a free market for the paper." . . . Thus, when a transferee takes an instrument from a holder in due course, the transferee takes free from all claims and defenses to the same extent as did the holder in due course even if the transferee is aware of those claims and defenses. If this [were] not the rule, a holder in due course could be deprived of a market for the instrument if the obligor widely disseminated notice of a claim or defense. Such a result would not benefit the obligor, who would still be liable to the holder in due course, but it would harm the holder in due course by destroying a market for the instrument. . . .

Under [§3-201], it is irrelevant that Finalco could not reacquire the note as a holder in due course. The shelter provision does not make the transferee a holder in due course; [except in circumstances not present here,] it transfers the freedom from claims and defenses of the original holder in due course to each succeeding transferee. Finalco was simply another transferee in a chain of transfers of the Roosevelt note. Where the transferee happens to have been a prior holder in due

CASE 33.3 Continued	course, it takes back from its transferor the same rights it transferred. Here, Finalco was in no better or worse position vis-a-vis Roosevelt's claims and defenses against Dover than if Finalco had originally retained possession of Roosevelt's note....
JUDGMENT	The judgment [of the trial court] is affirmed.

FTC LIMITS

Reasons for FTC Limits

In recent years, consumer groups have voiced strong opposition to holder-in-due-course status. They object to the idea that a maker or drawer of an instrument is not permitted to assert a legitimate defense—e.g., fraud in the inducement or breach of warranty—simply because the payee transfers a negotiable instrument for value to a third person. Especially upsetting is the impression that the courts have tended to resolve doubts against consumers and in favor of finance companies whose relationships with payees are clearly suspect, thus permitting or encouraging widespread fraud, shoddy work, excessive finance charges, and the like. Unsophisticated consumers are especially vulnerable to being exploited by unscrupulous sellers who set up a financing subsidiary as a holder in due course to receive consumer notes that the sellers know are subject to personal defenses of the consumers.

The courts have, of course, allowed consumers to assert personal defenses where the holder could be shown to lack holder-in-due-course status. Some courts have found a lack of good faith on the basis of such facts as the holder's probable awareness of suspicious circumstances surrounding the seller-payee's, or industrywide, business practices. The close business relationship between a seller and its financing subsidiary, unusually deep discounting of consumer notes, very speedy transfers of consumer notes from payee to transferee, and the fact that the transferee prepared note forms and other documents for the consumer to sign—the courts have considered all these factors and more when deciding whether a person is a holder in due course. In many close cases, judges have felt obliged to rule that a person was a holder in due course, even while expressing serious doubts about the transferee's status.

Because of inadequate or uneven protection of consumers by the courts, some state legislatures enacted statutes that deprived transferees of holder-in-due-course status or in some other way allowed consumers to assert their personal defenses. But only a few states enacted such statutes. So, in 1976, the Federal Trade Commission put into effect its Trade Regulation Rule 433 [16 C.F.R. §433].

The FTC Rule

In the typical consumer credit transaction, the consumer's installment note is promptly transferred to a finance company, which purchases the note at a discount. **FTC Rule 433** protects consumers by requiring a seller or a lessor of consumer goods or services to include in a consumer *credit* contract a prominently printed notice as follows:

NOTICE
ANY HOLDER OF THIS CONSUMER CREDIT CONTRACT IS SUBJECT TO ALL CLAIMS AND DEFENSES WHICH THE DEBTOR COULD ASSERT AGAINST THE SELLER OF GOODS OR SERVICES OBTAINED PURSUANT HERETO OR WITH THE PROCEEDS HEREOF. RECOVERY HEREUNDER BY THE DEBTOR SHALL NOT EXCEED AMOUNTS PAID BY THE DEBTOR HEREUNDER.

Failure of the seller to provide the required notice constitutes an unfair and deceptive practice within the meaning of Section 5 of the Federal Trade Commission Act. The notice requirement applies to all consumer credit contracts in or affecting commerce, including three common types: (1) a negotiable promissory note signed by the consumer, (2) an ordinary (nonnegotiable) consumer credit contract containing a waiver-of-defenses clause, and (3) a consumer credit loan arranged by the seller for the consumer-buyer.

The presence of this notice preserves all claims and defenses that a consumer may have, even against a good faith purchaser for value who is without notice of any defenses. A **consumer** is a person who acquires goods or services (e.g., automobiles, home improvements, and health spa memberships) for personal, family, or household use. Rule 433 does not cover purchases of real estate or securities, or purchases over $25,000; nor are contracts for public utility services (e.g., gas and electricity) affected by the rule. The rule also does not cover a purchase in which the consumer pays by check. A check is not a credit instrument and need not contain the notice.

A merchant may not circumvent the FTC rule by arranging for the consumer to borrow money from a lender and pay cash to the merchant. The rule provides specifically that when the merchant arranges for the loan, the credit instrument must contain the specified notice, and the lender has no greater rights against the consumer than the seller does. However, the rule does not apply to all lenders. A lender is required to include the notice (and is therefore deprived of holder-in-due-course status) only where the merchant *refers* consumers to the lender or *is affiliated* with the lender by control or by business arrangement.

Rule 433 puts upon purchasers of commercial paper (and other consumer credit contracts) the burden of policing consumer financing. If those purchasers are careful to check for fraud and other misconduct of their transferors, consumers will receive a protection not formerly available to them—the scrutiny by commercial paper buyers of business practices that the consumer once had to combat alone. If the policing activities are not effective, finance companies may pay less for consumer obligations, since the risk of nonpayment would be greater. Ultimately, sellers of goods or services may raise prices to consumers to compensate for a higher discount rate. To date, however, there is little evidence that prices have increased for this reason.

Rule 433 limits the protection that a consumer receives. The maker or drawer who has a defense may refuse to pay further sums on the instrument and may recover amounts previously paid. However, the consumer may not assert a claim against the holder of the instrument for damages in excess of the amount the consumer paid. A consumer who seeks a larger award—for example, for consequential damages—must institute an action in state court against the merchant who sold the goods or services.

BOX 33.3

Commercial Paper Law and Business Planning

You are the manager of Finance Co. It buys commercial paper, mostly promissory notes issued by small firms and consumers to pay for goods and services supplied by a variety of businesses called vendors. Finance Co. usually holds the paper for collection. Occasionally you and other employees of Finance Co. hear of dissatisfied customers of the vendors. Some of these customers have been so unhappy with goods and services that they have complained directly to Finance Co., the holder of their paper. Indeed, some have refused to pay when their notes fell due. As manager of Finance Co., what precautions should you take, regarding future commercial paper transactions, to minimize losses to Finance Co.? Consider the shelter provision and FTC Rule 433, and the fact that Finance Co. drafts many of the note forms that vendors have their customers sign. ∎

SUMMARY

Any holder of commercial paper can negotiate it and thereby enable a properly qualified transferee to become a holder in due course. The transferee, if he or she is a holder, may become a holder in due course by giving value for the instrument, taking it in good faith, and taking it without notice of defenses to payment, rival claims of ownership, or other problems surrounding its issuance, transfer, or collection.

A transferee of commercial paper receives whatever rights the transferor had. A holder who does not personally qualify as a holder in due course may receive the rights of one by assignment, under the shelter provision, the purpose of which is to assure a holder in due course of a market for the paper. However, a prior holder with notice of defenses cannot improve his or her position merely by selling an instrument to and repurchasing it from a holder in due course. Nor can a transferee who has been a party to any fraud or illegality affecting the instrument acquire the rights of a holder in due course.

FTC Rule 433 has, in effect, abolished holder-in-due-course status as to holders of certain consumer credit contracts, by imposing a notice requirement that preserves claims and defenses of consumer-makers. The rule puts the burden of policing consumer credit transactions on the purchasers of consumer credit contracts rather than on consumers alone.

REVIEW QUESTIONS

1. Explain whether the following statement is accurate: "A holder in due course is a holder who takes the instrument for value, in good faith, and without notice of any defense against it."

2. (a) Explain the following statement: "In the law of commercial paper, value is not the same thing as consideration." **(b)** John Doe deposits a check in his bank. Under what circumstances, and to what extent, does the bank become a holder for value of that item? **(c)** Explain the "first in, first out" rule.

3. Is the following statement accurate? "A holder lacks the good faith necessary to be a holder in due course only if the holder has knowledge of actual wrongdoing concerning the instrument."

4. (a) When is a check overdue? **(b)** When are other varieties of commercial paper overdue?

5. (a) What is "dishonor"? **(b)** How may a holder be on notice of dishonor?

6. Can a holder be on notice of defenses of a maker or a drawer even though the holder is not aware of any particular wrongdoing by the payee? Explain.

7. Ordinarily, the payee of a negotiable instrument is its holder. How might the payee also be a holder in due course?

8. (a) What is the purpose of the "shelter provision"? **(b)** What kinds of transferees may not benefit from the shelter provision?

9. (a) What is the justification for FTC Rule 433? **(b)** To what transactions does it apply? Not apply?

CASE PROBLEMS

1. Wesley Heights Realty drew a check for $1,400, payable to the order of a customer of Falls Church Bank. The customer deposited the check in his account, was given a provisional credit of $1,400, and was permitted to withdraw $140 immediately, before the bank discovered that Wesley Heights had stopped payment on the check. By the time the bank received the dishonored check, its customer had "skipped," leaving no credits in his account against which to charge the $140. Bank demanded $140 from Wesley Heights, which refused to pay because it had a personal defense against the customer. The trial court granted judgment to Wesley Heights, holding that the bank was only an agent for collection and "not a holder in due course for value." Bank appealed. If the bank gave value, the decision of the trial court should be reversed. Did the bank give value?

2. Girner issued a negotiable $5,000 promissory note to First Realty Corp. on September 25, 1980. A payment schedule was printed on the back of the note. Monthly payments were to begin on January 15, 1981. First Realty assigned the note to Bohra for value. On July 27, 1981, Bohra transferred the note to his attorney, Richardson, in payment for legal services. At that time, no payments had been recorded on the payment schedule. When Richardson tried to collect on the note, he learned that Girner had a personal defense. Girner refused to pay.

Richardson, alleging that he was a holder in due course, sued Girner for the amount of the note. Was Richardson a holder in due course?

3. Dr. Cecil R. Simmons bought a unit in East Pointe Land Partners, a limited partnership that invested in Texas real estate. He paid for it with a promissory note made out for $117,864 to Q-L Investments, Inc., the general partner. Q-L indorsed Simmons' note to its related company, Quinn-L Capital Corp., which indorsed it to the Bank of Commerce (BOC) as security for a $4 million loan to Quinn-L, which signed a promissory note of its own. For the Quinn-L loan, BOC was the "lead" bank, and Schwegmann Bank was a "funding" bank that agreed to a $1 million participation. When BOC experienced severe financial difficulties, Schwegmann took over the Quinn-L note and BOC indorsed to Schwegmann the investor notes such as Dr. Simmons' that secured it. After Quinn-L filed for bankruptcy and BOC went into receivership, Schwegmann demanded payment of the Simmons note. Simmons alleged that when Schwegmann received his note, Schwegmann knew certain facts that put it on notice of his defenses against Q-L: (1) The East Pointe project was not fully subscribed, and (2) Quinn-L had been experiencing financial difficulties. Would Schwegmann's knowledge of these facts deprive it of holder-in-due-course status?

4. Cochise College Park, Inc., of Arizona sold a lot to Vanotti, who signed a promissory note and mortgage for the purchase price of about $4,400. Three weeks later, Cochise sold the note to Salter for $2,760. Earlier, Salter had purchased seven notes from Cochise, each similar to Vanotti's. Salter received the note, Vanotti's original mortgage, the original Purchase and Sale Agreement, a copy of the Property Report required by a federal agency for interstate land sales, and a photocopy of a warranty deed showing a transfer of ownership from Cochise to Vanotti. However, no deed was ever delivered to Vanotti or recorded in Arizona. The Property Report granted Vanotti a 6-month period of inspection and a money-back guarantee. Federal law required that purchasers receive a copy of the Property Report at or before the sale. Vanotti denied receiving a copy, and Salter's copy did not include Vanotti's signature. After inspecting the lot, Vanotti tried to cancel the contract but could not locate any representative of Cochise, which was now in bankruptcy. Vanotti ceased making the monthly payments on the note, and Salter sued him for the balance due. The trial court held that Vanotti could exercise his right of cancellation because Salter was not a holder in due course. Salter appealed. Was Salter a holder in due course of Vanotti's note?

5. Impact Marketing, Inc., issued six postdated checks to Barry E. Bell for legal services to be performed in the future. Knowing that the checks were postdated and that the legal services had not yet been performed, Financial Associates purchased the checks from Bell at a discount. Impact paid four of the checks but stopped payment on the other two because Bell's services had been terminated. Financial sued Impact for the amount of the two dishonored checks. Is Financial entitled to payment?

6. Graff issued two promissory notes to Fred Klomann as payee. By special indorsement, Klomann gave the notes to his daughter, Candace. She examined the notes and handed them back to Fred for collection. Sometime later, Fred scratched out Candace's name in the special indorsement, inserted the name of his wife, Georgia, and delivered the notes to Georgia. When she brought suit to collect on the notes, the maker, Graff, defended on the ground that Georgia had no right, title, or interest in the notes and therefore had no standing to sue for collection. From a summary judgment for Georgia, Graff appealed. Was Georgia entitled to payment of the notes?

7. Samuel D. Lobmaster, the owner of Lobmaster Trailer Sales (LTS), owed Jefferson Bank (Bank) over $600,000. To pay the debt, he discounted to Bank his customers' notes representing trailer sales. As additional security, Lobmaster made Bank the main beneficiary of his $200,000 life insurance policy. Canyonville Bible Academy was entitled to any proceeds of the policy not needed to cover Lobmaster's debt to Bank. Then the *Lobe*masters (unrelated to

*Lob*master) bought a trailer from LTS and signed an installment note for $12,694.22. LTS endorsed the note over to Bank. Five days later, Samuel Lobmaster was killed in an airplane crash. About a year later, Lobemasters defaulted on their note, and Samuel Lobmaster's estate ended up owing Bank approximately $200,000. Bank charged defaulted obligations of LTS customers against the life insurance proceeds. Then Bank assigned the Lobemasters' note to Canyonville Bible Academy. Thus, the Academy received the defaulted note instead of the insurance proceeds that Samuel Lobmaster had intended the Academy to have as a gift. The Academy sued the Lobemasters for payment. The Lobemasters argued that a transferee of a note had to give value before he or she could receive the rights of the transferor. From a judgment for the Lobemasters, the Academy appealed. Was the Academy entitled to payment?

CHAPTER 34

Liability of the Parties; Discharge

Anyone who signs, transfers, or seeks payment of commercial paper can have two kinds of liability under the Uniform Commercial Code (UCC): contractual liability and warranty liability. Usually the liability is obvious and expected, as where a customer issues a check or a note to pay for something. Sometimes the liability comes as a surprise.

Most *signers* of commercial paper have **contractual liability** for the face amount, including any interest, because the Code imposes upon all signers except qualified indorsers an **engagement** (promise) to pay. So, if you issue a check or a note, or accept a draft naming you as drawee, you will be liable contractually ("on the instrument") for the stated amount. And when you indorse your paycheck to cash it, your unqualified indorsement makes you contractually liable to transferees (e.g., a bank or supermarket) if the drawee (your employer's bank) does not pay.

Because commercial paper is a type of property as well as a contract, the UCC imposes **warranty liability** too, on *signers* and *nonsigners* alike. Breach of a warranty may occur when a person transfers or seeks payment of an instrument that is defective in some way, as where a signature was forged.

A person who pays the amount specified in a negotiable instrument is **discharged** (freed) from liability. A person may also be discharged from liability by the actions of others. The contractual liability of the parties, their discharge from liability, and liability for breach of warranty are the main topics of this chapter.[1]

CONTRACTUAL LIABILITY OF THE PARTIES

Contractual liability is either primary or secondary. So a signer of commercial paper may be a **primary party** or a **secondary party.** The ultimate liability of primary and secondary parties is the same: to pay the face amount of the instru-

---

[1] A person who wrongfully possesses someone else's negotiable instrument may be liable for the tort of conversion. **Conversion** is the wrongful exercise of control over the personal property of another to the exclusion of the owner's rights, or in a manner inconsistent with those rights. A person who steals or who finds and sells bearer paper is a converter. A person who steals or finds order paper and forges an indorsement also commits conversion. So does a person who pays or buys an instrument containing a forged indorsement, even if that person has no knowledge of the forgery. And, as noted in Chapter 35, banks can commit conversion in a number of ways. A converter is liable to the true owner for the face amount of the instrument [3-419]. Thus, conversion is an important source of legal remedy for persons who have been wrongfully deprived of negotiable instruments.

ment. But, as is discussed later, the timing of primary liability differs markedly from that of secondary liability.

Recall from Chapter 31 that a **maker** is a person who issues a note or a certificate of deposit. A **drawer** is a person who issues a check or a draft. An **acceptor** is a drawee of a draft who signs the draft across its face and thereby agrees to pay it. And a **holder** is a person who possesses bearer or properly indorsed order paper, and who therefore appears to be the rightful owner, entitled to payment or acceptance.

Liability of Primary Parties

The *maker* of a note or certificate of deposit (CD) and the *acceptor* of a draft or check are primary parties. With one exception, primary parties have unconditional liability. This means that the holder of the instrument may sue the primary party for the face amount when the instrument comes due, without the need for any further action by the holder [3-122]. Consequently, when sued, a primary party cannot delay the lawsuit on the ground of the holder's failure to make presentment (demand) for payment. The exception is the certificate of deposit: When it comes due, the holder must demand payment before bringing suit. As a practical matter, however, holders of other kinds of notes normally demand payment before suing the maker, even though they are not required to do so.

When a draft or check is issued, there is no primary party (no maker or acceptor). The drawer is a signer, but is a secondary party; the drawee is not a signer and thus has no contractual liability to anyone. Of course, if the drawee later accepts the draft, the drawee becomes a primary party. **Certification** of a check by a drawee bank is a type of acceptance making the drawee bank liable as a primary party.

Liability of Secondary Parties

If a maker or drawee does not pay or accept as expected, the holder can collect from a secondary party (drawer or indorser)—but only if certain triggering "conditions" or events take place: presentment, dishonor, and notice of dishonor. **Presentment** is the holder's demand for payment or acceptance. **Dishonor** is a maker's or drawee's refusal to pay an instrument or the drawee's refusal to accept a time draft. **Notice of dishonor** is simply a message that dishonor has occurred, usually given by the holder.[2]

The conditional nature of secondary liability can be seen in the following illustrations.

1 You issue a check to Paula to pay for a tennis racket. Paula (or some transferee such as her bank) is required to seek payment from your bank (the drawee), not from you. Paula will be entitled to have payment directly from you, the drawer, only if the drawee does not pay. But to trigger your secondary liability, Paula must first present the check to the drawee for payment, undergo the unpleasant experience of having the check dishonored, and give you notice of dishonor.

2 You receive your paycheck, indorse it in blank, and cash it at Ned's Supermarket. Ned (or some transferee) is required to seek payment from the drawee (your employer's bank). Ned can have payment from you, the indorser, only if he presents the check to the drawee bank, the bank dishonors it, and Ned gives you notice of dishonor. Thus, like a drawer, an indorser is a secondary party and is not liable for the face amount unless the conditions of presentment, dishonor, and notice of dishonor have been met.

Requirement of Presentment. Since presentment is the required first step for holding a secondary party liable, holders need to know to whom, where, and when to present the instrument.

To whom to present: To hold secondary parties liable, a holder must first present the instrument to the party expected to pay or to accept.

---

[2]For instruments accepted or payable outside the United States—i.e., in international trade—a fourth triggering event, called protest, may be required. A **protest** is a document or certificate of dishonor signed and sealed by a public official such as a U.S. consul or a notary public authorized to certify that the instrument was dishonored.

> **BOX 34.1**
> **Liability of Indorsers among Themselves**
>
> Where one of several indorsers has paid the holder, may the one who paid have payment from some other indorser? Unless otherwise agreed among indorsers, an indorser's promise is made only to subsequent indorsers (those signing later) and to the holder [3-414(2)]. Thus, liability of indorsers to one another depends on the order of signing. Paul, the payee of a check, indorses and delivers it to Ben, who in turn indorses and delivers it to Cora. If Cora is unable to collect from the drawee bank, she may collect from Ben, and Ben in turn may collect from Paul. But if Cora had skipped Ben and had received payment from Paul, Paul could not collect from Ben because Ben's engagement as an indorser is made to subsequent indorsers (Cora), not prior ones (Paul). Paul's only recourse is to the drawer of the check.

Makers of notes, and drawees and acceptors of checks and drafts, are expected to *pay*. Drawees of drafts may be expected to *accept*. Presentment *for acceptance* is necessary for making drawers and indorsers liable where [3-501]:

1. The draft so provides.
2. The draft is payable at a place other than the residence or business of the drawee.
3. The date of payment depends on presentment (e.g., "Pay [this draft] 30 days after sight [by drawee]").

Where and how to present: A holder may make presentment in a variety of ways [3-504]:

1. In person. For example, by taking a check directly to the drawee bank. If a required place for presentment has not been stated, the holder ordinarily must present the instrument at the business or residence of the party who is to accept or pay.
2. By mail. A mailed presentment is effective upon receipt.
3. Through a clearinghouse. A **clearinghouse** is a place where banks exchange checks and drafts drawn on each other and thereby settle their daily balances. A clearinghouse would be involved where, for example, the holder and the drawer of a check do their banking business at different banks, both of which deal with the clearinghouse.

When to present—time limits: A holder's unexcused delay in making presentment always discharges indorsers from liability. In very rare circumstances involving a bank's insolvency, the holder's delay also discharges the drawer. What time limits must a holder observe to avoid discharging secondary parties?

Many instruments indicate a date for payment or acceptance. To avoid discharging secondary parties, the holder must make presentment on or before that date, unless presentment is **excused.** Presentment is excused where, for example, the secondary party waives (gives up the right to) presentment, or where the holder by reasonable diligence cannot make presentment.

If no date is specified, the holder must make presentment within a reasonable time [3-503]. The reasonable time for presentment to a *drawer* is measured from the date of the draft or its date of issue, whichever is later. The reasonable time for presentment to an *indorser* is measured from the time of indorsement. What constitutes a reasonable time varies according to the circumstances. A court might allow more time if great distances or unreliable communications are involved than if distances are short and communication is easy.

For an *uncertified check*—one that has not been accepted by the drawee bank—the reasonable time for presentment is presumed to be 30 days with respect to the drawer's liability and 7 days with respect to an indorser's liability [3-503(2)]. These time limits are intended to encourage prompt presentment of checks so that the check-clearing process will remain efficient. However, a holder may "rebut" (overturn) the presumption by proving that under the circumstances a longer time for presentment was reasonable.[3]

---

[3] The 1990 amendments increased the 7-day limit for making presentment to an indorser to 30 days, and this 30-day period is absolute, not presumptive [revised § 3-415(e)].

> **BOX 34.2**
> **The Two 30-Day Rules of Article 3**
>
> Recall from the preceding chapter that a person who takes a check for value more than 30 days after issue is presumed to be on notice that the check is overdue. A slow taker therefore cannot be a holder in due course. The 30-day *presentment* limit discussed in the preceding paragraph is different. The rule here concerns a timely taker, who usually *is* a holder in due course. However, even a holder in due course loses the liability of indorsers for making a slow *presentment*—and may lose the liability of the drawer too, if, as discussed later in Unexcused Delay, the drawee bank has become insolvent. ∎

Requirement of Dishonor. Dishonor is a refusal or failure to pay or to accept an instrument that the holder has properly presented for payment or acceptance [3-507]. Dishonor includes:

- Maker's refusal *to pay* a note or certificate of deposit on the due date
- Drawee's or acceptor's refusal *to pay* a draft or check on the due date
- Drawee's refusal *to accept* a time draft (e.g., one payable at a specified date after issue, or one payable "60 days after sight") if the holder presents it for acceptance before the due date

The drawee's refusal to accept a time draft is a dishonor because the holder needs to know early whether the drawee is willing to pay when the due date arrives. The drawee's refusal to accept shows unwillingness and allows the holder to establish the liability of secondary parties immediately. However, a drawee's refusal to accept a *demand* draft is not a dishonor, because the holder of a demand draft (including a check) is already entitled to payment in cash and does not face the uncertainty of payment facing the holder of a time draft that is not yet payable. Of course, a drawee's failure to *pay* a demand draft upon presentment is a dishonor.

Makers and drawees are entitled to assurances that a presentment is legitimate. So the following acts, among others, are *not* dishonors:

- Returning an instrument for lack of proper indorsement
- Refusing to pay or to accept because of an illegible signature, postdating, alteration of a payee's name, or evidence of forgery
- Requiring exhibition of the instrument, reasonable identification of the presenter, evidence of the presenter's authority to make presentment for another person, and presentment at the place, if any, specified in the instrument for payment or acceptance.

Requirement of Notice. After an instrument has been dishonored, secondary parties (drawers and indorsers) are entitled to timely notice of dishonor unless notice has been excused. Usually the holder gives notice, but it may be given by any party who can be compelled to pay, such as a prior indorser.

The notice must be given within time limits prescribed by the Code, usually 3 business days [3-508(2)].[4] Collecting banks have a shorter time to give notice of dishonor, up to 2 business days. The notice may be given in any reasonable manner, either orally or in writing. Unlike a presentment, a notice of dishonor sent by mail is given when sent, even though it may never reach the secondary party.

A person attempting to collect the amount of a dishonored check from an indorser must keep **two time limits** in mind: (1) the 7-calendar-day limit on the indorser's liability (which begins to run at the time of indorsement) and (2) the 3-business-day maximum time for giving notice of dishonor. The following examples illustrate the interplay between the two time limits.

1 On Monday, May 1, the following events occur: Dora makes a check out to Paul, Paul indorses it to Hal, Hal presents it to Dora's bank for payment, and Bank dishonors the check for

---

[4]The 3-day period ends at midnight of the third business day following (1) the day of dishonor (where the holder personally presented the instrument) or (2) the day the holder received notice of dishonor from another party.

insufficient funds. Paul is liable as indorser for 7 calendar days after his indorsement—through Monday, May 8. But Hal has only 3 business days after the day of the dishonor to notify Paul of it—i.e., until midnight of Thursday, May 4. If Hal waits until Friday to give notice, he is too late to have payment from Paul even though Paul may still be liable to others.

2 Hal receives the indorsed check on May 1. He waits until Friday, May 5, to present it for payment, and Bank dishonors it then. Hal's 3 business days for giving notice (ending at midnight Wednesday, May 10) will be cut short because Paul's 7-day indorser's liability expires on Monday, May 8.

> **BOX 34.3**
>
> **Revised Article 3**
>
> The 1990 amendments change the 7-day and 3-day time limits just discussed to 30 days each. So, in states adopting the amendments, an indorser is liable for 30 days after indorsing, and a holder has 30 days within which to give notice of dishonor. Collecting banks still must give notice within 2 days. ■

Case 34.1 discusses how long a payee has to collect a dishonored check.

CASE 34.1	**Harik v. Harik** • 861 F.2d 139 (6th Cir. 1988)
FACTS	On March 1, 1980, plaintiff Antoine Harik received from defendant Salim Harik a personal check for $50,000 drawn on the National Bank and Trust Company of Michigan. Payee Antoine presented it for payment on December 14, 1982. Because of an April 1980 stop payment order, Bank dishonored the check and marked it "stale dated." On July 8, 1987, plaintiff filed suit for payment of the check. Holding that plaintiff's claim was barred by the Michigan statute of limitations, the district court awarded judgment to defendant Salim. Antoine appealed.
OPINION	GUY, C. J. . . . [Plaintiff contends] that the district court erred in determining that plaintiff's claim is barred by the . . . Michigan statute of limitations. All parties agree that the [relevant statute] provides for a six-year [period] in which to bring an action on a personal negotiable instrument. . . . However, [the key issue is, on which date did the statute of limitations commence to run?] [W]e find that the statute of limitations commenced to run on December 14, 1982, and therefore plaintiff filed his complaint within the six-year limit. [The Michigan UCC clearly indicates when] a cause of action accrues against the drawer of a check. [Section 3-122] states: > . . . (3) A cause of action against a drawer of a draft or an indorser of any instrument accrues upon demand following dishonor of the instrument. Notice of dishonor is a demand. . . . A draft is an instrument in which a drawer orders a drawee to pay money to a payee. A check is a [demand] draft in which the drawee is a bank. . . . When plaintiff presented the check to the bank on December 14, 1982, and the bank dishonored the check, plaintiff then had notice of his cause of action against defendant, and the limitations statute commenced to run. Plaintiff was

**CASE 34.1
Continued**

excused from providing defendant with notice of dishonor . . . because defendant had placed a stop-payment order on the check and therefore had no reason to expect that the check would be paid by the bank. [Section 3-511], which excuses the requirement of demand, provides in part:

. . . (2) Presentment or notice . . . as the case may be is entirely excused when . . . (b) [the party to be charged] has himself dishonored the instrument or has countermanded payment or otherwise has no reason to expect or right to require that the instrument be accepted or paid. . . .

Defendant, however, argues that plaintiff was required to present the check to the bank within thirty days of the date of issue, which was March 1, 1980. [Section 3-503] provides: . . .

(2) . . . In the case of an uncertified check which is drawn and payable within the United States . . . the following are presumed to be reasonable periods within which to present for payment or to initiate bank collection:
   (a) with respect to the liability of the drawer, 30 days after date or issue whichever is later. . . .

The district court was apparently persuaded by this section, and held that, since the check should have been presented within thirty days, plaintiff's cause of action commenced to run on March 30, 1980, and therefore . . . was time-barred. However, [§ 3-503] must be read in conjunction with [§ 3-502], which sets forth the effect of presentment beyond the thirty-day period. Section [3-502] provides: . . .

(1) Where without excuse any necessary presentment or notice of dishonor is delayed beyond the time when it is due . . . (b) any drawer . . . of a draft payable at a bank . . . who because the drawee . . . bank becomes insolvent during the delay is deprived of funds maintained with the drawee . . . to cover the instrument may discharge his liability by written assignment to the holder of his rights against the drawee . . . in respect of such funds, but such drawer . . . is not otherwise discharged. . . .

Therefore, plaintiff's holding of the check beyond the thirty-day reasonable presentment period did not discharge the liability of defendant, the drawer of the check. The drawer would . . . be discharged from liability [only] if presentment was unreasonably delayed and the drawee bank became insolvent during the delay. . . .

We also reject defendant's contention that the statute of limitations began to run, at the latest, on April 7, 1980, when defendant placed a stop-payment order on the check. Plaintiff had no means of knowing that this stop-payment order was in effect until he presented the check at the bank on December 14, 1982, and thus the stop-payment order served as no notice to him that the check would be dishonored. . . .

JUDGMENT

The decision of the district court awarding summary judgment to the defendant is REVERSED.

[In a footnote, the court commented as follows: "The district court was apparently also influenced by the 'stale dated' notation on the check. Michigan's Stale

> **CASE 34.1**
> **Continued**
>
> Check Law states: . . . A bank is under no obligation to [its checking account customer] to pay a check . . . which is presented more than six months after its date. . . . This section [permits the drawee to decline payment of stale checks without liability to its customer, the drawer. However, the section] has no effect on the drawer's [ultimate] liability to the payee. . . .]

Liability of Accommodation Parties

An **accommodation party** is a person who signs an instrument for the purpose of lending his or her name (credit) to another party to the instrument [3-415]. Jorge wants to buy goods on credit and to give a promissory note in payment. The seller may refuse to extend credit if Jorge is a minor or has a poor credit rating, but may agree to deal with Jorge if someone with good credit will sign the note as an accommodation party.

Usually an accommodation party signs as either co-maker or indorser, but he or she may sign in any other capacity, including co-drawer or acceptor. A person signing as maker or acceptor has primary liability; a person signing as drawer or indorser has secondary liability (i.e., presentment, dishonor, and notice are required to establish liability).

An accommodation party has a signer's usual liability to a holder. However, an accommodation party who must pay has a right of recourse against the party accommodated. For example, Marian cosigns a note so her son Dom may buy a car, and must pay the note when Dom defaults. Marian may recover the amount from Dom.

Signatures by Agents and Forgers

Signature by Authorized Agent. Andy Agar is authorized to sign negotiable instruments on behalf of Pam Pell, his employer, and wishes to bind her as maker, drawer, acceptor, or indorser without binding himself on the instrument. The best way for Andy to do this is to sign the instrument

Pam Pell
By Andy Agar, Agent

Andy escapes liability as a signer because he (1) has named the person represented and (2) has made clear his representative capacity [3-403].

If Andy uses forms of signature that do not do *both* of these things, he may be held personally liable for the face amount of the instrument. The following examples illustrate the dangers of an agent's signing incorrectly. In the examples, Andy is authorized to sign a check for Pam, made out to Paul Payee in payment for goods delivered to Pam.

1 Andy signs "Andy Agar," or "Andy Agar, Agent." Andy is liable on the instrument. Pam is not liable to anyone *on the instrument* because her name does not appear on it. However, under agency law, Pam may be liable to Paul on the underlying contract, since she authorized it. If Andy must pay, Pam has a duty under agency law to reimburse him.

2 Andy signs both names as follows:

Pam Pell
Andy Agar

Andy is liable on the check because he did not reveal his representative capacity. Pam is liable on the check because she authorized Andy to sign for her. Parol evidence is admissible between the immediate parties (Paul and Andy) to show that Andy was not intended to be liable, but parol evidence is not allowed to defeat Andy's liability to subsequent parties.

3 Andy signs as follows:

Pell Industries, Inc.
Andy Agar, President

Has Andy signed in a representative capacity? He might have intended to sign as an accommodation party. The Code says he has signed as a representative "except as otherwise established" [3-403(3)]. This means that he has no liability on the instrument unless an interested party can prove that Andy intended to be liable.

Unauthorized Signature. Unauthorized signature includes both a forgery and a signature by an agent without actual, implied, or apparent authority to sign the principal's name. An unauthorized signature is not binding on the person whose name was signed, unless that person *ratifies* (later approves) the unauthorized signature or *is precluded* (prevented) by law from denying it—e.g., where the "signer's" negligence substantially contributes to its making [3-404]. An unauthorized signature *is* effective, however, to impose on the actual signer (forger or unauthorized agent) liability to persons who pay the instrument in good faith or take it for value.

How can a person be so negligent that his or her unauthorized signature will be binding? One way would be to hire a convicted thief and forger with a fabricated resume to manage millions of dollars in union funds, without conducting a background investigation. Actors Equity did this when it hired a new comptroller, who promptly forged the drawer's signature to a number of checks. The court held that the union's negligence precluded it from requiring the drawee bank to recredit the union's account for the amount of the forged checks.[5] More commonly, a firm authorizes an employee to sign checks on its behalf by means of a check-writing machine and negligently gives unauthorized persons access to it. If the negligence substantially contributes to an unauthorized signature, the firm cannot use lack of authority as a defense against a holder in due course or against a drawee who, observing reasonable banking standards, pays the instrument in good faith [3-406]. If the victim is *not* negligent, the usual rule continues to apply—an unauthorized signature provides the "signer" with a real defense that is good against even a holder in due course.

Effect of Indorsement by Imposter or Dishonest Agent

As noted in Chapter 32, a person ordinarily must be a *holder* to negotiate commercial paper, but there is one exception to this rule. The exception applies where, for example, a principal has been induced by the fraud of a dishonest agent to sign a negotiable instrument made out to a fictitious payee. Or an employer is induced by a dishonest agent to sign a payroll check made out to a nonexistent worker. Then the agent gets possession of the check, signs the name of the fictitious payee on the back of the check, and cashes it at a supermarket. The dishonest agent is not the payee. Ordinarily the agent would not be a holder, and the indorsement would be a forgery. However, UCC Sec. 3-405 specifically provides that the indorsement of such a dishonest person *is* effective as that of the payee. Thus, the dishonest agent has a Code-conferred holder status, and the supermarket can be a holder in due course entitled to payment. A similar principle applies where an imposter (a person pretending to be someone else) tricks the issuer of a negotiable instrument into thinking the imposter is the intended payee.

Why should these particular dishonest people be given holder status? The reason is that the issuer of an instrument is in a better position than is a subsequent holder or a drawee to prevent the padding of payrolls and similar dishonesty, and to check the identity of imposters. An employer is expected to take reasonable care in supervising employees or to cover any loss by fidelity insurance. Although Sec. 3-405 may seem to encourage dishonesty, the persons who do the defrauding are still subject to criminal penalties for their dishonesty, to civil suits for damages, and, as signers, to liability on the instrument.

> **BOX 34.4**
>
> ### Revised Article 3
>
> Under the pre-1990 Code, a drawee bank that pays an instrument in violation of reasonable banking standards loses, even as against negligent drawers. The 1990 revision of § 3-406 changes this by providing a **comparative negligence** standard. Under this standard, the loss is *allocated* between the parties to the extent that each contributed to it.

---

[5]*Fireman's Fund Ins. Co. v. Bank of New York*, 539 N.Y.S.2d 339 (N.Y. App. 1989).

Case 34.2 illustrates a fictitious payee situation, and discusses whether the dishonest agent's bank is liable to the drawer-employer for negligently paying the checks.

CASE 34.2 **Prudential-Bache Securities, Inc. v. Citibank**
• 536 N.E.2d 1118 (N.Y. 1989)

FACTS John Eflar embezzled approximately $18.9 million from his employer, Prudential-Bache Securities, Inc. (P-B), channeling $3.7 million through defendant Citibank.

As section manager of the Dividend Department, Eflar induced P-B to issue dividend checks to shell corporations set up and controlled by him and his co-conspirator, Lawrence Artese. To launder the proceeds, Artese opened accounts in the names of the shell corporations at Citibank's Hudson Street branch. The conspirators bribed two Citibank employees—Robert Hutchinson, an assistant manager, and Juanita Reyes, a customer service representative. They set up the checking accounts at Citibank without proper account records and with fictitious corporate officers. They also agreed not to prepare reports required by the Internal Revenue Service for cash transactions exceeding $10,000.

Within a few months, Artese personally deposited more than $3.7 million in P-B checks at the Citibank branch and withdrew the funds in cash. He wrote some 100 checks, often cashing several on a single day and leaving the branch with large quantities of currency. More than 40 of the checks were for over $10,000, some exceeding $50,000; no currency transaction reports were prepared. P-B alleged that other Citibank employees, including managers, were aware of these activities through conversations with Artese on his near-daily visits to the branch and through cash distributions at teller windows.

Eventually, on a tip, Efler's supervisor reviewed account records and the scheme was exposed. No internal audit of the Dividend Department had been conducted during the entire period of the fraud. The two Citibank employees were convicted of various crimes against Citibank.

P-B then sued Citibank for damages, alleging conversion and commercial bad faith. The Supreme Court (New York's trial court) dismissed P-B's complaint. The Appellate Division affirmed the trial court's decision, and P-B appealed.

OPINION KAYE, J. . . . [W]e conclude that no cause of action has been stated for conversion . . . but that plaintiff has . . . a cause of action for "commercial bad faith" against the bank. . . .

We first consider UCC 3-405(1)(c), which was a basis for dismissal of the complaint.

The [UCC], in its rules governing check fraud, assigns losses by the relative responsibility of the parties for the loss. Losses arising out of forged indorsements are allocated to the party best able to take precautions to prevent them. . . .

Ordinarily, an unauthorized indorsement—that is, either a forged indorsement or one made by an agent exceeding authority . . . —is ineffective to pass title or authorize the drawee bank to pay. . . . The check is not properly payable because an unauthorized signature is inoperative as that of the person whose

CASE 34.2 Continued

name is signed. . . . Consequently, the drawee bank generally may not debit the drawer's account when it pays such a check. . . .

UCC 3-405(1)(c) creates an exception to the general principle that a drawer is not liable on an unauthorized indorsement. Known as the "fictitious payee" or "padded payroll" rule, [it] provides that an "indorsement by any person in the name of a named payee is effective if . . . an agent or employee of the maker or drawer has supplied him with the name of the payee intending the latter to have no such interest." Thus . . . the indorsement is treated as effective even though . . . unauthorized, and the loss is allocated to the drawer-employer. . . .

UCC 3-405(1)(c) expresses a fundamental public policy determination. As [explained in a comment to that section,] "The employer is normally in a better position to prevent such forgeries by reasonable care in the selection or supervision of his employees, or, if he is not, is at least in a better position to cover the loss by fidelity insurance; and . . . the cost of such insurance is properly an expense of his business rather than of the business of the holder or drawee." . . .

[The Legislature intended] "to shift the balance in favor of the bank 'in situations in which the drawer's own employee has perpetrated the fraud or committed the crime giving rise to the loss.'" . . . As has been widely acknowledged, UCC 3-405 is "a banker's provision intended to narrow the liability of banks and broaden the responsibility of their customers." . . .

The facts of this case fit . . . within UCC 3-405(1)(c). It is undisputed that an "employee" (Efler) supplied the "maker or drawer" (P-B) with the name of ["payee" corporations]. The payees, who were fictitious customers not entitled to the dividend payments, were intended "to have no such interest" in the instruments issued. . . . [T]he practical, policy considerations that motivated UCC 3-405(1)(c) are evident in the facts of this case. . . . As is plain simply from the chronology of undisputed facts, P-B was in a position to prevent the massive losses in issue here, by supervising its employees, enforcing its rules and examining records relating to a fraud that had been in progress for nearly two years. Under UCC 3-405(1)(c), the loss occasioned by Efler's wrongdoing should thus fall to plaintiff, not Citibank.

[T]o avoid this result, P-B [argues] that a standard of care for banks should be read into UCC 3-405(1)(c) and [that] Citibank failed to meet it. . . . UCC 3-405(1)(c) itself specifies no duty of care. . . . While the Legislature might have . . . apportioned liability according to each party's actual fault in a particular transaction—as it did elsewhere in the Code—it chose [not to do so in] UCC 3-405(1)(c). . . . [A depositary] bank's [mere negligence] in handling a check . . . will not subject [it] to liability. . . .

Plaintiff urges, however, that an action lies outside the Code for "commercial bad faith." . . .

. . . Where a depositary bank acts dishonestly—where it has actual knowledge of facts and circumstances that amount to bad faith, thus itself becoming a participant in a fraudulent scheme—such conduct falls wholly outside the allocation of business risks that was contemplated by UCC 3-405(1)(c). . . .

[Plaintiff alleges] that Citibank, through its officers, agents and employees, actually knew of and thereby itself became a participant in the unlawful scheme to launder plaintiff's funds. . . . What plaintiff has pleaded is not merely a lapse

CASE 34.2
Continued

of "wary vigilance" . . . or even "suspicious circumstances which might well have induced a prudent banker to investigate." . . . Such assertions of bank negligence by a drawer would be insufficient to state a cause of action against a depositary bank. Instead, plaintiff has portrayed an embezzlement scheme of massive dimension. . . . [Plaintiff alleges] that . . . managerial employees [other than Hutchison and Reyes] knew of and thus participated in the scheme. [Plaintiff also] argues that . . . we must infer the participation of other employees from the frequency of Artese's visits to the branch, his repeated large cash withdrawals at teller windows, and his conversations with other Citibank employees.

[P]laintiff bears a heavy burden to sustain its assertions of bank dishonesty. . . . A showing short of the bank's bad faith will not suffice to shift the loss from plaintiff, where it has been squarely placed by the Legislature in UCC 3-405(1)(c). Great though plaintiff's burden may be, however, its assertions of bad faith are sufficient [to support its] complaint.

JUDGMENT

Accordingly, the order of the Appellate Division should be modified [and affirmed as modified].

BOX 34.5

Revised Article 3

Under the pre-1990 rule just discussed, an employer who issues a check to a fictitious payee or an imposter must bear the loss, even if the bank where the dishonest agent deposited the check was negligent in making payment. The 1990 revisions make substantial changes in the liability of persons like depositary banks in the fictitious payee/padded payroll cases. The employer may recover damages from the depositary bank not only for its "commercial bad faith" as before, but also for its **ordinary negligence,** "to the extent the failure to exercise ordinary care contributed to the loss" [revised § 3-405(b)]. ■

DISCHARGE FROM CONTRACTUAL LIABILITY

As people circulate negotiable instruments, the liability of various signers—makers, drawers, acceptors, and unqualified indorsers—may be discharged (terminated) in a variety of ways. In a lawsuit brought to compel a signer to pay, the signer may assert a discharge as a defense. Most discharges are personal defenses; a few are real.

This part of the chapter describes some common methods of discharge and the effect of a discharge on the rights of a holder in due course.

Common Methods of Discharge

Payment. A party who pays the amount of the instrument to a holder (and removes the instrument from circulation or cancels it by, for example, marking it "Paid") is completely discharged from liability on it [3-603(1)]. Discharge will not result, however, if the payment was made in bad faith, as where the person making payment knows that the holder acquired the instrument by theft. Nor will a payment that is inconsistent with a restrictive indorsement ordinarily discharge the person making payment.

The discharge of a party who has no recourse on the instrument (no valid claim against any other party) usually results in the discharge of all other parties [3-601(3)]. Thus, if a maker or drawer pays a holder and is thereby discharged, all others such as indorsers and accommodation parties are discharged too.

Usually an instrument is given for the purpose of discharging some underlying obligation. For example, a tenant mails the landlord a check for a month's rent. Unless otherwise agreed, the underlying obligation (here, to pay rent) is not discharged until the check is actually paid [3-802]. The landlord's taking the check, however, suspends the landlord's right to sue for nonpayment until the check is overdue or dishonored.

Fraudulent and Material Alteration. Sometimes a holder alters an instrument after it gets into circulation—by adding, deleting, or changing a term, or by completing an incomplete (but signed) instrument "otherwise than as authorized" [3-407]. An alteration, if fraudulent and material, *discharges* the party affected by it from any liability to the holder who made it, and from liability to subsequent assignees. Since a fraudulent and material alteration (hereafter called "material alteration") is a real defense, the affected party also receives appropriate protection from the claims of a holder in due course.

An alteration is **fraudulent** if the holder acts with a dishonest purpose. Ordinarily, a payee who raises the amount of a check acts fraudulently. In contrast, a holder who substitutes a lower interest rate to benefit the maker probably has not acted fraudulently. An alteration is **material** if it changes the *contract* of a party *in any respect*. The addition of 1 cent to the amount payable, or an advance of 1 day in the date of payment, is material. A change that does no more than correct an obvious error or a misspelling is not material.

A party whose contract is changed by a holder's material alteration is completely discharged from liability to (1) the holder who made the alteration, and (2) any other person who is merely an assignee of the altered instrument—unless, for example, the affected party assented to the alteration [3-407(2)(a)]. In addition, material alteration is a partial real defense as against a holder in due course, though it may be no defense at all. A holder in due course always may enforce the altered instrument against the affected party according to the original tenor (terms) of the instrument. And, where a signed but incomplete instrument has been completed, the holder in due course may enforce the instrument as completed [3-407(3)]. Furthermore, a holder in due course is entitled to enforce an instrument *as altered* (e.g., for a fraudulently raised amount)

where the affected party's negligence (here, the issuer's negligence) made alteration easy [3-406].

For example, Maria makes and delivers to Paul a note for $100, payable to Paul's order. Paul negotiates it to Art, who fraudulently raises the amount to $2,100 and then negotiates the note to Ben, a holder in due course. Maria and Paul are discharged from any liability to Art because Art's alteration was fraudulent and material. Maria and Paul are liable to Ben for $100, the amount originally specified in the note. But if in preparing the note Maria negligently left spaces in which additional words or figures could easily be inserted, Ben may recover the full $2,100 from Maria. Art, the defrauder, is liable to Ben for $2,100.

Where a holder makes an unauthorized *completion* of a signed, incomplete instrument and transfers it, the signer-issuer is discharged as to a mere holder, but is liable to a holder in due course for the amount of the instrument *as completed*. The loss should fall on the issuer whose conduct (issuing a signed but incomplete negotiable instrument) has made the holder's fraud possible, rather than on the innocent purchaser. Dora issues a paycheck to Paul but leaves the line for the amount blank for Paul to fill out for the amount she owes him, $200. Paul completes the check for $500. Dora is not liable on the instrument to Paul; but as to any holder in due course, Dora will be liable for $500.

Unexcused Delay. A holder's **unexcused delay** in making presentment or giving notice of dishonor completely discharges an *indorser* from liability on the instrument [3-501(1)]. In *Hanes v. Exten*,[6] for example, the Extens indorsed an installment note which stated that it became due 30 days after the maker's default. The maker defaulted. Hanes then acquired the note, held it for almost 18 months before presenting it to the maker for payment, and, being unable to collect, sued the Extens in their capacities as indorsers. The court held that the 18 months far exceeded the reasonable time allowed by the Code for presenting the note to the maker. The indorsers therefore were discharged from liability.

[6]259 A.2d 290 (Md. App. 1969).

Though unexcused delay in making presentment completely discharges an indorser, a holder's delay in presenting commercial paper for payment will not, by itself, discharge a *maker, drawer, or acceptor*. Ordinarily, these parties remain liable on the instrument for the full time prescribed by the applicable statute of limitations, despite the holder's delay in seeking payment. The purpose of this rule is to avoid imposing loss on holders whose delay is harmless and to avoid unjustly enriching parties who normally receive consideration for their instruments.

However, makers, drawers, and acceptors of instruments *payable at a bank* are protected where unexcused delay together with a bank failure causes them loss. Dora, the drawer of a check made out to Paul, has sufficient funds on deposit with the drawee bank to pay the check. Her bank becomes insolvent 32 days after the check is issued, and Paul presents the check for payment on the thirty-third day. Since 30 days after issue is presumed to be a reasonable time within which to present an uncertified check for payment, Paul's delay is unexcused. Dora, the drawer, may discharge her liability to Paul by *assigning in writing* to the holder (Paul) whatever rights regarding the deposited amount Dora might have against the insolvent bank [3-502]. Thus, where funds were available during the 30 days and the bank later failed, the holder must absorb any loss caused by the holder's unexcused delay in presenting the instrument for payment.

Cancellation. Perhaps to make a gift or to pay a creditor, the holder of an instrument may discharge any party (e.g., an indorser or a maker) by canceling the instrument or by canceling the party's signature [3-605]. Ordinarily, one cancels an instrument by intentionally destroying it or by marking it "Paid." A holder's canceling (crossing out) a signature discharges the liability of the favored person, but the holder still owns (has title to) the instrument and may negotiate or collect it.[7]

[7]*Accidental* destruction is not a cancellation; the owner may enforce a lost, destroyed, or stolen instrument by proving its terms and facts preventing its production [3-804].

Impairment of Recourse; Impairment of Collateral. An indorser who pays a dishonored instrument has a right of recourse (a right of payment) not only against the drawer, maker, or acceptor, but also against any prior unqualified indorser who has received timely notice of dishonor. However, if the holder of an instrument impairs (interferes with) an indorser's right of recourse against some other party, the indorser is discharged to the extent of the impairment.

Impairment of recourse takes many forms—for example, by a holder's discharging an indorser without the consent of subsequent indorsers. Martha issues a note to the order of Peter. The note is successively indorsed to Agnes, Ben, and Harold. Indorser Ben expects Agnes or Peter to pay if Martha does not. If Harold cancels Agnes' indorsement without Ben's consent, Harold has (by discharging Agnes) impaired Ben's right of recourse against Agnes and has discharged Ben too [3-606(1)].

An unjustifiable **impairment of collateral** has the same effect as impairment of recourse. It discharges the party whose rights against others are jeopardized. Suppose that when Martha issued the note to Peter, she also pledged shares of her stock to Peter to secure payment of the note. Then Peter indorsed the note and transferred the collateral to Agnes. Agnes, in turn, indorsed the note to Ben but, without Peter's consent, returned the stock to Martha. By returning the stock to Martha, Agnes has given up the creditor's security interest in it. Since Peter no longer has access to the stock in the event that he must pay the note, his collateral is thereby impaired, and he is discharged from liability.

Reacquisition of Instrument. A holder may negotiate an instrument to others and later reacquire it. The reacquisition discharges any intervening party from liability to the reacquiring party and subsequent holders not in due course [3-208]. Paul indorses a note to Andrew, who indorses it to Brent, who indorses it back to Paul. Paul's reacquiring the instrument discharges Andrew and Brent as to Paul. Were this not true, Paul would have recourse against Andrew and Brent if the note was not paid when due, and then Andrew and Brent each would have a cause of action against Paul on his original indorsement. To prevent such circular legal actions, the Code discharges intervening indorsers *as to reacquirers and assignees*. However, the intervening indorsers remain liable to subsequent holders in due course.

Other Methods of Discharge. There are numerous other methods of discharging a party from liability on the instrument. These include the methods (discussed in Chapter 13) that are recognized by the general law of contracts and that apply to negotiable instruments as well: mutual rescission, novation, accord and satisfaction, and so on. Other examples include a discharge in bankruptcy and, as noted in Chapter 35, the discharge that may result from certification of a check.

BOX 34.6

Payment-in-Full Checks and the 1990 Amendments

Ordinarily, a person who cashes a check marked "Payment in full" for a disputed debt is held to have accepted the check amount as full payment. This process is called an accord and satisfaction. Can the recipient of a payment-in-full check nullify the effect of that language by adding a statement such as "This check is cashed under protest," and thus reserve a right to collect the balance allegedly owed? At least for the sale of goods, Sec. 1-207 of the UCC seems to permit such action, and the New York courts have so held. The states of Delaware, Florida, Massachusetts, and New Hampshire may be in agreement with the New York position. The courts of *most* states, however, hold that Sec. 1-207 does *not* replace the accord and satisfaction rule applying to payment-in-full checks. The 1990 amendments to the UCC make clear that Sec. 1-207 is not meant to apply to payment-in-full checks [revised § 3-311]. ■

Effect of Discharge on Holder in Due Course

Generally, discharge of a maker, indorser, or other party is a personal defense that is not good against a subsequent holder in due course who is without notice of it [3-602]. Marty Maker pays Paul Payee the amount of a note before its maturity date and does not remove it from circulation or mark it "Paid." A subsequent holder in due course to whom Paul sells the note may require Marty to pay again. However, as noted in Chapter 32, a few discharges, such as a discharge in bankruptcy, are real defenses, good even against a holder in due course.

BOX 34.7

Test Your Knowledge

1. Dora, an employer, signs forty payroll checks but leaves them blank for her agent to fill out later, and places them in her office safe. That night a thief breaks open the safe, takes the signed checks, makes them out for $100 to himself as payee, and negotiates them to holders in due course. Is Dora discharged from obligation because of the unauthorized completions and her care in safeguarding the signed checks?

2. Marla buys a house from Peg and pays for it with a negotiable promissory note for $90,000. Peg indorses it to Al, who indorses it to Bea, who indorses it to Harriet. Harriet strikes out Al's indorsement and indorses the note to Xavier, a holder in due course. On its due date, he presents the note to Marla for payment but cannot collect because of Marla's bankruptcy. Xavier gives timely notice of dishonor to Peg, Al, Bea, and Harriet. Which indorsers, if any, are liable to Xavier? ■

WARRANTY LIABILITY

Because commercial paper is a type of property, the UCC imposes warranties (guarantees of the absence of certain defects) on people who *transfer* commercial paper or *present* it for payment of acceptance. Thus, there are **transfer warranties** and **presentment warranties.**

For wronged persons, warranty liability has several practical advantages over contractual liability:

- It exists in the absence of contractual liability. For example, qualified indorsers, people who negotiate bearer paper without indorsing it, and indorsers discharged by a holder's unexcused delay have warranty liability.
- Presentment, dishonor, and notice of dishonor are not required for a suit in warranty. Upon discovering a breach of warranty, a transferee may simply return the instrument to the transferor and receive back anything paid for it.
- The right to sue for breach of a warranty arises immediately upon discovery of the breach, even though the time for payment may not yet have arrived.

Transfer Warranties

Any person, including a thief, who transfers *and receives consideration for (sells)* a negotiable instrument makes the five transfer warranties discussed in the following paragraphs.[8] If the seller delivers the instrument without signing it (as in the transfer of bearer paper), the transfer warranties run only to the *immediate* transferee. If the transfer is by indorsement, they run to *any* subsequent holder [3-417(2)]. Table 34.1 summarizes who makes and receives transfer warranties.

[8] One who gives an instrument away makes no transfer warranties, but *does* make presentment warranties.

Warranty concerning title: A seller of a negotiable instrument warrants that he or she has good title to (owns) it, or is authorized to obtain payment or acceptance for the owner, and that the transfer is otherwise rightful. Breach of the warranty occurs under any of the following circumstances:

1. A finder or a thief of a bearer instrument sells it.
2. There is a sale of an order instrument on which a necessary indorsement has been forged.
3. An agent lacks authority to transfer an instrument for the principal, or the agent is authorized but the principal does not have good title.

Warranty concerning signatures: A seller of commercial paper warrants that all signatures are genuine or authorized. Thus, a wronged transferee may sue the seller or rescind the transfer if the signature of a maker, a drawer, an acceptor, or an indorser is forged or unauthorized.

Warranty concerning alterations: A seller of commercial paper warrants that the instrument has not been materially altered. Dan draws a check for $100 payable to the order of Pam; Pam indorses it in blank and delivers it to Amy; Amy raises the amount to $2,100 and, without indorsing, negotiates the check to Ben for $2,100. If Ben is a holder in due course, Pam and Dan are liable to Ben for $100, the original tenor of the instrument. But Ben also has a

Table 34.1 Transfer Warranties

Person Making Transfer Warranties	Person Receiving Transfer Warranties	Warranties Received
Any transferor *receiving consideration*	Where transferor *does not indorse* but receives consideration, only the *immediate transferee*	1. Title 2. Signatures 3. Against alterations 4. Against insolvency 5. Against defenses
	Where transferor *indorses* and receives consideration, *any subsequent transferee*	

cause of action against Amy for breach of warranty. When Amy transferred the check and received consideration, she warranted to her immediate transferee, Ben, that the check had not been materially altered. Amy's breach entitles Ben to his actual damages: here, $2,000 plus cost of litigation.

Warranty concerning insolvency proceedings: A seller of a negotiable instrument warrants that she or he has no knowledge of any insolvency proceeding instituted with respect to the maker, drawer, or acceptor.

Warranty concerning defenses: The warranty concerning real and personal defenses—infancy, fraud in the inducement, and so on—varies according to the type of seller. A seller who makes an *unqualified indorsement,* or who transfers without indorsement, warrants flatly that no defense of any party is good against him or her. But a seller who makes a *qualified* indorsement (one "without recourse") warrants only *no knowledge* of a defense.

Presentment Warranties

Presentment warranties (Table 34.2) run only to persons who pay or accept an instrument—i.e., only to makers, drawees, or acceptors [3-417(1)]. The presentment warranties are made by the person actually presenting the instrument for payment or acceptance *and* by *all prior* transferors (sellers and nonsellers) of that instrument. Thus, if someone breaches a presentment warranty, as by making a forged indorsement, a payor or acceptor may have recourse against a number of persons in addition to the actual presenter.

A presenter (or a prior transferor) warrants the following:

1. He or she has good title, or has authority to obtain payment or acceptance for a person who has title.
2. He or she lacks knowledge that the signature of the maker or drawer is unauthorized.
3. The instrument has not been materially altered.

A holder in due course acting in good faith does *not* make the last two warranties to makers, drawers, or acceptors. These parties are in a better position than a holder in due course to verify their own signatures or detect material alterations before payment.

How does a presentment warranty work? Dan issues a check to the order of Pam. A thief steals it, forges Pam's in-blank indorsement, and transfers the check to Amy as a gift. Amy then transfers it without indorsement to Ben, who presents it to Dan's bank (the drawee) and receives payment. Having forged Pam's signature, the thief acquired no title and could confer none on anyone else. So Ben, Amy, and the thief have all breached the presenter's warranty that he or she "has good title to the instrument," and the bank may recover from any of them the money it mistakenly paid Ben. Thus payors and acceptors shift such losses to others. Often, though, the forger escapes and the party taking from the forger must pay. This makes sense, because that party was in the best position to detect the forgery and prevent the loss.

The case that follows explains why an accommodation indorser may have no warranty liability.

Table 34.2 Presentment Warranties

Persons Making Presentment Warranties	Persons Receiving Presentment Warranties	Warranties Received
Actual *presenters*	Maker, drawee, acceptor	1. Title
All prior transferors		2. Signatures
		3. Against alterations

| CASE 34.3 | **Oak Park Currency Exchange, Inc. v. Maropoulos**
• 363 N.E.2d 54 (Ill. App. 1977) |
|---|---|
| FACTS | John Bugay possessed a check drawn to the order of Henry Sherman, Inc., and fraudulently indorsed "Henry Sherman" on the reverse side. To cash the check, Bugay sought the assistance of defendant, James Maropoulos. Maropoulos took Bugay to plaintiff Oak Park Currency Exchange, Inc., where Maropoulos was known. Oak Park agreed to cash the check if Maropoulos would indorse it. He indorsed the check, received the money, and gave it immediately to Bugay.

Oak Park then indorsed and deposited the check in Belmont National Bank. The indorsement "Henry Sherman" was later found to be a forgery. The bank sought and received payment back from Oak Park. Oak Park, in turn, sought payment from Maropoulos on his indorsement and for breach of warranty, and filed suit. From a directed verdict in favor of defendant, Oak Park appealed. |
| OPINION | GOLDBERG, P.J. [P]laintiff urges that defendant breached his warranty of good title when he obtained payment of a check on which the payee's indorsement was forged and that there was sufficient evidence to support a directed verdict in favor of plaintiff. . . . Defendant contends that an accommodation indorser does not make warranties under Section 3-417(1) and that the trial court properly directed a verdict for the defendant.

A party who signs an instrument "for the purpose of lending his name to another party to" that instrument is an accommodation party. . . . Such a party "is liable in the capacity in which he has signed. . . ." Therefore defendant is an accommodation indorser and would be liable to plaintiff under his indorser's contract, provided that he had received timely notice that the check had been presented to the drawee bank and dishonored. . . . Because these conditions precedent to the contractual liability of an indorser have not been met, defendant is not liable on his contract as an accommodation indorser.

Furthermore, the drawee bank, American National, did not dishonor the check but paid it. This operated to discharge the liability of defendant as an accommodation indorser.

The portion of the Code upon which plaintiff seeks to hold defendant liable . . . sets out warranties which run only to a party who "pays or accepts" an instrument upon presentment. We note that presentment is defined as "a demand for acceptance or payment made upon the maker, acceptor, drawee, or other payor. . . ." As applied to the instant case, the [presentment warranties] run only to the payor bank and not to any other transferee who acquired the check. In the case before us, [Oak Park] is not a payor or acceptor of the draft. . . . [Oak Park is] a transferee, not a [drawee] who paid or accepted the instrument. Thus it appears that reliance by plaintiff upon subsection 3-417(1) was misplaced. . . .

An additional theory requires affirmance of the judgment appealed from. Subsection 3-417(2) of the Code provides that one "who transfers an instrument and receives consideration warrants to his transferee" that he has good title. . . . The evidence presented in the case at bar establishes that defendant received no consideration for his indorsement. Though Mrs. Panveno [Oak Park's employee] testified that she saw Bugay hand defendant some money as the two left the cur- |

CASE 34.3 Continued	rency exchange, she also testified that defendant stated that he was doing a favor for his friend; that she was not paying close attention to the two men and that she did not watch them as they walked away from her. Thus her testimony was considerably weakened by her own qualifying statements, and it was strongly and directly contradicted by the positive and unshaken testimony of defendant that he received nothing in return for his assistance. The simple fact standing alone that this witness saw Bugay hand some money to defendant, even if proved, would have no legal significance without [proof] that the payment was consideration for defendant's indorsement.
JUDGMENT	Judgment affirmed.

SUMMARY

Most signers of commercial paper have contractual liability for the face amount of the instrument. The liability of makers and acceptors is primary; that of drawers and indorsers is secondary. A primary party is liable immediately and unconditionally when the instrument is due. A secondary party is liable only if the triggering events of presentment, dishonor, and notice of dishonor take place or are excused. The nature of an accommodation party's liability depends on the capacity in which the party signs—as a maker, an indorser, and so on. A secondary party who guarantees payment has a liability similar to that of a co-maker.

To avoid liability as a signer, an agent should name the person represented and show that the agent has signed in a representative capacity. Ordinarily an unauthorized signature has no effect as that of the person whose name is signed, but it does serve as the signature of the person acting without authority. An indorsement made by an imposter or by a dishonest employee in a "padded payroll" case *is* effective to negotiate the instrument.

The liability of signers may be terminated by a variety of methods, including fraudulent and material alteration and unexcused delay in making presentment. Generally, discharge is a personal defense, but a discharge in bankruptcy is a real defense.

Since commercial paper is property, there can be warranty liability. The UCC imposes transfer and presentment warranties.

REVIEW QUESTIONS

1. (a) Distinguish between primary and secondary liability on an instrument. **(b)** Do all instruments have primary parties? Explain.

2. Explain the meaning and purpose of **(a)** presentment, **(b)** dishonor, and **(c)** notice of dishonor.

3. How long, and why, may acceptance or payment be delayed without the delay's being considered a dishonor?

4. What two things must an agent's form of signature do if the agent is to avoid liability on the instrument?

5. John Doe receives a check made payable to his order. A thief steals it, indorses it in Doe's name, and transfers it for value to Henry Holder. **(a)** Is Doe liable on the instrument? Explain. **(b)** Is the thief?

6. Who is liable on an instrument made out to and indorsed by an imposter? Why?

7. (a) Under what circumstances will payment not discharge a maker, an acceptor, or an indorser of an instrument? **(b)** What effect does a person's taking a check have on the underlying obligation?

8. If an alteration discharges a party to the instrument, against whom will the discharge be effective? Against whom will it *not* be effective?

9. (a) Whom does unexcused delay in making presentment discharge completely? **(b)** Under what circumstances will unexcused delay discharge a maker, a drawer, or an acceptor?

10. Explain or illustrate how the following transfer warranties are breached: warranty of title, warranty concerning signatures, and warranty against alterations.

11. How does a qualified indorsement affect the warranty concerning defenses?

12. How do presentment warranties differ from transfer warranties with regard to **(a)** who makes them and **(b)** who receives them?

CASE PROBLEMS

1. Richard and Ronald Osofsky owned or worked for Integrated Agricultural Management Co., Inc. They bought some cattle for the company, paying with promissory notes signed as follows:

Integrated Agricultural Management Co., Inc.

(signed) Richard A. Osofsky, Secretary

(signed) Richard A. Osofsky

(signed) Ronald Osofsky

The notes were not paid when due, and Klapper, the payee, sued the Osofskys. They defended on the ground that the notes were corporate, not personal, obligations. Should the Osofskys be held personally liable?

2. Snug Harbor Realty Co., a construction company, employed Magee as its superintendent. One of his duties was to inspect work in progress and be sure that work was done or materials delivered before Snug Harbor issued checks in payment. On the basis of Magee's investigations and accurate reports, Snug Harbor issued a number of checks to various suppliers and subcontractors. Magee was to deliver the checks to the people entitled to them, but instead he forged the indorsements of 132 payees and cashed the checks himself. Snug Harbor brought suit against the drawee bank to recover from it the amounts of the checks. From a judgment for the bank, Snug Harbor appealed. Should the bank be required to recredit Snug Harbor's account?

3. In exchange for merchandise, Florida City Express, Inc. (Express), signed two negotiable promissory notes totaling about $7,000, payable to Latin American Tire Co. Latin American indorsed and discounted the notes to the Bank of Miami (Bank), which took them before maturity, for value, and without notice of any defenses to payment. Before and after Latin American negotiated the notes to Bank, Express paid all the amounts due to Latin American, but did not require that Latin American display or surrender the notes or make any notation on the notes of payments made. At the maturity date of each note, Bank, after making unsuccessful demands on Latin American, sought but was refused payment from the maker, Express. Bank sued Express on the notes. Express raised the defense of payment. From a judgment for Express, Bank appealed. Should the judgment of the trial court be upheld?

4. Litchfield Co. drew a check on Bankers Trust payable to the order of Jensen Farley Pictures. Jensen Farley negotiated the check to First American Bank for value, and First American forwarded the check to Bankers Trust for payment. Unknown to First American, Litchfield earlier that day had stopped payment on the check. Bankers Trust dishonored the check and returned it to First American. Three months later, after several attempts to collect from Jensen Farley, First American learned of Jensen Farley's pending bankruptcy and sought payment from the drawer, Litchfield. Alleging First American's unexcused delay in giving notice of dishonor, Litchfield refused to pay. First American brought suit. Must drawer Litchfield pay?

5. Martin Maker executed and delivered to Paula Payee a 30-day note in the amount of $195 payable to the order of Payee. Payee indorsed the note in blank, and "without recourse" and sold it to Alfred Anderson. Anderson indorsed the note in blank, and "without recourse" sold it to Betty Brown. Brown, without indorsing the note, sold it to Harold Holder.

After the due date of the note, Holder presented it to Maker for payment. Maker refused to pay, correctly stating that he had given the note to Paula Payee for a gambling debt and that a state statute made gambling instruments null and void. **(a)** Assume that Holder sued Brown for breach of warranty. Judgment for whom? **(b)** Assume that Holder sued Anderson for breach of warranty. Judgment for whom? **(c)** Assume that Holder sued Payee for breach of warranty. Judgment for whom?

6. Martin Maker executed a note payable to the order of Paula Payee. Payee lost the note. Fred Forger, the finder, forged Payee's indorsement and sold the note to Georgia Goodenough, who indorsed and sold the note to Harold Holder. Neither Goodenough nor Holder was aware of the forgery. Holder presented the note at maturity, and Maker paid it. Later Maker discovered that the signature on the instrument was a forgery. **(a)** Assume that Maker sued Holder for breach of warranty. Judgment for whom? **(b)** Assume that instead of suing Holder, Maker sued Goodenough for breach of warranty. What would the judgment be?

7. The Georgia Farm Bureau Mutual Insurance Co. (MIC) issued a check for $685.28 to Willie Mincey and itself (MIC) as copayees. Without indorsing it, MIC forwarded it to Mincey. He indorsed it and tried to cash it at First National Bank (FNB). Because Mincey was not known to FNB personnel, FNB refused to cash the check. Mincey returned to the bank with his uncle, Montgomery, who was known to FNB. FNB agreed to cash the check if Montgomery would indorse it. He did so, and Mincey received the cash. Eventually the check was returned to FNB for lack of MIC's indorsement. Mincey apparently was neither entitled to payment nor available for suit. Alleging that Montgomery was liable as an indorser, and had breached a transfer and a presentment warranty, FNB sued Montgomery for the amount of the check. Was Montgomery liable to FNB?

CHAPTER 35

Checks; Relationship between Bank and Customer; Electronic Funds Transfers

Most people have a checking account and, consequently, a continuing business relationship with a bank. Checking account customers pay debts by issuing checks drawn on their accounts. They also deposit for collection the **items** they receive—checks, drafts, matured bonds, interest coupons, and other instruments calling for payment in money.

Previous chapters dealt with many important aspects of checks: negotiable form; the liability of drawers and indorsers; the requirements of presentment, dishonor, and notice of dishonor for triggering the liability of secondary parties; the holder-in-due-course status of most people who cash checks; and other topics governed by UCC Article 3.

Additional laws, however, apply to checks and banks. For example, UCC Article 4, Bank Deposits and Collections, deals with the contractual relationship between a bank and its customers. Federal law applies to the computer-controlled **electronic funds transfer** (EFT) systems now widely used by consumers as a substitute for paper checks. And UCC Article 4A applies to large-scale commercial **funds transfers** (usually made electronically) between business and financial institutions.

The first part of this chapter discusses the special nature of checks and the uses of certified checks. The remainder of the chapter examines (1) the rights and duties of banks and their checking account customers and (2) the nature of computerized EFT and funds transfer systems.

CHECKS

Special Nature of Checks

Two features distinguish checks from other kinds of drafts: A check is always drawn on a bank, and a check is always payable on demand of the payee or other holder [3-104(2)]. Even a **postdated check** (one issued, say, on May 1 but dated May 5) is a demand instrument, though it does not become effective (payable) until the stated date arrives [3-114(2)]. The postdating simply postpones the time at which the holder may demand payment. When the stated day arrives, the drawee bank must honor the check upon the holder's demand unless there is some reason for dishonor, such as insufficient funds in the drawer's account.

Figure 35.1 illustrates the relationship among the persons normally involved in issuing and cashing a check. Usually the drawer (Dr) issues a check to the payee (Pe) to pay for something Dr bought. The resulting contract is the **underlying transaction** discussed in Chapter 31. After receiving the check from Dr, Pe might cash it at a supermarket, cash it at Pe's own bank, or present it directly to the drawee bank (De) for payment. Figure 35.1 shows Pe cashing the check at Pe's own bank (*selling* it, in effect) so that Pe's bank becomes a holder in due course (HDC). HDC will present the check (perhaps through a clearinghouse) to De for payment. In accordance with the **contract of deposit** between Dr and De, De will pay HDC the amount of the check, cancel it by marking it "Paid," and return it or otherwise make it available to Dr as a part of Dr's financial records.

A drawee bank has no liability to a presenting holder for dishonoring (refusing to pay) an uncertified check, because a check does not operate as an assignment (present transfer) of funds in the account [3-409]. Rather, a check is the drawer's instruction to the bank to pay the specified amount from the drawer's account when a holder presents the check to the bank. Since a check does not by itself transfer funds at the time of issue, the drawee bank has not violated the holder's property rights by dishonoring it. However, as discussed later in this chapter, a drawee who wrongfully dishonors a check may be liable to the drawer for breaching the contract of deposit.

Figure 35.1 Issue, transfer, payment, and return of check.

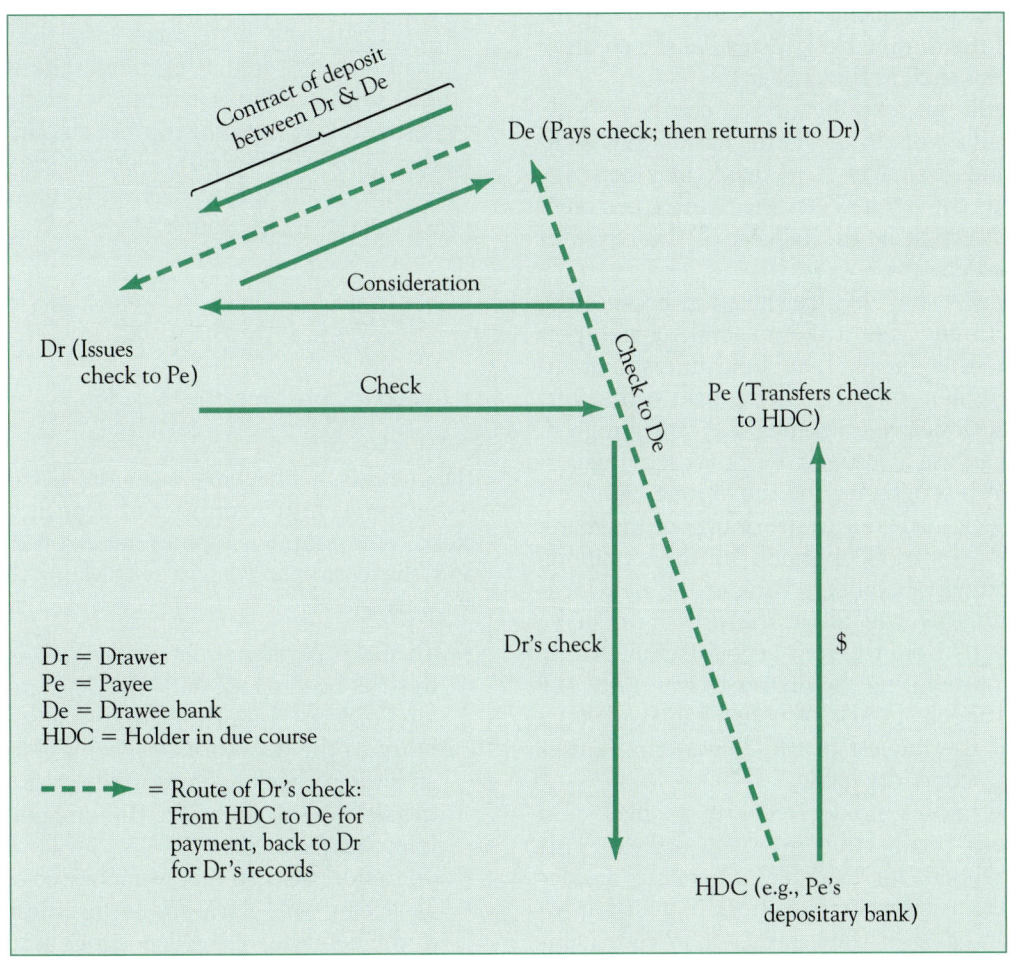

Certified Checks

A nonsigning drawee bank has no liability on a check when it is issued. However, to reduce doubts of the payee or a subsequent holder about its collectability, the drawee bank may be willing to certify it.

Certification is the acceptance of a check by a drawee bank [3-411]. A bank official usually certifies a check by stamping the word "accepted" or "certified" on its face and adding the date and the official's signature. Upon certifying a check, the drawee bank becomes primarily liable for the face amount. Ordinarily, the bank debits (charges) the drawer's account for the amount of the check before certifying it. But regardless of whether the bank actually debits the drawer's account, the bank, by certifying the check, makes an independent engagement (promise) to pay. Thus, subsequent holders may rely on the credit of the drawee bank instead of the credit of individuals such as the drawer.

A bank has no obligation to certify a check, but usually will do so if the drawer has sufficient funds to cover it. A bank may certify a check at the request of the bank's customer (the drawer) or at the request of the payee or other holder.

A drawer may seek certification because the payee has requested it. For example, a transport company that moves household furnishings interstate usually insists on being paid with a certified check before unloading the furnishings. A drawer can use a certified check for moving personal funds too, by having the drawee bank certify a check made out to the drawer or to a bank at a new location. Because of the certifying bank's primary liability, a bank at the new location ordinarily will allow the drawer to make withdrawals from the new account immediately instead of requiring the drawer to wait until the certified check "clears." Where a bank certifies a check at the request of the *drawer*, the drawer remains secondarily liable.

Sometimes a holder receives a check and then seeks certification from the drawee. This might happen, for example, where the holder would like to transport the check to a distant location and cash it there rather than cash it locally and carry the money. Where a bank certifies a check at the request of the *payee or holder*, the drawer and all prior indorsers are *discharged* from liability on the check [3-411]. Thus, the certifying bank is *substituted* as the party liable for payment.

BOX 35.1

Revised Article 3

Under the 1990 amendments, a bank's certifying a check or any other draft discharges the drawer (and prior indorsers), regardless of when or by whom certification was obtained [revised §§ 3-414, 3-415].

Suppose a person has a check certified, skillfully raises the amount, and negotiates the check to a holder in due course. What is the certifying bank's liability? Under revised § 3-413(b), the bank must pay the raised amount of any draft it certifies. The reasoning? Certifying banks can protect themselves by stating on the check the amount they agree to pay. If they fail to do so, the risk of subsequent alterations lies with them, not with holders in due course.

RELATIONSHIP BETWEEN BANK AND CUSTOMER

Contract between Bank and Customer

By opening a checking account, a bank customer enters into a **contract of deposit** with the bank. This contract imposes duties on the bank and the customer (depositor). Major duties of the *bank* are:

- To make payments out of the account only in strict accordance with the depositor's genuine orders. Thus, the bank has absolute liability to the depositor for paying a forged or an altered check and ordinarily must recredit the drawer's account for the amount of any improper payment.
- To honor the customer's timely stop orders.
- To act in good faith and with ordinary care in the handling of the depositor's account.

> **BOX 35.2**
>
> **Revised Article 3**
>
> A 1990 amendment changes the bank's duty of good faith—from "honesty in fact" to "honesty in fact and the observance of reasonable commercial standards of fair dealing." Thus, under the 1990 amendments, banks must observe the good faith standard applicable to merchants. ∎

Major duties of the *customer* are:

- To avoid negligence when drawing and issuing a check.
- To examine bank statements and canceled checks with reasonable care and to report forgeries and alterations promptly.

If the customer fails in these duties, the bank may be relieved of liability for an otherwise improper payment out of the customer's account, unless the bank is negligent. Then the bank's negligence nullifies the customer's negligence.

Most banks require their checking account customers to sign a **signature card** that includes some terms of the deposit contract. Often the signature card covers the bank's handling of items received for deposit or collection, the depositor's responsibility when requesting the bank to stop payment on a check, and the service charges imposed by the bank.

Banking is so complicated that it is not feasible to list all the parties' rights and duties on a signature card. Many are imposed by the UCC and other law. However, the parties are free to vary by contract the effect of a Code provision, except that, as Case 35.1 illustrates, no agreement can disclaim a bank's responsibility for its own lack of good faith or its failure to exercise ordinary care [4-103].

CASE 35.1 Stanek v. National Bank of Detroit • 430 N.W.2d 819 (Mich. App. 1988)

FACTS On February 18, 1985, plaintiff Helen Stanek drew a $197 check on defendant National Bank of Detroit, payable to Western Glass Company. At defendant's branch bank the next day, she issued a stop payment order at 9:35 a.m. Within 5 minutes, the stop payment order was entered into defendant's computer system. Later that day, Western Glass cashed the check at defendant's main office, and defendant debited Stanek's account.

Stanek sued to recover the $197, stating that when she told a bank employee she wanted to stop payment, the employee verified by computer that the check had not been cashed and said that because the stop payment order was entered on the computer, no one could cash the check from that time forward.

In support of its motion for summary judgment, defendant cited language appearing on the stop payment order:

> It is understood that this stop payment order is not effective if said check shall have been . . . cashed at any one of the Bank's offices . . . without actual notice of this stop payment order or before the Bank has a reasonable time to act under this order. It is agreed that "reasonable time" as used herein shall mean one (1) full banking day.

From district and circuit court judgments for defendant bank, Stanek appealed.

OPINION MacKENZIE, J. . . . It was defendant's argument, and the district court's holding, that the parties, by the language on the stop payment order, contracted to

**CASE 35.1
Continued**

define "reasonable opportunity to act" as one full banking day and that, therefore, one full banking day is the standard to which defendant is held as a matter of law. Defendant maintains that, even in the event of negligence on its part, any lack of ordinary care is excused for a period of one full banking day by virtue of the exculpatory language on the stop payment order.

We conclude that defendant's position must fail in light of § 4-103(1), which provides that "no agreement can disclaim a bank's responsibility for its own . . . failure to exercise ordinary care or can limit the measure of damages for such lack or failure." While there are no Michigan cases interpreting this language, courts in other jurisdictions have construed this section of the Uniform Commercial Code to void exculpatory clauses on bank forms. . . .

[The *Gillen* and *Levy* cases] held that no agreement between a bank and its depositor may relieve the bank of its responsibility for its own lack of good faith or failure to exercise ordinary care. While neither of these cases deals specifically with stop payment orders or the definition of reasonable opportunity to act, in the majority of states such exculpatory clauses are struck down for public policy or failure of consideration reasons. . . .

In this case, the language of the stop payment order attempts to absolve defendant from liability for payment over the stop order, even if due to its own lack of ordinary care, for a period of one full banking day. [On the basis of authority from] other jurisdictions, we conclude that this phrase is an exculpatory clause which should not be binding on the parties. Instead, it is for the trier of fact to determine what length of time constitutes a "reasonable opportunity to act" under § 4-403(1).

Courts in other jurisdictions which have addressed the question of what constitutes a reasonable opportunity for a bank to act on a stop payment order have determined that the reasonableness is dependent on the particular facts of each case. Less than one full banking day has been determined to be a reasonable opportunity to act. . . . In Chute, bank personnel testified that a stop payment order can be placed on an account by computer within a short time after it is received and that once it is placed on the computer the information is immediately available to all other branches of the bank. . . . Other cases also mentioned that the availability and use of computer technology by the bank may shorten the amount of time considered a reasonable opportunity to act. . . .

Case law from other jurisdictions suggests that this time limit definitely expires when the tellers have actual knowledge of the stop payment order. . . . In the Dunbar case, all tellers had been notified verbally of the stop payment order, and in Chute, the order had been entered in the computer system prior to the presentment of the check. Both Dunbar and Chute noted, however, that the question of what constitutes a reasonable opportunity to act is a question of fact to be determined by the trier of fact based upon factors such as those mentioned above. . . .

JUDGMENT

[T]he terms contained in the stop payment order were tantamount to an exculpatory clause which should not be binding between the parties. It was for the trier of fact to determine whether defendant had a reasonable opportunity to act under § 4-403(1). Accordingly, we reverse the orders of the district court and circuit court and remand for further proceedings. . . .

Nature of Bank-Customer Relationship

A bank and its checking account customer have a dual relationship: debtor and creditor, and principal and agent. When a customer deposits money, the bank becomes the customer's debtor for the amount, and the customer is the bank's general creditor with no claim to any specific funds. When a customer deposits a check or other item for collection, the bank is temporarily the customer's collecting agent. Upon receiving payment, the bank ceases being the customer's agent and becomes the customer's debtor for the amount collected. A bank also acts as its customer's agent in honoring checks that the customer has drawn against funds on deposit.

Check Collection Process

Usually, a person initiates the check collection process by depositing a check with his or her bank. Paul works in Fresno, California, for Dora, who owns a nationwide auto parts business headquartered in Massachusetts. Paul receives his paycheck in Fresno, but it is drawn on Boston Bank, where Dora has her payroll account. Paul has an account with Fresno Bank and deposits his paycheck there.

Fresno Bank has no direct dealings with Boston Bank. To collect the check for Paul, Fresno Bank will send it through a series of banks that collect checks for other banks. Paul's check may travel from Fresno Bank through some California state banks and the Federal Reserve Bank of San Francisco to the Federal Reserve Bank of Boston, which will present the check to Boston Bank for payment. A clearinghouse (a place where banks exchange checks and settle their daily balances) may be involved.

In Figure 35.2, the banks between Fresno Bank and Boston Bank are referred to collectively as "Fed Bank." Fresno Bank is the **depositary** bank; Fed Bank is the **intermediary** bank; and Boston Bank, the drawee, is the **payor** bank. Depositary and intermediary banks are also called **forwarding** or **collecting** banks.

Ordinarily, a collecting bank must forward a check no later than midnight of the banking day following the day of receipt—e.g., by midnight Tuesday for a check deposited on Monday [4-202]. This time limit is called the bank's **midnight deadline** [4-104].

Collection is accomplished through the use of accounts that banks maintain between themselves for collection purposes. Collection is based on a system of **provisional credits** that Paul and the collecting banks expect to become **final**. A collecting bank may allow its depositor to withdraw funds against a provisional (reversible) credit. However, until the depositor's provisional credit becomes final, the bank can recover the credited amount if the bank itself does not receive final settlement. This would happen where, for example, the payor bank dishonors the deposited check or becomes insolvent. When a provisional credit received by a collecting bank becomes final, the depositor's provisional credit in turn becomes final and the collecting bank becomes accountable to its customer for the amount.

Provisional credits become final when the *payor* (drawee) bank takes any of a variety of actions [4-213]. Among them are:

1. Paying the item (check) in cash.
2. Completing the process of posting the item to the drawer's account. **Posting** is the payor bank's act of deciding to pay an item and recording the payment in the account to be charged. Ordinarily, the process involves the verification of signatures, determining that the drawer has sufficient funds available, marking the check "Paid," and debiting the drawer's account.[1]
3. Failing to revoke a provisional credit within the time allowed by law—for example,

---

[1] Once, every deposit, withdrawal, or posting transaction was recorded laboriously by hand. Now, magnetically encoded checks and deposit slips enable computers to record account numbers, amounts of checks, and other information instantly, store it in memory, enter daily account information into individual customer accounts, and print out balances and statements. Checks must be physically sorted as a part of the posting process. Computerized sorters process thousands of checks per hour.

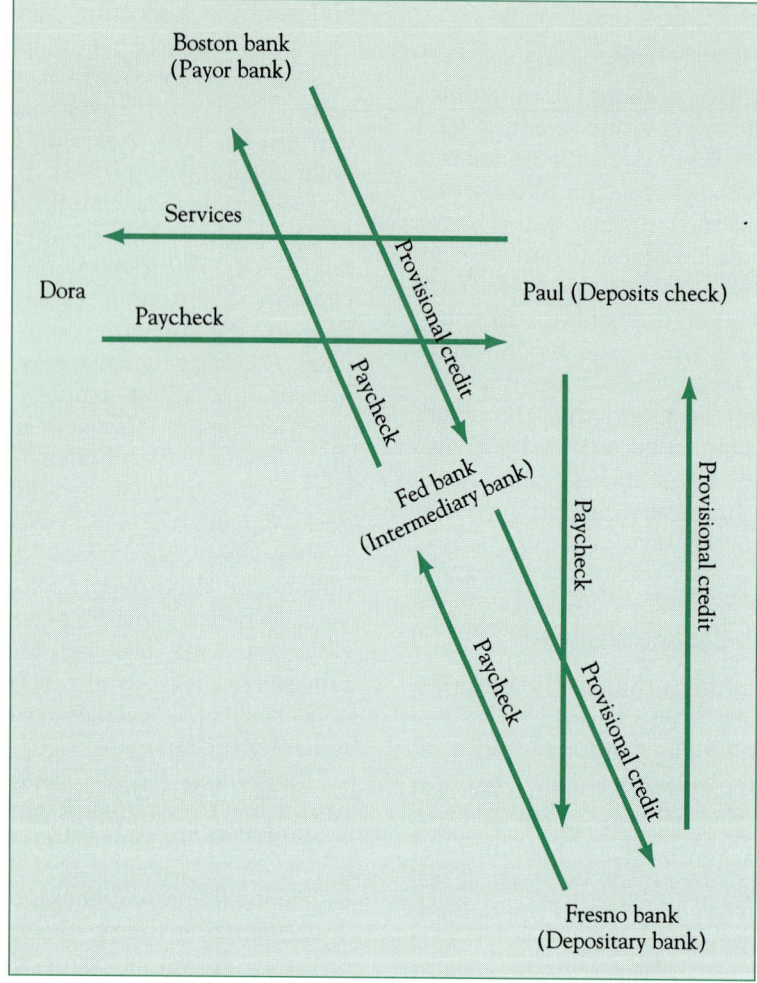

Figure 35.2 Banks in collection process.

in **deferred posting,** failing to revoke the credit by the payor bank's midnight deadline.[2]

So, as soon as Fresno Bank has had a reasonable time to learn that settlement for Paul's paycheck has become final, Paul has a right to withdraw the funds [4-213(4)]. However, in the past some banks delayed giving their customers access to collected funds, holding them for as much as two or three weeks and keeping the interest earned by the funds during that time. To prevent unreasonable delay in giving depositors access to collected funds, Congress enacted the **Expedited Funds Availability Act.**[3] Under the Federal Reserve Board's **Regulation CC,** which implements the Act, a bank must disclose its funds availability policy to existing and prospective customers. That policy must

[2] In deferred posting, which enables payor banks to distribute their workloads efficiently, a bank gives a provisional credit on the day a check is received and has until midnight of the following banking day (its midnight deadline) to complete the posting process. If the payor bank decides to dishonor a check and revoke the provisional credit it gave, it must do so before the midnight deadline; otherwise, the provisional credit becomes final [4-301].

[3] 12 U.S.C.A., Secs. 4001–4010 (1988).

conform to the *minimum* requirements of Regulation CC, which imposes the time limits listed in Table 35.1.

These federal rules are subject to exceptions intended to protect depositary banks from excessive risk. Longer hold periods apply to the following:

- *New accounts.* For the first 30 days of a new account (an account established by a new depositor), a bank may suspend the availability rules. This means, for example, that the bank may hold collected proceeds of ordinary checks for up to 30 calendar days. However, the bank must allow next-business-day withdrawal of cash deposits, wire transfer (electronic) deposits, and up to $5,000 in deposits of most government checks, cashier's checks, and the like. In this last category, amounts above $5,000 may be held for 9 business days. After the first 30 days, an account is no longer new, and the regular availability rules apply.
- *Large deposits* (non-new accounts). Amounts over $5,000 can be held for a reasonable time, usually 4 days.
- *Repeatedly overdrawn accounts.* Collected funds can be held for a reasonable time.
- *Unpaid, redeposited checks* (reasonable time).
- *Checks the bank reasonably considers uncollectable* (reasonable time).
- *Emergency situations* (e.g., reasonable time for power outage).

Whether a bank will impose these longer hold periods depends on its loss record, the amount of competition for new customers, and similar factors.

Table 35.1 Time Limits for Making Funds Available to Depositors

Type of Deposit	Available by START of
Cash deposited via human teller *Wire transfer*—e.g., direct deposit of payroll, social security payments *Government checks*—e.g., those drawn on U.S. Treasury, Federal Reserve Bank; some state checks *Cashier's, certified, and teller's checks* *Checks drawn on depositary bank* ("On us" checks) *First $100* per day of any check deposits	1st business day after day of deposit*
Local checks (those drawn in Federal Reserve area of depositary bank) *Automatic teller machine* (ATM) and mail deposits	2nd business day after day of deposit**
Nonlocal checks (those drawn in the United States, but outside Federal Reserve area of depositary bank)	5th business day after day of deposit**

*Funds from these deposits must be made available for either cash withdrawal or check writing.

**Funds from these deposits must be made available for check writing only. Cash withdrawals are limited to $400 (or the ATM maximum) and may be delayed until 5:00 p.m. of relevant day.

> **BOX 35.3**
>
> ### Test Your Knowledge
>
> You have been transferred from your job in Arizona to a new position in Boston. You make the following deposits in your account at Boston Local Bank. When can you withdraw funds?
>
> - $750 in cash deposited with the teller with whom you opened the account
> - Your last paycheck from your Arizona job, drawn on an Arizona bank and deposited when you opened the account
> - Your first paycheck from your new job, drawn on a Boston bank and deposited 2 weeks after you opened the account
> - A certified check for $27,000, the proceeds from the sale of your Arizona house, drawn on an Arizona bank and deposited 7 months after you opened the account
> - A federal tax refund check for $984, deposited a year after you opened the account

When Bank May Charge Customer's Account

When a bank honors a check properly drawn on the customer's account, or certifies a customer's check, it *debits* (charges) the customer's account for the amount of the check. However, the bank's right to charge the customer's account has limits.

Payment of Overdraft. In an ordinary checking account, a bank is not required to pay an **overdraft** (a check written without sufficient funds to cover it), but may do so if it wishes. If the bank honors an overdraft, the customer must reimburse the bank [4-401]. However, the bank is not allowed to charge the customer's account for interest on the overdraft amount.

For the benefit of both customer and bank, many banks offer a special ("ready reserve") checking account that allows the customer to overdraw it by a stated number of dollars. The amount of an overdraft in this type of account is considered a loan, and the customer is charged interest.

Payment of an Altered Check. A holder in due course who takes an altered instrument may enforce it according to its original tenor—i.e., for its original amount. The Code gives parallel protection to a drawee bank by providing that if the bank in good faith makes payment of an altered check, it may charge the customer's account according to the original tenor of the check [4-401(2)]. Alicia issues a check for $100, a holder raises the amount to $2,100, and the drawee bank pays the check in good faith. The bank may charge the drawer's account, but only for $100. The bank may charge Alicia's account with the *raised* amount, however, if (1) her *negligence substantially contributed* to the alteration, and (2) payment by the bank was made in good faith and in accordance with reasonable commercial standards in the banking business [3-406].

Payment of Check Incomplete When Issued. A check containing a material omission—e.g., lacking an amount or the payee's name—will not be honored by the drawee bank. However, the payee or holder of an incomplete check may fill in the missing information and present the check for payment. If the drawee in good faith pays the completed check, the drawee may charge the customer's account for the item as completed [4-401]. Otto signs a blank check and delivers it to Ella, telling her to "fill it in for the amount I owe you." She fills it in for twice the amount. If the bank in good faith pays the check, it may charge Otto's account with the amount of the check as completed. The bank is protected even if it knows of the completion—where, for example, Ella fills in the amount in the presence of a bank employee. The bank, however, is *not* allowed to charge Otto's account if the bank is on notice that the completion was improper.

Payment of a Stale Check. Checks that are outstanding for 6 months or more are called **stale** checks. For the protection of drawee banks and their customers, banks are not obligated to pay a check, other than a certified check, that is presented to it more than 6 months after issue. That is, the bank may dishonor a stale check without being liable to the drawer for wrongful dishonor. However, if the bank chooses to honor a stale check (as where a bank knows its corporate customer wants all dividend checks honored), it may charge the customer's account, provided the payment is made in good faith [4-404]. And, of course, unless the drawer has a good defense to payment, the drawer remains liable on the instrument.

Payment of a Postdated Check. Postdating a check has no effect on its negotiability [3-114]. A taker of a postdated check therefore may be a holder in due course. However, if a holder presents the check to the drawee bank for payment before the specified date, the bank may properly refuse payment. The refusal to pay is not a dishonor because the check is not due yet. Consequently, the refusal does not trigger the liability of secondary parties. The bank's refusal to pay is proper because the bank could be held liable to its customer for paying a postdated check early, charging the customer's account, and thereby reducing the balance in the account to a point where currently payable checks are wrongfully dishonored.

Bank's Liability for Wrongful Dishonor

A bank is liable to its customer for damages caused by the **wrongful dishonor** of (refusal to pay) the customer's check [4-402]. Since a bank is liable only for a *wrongful* dishonor, it is not liable where it dishonors a check for the drawer's lack of funds, or for lack of a necessary indorsement, or for other good reason such as staleness. A bank is liable for wrongful dishonor only to the drawer-customer, for breach of the contract of deposit. Others who may be harmed by the drawee bank's wrongful dishonor have no right of recovery against the bank.

Wrongful dishonor includes intentional refusal to pay a check, brought about by mistake. Where the dishonor occurs through mistake, the bank's liability is limited to "actual damages proved." The Code *rejects* the view that the wrongful dishonor of a check automatically defames the drawer by reflecting badly on the drawer's credit and therefore entitles the drawer to an award without proof that damage has occurred. The Code recognizes, however, that actual damages may include damages caused by an arrest or prosecution of the customer or, as Case 35.2 illustrates, other circumstances directly resulting from the wrongful dishonor.

CASE 35.2 Twin City Bank v. Isaacs • 672 S.W.2d 651 (Ark. 1984)

FACTS On Sunday, May 13, 1979, Kenneth and Vicki Isaacs discovered that their checkbook was missing. On Monday, May 14, they reported the loss to Twin City Bank (Bank), with which they had a checking account. Later they learned that two forged checks totaling $2,050 had been written on their account and honored by Bank on May 11 and 12. Bank decided to freeze the Isaacs' account, which had contained approximately $2,500 before the forgeries occurred. A few valid checks cleared Monday morning before the hold order was issued, leaving a balance of about $2,000. After the freeze, Bank dishonored the Isaacs' checks. In mid-June 1979, the Isaacs sued Bank for wrongful dishonor of their checks and wrongful withholding of their funds.

Bank froze the account because Mr. Isaacs had been convicted of burglary and Bank suspected that the Isaacs were somehow involved in forging the checks. The forger was charged and convicted soon after the forgeries occurred. On May

**CASE 35.2
Continued**

30, 1979, the police told Bank there was nothing to connect the Isaacs with the person arrested. Two weeks later the police notified Bank a second time that they could not connect the Isaacs to the forgeries. Nevertheless, Bank continued the freeze, denying the Isaacs their funds for some 4 years. At trial, the jury awarded the Isaacs $18,500 in compensatory damages and $45,000 in punitive damages. The trial court denied Bank's motion for a new trial, and Bank appealed.

OPINION

STEELE HAYS, J. . . . [B]ank maintains there was insufficient evidence to support the $18,500 award for mental anguish . . . [and] loss of credit and loss of the bargain on a house, [and] that the award of punitive damages should not have been given at all, as there was not only insufficient proof of actual damages but insufficient evidence of malice or intent to oppress on the part of the bank. The bank does not challenge the sufficiency of the evidence of its wrongful dishonor, but contends only that there was no evidence to support an award of damages. These arguments cannot be sustained. . . .

[T]here can be no serious question as to certain losses: the $2,000 wrongfully withheld by the bank for four years, and the value of two vehicles repossessed because the Isaacs did not have access to their funds, resulting in a loss of approximately $2,200. Additionally, after the account was frozen the bank continued to [impose] a service charge and overdraft fees on checks written before the forgeries but presented after the account was frozen. The bank does not refute these damages but argues [that] there is no showing of any financial deprivation from loss of credit or loss of the bargain on a house the Isaacs wanted to buy, and insufficient proof of mental anguish. We find, however, that . . . there was sufficient evidence to sustain damages for mental suffering, loss of credit, and sufficient demonstration of some loss attributable to the inability to pursue the purchase of a home. . . . In general, the type of mental anguish suffered under § 4-402 does not need to rise to the higher standard of injury for intentional infliction of emotional distress. Wrongful dishonors tend to produce intangible injuries similar to those involved in defamation actions. . . .

Decisions upholding recovery for mental suffering under the code have found injury resulting from circumstances comparable to this case. In Northshore Bank v. Palmer . . . , for example, a $275 forged check was paid from Palmer's account. After the bank knew or should have known the check was forged, it charged Palmer with the $275 check and later wrongfully dishonored other checks. Part of the actual damages awarded was attributed to mental suffering for the "embarrassment and humiliation Palmer suffered from having been turned down for credit for the first time in his life." . . . And in Farmers & Merchants State Bank of Krum v. Ferguson . . . , the plaintiff's account in the amount of $7,000 was frozen for apparently one month for reasons not stated. The plaintiff was awarded $25,000 for mental anguish, $3,000 for loss of credit based on a denial of a loan, $5,000 for loss of time spent making explanations to creditors, and $1,500 for loss of use of his money. The court justified the mental suffering award because the dishonor was found to be with malice—the bank had failed to notify Ferguson that the account was frozen, some checks were honored while others were not, and the bank continued to withdraw loan payments due it during the entire time.

**CASE 35.2
Continued**

In this case, prior to the forgery incident the Isaacs' credit reputation with Twin City Bank was described by the bank as "impeccable" and the freezing of their funds had a traumatic effect on their lives. They obviously lost their credit standing with Twin City, and were unable to secure credit commercially at other institutions because of their status at Twin City. The Isaacs had to borrow from friends and family, and were left in a precarious position financially. They did not have the use of their $2,000 for four years. The allegation relative to the loss of a house resulted from the dishonor of an earnest money check for a home they were planning to buy, ending prospects for the purchase at that time. Though there may have been insufficient proof of loss of the bargain on the house, as the bank argues, nevertheless this evidence was admissible as an element of mental suffering. . . . There was also testimony that the financial strain contributed to marital difficulties leading at one point to the filing of a divorce suit. . . . Finally, the Isaacs lost equities in two vehicles repossessed as a result of the withholding of their funds. One of these, a new van, was repossessed by Twin City in June, 1979, before a five day grace period for a current installment had expired.

. . . We recognize that our holding today presents some conflict with pre-code law by allowing recovery without exactness of proof as to damages. [However, § 4-402], although similar to its predecessor, has additional language which impliedly recognizes mental suffering and other intangible injuries . . . as recoverable under this statute. . . .

[Bank objected to the award of punitive damages. We] address only the question of the excessiveness of the verdict. . . . In Holmes v. Hollingsworth . . . we noted the elements that may be considered in assessing the amount of punitive damages, recognizing that the deterrent effect has some correlation to the financial condition of the party against whom punitive damages are allowed. In view of the circumstances in their entirety presented by this case, we cannot say the amount awarded was grossly excessive or prompted by passion or prejudice. . . .

JUDGMENT Affirmed.

Stop-Payment Order

As a part of the contract of deposit, a drawer has a right to stop payment of a check by issuing a **stop order**—an instruction to the drawee not to pay the check [4-403]. A stop order protects drawers in some situations but not in others.

Customer's Right to Stop Payment. Most states permit oral stop orders. In those states, an oral order is binding on the bank for 14 calendar days (1 day in the District of Columbia). To be binding for a longer time, the order must be confirmed in writing within the 14-day period [4-403]. A written stop order is effective for 6 months and can be renewed by the customer. In some states (Arizona, California, Florida, Texas, and Utah), a stop order must be in writing to be enforceable. In all states, to bind the bank, a stop order must be received in time to give the bank a reasonable opportunity to act on it before the bank certifies or pays the check.

After a bank has certified a check, the *drawer can no longer stop payment*. A certification is the bank's own engagement (promise) to pay, and the bank is not required to impair its own credit by refusing payment for the convenience of the drawer [3-403, comment 5]. Neither, in most states, may a bank stop payment of its own cashier's check. Certified checks and cashier's checks are readily accepted as substitutes for money because banks rather than individuals stand behind them. To allow drawers to stop payment on such checks would undermine public confidence in them and thus would impair their utility.

Bank's Liability for Paying a Stopped Check.
Suppose a bank pays a check contrary to a timely stop order and charges the drawer's account. Then the drawer demands that the bank recredit the account for the amount of the check. Must the bank do so?

Often, the answer is yes. A drawer's personal defense is good against anyone who is not a holder in due course or an assignee of one. You issue a check to Lowlife Carpets, which poorly installs defective carpet in your house. If, despite your timely stop order and personal defense of poor workmanship, your bank pays Lowlife and charges your account, the bank must recredit your account. Likewise, if you had a real defense such as a forged signature, and the bank paid a holder in due course despite your stop order, you would be entitled to a recredit.

However, if there is no legitimate basis for a stop order or if the drawer suffered no loss, the drawee is *not* required to recredit the drawer's account. Despite Joe's timely stop order, his bank pays TV Sales the amount of a check that Joe issued to it for a television set that works perfectly. Because Joe had no valid defense to payment, the bank need not recredit Joe's account. Even if Joe had a valid personal defense such as fraud in the inducement and the bank paid a holder in due course despite Joe's stop order, the result would be the same. Since a holder in due course could collect from Joe despite his personal defense, the bank's ignoring Joe's stop order caused him no loss, and the bank need not recredit his account.

Bank's Right to Retrieve an Improper Payment.
What if the drawee ignores a timely stop order and *is* required to recredit the customer's account? May the drawee retrieve the mistaken payment from the person who received it? Yes. The UCC confers upon the drawee bank several legal statuses that enable it to recover mistaken payments in a variety of situations. For example, where payee Lowlife Carpets receives payment despite your stop order and defense of poor workmanship, and the bank has to recredit your account, the bank "inherits" (is **subrogated** to) your right to sue the payee for breach of the underlying transaction. Thus, the bank can retrieve from the payee the amount the bank improperly paid.

Customer's Duty to Report Unauthorized Signature or Alteration

A bank that pays a forged or altered item usually must recredit the customer's account for the amount of an improper charge and to absorb the loss or collect the amount from someone else. However, the bank's liability depends in part on whether the customer gave timely notice of unauthorized signatures or alterations.

Banks generally furnish their checking account customers with monthly statements of account and supporting items such as canceled checks. A customer is required to examine them promptly and carefully, and to notify the bank promptly of any unauthorized signature or alteration [4-406(1)]. If the bank suffers loss from the customer's failure to inspect or give prompt notice, *and the bank itself has used ordinary care in paying the challenged items*, the customer may not assert against the bank the customer's own unauthorized signature or any alteration [4-406(2)]. The bank would suffer loss where, for example, the customer's failure to give prompt notice enabled a forger to "skip town" and avoid payment, or prevented the bank from suing the forger until he or she became insolvent.

If the customer can prove that the bank itself was negligent in not discovering an unauthorized signature or an alteration, the bank must recredit the customer's account for the amount of the unauthorized payment *even though* the customer was slow or negligent [4-406(3)].

The bank's liability for improper payments, and even for its own negligence, is subject to strict time limits. The customer must report his or her own unauthorized signature or any alteration within 1 year (60 days in the state of Washington) from the time the customer's state-

> **BOX 35.4**
>
> ### Revised Article 4
>
> The 1990 amendments *allocate* loss between customer and bank where both are negligent, instead of placing it solely on the negligent bank as before. The amount of loss that each must bear depends on how negligent each was. Revised 3-406, 4-406. ∎

ment is available to the customer. The customer must report an unauthorized indorsement within 3 years (1 year in California and Ohio) [4-406(4)]. Note that the times just mentioned are outer limits on the bank's liability for an improper charge. In reality, unless the bank was negligent, the customer has only a reasonable time to discover alterations and unauthorized signatures—not necessarily the full 1 or 3 years just discussed [4-406, comment 5].

Where a series of checks containing unauthorized signatures or alterations made by the same wrongdoer is paid by a nonnegligent bank and charged to the customer's account over a period of time, the customer has less time than usual to detect and report the wrongdoing. Where the same wrongdoer makes a series of forgeries or alterations, the customer has a reasonable time not exceeding 14 calendar days[4] to report the wrongdoing [4-406(2)(b)]. If the reasonable time (up to 14 days) expires, and if the bank pays a forged or altered item before receiving notice of earlier wrongdoing, the bank is not liable for the improper payments that occurred between the expiration of the reasonable time and the time that the bank received notice of the earlier wrongdoing.

Suppose, for example, that on the twenty-fifth of each month Carl's employee Amy skillfully forges Carl's signature to an extra monthly paycheck for 5 months in a row: May, June, July, August, and September. The bank pays all five checks in good faith, without negligence; and in late September Amy disappears. On June 1, Carl received his bank statement and canceled checks for the month of May. They reveal the first forgery. The statements and canceled checks for the following months reveal the other forgeries. However, Carl waits until December 1 before inspecting any of the records. Then, on December 1 Carl discovers all five forgeries, reports them to the bank immediately, and demands that the bank recredit his account for the amount of all five checks. What are the rights of Carl and the bank?

1 As to the first check, Carl has a reasonable time to discover the forgery of his signature—up to the outer limit of 1 year. Whether Carl's waiting 6 months to check for forgeries was reasonable is a question for a jury. If Carl's inspection and notice to the bank were "prompt," the bank must recredit Carl's account for the amount of the first check.

2 As to the other four checks, Carl is not entitled to a recredit. Because the five forgeries were made by the same wrongdoer (Amy), Carl is subject to the 14-day limit. Since he did not discover and report the first forgery within 14 calendar days after receiving the May statement, and since he did not give the bank notice of the first forgery before the bank paid Amy the amounts of the other forged checks, Carl must absorb the loss or pursue Amy for the amount of the last four checks.

Suppose now that Carl notified the bank of the first (the May) forgery on August 26, immediately after the fourth forgery, but the bank paid the fifth forged check anyway. If Carl's August 26 notice was prompt as to the May forgery, the bank must recredit his account for the May check, is not required to recredit the account for the next three checks (because Carl violated the 14-day rule), but must recredit the account for the fifth check because Carl gave notice of the earlier wrongdoing before the bank paid the fifth check, and did so in time for the bank to act on it.

If a customer promptly discovers and reports a check on which the amount has been raised by a wrongdoer and paid in good faith by the bank, the customer is entitled to, at most, a *partial* recredit. The bank may charge the customer's account according to the original tenor

---

[4] 30 days under the 1990 amendments.

of the altered item [4-401(2)(a)]. And, where the customer has signed and issued an *incomplete* item, the bank may charge the account according to the tenor of the item *as completed*, unless the bank has notice at the time of payment that the completion was improper [4-401(2)(b)]. Moreover, a bank acting carefully and in good faith may charge a customer's account for the whole amount of an altered item if the customer's own negligence substantially contributed to the alteration [3-406]. The customer's leaving open spaces on the face of the check so that alteration is easy is one example of such negligence.

Case 35.3 discusses whether a drawee bank observed reasonable commercial standards in paying forged checks by means of a computer without reviewing signatures individually.

CASE 35.3   **Medford Irrigation District v. Western Bank** • 676 P.2d 329 (Or. 1984)

FACTS   The bookkeeper for Medford Irrigation District (District) forged the name of its manager on several checks drawn on its account with defendant Western Bank. (Apparently the bookkeeper made the checks payable to herself or to a fictitious payee, forged the name of the manager as drawer, and cashed them at various places by providing the indorsement required by the particular forged check.) Western Bank, the drawee, paid the checks and debited District's account. District brought suit to recover the face value of the checks. From a summary judgment for District, Western appealed.

OPINION   RICHARDSON, P.J. . . . Ordinarily the law places the risk of loss from forgeries on the bank. Any unauthorized signature is generally "wholly inoperative as that of the person whose name is signed." UCC 3-404. Because a forged signature is wholly inoperative, a forged check is not "properly payable," UCC 4-401, and a bank cannot debit the depositor's account. If, however, the depositor's negligence substantially contributes to the forgery, the depositor is precluded from asserting the improper payment against a bank which pays the check in good faith and in accordance with reasonable commercial standards of the banking industry. UCC 3-406. Also, if the depositor fails to exercise reasonable care in examining its bank statement and promptly reporting any unauthorized debits to the bank, the depositor is precluded from asserting the unauthorized payment unless it establishes lack of ordinary care on the part of the bank in paying the check. UCC 4-406.

[Plaintiff District conceded for the purposes of the summary judgment motion that it was negligent in not supervising the bookkeeper and in not auditing the accounts and reviewing the bank statements, and that its negligence substantially contributed to the forgeries. However, District contended that Western did not follow reasonable commercial banking standards and failed to exercise ordinary care in paying the forged checks.]

Western . . . argues that there is a genuine issue of material fact as to whether it exercised ordinary care and whether its procedures comported with reasonable commercial banking standards. Western utilizes a computer check payment system. Checks for a face amount under $5,000 are paid without human intervention or "sight review" of the signatures. Checks are received for payment at Western's data processing center in Portland, and, unless there is a "hold" or a

**CASE 35.3
Continued**

"stop payment" order for a check, it is paid automatically by computer. The canceled checks are ultimately forwarded to the customers along with the bank statement. The computer is programmed to "kick out" checks with a face amount of $5,000 or more. Absent specific instructions from a customer, only checks of $5,000 or more are individually reviewed for authorized signatures or alterations.

Western . . . concluded that the cost of reviewing checks for unauthorized signatures greatly exceeded the benefits. . . . [A] small number of forgeries was detected by individual review of checks, while the cost of that review was approximately $200,000 per year. Western contends that the procedure it [uses conforms] with methods used by most banks of its size throughout the United States. It argues that it is a fact question whether its procedures comport with reasonable commercial standards and whether it exercised ordinary care. . . .

The reasonableness of commercial banking standards must be analyzed in the context of a bank's duty in relation to the depositor's account. Although a procedure may be common throughout the banking industry, it is not, by that fact alone, a reasonable procedure. Implied in the relationship between a bank and its checking account depositors is a contractual undertaking on the part of the bank that it will . . . discharge its obligation [only] on an authorized signature. Section 3-404 specifies that an unauthorized signature is wholly inoperative, and a check with an unauthorized signature is not properly payable by the bank. UCC 4-401. The responsibility of the bank is to use ordinary care in paying only checks with authorized signatures. Thus, the procedure utilized must reasonably meet that responsibility to be [consistent with] due care or reasonable commercial banking standards in the context of UCC 3-406 or 4-406.

The [UCC] does not set out particular procedures or standards that the banking industry must follow, or attempt to define what ordinary care or reasonable commercial standards are[, because, according to a comment to Section 4-103, due to the technical complexity of the field of bank collections, "it would be unwise to freeze present methods of operation by mandatory statutory rules"]. We do not hold that a bank must adopt a particular procedure, such as "sight review," in order to comply with the statutory mandate. We do hold that the procedure used must reasonably relate to the detection of unauthorized signatures in order to be considered an exercise of ordinary care or reasonable commercial banking standards. Western's approach is automatically to pay all checks under $5,000 without any procedure to detect unauthorized signatures on those items. While that approach, based on considerations of cost and efficiency, may be a prudent business decision and followed by most banks, it does not meet the bank's responsibility under the statutes. . . . We hold as a matter of law that the bank failed to exercise ordinary care and that the procedures adopted are not reasonable commercial practices. . . .

JUDGMENT

[B]ecause Western failed to exercise ordinary care or to follow reasonable commercial banking practices, it is foreclosed from asserting plaintiff's negligence and is liable for . . . the face amount of the forged checks. . . . The court did not err in granting summary judgment for plaintiff. . . . Affirmed.

Final Payment Rule

A drawee bank is not supposed to pay a check containing a forged signature, but if it *does* pay, it normally may not charge the customer's account. Instead, the bank must collect the amount of the mistaken payment from someone else or absorb the loss. From whom may the bank collect? The answer depends in part on whose signature was forged.

Forgery of Drawer's Signature. Where the *drawer's* signature was forged, the bank may not retrieve its payment from a "holder in due course," since the Code makes payment to such a person **final** [3-418].[5] X forges Dan Drawer's signature to a check made out to X; X indorses the check to Hal Holder (a holder in due course); and the drawee by mistake makes a "final" payment to Holder (i.e., does not make merely a provisional credit). Despite X's forging Drawer's signature, the drawee bank cannot recover from Holder the money paid by mistake *unless Holder breached a presentment warranty.* This he did not do, since a holder in due course does not warrant the authenticity of the drawer's own signature. Neither did Holder breach the presentment warranty of title, since that warranty pertains only to forged indorsements. However, the bank may collect the amount from X. Since forger X knows that Drawer's signature is unauthorized, X has therefore breached a presentment warranty.

Forgery of Payee's Signature. Drawer issues a check to the order of Payee, X steals the check from Payee and forges Payee's indorsement, and X sells the check to Watkins, who presents it to and receives payment from the drawee bank. The bank may recover the amount from either X or Watkins. X lacks title and therefore has breached the presentment warranty of title. Because the indorsement was forged, Watkins, too,

---

[5] The expression "holder in due course" used in § 3-418 may be misleading, since the forged signature often involved is inconsistent with holder status. The 1990 revision of § 3-418 describes the protected person more accurately as "a person who took the instrument in good faith and for value."

> **BOX 35.5**
>
> **Revised Article 3**
>
> **Computerized Check Sorting— Should There Be a Change in the Law?**
>
> Given the cost-effectiveness of computerized check sorting, will negligent depositors continue to enjoy the amount of protection given in *Medford* when their banks pay forged checks without inspecting them? There are strong indications that this protection is eroding, largely through a redefinition of what constitutes negligence by drawee banks. *Wilder Binding Co. v. Oak Park Trust and Savings Bank* (Ill. App. 1988, one judge dissenting) follows *Medford* in holding the bank negligent as a matter of law for paying forged checks without individually inspecting them for forgeries. In contrast, the court in *Rhode Island Hospital Trust National Bank v. Zapata Corp.* (1st Cir. 1988) held that failure to give each check individual scrutiny does not necessarily constitute bank negligence, given processing cost savings and a random inspection of about 1 percent of the otherwise uninspected checks. The dissenting judge in *Wilder* and the court in *Rhode Island* agree, in essence, that the question of bank negligence should be decided on a case-by-case basis, and that a failure to inspect each check should not, in itself, automatically constitute negligence.
>
> In defining "ordinary care," a 1990 amendment of Article 3 says, "In the case of a bank that takes an instrument for processing . . . by automated means, reasonable commercial standards do not require the bank to examine the instrument if the failure to examine does not violate the bank's prescribed procedures and the bank's procedures do not vary unreasonably from general banking usage. . . ." Revised 3-103(a)(7).
>
> Suppose computerized check sorting without individual inspection of checks for forgeries becomes "general banking usage." Should the practice be approved as nonnegligent? What factors should the courts consider? ■

lacks title and has breached the presentment warranty of title.

Effect of Customer's Death or Incompetence

A bank acts as the agent of its customer (the principal) in two ways: (1) as a collecting agent where the customer has deposited an item for collection and (2) as a paying agent when honoring checks drawn by the customer.

Ordinarily, a principal's death or the adjudication of his or her incompetency immediately terminates the agency relationship and, consequently, the authority of the agent to act for the principal, even before the agent learns of the terminating event. In banking, however, this rule would be unworkable. Given the tremendous number of items handled, banks cannot verify the continued life and competency of their customers. Accordingly, the UCC provides that neither the death nor the incompetency of a customer revokes a bank's authority to pay or collect an item until the bank knows of the death or adjudication of incompetence and has reasonable opportunity to act on it [4-405].

Furthermore, even if a bank knows of its customer's death, the bank may for 10 days after the date of death pay or certify checks drawn on or before that date. There is one *exception* to this rule: The bank may *not* pay or certify a check within the 10 days if it was ordered to stop payment by a person claiming an interest in the account, such as the executor of the decedent's estate or a person with whom the decedent had a joint account.

Bank's Liability for Conversion

Conversion is the act of handling or using someone else's property in a manner inconsistent with that person's ownership. A bank converts a negotiable instrument, and becomes liable to the wronged person for the face amount, in the following ways [3-419]:

1 Refusing, on demand by the rightful owner (usually a holder), to return a draft (or check) presented for acceptance
2 Refusing, on demand by the rightful owner, to pay or to return to the owner an item presented for payment
3 Paying an instrument on the basis of a forged indorsement

Dee issues a check to the order of Paul. Tom steals the check, skillfully forges Paul's indorsement, and cashes the check at Dee's bank. Tom is both a thief and a converter. As a converter, Tom is liable to Paul for the amount of the check. Dee's *bank* is also a converter because it paid Tom on the basis of the forged indorsement and thereby acted in a manner inconsistent with Paul's ownership.

ELECTRONIC FUNDS TRANSFERS

Since the 1970s, computers have revolutionized consumer and commercial banking. No longer do banks process the billions of paper checks and deposit transactions laboriously by hand. Nor are customers required to do all their banking in person and only during the "banker's hours" of 9:00 to 3:00. Today, most banks use computerized electronic funds transfer (EFT) systems in a variety of consumer and commercial applications.

A federal law, the Electronic Fund Transfers Act (EFTA),[6] governs electronic funds transfers involving consumer accounts—those established primarily for personal, household, or family purposes. It does *not* apply to funds transfers accomplished by paper checks and other traditional means. Article 4A of the Uniform Commercial Code (state law) governs commercial EFT transactions.[7] If the EFTA applies to any part of a transaction, it is excluded from Article 4A—that is, it is treated as a consumer transaction.

Consumer EFT Applications

Most familiar to bank customers are the nation's 87,000 automated teller machines (ATMs) used

[6]15 U.S.C.A., Secs. 1693a–1693r (1978).

[7]As of March 1993, Article 4A has been adopted in forty-two states and the District of Columbia.

for 24-hour-a-day, do-it-yourself banking. Fewer in number but growing in popularity are the point-of-sale terminals and the pay-by-phone bill-paying systems used in many parts of the country.

Automated teller machines, commonly located at banks, are operated by the customer's electronically encoded "debit card." When activated by the card and the **personal identification number** (PIN) that must be used for each transaction, the machine will dispense specified amounts of money and will debit (charge) the customer's account for the amount withdrawn. The customer can also make deposits at the ATM and transfer funds between savings and checking accounts. Although teller machines accept deposits at any time, the actual crediting of the customer's account is done only after bank personnel have verified amounts, reviewed indorsements, and so on.

Point-of-sale (POS) terminals are found in supermarkets and other businesses. They are similar in operation to automatic teller machines and accept the debit cards that customers use at their banks—ATM cards encoded for use with national or regional EFT networks such as CIRRUS, Plus, Magicline, and Interlink. To pay for a purchase, the customer simply hands the card to the store cashier and taps the PIN into a keypad at the counter. Customers thus debit their bank accounts and credit those of the merchants instantly.

Since many different banks belong to the same network, a variety of ATM cards work in the same POS terminal. Some businesses limit POS terminal payments to the amount of purchase. Others permit customers to receive as much as $200 in "change," thus allowing the POS terminal to serve as an ATM and saving the customer a trip to the bank.

Pay-by-phone bill-paying **systems** require the bank customer to authorize, in advance, a list of payees and amounts to be paid. Then the customer need only pick up a telephone, enter the proper identification data, and give payment instructions to the bank's computer. This kind of bill-paying system operates without the use of a debit card.

Most payments carried out by an **automated clearinghouse (ACH)** are consumer transactions covered by the EFTA—for example, the payments involved in the clearing of checks issued and received by consumers. ACHs are also used to facilitate **direct deposits** into consumers' accounts. Instead of sending thousands or millions of paper paychecks to employees, for example, large employers such as state governments send a magnetic tape containing payments information to an ACH. The ACH sorts the information according to the financial institutions in which the employees have accounts and, by electronic signals between computers, credits employee accounts, if the employee has previously authorized the direct deposit. ACHs are now widely used for such recurring payments as private and governmental payrolls, social security payments, mortgage payments, and insurance premiums.

As in the use of paper checks, there are many opportunities for an unauthorized person to make improper use of a customer's debit card or to order improper payments by phone. And banks sometimes make errors in crediting or debiting customers' accounts.

Under the EFTA, if a debit card is lost or stolen and used without the customer's permission, the customer is liable to the bank for a maximum of $50 worth of unauthorized use. The customer's loss is limited to $50 *only if* the customer gives the bank notice of the theft or loss within 2 business days after learning of it. The customer's liability is a maximum of $500 if the 2-day notice requirement is not met; if the customer does not give notice within 60 days after receiving his or her statement of account, the customer's liability is unlimited. In extenuating circumstances such as the customer's extended travel or hospitalization, the 2-day and the 60-day periods are increased to a reasonable time under the circumstances.

The customer must report the bank's errors in EFT record keeping to the bank within 60 days after receiving a statement of account. Then the bank has 10 days to investigate and correct them, or 45 days if within the 10 days the bank elects to provisionally recredit the customer's account. Upon determining that an error occurred, the bank has up to 1 business day to correct it. If the bank determines that an error did not occur, the bank must deliver or mail its findings to the customer within 3 business days after concluding the investigation, and must promptly document its findings upon the customer's request.

Commercial EFT Applications—Interbank Transfers and Article 4A

The largest of all banking transactions is the **wholesale wire transfer** between banks or other business or financial institutions, involving huge sums per transaction and, collectively, over a trillion dollars per day. FEDWIRE, the Federal Reserve System's wire transfer network, has a computerized switching center that enables its thousands of member banks to transfer funds between and within banks almost instantly. CHIPS, the Clearing House Interbank Payments System, serves the New York area. Other networks serve the international banking community.

Until recently, commercial wire transfer systems were governed largely by their own rules, Federal Reserve rules, and the common law of contracts and torts. There were gaps in coverage, and resulting uncertainty. Today, Article 4A of the UCC provides a comprehensive body of law defining the rights and obligations arising from wire transfers and nonconsumer ACH transactions.

Article 4A applies only to *commercial* transfers of funds—especially to wholesale wire (electronic) transfers between businesses such as banks, but also to nonelectronic transfers such as those handled by mail. Hence, Article 4A uses the broader term **funds transfer.** Article 4A does not apply to paper-based checks or credit cards, nor to electronically based consumer payments. Moreover, Article 4A does not apply to all commercial funds transfers. It applies only to so-called **credit transfers,** those in which the instruction to pay is given by the person making payment. Article 4A excludes *debit* transfers, those in which the instruction to pay is given by the person receiving payment.

A typical Article 4A transaction works this way: To pay a debt owed to Acme Corp., Debtor instructs Debtor's bank by means of a **payment order** to credit a sum of money to Acme's account in another bank. Debtor's bank carries out **(executes)** the instruction by issuing its own payment order to Acme's bank, thus instructing it to credit Acme's account with the amount Debtor requested. Debtor and Debtor's bank are the **senders** of their respective payment orders. Debtor's bank and Acme's bank are the respective **receiving banks.** Acme is the **beneficiary** of Debtor's order. Debtor is the **originator** of the funds transfer, Debtor's bank is the **originator's bank,** and Acme's bank is the **beneficiary's bank.** In more complex transactions, there may be one or more **intermediary banks.**

A receiving bank has no liability under a payment order until it **accepts** it. Debtor's bank accepts Debtor's payment order by sending the bank's own payment order instructing Acme's bank to credit Acme's account. Acme's bank, in turn, accepts Debtor's bank's payment order by paying Acme, notifying Acme of the receipt of the payment order, or receiving payment from the sending bank. A bank that executes a payment order is entitled to receive payment from the sender and may debit an authorized account of the sender.

SUMMARY

Since a check does not by itself transfer funds at the time of issue, the drawee is not liable to the payee or holder for refusing to pay it, but the drawee may be liable to the drawer for refusing to pay. A bank is not required to certify a check, but a certification at the request of the payee or a holder discharges the drawer and any prior indorsers.

A bank is the debtor of the customer as to money on deposit. But the bank is the agent of the customer for purposes of collecting items and paying checks drawn by the customer. Many difficulties confront banks as they honor checks of their customers. These difficulties usually involve the payment of overdrafts, altered or forged checks, checks that were incomplete when issued, stale checks, and postdated checks. A bank is liable to the customer for damages caused by a wrongful dishonor, but in many situations a bank may charge the customer's account even though there was a valid stop-payment order. Where a bank has no right to charge the customer's account, the bank may have a right of subrogation against the payee or a holder.

The bank may not charge the customer's account where there is an alteration or an unauthorized signature, but the customer must inspect bank statements and promptly notify the bank of any improper charges if the bank is to be held liable. A bank can be liable for the tort of conversion in a variety of ways.

Where consumer electronic funds transfer systems are in use, bank customers are liable in varying degrees for unauthorized use of lost or stolen debit cards. Banks are fully liable for their own EFT errors, however, if properly notified of them. Commercial funds transfers are governed by Article 4A of the UCC.

REVIEW QUESTIONS

1. What is the difference in legal effect between certification of a check at the request of the *holder* and certification at the request of the *drawer*?

2. (a) When and why is the relationship between a bank and its checking account customer that of principal and agent? **(b)** What is the significance in the collection process of a payor bank's midnight deadline? **(c)** How does a provisional credit become final? With what legal effect?

3. Under what circumstances may a bank that has paid a raised check charge the customer's account with the altered amount?

4. Explain why a bank may be liable to its customer for paying a postdated check before the specified date.

5. (a) Explain and give an example of a wrongful dishonor. **(b)** How are damages measured when a check is dishonored by mistake?

6. (a) How may a stop-payment order be made? **(b)** When must the order be received to be effective?

7. Explain in what way the following statement is inaccurate. "A bank by agreement with its depositor may absolve itself from liability for paying a check contrary to a stop order."

8. Suppose that a bank has paid a check over a stop order and must recredit the drawer's account. Illustrate how the bank may be subrogated to the rights of the drawer.

9. Give examples of situations where a payor bank may properly charge its customer's account for a check containing an unauthorized signature.

10. (a) Where a customer's EFT debit card was lost or stolen and used without authorization, what is the customer's liability to the bank? **(b)** Explain how a typical commercial funds transfer works.

CASE PROBLEMS

1. Dixon issued a check for $1,868.15 to Lloyd's Chevrolet-Olds. Later that day, Dixon called First State Bank, the drawee, to stop payment on the check. He gave Hargis, Bank's employee, the correct account number, check number, date, and payee of the check, but misstated the amount of the check as $1,828.73. When Dixon received his bank statement, he discovered that Bank had paid the check despite the stop order. Upon Bank's refusal to recredit his account, Dixon sued Bank for the amount of the check. At trial, Hargis testified that Bank's stop-payment requests were computerized, and Bank had to have the exact amount of a check in order to stop payment. From a judgment for Dixon, Bank appealed. Should the judgment be affirmed?

2. Giordano agreed to purchase two trucks for use in his business. National Newark & Essex Bank lent Giordano $9,500 for the purchase and drew a cashier's check on itself payable to the order of Fiero, the seller. Shortly after delivering the check to Fiero, Giordano discovered that the trucks were defective and asked Bank to stop payment on the check. Bank refused to do so. When Giordano later refused to repay the loan, Bank sued him for the amount.

Whether Giordano should be held liable depended on whether Bank had a duty to stop payment on the check. Was Bank required to stop payment?

3. USA Construction Co. drew a check for over $67,000 on its account with Palmetto Federal Savings Bank, payable to Specialty Flooring Co. On Friday, March 6, 1987, Specialty deposited the check in its own account with Palmetto. Before the bank opened on Monday, March 9, USA informed Specialty that Specialty's work was unacceptable and that USA was stopping payment on the check. That same morning, John Wingo, Specialty's owner, went to Palmetto and requested a cashier's check for $70,000. Palmetto issued instead a bank check (bank draft) for $70,000, drawn on its account with Citibank. Wingo paid for the bank check with his own check written on Specialty's account with Palmetto. Later that day, USA stopped payment on the $67,000 check. A few days later, upon learning of the stopped payment, Palmetto revoked the provisional credit it had given to Specialty for USA's check and charged back the $67,000. And, since Specialty's account now lacked sufficient funds to cover the $70,000 check that Specialty had given for Palmetto's bank check, Palmetto also stopped payment on its bank check. Specialty sued Palmetto, alleging that Palmetto had no right to stop payment of the bank check, and that Palmetto had breached its contract as drawer of the bank check. Should Specialty prevail?

4. Atlantic Telec, Inc., made out a check to Genesis as payee, in payment for "soil inoculant" that Atlantic intended to resell to farm operators. Alleging that Genesis had breached its contract with Atlantic, Atlantic ordered Bank to stop payment of the check. Genesis presented the check to Bank for payment. Despite the stop order, Bank paid the check; and Atlantic sued Bank for $13,000, the amount of the check. From a judgment for Atlantic, Bank appealed. Bank also appealed the trial court's dismissing Bank's third-party complaint against Genesis, which Bank wished to pursue if found liable to Atlantic. Assume that Atlantic had a personal defense against Genesis. **(a)** Was Bank liable to Atlantic? **(b)** If so, did Bank have a cause of action against Genesis?

5. Marlow crashed his car into the drive-in window facility of the Bank of Hartshorne, causing $1,200 damage to the facility. Marlow issued to Bank his check in payment for the damage. On May 30, Marlow died. On May 31, Cirar, Marlow's daughter, personally informed an official of Bank that her father had died. Although on notice of Marlow's death, Bank negotiated the check to the National Bank of McAlester on June 1, received the check back from the McAlester bank on June 3 for collection, and on June 4 paid the amount of the check to the McAlester bank, debiting Marlow's account. Alleging that Bank had made an improper payment from Marlow's account, Cirar, administratrix of Marlow's estate, sued the Bank of Hartshorne to recover the $1,200. Was the Marlow estate entitled to the $1,200?

ETHICS IN PRACTICE

Like the insurance industry, commercial paper is rife with temptation for people who would part others from their money. Practices that are obviously illegal, such as forgery and the fraudulent alteration of checks, have been discussed in the preceding chapters on commercial paper. The following problems focus more on ethical concerns than on the obviously illegal.

PROBLEMS IN ETHICS

1. Banks, finance companies, auto dealers, and other installment lenders sell credit-life and credit-health-and-accident insurance policies to borrowers to cover the amount of the loan should the borrower die or become disabled. Credit insurance is very profitable to companies that sell it. They typically pay out a small percentage of premiums in claims; yet credit insurance is priced many times higher than standard term insurance of the same face amount. Compared with the commissions that salespeople receive on other types of insurance, credit-insurance commissions are very high. Installment lenders receive commissions on credit insurance they sell. Some "pack" various credit-insurance policies into consumer-loan or installment-sales agreements, often without the customers' knowledge or consent. **(a)** Is it ethical for an installment lender to include credit-insurance charges without notifying the debtor? **(b)** Carsco advertises 4.9 percent financing on new cars, which is half to a third the rate charged by other new-car dealers: "Friday and Saturday only—instant financing." Unknown to customers who do not read the fine print in the ad, the low interest rate is contingent on the purchase of credit insurance. The credit insurance charges will add over $500 to the price of a $10,000 car, but the ad does not point this out and Carsco salespeople are instructed not to discuss the insurance charges unless asked. Is tying low interest rates to the sale of credit insurance in this manner ethical? If not, could "tying" somehow be made ethical?

2. Angela, a foreign student unfamiliar with U.S. banking law, has her checking account in a large American bank near campus. Angela's roommate steals Angela's checkbook from her desk, forges a check for $50, and cashes it at Angela's bank. Distressed by her roommate's dishonesty, Angela goes to the bank to close her account. Mary, Bank's employee, asks, "Why do you want to close your account? You just opened it." Explaining that her roommate forged Angela's name to a check and Bank cashed it, Angela replies, "I am from a very poor family. What else can I do?" Mary says, "Well, we can close your account as you ask and open a new one for you. Are you sure that's OK?" Angela says "Yes." Mary knows that Bank has a duty to recredit Angela's account for the $50, but she does not so inform Angela and Angela does not ask. **(a)** Has Mary committed a breach of ethics by not informing Angela of Bank's duty to recredit her account? **(b)** Has Bank itself acted unethically? What factors would bear on your answer?

3. Under UCC § 4-403, an oral order stopping payment of a check is binding on the drawee bank for 14 calendar days. Most states have adopted this rule, but five states require stop orders to be in writing to be enforceable. In those five states, therefore, a person who attempts to stop payment of a check by phone can be required to go to the bank to sign the stop order. In the meantime, the bank can legally honor a check, even if it knows that the customer wants the check dishonored. **(a)** What would cause a legislature to require stop orders to be in writing? **(b)** Does the law requiring a stop order to be written seem consistent with sound business ethics?

4. Under UCC § 4-103, a bank may not avoid liability for its own bad faith or for its negligence in the handling of its customers' accounts. Yet the signature cards and stop order forms of many banks contain clauses stating, in effect, "Bank shall not be liable for oversight or accident in making payments from this account." This clause, if enforceable, would protect a bank from the consequences of its own negligence. Assume that banks know that such clauses are not enforceable. **(a)** Why would a bank use a clause that it knows is not enforceable? **(b)** Is it ethical for banks to use such clauses?

PART EIGHT

Agency

CHAPTER 36
Nature of Agency Relationships

CHAPTER 37
Agency and Tort Liability

CHAPTER 38
Agents' and Principals' Duties to Each Other;
Termination of Agency

Ethics in Practice

CHAPTER 36

Nature of Agency Relationships

Before the industrial revolution, business was carried on largely by individual artisans in their homes and in small family-operated shops. As population and trade expanded, it became more complex to make and distribute goods. To keep up with demand, manufacturers and shopkeepers began to hire others to work for them. These helpers—or "servants," as they were called—performed whatever physical tasks were assigned to them, under the close personal supervision of the "master." Today the legal terms **master-servant** and **employer-employee** are used interchangeably. Over time, employers delegated a broader range of responsibilities to their employees—for example, by giving them authority to contract for raw materials, to sell finished products, and even to employ other workers. In these expanded roles, the employees became known as **agents,** and their employers were called **principals.**

An *agency is a consensual fiduciary relation in which one person, an agent, agrees to act on behalf of and under the control of another, who is called the principal*.[1] The required consent usually arises by contract between principal and agent—for example, a real estate agent's listing agreement to sell an office building. However, a contract is not essential to create an agency. You say to your sick neighbor, "Joe, let me do your grocery shopping," and he agrees. By mutual assent you have become his *purchasing agent,* even though you have no contract with him and will not be paid for your services.

Agency law pervades business and personal affairs. Whether you buy wholesale gems, machine tools, insurance, stock, real estate, or retail groceries, you commonly deal with agents authorized to make sales on behalf of their principals. Most people who work for others do so as agents or servants. Indeed, agency law is basic to daily business operations, especially so in negotiable instruments, real estate, partnerships, and corporations. Each partner acts as a *principal* in dealing with third parties on partnership business, but at the same time is acting as an *agent* for the partners who are not present. Even more significant are corporation employees, who constitute the largest number of agents in the United States. Because a corporation is a fictitious legal person, it can function only through employees who, as servants and agents, work on production lines, hire other workers, purchase supplies, and sell products. From the actions of the directors meeting in the boardroom to those

---

[1] *Restatement of the Law of Agency, (Second), Sec. 1(1)*. This authoritative summary of agency law is formulated by the American Law Institute.

of the janitor emptying the office wastebaskets, agency law governs the corporation's relationships.

Few areas in the entire field of law are fraught with so much danger for principals, who constantly face potential liability for contracts and torts of their agents. Principals' liability on contracts negotiated by their agents is based on the Roman **identity theory:** "He who acts through another acts for himself." This view that the principal and agent are virtually identical underlies another doctrine of agency law—*respondeat superior*—which says: "Let the principal respond in damages for the tortious acts of the agent within the scope of authority." Often called a **doctrine of vicarious liability,** *respondeat superior* holds that the principal who is personally without fault and innocent of wrongdoing nevertheless has liability because the agent's wrong is imputed to the principal. A company's purchasing agent might accidentally scald a supplier's representative with hot coffee. A salesclerk may argue with a customer and strike a physical blow. In each instance, the principal is vicariously liable for the agent's wrong.

This chapter discusses the general nature of the principal-agent relationship, some important agency law terminology, and the kinds of authority agents have when contracting on behalf of their principals. Chapter 37 looks at principals' liability for the torts of their agents. Chapter 38 deals with the obligations of principal and agent to each other, and with the termination of the agency relationship.

AGENCY RELATIONSHIPS

Agency law distinguishes three important relationships: (1) principal and agent, (2) employer and employee (also called master and servant), and (3) principal and independent contractor.

Principal and Agent

The principal-agent relation, defined at the beginning of this chapter, usually anticipates that the agent will represent the principal in contractual dealings with third parties. The principal may empower the agent to perform any activity in which the principal may legally engage, but for self-protection and to minimize liability to third parties, a principal may carefully define the scope of an agent's authority. It may be restricted to menial tasks not requiring skill or may be expanded to permit the agent to exercise a great deal of discretion, such as carrying on negotiations, entering into contracts, and buying and selling property on behalf of the principal. However, as we will see later, in many situations, agents who exceed their authority still have legal power to make their principals liable on contracts with third persons. Most problems discussed in this chapter involve contracts with third parties negotiated by an agent for, on behalf of, and in the place of the principal.

Employer and Employee

Although **employer-employee** is the preferred term today in law and business, many authorities still use the older **master-servant** expression. Section 2 of the American Law Institute's *Restatement (Second), Agency*, in defining the employer-employee relation, states:

(1) A master is a principal who employs an agent to perform service in his affairs and who controls or has the right to control the physical conduct of the other in the performance of his service.

(2) A servant is an agent employed by a master to perform service in his affairs whose physical conduct in the performance of the service is controlled or is subject to the right to control by the master.

The words "servant" and "physical" in the above definitions do not denote menial or manual service. Many servants, such as corporate officers or hospital interns, use much more brainpower than muscle. Rather, the terms denote that the master or employer has the right at all times to *control* the physical whereabouts and activities of the employee. Typical employees—whether they are bank tellers, salespeople, computer operators, or workers on a factory assembly line—must follow the employer's detailed instructions and explicit procedures. While under the direction and control of the employer (master), the employee (servant) may, but usually does not, represent the employer in dealings with third parties. In either case, the law of agency applies. Although the usual function of a servant is to perform noncontractual services, the servant's ability to subject the master to legal liability for torts (usually negligence) against third parties is prominent in litigation, and therefore is discussed separately in the next chapter. As a general rule, an employee must personally perform the work or service in question and cannot delegate those duties to another except in case of emergency when the principal cannot be reached.

Principal and Independent Contractor

An independent contractor is not an employee. Nor can the other party to the contract be the employer of the independent contractor, since there is no control over the independent contractor's physical conduct or performance of work. *Restatement (Second), Agency* § 2(3) defines an independent contractor as

... a person who contracts with another to do something for him but who is not controlled by the other nor subject to the other's right to control with respect to his physical conduct in the performance of the undertaking. He may or may not be an agent.

The statement that an independent contractor "may or may not be an agent" raises the question: When an agent, and when not an agent? There are two types of independent contractors: (1) professional agents (sometimes called nonservant agents or agent independent contractors and (2) nonagent independent contractors.

Independent Contractors as Professional Agents. Although most independent contractors are nonagents, others act in an agency capacity and are often referred to as professional agents. Examples abound:

- An attorney who represents clients in negotiations
- A certified public accountant who represents clients before the Internal Revenue Service
- An architect who agrees to represent the owner in arguments with the construction contractor
- A theatrical agent who agrees to place an actress in a drama or film
- A sports agent who undertakes to negotiate a football player's contract
- An auctioneer who agrees to sell a rare painting
- An employment agent who finds bilingual personnel for a multinational company
- An insurance broker who agrees to write a policy of auto insurance with a particular company
- A manufacturers' representative who agrees to sell a new factory's products in the Seattle area

All are examples of independent contractors who are also agents. They are agents because they agree to represent principals in dealings with third parties. Yet they are also independent contractors, not servants, because the principal *has no control over their physical conduct in the performance of their undertakings.* For example, if Paul engages Bob, a real estate broker, to find a buyer for his house, the broker is a **nonservant agent.** He is not an employee because Paul does not control Bob's activities during the day. Bob has listings with other property owners, and makes his own schedule of activities. He can choose to work on selling an office building and restaurant today, and may decide not to show Paul's home to prospective buyers until tomorrow. For convenience, this type of independent contractor is often called simply an "agent" rather than the more unwieldy term "nonservant agent," "agent independent contractor," or "professional agent." The relationships among these terms are shown graphically in Figure 36.1.

The distinction between servant and nonservant agent is significant in agency law. Although some servants contract on behalf of their masters—for example, corporate purchasing agents—contracting is not their usual work. In contrast, making contracts on behalf of principals *is* the main work of all the nonservant agents (professional agents) listed above.

Nonagent Independent Contractors. Most independent contractors are nonagents, and the

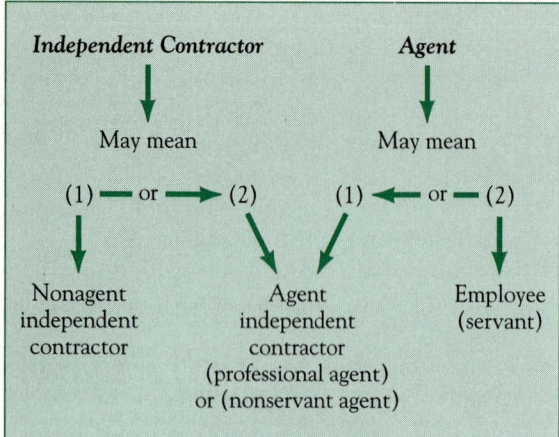

Figure 36.1 Meanings of "independent contractor" and "agent."

law of agency does not apply to them. Usually, they carry on a distinct occupation, at a separate place of business, with a separate business name and a number of other customers. They contract to produce a service or product according to specifications, but the other contracting party (called the principal in this discussion) has no control or authority to order exactly how the result will be produced—how the doctor will conduct the operation, or how the builder will physically build a house. Nonagent independent contractors do not represent or act for the principal in dealing with third parties. Unlike an employee, the contractor may delegate to other people any duties except those which require the exercise of personal judgment and discretion. For example, a building contractor may build a house alone, or may hire carpenters, plumbers, and subcontractors and delegate some of the work to them.

Independent Contractors Distinguished from Employees. The distinction between the employer-employee relation on the one hand and the principal–independent contractor relation on the other, is important for two reasons:

1 Major federal and state labor laws such as those regulating minimum wages, overtime pay, workers' compensation, social security, income tax withholding, workers' rights to organize labor unions, and age and sex discrimination (discussed in Chapter 48) generally apply only to the employer-employee relation, *not* to the principal–independent contractor relation.

2 *Respondeat superior* (which holds principals liable for torts of their agents while acting within the scope of authority) applies only to the principal-agent (including the employer-employee) relation, *not* to the principal–independent contractor relation.[2]

For example, if Tim retains Ned, a paint contractor, to paint his office building, and Ned carelessly tips a can of paint onto Ms. Rich's $20,000 chinchilla coat, Ned is liable for his negligence. However, *respondeat superior* does *not* apply to Tim because he is *not* a principal-employer and Ned is not his agent-employee: Ned is an independent contractor. (Vicarious liability of a principal for the torts of the agent under *respondeat superior* is discussed in detail in Chapter 37.)

Courts weigh all the factors listed in Table 36.1 in deciding whether a person is an employee or independent contractor. However, the employer's *control*, or ultimate *right to control*, the employee's activities is generally more important than the other factors in establishing an employer-employee relation. Sometimes the parties recite in a written agreement: "The relation intended to be created herein is that of two independent contractors, not principal-agent or employer-employee." Although such disclaimers are given some weight, they are not controlling if the other factors in the relationship clearly show a principal-agent relation.

Although certain occupations such as building construction contractors and subcontractors

---

[2] An exception arises where the principal engages an independent contractor to perform *ultrahazardous* or *intrinsically dangerous* work, such as a contractor's negligent blasting of rock in leveling a residential lot which injures a third party. The duty of a principal toward third persons who might be injured through such negligence is said to be *nondelegable*—that is, the principal cannot avoid liability by delegating this duty to an independent contractor. *Restatement (Second), Agency,* Sec. 214c; *Restatement of Torts,* Secs. 416–429.

Table 36.1 Factors Considered by Courts in Deciding Whether a Person Is an Employee or Independent Contractor

Factor	Employer–Employee Relation	Principal–Independent Contractor Relation
Degree of control exercised	Employer exercises high degree of control over employee conduct	Principal exercises no control over the means of accomplishing a result
Provision of tools/capital equipment	Furnished by employer, with few exceptions	Generally furnished by independent contractor
Mode of termination	Generally, an "at will" relationship and is terminable immediately by either party (e.g., "I quit," "you're fired")	Agreement between an independent contractor and principal usually provides for termination by notice, followed by a waiting period
Method of compensation	By hour, day, week, month, or other time period	Usually a lump sum or "fixed fee" but sometimes calculated on a time basis

typically function as independent contractors, and not employees, the distinction between the two relationships is not determined by the kind of business, profession, or activity that is involved. For example, one might ordinarily think of a janitor as an employee, not an independent contractor. Yet in major cities, such work in factories and office buildings is usually done by an independent contracting janitorial service that furnishes the necessary cleaning equipment and undertakes to produce a result—namely, changed light bulbs, cleaned rugs, emptied wastebaskets—for a lump-sum monthly fee, without supervision, after regular hours.

In the following case, the U.S. Supreme Court summarizes the agency law distinction between an employer-employee relation and that of a principal and independent contractor.

CASE 36.1   Nationwide Mutual Insurance Co. v. Darden • 117 L Ed 2d 581 (1992)

FACTS   Darden was an insurance "agent" selling insurance for Nationwide under a written contract in which Darden would be enrolled in a Nationwide retirement plan for agents but would forfeit plan benefits if, within a year of his termination and 25 miles of his prior business location, he sold insurance for Nationwide's competitors. After termination, Darden did begin selling for competitors, and Nationwide contended he had forfeited retirement benefits. Darden then sued for benefits under the Employee Retirement Income Security Act of 1974 (ERISA). The case turned on the question whether Darden was an employee or an independent contractor. If Darden was an employee he could properly sue for benefits under ERISA. If he was not, the "insurance agents retirement plan" was not subject to ERISA. ERISA contained no statutory definition of "employee" or of the "employer-employee" relation. The trial court, applying the common law distinction between the employer-employee relation and that of principal–

**CASE 36.1
Continued**

independent contractor, concluded that Darden was not an employee and granted summary judgment for Nationwide Insurance. The Court of Appeals reversed, holding that the common law definition of "employee" was not appropriate in an area where Congress had enacted labor laws such as the Fair Labor Standards Act that contained statutory definitions of "employee." Using such definitions from analogous labor laws, the Court concluded, contrary to the trial court, that Darden could qualify as an employee. The U.S. Supreme Court reversed, holding that when labor laws such as ERISA do not contain a statutory definition of "employer-employee," the common law definitions and standards should be used to determine if a person is an "employee" or "independent contractor."

OPINION

SOUTER, J. . . . We have often been asked to construe the meaning of "employee" where the statute containing the term does not helpfully define it. Most recently we confronted the problem in Community for Creative Non-Violence v. Reid, 104 L Ed 2d 811 (1989), a case which . . . ultimately turned on whether . . . [work] had been "prepared by an employee within the scope of his or her employment." Because the . . . [statute involved in the Reid case] nowhere defined the term "employee," we unanimously applied the "well established" principle that

> Where Congress uses terms that have accumulated settled meaning under the common law, a court must infer, unless the statute otherwise dictates, that Congress means to incorporate the established meaning of these terms. In the past, when Congress has used the term "employee" without defining it, we have concluded that Congress intended to describe the conventional master-servant relationship as understood by common-law agency doctrine.

. . . ERISA's nominal definition of "employee" as "any individual employed by an employer," is completely circular and explains nothing. . . . Thus, we adopt a common-law test for determining who qualifies as an "employee" under ERISA . . . :

> In determining whether a hired party is an employee under the general common law of agency, we consider the hiring party's right to control the manner and means by which the product is accomplished. Among the other factors relevant to this inquiry are the skill required; the source of the instrumentalities and tools; the location of the work; the duration of the relationship between the parties; whether the hiring party has the right to assign additional projects to the hired party; the extent of the hired party's discretion over when and how long to work; the method of payment; the hired party's role in hiring and paying assistants; whether the work is part of the regular business of the hiring party; whether the hiring party is in business; the provision of employee benefits; and the tax treatment of the hired party.

Since the common-law test contains no shorthand formula or magic phrase that can be applied to find the answer, all of the incidents of the relationship must be assessed and weighed with no one factor being decisive. . . . To be sure, the traditional agency law criteria offer no paradigm of determinacy. But their application generally turns on factual variables within an employer's knowledge, thus permitting categorical judgments. . . . Agency law principles comport, moreover, with our recent precedents and with the common understanding reflected

CASE 36.1 Continued	in those precedents of the difference between an employee and an independent contractor.
JUDGMENT	While the Court of Appeals noted that "Darden most probably would not qualify as an employee" under traditional agency law principles, it did not actually decide that issue. We therefore reverse and remand the case to that court for proceedings consistent with this opinion. So ordered.

ESTABLISHING AN AGENCY

The Principal-Agent Relationship

To establish a principal-agent relationship, four elements must be present: (1) parties who are competent to be principal and agent, (2) who mutually agree, (3) that the agent will act for or on behalf of the principal to accomplish a legal purpose, and (4) that the agent will be under the principal's control.

Capacity of Principal and Agent

Capacity of Principal. A principal must have, at least, the *capacity to give legal consent*. Clearly, any person who meets the somewhat higher standard of having capacity to enter into contracts (see Chapter 13) is qualified to be a principal. A corporation, partnership, or federal, state, city, or other governmental entity may be a principal. However, an unincorporated association, club, or society, not given by law the right to contract in its own name, is not a legal entity and cannot appoint an agent. Courts avoid this problem by holding that the individuals within the organizations who actually engage the services of agents, and those members who concur in that action, are the principals.

Even though minors lack capacity to contract except for necessities of life, they may still appoint agents with limited power to contract for such necessities. Since minors have the right to disaffirm contracts for nonnecessities, they also can disaffirm agreements employing agents to purchase such nonnecessities. An insane or incompetent person lacks capacity and cannot appoint an agent. Therefore, an agency does not result even though an insane person attempts to appoint as an agent a fully competent adult.

Capacity of Agent. Minimal legal capacity is required to be an agent or employee. All that is necessary is that the person have the mental and physical ability to do the tasks that he or she was appointed to perform. Virtually anyone can qualify as an agent-employee. The work or services may be quite simple, such as running an errand. Or the work or services may involve the exercise of a great deal of discretion and judgment affecting the principal's contractual relations with third parties. An agent need not be an individual; a corporation or a partnership may be an agent.

Any person who is able to comprehend the duties to be performed may be an agent even if such a person lacks the capacity to contract for himself or herself. Assume that a mother tells her 10-year-old son to go to the pet store, buy some dog food, and charge it to the parent's account, and that a state statute forbids minors to purchase goods on credit. The boy, although too young himself to purchase a nonnecessity such as dog food, can legally carry out the instructions as his mother's agent. He may make a binding contract of purchase between his mother and the storekeeper, because a contract made by an agent on behalf of a principal is considered to be the contract of the principal—not the agent.

Kinds of Agents

There are three kinds of agents: general agent, special agent, and gratuitous agent.

General Agent. An agent whose duties involve a continuity of service is a **general agent.** For example, John Smythe, permanently employed to seek out and buy good horses for Purebred Farms, is a general agent of Purebred Farms. Similarly, a person permanently employed by a big chain like J. C. Penney to find good shopping center locations for its new stores is a general agent.

Special Agent. A person who is employed to conduct a single transaction or a small group of related transactions is a **special agent.** The realtor whom you engage to sell your house is a special agent. The distinction between a general agent and a special agent rests upon the degree of continuity of the relationship rather than upon the extent of the agent's powers. These terms are also in common usage in some businesses; for example, in the insurance industry a general agent sells insurance policies of many different companies, while a special agent represents a single company.

Gratuitous Agent. It is not necessary that the services of an agent be compensated. An agent who receives no compensation is a **gratuitous agent.** Such an agent may affect the legal relations of the principal with third parties to the same extent as an agent who is paid to perform services. For example, if your neighbor offers to include your old furniture in her garage sale, she has the same authority as if she were a sales agent to whom you promised a commission. Accordingly, she has the power to transfer your furniture to buyers and accept payment for it.

The Principal-Agent Agreement

Mutual Assent. One party alone cannot establish the relation of principal and agent. Both parties must in some way assent. Since agency is a *consensual* relation, it is created by any express or implied conduct which shows that the agent is willing to act on behalf of the principal and that the principal assents to have the agent so act. Although most agencies arise from contract, a contract with consideration is not necessary. As we have seen, many gratuitous agencies are created each day.

Sometimes only conduct or actions of the agent will imply assent to an agency. For instance, Henry tells his neighbor, "Bob, when you go to the hardware store, I'd appreciate your buying me a rake. Charge it to my account." Bob says nothing but buys the rake. By his action, Bob became Henry's agent for that transaction. Henry, as principal, is bound to pay the hardware store for the rake.

In all cases, the mutual assent of the principal and agent must call for the agent to perform an act which is *legal*—that is, an act which is not criminal, tortious, or against public policy. An agency to perform such an act is void and unenforceable.

Contract to Create Agency. In the business world, employee agents, as well as professional agents, are willing to work only if they are paid a salary, fee, commission, or other form of compensation. Thus, with most agencies, the necessary mutual assent of the principal and agent arises from a contract between them. The agent agrees to furnish services in consideration of compensation paid by the principal.

Form of Agreement. Except in the special circumstances discussed later, no particular formality is needed to establish a principal-agent relationship. The agreement may be written or oral, or implied from the conduct of the parties. Usually, an agent is employed by an informal oral understanding—for example, a storekeeper asks, "Can you start on Monday as a salesperson at $400 a week?" Kim answers, "Yes, that's fine." An agency contract has been created. However, when an important position is involved, the terms of employment are usually formalized with a written contract. It protects the principal-employer by defining and appropriately limiting the agent's scope of authority. It protects the agent by clearly setting out the agent's duties and the benefits to which the agent will be entitled. In addition, it avoids misunderstandings between principal and agent.

When Agent's Authority Must Be in Writing; Equal Dignities. Most state statutes or court decisions have established the **equal dignities rule:**

Whenever the act of a person must be executed with certain formalities, the authority of the agent to perform the same act must be executed by the principal with the same formalities.

To illustrate the rule, suppose that Paula plans to travel, and while she is gone, she wishes to authorize Alvin, her real estate agent, to sell her home. Since the statute of frauds in all states requires contracts for the sale of land to be in writing, Paula, as principal, must execute Alvin's authorization to sell her land with the same formality—that is, Paula must put it in writing.

Assume that Paula gives Alvin written authority to sell her home, and he finds a buyer who arranges for the purchase money to be paid to Alvin as soon as he signs a deed to the property. Does Alvin have authority to sign the deed? In most states the answer is no. State recording statutes require signatures on deeds to be notarized. Therefore, under the equal dignities rule, Paula's authorization of Alvin to deed her property to a buyer must be *executed with the same formality*—that is, it must be notarized. Before leaving on her trip, Paula must appear before a notary and verify under oath the validity of her signature on the document that authorizes Alvin to deed her property. The equal dignities rule generally applies to all types of agency contracts that are required by the statute of frauds (see Chapter 15) to be in writing. Generally, in all such cases, the authority of the agent to negotiate for the principal must be in writing.

It is common for states to require particular types of agency contracts to be in writing even though neither the general statute of frauds nor the equal dignities rule applies. In California and many other states, for example, a real estate agent is not entitled to a commission for finding a buyer unless a written agreement between seller and agent establishes the agent's compensation.

Power of Attorney. The word "attorney" means agent. Hence, a **power of attorney** is simply a written agency authorization by which a principal appoints an agent to carry on some important activity or to execute for the principal an instrument to be recorded as a public record. The power of attorney defines the duties and activities of the agent and the length of time the power of attorney is to be effective, and may itself be recorded. A **general power of attorney** authorizes the agent to do anything that may be necessary to transact the principal's legal affairs. A **special power of attorney** gives the agent power to carry out only some particular duty or duties and normally is limited in time or in place. An individual who is designated an agent by a power of attorney is called an **attorney in fact.** An attorney in fact should be distinguished from an attorney at law, who is an agent licensed to practice law. A power of attorney form appears in Figure 36.2. Courts construe ambiguous provisions in powers of attorney strictly in favor of the principal and against agents and third parties.

POWER OF AGENT TO BIND PRINCIPAL IN CONTRACT

Many contracts in the business world, and all contracts of corporations, are negotiated and executed by agents. When a third party sues to enforce such a contract, the principal often argues that the contract is not binding because the agent lacked authority to enter into it or exceeded the limits of authority set by the principal. Therefore, it is crucial that the third party know with certainty that the agent's purported authority rests upon solid legal ground. The third party's remedy of suit for breach of the agent's implied warranty of authority is discussed later in this chapter. However, the third party's surest precaution is to have the principal verify the extent of the agent's authority.

An agent's authority to bind a principal in contract arises in various ways:

1 By **actual authority,** it is communicated or otherwise made known by the principal to the agent.

> State of _____
>
> County of _____
>
> Know all men by these presents, that I, _____, the undersigned of _____ [address], City of _____, County of _____, State of _____, hereby make, constitute, and appoint _____, of _____ [address], City of _____, County of _____, State of _____, my true and lawful attorney in fact for me and in my name, place, and stead, giving unto said _____ full power to do and perform all and every act that I may legally do through an attorney in fact, and every proper power necessary to carry out the purposes for which this power is granted, with full power of substitution and revocation, hereby ratifying and affirming that which _____ or his substitute shall lawfully do or cause to be done by himself or his substitute lawfully designated by virtue of the power herein conferred upon him.
>
> _____ [If period of power of attorney is to be limited, add: This power ends _____, 19 _____]
>
> Dated _____, 19 _____
>
> [Signature]
>
> [Acknowledged]

Figure 36.2 Power of attorney—short form.

2 By **apparent authority (estoppel),** it is made known *by the principal* to the third party in the transaction in which the agent is engaged.
3 By **ratification,** it is evidenced retroactively by the principal giving approval to an agreement which had been entered into by someone who, without prior authority of the principal, purported to act as an agent of that principal.
4 By **operation of law,** it is conferred through statutes or court decisions.

Agent's Actual Authority; Agent's Apparent Authority

Power of Agent Arising from Actual Authority. Actual authority may be conferred by a principal upon an agent either expressly or impliedly.

Express authority of agent. If a principal tells an agent, either orally or in writing, what to do, this is the agent's *express authority* to act for the principal in accordance with those instructions. For example, Sun Stables, Inc., tells Bret, a horse trainer, to buy a sound horse less than 3 years old for no more than $2,500. Bret has express authority to buy the horse within the limits set. When he buys it, Sun Stables must pay for the horse.

Implied authority of agent. When the agent's services will continue over an extended period of time, instructions are usually expressed in broad terms such as, "OK, you're hired as our football coach." When the agreement is in such general terms, *an agent has implied authority to do all acts that may be reasonably inferred from* (1) the principal's words and actions, (2) the circumstances surrounding the agency, (3) the customs of the trade or profession as well as of the community where the service is to be performed, and (4) the relations of the parties.

The authority that an agent reasonably infers from a principal's express words constitute an agent's **implied authority.** The law presumes that an employer intends its employees to have such powers as are reasonably necessary for them to carry on their assigned work. Powers "reasonably necessary" for agents to carry on their authorized work are not, however, without limitation. For example, as an attorney employed to file suit for $100,000 damages arising from an auto injury, Art has implied authority to agree with opposing counsel on routine matters that affect the trial of the case. But Art may not settle the case for $5,000 without his client's consent, because such settlement affects important substantive rights.

As another example, an agent hired to manage a dress shop may reasonably infer the power to do everything ordinarily required to operate the business, consistent with the location, size, and general character of the store and of the community it serves. This implied authority would empower the agent to contract for newspaper and radio advertising, to hire and fire employees, to make emergency repairs, to store windows and fixtures, and to order and pay for merchandise that a store of that kind usually sells in that community. However, the managing agent would not have implied authority to contract for all new carpeting and fixtures in the store, to move the store into a different building, or to order men's clothing to be sold in the store. To have power to do anything that is not part of the normal management of the store, the manager must first secure express authority from the principal.

Implied authority may arise in another way. If some **unforeseen emergency** occurs with respect to a matter covered by the agency and it is impracticable for the agent to communicate with the principal, the agent is authorized to do whatever is reasonably believed to be necessary in order to prevent the principal from suffering a substantial loss. For example, Bob drives a refrigerated truck that breaks down at night. If the truck is not repaired immediately, its load of meat will spoil. Bob tries but can't reach his employer, Pat, by telephone. Bob hires a towing service to take the truck to a garage for repairs, and orders the bills sent to Pat. Bob has implied authority to do these things because of the emergency. Pat must pay the bills.

Power of Agent Arising from Apparent Authority (Estoppel).

Unlike actual authority, which is based on what the principal communicates to the agent, apparent authority stems from what the principal communicates to a third party. *Apparent* or *ostensible* authority arises when a principal leads a third party reasonably to believe that an agency exists, or that an agent has a particular degree of power, under circumstances where there is no express or implied authority. Apparent authority is sometimes called *agency by estoppel* (discussed in Chapter 12) because it is based upon principles of estoppel which consist of (1) words or conduct of the principal which lead the third party to reasonably believe that an unauthorized person is an agent, (2) reliance by the third party upon the principal's conduct or statements, and (3) a loss suffered by the third party.

A principal may communicate apparent authority to a third party in several ways: (1) by making a direct statement to the third party; (2) by permitting someone to have a business title, to occupy a position, or to perform duties which lead the third party reasonably to believe that the individual has power to act for the principal; or (3) by remaining silent in certain situations, thereby clothing an unauthorized agent with apparent authority. Suppose, for example, that Al, who has no authority to contract for Paul, tells Tom that he is Paul's agent and wants to purchase some farm supplies. Paul is present, but says nothing while Tom fills the order. Paul is liable on the contract. His silence when there was a duty to speak has clothed Al with apparent authority to contract on Paul's behalf. If Tom sues to enforce the contract, Paul will be *estopped* (prevented) from claiming that he had not authorized the purchases by Al.

In this illustration, Tom, as third party, relied on the principal's representations of apparent authority to establish an agency where there was no agency—express or implied. However, more frequently third parties rely on the principal's representations to *expand* the authority of one who is already an agent, but who has exceeded the scope of actual authority. For example, a bank (principal) hires Alicia as receptionist (agent) with authority only to direct customers to other employees. When Alicia's desk must be moved for recarpeting, the bank tells Alicia to sit at the desk of the "new accounts" clerk, who is on vacation, but instructs Alicia not to attempt to open new accounts.

Ted, believing Alicia is the person in charge of new accounts, asks her to open one for him, and gives her $10,000 cash. Alicia gives Ted a receipt and absconds with the money. The bank, as principal, is bound by this transaction, and must credit Ted's account with $10,000. Alicia has apparent authority to handle new account transactions. This example also illustrates the rule that a principal's secret limitation upon the authority of an agent is not binding upon third parties.

The important factor in apparent authority is that it originates with the principal. The actions of the agent alone will not suffice. Whether or not apparent authority is conferred depends upon the facts in any particular case, but the key is whether the elements of estoppel are present—injurious reliance by a third party upon the representations of the principal.

The court in the next case based liability upon all three theories of agency authority—express, implied, and apparent.

CASE 36.2 **Tri-Circle, Inc. v. Brugger Corp.** • 829 P.2d 540 (Id. App. 1992)

FACTS The case concerns an action by Tri-Circle, Inc. (plaintiff), for materials and labor that were supplied to farm property owned by Brugger Corp. but that were ordered by J. Weimer, who leased and operated the farm. In 1987 Weimer met with Brugger Corp.'s manager to discuss a new lease of the farm. In negotiations, Brugger agreed to pay for necessary repairs on the irrigation system. Weimer then contracted with Tri-Circle to make the repairs, representing that he was authorized by Brugger to do so, and requesting that Tri-Circle bill the job to a separate account in Brugger Corp.'s name and send the bills to Weimer. After verifying the accuracy of the bills, Weimer told Tri-Circle that he would send them to Brugger for payment. In June, Weimer forwarded Tri-Circle's bill for $9,769 to Brugger Corp., which paid it by mailing a check to Tri-Circle. Later bills totaling $11,540 were approved by Weimer and sent to Brugger Corp., but were never paid. Tri-Circle sued Weimer and Brugger. The trial court found that Weimer was agent for Brugger Corp., a disclosed principal, and entered judgment against Brugger for $11,540. The suit as to Weimer was dismissed. The court also ordered Tri-Circle to pay Weimer's attorney's fees in defending the suit, because Tri-Circle should have known that Weimer, as agent of a fully disclosed principal, was not liable on the contract and should not have joined him in the suit. Brugger Corp. appealed, claiming that Weimer lacked authority to contract as its agent.

OPINION SILAK, J. . . . There are three separate types of agency, any of which are sufficient to bind the principal to a contract entered into by an agent with a third party. The three types of agencies are: express authority, implied authority, and apparent authority. Here, the district court specifically found that "evidence of all three types of agency exist in this case." . . . The district court had substantial evidence upon which to find an express agency relationship between Weimer and Brugger. Express authority may be found when there is evidence that the principal has explicitly granted the agent authority to act in the principal's name. Weimer testified that he had been explicitly authorized by Grant McQueen, an officer of Brugger, to purchase repairs in the name of Brugger. Three . . . invoices which Brugger paid expressly stated that the charges were for materials and labor sold to "Brugger Corp. c/o Jason Weimer." . . . All this

CASE 36.2 Continued

constitutes substantial competent evidence to support the trial court's finding that Weimer had been granted express authority by Brugger.

The trial court's finding of implied authority is also supported by substantial evidence. Implied authority refers to that authority which is necessary, usual, and proper to accomplish or perform the express authority delegated to the agent by the principal. . . . Weimer's opening of an account with Tri-Circle in the name of Brugger and charging repairs performed to that account, was necessary, usual, and proper in performing the expressly authorized act of purchasing irrigation system repairs.

Apparent authority differs from express and implied authority in that it is not based on the words and conduct of the principal toward the agent, but the principal's words and conduct toward the third party. Apparent authority may be found when a principal voluntarily places an agent in such a position that a person of ordinary prudence, conversant with the business usages and the nature of a particular business, is justified in believing that the agent is acting pursuant to existing authority. . . . The invoices Brugger received for Tri-Circle's services clearly stated that Weimer was obtaining irrigation repairs and charging them to Brugger. Based on Brugger's payment of these charges, the district court could find that Brugger had clothed Weimer with apparent authority by voluntarily placing him in such a position that Tri-Circle would justifiably believe that Weimer was acting pursuant to existing authority. . . . Based on the above, we conclude that the district court's findings as to agency were supported by substantial, competent evidence, and we will not disturb those findings on this appeal.

JUDGMENT   The judgment of the district court is affirmed.

Ratification of Agent's Acts

In contracting with a third party, even though an agent acts in excess of express, implied, or apparent authority, the principal may still be able to obtain the benefit of the contract by **ratification**. Ratification is the principal's affirmance of an agent's previously unauthorized contract or act.[3] Generally, after a ratification, the consequences of the original transaction are the same as if it had been authorized.

Requirements of Ratification. Typically, there are three steps in a ratification:

1. An agent, purporting to act on behalf of the principal, but acting in excess of his or her authority, enters into a contract with a third party.

2. The principal later acquires *full knowledge of all the relevant facts of the transaction* (or deliberately decides to approve the transaction without any knowledge of the facts).

3. By actions, statements, or conduct, the principal expressly or impliedly indicates an intention to be bound by the transaction.

Ratification is *express* when the principal says "I ratify that act" or words to the effect. More often, ratification is *implied* when the principal with full knowledge of all aspects of a transaction (1) accepts any of the benefits of the contract between the unauthorized agent and the third party; (2) fails in a timely way to repudiate the agent's act; or (3) brings a legal action to enforce it.

Often, the principal's intention to ratify the contract is demonstrated by simply paying the purchase price of goods that the agent, acting without authority, contracted to buy. For exam-

---

[3]*Restatement (Second), Agency,* Sec. 82.

ple, Agnes, the office manager of an oil company, has no authority to purchase for the firm. But learning of a low-priced computer that the company needs, she orders it and tells the president. When the bill for the computer arrives, the president pays it. He has now ratified Agnes' unauthorized contract.

Effect of Ratification. A transaction that has been ratified is treated as though it had been originally authorized. The principal may ratify without the knowledge or consent of the third party to the transaction. The principal must ratify the transaction entirely, or not at all. The reason for this rule is obvious. Ratification is approval of a transaction that has already taken place. Therefore, the principal has the power to approve the transaction only as it occurred, not to reconstruct it to suit present needs.

Sometimes this rule can be disastrous for the principal. Suppose that a principal-wholesaler says to Arnold, his agent who collects delinquent accounts: "Don't come back until you have collected the money Todd owes me." Arnold returns, tosses a $1,000 check on the principal's desk, and says: "I had to knock out a couple of teeth, but there is your money." The principal cashes the check. If Todd sues the principal for the tort of assault and battery, he is liable. Ratification of the agent's act of collecting the delinquent account also ratified the illegal assault that was part of the transaction.

Responsibilities of Principal and Agent after Ratification. Ratification brings about some interesting changes in the relationship of the parties and in their respective rights and obligations. Until the act is ratified, the "purported agent" has acted without authority and may be liable to the third party for breach of the implied warranty of authority or even for fraudulent representations. Because the agent acted without authority, neither the principal nor the third party is bound or required to perform the agreement made by the purported agent. *After* ratification, however, the situation changes. The transaction of the purported agent is now treated as authorized by the principal, the agent's liability to the third party disappears, and the principal and third party are bound to each other to perform the agreement made by the agent. The following case illustrates ratification.

CASE 36.3 — Progressive Casualty Ins. Co. v. Ehrhardt • 518 A.2d 151 (Md. App. 1986)

FACTS Robert Ehrhardt had a motorcycle liability insurance policy, issued by Progressive Casualty Insurance Company, which provided that coverage would cease at 12:01 a.m. on May 19, 1983, if the premium of $70.40 was not paid by that time. If Ehrhardt tendered payment after the expiration date, the policy would be renewed effective on the postmark date that the premium was mailed.

Robert failed to pay his premium and his policy lapsed on May 19. On May 25 he was in a motorcycle accident in which Judith Penn, his passenger, suffered serious injuries. The next morning (May 26) Robert's father paid the overdue premium to the Brown Agency, the insurance company's agent. On that same day, Judith's mother informed Progressive Casualty by telephone that on May 25 its insured, Robert Ehrhardt, had been in a motorcycle accident, in which her daughter was injured. On May 31 Robert notified Progressive of the accident. Upon receiving Ehrhardt's renewal premium on May 26, the Brown Agency immediately mailed it to Progressive's Richmond office. There the renewal was marked effective May 26, 1983, the date on which the envelope in which it was enclosed was postmarked. On June 2, Progressive's underwriting agent backdated its renewal from May 26 to May 19, 1983, and Robert

CASE 36.3 Continued

Ehrhardt received in the mail from Progressive a renewal policy effective May 19, 1983.

Judith filed a tort suit against Ehrhardt for her personal injuries. At trial, Progressive asked the court to declare that it had no duty to defend or indemnify Ehrhardt because its insurance policy was not in effect at the time of the accident. The court ruled otherwise and Progressive appealed.

OPINION

BISHOP, J. . . . This case . . . need not turn on the issue of whether Progressive's underwriter acted with apparent authority [when he backdated the renewal of the policy—an argument made by Judith Penn]. Even if the underwriter acted completely without authority, Progressive can nevertheless become liable if it ratifies the agent's conduct. . . . Ratification requires an intention to ratify, and knowledge of all material facts.

Intention to ratify may be inferred by words, conduct or silence on the part of the principal that reasonably indicates its desire to affirm the unauthorized act. . . . Circumstances that suggest an intent to ratify include: receipt and retention of the benefits of the unauthorized transaction, and a failure to make a timely disaffirmance of the unauthorized acts.

Applying these factors to the case at hand, the telltale signs of ratification are apparent. There is no doubt that Progressive received a benefit when it backdated Ehrhardt's policy from May 26 to May 19, 1983. . . . The practice of backdating policies results in financial gain to the insurer by creating a shorter period of coverage [because the policy will terminate at an earlier date but the insurer will be paid for the entire period]. While the amounts in any individual case are minor, if practiced on a larger scale, the financial gain can be significant. The practice, however, does have its perils as evidenced by the factual situation in this case.

Moreover, it is undisputed that Progressive retained the benefit and did not attempt to disaffirm the allegedly unauthorized act of its lead underwriter for over six months.

As to the second requirement [for ratification], we hold that Progressive acted with full knowledge of all material facts. The trial court explicitly found, and we affirm, that Progressive was on notice that a loss to its insured occurred during the defaulting period. Because of that knowledge, Progressive is in no position to deny the legal implications of its retention of the benefits of the transaction. Accordingly, we hold that Progressive's actions retroactively conferred authority on its agent, subjecting it to whatever liability that backdating the policy entails.

JUDGMENT

[The court affirmed the trial court's decision that Progressive Insurance had ratified its agent's backdating the policy and that the policy was in effect at the time of the accident.]

Agent's Authority by Operation of Law

In some situations, the agent's ability to bind the principal is referred to as authority by operation of law. Such authority is created by statute or by decisions of the courts. For example, some state statutes authorize a spouse to contract with third parties, especially for the necessities of life, and hold the nonacting spouse liable as principal. Other statutes bind the parents as principals on a minor child's contracts for the necessities of life. Many state statutes relating to the practice of law provide that an attorney, as agent for a client (the principal), has authority to bind the principal on certain matters, such as a stipulation (agreement) in open court. Even though the attorney (agent) was not specifically authorized to make such an agreement, the principal (client) is bound by it.

Figure 36.3, a bull's-eye chart of agency authority, summarizes the various legal theories that are used to establish that a principal has authorized an agent. In the course of almost any civil lawsuit, a question of agency authority will arise. Lawyers who claim agency have the burden of proving it exists. Figuratively speaking, they apply the chart as a checklist to the facts of any case. Facts supporting any *one theory* shown on the chart are sufficient to establish that an agency exists, or that the act of the agent was within the scope of authority.

CONTRACTUAL RIGHTS AND OBLIGATIONS OF PRINCIPAL, AGENT, AND THIRD PARTY

Sometimes principals do not wish third parties to know that contracts are being negotiated by agents acting on their behalf. At other times, even when the principal desires a full disclosure and carefully instructs the agent to advise third parties of the agency and the principal's identity, the agent may inadvertently or wilfully fail to do so. Therefore, depending upon how much of a disclosure the agent makes to the third party,

Figure 36.3 Kinds of agency authority.

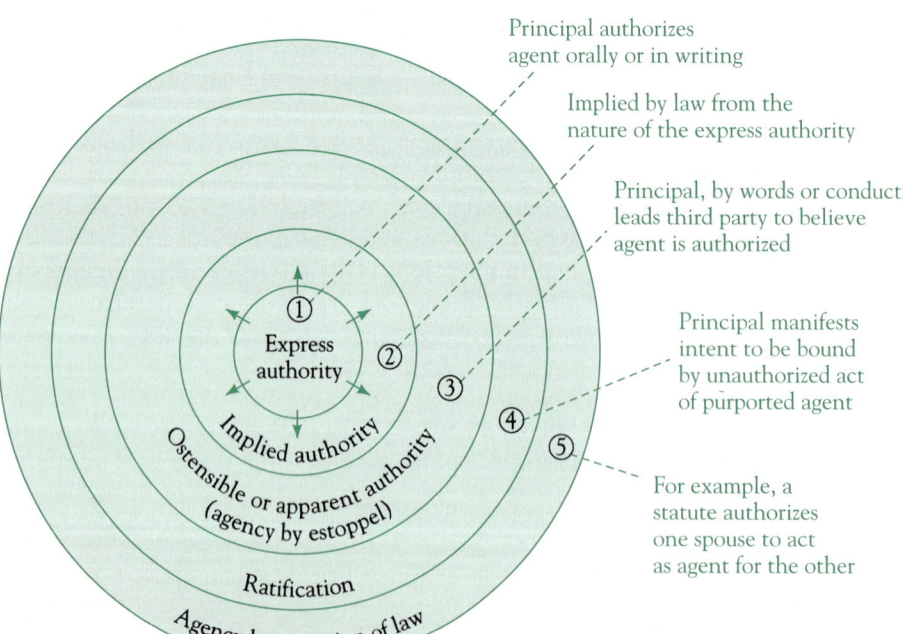

three distinct situations may arise, each with different legal consequences:

1. A disclosed principal
2. A partially disclosed principal
3. An undisclosed principal

Disclosed Principal

When the word *principal* is used by itself, it refers to a fully **disclosed principal**—that is, one whose identity and capacity as a principal is fully known to the third party at the time of the transaction. Assume that John Smythe is employed to purchase horses for Purebred Farms. Smythe's business card is shown in Figure 36.4. When Smythe gives his card to Adams, who sells horses, Adams knows that Smythe is acting for Purebred Farms. Purebred Farms is a *disclosed* corporate principal and Smythe is its agent. If he is writing a series of letters to the third party, he should sign each letter in the customary way that fully discloses the agency: "John Smythe, Agent for Purebred Farms, Inc." or "Purebred Farms, Inc., by John Smythe, Agent."

Agent Acting within Scope of Authority. Agency law evolved because agents were expected to stand in the shoes of their principals in dealing with third parties. Hence, the rule

---

JOHN SMYTHE

Horse Buyer for

PUREBRED FARMS, INC.

144 High Street
Lexington, Kentucky

Figure 36.4

quickly developed that when the agent, acting within the scope of a disclosed principal's authority, enters into a contract, it is a contract of the principal just as though the principal had negotiated it personally. The principal, not the agent, is the contracting party, is entitled to the benefits of the contract, and may enforce its performance. Likewise, it is the principal who must perform in accordance with the contract terms. The agent is only a go-between and, not being a party to the contract, can neither require performance nor be forced to make good if the principal fails to perform. The legal effect of the agent's contract with the third party is illustrated in the following case.

CASE 36.4	**Pfluger v. Colquitt** • 620 S.W.2d 739 (Tex. Civ. App. 1981)
FACTS	Pfluger, plaintiff, owned two antique Cadillac automobiles. The cars were displayed by Williams, who operated an antique automobile restoration business and museum. Colquitt, a customer, offered to purchase Pfluger's two cars for $14,500. Williams telephoned Pfluger, who agreed to the sale of the cars at that price. Colquitt gave Williams his check, received Williams's bill of sale, and took possession of the two cars. Pfluger still had the certificates of title, but Williams assured Colquitt that he would receive them from Pfluger as soon as Colquitt's check cleared the bank. After Colquitt's check cleared, Williams did not forward the funds to Pfluger, who therefore refused to deliver the certificates of title to Colquitt, and after demand for return of the cars was refused, Pfluger sued both Williams and Colquitt. Colquitt counterclaimed for title to the cars. The jury found that Williams was

CASE 36.4 Continued	acting as Pfluger's agent when he sold the cars. Judgment was rendered for Colquitt for title to the vehicles and for Pfluger against Williams for the purchase money. Pfluger was not satisfied; he wanted his cars back and appealed that part of the judgment that vested their title in Colquitt.
OPINION	GUITTARD, C.J. . . . The jury found that Williams was acting as Pfluger's agent in selling the vehicles, and since there is no attack on this finding, the transaction had the same effect as if Pfluger had dealt personally with Colquitt, because one who acts through a duly authorized agent is bound as if he had acted in person. . . . Therefore, Colquitt is entitled to demand a proper transfer of the title from Pfluger. This result is not affected by Colquitt's payment of the purchase price to Williams. Since Williams was found to be Pfluger's agent in making the sale, when Williams accepted the check, he did so as Pfluger's agent and became responsible to Pfluger for the money; thus, the payment had the same effect as a payment directly to Pfluger. . . . Williams's subsequent conversion of the money . . . could not adversely affect Colquitt's right to demand a proper transfer of the certificates from Pfluger. . . .
JUDGMENT	Affirmed in favor of the third party, Colquitt.

Agent Acting outside Scope of Authority When an agent of a disclosed principal acts *outside* the scope of his or her authority and the principal does *not* ratify the unauthorized act, the principal is not bound by it and is not obligated to the third party. Agents may exceed their authority for a number of reasons. Sometimes they simply have an exaggerated view of their importance and their authority. At other times, they may overstate their authority as part of a deliberate scheme to defraud. The fact that no rule of law requires third parties to take agents' representations of their authority at face value should serve as a warning that *third parties cannot afford the luxury of assuming that an agent's scope of authority is as large as he or she says it is.*

Court archives are full of cases where third parties have been denied recovery against principals whose agents have misrepresented their authority and absconded with funds. When in doubt, the best safeguard for third parties is to verify the scope of an agent's authority directly with the principal. A tactful way of doing this is to insist upon adding a clause to the contract providing that it shall not be effective until the principal has signed, or, if the principal is a corporation, until a certified copy of a directors' resolution authorizing officers to sign the contract, has been furnished to the third party.

Agents' Implied Warranty of Authority. In an effort to protect third parties, the law has developed a rule which holds that *agents impliedly warrant to third parties that they have the authority to do that which they undertake to do.*[4] If, in fact, agents of disclosed principals exceed their authority, third parties may bring suit against them for breach of this implied warranty, not breach of the contract itself. If agents' representations are intentional, the third party has an additional cause of action for fraud. Frequently, however, judgments against agents are an empty remedy, because the agents do not have sufficient assets to pay them.

[4]*Restatement (Second)*, Agency, Sec. 329.

Partially Disclosed Principal

A **partially disclosed principal** is one whose existence is confirmed by the agent, but whose identity is not revealed to the third party at the time of the transaction. Assume that John Smythe's business card reads as shown in Figure 36.5. A third party who reads this card knows that Smythe is an agent, but does not know the identity of his principal. Smythe is an agent for a partially disclosed principal. Wealthy principals often instruct agents not to reveal their identity so as to protect themselves from being gouged. For example, the Rockefeller family bought property in the heart of New York City through agents who did not disclose to the sellers the name of their famous principal. The property was then donated to the United Nations for its headquarters.

An agent for a partially disclosed principal is a party to the contract because it is likely that the third party is relying on the reputation and credit of the agent as well as the possible financial resources of the unknown principal. Hence, the partially disclosed principal *and* the agent may be required to perform the contract, and both are liable for its breach.[5] For example, assume that Central Purchasing Agency (CPA) buys a carload of tires from Firestone's factory without disclosing that Brown is the purchaser (principal) in this transaction. Firestone knows that CPA is buying tires for a customer but does not know who that customer is. Brown receives the tires, but Firestone is not paid. Firestone, in making the sale, relied upon the good credit rating of CPA as well as upon the assumption that the unknown, partially disclosed principal would also be responsible. Hence, CPA and Brown are liable for the bill, but Firestone can collect it only once.

If a third party fails to perform an agreement entered into with an agent acting for a partially disclosed principal, either the agent or the partially disclosed principal can require the third party to perform its part of the agreement. In the above example, if Firestone failed to deliver the tires, either CPA or Brown could demand that Firestone perform the contract.

Undisclosed Principal

An **undisclosed principal** is one whose very existence is not known to the third party at the time of the transaction. Thus, a third party who is handed a business card like that in Figure 36.6 is led to believe that Smythe is acting for himself. If Smythe is, in fact, acting for another, he is an agent for an undisclosed principal.

Rights of Undisclosed Principal against Third Party. Even though the third party to the agent's contract has no idea that someone else is involved in the transaction, agency law allows that unknown "someone" to come forward and

[5]*Restatement (Second), Agency,* Sec. 321.

Figure 36.5

JOHN SMYTHE

Purchasing Agent

144 High Street
Lexington, Kentucky

Figure 36.6

JOHN SMYTHE

HORSES BOUGHT & SOLD

144 High Street
Lexington, Kentucky

demand third-party performance of the contract. However, this rule has four exceptions.

1 When performance rendered to the principal would impose a greater burden on the third party than that required by the original contract, the third party is excused from the *additional* performance. For example, if Tom, the third party, agreed to deliver goods to the agent's address and the undisclosed principal's place of business is twice as far, Tom has the right to charge more for the extra distance or be relieved of any obligation to the third party.

2 If an undisclosed principal eventually appears and sues on the contract, a third party who had a defense against the agent can assert the same defense against the principal. For example, suppose the agent owed the third party a preexisting debt of $100, arising from a separate transaction. If the undisclosed principal comes forward and sues the third party for breach of contract, the third party can *set off* the $100 debt owed by the agent against the principal's claim for damages.

3 If the existence of the agency was *fraudulently concealed* from the third party prior to the agreement, the third party will not be required to perform the contract. A fraud may be perpetrated (1) if the agent, when asked by the third party, denies existence of the agency or (2) if a principal, knowing that a third party does not want to deal, attempts to deal through a secret agent.

4 If the contract calls for the agent to perform it personally, and the agent fails to do so, the third party is excused from performing its side of the contract. For example, suppose Ada, a famous landscape artist, who is also a commission agent for other artists, agrees to deliver a painting of the third party's ranch for $1,000, but secretly intends Pam, her undisclosed principal, to paint the landscape. Pam, as undisclosed principal, cannot identify herself and sue the third party for breach, because the third party's reasonable expectation and intent was that Ada personally would paint the landscape.

Rights of Agent of Undisclosed Principal against Third Party. An agent for an undisclosed principal is in a different legal position than an agent for a disclosed principal regarding rights against a third party. An agent for a *disclosed* principal is not a party to the contract, has no rights in the contract, and cannot require its performance. The agent who acts for an *undisclosed* principal *is* a party to the contract and has all the rights of a principal. Such an agent can enforce the contract, including the right to sue the third party for its breach.

Rights of Third Party against Undisclosed Principal or Its Agent. It would be unfair to give an undisclosed principal a right against a third party without giving a reciprocal right to the third party against the undisclosed principal. The common law therefore gives the third party the right, when the identity of the principal is revealed, to seek performance from either the agent *or* from the previously undisclosed principal, whichever one he or she chooses to hold responsible. Exercising this choice is called an "election."

Many courts are moving away from the common law principle of election and instead give the third party remedies against *both* the agent and the undisclosed principal, but permit only one satisfaction of the claim. The case which follows is illustrative of this modern but growing *minority* view.

CASE 36.5	**Crown Controls, Inc. v. Smiley** • 737 P.2d 709 (Wash. App. 1987)
FACTS	Jim Smiley was a manufacturer's representative and distributor. Identifying himself as an agent of Industrial Associates, he purchased from Crown Controls certain industrial equipment. At no time did Smiley disclose that he was acting on behalf of a corporation. Crown later learned that Industrial Associates was a trade name of North American Drill Supply, Inc. (NADS), a corporation of which Smiley was the president. Crown sued NADS and Smiley individually for the purchase price of the equipment. Crown secured a partial summary judgment against NADS and attempted to garnish its bank account, but the account had been closed. Trial of the action against Smiley continued. The court permitted Crown to vacate its partial summary judgment against NADS and to enter judgment only against Smiley. Smiley appealed, claiming that Crown, having elected to hold NADS liable as principal for the purchase price, could not hold him liable as agent.
OPINION	CHAN, J. . . . We agree that Crown Controls' . . . garnishing NADS' bank account constituted an election by Crown . . . to hold NADS liable instead of Smiley. However, we believe the election rule pertaining to agents and undisclosed principals is illogical and contrary to the policy of favoring full compensation of wronged parties. We therefore hold, for the reasons that follow, that Crown . . . may have judgment against both NADS and Smiley, although it may only have one satisfaction. . . . This court may abandon or modify a common law rule if, in the light of current conditions and thinking, the rule's precepts are incompatible with present-day society. . . .

A leading case abolishing the rule of alternative liability in the undisclosed principal context is *Grinder v. Bryans Road Bldg. & Supply Co., Inc.*, 290 Md. 687, 432 A.2d 453 (1981). . . . The *Grinder* court adopted the law of Pennsylvania as the better reasoned rule and the one endorsed by the legal commentators. Under that rule, the liability of the agent and previously undisclosed principal is joint and several rather than alternative.

Undoubtedly an agent who makes a contract in his own name without disclosing his agency is liable to the other party. The latter acts upon his credit and is not bound to yield up his right to hold the former personally, merely because he discloses a principal who is also liable. . . . But it does not follow that the agent can afterwards discharge himself by putting the creditor to his election. Being already liable by his contract, he can be discharged only by satisfaction of it, by himself or another. . . .

When it is recognized that the third person acquires several rights against the principal and agent, there does not seem to be any reason . . . why he should not have every advantage that accrues to anyone else who has more than one right. Specifically, his attempt to hold one obligor should not exonerate another obligor. . . .

We agree with this analysis and hold that a creditor is entitled to take judgment against both an agent and his previously undisclosed principal, although the creditor may have only one satisfaction. . . . |
| JUDGMENT | The judgment is affirmed. . . |

SUMMARY

Agency is a consensual agreement whereby one person (the principal) authorizes another (the agent) to act on the behalf of, and subject to the direction or control of, the principal. Depending upon the degree of control a principal exercises, an agent may be an independent contractor or an employee. Anyone may be appointed an agent, but only an individual capable of entering into a contract may be a principal. The principal-agent relationship may be created in writing or, unless statutes provide otherwise, may be established orally or implied from the conduct of the parties.

An agent has the power to bind a principal to legal obligations when acting within the scope of authority established by the principal. The principal may vest authority in the agent either by actual (express or implied) authority or by apparent (ostensible) authority. Actual authority arises expressly from the written or spoken words of the principal, or impliedly from the agent's reasonable inferences from those words. Apparent authority is based upon the elements of estoppel and results from words or conduct expressed *by the principal to a third party* that causes the third party reasonably to believe that a person has authority to act for the principal. When a person without authority purports to act for a principal, the principal may ratify that act by words or conduct manifesting an intention to be bound.

If a third party to a transaction knows the fact of agency and the identity of the principal, the latter is a **disclosed principal.** If the fact of agency is revealed but the principal's identity is withheld, the principal is a **partially disclosed principal.** When the third party knows neither the fact of agency nor the identity of the principal, the latter is an **undisclosed principal.** An agent acting within the scope of authority incurs no obligation on a contract entered into on behalf of a disclosed principal. The principal alone is responsible and may require performance by the third party. When an agent acting within the scope of authority enters into a contract for an undisclosed principal, both the principal and the agent are parties to the contract. Upon the third party discovering the identity of the undisclosed principal, the party can, with few exceptions, hold the principal or the agent liable on the contract. However, most courts require the third party to make an election at the time of trial. Either the principal or the agent can require performance from the third party unless the agent fraudulently concealed the fact of the agency, or unless the third party had a right to expect performance by the agent personally. In that event, only the agent can be required to perform.

REVIEW QUESTIONS

1. (a) Define agency. **(b)** State in general terms, or by examples, the importance of agency to the business community.

2. (a) What must the parties do to create a principal-agent relationship? **(b)** Is an individual who is qualified to be an agent also qualified to be a principal? Explain.

3. Distinguish an independent contractor from an employee.

4. Can a person who is hired as an employee bind his or her employer in contract? Explain.

5. (a) Distinguish between actual authority and apparent authority. **(b)** In what factual circumstances would one kind of authority exist without the other?

6. (a) What is meant by ratification? **(b)** What conditions must exist before an act can be ratified? **(c)** Does a third party have any recourse against either the principal or the agent if the principal does not ratify an agent's unauthorized act? Explain.

7. (a) Distinguish among a disclosed principal, a partially disclosed principal, and an undisclosed principal. **(b)** Does an agent for an undisclosed principal have a greater or lesser degree of apparent authority than an agent for a disclosed principal? Why?

8. (a) A third party, at the time of dealing with an agent for an undisclosed principal, has no idea that such a principal exists. Yet upon discovering the principal's identity, the third party receives a windfall by being permitted to hold the undisclosed principal liable. Why? **(b)** Under what circumstances would an undisclosed principal have a right of action against a third party who had entered into a contract with an agent for the undisclosed principal?

CASE PROBLEMS

1. Douglas, dressed in a doorman's uniform, was standing in front of Ajax Restaurant when Weingart stopped his car in front of the restaurant. Weingart handed Douglas his car keys and Douglas gave him a claim check. Later, when Weingart came out of the restaurant, Douglas could not find the car. When Weingart demanded that the restaurant pay him the value of the car, the restaurant owner refused, saying that Douglas was not an employee, although he (the owner) was aware that Douglas was working on his own parking cars for Ajax Restaurant as well as three other establishments on the block. Weingart then brought suit against Ajax Restaurant for compensation. What would the judgment be? Why?

2. Charles wanted to buy a harvester from Farmall Co., but he knew that Farmall would not do business with him because of past hostilities between them. Charles therefore arranged, for a small fee, to have Warren make the purchase for him without disclosing the agency. Charles agreed to give Warren the full purchase price and the promised fee as soon as the harvester arrived. Warren ordered the machine. A month later, when the machine was delivered to Warren, he received from Charles the money to send to Farmall plus his fee. However, Warren began using the machine himself and did not turn it over to Charles; nor did he pay Farmall. Farmall learned that Charles was the undisclosed principal in the transaction and sued him for the purchase price. What should be the outcome of the litigation?

3. Viti owned a filling station and hired Quinn as manager. Viti directed Quinn to buy all gasoline for the station from Newport Oil Co. but, because of changing prices, never to buy more than a week's supply at any one time. Viti told Newport to be sure to collect from Quinn for all purchases each week, since Viti did not want bills to accumulate. Viti received weekly reports showing the business condition of the station. Despite Viti's direction to Quinn and the warning to Newport, Quinn, instead of paying each week, ran up a sizable bill. Newport demanded payment from Viti, who sent a check for one week's gasoline purchase and refused to pay anything more. Does Newport have a cause of action against Viti? Explain.

4. Valley Corp., a building contractor, was an authorized distributor of Prefab Farm Buildings. Prefab's brochures said, "We back our buildings with a Local Independent Builder." Herman contracted with Valley Corp. to erect a Prefab building. Because of Valley's poor workmanship, the roof leaked when it rained. Herman sued both Prefab and Valley for the cost of repairing the leaks. Can Herman recover from both defendants? Explain.

5. Smith went to a hospital emergency room complaining of a sore throat. Dr. Henderson operated, but negligently failed to promptly administer oxygen, causing permanent brain damage and rendering Smith incompetent. Smith's guardian sued the doctor and hospital for malpractice. The hospital claimed it had contracted with an outside group of doctors to staff the emergency room, that Dr. Henderson was hired and paid by that group, that *respondeat superior* did not apply, and that it was not liable. Smith's lawyer argued that the doctor was the hospital's ostensible or apparent agent and that it was estopped by its conduct from denying the agency. Evidence showed that the hospital clerk at the admitting desk stated "one of our doctors is on duty"; there was nothing in the room to indicate whether the doctor was an independent contractor or an employee of the hospital; and the *hospital* billed Smith for the emergency room, including the doctor's services. **(a)** Was Dr. Henderson an apparent or ostensible agent of the hospital? **(b)** Because of its conduct, was the hospital estopped to deny that Dr. Henderson was its agent?

CHAPTER 37

Agency and Tort Liability

The previous chapter reviewed rights and liabilities of principals arising from contracts negotiated by their agents. In this chapter, the discussion begins by looking at the nature of a principal's liability to third parties for physical injuries resulting from an agent's torts. Then it focuses on principals' liability for agents' torts, such as fraud, that do not result in physical injury to third parties. We do not deal with employees' personal liability for their own torts—only with employers' *vicarious* (indirect) liability for agents' tortious acts.

The principal's tort liability hinges on two variables: (1) whether the victim of the tort suffered **physical** or **nonphysical** injury and (2) whether the tort was committed by **a nonservant independent contractor** or a **servant (employee).** The distinction between nonservant independent contractors (sometimes called agent independent contractors) and servants was presented in Chapter 36. It will be recalled that the essential difference between these two types of agents was that the master has *control* over the physical conduct of the servant but does *not* have such control over the activities of a nonservant independent contractor.

LIABILITY FOR TORTS RESULTING IN PHYSICAL INJURY

A principal is liable for the following torts that result in physical injury to third parties:

1. The principal's own torts.
2. Torts which the principal *directs* the agent to commit—for example, a principal bar owner who directs his bouncer to take a customer outside and "rough him up."
3. Torts, not directed by the principal, but committed by the agent while acting with the scope of authority.

Suppose a truck driver while making a delivery negligently hits an elderly woman in a crosswalk. She, as plaintiff, will normally seek and obtain judgment against both principal (master) and agent (servant) as **joint tortfeasors.** She ordinarily does not expect to collect the money judgment from the agent, since such persons are often "judgment proof"—that is, without assets that can be reached to pay the judgment. However, the plaintiff usually expects an employer to be covered by insurance and to have substantially more assets than the employee. Therefore, the employer is generally looked upon as the "deeper pocket" from which to pay the money judgment.

The principal has an additional kind of liability, discussed later in this chapter, for tortious acts of the agent, such as fraud, that do *not* cause physical injury to third parties.

Agent Independent Contractor's Torts Causing Physical Injury

Agency law holds that a principal is *not* liable for torts of an agent independent contractor resulting in physical injury to third parties. The reason for this rule is obvious. If the principal has no right to control the *physical conduct* of the agent independent contractor, the principal should not be liable for torts which the agent independent contractor commits while not under such control.

To illustrate, suppose you contract with Art, a real estate broker, to find a buyer for your office building. Art drives Ben, a prospective customer, to view the property. On the way, Art negligently crashes into another auto and injures Ben. Even though Art is your agent independent contractor, you would not be liable because at no time did you have control over Art's physical conduct. An exception to this rule, discussed later in this chapter, imposes strict liability upon the principal regardless of whether the work is done by an agent or a nonagent independent contractor.

Employees' Torts Causing Physical Injury

Suppose a delivery driver for a local pizza shop collides with your car, damaging it and injuring you. You learn that the driver had been drinking. Do you have any right to expect payment for your damages from the pizza shop, or must you look only to the driver? Since the driver is an agent employee, not an agent independent contractor, the employer *has the right to control* the manner in which the agent performs his or her duties. Therefore, under agency law, an employer, as a principal, is liable for the tort of the agent employee acting within the scope of employment that causes physical injury to a third party.

The employer does not have to be actually exercising control over an employee at the moment a tort is committed, so long as at that moment, the employer had the *right to exercise control*. To illustrate: Paul, who owns a four-story building, employs Archer as janitor. Paul has never given Archer instructions as to where to hang his pail while washing windows. One day Archer drops a pail from a fourth-floor window and injures Lisa, walking below. Paul, the employer, is liable to Lisa for the injury Archer, his employee, caused while acting within the scope of his employment even though Paul himself is innocent and did not personally participate in the accident. It is immaterial that Paul did not exercise his right to control Archer's performance by giving specific safety instructions about hanging his pail. The important factor is that Paul had the *right* to do so because Archer was in Paul's employ.

Master and Servant Defined. Since we have been discussing two kinds of agents—(1) employees and (2) agent independent contractors—it is useful to review some of the simple terminology discussed at the beginning of Chapter 36, and to identify each type of agent. Employee-type agents are also called **servants,** in which case their employers are called **masters.** Agent independent contractors are sometimes called **professional agents,** or **nonservant agents.** In this chapter we will follow the practice of most courts and use *employer-employee* interchangeably with *master-servant*.

Respondeat Superior. The liability of a master for loss or harm caused by a servant acting within the scope of employment is called *respondeat superior*. Essentially, it means "Let the master respond" in damages for the servant's torts committed within the scope of employment even though the master may have been personally free from fault. The tort may have been (1) unintentional negligence—the carelessness of a servant which causes physical harm or loss to a third person—or (2) an intentional act of a servant, such as assault and battery, in connection with employment which results in physical injury to another. As we have already seen, *respondeat superior* does *not* apply to physical torts of an independent contractor agent.

Reasons for *Respondeat Superior*. The doctrine of *respondeat superior,* first expressed in England in 1698, has been firmly fixed in our law ever since. It is unique to the law of agency. Courts and legal writers have given many reasons to justify this rule, which imposes on an otherwise innocent person vicarious liability to pay for another's fault. Among those reasons are:

1 A party who has the power to control another's acts should be held responsible for the results of those acts.
2 The master gets the benefits of a servant's acts, and so should bear the burden of them (the "benefits and burdens" theory).
3 Although a master may be without fault, the injured person may also be without fault, and as between two innocent people, an employer who places an employee in a position to cause injury in connection with that employment should bear the loss.
4 The master has the "deeper pocket" out of which to pay damages to a third party for an injury sustained by the latter.
5 Liability is imposed on masters for the privilege of using the services of others.
6 To make masters liable tends to make them more careful in selecting and supervising servants, thus benefiting the public.
7 Wrongful acts of servants in the course of employment are a *cost* of conducting business. One court has stated it this way:

The modern justification for the doctrine of *respondeat superior* is a rule of policy, a deliberate allocation of a risk. The losses caused by the torts of employees, which as a practical matter are sure to occur in the conduct of the employer's enterprise, are placed upon that enterprise; itself, as a required cost of doing business. It is just that the employer rather than the innocent injured plaintiff should bear the losses because the employer is better able to absorb them, and to distribute them, through prices, rates, or liability insurance, to the community at large.[1]

The costs which a master is required to bear are normally in the form of premiums paid for liability insurance. These premiums become an element calculated in the cost of the services or articles a master sells. The ultimate result is that in every purchase the consuming public pays some portion of a master's protection against tort liability.

Application of *Respondeat Superior*

While the definition of *respondeat superior* is simple, many complex legal questions arise in its application. For example, courts find it necessary, on a case-by-case basis, to decide:

1 Was the wrongdoer a servant or a nonservant agent?
2 If John, a servant of one master, is borrowed by a second master and, while temporarily working for the second master, John negligently injures a third party, does *respondeat superior* apply to the first master, the second, or both?
3 Was the servant acting within the scope of employment when the injury occurred?
4 Can a master be subjected to liability by ratifying a tort that the servant committed *outside* the scope of employment?

Each of these questions will now be considered.

Was the Wrongdoer a Servant? We have seen that the employer's *right to control the physical conduct* of a person is the chief determinant that such person is an employee. Since, at the moment an employee causes an accident or other tort, the employer usually is not present, and may not be actively and directly exercising the right of control over the employee's physical actions, it frequently is not clear whether the relationship involved is that of master-servant or principal–independent contractor. The courts must therefore consider all the circumstances

---

[1]*Lazar v. Thermal Equipment Corp.,* 195 Cal. Rptr. 890 (1983).

> **BOX 37.1**
> **IRS Slashes Number of Self-Employed Independent Contractors**
>
> A computer genius quits work at IBM, then agrees, as an independent contractor, to invent an improved chip. The IRS in 1991 reclassified over 100,000 contractors as employees and assessed employers over $135 million in proposed penalties. IRS continues an active campaign to cut thousands more from the list of such self-employed persons, saying more than 50 percent of them should not be classified as working for themselves. Why? If a person is an employee, the employer must pay the government withholding tax, half of social security deductions, and all unemployment taxes. An independent contractor must pay all such taxes; the employer only has to file a 1099 slip.
>
> Using a list of 20 common law factors that date from the Middle Ages to distinguish employees from contractors, the IRS finds in nine out of ten audits that the employer has misclassified employees as contractors. The IRS then assesses withholding taxes—taxes often already paid by the contractor. Officials at Treasury admit that the factors used to distinguish employees from contractors do not yield consistent results. How would you argue—for or against administering tax laws this way? ■

> **BOX 37.2**
> **Can an Employee Incorporate, Deal as Independent Contractor with a Former Employer, and Still Be an Employee?**
>
> To obtain certain pension benefits Frankel, age 61, formed a one-man corporation which then contracted with Bally, Inc., to furnish his services as a sales representative. When Bally terminated the contract, Frankel, claiming he was their employee, sued under the Age Discrimination in Employment Act (ADEA). The trial court dismissed his case, saying Bally had contracted with Frankel's corporation as an independent contractor to provide service—not with Frankel—and that he had no status as an employee of Bally. The circuit courts reversed. It said that a person who incorporates himself doesn't necessarily lose "employee" status under the ADEA. * ■
>
> *Frankel v. Bally, Inc., 987 F.2d 86 (2d Cir. 1993).

surrounding the employment in order to reach a decision.

In Chapter 36 we considered some of the characteristics of an independent contractor agent. Although the presence of these criteria does not necessarily prove that such an agency exists, courts generally weigh all of them in deciding on a case-by-case basis whether a particular relation is that of employer-employee or principal–independent contractor agent. Several factors normally, but again not necessarily, tend to show that a person is a servant:

1. The work is closely supervised, with a high degree of control by the employer.
2. The tools used in the work are supplied by the employer; the servant does not usually furnish them.
3. Payment is usually by the hour, day, week, or month.
4. The employee may not delegate work to someone else without the employer's permission.
5. The work of the employee is part of the employer's regular business.
6. The parties believe that they have a master-servant relationship.

It must be emphasized that the absence of one or more of these factors does not necessarily prove that a person is not a servant, nor does the presence of one or more of these factors necessarily prove that a person is a servant. For example, the Bar-Bell Company hires Strong as a full-time salesperson to sell its exercise equipment throughout the western half of the state. The agreement, prepared by Bar-Bell, specifies that Strong is an independent contractor. Bar-Bell, like many mistaken employers, recites that the parties intend an independent contractor relationship in the hope of avoiding, not only the liability of a master for the servant's torts, but also the impact of statutes that regulate the employer-employee relationship—such as federal withholding tax, social security deductions, workers' compensation costs, minimum wage-hour-overtime pay laws, and right-to-bargain-through-union laws. A court may find, as in Case 37.1, which follows, that under the particular facts before it, the salesperson was a servant, not an independent contractor, and Bar-Bell is therefore liable for Strong's negligent actions. Usually, when a court is required to determine whether someone is an independent contractor or a servant, the court must weigh conflicting factors in the light of the entire enterprise. It is not surprising, therefore, that different courts sometimes reach opposite conclusions when considering substantially similar facts.

How a court weighs the facts to determine whether a master-servant relationship exists and therefore *respondeat superior* applies, is demonstrated in the following case.

CASE 37.1   **Mustang Transp. Co. v. Ryder Truck Lines, Inc.**
• 523 F. Supp. 1097 (1981); Aff'd 688 F.2d 823 (1982)

FACTS   Henry Crowder operated a tractor-trailer truck under a lease agreement with Mustang Transportation Company (Mustang). The agreement described Crowder as an independent contractor. Crowder owned the tractor portion of the truck and Mustang owned the trailer. On behalf of Mustang and himself, Crowder entered into a one-way lease agreement with Ryder Truck Lines (Ryder) to transport a load of freight from New York to Michigan. Ryder paid Mustang for the use of the tractor-trailer in accordance with the lease agreement. In turn, Mustang paid Crowder in accordance with the terms of their agreement.

While carrying Ryder's goods, Crowder negligently caused his truck to collide with an automobile. As a result of the accident, one passenger in the car was killed and the driver and another passenger were injured. A dispute arose between Mustang's and Ryder's insurance carriers as to which was obligated to pay the damages occasioned by the accident. The matter was submitted to the court for trial without a jury. Pertinent portions of the court's findings of fact and conclusions of law follow.

OPINION   GREEN (CLIFFORD SCOTT), J. . . . The first issue to be resolved is the nature of the relationship of Henry Crowder to Mustang and to Ryder at the time of the accident. Disclaiming liability for the acts of Crowder, Mustang and Ryder each denies that he was its agent or employee (servant) at the time of the accident. In fact, each contends that the other was his principal or employer (master). . . .

The *Restatement, Second, Agency* characterizes a servant as "a species of agent" and defines it as:

> . . . an agent employed by a master to perform service in his affairs whose physical conduct in the performance of the service is controlled or is subject to the right to control by the master.

**CASE 37.1
Continued**

An agent who is not a servant is an "independent contractor." An independent contractor is one who "contracts to act on account of the principal." (Comment (b) to §2 of the *Restatement, Second, Agency*.) The distinction between the relationship of master/servant and that of principal/independent contractor, according to the *Restatement*, is that in the former situation, the master is responsible to third persons for the physical conduct of the servant. . . .

At the time of the accident, the relationship between Mustang and Crowder was defined by a lease agreement. Under Georgia law [applicable to the agreement] . . . if the employer has or assumes the right to control how the work shall be done, as distinguished from the mere right to require certain definite results in conformity to the contract, the relation is that of employer and servant rather than that of employer and independent contractor. . . .

If a written contract describes a party as an independent contractor, it is presumed that he is as designated. However, if other provisions of the agreement reveal that the employer has retained control over the time, manner and method of execution of the work, this presumption will not apply.

An examination of the lease agreement, which was drafted by Mustang, reveals that despite the description of Crowder as an independent contractor, Mustang maintained sufficient control over the execution of Crowder's work to establish a relationship of master and servant. For example, paragraph 10 of the agreement states: "The owner [Crowder] agrees that the vehicle(s) shall be operated in accordance with the rules, policies and practice of Mustang." Paragraph 2 provides in relevant part: "Any driver (including the owner if he shall drive himself) shall comply with all the safety regulations of Mustang. . . ." Similarly, Paragraph 5 states:

> Owner [Crowder] hereby agrees that no freight will be transported on said vehicle(s) while being used in the transportation of freight other than at the direction of Mustang, or with the knowledge and consent of Mustang, and that all freight transported therein will be transported pursuant to freight bills and bills of lading made out by or for and in the name of Mustang. . . .

While Mustang may have wished to limit its liability by describing Crowder as an independent contractor, these provisions show that it maintained too much control over the manner in which Crowder operated the tractor-trailer and transported freight to create a relationship of principal and independent contractor. . . .

Having determined that Crowder was the servant of Mustang, I now must decide Crowder's relationship to Ryder. . . . The lease agreement entered into by Crowder on behalf of Mustang and himself with Ryder . . . does not give Ryder any control over the manner in which Crowder was to operate the truck. . . . [T]he language focuses on Ryder's control over the shipment and not over the driver. . . . Because Ryder merely had the "right to require certain definite results under the contract" at the time of the accident Crowder's relationship with Ryder was that of independent contractor and principal under Georgia law. Thus no basis for liability of Ryder for the negligence of Crowder arises under state tort law.

JUDGMENT

[Having found that Mustang was the employer of Crowder and thus vicariously liable for his acts, the court entered judgment against both.]

Many times, particularly when a franchise arrangement is involved, it can be very difficult to determine whether it is proper to apply *respondeat superior*. Under a franchise arrangement such as a Chicken Delight or Taco Bell store or an Arthur Murray Dance Studio, a local firm **(franchisee)** pays a fee to a nationally operated organization **(franchisor),** takes its name, and does business under its rules. Whether such a business stands in relation to the franchising company as an independent contractor or as its servant is frequently litigated. Generally, courts look beyond franchise recitals that smugly declare the parties to be principal and independent contractor and examine their day-to-day relationship. If the national franchisor exercises a high degree of control—and many do—courts will not hesitate to hold that the franchisor and franchisee stand in the relation of principal and agent, and not principal and independent contractor.

Whose Servant Was the Wrongdoer? For the doctrine of *respondeat superior* to apply, not only must the tortfeasor (the one who commits the tort) be a servant, but he or she must also, at the time of the wrongful act, be a servant of the master who is to be charged with the vicarious liability. Such liability may depend upon (1) whether the servant was temporarily borrowed by another employer and while working for the temporary employer committed the tort which injured a third party or (2) whether the servant had temporarily employed someone else (called a **subservant**) to do the servant's work and the subservant committed the tort.

The borrowed servant problem. Because businesses and trades are becoming increasingly specialized in today's world of commerce, employees of different principals often work on the same premises at the same time. When the Jones Company lends its employee, Tom, to the Smith Company to do temporary work for the latter, the Jones Company is said to be Tom's **general employer,** the Smith Company is Tom's **special employer,** and Tom is called a **borrowed servant.**

The courts have not articulated a uniform test for determining whether the general or special employer is liable under *respondeat superior* for the tort of a borrowed servant. The traditional rule has been that the special employer, being the one benefited, is the one liable for the wrongful act. Some courts find a general employer liable if the servant (1) is paid by and can be discharged by the general employer, (2) is a skilled worker who has control over the operational details of the work, (3) is not engaged in the borrower's usual business, (4) is employed by the special employer for only a brief period of time, and (5) is using tools and equipment furnished by the general employer. Other courts, in deciding borrowed servant cases, apply a "whose business interest is being served" test, looking to see if the servant who is loaned to a special employer continues to further the interests of the general employer. If so, the general employer remains liable under *respondeat superior*. A view suggested by *Restatement (Second), Agency,* and followed by a growing number of courts, is to impose **dual liability** on both general and special employers, since the servant is actually serving both masters.

Two scenarios illustrate the borrowed servant problem.

1 Smith Company, located next door to Jones Moving Company, asks Jones to lend it an unskilled worker for 1 day because one of Smith's employees is ill. Jones (the general employer) agrees and directs Mark, its employee, to go to Smith Company (the special employer) and "do whatever they ask you to do." Jones Moving Company continues to carry Mark on its payroll. While temporarily working for Smith, Mark negligently injures a third party. When the tort was committed, Smith had control over Mark's physical actions in the performance of his work, all the tools and equipment belonged to Smith, and the work was entirely for Smith's benefit. Therefore, under the traditional view, Smith, the special employer, is the responsible master.

2 The problem becomes more complicated when heavy equipment, such as a tractor with an operator or an airplane with a pilot, is rented out. The equipment is of considerable value and the operator or pilot, a servant of the equipment

owner, is specially trained to take care of the equipment and to operate it in the manner established by the general employer. The party that rents the equipment (the special employer) tells the tractor operator where the machine is to be used, what earth to move, and where it should be piled, or tells the pilot what time to take off, where to go, and when to return. If, while complying with those directions, the tractor driver or the pilot operates the equipment negligently and injures someone or destroys property of a third party, the general employer would be liable under *respondeat superior*. This is because the borrowed servant (tractor operator or pilot) was still working for the benefit of the general employer, was performing the job in the manner required by the general employer, and was charged with the care of the equipment.

In the following case, the court applied Wisconsin's test, which imposes liability on the basis of which employer received the "primary benefit" of the borrowed servant's activity.

CASE 37.2   **Green v. United States** • 709 F.2d 1148 (7th Cir. 1983)

FACTS   Since 1969 Dr. Stanford had been chief of the Cardiothoracic Surgery Service at Lackland Air Force Base Hospital. His colleagues became concerned that his surgical skills were inadequate. The mortality rate for his patients was approximately four times the average mortality rate for the patients of the other surgeons at that hospital. To retrain in surgical procedures, Dr. Stanford applied for and received a temporary fellowship with Cardiovascular Surgery Associates (CVSA) in Milwaukee, Wisconsin. He remained on the Air Force payroll and received no pay from CVSA.

In 1978 Dr. Mullen of CVSA performed a coronary bypass operation on the plaintiff, Takuye Green. Dr. Stanford acted as Dr. Mullen's first assistant, being responsible for opening the patient's chest and connecting the lines between the patient and the heart-lung machine. In the course of preparing the patient for surgery, a physician's assistant (William Signorini) negligently reversed the arterial and venous lines that were to be inserted into the patient's chest. When the heart-lung machine was turned on, irregularities in the arterial and venous pressures were noted but it took 15 or 20 minutes before the error in the lines was discovered. As a result of the improper connection to the heart-lung machine, Mrs. Green suffered brain damage and became a blind quadraplegic. A malpractice suit against all participants in the surgery ensued. The United States was joined as a defendant under the Federal Tort Claims Act (FTCA), which authorizes suits against the government arising from negligence of its employees while acting within the scope of their employment. Applying comparative negligence rules, the district court found that Dr. Stanford was 62 percent negligent in causing Mrs. Green's injuries, Dr. Mullen was 16 percent negligent, and Signorini was 22 percent negligent. The court held that the United States, as Dr. Stanford's general employer, was liable for the negligence attributed to him. The United States claimed that it could not be held vicariously liable for Dr. Stanford's negligence, because at the time he operated he was CVSA's borrowed servant.

OPINION   BAUER and COFFEY, Circuit Judges, and BONSAL, Senior District Judge. . . . The FTCA requires us to apply the law of Wisconsin . . . as the accident occurred in that state. . . .

CASE 37.2 Continued

Wisconsin law, following the approach taken by the *Restatement of Agency*, ... starts with the inference that the employee remains in the employ of the general employer.... The mere fact that Dr. Stanford was working under the supervision of other physicians at CVSA at the time of the accident did not make him the borrowed servant of CVSA. Under Wisconsin law, the government must also show that the work done by Dr. Stanford was primarily for the benefit of CVSA, the special employer, rather than the Air Force.... The important question is whether ... [the employee] is acting "in the business of and under the direction of one or the other...." However, even if it were true that Dr. Stanford was acting both "in the business of" and "under the direction of" CVSA, the evidence simply does not support the conclusion that his work—however narrowly defined—was of primary benefit to CVSA.

While CVSA may have decided to offer Dr. Stanford a fellowship with the expectation that he would contribute something to the group's medical practice in exchange for the training provided him, it is clear that the fellowship was intended to benefit the government and Dr. Stanford more than CVSA.... Dr. Stanford himself sought the unpaid fellowship at CVSA in order to improve his surgical skills. While at CVSA he continued to receive his salary from the Air Force. While this ... does not necessarily show that the Air Force benefited more from Dr. Stanford's work in Milwaukee than did CVSA, it strongly suggests that this was the case. There can be no doubt that Dr. Stanford's fellowship suited the government's needs; it had the immediate advantage of forestalling an even greater controversy at [the Air Base] than has already arisen concerning his competence as a surgeon, and it had the long-term advantage of improving his skills....

Dr. Stanford himself was a board-certified thoracic surgeon; he went to CVSA as a fellow, not an employee; he was to remain there only a limited time and was not to be compensated by CVSA for his work; and the government, as distinguished from a private business enterprise, is not accustomed to loaning its employees to other employers.

We agree with the district court that Dr. Stanford's work at CVSA was not primarily for the benefit of CVSA. Therefore, under the law of Wisconsin Dr. Stanford was not the borrowed servant of CVSA and the United States remained liable for his negligence during the operation on Mrs. Green.

JUDGMENT

[Judgment of the trial court that Dr. Stanford was not the borrowed servant of CVSA and that the United States remained liable for his negligence was affirmed.]

Principal's liability for acts of subagent. If an agent has authority to hire subagents, the principal is liable for their acts. Suppose Paul, a principal who produces mousetraps, hires Arnold as agent in a distant city to sell his products, and authorizes him to "hire another salesperson if demand gets too big for you." Arnold hires Sam, who negligently injures a pedestrian in a crosswalk while in the scope of his employment. Paul is liable for the pedestrian's injuries under *respondeat superior*. In addition to the express authority that Paul gave to Arnold to hire subagents, there are three other situations where the principal is liable for acts of subagents because authority to appoint such subagents is implied by law:

1. The agent is appointed to a position, or in a place, where it is business custom to appoint subagents. (For example, a New Orleans cotton purchasing agent for a Boston textile manufacturer has authority to appoint a local cotton broker as subagent to complete the shipping details after a cotton purchase has been negotiated.)
2. Carrying on the principal's business reasonably requires the employment of other agents. (For example, a nationwide department store chain hires a branch manager.)
3. An unforeseen emergency makes it impracticable to communicate with the principal, and appointment of a subagent is reasonably necessary to protect the interests of the principal that are entrusted to the agent.[2]

In all these situations, the principal is liable for the tortious acts of subagents whose appointment the principal had authorized. Conversely, if the appointment of the subagents was not authorized, the agent alone is responsible for their actions and the agent is, in effect, a principal in relation to the subagents.

Subservants. A servant has no authority to delegate the work to others without the master's permission. If, without that permission, a servant gets another (a **subservant**) to perform his or her work, the servant becomes the master of the subservant, and as such, the servant has the liability of a master under *respondeat superior* for any wrongful act the subservant may commit in the course of the work. The reason for this is that the servant has the *right to control* the subservant in the performance of that work. To illustrate, suppose Harry is employed to drive a delivery truck for the Apex company. Harry, an avid baseball fan, without Apex's permission asks his brother, Bob, to drive the truck for him one day so that he (Harry) can go to the ball game. Bob accommodates his brother but unfortunately drives negligently and injures a pedestrian. Harry, as Bob's master, is liable under *respondeat superior*.

If, however, the employer *authorized* the servant to employ a subservant—as for instance, in an emergency—only the original master is responsible under *respondeat superior* for a tort committed by the subservant.

Was the Servant within the Scope of Employment?

In order for a master to be liable for the tort of a servant, the tort must occur while the servant is acting within the scope of his or her employment. The *Restatement (Second), Agency,* Sec. 228, provides that the phrase "in scope of employment" means that an act (1) is of the same general nature as, or is incidental to, the authorized work; (2) has a reasonable connection in time and place with such work; and (3) is intended by the servant, at least in part, to serve the master. Stated negatively, a servant is not acting within the scope of employment where the act is greatly different from that authorized, or is far beyond the time and place limits, or is too little motivated by a purpose to serve the master.

A growing number of courts have simplified the test of scope of employment to this: A servant's actions are within the scope of employment if they can reasonably be foreseen by the employer. In *Lazar v. Thermal Equipment Corp.*,[3] the employer permitted its engineer to garage its truck at his home, from which he drove to different jobs the next day. Driving toward a store where he intended a personal purchase before going home, he injured the plaintiff. The court held that the employer could foresee that personal errands might be mixed with company business. It said:

> Where the servant is combining his own business with that of his master or attending to both at substantially the same time, no nice inquiry will be made as to which business the servant was actually engaged in when a third person is injured. Where as here, the deviation is insubstantial and foreseeable, the doctrine of *respondeat superior* will apply.

General nature of the work. A servant is acting within the scope of employment when he or she is engaged in any activity that can reason-

---

[2] *Restatement (Second), Agency,* Secs. 79, 80.

[3] 195 Cal. Rptr. 890 (Cal. App. 1983).

ably be regarded as incidental to the work that the servant was authorized to perform. Suppose that a debt collector uses abusive language and threats in order to intimidate a customer into paying a bill. As a result, the customer suffers emotional distress and sues the employer. A court would consider whether the act was incidental to the servant's employment; whether it was commonly done by the servant or by others in the master's employ; whether the act was within the master's business and, if so, whether the master had ever permitted such an act to be performed by a servant; whether the harm caused by the servant was done by tools or equipment furnished by the master; and whether the master could have reasonably anticipated the servant's actions.

Time and place of the act. For the doctrine of *respondeat superior* to apply, a servant's tortious act must have a reasonable connection in time and place with authorized work. Generally, a tort that occurs going to and from work (the so-called **going-and-coming rule**) is not within the scope of employment. Therefore, when the employee is not being compensated for the journey, the master is not liable if the servant drives negligently and has an accident because of rushing to get to work on time, or because of falling asleep at the wheel on the way home after a hard day's work.

But, as with many rules, there are exceptions to the going-and-coming rule. The fact that the act occurs before or after normal working hours does not necessarily preclude the master's responsibility. For instance, an employer asks Bob, an employee, to mail a package at the post office on his way home from work. While driving to the post office Bob has an accident. Because he was then acting in the dual purpose of serving the master as well as going to his home, the **dual purpose rule** applies and he was within the scope of his employment. Had the accident occurred after Bob left the post office, he would no longer have been serving a dual purpose and he would not have been within the scope of employment.

Under the so-called **lunch hour rule,** if, while strictly on his own business, Bob is away from his employer's premises for lunch, he is not within the scope of employment. However, if Bob takes his lunch or coffee break on his employer's premises (or if he goes to a restroom provided by the employer), Bob remains within the scope of his employment.

Even though a servant's act may have occurred outside working hours, if the employer is being served it may still be within the scope of employment. For example, assume that Eve, a store employee, is directed by her employer to close the store at 5:00 p.m. and not to admit any customers after that hour. After the store is closed, Eve opens the door and allows another customer to enter. Eve may be within her scope of employment if, in an ensuing argument over returned merchandise, she assaults the customer. The store may be liable for Eve's tortious act even though it was outside her regular hours of duty.

The time and place of a tort are important considerations in the application of *respondeat superior*. This is reflected in the series of cases which hold that employees are within the scope of employment when they are on the way home from an office party which they are expected to attend. When an office party is held after working hours and away from the regular place of work, the fact that the employer mandated the employees' presence removes the circumstances from the going-and-coming rule and *respondeat superior* applies.

In the next case, which also involves employees who are partying, the court applies the **enterprise theory** to test whether an employee is within the scope of employment.

CASE 37.3 Henderson v. Professional Coatings Corp. • 819 P.2d 84 (Haw. 1991)

FACTS Plaintiff Mary Henderson sued Professional Coatings Corp. for injuries sustained in a head-on collision with a car rented by Professional Coatings and driven by its employee, J. Hughes. Before the accident, John Phelps, part-owner of Professional Coatings, and a crew of employees, including J. Hughes and J. McLean, had flown from the island of Oahu to Kauai to work on a month-long paint job. At Kauai the crew moved into quarters which the employer rented for the duration of the job. The day after arriving, Phelps permitted McLean, Hughes, and two other employees to use the rental car to visit a friend. McLean drove to Hanalei Beach Park, where Hughes met a woman who then accompanied the group to a barbecue party at the home of McLean's friend. Both McLean and Hughes drank heavily at the party. McLean became so drunk he could not drive and decided to sleep at his host's home. He entrusted the car to Hughes, who was also drunk. Hughes and his female companion went to her home and spent several hours there. When Hughes left to return to the party, the collision occurred. Henderson claimed that Professional Coatings was liable under *respondeat superior* for Hughes' negligence, which caused the accident. The trial court held that at the time of the accident, Hughes was not within the scope of his authority, and Henderson appealed.

OPINION MOON, J. . . . Under the doctrine of *respondeat superior* the employer is held accountable and liable for the negligent acts of its employees. However, recovery under the doctrine requires that the employee's act complained of must have been within the scope of the employment. The *Restatement (Second) of Agency* § 228 delineates the scope of employment in pertinent part as follows:

(1) Conduct of a servant is within the scope of employment if, but only if:

    (a) it is of the kind he is employed to perform;
    (b) it occurs substantially within the authorized time or space limits; and
    (c) it is actuated by a purpose to serve the master.

(2) Conduct of a servant is not within the scope of employment if it is different in kind from that authorized, far beyond the authorized time or space limits, or too little actuated by a purpose to serve the master.

Although generally whether the employee is acting within the scope of his employment is a question of fact to be determined in the light of the evidence of each particular case, where the facts are susceptible of but one reasonable conclusion, the question may become a question of law for the court. . . . We find that the facts of the case before us lead only to the conclusion that neither Hughes nor McLean was acting within the scope of their respective employments when committing the allegedly negligent acts.

. . . In this case, Hughes was driving a car rented by his employer. He was on Kauai for a limited time of one month and lived with his co-workers in a condominium supplied by his employer. Based on these facts, Henderson argues that Professional Coatings had potential control over its employees during off work hours. We do not agree. Instead, we find [that] . . . the liability imposed upon

**CASE 37.3
Continued**

the employer is not open-ended and unlimited. The employer's liability is limited by . . . "enterprise theory" which finds liability if the enterprise of the employer would have benefited by the . . . act of the employee but for the unfortunate accident.

We conclude that here . . . the only reasonable result is that the employer is not vicariously liable for the acts of the employees. Neither the act of McLean in entrusting the car to Hughes so that he could spend time with a female acquaintance, nor the act of Hughes in driving the car to return to the party after spending time with the woman in question, was within the course and scope of their respective employments. The acts involved were not of the kind that Hughes or McLean were employed to perform, did not occur within authorized work hours, and were not actuated, even in part, by a purpose to serve their employer. . . . There was no intention to act in the employer's interest, nor was there any direct benefit to the employer. . . . We do not believe that the *respondeat superior* doctrine is so pliant that where an employee is hired in one locality and relocated to another by his employer for an indefinite period of time, any act of the employee before, during or after his working hours is one within the scope of his employment as long as he works for the employer in the latter locality.

In the present case, there is no evidence to support Henderson's assertion that Professional Coatings had the potential, or even the desire, to control the behavior of its employees outside of work hours. . . .

JUDGMENT We hold that summary judgment was properly granted [in favor of Professional Coatings, the employer].

Frolic and detour. Often an employee is required to drive a company vehicle on a prescribed route or between specific locations. What if the servant does not follow instructions and deviates from the assigned course? The liability of a master for a tort committed by the servant while on a deviation depends upon whether the servant is engaged in a **detour** or a **frolic**.

A **detour** consists of a slight deviation from an employee's duties, in which event the employee is still said to be within the scope of employment. Suppose Tom, a delivery driver, is directed not to drive the company pickup on Main Street but to use a nearby parallel road because his boss does not want the vehicle to add to downtown congestion. Tom disregards the instruction and drives down Main Street in making his rounds. Tom's deviation from the prescribed route would be but a slight departure from his assigned duties. He would therefore be considered to have been on a detour and still within his scope of employment. If he negligently runs down a pedestrian on Main Street, the employer is liable under *respondeat superior*.

A **frolic** is a substantial deviation from an assigned route. A master is not liable for the torts of a servant while on a personal frolic, because he or she is outside the scope of employment. For example, Tom, instead of delivering packages, goes to the racetrack to see his favorite horse run, intending to resume his work immediately after the race. His driving to the racetrack constitutes a frolic; and if he has an accident on the way, he is not within the scope of employment.

The courts have given no clear rule as to where a detour ends and a frolic begins, but they have developed rules concerning when a frolic ends. Most courts hold that a servant reenters the scope of employment when he or she is again reasonably near the authorized route and the servant, within the time limits of the employment, is once again acting with intent to serve the master. For example, suppose Tom after making the delivery to the freight office, and without permission of his employer, drives 15 miles beyond to visit his sister. After the visit, he returns toward the freight office and when he is a half-mile away, he has an accident. As Tom is not far from his authorized route, intended to return to his workplace, and obviously is within his work hours, a court would probably hold that Tom is within his scope of employment and the master is liable.

The next case deals with the question of whether smoking on the job can be a deviation from the scope of employment.

> **BOX 37.3**
> **Law in Action: Frolic or Detour?**
>
> "One of the useful guidelines for assessing whether the conduct of a particular employee falls within the scope of employment for *respondeat superior* purposes is the extent of departure from normal methods of performance. It is our view that an employee's trip to a nearby store during his coffee break to purchase soda and chips for his own consumption was a substantial departure from the normal methods of performing duties as a yardman."*
>
> *Overton v. Ebert*, 590 N.Y.S.2d 508 (1992).

CASE 37.4 Edgewater Motels Inc. v. A. J. Gatzke • 277 N.W.2d 11 (Minn. 1979)

FACTS Gatzke, a district manager for the Walgreen Company, was in Duluth, Minnesota, to supervise the opening of a new Walgreen restaurant. While there, he stayed at the Edgewater Motel. His company, Walgreen, paid all his motel, laundry, living, and entertainment expenses. While in Duluth Gatzke worked 15 hours each day and remained on call 24 hours per day to handle problems arising in other Walgreen restaurants in his district. On August 23, 1977, Gatzke worked at the restaurant for about 17 hours. About midnight, he, together with his regional supervisor and a manager from another district, left the restaurant and went to the vicinity of the Edgewater, where they each had rooms. Before turning in, Gatzke and the other manager went across the street to a bar, where they talked about company business. Gatzke had four brandy Manhattan cocktails and talked with the bartender about mixing drinks to gather information for the new Walgreen restaurant, which also served liquor. About an hour later they returned to their rooms at the Edgewater. Gatzke smoked a cigarette while filling out his expense account and then went to bed. A fire soon broke out and the motel was extensively damaged. It was later determined that the fire started in the wastebasket in Gatzke's room. Edgewater sued Walgreen, claiming that Gatzke was within the scope of his employment when he negligently started the fire. After finding for the plaintiff, the court granted Walgreen's motion for judgment in its favor notwithstanding the verdict, and Edgewater appealed.

OPINION SCOTT, J. . . . The question raised here is whether the facts . . . reasonably support the imposition of vicarious liability on Walgreen's part for the conceded negligent act of its employee. . . . To support a finding that an employee's negligent act occurred within the scope of employment, it must be shown that his conduct was, to some degree, in furtherance of the interests of his employer. . . . Other factors to be considered are whether the conduct is of the kind that the

**CASE 37.4
Continued**

employee is authorized to perform and whether the act occurs substantially within the time and place restrictions [of the employment]. . . . No hard and fast rule can be applied to resolve the "scope of employment" inquiry. Rather, each case must be decided on its own individual facts. The initial question . . . is whether the employee's smoking a cigarette can constitute conduct within his scope of employment. . . . A number of courts . . . have ruled that the act of smoking, even when done simultaneously with work-related activity, is not within the employee's scope of employment because it is a matter personal to the employee which is not done in furtherance of the employer's interests. . . . Other courts . . . have reasoned that the smoking of a cigarette, if done while engaged in the business of the employer, is within an employee's scope of employment because it is a minor deviation from the employee's work-related activities, and thus merely an act done incidental to general employment. . . .

. . . [W]e are persuaded by the reasoning of the courts which hold that smoking can be an act within an employee's scope of employment. It seems only logical to conclude that an employee does not abandon his employment as a matter of law while temporarily acting for his personal comfort when such activities involve only slight deviations from work that are reasonable under the circumstances, such as eating, drinking, or smoking. We . . . hold that an employer can be held vicariously liable for his employee's negligent smoking of a cigarette [if] he was otherwise acting in the scope of his employment at the time of the negligent act.

The record indicates that Gatzke was an executive type of employee who had no set working hours. . . . It was therefore . . . reasonable for the jury to determine that the filling out of his expense account [and the smoking] was done within the authorized time and space limits of his employment. . . .

JUDGMENT

We set aside the trial court's grant of judgment for Walgreen's and reinstate the jury's determination that Gatzke was working within the scope of his employment at the time of the negligent act.

Was the Act Intended to Serve the Master? The last requirement for *respondeat superior* is that a servant's act must be undertaken with the intent, at least in part, to serve the master or that the act, if negligent or intentional, must be connected with and grow out of the employment.

Negligent act. Generally, a negligent act is considered to be within the scope of employment when (1) it occurs during working hours at the prescribed place of work or (2) while away from the workplace in the course of a servant's employment or pursuant to the employer's directions, unless the servant is on a personal frolic. But even where a servant is on the employer's premises, a servant is outside the scope of employment if the act is undertaken *solely* to satisfy the servant's own purpose. Assume that a factory maintains a parking lot for visitors but forbids factory employees to park in that lot. One day Cy arrives late to work, parks his car in the lot, punches the time clock, and returns to the parking lot to move his car to a street near the factory. In the process of moving his car and while still on factory grounds, Cy drives his car negligently into a visitor's parked car. At that time, Cy was moving his car solely to satisfy his own purposes and *respondeat superior* does not apply.

Intentional act. Thus far, we have been looking at a servant committing the uninten-

> **BOX 37.4**
>
> **A Question of Law**
>
> The owner of Macon Hardwood told his son, Tom, a foreman, "Drive to Nashville's auto auction, and if you find a good used truck, buy it for the business." Tom agreed, saying he might also buy a car for himself while there. Tom's father knew that Tom planned to drive to the auction with Smith, a used car dealer, who often took friends to the auction to help drive cars he bought back to his lot. At the auction Tom didn't buy a vehicle, but Smith bought a Buick. Tom was anxious to go home early to celebrate his birthday, and Smith agreed to let him drive the Buick, telling Tom to use a different route home. While doing so, Tom negligently crashed head on with Linda's car. Macon's and Smith's insurers asked the court to decide whether Tom was the agent of Macon or Smith, or both, at the time of the crash. Decision?

> **BOX 37.5**
>
> **A Not-So-Friendly Restaurant**
>
> Brenda, a uniformed waitress of Friendly Restaurant, while on her 15-minute paid break, went outside with Neal an off-duty soda jerk, and the two were hitting each other in a playful manner. Going back into Friendly's, as Neal headed for the restroom, he poked Brenda in the arm. She grabbed some water from a table and, without looking, threw it at Neal, striking Dixie, a customer, and causing her to fall and sustain injury. When Dixie sued, Friendly claimed that at the time of the incident, Brenda was outside the scope of her employment. The court gave summary judgment for Friendly, and Dixie appealed. Decision?

tional tort of *negligence*. However, a servant can inflict physical injury by committing an *intentional* tort which will be within the scope of employment if it (1) was intended to serve the master or (2) was connected with and grew out of the employment in a sudden outburst of anger stemming from the frustrations and pressures of the job. In either event, the tortious act must not be so violent as to be outrageous. If a servant's intentional tortious act is reasonably within the authorized duties of a servant, the action is within the scope of employment and the master is liable.

A recent court decision illustrates how *respondeat superior* may be applied to the intentional tort of assault and battery: King parked his truck at a supermarket to load empty Coca-Cola bottles. Campanale drove up in another truck and asked King to move out of the parking space so that he (Campanale) could park there and make an urgent delivery. King refused to move his truck and Campanale punched him in the face. The act, although clearly wrongful and unauthorized, was committed by Campanale in an effort to overcome an obstacle in the way of doing his master's work. The wrongful act was not held to be so "outrageous" under the circumstances as to take Campanale out of his scope of employment. His employer was liable to King.

What justification can be argued for a rule that makes an innocent employer liable for a pugilistic servant's assault and battery? The most widely quoted argument is called the *economic responsibility doctrine*. It forthrightly holds that the wrongful acts of employees in the course of employment are simply a cost of conducting business that the employer is best able to bear.

The principal is not liable for the servant's intentional tort when it bears no relation to his or her duties but takes place only because of personal animosity. Suppose Bill, a lathe operator at the Square Deal factory, without the knowledge of his employers, runs a football pool. During working hours he collects bets and pays off winners. Jim, employed at a plant next door, invests in Bill's pool. One day, during working hours, Jim comes to Bill's workplace and claims that Bill has withheld winnings that should be paid. In the ensuing fight, Bill breaks Jim's jaw. *Respondeat superior* does not apply and Square Deal is not liable.

Can an Agent's Wilful Tort Outside Scope of Employment Be Ratified?

Just as a principal can become liable by ratifying an unauthorized contract entered into by an agent, so a master can incur liability by ratifying a wilful tort committed by a servant outside the scope of employment. For example, Fred fraudulently acquired money from Sarah and turned it over to his employer as a credit against a shortage in his (Fred's) accounts. The employer retained the money after learning that it had been fraudulently acquired. A court held that the employer had ratified Fred's tort and was liable to Sarah for the money.

Strict Liability of Principal. Earlier in this chapter it was noted that there are certain types of activities which impose **strict liability** upon the principal even when the work is performed by a nonagent independent contractor. The principal's strict liability for ultrahazardous activity undertaken by an independent contractor is an exception to the general rule that the principal is not liable for the torts of an independent contractor resulting in physical injury to third parties. Often state statutes will impose strict liability on certain classes of principals engaging in businesses which affect the public interest. For example, there is strict liability if a third party suffers injury or damage when work is performed by an independent contractor (1) for a principal holding a governmental license or franchise, such as that held by a gas company which digs a ditch along a street in order to lay its gas lines, or (2) for a principal who is required by statute to maintain precautions for the protection of the public, such as a railroad company at its crossings, or (3) for any principal engaging in *inherently dangerous or ultrahazardous work*, such as blasting in a populated area or fumigating with a deadly poison.

Any principal who undertakes such **inherently dangerous or ultrahazardous activity** is said to have a **nondelegable duty of care**. If, when engaging in such activity, the principal's duty of care is nondelegable, it follows that

---

> **BOX 37.6**
> ### The Case of the Doberman Pinscher
> After two men, repossessing Sanchez's car, ignored her order to get off her property, Sanchez locked herself inside the car. The men, hired by the bank as independent contractors, towed the car to a fenced storage yard and locked the gate, leaving Sanchez alone inside the car with a Doberman pinscher outside. After her rescue, she sued the bank, which argued: "A principal is not liable for torts of nonagent independent contractors." But Sanchez argued the exception: "Not if they are engaged in inherently dangerous activities which impose duties of care on the bank that it cannot delegate to a contractor." What do you think? Is repossessing autos an inherently dangerous activity like blasting or high-voltage wiring?*
>
> *MBank v. Sanchez*, 836 S.W.2d 151 (Tex. 1992).

---

whether the principal does the work personally, or hires an agent or a nonservant independent contractor to do the work, the principal continues to be liable for any failure to exercise due care. The court, in *Hofstetter v. Union Electric Company*,[4] explained the meaning of the phrase "inherently dangerous":

To be inherently dangerous, the work being done must, by its very nature, involve some "peculiar risk" of physical harm. A peculiar risk is differentiated from a "common risk" in that common risks are those to which persons in general are subjected by the ordinary forms of negligence which are typical in the community. . . . The theory of liability for an inherently dangerous activity is not applicable where the negligence of the independent contractor creates a new risk, not intrinsic in the work itself, which could have been prevented by routine precautions of a kind which any careful contractor would be expected to take.

The next case deals with a principal's strict liability for inherently dangerous work performed by an independent contractor.

[4] 724 S.W.2d 527 (1986).

| CASE 37.5 | **Erickson v. Monarch Industries, Inc.** • 347 N.W.2d 99 (Neb. 1984) |

FACTS Monarch Industries, Inc., defendant, was the general construction contractor of a facility for the storing, drying, and processing of grain. Walters-Heiliger Electric, Inc., was its subcontractor and also a defendant. It performed electrical work at the facility, furnishing and installing a large transformer.

After the facility's completion, Loyal Erickson, a night operator, was found dead in 1977—killed when an explosion occurred in the transformer installed by the subcontractor. Erickson's administrator sued the general contractor and the subcontractor for the wrongful death, claiming that the transformer had inadequate capacity and was improperly connected, causing it to overheat. As a result, materials surrounding the wiring melted, forming flammable gas, which exploded. The explosion blew the doors off the transformer cabinet, which struck and killed Erickson. A key issue was whether the general contractor was responsible for negligence of its subcontractor. The lower court entered a verdict for the plaintiff against both defendants and they appealed.

OPINION BOSLAUGH, J. . . . Monarch contends that it cannot be held liable for the negligence of Walters-Heiliger [the subcontractor]. Monarch relies on the general rule that the employer of an independent contractor is not liable for physical harm caused to another by the acts or omissions of the contractor or his servants. . . .

There are exceptions to this rule of nonliability. The general contractor remains liable for the negligence of the subcontractor if he retains "control" of the work—or if, by rule of law or statute, the duty to guard against the risk is made "nondelegable." . . . In the present case Monarch had a nondelegable duty to provide a facility which was safely wired. The nondelegable duty exception is based upon the theory that certain responsibilities of a principal are so important that the principal should not be permitted to bargain away the risks of performance. . . .

> We believe that an essential element of the doctrine [of nondelegable duty] is the failure of the principal to see that all appropriate precautions are taken by the one to perform the inherently dangerous task. The doctrine, in short, says that the principal is negligent, and hence liable, because it has allowed the independent contractor to be negligent in performing the job. There is a nondelegable duty to see that the work is done with the requisite degree of care; when the contractor fails in fulfilling its duty of care, the principal has breached its own precautionary duty. . . . The person on whom the duty devolves is not excused from taking the necessary precautions by contracting with or relying on others to take necessary precautions. . . .

In the present case Monarch entered into an agreement to construct the grain-drying facility. Monarch employed Walters-Heiliger to perform the necessary electric wiring. W-H was required to exercise utmost care and skill in providing the proper components and in wiring the facility, as it was providing a dangerous commodity. . . . Monarch could not delegate its duty to provide a facility that was wired safely. . . . Moreover, the installation of the electrical

CASE 37.5 Continued	transformer was an inherently dangerous task such that the law will not relieve the contractors' liability for their negligence. . . .
JUDGMENT	The judgment of the district court in favor of the plaintiffs and against the defendants Monarch and Walters-Heiliger is affirmed. . . .

LIABILITY FOR TORTS NOT RESULTING IN PHYSICAL INJURY

Thus far in this chapter, we have considered a principal's liability for the torts of servant and nonservant agents which result in physical injury to third parties. We now consider a principal's liability for those torts which do not result in physical harm—torts such as fraud, deceit, and defamation. A principal is liable when such torts are committed by either a servant or nonservant agent who is acting in the course of a transaction authorized or apparently authorized by the principal. For example, in one case, Frank was foreman for Hi-Flier, a trucking company. One morning the truck drivers assembled in the company yard, threatening a strike to protest a new company rule prohibiting drivers from patronizing Smiley's Truck Stop. To justify the Hi-Flier rule and to quiet the men, Frank said: "We all know Smiley's Truck Stop is just another brothel." Smiley's Truck Stop sued Hi-Flier and Frank for the tort of slander. The court held that Hi-Flier, as principal, was liable under *respondeat superior*. Frank was within the scope of his employment because his statement was made while exercising his implied authority to maintain harmony among the truck drivers.

Liability is not restricted to situations where an agent commits a tort for the principal's benefit but may extend to a situation where the agent, in conjunction with the employment, commits an economic tort for his or her own benefit. For example, assume that the Tent City Company manufactures tents and has been selling them through a sales agency. The agency, in order to earn quick commissions after learning that Tent City will soon use a different sales agency, falsely represents to purchasers that the tent material is fireproof. Tent City had not authorized the sales agency to make such a representation and, in fact, the material is not fireproof. However, Tent City must bear legal responsibility for the agency's fraudulent representations.

Basis of Principal's Liability

When no physical harm results from an agent's tort, the basis of the principal's liability rests upon ordinary rules of actual and apparent authority. Thus, when a principal appoints an agent and clothes him or her with authority, the

> **BOX 37.7**
> **Principal Bound by Agent's Fraud?**
>
> On the same day that Una put her husband, Floyd, in the hospital, she phoned Johnson's insurance agency to come to her home to discuss a "nursing home policy." Johnson knew Floyd was hospitalized, and fraudulently had Una sign a blank insurance application which he later filled out with answers that he knew were untrue but that would persuade Pioneer Insurance to issue the policy. Pioneer canceled it 6 months later, when Una first filed claims. Una sued, claiming Pioneer, as principal, was bound by the fraudulent acts of the agent, even though he was acting for his own interest and against the interests of the company, and asked the court to rule that the policy was in effect. On previous occasions, Pioneer knew Johnson had problems selling insurance because of his "dope smoking." Is Pioneer bound by the fraudulent statements Johnson wrote into the Insurance application? ∎

principal is liable for any loss to a third party caused by the agent's economic tort in the exercise of such authority. The reasoning behind this is that public policy dictates that a loss should be borne by the one who made the tort possible (the principal) as well as by the one who committed it (the agent), rather than be borne by the victim of the tort. The principal's liability for the agent's economic torts also rests upon the time-honored theory that, since the principal receives the benefits of the agent's activities, he should also bear the burdens. In *Gilmore v. Constitution Life Ins.*,[5] the court summarized this "benefits-burdens" theory as follows:

> A principal may not accept the benefits of its agent's endeavors and reject out of hand detriments arising therefrom. A principal may not turn loose his agent on the general public, and then merely sit back and exercise little or no supervision [over the agent].

When a stock brokerage employee takes funds from a customer's account and trades in the market for his own benefit, can the principal-employer be held liable for the loss and for punitive damages as well? The court had to decide this issue in the following case of the crooked account executive.

[5] 502 F.2d 1345 (10th Cir. 1974).

CASE 37.6   Pusateri v. E. F. Hutton & Co. • 180 Cal. App. 3d 247 (1986)

FACTS   Mr. and Mrs. F. Pusateri deposited $196,000 with E. F. Hutton & Co., a stock brokerage firm. The Pusateris advised orally and confirmed with a standard Hutton written form delivered to Johnson, their account executive, that they wanted to maintain a conservative account and investment program, from which they would receive a monthly income of $2,000 to $2,500. Later Johnson had the Pusateris sign margin authorization and stock option forms without explaining the high risk of their use. Then, without the Pusateris' knowledge, Johnson engaged in more than 130 transactions involving purchases and sales for their account, thereby generating sizable monthly commissions for himself. Such an activity, called "churning," violates the rules of the stock exchange and is illegal. Nee, the office manager, noted in reviewing the monthly reports that Johnson had average commissions of more than $2,000 per month from the Pusateri account—an indication that the account was not being handled conservatively. Nee conferred with Johnson about the account and asked Pusateri only if he was satisfied with his account executive, but Nee did nothing more about Johnson's handling of the account.

Johnson left Hutton's employ in February 1982 and the account was assigned to another executive. In March the Pusateris, in reading their income tax return prepared by their accountant, first learned that they owed Hutton $3,600 on a margin account and that the value of their original investment of $196,000 had shrunk to $96,800. The Pusateris filed suit against E. F. Hutton and Johnson. The jury awarded plaintiffs $45,000 in compensatory damages against both defendants and $160,000 in punitive damages against Hutton. Hutton appealed the punitive damages award.

OPINION   RACANELLI, P.J. . . . In applying the standard for awarding punitive damages against employers, courts have generally required a showing that a corporate defendant either itself committed acts of oppression, fraud or malice, or that it authorized or ratified such acts on the part of its employees. . . .

CASE 37.6 Continued

Failure to dismiss an employee after the commission of oppressive acts is evidence of ratification if the managing agent has knowledge of, or the opportunity to learn of, the misconduct and fails to investigate. . . . Nee was aware of the excessive activity in plaintiffs' account and their conservative investment goals, yet he failed to inspect the Pusateris' portfolio. . . . Nee admitted the large number of trades and amount of commissions prompted his November contact with Pusateri and his discussion of the account with Johnson. In thirteen months over $47,000 in interest and commissions was generated. . . . Nee also admitted that he never mentioned the condition of the account [to Pusateri] or the fact that [at one time] nearly $200,000 was owed to Hutton on margin purchases. Nee agreed that the level of activity in the account indicated a need for his review. . . . In the succeeding months that Johnson continued to mishandle the account, Nee—inexplicably—did nothing to determine whether the unsuspecting clients were even aware of what was happening. Thus, although Nee did not testify directly that he knew of Johnson's activity and nonetheless approved it, there was sufficient circumstantial evidence from which the jury could conclude that this was true. From the sum of such persuasive evidence, together with Nee's direct knowledge of the status of the account, the jury was entitled to find that Nee consistently ratified Johnson's outrageous and oppressive conduct justifying the award of punitive damages against his corporate employer.

JUDGMENT

[The judgment of $205,000 compensatory and punitive damages in favor of the Pusateris was affirmed.]

Remedies of Principal against Agent

Being anxious to make a sale or to carry a transaction to a successful conclusion, an agent, consciously or unconsciously, may misrepresent or conceal some element of the deal and, as noted above, the principal may be bound to the third party by those misrepresentations. In an effort to minimize the risk of liability to third parties for agents' fraud, it is common practice for principals to insert protective clauses in contracts or order blanks that they furnish to agents for use with customers. Such provisions, called **disclaimers** or **exculpatory clauses,** are designed to notify third parties that the agent has no authority to make representations other than those printed on the contract or order blank.

A typical disclaimer clause might read as follows: "There are no understandings, agreements, or representations between the parties other than those stated in this written contract." What happens if the buyer relies on the agent's false representations and signs the contract without reading the disclaimer clause? Most courts hold that even where a third-party buyer has signed a purchase contract containing a disclaimer clause without first reading it, but has, in fact, been deceived by the agent's unauthorized false statements, such third party may sue the principal and rescind the contract for fraud. However, a majority of courts will restrict the buyer's remedy to getting out of the contract (rescission) and recovering the purchase price. In such cases where a third-party buyer has carelessly not read the contract, most courts refuse to permit such buyer to sue the principal for the tort of fraud and deceit in an attempt to recover punitive damages far above the buyer's out-of-pocket loss.

If the agent's fraud, or other tort not involving physical injury, causes loss or damage, the injured principal has a right of action against the agent to secure reimbursement for the loss sustained. Whether the principal will collect on the judgment depends, of course, upon the financial resources of the agent.

SUMMARY

A principal who has the *right to control* the manner in which duties are performed by an agent is called a master and the agent is called a servant. *Respondeat superior* is a rule which holds that a master is liable for physical harm to third parties caused by a servant who is within the scope of employment even if the servant is acting contrary to instructions.

In general, a servant is acting within the scope of employment if the act (1) is of the same general nature as, or is incident to, authorized work; (2) is reasonably connected with the work in time and place; and (3) is intended by the servant to be a part of the work. A servant does not necessarily leave the scope of employment when there is a slight departure (detour) from the prescribed work or specified route; hence, if the servant is negligent during a detour, the master is liable under *respondeat superior*. However, the master is *not* liable if there is a substantial deviation amounting to a frolic. Courts do not agree as to when the servant, returning from a frolic, reenters the scope of employment. Most courts hold it a reentry if the servant is reasonably close to the authorized route and intends to reengage in work.

Under the dual purpose rule, if a servant is engaged in an activity in which the interests of the master are being satisfied to some substantial degree at the same time that the servant is acting for himself, the servant is still considered to be within the scope of employment. A master may be liable for a servant's *intentional* tort if (1) it results in physical injury to a third party, (2) the tort is not outrageous, and (3) it is committed within the agent's scope of employment or arises from job frustration reasonably related to authorized work.

The principal has strict liability for injury or damage to a third party caused by a nonagent independent contractor negligently discharging nondelegable duties that involve ultrahazardous activity. A principal is also liable for a tort which does not result in physical injury to a third party if the tortious act is committed by either a servant or nonservant agent within the scope of the agent's express or apparent authority. Among such torts are fraud, deceit, and defamation. Principals, to minimize liability for agents' fraud, include exculpatory statements in their contract forms, thus giving notice that the agent lacks authority to make representations other than those printed on the form. However, if the agent actually engages in such fraud, the third party can rescind.

REVIEW QUESTIONS

1. When is the principal liable for an agent's tort?

2. Jones, a salesman, works in a city far removed from the "home office." Is the employer liable for a physical tort that Jones commits in the performance of his duties? Why or why not?

3. (a) Explain the doctrine of *respondeat superior*, **(b)** the chief reasons for it, and **(c)** the problems it presents.

4. Distinguish a servant from an independent contractor agent.

5. For protection from vicarious liability, an employer should have a standard clause in all employment contracts saying: "The parties agree that they have established a principal-agent relationship and not one of master and servant." Do you agree?

6. A servant is lent by her employer to another employer for one day, being subject to the temporary employer's orders. While working for the "temporary boss" the servant commits a tort. What tests will determine which employer is liable for the tort?

7. (a) What is meant by "scope of employment"? **(b)** How is "foreseeability" related to scope of employment?

8. If May gives clear, strict directions as to the care that John, her servant, must exercise, how does it affect her liability if John acts negligently in the course of his work?

9. Explain why the *time* and *place* where servants commit torts are important factors determining scope of employment.

10. Define the going-and-coming, dual purpose, and lunch hour rules.

11. (a) Distinguish between a detour and a frolic. (b) Joe, a TV delivery employee, in between job service calls, stops at a nearby playground to watch his son play little league baseball. In attempting to get his car out of the playground's parking lot, Joe runs into your car and damages it. To whom can you look for compensation? Why?

12. (a) Mike, a nightclub bouncer, injures an unruly patron while forcefully ejecting him. Is the master liable? (b) Amy, a salesclerk, showed 30 pairs of shoes to a customer who tried them all on but didn't buy any. Amy became angry and used insulting language to the customer, who sued for defamation. Would the master be liable for Amy's tort? Why or why not?

13. (a) Explain when and how a principal may be liable for an independent contractor's tort resulting in physical injury to a third party. (b) For a tort not resulting in physical injury.

14. Can an employer be liable for fraud of a nonservant agent who personally benefits from the tort? If so, on what theory?

15. (a) Explain the use of exculpatory clauses in sales contracts. (b) How much does such a clause protect a principal?

CASE PROBLEMS

1. LeFevre, a contractor, rented from To-Bi-Too a back hoe and an operator (Malcolm) to dig a ditch for a water line in Alaska. When Malcolm started digging a 5-foot ditch, LeFevre told him to enlarge it to a 6-foot ditch and not to worry about shoring it up—LeFevre would take care of that later. The ditch collapsed, injuring Kastner, whom LeFevre had hired to lay pipe in the ditch. Kastner sued To-Bi-Too, claiming it was vicariously liable for Malcolm's negligence. The court's summary judgment for To-Bi-Too found Malcolm to be a borrowed servant, and held that only LeFevre as special employer should be liable. Is To-Bi-Too, as general employer, also vicariously liable?

2. Dolores, who worked for a firm that cleaned offices, was driving home from work at high speed in congested traffic. When the car ahead slowed down and Dolores finally applied the brakes, her car skidded across the road into another car, injuring its driver. He sued Dolores' employer, claiming she was within the scope of her employment at the time of the accident, since she was going home from work, and had cleaning materials in her car which she intended to use the next day in her work. Is the employer liable? Why or why not?

3. The Ideal Heating Corp. had a rule that no employee could smoke in the work area. It was the practice of Lupella, an employee, to go to the washroom four or five times a day to smoke. On one of his trips to the washroom, he passed a large drum of highly flammable paint thinner outside the painting area (his work did not involve painting). Seeing a chance to fill his cigarette lighter, he opened the spigot of the drum, holding his lighter under it. Lupella was unable to turn off the spigot and a fire ensued. Ideal's plant and that of Artcraft Co. next door were severely damaged. Artcraft sued Ideal for its fire damage. Should Artcraft prevail? Why or why not?

4. Lambert, an installer-repairman for the telephone company, installed a telephone in the home of the plaintiff and then physically attacked her. Plaintiff sued the telephone company on the theory of *respondeat superior*. Lambert had never previously been charged with having committed any crime, and no complaint had ever been lodged by a customer against him. Is the telephone company liable? What are the reasons for your answer?

5. McCutcheon, a police officer for the city of Philadelphia, had just gone off duty and was still in uniform when he got into a hot argument with his neighbor, Fitzgerald. McCutcheon drew his service revolver and shot and wounded Fitzgerald. Fitzgerald sued Philadelphia for the injuries inflicted on him by its agent, McCutcheon. Should Fitzgerald recover? Why or why not?

6. A family of beavers had built a dam in a stream alongside a road. The county engineer decided the dam should be blasted open to prevent erosion of the roadbed by water backed up by the dam. An independent contractor was hired by the county to open the dam. The blasting deposited a quantity of mud on the road. The contractor did not remove the mud or put warning signs on the road. Westby, driving his car along the road, suddenly came upon the muddy surface. Unable to slow the car down, he skidded, turned over, and was severely injured. Who is liable for Westby's injuries? Why?

7. Gilmore was employed by Beacon Kitchenware Products to sell its No Stickum pots and pans. Gilmore was supposed to send his orders to the company, which would ship the merchandise to the buyer COD. One day Gilmore sold a large order of kitchenware to Agnes. He told her that he could allow a 25 percent discount if she paid in advance. Agnes paid Gilmore the full purchase price less the discount. Gilmore never placed the order, kept the money, and destroyed the order form. When she failed to receive the kitchenware, Agnes demanded that Beacon either deliver it or refund the money she had paid. Beacon replied that Gilmore no longer worked there; that he had acted illegally and outside the scope of his employment when he took Agnes' order; that Beacon never allowed discounts of the kind Gilmore had promised; that *respondeat superior* did not apply; and that Beacon was not obligated to Agnes in any way. Would a court hold Beacon liable under *respondeat superior*? Why or why not?

CHAPTER 38

Agents' and Principals' Duties to Each Other; Termination of Agency

Whenever an agent is hired, the principal takes a financial risk. The agent who acts foolishly or fails to follow instructions may bind the principal to a ruinous contract. The agent who negligently runs down a pedestrian with the company truck, or who exercises bad faith while dealing with company customers, can cost the principal millions. (It will be recalled that the oppressive tactics of the insurance agent in Case 27.3 cost his principal $5 million in punitive damages.) Because such liabilities can be thrust upon principals by agents, the law imposes upon them a broad range of duties toward their principals. Conversely, since principals are normally the source of agents' livelihood, the law also places definite obligations upon principals toward their agents. The entire principal-agent relationship rests upon this ethical foundation.

This chapter examines (1) duties of principals and agents to each other and their legal remedies when those duties are violated and (2) termination of the agency relationship. Hereafter, we will not distinguish between servant and nonservant agents because the obligations existing between master and servant are essentially the same as those which exist between principal and nonservant agent.

DUTIES AGENTS OWE TO PRINCIPALS

An agent who undertakes to perform work or services owes the principal the following duties:

1. **Duty to perform work with normal care and skill**, and without negligence
2. **Duty of obedience** to the principal's reasonable instructions
3. **Duty to perform services** *personally*
4. **Duty to communicate** all pertinent information
5. **Duty to account for all receipts** of funds and give them to the principal
6. **Fiduciary duty of loyalty**—to act with the *utmost good faith,* and solely for the interest of the principal

Whether compensated or not, the agent has the obligation to observe all these duties. Although listed separately, they overlap and the distinctions between them are sometimes blurred in court decisions. For example, the agent's fiduciary duty essentially arises from the *confidence and trust* that the principal places in the agent. Suppose, in breach of that trust, the agent makes a secret profit at the principal's expense; the agent must give an *accounting* and pay the profit to the principal. The secret profit is realized because the agent failed to *communicate* with the principal, and did not act in *obedience* to instructions to turn over all receipts to the principal. The agent may have failed to exercise *normal care and skill*, and owing to an error in simple addition, negligently overcharged a customer $100, later deciding to keep it rather than admit a mistake. Thus, breach of all duties of an agent listed above may also involves breach of the fiduciary duty. For analysis, however, we will treat the listed duties as mutually exclusive.

Duty to Perform Work with Care and Skill

An agent impliedly assures the principal that he or she has the knowledge and skill to do the assigned work and will use reasonable care and diligence in its performance. Normally there is no guarantee that the agent has the *highest* degree of skill and diligence or will make no mistakes in the work. The law contemplates only that a principal can expect from an agent (1) the exercise of reasonable care and skill and (2) the degree of ability that is standard in the locality for the kind of work the agent undertakes to perform.

Some agents hold themselves out as experts. If so, they must have the additional knowledge and use the care and skill usually possessed by such experts in that community. An agent practicing a profession which requires extensive education and special license from the state is generally considered to be an expert. Therefore accountants or attorneys who give clients advice on tax matters or estate planning impliedly represent that they are conversant with relevant tax law and regulations.

Duty of Obedience to Principal's Instructions

An agent is under a duty to obey the reasonable instructions of the principal. A corollary rule requires an agent to refrain from doing acts that the principal has not expressly or impliedly authorized. For example, if a sales agent is instructed to accept only cash payments, acceptance of a check breaches the agent's duty to obey the principal's reasonable instructions—even if the agent believes in good faith that the check is valid and that accepting it would bring profit to the principal. Of course, if the check "bounces" the agent must make it good, because the rule is: The agent is liable to the principal for any loss resulting from failure to obey reasonable instructions.

In *emergency situations* there is an exception to the rule of obeying reasonable instructions. If there is a good faith belief that deviation from instructions is necessary to protect the principal's interests in an emergency, the agent may do so. An emergency is one that the agent reasonably believes was unforeseen by the principal and that requires action before the agent has an opportunity to inform the principal and to ask for revised instructions. For example, John, the manager of a grocery store, instructs employees not to contract any purchases. On a hot day, the frozen food unit breaks down while John is away and cannot be reached. Mary, a clerk, calls a repairman to fix the refrigeration before the food spoils. The store must honor that contract and pay for the repairs.

The following case illustrates the obligation of an agent to exercise professional skill and the agent's duty to carry out diligently the instructions of the principal.

CASE 38.1   Quechee Lakes Rental Corp. v. Boggess • 608 A.2d 39 (Vt. 1992)

FACTS Mr. and Mrs. Stephen Boggess (plaintiffs) listed a condominium with Quechee Lakes Rental Corp. (QLRC), a licensed real estate corporation, at a sale price (furnished) of $289,500 and agreed to pay an 8 percent commission. Ms. Bacon, a licensed real estate salesperson employed by QLRC, produced buyers who of-

CASE 38.1 Continued

fered $281,000, which Stephen Boggess turned down. QLRC then informed the buyers that if they made a $289,500 offer, QLRC would pay the buyers $8,500 for the furnishings in the apartment. Thus the buyers would still be paying $281,000 and in effect, the difference was made up by real estate broker, QLRC. QLRC did not tell the Boggesses about their offer to purchase the furniture.

When they received the offer of $289,500 the Boggesses made a counteroffer with such harsh terms that the buyers started looking at other property. QLRC then reminded the Boggesses that they had contractually agreed to pay an 8 percent commission if QLRC found buyers ready, willing, and able to buy for $289,500, which QLRC had done, and that the Boggesses would have to pay them a commission, regardless of whether they went through with the sale. The Boggesses then quickly accepted the buyers' offer, but Ms. Bacon waited 3 days to tell the buyers because QLRC had them interested in a higher-priced condo which they bought for $385,000. QLRC then sued the Boggesses for its commission on the theory that it had produced a buyer ready, willing, and able to buy. The trial court found that QLRC was not entitled to commissions because it breached its fiduciary duty in not disclosing its deal to buy furniture, and not basing its commission on 8 percent of $281,000 instead of $289,500. It held QLRC negligent in not immediately communicating the seller's acceptance of the buyers' offer of $289,500. QLRC appealed.

OPINION

JOHNSON, J. . . . A real estate broker, as an agent, must act with the utmost good faith and loyalty for the furtherance and advancement of the interests of his or her principals. A person employing a broker to negotiate a sale bargains for the disinterested skill, diligence and zeal of the broker for his or her own exclusive benefit. Part of this duty requires that a broker disclose all matters that are material to, and might affect, the principal's actions. . . .

Contrary to the trial court, however, we conclude that the material breach to be drawn from the facts is Bacon's failure to immediately communicate to the buyers that Boggess had rescinded his counteroffer and was willing to accept the last offer made by the buyers. It is the general rule that a real estate agent must act in compliance with the instructions of his principal. A broker cannot be controlled by his own judgment, rather than that of his principal. . . . To make matters worse, Bacon's reason for waiting was out of concern for the buyers, and not in furtherance of some purpose consistent with that of her principals. We can think of few matters more important to be immediately disclosed on behalf of a seller than acceptance of an offer, and Bacon's failure to disclose it breached her fiduciary duty to the Boggesses. . . . Later QLRC's actions were directed at retaining the buyers as customers, rather than selling the Boggess property, and their efforts were successful.

. . . QLRC argues that, whatever its conduct, it produced a buyer prepared to purchase the property at the full listed price, and, therefore, it is entitled to its commission. We are not willing to hold, however, that QLRC's breach of its fiduciary duty . . . carries no penalty. We apply the well-settled rule of agency law that an agent who conceals material information from a principal, or does not otherwise comply with the principal's intentions, is not entitled to collect a commission on the sale. *Restatement, Second, Agency,* §469, Comment a:

CASE 38.1 Continued	An agent who, without the acquiescence of his principal acts for his own benefit or for the benefit of another in antagonism to or in competition with the principal in a transaction is not entitled to compensation which otherwise would be due him because of the transaction. This is true even though the conduct of the agent does not harm the principal, and even though the agent believes that his conduct is for the benefit of the principal and that he is justified in so acting.
JUDGMENT	We hold that when a real estate broker breaches a fiduciary duty to a principal, the broker is not entitled to receive a commission if some potential harm to the principal may have been caused by the breach, even though no actual harm is shown. Affirmed.

Duty to Perform Services Personally

A person appointed by an agent to assist with the agency is called a **subagent.** If an agent who is a servant (employee) appoints an assistant, such person is called a **subservant.** Unless an agent has the principal's express or implied authority to delegate work to a subagent, the agent must *personally* perform the work he or she was hired to do. The reason for this rule is obvious: Principals should assume the substantial risk of employing agents only when they are served by agents they have chosen. However, duties of an employee may be delegated (1) when the act that the employee seeks to delegate is purely clerical (e.g., filing papers) or (2) when the employer knows or has reason to know that it is impractical for the employee to perform the duty personally (e.g., the work can be done only by a crew). When the agent has authority to appoint subagents, they owe the duties of an agent to the person who appointed them as well as to the principal.

A *nonservant agent* (an independent contractor) has even greater authority and can delegate so much of the work as does not involve the exercise of discretion, but must perform all work requiring discretionary judgment.

What is the distinction between the delegable and nondelegable duties of a nonservant agent (independent contractor)? Assume that you hire Jane, a real estate broker (a nonservant independent contractor), to submit on your behalf an offer to purchase Green Acres. Jane may delegate to subagents such jobs as finding out how much the current owner paid for Green Acres, whether there have been recent offers for its purchase and, if so, for how much, and for what prices comparable properties have recently been sold. However, Jane may *not* delegate to others the duty to decide the price or terms of payment she will recommend that you offer for the property. Neither can Jane delegate to subagents the task of negotiating the purchase. These duties are nondelegable because they require the exercise of judgment and discretion on the part of the agent herself.

Duty to Communicate Pertinent Information

An agent, whether servant or nonservant, has the duty to keep the principal fully and promptly informed of all facts that are relevant to the subject matter of the agency. The need to fulfill this duty is underscored by a corollary rule: Knowledge or information that the agent acquires is imputed to the principal—that is, the principal is presumed to know it. It follows that the disclosure of information that the agent has is critical because the principal is legally chargeable with such notice and knowledge, regardless of whether he or she has been told.

Information learned by an agent is classified either as **knowledge** or **notice.** *Knowledge* is any information of importance which an agent acquires concerning matters in which the agent has the power to bind the principal. For example, assume that Paul Principal authorizes Art

Agent to negotiate with Tom, a third party, to buy a tractor for him. Before buying the tractor, Tom tells Art that the reverse gear doesn't work. However, thinking it can be fixed, Art buys the tractor and takes it to Paul. Paul is unhappy with the reverse gear, and attempts to rescind the contract with Tom for fraud. Paul cannot use the defective gear as a basis for backing out of the deal. Art's knowledge of the tractor defect acquired *before* the purchase is *imputed* to Paul, the principal. Because "knowledge of the agent is knowledge of the principal," Paul is deemed to have been aware of the defect before the tractor was purchased.

Notice is knowledge that a third party communicates to a principal through an agent. The law assumes that an agent performs the duty of conveying to the principal all notices received for the principal. This assumption is binding upon the parties even if, in fact, an agent neglects to convey to the principal the notice the agent received. As a result the rights and liabilities of a principal with regard to a third party are the same as if the principal had *personally* received the notice. To illustrate, assume that Paul owns apartments and leases one to Tina for a year. The lease expires May 1, but states that it may be extended for another year at the same rent if Tina notifies Paul before March 30. March 25, Tina pays her rent to Art, the agent managing Paul's apartments, and tells him that she is extending her lease for another year. Although Art neglects to give Paul the message, the law presumes that notice to Art as agent is notice to his principal, Paul. Tina's notice to Art renewed the lease. The following case shows us how the principal can be bound by the knowledge of the agent.

CASE 38.2   Gering v. Smith Company • 337 N.W.2d 747 (Neb. 1983)

FACTS The City of Gering awarded a contract to the Smith Company for the construction of Phase IV of a gravity-flowing sewer system. Schaff, employed as City engineer, designed the system. During the work it was observed by at least one construction engineer working on the job under Schaff that the sewer line had a "sag" in it. The sag was noted on a set of "as-built plans" drawn by Schaff's staff, but it was not shown to City officials.

In November 1976 the sewer line was finished, and Schaff filed a certificate of completion stating "I hereby certify that Outfall Sewer–Phase IV . . . has been fully completed according to the terms and conditions of the contract, and I recommend that the work be accepted." The City of Gering accepted the work and Smith was paid. It later became evident that further work would be required to correct the sag in the line. The City sued Smith for the cost of the corrective repair work. Smith appealed from a judgment for the City, maintaining that the City, through its engineer, accepted the work with knowledge of its defect and that therefore the City had waived any right to damages.

OPINION KRIVOSHA, C.J. . . . Knowledge of the agent Schaff was knowledge of the principal, City of Gering. . . . It is the duty of an agent to communicate to his principal all the facts concerning the service in which he is engaged that come to his knowledge in the course of his employment, and this duty, in a subsequent action between the principal and a third person, . . . [the agent] is conclusively presumed to have performed. This is the foundation of the doctrine . . . that notice to an agent is notice to his principal. Thus, in the instant case, the knowledge of the engineer, acting as agent of the City, is knowledge to the City. . . .

CASE 38.2 Continued	The finding of the trial court . . . that the officials of the City did not see the "as-built plans" or have actual knowledge of the sag does not affect the matter of waiver where the uncontroverted evidence is that with knowledge of that fact the engineer for the City executed the certificate of completion. . . . The City may have some quarrel with its engineer, a fact we do not decide. What is clear, however, is that there was acceptance with knowledge and therefore waiver. . . .
JUDGMENT	Judgment reversed in favor of Smith Company.

There are two exceptions to the rule that an agent is presumed to have given the principal all notices and information pertinent to an agency:

1   A principal is not presumed to have knowledge of any information the agent acquires in confidence. For example, if attorney Ruth, in the course of representing her client Fox learns from him in confidence that he contemplates going out of business, she may not reveal this information to another client, Hall, even though that information would be valuable to Hall. Ruth acquired the information outside the scope of her agency relationship to Hall and, therefore, has no duty to communicate it to him. Although the knowledge that Fox is going out of business is in Ruth's mind, the law does not presume that Hall knows that information, because Ruth acquired it in confidence and outside the scope of her agency relation to Hall.

2   A principal is not presumed to have knowledge that an agent acquires when acting adversely or fraudulently against the principal. For example, if agent Art steals from his principal, the principal is not presumed to know of the embezzlement.

Duty to Keep and Render Accounts

If an agent's duties require receipt of money or other property for the principal, the agent must keep accurate records of those receipts. All such money or property must be turned over to the principal within a reasonable time unless otherwise provided in the agency agreement. The principal's money should never be mixed with funds of the agent. If an agent fails to account,

> **BOX 38.1**
>
> **Point of Law**
>
> Hibberd gave Paine-Webber his check to cover an open order to buy stock if the price dropped to 68. P-W deposited the check, as Hibberd expected the company to do, in a regular brokerage bank account, so that if P-W eventually bought the stock, it would pay the seller with a P-W check—not Hibberd's. The bank failed and depositors eventually received only 40 percent of their money. P-W refunded Hibberd 40 percent of his original check. He sued for the balance, claiming that, as his agent, P-W, by mingling his funds in a bank account with its own money, had created a debtor-creditor relationship; the loss was entirely P-W's and the company owed him the full amount of his check. Did P-W, as agent, have a duty to pay Hibberd the 60 percent that was lost when the bank failed?

the principal has a right to sue the agent for an accounting in a court of equity. The court typically will order the agent to submit a complete accounting and, after trial, enter judgment for any balance that is shown to be owing to the principal. In addition, the principal may recover from the agent any profit the agent personally made from the use of the money or property.

Fiduciary Duty of Loyalty

The most far-reaching obligation of an agent to a principal is the duty to be loyal. It is the chief characteristic of the fiduciary relationship between principal and agent. The term *fiduciary* comes from *fides*, a Latin word meaning trust or confidence. A principal places trust and confidence in, and reliance upon, the agent to act solely for the principal's benefit in all matters involving the agency. An agent must carry out the fiduciary duty by exercising the *utmost good faith*. This demands avoidance of any conflict between the agent's interests and those of the principal, or between the principal's interests and those of other principals that the agent represents. (See Case 38.1.)

To exercise the utmost good faith an agent, when in doubt, must make *full disclosure* of every relevant fact which he or she knows that might adversely affect the principal's interest. By making disclosure and obtaining the principal's approval before entering into transactions, agents can virtually be certain that their fiduciary duties have not been breached.

Case law has expanded the concept of the agent's fiduciary duty of loyalty to include (1) the duty not to take secret benefits or profits in transactions that the agent undertakes for the principal, (2) a broad duty not to act adversely against the interests of the principal, and (3) a duty not to reveal or use confidential information. When a particular type of agent wrongdoing recurs frequently, courts develop rules to deal with it. One such rule forbids an agent from making a secret profit.

Duty Not to Make a Secret Profit or Benefit.

To minimize the danger of divided loyalties, the law forbids agents (1) to make a secret profit on a principal's transaction or (2) to accept any kind of payment or benefit from someone who might influence the agent against the principal's interests. A few examples will illustrate.

1 P authorizes A to sell P's car for $1,000, telling A he will give him a $100 commission. A sells the car for $1,500 and gives P $900. A has made a secret profit of $500. In an equity court P can get an accounting from A, judgment for the $500 secret profit, and judgment for $100 because agents who breach their fiduciary duty have not earned their compensation and forfeit it.

> **BOX 38.2**
>
> ### An Ethical Point to Consider
>
> Lawyers and accountants who persist in breaching their fiduciary duties and ignoring ethical standards may end up *doing* time instead of *billing* it.
>
> Once regarded as one of the top trial attorneys in the United States, Harvey D. Myerson, on November 16, 1992, was sentenced to 70 months in prison for overbilling clients and then not reporting to the IRS $1.2 million of the overbillings. At one time, Myerson represented Donald Trump and the U.S. Football League. Forfeiture proceedings were commenced against Myerson's home in Key West, Florida. U.S. District Court Judge Korman rejected Myerson's request for a shorter sentence, citing his "lack of remorse." ∎

2 A is a purchasing agent for P corporation. T promises A $500 plus a new TV set if he will order T's products. A must make a full disclosure of this offer to P and can accept the cash and TV set only if P consents. If A secretly accepts these items, they are P's property. P can also discharge A for breach of the fiduciary duty.

3 P oil refinery asks A, a real estate broker, to find profitable lease locations for service stations. A buys lots in the name of a dummy and negotiates leases between the dummy and P, with all rentals secretly coming to himself. A has breached his fiduciary duty. P can terminate A as a broker, refuse to pay any commissions, and rescind all the leases because of A's fraud. If A honestly believes his lots would be profitable for P, he must make a full disclosure of all facts, and obtain P's approval of the transactions before entering into them.

Duty Not to Act Adversely to Principal.

When agents are disloyal, it is clear they are also acting adversely to the interests of their principals. Examples are endless. One of the most common forms involves an agent secretly operating a competing business. Often the disloyalty develops because the agent learns of an attractive **economic opportunity** through employment. The fiduciary duty requires that this opportunity be brought to the attention of the principal. Instead, the agent personally seizes and develops it for his or her own benefit. If the principal seeks it, a court will impose a constructive trust on any profits and property gained from the opportunity and order the agent to turn them over to the principal. A variation of this rule, called the **corporate opportunity doctrine,** prohibits corporate officers (agents) from secretly grabbing such economic advantage for themselves. (See Chapter 44.) As always, if the agent makes a *full disclosure* of all the facts to the principal *before* the transaction, and the principal rejects the opportunity, the agent then is free to appropriate it.

Another frequently recurring breach of fiduciary duty involves the agent who not only represents a principal in dealing with a third party but also attempts to represent the third party. Again, such conduct becomes permissible if there is full disclosure in advance and *both* principals know about the dual representation and consent to it.

Dual representation of conflicting parties, however, is distinguishable from situations that sometimes arise where an agent "stands in the middle" between potential contracting parties, speaking for neither of them and not attempting to settle price or terms. In that posture, the agent does not violate any confidences and does not represent conflicting interests so long as no position is taken for or against either principal. Real estate and escrow agents often occupy such middle ground between buyer and seller in real property transactions.

In the event an agent represents principals on both sides of a transaction without obtaining their consent or making full disclosure, either principal may (1) refuse to pay the agent (even when, though the agent negotiated a fair agreement), (2) rescind the agreement that was negotiated by the agent, (3) recover any money damages from the agent, and (4) terminate the agency. These remedies can be used only by a principal who was unaware of the dual representation. Such party might also have a right of action for damages against the other principal who was secretly collaborating with the agent.

The agent's duty not to secretly sell or buy from the principal is another milestone of case law adding precise definition to the concept of an agent's fiduciary duty. In essence, this rule holds that an agent may not, without the consent of the principal, play the dual role of agent and third party. It is immaterial that the agent innocently believes that the acts are in the best interests of the principal. Accordingly, an agent who buys for a principal may not, without the principal's full knowledge, sell the agent's own property to the principal. An agent who does so is acting as a third party and could take unfair advantage of the principal. For instance, the agent could deliver an inferior article, or charge the principal an inflated price, or buy items with personal funds on the open market, and then sell to the principal at a profit.

Similarly, an agent who is *selling* articles for a principal may not, without full disclosure to the principal, buy one personally unless the principal had placed a firm price upon the article. The following case reflects the strict interpretation that courts give to the rule that the agent who has agreed to sell property for the principal may not secretly buy it.

CASE 38.3 Sierra Pacific Industries, Inc. v. Carter • 163 Cal. Rptr. 764 (Cal. 1980)

FACTS Sierra Pacific (plaintiff) wanted to sell land that it owned. Relying on the representation of Carter (defendant), a real estate agent, that it was worth $85,000, the plaintiff orally commissioned him to sell it for that amount, agreeing that Carter would receive a fee of $5,000. After unsuccessfully showing the property to several prospective customers, Carter sold the property for $85,000 to his

CASE 38.3 Continued

daughter and son-in-law. Carter retained his agreed $5,000 commission and turned the balance over to the plaintiff, without telling him of his relationship to the buyer.

When Sierra Pacific discovered that Carter's daughter and son-in-law were the purchasers, it brought suit against Carter, alleging that he had breached his fiduciary duty as agent and sought recovery of the $5,000 commission retained by him. After a verdict for Carter, the court granted Sierra Pacific's motion for a new trial, and Carter appealed.

OPINION

RHODES, Assoc. J. . . . An agent bears a fiduciary relationship to his or her principal which requires . . . disclosure of all information in the agent's possession relevant to the subject matter of the agency. . . . An agent may not compete with the principal, nor . . . act as agent for another whose interests conflict with those of the principal. . . .

In the context of an agreement to sell land on another's behalf, the general duties inherent in every agency become more specific. A real estate agent must refrain from dual representation in a sale transaction unless he or she obtains the consent of both principals after full disclosure. . . . This means under most circumstances that if the agent is related to the buyer in a way which suggests a reasonable possibility that the agent . . . could indirectly be acquiring an interest in the subject property, the relationship is a material fact which must be disclosed.

There is no question that Carter concealed information material to this transaction from his principal, Sierra Pacific. He claims that he was exempted from the disclosure requirement, however, on the basis of a so-called "net listing." Under a net listing agreement the seller agrees to take a fixed sum of money for his property and the broker is entitled to all additional sums as his commission. It is true that under this type of arrangement, a broker may not be obligated to disclose any relationship he has to the buyer. . . .

In order to exempt a broker from the strict requirement of disclosure a real estate sales agreement must include a net sale price determined by the seller *without influence by the agent.* . . . Here, uncontradicted evidence shows that Sierra Pacific officials agreed to the $85,000 figure based on an estimate Carter made at their request. . . . The key factor in permitting the real estate broker this relief [under the net listing exemption] is the independent and completely uninfluenced determination of the net sales price by the seller. . . .

It is thus evident that Carter owed a duty of disclosure to his principal, Sierra Pacific. It is equally evident that the duty was breached. . . . Sierra Pacific was entitled to recover the commission it paid to Carter. . . . By misconduct or willful disregard in a material respect of an obligation imposed upon him by the law of agency, he may forfeit his right to compensation. . . . We thus are led to the inescapable conclusion that Carter is liable to Sierra Pacific as a matter of law for a minimum of $5000 and that the jury's verdict to the contrary is in error. . . .

JUDGMENT

[The court ordered a new trial on the sole issue of the extent of the plaintiff's damages.]

Duty Not to Use Confidential Information.
All agents owe a duty not to use confidential information for the benefit of themselves or others, unless the principal's consent is obtained. The duty not to use confidential information is imposed by law and need not be spelled out in the employment contract. Nevertheless, firms often require employees to sign *secrecy agreements* so as to remind them of the nondisclosure duty and to make it easier to sue in case of breach. Unlike agents' other obligations already discussed, the prohibition against disclosing confidential information continues even after the agent ceases to work for the principal.

Trade secrets. Some kinds of confidential information, called **trade secrets,** consist of any information that gives a firm an advantage over its competitors, such as chemical formulas, manufacturing processes, or pricing lists. An employee has no right to use or to disclose trade secrets learned in employment. However, when employees change employment, they inevitably bring to the new job knowledge gained from the former one. Although they may not disclose previously learned trade secrets to the new employer, they do have the right to use the skills and knowledge they have acquired. The distinction between learned skills and a former employer's trade secret is often blurred, and the decisions are varied and conflicting.

Customer lists. A **customer list** is a compilation of names and addresses of potential purchasers of particular services or articles. For example, retailers keep lists of their charge account customers, banks have lists of Visa card holders, stockbrokers compile lists of people interested in financial matters, and a mail order firm keeps a running list of its customers and their buying preferences. Customer lists are costly to develop and are valuable assets. Consequently, anyone who starts a new business using a former employer's confidential list to solicit customers risks a lawsuit. Courts dealing with such cases weigh the former employee's right to become an entrepreneur against the former employer's right to protect its property. Generally, the law permits solicitation of customers of a former employer if the employee knew the names of such customers from having personally dealt with them during employment. One court tersely explained the reason for the rule: "Equity has no power to compel a man who changes employers to wipe clean the slate of his memory."[1]

Customers of former employers may also be solicited if they are openly engaged in business or if their names can be discovered from business directories such as a telephone book's Yellow Pages. However, it is a breach of fiduciary duty for agents to bring to a new employer partially completed customer contracts on which they had been working with a former employer. In such cases, the former employer, as principal, may sue both agent and third parties who knowingly used the information, enjoin them from its future use, and recover profits made from past misuse.

> **BOX 38.3**
>
> ### A Point of Ethics
>
> Recently, an Oklahoma state court jury awarded a $120 million verdict against a lawyer accused of doublecrossing his client. Adco Oil, a small company, retained the lawyer to appear before the state's oil and gas regulatory board and to persuade it to permit the firm to drill for oil in a proposed locale. However, the jury found that the lawyer, at the time he was retained, represented a rival company and informed them of his client's pending petition, thus giving the rival time to effectively block his client's drilling project. The judge told the jury that the case presented it with an opportunity to send lawyers a message about the consequences of breach of the fiduciary duty. Seeking punitive damages, plaintiff's lawyer told the jury that the case would give them an opportunity to "fire a shot that would be heard in all lawyerdom." The jury awarded $20 million of its total verdict as punitive damages. The lawyer is considering whether to appeal the case.

---

[1] *Peerless Pattern Company v. Pictorial Review Co.*, 132 N.Y.S. 37, 39 (N.Y. App. 1911).

The shop-right privilege. Sometimes, an employee whose duties do not include research or invention perfects an invention while using the employer's facilities, materials, or equipment. The **shop-right privilege** is a variant of an agent's obligation to turn over to the employer all information relating to the agency. The employee is the owner of the invention but the employer has a *shop-right* interest in it—that is, the right to use the invention without paying a royalty. However, if employees' duties are to conduct research or to invent, their work product, including any patents, is the employer's property.

OBLIGATIONS OF PRINCIPALS TO AGENTS

Just as agents owe duties and obligations to principals, so principals have parallel obligations to agents. Some of those obligations may be spelled out in the agreement; others are implied. In suits to enforce these rights, most state laws provide that if the principal is shown to have used "malice, oppression, or fraud," juries may award punitive damages. A principal has the obligation:

1. To compensate the agent for services (unless otherwise agreed)
2. To keep and render accounts
3. To provide the agent with means to accomplish the work
4. To continue the employment of the agent for such period of time as had been agreed upon between them

If the agent is a servant (employee), then the principal has two additional statutory obligations: (1) to provide a safe workplace (required by state statutes and the federal Occupational Safety and Health Act) and (2) to ensure that the employee will be compensated for injuries sustained in the course of the employment, as required by state workers' compensation laws and the federal Jones Act.

Duty to Compensate Agent

Principals' obligations to agents primarily focus on the duty to compensate them for services rendered (unless they have agreed to serve gratuitously). If a servant-type agent is employed and the rate of compensation is not specified, then the employee is entitled to the reasonable value of the services. All states have laws which penalize employers who are delinquent in paying wages owed to their employees or who pay less than the legal minimum wage.

Compensation of a nonservant agent (independent contractor) is fixed by the parties' agreement, and if none exists, the agent is entitled to the reasonable value of the services. If compensation is dependent upon results attained, the agent may be paid a commission, fee, or bonus. In the real estate business, unless some other agreement is made, a real estate broker employed by an owner to sell a property undertakes to find a buyer who is *ready, willing, and able* to buy on terms and price specified. If the agent finds such buyer, the agent is entitled to a commission regardless of whether the owner goes through with the sale.

A principal is also obligated to compensate or indemnify an agent for costs reasonably expended on behalf of the principal in carrying out the purpose of the agency. The following might be called the case of the unprincipled principal. When he caused an auctioneer (agent) to misrepresent the goods, the court had to decide whether the principal should reimburse the agent for the damages he sustained because of the principal's fraud.

CASE 38.4   Castille v. Folck • 338 So. 2d 328 (La. 1976)

FACTS   Navarre, the owner of a mare named Flying Cobre, consigned the horse to auctioneer Folck to sell at auction. Navarre told Folck the horse had a "negative Coggins test" and that a laboratory certificate would be given the purchaser attesting that the horse did not have swamp fever. Folck, relying on this representation, repeatedly told the bidders during and after the sale that Flying Cobre had a favorable Coggins test certificate. Navarre attended the auction but did not correct Folck's statements about the Coggins test. Relying on Folck's representations while conducting the sale, plaintiff Castille made the high bid and bought the mare. In fact, Flying Cobre had not had a Coggins test. When Castille was not given the laboratory certificate as promised, he sued Folck for rescission of the sale, return of the sale price, and damages.

Folck deposited into court the purchase price (which had not yet been paid to Navarre) and brought Navarre into the suit as a third-party defendant, claiming that, as Navarre was the principal and Folck was his agent, Navarre was responsible for any judgment which might be rendered against Folck growing out of the transaction. The trial court ordered the sale rescinded and Folck was directed to compensate plaintiff Castille for the damages he sustained. In addition, Navarre was ordered to reimburse Folck. Navarre appealed.

OPINION   GUIDRY, J. . . . The trial court determined that a principal-agent relationship existed between Folck and Navarre. Prior to and up until the time of sale Navarre assured Folck that the brood mare "Flying Cobre" had been Coggins tested and that a Coggins certificate would be furnished to the purchaser. . . . A principal is under a duty to reimburse his agent for payment of damages which the agent is required to make to third persons on account of the authorized performance of an act which constitutes a tort or breach of contract. . . .

The trial court found, and we believe correctly so, that although Mr. Folck did misrepresent to prospective purchasers before and at the time of sale that the brood mare Flying Cobre had been Coggins tested, he did so based upon assurances to that effect from his principal. . . . The third party defendant, Navarre, is obligated to reimburse his agent, Folck, for the amount of damages finally determined to have been incurred by plaintiff.

JUDGMENT   Judgment affirmed.

Duty to Keep and Render Accounts

A principal must keep whatever accounts are necessary to establish the amount of money due an agent for services rendered. In the event a principal fails to keep proper accounts, the agent may sue and ask a court of equity to order the principal to render an *accounting*. When the accounting is submitted, the principal is ordered to pay the agent the amount due.

Duty to Provide Means to Accomplish the Work

Normally, a principal need not furnish a nonservant agent with the means to accomplish the agent's task. However, a master (employer) is obligated to furnish a servant-type agent (employee) with the means necessary to accomplish the task for which he or she is hired in situations where the agent's compensation depends upon the results to be accomplished. For example, a salesperson on commission should usually be furnished with samples or descriptive literature; and a brickmason who is paid by the number of bricks laid in a day should be supplied with the bricks, mortar, and scaffolding required to do the job. An employer who does not furnish an employee with the means to do the work breaches the employee's contract of employment.

A principal must not place any agent (either servant or nonservant) in a position that jeopardizes the agent's future employment. For instance, a principal may not require an agent to perform an illegal or unethical act. If the principal tries to do so, the agent may refuse to obey such instructions without violating his or her agency obligations to the principal.

Duty to Continue Employment of Agent; Wrongful Discharge

Among the obligations that a principal owes is the duty to retain the agent in employment for the period agreed upon when the agent is hired. This is called an **agency for a term.** If there is no understanding as to the length of the employment, an **agency at will** is established.

The tenure of a *nonservant* agent is generally fixed by oral or written agreement with the principal. The employment period of a *servant* agent is generally determined in one of four ways: (1) by an oral understanding; (2) by the time interval for which the employee is to be paid—e.g., if payment is by the week it is understood the employee will be retained for at least that length of time; (3) by the established employment practices of the employer; or (4) by the completion of the work the employee was hired to perform.

When an employer hires an employee *at will*, it generally is understood to mean that the employee may quit at any time, and in like manner, the employer may terminate the employment at any time. An appellate court recently stated the traditional rule:

An employment contract at will may be terminated by either party with or without cause or justification. A party may be discharged for a good reason, a wrong reason, or for no reason at all.[2]

This once-dominant rule that employers could summarily dismiss workers not protected by union contracts has been significantly modified in varying degrees by the courts of at least forty states, which now grant relief for "wrongful discharge." The trend has been to modify the at-will doctrine by developing four major exceptions to its operation:

1 An *express contract*, such as a union contract, contains a guarantee of employment for a stated period.

2 The *implied contract* exception relies upon proof of an implied promise of continued employment subject only to termination for "just cause." Since at-will employment is *contractual*, the presumption that employment contracts of indefinite duration are terminable at will can be modified by the parties, just as other contracts are modified. One widely accepted means of modifying the at-will understanding is by use of personnel manuals, guides, or rules by employers. Representations set out in these publications can become terms of the employment contract and limit an employer's ability to discharge employees. In addition, a *prior course of employer conduct* can create an implied agreement that at-will employees may be discharged *only for cause* and that the decision to fire employees can be made only after an impartial hearing. "Help wanted" ads can also modify the presumption of at-will employment. Statements such as "This position offers a career opportunity" and "Excellent pension benefits" are often used as evidence of the employer's intent to provide permanent employment with the legal effect of restricting the employer's right to fire a job applicant except for cause.

3 *Bad faith breach of an implied covenant of good faith and fair dealing* is recognized by courts to prevent discharge by employers acting in bad faith—usually evidenced by oppression,

---

[2]*McCluskey v. Unicorn Health Facility, Inc.*, 484 So. 2d 398 (Ala. App. 1986).

fraud, malice, or artifice. Exercising such bad faith is a *tort*.[3]

4 *The public policy tort exception* permits recovery where the employer's conduct (usually a retaliatory discharge) undermines public policy. Underlying this exception is the view that workers should not have to forfeit their jobs because they have supported some important public policy principle such as refusing to participate in illegal behavior, performing a public obligation such as jury duty, exercising a legal right such as filing a workers' compensation claim, signing a union membership application, or exposing employer wrongdoing ("whistle blowing").

Actions for wrongful discharge in breach of public policy essentially involve employer breaches of duty imposed by law, and most court decisions treat them as actions in tort rather than contract. The public policy exception includes a variety of employee acts resulting in discharge which often subjects the employer to statutory penalties.

Some of these statutes may also reward the employee. For example, the **False Claims Act** permits employees of a defense contractor to sue the employer on behalf of the government to recover damages caused by the employer's falsified claims and billings against the federal government. If the civil suit is successful the whistleblowing employees are entitled to 15 percent to 25 percent of the damages assessed against the contractor.

---

[3]The effect of Title VII of the 1964 Civil Rights Act upon discrimination in the workplace is taken up in Chapter 48.

CASE 38.5	Wallace v. Milliken & Co. • 406 S.E.2d 358 (S.C. 1991)
FACTS	In July 1986 Jimmy Wallace injured his hand while working as a machine operator for Milliken & Co. He filed a workers' compensation claim and received temporary and total permanent disability benefits. After hospitalization and several operations, he returned to light duty work in December, at which time he was terminated. He filed suit, alleging that his discharge was in retaliation for filing the claim. The court of appeals affirmed the trial court's award of $12,500 damages and order of reinstatement. The employer appealed.
OPINION	CHANDLER, J. . . . Three different causation tests are applied by courts in retaliatory discharge cases: (1) *Sole factor,* which places the greatest burden on the employee. It requires proof that the *only* motivating factor for discharge was filing of the claim. (2) *Substantial factor,* which places the least burden on the employee. It requires proof that filing of the claim constituted an *important* or *significant* motivating factor for discharge. (3) *Determinative factor,* which places a burden on the employee more stringent than *substantial factor,* but less stringent than *sole factor.* It requires proof that the employee would not have been discharged "but for" the filing of the claim. . . . We here adopt the *determinative factor* test. . . . While the employer has the burden of proving its affirmative defenses, the ultimate burden is, throughout, upon the employee. . . . The burden of persuasion never shifts and the employee bears the burden of persuasion that the reason given for termination was

CASE 38.5 Continued	pretextual. . . . We affirm that the reason offered by the company, violation of company policy, was pretext.
JUDGMENT	[The Supreme Court affirmed the court of appeals' holding that there was a wrongful, retaliatory discharge.]

As a result of limitations placed by the courts on the firing of employees, disgruntled former employees with increasing frequency are filing suit and demanding huge awards, not only for lost wages but also for emotional distress and punitive damages. Six-figure judgments are common in many states. Employers recently have asked legislatures for relief. For example, Montana has enacted laws that protect employees against arbitrary dismissal and limit damages when employees successfully sue former employers. The case which follows illustrates how high the cost of a high-handed discharge can go.

CASE 38.6	**Western States Minerals Corp. v. Jones** • 819 P.2d 206 (Nev. 1991)
FACTS	Robert Jones (plaintiff) was employed by Western States (defendant). He operated heavy equipment, and when it broke down he was sent to work in the cyanide leach pit. Jones had attended one of Western States' required safety courses and had learned about cyanide absorption risk and the need to protect unhealed wounds from cyanide exposure. Still under a doctor's care, and recovering from an unclosed surgical wound, Jones respectfully advised the company of the medical necessity of not working near cyanide. He was fired for "insubordination." A jury found the discharge wrongful, and gave a verdict against the company of $151,150 in lost wages and $100,000 in punitive damages—a *total of $251,150*. Western States appealed to the Nevada Supreme Court.
OPINION	SPRINGER, J. . . . The law relating to claims by employees against their employers for wrongful discharge is rapidly evolving and is often lacking in the clarity one would expect to find in the more static areas of judicial decisionmaking. For this reason . . . [it is] useful to give a preliminary overview of the three claims for relief . . . namely, a claim for breach of contract, a claim for the tortious breach of the implied covenant of good faith and fair dealing which can arise out of certain employer-employee relationships (sometimes called a "bad faith discharge tort"), and tortious discharge (sometimes called a "public policy tort"). **Breach of Employment Contract** Employment contracts are ordinarily and *presumably* contracts which are terminable at will; however, an employer may expressly or impliedly agree with an employee that employment is to be for an indefinite term and may be terminated only for cause or only in accordance with established policies or procedures. We have called this a contract of "continued employment," a contract which an employee can enforce in accordance with its terms.

**CASE 38.6
Continued**

Bad Faith Discharge Tort

This tort is committed when an employer, acting in bad faith, discharges an employee who has established contractual rights of continued employment and who has developed a relationship of trust, reliance and dependency with the employer. By its nature this kind of employer-employee relationship cannot develop in at-will employment; consequently, a bad faith discharge tort cannot be committed against an at-will employee as can a tortious discharge.

Tortious Discharge

This tort, the so-called public policy tort, is the simpler of the two subject employment torts. An employer commits a tortious discharge by terminating an employee for reasons which violate public policy. Although this kind of public policy tort cannot ordinarily be committed absent the employer-employee relationship, the tort, the wrong itself, is not dependent upon or directly related to a contract of continued employment such as that existing in the present case. Discharging an employee for seeking industrial insurance benefits, for performing jury duty, or for refusing to violate the law are examples of tortious discharge.

[The court then confirmed the findings of the lower court that (1) the employees' manual reflected an intent for continued employment terminable *only* for cause, which the employer breached by discharging Jones; (2) the jury verdict clearly established that Jones was *not* insubordinate and, therefore, was wrongfully discharged; and (3) there was no merit to that part of Jones' claim relating to tortious bad faith discharge because the employer in this case was not guilty of artifice, fraud, misrepresentation, or betrayal of the kind required to sustain a claim for tortious bad faith discharge. The court then continued discussion of the public policy tort.]

The essence of a tortious discharge is the wrongful, usually retaliatory, interruption of employment by means which are deemed to be contrary to the public policy of this state. . . . We conclude that it is violative of public policy for an employer to dismiss an employee for refusing to work under conditions unreasonably dangerous to the employee. The Nevada Occupational Safety and Health Act states that "the legislature finds that such safety and health in employment is a matter greatly affecting the public interest of this state." . . . The public policy thus implicated extends beyond the question of fairness to the particular employee; it concerns protection of employees against retaliatory dismissal for conduct which, in light of the statutes, deserves to be encouraged, rather than inhibited. . . . This being the case, we hold that dismissal of an employee for seeking a safe and healthy working environment is contrary to the public policy of this state. . . . Here, Jones had no comprehensive statutory or other tort remedy available to compensate him for the civil wrong committed against him by Western States. He was, therefore, entitled to pursue an action for tortious discharge against his employer. . . . [The trial] Judge instructed the jury that it could assess punitive damages against the employer if it found "fraud, oppression or malice, express or implied." There is evidence to support a jury finding that Western States was guilty of the intentional public policy tort, tortious discharge; . . . that the charge of "insubordination" was a contrivance and a fraud.

CASE 38.6 Continued	There is evidence to support malicious intent and oppressiveness on the part of Western States. Therefore, we may not disturb the trial court's determination that the punitive damage award will be upheld.
JUDGMENT	The judgment of the trial court is . . . affirmed.

Duty to Provide a Safe Workplace

Of even greater importance than furnishing employees the means to accomplish their work is the requirement that all employers must furnish employees with a safe workplace in compliance with state safety laws. In addition, the Occupational Safety and Health Act (OSHA) of 1970 authorized the Secretary of Labor to establish federal health and safety standards that keep workplaces free from hazards likely to cause sickness, injury, or death to employees. Employers must comply with these standards.

Duty to Compensate Agent for Injuries

Servant agents have the right to be compensated for injuries suffered in the course of employment because the principal (master) has the right to control their physical activities. However, nonservant agents (independent contractors) are *not* entitled to compensation for injuries sustained while performing services for a principal because the principal does not have the right to control their physical activities. (See Chapters 36 and 37.) Two examples are illustrative.

1. You employ a real estate agent, Ruth, to sell your house. She is injured in an auto accident while taking a prospective customer to view your property. Ruth is a nonservant agent (independent contractor). You are not liable for Ruth's injury.
2. A physical education teacher, showing his class how to "slam dunk" a basket on a concrete court, fractures his leg. He is a servant. The school district must provide compensation.

Under the common law, a servant agent injured in the course of employment had great difficulty obtaining compensation for work-related injuries. If the claim went to trial, the worker had two almost insurmountable obstacles: (1) the fellow-servant rule ("You can't recover from the employer if a fellow worker caused your injury") and (2) the assumption-of-risk rule, which held that the worker impliedly assumed all risks of the workplace, including tools and machinery. Therefore, if the injury was, for example, sustained from a drill press with no guard rail or from a workroom that was poorly lit, the worker was deemed to have assumed the risk of injury from those conditions.

All states now have workers' compensation laws which supplant the common law, abolish the fellow-servant and assumption-of-risk defenses, and assure *without litigation* that workers will be compensated for injury or disease growing out of their employment. Special commissions decide the degree and permanence of injuries and apply an established compensation schedule. However, compensation under such schedule does not include payment for pain and suffering, and the amounts allowed are far less than the recovery that could be expected from a jury trial if identical injuries were the subject of a tort lawsuit. (Chapter 48 presents a full discussion of workers' compensation.)

REMEDIES OF PRINCIPALS AND AGENTS FOR BREACH OF OBLIGATIONS

When the obligations that principals and agents owe to each other are breached, many remedies are available and often several may be applied at the same time. Most of these remedies have been illustrated in this series of chapters on agency law. Remedies of principals against agents are summarized in Table 38.1, and reme-

Table 38.1 Remedies of Principals against Agents

For breach of obligations by an agent, a principal may:

1. Discharge the agent
2. Withhold compensation
3. Recover any secret profit made by the agent
4. Restrain the agent by court injunction from continuing to breach his or her agency obligations
5. Recover damages from the agent for breach of the contract of employment
6. Secure reimbursement from the agent for any damages owing to a third party assessed against the principal because of the agent's wrongdoing
7. Rescind a contract entered into by an agent for the principal in which there was a bribe or other improper inducement offered or paid to the agent by a third party

---

dies of agents against principals appear in Table 38.2. Where the agency consists of the master-servant relationship, the legal rights of the principal and agent are more significantly affected by statute than are other types of agency.

TERMINATION OF AGENCY

Methods of Termination

An agency relationship may terminate (1) when its purpose is accomplished or its term has expired, (2) by subsequent mutual assent, (3) by decision of one of the parties, or (4) by operation of law.

Termination by Provision in Agency Agreement. When an agency is created for a specified purpose, the agency terminates automatically once that purpose has been accomplished. If John is hired to remodel a kitchen, his employment ends when the kitchen is remodeled. Similarly, if the agreement states that the agency terminates after a month, the agency terminates automatically when that time has run out.

Table 38.2 Remedies of Agents against Principals

For breach of obligations by a principal, an agent may:

1. Refuse to continue his or her employment
2. Bring legal action to force his or her reinstatement in employment
3. Recover damages for the principal's breach of the employment contract
4. Rescind the employment agreement and recover the value of any services rendered
5. Bring an action for an accounting
6. Secure reimbursement for payments made by the agent for his or her principal
7. Secure indemnity for personal liability sustained while performing an authorized act for the principal
8. Seek administrative or statutory relief from appropriate governmental agencies

Termination by Mutual Assent. Since an agency is created by mutual assent, it can be terminated by mutual assent.

Termination by Decision of One Party. Because an agency is a consensual arrangement, either a principal or an agent may terminate it orally, in writing, or through actions which demonstrate that the agency relationship no longer exists. However, if the principal or agent breaches the agreement by terminating the agency before the agreed-upon time, such breaching party will be liable to the other in damages. If a servant improperly terminates the agency relationship, the employer cannot force the employee to continue to work, since that would amount to involuntary servitude and is prohibited by the Thirteenth Amendment of the U.S. Constitution. However, an *employer* who improperly terminates employment may be required to continue the employment of that agent, or to pay damages. An exception to the rule permitting a principal to terminate an agency arises where there is an **agency coupled with an interest,** discussed below.

Termination by Operation of Law. Termination by operation of law is a cessation of agency for reasons beyond the decision of one or both of the parties. It may occur in the following ways.

Death or insanity of principal or agent. The general rule is that an agent's power to act for a principal ceases when the principal dies or becomes insane. Since it is impossible to be an agent without a principal, any contract entered into with a third party on behalf of a deceased principal is void even if the agent had no knowledge of the death. Since the agreement is void, it follows that the third party, even though unaware of the principal's death, cannot sue the principal's estate to enforce its performance. Because of this hardship, some state laws now provide that if both the agent and the third party had no knowledge of the principal's death when they entered into their agreement, the estate of the deceased principal may be required to perform. The *agent's* death or insanity also terminates the agency.

Agency coupled with an interest. An exception to the rule that death of the principal terminates the agency arises where there is an **agency coupled with an interest**—that is, where the agent has an *economic* or *property* interest in the subject matter of the agency. This property interest must be more than the agent's interest in a commission from the sale, or a share in the profits of a transaction. For example, suppose P sells her stock to A, and P signs the printed power of attorney (agency) on the back authorizing A as agent to request the corporation to transfer the certificate of stock on its books into A's name. P's death does not terminate the agency because A's power of attorney was given to permit A to transfer title to his property into his name. A has a *power coupled with a property interest in the subject matter of the agency.*

Permanent disability of principal or agent. If a permanent disability prevents either a principal or an agent from being able to function as such, the agency terminates.

Loss of qualification of principal or agent. The failure of a principal or agent to obtain or retain a required franchise or license may result in the termination of the agent's authority. For instance, if Pauline employs Agnes as her attorney (agent), a later disbarment of Agnes terminates her authority to represent Pauline.

Bankruptcy. Bankruptcy or insolvency of the principal or agent may terminate the agency depending upon the facts in each case. There may be circumstances where it is still reasonable and practical to continue an agency notwithstanding bankruptcy of either party. For example, suppose Cityflite, a domestic airline, has a commission agency agreement with Global Air, an international carrier, to write and sell Global tickets to Cityflite customers requesting international flights. If Cityflite is in Chapter 11 bankruptcy, which allows it to continue operating, both Cityflite as agent and Global as principal are benefited by continuing the agency relation. Similarly, if principal Global Air went into Chapter 11, the same conclusion would be reached. On the other hand, assume that Help, Inc., a worldwide humanitarian charitable corporation, has a large endowment fund and employs ABC, a stock brokerage firm, to advise it on its securities investment program. If ABC becomes insolvent or bankrupt, case decisions hold that the agency is terminated by operation of law, because the principal would suffer unreasonable injury if the agency were to continue.

Impossibility of performance. An agent's authority is terminated when the accomplishment of the agency purpose becomes impossible. Thus, if Carl is employed to sell Dan's automobile, its destruction would terminate Carl's authority.

Subsequent illegality. A change of law that makes performance of an agent's duties illegal also terminates the agency relationship. Suppose Alice is a national distributing agent for Games, Inc., a slot machine manufacturer. Subsequent enactment of a federal law making the interstate shipment of slot machines illegal would terminate the agency relationship.

Important change of circumstances. The authority of an agent also terminates when there is such a change in the affairs of the principal, or in the subject matter of the agency, or in external events, that the agent should reasonably infer that the principal would not desire the agent to act under the changed circumstances. Suppose a farmer employs an agent to sell his farm because he can't pay his bills. If the agent learns that oil has been discovered on the farmer's land, the changed circumstance will revoke the agent's authority.

Notice to Third Parties of Termination

Many principals have discharged a dishonest agent only to sustain serious financial loss because of failure to notify third parties that the agent's authority had been terminated.

Notice When Termination Is by Act of Principal or Agent.
When an agency is terminated by one or both of the parties to an agency agreement, the principal should give prompt notice of the termination to all persons who did business with the agent or who may have known of the agency. Failure to do so may leave the agent with *apparent authority* to continue to represent the principal and to have the *power* (though not the *right*) to bind the principal contractually to a third party who reasonably relies upon that apparent authority. (Apparent authority is explained in Chapter 36.)

To illustrate: A is employed as a salesman by Hi-Style, a shoe manufacturer. A has sold shoes to ShoeMart, a nationwide retailer, and Hi-Style has always shipped shoes in accordance with the orders secured by A. Hi-Style has thereby clothed A with apparent authority to act for it in transactions with ShoeMart. If Hi-Style discharges A and terminates the agency, A still has the *apparent authority* to act as Hi-Style's agent and to bind it in transactions with ShoeMart unless ShoeMart in some way learns or is notified that the agency no longer exists. Thus, if A, after being fired, with no notice being given to Shoemart, takes a big order from ShoeMart and absconds with the cash down payment, Hi-Style is legally bound to ship the shoes to ShoeMart and to credit it with the cash that A stole. Of course, Hi-Style can sue A to recover the money he took, but all too often in real life, the agent is in hiding, in jail, broke, or just plain dead. How much simpler it would be for Hi-Style to notify all of A's customers, including ShoeMart, that A no longer represented the firm.

In order to bring an end to an agent's apparent authority when an agency is terminated by the parties, the principal must give *two* kinds of notice:

1. *Actual* notice of the termination should be sent to all persons who dealt with the agent prior to his or her termination.
2. *Constructive* notice should be given to those parties who might have known of the agency but who had not previously done business with the principal through the agent. *Constructive notice* is given by publication in the "Legal Notices" column of a newspaper of general circulation in the area where the agency business is regularly carried on. The notice states that the named agent is no longer employed by the principal. This notice is binding even upon those third parties who did not see it or read it.

Notice When Termination Is by Operation of Law. The general rule is that when an agency terminates by operation of law, apparent authority automatically ceases without the need for any notice being given to third parties.

SUMMARY

In return for the trust and confidence a principal reposes in an agent, an agent owes duties, including the duty (1) to use ordinary care and skill in the work unless the agent undertakes to perform to a higher standard, (2) to obey the principal's reasonable instructions, (3) to perform the work or service personally, (4) to communicate to the principal any notice received for the principal or any knowledge of matters concerning the agency which the agent ought reasonably to know would be of interest to the principal, (5) to keep and render such accounts as the work or service requires, and (6) to be loyal.

This **fiduciary duty** of loyalty means that an agent may not act adversely to the principal's interest, make a secret profit, or represent both a principal and third party to a transaction unless both of those parties consent. An agent may not become the third party to a transaction carried on for a principal without the latter's consent. An agent engaged to sell an item may not buy it without the principal's consent. An agent whose duty it is to buy may not sell his or her own property to the principal. Agents cannot use for their own benefit trade secrets or other confidential information belonging to their principals.

When an agent violates fiduciary duties, a principal may (1) terminate the agency, (2) withhold compensation, and (3) recover such damage as the agent may have caused. A principal may also rescind a contract made by an agent with a third party who paid a bribe or used other illegal means to induce the agent to enter into the contract.

A principal's obligations to an agent involve the duty (1) to pay the agent compensation as agreed, (2) to keep and render accounts, (3) to continue the agent's employment as agreed, and (4) to provide a servant agent with the means to accomplish the work, a safe workplace, and compensation for injuries arising out of employment.

An agency agreement terminates at the will of either party or when its purpose is accomplished. It is terminated by operation of law when either party dies or becomes permanently incapacitated, or when either party ceases to be qualified to act, or when the purpose of the agency becomes impossible to perform or illegal.

An agent's apparent authority to act may sometimes continue after his or her actual authority has ceased. To terminate a continuing apparent authority, the principal must supply actual notice to third parties who did business with the agent as well as constructive notice (by publication) to those who may have known of the agency but had not previously done business with the agent.

REVIEW QUESTIONS

1. (a) Why is the distinction between servant and nonservant agent, which was so important in the previous agency chapters, relatively unimportant when analyzing principals' and agents' obligations to each other? (b) Why does the law hold principals and agents to high ethical standards toward each other?

2. Explain principals' and agents' fiduciary relationship.

3. Distinguish between the degree of care owed by an agent who is an expert and an agent who is not an expert.

4. Can (a) servants or (b) nonservants delegate their duties?

5. (a) What is the difference between "knowledge" and "notice" in the law of agency? (b) Do you think the duties owed by an agent concerning the communication of information to his or her principal are fair and reasonable? Why or why not?

6. (a) What is meant by the duty of loyalty that agents owe to their principals? (b) Is the duty of loyalty consistent with employees' arm's-length bargaining with employers for better wages and working conditions? Give reasons for your answer.

7. Assume that agent Art is hired to sell land for his principal. Without the principal's knowledge, Art gives advice to the buyer by suggesting a price to offer for the property. The principal accepts the buyer's offer, but later discovers that the agent had also acted for the buyer. Would the principal be acting both legally and ethically if she refused to pay the agent's regular commission on the sale? Why or why not?

8. Can Henry apply in his own business any information that he gained while working for someone else? Explain.

9. Define (a) trade secret and (b) shop-right privilege.

10. (a) Give an illustration of an economic opportunity. (b) How can an agent legitimately seize an economic opportunity that develops during the course of employment?

11. What obligations does a principal owe to the agent?

12. (a) May an agency created by *written* instrument be terminated before its normal conclusion by one party's *oral* notice of revocation to the other? (b) What might be the consequences?

13. You have a jewelry store in Boston. Tom, who lives in Iowa, has left with you a valuable necklace to sell on commission. You sell and deliver it to Mrs. Jones, who pays you cash. You then send the money you received, less your commission, to Tom. However, unknown to you or to Mrs. Jones, Tom died 3 days before the sale. (a) Is Tom's estate bound by the sale of the necklace? (b) Suppose the executor of Tom's estate is unhappy with the sale and offers to refund the purchase price if Mrs. Jones returns the necklace. What are the rights and liabilities of all parties?

14. When a principal gives notice to a third party that an agent is no longer employed by the principal, how is the notice given?

CASE PROBLEMS

1. Art, employed as a driver by Tanksley Trucking, was driving a company truck behind a car driven by Garcia. Art repeatedly blew his horn, in effect asking Garcia to move to his right so that Art could pass. After some delay, Garcia finally moved to the right, giving Art room to pass. Art, angry by this time, passed so closely that he scraped and damaged Garcia's car. Garcia sued Tanksley Trucking and secured a judgment. Art's employer, without his consent, withheld a portion of Art's pay each week in order to reimburse itself for the sum it had to pay to satisfy the judgment. A few weeks later, Art quit his job and sued Tanksley Trucking to recover the amounts withheld from his pay. Should Art succeed? Why or why not?

2. In order to buy a house, Miles arranged a loan from Perpetual Savings, which also agreed to handle the escrow closing (completion) of Miles' purchase of the property. As one element of the closing, Perpetual secured a termite inspection of the property, showing that the house was infested with termites and that it would cost $450 to remove them. Perpetual tried without success to have the seller of the house pay for termite removal, but did not notify Miles of the report. When Miles moved into the house, he found the termites, spent $450 to remove them, and asked for reimbursement from Perpetual. The bank replied that its duty was only to handle the "closing" of the sale escrow and that it had performed that duty. Perpetual also stated that Miles should look to the seller to repay the termite bill. Was Perpetual correct?

3. Burg was employed "at will" as department manager of Precision Tool. He was authorized in emergencies to buy production parts from outside manufacturers. Without his employer's knowledge, he organized a small machine shop (with his friend Ted as its manager), from which Burg bought needed supplies for Precision Tool. When Burg's employer learned of the arrangement, he was fired. Burg sued Precision, saying that he was wrongfully fired because he never charged Precision more than the going market price for supplies he purchased from his company. Should Burg recover? Discuss.

4. Crain, Inc., required new employees to sign a receipt for a personnel handbook. The handbook stated that if there was a layoff, it would be according to seniority (the last hired would be the first laid off). Crain later revised the handbook by adding this statement: "I understand that the Company Handbook is *not* a contract of employment and management reserves the right to change it at any time." The revision was not distributed to current employees. Crain then laid off six employees with more seniority than employees who were not laid off. The six who were laid off sued Crain, claiming its statement of layoffs according to seniority was part of the employment contract which Crain had breached. Crain contended that the six were at-will employees and that it could lay off whomever it wanted to. Decision?

5. Johnson worked as inspector for Thiokol for 9 years. During that period, Thiokol distributed a handbook to employees describing company policy concerning discipline, employee evaluation, and grievance procedures. In the front of the handbook was a clear and conspicuous statement: "The provisions of this manual are not intended as terms of an employment contract. Your employment is for no set period and may be terminated without notice and at will at any time by you or by the company." Because of inadequate inspection by Johnson, a rocket motor malfunctioned, causing a 20-day delay in a NASA rocket program and adverse national publicity. Following procedures in the handbook, Thiokol terminated Johnson for "careless performance of duty." He sued, claiming he was fired in breach of an implied contract not to terminate him except for cause. Decision?

6. Colquin sold insurance for Group Plans, Inc. The sale of group insurance requires much effort. Colquin asked for a raise in salary. When Group Plans refused, he quit and went to work for a competitor. Colquin continued his sales efforts among a number of customer firms with whom he had negotiated partially completed contracts for Group Plans, but with the goal of selling those firms his new employer's policies. He concluded two such contracts for his new company. Group Plans sued Colquin and his new employer to enjoin them from soliciting former clients and to obtain damages. Should Group Plans succeed? Why or why not?

7. Jose Davos was the grounds keeper of the newly remodeled Bay View Golf Club. He had so improved the course that he was given a new 3-year contract of employment with a raise in pay. The contract stated that the golf club would not reduce or modify the authority of Jose and he, in turn, agreed to continue in Bay View's employ for the full 3 years. Six months after signing the employment contract Jose was offered the grounds keeper's job at Queen's Golf Club at a higher salary. Jose left Bay View to work for Queen's. What should be the outcome of Bay View's suit to enjoin Jose's breach of his employment obligation? Why?

8. Hope Lumber employed Pearson "at will." Because of repeated inventory shortages, Hope asked all employees to sign a waiver or release of liability and then submit to a polygraph (lie detector) test. Pearson refused to take the test and was fired. He sued Hope Lumber, claiming that his discharge was wrongful because it was against public policy to require polygraphs. The Federal Employee Polygraph Protection Act (29 USC, Secs. 2001–09) was not yet in effect in Oklahoma, and even if it were, Pearson was not under its federal jurisdiction. Was Pearson's discharge wrongful because it was against public policy? Discuss fully.

ETHICS IN PRACTICE

Like other areas of law, agency law reflects ethical norms. For example, a master's liability for the servant's torts is consistent with the widely held belief that a person should refrain from harming others without justification. The law of labor and employment, a close relative of agency law, also reflects ethical concerns. Workers' compensation acts, federal labor legislation, the Civil Rights Act, and laws concerning equal pay for equal work, occupational health and safety, and pension reform express or imply value judgments about what is right in the workplace and appropriate for mitigating its harshness and inequities.

Agency law not only reflects ethical norms; it incorporates them as part of the law. For example, parties to ordinary business transactions deal with each other at arm's length—i.e., as wary strangers. In arm's-length transactions, a party sometimes can act unethically without violating the law. In contrast, in agency law a fiduciary relationship exists between principal and agent. Ethical and legal obligations merge, and conduct that breaches ethical standards—especially those pertaining to the agent's duty of loyalty and the principal's duties of fair dealing—also violates the law.

The following problems deal with ethical dilemmas typical of principal-agent relations. Problems relating to labor and employment law are addressed in Part Ten.

PROBLEMS IN ETHICS

1. In his "Managing People" column, Andrew Grove, CEO of Intel, describes the following incident: A secretary in a firm with fourteen other secretaries was bothered that her boss and the boss's supervisor recruited the secretaries to sell products for an outside door-to-door sales organization. The secretary had two main concerns: First, she felt that secretaries who joined the bosses' sales organization were given preferential treatment over those who did not join. Second, the bosses spent a couple of hours per day on the phone attending to their "extracurricular" sales activities. Grove agreed that discrimination against the nonjoiners was wrong and that the secretary had a valid complaint that she should pursue. But as to the charge that the bosses were wasting company time on outside activities, he said, "That's not really your business but the business of their management," implying that the secretary had no valid interest in the matter, or at least should not pursue it. If Grove meant that the bosses' wasting company time was of no legitimate concern to the secretary, do you agree?

2. You are a financial planner who advises a number of unsophisticated investors of modest means. Your main source of income is the commissions you receive from the sale of financial products that you recommend to your clients, who never inquire about commission rates. Commissions vary considerably among the products you sell. On a client investment of $10,000, you would receive the following commissions: limited partnership, $600–$1,000; common stock newly issued to the public, $300–$1,000; annuities and life insurance products, $400–$600; common stock traded on the New York Stock Exchange, $200–$250; U.S. government securities, $50. Risk of loss to your clients is greatest for limited partnerships and least for government securities. **(a)** Does this commission structure pose an ethical problem for you? **(b)** If so, how would you resolve it?

3. Bob is employed as a salesperson for Best Electrical Company. He is told by his superior that Best Electrical is working on an electric light bulb which will have a practically indestructible lighting element. Although the new bulb has not yet reached the testing stage, Bob is given literature and told to take orders for the bulb and to receive a 10 percent deposit with each order. Bob knows Best Electric is undercapitalized and is asking for the deposit money in order to secure funds with which to complete the bulb's development. Bob is instructed not to reveal this to his customers. Bob has reason to believe that the bulb cannot be perfected and that the customers who have paid deposits will most likely not be able to get refunds. What should Bob do? Why?

4. According to a survey conducted by *Macworld* magazine, about 22 percent of U.S. employers monitor at least occasionally the computer files, electronic messages, and voice mail of their employees, while over 34 percent of employers believe it's "never acceptable" to monitor workers electronically. Another report says that employers used several types of electronic devices for worker surveillance—hidden video cameras and devices that allow employers to listen in on phone calls, count keystrokes, and calculate the amount of time workers spend on transactions. Many employers monitor secretly. Others warn their workers. Some use a combination of secret and nonsecret monitoring. Is it ethical for employers to engage in electronic surveillance of workers?

5. Sam, a grocery store manager, was fired for overpricing more than 2,000 items stocked by the store chain. Alleging that he was simply acting on orders from higher management, Sam sued the chain for wrongful termination of employment. The jury awarded Sam $832,826 damages as compensation for past and future wages. **(a)** What is the ethical quality of Sam's conduct? Of the former employer's conduct? **(b)** If Sam acted unethically, did his winning the lawsuit make his conduct ethical?

PART NINE

Business Organizations

CHAPTER 39
Introduction to Business Organizations; Formation of Partnerships; Rights and Duties of Partners

CHAPTER 40
Termination of Partnerships

CHAPTER 41
Limited Partnerships and Limited Liability Companies

CHAPTER 42
Nature and Formation of Corporations

CHAPTER 43
Financing Corporations

CHAPTER 44
Management of Corporations

CHAPTER 45
Shareholders' Powers, Rights, and Liabilities

CHAPTER 46
Securities Regulation: Protecting Investors

CHAPTER 47
Accountants' Liability

Ethics in Practice

CHAPTER 39

Introduction to Business Organizations; Formation of Partnerships; Rights and Duties of Partners

INTRODUCTION TO BUSINESS ORGANIZATIONS

If you decide to start a business, one of the first steps you must take is to determine what kind of business organization it will be. Practically speaking, you have five different forms of business structure to choose from. Which form you choose requires careful weighing of important factors: the extent of liability of yourself and possibly other investors for the organization's debts, tax advantages and disadvantages, the expense of forming and operating the organization, the complexity of the management structure, difficulty of raising capital with the particular form of organization, and the ease of preserving continuity of control in the event a key manager or owner should die.

Five Common Forms of Business Organization

Chapters 40 to 46 examine the five most common forms of business organization and discuss the rights, duties, and liabilities of members of those firms. These five business structures, listed in descending order of personal liability for firm debts, but ascending order of complexity, are: (1) sole proprietorship (the simplest form, in which the owner has maximum liability for debts), (2) general partnership (including joint venture), (3) limited partnership, (4) limited liability company, and (5) corporation (the most complex form, with the least degree of personal liability for firm debts).

From a standpoint of *ownership and management*, these types of business organization range from a sole proprietorship, with ownership and management merged in a single person, to the giant publicly held corporation, with thousands of owners (stockholders) who are usually separated from the salaried officers, executives, and directors that run the business from day to day.

Sole Proprietorship. When you are the sole owner (proprietor) of a business, the state exercises a minimum of control over how you operate that business. But the trade-off for maximum personal control over the enterprise is that you are subject to full personal responsibility for all its debts.

With few exceptions if you are a sole proprietor you may engage in any type of business you choose. You will merely be obligated to pay a license fee required of all businesses and to comply with any laws that may be applicable to the type of business you operate. Such laws regulate, for example, advertising signs, zoning, workers' compensation, employee wages and hours, and payroll taxes. As sole proprietor, you are in complete charge of your company's operations. If you require additional funds to carry on the business, you may borrow from a bank or other lender. You may also pledge the assets of the business as security for repayment of your loans or you may be required to pledge your house or other personal assets. You are entitled to all the profits the business makes, and you must pay for all the losses. To put it succinctly, it is *your* business.

The chief drawback to doing business as proprietor is that, as sole owner, you alone are personally liable for all debts the business incurs, and you may not have the capital or credit that is needed for an expanding business.

Partnership. If you still desire substantial control of the business, but need to bring in other associates to increase your capital, your next step may be to consider formation of a **general partnership** or a **joint venture.** With more than one person involved in the ownership of the business, the organization is more complex than that of a sole proprietorship. You and your partners assume duties and obligations which are not present in a sole proprietorship. Chief among these is the *fiduciary duty* that the partners owe to one another. It will be recalled from agency law that the fiduciary duty of mutual trust and confidence is a serious responsibility.

If you form a **general partnership,** you and your partner(s) may carry on almost any kind of business activity that you wish—again with only a minimum of governmental control. This type of organization is particularly appropriate for a small business owned by two or more people, each of whom desires to have a voice in management. Usually, each member invests in the enterprise, money, some property, work, or service. Like a sole proprietor, each partner is personally liable for all the company's debts and each partner owes special legal obligations to the other copartners. There is no federal income tax, as such, on a partnership. Rather, each partner declares a pro rata share of the firm's profits on his or her personal income tax return.

A **joint venture** differs from a general partnership in that its business is of shorter duration and narrower in scope. It is usually organized to carry out a single project or series of related projects with a fairly short life span. Laws governing general partnerships generally apply equally to joint ventures.

Limited Partnership. In a **limited partnership,** one or more of the partners (the general partners) manage the business while others (the limited partners) merely invest in the enterprise and have very limited rights in its management. The general partner of a limited partnership, like the partner in an ordinary partnership, is personally liable for the firm's debts. If you become a limited partner, however, you have no personal liability beyond your capital investment. Essentially, you will be only an investor in the firm, with a slight voice in its management. Limited partnerships are discussed in Chapter 41.

Limited Liability Company. Very recently fifteen states have enacted laws permitting formation of a new business entity called a **limited liability company** (LLC). An LLC differs from a limited partnership in a very important respect: *All its members, whether active in management or not, have their liability limited to the amount of their capital investment.* Thus, in an LLC, there is no counterpart to the general partner of a limited partnership, who puts all personal assets at risk to satisfy creditors. As in a partnership, each member's pro rata share of the firm's profits is taxed on his or her personal federal income tax return, but there is no tax against the LLC as such. Federal tax law also permits *passive losses* of an LLC to be deducted from other personal income on the individual member's return—a distinct tax advantage over the general partnership. LLCs are discussed in Chapter 41.

Corporation. Instead of establishing a sole proprietorship or a business in one of the partnership forms, you may find that a corporation best suits your needs. Of the five types of business organizations, the **corporation** has the most complicated structure. A corporation is established by charter from the state and is a separate legal entity apart from its owners. This form of organization is particularly suited to large and complex enterprises. It may also be the organization of choice if the parties do not want to place their personal resources at risk in the event that the business should fail. The shareholders of a corporation, who may number in the thousands, are its owners. They have no voice in day-to-day management and no liability for debts; but they do share in company earnings. Unlike partnerships or LLCs, corporations are subject to double federal and state taxation of the same earnings—first, by the corporate income tax, and again when the same earnings are passed on as dividends to the stockholder, who pays personal income tax on the additional income.

Recent decades have witnessed rapid growth of the **close corporation**—that is, a small corporation with usually fewer than thirty stockholders who also serve as directors, officers, and employees. This device combines some of the best features of the other four types of organizations previously discussed. First, like its big brother, a close corporation offers the advantage of *limited liability*. If the close corporation elects to acquire **S corporation** status (under Subchapter S of the Internal Revenue Code), it is also *taxed like a partnership*—that is, the net income of the business is declared on the personal tax returns of the stockholders in proportion to their shares in the corporation.

The above five types of business organizations are summarized here in outline form and examined in greater detail in the chapters which follow. Chapter 42 presents a comparative chart showing the major features of each type of organization (Table 42.2).

This chapter discusses the organization of general partnerships (including joint ventures) and the rights and duties of partners; Chapter 40 deals with the dissolution and termination of partnerships; limited partnerships are described in Chapter 41; and Chapters 42 through 46 explore corporations.

FORMING A PARTNERSHIP; RIGHTS AND DUTIES OF PARTNERS

The partnership form of business organization is of ancient legal lineage. It was used in classical Greece and Rome. The early common law of England included partnership law. In the United States the partnership has been modernized and codified in the Uniform Partnership Act (UPA), which has been adopted by all states except Louisiana. In 1992, the National Conference of Commissioners on Uniform State Laws prepared a revised UPA which appears as Appendix 3. It is reasonably predictable that a majority of the states will also adopt the revised UPA. The UPA does not completely cover all aspects of partnership law. On questions where the Act is silent and there is no applicable state law, the common law still governs.

Agency law is the cornerstone upon which partnership law is erected. For example, if you are a partner dealing with third parties, you are acting as a principal for yourself and as an agent for your other, nonacting partners who are not present or participating in the transaction. Another important axiom of partnership law is that each partner has authority to contract with third parties on all matters within the *scope of the partnership business*. Here again, a familiar agency law concept—scope of authority—comes into play.

Is a Partnership an Entity or an Aggregate?

Two theories have developed to explain the nature of a partnership. The **entity theory,** followed by the civil law and a few states, holds that a partnership has a separate legal personality, apart from the members, in much the same way that a corporation is considered to be a separate legal person. Thus, in going about partnership business, each partner acts as agent for an abstract partnership entity (the principal).

The prevailing view, followed by the common law and many sections of the UPA, is the **aggregate theory.** It views a partnership merely as an *aggregate* of individuals. Hence, in dealing with third parties a partner cannot act as agent of the partnership, but acts as a principal for his or her own interests and as an agent for the nonacting partners.

Examples of the Aggregate Theory. Many aspects of partnership law are based upon the aggregate theory:

1 A partnership legally dies when one of its member dies. In contrast, a corporation continues in perpetuity as an *entity* and is not affected by the death of one or more stockholders. If the surviving partner continues to carry on the business, the new organization is a sole proprietorship. If several former members continue, a new partnership has been formed.

2 Logically, if a partnership is an aggregate of individuals, it cannot sue or be sued in the name of an abstract partnership entity. Suit for or against the partnership must be brought in the names of the individual partners. However, special statutes in many states, including even those that follow the aggregate theory, recognize a partnership as an entity for special purposes such as suing or being sued in the partnership name.

3 Each partner is *personally* liable for the firm's debts.

Examples of Entity Theory. For some purposes, the view that a partnership is an abstract entity is still used. For example:

1 The UPA [8(3,4), 10] provides that the partnership may acquire and convey title to real property in the partnership name, and that the entity "owns" specific personal property (UPA 25).

2 In a few specific situations, federal statutes and court rules treat a partnership as an entity and permit it, in its own name: (a) to sue and be sued, (b) to file a bankruptcy petition, and (c) to report partnership profits to Internal Revenue Service on a federal income tax "information return." However, no tax is paid by the partnership; instead, its profit (or loss) passes through to each partner, who then shows a pro rata share on his or her individual tax return and pays personal income taxes on such share.

The IRS follows the entity theory with respect to the partnership information return, but the aggregate theory for purposes of assessing and collecting income taxes from the individual partners. Courts likewise are not consistent in following the entity or aggregate approach.

What Is a Partnership?

The UPA defines a partnership as "an association of two or more persons to carry on as co-owners a business for profit." This definition has three elements: (1) **joint ownership,** (2) **joint management,** and (3) **profit motive.** If any one element is absent, a partnership has not been formed, even if one was intended. Conversely, if a relationship between parties meets these three requisites, a partnership has been formed even if the parties did not intend to create a partnership.

Business participants need to know what is, and what is not, a partnership in order to avoid litigation. A surprising number of relationships, such as employer-employee, husband-wife, landlord-tenant, cotenants of land, and franchisor-franchisee, raise questions as to whether a partnership does or does not exist. Such ambiguity can usually be avoided if the parties are aware of the legal elements of a partnership and express their intent clearly in writing.

"Carrying on as Co-owners." For a business to be a partnership, the members must agree that all are co-owners of the business. Co-ownership involves sharing (1) the profits and losses of the enterprise and (2) the right to manage unless otherwise agreed. Receipt of a share of the profits of a business is prima facie evidence that the individual is a partner in the business. However, the UPA provides that no such inference can be drawn in business situations where receipt of a share of profits is not intended to create partnership status but is given as payment for debt, rent, wages, or interest on a loan, as an annuity to the spouse or estate of a deceased partner, as payment for purchase of goodwill, or as a distribution to someone who is not responsible for the concern's debts and obligations [UPA 7(4)].

How much of an investment must one make to be a co-owner within the meaning of the UPA? A partnership may begin business with any amount of capital or with no capital. Contributions of partners vary widely: They may consist of money, services, property of any kind, a patent, a license, some kind of know-how or skill, the value of a person's name or credit standing, or only the joint desire of the members. But the law does not require any capital contribution in order to become a partner.

How long do partners have to "carry on as co-owners" in order to qualify as partners under the UPA? They may operate from day to day, agreeing that the arrangement can be terminated at any time (a *partnership at will*), or it can be for an agreed-upon term.

"A Business for Profit." Not only must the partners be co-owners, but as co-owners they must carry on *a business* for profit. Many forms of co-ownership do not involve carrying on a business for profit. For example, suppose Bill and Ada co-own Greenacres as tenants in common and lease it to an oil company that pays them $40,000 a year in oil royalties. Bill agrees that each year he will obtain a public liability insurance policy on the land; Ada agrees to pay the taxes. They both will be reimbursed from oil royalties and then split the royalty income equally. They are not partners because they are not *carrying on a business* for profit. Instead, they simply co-own a passive asset that produces income. However, if they co-own a huge apartment complex so that they are engaged full time with bookkeeping, repairs, and rent collection, they are partners carrying on a business for profit.

Court decisions supplement the UPA requirement that the parties carry on a business for profit by holding that there must also be intent to *share losses*. Often in business, a percentage share of *gross* income will be paid (1) to a manager as incentive compensation, (2) to a franchisor such as Taco Bell for the privilege of operating a local franchise, or (3) to a shopping center lessor as a part of the rent. Such payments do not create a partnership because the UPA requirement that two or more persons carry on a business for profit refers to *net profit*—not gross profit. In addition, such arrangements do not create a partnership because the parties do not intend to *share losses*.

True partners *intend* their business to make a profit even if, in fact, no profit is earned. UPA 2 defines business to include every trade, occupation, or profession. Therefore, any profit-oriented enterprise undertaken jointly by two or more parties is subject to partnership law. On the other hand, religious, patriotic, charitable, civic, fraternal, or other nonprofit organizations such as hospitals and orphanages cannot qualify as partnerships.

The following case, involving a couple who operated a restaurant together, raises the classical UPA question: Did they intend to carry on as co-owners a business for profit?

CASE 39.1 **Bass v. Bass** • 814 S.W.2d 38 (Tenn. 1991)

FACTS William Bass and Linda Bass, after dating each other for a year, started living together in 1975, at which time she was employed full time, and he was unemployed. A year later, he leased a restaurant. Initially, Linda operated it alone, working 17-hour days by herself, taking orders, cooking, cleaning, and running the cash register. When William began working with Linda, each worked a 12-hour shift, keeping the restaurant open 24 hours a day. Linda worked 5 years without any pay. The restaurant burned down, and William started a video amusement game business. The couple married in 1980 and divorced the same

CASE 39.1 Continued

year, after which they resumed living together. The video game business prospered, expanding to sixty-five machines in eighteen locations, which Linda helped service. She collected and banked game proceeds, kept books for all the games, wrote and signed most checks, and worked on the video machines. She was listed on all business licenses as partner or co-owner. However, bank accounts, safety deposit box, and real estate were all in William's name. He also bought a convenience market along with a used car business, and built a large home on his property, where the two resided until he died intestate in 1986. His brother James and Linda were appointed co-administrators of his estate. Linda asked the court to be declared William's surviving spouse or, alternatively, his partner. The judge ruled that since William had held himself out as Linda's husband, the estate was estopped to deny the marriage. The court of appeals reversed. The judge then found that Linda was William's business partner, entitled to half of all partnership assets. From another appellate reversal, Linda appealed to the Tennessee Supreme Court.

OPINION

DROWOTA, J. . . . In Tennessee [which has adopted the UPA] a partnership is defined as an association of two or more persons to carry on as co-owners a business for profit, and the receipt of a share of the profits of that business is prima facie evidence that a partnership exists. In determining whether one is a partner, no one fact or circumstance may be pointed to as a conclusive test, but each case must be decided upon consideration of all relevant facts, actions, and conduct of the parties. If the parties' business brings them within the scope of a joint business undertaking for mutual profit—that is to say if they place their money, assets, labor, or skill in commerce with the understanding that profits will be shared between them, the result is a partnership whether or not the parties understood that it would be so.

Moreover, the existence of a partnership depends upon the intention of the parties, and the controlling intention in this regard is that ascertainable from the acts of the parties. . . . It is not essential that the parties actually intend to become partners. . . . It is the intent to do the things which constitute a partnership that determines whether individuals are partners. . . . [T]here is ample evidence in the record to support the disposition of this case made by the trial court. There is no question that Linda and William Bass carried on as co-owners a business for profit. The parties pooled their money to purchase food [for the restaurant], to pay bills, and most importantly, to lease the restaurant. . . . Linda made a significant financial contribution, particularly when the couple began . . . the restaurant. . . . The existence of a partnership may be implied from the circumstances where it appears that the individuals involved have entered into a business relationship for profit, combining their property, labor skill, experience, or money. This is precisely what the parties involved in this did. . . .

JUDGMENT

For the foregoing reasons the judgment of the Court of Appeals is reversed, and that of the trial court [holding that Linda was a partner] is reinstated.

Establishing the Partnership Agreement

A partnership agreement may be oral, written, or implied from the parties' conduct, as in Case 39.1. However, because disputes easily develop over oral agreements, partners should have a written agreement. No particular form need be used. A well-drawn partnership agreement describes the firm's activities, the partners' duties, hours, compensation, capital contributions, mode of termination, and disposition of assets upon termination, whether by retirement, incapacity, or death. Most partnership agreements are complex, so the help of a lawyer is advisable. Figure 39.1 is a sample agreement.

Partnership Name. A firm may carry the names of the partners who own it (Smith & Jones) or a fictitious name (Ideal Bakery). The use of "& Co." after the name of one of the partners (Smith & Co.) establishes prima facie the existence of a partnership. Using a fictitious firm name instead of the partners' real names has an advantage: It enhances the future sale price of the business, including goodwill, by ensuring that the firm will not have to substitute names of the new owners when the selling partners leave. When adopting a fictitious firm name, partners must comply with the state fictitious firm name statute, which requires publication of the fictitious name and the owners' names so as to enable creditors to identify and locate them.

Who May Be a Partner?

Any person who has legal capacity to contract can be a partner. "Person" includes an individual, a corporation (if its charter does not forbid it to be a partner), or a partnership. Thus, a partnership may itself act as one of the partners in another partnership. For example, suppose Ajax Tool Co. has two partners, Smith and Jones. Ajax Tool Co. can also be a partner in Peerless Distributors, a three-way partnership in which the other two partners are John Brown, an individual, and Kraftco, Inc., a corporation.

No one can become a member of a partnership that is being formed, or join an already existing partnership, without consent of *all* members of the organization. This principle of *delectus personae* (Latin for "choice of person") requires consent of everyone because each partner should have the right to choose each of the other partners whose torts or other possible wrongdoing could cause great personal financial loss.

Minors as Partners. Just as minors are permitted by law to enter into contracts, so they can enter into partnership agreements with adults or with other minors. A minor has the same rights as the other partners in the management of the business, including the right to incur debts for the partnership and to share in its profits. However, the contract law rule that a person, during minority, may disaffirm ("get out of") a contract also applies to a minor's participation in a partnership. Thus a minor can disaffirm and withdraw from the partnership without liability for breach of contract. However, the minor's contributions to partnership assets remain subject to claims of any creditors who extended credit to the partnership while the minor was with the firm.

Partner by Estoppel. Under certain circumstances a person who is not a partner can be subject to liability as a **partner by estoppel** (UPA 16). A *partner by estoppel* (also called an *ostensible partner*) is really not a partner at all, but a person who (1) represents to a third party that he or she is a partner or (2) consents to a partner making such representation. If, in reliance upon that representation, a third party extends credit to the partnership, both the partnership and the partner by estoppel are liable to the third party. The following case is illustrative. It also shows how partnership law is equally applicable to a joint venture.

This agreement, made and entered into this ___day of ____199____by and between J. Smith and T. Jones (hereafter referred to as Partners).

RECITALS

WHEREAS, the PARTNERS desire to form a general partnership ("The Partnership") for the term and upon the conditions hereinafter, and

WHEREAS both Smith and Jones have each had 15 years' experience in the widget manufacturing business,

NOW, THEREFORE, in consideration of the mutual covenants herein contained and for other good and valuable consideration, receipt of which is hereby acknowledged, the parties agree as follows:

1. **Name and Purpose.** The partnership business shall be conducted under the fictitious firm name and style of Kwalitee Widgets Mfg. Co. The PARTNERS agree forthwith to cause to be published a Notice of Doing Business Under Fictitious Firm Name, in compliance with the laws of the State of _____. The partnership will primarily engage in the manufacture of widgets.

2. **Place of Business.** The principal office and manufacturing plant of the Partnership shall be at _____, City of _____, County of _____, State of_____, or such other location as the Partners shall agree upon from time to time.

3. **Term.** The Partnership will commence on_____and continue for a period of _____5 years_____ until terminated: (1) upon __360 days'__ notice by either Partner to the other, or (2) by death or disability of a partner, or (3) expulsion of a partner for cause, or (4) by mutual agreement of the Partners

4. **Approval of Prior Transactions.** The Partners hereby approve, ratify, and adopt the duties and benefits of all prior executory agreements by and between them prior to the execution hereof, and hereby agree to perform all of these obligations, and the debts and liabilities as well as the income and property from said transactions as set forth in financial report dated ___,199__ and incorporated herein by reference are hereby assumed by the Partnership.

5. **Capital Contributions.** The Partnership shall be capitalized at $100,000, consisting of $50,000 contributed by Smith for a __50%__ interest in the partnership; Jones hereby contributes manufacturing machinery, tools, and inventory, office furniture and equipment, with an agreed-upon value of $50,000 for a __50%__ interest in the partnership. Additional capital contributions, proportional to the interest of each Partner, may be made hereafter, provided Partners agree that such additional contribution should be assessed. Additional capital may be loaned to the Partnership by either partner only if approved in advance by both partners. Any such loan shall bear interest at 6% per annum, and shall be repaid with interest prior to any return of any capital. Any return of capital contributions shall be in the same ratio as the respective interests of the Partners in the Partnership, and shall bear no interest. Neither partner shall be entitled to demand a return of his capital contribution except as provided hereinafter.

6. **Duties and Salaries.** Each Partner shall devote substantially full time to the business, to wit, 40 hours per week. However, it is agreed that Jones will work additional time on Saturday of approximately 8 hours. Each of the partners will be entitled to draw a salary of $3,000 per month; all salaries shall be charged and deducted as an expense to the Partnership before any distribution of Profits, and shall not be considered an advance against profits. Jones, however, shall be entitled to draw an additional $1,000 per month as additional salary for said Saturday work in excess of the common time expenditure for the Partners. It is agreed that Smith will be responsible for the office management, personnel, accounting, sales, and billing. Jones will be responsible for production, purchasing, shipping and receiving, and inventory control. While there will not be regular meetings, the partners will consult and agree before initiating any new policies or major changes in the usual manner of doing business.

Figure 39.1 Sample partnership agreement.

7. Profits and Losses. The fiscal year shall run from January 1 to December 31. No later than 30 days after the close thereof, statement of income and expense, and balance sheet shall be prepared and annual profits shall be distributed to the Partners in proportion to their interest in the partnership, which as of the date hereof, is a 50% interest in each partner. Annual losses shall be assessed in proportion to each Partner's interest in the Partnership and shall be paid into the Partnership no later than March 1 following the close of the fiscal year. If either partner fails to pay his contributive share of such loss, the other partner may pay it for him, whereupon the Capital Account of such partner shall be credited with said amount, and the Capital Account of the other partner debited with said amount.

8. Books and Accounting. Smith shall keep current and complete books showing all business receipts and expenditures, for which there shall be a certified audit by a CPA after the close of each fiscal year.

9. Breach, Expulsion, Resignation. In event a partner materially breaches this agreement, voluntarily resigns prior to the expiration of the term hereof, is expelled from the partnership for just cause, or is the subject of a bankruptcy proceeding, whether voluntary or involuntary, such partner hereby gives an option to the other partner, exercisable no later than 60 days from any of said events, to buy his interest in the partnership at a price equal to 50% of the value of the partnership as shown on Exhibit A attached hereto, exclusive of goodwill, less any offsetting damage suffered by the other partner by reason of such breach, it being agreed that the breaching, expelled, or resigning partner gives said option in addition to his obligation as a partner to indemnify the partnership and the other partner for any loss or damaged suffered by reason of his personal debts or liabilities, including but not limited to liability for torts.

10. Death or Disability. (a) In the event a partner dies or becomes, incompetent, or permanently and totally disabled, the surviving or continuing partner is hereby given the preemptive right and option to purchase the deceased or disabled partner's interest in the partnership at 50% of the price set forth in Exhibit A, including the price representing the valuation of the good-will of the partnership. (b) Said option may be exercised no later than 60 days from date of death or disability by giving notice to the deceased partner's personal representative, guardian, or to the disabled partner. The continuing partner shall have 60 days thereafter to complete the purchase. At the end of each fiscal year, the partners shall review the Partnership financial statements, and agree on the valuation of the partnership for that year and write such valuation into said Exhibit A and sign same. They shall also write in Exhibit A, and sign, a separate valuation for the good-will of the Partnership. If in any year the partners fail to write a valuation for the partnership into Exhibit A, the dollar amount for the last year that was written into Exhibit A shall be used for purposes of Paragraph 9 and 10.

11. Assignment. During the term hereof, neither partner shall pledge, hypothecate, transfer, assign, his interest in the partnership without the other partner's prior written consent. Neither partner shall attempt to sell his interest in the partnership until he has extended a right of first refusal to the other partner, offering to sell said interest to said partner on the same terms as offered by an outside buyer. Should either partner violate this covenant, it shall be considered just cause for expulsion, and give rise to the option to purchase described in Paragraph 9 above.

12. Construction, Arbitration. This agreement shall be interpreted in accordance with the laws of the State of____, and any dispute shall be resolved by arbitration in accordance with the rules of the American Arbitration Association. This agreement shall bind and inure to the benefit of the heirs, executors, and administrators of the parties. Any notice required hereunder shall be given by mailing, registered mail, to the partner's last known address.

IN WITNESS WHEREOF, the parties have set their hands and seals the day and year first above written.

_____   _____
            J. Smith   T. Jones

CASE 39.2	**Friedman v. New Westbury Village Associates** • 787 S.W.2d 154 (Tex. App. 1990)
FACTS	Ben and Susanna Friedman owned a 12.5 percent interest in New Westbury Village Associates (NWV), a joint venture apartment project. The joint venture agreement provided that the managing partner could call upon the joint venturers (partners) to make capital contributions as funds were needed for construction or to pay off loans due at the bank, and that if a partner failed to pay a contribution when called for, the other partners could advance it. If they were not repaid within 6 months, the interest of the defaulting partner would be forfeited to those partners who made the advance. The agreement also stated that a joint venturer could transfer his interest to a member of his family, who would be entitled to full voting privileges held by the transferor. Ben and Susanna Friedman entered into a divorce agreement that awarded an undivided 7 percent interest in NWV to Susanna and a 5.5 percent interest to Ben. The agreement also provided that "each party, as transferee, hereby assumes and promises to pay the debts, encumbrances and liens of the joint venture, in proportion to their percentage." Although Susanna had never signed the joint venture agreement, in April 1985 she did sign a document describing her as a "joint venturer of NWV with a 7% interest," together with other joint venturers, which authorized the managing partner to sign notes and borrow from the bank for the project. The document also contained a continuing guarantee of all such bank loans. Partnership information tax returns, filed for 1985 to 1987, showed Susanna Friedman as owning a 7 percent interest in the joint venture. Susanna never objected to these returns. The joint venture became insolvent, and after the bank had foreclosed on the apartment project, there remained $87,000 still owing. The joint venturers paid it off and then sued Ben and Susanna on their pro rata guarantee. The trial court found Susanna was a partner by estoppel and entered judgment of joint and several liability against Ben and Susanna. Susanna appealed.
OPINION	BASS, J. . . . Mrs. Friedman asserts that she is not liable because she did not sign the joint venture agreement or the $300,000 note to the bank. . . . However, even if Susanna was not a partner in the joint venture, at the very least, there is evidence to support a finding of partnership by estoppel. Texas . . . [has adopted the UPA and] § 16(1)(a) provides that a person is liable as though she were an actual member of the partnership, where she represents herself to be a partner in an existing partnership, and another party has extended money in good faith on the basis of the representation. Mrs. Friedman signed an agreement [which referred to her] as a partner with a seven percent interest in the joint venture. . . . She also agreed to contribute her pro rata portion of seven percent of the amount needed in the event of a shortage of capital. A $50,000 loan was obtained from the Bank of Houston pursuant to that agreement. A $300,000 loan was subsequently obtained from the Bank on July 16, 1986, long after Mrs. Friedman signed the authorization for the $50,000 loan. Therefore, Mrs. Friedman had already represented herself to the Bank of Houston as a joint venturer in NWV by the time [the $300,000 note

CASE 39.2 Continued	was executed]. . . . Finally, Mrs. Friedman never objected to the partnership's filing of tax returns on her behalf, which indicated her 7% interest in the joint venture.
JUDGMENT	The Judgment [holding Susanna liable as a partner by estoppel] is affirmed.

PARTNERSHIP PROPERTY

A major objective of the UPA was to permit a partnership as a legal entity to receive or convey title to real property in its own name. The UPA attains this objective by defining the true nature of a partner's property as a form of *intangible personal property* called an "interest in the partnership" and treating that interest as distinct from any rights to specific real or personal property of the firm.

Partner's Interest in the Partnership

Each partner's *interest in the partnership* consists of his or her share of the profits and of its surplus when the business comes to an end. A partner's *interest in the partnership* is always treated as *personal property*. The status of a partner's interest as personal property becomes important in many contexts. For example, partner Tom's will leaves "all my real property to my son Jack, and all my personal property to my daughter Jill." Tom's estate consists of a $100,000 residence and a half-interest in a partnership that owns land with a value of $1 million. Jack gets the real estate—the $100,000 home. And Jill gets the personal property—Tom's interest in the partnership whose only asset is a $1 million parcel of land!

Assignment of Partnership Interest. Since a partner's interest in a partnership is *personal property*, not real property, even when the partnership owns only land, that interest is transferred by **assignment** or **bill of sale**—not by deed, which is used for conveying land rather than personal property. A partner may sell that interest (1) to the partnership, (2) to another partner in the firm, or (3) to a third party. Most partnership agreements provide that the partners have the right to buy a withdrawing partner's interest that is offered for sale (**preemptive right,** also sometimes called a **right of first refusal**) before the interest may be sold to third parties. (See Figure 39.1, ¶ 11.)

Assume that partner Ann desires to leave her partnership permanently. She sells her interest in the partnership outright, giving the buyer a **permanent assignment.** The assignee will receive Ann's share of the profits until the dissolution of the partnership. At dissolution the permanent assignee is also entitled to receive the value of Ann's interest. However, under the principle of *delectus personae*, discussed earlier, unless *all* partners agree, the assignee cannot become a partner in the firm, share in management, or inspect partnership books.

Heirs' Rights to a Partner's Interest. If partner Tom dies his *interest in the partnership* is included in his estate. It is personal property, and goes to heirs named in Tom's will or, if none exist, then to his heirs according to state inheritance laws. (See Chapter 26.) Whoever inherits Tom's partnership interest does not automatically become a partner in the firm but has only the rights of an assignee discussed above. Many partnership agreements give surviving partners a **preemptive right**—an option to buy the deceased partner's interest. (See Figure 39.1, ¶ 10.)

Creditors' Rights against Partner's Interest. If Sam is a partner in a business and owes a creditor money on a personal debt, under the UPA, there is only one way that Sam's partnership interest can be reached to satisfy the debt. The creditor must secure a **charging order** (in the nature of an attachment) from the court (UPA 28). The court appoints a receiver, who collects and turns over to the creditor, partnership profits that would otherwise be paid to Sam. If the debt is not repaid, the creditor may foreclose the charging order (similar to a mortgage foreclosure), causing Sam's partnership interest to be sold at a public auction. The proceeds will be used to pay Sam's debt, with any excess going to Sam. The purchaser of Sam's interest does not become a partner in the firm, but has only the limited rights of an assignee described above.

Partner's Rights in Specific Partnership Property

What Is Specific Partnership Property? Partnership property under the UPA consists of (1) real and personal property contributed by the partners to the firm's capital assets, (2) property acquired with partnership funds, (3) property created or manufactured by the partnership business, and (4) profits of the partnership (UPA 8). *Specific partnership property* means any particular property a partnership owns such as bank accounts, a building, an automobile, a crane, or a computer.

Departing from the common law view that partners *directly* own property, the UPA provides that the *partnership* owns property, and a partner only *indirectly* owns specific partnership property by owning an interest in the firm. However, it is often unclear whether the partnership or an individual partner is the owner of property because the UPA allows partnership property to be held either in the name of the partnership or of a partner. Confusion often arises when partners loan personal property to the firm without intending to transfer ownership.

Whether the partnership or one of its partners owns specific property becomes critical when (1) a partnership is dissolved and its assets are being divided; (2) a creditor attempts to attach or to levy upon the property; (3) personal creditors want to reach the property of a partner who is in personal bankruptcy; or (4) the estate of a deceased partner claims ownership of the property.

Suppose the Tom & Jerry Co. uses partnership funds to buy a Rolls Royce for each partner, and Tom and Jerry each takes title to a car in his own name. Tom dies and his widow claims that the Rolls Royce is part of his estate—that the partnership funds used to buy the car were really an equal distribution of profits to each partner. Jerry claims that the autos are partnership property. Is Tom's estate or the partnership the true owner? Courts use two rules to resolve such issues: (1) Partnership property is that which the partners *intend* to be partnership property; and a corollary: (2) To ascertain the parties' intent, courts will look to surrounding circumstances, such as:

1. Were partnership or personal funds used to buy it? If partnership funds were used to buy it, it is presumed to be partnership property.
2. On whose books is the property carried? (e.g., Is depreciation claimed on the partnership tax return?)
3. How is the property used?
4. Who pays the state and federal taxes, insurance premiums, and upkeep charges on it?
5. Who has made claims if the property was damaged—the partnership or the individual?

Partner's Personal Use of Partnership Property. An individual partner is only a tenant in partnership in the property with the other copartners. **Tenancy in partnership** is a new form of legal interest created by the UPA (see Chapter 25). Under such tenancy, a partner's rights in any particular item of partnership property are sharply limited. Thus a partner has almost no right *personally* to use or control partnership property. If a partner wants to make personal use of specific partnership property, the other partners must first consent.

Partner's Attempted Sale of Partnership Property. Under a tenancy in partnership, a partner has no right to sell or assign any particular item of partnership property unless (1) all partners consent or (2) the sale or assignment is simply carrying on the partnership business in the usual way.

Heirs' Rights in Specific Partnership Property. If partner Ted dies, his estate does not acquire Ted's right as a tenant in partnership to specific partnership property, nor can spouse, heir, or any other beneficiary claim any right to specific partnership property. When partner Ted dies, all he leaves behind is an item of intangible personal property called his *interest in the partnership* which his executrix lists as an estate asset in probate court. If the partners have all been prudent, their agreement gives surviving partners the *preemptive right* to buy deceased partner Ted's interest at a price computed by formula contained in the agreement. The most common practice is to attach a valuation schedule to the agreement, to review partnership net income at the end of each year, and to insert an agreed-upon value of the business, including the goodwill. (See Figure 39.1, ¶ 10.)

The rest goes smoothly. The surviving partners offer the agreed-upon value to the widow, she accepts, routinely obtains court approval of the sale, the partners pay her the money and the she gives them a bill of sale of the decedent's interest in the firm. The partners' purchase monies are usually obtained from reciprocal life insurance policies that each partner has on the life of the other partners. Thus, by dealing in the agreement with the problem of transfer of a partner's interest at death, the parties avoid the traditional war between widow and surviving partners over the value of the business.

Specific Partnership Property—Immunity from Creditors. A creditor trying to reach a debtor's property can have no greater rights than the rights of the debtor. Since a partner has no *personal* right to specific partnership property, his or her creditor can only acquire the same rights. Therefore, a creditor cannot reach specific partnership property by obtaining a charging order against the partner-debtor. The charging order can reach only a partner's *interest in the partnership*.

RIGHTS AND DUTIES OF PARTNERS

A member of a partnership has well-defined legal rights and duties with respect to the other partners, the partnership, and third parties who do business with the firm. The partnership agreement can limit partners' rights and impose duties that each must perform. However, such agreements among themselves cannot alter partners' legal obligations to third parties.

Fundamental to a partner's rights and duties is the fact that he or she owns an undivided interest in the partnership business and is a principal in the enterprise. Accordingly, each partner personally is liable for the contract and tort obligations incurred by the partnership. At the same time, since more than one individual owns the partnership business, each partner as well as being a principal is also an *agent* of the other co-partners with the duties and obligations that agency law imposes.

Rights of Partners among Themselves

Each partner has the right (1) to participate in the management of the firm, (2) to have access to its books, (3) to share in its profits, and (4) to be reimbursed for personal expenditures made on behalf of the partnership.

Management. The right to participate in the firm's management is not determined by the value or kind of contribution each partner makes to the firm. Unless otherwise agreed, each partner has an *equal* right with the other co-partners to manage the firm's business. With an odd number of partners, issues are settled by majority vote. If the number is even, the partners must agree on arbitration or some other method to settle their disputes. (See Figure 39.1, ¶ 12.)

UPA 301 provides that every partner is an agent of the partnership, and the act of every partner "for apparently carrying on in the usual way the business of the partnership of which he is a member binds the partnership. . . ." The time-honored **trading partnership rule** held that any one partner of a trading partnership (one that buys and sells) has authority to borrow money and execute negotiable instruments. In contrast, a member of a nontrading partnership (for example, one engaged in practicing law, accounting, or insurance) did not have such authority. More recently, however the distinction has become blurred. Today, partners, whether trading or nontrading, are held by courts to be "apparently carrying on in the usual way the business of the partnership" when they buy and sell goods, hire and fire employees, receive money or property from nonpartners, contract credit, or execute negotiable instruments.

Limitations on authority of a partner. Notwithstanding a partner's right to an equal voice in management, the partners may agree among themselves to limit the sphere in which each will work. In addition, partners may also agree to limit the authority of a member to deal with third parties. However, any such limitation on a member's authority cannot diminish that partner's power to bind the partnership in transactions with third parties who have no knowledge of the limitation. In the next case, partnership liability for $65,000 turned on whether the bank knew of limits on a partner's authority to borrow.

CASE 39.3 **First Nat. Bank & Trust v. Scherr** • 467 N.W.2d 427 (N.D. 1991)

FACTS In September 1981, Pius and Albinius Scherr formed a general partnership to construct buildings. They opened a partnership bank account, and both signed the signature card authorizing the bank to accept checks, notes, or other instruments for deposit or withdrawal of funds, and to borrow money on notes signed by either partner. Not until December did they both sign a formal partnership agreement and deliver a copy to the bank. The agreement required signatures of *both* partners to borrow money or execute notes.

During the next 3 years the partnership borrowed large sums to buy land and construct buildings, with both partners signing the documents. In October 1983, Pius Scherr alone signed a short-term partnership note for $65,000. The partnership defaulted on all loans, the bank foreclosed on all secured loans, and the bank then sued the partnership on the $65,000 note. The trial court granted judgment against Pius Scherr individually. However, it held that Albinius and the partnership were not liable on the note because the bank had received a copy of the partnership agreement containing the restriction on Pius' authority to borrow. Albinius argued that receipt of the partnership agreement put the bank on notice that Pius could not bind the partnership with a one-signature loan. The bank appealed to the supreme court.

OPINION MESCHKE, J. . . . North Dakota has adopted the Uniform Partnership Act, as have nearly all states. [Our statute which corresponds to UPA § 9(1)] says:

1 Every partner is an agent of the partnership for the purpose of its business, and the act of every partner, including the execution in the partnership name of any instrument, for apparently carrying on in the usual way the business of the partnership . . . binds the partnership, unless the partner so acting has in fact no authority to act for the partnership in the particular matter, and the person with whom he is dealing has knowledge of the fact that he has no such authority. . . .

4 No act of a partner in contravention of a restriction on authority shall bind the partnership to persons having knowledge of the restriction.

As this statute pronounces, a partner's liability to a third person is largely fixed by the law of agency. . . . Agency law, then, controls this case. A partner, as an agent of the partnership, normally binds the partnership by executing any instrument that carries on the business of the partnership in the usual way. But, as with

CASE 39.3 Continued

any agent, that is not so if the partner's authority is restricted, and if the restriction is known to the person with whom the partner deals.

Many decisions by other courts . . . demonstrate that knowledge of a restriction on, or revocation of, an individual partner's authority controls over a preexisting arrangement with a creditor. . . . "If a person dealing with an agent has notice that the agent's authority is created or described in a writing which is intended for his inspection, he is affected by limitations upon the authority contained in the writing, unless misled by conduct of the principal." *Restatement (Second) of Agency* § 167. [Our statute provides:]

> A person has notice of a fact within the meaning of this title when the person who claims the benefit of the notice . . . delivers through the mail, or by other means of communication, a written statement of the fact to such person or to a proper person in his place of business . . .

The signature card did not stand alone. After the signature card, the Bank sought, received, and knew about a later partnership agreement that restricted one partner's power to borrow for the partnership without the consent of the other partner. . . . The trial court's finding, that the Bank was bound by its knowledge of the restriction in the written partnership agreement delivered to the Bank after the signature card, was not . . . erroneous.

JUDGMENT [The trial court's judgment that the partnership was not bound by Pius' one-signature note was affirmed.]

Deciding extraordinary issues. With certain matters unanimous action of *all* partners is necessary: to confess a judgment, submit a partnership claim to arbitration, dispose of the goodwill of the business, or do any other act which would make it impossible to carry on the ordinary business of a partnership. When a question not ordinarily connected with the partnership business is in issue, such as a proposed change in the partnership agreement or whether a new partner should be admitted to the firm, the partners must arrive at a unanimous decision. If this is impossible, any partner can sue and obtain a court order dissolving the partnership. The grounds for dissolution of a partnership are discussed in Chapter 40.

Access to Partnership Books. Each partner has the right to inspect the partnership books at any reasonable time and to copy from them (UPA 19). Books should be kept at the partnership's principal place of business unless otherwise agreed.

Right to Share in Profits. Each partner is presumed to have an equal share in the profits in the absence of an agreement to the contrary [UPA 18(a)]. This presumption of equality exists even though the individual contributions to the firm differ considerably in amount and character. Therefore, if profits are to be divided in unequal proportions, that fact should be carefully spelled out in the partnership agreement.

Right to Be Compensated for Services. The UPA provides that "no partner is entitled to remuneration for acting in the partnership business." The only compensation that is to be received is each partner's share of the profits. Here again, if a partner is expected to devote more time to the firm's business than the others, the agreement should provide an appropriate compensation differential for the more active partner. (See Figure 39.1, ¶ 6).

Right to Be Repaid Personal Expenditures. A partner who expends personal funds, beyond the initial capital contribution, to pay partnership debts, or as a loan to enable the partnership to carry on its ordinary business, is entitled to repayment with interest before any other payments are made to the partners out of the firm's capital. Courts often cite Case 39.4 as precedent for the partnership's obligation to repay partner's advances.

CASE 39.4   Levy v. Leavitt • 178 N.E. 758 (N.Y. 1931)

FACTS   Levy (plaintiff) and Leavitt (defendant) purchased a large quantity of bacon from the government, hoping to sell it overseas at a profit. Leavitt was in sole charge of the enterprise; Levy was only an investor. After the bacon was purchased, government delay of export licenses caused it to spoil. Leavitt persuaded Congress to enact a law permitting suit for the loss; he filed the suit and won, forcing the government to pay the claim. In all these actions Leavitt spent his own funds. Levy sued for an accounting of the joint venture's affairs. Leavitt claimed he was entitled to repayment, with interest, of personal funds he had advanced, and also to payment for the reasonable value of his extraordinary services to rescue the venture from total loss. The court denied the claims and Leavitt appealed.

OPINION   LEHMAN, J. . . . The partnership agreement was oral and informal. There is nothing to show that the parties considered or discussed whether Leavitt should be entitled to compensation for his services or to any interest for moneys he might furnish.

. . . [As to] Leavitt's right to charge against Levy's share in the partnership funds, interest on moneys furnished by Leavitt . . . the Partnership Law . . . provides:

> . . . A partner, who in aid of the partnership makes any payment or advance beyond the amount of capital which he agreed to contribute, shall be paid interest from the date of the payment or advance.

. . . Where the express contract of partnership fails to provide for payment of special compensation for services rendered, the burden of proving that the parties intended such payment rests upon the person claiming such compensation. Where the express contract fails to provide for payment of interest on moneys furnished by a partner beyond the amount which he agreed to contribute, the burden of proving that the parties intended that no such interest should be paid rests upon the other partners. . . . The distinction . . . rests upon an inherent difference between the obligation of a partner to render services in the partnership business and the obligation to provide capital. . . . [Thus,] where a partner pays money to the partnership beyond his partnership obligation, it is a reasonable inference that the parties intended that such payment should be a loan and should bear interest.

JUDGMENT   [The judgment was modified to include interest to Leavitt on the sums he advanced to sue the government.]

Duties of Partners

Each partner undertakes (1) to serve the partnership according to the terms of the agreement, (2) to share in the losses of the enterprise, and (3) to discharge fiduciary duties owing to copartners.

Duty to Serve. Partnership agreements usually define partners' duties and the amount of time each will devote to the business. Even when a partner spends more time than the others, the UPA provides that such member is *not* entitled to extra compensation beyond a regular share of the profits unless the partnership agreement provides for it. If partners fail to perform their agreed-upon duties or otherwise act contrary to the partnership agreement, the sole legal remedy is suit for dissolution of the partnership accompanied by a claim for damages for the breach. The outcome depends upon the provisions of the agreement and whether the breach is intentional. (See Figure 39.1, ¶ 6.)

Duty to Share Losses. Just as partners share profits equally, or in whatever ratio is fixed in the agreement, so each has a parallel duty to share losses in the same ratio as the agreement provides for sharing profits. If the partnership lacks funds to cover its losses, they must be covered from the partners' personal funds. How losses are distributed among partners is discussed fully in Chapter 40.

Duty to Inform. Upon demand from any member, the UPA requires each partner to furnish complete information concerning all things affecting the partnership. This obligation is reinforced by a partner's fiduciary duty, which is often described as a duty to voluntarily disclose every material fact that might adversely affect the partnership. Every partner, as a co-manager, is entitled to equal knowledge of partnership affairs. In the next case we see the high cost an unethical partner had to pay for ignoring his fiduciary duty.

CASE 39.5 **Marsh v. Gentry** • 642 S.W.2d 574 (Ky. 1982)

FACTS Marsh (plaintiff) was a partner with Gentry (defendant) in the business of buying and selling racehorses. The firm owned a mare named Champagne Woman (which cost the partnership $155,000) and her foal Excitable Lady. The partners agreed to sell Champagne Woman at an auction which both Gentry and Marsh attended. Champagne Woman was sold at the auction for $135,000. Gentry's agent secretly bought the horse; but Gentry never told Marsh, and Marsh did not find out until 11 months later.

Next, Gentry proposed that he sell Excitable Lady at private sale, and Marsh agreed. Later, Gentry told Marsh that the horse had been sold to someone in California at the price he and Marsh had established. Gentry gave Marsh his proper share of the sale price, but Gentry refused to reveal the name of the buyer. A year later, when Excitable Lady won a big race, Marsh discovered that Gentry was the owner of the horse.

Marsh brought suit against Gentry for an accounting based upon Gentry's breach of his partnership obligation to make full disclosure to his copartner concerning both sales. The trial court held for the defendant (Gentry) and Marsh appealed.

OPINION O'HARA, J. . . . The controlling statute which is dispositive of this case is . . . [UPA 21], a codification of the common law. . . . :

<blockquote>

CASE 39.5 Continued

Every partner must account to the partnership for any benefit and hold as trustee for it any profit derived by him *without the consent of the other partners from any transaction connected with the formation, conduct, or liquidation of the partnership or from any use by him of its profit.*

Applying the clear and unambiguous language of the statute to the facts of this case, it becomes instantly apparent that Gentry did not comply with the evident intent of the law when he withheld [information about the sale of the horses] and misled his partner concerning the two "transactions." . . .

The actual bidding [at auction of Champagne Woman] was done by a secret agent of Gentry without the knowledge of Marsh. In addition, when the auction was completed, the sale was listed in the name of a third party. . . . As it turns out, the purchaser was Gentry himself. Admittedly, at an auction sale, the specific identity of the purchaser cannot be ascertained before the sale, but the [Partnership Act] . . . required a full disclosure by Gentry to Marsh that he would be a prospective purchaser.

As to the private sale of Excitable Lady, . . . even though Marsh obtained the stipulated price, a partner has an absolute right to know when his partner is the purchaser. Partners scrutinize buy-outs by their partners in an entirely different light than an ordinary third party sale. . . . The requirement of full disclosure among partners as to partnership business cannot be escaped. . . . Had Gentry made a full disclosure to his partner of his intentions to purchase the partnership property, Marsh would not later be heard to complain of the transaction.

JUDGMENT Accordingly, the judgment was reversed and the case remanded for the trial court to determine the sum due Marsh.

</blockquote>

Fiduciary Duties. Because of the close personal nature of a partnership and the dual capacity in which each partner functions as both principal and agent, each partner owes the fiduciary duty to act with the utmost good faith and loyalty toward the other partners. Among the most important elements of the fiduciary duty are: (1) the duty not to profit secretly from any business connected with the partnership and (2) the duty of a member not to compete with the partnership.

Secret profit. A partner must not secretly use partnership property or funds for private benefit or for payment of personal debts. If a partner engages in any such wrongful use, not only must the value of the "borrowed" item be accounted for, but also any secret profit must be accounted for and turned over to the partnership. Suppose partner Tom "borrows" $20,000 from the partnership bank account, invests in Goldgulch mining stock, which doubles in value. Tom sells the shares and redeposits the $20,000 in the partnership account. The partnership is entitled to the $20,000 profit Tom made with the partnership's funds and can also dissolve the partnership for breach of fiduciary duty.

Duty not to compete. A partner's fiduciary duty also includes the duty not to compete with the partnership unless it is fully informed and the other partners approve. Thus, a partner may not take personal advantage of an economic opportunity that is within the ambit of the partnership business. For instance, in the landmark case of *Meinhard v. Salmon*, it was held that a partner could not renew in his own name a lease to property occupied by his partnership even though the new lease was not to begin until after the partnership agreement terminated. Fiduciary obligations do not preclude a partner from any activity that is separate and distinct from partnership affairs. For example, assume that Bill and Ray, as partners, operate a laundry. When Bill has no duties to perform there, he may work at, or even be a partner in, a nearby shoe store without accounting to the laundry partnership because the two firms do not compete. In contrast, the next case shows how strictly courts view a partner who claims "after-hours" work does not compete with the firm.

> **BOX 39.1**
>
> **A Point of Ethics**
>
> In one of the most celebrated opinions in the annals of civil law, Judge Benjamin Cardozo, with timeless eloquence, defined the fiduciary duty and ethical standard that a partner must observe:
>
> "Many forms of conduct permissible in a workaday world, for those acting at arm's length, are forbidden to those bound by fiduciary ties. A . . . [partner] is held to something stricter than the morals of the market place. Not honesty alone, but the punctilio of an honor the most sensitive, is the standard of behavior. As to this there has developed a tradition that is unbending and inveterate."*
>
> *Meinhard v. Salmon, 164 N.E. 545 (N.Y. 1928).

CASE 39.6 **Veale v. Rose** • 657 S.W.2d 834 (Tex. App. 1983)

FACTS Rose, Veale, and others formed a partnership of certified public accountants. Their written agreement allowed partners to pursue and receive pay for other business activities so long as those activities did not conflict with the partnership practice and did not interfere with partners' duties to the firm. Without approval of all partners, no partner could practice *any* public accounting other than for the partnership.

Partner Rose was an officer in Right Away Foods, which paid him for providing basic accounting services that did not require the accountant to be a CPA. He also did accounting "after hours" for another firm for which he received pay. When Rose left the partnership, his partners disputed the amount the firm owed him. Rose sued the partners for an accounting and for the money due under the partnership agreement. Veale and the other partners counterclaimed for money due them for the accounting services which Rose carried on in competition with the partnership. The jury found that Rose did no accounting work in competition with the partnership. The partners appealed.

OPINION NYE, J. . . . Partners may be said to occupy a fiduciary relationship toward one another which requires of them the utmost degree of good faith and honesty in dealing with one another. . . . Breaches of a partner's duty not to compete with the partnership are compensable at law by awarding to the injured partners their proportionate share of the profits wrongfully acquired by the offending partner. . . .

It is undisputed that while a partner of Veale and Company, Rose rendered accounting services for Right Away Foods for which he billed and received pay-

> **CASE 39.6 Continued**
>
> ment personally. It is also undisputed that the partnership did not share in the proceeds. . . . Rose also admitted that he performed [other] accounting services during his tenure as a partner at Veale for which he billed and received payment personally. . . . His later testimony that he performed these services, in effect after hours, or in addition to his duties to the partnership, is of no value in light of the obligation imposed by the partnership agreement and by the common understanding of the term "competition."
>
> The misappropriation by one partner to his own use of property of the partnership is considered in law as constructive if not actual fraud on the partnership, and is actionable. . . . Again the record is replete with Rose's admissions that he used [partnership] employee and computer time and that he had not billed [his private client] for those services. . . .
>
> **JUDGMENT** [The partners' counterclaim against Rose was upheld.]

When a partner breaches partnership duties, the other members have a right (1) to recover from the wrongdoing partner any monetary losses sustained, (2) to secure an injunction when circumstances justify it, and (3) to use the breach as a basis to secure the dissolution of the partnership.

POWER OF PARTNERS TO OBLIGATE PARTNERSHIP AND COPARTNERS

We have already seen that each partner acts concurrently both as (1) a principal and (2) an agent of the other copartners. Accordingly, even when the other partners have limited a partner's authority, if it appears to a third party that the partner is carrying on the business of the partnership in the usual way, that partner has the power (but not the right) to obligate the partnership and the other copartners. This power to obligate the partnership may involve: (1) engaging in a contract for the partnership, (2) making admissions or representations against the interests of the partnership, (3) receiving information or notice binding on the partnership, and (4) committing tortious acts for which the partnership is liable.

Power to Obligate by Contract

A partner may obligate the partnership and copartners by contract (1) when specifically authorized by the partnership agreement to do so, (2) when the other partners either actually or impliedly consent to the action, or (3) when the partner is apparently carrying on the business of the partnership in the usual manner.[1]

Power to Obligate by Statement against Interest

A statement by a partner against the interest of the partnership may be used against the firm if it is made while carrying on the business of the partnership. Suppose Partner Tom, while making a delivery in the partnership van, negligently drives into Andy's auto, and says: "I'm sorry—it was all my fault." Tom's admission may be used as evidence against the partnership if it later denies liability.

Power to Obligate by Notice or Knowledge

All partners are charged with notice of any matter relating to partnership affairs that comes to the attention of any of its members. For example, city health officials hand a notice to Jack of the Jack, Jill & Jane Bakery, notifying the firm that their leaky drain pipe is flooding city land, and if not repaired, the city will file suit. All

---

[1] Chapter 36 examines at length the meanings of "apparent authority" and "implied authority."

partners are deemed to have received such notice when it is delivered to Jack, even if he throws it away and doesn't inform them. Jack has violated his duty to inform partners and is liable for any resulting loss.

Paralleling a partner's duty to communicate *notices* to the other partners is the duty to share any *knowledge* pertinent to partnership affairs. Such knowledge is imputed to the partners even if it is not communicated to them. For example, suppose partner Rod, while testing the partnership's product—a skateboard—learns that a defectively designed washer can cause the wheels to lock, creating a hazard to users of the product. That knowledge is imputed to all the other partners. However, an exception to the rule arises where a partner acts *adversely or fraudulently* against the interests of the partnership. Thus, if a partner steals partnership money, the copartners are not presumed to have knowledge of the theft.

Power to Obligate by Tortious Act

Under the UPA, each partner is liable for a copartner's torts committed within the scope of the partnership business. Often, partners who are innocent of wrongdoing are, nevertheless, liable not only for the unintentional tort of negligence, but also for intentional torts such as fraud, illustrated in the case below. An ethical proverb emerges from the case: "If your brother is a fraud, don't form a partnership with him."

CASE 39.7   **Bergh v. Mills** • 763 P.2d 214 (Wyo. 1988)

FACTS   Leslie Bergh and two employees decided to build a Billys Country Music Emporium (Billys). They formed a corporation, Billys, Inc., issuing stock to themselves in exchange for promissory notes in violation of Wyoming law. About the same time, Leslie Bergh and his brothers Milton and Raymond formed a partnership, Khybur Investments, to acquire land and construct the building for the saloon-dance hall. Needing more funds to complete the hall, Bergh met with his friend and drinking companion, John Mills. Bergh gave Mills a prospectus projecting $1 million net profit the first year. Bergh did not tell Mills that the project was already over budget, that the others had "purchased" their stock with promissory notes at a price which was less than half of what they were offering Mills, and that the corporation was already insolvent. Mr. and Mrs. Mills mortgaged their home to buy $150,000 of stock and later advanced additional sums. Billys opened, but owing to insolvency, closed. Mills sued Bergh's corporation and partnership. The trial court found that Leslie Bergh had defrauded Mills, and gave $286,000 judgment against the three brothers. They appealed.

OPINION   CARDINE, C. J. . . . We affirm the court's extension of liability to Khybur Investments and Raymond and Milton, Leslie Bergh's brothers and copartners. . . . [Wyoming's statute adopting the UPA] provides:

> Where by any wrongful act or omission of any partner acting in the ordinary course of the business of the partnership, or within the authority of his co-partners, loss or injury is caused to any person, not being a partner in the partnership, or any penalty is incurred, the partnership is liable therefor to the same extent as the partner so acting or omitting to act.

Khybur Investments was formed by Leslie Bergh and his two brothers for the sole

CASE 39.7 Continued	purpose of purchasing the land and the building for Billys. The necessary funds were borrowed [by the partnership] and the real estate was leased to Billys, Inc., for an amount sufficient to cover Kybur Investment's loan payments. When the meeting [with Mills] was held, Billys, Inc., needed funds to cover its obligations, which included the lease payments to Khybur. The evidence was sufficient to support an inference that Leslie Bergh was acting for the benefit of the partnership in the ordinary course of the partnership's business when he met with Mills. Consequently, the partnership is liable for the fraud committed by Leslie Bergh at that meeting. Raymond and Milton Bergh, partners in Khybur Investments, are liable by virtue of [Wyoming's UPA statute,] which provides: All partners are liable: (i) Jointly and severally for everything chargeable to the partnership under sections 13 and 14. The effect of this section of the Uniform Partnership Act is to impose individual liability against the members of a partnership when another partner commits a tortious act within the scope of partnership business. Fraud is among the tortious acts included within the scope of this section.
JUDGMENT	The judgment of the trial court [holding Raymond and Milton Bergh, the non-acting partners, liable for the fraud of Leslie, the acting partner] is affirmed.

Actions to Enforce Partnership Obligations. At common law, suit must be brought against the members of a partnership personally and not against the firm as such. Today, many states permit direct suit against a partnership as though it were a legal entity.

At common law and under the UPA all members of a partnership are: (1) *jointly* liable on obligations arising out of *contract*; hence, an outside third party must bring any suit against all the partners by name; and (2) *jointly and severally* liable for a partner's *tort* committed within the scope of the business. This means that the suit may be brought against all

> **BOX 39.2**
> **Are Innocent Partners Liable for Punitive Damages against a Fraudulent Partner?**
>
> Melvin and his copartners Bonnie, Frank, and Dorothy were real estate brokers. Duncan sued the partnership for fraudulently inducing her to buy real estate, alleging the acts were wanton, malicious, and oppressive. The court awarded compensatory damages, punitive damages, attorney's fees, and costs against Melvin but none against the three partners, finding they had "committed no fraud." On appeal, the New Mexico Supreme Court held that under the UPA, since partners are jointly and severally liable for the tort of a partner the judgment for compensatory damages should be against all four partners. However, since the purpose of *punitive damages* is to punish the wrongdoer, punitive damages cannot be awarded against innocent partners unless it is shown that they "ratified, authorized, controlled, or participated in the tortious act."*
>
> *Duncan v. Hennington*, 835 P.2d 816 (N.M. 1992).

the partners or against any one or more of them, and that the judgment can be satisfied against any one of them. A growing number of states, by statute or judicial interpretation, make no distinction between contract and tort actions—all liabilities are considered joint and several.

Generally, courts will not hear a dispute between partners unless it rises to the level of a suit for dissolution of the partnership and an accounting. Basically, such an action is the only remedy available to quarreling partners (see Chapter 40).

SUMMARY

The most common types of business organization are (1) sole proprietorship, (2) general partnership or joint venture, (3) limited partnership, (4) limited liability company, and (5) a corporation. In a sole proprietorship, one person owns the business and is personally liable for all debts. Two or more persons own a partnership; each has the right to manage but is personally liable for the firm's debts. A joint venture is formed to conduct one or a few business transactions. A limited partnership is managed by general partners who are personally liable for the firm's debts. The firm's limited partners have few managerial rights and no personal liability for the firm's debts beyond their investment. Similarly, members of a limited liability company are not liable for its debts beyond their capital investment.

Most large businesses incorporate. Owners (shareholders) have no control of management and no personal liability for debts. A partnership is an association of persons carrying on a business for profit as co-owners. Any person who is competent to contract may become a partner, but all partners must consent.

Partners may, by agreement, set up rights and obligations among themselves that differ from those set out in the UPA. They may not, however, diminish the obligations owed by the partners to third parties. Unless otherwise agreed, partners (1) share equally in the profits of the firm; (2) are each obligated to pay, in the same proportion as they share in the profits, any losses the firm sustains; and (3) receive no compensation for their services to the firm, other than their share of profits. Each partner is a principal in the firm and an agent of the copartners. Therefore, unless otherwise agreed, all partners have equal rights in management and personal liability for debts. A partner, like any other agent, may bind the partnership if the partner has express or apparent authority (based on estoppel). Partners have apparent authority if it reasonably appears that they are carrying on the business in the usual way.

Each partner must serve the partnership faithfully and furnish to the others all information about matters which might affect the partnership. In addition, a partner owes the other partners a fiduciary duty of loyalty, not to take secret profits from the partnership, and not to compete with it.

REVIEW QUESTIONS

1. (a) What are the principal forms of business organization? **(b)** What are some advantages and disadvantages of each form?

2. How do a *general* partnership, a *limited* partnership, and a *joint venture* differ?

3. (a) How does the UPA define partnership? **(b)** How many people constitute a partnership? **(c)** What is the maximum length of time a partnership can exist?

4. (a) How is a partnership formed? **(b)** How much "capital investment" is required to form a partnership?

5. (a) "A partnership can exist even though the parties do not know they are doing business as a partnership." Do you agree? **(b)** Why is it important that people doing business know whether or not they have formed a partnership?

6. "A person may participate in the profits of a business without being a partner in the business." True or false? Explain.

7 A person cannot become a partner unless all the partners already in the business give their consent. Why?

8. Define partner by estoppel and give an example of one.

9. (a) Distinguish between an interest in a partnership and a partner's rights in specific partnership property. (b) How does a judgment creditor of a partner reach a partner's interest in a partnership to obtain payment of the judgment debt?

10. When partner Tom dies what rights does his surviving spouse have to his interest in the partnership?

CASE PROBLEMS

1. Art, opening his new accounting office, asked Bryan, a lawyer, to share office space and "split" secretarial and rental costs with him. Bryan agreed. Art signed a lease for the rooms, and they conducted their respective practices there. Bryan won a lawsuit, earning a large fee. Arthur claims a share of that fee, asserting that they had, by their arrangements, established a partnership. Was he correct? Why or why not?

2. Able and Baker were partners, making a prototype of Baker's invention. Short of working capital, they asked Oscar to invest $10,000 in the project, and promised him a 25 percent interest in the venture and the prospect of "making a lot of money." Oscar gave Able and Baker the money. Although Oscar was told that he had nothing to do with the management of the enterprise, he frequently helped in the work by preparing brochures for use in sales and furnishing his own employees and equipment for rush jobs on the invention. He cosigned with Able and Baker an application for a loan which was not granted. They told Oscar that they needed more funds to develop the invention and that profits would be split three ways. Oscar invested an additional $10,000. They spent much time on the project, but with no progress. Able and Baker spent most of the partnership funds for secondhand equipment which malfunctioned. Oscar sued Able and Baker for return of his money, claiming that their negligence caused the venture to fail and that, as a passive investor—not a partner—he was entitled to the return of his money. Should he recover? Why?

3. Rice and Smith, by written agreement, formed R&S partnership, each owning 50 percent. The partnership owned and operated a large apartment house in New York. Their agreement said in part:

Art. 12. It is agreed that neither partner shall have the authority to sell or assign any interest in this partnership before offering it to the other party for purchase, except that either party may assign a part or all of his share to a member of his immediate family who attains the age of 21 years.

In 1983, Rice transferred one-half of his partnership share to his 22-year-old daughter, Alice. Rice said that Alice was now a partner in the firm, with a 25 percent interest. Smith refused to treat Alice as a partner. Was Rice or Smith correct? Why?

4. Smith and Lea were logging partners. Redd talked to them about starting a sawmill, and said he would train them to operate it. They brought all their logging equipment, built a mill, an office building, and regularly worked a 65-hour week. Redd paid them low wages and no overtime, from which withholding and social security taxes were deducted. Smith and Lea supervised and hired and fired other workers. After 5 years, Lea left and Redd paid him $20,000, saying to Smith, "His leaving means more for us." He promised Smith "a third to a half" of the business when the bank loan was paid off, and when he had recouped his $400,000 investment. By 1988, Redd had paid himself $500,000 from the business, and although there was enough cash, Redd declined to pay off the bank. Smith sued Redd for dissolution of partnership and payment of his interest. Redd denied that a partnership existed. Was there a partnership?

5. Ethel owned 10 percent, Dorothy 10 percent, and Sarah 80 percent of Hi-Time Liquors, a partnership. A personal creditor obtained judgment against Sarah. A charging order was entered against her partnership interest. A court-appointed receiver held a judicial sale at which Audrey bought Sarah's partnership interest. When Hi-Time's liquor license needed to be renewed, Audrey applied for it, as new owner of 80 percent of the partnership. Ethel and Dorothy also applied for the renewal, contending that Audrey had no right to apply for it. To whom should the license be issued? Why?

6. Martin complained of stomach pain to Dr. Barbour, who examined him and then operated, negligently severing a muscle. Dr. Barbour's partner, Dr. Egle, handled postoperative care. Dr. Egle had not seen Martin before or during the operation. Martin sued Dr. Barbour and Dr. Egle for malpractice. Dr. Egle asked to be dismissed from the case, as he was not a surgeon nor was he involved in the operation. Should he be dismissed? Explain.

CHAPTER 40

Termination of Partnerships

The UPA definition of partnership, which begins with the phrase "an association . . ." might also be described as a *close association*. Often, the relationship is closer than partners realize, and when misunderstanding develops, partners argue over many of the same things that divorcing couples argue over, with a similar legal outcome—dissolution. Whatever the cause—unhappy differences, death, or simply a mutual desire to part peacefully—partnerships do end.

When partners are amicable, formal dissolution and winding up are usually not necessary. Instead, the partners mutually settle their accounts and business affairs and pay off the withdrawing partner, estate of a deceased partner, or creditors. The business is then carried on by a remaining partner as a sole proprietor or by a new partnership of the remaining partners with or without new members.

In more formal, adversary, or hostile situations, a partnership ends through a three-step process: (1) **dissolution;** followed by (2) a period of formal **winding up** of the business; resulting in (3) its final **termination.** Dissolution and termination, then, are two moments in time, with winding up as the *period of time* in between.

The first part of this chapter considers the circumstances which bring about dissolution as well as the process of winding up a partnership. The second part looks at scenarios in which the partnership business may be continued without winding up.

DISSOLUTION OF PARTNERSHIPS

The Uniform Partnership Act (UPA) defines **dissolution** as "the change in the relation of the partners caused by any partner ceasing to be associated in the carrying on . . . of the business."

Dissolution must not be confused with termination. When a partnership is dissolved it does not mean that it is terminated (ended) at that moment in time. Dissolution means that the partnership cannot continue to carry on business in the normal way. Instead, a dissolved firm generally enters into a period of winding up, during which the partnership is liquidated. Current contracts are completed, debts collected, bills paid, and remaining assets, if any, distributed among the partners. Only then is the partnership *terminated*. However, liquidation is not the only alternative. For example, if death of a partner dissolves the partnership, the surviving partners could simply vote to continue the business as a partnership consisting only of the surviving partners.

> **BOX 40.1**
>
> **Can the Uniform Partnership Act Be Used to Dissolve a Corporation? A Virginia Court Says "Yes!"**
>
> After practicing law for 10 years as part of a professional corporation, four lawyers left Boyd and the old corporation to start a new one of their own. Boyd and the old corporation sued the four, claiming they had collected fees and funds that belonged to it. The four lawyers replied that it was true they had incorporated, but only for a tax shelter, and for the entire 10 years they really had operated as a partnership. When a new member had joined, no stock certificate was issued. They referred to themselves as "partners," and filed partnership tax returns.
>
> The court held that the final accounting should be settled on the basis of the UPA and partnership law—not corporation law. In the court's view, "it is not inconsistent with close corporation law for its member-stockholders to disregard the corporation and conduct internal affairs as a partnership."* ∎
>
> *Boyd P.C. v. Payne P.C., 422 S.E.2d 784 (1992).

Dissolution Pursuant to Terms of the Agreement. When a business is organized as a partnership, it is common practice to limit its life to a fixed term. (See Figure 39.1, ¶ 3.) Thus, if partners agree to operate for 5 years and during that time do not extend the term, upon its expiration the partnership will automatically dissolve. Partners may also condition the life of their partnership upon the completion of a stated purpose or upon the occurrence of a particular event. For example, a partnership (or joint venture) formed to race Hi-Flyer, a stallion, is dissolved if the horse dies.

Since a partnership comes into existence by voluntary agreement of its members, the partners may likewise, by unanimous assent, at any time dissolve it without regard to the term or purpose for which it was originally formed. Partnership agreements usually spell out what happens when partners die, become disabled or incompetent, or withdraw and retire after reaching a stated age—all of which cause dissolution of the partnership without violating its terms. (See Figure 39.1, ¶ 10.)

Older case law considered a partnership dissolved when the partners added a new member. It was reasoned that by unanimous agreement the partners had terminated the first firm and established a new one with the new member. The modern and growing view is that a partnership agreement may permit a new partner to enter without dissolving the firm. Some courts reason that the old partnership has not dissolved because the original partners continue to be associated in the business. Other courts, as in the case which follows, interpret the UPA as not requiring dissolution unless the agreement provides otherwise.

Dissolution may be (1) not in violation of the terms of the partnership agreement, (2) in violation of the partnership agreement, (3) by operation of law, or (4) by court decree.

Dissolution Not in Violation of Partnership Agreement

A dissolution that does not violate the partnership agreement may arise in several ways.

CASE 40.1   **Brookfield Associates v. Estate of Bacon** • Lexis 561 (Conn. Super. 1993)

FACTS   E. McCarty and Frank Bacon signed a written partnership agreement in 1988. Paragraph 14, a "buyout" provision, gave a surviving partner the right to purchase the deceased partner's interest at a price equal to the decedent's capital account at prior calendar year end, increased by his share of profits and decreased by his withdrawals up to date of death. As of date of death, Bacon had over-

CASE 40.1 Continued

drawn his capital account by $14,180. McCarty notified Margaret Bacon as executrix of her husband's estate that since the capital account was overdrawn, McCarty had fully performed under the agreement for the transfer of the decedent's partnership interest. After demand for repayment of the overdrawn capital account was refused, McCarty sued the estate.

The executrix claimed that the addition of two new partners (the Taorminas) *after* the date of the McCarty-Bacon agreement had the legal effect of dissolving the old partnership and substituting a new, oral, at-will partnership in its place. Finally, the executrix argued that the new partnership should be governed by the UPA—not the former agreement. The validity of this argument was reviewed on appeal.

OPINION

McGRATH, J. . . . Where the UPA is in effect, the dissolution of a partnership can only be brought about as the Act provides, in the absence of specific provisions in a partnership contract governing the termination of partners' interests by dissolution, or expressly providing that the partnership will continue and dissolution and winding up are not required on the occurrence of certain events. The courts recognize, however, that dissolution may take place under certain circumstances not specifically enumerated in the Uniform Act, including, for example, the admission of a new partner to the firm, or a partner's withdrawal from the firm.

The Uniform Partnership Act does not appear to make the admission of a new partner a ground for dissolution. Several provisions of the Act support this proposition:

(a) the general definition appears to require that there be a partner who ceases to be associated in carrying on the business, and this does not necessarily occur when a new partner is admitted;

(b) admission of a new partner is not listed as either a cause of dissolution by operation of law or a ground for obtaining a judicial decree of dissolution; and

(c) the Act provides that no person can become a member of a partnership without the consent of all the partners, thus apparently recognizing the admission of a partner into a continuing partnership.

Admission of a partner is not included among the U.P.A. causes of dissolution and is not within the definition of dissolution under U.P.A. Sec. 29 as involving a dissolution. Although there is some authority supporting dissolution in this situation, nondissolution upon admission of a partner is clearly the better rule. The only justification for dissolving upon admission of a partner is that a new partner changes the close-knit relationship of a small partnership. In a very closely held partnership, however, each partner will ordinarily be able to veto admission of a new partner, so dissolution is not necessary. The power to veto new members is most likely to have been altered by contrary agreement only in the larger firms; in this type of firm, dissolution for admission of a new partner is unnecessary, potentially disruptive, and probably contrary to the expectations of the partners.

JUDGMENT

[The court held that a partnership is not dissolved by admission of a partner unless the agreement provides otherwise.]

Dissolution by Withdrawal from At-Will Partnership. A partnership at will is one in which the partnership agreement does not specify any date or circumstance for its dissolution. Since the partners have not agreed to continue the partnership for any fixed period of time, each partner has the right to withdraw "at will"—that is, at any time. Ordinarily, the withdrawing partner does not breach the partnership agreement even if the firm is operating profitably and its dissolution results in monetary loss to the other partners. However, a partner such as the defendant in the next case, who terminates an at-will partnership in *bad faith*, faces liability for tortious breach of the implied covenant of good faith.

CASE 40.2 **Wilensky v. Blalock** • 414 S.E.2d 1 (Ga. 1991)

FACTS Blalock and Arford were at-will partners in a firm that located borrowers, originated mortgage loans, and sold them to Gulf States Mortgage Company, Inc. (Gulf), of which Wilensky was an officer. The partnership and Gulf offices were in the same building. After a dispute developed and Arford physically ejected Blalock from the partnership business, Wilensky urged Arford to terminate the partnership and to keep for himself its material assets and its profitable relationship with Gulf. Wilensky, at one point, threatened to change the locks on the building if Blalock didn't stay out. Blalock sued Arford, Wilensky, and Gulf. After jury trial, the court entered judgment against Arford and Gulf. On appeal, the court affirmed as to Arford, but held that Gulf could not be liable for terminating the relation between Gulf and the partnership since that relation was terminable at will. The court also held that Wilensky was liable for the tort of interfering with the Arford-Blalock's partnership agreement. Arford and Wilensky appealed to the Georgia Supreme Court.

OPINION BENHAM, J. . . . Arford has argued that he can have no liability in contract for the termination of the partnership because the relationship was terminable at will. According to his approach . . . the fact that the oral agreement was terminable at will meant that from the moment that he declared the relation to be ended, he had no further contractual duties which could be breached. We believe that the obligations of partners can reach beyond that moment and that the jury and the Court of Appeals correctly determined that such was the case in the present matter.

Laws in existence at the time a contract is executed are part of that contract. Already in existence at the time the partnership . . . was created was the provision in . . . [Georgia statutes] that partners owe a duty to act in the utmost good faith with regard to each other. Therefore, it follows . . . that the partnership agreement here included, as a matter of law, an agreement that Arford and Blalock, would act in utmost good faith toward one another. . . . We accordingly adopt the reasoning of the Court of Appeals on this issue in the case:

> Even though a partner has a right to dissolve the partnership, if it is proved that the partner acted in bad faith and violated his fiduciary duties by attempting to appropriate to his own use the prosperity of the partnership without adequate compensation to his copartner, the dissolution would be wrongful and the partner would be liable as

> **CASE 40.2 Continued**
>
> provided by the section of the Uniform Partnership Act defining the rights of partners upon wrongful dissolution for violation of the implied agreement not to exclude the other partner wrongfully from the partnership business opportunity.
>
> . . . A review of the testimony at trial [justified the jury in concluding] . . . that Arford kept for himself all the partnership's material assets and continuing income from its mortgage origination business, that Arford's conduct was a breach of the implied duty of good faith in the oral partnership agreement, and that the breach of that agreement caused Blalock damages.
>
> **JUDGMENT** [Judgments against Arford and Wilelnsky were upheld.]

Dissolution by Expulsion of a Partner. The partnership agreement may authorize members to expel a partner for breach of the obligation to perform listed duties or for engaging in prohibited conduct. (See Figure 39.1, ¶ 9.) Conduct that is often defined as a breach of the agreement, for example, includes failure to pay one's share of a partnership obligation, exceeding or ignoring limitations on one's authority, or being convicted of a felony. Note, however, that *if the agreement does not provide for expulsion, partners are without authority to expel a wrongdoing partner.* To escape from the unpleasant association they must seek judicial dissolution of the partnership.

When the partnership agreement provides for expulsion of a partner and the majority decide to take that action, they must follow the procedures set out in the agreement. They must act to serve the best interests of the partnership. Partners cannot, by expelling a member of the firm, cause the loss of the expelled partner's investment in the firm. The UPA provides that the expelled partner should be "discharged from all partnership liabilities . . . [and] receive in cash . . . the net amount due him from the partnership." Since each partner has personal liability for partnership debts incurred while a member of the firm, anyone expelled from a partnership remains subject to the claims of those who were then the firm's creditors. How these obligations are discharged is discussed later in this chapter.

In the following case, a group of doctors exercised their contractual right to expel a copartner against his wishes.

> **CASE 40.3** **Gelder Medical Group v. Webber** • 363 N.E. 2d 573 (N.Y. 1977)
>
> **FACTS** In 1974, Dr. Webber joined the Gelder Medical Group, a partnership of several doctors. The partnership agreement stated that a majority vote of partners could request any member to withdraw from the group effective immediately; that the expelled member would be paid his share of the profits to date of termination; and that he would not "for five years after any voluntary or involuntary termination . . . practice his profession within . . . thirty miles of the Village of Sidney, . . . without consent . . . of the Gelder Medical Group."
>
> After a few months, a majority of the doctors reached the conclusion that Dr. Webber was an embarrassment to them. When they asked him to withdraw from the partnership, he refused. Following the procedures specified in the partnership agreement, Dr. Webber was formally notified that effective immediately his asso-

CASE 40.3 Continued

ciation with the partnership was terminated and, after an accounting, he was paid $18,568.41. Thereafter, disregarding the prohibition in the agreement against practicing medicine in the vicinity of Sidney, he opened a medical office there. The medical group sued to enjoin Dr. Webber from practicing medicine in Sidney. In reply, Dr. Webber claimed that the group acted in bad faith and therefore had wrongfully expelled him from the partnership. The trial court held for the medical group, the supreme court affirmed, and Dr. Webber appealed to the court of appeals, the highest appellate court in New York State.

OPINION

BREITEL, C.J. . . . Covenants restricting a professional, and in particular a physician, from competing with a former employer or associate are common and generally acceptable. . . . If they are reasonable as to time and area, necessary to protect legitimate interests, not harmful to the public, and not unduly burdensome, they will be enforced. . . .

Similarly common and acceptable are provisions in a partnership agreement to provide for the withdrawal or expulsion of a partner. While there is no common-law or statutory right to expel a member of a partnership, partners may provide, in their agreement, for the involuntary dismissal, with or without cause, of one of their number. . . .

. . . When, as here, the agreement provides for dismissal of one of their number on the majority vote of the partners, the court may not frustrate the intention of the parties at least so long as the provisions for dismissal work no undue penalty or unjust forfeiture, overreaching, or other violation of public policy. . . . It was important . . . in the group's eyes . . . that it be disassociated from the new member's conflict-producing conduct. Indeed, at the heart of the partnership concept is the principle that partners may choose with whom they wish to be associated. . . .

JUDGMENT

Accordingly, the order of the Appellate Division [upholding the expulsion of Dr. Webber] should be affirmed.

Dissolution in Violation of Partnership Agreement

Because a partnership is a voluntary association of its members, any partner has the *power* to dissolve the association at any time. The partnership agreement merely puts contractual limits on the *right* of a partner to exercise that power. The partner who exceeds those limits is said to dissolve the partnership in *violation* of the agreement. Such dissolution occurs most frequently when a partner withdraws from the firm before expiration of the agreed-upon term. Of course, withdrawal of at-will partners generally does not violate the partners' agreement.

Does Assignment of Interest in the Partnership Dissolve It? An assignment of a partner's interest in the partnership does not automatically dissolve the partnership unless there is some evidence that the partner intends to leave the firm. If there is intent to leave, normally the departing partner will express it either orally or in writing to the remaining partners. For example, if Ann assigns her partnership interest to a bank as security for a loan, but continues to perform her partnership duties, clearly she has not evidenced intent to withdraw, and automatic dissolution has not come about. However, if Ann at the time of assignment, tells her partners that she is leaving the partnership and wants to be paid for the value of her interest in the firm, she has caused dissolution. Of course, if the partnership agreement forbids assignment and declares it to be grounds for expulsion, it would bring about dissolution should the partners decide to expel. For example, suppose partner Ted assigns his partnership interest in violation of the agreement which prohibits it, but does not express intent to withdraw and continues to participate in the business. Such conduct might not result in automatic dissolution of the partnership. However, the other partners could use Ted's act as grounds for a court-ordered dissolution, discussed later in this chapter.

What if a partner is convicted of a felony, and the partnership agreement provides that such conduct will automatically dissolve the partnership? When a partner's wrongful act in contravention of the partnership agreement triggers dissolution, the remaining partners have the option of continuing the partnership business or of winding it up. In either event, the withdrawing partner is entitled to receive payment of the value of his or her interest, but that value is diminished by whatever damages the innocent partners may have suffered.

Suppose the partnership agreement defines a partner's failure to meet a capital call as a wrongful act that automatically causes dissolution. Assume further that the agreement has a "liquidated damages" clause, which declares that all the defaulting partner's previous capital contributions are forfeited to the partnership as liquidated (contractually agreed-upon) damages. Under the UPA, can the defaulting partner not only be thrown out of the partnership but also forced to lose his or her investment? The next case answers that question.

CASE 40.4 **Hindman v. Salt Pond Associates** • Lexis 265 (Del. Ch. 1991)

FACTS Fifteen persons formed a general partnership, Salt Pond Associates, to develop commercial property. The agreement required additional capital contributions if approved by partners with 70 percent interest. In 1990 the partners met and voted to call for an additional capital contribution of $800,000. Hindman was notified that his share was $80,000, but failed to pay it. The partnership agreement provided:

> If any additional capital contribution that is not received by the partnership on or before 90 days from the date of authorization, the partner failing to make the additional capital contribution shall be deemed to be in a material default of its obligation and responsibilities as a partner and all of the defaulting partner's interest in the partnership shall be automatically transferred to the partnership itself and the defaulting partner shall forfeit all rights as a partner including future income from the partnership.

After receiving notice from the partnership that because of his default on the capital call, his initial $10,000 investment was forfeited to the partnership, Hindman (plaintiff) sued, asking the court to order the partnership to pay him the value of his interest in the partnership.

OPINION CHANDLER, J. . . . Plaintiff compares the Agreement to a high stakes poker game, with the other partners increasing the stakes through capital contributions, effectively forcing out minority partners who could no longer afford to participate. The plaintiff, however, does not allege that he was induced, by trickery or deception, to enter into an agreement that included a provision al-

CASE 40.4 Continued

lowing partners of superior resources to exert economic power unfairly against financially weaker, minority partners. Nor has the plaintiff alleged that he did not read or understand the Agreement's provisions regarding capital contributions. . . . Our law respects bargained-for contractual provisions as long as they do not violate our statutes or public policy. The question then becomes whether an agreement that permits, in certain circumstances, a partner's interest to be forfeited to the partnership, contravenes public policy or our statutes. . . .

When the parties in unambiguous language write into their agreement a provision for forfeiture, the courts will enforce the provision. . . . Plaintiff argues that he was not aware that he could be required to pay additional capital contributions and that such a large contribution was not anticipated. Ignorance of specific contractual terms, plainly presented in the contract and freely and voluntarily accepted, has no legal weight in determining the validity of a contract. . . . Using plaintiff's own "poker game" analogy, a party who knowingly takes a seat at a "no raise limit" poker game accepts the risk of elimination from the game when he cannot meet the "raise." . . .

Under the Agreement, plaintiff forfeited his interest upon his failure to meet the additional capital contribution, making the value of his interest zero upon dissolution. Therefore, the remaining partners are required to pay plaintiff nothing, per the forfeiture provision in the Agreement. His forfeited interest was in practice a form of liquidated damages for failure to provide capital as required by the Agreement. Nonetheless, consistent with . . . [UPA § 38 (b) (2)] if the remaining partners wish to continue the business of Salt Pond Associates, they must indemnify plaintiff against any Partnership liabilities that develop subsequent to his expulsion.

JUDGMENT [Summary judgment for the partnership was ordered.]

Dissolution by Operation of Law

Dissolution by Death of a Partner. As a general rule, death of a partner automatically dissolves the partnership. Some partnerships, particularly those in accounting, law, and finance, may have several hundred partners in a single firm. To forestall an unbroken chain of dissolutions and litigation, these large partnerships, as well as many smaller firms, have modified their agreements to provide that "neither withdrawal nor death of a partner, nor the admission of any new partner shall dissolve or terminate the partnership." In addition, "buy/sell" clauses are included in the agreements, which obligate the continuing partners to purchase the interest of a member who dies, retires, or otherwise leaves the firm. (See Figure 39.1, ¶ 10.) In this way, dissolution of the firm is not automatic upon death of a partner. Such provisions add flexibility to the partnership organization, and make it possible to continue under its original firm name even when partners whose names the firm bears are no longer alive. Recent cases are giving effect to such partnership agreements, and a few states have laws which give those agreements a clear legal foundation.

Dissolution by Bankruptcy. Dissolution also automatically results from bankruptcy of a partnership or of an individual partner. A partner in a successful partnership might still incur large personal debts, such as medical bills or credit card purchases, and see no way out but personal bankruptcy. Unfortunately for partners, bankruptcy results in the automatic dissolution of the partnership. As explained in Chapter 26 on bankruptcy law, if assets of a partner in personal bankruptcy are not sufficient to discharge personal debts, the partner is nevertheless relieved from any additional obligations, including those arising out of membership in the partnership. This protection afforded by the bankruptcy act takes precedence over the fundamental partnership concept that all partners are equally responsible for their firm's obligations.

Dissolution by Subsequent Illegality. Any event which makes it unlawful for a partnership business to continue, or for any of its members to engage in the business, automatically dissolves the firm. For example, assume that a partnership is in the business of selling intoxicating liquor at retail. A new state law makes the retail sale of intoxicating liquor illegal. Upon the effective date of that law, the partnership is dissolved.

Dissolution by Court Decree

Courts are reluctant to settle disputes between partners concerning the firm's business affairs. Furthermore, partners have the power to dissolve a partnership without recourse to court assistance. It follows that asking a court to order a partnership dissolved is unnecessary, expensive, and time-consuming. However, a partner whose other partners oppose dissolution may justifiably ask a court to decree dissolution because of (1) incapacity of a partner to perform his or her duties, (2) misconduct of a partner, (3) the fact that the continuation of the business can result only in financial loss, or (4) any other circumstance which would justify a court in finding dissolution to be equitable.

Dissolution for Incapacity of a Partner. The temporary incapacity of a partner does not cause dissolution of a partnership nor does it furnish grounds for the member to be expelled from the firm. However, a partner's continuing mental or physical incapacity to perform partnership duties is a basis for a court-ordered dissolution.

If a court declares a partner mentally unsound and unable to manage business affairs, there is clear ground for dissolution by court order. A more troublesome problem arises when a partner suffers disability which prevents performance of duties, but which is uncertain as to its duration. If partners cannot settle the issue amicably, a court must rule whether the partner is competent to continue in the firm. Partnership agreements usually cover such problems with provisions defining permanent disability and establishing fair procedures for a "buyout" of the incapacitated partner's interest.

Dissolution for Misconduct of a Partner. An equity court will order dissolution of a partnership upon proof that (1) one of the partners has been guilty of conduct which tends to prejudice the carrying on of the partnership business, (2) one of the partners has wilfully or persistently breached the partnership agreement, or (3) one or more partners find it is not reasonably practicable to continue in business with one or more of the other partners.

Because it is judicial policy not to interfere in minor internal partnership affairs, the intervention of a court is not warranted if financial loss to the partnership results from an incident in which a partner made an honest error in judgment (such as extending credit to an unworthy purchaser), or if the objectionable conduct is only trifling (e.g., a partner grumbles every time a bill must be paid). But innocent partners can obtain dissolution by court decree where wrongdoing is continuing and egregious—for example, where a partner:

1. Deals fraudulently with purchasing agents
2. Refuses to explain or justify checks drawn against the partnership account
3. Persists in dealing with customers in a manner that results in permanent injury to the partnership business
4. Causes the firm to be brought into such public disrepute or ridicule that its credit and goodwill are impaired

Dissolution for Unprofitable Business. Since partners intend the firm to be profitable, they will usually agree to dissolve a partnership that can only operate at a loss. However, if dissolution is opposed by partners who think success is "around the corner," a court must decide the issue.

Dissolution for Other Circumstances. If it is equitable and fair to all parties, a court may order dissolution in circumstances other than those discussed above—for example, where partners have irreconcilable differences as to how to run the business or how much to spend on advertising; or where a partner has made a secret profit or seized a partnership opportunity for personal advantage.

WINDING UP OF PARTNERSHIPS

The dissolution of a partnership brings to an end the normal working relationships of the partners. However, the partnership continues to exist after dissolution and must go through another step—winding up—before it is terminated.

Who Conducts the Winding Up? Compensation

If a partnership is dissolved because its agreed-upon term has ended, or its purpose has been accomplished, or because the partners agree to dissolution, all the partners are entitled to participate in the winding up. However, they usually entrust that function to one of their number or to some third party designated by all. If the partners cannot agree upon who will conduct the winding-up process, or a dissolution is ordered by judicial decree, a court will appoint a receiver to take charge of the winding up. Neither a member who has caused dissolution by wrongfully withdrawing from the partnership nor a partner whose bankruptcy caused the dissolution may conduct the winding up.

If dissolution comes about because a partner has died and the surviving partners have decided not to continue the business, the winding up is done as described above with one exception: Some states require the executor or administrator of the deceased partner's estate to wind up the partnership so that the decedent's interest in it will be properly protected.

Because sooner or later every partnership business comes to an end, the winding-up process (except if a partner dies) is considered to be a normal partnership function. Consequently, the partner or partners who conduct it are not entitled to compensation unless the other partners agree to pay it. But if the dissolution occurred because of a death, the winding-up partners are entitled to compensation.

Some states impose a statutory duty upon a surviving partner to wind up the partnership and render an accounting within 2 years from the date of the deceased partner's death. The case below points out how failure to carry out the duty to wind up can lead to serious financial loss. It also clarifies the different, but parallel, roles of (1) the surviving partner winding up partnership business and (2) the surviving personal representative (executor or administrator) winding up matters involving a decedent's property *other* than partnership property.

CASE 40.5   **Darlage v. Crane** • 576 N.E. 2d 1303 (Ind. App. 1991)

FACTS   George Darlage and his son, Joseph, operated Darlage Crane and Earthmoving Service, a partnership. In April 1983, Joseph died in a car accident. The probate court appointed his sister, Jane, as executrix of his will, which left his estate to his two minor children by his divorced wife, Cheryl. Jane, as executrix, obtained probate court approval of her petition to continue Joseph's portion of the partnership business. George continued the business until mid-December. He then gave Jane a list of equipment and liens and paid the estate $14,487 for Joseph's

CASE 40.5 Continued

interest in the partnership; at the same time, he handed Jane a claim against Joseph's estate for $14,937, which Jane paid from estate funds. Jane never asked for or obtained probate court approval of this transaction. Indiana law imposed on a surviving partner a duty to wind up partnership affairs in 2 years, but George gave no accounting for over 7 years.

In 1985 Cheryl, as guardian ad litem (guardian for purposes of litigation) for the minor children, obtained from the probate court a judgment for her claim against the estate for alimony and child support prior to Joseph's death, but there were no funds in Joseph's estate to pay this. Cheryl then commenced suit in probate court against George, to collect Joseph's share of partnership assets, which Cheryl claimed George had never accounted for. Cheryl also sued on behalf of the minor children for their just inheritance, which she claimed George was wrongfully withholding. At trial, evidence showed that in 1984 he had sold a partnership landfill contract to another earthmoving company for $100,000. Based on expert accounting testimony, the court found that Joseph's interest in the partnership was valued at $90,061, which with interest from 1983 to 1989 at 8 percent amounted to $138,126.67. Judgment for that amount was given in favor of Cheryl on her claim combined with that on behalf of the minor children. George Darlage appealed.

OPINION

RATLIF, J. . . . In its judgment, the trial court observed that the transaction between Jane and George purporting to settle the partnership business between the partners was "poisonous" in its tendencies, even though no actual fraud could be shown. We agree. A delay of more than seven years after a partner's death with no filings and accountings by the surviving partner as required by statute, an executrix who has failed to enforce actively the deceased partner's rights against the surviving partner, and the familial relationship between the executrix and the surviving partner make any real resolution of the partnership business at any time in the future dubious at best. Cheryl, as creditor of the estate and as the guardian of the estate's heirs [the minor children] . . . has standing to assert this claim. . . .

George claims that there was a binding . . . settlement between himself and Joseph's estate as a matter of law. We find that no such settlement occurred. . . . The probate code specifies the procedure to be used when settling a decedent's estate. In part, it provides that an executrix may make compromises with any of the estate's debtors, if such action is in the "best interest" of the estate, and on "court order." Any settlement must be "fair and reasonable." The record shows that the purported settlement between George and Joseph's estate, through Jane, was neither in the best interest of the estate, nor on court order. Jane paid George's claim against the estate when the estate was insolvent, and prior to any order by the court sanctioning such payment. As such, it cannot be characterized as fair or reasonable, and is in direct violation of the statute. Any payment made in violation of the statute is not binding on the estate.

JUDGMENT

[The court affirmed the judgment of $138,126 against George, to settle Joseph's interest in the partnership, payable through the estate to Cheryl in satisfaction of her claim, with the balance representing the inheritance of the minor children.]

Table 40.1 Steps in Winding Up a Partnership under UPA

1. **Preserve partnership assets**—verify insurance coverage of partnership property.
2. **Complete unfinished business**—person winding up has no authority to commence new business, but must complete executory contracts, including payment of inventory purchase contracts; may borrow working capital from bank to complete unfinished contracts.
3. **Collect all debts owed to partnership**—collect receivables and other debts; sue to collect valid claims; make reasonable compromise settlements of disputed claims.
4. **Reduce assets to cash and pay debts first.**
5. **Render accounting to partners**—if dissolution was due to death of partner, submit copy to executor of estate and to probate court, if required; if surviving partners are buying decedent's interest in partnership, obtain court approval, pay executor the buyout price, and receive back a bill of sale.
6. **Distribute assets to partners**—according to their respective interests.

The Winding-Up Process

Winding up means the liquidation of the partnership business. The steps in winding up are shown in Table 40.1.

Reducing Assets to Cash, Paying Debts. Since the most ready buyers of partnership property are often the partners themselves, remaining partnership property may, with the consent of all partners, be sold to one or more partners; or the property may be transferred to them to satisfy partnership debts owing to such members. Any debts incurred in winding up or completing unfinished business at the time of dissolution are chargeable to the partnership and its members.

Accounting. As the winding-up process comes to a close, the person in charge of it must render an **accounting,** which is a financial statement setting out all transactions that were involved. It shows the total assets, debts, and equity of the firm at the date of dissolution and at the conclusion of the winding up. If, after all receipts and disbursements are accounted for, partnership assets are exhausted and unsatisfied claims still remain against the partnership, the accounting will state how much each partner is required to pay the remaining creditors. On the other hand, after all obligations are paid, if assets remain, the accounting will show how they will be distributed among the partners.

Limitation on Partners' Powers during Winding Up

Except in matters connected with winding up a partnership, its dissolution terminates authority of all partners to act for it. However, although partners have no actual authority after dissolution, they may still have *apparent authority* to bind a dissolved partnership. Apparent authority exists when (1) the nature of the transaction is such that the partnership would be bound if the dissolution had not taken place, and (2) the *third party had no knowledge or notice of the dissolution.* To illustrate this rule, suppose Abe, Bob, and Cal are partners in a home construction business. Abe dies, and Bob has been designated to wind up the partnership. Cal regularly purchases home appliances on partnership credit from Jiffy Supply in another city, and the Jiffy people do not know of Abe's death. Cal knows that no additional fixtures are needed to complete the homes under construction at the time of Abe's death, but he has a scheme. Cal buys on partnership credit $30,000 worth of kitchen, bath, and heating appliances, loads them on his truck, and drives off into the sunset. Cal had apparent authority to buy on partnership credit. Jiffy can hold the partnership liable on the contract. To safeguard against liability for unauthorized transactions, partners must give third parties prompt notice of dissolution. Under UPA 35, two different kinds of notice must be given—one for each of the two classes of creditors that are involved in a dissolution:

1 *Predissolution creditors* are third parties such as merchants and tradespeople who had actually extended credit to the partnership prior to the dissolution; for this class of creditors, "notice" means *actual notice*. A safe way to effect it is to send written notice of dissolution to each former creditor, by return-receipt certified letter.

2 *Postdissolution creditors* are third parties who knew of the partnership but had not extended credit to it prior to dissolution. For this class of creditors, *constructive notice* is sufficient. The required constructive notice may differ from state to state. However, it generally is sufficient to publish (in some states, several times) notice in a newspaper of general circulation stating that the partnership has been dissolved. The postdissolution creditors are deemed to be constructively notified of the dissolution even if they did not see the publication or read it.

Settlement of Partnership Accounts

The ultimate objective of winding up is to pay all partnership debts and then repay partners their capital contributions together with their respective share of remaining assets. The order of payment of a dissolved partnership's liabilities appears in Table 40.2.

Ratio of Distribution of Assets to Partners. Unless the agreement provides otherwise, partners share *equally in profits*, even if their investments (capital contributions) to the partnership were unequal amounts. If a dissolved partnership does not have enough assets to pay all creditors or to return to the partners their contributions to

Table 40.2 Order of Payment of Liabilities upon Dissolution of Partnership under UPA*

1 Those owing to partnership creditors other than to the partners themselves
2 Those owing to partners for loans or advances made to the partnership
3 Those owing to partners as repayment of their capital contributions
4 Those owing to partners as their share of profits, if any

*The partners may agree among themselves to change the order of payment of items 2, 3, and 4.

the firm's capital, then all partners must contribute toward paying off those losses. Generally, each partner is obligated to contribute sufficient money so that they all suffer the same ratio of loss as the ratio in which each was entitled to receive profits [UPA 18 (a), 34, 40]. If one partner is unable to pay his or her obligation to creditors, the other partners who are able must pay it.

The computation of how much each partner must contribute when partners who are entitled to *share equally* in profits have *contributed different amounts to the capital account* of the firm is best explained by illustration. Assume that partner Art made a capital contribution of $10,000; partner Bob made a contribution of $5,000 and services; and partner Clara's contribution was her expert knowledge. Although it was important to the firm, it was never given a dollar value, and so never became part of her contribution to capital. It was understood that the three partners were to share equally in the profits. Assume further that upon dissolution, the partnership paid all but two bills, which remain outstanding: $2,500 to creditor Judy and $1,100 to partner Clara, who had loaned that amount to the business. The firm has no money or property. Most courts would compute the partnership accounts of this firm as shown in Table 40.3.

A few states, such as California, would distribute the loss only among partners Art and Bob and assess no monetary contribution against Clara, because Clara contributed services but no money to the partnership.

Table 40.3 Calculation of Partners' Contribution to Losses upon Dissolution

Obligations of the firm:

To Judy	$2,500	(for amount due on loan)
To Clara	1,100	(for loan to partnership)
To Art	10,000	(for return of capital contribution)
To Bob	5,000	(for return of capital contribution)
To Clara	0	(no capital contribution made)
	$18,600	Total obligations

Contributions required:

Since the partners had agreed to share equally in the profits, they must contribute equally to cover the losses. Therefore, Art, Bob, and Clara must equally share the loss of $18,600, or $6,200 each, distributed as follows:

Art	$0	no new contribution (original contribution $10,000; loss $6,200; balance due Art $3,800)
Bob	1,200	additional contribution (original contribution $5,000; loss $6,200; balance due $1,200)
Clara	6,200	(no original contribution)
	$7,400	Contributions required

Distribution of total contributions of $7,400:

To Judy	$2,500	(to pay creditor's bill)
To Clara	$1,100	(to repay loan)
To Art	$3,800	(partial return of contribution)

Therefore all partners share equally the loss of $18,600:

Art	loses	$6,200 ($10,000 original contribution less $3,800)
Bob	loses	$6,200 ($5,000 original contribution plus new contribution of $1,200)
Clara	loses	$6,200 ($6,200 new contribution)

Settlement of Accounts with Creditors. Each partner is personally liable for all partnership obligations—its debts, unperformed contracts, and tort claims (UPA 15, 36). Each partner also probably has personal debts for credit card purchases, house mortgage payments, car payments, and so on. If a partner does not have sufficient resources with which to pay both the partnership debts and his or her own debts, and legal actions are brought against the partner, the question arises whether the personal creditors of the partner or the partnership creditors are entitled to be paid first out of the partner's funds. Here a formula informally called the "jingle rule" applies. Under that rule, a partner's *personal assets* are first used to pay *personal debts*, while *partnership assets* are first used to pay *partnership debts*.

The jingle rule had been recognized under federal bankruptcy law until the Bankruptcy Reform Act of 1978, which reversed the rule so that it does not apply when a partnership is in bankruptcy. Now, under Sec. 723 of that Act, partnership creditors can recover payment from the individual partners at the same time as the partners' personal creditors. To illustrate, assume that a partnership of Art and Ben is in bankruptcy and does not have assets with which to pay $6,000 owing its creditors. Partner Art has no personal assets; but partner Ben has personal assets of $4,000, and he owes Doris a personal debt of $2,000. Since Art has no assets, Ben's $4,000 must in some way be applied toward both the partnership debt of $6,000 and his private debt to Doris of $2,000. As these two debts are treated equally, Ben's $4,000 is divided between the partnership creditors and Doris in the proportion that each of their claims bears to the $8,000 *total* debt. Therefore, the partnership creditors receive $3,000 (six-eighths of Ben's $4,000) and Doris receives $1,000 (two-eighths of the $4,000).

Partners' Fiduciary Responsibilities during Winding Up

During winding up, a partnership is still an existing business organization, and partners owe to one another the normal fiduciary obligations of partners, as discussed in Chapter 39.

The most common fiduciary problems which arise during the winding-up process involve: (1) improper exercise of winding-up duties, (2) improper purchase by a partner of partnership property, and (3) the seizure for personal gain of partnership legal rights or opportunities. (See Case 40.2.)

Partners must exercise the utmost good faith in winding up. Their fiduciary duty requires that they protect partnership assets, collect monies due the partnership without secretly profiting, settle debts and obligations honestly, and distribute fairly to the partners any profits which remain after liquidation is completed. Winding-up partners who negligently or dishonestly perform their duties so as to injure other partners are liable to them in an **action for an accounting.**

Frequently during the winding-up process, a partner will want to acquire partnership property that is being liquidated. Such partner must deal fairly with the others and fully disclose everything known about the value of the property. If the purchasing partner fails to reveal all such information or conceals the fact that the purchase is being made through a secret agent, then the purchasing partner has breached his or her fiduciary duty to the others, who can void the sale.

A partner may not, during the winding-up process, seize partnership legal rights or opportunities that are part of the partnership's assets. If such seizure is challenged, an equity court will order that the value of such asset be accounted for in the final computation of the amounts of money owing to the partners. The following case illustrates a partner's fiduciary responsibilities during the winding-up process.

CASE 40.6   Hooper v. Yoder • 37 P.2d 852 (Colo. 1987)

FACTS   Steven Hooper and David Yoder formed a partnership to manufacture and sell frozen yogurt bars. They agreed to share equally in the financial risk, workload, and potential profits of the business, but no formal written partnership agreement was drawn up. In 1977 they formed Beautiful Daydreams, Inc. (Daydreams), to take over the partnership business. Hooper was president and treasurer of the corporation and Yoder vice president and secretary. The two men, who composed its board of directors, agreed to defer issuance of corporate stock.

Market West, a food brokerage firm, agreed to accept stock in Daydreams as part payment of a loan that Market West had made to Daydreams, and in October 1978 Hooper and Yoder elected Brian Bradley of Market West to the Daydreams board of directors. A month later, Hooper scheduled a directors' meeting

**CASE 40.6
Continued**

while Yoder was out of town and unable to attend. At the meeting, Hooper and Bradley authorized the issuance of 95 shares of corporate stock to Hooper and 5 shares to Market West. At a directors' meeting the following month, Hooper and Bradley told Yoder that because of the financial condition of the company, neither Hooper nor Yoder would receive a salary.

In January 1979, Hooper and Market West, without notifying Yoder and acting as the sole shareholders of Beautiful Daydreams, Inc., removed the entire board of directors of the company, elected Hooper and Bradley as its only directors, and also named Hooper as president and Bradley as vice president. Yoder was then notified that his services were terminated. Later, Yoder found out that corporate stock had been issued to Hooper and to Market West; that he (Yoder) was no longer an officer of the corporation; and that Hooper had received the sum of $141,500 as salary from 1979 to 1982.

Yoder filed suit against Hooper and Daydreams. The trial court entered a judgment in favor of Yoder for $70,750 (one-half of the salary paid Hooper beginning in 1979) and directed Hooper to transfer to Yoder 47 1/2 shares of the stock held by him in Daydreams. The court of appeals affirmed the judgment. Hooper then appealed to the Colorado Supreme Court.

OPINION

LOHR, J. . . . As a general rule, when partners organize a corporation to operate the business of the partnership and transfer the assets to the corporation, the partnership is dissolved. This is because such action usually reflects the express will of the parties that the partnership be dissolved. . . . The dissolution of a partnership, however, does not automatically terminate the existence of the partnership. The Uniform Partnership Act provides that "on dissolution the partnership is not terminated but continues until the winding up of partnership affairs is completed." The winding up includes the entire process of settling the partnership affairs after dissolution.

When partners organize a corporation to continue the business of the firm, the winding up of the partnership includes the transfer of the partnership assets to the corporation in exchange for corporate stock. Here the winding up of the partnership remained incomplete pending issuance of corporate stock to Hooper and Yoder in equal amounts pursuant to the agreement they made as partners prior to incorporation. Because there were no shares of stock issued upon incorporation of Beautiful Daydreams, it cannot be said that the property of the partnership was exchanged for stock in the corporation and that the stock was then distributed to the partners, thereby winding up the partnership affairs. The circumstances of this case bring us to the conclusion that the winding up of the partnership was not accomplished upon incorporation and, therefore, the partnership continued to exist.

Because the partnership continued to exist, so did the fiduciary duties that one partner owes to another. Partners in a business enterprise owe to one another the highest duty of loyalty; they stand in a relationship of trust and confidence to each other and are bound by standards of good conduct and square dealing. Each partner has the right to demand and expect from the other a full, fair, open and honest disclosure of everything affecting the relationship. During the winding up of partnership affairs, the partners continue to owe to each other the same duty of loyalty and fair dealing.

> **CASE 40.6 Continued**
>
> . . . Hooper's actions in causing the issuance of 95 shares of stock to himself and none to Yoder and in drawing a salary from the business without the assent or knowledge of Yoder are the very antithesis of the type of fair dealing required between partners in winding up a partnership. . . .
>
> The trial court provided appropriate remedies for breaches [of Hooper] by . . . requiring Hooper to share the stock and salary equally with Yoder in accordance with the partnership agreement between them.
>
> **JUDGMENT**   Judgment [in favor of Yoder] affirmed.

CONTINUATION OF PARTNERSHIP BUSINESS WITHOUT WINDING UP

The dissolution and winding up of a partnership involves some measure of forced sale at which it is highly probable that some or all of the partnership property will be sold for less than its true value. Liquidation of a partnership business may also result in the loss of the value of the firm's goodwill. Therefore innocent partners who did not cause the dissolution are likely to be faced, through no fault of their own, with financial loss if there is a winding up and forced liquidation of the business. To protect innocent partners, the law allows a partnership business to be continued without a winding up when (1) a partner has wrongfully withdrawn or has been expelled, or (2) a partner has retired or died.

If a partnership business is to be continued in place of a winding up, instead of the physical liquidation of its assets, there is an accounting of its affairs as of the date of the dissolution. In the accounting, all the assets and liabilities of the partnership including the value of its goodwill are comprehensively reviewed and evaluated, and the value of each partner's interest is mathematically determined as *of date of dissolution*. Note that when there is a winding up, the value of each partner's interest is determined *at the end of the winding up* when the liquidation of the business has been completed (not the date of the dissolution).

When a partnership business is continued, the dissolved partnership is not the owner of the continuing business, unless the original partnership agreement and state law so provide. In the absence of that rare circumstance, the partners who carry on the business do so either (1) as a sole proprietorship, if only a single partner remains to operate the business, or (2) as a new partnership if more than one of the partners of the dissolved partnership carry on the business.

The two situations in which a partnership business can be carried on without a winding up—(1) after a wrongful withdrawal or expulsion of a partner or (2) after death or retirement of a partner—will be discussed separately, since different rules will apply in these two situations.

Continuation after Wrongful Withdrawal or Expulsion of Partner

When a partnership is dissolved because a partner has wrongfully withdrawn from the firm or because a member is expelled as authorized by the agreement, the remaining partners must unanimously elect either (1) to wind up the partnership business or (2) to continue the partnership business. Neither the wrongdoing partner nor the expelled partner has a voice in that decision. If the remaining partners elect to wind up the partnership, then the partnership is wound up in the manner outlined in the first portion of this chapter. If they elect to continue the business, the value of the withdrawing or expelled partner's interest is computed by deducting the firm's total liabilities from the value of its total assets. The departing partner is then due the value of his or her interest in the partnership, less, however, any damage he or she may have caused the partnership. In the computation of the value of a *withdrawing* partner's interest, no credit is given for the value of the partnership goodwill, for such partner has literally "walked away" from that partnership asset. In the case of an *expelled partner,* if there is nothing to the contrary in the partnership agreement, the value of partnership goodwill is included in calculating the value of the share.

A partner who wrongfully withdraws or is expelled is entitled to be paid in cash the computed value of his or her interest unless the partnership agreement provides otherwise. If full cash payment is not made, the departing partner may require the unpaid balance to be secured by court-approved bond. A wrongfully withdrawing partner or an expelled partner ceases to be a member of the partnership and is not liable for partnership obligations thereafter incurred.

Continuation after Retirement or Death of a Partner

Effect of Partnership Agreement. Partners may agree when the firm is organized, or at a later time, that if one of their members retires or dies, the surviving partner(s) may, at that time, decide whether to continue the business without going through a winding up, or to wind up and liquidate it. Typically, such an agreement will give the remaining partners the right to buy the interest of the member who retires or dies, setting out the method for determining the purchase price. If no such formula had been established and the remaining partners want to continue the business, an accounting of the partnership affairs must be conducted, including its goodwill, as of the date of the dissolution. The retired partner or deceased partner's estate must be paid the share that is computed in the accounting.

A different situation exists if the partners had not previously agreed that the remaining partner(s) may continue the business without a winding up. In that event, when a partner retires or dies, the surviving or remaining partner(s) must secure the consent of the retiring partner or of the personal representative of the deceased partner to continue the business without a winding up. If that request is denied, the partnership must be wound up, regardless of the remaining partners' wishes.

Payment of Value of Partner's Interest. When a partnership business continues without a winding up after death or retirement of a partner, the deceased partner's personal representative (executor or administrator) or the retired partner is entitled to receive in cash such partner's share of the computed value of the partnership, including the value of its goodwill. However, it may be that the remaining partners are unable immediately to pay the retiring partner or the estate of the deceased partner the value of his or her interest. Or it may be that instead of receiving payment, the retiring partner or the

---

BOX 40.2

Can a Court Ignore Business Profitability in Fixing the Value of a Withdrawing Partner's Interest?

Jones and Smith, as partners, owned and operated the Clarette Club, a private night spot. When it began to lose money, suit for dissolution of the partnership was filed. The court awarded Jones the nightclub, fixing the value of Smith's interest at $20,000, and giving Smith judgment in that amount. Jones appealed, claiming that the court should have ordered an audit of the books before valuation of Smith's interest; and that if it had done so, the court would have found the business so unprofitable that it would have reduced the $20,000 judgment to a lower figure.

The court upheld the trial judge, citing the record, which showed that Smith, Jones, and the bookkeeper had for months been skimming profits from the club and not reporting them to IRS. The court said such illegal conduct would make an audit useless, and added that the right to an accounting may be denied upon the maxim, "He who comes into equity must do so with clean hands."*

*Smith v. Jones, 794 P.2d 1178 (Kan. App. 1990).

deceased partner's representative may want to leave that share in the partnership business as an investment. In that event, if the continuing partners agree, the retiring partner or the representative of the deceased partner must, under the UPA, elect whether to be paid (1) interest upon the share left in the firm or (2) so much of the profits of the continuing business as that share earns. This election to receive interest or profits may be made only one time.

When a retiring partner, or the surviving spouse of a deceased partner, leaves the partnership share in the business, he or she becomes an ordinary creditor of the partnership in that amount, but in event of insolvency, the claims of other creditors against the partnership have priority.

The next case illustrates the application of the UPA to the rights of retired and deceased partners when a partnership business continues.

CASE 40.7 **Matter of Trust Estate of Schaefer** • 283 N.W.2d 410 (Wis. 1979)

FACTS Ben Schaefer owned thirteen parcels of real estate in partnership with Arthur Schaefer. Ben died in 1969; Arthur, the surviving partner, began to wind up the partnership. Ben's widow sued, challenging the existence of the partnership and claiming that all the property belonged to Ben's estate. Because of the suit, Arthur kept partnership affairs unchanged. He stopped liquidating assets, incurred no new debts, and bought no new properties. Eight years later the state high court decided that the land was partnership property. Thereupon, the executor of Ben's estate and trustee under Ben's will brought an action asking the court to declare whether the interest of Ben's estate in the property was (1) 50 percent of its valuation at the date of his death plus 50 percent of the profits from the date of death until final settlement of the partnership, or (2) 50 percent of its valuation at final settlement of the partnership accounts, which had not as yet occurred. Since Ben's death, the property had appreciated in value so that the second method of valuation would be more beneficial to the estate. The probate court determined that UPA 42 controlled, and therefore the trustee's interest was limited to 50 percent of the partnership assets valued at the date of death plus the interest or profits accruing since then until date of final settlement. The trustee appealed.

OPINION BROWN, J. . . . When a partner dies, the partnership is dissolved. . . . On dissolution, however, the partnership is not terminated; it continues until the wind-up of the partnership affairs is completed. . . . Winding up is the process of settling partnership affairs after dissolution. Partners, or those claiming through a deceased partner, may agree to settle the partnership affairs without a liquidation of the assets (by agreeing to a cash settlement or in-kind distribution). However, absent an agreement, winding up involves reducing the assets to cash (liquidation), paying creditors, and distributing to partners the value of their respective interests. . . .

Ordinarily, upon distribution due to death of a partner, it is the duty and responsibility of the surviving partner to wind up the partnership with due diligence and pay the estate of the deceased partner the value of his interest in the partnership. . . . The surviving partner, however, need not wind up the partnership if he has a right to continue the business . . . [when] the legal representative of

> **CASE 40.7**
> **Continued**
>
> the deceased partner consents to the continuation without liquidation of the partnership affairs. . . . The record is clear that the legal representative did not consent to or acquiesce in the continuation of the business. . . . Therefore, . . . the business was not continued . . . but was instead a slow wind-up due to the pending litigation [brought by Ben's widow]. . . .
>
> If a partnership is seasonably wound up after dissolution, *profits and losses* during liquidation are shared by the partners in proportion to their predissolution ratios unless they have agreed otherwise. . . . Where the business is continued, the value of the deceased partner's interest may be different. Under Section 42 of the Uniform Partnership Act . . . the non-continuing partner (or his representative) has a *first election* between two basic alternatives, either of which can be enforced in an action for an accounting. He can force a liquidation, taking his part of the proceeds. . . . Alternatively, he can permit the business to continue (or accept the fact that it has continued) and claim as a creditor (though subordinate to outside creditors) the value of his interest at dissolution. This gives him a participation in all values at dissolution. . . . If he takes the latter route, he has a *second election* to receive in addition either interest (presumably at the local legal rate) or profits from date of dissolution.
>
> Where the business is wound-up, the deceased partner's interest is not determined until the wind-up is complete. After the creditors have been paid, all profits are shared by the surviving partner and the deceased partner, as well as losses based on their predissolution ratios (in this case 50%). Therefore, where the business is wound up rather than continued under the conditions set forth in [UPA §42] the deceased partner's interest is the value of his interest at the date of liquidation (when wind-up is complete). This value includes asset appreciation during the winding-up period and is subject to any losses incurred during that time. . . .
>
> In the present case, . . . there was no agreement to continue the business. . . . Therefore, [UPA 42] does not apply. [UPA 38] applies and the estate is entitled to 50% of the proceeds, including asset appreciation, at the time of liquidation or final settlement. . . .
>
> **JUDGMENT**   Decree reversed and case remanded for liquidation of all assets and distribution of the surplus, after payment to creditors, to the deceased partner's estate and the surviving partner, 50% to each, unless otherwise agreed.

Creditors' Rights against Continuing Partners

When the business of a partnership is continued without a winding up of its affairs, creditors of the dissolved (original) partnership become creditors of the new (continuing) partners and partnership, standing in an equal position with the new creditors of the continuing partnership.

If new members are added to a continuing partnership, their contributions to capital may be used to pay partnership debts incurred *before or after* they joined the firm. However, the new members are *not liable personally* for partnership debts incurred *before* joining the firm.

Creditors' Rights against Departed Partners

After dissolution, each partner remains personally liable for all obligations of the partnership incurred while such partner was a member. For example, Tom, a partner in the Acme Partnership, died last April, and the partnership was wound up. His estate (along with the other Acme partners) remained legally liable to pay partnership creditors for all debts that were incurred up to the time the winding up was concluded.

When there is a dissolution *without* a winding up, a partner who leaves the firm may have to pay the same partnership debt twice. For example, suppose Al, Ben, and Chad are partners in ABC Bakery, and the value of each partner's interest is $11,000. Al retires, at which time the firm's only debt is $3,000 owed to creditor Smith. Except for that debt, the value of Al's interest in the partnership would be $11,000. However, because of the $3,000 debt, the value of Al's interest at his retirement is reduced by $1,000 (one-third of the $3,000 Smith debt). Accordingly, Al is paid $10,000 when he retires from the partnership. Now assume further that the partnership does not pay the Smith debt. A year after Al's retirement, Smith demands payment of his $3,000. If ABC Bakery cannot pay him, Ben and Chad (the partners continuing in the business) and Al (because the debt existed while Al was still a partner) must each contribute one-third ($1,000) out of their own personal resources to discharge the Smith debt. Furthermore, in the event Ben or Chad (or both of them) cannot pay their share of the debt, Al would be liable for the unpaid portion.

To offset the possibility of the liability which a retiring partner like Al now faces, partners generally enter into an **indemnification agreement** when a partner leaves the firm. By such agreement the continuing partners agree to reimburse whatever amount a departing partner is later forced to pay to creditors of the dissolved partnership. Sometimes a different device, called a *novation*, is used. In a novation agreement: (1) the creditor agrees to discharge the departing partner of any liability, and to look solely to the continuing partners to pay the debt, and (2) the continuing partners agree to pay the entire debt.

SUMMARY

When partners no longer carry on business together, their firm is automatically dissolved. After dissolution, either the partnership may be wound up (i.e., liquidated) or the business may be continued by the remaining partner(s) after an accounting of the interest of each partner. A partnership is dissolved (1) by the agreement of all the partners, as expressed in the partnership agreement or at a later date; (2) by withdrawal of a partner in a partnership at will; (3) by an act in violation of the partnership agreement, such as the wrongful withdrawal of a partner; (4) by automatic operation of law, as when a partner dies; or (5) by court decree for any reason a court finds proper.

A partnership does not cease to exist when it is dissolved. Its existence ends when the winding up is complete—that is, when all money owing to the partnership has been collected, all debts have been paid, partnership contributions have been returned, and remaining assets have been distributed among the partners in the same ratio that they shared in the profits. If there are insufficient assets to pay all obligations, partners must contribute from their own personal funds to share losses in the same ratio that they would have shared in the profits.

A partner who caused dissolution by wrongful breach of the partnership agreement, or because of personal bankruptcy, may not conduct the winding up. The person who conducts the winding up completes the firm's ongoing contracts but may not make new ones except to implement the winding up. During the winding up the partners still owe fiduciary obligations to one another.

Unless the partnership agreement provides otherwise, a retiring partner or the personal representative of a deceased partner must consent if the remaining partners want to continue the business after dissolution without a winding up. The departing partner (or personal representative of a deceased partner) must then elect whether to receive his or her share in the firm in cash or to leave that share in the business as an investment. If it is left in the business, there must be a further election whether to receive interest on the money left in the business or to receive a share of the firm's profits.

Dissolution of a partnership for any cause does not free a withdrawing or retiring partner or a deceased partner's estate from liability for debts of the firm which existed when that partner was still a member of the firm.

REVIEW QUESTIONS

1. Distinguish among dissolution, winding up, and termination of a partnership.

2. Does addition of a new partner dissolve an existing firm?

3. What is a partnership at will?

4. When a partner wrongfully withdraws from a firm, what happens to the capital contribution he or she made?

5. What does "dissolution by operation of law" mean?

6. Assume a partner suffers a stroke and as a result is unable to walk. Discuss the effect of this event upon the partnership.

7. What effect, if any, does the dissolution of a partnership have on **(a)** its rental obligation under an unexpired lease, **(b)** a debt that is owed to the partnership, and **(c)** a contract to build a house which the partnership has half completed?

8. (a) When a winding up is concluded, in what order are partnership assets distributed? **(b)** What action is taken if the assets are not sufficient to pay all the partnership debts?

9. When can a partnership continue business and not wind up?

10. If a dissolved partnership business is continued without a winding up, does this mean that the original partnership is continuing the business? Explain.

11. When a partnership is continued without a winding up, what rights do the creditors of the dissolved partnership have?

CASE PROBLEMS

1. Stark and Henning, as partners, operated a sales agency. One of their accounts was Utica Co. Stark left the partnership, thereby causing its dissolution, and went to work for Utica Co. Henning claimed that Utica Co. still owed the former partnership commissions for sales that the partnership had made. He sued Utica Co. in the partnership name (which was permitted in that state). Stark did not join in the suit. Utica claims the suit should be dismissed because both partners did not join in filing the action. Discuss the issues and decide.

2. Jerry, Nick, and Lorenzo, as partners, owned an orange juice factory. Their term had 4 years to run. Their agreement had no provision for expulsion of a partner. Lorenzo's outspoken political views became so obnoxious to Jerry and Nick that, in Lorenzo's absence, they changed factory locks and denied him entry. They told him they had dissolved the partnership, that the two of them were going to carry on the business, and that they would pay him "every penny he had coming to him." Lorenzo sued for a court decree of dissolution, and asked that he be appointed to wind up the partnership. Decision?

3. Deck and Tread, as partners, managed Deck & Tread Electric. They agreed to dissolve, with Deck conducting the winding up and then continuing the business as sole proprietor. No notice of dissolution was given to any supplier. A week after dissolution and before termination, Deck bought electric wire from Hecla Wire Co. Some of the wire was necessary to fill an order that the partnership had received prior to dissolution; the rest of the wire was put in stock for use after Deck became sole owner of the business. When Hecla Wire was not paid, it sued the Deck & Tread partnership and the partners individually. Tread claimed that he was not obligated to pay for any of the wire. Decision?

4. Axel and Len, an oral at-will partnership, started a café business. They contributed equally to the firm's capital, agreed to both work full time, and to share profits equally. After a year, the two argued so much they could not work together and Axel, on January 5, ceased to go to the café. Len continued to run the business, retaining the profits that were made. Several times Axel asked when the business was going to be wound up. In August, Len sold the café. Axel immediately sued for an accounting, and asked for half the money Len had received on the sale. Len offered to pay Axel half the value of the café as of January 5, when the partnership dissolved, but Axel refused to accept. Was Axel or Len correct?

5. Art, Ben, Charles, and Doris conducted an at-will partnership law practice called ABCD. Art and Ben were in charge of a multimillion-dollar suit for Pluto Co., the firm's client. The ABCD law firm's fee was thirty five percent of any recovery. From that gross fee, 15 percent was to go to Art and 15 percent to Ben, based on the firm's past practice. Just before trial of the case, Art and Ben asked for 25 percent each, but Charles and Doris refused to modify their past office practice. Art and Ben left ABCD, thereby dissolving it, and formed a new two-partner firm. Before any winding up of ABCD had commenced, Pluto discharged ABCD as its law firm and hired the new Art-Ben partnership to handle the suit. Before ABCD had been wound up, Art and Ben won a huge judgment in Pluto's favor. They claim that because ABCD was dissolved and the client had discharged it, ABCD had no claim to any part of the fee. Were Arthur and Ben correct? Explain.

6. Turner, Kaplan, and Hoffman were partners. When Turner retired, Kaplan and Hoffman asked him to leave his $35,000 partnership interest in the business, which they continued to operate. They agreed that Turner would receive annual payments representing the profits his share earned. The next year Turner received a good return on his investment but thereafter the partners paid him nothing, saying that they would pay him his share of the profits "after first clearing up the old partnership bills." Turner replied that if they paid those creditors before paying him, they would be acting illegally. Do you agree or disagree?

CHAPTER 41

Limited Partnerships and Limited Liability Companies

While reading the last two chapters on general partnership law, you may have noticed red lights flashing a warning every few pages: "Danger! Unlimited Liability Ahead." Most people launching into business do not want to assume the risk of unlimited liability. Instead, they look for an entity which can guarantee that liability will be *limited* to the amount of their investment, and that their homes, personal estates, and savings will not be at risk. As you will see in the next five chapters, a corporation will serve that end, but one of its shortcomings is the problem of double taxation—the corporation pays an income tax, then when it distributes that income as dividends to the shareholders, they pay income tax on the same money a second time.

Halfway between a general partnership and a corporation is the limited partnership, consisting of limited partners—whose liability is limited to their investment—and one or more general partners who have unlimited liability. This form offers to its limited partners the corporation's advantage of liability limited to the amount of their capital contribution, and yet the advantage of being taxed like a partnership. However, the general partners' personal assets are still at risk because they have unlimited liability for the debts of the enterprise. An addi-

> **BOX 41.1**
>
> ### The Limited Liability Company: A Radically New Business Entity
>
> Fifteen states have pioneered a bold new business entity that is flourishing across America—the limited liability company (LLC). A cross between the corporation and the limited partnership, it offers the best features of both—limited liability for *all* members, including the managing members, with the tax structure of a partnership. Best of all, active members can offset losses against ordinary income.

tional drawback is that limited partners lose their limited liability and take on the unlimited liability of a general partner if they *participate in the management of the firm*.

To solve this problem, a new entity has developed in the last 5 years—the **limited liability company** (LLC). It has the advantage of having its income taxed only once—to the individual members of the company in the same way as a partnership. But its umbrella of *limited liability extends to all members, including those actively engaged in managing the enterprise*. No one in an LLC has unlimited liability. LLC statutes have been enacted in fifteen states and are pending in fourteen others.

The first part of this chapter deals with the limited partnership. The last part will tell you more about this most recent creature of state legislation—the limited liability company.

LIMITED PARTNERSHIPS

Julie breeds racehorses. She learns that Flasher, a very desirable colt, is for sale, but she lacks funds with which to buy him. Julie secures an option to buy Flasher and then sets out to raise the purchase price of $20,000 and an additional $10,000 to cover the initial costs of raising and training the horse. Julie forms a limited partnership. She is the general partner, and she sells limited partnership interests in units of $3,000 to ten investors, thereby raising the necessary $30,000.

As the general partner in the enterprise, Julie will run the business and make all required decisions; the limited partners will have no managerial responsibilities. If the colt lives up to Julie's expectations, the limited partners stand to earn back many times their investments by sharing with Julie the income from the winnings, stud fees, or the sale of Flasher for a high price—or from all these sources. Of course, the limited partners' profits will depend upon the success of the venture.

Julie buys the colt, hires a trainer, and pays all the bills. But alas, shortly after his first race, which he wins handily, Flasher falls, breaks a leg, and must be destroyed. Julie has used up all the capital investment obtained from the limited partners and still has many unpaid bills from the feed store, the veterinarian, the trainer, the blacksmith, and others. Because the enterprise was a limited partnership, Julie, the general partner, is *personally liable* for all the debts. But although the limited partners risked and lost their investments, they have no personal liability to any of the creditors.

The limited partnership was devised to satisfy the need of businesspeople and investors for an entity that would resemble a partnership, yet not subject **pure investors** (those not participating in management) to risk of personal liability for the firm's debts. It is true that the corporate form (discussed in the next five chapters) also offers the opportunity to invest funds without participating in management as well as freedom from liability for the firm's debts. However, members of a limited partnership who desire a firm with restricted duration and a small number of managers frequently object to the corporate form as too unwieldy and too heavily regulated by government.

A limited partnership fills the business organizational gap between a general partnership and a corporation, and it has characteristics of both types of organization. Limited partnerships are popular with investors because they sometimes offer attractive returns, they often provide tax savings, and their downside risk is limited to the amount invested. In addition, this type of business organization is a vehicle which encourages investment in new and sometimes novel ventures. Limited partnerships may be organized for any lawful business purpose. They have been formed, for example, to purchase calves to be fattened and sold as beef cattle; to drill wildcat oil wells; to own and rent railway boxcars, locomotives, ice vending machines, and computers; to film and distribute motion pictures; and to purchase land for subdivision and sale as residential lots.

Nature and Development of Limited Partnerships

What Is a Limited Partnership? A limited partnership is a partnership formed by two or more persons in the manner prescribed by law, which has one or more general partners and one or more limited partners. The general partners conduct the business of the venture and have unlimited personal liability to creditors for its obligations; the limited partners have very limited rights to participate in the management of the business, and the extent of their personal liability lies only in the risk of loss of their investments. Limited partners will be entitled to profits as set forth in the partnership agreement. For example, the agreement might say that 80 percent of the profits will be divided among the limited partners and the remainder will be divided among the general partners.

Legal Development of Limited Partnerships.

Limited partnerships were developed in the Middle Ages to enable the nobility and clergy to make quiet investments without being criticized for engaging in trade. The untidy business of trade was left to the general partners in the merchant class. The limited partnership idea never became part of the common law, however, and within the United States it is solely a creature of state statutes.

Because limited partnerships had no foundation in the common law, the statutes authorizing this organizational form usually were very strictly construed, with some courts holding that even minor or trivial departures from the statutory requirements subjected the limited partners to the same personal liability as that of general partners. This strict construction tended to inhibit realization of the liberal purposes intended by these laws. Therefore the National Conference of Commissioners on Uniform State Laws in 1916 prepared a Uniform Limited Partnership Act (ULPA). It was adopted by all states except Louisiana, which has its own form of limited partnership. Over the years, the Act was criticized for not permitting limited partners to exercise a greater degree of control in management. To further this objective, the Revised Limited Partnership Act of 1976 (RULPA) was developed. In 1985 the Conference of Commissioners drafted a superseding version. Adopted by 31 states, it is cited in this chapter as ULPA and is reprinted in Appendix 4.

Application of the UPA to Limited Partnerships.

While a limited partnership is distinct from an ordinary partnership, the two have many characteristics in common. In fact, the Uniform Partnership Act (UPA) applies to limited partnership matters wherever the ULPA is silent. UPA 6(2) provides, ". . . this Act shall apply to limited partnerships except insofar as the statutes relating to such partnership are inconsistent herewith"; and ULPA 1105 states, "In any case not provided for in this Act the provisions of the Uniform Partnership Act govern." Accordingly, if questions of law arise—for example, on the powers and liabilities of a general partner—reference must be made to the UPA for the answer.

Formation of Limited Partnerships

Requirements for Formation.

To establish a limited partnership the ULPA dictates that the firm must consist of at least one general partner and at least one limited partner and that a *certificate of limited partnership* must be filed with the secretary of state of the state in which it is organized (ULPA 201).

Certificate of Limited Partnership.

As we saw in Chapter 39, all that is required to organize an ordinary business partnership is an oral or written agreement of two or more persons to be associated together as co-owners to carry on a business for profit. The organization of a limited partnership is more formal. It comes into existence only when a proper *certificate*, signed by all the firm's general partners, is filed as a public record. In addition, all the parties (the limited partners as well as the general partners) become bound by an *agreement of limited partnership* which is not made a public record.

Contents of certificate. The Uniform Limited Partnership Act and state laws dictate that a certificate of limited partnership must contain (1) the name of the limited partnership, (2) the address of its office and the name and address of its agent for service of process, (3) the name and address of each general partner, (4) the latest date upon which the limited partnership is to dissolve, and (5) any other matters the general partners wish to include. Figure 41.1 is a sample certificate of limited partnership.

Filing of certificate. It is required that the certificate of limited partnership and any amendments to it, signed by the general partner(s), be filed in the office of the secretary of state in the state where the partnership is formed. Should the partnership desire to do business in any other state, it is required to register as a foreign limited partnership with the secretary of state of that state (ULPA 902).

If parties engage in a business which purports to be a limited partnership without signing and filing a certificate, a limited partnership is not formed but, instead, the organization is treated as an ordinary business partnership. In that event all its members—general partners as well

> We, the undersigned, desiring to form a limited partnership pursuant to the Uniform Partnership Act as set forth in _____ (cite the statute) of the State of _____ , do hereby certify:
>
> 1. The name of the limited partnership is _____
> _____
>
> 2. The address of the office of the limited partnership is _____
> _____
> City of _____ County of _____
> State of _____ Zip _____
>
> 3. The name and address of the agent for the service of process on the limited partnership is :
> _____
> _____
>
> 4. The name and the business address of each general partner in the limited partnership is:
>
> Name   Business Address
> _____   _____
> _____   _____
>
> 5. The latest date upon which the limited partnership is to dissolve is _____ . [insert terminating date or event]
>
> In Witness Whereof the undersigned have executed this certificate this the _____ day of 19____ .
>
> _____
> General Partner
>
> _____
> General Partner
>
> (Notary acknowledgment optional)

Figure 41.1 Form of certificate of limited partnership.

as limited partners—are personally liable for the firm's debts and obligations as though they were all general partners. However, the limited partner is liable *only* if the third party believed in good faith that the person was a general partner (ULPA 304).

Thus, if Pam purchases a limited partnership interest in a nonexistent limited partnership (because a certificate was not filed), believing there was no personal liability, she could find herself liable as a general partner for all the firm's debts. To avoid such liability Pam, or any cautious investor, should insist on seeing the certificate and proof of filing, or alternatively, withdraw from the organization in writing, renounce future participation in firm profits or income, and file with the secretary of state a certificate declaring such withdrawal (ULPA 304). However, such filing does not insulate Pam from liability to creditors who had already transacted business with the firm believing in good faith that she was a general partner.

The case below illustrates what constitutes filing a certificate of limited partnership and the potential liability of limited partners when a certificate has not been filed.

CASE 41.1 Fabry Partnership v. Silver Queen Limited Partnership
• 794 P.2d 719 (Nev. 1990)

FACTS

On April 24, 1980, the Silver Queen Motel was bought by Silver Queen Limited Partnership from Fabry Partnership (Fabry) for $3.1 million. Silver Queen Limited Partnership paid $500,000 cash and signed a $2.7 million note secured by trust deed (mortgage) on the property. Before the sale, a certificate of limited partnership was signed by the four general partners, and between April and June thirty limited partners signed the signature page of the certificate of limited partnership, contributed equal capital, and understood that they were limited partners. The limited partnership certificate was dated April 1, 1980, and became effective April 24, 1980—the date of sale. However, the certificate was not recorded with the county until December 29.

Silver Queen Limited Partnership made payments on the note for 2 years, during which time the motel was operated by the general partners, without participation or control by any of the limited partners. When the limited partnership defaulted on the note, Fabry foreclosed, and was the high bidder at the public sale. Because the amount of the remaining debt exceeded the sale price of the motel, Fabry sued the general partners and the limited partners for the deficiency on the note. The trial court granted summary judgment dismissing the limited partners from the suit, and Fabry appealed to the Nevada Supreme Court.

OPINION

PER CURIAM . . . Fabry contends that the limited partners failed to comply with the statutory requirements for the creation of a limited partnership. . . . [The Nevada Limited Partnership Statute] states in part:

1. Two or more persons desiring to form a limited partnership shall:

    (a) Sign and acknowledge a certificate. . . .

    (b) File the certificate for record in the office of the recorder of the county in which . . . the principal place of business of the partnership is maintained, file a certified copy of the original for record in the office of the recorder of each other county in which the partnership maintains a place of business.

Fabry contends that the limited partners failed to comply with the statute because no certificate was filed with the Nye County Recorder at the time of the transaction between Fabry and the Limited Partnership. Fabry further argues that the filing of the certificate of limited partnership in December of 1980 cannot relate back to the April transaction. We disagree. Specifically, two provisions in the Nevada Partnership Act militate against Fabry's position. First, . . . [it] provides:

> A limited partnership is formed if there has been substantial compliance in good faith.

Therefore, it appears that substantial compliance is sufficient for the formation of a limited partnership. Second, . . . [our statute] provides for a liberal construction of the Act. It states:

> The rule that statutes in derogation of the common law are to be strictly construed shall have no application to this chapter.

> **CASE 41.1 Continued**
>
> Based upon the aforementioned statutes, we are persuaded that the trial court properly entered summary judgment dismissing the limited partners from the action below. There was substantial compliance with the Act by the limited partners, and the certificate was filed within a "reasonable time."
>
> Furthermore, in the instant case, Fabry knew from the outset that the sale of the Silver Queen Motel involved a limited partnership. This knowledge is supported by the note and deed of trust which clearly identified the Silver Queen Limited Partnership as the purchaser of the motel. Additionally, the business relationship between the parties continued without protest for nearly two years after the filing of the certificate and before default was declared. Fabry cannot now circumvent the Limited Partnership in an attempt to impose individual liability on the limited partners.
>
> **JUDGMENT**
>
> We affirm the trial court's entry of summary judgment in favor the limited partners. As a matter of law, they cannot, under the facts presented on this appeal, be held individually liable as general partners.

Limited Partnership Agreement. In addition to the ULPA requirement that a certificate of limited partnership be signed by the general partners, all the partners, limited as well as general, either expressly or impliedly, must join in a limited partnership agreement covering the operations of the enterprise.

Form of agreement. The ULPA prescribes neither the form nor the content of the agreement; nor does it require a written statement. However, because arrangements between the partners may be complex, prudent organizers will have an agreement in writing, prepared by a lawyer, and signed by all partners.

Content of agreement. A partnership agreement usually covers how the business will be conducted and the relationship of the partners, both general and limited, to the firm. It normally includes such information as (1) the business to be conducted by the partnership, (2) the functions and duties of the general partners and whether they may engage in competing enterprises, (3) the contributions to be made by the partners, (4) restrictions upon business transactions between partners and the partnership (e.g., whether a partner may sell something to the partnership), (5) conditions under which an investor may acquire a limited partnership interest after the organization has been established, and (6) the rights of limited partners to vote on partnership matters.

The agreement should include provisions governing the conduct of the business in the event a general partner should die or cease to perform duties and how profits will be allocated (divided) among the general and the limited partners. The allocation may be (1) on the basis of the value of each member's contribution to the firm (not including promises of future contribution) or (2) by some other formula set out in the agreement.

Business of a Limited Partnership; Duration. Limited partnerships, like general partnerships, may carry on any business unless the statute under which they are organized provides otherwise. Many states require that certain regulated industries, such as banking and insurance, be conducted only by corporations that are organized under special statutes; limited partnerships normally do not qualify under such laws.

A limited partnership terminates at the time and under the conditions stated in its certificate. However, if the date of termination is approaching and the objective of the business has not yet been reached, the partners may file an amended certificate establishing a new termination date.

Name of a Limited Partnership. Every limited partnership must have a name which includes, without abbreviation, the words "Limited Partnership" (ULPA 102). The name may not be deceptively similar to the name of any other firm organized under the laws of that state. In addition, a limited partnership may not have the same name as the surname of one of its limited partners unless one of the general partners bears the same surname. For instance, if Henry Hill is to be a limited partner, the business may not be named "Hill Properties, a Limited Partnership," unless at the time the firm is organized one of the general partners is also named Hill. Without this rule, a third party that does business with the firm might improperly have the impression that Henry Hill is actually a general partner and rely upon his financial resources in extending credit to the firm.

A limited partner who knowingly permits his or her surname to be used in the partnership name is liable to creditors who extend credit to the partnership in the belief that the limited partner is a general partner. If a general partner whose name is also part of the firm name leaves, and the partnership continues in business, the firm name need not be changed unless the agreement requires it.

Contributions to a Limited Partnership. The **contribution** of a partner to a limited partnership may be in the form of cash, property, services performed, a promissory note, or a written obligation to make a future contribution [ULPA 101(2)]. The following examples illustrate how services may be treated as contributions to capital:

1. Ned decides to form a limited partnership, does all the work required to bring a viable business into existence, and is its sole general partner. He lists the value of those services as part of the firm's capital. Although Ned could arbitrarily place a very high value upon those services, he is not likely to do so because, if he does, he would be entitled to such a large share of the profits that potential investors would not be attracted to purchase limited partnership interests in his firm.

2. In the organization of his enterprise Ned asks Beth, a lawyer, to perform all legal services involved. She agrees to accept a limited partnership interest as her fee. The value of her services becomes her contribution to the firm.

When a limited partner fails to make a contribution (cash, property, or services) that has been promised *in writing* (ULPA 502), the partnership may by legal action force that partner (or the estate of a deceased partner) to pay the value of the promised contribution in cash [ULPA 502(b)]. A defaulting partner's debt may, by consent of all partners, be compromised—that is, a smaller sum may be accepted in full payment. Regardless of any such compromise, a creditor who extended credit to the partnership may enforce payment of the full amount that the defaulting partner originally promised.

The next case emphasizes the seriousness of entering into a limited partnership agreement that gives the general partner the right to call for additional capital contributions later on. The case also cautions prospective partners to read a limited partnership agreement carefully before signing it.

CASE 41.2 Continental Ill. Natl. Bank v. Allen, et al. • 811 P.2d 168 (Utah 1991)

FACTS Color Craft was organized in 1979 as a limited partnership. Cullimore was an officer of a corporation which was one of the general partners. In June 1980, Color Craft sent out to all limited partners and potential new investors an amended limited partnership agreement proposing to buy a new "press B" for $6.9 million and to create a new Class B group of limited partners to raise the money. The amended agreement stated:

CASE 41.2 Continued

> 7.5 Class B. The Class B Limited Partners *hereby agree to contribute to the Partnership, in their Distribution Ratio, the amounts of principal and interest on financing for the acquisition of Press B as such payments come due to the extent that the Partnership does not have sufficient cash from other sources to make such payments. . . . The Class B Limited Partners agree to personally guarantee repayment of indebtedness incurred by the Partnership to acquire Press B. . . .*

The amended partnership agreement was sent to the partners with a letter repeating that limited partners would be guaranteeing the debt incurred to purchase Press B, that instalment payments would total $5,903,254, that Cullimore would personally guarantee 100% of the indebtedness, and that each partner had the option to withdraw from the partnership. None withdrew. Fifty investors became Class B limited partners. In October 1980, the general partner purchased Press B for $6.9 million. Continental Bank (Bank) financed the unpaid time balance, but insisted that Color Craft have each limited partner sign its form guaranteeing "up to the original aggregate principal amount of $1,485,028."

Color Craft filed for bankruptcy. At the bankruptcy trustee's public sale, Bank bought Color Craft's right to make additional capital calls on its limited partners as set forth in the partnership agreement. The bank repossessed Press B, sold it, applied the proceeds to reduce the debt, and then made a call for capital contribution on all limited partners. When they refused, Bank sued Allen and 45 other limited partners for the unreimbursed balance of its loan. At trial, the court held that the amended limited partnership agreement was made for the benefit of Bank as the creditor that financed Press B, and that Bank could sue as third-party beneficiary and enforce the agreement. Bank obtained judgment against the general partner and limited partners, and they appealed.

OPINION

HOWE, J. . . . In the instant case, the limited partners promised Color Craft additional capital contributions. Color Craft became bankrupt. The Bank could not collect the debt from Color Craft, but was the intended beneficiary of the limited partners' agreement to make additional capital contributions toward the indebtedness incurred by the acquisition of press B.

Similarly, the Bank is also a third-party beneficiary of the latter part of paragraph 7.5 of the partnership agreement. There, the limited partners agree to personally guarantee payment of a portion of the indebtedness incurred by Color Craft to acquire press B from [the vendors,] Roberts and Porter, Inc. Clearly, Roberts and Porter, Inc., was a third-party beneficiary, and the Bank became a beneficiary when it took an assignment of Roberts and Porter's rights under the purchase contract. Further, in the last sentence of paragraph 7.5, reference is made to a "lender" in connection with the acquisition of the press. The limited partners agree to execute such additional documents which the lender may require to evidence their guaranty. . . . The trial court concluded that recognition of a right of performance in Bank on the partnership agreement as third-party beneficiary was appropriate to effectuate the intention of the parties.

. . . Under the partnership agreement the Bank is entitled to recover under section 7.5 on both the provisions for an additional capital contribution and on the guaranty.

JUDGMENT

[Judgment against the limited partners was affirmed.]

General Partners

Who May Be a General Partner? Any person legally capable of contracting who meets the qualifications stated in the limited partnership agreement may be a general partner. Another partnership, or even a corporation (if its charter permits), may be a general partner in a limited partnership. Where a corporation is general partner, as in *Continental Bank v. Allen,* above, it provides a form of *limited liability even for the general partner.* This is true because the general partner's liability is still limited to the assets of the corporate general partner.

There is no limitation upon the number of general partners in a limited partnership. However, they tend to be few in number because general partners are reluctant to share managerial authority while the limited partners prefer to hold one or a few persons responsible for management decisions. A general partner may make contributions to the limited partnership and may also contribute (invest) as a limited partner. Thus, one who is both general and limited partner in the same partnership has a general partner's liabilities and a limited partner's rights. If partners anticipate admitting additional general partners into an existing limited partnership, they should provide for it in the partnership agreement. If the agreement does not provide for admission of additional general partners, written consent of *both* limited and general partners is required (ULPA 401).

Powers of General Partners. A general partner in a limited partnership has all the powers and is subject to the same rights, restrictions, and liabilities as a partner in an ordinary business partnership (ULPA 403). A general partner is the manager of the enterprise, conducting its business and executing in the partnership name any instrument necessary to carry on partnership affairs. Accordingly, a general partner may buy and sell partnership property without the knowledge or consent of the limited partners if such actions are in furtherance of partnership purposes and are not in conflict with the partnership agreement. If the general partner wishes to act beyond the scope of authority that is set out in the agreement, then all the partners—general and limited—must first give written consent. Thus, general partners in a firm organized to construct a boat marina have authority to buy necessary building material, but if they plan to buy a hospital, they must obtain written consent from the other partners. A general partner may personally do business with the firm or lend the partnership money if the transaction does not violate the partnership agreement. For example, a firm may agree to pay general partner Sue for running its advertising campaign. How-

---

BOX 41.2

A Question of Business Planning

Should you be an officer of a corporation that is the general partner and be a limited partner at the same time?

Gonzalez remodeled an apartment house of Excel Associates, a limited partnership. When his bill for $55,000 went unpaid, he sued the corporate general partner, Tribute, Inc., and the sole limited partner, Edward Chalpin. Chalpin was also president and sole stockholder-director of Tribute, Inc. He defended on the ground that, although he was very active as CEO for Tribute, Inc., which ran Excel's business as general partner, *all* of his acts on Excel's behalf were performed only in his capacity as an officer of Tribute. However, he was not able to produce evidence to clearly link his actions with Tribute, Inc., or to disprove Gonzalez's theory that Chalpin was active in his capacity as a limited partner and should therefore have unlimited liability.

In sustaining judgment against Chalpin, the court said: "A limited partner who assumes such a dual capacity rightly bears a heavy burden when seeking to elude personal liability. The clinching documentary evidence shows Chalpin signing Excel's checks in payment to Gonzalez in his own name and without naming Tribute or indicating that he was signing in any representative capacity."*

*Gonzalez v. Chalpin, 564 N.Y.S.2d 702 (N.Y. App. 1990).

Table 41.1 Fiduciary Duties Owed by General Partner to Limited Partners

1. Duty to exert best efforts to assist the partnership in accomplishing the purposes for which it was formed
2. Duty to devote partnership funds to the purposes for which it was organized and to render to all the limited partners, on demand, full information about the firm's financial condition and affairs
3. Duty to comply with state and federal securities laws
4. Duty, where general partner or partnership is purchasing a limited partner's interest, to fully disclose all relevant information pertaining to the value of the seller's interest, and if payment is not cash, the value of the offered consideration
5. Duty not to acquire a business opportunity which rightfully should be taken for the partnership

---

ever, to avoid later charges of self-dealing, the firm should include the details of her employment in the partnership agreement.

Fiduciary Duty of General Partners. A general partner, being in full charge of the partnership business, must act with the utmost good faith toward the limited partners, who have no option but to rely on his or her integrity. Table 41.1 summarizes a range of fiduciary duties that the general partner owes to the limited partners. The most flagrant breaches of fiduciary duty involve self-dealing. The varieties of this dishonest conduct are limited only by human ingenuity. For example, suppose that Hal is general partner in Deep Gold Limited Partnership, formed to develop its ore property. He learns that Jim, a prospector, has filed a mining claim close to Deep Gold's properties. Hal buys the claim from Jim, then sells it to his partnership at a handsome profit. If Hal had not been general partner, the sale to the partnership would have been proper. But as general partner, Hal has a fiduciary obligation to give his firm the opportunity to buy the claim directly from Jim at the lower price.

To what extent does a general partner's fiduciary obligation require him to guarantee that the venture will be profitable? The judge decided that issue in the next case.

CASE 41.3 **Wyler v. Feuer** • 149 Cal. Rptr. 626 (Cal. App. 1978)

FACTS Cy Feuer and Ernest Martin and their corporation, Feuer and Martin Productions, Inc. (defendants), had produced successful Broadway musical comedies such as *Guys and Dolls*, and their first motion picture, *Cabaret*, received eight Academy Awards. Martin acquired worldwide picture rights to a book about the famous French singer Edith Piaf. Feuer and Martin formed a limited partnership in which they were general partners and Wyler (who had no prior movie experience) was a limited partner. The sole purpose of the firm was to make a film based on the book.

Wyler contributed the entire $1,512,000 it cost to produce the motion picture. When released, the film was a failure. The partners had overestimated the

**CASE 41.3
Continued**

public's interest in the subject matter and had weakened the film's chances by employing an unknown French actress as the lead. Wyler sued the defendants for mismanagement of the business of the limited partnership. The trial court entered a nonsuit on that cause of action. Plaintiff Wyler appealed.

OPINION

FLEMING, Assoc. J. . . . Wyler alleged excessive costs of production, . . . failure to produce a marketable English version, improvident selection of actors, unseasonable scheduling of photography, failure to obtain production financing, and procurement of unfavorable distribution contracts.

A limited partnership affords a vehicle for capital investment whereby the limited partner restricts his liability to the amount of his investment in return for surrender of any right to manage and control the partnership business. . . . In a limited partnership the general partner manages and controls the partnership business. . . . In exercising his management functions the general partner comes under a fiduciary duty of good faith and fair dealing toward other members of the partnership. . . .

Three characteristics—limited investor liability, delegation of authority to management, and fiduciary duty owed by management to investors—are similar to those existing in corporate investment where it has long been the rule that directors are not liable to stockholders for mistakes made in the exercise of honest business judgment. . . . By this standard a general partner may not be held liable for mistakes made or losses incurred in the good faith exercise of reasonable business judgment.

We agree with the trial court that plaintiff did not produce sufficient evidence to hold the defendants liable for bad business management. Plaintiff's evidence showed that the Piaf picture did not make money, was not sought after by distributors, and did not live up to its producers' expectations. The same could be said of the majority of motion pictures made since the invention of cinematography. . . . The good faith business judgment and management of a general partner need only satisfy the standard of care demanded of an ordinary prudent person, and will not be scrutinized by the courts with the cold clarity of hindsight. The trial court correctly granted a nonsuit on the mismanagement cause of action.

JUDGMENT

The judgment is affirmed.

General Partner's Liability to Third Parties.

Each general partner is personally liable to third parties for the debts and obligations of the firm. This liability is similar to the personal liability of partners in an ordinary business partnership [ULPA 403(b); UPA 15]. A third party can reach a general partner's interest in the firm only by a charging order. A general partner is also liable to anyone who suffers a loss as a result of having relied upon a statement in the certificate of limited partnership *which the general partner knew or should have known to be false*. For example, a general partner in a limited partnership is personally liable to repay a bank loan to the partnership if, at the time of the loan, the bank relied on a statement in the signed partnership certificate which the general partner knew or should have known to be false.

Compensation of General Partner. A limited partnership agreement may provide for compensation to a general partner (in addition to a share of profits) for managing the firm's affairs. There is no standard formula for fixing a managing general partner's compensation. It may be fixed by (1) a management fee representing a certain percentage of the partnership's annual income, (2) an agreed percentage of the total capital of the firm, (3) a reimbursement of money for reasonable managerial expenses incurred, (4) a salary or a fixed fee, or (5) some other formula. Regardless of the method used, general partners, in organizing a firm, try to adopt compensation plans that appear reasonable to investors.

Termination of General Partner's Status. ULPA 402 provides that membership in a limited partnership ceases when the general partner (1) withdraws from the partnership, (2) assigns his or her interest, (3) is removed by the limited partners in accordance with the limited partnership agreement, (4) files a petition in bankruptcy, (5) is adjudged incompetent to manage his or her affairs, or (6) dies.

Withdrawal. A general partner may at any time withdraw from the partnership by giving written notice to all other partners (ULPA 602). Generally, the withdrawal of a general partner will dissolve a limited partnership unless (1) there is at least one other general partner and the written provisions of the limited partnership agreement permit the business to be carried on by the remaining partner, or (2) within 90 days *all* partners agree in writing to continue the business, and appoint another general partner if necessary (ULPA 801).

If there is a wrongful withdrawal, the general partner of a limited partnership, like the partner of a general partnership, is liable to the other partners. In contrast, limited partners generally have the right to withdraw at any time.

Assignment of interest. A general partner who assigns his or her general partnership interest to someone else ceases to be a general partner in the firm. The assignee does not thereby become a new general partner unless all the limited partners consent in writing or unless admission is so authorized by the limited partnership agreement. The assignee who is not admitted as a partner is merely entitled to receive that portion of profits or assets to which the assigning partner would have been entitled. Here again, the general partner's rights to assign contrast with those of limited partners, who can freely assign their interests. A general partner who also owns a limited partnership interest in the firm may assign that interest without affecting his or her general partnership interest or status.

Removal. A general partner may be removed if the limited partnership agreement sets out the conditions under which that action may be taken. For example, if a partnership agreement states that Ned, the sole general partner, can be removed if he does not sell the firm's building within 18 months and he fails to do so, then the limited partners may remove him.

Limited Partners

Who May Be a Limited Partner? Any "person"—defined by the ULPA as an individual, a partnership, a limited partnership, a corporation if its charter permits, an estate, an association, or a general partner—may be a limited partner. In every limited partnership there must be at least one limited partner, but the law sets no limit on the number there may be. The number of limited partners in a firm depends primarily upon the financial needs and the character of the business in which the partnership is engaged. Some limited partnerships, such as those organized to drill for oil or to trade in real estate on a large scale, have been given the popular name of **master limited partnerships** because they have hundreds of limited partners (investors) scattered all over the country. These interests are traded on financial stock exchanges and thus have a ready market for purchase and sale. By way of example, the following four are master limited partnerships: Mesa Limited Partnership and Apache Petroleum Company Limited Partnership, both of which explore and drill for oil; Allstar Inns Limited Partnership, which owns and operates motels; and Maritrans Partners Limited Partnership, which transports crude oil products by sea. Generally, corpora-

Table 41.2 Three Ways of Adding Limited Partners to a Limited Partnership (ULPA 301; 704)

1. By acquiring an interest directly from the firm in the manner provided in the partnership agreement; if it has no provision, then written consent of all partners is required
2. By assignment of a limited partner's interest, *if* the partnership agreement provides that a limited partner has the power to give the assignee standing as a limited partner
3. With written consent of all partners

tions that have changed into master limited partnerships have done so for tax reasons.

Most limited partnerships are not nearly so huge or ambitious as master limited partnerships. Usually, no more than thirty-five limited partnership interests are offered for sale in any one enterprise, because when that number is exceeded the firm is required to comply with stringent federal securities laws. Each state also imposes restrictions on the sale of limited partnership interests. For example, in order to protect unsophisticated investors from exploitation by promoters, a state may require that sale of a limited partnership interest be restricted to investors who possess a specified minimum net worth. After a limited partnership has been organized, new limited partners may be added in various ways, as shown in Table 41.2.

Powers of Limited Partners. While limited partners are *members* of the limited partnership, they are not *partners* in the full sense in which that word is normally used. A limited partner is only an investor in the firm, receiving (if the firm is successful) income from that investment while having but slight authority to participate in the management of the enterprise. Like any stranger to the firm, a limited partner may be hired by the partnership as an employee or independent contractor. For example, Art, a limited partner, may be paid to superintend a partnership construction job, and Sue, another limited partner, may be hired as its chief accountant. However, in performing these functions, the limited partner risks the unlimited liability of a general partner if he or she exercises control or managerial responsibility. Unless prohibited by the partnership agreement, a limited partner may also transact business with the partnership (ULPA 107). Thus if Ted owns a heating company, he may sell his products to Greenacres Estates, a home-building limited partnership in which Ted is a member; and Ben, still another limited partner, may lend the firm money at interest. None of these or similar transactions will affect the limited partner's status in the firm.

A limited partner, unless specifically designated to act as an agent of the partnership, has no authority to bind the partnership either by contract or by tortious conduct. For example, Ann, a limited partner, cannot obligate the partnership to pay a roofer to fix a leak in the firm's roof unless she is authorized by a general partner to hire the roofer. Similarly, limited partner Hal, who is not employed by the partnership, does not make the firm liable for a slander he commits against a competitor unless a general partner authorized it.

Rights. Limited partners have threefold rights:

1. To share in the firm's profits and distribution of assets (ULPA 503; 504)
2. To secure information about the business (ULPA 105)
3. To participate to a limited extent, as set forth in the partnership agreement and the ULPA, in the control of the partnership (ULPA 302)

A limited partner has the right to share in the firm's profits and in the distribution of its assets as provided in the partnership agreement.

Limited partners are also entitled to inspect and copy any partnership books. In addition, they may obtain from the general partner upon reasonable demand (1) information regarding the financial condition of the partnership business, (2) copies of its federal, state, and local income tax returns, and (3) other information regarding its affairs.

In the next case the court had to decide a tug-of-war between limited partners, who demanded partnership information, and the general partner, who was trying to withhold it.

CASE 41.4 McCain v. Phoenix Resources, Inc. • 185 Cal. App. 3d 575 (Cal. 1986)

FACTS Valley Investors was a limited partnership formed to own and develop land in California. The managing general partner was a corporation, Phoenix Resources, Inc. (defendant). McCain and Howell (plaintiffs) were the limited partners. They questioned the manner in which the Phoenix corporation was conducting partnership affairs and sought to examine partnership books and records. Phoenix consented to the inspection of only financial and accounting records, legal documents such as contracts, and minutes of limited partnership meetings. Plaintiffs demanded to see additional partnership records and Phoenix refused. Plaintiffs sued, and the court granted their request to order all partnership records to be available for inspection and copying. Phoenix appealed.

OPINION LOW, P.J. . . . It should be noted that a partner's statutory right of inspection can be exercised *without* a showing of either good cause or proper purpose. . . . A managing partner has a legal duty to disclose to copartners "matters affecting their business relationship" . . . [including] a duty to make a full disclosure of all matters substantially affecting the value of the partnership. . . . Because of their fiduciary relationship, the records sought by plaintiffs herein were not the private property of defendant, but were subject to the rights guaranteed to the other partners to have access to all information pertaining to partnership affairs.

Although a partnership should be protected from harassment by placing reasonable time, place, and manner restrictions on a partner's right of inspection, the statutory language demonstrates that a partner is entitled to have broad access to partnership information. . . .

Defendant also resists disclosure of any information [concerning the partnership] in the possession of the two law firms [employed by Phoenix]. . . . Defendant argues that "[t]he right of inspection applies only as against partners" and alleges there is "no authority that would support a right of inspection against a law firm or any other third party as an adjunct of [plaintiffs'] right of inspection. . . ." A partnership can be a client of a law firm and a lawyer may transact business on behalf of the partnership. . . . Under such circumstances, it is foreseeable that a law firm would have information in its possession relating to partnership affairs. . . .

JUDGMENT [The order requiring the general partner to submit all records for the limited partners' inspection was affirmed.]

Restrictions on Right of Limited Partner to Manage. The philosophy underlying a limited partnership is that an investor, as a limited partner, gives up the right to participate in management in exchange for freedom from personal liability for the debts and obligations of the firm. In the original (1916) version of the ULPA, a limited partner who took part in management of the firm lost that immunity and became subject to the same liability as a general partner for all partnership obligations.

However, over the years, business experience has demonstrated that a limited partner should have a restricted right to participate in some elements of control of the business without being subjected to personal liability. The drafters of the later versions of the ULPA concluded that it is contrary to sound public policy to hold a limited partner who did not participate in the creation of partnership obligations to be held liable for them. However, it was also determined that limited partners should be liable to persons transacting business with the partnership where their conduct leads such persons to reasonably believe that they are general partners.

To illustrate this concept: Ted, a limited partner in the Otis Limited Partnership, is an engineer. The partnership contemplates buying a new piece of equipment from Castwell, Inc. Ted helps the general partner decide upon the equipment to buy. Ted is not liable as a general partner. However, in helping the general partner to decide what equipment to buy, Ted meets daily with Castwell's salespeople and discusses the merits and drawbacks of various models. Finally, when he is satisfied that he has selected the best model for the Otis partnership to buy, Ted says to Castwell: "Model X is best—ship it to us." Ted has led Castwell to reasonably believe he is a general partner. Later, if Otis defaults on the bill, Castwell, Inc., may hold Ted personally liable to pay it, along with Otis' general partner.

What if Ted never had any direct contact with Castwell? Is it still possible for him to end up with the liability of a general partner? In the following case, the limited partner actively engaged in day-to-day management of partnership affairs, but had *no direct contact with the third-party creditor*. However, the creditor, in dealing with the firm, relied on the representations of the *general partner* that his credit purchases were being financially backed by an affluent limited partner. Note that the Arizona court is interpreting RULPA as enacted by its legislature with modifications. The case raises an important point: It is not enough to know that one's state has adopted ULPA or RULPA; one must also know what *modifications* were adopted.

CASE 41.5 **Gateway Potato Sales v. G.B. Investment Co.**
• 822 P.2d 490 (Ariz. App. 1991)

FACTS Two corporations—Sunworth Corporation and G.B. Investment Co.—formed a limited partnership called Sunworth Packing. Sunworth Corporation was to be the general partner, and G.B. Investment was the limited partner. In 1985, R. Ellsworth (president of Sunworth Corporation) contracted on behalf of the limited partnership to buy potatoes from Gateway Potato Sales. Knowing that Ellsworth had undergone bankruptcy, Gateway was reluctant to extend credit, but Ellsworth assured Gateway that he was in partnership with a large financial institution, G.B. Investment Co., which not only provided financing but was actively involved in the operation of the business and had approved purchase of the potatoes. At all times while filling the order, Gateway believed that it was doing business with a general partnership (i.e., Sunworth Packing, formed by Sunworth Corporation and G.B. Investment as the two partners).

CASE 41.5 Continued

Gateway's manager had no contact of any kind with G.B. Investment prior to the sale of the potatoes. Sunworth never paid its bill, and Gateway sued both the general and limited partners, contending that it had relied on the belief that Sunworth Packing was a general partnership, and that G.B. Investment was one of the partners. G.B. Investment moved for summary judgment. Gateway, in opposition, produced the affidavit of R. Ellsworth (president of the corporation that was general partner), which stated that two of G.B. Investment's employees controlled the day-to-day affairs of the limited partnership, made Ellsworth account to them for nearly everything he did, and approved most important operational decisions, expenditures, and the use and management of partnership funds without Ellsworth's involvement.

The trial court granted G.B. Investment's motion for summary judgment, basing its decision on the belief that, as a limited partner, G.B. Investment could never be liable under the statute unless the creditor (Gateway) had contact with the limited partner and learned directly from G.B. Investment of its control and participation in the business. Gateway appealed.

OPINION

TAYLOR, J. . . . To the extent that the trial court's ruling may have been based on a belief that a limited partner could never be liable under the statute unless the creditor had contact with the limited partner and learned directly from him of his participation and control of the business, we believe the [trial court's] ruling to be in error.

[In adopting ULPA 303(a) for the state of Arizona,] . . . the legislature stopped short of expressly stating that if the limited partner's participation in the control of the business is substantially the same as the exercise of the powers of a general partner, he is liable to persons who transact business with a limited partner even though they have no knowledge of his participation and control. It has made this statement by implication, though. . . . We believe this interpretation is strengthened by an examination of the legislative history of Arizona's limited partnership statute. . . .

Presently [the Arizona statute] dealing with a limited partner's liability to third parties is very similar to the 1976 version of section 303(a) of the RULPA which stated:

> Except as provided in subsection (d), a limited partner is not liable for the obligations of a limited partnership unless he is also a general partner or, and in addition to the exercise of his rights and powers as a limited partner, he takes part in the control of the business. However, if the limited partner's participation in the control of the business is not substantially the same as the exercise of the powers of a general partner, he is liable only to persons who transact business with the limited partnership with actual knowledge of his participation and control.

In 1985, the drafters of the RULPA backtracked from the position taken in section 303(a) of the 1976 Act. The new amendments reflect a reluctance to hold a limited partner liable if the limited partner had no direct contact with the creditor. The 1985 revised RULPA section 303(a) was amended to provide as follows:

> . . . However, if the limited partner participates in the control of the business, he is liable only to persons who transact business with the limited partnership reasonably

> **CASE 41.5**
> **Continued**
>
> *believing, based upon the limited partner's conduct, that the limited partner is a general partner.* . . .
>
> The Arizona legislature, however, has not revised . . . [its statute] to correspond to the section 303 amendments. The Arizona statute continues to impose liability on a limited partner whenever the "substantially the same as" test is met, even though the creditor has no knowledge of the limited partner's control. It follows that no contact between the creditor and the limited partner is required to impose liability.
>
> Moreover, whereas section 303 of the RULPA states that the creditor's reasonable belief must be "based upon the limited partner's conduct," under . . . [the Arizona statute] the only requirement is that the creditor has had "actual knowledge of the limited partner's participation in control." The statute does not state that this knowledge must be based upon the limited partner's conduct. The comments to . . . section 303 of the RULPA from which Arizona's statute is taken, make it clear that only when the "substantially the same as" test is met is direct contact not a requirement. Conversely, if the "substantially the same as" test is not met, direct contact is required. [G.B. Investment never had any contact with Gateway.] We conclude, therefore, that G.B. Investment would be liable only if the "substantially the same as" test was met. . . .
>
> **JUDGMENT** We conclude that Gateway is entitled to a determination by trial of the extent of control exercised by G.B. Investment over Sunworth Packing. . . . We reverse the judgment of the trial court and remand for further proceedings.

The above case explored the circumstances under which a limited partner is *liable* as a general partner under ULPA 303(a). Table 41.3 lists a number of situations under ULPA 303(b) where the limited partner *is not* liable as a general partner. In their comments concerning this section, the drafters of the ULPA revision stated that they had extended the enumeration to assure that limited partners would not be subjected to general liability where it is not appropriate.

A limited partner is also allowed to bring a **derivative action** on behalf of the partnership without being deemed to have participated in the firm's management. As applied to a limited partnership, a derivative action is a lawsuit in the partnership name brought by one or more of the limited partners in order to protect or enforce partnership rights when the general partner refuses to take appropriate action (ULPA 1001).

A derivative action may, under appropriate circumstances, be brought against a third party, a general partner, or a limited partner. Such a suit would be appropriate, for instance: (1) to

Table 41.3 Safe Harbor Situations Where a Limited Partner Is Not Liable as a General Partner [ULPA 303(b)]

Where the limited partner:

1. Acts as a contractor for, or an agent or employee of, the limited partnership
2. Advises a general partner with respect to the business of the firm
3. Acts as surety for the partnership
4. Votes upon such matters as dissolution and winding up of partnership, or a change in the nature of its business, or the admission or removal of a general or limited partner, or amendment to the partnership agreement

Table 41.4 Situations Where a Limited Partner Has the Liability of a General Partner [ULPA 303(a)]

1. The limited partner participates in the firm's control of the business beyond the boundaries permitted by the ULPA or the partnership agreement.
2. No limited partnership certificate has been filed with the secretary of state.
3. The limited partner knowingly permits his or her surname (a different name from that of any of the general partners) to be used as part of the name of the limited partnership.

---

force a landlord to comply with his or her promise to extend a lease on premises occupied by the limited partnership and necessary for the continuation of its business, (2) to force a general partner to turn over to the limited partnership monies collected by that partner which rightfully belong to the partnership, or (3) to force a limited partner to pay a long-past-due promissory note given to the partnership as a capital contribution to the firm. Limited partners often use derivative suits to protect their interests in the enterprise.

Liability of Limited Partners. Generally, the only financial risk that limited partners take is the possibility of losing their investment in the firm. The three situations shown in Table 41.4, however, impose upon the limited partner the same burden of unlimited liability that the general partner must bear.

Fiduciary Duties of Limited Partners. By definition, limited partners have a relatively inactive role in the partnership business, and the opportunities for self-dealing or seizing a partnership opportunity are not available to them, as they would be to the general partner. Nevertheless, in the limited area where limited partners function, they have fiduciary duties. This follows from the fact that where the ULPA is silent (as it is concerning fiduciary duties of limited partners), the UPA, which imposes a fiduciary duty on all partners, would apply.

Action by Third Party against Limited Partner. A creditor who has a judgment against a limited partner arising out of a personal obligation can reach the limited partner's interest only by securing a court charging order in the same manner as with a general partnership. If the charging order is foreclosed, the purchaser at the foreclosure sale becomes an assignee of that portion of the partner's interest so purchased.

Assignment of Limited Partnership Interest. A limited partner, being only an investor in the firm, may at any time assign (sell or give away) all or a portion of his or her partnership interest without causing a dissolution of the firm. The assignee becomes entitled to the same distribution that the assigning partner would have been entitled to receive.

A person who acquires either all or part of a limited partner's interest does *not* automatically become a limited partner. If the partnership agreement permits, the one who assigns the interest may designate the recipient as a limited partner. If there is no such provision in the agreement, then the consent of all the limited partners is required before the assignee becomes a limited partner. An assignee who has become a limited partner is subject to the restrictions and liabilities imposed by the partnership agreement upon limited partners. However, the assignee is not obligated for liabilities unknown at the time when the assignee became a limited partner.

Withdrawal or Death of a Limited Partner. A limited partner may withdraw from the partnership at the time and upon the conditions set forth in the partnership agreement. At the time of withdrawal, the limited partner is entitled to receive whatever distribution is provided in the partnership agreement. If the agreement contains no provision for withdrawal, a limited partner may withdraw after giving at least 6 months' written notice to each of the general partners. Within a reasonable time after withdrawal, the partnership must pay the fair value of the limited partner's interest as of the date of withdrawal.

If a limited partner dies, the personal representative of the estate (executor or administrator) may exercise all the rights to which the deceased limited partner was entitled.

Winding Up and Termination of Limited Partnerships

A limited partnership, similar to a general partnership, must go through the process of dissolution and winding up before it is terminated. Grounds for dissolution of a limited partnership appear in Table 41.5.

After its dissolution, a limited partnership is wound up by a general partner who has not caused the dissolution. If there is no general partner to conduct the winding up, it may be performed by the limited partners or by some person, usually a receiver, designated by a court.

Table 41.5 Grounds for Dissolution of a Limited Partnership (ULPA 801; 802)

A limited partnership is dissolved when any of the following events happen:

1 The time or the event specified in writing in the limited partnership agreement occurs.

2 All the partners, in writing, agree to the dissolution.

3 A general partner dies or withdraws from the partnership, unless (a) the written provisions of the agreement permit the business to be carried on by the remaining general partners (if any), or (b) if there is no remaining general partner, the limited partners, within 90 days, agree in writing to continue the business and appoint one or more new general partners.

4 The partnership is dissolved by court order. Any general or limited partner may ask the court to dissolve the partnership when it cannot carry on business as intended—for example, if (a) there is no profitable market for the firm's products or services, (b) a general partner is acting fraudulently or violating his or her fiduciary duties, or (c) the general partner is not properly managing the partnership property.

Table 41.6 Order of Distribution of Assets of Limited Partnership after Winding Up (ULPA 804)

1 To the firm's creditors, including partners who are creditors

2 To partners and former partners for distributions previously due them and unpaid, except as otherwise provided in the partnership agreement

3 To the partners for the return of their contributions, except as otherwise provided in the partnership agreement

4 Any remaining balance to the partners according to the partnership agreement formula

As in the winding up of an ordinary general partnership, the individual who conducts the winding up collects all debts owing to the partnership, sees that the partnership's existing contracts are performed, and turns its assets into cash. At the conclusion of the winding up, any remaining assets are distributed as shown in Table 41.6. The completion of the distribution terminates the limited partnership.

LIMITED LIABILITY COMPANIES

As we have seen, the limited partnership is an attractive alternative to the general partnership because liability of limited partners is limited to the amount they invest. Unfortunately, however, the general partner's personal estate is still at risk whenever assets of the limited partnership are not sufficient to satisfy creditors. To remedy this shortcoming of the limited partnership, as well as to offer tax advantages, fifteen states have enacted statutes authorizing two or more "members" to form a *limited liability company* *(LLC)*.[1] Unlike a limited partnership, where the general partner has unlimited liability, *all members of an LLC have liability limited to the amount of their capital investment.* Yet an LLC, for federal income tax purposes, is taxed like general and

[1]The states are Arizona, Colorado, Florida, Iowa, Kansas, Louisiana, Maryland, Minnesota, Nevada, Oklahoma, Texas, Utah, Virginia, West Virginia, and Wyoming.

limited partnerships—that is, the income of an LLC "passes through" pro rata to the members, in proportion to their capital investment. They then declare that income on their personal income tax returns.

What Is a Limited Liability Company?

Although state statutes differ in detail, generally they provide that (1) an LLC may be formed by two or more "members," (2) there must be a stated term of not more than 30 years' duration, (3) all members have liability limited to the amount of their invested capital plus any additional capital contribution contractually promised to be paid in the future, (4) members' shares are not freely transferable, and (5) centralized management shall be elected by the members.

What Are the Tax Advantages of a Limited Liability Company?

Essentially, an LLC has two major tax advantages. First, it is taxed as a partnership so that, unlike a corporation, taxes on its income are paid only once—by the members who declare their pro rata share of LLC income on their personal income tax returns. Second, LLC members who actively participate in management may treat losses of the enterprise as "active losses,"[2] which can be offset against other income (including wages and salaries) on their personal income tax return.

Taxation of LLCs contrasts sharply with the tax treatment of limited partnerships. A limited partner, by definition, does *not* and cannot materially participate in management.[3] Therefore, a limited partner's pro rata share of any loss is treated for tax purposes as a *passive activity loss*. The Internal Revenue Code (IRC) defines a passive activity as any rental activity or any trade or business involvement in which the taxpayer (e.g., a limited partner) does not actively participate. A serious disadvantage results from classifying the limited partner's loss as a passive activity loss, because *such a loss can be offset only against passive income*. Unfortunately, many small investors in limited partnership interests do not have other passive income, and thus get no tax benefit out of a limited partnership loss. The rule that passive losses can be offset only against passive income has been a significant disincentive to the formation of limited partnerships.

Qualifying an LLC to Be Taxed as a Partnership

Under the Internal Revenue Code a business entity is taxed according to its *characteristics*, not the label that is used to describe it. It follows that not all LLCs are routinely taxed as partnerships, but only those that *lack the characteristics of a corporation*. Federal tax authorities list six identifying characteristics of a corporation: (1) associates who have (2) the objective to carry on business and divide profits, (3) continuity of life, (4) centralized management, (5) limited liability for corporate debts, and (6) free transferability of ownership interests in the enterprise.[4] Since the first two items are found in all business organizations, the Internal Revenue Service focuses on items 3 through 6 for purposes of distinguishing a partnership from a corporation. A business entity that *lacks any two of these items* will be treated as a partnership and will not be subject to corporate income taxes.

The characteristics of an LLC are found by examining the LLC's articles of organization, which are similar to articles of incorporation, and must meet the requirements of the state statute. Since LLC articles of organization, formed under most state statutes, contain provisions that (1) limit the life of the organization to a stated term of years (usually less than 30) and (2) significantly restrict transferability of shares, it can be said that, LLCs will generally

---

[2] IRC Sec. 469.

[3] IRC Sec. 469(h), in effect, declares that all losses of a limited partner are "passive activity losses" by specifically stating that "no interest in a limited partnership as a limited partner shall be treated as an interest with respect to which a taxpayer materially participates."

[4] IRC Sec. 301.7701-2(a)(1); 41-43 301.7701-3(b)(1).

lack these two corporate characteristics, and will therefore qualify to be taxed as partnerships. However, numerous IRS rulings decide whether a particular LLC lacks any two of items 3 through 6, listed above, so as to qualify as a partnership for tax purposes. Investors contemplating an LLC structure should give careful attention to these factors and to the rulings relating to them.

LLCs—A Viable Hybrid

The growing popularity of LLCs stems from widespread recognition that they are an important alternative form of business organization. They are unique in combining the income tax status of a partnership with the advantage of limited liability for *all* members—a feature that is not available in a limited partnership. In a sense, LLCs represent a form of organization that stands somewhere between the limited partnership and the corporation. Because most LLCs severely restrict transferability of shares, they are not adaptable where a large number of investors is contemplated. Similarly, if continuity in perpetuity is desired, a corporation is the only option.

SUMMARY

A limited partnership (authorized by the ULPA) is a business organization composed of at least one general partner and at least one limited partner. The general partner or partners manage and operate the partnership business. They have all the rights and liabilities of partners in an ordinary business partnership. The limited partners are investors in the firm and normally exercise no control over management. A limited partner is not personally liable for the firm's debts unless he or she participates in the control of the business.

A limited partnership may carry on any lawful business not in conflict with state law. A limited partnership comes into existence when a certificate of limited partnership is filed with the office of the secretary of state in the state where the partnership is organized. In addition, the parties either orally or in writing enter into a partnership agreement. The ULPA does not prescribe the content of the agreement, but it usually deals with capital contributions of the partners, the authority of the general and limited partners, and distribution of partnership income and assets.

Each limited partner and general partner may make a contribution of cash, property, or services to the capital of the partnership. If the agreement states no formula for the allocation of income, then the profits and losses are distributed in the same ratio as each partner's contribution bears to the total contributions received by the partnership.

A general partner or a limited partner ceases to be a member of the partnership upon assigning (selling or giving away) his or her entire partnership interest. In the event that a general partner withdraws, the remaining general partner(s), if any, may continue to carry on the partnership business if the partnership certificate so provides. Absent such a provision, the limited partners may agree that the remaining general partner will continue the business. If no general partner remains, the limited partners may either appoint a new general partner or dissolve the partnership.

When a limited partnership is dissolved, it goes through a winding-up process similar to the winding up of an ordinary business partnership. After the assets have been gathered together and turned into cash and all the creditors have been paid, the remaining assets are divided among the partners according to the formula set forth in the partnership agreement, and the partnership terminates.

Fifteen states have enacted laws authorizing formation of a new kind of business entity—the limited liability company (LLC). For small groups of investors, it offers an advantage over the limited partnership because *all* investors have limited liability—yet it is taxed as a partnership if it lacks any two of the following features: continuity of life, centralized management, limited liability, and transferability of shares. In addition, investors that actively engage in the business can offset partnership losses against other income because such losses are not classified by federal tax authorities as passive activity losses.

REVIEW QUESTIONS

1. Why would you want to invest in a limited partnership?

2. (a) How is a limited partnership formed? (b) How does its formation differ from that of a general partnership? (c) What limitations are there in adopting a limited partnership name?

3. (a) What is a certificate of limited partnership? (b) What, in general terms, does this document contain? (c) What are the consequences of not filing a limited partnership certificate?

4. (a) What is a limited partnership agreement? In general terms, what might such an agreement contain? (b) If there is a limited partnership agreement, must there also be a certificate of limited partnership? Explain.

5. Assume a limited partner promises to make a contribution of $5,000 to a limited partnership and fails to do so. (a) What rights does the partnership have with respect to that promise? (b) What rights does a creditor of the limited partnership have with respect to that promised contribution?

6. May an already organized limited partnership admit (a) a new general partner? (b) A new limited partner? Explain.

7. Describe a general partner's powers in a limited partnership.

8. What are a general partner's duties and obligations toward the limited partnership and toward the limited partners?

9. What are the duties and obligations of a limited partner?

10. Discuss a limited partner's participation in the business.

11. What is the purpose of a limited partner's derivative action suit?

12. (a) Describe a limited liability company's characteristics. (b) Explain the advantages and limitations of LLCs.

CASE PROBLEMS

1. Betz and Kinn were general partners and Twitch and seven others were limited partners in Chena Resort, a Limited Partnership. Twitch owned only a 5 percent interest in the partnership and was entitled to 5 percent of its profits. The general partners neglected to file a certificate of limited partnership with the secretary of state. A creditor of Chena Resort sued all the general and limited partners for the unpaid purchase price of goods bought by Chena. Twitch claimed that the creditor's suit should have been against the general partners only or, as an alternative, against the general and limited partners in proportion to their interests in the limited partnership. Was Twitch correct? Explain your answer.

2. In February, Gray Electric Company extended credit to Blom Electric, a limited partnership in which Blom and Preston were the general partners and Lowe was the sole limited partner. Blom Electric had not filed the required certificate of limited partnership, but Gray did not know this. Gray knew, however, that Lowe was only a limited partner. In April, by letter to Gray, Lowe renounced any interest in Blom Electric. Almost a year later Gray, not having been paid and ascertaining that no limited partnership certificate had been filed, sued Preston, Blom, and Lowe for the unpaid bills. Gray claimed that Lowe was liable as a general partner because no certificate was on file. Is Lowe liable to Gray? Explain.

3. The limited partnership agreement of Spira-Mart showed that the limited partners were to contribute to the partnership various sums of capital totaling $250,000. In fact, however, they contributed a total of only $74,000. A partnership creditor sued to collect from the delinquent limited partners an amount sufficient to discharge the creditor's judgment against Spira-Mart. Is the creditor entitled to this remedy? Explain.

4. The Meadows was a limited partnership to develop sixty-five acres into an industrial park. Each of thirty-two limited partners contributed

$50,000 to the firm. The limited partnership agreement did not state what portion of the enterprise's net profits would be distributed to the limited partners each year. However, the general practice of other successful limited partnerships in that area was to distribute all net profits annually. At the end of the first year, Meadows' general partner distributed only 50 percent of net profits to the limited partners as dividends. He told the limited partners that the balance was being retained against the possibility of future partnership needs. As a result, each limited partner's investment produced only a 5 percent return. The limited partners petitioned the court to force the general partner to make a supplemental distribution. Will the limited partners be successful in the litigation? Why or why not?

5. Alice was general partner in Sea Boutique, a limited partnership. Larry and Winnie were the limited partners, each contributing $10,000 to the firm. After 2 months Larry decided to invest elsewhere, and he asked Alice to buy him out. Alice offered $10,000, the amount he had invested, and he agreed, was paid, and withdrew from the partnership. Two months later, Larry learned that the boutique was very successful and that his interest was worth double his sale price. He complained to Alice. She said that selling was his idea, and he could have refused her offer. Does Larry have a cause of action against Alice?

6. Ozark Skyrise was a limited partnership organized to operate a resort at Lake of the Ozarks. Seymour was general partner and there were six limited partners. Seymour learned of an opportunity to purchase a motel at a low price near Kansas City, 100 miles away from the partnership's resort. Seymour thought it an excellent investment and, since the partnership had enough cash to make a down payment, he bought the motel in the partnership's name. When the limited partners learned of the purchase, they demanded that Seymour dispose of the motel and reimburse the partnership for the funds he had expended. Were the limited partners legally justified to make that demand? Discuss fully.

7. Block and Dardan entered into a limited partnership to operate a café. Dardan was the general partner and Block the limited partner. The café opened on May 1, 1980, and Dardan put his son in charge of it. Dardan himself seldom went to the café. After a year, Dardan told Block: "The café has not made any money, but I think it will next year." Block asked for an accounting, but Dardan stalled. Block sued for dissolution of the partnership. Can Block, as limited partner, properly file such a suit? Explain.

CHAPTER 42

Nature and Formation of Corporations

The corporation is the most important form of business organization in the United States. Since World War II, corporations have been formed five times faster than partnerships. A corporation is equally suitable for a complex multimillion-dollar business as for a small family enterprise in which the participants simply don't want the risk of personal liability.

This chapter briefly traces the development of corporation law and discusses important legal principles relating to the nature and formation of modern business corporations. Later chapters in this part of the book deal with the financing, management, and regulation of business corporations.

WHAT IS A CORPORATION?

A corporation is an artificial "person" created by the state. Although you can't touch or see a corporation, the law recognizes it as a living entity that exists separate and apart from anyone else. Its existence is even independent of its owners—that is, the people who own its stock. A corporation conducts business, enters into contracts, buys and sells property, and sues and is sued as though it were a living, breathing person. It pays taxes and is subject to criminal prosecution and fine. Its debts are the obligations of the corporate entity—not of its individual owners, the shareholders. A corporation's decision-making structure appears in Figure 42.1.

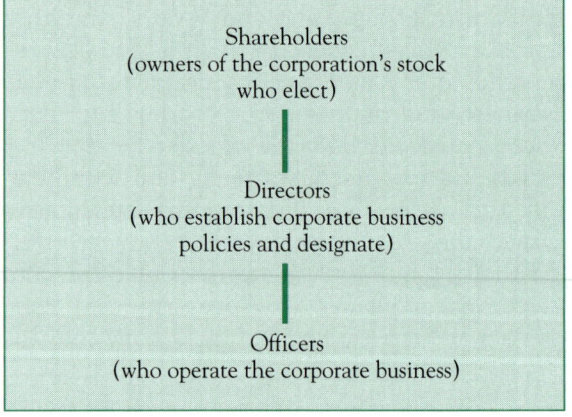

Figure 42.1 The decision-making structure of a corporation.

DEVELOPMENT OF MODERN CORPORATION LAW

The idea that a sovereign government can breathe life into a fictitious legal person known as a corporation originated in ancient Rome, spread to England, and from there migrated to the American colonies. Initially, U.S. corporations were formed by special acts of various state legislatures to carry on projects having some public purpose, such as building canals or toll bridges.

State Incorporation Laws

As the industrial revolution advanced, all kinds of businesses sought special legislative action to allow them to incorporate. Responding to such pressure, the states, beginning with New York in 1811, enacted general incorporation laws called **enabling acts.** These statutes permitted any lawful business to incorporate by complying with simple procedures supervised by state administrative officials. As a result, special acts of the legislature are no longer necessary to incorporate. General incorporation laws also define rights and duties of directors and shareholders and establish rules for financing and dissolving corporations.

In the course of the nineteenth century, the restrictions on incorporation were relaxed as the states began to compete for the taxable income and employment opportunities generated by the larger companies. In 1899 the *Delaware General Corporation Law* was revised to offer corporations maximum freedom from restriction. Today, about half of the nation's Fortune 500 companies and 40 percent of the companies listed on the New York Stock Exchange have incorporated under the laws of Delaware.

Commencing in 1933, the American Bar Association published and periodically revised the Model Business Corporation Act as a suggested guide for state corporation statutes. The Model Act was designed to meet the needs of large, small, and close corporations and to encourage unanimity in state corporation laws. Major revisions of the Model Act were made in 1969 and in 1984. The 1984 Revised Model Business Corporation Act, referred to here as the Revised Model Act (RMA), appears at the end of this text as Appendix 5. Thirty-nine states[1] and the District of Columbia have adopted the 1969 or the 1984 Act, but they have used it only as a guide and have modified it extensively. No state has adopted either the 1969 or 1984 Act in its entirety. Therefore, even if a state has followed the Model Act, its statutes must be consulted to find the precise incorporation requirements.

Each state also has a variety of regulatory statutes that govern and often restrict the business activity of corporations. These include **blue sky** laws, regulating the issuance and sale of corporate securities, laws regulating special corporations such as banks and public utilities, laws dealing with transfers of stocks and bonds, laws setting out rules for making loans with corporate securities as collateral (Articles 8 and 9 of the Uniform Commercial Code), tax laws, and laws regulating **foreign corporations** (corporations organized in another state or foreign country) that enter the state and commence to do business there.

Federal Laws Affecting Corporations

There is no federal general law under which businesspeople can incorporate, although Congress from time to time may organize a corporation, such as the Federal Deposit Insurance Corporation, to carry out some governmental objective. Therefore, one who wishes to form a corporation must secure the charter from the secretary of state where the company will be organized. Once a corporation is formed, it is subject to federal laws, regulations, and court decisions, which are often called "federal corporation law."

---

[1] The states are Alabama, Alaska, Arkansas, Arizona, Connecticut, Colorado, Florida, Georgia, Illinois, Iowa, Kansas, Kentucky, Louisiana, Maine, Maryland, Massachusetts, Michigan, Mississippi, Missouri, Montana, Nebraska, New Jersey, New Mexico, New York, North Carolina, North Dakota, Oregon, Rhode Island, South Carolina, South Dakota, Tennessee, Texas, Utah, Vermont, Virginia, Washington, West Virginia, Wisconsin, and Wyoming.

NATURE OF MODERN CORPORATIONS

As discussed under limited liability companies in Chapter 41, U.S. tax authorities use six characteristics to identify a "pure" corporation. We now take a closer look at these and other corporate characteristics.

Characteristics of Corporations

The following features distinguish corporations from other types of business organizations.

Legal Entity. Corporation means *body*. A corporation may therefore be thought of as a legal body or an artificial person whose rights and obligations are separate and distinct from those of its shareholders. Since it is a legal entity, a corporation is protected as a natural "person" in most situations arising under the Constitution. Under the First Amendment, a corporation has a right of freedom of speech. It is protected from unreasonable searches and seizures under the Fourth Amendment, and has the right under the Fifth Amendment not to be tried twice for the same offense (double jeopardy). Under the Fifth and Fourteenth Amendments, property rights of a corporation cannot be denied without due process of law, and it is entitled to equal protection of the laws.

A Creature of the State with Broad Purpose and Powers. In 1819 Chief Justice John Marshall said:

> A corporation is an artificial being, invisible, intangible, and existing only in contemplation of law. Being a mere creature of law, it possesses only those properties which the charter of its creation confers upon it, either expressly or as incidental to its very existence.[2]

Unlike a partnership, which springs from an agreement between partners, a corporation comes into existence only after full compliance with the state enabling act that authorizes its creation. In earlier years, states required the articles of incorporation (charter) to state fully the purpose of the corporation being formed, and it could not carry on any different or additional business. As a result, incorporators began to list every conceivable activity as a possible purpose of the corporation. In a move toward simplification, most state statutes and the Revised Model Act now allow articles of incorporation to state that the corporation is being organized to engage in "any lawful business." The RMA also provides that a corporation has the same powers as an individual to do anything necessary to carry on its business and affairs. However, all states reserve the power to amend or repeal the Act at any time and thereby may modify or withdraw powers previously granted to a corporation. Corporate powers are discussed fully in Chapter 44.

Perpetual Existence. A corporation continues in existence indefinitely unless it is given shorter life by its articles of incorporation or is dissolved by action of the state. The death, illness, or withdrawal of a shareholder, officer, or director does not affect the life of a corporation. Statutes in most states permit shareholders to force dissolution of a corporation (RMA 14.30). This action, however, is rarely taken.

Limited Liability of Shareholders. Probably the most important characteristic of a corporation is **limited liability**—that is, the shareholders' liability is limited to the amount of their capital investment. Normally, the shareholders of a corporation are not personally liable for its debts and obligations. Therefore, except in unusual circumstances, the only financial hazard involved in becoming a shareholder is the risk of losing one's investment in the corporation. Billions of dollars of capital are raised for new investment each year primarily because limited liability makes ownership of corporate shares the most attractive form of investment throughout the world. Unlike partners in a partnership, neither officers nor directors of a corporation are personally liable for the firm's debts and obligations. Because of this feature, people about to start a new and perhaps risky venture prefer a corporation.

---

[2]*Dartmouth College v. Woodward*, 17 U.S. 518 (1819).

Free Transferability of Shares. A share of stock is a pro rata ownership interest in a corporation. Some corporations issue millions of shares; others issue fewer than a dozen. Table 42.1 lists the number of shares issued by five representative giant American corporations. The owner of shares of stock, unless restricted by contractual agreement, may freely transfer those shares to anyone. Permission from the corporation, the shareholders, or any other authority is not necessary. Transfer of share ownership in no way affects the legal existence of the corporation. The free transferability of shares is a major factor in the development of national stock exchanges and the enormous expansion of American industry.

Centralized Management. A corporation's management and control are centralized in a shareholder-elected board of directors. Directors adopt resolutions establishing corporate policies and appoint officers to carry them out. This centralized management enables a huge corporation to act with maximum efficiency to benefit its owners—the shareholders. In larger firms directors are selected for their diversified business experience. Although the shareholders elect the board of directors, in an ordinary publicly held corporation they do not dictate the board's decisions and activities. However, as we will soon see, in a small, closely held corporation the shareholders also generally serve as its directors.

Comparison with Other Business Organizations. The principal elements of a corporation just reviewed may now be compared and contrasted with the main features of partnerships, limited partnerships, and limited liability companies. Essential characteristics of these four forms of business organization are summarized in Table 42.2.

Kinds of Corporations

Corporations may be classified in several ways. They may be seen as (1) corporations organized for public or private purposes, (2) corporations organized for profit or not for profit, (3) publicly or privately held corporations, and (4) domestic or foreign corporations. However, such classifications should not be thought of as mutually exclusive. For example, a corporation may be at the same time private, for profit, publicly held, and domestic.

Corporations Organized for Public or Private Purposes. A **public corporation** is created by state legislature or by Congress for governmental purposes. Clearly, an incorporated city or town, generally referred to as a municipal corporation, is a public corporation. States also create other kinds of public corporations, such as hospitals for the mentally ill, state bar associations, sanitation services, irrigation districts, and government-owned utilities.

From time to time the U.S. Congress creates corporations to satisfy some public need. For instance, in 1846 it created the Smithsonian Institution as a public corporation. In 1933 Congress incorporated the Tennessee Valley Authority to develop that area. More recently Congress created as corporate entities the United States

Table 42.1 Outstanding Common Stock Issued by Large American Corporations

Company	Outstanding Shares	As of
International Business Machines	769,000	Mar. 1992
General Motors	910,000	Dec. 1991
General Electric	480,525	June 1992
Exxon Corporation	690,000	June 1992
American Telephone & Telegraph	2,366,997	Oct. 1992

Table 42.2 Characteristics of Corporations, General Partnerships, Limited Partnerships, and Limited Liability Companies

Organizational Characteristic	Corporation	General Partnership	Limited Partnership	Limited Liability Company (LLC)
Entity	A separate legal entity and taxed as such.	Not a legal entity but has certain characteristics of one; consists of two or more partners who share equally in profits unless otherwise agreed.	Has many characteristics of a legal entity; partnership income belongs to its members in agreed percentages. Has two classes of partners: general and limited.	Has many characteristics of a legal entity—most notably, limited liability of *all* its members.
Creation	Created by the state upon application in required legal form; creation evidenced by charter or articles of incorporation.	Created by formal or informal agreement of its members; no state action involved.	Created by filing certificate of limited partnership with the state; also has, but not filed, an informal or formal limited partnership agreement.	Created by the state upon filing articles of organization, and compliance with IRS Revenue Procedure 89-12 to be taxed like a partnership.
Duration	Perpetual corporate life unless limited by articles of incorporation or bylaw, but life may be terminated by state or by shareholders as provided by law.	Life limited to term set by partnership agreement but is dissolved before expiration of term if for any reason partners cease to be associated in business together (e.g., death).	For the time or purpose specified in agreement, but may be dissolved earlier as specified therein.	Duration is limited by state statute—most commonly to less that 35 years; but term can be extended by unanimous written consent of members if statute and articles so provide.
Purposes and powers	Limited as stated in articles and state law; under Revised Model Act may engage in any lawful business with same powers as an individual.	To carry on any legal business agreed to by partners, generally state approval not necessary.	To carry on business specified in certificate and in agreement.	To carry on any lawful business; especially suited for real estate and oil and gas development because of the limited liability of *all* members.

Table 42.2 (continued)

Ownership	By shareholders evidenced by shares of stock held.	By individual partners in proportions agreed.	By general and limited partners as specified.	By individual members in the proportions agreed. Issuance of shares of stock not involved.
Transfer of ownership	Shares normally transferred at will of shareholder; consent of corporation or other shareholders not necessary.	Partnership interest may be transferred at will of partner but assignee does not become a partner unless all partners agree; transfer of entire interest dissolves partnership.	General partner may transfer interest with effect specified in agreement. Limited partner may transfer all or part of interest at any time; assignee becomes a limited partner only as specified in agreement.	Members may transfer all or part of interest at any time, but statutes permit transferee to participate in management only after obtaining unanimous consent of all members.
Liability of owners	Shareholder has no personal liability for corporate obligations; only risk is loss of investment.	All partners personally liable for partnership obligations; liability not limited to investment in partnership.	General partner has all the liability of a partner in a general partnership. Limited partner generally has no personal liability for partnership obligations.	As in a corporation, *all* members have liability limited to the amount of their investment and their capital commitments.
Management	By board of directors and officers acting under it; shareholder is generally limited to voting in election of directors and on amendments to articles and certain extraordinary matters.	All partners have right to manage the business; each is the agent of partnership and of his or her copartners.	General partners manage the business; limited partners have only a limited right to assist management or to vote on changes of partnership organization.	Management is vested in LLC members in relation to their respective pro rata capital contributions; members can participate in management without jeopardizing their limited liability.

Postal Service, Comstat (to build a communications satellite system), and Amtrak (to operate a passenger railroad service).

A **private corporation** is one that is organized by private individuals for private purposes, usually to earn profits, but it may also be organized for nonprofit purposes.

Corporations for Profit or Not for Profit. Most corporations are **for profit.** They are organized with the intent (1) to engage in a business which earns a profit, and (2) to distribute to the shareholders, as dividends, as much of that profit as the board decides. With increasing frequency, private corporations for profit are widely regulated by state and federal laws in areas such as issuance and sale of corporate securities, environmental control, and monopolistic practices. These laws and regulations are discussed in detail in later chapters.

State statutes prescribe how **nonprofit** corporations may be organized. There is a Model Nonprofit Corporation Act which some states have used as a guide in drafting the appropriate legislation. Like a corporation for profit, a nonprofit corporation is managed by officers who carry out policies laid down by the board of directors, but normally the nonprofit corporation has **members** instead of shareholders. Many state laws direct that an individual may hold no more than one membership in a nonprofit corporation.

Under the Internal Revenue Code, nonprofit corporations are generally tax-exempt when they use their income in charitable, religious, educational, or fraternal activities. Such favorable tax laws have encouraged formation of hundreds of nonprofit corporations. The term **nonprofit corporation** means only that this type of corporation, which may be very profitable, does not *distribute* its profits in the same manner as do ordinary for-profit corporations. Instead of being distributed to the members, profits are spent to further the corporation's stated purposes and its assets can be distributed to its members only when the corporation is dissolved. However, in order to retain their tax-exempt status, nonprofit **charitable** corporations, such as missions for the homeless, must provide in their charter that assets upon dissolution will be distributed to another charitable tax-exempt corporation, and not to the members. Larger nonprofit corporations are often organized as **foundations,** such as the Ford and Rockefeller foundations. They often receive huge blocks of business corporation stock as gifts. For example, Howard Hughes donated all the shares of Hughes Aircraft Corporation to Hughes Medical Foundation. After his death, the foundation sold those shares to General Motors Corporation for $5 billion, receiving an additional windfall that is typical for nonprofit charitable corporations: No tax is paid on the capital gain realized from such sales.

Publicly Held or Closely Held Corporations. A **publicly held corporation** (also called a **publicly traded corporation**) is one in which a large number of people own the shares and trade them on the New York or American stock exchanges or on the over-the-counter market, called NASDAQ (National Association of Securities Dealers Automated Quotations), whose share price quotes are regularly published. Shares of hundreds of companies are regularly listed and sold on these exchanges.

Publicly held corporations are vastly outnumbered by the multitude of small businesses whose shares are owned by a single individual, by family members, or by only a few people. These corporations are called **close corporations,** or **closely held corporations,** or **closed corporations.** In virtually all these small corporations, the shareholders do not intend to be mere passive investors, as are the shareholders in publicly held corporations. Working alone or with a few close associates, they seek primarily to establish a business in which (1) they have personal control of the corporation's policies, (2) they can have pension and tax benefits available through the corporation, and (3) they can obtain the benefit of limited liability so that their personal assets are not at risk if the business fails.

Many characteristics of sole proprietorship or a partnership are to be found in a close corporation. Typically:

- It has relatively few shareholders.
- Most or all of its shareholders participate in the management of the company.
- Its shares are not listed or traded on any stock or over-the-counter market.
- There may be company-imposed restrictions on the transfer of shares and on the admission of new shareholders.

Although the Revised Model Act is written in sufficiently broad language to accommodate both publicly held and closely held corporations, a number of states still have no special statutes for the latter. However, a body of case law has arisen which specifically responds to the needs of closely held corporations. In 1982 the American Bar Association published a Close Corporation Supplement to the Model Business Corporation Act which is designed to be integrated with the Revised Model Act. Many states have adopted the Close Corporation Supplement or have enacted laws similar to it. These are discussed in Chapter 44.

S Corporations. Stockholders of a firm that qualifies under Subchapter S of the Internal Revenue Code can, by unanimous vote, elect to become an **S corporation.** It is then treated as a partnership for federal income tax purposes without losing the advantages of a corporation. The corporation's net income is pro-rated to the stockholders, who then pay personal income taxes on their respective shares of such profits, regardless of whether the profits are actually received. Thus, corporations with thirty-five or fewer stockholders (counting a husband and wife as a single shareholder) can avoid the burden of being taxed twice on the same dollar—once when the corporation earns it and again when it is distributed to the shareholder as dividends. The qualifications of an S corporation are set out in Table 42.3.

An additional advantage to shareholders is that they can offset the losses of an S corporation against other personal income. For example, if Beth has a pro rata S corporation loss of $3,000, she can deduct it from her $25,000-a-year salary and pay her yearly income tax only on the remaining net of $22,000. However, a major drawback of an S corporation is that, even though it can tax-deduct the cost of fringe benefits (e.g., health insurance) for the corporation's employees, shareholders who own more than 2 percent of the corporation's stock *must declare the value of those benefits as income and pay personal income tax on that value each year.* An even more serious disadvantage: Federal tax authorities interpret qualifying standards for an S corporation so strictly that shareholders often are dismayed to learn that their firm has not qualified as an S corporation and is therefore subject to corporate income taxes. In contrast, a limited liability company (LLC), discussed in Chapter 41, does not appear to have the same difficulty qualifying for favorable partnership-like tax treatment, yet all members enjoy limited liability.

Professional Corporations. Several decades ago accountants, lawyers, doctors, and other professionals joined in an outcry for state legislation

Table 42.3 Qualifications of an S Corporation

Corporation Must	Corporation Must *Not*
Be a domestic corporation with no shareholders who are nonresident aliens	Be an affiliate in a group of corporations
Have shareholders who are individuals, decedents' estates, or qualifying trusts	Have any shareholders who are corporations, partnerships, or non-qualifying trusts
Have only one class of stock, although voting rights may vary	Have more than thirty-five shareholders

permitting them to incorporate. Their chief objective was to obtain for themselves the same tax benefits that IRS regulations gave to other kinds of corporations. These benefits included tax-deductible life and health insurance programs as well as retirement pension plans. Most states responded to this demand by adopting enabling acts permitting professional persons to incorporate. Today, it is commonplace to read on professional office doors "Jane Jones, M.D., a Professional Corporation," or "Joe Doakes, a Law Corporation." Most state statutes provide that members of professional corporations continue to be personally liable for professional acts they perform. Thus, shareholders of professional corporations, unlike other shareholders, do not have liability limited to their capital investment.

Domestic or Foreign Corporations. A corporation is described as **domestic** within the state of its incorporation, regardless of the residence of its shareholders. In other states where it may be doing business it is referred to as a foreign corporation. Thus, if X-Cel, Inc., is chartered in Idaho but does business in Texas by having a sales office there, it is a domestic corporation in Idaho but is treated as a foreign corporation in Texas. X-Cel's charter authorizes it to do business in Idaho, but it cannot grant privileges or the right to do business in another state (called a **host state**) without that state's permission.

Each state where a foreign corporation proposes to do business requires it to qualify by obtaining from the secretary of state a **certificate of authority** [RMA 15.01(a)]. Until the certificate is obtained, a foreign corporation may not file lawsuits in the host state's courts and it may also be liable for civil penalties. In addition, a foreign corporation may have its certificate of authority revoked if it fails to maintain a registered agent and office, or to file an annual report within 60 days after the due date, or to pay franchise taxes.

The Supreme Court has developed a large body of case law to decide a crucial question: What is "doing business" within a state? In *International Shoe Co. v. State of Washington*,[3] the Court extended state jurisdiction over a foreign corporation whenever the corporation maintained certain **minimum contacts** within the host state and received **benefits and protection** from that state. For example, maintaining a warehouse or sales office in a state is enough contact to require a foreign corporation to qualify to do business. In other situations where corporate contacts are negligible, for example, Ford's shipping automobiles from Michigan to a dealer in Idaho, the Court has held that the foreign corporation is not doing business within the state, but is simply exercising its right to engage in interstate commerce.

FORMATION OF CORPORATIONS

Three steps are involved in the formation of a corporation: (1) engaging in preincorporation activities, (2) filing the articles of incorporation, and (3) holding the organizational meeting.

Preincorporation Activities

A business corporation originates as an idea. Preincorporation activities transform that idea into a reality. The individual who carries on these activities is called a **promoter.** Although there have been dishonest promoters, in corporation law a promoter performs the legitimate and necessary function of organizing the corporation. An individual (often an incorporator), a partnership, another corporation, or some other entity may be a promoter of a new corporation.

Fred, an engineer with limited finances, has just patented a superconductor manufacturing process. He wants to incorporate and use the patent to manufacture electric motors. He knows that capital of $1 million must be raised by selling stock. Fred is thinking about retaining a promoter to start the enterprise. If hiring a promoter is too costly, Fred may call upon a friend, or decide to be the promoter himself. The promoter might perform any or all of the duties shown in Table 42.4.

[3] 326 U.S. 310 (1945).

Table 42.4 Functions of a Corporate Promoter

1. Verifies economic feasibility of the enterprise and its proposed project
2. Brings together incorporators who will sign the certificate of incorporation
3. Finds subscribers who agree to buy the new corporation's shares of stock
4. Arranges for necessary financing and may be required to:
   - Contract for factory space, manufacturing equipment, and materials necessary to commence production
   - Recruit people as officers and key employees of the firm

Liability for Preincorporation Contracts. After the new corporation is organized, one of its first problems is to decide what to do about preincorporation contracts which the promoter may have entered into but which have not been fully performed. The promoter or the corporation after it comes into existence, or both, may be liable for contracts that the promoter made on behalf of the corporation before it was chartered.

Promoter's liability for preincorporation contracts. If a promoter promises personally to pay for goods or services that will benefit a future corporation, the promoter is, of course, liable. But even when the promoter makes no such promise, if the newly formed corporation does not pay for the goods or services, the promoter must pay for them (RMA 2.04). The logic is simple. At the time a third-party contract is entered into, the promoter is purporting to act for a principal, even though that principal—the corporation—is not yet in existence. It is basic agency law that one who acts for a nonexistent principal is personally liable on the contract. Of course, the promoter and third-party supplier may agree that only the proposed corporation will be bound by the contract. However, suppliers will seldom risk such a contingency.

The next case involves the liability of a promoter who made a contract on behalf of a corporation before it had been formed.

CASE 42.1   **Ratner v. Central National Bank of Miami**
- 414 S.2d 210 (Fla. App. 1982)

FACTS   Joel Ratner was the promoter of Stereo Corner, Inc. He signed a merchant's Mastercharge agreement with Central National Bank of Miami: "The Stereo Corner, Inc., by Joel Ratner." Stereo Corner was not incorporated by Ratner, its promoter, until 8 months later, although it did business in the interim. Both before and after Stereo Corner was incorporated, one of its employees forged a series of sales drafts (Mastercharge customer vouchers) which were deposited and credited to Stereo Corner's account. The Mastercharge agreement provided that the company warranted each sales draft and agreed to be liable for any that were improperly or fraudulently executed. When the bank was unable to collect on the forged vouchers, it charged Stereo the amounts due. Stereo became insolvent and the bank sued Ratner, claiming that he was individually liable on the Mastercharge agreement. Ratner claimed that the bank intended to contract with Stereo Corner as a corporate entity and not with him individually. He also claimed that Stereo Corner ratified the agreement, thereby making it its own. After judgment was entered for the bank, Ratner appealed.

OPINION   FERGUSON, J. . . . The Florida law and general rule is that the promoter of a corporation is liable on his contract although the contract was made on behalf of

> **CASE 42.1**
> **Continued**
>
> the corporation to be formed, unless the other party agrees to look to another fund for payment. . . . The later formation of the corporation and subsequent adoption or ratification of the contract by the corporation does not necessarily release a promoter from liability, but may result in joint liability of the promoter and corporation, absent a novation or express release by the other party to the contract. . . . Moreover, where the promoter does not make it clear that he is acting as a promoter and misrepresents—even if unintentionally—that the corporation is already in existence, thereby causing the other party to enter the contract without knowledge that the entity has not yet been incorporated, the later formation of the corporation and subsequent ratification of the contract, will not by itself, relieve the promoter of liability.
>
> In this case . . . there is no evidence that Central [Bank] agreed to look solely to the corporation. . . .
>
> **JUDGMENT** Affirmed.

Corporate liability for preincorporation contracts. A newly formed corporation does not *automatically* become a party to a preincorporation contract made on its behalf by a promoter. The legal reasoning behind this is twofold: (1) The promoter, when engaging in the contract, could not act as the agent of the corporation because the corporation had not yet come into existence and it therefore could not have been a principal. (2) Once the corporation is organized, it is a legal entity separate from its promoter, with independent rights and duties. Accordingly, it is privileged to choose which of the preexisting contracts it will assume and which it will reject. However, some states require a corporation to adopt promoter's contracts made on its behalf.

A corporation adopts a preincorporation contract either expressly or impliedly. It **expressly adopts** it by passing a resolution to that effect at a directors' or shareholders' meeting. It **impliedly adopts** a preincorporation contract by accepting its benefits or by performing according to its terms. In either event, the promoter remains liable jointly on the contract unless the newly incorporated company and the creditor enter into a **novation.** Under such an agreement the creditor substitutes the corporation as contracting party in place of the promoter, who is then released.

Fiduciary Duty of Promoters. A promoter is not the agent of the corporation being formed nor is the promoter the agent of individuals brought into the venture. Nonetheless, the promoter owes a fiduciary duty to the future corporation, to the subscribers of its shares, and to its future shareholders. This fiduciary duty requires fair dealing, the utmost good faith, and a full disclosure of all material facts concerning transactions that have been made on behalf of the future corporation.

Typically, the duty of disclosure comes into play when the promoter's own property is proposed to be sold to the corporation or exchanged for shares of the corporation's stock. Suppose Ted, a promoter, owns land he wants to sell to the new corporation, either for cash or for stock. To make the sale or exchange legally, Ted must fully disclose all elements of the deal to the board of directors. However, if they are **dummy directors** who are completely under Ted's control, he must make the disclosure to all the *shareholders.* This procedure protects the new corporation from paying Ted an exorbitant price for his land. If Ted fails to make a disclosure, the corporation can rescind the deal or keep the land and recover any secret profit that Ted made.

Subscription to Shares of Stock. Unless a corporation is to be closely held, one of the promoter's duties is to recruit investors in the new enterprise. The promoter does this by securing from potential investors a **subscription**—that is, an offer to purchase shares of stock of the proposed company at an agreed price—payable at an agreed future time. Anyone who offers to purchase shares of stock in a future company is called a **subscriber.** How corporations, once formed, go about issuing shares is discussed in Chapter 43.

About this time a hand goes up in the class, and one of the alert students asks an incisive question: "The *big* idea is for the corporation to get stockholders lined up in advance, right? But the corporation is not yet formed—it doesn't exist yet, right?" Now the coup de grace: "Then how can the corporation, *after* it comes into existence, enforce the contract promise that a prospective stockholder made to it when it hadn't arrived in the world yet, when it was a total nonentity—a zero?"

After a sentence or two of filibustering to buy time while working on the answer, the professor comes up with a really good explanation: "A majority of courts look at the subscription agreement as *a continuing offer to purchase shares*—an offer that may be revoked by the subscribing offeror at any time before acceptance. As a practical matter, this means that the offer is dangling in midair until the corporation is formed and the directors finally get around to passing a resolution *accepting the offer*. If they do so, we then have an *offer and acceptance—a contract*—and both sides are legally bound."

A minority of courts regard a subscription as a *present, binding contract between subscribers* which is irrevocable unless all the subscribers consent to modify or revoke it. This contract between prospective shareholders is independent of the corporation to be formed in the future. Later on, when it is formed, the corporation can come along and take advantage of the subscription pledge, and even enforce it as a *third-party beneficiary.*

Finally, a compromise between these two attempts to define the very last moment a shareholder can revoke a subscription offer to buy stock is to be found in the Revised Model Act. It provides that a subscription for shares is irrevocable for 6 months unless otherwise provided in the agreement or unless all the subscribers consent to the revocation [RMA 6.20 (a)].

There is conflict also as to what constitutes acceptance of a preincorporation share subscription. The majority view is that completion of the incorporation process amounts to an automatic acceptance of the subscriber's offer. The minority view is that the corporation must perform some act of acceptance, such as listing the subscriber as a shareholder in the corporation records.

A subscription agreement obligates the subscriber to pay cash at the time stated in the agreement or, if no time is stated, at such time as is fixed by the board of directors. If the subscriber defaults on a payment, the corporation may proceed to collect the amount due in the same manner it collects other debts. If the subscription is payable in installments, the subscriber is not a shareholder until the full amount is paid.

Creating the Corporation

The kinds of questions that must be answered and decisions that must be made in forming a corporation depend upon its size and complexity. All corporations, however, face certain key issues.

Selection of State of Incorporation. If a corporation is to operate chiefly within one state, the firm normally is incorporated in that state. But because corporations may operate in a number of states, and a great many do, important factors must be taken into account in selecting the state of incorporation. The selection might depend on the relative flexibility and freedom from restrictions offered by the corporation statutes, or the relative severity of state taxes and fees on corporations. States vary greatly in the organization fees, franchise taxes, income taxes, and stock issuance and transfer taxes they impose. The corporation must also take into account the hurdles involved in qualifying to do business in each state or foreign jurisdiction where it will operate. Finally, it is desirable to select a state, such as Delaware, with a sound body of court decisions that give its corporation law a clear meaning.

Preparation of Articles of Incorporation. Incorporation requirements differ from state to state, but the first step always is to draft and file the **articles of incorporation.** The promoter prepares or has a lawyer prepare the articles. They may be likened to a self-imposed constitution. The articles, together with the applicable statutes of the state of incorporation, provide the legal framework within which the corporation must operate. The trend of states toward simplicity is illustrated by the articles of incorporation in Table 42.5, which meet the minimum statutory requirements of California as well as the Revised Model Act (2.02). In addition, the articles may include other relevant corporate information, such as names and addresses of the individuals who are to serve as the initial directors, the purpose(s) for which the corporation is organized, and provisions regarding managing the business and regulating its affairs. In some states the articles must list powers that the corporation will use and its duration.

Corporate name. The corporation name must contain the word or the abbreviation for corporation (Corp.), incorporated (Inc.), company (Co.), or limited (Ltd.) (RMA 4.01). The name chosen must be distinguishable from the name of any domestic or foreign corporation authorized to transact business within the state. Care must be taken in the choice of name if it is expected that the corporation will transact business in states other than the state of its incorporation. In that case, the organizers should verify with each secretary of state that the name selected is not confusingly similar to the name of a corporation already doing business in that state. If the names are similar, a firm that previously has been using the name may ask a court to enjoin its use by the new corporation.

Incorporators. An incorporator's sole function is to sign the articles, usually before a notary public. The promoter may sign the articles as incorporator—or may be one of the incorporators if the state of incorporation requires more than one. Some states require three incorporators, but a majority of states require only one (RMA 2.01). Statutory qualifications of incorporators vary. A few states impose citizenship or residence, or require incorporators to subscribe for shares. Many states permit a domestic or foreign corporation to be an incorporator, and Delaware even extends the privilege to a partnership or association. As a general rule, an incorporator who takes no part in company management has no legal liability.

Registered office and agent. A corporation must have, within the state of incorporation, a registered office with a registered agent (RMA 5.01). That office is not necessarily the corporation's business office although frequently it is. The registered office and agent must be maintained so that there is always someone available upon whom legal process may be served and to which official state notices may be sent.

Filing articles of incorporation. The signed articles of incorporation together with the required filing fees are forwarded to the designated

Table 42.5 Articles of Incorporation of Hi-Tech, Inc.

I

The name of this corporation is HI-TECH, Inc.

II

The purpose of this corporation is to engage in any lawful act or activity for which a corporation may be organized under the General Corporation Law of California other than the banking business, trust company business, or practice of a profession permitted to be incorporated by the California Corporations Code.

III

The name and address in the State of California of this corporation's initial agent for service of process is:

Name: <u>John Smith</u>

Address: <u>1234 Main Street, Fresno, Cal.</u>

The corporation's initial place of business and registered office is at the above address.

IV

This corporation is authorized to issue only one class of shares of stock; and the total number of shares which this corporation is authorized to issue is 1,000.

John Smith, Incorporator

state official, usually the secretary of state. The articles are there reviewed and if for any reason they do not conform to state law or if the name selected is similar to a name already in use, the articles are returned to the sender. If the state officials determine that the articles of incorporation fully comply with statute, they are then officially **filed. Filing** technically means state approval of the articles as evidenced by some state action—it may be by the issuance of a formal certificate of incorporation, by affixing of an official stamp acknowledging the filing, or by the mere issuance of a dated receipt of the filing fee. Normally, a corporation's life begins when the articles are filed with the secretary of state. Some states require additional filing in specified counties. For example, Delaware requires a certified copy of the articles to be filed in the county where the corporation's registered office is located even though corporate existence commences when articles are filed with the secretary of state. A few states condition corporate existence upon completion of all supplemental filing requirements.

The Organizational Meeting: Agenda and Bylaws

Once the corporation has been chartered, if its board of directors had not been named in the articles of incorporation, the initial incorporator(s) elect members of the board and then resign. The directors then hold an organizational meeting to get the newly formed corporate entity under way (RMA 2.05). At this meeting, the board of directors acts on the agenda shown in Table 42.6.

Bylaws got their name from the fact that in early England a small village was called a **bye.** Bye laws were the laws of the bye, and the term, made into one word, has come down to us from that time. Corporate bylaws are rules for the conduct of the company's operations. They must

Table 42.6 Agenda of Hi-Tech, Inc., a Delaware Corporation

First Meeting of Board of Directors

1 Adopt bylaws which will govern the internal management of the corporation.
2 Elect officers—president, vice president, secretary, and treasurer—and fix salaries.
3 Transact other necessary business such as adopting a resolution authorizing lease of a factory building or rental of office space.
4 Adopt resolutions selecting corporation's bank, and designating officers authorized to draw checks.
5 Adopt or reject each preincorporation contract or promoter's commitment on behalf of firm.
6 Adopt form of certificate representing shares of the corporation's stock which will be issued to shareholders.
7 Adopt corporate seal to impress on corporate documents, deeds, and certified copies of corporate resolutions.
8 Adopt resolution directing treasurer to call and collect preincorporation subscriptions.

not be inconsistent with state law or with the articles of incorporation. They are, in effect, private laws which govern corporate internal affairs. Bylaws are binding upon directors, officers, and shareholders regardless of whether these corporate members have read them. However, *bylaws are not binding upon persons outside the corporation.* For example, the bylaws of XYZ, Inc., might provide that any purchase order over $500 must be approved by the company's treasurer. However, XYZ, Inc., must pay for any unapproved purchase amounting to $501 or more made by its purchasing agent if the seller had no knowledge of the bylaw limitation on the purchasing agent's authority. The next case illustrates the importance and function of bylaws.

CASE 42.2   Centaur Partners v. National Intergroup, Inc. • 582 A.2d 923 (Del. 1990)

FACTS At the 1984 annual meeting, National's stockholders had voted to amend Article Eighth of the corporate charter by (1) providing for a "classified" board divided into three groups, with only one group of directors elected each year to serve a 3-year term, and (2) providing that an affirmative vote of holders of 80 percent or more of the voting power of the shares outstanding be required to amend the provision *"or any similar provision"* in the bylaws of the corporation. The stockholders also adopted a parallel amendment to the bylaws with the same two provisions.

Centaur was an investment partnership that owned 16 percent of the outstanding shares of National Intergroup. Centaur wanted National to sell its assets and distribute the proceeds to the stockholders. Since National's existing board of directors was opposed to liquidating the corporation's assets, Centaur sought in 1990 to amend National's bylaws to enlarge the board from 9 to 15 members and then, at the annual meeting, run its slate of new directors pledged to liquidate the company's assets. Anticipating that the board of directors would oppose it, Centaur filed a declaratory relief action, asking the court to rule that at the forthcoming annual meeting, only 50.1 percent of the outstanding shares would be required to amend the bylaws. National argued that the bylaws required an 80 percent supermajority vote to change the number of directors. Centaur claimed that the "or any similar provision" language of Article Eighth was ambiguous and that, in the face of such ambiguity, majority vote must control. The trial court ruled that a supermajority 80 percent vote would be required to increase the board, and Centaur appealed.

OPINION WALSH, J. . . . Corporate charters and by-laws are contracts among the shareholders of a corporation and the general rules of contract interpretation are held to apply. In the interpretation of charter and by-law provisions, courts must give effect to the intent of the parties . . . and the circumstances surrounding their creation and adoption. Therefore, the intent of the stockholders in enacting particular charter or by-law amendments is instructive in determining whether any ambiguity exists.

. . . The proxy materials which were distributed to the stockholders prior to the 1984 annual meeting . . . state:

> The Board of Directors has unanimously adopted resolutions recommending that the stockholders amend the Corporation's Certificate of Incorporation and the Corporation's By-laws to provide for the division of the Corporation's directors into three classes, the directors in each class to serve for a term of three years. The proposed amendments also contain a provision which, if adopted, shall provide that the affirmative vote of the holders of 80% or more of the outstanding stock of the Corporation be required to amend or repeal these new provisions in the Certificate of Incorporation and the By-Laws.

This explanation illustrates the intended result of the proposed combined change in the charter and by-laws that the board be classified and that a supermajority vote of 80% or more be required to amend any portion of these two provisions. The classification of the board and the 80% supermajority vote are de-

**CASE 42.2
Continued**

signed to insure continuity in the board of directors and avoid hostile attempts to take over the corporation. As the proxy materials recite:

> A further purpose of the proposed change is to discourage unfriendly takeovers of the Corporation. The attempts to seize control of public companies through the accumulation of substantial stock positions followed by a tender offer and squeeze-out merger are well known today. These transactions are often followed by a substantial restructuring of the company, a significant disposition of assets or other extraordinary corporate action.

Given the clear language of the proxy materials, the conclusion is inescapable that the stockholders, in adopting these two provisions evidenced an intent to classify the board and impose an 80% supermajority requirement on amendments to these sections in order to thwart attempts to seize control of National.

JUDGMENT

We conclude that the Court of Chancery correctly determined that Article Eighth of National's charter was clear and unambiguous in requiring that an 80% supermajority would be needed to amend the by-laws of National, thereby overcoming the presumption of majority rule. Accordingly, we affirm the decision of the Court of Chancery.

LIABILITY OF CORPORATE MEMBERS

Shareholders' freedom from personal liability for corporate debts depends upon whether (1) it is a *bona fide* corporation—that is, whether it was formed in compliance with state incorporation statutes, and (2) whether the doctrine of **piercing the corporate veil** (discussed later in this chapter) applies so that a court can go behind the corporation and hold the owners liable.

If a corporation is organized in full compliance with state law, its "corporateness" is impregnable. Its shareholders are not liable for corporate debts (RMA 6.22) except in unusual cases involving piercing the corporate veil. What happens if the corporation is *not* organized in strict compliance with the state incorporation statute?

A *defective* corporation is open to attack on all sides. Creditors may contend that the business does not exist as a corporation and that its shareholders are, in effect, partners with unlimited personal liability for the debts of the enterprise. Debtors who are sued by a defective corporation may challenge its capacity to contract or to sue. Subscribers to the corporation's shares may seek to escape liability on their subscription contracts by asserting that the proposed corporation never came into existence. The corporation itself may deny its own "corporateness" in order to avoid liability to creditors. Lastly, the state may cite failure to comply with statutory requirements for incorporation as the basis for a court order requiring the corporation to forfeit its charter or to cease operations.

RMA 2.03(b) and many state statutes now provide that the secretary of state's *filing of the articles of incorporation* is conclusive proof that the incorporators satisfied all conditions necessary to incorporate. Accordingly, in states where that rule applies, once articles of incorporation are filed in the office of the secretary of state, the question of corporate existence should seldom arise. However, in states that do not follow the Revised Model Act, courts continue to recognize corporate existence in three distinct situations: de jure corporations, de facto corporations, and corporations by estoppel.

De Jure Corporation

A **de jure corporation** is one organized in compliance with state laws. It is a legal fortress which shields its shareholders from personal liability for corporate obligations. In states following the Revised Model Act, a de jure corporation is formed upon the filing of its articles of incorporation. In states not following the RMA, the conditions shown in Table 42.7 must be met in order to establish a de jure corporation. In varying degrees, courts adopt the view that a minor defect in complying with the enabling statute should not defeat or diminish the limited liability of shareholders. Some courts hold that all the provisions of the incorporation statute are *mandatory* and must be strictly complied with in all particulars in order to establish a de jure corporation. Others take a more liberal view and consider some of the statutory requirements to be *directory*, meaning that only *substantial compliance* is necessary. Whether the incorporation effort in a particular case constitutes substantial compliance is a question that the courts decide on a case-by-case basis, the answer depending upon individual circumstances. For instance, articles of incorporation must be signed and the address of the individual who signs must be stated. The signing of the articles is a mandatory requirement which must be strictly complied with. If a signature is lacking, a de jure corporation is not formed. On the other hand, a court might hold that if the only claimed defect is a wrong address, there has been substantial compliance with the statute (since some address is given).

De Facto Corporation

Sometimes organizers fall short of substantially complying with the mandatory requirements of the corporation enabling statute. For example, they might fail to publish the articles of incorporation in the county where the corporation commences to do business, as required by some state statutes. Although a de jure corporation has not been formed, it is still probable that courts will recognize the validity of its existence as a **de facto corporation** if the three requirements shown in Table 42.7 are met.

Courts often utilize the de facto doctrine to protect innocent shareholders from creditors' attempts to hold them personally liable for the corporate debts. In the typical situation, a zealous creditor has searched the statehouse records for a technical defect in the incorporation process in order to claim that the shareholders are really partners with unlimited liability. Since, at the time of extending credit, the creditors were advised that they were dealing with *a corporation*, they should not later be allowed to recover from shareholders on the theory that they are partners. To permit such recovery would give creditors a windfall they had never bargained for. In addition, courts reason that injustice should not result from honest mistakes or omissions. In states that have adopted and strictly follow the Revised Model Act, there can

Table 42.7 Requirements for Recognition as a Corporation (in Non-RMA States)

De Jure Corporation	De Facto Corporation
A constitutionally valid enabling statute under which a corporation can be formed (all states meet this requirement)	A state statute under which the organizers could have validly incorporated (all states have such statutes)
Substantial compliance with the statutory requirements	A *good faith* attempt by the organizers to comply with the mandatory requirements of the statute—even if the attempt falls short of compliance
	Corporate user status—that is, the organizers commenced to do business as a corporation and held themselves out to the world as a corporation

be no de facto corporation—a corporation is either de jure or no corporation at all. For example, in *Bowers Building Co. v. Altura Glass Co.*,[4] a general contractor sued his subcontractor for breach of contract to install windows. The subcontractor's president argued that he was insulated from personal liability because he had mailed the articles of incorporation to the secretary of state on the same day that he signed the contract on behalf of his "corporation." However, the secretary of state did not issue the certificate of incorporation until 4 days later. The court denied corporate existence and held the "president" personally liable, stating:

Under the Model Act a corporation comes into existence only when the certificate of incorporation has been issued and, until issuance of the certificate, there is no corporation de jure [or] de facto. . . .

In states that do not follow the Revised Model Act but do recognize de facto corporations, once the existence of a de facto corporation has been established, no one, including creditors, can challenge its legal existence. Of course, the *state* always has the power to challenge a corporation's right to exist and often does so by initiating a *quo warranto* proceeding, which literally asks the corporation: "By what authority are you doing business?" However, it is improbable that the state would attempt to take the life of a de facto corporation unless it is no longer carrying out the purpose stated in its charter, or is engaging in criminal activity.

Corporation by Estoppel

Under certain circumstances a party in a lawsuit is estopped (prevented) from claiming that a corporation does not exist as a legal entity even though the purported corporation does not meet the de jure or de facto tests. A **corporation by estoppel** is said to exist where, for example, (1) an improperly organized corporation attempts to escape contractual liability by denying its own corporateness, or (2) a person contracting with such a corporation tries to avoid liability by claiming that the corporation does not legally exist. There are three elements of a corporation by estoppel:

1. A representation by an enterprise that it is a corporation
2. A reasonable reliance on that representation by another party (usually a creditor) resulting in damage
3. Fair and equitable conduct by the party asserting the estoppel

Suppose the ABC Company, a defectively formed corporation, buys in the corporate name a boat from Smith but fails to pay for it. When Smith sues ABC, it denies liability, claiming that it is not a corporation. The court will not allow ABC to escape responsibility for its legitimate debts by denying its corporate existence.

The essential difference between a de facto corporation and a corporation by estoppel is this: A court's finding that a firm is a de facto corporation is binding upon everyone (except the state) who does business with it; but a finding that a corporation by estoppel exists affects only the parties to that suit.

Liability of Members of Firm Improperly Labeled a Corporation

A corporate legal entity does not exist (1) when an incorporation effort is so defective that neither a de jure nor a de facto corporation is established or (2) when the business associates operate as a corporation without any intention of complying with the incorporation statutes. In either of these situations, and if corporation by estoppel does not apply, the supposed corporation form under which the association is doing business does not shield its members against personal liability from third-party claims arising out of transactions with the association. Most courts will subject each member of the purported corporation to personal liability as though the enterprise were a general partnership and all its "shareholders" were partners within it. Other courts will impose partnership liability only on those who *actively* engage in the promotion or management of the business and will limit the liability of the *inactive* members to their capital investments.

---

[4] 694 P.2d 876 (Col. App. 1984).

Disregarding Corporateness—Piercing the Corporate Veil

Having seen how quickly courts apply the de facto doctrine to declare defectively formed corporations legal when justice demands it, let us now look at the other side of the coin. Courts just as quickly will refuse to recognize a *perfectly formed* corporation and will disregard the corporate entity in order to expose to view the fraud and unfair conduct of the owners who are hiding behind the corporate shell. When an equity court thus ignores the separateness of the corporation from its shareholders, it is said to be **piercing the corporate veil** in order to hold the owners personally liable for using the corporate entity to perpetrate fraud, promote injustice, evade a statute, avoid a contract obligation, or otherwise engage in unfair wrongdoing or sharp practice. In such situations the courts ignore the cries of the shareholders that corporation law shields them from liability.

Disregard of Close Corporation Entity; Alter Ego Doctrine. Equity courts have often pierced the veil of corporations that consist of a single person or a few family members. The resulting case law has developed the **alter ego doctrine,** which is applied when two requirements are met:

1 There is such a *unity of interest* between the personal and corporate actions of the dominant shareholder that corporate activities cannot be distinguished from personal activities. The corporation is literally the alter ego, the "other self" of the dominant shareholder, so that separateness does not exist. The following facts tend to show unity of interest and lack of separateness between personal and corporate affairs:
   - The corporation is inadequately capitalized to meet the reasonably anticipated needs of the business.
   - The assets of the corporation and of a shareholder are commingled, no adequate record is kept to distinguish between the two, and corporate funds are used for the payment of private debts or for other private purposes.
   - No minutes book or other record of corporate activities is kept, there is no annual election of directors or appointment of officers,[5] and other corporate formalities are ignored.
   - The shareholder uses the corporation as an instrument to engage in economic ventures without risk, taking personal advantage of the gains which accrue and leaving to the corporation the payment of debts incurred.
   - The corporation was established for a sham purpose.

2 *Fraud* or *injustice* would be promoted if the corporation were used as a shield to protect the shareholder(s) from liability.

In short, if the corporation is merely an alter ego or facade to hide the wrongful conduct of the dominant shareholders, creditors will be permitted to hold them liable for the debts and torts of the business. The alter ego doctrine may also be applied in reverse: Not only can the shareholder be held liable for the corporation's debts and torts, but in certain instances the corporation can be held liable for the shareholder's debts and torts. In the next case, a shareholder used his corporation to avoid a contract.

---

[5] The Close Corporation Supplement and statutes of a number of states that have not adopted the supplement are an exception. For example, the California close corporation law provides that shareholders of a close corporation may agree to manage it like a partnership, and that failure to observe corporate formalities relating to directors' and shareholders' meetings "shall not be considered a factor tending to establish that the shareholders have personal liability for corporate obligations."

CASE 42.3	**United Elec. Contractors, Inc. v. Prog. Builders, Inc.** • 603 A.2d 1190 (Conn. App. 1992)
FACTS	Plaintiff United Electrical Contractors, Inc. (United), under a contract with Progress Builders, Inc. (Progress), did all electrical work on a home being built on land owned by Edgecliffe Corporation. K. Mahler was president, director, and stockholder of both Progress and Edgecliffe. To put the house and lot beyond reach of United, Mahler caused Edgecliffe to deed the property to his wife, Jane. When Progress refused to pay for the work, United sued Progress and Edgecliffe, and also asked the court to pierce their veils and hold the Mahlers liable as sole stockholders. The trial court entered judgment against Progress and Edgecliffe, but it refused to pierce their veils to hold the Mahlers liable. United appealed.
OPINION	NORCOTT, J. . . . When the statutory privilege of doing business in the corporate form is employed as a cloak for the evasion of obligations, as a mask behind which to do injustice, or invoked to subvert equity, the separate personality of the corporation will be disregarded. . . . Under Connecticut law, the corporate veil may be pierced under either the "instrumentality" or "identity" rules. Under the instrumentality rule, in any case but that of express agency, proof of three elements is required: (1) Control, not mere majority or complete stock control, but complete domination, not only of finances but of policy and business practice in respect to the transaction attacked so that the corporate entity as to this transaction had at the time no separate mind, will, or existence of its own; (2) that such control must have been used by the defendant to commit fraud or wrong, to perpetrate the violation of a statutory or other positive legal duty, or dishonest or unjust act in contravention of plaintiff's legal rights; and (3) that the aforesaid control and breach of duty must proximately cause the injury or unjust loss complained of. Under the "identity" rule, the corporate veil may be pierced when the plaintiff shows such a unity of interest and ownership that the independence of the corporation had in effect ceased or had never begun and that an adherence to the fiction of separate identity would serve only to defeat justice and equity by permitting the economic entity to escape liability arising out of an operation conducted by one corporation for the benefit of the whole enterprise. A key factor in determining whether the corporate shield should be disregarded is the degree of control or influence exercised over the corporation by the individual sought to be held liable. The identity rule primarily applies to prevent injustice in the situation where two corporate entities are, in reality, controlled as one enterprise because of the existence of common owners, officers, directors, or shareholders and because of the lack of observance of corporate formalities between the two entities. Here . . . the record clearly discloses that Mahler did control the business affairs of both Progress and Edgecliffe with respect to the debt Progress owed the plaintiff and Edgecliffe's transfer of the lot to Jane Mahler. Neither corporation had a separate mind, will or existence of its own. They shared the same officers, directors and shareholders, and conducted joint meetings at which no minutes were taken and only Keith Mahler was present. It is also clear from the record

CASE 42.3 Continued	that he used these corporations as intermediaries in breaching his duty to the plaintiff, thereby proximately causing its injury. In light of these facts, it is manifest that the trial court should have pierced the corporate veils of Progress and Edgecliffe under either the "instrumentality" or "identity" rule.
JUDGMENT	[The judgment of the trial court that the corporate veils of Progress and Edgecliffe should not be pierced was reversed.]

Parent-Subsidiary Corporations. By applying the alter ego doctrine, courts may pierce the corporate veil of a wholly owned subsidiary and impose on its more affluent parent corporation liability for the subsidiary's obligations if there is:

1. Unity of interest and ownership between the parent and its subsidiary. The key words here are *agency*, *identity*, and *instrumentality*, which means that the parent is using the subsidiary as an *agent*; there is such a unity of interest that the parent and subsidiary have virtually the same *identity*; or the parent is using the subsidiary as its *instrumentality*.

2. Use of the subsidiary to promote fraud, sharp practice, unfair advantage or illegality, or to evade a statute or contractual obligation; or inadequate capitalization of the subsidiary to meet its normally anticipated business needs.

In the following case, the court's opinion lists in points (a) through (i) the factors that are weighed to determine if the subsidiary is an agent or instrumentality of the parent, or is so nearly identical with the parent that it is not a separate entity.

CASE 42.4	**Glanzer v. St. Joseph Indian School** • 438 N.W.2d (S.D. 1989)
FACTS	The Glanzers made and sold fishing tackle out of their home. In June 1984, Dehon Industries, Inc. (Dehon), and the Glanzers formed a limited partnership, Glanzer Tackle Company, with Dehon as general partner and the Glanzers as limited partners. Dehon was to pay $30,000 cash into the partnership, provide accounting services, furnish space, and pay utilities for a year. For transferring the business to the partnership, the Glanzers were to be paid $20,000—$10,000 in cash immediately, and the remaining $10,000 in a year—but Dehon never paid it. Although Alan Glanzer was to be employed in the business for 3 years, Dehon terminated him after 13 months. Glanzer sued Dehon Industries, Inc., and also St. Joseph Indian School, a nonprofit corporation, on the theory that Dehon Industries, Inc., was at all times acting as agent for, and an instrumentality of, St. Joseph as parent corporation. The jury verdict was against Dehon, but the trial judge granted summary judgment dismissing St. Joseph from the case. The Glanzers appealed.
OPINION	TIMM, C.J. . . . A parent corporation is liable for the acts of its subsidiary under the instrumentality exception when (1) the parent controls the subsidiary to such a degree as to render the latter the mere instrumentality of the former, and (2) adherence to the rule of corporate separateness would produce injustice and

**CASE 42.4
Continued**

inequities. Similarly, a parent corporation is liable for acts of its subsidiary if an agency relation exists.

Under the first leg of the instrumentality exception, a number of factors have been identified which indicate the degree of control necessary to hold the parent liable: (a) The parent corporation owns all or most of the capital stock of the subsidiary. (b) The parent and subsidiary corporation have common directors or officers. (c) The parent corporation finances the subsidiary. (d) The parent corporation subscribes to all the capital stock of the subsidiary or otherwise causes its incorporation. (e) The subsidiary has grossly inadequate capital. (f) The parent corporation pays the salaries and other expenses or losses of the subsidiary. (g) The subsidiary has substantially no business except with the parent corporation or no assets except those conveyed to it by the parent corporation. In the papers of the parent corporation or in the statements of its officers, the subsidiary is described as a department or division of the parent corporation, or its business or financial responsibility is referred to as the parent corporation's own. (i) The parent corporation uses the property of the subsidiary as its own. (j) The directors or executive of the subsidiary do not act independently in the interest of the subsidiary but take their orders from the parent corporation in the latter's interest. (k) The formal legal requirements of the subsidiary are not observed. . . . The second leg of the instrumentality exception is established where the wrong alleged is a result of fraudulent, unjust, or illegal acts.

Liability on the agency theory is established if the following factual elements are present: (1) manifestation by the principal that the agent shall act for him; (2) the agent's acceptance of the undertaking; and (3) the understanding of the parties that the principal is to be in control of the undertaking.

With these theories in mind we turn to the facts presented by St. Joseph's to the trial court. . . . Father Cassidy was superintendent of St. Joseph's . . . and president of the board of directors of Dehon; . . . employees of St. Joseph were currently serving as directors and officers of Dehon. . . . Father Westhoven was Director of Development of St. Joseph's and Treasurer of the Board of Directors of Dehon. . . . Cy Maus was Senior Executive Officer for Development at St. Joseph's . . . and Secretary of the Board of Directors of Dehon. The manager of Glanzer Tackle Company was an employee of St. Joseph's, receiving compensation solely from St. Joseph's. Glanzer Tackle Company was located in the same building as St. Joseph. . . . Dehon was incorporated to develop Indian-oriented business ventures. . . . Cy Maus testified that the sole intent in creating Glanzer Tackle Company was to provide income, employment and business outlets for Indian people. . . . Glanzers were insured through St. Joseph's medical insurer. . . . Alan Glanzer's W-2 for 1984 listed St. Joseph's as his employer. Alan Glanzer was paid for work done for Glanzer Tackle Company by checks drawn on St. Joseph's account. . . . St. Joseph's in exchange for stock, capitalized Dehon. . . . Dehon used St. Joseph's stationery in transacting business. . . . The evidence before the trial court on St. Joseph's control of Dehon, Dehon's mismanagement of Glanzer Tackle Company, failure to meet financial obligations to Glanzers, and self-dealing raises questions of injustice and inequity were St. Joseph's not held liable for the acts of Dehon.

> **CASE 42.4 Continued**
>
> ... [Regarding the] Glanzers' agency theory ... the evidence demonstrates issues of material fact as to Dehon's status as an instrumentality or agent of St. Joseph's. ... St. Joseph's failed to shoulder its burden of presenting a prima facie case for summary judgment.
>
> **JUDGMENT** The trial court erred in granting summary judgment. On remand, the question of St. Joseph's liability as parent for acts of Dehon as agent or instrumentality must go to the jury.

Undercapitalized Corporations. Although a corporation's undercapitalization is not, in itself, sufficient to justify disregard of the corporate entity, it is a factor that a court may consider in deciding whether to pierce the corporate veil. If the corporation's capitalization is very small in relation to the proposed business it intends to carry on and to the risks that the business necessarily entails, a court may find that the corporation was organized and carried on its business with a capital investment far less than its shareholders should reasonably have anticipated as necessary to meet its obligations. Under such circumstances, a court may pierce the corporate veil to protect creditors.

TERMINATION OF CORPORATIONS

Under the Revised Model Act and in most states, a corporation loses its authority from the state to continue doing business as the result of a two-step process: (1) **dissolution,** followed by (2) a period of **winding up and liquidation** (RMA 14.05). Dissolution can be **voluntary** or **involuntary,** and can occur in a number of ways:

Voluntary Dissolution

1. By resolution of the directors and shareholders followed by filing articles of dissolution with the secretary of state (RMA 14.02)
2. In many states, by unanimous approval of the shareholders

Involuntary Dissolution

3. By court decree as the result of a *quo warranto* action by the attorney general of the state seeking forfeiture of the corporate charter because of *ultra vires* acts or other abuse of charter privileges
4. By court decree, pursuant to a suit by shareholders seeking dissolution because directors are deadlocked on policy issues, or are so hostile or opposed to one another that the corporation can no longer function as a going business
5. By action of the secretary of state in carrying out an **administrative dissolution** for nonfeasance or misfeasance of the corporation—e.g., nonpayment of annual franchise taxes (RMA 14.20–14.21).
6. By expiration of the period of its duration stated in its articles or certificate of incorporation

The common law view that a corporate dissolution, like a natural person's death, extinguished the corporation's existence has been replaced by the current view which the California Supreme Court recently summarized as follows:

Modern survival statutes provide that a dissolved corporation nevertheless continues to exist for the purpose of winding up its affairs, prosecuting and defending actions by or against it and enabling it to collect and discharge obligations, dispose of and convey its property, and collect and divide its assets, but not for the purpose of continuing business except so far as necessary for winding up thereof.[6]

The Revised Model Act requires a dissolved corporation to give notice in writing to *known* creditors, and to give notice by newspaper publication to *unknown* creditors. Five years after

---

[6]*Penasquitos v. Superior Court,* 812 P.2d 154 (Cal. 1991).

such publication, creditors who have not commenced suit against the dissolved corporation are barred from recovery (RMA 14.06–14.07).

Most states that have not adopted the Act use the **trust fund doctrine,** illustrated by the following case.

CASE 42.5 Carson v. Davidson • 808 P.2d 1377 (Kan. 1991)

FACTS Tuttle Creek Development, Inc. (TCD), was a Kansas close corporation in which Davidson and Martin were the sole officers, directors, and 50 percent stockholders. In 1983 TCD sold its only asset, a mobile home park, to William and Norma Carson (plaintiffs). In July 1984 the corporation's charter was revoked by the secretary of state of Kansas for failure to file a 1983 annual report. In July 1983, TCD filed for an Internal Revenue Code Sec. 337 liquidation. In 1986 the Carsons sued TCD, and officers Davidson and Martin, and obtained a judgment for breach of their contract with TCD. They attempted to levy execution on the corporate assets, and upon finding there were none, sued Davidson and Martin personally as former shareholders of the dissolved corporation. Davidson and Martin claimed they were not liable since the corporation was dissolved.

OPINION McFARLAND, J. . . . Where the assets of a dissolved corporation have been distributed among the stockholders, a creditor of the dissolved corporation may follow such assets as in the nature of a trust fund into the hands of stockholders. The creditors have the right to subject such assets to their debts, and for that purpose the stockholders hold them as though they were trustees. In other words, the assets of the dissolved corporation are a trust fund against which the corporate creditors have a claim superior to that of the stockholders. . . .

JUDGMENT [The supreme court set aside the trial court's summary judgment, and held that Davidson and Martin were liable to satisfy the judgment against the corporation to the extent of the assets they had received from it at the time of its dissolution.]

SUMMARY

The corporation for profit is the form of business organization used by most large and small firms. Many state corporation statutes follow the Revised Model Business Corporation Act. The chief characteristics of a business corporation are (1) its status as a legal entity, (2) its creation by the state with broad purposes, (3) its perpetual life, (4) centralization of management in a board of directors, (5) free transferability of shares of stock, and (6) limitation of liability to shareholders' capital investment. There are various kinds of corporations: public or private, for-profit or nonprofit, public or closely held, professional, domestic, foreign, and Subchapter S.

Promoters create many corporations, finding stock subscribers, drafting articles of incorporation, and securing the financing and personnel necessary to begin business. The promoter has a fiduciary duty to subscribers, shareholders, and the corporation itself.

A corporation is not automatically liable on a promoter's preincorporation contract made in the name of a future corporation. Even if a corporation adopts such a contract expressly or impliedly, the promoter is still liable to the creditor unless liability is waived. To incorporate under the Revised Model Act, a firm's organizers must submit signed *articles of incorporation* to the secretary of state. These must contain (1) a proposed corporate name different from names of other corporations, (2) a statement of powers and purposes, (3) description of number and kinds of shares of stock authorized to be issued, (4) name and address of original incorporator(s), (5) address of the corporation's registered office, and (6) name of its registered agent. If the articles are legally in order, the secretary of state issues a certificate of incorporation which begins the firm's existence as a corporation. Directors then hold an organizational meeting, adopt bylaws and a corporate seal, appoint officers, authorize stock issuance, and other needed steps. A de jure corporation fully complies with requirements of the incorporation statute; a de facto corporation is formed where there is a good faith attempt at such compliance and a corporate user; no one can attack it except the state. A corporation by estoppel is not de jure or de facto, but is recognized by the courts as a corporation in order to serve justice in a particular lawsuit.

Courts will disregard corporateness and pierce the corporate veil to hold stockholders behind the corporation liable for its debts (1) if there is a unity of interest so that the corporation is indistinguishable from its controlling shareholder (alter ego)—or a subsidiary corporation is being used in an agency relation to the parent company, or has the same identity as the parent, or is being used as an instrumentality of the parent; and (2) if the corporation is being used to promote fraud or other inequitable conduct. Where these elements are present, a court may hold the shareholders liable for debts or torts of the corporation.

REVIEW QUESTIONS

1. Distinguish between state and federal corporation laws.

2. Explain the origin and meaning of "federal corporation law."

3. Explain **(a)** the chief characteristics of business corporations and **(b)** the advantages that arise from each characteristic.

4. What are the chief differences among a corporation, limited liability company, limited partnership, and a partnership?

5. "There is no longer a place for a limited partnership or a partnership in the American economy." Do you agree or disagree? Discuss.

6. Compare these kinds of corporations: **(a)** private and public, **(b)** publicly traded and close, and **(c)** domestic and foreign.

7. Explain **(a)** promoters' fiduciary duties to future shareholders and **(b)** how a corporation accepts a share subscription.

8. What facts are generally required in articles of incorporation?

9. Compare a de jure corporation, de facto corporation, and corporation by estoppel.

10. When is the veil of a close corporation pierced? Of a subsidiary?

CASE PROBLEMS

1. The Rippee brothers, as agents of Northwest Tech, Inc., signed two 2-year commercial leases with Heintze Corp. as lessor. Heintze was unaware that Northwest was not incorporated when the first lease was signed on May 1. Northwest completed its incorporation on June 17. The second lease was signed July 15. Northwest paid rent on both leases for a year and then stopped. Heintze sued Northwest *and* the Rippee brothers to recover unpaid rent. **(a)** Can Heintze recover from Northwest on either or both leases? **(b)** Are the Rippee brothers personally liable on either or both leases?

2. Emmick was the promoter of O.K. Enterprises, Inc. At the corporation's organizational meeting, attended by Emmick and his engineer Fosdick, who was the initial incorporator, Emmick exchanged his farm for 2,000 shares of the corporation's stock. Thereafter, individuals who had subscribed to stock were issued their shares. Some of those shareholders, upon learning that

Emmick had traded his farm for shares, believed his farm had been grossly overvalued. They want to compel Emmick to return to the corporation some of the shares issued to him. Do they have a cause of action? Explain.

3. The general corporation law of Kansas provides that corporate existence commences after (1) filing articles of incorporation with the secretary of state and (2) filing a certified copy of the articles with the local county register of deeds. Allen, an officer and organizer of Constructors, Inc., filed proper articles with the secretary of state but never filed a copy with the county register of deeds. The state of Kansas sued the corporation for delinquent unemployment taxes and also sued Allen for personal liability as the operator of a defectively formed corporation. Allen claimed that (1) there was substantial compliance with the statute so that a de jure corporation was formed and, alternatively, (2) even if Constructors, Inc., was not de jure, it was a de facto corporation so that he was shielded from personal liability for the company's taxes. Was the corporation de jure or de facto so as to shield Allen personally?

4. Baker owned a farm that had financial problems. He agreed to form a corporation with two investors who were to buy stock for cash sufficient to pay off the debts that Baker owed. Baker agreed to deed the farm as his capital contribution to the corporation, and recorded the deed *before* the articles of incorporation had been filed with the secretary of state. Thus, at the time of the deed, the corporation was neither de jure nor de facto. After the corporation was formed, Baker was active in the corporate farming business as an officer, director, and stockholder. He later claimed that since the corporation did not exist at the time of the deed, it was a nullity and that title to the farm remained with him. The corporation claimed that Baker should be estopped to deny the corporate existence because before and after incorporation, he dealt with it as a corporation. Is Baker estopped to deny corporate existence at the time he deeded the farm?

5. Emma and Robert Butler bought a motel and incorporated it as Yacht Club Vista, Inc., in order to convert it into condominiums for sale to the public. As the condos were sold, buyers were required to join a condo owners' association. When complaints of construction defects began coming in, the Butlers started depleting the assets of the corporation. George Terren, buyer of six condo units, after complaining unsuccessfully about construction defects, commenced an action against the Butlers and their corporation. The condo owners' association members also were discovering defects and they joined in the suit. The trial court gave judgment of $319,428 against Butlers' corporation, but finding it had only $100,000 of assets, the court pierced the corporate veil and entered a personal judgment against the Butlers. They appealed. Was it proper to disregard Yacht Club Vista, Inc., and hold the Butlers liable?

CHAPTER 43

Financing Corporations

The most common cause of business failures is underfinancing. A corporation, like any other business, must have working capital to begin business and to expand. Two methods of raising funds are unique to business corporations: issuing and selling (1) **bonds** and (2) **stock.** Although a few states permit formation of nonstock corporations for profit, most states do not treat formation of a corporation as complete until it issues and sells stock. Selling stock is called **equity financing** because the corporation is selling an *ownership* interest—an **equity**—in the business. For this reason stocks are often referred to as **equity securities.** The sale of bonds is called **debt financing** because a bond is a certificate evidencing long-term debt owed by the corporation to the purchaser of the bond; the bond also contains the corporation's promise to repay the indebtedness together with interest. That is why bonds are also called **debt securities.**

DEBT FINANCING; BONDS

Debt financing simply means borrowing money. As a general rule, state statutes give corporations the power to borrow money, and to issue notes, bonds, and other obligations; no special enabling provision in the articles of incorporation is necessary.[1] In general, debt financing may be treated as either short term or long term.

Short-Term Financing

Short-term financing takes many forms, such as securing favorable bank credit, assigning accounts receivable, pledging some or all of the corporation's properties, purchasing equipment on installment, selling (or leasing back) machinery, and issuing promissory notes for cash. A promissory note is an instrument by which a corporation expresses its promise to repay, with interest, a sum of money it borrows. Promissory notes, as a form of commercial paper, are explained in Chapter 31.

When a corporation is newly formed or does not have well-established credit or sufficient collateral to secure a loan, the lender may require a corporate officer or major shareholder to guarantee repayment personally. If the corporation defaults on the loan, the lender may go against the guarantor. A *secured* lender may take possession of the collateral, sell it, and apply the proceeds to the debt. An *unsecured* lender has

---

[1] For example, see Sec. 3.02 of the Revised Model Business Corporation Act, hereafter referred to as the Revised Model Act (RMA).

no claim on specific corporate property but must obtain a judgment on the claim and then levy execution on whatever corporate assets can be found. If the corporation is in bankruptcy, the unsecured lender must "stand in line" with other unsecured creditors.

Long-Term Bond Financing

In addition to selling stock, a corporation can obtain long-term financing by selling bonds. A bond is a corporate promissory note, usually secured by a mortgage on the corporation's assets, promising to pay the bondholder (1) the amount of the bond at a distant future time, sometimes 30 or 40 years from the date of issue, and (2) a fixed rate of interest, usually payable semiannually. The specific terms of a bond issue are set out in a lending agreement, called a **bond indenture,** between the issuing corporation and a trustee, often a commercial bank or trust company, acting on behalf of the investors who buy the bonds after they are issued. Each bond, generally in the sum of $1,000, is a negotiable debt security and is a part of a large corporate bond issue sold to buyers through stockbrokers. The characteristics of negotiability of securities are discussed later in this chapter.

The many possible combinations of bond provisions often result in varieties of bonds that defy easy classification. The major types of bonds issued by corporations are (1) debentures, (2) mortgage bonds, (3) equipment trust certificates (bonds), (4) convertible bonds, and (5) callable or redeemable bonds. The characteristics of these kinds of bonds are shown in Table 43.1.

During the 1980s, the term **junk bonds** was coined by the securities industry to denote any bond below "investment-grade quality" as determined by standards set by securities rating firms. The term was associated particularly with bonds issued by an aggressor corporation to accomplish a **leveraged buyout (LBO)** of a target corporation. Junk bonds were issued with fixed interest charges far in excess of many corporations' ability to pay. Many such issuers went into bankruptcy, and thousands of bondholders lost their investment during this era.

Registered Bonds. Most corporate bonds are registered. The term **registered bond** means a bond issued to an owner whose name is stated on the face of the bond and registered on the records of the issuing corporation. The corporation undertakes to pay the stated principal and interest to the registered owner.

Bearer Bonds. A **bearer bond** has no registered owner. The issuing corporation agrees to pay anyone who is the bearer in possession of it. In 1983, the Internal Revenue Code was amended to impose stiff penalties on corporations issuing bearer bonds; ever since then, all new bond issues have been registered. The new law discourages tax evasion, since the IRS can now easily learn from corporate records who owns a bond and how much interest income the owner has received from it. Foreign corporations, however, continue to issue bearer bonds, which are traded in global markets. Registered bonds offer one important advantage: If they are lost or stolen, the issuing corporation must replace them.

EQUITY FINANCING—STOCKS

A corporation's initial stock issue usually provides most of the capital needed to commence business. The sale of additional stock or issuance of a new series of shares may be required to provide the financing needed for later business expansion.

Nature of Shares of Stock

With any investment, the rate of return is a function of risk—the greater the risk, the greater the rate of return that is offered to induce investors to part with their savings. **Shareholders** (also called **stockholders**), as *owners* of the corporation, are the risk takers. Consequently, after the corporation has paid its creditors, suppliers, employees, and bondholders, what is left is available for the shareholders—but only if the board of directors decides to declare a dividend. If no dividends are declared, the shareholders receive no income from their ownership. However, if all goes well, the share-

Table 43.1 Characteristics of Major Bond Issues

Type	Characteristics
Debentures	These instruments are unsecured by any pledge of corporate assets and are backed only by general assets and the credit standing of the corporation.
Mortgage bonds	Repayment is secured by a mortgage of corporate real or personal property; upon default, the property is sold for cash to reimburse the bondholders.
Equipment trust certificates (bonds)	These instruments are sold to finance the purchase of heavy equipment, such as railroad rolling stock; legal title is held by a trustee until principal and interest are repaid. Upon default, the trustee sells the equipment and uses the proceeds to pay off certificate holders. In effect, an equipment trust certificate is much like a chattel mortgage bond that is secured by personal property of the corporation.
Convertible bonds	At the option of the bondholder, this instrument may be exchanged for a specified number of shares of the corporation's stock. If the market price of the stock rises, the bondholder exercises the conversion privilege and sells stock at a profit; if the stock price drops, the bondholder keeps the instrument as a bond and it continues as a debt that must be repaid at face value together with interest.
Callable (redeemable) bonds	These instruments are callable before maturity at the option of the corporation. The callable feature, a part of the bond indenture (or contract), permits the firm to call in and redeem bonds sold in a high interest rate period, and pay for the redemption cost by floating a new bond issue at lower interest rates.

holders receive generous cash dividends. Even if corporate profits are plowed back into the business, the per-share value of the shareholders' stock will increase to reflect the retained earnings. Bondholders, as *creditors* of the business, assume much less risk than stockholders, and so their rate of return is usually less. Even if the corporation is not profitable, bondholders are entitled to be paid back principal plus the interest called for in their bonds.

Stock ownership typically includes a right to participate in corporate earnings through dividends, to share in the corporation's net assets upon liquidation, and to vote in the election of directors and in certain extraordinary matters, such as deciding whether to dissolve or to merge with another corporation. Bondholders, in contrast, receive no dividends and have no voting rights.

A share of stock does not confer upon the holder a vested title to any specific property owned by the corporation. Rather, a share of stock represents a proportionate ownership interest in the net worth or equity of the corporation. Net worth and equity are used here in the accounting sense to mean assets minus liabilities. In the event of bankruptcy or liquidation, claims of creditors, bondholders, and employees rank ahead of shareholders. If any corporate assets remain, they are distributed to shareholders. Table 43.2 contrasts the rights of bondholders and stockholders.

Table 43.2 Rights and Risks of Bondholders and Stockholders

Bondholders	Stockholders
Are *creditors*	Are *owners*
Investment earns *interest*, which must be paid regardless of whether any profit is earned	Investment earns *dividends* only if (1) corporation earns profits and (2) board of directors declares dividends
Generally have no voting rights or right to participate in management unless bonds are in default	Elect board of directors, which operates the corporation, and vote on extraordinary matters such as mergers
Investment is returned at maturity date, when face value of the bond is repaid	Stock does not have a maturity date; corporation usually does not repay stock unless it repurchases treasury stock
As creditors, can exhaust corporate assets to pay principal and interest before distributions are made to stockholders	Have a right to claim assets, income, and property only after bondholders and other creditors are paid

A shareholder's interest is generally evidenced by a *stock certificate* for a stated number of shares of a designated type. However, RMA 6 provides that

unless the articles of incorporation or bylaws provide otherwise, the board of directors of a corporation may authorize the issue of some or all of the shares of any or all classes or series without certificates. . . .

A few states, following this section of the Revised Model Act, have enacted statutes which permit the issuance of uncertificated shares—that is, shares not represented by stock certificates. Instead, a record of shareholders' ownership is maintained by a bank, stock brokerage house, or registrar of the stock.

Issuance of Shares

Authority to Issue Shares. A business corporation can offer and sell only the classes of shares, and only the maximum number of shares of each class, that are authorized in its articles of incorporation (RMA 6.01). An overissue is void. Each proposed issue must also satisfy state and federal statutes designed to protect the public from fraudulent stock schemes.

Issuance for Cash. Generally, shares of stock are sold by a corporation for cash at the value fixed by the articles or the directors (RMA 6.21). If a stock subscription is payable in installments, a certificate cannot be issued and delivered to the subscriber until the shares represented by the certificate are fully paid.

Issuance for Property. Tangible or intangible property may be accepted by a board of directors as adequate consideration for the issuance of shares of the corporation's stock. For example, a person may offer to transfer to the corporation such tangible property as a parcel of land, a piece of machinery or equipment, or a vehicle in return for a certain number of its shares of stock. Intangible property, such as trade secrets, goodwill of a going business, accounts receivable, and patents, may also be used as consideration for the purchase of shares.

In some states, a corporation is precluded from issuing its stock in exchange for an unsecured promissory note, since such a note basically is a promise to pay money in the future. Suppose, however, that Al gives Beth his promissory note for $10,000, due in 6 months. Beth wishes to buy Ajax Corporation shares, but she has no cash. She offers to endorse Al's note over to the corporation in return for $10,000 of its stock. Under some state laws, a third-party note (such as Al's note) is legal consideration for the issuance of stock. RMA 6.21(b) goes further and permits the directors to authorize issuance of stock in return for the personal unsecured note of the shareholder.

Issuance for Services. In most states, a corporation may issue stock in return for *past* services that benefited the corporation. Such an event would occur when a corporation issues stock to a promoter for services rendered in organizing the corporation. Many states, on the other hand, prohibit the issuance of stock in consideration of *future* services, even though the obligation to perform is evidenced by a contract. However, the Revised Model Act permits the board of directors to issue stock in exchange for a contract to perform future services.

Valuation of Consideration. The board of directors fixes the value of the consideration offered to the corporation in exchange for shares of its stock. Problems may arise in determining the valuation when the consideration is property or services. Opinions regarding the value of intangible property or of the services of a promoter may differ. A shareholder of a corporation may contend that its directors issued an excessive amount of stock in exchange for the consideration received and thus violated the fiduciary obligations they owed to the corporation. To avoid time-consuming and expensive litigation, many state statutes provide that the board of directors' valuation of the consideration accepted in exchange for shares shall, in the absence of fraud, be conclusive. RMA 6.21 also takes a liberal stance, requiring only that if directors determine that the consideration received for shares is *adequate*, their determination is conclusive.

Watered Stock. When shares are issued for the full consideration fixed by the directors or the shareholders, they are properly issued, fully paid, and nonassessable [RMA 6.21(d)]. Shares issued to persons for less than full consideration are said to be **discount** shares; if issued for no consideration at all, they are **bonus** shares, and if issued in exchange for property that is overvalued, they are referred to as **watered stock.**

In the nineteenth century, western land developers were notorious for stock-watering schemes. In the classic example, promoters formed a corporation and transferred worthless land to it in exchange for stock with a total par value of, say, $1 million. Then they had the corporation issue another $1 million of stock to the public for cash. Since they held half the outstanding stock, they fraudulently acquired the right to $500,000. The evil of watered stock is obvious. It injures creditors who, relying upon an inflated capitalization, extend credit to the corporation, and it erodes the equity of the honest stockholders who pay cash for their shares. Modern state and federal securities regulation has substantially curtailed such fraud.

Illegal Issuance. If a corporation issues stock in violation of state corporation laws, the issuance is illegal and is *voidable* at the option of the shareholder who receives the shares. Thus, the purchaser may choose either to keep the stock and comply with the terms of his or her agreement or to rescind the transaction, return the shares, and recover the consideration given to the corporation.

The following case answers the question whether shares of common stock issued for unsecured promissory notes, due on demand, are void or only voidable.

CASE 43.1	**Kirk v. Kirk's Auto Electric, Inc.** • 728 S.W.2d 529 (Ky. 1987)
FACTS	Kirk's Auto Electric, Inc., issued eleven shares of its common stock to Billy Bone. Six years later, it issued ten shares of its common stock to Andre Bone and five shares to Joe Bone. In exchange for these shares, the Bones each delivered to the corporation unsecured, interest-bearing promissory notes payable on demand. At the time the shares were issued, Billy Bone was a director and president of the corporation, and Kirk was a director and its secretary. Billy Bone and Kirk each signed the certificates on behalf of the corporation. No payment was made upon the notes, and Kirk brought action to have the court declare void the shares of stock issued in exchange for the notes. The lower court held the stock to be voidable but not void, and Kirk appealed.
OPINION	LAMBERT, J. . . . Section 193 of the constitution of Kentucky states:

> No corporation shall issue stock or bonds, except for an equivalent in money paid or labor done, or property actually received. . . .

. . . In 1972 the General Assembly adopted the "Kentucky Corporations Act" . . . as follows:

> Payment for shares. (1) The consideration for the issuance of shares by a corporation may be paid only by an equivalent in money paid or labor done, or property actually received and applied for the purpose for which such corporation was created, and neither labor nor property shall be received in payment of consideration for the issuance of shares at a greater value than the market price at the time such labor was done or property delivered. . . .
>
> (2) In the absence of fraud in the transaction, the judgment of the directors or the shareholders, as the case may be, as to the market price of the consideration received for shares shall be conclusive unless the person questioning the market price shall by clear preponderance of the evidence establish a different market price.

This statute applies to stock issued to Andre Bone and Joe T. Bone. [The above statute was replaced by a new but similar statute which was applied to the shares issued to Billy Bone.] The constitutional and statutory provisions quoted herein evince a strong policy in this commonwealth toward protecting corporations, shareholders, and corporate creditors from the dissipation of corporate assets. The issuance of shares must be attended by good faith and the corporation must receive value not disproportionate to the value of the shares issued. . . .

The promissory notes received by Kirk's Auto Electric, Inc. were unsecured and were payable only upon demand. The only persons eligible to demand payment from the makers of the notes were the members of the board of directors, appellant, Kirk, and appellee, Billy H. Bone, the same persons who authorized issuance of the shares and acceptance of the unsecured notes. Appellee, Billy H. Bone, was himself maker of one of the notes. Therefore, appropriate vigilance would be less than assured. This transaction well illustrates the need for strict enforcement of the constitutional and statutory requirements.

Our holding in this case may appear to be too restrictive and represent an interference with the power of a corporation to conduct its business affairs. In ordi- |

CASE 43.1 Continued

nary commercial transactions, unsecured promissory notes are essential and undoubtedly constitute valuable consideration. Nevertheless, the constitutional and statutory provisions are impressed with a public interest and their primary purpose is to prevent fraud and to protect creditors or purchasers of stock or securities of corporations. If the public interest is to be protected, strict adherence to the law must be required.

We believe Section 193 of the constitution of Kentucky is plain and unambiguous. Stock issued by a corporation must be "for an equivalent in money paid or labor done, or property actually received." Otherwise, stock issued by a corporation is a "fictitious increase" which is void. . . .

JUDGMENT The judgment of the Court of Appeals is reversed. . . .

DISSENT LEIBSON, J. . . . I would adopt [the] Court of Appeals' opinion to the effect that the stock issued to the Bones' was voidable, but Kirk has *no standing* to have the stock declared void because he actively participated in causing it to be issued.

Classes of Shares

Shares of stock may be issued as one class or may be divided into two or more classes. The two principal classes of stock are common and preferred, but there are many kinds of common and preferred shares. Articles of incorporation set forth the designations, preferences, limitations, and relative rights of each class of authorized stock.

Common Stock. **Common stock** is the basic stock issued by a corporation. Such shares represent an ownership interest. If a corporation has only one class of stock, it is *common stock,* even if the articles of incorporation do not use that term. State statutes typically permit corporations to issue classes of common stock with different rights or privileges. For example, a corporation may issue *Class A common stock* with voting rights and *Class B common stock* with no voting rights. A corporation may also issue one class of common stock with multiple votes per share (to be held by key officers and directors of the corporation) and another class with but one vote per share (to be held by the public). However, if only one class of common stock is issued, each common share must be treated equally with every other share issued.

Preferred Stock. **Preferred stock** gains its name because these shares have preferential rights over other classes of stock. Generally, the preference is the right to receive (1) dividends at a specified rate stated on the face of the shares, such as a stated number of dollars or a stated percentage of the par value of the shares, before any dividends are paid to the common stockholders, and (2) distribution of assets upon dissolution or liquidation, ahead of any distribution to the common stockholders.

Despite the preferences given to preferred shares, they represent a *nonvoting* ownership interest in the corporation and are not considered to be a part of the company's debt. Designating shares as *preferred* has no legal effect unless the articles of incorporation authorize the preference.

If a board is authorized to issue preferred shares, it may do so at its option. If the board does decide to issue preferred shares, it may establish different classes or series of such shares, fixing their terms and assigning to each series independent rights, dividend rates, and redemption prices (RMA 6.01).

The common types of preferred shares are (1) cumulative, (2) participating, (3) convertible, and (4) redeemable.

Cumulative preferred stock. Dividends on preferred shares may be **cumulative** or **noncumulative.** Cumulative shares give the holder the right to receive the stated dividend in full each year. If there is a nonpayment in any year, that right is not lost but the unpaid cumulative preferred dividends cumulate and must be paid in full to the holders of such shares in the future before any dividends may be paid to the holders of the corporation's common shares. This inherent characteristic of cumulative preferred shares prevents directors (who are elected by the common shareholders) from intentionally failing to declare preferred dividends for several years and then declaring a large dividend payable to the common shareholders.

Holders of *noncumulative* preferred shares are not entitled to payment of past-due dividends, and any unpaid dividends need never be made up. To avoid the danger of a board of directors intentionally failing to declare dividends on the corporation's noncumulative preferred stock in order to create a greater fund for its common shareholders, articles of incorporation often provide that if preferred dividends are not declared for a specified period of time (e.g., eight quarters), the preferred shareholders have the right to replace a majority of the board of directors.

Participating preferred stock. If a corporation has unusually high earnings, owning **participating preferred** shares may be quite beneficial because the holder of such preferred shares has two "bites" at the dividend "apple." In addition to being entitled to the stated dividend before any dividend can be paid to the common shareholders, the holders of participating preferred shares participate with the common shareholders in the receipt of any remaining funds that are set aside for dividend purposes. Because such participation reduces the dividends that otherwise might be paid the common shareholders, most corporations do not give their preferred shares the right to participate.

Convertible preferred stock. **Convertible preferred** shares are similar to convertible bonds in that the holder of these shares has the option of converting them into shares of another class of stock of the corporation (usually common stock) at a predetermined ratio. If the shares to which they may be converted rise in value, the convertible preferred shares ordinarily would also rise in value.

Redeemable preferred stock. **Redeemable preferred** shares are issued with the condition that they may be repurchased (i.e., redeemed) by the issuing corporation at a stated price and time. It is not unusual for the issuing corporation to establish a sinking fund, separate from funds available for dividends, for redemption purposes. If the market value of the redeemable preferred shares rises above the redemption price, the directors can be expected to exercise the corporation's right of redemption. When a corporation repurchases its preferred stock, the common shareholders benefit because stock with a priority claim on dividends and liquidation proceeds has been canceled or returned to the corporate treasury.

Par and No-Par Stock. The Revised Model Act and statutes of many states no longer permit par-value stock. These statutory changes do not affect companies already formed. Many of the companies listed on the New York Stock Exchange continue to issue par-value stock. **Par value** is a dollar amount, stated in the articles, below which the shares may not be sold by the issuing company. After the shares have been issued and sold, their par value becomes irrelevant, as the share price thereafter is fixed by the market.

If shares are sold by a corporation as fully paid but the consideration received by it was less than their par value, the shares are watered to the extent the par value was not received by the corporation. For example, assume that shares have a par value of $100. In order to sell them to the public, the corporation accepts $75 for each share. Thus, each share is watered to the extent of $25. In most states, ordinarily neither the corporation nor minority shareholders may complain of stock watering. But, as noted earlier, if the corporation becomes insolvent, creditors may have a right of action against the shareholders to recover an amount equal to the "water" in their shares.

Stock that is issued without a stated (par) value is said to be **no-par value stock.** All states

Table 43.3 Characteristics of Stock Issues

Type	Characteristics
Common	Basic stock issued by a corporation with a rank below all other classes of stock regarding dividends and distribution of assets upon dissolution
Common, Class A Class B	Shares of common divided into two classes—Class A voting and Class B nonvoting—with Class A holders having *control*
Preferred	Shares that have preferential rights over other classes of stock in two ways: (1) dividends payable at stated rate and (2) distribution of assets upon liquidation
Convertible preferred	Shares that at holder's option may be converted into shares of another class—usually common
Cumulative preferred	Holder has right to receive stated dividend each year; unpaid dividends cumulate from year to year and must be paid before dividends can be paid on common
Callable (redeemable) preferred	Stock that corporate issuer has a right to "call" (repurchase) at stated time and price
Par value	The price fixed in articles below which par stock must not be issued and sold
No par value	Stock issued without par and sold at a price fixed by directors or articles
Bonus	Stock issued for which the corporation receives no lawful consideration
Discount	Stock issued for a cash price less than the full consideration fixed by directors
Watered	Stock issued in exchange for property worth less than the consideration fixed by the board (the term may also refer to bonus or discount shares)
Incentive stock option	An option given executives to buy stock at a given price—to be exercised later when prices are higher

authorize the issuance of no-par value stock, which is sold by the issuing company at whatever price the board of directors determines is reasonable. In the absence of fraud or self-dealing, the board's determination of the reasonableness of the consideration—i.e., the **stated** value of the shares—will be upheld. Characteristics of types of stock are summarized in Table 43.3.

THIN CORPORATIONS

As noted above, a corporation's financial structure usually includes both equity and debt financing. A **thin corporation** is one financed with a relatively high ratio of debt compared with equity. In other words, it has an excessive amount of debt in its capitalization. What is

Table 43.4 Balance Sheet Headings

Assets	Liabilities (Debt financing)	Stockholders' Equity
Plant	Notes payable	Common stock
Equipment	Bonds payable	Retained earnings
Patents		
Cash		
Accounts receivable		
Inventory		

considered excessive depends upon the facts in each particular case. One commonly used test holds that when debt equals or exceeds four times equity, it is a thin corporation. To understand when and why a corporation is thin, we can add hypothetical numbers to the corporate balance sheet headings in Table 43.4. For example, suppose that assets total $100,000, and liabilities are $90,000 and stockholders' equity is $10,000. The hypothetical corporation's debt-equity ratio is 9 to 1. It is a thin corporation.

In close corporations there are several incentives for shareholders to thinly incorporate. First, investors in a close corporation naturally desire to recoup their capital investment without giving up control of the business. Suppose investors put $100,000 of start-up capital into our hypothetical corporation, taking back common stock. The only way they could get their capital back would be to sell their stock. This is undesirable, because the shareholders do not want the business to be owned by outsiders, nor do they want to give up their positions in the corporation. If, on the other hand, the investors are issued stock of the stated value of $10,000, and notes or bonds for $90,000, the latter amount is a *debt* the corporation owes. The corporation can repay the $90,000 debt, and the investors will still retain full ownership interest in the corporation.

Another incentive to create a thin corporation is that it may reduce corporate federal income tax. Thin corporations attempt to do so on their tax returns by deducting interest payments to creditors, including owners who, claiming to be creditors, have made "loans" to the corporation. In contrast, corporate payments of dividends to shareholders are *not* deductible. Thus, if our hypothetical thin corporation declares a dividend of 6 percent upon the $10,000 stock issue, that $600 dividend is *not* tax-deductible. But if the corporation also pays 6 percent interest on the $90,000 loan, it can try to claim the $90,000 as a bona fide loan and deduct the $5,400 as an interest payment on a legitimate debt.

One of the dangers of thin corporations is that the IRS tends to scrutinize such arrangements carefully, since the government stands to lose potential tax revenue. In our hypothetical case, it is probable that the IRS would find the debt-equity ratio "too thin" and would (1) treat the shareholders' "loans" as capital *contributions* to shareholders' equity and (2) disallow the interest payments by the corporation to its shareholders, instead treating those payments as nondeductible dividends. As a result, the corporation would be required to pay income tax on the $5,400 it incorrectly treated as interest. Thus, corporations financed with a mixture of debt and equity must be carefully monitored to ensure that they are not "too thin."

A second danger of thin incorporation, discussed in Chapter 42, is that inadequate initial equity capitalization is one factor considered by the courts in applying the *alter ego doctrine* to pierce the corporate veil and hold the shareholders personally liable for the company's debts.

A third possible danger facing shareholders of a thin corporation arises if the business becomes insolvent or bankrupt with liabilities owing *both* to shareholders and to outside creditors. In such situations, courts generally refuse to treat those liabilities equally but instead give to the outside creditors first claim against the corporate assets. This is an equitable principle known as the **deep-rock doctrine**.[2] In applying the doctrine, the court considers the corporation's debt-equity ratio as a major factor, as illustrated by the following case.

[2] The name is derived from the subsidiary corporation in *Taylor v. Standard Gas and Elec. Co.*, 306 U.S. 307 (1939).

CASE 43.2 Tanzi v. Fiberglass Swimming Pools, Inc. • 414 A.2d 484 (R.I. 1980)

FACTS In 1968, Richard Tanzi and his parents formed Fiberglass Swimming Pools, Inc., with a capital stock investment of $3,000. In the spring of each year, when swimming pool construction commenced, Richard met the operating capital needs of the business by advancing his personal funds to Fiberglass. In 1972, Richard and his mother advanced $43,000 in personal funds to Fiberglass to purchase excavating equipment. Not until a year later did the corporation issue promissory notes in the amount of their advances.

Fiberglass went into receivership in 1976, and after liquidating the corporate assets, the receiver proposed to distribute them pro rata to the creditors exclusive of the Tanzis. The Tanzis filed a petition of objections with the court, claiming that their loans to the corporation were bona fide and that the loans should be included with the claims of outside creditors. The trial court held that their loans were "contributions to capital used to operate the corporation" and rejected the theory that the Tanzis were creditors. The Tanzis appealed.

OPINION KELLEHER, J. . . . We have not previously articulated standards regarding the distinction between a bona fide debt and a contribution to capital. . . . *In re Mader's Store for Men*, 254 N.W.2d 171 (1977), the court collected and analyzed cases in which advances to a corporation were subordinated on the capital contribution theory and extracted the following relevant factors: (1) was the claimant in a position to control corporate affairs "at least to the extent of determining the form of the transaction"; (2) were the advances intended to be repaid in the ordinary course of the corporation's business; and (3) was the paid-in stated capital "unreasonably small in view of the nature and size of the business in which the corporation was engaged." In our view, the *Mader* court correctly indicated that a breach of fiduciary duties was not a prerequisite to treating shareholder advances as capital contributions. . . . "Inequity enough to justify subordination exists when it is shown that a claim which is in reality a proprietary interest is seeking to compete on an equal basis with true creditors' claims." . . . [Court decisions establish the following criteria] in determining the treatment of disputed advancements: the adequacy of capital contribution, the ratio of shareholder loans to capital, the amount of shareholder control, the availability of similar loans from outside lenders, and certain relevant questions such as whether the ultimate financial failure was caused by undercapitalization, whether the note included repayment provisions and a fixed maturity date, whether a

> **CASE 43.2 Continued**
>
> note or debt document was executed, whether proceeds were used to acquire capital assets, and how the debt was treated in the corporate records.
>
> Applying the criteria . . . to the facts in this case, we conclude that the trial court was justified in finding that the cash advancements to Fiberglass were contributions to risk capital rather than bona fide loans to the corporation. We feel that the initial risk capital of $3,000 was inadequate to sustain corporate sales in excess of $200,000. . . . On balance, the transaction itself bore very few earmarks of an arm's length bargain. The note lacked either interest, repayment, or default provisions and had no fixed maturity date. . . . Finally, the belated execution of the promissory note strongly suggests that it was an attempt in form rather than in substance to protect the family investment. . . . The Tanzis' "loan" therefore, qualified as a contribution to capital that was correctly subordinated to the claims of the general creditors.
>
> **JUDGMENT** Accordingly, the Tanzis' appeal is denied and dismissed, and the judgment appealed from is affirmed.

TRANSFER OF SECURITIES

All investors have the right to transfer their securities by sale, pledge, gift, or terms of a will. A bearer bond is transferred by *mere delivery* of the instrument. The transfer of registered securities (stocks and bonds) requires *indorsement and delivery* of the certificates to the new owner. In this context, "registered securities" means that the owner's name appears on the face of the security and is registered on the corporate books, as distinguished from the term's second meaning—an issue of securities that is **registered** (filed) with the Securities and Exchange Commission and is approved by that federal agency. The new owner of a security in registered form should register the transfer on the books of the issuer, but failure to do so will ordinarily not affect the new owner's title to the transferred shares. However, until a transfer is recorded, the corporation continues to recognize the transferor when it pays dividends, sends notices of meetings, or determines voting eligibility.

Indorsements Required

Indorsements of securities can be made on an assignment form printed on the reverse side of the certificate or on a separate document, called a **stock power** or **bond power,** which must then be delivered with the certificate. In either event, the transferor may indorse in one of two ways: in blank or special. Indorsement **in blank** occurs when the transferor simply signs his or her name without any additional language. For example, the owner may sign his name "Charles Smith" on the back of the certificate or on a stock or bond power. The effect of such a blank indorsement is to make the security into **bearer paper**—that is, anyone who has possession of the instrument may exchange it for cash.

A **special indorsement** occurs when the transferor signs his or her name and also names a specific transferee. For example, the owner may sign the back of the certificate or the stock or bond power, "I hereby assign and transfer to Alan Jones my 100 shares of Ajax Corporation common stock. (Signed) Amy Smith." The effect of a special indorsement is that in order to further transfer or sell the securities, the signature of the named transferee is required. Thus, in this example, if the certificate is lost or stolen, a finder or thief, in order to sell and transfer the stock, would have to forge the signature of Alan Jones and also persuade a bank or trust company to guarantee that signature. As an additional precaution, corporations, or the **transfer agents** that provide the service of transferring their securities from one stockholder to another, customarily require such guaranteed signatures in order to discourage forged or unauthorized indorsements. To obtain a signature guarantee, the owner of the shares goes to his or her bank and asks that the document be stamped "Signature Guaranteed" next to the owner's signature and that it be signed by a bank officer.

The following case illustrates the legal necessity of *delivery* of the certificates representing shares in order to transfer legal title to them.

CASE 43.3   Bankwest, N.A. v. Williams • 347 N.W.2d 163 (S.D. 1984)

FACTS   In January 1981, Tane Williams was divorced from his wife, Pamela. Several weeks later, in lieu of alimony payments for the year, Tane, by a separate written assignment, transferred to Pamela 317 shares of stock. However, the share certificates were not delivered to Pamela because Tane had previously signed them in blank and delivered them to Bankwest as collateral for a loan. Pamela did not notify the bank of the assignment or ask it to transfer the stock to her. When Tane defaulted on the loan, the bank sold the shares at private sale. The proceeds were then applied to pay off the loan for which the shares were pledged as collateral, and the bank paid the surplus into court for distribution. Bankwest asserted it could levy execution upon the surplus to satisfy a judgment that the bank had on two other notes executed by Tane that were unsecured. Pamela claimed she had sole right to the proceeds of the sale of the certificates over the amount canceling the indebtedness on the one loan for which they were held as security. The trial court gave judgment for Bankwest, and Pamela appealed.

OPINION   HENDERSON, J. . . . As these stock certificates are negotiable instruments, resolution of this matter is governed by . . . the [South Dakota] U.C.C. Sections 8-102(1) and 8-105(1). "Delivery" with respect to instruments . . . means voluntary transfer of possession. Section 1-201(14).

> (1) Delivery to a purchaser occurs when (a) He or a person designated by him acquires possession of a security; or . . . (d) With respect to an identified security to be delivered while still in the possession of a third person when that person acknowledges that he holds for the purchaser; or (e) Appropriate entries on the books of a clearing corporation are made under 8-320. . . .

Pamela did not acquire possession of the security, for it was being held by . . . [the bank]; thus there was no delivery under item (a). Neither did the bank acknowledge it was holding the certificates for Pamela. In point of fact, it was never notified of the agreement transferring the stock. Pamela also testified that she did not notify . . . [the corporation that had issued the stock] of the agreement, nor did she request a change of name on its books. There was, then, no delivery under provisions (d) and (e). Without delivery, the agreement, in itself, could not act to validly transfer ownership of the stock. When a transfer is by separate document, Section 8-309 specifically states:

| CASE 43.3 Continued | An indorsement of a security whether special or in blank does not constitute a transfer until delivery of the security on which it appears or if the indorsement is on a separate document until delivery of both the document and the security. . . .

The execution of the . . . 1981 agreement between Tane and Pamela did not constitute an effective delivery transferring ownership of the 317 shares of stock. The stock remained in the name of Tane. Bankwest, having a valid judgment against Tane, could lawfully execute upon the proceeds arising from the sale of the stock to satisfy its claim. |
|---|---|
| JUDGMENT | Affirmed. |

Lost or Stolen Certificates

Suppose Alice loses her certificate and Carol purchases it from the finder or a thief. What are the rights of the parties? Under Article 8 of the Uniform Commercial Code (the law governing the transfer of securities), a **bona fide purchaser** acquires ownership of a security free from any adverse claim—for example, a claim that someone else is owner. A *bona fide purchaser* is essentially a good faith buyer who takes delivery of a bearer certificate (or a properly indorsed registered certificate) without notice of an adverse claim.

Suppose Bill steals Alice's registered certificate that she has indorsed "in blank" and sells it to Carol, who has no knowledge of the theft. As a bona fide purchaser, Carol acquires the certificate free from Alice's claim of ownership. Carol also has a right to have the securities transferred into her name on the books of the corporation, and to receive a new certificate in her own name. Why does the law favor Carol as owner of shares that were stolen from Alice? The reason most often cited by courts is the time-honored **two innocent parties rule:** As between two innocent parties, the one whose negligence most nearly caused the loss will bear the burden. Alice and Carol are both innocent; but Alice, by negligently indorsing the certificate, led Carol, as a good faith purchaser, to believe that Alice had intentionally parted with ownership.

The situation is quite different where Bill steals Alice's *unindorsed* registered certificate and forges her indorsement. Only Alice or some authorized person can make an effective indorsement. Because Bill's forgery is ineffective to confer ownership rights on Carol, Alice is entitled to recover the certificate from Carol. Or, Alice may receive a new certificate from the corporation by following the procedure set out in Article 8 of the UCC for lost, destroyed, or stolen certificates. To obtain the new certificate, Alice must, for example, inform the corporation of the loss within a reasonable time after she has notice of it.

What happens if Alice properly obtains a substitute certificate, but in the meantime the corporation mistakenly issues a new certificate to Carol on the basis of the forged indorsement? The corporation must honor both certificates. Since both Alice and Carol are entitled to the shares specified in their certificates, the corporation must supply the required number of shares or absorb any loss—e.g., by pursuing the thief (Bill) or anyone, such as a transferring broker, who guaranteed the forged signature.

Restrictions on Transfer

A corporation has a duty to transfer a registered security into the name of a new owner upon request of the new owner. The corporation must record the transfer on the corporate books, cancel the surrendered certificate, and issue and deliver a new certificate registered in the transferee's name. If the corporation fails to do so, the new owner may recover damages for conversion or, in some instances, may obtain a decree compelling transfer. The new owner may also hold the corporation liable for unreasonable delay. Nevertheless, the corporation has a duty to inquire into any adverse claim if timely written notice is received before the transfer is recorded. This duty of inquiry may be discharged by any reasonable means.

As a general rule, securities are freely transferable. However, when stock of a corporation is closely held, the shareholders often wish to restrict the transfer of stock to others. Restrictions on future dispositions of stock are necessary to preserve continuity of control, an important factor in close corporations. Three conditions must be met in order to restrict the transfer of stock:

1. The restriction must be *reasonable*. For example, sales of close corporation stock to outsiders are usually restricted by providing that each shareholder must first offer his or her stock to the corporation or to the remaining shareholders or both. Such a provision is reasonable and is called a **right of first refusal.** If the offer is refused by the corporation and other shareholders, the person may then sell to an outsider. Ordinarily such restrictions do not prohibit a shareholder from transferring shares by gift or by will. The beneficiary will take the shares subject to the same restrictions. In addition, the shareholders of a close corporation sometimes decide to create a mandatory buy-sell provision by mutually agreeing to buy the shares of persons who die or who may simply desire to cash out their investment.
2. Restraints on transfer must be contained in the articles or bylaws, or in an agreement among stockholders.
3. Reference to the restrictions on transfer must be noted *conspicuously* on the stock certificate.

Unless conspicuously noted on the certificate, any restriction imposed by the issuing corporation is ineffective "except against a person with actual knowledge of it" (UCC 8-204). Generally, the full terms of the restriction do not appear on the face of a certificate, but a statement is printed in distinctive type that indicates where the full provision may be found.

DIVIDENDS AND OTHER CORPORATE DISTRIBUTIONS

The three most important and commonly used ways that a corporation distributes cash or property to its shareholders are (1) cash dividends in proportion to the shareholder's shares in the corporation, (2) stock dividends, and (3) cash distributed to the stockholder at the time a corporation redeems or repurchases its securities.

Dividend Distributions

A corporation for profit is distinguished from a nonprofit or a public corporation by the fact that it has shareholders who expect to receive dividends. However, corporations may refrain from declaring dividends for a variety of reasons. New corporations usually reinvest most of their earnings in the business—sometimes setting aside millions of dollars for capital expansion, research, or acquisition of another corporation. More mature publicly held corporations may regularly distribute a substantial dividend quarterly to their shareholders, who look upon their investment as **income stock.** Other companies distribute only nominal dividends—or none at all—because they want the stock market to view their securities as **growth stocks.** Investors in such shares wish to avoid income taxes on dividends in the near term; then in retirement years when they are in lower income tax brackets, they plan systematically to sell the shares. Meanwhile, their expectation and hope is that the stock will appreciate faster than the inflation rate as a result of the corporation's regular policy of plowing most of its earnings back into the business.

Cash and Property Dividends. Dividends usually are paid in cash and, less frequently, in property. A corporation sends cash dividends each quarter to the shareholders registered on its books. On rare occasions a corporation will make a distribution of its assets—for example, a portion of its inventory or shares of stock it owns in another corporation. Such a dividend is called a "property dividend," or a "dividend in kind."

Authority to Declare Dividends; Business Judgment Rule. Most state statutes give corporate directors exclusive power to declare dividends as long as they, in good faith, exercise sound business judgment. This is a variant of the **business judgment rule,** discussed at length in Chapter 44. A court will not substitute its own judgment for that of directors unless the board on which they sit acts arbitrarily, fraudulently, or in bad faith. The business judgment rule also applies to the declaration of dividends on preferred shares. Directors may, acting reasonably and in good faith, decide not to declare a dividend at a time when it would normally fall due. The board's business judgment will be upheld in the event a shareholder sues to compel declaration of a dividend.

The following case, one of the most unusual in legal history, raised the question: When should a court substitute its judgment for the board of directors regarding declaration of a dividend? The future of the Dodge automobile hung on the court's decision.

CASE 43.4 Dodge v. Ford Motor Co. • 170 N.W. 668 (Mich. 1919)

FACTS The Ford Motor Co. in 1903 issued 1,000 of its authorized $100 par-value shares. In 1908, 19,000 shares were distributed to the shareholders as a stock dividend, thereby increasing the company's stated capital to $2 million. From 1911 to 1916, the Ford company paid dividends equal to 5 percent of its stated capital each month and also paid twelve special dividends totaling $41 million (a return of 410 to 1 on the original shares). The directors continued to declare regular monthly dividends of 5 percent, but in 1916 they discontinued the special dividends. In that year, the company had $53 million cash on hand. Total liabilities were $18 million, there was a surplus of $112 million, and anticipated annual profits were $60 million.

Originally, the Ford car sold for $900, but by 1916 the price had been reduced to $440. The directors justified their refusal to declare further special dividends by stating that they wished to lower the price of Ford cars to $360 and that they intended to construct a smelting plant and a steel plant to produce steel products to be used in manufacturing their cars. The cost of these facilities was estimated to be $24 million. John F. Dodge and Horace E. Dodge, owners of 2,000 shares of Ford Motor Co. stock, objected to the expansion of the business as unwise and to the retention of profits which, they contended, should be distributed to the company's shareholders. They filed an action to compel the Ford directors to declare a special dividend.

The trial court ordered the directors to pay a special dividend of $19 million. Ford appealed.

OPINION OSTRANDER, C.J. . . . The case for . . . [Dodge] must rest upon the claim . . . that . . . the withholding of the special dividend . . . is [an] arbitrary action of the directors requiring judicial interference. . . . This court in *Hunter v. Roberts, Throp & Co.*, 47 N.W. 131, . . . [said]

> it is a well-recognized principle of law that the directors of a corporation, and they alone, have the power to declare a dividend. Courts of equity will not interfere unless [the directors] refuse to declare a dividend when the corporation has a surplus of net profits which it can, without detriment to its business, divide among its shareholders,

CASE 43.4 Continued

and when a refusal to do so would amount to such an abuse of discretion as would constitute a fraud, or breach of that good faith which they are bound to exercise towards the stockholders.

Mr. Henry Ford is the dominant force in the business of the Ford Motor Company. . . . The record . . . convinces that he has the attitude towards shareholders of one who has distributed to them large gains and that they should be content to take what he chooses to give. His testimony creates the impression also that he thinks the Ford Motor Company has made too much money, and that, although large profits might be still earned, a sharing of them with the public, by reducing the price of the output of the company, ought to be undertaken. . . .

There should be no confusion . . . of the duties which Mr. Ford conceives that he and the stockholders owe to the general public and the duties which in law he and his codirectors owe to protesting, minority stockholders. A business corporation is organized and carried on primarily for the profit of the stockholders. The powers of the directors are to be employed for that end. The discretion of directors is to be exercised in the choice of the means to attain that end, and does not extend to a change in the end itself, to the reduction of profits, or to the nondistribution of profits among stockholders in order to devote them to other purposes. . . . [N]o one will contend that, if the avowed purpose of the defendant directors was to sacrifice the interests of the shareholders, it would not be the duty of the courts to interfere. . . .

Assuming the general plan and policy of expansion . . . [to be] for the best ultimate interest of the company and therefore of its shareholders, what does it amount to in justification of a refusal to declare and pay a special dividend or dividends? . . . If the total cost of proposed expenditures had been immediately withdrawn . . . from the cash surplus . . . on hand . . . there would have remained nearly $30,000,000. . . . Moreover, the contemplated expenditures were not to be immediately made. The large sum appropriated for the smelter plant was payable over a considerable period of time. So that, without going further, it would appear that, accepting and approving the plan of the directors, it was their duty to distribute on or near the 1st of August, 1916, a very large sum of money to the stockholders.

JUDGMENT The decree of the court below fixing and determining the specific amount to be distributed to stockholders is affirmed. . . . [The Dodge brothers used the money from their dividends to begin the Dodge Motor Company.]

Persons Entitled to Dividends. The directors ordinarily close the stock transfer books for a stated period and fix a future "record date" to determine which shareholders are entitled to receive a dividend. The corporation may pay dividends to shareholders "of record" on that date without liability to transferees whose interests are unknown to the corporation [UCC 8-207(1)]. Nevertheless, the recipient may be required to pay the dividend to others who have purchased the shares. A seller and buyer can contractually agree to the disposition of a particular dividend. If there is no agreement to the contrary, the seller (transferor) is entitled to dividends declared before the transfer. The buyer (transferee) is entitled to dividends declared after the transfer. However, listed stock purchased during the 5 business days prior to the record date is *ex dividend* (without dividend) to the buyer.

For example, suppose that on May 1 (the declaration date), Ajax Corporation declares a dividend payable on June 15 to shareholders of record on June 1 (the record date). On June 3, Clara sells her 100 shares of Ajax stock to Carlos, but Ajax had already closed its shareholders' ownership books. Because Carlos was not an owner of record on June 1, Ajax will pay the dividend to Clara, the record holder, and not to Carlos. In these circumstances, doubtless Clara and Carlos had adjusted the selling price of the shares to take into account the shares that were being sold *ex dividend*.

Directors of closely held corporations often do not fix a record date for dividend distribution. In that event, the date dividends are declared is treated as the record date for determining which shareholders are entitled to the dividend. The entitlement of a shareholder to receive a declared dividend on the record date and not on the date of declaration is explained in the next case.

> **BOX 43.1**
>
> ### A Very Taxing Matter
>
> If your corporation is retaining earnings to reinvest in the business—whether for inventory, machinery, a new building, or research—be sure to have the directors adopt a resolution stating *all the reasons that earnings are being retained.* Why? Because large reserves of unexplained cash can invite a shareholder suit asking the court to order a dividend. Even more important, the Internal Revenue Service imposes severe penalties for retaining earnings without a clearly stated purpose—the IRS wants earnings distributed as dividends to the shareholder, who then has to pay income taxes. Waiting for a tax audit may be too late—often, the first thing the IRS asks to see is whether the corporate minute book has a resolution explaining the purpose for retaining earnings. ∎

CASE 43.5 **Caleb & Co. v. E. I. Du Pont de Nemours & Co.**
• 615 F. Supp. 96 (D.C. N.Y. 1985)

FACTS E. I. Du Pont de Nemours and Co. (Du Pont) made a tender offer for the shares of Conoco, Inc., agreeing to pay for all of the Conoco shares tendered through First Jersey National Bank before August 17, 1981. On July 31, Conoco declared a per-share dividend of 65 cents, payable September 14 to stockholders of record August 14. On August 5, Du Pont accepted the shares that had been tendered to the bank. Plaintiff filed suit to bar the takeover, claiming that the First Jersey Bank improperly permitted Du Pont to acquire the shares prior to paying for them, thereby improperly becoming entitled, as the shareholder of record on August 14, to the dividend on those shares.

OPINION SWEET, D.J. . . . Du Pont's acceptance of tendered shares on August 5 vested in Du Pont the right to be considered the record owner on August 14, even though payment for the shares postdated August 14. The principle was explained and held to be uniformly applicable by Professor Williston, who stated:

> . . . the purchaser of shares, absent any agreement to the contrary, is generally entitled to dividends, rights, and all the privileges of a shareholder, except voting power, from the time he makes the purchase contract *whether or not he has made payment,* has

**CASE 43.5
Continued**

taken legal title or has been registered on the corporation records as a shareholder. 8 Williston on Contracts § 953 at 320-321.

An examination of the Delaware authorities . . . establishes that an owner as of the record date but not the declaration date is the beneficiary of the dividend. A sale between the declaration and record dates causes the dividend to inure to the benefit of the purchaser.

. . . Before the record date problem arose the courts with very few exceptions held that dividends belonged to the owner of the stock on the date the dividend was declared. However, the practice of most corporations today is to declare the dividend to be payable to shareholders on a date of record between the declaration date and the date set for payment. The original purpose of such a practice was undoubtedly to protect the corporation, so that when it paid a dividend to the person registered on the books on the record date, no liability would fall on the corporation if such person were not the actual owner on that date. . . . [The numerical majority of the] courts have held that the record date is the effective date of the dividend and the actual owner on the date of record is entitled to the dividend even though he may not be the owner registered on the books of the corporation. . . .

When there is both a declaration date and a record date, the declaration of the dividend creates a debtor-creditor relationship between the corporation and the owner of the stock on the date of declaration. . . . And if such dividend is not paid when due it may be recovered in an appropriate action by the shareholders. . . . However, the ultimate beneficiary of the dividend will still be controlled by the owner of the stock on the record date. As the court explained in *Wilmington Trust*, 15 A.2d 665, 667 (1940), the debtor-creditor relationship between the corporation and stock owner arising at the time of declaration of the dividend [is] not ultimately controlling.

JUDGMENT

I conclude that [the] clear implication [of the Delaware Code and of the majority of the decided cases] is that the owner as of the record date is the proper recipient of the dividend. Caleb's final cause of action is therefore dismissed. . . .

Legal Restrictions on Dividend Declaration. While the declaration of dividends is essentially the responsibility of a corporation's board of directors in the exercise of good business judgment, sometimes because of legal restraints they may not do so. Such restraints may be found in

- Its articles of incorporation
- Its preferred-share agreements
- Its bond indentures and loan contracts that prohibit dividends until the corporation repays the lender
- SEC rules that bind the corporation

The directors must also comply with statutory restrictions on payment of dividends imposed by the state of incorporation. These statutes are designed to protect the interests of creditors and shareholders by preserving the capital strength required by a corporation to carry on its business. These rules essentially present accounting rather than legal problems. However, the complexity of modern corporate balance sheets sometimes makes it difficult for directors to determine the precise source of cash that is proposed to be used for dividends. The primary statutory restrictions are:

1. All states provide that a dividend may not be paid if the corporation is insolvent or, as a result of the payment, would become insolvent.
2. The majority of states say that dividends must be paid out of surplus—i.e., out of the excess of total assets over total liabilities—and that dividends may not be paid out of a corporation's stated capital.
3. The minority have adopted a more liberal stance and permit payment of dividends (sometimes called "nimble dividends") out of current net profits, regardless of its effect on the corporation's capital account. Such dividends may be paid even if there was an earnings deficit in prior years. A variant of that flexible approach is the California rule that permits a corporation to pay a dividend as long as (1) its total assets, after the dividend payment, are at least equal to 125 percent of its liabilities, and (2) its current assets are at least equal to its current liabilities.
4. The Revised Model Act [6.40(c)], in substance, precludes payment of dividends, contrary to restrictions in the articles of incorporation, or if (1) as a result of the payment the corporation would not be able to pay its debts as they become due in the usual course of business, or if (2) the corporation's total assets would then be less than its total liabilities.

Other Corporate Distributions

Stock Dividends. A corporation may issue new shares to its existing stockholders as a "share" or "stock" dividend. The dividend shares are usually of the same class as the shares entitled to the dividend and are distributed in a fixed ratio. For example, if a 5 percent stock dividend is declared on common stock, one share of common will be issued and distributed for each block of twenty shares owned by holders of common stock. Dividend shares may be of another class or series if authorized by the articles or by the holders of a majority of outstanding shares of the same class as the proposed dividend.

The shareholders receive certificates evidencing the dividend shares, but the corporation does not, in fact, distribute any of its cash or assets. Stated capital is increased in the corporate books by the total amount of the stock dividend, and retained earnings are reduced by the same amount. Thus, *when there is a stock dividend, the shareholder's proportionate ownership in the corporation is unchanged.* Stock dividends are not taxable as income by the recipients until the shares are sold. A stock dividend, therefore, may be considered to be merely a psychological dividend, but such dividends are gratefully received by the shareholders, being viewed as a substitute for a cash dividend which may be sold for cash at whatever price is established by the marketplace.

Stock Splits. A **stock split** is the division of each share of a class of stock into two or more parts. For example, if you hold ten shares of Ajax stock, and the stock is split 2 for 1, the corporation will send you an additional ten shares—one share of stock for each share you hold. It follows that the market price of each share will be adjusted accordingly. A stock split resembles a stock dividend in that the new shares do not increase a shareholder's proportionate ownership. However, a stock split does not increase the corporation's stated capital, whereas with a stock dividend there is an increase in stated capital and a decrease in retained earnings by a corresponding amount. Moreover, to effect a stock split, a corporation need not have retained earnings or meet any of the other statutory dividend tests. In addition, a stock split is usually accompanied by a change in the dividend rate per share. Typically, a stock dividend does not bring about a change in the per-share dividend rate.

A stock split is accomplished in a manner that is completely different from that of a stock dividend. The directors propose to the shareholders a stock split in some ratio, such as 2 for 1 or 3 for 2. The shareholders then must vote to amend the articles of incorporation to reduce the par value of the shares being split. If 100 shares of $100-par stock are split into 200 shares of $50-par stock, the total stated capital ($10,000) remains the same but more shares are

> **BOX 43.2**
> **Two Questions of Law**
>
> 1 Should the court split a stock split and award it to a divorcing wife?
>
> 2 Is an unexercised stock option a property right or only an expectancy?
>
> Shelly and Eric were parties to a marriage dissolution in 1991. In 1989 Wal-Mart granted Eric an option to buy 500 shares of its common stock in 8 annual installments of 55 shares each. The option to buy 55 shares in one year could be carried over to the next year. At the time of trial, Eric had 30 shares carried over from the preceding year in which Wal-Mart had a stock split, which increased his option to 60 shares. He also had future options to purchase 840 shares, but if his employment terminated the employer could revoke the options. Shelly claimed (1) the court should divide the total shares equally after the stock split and award her half, or equivalent value, and (2) the court should determine the value of the 840 future options and award her half. On appeal, the court held that the value of the 60 shares (after the split) should be awarded to Shelly, but *not* the future options because Eric's right to exercise them "is uncertain and could only be classified as a contingent expectancy."*
>
> *Hutto v. Hutto*, Lexis 523 (Ark. App. 1992).

outstanding. The chief purpose of a stock split is to reduce the market price of shares to the customary price range of $20 to $75 per share. If the market price of a stock falls below that range, a **reverse stock split,** in which two or more shares become one, may be employed to increase the market price of the shares.

Redemption or Repurchase of Outstanding Shares. A corporation may reacquire shares of its stock in two ways: (1) by **redemption** and (2) by **repurchase.** In order to create a right of *redemption* the articles of incorporation must authorize redemption of a designated class of shares (usually preferred stock). The corporation's right of redemption is exercisable at the option of the directors and initiates an *involuntary* sale by the shareholders. The price and terms are fixed in the articles.

A *repurchase,* on the other hand, is a voluntary sale to the corporation by holders of the class of shares repurchased. Price and terms are not fixed, but they are negotiable between the corporation and the selling shareholder. The corporation may repurchase its preferred stock as well as its common stock.

In order to reacquire stock by redemption or purchase, the corporation ordinarily pays cash to the shareholder. It follows that a corporation's power to reacquire shares is restricted by statutes, similar to those discussed above, which limit dividend distributions. Thus, the corporation must have sufficient retained earnings, current earnings, or balance sheet surplus, and it must remain solvent after the acquisition.

A corporation may cancel repurchased shares or may hold them as treasury stock. Treasury shares cannot be voted and are not entitled to dividends. The benefit to the corporation of treasury shares is that they can be sold below par. RMA 6.31(a) and several states no longer recognize treasury shares but provide that reacquired shares revert to the status of "authorized but unissued" shares. In contrast to purchased shares, redeemed shares cannot be reissued and must be canceled.

SUMMARY

Corporations raise capital by borrowing funds from traditional business sources, by issuing and selling bonds (debt financing), and by selling stock (equity financing). In order to raise money for short periods of time (e.g., a few months), corporations normally issue promissory notes; for long periods of time they issue bonds. Bonds are obligations which create a debtor-creditor relation between the corporation and the bondholder. There are many types of bonds. Unsecured bonds are called debentures. A share of stock is a proportionate ownership interest in a corporation. Before the corporation can issue a stock certificate, the prospective shareholder must make payment in full for the shares in cash (usually in property other than promissory notes) or in services. There are two principal classes of stock: common and preferred. Common stock is subordinate to the liquidation and dividend preferences of preferred stock. Common stock ordinarily gives the holder the right to vote. Preferred stock has no voting rights except in extraordinary situations. There are many types of preferred stock.

Common stock may be issued with a par value or without a par value (no-par stock). The par value is the minimum price at which shares may be sold by the corporation. The par value of a share (fixed in the articles of incorporation) or the stated value of a no-par share bears no relation to the market value of the share, which is determined in the stock market. The Revised Model Act and the statutes of many states have done away with the concept of par-value stock.

Thin incorporation refers to a high debt-equity ratio. Tax authorities will disallow interest deductions on debts owed to shareholders if the corporation's debt-equity ratio is "too thin." In addition, thin incorporation is a factor that courts consider in applying the alter ego doctrine to pierce the corporate veil; under the deep-rock doctrine courts rank outside creditors' claims ahead of debts owing to controlling shareholders.

Transfer of securities issued in bearer form is completed by delivery to the transferee, but transfer of registered securities (i.e., stocks or bonds having the owner's name on the certificate) requires the registered owner's indorsement and delivery of the certificate. If a certificate is lost or stolen, the legal result varies. Under the Uniform Commercial Code, if the original owner promptly notifies the corporation when the loss becomes apparent and satisfies other requirements, the corporation will issue to the original owner an equivalent number of shares.

Courts will enforce agreements restricting share transfers if the restrictions are (1) reasonable, (2) set forth in the articles or bylaws or in a contract between the shareholders, and (3) noted conspicuously on the certificates.

Typically, subject to certain statutory restrictions, directors have the discretion to declare dividends and may not be forced to pay dividends unless they act arbitrarily, fraudulently, or in bad faith. A stock dividend creates the illusion of a property distribution but is not a true dividend. Retained earnings are reduced, and stated capital is increased without altering the shareholders' proportionate interests, which are merely represented by more shares. A stock split reduces the par value of outstanding shares and increases their number proportionately so that total stated capital is unchanged. No dividend test need be met in order to declare a stock split.

The use of corporate funds to redeem or to repurchase a corporation's own stock is restricted by statutes similar to those governing dividend distributions. Redeemed shares must be canceled, but in most states repurchased shares may be either canceled or held as treasury stock. Treasury stock held by the corporation has no dividend or voting rights, but it may be resold below par.

REVIEW QUESTIONS

1. Explain the difference between a secured and an unsecured note.

2. Contrast a registered bond and a bearer bond as to **(a)** payment of interest and **(b)** effect of theft or loss of the bond.

3. Describe the uses of **(a)** redeemable and **(b)** convertible bonds.

4. (a) What is a share of stock? **(b)** How does a shareholder's relation to the corporation differ from that of a bondholder?

5. Explain why you agree or disagree with the following statement: "A corporation may issue stock in return for future services."

6. (a) What are the major advantages of owning common stock? **(b)** Does common stock always have voting rights? Explain.

7. Distinguish between **(a)** cumulative and noncumulative preferred stock, and **(b)** participating and nonparticipating preferred stock.

8. (a) Explain the meaning and purpose of stock with par value. **(b)** What is the benefit to directors of having no-par stock?

9. Explain **(a)** thin incorporation, **(b)** risks that stockholders take when using it, and **(c)** two incentives for thinly incorporating.

10. (a) What is required to transfer a bearer instrument? **(b)** What is required to transfer registered bonds and shares?

11. Should new registered-share owners transfer them on the corporate books? Why or why not?

12. What three conditions must be met in order to restrict the transfer of shares of stock?

13. (a) Explain the primary purpose of statutory restrictions on dividends. **(b)** Discuss four statutory tests of a valid dividend.

14. (a) Why is a *record date* important in declaring dividends? **(b)** Explain rights of transferees-not-of-record upon dividend payment.

15. Compare and contrast a stock dividend and a stock split.

16. Compare and contrast corporate redemptions and share purchases.

CASE PROBLEMS

1. Haselbush agreed to buy 10,000 shares of XYZ, Inc., for $20,000, giving the corporation his promissory note for that sum. The purchase was entered on XYZ, Inc.'s, books, but the certificate of stock was not issued to Haselbush pending payment of the note. Haselbush failed to pay the note and XYZ, Inc., sued to collect. Haselbush claimed the transaction was illegal and thus voidable and asked the court to cancel the note. Should the note be canceled?

2. Realty Co. was incorporated by eight doctors to build a medical building. Each doctor purchased common stock and bonds of the corporation. The bonds had a fixed maturity date, and no provision was made for their earlier redemption. If the corporation were to default on its bond payments, individual bondholders could not enforce payment without the consent of a majority of the eight doctors who were the bondholders. In addition, the rights of the bondholders were subordinate to the rights of outside creditors. For 7 years Realty Co. deducted on its income tax return the accrued but unpaid bond interest. The IRS construed the bonds as shares and disallowed the interest deductions. Was the IRS correct?

3. The articles of incorporation of Spaziani Bakery state, "No certificate of stock of this corporation shall be transferred to any person until it has first been offered for sale to this corporation." Vince Spaziani, an original incorporator, died. His two heirs demanded that Vince's shares be distributed to them. The corporation claims first right to purchase the shares. Decision?

4. On December 6, 1986, Zobrist delivered two stock certificates, each for 100 shares of KFC stock, to Schwabacher, a stockbroker, for him to sell. Schwabacher sold the shares. The sale of 100 shares was registered on KFC Corporation's books immediately, but the sale of the remaining 100 shares was not recorded until January 3, 1987. On December 5, 1986, KFC declared a 2-for-1 stock split effective on December 15, 1986, the record date. On December 16, 1986, Zobrist received a certificate for 200 new shares of KFC stock, which he held until the following September, at which time he sold them for $14,797. Schwabacher discovered what had happened and, on behalf of the buyer of the stock, sued Zobrist for the $14,797. Should Zobrist be forced to give up the money?

5. In July 1977, Wright became a marketing consultant for Anacomp, Inc. It was agreed that in September 1977 the parties would reach a definitive agreement whereby Wright would be employed as an Anacomp executive for 5 years. As a part of the original understanding **(a)** Wright paid Anacomp $26,000 and received 3,000 shares of Anacomp stock, **(b)** but if no definitive employment agreement were reached, Anacomp would repurchase the 3,000 shares from Wright at the price she had paid. Wright ceased to work for Anacomp in 1979 when negotiations for the definitive employment agreement broke down. As originally agreed, Anacomp repaid Wright the $26,000 she had paid for the 3,000 shares and asked for their return together with the additional 3,000 shares of Anacomp's common stock that Wright had received as stock dividends on the 3,000 shares. Anacomp sued Wright for return of the additional 3,000 shares. Must Wright return them to Anacomp?

CHAPTER 44

Management of Corporations

The external and internal sources of power of managers to operate a corporation may be seen as a pyramid. At the top are state and federal *statutes*, which in a very real sense are sovereign delegations of power that may be exercised by a business that is incorporated under state law. Next, moving downward, a corporation's powers are spelled out and made more definite by the *charter* issued to it when the state gives life to the corporation. At the next lower level of the pyramid are the corporation's *bylaws*, a set of self-developed rules for the internal governance of the corporation's shareholders, directors, and officers. At the next lower level of the pyramid are the *policies* established by resolutions adopted by the board of directors who are elected by the corporation's owners—the shareholders.

Because a corporation is an inanimate entity, it must, in order to utilize and implement its powers, act through living individuals. Its directors appoint officers who, in turn, hire employees to carry on the business of the corporation within the limits of its powers and policies fixed by the board of directors.

This chapter first discusses the powers under which a corporation operates, the managerial roles of corporate directors and officers, and the kinds of legal liability which they face. The final part of the chapter deals with the special management problems that arise in close corporations.

THE CORPORATE ENTITY: POWERS AND LIABILITIES

Sources of Corporate Powers

The term *corporate powers* refers to a corporation's legal ability to carry out the business purposes defined in its charter. A corporation's powers may be express or implied.

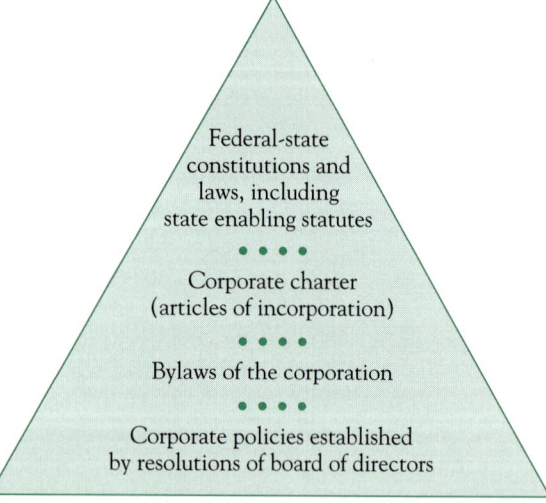

Figure 44.1 The power structure of a corporation.

Express Powers. Sources of **express powers** of a corporation are: federal-state constitutions and statutes, articles of incorporation (charter), by-laws, and resolutions adopted by the board of directors. Some states, particularly those which follow the Revised Model Business Corporation Act,[1] grant corporations the same broad powers that are possessed by individuals to do whatever is necessary and convenient to carry out their business affairs. In most states, corporations are given the power to exist in perpetuity; to sue and to be sued; to acquire or transfer real and personal property; to have a seal; to make by-laws; to make gifts for charitable or educational purposes; to adopt profit-sharing, pension, or stock option plans as incentive compensation for directors, officers, or employees; to be a partner or joint venturer; and to guarantee obligations of others. However, federal law prohibits corporations from contributing to federal election campaigns.[2]

Under state law, the articles of incorporation must set forth the corporation's business purposes, but they may usually be given in broad terms such as "to engage in any lawful business" without restating all the powers listed in the incorporation statute. Some businesses, such as banks, insurance companies, and utilities, are so closely tied to the public interest that their powers are subject to special limitations. For instance, laws provide that these businesses may not engage in manufacturing, retail sales, and other commercial enterprises. Likewise, because a professional corporation is unique in nature, its only permitted business activity is to perform the professional services for which it was incorporated.

Implied Powers. Courts generally interpret broadly the powers stated in a corporation's charter. They hold that a corporation has, in addition to its expressly stated powers, **implied powers** to perform all acts reasonably necessary to accomplish the purposes stated, provided of course, they are not unlawful. For example, Smith organizes a corporation. Its charter states simply that it has the power to operate a service station. The corporation has the implied power to buy equipment, to buy and sell supplies for cash or credit, and to hire mechanics who will repair cars.

What can be construed as an implied power depends upon the wording of the corporation's charter and the statutory provisions under which the corporation is organized. For example, in *Blue Cross and Blue Shield of Connecticut v. Mike*,[3] the court held that the corporation's charter empowered it to establish comprehensive health plans but did not include the implied power to own and operate an insurance company.

Ultra Vires Acts

A corporation that through its officers or employees acts in excess of its express or implied powers is acting *ultra vires,* or beyond the powers of the corporation. The term refers to acts prohibited by the charter, as well as to acts in excess of granted powers. Thus, an *ultra vires* act would take place if the president of a corporation that was chartered to operate a restaurant should buy a fleet of autos and start a car rental business. If a salesclerk commits the tort of negligence by carelessly injuring a customer, or an intentional tort such as assault and battery, such an act is beyond the corporation's powers, even though the corporation can be held liable for it. Whenever directors or officers commit a crime, such as engaging in unlawful price fixing or bribing a public official, it is clearly an *ultra vires* act.

In the case below, the court held that a corporation cannot justify an *ultra vires* act even if it is intended to accomplish a lawful purpose.

---

[1] See Chapter 42. The Act is referred to as the Revised Model Act (RMA) throughout this chapter. Section citations are given in parentheses or brackets. The text of the RMA appears in Appendix 5.

[2] 18 USCA 321.

[3] 439 A.2d 1026 (Conn. 1981).

| CASE 44.1 | **Lovering v. Seabrook Island Property Owners**
• 352 S.E.2d 707 (S.C. 1987) |
|---|---|
| FACTS | The Seabrook Island Property Owners Association (Association) assessed its members to pay for bridge repairs and improvements to the beach within the Association's property. The petitioners, members of the Association, challenged the validity of the assessment as an *ultra vires* action. The trial court gave summary judgment for the Association; the court of appeals reversed, and the Association and the Seabrook Island Company, which owned the bridges and the beach, appealed to the South Carolina Supreme Court. |
| OPINION | PER CURIAM . . . The Association had no express power to impose the assessment in issue. The Association and the Company argue, however, that the power to levy this special assessment was an implied or incidental power of the Association's authority under its Bylaws to maintain and preserve the amenities and values of the development.
    Implied or incidental powers are those which are reasonably necessary to the exercise of the corporation's express powers, not those which are merely convenient or useful. . . . Assuming, without deciding, that the Association had the responsibility of maintaining the streets and the beach, the Bylaws provided the mechanism of an annual maintenance charge to finance the necessary repairs. Furthermore, the Association could have financed the repairs by use of its statutory authority to borrow funds . . . , a course of action the Association apparently considered and rejected. Since the power to levy a special assessment was not *necessary* for the Association to carry out its express powers, even if more convenient than the available fund raising methods, it could not be an implied or incidental power. . . . The Court of Appeals correctly held that the imposition of the special assessment was *ultra vires*. |
| JUDGMENT | Affirmed . . . |

Suits against a Corporation for *Ultra Vires* Acts. In rare situations, the attorney general of the state of incorporation may sue in a ***quo warranto*** action to enjoin or dissolve a corporation engaged in *ultra vires* acts beyond the powers stated in the charter. More commonly a shareholder may, by means of a **derivative suit** on behalf of the corporation, ask a court to restrain *ultra vires* acts of directors and officers and to recover damages from them on behalf of the corporation. For example, the *Lovering* case above was a derivative suit successfully brought by a shareholder seeking an injunction against the corporation's *ultra vires* act (attempting to levy a special assessment on the members).

***Ultra Vires* Defense by a Corporation.** A corporation may not escape liability on a contract by arguing that its charter did not permit it to enter into such contract—in other words, by claiming that entering into the contract was an *ultra vires* act. The practical result of this rule is that a corporation may enter into valid contracts in excess of its powers. For example, suppose the president of a corporation, chartered only to manufacture automobiles, should contract to purchase 1,000 propellers preparatory to manufacturing airplanes—an *ultra vires* act beyond the corporation's express or implied powers. If the supplier sues the corporation for the purchase price, *ultra vires* is not a defense. Of course, the president may be liable to the corporation for the wrongful *ultra vires* act of guaranteeing a personal note.

Suits by a Corporation. Assume the same facts as in the above example, but the airplane propellers are defective and worthless, and the corporation sues the supplier for breach of contract. Can the supplier argue *ultra vires* to persuade the court that the corporation should not recover for breach of a contract that it did not have the power to make? Courts, statutes, and the Revised Model Act hold that no corporation's action is invalid simply because it lacked power to act, except in unusual cases such as (1) a shareholder suit against the corporation to enjoin an *ultra vires* act, as in *Lovering* above, (2) a suit by a corporation against present or former directors for damages arising from their *ultra vires* acts, or (3) a *quo warranto* suit by the state attorney general either to enjoin unauthorized activity or to dissolve the corporation (RMA 3.04).

Liability for Crimes and Torts. The American Law Institute's Model Penal Code permits conviction of a corporation for the crimes of agents and servants within the scope of their authority (1) where the criminal statute reflects a legislative intent to hold corporations liable, (2) where the law subjects a corporation to an affirmative duty (e.g., to install safety equipment in a coal mine), and defines a breach of that duty as a criminal offense, and (3) where a corporate **high managerial agent** (called a **vice principal**) ordered, authorized, committed, or recklessly tolerated the crime.

If a corporation is sued, under the agency law doctrine of *respondeat superior*, for torts of employees committed within the scope of their authority, the corporation cannot successfully raise *ultra vires* as a defense. The laws of agency (discussed in Chapters 36 and 37) are applicable to the torts of corporate employees who act within the scope of their employment. Under the doctrine of *respondeat superior*, an injured party may hold a corporation liable for the wrongful acts of employees acting within the general scope of their employment, even if the corporate employer had instructed the employees not to com-

> **BOX 44.1**
>
> ### Law in Action: Corporate Criminal Liability
>
> General Electric Co. on July 22, 1992 pleaded guilty to criminal charges of defrauding the federal government in the U.S. District Court, Cincinnati, and agreed to pay $59.5 million in settlement of the charges. In addition, a fine of $9.5 million was imposed by Judge Carl Rubin. The firm was charged with conspiracy, money laundering, and submitting false claims. U.S. Attorney Michael Crites said the case was the largest ever prosecuted in the government's foreign military aid program, and the first time a defense contractor was charged under the Money Laundering Control Act of 1986.
>
> In civil charges, G.E. was accused of defrauding the Pentagon and the Israeli Defense Ministry by filing more than $40 million in false claims. Brain Rowe, General Electric's CEO, said: "The company has accepted responsibility for the actions of its employees." The Justice Department took the case over from a whistle-blower lawsuit commenced by an employee. Under the False Claims Act, a person who blows the whistle on a false claim receives a percentage of the recovery.

mit the tort. The rule of *respondeat superior* imposes liability upon a corporation for employees' unintentional torts of negligence as well as for *intentional* torts, such as trespass, fraud, and conversion. The employee's wrongful intent, by operation of law, is deemed to be the wrongful intent of the corporation. Stated differently, the employee's wrongful intent is *imputed* to the corporate employer—that is, theoretically, put over to the account of the innocent corporation so that in the eyes of the law the corporation itself had a wrongful intent.

Whether a corporation can be liable for *punitive* (exemplary) damages for wilful, wanton, or malicious torts of employees within the scope of their authority or employment has led to conflicting decisions. Corporations have contended that they cannot be liable for such acts because they did not intend the wrong. A growing minority of courts hold, as in *Robinson v. Winn-Dixie Stores, Inc.*,[4] that if there is *some fault* on the part of the corporate management which foreseeably contributed to the plaintiff's injury, the corporation is liable for punitive damages. This conclusion is reached even though the corporation's fault was merely the result of negligence and was not wilful or malicious. The following case, representing the majority view, holds that punitive damages may be assessed against a corporation only when its agents have "evil motive or intent" or "reckless or callous indifference to the federally protected rights of others."

[4] 447 So. 2d 1003 (Fla. App. 1984).

CASE 44.2

Shearson Lehman Hutton, Inc. v. Tucker
• 886 S.W.2d 94 (Tex. App. 1991)

FACTS Stuart Tucker (plaintiff) sued Shearson Lehman Hutton, Inc. (Shearson), for slander, alleging that its senior vice president of sales, Jonathon Wilde, had made statements that Tucker (1) was going to lose his license as a broker, (2) was in big trouble with the Securities and Exchange Commission, and (3) would never work again as a broker. A jury found the statements were false, slanderous, and malicious. The jury awarded $212,875 for past and future damage to Tucker's reputation, $84,525 for lost earnings, $19,791 for mental anguish, humiliation, and embarrassment, and $1 million in exemplary damages. Shearson appealed.

OPINION DORSEY, J. . . . Unlike an award of compensatory damages against an employer for the torts of an employee committed in the course and scope of his employment, liability for punitive damages does not flow from the employment relationship through the doctrine of respondeat superior. Rather, the employer must have either some direct culpability, such as ratification of the act, or recklessness in retaining or hiring the employee, or the agent must have more authority than a mere employee such as either a manager or vice-principal. . . . Thus, we must determine whether the evidence is sufficient to find that Wilde was a vice-principal of Shearson or that Shearson authorized Wilde's actions. . . .

Wilde was a senior vice-president of sales with Shearson. He was one of only two brokers in the Shearson office who had such a title among as many as fourteen Shearson brokers. Moreover, the evidence showed that Wilde was acting within the scope of his employment when he made the [slanderous] statements . . . during a sales call on behalf of Shearson. . . .

We find that the above evidence is sufficient to support a . . . finding that Wilde was a vice-principal of Shearson and that Shearson authorized Wilde's acts. First, the undisputed evidence showed that Wilde was a senior vice-president of sales at Shearson. A vice-president is one who acts in the stead or place of the president. This is sufficient evidence from which the trial court could find that Wilde, being a corporate officer, had managerial responsibilities at Shearson. Indeed, Wilde's testimony was that he had a role in the recruiting of employees and his title suggests that he was given authority over

CASE 44.2 Continued

the sales division of Shearson. Moreover, Wilde's testimony that Shearson authorized him to say whatever he did say is some evidence that Shearson authorized his acts. . . . We find the evidence sufficient for the trial court to have found that the status of Wilde was that of manager or vice-principal. Thus we find the issue of Shearson's liability for Wilde's acts deemed in conformity with the trial court's judgment.

JUDGMENT The judgment of the trial court is affirmed.

CORPORATION DIRECTORS AND OFFICERS

A corporation, being an inanimate entity, cannot itself utilize its powers nor can it establish or implement policy. All this must be accomplished by people who act for the corporation. The powers of a corporation, set forth in statutes and in its charter, are exercised by its board of directors, which is charged with the management of the corporation's business affairs. The board makes overall corporate policy; the officers and employees implement it.

Directors

Ten states require a minimum of three directors,[5] and twelve states follow the Revised Model Act (8.03), which requires only one director.[6] The remaining states offer a compromise, particularly to accommodate close corporations with but a single shareholder. These states provide that although there is a general requirement of three directors, the number of directors need not exceed the number of shareholders. Thus, if there is only one shareholder, there may be a single director. A company's articles of incorporation or its bylaws must fix the number of directors but need not set out their qualifications.

Election and Removal of Directors. Prior to the annual meeting of shareholders, the directors send them nominations for the board of directors. The shareholders may also submit names of their own nominees. Unless a corporation's articles or bylaws provide otherwise, a director need not be a shareholder. The shareholders, by plurality vote, elect directors.

Typically, a director serves a 1-year term, although a corporation's articles or bylaws may specify a longer period. If a director dies or resigns, the board of directors can elect a director to fill the vacancy, thus obviating the necessity of calling a special meeting of the shareholders. A corporation's articles or bylaws may also give the directors power to increase the size of the board. When directors do so, they can temporarily fill the "vacancies" created until the next shareholder election of directors.

Most statutes permit the board to remove a director who has been declared insane or convicted of a felony, and corporate articles or bylaws seldom permit the directors to remove a board member for any other reason. The shareholders, however, have the inherent power at any time to remove a director for cause or without cause. In many states, after a legal action, a board member may be removed by court order (RMA 8.09).

Authority of Directors. The business affairs of the corporation are managed by a board of directors charged with the following functions:

1 It establishes and reviews the company's principal goals, objectives, and policies.

---

[5]The ten states are Alabama, Colorado, Hawaii, Maryland, Mississippi, Montana, New Hampshire, North Dakota, Oklahoma, and Utah.

[6]The twelve states are Arizona, Delaware, Florida, Michigan, Missouri, New Jersey, New Mexico, Oregon, South Dakota, Texas, West Virginia, and Wisconsin.

2 It reviews and approves major programs, budgets, and plans, and it monitors the financial and operating functions of the company.
3 It can authorize the issuance of shares of stock and, in the corporate name, it can repurchase shares already issued.
4 It fills vacancies on the board by electing directors who hold office until the next annual meeting of the shareholders.
5 It appoints and removes officers, authorizes important actions by officers, and reviews their performance.
6 It may acquire the business of another corporation.
7 It declares dividends to shareholders and fixes payment dates.
8 It may adopt, amend, or repeal bylaws, unless the articles of incorporation reserve this power to the shareholders.
9 It may recommend dissolution to the shareholders.

Compensation of Directors. In publicly held corporations, most members of boards of directors are neither officers nor employees of the company but are knowledgeable, competent businesspeople outside the company who are asked to bring to the board room their unbiased expertise in particular fields. A director who is not an officer or employee of the corporation is called an **outside member of the board.** An outside director does not necessarily own any stock of the corporation. To encourage highly experienced people to accept a director's responsibility and exposure to shareholder lawsuits, boards usually pay substantial sums to outside directors. Payment is usually an annual cash retainer plus a per diem payment for attending board or committee meetings. This may be supplemented with stock options or other perquisites **(perks).**

Actions by Boards of Directors. A board of directors generally must meet formally in order to act in behalf of the corporation. Such meetings are held at fixed intervals established in the bylaws or in a standing resolution. Special meetings may be held after notice to all directors as prescribed in the bylaws.

There is a growing tendency for state statutes, articles of incorporation, and bylaws to permit boards to act also through simultaneous telephonic conferences, through video teleconferences, or even without a meeting through a **unanimous written consent resolution,** which is usually circulated by mail to the directors' for signature. Unless specified in statutes or bylaws, there is no requirement that directors meet at the corporate offices or even in the state of incorporation. Not surprisingly, directors often schedule meetings (usually tax-deductible) at attractive resorts or even aboard cruise ships.

Directors' actions during a meeting are expressed in formal **resolutions** adopted by a majority of a quorum of the board. A **quorum** is the minimum number of persons required to be present in order to legally transact the board's business. Statutes and bylaws may differ as to the total number of directors upon which a quorum is computed—it may be (1) the number of directors *authorized* in the charter or bylaws or (2) the number of *current* board members, owing to existing vacancies on the board. Generally, a quorum consists of a majority of the members of the board [RMA 8.24(a)]. A director is not allowed to vote by proxy and must attend the meeting in person in order to be counted for quorum purposes. A **proxy** is a person authorized to vote someone else's shares. (The word may also refer to the document granting authority to a specified individual to vote in someone's stead.) For a resolution to be adopted, ordinarily a majority of those present must concur. Thus, if an eleven-member board duly calls a meeting to elect a treasurer and six attend, there is a quorum. If four vote for Jan, she is the newly elected treasurer even though much less than a majority of the board voted for her. If the full board is deadlocked on an important issue, such as a proposed merger, courts in some states may appoint a provisional director to serve until the deadlock is broken.

Committees of Boards of Directors. As a company grows in size and complexity, the responsibility of its board of directors increases apace. To operate more efficiently, a board may create committees composed of its members to study continuing problems and submit reports and recommended actions to the board. The board may also delegate to an **executive committee** authority to act for the board during intervals between meetings. Committees must exercise powers delegated to them strictly within the limits of the board resolutions which established them.

New York Stock Exchange rules require every listed corporation to have an audit committee consisting of outside directors. They have the duty of reviewing with the corporation's independent public accountants the annual and special audit reports, along with the internal accounting and financial controls of the company, and recommending actions deemed necessary. Large corporations have gone beyond the NYSE's audit committee requirement; they normally establish additional board committees in other areas of responsibility. Table 44.1 lists the committees of the boards of three large corporations.

Officers

A corporation's officers actively control and manage the company's business activities. They act under authority given by the board of directors and they carry out its announced policies.

Election. Officers are elected by the directors and hold office at the pleasure of the board,

Table 44.1 Committees of the Board of Directors

Corporation	Committees of the Board
Exxon	
18 board members	Audit committee
7 company officers	Advisory committee on contributions
11 outside members	Compensation committee
	Executive committee
	Finance committee
	Nominating committee
General Electric	
19 board members	Audit committee
3 company officers	Finance committee
16 outside members	Management compensation committee
	Nominating committee
	Operations committee
	Public responsibilities committee
	Technology and science committee
General Motors	
22 board members	Audit committee
9 company officers	Executive committee
13 outside members	Finance committee
	Incentive and compensation committee
	Nominating committee
	Public policy committee

which also fixes their salaries. If the board by contract establishes the tenure of officers, they still serve only at the board's pleasure. Of course, if they are discharged before the end of their contract period, the corporation could be liable for breach of contract.

Generally, bylaws provide for a president, one or more vice presidents, a secretary, and a treasurer. The bylaws also describe general duties and authority of each officer, and the board assigns additional duties from time to time. One person may hold more than one office, but in most states the same person cannot be both president and secretary. However, a growing minority of states have eliminated this prohibition to accommodate the needs of close corporations. In large, publicly held corporations, the board may designate a **chief executive officer (CEO)**. If such an office is created, it is generally filled by the president or by the chairperson of the board.

Authority of Officers. Corporate officers are employees of the corporation and, as its agents, may bind the corporation in contract and in tort when acting within the scope of their authority. On the other hand, directors are *not* agents of their corporation except when they meet and act as a board.

Authority of an officer may be express, implied, or apparent. An officer's *express authority* arises out of statements of authority set out in the company's bylaws and in specific directions from the board often contained in formal resolutions. An officer's *implied authority* may stem from a reasonable understanding of the meaning and application of that express authority, from the powers previously exercised by an occupant of that office, or from the powers generally exercised by the incumbent of a similar office in another corporation in that general region. *Apparent authority* of an officer is the name given to the authority, whether or not it is express, that the corporation's actions lead a third party to believe the officer possesses. For example, a vice president in charge of rocket booster development would appear to third parties to have authority to approve a contract to buy rocket fuel even though internal rules of the corporation prohibit such authority. Nevertheless, because of *apparent authority*, the corporation is bound if the vice president contracts to purchase fuel from a supplier that had no notice or knowledge of the lack of authority. Under agency law (see Chapter 36), an unauthorized act of an officer will also bind the corporation if it later ratifies the act.

Duties Owed by Directors and Officers

In exercising their management functions, directors and officers owe a **duty of care** in the performance of their responsibilities and a **duty of loyalty** to the corporation [RMA 8.30(a), 8.42(a)].

Duty to Act with Due Care. Directors and officers may be liable to the corporation and to its shareholders if they do not exercise the proper degree of care in the performance of their duties. The test of what constitutes due care has been stated in several ways. The Revised Model Act (8.30) provides that a director shall discharge his or her duties

- In good faith
- With the care that an ordinarily prudent person in a like position would exercise under similar circumstances
- In a manner he or she reasonably believes to be in the best interests of the corporation

Some courts express the duty of care more strictly by holding that the care and skill must be what *ordinarily prudent persons* would exercise had they been *acting for themselves* at the time. Either standard of care may be difficult to apply to a business risk, so frequently taken by a director, where there is no known precedent to apply. For instance, suppose director Jones introduces a resolution authorizing the corporation to market a new product which he has researched and is certain will be successful. It will cost $2 million to test-market the product. Although Smith was absent from the previous directors' meeting when the product was fully discussed, at a later meeting she casts the deciding vote in its favor because she is a personal friend of Jones. Alas!

The project fails, $2 million is lost, and the corporation's shares go down in value. Are directors Jones and Smith liable to the corporation and shareholders for the losses sustained—on the theory that a prudent person would have voted against the project?

Business judgment rule. In the event Jones and Smith are sued, they will probably deny liability, claiming they had used the due care required of a director under the **business judgment rule** in a matter where no one could guarantee success or failure. The business judgment rule applies to directors and officers who must make business decisions, and holds that a director or officer who acts in good faith is not liable for a business decision which causes loss to the corporation if (1) the decision was not induced by any element of fraud, conflict of interest, or other illegality, and (2) there was no *gross negligence* in reaching that decision.

As a member of a policymaking board, a director must be fully informed of company affairs and make rational decisions founded upon reasonable information. The information may be furnished by other directors, officers, or employees of the corporation, by its legal counsel, by accountants or other professional experts, by committees of the board, or by a director's independent reasonable investigation to discover the relevant facts. Directors have failed to exercise the required care if:

- They repeatedly fail to attend meetings of the board
- In preparation for a meeting, they fail to analyze the corporation's latest financial statements prepared by in-house and independent auditors or to review legal opinions of its attorneys pertinent to the corporation's activities
- They do not become conversant with available information relevant to their duties

If, because of such omissions, the corporation suffers financial loss, the director may be liable in damages to the corporation or to its shareholders, but the negligent director is not liable to creditors of the corporation who are only indirectly injured. From the foregoing, we can conclude that director Jones in the example above has the business judgment rule shielding him from liability, but director Smith may not be so fortunate.

Business judgment rule in hostile takeovers. In the following case, Delaware's supreme court held that a board's defensive actions in response to a hostile takeover must be "reasonable in relation to the threat posed" in order to come within the ambit of the business judgment rule. But if the board has the firm up for sale, the business judgment rule requires directors to maximize share price for the benefit of stockholders.

CASE 44.3   **Paramount Communications v. Time, Inc.** • 571 A.2d 1140 (Del. 1989)

FACTS   Beginning in 1983 Time's board developed a long-term plan to move into video and filming. In 1989, Time proposed to Warner Communications a stock-for-stock trade, with the two firms' CEOs co-managing the merged companies for 5 years. Warner would merge into a Time subsidiary, and Warner would be the surviving corporation with a 24-member board, 12 to be named by Time and 12 by Warner. The new board was to create an entertainment committee with a majority from Warner, and a publishing committee with a majority from Time. Time agreed to a "no shop" clause giving up its power to consider any other merger proposals. Time's and Warner's boards approved the merger. Time set its stockholder vote for June 23 and sent out proxy statements urging approval of a merger that would combine $30 billion of corporate assets.

CASE 44.3 Continued

On June 7 Paramount Communications announced an all-cash offer of $175 per share to Time stockholders. The following day, Time stock shot up from $126 to $170 per share, and later to $182. On June 8, Time's board rejected Paramount's offer, and voted that merger with Warner was the better course. The board also debated but rejected a proposed "Pac Man defense," whereby Time would launch a tender offer for Paramount's stock, thus consuming its rival. The board then voted to restructure the Warner deal with a cash offer to buy 51 percent of Warner's stock for $70 per share, purchasing the rest later by incurring a $7 billion to $10 billion debt. On June 23 Paramount raised its offer to buy Time stock to $200 per share. Time's board again voted to reject the bid and concluded that Warner offered a greater long-term value for stockholders. Paramount and a group of Time shareholders filed suit to enjoin Time's proposed merger with Warner. The injunction was denied, and Paramount appealed to the Delaware Supreme Court.

OPINION

HORSEY, J. The Shareholder plaintiffs . . . argue that Time's board's decision to merge with Warner imposed a fiduciary duty to maximize immediate share value and not erect unreasonable barriers to further bids [from other corporate suitors]. Paramount contends that the Chancellor [a judge in a court of equity] . . . erred in finding that Time's board had reasonable grounds to believe that Paramount posed both a . . . threat to Time shareholders and a danger to Time's corporate policy and effectiveness. Paramount also contests the court's finding that Time's board made a reasonable and objective investigation of Paramount's offer so as to be informed before rejecting it. . . .

Paramount argues that the underlying motivation of Time's board in adopting these defensive measures was management's desire to perpetuate itself in office. The Court of Chancery posed the pivotal question presented by this case to be: Under what circumstances must a board of directors abandon an in-place plan of corporate development in order to provide its shareholders with the option to elect and realize an immediate control premium? As applied to this case, the question becomes: Did Time's board, having developed a strategic plan of global expansion to be launched through a business combination with Warner, come under a fiduciary duty to jettison its plan and put the corporation's future in the hands of its shareholders?

. . . Directors, generally are obliged to charter a course for a corporation which is its best interest. . . . A board of directors, while always required to act in an informed manner, is not under any per se duty to maximize shareholder value in the short term, even in the context of a takeover. . . . The pivotal question presented by this case is: Did Time by entering into the proposed merger with Warner, put itself up for sale? [Whenever a corporation (1) initiates active bidding to sell itself, (2) seeks reorganization, or (3) in response to a bidder's offer, abandons long-term strategy in favor of alternatives that involve a breakup of the company] . . . we impose upon the board a duty to maximize immediate shareholder value and an obligation to auction the company fairly. . . . We do not find in Time's recasting of its merger agreement with Warner from a share exchange to a share purchase a basis to conclude that Time had either abandoned its strategic plan or made a sale of Time inevitable. . . . Our task is sim-

**CASE 44.3
Continued**

ply to review the record to determine whether there is sufficient evidence to support the Chancellor's conclusion that the initial Time-Warner agreement was the product of a proper exercise of business judgment. . . . In *Unocal Corp. v. Mesa Petroleum Co.*, 493 A.2d 946 (1985), we held that before the business judgment rule is applied to a board's adoption of a defensive measure, the burden will lie with the board to prove (a) reasonable grounds for believing that a danger to corporate policy and effectiveness existed; and (b) that the defensive measure adopted was reasonable in relation to the threat posed.

In this case, the Time board reasonably determined that inadequate value was not the only . . . threat that Paramount's all-cash, all-shares offer could present. . . . One concern was that Time shareholders might elect to tender into Paramount's cash offer in ignorance or a mistaken belief of the strategic benefit which a business combination with Warner might produce.

Paramount also contends that the Time board had not duly investigated Paramount's offer. The record does, in our judgment, demonstrate that Time's board was adequately informed of the potential benefits of a transaction with Paramount. . . . The fiduciary duty to manage a corporate enterprise includes the selection of a time frame for achievement of corporate goals. That duty may not be delegated to the stockholders. Directors are not obliged to abandon a deliberately conceived corporate plan for a short-term shareholder profit unless there is clearly no basis to sustain the corporate strategy. . . . Time's responsive action to Paramount's tender offer was not aimed at "cramming down" on its shareholders a management-sponsored alternative, but rather had as its goal the carrying forward of a pre-existing transaction in an altered form. Thus, the response was reasonably related to the threat. . . . Finally we note that although Time was required, as a result of Paramount's hostile offer, to incur a heavy debt to finance its acquisition of Warner, that fact alone does not render the board's decision unreasonable so long as the directors could reasonably perceive the debt load not to be so injurious to the corporation as to jeopardize its well being.

JUDGMENT [The Supreme Court affirmed the Chancellor's denial of an injunction against the Time-Warner merger.]

"Other Constituency Laws" Effect on Business Judgment Rule. The above case highlights a century-old conflict concerning the appropriate standard for directors' decisions. The traditional view, stated by the American Law Institute in 1984, is that a corporation's primary objective should be enhancement of "corporate profit and shareholder gain," although it *may* devote a "reasonable amount of resources to public welfare, humanitarian, educational, and philanthropic purposes." An opposing view is that directors in their deliberations should take into account "other constituencies" such as employees, suppliers, or even a community at large. To obstruct attempted takeovers in the past decade, over eighty major American corporations have amended their articles to require directors to weigh interests of "other constituencies" when considering a business combination. Such provisions make it easier for a board to resist a Paramount-type takeover, particularly when the board has to explain to its shareholders why it opposes a very attractive cash offer to buy their stock. Half of the states

> **BOX 44.2**
>
> **A Question of Ethics**
>
> Where would you invest your savings dollars? In stock of a corporation whose directors are committed to the principle of:
>
> - Maximizing profit and stockholders' per-share value, with *permissive* discretion to donate corporate funds to educational, charitable, and humanitarian causes
>
> *or*
>
> - Furthering interests of shareholders and "other constituencies," including employees, creditors, customers, suppliers, and the community.

have now adopted **other constituency** statutes.[7] Delaware has not, but the decision in *Paramount* affirmed directors' right to look beyond the short-term interests of shareholders when considering an attractive tender offer. All other constituency statutes permit directors to consider nonstockholder constituencies such as employees, customers, creditors, suppliers, and national, state, and community economies, as well as long- and short-term interests of the corporation and shareholders. Connecticut law provides that boards *must* consider other constituencies, but the remaining state statutes provide that boards *may* consider them. The greater discretion given boards under these statutes will doubtless encourage directors to resist attractive takeover offers by lessening their fear of shareholder suits for doing so. On the other hand, it may be argued that a corporation's stock values can decline if investors are reluctant to buy stock in a company whose board of directors is not bound to the traditional standard of maximizing profit and per-share stock value.

---

[7]The states are Arizona, Connecticut, Florida, Georgia, Hawaii, Idaho, Illinois, Indiana, Iowa, Kentucky, Louisiana, Maine, Massachusetts, Minnesota, Missouri, Nebraska, New Jersey, New Mexico, New York, Ohio, Oregon, Pennsylvania, Tennessee, Wisconsin, and Wyoming.

In recent years, increasing awareness of the standard of care that directors must observe under the business judgment rule has prompted shareholders to initiate a flood of litigation claiming gross negligence against directors in the discharge of their duties. Most states have enacted statutes that permit their domestic corporations to indemnify (reimburse) directors for the expenses, settlement payments, and other costs they must pay in defending themselves in this type of litigation. Corporations generally purchase insurance as protection against such expenses. However, because of the difficulty in procuring adequate insurance and because of the increase in premium costs when coverage is obtainable, Delaware, effective July 1, 1986, amended its General Corporation Law in Sec. 102(b)(7). That section allows a certificate of incorporation to contain a provision *eliminating or limiting the personal liability of a director to the corporation or to its shareholders arising out of breach of duty of due care*. As a result, insurance coverage should be more procurable. In addition, the Delaware law broadens a corporation's authority to indemnify its directors for damages imposed upon them by third-party suits arising out of their performance of corporate duties. The limitation on liability does *not*, however, apply to:

- A breach of duty of loyalty to the corporation
- Acts or omissions not in good faith
- Intentional misconduct or a knowing violation of law
- Paying a dividend or making a stock purchase in violation of law
- A transaction from which the director derived an improper personal benefit

Other states are fast following Delaware's lead, and corporations are hastening to amend their articles accordingly, stating in their annual reports, in substance, "the board of directors believes that to continue to attract and retain qualified directors, the company must act to reduce the personal risk of a director."

Duty of Loyalty. Directors and officers stand in a *fiduciary* relationship to the corporations they serve. (The Latin root for fiduciary, *fides,* means faith, trust, or public confidence.) Investors who buy a corporation's stock place trust and confidence in the directors and officers, expecting them to manage and work for the corporation to make it profitable. This requires, in addition to the duty of due care, a duty of loyalty. If directors or officers act so as to create a conflict of interest between themselves and the corporation, they have breached their fiduciary duty. In closely held corporations that are operated much like partnerships, where shareholders are also directors and officers, there exists an even higher degree of trust and confidence. Nevertheless, the fiduciary duty is often breached in an endless variety of ways.

Doing business with a corporation. If a director or an officer sells property to the corporation, the possibility exists that such self-dealing has led the corporation into an unfavorable transaction. Some courts follow the common law view that such a purchase is *voidable* at the option of the corporation. The modern view, however, is that the transaction is *not* voidable (1) if the contract is fair to the corporation or (2) if the conflict is fully disclosed or known to the *disinterested* directors or to the shareholders, and without counting the vote or consent of the *interested* parties, either body approves or ratifies the transaction (RMA 8.31). Some courts are even stricter in applying this rule and require that the transaction must be *just and reasonable* in addition to being fully disclosed. The corporation may rescind any contract between it and its directors or officers that is neither fair nor approved by disinterested directors or shareholders. Alternatively, the contract may be affirmed, and any damages that the corporation may have sustained may be recovered from the wrongdoing director or officer.

Fixing one's own compensation. In large corporations, salaries of officers are fixed by a committee of outside directors; therefore, although the entire board approves the salaries, a director who is also an officer of the corporation is protected from the charge of self-dealing. However, self-dealing is unavoidable in a case where the majority of the board of directors are outside members who fix their own compensation. If directors' compensation does not bear a reasonable relation to the services they are required to render, shareholders may bring a successful suit to limit or deny that amount. Court rulings in these suits are often based upon the premise that directors do not have unlimited freedom to give away corporate property against loud shareholder protests.

In closely held corporations, since directors and shareholders are usually one and the same, there is generally no legal problem of compensation. However, a minority member of the board may bring action if the remuneration bears no reasonable relation to the services the individuals are to perform.

Competing with a corporation. Directors or officers of a corporation who either personally or through another business compete with their corporation may or may not be breaching a fiduciary duty, depending upon the particular facts. For example, it would be bad faith and a breach of duty if a director or officer used influence to prevent the corporation from competing with a private business concern in which the director had a personal interest, or used corporate employees in a personal venture in which the corporation had no interest, or accepted secret profits or commissions, or revealed trade secrets to outsiders.

A similar type of conflict of interest may arise where five or six persons participate as directors on the boards of *two* corporations which contract with each other (called **interlocking directorates**). In effect, the directors are acting as advisors to a competing entity, and because a conflict of interest is presumptively present, interlocking directorates are viewed with suspicion. Courts apply the same standard of fairness as in the case of directors pursuing their own personal interest.

Seizing corporate opportunity. Directors or officers improperly compete with the corporation when they personally take advantage of an economic or business opportunity which rightfully belongs to the corporation. The **corporate opportunity doctrine** holds that when a business opportunity comes to the attention of directors or officers, they must first submit it to the corporation, and only when the company refuses the opportunity can they utilize it themselves. Generally, the corporate opportunity rule applies when

- A director or an officer becomes aware of the opportunity in his or her corporate capacity
- The corporation customarily deals in such an opportunity
- The opportunity is developed with corporate capital, facilities, or personnel

A corporate opportunity is *not* usually held to exist if

- The corporation cannot obtain necessary financing despite the directors' best efforts
- Involvement by the corporation would be *ultra vires*
- The director or officer who discovers the opportunity submits it to his or her company and a majority of the *disinterested* directors votes against the proposal

In the case below, two controlling directors squeezed out the third director and seized the corporate opportunity for themselves.

CASE 44.4 J. Bar H, Inc. v. Johnson • 822 P.2d 849 (Wyo. 1991)

FACTS In 1976 Joanna Johnson created J Bar M, a game-processing business which she operated as a sole proprietorship. In 1983, she and Donald and Irene Harger incorporated as J Bar H, Inc., and 50 percent of the stock was issued to her and 50 percent to the Hargers. A stock restriction agreement was signed, naming as directors the two Hargers and Johnson, but gave her the right to name a fourth director so long as she was a stockholder. The agreement set forth with specificity the managerial duties of each party.

The parties had very different backgrounds. Johnson had experience in game processing but never before served on a corporate board. Mr. Harger had management experience in several large corporations. He became increasingly dictatorial, and in 1986 began to squeeze Johnson out of the business. He terminated her, cut off her salary, changed the locks on the business, and told employees not to allow her to enter. Since the business was losing money, in May 1988 the Hargers, without consulting Johnson, adopted a resolution in which J Bar H, Inc., borrowed $247,000 from themselves in exchange for corporate notes. After the squeeze-out, Johnson started another meat-processing business and solicited business from many of the outfitters who were J Bar customers. The Hargers filed a shareholders' derivative suit on behalf of the corporation, claiming that Johnson had seized the corporate opportunity of J Bar H for herself, and asked for an injunction restraining her from running a competing business. Johnson cross-filed for dissolution of the corporation. The trial court found that Johnson had breached her fiduciary duty by commencing a competing business, but only because she had been squeezed out of J Bar H and, therefore, there was no damage. The Hargers appealed to the Wyoming Supreme Court.

OPINION CARDINE, J. This case presents a textbook example of oppression and deadlock in a small, closely-held corporation. The trial court ordered the corporation dissolved and a receiver appointed. It found that money loaned to the corporation [by the Hargers] was not a valid debt of the corporation. It also refused to order relief in the corporation's derivative action against Johnson for starting a competing business. . . .

CASE 44.4 Continued

Corporate officers and directors have a fundamental duty of loyalty and fiduciary responsibility to the corporation they manage. In the small, closely-held corporation, this duty is also reciprocal between the officers/directors of the corporation. The Hargers violated their fiduciary duty to Johnson when they performed a classic "squeeze-out" against Johnson's interests in the corporation. In their treatise on oppression . . . O'Neal and Thompson describe some of the harms which a minority shareholder may endure when "squeezed out" of participation in a closely-held corporation:

> The losses which a minority shareholder suffers in a squeeze-out are sometimes catastrophic. He may be deprived of any effective voice in the making of business decisions. Not only that, he may be locked out of the company's premises; and majority participants may be able to withhold from him information on the affairs of the business and on policies being adopted and decisions being made. . . .
>
> Quite commonly when a participant invests in a close corporation he expects to work in the business on a full-time basis. He may put practically everything he owns into the business and expect to support himself from the salary he receives as a key employee of the company. Whenever a shareholder is deprived of employment by the corporation . . . he may be in effect deprived of his principal means of livelihood.

. . . It has been generally held that in the absence of a contractual provision to the contrary, corporate fiduciaries, including directors and officers, are free to resign and form a competing enterprise. They must not, however, form a competing enterprise while serving as directors. . . . This case is subtle, because although Johnson was nominally an officer and director of J Bar H when she began her competing business, she had also been squeezed out of a managerial role. . . . From an equitable standpoint, we must treat this case as if Johnson had resigned her offices in the corporation when she was shut out of the exercise of them. As a "former" director and officer, Johnson was under no obligation not to compete when she formed her business. The Hargers have claimed that Johnson improperly appropriated the customer list for J Bar H. However, . . . most of the customers . . . had known her for many years.

JUDGMENT [The supreme court affirmed the trial court's order denying the Hargers damages for Johnson's starting a competing business, and ordering corporate dissolution.]

Statutory Obligations. Statutes direct that all dividends or distributions to shareholders must be paid out of corporate earnings and not out of corporate capital. In addition, the Revised Model Act (6.40, 8.33) and state statutes prohibit distributions or dividends if they would cause the corporation not to be able to pay its debts as they became due. If directors declare dividends or distributions in violation of such statutes, they are liable personally along with the corporation for any illegal payment.

Federal laws restrict directors when trading in their own company stock, and impose severe penalties on directors who negligently or intentionally misrepresent facts in a prospectus distributed to attract buyers of a new corporate stock issue. Federal law also imposes heavy fines and even prison terms for directors who disclose confidential inside information or engage in illegal insider trading. These federal laws are discussed in Chapter 46.

Protection against Takeover

Another side of management that has become important in recent years involves managerial decisions during an attempted takeover. A takeover means that an entity, by itself or with others, acquires control of a corporation by purchase or by otherwise controlling sufficient shares of its stock to take over its management. As we saw in *Paramount Communications v. Time, Inc.* (Case 44.3), the business judgment rule protects directors of a target company if (1) they believe the takeover threatens established policies and (2) their actions are reasonably calculated to counter that threat. On the other hand, *Paramount* also held that when it becomes clear to directors that their corporation will break up, their duty is to maximize per-share selling price.

Directors face other serious decisions in a takeover: (1) terms and conditions under which the corporation should accede to a friendly takeover by another entity, (2) what action the corporation should take to frustrate an unwelcome takeover, and (3) whether to provide special financial protection to the corporation's principal officers in event the company is taken over. Many decisions require shareholder approval at special meetings. Directors who believe that their corporation may be a takeover target may modify the corporation's financial structure in such a way as to ward off the takeover attempt. This restructuring is often referred to as **shark repellent** or as a **poison pill.** The usual device is issuance of a new class of preferred shares which must be repurchased from the shareholders by the aggressor corporation at a high price in the event the target is subjected to an unfriendly takeover. As a result, the cost of an unfriendly acquisition is increased so much that the corporation is "poisoned" and its takeover becomes economically unattractive.

Instead of fighting an unfriendly takeover, directors may decide to seek a friendly sale of the corporation to another company on terms and conditions more agreeable than those offered by the unfriendly suitor. When a suitable buyer is found (called a **white knight**), the directors conclude an amicable takeover agreement.

Yet another management ploy is used to defeat an unwelcome takeover when the holder of a block of the corporation's shares is threatening to gain control. The directors can authorize their corporation to purchase the aggressor's shares at a premium price in exchange for an agreement to discontinue the takeover attempt. Such a price, appropriately enough, is called **greenmail.** A related tactic involves the **Pac Man defense.** If the aggressor corporation's stock is widely held in the market, the target corporation can make a tender offer to purchase its controlling shares in an effort to defeat the adversary by simply swallowing it.

Top-echelon officers of large corporations hold lucrative positions. When a company is taken over by another corporation, there is likely to be a change in personnel at the top. To protect a key executive against that eventuality, the directors may give the executive a contract called a **golden parachute,** which provides special benefits if the corporation is taken over and the executive voluntarily leaves the corporation or is forced out. The extra benefits are often in the form of sizable severance fees, often two or three times an officer's annual salary. Directors may be personally liable to the corporation and to its shareholders if they authorize payment of greenmail or a golden parachute under such circumstances or in such amounts as not to be protected by the business judgment rule.

BOX 44.3

A Question of Ethics

Which, if any, of the following tactics during a corporate raid involve questionable ethics?

Tiger, Inc., attempts a tender offer takeover of Bambi, Inc. Bambi's directors quickly pass resolutions authorizing:

- White knight takeover
- Poison pill
- Golden parachute
- Pac Man defense
- Shark repellent

UNIQUE MANAGEMENT PROBLEMS OF CLOSE CORPORATIONS

As discussed in Chapter 42, a closely held corporation's management strongly resembles that of a partnership, and shareholders in a close corporation owe to their coshareholders fiduciary obligations similar to those of partners. If irreconcilable differences arise within a partnership as to how it will be operated, a partner, as a last resort, may cause its voluntary dissolution. But a minority shareholder cannot as readily dissolve a profitable close corporation, particularly in the absence of fraud by its majority shareholders. Special management problems frequently develop in close corporations because their structure differs significantly from that of publicly held corporations. Table 44.2 summarizes the differences between publicly and closely held corporations with respect to shareholder rights and management policies.

Management Problems of Close Corporations Analyzed

The management problems unique to close corporations can best be understood by examining

Table 44.2 Contrast between Shareholder Rights in Publicly Held Corporations and in Closely Held Corporations

Shareholder Right	Publicly Held Corporations	Closely Held Corporations
Transferability of shares	Most shares are freely transferable with little or no impact on the control of the corporation. No permission to effect transfer is required from the other shareholders.	The transfer may seriously disturb the balance of management control. To preserve such continuity, restrictions upon share transfer to outsiders are usually imposed by the bylaws or by agreement of the shareholders.
Marketability of shares	Shares can be readily sold on a securities exchange or in the over-the-counter market.	Because of the restrictions on share transferability, minority interests often cannot be sold except at a price far below their true going-concern value.
Shareholder control of corporation	Normally, a majority of the owners of outstanding shares elects the board of directors, who, by majority vote, manage the corporation.	Shareholders normally are also the directors and officers. The majority shareholders may adopt policies which would work to the disadvantage of the minority.
Dividend policy	A majority of the board determines when to declare a dividend and the amount of any dividend. A decision not to declare a dividend will generally not be disturbed by the courts.	Majority shareholders may vote themselves disproportionately large salaries and not declare dividends. They may also attempt to freeze out a minority shareholder.

the troubles of Hi-Tech, Inc., a hypothetical company. Al, Bob, and Carol formed Hi-Tech, Inc., each holding a third of its shares. The three were also the corporate directors and officers. Each was employed by the corporation: Al in production, Bob in sales, and Carol in accounting. Hi-Tech, Inc., was very successful. In 5 years each shareholder's equity grew to $150,000. Then friction began.

Voting Control Problem. Al and Bob consistently outvoted Carol on policy matters in directors' meetings. Al, with Bob's concurrence, has given Al's cousin Dan a job as Carol's assistant. Carol insists she needs no assistant. She is certain that Al and Bob intend to ease her out of her job and to ease Dan in. She has suggested long-term employment contracts for each shareholder, but the two men delay acting on the idea. Carol's attorney tells her that a majority of shares elects the board, and that a majority of the board makes policy. He says he can do nothing to assure her job security, as the other directors have not breached their duty.

Marketability-of-Shares Problem. Bob's wife holds a lucrative job with another company. She believes she will be transferred to another city. Bob, in anticipation of the move, asks his banker and stockbroker if they can sell his Hi-Tech shares. They say there is no ready market for them, that his best bet is to sell the shares to Hi-Tech, Inc., or to the other two shareholders. Bob lays his problem before Al and Carol and asks them if they or the corporation would buy his shares if he had to move. They give evasive answers.

Declaration-of-Dividend Problem. Al is planning retirement and has been sure his two co-owners would assist him in his retirement years by adopting a liberal dividend policy and a program for the firm's purchase of his shares over a period of time. Bob and Carol have ignored his proposal. They fear that if dividends are raised, they will have to pay more personal income taxes, and they want to continue the directors' policy of reinvesting profits for company growth. Bob does not agree to the corporation's buying Al's shares. That arrangement would block Bob's plan to have the company buy his shares. Al is angry and threatens to sell his shares to Dan.

Interruption-of-Continuity-of-Control Problem. Meanwhile, Al and Bob have good reason to suspect that Carol has a serious health problem and they fear this might result in an interruption of control of the corporation's affairs. Often, Carol has talked of making a gift of some of her shares in the company to relatives, and she says that in her will she is giving the remaining shares to her husband. Al and Bob do not relish a business relationship with Carol's husband. They are also concerned about company shares falling into the hands of Carol's relatives, who, they believe, would be neither cooperative nor competent businesspeople.

Freeze-Out Problem. Carol's freeze-out problem worsens. She knows that if Al sells his shares to Dan, Bob and Dan will then control the board of directors. She fears that they will freeze her out of the company altogether. She expects that they will terminate her employment; then, knowing she will need funds and that there is no market for her shares, they will likely offer to buy her shares at a ridiculous rock-bottom price.

What's that? You think Al, Bob, and Carol's problems are nothing but pure academic theory? Then you must read the next case. And as you do, keep in mind that it involved a courtroom battle royale between businesspeople whose problems were like those of Al, Bob, and Carol, with one difference: The problems in Case 44.5 were *very real* and *very* costly.

CASE 44.5   Wilkes v. Springside Nursing Home, Inc. • 353 N.E.2d 657 (Mass. 1976)

FACTS   Wilkes, Quinn, Connor, and Riche were the sole shareholders, directors, and officers of Springside Nursing Home, Inc. Each actively participated in the close corporation's management and received weekly salaries. Friction developed between Quinn and Wilkes. At a directors' meeting, new weekly salaries for Quinn, Riche, and Connor were established, but no provision was made for a salary for Wilkes. A short time later, at the annual shareholders' meeting, Wilkes was not reelected a director or an officer of the corporation. The other three then told him that they no longer desired his services or his presence at the nursing home.

Wilkes sued for damages in the amount of the salary he would have received had he continued as an officer and director of the corporation. A judgment was entered dismissing Wilkes's action. He appealed, claiming the majority shareholders had frozen him out in breach of their fiduciary duty to him as minority shareholder.

OPINION   HENNESSEY, C.J. . . . Wilkes's claim for damages [is] based on a breach of the fiduciary duty owed to him. . . . We do not consider it vital to our approach to this case whether the claim is governed by partnership law or the law applicable to business corporations. . . . Springside was at all times . . . a close corporation. . . . In *Donahue v. Rodd Electrotype Co. of New England, Inc.*, 328 N.E.2d 505 (Mass. 1975), we held that

> stockholders in the close corporation owe one another substantially the same fiduciary duty in the operation of the enterprise that partners owe to one another. [They must exercise] utmost good faith and loyalty. . . . They may not act out of avarice, expediency or self-interest in derogation of their duty of loyalty to the other stockholders and to the corporation.

In the *Donahue* case, we recognized that one peculiar aspect of close corporations was the opportunity afforded to majority stockholders to oppress, disadvantage, or "freeze out" minority stockholders. In *Donahue* itself . . . the net result . . . was that the minority could be forced to "sell out at less than fair value," . . . since there is by definition no ready market for minority stock in a close corporation.

"Freeze outs," however, may be accomplished by the use of other devices. One such device which has proved to be particularly effective in accomplishing the purpose of the majority is to deprive minority stockholders of corporate offices and of employment with the corporation. . . . The denial of employment to the minority at the hands of the majority is especially pernicious in some instances. A guarantee of employment with the corporation may have been one of the "basic reasons why a minority owner has invested capital in the firm. . . ." The minority stockholder typically depends on his salary as the principal return on his investment, since the "earnings of a close corporation . . . are distributed in major part in salaries, bonuses and retirement benefits." . . . In sum, by terminating a minority stockholder's employment or by severing him from a position

> **CASE 44.5 Continued**
>
> as an officer or director, the majority effectively frustrate the minority stockholder's purposes in entering on the corporate venture and also deny him an equal return on his investment.
>
> It is an inescapable conclusion . . . that the action of the majority stockholders here was a designed "freeze out" for which no legitimate business purpose has been suggested. Furthermore, we may infer that a design to pressure Wilkes into selling his shares to the corporation at a price below their value may well have been at the heart of the majority's plan.
>
> **JUDGMENT** . . . So much of the judgment as dismisses Wilkes's complaint . . . is reversed.

Some Solutions to Close-Corporation Problems

The major concerns of close-corporation owners, illustrated in the hypothetical case history of Al, Bob, and Carol and in *Wilkes*, reveal that all close-corporation shareholders have conflicting but related goals. On the one hand, they want their shares to be readily marketable at a fair price, and on the other, they do not want harmony and continuity of control of the corporation to be upset by inside shareholders transferring their shares to outsiders. Several devices are used to reconcile these objectives.

First Refusal Agreements.
In Chapter 43 we examined restrictions on transfer of shares of stock. A first refusal agreement may give the corporation (and then the inside shareholders) the right to purchase shares of a withdrawing shareholder at the same price and on the same terms as those offered to the seller by a legitimate outside purchaser of those shares. Such an agreement preserves continuity of control among the insiders, but for one or more of the following reasons it may not be the expected solution:

- The selling shareholder would most likely get only a very low price offer from an outsider. The outsider would not be willing to pay much for a minority interest in a closely held corporation whose majority shareholders might effectively engage in freeze-out tactics. Therefore, the low matching price that the corporation could rightfully offer would probably be unsatisfactory to the selling shareholder.
- Most states do not permit a corporation to repurchase its shares from any funds other than retained earnings. Therefore, if a corporation has insufficient retained earnings, it will not be able to buy the shares.
- If the corporation cannot purchase the shares, there is no assurance that the inside shareholders who have the opportunity to do so will have the funds to make the purchase or will want to add to their shares if they already have effective control of the corporation.

Thus, a first refusal agreement may effectively assure continuity of control, but it does not assure a market for a seller's shares.

Offer to Sell and Obligation to Purchase.
In some situations an *obligation* may be placed upon the corporation or on continuing shareholders *to purchase* the withdrawing shareholder's shares. When a seller of shares has a contractual right to *compel* a buyer to purchase, such right is called a **put**. The price is usually established annually according to a formula agreed to by the shareholders rather than by an offer from some outsider. A put provision in a stockholders' agreement normally establishes a reduced price for the shares, such as book value without allowance for goodwill. The reasoning behind this practice is simple. Since it is almost always inconvenient for the buying shareholders to be required to raise cash to accommodate the selling

shareholder, the *put price* should be attractive enough to reward buying shareholders for their inconvenience. A put clause in the shareholders' agreement assures them of an ever-ready market for their stock at a price that they have agreed is fair.

Transfer of Shares upon Death. The put clause in a stock restriction agreement or corporate bylaw is often supplemented with a provision for a similar arrangement when one of the parties dies. Because the shareholders do not know which of them will die first, each one is willing to accept an arrangement which obligates the survivors to pay a price per share closely approximating its market value. Therefore, the pricing formula generally includes the value of the firm's goodwill.

A surviving spouse or an heir may elect not to sell to the remaining shareholders the inherited shares, preferring to receive dividends on those shares and to benefit from a possible later appreciation in their value. To avoid such a situation, some agreements or bylaw provisions require the estate of a deceased shareholder to sell the shares to the corporation or to the surviving shareholders, with the reciprocal obligation upon the corporation or the surviving shareholders to buy them.

CASE 44.6   **Dixie Pipe Sales, Inc. v. Perry** • 834 S.W.2d 491 (Tex. App. 1992)

FACTS   Dixie Pipe Sales, Inc. (DPS), had a bylaw giving the closely held corporation the right of first refusal on a stock transfer. Rebecca Thompson Perry and her brother, Edward Thompson, each inherited 2,000 shares of DPS stock and presented the certificate to the corporate secretary for transfer on the books of the corporation. The corporation refused to transfer the shares. Instead, it claimed a right of first refusal under a provision in its bylaws and offered to purchase the shares, tendering to Rebecca and Edward the book value of the shares, in the sum of $800,000 each. When Perry and Thompson refused, the corporation sued for declaratory relief, asking the court to enforce the corporate bylaw. The court ruled for Rebecca and Edward and held that the first refusal provision did not apply to inheritance stock. DPS appealed.

OPINION   MURPHY, J. . . . Under article 2.22, the bylaw restriction "shall" apply to the transfer from the holder of the stock, including an executor, to a beneficiary under a will. There is no dispute that the restriction is noted conspicuously on the stock certificate. The only question remaining is whether the restriction is reasonable.

The provision in Dixie's bylaws is not unreasonable, but is calculated instead to advance legitimate objectives of both the corporation and its individual stockholders, that is, to keep the stock in the family. Such a restriction is inherently more "reasonable" when applied to the stock of a corporation having only a few shareholders who are active in the business and members of the same family, than when imposed on the stock of a corporation that has many shareholders who are not only unrelated to one another, but who, ordinarily, do not participate actively in the day-to-day management of the corporation. The restriction found in Dixie's bylaws is a reasonable restriction and is applicable to any disposition of Dixie's stock, including that made under a will.

JUDGMENT   [The court held for DPS and reversed the trial court.]

Remedies When Directors Are Deadlocked. The above case, as well as previous discussion, emphasizes the importance of shareholder-directors of a close corporation entering into a stock restriction agreement covering the problems of (1) guaranteeing continuous employment, (2) transfer of shares upon death, and (3) buy-sell provisions that guarantee a market for shares as well as a right of first refusal for continuing shareholders to buy the shares of a withdrawing shareholder. If shareholder-directors fail to take these precautions, they have five alternatives as their ultimate recourse: (1) to dissolve the corporation if it is so provided for in the firm's articles; (2) to seek a judicial dissolution of the corporation (see Chapter 42); (3) to seek, in the states which so allow, the appointment of an additional director to resolve the deadlock; (4) to resort to arbitration if that procedure is authorized in the corporation's articles or bylaws, or in a shareholder agreement; or (5) to agree that one group of shareholders will buy out the other.

SUMMARY

A corporation is limited by the powers in its charter. A corporation's express powers are conferred by state statutes and articles of incorporation. The corporation also has implied powers to do what is reasonably necessary to carry out its express powers. A corporation and its officers may be liable in damages for *ultra vires* acts that exceed its corporate powers. Under agency law, a corporation is also liable as employer for the wrongful acts of its employees in the scope of their authority. Similarly, a corporation has vicarious liability for crimes of high managerial agents committed in the course of authorized corporate business.

Corporate affairs and policies are controlled by a board of directors. In publicly held corporations, the directors consist of some individuals who have no other connection with the corporation (outside directors) and some who are primary officers within the corporation (inside directors). In closely held corporations, the directors are also shareholders and usually officers of the corporation. In both kinds of corporations, shareholders elect directors. The number of directors is fixed in the articles of incorporation. A board of directors acts by formal resolution adopted by a majority voting at a regular or special meeting at which a quorum is present, or by unanimous written consent without a meeting. The board may also act in special areas through committees composed of board members. Directors establish policy that is carried out by officers whom the board elects.

Directors must act with due care, in good faith, in accord with the business judgment rule, after becoming reasonably acquainted with all the facts involved in a particular matter. A director also owes the corporation a fiduciary duty of loyalty—that is, a duty not to act adversely to the corporation. Conflicts of interest may arise in doing business with the corporation, competing with it, or seizing an economic opportunity which rightfully belongs to the corporation. However, a director may contract with the corporation if the contract is fair and reasonable, or if disinterested directors or shareholders know of the conflict of interest and either body approves the transaction.

A close corporation has only a few members, all of whom are usually officers, directors, and shareholders. Because of this joinder of management and ownership, a close corporation resembles a partnership; hence, management problems not found in publicly held corporations may result. These problems usually center around conflict in voting control, lack of marketability of shares, and interruption of continuity in control of the business. In addition, a shareholder-employee-director may be discharged and removed as a director as a result of "freeze-outs" by the majority. Unfair freeze-out tactics may ultimately force shareholders to sell their shares at unreasonably low prices. However, courts will enjoin such tactics because of the fiduciary duty majority shareholders owe the minority.

REVIEW QUESTIONS

1. Explain **(a)** the sources of corporate power and **(b)** the limits upon it.

2. Distinguish between express and implied powers of a corporation.

3. What is meant by an *ultra vires* act of a corporation?

4. Can a corporation be liable for a tort or crime? Explain.

5. Distinguish among shareholders, directors, and officers.

6. (a) How does one become a corporate director? (b) How does one become an officer? (c) Who serves on board committees? How do they function?

7. Discuss four management problems of close corporations.

8. Define (a) corporate opportunity, (b) poison pill, and (c) greenmail.

9. Explain the business judgment rule, and the reasons for it.

10. What is meant by fiduciary duty? Explain your answer.

CASE PROBLEMS

1. After buying sheet panels, E. Ramos accompanied a K-Mart clerk to the loading area. The clerk unlocked a double-roller gate, which came off its track as he pushed it open and struck Ramos, causing severe head injuries. The court found it necessary to appoint a guardian to look after Ramos' affairs. Ramos' guardian, Pauletta Pearson, sued for gross negligence. The evidence showed that K-Mart's management (1) knew long before that the 100-pound gate tended to come off track, fall, and hit the ground, and was dangerous; and (2) had the ability to warn invitees of the danger and did not. After receiving detailed instructions from the court, a jury returned a verdict for $1.7 million in compensatory damages and $2.2 million in punitive (exemplary) damages. K-Mart appealed, claiming (1) that in view of its annual sales of $27 billion in 1988 and its net aftertax income of $803 million, the punitive damage verdict was excessive, and (2) that the verdict violated the due process clause of the Fifth and Fourteenth Amendments of the U.S. Constitution, since it amounted to an arbitrary fine. Should K-Mart prevail on either argument?

2. The bylaws of American Insurance provided for a board of eight directors and a quorum of at least five directors. A contract with Management Corp. was approved by a unanimous vote of six directors, the total number present at a meeting of American's board. Three of the directors who voted were also on the board of Management. Two of the three were the president and secretary, respectively, of both corporations. American later decided that the contract was against its best interests and gave Management notice of its termination. Management sued American for breach of contract and $90,000 in damages. American argued that the contract was voidable because a quorum of disinterested directors had not approved it. Is Management entitled to recover from American?

3. Ed Ash and his wife, Fay, owned 74 percent of Lumber Co., Inc., stock. The corporation borrowed $240,000 in exchange for demand notes payable to Ed, who was board chairman and president of the corporation. Ed was very wealthy and never required substantial payments on the notes, but when Fay filed for divorce, Ed stated: "I'll run the corporation into the ground as long as Fay has an interest in it." That year, Ed enforced payment of $140,000 on the notes. He then used his influence to cause the corporation (which was left with a deficit of $120,000) to file a notice of election to dissolve. Fay filed a derivative shareholder suit against Ed for breach of fiduciary duty to the corporation and its shareholders. Is Fay entitled to judgment on behalf of the corporation?

4. Arn and Ball organized Supply, Inc., and served as its directors and officers. Arn was the sole stockholder and personally guaranteed a $20,000 loan made to the corporation. No capital was invested by Ball. The corporation wanted to buy a building, but it did not have the required cash or credit, so Arn bought the building for its benefit. He obtained financing and "temporarily" took title in his own name. Ball knew that the corporation was making the monthly loan payment of $500 and entering it in the books as rent. The payments were shown as income on Arn's tax return. He also took the

depreciation and listed the building as a personal asset on his financial statements. The corporation went into receivership. The receiver sued Arn, claiming his building was a corporate opportunity which Arn had seized in breach of his fiduciary duty. Should the court order Arn to deed the building to the corporation, subject to the existing mortgage?

5. Emory, Arnold, Rose, and Sam each hold an equal number of shares in a closely held family corporation. They are the directors and officers of the corporation and are employed by it. It had been the practice of the board to retain all earnings in the business rather than to distribute profits as dividends. Arnold resigned from his positions as officer, director, and employee of the firm, but he retained his shares in the company. He told the board of his need for income and asked that the corporation begin to pay reasonable dividends. The directors declared very small dividends. Arnold contends that the directors declared the dividends, not in good faith, but only to "get even" with him, and hence breached their fiduciary duties. He claimed that the small dividends showed a concerted effort by the directors to deprive him of his right to a fair proportion of the profits of the business. On the basis of these facts, should Arnold expect to recover?

6. Long was president and sole stockholder of Longfield Corp., which had gone bankrupt. When the bankruptcy closed, the trustee let title to six parcels of worthless land revert to the corporation. Harrisburg City filed seven citations against the corporation for failure to cut weeds and grass on the properties. There was no evidence that Long intentionally neglected the properties. The trial judge found Long personally guilty for failing to comply with the citations issued against the corporation. On appeal, the court affirmed Long's guilt because

> individuals are subject to indictment in the criminal sphere, for acts done under the guise of a corporation. Long is the lone person left aboard an otherwise deserted ship. Under such circumstances it makes little difference if the sole occupant of the vessel is a rear admiral or a cabin boy; the mere fact of his solitude makes him the one who dominates and controls the vessel.

Should the state supreme court also pierce the corporate veil and hold Long personally guilty of the misdemeanor?

CHAPTER 45

Shareholders' Powers, Rights, and Liabilities

While the preceding three chapters focused on the formation, management, and financial structure of corporations, there has been an underlying theme: In a corporation for profit, the investing shareholders are of central importance. Although shareholders are the ultimate owners of publicly held corporations, they have only limited power to control corporate management. On the other hand, in closely held corporations, shareholders typically are active in daily management because they are also directors and officers. People become shareholders in publicly held corporations because they expect a return on their investment, and because if they need cash, they know they can quickly sell their shares—hopefully, at a profit. People become shareholders in close corporations because they want to be in business for themselves.

As discussed in Chapter 44, directors and officers manage corporations daily without consulting shareholders. Nevertheless, state and federal laws require shareholder approval of various extraordinary proposals that are of major importance to the corporation, such as electing and removing directors, amending the articles of incorporation, and approving a merger. This chapter reviews how shareholders function in a corporation and examines their powers, rights, and liabilities.

POWERS OF SHAREHOLDERS

Shareholders' powers are found in the state general incorporation law, in the corporation's articles and bylaws, and in the provisions of their stock certificate—which is a contract between the shareholders and the corporation.

Election and Removal of Directors

Shareholders meet annually and elect directors by a majority of the shares voted. The directors hold office until the next such meeting or until their successors are elected and qualified. If the directors serve staggered terms, the shareholders vote on the directorships that are vacated as of each annual meeting. For example, if there is a nine-person board, with three directors elected each year for a 3-year term, at each annual meeting there would be three vacancies which the shareholders would fill by election.

Under the Revised Model Business Corporation Act,[1] shareholders have the power to remove any or all of the directors (8.08). In most states, a majority of the shareholder votes cast at a duly called meeting may remove a director at

---
[1] Hereafter referred to as the Revised Model Act (RMA). Section numbers are given parenthetically or in brackets.

any time and no reason need be given for doing so unless the articles provide that a director can be removed only for cause. Often, in a closely held corporation one or two persons may effectively control the directors and thus have an indirect influence on corporate policy. In publicly held corporations, one or two persons may obtain control by soliciting proxies from other shareholders until they have a majority.

Sometimes majority shareholders will conspire *not* to remove a wrongdoing director. However, if there is cause for removal, the Revised Model Act (8.09) permits holders of 10 percent of the outstanding shares of any class to petition a court to remove a director for "fraudulent or dishonest conduct, or gross abuse of authority or discretion." The court may also bar a director from being reelected for a prescribed period of time. Many states that have not adopted the Revised Model Act, such as California and New York, have nevertheless enacted similar statutes that permit a 10 percent minority of shareholders to remove a director for cause.

Amendment of Articles

Articles of incorporation and state statutes establish how the charter may be amended (RMA 10.01 *et seq.*). There are many reasons for amending articles. Among them are (1) to change a corporation's name, (2) to change the number or par value of authorized shares, (3) to change the relative rights and preferences of issued or unissued shares, (4) to create new classes of shares, and (5) to grant or deny shareholders the right to acquire additional shares from the corporation (although any such provision cannot affect a stockholder's right to buy shares in the open market).

Shareholders must approve amendments to the articles, but ordinarily they do not initiate an amendment. Typically, the board of directors recommends to shareholders all proposals to amend the articles of incorporation. Generally, the board itself cannot amend the articles. In most states, a majority of the holders of the corporation's voting stock must approve an amendment to the articles. In addition, if an amendment will adversely affect a particular class of outstanding shares, a majority of that class also must approve the amendment.

> **BOX 45.1**
>
> ### A Question of Law
>
> Can an owner of 100 percent of the outstanding shares of a corporation dominate dividend policy of the board of directors by the terms of his will?
>
> Edwin died in 1962 owning all 110 shares of a family corporation. The will gave a close relative, Lily, a life income in 20 shares, and on her death, the remainder to go to Edwin's grandchildren. Edwin's daughter-in-law Madeline was controlling shareholder and she and her daughter and son-in-law were the officers and directors. For two years after Edwin died, the board distributed 100 percent of the corporate income to the shareholders, then suddenly reduced this to 60 percent. As a result, by 1989 the corporation had retained earnings of $10 million, and in that year the officers and directors received $2 million in salaries. Lily, age 82, sued for an order to carry out Edwin's testamentary intent, by declaring 100 percent of earnings as dividends. The court declined, saying: "A testator even though owner of all outstanding shares of a corporation cannot by testamentary device set a dividend policy for the board of directors elected subsequent to his death. Corporate policy cannot be run from the grave." However, the court did order trial on whether the majority breached their fiduciary duty to the minority by receiving excessive salaries.*
>
> *Winter v. Bernstein*, 566 N.Y.S.2d 1012 (N.Y. Misc. 1991).

Acquisitions by Merger or Consolidation

In the 1980s, the number of mergers and consolidations of major American corporations increased dramatically. Such amalgamations were encouraged by the structure of the U.S. income tax laws and by major financial considerations. During this period, courts interpreted antitrust laws liberally, and federal agencies regulated in such a manner that few mergers were prohibited. Laws concerning mergers and consolidations are complex and vary greatly from state to state.

A **merger** occurs when an existing and usually large corporation acquires all the assets and assumes all the liabilities of another, smaller corporation which then ceases to exist. The **surviving** corporation usually exchanges its securities or cash for the outstanding shares of the **disappearing** corporation, whose shareholders in turn receive cash or shares of the survivor. For example, in 1987 Chrysler Corporation by merger acquired American Motors Corporation. If you had owned shares of American Motors stock, you would now own shares of Chrysler Corporation.

A **consolidation** occurs when a new corporation is created for the express purpose of consolidating the assets and liabilities of two or more constituent corporations which then cease to exist. Their outstanding shares are usually exchanged for securities issued by the consolidated corporation. For example, X Corp. and Y Corp. exchange their stock for stock in Z Corp.

Both mergers and consolidations require shareholder approval. In many states, such as California, a majority of shareholders of each class of stock of both corporations must approve the amalgamation. Obtaining approval is a greater burden when giant corporations, such as General Electric and RCA, seek to merge, because their shareholders number in the millions.

Sale of All Assets of a Corporation

Under the statutes of most states a proposal by the directors to sell, lease, or exchange all, or substantially all, of the corporation's assets must be approved by a majority of voting shares. The directors have the power to sell, lease, or exchange corporate assets in the ordinary course of business. However, when the corporation owns only one major asset, the directors may no longer act alone. For example, suppose that the only asset of Ajax, Inc., is a hotel which Hilton, Inc., has agreed to buy. The sale is not in the ordinary course of business, and Ajax shareholders must approve it.

Typically, in a sale-of-assets transaction the purchaser does not assume any of the liabilities of the selling corporation. For this reason, a major corporation might choose not to acquire a small corporation by merger or consolidation; instead, it might choose to buy that corporation's prime assets with cash or stock. Another advantage of avoiding merger or consolidation is that no approval is required by the share-

---

BOX 45.2

A Question of Law

Under the Revised Model Act, the appraisal rights of a dissenting stockholder who is *adversely* affected by *amendments to the articles of incorporation* raise an important legal question: How adversely does a stockholder have to be affected to be entitled to appraisal rights?

Richard was a 36 percent minority shareholder in a Minnesota closely held corporation. Its 51 percent directors amended the articles to (1) delete a requirement of 30 percent shareholder approval for certain decisions, (2) reduce the number of directors from five to three so that the minority even with cumulative voting could elect only one director instead of two, (3) delete a 75 percent supermajority vote required to amend bylaws (thus deleting, a *veto power* for the minority).

The appeals court held that there was "not enough adversity to justify appraisal rights" but the Minnesota Supreme Court disagreed. Interpreting the Revised Model Act, the court said: "The amendments fundamentally altered Richard's rights such that he is entitled to be paid the fair value of his shares. . . . The difficulty of disposing of an investment in a close corporation . . . increases the desire of minority shareholders for a veto over corporate decisions."*

*Whetstone v. Hossfeld Mfg. Co., 457 N.W.2d 380 (Minn. 1990).

holders of the acquiring corporation. Following a sale of all its assets, the selling corporation may dissolve and distribute to its shareholders the cash or stock received from the purchasing corporation. Alternatively, the selling corporation could use its cash or stock to start a new business.

Appraisal Rights of Dissenting Shareholders

A shareholder who objects to a merger, consolidation, or extraordinary sale of assets and is outvoted by the majority can sell the stock on the open market. In the case of a merger or consolidation, if there is no market in the disappearing corporation's stock because it is closely held, the stockholder must accept stock in the acquiring or surviving corporation. When the majority votes to sell all the assets of a closely held corporation, the minority shareholder has no opportunity to sell or exchange his or her stock. However, most states today provide a remedy for the objecting shareholder, called *appraisal rights*. The Revised Model Act [13.02(a)(4)] also extends appraisal rights to shareholders who are adversely affected by amendments to the articles of incorporation.

In the exercise of appraisal rights, dissatisfied shareholders who object to a proposed merger, a consolidation, or an extraordinary disposition of corporate assets have a right to demand in writing that their shares be appraised and purchased by the corporation at a fair value. The corporation responds by making a written offer to purchase the shares. If the offered price is unacceptable to a shareholder, the corporation or dissenting shareholder may file suit for judicial appraisal and ask the court to appoint an appraiser to determine the fair value of the shares. The valuation approved by the court is binding upon the parties.

Although courts and legislatures have tended to view dissenting stockholders' rights as a perfect remedy, the system has flaws. For one, it tempts majority shareholders to try to oppress the minority, or even to squeeze them out of the company with the blessing of the courts. This problem is emphasized by the dissenting opinion in the following case.

CASE 45.1 **Stringer v. Car Data Systems, Inc.** • 841 P.2d 1183 (Ore. 1992)

FACTS Stringer and several others held 43 percent of the shares in Consumer Data Systems, Inc. (CDS), a close corporation. They sued thirty-two defendant shareholders (holding 57 percent of outstanding shares), including six directors of CDS led by Smith (Smith group). The Stringer group claimed that, incident to a cash-out merger (also called a squeeze-out or freeze-out merger) by CDS into Car Data, another corporation, the Smith group breached the fiduciary duty that a close corporation's majority stockholders owe to the minority. Stringer's complaint alleged that in 1989, Smith, CDS directors, and several large stockholders decided to squeeze the minority shareholders out of their ownership and offer them a sum for their stock far below its fair market value. The Smith group formed a new corporation, Car Data, and transferred all their CDS stock to it, in exchange for new Car Data stock. Car Data then held 57 percent (still a majority) of CDS shares, thereby ensuring that the Smith group's directors were still in control of CDS. Car Data shareholders next voted a merger with CDS, with Car Data to be the surviving corporation. Car Data then offered the Stringer group $ .002 per share, which they rejected, countering with a demand for $.10 per share. Car Data then commenced dissenter appraisal proceedings so that the Stringer group would be paid off and the Smith

CASE 45.1
Continued

group would have 100 percent of all stock in Car Data. The Stringer minority then filed an action against the Smith group and Car Data, claiming breach of fiduciary duty, and asking that the merger be rescinded and the corporation liquidated so as to maximize the return on their shares. The court of appeals affirmed the trial court's dismissal of the suit, and plaintiffs appealed to the Oregon Supreme Court.

OPINION

PETERSON, J. . . . A brief summary of cash-out mergers is appropriate. At common law, each shareholder of a corporation was considered to have a "vested right" in the corporation. As a result, the rule in many jurisdictions was that a single shareholder could veto a proposed business combination. Legislatures, courts, and commentators found that the right of a single shareholder to veto business transactions trammeled the concept of corporate democracy. The veto was therefore eliminated. The general rule today is that decision-making by the majority must take precedence over the objection of a lone dissenter. See Revised Model Business Corporation Act §12.01 (The Model Act).

The rejection of a minority veto and the recognition of a majority rule has not occurred without regard for the potential abuses of a majority's power directed against minority interests. . . . One device commonly used to eliminate minority shareholders who disagree with the majority shareholders about corporate decision-making is the cash-out merger. . . . Controlling shareholders often utilize a statutory merger as an instrument for squeezing out minority shareholders or altering their rights and preferences. . . . Undeniably, such mergers have a coercive element.

The Oregon statutes that permit cash-out mergers contain procedural protections for minority shareholders. . . . Dissenters from a proposed merger have a right to demand payment for their shares. . . . The appraisal procedure is the sole remedy for dissenting shareholders in the absence of "unlawful or fraudulent" conduct. . . . The dispositive question here is whether plaintiffs have alleged facts that would establish that defendant's conduct was "unlawful or fraudulent" within the meaning . . . [of Oregon's statute].

We start with the observation that this court may not question the wisdom of the Legislative Assembly in enacting the Oregon Business Corporation Act. That law drew upon the Model Business Corporation Act and contains procedures for majority shareholders to "squeeze out" minority shareholders.

> The accompanying proposals as a whole are designed to benefit both minority shareholders and controlling shareholders. Minority shareholders benefit because the assertion of their rights is made easier, and penalties are introduced for vexatious obstruction by corporate management. Controlling shareholders benefit directly and indirectly. They benefit directly by the added incentives for dissenters to settle without a judicial appraisal. They benefit indirectly because the provision of an adequate appraisal right diminishes the justification for courts to enjoin or set aside corporate changes because of the absence of an "adequate remedy at law," or because the corporate action "would operate as a fraud."

. . . A dissenting shareholder is entitled to payment for that which has been taken, the fair value of the stock. In determining the fair value of a stock immediately before the merger, many factors are relevant, including . . . the

CASE 45.1 Continued

price at which the shares had been selling; the amount, if any, of present share value increase or decrease because of anticipated future earnings of the corporation; corporate assets; corporate earnings or losses; corporate reputation; anticipated competition. . . .

Cases such as this are the very kind addressed by the statutory scheme. . . . Where the allegations show only a disagreement as to price, however, with no allegations that permit any inference of self-dealing, fraud, deliberate waste of corporate assets, misrepresentation, or other unlawful conduct, the remedy afforded by . . . [the Oregon statute] is exclusive. That is true even if the majority shareholders acted arbitrarily or vexatiously or not in good faith.

JUDGMENT

The decision of the Court of Appeals is affirmed.

DISSENT

UNIS, J. . . . None of the fiduciary obligations owed by corporate directors and majority shareholders were satisfied in this case. Plaintiffs . . . alleged that the directors of CDS, acting with three certain larger CDS shareholders, developed a plan to squeeze out plaintiffs for a nominal sum, a sum significantly below the fair market value of plaintiffs' shares. The squeeze-out merger was implemented just after the majority shareholders had rejected a third-party offer to purchase substantially all of CDS assets at a price substantially greater than the $.002 per share price set in the squeeze-out merger. The squeeze-out merger would have permitted the majority shareholders, which includes the six directors of CDS, to sell the CDS assets at this higher price without sharing any of the proceeds with the minority shareholders. . . .

The inference fairly drawn from the complaint is that . . . Car Data was no more than the alter ego of CDS's own directors and several of its largest shareholders. Its purpose . . . was to create a majority voting block to devalue the corporation's stock.

Had the three larger majority shareholders conspired with the CDS directors to reject a legitimate purchase offer and then sold all CDS's assets to Car Data at far below market value so that they could resell Car Data at a windfall price, I do not believe that the majority would find it as difficult to find "overreaching." Yet, in this case, an allegation that certain shareholders and the directors of CDS created a paper corporation in order to accomplish the same result through a "merger" is considered insufficient. I do not believe that the drafters of the RMBCA or the Oregon legislature intended to create a vehicle for this kind of business practice simply because they wished to facilitate legitimate business mergers when there is a disagreement among shareholders over the wisdom of the merger. [Fadeley, J. concurred in the dissent.]

Corporate Dissolution

A corporation may dissolve (sell its assets, pay its debts, and terminate business) either (1) voluntarily or (2) pursuant to court order. In most states, a majority of a corporation's voting shares has the power to voluntarily dissolve the corporation at any time. Thus, a majority of shareholders may choose to dissolve a corporation that is profitable and paying dividends.

An involuntary dissolution is more difficult to achieve. A shareholder must petition a court and set out facts that justify a judicial dissolution. The Revised Model Act [14.30(2)] and typical state statutes set forth grounds for court dissolution of a corporation upon petition of a shareholder:

- The directors are deadlocked in the management of corporate affairs, and irreparable injury to the corporation is threatened or corporate business can no longer be conducted to the advantage of shareholders.
- Those in control of the corporation have acted in a manner that is illegal, oppressive, or fraudulent.
- Corporate assets are being misapplied or wasted.

As a general rule, if the court grants a petition for involuntary dissolution, it will appoint a receiver to take over the management of a corporation. The receiver will proceed to sell all the assets of the corporation, pay its creditors, and distribute any remaining funds to shareholders. The following case discusses the grounds for involuntary dissolution of a corporation.

CASE 45.2   **Matter of Villa Maria, Inc.** • 312 N.W.2d 921 (Minn. 1981)

FACTS   John Mondati and James Sheehan formed Villa Maria, Inc., to construct and operate a nursing home. Each owned 50 percent of the outstanding stock. The board of directors consisted of Mondati and his lawyer and Sheehan and his brother. The two Sheehan brothers secured, and personally guaranteed, a $650,000 loan for construction of the home. Mondati secretly caused a corporation that he owned to purchase land next to the home and then, as president, arranged for Villa Maria to lease the property as a parking lot. Mondati refused to call special board meetings when the Sheehans requested them, and refused to attend meetings when the Sheehans called them, thus preventing action because of lack of a quorum. Mondati received offers to purchase the home but never told the Sheehans. He never gave them financial statements for the corporation. He refused to declare dividends, although requested to do so. A shareholder agreement between Mondati and Sheehan provided that if either shareholder wished to sell his stock, the other had the right to buy the shares at book value.

Sheehan brought suit in equity for a statutory dissolution. The trial court ordered dissolution and liquidation of the corporation's assets or, alternatively, gave Mondati the option to buy Sheehan's shares at appraised fair market value—not book value as provided in the shareholder agreement. Mondati appealed.

OPINION   OTIS, J. . . . The power of the courts to grant an involuntary dissolution of a corporation is governed by [the Minnesota statute enacted in 1980,] . . . which states in part:

> A corporation may be dissolved by involuntary proceedings in the discretion of the court when it is made to appear: . . .
>
> (3) that the directors or those in control of the corporation have been guilty of fraud or mismanagement, or of abuse of authority, or of persistent unfairness toward minority shareholders; or
>
> (4) that there is internal dissension and that two or more factions of the shareholders in the corporation are so deadlocked that its business cannot longer be conducted with advantage to its shareholders; . . .

**CASE 45.2
Continued**

The law is clear that "one entrusted with the active management of a corporation, such as an officer or director, occupies a fiduciary relationship to the corporation and may not exploit his position as an 'insider' by appropriating to himself a business opportunity properly belonging to the corporation." . . . By purchasing the land and then arranging for the terms of the lease between two companies in which he had an interest, Mondati breached his fiduciary obligation. . . .

We cannot escape the conclusion that Mondati used his position as president to run Villa Maria as he pleased and that in doing so he acted unfairly toward the Sheehans. The Sheehans personally guaranteed the loans which made it possible to build Villa Maria. They have seen no return on an investment they made in 1965 and have never received financial statements indicating the corporation's status. There have been no meetings, no consultations, and Mondati has refused to consider issuing dividends. The district court has the equitable power to adjudge the dissolution of a domestic corporation where there is prejudicial mismanagement by those in control. . . . The court was fully justified in ordering dissolution and therefore Mondati's rights were no longer governed by contract but were limited to the liquidation assets available under the statute. . . . Mondati's high-handed manner in running Villa Maria as though it were his own business and his failure to consider the interests of the other shareholder justifies Sheehan's avoiding the agreement.

JUDGMENT Affirmed.

SHAREHOLDERS' MEETINGS

Annual and Special Meetings

State statutes provide for two types of shareholder meetings: annual and special. A corporation's bylaws fix a time for the **annual shareholders' meeting,** the primary purpose of which is to elect the board of directors or to fill a vacancy in the membership of the board, and to review corporate operations of the previous year. Annual meetings tend to be routine and boring. Only occasionally will a meeting become lively by a shareholder questioning management's expenditure of funds or offering a resolution concerning the effect of the corporation's business on current social or political issues. If a place is not designated in the bylaws, meetings are held at the corporation's principal place of business. Any shareholder may seek a court order to compel the holding of an annual meeting if none is called by the board of directors after the lapse of a period of time stated in the articles, bylaws, or statute—e.g., 13 months after the last annual meeting or, if the Revised Model Act [7.03(a)(1)] is applied, the earlier of 6 months after the end of the corporation's fiscal year or 15 months after its last annual meeting.

As a general rule, a **special shareholders' meeting** may be called by holders of 10 percent or more of the shares entitled to vote, or by the president of the corporation. Special meetings are called infrequently, usually to consider matters requiring action before the next annual meeting, e.g., to remove a director, to consider a merger, or to change company auditors.

Notice of Meetings; Waiver of Notice

Most states require that the shareholders who are eligible to vote at an annual or a special meeting receive timely written notice of the place, day, and hour of the meeting and of the proposals which the shareholders are to consider. Timely notice usually means at least 10 days prior to the date of the meeting. At an annual meeting, shareholders may consider matters outside the scope of proposals stated in the notice. However, a different rule exists with regard to special meetings. Any action on a proposal not listed in the notice of a special meeting is void. Thus, for example, if a special meeting is called to approve a new stock option plan for key officers, a resolution increasing the number of directors on the corporation's board may not be presented to shareholders for their approval or disapproval.

Many states and the Revised Model Act (7.04) permit shareholders to take corporate action under certain circumstances without strict compliance with all the procedural requirements of a formal meeting:

- Lack of notice or defective notice may be waived if (1) all the shareholders attend the meetings in person or by proxy, and no one objects, or (2) not all shareholders attend the meeting but the absent shareholders, before or after the meeting, sign a written waiver of notice.
- Shareholders may take action *without a meeting* if all shareholders entitled to vote on the action sign written consents which are filed with the corporate minutes or records.

Obviously, these methods of informal action are not suited to publicly held corporations. They are especially useful to closely held corporations with few shareholders.

Proxy Voting

A shareholder may vote his or her shares in person or appoint another to do so. The appointee and the authorization which the shareholder signs are both referred to as a *proxy*. Most statutes require a proxy to be in writing, and, unless the proxy declares otherwise, its duration is limited to 11 months. Proxies can be limited to a particular transaction, but most proxies authorize the appointee to vote on all matters submitted to the shareholders. Most publicly held corporations send a proxy form with the notice of annual or special meeting and ask the shareholder to mark "yes" or "no" in regard to specific issues and to return the completed proxy before the announced date of the meeting. Solicitation of proxies by contending groups often is expensive and involves professional experts skilled in the strategies of vote accumulation.

Since a proxy is fundamentally an agency relationship for the purpose of casting a vote, proxies are governed by agency law rules. Unless a proxy is "coupled with an interest," it is revo-

---

BOX 45.3

A Question of Law

Should the court let a condominium project go to the dogs?

El Dorado Estates was an incorporated association with each condominium owner having one vote. Article VII of the bylaws permitted pet ownership. Notice of the 1979 annual meeting was sent to members stating there would be "Proposed Amendments to the Bylaws" without describing them. At the meeting Article VII was repealed and an amendment passed prohibiting pets anywhere on the premises. The Association sued Jim Carroll and others for a court order to remove their dogs from their units. Jim argued that the adoption of the "no dogs" amendment was void because notice of the meeting did not state the nature of the amendment prohibiting pets. Noting that Alaska's version of the Model Bus. Corp. Act did not require that notice of the annual meeting state the purpose, the Supreme Court made case law on the point. It said that since members of a condo association have a heightened interest in the corporation as compared to shareholders of other business corporations, a "higher standard of notice is therefore appropriate." Noting also that the Uniform Condominium Act (adopted by many states) requires notice to include items on the agenda, the Court held that the bylaw amendment was invalid so that, in effect, the dogs had at least a temporary stay of execution.*

*Carroll v. El Dorado Estates, 680 P.2d 1158 (1984).

cable at any time. Revocation occurs if the shareholder (1) dies, (2) attends a shareholders' meeting in person and votes the shares, or (3) signs a later proxy for the same shares. The rule that the last proxy signed is the one that is counted is important in the strategy of proxy fights for control of a corporation. A proxy is *coupled with an interest* if, for example, a shareholder pledges shares as security for a loan and, in conjunction with the loan, gives a proxy to the lender. The proxy is coupled with an interest because it is part of the lender's property interest in the shares, and, as long as the loan is unsatisfied, it cannot be withdrawn by the borrower without the lender's consent.

Quorum and Voting Requirements

A quorum is the minimum number required to conduct a meeting. Most states provide that a majority of the outstanding shares constitutes a quorum in the absence of some other figure specified in a corporation's articles or bylaws. A quorum may be achieved by shareholders attending the meeting in person or by proxy. In many major corporations it would be impossible to achieve a quorum without proxies because so few shareholders attend meetings in person.

Once a quorum is present, proposals may be approved by simple majority of the voting shares present. Of course, the articles or bylaws may specify that certain actions (e.g., a corporate purchase of real estate) require the approval of more than a simple majority of voting shares. In addition, many statutes require that certain actions (e.g., mergers and amending the articles) be approved by a majority of *outstanding* voting stock.

Voting Eligibility

Only holders of voting shares as of the record date fixed by the bylaws or by the board of directors have the right to vote at shareholders' meetings. In most states the corporation can establish a record date any time between 10 and 70 days prior to the meeting. The record date serves the dual purpose of determining those to whom the corporation will mail a notice of the meetings and those who are eligible to vote at the meeting. If you buy stock after the record date, you cannot vote unless you get a proxy from the seller.

Election of Directors; Cumulative Voting

An annual meeting of shareholders is held to elect the corporation's directors, who generally serve 1-year terms. Voting may be either straight or cumulative. Most corporations adopt a *straight voting system* whereby the holder of each share is entitled to one vote in filling each vacancy on the board. Thus, if you hold 100 shares of Ajax stock and there are several nominees for two director openings, you may cast your 100 votes for each of the two nominees you desire to serve on the board. Normally, a simple majority of the shares voting at a meeting at which a quorum is present can elect all the directors.

Under the *cumulative voting system*, shares may be bunched together and the total votes can be cast for a single director. For instance, assume that there are 100 voting shares at the meeting and that two slates of five directors each are nominated for five directorships. Assume further that the holders of 70 shares want one slate and the holders of 30 shares want the other slate. Under cumulative voting, each shareholder may cast 5 votes (5 directors × 1 vote per share) in any manner he or she wants, such as casting a single vote for each of 5 nominees, casting all 5 votes for a single nominee, or making any other desired division of his or her votes. If straight voting is used, the 70-share majority will elect its entire slate of directors. But if cumulative voting is used and the majority spreads its 350 votes (70 shareholders × 5 votes each) evenly over its slate of five directors, each nominee receives 70 votes. The minority shareholders can "single shot" their slate and cast their 150 votes (30 shareholders × 5 votes each) cumulatively for just one of their nominees, or they may divide their cumulative vote among two of their nominees, giving each 75 votes. In this way, the minority is assured of at least some representation on the board of directors.

Often, special-interest groups of a large publicly held corporation will attempt to buy or secure proxies for sufficient shares to elect one or more representatives to the board. Sometimes, several such rival groups become locked in a conspiratorial combat for control. When this happens, a drama of artifice and stratagem unfolds that even Machiavelli would find intriguing.

Corporations that adopt a cumulative voting system often diminish its effectiveness by permitting directors to be elected for longer, staggered terms. Suppose, in the above illustration, the articles are amended to provide for 3-year staggered terms, two directors to be elected in the first and second years, and one director in the third year. In the years that two directors are to be elected, if the minority cumulates its votes, it has 60 votes (2×30). The majority has 140 votes (2×70). Even if the minority casts all its votes for one candidate, the majority is able to cast 70 votes for each of two candidates and defeat the minority. With staggered terms the minority is frozen out and could never gain representation on the board.

SHAREHOLDERS' RIGHTS

Shareholders have a sizable bundle of rights that are conferred upon them by state statutes. In the preceding section we examined the shareholder's critically important right to vote. Other fundamental shareholder rights include (1) preemptive rights, (2) the right to inspect the corporate books, and (3) the right to go to court and bring certain causes of action against the corporation or controlling shareholders.

Preemptive Rights

Preemptive rights mean that shareholders have a right to preserve their proportionate stock interests by purchasing shares of a new issue ahead of other investors. The use of preemptive rights is designed to prevent the dilution of the existing shareholders' equity in a corporation when additional shares are issued. For example, suppose you own 15 percent of the XT Corporation and the board decides to issue 10,000 new shares to Dodd. Your 15 percent will be diluted and you will have a smaller percent of the total outstanding shares. A *preemptive right* means that you have first option to buy up to your percentage of the new issue (15 percent). If you decide not to, then Dodd can buy the shares.

All states, except New Hampshire, recognize preemptive rights, but most states permit the articles to limit or deny such rights. In some states, including California, Delaware, New Jersey, Michigan, Massachusetts, and Pennsylvania, preemptive rights are recognized only if they are established in the articles. There are several exceptional situations where courts will not apply preemptive rights, the most important being reissue of treasury stock.

The size of a corporation often determines whether its charter should authorize preemptive rights. Shareholders of closely held corporations may find that preemptive rights are crucial to voting control. Even where the articles do not protect preemptive rights, if directors propose a new stock issue so as to fraudulently seize voting control or oppress minority shareholders, equity courts in many states will invoke "quasi-preemptive rights" and enforce them in order to protect victims of wrongdoing. On the other hand, in publicly held corporations most shareholders own only a very small proportion of outstanding shares and are, therefore, unconcerned about preemptive rights.

Large corporations sometimes protect their shareholders in a manner which is similar to preemptive rights by issuing to their shareholders options to buy the corporation's shares at a stated price. Sometimes such options are issued as a substitute for a dividend. The options may take the form of *stock rights* or *warrants*. The option under a stock right expires within a relatively short time if it is not exercised. A warrant is a long-term option to buy a certain number of the corporation's shares at a stated price. Warrants are freely transferable and are frequently traded. Their value depends upon the option price specified compared with the market price of the corporation's shares.

The following case discusses the rights of shareholders in a closely held corporation when treasury shares are reissued.

CASE 45.3 Schwartz v. Marien • 373 N.Y.S.2d (N.Y. App. 1975)

FACTS Smith, Marien, and Dietrich each owned one-third (fifty shares) of the outstanding stock of Superior Engraving Co. When Smith died in 1959, the corporation purchased his shares as treasury stock. When Marien died in 1961, his shares passed to his wife and three sons. Thereafter, Dietrich, his daughter Margaret Schwartz, and two of Marien's sons constituted the four-member board. When Dietrich died in 1968, the three Marien directors called a special board meeting and the third Marien son was elected to fill the Dietrich vacancy. The three Marien directors then voted to have the corporation sell one share of treasury stock to each of them. The three treasury shares gave voting control of the corporation to the Marien family. Margaret Schwartz was denied the right to buy treasury shares to equalize the Dietrich holdings.

Schwartz sued the Marien brothers for breach of their fiduciary duty as directors and controlling shareholders. Schwartz's motion for summary judgment was denied, and she appealed.

OPINION JONES, J. . . . While preemptive rights as such do not attach to treasury stock in the absence of specific provision in the certificate [articles] of incorporation, members of a corporate board of directors nevertheless owe a fiduciary responsibility to the shareholders in general and to individual shareholders in particular to *treat all shareholders fairly and evenly.*

Departure from precisely uniform treatment of stockholders may be justified where a bona fide business purpose indicates that the best interests of the corporation would be served by such departure. The burden of coming forth with proof of such justification shifts to the directors, where, as here, a prima facie case of unequal stockholder treatment is made out. Particularly is this so, when it appears that the directors favored themselves individually over the complaining shareholder. Additionally, disturbance of equality of stock ownership in a corporation closely held for several years by the members of two families calls for special justification in the corporate interest; not only must it be shown that it was sought to achieve a bona fide independent business objective, but as well that such objective could not have been accomplished substantially or effectively by other means which would not have disturbed proportionate stock ownership.

JUDGMENT [The case was remanded to the trial court with instructions to proceed in accordance with the above opinion.]

Right to Examine Corporate Books

Shareholders, as ultimate owners of the corporation, have the right to inspect corporate records. However, since undue demands could be made on the corporation, limitations may be imposed on the exercise of the right. The records which shareholders most often wish to inspect are minutes of meetings, books of account, corporate contracts, correspondence, and lists of shareholders. As a general rule, shareholders may inspect these records, subject to two conditions: (1) the inspection must be at the corporation's home office during usual business hours, and (2) the inspection must be for a proper purpose. The latter requirement has caused considerable litigation. A proper purpose would include the right to inspect the records in order to determine the corporation's financial condition or the propriety of dividends, and to discover mismanagement. Some courts limit inspection rights by holding that a proper purpose must be related to the shareholder's economic interest in the corporation. In many states the rule is that if the shareholder alleges a proper purpose, the corporation has the burden of proving the shareholder has an improper purpose. Thus, a denial of inspection rights will be upheld only if the corporation proves that the shareholder has an ulterior motive, such as to aid a competitor, to discover trade secrets, or simply to harass management.

Management often tries to deny a shareholder a list of names and addresses of all other shareholders in the corporation, citing as an excuse the expense of preparation. The real reason may be self-defense—namely, to protect the position of incumbent directors and officers. Courts have upheld the right of a shareholder to secure a copy of a shareholder list even if the avowed purpose is to start a proxy fight. A proper purpose does not include developing a mailing list of well-to-do persons to sell to mail solicitation firms. Some statutes attempt to reduce capricious demands by limiting the right of inspection to shareholders who have owned their shares for 6 months or to holders of 5 percent of outstanding shares. However, Delaware gives shareholders the right of inspection regardless of the size or duration of their holdings.

An inspecting shareholder may be accompanied by an attorney, an accountant, or another agent. The shareholder is entitled to copies of documents, for which the corporation may make a reasonable charge. The following case illustrates a shareholder suit to enforce his right of inspection.

CASE 45.4 **Wrights Beauty College v. Bostic** • 576 N.E.2d 626 (Ind. App. 1991)

FACTS In 1978 Wrights Beauty College, a corporation, appointed Bostic director of one of its schools. In 1984 Bostic and his wife acquired stock and joined Martin and Vicky Wagoner as the only shareholders. In February 1990 the corporation discharged Bostic. At that time, in addition to the Wagoners and Bostics there was one other shareholder, Don Wagoner. After dismissal, Bostic asked to review corporate documents, but was permitted to see only a few of them. Bostic then made written request for corporate records relating to bank loans, real estate mortgages, certain contracts and leases, and all transactions with Don Wagoner. Upon refusal, Bostic filed suit. In his complaint he identified three reasons for his request to view the records: (1) to fulfil his obligations as a member of the board of directors, (2) to determine whether he had any individual liability for loans for which he had signed both individually and as an officer of the corporation, and (3) to evaluate his holdings in the corporation in order to determine if the corporation's offer to buy his shares was fair. Under a bylaw provision, the corporation had a right to purchase as much of his stock as it desired, but if the price offered by the corporation was disputed, the matter would go to arbitration. The corporation argued that these were not proper purposes for inspection.

OPINION SHARPNACK, J. . . . Under the common law of this state, a shareholder had the right to inspect corporate documents upon a showing of a proper purpose related to the interests of the shareholder. Modern statutes, like the common law, impose the requirement that the request be related to a proper purpose. . . . Our research reveals that a majority of states have determined that valuation is a

> **CASE 45.4 Continued**
>
> proper purpose. In *Helmsman Management Services, Inc. v. A & S Consultants, Inc.* (1987) 525 A. 2d 160, the court considered whether the valuation for sale of the stock of a corporation where the stock was closely held and not publicly traded, and where the corporation had the right of first refusal in any stock sale, constituted a proper purpose for inspection of the corporate records. The court . . . held that valuation was normally a proper purpose, and could be a proper purpose even where the shareholder had not yet definitely decided to sell the stock. . . .
>
> **JUDGMENT** Because we hold that valuation is a proper purpose for inspecting corporate documents under the terms of our statute, the court's finding that the documents are necessary for valuation supports its judgment ordering the corporation to allow inspection and copying. . . . We affirm the judgment of the trial court.

Rights of Action

Individual Suits and Class Actions. An *individual* shareholder may sue a corporation to enforce preemptive rights, inspection rights, or other rights to which the shareholder is entitled. Individual suits are also filed to recover dividends declared but unpaid, or to enjoin *ultra vires* acts. A group of shareholders may collectively pursue individual causes of action arising out of the same transaction by bringing a *class* action against the corporation. The individuals joining in the suit commence the action in their own names and on behalf of "all others similarly situated." There are two major requirements for a class action: (1) a common question of law needs to be resolved (e.g., Can directors be forced to pay a dividend to all shareholders of a class?) and (2) the class is so large as to make it impractical for the courts to handle multiple individual suits (e.g., a million shareholders in General Motors suing for a $10 dividend each). Other class members must usually be given notice of the pending suit and may elect to benefit from the judgment by paying a pro rata share of litigation costs.

Shareholders' Derivative Suits. If a third party or an insider wrongs a corporation and the value of its shares is depreciated, each shareholder suffers a pro rata share of the damage. If the corporation does not file an appropriate action, a shareholder may file a *derivative suit*, which is a legal action to recover for the wrong done to the corporation. The wrong may have been committed (1) by a third party, such as a customer who has failed to pay money owed to the corporation or who has infringed its patents, or (2) by a corporate insider, such as an officer who has looted the corporate treasury and seized a corporate opportunity, or has violated federal security laws to the damage of the corporation. The suit is for the benefit of the corporation, and the recovery belongs to it—not to the shareholder who brings the action. Therefore, a derivative suit protects the corporation and its creditors and equally benefits all shareholders because a recovery appreciates the value of all outstanding shares.

At times shareholders have used derivative suits to harass directors and officers with unwarranted accusations of mismanagement. These tactics have been used to intimidate management into making a lucrative out-of-court settlement or purchasing the complaining shareholder's stock at a favorable price. Abuse arising from such "strike" suits has led to restrictive statutes and court rules. Today, in most states in order to file a derivative suit, shareholders must meet several requirements. They must (1) own their shares at the time of the wrongdoing; (2) show that a demand was made on the directors (and in some states, the shareholders) to commence suit on behalf of the corporation; (3) show that the directors refused to sue; and (4) show that the directors' refusal was in bad faith. If steps 2, 3, and 4 would be futile, the courts often waive them. If no demand has been made on the board for action, the burden is on the shareholder to prove that such a demand would have been futile. For instance, a demand would be futile if members of a board were involved in a wrong to such an extent that the board's interests were antagonistic to those of the corporation. To be excused from going through the motions of a demand and refusal from the board, the shareholder must claim that directors were engaged in something more than mere negligence or even recklessness in their actions. The shareholder must claim that the directors are guilty of such intentional wrongdoing that it would be pointless to demand that they correct the situation.

In the event of a favorable judgment, a shareholder can generally recover reasonable litigation expenses from the corporation, but not anything for his or her time. Thus, a shareholder bringing a derivative suit must be a "crusader" type. Derivative suits and class actions are both initiated by stockholders, but there is an important difference: A derivative suit is commenced *on behalf of the corporation,* and the judgment recovered is the property of the corporation. A class action is a direct suit *against* the corporation for invasion of its shareholders' rights, and if a judgment is recovered, it directly benefits the shareholders.

The following case involves a derivative suit filed to recover "greenmail" paid to a well-known corporate raider.

CASE 45.5 **Samuel M. Feinberg Testamentary Trust v. Carter**
• 652 F. Supp. 1066 (S.D. N.Y. 1987)

FACTS In 1984, Carl Icahn informed the directors of B. F. Goodrich Company that he had acquired 1,171,700 shares, or 4.9 percent, of Goodrich's common stock and that he planned to acquire control and obtain seats on its board of directors. Icahn also offered to sell to the corporation his stock at $35 per share. The market price of Goodrich was then about $28 per share. On November 5, the directors accepted Icahn's offer and purchased his stock. Icahn agreed to abstain from acquiring any Goodrich stock for 5 years and agreed not to disclose the repurchase unless required by law. Goodrich announced the repurchase of stock in very general terms, but it did not disclose that the shares were purchased at a price significantly above the market price or that the shares were purchased from one individual. A similar general notice was given to the Securities and Exchange Commission in March 1985.

Two shareholders filed a derivative suit against the board of directors and Icahn, asking for various remedies, including rescission of the $41 million payment for Icahn's shares. The defendants moved for a dismissal of the suit on the ground that there was no demand on the directors to take appropriate action. The shareholders replied that such demand would have been futile.

OPINION WALKER, J. . . . The . . . purpose of the "demand" rule is to give the derivative corporation itself the opportunity to take over a suit which was brought on its behalf in the first place, and thus to allow directors the chance to occupy their normal status as conductors of the corporation's affairs. . . . However, such a demand is excused if the demand would be "futile," "useless" or "unavailing"; if the directors are "antagonistic, adversely interested, or involved in the transaction attacked, a demand on them is presumptively futile and need not be made.". . .

**CASE 45.5
Continued**

The Defendant Directors posit no proper business justification for their purchase of Icahn's stock at $35 per share, when this stock possessed a market value of $28 per share. This repurchase cost Goodrich a total of $41 million, or about $8 million more than a purchase of the same volume of stock in the open market. In return for this $8-million premium, Goodrich received nothing more than the 4.9 percent shareholder interest in Icahn's hands, his promise that he would not acquire shares of Goodrich stock for five years, and his promise of silence about the transaction.

. . . [Defendants] have pointed to no evidence indicating that elimination of Icahn as a shareholder would so improve the company's financial position to justify an $8-million premium. . . .

However, while the removal of Icahn as a potential Goodrich stock purchaser at an $8-million premium could only be accomplished at the expense of the individual shareholders, the same transaction would significantly benefit board members by securing the continued possession of their director positions. For, if Icahn in fact had consummated his proposed takeover, a change in Goodrich management, including the board of directors, was possible. With such a turnover, board members would lose the benefits they receive as Goodrich directors. Not only did such directorships carry with them an intangible benefit of prestige, they included significant financial rewards as well. Each of the directors received more than $200,000 in annual salary, with Defendants Carter and Patrick Ross receiving more than $300,000, and Defendant Ong receiving more than $500,000. If any director served on the board for five years, he was entitled to receive a yearly pension equaling at least half of his compensation during his final year on the board. The directors' desire to retain their positions furnishes the requisite "adverse interest" indicating that any plaintiff demand on the Goodrich board of directors would have proven futile. . . .

The adverse interest of the Goodrich directors is further indicated by their subsequent failure to disclose the Icahn transaction to the public and the shareholders. . . . The Court views the instant case as an atypical situation where the self-interest of corporate directors may well have dominated other considerations.

JUDGMENT

For the reasons set forth above, this Court finds that any plaintiff attempt to make demand in the instant case would prove futile. Defendants' motion to dismiss for failure to make demand is denied. . . .

SHAREHOLDERS' LIABILITIES

The fact that a shareholder's liability is limited to his or her capital investment is perhaps the most important reason that businesspeople form corporations instead of partnerships. Nevertheless, there are exceptions to the principle of limited liability. For example, in newly formed close corporations where shareholders are also usually officers, lenders and other creditors generally insist that loans or other credit extended to the corporation be *personally* guaranteed by the stockholders. Thus, as a practical matter, the corporation does not insulate them from personal liability. There can also be personal liability if, as discussed in Chapter 41, creditors prove that shareholders are abusing the corporate privilege and "pierce the corporate veil." Other liabilities which frequently arise are discussed in the following paragraphs.

Liability for Unpaid Subscriptions

Stock subscriptions are discussed in Chapter 42. Some subscriptions provide that the subscriber will pay for the stock by making installment payments. If the corporation becomes insolvent or bankrupt, the subscriber remains liable for the unpaid balance owing on the subscription. If the subscriber dies, his or her estate is liable for the balance due.

Liability for True Value of Shares

Shares are sometimes issued for overvalued property. If there has been fraud on the part of the shareholder or bad faith on the part of the directors, the shareholder is liable for the amount of any underpayment that results. In such cases the stock is called "watered stock." Courts have used a variety of theories to impose liability on the stockholder but the end result, in most cases, is to hold the shareholder liable to the corporation (or to its creditors) for the difference between the inflated value and the true value of the property—that is, for the "water." Stated another way, the shareholder must pay the difference between the true value of the property and the issuance price of his or her shares.

As noted in Chapter 43, a corporation is not permitted to issue stock (other than treasury stock) at a price below par value. Thus, for example, if stock has a par value of $10 per share, the corporation should receive for each share $10 in cash, property, or services. In many states an exception is made where the directors in good faith attempt but are unable to find anyone who will pay the full par value. In such a case, the corporation may issue shares at a "discount," show them as fully paid, and disclose both the discount and the value of the consideration on its balance sheet. This is not a watered stock transaction, and the shareholder is not liable to the corporation or its creditors even though he or she pays less than par value. In any case, whether the sale was fraudulent or made in good faith, an innocent purchaser of stock from the initial shareholder is not liable for any deficiency.

Liability for Unlawful Dividends and Distributions

Many states permit a corporation to recover from shareholders who know that a dividend or another corporate distribution is unlawful. Rules governing the declaration of dividends by directors are discussed in Chapter 43. Of course, the obvious problem is proving that a shareholder *knows* of the illegality. In a closely held corporation, the corporation (or creditors) might have a chance to prove such knowledge, since shareholders in a closely held corporation typically are active in the business as officers and directors. A shareholder with knowledge may be held liable for unpaid debts of the corporation, up to the amount received as an illegal dividend or distribution. For example, suppose Ann knowingly receives an illegal dividend of $1,000 and the corporation becomes insolvent with $50,000 of unpaid liabilities. Ann may be compelled to return the $1,000. However, she is not liable for the remaining corporate liabilities.

Liability of Controlling Shareholders

In addition to *liability to the corporation or creditors*, shareholders may have *liability to one another*. Normally, one shareholder is not liable to another shareholder. But if a shareholder owns enough stock to control the corporation (either by outright ownership or by proxies), a fiduciary or quasi-fiduciary duty may be owed. The courts have not clearly defined the duties that controlling shareholders owe to minority stockholders. One problem that arises frequently, especially in closely held corporations, involves the injuries suffered by minority shareholders as the result of the sale of controlling shares. In a number of cases, the selling price of controlling shares is in excess of their fair market value because the price includes a premium to obtain voting control of the corporation. A growing number of courts will compel majority shareholders to disgorge the premium paid to them for control and will redistribute the amount of the premium ratably among *all* shareholders. The following case illustrates the fiduciary duty owed by a controlling shareholder to the minority shareholders.

| CASE 45.6 | **DeBaun v. First Western Bank & Trust Co.**
• 46 Cal. App. 3d 686 (Cal. App. 1975) |
|---|---|

FACTS In 1955, Johnson formed Alfred S. Johnson, Inc. Johnson initially owned all the corporation's outstanding stock (100 shares), but he later sold 10 shares to Stephens and 20 shares to DeBaun. When Johnson died in 1965, he left his 70 controlling shares to First Western Bank & Trust Co. (Bank) as trustee of a trust created by his will. DeBaun and Stephens continued to run the business, and profits rose steadily. By 1968, Alfred S. Johnson, Inc. (Corporation), had $198,000 of liquid assets and a net worth of $220,000.

Raymond Mattison owned S.O.F. Fund, Inc., and offered to have it purchase the Johnson shares, which Bank held as trustee. The down payment was to be $50,000. The balance of $200,000 was to be paid over 5 years, and payment was to be secured by Corporation's assets. Bank's decision to accept the offer was based on Mattison's "friendly reception by fellow Jonathan Club members." A Dun & Bradstreet report suggested that S.O.F. Fund no longer existed and indicated that Mattison and his other entities had a history of financial failures and legal troubles. Bank held an unsatisfied judgment against Mattison, and it asked Mattison's attorney about pending litigation. His attorney referred Bank to courthouse records. The courthouse records, which Bank failed to check, showed that Mattison and his entities had potential liability exceeding $1 million under thirty-eight unsatisfied judgments, twenty-two recorded abstracts of judgment, fifty-four pending suits, and eighteen tax liens.

Bank's staff doubted that it was legal to permit Mattison, as a shareholder, to secure his personal obligation arising from the purchase of Johnson's stock with Corporation's assets. However, Bank concealed these facts to induce DeBaun and Stephens (as stockholders and directors) to approve the sale to Mattison. Bank then gave Mattison a proxy to vote the 70 shares held by it in trust but retained them as additional security. Bank soon learned that Mattison was looting the corporation but took no action until Corporation was hopelessly insolvent. Pursuant to the security agreement, Bank sold Corporation's remaining assets for $60,000. After tax liens were satisfied, only $35,000 remained in the Johnson trust.

DeBaun and Stephens brought a derivative action on behalf of Corporation against Bank to recover damages resulting from its sale of controlling shares to Mattison. The trial court held Bank liable to Corporation for $473,836 in damages (the corporation's net worth as of transfer date plus 10 years of projected aftertax earnings). Bank appealed.

OPINION THOMPSON, J. . . . "In any transaction where the control of the corporation is material," the controlling majority shareholder must exercise good faith and fairness "from the viewpoint of the corporation and those interested therein." *Remillard Brick Co. v. Remillard-Dandini Corp.,* 109 Cal. App. 2d 405, 420; 241 P.2d 66. That duty of good faith and fairness encompasses an obligation of the controlling shareholder in possession of facts sufficient to awaken suspicion that a potential buyer of his shares may loot the corporation, . . . to conduct a reasonable and adequate investigation of the buyer. [As trustee of Johnson's shares,]

**CASE 45.6
Continued**

Bank was the controlling majority shareholder. It became directly aware of facts that would have alerted a prudent person that Mattison was likely to loot the corporation. . . . Armed with knowledge of those facts, Bank owed a duty to Corporation and its minority shareholders to act reasonably with respect to its dealings in the controlling shares with Mattison. It breached that duty. Knowing that the information could be discovered from the public records, Bank closed its eyes to that obvious source. . . . Had Bank investigated, as any prudent man would have done, it would have . . . precluded its dealings with [Mattison].

Bank, however, elected to deal with Mattison in a fashion that invited his looting of Corporation's assets. . . . By fraudulently concealing its nature from DeBaun and Stephens, Bank obtained corporate approval of a security agreement which hypothecated corporate assets to secure Mattison's obligation to it. Thus, to permit it to sell its majority shares to Mattison, Bank placed the assets and business of Corporation in peril. . . .

JUDGMENT   The judgment is affirmed.

SUMMARY

Shareholders exercise indirect control over corporate policies by electing or removing directors. Directors are elected for designated terms, but they may be removed with or without cause by a majority of the shares voted at a meeting called for that purpose. Shareholders may also amend articles in order to change the corporate name or to alter the number, par value, rights, or classes of authorized shares. Other extraordinary transactions which require shareholder approval include merger, consolidation, sale, or lease of substantially all corporate assets *not* in the ordinary course of business, and voluntary and involuntary dissolutions.

Shareholders exercise their power by voting in annual or special meetings. Shareholders may vote in person or by proxy. Proper notice of shareholders' meetings must be given, but in closely held corporations there are several methods of informal shareholder action. With certain statutory exceptions, actions are usually effected by majority vote of shares represented at any meeting in which a quorum (a majority of outstanding voting shares) is present.

A shareholder is entitled to one vote for each voting share held as of a fixed record date preceding a shareholders' meeting. Cumulative voting for directors is allowed in most states and required in a few. Such voting gives minority shareholders greater influence by permitting their votes (shares owned × number of directors to be elected) to be cumulated for a single candidate.

Shareholders possess several rights in addition to the right to vote. Among them are preemptive rights, which give shareholders first preference in buying a new stock issue in order to preserve their proportionate stock interests and voting rights; preemptive rights may be limited or denied in the articles. In addition, shareholders have a right to

- Inspect corporate books and records
- Institute individual suits and class actions
- Initiate derivative suits in the corporation's name to enforce its rights against third parties (if directors fail or refuse to do so)

Under certain circumstances, a shareholder may be held liable for unlawful dividends or distributions and for the "true value" of shares acquired in exchange for overvalued property. Controlling shareholders of close corporations may also be liable for the sale of controlling shares involving fraud or wrongful purpose.

REVIEW QUESTIONS

1. How do shareholders exercise their managerial power?

2. What are some of the reasons for amending a charter?

3. Explain the difference between a merger and a consolidation.

4. (a) Explain requisites for dissenting shareholders' appraisal rights. **(b)** Why are such rights important?

5. Distinguish between voluntary and involuntary dissolution.

6. (a) How do shareholders know when and where the annual meeting will be held? **(b)** When can shareholders compel such a meeting?

7. (a) What would happen if shareholders were given notice 8 days prior to a meeting? **(b)** What are the three methods of informal shareholder action?

8. (a) What is a proxy? **(b)** How long does a proxy last?

9. At shareholders' meetings, what is the Revised Model Act requirement **(a)** for a quorum? **(b)** For an affirmative vote of shareholders?

10. How does cumulative voting benefit minority stockholders?

11. Define **(a)** preemptive rights, **(b)** stock rights, and **(c)** warrants.

12. List requirements for **(a)** a class action and **(b)** a derivative suit.

13. (a) When are shareholders personally liable for difference between the par value of their stock and the value placed on property exchanged for that stock? **(b)** When are they liable for an unlawful dividend?

CASE PROBLEMS

1. Camp and his group rounded up the majority shares in Woodmere, Inc., a close corporation, and called a special shareholders' meeting for December 9 to elect their own board, and to remove McMath and his existing board, which collectively had support of only the minority shares. McMath's group scheduled a board meeting for December 8 and planned two strategies: (1) to amend the bylaws, eliminating the provision for preemptive stock rights, and then (2) to vote to issue enough additional shares to be purchased by McMath's group so that it would have majority control. The Camp group sued the McMath group and asked the court to enjoin it from holding the December 8 meeting until after the December 9 meeting. Should the court grant the injunction?

2. Baggs formed Auto West, Inc., to operate a Volkswagen automobile dealership. Auto West encountered serious financial difficulties, and Baggs sold to Bryan and Graff 80 percent of the stock of Auto West. They became the officers and directors of the corporation. Baggs retained 20 percent of the stock and remained as general manager. Volkswagen would not agree to the change in ownership of Auto West unless Baggs had a majority of the voting rights. To satisfy Volkswagen, Graff and Bryan executed irrevocable proxies to Baggs for an indefinite period. The parties later disagreed over Baggs' operation of the dealership, and the directors fired him. Graff and Bryan, together with Auto West, filed suit to terminate the proxies. Baggs claimed that the proxies were irrevocable and that he still had majority voting rights. Was Baggs' claim correct?

3. Bruce Stancil and his brother Howard each owned 12,500 shares of the common stock of Stancil Refrigeration, Inc. An annual shareholders' meeting was held to elect members of the corporation's board of directors. The bylaws provided for cumulative voting. Three directors were to be elected, and Bruce Stancil nominated himself, Sarah Barnes, and Eva Stancil. Howard Stancil nominated himself, Clara Stancil, and Henry Babb. Since cumulative voting was authorized, Bruce cast 12,500 votes for each of his nominees, thus casting a total of 37,500 votes. **(a)** How would you advise Howard to cast his votes? **(b)** Why?

4. Pillsbury, who had no interest in Honeywell, Inc., learned that Honeywell was manufacturing bombs to be used in the Vietnamese war. Pillsbury was opposed to the war and bought one share of Honeywell stock in order to make his views known to its management and stockholders. Pillsbury demanded shareholders' lists and all corporate records dealing with munitions produced by the company. When Honeywell failed to comply, Pillsbury sued. Should the court compel Honeywell to make the records available for inspection?

5. Harff owned convertible debentures of MGM, Inc. The board of directors declared a large cash dividend on the corporation's common stock. Harff filed a derivative action against the directors to recover for the corporation the amount of the dividend. The complaint claimed that the dividend was self-serving on the part of the directors, who owned common shares, and that it undermined the value of the corporation's debentures by reducing the market value of the common stock into which the debentures could be converted. Do these facts satisfy the requirements for a derivative action?

CHAPTER 46

Securities Regulation: Protecting Investors

America's phenomenal industrial growth after the Civil War was made possible by the sale of corporate stocks and bonds to millions of investors. Not surprisingly, unscrupulous swindlers also became a part of the scene, employing an ingenious variety of fraudulent practices to victimize unwary investors.

STATE SECURITIES REGULATION

Commencing with Kansas in 1911, states began enacting **blue-sky laws** aimed at preventing fraudulent practices. Although all states have such statutes, lack of uniformity is a serious problem for corporations desiring to qualify securities issues for sale in more than one state. Some states, such as Delaware and Connecticut, have opted for minimal blue-sky regulation. Others, such as New York and California, exert maximum regulatory authority. Most state blue-sky laws are based upon the Uniform Securities Act, published in 1956. These laws typically require:

- Registration of securities issues of domestic corporations as well as foreign corporations that plan to issue and sell securities within the state. Registration means applying to a state corporations commissioner to qualify and approve a proposed issuance of securities before it can be sold.
- Registration and licensing of securities brokers and dealers.
- Distribution by corporations to prospective buyers of basic information about the proposed issue, as well as the corporation (which is called an issuer), its directors, officers, and financial condition, before offering to sell securities.

In addition, blue-sky laws prohibit fraud in the sale of securities and impose severe penalties for falsifying registration data.

FEDERAL SECURITIES REGULATION

During the Great Depression, congressional investigating committees found that one of the causes of the depression was the corps of smooth-talking sales representatives who had combed the countryside, high-pressuring prospective stock buyers with get-rich-quick schemes aimed at selling them shares in everything from mousetraps to the blue sky. It was also concluded that state blue-sky regulation was ineffective in stopping nationwide stock frauds. "Fast-buck swindle schemes," coupled with a decade of "easy" bank credit during the 1920s, fueled a frenzy of buying worthless stock at inflated values.

> **BOX 46.1**
>
> **A Uniquely American Business Term: Fast-Buck Blue-Sky Scheme**
>
> If you are warned to watch out for a "fast-buck blue-sky scheme," what does the term mean? On the early American frontier, a buckskin was traded for a dollar. The person who harvested a lot of deerskins had a lot of "bucks." In *Hall v. Geiger-Jones Co.*, 242 U.S. 539 (1917), the U.S. Supreme Court attacked stock swindles that had no more basis than "so many feet of blue sky." The phrase has been used ever since to describe a crooked stock promotion scheme. ∎

When inevitable collapse and the Great Depression came, Congress swiftly enacted two laws of major importance: (1) the Securities Act of 1933 and (2) the Securities Exchange Act of 1934, which created the Securities and Exchange Commission.[1] The SEC is an independent agency of five commissioners appointed by the President with staggered terms over 5 years. Table 46.1 shows their chief responsibilities.

The 1933 and 1934 Acts were adopted to ensure that (1) accurate information is available to individual and institutional investors concerning any company that issues a security and the risks involved in its purchase, (2) the securities market is not manipulated at the expense of unwary investors, and (3) individuals and firms engaged in selling securities maintain proper business standards. The Acts also provided punishment for securities law violators.

The Securities Act of 1933 was designed to regulate the *issuance of new securities*. The Securities Exchange Act of 1934 was designed to regulate the *trading* (purchase and sale) *of existing securities*. Both Acts contain registration and antifraud provisions. Their approach is to furnish potential investors with information from which they can decide whether to purchase a security. Neither of the Acts guarantees an investor that the security is a sound investment. Because the public buys corporate shares throughout the country, their issuance and sale usually affects interstate commerce. Congress' constitutional authority to regulate interstate commerce is the basis for legislation regulating the issuance and sale of securities. However, the federal government recognizes that states also have jurisdiction over securities. As a result, the issuance of securities is subject to *both* state and federal control.

Table 46.1 Major Functions of the Securities and Exchange Commission

1. To enforce federal securities laws by investigating violations, holding adjudication hearings, and imposing fines where proper
2. To make rules to regulate issuance and sale of securities and to ensure that shareholders receive basic information
3. To regulate trading on the national and regional securities exchanges as well as over the counter
4. To enforce rules requiring filing of periodic reports with the SEC by corporations, stock exchanges, brokers, dealers, investment advisors, mutual funds, attorneys, and accountants
5. To approve or reject corporate registration statements filed with the SEC seeking permission to issue stocks or bonds
6. To issue and administer regulations relating to mutual funds, and to act as regulatory superviser of the securities industry
7. To issue press releases, policy statements, interpretative regulations, guidelines to compliance with regulations, and "no action" letters when asked for interpretations of SEC rules

DEFINITION OF A SECURITY

People who decide to sell an interest in their business to a group of buyers need to ask: "Are we selling a 'security' as the SEC defines it?" If so,

---

[1] The following federal statutes applying to securities of particular industries are not discussed: Public Utility Holding Company Act of 1935, Trust Indenture Act of 1939, Investment Company Act of 1940, Investment Advisors Act of 1940, and Securities Investor Protection Act of 1970.

and if the contract with the buyer is not *registered*, there could be serious trouble. The SEC has convicted managers of large and small firms, reduced or eliminated their fortunes with fines and forfeitures, and sent them to prison for selling unregistered securities. To play it safe, one needs to know what the law says a "security" really is. The Securities Act of 1933[2] and the Securities Exchange Act of 1934[3] define a security as

> any note, stock, treasury stock, bond, debenture, certificate of interest or participation in any profit-sharing agreement or in any oil, gas, or other mineral royalty or lease, any collateral-trust certificate, preorganization certificate or subscription, transferable share, investment contract, voting-trust certificate, certificate of deposit, for a security, any put, call, straddle, option, or privilege on any security, certificate of deposit, or group or index of securities (including any interest therein or based on the value thereof), or any put, call, straddle, option, or privilege entered into on a national securities exchange relating to foreign currency, or in general, any instrument commonly known as a "security"; or any certificate of interest or participation in, temporary or interim certificate for, receipt for, or warrant or right to subscribe to or purchase, any of the foregoing, but shall not include currency or any note, draft, bill of exchange, or banker's acceptance which has a maturity at the time of issuance of not exceeding nine months. . . .[4]

Court interpretation has broadened this statutory definition in order to carry out the objective of the 1933 and 1934 Acts—to protect the unwary. For example, the word "securities" generally calls to mind a set of stock certificates with fancy engraving around the sides and a bald eagle landing on the company name in the middle of the paper. Certainly, bottled whiskey and a herd of cattle in Texas do not come to mind. Yet the U.S. Supreme Court has held them to be securities. In the leading case of *Securities and Exchange Commission v. W. J. Howey Co.*,[5] the Court held that sale to the public of parcels of orange orchard land in Florida, coupled with "service contracts" that charged a "management fee" to harvest and market the crops, constituted the sale of securities within the meaning of the law. The *Howey* definition, expanded by later decisions, appears in the accompanying box. Only recently, the High Court said: "Congress' purpose in enacting the securities laws was to regulate *investments*, in whatever form they are made and by whatever name they are called."[6] This view is reinforced in Case 46.1 below. It reaffirmed the *Howey* test as a technique to identify a security but supplemented it with a new "strong family resemblance" test to determine when a *promissory note* is a security and when it is not.

[2] 15 USC 77a *et seq.*
[3] 15 USC 78 *et seq.*
[4] 15 USC 78c(a)(10); 1934 Act, Sec. 3(a)(10).
[5] 328 U.S. 293 (1946).
[6] *Reves v. Ernst & Young*, 108 L. Ed. 2d 47 (1990).

BOX 46.2

The Supreme Court Answers the Question: What Is a Security?

Every transaction involves a security when:

1 A person invests money
2 In a common enterprise
3 With a reasonable expectation of profits
4 To be derived *primarily and substantially* from the managerial or entrepreneurial efforts of others.*

Examples from case law include "sales," coupled with agreements to manage assets sold, of:

- A Florida orange orchard
- Limited partnership interests
- A franchise to sell cosmetics
- Contracts selling chinchillas and fishing worms for breeding purposes, coupled with promises to repurchase the increase

*SEC v. W. J. Howey Co., 328 U.S. 293 (1946).

CASE 46.1	**Reves v. Ernst & Young** • 108 L. Ed. 2d 47 (1990)
FACTS	Farmer's Cooperative (Co-op) with 23,000 members, sold demand notes to support its business operations. Its newsletter ads said: "Your Co-op has more than $11 million in assets to stand behind your investment. . . . It is . . . Safe . . . Secure . . . and available when you need it." When Co-Op filed for bankruptcy in 1984, over 1,600 people held notes worth $10 million. Reves, and others as note holders, brought a class action against Arthur Young & Co. (predecessor to Ernst & Young) under the antifraud provisions of the 1934 Securities Exchange Act. The suit claimed that Arthur Young & Co. had failed to follow generally accepted accounting principles (GAAP) in its audit regarding valuation of Co-Op's major asset—a gasohol plant. Had the plant been valued properly, plaintiffs would not have purchased demand notes because Co-Op's insolvency would have been apparent. Arthur Young & Co. appealed from a judgment of $6.1 million, claiming that the demand notes were not "securities" under the 1934 Act. This was a logical defense, because if plaintiffs' notes were *not* securities, there obviously wasn't any case for violating securities laws. Reves insisted that the rates were securities.
OPINION	MARSHAL, J. . . . The fundamental purpose undergirding the Securities Acts is to eliminate serious abuses in a largely unregulated securities market. In defining the scope of the market that it wished to regulate, Congress painted with a broad brush. It recognized the virtually limitless scope of human ingenuity, especially in the creation of "countless and variable schemes devised by those who seek the use of the money of others on the promise of profits." *SEC v. W. J. Howey Co.* [After noting that the *Howey test* is inapplicable to promissory notes, the Court proposed a new test:] The Second Circuit's "family resemblance" approach begins with a presumption that any note with a term of more than nine months is a "security." Recognizing that not all notes are securities, however, the Second Circuit has also devised a list of notes that it has decided are obviously not securities. Accordingly, the "family resemblance" test permits an issuer to . . . [treat the instrument as a note if it] "bears a strong family resemblance" to an item on the judicially crafted list of exceptions. . . . . . . We reject the approaches of those courts that have applied the Howey test to notes; Howey provides a mechanism for determining whether an instrument is an "investment contract." . . . To hold that a "note" is not a "security" unless it meets a test designed for an entirely different variety of instrument would make the [Securities] Acts' enumeration of many types of instruments superfluous. . . . . . . Because we think the "family resemblance" test provides a more promising framework for analysis, however, we adopt it. The test begins with the language of the statute; because the Securities Acts define "security" to include "any note" we begin with a presumption that every note is a security. . . . [However,] . . . the Second Circuit has identified a list of instruments commonly denominated "notes" that nonetheless fall without the "security" category. Types of notes that are not "securities" include

**CASE 46.1
Continued**

the note delivered in consumer financing, the note secured by a mortgage on a home, the short-term note secured by a lien on a small business or some of its assets, the note evidencing a "character" loan to a bank customer, short-term notes secured by an assignment of accounts receivable, or a note which simply formalizes an open-account debt incurred in the ordinary course of business (particularly if, as in the case of the customer of a broker, it is collateralized) . . . [and] notes evidencing loans by commercial banks for current operations.

We agree that the items identified by the Second Circuit are not properly viewed as "securities." More guidance, though, is needed. . . . Thus, some standards must be developed for determining when an item should be added to the list. . . . First, we examine the transaction to assess the motivations that would prompt a reasonable seller and buyer to enter into it. If the seller's purpose is to raise money for the general use of a business enterprise or to finance substantial investments and the buyer is interested primarily in the profit the note is expected to generate, the instrument is likely to be a "security." If the note is exchanged to facilitate the purchase and sale of a minor asset or consumer good, to correct for the seller's cash-flow difficulties, or to advance some other commercial or consumer purpose . . . the note is less sensibly described as a "security." . . . Second, we examine the "plan of distribution" of the instrument to determine whether it is an instrument in which there is "common trading for speculation or investment." Third, we examine the reasonable expectations of the investing public: The Court will consider instruments to be "securities" on the basis of such public expectations, even where an economic analysis of the circumstances of the particular transaction might suggest that the instruments are not "securities" as used in that transaction. Finally, we examine whether some factor such as the existence of another regulatory scheme significantly reduces the risk of the instrument, thereby rendering application of the Securities Acts unnecessary.

We conclude, then, that in determining whether an instrument denominated a "note" is a "security," courts are to apply the version of the "family resemblance" test that we have articulated here: a note is presumed to be a "security," and that presumption may be rebutted only by a showing that the note bears a strong resemblance (in terms of the four factors we have identified) to one of the enumerated categories of instrument. . . .

Applying the family resemblance approach to this case, we have little difficulty in concluding that the notes at issue here are "securities." [The Court then applied the four prongs of the "family resemblance" test to Co-Op's notes, finding that (1) Co-Op sold them to raise capital and buyers bought them to profit from the high interest rate offered; (2) the notes were sold to a broad segment of the general public; (3) the public perceived the notes to be "securities"; and (4) there was no risk-reducing factor such as collateralization of the notes to disqualify them as securities.]

JUDGMENT

We conclude that the demand notes at issue here fall under the "note" category of instruments that are "securities" under the 1933 and 1934 Acts. [The Court also concluded that the demand notes did not fall within the short-term note exclusion of Section 3(a)(10). The judgment was for Reves.]

THE 1933 ACT: REGULATING NEW ISSUES OF SECURITIES

Registration Requirements

The Securities Act of 1933 requires that any security which does not qualify for exemption must first be *registered* before it may be offered to the public through the use of mails, telephones, or any other interstate commerce facility. An *issuer* (a firm proposing to issue securities) commences the registration process by filing with the SEC a *registration statement* containing detailed data sufficient to enable the investing public to judge the financial soundness of the issuer and the quality of the proposed security. If the SEC makes no objections, on the twentieth day after filing the registration statement, the issuer may commence selling the security to the public, but must first furnish buyers with a *prospectus*, approved by the SEC, giving enough information about the security to enable the investor to evaluate the risk. Registration does *not* mean that the SEC has found the security to be risk-free, fairly priced, or a "winner" as an investment. Registration simply ensures that sufficient disclosure is made.

Content of Registration Statement. Table 46.2 lists the general contents of a registration statement. The 1933 Act provides that falsification or omission of material facts in the registration statement is not only a crime but also voids the security issue, entitling the buyers to recover their purchase money from directors, officers, underwriters, attorneys, accountants, and others. Case 46.2 tells that story, later in this chapter.

Activities before, during, and after Registration. *Before* filing the registration statement, which includes the prospectus, with the SEC, the issuing corporation is permitted to retain an *underwriter* to distribute (sell) the proposed issue, but not to make public statements about the issue or offer to sell them to the public. *During* the 20 days after filing, the issuer and interested investors may exchange oral offers to buy and sell the proposed securities, but no sale may be consummated. In this period leaflet notices are restricted to a *red herring prospectus*, so

Table 46.2 What Does an SEC Registration Statement Contain?

Part I Prospectus
1 Balance sheet
2 Statement of income and expense
3 Other data

Part II Details
1 Description of the main features of the security; the plan for marketing it, including underwriting and selling costs; how the proceeds of the sale will be used
2 The names and compensation of directors, principal officers, and persons who control the company or who own 10 percent or more of its securities; details of material transactions between any such persons and the company
3 Details of pending legal proceedings by or against the company
4 Detailed certified financial statements (for the past 3 years)

named because SEC Rule 430 requires the title page to carry a warning in conspicuous red print that, although filed, the registration statement has not yet become effective. Under SEC Rule 134, newspaper publicity is limited to publication of *tombstone ads*, so-called because their black border and brevity resemble grave markers. Figure 46.1 shows a typical tombstone ad that appeared in *The Wall Street Journal*. After the effective date, the securities covered in the registration statement may legally be offered and sold provided a prospectus is first delivered to each investor.

Shelf Registration. Under new SEC Rule 415, larger companies that regularly issue new securities can avoid the burden of preparing repeated registration statements by using a *shelf registration*. A firm files a single registration statement describing long-range plans to issue securities, supplemented by updated periodic reports. In this way, a registration statement is always available "on the shelf" so that the firm can issue securities without further SEC approval.

This announcement is under no circumstances to be construed as an offer to sell or as a solicitation of an offer to buy any of these securities. The offering is made only by the Prospectus.

June 29, 1993

6,500,000 Shares

Hospitality Franchise Systems, Inc.

Common Stock

Price $32 Per Share

Copies of the Prospectus may be obtained in any State or jurisdiction in which this announcement is circulated from only such of the undersigned or other dealers or brokers as may lawfully offer these securities in such State or jurisdiction.

5,560,000 Shares

The above shares were underwritten by the following group of U.S. Underwriters.

Merrill Lynch & Co.

Montgomery Securities

The Nikko Securities Co.
International, Inc.

Alex. Brown & Sons	The First Boston Corporation	BT Securities Corporation	Kidder, Peabody & Co.
Incorporated			Incorporated
Lehman Brothers	PaineWebber Incorporated	Prudential Securities Incorporated	Salomon Brothers Inc
Smith Barney, Harris Upham & Co.	S.G. Warburg Securities		Dean Witter Reynolds Inc.
Incorporated			
Advest, Inc.	J. C. Bradford & Co.	The Buckingham Research Group	Cowen & Company	Dain Bosworth
		Incorporated		Incorporated
First of Michigan Corporation	Interstate/Johnson Lane		Janney Montgomery Scott Inc.
	Corporation		
Kemper Securities, Inc.	Ladenburg, Thalmann & Co. Inc.		C. J. Lawrence Inc.
Legg Mason Wood Walker	Morgan Keegan & Company, Inc.		Neuberger & Berman
Incorporated			
Piper Jaffray Inc.	Rauscher Pierce Refsnes, Inc.		Raymond James & Associates, Inc.
The Robinson-Humphrey Company, Inc.	Rodman & Renshaw, Inc.	Stephens Inc.	Wheat First Butcher & Singer
			CAPITAL MARKETS

940,000 Shares

The above shares were underwritten by the following group of International Underwriters.

Merrill Lynch International Limited

Montgomery Securities

Nikko Europe plc

Banque Indosuez	Dresdner Bank	NatWest Securities Limited
	Aktiengesellschaft	
	Paribas Capital Markets	S.G. Warburg Securities

Figure 46.1 A typical tombstone advertisement.

Disclosure and Integrated Registration

Section 12 of the 1934 Act requires all companies whose securities are traded on the national exchanges as well as other companies with 500 shareholders or more and over $5 million in assets to register their securities with the SEC and to comply with periodic reporting requirements. For years these "Section 12 companies," which had regularly filed the 1934 Act's required periodic reports, were angered whenever they applied to the SEC under the 1933 Act to register a proposed public issue of securities. At that time they were told they had to file the usual registration statement under the 1933 Act even though much the same information had been furnished to the SEC in the periodic reports. To quell criticism, the SEC in 1982 established uniform disclosure requirements under the 1933 and 1934 Acts. The new rules simplify registration under the 1933 Act by giving firms leeway, depending on size, to incorporate by reference data previously filed under the 1934 Act.

Offer and Sale of Securities

The SEC and the courts broadly define what constitutes an offer or sale of a security that must be preceded by a registration statement. An *offer* of a security includes any attempt or proposal to dispose of a security for value. Solicitation of an offer to buy a security is also included within the meaning of the term. A *sale* of a security includes every contract for the sale or disposition of a security for value. Even shares pledged as collateral for loans have been held to constitute an "offer" or "sale."

A *public offering* involves a *distribution* of securities to the general public. It is generally made in either of two ways: (1) the issuer sells the securities directly to the public, or (2) the issuer enlists the services of an investment banking firm, called an *underwriter*. One or more underwriters usually agree to sell securities for the issuer on a "best efforts" basis, incurring no liability for unsold shares. Alternatively, underwriters *purchase* an issuer's securities and resell them to the investing public.

Underwriters should be distinguished from securities dealers (brokers) who execute orders to buy or sell securities on a commission basis for the account of others. A dealer or broker may also act as an underwriter for particular shares. For example, in the Figure 46.1 tombstone advertisement Merrill Lynch & Co., Montgomery Securities, and Nikko Securities Co. were lead underwriters, while the listed brokers had limited participation.

Exemptions

Corporations seek exemption from registration for their securities to avoid (1) high registration costs and (2) the burdensome reporting requirements of the 1934 Act (discussed later in this chapter). The 1933 Act sets out two classes of exemption from registration: (1) *exempted securities* which are not required to be registered at any time, and (2) *exempted transactions* in securities which require no initial registration but require one for any later transfer of the security. There are no exemptions from the SEC's antifraud laws and regulations.

Exempted Securities. Securities exempt from registration are shown in general terms in Table 46.3.[7]

[7]15 USC 77c.

Table 46.3 Securities Exempt from Registration under the 1933 Act

1. Securities issued or guaranteed by the U.S. government or by state or local governmental agencies.
2. Securities issued by banks and savings and loan associations.
3. Securities issued by religious and charitable organizations.
4. Insurance policies and annuity contracts.
5. Commercial paper not advertised for sale to the public **(a)** arising from current business transactions and **(b)** having a maturity of not more than 9 months, including instruments having a "strong family resemblance" to commercial paper. (See Case 46.1 above, and Chapter 31.)
6. Intrastate exemption—offerings solely to residents of the state in which entity is incorporated. (This exemption is burdensome and rarely used because most local offerings are exempt transactions under SEC Regulation D.)

Table 46.4 Overview of Transactions (Distributions by Issuers[f]) Exempt from Registration Under 1933 Securities Act and 1934 Securities Exchange Act[e]

Exemption (Statute or Rule)	Limit on Total Offering Price	Number of Investors	Qualifications of Investors	Solicitation and Advertising Limitations	Resale Restrictions and Manner of Offering	Disclosure Requirements	Notice to the SEC
Small or limited offerings Regulation D[g] Rule 506[a] (17 CFR, § 230.506) "private placement exemption" [§ 4(2)]	Unlimited	Unlimited but no more than 35 non-accredited investors	Only sophisticated (e.g., accredited) investors[b]	No public offering or general solicitation	Restricted (Rule 144)[c] Issuer must take precautionary steps against resale[h]	None if purchased solely by accredited investors; if any buyers are non-accredited, disclosure to *all* purchasers under Rule 502 must be made[d]	Yes (Rule 503)
Rule 505 (17 CFR § 230.505)	$5 million in any 12-month period; cannot be an investment company offering	Unlimited but no more than 35 nonaccredited investors	Accredited investors as defined in note b; issuer is not required to believe each unaccredited investor is knowledgeable enough to evaluate risk	No general solicitation or advertising; no public offerings	Restricted (Rule 144)[3] Issuer must take precautionary steps against nonexempt, unregistered resales.[8]	If any buyers are nonaccredited, disclosure must be made to *all* purchasers; however, issuer *not* required to believe each unaccredited investor is knowledgeable enough to evaluate the risk (17 CFR §230.505)	Yes (Rule 503)
Rule 504 (17 CFR § 230.504)	$1 million in any 12-month period so long as no more than $500,000 sold without registration under state blue-sky laws (must be non-investment company offering).[e]	Unlimited	None	No general solicitation or advertising Restrictions on unregistered resales and on advertising not applicable if offering is solely within a state with registration and disclosure laws, and issuer has complied with such laws	Issuer must take precautionary steps against non-exempt and unregistered resales[h]	No prospectus or information need be furnished to investors	Yes (Rule 503)

1026

Regulation A **Rules 251–264** (17 CFR § 230, 251–264); § 3(b) 1933 Act 15 USC § 77c(b)	Offer up to $1.5 million in any 12-month period	Unlimited	None	Because offering circular must be given buyer before sale, limited advertising is permitted	None	If offering exceeds $100,000, 10 days after filing offering statement with SEC; if no objection, must then give buyer offering circular *before* any sale	Must file an offering statement with SEC (much less than full-blown registration statement) Yes
§4(6) 1933 Act [amendment added in 1980 15 USC § 77 (d)(6)]	Up to $5 million	Unlimited number of accredited investors	Only accredited investors	No general solicitation	Restricted	None required	
Intrastate offerings §3(a)(11) 1933 Act; 15 USC § 77(c)(a)(11); SEC **Rule 147** ("safe harbor" rule)	Unlimited	Unlimited	All buyers as well as offerees must be residents of issuer's state of incorporation; 80 percent of issuer's assets must be in-state; 80 percent of gross revenue must come from in-state; 80 percent of proceeds of sale of issue must be used in-state (the 80 percent criteria are part of Rule 147, which provides a "safe harbor")	Can be private or public offering	No limit on resales to residents; after 9 months resales can be made to non-residents. Precautionary steps[h] against unregistered resales must include investors' verifying state residence in writing	If a public offering, state blue-sky laws are applicable	No

[a]Rule 506 is described as a "safe harbor" rule because compliance with it assures the issuer entitlement to the exemption.

[b]Under Rule 501, **accredited investor** includes all types of institutional investors such as banks, credit unions, insurance companies; directors, executive officers, general partners of the issuer; certain corporations and trusts whose assets exceed $5 million; and a "big ticket" purchaser who buys at least $150,000, which amount does *not* exceed 20 percent of the purchaser's net worth; a person whose net worth at the time of purchase exceeds $1 million is also an accredited investor. A **nonaccredited investor** alone, or with a representative, must have sufficient financial knowledge or experience to evaluate the risks of the investment. The issuer determines whether a purchaser qualifies as an accredited or nonaccredited investor; the test is subjective, requiring the issuer to act reasonably in its classification.

[c]Rule 144 is a guide to tell when a registration statement must be filed with the SEC for a *secondary distribution*—that is, transactions by persons other than issuers, underwriters, or dealers. It answers the question: When can a buyer of securities in one of the above *exempt transactions* resell the securities? In general, the rule requires the person reselling securities to (1) hold them 2 years, then sell in a 3-month period (a) shares not exceeding 1 percent of the outstanding shares or (b) average weekly trading volume for previous 4 weeks, whichever is greater; (2) effect such sale through a broker or dealer; and (3) notify the SEC of the sale. This is sometimes called the **"2-year-and-dribble" rule.**

[d]If there are any nonaccredited buyers, the issuer must reasonably believe that the buyer alone or with a representative "has such knowledge and experience in financial and business matters that he is capable of evaluating the merits and risks of the prospective investment." The issuer must also provide *all* purchasers with material information about the issue *before* the sale. This **"private placement" exemption is probably the most popular of the exemptions.** It is often used to sell big blocks of shares to institutions or to small groups of private individuals. See full text of Rule 502.

[e]The Regulation 504 exemption is not available to companies subject to registration and reporting provisions of the 1934 Act. This limitation restricts the exemption of Rule 504 to smaller firms.

[f]Most securities sold under a *transactions* exemption, unlike the *securities* exemption, may not be resold without registration or compliance with another exemption, such as Rule 144. (Note c above.)

[g]Restrictions on resale and manner of offering covered by Regulation D are not applicable to sales that comply with a state's blue-sky law, which requires securities registration and delivery of disclosure prospectus to buyer prior to sale. Neither is Regulation D applicable if sales do not exceed $500,000 in states having no blue-sky laws, provided the securities are sold in at least one state in compliance with its registration and disclosure statute and a copy of the prospectus is given buyers in all states having no blue-sky laws.

[h]Precautionary steps against resale of nonexempt unregistered securities include requiring the investor to verify that the purchase is not for account of others, warning each buyer in writing that the unregistered securities cannot be resold except under an exemption such as Rule 144, and stamping "Restricted" on the security.

Exempted Transactions; Regulation D. Table 46.4, an overview, shows the principal features of each of the major *exempted transactions*. SEC Regulation D exempts *private offerings* or *private placements*, which are the most widely used transactional exemptions. The overall philosophy of the private placement exemption is that the general public will not be harmed by small issues of stock to a limited number of sophisticated investors. Regulation D has two classes of sophisticated investors: (1) accredited and (2) unaccredited, as defined under Rule 501 (Table 46.4, note b). Generally, both classes consist of persons who have sufficient financial knowledge or experience to evaluate the risks of the investment. Regulation D has a number of rules, the most important of which are Rules 505 and 506, shown in Table 46.4. The two rules have these chief differences:

1. Rule 505 limits the issue to $5 million, whereas Rule 506 has no limit on the dollar amount of securities offered.
2. Rule 505 permits sale to thirty-five *nonaccredited* investors (Table 46.4, note b) who probably lack financial background and knowledge to evaluate the merits and risks of the investment. Therefore, Rule 505 requires that information about the issuer that is normally in a registration statement be supplied to nonaccredited investors. Rule 506, in contrast, requires only that investors be "sophisticated" enough to judge the merits and the risks of the investment. The issuer must act reasonably in differentiating between those unaccredited investors who are "sophisticated" and those who are not. The issuer usually qualifies sophisticated investors by requiring written answers to questions concerning their financial worth.

Summary of 1933 Act; the Secondary Trading Exemption. Let's pause a moment to review our odyssey through the Securities Act of 1933. It started by requiring registration of *all* issues of securities, unless exempted. Then Section 3(a) came along with exempt *securities* such as government bonds, Treasury bills, insurance company annuities, and ordinary promissory notes. Next, we saw how Regulations A and D and Section 3(a)(11) provided for *transactions* exemptions, through which issuers can make limited or intrastate offerings without SEC registration. Yet both *securities exemptions* and *transactions exemptions* involve corporate distributions of *new stock*.

How do the billions of dollars of daily transactions in *existing* shares that are offered and sold on the national stock exchanges fit into this regulatory scheme? The answer brings us to the *secondary trading exemption*. Section 4(3) of the 1933 Act exempts transactions by securities dealers (but not sales of new corporate stock issues). Section 4(4) exempts brokers' transactions on a securities exchange or on the over-the-counter market. The net effect of these laws is to exempt daily trading by dealers and brokers on behalf of investors in secondary markets for stocks that have already been issued.

Resale of Restricted Securities. Generally, however, underwriters and issuers, as well as *controlling persons*,[8] remain subject to the 1933 Act's registration requirements unless an exemption applies. The 1933 Act accomplishes the objective of requiring registration by controlling persons who intend resale of new-issue shares by defining an issuer as *anyone who purchases a new issue with intent to distribute the shares*. This definition clearly includes controlling persons who intend resale, and they are thus subject to the Act's requirement of registration by issuers.

Suppose an issuer sells shares in an exempt transaction under Rule 506 of Regulation D (Table 46.4). Shares so issued and sold are stamped "Restricted." What does this mean? Under Rule 144 (1) issuers are restricted from advertising the offering and (2) buyers are restricted from immediately reselling the securities. Instead, the buyers must hold the shares for at least 2 years before sale. Even after the 2-year waiting period, the holder may sell only a few shares each calendar quarter (Table 46.4, note c). Thus, Rule 144 has been dubbed the

---

[8]SEC Rule 405 defines "controlling persons" as those who have the power to direct management policies.

"2-year-and-dribble rule." However, the rule permits resale during the 2-year holding period if the issuer files a registration statement with the SEC or if the resale otherwise qualifies for exemption under Rule 505 or Rule 506. In this way, over time, unregistered restricted new securities can eventually be traded on exchanges.

Enforcement of the 1933 Act

The SEC and injured investors have many available enforcement tools. Under Section 8 of the 1933 Act, the SEC can issue a *refusal order* to stop the time running on the 20-day automatic approval of a registration statement. After the effective date of a registration statement, it can issue a *stop order* which in effect prohibits any sales of the described securities. Section 11, as illustrated in Case 46.2, authorizes injured investors to rescind their securities purchases and recover from directors, officers, attorneys, and others. However, an expert is liable for so much of the registration statement as he or she prepared or certified. Section 12 permits investors to recover for false representations made in a prospectus, or oral misrepresentations made outside of the prospectus. Section 17(a) imposes civil liability on those who perpetrate, aid, or abet any fraud in connection with an offer or sale of securities. Under Section 24, there is criminal liability for *wilful violation of any part of the 1933 Act.*

CASE 46.2   **Escott v. BarChris Construction Corp.** • 283 F. Supp. 643 (S.D. N.Y. 1968)

FACTS   BarChris Construction Corp. built bowling alleys during the postwar bowling boom of the 1950s. To finance its rapid expansion, it decided to sell convertible debenture bonds and filed a registration statement with the SEC. The statement overstated current assets by $609,000; understated contingent liabilities by $618,000; and did not disclose the corporation's liability as *contingent guarantor* of new bowling alley leases of $1,350,000. Unable to pay bond interest, the firm went into bankruptcy.

Escott brought a class action lawsuit under Section 11 of the 1933 Act against (1) directors, officers, and the attorney who signed the registration statement, (2) the eight underwriting firms that distributed the issue, and (3) the outside auditors and accountants (Peat, Marwick, Mitchell & Co.) that prepared financial statements. Escott claimed the registration statement contained false statements, omitted material facts, and was misleading, in violation of Section 11 of the 1933 Act. Each defendant responded with the defense that "due diligence" had been used in verifying all "material" facts in the registration statement. All defendants were found liable. The court's opinion denying a motion to dismiss follows.

OPINION   McLEAN, J. . . . It is a prerequisite to liability under Section 11 of the [Securities Act of 1933] that the fact which is falsely stated in a registration statement, or the fact that is omitted when it should have been stated to avoid misleading, be "material." . . . Judged by this test, there is no doubt that many of the misstatements and omissions in this prospectus were material.

**CASE 46.2
Continued**

[Liability of Underwriters]

... The *underwriters* [of the debentures] ... say that the prospectus is the company's prospectus, not theirs. Doubtless this is the way they customarily regard it. But the Securities Act makes no such distinction. The underwriters are just as responsible as the company if the prospectus is false. And prospective investors rely upon the reputation of the underwriters in deciding whether to purchase the securities. ... The purpose of Section 11 is to protect investors. To that end the underwriters are made responsible for the truth of the prospectus. If they may escape that responsibility by taking at face value representations made to them by the company's management, then the inclusion of underwriters among those liable under Section 11 affords the investors no additional protection. ... In order to make the underwriters' participation in this enterprise of any value to the investors, the underwriters must make some reasonable attempt to verify the data submitted to them. They may not rely solely on the company's officers or on the company's counsel. ... In the present case, the underwriters' counsel made almost no attempt to verify management's representation. I hold that was insufficient. ... Hence they have not established their due diligence defense.

[The Officers and Directors]

Vitolo was president and Pugliese was vice president [of BarChris]. Vitolo and Pugliese are each men of limited education. It is not hard to believe that for them the prospectus was difficult reading, if indeed they read it at all. But whether it was or not is irrelevant. The liability of a director who signs a registration statement does not depend upon whether or not he read it or, if he did, whether or not he understood what he was reading.

And in any case, Vitolo and Pugliese were not as naive as they claim to be. They were members of BarChris's executive committee. At meetings of that committee BarChris's affairs were discussed at length. They must have known what was going on. Certainly they knew of the inadequacy of cash in 1961. They knew of their own large advances to the company which remained unpaid. They knew that they had agreed not to deposit their checks until financing proceeds were received. They knew and intended that part of the proceeds were to be used to pay their own loans. ... They could not have believed that the registration statement was wholly true and that no material facts had been omitted. And in any case, there is nothing to show that they made any investigation of anything which they may not have known about or understood. They have not proved their due diligence defenses.

[The Independent Auditors—Peat, Marwick, Mitchell & Co.]

... Section 11(b) provides:

... no person shall be liable as regards any part of the registration statement purporting to be made upon his authority as an expert ... [if] he had, after reasonable investigation, reasonable ground to believe and did believe, at the time such part of the registration statement became effective, that the statements therein were true and that there was no omission to state a material fact required ... to make the statements therein not misleading.

> **CASE 46.2 Continued**
>
> This defines the due diligence defense for an expert. Peat, Marwick has pleaded it. . . . Most of the actual work was performed by a senior accountant, Berardi, who had junior assistants. Berardi was. . . not yet a C.P.A. This was his first job as a senior accountant. He hardly could have been given a more difficult assignment. . . .
>
> [Berardi failed to discover that certain of BarChris's bowling alleys had been sold; he made errors in calculating BarChris's current assets and in computing its contingent liabilities, its 1960 sales figures, and its cash position; and he did not follow the written program prepared by Peat, Marwick for the review. . . .] In substance, he asked questions, he got answers which he considered satisfactory, and he did nothing to verify them. . . . Berardi had no conception of how tight the cash position was. He did not discover that BarChris was holding up checks in substantial amounts because there was no money in the bank to cover. . . . His review was useless.
>
> Accountants should not be held to a standard higher than that recognized in their profession. I do not do so here. Berardi's review did not come up to that standard. He did not take some of the steps which Peat, Marwick's written program prescribed. He did not spend an adequate amount of time on a task of this magnitude. Most important of all, he was too easily satisfied with glib answers to his inquiries. . . . There were enough danger signals in the materials which he did examine to require some further investigation. Generally accepted accounting standards require such further investigation under these circumstances. . . . I conclude that Peat, Marwick has not established its due diligence defense.
>
> **JUDGMENT** Defendant's motions to dismiss this action. . . are denied. [The court also found that BarChris's controller, its in-house counsel, its lawyer-director, a director-underwriter, and the underwriters consisting of eight investment banking firms led by Drexel & Co. had all failed to establish the due diligence defense.]

THE SECURITIES EXCHANGE ACT OF 1934

The 1933 Act monitors *issuance of new securities*. It is augmented by the Securities Exchange Act of 1934, which regulates *trading* in securities *after initial issuance*. Major features of the 1934 Act include:

1 Reporting requirements
2 Standards for fair dealing in securities marketplaces:
   (a) A ban on trading based upon "inside information"
   (b) Rules against keeping any "short-swing" profits
   (c) A code of fair practices for takeover of companies by corporate raiders

Reporting Requirements under the 1934 Act

Under the 1934 Act, "Section 12 companies," defined in Table 46.5, must file a *registration statement,* not to be confused with the registration statement required for new issues of stock under the 1933 Act. The registration statement under the 1934 Act must include the structure of outstanding securities, the background and compensation of directors and officers, certified financial statements for the past 3 fiscal years, and a variety of other matters. In addition, under Section 13 of the 1934 Act, Section 12 companies must file the periodic reports described in Table 46.5. All such reports are subject to the antifraud provisions of the 1934 Act. As of January 1993, over 10,000 *Section 12 com-*

Table 46.5 Periodic Reports That Section 12 Companies Must File with the SEC*

Report	Description
Form 10-K	Annual report about the corporation's current management, outstanding securities, business operations, and certified financial statement for the preceding fiscal year, and an update of the firm's 1934 Act registration statement
Form 10-Q	Quarterly operating statement and certified statement of financial condition, together with disclosure of recent stock sales and purchases by officers and directors
Form 8-K	"Early warning" report to be filed within 15 days of "any materially important event" affecting the corporation (e.g., a change of auditors, an offer to take over the corporation, or a major write-off of bad debts)

*A "Section 12" company under the 1934 Act is one whose registered securities trade on national exchanges or one that has 500 or more shareholders and assets over $5 million even though its securities are not registered under the 1933 Act.

panies were registered and reporting under the 1934 Act. The Section 12 reports are public records that potential investors may analyze before buying securities. In addition, the SEC examines the reports for securities law violations. The 1934 Act also requires securities exchanges, national securities associations, brokers, and dealers to register with the SEC.

Antifraud Section 10(b) and Rule 10b-5; Insider Trading

Rule 10b-5. Implementing the 1934 Act's Section 10(b) is Rule 10b-5:

It shall be unlawful for any person directly or indirectly, by use of any means or instrumentality of interstate commerce, or of the mails, or of any facility of any national securities exchange,

(1) to employ any device, scheme, or artifice to defraud,
(2) to make any untrue statement [written or oral] of a material fact or to omit to state a material fact necessary in order to make the statements made in the light of circumstances under which they were made, not misleading, or
(3) to engage in any act, practice, or course of business which operates or would operate as a fraud or deceit upon any person

in connection with the purchase or sale of any security.

Rule 10b-5 is the general antifraud provision of the 1934 Act and is used to prosecute a wide variety of deceptive practices. It generates more securities litigation than any other SEC rule. Insider trading isn't mentioned specifically, but courts use Rule 10b-5 as the chief weapon against insider wrongdoing in civil and criminal actions.

Purpose of Rule 10b-5. Corporate insiders—directors, officers, and key employees—have constant access to information that affects the value of the company's stock. If insiders could buy or sell company shares without disclosing such nonpublic information, they could clearly have an unfair advantage over other shareholders and the public at large. Under Section 10(b) and Rule 10b-5 it is unlawful for corporate insiders to trade in their company's shares on the basis of material (relevant) advance, nonpublic information—that is, information not available to the other party or to securities traders generally. Advance information is material when its disclosure to the public could lead to an immediate rise or fall in the share price. Clearly nothing is unfair about a corporate insider trading on the basis of information that is public, since the party with whom the insider is dealing has access to the same information. Thus the SEC's disclose-or-abstain doctrine requires insiders to abstain from trading in their company's securities until the inside information has been disclosed, and the public has had reasonable time to react to it.

Persons and transactions covered. Rule 10b-5 is *not* restricted to corporate directors, officers, or major shareholders who have inside information that could affect the price of the company's shares. Courts have extended the rule to include

1 An employee of the corporation
2 Outside attorneys, accountants, or investment bankers; their employees; others who have access to inside information; and any person who acts on a tip (*a tippee*) from a corporate insider (*a tipper*), knowing that the information is not available to the investing public

Rule 10b-5 applies to all transactions, regardless of size, where mail, telephone, or other instrumentalities of interstate commerce are involved, and irrespective of whether the transaction is made privately or on a stock exchange, or whether the securities are registered under the 1933 Act or are Section 12 securities under the reporting and registration requirements of the 1934 Act.

Cases interpreting Rule 10b-5. The SEC framed Rule 10b-5 in broad terms, leaving the federal courts with the task of developing its precise meaning in a series of important decisions.

Rule 10b-5 does *not* cover *negligence*. For example, when accountants carelessly (but not fraudulently) prepare misleading financial statements that cause loss, there may be liability for negligence under state law, but federal Section 10(b) and Rule 10b-5 do not apply. In *Ernst & Ernst v. Hochfelder*,[9] a brokerage president induced clients to mail in funds which were to be invested in fictional high-yield accounts, but which he lost in speculation. His suicide note told of the fraud, which was not discovered because of his "mail rule" that only he could open mail. One of the victims, Hochfelder, sued the accounting firm, claiming that negligent failure of their annual audit to uncover the mail rule had damaged him in violation of Rule 10b-5. The Supreme Court held that words in Section 10(b) such as "manipulative," "device," and "contrivance" reflect congressional intent to ban intentional fraud—not loss from ordinary negligence.

In a landmark case, *Securities and Exchange Commission v. Texas Gulf Sulphur Co.*,[10] company geologists reported one of the richest mining strikes in modern history. Carefully guarding the secret, directors and officers issued deceptive press releases contradicting rumors of the discovery. They and their tippees then quietly increased their holdings from 1,100 to more than 12,000 shares. When the price of Texas Gulf rose from $18 to $58 per share, the SEC sued to compel insiders and tippees to disgorge the profits made from the inside information. The appellate court upheld the trial court's order that defendants repay $2.7 million to the victims who had sold their shares in ignorance of the inside information. The court said:

Anyone who, trading for his own account in the securities of a corporation has access, directly or indirectly, to information intended to be available only for a corporate purpose and not for personal benefit, may not take advantage of such information knowing it is unavailable to those with whom he is dealing, i.e. the investing public.

After *Texas Gulf*, a new question arose: Does an *outsider* who trades while having material nonpublic information owe a duty of disclosure to *everyone* in the marketplace? In *Chiarella v. United States*,[11] Chiarella was employed by printers that prepared confidential tender offer materials for lawyers of the offering companies. He learned the names of target companies in pending mergers and made over $30,000 trad-

---

[9] 425 U.S. 185 (1976).

[10] 446 F.2d 1301 (2d Cir., 1971).

[11] 100 S. Ct. 1108 (1980).

ing in their stock. Convicted on seventeen counts of violating Rule 10b-5, Chiarella appealed. The Supreme Court rejected the notion that mere use of nonpublic material information is fraudulent. Chiarella's use of the information was not a fraud unless there was a duty to speak, the Court said. Such a duty must arise from a *prior relation with the sellers*—which Chiarella did not have. He had bought shares in an impersonal stock market, and had no prior dealings with the sellers. "He was not their agent, he was not a fiduciary, he was not a person in whom the sellers had placed their trust and confidence." The *misappropriation theory*, discussed below, was developed to deal with the Chiarella-type situation where no fiduciary duty was owed to the shareholders.

In an important sequel, *Dirks v. Securities and Exchange Commission*,[12] the Court faced another new problem: Should there be liability if the insider does *not trade directly but simply passes a tip to others?* Secrist, a former officer of Equity Funding, reported its big-scale fraud to Dirks, an investment analyst. Dirks waited 20 days before telling a *Wall Street Journal* reporter, who advised the SEC. During that time, Dirks advised sale of Equity shares to his client-tippees. The SEC sued them and Dirks, claiming that his selective private disclosure to clients before public disclosure was a "deceptive device" in violation of Rule 10b-5. The Supreme Court held that liability turns on whether the insider breached a fiduciary duty to the corporation's shareholders, and this in turn depends on a "personal benefit" test. Here Secrist (the tipper) had not received any personal benefit, and had not breached his fiduciary duty. The duty of Dirks (the tippee) to disclose or abstain is derived from the insider's duty—the tippee cannot violate Section 10(b) if the tipper does not. The Court concluded that since Secrist, as tipper, received no personal benefit and had not breached his fiduciary duty, Dirks, as tippee, had no derivative liability.

In *Bateman Eichler, Hill Richards, Inc. v. Berner*[13] a stockbroker (tipper) claimed he had inside information that the firm had a rich gold strike abroad. Relying on it, plaintiff (tippee) bought the stock, which dropped drastically in price. The buyer-tippee then sued the broker (tipper), who argued that the tippee had no standing to sue because he was equally guilty (*in pari delicto*) of any wrongdoing in that he had traded on the information. Upholding the tippee's right to sue, the Supreme Court noted that a tippee is not as culpable as a tipper whose breach of duty gave rise to the tippee's loss in the first place. The Court concluded:

> Denying the *in pari delicto* defense will best promote the primary objective of the federal securities laws—protection of the investing public. . . .

Facts in *Securities and Exchange Commission v. Materia*[14] were similar to those in *Chiarella*. A printing employee obtained tender offer information from his employer and bought and sold target company stock, realizing a profit of over $100,000. Instead of a criminal prosecution, which was unsuccessful in *Chiarella*, the SEC brought a *civil* action under Rule 10b-5. The appeals court upheld an order for Materia to disgorge his profits and announced a new *misappropriation theory* of Rule 10b-5 liability:

> One who misappropriates nonpublic information in breach of a fiduciary duty and trades on that information to his own advantage violates Section 10(b) and Rule 10b-5.

In 1987, the U.S. Supreme Court had before it a similar question arising from an appeal from criminal convictions for violating Rule 10b-5.[15] Winans, a reporter for *The Wall Street Journal*, wrote a column "Heard on the Street" in which he gave positive and negative information about selected stocks. Violating the *Journal*'s policy of not revealing confidential information prior to publication, Winans tipped off Carpenter and other defendants about what would appear in his column. In 4 months the defendants netted $690,000 in stock trades on the basis of information that was about to appear in Winans'

---

[12]103 S. Ct. 3255 (1983).
[13]472 U.S. 299 (1985).
[14]745 F.2d 197 (2d Cir. 1984).
[15]*Carpenter v. United States*, 108 S. Ct. 316 (1987).

columns. Under the misappropriation-of-confidential-information theory, the defendants were convicted of violating the securities laws and of mail and wire fraud. The defendants appealed. The Supreme Court was evenly divided with respect to the convictions based on *applying the misappropriation theory to Rule 10b-5*. Thus, in effect, it approved the theory.

Insider Trading Sanctions Act of 1984. The Insider Trading Sanctions Act[16] strengthens Rule 10b-5 by empowering an SEC civil penalty suit against anyone who purchases or sells securities from or through a broker using a national securities exchange while in possession of material nonpublic information. The Act empowers a court to assess a penalty payable to the United States of up to three times the violator's profit (or loss that was avoided). The Act did not eliminate the need to prove the violator owed a fiduciary duty.

Insider Fraud in Corporate Takeovers in the 1980s. During 1986 and 1987, a flood of corporate takeovers spurred the SEC to ferret out insider trading. The SEC identified heavy trading in shares of firms rumored to be takeover targets. Resulting investigations led to the arrest of persons who had actively traded in shares of corporate targets on the basis of insider information. Prestigious lawyers, investment bankers, and stockbrokers were among those arrested and convicted of securities fraud. One big trader, Ivan Boesky, was fined $100 million by the SEC and was sent to prison. In 1992, Michael R. Milken and other former employees of the underwriting firm of Drexel Burnham Lambert Inc. settled more than 160 consolidated securities fraud lawsuits for $1.3 billion—perhaps the largest settlement of its kind in history. Milken paid $900 million of the settlement in addition to serving a prison sentence.

Insider Trading and Securities Fraud Enforcement Act (1988). To discourage insider trading, Congress enacted the Insider Trading and Securities Fraud Enforcement Act. It provides for up to 10 years' imprisonment for insider traders and those who aid them in violating the 1934 Act or SEC rules. In addition, fines may be imposed up to $1 million. Corporation or partnership violators may be fined up to $2.5 million. The SEC may also impose *civil* fines against insider traders or companies that knowingly or recklessly fail to detect or prevent insider trading by employees. A firm entrusted with confi-

---

[16]15 USC 78u(d)(2)(A).

> **BOX 46.3**
> **When Is a Tippee Liable under Rule 10b-5? Meet at the Monkey Farm Café to Find Out**
>
> Dillon noticed that when *Business Week*'s "Inside Wall Street" column hit the newsstands Thursdays at 5:00 p.m., prices of the analyzed stocks rose. He bribed employees to meet him Thursday morning at Monkey Farm Café with a copy smuggled out of the printing plant against strict company rules and signs posting warning of the dangers of insider trading. Stock trading profits were so good that Libera, Dillon's friend, joined him at the Monkey Farm Café and began trading, making over $90,000 in 5 months. Libera shared his secret with his attorney, Sablone, who made fifty-seven trades for a profit of $36,000. Dillon pleaded guilty to wire fraud.
>
> A jury convicted Libera and Sablone each on fifty-six counts of securities fraud and fifty of mail fraud. Affirming on appeal, the court held that the misappropriation doctrine prohibits trading in securities based on material, nonpublic information acquired in breach of a duty to any owner of such information. The defendants knew that the information was obtained by employees in breach of their fiduciary duty. The court also ruled that it is not necessary to a tippee conviction to prove that the tipper knew the leak of confidential information would lead to the tippee's trading on the misappropriated information.*
>
> **United States v. Libera*, 989 F.2d 596 (1993).

dential matters about a corporation or its securities must establish procedures to insulate that part of its office dealing in such matters from other areas. As a further sanction, the 1988 Act authorizes SEC payment of bounties to reward informers whose tips lead to imposition of insider trading convictions. The Act also gives victims of insider trading new rights of legal action against violators in addition to suits under Rule 10b-5.

Short-Swing Insider Trading and Reporting; Section 16(b)

Another kind of insider trading occurs when any officer, director, or beneficial owner of more than 10 percent of his or her corporation's shares, within any 6-month period, buys and sells corporate stock and makes a profit. Sections 16(a) and 16(b)[17] of the 1934 Act were enacted to discourage insiders from short-term trading by forcing them to return to their corporation all such short-swing profits. The sections are *based not on fraud* but simply on the *length of time a security is held*.

Section 16(b) also applies to a *sale and purchase*, since insiders can profit by selling shares at high prices and buying back again when they drop. Section 16(a) requires directors and other covered persons to file with the SEC, and with the national exchange on which the stock is traded, reports showing the number of corporate shares owned directly or beneficially as well as any change in those holdings. Courts apply Section 16(b) mechanically to insider stock trading—neither *scienter* (intent to violate the statute) nor the use of nonpublic information is an element of the offense, nor does it matter that the defendant acted in good faith. All that the corporation or private plaintiff must prove is that the director, officer, or 10 percent stockholder purchased and sold company stock at a profit within the 6-month period. Courts have interpreted Section 16(b) liberally in order to deter insiders from profiting from their own companies. Short-swing reports are public records and may be inspected by the SEC staff or "bounty hunters" searching for violations. If a violation is discovered, and the corporation fails to recover the short-swing profit, a shareholder may do so by filing a derivative suit on behalf of the corporation. The SEC has no authority to enforce Section 16(b).

BOX 46.4

Test Your Knowledge: An $83 Million Question

When a corporate raider that owns more than 10 percent of the shares of a target company collects greenmail in a 4-month period by selling the target's shares back to it in exchange for bonds which are then sold for cash, is the resulting gain a short-swing profit under Section 16(b) of the 1934 Act?

By April 1985, Mesa Partners II, formed by T. Boone Pickens and others, had acquired 23.7 million shares, or 13.6 percent, of Unocal stock, and made a tender offer of $54 per share to shareholders of Unocal. Unocal then offered its own shareholders $72 per share. In May, Unocal and the Pickens group made a deal: Mesa would not acquire Unocal shares or solicit proxies for 25 years, and Mesa exchanged 7.8 million shares of its Unocal stock for Unocal debt securities, which it promptly sold for $589 million. A Unocal shareholder filed a derivative suit claiming that all of Mesa's cash profit on the deal should be paid to Unocal because the trade of its Unocal stock for debt securities was, under Section 16(b), a "sale" by a beneficial owner of more than 10 percent of Unocal shares, and that the short-swing profit ($83 million) belonged to the corporation—Unocal. When the Pickens group traded its stock for bonds and sold the bonds, was its profit the result of a "sale" and, therefore, a short-swing profit?*

*Unocal v. Mesa Petroleum, 951 F.2d 1512 (1991).

---

[17]15 USC 78l.

Proxy Statements

Section 14(a) of the 1934 Act[18] governs solicitation of proxies from shareholders of Section 12 companies. A *proxy* is a written authorization by which a stockholder gives to another person the authority to vote the stockholder's shares. The term is also used to refer to the *person* appointed in the written proxy. Prior to the annual meeting of shareholders, companies customarily solicit proxies from their shareholders. Such proxies authorize one or more directors to vote the stockholders' shares for reelection of the board, approval of the corporation's auditors, and a variety of other management proposals. SEC Rule 14a-9 (illustrated in Case 46.3 below), like Rule 10b-5, prohibits fraudulent statements or omissions in a proxy solicitation by management or by minority shareholders and requires full disclosure of all material facts pertaining to the matters on which shareholder votes are solicited. SEC rules require Section 12 companies to submit prescribed financial statements to stockholders at the time their votes are solicited for election of directors.

SEC regulations have steadily increased shareholders' rights to be heard on matters affecting corporate profitability as well as social responsibility. For example, in 1992 the SEC ruled that shareholder proposals concerning compensation of directors and senior executives are no longer excludable from a company proxy statement under Rule 14a-8(c)(7). This ruling opens the door for shareholders to force non-binding "straw votes" on resolutions that propose to limit or reduce compensation of top executives, or to propose measures that would link compensation with profitability and performance. The policy was adopted in response to public furor over what was regarded as excessive pay in the top echelons of corporate America. Mutual funds and pension funds, which now virtually own many American corporations, are also using the new rules to play a more active role as principal shareholders in curbing corporate excesses and demanding greater economy and efficiency. A revised SEC rule is pending that will also require a more complete disclosure of executive compensation in the proxy statement in the form of a table showing cash compensation as well as the *value of stock options* granted that year, and a comparison schedule showing increases or decreases in total compensation for a period of years. The new rule will also require the board to describe the criteria used in awarding incentive compensation.

[18] 15 USC 78n(a).

CASE 46.3 **Virginia Bankshares, Inc. v. Sandberg** • 114 L. Ed. 929 (1991)

FACTS A bank holding company began a freeze-out merger of a target bank into a wholly owned subsidiary of the holding company. The subsidiary owned 85 percent of the shares of the target bank, the remaining 15 percent being held by minority shareholders who were to lose their interest after the merger because state law permitted the acquiring corporation to buy minority shares in such a merger. An investment banking firm advised the target bank that $42 a share would be a fair price for minority stock, and the target bank's board approved the merger proposal at that price. The target bank's directors solicited proxies for the annual meeting, urging a "yes" vote on the proposal and stating that the board had approved the merger because it provided a "high" value for minority shareholder stock. Sandberg refused to give her proxy and sued the holding company, the subsidiary, and directors of the target bank, claiming that they violated Section 14(a) of the 1934 Act and Rule 14a-9 by circulating proxy solicitation material that falsely stated a high price of minority shares when the directors did not believe it and by

**CASE 46.3
Continued**

approving the merger because it was the only way they could retain their jobs as directors on the target bank's board. Sandberg also claimed that this conduct amounted to breach of the directors' fiduciary duties under state law.

A jury found $60 a share to be a fair value, and awarded Sandberg the difference between that sum and the $42 she was paid, or $18 per share. The court of appeals affirmed and defendants appealed. The U.S. Supreme Court considered two issues: (1) whether directors' statements of *beliefs* are statements with respect to *material facts* under Rule 14a-9, and (2) whether a suit by minority shareholders was proper even though their vote was not needed to carry the merger proposal.

OPINION

SOUTER, J. [D]irectors' statements of reasons or belief . . . are factual in two senses: as statements that the directors do act for the reasons given . . . and as statements about the subject matter of the reason or belief expressed. . . . There was indeed evidence of a "going concern" value for the Bank in excess of $60 per share of common stock, . . . [a] fact never disclosed. . . . Under §14(A), then, a plaintiff is permitted to prove a specific statement of reason knowingly false or misleadingly incomplete, even when stated in conclusory terms.

. . . But not every mixture with the true will neutralize the deceptive. If it would take a financial analyst to spot the tension between the one and the other, whatever is misleading will remain materially so, and liability should follow. . . .

The second issue before us . . . is whether causation of damages compensable through the implied private right of action under §14(a) can be demonstrated by a member of minority shareholders whose votes are not required by law or corporate bylaw to authorize the transaction giving rise to the claim. . . . The rule that has emerged . . . is that recognition of any private right of action for violating a federal statute must ultimately rest on congressional intent to provide a private remedy. [The Court then reviewed House and Senate debates on the statute and concluded there was no evidence that Congress intended to create a private right of action in situations where misleading premerger proxy solicitations are sent to shareholders whose vote is not needed to effect the merger. . . .] Assuming the . . . proxy statement as materially misleading, the very terms of the Virginia statute indicate that a favorable minority vote induced by the solicitation would not . . . [prevent the minority from attacking the merger under state law based upon the directors' conflict of interest]. . . . There was no loss of state remedy to connect the proxy solicitation with harm to minority shareholders. . . .

JUDGMENT

[The judgment of the court of appeals was reversed, with the Supreme Court holding that (1) plaintiff shareholders are unable to prove the necessary causal link between misleading proxy statements and their vote for a merger where, under state law, the merger would be approved without their vote; (2) suits to set aside mergers, or for damages resulting from misleading proxy statements, should not be expanded beyond the limits that Congress intended in enacting Section 14(a) of the 1934 Act; and (3) where, under state law, minority shareholder votes could not prevent a merger, and there is an adequate remedy under state law for misleading proxy statements, minority shareholders may not bring an action under Section 14(a) and Rule 14a-9.]

Corporate Takeovers

Throughout the 1980s and into the 1990s, corporate takeovers have been very much in the news. For example, in 1991 bank mergers and takeovers smashed all previous records, with private sector deals exceeding $20 billion—almost five times the $4.3 billion total in 1990.

Purpose of Takeovers. A *takeover* may be for several purposes and may take several forms:

1. One corporation may take over another to enhance its business by acquiring the other corporation's skilled personnel and management, its patents, secret processes, or market share.
2. The takeover may be a *leveraged buyout*. This involves the purchase of all the corporation's shares of stock, generally by some members of the top management of the company together with others. The transaction is complex. Purchasers borrow the necessary funds and pledge, as security for the loan, all of the assets of the corporation purchased.
3. The corporation may be the target company of a corporate raider. The raider may intend to continue operating the corporate business, to merge the corporation into another corporation, or even to dismantle the corporation and sell its component parts, distributing the proceeds to itself—the raiding corporation—as well as to any other shareholders.

It is debatable whether takeovers or mergers benefit the target company shareholders. Some raiders claim that the target shares are increased in value by improved efficiency, and the tender offer price often is higher than the market value. Others, however, feel that more economic harm than good comes from most takeovers or mergers; they see them as a prelude to permanent closure of plants and elimination of jobs, and argue that the huge corporate debt often incurred in leveraged buyouts can saddle a corporation with fixed interest costs that impair its credit and its ability to borrow for capital expansion.

Tender Offer. A corporate raider often gains control of a target company by soliciting proxy approval from its shareholders for the election of the raider's own slate of directors or for the merger of the target company into a company controlled by the raider. As an alternative, the raider may make a *tender offer*—that is, an offer to the shareholders of the target company to buy their shares at a price the raider establishes. If the attempt succeeds, the raider acquires controlling interest in the target corporation. In order to induce the target company's shareholders to sell their shares, the raider offers a price

---

Table 46.6 Tender Offer Information to Be Filed with the SEC by Acquirors of More Than 5 Percent of a Corporation's Securities

1. The purchasers' names and background
2. The source of the funds used for the acquisition
3. The purpose of acquiring the shares
4. The purchasing entity intending to make a tender offer must, in addition, also file with the SEC and with each offeree a report containing:
   a. Details of any planned merger or other disposition of the target company's assets
   b. Information as to past dealings among the offeror, the target corporation, and those holding important positions in the target corporation
   c. Financial statements
   d. Any special agreements made with shareholders to obtain their support for the tender offer

well above the market value of the shares. This anticipated spread between the offered price and the market price induces speculators to buy shares of a takeover target in the hope of selling them at a profit to the raider or on the open market at the time of tender.

Williams Act. Neither the 1933 Act nor the 1934 Act required corporate raiders to give target company shareholders advance information about a proposed takeover. To forestall typical abuses that arose from this oversight, Congress in 1968 enacted the Williams Act to amend the 1934 Act and amended the Act again in 1970. These amendments and SEC Rules 13(d) and 14(d) require that any entity acquiring beneficial ownership of more than 5 percent of a corporation's securities must, within 10 days, file a report with the SEC and with the corporation whose securities have been acquired, including the information listed in Table 46.6.

To ensure equal treatment of shareholders and to discourage them from rushing in panic to accept a tender offer, shareholders' tenders of their stock are not accepted on a first-come, first-served basis. Instead, if more shares are tendered than the raider offered to purchase, the raider must purchase the tendered shares on a pro rata basis, paying the same price for all purchases. The Williams Act prohibits misrepresentation or omission of facts in proxy or tender offer solicitations that are likely to influence a reasonable shareholder's decision to sell shares. Any offer to pay holders of large blocks a higher price for their shares than that offered to other shareholders is prohibited.

Tender offers may be either friendly or hostile. If the target corporation doesn't object to the takeover, it is friendly. But when target directors conclude it is *not* in their corporation's or shareholders' best interests to sell controlling shares and the offeror persists, then the tender offer is hostile. In that event, target company directors may take one or more of the defensive steps discussed in Chapter 44. These include using the *poison pill,* paying *greenmail* to the raider, and finding a *white knight,* as in Case 46.4 below. So long as the information required by the Williams Act is furnished, the Act does not bar a hostile takeover.

During takeover negotiations, if either the acquiring corporation or the target corporation conceals material facts or makes false representations, shareholders are not hesitant to bring class actions under SEC Rule 10b-5. Thus, in the following case, plaintiff claimed that he was injured by the target corporation's violation of Rule 10b-5 in falsely denying a pending merger. The case illustrates how the Supreme Court has expanded Rule 10b-5 to grant shareholders damages for fraud without proving their *reliance* on fraudulent statements. The Court reached this conclusion by using the relatively new *fraud-on-the-market* theory.

CASE 46.4 — Basic Incorporated v. Levinson • 108 S. Ct. 978 (1988)

FACTS In 1976, Combustion Engineering, Inc., commenced merger discussions with Basic's officers. In the next 2 years, Basic issued three public statements denying involvement in merger negotiations: (1) In 1977, a newspaper quoted Basic's president as stating: "No negotiations are under way with any company for a merger." (2) In 1978, a Basic release said: "Management is unaware of any present or pending company development that would result in the abnormally heavy trading activity and price fluctuations in company shares." (3) On November 6, 1978, Basic repeated the statement in its report to shareholders. On December 18 Basic advised the New York Stock Exchange that it had been contacted about a merger, and asked the exchange to suspend trading in its shares. On December 20, Basic announced its approval of Combustion Inc.'s tender

**CASE 46.4
Continued**

offer of $46 per share. Levinson and others, in a class action against Basic and its directors (defendants), claimed that they violated Rule 10b-5 by issuing the three false statements; and that plaintiffs' *reliance* on the statements had caused them to sell their stock at low prices, thereby suffering damage. The trial court ruled that under the fraud-on-the-market theory, there was a rebuttable presumption that plaintiffs had relied on the statements and no further proof of reliance was necessary unless defendants came forward with evidence showing plaintiffs did *not* rely on the statements that merger negotiations were not going on. However, the trial court ruled that Basic's statements were not material or relevant to plaintiffs' decision to sell their stock, and granted summary judgment for Basic. The court of appeals reversed, and Basic appealed to the U.S. Supreme Court.

OPINION

BLACKMAN, J. . . . To fulfill the materiality requirement "there must be a substantial likelihood that the disclosure of the omitted fact would have been viewed by the reasonable investor as having significantly altered the 'total mix' of information made available.". . . We turn to the question of reliance and the fraud-on-the-market theory. Succinctly put:

> The fraud on the market theory is based on the hypothesis that, in an open and developed securities market, the price of a company's stock is determined by the available material information regarding the company and its business. . . . Misleading statements will therefore defraud purchasers of stock even if the purchasers do not directly rely on the misstatements. . . . The causal connection between defendants' fraud and the plaintiffs' purchase of stock in such a case is no less significant than in a case of direct reliance on misrepresentations. *Peil v. Speiser*, 806 F.2d 1154 (1986).

Our task, of course, is. . . to consider whether it was proper for the courts below to apply a rebuttable presumption of reliance, supported in part by the fraud-on-the-market theory. . . . [Basic] complains that the fraud-on-the-market theory effectively eliminates the requirement that a plaintiff asserting a claim under Rule 10b-5 prove reliance. . . . Modern securities markets . . . differ from the face-to-face transactions contemplated by early fraud cases, and our understanding of Rule 10b-5's reliance requirement must encompass these differences.

> The market is interposed between seller and buyer and, ideally, transmits information to the investor in the processed form of a market price. Thus the market is performing a substantial part of the valuation process performed by the investor in a face-to-face transaction. The market is acting as the unpaid agent of the investor, informing him that given all the information available to it, the value of the stock is worth the market price.

. . . The courts below accepted a presumption, created by the fraud-on-the-market theory and subject to rebuttal by [Basic] that persons who had traded Basic shares had done so in reliance on the integrity of the price set by the market, but because of [Basic's] material misrepresentations that price had been fraudulently depressed. . . . An investor who buys or sells stock at the price set by the market does so in reliance on the integrity of that price. Because most publicly available information is reflected in market price, an investor's reliance on any public material misrepresentations . . . may be presumed for purposes of a Rule 10b-5 action. . . .

> **CASE 46.4**
> **Continued**
>
> **JUDGMENT** [The trial court's judgment was vacated. The Supreme Court upheld the court of appeals' decision favoring Levinson and held that (1) the false press releases were material misrepresentations and (2) in a tender offer, if directors give false information to the public, under Rule 10b-5 there is a rebuttable presumption that a plaintiff who sold his or her shares relied on that information, because the directors' misrepresentations are a fraud on the market of which the selling plaintiff is a part.]

Enforcement of the 1934 Act

The 1934 Act imposes civil and criminal liabilities on directors, officers, and others who participate in deceptive or manipulative practices or who commit fraud in connection with securities transactions. One who aids and abets such wrongdoing or who knowingly benefits from a securities violation is subject to civil penalty.

After a hearing, the SEC may impose civil penalties such as denying lawyers or accountants the privilege of representing clients before it, revoking securities registrations, or imposing civil fines—such as the $900 million payment by Michael Milkin to settle the SEC's suit for insider trading violations, or the $650 million in criminal and civil penalties required of Drexel Burnham Lambert Inc. To wilfully violate any federal statute monitored by the SEC is a crime subject to fine and imprisonment.

SUMMARY

Federal and state governments have enacted laws controlling issuance and sale of securities. The Securities Act of 1933 governs registration of *new* securities. The Securities Exchange Act of 1934 regulates national stock exchanges and the sale of securities *after* issuance. The 1934 Act set up the SEC to monitor federal securities laws. State blue-sky laws augment the federal laws and SEC rules.

The 1933 and 1934 Acts and SEC rules aim to reduce fraud and unfair dealing in the issuance and sale of securities, and to preserve orderly markets for purchase and sale of securities.

Under the *Howie* test, a security is any investment contract in a common enterprise where management is separate from an investor who expects a profit primarily from the efforts of others. Notes that bear a "strong family resemblance" to those listed in federal court decisions are not securities; all others are. Securities must be registered with SEC before being offered for sale. The registration statement includes a prospectus and a Part II, with additional data. Section 11 of the 1934 Act provides that a company's directors, officers, attorneys, auditors, and underwriters have criminal and civil liability for material false statements or omissions in the registration statement. A purchaser of the security may also sue and recover damages. Issuers under the 1933 Act, and Section 12 firms under the 1934 Act, must file periodic financial reports.

Exempted securities and exempted transactions are not subject to the registration requirements of the 1933 Act. Securities issued as part of an exempted *transaction* are "restricted" so that resales are subject to extensive SEC regulation.

A major purpose of the 1934 Act is to assure that traders of securities have equal access to information regarding its value. Hence, insiders possessing material nonpublic information have both criminal and civil liability when, with scienter (intent to defraud), they violate a fiduciary duty and trade on the basis of that information. Generally, tippees who trade on the basis of information from such insiders (the tippers) are liable as well. The 1934 Act also requires directors, officers, or more than 10 percent stockholders of any Section 12 corporation to pay to it short-swing profits made within a 6-month period.

REVIEW QUESTIONS

1. Compare and contrast the 1933 Act and the 1934 Act.

2. What controls do states exercise over the sale of securities?

3. (a) What is the SEC? (b) What is its function?

4. Define (a) prospectus, (b) tombstone ad, and (c) underwriter.

5. (a) What kinds of securities must be registered? (b) What information should be included in a registration statement?

6. Your corporation proposes to sell securities. What activities are permitted (a) prior to filing a registration statement? (b) during the postfiling waiting period? (c) after registration?

7. Compare and contrast exempt security and exempt transaction.

8. (a) Define accredited investor and unaccredited investor. (b) What securities can each buy? (c) Why did the SEC create the terms?

9. (a) How does Rule 10b-5 affect insider trading? (b) Under what circumstances is a tippee precluded from trading in a security? (c) Why does the SEC endeavor to prevent insider trading?

10. (a) Who is affected by the 1934 Act's ban on insider short-swing trading—Section 16(b)? (b) What is the section's purpose?

CASE PROBLEMS

1. For $1.8 million, Reynolds sold 245 investors a "Gold Program" in which they bought gold ore coupled with a contract to mine and refine it at an indefinite future date. The SEC sued Reynolds, alleging he made false representations in violation of Section 10(b) and had offered and sold unregistered securities. Reynolds argued that the Gold Program did not involve the sale of a security. Was the Gold Program a security? Why or why not?

2. Ira Walbaum, a supermarket chain's controlling shareholder, accepted a tender offer from A&P, Inc., to buy his shares and informed his sister that the deal would close 2 days later, cautioning her not to tell anyone. Ira's sister told her daughter, who told her husband, Keith Loeb, who told his broker, Robert Chestman. Chestman knew that Loeb had married into the Walbaum family. A day before the tender offer was publicly announced, Loeb bought 1,000 shares and Chestman purchased 11,000 shares. After the public announcement, the price rose from $24 to $50. Chestman appealed from a 10-count criminal conviction for fraud under SEC Rule 14e-3. He claimed that the rule exceeded the authority Congress delegated to the SEC under the Williams Act. Under Rule 14e-3, "it is unlawful for any person to engage in fraudulent, deceptive, or manipulative practices in connection with any tender offer." Should the court uphold Chestman's conviction?

3. Fond Hope Genetic, Inc., makes and sells sophisticated pharmaceuticals. Arthur, a biologist, is vice president for blood pressure research. Each of the firm's three other vice presidents oversees a specialized area of scientific research. Arthur occasionally buys and sells shares of Fond Hope's stock, which is actively traded on a stock exchange. On January 12, 1988, Arthur borrowed funds and bought 1,000 shares of Fond Hope stock. On June 1, 1988, he sold 500 of those shares and made a profit of $10,000, which the company treasurer says Arthur must turn over to it because he is an officer. Arthur says that the rise in the firm's share price was not related to any research carried on by his department; that he knew nothing of the firm's other research activities or why the share price rose. Must Arthur give his profit to the company? Why or why not?

4. Burlington Northern, Inc., made a hostile tender offer for 25 million El Paso Gas Co. shares at $24 per share. A majority of El Paso's shareholders subscribed to the offer. Burlington then withdrew its offer and announced it had made a new and friendly takeover agreement with the El Paso directors. The agreement provided that Burlington would buy 21 million shares at $24 per share and recognized "golden parachute" contracts between El Paso and four

of its senior officers. The new offer was oversubscribed and the takeover completed, but Burlington bought fewer shares than it would have purchased under the original tender offer. Plaintiff and other similarly situated shareholders brought suit, claiming that Burlington, El Paso, and El Paso's board of directors had violated Section 10(b) of the 1934 Act, which bans "fraudulent, deceptive, or manipulative acts," in connection with any tender offer. The district court dismissed the suit, saying no misrepresentation was involved, and appeal was taken to the Supreme Court. What was the Court's decision?

5. Plaintiff Berner and other investors traded through Lazzaro, a registered securities broker employed by a stock brokerage firm. Lazzaro told them that insiders of TONM Exploration Inc. (TONM) had told him that TONM had made a big gold strike in Surinam, where it had options for thousands of acres of gold-bearing land. Lazzaro also said that when the information became public, TONM's shares, then selling for $1.50 to $3, would go to $10 or $15 and might increase to $100 in a year. When a few plaintiffs asked TONM's president if the tip was accurate, he said that the information was "not public knowledge; I will neither confirm nor deny these claims," but allegedly he added, "Lazzaro is very trustworthy and a good man." Plaintiffs bought TONM's stock—and its price dropped to new lows. Plaintiffs sued, asking damages for lost profits and claiming Lazzaro and TONM's president violated Section 10(b) of the 1934 Act by making intentional untrue representations to induce plaintiffs to purchase the stock. The trial court dismissed the complaint, holding that plaintiffs themselves traded on inside information and should be denied recovery. On appeal, did the Supreme Court agree with the trial court? Why or why not?

6. Smith & Smith, certified public accountants, performed audits on XYZ Corporation. The corporation's controller fraudulently concealed kickbacks given by the corporation to foreign purchasers. A shareholder sued Smith & Smith for aiding and abetting the fraud, claiming its failure to discover the fraud during its audit was a negligent violation of SEC Rule 10b-5. Are the accountants liable?

CHAPTER 47

Accountants' Liability

Accounting is a systematic process of compiling, recording, and presenting financial information on business firms and nonbusiness entities. The availability of reliable information facilitates the decision making of business managers, creditors, investors, and others in the general public. By supplying it, the accounting profession enhances the overall efficiency of the market and thus serves an important function in our economy.

A comprehensive regulatory framework exists, both private and public, to monitor the accounting profession in the performance of its informational function. A national association, the American Institute of Certified Public Accountants (AICPA), has been instrumental in developing the technical and ethical standards for the accounting profession. It also serves as a private regulatory body to ensure that public accountants maintain high standards of competence and integrity.

Public regulation of accountants is both state and federal. Although public accountants are licensed by state boards of accountancy, federal agencies such as the Securities and Exchange Commission and the Internal Revenue Service play a major role in the regulation of public accounting. The common law of torts and contracts provides the rules for accountants' malpractice liability, which parallel the liability standards for other professions. Accountants are also exposed to civil and criminal liability under state and federal statutes, particularly the federal securities laws.

Lawsuits and jury awards against accountants have dramatically increased in recent years. In 1991, for example, the industry spent $477 million, or 9 percent of accounting revenues in the United States, to settle and defend liability suits. In 1992, that figure increased to $783 million, representing 14.3 percent of the industry's revenues. The major accounting firms, the "Big Six,"[1] estimated in 1992 that the profession was facing $30 billion in damage claims.[2] Generally such liability suits result from accountants' work as auditors. For example, in 1992 a jury rendered one of the largest verdicts ever in an auditor lia-

---

[1] The Big Six firms are Arthur Andersen & Co., Ernst & Young, Coopers & Lybrand, KPMG Peat Marwick, Deloitte & Touche, and Price Waterhouse.

[2] Arthur Andersen & Co., Coopers & Lybrand, Deloitte & Touche, Ernst & Young, KPMG Peat Marwick, and Price Waterhouse, "The Liability Crisis in the United States: Impact on the Accounting Profession" (August 6, 1992).

bility lawsuit,[3] awarding bondholders of MiniScribe Corp., a bankrupt computer parts maker, $200 million against the company's independent auditor, Coopers & Lybrand. Managers of the company had committed fraud by inflating their sales and inventory, including shipping boxes of bricks to distributors as disk drives and counting them as sales. The plaintiffs alleged that Coopers & Lybrand conducted a faulty audit by overlooking the improper sales and inventory values. Coopers & Lybrand later settled the case for a reported $45 million and also paid $95 million to the bankruptcy trustee of MiniScribe for the benefit of its creditors.

The savings and loan crisis has also resulted in liability actions against accountants as injured investors and the government seek to recover their losses from the auditors of failed institutions. Recently, Ernst & Young and Arthur Andersen agreed to pay $63 million and $22 million respectively to settle claims arising out of the collapse of the notorious Lincoln Savings & Loan. And in 1992, Ernst & Young reached a comprehensive settlement with the federal government, paying $400 million to resolve all government claims relating to the failure of banks and other depository institutions. Because of the rise in lawsuits, accountants face increased litigation expenses, escalating insurance premiums, and a decline in revenue from audit work. The legal standards for accountants' liability are, therefore, a major concern of the profession.

Understanding the legal environment of accounting is important for both accounting and other business students. Accountants need to understand the professional standards to which they will be held and the legal liabilities they face if they fail to live up to those standards. Business managers should understand the nature of the accountant-client relationship and the extent to which they can rely on accounting information in their decision-making process. The first part of this chapter addresses the nature of the accountant-client relationship. Next, the chapter examines the civil liability of accountants—first the common law and then statutory liability. Finally, criminal and administrative liabilities of accountants are described.

THE ACCOUNTANT-CLIENT RELATIONSHIP

Businesses and individuals rely on accountants to perform audits of their firms, to provide advice and planning on complicated tax laws and regulations, and to give advice on a range of management decisions and business plans. The accountant-client relationship is usually established when the parties enter into a binding contract in an engagement letter. The engagement letter sets forth the parameters of the services to be rendered and the duties assumed by the accountant.

An accountant is in a relation of trust with his or her client, a relation that requires a strict duty of confidentiality. Disclosure of confidential information without the consent of the client can result in both civil liability for damages and sanctions for unethical conduct. However, accountants can be compelled to disclose confidential information and their working papers in a court of law, since most jurisdictions do not recognize an accountant-client privilege.

Nature of Accounting Services

Public accounting firms are primarily engaged in three services: tax preparation and planning, management advisory services, and auditing. Tax work is a traditional area of practice for accountants. CPA firms regularly prepare state and federal tax returns for their clients and engage in tax and estate planning. Management advisory services is the fastest growing area of accounting. It includes a variety of consulting activities, including business planning, investment advice, development of computer systems, and litigation assistance services. Auditing is

---

[3] The largest verdict ever, $383 million, was awarded in May of 1992 to Standard Chartered in its lawsuit against Price Waterhouse. Standard Chartered claimed that it was damaged by the accounting firm's negligence in the audit of United Bancorp, a company that Standard purchased and later sold at a substantial loss. The verdict was later set aside by the trial court.

the practice area in which public accounting firms derive most of their income (approximately 60 percent) and for which there is the greatest liability exposure.

Auditing is the process of examining the financial statements provided by the management of a business firm to determine whether the reported information is consistent with the actual financial condition of the firm. The **financial statements** consist of the balance sheet, income statement, statement of changes in shareholders' equity, and statement of cash flow. Clients need audits for a variety of reasons. Audited or **certified financial statements** may be needed to lawfully sell securities to investors, to secure business financing from banks and trade creditors, and to provide managers and shareholders with information on the financial health of the firm.

In auditing financial statements, an accountant conducts an investigation of the firm and its accounting procedures. The investigation must comply with the AICPA's **generally accepted auditing standards (GAAS).** The GAAS, which are set forth in Table 47.1, require, for example, that the auditor gain an adequate understanding of the internal control structure of an organization so as to adequately plan the audit work and to secure sufficient information, through sampling of records and physical observations, to render an opinion on the financial statements under review. The auditor must determine whether the financial statements, which are provided by and are the responsibility of management, conform to **generally accepted accounting procedures (GAAP),** the professional standards for reporting accounting information. GAAP will gov-

Table 47.1 Generally Accepted Auditing Standards (GAAS)

General Standards

1. The audit is to be performed by a person or persons having adequate technical training and proficiency as an auditor.
2. In all matters relating to the assignment, an independence in mental attitude is to be maintained by the auditor or auditors.
3. Due professional care is to be exercised in the performance of the audit and the preparation of the report.

Standards of Field Work

1. The work is to be adequately planned and assistants, if any, are to be properly supervised.
2. A sufficient understanding of the internal control structure is to be obtained to plan the audit and to determine the nature, timing, and extent of tests to be performed.
3. Sufficient competent evidential matter is to be obtained through inspection, observation, inquiries, and confirmations to afford a reasonable basis for an opinion regarding the financial statements under audit.

Standards of Reporting

1. The report shall state whether the financial statements are presented in accordance with generally accepted accounting principles.
2. The report shall identify those circumstances in which such principles have not been consistently observed in the current period in relation to the preceding period.
3. Informative disclosures in the financial statements are to be regarded as reasonably adequate unless otherwise stated in the report.
4. The report shall contain either an expression of opinion regarding the financial statements, taken as a whole, or an assertion to the effect that an opinion cannot be expressed. When an overall opinion cannot be expressed, the reasons therefore should be stated. In all cases where an auditor's name is associated with financial statements, the report should contain a clear-cut indication of the character of the auditor's examination, if any, and the degree of

ern, for example, how an entity should report sales, leases, taxes, costs, and other assets and liabilities.

The auditor prepares a report in which he or she expresses an opinion on whether the financial statements conform to GAAP and whether the statements accurately reflect the condition of the firm. If the auditor concludes that the financial statements comply with GAAP, the auditor issues an **unqualified** or **clean** opinion. The audit report will contain qualifications or explanatory paragraphs if the financial statements depart from GAAP or uncertainty exists as to future events—e.g., a pending multimillion-dollar lawsuit against the firm. An audit gives the client and other users a high degree of assurance (but not a guarantee) that the financial statements of a firm accurately reflect its condition.

Because audits are expensive, accountants provide their clients with two alternatives—unaudited reports of financial statements called **reviews** and **compilations.** An accountant performing an audit investigates the firm's accounting procedures, whereas an accountant performing a review merely questions management concerning the reporting of financial information. On the basis of such inquiries and a review of the financial statements, the accountant will render an opinion. The opinion will assure the client and other users only that the accountant is not aware of any material inaccuracies in the financial statements. A review provides some assurance that the financial statements fairly represent the entity's condition. In contrast, a compilation provides no assurance to clients or other users. In a compilation, the accountant simply writes up the information provided by the client in the format generally used for financial statements. Accordingly, the standard compilation report contains a disclaimer that the accountant has not audited or reviewed the financial statements and thus expresses no opinion as to their accuracy.

The Contract between Accountant and Client

Unless an accountant provides free services for another, the relationship between accountant and client is contractual. The elements of a contract discussed in Chapter 10—mutual assent, consideration, capacity of parties, and legal objective—are thus necessary for an enforceable agreement for accounting services. Also, the general common law rules relating to the formation, performance, interpretation, and breach of a contract are applicable to the accountant-client contract.

In addition, there are some particular applications of contract law to the accounting services contract. The contract between accountant and client, being one for personal services, does not come under the statute of frauds, and thus need not be in writing. Frequently, however, the contract will be in the form of an **engagement letter.** The engagement letter will set forth the professional services to be performed by the accountant. The client's signature on the letter constitutes an acceptance of the engagement. The scope of the accountant's work, and thus the performance required under the contract, is determined by the terms of the engagement letter. For example, the engagement letter should indicate whether the accountant is performing an audit, review, or compilation of a client's financial statements and should state the other material terms of the engagement.

The engagement letter will be interpreted in light of the reasonable expectations of the parties. Suppose that an accountant undertakes to audit the financial statements of a firm. A general audit is not specifically designed to uncover fraud by management or embezzlement by employees; thus a failure to uncover such wrongdoing would not necessarily be a breach of the accountant's duties. However, an accountant who undertakes a **fraud audit** has a duty to take steps to uncover any wrongdoing. In that case, the engagement letter should indicate that the accountant is obligated to perform services more extensive than those required in a standard audit engagement.

Duty of Confidentiality

Confidential Communications and Working Papers. In the performance of his or her work, an accountant acquires confidential information

> **BOX 47.1**
>
> ### A Question of Ethics
>
> Public accounting firms derive a substantial part of their income from audit work. Auditors thus have a vested interest in maintaining good relations with their clients. While the auditor is under a professional obligation to be independent and to present an accurate appraisal of the firm, managers of a business frequently want the auditor to paint an unrealistic picture of the firm's financial condition. This may cause a conflict between management and the auditor and place pressure on the auditor to distort the audit report. What steps should auditors take when pressured to alter their audit reports? Can auditors ever be truly independent when they are being paid by and may derive future income from businesses they are auditing? ∎

concerning a client's business and activities. To protect their clients' interests, accountants have a legal obligation to maintain the confidentiality of client communications and secret information. This duty of confidentiality extends to **working papers**—documents such as audit papers and notes prepared by an accountant. The law recognizes that the accountant is the owner of the working papers, but the client has the right to control the disclosure of their contents to third parties.

Disclosing confidential information may also violate professional ethics. Under Rule 301 of the AICPA Code of Professional Responsibility, a public accountant is prohibited from disclosing any confidential information without the explicit consent of the client. However, disclosure of confidential information *is* ethical when:

- Professional standards mandate disclosure—e.g., when GAAS or GAAP requires its disclosure in an audit of a firm
- A lawful court order or subpoena requires disclosure
- The information is sought by a legitimate investigatory or disciplinary body such as a state board of accountancy
- Information is needed as part of a peer review or quality review by the AICPA or state CPA society

In all other circumstances, disclosure of confidential information by the accountant without a client's consent is unethical.

Accountant-Client Privilege. The common law does not recognize a privilege that would prevent an accountant from disclosing a client's confidential communications in a court of law. Thus, unlike an attorney whose communications with a client are protected under the attorney-client privilege, an accountant can be compelled to testify against a client in most state courts. Federal law also fails to recognize an accountant-client privilege. Consequently, securities and tax accountants can be forced to divulge confidential client communications and working papers to the government.

In contrast to common law and federal law, a minority of states have established a limited, statutory accountant-client privilege. Under these privilege statutes, a client has the right to prevent an accountant from testifying regarding confidential matters. The privilege is not absolute, however. Many statutes contain exceptions; for example, a statute may permit an accountant to testify against a client in a criminal prosecution. And the privilege, being for the protection of the client's interests, belongs to the client, not the accountant, who can choose to assert or waive it in court.

In Case 47.1, the court discusses the accountant-client relationship, the duty of confidentiality, and the accountant's liability for damages if confidential information is improperly disclosed to third parties.

CASE 47.1	**Wagenheim v. Alexander Grant & Co.** • 482 N.E.2d 955 (Ohio App. 1983)
FACTS	Joel Wagenheim established Consolidata Services, Inc. (CDS), in 1970 to provide bookkeeping services to small and medium-sized businesses. CDS later started handling company payroll distributions. Payroll clients of CDS would deposit monies with CDS in an amount sufficient to cover the monthly payroll checks. CDS did not segregate the deposits. If a customer terminated its contract with CDS, CDS was obligated to return the amounts the client deposited.
	Alexander Grant & Co., an accounting firm, provided services to CDS. Many of the clients of CDS were also clients of Alexander Grant. In January 1978, Tom Ryan, the president of CDS, provided Alexander Grant with a financial statement that revealed a shortage of $150,000 in the payroll accounts based upon the payroll amounts owed and received. The accountants, acting on the advice of their in-house attorney, asked CDS to disclose the cash flow problem to their mutual clients before receiving any further client monies. Ryan declined to make the disclosures and suggested that Wagenheim be informed of the problem. At a second meeting on February 6, 1978, between Ryan and the accountants of Alexander Grant with Wagenheim present, the accountants again requested that CDS disclose the problem to the mutual clients. Wagenheim requested time to formulate a plan to correct the problem. Ryan resigned as sole officer and director of CDS.
	The next day the accountants began to contact the mutual clients of Alexander Grant and CDS and to advise them not to send additional payroll funds to CDS. Most of the clients refused to continue their relationship with CDS and, subsequently, canceled their contracts. On February 9, 1978, CDS and Wagenheim received a letter from Alexander Grant terminating its accountant-client relationship with CDS. As a result of Alexander Grant's contacts with the mutual clients, CDS ceased operations and was forced into receivership. CDS sued Alexander Grant and a jury awarded the plaintiff $350,000 in compensatory damages. From an order denying Alexander Grant's motion for a new trial, Alexander Grant appealed.
OPINION	STRAUSBAUGH, J. . . . [Alexander Grant] asserts . . . that no cause of action exists placing liability upon an accountant for the disclosure of confidential information obtained from a client during their association in order to protect the interests of certain third parties. . . .
	[T]his case appears to be one of first impression in the United States. However, this court recognizes that the legal basis upon which such liability could be established exists. . . .
	A contractual relationship exists between an accountant and his client and . . . an accountant's liability to his client is determined by the extent of their contractual relationship and the duties imposed by law upon accountants. . . . [W]e find that an accountant-client relationship existed between Alexander Grant and CDS and continued . . . up to the time that the defendant notified the plaintiff by letter, on February 9, 1978, terminating their relationship. . . .
	The legal obligations that flow from an accountant's business relationships necessarily arise from an understanding between the parties of the objectives to

CASE 47.1 Continued

be achieved and the expectations that govern their achievement. As has been [done] in both the legal and medical professions, the State Accountancy Board has promulgated its own code of professional conduct. . . .

Ohio Adm. Code 4701-11-02(A), confidential client information, states:

> The certified public accountant or public accountant shall not disclose any confidential information obtained in the course of a professional engagement except with the consent of the client. . . .

[T]here is a reasonable expectation that Alexander Grant in providing accounting services to the public will conduct itself in a professional manner consistent with those standards established within the state. As a result, there is a legal obligation existing in every accountant-client relationship in which it participates, unless specifically excluded, that all information communicated to [Alexander Grant] by its client in confidence should not be disclosed without the client's prior consent. . . .

While [it] did not specifically disclose any confidential communications concerning CDS to its clients, the advice that it gave was based upon such information. Because of its superior knowledge, the warnings given by Alexander Grant were heeded with almost no hesitation by its clients and reasonably so. Thus, by using the confidential information obtained from CDS, and advising its clients to cease any further business dealings with the plaintiff, its actions were equivalent to, or perhaps even worse than, a complete disclosure of CDS's financial status to the mutual clients—because, without a complete disclosure, the mutual clients were unable to make an independent evaluation as to what course of action should be pursued.

Although the duty of confidentiality implied in an accountant-client relationship is favored, this court recognizes that such duty is not absolute. Overriding public interests may exist to which confidentiality must yield. [Alexander Grant] asserts that the disclosures were necessary and justified because they were made to protect the overriding interests of the mutual clients. [It] cites the insolvency of CDS, the absence of any officers or directors after Ryan's resignation, and certain questionable activities within the corporation as the bases for disclosures. . . .

The mere fact that CDS was insolvent does not itself justify the disclosure of that corporation's financial status . . . to CDS's clients, without some further investigation into the business activities of the corporation to determine if, indeed, a fraud was being committed upon the mutual clients and if they were in immediate danger of suffering significant financial losses from a continued association with CDS. . . . Certainly, if CDS were so insolvent that it had no reasonable expectations or intentions of fulfilling its contractual obligations, then it would be fraud for CDS to fail to disclose its insolvency. . . . In this case, although there was some evidence presented by [Alexander Grant] that it knew or could reasonably have believed that CDS was irretrievably insolvent and had no reasonable expectation of fulfilling its contractual obligations with its payroll clients, we find that there was sufficient evidence in the record that CDS could have regained its solvency and obtained the cash needed to balance the accounts of its payroll clients.

JUDGMENT

Affirmed in part and remanded to the trial court for a new trial limited to the determination of damages only.

COMMON LAW LIABILITY OF ACCOUNTANTS

Accountants, like other individuals, are subject to civil liability under the common law of contracts and torts. The engagement letter creates an enforceable contract between the parties, the breach of which gives rise to an action for damages against the accountant. The contract also creates a duty on the part of the accountant to exercise professional care and skill in the performance of the services. Thus, if an accountant fails to act in a reasonable and careful manner, the breach of duty constitutes the tort of negligence. Accountants can also be sued for the tort of fraud if they knowingly or recklessly misrepresent facts upon which others rely to their detriment. An accountant's common law liability may extend beyond his or her client to other users of the accountant's work product.

Contract Liability and Breach of Fiduciary Duty

An accountant who fails to perform the services expressly agreed to under the engagement can be liable for breach of contract. If the breach is material, the accountant is liable for actual damages caused by the breach and may also forfeit his or her right to compensation. In one case, for example, an accountant failed to file a client's corporate income tax return as required by their contract. The court held the accountant liable for the cost of having another accountant prepare and file the return, and denied the breaching accountant any payment for his services.

An accountant is generally considered to be in a confidential relationship with his or her client, a relationship requiring the accountant to make full disclosure of all material facts and to act in the client's best interests. An accountant can be sued for breach of fiduciary duty if he or she does not comply with this strict obligation of loyalty and good faith. Suppose that ABC Investments hires Jane Thompson, CPA, to advise the firm on the purchase of a computer system. Jane has a legal obligation to act solely in the best interests of ABC in providing advice on the system. If Jane advises ABC to purchase a system from a company that Jane owns without disclosing that interest to her client, she breaches her duty of loyalty and is liable to her client for damages.

Liability for Fraud

An accountant makes a variety of statements, representations, and assertions in giving advice and information to his or her client. In an audit, for example, the accountant certifies that the financial statements of the firm fairly represent its financial condition. If the accountant's assertions are false, the client can bring an action for actual fraud, constructive fraud, or negligence, depending upon the mental state of the accountant.

Actual Fraud and Scienter. As noted in Chapter 6, to recover in an action for the tort of fraud, the plaintiff must prove that (1) the defendant made a false representation of material fact, (2) the defendant had knowledge that the representation was false and intended another to act upon the representation, and (3) the plaintiff justifiably relied on the representation and suffered injury resulting from such reliance. The mental state required for actual fraud—knowledge of falsity—is called *scienter*. An accountant who knowingly misrepresents the financial condition of a firm commits actual fraud and is liable to the client for both compensatory and punitive damages.

Constructive Fraud and Gross Negligence. An accountant who recklessly makes false statements that a client justifiably relies on is liable for **constructive fraud.** The mental state required for constructive fraud is **gross negligence,** a reckless indifference to the truth or falsity of the matter asserted. Suppose that Mario, an accountant engaged to perform an audit, makes no examination or investigation of the financial statements provided by the management of a firm. Relying solely on the assertions of management, he certifies that the statements fairly represent the condition of the firm. Because he did not know the statements were false, he did not commit actual fraud. Yet his lack of a basis for asserting that the financial statements were accurate is sufficient to constitute gross negligence, which will support an action for constructive fraud against him.

Liability for Professional Negligence

An accountant may be liable for professional negligence in the performance of his or her work. This is often referred to as accounting malpractice. In order to establish professional negligence, the plaintiff is required to prove four elements:

1 *Duty.* The accountant owed the plaintiff a duty to exercise reasonable care and skill in the performance of the work.
2 *Breach of duty.* The accountant failed to exercise professional care and skill in the work.
3 *Causation.* The accountant's breach of duty was the actual and proximate cause of the plaintiff's damages.
4 *Damages.* The plaintiff suffered losses or damages.

In a negligence action, plaintiff's theory of recovery will often be that the accountant made negligent misrepresentations—that is, that the accountant was negligent in giving false or misleading advice or information to his or her client or others who acted upon that advice or information and were damaged. For **negligent misrepresentation,** many jurisdictions have adopted the standards of Section 552(1) of the *Restatement (Second), Torts,* as set forth in Table 47.2. Although these standards are similar to the elements of negligence, causation under Section 552 requires that the client justifiably rely on the misrepresentations of the accountant. Thus, in states that follow Section 552, an accountant is liable for negligent misrepresentation only when the plaintiff actually relied on the information supplied by the accountant and this reliance was reasonable. If, for example, a bank extended credit to a firm knowing that the firm was insolvent and the certified financial statements were false, any reliance on the auditor's report would be considered unreasonable.

Table 47.2 *Restatement (Second), Torts, Section 552*

1 One who, in the course of his business, profession or employment, or in any other transaction in which he has a pecuniary interest, supplies false information for the guidance of others in their business transactions, is subject to liability for pecuniary loss caused to them by their justifiable reliance upon the information, if he fails to exercise reasonable care or competence in obtaining or communicating the information.

2 Except as stated in Subsection (3), the liability stated in Subsection (1) is limited to loss suffered

   a by the person or one of a limited group of persons for whose benefit and guidance he intends to supply the information or knows that the recipient intends to supply it; and

   b through reliance upon it in a transaction that he intends the information to influence or knows that the recipient so intends or in a substantially similar transaction.

The Reasonable Accountant Standard. As in other professions, accountants are held to a professional standard of care. They are expected to exercise that degree of care, skill, and diligence exercised by reasonably prudent members of the accounting profession. This does *not* mean that accountants "insure" their work. Just as doctors do not guarantee a cure, accountants do not guarantee the accuracy of the information or advice they provide. If they perform *negligently,* however, they are liable for all the damages they proximately cause.

The scope of the work that the accountant engages to perform affects the degree of care owed to the client. For example, an accountant assumes a higher level of professional responsibility in an audit than in a review or compilation engagement. In a review or compilation, the accountant relies heavily on management for information about the firm, but in an audit the accountant personally conducts or oversees a probing examination of the firm's financial records. Irregularities that a properly conducted audit would reveal may not be reasonably discoverable in a review engagement. Thus, a failure to uncover irregularities may breach the duty of reasonable care in an audit engagement, but not breach the duty of care that applies to a review or compilation engagement.

Whatever the terms of the engagement, accountants must disclose any material irregularities or wrongdoing that they discover in the course of their work. If during a compilation Maria uncovers employee wrongdoing, she must so inform her client. Failure to do so constitutes negligence even though she merely undertook to compile the financial statements of the firm.

GAAP and GAAS. Because an accountant is held to a professional standard of care, the standards of the industry, including GAAS and GAAP, are critical in determining whether an accountant breached his or her duty of care. In most jurisdictions, the jury can infer (presume) negligence if it finds that an accountant did not comply with the applicable professional standards. Since malpractice actions against accountants will frequently turn on whether the accountant complied with GAAP or GAAS, the plaintiff will generally need expert testimony to establish both the relevant professional standards under the circumstances and the accountant's failure to comply with those standards.

In contrast, an accountant does not necessarily exercise due care simply by complying with GAAP and GAAS. As the next case demonstrates, most jurisdictions recognize that the professional accounting standards are not determinative of the due care issue.

CASE 47.2   **Maduff Corporation v. Deloitte Haskins & Sells**
• 779 P.2d 1083 (Or. App. 1989)

FACTS   Maduff Mortgage Corporation, a subsidiary of Maduff Group, Inc., provided construction loan financing to builders of residential housing using a line of credit guaranteed by Maduff Group. Maduff Mortgage generally required builders to secure contracts from buyers called "presale agreements" and disbursed construction loans only as the work progressed. In 1981 and 1982, Maduff Mortgage began making construction loans to Macal Development, a Portland developer. By September of 1982, there were serious problems with the Macal loans. The loans were overdisbursed, presale agreements were nonexistent or were forged, and construction loan proceeds were improperly diverted by Macal. There was evidence that employees and officers of Maduff Mortgage assisted Macal in committing these wrongful acts.

The accounting firm of Deloitte Haskins & Sells (Deloitte) audited the financial statements of Maduff Mortgage for the years ending 1979–1982, but its audits failed to uncover the Macal irregularities. By the time the problems were discovered in May of 1983, Maduff Mortgage was financially unable to continue in business. Maduff Mortgage and Maduff Group sued Deloitte for professional negligence. The jury found the accounting firm negligent, and the court granted money judgments to Maduff Mortgage and Maduff Group for $669,000 and $1,056,000 respectively. Deloitte appealed.

OPINION   RIGGS, J. . . . Deloitte first assigns as error the trial court's failure to give its requested instruction on an auditor's responsibility for detecting fraud. . . . Deloitte's requested instruction in effect states that an auditor is not liable for failing to detect fraud unless it has failed to comply with generally accepted auditing standards:

> **CASE 47.2**
> **Continued**
>
> An ordinary audit cannot be relied upon to assure that fraud or deliberate misrepresentations by plaintiff's management will be discovered. The defendant is not an insurer or guarantor if it turns out that fraud occurred and the defendant did not discover it. The defendant does have a responsibility for failing to detect fraud when such failure clearly results from the defendant's failure to comply with Generally Accepted Auditing Standards. The subsequent discovery of fraud does not of itself mean that the defendant's examination was negligently done.
>
> Deloitte contends that the standards promulgated by the American Institute of Certified Public Accountants (AICPA) are the generally accepted auditing standards against which an auditor's examination must be evaluated and that its requested instruction incorporates those standards. . . . The requested standards were admitted as evidence, but not given as instructions. Deloitte argues that, without an instruction on those standards, a jury would not understand that a finding that there was fraud that Deloitte did not discover would not necessarily mean that the audit was inadequate.
>
> [Maduff Mortgage] argues that the AICPA standards are only evidentiary. We agree. They are principles and procedures developed by the accounting profession itself, not by the courts or the legislature. They may be useful to a jury in determining the standard of care for an auditor, but they are not controlling. The amount of care, skill and diligence required to be used by defendant in conducting an audit is a question of fact for the jury, just as it is in other fields for other professionals.
>
> **JUDGMENT** Affirmed.

Contributory and Comparative Negligence. To what extent can an accountant use the negligence of a client as a defense to the client's claim that the accountant was negligent? Auditors sometimes attempt to avoid liability for failing to uncover internal wrongdoing by arguing that the client's damages were actually caused by poor business practices. In most jurisdictions, the client's negligence is not a defense unless it contributed to the accountant's failure to perform the contract and report the truth. For example, an auditor who negligently fails to uncover employee embezzlements cannot use the client's inadequate internal controls as a defense. A client failure of this sort ordinarily would not prevent a careful auditor from uncovering the thefts and reporting the truth. On the other hand, a growing number of states apply comparative negligence, allowing the jury to compare the client's fault with that of the accountant's and to reduce the client's damages according to the percentage of fault attributable to the client. In these states, the client will recover only those damages that the jury attributes to the accountant's negligence.

Liability to Third Parties

An accountant's liability to third parties—persons other than the client—is a major area of concern to the accounting profession. Clients have a right to sue accountants for malpractice because the engagement contract imposes a duty on the accountant to exercise due care for the client's protection. But what about third parties who may rely on the accountant's work product in making important business decisions? Since audited financial statements may be relied on by a client's creditors, potential investors in or purchasers of the client's business, or others to whom the client provides the information, the range of third-party users to whom an accountant owes a duty of care can be critically important to the accountant's financial health.

In general, accountants are liable to *all users* for any fraud, actual or constructive. For negligence, however, the courts have restricted accountants' liability to third parties, though in varying degrees among the states. Collectively, the courts have adopted three different standards to determine the accountant's negligence liability to third parties: the primary beneficiary rule, the known-class-of-users rule, and the foreseeable users rule.

Ultramares **and the Primary Beneficiary Rule.** The landmark case on accountants' liability to third parties for negligence is the 1931 decision of the New York Court of Appeals in *Ultramares Corporation v. Touche*.[4] In *Ultramares*, the accounting firm of Touche, Niven & Co. audited the balance sheet of its client, Fred Stern & Co., which used the certified balance sheet to secure credit from Ultramares. Fred Stern & Co. was insolvent and ultimately went into bankruptcy. Ultramares sued Touche, claiming negligence and fraud. Justice Cardozo, speaking for the court in *Ultramares*, concluded that an accountant has no liability to third parties for professional negligence because the accountant owes a duty of care only to persons in privity of contract—that is, the client. He reasoned that to allow negligence suits by third parties not in privity or in a relationship bordering on privity would open a floodgate of lawsuits exposing the accountant to "liability in an indeterminate amount for an indeterminate time to an indeterminate class."

The *Ultramares* rule with some modification is still followed in a number of jurisdictions either by common law decision (e.g., New York) or under a statute limiting the liability of accountants (e.g., Illinois). In general, the modern formulation of *Ultramares* allows negligence actions only by a third party for whose primary benefit the accounting work was undertaken. A person is a **primary beneficiary** of an accountant's work when the accountant (1) knew the specific party intended to be benefited by the work, (2) knew the specific purpose for which the work was to be used, and (3) took actions that indicated an understanding that the identified third party was relying on his or her work.

For example, assume that Ultimate Design Inc. is in need of a $1 million operating loan. Its bank, First Fidelity, is willing to make the loan if Ultimate provides certified financial statements. Ultimate engages its accountant, Jackson, to conduct an audit for that purpose, informing Jackson that the audit is required by First Fidelity for the loan. Jackson provides a copy of the audit report to First Fidelity and discusses the financial statements with bank officers in charge of the loan. On the basis of the audited financial statements, First Fidelity loans the money to Ultimate. Under the circumstances, First Fidelity is a primary beneficiary of the accountant's work and can sue Jackson for negligence. Jackson knew the specific party (First Fidelity) for whose benefit the audit was being done and the specific purpose of the work (the $1 million operating loan to Ultimate Design). By providing the audit report to First Fidelity and discussing the financial statements with the bank, Jackson understood that First Fidelity was relying on the audit. Note that other third parties relying on Jackson's audit, including other banks making an operating loan to Ultimate Design, would not be considered primary beneficiaries and would have no right to sue the accountant for negligence.

The *Restatement (Second)* Known-Class-of-Users Rule. The prevailing modern rule on accountants' negligence liability to third parties is the **known-** or **foreseen-class-of-users** rule, which is set forth in Section 552 of the *Restatement (Second), Torts* (see Table 47.2). A third party is within a known class of users when he or she is "one of a limited class of persons for whose benefit and guidance [the accountant] intends to supply the information or knows [the client] intends to supply it" and when the third party relies on the information "in a transaction that [the accountant] intends the information to influence or knows that [the client] so intends

[4]174 N.E. 441 (N.Y. Ct. App. 1931).

or in a substantially similar transaction." Under this rule, an accountant's liability to third parties is not limited to identified beneficiaries but extends to any user of the accountant's work who was one of a group of persons the accountant *knew* would receive and rely on the information in a particular transaction. The accountant must have knowledge of (1) the class of persons who may use his or her work and (2) the nature of the transaction for which the work will be used.

For example, assume that Alvarez decides to sell her business, Northern Enterprises, and engages a public accounting firm, Hallen & Flamm, to audit Northern's financial statements for use in the sale. Hallen & Flamm is informed that the audit report will be shown to prospective purchasers as evidence of the value of Northern Enterprises. Price purchases Northern Enterprises relying on the audited financial statements. Because Hallen & Flamm knew the class of users who would receive its audit report (prospective purchasers of the business) and the transaction for which the work would be used (the sale of Northern Enterprises), any person relying on the financial statements in the purchase of the business (including Price) would be within the known class of users and could sue Hallen & Flamm for negligence under the *Restatement* rule. Other third parties who receive and rely on the audited financial statements (e.g., creditors of the business) would have no claim against Hallen & Flamm.

The Foreseeable Users Rule. A small number of states hold that an accountant is liable to all **foreseeable users.** Under this most liberal rule, if the accountant *should have known* of the use of his or her work product by particular third parties, the accountant is liable to them for negligence. Thus, an accountant performing an audit, for example, must anticipate the users of his or her report and exercise due care for their protection. An accountant need not know the person or class of persons who will rely on the work product as long as the person's use of the work is reasonably foreseeable.

In Case 47.3, the court discusses the alternative tests for third-party liability and adopts the *Restatement* rule on policy grounds.

CASE 47.3 **Raritan River Steel Co. v. Cherry, Bekaert & Holland**
• 367 S.E.2d 609 (N.C. 1988)

FACTS Raritan River Steel Company and Sidbec-Dosco, Inc., were creditors of Intercontinental Metal Corporation (IMC). The public accounting firm of Cherry, Bekaert & Holland audited the financial statements of IMC for the years 1980 and 1981. Sidbec-Dosco claimed that it extended substantial unsecured credit to IMC in 1982, relying directly on the audited financial statements. Contending that the net worth of IMC was overstated in the audit reports and that the overstatement caused it damages, Sidbec-Dosco sued the accountants. From a dismissal of their complaint, the creditor appealed. The court of appeals reversed the trial court's decision, and the defendant accountants requested and were granted review by the Supreme Court of North Carolina.

OPINION EXUM, C.J. . . .

The Sidbec-Dosco Claim

The . . . difficult question raised by Sidbec-Dosco's complaint is whether it alleges enough to show that defendants owed it a duty of care.

**CASE 47.3
Continued**

The complaint specifically states [t]hat at the time the Defendant prepared the audited financial statements for IMC, the Defendant knew that such financial statements would be used for, among other purposes, general representations by the company of its financial condition, and that extensions of credit to IMC and its affiliated companies would be based upon such statements. . . .

Courts in our sister states have recognized . . . different approaches to determine the scope of an accountant's liability for negligent misrepresentation in the context of financial audits. The most restrictive standard was first enunciated [in *Ultramares*] in an opinion by then Chief Judge Cardozo of the New York Court of Appeals, in which the Court concluded that to be liable for negligent misrepresentation, an accountant must be in privity of contract with the person seeking to impose liability or there must be "[a] bond . . . so close as to approach that of privity."

A less restrictive rule is set forth in the Restatement (Second) of Torts 552 (1977). . . . [U]nder the Restatement approach an accountant who audits or prepares financial information for a client owes a duty of care not only to the client but to any other person, or one of a group of persons, whom the accountant or his clients intends the information to benefit; and that person reasonably relies on the information in a transaction, or one substantially similar to it, that the accountant or his client intends the information to influence. [T]he accountant must know of his client's intent at the time the accountant audits or prepares the information.

The courts of three states have recently adopted a position which extends an accountant's liability to all persons whom the accountant should reasonably foresee might obtain and rely on the accountant's work. . . .

We reject the *Ultramares* "privity or near-privity" approach . . . because it provides inadequately for the central role independent accountants play in the financial world. Accountants' audit opinions are increasingly relied upon by the investing and lending public in making financial decisions. . . . Because of this heavy public reliance on audited financial information we believe an approach that protects those persons, or classes of persons, whom an accountant knows will rely on his audit opinion, but who may not otherwise be in "privity or near privity," with him is desirable.

Although the *Ultramares* approach to accountants' liability seems unduly restrictive, we also decline to adopt the "reasonably foreseeable" test because it would result in liability more expansive than an accountant should be expected to bear. . . .

An accountant performs an audit pursuant to a contract with an individual client. The client may or may not intend to use the report for other than internal purposes. It does not benefit the accountant if his client distributes the audit opinion to others. Instead, it merely exposes his work to many whom he may have had no idea would scrutinize his efforts. We believe that in fairness accountants should not be liable in circumstances where they are unaware of the use to which their opinions will be put. Instead, their liability should be commensurate with those persons or classes of persons whom they know will rely on their work. With such knowledge the auditor can, through purchase of liability insurance, setting fees, and adopting other protective measures appropriate to the risk, prepare accordingly. . . .

> **CASE 47.3**
> **Continued**
>
> We conclude that the standard set forth in the Restatement (Second) of Torts 552 (1977) represents the soundest approach to accountants' liability for negligent misrepresentation. . . . [It] balances . . . the need to hold accountants to a standard that accounts for their contemporary role in the financial world with the need to protect them from liability that unreasonably exceeds the bounds of their real undertaking. . . .
>
> Applying the Restatement test to Sidbec-Dosco's complaint, we conclude Sidbec-Dosco has stated a legally sufficient claim against defendants for negligent misrepresentation. Sidbec-Dosco alleges that when defendants prepared the audited financial statements for IMC they knew: (1) the statements would be used by IMC to represent its financial condition to creditors who would extend credit on the basis of them; and (2) plaintiff and other creditors would rely upon these statements. These allegations are sufficient to impose upon defendants a duty of care to Sidbec-Dosco under the Restatement approach as we have interpreted and adopted it herein.
>
> **JUDGMENT** Affirmed.

FEDERAL STATUTORY LIABILITY OF ACCOUNTANTS

In addition to common law liability for breach of contract, negligence, and fraud, an accountant can be sued under various federal statutes that provide civil remedies. The most expansive area of accountant liability is under the federal securities laws discussed in detail in Chapter 46. An accountant can be sued by securities investors under Section 11 of the Securities Act of 1933 and under Rule 10b-5 of the Securities Exchange Act of 1934. Other federal laws, such as RICO, provide civil liability provisions under which accountants can be held liable.

Liability under the Securities Act of 1933

The Securities Act of 1933 governs the initial issuance of securities to the public. It was designed to provide investors with relevant information upon which to base their investment decisions. The Act achieves that objective by requiring an issuer of securities to file a detailed registration statement with the SEC and to provide a prospectus to investors. The registration statement includes certified financial statements on the issuer; therefore, accountants are employed by issuing companies to audit the financial statements in connection with a sale of securities under the Securities Act. Accountants can be held civilly liable to investors under several sections of the Act, the most important being Section 11.

Section 11. Section 11 imposes civil liability when a registration statement is materially false or misleading. Accountants can be held liable for inaccuracies in that part of the registration statement for which they act as experts—the certified financial statements. To hold an auditor liable under Section 11, investors must prove the following elements: (1) the financial statements contained a false statement or omission of material fact at the time the registration statement became effective, and (2) the plaintiff purchased the security and suffered a loss. The investors need not establish that they relied on the financial statements (or even read them) or that the accountant knew that the statements were false. Damages recoverable by the plaintiff are usually based on the difference between the purchase price of the security and its actual value.

Due Diligence Defense. Investors suing under Section 11 need not prove that the accountant was negligent in the audit of the financial statements. The burden is on the accountant to show that he or she exercised reasonable care and skill in conducting the audit—that is, that he or she exercised **due diligence.** Under the due diligence defense, an accountant is not liable if he or she establishes that a reasonable investigation was conducted and that he or she reasonably believed that the financial statements were accurate. In addition, the auditor must show that he or she reasonably believed that the financial statements were not materially false at the time the registration statement became effective. A registration statement does not become effective until at least 20 days after it is filed with the SEC. Because the effectiveness date is after the date when the auditor certifies that the statements are accurate in his or her report, the auditor must conduct a reasonable postaudit review. In the *BarChris* case discussed in Chapter 46, the leading case on both Section 11 and the due diligence defense, the auditors failed to prove due diligence in part because they failed to conduct a proper postaudit review.

Privity is not a defense under Section 11 or under the securities laws in general. However, it is a defense to Section 11 if (1) the investors knew of the misstatement in the financial statements, (2) the decline in the value of the security purchased was caused by factors unrelated to the false financial statement (e.g., a general decline in the stock market), or (3) the investors fail to sue within the statutory limitation period, which is 1 year from the time the falsity was or should have been discovered but no longer than 3 years from the time the security was offered to the public.

Liability under the Securities Exchange Act of 1934

The Securities Exchange Act of 1934 regulates the secondary trading of securities. Firms having 500 or more shareholders and assets of more than $5 million and firms whose securities are traded on a national exchange are required to file a registration statement and make periodic filings with the SEC. Some of the reports under the Act contain certified financial statements. For example, the 10K annual report includes audited financial statements of the filing company. Accountants can incur civil liability in connection with the registration of securities under the 1934 Act as well as under the general antifraud provisions of the law.

Section 10b and Rule 10b-5. The Securities and Exchange Commission has promulgated Rule 10b-5, the antifraud provision under which accountants can be held civilly liable to injured investors. As noted in Chapter 46, to recover under Rule 10b-5, an injured party must prove that the defendant made a material misrepresentation or omission of a material fact in connection with the purchase or sale of a security, that the defendant acted with scienter, and that the plaintiff justifiably relied upon the misrepresentation and suffered damages.

The landmark case under Rule 10b-5 is *Ernst & Ernst v. Hochfelder*.[5] In *Hochfelder*, customers defrauded by First Securities Co. of Chicago brought a lawsuit against Ernst & Ernst claiming a violation of Rule 10b-5. Leston Nay, the president and primary shareholder of First Securities, a Chicago brokerage firm, induced his customers to invest monies in what he claimed were high-yielding "escrow" accounts. The transactions were not handled in the same manner as ordinary transactions of First Securities. Rather, the customers sent funds directly to Nay, who converted the monies to his personal use and concealed the phony investments. The fraud went undetected until Nay committed suicide and left a note revealing the scheme. The customers claimed that Ernst & Ernst was liable under Rule 10b-5 because it negligently failed to uncover the fraud. The U.S. Supreme Court concluded that Ernst & Ernst was not liable and that mere negligence was not sufficient to impose liability for securities fraud. It held that scienter is an essential element of a claim under Rule 10b-5. The Supreme Court left open the possibility that reckless conduct would be sufficient to constitute scienter, and in subsequent cases, federal courts have concluded that recklessness can satisfy the mental state required under Rule 10b-5.

[5]425 U.S. 185 (1976).

Although the *Hochfelder* case limited an accountant's liability for securities fraud, accountants continue to have significant exposure under Rule 10b-5. An accountant can be held secondarily liable for a Rule 10b-5 violation committed by his or her client if the accountant aids and abets in the commission of a securities fraud. To aid and abet, the accountant must knowingly and substantially assist a client in the commission of a Rule 10b-5 violation.

An accountant may also be guilty of securities fraud for a failure to disclose wrongdoing by a client. Because Rule 10b-5 liability can be based on an "omission" of material facts, a failure to reveal material information by a person under a duty to speak constitutes securities fraud. A major area of uncertainty exists regarding the circumstances under which an accountant is under a duty to disclose a client's wrongdoing. Some courts hold that accountants are not under a duty to "blow the whistle" on their clients, reasoning that accountants have no fiduciary duty to investors in the securities markets. The next case represents a contrary position on this issue.

CASE 47.4   Rudolph v. Arthur Andersen & Co. • 800 F.2d 1040 (11th Cir. 1986)

FACTS   In 1978, John DeLorean attempted to establish a new automobile manufacturer. He set up a limited partnership, DeLorean Research Limited Partnership (DRLP), to raise research and development funds for the new DeLorean sports car. In March of 1978, Delorean sold limited partnership interests under a "private placement memorandum" which represented that the funds would be used for research and development of the new DeLorean car. This representation was important to investors, because the success of the enterprise was linked to research and there were tax benefits associated with the research and development activities. The memo contained audit reports prepared by Arthur Andersen concerning the past financial condition of DeLorean entities for the years 1976 and 1977. DeLorean initially intended to locate the production facility in Puerto Rico, but before the sale of the limited partnership interests was completed, he decided to set up the manufacturing plant in Northern Ireland. Because the financial benefits from locating in Northern Ireland made the research and development funds unnecessary, DeLorean diverted the limited partnership funds to other uses. The DRLP investors were not informed of this change.

When DeLorean's automobile venture collapsed, investors in DRLP lost their money. One of the investors, Sidney Rudolph, and the liquidating trustee for DRLP filed a lawsuit against Arthur Andersen & Co., the accounting firm for DeLorean and his businesses. During the period from the issuance of the placement memo to the diversion of the funds by DeLorean, Arthur Andersen was performing nonauditing services for DeLorean's businesses. The complaint claimed that Arthur Andersen violated Rule 10b-5 by wilfully or recklessly failing to disclose the alleged fraud perpetrated by DeLorean. From a district court dismissal of the complaint for failure to state a claim under Rule 10b-5, the plaintiffs appealed.

OPINION   VANCE, Cir. J. . . . [Under] Rule 10b-5 . . . a defendant's omission to state a material fact is proscribed only when the defendant has a duty to disclose. Such

**CASE 47.4
Continued**

a duty may exist "where the law imposes special obligations, as for accountants, brokers, or other experts, depending on the circumstances of the case.". . . In evaluating the circumstances [to determine whether there is a duty of disclosure]

> we consider the relationship between the plaintiff and defendant, the parties' relative access to the information disclosed, the benefit derived by the defendant from the purchase or sale, defendant's awareness of plaintiff's reliance on defendant in making its investment decision, and defendant's role in initiating the purchase or sale. . . .

A duty to disclose may also be created by a defendant's previous decision to speak voluntarily. Where a defendant's failure to speak would render the defendant's *own* prior speech misleading or deceptive, a duty to disclose arises. . . .

We have not held these factors to be exclusive. . . . For instance, the extent of defendant's knowledge and the significance of the misstatement, fraud, or omission might be relevant.

Although this court has not considered the issue, other courts have held that accountants "have a duty to take reasonable steps to correct misstatements they have discovered in previous financial statements on which they know the public is relying.". . .

On the other hand, courts have refused to hold accountants liable for not disclosing ordinary business information discovered after the completion of a report, where the information did not indicate that the report was inaccurate as of the date it was issued. . . .

The rule that an accountant is under no duty to disclose ordinary business information, unless it shows a previous report to have been misleading or incorrect when issued, is a sensible one. It would be asking too much to expect accountants to make difficult and time-consuming judgment calls about the nature of routine facts and figures turned up after a report has been completed. The situation is quite different, however, where the issue is the disclosure of actual knowledge of fraud. Standing idly by while knowing one's good name is being used to perpetrate a fraud is inherently misleading. An investor might reasonably assume that an accounting firm would not permit inclusion of an audit report it prepared in a placement memo for an offering the firm knew to be fraudulent, and that such firm would let it be known if it discovered to be fraudulent an offering with which it was associated. It is not unreasonable to expect an accountant . . . to disclose fraud in this type of circumstance, where the accountant's information is obviously superior to that of the investor, the cost to the accountant of revealing the information minimal, and the cost to investors of the information remaining secret potentially enormous. . . .

Our only task is to determine whether plaintiffs could . . . prove facts under which we would hold that Andersen had a duty [to disclose]. . . .

The complaint . . . alleges that Andersen performed non-auditing services for DeLorean. Plaintiffs could possibly prove that through these services Andersen was involved in the fraud itself. It is also likely that the evidence will show that Andersen had spoken previously with respect to the DRLP offering, through its audit reports and statements included in the placement memo, and that Andersen knew investors would rely to some extent on those reports and state-

CASE 47.4 Continued	ments. Plaintiffs might also prove that Andersen failed to disclose DeLorean's fraud even though it had *actual knowledge* of that fraud, and that Andersen's access to information concerning the fraud was far greater than plaintiffs'. Proof of these circumstances would be sufficient to establish that Andersen had a duty to disclose. Plaintiffs' proposed complaint also states a valid claim for aiding and abetting securities violations by DeLorean. . . . [P]laintiffs could . . . prove at trial that DeLorean committed securities violations, that Andersen knew about DeLorean's fraudulent scheme, that Andersen did not disclose the scheme, and that in doing so Andersen violated a duty to disclose. Proof of such facts . . . could . . . suffice to prove aiding and abetting. . . .
JUDGMENT	Reversed and remanded.

Section 18. An accountant can also be sued under Section 18 of the 1934 Act. This provision imposes liability on an accountant for material misstatements or omissions in the registration filings under the Act. The standards for liability under Section 18 are more stringent than the liability standards under Section 11 of the 1933 Act. Under Section 18, the plaintiff must prove that the plaintiff relied on the misstatements or omissions in materials filed with the SEC in purchasing or selling a security and that the price of the security was "affected by" the misstatements or omissions resulting in plaintiff's damages. Assume that Wilson claimed that she was damaged because the certified financial statements in the annual 10K statement of Alexander & Co. were false. To prevail under Section 18, she would have to establish that the misstatements were material, that she read the 10K report and relied on it, and that the misstatements inflated the market price of the securities, causing her damages.

An accountant sued under Section 18 also has an affirmative defense if it can be proved that he or she acted in good faith and had no actual knowledge of the misstatements or omissions in the registration filings. Under this good faith defense, the accountant will not be liable unless he or she was grossly negligent or fraudulent in making the statements. Negligence on the part of the accountant, standing alone, will not be sufficient to hold the accountant liable under Section 18.

RICO

As discussed in Chapter 9, a person may be civilly and criminally liable under the Racketeer Influenced and Corrupt Organizations Act (RICO). RICO makes it a crime, for example, to use monies derived from a "pattern of racketeering activity" to secure an interest in an enterprise engaged in interstate business or to acquire an interest in such an interstate business through a "pattern of racketeering activity." To be guilty of a "pattern of racketeering activity," a person must commit at least two predicate acts, violations of certain federal and state criminal laws (including white-collar offenses such as wire fraud, mail fraud, securities fraud, and commercial bribery), within a 10-year period.

RICO provides a civil remedy under which a person injured by a violation can sue for treble damages (three times the actual damages), costs, and attorney's fees. Accountants have been sued under RICO by plaintiffs in securities and tax fraud cases. Recently, the Supreme Court in *Reves v. Ernst & Young*[6] substantially limited an accountant's liability under RICO. A section of RICO makes it an offense for a person associated with a enterprise to "conduct or participate in" the affairs of the enterprise through a "pattern of racketeering activity." In *Reves*, an auditor was sued under that provision by the trustee

---

[6]116 S. Ct. 1163 (1993) (Reves II). (See the discussion of Reves I [Case 46.1] in Chapter 46.)

CRIMINAL AND ADMINISTRATIVE LIABILITY

Accountants are regulated at both the state and federal levels, and the regulatory agencies have the power to impose administrative penalties on accountants under appropriate circumstances. Accountants who violate the law with the necessary criminal mental state may also face criminal prosecution and punishment.

State Law

Certified public accountants are required to be licensed by the state in order to engage in public accounting. Accountants are prohibited from engaging in auditing, for example, unless they are licensed CPAs. State boards of accountancy have been established to oversee the public accounting profession and to license and discipline its members. The state boards have the power to impose administrative sanctions on CPAs who violate the codes of conduct established by the board or by state law. Administrative penalties include reprimands, probation, and for egregious violations, suspension or revocation of a CPA's license.

Accountants also face potential criminal liability under state law. For example, a practitioner can be prosecuted under state securities laws or under statutes prohibiting the unauthorized practice of law.

Federal Law

The IRS and the Internal Revenue Code. Accountants who violate federal tax laws and regulations are subject to civil and criminal penalties. In addition, the Internal Revenue Service has the authority to seek injunctive relief against accountants for violating the income tax laws.

Administrative penalties. Accountants frequently prepare income tax returns for their clients. Under the Internal Revenue Code, a tax preparer is defined as a "person who prepares for compensation . . . any return of tax imposed . . . or any claim for a refund." Tax preparers are under specific duties to the tax-

---

> **BOX 47.2**
> **A Question of Policy:**
> **Joint and Several Liability**
>
> The common law rule of "joint and several" liability applies to cases involving more than one wrongdoer—joint tortfeasors who cause the plaintiff's injuries. The rule imposes separate liability upon each of the joint tortfeasors for the entire amount of the plaintiff's injuries, regardless of their relative share of the fault. If one of the tortfeasors is insolvent, the other tortfeasors must pay the entire judgment.
>
> The rule of joint and several liability generally applies to common law and securities actions against accountants. The accounting profession has criticized this rule in the auditor liability context because frequently the accountant is the only solvent defendant in such a case (the business is often bankrupt), leaving the auditor to pay the entire judgment. The rule thus encourages plaintiffs to go after the auditor, the only defendant with a "deep pocket," even if the accountant was minimally at fault.
>
> The industry has proposed that the rule be replaced with "proportionate" liability in accountant liability cases under which a joint tortfeasor would be liable only for its relative share of fault as determined by the jury. Should this proposal be adopted by the states or the federal government? What policy reasons justify a rule of joint and several liability? Is the proportionate liability rule fairer? To whom? ■

---

of a bankrupt agricultural co-op on behalf of the holders of securities who were misled by inaccurate audited financial statements. The Court held that the auditor could not be held liable under that section of RICO, reasoning that the language "conduct or participate in" requires that a person participate in the "operation or management" of the enterprise. Since the auditor did not manage or operate the co-op, it could not be held liable under that section. The opinion in *Reves* is a major victory for the accounting profession.

payer-clients for whom they prepare returns. Tax preparers are required to sign the returns, provide their clients with completed copies of the returns, and maintain a list of tax clients or a copy of their returns for 3 years. Failure to comply with these obligations can result in a penalty of $50 per violation.

The IRS also imposes administrative penalties on accountants for negligently or wilfully understating the tax liability of clients. A $250 penalty can be assessed for an understatement where the accountant took a legal position under the return that was not supported by the tax laws and regulations. The accountant has a defense to the civil penalty if he or she had a reasonable basis for the position taken and acted in good faith. If the understatement resulted from a "wilful" attempt to misrepresent the tax liability of a client, the penalty is $1,000.

Criminal liability. An accountant commits a felony by wilfully aiding a client in the preparation of a fraudulent return or by subscribing to a document made under oath which the accountant knows is not true and correct. For example, an accountant who intentionally prepares a tax return that he or she knows is materially false commits a criminal violation and is subject to a fine of $100,000 and up to 3 years' imprisonment.

The SEC and the Securities Laws

Administrative sanctions. The SEC, as the federal agency empowered to regulate the securities marketplace under the 1933 and 1934 acts, has the authority to control the accountants who practice before it. Under Rule 2(e) of the SEC's Rules of Practice, the SEC may deny an accountant the right to perform audits for securities clients if the accountant is lacking in character or integrity, has engaged in unethical or improper professional conduct, or has violated the securities laws or regulations. For example, the SEC recently imposed a 2-year suspension on two partners of Coopers & Lybrand for failing to comply with GAAS in conducting the audit of Savin Corporation. The SEC upheld a finding by an administrative law judge that Savin materially violated GAAP by deferring over a 4-year period $37 million in costs incurred in the failed development of a line of photocopiers. Such costs should have been expensed as research and development, and the auditor should have qualified its opinion relative to compliance with GAAP. The SEC also reaffirmed its position that scienter is not a requirement for imposing a sanction under Rule 2(e); negligence is sufficient to impose a suspension.

Criminal liability. A person who wilfully violates any federal statute administered by the SEC is also subject to criminal penalties of fine and imprisonment. Under Section 32 of the Securities and Exchange Act of 1934, a person who "wilfully" and "knowingly" makes a false or misleading statement in a report filed under the Act is guilty of a criminal offense. So, for example, an accountant who intentionally certifies a false financial statement in a 10K annual report violates Section 32 and is subject to a $1 million fine and 10 years' imprisonment.

SUMMARY

Accounting serves an important informational role in our society by providing managers, creditors, investors, and members of the general public with reliable information upon which to make important economic decisions. Accountants face a legal environment in which their work product will expose them to substantial damage claims. At common law, a client can sue an accountant for breach of contract or fiduciary duty, professional negligence, and actual or constructive fraud. In a professional negligence action, the critical issue will generally be the accountant's compliance with GAAP and GAAS, since these professional standards have a significant (but not controlling) effect on the issue of due care. Accountants' liability for negligence may also extend to third-party users of their work. When an accountant knows that his or her work product will be received and relied upon by a limited group of persons, anyone within that known class of users can sue the accountant under the prevailing rule. This modern rule expands the negligence liability of accountants, which under common law was generally limited to persons in privity with the accountant.

Injured investors can assert federal securities claims against accountants. Under Section 11 of the Securities Act of 1933, accountants are liable if (1) a purchaser of securities establishes that there were misstatements or omissions of material fact in the audited financial statements contained in the registration filing and (2) the accountant fails to establish a due diligence defense. Similarly, Rule 10b-5 of the Securities Exchange Act of 1934 imposes liability on accountants for fraud in connection with the sale of securities. Material misrepresentations or omissions by the accountant can result in either primary liability or secondary liability for aiding and abetting. However, accountants can be held liable under Rule 10b-5 only if scienter—a higher standard of culpability than the negligence standard of Section 11—can be established.

REVIEW QUESTIONS

1. How do an audit, a review, and a compilation differ?

2. Why is an engagement letter important to the contracting accountant? To the client?

3. Under what circumstances is it ethical for an accountant to disclose confidential client information to third parties?

4. Should the law recognize an accountant-client privilege? Explain the policy arguments for and against such a privilege.

5. Explain the differences among actual fraud, constructive fraud, and negligent misrepresentation.

6. Explain the three rules that the courts have developed to determine the negligence liability of accountants to third parties. From a policy perspective, which is the best rule? Why?

7. What is the prevailing rule on the defense of contributory negligence in an action against an accountant for professional negligence? Should this rule be changed? Why?

8. Explain the liability standards under Section 11 of the Securities Act of 1933 and the due diligence defense. How is Section 11 different from common law negligence?

9. Under what circumstances should Rule 10b-5 require an accountant to disclose information to investors concerning his or her client's business?

10. What steps should public accounting firms take to prevent administrative liability under SEC Rule 2(e)?

CASE PROBLEMS

1. Fund of Funds, Ltd. (FOF), a mutual fund, established a specialized investment account called the Natural Resources Fund Account. FOF entered into an agreement with King Resources Corporation regarding the purchase of oil, gas, mineral, and other natural resource properties for the Natural Resources Fund. King Resources agreed to sell natural resource properties to the fund at "prices no less favorable . . . than the prices charged by King to its . . . industrial and other purchasers." Arthur Andersen & Co., a public accounting firm, was the auditor for both FOF and King Resources. During the 1968 audit of FOF, Arthur Andersen learned that King Resources overcharged FOF on sales of natural resources but failed to disclose the overcharges to FOF. When the overcharges were subsequently discovered by FOF, it sued Arthur Andersen under common law and securities grounds. Arthur Andersen argued that FOF had no right to know the costs to King Resources of the natural resource properties sold to FOF, and that Arthur Andersen could not legally disclose that confidential information to FOF. Did Arthur Andersen breach its duty to FOF by failing to disclose the overcharges? Would such a disclosure have been a breach of Arthur Andersen's duty of confidentiality to King Resources? What steps short of disclosure of the information could Arthur Andersen have taken to avoid the conflict of interest created by the overcharges?

2. Intermountain Merchandising Inc., a Montana corporation formed by Eugene Thayer and Robert Hicks, acquired and operated several retail stores and a wholesale art, craft, and hobby supplier. Hicks proposed to sell his interest in the business to Thayer. After the acquisition, Thayer's separate company, Montana Merchandising, would provide additional capital for Intermountain. Allen Bloomgren was hired by Hicks to perform an audit of Intermountain to determine its value for the buyout. Bloomgren was aware that the audit was to be used to determine the buyout price and that the reason for the purchase was to secure capital for Intermountain from Montana Merchandising. Bloomgren also met with the controller and attorney for Intermountain during the course of the audit. The audit showed a positive shareholder equity of $112,000, and Thayer purchased Hicks' interest in the business. After the purchase, Montana Merchandising advanced monies to Intermountain and guaranteed loans of Intermountain in the sum of $1 million. When a second audit by another public accounting firm established material errors in the Bloomgren audit and showed that Intermountain was insolvent at the time of the buyout, Montana Merchandising liquidated Intermountain. The liquidation reduced Intermountain's bank debts to $338,000, which Montana Merchandising was required to pay to the banks under the guarantees. Thayer and Montana Merchandising sued Bloomgren for that amount, alleging negligence in the audit. The jury was instructed that Bloomgren was liable to Montana Merchandising only if he "had reason to know that Montana Merchandising would rely upon the audit." The jury was further instructed that if it found that Bloomgren failed to comply with GAAS or GAAP, Bloomgren was presumed as a matter of law to have committed negligence. On appeal, the Montana Supreme Court adopted the primary beneficiary test for third-party liability. Was the jury instruction on third-party liability proper under the primary beneficiary rule? Given the facts, was Bloomgren liable to Montana Merchandising and Thayer under this rule? Was the instruction on the effect of Bloomgren's failure to comply with GAAP and GAAS correct? If not, how should the jury have been instructed on GAAP and GAAS?

3. Baumann-Furrie & Co., a public accounting firm, provided accounting services to plaintiff, Halla Nursery, Inc., during the years 1983–1985. Halla's bookkeeper embezzled some $135,000 from the company during that period of time. In 1986, Halla brought a malpractice action against Baumann-Furrie, alleging negligent performance of the accounting services because of Baumann-Furrie's failure to detect the embezzlement. Baumann-Furrie raised the affirmative defense of Halla's contributory negligence, claiming that Halla failed to put in place internal financial controls to protect the company. At trial, the jury was instructed to compare the negligence of the two parties and attribute a percentage of fault to each. The jury found Halla 80 percent at fault, and Baumann-Furrie 20 percent at fault. Because Halla's fault was greater than Baumann-Furrie's, the trial court ordered judgment of no recovery. (Under Minnesota law, a plaintiff must establish that the defendant was at least 50 percent at fault to recover any damages.) Halla moved for a new trial, arguing that the jury should have been instructed that Halla's contributory negligence was a defense only if it directly interfered with Baumann-Furrie's ability to perform the contract in accordance with GAAP. Is Halla entitled to a new trial?

4. American Solar King Corporation manufactured collectors for the solar heating of water in residential homes. In 1982, it entered the industrial solar heating market with the distribution of solar collectors to apartment complexes and industrial users. Under its distribution system, an industrial user did not purchase the system but rather guaranteed to pay for energy used, up to 80 percent of prior fuel costs. One day before the end of fiscal 1982, a sale was made to a Wisconsin meat packer, Provimi, at a price of $1,750,000—$20,000 in cash and the balance under the terms of two notes. As a result of the $964,000 profit from the Provimi sale, the financial statements of American Solar reported a profit for the quarter and a small loss for the year; without it, a significant loss would have been reported. An audit memorandum, prepared by the public accounting firm of Main Hurdman, indicated that American Solar's reserve for doubtful accounts should have been increased by $200,000 to $300,000, but that the client would not consider such an adjustment because it had a bad year. It was decided that a qualified opinion would be issued on the accounts receivable issue. The qualifying paragraph read as follows:

While management is of the opinion that the allowance for doubtful trade accounts and notes receivable is adequate at July 31, 1982, we are unable to determine the adequacy of the provision for uncollectible accounts.

Investors who purchased stock in American Solar after October 28, 1982, the date on which the 10K report containing the audited financial statements of American Solar was filed with the SEC, sued Main Hurdman, the public accounting firm that issued the qualified opinion on the financial statements, for violations of Section 10b and Rule 10b-5 of the Securities Exchange Act of 1934. The trial court granted summary judgment for Main Hurdman, concluding that there was not a triable issue of fact on scienter. The investors claimed that Main Hurdman acted with recklessness in certifying the financial statements with the qualifying language. Was there sufficient evidence of scienter?

5. On December 22, 1970, Zeron Systems offered 350,000 shares to the public under a registration filed with the SEC. Myers & Johnson, a public accounting firm, performed the audit and issued an unqualified opinion on the financial statements of Zeron. After the sale of the securities to the public, an SEC investigation of Zeron Systems revealed that the registration statement contained material misstatements and omissions. Specifically, the financial statements overstated the amount of back orders from Zeron customers by $2 million and failed to disclose that the backlog customers were unlikely to receive their orders because of financial difficulties. When Zeron went into bankruptcy, the purchasers of its stock under the registration statement sued Myers & Johnson under Section 11 of the Securities Act of 1933. Myers & Johnson presented an affidavit from its audit manager that the Zeron audit had been conducted in accordance with GAAS and that the backlog was not susceptible of audit. (An AICPA accounting standard directed accountants not to comment on backlogs.) In a responsive affidavit submitted by the plaintiff-investors, it was established that Myers & Johnson may have known that the backlog figures were misleading. Myers & Johnson argued that compliance with GAAS and GAAP satisfied the "due diligence" defense under Section 11. Under the circumstances, can the investors establish the elements of a Section 11 claim? Explain. Assuming that the accountants complied with GAAS and GAAP, did Myers & Johnson conclusively establish its "due diligence" defense? Would the result of the case change if the accountants were sued under Rule 10b-5? Why?

ETHICS IN PRACTICE

Although partnerships and corporations differ structurally, many ethical norms apply to both types of organizations. For example, partners in an ordinary partnership are agents of one another, and each has fiduciary obligations to the others. Similarly, corporate officers, as agents of their corporations, have fiduciary obligations to their corporate employers; and corporate directors, although not agents of the corporations they serve, owe fiduciary obligations to their corporations and to the shareholders.

As noted in Chapter 5, the main obligation of corporate management (officers and directors) under classical economic theory is to maximize profits for the shareholders. But many commentators and business leaders believe that corporations and their managers have broader responsibilities. Corporations have great impact on the users of their products and services worldwide and on the economic, social, and physical well-being of the communities in which their plants and offices are located. To restrain the negative forces that corporations have the power to generate and to enhance the positive forces, new ethical norms have arisen, contributing to a body of ethical thought called "corporate social responsibility."

Proponents of corporate social responsibility argue that corporations are more than just privately owned economic entities—they are also citizens with rights and duties, and social actors whose conduct can affect millions of people. Consequently, managers have responsibilities not only to shareholders but also to other stakeholders such as employees, consumers, and the communities in which corporations operate. Managers should do more than lawfully generate profits; they should spend corporate time and money on social concerns such as environmental pollution, unemployment arising from plant relocation, industrial hazards to employee health, and improvement of the quality of life in the host communities.

In recent decades many ethical norms, such as those condemning environmental pollution, racial discrimination in employment, and unwarranted threats to employee safety and health, have been incorporated into statutory law or administrative regulation and have become legal norms as well. Other concerns, such as improving the quality of life in the host community, remain largely if not exclusively a matter of moral obligation. Today, many corporations, large and small, accept the idea of corporate social responsibility (often seen as a desirable alternative to governmental regulation) and are enthusiastically implementing it. Others actively resist it, doing only the minimum required by law.

The problems that follow present a number of ethical dilemmas relating to internal or external corporate operations, or to both.

PROBLEMS IN ETHICS

1. A corporation asked its employees to buy U.S. savings bonds as part of a company-sponsored bond drive. The company president wanted total participation. Employees were shown movies and given presentations. Management made lists of employees who had not participated, and supervisors contacted them individually. When asked if nonparticipation would hurt employees' chances for promotion, management did not say no. Participation in the bond drive was high, but some employees felt that management's conduct was inappropriate. Is it ethical for corporate management to use work-related authority to force participation in bond drives, United Way campaigns, and the like?

2. In a September 1992 issue, *Time* notes:

Nothing is as bothersome to corporate CEOs as the annual ritual of subjecting their compensation to outside scrutiny. Disclosures of king-size pay packages and royal perks regularly rouse public resentment and shareholder revolts, not to mention congressional calls for reform. Unable to cap the criticism, the bosses are moving quietly but aggressively to plug the flow of information. In their cross hairs are the compensation consultants who prepare the data under contract with big corporations. Led by the Business Roundtable, the captains of industry have issued veiled threats to consultants who share information with journalists, financial analysts and regulatory authorities. The message: Stop cooperating or lose future business.

What are the ethics of this CEO conduct? Of what concern to the public is the pay of CEOs? Does it matter that large-company CEO compensation reportedly rose from 40 times the wages of the average factory worker in 1980 to about 93 times as much in 1989? Consider a comment attributed to corporate raider T. Boone Pickens: "The problem is that there is very little difference between the pay of CEOs who are performing for shareholders and those who are not. Compensation policies at most companies . . . reward the CEO simply for reaching the top, rather than basing pay on what the executive does once he gets there."

3. Columnist Anna Quindlen is troubled by the tobacco industry's use of its money. She writes, "The Coalition for the Homeless doesn't take money from the tobacco industry anymore" (Philip Morris once donated $100,000). The reason? A public relations firm representing the industry asked the Coalition's executive director to help kill a bill mandating anti-smoking ads by demanding that the City Council focus on more important issues, like her own.

". . . [T]he tobacco companies are everywhere," giving enormous sums to both Republican and Democratic war chests and to senators liberal and conservative. "[As makers] of a product that, when used as directed, causes death, they must be intensely political. And intensely philanthropic as well." Tobacco companies contribute to most of America's best-known nonprofit organizations. Among them: the Partnership for a Drug-Free America, the American Civil Liberties Union, the NAACP, the Urban League, the National Women's Political Caucus, and the Poetry Society of America, children's charities, environmental groups, even health organizations. Worthy organizations get something they richly deserve—money for their work; tobacco companies get something entirely undeserved—the chance to suggest that they're not such bad guys after all.

"This is money laundering," Quindlen contends. Tobacco money that charities receive is tainted by death and disease; money they spend is gilded by good works. Organizations that work tirelessly to make life better pay for their works with profits on a product that kills almost 440,000 Americans every year. "It's a peculiar equation," she says, that she can't quite get to add up.

(a) Is Ms. Quindlen being fair to the tobacco industry? Isn't the industry's largesse simply an act of corporate social responsibility? Or is it a sinister, subversive act—the buying of silence to assure the survival of a deadly product? **(b)** Is it ethical for charities, especially those concerned about public health, to take tobacco industry money?

4. In March 1990, securities analyst Marvin Roffman, an employee of Janney Montgomery Scott, a Philadelphia brokerage firm, told *The Wall Street Journal* that Donald Trump's Taj Mahal Casino Resort in Atlantic City, N.J., could encounter financial trouble because its economics were flawed. In a 1989 report published by his employer, Roffman had called the Taj Mahal impressive but had expressed concern about its high debt and payroll costs. After the March 1990 comments, Trump threatened Janney Montgomery Scott with a lawsuit unless Roffman publicly retracted his comments. Roffman signed a letter of apology, repudiated it in a second letter, and was fired. Later Trump did face a cash crunch because of his debt obligations and had to renegotiate financing on another casino. Given the function that a securities analyst serves, did Janney Montgomery Scott act ethically in firing Roffman?

PART TEN

Government Regulation; Computer Law; International Business Law

CHAPTER 48
Law of Labor and Employment

CHAPTER 49
Consumer Law

CHAPTER 50
Computer Law

CHAPTER 51
Law and the Environment

CHAPTER 52
Introduction to Antitrust Law;
The Sherman Act

CHAPTER 53
The Clayton, Robinson-Patman, and
Federal Trade Commission Acts

CHAPTER 54
Business Law in a Global Economy

Ethics in Practice

CHAPTER 48

Law of Labor and Employment

Laws affecting employment and the workplace in America have been evolving for more than two centuries. In colonial times, employers, legislatures, and courts maintained an unfriendly environment for workers. In the country's first labor litigation, Philadelphia cordwainers (shoemakers) were found guilty of criminal conspiracy for refusing to work unless paid higher wages.[1] Employers and courts looked upon strikes and picketing as civil wrongs for which unions had to answer in damages. Although in 1842 *Commonwealth v. Hunt*[2] upheld the legality of unions, strife and violence continued. Employer groups hired Pinkerton detectives and brought in police to break up strikes or to protect **scabs** hired to replace strikers. In 1886, during the nationwide general strike for an 8-hour workday, Chicago's Haymarket Riot broke out; a police officer was killed, and four "anarchists" were arrested and executed. When Eugene Debs led the 1894 strike against Pullman Company, President Cleveland called in federal troops. Debs was arrested and sent to prison.

Post–Civil War federal courts continued to back employers by enjoining strikes and enforcing **yellow dog contracts** (in which employees promise not to join a union). Although the Sherman Act of 1890 was created to attack monopolies, federal courts used it to suppress unions by ruling that they were prohibited "combinations in restraint of trade." Sections 6 and 20 of the 1914 Clayton Act were designed to forbid injunctions against unions, but the Supreme Court interpreted these sections to permit that which they were supposed to prevent—use of injunctions to attack organized labor. Long overdue, the Norris-La Guardia Act[3] of 1932 severely limited federal court power to issue injunctions in labor disputes and banned further enforcement of yellow dog contracts.

The Great Depression of the early 1930s brought unprecedented labor strife, violence, **sit-down strikes,** and property destruction. Congress responded with the Wagner and Taft-Hartley Acts guaranteeing workers' right to organize unions. In the 1960s and 1970s laws were enacted to provide a safer workplace and to attack discrimination based upon race, sex, or religion. Major landmarks in labor law appear in Table 48.1.

---

[1]*Commonwealth v. Pullis,* 3 Commons & Gilmore (Philadelphia Mayor's Court, 1806).
[2]4 Metcalf 111 (Mass. 1842).
[3]29 USC 101.

Table 48.1 Landmarks in Labor Law

Year	Court Decision, Legislation, or Other Event	Significance
1842	*Commonwealth v. Hunt*, 4 Metcalf 11 (Mass.)	Held that a labor union is not a conspiracy and is illegal only if it uses unlawful means (e.g., violence)
1890	Sherman Antitrust Act	Ostensibly passed to check monopolies but more widely used to enjoin union strikes, which courts declared were "combinations in restraint of trade"
1914	Clayton Act, Secs. 6 and 20	Declared that "labor is not a commodity" and purported to restrict use of injunctions in labor disputes; prohibited enforcement of yellow dog contracts
1917	*Hitchman Coal & Coke Co. v. Mitchell*, 245 U.S. 229	Held that mine workers' union should be enjoined from interfering with yellow dog contract
1926	Railway Labor Act	Recognized right of railway employees to organize unions without fear of retaliation
1932	Norris-La Guardia Act	Legally recognized the right to strike and peacefully picket; limited greatly power of federal courts to enjoin labor disputes; prohibited enforcement of yellow dog contract
1936	National Labor Relations Act (NLRA); also called Wagner Act	Labor's Magna Carta: created NLRB to conduct employee elections to select union or "no union" as bargaining representative; required union and management to bargain in "good faith"; authorized NLRB to prosecute unfair labor practices
1940	*Thornhill v. Alabama* 310 U.S. 88	U.S. Supreme Court held that peaceful picketing is protected as First Amendment free speech
1947	Labor-Management Relations Act (LMRA); also called Taft-Hartley Act	Prohibited unions from engaging in unfair labor practices; prohibited closed shop and secondary boycott; protected employer right of free speech and employee right not to participate in union activity
1959	Labor-Management Reporting and Disclosure Act (LMRDA); also called Landrum-Griffin Act	Regulated internal union conduct; required record keeping aimed at corruption and fraud; adopted reforms for union elections

This chapter surveys the impact of state and federal legislation in the twentieth century upon employment and business. The first part analyzes labor-management relations, including collective bargaining. Later parts examine how federal laws dealing with equal employment opportunity, workers' compensation, and other labor issues affect managerial decisions.

Generally all state and federal labor laws apply only to the employer-employee relationship. This fact underscores the importance of making a threshold determination that the relationship involved in a particular case is, in fact, an employer-employee relation and not that of employer and independent contractor. The distinction, discussed in Chapter 36, is sometimes difficult to draw. Nevertheless, employers *must* distinguish correctly because, if a person is an employee, the employer must comply with the employment laws discussed in this chapter. Administrative agencies and courts always determine whether persons are employees or independent contractors when considering if a given labor law has been violated. Such agencies or courts will base their decisions on the control test and other factors discussed in Chapter 36.

LABOR-MANAGEMENT RELATIONS

In the nineteenth century, labor-management relations were characterized by violence because employers refused to recognize unions and denied their right to exist. Beginning with the Railway Labor Act (1926), Congress developed the notion that if the law required employers to recognize unions, there would be less fighting and more negotiation of compromise. The Act first recognized employees' right to organize into unions without fear of reprisal and the right to bargain collectively free from interference or coercion. The statute also outlawed yellow dog contracts. Next came Section 7(a) of the National Industrial Recovery Act of 1933[4] (NIRA), which held that

> employees shall have the right to organize and bargain collectively through representatives of their own choosing, and shall be free from interference, restraint, or coercion of employers. . . .

The Supreme Court declared the NIRA unconstitutional in 1935.[5]

---
[4]48 Stat. 195.
[5]*Schechter Corporation v. United States*, 295 U.S. 495 (1935).

Table 48.2 Unfair Labor Practices Prohibited by the National Labor Relations Act as Amended

1 *Interfering with workers' rights to organize*, as guaranteed in Section 7. Example: hiring spies to report union plans and organizing activities [Section 8(a)(1)].

2 *Dominating an employee organization or contributing financial support to it.* Example: forming a company union or assisting unions financially [Section 8(a)(2)].

3 *Discriminating against employees for the purpose of discouraging or encouraging union membership.* Example: denying promotions or wage increases, or firing an employee, because of union activity [Section 8(a)(3)].

4 *Discriminating against employees who have given testimony or filed charges under the Act.* Example: discharging an employee in retaliation for union activity [Section 8(a)(4)].

5 *Refusing to bargain in good faith with employee representatives (ordinarily unions)* [Section 8(a)(5)].

The National Labor Relations Act

The Great Depression's continued industrial conflict and economic upheaval prompted Congress to enact the National Labor Relations Act[6] (NLRA), also called the Wagner Act after its chief sponsor. The Act extends legal protection to unionizing efforts of employees and encourages collective, rather than individual, bargaining.

Coverage. The Act's key provision, Section 7, guarantees employees the right

> to form, join, or assist labor organizations, to bargain collectively through representatives of their own choosing, and to engage in other concerted activities for the purpose of collective bargaining or other mutual aid or protection. . . .

Section 8 of the NLRA protects employee rights guaranteed in Section 7 by *prohibiting* "unfair labor practices," as described in Table 48.2.

---
[6]29 USC 151.

The NLRB. The Wagner Act also established a new administrative agency, the National Labor Relations Board (NLRB), to (1) *conduct elections* among workers to select a union representation; (2) *certify* the duly elected union as bargaining agent; (3) *investigate* charges of unfair labor practices; and (4) *prosecute* and *adjudicate* violations. The NLRB also has power to impose remedies such as orders for new elections, reinstatement, back pay, and cease-and-desist orders. NLRB orders are enforced by federal courts of appeal, as demonstrated in Case 48.1.

CASE 48.1 **Lechmere, Inc. v. National Labor Relations Board** • 117 L. Ed. 79 (1992)

FACTS Lechmere, Inc., operated a retail store in a shopping plaza and jointly owned the plaza's parking lot in Hartford, Connecticut. Organizers for the United Food and Commercial Workers Union, not employees of Lechmere, distributed handbills to cars parked in the plaza, but each time, store personnel asked them to leave and removed the handbills. After picketing for 7 months in the grassy area between the parking lot and highway, sending mailings to store personnel, and contacting forty-one employees, the organizers obtained only one signed union authorization card. The union filed an unfair labor practice charge, claiming Lechmere had violated Section 8(a)(1) of the NLRA by barring the organizers from the parking lot. The administrative law judge (ALJ) ruled for the union; the NLRB (Board) affirmed and ordered Lechmere to cease and desist its efforts to prevent the union from using the parking lot. The court of appeals enforced Board's order, and Lechmere appealed to the U.S. Supreme Court.

OPINION THOMAS, J. . . . This case requires us to clarify the relationship between the rights of employees under Sec. 7 of the National Labor Relations Act and the property rights of their employers. . . . [In] *NLRB v. Babcock Wilcox Co.*, . . . we explained that the Board had erred by failing to make the critical distinction between the organizing activities of employees (to whom Sec. 7 guarantees the right of self-organization) and nonemployees (to whom Sec. 7 applies only derivatively). . . . As a rule, an employer cannot be compelled to allow distribution of union literature by non-employee organizers on his property. As with many other rules, however, we recognized an exception. Where "the location of a plant and the living quarters of the employees place the employees beyond the reach of reasonable union efforts to communicate with them," employers' property rights may be "required to yield to the extent needed to permit communication of information on the right to organize." . . .

The threshold inquiry in this case, then, is whether the facts here justify application of *Babcock*'s inaccessibility exception. The ALJ below observed that "the facts herein convince me that reasonable alternative means [of communicating with Lechmere's employees] were available to the union." . . . However, the Board reached a different conclusion on this point, asserting that "there was no reasonable, effective alternative means available for the union to communicate its message to [Lechmere's] employees." We cannot accept the Board's conclusion because it rests on erroneous legal foundations. As we have explained, the exception to *Babcock*'s rule is a narrow one. It does not apply wherever non-trespassory access to employees may be cumbersome or less-than-ideally effec-

CASE 48.1 Continued	tive. Classic examples include logging camps, mining camps, and mountain resort hotels. . . . Because [Lechmere's] employees do not reside on Lechmere's property, they are presumptively not "beyond the reach" of the union's message. Although the employees live in a large metropolitan area, that fact does not in itself render them "inaccessible". . . . Access to employees, not success in winning them over, is the critical issue. . . .
JUDGMENT	Because the union in this case failed to establish the existence of any "unique obstacles" that frustrated access to Lechmere's employees, the Board erred in concluding that Lechmere committed an unfair labor practice by barring the nonemployee organizers from its property. The judgment of the First Circuit is therefore reversed, and enforcement of the Board's order denied.

The Taft-Hartley Act

Under the protection afforded by the Wagner Act, the balance of power between employers and employees began to shift in favor of unions. Moreover, the NLRB came under criticism as possessing too much authority and displaying antiemployer bias. To curb union and NLRB excesses, Congress in 1947 amended the Wagner Act by enacting the Labor-Management Relations Act (LMRA), or Taft-Hartley Act.[7]

The Taft-Hartley Act did not take away any of the protection guaranteed unions by the Wagner Act; instead, it added protections for employers and for individual employees. One addition was a guarantee of free speech for employers, permitting them to state opinions freely and to campaign actively against unions organizing employees so long as there was no "*promise of benefit or threat of reprisal.*"

Section 7 was amended to give employees the right to abstain from union organizing activities, and a Section 8 amendment created **union unfair labor practices.** (See Table 48.3.) The LMRA also banned the **closed shop**—a labor contract which required, as a condition of hiring, that all employees be members of the union in good standing. Instead, the Act permitted a **union shop,** which allows the employer to hire anyone, regardless of union status, but requires that within 30 days the employee (1) join the union or (2) decide not to join but nevertheless

Table 48.3 Union Unfair Labor Practices under Labor-Management Relations Act of 1947

1. *Restraining or coercing employees in the exercise of rights guaranteed in Section 7.* For example, it is an unfair labor practice for a union to intimidate nonstrikers who seek to enter a struck plant [Section 8(b)(1)(A)].

2. *Discriminating against nonunion employees or causing employers to discriminate against them.* Unions may not discriminate against nonunion employees, except to enforce union shop contracts [Section 8(b)(2)].

3. *Refusing to bargain in good faith with employers* [Section 8(b)(3)].

4. *Engaging in secondary boycotts*—that is, pressuring one employer to stop doing business with another employer with which the union has a dispute [Section 8(b)(4)].

5. *Imposing excessive initiation fees* [Section 8(b)(5)].

6. *Forcing an employer to pay for work not performed (featherbedding)* [Section 8(b)(6)].

7. *Striking, picketing, or boycotting for an illegal purpose.* Illegal purposes include forcing an employer to bargain with a union other than the one which has been certified as the employees' representative, and forcing an employer to assign work to one union rather than another [Sections 8(b)(4) and 8(b)(7)].

---

[7]29 USC 141.

pay regular dues to the union. After 30 days, a new employee who fails to comply must be discharged by the employer if the union requests it. Thus it is lawful for an employer and a union to discriminate against a new employee who doesn't pay dues; but all other discrimination by unions against nonunion employees is prohibited (See item 2 in Table 48.3.)

The Taft-Hartley Act reduced the authority of the NLRB by empowering federal courts of appeals to review and overturn NLRB unfair labor practice decisions. It also separated the NLRB's prosecutorial and adjudicatory functions, which formerly were combined. In addition, the Act created the Federal Mediation and Conciliation Service to assist employers and unions in voluntarily resolving disputes. It also established an 80-day "cooling-off period" to delay strikes which the President believes will threaten national safety.

The Landrum-Griffin Act

Congress further amended the Taft-Hartley Act by passing the Labor-Management Reporting and Disclosure Act (LMRDA), or Landrum-Griffin Act,[8] in 1959. The LMRDA was intended to promote democracy and honesty in internal union affairs after congressional hearings revealed serious corruption and abuses in labor union conduct. The Act added new union unfair labor practices, including a prohibition on **hot cargo contracts**—agreements whereby *employers* promise not to handle, use, or deal in the goods of nonunion employers. Such contracts, although a type of secondary pressure, were not outlawed by the Taft-Hartley Act, which had prohibited unions from inducing *employees* (but not *employers*) to join secondary boycotts. The LMRDA also established a "bill of rights" for union members and imposed financial reporting and disclosure requirements upon unions and union officials.

[8]29 USC 153.

> **BOX 48.1**
>
> ### You Be the Judge
>
> In 1989 the textile workers union narrowly won an NLRB election at Reef Industries. Reef filed an unfair labor practice charge against the union in an effort to set aside the election results. The hearing was a credibility contest between Reef's election observer and the union observer. To prove its witness was more reliable, Reef noted that he had a twelfth grade education, and to show that the union witnesses were not reliable, Reef personnel manager Diane Schulz testified that the men in the plant had a tenth grade education.
>
> The dispute irked Dillard, a warehouse employee, who, with his flair for cartooning, sketched a cross-eyed, head-scratching dumb duck on a T-shirt with the caption: "Duh. I dunno. I got a tenth grade education." The men in the plant sent the T-shirt to Schulz as a token of "our esteem graditude." Reef fired Dillard, and his union filed an unfair labor practice charge with the NLRB.
>
> Was Dillard's dumb duck a protected activity under the NLRA? Did Reef commit an unfair labor practice?*
>
> *Reef Ind. Inc. v. National Labor Relations Board, 925 F.2d 830 (Fifth Cir. 1991).

Case decisions under the LMRDA have expanded individual union members' legal rights. For example, courts have held that the constitutions of the local union and its international affiliate are *contracts* and where they confer benefits and rights on individual members, such members can sue the local or international or both to enforce their benefits and rights. Case 48.2 reflects LMRDA policy toward union elections.

CASE 48.2 Masters, Mates & Pilots v. Brown • 112 L. Ed. 2d 991 (1991)

FACTS Brown, an unsuccessful candidate in prior elections of the Masters, Mates & Pilots Union (Union), announced that he would be a candidate in the upcoming 1988 election and asked Union for mailing labels so he could send a timely mailing of campaign materials to the membership before Union's forthcoming nominating convention. The request was denied because preconvention mailings were against a union rule. Brown sued under LMRDA Section 401(c), which imposes on every union

> a duty enforceable at the suit of any bona fide candidate . . . to comply with all reasonable requests of any candidate to distribute by mail or otherwise at the candidate's expense campaign literature. . . .

The district court granted an injunction ordering Union to furnish the membership list and labels. It ruled that the clear language of Section 401(c) required the court to focus on the reasonableness of Brown's request, not on the reasonableness of the union rule under which the request was denied. The court of appeals affirmed, and Union appealed to the U.S. Supreme Court.

OPINION STEVENS, J. Labor unions have a statutory duty to distribute campaign literature to their membership in response to the reasonable request of any candidate for union office. The question presented is whether a court must evaluate the reasonableness of the Union's rule before it decides whether the candidate's request was reasonable. . . .

The text, structure and purpose of Title IV of the LMRDA all support the conclusion that our inquiry should focus primarily on the reasonableness of the candidate's request rather than on the reasonableness of the Union's rule curtailing the period in which campaign literature may be mailed. . . . The language of the statute plainly requires unions to comply with "all reasonable requests," and just as plainly does *not* require union members to comply with "all reasonable rules" when making such requests. . . . Thus, as the language of the statute suggests, Congress gave this right pertaining to campaign literature a special status that it did not confer upon other rights it granted to union members. . . .

The special purpose of Title IV was to insure free and democratic union elections. The statutory guarantees are specifically designed to offset the "inherent advantage over potential rank and file challengers" possessed by incumbent union leadership.

JUDGMENT The judgment of the Court of Appeals is affirmed. [The injunction issued by the trial court ordering Union to furnish membership mailing lists and addresses to Brown was upheld.]

Coverage of Wagner Act as Amended. The NLRA as amended by the LMRA and LMRDA applies, with certain exceptions, to employers engaged in business affecting interstate commerce. Railroads and interstate airlines, which are governed by the Railway Labor Act,[9] are excluded, as are local, state, and federal government employers. The amended NLRA extends protection to *employees* but excludes certain groups such as domestic servants, supervisors, independent contractors, and agricultural laborers.

The Collective Bargaining Process

The chief aim of the NLRA as amended is to promote industrial peace by substituting collective bargaining for individual bargaining in the workplace. Implementing this goal requires employees to (1) choose a bargaining representative, (2) bargain in good faith for a contract covering wages, hours, and working conditions, and (3) monitor the union contract throughout its term.

Choosing a Bargaining Representative. Section 9 of the NLRA sets out the *procedure* for employee selection of a bargaining representative. Suppose Al, a welder for an auto parts maker, has just read Section 9. He is concerned because his 100 co-workers are unhappy with their employer's arbitrary and harsh treatment. He contacts representatives of the International Machinists Union for information on how to form a local. They give him 100 cards for the workers to consider signing. The cards authorize the Machinists Union as the workers' bargaining representative. At the same time Ben, a co-worker, takes the organizing problem to the United Auto Workers (UAW), which also gives him 100 cards. Al and Ben talk to their co-workers and pass out the cards. Machinists cards are signed by 31 workers and UAW cards by 40 workers. Al and Ben take these to the local NLRB office, which checks the cards against employer payroll records and concludes that both unions have obtained more than the required 30 percent "showing of interest." The NLRB then defines the **appropriate bargaining unit**— the group of employees eligible to vote— in this case, "all production and maintenance employees."

The campaign to win the election begins, with the employer taking full advantage of the Taft-Hartley free speech guarantee. Employer and union **election observers** are appointed to oversee the voting. At the NLRB-supervised election by secret ballot, 30 workers vote for the Machinists Union, 33 for the UAW, and 37 for "no union." The NLRB drops the low candidate and holds a runoff election between the UAW and "no union." A majority votes "no union," but 2 days later the UAW files an unfair labor practice complaint with the NLRB. It claims that the employer interfered with the voting process by giving each worker a turkey just before election time and asks that the election be set aside. Case 48.3 presents a similar set of circumstances, to which the Supreme Court responds.

[9] 45 USC 151.

CASE 48.3	**National Labor Relations Board v. Exchange Parts Co.**
	• 375 U.S. 405 (1964)
FACTS	After a 30 percent showing of interest by the boilermakers (AFL-CIO), the NLRB scheduled an election on March 18, 1960, for workers of Exchange Parts Co. Six days after the NLRB ordered an election, the firm's vice president held a dinner for the employees, announced an additional vacation day, and told them they could decide whether it would be a "floating holiday" or their birthday. He said the union had slanted the facts; without a union there were many benefits to be gained by the employees. In a letter to them before the election he said:

**CASE 48.3
Continued**

It is the Company that puts things in your envelope. . . . The Union can't put any of those things in your envelope. . . . It didn't take a Union to get any of those things and . . . it won't take a Union to get additional improvements in the future.

Included in the letter was a new system for computing overtime during holiday weeks, which had the effect of increasing wages, and a new vacation schedule, which enabled employees to extend vacations by sandwiching them between two weekends. The union lost the election and filed a complaint charging the employer with an unfair labor practice in violation of Section 8(a)(1) of the NLRA. The NLRB found unfair labor practices, the court of appeals reversed, and the union appealed to the U.S. Supreme Court.

OPINION

HARLAN, J. This case presents a question concerning the limitations which §8(a)(1) . . . places on the right of an employer to confer economic benefits on his employees shortly before a representation election. . . . We think the Court of Appeals was mistaken in concluding that the conferral of employee benefits while a representation election is pending, for the purpose of inducing employees to vote against the union, does not "interfere with" the protected right to organize.

The broad purpose of §8(a)(1) is to establish the right of employees to organize for mutual aid without employer interference. We have no doubt that it prohibits not only intrusive threats and promises but also conduct immediately favorable to employees which is undertaken with the express purpose of impinging upon their freedom of choice for or against unionization and is reasonably calculated to have that effect. . . . The danger inherent in well-timed increases in benefits is the suggestion of a fist inside the velvet glove. Employees are not likely to miss the inference that the source of benefits now conferred is also the source from which future benefits must flow and which may dry up if it is not obliged. The danger may be diminished if, as in this case, the benefits are conferred permanently and unconditionally. . . . We cannot agree with the Court of Appeals that enforcement of the Board's order will have the "ironic" result of "discouraging benefits for labor." The beneficence of an employer is likely to be ephemeral if prompted by a threat of unionization which is subsequently removed. Insulating the right of collective organization from calculated good will of this sort deprives employees of little that has lasting value.

JUDGMENT

Reversed. [The election results were set aside and a new election ordered. Note that the NLRB also has authority to order bargaining despite election results, or to mandate bargaining where there has been no election if it thinks unfair labor practices during the campaign have precluded a fair election.]

Duty to Bargain in Good Faith. If employees vote against a union, no new organizing effort can be initiated for at least a year. When employees do select a union, its primary function is to represent them in *collective bargaining*. Usually, the immediate objective of the employees and their new union is to negotiate and sign a labor agreement. The Wagner Act requires both sides to *bargain in good faith*. This does not mean that they must agree; either party can resort to an economic weapon such as a strike or lockout if all genuine efforts to reach agreement fail. Furthermore, the NLRB cannot force an agreement upon the parties when their bargaining is unsuccessful. The duty to bargain in good faith extends to "wages, hours, and other terms and conditions of employment." These are called **mandatory** subjects of bargaining and include all forms of compensation and working conditions which concern the employment relationship. Fringe benefits such as health insurance, vacation pay, and profit-sharing plans are mandatory subjects of bargaining, as are matters ranging from shift starting time to grievance procedures and work rules. Refusing to bargain or making unilateral decisions on mandatory subjects is an unfair labor practice [Sections 8(a)(5); 8(b)(3)].

Other subjects are **permissive**— that is, the parties *may*, but need not, bargain about them. Either party can act unilaterally in these areas. Matters which are not essentially related to employment—for example, those which are managerial or entrepreneurial in nature—are permissive subjects. However, the distinction between mandatory and permissive subjects remains a crucial issue, as illustrated in Case 48.4.

CASE 48.4

First National Maintenance Corporation v. National Labor Relations Board • 108 S. Ct. 2573 (1981)

FACTS

First National Maintenance (plaintiff) provided maintenance services for commercial customers. It had a maintenance contract with a nursing home. After a dispute with the home over the size of its fee, plaintiff terminated the contract. Upon learning of plaintiff's intention to discharge its employees, the union requested a delay for the purpose of bargaining, but plaintiff refused. The union then filed an unfair labor practice charge, claiming that the plaintiff had violated its duty to bargain in good faith. The NLRB upheld the charge and ordered plaintiff to reinstate the employees if the nursing home contract was renewed, or to offer equivalent jobs elsewhere. Appeal was taken to the Supreme Court.

OPINION

BLACKMUN, J. . . . Must an employer, under its duty to bargain in good faith "with respect to wages, hours, and other terms and conditions of employment," negotiate with the certified representative of its employees over its decision to close a part of its business? . . . Although parties are free to bargain about any legal subject, Congress has limited the mandate or duty to bargain to matters of "wages, hours, and other terms and conditions of employment." . . . In establishing what issues must be submitted to the process of bargaining, Congress had no expectation that the elected union representative would become an equal partner in the running of the business enterprise in which the union's members are employed. Despite the deliberate open-endedness of the statutory language, there is an undeniable limit to the subjects about which bargaining must take place. . . .

Some management decisions, such as choice of advertising and promotion, product type and design, and financing arrangements, have only an indirect and attenuated impact on the employment relationship between employer and employee. Other management decisions, such as the order of succession of layoffs and recalls, production quotas, and work rules are almost exclusively an aspect of

| CASE 48.4 Continued | the relationship between employer and employee. The present case concerns a third type of management decision, one that had a direct impact on employment, since jobs were inexorably eliminated by the termination, but had as its focus only the economic profitability of the contract with [the nursing home], a concern under these facts wholly apart from the employment relationship. This decision, involving a change in the scope and direction of the enterprise, is akin to the decision whether to be in business at all, not . . . primarily about conditions of employment. . . . At the same time, this decision touches on a matter of central and pressing concern to the union and its member employees: the possibility of continued employment and the retention of the employees' very jobs.

. . . Moreover, the union's legitimate interest in fair dealing is protected by Section 8(a)(3), which prohibits partial closings motivated by antiunion animus, when done to gain an unfair advantage. Under Section 8(a)(3) the Board may inquire into the motivations behind a partial closing. An employer may not simply shut down part of its business and mask its desire to weaken and circumvent the union by labeling its decision "purely economic." . . .

Management's interest in whether it should discuss a decision of this kind is much more complex and varies with the particular circumstances. If labor costs are an important factor in a failing operation and the decision to close, management will have an incentive to confer voluntarily with the union to seek concessions that may make continuing the business profitable. At other times, management may have great need for speed, flexibility, and secrecy in meeting business exigencies. It may face consequences that hinge on confidentiality, the timing of a plant closing, or a reorganization of the corporate structure. The publicity incident to the normal process of bargaining may injure the possibility of a successful transition or increase the economic damage to the business. The employer also may have no feasible alternative to the closing, and even good-faith bargaining over it may be both futile and cause the employer additional loss. . . .

We conclude that the harm likely to be done to an employer's need to operate freely in deciding whether to shut down part of its business purely for economic reasons outweighs the incremental benefit that might be gained through the union's participation in making the decision, and we hold that the decision itself is not part of Section 8(d)'s "terms and conditions," over which Congress has mandated bargaining. |
|---|---|
| JUDGMENT | The judgment of the Court of Appeals . . . is reversed. . . . |

The Collective Bargaining Agreement. Most union contracts with management are for a 1-year period, although in some industries a 3- or even 5-year agreement may be negotiated covering all terms of employment other than wages. A special "reopener" clause is used to permit annual negotiation of the wage issue. At the commencement of bargaining, the parties usually agree in writing that they do not intend a contract to come into existence until all issues on the bargaining agenda are resolved, reduced to writing, and signed by the parties. This procedure prevents disputes based on claims that an *oral agreement* was entered into at some stage of discussions. During negotiations, minor differences are usually resolved first and the "big ticket" items last. One such item is a *no strike–no lockout* clause, which in effect is an agreement to buy peace for another year. With such a clause, any strike or lockout in the ensuing term is a breach of contract.

Another provision that is usually important to both parties is grievance procedure, in which the last step is usually to refer an unresolved matter to **arbitration** for hearing and final decision by an impartial arbitrator. Arbitration is invaluable for resolving minor differences over such matters as vacation and holiday pay, seniority, layoffs, promotion, and transfer. Such issues usually do not warrant the time or expense of litigation, yet they still must be resolved before escalating into a major controversy. However, both unions and employers are usually unwilling to delegate to an arbitrator the authority to settle major issues such as wages or a cost-of-living adjustment (COLA).

> **BOX 48.2**
> **A Mandatory or Permissive Bargaining Issue?**
>
> Some months ago, management of Boston's sumptuous Copley Plaza Hotel ordered its chambermaids to lay their mops aside and scrub floors by hand. Irate union leaders from the Boston Hotel and Restaurant Workers Union protested that this was demeaning. Alan Tremain, president of Hotels of Distinction, which manages the Copley Plaza for the owner, said "a maid is a maid, and that is what she has to do." He added that with rooms costing from $140 to $195 per night, the hotel caters to an elite clientele and must therefore pay attention to detail. "Even the silver is polished before it is put on the table," he said, adding that he believes the union protested the order because of forthcoming contract negotiations.
>
> Under the Wagner Act as amended, if the contract is silent on the subject, does management have the right to order the maids to work on their knees? When the contract comes up for renewal, is this a mandatory or permissive bargaining matter? ■

Because there is a range of uncertainty between mandatory and permissive bargaining issues, employers usually demand that the contract include specific "management rights" clauses which spell out in detail the matters which the union agrees are the exclusive province of the employer during the life of the contract.

Recently, a variation of Japan's worker-employer team approach to industrial organization has appeared in the United States in the form of *employee participation programs* (EPPs). It is estimated that 80 percent of Fortune 1000 companies have EPPs. In 1989 Electromation, Inc., a firm with 200 employees, sought to reduce costs and improve efficiency by creating four "action committees" of workers and management to deal with absenteeism, attendance bonus plans, and a no-smoking policy. The committee members met during work hours, receiving their regular pay. The union filed unfair labor practice charges, claiming (1) the committees were in effect a *company union* (i.e., an employer-sponsored labor organization) and (2) the employer had dominated and interfered with the formation and administration of the EPP in violation of Sections 8(a)(1) and 8(a)(2). The National Labor Relations Board held for the union, and the case was appealed to the federal courts. The issue has drawn the attention of members of Congress, who have announced plans to sponsor legislation amending the NLRA to permit EPPs.

Strikes and Lockouts. If an existing contract is expiring and collective bargaining has not resolved the differences between the parties, the union or the employer may decide to put pressure on its opponents. The union may call an *economic strike* and keep its labor away from the plant, or the employer may shut down (a lockout) and keep the plant away from labor. Either action is lawful. The NLRA as amended permits the employer to notify workers that if they do not return to work at a set time, they will be *permanently replaced*. If the employer hires replacements **(scabs),** it is an unfair labor practice for striking workers to intimidate them as they cross the picket line to work. When the strike is over, the employer does not have to fire permanent replacements hired during the strike in order to make room for returning economic strikers. However, such strikers have not lost all rights as employees. If they have not found work and a *vacancy* occurs, and if they apply for it unconditionally, the employer must rehire them.

Illegal Strikes. In addition to *lawful strikes*, there are many kinds of *illegal strikes*, as detailed in Table 48.4. In Case 48.5, the Boich Company claimed that the union was conducting an illegal strike because its real fight was with Aloe, a different company. If Aloe was, in fact, a different company, then under Section 8(b) the union was illegally striking in support of an unlawful secondary boycott. The big question: Was Aloe a different firm?

Table 48.4 Illegal Strikes under the National Labor Relations Act as Amended

1. *Strike within 60 days of contract's end.* Section 8(d) requires the union and employer to notify the other of intent to modify or terminate an existing contract 60 days before expiration. The idea is to have a cooling-off period during which the union and employer will work out differences. Those striking during this period lose their status as employees—thus, the employer may permanently discharge them.

2. *Strike in breach of existing contract.* If a union strikes while a no-strike clause is in effect, it is a breach of contract and therefore unlawful. It gives the employer a right to discharge or discipline striking employees.

3. *Strike in support of secondary boycott.* Employees are assured the right to strike only against their *primary employer* (Section 13) but generally, it is illegal under Section 8(b) to strike or picket in support of a secondary boycott. This occurs when the union exerts pressure on employers *other* than the primary employer to cease doing business with the primary employer. It is also an illegal secondary boycott for a union and employer to make a hot cargo contract in which the employer agrees not to handle products of firms with which the union has a dispute.

4. *Strike during national emergency.* In case of a national emergency, the President can obtain an 80-day injunction restraining the strike. During this cooling-off period, a strike is unlawful.

5. *Violent strike.* A strike that is enmeshed with violence is unlawful and both federal and state courts will not hesitate to enjoin it. Violence can include physical assault, or wilful destruction of property (trespass), or simply wrongful possession of property, such as a sit-down strike in which the workers refuse to leave the workplace.

6. *Wildcat strike.* Although there are a few independent unions, most local unions are affiliated with an international union. Its constitution, as well as those of local unions, calls for a majority membership vote to approve a strike. When minority employees decide unilaterally to strike without such a vote, they are engaging in a wildcat strike. Since constitutions are contracts with the members, those who strike contrary to the restrictions in their constitution are breaching their contract and therefore engaging in an unlawful strike.

CASE 48.5	**Boich Mining Company v. National Labor Relations Board** 955 F.2d 431 (6th Cir. 1992)
FACTS	Boich Mining (an Ohio corporation) operated a coal mine. Thirty miles away, Aloe Coal Company (a Pennsylvania corporation) also operated a coal mine. Both corporations were wholly owned subsidiaries of Aloe Holding Company. United Mine Workers (UMW) represented production workers of both corporations under separate union contracts with different expiration dates. On July 11, 1989, Aloe's contract expired. Unable to agree on a new contract, UMW went on strike. Although Boich's contract was still in effect, UMW called upon Boich employees to strike in support of the strike against Aloe. Boich filed an unfair labor practice charge against UMW, claiming that it was engaging in an unlawful secondary boycott in violation of Section 8(b)(4)(i) of the NLRA. The administrative law judge (ALJ) of the NLRB (Board) found that Boich was not a neutral employer and dismissed the complaint. Boich appealed.
OPINION	BOGGS, NORRIS, and TIMBERS, Cir. Js. Section 8(b)(4), known as the secondary boycott section, makes it unlawful for a labor organization to picket or otherwise pressure an employer with whom it has no dispute. The purpose of this statutory provision is to preserve the rights of employees to strike against their employers with whom they have a legitimate dispute, while protecting other neutral or secondary employers from becoming enmeshed in the dispute because they happen to conduct business with the employer being struck. As a result, the provision makes it unlawful to resort to a secondary boycott to injure the business of a third person who is wholly unconcerned or not involved in any way in the dispute between an employer and his employees. The Board, however, has held consistently that an otherwise neutral employer may lose this protection if that employer becomes somehow "allied" with the primary employer. Under this "ally doctrine," a neutral employer may be stripped of its neutral status (1) if it performs "struck work" for the employer, i.e. work that it otherwise would not perform absent a strike, or (2) if the two employers become so closely entwined as to function essentially as a single entity. In both instances, the union bears the burden of establishing that the two employers are allies under the Act. The Board and the courts have enunciated four criteria to determine whether two employers should be treated as a single entity: (1) common ownership; (2) common management; (3) centralized control of labor relations; and (4) interrelationship of operations. . . . Applying these considerations to the relationship between Boich and Aloe, we hold that the union's efforts to ally the two coal companies constitute a violation of §§ 8(b)(4)(i) and (ii)(B). It is true that both Boich and Aloe are wholly owned subsidiaries of Aloe Holding Company. It is not unusual, however, to find that two companies are not allied simply because they are under common ownership. . . . This is particularly true where the management operations of the subsidiaries are kept separate intentionally. In the instant case, Boich and Aloe each has a separate management. At each company, labor relations are entirely separate. Each company's operations are completely separate. Aloe and Boich maintain separate offices,

CASE 48.5 Continued	payroll systems, bank accounts, financial and accounting operations. There is no interchange of either employees or supervisors. The two companies do not sell coal to the same . . . customers.
JUDGMENT	We hold that the Board's decision affirming the ALJ's finding that Boich was not a neutral employer . . . is not supported by the evidence. [The case was remanded to the NLRB with instructions to issue a cease-and-desist order against the UMW's boycott.]

EQUAL EMPLOYMENT OPPORTUNITY

State and federal employment discrimination law is perhaps today's most hotly debated labor issue. Since most laws discussed in this section permit the plaintiff in a successful discrimination suit to recover attorney's fees, the statutes have been applauded by both lawyers and clients, and the size of recent judgments has compelled employers to take discrimination laws seriously.

The civil rights movement of the 1950s and 1960s ended with enactment of the Civil Rights Act of 1964. During the next three decades, the act fueled passage of a host of supplemental antidiscrimination laws, listed in Table 48.5.

During the same period, many states enacted employment discrimination laws along the federal pattern. Some state laws are even stricter. California, for example, prohibits discrimination not only on the bases covered by federal law but also on the bases of marital status, physical handicap, medical condition, and age over 40—with no upper limit. Federal agencies ordinarily permit states having an enforcement agency to conduct the investigation and conciliation effort.

Title VII

The Civil Rights Act of 1964 broadly prohibits discrimination on the basis of race, color, religion, sex, or national origin in providing accommodations, education, and economic opportunity. The Act created the Equal Employment Opportunity Commission (EEOC) to administer and enforce Title VII. Headed by a five-member group appointed by the President, the agency has the authority to issue binding regulations. It also investigates, conciliates, and prosecutes claimed violations of the Act.

Coverage. Title VII prohibits discrimination in employment.[10] It applies to all employers of fifteen or more employees whose business affects interstate commerce, to labor unions that have fifteen or more members or operate a hiring hall, and to employment agencies. Unions are forbidden to discriminate not only in membership but in grievance representation and in referral for employment and apprenticeship programs. Employment agencies cannot discriminate in making referrals, in interviewing, or in advertising. As amended in 1972, Title VII also covers state, federal, and local employees. Title VII prohibits discrimination at all points in the employment scene, including hiring, fixing compensation, promotion, seniority, assignment of work, transfer, layoff, discharge, and any other "term, condition or privilege" of employment.

"Protected Class." Not all discrimination is forbidden—only that against members of a *protected class*, which is one based upon *race, color, sex, religion, or national origin*. For example, Title VII does not list married persons, or homosexuals, as a protected class. If an employer engages in prohibited discrimination against persons in a protected class, they may file a class action on behalf of themselves and "all other persons

---

[10] 42 USC 2000(e).

Table 48.5 Evolution of Fair Employment and Equal Employment Opportunity Laws

Date	Decision or Statute	Significance
1937	*West Coast Hotel v. Parrish* (300 U.S. 379)	Supreme Court upheld state minimum wage laws
1938	Fair Labor Standards Act	Federal minimum wage and overtime pay law enacted
1944	*James v. Marinship Corp.* (25 Cal. 2d 721)	Union can't restrict membership on account of race
1963	Equal Pay Act	Bans discrimination in pay because of sex
1964	Civil Rights Act, Title VII	Bans discrimination based on race, color, religion, sex, or national origin
1967	Age Discrimination in Employment Act (ADEA)	Bans discrimination based on age
1973	Rehabilitation Act of 1973	Bans discrimination by federal agencies and contractors against handicapped
1978	Pregnancy Discrimination Act	Bans discrimination based on a woman's ability to become pregnant
1991	Civil Rights Act of 1991	Eases employee's burden of proof in Title VII case
1992	Americans with Disabilities Act (ADA)	Bans employers of 25 or more from discriminating against disabled persons
1993	Family Leave Act	Employer of 50 or more full-time workers must grant up to 12 weeks unpaid leave for family emergencies

similarly situated." If the suit is successful, the court permits such others in the class to join the lawsuit and become claimants against the offending employer and participate in the judgment as well as in the costs of the suit.

Enforcement. If an investigation discloses a Title VII violation, the EEOC attempts **conciliation.** If this fails, the EEOC may file a discrimination suit, but typically it issues a "right to sue" letter to the complaining party, who then commences a private suit independent of the EEOC. The EEOC must issue the letter within 180 days from receipt of the complaint.

Proving Discrimination. It is not illegal discrimination to treat employees differently; it is treating an employee or group of employees differently *because of* their race, color, religion, sex, or national origin that violates Title VII. To promote a white male over a white male is to discriminate between them but is not illegal because such discrimination is not prohibited by Title VII. Even to promote a white male over a black female does not violate Title VII unless it is for a prohibited discriminatory reason—such as race or sex. Illegal discrimination may be proved by showing (1) **disparate treatment** or (2) **disparate impact.**

> **BOX 48.3**
>
> ### Discrimination Can Be Costly: Can Business Planning Avoid It?
>
> To Guy Saperstein, a plaintiff's lawyer who specializes in employment discrimination cases, civil rights law is more than a mission—it can be a profitable business. Noticing that State Farm's district managers (whose pictures appeared in local newspaper ads) were all men, he had himself quoted in local papers decrying sex discrimination in the insurance industry. A reader, Muriel Kryszewski, who State Farm had not promoted, came to see Saperstein. He filed a class action for her, and acting on behalf of all others similarly situated. After 13 years of weary litigation, in 1993 Saperstein negotiated a $239 million settlement which State Farm paid to put an end to mounting legal fees. Shoney's Inc. has agreed to pay $132.5 million in a racial bias suit, and Saperstein's twenty-four-lawyer firm has settled with Lucky Stores for about $100 million. The law firm's fees are 20 to 30 percent of the recovery. Its recent 5-year net income was in the $25–$35 million range on revenue of $80 million. Coming up is a another trial that Saperstein hopes will bring a $1 billion jury verdict.
>
> #### Three Critical Thinking Questions
>
> 1. If you were on the board of one of these giant corporations, what business planning steps would you take to avoid running afoul of a Saperstein suit?
> 2. With a twelve-person jury, most of whom are *employees*, is there any possibility for justice to miscarry in a suit by employees against a large corporation?
> 3. If a large company such as Lucky Stores is hit with a $100 million judgment, could this adversely affect employment? How?

Disparate treatment discrimination. **Disparate treatment,** which simply means "different treatment," is proved when plaintiffs show that they have been treated differently from persons not of the same race, color, religion, sex, or national origin who are in simiilar circumstances. A black male who was terminated for excessive absences, for example, would establish "disparate treatment" if he showed that his employer did not terminate a white male who had a similar attendance and work record.

Because it is impossible to prove by direct evidence that an employer's undisclosed inner motive for an employment decision was discriminatory, courts allow plaintiffs to prove disparate treatment discrimination indirectly. In a series of decisions beginning with *McDonnel Douglas Corp. v. Green*,[11] the Supreme Court listed the **requirements for indirect proof of disparate treatment,** described in Table 48.6.

Disparate impact discrimination. The Title VII violation of **disparate impact discrimination** refers to illegal discrimination in which the employer establishes a seemingly neutral job requirement or test that has a disproportionate effect on members of a particular group. For example, a general requirement that an applicant for a job possess a minimum height or weight has been found to disproportionately exclude women and certain minorities from job opportunities. When these or other requirements such as education, experience, or test scores are really unrelated to performance of the job in question, they violate Title VII. In such cases, proof of intent to violate the statute is not required. The rule that job qualifications which the employer establishes must truly have "job-relatedness" was first articulated by the Supreme Court in the landmark case *Griggs v. Duke Power*.[12] The company had restricted employment in its higher-paying departments to persons with high school diplomas. Plaintiffs, a group of black employees, proved that such a requirement had a disproportionately negative effect on blacks, who (at that time and in that area) were less likely than whites to possess high school diplomas. The Court held the requirement to be illegal because it was not related to the jobs in question or required by business necessity. The Court stated:

[11] 411 U.S. 792 (1973).
[12] 401 U.S. 424 (1971).

Table 48.6   How to Prove Disparate Treatment in a Sex Discrimination Suit* (The Case of Wendy the Welder)

1 *Plaintiff must establish a prima facie case.* (Wendy applies for job of welder and is rejected.) As plaintiff Wendy must show that:

   a Plaintiff is a member of one of the groups protected by Title VII (race, sex, color, religion, nationality).

   b Defendant had a job vacancy (welder).

   c At all times plaintiff was capable of performing the job, and applied for it (Wendy is a certified welder).

   d Plaintiff was, in fact, not hired, but the job was filled by a person not in the protected group.

   (Assume Wendy has proved the above—she has made a prima facie case of illegal discrimination. The ball is now in the employer's court.)

2 *Defendant employer has the burden of offering a legitimate nondiscriminatory reason for its actions in rejecting plaintiff.* If it fails to do so, plaintiff wins. (The employer claims, "Women aren't physically able to weld an 8-hour day.")

3 *If employer offers a nondiscriminatory reason for rejection, plaintiff must then carry the burden of proving it is a pretext, masking an illegal motive.* (Wendy shows she welded an 8-hour day for 5 years on ships; and a direct competitor has four women welding an 8-hour day; hence, the employers "reason" is a pretext and an excuse.)

4 *The burden again shifts to the employer to prove either or both of the following defenses:*

   a *BFOQ defense.* Here the employer admits the discrimination, but argues that a bona fide occupational qualification required it. (The employer states that this particular job calls for a heliarc welder part of the time and a sigma welder the other part, while Wendy is only a heliarc welder.) The BFOQ defense is: two types of skills are required by the job.

   b *Business necessity defense,* in which the employer shows that it has a nondiscriminatory reason for not hiring plaintiff. (The welders are sent for 6 months each year to weld Arab oil rigs under Arab supervision, and a female welder in the Middle East would be culturally unacceptable and fatal to obtaining a maintenance contract.)

**McDonnel Douglas Corp. v. Green*, 411 U.S. 792 (1973).

Nothing in the Act precludes the use of testing procedures; obviously they are useful. What Congress has forbidden is giving these devices and mechanisms controlling force unless they are demonstrably a reasonable measure of job performance. Congress has not commanded that the less qualified be preferred over the better qualified simply because of minority origins. Far from disparaging job qualifications as such, Congress has made such qualifications the controlling factor, so that race, religion, nationality, and sex become irrelevant. What Congress has commanded is that any tests used must measure the person for the job and not the person in the abstract.

Griggs, later decisions, and the Civil Rights Act of 1991 summarize steps that must be taken to prove disparate impact. (See Table 48.7.)

Civil Rights Act of 1991. In *Wards Cove Packing Co. v. Atonio,*[13] the Supreme Court substantially eroded plaintiffs' ability to prevail in disparate impact cases by increasing their burden of proof and by expanding employer defenses. Congress responded 2 years later with the Civil Rights Act of 1991. It codified the cause of action for disparate impact discrimination and expressly denounced *Wards Cove* procedures, reverting to the procedures established by the four decisions cited in Table 48.7. The bill was hotly debated, one side focusing on eliminating discrimination, the other on the economic viability of subjecting small business to the cost of such litigation. To obtain enough

[13]490 U.S. 642 (1989).

Table 48.7 Proving Disparate Impact in a Discrimination Case

1 *Plaintiff has the burden of making a prima facie case of discrimination.* For example, the plaintiff may show that a test score, educational experience, or other personnel policy requirement has an adverse and disparate impact on the plaintiff's protected group compared with other groups.

2 *If the plaintiff succeeds with the prima facie case, the burden shifts to the defendant to show business necessity for the personnel practice or test by proving that the test measured performance for the specific job for which it was used.**

3 *If the defendant shows business necessity that validates the hiring practice or other personnel policy, the burden shifts again to the plaintiff to show that there are other policies and practices that are less discriminatory that would still carry out the employer's objective.*

*Civil Rights Act of 1991 (42 U.S.C.A. Secs. 2000e *et seq.*) merely states that an unlawful employment practice is established when the plaintiff makes out a prima facie case of discrimination, "and the respondent fails to demonstrate that the challenged practice is job related for the position in question and consistent with business necessity" (Sec. 2000e-2).

Source: *Griggs v. Duke Power*, 401 U.S. 424 (1971); *Patterson v. McLean Credit Union*, 491 U.S. 164 (1989); *Lorance v. AT&T Technologies, Inc.*, 490 U.S. 900 (1989); *Martin v. Wilks*, 490 U.S. 755 (1989).

votes to enact the bill, congressional sponsors watered it down to a nullity. The "business necessity" defense was left undefined. The result: Both sides proclaimed victory in the final bill, but its ambiguous terms require continued interpretation by the Supreme Court. Many experts predict that the Court again will construe the statute strictly so as to diminish plaintiffs' ability to win. Meanwhile, plaintiffs and their lawyers are following the procedures shown in Table 48.7.

Religious Discrimination. Under Title VII, discrimination because of religion is unlawful in hiring, promotion, layoff, or discharge. However, the statute exempts religious organizations as well as the businesses they own. A serious problem for secular businesses is that, often, to treat all employees alike is to discriminate against persons whose religious beliefs require out-of-the-ordinary considerations.

What does the employer do when a person's religion forbids work after sundown on Friday but the workweek includes Saturday? The courts' solution has been to require "accommodation" of religious beliefs. This means that employers must make a *reasonable effort* to work around employees' religious requirements. In *Trans-World Airlines, Inc. v. Hardison*,[14] however, the Supreme Court held that employers need not accommodate contrary to union agreements or where costs are more than minimal.

Pregnancy Discrimination Act of 1978. In 1978, Congress enacted the Pregnancy Discrimination Act as a new section of Title VII. It provides that Title VII's forbidden discrimination on the basis of sex shall include "pregnancy, childbirth, or related medical conditions." Accordingly, employer programs such as disability or leave plans that treat pregnancy differently from other conditions violate Title VII. Subsequent to passage of the Act, the Supreme Court held in *Newport News Shipbuilding & Dry Dock Co. v. EEOC*[15] that an employer's health plan which provided fewer pregnancy-related hospitalization benefits for spouses of male employees than for female employees discriminated against male employees in violation of Title VII. In the following discrimination case, the U.S. Supreme Court considered whether a fetal protection program for pregnant women unlawfully discriminates against them because of their sex. The Court also explains the "business necessity" and BFOQ defenses.

[14] 432 U.S. 63 (1977).

[15] 462 U.S. 669 (1983).

CASE 48.6   Auto Workers v. Johnson Controls • 113 L. Ed. 2d 158 (1991)

FACTS   Johnson Controls manufactured lead batteries. In 1982, after eight of its pregnant employees showed blood lead above safe levels set by the Occupational Safety and Health Administration (OSHA) for a worker planning to have a family, Johnson announced that women "who are pregnant or who are capable of bearing children will not be placed into jobs involving lead exposure." . . . "Women capable of bearing children" were defined as "all women except those whose inability to bear children is medically documented." United Auto Workers (UAW) filed a class action on behalf of all production employees challenging Johnson's fetal protection policy as sex discrimination in violation of Title VII. The court of appeals upheld judgment for Johnson, and UAW appealed to the U.S. Supreme Court.

OPINION   BLACKMUN, J. . . . Applying [the] business necessity defense, the Court of Appeals . . . concluded that there was no genuine issue . . . about the substantial health-risk factor because the parties agreed that there was a substantial risk to a fetus from lead exposure. . . . Having concluded that the business necessity defense was the appropriate framework and that Johnson satisfied that standard, the court proceeded to discuss the BFOQ defense and concluded that Johnson met that test, too. The *en banc* majority ruled that industrial safety is part of the essence of Johnson's business and that the fetal-protection policy is reasonably necessary to further that concern. The majority emphasized that, in view of the goal of protecting the unborn "more is at stake" than simply an individual woman's decision to weigh and accept the risks of employment. . . .

The bias in Johnson's policy is obvious. Fertile men, but not fertile women, are given a choice as to whether they wish to risk their productive health for a particular job. The Civil Rights Act of 1964 prohibits sex-based classifications in terms and conditions of employment, in hiring and discharging decisions, and in other employment decisions that adversely affect an employee's status. Johnson's fetal-protection policy explicitly discriminates against men on the basis of their sex. The policy excludes women with child-bearing capacity from lead-exposed jobs and so creates a facial classification based on gender. . . .

Nevertheless, the Court of Appeals assumed, as did the two appellate courts who had already confronted the issue, . . . that because the asserted reason for the sex-based exclusion (protecting women's unconceived offspring) was ostensibly benign, the policy was not sex-based discrimination. That assumption, however, was incorrect. . . . Johnson's policy classifies on the basis of gender and childbearing capacity, rather than fertility alone. . . . Despite evidence in the record about the debilitating effect of lead exposure on the male reproduction system, Johnson Controls is concerned only with the harms that may befall the unborn offspring of its female employees. . . . Johnson's policy is facially discriminatory because it requires only a female employee to produce proof that she is not capable of reproducing. Our conclusion is bolstered by the Pregnancy Discrimination Act of 1978 (PDA) in which Congress explicitly provided that for purposes of Title VII, discrimination "on the basis of sex" includes discrimination "because of or on the basis of pregnancy, childbirth, or related medical conditions." . . .

**CASE 48.6
Continued**

We hold that Johnson Controls' fetal-protection policy is sex discrimination forbidden under Title VII unless Johnson can establish that sex is a "bona fide occupational qualification."

Under Title VII, an employer may discriminate on the basis of "religion, sex, or national origin in those certain instances where religion, sex, or national origin is a bona fide occupational qualification reasonably necessary to the normal operation of that particular business or enterprise."

. . . Johnson argues that its fetal-protection policy falls within the so-called safety exception to the BFOQ. Our cases have stressed that discrimination on the basis of sex because of safety concerns is allowed only in narrow circumstances. In *Dothard v. Rawlinson*, 433 U.S. 321, this court . . . allowed the employer to hire only male guards for contact areas of maximum-security male penitentiaries only because more was at stake than the "individual woman's decision to weigh and accept the risks of employment." We found sex to be a BFOQ inasmuch as the employment of a female guard would create real risk of safety to others if violence broke out. . . .

The PDA's amendment to Title VII contains a BFOQ standard of its own: unless pregnant employees differ from others "in their ability or inability to work," they must be "treated the same" as other employees "for all employment-related purposes.". . .

We have no difficulty concluding that Johnson Controls cannot establish a BFOQ. Fertile women, as far as appears in the record, participate in the manufacture of batteries as efficiently as anyone else. Johnson Controls' professed moral and ethical concerns about the welfare of the next generation do not suffice to establish a BFOQ of female sterility. Title VII, as amended by the PDA, mandates that decisions about welfare of future children be left to the parents who conceive, bear, support and raise them rather than to the employers who hire those parents or the courts.

JUDGMENT

Our holding today that Title VII . . . forbids sex specific fetal-protection policies is neither remarkable nor unprecedented. . . . Congress in the PDA prohibited discrimination on the basis of a woman's ability to become pregnant. We do no more than hold that the Pregnancy Discrimination Act means what it says.

Sexual Harassment. Another issue often raised under Title VII is sexual harassment, which the EEOC defines as any unwelcome sexual conduct that "has the purpose or effect of unreasonably interfering with an individual's work performance or creating an intimidating, hostile, or offensive work environment," including making sexual advances toward a person in exchange for promises of getting or keeping a job or a raise in pay. Liability usually arises when a supervisor or other agent makes advances or demands for sexual favors in return for job benefits. The Civil Rights Act of 1991 has increased the penalties for this form of discrimination.

In its first decision on the subject, the Supreme Court held in *Meritor Savings Bank v. Vinson*[16] that sexual harassment in violation of Title VII not only involves conduct that injures the plaintiff economically, such as loss of a promotion or salary increase, but also occurs when harassment creates a *hostile or abusive work envi-*

---

[16]106 S. Ct. 2399 (1986).

ronment. The *Meritor* court also held that, under general principles of agency law, corporate top management can be held liable in damages for sexual discrimination of a subordinate supervisor if it knew or should have known of the misconduct. The case suggests that the employer might avoid such liability by creating grievance procedures to hear employee complaints and by acting promptly to discipline offending supervisors. In *Harris v. Forklift Systems, Inc.*, U.S. Lexis 7155 (1993), the Supreme Court made it easier for women to win suits for sexual harassment by holding that it does not have to result in psychological harm or cause injury. All that must be proved is that a "reasonable person" would find the offensive conduct produced a hostile or abusive work environment.

Affirmative Action Programs. Affirmative action programs give preference in employment decisions to women and minorities, based on the assumption that such preference is necessary to correct past discrimination against them. In contrast, Title VII's prohibition of discrimination is perfectly neutral; it protects whites as well as blacks, men as well as women. Thus, *there is clear conflict between Title VII's duty not to discriminate and affirmative action's preference for victims of past discrimination.* Affirmative action programs that favor minority interests over the majority are sometimes loosely referred to as **reverse discrimination.**

There are three kinds of affirmative action: (1) programs initiated by special statute or executive order, (2) voluntary programs, and (3) court-ordered programs to cure past discriminations. Courts evaluate the legality of these three types of programs differently, depending on such factors as whether

1 There was clearly past discrimination
2 The requirements of the plan are absolute or flexible
3 Seniority is involved

Statutory affirmative action. An example of affirmative action initiated by statute or executive order is the **Rehabilitation Act of 1973,** which requires federal agencies and contractors to set up affirmative action programs for handicapped persons and bans discrimination against them. Executive Order 11246 requires contractors and subcontractors to refrain from discrimination and to take affirmative action to advance women and minorities.

Voluntary affirmative action. United Steelworkers of America v. Weber[17] involved a clause in an agreement between the union and Kaiser Aluminum which reserved 50 percent of the openings in Kaiser's training programs for blacks. Weber, a white male, sued for reverse discrimination when blacks with less seniority were accepted ahead of him into the program. The Supreme Court held that Title VII does not prohibit *voluntary affirmative action to abolish traditional patterns of race discrimination.* Although the Court did not draw a line between permissible and impermissible affirmative action, it said that Kaiser's plan was acceptable because it was voluntary and temporary, and did not abrogate preexisting rights or create an absolute bar to advancement of whites.

In *Firefighters Local Union No. 1784 v. Stotts,*[18] however, the Supreme Court limited affirmative action by holding that a district court could not order a city to depart from its seniority system in a layoff in order to preserve the status of blacks recently hired under an affirmative action plan. The city had voluntarily adopted the plan, which did not contain a provision for overriding white employees' seniority. The Court held that district courts have no power to invent such an override under the mantle of "affirmative action."

Court-imposed affirmative action. Notwithstanding the potential for reverse discrimination, courts have imposed affirmative action as a remedy for proven violations of Title VII, and many employers and unions have adopted it voluntarily in order to avoid discrimination lawsuits. But courts have not as yet offered clear solutions in reverse discrimination cases. In

---

[17]433 U.S. 193 (1979).
[18]467 U.S. 561 (1984).

Regents of the University of California v. Bakke,[19] a white male sued for race discrimination under the equal protection clause of the Fourteenth Amendment when the University of California medical school rejected his application for admission but accepted sixteen blacks whose credentials were inferior to his. The Supreme Court held that *quota systems that make race the sole criterion for a preference are illegal in the absence of a finding of past discrimination, but that race may be considered* in a university's admissions process.

At present, then, it is clear from the cases that voluntary affirmative action in some form is legally permissible. But given the conflict between affirmative action and nondiscrimination, courts will continue to establish and enforce limits on the use of the doctrine. The Supreme Court provided significant guidance for legal affirmative action in 1987. In *Johnson v. Transportation Agency, Santa Clara County*,[20] the Court held that a county agency did not violate Title VII by promoting a female over a male employee with a higher test score because (1) an affirmative action plan required sex or race to be considered as a factor to rectify underrepresentation of women and minorities in jobs that were traditionally segregated, and (2) the plan did not necessarily eliminate the rights of male employees. In validating the county's decision and plan, the Court said that an employer need not prove actual prior discrimination but only *conspicuous imbalance* in a traditionally segregated job category in order to establish a legal affirmative action plan. It would appear that without evidence of such *conspicuous imbalance* in the past, a voluntary affirmative action plan might not be upheld.

In *United States v. Paradise*[21] the Court ratified an affirmative action plan fashioned by a district court that required 50 percent of promotions of new state trooper corporals to be awarded to blacks until approximately 25 percent of the corporal rank was composed of blacks. The plan was challenged as a violation of the Fourteenth Amendment's equal protection clause, but the Court said that the plan was justified by a compelling governmental interest in eradicating discriminatory exclusion of blacks and was narrowly tailored to serve that purpose. Thus, even *quantified* goals can be appropriate in some circumstances. However, Title VII amendments prohibit **race-norming,** the practice of arbitrarily adding points to the test scores of racial groups who have suffered past discrimination.

Courts have made it clear that moderate affirmative action programs instituted on a case-by-case basis are fully consistent with Title VII. Most voluntary affirmative action programs have been upheld by the courts, and they are attractive to many employers because broad discretion can be exercised in creating them.

Other Sources of Employment Discrimination Law

Although Title VII of the 1964 Civil Rights Act is the chief equal employment opportunity law, the duty not to discriminate arises from other sources as well.

Age Discrimination in Employment Act.[22]

The ADEA protects employees over the ages of 40 from discrimination on the basis of age. ADEA is not under Title VII, but is administered by the Equal Employment Opportunity Commission (EEOC). The Act applies to unions, employers, and employment agencies and covers age discrimination in hiring, firing, promotion, and layoff. In layoff cases, the employer's most frequent defense is that the layoff was part of a general reduction in the work force or that a maximum limit on age is required by the job, as is the case with airline

---

[19]438 U.S. 265 (1978). The case did not involve employment discrimination under Title VII, but arose under Title VI of the Civil Rights Act, which bans discrimination by institutions such as universities that receive federal funds.

[20]107 S. Ct. 1442 (1987).

[21]107 S. Ct. 1053 (1987).

[22]29 USC 621.

pilots.[23] ADEA claims are relatively unsuccessful. A random review of 100 court of appeals decisions in 1992–1993 showed that more than 90 percent either dismissed the plaintiff's complaint or gave summary judgment for the employer without trial. ADEA also provides for attorney's fees, injunctive relief, and if discrimination is "wilful," punitive damages equal to compensatory damages. For example, in *Malarkey v. Texaco, Inc.*,[24] after 10 years of litigation a jury found that the employer had wilfully failed to promote a secretary in retaliation for filing an EEOC claim, and assessed damages of $65,000. The court doubled it to a judgment of $130,000, awarded $268,000 in attorney's fees, and ordered the employer to reinstate the secretary's job two grades above the level she was at when discharged. On appeal, Texaco argued that it was arbitrary for the court to assume the plaintiff would have had two promotions in the 10-year period, but the court said:

There is no exacting calculus that can be employed to pinpoint the correct remedy. Rather, this is a process where uncertainties are endemic. . . . Any uncertainty as to how far the remedy should reach in order to provide relief is the result of Texaco's unlawful retaliation; Texaco should not be the beneficiary of that uncertainty. The wrongdoer does not become the beneficiary of his own wrongful conduct.

Equal Pay Act. The Equal Pay Act of 1963[25] addresses only the narrow issue of discrimination in compensation because of sex. It was enacted to end the common practice of paying women less than men working the same jobs and mandates *equal pay for equal work regardless of sex*. "Equal" means *substantially equal*, not identical. Equal work means work requiring substantially similar "skill, effort, and responsibility" that is performed under similar working conditions. Thus, under the Act, male and female flight attendants must be paid the same (with certain permissible differences for non-sex-related factors such as seniority or merit) but male truck drivers and female secretaries need not be. The EEOC enforces the Equal Pay Act, and violations are a type of sex discrimination actionable under Title VII.

Comparable worth. The Equal Pay Act requires equal pay for *equal* work—not for *comparable* work. The *comparable worth theory* (also called "pay equity") holds that certain jobs have traditionally been underpaid because they have been held largely by women. Advocates of comparable worth argue that it is illegal sex discrimination to continue to pay "women's jobs" less than jobs that are different (and thus not addressed by the Equal Pay Act) but that require no more skill, effort, or responsibility. The Supreme Court has not yet resolved the question. But in *County of Washington v. Gunther*,[26] the Court at least opened the door to the comparable worth theory by holding that sex discrimination claims under Title VII are not limited to those recognized by the Equal Pay Act, and that sex discrimination in compensation could exist even where the jobs being compared are not substantially equal as required by the Act. To date, courts have frowned on comparable worth theory.

Americans with Disabilities Act (ADA). Effective in 1992, employers of fifteen or more persons may not refuse to hire a disabled person unless the applicant cannot perform the essential functions of the job. Fear of absenteeism or increased insurance costs is not a basis for refusal to hire. However, after a job offer has been extended, the employer may require a medical exam to determine if the applicant can perform the essential job functions, and if not, the offer of employment may be rescinded. The ADA defines disability as (1) a physical or mental impairment that substantially limits one or more

---

[23]*Western Air Lines Inc. v. Creswell*, 472 U.S. 400 (1985), upheld employer policy and FAA regulations establishing mandatory retirement at age 60 for pilots and engineers as a bona fide occupational qualification (BFOQ) based on safety considerations. ADEA Sec. 4(f)(1) provides an exception to coverage of the Act where age is a BFOQ reasonably necessary to the normal operation of a particular business.

[24]983 F.2d 1204 (Cal. 2d 1992).

[25]29 USC 49.

[26]452 U.S. 151 (1981).

major life activities, (2) a *record* of such impairment, or (3) *being regarded* as having such impairment. AIDS is specifically covered as a disability but conditions arising from illegal drug use are not.

An employer must provide a disabled person reasonable accommodation (if it is available to the employer without undue hardship) in order to enable the disabled person to perform the job—for example, installing ramps and bathroom aids. EEOC rules, issued to implement the ADA, bar employers from providing unequal health benefits to employees with disabilities or chronic illnesses. EEOC filed the first suit to enforce its rules (the day after they were announced) on behalf of a man with AIDS.

The ADA requires employers to focus on people's *abilities* rather than on their disabilities. For example, an employer who asks job applicants to respond orally or in writing to inquiries about past medical history—including treatment for drug abuse or alcoholism, previously filed workers' compensation or health insurance claims, absenteeism because of illness, or treatment for mental illness—risks being charged with discrimination against persons with disabilities. In any formal hearing on such charges, asking such questions may be cited as evidence of intent to discriminate. Officials administering the ADA have suggested that even running a "help wanted" newspaper ad listing only a telephone number could be cited in a lawsuit as evidence that the employer has a bias against the hearing-impaired. It is predictable that the ADA will be much litigated in the future.

Wrongful Discharge. **Wrongful discharge** cases fall into three categories: (1) breach of written contract, (2) bad faith breach of contract, and (3) tortious discharge, which includes public policy violations. Among the states there are many statutes and some court decisions which prohibit discharges in retaliation for a variety of employee actions, including filing workers' compensation claims and **whistle blowing** (reporting an employer violation of law to government officials). These categories are discussed in Chapter 35.

Many federal laws that create regulatory agencies impose penalties on employers who engage in retaliatory discharge for a protected employee action such as refusing to operate unsafe equipment or reporting violations of the minimum wage law.

WAGE AND HOUR LAWS

In addition to collective bargaining and equal employment, state and federal laws regulate wages and working conditions.

The Fair Labor Standards Act of 1938 (FLSA)[27] establishes a federal minimum wage, mandates extra pay for overtime work, and regulates the employment of children. It applies to all employers whose business affects interstate commerce, but it exempts certain employees from its minimum wage and overtime provisions. These employees include executive, administrative, and professional personnel, outside salespeople, and the employees of certain small retail establishments and farms. Congress periodically adjusts the minimum wage rate, which was fixed at $4.25 per hour as of 1991. Employers must pay employees at least that amount per hour for the 40 hours in a workweek. Overtime hours—that is, hours in excess of 40 per week—must be compensated at one and a half times the employee's regular rate of pay, whether that rate is minimum wage or higher. In the calculation of hours worked, employers must include all hours "suffered or permitted to be worked," not just those formally scheduled or reflected on a time clock.

The child labor provisions of the FLSA are designed to protect minors from dangerous or unduly rigorous working conditions and to ensure that they have an opportunity to pursue their education. The Act, with certain limited exceptions, altogether prohibits the employment of children under the age of 14 and forbids the employment of children under 18 in hazardous occupations.

The FLSA is enforced by the Department of Labor and by private suits in federal or state courts. Employers who violate the minimum

[27]29 USC 201.

wage and overtime provisions of the Act must pay injured employees all back wages due, with an additional, equal sum as liquidated damages. Wilful violations of any FLSA provisions are punishable by fines and even imprisonment. In *Donovan v. Hudson Stations, Inc.*[28] the Secretary of Labor obtained a $10 million judgment against the employer for wilful violations of the FLSA—one of the highest awards ever obtained.

WORKERS' COMPENSATION

Before enactment of workers' compensation laws, employees who were injured in the workplace or who contracted job-related diseases received no monetary compensation unless they could prove their employer's negligence and, in addition, overcome three iron-clad employer defenses: (1) the employee, as an implied covenant of the employment contract, had *assumed the risk* and hazards of the job; (2) the accident was caused by a *fellow servant*, not the employer; and (3) the employee's own *contributory negligence* was a cause of the accident. All states responded to this injustice by passing workers' compensation laws.

Coverage; AOE and COE

Generally, the workers' compensation laws reimburse employees for losses sustained because of work-related injury or disease regardless of who, if anyone, was at fault. Under most statutes, a work-related injury is defined as one *arising out of employment (AOE)* and in the *course of employment (COE)*. These terms are similar to *scope of employment* in agency law (see Chapter 38) but with this important difference: *Because the statutory policy of workers' compensation laws is to provide extensive coverage, courts interpret AOE and COE much more broadly than the agency law concept of "scope of employment."* For example, an intercity truck driver who was struck and injured by an auto after leaving his truck and crossing the street to a café for lunch has been held to be AOE and COE and entitled to workers' compensation. If the driver had been an office employee crossing the street to the same café, under the "lunch hour" rule of agency law, he would have been outside the scope of his authority in most states.

Fraud on the part of the worker may also result in ineligibility to receive workers' compensation benefits. In *Shaw's Supermarkets, Inc. v. Delgiacco*,[29] the employer told the worker that the job required a "strong, healthy back and involved repetitive heavy lifting." On his questionnaire, the employee answered no to questions asking if he had back pains, or ever had a back problem. In truth, he had previously filed and collected from six workers' compensation claims for his back. The court held that *where the employee knowingly makes fraudulent representations concerning his health, which are relied upon by the employer in hiring, and there is a causal link between the misrepresentation and the injury, the employee may not receive compensation, and can be ordered to reimburse previous payments based on his fraudulent claim.*

Amount of Compensation

There are two kinds of payments to disabled or injured workers: (1) *temporary disability payments*, which cover costs of medical care, lost income, and rehabilitation expenses, and (2) a *permanent disability award*, which is paid in a lump sum at the time the injured worker's condition has become stationary. At that time a disability rating is assigned to determine the amount of the award. The laws also provide for continuing benefit payments to spouses and children of workers who die from occupational disease or injury.

Exclusions

Workers' compensation laws apply to virtually all industrial and service employees as well as to state and local government employees. The major exclusions from coverage are of agricultural, domestic, and casual employees who may be working for more than one employer or whose work is sporadic.

---

[28] 26 WH Cases 795 (D.C. Kans. 1983).

[29] 575 N.E.2d 1115 (Mass. 1991).

Funding

The expense of workers' compensation is borne by employers, who ordinarily meet their obligation through purchase of insurance from private carriers. A few states require employers to insure in a state-operated insurance fund that apportions costs based on claims experience. Almost all states also allow employers to "self-insure"—that is, to establish, according to state regulations, a reserve fund from which claims are paid. Ordinarily, however, only large employers can afford to elect this method.

OCCUPATIONAL SAFETY AND HEALTH

Unlike workers' compensation statutes, which are designed to reimburse employees once workplace injuries have occurred, safety and health laws are intended to prevent injuries and promote job safety. The basic federal legislation is the Occupational Safety and Health Act (OSHA), which Congress enacted in 1970. OSHA's coverage is broad: It applies to virtually all private sector employees, with the exception of atomic energy workers and employees of very small agricultural enterprises. However, it does not apply to state and local government employees.

OSHA takes a comprehensive approach to workplace safety. It mandates the development of detailed health and safety standards by the Occupational Safety and Health Administration (also called OSHA), which is authorized to enforce such standards through complaint, inspection, and investigation procedures. The Act also established the National Institute for Occupational Safety and Health, which researches and develops standards and provides education and training in the safety field. The Act encourages each state to adopt proper standards; once it does, OSHA transfers jurisdiction to the state.

OSHA places employers under the general duty to provide a workplace free from "recognized hazards" that are causing or may cause death or serious physical harm. Recognized hazards include, for example, undue exposure to toxic substances and inoperable safety equipment. Employers must also conform to workplace air quality, noise level, and other standards. In addition, they must keep detailed records of job-related injuries and report serious accidents to OSHA, which may conduct unannounced workplace inspections to monitor compliance with the Act. Since the Supreme Court's decision in *Marshall v. Barlow's, Inc.*,[30] a search warrant is required for such inspections, if one is demanded by the employer.

OSHA inspectors can order immediate correction of violations or can issue citations fixing a date for correction. The law authorizes penalties up to $1,000 for each violation and as high as $10,000 for repeated or wilful violations. Employers can defend a charge before an administrative law judge, and then before the OSHA Review Commission, with a right to judicial review by the circuit court of appeals.

OSHA imposes responsibilities upon *employees*, who can be discharged for failure to comply with safety standards, but the Act protects employees' rights as well. Employees may not be discharged or discriminated against for filing a complaint, testifying, or exercising any other right under the Act. OSHA also enforces an employee's right to refuse to perform a task reasonably believed to pose serious risk of injury or death.[31]

SUMMARY

In the interest of industrial peace, between 1930 and 1960 Congress passed the Norris-La Guardia Act to restrict injunctions and the NLRA (Wagner Act), as amended by the LMRA (Taft-Hartley Act) and LMRDA (Landrum-Griffin Act), to foster collective bargaining.

The 1964 Civil Rights Act (Title VII) bans discrimination in employment because of race, color, religion, sex, or national origin. It is proved by "disparate treatment" or "disparate impact" theories. Other acts—such as ADEA, EPA, ADA, and the Rehabilitation Act of 1973 as amended—also are aimed at discrimination. The FLSA establishes a minimum wage, requires

---

[30] 436 U.S. 307 (1978).

[31] *Whirlpool Corp. v. Marshall*, 445 U.S. 1 (1980).

overtime pay for hours worked in excess of 40 per week, and regulates the work of minors.

Workers' compensation laws reimburse employees, regardless of fault, for losses from work-related disease and accidents, and provide benefits to the spouses and families of workers who die from occupational disease or injury. OSHA focuses on workplace safety and requires employers to maintain a working environment that conforms to safety standards. The Occupational Safety and Health Administration enforces the Act, and encourages the states to adopt safety standards.

REVIEW QUESTIONS

1. What was the purpose of the Norris-La Guardia Act?

2. (a) What was the goal of the NLRA? (b) How was it accomplished?

3. How was the NLRA changed by (a) the Taft-Hartley Act and (b) the LMRDA?

4. (a) What are unfair labor practices? (b) Give five examples.

5. Distinguish between mandatory and permissive bargaining subjects.

6. Define "discrimination in employment."

7. How do disparate treatment and disparate impact differ?

8. (a) Differentiate between Title VII's duty not to discriminate and affirmative action. (b) What is "reverse discrimination"?

9. (a) Distinguish between "equal pay for equal work" and "equal pay for comparable work." (b) Which is legally mandated?

10. What duties does OSHA impose on employers and on employees?

CASE PROBLEMS

1. Wood, a member of Local Union, filed suit claiming that because of his opposition to union actions, Local had violated his rights under the LMRDA by discriminating against him in job referrals at its hiring hall. He also claimed that such conduct violated the International Constitution as well as Local's bylaws, and claimed that as a union member he had a right to sue for breaches of the constitution and bylaws, since they were contracts conferring benefits on him. The trial court dismissed all claims against Local, and Wood appealed. Did Wood have a right to sue Local for breach of contract under the LMRDA?

2. After an election campaign, Drivers Union became the bargaining representative for Otis Co. production employees. Bargaining between company and union led to a tentative agreement for a wage increase. The union representative told the company's employees that the raise would not become effective until the contract was signed and that the contract would not be signed until 80 percent of the employees completed applications for union membership and checkoff dues authorizations (instructions to the company for automatic payroll deduction of union dues). Out of eighty-three workers, sixty-two joined Drivers and signed checkoff authorizations. Did the union commit an unfair labor practice? If so, what type?

3. Litton, Inc.'s, company policy was not to employ persons who had been arrested several times for other than minor traffic offenses. The policy applied to all applicants regardless of race. Gregory, a black, applied for employment as a mechanic and was hired. When he disclosed the fact that he had been arrested fourteen times, Litton withdrew its offer. Gregory claimed a violation of Title VII in that Litton's seemingly neutral policy had the effect of denying black applicants an equal opportunity for employment. At trial, Gregory proved that blacks are arrested substantially more often than whites in proportion to their numbers. What must Litton prove to negate the inference of discrimination? Decision? Explain.

4. Matthews, Hampton, Slack, and Murphy were employees in the bonding and coating department of Havens, Inc. Although their work ordinarily involved only light cleanup, one day their supervisor told them to suspend production and begin a general cleanup of the bonding and coating department. The assignment involved hard and possibly dangerous work such as cleaning light fixtures and scraping hard resin off the floor. The supervisor excused Murphy, who was white and had less seniority than the others, who were black; he then called in another employee, Hale, who was also black, to perform the cleanup work. When the four refused, they were fired. Did Havens discriminate illegally against the employees because of race?

5. Ron Brook was a schoolteacher and member of a church whose tenets require members to refrain from secular employment during designated holy days, a practice that caused him to miss approximately 6 days of school per year. Under the collective bargaining agreement between the school board and Brook's union, teachers were granted 3 days' annual leave to observe religious holidays but were not permitted to use for religious observance any accumulated sick leave, 3 days of which were normally available for other "necessary personal business." Accordingly, Brook had to either work or take unpaid leave for three additional religious holidays. When the school board rejected Brook's repeated requests to use personal business leave for the extra religious days or to receive full pay while bearing the cost of a substitute himself, Brook filed suit alleging that the school board had failed to reasonably accommodate his religious observance. How did the Supreme Court rule, and why?

6. Security officers and housekeeping employees of Mercy Hospital were required to change into uniforms on the hospital's premises. The employees were required to wear their uniforms while at work but were not permitted to wear their uniforms to work. Does the FLSA require compensation for the time spent changing clothes?

7. Osborne, Inc., was charged with an OSHA violation when an employee working on a scaffold four floors above the ground without a safety belt fell to his death during a gust of wind. The employer proved that: it provided safety belts on its scaffolds, its work rules required their use, its regular safety meetings stressed the importance of safety belt requirements, and it terminated employees for noncompliance with the rules. Did the employer violate OSHA?

CHAPTER 49

Consumer Law

As measured by the value of goods and services sold, the United States is without question the largest consumer market in the world. Sheer market size alone creates an indirect relationship between the producer of goods and services and the consumer.

Complicated, multichanneled systems of delivering goods and services encircle the U.S. consumer landscape. A single, mundane consumer purchase, such as a tube of toothpaste, involves a multitude of market participants that help make the transaction possible—from the toothpaste producer, through layers of distributors and wholesalers, possibly through a chain food or drug warehousing system, ultimately to the retail shelf and to the consumer. Simultaneously, other market participants are likely to be involved—such as advertising firms, market research firms, firms handling consumer database information, and promotion and fulfillment houses.

In a market environment with so many participants, things can and do go wrong in the delivery of consumer satisfaction. Usually, when things go awry, standing systems created by the participants themselves rectify the problem. For example, a majority of companies with sales over $10 million annually have 800 telephone numbers to handle consumer gripes.[1] Because the success of most ongoing businesses depends on repeat business and a good reputation, market pressures enforce good conduct on most market participants.

Unfortunately, market pressures alone have shown themselves to be insufficient to protect consumers. The market power of an individual consumer is minuscule when compared with the market power of even a single large producer. Such disparity of power can lead to dissatisfied and injured consumers. Moreover, modern communications and computer technology has contributed to a disparity between the consumer's ability and that of other market participants to collect and disseminate information, a situation which has resulted in consumer abuse and injury. Accordingly, there is an accumulating body of laws that can be variously deemed consumer law.

These laws are not to be confused with laws which address harms to the marketplace, such as monopolies and unfair competition, as covered in previous chapters. Rather, the laws organized around the *concept of consumer injury*

[1] P. Sellers, "How to Handle Consumer Gripes," *Fortune* (October 24, 1988), p. 92.

focus on the nonbusiness buyer or end user of goods and services—the consumer. The concept encompasses not only physical harm to consumers but also harms to consumers' economic interests (e.g., a home improvement swindle) and right-based interests (e.g., a personal privacy invasion by a debt collector). The scope of the concept of consumer injury is very broad. At the one extreme, it includes substantial physical, economic, or right-based harm to an individual consumer or a few consumers, such as a rare, but life-threatening allergic reaction arising from the mislabeling of a food ingredient. At the other extreme, it includes minor injury to many consumers, such as the inconvenience caused by broad-scale use of automated telephone solicitations during evening and night hours. The consumer injury can arise from market participants in the direct trail of delivery of goods and services to the consumer or from market participants that provide supplies or services to those in the trail. Examples of the latter are debt collectors, credit reporting firms, and marketing research firms.

This chapter is divided into two sections—state consumer laws and federal law and regulation. As you read the chapter, keep in mind that many state and federal laws overlap. Consequently, it is possible for a business to run afoul of more than one law for the same act causing consumer injury. Moreover, it is common for state laws to be more stringent than federal laws, but such state-to-state variations in the law will not be covered here.

STATE LAW

Historically, states and localities were the principal regulators of commercial activities within their borders. Unless a law was particularly onerous so as to infringe upon a federally protected right or to restrict interstate commerce, states and localities were basically free to set the rules under which business could be conducted. Such laws are many and varied. This section outlines the major areas of state law which are used to address consumer injury.

Common Law

An action in common law is perhaps the most long-standing legal avenue for redress of consumer injury. Common law actions, however, are best suited for dealing with substantial individual consumer injury or for class actions which represent groups of consumers who have suffered basically the same injury. Class actions are particularly suitable when each individual consumer injury is relatively minor but when compounded becomes a sufficiently large injury to a group of consumers as to merit a lawsuit. Additionally, common law concepts are often the basis upon which consumers secure redress in small claims courts.

Among the most frequently brought common law causes of action to redress consumer injury are ones involving (1) misrepresentation, (2) breach of contract, and (3) products liability. Parts Two and Three of this text deal extensively with common law tort and contract concepts. Chapter 22 addresses the law of products liability. This subsection will provide some additional remarks either to clarify or reemphasize some important points.

Misrepresentation. In the consumer law context, it should be no surprise that misrepresentation is a frequent basis for a lawsuit. At bottom, such a cause of action arises when a consumer did not get what the consumer reasonably expected to get, and hence was injured. Misrepresentation can be either intentional (also known as common law "deceit" or "deception") or unintentional. Perhaps the most important element to keep in mind in this cause of action is that, whether the misrepresentation was intentional or not, the consumer must have *justifiably relied* on the material facts presented by a seller or provider and the injury must have occurred as a result of that reliance.

Let's say that Hapless invites BestX Exterminators to provide a quote for eradicating termites from Hapless's garage. While making the sales pitch, a representative from BestX tells Hapless that the television celebrity Talking Head also used BestX Exterminators for his

Hollywood home. After getting quotes from other exterminators, Hapless retains BestX for the extermination job on the basis of price, and BestX performs a satisfactory job. Sometime later, Hapless sees a television commercial in which Talking Head endorses one of BestX's competitors, reporting what a good job the competitor did at Talking Head's home. Even though the BestX representative made false statements to Hapless about Talking Head, Hapless does not have a cause of action against BestX because Hapless did not rely—and hence was not injured from—the false representation.

Unintentional misrepresentation (including unintentional nondisclosure) is different from intentional misrepresentation in more ways than the presence or absence of scienter (i.e., knowledge of making a false statement). And the difference can sometimes be confusing for the business law student. Unintentional misrepresentation seems like it ought always to be classified as a tort. In Chapter 22, for example, negligent misrepresentation is treated as a tort, but in that chapter the focus is upon products—goods. While it may seem logical to think about unintentional misrepresentation as something like the tort concept of negligence (injury resulting from an unintentional breach of a duty), modern courts generally treat unintentional misrepresentation involving the sale of consumer services as arising out of contract and warranty notions—even when there is no privity between the parties. (Privity refers to the relationship between contracting parties which historically was required for a cause of action in contract.)

In summary, intentional misrepresentation of a material fact upon which a consumer justifiably relies and which causes injury is a tort—common law deceit or deception. Unintentional misrepresentation which similarly causes consumer injury can be viewed either as a tort or as arising out of a breach of warranty or contract. Generally, if it involves chattels (goods), the action will sound in tort; if consumer services are involved, the action will sound in common law contract or warranty.

Common Law Contract. Consumer expectations are also based on contract and warranty, the breach of which can cause consumer dissatisfaction and injury. Causes of action and remedies for damages from such breaches can be based on common law contract concepts.

Part Three of this text covers common law contracts comprehensively. Worthy of reemphasis in this chapter on consumer law is that contracts for consumer services are governed by common law. Contracts for the sale of goods, however, are governed by the Uniform Commercial Code in all states but Louisiana.

Products Liability. Though the category of possible consumer legal action is organized under state common law in this chapter, the law of products liability is really an integrated body of law encompassing torts (negligence, strict liability, and misrepresentation theories) and sales law (the Uniform Commercial Code).

Worthy of reemphasis here is that the law of products liability is applicable for providing legal remedies for economic and physical injuries caused by defective goods—not services.

Statutes

Uniform Commercial Code. Part Three of this text devotes several chapters to the Uniform Commercial Code (UCC), which applies exclusively to goods, not services. Worth highlighting in this section are three important consumer-related aspects of the UCC.

1. *Good faith requirement.* Section 1-203 imposes an obligation of good faith in the performance or enforcement of every contract or duty within the UCC. While much attention is given to contracts between merchants in Part Three of this text, the good faith requirement also applies to sales contracts between merchants and consumers.

2. *Express and implied warranty provisions.* Sections 2-312 through 2-318 cover express and implied warranties. The Magnuson-Moss Warranty Act, discussed later in this chapter, makes specific provision for the operation of state law; most notably, it requires that warrantors advise consumers that state law (UCC) may prohibit certain warranty exclusions and may impose certain implied warranties. For a full understanding

of how the Magnuson-Moss Warranty Act operates, refer to pertinent sections of Part Three of this text.

3. *Nonenforcement of unconscionable contracts.* Section 2-302 of the UCC provides for a court to refuse to enforce or to limit the application of a contract which it finds, as a matter of law, unconscionable. Unconscionability has been defined in various ways. For purposes here, think of a contract as unconscionable if, in light of general business practices and needs of the marketplace, the contract is so one-sided as to shock the conscience. The principle upon which nonenforcement of unconscionability rests is one of avoiding oppression and unfair surprise in contractual relations.

Little FTCs. In 1970, the Council of State Governments recommended for adoption by individual states the Unfair Trade Practices and Consumer Protection Act. Similar to and overlapping with federal legislation on the subject, the Act provides for public enforcement against unfair and deceptive practices within the states themselves, and also provides for private remedies. The Unfair Trade Practices and Consumer Protection Act is often referred to as the Little FTC Act, since it creates within adopting states mini versions of the Federal Trade Commission, or "little FTCs." A majority of states have enacted laws the same as or similar to this legislation.

Lemon Laws. For most consumers, the purchase of a new automobile represents one of the single largest expenditures for a consumer product. When things go wrong that are not fixed satisfactorily by the auto manufacturer or its agent, the economic injury to a single consumer can be substantial. Reacting to a public outcry for better consumer protection in automobile purchases, all but six states have adopted what are known as Lemon Laws to provide consumers with remedies over and above other legal remedies when manufacturers do not comply with their *express* warranties.

Lemon Laws vary from state to state and have been challenged on constitutional grounds several times, most notably as representing a burden upon interstate commerce. To date, Lemon Laws have survived all constitutional challenges.

A criticism of Lemon Laws is that in practice they discourage consumers from bringing formal legal action because it takes too long to secure remedy through the courts. In the case that follows, note that the automobile in question was purchased in late 1985, a request of refund was made in early 1986, but hearings on the legal claim in court did not take place until 1991.

CASE 49.1 **Harmon v. Chrysler Corporation** • 598 A.2d 696 (Del. Super. 1991)

FACTS The plaintiff, Joyce A. Harmon, a resident of Delaware, purchased a new 1985 Plymouth Horizon in September 1985 from a Pennsylvania dealership, but registered the new car in Delaware. Harmon soon began having trouble with the car stalling. By November 1985 she had returned the car five times to correct the stalling problem. In January 1986 she asked Chrysler to accept return of the car and to refund the price. She also requested arbitration, which resulted in an arbitration order in March 1986 for Chrysler to repair the car. In May 1986 Harmon reported that the condition had not been corrected. A second arbitration, in July 1986, resulted in a second order to repair the car. In September 1986 Harmon's attorney demanded refund, and Chrysler refused to refund or replace the car. In October 1986 the car was returned for repairs and remained in repair for 38 days. In November 1986 the car was towed in for repairs, and was not returned for a month. On the day of its return, the car stalled, causing the brakes to fail which

CASE 49.1 Continued

then caused an accident in which Ronald Harmon, husband and co-plaintiff, was injured. The car was towed to a Chrysler dealer in Delaware, where it remained until the car was repossessed by Chrysler Credit Corporation and subsequently sold.

The Harmons brought this action in Delaware Superior Court against Chrysler and various dealerships. Defendants moved for summary judgment on several grounds, including inapplicability of the Delaware Lemon Law and non-return of the automobile in question.

OPINION

TAYLOR, J. . . . The first issue is whether the Delaware Lemon Law applies to this car. [The Pennsylvania] salesman who handled the sale of the car knew that [Harmon] was a Delaware resident, that the car was to be titled in her name in Delaware, to be used for her personal and family use, and that [the Pennsylvania dealership] processed the paperwork for registering the car in Delaware. This is not denied.

The Lemon Law applies to "any passenger motor vehicle, except motorcycles, which is leased or bought in Delaware or registered by the Division of Motor Vehicles . . . [in Delaware]." . . . [T]his car is subject to the Lemon Law since . . . the sale contemplated registration of the car in Delaware. Therefore, this new car . . . is within the protection of the Delaware Lemon Law.

. . . [Chrysler's] position is [also] that [the Harmons] are not entitled to recover under the Lemon Law because they have not returned the car. . . .

It is true that the specific relief under the statute, [a refund of the price], is dependent upon the return of the car. However, each time [Harmon] made her request for refund, Chrysler denied the request and undertook to make further repairs. This happened on at least three occasions. While [Delaware law] does not permit an informal settlement procedure to be established by a manufacturer which a customer must follow before [getting a refund], the bar [against refund] is based upon the customer having "first resorted to such a procedure." It does not require repeated resort to such procedure which has proved ineffective. In a case such as this, after resorting to such procedure without relief, the manufacturer had a duty to accept the car and either refund the adjusted purchase price or replace the car with a new one. Upon receipt of the request from the plaintiffs, Chrysler had a duty to acknowledge that duty and provide plaintiffs with instructions on how and when to return the lemon car.

Under the Delaware Lemon Law after the manufacturer has attempted to repair the defect four times or has had the car for repair for a cumulative total of more than 30 days, the purchaser is entitled to either a new car or refund of the purchase price, at the election of the purchaser.

. . . Where a manufacturer breaches [the duty to instruct the purchaser on how and when to return the lemon car], it should not be permitted to assert the failure of the purchaser to return the car as a ban to the purchaser's suit for the benefits provided by the Lemon Law.

Based on the foregoing . . . , I conclude that defendants have failed to establish that they are entitled to summary judgment on the issues raised.

JUDGMENT

Motion denied.

Uniform Consumer Credit Code. Intended to bring uniformity to state consumer credit laws, the Uniform Consumer Credit Code (UCC) has been adopted in a minority of states. In the adopting states, this law governs interest rates, credit information disclosure (overlapping with the federal Truth in Lending Act, discussed later in the chapter), garnishment, door-to-door credit sales, and remedies.

In addition, all states regulate interest rates in credit transactions occurring within their borders. These laws, called Usury Laws, specify a maximum allowable interest rate, and such interest rates vary from state to state.

FEDERAL LAW AND REGULATION

Product Warranty—Magnuson-Moss Warranty Act

While the warranty provisions of the Uniform Commercial Code have proved to be beneficial, particularly in cases involving products liability, the UCC requirements fall short of making product warranties "consumer friendly." Specifically, the UCC does not require warranties to be stated in language that is easily understandable by nonlawyers. As a consequence, it is possible for a seller of goods to state warranties that conform to the UCC but that simultaneously are confusing and misleading—even deceptive—to ordinary consumers.

To rectify this possibility and to eliminate abuses in the marketplace, Congress enacted the Magnuson-Moss Warranty Act in 1975. The Act has two broad purposes:

1 To improve the adequacy of warranty information available to consumers, to prevent deception, and accordingly to improve competition in the marketing of consumer products
2 To encourage product warrantors to establish procedures for the informal settlement of disputes with consumers

The Magnuson-Moss Warranty Act applies *only* to consumer products, defined as any items of tangible personal property that are distributed in commerce and are normally used for personal, family, or household purposes. This definition is also intended to include products which are to be attached or installed in real property, such as a water heater or a cooking range. While this law enables the Federal Trade Commission (FTC) with rulemaking and enforcement powers, a person—whether as an individual or a class—may bring suit in state or federal court for actual damages and other appropriate remedies. However, if a product warrantor has established informal settlement procedures which under warranty require that a consumer use such procedures before going to court, the consumer is bound to the requirement. The Act also empowers the FTC and the U.S. Attorney General to bring suit to enjoin a warrantor from making a deceptive warranty or from violating any other prohibitions contained in the Act.

The most important requirements of the Magnuson-Moss Warranty Act are summarized below. Note that the Act *does not* require that a consumer product or any of its components be warranted. If a seller does provide a warranty, then the Act's requirements are imposed. Nor does the Magnuson-Moss Warranty Act replace the warranty provisions of the UCC; basically it operates in addition to the UCC. However, the Magnuson-Moss Act nullifies any conflicting warranty legislation.

Disclosure Requirements—Contents and Time of Disclosure. The Magnuson-Moss Warranty Act requires the maker of a written warranty on a consumer product to disclose fully and conspicuously in a single document in simple, understandable language the items of information required by the FTC. Specifically, for products costing more than $15, the FTC requires the following information:

1 If the written warranty is not to be extended to every consumer who owns the product during the term of the warranty, the identity of the person or persons (e.g., "original owner") to whom the warranty is extended.
2 A clear description of the parts or product characteristics covered and, where necessary for clarification, what is excluded from the warranty.

3 A statement of what the warrantor will do to correct a defect, malfunction, or failure of the product to conform to the warranty, including items and services the warrantor will provide or pay for. For clarification, the warrantor must state the items or services that it *will not* pay for or provide.
4 The warranty start date (if different from the purchase date) and the duration of the warranty term.
5 A step-by-step explanation of how the consumer may obtain warranty service. If the consumer is required to register the warranty in writing (such as with a registration form), the warranty must disclose this fact.
6 Information about any informal dispute settlement procedure (such as arbitration) used by the warrantor.
7 Any limitations on the duration of implied warranties (such as those arising from the Uniform Commercial Code), together with the following statement:

> Some states do not allow limitations on how long an implied warranty lasts, so the above limitation may not apply to you.

> A limitation on the duration of an implied warranty must appear on the face of the written warranty.

8 Any limitations or exclusions of damages, together with a statement that some states do not permit such limitations.
9 The following statement:

> This warranty gives you specific legal rights, and you may also have other rights which vary from state to state.

The text of a warranty must be made readily available to a prospective buyer *prior to the sale*. The availability of this warranty applies to all sellers—including door-to-door salespeople—of the warranted consumer product.

Labeling Requirement—"Full" versus "Limited" Warranty.
The Magnuson-Moss Warranty Act also requires that any written warranty of a consumer product costing more than $10[2] be clearly and conspicuously designated as either a "full warranty" or a "limited warranty," unless otherwise exempted by a FTC rule.

A consumer product can be labeled as having a "full warranty" if it meets four minimum standards:

1 Where the product is defective or fails to conform to the written warranty, the warrantor must remedy the product within a reasonable time and without charge.
2 The warranty *may not* impose any limitation of the duration of any implied warranty (e.g., UCC-implied warranties). The warranty, however, may limit the duration of the warranty term (e.g., "full 12-month warranty").
3 Any clause excluding or limiting consequential damages for breach of warranty must conspicuously appear on the face of the warranty.
4 If the product (or a component part) contains a defect or continues to malfunction after a reasonable number of attempts by the warrantor to remedy the product, the warrantor must permit the consumer to elect either a refund of the purchase price or a replacement of the product (or component part).

A written warranty of a consumer product that does not conform to the four minimum standards is a "limited warranty" and must be so labeled. For example, if a consumer is required to fill out and return a warranty registration, it is a limited warranty. Similarly, if a consumer is required to pay for any service or part, the warranty is limited.

Product Integrity

The product integrity area of federal regulation contains perhaps the most long-standing of federal consumer protection laws—those governing

---

[2]This $10 cost threshold is established in the Act itself. Earlier in this section, the cost threshold for disclosure requirements was stated as $15. The $15 amount is set by FTC rule as allowed by the Act, which itself specifies a minimum $5 cost threshold but also allows the FTC to set a higher threshold amount.

foods and drugs. Treated as a single category, foods and drugs are important not only because consumers ingest them but also because the category today accounts for roughly one quarter of consumer retail spending. Statutory provisions date back to almost a century ago. More recently, in the early 1970s, additional laws dealing with the safety of nonfood products were put into place.

Safety of Food, Drugs, and Cosmetics. Described as an "amalgam of provisions enacted by Congress over a period of almost 80 years,"[3] current statutes governing food, drugs, and cosmetics find their origins in the 1890s and early 1900s in the political response to muckraker reports of unsanitary food handling and to scientific reports on harmful preservatives used in foods. The first federal legislation in the area was the Pure Food and Drug Act of 1906. However, because the 1906 statute was vague in its provisions and because it did not include the product category of cosmetics, Congress enacted the Food, Drug, and Cosmetic Act of 1938. The Food and Drug Administration (FDA) draws most of its legal authority from this Act and subsequent amendments. In short, the FDA is charged with the task of ensuring that foodstuffs are safe and wholesome; that drugs are not only safe but also effective; and that foods, drugs, and cosmetics are produced in sanitary conditions.

The FDA is given broad standard-setting, inspection, and enforcement authority, and is also given authority to regulate the marketing and labeling of foods,[4] prescription and over-the-counter drugs, cosmetics, medical devices, food ingredients, and additives.

The enforcement authority of the FDA includes product seizure, product recall, injunctions, and criminal prosecution. In addition, because statutes covering foods, drugs, and cosmetics impose various duties upon those in the production and marketing of such products, these statutes also provide the basis for private rights of action against nonconforming producers and sellers.

Product Safety. Enacted in 1972, the Consumer Product Safety Act created the Consumer Product Safety Commission (CPSC), which is responsible for creating and issuing product safety standards, gathering information about product hazards, and enforcing those standards. The jurisdiction of the CPSC extends to all consumer products except ones specified by law as under the jurisdiction of other federal agencies—products such as foods, drugs, cosmetics, tobacco, firearms, alcohol, motor vehicles, and pesticides.

An unusual feature of the regulatory scheme of the CPSC is that it maintains databanks on consumer injuries from products—information accumulated from consumers, producers, and sellers. The CPSC uses this information for formulating standards and for substantiation when issuing bans on the distribution and sale of dangerous products.

Moreover, the Consumer Product Safety Act obligates retailers, distributors, and manufacturers with the affirmative duty to report product hazards to the CPSC, a duty the failure of which can result not only in civil penalties but also in criminal penalties.

Similar to the FDA, the CPSC has a wide range of enforcement options, including product seizure and bans. The statute also allows for private rights of action to sue for enforcement of CPSC rules and for recovery of damages over statutorily specified amounts.

Credit

With the rapid growth and acceptance of the credit card and other convenient forms of consumer credit in the last two decades, credit itself has become a consumer product. Before the late 1960s, when the federal government began enacting legislation involving various aspects of credit, state laws governed the area. Those state laws, however, were insufficient to handle marketplace abuses involving credit transactions. The following are among the most important federal laws in this area.

---

[3] Richard Merrill and Peter Hutt, FOOD AND DRUG LAW (1980), p. 2.

[4] The U.S. Department of Agriculture, however, has jurisdiction over fish, meat, and poultry.

> **BOX 49.1**
> **The Consumer Product Safety Commission Takes Action on Disposable Lighters**
>
> After a final round of comment and rulemaking on a proposed rule,* the CPSC voted unanimously in June 1993 to require that manufacturers make disposable butane lighters child-resistant. Hailed by observers as the single most life-saving and injury-avoiding action in the commission's history, the rule will take effect in the summer of 1994.
>
> The Commission estimated that between 1980 and 1985 residential fires caused by children playing with disposable butane lighters resulted in an annual average loss of 120 lives and 750 injuries. Other sources estimate even higher incidence of injury and death from fires caused by disposable lighters.†
>
> Accounting for 95 percent of the 500 million lighters sold annually in the United States, disposable butane lighters may end up costing between 5 cents to 20 cents more to accommodate the new safety regulations.‡ ∎
>
> *16 CFR Part 1145, Proposed Rule to Regulate under the Consumer Product Safety Act Risks of Injury Associated with Lighters That Can Be Operated by Children, August 17, 1992.
>
> †See, e.g., "Briefly," *Los Angeles Times* (June 10, 1993), Part 2, p. 2, col. 1. The article reports 150 deaths and more than 1,000 injuries annually.
>
> ‡"Short Cuts," *Newsday* (June 10, 1993), p. 46.

Truth in Lending Act. Until the enactment of the Truth in Lending Act (TILA) in 1968, consumer credit firms had wide latitude on how they could represent the terms of their credit lending in loan contracts and in other communications—namely, for advertising and promotion of consumer credit products. In those pre-TILA days, consumers were often confused about the credit terms offered and encountered difficulty in comparison of credit terms when choosing among consumer lenders.

The principal features of TILA are that it governs both the content and style of communication that a consumer lender can make. TILA imposes requirements on what information must be disclosed, and the format of such disclosures—not only in the lending agreements themselves, but also in advertising and promotional representations. The objective served by the law is to facilitate greater consumer understanding—through disclosure and uniformity of disclosure—of the credit arrangements that consumers enter into and to avert consumer injury caused by lenders that would otherwise take advantage of consumer misunderstanding of and confusion over credit terms.

TILA applies to consumer creditors such as banks, savings and loan associations, credit card companies, and businesses that extend credit to consumers for the purchase of the business's goods or services. Also, TILA applies only to debtors who are natural-born persons, and accordingly does not apply to business debtors such as corporations and partnerships. Except in situations discussed later in this subsection, extensions of credit greater than $25,000 are exempted from TILA requirements.

The Federal Reserve Board is the federal agency responsible for issuing the rules and regulations under TILA. The most important disclosure rules are contained in Regulation Z.

Regulation Z. The precise disclosure requirements for consumer creditors set out by Regulation Z vary according to the type of credit arrangement—slightly different rules apply to revolving credit, for example, than to an installment car loan. Common to all credit arrangements, however, is the requirement that disclosures be made clearly and conspicuously and be in a form that consumers may retain for their own records. Additional requirements pertain to the reporting of:

- Finance charges, including the annual percentage rate (APR)
- The amount or amounts being financed
- Penalties—either for prepayment or for late payment
- Terms and dates of payment
- Methods of computing charges

Exceptions to the $25,000 maximum. As noted earlier, TILA applies to consumer credit transactions involving amounts less than

$25,000. However, TILA applies to amounts greater than $25,000 if the credit transaction involves (1) the sale of real estate, (2) the taking of a security interest in real property (e.g., a home equity loan or a loan for home improvements provided by the developer), or (3) the taking of a security interest in personal property which is used as a dwelling (e.g., a mobile home).

Additional rights and protections. Though TILA is principally a consumer credit disclosure law, it also provides for other rights and protections. Important among them are the following:

1 *Specific rescission rights.* For credit arrangements involving a creditor's taking of a security interest in real or personal property which serves as the debtor's dwelling, TILA provides for a 3-day rescission right. This right allows the potential debtor to rescind the credit transaction within 3 business days, a sort of cooling-off period. However, the right does not apply to home mortgages or to loans intended for the acquisition or construction of a home. This rescission right is intended to protect a consumer from being "hyped" into the purchase of home improvement materials and services which are financed by credit arrangements whereby the seller takes a security interest in the consumer's dwelling. The 3-day period gives the consumer time to think things over without the immediate pressure of a salesperson.
2 *Credit card protection.* TILA places a cap of $50 on the maximum liability a consumer faces in the event of unauthorized use of a credit card.
3 *Advertising regulation.* Regulation Z provides rules which apply to the advertising of consumer credit products.
4 *Credit card billing errors and disputes.* An amendment to TILA, also known as the Fair Credit Billing Act of 1974, specifies requirements that a credit card issuer must follow in resolving billing disputes and fixing billing errors.

The principal federal enforcer of TILA is the FTC. However, TILA also allows private individual and class actions as well as enforcement from other federal agencies (such as the Department of Justice), particularly in situations involving intentional violations which carry criminal sanctions.

Debt Collection—The Fair Debt Collection Practices Act. In response to public outcry over abusive debt collection practices, Congress enacted the Fair Debt Collection Practices Act (FDCPA) in 1977. Intended to curb bullying practices of bill collectors (such as threats or harassing contact by telephone, in person, or to one's employer), the Act specifies prohibited debt collection conduct. However, the FDCPA generally does not apply to those who collect debts arising from their own consumer-oriented businesses (e.g., a retailer collecting on its own accounts). Rather, it focuses on those engaged in the consumer (versus commercial) debt collection business (e.g., the professional bill collector).

The FDCPA contains several important prohibitions and requirements:

1 If a consumer puts a debt collector on written notice (i.e., notifying in writing versus notifying by telephone), the collector must stop communication intended to persuade the consumer to pay the debt.
2 The bill collector is required to provide essential information promptly regarding the debt in question. Moreover, if a consumer challenges the debt in writing and within 30 days, the collector is prohibited from attempting to collect the debt until the consumer is provided with a written verification of the debt.
3 Bill collectors are generally prohibited from communicating with a debtor's friends, family, neighbors, and employers—except for the purpose of locating the debtor.
4 Once a bill collector is made aware that a consumer debtor is represented by an attorney, the bill collector is prohibited from communicating with the debtor.
5 Unless a debtor consents, bill collectors are prohibited from communicating with the debtor at work, at inconvenient times and places, and in unusual circumstances.

6. Threats from bill collectors are generally prohibited. Any threat of violence is strictly prohibited. Intimidations—such as threats to inform employers, relatives, or friends of the unpaid debt—are also prohibited.
7. Harassment is prohibited. Conduct such as repeated visits to a debtor's home or repeated telephone calls are forbidden. Abusive activities, such as slurs of moral character or offensive language, are also prohibited.
8. In communicating with a debtor, bill collectors are prohibited from using any language or symbol on envelopes or telegrams which shows that they are in the debt collection business. This prohibition is intended to avoid injury to a consumer's reputation resulting from third parties (e.g., neighbors) seeing an envelope and forming an adverse opinion.
9. Bill collectors are prohibited from using false or misleading materials or practices. For example, it is unlawful for a bill collector to pose as an opinion pollster in order to gain access to a debtor and then to attempt to collect the debt.

The FTC is the principal federal enforcement agency of this law. However, the FDCPA provides for consumers to have a private right of action and includes provisions for recovery of attorney's fees.

Equal Credit Opportunity Act. Congress passed the Equal Credit Opportunity Act (ECOA) in 1974 to prohibit discrimination on the basis of sex or marital status in credit transactions. The law was later amended to also prohibit discrimination on the basis of race, age, national origin, and religion. In addition, it prohibits economic discrimination against persons who derive their income from public assistance.

As with TILA, rules under the ECOA are issued by the Federal Reserve Board and enforced principally by the FTC.

Unfair and Deceptive Practices

The Federal Trade Commission (FTC) was created in 1914 by the Federal Trade Commission Act, but it was not until 1938, with the passage of the Wheeler-Lea Amendments, that the FTC was granted jurisdiction over protecting consumers from injury caused by unfair and deceptive commercial practices. Before these amendments, the FTC was required by law to establish that trade practices were anticompetitive in order to impose its regulatory sanctions.

The FTC, moreover, has long been viewed as one of the most political of administrative agencies. Though the FTC has broad enforcement discretion of its comprehensive trade regulations, the agency's history has been marked by politically motivated funding cutbacks and congressional trimming of its authority. Most notably, in the FTC Improvements Act of 1980, Congress, among other things, restricted the agency's rulemaking powers over television advertising to children and also restricted the agency's power to regulate the funeral industry.

Under its power to make rules and to enforce against unfair and deceptive practices, the FTC has established a large body of trade regulation rules (TRRs) which govern many things. For example, there are rules which regulate the use of the words "new" and "free" in advertising and on package labels. Similarly, there are rules prohibiting "bait-and-switch" practices, in which a seller lures a prospective customer by advertising a particular product at an attractive price and once the customer is in the store substitutes a different product for the advertised one or persuades the customer to buy a different product, one usually more profitable to the seller.

In addition to technical TRRs, the FTC employs two overarching standards, one for deception and another for unfairness. These have been in effect since the early to mid-1980s and reflect the policies of President Reagan and President Bush. Critics of the unfairness and deception standards have asserted that they may be too lenient on business and not protective enough of consumers. Under the Clinton administration, politics may again change the FTC's standards for deception and unfairness. What follows are the current standards.

FTC Deception Standard. "[T]he Commission will find deception if there is a representation, omission or practice that is likely to mislead the consumer acting reasonably in the circumstances, to the consumer's detriment."[5]

In explaining this policy, the FTC has identified the three key elements of deception. They are:

1. Likelihood of misleadingness of a representation, omission, or practice. Specific examples include false statements, misleading price claims, sales of systematically defective or hazardous products, inadequate disclosure, bait-and-switch practices, and contract or warranty breaches.
2. Reasonableness of the consumer under the circumstances. Consumer reasonableness derives from what is commonly known as the "fool's test"—that is, if only a fool would believe it, it is not deceptive. This consumer reasonableness element eliminates absurd consumer claims as a basis for serious deception cases. In addition, it eliminates mere "puffing" in advertising and sales pitches as a deceptive practice. An example of mere "puffing" or "puffery" is a claim such as "Best Hot Dog in Town."
3. Materiality of the representation, omission, or practice. A representation, omission, or practice has to matter—to be important—to a consumer decision before it can be considered a source of injury or likelihood of injury.

Case 49.2, at the end of this section, illustrates an application of the FTC's deception standard.

FTC Unfairness Standard. "Unfairness analysis focuses on three criteria: (1) whether the practice creates a serious consumer injury; (2) whether this injury exceeds any offsetting consumer benefits; and (3) whether the injury was one that consumers could not reasonably have avoided."[6]

Unfairness analysis differs significantly from deception analysis. Unfairness, under the above standard, deals only with serious injury that consumers cannot reasonably avoid; more significantly, the standard imposes a cost-benefit balancing similar to risk utility in products liability law, as discussed in Chapter 22. Instead of balancing the risk of injury from a product with society's utility for that product, the FTC's unfairness test weighs the trade-offs involving compliance costs (such as the costs of providing more information to consumers) against countervailing benefits to competition and consumers. For example, a company would fail this balancing test if the extent of injury to consumers were greater than the cost of avoiding the injury.

Upon a finding of either unfairness or deception, the FTC has a number of remedies at its disposal. Among these remedies are (1) cease-and-desist orders; (2) consent orders (in which the party against which action is taken basically agrees to compliance before full adjudication takes place); (3) orders for corrective advertising (e.g., Warner-Lambert was ordered to advertise that its mouthwash Listerine did not cure colds after it was found that previous advertising contained unsubstantiated cold curative claims[7]); (4) monetary penalties; (5) restitution; and (6) specific injunctions.

---

[5]*Federal Trade Commission Policy Statement on Deception*, 45 Antitrust & Trade Reg. Rep. (BNA) 689 (1983).

[6]*In re International Harvester Company*, 104 FTC 949 (1984).

[7]See *Warner-Lambert Co. v. FTC*, 562 F.2d 749 (D.C. Cir. 1977). Some observers describe an order for corrective advertising as actually "a creative cease-and-desist order." See, e.g., Edmund Kitch and Harvey Perlman, LEGAL REGULATION OF THE COMPETITIVE PROCESS (1991), pp. 239–240.

CASE 49.2 In the Matter of Kraft, Inc.
• FTC Docket No. 9208 (1991 FTC LEXIS 38), January 30, 1991

FACTS Kraft, Inc., one of the largest food products companies in the United States, produces and markets a broad line of cheese and dairy products. One such product is Kraft Singles American Pasteurized Process Cheese Food (Kraft Singles), which consists of individual cellophane-wrapped slices of pasteurized process cheese food sold in various count packages.

Kraft is charged with violating Sections 5 and 12 of the Federal Trade Commission Act by materially misrepresenting the calcium content and relative calcium benefit of Kraft Singles in a series of nationally disseminated broadcast and print advertisements that ran from early 1985 through mid-1987.

The challenged advertisements are known as "Skimp" and the "Class Picture/5 ounce" ads, which were developed as part of Kraft's overall "Five Ounces of Milk" advertising campaign. Most advertisements in the "Five Ounces of Milk" campaign focused on the theme that a slice of Kraft Singles has five ounces of milk as an ingredient, while imitation slices use very little milk, or are made predominantly from vegetable oil and water.

The "Skimp" ads ran nationally, and featured the message that Kraft Singles have five ounces of milk per slice while imitation slices use "hardly any milk." The ads were designed to communicate the nutritional benefit of Kraft Singles by referring expressly to calcium in the ad copy as the key nutritional ingredient.

The "Class Picture/5 ounce" ads reflected a different creative strategy from the "Skimp" ads, and were intended to communicate that Kraft Singles are an "excellent source of calcium." These ads are not expressly comparative in that they do not mention imitation or substitute slices.

After administrative hearings, the administrative law judge (ALJ) found Kraft liable for making both of the alleged calcium claims, holding that the claims were material because they involved important health concerns, that the claims were objective product claims, and that they were false and unsubstantiated.

Kraft appealed from the ALJ's initial decision and order.

OPINION OWEN, Commissioner . . . We affirm liability under Sections 5 and 12 of the FTC Act.

Our analysis of the issues on appeal is presented below:

• • •

II. WERE THE CLAIMS MADE?

The Commission will deem an advertisement to convey a claim if consumers, acting reasonably under the circumstances, would interpret the advertisement to contain that message. For analytic purposes, the Commission often distinguishes between express claims and implied claims. . . . Express claims directly state the representation at issue. Implied claims are any claims that are not express. . . . Both express and implied claims can be deceptive.

Advertisers can be liable for misleading consumer by innuendo as well as by outright false statements.

**CASE 49.2
Continued**

The primary evidence of what claims an advertisement can convey to reasonable consumers consists of the advertisement itself. . . . We are often able to conclude that an advertisement contains an implied claim by evaluating the content of the ad and the circumstances surrounding it.

The challenged "Skimp" and "Class Picture/5 ounce" ads do not expressly state the alleged calcium claims.

The ALJ found that the reference in the "Skimp" ad copy to the precise amount of milk in a Kraft Single, together with the reference to calcium, can be interpreted as implying that a slice of Kraft Singles contains the same amount of calcium as five ounces of milk; because there is no mention that calcium is in fact lost in the processing of cheese, the "Skimp" ads convey the milk equivalency claim.

We agree that . . . the "Skimp" series . . . conveys an overall net impression that Kraft Singles contain the same amount of calcium as five ounces of milk.

We agree that the "Class Picture/5 ounce" ads contain elements substantially similar to the "Skimp" ad elements that convey the impression of milk equivalence.

• • •

III. WERE THE CLAIMS LIKELY TO MISLEAD REASONABLE CONSUMERS?

The standard by which advertising is judged is whether it is likely to mislead reasonable consumers; proof of actual deception is not required.

[W]e agree with the ALJ that it is reasonable to presume that a significant number of consumers are not aware that the calcium in five ounces of milk is reduced or lost during . . . processing . . . , and that they are also not aware that imitation cheese slices may be fortified with calcium. The implied calcium claims . . . are credence claims because consumers cannot readily determine . . . whether or not they are in fact providing the amount of calcium benefit implicitly promised. Therefore, a reasonable consumer would not be aware of these facts.

• • •

IV. WERE THE CLAIMS MATERIAL?

. . . A "material" misrepresentation is one that involves information that is important to consumers, and that is therefore likely to affect a consumer's choice of or conduct regarding a product. Proof of actual consumer injury is not required. The Commission presumes several types of claims to be material: express claims; implied claims where there is evidence that the seller intended to make the claim; and claims or omissions that significantly involve health, safety, or other areas with which reasonable consumers would be concerned.

The ALJ concluded that the calcium claims in the challenged advertisements are significant health claims and thus presumptively material.

We conclude that each of the implied calcium claims in this case is material.

JUDGMENT Affirmed. Cease-and-desist order issued.

Consumer Information and Privacy

The newest developments in consumer law center on information gathering and the individual's right to privacy. Issues involving how consumer information is gathered and used are presently making headlines.[8] In addition, consumers have become more militant in their intolerance of telemarketing intrusions into their homes, a development which has resulted in new federal laws.

Credit Reporting. In the past few years, federal laws relating to consumer credit information gathering and reporting have come under severe criticism by consumer groups.

As consumers in the United States have become more dependent upon consumer credit and have become more demanding of credit organizations to provide fast approvals of credit accounts, the credit reporting business has grown to more than $1 billion annually. Moreover, credit reports are also used in analyzing a person's suitability for employment, housing, and insurance—and for other types of decisions involving the person's record of financial responsibility. In the U.S. marketplace, unfortunately, consumers have been injured by inaccurate credit reporting and by abuses of the private information contained in such reports.

The principal federal law governing the conduct of credit gatherers, reporters, and users—the Fair Credit Reporting Act (FCRA) of 1970, with amendments—remains in force today. However, various bills to create new laws and substantial amendments to the FCRA have been put before Congress, thus far without success. Today intense social pressures are being placed on credit reporting companies to fix the credit reporting business and on government to change the laws which govern them.

Notwithstanding the possibility of change, we will examine the major contours of the existing Fair Credit Reporting Act. Keep in mind that at the time the FCRA was enacted, the issue of consumer privacy was not in the national forefront as it is today; the original purpose of this law was to protect consumers against inaccurate reporting of their credit information.

The FCRA imposes certain responsibilities on providers of credit information—credit agencies and companies which perform similar functions. One area of responsibility is that such providers must use reasonable procedures to safeguard consumers in three sensitive aspects of the credit reporting business:

1. *Legitimate business need.* Users of the credit information should have a "legitimate business need" for the credit information.
2. *Old or obsolete information.* Reports should not contain information which is beyond the reporting period of a credit report.
3. *Accuracy.* Reports should be as accurate as possible. (There is no requirement that the report indeed be absolutely accurate, but rather that the reporting firm have procedures in place to minimize mistakes.)

If a reporting firm is supplying a report which is essentially a background check—one that goes beyond credit reporting and contains personal information collected from sources such as friends, former employers, neighbors, and public records—the FCRA imposes additional responsibilities. The reporting firm must (1) notify the person who is the object of the report that a report has been requested; (2) inform the person of the nature of the information gathered; and (3) inform the person of his or her rights to disclosure of information in the report.

A consumer who has been adversely affected by a credit report (such as being refused credit or rejected for insurance) is entitled to a copy of the credit report at no charge. Consumers who have not been adversely affected by a report are entitled by law to be able to purchase the report at reasonable cost.

The chief governmental enforcer of the FCRA is the FTC. In fact, in recent years the largest single category of complaints from consumers to the FTC has been in the area of credit reporting. In addition, the FCRA allows for private civil actions and class actions

---

[8] See, e.g., "Consumer Enemy No. 1," *Newsweek* (October 28, 1991), p. 42 (lead business story); and "Somebody's Watching," *Time* (November 11, 1991), pp. 34–40 (cover story).

BOX 49.2

Are Credit Reporting and Consumer Privacy Laws in for More Change?

In late 1991, a large national survey of American adults* reported findings which hint at the trends that future laws affecting credit reporting and privacy might take. The survey asked about consumers' attitudes and beliefs about privacy as it pertains to business practices and law. Among the survey's findings are the following:

1. Americans' concern about threats to privacy is high—79 percent of respondents say that they are "very concerned" or "somewhat concerned."
2. Most respondents—71 percent—believe that consumers have lost all control over how personal information about them is circulated and used by companies.
3. A majority of Americans—58 percent—now believe that consumers' privacy rights in credit reporting are not adequately protected by law and business practice.
4. The number of people who see either telephone calls or direct mail as an invasion of privacy—27 percent of respondents—is much smaller than the number who think of them as a nuisance—55 percent of respondents.

Also, in 1991, the Consumers Union published a full-length feature article on the subjects of privacy and credit reporting.† The article took aim at the Fair Credit Reporting Act and pointed to its shortcomings. The current law, the feature assessed, was written when credit reporting information was manually kept on file cards and stored in well-guarded filing cabinets. Modern computer technology has made information not only easier to process and store than paper file systems but also easier to access and use—sometimes not in the interests of consumers. "[A]nyone who has a personal computer a nd a modem," the feature stated, "can link up to one of the credit bureaus." The article also projected that of the 400 million credit reports maintained by the three largest credit bureaus, as many as 172 million of them probably contain errors.

The Consumers Union article also assessed the Fair Credit Reporting Act's requirement that a business seeking access to a consumer's credit report first show "legitimate business need." The definition of "legitimate business need" was characterized as "loose" and included businesses "that want to sell things to you—not just creditors." The article gave the example of an automobile salesperson who can call up a credit report "while you're in the lot just browsing."

Improvements in the Fair Credit Reporting Act that the Consumers Union would support include:

1. Imposing civil penalties on bureaus and companies that supply incorrect information
2. Requiring that consumers be notified when negative information enters their files
3. Reducing or eliminating fees that consumers must pay to see their credit reports
4. Disclosing information in credit reports only if the consumer authorizes the disclosure
5. Allowing a maximum of 30 days for credit reports to investigate when a consumer asks for a file to be checked for accuracy
6. Disclosing to consumers exactly how bureaus investigate possible errors

*HARRIS-EQUIFAX CONSUMER PRIVACY SURVEY 1991 (privately published and released to the press in report form by Equifax, Inc., and conducted by Louis Harris and Associates).

†"What Price Privacy?" *Consumer Reports* (May 1991), p. 356.

against violators of the Act and has provisions for allowing punitive damage awards for intentional violators.

Telephone Protection—Telephone Consumer Protection Act. The newest of federal consumer protection laws reveals the tensions between the interests of business and the interests of consumers. Enacted in 1991, the Telephone Consumer Protection Act (TCPA) went into effect on December 20, 1992. Two days later, a federal district court preliminarily enjoined the government from enforcing the Act.[9]

At this writing, the issue remains whether the Telephone Consumer Protection Act will survive the legal challenges being mounted by telemarketing businesses. Since the law seems indicative of the trends that consumer protection laws will take, it will be discussed somewhat differently from other statutes in this chapter and in this book. The surrounding controversy gives the business law student an opportunity to appreciate the dimensions of unsettled, but possibly very important, law. Discussion will be broken into two parts: background of the law and the statute itself.

Background. Telemarketing in the United States has emerged as a huge business, accounting for an estimated $435 billion in generated sales in 1990. More than 30,000 businesses use telemarketing techniques in the sale of their goods and services to consumers. Compared with the expense associated with door-to-door selling and other sales methods, telemarketing has proved to be exceptionally cost-effective for many businesses.

However, consumers are not as happy with telemarketing as business is. The sheer quantity of telephone solicitation to consumers' homes is enormous—an estimated 6.5 billion calls annually, or 18 million calls a day. Among the findings behind the passage of the TCPA, according to Congress, was that many consumers were "outraged over the proliferation of intrusive, nuisance calls to their homes from telemarketers."[10]

An additional concern for Congress was that some telemarketing techniques resulted in putting emergency and medical telephone services at risk. Of particular concern was the use of telephone technology which could place many calls simultaneously and tie up the lines going to emergency services. Thus public health and safety—in addition to the rights of business and consumers—were at issue in the creation of the TCPA.

The economic climate during the making of this law encouraged Congress to recognize that regulations which inhibit commerce will also contribute adversely to national job growth and economic recovery. Yet the tension lines between business and consumers grew tighter.

Congress concluded that in the making of the TCPA, "privacy rights, public safety interests, and commercial freedoms of speech and trade must be balanced in a way that protects the privacy of individuals and permits legitimate telemarketing practices."[11]

The final law took drastic measures against automated telemarketing techniques while allowing in-person telemarketing practices. Business-to-business telemarketing (telephone sales calls from one business to another) remained basically unaffected, except for prohibiting the making of simultaneous calls to the same business so as to tie up telephone lines. Key features of this new law now follow.

The statute. The Telephone Consumer Protection Act imposes four prohibitions on the use of automated telemarketing equipment.

1. It is unlawful to use any automatic telephone dialing system or an artificial or prerecorded voice to make a call (a) to any emergency line (e.g., 911) or to any emergency line for medical services (e.g., hospitals, clinics) or private fire and police lines; (b) to any line of any guest room at a hospital or health care facility or similar establishment; or (c) to any number assigned to a paging service or cellular carrier service or to any service for which the called party is charged for the cost of the call.

---

[9]*Moser v. Federal Communications Commission,* D.C. Ore., No. 92-1408-AS, December 22, 1992.

[10]Pub. Law 102-243, Sec. 2(6).

[11]Pub. Law 102-243, Sec. 2(9).

2. It is unlawful to initiate any call to a residential phone.
3. A telephone facsimile machine (fax), computer, or other device may not be used to send an unsolicited advertisement to another fax.
4. An automatic dialing system may not be used in such a way that two or more telephone lines of a multiline business are engaged simultaneously.

This statute excludes tax-exempt not-for-profit organizations that use automated telemarketing equipment to deliver noncommercial messages to residential phone numbers.

The TCPA also delegated to the Federal Communications Commission (FCC) rulemaking authority for the protection of telephone subscriber rights. Under this authority, the FCC is charged to create rules concerning the use of telephone number databases and the creation of a database in which consumers can be listed as not wanting solicitation on their home phones. The TCPA also directs the FCC to consider and to recommend any other restrictions on telephone solicitation that the FCC deems appropriate.

The FCC is to be the chief federal enforcer of this law. The TCPA provides for persons or classes to have a private right of action against violators of the Act, and for states to be able to bring action against violators as well.

SUMMARY

As the U.S. market for consumer goods and services has grown larger and more complex, laws intended to offer greater consumer protection have also grown in number and in scope.

Historically, state law provided the chief avenue for redress of consumer injury. Common law tort and contract remain today in the array of bases for consumer-related causes of action. In addition, the Uniform Commercial Code, Lemon Laws, little FTCs, the Uniform Consumer Credit Code, and Usury Laws operate to either avoid or rectify consumer injury.

Federal law and regulation also govern several aspects of goods and services marketed to consumers. The Magnuson-Moss Warranty Act provides for more "consumer friendly" warranties of products. The FDA regulates the safety and purity of food, drugs, and cosmetics. The Consumer Product Safety Commission creates and issues product standards and removes dangerous products from the marketplace. Several laws relate to consumer credit, including the Truth in Lending Act, the Fair Debt Collection Practices Act, and the Equal Credit Opportunity Act. The FTC regulates trade practices and enforces against unfair and deceptive practices. Finally, protection of consumer information and consumer privacy is an emerging area of federal law.

REVIEW QUESTIONS

1. Compare the common law tort of misrepresentation with the Federal Trade Commission's standard of deception. Are they significantly different? If so, explain.

2. How do the provisions of the Uniform Commercial Code on express and implied warranties operate in conjunction with the federal Magnuson-Moss Warranty Act? Explain.

3. (a) Under the Magnuson-Moss Warranty Act, must every product seller provide a written warranty? If not, explain those circumstances under which the warranty must be written and what must be contained in the warranty. **(b)** What is the difference between a full warranty and a limited warranty? Are the requirements different for such warranties?

4. What is Regulation Z? What does it regulate? What federal agency is responsible for issuing rules under Regulation Z? Is this the same federal agency which enforces the regulations?

5. Does the Fair Debt Collection Practices Act apply to all businesses which collect debt? If not, explain.

6. Under the Fair Debt Collection Practices Act, are debt collectors absolutely forbidden to communicate with a debtor's family, friends, neighbors, or employer? If not, under what circumstances is such communication permissible?

7. Compare and contrast the Federal Trade Commission's standards for deception and unfairness. How are they different?

8. What is the purpose of the Fair Credit Reporting Act? What responsibilities does it impose on credit reporting businesses?

CASE PROBLEMS

1. From 1966 to 1975, Orkin Exterminating Company sold its pest control and exterminating services under standard form contract along with guarantees for the lifetime of the treated structure as long as the consumer paid a specified annual renewal fee. In 1980, because of rising costs, Orkin decided to raise the renewal fees on these contracts (approximately 207,000 of them), despite the fact that the contracts contained no express language authorizing such an increase. Orkin's announcement of increased renewal fees brought consumer complaints against the company to the FTC. On what grounds could the FTC take action against Orkin? Explain and analyze those grounds.

2. American Motors Company, which was succeeded by the Jeep Eagle Corporation, manufactured, distributed, and sold Renault Alliance and Renault Encore automobiles. Variously between model years 1983 and 1985, American Motors issued warranties on these cars consisting of a 12-month/12,000-mile full warranty and a 24-month/24,000-mile limited warranty. Consumers complained that on a significant number of occasions, Renault-authorized dealers failed to correct automatic transmission fluid or engine oil leaks and related problems within a reasonable time after delivery of the vehicles to the dealers for repair. What laws—state and federal—could be applicable in either private or public legal actions involving these complaints? Explain.

3. Cliffdale Associates, Inc., made and distributed the Ball-Matic Gas Saver Valve. In advertisements and in sales promotion materials, Cliffdale made claims that the product was a new, significant, and unique invention which when installed in a typical automobile and used under normal driving conditions would significantly improve fuel economy—specifically, by 20 percent or more. Moreover, the advertisements and materials represented directly or by implication that competent scientific tests proved the fuel economy claims. Cliffdale's advertisements and promotional materials also carried consumer endorsements by persons claiming to have benefited from improved fuel economy from the product. In fact, the product was not new, significant, or unique. No competent scientific tests supported the product claims, and some of the endorsements came from persons who did not give permission for such endorsement, who did not use the product at the time of the endorsement, or who have not used the product in the recent past. Upon what basis can the FTC take action against Cliffdale? Explain.

4. Near the end of her senior year in college, Rita Donohue was offered a credit account at Campus Apparel retail store. The account limit was for $2,500. As Donohue prepared herself to interview for jobs at advertising agencies, she spent $2,200 for a new wardrobe at Campus Apparel and charged it to her new account. The job market, however, produced no jobs for her whatsoever, and she was soon 90 days overdue on her account. Donohue moved to New York City to try to find a job there, but listed her parents' home as a forwarding address. In an attempt to locate Donohue, the credit collection department of Campus Apparel tried several means—including writing and talking to her parents and locating friends who were Donohue's neighbors at school. In its communications, Campus Apparel's collection department revealed Donohue's past-due status to her family and friends. Donohue's mother gave the collection department Donohue's New York telephone number. When an officer of the collection department called Donohue in New York, she became frustrated and angry and told the collection officer never to call her again at home. However, the officer and others continued to call repeatedly. What federal law, if any, can help Rita Donohue put a stop to the calls?

CHAPTER 50

Computer Law

Of the many technological advances of the twentieth century, none has had such a dramatic impact on society as the computer. Computer technology has changed our personal lives and the way we do business. Computers now dominate the workplace, allowing employees to prepare letters, reports, and documents using sophisticated word processing and graphics. Business has achieved greater efficiencies in accounting, inventory control, and records storage. Computer technology has resulted in new products and innovative services. It has transformed our money, banking, and financial markets and led to significant advances in science, engineering, and medicine. Our educational institutions are now employing computer technologies for learning in the informational age.

The advent of the computer has not, however, been without its social costs and legal problems. Computer crime costs businesses and consumers millions of dollars each year. The unauthorized and unlawful copying of software has become a major problem in the marketing of computer technology. In addition, abuses and unfair competition occur at the development stage of computer technology. The misappropriation of a computer firm's creative works or trade secrets by competitors in the industry is of significant concern to computer developers. Finally, because of the sophisticated nature of computer technology, and the reliance of novices on computer specialists, businesses and individuals have suffered substantial losses when improperly designed computer technology failed to perform its intended functions.

Although the legislatures have adopted some statutes that are specifically applicable to computers, the courts have generally utilized existing substantive law to resolve issues involving this new technology. The legal environment of computers is a combination of intellectual property, contract, tort, and criminal law principles. In the sections that follow, we will explore contemporary issues of computer law. The first section examines property law rights in computer technology. Those who create computer hardware and software are protected under copyright, patent, and trade secret law. The next section addresses issues in computer transactions, including contracts for the sale of computer hardware and software and agreements for the development of computer systems. We then look at computer tort liability—a computer firm's liability for product defects or a nonperforming system. We then examine computer crimes and their implications for business. Finally, we discuss computers and privacy.

PROPERTY RIGHTS IN COMPUTER TECHNOLOGY

The creation and development of computer technology is a time-consuming and expensive endeavor. The computer marketplace is becoming increasingly competitive, and the life span of computer technology tends to be fairly short. Technological innovations and illegal copying of a program may strip a product of its value before the owner has an opportunity to recoup the investment. In a highly competitive environment, computer developers need to protect their legal rights in their creative works. The primary legal protection for computer technology is the law of intellectual property, particularly the law of copyright, patent, and trade secrets. The application of intellectual property law to computer technology is examined in this section.

Copyrights of Computer Technology

As you recall from Chapter 8, federal copyright law protects original "works of authorship" such as movies, books, and recordings. In 1980, Congress added computer programs to the list of works protectible under the Copyright Act. **Computer programs** are defined as "a set of statements or instructions to be used directly or indirectly in a computer in order to bring about a certain result." Copyright protection provides the owner with the exclusive right to reproduce and market the computer program (and any derivative works). Most computer copyrights, being owned by high-tech firms rather than natural persons, last for 75 years.

Copyright law protects the expression of an idea, not the idea itself. With computer programs, this idea/expression distinction is not an easy one to make. For example, does a computer copyright protect only the "literal" aspects of a computer program (the programming codes), or does it extend to the "nonliteral" elements (such as the organization, sequence, and structure) as well? The courts have recognized that the literal elements of a program, including the programming codes and flowcharts, are protected under a software copyright. In contrast, the courts have reached inconsistent rulings on the question of copyright protection for the "nonliteral" aspects of a program.

This issue is a complex one involving a balancing of interests—the developer's interest in a return on investment against society's interest in competition and the advancement of computer technology. One recent case in which the court struck the balance in favor of the developer involved Lotus Development and its popular spreadsheet program, Lotus 1-2-3.[1] A competitor, Paperback Software International, created a spreadsheet program "clone" of Lotus 1-2-3, the VP-Planner. The VP-Planner did not copy the literal codes of Lotus 1-2-3, but it replicated the commands and menus so that the program was interchangeable with Lotus 1-2-3. Potential users would be able to use the VP-Planner without any training, and Paperback Software marketed its program as compatible with Lotus 1-2-3. A federal district court ruled in favor of Lotus Development, concluding that the nonliteral elements of Lotus 1-2-3 were protected under its program copyright.

The following case involves a similar issue that arose between two giants of the industry, Apple Computer and Microsoft Corporation.

[1]*Lotus Development Corporation v. Paperback Software International*, 740 F. Supp. 37 (D. Mass. 1990).

CASE 50.1   **Apple Computer, Inc. v. Microsoft Corporation**
• 799 F. Supp. 1006 (N.D. Cal. 1992)

FACTS   Apple's Macintosh microcomputer was one of the major commercial triumphs of the 1980s. Its success was based, in part, on the visual displays or images which the Macintosh generated on its computer screens. When the user interface (the com-

**CASE 50.1
Continued**

bination of user command functions and visual displays) incorporates significant graphical elements, as does the Macintosh, it is referred to as a graphical user interface (GUI, or "gooey"). On the Macintosh, the screen displays include icons or symbols to represent programs or information; pull-down menus or lists of commands or information; use of windows to display information; the ability to move, resize, open, or close the windows to retrieve, put away, or modify information; and a display of text by a proportionally spaced font in all menu items, title bars, icon names, and text directories for a consistent and distinctive appearance.

Microsoft developed and, in 1985, introduced its Windows 1.0 software, which operated on IBM-compatible machines. Later versions of Windows generated complex visual displays and a graphical user interface that resembled the Macintosh, including the use of windows to display multiple images on a computer screen and the use of icons to facilitate organization of information stored in the computer's memory. Because IBM and especially IBM-compatible hardware had consistently been less expensive than comparable Macintosh hardware, and IBM-compatible users were interested in protecting their investments in such hardware, Windows proved a hugely formidable force in the software market.

Apple filed a copyright infringement action against Microsoft Corporation on March 17, 1988, claiming that Microsoft's Windows computer software infringed seven Apple copyrights protecting the audiovisual works for the graphical user interface of its Macintosh computer. In resolving pretrial motions, the court addressed the issue of the extent to which the copyrights protected the Macintosh graphical user interface.

OPINION

WALKER, J. . . . Apple contends that to "understand" the distinctive appearance of the Macintosh interface, "one needs to consider not only the individual elements that make up the appearance of the interface but also the way those elements are arranged and interact with one another to create the consistent and distinctive Macintosh interface." The claimed unifying idea of the . . . Macintosh works is "an interface suggestive of an office environment with a desktop background, implementing through animated graphical images and fanciful symbols what has been referred to as a 'desktop metaphor.'" . . .

Apple's expert . . . isolate[d] the general concepts or ideas that make up the "desktop metaphor" . . . includ[ing] multiple windows that serve as separate workspaces or mini-screens unto themselves; the ability to open and close these windows; icons that represent programs, files and documents; the use of a mouse to manipulate directly these visual displays; menu bars dedicated to an array of choices. . . .

But Apple goes further than simply claiming that the Macintosh interface expresses these ideas. To the extent the individual features of the Macintosh interface are . . . unprotectible they are together, or in conjunction with the protectible features, claimed as a copyrightable arrangement—a "look and feel" which constitutes protectible expression apart from its individual elements. . . .

The elements of such an arrangement serve a purely functional purpose in the same way that the visual displays and user commands of the dashboard, steering wheel, gear shift, brakes, clutch and accelerator serve as the user interface of

**CASE 50.1
Continued**

an automobile. Purely functional items or an arrangement of them for functional purposes are wholly beyond the realm of copyright as are other common examples of user interfaces or arrangements of their individual elements—the dials, knobs and remote control devices of a television or VCR, or the buttons and clocks of an oven or stove. . . .

The similarity of such functional elements of a user interface or their arrangement in products of like kind does not suggest unlawful copying, but standardization across competing products for functional considerations. . . .

Some visual displays are or become so closely tied to the functional purpose of the article that they become standard. If "market factors play a significant factor in determining the sequence and organization" of a computer program, then those patterns may well be termed ideas beyond the ownership of any one seller. No better evidence of "market factors" (i.e., expectations of users) accounting for the features of computer user interfaces can be found than the almost invariable incorporation of those features in most graphical user interfaces. . . .

By virtue of having been the first commercially successful programmer to put these generalized features together, Apple had several years of market dominance in graphical user interfaces until Microsoft introduced Windows 3.0, the first DOS-based windowing program to begin to rival the graphical capability of the Macintosh. The Macintosh still to this day offers graphical features that translate into competitive advantages. To accept Apple's "desktop metaphor"/"look and feel" arguments would allow it to sweep within its proprietary embrace not only Windows . . . but, at its option, also other desktop graphical user interfaces which employ the standardized features of such interfaces. . . . Apple's copyrights would hold for programs in existence now or in the future—for decades. One need not profess to know for sure where should lie the line between expression and idea, between protection and competition to sense with confidence that this would afford too much protection and yield too little competition.

The court declines Apple's invitation to use the advent of the microcomputer and its interface to abandon traditional standards which govern copyrights and invent some new law based on highly indefinite constructs such as "look and feel." . . .

JUDGMENT

[The court ruled against Apple and in favor of Microsoft, holding that most of the similarities between the parties' programs were not protected under the Copyright Act.]

Copyright Licenses of Software. To protect copyrighted software, computer firms have generally licensed their programs, rather than sell them. Under a **license,** the licensee acquires only a personal, nontransferable right to use the software, not title or ownership rights to the program copy. This widespread practice was an attempt by the computer industry to prevent the application of the **"first-sale doctrine."** Under the first-sale doctrine, which is codified in the Copyright Act, when a copyright owner sells a copy of a work, such as a book, the purchaser has a right to sell or transfer his or her copy of the book without the copyright owner's consent. Rental stores could, therefore, acquire a copyrighted computer program and lease it to others, who would invariably make an illegal copy of the program. To stop this practice and thereby recoup lost income from the leasing and unlawful copying of software, computer developers adopted the license arrangement as the means to market computer software.

Congress later responded to this problem with the passage of the Computer Software Rental Amendments Act of 1990, which allows only nonprofit libraries and educational institutions to lease or lend copies of protected computer programs. The "purchaser" continues to have the right to make copies to utilize the program in his or her computer and for archival purposes. The user can also sell his or her copy without the consent of the copyright owner.

Work-for-Hire Rule. Copyright protection is given to the "author" of the original work. Computer programs are often developed by high-tech firms that employ programmers to create the work. Who is entitled to the copyright on the program, the employer or the employee? The employer is generally entitled to the copyright under the **work-for-hire** provision of the Copyright Act, which provides as follows:

In the case of a work made for hire, the employer or other person for whom the work was prepared is considered the author for purposes of this title, and, unless the parties have expressly agreed otherwise in a written instrument signed by them, owns all of the rights comprised in the copyright.

The work-for-hire rule applies to programs developed by employees, not independent contractors. To determine whether an employer-employee relationship exists, the Supreme Court has adopted the common law "right to control" test, under which an individual is considered an employee, and not an independent contractor, when the employer has the "right to control the manner and means by which the work is accomplished." Recently, a federal district court applied this test to determine who owned the copyright on an accounting program developed for a swimming pool retailer by a computer engineer. Although the work was directed by the retailer, the court held that the programmer was an independent contractor because he received no employee benefits and was not treated as an employee for state and federal tax purposes.

Patents on Computer Technology

A federal patent can be secured for any "new and useful process, machine, manufacture or composition." Computer hardware and software can be patented if the computer technology is *useful*, *novel*, and *nonobvious* (not an obvious variation of existing technology), the three requirements for patent protection. A patent, which gives the holder a monopoly for 17 years, is a valuable form of legal protection for computer technology and an asset to the computer firm in the marketplace. The patent holder can either directly control the market for the product or derive income from licensing the patent to others.

The Semiconductor Chip Protection Act of 1984 protects a new form of intellectual property in "mask work" (the primary device used in the manufacture of a semiconductor chip). The creator of mask work is given the exclusive right for 10 years to reproduce and distribute the mask or chip. The purpose of the Act is to combat the unauthorized duplication of semiconductor chips used in a wide variety of products, ranging from computers and sophisticated weapons systems to kitchen products and video games, and thereby to encourage further research and investment in this high-tech field.

Computer Trade Secrets

Trade secret law provides another important protection for computer technology. Unlike federal patent and copyright law, trade secret law is governed by state common law or statute. Many states have adopted the Uniform Trade Secrets Act, which defines a trade secret as follows:

A trade secret may consist of any formula, pattern, device, or compilation of information which is used in one's business and which gives the business an opportunity to obtain an advantage over competitors who do not know or use it.

In determining whether a particular computer technology is a trade secret, the courts look to a number of factors, including the time and money that went into its development, its value to the owner, and the extent to which the owner has taken steps to keep the technology

> **BOX 50.1**
>
> ### Developments in the Law: Fair Use and Reverse Engineering
>
> To what extent is the "reverse engineering" of a copyrighted computer program a permissible fair use? As you recall from Chapter 8, the Copyright Act contains a fair use provision under which certain unauthorized copying of a copyrighted work is lawful. For example, the fair use defense is often available to those who copy a part of a work for purposes of scholarly criticism, news reporting, or educational use. In the computer software industry, it is possible to learn the programming codes of a program through a reverse engineering process known as "disassembly" or "decompiling." In that process, however, copies are made of the software's programming codes. Thus, the issue arises whether the disassembly or decompiling of a computer program is a fair use under the Copyright Act.
>
> This issue was addressed in the recent litigation involving Sega Enterprises Ltd., the manufacturer of the Genesis video game console, and Accolade Inc., an independent producer of computer entertainment software, including game cartridges. Sega produces games for its Genesis console and also licenses other developers of computer games to create Genesis-compatible games. Accolade did not want to enter into a license agreement to produce compatible games because Sega's licensing agreement provided that it was the exclusive manufacturer of Genesis-compatible games. So, to make its games work on the Genesis console, Accolade reverse engineered Sega's video game programs. It used a decompiler on the console to transform the "object" codes of three Sega games into their "source" codes. Accolade's engineers then studied printouts of the source codes and with further experimentation created a program that made its games compatible with the Genesis console.
>
> Sega sued Accolade in federal court for copyright infringement and the case ultimately reached the Ninth Circuit Court of Appeals. In *Sega Enterprises Ltd. v. Accolade, Inc.*, 977 F.2d 1510 (9th Cir. 1992), the court held that Accolade's reverse engineering was a fair use of the Sega programs. It reasoned that reverse engineering of the computer programs was necessary for Accolade to understand the compatibility requirements of the Sega programs—functional aspects of the program that are not protected under the Copyright Act. It further concluded that decompiling was the only method whereby those functional requirements of compatibility could be discovered. Finally, it noted that the games produced by Accolade were apparently not copies of those produced by Sega, and thus Accolade used only those functional aspects of the program that were necessary for the game to work on the Genesis console. It concluded that:
>
> [W]here disassembly is the only way to gain access to the ideas and functional elements embodied in a copyrighted computer program and where there is a legitimate reason for seeking such access, disassembly is a fair use. . . .
> 977 F.2d at 1527-28.
>
> Should reverse engineering of a computer program be considered a fair use under the Copyright Act? What do you think about the *Sega* court's approach to this issue? Does it give too little protection to copyrighted computer programs?

secret. Trade secret law is separate from copyright and patent protection; therefore, computer technology may be a trade secret even when it is not patentable or copyrightable.

Protection under trade secret law is particularly important in preventing the use or disclosure of the technology by former employees and insiders of a firm. Companies employ noncompetition agreements and other contractual nondisclosure promises to ensure that employees do not misappropriate trade secrets. However, trade secret law will not protect the technology

> **BOX 50.2**
>
> **Point to Consider: Trademark Protection for Windows**
>
> Microsoft Corporation claims a trademark on the word "Windows" for its highly successful software programs, and it applied to the U.S. Patent & Trademark Office to register Windows as a trademark. In 1993, the PTO rejected the application, finding that the term had been used by other firms prior to Microsoft's adoption of the mark in 1983 and that in the software industry, windows was a generic term used to describe any software using a windowed graphical interface. As we noted in Chapter 8, generic words, words that describe a type or category of product, cannot be protected as a trademark because they are not distinctive.
>
> Microsoft Corporation intends to appeal the decision. What is the likely outcome on appeal? Should other competitors be able to use the word in connection with their software or has windows acquired a secondary meaning in the software marketplace because consumers associate the word with the software of Microsoft? What economic effect would a ruling in favor of Microsoft have on the software market? How do you think this issue should be resolved?

noted in the preceding section, computer software is typically transferred to the user under a nontransferable license agreement, rather than under a sale.

Businesses may have more extensive needs for computer systems than do consumer users. A business may hire a consultant to study its computer information needs and recommend appropriate hardware and software. Or a business may hire a computer specialist to design and set up a working computer system that incorporates the necessary computer technology. Such a contract may also involve training of employees and maintenance of the system—or these functions may be handled under a separate contract. The acquisition of computer hardware and software may be accomplished by a sale or lease and may be financed through a secured transaction. Along with contracts at the user level, computer transactions will be entered into between producers, suppliers, and retailers, and will occur at the initial developmental and design stage. Given the wide range of computer transactions, our discussion will focus on the law relating to computer transactions with consumer and business users.

Governing Law—Sales or Contract Law?

The rights and duties of the parties to a computer transaction are determined by the terms of the agreement and the law governing that contract. In computer transactions, the relevant law of the contract will either be the Uniform Commercial Code (UCC) or the common law of contracts. Contracts for the sale of goods are governed by Article 2 of the UCC, the particular rules of which are discussed in detail in Chapters 18–22. On the other hand, contracts for services and nongoods transactions are governed by the common law of contracts, discussed in Chapters 10–17. The choice of relevant law may be important for a number of reasons. For example, the UCC provides purchasers with protection from defective products under its implied and express warranty provisions, whereas the common law does not impose warranties in a services contract. In a lawsuit

from its appropriation by a competitor that uses no improper means to learn the secrets. Reverse engineering, for example, is considered a legitimate method of learning trade secrets.

COMPUTER TRANSACTIONS

Individuals and businesses enter into a wide variety of computer transactions. An individual may purchase a computer for use in his or her home. The purchase may involve computer hardware—the central processing unit (CPU), the monitor, and the keyboard—as well as accessories such as a printer, a modem, and a mouse. The consumer may also acquire software—programs necessary for the computer to perform word processing and other functions. As over defective computer technology, the warranty rules will govern if the UCC applies to the transaction.

In determining whether the UCC or the common law governs a particular computer transaction, the courts consider two important issues. First, is the subject matter of the contract *goods?* The UCC applies only if the contract involves movable, personal property. Second, is the computer contract a *transaction* in goods? The UCC applies to sales and other "transactions in goods." Because computer technology may be leased or transferred under a license agreement, the courts must resolve the legal issue whether there is a UCC "transaction."

Contract for Goods? Under the UCC, goods means "all things (including specially manufactured goods) which are moveable at the time of identification to the contract." Goods clearly includes computer hardware and the courts have so held. In contrast, a contract to hire a computer consultant to give advice on a computer system is a services contract. Computer software contracts present a difficult question. In the sense that most computer software is transferred on a disk or in some other tangible form, the software is a good. But the program's value to the owner lies in the functions performed by the software and thus is an intangible form of property, one that cannot be reduced to physical possession. Thus, the argument can be made (and has been made) that computer software is not a good. The courts have generally held, however, that the sale of prepackaged computer software is a goods transaction subject to the Code. Similarly, a contract for the sale of a hardware and software package is generally deemed a goods transaction.

Contracts for specially designed computer software developed for a particular business presents a closer question. The courts have sometimes ruled that such contracts are for goods, but in other cases have held that such transactions are for services. The courts apply the **predominant factor** test to mixed or hybrid transactions that involve both goods (hardware or software or both) and services (e.g., design or development work). Under the predominant factor test, the court determines whether the goods are the primary aspect of the transaction and the services merely incidental, or whether the labor is the predominant aspect and the goods merely incidental. In a computer maintenance contract, for example, under which the contractor's sole obligation is to repair and maintain the system, the contract would be considered a services contract despite the incidental goods that the contractor may sell as part of the contract. The following case presents this issue in terms of a contract for the development of a **turnkey** system for a business.

CASE 50.2 Neilson Business Equipment Center, Inc. v. Monteleone
• 524 A.2d 1172 (Del. 1987)

FACTS Dr. Monteleone, a neurologist, began investigating various computer information systems in 1982; before that time, his office record keeping was entirely manual. Toni Reed, his bookkeeper and office manager, chose Neilson Business Equipment Center, Inc., in part because she had previously purchased an office photocopier from defendant with satisfactory results.

The parties signed a lease/purchase option agreement covering hardware equipment and software. As part of the agreement, Neilson agreed to customize the computer system to meet Dr. Monteleone's needs. The purchase price was $18,995, but Dr. Monteleone chose to lease the equipment with an option to purchase in order to obtain a favorable cash flow and tax benefits. The total of all lease payments amounted to $32,800.80.

**CASE 50.2
Continued**

The computer was delivered in July 1982, and problems immediately developed. For example, the system printed a separate bill for each treatment rather than one bill encompassing the doctor's services to a patient for a specific period; the bills and medical insurance forms were not compatible with Dr. Monteleone's records; patient information was not as detailed as required; and incorrect balances appeared in the accounts receivable register. When attempts to modify the system failed, Dr. Monteleone brought suit against Neilson for breach of warranty.

The trial court ruled that the transaction involved goods and applied the warranty provisions of the Uniform Commercial Code. It found that Neilson had breached the implied warranties of merchantability and fitness for a particular purpose, and awarded Dr. Monteleone damages totaling $34,983.42, with interest from March 11, 1983. Neilson appealed to the Delaware Supreme Court.

OPINION

MOORE, J. . . . The central issue before us is whether a contract for a computer system consisting of computer hardware, software and services constitutes "goods" under the Uniform Commercial Code. In our opinion, the parties agreed to a lease/purchase of a turn-key computer system which may properly be classified as a package constituting goods. . . .

Article Two of the Uniform Commercial Code applies to "transactions in goods." The contract between Dr. Monteleone and Neilson is a mixed contract for both goods and services. When a mixed contract is presented, it is necessary for a court to . . . determine whether the contract is predominantly or primarily a contract for the sale of goods. If so, the provisions of Article Two of the Uniform Commercial Code apply.

Neilson urges us to separate the contract into three distinct subparts—hardware, software and services. Defendant contends that only the hardware can be classified as "goods" under the Code, that there was nothing defective about the hardware, and thus plaintiff's claims for breaches of implied warranties fail. Neilson further argues that software is an intangible, and that intangibles do not constitute "goods" subject to the Code.

That argument is innovative, but unpersuasive. Neilson contracted to supply a turn-key computer system; that is, a system sold as a package which is ready to function immediately. The hardware and software elements are combined into a single unit, the computer system, prior to sale. The trial court's factual conclusion that the computer system is predominantly "goods" is supported by substantial evidence. Dr. Monteleone did not intend to contract separately for hardware and software. Rather, he bought a computer system to meet his information processing needs. Any consulting services rendered by Neilson were ancillary to the contract, and cannot reasonably be treated as standing separately to escape the implied warranties of the Uniform Commercial Code.

Here, the parties cast their agreement in terms of a lease with an option granted Dr. Monteleone to purchase the computer system later. Although structured as a lease, it is clear that the parties intended to enter into the equivalent of a purchase and sale. . . .

Every contract of sale entered into by a merchant includes an implied warranty that the goods sold be "merchantable." There is no dispute that the computer system failed in that regard. . . .

**CASE 50.2
Continued**

An implied warranty of fitness for a particular purpose arises when a seller, at the time of contracting, has reason to know a particular purpose of the buyer's for which the goods are required, and has reason to know that the buyer is relying on the seller's skill or judgment to select or furnish suitable goods. . . .

Here, Neilson knew that Dr. Monteleone, through his assistant, Ms. Reed, sought a computer system to meet specific information processing needs. Neilson admits that it was responsible for selecting the proper equipment, and also agreed to customize the software so that the computer system would be compatible with Dr. Monteleone's manual records. There could hardly be a clearer case where a buyer relies on the professional expertise of the seller than that presented here. Dr. Monteleone needed a system that would perform specific functions, and relied on Neilson's professional expertise and experience in the computer and information processing field to develop and deliver a satisfactory computer system. Neilson clearly had reason to know of Monteleone's reliance on the company's expertise and breached the warranty of fitness for a particular purpose. Its liability is established under the Uniform Commercial Code.

JUDGMENT [Affirmed but remanded for proper determination of damages.]

Transaction in Goods? A related but separate issue is whether the computer contract is a *transaction* in goods subject to the UCC. The Code applies only to "transactions in goods." Computer hardware and software may be sold or leased. The sale is governed by the UCC, but is the lease governed by Article 2 of the Code? In the thirty jurisdictions that have adopted Article 2A of the UCC, which applies to leases of goods, that article will govern the lease of a computer. But in the remaining jurisdictions that have not adopted Article 2A, this issue must be resolved. If the lease contains an option to purchase for a nominal amount, the courts will generally view it as a sale. In contrast, the courts have held that a lease under which the lessee is required to surrender the computer hardware and software at the end of the lease term is not a transaction in goods under the UCC.

Another recurring question concerns the applicability of the Code to a license agreement. Prepackaged computer software is usually licensed rather than sold. Is the license a transaction in goods? Broadly construing the UCC language, many courts have held that a license of prepackaged software is a transaction in goods.

Formation and Terms of the Computer Transaction

Formation of a computer contract, and the terms and conditions of the agreement, will thus be determined by the common law or UCC rules regarding the offer and acceptance, consideration, parties, and subject matter. One important difference between the UCC and the common law in terms of the contract rules is the requirement of a writing under the statute of frauds. If a computer transaction is a sales transaction, the Code requires a written memorandum of the agreement when the price is $500 or more. Article 2A requires a written contract when the lease payments are $1,000 or more. In contrast, a computer contract for services (e.g., consulting or maintenance) without a set term, need not be in writing. However, when parties to a computer transaction enter into a services contract that cannot be performed within a year from the date the contract is entered into, the statute of frauds requires a written memorandum. Documentation of a computer transaction may be important, not only to have written evidence of the parties' agreement but also to ensure that the contract is enforceable.

Shrinkwrap or Box-Top Licenses. To protect their copyright interests, producers of mass-marketed computer software developed a method of licensing the software to the "purchaser." The producer shrinkwraps the software in cellophane with the terms of the license printed on the box (the so-called **box-top license**) and provides a written notice on the package that opening it constitutes an acceptance of the terms of the license agreement. An example of a shrinkwrap license agreement is contained in Figure 50.1. Its terms are very broad. The sample agreement provides for a limited, 90-day warranty, disclaims all other express and implied warranties, and limits the remedy of the licensee to a replacement of any defective disk. Many license agreements also contain an integration or merger clause providing that the box-top license is the complete and total agreement of the parties. This is an attempt to render inadmissible any parol evidence of an agreement between the parties or oral representations of the seller that changes or adds to the license agreement.

The enforceability of a shrinkwrap agreement is important both to the "purchaser" and the computer vendor because it will limit the potential exposure of the seller for defective software and impose the risk of most software defects on the "purchaser." The validity of such agreements is subject to question, however. Many commentators have argued that the shrinkwrap license is a standard-form "contract of adhesion," which is unconscionable under the UCC or the common law. Another objection to the shrinkwrap agreement relates to whether its terms are part of the parties' agreement. Since the buyer does not sign any agreement, it is argued that the buyer's silence cannot be a sufficient acceptance of the vendor's offer. And even if there is an implied acceptance by the purchaser, do the terms of the license agreement, which may become known to purchaser after the sale is made, become part of the contract between the parties?

Section 2-207 provides the UCC rules relating to the offer and acceptance and whether particular terms are part of the parties' contract. This section, which is discussed at length in Chapter 18, provides as follows:

§ 2-207. Additional Terms in Acceptance or Confirmation.

(1) A definite and seasonable expression of acceptance or a written confirmation which is sent within a reasonable time operates as an acceptance even though it states terms additional to or different from those offered or agreed upon, unless acceptance is expressly made conditional on assent to the additional or different terms.

(2) The additional terms are to be construed as proposals for addition to the contract. Between merchants such terms become part of the contract unless:

    (a) the offer expressly limits acceptance to the terms of the offer;
    (b) they [the additional terms] materially alter it; or
    (c) notification of objection to them has already been given or is given within a reasonable time after notice of them is received.

(3) Conduct by both parties which recognizes the existence of a contract is sufficient to establish a contract for sale although the writings of the parties do not otherwise establish a contract. In such case the terms of the particular contract consist of those terms on which the writings of the parties agree, together with any supplementary terms incorporated under any other provisions of this Act.

In the next case, the court applies Section 2-207 to determine whether the box-top terms became part of a computer contract.

Figure 50.1 Example of a shrinkwrap license agreement.

Important - Read this before breaking the seal on your WINFAX PRO diskettes. If you do not agree to these terms and conditions, return the intact package, containing the diskettes, together with the other components of the product to the place of purchase and your money will be refunded. No refunds will be given for products which have the diskette seals broken or missing components.

This program and any accompanying documentation are proprietary products of Gateway 2000 and are protected under international copyright laws. Title to the program, or any copy, modification or merged portion shall at all times remain with Gateway 2000.

Permitted Uses
You may use the enclosed software on a single computer that you own or use. Under no circumstances may you use it on more than one machine at a time. You may make a copy of the software for backup purposes, provided that you reproduce and place our copyright notice on the backup copy.

You may transfer this program and documentation together with this license to another party, but only if the other party agrees to accept wholly the terms and conditions of this license and if you notify Gateway 2000 of the name and address of the other party. All copies must be transferred to the same party, or you must destroy those copies not transferred. any such transfer terminates your license.

Nonpermitted Uses
Without the express permission of Gateway 2000, you may not:

1. Use the software in a computer service business including rental, networking or timesharing software, not may you use it for multiple user, or on multiple computer system applications in the absence of individual licenses with Gateway 2000.

2. Use, copy, modify, alter or transfer electronically or otherwise, the software or documentation except as expressly allowed this agreement.

3. Translate, reverse program, de-assemble or decompile the software.

4. Sublicense or lease this program or its documentation.

Term
This license is effective from your date of purchase and shall remain in force until terminated. You may terminate the license and this agreement any time by destroying the program and its documentation, together with all copies in any form.

Gateway 2000 may terminate this agreement if you fail to comply with any of the terms and conditions of it. Upon any termination of this license, you agree to destroy the licensed software, and its documentation together with all copies, modifications or portions of the them in any form. You must provide us, on our request, written certification of such destruction.

Limited Warranty
Gateway 2000 warrants that, for a period of ninety (90) days of normal use from the date of original purchase, the diskettes on which the software is recorded will be free from defects in materials and faulty workmanship and the software will function substantially as described in the enclosed program documentation.

EXCEPT FOR THE AFORESAID WARRANTY, ALL PRODUCTS DELIVERED PURSUANT TO THIS AGREEMENT ARE DELIVERED ON AN "AS IS" BASIS AND GATEWAY 2000, ITS DEALERS AND DISTRIBUTORS, EXPRESSLY DISCLAIM ANY AND ALL OTHER WARRANTIES, EXPRESSED OR IMPLIED, INCLUDING, WITHOUT LIMITATIONS, IMPLIED WARRANTIES OR CONDITIONS OR MERCHANTABLE QUALITY OR FITNESS FOR A PARTICULAR PURPOSE.

Limitation on Liability
Gateway 2000's entire liability and your exclusive remedy for breach of the limited ninety (90) day warranty herein before provided for shall be the replacement of any diskette or program documentation not meeting with such warranty which is returned to Gateway 2000 or to one of the authorized dealers or distributors, together with a copy of your paid receipt. IN NO EVENT SHALL GATEWAY 2000, ITS DEALERS OR DISTRIBUTORS, BE LIABLE FOR LOST PROFITS, DATA OR INFORMATION OF ANY KIND OR FOR CONSEQUENTIAL, SPECIAL, INDIRECT, INCIDENTAL, PUNITIVE OR OTHER DAMAGES THAT MAY ARISE THROUGH USE OF THE PRODUCT LICENSED THEREUNDER, EVEN IF GATEWAY HAS BEEN INFORMED OF THE POSSIBILITY OF SUCH DAMAGES. THIS WARRANTY GIVES YOU SPECIFIC LEGAL RIGHTS AND YOU MAY ALSO HAVE OTHER RIGHTS WHICH MAY VARY FROM JURISDICTION TO JURISDICTION.

Governing Law
This license agreement shall be governed by the laws of the state of South Dakota. Gateway 2000/610 Gateway Drive/North Sioux City, SD 57049/U.S.S.

| CASE 50.3 | **Step-Saver Data Systems, Inc. v. The Software Link, Inc.**
• 939 F.2d 91 (3d Cir. 1991) |
|---|---|
| FACTS | Beginning in 1981, Step-Saver developed computer systems for business customers. It evaluated the available technology and combined hardware and software to satisfy the word processing, data management, and communications needs for offices of physicians and lawyers. Step-Saver originally marketed single computer systems, but it later marketed a multiuser system—a system with terminals attached to a single computer.

Step-Saver contacted The Software Link (TSL) about TSL's operating system for a multiuser system, known as Multilink Advanced. TSL sales representatives made representations concerning the capabilities of Multilink Advanced, including the assurance that the software was compatible with 90 percent of the programs available "off the shelf" for computers using MS-DOS. On the basis of these representations, Step-Saver sold 142 multiuser systems with Multilink Advanced to law and medical offices before terminating sales of the system in March 1987. Almost immediately upon installation of its multiuser systems, Step-Saver began to receive complaints from customers.

Step-Saver sued TSL for breach of express and implied warranties. TSL defended, relying in part on its box-top license, which disclaimed all express and implied warranties except for a warranty that the disks contained in the box were free from defects. Step-Saver contended that it placed its orders by telephone, and sent a purchase order containing the quantity, price, shipping, and payment terms. TSL then shipped the order promptly, along with an invoice containing terms essentially identical to those on the purchase order. No reference was made during the telephone calls, or on either the purchase orders or the invoices, to a disclaimer of any warranties. The district court ruled in favor of TSL, holding that the box-top license was the complete agreement of the parties, and Step-Saver appealed. |
| OPINION | WISDOM, J. . . . The "Limited Use License Agreement" printed on a package containing a copy of a computer program raises the central issue in this appeal.

Step-Saver contends that the contract for each copy of the program was formed when TSL agreed, on the telephone, to ship the copy at the agreed price. The box-top license, argues Step-Saver, was a material alteration to the parties' contract which did not become a part of the contract under UCC § 2-207. . . .

TSL argues that the contract between TSL and Step-Saver did not come into existence until Step-Saver received the program, saw the terms of the license, and opened the program packaging. . . .

As a basic principle, we agree with Step-Saver that UCC § 2-207 governs our analysis. . . . TSL has shipped the product, and Step-Saver has accepted and paid for each copy of the program. The parties' performance demonstrates the existence of a contract. The dispute is, therefore, not over the existence of a contract, but the nature of its terms. . . .

. . . TSL never mentioned during the parties' negotiations leading to the purchase of the programs, nor did it, at any time, obtain Step-Saver's express as- |

CASE 50.3 Continued

sent to, the terms of the box-top license. Instead, TSL contented itself with attaching the terms to the packaging of the software, even though those terms differed substantially from those previously discussed by the parties. . . .

Under § 2-207, an additional term detailed in the box-top license will not be incorporated into the parties' contract if the term's addition to the contract would materially alter the parties' agreement. Step-Saver alleges that several representations made by TSL constitute express warranties, and that valid implied warranties were also a part of the parties' agreement. . . . [A]ssuming that these warranties were included within the parties' original agreement, we must conclude that adding the disclaimer of warranty and limitation of remedies provisions from the box-top license would, as a matter of law, substantially alter the distribution of risk between Step-Saver and TSL. Therefore, under UCC § 2-207(2)(b), the disclaimer of warranty and limitation of remedies terms of the box-top license did not become a part of the parties' agreement.

JUDGMENT [W]e reverse the trial court's holding that the parties intended the box-top license to be a final and complete expression of the terms of their agreement. . . . We remand for further consideration of the express and implied warranty claims against TSL.

Warranty Liability

Unless properly disclaimed, warranties exist in a computer transaction governed by the Code. Because a breach of the warranties provides the purchaser with an action for damages, warranty liability gives computer purchasers a remedy when the computer technology is defective or fails to perform up to their expectations. Two types of warranties provide relief to purchasers under the Code: **express** and **implied** warranties. For a detailed discussion of these warranties, see Chapter 22.

Express Warranties. Express warranties are based upon the seller's representations concerning the goods. They may be created by (1) a statement of fact or promise relating to the goods, (2) a description of the goods, or (3) a sample or model. In the context of a computer transaction, aggrieved purchasers may be able to establish that an express warranty was created by the seller's advertising, oral representations, or written warranty provisions in the contract. For example, in Case 50.3, plaintiff claimed an express warranty on the basis of defendant's statements that its software was compatible with 90 percent of the "off the shelf" programs for computers using MS-DOS. The statement is both an affirmation of fact and a description of the goods sufficient to form an express warranty.

Implied Warranties. There are two warranties of quality implied by law under the UCC: the implied warranty of **merchantability** and the implied warranty of **fitness for a particular purpose.** Whenever a merchant makes a sale, the implied warranty of merchantability is created. It means that the seller warrants that the goods are fit for the ordinary purposes intended for such goods. This general warranty will protect a purchaser when the computer technology fails to perform its intended functions. The implied warranty of fitness for a particular purpose is created when the buyer has a particular need for the goods, the seller is aware of those needs, and the buyer is relying on the seller to select goods to meet those needs. This warranty has particular application to contracts for the custom design of computer systems. As noted in Case 50.2, a computer specialist that undertakes to

> **BOX 50.3**
> ## A Question of Policy: Shrinkwrap Licenses and Mass-Marketed Software
>
> In the *Step-Saver* case, the parties had direct communications before the sale and delivery of the software to the purchaser. But in most sales of software, the purchaser will acquire the software at a computer store or from a seller without any prior discussions with the seller or producer. Thus, the *Step-Saver* decision does not clearly resolve the issue of the enforceability of the shrinkwrap license in the context of mass-marketed software. Will the courts applying § 2-207 enforce a shrinkwrap license when a consumer purchases a software program at a computer superstore? Should it make a difference whether the box-top license terms are on the box rather than inside the package on a separate writing? Why?
>
> In *Step-Saver*, The Software Link made a policy argument in support of the enforceability of the shrinkwrap agreement, contending that the widespread practice of marketing software using the shrinkwrap license method was essential to the growth and development of the computer software industry. The court rejected that contention, reasoning as follows: "We are not persuaded that requiring software companies to stand behind representations concerning their products will inevitably destroy the software industry." What do you think about the policy implications of enforcing or not enforcing shrinkwrap licenses? Is the shrinkwrap license essential to the health of the computer software industry? From a policy standpoint, what is the preferable resolution of this issue? ∎

design a computer system for a particular business may create a warranty that the system will meet the special needs of the purchaser.

Disclaimers of Warranties. Purchasers of computer technology relying on the seller's representations or the implied warranties provided by the Code must be cautious of disclaimers of those warranties and limitations of remedies. The written contract between the parties may contain a disclaimer clause that limits or wholly eliminates express and implied warranties. To be enforceable, disclaimers must be conspicuous in the contract. To disclaim merchantability, the clause must use the term "merchantability." To disclaim the fitness warranty, the disclaimer must be in writing. Prior oral statements and representations of the seller creating an express warranty can also be disclaimed in the written contract. Purchasers must be careful that the contract includes any warranties given and does not exclude the protections under the implied warranties of the Code. The Magnuson-Moss Warranty Act may also protect the purchaser when the computer transaction involves consumer goods.

Limitations of remedies are also permitted under the Code. Computer contracts frequently limit the purchaser's remedy to a replacement of defective software. Unless the exclusive remedy "fails of its essential purpose" by not providing a remedy, it is enforceable.

COMPUTER TORT LIABILITY

Negligence and Computer Malpractice

Can the purchaser of computer technology sue the seller or developer for negligence? If so, will a computer specialist be held to a professional standard of care? In other words, can he or she be sued for **computer malpractice?** Courts have grappled with the question of the computer firm's liability for malpractice. Many courts have refused to allow a suit for malpractice on the theory that there is no professional relationship between the computer developer and the buyer or on the grounds that the courts should not recognize a "new tort" for computer malpractice. Other courts have simply applied traditional negligence principles to computer transactions in which the computer firm acts as a consultant or custom-designs a system for the purchaser. In the case that follows, the court recognizes a claim for negligence and holds the computer consultant to a professional standard of care.

CASE 50.4	**Diversified Graphics, Ltd. v. Ernst & Whinney** • 868 F.2d 293 (8th Cir. 1989)
FACTS	Diversified Graphics, Ltd. (D.G.), a screen printer and apparel manufacturer, hired Ernst & Whinney (E&W) to assist it in obtaining a computer system to fit its data-processing needs. E&W promised to locate a turnkey system which would be operational without the need for extensive employee training. The system that D.G. received, however, was difficult to operate and did not meet the needs of the company. It sued E&W in federal district court, asserting claims of negligence, breach of fiduciary duty, and breach of contract. At trial, the jury found in favor of D.G. on its negligence claim and awarded the plaintiff $82,500. E&W appealed to the Eighth Circuit Court of Appeals, arguing that the trial court improperly held it to a professional standard of care.
OPINION	LAY, J. . . . E&W argues that it should have been held to an ordinary, rather than a professional, standard of care. . . . A breach of a professional standard is more exacting and difficult to prove than breach of ordinary care. Accordingly, it would appear that a finding that E&W breached the former standard would necessarily encompass a finding that it failed to exercise ordinary care. In any event, D.G. presented sufficient evidence to support the jury's finding of lack of professional care. D.G.'s theory for recovery based on negligence encompasses the notion of a consultant-client relationship and therefore the existence of a professional standard of care: E&W failed to act reasonably in light of its superior knowledge and expertise in the area of computer systems. . . . D.G. claims that it retained E&W as a consultant during its purchase and implementation of an in-house data processing system. It is implicit in alleging the existence of an agreement that D.G. anticipated that E&W possessed superior knowledge in this area; D.G. contracted for the benefit of E&W's expertise. Based on D.G.'s allegations, E&W was properly held to a professional standard of care. The degree of skill and care that may be required of a professional is a question of fact for the jury. In the instant case, E&W argues that D.G. did not make a submissible case on negligence because D.G.'s expert, Norton Lee Hoffman, failed to both state the applicable professional standard and explain how E&W had violated that standard. . . . [W]e must agree with E&W that Hoffman could have stated the professional standard of care required of a computer systems consultant in a more straightforward manner. . . . Hoffman's testimony nonetheless contained significant discussion of the applicable professional standard of care and E&W's actions in relation to that standard. Furthermore, we find that there was substantial evidence elsewhere in the record regarding the applicable standards of a professional consultant. . . . The record reflects that D.G. had determined that it required a "turnkey" computer system that would fully perform all of its data processing in-house. The term "turnkey" is intended to describe a self-sufficient system which the purchaser need only "turn the key" to commence operation. The record makes clear that

CASE 50.4 Continued

the purchaser should not have to hire programmers and that current employees should not have to undergo extensive training to be able to operate the system. The evidence shows that to procure this type of customized and fully operational system, great care must be taken to carefully detail a business' needs and to properly develop specifications for the computer system. Potential vendors must be carefully scrutinized to discover all the inadequacies of their data processing systems. Once a vendor is chosen, proper implementation is imperative to ensure that the purchaser truly need only "turn the key" to commence full operation of the system. A fundamental part of the implementation involves testing the system through parallel data processing operation. Finally, the existence of adequate documentation regarding the operation of the system is crucial once the system is up and running. As previously stated, employees will have had only minimal training and will depend heavily on the instructions for operation. Moreover, documentation is particularly important because this type of system is highly customized and standard instruction sources will have only limited value.

Thus, the record reflects sufficient information from which a jury could determine the applicable professional standard of care and upon which the jury could conclude that E&W's conduct fell short of adhering to that standard. The record also contains sufficient evidence to support the jury's findings that the inadequacies of the data processing system caused D.G. to incur considerable expense necessary for modifications, employee training, and additional staffing and consultation.

JUDGMENT We therefore affirm the judgment entered by the district court insofar as it awards D.G. $82,500 for its negligence claim.

Strict Liability and Fraud

In most computer transactions, strict products liability will not be a viable theory of recovery. In the vast majority of jurisdictions, strict products liability applies only to "unreasonably dangerous" products that cause personal injuries or physical property damage. A plaintiff who suffers only economic losses (e.g., lost income or increased business expenses) as a result of a defective product cannot sue on the basis of strict liability. Thus, because most computer tort cases arise when an individual or business suffers economic losses as a result of a nonperforming system, strict liability is not a remedy for a defective computer system.

An injured party in a computer transaction can, however, sue for fraud when the computer developer has made fraudulent representations about the computer technology. The plaintiff must establish that the misrepresentations of the computer vendor were made knowingly and intentionally, and that the injured party reasonably relied on the representations to his or her damage. Despite the difficulties of proving the elements of fraud, individuals and businesses have been successful in suing for fraud in connection with a computer transaction. When the computer specialist undertakes to provide advice and information to a business or individual regarding the appropriate computer technology, a suit for negligent misrepresentation may also be available. For a thorough discussion of the torts of fraud and negligent misrepresentation, see Chapters 6 and 7.

COMPUTER CRIMES

Computer-related offenses have become a particularly troublesome type of white-collar crime. Today, computers process the financial transactions of government and of practically all business enterprises, large and small. Money circulates not physically but in the form of binary digital information. Computers perform the most intricate calculations and business tasks; some computers print out negotiable instruments; many write checks; others maintain inventories and place and fill orders. In addition, computer memory banks are repositories for trade secrets and other confidential business information such as customer lists and pricing formulas.

An unscrupulous individual who possesses the inventiveness to discover the required commands can, using his or her personal computer and telephone lines, unlawfully gain access to large corporation and government computers which are served by many terminals. Such an individual can unlawfully extract confidential information from the computer, rearrange its data, alter the accounts stored in its memory, or transfer money that the machine controls.

A number of computer programming whizzes, called hackers, intrigued by the challenge, set out to discover how to gain access to computers of large corporations and of government agencies using only their own personal computers and telephone hookups. Many hackers, including high school students, have succeeded. For example, four teenagers, one of them only 13 years old, illegally gained access to two computers at NASA's Marshall Space Center. Their unauthorized entry destroyed records and blocked scientists from using the government computers. Hackers have also illegally gained credit card numbers and infiltrated computerized files of colleges and universities, changing grades and even creating phony degrees. The government has fought back. Recently, two computer hackers pled guilty to gaining illegal access to the computers of Bank of America, Southwestern Bell, and TRW Information Services. They were part of a group called MOD, Masters of Disaster (or Deception), which used personal computers and modems to break into computer systems.

Computer viruses and worms present a means to damage or destroy computer technology. For example, a computer whiz graduate student at Cornell University created a computer program by which, using the electronic mail system, he entered into the unclassified nationwide Pentagon network called Internet. The electronic worm interfered with the operations of about 6,000 computers across the country until it was detected and removed. Fortunately, the worm caused no lasting damage.

Thefts running into millions of dollars have been committed by computer manipulation. Some experts estimate that computer crimes cost the public at least $10 billion a year. The report of the legislative hearings upon the bill which became the Small Business Computer Security and Information Act of 1984 states in part:

Many small businesses have yet to learn . . . how to protect their information, and how to safeguard their computers from accidental or deliberate misuse. . . . The stakes are high. According to FBI statistics, the average bank robbery is $10,000. The FBI estimates that the average computer crime is over $400,000. According to one expert on computer crime, only one of the estimated 200,000 computer crimes committed each year is likely to be prosecuted. Few companies want to admit they were victims of computer theft because it would devastate a firm's image. . . .

Kinds of Computer Crime

Businesspeople should know that a computer may be used for criminal purposes in many ways. For example, false information may be inserted into the machine to alter data in the computer's memory; programming orders given to a computer may be wrongfully modified; or a wrongdoer may withdraw from a computer's memory and improperly use information stored within it. Illustrative of such computer crimes are the following occurrences.

1 A bank official introduced into a computer false debits and credits at such intervals that the bank's internal security system did not detect the fraud for a considerable time. As a result, the official succeeded in embezzling $21 million from the bank before he was caught.

2 By telephone, a man not connected with a company instructed its computer to deliver supplies of wire, cable, and other costly equipment to locations he selected. The deliveries were made, and he subsequently unlawfully sold more than $1 million of the company's products.

3 In the now-famous *Equity Funding* case, the management of a large finance company which controlled a mutual fund and an insurance company inflated its assets by programming its computer to show ownership of about 50,000 fictitious insurance policies reputed to be worth about $2 billion. Other insurance companies, in legitimate transactions called "reinsurance," purchased many of the fictitious policies. The purchasers relied upon computer printouts furnished them to establish the authenticity and current status of the nonexistent policies. Millions of dollars were lost through the far-reaching swindle.

4 An employee in the accounting department of a large company was authorized to "round out" employees' net salaries down to two decimal places. When he did so, using the computer, he wrongfully transferred the tiny remainder amounts to his own salary account. Over a period of time he thereby "earned" thousands of dollars.

Laws Applicable to Computer Crimes

Statutes which prohibit the theft of property, unlawful destruction of property, mail fraud, wire fraud, and theft of trade secrets were enacted long before computers came upon the scene. Now, with the advent of the computer age, the question has arisen whether computer software, information, and services are covered by the terms used in the precomputer statutes, and whether unauthorized access and other computer abuses fall within the prohibition of the statutes. Although that question has generally been answered in the affirmative, and the government has been able to successfully prosecute individuals under these criminal laws, some persons misusing computers or computer information have escaped prosecution.

As a result, and to remove any doubt as to whether "old" criminal statutes apply to computer activities, most states have enacted laws specifically defining computer crimes. The federal government has also passed several statutes prohibiting computer frauds and wrongs.

State Computer Crimes. Almost all states have passed statutes prohibiting various computer wrongs, including computer theft and unauthorized access to computers. A common offense is **computer fraud** or **computer theft,** frequently defined as using a computer—or accessing a computer, computer system, or computer network—for the purpose of (1) devising or executing any scheme to defraud or (2) obtaining money, property, or services by means of false conduct, practices, or representations.

Some states have delineated specific computer crimes to cover various types of computer abuse. An example is the Georgia statute which prohibits (1) computer theft; (2) **computer trespass** (unauthorized use of a computer to delete, remove, obstruct, interrupt, interfere, alter, or damage a computer, computer network, computer data, or program); (3) **computer invasion of privacy** (unauthorized use of a computer to examine any employment, medical, salary, credit, or financial or personal data on another person); (4) **computer forgery;** and (5) **computer password disclosure** (unauthorized disclosure of a number, code, password, or other means of access to a computer). Connecticut along with several other states has passed a comprehensive statute which outlaws the following crimes:

- Unauthorized access to a computer system—knowingly accessing a computer without authority
- Theft of computer services—accessing a computer system with the intent to obtain unauthorized computer services
- Interruption of computer services—intentionally degrading or disrupting a computer system or access to it
- Misuse of computer system information—accessing a computer or a computer system and

intentionally altering, deleting, adding, destroying, intercepting, using, or disclosing data in the system
- Destruction of computer equipment—intentionally tampering with, taking, transferring, concealing, altering, or damaging computer equipment

Federal Computer Crimes. The federal government has also passed several statutes to deal with computer crimes. The most important is the Computer Fraud and Abuse Act. This law makes it a federal crime to:

- Knowingly access a computer and without authority secure information that has been restricted by the federal government
- Intentionally access a computer and without authority obtain financial records of a financial institution or credit card issuer or secure information in a consumer's file from a consumer reporting agency
- Intentionally and without authority access any computer that is exclusively used by an agency of the federal government
- Knowingly and with intent to defraud gain access to a "federal interest computer" (a computer used exclusively by a financial institution or the federal government) and further the fraud by some act
- Intentionally access a federal interest computer and without authority alter, damage, or destroy information, or prevent authorized use and cause losses of $1,000 or more

Also, it is estimated that there are forty provisions of the federal criminal code (Title 18, U.S. Code) which may be applicable to the misuse of computers. These are particularly 18 USC 1029, which prohibits fraud and related offenses involving counterfeit and unauthorized credit cards and other "access devices"; 18 USC 641, which prohibits theft of government property and related offenses; 18 USC 1341, which prohibits mail fraud; and 18 USC 1343, which prohibits fraud by wire. Of importance, too, is the Electronic Funds Transfer Act (15 USC 1693), which concerns the making of payments and deposits electronically.

COMPUTERS AND PRIVACY

Although our society has reaped the social and economic benefits of computers, it has also had to face the dangers to privacy posed by the use of computers and related technologies. Individual privacy is threatened by the pervasive use of computers in gathering and storing private information and by the intrusive nature of computer-based technologies. Traditional privacy laws have proved to be inadequate to protect individual privacy in the computer age. State privacy laws provide only a modicum of protection from invasions of privacy involving computer technology. The tort of invasion of privacy discussed in Chapter 6 protects individuals from unreasonable intrusion into their private affairs and from the public disclosure of private facts. Thus, some forms of unauthorized access to computers and disclosure of private information may fall within the parameters of the invasion of privacy tort. To strengthen the traditional protections for privacy, both the states and the federal government have passed laws to control access to private information stored in public and private data banks, to protect electronic communications, and to restrict computer telemarketing. These laws are examined in the following discussion.

Access to Private Information

Computer technology has allowed the government and businesses to create massive data banks of information on individuals. Because public and private data banks contain a great deal of sensitive information—private information on a individual's credit history, medical records, bank accounts, and personal life—laws have been enacted to control the use of and access to this information. For example, the Right to Financial Privacy Act of 1978 prohibits the federal government from gaining access to a person's records at a financial institution without his or her consent or a warrant. Many states have similar state laws controlling access to financial records by state government agencies. Access to student records at colleges and universities is restricted by the Family Educational Rights and Privacy Act, and video rental stores and public libraries cannot disclose a customer's choice of movie rentals under the Video Privacy Protection Act of 1988. The Computer Fraud and Abuse Act prohibits various forms of unauthorized access to the federal government's computer system. It also specifically prohibits anyone from gaining access to a computer and securing a person's records at a financial institution or credit card issuer or a consumer's file at a consumer reporting agency.

E-Mail and Computer Communications

Computers have changed the way we talk to each other; E-mail and computer bulletin boards have become modern high-tech modes of communication. Congress has passed several statutes to protect electronic communications from eavesdropping and snooping by others. The Electronic Communications Privacy Act of 1986 prohibits any third party, government or private individual, from intercepting a computer communication or disclosing the contents of such communications without authorization. The law does not, however, prohibit employers from intercepting their employees' electronic communications at work. The law is supplemented by the Stored Wire and Electronic Communications and Transactional Records Act. The Stored Wire Act generally prohibits anyone from intentionally and without authority gaining access to or disclosing the contents of electronic communications in electronic storage.

Computer Telemarketing

Computer-generated telemarketing systems (**autodialers**) automatically dial telephone numbers and leave prerecorded sales messages with consumers. Autodialers provide the benefits of telemarketing without the cost of live operators, furnishing an efficient and inexpensive means of marketing products and services. Although they are particularly attractive to small businesses, consumers and others have complained about this new technology. Autodialers have tied up telephone lines when they failed to disconnect, including emergency numbers and medical facilities, and some consumers find the impersonal calls annoying and intrusive. In response, the federal government and the states have acted to curtail the use of autodialers. Forty states have passed laws that either regulate the timing and content of computer-generated calls or that ban the calls altogether. Recently, Congress passed the Telephone Consumer Protection Act of 1991 prohibiting computer-generated commercial solicitations without the prior consent of the person called. The constitutionality of the restrictions on autodialers is open to question, however, because the laws restrict commercial free speech. (See discussion of commercial speech in Chapter 3.)

Computer Monitoring

Businesses are increasingly using **electronic monitoring** of their employees to achieve better supervision and increased productivity. Electronic monitoring involves the use of computer technology to gauge the performance of workers on computer terminals. Such monitoring is used extensively in service businesses to oversee clerical workers, telephone operators, and customer services employees. The use of such surveillance techniques has come under criticism by those who contend that monitoring is an unreasonable intrusion into workers' privacy and causes undue stress on employees. Although few legal restrictions apply to these practices, legislation has been proposed at the state and federal levels. Congress is considering the Privacy for Consumers and Workers Act which would place significant limits on employers' use of electronic monitoring. The law would require employers to notify employees of the types and frequency of electronic monitoring and give workers access to the information collected. It would also restrict employers' internal use of the information and the disclosure of it to third parties. Some states are considering similar legislation to protect workers' privacy interests.

SUMMARY

Computer law is the application of intellectual property, contract, tort, and criminal law to computer technology. Computer firms have protected property rights in their work products. Computer programs can be copyrighted under federal law. The copyright owner may license others to use the program and prevent the unlawful infringement of his or her copyright. Protection will cover the literal elements of a program and may extend to some nonliteral aspects as well. Patents provide an alternative vehicle to protect computer hardware and software. To secure such protection, however, the developer must establish that the computer innovation is useful, novel, and not an obvious variation of existing technology. Even in the absence of patent or copyright protection, state trade secret law will protect computer developers when their technology is kept secret and gives them a competitive advantage in the marketplace. Firms can thus prevent the misappropriation of trade secrets by former employees of the firm.

Computer transactions are usually governed by the UCC or the common law of contracts. Sales law governs when the transaction involves goods (e.g., hardware and prepackaged software) and the agreement is a sale or other "transaction" in goods. When sales law applies, the purchaser's primary remedy for defective software is a suit for breach of the express and implied warranties of the Code. Vendors will often defend on the basis of disclaimers or limitation of remedies in the computer contract. They may also attempt to rely on a box-top license, although the validity and binding effect of such "shrinkwrap" agreements is open to question. Tort theories provide an alternative ground upon which to hold a computer firm liable for defects in computer technology, particularly in the context of contracts for computer consulting and for custom-designed systems. The courts are divided, however, on the availability of computer malpractice or negligence claims. Fraud and negligent misrepresentation provide other grounds to sue a computer developer.

Computer crimes are a significant social problem. The states and the federal government have responded to the computer crime problem by passing specific laws tailored to computer crimes and by enforcing existing criminal statutes against violators. Laws have also been passed to protect privacy from intrusions involving computer technology.

REVIEW QUESTIONS

1. (a) Why is it important for a computer developer to protect its computer technology under copyright or patent law? (b) How does copyright protection differ from patent protection?

2. (a) Should copyright law protect the nonliteral aspects of computer programs? (b) Explain the policy reasons for and against such protection.

3. (a) What is the work-for-hire rule under the Copyright Act? (b) If a business hires an independent contractor to create a program, how can it preserve its copyright in the program?

4. Explain the concept of a trade secret and the application of trade secret law to computer technology.

5. (a) What types of computer transactions are governed by the UCC? (b) What types are governed by the common law?

6. (a) When does a computer transaction have to be in writing to be enforceable? (b) What are the advantages of a written contract? (c) From a vendor's perspective, what terms should be contained in the computer contract?

7. What is a "shrinkwrap" agreement?

8. (a) What warranties will protect the purchaser of computer technology? (b) How can those warranties be limited?

9. (a) Should the courts recognize a tort of computer malpractice? (b) If so, in what types of computer transactions should a suit for malpractice exist?

10. (a) Identify the different types of computer crimes that may be committed against a business. (b) What laws exist to control those crimes?

CASE PROBLEMS

1. Nintendo of America Inc. produces and sells the popular Nintendo Entertainment System (NES), a home video game system. It designed a computer program, the 10NES, which prevented the system from accepting unauthorized game cartridges. Atari, a competitor, attempted to analyze and duplicate the 10NES security system. It secured a reproduction of the 10NES program from the U.S. Copyright Office by falsely stating that it was a defendant in a copyright infringement action and needed the program for that litigation. After obtaining the source code, it was able to decipher the object code of the program. Atari then developed its own program, called Rabbit, to unlock the NES system, and allow Atari access to Nintendo owners without having to pay a license fee to Nintendo. Rabbit employed a different programming language from the 10NES, but it generated signals that were indistinguishable from the Nintendo program. Nintendo sued Atari for copyright infringement. Atari claimed that it broke the 10NES code by reverse engineering, and that its program was not substantially similar to Nintendo's. How will the copyright issues be resolved in this case? Explain. Is it significant that Atari improperly secured the code for the 10NES from the Copyright Office? Why?

2. Vault Corporation copyrighted a computer program called PROLOK that prevents the copying of software programs. It sold PROLOK to software manufacturers and others under a box-top license agreement providing that the software could not be transferred, copied, decompiled, or disassembled. Quaid Software manufactured CopyWrite, a segment of which allowed a user to make a copy of software programs on a PROLOK disk. It had acquired the PROLOK disk by mail, and from an analysis of the program, developed the CopyWrite program. Vault Corporation sued Quaid Software to stop its sales of CopyWrite, claiming a breach of its licensing agreement and a misappropriation of its trade secrets. Vault relied on the Louisiana Software License Enforcement Act (SLEA) which allowed software sellers to bind purchasers to the terms of a box-top license agreement. It argued that by reverse engineering the PROLOK program, Quaid had violated the SLEA and thus used an improper means to discover Vault's trade secrets in its PROLOK program. It also argued that Quaid infringed or contributed to others' infringing its copyrights. Quaid defended on the grounds that CopyWrite enabled software owners to make lawful archival copies of the PROLOK program. It also contended that the SLEA was preempted by the Copyright Act because the SLEA conflicted with the rights of program purchasers to make lawful archival copies of their program copies. Who is likely to prevail on these issues? Explain.

3. Howard Rubin developed a computer program that estimates the time, staff, risks, money, and type of hardware required to develop new software or modify existing software. Rubin developed the program by scanning existing research, acquiring his own data, and using an IBM manual. Computer Associates acquired the rights to the software and marketed it under the trademarks CA-Estimacs and CA-Planmacs. Computer Associates sold over 17 million of the programs under license agreements providing that title remained with Computer Associates, that the program was a trade secret, and that the licensee was under a strict duty of confidentiality. Employees of the firm were required to sign employment contracts containing promises not to disclose any trade secrets of the company, and upon termination to sign a promise of confidentiality. One of the employees, David Bryan, worked for the company for 7 years. He became an expert on the Estimacs systems and learned of confidential customer feedback on the programs. He left the company and developed a competing estimating program using his knowledge of Computer Associates' programs. Computer Associates and Rubin sued him for misappropriating trade secrets. Bryan defended, claiming that the Rubin programs were developed from public sources and, therefore, not trade secrets. He also argued that his employment agreement with Computer Associates was unconscionable. Are the programs developed by Rubin legitimate trade secrets? Why? Who is likely to prevail in the lawsuit? Explain.

4. Cricket Alley Corporation operates seven women's clothing stores with headquarters in Wichita, Kansas. The company had a Wang computer, but its computerized cash registers could not communicate with the computer. As a result, the company had to manually enter cash register information on the main computer. It wanted to secure a modern system in which the computerized cash registers could communicate with the main computer. Cricket Alley's president, Robert Harvey, saw an advertisement in a retail trade magazine showing Wang computers communicating with computers manufactured by Data Terminal Systems (DTS). Later, at a retail merchants' convention, Harvey saw a DTS display in which Wang computers were working with DTS cash registers. He was told by a DTS representative at the display that the DTS machines could communicate with the Wang computers. Cricket Alley purchased ten DTS cash registers, but the company was never able to get the DTS machines to consistently work with the Wang computer. Eventually it replaced the equipment with IBM machines, which functioned with the Wang as a system, and sued DTS for breach of warranty. Can Cricket Alley sue for breach of warranty? Explain. What warranties were created by the sale? Explain. What warranties were breached? Explain.

5. In 1980, Invacare Corporation decided to purchase a computer system capable of coordinating its accounting and manufacturing systems. Sperry Corporation sent a team of manufacturing specialists to examine Invacare's operations and recommend a particular computer. Sperry recommended the purchase of a Univac System 80 computer along with programs and data-processing products from Sperry. Invacare purchased the system. It alleged that the Univac System 80 was incapable of operating the Sperry programs, and that the products were incapable of fulfilling Invacare's needs. Invacare sued Sperry, claiming that Sperry was negligent in recommending the Univac System 80 and in advising Invacare to acquire the program when it knew or should have known that the system wouldn't meet Invacare's needs. Sperry made a motion to dismiss the suit, contending that the negligence claim was for computer malpractice and not a valid claim. Assuming that the facts are true, will the court allow a claim against Sperry for negligence? Explain. Upon what other grounds can Invacare sue Sperry?

CHAPTER 51

Law and the Environment

The emergence and accumulation of laws intended to protect the environment coincide with society's growing awareness in the late twentieth century that human activity can greatly affect the air we breathe, the water we drink, the wildlife we enjoy—the viability of our very own existence.

Until recent decades, our laws reflected society's view that natural resources such as clean air and water were inexhaustible, and that nature would cleanse itself somehow. In addition, our laws and customs concerning the use and disposal of property, both real and personal, were guided almost exclusively by the free market "invisible hand" notion, a notion which holds that the most efficient use and allocation of resources, especially those associated with private property, occurs when individuals act in their own self-interest and without government intervention.

Accordingly, older laws that could today be considered environmental in nature were based on the common law, principally property law and tort law, which offered remedies in money damages and in equity—injunctions and orders. These traditional laws, in order to address environmental concerns, relied on individuals to take legal action to assert their own interests in their own legally protected rights in property and person.

The traditional laws, however, were not geared for providing private redress to stem environmental destruction caused by complex processes involving many, perhaps uncountable, enterprises and individuals. One such set of complex processes concerns those believed to lead to acid rain, a phenomenon created when smokestack operations in one region of the United States emit chemical compounds which come down as acid in the rainfall of other regions, causing damage to forests, wetlands, lakes, and associated wildlife. Under traditional laws, those whose property or person is injured by acid rain cannot sue a whole manufacturing region. There would be plainly too many defendants, and moreover it would be impossible to provide legal evidence of direct causation of private injury by identifiable defendants.

As modern economists have pointed out, the traditional laws provided no means for assigning the costs of "externalities" to those who injure the quality of the environment. Generally defined, externalities are those effects that go along with a particular activity or process. In the context of environmental concerns, an externality might be the accompanying degradation of air quality associated with a manufacturing plant's operation of a smokestack. Under traditional laws, the manufacturer pays no direct cost for injuring the environment by emitting smoke; yet there is the external cost of diminished air quality to be paid by those who are not the manufacturer.

As society began to recognize that natural resources are indeed exhaustible and that natural processes cannot clean the environment as fast as people can pollute it, contemporary federal and state regulation was created in an attempt to better assign the cost of environmental injury to those who commit the injury and to discourage environmentally destructive activities. This modern regulation is far reaching and governs many activities.

Both the traditional laws and modern regulation are in effect today. Recent cases in New Jersey[1] and some other states suggest that a period of expansion of tort liability for environmental injurers may lie ahead. Accordingly, this chapter will first cover the traditional legal approach to remedy environmental injury, coverage expanded beyond what is generally found in business laws texts, and then provide discussion of state and federal law and regulation.

THE TRADITIONAL APPROACH

The traditional approach relies on common law and equity theories which have evolved through the centuries. Recall from the introductory chapters of this text that in the United States, actions in common law and in equity are generally heard in the same court and do not require separate proceedings. In private legal actions to remedy an environmental injury, the distinction between common law and equity is quite important. This chapter will not devote a special discussion section to the distinction, but the following simple test can be used to determine whether a suit sounds in common law or in equity or both. The test relies on the nature of the remedy sought—whether the plaintiff wants money damages or whether the plaintiff is asking the defendant either to stop a particular activity (an injunction) or to perform specific actions (specific performance). If the plaintiff is after money damages, the action is in common law. If an injunction or order of specific performance is sought, the action is in equity.

The distinction between common law and equity is a very practical one in environment-related lawsuits. A defendant who has lost a common law action fulfills his or her legal obligations by paying the money damages. If the defendant continues the environmentally injurious activity, the plaintiff would have to sue again. However, a legal action in equity which results in, for example, an injunction against a defendant imposes a legal obligation on the defendant not to engage in the injurious activity. The practicality of the distinction is that common law remedies allow businesses to assess the relative costliness of their actions. If money damages are minor, an enterprise may simply consider those damages as the cost of doing business. Common law remedies also include punitive damages for intentional harm. By contrast, an equity remedy—an injunction or order—either forbids a certain activity altogether or orders that certain actions be taken. An injunction or order could suspend or even shut down business operations altogether.

Though legal actions based on traditional approaches may be variously limited by federal and state statutes, common law environmental suits continue to be a part of the legal apparatus used to compensate injured plaintiffs and to discourage future environmental injury. For instance, part of the litigation surrounding the 1989 *Exxon Valdez* oil spill off the coast of Alaska included suits by private parties (local businesses, outdoor photographers, outdoor sportspeople, fish processors, and others) on common law grounds.[2]

---

[1] *Rubanick v. Witco Chemical Corp.*, 125 N.J. 421 (1991); *T & E Industries, Inc. v. Safety Light Corporation*, 123 N.J. 371 (1991). In these two trend-setting tort cases, the New Jersey Supreme Court gave favor to environmental protection, with the cost of protection to be paid by industry.

[2] See *In re Exxon Valdez*, 767 F. Supp. 1509 (D. Alaska 1991), in which the court denied dismissal of state common law claims, allowing the case to proceed on complaints of negligence, nuisance, misrepresentation, and tortious interference with contract, as well as on strict liability claims as limited by state statute.

Depending upon the nature of the injury to person or property and the type of remedy sought, a legal action for environmental harm could be based on any of a number of common law concepts. In this section, four of the more common bases for legal action will be discussed: (1) intentional interference with property or person, (2) nuisance, (3) negligence, and (4) strict liability.

Intentional Interference with Property or Person

Intentional interference is among the oldest bases for legal action in common law. It is based on society's recognition of a personal freedom from purposeful interference with exclusive use of one's property and from unwanted contact with one's body. The origins of this legal action come from the thirteenth-century notion of "trespass," or intentional, direct injury to people or property. The term lives in the law today, as the case at the end of this section illustrates, and the associated concept provides a basis for private parties to obtain legal remedy for environmental injury which affects them directly.

Chapters 6 and 7 provide general discussions on the elements of torts. In this chapter, two aspects of an important element of trespass—intent—merit reemphasis in an environmental law context. First, a common requisite for a jury or court to award punitive damages is intent. Punitive damages, as the name indicates, offer civil punishment for defendant's wrongdoing and operate over and above the actual damages a plaintiff may have suffered. Especially in environmental legal actions, the provable actual damages can be very small indeed—perhaps only some annoying dust or smoke, or perhaps a day of physical discomfort such as watery eyes or merely an off-taste in well water with no provable lasting effects or threats to health. Merely to award minor actual damages would provide little economic incentive for an offending enterprise not to pollute repeatedly. Substantial punitive awards assist in removing profitability from those who would otherwise cause environmental injury.

The second aspect of intent to be reemphasized here is that the application of the concept goes beyond the word's common meaning. More than "meaning to do harm," the concept of intent goes directly to whether one meant to do the *actions* which resulted in harm. So, for example, an operator of an auto body shop who sprays paint on repaired cars in the open air might not intend that benzene (a common paint component) be inhaled by passersby or that fine particles settle and dry on nearby property; but this operator's conduct could be determined as intentional—because he purposefully sprayed the car in a way that certain and expected consequences of the conduct will be harmful.

Trespass. The modern articulation of **trespass,** generally adopted in most states, appears in the *Restatement (Second), Torts* (1965), Section 158, which states:

One is subject to liability to another for trespass, irrespective of whether he thereby causes harm to any legally protected interest of the other, if he intentionally (a) enters land in the possession of the other, or causes a thing or third person to do so, or (b) remains on the land and, or (c) fails to remove from the land a thing which he is under a duty to remove.

In environmental law, the nature of the entrance on land by a trespasser is particularly relevant, and application of the rule (in addition to the other standard elements of trespass) revolves around the causing of a "thing" to enter the land. What is a thing? The common law in most states requires that a thing be a perceivable object of some sort. For instance, in the earlier example involving the auto body operator, the fine but perceivable mist of paint settling on nearby property could be determined as sufficient to constitute trespass. However, from state to state there is no uniform agreement in the common law on what a thing is. In some states, the mere stirring up of dust on one property which then settles on another is not trespass,[3] though dust is indisputably composed of many

---

[3] See *Padilla v. Lawrence*, 101 N.M. 556 (1984), in which the court held that dust from a manure plant was not trespass, unless the amount was measurable.

minuscule, but perceivable, objects. Frequently, courts will not determine a trivial entrance upon property as trespass. However, an emerging feature—perhaps a future trend—in the common law is to recognize invisibly small objects as things, some totally lacking in physical substance. A small number of recent cases have recognized intangible intrusions on property—such as radioactive emissions[4] and damage-causing vibrations[5]—to be trespass.

Battery. The essence of the notion of **battery** is the intentional infliction of harm by an unwanted touching. The *Restatement (Second), Torts* (1965), Section 13, states that one is liable for battery if:

(a) he acts, intending to cause a harmful or offensive contact with another, or if there is an imminent apprehension of such a contact, and (b) a harmful contact with another directly or indirectly results.

The classic battery is a punch in the nose, but in the context of environmental law the unwanted touching is more subtle. Essentially, the unwanted touching is accomplished indirectly, with a person setting off forces or objects in force which result in harm to another—such as discharging chemicals into the air or water and ultimately into contact with people or setting off explosions or vibrations.

In a legal action alleging battery, showing that a polluter intended to do harm is a practical difficulty. The doctrines surrounding "intent" in a battery action are more stringent than those in trespass actions; and though common law cases may start with complaints of battery, they more often proceed on the basis of aggravated negligence employing a "wilful and wanton" or "reckless" standard, which like an intentional tort allows plaintiffs to seek punitive damages.

---

[4]*Maryland Heights Leasing, Inc. v. Mallinckrodt, Inc.*, 706 S.W.2d 218 (Mo. App. 1985).

[5]See *Wilson v. Interlake Steel Co.*, 649 P.2d 922 (Cal. 1982), in which the court held that vibrations by themselves are not trespass, but damage-causing intangible intrusions may constitute trespass.

Nuisance

Nuisance is the interference with one's right to use and enjoy one's property. A tort, nuisance can be either intentional or negligent, but generally speaking only a finding of intentional nuisance also carries the possibility that a plaintiff may seek punitive damages.

The nonpunitive remedies for nuisance that plaintiffs may seek are actual damages (which may include both current and future economic losses) and injunctions—legal orders which put a stop to offending conduct. However, courts are often reluctant to issue blanket injunctions in nuisance actions, and even though the legal action is between two private parties, courts often weigh competing social interests of third parties before issuing an injunction. For example, a solitary plaintiff with an undisputed nuisance claim against a manufacturer whose factory is the area's largest employer is unlikely to be successful in getting an injunction to shut down the factory. A court will likely balance the interests of the community with the interests of the plaintiff. Since more persons (third parties, such as factory employees and local retailers) would be harmed by an injunction than a solitary plaintiff would be helped, a court would probably opt to grant only money damages.

At first glance, an action in nuisance against an environmental injurer may seem like an action in trespass—because both actions protect the exclusive right to use and enjoy personal property. But nuisance and trespass are fundamentally different. Whereas trespass is based upon a physical invasion onto property, nuisance is not. Nuisance involves nonphysical interferences—noise, smells, light (or obstruction of it), and the like.

Accordingly, if there has been a physical invasion onto land, a plaintiff may sue the party causing the invasion both in trespass and in nuisance, but without a physical invasion, only a nuisance action is available.

Case 51.1, at the end of this section, addresses nuisance and distinguishes it from trespass.

Negligence

Common law **negligence** operates in environmental law the same as it does in any other setting. Negligence revolves around a party's failure to meet a duty to act reasonably which results in harm or a failure to use reasonable care to avoid a foreseeable harm.

The modern proliferation of federal, state, and local environmental statutes and regulations has, in part, assisted injured plaintiffs in mounting negligence actions against environmental tortfeasors. By articulating specific mandatory conduct and prohibited conduct for businesses to follow in protecting the environment, these modern environmental statutes and regulations have established legal duties, the breach of which can give rise to a common law cause of action in negligence.

In addition, while damages for negligence are usually for actual damages, circumstances can arise for awards of punitive damages for gross negligence. Generally, punitive damages in tort arise in situations in which the tortfeasor's conduct was intentional. Negligence, by conventional legal categorization, is an unintentional tort. However, some negligent and harmful conduct, though unintentional, can be so unreasonable that it is legally deemed "wilful and wanton" or "reckless" and rises to what could be called "quasi-intent"[6] (i.e., similar to but not the same as legal intent), and accordingly can be the appropriate basis for a punitive award. In a somewhat celebrated case,[7] a class of plaintiffs sued a chemical company for injuries resulting from the company's burying of more than 300,000 drums of toxic chemicals which contaminated the plaintiffs' drinking water. The plaintiffs sought $1.5 billion in compensatory damages and $1 billion in punitive damages, but after 8 years of litigation, the court awarded $5.3 million in compensation, $8.9 million in back interest, and $7.5 million in punitives based in large part on what the court called "gross, wilful and wanton disregard for the health and well-being of the plaintiffs."

Strict Liability

Strict liability, as applied in the environmental setting, resembles strict liability in products law. Businesses which place "unreasonably dangerous products" in the flow of commerce can be held liable for injuries caused by those products, regardless of fault. Similarly, business which engage in "abnormally dangerous" or "ultrahazardous" activity can also be held strictly liable for injuries caused by the activity.

The common law of ultrahazardous or abnormally dangerous activities is stated in the *Restatement (Second), Torts* (1977), Sections 519 and 520, as follows:

519. General Principle
(1) One who carries on an abnormally dangerous activity is subject to liability for harm to the person, land or chattels of another resulting from the activity, although he has exercised the utmost care to prevent the harm. . . .
520. Abnormally Dangerous Activities
In determining whether an activity is abnormally dangerous, the following factors are to be considered:
  (a) existence of a high degree of risk of some harm to the person, land or chattels of others;
  (b) likelihood that the harm that results from it will be great;
  (c) inability to eliminate the risk by the exercise of reasonable care;
  (d) extent to which the activity is not a matter of common usage;
  (e) inappropriateness of the activity to the place where it is carried on; and
  (f) extent to which its value to the commnity is outweighed by its dangerous attributes.

This type of strict liability is applied when harm occurs as a result of businesses engaging in the making and transportation of toxic chemicals, explosives, radioactive materials, and similarly ultrahazardous substances and related operations.

---

[6]W. Prosser, LAW OF TORTS 184-6 (4th ed., 1964), describes quasi-intent as "[l]ying between intent to do harm . . . and the mere unreasonable risk of harm to another involved in ordinary negligence."

[7]*Sterling v. Velsicol Chemical Corp.*, 647 F. Supp 303 (W.D. Tenn. 1986), aff'd in part, rev'd in part, 855 F.2d 1188 (6th Cir. 1988).

CASE 51.1 **Bradley v. American Smelting and Refining Company**
• 104 Wash. 2d 677, 709 P.2d 782 (1985)

FACTS Michael and Marie Bradley own and occupy real property on Vashon Island in King County, Washington. Four miles to the south of the Bradleys, American Smelting and Refining Company (ASARCO) operates a primary copper smelter in Ruston, Washington, near Tacoma.

The ASARCO smelter meets the National Ambient Air Quality Standards, both primary and secondary, for both sulfur dioxide and particulate matter. The smelter is also in compliance with the Puget Sound Air Pollution Control Agency's Regulation I concerning particulate emissions.

As part of the industrial process of smelting copper, various gases such as sulfur dioxide and particulate matter (including arsenic, cadmium, and other metals) are emitted. The particulate matter is composed of distinct particles of matter other than water which cannot be detected by the human senses. ASARCO was aware since 1905, when it acquired the smelting plant, that the wind on occasion does cause smelter particulate emissions to blow over Vashon Island.

In 1983, the Bradleys brought an action in King County Superior Court against ASARCO alleging intentional trespass and nuisance. The case was removed to the U.S. District Court, and upon certification came before the Supreme Court of Washington to resolve questions of state law to be applied to the case.

OPINION CALLOW, J. . . . For the purposes of resolving the certified questions, the parties stipulate [agree] that some particulate emissions of both cadmium and arsenic from the Tacoma smelter have been and are continuing to be deposited on plaintiff's land.

1. Did the defendant have the requisite intent to commit intentional trespass as a matter of law? . . .

Addressing the definition, scope and meaning of "intent," Section 8A of the *Restatement (Second) of Torts* says:

> The word "intent" is used . . . to denote that the actor desires to cause consequences of his act, or that he believes that the consequences are substantially certain to result from it. . . .
>
> Intent is not, however, limited to the consequences which are desired. If the actor knows that the consequences are certain, or substantially certain, to result from his act, and still goes ahead, he is treated by the law as if he had in fact desired to produce the result.

ASARCO has know for decades that sulfur dioxide and particulates of arsenic, cadmium, and other metals were being emitted from the tall smokestack. It had to know that the solids propelled into the air by the warm gases would settle back to earth somewhere. It had to know that the purpose of the tall stack was to disperse gas, smoke and minute solids over as large an area as possible as far away as possible, but that while any resulting contamination would be diminished as to any one area or landowner, that nonetheless contamination, though slight, would follow. . . .

**CASE 51.1
Continued**

We find that ASARCO had the requisite intent to commit intentional trespass as a matter of law.

2. Does an intentional deposit of microscopic particulates, undetectable by the human senses, upon a person's property give rise to a cause of action for trespassory invasion of the person's right to exclusive possession of property as well as a claim of nuisance?

The courts have been groping for a reconciliation of the doctrines of trespass and nuisance over a long period of time and, to a great extent, have concluded that little of substance remains to any distinction between the two when air pollution is involved. . . .

The first and most important proposition about trespass and nuisance principles is that they are largely coextensive. Both concepts are often discussed in the same cases without differentiation between the elements of recovery. . . . It is also true that in the environmental arena both nuisance and trespass cases typically involve intentional conduct by the defendant. . . . The principal difference in theories is that the tort of trespass is complete upon a tangible invasion of plaintiff's property, however slight, whereas a nuisance requires proof that the interference with use and enjoyment is "substantial and unreasonable." . . .

We hold that theories of trespass and nuisance are not inconsistent, that the theories may apply concurrently, and that the injured party may proceed under both theories when the elements of both actions are present.

3. Does the cause of action for trespassory invasion require proof of actual damages?

When airborne particles are transitory or quickly dissipate, they do not interfere with a property owner's possessory rights and, therefore, are properly denominated as nuisances. When, however, the particles or substance accumulates on the land and does not pass away, then a trespass has occurred. While at common law any trespass entitled a landowner to recover nominal or punitive damages . . . , such a rule is not appropriate under the circumstances before us. No useful purpose would be served by sanctioning actions in trespass by every landowner within a hundred miles of a manufacturing plant. Manufacturers would be harassed and the litigious few would cause the escalation of costs to the detriment of the many. The elements that we have adopted for an action in trespass . . . require that a plaintiff has suffered actual and substantial damages. Since this is an element of the action, the plaintiff who cannot show that actual and substantial damages have been suffered should be subject to dismissal of his cause upon a motion of summary judgment. . . .

JUDGMENT

Returned to District Court for further action.

ENVIRONMENTAL STATUTES AND REGULATION

Because of the vast enormity of detailed state and federal law and regulation on matters involving the environment, it is impossible to provide the business law student with the same level of coverage of substantive law in this area as is found in earlier chapters devoted to other subjects. Accordingly, this section is primarily intended to provide (1) a general understanding of the legal and regulatory framework governing activities which affect the environment, and (2) familiarity with the goals and objectives of specific environmental laws.

State and Local Environmental Control

To varying degrees, states and localities regulate activities which have environmental consequences. The sheer quantity of state and local laws prohibits extensive discussion of them here. Such laws range from long-standing local "washday" laws,[8] which restrict commercial and individual incineration to specified days of the week, to complicated laws regulating land use.

To the extent that enforceable state laws cannot be more lenient than federal environmental laws, many individual states also regulate air and water pollution, waste disposal, auto emissions, pesticide use, and so forth. States also have laws which govern wildlife and habitat.

The common types of local (county, city, township, village) law which reflect environmental concerns govern waste disposal, recycling, zoning, noise, commercial activity, parks, and more recently indoor working environments. This list, however, is far from exhaustive. Local environmental laws affect a wide range of private and commercial activities. For example, local regulations which require cemeteries not to allow burial without sealed vaults may reflect the community's protection against anaerobic bacterial contamination of groundwaters upon which the local well-water supply depends.

In addition, many federal laws affecting the environment direct the states to carry out the mandate of those laws while other federal laws work in tandem with state laws.

Federal Environmental Laws and Regulation

The body of federal statutes and regulation governing activities which affect the environment is immense. The creation of federal regulation is performed exclusively by federal administrative agencies. Accordingly, you may want to review Chapter 4 on administrative agencies and process before reading this section. Aspects of rule creation and administrative hearing processes are of particular relevance in this chapter, as are aspects of judicial review. The Administrative Procedure Act (APA) specifies federal agency procedures unless other procedures are specified in statutes that agencies are directed to administer. Many of the statutes which follow delineate procedures that depart from APA procedures, the details of which will not be covered here.

The Environmental Protection Agency. Created in 1970 by executive order, the Environmental Protection Agency (EPA) was initially intended to coordinate federal activities and assist in performing the executive functions related to existing federal law on environmental protection. Since the EPA's creation, Congress has passed several major environmental laws (and amended those laws many times as well) and has so expanded the responsibilities of the EPA that it is today the key administrative agency on matters of the environment.

The EPA, however, is not the only federal agency involved in environmental protection and directed by law to perform environmental control responsibilities. The list of such other federal agencies is long, but significant among them are the Nuclear Regulatory Commission, the Department of Defense (the Army Corps of Engineers), the Department of Justice (criminal prosecution of environmental law offenders), the Department of the Interior, and the Food and Drug Administration.

In the description of federal environmental laws which follows, the involvement of other federal agencies will be discussed where appropriate.

Air Pollution—The Clean Air Act. First enacted in 1970, the Clean Air Act has been significantly modified by Congress twice—in 1977 and in 1990. The 1970 and 1977 versions of the law laid out the regulatory scheme for control-

---

[8]"Washday" laws were originally created to prohibit incineration on a certain day of the week, typically a Monday, so that soot and particulates would not soil household laundry drying on outside clotheslines.

ling air pollution, provided for the setting of air quality standards, and included further enactments to stem air quality degradation in areas where air quality is already better than standards set by federal law. In 1990, amendments included provisions to address acid rain, toxic air pollutants, and smog.

Stationary sources. Under the Clean Air Act, the EPA was directed to set **national ambient air quality standards,** or NAAQS. The resulting standards were divided into two tiers—primary and secondary. The primary standards are focused on protection of the public's health. The secondary standards are focused on protection of other concerns—climate, vegetation, visibility, and so forth. In addition, the EPA has set air quality standards for specific substances such as ozone, lead, carbon monoxide, nitrogen oxide, and particulates—standards which also apply to regulation of mobile sources of air pollutants, discussed under Mobile Sources below.

Imposition of the EPA's standards is accomplished by a segmented regulatory scheme. Specifically, areas of the United States are segmented according to existing air quality. Then each area or region is to prepare and execute what is called a **state implementation plan,** or SIP. Each state is then required to improve (or maintain) air quality consistent with these plans.

For stationary sources such as factories and utilities, states are required to assess not only the numbers and types of polluters, but also the total amount of air pollution they create. Having made this assessment, the states then require polluters to reduce their emissions commensurate with or greater than what is needed to accomplish achievement of the area's NAAQS.

In addition, so that the law and regulation do not work to encourage polluting industries merely to relocate to areas having more lenient NAAQS, the Clean Air Act requires that new plants and factories use the "best available technology" for abatement of air pollution.

Mobile sources. Under a similar legal and regulatory scheme as that governing stationary sources of air pollution, control of emissions from mobile sources such as cars and trucks is also addressed by the Clean Air Act. The United States is segmented according to "attainment" or "nonattainment" areas for each pollutant—such as carbon monoxide, ozone, lead, sulfur oxides, nitrogen oxides, and particulates—for which there is a standard (NAAQS).

The 1990 amendments to the Clean Air Act listed, for example, thirty-nine metropolitan areas that failed the NAAQS for carbon monoxide and ordered forty-two areas to allow sale of only gasoline which has at least 2.7 percent oxygen content in winter in order to reduce carbon monoxide emissions caused by "cold starts." In those same amendments, ninety-seven metropolitan areas were cited for nonattainment of the ozone NAAQS. According to a late 1992 report,[9] forty-one of those areas are now in compliance with ozone standards.

Separately, vehicle manufacturers are mandated by the Clean Air Act 1990 amendments to have their new cars and trucks meet various emission standards according to specified timetables. As an example, all cars manufactured in 1996 must meet the carbon monoxide standards, whereas in 1994 only 40 percent of cars and trucks must be in compliance according to timetable.

Acid rain and toxic air pollutants. The 1990 Clean Air Act amendments addressed two additional concerns in improving air quality.

One of the concerns was to rectify what economists and public policy experts would term a "perverse effect" of the 1970 Act. A perverse effect is an outcome which is opposite to that intended. Though the 1970 Act intended to encourage practices which would improve air quality, it also encouraged plants and utilities to employ facilities which, while improving local air quality and bringing operations into local compliance, spread pollutants over much broader areas—sometimes hundreds of miles. Specifically, some emissions from tall smokestacks not only chemically changed while airborne, but also came down as acids when mixed with rain.

[9] Pendleton, "Cities Have Cleaner Air Due to New Cars on Road," *The Christian Science Monitor* (December 4, 1992), p. 8.

Consequently, the 1990 amendments specify initial maximum limits and then subsequent reductions of the harmful emissions—principally sulfur and nitrogen oxides—over a two-decade period. A controversial provision of the 1990 amendments of the Clean Air Act, however, allows companies essentially to buy and sell air pollution rights. This provision would let a company which has achieved controlling its emissions of, for example, sulfur oxides at levels below regulatory standards to sell the amount of its overachievement to a company which has not yet complied with standards. The idea behind this provision is that strict enforcement would hurt industries in which compliance would be difficult to achieve and that, over time, total air pollution will be reduced and the reduction period hastened by providing further economic incentives for compliance to those companies better situated to accomplish it.

The second additional concern addressed by the 1990 amendments was the control of toxic air pollutants. Though the 1970 Act mandated the EPA to regulate air toxics, the agency set standards for only a handful of chemicals and substances. In 1990, Congress directed the EPA to create and issue regulations governing a list of toxic air pollutants, the control of which is to be accomplished within 10 years.

Water Pollution. The most long-standing area of federal control of pollution is water pollution. The first legislation, the Rivers and Harbors Act, dates back to 1886. However, the great bulk of law and regulation over protecting American waters, drinking water, and wetlands has been created since 1970.

The Clean Water Act. Though the 1948 federal legislation, the Federal Water Pollution Act, and four subsequent sets of amendments addressed control of water pollution, it was not until 1972 that comprehensive additional amendments were passed to create what is referred to today, along with subsequent further amendments, as the Clean Water Act (CWA). The name of the Act officially changed with the passage of the 1977 amendments.

The 1972 amendments set initial deadlines, now long passed, which have been twice modi-

---

BOX 51.1

A Question of Ethics

Critics of the 1990 amendments to the Clean Air Act assert that the new provisions, which allow the buying and selling of air pollution rights, encourage what economists call "rent-seeking behavior." In a legal context, "rent seeking" is using new or changed laws as a basis for profit or competitive advantage.

Economists will also tell you that in order for buying and selling of anything to occur, there must also be a "market" of some kind.

What concerns (other than legal concerns) should individuals and society have over the creation of a market which essentially allows polluters to buy rights to injure the environment?

Imagine yourself as an employee of a firm which serves as a profit-making clearinghouse for the buying and selling of air pollution rights. What ethical and moral justifications do you have for your occupation?

Imagine that you are president of a company which has overachieved abatement of air pollution at its plants and now could sell pollution rights. What ethical issues confront you and how would you resolve them? Would it make a difference to your resolution of issues if your company's air pollution program was planned, in part, to be funded by the proceeds of selling air pollution rights? ■

---

fied by Congress. Initially, the 1972 amendments set two goals. The first goal was for the country to achieve, by 1983, sufficiently clean water for human outdoor recreation and water sufficiently clean to protect and sustain fish and wildlife. The second goal, to be achieved by 1985, was to have no water pollutant discharges.

While these goals have not been totally accomplished, much progress has been made. Today, under the Clean Water Act, individual states enforce water quality standards according to the water's designated use and according to federal directives. In addition, through the National Pollutant Discharge Elimination System (NPDES), effluents through what are termed "point sources" (water ditches, pipes, and channels, but not natural water run-off) are controlled through a permit system. Both public and private entities which empty discharges through a point source are required to get a permit from the EPA or an approved state program. The EPA is also charged with setting the effluent limitations that may be discharged under a permit.

Under the Clean Water Act, the definition of pollutant is broad and includes "dredged spoil, solid waste, incinerator residue, sewage, garbage, sewage sludge, munitions, chemical wastes, biological materials, radioactive materials, heat, wrecked or discarded equipment, rock, sand, cellar dirt and industrial, municipal, and agricultural waste discharged into water." While the EPA and the states are responsible for control of most of these pollutants, the Army Corps of Engineers—by virtue of its jurisdiction over U.S. waterways—is responsible for wetland protection (with EPA involvement) and manages a permit system affecting the dredging or filling of wetlands connected to U.S. jurisdictional waters. Before a party can dredge or fill a wetland, it must first secure a permit from the Army Corps of Engineers.

Similar to requirements for new plants and factories under the Clean Air Act which mandate that they must install the "best available [control] technology," the Clean Water Act specifies that the "best available demonstrated control technology" be used for all new water pollution sources.

Citizens may take court action against the EPA for failure to enforce this law. Moreover, citizens may sue violators (both public and private) of this law, an EPA order, or a state order. The following case illustrates a citizen-initiated suit involving a dispute over wetland drainage.

CASE 51.2 **Save Our Community v. U.S. Environmental Protection Agency**
•971 F.2d 1155 (5th Cir. 1992)

FACTS Save Our Community (SOC) is an unincorporated association of persons organized to oppose the expansion of a landfill, called Skyline Landfill, near Ferris, Texas. The landfill is operated by Trinity Valley Reclamation, Inc. (Trinity), which is a wholly owned subsidiary of Waste Management of North America, Inc.

In contemplation of expanding Skyline Landfill, Trinity solicited an opinion from the Army Corps of Engineers (the Corps) in May 1987 to determine whether the Corps had jurisdiction over the expansion area as constituting U.S. waters, and thus whether the area was a wetland. The landfill expansion area included seven artificial ponds. The Corps determined that the ponds were indeed waters of the United States and were covered by the Clean Water Act (CWA). Later, the EPA advised Trinity that it agreed with the Corps and that a permit was needed if any discharge into these ponds was contemplated.

Since filling in the ponds would violate the CWA, Trinity began draining the ponds instead. Trinity used the waters to irrigate sod covering the existing landfill. The result of the pumping reduced the surface area of the ponds from 20 acres to 10. Trinity applied to the Texas Department of Health for a permit to expand the landfill, and the Texas authorities referred the application to the U.S. Fish and Wildlife Service (FWS), which concluded that the permit be denied and that there was "an apparent attempt [by Trinity] to circumvent the regulations." However, the Corps, the EPA, and the FWS advised Trinity that no permit was required as long as Trinity did not discharge any pollutants into any jurisdictional waters.

CASE 51.2 Continued

In 1990, SOC and the City of Ferris sued Trinity in U.S. District Court and secured a preliminary injunction to stop further removal of water from the ponds.

Trinity and the EPA appealed, and challenged the district court's interpretation of the CWA, which did not take into account whether the draining of wetlands involves discharges of pollutants in order to require a permit.

OPINION

PER CURIAM . . . In interpreting the statute . . . , we begin, of course, with the words [of the Clean Water Act]. . . . Our function is to construe the language so as to give effect to the intent of Congress. The district court, in its interpretation of the CWA, relied heavily, if not entirely upon . . . legislative history. . . . However, the most persuasive evidence of Congressional intent is the wording of the statute.

. . . [T]he CWA proscribes "the discharge of any pollutant by any person" into the waters of the United States. It then specifically requires a permit . . . "for the discharge of dredged or fill material" into these waters. The conclusion is inescapable. The existence of discharge is critical. The discharge must be of effluent or dredged or fill material. . . .

Determining whether a discharge of effluent occurred in this case, therefore becomes crucial. The activity at issue here involved the draining of wetlands via . . . a mechanical pump.

. . . According to SOC, the district court made a finding of fact that there were some "minor" discharges. SOC relies primarily on two observations by FWS. . . .

. . . Trinity . . . urges that a genuine dispute concerning material facts remains on the issue as to whether any discharge at all occurred.

We hold that the wetlands draining activity per se does not require a . . . permit under the CWA, as only activities involving discharges of effluent necessitate obtaining such a permit. Consequently, we dissolve the injunction. . . . [W]e [also] conclude that there are disputed issues of material fact regarding . . . discharge[s].

JUDGMENT

Reversed and remanded.

Safe Drinking Water Act. To address the protection and improvement of the quality of the nation's drinking water, the Safe Drinking Water Act was passed by Congress in 1974. This Act directed the EPA to create minimum standards of quality for water intended for human consumption. As in other pollution control legislation, facilities providing public water supplies must use the "best available technology" to meet the drinking water standards. Individual states are principally responsible for enforcing these standards.

Of particular concern to the EPA under this Act are underground sources of drinking water contamination. Groundwater that is a source of drinking water in a majority of states is known to contain pollutants believed to adversely affect human health.

Marine Protection, Research, and Sanctuaries Act. First passed in 1972 and subsequently amended several times, this Act addresses the pollution of ocean waters and specifically prohibits all ocean dumping of various hazardous substances such as radioactive and chemical wastes. Except under permit and in tandem with other environmental regulation and law, the dumping and transportation of other materials is also prohibited.

Radiation and Toxic Chemical Pollution

Nuclear Regulatory Commission and Nuclear Waste Policy Act. The principal regulator of high-level radioactive wastes is the Nuclear Regulatory Commission (NRC). Though the mishandling of radioactive wastes or an accident in the operation of a nuclear power plant can cause serious devastation to the environment and human health (e.g., the 1986 Chernobyl accident in the former Soviet Union), the EPA is at most only tangentially involved in controlling this form of pollution.

Established during the early days of the Cold War era when control of nuclear technology was considered particularly important to the national defense, the Nuclear Regulatory Commission (formerly the Atomic Energy Commission, enabled under the Atomic Energy Act of 1954) has the exclusive responsibility for regulating the private nuclear industry. The NRC establishes rules and regulations over the private use of nuclear materials, issues operating permits, issues permits for the disposal and/or storage of both high-level and low-level radioactive wastes, and assesses the environmental impact of new plants and of modifications to older plants.

The Nuclear Waste Policy Act of 1982, among other things, authorizes site selection and development of a permanent high-level radioactive disposal facility. Though the nuclear waste repository is not targeted to commence operations until after 2000, site selection by itself has stirred much controversy.

Toxic Substances Control Act. Passed in 1976, the Toxic Substances Control Act (TSCA) requires that the EPA assemble lists of all chemicals. A manufacturer that intends to put into commercial use any chemical not on the list must give the EPA notice of the chemical and its use within a specified time in advance of actual commercial production. A manufacturer that intends to use an EPA-listed chemical in a new manner must similarly provide the EPA with advance notice.

The advance notice provision of the TSCA, however, is not an approval or licensing regulatory system. If the EPA challenges the safety of a substance, the ultimate burden is upon the manufacturer to establish that the substance presents no unreasonable risk either to human health or to the environment.

Under the TSCA, the EPA is given broad powers—it can delay, restrict, or prohibit altogether the use of any substance that the agency determines to be hazardous to health or injurious to the environment.

Federal Insecticide, Fungicide, and Rodenticide Act. Though the Federal Insecticide, Fungicide, and Rodenticide Act (FIFRA) was put into law in 1947, before the creation of the EPA, the agency today is responsible for enforcement of its provisions.

Similar to the Toxic Substances Control Act (which the EPA uses in tandem with FIFRA to regulate agricultural chemicals), FIFRA requires a manufacturer to submit registration of a pesticide before it can be put into use. Upon EPA determination, depending upon the health and environmental risks, a registration may be for general or restricted use.

Once a pesticide has been registered, the EPA can cancel the registration after a finding that the pesticide presents unreasonable risks. The burden of establishing a pesticide's safety is upon the manufacturer.

Unlike the TSCA, FIFRA requires that a pesticide registration be reviewed every 5 years.

Waste Disposal—Resource Conservation and Recovery Act.
Administered by the EPA, the Resource Conservation and Recovery Act (RCRA) requires permits for the handling—generation, treatment, storage, transportation, and/or disposal—of hazardous wastes. Enacted in 1976, the law reflects the nation's concern in the late 1970s with averting environmental disasters such as the one that occurred at Love Canal, New York, where residents and schoolchildren were exposed to toxic chemicals leaching from an old dumpsite buried under a housing development and school.

Requirements of permit holders under the RCRA cover detailed record keeping of all facets of handling hazardous waste, including proper transportation and location of hazardous waste disposal; monitoring of operations and disposal facilities; and insurance for possible liabilities.

The definition of hazardous waste in the RCRA is intentionally general to encompass any substance which "because of its quantity, concentration, or physical, chemical, or infectious characteristics may . . . pose a substantial present or potential hazard to human health to the environment. . . ."

Superfund—Comprehensive Environmental Response Compensation and Liability Act.

The Love Canal disaster, in part, also gave rise to the passage of the Comprehensive Environmental Response Compensation and Liability Act of 1980 (CERCLA). Not only were future hazardous waste disasters to be prevented (the purpose of the RCRA), but also existing messes which continued to threaten human health and the environment had to be cleaned up.

Consequently, CERCLA and its subsequent amendments created a system for identifying and cleaning up previously uncontrolled public and private hazardous waste disposal sites, abandoned disposal and storage sites, and sites contaminated accidentally from spills or leakage of hazardous substances.

Under this law, the EPA was directed to identify such contaminated sites and to rank them according to priority of cleanup, with the highest priorities placed on the EPA's "National Priorities List." In 1992, the total number of cleanup sites on the National Priorities List was 1,200. Since enactment of CERCLA, however, only about 70 sites have been cleaned up through mid-1992.

Moreover, the definition of hazardous substances in CERCLA is the broadest definition of all major federal environmental statutes. CERCLA defines hazardous substances as those deemed hazardous under the Clean Air Act, the Clean Water Act, the Toxic Substances Control Act, and the Resource Conservation and Recovery Act.

To finance the expensive cleanups, CERCLA created the Hazardous Substance Response Trust Fund, also known as the Superfund. Initially, the Superfund received an allocation of $1.6 billion. After this initial allocation, the operating fund is to be replenished by two means—by taxes on certain substances and corporations in general and by direct recovery from parties responsible for creating the need for site cleanup.

BOX 51.2
Should the Superfund Be Reconceived?

The idea behind the Superfund was to create a large pool of funds to clean up environmentally contaminated sites. However, it is estimated that from the time of CERCLA's creation (1980) up to 1992, 80 to 90 percent of Superfund funds have not been spent on environmental cleanup. Rather, the funds have gone to litigation and legal fees.

Some critics—including a candidate for the presidency of the American Bar Association*—have asserted that lawyers, not the environment, have cleaned up from the Superfund. Vice President Gore has raised the same criticism.

CERCLA may be facing substantial amendments during the Clinton administration.

*"Shestack on American Justice," *Focus* (February 1, 1993), p. 18.

Under CERCLA, which provides for the EPA to bring legal actions in strict liability, the EPA may sue for recovery of cleanup costs incurred by the Superfund, and all responsible parties are jointly and severally liable for all costs. CERCLA specifies that the EPA may sue those who are designated under the statute as "Potentially Responsible Parties."

The following case discusses Superfund recovery, the basis on which a CERCLA action may be brought, and what constitute "Potentially Responsible Parties."

CASE 51.3 United States v. Amtreco, Inc.
• No. C.A. 90-31-VAL, slip op. (M.D. Ga. 1992)

FACTS James Dickerson incorporated Amtreco, Inc., in 1977. Amtreco's business was the treatment and sale of wooden fence posts. Dickerson was the company's president, sole shareholder, and sole director.

Amtreco's plant was constructed on land owned by Dickerson—a 5.6-acre tract in Homerville, Georgia. Between September 1977 and March 1978, when Dickerson conveyed the property to the company, thousands of gallons of creosote, classified as a hazardous substance, were delivered to the Amtreco site. It is unclear whether Amtreco began wood-treatment operations before or after the conveyance of the property.

In 1980, Amtreco was forced to close because of financial hardship. In 1984, the Georgia Department of Natural Resources inspected and tested the Amtreco site and notified the EPA. After an investigation, the EPA determined that hazardous wastes were present and should be removed from the site.

In July 1984, the EPA issued an administrative order requiring Dickerson and Amtreco to initiate cleanup of the site, and giving them 42 days to do so. After rejecting their various proposals for cleanup, the EPA informed Dickerson and Amtreco that the agency itself would begin a cleanup in September 1984, using Superfund funds.

While related litigation took place, actual cleanup occurred between August 1987 and March 1988.

In April 1990, the United States sued for recovery of all costs connected with the cleanup—in excess of $1,079,955—and sought civil penalties as well.

The defendants, Amtreco and Dickerson, denied all liability and moved for summary judgment on all issues.

OPINION OWENS, J. . . . The Comprehensive Environmental Response, Compensation, and Liability Act (CERCLA) . . . authorizes the EPA to respond to releases or threatened releases of hazardous substances . . . through means of investigation, evaluation, and cleanup. CERCLA also establishes the Hazardous Substances Trust Fund ("Superfund") to fund these EPA responses.

In addition, CERCLA provides that the EPA can recover the costs of its response activities from responsible parties. This provision serves not only to replenish the Superfund for future cleanup activities, but also to place the ultimate responsibility for cleaning up hazardous waste problems upon those who created [them]. . . .

LIABILITY UNDER CERCLA

In order to establish liability under CERCLA, the United States must prove the following four elements:

1 The Amtreco site is a facility as defined [in the statute].
2 There was a release or threatened release at the site.
3 The government incurred response costs as a result of the release or threatened release.

**CASE 51.3
Continued**

4 Defendants are potentially responsible persons as defined [by the statute].

A. The Amtreco Site Is a Facility.

. . . CERCLA defines "facility" as follows:

(A) any building, structure, installation, equipment, pipe or pipeline (including any pipe into a sewer or publicly owned treatment works), well, pit, pond, lagoon, impoundment, ditch, landfill, storage container, motor vehicle, rolling stock, or aircraft, or (B) any site or area where a hazardous substance has been deposited, stored, disposed of, or placed, or otherwise come to be located; . . .

Since creosote and other hazardous wastes were present on the Amtreco site prior to the EPA cleanup, the Amtreco site is a facility under CERCLA.

B. A Release or Threatened Release Occurred at the Amtreco Site.

. . . [An EPA] inspection . . . revealed the presence of two hundred and fifty-two drums in various conditions containing creosote constituents and hazardous solvents . . . , two 20,000 gallon tanks and one 10,000 gallon tank, all of which contain, in various amounts, waste creosote. The site also contains two large, unlined surface impoundments, that contain large quantities of waste creosote.

. . . While this court is not completely convinced that the site in question is an imminent and substantial danger to public health or welfare, it appears that Congress has already determined that substances classified as hazardous . . . meet that criterion as a matter of law, and thus, since the EPA contends that hazardous substances have been and continue to be released at the Homerville site, the EPA need only demonstrate that there has been a release or may be a release. . . . It is undisputed that creosote is a known carcinogen and has been classified by Congress as being hazardous. This fact . . . leaves this court with the inescapable duty of concluding that the EPA is authorized to conduct a response action at the site. . . .

C. The United States Incurred Costs Due to the Release or Threatened Release at the Amtreco Site.

It is undisputed that the United States has incurred extensive costs . . . for monitoring, assessing, and evaluating the release of hazardous substances at the Amtreco site. . . . It is of no consequence that some of these costs are not recoverable from the defendants; for purposes of liability, the United States need only show that it has incurred some costs.

D. Defendants Amtreco and Dickerson Are Potentially Responsible Parties.

. . . Under [the statute], "the owner and operator of a vessel or a facility" are liable for costs incurred . . . in a response action.

1. Defendant Amtreco

There is no dispute that Amtreco was both the owner and operator. . . . Moreover, Amtreco still holds fee simple title to the Amtreco site. . . .

2. Defendant Dickerson

Another potentially liable person under CERCLA is defined [in the statute] . . . as "any person who at the time of disposal of any hazardous substance owned or operated any facility at which such hazardous substances were disposed of." Dickerson owned the Amtreco site until he conveyed the property to Amtreco. . . .

CASE 51.3 Continued	This court agrees with [a case in another federal circuit] and finds that the term "owner" in CERCLA should be construed broadly such that a sole stockholder [such as Dickerson] who actively participates in the management of the corporation is personally liable under CERCLA as owner and operator. . . .
	CONCLUSION . . . Defendants Dickerson and Amtreco are liable for all recoverable costs incurred during the cleanup of the Amtreco site. The amount of these recoverable costs will be determined at a later trial.
JUDGMENT	Defendant's motion of summary judgment denied.

National Environmental Policy Act. Unlike the other statutes discussed in this chapter, the National Environmental Policy Act (NEPA), enacted in 1970, addresses the environmental impact of federal government activities.

Specifically, NEPA imposes a duty on federal agencies to assess every federal project or legislative proposal in light of its impact on the environment. The assessment is called an **environmental impact statement** and is required for every project administered by the U.S. government.

Though NEPA is focused on federal activities, it also indirectly affects other enterprises. In particular, private activities which either are federally funded or operate under a permit or license from the U.S. government also fall under the requirements of NEPA. Accordingly, such private activities, before they are initiated, must go through the environmental assessment process, and environmental impact statements must be prepared and submitted for them.

> **BOX 51.3**
> **Business Planning Question**
>
> Fortuna, an entrepreneur, identified a possible opportunity for a new business. A parcel of Wild West National Park along a road within the park had been recently approved for commercial development, to serve the growing numbers of tourists. A hotel and a fast-food business had already secured leases from the federal government for land on this parcel. Other sorts of tourist-oriented businesses were seeking similar leases. Fortuna, however, noticed that no laundromats or self-serve dry cleaners had plans to enter the new development. So Fortuna applied to get a federal lease for parkland upon which to start a combination laundromat/self-serve dry cleaner. What environmental law questions, if any, should Fortuna ask a lawyer regarding startup, operation, and profitability of the proposed laundromat/dry-cleaning business?

SUMMARY

Though the great bulk of laws which govern activities that affect the environment have been created within the last few decades, common law and equity concepts operated for centuries to stem private environmental injury (though not labeled as such). Long-standing legal remedies—such as actual and punitive damages and injunctions—can act to discourage environmentally harmful conduct. The most common bases for common law actions in the environmental context are intentional harm to person or property, nuisance, negligence, and strict liability.

Since the early 1970s, the federal government has been an active participant in the environmental arena. Congress has passed many far-reaching laws to enhance human health and the quality of the environment. Those laws, which also involve the states as well, are intended to improve air and water quality; to prohibit injurious use of chemicals, pesticides, and radioactive substances; to protect wetlands and wildlife; and to provide mechanisms whereby the federal government can clean up environmental messes left by both private and public entities and place the costs and liabilities upon those responsible for the pollution.

REVIEW QUESTIONS

1. (a) What is an "externality"? (b) How is the concept of externality relevant to modern environmental law and regulation?

2. (a) What are the most common private common law causes of action for environmental injuries? (b) Describe those common law causes of action.

3. Why is the distinction between common law and equity important in an environmental law context? Explain.

4. (a) What is the difference between trespass and nuisance? (b) Under what conditions may a plaintiff bring causes of action based on both trespass and nuisance? (c) Under what conditions may a plaintiff bring only one cause of action? Which one? Why?

5. How is strict liability for environmental injury similar to strict liability in products law? Explain.

6. (a) Explain the meaning of intent. (b) Compare "intentional" and "wilful and wanton" disregard.

7. Discuss whether the Environmental Protection Agency (EPA) is the only federal agency regulating the environment. Provide specific examples.

8. Compare and contrast the regulation of air pollution from stationary sources with regulation from mobile sources.

9. (a) What is the definition of "pollutant" in the Clean Water Act? (b) What is a "point source" and why are point sources important to implementing environmental control laws?

10. Identify and discuss which federal environmental laws operate under a permit system and/or a registration system.

11. Discuss and provide support for your answer to the following: Before prohibiting or restricting use of a substance under various environmental laws, the EPA is ultimately required to prove that the substance is hazardous. True, partly true, or false?

12. Explain how funding for cleanup of sites posing real or threatened hazards to the environment is accomplished.

CASE PROBLEMS

1. William Ellen, a marine engineer who had 15 years of experience in wetlands work, was hired to build a 3,272-acre hunting preserve for a wealthy business executive. Ellen was responsible, among other things, for securing all the appropriate permits for the preserve. Part of the work for creating the hunting preserve was the filling in of 86 acres of federally protected wetlands, for which Ellen did not secure permits. When inspectors visited the site and determined that the wetlands in question were being filled in, a cease-and-desist order was issued, an order which Ellen ignored. However, though Ellen's work on the preserve involved the destruction of protected wetlands, the end result of the project was the creation of more wetlands than had been destroyed. Ellen was charged with six criminal violations of the Clean Water Act and was convicted of five, all involving the destruction of protected wetlands. Ellen was sentenced to 6 months' imprisonment in a federal penitentiary and 1 year of supervised release, including home detention. Upon appeal, the federal circuit court upheld the conviction and sentence. One of the issues at trial was that the creation of more wetlands would attract ducks, which in turn would defecate in the waters and consequently reduce water quality in the wetlands. Another goal of the Clean Water Act, however, is to protect and enhance environments which can sustain wildlife—a policy goal served by Ellen's work on the hunting preserve. The U.S. Supreme Court declined to hear the case, and

Ellen sought pardon from the President of the United States. How should the President decide? Supporters of Ellen assert that his conviction was a result of overzealous prosecution, and that street criminals convicted of violent crimes and drug offenses often get more lenient sentences than Ellen received. Should the severity of the sentence affect the President's decision? What arguments support the imposition of similar or greater criminal punishment for environmental offenses than for other crimes?

2. A pharmaceuticals company, NEPACCO, manufactured hexachlorophene in a factory in Missouri. The manufacturing process produced a variety of hazardous wastes, including dioxin, which is a highly toxic chemical. NEPACCO disposed of more than eighty large drums of hazardous wastes by dumping them into a trench on a nearby farm. Many of the drums had deteriorated before disposal and broke open when they were dumped into the trench, producing a strong chemical odor at the farm site for several months. NEPACCO hired IPC, a subcontractor, to dispose of other hazardous wastes containing dioxins. IPC subcontracted yet another service supplier—Mr. Bliss—to actually dispose of the wastes. Bliss transported and sprayed the hazardous wastes, mixed with waste oil as a dust suppressant, on the grounds of Bubbling Springs Stables, also in Missouri. After this, a Mr. Minker purchased dirt from Bubbling Springs Stables to use as landfill on Minker's property. What causes of action—both private and regulatory—can be brought against whom for what? Who can bring those causes of action? What federal environmental laws are likely to be relevant?

3. Mr. and Mrs. Seal bought 15 acres of property in Washington State in 1955. The property was bisected by an irrigation canal owned by the local irrigation district. In 1976, the Seals planted more than 450 cherry trees on this property. However, sometime in the late 1970s, the canal started to seep water onto the Seals' property, flooding it in the spring. While the canal appeared to have sealed itself at that time, other spontaneous leaks and seeping occurred. Both the Seals and the irrigation district attempted to fix the situation, but the seeping continued. By 1980, the Seals noticed a decrease in fruit production and other problems with their cherry trees. The Seals determined that a fungus, caused by the canal seepage, was killing their cherry trees by stopping the flow of nutrients to the trees. What private causes of action do the Seals have against the irrigation district? Explain.

CHAPTER 52

Introduction to Antitrust Law; The Sherman Act

Antitrust law refers to a broad system of federal and state law which seeks to promote business competition and to prohibit monopoly power. **Monopoly** means "a single seller." **Monopoly power** may therefore be defined as the *power of a single large seller to use predatory means to exclude competitors from a market or to fix prices at arbitrarily high levels.* Underlying antitrust law is a fundamental precept of capitalism: Scarce resources can be allocated most efficiently to satisfy consumer wants at the lowest price through a competitive free enterprise system. Such a system is incompatible with monopoly power and high prices that result from the abuse of such power.

This chapter briefly traces early English common law origins of antimonopoly sentiment, the Sherman Antitrust Act, and the U.S. Supreme Court's interpretations of that Act. Chapter 53 then looks at the other federal antitrust laws—the Clayton, Robinson-Patman, and Federal Trade Commission Acts—and their impact on business.

DEVELOPMENT OF ANTITRUST LAW

Antecedents of modern antitrust legislation are found in the early English common law. In *Dyer's case*,[1] the court held that a dyer's agreement not to work in the town violated the policy of the common law rule against restraints on competition. In 1623, Parliament's Statute of Monopolies declared "that all monopolies are contrary to the laws of this realm, and so . . . shall be void." In the famous case of *Mitchel v. Reynolds*,[2] when Reynolds sold his bakery to Mitchel, he promised not to compete for 5 years but then did so. Mitchel sued and won; the court said that only *total* restraints on trade are unlawful. If a *partial restraint* contained in an agreement was *reasonable*, it would be enforced. The case is an important precedent for the Supreme Court's rule of reason, discussed later in this chapter.

The Rise of Trusts in the United States

Rapid expansion of industry and national markets after the Civil War spurred large corporations to form industrial combines, or **trusts,** to fix prices, control production, divide markets, and freeze out competitors. The trusts were easily formed: Each corporation would cause a ma-

---

[1] Y.B. 2 Hen V., vol. 5, pl. 26.
[2] 1 P. Williams 181, 24 Eng. Rep. 347 (K.B. 1711).

jority of its stockholders to transfer their shares to a board of trustees which included a representative from each company that was a party to the combine. The board then issued the stockholders trust certificates in exchange for their shares. These certificates gave owners the right to dividends declared by the trustees out of the combine's pooled earnings. With a majority of the outstanding shares of each member corporation in hand, the board could control elections of the directors of each member company. Anticompetitive policies of the trust were then uniformly imposed upon all member firms. Yet each company had a separate identity and controlled everything but the trust's monopolistic goals.

Enactment of Laws to Promote Competition

In the post–Civil war period, trusts began controlling railroads, fuel oil, sugar, whiskey, and other commodities. The "captains of industry" who operated these trusts became ruthless. They cut prices below costs of production in areas where small competitors operated, forced them out of business, and then boosted prices to monopoly levels. Responding to public outcry for regulation, a few state legislatures enacted "antitrust" laws aimed at monopolies, such as John D. Rockefeller's Standard Oil Co., which used the trust device. Today, however, antitrust legislation is not limited to trusts but regulates a wide variety of practices that have the same anticompetitive effect. These include industrial combination devices such as holding companies, interlocking directorates, corporate mergers, formal or informal agreements between companies, and "understandings" between members of a trade association.

THE SHERMAN ANTITRUST ACT

Since monopolistic practices were nationwide in scope, the common law as well as antitrust legislation of the states was largely ineffective in combating the trusts. Rising clamor for national corrective regulation drove Congress to enact the Sherman Antitrust Act (1890), aimed at the anticompetitive practices of the industrial trusts and monopolies. Most states enacted new antitrust laws based on the federal model to ban intrastate combinations. The Supreme Court, summarizing the Sherman Act's impact,[3] said:

> Antitrust laws in general, and the Sherman Act in particular, are the Magna Carta of free enterprise. They are as important to the preservation of economic freedom and our free-enterprise system as the Bill of Rights is to the protection of our fundamental personal freedoms. And the freedom guaranteed each and every business, no matter how small, is the freedom to compete. . . .

Purpose and Scope of the Act

Purpose. An immediate aim of the Sherman Act was to curb the anticompetitive practices of Rockefeller's oil empire. The main congressional purpose was to promote competition by slowing down the trend toward concentration in industry. Another congressional goal was to create

---

BOX 52.1
Monopoly and the American Revolution

Opposition to monopoly is part of a long American tradition. England's Tea Act of 1773 gave the East India Company a legal monopoly on tea for all British colonies. Because the East India Company had an 18-million-pound tea surplus at the time, the *net effect of the Act was to reduce the price of tea* below even the price of Dutch tea, which the angry colonists had been using. But the colonists were still angry—they saw the Act as threatening a *complete British economic monopoly over the colonies*. On December 16, 1773, after an overflow crowd gathered at Old South Meeting House with cries of "down with monopoly," over 100 angry patriots of the Boston Tea Party dumped 110 chests of tea, each weighing 340 pounds, into Boston Harbor. The war against monopoly had started!

---

[3]*United States v. Topco Associates, Inc.*, 405 U.S. 596 (1974).

broad federal court jurisdiction to build a new body of antitrust law that would not be bound by common law rules.

Scope. The two basic sections of the Sherman Act[4] are:

1. Every contract, combination in the form of trust or otherwise, or conspiracy, in restraint of trade or commerce among the several states, or with foreign nations, is hereby declared to be illegal. . . .

2. Every person who shall monopolize, or attempt to monopolize, or combine or conspire with any other person or persons, to monopolize any part of the trade or commerce among the several States, or with foreign nations, shall be deemed guilty of a felony. . . .

Congress did not define such key terms as "restraint of trade," "combination," and "monopolize" and left to the courts the task of developing the legal meaning of these words on a case-by-case basis. Since the Sherman Act was an exercise of congressional power to regulate interstate commerce, it remained for courts to say at what point a local contract restraining trade *substantially affects interstate commerce* so as to violate the Act.

Sections 1 and 2 of the Sherman Act provide that violations are punishable as crimes. Both sections are *proscriptive* rather than *prescriptive*—that is, they tell business what it cannot do, rather than what it can do. In 1914, the Federal Trade Commission was created to administer the Sherman Act.

Exemptions. *Express exemptions* to antitrust law are set out in the Sherman Act and other federal statutes. *Implied exemptions* are found in court decisions. Major exemptions appear in Table 52.1.

Enforcement of the Act

The provisions of the Sherman Act and other federal antitrust laws are enforced by private or governmental *civil suits*. The government may also bring *criminal actions* against violators. The Antitrust Division of the Department of Justice and the Federal Trade Commission are jointly responsible for antitrust enforcement.

Table 52.1 Major Exemptions from Antitrust Laws

1. Labor unions
2. Agricultural, livestock, and fishery cooperatives
3. Public utilities such as gas and electric companies
4. State government and its "actively supervised" industry price-regulating programs (banking, insurance, wine and liquor, milk production, raisin farming, etc.)
5. Monopoly privileges arising from patents and copyrights
6. Professional baseball
7. Most American–foreign joint ventures
8. American exporters subject to Export Trading Company Act

Private Actions; Standing to Sue. Most antitrust cases in the federal courts are commenced by private parties, not government. Special statutes authorize private enforcement by empowering any person "injured in his business or property by reason of anything forbidden in the antitrust laws"[5] to bring a *private action* to recover treble damages plus reasonable attorney's fees. Private litigants may also ask the court to grant injunctive relief against violations.[6] Damage awards can be very substantial. For example, in *Trans World Airlines, Inc. v. Hughes*,[7] the damage award was $137 million after trebling, and attorney's fees totaled $7.5 million.

To prevail in a private treble damage suit, a plaintiff must have standing to sue. That is, the plaintiff must be able to prove that:

1. The defendant violated the antitrust laws
2. The violation was a substantial or direct cause of plaintiff's injury which can be measured in money terms

---

[4]15 USCA 1–7.
[5]Clayton Act 4; 15 USC 15.
[6]15 USC 26.
[7]409 U.S. 363 (1973).

3 Defendant's illegal act adversely affected activities of the plaintiff that are specifically protected by the antitrust laws

In determining whether a plaintiff has standing to sue, courts focus on the *directness* of the plaintiff's injury as a result of the defendant's wrongful antitrust violation. For example, courts have held that creditors of a corporation claiming to be hurt by its antitrust violations lacked standing to sue because their damage was too indirect.

Government Enforcement. The Sherman Act gives the federal government a wide variety of enforcement laws, as shown in Table 52.2.

Table 52.2 Antitrust Enforcement Devices

1 Under Sections 1 and 2, restraints and monopolies are felonies, punishable by fine of up to $1 million against a corporation or $100,000 against an individual or 3 years' imprisonment, or both. The Justice Department proceeds criminally against "hard core" violators engaged in price fixing, bid rigging, and market and territorial allocation schemes. Lesser offenders may enter nolo contendere (no contest) pleas, resulting in judgments that are not admissible to prove liability in a later civil suit—for example, a suit filed by a competitor.

2 Section 4 empowers the Justice Department to bring a *civil action for injunction*, restraining violations of any provision of the Sherman Act.* Courts have used injunctive power to order a firm to divest itself of ownership of another company *(divestiture)*, to dissolve itself as a corporation, or to cease from restraining trade.

3 Property being transported in interstate or foreign commerce under a contract or conspiracy that violates Section 1 may be *seized by and forfeited* to the United States.

4 Each state's *attorney general is authorized to commence civil treble damage actions*, in the name of the state, to recover for antitrust injury to its residents.

*15 USC 4.

Proving "Commerce" Jurisdiction under Sections 1 and 2. Under the Constitution, Congress can regulate only *interstate* commerce, not intrastate commerce. Therefore, federal courts are without jurisdiction to decide an antitrust case unless the restraint has a significant impact on interstate or foreign commerce.

Either of the two tests in Table 52.3 may be used to meet the interstate commerce jurisdiction required by the Sherman Act. In practice, a relatively small amount of direct or indirect interstate activity will be held to "substantially affect" interstate commerce. The Supreme Court has held that even if a manufacturer's conspiracy to boycott a single retailer would only slightly reduce shipments in interstate commerce, it is still enough to warrant "commerce" jurisdiction.[8] In Case 52.1 the U.S. Supreme Court applies both the "flow of commerce" and the "effects on commerce" tests in determining Sherman Act jurisdiction.

[8]*Klor's Inc. v. Broadway-Hale Stores, Inc.*, 359 U.S. 207 (1959).

Table 52.3 "Flow of Commerce" and "Effects on Commerce": The Supreme Court's Two Tests for Sherman Act Jurisdiction

1 Did the activities occur within the *flow of commerce*? This test applies only if a restraint is imposed directly upon goods or services while moving in interstate commerce. Hence, under this test, volume or size of the restraint may be relatively small.*

2 Did the activities have *substantial* and adverse *effect* on commerce? Even a wholly intrastate activity will meet the jurisdictional requirement if it substantially affects interstate commerce and is not merely inconsequential or remote.† "The test of jurisdiction is not that the acts complained of affect a business engaged in interstate commerce, but that the conduct complained of affects the interstate commerce of such business."‡

*United States v. Yellow Cab Co., 332 U.S. 218 (1947).

†Northern Cal. Pharmaceutical Ass'n v. United States, 306 F.2d 379 (1962).

‡C.A. Page Publ. Co. v. Work, 178 F. Supp. 184 (S.D. Cal. 1959).

CASE 52.1 — McLain v. Real Estate Board of New Orleans • 444 U.S. 232 (1980)

FACTS McLain and other real estate vendors (petitioners) instituted a treble damage private antitrust class action against an association of real estate brokers in New Orleans (respondents), claiming that they had conspired to fix prices (broker's commissions) in violation of Section 1 of the Sherman Act. The trial court dismissed the complaint for lack of "commerce" jurisdiction, the U.S. Court of Appeals affirmed, and McLain appealed to the U.S. Supreme Court.

OPINION BURGER, C.J. . . . Petitioners advance two independent theories to support federal jurisdiction: (1) that respondents' activities occurred within the stream of interstate commerce; and (2) that even if respondents' activities were wholly local in character they depended upon and affected the interstate flow of both services and people. . . . The jurisdictional requirement of the Sherman Act may be satisfied under either the "in commerce" or the "effect on commerce" theory. . . .

It is clear that an appreciable amount of commerce is involved in the financing of residential property in the Greater New Orleans area and in the insuring of titles to such property. The presidents of two of the many lending institutions in the area stated in their deposition testimony that those institutions committed hundreds of millions of dollars to residential financing during the period covered by the complaint. The testimony further demonstrated that this appreciable commercial activity has occurred in interstate commerce. Funds were raised from out-of-state investors and from interbank loans obtained from interstate financial institutions. . . . Mortgage obligations physically and constructively were traded as financial instruments in the interstate secondary mortgage market. Before making a mortgage loan in the Greater New Orleans area, lending institutions usually, if not always, required title insurance, which was furnished by interstate corporations.

To establish federal jurisdiction in this case, there remains only the requirement that respondents' activities which allegedly have been infected by a price-fixing conspiracy be shown "as a matter of practical economics" to have a not insubstantial effect on the interstate commerce involved. It is clear, as the record shows, that the function of respondent real estate brokers is to bring the buyer and seller together on agreeable terms. . . . Whatever stimulates or retards the volume of residential sales, or has an impact on the purchase price, affects the demand for financing and title insurance; those two commercial activities that on this record are shown to have occurred in interstate commerce.

JUDGMENT [The Court held that buying and selling real estate and the related title insurance, mortgage financing, and services of brokers meet both the "flow of commerce" and "substantial effect on commerce" tests for determining Sherman jurisdiction.]

Restraints which affect the flow of services or goods imported into the United States, or exported from it, meet the jurisdictional requirement of "commerce . . . with foreign nations." Once such a flow of imports or exports that affect competition in the United States is established, the Sherman Act will apply to activities of U.S. citizens or foreign nationals, within the United States or within a foreign country, and before or after the goods actually flow in commerce. Generally, the Sherman Act will not be enforced against an act of a foreign nation or its agent. However, the Foreign Sovereign Immunities Act of 1976[9] applies the Sherman Act to a foreign state's "commercial activities" which have a "direct effect" in the United States. These activities are covered in Chapter 54.

Proving Conspiracy under Section 1. The words "contract, combination . . . or conspiracy" clearly require proof that at least *two* persons agreed to act in concert so as to restrain trade. A corporation is a separate legal person, and, because it can act only through its agents, it is incapable of conspiring with its officers or employees. Hence, any such "conspiracy" does not meet the two-actor requirement of Section 1. Since corporations are separate entities, logic would suggest that two wholly owned subsidiaries might conspire between themselves or with the parent corporation to violate Section 1. However, the modern economic reality is that parent-subsidiary corporations function as a single unit, and the Supreme Court, after noting that fact, has held that such a unit of affiliated companies is unable to conspire with itself.[10]

Under well-established doctrines of criminal conspiracy, a convicted defendant is liable for all the acts of any co-conspirators. As long as a defendant is active in the conspiracy, he or she is liable for the actions of others which occur *before or after* the defendant's participation.

Courts have used "combination" and "conspiracy" interchangeably,[11] and because it is often impossible to obtain direct evidence of a combination, or conspiracy to restrain trade, circumstantial evidence is sufficient.[12] For example, a conspiracy to boycott was inferred when a dealers' association distributed to its members a list of wholesalers that sold directly to consumers, and thereafter the members ceased to deal with the listed wholesalers.[13]

Consciously parallel behavior—that is, uniform business conduct by competitors that are aware of one another's actions—would seem to be circumstantial evidence from which an agreement could be inferred. However, standing alone, it is generally insufficient to prove a conspiracy.[14] In *Theatre Enterprises, Inc. v. Paramount Film Distrib. Corp.*[15] plaintiff exhibitor claimed a boycott conspiracy among defendant film distributors that refused to lease him films, but he proved only parallel behavior. In affirming a jury verdict for the defendants, the Supreme Court said:

This court has never held that proof of parallel business behavior conclusively establishes an agreement, or . . . that such behavior itself constitutes a Sherman Act offense.

However, conscious parallelism, together with evidence of exchange of pricing data at meetings or by correspondence, is enough to infer a conspiracy.[16]

Court Interpretations of Section 1

In the 100 years since the Sherman Act of 1890 was enacted, U.S. Supreme Court interpretations have traveled full circle. In the

---

[9]38 USC 1602–1611.

[10]*Copperweld Corp. v. Independence Tube Corp.*, 104 S. Ct. 2731 (1984).

[11]*Perma Life Mufflers, Inc. v. International Parts Corp.*, 392 U.S. 134 (1968).

[12]*United States v. General Motors Corp.*, 384 U.S. 127 (1966).

[13]*Western States Retail Lumber Dealers' Ass'n v. United States*, 234 U.S. 600 (1914).

[14]*Federal Trade Commission v. Lukens Steel Co.*, 454 F. Supp. 1183 (D.D.C. 1978).

[15]346 U.S. 537 (1954).

[16]*Gainesville Utilities Dept. v. Florida Power & Light Co.*, 573 F.2d 292 (5th Cir. 1978).

> **BOX 52.2**
>
> **Test Your Knowledge: Does Conscious Parallelism Violate Section 1?**
>
> You meet your friendly competitors at the seventh hole on the golf course and say, "Tomorrow I'm raising the price of all my products $10." Next day you find they have all raised their prices $10, but you needn't worry about antitrust violations, right? Wrong.
>
> Conscious parallelism, and nothing more is not proof of a conspiracy. But here there is something more, and it is up to a jury to decide if you and your competitors had an implicit conspiracy going on at the seventh hole. If the jury decides you did, and you're guilty of the crime, what are your chances on appeal?
>
> In *Esco Corp. v. United States*,* upholding a jury conviction on similar evidence, the court said: "Any conspiracy can ordinarily only be proved by inferences drawn from . . . circumstantial evidence, including the conduct of the defendants charged. A knowing wink can mean more than words . . . [and] it remains a question for the jury."
>
> *300 F.2d 1000.

early years, the Court took such a narrow view of interstate commerce that very few monopolies were held to be within the jurisdiction of the Act. Then, in 1897, the Court took the astounding view that *every* restraint of trade was a violation of the Sherman Act. Such a rigid interpretation could be used to invalidate every normal business deal by arguing that it restrains trade because the contractually obligated parties are no longer free to deal with others. The Court's inevitable retreat from this position came when it decided *Standard Oil Company of New Jersey v. United States*.[17]

The Rule of Reason. In *Standard Oil*, the Court rejected its earlier position that *all* contracts in restraint of trade were prohibited by the Sherman Act and announced a principle of antitrust law that would prevail for the next century— the **rule of reason.** The Court held that Congress did not intend to prohibit *reasonable restraints of trade*—only contracts that *unreasonably* restrained trade. This rule of reason— that is, the requirement of determining whether the defendant's conduct is so anticompetitive that it constitutes an "unreasonable restraint"— is very much a part of Section 1 antitrust cases today.

Doctrine of Per Se Unreasonableness. Some types of agreements are so inherently anticompetitive that it can be said as a matter of law that they unreasonably restrain trade and are therefore illegal under Section 1 of the Act. If an activity is illegal **per se,** proof of that activity is sufficient to establish its anticompetitive nature, and it is not necessary to present evidence that the activity unreasonably restrained trade. Obviously, per se claims are easier to win because they take less effort to establish than do other Section 1 cases where additional proof must be presented that the restraint is unreasonable. Even if firms collusively fix prices at reasonable levels, the act is still an unreasonable conspiracy to restrain trade under Section 1. In *United States v. Trenton Potteries Co.*,[18] the Court said:

> The aim and result of every price-fixing agreement, if effective, is the elimination of one form of competition. The power to fix prices, whether reasonably exercised or not, involves power to control the market and to fix arbitrary and unreasonable prices. The reasonable price fixed today may through economic and business changes become the unreasonable price of tomorrow . . . Agreements which create such potential power may well be held to be in themselves [per se] unreasonable or unlawful restraints without . . . placing on the government in enforcing the Sherman law the burden of ascertaining from day to day whether they have become unreasonable. . . .

Thirty years after *Trenton*, when the per se doctrine was fully developed, the Supreme Court summarized it:

[17] 221 U.S. 1 (1911).

[18] 273 U.S. 392 (1927).

There are certain agreements or practices which because of their pernicious effect on competition and lack of any redeeming virtue are conclusively presumed to be unreasonable and therefore illegal without elaborate inquiry as to the precise harm they have caused or the business excuse for their use. This principle of *per se* unreasonableness . . . avoids the necessity for an incredibly complicated and prolonged economic investigation into the entire history of the industry involved, as well as related industries, in an effort to determine at large whether a particular restraint has been unreasonable—an inquiry so often wholly fruitless when undertaken. . . .[19]

It is only after considerable experience with certain business relationships that courts classify them as per se violations of the Sherman Act.[20] Joint activities in interstate commerce that are regularly recognized as per se violations appear in Table 52.4. Generally, all kinds of anticompetitive restraints that are not per se violations are judged under the rule of reason to determine if the particular restraint is unreasonable and therefore unlawful.

Horizontal price fixing. When two or more competitors at the same level—such as two manufacturers, two wholesalers, or two retailers—agree to establish a minimum or maximum price or a set price for a product, the result is a **horizontal price-fixing agreement.** Such an agreement

[19]*Northern Pac. Railway Co. v. United States*, 356 U.S. 1 (1958).
[20]*United States v. Topco Associates, Inc.*, 405 U.S. 596 (1972).

Table 52.4 Per Se Violations of Antitrust Law

1 Horizontal price fixing
2 Vertical price fixing
3 Restricting production
4 Horizontal division of geographic markets or customers
5 Group boycotts where coercion is involved (concerted refusals to deal)
6 Most reciprocal dealing arrangements (where coercion is present)
7 Most tying contracts (where there is strong market power over tying product)
8 Collusive bid rigging and similar restraints
9 Agreements to refrain from advertising prices

by its very nature eliminates price competition and is the most common per se violation of the antitrust law. Once the prosecution has proved the existence of horizontal price fixing, it is no defense to argue that such action was necessary to prevent "ruinous competition," "financial disaster," or the "evils of price cutting." In addition, the fact that the prices fixed are equal to the fair market price or are otherwise reasonable is considered irrelevant. In Case 52.2, the Supreme Court ponders whether a wholesalers' horizontal agreement to deny credit to retailers is equivalent to an agreement to fix prices, and if the per se doctrine applies.

CASE 52.2 **Catalano, Inc. v. Target Sales • 446 U.S. 635 (1988)**

FACTS Beer retailers (plaintiffs) in the Fresno, California, area brought a class action for treble damages and injunctive relief against a group of wholesalers (defendants), claiming that they had violated Section 1 of the Sherman Act by horizontally conspiring to eliminate the industry practice of granting short-term credit to retailers on beer purchases. The trial and appellate courts rejected plaintiffs' claim that the credit restriction was a per se violation of Section 1. Plaintiffs appealed to the Supreme Court.

OPINION PER CURIAM . . . Prior to the agreement wholesalers had competed with each other with respect to trade credit, and the credit terms for individual retailers

**CASE 52.2
Continued**

had varied substantially. After entering into the agreement, respondents uniformly refused to extend any credit at all. . . . Certain agreements or practices are so plainly anticompetitive and so often lack any redeeming virtue that they are conclusively presumed illegal without further examination under the rule of reason generally applied in Sherman Act cases. A horizontal agreement to fix prices is the archetypal example of such a practice. It has long been settled that an agreement to fix prices is unlawful *per se*. It is no excuse that the prices fixed are themselves reasonable.

 . . . It is virtually self-evident that extending interest-free credit for a period of time is equivalent to giving a discount equal to the value of the use of the purchase price for that period of time.

 . . . An agreement to terminate the practice of giving credit is thus tantamount to an agreement to eliminate discounts, and thus falls squarely within the traditional *per se* rule against price fixing.

 . . . An agreement among competing wholesalers to refuse to sell unless the retailer makes payment in cash either in advance or upon delivery is plainly anticompetitive. Since it is merely one form of price fixing, and since price fixing agreements have been adjudged to lack any "redeeming virtue," it is conclusively presumed illegal without further examination under the rule of reason.

JUDGMENT [The Court held the wholesalers' agreement that uniformly denied credit to retailers was a per se violation of Section 1.]

Vertical price fixing. If a manufacturer sells to a wholesaler (or a wholesaler sells to a retailer) on condition that the buyer will not resell the product below a set minimum price, or on condition that the buyer will only resell at a stated fixed price, the contract is called a **vertical price-fixing agreement.** This process, whereby a seller at one level of the chain of distribution fixes the resale price terms of a buyer at a different level, is also called **resale price maintenance.** Until 1937, the Supreme Court held that resale price maintenance contracts in interstate commerce were per se violations of Section 1 even though the buyer's state legislature had enacted a *fair trade law* permitting such contracts. However, in that year Congress enacted the Miller-Tydings Act exempting resale price maintenance contracts from the Sherman law *if* there was a fair trade law in effect in the buyer's state. Since most states had fair trade laws, the effect of Miller-Tydings was to legalize most resale price maintenance contracts.

In 1976, Congress repealed the Miller-Tydings Act with the result that resale price maintenance in interstate commerce once again constituted a per se violation of Section 1. Today, such vertical price-fixing agreements are unlawful to the same extent as before 1937. Thus, it is a violation of the Sherman Act for a manufacturer to establish suggested retail prices and then refuse to sell to wholesalers selling to retailers that do not observe such prices. Often, such pricing policies are accompanied by a network of cooperating retailers and wholesalers that report "price cutters" to the manufacturer, which swiftly terminates their distributorship privileges.

In a slightly different situation, it is still lawful for a seller to establish suggested resale prices and to *unilaterally* announce in advance (e.g., a manufacturer announcing to wholesalers) that it will refuse to sell to *immediate customers* who do not maintain such prices. The theory underlying this "*Colgate* exception"[21] is that a single seller's unilateral announcement that it will sell only to dealers following its suggested resale prices cannot violate the law because there is no *concerted* action by two or more actors, as required under Section 1—only the seller's unilateral action.

There is an important distinction between vertical price fixing and other vertical nonprice restraints. Generally, **vertical nonprice restraints**—for example, a manufacturer's allocation of market territory among franchised retailers—are subject to the rule of reason, and are not per se violations.[22]

Restricting production. Competition theory holds that many producers competing with one another will maximize production at minimum prices. However, if producers combine and agree to fix prices, the scheme cannot be effective unless the producers also agree to restrict production and sales. Since price fixing and regulating production are closely related, agreement to manipulate production for an anticompetitive goal is a per se violation.[23]

Dividing markets or customers. It is illegal per se for *horizontal* competitors (those at the same level) to apportion market territory geographically among themselves, to allocate customers while agreeing not to solicit one another's customers, or to divide product markets.

---

[21]*United States v. Parke, Davis & Co.*, 362 U.S. 29 (1960); *Federal Trade Commission v. Beech-Nut Packing Co.*, 257 U.S. 441 (1922). In *United States v. Colgate & Co.*, 250 U.S. 300 (1919), the Supreme Court affirmed dismissal of an indictment against Colgate for merely announcing in advance the prices at which its goods could be resold and refusing to deal with wholesalers and retailers that did not conform to such prices.

[22]In *Business Electronics Corp. v. Sharp Electronics Corp.*, 485 U.S. 717 (1988), the Court held that a vertical restraint of trade is not per se illegal under Section 1 unless it includes some agreement on price or price levels.

[23]*United States v. Addyston Pipe & Steel Co.*, 85 F. 271 (6th Cir. 1898); *Hartford-Empire Co. v. United States*, 323 U.S. 386 (1945).

CASE 52.3	**Palmer v. BRG of Georgia** • 112 L. Ed. 2d 349 (1990)
FACTS	From 1976 to 1979, BRG of Georgia, Inc. (BRG), was in intense competition with Harcourt Brace Jovanovich Legal and Professional Publications (HBJ), the nation's largest provider of bar review materials. In 1980 BRG and HBJ agreed that BRG would have an exclusive license to market HBJ's material in Georgia and to use its trade name; HBJ would not compete with BRG in Georgia and BRG would not compete with HBJ outside of Georgia. HBJ received $100 per student enrolled by BRG and 40 percent of all revenues over $350. Immediately after the agreement, BRG raised its bar review course price from $150 to over $400. Petitioners, bar review students, alleged that BRG had increased prices pursuant to an unlawful violation of Sherman Section 1. The trial court and court of appeals ruled the agreement lawful. Petitioners appealed to the U.S. Supreme Court.
OPINION	PER CURIAM. In *U.S. v. Socony-Vacuum Oil Co.*, we held that:

> Under the Sherman Act a combination formed for the purpose and with the effect of raising, depressing, fixing, pegging, or stabilizing the price of a commodity in interstate or foreign commerce is illegal per se.

The revenue-sharing formula in the 1980 agreement between BRG and HBJ, coupled with the price increase that took place immediately after the parties

CASE 52.3 Continued	agreed to cease competing with each other in 1980, indicates that this agreement was "formed for the purpose and with the effect of raising" the price of the bar review course. In *United States v. Topco Associates, Inc.*, 405 U.S. 596 (1972), we held that agreements between competitors to allocate territories to minimize competition are illegal: > One of the classic examples of a per se violation of §1 is an agreement between competitors at the same level of the market structure to allocate territories in order to minimize competition. . . . This Court has reiterated time and time again that horizontal territorial limitations . . . are naked restraints of trade with no purpose except stifling of competition. Such limitations are per se violations of the Sherman Act. . . . Here, HBJ and BRG had previously competed in the Georgia market; under their allocation agreement, BRG received that market, while HBJ received the remainder of the United States. Each agreed not to compete in the other's territories. Such agreements are anticompetitive regardless of whether the parties split a market within which both do business or whether they merely reserve one market for one and another for the other. Thus the 1980 agreement between HBJ and BRG was unlawful on its face.
JUDGMENT	[The Supreme Court reversed the appellate court's decision, holding that the agreement to raise prices of the bar review course and to divide territory was unlawful per se.]

Although the *Palmer* decision above reaffirmed the long-standing rule that *horizontal* division of market territory is a per se violation of Section 1, *vertical* division of markets or customers is *not* a per se violation, but is evaluated under the rule of reason. In the following case, the Supreme Court argues that the test of reasonableness of a vertical nonprice restraint is *whether the procompetitive effect of the restraint on interbrand competition* (with RCA, Sony, Zenith) *outweighs the anticompetitive effect of eliminating intrabrand competition* (between Sylvania dealers).

CASE 52.4	Continental TV, Inc. v. GTE Sylvania, Inc. • 433 U.S. 36 (1977)
FACTS	Commencing in 1962, Sylvania ceased marketing its TV products through distributors and sold direct to franchised retailers such as Continental TV (plaintiff). The retailers were restricted to selling only from locations at which they were franchised. The franchise agreements did not establish exclusive territory, and Sylvania retained sole discretion to increase the number of retailers in an area depending on success or failure of existing retailers in developing their market. Sylvania's franchise program increased its market share of national television sales from 1 percent in 1962 to 5 percent in 1965. Continental was one of the more successful franchise retailers in the San Francisco area. When Sylvania refused Continental's request for a franchise to open a new retail outlet in Sacra-

**CASE 52.4
Continued**

mento, Continental announced it would go ahead without a franchise. Sylvania then terminated Continental's San Francisco franchise. Continental sued Sylvania, claiming that forcing franchised retailers to sell only from specified locations (a "location restriction") was a per se violation of Section 1.

The trial court relied on *Schwinn & Co. v. United States*, 388 U.S. 365, which held that vertical market restraints imposed by sellers were per se violations of Section 1, regardless of the reasonableness of such restraints. Accordingly, the jury was instructed that once Sylvania had parted with title to its products any attempt to control their resale, including the location restriction on dealers, was a violation of Section 1 of the Sherman Act, regardless of the reasonableness of the restriction. Based on those instructions, the jury awarded Continental TV $1,774,515 in damages. The court of appeals reversed, stating that the sales location limitation clause should be judged under the rule of reason and that the provision did not constitute a per se violation. Continental appealed.

OPINION

POWELL, Assoc. J. . . . Sylvania argues that if *Schwinn* cannot be distinguished, it should be reconsidered. Although *Schwinn* is supported by the principle of *stare decisis*, we are convinced that the need for clarification of the law in this area justifies reconsideration. . . .

The market impact of vertical restrictions is complex because of their potential for a simultaneous reduction of intrabrand competition and stimulation of interbrand competition. . . . Vertical restrictions reduce intrabrand competition by limiting the number of sellers of a particular product competing for the business of a given group of buyers. Location restrictions have this effect because of practical constraints on the effective marketing area of retail outlets. . . .

Vertical restrictions promote interbrand competition by allowing the manufacturer to achieve certain efficiencies in the distribution of his products. These "redeeming virtues" are implicit in every decision sustaining vertical restrictions under the rule of reason. Economists have identified a number of ways in which manufacturers can use such restrictions to compete more effectively against other manufacturers. For example, new manufacturers and manufacturers entering new markets can use the restrictions in order to induce competent and aggressive retailers to make the kind of investment of capital and labor that is often required in the distribution of products unknown to the customer. Established manufacturers can use them to induce retailers to engage in promotional activities or to provide service and repair facilities necessary to the efficient marketing of their products. Service and repair are vital for many products, such as . . . major household appliances. . . . Certainly, there has been no showing in this case, either generally or with respect to Sylvania's agreements, that vertical restrictions have or are likely to have a "pernicious effect on competition" or that they "lack . . . any redeeming virtue." Accordingly, we conclude that the *per se* rule stated in *Schwinn* must be overruled. In so holding we do not foreclose the possibility that particular applications of vertical restrictions might justify *per se* prohibition. . . . But we do make clear that departure from the rule of reason standard must be based upon demonstrable economic effect rather than—as in *Schwinn*—upon formalistic line drawing.

> **CASE 52.4**
> **Continued**
>
> In sum, we conclude that the appropriate decision is to return to the rule of reason that governed vertical restrictions prior to *Schwinn*. When anticompetitive effects are shown to result from particular vertical restrictions they can be adequately policed under the rule of reason, the standard traditionally applied for the majority of anticompetitive practices challenged under Section 1 of the Act.
>
> **JUDGMENT**
>
> [The Supreme Court affirmed the appellate court's view that vertical nonprice restraints should be judged under the rule of reason, and held that the trial court was in error in ruling that Sylvania's location restriction was a per se violation of Section 1. The Court also noted that horizontal restrictions and vertical resale price maintenance would remain per se illegal. On further hearing, the district court found that Sylvania's location restriction had procompetitive effects on interbrand competition that outweighed the anticompetitive effects on intrabrand competition. 461 F. Supp. 1046 (1978).]

Sylvania was a watershed decision that marked retreat from the per se analysis of anticompetitive restraints. It also began a trend toward expanding the use of the rule of reason to evaluate challenged restraints by weighing their procompetitive and anticompetitive effects. Thus, in *Monsanto Co. v. Spray-Rite Service Corp.*[24] the Court addressed the problem of a manufacturer terminating a distributor whose "price-cutting" tactics were objected to by other distributors. In affirming a $10.5 million jury award against the manufacturer, the High Court discussed the proper standard of proof required to establish price-fixing conspiracy between manufacturer and distributors.

The Supreme Court first noted that in distributorship termination cases, illegal price fixing must be distinguished from two activities that are *not* unlawful: (1) independent action by the manufacturer in publishing suggested resale prices together with a unilateral announcement that it will refuse to sell to distributors that do not conform to the resale prices—a policy which is permissible under the *Colgate* doctrine; and (2) vertical *nonprice restraints*, which are judged under the rule of reason—and not as per se violations. More is required to prove a Section 1 violation than mere "rumors" of price cutting followed by distributor termination. There is danger of injustice if price-fixing conspiracy is grounded on nothing more than rumor. Competitors are always grumbling to manufacturers about price-cutting distributors.

The Court then restated the proper standard of proof required to sustain a price-fixing conspiracy:

The antitrust plaintiff should present direct or circumstantial evidence that reasonably tends to prove that the manufacturer and others had a conscious commitment to a common scheme designed to achieve an unlawful objective.

Monsanto provides an important addition to current antitrust law: Where price fixing is mixed with nonprice vertical restraints, such as a location restriction, the price-fixing conspiracy will continue to be treated as a per se violation if the evidence shows "a conscious commitment to a common scheme designed to achieve an unlawful objective," and the vertical nonprice restraints will continue to be judged under the rule of reason after procompetitive and anticompetitive effects of the restraint are weighed to determine whether it is "reasonable."

Jointly refusing to deal—group boycotts. Joint actions for the purpose of restricting a competitor's access to markets or sources of supply are per se violations of Section 1. Examples of ille-

[24]104 S. Ct. 1464 (1984).

gal per se group boycotts include refusals to sell, refusals to buy,[25] picketing by a trade association to force retailers to remove a competitor's product, joint cancellation of advertising in a local newspaper in order to eliminate competition against the sole remaining newspaper,[26] an agreement among member teams of a sports association that they will not negotiate with prospective players until 4 years after high school graduation,[27] and the lawyers' boycott of a court system discussed in Case 52.5 below.

[25]*United States v. Hilton Hotels Corp.*, 467 F.2d 1000 (9th Cir. 1972).

[26]*Greenspun v. McCarran*, 105 F. Supp. 662 (D. Nev. 1952).

[27]*Denver Rockets v. All-Pro Management, Inc.*, 325 F. Supp. 1049 (C.D. Cal. 1971).

CASE 52.5   **Federal Trade Commission v. Superior Court Trial Lawyers Association**
• 107 L. Ed. 2d 851 (1990)

FACTS   The District of Columbia Criminal Justice Act (CJA) authorized payment of $30 per hour in legal fees for court time and $20 per hour for out-of-court time to approximately 100 private lawyers to represent indigent clients in criminal cases, thus supplementing the public defender's heavy caseload. In 1982 the lawyers organized the Superior Court Trial Lawyers Association (SCTLA), and its officers asked the District of Columbia to increase the rates. When their demands were rejected, they formed a "strike committee," refused to take court assignments of cases, and demanded hourly rates of $45 out of court and $55 in court. A month after the strike, the City Council for the District of Columbia authorized an increase in the hourly rate to $35, which SCTLA accepted. The Federal Trade Commission (FTC) then filed a complaint against SCTLA and its officers, claiming an unlawful conspiracy to boycott and to fix prices in violation of Section 5 of the FTC Act. A violation of Sherman Section 1 is automatically a violation of FTC Section 5, which prohibits "unfair competition." The court of appeals reversed the FTC's finding that the lawyers' group boycott was a per se unlawful restraint on trade, and the FTC appealed to the Supreme Court.

OPINION   STEVENS, J. . . . Respondent's boycott constituted a classic restraint of trade within the meaning of Section 1 of the Sherman Act. As such, it also violates the prohibition against unfair methods of competition in §5 of the FTC Act. Prior to the boycott, CJA lawyers were in competition with one another, each deciding independently whether and how often to offer to provide services to the District at CJA rates. . . . This constriction of supply is the essence of price-fixing, whether it be accomplished by agreeing upon a price, which will decrease the quantity demanded, or by agreeing upon an output, which will increase the price offered. The horizontal arrangement among these competitors was unquestionably a "naked restraint" on price and output.

Respondent's argument . . . ultimately asks us to find that their boycott is permissible because the price it seeks to set is reasonable. But it was settled shortly after the Sherman Act was passed that it "is no excuse that the prices fixed are themselves reasonable." . . . Every such horizontal arrangement among competi-

CASE 52.5 **Continued**	tors poses some threat to the free market. . . . Whatever economic justification particular price-fixing agreements may be thought to have, the law does not permit an inquiry into their reasonableness. They are all banned because of their actual or potential threat to the central nervous system of the economy. . . . Conspirators need not achieve the dimensions of a monopoly, or even a degree of market power any greater than that already disclosed by this record, to warrant condemnation under the antitrust laws.
JUDGMENT	The judgment of the Court of Appeals is accordingly reversed insofar as that Court held that per se rules inapplicable to the lawyers' boycott. The case is remanded. . . .

The size of a group boycott does not affect its illegality. In *Klor's Inc. v. Broadway-Hale Stores, Inc.*[28] plaintiff Klor's, a retail appliance store, brought an antitrust action against its next-door competitor Broadway-Hale and ten national appliance manufacturers and their distributors, claiming they entered into a group conspiracy not to sell to Klor's. The Supreme Court held such actions to be an unlawful group boycott prohibited by Sherman Sections 1 and 2—actions that were "not to be tolerated merely because the victim is just one merchant whose business is so small that his destruction makes little difference to the economy." The Court added:

The Sherman Act has consistently been read to forbid all contracts and combinations which tend to create a monopoly, whether the tendency is a creeping one or one that proceeds at a full gallop.

Not all group boycotts are per se violations of Section 1. If coercion is not present, or if the anticompetitive impact of a particular group practice is not obvious, the joint activity will be evaluated by the courts under the rule of reason. Case 52.6, involving a boycott by a group of dentists, is illustrative.

[28] 359 U.S. 207 (1959).

CASE 52.6	**Federal Trade Commission v. Indiana Federation of Dentists** • 90 L. Ed. 2d 445 (1986)
FACTS	A group of dentists, with a large majority of their profession in two cities, formed a "union" called the Indiana Federation of Dentists. It then adopted a "work rule" requiring member dentists to withhold x-rays requested by insurance carriers for use in evaluating patients' claims for reimbursement for dental care. Member dentists did not wish to have dentists hired by the insurers review the x-rays to determine that a less expensive dental procedure would have been appropriate. The Federal Trade Commission (FTC), after a full evidentiary trial-type hearing, issued a cease and-desist order against further union organizing efforts. The FTC found the work rule to be an unreasonable horizontal restraint of trade in violation of Sherman Section 1 and therefore automatically a violation of FTC Section 5, which prohibits unfair methods of competition. The appellate court vacated the FTC's order, finding it unsupported by substantial evidence. The FTC appealed.

**CASE 52.6
Continued**

OPINION

WHITE, J. The issue is whether the Commission erred in holding that the Federation's policy of refusal to submit x-rays to dental insurers for use in benefits determinations constituted an "unfair method of competition." . . . The relevant factual findings are that the members of the Federation conspired among themselves to withhold x-rays requested by dental insurers for use in evaluating claims for benefits, and that this conspiracy had the effect of suppressing competition among dentists with respect to cooperation with the requests of the insurance companies. . . . One of the primary reasons . . . for the Federation's existence was the promulgation and enforcement of the so-called "work rule" against submission of x-rays in conjunction with insurance claim forms. . . .

The Commission's findings that "in the absence of . . . concerted behavior, individual dentists would have been subject to market forces of competition, creating incentives for them to . . . comply with the requests of patients' third-party insurers," finds support not only in common sense and economic theory, . . . but also in newsletters circulated among Indiana dentists, revealing that Indiana dentists themselves perceived that unrestrained competition tended to lead their colleagues to comply with the insurers' requests for x-rays. Moreover, there was evidence that outside of Indiana, in States where dentists had not collectively refused to submit x-rays, insurance companies found little difficulty in obtaining compliance by dentists with their requests. A "reasonable mind" could conclude on the basis of this evidence that competition for patients . . . would lead dentists in Indiana (and elsewhere) to cooperate with requests for information by their patients' insurers.

The policy of the Federation with respect to its members' dealings with third-party insurers resembles practices that have been labeled "group boycotts": The policy constitutes a concerted refusal to deal on particular terms with patients covered by group dental insurance. Although this Court has in the past stated that group boycotts are unlawful per se, we decline to resolve this case by forcing the Federation's policy into the "boycott" pigeon-hole and invoking the per se rule. . . . The category of restraints classed as group boycotts is not to be expanded indiscriminately, and the per se approach has generally been limited to cases in which firms with market power boycott suppliers or customers in order to discourage them from doing business with a competitor—a situation obviously not present here. . . . Thus, we evaluate the restraint at issue in this case under the Rule of Reason rather than a rule of per se illegality.

Application of the Rule of Reason to these facts is not a matter of any great difficulty. The Federation's policy takes the form of a horizontal agreement among the participating dentists to withhold from their customers a particular service that they desire—the forwarding of x-rays to insurance companies along with claim forms. While this is not price fixing as such, no elaborate industry analysis is required to demonstrate the anticompetitive character of such an agreement. . . . Absent some countervailing procompetitive virtue . . . such an agreement limiting consumer choice by impeding the ordinary give and take of the market place, cannot be sustained under the Rule of Reason. No credible argument has been advanced for the proposition that making it more costly for the

CASE 52.6 Continued	insurers and patients who are the dentists' customers to obtain information needed for evaluating the dentists' diagnoses has any procompetitive effect. . . . The Federation is not entitled to preempt the working of the market by deciding for itself that its customers do not need that which they demand. . . .
JUDGMENT	The factual findings of the Commission regarding the effect of the Federation's policy of withholding x-rays are . . . sufficient as a matter of law to establish a violation of Section 1 of the Sherman Act, and hence, Section 5 of the Federal Trade Commission Act. . . . [T]he Commission's order must be sustained. The judgment of the Court of Appeals is accordingly reversed.

Reciprocal dealing. Sometimes a company buys large quantities of goods from a supplier that also needs the products of the company it supplies. For example, an automobile manufacturer may buy large quantities of steel from a supplier whose nationwide selling organization regularly needs automobiles. If the automobile manufacturer uses its purchasing power leverage to coerce the steel supplier to buy its automobiles, the arrangement is called *reciprocal dealing* or *reciprocity.* The basic evil is that such an arrangement forecloses other auto manufacturers from competing for the steel supplier's car purchases. Reciprocity arising from coercion, or even a "voluntary" reciprocal buying arrangement in which one of the parties departs from the usual criteria of product selection (quality, price, service, time of delivery), can be a per se violation of Section 1 of the Sherman Act. In determining whether reciprocity is illegal per se, courts consider factors such as (1) the relative size and purchasing volume of the parties; (2) the existence of power to exert "leverage" pressure on a supplier, regardless of whether leverage was actually used in a purchasing agreement; and (3) maintenance of facilities such as a "trade relations department" to use coercion.

Other per se violations. There are other joint per se restraints that occur less frequently than those discussed. For example, collusive bidding ("bid rigging") includes selecting one bidder from a group to make the lowest bid while the others refrain from bidding, comparing bids prior to submission, creating a bid depository where competitors compare bids and fix the bid price, or splitting the profits made by the successful bidder. In addition, arrangements to refrain from advertising prices and most tying contracts are per se unreasonable restraints. To establish an unlawful tying arrangement, three elements must be proved:

1. The scheme in question involves *two distinct* items and provides that one (the tying product) may not be obtained unless the other (the tied product) is also purchased.
2. The tying product possesses sufficient economic power to restrain competition in the tied product market.
3. A "not insubstantial" amount of commerce is affected by the arrangement. It has been held that a trademark can be a tying product. Tying contracts may also violate the Clayton Act, discussed in Chapter 53.

Decline of the Per Se Doctrine. *Sylvania* (Case 52.4) and *Federation of Dentists* (Case 52.6) reflect the growing reluctance of the Supreme Court to decide antitrust cases under the per se analysis and the Court's increasing tendency to judge borderline restraints under the rule of reason. This trend reflects the influence of antitrust scholars from the University of Chicago (the "Chicago School"), who emphasize *economic efficiency* as the chief standard for judging antitrust challenges. For example, the Court refused to apply per se analysis to an out-and-out price-fixing agreement between composers and a broadcasting company. In-

> **BOX 52.3**
>
> **Test Your Knowledge**
>
> *What is the Supreme Court's rule of reason?*
> Answer: Only "unreasonable" restraints on trade are unlawful" under Sherman Section 1.
>
> *What restraints are judged under the rule of reason?*
> Answer:
>
> - Restraints in most Section 1 cases
> - All restraints other than per se restraints
> - Vertical nonprice restraints, including vertical division of markets and vertical location restrictions
> - Group boycotts (with little or no coercion and limited market power)
>
> *How does a court decide if a restraint is reasonable?*
> Answer: The court balances the procompetitive effects of the restraint against the anticompetitive disadvantages, considering "the facts peculiar to the business to which the restraint is applied; its condition before and after the restraint was imposed; the nature of the restraint and its effect . . . the history of the restraint, the evil believed to exist, the reason for adopting the particular remedy, the purpose or end sought to be attained."*
>
> *Chicago Board of Trade v. United States, 246 U.S. 231 (1918).

stead, the Court judged the agreement under the rule of reason and found that it would increase economic efficiency and did not violate Sherman Section 1.[29]

Proving Monopolization under Section 2

Sherman Section 2 lists three distinct offenses: to "monopolize," "attempt to monopolize," or "combine or conspire . . . to monopolize" any part of interstate or foreign commerce. Unlike the prohibitions of Section 1, which always require at least two actors, a violation of Section 2 can result from a *single firm's* outright acquisition of a monopoly position or attempt to monopolize. However, a Section 2 violation can also result from a plurality of actors—as, for example, when two companies combine or conspire to monopolize. It is also possible that two companies can conspire to restrain trade so as to violate Section 1 but not Section 2, because the amount of trade they are restraining is not sufficient to constitute a monopoly or an attempt to monopolize their industry. On the other hand, any conspiracy or combination to monopolize necessarily is a conspiracy in restraint of trade, which also violates Section 1. Two elements are necessary to establish criminal or civil liability for monopolization under Section 2:

1. The *acquisition of monopoly power*—that is, the power to control prices or exclude competitors in a relevant market
2. Deliberateness or a *general intent to monopolize*

To clarify the nature of a monopolist's power to control prices and exclude competitors, the courts have endeavored to incorporate basic economic theory into antitrust principles of law.

Monopoly Power in a Relevant Market. Courts consider many factors in determining whether a firm has the monopoly power to control prices or exclude competitors in a relevant market. They are (1) the size of the market share; (2) whether the size of the firm was achieved through "natural growth" or by acquiring competitors; (3) the number of competitors and their financial strength; (4) whether the firm engaged in unlawful exclusionary practices to prevent market entry by potential competitors; and (5) the extent to which the firm used unduly coercive tactics to suppress competition.[30] The most important of these factors is *size of market share*. Although there are no judicially approved precise formulas, 80 percent or more of the market is generally considered to consti-

[29] *Broadcast Music, Inc. v. Columbia Broadcasting System, Inc.*, 441 U.S. 1 (1979).

[30] *United States v. Aluminum Co. of America*, 148 F.2d 416 (2d Cir. 1945).

tute market power and 50 percent or less is insufficient evidence that such power exists. If a defendant has 50 to 80 percent of the market share, courts will then examine the other factors more closely in order to decide whether the defendant has market power.[31]

The relevant market generally consists of (1) a *geographic market*—the geographic area of effective competition in which a particular product is traded—and (2) the *product market*—the market area for a given product and for other substitute products with which the given product is interchangeable. In the terminology of economists (who are often used as expert witnesses in antitrust cases), product interchangeability is known as *cross-elasticity of demand*—that is, the degree to which users of product X will shift to buying product Y in response to a drop in the price of Y. If the number of users of X that shift to purchasing Y is relatively high, it is said that X and Y have a high degree of cross-elasticity of demand or, in the terminology of the courts, a high degree of interchangeability.

The terms "monopoly power," "relevant market," and "cross-elasticity of demand" were applied by the Supreme Court in *United States v. E.I. du Pont de Nemours & Co.*,[32] in which the United States brought a Section 2 civil suit charging du Pont with monopolizing the cellophane industry. In the period involved, du Pont produced almost 75 percent of the cellophane in the United States, but cellophane constituted less than 20 percent of all "flexible packaging material" sales. The central question was: Does the "relevant market" include only cellophane, or is du Pont competing in a larger market of "flexible packaging materials" (such as Saran, foil, and wax paper) that are interchangeable?

The court found that du Pont cellophane was competing in the larger market and that the interchangeable products in that market had a high degree of cross-elasticity of demand. Pointing out that du Pont furnished less than 7 percent of wrappings for bakery products, 25 percent for candy, 32 percent for snacks, and 35 percent for meat and poultry, the trial court concluded that du Pont did not have monopoly power in the flexible packaging material market. Upholding the decision, the Supreme Court said:

The "market" which one must study to determine when a producer has monopoly power will vary with the part of commerce under consideration. The tests are constant. That market is composed of products that have reasonable interchangeability for the purposes for which they are produced—price, use, and qualities considered. While the application of the tests remains uncertain, it seems to us that du Pont should not be found to monopolize cellophane when that product has the competition and interchangeability with other wrappings that this record shows.

General Intent to Monopolize

Conduct That Is Not Monopolization. Monopoly power may be lawfully obtained through superior business acumen or product, or as the result of historic accident. However, size alone does not violate the Sherman Act. As Judge Hand put it:

Persons may unwittingly become monopolists by force of accident. A single producer may be the survivor out of a group of active competitors merely by virtue of his superior skill, foresight and industry. The successful competitor, having been urged to compete, must not be turned upon when he wins.[33]

A defendant firm that has acquired monopoly power in this manner usually argues that its monopoly position was "thrust upon" it and that its market dominance did not come about as the result of any wrongful conduct under Section 2. For example, in the *du Pont* case discussed above, the Supreme Court found the company's bigness to be lawful because it resulted from investing millions of dollars in research over 40 years to develop a viable cellophane product in a very competitive market for flexible wrapping materials.

---

[31]*Yoder Bros. Inc. v. California-Florida Plant Corp.*, 537 F.2d 1347 (5th Cir. 1976).

[32]351 U.S. 377 (1956).

[33]*United States v. Aluminum Co. of America*, 148 F.2d 416 (1945).

Oligopoly. In the absence of concerted action to fix prices or engage in other anticompetitive conduct, the "thrust upon" or "historic accident" defense to monopolization charges is probably available in most industries characterized by **oligopoly** (literally, "a few sellers"), in which a small number of firms account for substantially all of an industry's output. Oligopoly often arose in American industry because of historical accident, ownership of a valuable patent, or natural growth up to the point where a few firms found themselves participating in what is sometimes called a "shared monopoly." The mere size of firms that grew in this manner does not, of itself, violate Section 2. However, if firms in an oligopoly jointly participate in predatory activity which poses a *probability of creating monopoly power,* Section 2 has been violated.

Specific Intent to Monopolize Required by Section 2. In the leading Section 2 cases,[34] the "thrust upon" defense was not successful in avoiding the charge of monopolization because the growth to market power was always accompanied by *predatory practices*. These include such activities as injuring competitors, engaging in coercion, excluding potential competitors, erecting barriers to entry into the market ("limit pricing"), and refraining from maximizing profits until competitors are driven out of the market ("predatory pricing") after which there is a **recoupment** obtained by charging monopoly prices.

Any deliberate conduct, the probable result of which leads to monopoly, meets the "general intent" necessary to establish Section 2 liability. An *attempt to monopolize* is proved when it is shown that the defendant employed "methods, means and practices which would, if successful, accomplish monopolization, and which, though falling short, nevertheless approach so close as to create a dangerous probability of it."[35] If a firm has substantial market power, a court may interpret a commonplace business decision as proof of intent to monopolize. In the classic Section 2 *Aluminum Co. of America* case, the Court held that the relatively innocent act of expanding plant capacity at times of slack demand could be construed as intent to monopolize through an ongoing program of discouraging potential entrants into the market. Obviously, if a firm acquires monopoly power while restraining trade in violation of Section 1, it has also clearly violated Section 2.

The following case involves the application of antitrust law to **aftermarkets,** or secondary markets created by demand for a new product—for example, blades are an aftermarket for razors. Eastman Kodak manufactured photocopiers, for which the aftermarket was photocopier repair and service. A group of independent service organizations accused Kodak of tying the sale of parts (the tying product over which it was claimed Kodak had market power) to the sale of service (the tied product). The case raised novel questions: If a producer lacks power in the market for its primary product, can it have power in the aftermarket? Is the aftermarket inseparable from the primary market, or should the aftermarket be considered a wholly independent market?

---

[34]*United States v. Aluminum Co. of America,* 148 F.2d 416 (2d Cir. 1945); *United States v. Grinnell Corp.,* 384 U.S. 563 (1966).

[35]*American Tobacco Co. v. United States,* 221 U.S. 106 (1911).

CASE 52.7	**Eastman Kodak Company v. Image Technical Services Inc.** • 112 S. Ct. 2072 (1992)
FACTS	Kodak manufactures photocopiers which compete with other photocopiers such as Xerox. Eighteen independent service organizations (ISOs) began servicing Kodak's photocopiers. Kodak then adopted policies to limit the availability to ISOs of replacement parts for its equipment, and to make it more difficult for ISOs to compete with it in servicing such equipment. The ISOs sued, claiming violations of Sherman Sections 1 and 2 (attempting to monopolize and unlawful monopolizing). The trial court granted Kodak's motion for summary judgment, the court of appeals reversed, and Kodak appealed to the Supreme Court, claiming that a firm with no power in the equipment market must be assumed to lack power in the service repair aftermarket.
OPINION	BLACKMUN, J. . . . Beginning in the early 1980s, ISOs began repairing and servicing Kodak equipment. They also sold parts and reconditioned and sold used Kodak equipment. . . . Some of the ISOs' customers purchase their own parts and hire ISOs only for service. In 1985 and 1986 Kodak implemented a policy of selling replacement parts . . . only to buyers of Kodak equipment who use Kodak service or repair their own machines. As part of the same policy, Kodak sought to limit ISO access to other sources of Kodak parts. Kodak and its original-equipment manufacturers (OEMs) agreed that the OEMs would not sell parts that fit Kodak equipment to anyone other than Kodak. . . . Kodak intended through these policies, to make it more difficult for ISOs to sell service for Kodak machines. . . . [To prove a tying arrangement, it must be shown] . . . first, that service and parts are two distinct products, and, second, that Kodak has tied the sale of the two products. For service and parts to be considered two distinct products, there must be sufficient consumer demand so that it is efficient for a firm to provide service separately from parts. Evidence in the record indicates that service and parts have been sold separately in the past and still are sold separately to self-service equipment owners. . . . Kodak's assertion also appears to be incorrect as a factual matter. At least some consumers would purchase service without parts, because some service does not require parts, and some consumers, those who self-service for example, would purchase parts without service. Enough doubt is cast on Kodak's claim of a unified market that it should be resolved by the trier of fact. . . . Kodak contends that there is no need to examine the facts when the issue is market power in the aftermarkets. A legal presumption against a finding of market power is warranted in this situation, according to Kodak, because the existence of market power in the service and parts markets absent power in the equipment market "simply makes no economic sense." . . . The extent to which one market prevents exploitation of another market depends on the extent to which consumers will change their consumption of one product in response to a price change in another, i.e., the "cross-elasticity of demand." Kodak's proposed rule rests on a factual assumption about the cross-elasticity of demand in the equipment and aftermarkets: "If Kodak raised its parts or

> **CASE 52.7 Continued**
>
> service prices above competitive levels, potential customers would simply stop buying Kodak equipment." Kodak argues that the Court should accept, as a matter of law, this "basic economic reality," that competition in the equipment market necessarily prevents market power in the aftermarkets. . . .
>
> We conclude . . . that Kodak has failed to demonstrate that respondents' inference of market power in the service and parts markets is unreasonable. . . . It is clearly reasonable to infer that Kodak has market power to raise prices and drive out competition in the aftermarkets, since respondents offer direct evidence that Kodak did so. It is also plausible . . . to infer that Kodak chose to gain immediate profits by exerting that market power where locked-in customers, high information costs, and discriminatory pricing limited and perhaps eliminated any long-term loss. Viewing the evidence in the light most favorable to respondents, their allegations of market power "make . . . economic sense."
>
> **JUDGMENT** [The Court upheld a denial of summary judgment for Kodak, requiring that the case go to a full-fledged trial.]

In the *Eastman* ruling, although plaintiff ISOs conceded that Kodak lacked power in the market for its manufactured photocopiers, the Court refused as a matter of law to rule that it therefore lacked power in the aftermarket for photocopier repair service. Stanford's Professor Baxter, former federal antitrust czar, has criticized the decision for not recognizing the interdependency of the service aftermarket with the primary market for photocopiers, and for treating aftermarkets as a wholly independent market. Many observers predict that in the future judges will be more hesitant to dismiss a case on motion for summary judgment even when it is based upon a wholly implausible economic theory.

SUMMARY

The Sherman Act was passed to promote competition, retard concentration in industry, and develop a new body of antitrust law. Section 1 prohibits contracts or conspiracies in restraint of trade, and Section 2 prohibits monopolization. The Act is enforced in three ways:

1 By civil treble damage suits brought by private parties having standing to sue—that is, having injury causally and directly linked to the defendant's wrongful antitrust conduct

2 By the government in civil suits for injunction and damages, or in criminal proceedings punishable by fine of up to $1 million against a corporation or $100,000 against an individual, or 3 years' imprisonment, or both

3 By forfeiture to the United States of property transported interstate in a conspiracy that violates Section 1

To establish "commerce" jurisdiction in Section 1 and 2 cases, it must be proved that defendant's activities either (1) were within the *flow of commerce* or (2) had a substantial and adverse *effect on commerce*. In all cases there must be proof of *intent* to contract, combine, or conspire (Section 1) or to monopolize (Section 2). Intent may be inferred by circumstantial evidence. By itself, consciously parallel behavior is insufficient to prove conspiracy.

In *Standard Oil*, it was held that Section 1 forbade only contracts that *unreasonably* restrain trade. Under this rule of reason, if a restraint was reasonable, it was lawful. Most Section 1 cases are judged under this rule of reason. However certain agreements or practices are deadly to competition, are presumed unreasonable, and are therefore illegal without need for proof. Such per se violations include horizontal or vertical price fixing, restriction of production, division of markets or customers, group boycotts (refusal to deal), reciprocal dealing arrangements, and most tying contracts. However, vertical nonprice restraints, such as allocation of market territory to franchised retailers, are under the rule of reason.

Two elements are required to prove violation of Section 2. First, plaintiff must show that the defendant acquired monopoly power to control prices or exclude competitors in a relevant market. (To determine a relevant market, courts define the product and then the geographic area of effective competition in which the product, and any interchangeable substitute, are traded.) Second, plaintiff must show that the defendant had a general intent to monopolize, as indicated by predatory activities such as injuring or excluding competitors, blocking entry, or "predatory pricing."

Monopoly power may be reached lawfully if superior business acumen or historic accident "thrust it upon" the defendant. The "thrust upon" defense is not successful if predatory practices are found to have accompanied the firm's growth. If there is no predatory activity, the defense is available to most oligopolies.

REVIEW QUESTIONS

1. Explain the meaning of antitrust law.

2. What economic forces fostered American antitrust law?

3. "The trust device can control a group of corporations." Explain.

4. What was the chief objective of Congress in passing the Sherman Act?

5. What activities are prevented under Section 1 of the Sherman Act? Under Section 2?

6. List three ways to enforce the Sherman Act. Which is the most commonly used?

7. (a) How does the doctrine of per se unreasonableness relate to the rule of reason? **(b)** What is the advantage of proving per se violations?

8. What factors do courts consider in judging whether a firm has monopoly power to control prices in a relevant market?

9. (a) What evidence do courts consider relevant to prove intent to monopolize? **(b)** How can monopoly power be lawfully achieved?

CASE PROBLEMS

1. Unions filed a Sherman Section 1 suit against Employers, a multiemployer association. Unions sought treble damages, claiming that Employers coerced certain third parties as well as Employers' members to enter into relationships with nonunion contractors and subcontractors and thus adversely affect the trade of unionized firms and of Unions' business activities. Employers argued that under antitrust law, Unions had no standing to sue. Do you agree? Explain.

2. Checker Corp. manufactured taxicabs. Yellow Cab Co. and other cab companies operating in New York, Chicago, Pittsburgh, and Minneapolis agreed to buy their cabs exclusively from Checker. The agreement involved the purchase of only 5000 cabs in the four cities. Collectively these purchases constituted a very small percentage of all cabs bought in the United States. The government brought a civil suit against Checker and Yellow Cab Co., charging them with violating Section 1 of the Sherman Act. The trial court dismissed the action for failure to state facts showing that interstate commerce was affected. The government appealed. Decision?

3. Thirty-five of thirty-eight savings and loan associations in Richmond, Virginia, used the "escrow accounting method" for prepayments of insurance and taxes advanced by mortgage borrowers. Eight of these firms had changed to the escrow method from the "capitalization method" within the previous 3 years. Brown, a borrower, brought an action against the savings and loan associations claiming violations of Section 1 of the Sherman Act. Brown noted that lending institutions must pay more interest on borrowers' advances under the capitalization method, and that its elimination was therefore an economic motive for conspiring to use the escrow method. Brown also claimed that parallel behavior of the associations established intent to restrain trade. Although most of the defendant firms belonged to the same trade association, there was no evidence that they had exchanged information on accounting methods. Did the defendant savings and loan associations conspire to violate Sherman Section 1?

4. Copperweld, Inc.'s, wholly owned subsidiary, Regal, Inc., manufactured steel tubing. XYZ, Inc., was formed by a former Copperweld officer in violation of a noncompetition agreement. XYZ Inc., ordered a tube mill from Yoder. Copperweld sent Yoder a letter threatening suit unless Yoder refused to fill the order of XYZ, Inc. Yoder voided the order. XYZ, Inc., sued Copperweld, Regal, and Yoder, alleging their conduct was an unlawful group boycott in violation of Section 1 of the Sherman Act. The jury returned a verdict of $7.5 million against Copperweld and Regal, for conspiring against XYZ, Inc., but found that Yoder was not a part of the conspiracy. Copperweld and Regal appealed, claiming that a parent and its wholly owned subsidiary corporation are a "single entity" and as such are not capable of "conspiring" in violation of Section 1. Are Copperweld and Regal a single entity?

5. Paper Companies was a group of ten manufacturing firms that accounted for 90 percent of the shipments of corrugated containers from plants in the southeastern United States. From 1955 to 1963, these firms regularly exchanged price information among themselves, but no agreements to adhere to a price schedule were made. When a seller requested and received price information from a competitor, it affirmed its willingness to furnish such information in return. Frequently, after two competitors exchanged price information, they would quote the same price to a buyer. The exchange of price information had the effect of stabilizing prices in a narrow range, but with supply exceeding demand in the container market, prices drifted downward over an 8-year period. Did Paper Companies violate the price-fixing prohibition of Sherman Section 1?

6. Chicken Delight, a fast-food franchising company in interstate commerce, required its franchisees to purchase certain essential cooking equipment, dry-mix food items, and trademark-bearing packaging exclusively from Chicken Delight as a condition of getting a franchise and trademark license. A class action filed against Chicken Delight claimed violation of Sherman Section 1 for an unlawful tying arrangement. Chicken Delight said that the trademark and franchise license were not separate and distinct from food items, packaging, and equipment, but that all of these constituted an integrated franchise system to be treated as a combined sale. Was the franchise system an unlawful tying arrangement?

7. In 1981, the NCAA adopted a plan to stem the loss of attendance at its member college football games as a result of television. The plan limited the total number of games that could be televised and the total number of games any one college could televise. It also prohibited any NCAA member from selling television rights except in accordance with the plan. The NCAA then made separate agreements with ABC and CBS television networks for the right to televise the games. Oklahoma University and other members of the NCAA formed the College Football Association (CFA) and contracted with NBC for increased revenues and televising more games. When the NCAA then threatened disciplinary action against members that had joined the CFA, Oklahoma University and other CFA universities sued the NCAA, claiming violations of Sherman Section 1. The trial court rejected the NCAA's claim that it was a joint venture and therefore a single entity unable to conspire. Using the rule of reason, the court also found live college football television to be "the relevant market" and held that competition had been unlawfully restrained by (1) the NCAA's fixing prices for particular broadcasts, (2) the exclusive contracts with ABC and CBS, which amounted to a group boycott of all other potential television broadcasting competitors, and (3) the NCAA plan which placed an artificial limit on production of televised college football. The circuit court held that the three practices were per se violations of Section 1. How should the High Court decide? **(a)** Is the NCAA a "single entity" joint venture? **(b)** Did it violate Section 1? **(c)** Does the rule of reason or per se standard apply?

CHAPTER 53

The Clayton, Robinson-Patman, and Federal Trade Commission Acts

For 25 years following the Sherman Act of 1890, critics relentlessly attacked its shortcomings. The Act did little or nothing to stop anticompetitive practices in their beginning stages. Labor protested that injunctions authorized by the Act to combat monopolies had been twisted by the courts into tools for suppressing strikes, pickets, and boycotts. Others argued that conflicting court interpretations made it impossible to know what the Act prohibited. Still others said it hadn't stopped corporate concentration.

Congress responded in 1914 by passing two laws: the Clayton Act, amended in 1936 by the Robinson-Patman Act, and the Federal Trade Commission Act, which created the Federal Trade Commission (FTC) to administer parts of the antitrust laws.

THE CLAYTON ACT

Purpose and Scope of the Clayton Act

The Clayton Act[1] was enacted to prohibit four types of anticompetitive business practices involving interstate commerce:

1 Price discrimination (Section 2)

[1] 15 USC 12-27.

2 Exclusive dealing and tying contracts (Section 3)
3 Anticompetitive corporate mergers (Section 7)
4 Interlocking directorates (Section 8)

Because the Act's underlying philosophy was to strike monopolistic practices in their *incipiency*, each of the four prohibited acts is unlawful only if it *tends* "to substantially lessen competition."

The Act authorized civil sanctions, most notably private treble damage suits against violators. In addition, the FTC could issue cease-and-desist orders to restrain anticompetitive practices, and the Antitrust Division of the Justice Department could sue for injunctive relief against violators. Since the Act focused on practices that *tend* to lessen competition, challenges to anticompetitive conduct could now prevail even when the evidence showed only probable future injury but fell short of showing actual present injury. For this reason, criminal penalties were not imposed against violators until the later Robinson-Patman Act amended Section 2 of the Clayton Act to provide for criminal sanctions.

Section 2—Price Discrimination

The Robinson-Patman Act in 1936 amended the Clayton Act's Section 2 to prohibit **price**

discrimination, which occurs when a seller charges different buyers different prices for the same merchandise. As a hypothetical example, if Goodyear sells 1,000 tires to Montgomery Ward and 1,000 to Sears, but charges Sears $2 per tire more, it is illegal price discrimination under Section 2(a), provided that the seller:

1. Is engaged in interstate commerce—that is, at least one of two or more sales must be to a competing buyer in a state other than that of the seller (the transaction must involve two or more states)
2. Sells goods, wares, or merchandise (not services) of like grade and quality, at or about the same time
3. Charges prices that discriminate between two or more buyers
4. Is engaging in price discrimination that may substantially lessen competition or tend to create a monopoly

Three important exceptions are that (1) any seller can refuse to sell to a buyer if such refusal is not designed to restrain trade; (2) a seller can change prices in response to market conditions such as deterioration of perishable goods, obsolescence of seasonal goods, distress sales under court process, or "going out of business"; and (3) the Act does not apply to sales to end users. The underlying reasoning is that with competition keen at the retail level it is unlikely that a local stereo dealer will sell the same speaker to two customers at a different discriminatory price on the same day.

"Like Grade and Quality." Obviously a difference in price based upon a difference in grade is not discriminatory—large eggs appropriately sell for more than small; but determining if goods are of like grade and quality is not always easy. Often, sellers package under private label a product that is identical to their well-known brand product and then sell it to chain stores at a discounted price. However, the Supreme Court has held that in interstate commerce such practices violate Section 2(a).[2] On the other hand, even when the products have the same brand, if there is an actual difference in grade or quality, the seller may charge whatever different prices it chooses, regardless of whether the prices are proportionate to the differences in the seller's costs.

Functional Discounts. Competitive injury generally does not result when a supplier sells at different prices to buyers that are differentiated by *function*. For example, a supplier of tires may sell at a given price to wholesalers of replacement tires but sell at a lower price to an automobile manufacturer that markets the tires as part of a car in a different functional distribution system. Functional discounts may also reflect, in a general way, services performed by the purchaser for the supplier. The decisive test in functional discount cases is: Does the price differential have a significant anticompetitive effect?

Proving Injury to Competition. Under Section 2(a) price discrimination is not automatically illegal but requires proof that it may "tend to create a monopoly in any line of commerce, or to injure, destroy, or prevent competition." The Act is aimed at preventing probable injury to competitors of the seller **(primary line injury)**, to buyers **(secondary line injury)**, to customers of buyers **(tertiary line injury)**, and even to competitors of the buyer's customer **(fourth line injury)**, according to the U.S. Supreme Court. In *Perkins v. Standard Oil Company of California*,[3] Standard sold gasoline at a favored price to another oil company, Signal. Signal resold to its subsidiary Western Hyway, which in turn sold to its subsidiary Regal, whose sales at cut-rate prices caused injury to Regal's competitor Perkins. The court of appeals termed Regal's harm to Perkins "fourth level injury" and held that since Section 2(a) lists only three levels of injury, Perkins was not entitled to recover under the Act. The Supreme Court reversed and in ruling for Perkins pointed out that "the competitive harm done him by Standard is certainly no less because of the presence of an additional link in this particular distribution chain."

---

[2] *Federal Trade Commission v. The Borden Co.*, 383 U.S. 637 (1966).

[3] 89 S. Ct. 1871 (1969).

Two customers situated in *different* geographic markets are clearly not competing and cannot suffer competitive injury if one of them receives a favored price from a discriminating supplier. For example, a manufacturer that sells a can opener to a retailer in Boston for $1 does not injure a Seattle retailer that is charged $2 but is not competing in the Boston market.

How small business proves that price discrimination has caused competitive injury is seen in *Utah Pie Co. v. Continental Baking Co.*[4] Utah Pie, a Salt Lake City bakery, by investing in a new plant, captured 45 to 60 percent of the frozen pie market in the local area. Three national firms—Carnation, Pet Milk, and Continental Baking—decided to undercut Utah Pie, and for 2 years flooded the local market with frozen 22-ounce pies, many priced as low as 24 cents each—far lower than their prices in other regions of the United States and, on a number of occasions, far below costs of production. Hence, the pricing was not only discriminatory under Robinson-Patman, but also *predatory*. In sustaining a jury verdict of discrimination in violation of Clayton Section 2(a), the U.S. Supreme Court observed that the Act is aimed as much at price discrimination that slowly erodes competition as at price discrimination that has an immediate destructive impact.

Defenses to Liability under the Act

Defenses to Liability under Section 2(a). The Clayton Act provides sellers with two defenses to a price discrimination suit:

1. *Cost justification defense* is based on the theory that price differentials are justified by "differences in the cost of manufacture, sale, or delivery resulting from the differing methods or quantities" involved.
2. *Meeting competition defense* is grounded on the principle that lowering the "price or furnishing of services or facilities . . . was made in good faith to meet an equally low price of a competitor. . . ."

The burden of proving a defense rests upon the party claiming it.

[4]386 U.S. 685 (1967).

BOX 53.1

The Supreme Court Makes It Tough for Robinson-Patman Plaintiffs

In a sequel to *Utah Pie Co. v. Continental Baking Co.*, Brooke Group Ltd., a maker of generic cigarettes packaged in black and white, by a 6-to-3 vote, lost its appeal to the Supreme Court to reinstate a $150 million lower-court antitrust verdict. In 1980, Brooke tried to revive sagging cigarette sales by bringing out the lower-priced generic brand. Brown & Williamson (B&W), another manufacturer, responded by marketing its own generic and giving distributors deep price discounts. Brooke sued under Robinson-Patman, claiming B&W had slashed prices *below* cost of production to put Brooke out of business, intending to later raise its prices and recoup its lost profits. The Supreme Court said a Robinson-Patman plaintiff claiming predatory pricing must prove as in a Sherman Section 2 case that (1) "the prices complained of are *below* . . . the rival's costs, and (2) that the competitor [monopolist] had a reasonable prospect of later *recouping* its investment in below-cost prices." Brooke failed to do this.

The Court held that juries should not be permitted to rule on such unsupported predatory pricing claims. The claims are "implausible" because if an oligopolist such as B&W drops its price *below* cost to discipline Brooke, it has no assurance that other oligopolists would cooperate. Rather, they too would cut costs to retain their market shares, and if the target went under, all the oligopolists would raise their prices together so that B&W would have no assurance of recouping what it had invested in a predatory pricing program. The Court also justified the decision as one favoring low consumer prices, even if they hurt small competitors. The High Court said that the purpose of antitrust laws "is to promote consumer welfare, not protect competitors."*

*Brooke Group v. Brown & Williams, Lexis 4245 (1993).

"Cost justification" under Section 2(a). A seller accused of discrimination for charging larger chain stores lower prices than small retailers may defend itself by showing that economies realized in large-quantity sales justify the lower per-unit selling price. The FTC and courts permit sellers to group customers according to dollar volume of purchases and to average costs for each group. However, an arbitrary cost-averaging system was rejected in *United States v. Borden Co.*[5] Borden sold milk at an 8.5 percent discount to two large grocery chains, but gave independent stores discounts of only 5.5 percent or less. In a price discrimination suit under Clayton Section 2(a), Borden's defense was that lower costs from the chains' quantity purchases justified the lower prices. However, some independents had larger dollar volumes than chain stores. The Supreme Court held that it was arbitrary discrimination to group buyers as "chain stores" or "independents" rather than on the basis of a cost-saving factor such as volume of purchases. Recognizing the complexity of defining cost, the Supreme Court has noted the "elusiveness of cost data," and many lawyers doubt the effectiveness of the defense for the same reason.

"Meeting competition" under Section 2(b). Clayton Section 2(b) allows a seller to rebut a price discrimination charge by showing that the lower price was made in *good faith to meet an equally low price of a competitor.* This "meeting competition" defense cannot be used by a seller that knowingly goes *below* the competitor's price by undercutting it. Courts and the FTC have consistently denied the defense to sellers whose products, because of intrinsic superior quality or intense public demand, normally command a price higher than that received by sellers of competing goods. For example, the defense was denied when the price of Lucky Strikes was dropped to the level of a "poorer grade of cigarettes."[6] Similarly, it is no defense if the seller meets the price the competitor quoted for goods in much larger quantities. However, a seller is permitted to make a good faith competitive price reduction to retain an old customer, and to quote the same price to take a new customer away from a competitor.[7] The seller may only *reasonably rely* on a buyer's representations as to the low prices quoted by competitors; but the buyer that lies about competitors' low prices violates Section 2(f) by *inducing and receiving an illegal discriminatory price from the seller.*

Unlawful Brokerage, Promotional Allowances, and Services. A supplier that leans toward illegal price discrimination might try to evade Section 2(a) by charging uniform prices to all customers while secretly paying a phony "brokerage" commission to a favored buyer's agent or by paying a buyer a fictitious "promotional allowance." The Robinson-Patman amendments in Table 53.1 block such evasion.

Courts hold that the "meeting competition" defense of Section 2(b) also applies to 2(d) and (e). Thus, if Ted, a supplier, pays a favored buyer a larger sum for advertising than he pays his other customers, he can avoid liability by showing that he made the payment to meet a competitor's offer to pay the buyer a like amount.

Exclusive Dealing

Section 3 applies to **exclusive dealing contracts**—that is, to sales of goods on condition that the buyer will not *use or deal in goods of the seller's competitor.* As in all Clayton Act violations, such arrangements are prohibited only if they will "substantially lessen competition or tend to create a monopoly in any line of commerce." The typical form of exclusive dealing is an agreement between a supplier and distributor which bans the distributor from dealing in goods of the supplier's competitors. Such an agreement should be distinguished from an **exclusive distributorship,** in which a supplier agrees to deal with a single distributor in a given territory. One of the most common exclusive dealing arrangements is a **requirement**

---

[5] 383 U.S. 637 (1966).
[6] *Porto Rican American Tobacco Co. v. American Tobacco Co.*, 30 F.2d 234 (2d Cir. 1929).

[7] *Sunshine Biscuits, Inc. v. Federal Trade Commission*, 306 F.2d 48 (7th Cir. 1962).

Table 53.1 Illegal Brokerage Commissions, Promotional Allowances, and Services Prohibited by Robinson-Patman Amendments

1. Section 2(c) bans sellers from paying brokerage commissions to the buyer or buyer's broker. To do so is a per se violation for which an injured competitor can bring a treble damage suit, without proof of injury to competition. Section 2(c) also prohibits a seller from paying brokerage to an intermediary acting for the buyer.

2. Section 2(d) makes it a per se violation for the seller to pay the buyer for promotional services, unless such payment is available on "proportionately equal terms" to all other customers. This section ensures that promotional allowances such as advertising, giveaway samples, and merchandise displays, or direct payments to customers to engage in such activities, will be made available uniformly to all customers.

3. Section 2(e) makes it a per se violation for the seller to furnish services to a buyer in connection with a sale unless the same services are made available uniformly to all buyers on "proportionately equal terms."

4. Section 2(f) prohibits buyer-induced discrimination, which makes it unlawful for any person knowingly to induce or receive a price that is discriminatory under Clayton Section 2.

---

contract, which provides that all a buyer's requirements for a product will be purchased from a single supplier. Exclusive distributorships and requirement contracts are illegal *only if they are anticompetitive*.

Exclusive dealing arrangements may hurt distributors, because they are banned from buying on more favorable terms elsewhere. Such contracts also can hurt the seller's competitors, because they are denied the opportunity to sell their products to the exclusive distributor. To determine if such contracts will "substantially lessen competition or tend to create a monopoly" under the Clayton Act, courts first define the **relevant market** and then attempt to measure the effect of the exclusive dealing arrangement on competition in that market. This approach is the same as that used in Sherman Section 1 cases. Courts measure competitive effect with two tests: (1) a quantitative substantiality test and (2) a qualitative substantiality test.

Under the **quantitative substantiality test,** if the exclusive dealing contract covers a *substantial quantity of the relevant market*, it is held to substantially lessen competition and there is no need for further inquiry. The test is used primarily to evaluate exclusive dealing contracts when the defendant dominates the relevant market.

A **qualitative substantiality test** was adopted by the Supreme Court in *Tampa Electric Co. v. Nashville Coal Co.*,[8] a case involving a contract to supply a power company's coal requirements. The Court required a *qualitative economic evaluation* of anticompetitive effects to consider (1) the relative market strength of the parties, (2) the contract volume of trade compared with total volume in the relevant market, (3) the contract's probable immediate and future effect on competition, and (4) whether competition prospered despite the restrictive agreement. Weighing these factors, and stressing the small percentage of the coal market that was involved, the Court held that the exclusive contract to supply Tampa's coal needs for 20 years was not anticompetitive. The qualitative test is favored where the seller does not dominate the market and a small amount of competitors' business is foreclosed from it.

Tying Arrangements

Section 3 also prohibits **tying contracts,** in which a seller will sell a product (the tying product) only if the buyer agrees to buy a second, distinct product which the buyer often does not want (the tied product). Table 53.2 lists the three factors which must be present for a tying arrangement to be illegal. When these three requirements are met, tying contracts (unlike other forms of exclusive dealing, which are judged under the rule of reason) almost always are per se violations, especially where there is strong market power over a tying product.

[8] 365 U.S. 320 (1961).

Table 53.2 Elements of an Unlawful Tying Arrangement under Clayton Section 3

1. *Two distinct products.* Is a flashlight with batteries one product or two? In deciding whether two products are different, courts consider whether the products are priced separately, are physically separate, or have separate markets, and whether consumers view them as separate items.

2. *Market power.* The seller must have sufficient market power with respect to the tying product to force the purchase of the tied product, and thus appreciably restrain free competition in the market for the tied product.*

3. A *"not insubstantial effect on commerce."* The tying arrangement must affect interstate commerce adversely. Presumably the Clayton Section 3 requirement ("affects a not insubstantial amount of commerce") requires less evidence than would be required to show that the arrangement had a "substantial effect on commerce"—the Sherman Section 1 test.†

*Northern Pac. Ry. v. United States, 336 U.S. 1 (1958).
†United States Steel Corp. v. Fortner Enterprises, Inc. 429 U.S. 610 (1977).

Section 1 of the Sherman Act (discussed in Chapter 52) also prohibits exclusive dealing contracts and tying arrangements. Generally, the tests of legality of tying arrangements are the same regardless of whether the plaintiff sues under Section 1 of the Sherman Act or Section 3 of the Clayton Act. However, there are important differences in how the two laws treat exclusive dealing and tying contracts, as shown in Table 53.3.

Corporate Mergers—Section 7

The "antimerger section" of the Clayton Act, as amended in 1950, was enacted to halt the national trend toward concentration of market power.

Scope. Section 7 prohibits one business (a proprietorship, partnership, or corporation) from acquiring the *stock* or *assets* of another firm where the effect "may be substantially to lessen competition, or to tend to create a monopoly." Mergers may be challenged by both the FTC and the Justice Department. In 1992, the two agencies jointly issued *Horizontal Merger Guidelines*. Since 1950, a large body of case law has developed from private Section 7 suits against mergers. Kinds of mergers are defined in Table 53.4.

The Antitrust Improvement Act of 1976 requires corporations with sales or assets over $100 million to give advance notice to the Department of Justice and the Federal Trade Commission of any acquisition of a corporation with sales or assets of $10 million or more. These notices, called Hart-Scott-Rodino filings, permit the regulatory agencies to advise in advance whether a merger will be challenged, thus avoiding mergers that later have to be undone. The Antitrust Procedural Improvement Act (1980) enlarges the Justice Department's enforcement powers.

Relevant Market under Section 7. As noted in Chapter 52 in the discussion of Sherman Section 2 monopolization cases, anticompetitive behavior always occurs in a *market*. Therefore, analysis of a merger's anticompetitive effects under Clayton Section 7 must begin by defining the firm's *relevant product and geographic market*. In a proposed merger, a narrowly defined product or geographic market will result in greater anticompetitive effect. Conversely, a broadly defined product line or geographic market will result in a smaller adverse effect on competition. Thus, the entire issue of probable anticompetitive effect of a merger often depends upon the relevant "product" and "geographic" market definitions used by the trial court.

The Supreme Court defined product and geographic market in a classic case involving a proposed merger between Brown Shoe Co. and G. R. Kinney Company.[9] Since both were manufacturers that operated chains of retail shoe stores, the proposed merger was both vertical and horizontal. The Supreme Court outlined the steps to follow in defining the product and

[9] *Brown Shoe Co. v. United States*, 370 U.S. 294 (1962).

Table 53.3 Sherman and Clayton Acts Compared and Contrasted

	Sherman Act	Clayton (Robinson-Patman) Act
Scope	Covers broader range of activity, including real estate transactions and services (e.g., advertising, radio, TV, electric power).	Applies only to "sales or leases" of "goods, wares, merchandise, machinery, supplies or other commodities."
"Commerce" jurisdiction	Defendant's acts must be in "flow of commerce or have a substantial and adverse effect on commerce"—much broader than Clayton.	Applies only to one who acts "in the course of commerce"—a narrower "commerce" definition than the Sherman Act.
Exclusive dealing	To be unlawful, the exclusive dealing or tying arrangement must "actively and unreasonably restrain trade."	Plaintiff must show only that the exclusive dealing or tying arrangement might tend to lessen competition or create a monopoly.*
Tying arrangements	The tying product and tied product can be two goods, two services, or a service and a good (e.g., electric service tied to light bulb sales).	Both the tying and tied products must be "goods, wares, and merchandise" (a "good" cannot be tied to a "service").

*For example, a plaintiff may sue under Sherman Section 1 and Clayton Section 3 and not have enough proof to prevail on Sherman Section 1, but still have enough proof to prevail on Clayton Section 3.

geographic market: First, it defined the *product line* as "shoes" but broke it down into subcategories such as "men's, women's, children's." Second, it defined an *outer-boundary market*, which was determined to be the United States. Third, it defined *geographic submarkets*, which were determined to be every city in the United States with a population of 10,000. The Court then said, "[I]t is necessary to examine the effects of a merger in each such economically significant submarket to determine if there is a reasonable probability that the merger will substantially lessen competition." After analyzing the two firms' market shares before merger, the Court held that the merger's vertical and horizontal aspects both violated Clayton Section 7.

The definition of product line is also crucial to the outcome of a Section 7 merger. For example, in *United States v. E. I. du Pont de Nemours & Co.*[10] the government charged du Pont with a violation of Section 7 by reason of its acquisition of 23 percent of the stock of General Motors (GM). Du Pont sold paint to GM as well as to many industrial users other than auto manufacturers. The case turned on whether du Pont's product line was paint in general or automotive paint. If it was paint in general, GM's purchases were foreclosing competitors of du Pont from only 3.5 percent of the total industrial paint market—an inconsequential amount. On the other hand, if du Pont's product line was automotive paint, GM's purchases were 24 percent of total automotive uses. The Supreme Court ruled that the "line of commerce" was automotive paint, thus greatly expanding the impact of the merger upon du Pont's competitors. Having

[10] 353 U.S. 586 (1957).

Table 53.4 Kinds of Mergers

Horizontal	Vertical	Conglomerate
A merger between competitors (e.g., two shoe wholesalers or two supermarket chains). Most often challenged under antitrust law.	*Forward merger*—also called a *downstream vertical merger*—occurs when a firm acquires a customer. *Backward merger*—also called an *upstream vertical merger*—occurs when a firm acquires a supplier.	A joinder of two firms that have unrelated, noncompeting products. The Justice Department defines it as "any merger that is not horizontal or vertical." Also includes a *market extension merger*—a joinder of two firms selling the same product in different geographic markets; and a *product extension merger*—a joinder in which the product of the target firm is in the same general category as the product of the acquiring firm.

adopted the narrower product line definition, the Court found that the merger foreclosed a substantial share (24 percent) of the market, and that the acquisition was unlawful.

Proving Substantial Lessening of Competition. After defining the relevant product line, geographic market, and submarkets, a Section 7 plaintiff must prove that the effect of the merger "may be substantially to lessen competition, or to tend to create a monopoly." Generally, the FTC, the Department of Justice, and the courts are to examine market concentration as measured by market share percentages of the merging firms before and after the merger. Since the percentage of market share allowed depends on whether the merger is horizontal, vertical, or conglomerate, each type of merger must be evaluated separately. Although corporate combinations may also violate Sections 1 and 2 of the Sherman Act, most challenges are made under the easier-to-prove Clayton Section 7.

Horizontal mergers. If **horizontal mergers** (defined in Table 53.4) result in a significant increase in concentration as measured by market share, they are likely to be challenged by the Department of Justice, which has primary enforcement responsibility in merger-acquisition cases. Its *Merger Guidelines* (1984, 1993) utilizes a statistical Herfindahl-Hirschman Index (HHI) for testing whether to challenge horizontal mergers. Under the HHI formula, the postmerger market share of each firm in the relevant market is squared, and the squares are added. If postmerger HHI total for all firms in the relevant market is under 1,000, the merger is not likely to be questioned; if it is between 1,000 and 1,850, it is more likely to be challenged, particularly if (1) the remaining market is highly concentrated, (2) there is a continuing trend in the industry toward concentration, or (3) there are very high entry barriers to potential competitors. An HHI above 1,850 means a concentrated market with merger likely to be challenged.

Consider, for example, a proposed merger of 2 companies in a relevant market of 20 firms, each having a 5 percent market share.

The premerger HHI is $20 \times 5^2 = 500$. The postmerger HHI is $18 \times 5^2 = 450$ plus $1 \times 10^2 = 100$, for a total of 550. Since the HHI total is only 550, the merger is not likely to be challenged. Moreover, even at HHI totals of up to 1,800, mergers increasing the market's HHI by less than 100 points are unlikely to be challenged. In Case 53.1 the court applied HHI indices to a horizontal merger under Clayton Section 7.

CASE 53.1 **Federal Trade Commission v. PPG Industries, Inc.**
• 798 F.2d 1400 (D.C. Cir. 1986)

FACTS PPG Industries, the world's largest producer of aircraft transparencies (windows and mixed glass-acrylic windshields), proposed a horizontal merger with Swedlow Inc., the world's largest manufacturer of acrylic (but not glass) aircraft transparencies. The two firms were frequent competitors in bidding for major U.S. airframe manufacturers contracts. Functionally, glass and acrylic transparencies are interchangeable. The FTC (Commission) sued under Clayton Section 7, seeking an injunction against the merger on the ground that it would "substantially lessen competition." The trial court ruled that the Commission had a substantial likelihood of prevailing at trial, but made a "hold separate order," which required the companies to operate separately so that divestiture of Swedlow could be implemented if the FTC won its case at trial. The FTC appealed, claiming that since the court found the Commission was likely to prevail, it should enjoin merger pending trial.

OPINION BORK, J. . . . The Commission's challenges are supported by the record. . . . This conclusion requires us to reverse the district court's entry of a hold separate order and to remand the case with instructions to enter a preliminary injunction barring consummation of the merger pending completion of the proceedings. . . .

The relevant geographic market was found to be the United States for such aircraft transparencies. Because it had no accurate figures for the emerging high technology market, the court used the closest relevant market, that for all transparencies, and noted that this market is already highly concentrated with the top four firms accounting for over 80% of all sales in 1984 . . . which yields a 1943 on the Herfindahl-Hirschman Index ("HHI"). The merger of PPG, the largest manufacturer with a 30% market share, and Swedlow, the second largest manufacturer with a 23% market share, would create an entity with a combined market share two-and-one-half times larger than the nearest competitor and raise the HHI to 3295.

Market power or the lack of it is often measured by the HHI. The FTC and the Department of Justice, as well as most economists, consider the measure superior to . . . cruder measures. . . . The Department of Justice Merger Guidelines define as "unconcentrated" a market with an HHI below 1000, as "moderately concentrated" a market with an HHI between 1000 and 1800, and as "highly concentrated" a market with an HHI over 1800. The pre-acquisition HHI calculated by the district court shows that the relevant market, as the

CASE 53.1 **Continued**	court defined it, is already "highly concentrated" and the effect of the acquisition would be a dramatic increase in concentration. . . . PPG and Swedlow maintain that they do not compete, because their businesses are largely complementary . . . [but] the evidence that PPG and Swedlow are competitors is overwhelming.
JUDGMENT	[The court of appeals remanded the case to the trial court, instructing it to enter a preliminary injunction against merger.]

Additional Tests of a Merger's Anticompetitive Effect. Both the Department of Justice and the FTC consider factors other than HHI calculations in deciding whether to challenge a merger. For example, if the acquiring firm is double the size of the next largest firm in the industry and has 35 percent or more of the market, *Merger Guidelines* indicates that the acquiring firm's proposed merger, even with a firm having only a 1 percent market share, will be challenged. In addition, other nonmarket share factors are weighed, such as whether (1) the acquiring firm has a history of merger expansion; (2) the target firm has been a significant competitive influence in the market; (3) in the past most of the industry firms have pursued anticompetitive activities such as exchanging price information, following a "delivered price" system, or joining in such horizontal "cooperation" as price fixing or dividing customers or markets; and (4) there is a trend toward concentration in the industry. In the following case, the court relied on the Justice Department's "five percent test" of cross-elasticity of demand to assist the FTC in defining the product market.

CASE 53.2	**Olin Corporation v. Federal Trade Commission** • 986 F.2d 1295 (9th Cir. 1993)
FACTS	Olin manufactured 84 percent of the nation's calcium hypochloride (CAL/HYPO), one of two dry sanitizers for killing algae and bacteria in swimming pools. The other is isocyanurates (ISOS), which Olin did not produce but bought and repackaged for resale to the swimming pool market. In 1985 Olin agreed to buy FMC's plant for manufacturing ISOS. The FTC (Commission) allowed Olin to complete the deal under a "hold separate" order. After hearing, the administrative law judge (ALJ) found that a merger would likely lessen competition. The FTC affirmed and ordered divestiture. Olin appealed, arguing that the product market was the "ISOS-only" market, but the FTC claimed that the relevant market was "dry sanitizers," which consisted of ISOS and CAL/HYPO.
OPINION	TANG, J. . . . There is no dispute in this case that the geographic market relevant to this case is the entire United States. The parties have further stipulated that one relevant United States product market consists solely of ISOS (the "ISOS-only" market). The Commission also identified over Olin's objection a second relevant United States product market, one comprised of both ISOS and CAL/HYPO (the "dry sanitizers" market). . . . In analyzing the post-acquisition

**CASE 53.2
Continued**

dry sanitizers market, the Commission concluded that Olin's production capacity would be 57% of a market in which the "four-firm concentration ratio" was 95%. Nevertheless, there is evidence supporting the Commission's conclusion regarding likely anti-competitive effect on the ISOS-only market. It appears that Olin's post-acquisition share of production capacity in an ISOS-only market would be 48%, with a "four-firm concentration ratio" of 99.7%. . . .

We recently described the process of product market definition. . . . The boundaries of such markets are determined by examining such practical indicia as: industry or public recognition . . . as a separate economic entity, the product's peculiar characteristics and uses, unique production facilities, distinct customers, distinct prices, sensitivity to price changes, and specialized vendors. . . .

To aid in product market definition, the Department of Justice has promulgated the "five-percent test." . . . The Department will begin with each product produced or sold by each merging firm and ask what would happen if a hypothetical monopolist of that product imposed a "small but significant and nontransitory" increase in price. If the price increase would cause so many buyers to shift to other products that a hypothetical monopolist would not find it profitable to impose such an increase in price, then the Department will add to the product group the product that is the next-best substitute for the merging firm's product and ask the same question again. This process will continue until a group of products is identified for which a hypothetical monopolist could profitably impose a "small but significant and nontransitory" increase in price. The Department generally will consider the relevant product market to be the smallest group of products that satisfies this test. . . . In attempting to determine objectively the effect of a "small but insignificant and nontransitory" increase in price, the Department in most contexts will use a price increase of five percent lasting one year.

In conducting its product market analysis for swimming pool sanitizers, the Commission . . . observed that similarities "predominate over the minor physical differences" between ISOS and CAL/HYPO. . . . (1) Both products are used to deliver chlorine to swimming pools; (2) each product is able to deliver chlorine with about the same efficiency—although a pool chlorinated with ISOS will remain chlorinated longer; (3) by virtue of both products' stability and other characteristics, "a pool owner can purchase a year's supply of either product in a single trip to the store"; and (4) both products are available to consumers in the same forms. . . . Olin could not profitably impose a small but significant and nontransitory increase in the price of CAL/HYPO because of the danger that consumers would then switch to ISOS. Given this indicator of cross-elasticity of demand, the Commission concluded that ISOS and CAL/HYPO together compose a relevant product market, i.e. the dry sanitizers market. . . . In sum, we find adequate support for the Commission's finding of cross-elasticity between ISOS and CAL/HYPO.

JUDGMENT

. . . We conclude that there is substantial evidence on which the Commission could base its identification of a relevant "dry sanitizers" market composed of ISOS and CAL/HYPO. [The Court upheld the FTC's order that Olin divest itself of the FMC acquisition.]

Horizontal Bank Mergers. In recent years there has been a significant increase in horizontal bank mergers. The Bank Merger Acts of 1960 and 1966 require that mergers involving national banks receive prior approval of the Comptroller of Currency, and mergers of member state banks must be approved by the Federal Reserve Board. Most banks are insured by the Federal Deposit Insurance Corporation (FDIC), so its approval is also required. When the proper regulatory agency is reviewing proposed mergers, it must consider anticompetitive effects, public convenience, and need for banking service. If approved, such proposed mergers may still be challenged by the Justice Department, which applies the principles and standards of Sherman Sections 1 and 2 as well as Clayton Section 7. The Justice Department challenged a proposed merger in *United States v. Philadelphia National Bank*.[11] In that case, the postmerger market share was 30 percent of the relevant market. The Supreme Court held that the proposed merger would result in excessive concentration and should be enjoined as a violation of the antitrust laws.

Vertical Mergers. **Vertical mergers** arise when a firm at one level, such as a manufacturer, acquires a firm at a different level, such as a wholesaler or a supplier. In contrast to horizontal mergers, vertical mergers generally do not increase concentration. However, they can adversely affect competition in several ways. These are illustrated by *Brown Shoe*, discussed above, in which two shoe manufacturers proposed to acquire two retail chain shoe stores:

1. The merged retail stores can no longer compete among manufacturers for the purchase of shoes for distribution in their outlets.
2. Competing shoe manufacturers are foreclosed from distributing their shoes through the two merged retail chains.
3. Potential manufacturers and retailers may be discouraged from entering the field and competing because of the postmerger market power of the combined firms.

As *Merger Guidelines* suggests, both antitrust enforcement agencies have eased scrutiny of vertical and conglomerate mergers. Since 1982 some of the largest mergers of corporations in the nation's history have taken place. According to FTC policy concerning a **failing company,** if a merging firm faces a clear probability of failing and has made a good faith effort to be acquired by a firm that would not produce anticompetitive effects (e.g., a conglomerate), then the merger will ordinarily not be challenged. The new merger guidelines evaluate vertical and conglomerate mergers on the basis of whether a significant market share will be foreclosed to competition. If so, other anticompetitive factors will be scrutinized: the existence of barriers to entry that restrict a potential competitor's equal access to customers or to suppliers, and whether the industry reflects a trend toward vertical integration.

Conglomerate Mergers. **Conglomerate mergers** and their subsets, **market extension** and **product extension mergers,** are defined in Table 53.4. They arise when there is little or no visible relation between the business of two uniting firms. Even in a product extension merger, products of the two firms do not *directly* compete. Two types of conglomerate mergers likely to be challenged as being anticompetitive are (1) mergers creating danger of reciprocal buying and (2) those involving a potential entrant into the market.

Potential Entrant Doctrine. The **potential entrant doctrine** (also called **potential competitor doctrine**) holds that the forbidden anticompetitive effect may exist if one of the two merging firms is a potential entrant into the market. Prohibiting such a merger increases the chances that the potential entrant will stimulate competition by entering the market de novo (as a new entrant). The fact that it is on the edge of the market also has a stimulating effect on competition among firms that are already there. In *Marine Bancorporation*,[12] the most recent case on the potential entrant doctrine, the Supreme Court said:

---

[11] 374 U.S. 321 (1963).

[12] *United States v. Marine Bancorporation, Inc.*, 418 U.S. 602 (1974).

The principal focus of the doctrine is on the likely effects of the premerger position of the acquiring firm on the fringe of the target market. . . . A market extension merger may be unlawful if the target market is substantially concentrated, if the acquiring firm has the characteristics, capabilities, and economic incentive to render it a perceived potential de novo entrant, and if the acquiring firm's premerger presence on the fringe of the target market . . . [is likely to present] the "wings effect"—the probability that the acquiring firm prompted premerger procompetitive effects within the target market by being perceived by the existing firms in that market as likely to enter de novo. The elimination of such present procompetitive effects may render a merger unlawful under § 7.

The potential entrant doctrine has also been applied to large conglomerate firms that could potentially enter a new product market. Antitrust policy is concerned that market dominance may result from merger with a powerful conglomerate because (1) its strength may enable it to sell below cost in a product or geographic market and drive out weaker competitors; (2) economies of scale may enable it to eliminate smaller competitors by underpricing them even without selling below cost; (3) the danger of reciprocal buying is increased, foreclosing suppliers from competing to meet the needs of either merging firm; (4) barriers to entry are potentially increased; and (5) the merger has potential for accelerating the trend toward concentration in industry with all its related evils. On the other hand, anticompetitive effects of conglomerate mergers are not readily visible or measurable. By definition the firms are in separate markets, so merger cannot *directly* affect competition, and the number of postmerger competitors in the market is unchanged.

Section 8—Interlocking Directorates. Clayton Section 8 attacked the potential anticompetitive effects of interlocking directorates by providing that "no person at the same time shall be a director in any two or more corporations, if any one of them has capital, surplus, and undivided profits aggregating more than $1 million" and if antitrust law would be violated by eliminating competition between the corporations. Inasmuch as one legal test is whether a hypothetical merger of the two companies would tend to reduce competition with other firms, there often is sufficient cross-elasticity (interchangeability) of demand for the products of two apparently noncompeting companies to prohibit the same director from serving on both boards. For example, in *United States v. Sears, Roebuck & Co.*,[13] the government sued under Section 8 to enjoin a director from serving on the board of Sears and B. F. Goodrich. Both companies competed in retail sales of refrigerators, washers, automotive supplies, and TV sets. The court found the two companies were competitors, and ordered the director to resign, saying:

> Since a price fixing or division of territory agreement would eliminate competition between them, and since such an agreement would *per se* violate at least one of the provisions of the antitrust laws, namely § 1 of the Sherman Act, it follows that § 8 forbids defendant to be a director of both corporations.

Today the hazard of a Section 8 violation, coupled with growing popularity of stockholders' derivative suits[14] against directors for negligence or breach of duty, has discouraged corporate boards from recruiting officers or directors from another corporation.

Private Enforcement of the Clayton Act

Competitors often sue horizontally merging firms, claiming injury from the merger's anticompetitive effect. Clayton Sections 4 and 16 authorize persons or firms that *suffer injury arising from a violation of antitrust law* to bring civil suits for treble damages plus attorney's fees, and to restrain the merger or other anticompetitive conduct. However, in 1977 the Supreme Court's *Brunswick* rule limited private plaintiffs' suits under Section 4 by requiring them to prove *antitrust injury*—that is, *injury that flows from the defendant's conduct which the antitrust laws were intended to prevent.* The rule was extended in the following case, in which the Supreme Court held that a private plaintiff's treble damage suit under Clayton Section 4 for per se violations of Sherman Section 1 must still prove antitrust injury.

---

[13] 111 F. Supp. 14 (S.D. N.Y. 1953).

[14] Derivative suits are defined and explained in Chapter 45.

| CASE 53.3 | ARCO v. USA Petroleum • 109 L. Ed. 333 (1990) |

FACTS Early in 1982 petitioner Atlantic Richfield Company (ARCO) increased its retail gasoline sales and market share by encouraging its dealers to match prices of independent dealers such as USA Petroleum (respondent). ARCO encouraged its dealers to match the retail gas prices offered by independents by making available to its dealers and distributors short-term discounts, as "temporary competitive allowances" and "temporary volume allowances," and reducing costs by eliminating credit sales. ARCO *did not drop its prices below the cost of production* (predatory pricing). When sales of USA (ARCO's competitor) dropped, USA brought a private plaintiff's treble damage action under Clayton Section 4, charging ARCO with vertical maximum price fixing—a per se violation of Sherman Section 1.

USA charged that ARCO had "drastically lowered its prices to appeal to price-conscious consumers," and had conspired with retail service stations selling ARCO gasoline to fix prices at *below-market* (not below cost) levels. The trial court in summary judgment said:

> Even assuming that USA can establish a vertical conspiracy to maintain low prices USA cannot satisfy the "antitrust injury" requirement of Clayton Act § 4 without showing such prices to be predatory [i.e., *below* ARCO's cost of production].

The court concluded that USA could make no such showing of predatory pricing because ARCO's market share was minimal, and there was ease of entry into the market with the result that ARCO was in no position to exercise market power. The court of appeals reversed, and ARCO appealed to the Supreme Court.

OPINION BRENNAN, J. . . . A private plaintiff may not recover damages under §4 of the Clayton Act merely by showing injury causally linked to an illegal presence in the market. Instead, a plaintiff must prove the existence of "antitrust injury, which is to say injury of the type the antitrust laws were intended to prevent and that arises from that which makes defendant's acts unlawful." . . . [Injury] will not qualify as "antitrust injury" unless it is attributable to an anticompetitive aspect of the practice under scrutiny since it is inimical to the antitrust laws to award damages for losses stemming from continuing competition." . . . Respondent [USA] argues that, as a competitor, it can show antitrust injury from a vertical conspiracy to fix maximum prices that is unlawful under § 1 of the Sherman Act, even if the prices were set above predatory levels. In addition, [USA] . . . maintains that any loss flowing from a per se violation of § 1 automatically satisfies the antitrust injury requirement. We reject both contentions and hold that respondent has failed to meet the antitrust injury test in this case. We therefore reverse the judgment of the Court of Appeals.

. . . A firm complaining about the harm it suffers from nonpredatory price competition is really claiming that it is unable to raise prices. This is not antitrust injury; indeed, cutting prices in order to increase business often is the very essence of competition. The antitrust laws were enacted for "the protection of competition, not competitors." . . . Although a vertical, maximum price-fixing agreement is unlawful under § 1 of the Sherman Act, it does not cause a com-

CASE 53.3 Continued

petitor antitrust injury unless it results in predatory pricing. . . . Low prices benefit consumers regardless of how those prices are set, and so long as they are above predatory levels, they do not threaten competition. Hence, they cannot give rise to antitrust injury. . . .

. . . Thus, proof of a per se violation and of antitrust injury are distinct matters that must be shown independently.

JUDGMENT

[The Supreme Court reversed the court of appeals finding and upheld the trial court's summary judgment in favor of ARCO.]

THE FEDERAL TRADE COMMISSION ACT

Simultaneously with passage of the Clayton Act in 1914, Congress enacted the Federal Trade Commission Act,[15] which created the Federal Trade Commission (FTC). A bipartisan agency established to provide day-to-day enforcement of antitrust law, the FTC was specifically charged with enforcement of Sections 2, 3, 7, and 8 of the Clayton Act. Section 5 of the FTC Act conferred upon the FTC broad authority to proceed against "unfair methods of competition and unfair or deceptive acts or practices."[16] In adopting Section 5, Congress recognized the limitless ingenuity of businesspersons to circumvent existing laws with anticompetitive practices not specifically forbidden by the antitrust statutes. Therefore, the FTC was given (subject to court review) broad authority to prosecute *any* practice that it considered anticompetitive. In *FTC v. Sperry & Hutchinson Co.*[17] the Supreme Court held that the FTC has power to prohibit practices that are unfair or deceptive in their effect upon consumers, regardless of their effect on competition. Thus, it is not necessary for the FTC to prove an anticompetitive effect when prosecuting unfair competition under Section 5.

In exercising this broad authority, the FTC considers whether the particular practice (1) offends public policy; (2) is immoral, unethical, oppressive, or unscrupulous; or (3) causes substantial injury to consumers, particularly with respect to purchases of necessities of life. Courts have also interpreted Section 5 to authorize the FTC to file civil suits against *any* violation of antitrust law, and against activities constituting unfair competition, even though such activities do not violate antitrust law. However, private treble damage suits cannot be brought under Section 5. Since 1914, many statutes have expanded FTC jurisdiction into consumer protection areas.

NATIONAL COOPERATIVE RESEARCH ACT—JOINT VENTURES WITH COMPETITORS

Joint Ventures and JRDVs; National Cooperative Research Act

With increasing frequency, competitors form joint ventures, particularly **joint research and development ventures (JRDVs).** In legal effect, a JRDV is a partnership, often between two corporations—one American and one foreign—for the purpose of research, development, and international marketing of a product. In order to encourage the formation of JRDVs, by reducing fear and uncertainty of their possible violation of antitrust laws, Congress enacted the National Cooperative Research Act in 1984. The Act creates special rules for suits against JRDVs to make it easier for them to combine without threat of antitrust liability.

The Act defines JRDVs to include pure and applied research and marketing of the resulting products or technologies through licensing agreements. Firms planning a JRDV are re-

---

[15] 15 USC 41-58.
[16] The Wheeler-Lea amendment added this phrase in 1938.
[17] 405 U.S. 233 (1972).

BOX 53.2
FTC Dusts Off 80-Year-Old Law

Frustrated by business practices that appeared to be questionable yet not specifically banned by any law, the FTC in 1992 dragged out an old statute—Section 5 of the Federal Trade Commission Act of 1914—and raised several questions. Does the statute apply to:

1. A manufacturer that proposes a price-fixing plan to a competitor that refuses and then notifies the FTC?
2. A supermarket chain with market power that sells one store in that market and buys three others?
3. A pharmaceuticals manufacturer that lets competitors know its bid on infant formula contracts in a sealed bidding situation by writing letters to officials in four states?

Charging violations of Section 5, the FTC succeeded in settling all three cases with nolo contendere pleas by Quality Trucking Corp., Von's Grocery, and Mead Johnson & Co., all of whom denied liability. Said an FTC official: "We plan to expand the use of Section 5 on a selective basis in the future." ∎

---

quired to give advance notice to the Federal Trade Commission and the Justice Department. Once a firm fits the definition and gives notice, it has special protection of the Act. Responding to growing criticism of treble damages plus attorney's fees awarded by the antitrust laws, the Act allows only *single* damage awards and further provides that if the JRDV wins the suit, it can recover its attorney's fees from the unsuccessful challenger. The Act also provides that any antitrust case filed against a JRDV is to be judged under the rule of reason—making it more difficult for plaintiffs to prove their case, since a per se liability theory is unavailable.

ANTITRUST EXEMPTIONS AND EXTRATERRITORIALITY

Approximately one-fourth of America's national income originates in sectors of the economy that are exempt from antitrust laws. There are two types of exemptions from antitrust: *express* and *implied*. **Express exemptions** are found in the antitrust statutes or in regulatory statutes for certain industries, particularly public utilities. Since a competitive economic system is the policy objective of antitrust law, courts interpret the law liberally to provide the broadest possible coverage; exemptions are construed strictly to limit them as much as possible. **Implied exemptions** arise from court interpretations that must reconcile conflict between antitrust law, other statutes, or the Constitution.

Express Exemptions

Labor Organizations. Section 6 of the Clayton Act exempted labor unions from the antitrust laws, and Section 20[18] granted unions relief from some injunctions. However, federal court injunctions against unions were not effectively limited until the Norris-La Guardia Act of 1932.[19] Today, unions have immunity from antitrust law only in *labor disputes* as defined in the Act. A union also loses its exempt status if its primary intent is to restrain trade or to conspire with nonlabor groups to monopolize. In *Allen Bradley*,[20] electrical contractors, suppliers, and a union all agreed that (1) contractors would hire union labor and buy only from the suppliers, and (2) suppliers would sell only in New York to contractors who hired union labor. The Supreme Court held the agreement to be an unlawful conspiracy that violated Sherman Section 1. It said that when unions combine with business to fix prices, the labor exemption is lost.

The labor exemption of the Clayton Act has been held not to apply to organizations representing learned professions, because the members are usually independent contractors rather than employees. Thus a lawyers' group publica-

---

[18] 29 USC 52.

[19] 29 USC 101–115; *United States v. Hucheson*, 312 U.S. 219 (1941).

[20] *Allen Bradley Co. v. Local Union No. 3, International Brotherhood of Electrical Workers*, 325 U.S. 797 (1945).

tion of minimum fee schedules[21] and a ban on competitive bidding by a professional engineers' association[22] have been held to be nonexempt violations of the antitrust laws. Even professional sports are subject to the Sherman Act, with the notable exception of baseball.[23]

Agricultural Cooperatives. Both Section 1 of the Clayton Act and Section 1 of the Capper-Volstead Act[24] establish an exemption for farmers' cooperative associations that are formed to market agricultural products. Like the labor exemption, the agricultural exemption is lost if the organization combines with outside firms to restrain trade.[25]

Patents and Copyrights. Federal legislation enacted under constitutional authority[26] expressly confers limited monopoly privileges on those who invent or publish. Although such rights conflict with the antitrust objective of promoting competition, they are recognized to encourage innovative inventions and publications.

Generally, courts have resolved conflicts between Sherman's competition goals and the monopoly objectives of patent law by interpreting patent and copyright privileges narrowly and by rejecting owners' attempts to expand such privileges into familiar areas of anticompetitive behavior. For example, in *Morton Salt Co. v. G. S. Suppiger Co.*,[27] Suppiger owned a patented machine used by the canning industry for depositing proper amounts of salt tablets into the contents of cans. It licensed the machine to canneries on condition that they buy their salt tablets from Suppiger. Morton sued under Clay-

---

[21]*Goldfarb v. Virginia State Bar*, 421 U.S. 733 (1975).
[22]*United States v. Nat'l Soc'y of Professional Engineers*, 404 F. Supp. 457; aff'd 55 L. Ed. 2d 637 (1978).
[23]*Toolson v. New York Yankees, Inc.*, 346 U.S. 356 (1953).
[24]7 USC 291–292.
[25]*Case-Swayne Co. v. Sunkist Growers, Inc.*, 389 U.S. 384 (1967).
[26]U.S. Constitution, Art. 1, Sec. 8, clause 8.
[27]314 U.S. 488 (1942).

> **BOX 53.3**
>
> **You Be the Judge: Football Strikes Out—But Is Baseball "Home Free"?**
>
> Whenever the nation's football leagues have filed antitrust suits, federal courts have held they are subject to such laws (*Los Angeles Coliseum Comm. v. National Football League*, 726 F.2d 1381, cert. denied). The same has not been true for baseball. In *Federal Baseball Club of Baltimore v. National League of Professional Baseball Clubs*, 259 U.S. 200 (1922), the Supreme Court ruled: "The business of providing public baseball games for profit between clubs of professional baseball players is not within the scope of the federal antitrust laws." Thirty years later, when asked to overrule the decision, the Court said: "We think that if there are evils in this field which now warrant application to it of the antitrust laws it should be by legislation."
>
> Angered by the "arrogance" of baseball owners, Congress has held hearings to consider amendments to the Sherman Act to bring baseball under its jurisdiction. James Michner, author of *Sports in America*, says, "Break up the illegal monopoly. Bring common sense back to the game."
>
> Should baseball be subject to antitrust law?

ton Section 3, claiming these were unlawful tying contracts that tended to lessen competition. The Supreme Court struck down the tying contract. Sidestepping the issue of whether Section 3 was violated, the Court said that it is against public policy for the courts to protect a patent monopoly when the owner is misusing it as a means of restraining competition with a tie-in sale of an unpatented article. This **patent misuse doctrine** blocks attempts to enjoin infringement if the patent is being used to suppress competition.

Implied Exemptions

State-Action Defense—The *Parker-Brown* Doctrine. In addition to the express exemptions discussed, many federal statutes provide limited exemptions for industries affecting the public interest—such as telephones, railroads, television and radio broadcasting, interstate pipelines, stock and grain exchanges, insurance, and ocean shipping. However, the trend continues toward deregulation.

Most industries affecting the public interest are regulated by commissions established by state law. A broad implied exemption for such "state action" was established by the Supreme Court in *Parker v. Brown*.[28] In that case, a raisin packer sued under Sherman Section 1 to enjoin the California director of agriculture from conducting a statutory price-fixing program for marketing raisins. The program involved pro rata restrictions on sales, first proposed by the producers but modified and formalized by the state. In holding such state action exempt from antitrust law, the Court emphasized that the program came from "legislative command of the state and was not intended to operate . . . without that command."

In *Goldfarb* (note 21 above), the Court held that a minimum lawyer's fee schedule approved by the state bar (an arm of the judicial branch of government) was nevertheless subject to the Sherman Act: "The fact that the State Bar is a state agency for some limited purposes does not create an antitrust shield that allows it to foster anticompetitive practices for the benefit of its members." The Court's current view is that a company affecting the public interest such as a utility can have its natural monopoly powers regulated by the state and simultaneously be required to comply with antitrust standards in other areas of business activity in the competitive sector of the economy.

In *Town of Hallie v. City of Eau Claire*,[29] the town sued an incorporated city, alleging that its policy of refusing to provide sewage treatment to county residents unless they voted to annex to the city violated the Sherman Act. The Supreme Court held that the city's allegedly anticompetitive conduct fell within the state-action exemption, but to obtain the exemption, the city had to prove it was engaging in the challenged activity pursuant to a "clearly articulated" state policy. Unlike a private party, a city is not required to show that the state "compelled" it to act, nor is active state supervision required where the actor is a city. The Local Government Antitrust Act of 1984 exempts local governments and their officers from money damages in antitrust suits.

Lobbying: The *Noerr-Pennington* Exemption. The First Amendment right of citizens to petition the government has been interpreted by courts to imply an antitrust exemption for lawful lobbying to obtain legislative or executive action, even if such lobbying is intended to restrain trade or eliminate competition. However, this *Noerr-Pennington* exemption[30] is lost if lobbying is used as a sham to cover other activities that directly restrain trade.

The following capstone case illustrates how the U.S. Supreme Court applies antitrust law to three issues discussed throughout this chapter—horizontal price fixing, unfair competition suits under the Federal Trade Commission Act, and the state-action doctrine.

---

[28]317 U.S. 341 (1943).

[29]471 U.S. 34 (1985).

[30]*Eastern Railroad Presidents Conference v. Noerr Motor Freight, Inc.*, 365 U.S. 127 (1961); *United Mine Workers v. Pennington*, 381 U.S. 657 (1965).

CASE 53.4 Federal Trade Commission v. Ticor Title Ins. Co.
• 119 L. Ed. 2d 410 (1992)

FACTS The FTC filed an administrative complaint charging the nation's five largest title insurance companies with horizontal price fixing of title search fees in violation of Section 5(a) of the Federal Trade Commission Act, which prohibits "unfair methods of competition in or affecting commerce." Title insurance is the business of insuring record title of realty for owners, occupiers, and lenders. A title insurance policy insures against certain losses or damages arising from defects in title not shown on the policy or title report. Before issuing a title policy, the insurance company performs a title search. The five insurers (respondents) accounted for over half the nation's title business. They charged uniform rates for title searches in Arizona, Connecticut, Montana, and Wisconsin. Each state licensed "rate bureaus" employed by the title companies. Uniform title search rates were proposed to the state insurance commission, and if there was no objection within a set period—often 30 days—the rates were deemed approved.

In the hearing before the administrative law judge (ALJ), the insurers' major defense was that their rate-making activities were entitled to state-action immunity, which permits anticompetitive conduct if it is authorized and supervised by state officials.

At the hearing, the ALJ developed a record of facts relative to the Supreme Court's rule on antitrust immunity, which requires that (1) *the state must articulate a clear and affirmative policy to allow the anticompetitive conduct, and (2) the state must provide active supervision of anticompetitive conduct undertaken by private actors.* In reviewing the record, the FTC held that none of the four states had conducted sufficient supervision and that the title companies were not entitled to immunity. The court of appeals reversed. The insurers (respondents) appealed to the Supreme Court.

OPINION KENNEDY, J. . . . While a State may not confer antitrust immunity on private persons by fiat, it may displace competition with active state supervision if the displacement is both intended by the State and implemented in its specific details. Actual state involvement, not deference to private price fixing arrangements under the general auspices of state law, is the precondition for immunity from federal law. . . .

The active supervision requirement . . . is designed to ensure that the state-action doctrine will shelter only the particular anticompetitive acts of private parties that, in the judgment of the State, actually further state regulatory policies. To accomplish this purpose, the active supervision requirement mandates that the State exercise ultimate control over the challenged anticompetitive conduct. The mere presence of some state involvement or monitoring does not suffice. . . . [S]tate officials [must] have and exercise power to review particular anticompetitive acts of private parties and disapprove those that fail to accord with state policy. Absent such a program of supervision, there is no realistic assurance that a private party's anticompetitive conduct promotes state policy, rather than merely the party's individual interests. . . . The purpose of the active supervision inquiry . . . is to determine whether the State has exercised suf-

CASE 53.4
Continued

ficient independent judgment and control so that the details of the rates or prices have been established as a product of deliberate state intervention, not simply by agreement among private parties. . . . The question is not how well state regulation works, but whether the anticompetitive scheme is the State's own. . . .

The respondents point out that in Wisconsin and Montana the rating bureaus filed rates with state agencies and that in both States the so-called negative option rule prevailed. The rates became effective unless they were rejected within a set time. It is said that as a matter of law in those States, inaction signified substantive approval. This proposition cannot be reconciled however with the detailed findings, entered by the ALJ and adopted by the Commission, which demonstrate that the potential for state supervision was not realized in fact. The ALJ found . . . that at most the rate filings were checked for mathematical accuracy. Some were unchecked altogether. In Montana, a rate filing became effective despite the failure of the rating bureau to provide additional requested information. In Wisconsin, additional information was provided after a lapse of seven years, during which time the rate filing remained in effect. These findings are fatal to respondents' attempts to portray the state regulatory regimes as providing the necessary component of active supervision.

. . . No antitrust offense is more pernicious than price fixing. In this context, we decline to formulate a rule that would lead to a finding of active state supervision where in fact there was none. Our decision should be read in light of the gravity of the antitrust offense, the involvement of private actors throughout, and the clear absence of state supervision. . . . We conclude that the acts of the respondents . . . are not immune from antitrust liability.

JUDGMENT The judgment of the court of appeals is reversed and the case is remanded for . . . proceedings consistent with this opinion.

Extraterritoriality of Antitrust Laws

Generally, agreements by American firms to divide world markets, assign export quotas, or fix prices overseas are subject to antitrust law. Beginning in the 1940s, the Department of Justice sought to break up large international cartels of American and foreign companies dominating markets for magnesium alloys, roller bearings, and other commodities. Enforcement has focused primarily on foreign activity by American or foreign firms that has a serious anticompetitive effect within the United States. The Justice Department and private plaintiffs are now giving increasing attention to extraterritorial (outside the United States) anticompetitive activities of multinational corporations.

Effect of Antitrust Law on American Competition Abroad. American antitrust policy conflicts sharply with the views of many other free world nations which hold that antitrust notions should be discarded in the highly competitive areas of world trade. The United States is virtually alone among major trading nations in the extent to which it imposes a variety of antitrust restrictions on exporters wishing to combine to penetrate foreign markets.

In contrast with American efforts to give antitrust laws extraterritorial effect, many foreign governments openly encourage export cartels by offering antitrust exemption, outright subsidies, or tax incentives. Such foreign export monopolies have an advantage over small and medium-sized American firms, which are prevented by the antitrust laws from combining to meet world competition. The extent to which joint research and development ventures (JRDVs), discussed above, will improve this situation remains to be seen.

Webb-Pomerene and Export Trading Company Acts. In token recognition of the competitive disadvantage of American firms in world markets, Congress in 1918 passed the Webb-Pomerene Export Trade Act,[31] which attempted to exempt from the Sherman Act an export trade association. However, the Act contained so many restrictions that trade associations organized under it accounted for only 3 percent of total American exports.

In an effort to improve the bargaining position of American sellers in international markets, Congress enacted the Export Trading Company Act of 1982.[32] It authorizes the Commerce and Justice Departments to establish antitrust standards that will be applied to export trading companies and to certify that a particular applicant meets those standards. These standards specify, as antitrust criteria, that there be no (1) substantial lessening of competition in the United States, (2) unreasonable upward pressure on prices in the United States, (3) unfair methods of competition, and (4) resale or consumption of exported goods in the United States. A certificate holder has complete immunity from U.S. antitrust laws *except* for civil lawsuits for injunctive relief and actual damages. However, to bring an allowable civil suit, a plaintiff must show that the trading company violated one of the above specific standards. In such civil suits there is a presumption of compliance by the defendant trading company, and if the court finds that the defendant complied with the antitrust standards, the plaintiff may be required to reimburse costs of suit and defense attorney's fees.

The new Act includes services, whereas Webb-Pomerene continues to apply to commodities only. The new Act also provides exemption from Section 5 of the FTC Act and from state antitrust laws.

Foreign Trade Antitrust Improvements Act. The Foreign Trade Antitrust Improvements Act[33] of 1982 was a companion bill to the Export Trading Company Act. The key provisions are contained in Title IV, which is designed to free American businesses from excessive antitrust regulation of export activities and overseas joint ventures. To achieve this goal, Congress attempted to codify and define the extraterritorial reach of the antitrust laws, as reflected in two landmark court decisions: *Timberlane*[34] and *Mannington Mills*.[35] The *Timberlane* court established an **effects test** of jurisdiction over international antitrust cases. The test required the trial court to make a preliminary ruling on the basis of three factors:

1 The court should decide if the conduct affected U.S. commerce.
2 The court should find whether the conduct was of a type or size that amounted to violation of antitrust law.
3 The court should decide whether to refuse jurisdiction for reasons of **comity**—that is, respect for the sovereignty of other nations.

The *Timberlane* effects test was supplemented by the *Mannington Mills* court. It listed ten factors to be weighed in balancing interests of the United States and a foreign government in order to decide whether to abstain from asserting jurisdiction for reasons of comity.

Essentially, Title IV reflects the "effects-balancing" standards of *Timberlane–Mannington Mills* so that U.S. courts in a proper case can abstain from exercising jurisdiction in deference to foreign interests. Under Title IV, there is no antitrust jurisdiction over conduct affecting wholly foreign commerce. Only U.S. exporters that suf-

---

[31]15 USC 61–66.
[32]15 USC 4001–4021.
[33]15 USC 6(a)(1), 45(a)(3)(A).
[34]*Timberlane Lumber Co. v. Bank of America*, 549 F.2d (9th Cir. 1976).
[35]*Mannington Mills, Inc. v. Congoleum Corp.*, 595 F.2d 1287 (3rd Cir. 1979).

fer injury—not foreign competitors—are entitled to file suit. The Act has been criticized on several grounds.

1. It does not modify existing case law or expand antitrust exemption sufficiently to stimulate export trade.
2. It deals primarily with exporters' antitrust exemptions without reaching the major source of conflict between the United States and foreign countries—namely, *imports* that affect American competition.
3. Owing to comity, it does not deal with commercial activities of *foreign states* that affect American domestic competition.

However, the Justice Department's 1988 *Merger Guidelines* shields most foreign investors and American-foreign joint ventures from antitrust enforcement actions unless such international business ventures have a direct, substantial, and reasonably foreseeable anticompetitive effect on American consumers. The guidelines also stress that patents, licenses, and other intellectual property rights—previously assumed to conflict with antitrust laws and promote monopolies—now will be considered procompetitive by the Justice Department, because they encourage efficient development of innovative technology. Although not binding on American courts, the guidelines give antitrust enforcers greater discretion to consider comity, diplomacy, foreign policy, and other noneconomic factors in deciding whether to tolerate certain activities by foreign companies doing business in the United States.

SUMMARY

The Clayton Act was passed to halt anticompetitive practices in their incipiency. The Act and its Robinson-Patman amendments prohibit price discrimination (Section 2), exclusive dealing and tying contracts (Section 3), mergers (Section 7), and interlocking directorates (Section 8). The Clayton Act applies only to activities that occur "in the course of commerce" and that "tend to substantially lessen competition, or to create a monopoly."

In applying this standard to exclusive dealing and tying contracts, courts use (1) the quantitative substantiality test, which is met if a contract covers a substantial quantity of the relevant market, and (2) the qualitative substantiality test, which looks at the contract's anticompetitive effect on the parties' market strength, and how competition is flourishing. Most tying contracts are held to be per se violations if (1) the seller has market power over the tying product, and (2) the arrangement affects a "not insubstantial amount of commerce." There must also be two distinct commodities.

Under Section 7, a firm is prohibited from acquiring the stock or assets of another if the acquisition would tend to create a monopoly or lessen competition. A product, its relevant geographic market, and submarkets must be defined in order to evaluate anticompetitive effects of a merger. Then the focus is on whether competition in each submarket will be lessened. HHI indices are used to evaluate horizontal mergers. An anticompetitive effect may be found if, by not merging, a firm is a *potential entrant* into the market. This doctrine encourages expansion by branching de novo.

The Clayton Act is enforced by private civil treble damage suits in which the plaintiff must show antitrust injury, by FTC cease-and-desist administrative proceedings, and by Justice Department civil suits and criminal proceedings. Section 2(a) of the Robinson-Patman amendments prohibits price discrimination among different purchasers of commodities of like grade and quality. To prove violation, there must be two sales of goods in two or more states to two or more purchasers at about the same time, at discriminating prices. Section 2 is aimed at preventing injury to competitors of the seller (primary line), to buyers (secondary line), to customers of buyers (tertiary line), and to competitors of the buyer's customer (fourth line). Defenses under Section 2(a) include (1) *cost justification* and (2) *meeting competition*—that prices were lowered in good faith to meet an equally low price of a competitor. Unlawful *brokerage commissions, kickbacks, or promotional services or allowances* are prohibited by Sections 2(c) and (e). Section 2(f) forbids buyers to induce or receive a discriminatory price.

The Federal Trade Commission Act of 1914 created the FTC to enforce the Clayton Act and to ban "unfair methods of competition or deceptive acts or practices." The National Cooperative Research Act spurs joint research and development ventures (JRDVs), which are judged under the rule of reason and are subject only to single damages.

Exemptions to antitrust law are *express* (for labor unions, agricultural cooperatives, and patents or copyright owners) or *implied* as a result of case law. An example of the latter is the *Parker-Brown* doctrine, which holds that state action is immune from the antitrust laws. The *Noerr-Pennington* rule exempts lawful lobbying from the antitrust laws, even if it is intended to restrain trade.

Agreements by American firms to divide world markets, as well as foreign activity that has an anticompetitive effect in the United States, are subject to antitrust law. To cure defects of the Webb-Pomerene Export Trade Act, Congress in 1982 enacted the Export Trading Company Act and the Foreign Trade Antitrust Improvements Act.

REVIEW QUESTIONS

1. (a) What Sherman Act defects did the Clayton Act aim to cure? (b) How well did Clayton Sections 2, 3, 7, and 8 cure these flaws?

2. (a) Define exclusive dealing and tying contracts. (b) Compare Sherman Section 1 and Clayton Section 3 as to (i) "commerce" and (ii) coverage.

3. Explain how the (a) quantitative and (b) qualitative substantiality tests are used in Clayton Section 3 cases.

4. Explain the different kinds of (a) plaintiffs, (b) remedies, and (c) proceedings for violations of the Clayton Act.

5. In broad terms, explain the scope of the Robinson-Patman Act.

6. Explain the "cost justification" and "meeting competition" defenses.

7. How does the Clayton Act prevent indirect price discrimination?

8. (a) What groups are expressly exempted from antitrust law? (b) How have court decisions limited these exemptions?

9. Explain the state action needed for *Parker-Brown* antitrust exemption.

CASE PROBLEMS

1. Polaris manufactures snowmobiles and all-terrain vehicles (ATVs), selling them through Western Power Sports. In 1989 Polaris advised Western that it had to purchase a specified quota of ATVs and that if it failed to do so, its snowmobile distributorship agreement would be terminated. When the market for ATVs had a downturn, Western refused to purchase the allotted quota of ATVs, and Polaris terminated its distributorship contract. Western sued Polaris, claiming it imposed an illegal tying contract in violation of Section 3 of the Clayton Act. Western offered proof that Polaris had 100 percent of the market for snowmobiles. The trial court gave summary judgment for Polaris. Has Western stated a case for a Clayton Section 3 violation?

2. Five cemeteries (Cemetery Group) had a pattern of selling burial lots only on condition that buyers purchase a grave marker (and service to install it) from the cemetery. Moore, a gravestone maker, in a private antitrust suit claimed that these arrangements were illegal tie-ins under Clayton Section 3 and Sherman Section 1. Cemetery Group claimed that (1) lots and grave markers are not two distinct products but must be sold as a single product, and (2) such combined sales were needed to retain aesthetic quality control of the grounds. Assume there is "commerce" jurisdiction, and that a noncompetitive higher price is charged by Cemetery Group for grave markers because of its market power over cemetery lots. (a) Are cemetery lots sold with grave markers and installation services distinct products? (b) Is there a possible tying contract that violates Clayton Section 3 or Sherman Section 1? (c) Assume that the sale of lots and grave markers is a tie-in. Is it justified to promote goodwill by favorably impressing customers with the aesthetic neatness of the grounds?

3. Bank A (acquiring bank) proposed to acquire Bank T (target bank). Bank Merger Act required FDIC regulators to evaluate the merger according to antitrust standards under Clayton Section 7. The "line of commerce" (product) was demand deposits. However, a dispute arose as to the geographic market. A survey showed that Bank A had 91 percent of its demand deposits in the southern half of Pike County and 6 percent in the northern half. Bank T had 95 percent of its demand deposits in the northern half and 3 percent in the southern half. Competition from other banks in northern Pike County was strong. Freeway access to all parts of the county was good. The evidence showed that small demand depositors tend to bank near their residences. Banks A and T claimed that the northern and southern halves of the county were separate geographic markets, but the FDIC argued it was all of Pike County. The FDIC also argued that if Bank A remained a separate entity in the southern half of Pike County, it would be an "actual potential entrant" into the northern half and would therefore have a procompetitive effect on the entire county. Evidence showed that it was not viable for Bank A to enter the northern half by establishing branches because of strong competition there. **(a)** What is the appropriate "geographic market"? **(b)** Should the merger be approved or denied? Explain fully.

4. Texaco sold gasoline directly to independent retailers in Spokane, Washington, at the supplier's retail tank wagon price, but granted big discounts to two distributors that engaged in retail operations as well, thus substantially increasing their sales. Hasbrouck and other independent retailers sued Texaco, claiming that its distributor discounts violated Section 2(a) of the Clayton Act. Texaco's defense was that it had granted legitimate functional discounts. One distributor was paid separately for its hauling function, neither distributor maintained storage facilities, and both resold most gas directly to consumers. Did the functional discount violate Section 2(a)?

5. A&P, a grocery chain, asked Borden Co. to supply milk. A&P turned down Borden's initial offer, and obtained a lower offer from a competitor. A&P told Borden that a $50,000 drop in price wouldn't be "a drop in the bucket." Borden then, in good faith, submitted a new offer *below* the competitor's offer, and A&P accepted. Borden did not know its new offer was lower than the competitor's. The FTC charged A&P with violating Section 2(f) of the Robinson-Patman Act by misleading Borden (in not revealing that the second offer was lower than the competitor's) and thus knowingly inducing or receiving a discriminatory price. A&P argued that Borden's cut in price was made to "meet competition," and since Borden could not be liable under Sections 2(a) and (b) for discrimination, A&P could not be liable under Section 2(f). The FTC claimed that A&P could not use Borden's "meeting competition" defenses. Did A&P induce unlawful discrimination?

6. Fire Protection Assn. (Association), a private group of members from industry, labor, academia, insurance, and medicine, publishes fire protection codes and standards. Its electrical code is routinely adopted into law by state and local government, and is widely adopted by insurers, electrical contractors, and inspectors. Steel, Inc., made steel electrical conduit, approved by the code. Plastic, Inc., applied to Association to have plastic pipe added as a code-approved conduit. Steel, Inc., packed Association's annual meeting with members whose only function was to vote against plastic conduit. Plastic, Inc., sued Association under Sherman Section 1 for restraining trade, and Association claimed immunity under the *Noerr* doctrine, because its annual meeting actions were routinely approved by governments. Was Association entitled to Sherman Act immunity under the *Noerr* doctrine?

7. Trucking Unlimited (TU) a truckers' group, sued Cal Motor Assn. (CMA), a competing motor carrier, claiming that CMA violated Sherman Section 1 by commencing proceedings in California, and in federal courts as well as agencies regulating the trucking industry, to defeat TU's applications to acquire or transfer operating rights. TU also complained that CMA filed unmeritorious actions without probable cause to prevent TU from having access to the administrative agencies and the courts, intending to put TU out of business and to monopolize the highway common carrier business. CMA said that the *Noerr* doctrine gave it First Amendment rights to petition government through the courts; and, regardless of goals, it was immune from Sherman Act liability. Assuming TU's claims are true, is CMA exempt from the Sherman Act?

CHAPTER 54

Business Law in a Global Economy

Increasingly, U.S. citizens find themselves doing business in foreign countries. Conducting business internationally can be complex, but it need not be daunting. A basic knowledge of international business procedures, cultural variations, and regulatory approaches of different countries will remove much of the mystery. This chapter surveys the legal aspects of international business transactions.

THE NATURE OF INTERNATIONAL BUSINESS TRANSACTIONS

Mauro Robles runs a successful tortilla manufacturing business in East Los Angeles. With branch bakeries already in San Francisco and Seattle, Robles now plans to establish a ten-oven factory in Vancouver, Canada. His use of conveyer belts to produce more than a million tortillas a day has interested businesspeople in Mexico City. They have asked Robles for a franchise that includes the transfer of his manufacturing technology. In addition, a mill in Mexico recently offered to ship Robles flour at attractive prices. Looking beyond Mexico City, Robles sees a market for his products in Honduras, Nicaragua, and Costa Rica.

Can Robles Market His Tortilla Technology on a Global Basis?

Like many other American firms, Robles's company has suddenly found itself conducting business in a global economy. But Robles is also discovering that operating an international business is much more complex than running a firm within the boundaries of a single country with a single system of laws and currency. Before Robles can proceed, he needs to know if his California corporation can legally do business in Canada; whether Canada will impose prohibitive tariffs on the ovens he plans to ship there; whether California health authorities can block the importation of Mexican flour; and what steps he should take to avoid injury if Mexico further devalues the peso. There are other questions: What effect, if any, will the free trade agreement between the United States, Mexico, and Canada have on Robles's contemplated expansion? What will he do if the Mexican government subsidizes flour tortilla exports and captures his American and Canadian markets with a cheaper product? If the Mexican franchisee should sell his technology and trade secrets to Japan or India, does he have an effective legal remedy? How does the Central American Common Market affect Robles's plan to expand to that area?

Emerging Global Competition

The past decade has witnessed astonishing political and economic changes. Twenty-four nations, emerging from the former Soviet empire, have now declared independence and are moving steadily toward market economies. Twelve other nearby countries that fought as enemies in two world wars have now banded together into the world's largest single currency market—the European Economic Community (EEC). Atlantic seaboard nations, after dominating world trade for 500 years, have quietly yielded that leadership position to Pacific Rim countries. In the Western Hemisphere, the United States, Canada, and Mexico move toward establishing the largest trading bloc in the world. The reunification of Germany and the emergence of postwar Japan as a major industrial nation are two other significant developments. These events mark the birth of a global economy in which the success—or even survival—of many businesses will require that they compete effectively in international markets. Ever since World War II, the United States has had an active role in this growing global economy. Its steady increase in world trade has been matched with a corresponding decrease in self-sufficiency.

Free Trade or Economic Nationalism?

In international business, two powerful but conflicting forces are at work. One force constantly moves toward global free trade and competitively determined prices. An opposing force presses for protection from foreign competition. Sometimes, but not always, protectionism reflects a desire to foster an economy characterized by **monopoly** or **oligopoly** (a few sellers) and maintenance of prices at arbitrarily high levels. At other times, local businesses may simply seek as much governmental protection from foreign competition as possible. Thus, the goal of international free trade is resisted by varying degrees of *economic nationalism* and its classic policies of high tariffs (import duties), limitation of imports, and government-sponsored monopoly.

Because world trade is vital to most countries, individual nations increasingly will disregard the desire of their local business constituencies to monopolize or to be sheltered under protective tariffs, and will enter into regional or multilateral treaties that establish free trade. The 108-nation General Agreement on Tariffs and Trade (GATT) and the European Economic Community's "competition" law (Articles 85 and 86 of the Treaty of Rome) are examples. Yet, because of internal political and cultural forces, nearly all countries also have protectionist laws aimed at limiting competition—especially *foreign* competition.

BOX 54.1

Points to Consider

Throughout this chapter you will find that most international laws either facilitate or restrict competition. As a businessperson or consumer who may be helped or hurt by a particular international law, you should find it useful to ask yourself a few critical questions:

- Does this law facilitate or restrict international competition?
- What special-interest group(s) pushed for passage of this law? Why?
- Does the law hurt or help me as a consumer? As a person engaged in business?
- Will this law increase or decrease international tension and hostility, thereby increasing (or decreasing) prospects for international war?

Recent legislation proposed in the U.S. House of Representatives would limit the number of Japanese-manufactured automobiles that could be imported into the United States each year. How would you answer each of the above questions as it applies to such legislation?

NATURE AND SOURCES OF INTERNATIONAL LAW

The legal environment of international business consists basically of public international law and private international law. **Public international law** governs the *relationship between nations*. **Private international law** is the internal or domestic law of a country governing *suits between persons domiciled within its borders and persons (or corporations) in other countries*.

Sources of Public International Law

There are four major sources of public international law: (1) custom, (2) bilateral and multilateral treaties, (3) regional multilateral agreements establishing trading communities, and (4) international organizations.

Custom. The oldest source of public international law is **custom**—that is, the time-honored observances of nations in their dealings with one another that eventually became "general practice accepted as law."[1] Many of these customs have been crystallized into recognized principles of international law by decisions of the World Court, which was created after World War I and later replaced by the United Nations International Court of Justice.

Bilateral and Multilateral Treaties. A second source of public international law is *bilateral trade treaties* between two nations. Since 1946, the United Nations Secretariat has registered and published over 30,000 international treaties that directly or indirectly affect international business. Businesses particularly want bilateral treaties in which a foreign nation guarantees the same rights that it grants its own citizens.

Treaties among three or more countries are **multilateral.** Multilateral treaties deal with matters ranging from communications satellites to commercial fisheries. Many are "open-ended," to permit ongoing ratification by nations electing to adopt them.

Regional Multilateral Trading Communities; EEC and GATT. In the past three decades, multilateral treaties have increasingly been used to create **regional trading communities.**

Many of these communities have extensive authority to regulate trade among member nations and hence are a major source of transnational business law and regulation. The Association of Southeast Asian Nations, for example, adopts uniform import duties (tariffs) and trade rules governing its member nations—Thailand, Singapore, the Philippines, and Malaysia. The five-country Andean Common Market in South America has a similar function. Other regional trade communities have appeared among the nations of Africa, the Caribbean, and the Arab Middle East. The United States, Canada, and Mexico recently negotiated the North American Free Trade Agreement. If ratified, it would create the largest common market in the world. These trading communities of the world are similar: They all have a policymaking body of delegates from member nations, a central administrative authority to develop uniform tariffs among member nations, and uniform trade policies toward nonmember nations. Most regional communities have their own judicial systems to resolve treaty-related trade disputes.

The European Economic Community (EEC). The most significant regional multilateral agreement is the *Treaty of Rome* (1957), which established the European Economic Community. The EEC is crucial to American business because it is the largest importer of American products in the world. In effect, the EEC is an economic United States of Europe, with a Parliament to make trade rules that are binding on member nations, a Court of Justice to enforce them, a policy of free trade and travel of workers within its boundaries, and a unified currency (the ECU) to be in effect by 1995. The EEC now includes twelve nations. Other countries have asked to join, including Austria, Turkey, Switzerland, Sweden, and a few nations that reappeared in eastern Europe after the collapse of the Soviet Union.

The EEC's Court of Justice interprets the Treaty of Rome, resolves conflicts between its provisions and the laws of member nations, and decides conflicts between the constituent bodies that make up the EEC. The court plays a key role because its decisions become law, to be im-

---

[1] Statute of the International Court of Justice, Article 38(1).

plemented and followed by the member states. Under the *supremacy of European law doctrine,* Community law prevails if it conflicts with domestic law. This principle is supplemented by the *doctrine of direct effect,* which holds that EEC and Court of Justice rules apply directly to citizens of member nations, without need for the nations first to ratify such rules.

The EEC **competition law,** set out in Articles 85 and 86 of the treaty, is the counterpart of American antitrust law. Its provisions, among the most crucial of the EEC, have far-reaching impact on American and other nonmember businesses engaged in commerce with member nations or their citizens. Article 85(1) prohibits all agreements which have as their object the prevention, restriction, or distortion of competition within the EEC.

With limited exceptions, agreements that violate Article 85 are null and void and subject to large fines. For example, suppose an American computer manufacturer appoints a Dutch distributor under an **exclusive dealing contract** in which the distributor agrees not to deal in or sell competing computers. Such an agreement might significantly distort competition or violate Article 85, and thus subject the American manufacturer or the distributor to costly sanctions. Article 85 expressly prohibits price fixing, limiting production, or applying unequal terms to parties that pay the same price.

General Agreement on Tariffs and Trade (GATT). The GATT, a multilateral treaty ratified by 108 member nations, has had a tremendous impact on international business. The agreement (1) states much of the substantive law of international trade, (2) provides a mechanism for settling trade disputes through panels of experts, and (3) establishes an international organization to promote free trade by reducing tariff and nontariff trade barriers. The GATT nations hold **rounds** (conferences) every few years to negotiate lower tariffs. The most recent Uruguay round focused on agriculture and services, such as construction contracts. Since its formation in 1947, the GATT has been the most notable force in world history to move toward freer trade.

One important means of promoting free trade is through **most favored nation** provisions, which require each member state to extend the same tariff rates to all members as it extends to its most favored nation. The GATT has also developed two important self-help measures—antidumping and countervailing duties—to aid member nations in defending themselves against unfair trade practices. Thus, where an exporting country **dumps** its products in an importing country at below-market prices, the importing country can impose an **antidumping duty** (tariff) to equalize the price with the fair market price in the exporting country. Sometimes the government of an exporting nation will **subsidize** an industry so that its exports may be sold at disruptively low prices to importing countries. In such cases, the importing country may levy a **countervailing duty** so that the import price plus the duty will equal the domestic price of the importing country's competing products.

International Organizations. Finally, the policy statements and resolutions of international organizations are a source of international law that profoundly affects global business transactions. For example, United Nations Security Council Resolution 692 (1991) declared Iraq liable under international law for any loss, damage, or injury to foreign governments, nationals, and corporations as a result of the unlawful occupation of Kuwait. The resolution created a fund from Iraqi oil revenues and ordered a compensation commission to pay claims from it. A separate organization, the United Nations International Court of Justice, at the Hague in Holland decides disputes, including trade controversies, that nations *voluntarily* bring before the court. The short history of this tribunal has witnessed a surprising number of nations submit disputes to the court and comply with its judgments.

Two other international organizations are important sources of international business law: the International Monetary Fund (IMF) and the International Bank for Reconstruction and Development (World Bank). Their rules and regulations, which have the force of law, can affect international business in a variety of ways. Recently, for example, the World Bank refused economic development loans to several countries that abuse human rights or deny free multiparty elections.

Sources of Private International Law—Conflict of Laws

There remains a large area of law affecting international business—namely, the internal or domestic laws of a nation that determine how suits over contracts, property, or torts are resolved between parties from different countries. For example, suppose an American exporter sues a Kenya importer for breach of contract, and under Kenya law, no contract was formed because the Kenya importer's acceptance was not a "mirror image" of the American exporter's offer. When the rules of law of the two countries conflict, which law should be applied?

Principles for Resolving Conflicts of Laws. The terms **conflict of laws** and **private international law** are used interchangeably to mean the internal system of rules of law that a nation uses to resolve conflicts about (1) which country's courts will be used and (2) which country's law will be followed. To discourage "forum shopping" (choosing courts of the nation whose laws are most favorable as the place to file a lawsuit), American courts balance the conflict-of-laws principles shown in Table 54.1 in an effort to reach a decision that the community of nations will regard as fair.

Table 54.1 Principles for Resolving Conflict-of-Laws Problems

An American wants to sue a Dutch national for breach of contract. In what court is the lawsuit filed?

If a suit is filed in an American court, that court will decide whether to take the case or let it be heard in Holland by applying the following principles of "private international law" (also called conflict-of-laws) principles:

Territorial principle	Suit should be brought in the territory of the country where the wrongful conduct, breach, or injury occurred.
Nationality principle	The matter should be litigated in the wrongdoer's country of citizenship.
Protective principle	Suit should be brought in the country whose basic national policy has been injured by the wrongdoer's conduct. For example, suit on a contract that violates the EEC competition law should be brought in Europe.
Reasonable expectation principle	The forum should be selected which appears to best carry out the reasonable expectations of the parties. For example, if the parties enter an agreement expecting any disputes to be settled by arbitration, a court should honor this expectation.
Comity principle	When deciding on the forum, a court should respect the sovereignty and basic values of the other country, and base its decision on principles internationally recognized as equitable.

Forum Non Conveniens. International business disputes often can be brought before courts of different jurisdictions. For example, where a corporation has a home office in the United States and is sued in a foreign country for alleged misconduct, jurisdiction may rest with a U.S. court because the United States is the corporation's residence, but the foreign country may also have jurisdiction because the alleged misconduct occurred there. The common law doctrine of *forum non conveniens* permits a court to dismiss an action where, even though it has jurisdiction, the case would be better tried in a court elsewhere.

The following case illustrates application of the doctrine of *forum non conveniens* in an international business context involving tort claims for negligence. Plaintiff, the government of India, representing victims of the Bhopal disaster, sought a civil jury trial in the United States—probably on the belief that a civil trial by jury in America would result in a much larger damage award than a trial by court. Civil jury trials are generally not available in England or any member of the British Commonwealth, including India.

CASE 54.1 **In re Union Carbide Corporation Gas Plant Disaster**
• 634 F. Supp. 842 (S.D. N.Y. 1986)

FACTS On December 3, 1984, the worst industrial disaster in history occurred in Bhopal, India, at a chemical plant owned and operated by Union Carbide India Limited (UCIL). It was incorporated under Indian law in 1934, with 50.9 percent of its stock being owned by defendant Union Carbide Corporation, the parent New York corporation. At the request of India, UCIL's plant manufactured pesticides, using deadly gas known as methyl isocyanate (MIC). On the night of the tragedy, for reasons yet unknown, huge amounts of MIC leaked from the plant. Prevailing winds blew the gas into the city, killing over 2,100 people, injuring over 200,000 more, and destroying cattle and crops.

In 1985 India's Parliament enacted the Bhopal Gas Leak Disaster Act, giving the Indian government exclusive right to represent Indian victims of the tragedy. The Indian government (plaintiff) filed suit on 487,000 Indian claims in the U.S. District Court. Defendant Union Carbide (the New York parent corporation) moved to dismiss, arguing *forum non conveniens.*

OPINION KEENAN, D.J. The doctrine of *forum non conveniens* allows a court to decline jurisdiction, even when jurisdiction is authorized by . . . statute. . . . A change of forum might frequently involve an unfavorable change of law for foreign defendants [e.g., by suing in the United States instead of India, Union Carbide would have much greater potential liability]. . . . Consequently, if the unfavorable change in law [greater potential liability under American law] were a major factor in the analysis, the American courts, which are already extremely attractive to foreign plaintiffs, would become even more attractive. The flow of litigation into the United States would increase and further congest already crowded courts. . . . Of course, if the remedy provided by the alternative forum [Indian courts] is so clearly inadequate or unsatisfactory that it is no remedy at all, the unfavorable change in law [by using courts in India instead of America] may be given substantial weight; the district court may conclude that dismissal would not be in the interests of justice.

**CASE 54.1
Continued**

This Court acknowledges that delays and backlog exist in Indian courts, but United States courts are subject to delays and backlog too. . . . However, the Bhopal Act permits the cases to be treated "speedily, effectively, equitably and to the best advantage of the claimants" . . . [so that] the most significant, urgent and extensive litigation ever to arise from a single event could be handled through special judicial accommodation in India. . . .

To sum up the discussion to this point, the Court determines that the Indian legal system provides an adequate alternative forum for the Bhopal litigation. . . . Differences between the two legal systems, even if they inure to plaintiffs' detriment, do not suggest that India is not an adequate alternative forum. . . . The inquiry now turns to a weighing of the public and private interest factors.

Private Interest Concerns

. . . The first example of a private interest consideration . . . is "relative ease of access to sources of proof." . . . Union Carbide argues that virtually all of the evidence which will be relevant at a trial in this case is located in India. . . . [M]ost of the documentary evidence concerning design, training, safety, and . . . matters bearing on liability, is to be found in India.

A second important consideration . . . [is] "availability of compulsory process for attendance of willing, and the cost of obtaining attendance of unwilling, witnesses." . . . [M]ost witnesses whose testimony would relate to questions of causation and liability are in India.

The third private interest factor . . . is the ease of arranging for a view of the premises around which the litigation centers. . . . An Indian court is in a far better position than this Court to direct and supervise such a viewing. . . .

Public Interest Concerns

Certain . . . administrative difficulties follow for courts when litigation is piled up in congested centers instead of being handled at its origin. Jury duty is a burden that ought not to be imposed upon the people of a community which has no relation to the litigation. . . . There is a local interest in having local controversies decided at home. There is an appropriateness, too, in having . . . a forum that is at home with the . . . law that must govern the case. . . . The substantial administrative weight of this case should be centered on a court with the most significant contacts with the event. Thus, a court in Bhopal, rather than New York, should bear the load. In addition taxpayers of this State should not be compelled to assume the heavy financial burden attributable to the cost of administering the litigation contemplated when their interest in the suit and the connection of its subject matter . . . is so ephemeral. Administrative concerns weigh against retention of this case. The Indian government, which regulated the Bhopal facility, has an extensive and deep interest in ensuring that its standards for safety are complied with. . . .

The Court concludes that the public interest of India in this litigation far outweighs the public interest of the United States. This litigation offers a developing nation the opportunity to vindicate the suffering of its own people within the framework of a legitimate legal system. . . .

JUDGMENT Therefore, the consolidated case is dismissed on the grounds of *forum non conveniens*. . . .

Unfortunately, courts throughout the world are not uniform in their decisions about which national court has the best claim to jurisdiction in a particular case. However, in recent years, the United States has ratified a number of multilateral treaties that harmonize private international law on such matters as obtaining legal evidence abroad and serving legal process on persons in foreign countries. Many of these treaties reflect the rules proposed in *Restatement (Third) of the Foreign Relations Law of the United States,* an unofficial but authoritative work.

THE INTERNATIONAL CONTRACT

Although there are many methods of conducting business abroad, one step is unavoidable: the negotiation and signing of a contract to reflect terms and conditions of the transaction. In developing the contract, one should think about several points: content, choice of law, choice of forum, arbitration, and, often, how the contract is affected by the Convention on Contracts for the International Sale of Goods (CISG).

Content

Points commonly covered in an international agreement are shown in Table 54.2. The agreement must contain the essential elements of a contract discussed in Chapters 10–17. One of these elements, *legality of object,* can be troublesome in transnational business agreements, because the internal laws of two nations may be involved. Suppose an Arab exporter from Dubai asks you to sign an agreement to buy crude oil delivered to you in New York at a good price. You say to yourself: "It's legal in Dubai to export oil and legal in the United States to import it." So you sign. But is it *really* legal? If the seller fails to deliver and you sue in Dubai for breach, you might find that Dubai's exporter can successfully claim that the shipment is illegal under Dubai law because it exceeds Dubai's oil quota established by an OPEC treaty. If you sue in a U.S. court, you might find that you had inadvertently signed a "standard form" contract with a clause, commonly used by oil-exporting Arab countries, stating that you agree not to conduct business with Israel. Such clauses are illegal under U.S. statutes. Clearly, advice of an international lawyer would have been useful.

Table 54.2 Checklist for Contracting Abroad

The contract should:
- Clearly define any terms that are ambiguous
- Be in writing and specify an official language that will be used in resolving conflicts
- Designate the currency to be used for payment and the time payment is due
- Contain a choice-of-law clause specifying which nation's law will govern if the parties have a dispute
- Include a choice-of-forum clause specifying which nation's courts will be used if a dispute develops (cheaper alternative: use an arbitration clause)
- Contain a force majeure provision excusing performance owing to an unforeseeable event beyond a party's control

Choice-of-Law, Choice-of-Forum Clauses

Parties to an international business contract often decide by agreement how, when, and where disputes over the contract will be resolved and who will resolve them. A **choice-of-law clause** provides that any dispute will be resolved by applying the law of a specified jurisdiction. For example, an American exporting firm that anticipates disagreement on the quality of goods shipped to a Dutch buyer may negotiate a choice-of-law provision that American law will be applied in event of a dispute. Similarly, a **choice-of-forum clause** in a contract can settle the question of *where* legal issues will be resolved if a dispute arises.

BOX 54.2
A Matter of Ethics

In 1993 Baxter International Inc., the world's largest hospital supply company, became the first firm to plead guilty to a felony charge of violating the U.S. law against supporting the Arab boycott of Israel. Trying to get off an Arab blacklist of firms doing business with Israel, Baxter's attorney G. M. Abbey pledged to "confer a benefit" on selected Arab states of $2.25 million. Baxter and Mr. Abbey agreed to pay $6.6 million in criminal and civil fines—the largest ever imposed under the boycott law. To deal with Arab countries that support the Israel boycott, a firm must promise not to invest in or deal with Israel.

Apart from the law, is it unethical for an American firm to make such a pledge? Why or why not?

Convention on Contracts for the International Sale of Goods

In 1980, sixty-two countries working for decades through the United Nations completed the Convention on Contracts for the International Sale of Goods (CISG). This treaty provides uniform rules for international sales of goods. Seventeen nations have ratified it, including the United States. Because of widespread participation in its development, the CISG is expected to become the international sales law of the future.

In many respects the CISG is an international version of Article 2 of the Uniform Commercial Code (UCC), particularly in establishing rules that apply when the parties have left certain terms open. Its rules attempt to give full effect to the intention of the parties consistent with the normal expectations of other business enterprises in the same trade. Under the CISG, there is a presumption that the parties have intended to follow normal trade usage and practices. The CISG also provides that in the absence of a contrary agreement, the goods being traded are fit for the purpose intended, or fit for any particular use known to the seller or contemplated by the parties.

Notwithstanding many similarities between the UCC and the CISG, there are important differences, including the following:

1. The CISG does *not* apply when the contracting parties agree that different law applies (e.g., UCC Article 2). It *does* apply only to parties in different nations *both* of which have ratified the CISG.
2. The CISG does not apply to consumer transactions.
3. Under the CISG, if the acceptance is not a mirror image of the offer, it will be considered a counteroffer and no contract arises (in contrast to UCC 2-207).
4. The CISG has no statute of frauds—hence, sale-of-goods contracts need not be in writing to be enforceable.
5. Under the CISG, a contract is formed upon *receipt* of acceptance rather than upon dispatch as under UCC 2-206.

Commercial Arbitration Clauses

The parties to an international contract may agree to be bound by *arbitration* in the event of a dispute. **Arbitration,** discussed in Chapter 2, is a process by which contractual disputes are resolved by an agreed-upon third party or tribunal other than a court. Arbitration is faster and less costly than court litigation, and a knowledgeable arbiter may prove to be an expert better qualified than a judge to hear and decide the case.

Arbitration does have disadvantages—for example, the arbiter has no power to subpoena or compel testimony of witnesses, or any means to enforce the arbitration award. However, enforcement of arbitration decisions was significantly improved by the United Nations Convention on Recognition and Enforcement of Foreign Arbitral Awards, which has been ratified by major industrial nations, including the United States. It provides that, once the arbitration award has been filed together with the contract calling for arbitration, the court of any nation can enforce the award. International commercial arbitration is so popular that a number of organizations have been formed to implement it, including the American Arbitration Association, Japan Commercial Arbitration Association, London Court of Arbitration, International Chamber of Commerce, and Inter-American Commercial Arbitration Commission. These organizations furnish printed procedures and rules, sample arbitration agreements, and lists of arbiters available to hear and decide cases.

The following case shows how both Congress and the Supreme Court encourage arbitration as an alternative to filing lawsuits.

CASE 54.2 **Mitsubishi Motors v. Soler Chrysler-Plymouth** • 87 L. Ed. 2d 444 (1985)

FACTS Mitsubishi Motors Corporation (plaintiff), an automobile manufacturer, was a joint venture owned by a Japanese parent corporation and by Chrysler International, SA (Chrysler), a Swiss corporation. The joint venture was formed to distribute Mitsubishi-Chrysler vehicles through Chrysler dealers outside of the United States. In 1979, Soler Chrysler-Plymouth (defendant), a Puerto Rican car dealer, contracted with Chrysler and Mitsubishi to buy their products for resale to consumers. Paragraph VI of the sales agreement stated that all disputes would be settled by arbitration "in Japan in accordance with the rules and regulations of the Japan Commercial Arbitration Association." In 1982, Soler disclaimed any responsibility for failing to sell cars under its contract. Mitsubishi sued in the U.S. District Court in Puerto Rico under the federal Arbitration Act and the Convention on Recognition and Enforcement of Foreign Arbitral Awards. It asked the court to compel arbitration. Soler counterclaimed against Mitsubishi and Chrysler, claiming breaches of contract and conspiracy to divide markets in violation of antitrust laws. The district court ordered Soler to arbitrate, even as to the antitrust claims, but the court of appeals reversed. Soler then appealed to the U.S. Supreme Court.

OPINION BLACKMUN, J. . . . [W]e find no warrant in the Arbitration Act for implying in every contract . . . a presumption against arbitration of statutory claims. . . . The "liberal federal policy favoring arbitration agreements," . . . manifested by the Act as a whole, is at bottom a policy guaranteeing the enforcement of private contractual arrangements. . . .

The international arbitral tribunal . . . is bound to effectuate the intentions of the parties. Where the parties have agreed that the arbitral body is to decide a defined set of claims which includes, as in these cases, those arising from the application of American antitrust law, the tribunal therefore should be bound to decide that dispute in accord with the national law giving rise to the claim. . . .

As international trade has expanded in recent decades, so too has the use of international arbitration to resolve disputes arising in the course of that trade. The controversies that international arbitral institutions are called upon to resolve have increased in diversity as well as in complexity. Yet the potential of these tribunals for efficient disposition of legal disagreements arising from commercial relations has not yet been tested. If they are to take a central place in the international legal order, national courts will need to "shake off the old judicial

CASE 54.2 Continued	hostility to arbitration" . . . and also their customary and understandable unwillingness to cede jurisdiction of a claim arising under domestic law to a foreign or transnational tribunal. To this extent, at least, it will be necessary for national courts to subordinate domestic notions of arbitrability to the international policy favoring commercial arbitration.
JUDGMENT	Accordingly, we require this representative of the American business community to honor its bargain, by holding this agreement to arbitrate "enforce[able] in accord with the explicit provisions of the Arbitration Act.". . .

ALTERNATIVE WAYS OF DOING BUSINESS ABROAD

If a Vermont clock manufacturer decides to market its products in France, it faces problems considerably more complex than selling the same goods to a buyer located in New York. First, because the transactions are international, they may often involve people who speak different languages and adhere to different business customs. Second, the business must find a means to assure itself of payment. If payment is in foreign currency, how will exchange into American dollars be accomplished, and what problems are presented by fluctuating exchange rates?

A *multinational enterprise*—any business established to move goods, services, information, people, and money across national borders—must choose among alternative methods of doing business. If the sale of goods is the objective, investment in foreign markets might be limited to direct sales efforts, or a seller might arrange for a foreign distributor or franchisee to sell its products in exchange for a percentage of profit or gross income.

A more intensive form of investment is a **joint venture** with a foreign business partner. For many American investors, a joint venture will be unacceptable if it is located in one of the many nations that restrict ownership by foreigners to less than majority control (e.g., 49 percent ownership by the foreign investor and 51 percent by a business entity in the host country). Then, too, certain types of joint venture agreements may violate American antitrust laws (see Chapter 53). The most extensive form of foreign business investment occurs when a *transna-*

> **BOX 54.3**
> Toward a Global Economy
>
> June 1992 was a turning point in history, not just because a Russian leader addressed the U.S. Congress for the first time, but because nuclear proliferation and the cold war were downgraded in favor of bilateral investment treaties, trading privileges, and a $24 million U.S. aid grant to assist Russia's conversion to a market economy, followed by a May 14, 1993, declaration of economic union of the Commonwealth of Independent States.

tional corporation operates through a wholly owned foreign subsidiary. Firms that do so can exercise a great deal of control over production and distribution in the foreign market.

Commonly, an expanding multinational enterprise develops foreign trade through a sequence of stages. First, it simply exports goods to foreign markets through direct-sales efforts. Next, it establishes a sales organization or other marketing arrangement on foreign soil. Eventually, the firm develops foreign production capabilities, first by licensing its patents and later by setting up its own manufacturing facilities. The types of legal problems that arise depend on the degree of investment.

Direct Sales

Most international business is transacted by means of direct sales. An American exporter contracts to sell computers to a French importer.

Both parties have many worries and risks. The American seller does not want to deliver the goods until payment is made. The French buyer doesn't want to part with the purchase price until delivery of the goods is assured.

Irrevocable Documentary Letter of Credit. Sellers' and buyers' concerns are eased by providing in the sales contract that payment of the purchase price and delivery of the goods will be made through intermediary banks, using an **irrevocable documentary letter of credit.** In this time-honored arrangement, buyer and seller, who are often unknown to each other, use trustworthy banks as neutral agents to assure payment of the purchase price to seller and delivery of the goods to buyer. How a French importer uses a letter of credit to finance a purchase of computers from an American exporter is illustrated in Table 54.3.

In essence, a letter of credit is a statement signed by an *issuing bank* in the buyer's country that it will pay the sales price to the seller when the seller presents to a *confirming bank* in the seller's country documents showing shipment of the goods via the carrier. These documents usually consist of an insurance policy, bill of lading, and certificate of customs clearance. When the confirming bank presents these documents, the issuing bank is contractually bound to pay the purchase price to the confirming bank, and this obligation is separate and independent from the contract between the exporting seller and the importing buyer. Because sellers are wary of a foreign bank's promises, they usually require a local nearby bank to *confirm* that it will honor the letter of credit issued by the buyer's bank. The overall effect of using irrevocable documentary letters of credit is to reduce both risk of nonpayment for goods (the exporting seller's risk) and risk of nondelivery of goods (the importing buyer's risk). Delay between time of shipment and payment is reduced. Buyer and seller each relies upon its contract rights with a local bank—rights that may be asserted and determined within each party's own country. International contractual risk is largely assumed by banks that regularly deal with each other.

Table 54.3 Itinerary of a Letter of Credit: Key to Safe International Buying and Selling

How does Pierre in Paris, use an *irrevocable documentary letter of credit (LC)* to finance the purchase of computers from an American seller, Hank of Houston, Texas?

The journey begins	Pierre contracts with his *issuing* bank in Paris for an LC in which bank agrees to pay the American *(correspondent or confirming)* bank when it forwards to the issuing bank documents showing ownership of the goods (computers).
First stop	The Paris issuing bank sends the LC to Bank of Houston and . . .
Second stop	Bank of Houston (as corresponding and confirming bank) forwards the LC to Hank of Houston.
Third stop	Hank of Houston now knows that a creditworthy Paris bank has issued a letter of credit and delivers the computers to ocean carrier in Houston, obtaining the necessary documents: *bill of lading* (document of title and proof of delivery to carrier), an insurance policy covering goods in transit, customs certificate of clearance for export, and his invoice.
Fourth stop	Hank takes the documents to correspondent Bank of Houston, which scrutinizes them to "confirm" that they meet the conditions set forth in the LC, and finding they do so, it pays Hank.
Fifth stop	Correspondent Bank of Houston sends documents to issuing Paris bank, which finds them in order, debits Pierre's account with sale price, delivers documents to him, and pays Bank of Houston.
Sixth stop	Pierre takes documents, including bill of lading, to carrier; gets computers.

Although UCC Article 5 determines the rights of parties to letters of credit within the United States, in global trade the International Chamber of Commerce's Uniform Customs and Practice for Documentary Credits (UCP) is the guide most widely used. Many international banks and contracting buyers and sellers specify that its terms will control the rights of the parties. A few state statutes permit buyers and sellers to substitute the UCP for the UCC in their letter-of-credit transactions.

Standby Letter of Credit. Unlike the ordinary letter of credit furnished by a buyer to finance the purchase of goods, a **standby letter of credit** is furnished by a *seller of services* to guarantee that they will be performed in accordance with the contract. If the contract to render services includes a liquidated damages clause and the seller breaches the contract, the purchaser of the services can recover damages from the bank that issued the standby letter. Suppose Builders, Inc., an American firm, contracts to build an office complex for Porsche in Frankfurt, Germany, and breaches its agreement by installing a leaky roof. Upon proof of loss as called for in the construction contract, Porsche can recover its damages from the bank that issued the standby letter of credit.

Distributorships and Licensing Arrangements

An American business that decides to invest in more than just direct sales may enter into distributorship or licensing arrangements with a business associate in a foreign country.

Distributorship. In a **distributorship,** an exporter agrees to market its products through the sales effort of a foreign-based distributor. If the distributor has exclusive rights to market the product in exchange for sharing profits with the exporter, the arrangement is an *exclusive distributorship*. Exclusive distributorships do not violate American antitrust laws because they do not affect competition within the United States or impair efforts of other American exporters to sell their products abroad. However, such arrangements might violate antitrust laws in the distributor's country.

One type of distributorship might be challenged under American antitrust laws: the *exclusive dealing arrangement,* in which the foreign distributor agrees not to distribute the products of any competing manufacturer. Assume that a German distributor has substantial control of the German market for personal computers and agrees to deal exclusively in the products of a particular American manufacturer. Other American manufacturers could be foreclosed from the market and antitrust violations under American law might result.

Licensing, Franchising, and Transfers of Technology. An owner of an intangible asset such as a production technology, patent right, innovative product, manufacturing technique, copyright, or trademark might want to **license** or **franchise** it to a foreign business. The foreign business usually agrees to pay royalties for the license. Licensing is the major means of transferring technology across national borders. In the past decade, a wave of trademark franchising of fast-food and convenience store outlets has swept overseas markets. The tourist encounters McDonald's from Moscow to Mexico City. And, of course, hundreds of foreign businesses have licensed their products and services to distributors in this country. A major problem of transferring patent rights abroad is that American patent law protects patented items in domestic markets, but does not protect them from competition of infringing products in foreign markets.

Joint Ventures

An *international joint venture* (IJV) is formed when a corporation from one country and a firm situated in a foreign host country agree to jointly operate an enterprise there. The IJV is perhaps the most popular form for doing business abroad. Forming an IJV with a local foreign firm offers many advantages. Among them are (1) local identity and management assistance as well as instant access to information about suppliers, customers, and political conditions; (2) one or more "partners" in the host country that can share the burden of raising capital as well as the risk; (3) an affiliate that often can be a steady purchaser of technology, capital equipment, or even end products of the American "partner"; (4) ability to fulfill requirements of most developing nations that their citizens have substantial participation in local ownership and management.

Transnational Business Corporations

A *transnational business corporation* (TNC), sometimes loosely referred to as a "multinational enterprise," is one that establishes at least one wholly owned foreign affiliate. The fact that a TNC operates in more than one country can be advantageous. By using choice-of-law clauses in various contracts, a TNC can choose a country's law that is most favorable to current business objectives. Also, a TNC can maximize tax advantages by controlling inventory buildups and sales prices among subsidiaries in different host countries with different tax rates. And TNCs have an advantage in negotiating labor contracts. If labor costs in one country become excessive, a TNC can set up or expand an affiliate in a different country where labor costs are lower. By operating in several countries, TNCs can optimize production and profits by efficiently matching capital, technology, and labor.

In recent years, some TNCs have been insensitive to the impact of their policies on a host country's local environment, economy, and culture. Sometimes, for example, local employees and their families have been exploited by extremely low wages. Reacting to such indifference and exploitation, many developing countries and international organizations have established codes of conduct to regulate TNCs.

SOVEREIGN REGULATION OF INTERNATIONAL TRADE

Why a Country Regulates International Trade

National governments regulate international trade for a variety of reasons. Many countries *restrict* trade to prevent foreign exporters from gaining allegedly unfair trade advantages by flooding local markets with products priced below the local costs of production. Most nations also restrict trade to further their national security—for example, by prohibiting export of military technology or products that might compromise national defense. A country might also prohibit imports of military weapons so that domestic firms can manufacture them without competition. Many developing nations promote international trade to spur economic growth. They appeal to foreign firms to bring in new industries, products, and technologies by offering cheap land, tax benefits, or monopoly privileges. Developed countries promote international trade to expand markets and to meet their own consumers' demand for foreign products. Sometimes a country regulates international trade to implement a foreign policy it considers important. For example, laws of the United States prohibit exports to communist Cuba.

Regulation of Imports— Protectionism or Consumerism?

A country's regulation of imports usually reflects an attempt to balance two conflicting policies. On the one hand, local business exerts pressure to "protect" it from what it describes as "cut-throat" foreign competition. The American auto industry's complaint against Japanese competition is an example. Responding to such complaints, global governments restrict competition by imposing import tariffs or by adopting nontariff restraints. Among the latter are prohibiting imports, establishing import quotas, and imposing burdensome manufacturing standards or complex customs or other taxes. For example, Canada recently imposed a 10 percent tax on beer cans—but no other cans—because American exported beer is canned whereas local Canadian beer is bottled. A government may also attempt to persuade foreign countries voluntarily to restrain exports. A more subtle import barrier arises when a government grants **subsidies** to its local producers (e.g., by absorbing part of the cost of production) so that they can secure a price advantage over foreign competitors.

On the other hand, many nations, particularly democracies, have a strong desire to benefit consumers. Achieving this goal calls for policies that encourage foreign competition so as to lower prices and improve quantity and quality of available products. Foreign competition is encouraged by lowering tariff barriers and abolishing import quotas and other trade restrictions.

Customs Inspection, Classification, and Valuation. To enforce import bans, quotas, and collection of duties, and to ensure compliance with other import regulations, all nations require that incoming products from another country pass through **customs inspection.** In the United States this involves several steps. Customs officials must classify goods for purposes of determining whether tariffs apply. **Classification** can be difficult. For example, a set of wooden bookends might be classified as an "art object," a "forest product," or simply "personal effects." The tariff charged depends on the classification used.

After a good is classified by customs officials, its **transaction value** must be determined—that is, the price actually paid for the merchandise when it was sold for export to the United States. Classification and valuation together are used to determine the amount of any import duties. U.S. customs officials' administrative decisions on these matters may be reviewed in the federal Court of International Trade. Customs officials must also determine the product's **country of origin,** since the products of some countries are subject to import restrictions. A product is said to originate in a particular country if it is wholly grown, produced, or manufactured in that country or has been transformed into a new and different article while there.

Dumping. Many countries impose special tariffs or other restrictions on products that are "dumped" in the country of importation at a price below that charged for the same product in the country of origin. A foreign firm often engages in dumping to increase its market share in the importing country. In the United States, the Antidumping Act[2] permits a U.S. firm or industry to complain before the U.S. International Trade Commission (ITC) if it is materially injured by imports from abroad that are sold at "less than fair value"—that is, at a price below that charged in the exporting country. If the ITC finds that unlawful dumping has harmed firms or industries, it can authorize the Secretary of the Treasury to levy a protective antidumping duty equal to the difference between the prices charged in the two countries. Foreign governments often subsidize their own manufacturers to give them a competitive edge in a targeted foreign market.

If U.S. firms or industries complain, the ITC investigates and holds hearings. If the ITC finds that such subsidies are injurious, a **countervailing duty** is imposed on the subsidized imports. Appeal from the administrative decisions of the ITC are taken directly to the U.S. Court of International Trade, recently created by Congress. The case below shows how the ITC investigates and adjudicates claimed violations of U.S. import regulations under the Trade Agreements Act of 1979.

BOX 54.4

Big Three Lose Dumping Claim

On June 25, 1992, the U.S. International Trade Commission, in a stunning setback, ruled 4 to 2 that General Motors, Ford, and Chrysler did not suffer any "material injury" from "dumping" of minivans by Toyota, Mazda, and other Japanese automakers, even though the Department of Commerce had agreed earlier that the vans were selling at unfairly low prices. The ITC decided that no additional import duties will be levied on Toyota's Previa or MPV of Mazda. One of the commissioners said the Big Three hurt themselves by signing a deal with the United Auto Workers that blocked cost-cutting layoffs, and by pushing used fleet sales at the expense of minivan sales.

U.S. industry still has an 80 percent share of the minivan market. Do you agree with the ITC decision? Why or why not?

---

[2] 19 USC 160.

CASE 54.3   **PPG Industries, Inc. v. United States**
• 781 F. Supp. 781 (U.S. Ct. of Int. Trade 1991)

FACTS   PPG Industries, Inc. (PPG), petitioning for itself and other U.S. auto glass makers, asked the U.S. Court of International Trade to review an administrative decision of the International Trade Administration of the Department of Commerce (Commerce). Commerce's decision was that the Mexican government had not subsidized Mexican producers and exporters of automotive glass and that therefore no countervailing duties should be levied on imports of such glass to the United States. After making this finding, Commerce had instructed the U.S. Customs Department (Customs) to refund Mexican exporters all deposits they had made to cover countervailing duties that might be assessed, and to discontinue further collection of any such deposits. PPG then asked for and obtained a court injunction restraining Customs from complying with Commerce's order.

In its administrative proceeding, Commerce found that none of the following Mexican government actions constituted a subsidy of Mexico's auto glass industry: (1) Mexico's pool of funds created to help Mexican firms refinance their foreign loans; (2) Mexico's low natural gas rate charged to its automotive glass fabricators; or (3) Mexico's program of giving tax rebates to exporters. PPG claimed that each of these activities subsidized the Mexican auto glass industry and that the United States should levy countervailing duties on imported auto glass.

OPINION   CARMAN, C.J. . . . Commerce's interpretations of the countervailing duty laws are accorded substantial deference and will be upheld as in accordance with law unless the interpretation is "unreasonable and plainly inconsistent with the statute, and unless weighty reasons require otherwise." . . .

Debt Refinancing Program

. . . This Court concludes that it was reasonable for Commerce to rely upon the statements of the Mexican government that it did not [discriminate in favor of its auto glass exporters in administering its debt refinancing program].

Natural Gas Program

PPG has not provided any new evidence that natural gas provided at government-controlled prices to all industrial users confers a countervailable benefit. We have repeatedly held that the provision of natural gas on these terms does not confer countervailable benefits. . . .

Mexico's Program of Rebating Taxes to Exporters

[None of the Mexican glass exporters] directly received . . . [tax rebates] during the administrative review period. Commerce's verification of this fact was based not only upon the verification conducted in Mexico City before Mexican government officials; it also examined the company records . . . as well as their

CASE 54.3 Continued	tax returns. . . . Commerce's determination that [the Mexican glass exporters] did not receive either direct or indirect benefits from [Mexico's tax rebate program] must be upheld as supported by substantial evidence on the record and as otherwise in accordance with law.
JUDGMENT	Commerce's determination that zero countervailable benefits were bestowed upon producers of fabricated automotive glass from Mexico . . . is sustained. . . . Action dismissed.

BOX 54.5
A Question of Ethics: "Social Dumping"

Environmental groups have recently protested the evils of "social dumping" to Congress in an effort to modify international trade law so as to force governments of foreign countries to institute costly environmental cleanup programs. When a foreign industry has no expense to comply with environmental regulation, it is able to sell its products in the United States at prices below U.S. prices, which include the costs of environmental regulation. This is equivalent to dumping at less than full cost, the argument goes, because a foreign industry's *real cost* should include (but does not) the same environmental regulatory costs that U.S. industry is paying. Hence, in theory, a countervailing duty should be charged equal to estimated costs that foreign exporters should be (but are not) spending to clean up the environment.

Do you think such a countervailing duty is justified? Is it a smokescreen for American producers to obtain tariff protection? If you were the ITC how would you estimate the cost of a theoretical environmental cleanup program in a foreign country?

Regulation of Exports—Licensing and Other Controls

National governments may also *restrict* the export of goods to other countries. Because sales abroad benefit domestic businesses, however, governments generally use export controls sparingly, and only after careful policy deliberation.

In general, exporting is subject to licensing. In the United States, export licenses are obtained from the Secretary of Commerce. Enforcement of export controls and export licensing is the responsibility of customs officials at the point of departure. Export controls may take the form of a complete ban on a product, of export quotas, or of export duties that must be paid before goods leave the jurisdiction. In the United States, the Export Administration Act limits export controls to special situations: (1) where the export will harm national security by contributing to the military potential of another country, (2) where the restriction will further the foreign policy of the United States or fulfill international treaty obligations, and (3) where control is needed to prevent a drain of scarce materials.

Regulation of Money across International Borders

For a variety of reasons, many countries prohibit or regulate transportation of cash across national boundaries. For example, to curtail international flow of drug traffic money, American law prohibits a person from carrying more than $10,000 of undeclared cash out of the United States. To protect its economy, a developing country may establish an official exchange rate for its currency in relation to other currencies, require mandatory currency exchange through its central bank, and enforce the established rate through stringent criminal laws and licensing requirements. Such strict currency control systems discourage currency exchanges in the country's "black market" at unofficial rates, thus compelling foreigners to buy currency from the central bank, often at unfavorable official rates of exchange.

Hedging against Fluctuating Exchange Rates.
International trade involves a risk that profits may be reduced by fluctuations in the currency exchange rate. For example, assume that an American importer agrees to pay a given amount in francs for a shipment of French wine. At the time of contracting, 1 American dollar is worth 9 French francs. By the time payment is due under the contract, 1 dollar is worth 8 francs. The American importer must now spend more dollars to obtain the francs needed to pay the French wine exporter than was contemplated at the time of the contract. The additional expense, due solely to fluctuating currency exchange rates, may convert an anticipated profit into a loss. A business can protect itself against such fluctuations by contracting with a bank that deals in foreign exchange for delivery (at a set price in dollars) of whatever francs are needed on the date payment is due. The risk of fluctuating exchange rates is thus passed on to the bank, which usually can offset losses against gains made in other foreign exchange transactions.

Repatriation of Capital Investment and Profits.
Other monetary concerns arise where a country places limits or conditions on foreign investors' removal of business earnings. Such laws are meant to discourage foreign investors from exploiting the country's resources or market potential without leaving behind some of the benefits derived from the opportunity to do business there. Some countries place strict limits on the percentage of a foreign firm's investment that may be *repatriated* (returned to the investor's country). Other countries levy graduated taxes on repatriated earnings, taxing higher earnings at higher rates.

The Foreign Corrupt Practices Act (FCPA).
The Foreign Corrupt Practices Act requires American firms to account for expenditures made in the pursuit of international business. A firm must keep financial records that accurately reflect the disposition of assets and assure that expenditures accord with management's authorization. Key criminal provisions of the FCPA prohibit any American business or its agents from giving or paying "anything of value" to "any foreign official for the purpose of influencing any act or decision of such official." Businesses may be fined up to $1 million and individuals may be fined up to $10,000 and imprisoned up to 5 years for violating the law.

> **BOX 54.6**
> **A Question of Ethics: Ban on Bribery Hurts Sales of U.S. Companies Overseas**
>
> "American companies say they have a definite disadvantage because of the Foreign Corrupt Practices Act. The companies from other countries don't have that," says a senior Energy Department official touring the Persian Gulf to drum up business for U.S. oil field service companies. "That's a fair statement," added an oil industry spokesperson. "What we call a corrupt practice is another country's standard operating procedure."
>
> Do you agree that the FCPA should prohibit giving money to a foreign government's procurement agent in order to induce the sale of oil-drilling services, or an aircraft? Why or why not?

The FCPA antibribery provisions are viewed by some international businesses as an effort to impose American values in foreign countries where different ethical standards often prevail. In some countries, payment of bribes to foreign officials may be an accepted way of obtaining or retaining business. In such contexts, the FCPA may be viewed as creating competitive disadvantages for U.S. firms by making such payments illegal. However, American courts have interpreted the FCPA antibribery provisions as a legislative effort to protect American shareholders and to avoid "a decline of foreign esteem for the United States." This goal is realized by discouraging American firms and businesspersons from bribing to get business and by requiring full disclosure and accountability of corporate outlays abroad.[3]

[3] *Clayco Petroleum Corp. v. Occidental Petroleum Corp.*, 712 F.2d 404 (9th Cir. 1983).

Extraterritoriality of Sovereign Business Regulations

How far can a country's trade laws reach? It is widely accepted in international law that a country cannot assert and enforce its laws in the territory of another country without that country's permission. Nevertheless, American courts have taken the view that

> if Congress has expressly prescribed a rule with respect to conduct outside the United States, even one going beyond the scope recognized by . . . foreign relations laws, a United States court would be bound to follow the Congressional direction unless this would violate the due process clause of the Fifth Amendment.[4]

Attempts by the United States and other governments to enforce laws governing international business transactions beyond their own borders meet strong resistance from other nations.

Antitrust. American antitrust law, like the "competition law" of the European Economic Community, seeks to promote vigorous markets by prohibiting monopoly and other anticompetitive practices. Historically, transnational corporations have actively engaged in monopolistic conduct, including the formation of international cartels to divide world markets and fix prices. For this reason, any collective effort to develop an international free trade would be seriously hampered without a program of vigorous antitrust enforcement.

In recent decades, efforts of American prosecutors and courts to give extraterritorial effect to U.S. antitrust laws have met with a cool reception abroad, and have often provoked other nations to enact retaliatory "clawback" legislation. For example, the United Kingdom has enacted legislation that forbids English courts from fully enforcing antitrust judgments of American courts. However, Congress made an effort toward reconciliation with American trading partners abroad by enacting the Foreign Trade Antitrust Improvements Act of 1982. The Act limits the extraterritorial application of U.S. antitrust laws to situations where the conduct has a direct, substantial, and reasonably foreseeable effect on import or export activities in the United States. In 1991, the United States and the EEC agreed to cooperate in enforcement of American antitrust and EEC competition law.

Taxes. In some situations, the United States has also given extraterritorial effect to its laws pertaining to taxation. For example, for many years the government has claimed the right to inspect records held abroad by foreigners who do business in the United States. Income of a U.S. corporation's foreign subsidiary is also subject to federal corporate income taxes, although not until the subsidiary remits its earnings to the parent stockholder.

Foreign Government Takeovers of Foreign Investments

Conversion of privately owned businesses into governmentally owned businesses is called **nationalization.** It is most likely to occur in unstable developing countries. By the beginning of the twentieth century, the Permanent Court of International Justice had adopted the consensus view of most nations that a government's taking of foreigners' property located there could be legitimate, but required full compensation. The consistent position of the United States in foreign government takeovers of American firms has been that "full compensation" means *prompt, adequate, and effective compensation.* Unfortunately, that standard has not been observed in a number of takeovers, including the Bolshevik revolution in Russia (1917) and Castro's revolution in Cuba (1959).

Expropriation; Confiscation. Expropriation is a country's taking over a business owned by foreign investors. Expropriation is considered legitimate if the foreign government's actions comply procedurally with its established law, the taking of the property serves a valid public purpose, and compensation paid by the expropriating government is "just" relative to the investment.

A governmental taking that neither serves a public purpose nor is justly compensated is a **confiscation.** Confiscations violate international

---
[4]*Leasco Data Processing Equipment Corp. v. Maxwell,* 468 F.2d 1326, 1334 (2d Cir. 1972).

law. For example, Idi Amin, the former military dictator of Uganda, drove over 100,000 alien Asians of Indian descent from the country and confiscated their textile mills, factories, retail shops, and other businesses without compensation. Confiscation includes governmental action that (1) forces aliens to flee and leave their property, (2) denies businesspeople access to profits or the right to take them abroad, (3) oppresses or persecutes owners to force them to sell businesses far below their value, or (4) taxes or bureaucratically harasses a foreign business in a way that prevents it from operating.

Overseas Private Investment Corporation (OPIC). American business investors who wish to hedge against the chances of expropriation or confiscation by foreign host governments may be able to insure against such risks through U.S. government-backed insurance. Overseas Private Investment Corporation, a U.S. agency, was created in 1969 with authority to insure American citizens' and corporations' private investments abroad. OPIC insurance covers only *new* investments which OPIC and the host country have *first* approved, and is available only for investments in the 100 nations that have investment guarantee treaties with the United States.

Judicial Limits on Extraterritorial Business Regulation

A business that wants to use the U.S. courts to contest a confiscation or to dispute the amount received in an expropriation of its assets may face a losing battle because of two key international law doctrines: (1) the doctrine of sovereign immunity and (2) the act-of-state doctrine. These doctrines apply to a wide variety of international trade issues.

Doctrine of Sovereign Immunity. The doctrine of sovereign immunity (meaning that a government cannot be sued without its consent) prohibits the courts of one country from acting against another country's government within that government's own borders. An important exception to the doctrine arises where the foreign government is acting out of a *commercial or business interest*. Then that government can be sued as if it were an ordinary business. However, if a foreign government acts officially with an expressed public or governmental purpose, and not a commercial purpose, a foreign court will apply the doctrine of sovereign immunity and nullify an attempt to sue such government. Therefore, those who feel wronged by a foreign government's act may fail to convince their home court that it has jurisdiction.

In the United States, the Foreign Sovereign Immunities Act (FSIA) limits the circumstances in which U.S. courts will recognize a foreign country's claim of sovereign immunity. The FSIA is applied in the following case, an appeal resulting from one of the most enormous commercial disputes in history.

CASE 54.4   **Texas Trading & Milling Corp. v. Federal Republic of Nigeria**
• 647 F.2d 300 (1981)

FACTS   Nigeria, with huge profits from high-grade oil exports, contracted to buy large quantities of Portland cement for construction of its infrastructure. It overbought and its harbors became clogged with ships waiting to unload. Unable to accept delivery, Nigeria repudiated its contracts. Plaintiffs, disgruntled suppliers, sued in the U.S. District Court, and Nigeria claimed sovereign immunity. The court dismissed the suit. On appeal, the U.S. suppliers argued that Nigeria should not enjoy sovereign immunity because it breached a *commercial contract*. To find the answer, the Circuit Court of Appeals looked to the Foreign Sovereign Immunities Act of 1976.

CASE 54.4 Continued	
OPINION	KAUFMAN, Cir. J. . . . [The FSIA provides that] a foreign state shall not be immune from the jurisdiction of the courts of the United States . . . in any case in which the action is based upon a commercial activity carried on in the United States by a foreign state; or upon an act performed in the United States in connection with commercial activity of the foreign state elsewhere; or upon an act outside the territory of the United States in connection with a commercial activity of the foreign state elsewhere [if] that act causes a direct effect in the United States. If the activity is not "commercial" but, rather, is "governmental," then the foreign state is entitled to immunity. Unfortunately, the definition of "commercial" is the one issue on which the Act provides almost no guidance at all. The first source [of guidance] is statements contained in the legislative history itself. The second source for interpreting the phrase "commercial activity" is the "very large body of case law which existed" in American law upon passage of the Act in 1976. Finally, current standards of international law concerning sovereign immunity add content to the "commercial activity" phrase of the FSIA. Under each of these three standards, Nigeria's cement contracts qualify as "commercial activity." Nigeria's activity here is in the nature of a private contract for goods. Its purpose—to build roads, army barracks, whatever—is irrelevant.
JUDGMENT	[The trial court's order dismissing the complaint for lack of jurisdiction was reversed, and the case remanded.]

Act-of-State Doctrine. Under the doctrine of sovereign immunity, a foreign government's actions cannot be judged by a domestic court because it *lacks jurisdiction*. In contrast, the act-of-state doctrine applies where a domestic court has jurisdiction but chooses not to rule on the case *because of self-imposed judicial restraint*. The doctrine is based on the idea that if courts interfere when a foreign government acts within its own territory, it might impair international relations between the countries and their respective citizens.

The reluctance of the courts of one country to sit in judgment on the acts of another that occur within that country's own territory is said to be a matter of **comity**—that is, a court's voluntary recognition of the sovereignty of another country, leading to a deliberate decision not to exercise jurisdiction. For example, in 1981 when Costa Rica was in serious economic crisis, its president issued a decree forbidding any bank from making an external debt repayment. A New York bank sued three Costa Rica banks to recover on their promissory notes. The U.S. court declined to accept jurisdiction, stating that judgment for the New York bank would

constitute a judicial determination that defendant [banks] make payments contrary to the directives of their government. This puts the judicial branch of the United States at odds with policies laid down by a foreign government on an issue deemed by that government to be of central importance. Such an act by this court risks embarrassment to the relations between the executive branch of the United States and the Government of Costa Rica.[5]

---

[5]*Allied Bank International v. Banco Credito Agricola de Cartago*, 566 F. Supp. 1440 (1983).

SUMMARY

Today, national and international laws reflect the ongoing tension between the goal of free trade on the one hand and monopolistic price fixing and high tariff barriers on the other. Global business is affected by *public* and *private* international law. Public international law is founded upon customs between nations, bilateral and multilateral treaties such as GATT, regional trading communities such as the EEC, and international organizations such as the United Nations, World Bank, and International Monetary Fund (IMF). Private international law, more recently called *conflict of laws*, is the substantative internal law of each nation that is used to resolve conflicts between parties from different countries. Territorial, nationality, protective, comity, and reasonable expectation principles are used by various national courts to decide conflict-of-laws problems. Under *forum non conveniens*, a court may dismiss a case so it may be tried in a foreign jurisdiction where the interests of justice require it.

In drafting international contracts, parties should pay attention to the official language, currency to be used for payment, choice-of-law and choice-of-forum clauses, arbitration clauses, and the legality of the object under the law of the parties' countries. The provisions of the Convention on Contracts for International Sale of Goods apply where parties have failed to express their intent and their countries have both signed the CISG. Methods of doing business abroad include direct sales with payment implemented by irrevocable documentary letters of credit, distributorship and licensing agreements, joint ventures, and transnational business corporations. Each method has advantages and disadvantages.

Sovereign nations regulate international trade to implement foreign policy, to "protect" domestic business by tariffs and import quotas, and to improve market share by dumping—a practice which may provoke countervailing duties by the injured country. Nations also regulate the flow of their money abroad, and their currency exchange rates. The American Foreign Corrupt Practices Act prohibits bribes to foreign officials to obtain business. Hazards of doing business in unstable countries include nationalization, expropriation, and confiscation. Risk of losing a foreign investment by expropriation can be reduced by insuring with OPIC. The Foreign Sovereign Immunities Act denies U.S. court jurisdiction over suits against foreign countries arising from their *noncommercial* official acts. The act-of-state doctrine holds that even where a court does have jurisdiction, it may dismiss the case for reasons of comity, or respect for a foreign nation's sovereignty coupled with a desire not to encroach on the U.S. executive branch's power to manage foreign relations.

REVIEW QUESTIONS

1. Compare and contrast free trade and protectionism.

2. (a) What are the chief sources of public international law? **(b)** Explain the term "private international law" and the principles used to resolve conflicts between domestic laws of different nations.

3. Explain the advantages of using choice-of-law, choice-of-forum, and arbitration clauses in international contracts.

4. How is American business affected by GATT? By the EEC?

5. Explain the significance of the doctrine of **(a)** *forum non conveniens*, **(b)** act of state, **(c)** sovereign immunity.

6. What advantages do transnational corporations have over multinational firms regarding labor cost, taxes, and profits?

7. How are American notions of extraterritoriality reflected in **(a)** antitrust law and **(b)** taxation?

8. What advantages might a country gain by restricting the transfer of currencies across its borders?

9. Explain how an irrevocable documentary letter of credit is used in an international business transaction.

CASE PROBLEMS

1. Kirkpatrick Corp. obtained a construction contract from Nigeria by bribing Nigerian officials. Nigerian law prohibits both the payment and receipt of such bribes. Tectonics Corp., an unsuccessful bidder for the contract, sued Kirkpatrick for damages under various federal and state laws. In a letter to the U.S. District Court, the Department of State advised that it would not be embarrassed nor would foreign affairs be hampered by court inquiry into the facts relating to the bribery. However, the court dismissed the suit on the ground that the act-of-state doctrine precluded judicial inquiry into the motivation of a sovereign act that would result in embarrassment to the sovereign, or constitute an interference with the conduct of U.S. foreign policy. The court dismissed because it concluded that resolution of the case in favor of Kirkpatrick would require imputing to foreign officials an unlawful motivation (the obtaining of bribes) and accordingly might embarrass the U.S. executive branch in its conduct of foreign affairs. Should the suit be dismissed because of the act-of-state doctrine?

2. Country A expropriates the property of a business that is incorporated in Country A but whose principal shareholders are residents of Country B. The state designates the corporation as an official instrumentality of Country A. The shareholders file suit in Country B to recover lost proceeds from the corporation. Will the court in Country B proceed to rule on the merits of the case? What reasoning may the court use to justify its decision?

3. Universe Tankships, defendant, chartered a cargo ship which was used to transport wheat from the United States to Egypt. Plaintiff Ministry of Supply, Cairo, the purchaser of the wheat, found that the wheat was damaged upon its arrival in Cairo and halted the discharge of the cargo for 81 days. Plaintiff then filed an action for cargo damages against defendant in the U.S. District Court having jurisdiction where the contract arose. Defendant counterclaimed for losses stemming from plaintiff's wrongful halting of the wheat offloading. It is conceded that plaintiff is an "agency or instrumentality" of Egypt within the meaning of the Foreign Sovereign Immunities Act of 1976. Plaintiff argues that defendant's counterclaim is barred on the ground of sovereign immunity. Is this argument likely to succeed? Why or why not?

4. A British supplier of massage appliances licensed a German importer as the sole distributor of its products in France and Germany. Subsequently, the German importer entered into a separate agreement with a French firm to became the sole distributor of the electric massage appliances in France. The French distributor began selling appliances, but when similar massage instruments appeared in French markets, the French firm broke its agreement with the German distributor. The German distributor then sued the French firm to recover damages for breach of contract. The French distributor claimed that its agreement with the German firm was null and void because it violated Article 85, paragraph 1, of the Treaty of Rome and thus could not be a basis for claiming damages. Does the Treaty of Rome apply to the facts in this case? If so, which party will prevail? Why?

5. Deepsouth Packing Company and Laitram Corporation each held patents on shrimp-deveining machines. Although Laitram's patent prevented Deepsouth from selling its machines in the United States, Deepsouth began selling its machines outside the United States. Laitram sued, asserting that its patent rights should prevent sales of Deepsouth machines abroad. Do you agree?

ETHICS IN PRACTICE

The ethical quality of an act cannot be determined without considering the social or legal context within which the act occurred. In the United States, the major regulatory statutes reflect legislative policy choices that most members of the informed public seem to accept as reasonable and right. The Sherman Antitrust Act controlling monopolistic practices, the Federal Trade Commission Act forbidding unfair and deceptive trade practices, the National Labor Relations Act banning unfair labor practices, and many other state and federal statutes set legal standards of business conduct that are consistent with most people's ideas of ethical behavior. If a person or business commits an unlawful act commonly accepted as wrongful, there is little doubt about the ethical quality of the act—it is both illegal and unethical.

Assessing ethical quality is not so easy where an act or practice is not expressly identified as against the law. An act that violates nonlegal ethical standards may be tolerated because law does not forbid it. Then the question is whether the offensive practice should be made illegal. Much law is stated in general terms so that administrative agencies and courts can apply it to a variety of suspect business practices that might later develop. In the meantime, harmful practices may flourish.

International business is perhaps the most difficult area in which to develop and apply consistent standards of business ethics. Differences in language, customs, and traditions account for the wide divergence of ethical principles encountered throughout the world. For example, in many countries officials routinely seek secret payments in exchange for directing government business to a particular firm or facilitating the flow of goods across a border. To much of the population, such payoffs are accepted as a customary means of doing business.

This view contrasts sharply with ethical standards in other countries. In the United States, for example, commercial bribery is thought to have so many harmful effects as to be difficult to justify morally. If corporate executives were allowed to disburse secret funds for bribes, they would have no accountability to the shareholders and could misappropriate corporate funds for their own use. If bribing foreign officials were acceptable, it would also be acceptable to bribe foreign customers and to receive return bribes in the form of kickbacks from foreign suppliers. Business decisions would then turn on the size of the bribe rather than the quality of goods and services, and consumers here and abroad would face increased costs and danger to their health and safety.

The problems that follow are from news accounts of actual happenings. Your objective should be to evaluate the ethical quality of the action taken.

PROBLEMS IN ETHICS

1. Railco, a railway company, believes it has too many railroad clerks in its work force. The current union contract allows Railco to reduce the number of clerks up to 4 percent overall, but requires Railco to "buy out" each clerk's position with a year's severance pay. Railco is willing to continue the buyouts, but wants a much greater reduction in clerk positions than the union contract allows. To save jobs, the union refuses to agree to more buyouts. Apparently in an attempt to get workers to pressure the union for broader buyouts, Railco has put clerks in various former lunchrooms throughout the system with nothing to do but read company rules and timetables. Has Railco acted ethically? Has the union?

2. A developer was to build a paint-manufacturing plant for Benjamin Moore Co. and intended to use nonunion labor. Instead of fighting the project with the usual boycotts and picket lines, the United Association of Plumbers and Steamfitters forced a detailed review of possible environmental problems. Faced with long and costly regulatory proceedings in a deteriorating economy, Benjamin Moore decided not to build the plant. According to developers, the union strategy is to delay projects, drive the price up, and thus make nonunion labor uncompetitive—to force through misuse of the regulatory process what it cannot get at the bargaining table. The environmentalists involved here, however, welcomed the help of the union. What are the ethics of the union strategy?

3. Tony, a farmer in a western state, planted 40 acres of grain for use as silage for livestock. Just before harvest time, tricolored blackbirds moved in to nest. Because of their large numbers, tricolored blackbirds are not protected under the federal Endangered Species Act, and are not a threatened species. Yet the International Migratory Bird Treaty Act prohibits farmers from harming or harassing the birds after they begin nesting. The U.S. Fish and Wildlife Service required Tony to stay out of his field until May 10, when the baby birds would be able to fly out. By then the crop was worthless. After considerable effort and worry, Tony learned that the government would pay for the lost crop, valued at about $6,000. What are the ethics of the Migratory Bird Treaty Act as applied to tricolored blackbirds?

4. A restaurant critic writing for a newspaper under an assumed name allegedly gave a bad review of a good restaurant, mistaking a fine loin of veal for a veal patty, complaining about the restaurant's *bagna cauda* (an elegant oil-and-anchovy dip) because he was expecting a more pedestrian dip, and incorrectly suggesting that its Bolognese sauce was tomato based and flavored with cheese when it was actually a pork sauce flavored with a little tomato. Complaining that the inaccurate reviews cost her business to drop 15–20 percent, the owner asked the state restaurant association to seek legislation requiring the licensing of restaurant critics through the Department of Consumer Protection. The proposed license requirements include experience in food service operation and management, graduation from a recognized culinary arts degree program, or a combination of at least 6 years of experience and formal training. "Licensing opinions is kind of silly," said the critic. Neither he nor the newspaper would reveal his real name. Is the proposed legislation a good idea? Is it ethical for a critic to use an assumed name?

5. In 1975, the Boston fire department rejected identical twins Phillip and Paul for employment because of poor exam scores. On their applications, they identified themselves as white candidates, but scored only 57 percent and 69 percent on the exam, well short of the 82 percent required of whites. In 1977 they applied again, this time declaring that they were black, and were hired. The department was under pressure to hire more minority fire fighters, and under a court-ordered affirmative action plan, the lower scores were overlooked for minorities. Ten years later, never having been officially questioned about their race, the twins were listed among black fire fighters proposed for promotion to lieutenant. The fire commissioner thought the twins were white; suspicions aroused, he asked the state department of personnel administration to check out their status. Informed of the investigation, a black city council member asked, "How could twins with Irish names, Caucasian features and no black identification from any perspective get onto the force and stay on without collusion?" The twins claimed that they did not learn they were black until 1976, when their mother discovered a sepia photograph of a pale-looking woman she said was their black great-grandmother. After an investigation, the twins were fired. The mayor recently disclosed that at least five other fire fighters will be asked to prove they are not white. What is the ethical quality of the twins' conduct?

6. Eli Lilly manufactures Spike, a herbicide that destroys coca bushes, the source of illegal cocaine. In cooperation with the Peruvian government, the U.S. government wishes to buy a large quantity of Spike to spread on 120 square miles of coca bushes in the Andes' Huallaga Valley, the world's number-one source of cocaine. Lilly fears that if it permits export of its product to Peru, it may become subject to suits such as those against the makers of Agent Orange, in which it was alleged that Agent Orange caused cancer in people who came into contact with it. Lawsuits and adverse publicity might arise if local workers in Peru came into contact with Spike or if it was improperly applied. Dow Chemical manufactures another herbicide, Garlon-4, that also destroys coca bushes. Dow shares Lilly's concern that misapplication of the product could raise complex environmental and health controversies in a tropical country where the herbicide has not previously been used. Each company fears potential terrorist reprisals if its product is sold and used to eradicate lucrative coca crops that belong to large organized-crime syndicates. Neither company believes that the profit on the sale would justify the potential risks. With proper application, both products have been used safely in the United States to kill brush along utility rights-of-way. The managements of Lilly and Dow recognize the importance of the war on drug trafficking, but refuse to sell the herbicides to the government. **(a)** Does the concept of corporate social responsibility (see Ethics in Practice for Part Nine) require Lilly and Dow to sell their products for drug eradication in Peru? **(b)** Suppose that the U.S. or the Peruvian government would be willing to indemnify Lilly and Dow for any losses resulting from herbicide-related lawsuits. Would this fact change your assessment of their corporate social responsibility? **(c)** The U.S. government has threatened to take away Lilly's patent for Spike and give it to a more cooperative firm. Although the legality of such a move is in doubt, Lilly could incur substantial costs in defending against the government's action. Is the government acting ethically in making the threat?

APPENDIXES

1
The Constitution of the United States of America

2
Uniform Commercial Code, 1978 Text
with 1990 Amendments

3
Uniform Partnership Act, 1992

4
Uniform Limited Partnership Act (1976),
with 1985 Amendments

5
Revised Model Business Corporation Act (1984) (Excerpts)

APPENDIX 1

The Constitution of the United States of America

PREAMBLE

We the People of the United States, in Order to form a more perfect Union, establish Justice, insure domestic Tranquility, provide for the common defence, promote the general Welfare, and secure the Blessings of Liberty to ourselves and our Posterity, do ordain and establish this Constitution for the United States of America.

ARTICLE I

Section 1. All legislative Powers herein granted shall be vested in a Congress of the United States, which shall consist of a Senate and House of Representatives.

Section 2. [1] The House of Representatives shall be composed of Members chosen every second Year by the People of the several States, and Electors in each State shall have the Qualifications requisite for electors of the most numerous Branch of the State Legislature.

[2] No Person shall be a Representative who shall not have attained to the Age of twenty five Years, and been seven Years a Citizen of the United States, and who shall not, when elected, be an Inhabitant of that State in which he shall be chosen.

[3] [Representatives and direct Taxes shall be apportioned among the several States which may be included within this Union, according to their respective Numbers, which shall be determined by adding to the whole Number of free Persons, including those bound to Service for a Term of Years, and excluding Indians not taxed, three fifths of all other Persons.] The actual Enumeration shall be made within three Years after the first Meeting of the Congress of the United States, and within every subsequent Term of ten Years, in such Manner as they shall by Law direct. The Number of Representatives shall not exceed one for every thirty Thousand, but each State shall have at Least one Representative; and until such enumeration shall be made, the State of New Hampshire shall be entitled to chuse three, Massachusetts eight, Rhode Island and Providence Plantations one, Connecticut five, New York six, New Jersey four, Pennsylvania eight, Delaware one, Maryland six, Virginia ten, North Carolina, five, South Carolina five, and Georgia three.

Note: *The clause of this paragraph inclosed in brackets was amended, as to the mode of apportionment of representatives among the several states, by the Fourteenth Amendment, §2, and as to taxes on incomes without apportionment, by the Sixteenth Amendment.*

[4] When vacancies happen in the Representation from any State, the Executive Authority thereof shall issue Writs of Election to fill such Vacancies.

[5] The House of Representatives shall chuse their Speaker and other Officers; and shall have the sole Power of Impeachment.

Section 3. [1] The Senate of the United States shall be composed of two Senators from each State, [chosen by the Legislature thereof,] for six Years; and each Senator shall have one Vote.

Note: *This paragraph and the clause of following paragraph inclosed in brackets were susperseded by the Seventeenth Amendment.*

[2] Immediately after they shall be assembled in Consequence of the first Election, they shall be divided as equally as may be into three Classes. The Seats of the Senators of the first Class shall be vacated at the Expiration of the Second Year, of the second Class at the Expiration of the fourth Year, and of the third Class at the Expiration of the sixth Year, so that one third may be chosen every second Year; [and if Vacancies happen by Resignation, or otherwise, during the Recess of the Legislature of any State, the Executive thereof may make temporary Appointments until the next Meeting of the Legislature, which shall then fill such Vacancies.]

[3] No Person shall be a Senator who shall not have attained to the Age of thirty Years, and been nine Years a Citizen of the United States, and who shall not, when elected, be an Inhabitant of that State for which he shall be chosen.

[4] The Vice President of the United States shall be President of the Senate, but shall have no Vote, unless they be equally divided.

[5] The Senate shall chuse their other Officers, and also a President pro tempore, in the Absence of the Vice President, or when he shall exercise the Office of President of the United States.

[6] The Senate shall have the sole Power to try all Impeachments. When sitting for that Purpose, they shall be an Oath or Affirmation. When the President of the United States is tried, the Chief Justice shall preside; And no Person shall be convicted

without the Concurrence of two thirds of the Members present.

[7] Judgment in Cases of Impeachment shall not extend further than to removal from Office, and disqualification to hold and enjoy an Office of honor, Trust, or Profit under the United States; but the Party convicted shall nevertheless be liable and subject to Indictment, Trial, Judgment, and Punishment, according to Law.

Section 4. [1] The Times, Places and Manner of holding Elections for Senators and Representatives, shall be prescribed in each State by the Legislature thereof; but the Congress may at any time by Law make or alter such Regulations, except as to the Places of chusing Senators.

[2] The Congress shall assemble at least once in every Year, and such Meeting shall [be on the first Monday in December,] unless they shall by Law appoint a different Day.

Note: *The part included in brackets was changed by Section 2 of the Twentieth Amendment.*

Section 5. [1] Each House shall be the Judge of the Elections, Returns, and Qualifications of its own Members, and a Majority of each shall constitute a Quorum to do Business; but a smaller Number may adjourn from day to day, and may be authorized to compel the Attendance of absent Members, in such Manner, and under such Penalties as each House may provide.

[2] Each House may determine the Rules of its Proceedings, punish its Members for disorderly Behavior, and, with the Concurrence of two thirds, expel a Member.

[3] Each House shall keep a Journal of its Proceedings, and from time to time publish the same, excepting such Parts as may in their Judgment require Secrecy; and the Yeas and Nays of the Members of either House on any question shall, at the Desire of one fifth of those Present, be entered on the Journal.

[4] Neither House, during the Session of Congress, shall, without the Consent of the other, adjourn for more than three days, nor to any other Place than that in which the two Houses shall be sitting.

Section 6. [1] The Senators and Representatives shall receive a Compensation for their Services, to be ascertained by Law, and paid out of the Treasury of the United States. They shall in all Cases, except Treason, Felony and Breach of the Peace, be privileged from Arrest during their Attendance at the Session of their respective Houses, and in going to and returning from the same; and for any Speech or Debate in either House, they shall not be questioned in any other Place.

[2] No Senator or Representative shall, during the Time for which he was elected, be appointed to any civil Office under the Authority of the United States, which shall have been created, or the Emoluments whereof shall have been increased during such time; and no Person holding any Office under the United States, shall be a Member of either House during his Continuance in Office.

Section 7. [1] All Bills for raising Revenue shall originate in the House of Representatives; but the Senate may propose or concur with Amendments as on other Bills.

[2] Every Bill which shall have passed the House of Representatives and the Senate, shall, before it become a Law, be presented to the President of the United States; If he approves he shall sign it, but if not he shall return it, with his Objections to the House in which it shall have originated, who shall enter the Objections at large on their Journal, and proceed to reconsider it. If after such Reconsideration two thirds of that House shall agree to pass the Bill, it shall be sent together with the Objections, to the other House, by which it shall likewise be reconsidered, and if approved by two thirds of that House, it shall become a Law. But in all such Cases the Votes of both Houses shall be determined by Yeas and Nays, and the Names of the Persons voting for and against the Bill shall be entered on the Journal of each House respectively. If any Bill shall not be returned by the President within ten Days (Sundays excepted) after it shall have been presented to him, the Same shall be a Law, in like Manner as if he had signed it, unless the Congress by their Adjournment prevent its Return in which Case it shall not be a Law.

[3] Every Order, Resolution, or Vote, to Which the Concurrence of the Senate and House of Representatives may be necessary (except on a question of Adjournment) shall be presented to the President of the United States; and before the Same shall take Effect, shall be approved by him, or being disapproved by him, shall be repassed by two thirds of the Senate and House of Representatives, according to the Rules and Limitations prescribed in the Case of a Bill.

Section 8. [1] The Congress shall have Power To lay and collect Taxes, Duties, Imposts and Excises, to pay the Debts and provide for the common Defence and general Welfare of the United States; but all Duties, Imposts and Excises shall be uniform throughout the United States:

[2] To borrow money on the credit of the United States;

[3] To regulate Commerce with foreign Nations, and among the several States, and with the Indian Tribes;

[4] To establish an uniform Rule of Naturalization, and uniform Laws on the subject of Bankruptcies throughout the United States;

[5] To coin Money, regulate the Value thereof, and of foreign Coin, and fix the Standard of Weights and Measures;

[6] To provide for the Punishment of counterfeiting the Securities and current Coin of the United States;

[7] To Establish Post Offices and Post Roads;

[8] To promote the Progress of Science and useful Arts, by securing for limited Times to Authors and Inventors the exclusive Right to their respective Writings and Discoveries;

[9] To constitute Tribunals inferior to the Supreme Court;

[10] To define and punish Piracies and Felonies committed on the high Seas, and Offenses against the Law of Nations;

[11] To declare War, grant Letters of Marque and Reprisal, and make Rules concerning Captures on Land and Water;

[12] To raise and support Armies, but no Appropriation of Money to that Use shall be for a longer Term than two Years;

[13] To provide and maintain a Navy;

[14] To make Rules for the Government and Regulation of the land and naval Forces;

[15] To provide for calling forth the Militia to execute the Laws of the Union, suppress Insurrections and repel Invasions;

[16] To provide for organizing, arming, and disciplining the Militia, and for governing such Part of them as may be employed in the Service of the United States, reserving to the States respectively, the Appointment of the Officers, and the Authority of training the Militia according to the discipline prescribed by Congress;

[17] To exercise exclusive Legislation in all Cases whatsoever, over such District (not exceeding ten Miles square) as may, by Cession of particular States, and the Acceptance of Congress, become the Seat of the Government of the United States, and to exercise like Authority over all Places purchased by the Consent of the Legislature of the State in which the Same shall be, for the Erection of Forts, Magazines, Arsenals, dock-Yards, and other needful Buildings;—And

[18] To make all Laws which shall be necessary and proper for carrying into Execution the foregoing Powers, and all other Powers vested by this Constitution in the Government of the United States, or in any Department or Officer thereof.

Section 9. [1] The Migration or Importation of Such Persons as any of the States now existing shall think proper to admit, shall not be prohibited by the Congress prior to the Year one thousand eight hundred and eight, but a Tax or duty may be imposed on such Importation, not exceeding ten dollars for each Person.

[2] The privilege of the Writ of Habeas corpus shall not be suspended, unless when in Cases of Rebellion or Invasion the public Safety may require it.

[3] No Bill of Attainder or *ex post facto* Law shall be passed.

[4] No Capitation, or other direct, Tax shall be laid, unless in Proportion to the Census or Enumeration herein before directed to be taken.

Note: *See also the Sixteenth Amendment.*

[5] No Tax or Duty shall be laid on Articles exported from any State.

[6] No Preference shall be given by any Regulation of Commerce or Revenue to the Ports of one State over those of another; nor shall Vessels bound to, or from, one State be obliged to enter, clear, or pay Duties in another.

[7] No money shall be drawn from the Treasury, but in Consequence of Appropriations made by Law; and a regular Statement and Account of the Receipts and Expenditures of all public Money shall be published from time to time.

[8] No Title of Nobility shall be granted by the United States; And no Person holding any Office of Profit or Trust under them, shall, without the Consent of the Congress, accept of any present, Emolument, Office, or Title, of any kind whatever, from any King, Prince, or foreign State.

Section 10. [1] No State shall enter into any Treaty, Alliance, or Confederation; grant Letters of Marque and Reprisal; coin Money; emit Bills of Credit; make any Thing but gold and silver Coin a Tender in Payment of Debts; pass any Bill of Attainder, *ex post facto* Law, or Law impairing the Obligation of Contracts, or grant any Title of Nobility.

[2] No State shall, without the Consent of the Congress, lay any Imposts or Duties on Imports or Exports, except what may be absolutely necessary for executing its inspection Laws; and the net Produce of all Duties and Imposts, laid by any State on Imports or Exports, shall be for the Use of the Treasury of the United States; and all such Laws shall be subject to the Revision and control of the Congress.

[3] No State shall, without the Consent of Congress, lay any Duty of Tonnage, keep Troops, or Ships of War in time of Peace, enter into any Agreement or Compact with another State, or with a foreign Power, or engage in War, unless actually invaded, or in such imminent Danger as will not admit of delay.

ARTICLE II

Section 1. [1] The executive Power shall be vested in a President of the United States of America. He shall hold his Office during the Term of four Years, and, together with the Vice President, chosen for the same Term, be elected, as follows:

[2] Each State shall appoint, in such Manner as the Legislature thereof may direct, a Number of Electors, equal to the whole Number of Senators and Representatives to which the State may be entitled in the Congress; but no Senator or Representative or Person holding an Office of Trust or Profit under the United States, shall be appointed an Elector.

[3] [The Electors shall meet in their respective States, and vote by Ballot for two Persons, of whom one at least shall not be an Inhabitant of the same State with themselves. And they shall make a List of all the Persons voted for, and of the Number of Votes for each; which List they shall sign and certify, and transmit sealed to the Seat of Government of the United States, directed to the President of the Senate. The president of the Senate shall, in the presence of the Senate and House of Representatives, open all the Certificates, and the Votes shall then be counted. The Person having the greatest Number of Votes shall be the President, if such Number be a Majority of the whole Number of Electors appointed; and if there be more than one who have such Majority, and have an equal Number of Votes, then the House of Representatives shall immediately chuse by Ballot one of them for President; and if no Person have a Majority, then from the five highest on the List the said House shall in like Manner chuse the President. But in chusing the President, the Votes shall be taken by States, the Representation from each State having one Vote; A quorum for this Purpose shall consist of a Member or Members from two thirds of the States, and a Majority of all the States shall be necessary to a Choice. In every Case, after the Choice of the President, the Person having the greatest Number of Votes of the Electors shall be the Vice President. But if there should remain two or more who have equal Votes, the Senate shall chuse from them by Ballot the Vice President.]

Note: *This paragraph, enclosed in brackets, was superseded by the Twelfth Amendment.*

[4] The Congress may determine the Time of chusing the Electors, and the Day on which they shall give their Votes; which Day shall be the same throughout the United States.

[5] No person except a natural born Citizen, or a Citizen of the United States, at the time of the Adoption of this Constitution, shall be eligible to the Office of President; neither shall any Person be eligible to that Office who shall not have attained to the Age of thirty five Years, and been fourteen Years a Resident within the United States.

[6] In case of the removal of the President from Office, or of his Death, Resignation or Inability to discharge the Powers and Duties of the said office, the Same shall devolve on the Vice President, and the Congress may by law provide for the Case of Removal, Death, Resignation or Inability, both of the President and Vice President, declaring what Officer shall then act as President, and such Officer shall act accordingly, until the Disability be removed, or a President shall be elected.

[7] The President shall, at stated Times, receive for his Services, a Compensation, which shall neither be increased nor diminished during the Period for which he shall have been elected, and he shall not receive within that Period any other Emolument from the United States, or any of them.

[8] Before he enter on the Execution of his Office, he shall take the following Oath or Affirmation: "I do solemnly swear (or affirm) that I will faithfully execute the Office of President of the United States, and will to the best of my Ability, preserve, protect and defend the Constitution of the United States."

Section 2. [1] The President shall be Commander in Chief of the Army and Navy of the United States, and of the militia of the several States, when called into the actual Service of the United States; he may require the Opinion, in writing, of the principal Officer in each of the Executive Departments, upon any Subject relating to the Duties of their respective Offices, and he shall have Power to grant Reprieves and Pardons for Offenses against the United States, except in Cases of Impeachment.

[2] He shall have Power, by and with the Advice and Consent of the Senate, to make Treaties, provided two thirds of the Senators present concur; and he shall nominate, and by and with the Advice and Consent of the Senate, shall appoint Ambassadors, other public Ministers and Consuls, Judges of the supreme Court, and all other Officers of the United States, whose Appointments

are not herein otherwise provided for, and which shall be established by Law; but the Congress may by Law vest the Appointment of such inferior Officers, as they think proper, in the President alone, in the Courts of law, or in the Heads of Departments.

[3] The President shall have Power to fill up all Vacancies that may happen during the Recess of the Senate, by granting Commissions which shall expire at the End of their next Session.

Section 3. He shall from time to time give to the Congress Information of the State of the Union, and recommend to their Consideration such Measures as he shall judge necessary and expedient; he may, on extraordinary Occasions, convene both Houses, or either of them, and in Case of Disagreement between them, with Respect to the Time of Adjournment, he may adjourn them to such Time as he shall think proper; he shall take Care that the laws be faithfully executed, and shall Commission all the Officers of the United States.

Section 4. The President, Vice President and all civil Officers of the United States, shall be removed from Office on Impeachment for, and Conviction of, Treason, Bribery, or other high Crimes and Misdemeanors.

ARTICLE III

Section 1. The judicial Power of the United States, shall be vested in one supreme Court, and in such inferior Courts as the Congress may from time to time ordain and establish. The Judges, both of the supreme and inferior Courts, shall hold their Offices during good Behaviour, and shall, at stated Times, receive for their Services a Compensation, which shall not be diminished during their Continuance in Office.

Section 2. [1] The judicial Power shall extend to all Cases, in Law and Equity, arising under this Constitution, the laws of the United States, and Treaties made, or which shall be made, under their Authority;—to all Cases affecting Ambassadors, other public Ministers and Consuls;—to all Cases of admiralty and maritime Jurisdiction;—to Controversies to which the United States shall be a Party;—to Controversies between two or more States;—between a State and Citizens of another State;*—between Citizens of different States;—between Citizens of the same State claiming Lands under the Grants of different States, and between a State, or the Citizens thereof, and foreign States, Citizens or Subjects.

[2] In all Cases affecting Ambassadors, other public Ministers and Consuls, and those in which a State shall be a Party, the supreme Court shall have original Jurisdiction. In all the other Cases before mentioned, the supreme Court shall have appellate Jurisdiction, both as to Law and Fact, with such Exceptions, and under such Regulations as the Congress shall make.

[3] The Trial of all Crimes, except in Cases of Impeachment, shall be by Jury; and such Trial shall be held in the State where the said Crimes shall have been committed; but when not committed within any State, the Trial shall be at such Place or Places as the Congress may by Law have directed.

Section 3. [1] Treason against the United States, shall consist only in levying War against them, or, in adhering to their Enemies, giving them Aid and Comfort. No Person shall be convicted of Treason unless on the Testimony of two Witnesses to the same overt Act, or on Confession in open Court.

[2] The Congress shall have Power to declare the Punishment of Treason, but no Attainder of Treason shall work Corruption of Blood, or Forfeiture except during the Life of the Person attained.

ARTICLE IV

Section 1. Full Faith and Credit shall be given in each State to the public Acts, Records, and judicial Proceedings of every other State. And the Congress may by general Laws prescribe the Manner in which such Acts, Records and Proceedings shall be proved, and the Effect thereof.

Section 2. [1] The Citizens of each State shall be entitled to all Privileges and Immunities of Citizens in the several States.

[2] A Person charged in any State with Treason, Felony, or other Crime, who shall flee from Justice, and be found in another State, shall on demand of the executive Authority of the State from which he fled, be delivered up, to be removed to the State having Jurisdiction of the Crime.

[3] [No Person held to Service or Labour in one State, under the Laws thereof, escaping into another, shall, in Consequence of any Law or Regulation therein, be discharged from such Service or Labour, but shall be delivered up on Claim of the Party to whom such Service or Labour may be due.]

Note: This paragraph has been superseded by the Thirteenth Amendment.

Section 3. [1] New States may be admitted by the Congress into this Union; but no new State shall be formed or erected within the Jurisdiction of any other State; nor any State be formed by the Junction of two or more States, or Parts of States, without the Consent of the Legislatures of the States concerned as well as of the Congress.

[2] The Congress shall have Power to dispose of and make all needful Rules and Regulations respecting the Territory or other Property belonging to the United States; and nothing in this Constitution shall be so construed as to Prejudice any Claims of the United States, or of any particular State.

Section 4. The United States shall guarantee to every State in this Union a Republican Form of Government, and shall protect each of them against Invasion; and on Application of the Legislature, or of the Executive (when the Legislature cannot be convened) against domestic Violence.

ARTICLE V

The Congress, whenever two thirds of both Houses shall deem it necessary, shall propose Amendments to this Constitution, or, on the Application of the Legislature of two thirds of the several States, shall call a Convention for proposing Amendments, which, in either Case, shall be valid to all Intents and Purposes, as part of this Constitution, when ratified by the Legislatures of three fourths of the several States, or by Conventions in three fourths thereof, as the one or the other Mode of Ratification may be proposed by the Congress; Provided that no Amendment which may be made prior to the Year One thousand eight hundred and eight shall in any Manner affect the first and fourth Clauses in the Ninth Section of the first Article; and that no State, without its Consent, shall be deprived of its equal Suffrage in the Senate.

ARTICLE VI

[1] All Debts contracted and Engagements entered into, before the Adoption of this Constitution, shall be as valid against the United States under this Constitution, as under the Confederation.

---

* This clause has been affected by the Eleventh Amendment.

[2] This Constitution, and the Laws of the United States which shall be made in Pursuance thereof; and all Treaties made, or which shall be made, under the Authority of the United States, shall be the supreme Law of the Land; and the Judges in every State shall be bound thereby, any Thing in the Constitution or Laws of any State to the Contrary notwithstanding.

[3] The Senators and Representatives before mentioned, and the Members of the several State Legislatures, and all executives and judicial Officers, both of the United States and of the several States, shall be bound by Oath or Affirmation, to support this Constitution; but no religious Test shall ever be required as a Qualification to any Office or public Trust under the United States.

ARTICLE VII

The Ratification of the Conventions of nine States shall be sufficient for the Establishment of this Constitution between the States so ratifying the Same.

Done in Convention by the Unanimous Consent of the States present the Seventeenth Day of September in the Year of Our Lord one thousand seven hundred and Eighty seven and of the Independence of the United States of America the Twelfth. IN WITNESS whereof We have hereto subscribed our Names,

Go. Washington—Presidt.
and deputy from Virginia

New Hampshire
John Langdon
Nicholas Gilman

Massachusetts
Nathaniel Gorham
Rufus King

Connecticut
Wm. Saml. Johnson
Roger Sherman

New York
Alexander Hamilton

New Jersey
Wil: Livingston
David Brearley
Wm. Paterson
Jona: Dayton

Pennsylvania
B. Franklin
Thomas Mifflin
Robt. Morris
Geo. Clymer
Thos. FitzSimons
Jared Ingersoll
James Wilson
Gouv Morris

Delaware
Geo: Read
Gunning Bedford Jun
John Dickinson
Richard Bassett
Jaco: Broom

Maryland
James McHenry
Dan of St. Thos. Jenifer
Danl. Carroll

Virginia
John Blair
James Madison, Jr.

North Carolina
Wm. Blount
Richd. Dobbs Spaight
Hu Williamson

South Carolina
J. Rutledge
Charles Cotesworth Pinckney
Charles Pinckney
Pierce Butler

Georgia
William Few
Abr Baldwin

Attest William Jackson
Secretary

AMENDMENTS TO THE CONSTITUTION OF THE UNITED STATES

Amendment I [1791]

Congress shall make no law respecting an establishment of religion, or prohibiting the free exercise thereof; or abridging the freedom of speech, or of the press; or the right of the people peaceably to assemble, and to petition the Government for a redress of grievances.

Amendment II [1791]

A well regulated Militia being necessary to the security of a free State, the right of the people to keep and bear Arms, shall not be infringed.

Amendment III [1791]

No Soldier shall, in time of peace be quartered in any house, without the consent of the Owner, nor in time of war, but in a manner to be prescribed by law.

Amendment IV [1791]

The right of the people to be secure in their persons, houses, papers, and effects, against unreasonable searches and seizures, shall not be violated, and no Warrants shall issue, but upon probable cause, supported by Oath or affirmation, and particularly describing the place to be searched, and the persons or things to be seized.

Amendment V [1791]

No person shall be held to answer for a capital, or otherwise infamous crime, unless on a presentment or indictment of a Grand Jury, except in cases arising in the land or naval forces, or in the Militia, when in actual service in time of War or public danger; nor shall any person be subject for the same offence to be twice put in jeopardy of life or limb, nor shall be compelled in any criminal case to be a witness against himself, nor be deprived of life, liberty, or property, without due process of law; nor shall private property be taken for public use, without just compensation.

Amendment VI [1791]

In all criminal prosecutions, the accused shall enjoy the right to a speedy and public trial, by an impartial jury of the State and district wherein the crime shall have been committed; which district shall have been previously ascertained by law, and to be informed of the nature and cause of the accusation; to be confronted with the witnesses against him; to have compulsory process for obtaining witnesses in his favor, and to have the Assistance of Counsel for his defence.

Amendment VII [1791]

In Suits at common law, where the value in controversy shall exceed twenty dollars, the right of trial by jury shall be preserved, and no fact tried by jury shall be otherwise reexamined in any Court of the United States, than according to the rules of the common law.

Amendment VIII [1791]

Excessive bail shall not be required, nor excessive fines imposed, nor cruel and unusual punishments inflicted.

Amendment IX [1791]

The enumeration in the Constitution, of certain rights, shall not be construed to deny or disparage others retained by the people.

Amendment X [1791]

The powers not delegated to the United States by the Constitution, nor prohibited by it to the States, are reserved to the States respectively, or to the people.

Amendment XI [1798]

The Judicial power of the United States shall not be construed to extend to any suit in law or equity, commenced or prosecuted against one of the United States by Citizens of another State, or by Citizens or Subjects of any Foreign State.

Amendment XII [1804]

The electors shall meet in their respective states and vote by ballot for President and Vice-President, one of whom, at least, shall not be an inhabitant of the same state with themselves; they shall name in their ballots the person voted for as President, and in distinct ballots the person voted for as Vice-President, and they shall make distinct lists of all persons voted for as President, and of all persons voted for as Vice-President, and of the number of votes for each, which lists they shall sign and certify, and transmit sealed to the seat of the government of the United States, directed to the President of the Senate;—The President of the Senate shall, in the presence of the Senate and House of Representatives, open all the certificates and the votes shall then be counted;—The person having the greatest number of votes for President, shall be the President, if such number be a majority of the whole number of Electors appointed; and if no person have such majority, then from the persons having the highest numbers not exceeding three on the list of those voted for as President, the House of Representatives shall choose immediately, by ballot, the President. But in choosing the President, the votes shall be taken by states, the representation from each state having one vote; a quorum for this purpose shall consist of a member of members from two-thirds of the states, and a majority of all the states shall be necessary to a choice. [And if the House of Representatives shall not choose a President whenever the right of choice shall devolve upon them before the fourth day of March next following, then the Vice-President shall act as President, as in the case of the death or other constitutional disability of the President.] The person having the greatest number of votes as Vice-President, shall be the Vice-President, if such number be a majority of the whole number of electors appointed, and if no person have a majority, then from the two highest numbers on the list, the Senate shall choose the Vice-President; a quorum for the purpose shall consist of two-thirds of the whole number of Senators, and a majority of the whole number shall be necessary to a choice. But no person constitutionally ineligible to the office of President shall be eligible to that of Vice-President of the United States.

Note: *The part included in brackets has been superseded by section 3 of the Twentieth Amendment.*

Amendment XIII [1865]

Section 1. Neither slavery nor involuntary servitude, except as a punishment for crime whereof the party shall have been duly convicted, shall exist within the United States, or any place subject to their jurisdiction.

Section 2. Congress shall have power to enforce this article by appropriate legislation.

Amendment XIV [1868]

Section 1. All persons born or naturalized in the United States, and subject to the jurisdiction thereof, are citizens of the United States and of the State wherein they reside. No State shall make or enforce any law which shall abridge the privileges or immunities of citizens of the United States; nor shall any State deprive any person of life, liberty, or property, without due process of law; nor deny to any person within its jurisdiction the equal protection of the laws.

Section 2. Representatives shall be apportioned among the several States according to their respective numbers, counting the whole number of persons in each State, excluding Indians not taxed. But when the right to vote at any election for the choice of electors for President and Vice President of the United States, Representatives in Congress, the Executive and Judicial officers of a State, or the members of the Legislature thereof, is denied to any of the male inhabitants of such State, being twenty-one years of age, and citizens of the United States, or in any way abridged, except for participation in rebellion, or other crime, the basis of representation therein shall be reduced in the proportion which the number of such male citizens shall bear to the whole number of male citizens twenty-one years of age in such State.

Section 3. No person shall be a Senator or Representative in Congress, or elector of President and Vice President, or hold any office, civil or military, under the United States, or under any State, who, having previously taken an oath, as a member of Congress, or as an officer of the United States, or as a member of any State legislature, or as an executive or judicial officer of any State, to support the Constitution of the United States, shall have engaged in insurrection or rebellion against the same, or given aid or comfort to the enemies thereof. But Congress may by a vote of two-thirds of each House, remove such disability.

Section 4. The validity of the public debt of the United States, authorized by law, including debts incurred for payment of pensions and bounties for services in suppressing insurrection or rebellion, shall not be questioned. But neither the United States nor any State shall assume or pay any debt or obligation incurred in aid of insurrection or rebellion against the United States, or any claim for the loss or emancipation of any slave; but all such debts, obligations and claims shall be held illegal and void.

Section 5. The Congress shall have power to enforce, by appropriate legislation, the provisions of this article.

Amendment XV [1870]

Section 1. The right of citizens of the United States to vote shall not be denied or abridged by the United States or by any State on account of race, color, or previous condition of servitude.

Section 2. The Congress shall have power to enforce this article by appropriate legislation.

Amendment XVI [1913]

The Congress shall have power to lay and collect taxes on incomes, from whatever source derived, without apportionment among the several States, and without regard to any census or enumeration.

Amendment XVII [1913]

The Senate of the United States shall be composed of two Senators from each State, elected by the people thereof, for six years; and each Senator shall have one vote. The electors in each state shall have the qualification requisite for electors of the most numerous branch of the State legislatures.

When vacancies happen in the representation of any State in the Senate, the executive authority of such State shall issue writs of election to fill such vacancies: *Provided,* That the legislature of any State may empower the executive thereof to make temporary appointments until the people fill the vacancies by election as the legislature may direct.

This amendment shall not be so construed as to affect the election or term of any Senator chosen before it becomes valid as part of the Constitution.

Amendment XVIII [1919]

Section 1. [After one year from the ratification of this Article the manufacture, sale, or transportation of intoxicating liquors within, the importation thereof into, or the exportation thereof from the United States and all territory subject to the jurisdiction thereof for beverage purposes is hereby prohibited].

Section 2. [The Congress and the several States shall have concurrent power to enforce this article by appropriate legislation].

Section 3. [This article shall be inoperative unless it shall have been ratified as an amendment to the Constitution by the legislatures of the several States, as provided in the Constitution, within seven years from the date of the submission hereof to the States by the Congress].

Note: *The Eighteenth Amendment was repealed by the Twenty-first Amendment to the Constitution of the United States.*

Amendment XIX [1920]

The right of citizens of the United States to vote shall not be denied or abridged by the United States or by any State on account of sex.

Congress shall have the power to enforce this Article by appropriate legislation.

Amendment XX [1933]

Section 1. The terms of the President and Vice President shall end at noon on the 20th day of January, and the terms of Senators and Representatives at noon on the 3d day of January, of the years in which such terms would have ended if this article had not been ratified; and the terms of their successors shall then begin.

Section 2. The Congress shall assemble at least once in every year, and such meeting shall begin at noon on the 3d day of January, unless they shall by law appoint a different day.

Section 3. If, at the time fixed for the beginning of the term of the President, the President-elect shall have died, the Vice President-elect shall become President. If the President shall not have been chosen before the time fixed for the beginning of his term, or if the President-elect shall have failed to qualify, then the Vice President-elect shall act as President until a President shall have qualified; and the Congress may by law provide for the case wherein neither a President-elect nor a Vice President-elect shall have qualified, declaring who shall then act as President, or the manner in which one who is to act shall be selected, and such person shall act accordingly until a President or Vice President shall have qualified.

Section 4. The Congress may by law provide for the case of the death of any of the persons from whom the House of Representatives may choose a President whenever the right of choice shall have devolved upon them, and for the case of the death of any of the persons from whom the Senate may choose a Vice President whenever the right of choice shall have devolved upon them.

Section 5. Sections 1 and 2 shall take effect on the 15th day of October following the ratification of this article.

Section 6. This article shall be inoperative unless it shall have been ratified as an amendment to the Constitution by the legislatures of three-fourths of the several States within seven years from the date of its submission.

Amendment XXI [1933]

Section 1. The eighteenth article of amendment to the Constitution of the United States is hereby repealed.

Section 2. The transportation or importation into any State, Territory, or possession of the United States for delivery or use therein of intoxicating liquors, in violation of the laws thereof, is hereby prohibited.

Section 3. This article shall be inoperative unless it shall have been ratified as an amendment to the Constitution by conventions in the several States, as provided in the Constitution, within seven years from the date of the submission hereof to the States by the Congress.

Amendment XXII [1951]

Section 1. No person shall be elected to the office of the President more than twice, and no person who has held the office of President, or acted as President, for more than two years of a term to which some other person was elected President shall be elected to the office of President more than once. But this Article shall not apply to any person holding the office of President when this Article was proposed by the Congress, and shall not prevent any person who may be holding the office of President, or acting as President, during the term within which this Article becomes operative from holding the office of President or acting as President during the remainder of such term.

Section 2. This Article shall be inoperative unless it shall have been ratified as an amendment to the Constitution by the legislatures of three-fourths of the several States within seven years from the date of its submission to the States by the Congress.

Amendment XXIII [1961]

Section 1. The District constituting the seat of Government of the United States shall appoint in such manner as the Congress may direct:

A number of electors of President and Vice President equal to the whole number of Senators and Representatives in Congress to which the District would be entitled if it were a State, but in no event more than the least populous state; they shall be in addition to those appointed by the States, but they shall be considered, for the purposes of the election of President and Vice President, to be electors appointed by a State; and they shall meet in the District and perform such duties as provided by the twelfth article of amendment.

Section 2. The Congress shall have power to enforce this article by appropriate legislation.

Amendment XXIV [1964]

Section 1. The right of citizens of the United States to vote in any primary or other election for President or Vice President, for electors for President or Vice President, or for Senator or Representative in Congress, shall not be denied or abridged by the United States or by any State by reason of failure to pay any poll tax or other tax.

Section 2. The Congress shall have power to enforce this article by appropriate legislation.

Amendment XXV [1967]

Section 1. In case of the removal of the President from office or of his death or resignation, the Vice President shall become President.

Section 2. Whenever there is a vacancy in the office of the Vice President, the President shall nominate a Vice President who shall take office upon confirmation by a majority vote of both Houses of Congress.

Section 3. Whenever the President transmits to the President pro tempore of the Senate and the Speaker of the House of Representatives his written declaration that he is unable to discharge the powers and duties of his office, and until he transmits to them a written declaration of the contrary, such powers and duties shall be discharged by the Vice President as Acting President.

Section 4. Whenever the Vice President and a majority of either the principal officers of the executive departments or of such other body as Congress may by law provide, transmit to the President pro tempore of the Senate and the Speaker of the House of Representatives their written declaration that the President is unable to discharge the powers and duties of his office, the Vice President shall immediately assume the powers and duties of the office as Acting President.

Thereafter, when the President transmits to the President pro tempore of the Senate and the Speaker of the House of Representatives his written declaration that no inability exists, he shall resume the powers and duties of his office unless the Vice President and a majority of either the principal officers of the executive department or of such other body as Congress may by law provide, transmit within four days to the President pro tempore of the Senate and the Speaker of the House of Representatives their written declaration that the President is unable to discharge the powers and duties of his office. Thereupon Congress shall decide the issue, assembling within forty-eight hours for that purpose if not in session. If the Congress, within twenty-one days after receipt of the latter written declaration, or, if Congress is not in session, within twenty-one days after Congress is required to assemble, determines by two-thirds vote of both Houses that the President is unable to discharge the powers and duties of his office, the Vice President shall continue to discharge the same as Acting President; otherwise, the President shall resume the powers and duties of his office.

Amendment XXVI [1971]

Section 1. The right of citizens of the United States, who are eighteen years of age or older, to vote shall not be denied or abridged by the United States or by any State on account of age.

Section 2. The Congress shall have the power to enforce this article by appropriate legislation.

Amendment XXVII [1992]

No law, varying the compensation for the services of the Senators and Representatives, shall take effect, until an election of Representatives shall have intervened.

APPENDIX 2

Uniform Commercial Code, 1978 Text with 1990 Amendments

Note: The 1978 text of the UCC has been updated to reflect the 1990 amendments of Article 3. So, in this appendix you can read either the 1978 version of the UCC or the 1991 version.

To update the UCC, the drafters used brackets ([ ]) to indicate deleted words, and underscoring (____) to indicate added words. If you want to use the 1978 text, read the ordinary type plus the bracketed words. If you want to use the 1991 text, read the ordinary type plus the underscored words (but minus the bracketed words).

ARTICLE 1: GENERAL PROVISIONS

Part 1: Short Title, Construction, Application and Subject Matter of the Act

§1-101. Short Title. This Act shall be known and may be cited as Uniform Commercial Code.

§1-102. Purposes; Rules of Construction; Variation by Agreement.
(1) This Act shall be liberally construed and applied to promote its underlying purposes and policies.
(2) Underlying purposes and policies of this Act are
(a) to simplify, clarify and modernize the law governing commercial transactions;
(b) permit the continued expansion of commercial practices through custom, usage and agreement of the parties;
(c) to make uniform the law among the various jurisdictions.

(3) The effect of provisions of this Act may be varied by agreement, except as otherwise provided in this Act and except that the obligations of good faith, diligence, reasonableness and care prescribed by this Act may not be disclaimed by agreement but the parties may by agreement determine the standards by which the performance of such obligations is to be measured if such standards are not manifestly unreasonable.

(4) The presence in certain provisions of this Act of the words "unless otherwise agreed" or words of similar import does not imply that the effect of other provisions may not be varied by agreement under subsection (3).

(5) In this Act unless the context otherwise requires

(a) words in the singular number include the plural, and in the plural include the singular;
(b) words of the masculine gender include the feminine and the neuter, and when the sense so indicates words of the neuter gender may refer to any gender.

§1-103. Supplementary General Principles of Law Applicable. Unless displaced by the particular provisions of this Act, the principles of law and equity, including the law merchant and the law relative to capacity to contract, principal and agent, estoppel, fraud, misrepresentation, duress, coercion, mistake, bankruptcy, or other validating or invalidating cause shall supplement its provisions.

§1-104. Construction Against Implicit Repeal. This Act being a general act intended as a unified coverage of its subject matter, no part of it shall be deemed to be impliedly repealed by subsequent legislation if such construction can reasonably be avoided.

§1-105. Territorial Application of the Act; Parties' Power to Choose Applicable Law.
(1) Except as provided hereafter in this section, when a transaction bears a reasonable relation to this state and also to another state or nation the parties may agree that the law either of this state or of such other state or nation shall govern their rights and duties. Failing such agreement this Act applies to transactions bearing an appropriate relation to this state.

(2) Where one of the following provisions of this Act specifies the applicable law, that provision governs and a contrary agreement is effective only to the extent permitted by the law (including the conflict of laws rules) so specified:

Rights of creditors against sold goods. Section 2-402.
Applicability of the Article on Bank Deposits and Collections. Section 4-102.
Bulk transfers subject to the Article on Bulk Transfers. Section 6-102.

Applicability of the Article on Investment Securities. Section 8-106.

Perfection provisions of the Article on Secured Transactions. Section 9-103.

§1-106. Remedies to Be Liberally Administered.

(1) The remedies provided by this Act shall be liberally administered to the end that the aggrieved party may be put in as good a position as if the other party had fully performed but neither consequential or special nor penal damages may be had except as specifically provided in this Act or by other rule of law.

(2) Any right or obligation declared by this Act is enforceable by action unless the provision declaring it specifies a different and limited effect.

§1-107. Waiver or Renunciation of Claim or Right After Breach. Any claim or right arising out of an alleged breach can be discharged in whole or in part without consideration by a written waiver or renunciation signed and delivered by the aggrieved party.

§1-108. Severability. If any provision or clause of this Act or application thereof to any person or circumstances is held invalid, such invalidity shall not affect other provisions or applications of the Act which can be given effect without the invalid provision or application, and to this end the provisions of this Act are declared to be severable.

§1-109. Section Captions. Section captions are parts of this Act.

Part 2: General Definitions and Principles of Interpretation

§1-201. General Definitions (1987 and 1990 Amendments). Subject to additional definitions contained in the subsequent Articles of this Act which are applicable to specific Articles or Parts thereof, and unless the context otherwise requires, in this Act:

(1) "Action" in the sense of a judicial proceeding includes recoupment, counterclaim, set-off, suit in equity and any other proceedings in which rights are determined.

(2) "Aggrieved party" means a party entitled to resort to a remedy.

(3) "Agreement" means the bargain of the parties in fact as found in their language or by implication from other circumstances including course of dealing or usage of trade or course of performance as provided in this Act (Sections 1-205 and 2-208). Whether an agreement has legal consequences is determined by the provisions of this Act, if applicable; otherwise by the law of contracts (Section 1-103). (Compare "Contract".)

(4) "Bank" means any person engaged in the business of banking.

(5) "Bearer" means the person in possession of an instrument, document of title, or certificated security payable to bearer or indorsed in blank.

(6) "Bill of lading" means a document evidencing the receipt of goods for shipment issued by a person engaged in the business of transporting or forwarding goods, and includes an airbill. "Airbill" means a document serving for air transportation as a bill of lading does for marine or rail transportation, and includes an air consignment note or air waybill.

(7) "Branch" includes a separately incorporated foreign branch of a bank.

(8) "Burden of establishing" a fact means the burden of persuading the triers of fact that the existence of the fact is more probable than its non-existence.

(9) "Buyer in ordinary course of business" means a person who in good faith and without knowledge that the sale to him is in violation of the ownership rights or security interest of a third party in the goods buys in ordinary course from a person in the business of selling goods of that kind but does not include a pawnbroker. All persons who sell minerals or the like (including oil and gas) at wellhead or minehead shall be deemed to be persons in the business of selling goods of that kind. "Buying" may be for cash or by exchange of other property or on secured or unsecured credit and includes receiving goods or documents of title under a preexisting contract for sale but does not include a transfer in bulk or as security for or in total or partial satisfaction of a money debt.

(10) "Conspicuous": A term or clause is conspicuous when it is so written that a reasonable person against whom it is to operate ought to have noticed it. A printed heading in capitals (as: NON-NEGOTIABLE BILL OF LADING) is conspicuous. Language in the body of a form is "conspicuous" if it is in larger or other contrasting type or color. But in a telegram any stated term is "conspicuous". Whether a term or clause is "conspicuous" or not is for decision by the court.

(11) "Contract" means the total legal obligation which results from the parties' agreement as affected by this Act and any other applicable rules of law. (Compare "Agreement".)

(12) "Creditor" includes a general creditor, a secured creditor, a lien creditor and any representative of creditors, including an assignee for the benefit of creditors, a trustee in bankruptcy, a receiver in equity and an executor or administrator of an insolvent debtor's or assignor's estate.

(13) "Defendant" includes a person in the position of defendant in a cross-action or counterclaim.

(14) "Delivery" with respect to instruments, documents of title, chattel paper, or certificated securities means voluntary transfer of possession.

(15) "Document of title" includes bill of lading, dock warrant, dock receipt, warehouse receipt or order for the delivery of goods, and also any other document which in the regular course of business or financing is treated as adequately evidencing that the person in possession of it is entitled to receive, hold and dispose of the document and the goods it covers. To be a document of title a document must purport to be issued by or addressed to a bailee and purport to cover goods in the bailee's possession which are either identified or are fungible portions of an identified mass.

(16) "Fault" means wrongful act, omission or breach.

(17) "Fungible" with respect to goods or securities means goods or securities of which any unit is, by nature or usage of trade, the equivalent of any other like unit. Goods which are not fungible shall be deemed fungible for the purposes of this Act to the extent that under a particular agreement or document unlike units are treated as equivalents.

(18) "Genuine" means free of forgery or counterfeiting.

(19) "Good faith" means honesty in fact in the conduct or transaction concerned.

(20) "Holder" [means a person who is in possession of a document of title or an instrument or a certificated investment security drawn, issued, or indorsed to him or his order or to bearer or in blank] with respect to a negotiable instrument, means the person in possession if the instrument is payable to bearer or, in the case of an instrument payable to an identified person, if the identified person is in possession. "Holder" with respect to a document of title means the person in possession if the goods are deliverable to bearer or to the order of the person in possession.

(21) To "honor" is to pay or to accept and pay, or where a credit so engages to purchase or discount a draft complying with the terms of the credit.

(22) "Insolvency proceedings" includes any assignment for the benefit of creditors or other proceedings intended to liquidate or rehabilitate the estate of the person involved.

(23) A person is "insolvent" who either has ceased to pay his debts in the ordinary course of business or cannot pay his debts as they become due or is insolvent within the meaning of the federal bankruptcy law.

(24) "Money" means a medium of exchange authorized or adopted by a domestic or foreign government [as a part of its currency] and includes a monetary unit of account established by an intergovernmental organization or by agreement between two or more nations.

(25) A person has "notice" of a fact when

(a) he has actual knowledge of it; or
(b) he has received a notice or notification of it; or
(c) from all the facts and circumstances known to him at the time in question he has reason to know that it exists.

A person "knows" or has "knowledge" of a fact when he has actual knowledge of it. "Discover" or "learn" or a word or phrase of similar import refers to knowledge rather than to reason to know. The time and circumstances under which a notice or notification may cease to be effective are not determined by this Act.

(26) A person "notifies" or "gives" a notice or notification to another by taking such steps as may be reasonably required to inform the other in ordinary course whether or not such other actually comes to know of it. A person "receives" a notice or notification when

(a) it comes to his attention; or
(b) it is duly delivered at the place of business through which the contract was made or at any other place held out by him as the place for receipt of such communications.

(27) Notice, knowledge or a notice or notification received by an organization is effective for a particular transaction from the time when it is brought to the attention of the individual conducting that transaction, and in any event from the time when it would have been brought to his attention if the organization had exercised due diligence. An organization exercises due diligence if it maintains reasonable routines for communicating significant information to the person conducting the transaction and there is reasonable compliance with the routines. Due diligence does not require an individual acting for the organization to communicate information unless such communication is part of his regular duties or unless he has reason to know of the transaction and that the transaction would be materially affected by the information.

(28) "Organization" includes a corporation, government or governmental subdivision or agency, business trust, estate, trust, partnership or association, two or more persons having a joint or common interest, or any other legal or commercial entity.

(29) "Party", as distinct from "third party", means a person who has engaged in a transaction or made an agreement within this Act.

(30) "Person" includes an individual or an organization (See Section 1-102).

(31) "Presumption" or "presumed" means that the trier of fact must find the existence of the fact presumed unless and until evidence is introduced which would support a finding of its non-existence.

(32) "Purchase" includes taking by sale, discount, negotiation, mortgage, pledge, lien, issue or re-issue, gift or any other voluntary transaction creating an interest in property.

(33) "Purchaser" means a person who takes by purchase.

(34) "Remedy" means any remedial right to which an aggrieved party is entitled with or without resort to a tribunal.

(35) "Representative" includes an agent, an officer of a corporation or association, and a trustee, executor or administrator of an estate, or any other person empowered to act for another.

(36) "Rights" includes remedies.

(37) "Security interest" means an interest in personal property or fixtures which secures payment or performance of an obligation. The retention or reservation of title by a seller of goods notwithstanding shipment or delivery to the buyer (Section 2-401) is limited in effect to a reservation of a "security interest". The term also includes any interest of a buyer of accounts or chattel paper which is subject to Article 9. The special property interest of a buyer of goods on identification of such goods to a contract for sale under Section 2-401 is not a "security interest", but a buyer may also acquire a "security interest" by complying with Article 9. Unless a [lease or] consignment is intended as security, reservation of title thereunder is not a "security interest", but a consignment [is] in any event is subject to the provisions on consignment sales (Section 2-326).

Whether a [lease is intended as] transaction creates a lease or security interest is [to be] determined by the facts of each case; however, [(a) the inclusion of an option to purchase does not of itself make the lease one intended for security, and (b) an agreement that upon compliance with the terms of the lease the lessee shall become or has the option to become the owner of the property for no additional consideration or for a nominal consideration does make the lease one intended for security.] A transaction creates a security interest if the consideration the lessee is to pay the lessor for the right to possession and use of the goods is an obligation for the term of the lease not subject to termination by the lessee, and

(a) the original term of the lease is equal to or greater than the remaining economic life of the goods,
(b) the lessee is bound to renew the lease for the remaining economic life of the goods or is bound to become the owner of the goods,
(c) the lessee has an option to renew the lease for the remaining economic life of the goods for no additional consideration or nominal additional consideration upon compliance with the lease agreement, or
(d) the lessee has an option to become the owner of the goods for no additional consideration or nominal additional consideration upon compliance with the lease agreement.

A transaction does not create a security interest merely because it provides that

(a) the present value of the consideration the lessee is obligated to pay the lessor for the right to possession and use of the goods is substantially equal to or is greater than the fair market value of the goods at the time the lease is entered into,
(b) the lessee assumes risk of loss of the goods, or agrees to pay taxes, insurance, filing, recording, or registration fees, or service or maintenance costs with respect to the goods,
(c) the lessee has an option to renew the lease or to become the owner of the goods,
(d) the lessee has an option to renew the lease for a fixed rent that is equal to or greater than the reasonably predictable fair market rent for the use of the goods for the term of the renewal at the time the option is to be performed, or
(e) the lessee has an option to become the owner of the goods for a fixed price that is equal to or greater than the reasonably predictable fair market value of the goods at the time the option is to be performed.

For purposes of this subsection (37):

(x) Additional consideration is not nominal if (i) when the option to renew the lease is granted to the lessee the rent is stated to be the fair market rent for the use of the goods for the term of the renewal determined at the time the option is to be performed, or (ii) when the option to become the owner of the goods is granted to the lessee the price is stated to be the fair market value of the goods determined at the time the option is to be performed. Additional consideration is nominal if it is less than the lessee's reasonably predictable cost of performing under the lease agreement if the option is not exercised;

(y) "Reasonably predictable" and "remaining economic life of the goods" are to be determined with reference to the facts and circumstances at the time the transaction is entered into; and

(z) "Present value" means the amount as of a date certain of one or more sums payable in the future, discounted to the date certain. The discount is determined by the interest rate specified by the parties if the rate is not manifestly unreasonable at the time the transaction is entered into; otherwise, the discount is determined by a commercially reasonable rate that takes into account the facts and circumstances of each case at the time the transaction was entered into.

(38) "Send" in connection with any writing or notice means to deposit in the mail or deliver for transmission by any other usual means of communication with postage or cost of transmission provided for and properly addressed and in the case of an instrument to an address specified thereon or otherwise agreed, or if there be none to any address reasonable under the circumstances. The receipt of any writing or notice within the time at which it would have arrived if properly sent has the effect of a proper sending.

(39) "Signed" includes any symbol executed or adopted by a party with present intention to authenticate a writing.

(40) "Surety" includes guarantor.

(41) "Telegram" includes a message transmitted by radio, teletype, cable, any mechanical method of transmission, or the like.

(42) "Term" means that portion of an agreement which relates to a particular matter.

(43) "Unauthorized" signature [or indorsement] means one made without actual, implied, or apparent authority and includes a forgery.

(44) "Value". Except as otherwise provided with respect to negotiable instruments and bank collections (Sections 3-303, 4-208 and 4-209) a person gives "value" for rights if he acquires them

(a) in return for a binding commitment to extend credit or for the extension of immediately available credit whether or not drawn upon and whether or not a chargeback is provided for in the event of difficulties in collection; or

(b) as security for or in total or partial satisfaction of a preexisting claim; or

(c) by accepting delivery pursuant to a pre-existing contract for purchase; or

(d) generally, in return for any consideration sufficient to support a simple contract.

(45) "Warehouse receipt" means a receipt issued by a person engaged in the business of storing goods for hire.

(46) "Written" or "writing" includes printing, typewriting or any other intentional reduction to tangible form.

§1-202. Prima Facie Evidence by Third-Party Documents. A document in due form purporting to be a bill of lading, policy or certificate of insurance, official weigher's or inspector's certificate, consular invoice or any other document authorized or required by the contract to be issued by a third party shall be prima facie evidence of its own authenticity and genuineness and of the facts stated in the document by the third party.

§1-203. Obligation of Good Faith. Every contract or duty within this Act imposes an obligation of good faith in its performance or enforcement.

§1-204. Time; Reasonable Time; "Seasonably".

(1) Whenever this Act requires any action to be taken within a reasonable time, any time which is not manifestly unreasonable may be fixed by agreement.

(2) What is a reasonable time for taking any action depends on the nature, purpose and circumstances of such action.

(3) An action is taken "seasonably" when it is taken at or within the time agreed or if no time is agreed at or within a reasonable time.

§1-205. Course of Dealing and Usage of Trade.

(1) A course of dealing is a sequence of previous conduct between the parties to a particular transaction which is fairly to be regarded as establishing a common basis of understanding for interpreting their expressions and other conduct.

(2) A usage of trade is any practice or method of dealing having such regularity of observance in a place, vocation or trade as to justify an expectation that it will be observed with respect to the transaction in question. The existence and scope of such a usage are to be proved as facts. If it is established that such a usage is embodied in a written trade code or similar writing the interpretation of the writing is for the court.

(3) A course of dealing between parties and any usage of trade in the vocation or trade in which they are engaged or of which they are or should be aware give particular meaning to and supplement or qualify terms of an agreement.

(4) The express terms of an agreement and an applicable course of dealing or usage of trade shall be construed wherever reasonable as consistent with each other; but when such construction is unreasonable express terms control both course of dealing and usage of trade and course of dealing controls usage of trade.

(5) An applicable usage of trade in the place where any part of performance is to occur shall be used in interpreting the agreement as to that part of the performance.

(6) Evidence of a relevant usage of trade offered by one party is not admissible unless and until he has given the other party such notice as the court finds sufficient to prevent unfair surprise to the latter.

§1-206. Statute of Frauds for Kinds of Personal Property Not Otherwise Covered.

(1) Except in the cases described in subsection (2) of this section a contract for the sale of personal property is not enforceable by way of action or defense beyond five thousand dollars in amount or value of remedy unless there is some writing which indicates that a contract for sale has been made between the parties at a defined or stated price, reasonably identifies the subject matter, and is signed by the party against whom enforcement is sought or by his authorized agent.

(2) Subsection (1) of this section does not apply to contracts for the sale of goods (Section 2-201) nor of securities (Section 8-319) nor to security agreements (Section 9-203).

§1-207. Performance or Acceptance Under Reservation of Rights.

(1) A party who, with explicit reservation of rights, performs or promises performance or assents to performance in a manner demanded or offered by the other party does not thereby prejudice the rights reserved. Such words as "without prejudice", "under protest" or the like are sufficient.

(2) Subsection (1) does not apply to an accord and satisfaction.

§1-208. Option to Accelerate at Will. A term providing that one party or his successor in interest may accelerate payment or performance or require collateral or additional collateral "at will" or "when he deems himself insecure" or in words of similar import shall be construed to mean that he shall have power to do so only if he in good faith believes that the prospect of payment or performance is impaired. The burden of establishing lack of good faith is on the party against whom the power has been exercised.

§1-209. Subordinated Obligations. An obligation may be issued as subordinated to payment of another obligation of the person obligated, or a creditor may subordinate his right to payment of an obligation by agreement with either the person obligated or another creditor of the person obligated. Such a subordination does not create a security interest as against either the common debtor or a subordinated creditor. This section shall be construed as declaring the law as it existed prior to the enactment of this section and not as modifying it.

Note: *This new section is proposed as an optional provision to make it clear that a subordination agreement does not create a security interest unless so intended.*

ARTICLE 2: SALES

Part 1: Short Title, General Construction, and Subject Matter

§2-101. Short Title. This Article shall be known and may be cited as Uniform Commercial Code—Sales.

§2-102. Scope; Certain Security and Other Transactions Excluded from This Article. Unless the context otherwise requires, this Article applies to transactions in goods; it does not apply to any transaction which although in the form of an unconditional contract to sell or present sale is intended to operate only as a security transaction nor does this Article impair or repeal any statute regulating sales to consumers, farmers or other specified classes of buyers.

§2-103. Definitions and Index of Definitions.
(1) In this Article unless the context otherwise requires

(a) "Buyer" means a person who buys or contracts to buy goods.
(b) "Good faith" in the case of a merchant means honesty in fact and the observance of reasonable commercial standards of fair dealing in the trade.
(c) "Receipt" of goods means taking physical possession of them.
(d) "Seller" means a person who sells or contracts to sell goods.

(2) Other definitions applying to this Article or to specified Parts thereof, and the sections in which they appear are:

"Acceptance"	Section 2-606
"Banker's credit"	Section 2-325
"Between merchants"	Section 2-104
"Cancellation"	Section 2-106(4)
"Commercial unit"	Section 2-105
"Confirmed credit"	Section 2-325
"Conforming to contract"	Section 2-106
"Contract for sale"	Section 2-106
"Cover"	Section 2-712
"Entrusting"	Section 2-403
"Financing agency"	Section 2-104
"Future goods"	Section 2-105
"Goods"	Section 2-105
"Identification"	Section 2-501
"Installment contract"	Section 2-612
"Letter of credit"	Section 2-325
"Lot"	Section 2-105
"Merchant"	Section 2-104
"Overseas"	Section 2-323
"Person in position of seller"	Section 2-707
"Present sale"	Section 2-106
"Sale"	Section 2-106
"Sale on approval"	Section 2-326
"Sale or return"	Section 2-326
"Termination"	Section 2-106

(3) The following definitions in other Articles apply to this Article:

"Check"	Section 3-104
"Consignee"	Section 7-102
"Consignor"	Section 7-102
"Consumer goods"	Section 9-109
"Dishonor"	Section 3-507
"Draft"	Section 3-104

(4) In addition Article 1 contains general definitions and principles of construction and interpretation applicable throughout this article.

§2-104. Definitions: "Merchant"; "Between Merchants"; "Financing Agency".
(1) "Merchant" means a person who deals in goods of the kind or otherwise by his occupation holds himself out as having knowledge or skill peculiar to the practices or goods involved in the transaction or to whom such knowledge or skill may be attributed by his employment of an agent or broker or other intermediary who by his occupation holds himself out as having such knowledge or skill.
(2) "Financing agency" means a bank, finance company or other person who in the ordinary course of business makes advances against goods or documents of title or who by arrangement with either the seller or the buyer intervenes in ordinary course to make or collect payment due or claimed under the contract for sale, as by purchasing or paying the seller's draft or making advances against it or by merely taking it for collection whether or not documents of title accompany the draft. "Financing agency" includes also a bank or other person who similarly intervenes between persons who are in the position of seller and buyer in respect of the goods (Section 2-707).
(3) "Between merchants" means in any transaction with respect to which both parties are chargeable with the knowledge or skill of merchants.

§2-105. Definitions: Transferability; "Goods"; "Future" Goods; "Lot"; "Commercial Unit".
(1) "Goods" means all things (including specially manufactured goods) which are movable at the time of identification to the contract for sale other than the money in which the price is to be paid, investment securities (Article 8) and things in action. "Goods" also includes the unborn young of animals and growing crops and other identified things attached to realty as described in the section on goods to be severed from realty (Section 2-107).
(2) Goods must be both existing and identified before any interest in them can pass. Goods which are not both existing and identified are "future" goods. A purported present sale of future goods or of any interest therein operates as a contract to sell.
(3) There may be a sale of a part interest in existing identified goods.

(4) An undivided share in an identified bulk of fungible goods is sufficiently identified to be sold although the quantity of the bulk is not determined. Any agreed proportion of such a bulk or any quantity thereof agreed upon by number, weight or other measure may to the extent of the seller's interest in the bulk be sold to the buyer who then becomes an owner in common.

(5) "Lot" means a parcel or a single article which is the subject matter of a separate sale or delivery, whether or not it is sufficient to perform the contract.

(6) "Commercial unit" means such a unit of goods as by commercial usage is a single whole for purposes of sale and division of which materially impairs its character or value on the market or in use. A commercial unit may be a single article (as a machine) or a set of articles (as a suite of furniture or an assortment of sizes) or a quantity (as a bale, gross, or carload) or any other unit treated in use or in the relevant market as a single whole.

§2-106. Definitions: "Contract"; "Agreement"; "Contract for Sale"; "Sale"; "Present Sale"; "Conforming" to Contract; "Termination"; "Cancellation".

(1) In this Article unless the context otherwise requires "contract" and "agreement" are limited to those relating to the present or future sale of goods. "Contract for sale" includes both a present sale of goods and a contract to sell goods at a future time. A "sale" consists in the passing of title from the seller to the buyer for a price (Section 2-401). A "present sale" means a sale which is accomplished by the making of the contract.

(2) Goods or conduct including any part of a performance are "conforming" or conform to the contract when they are in accordance with the obligations under the contract.

(3) "Termination" occurs when either party pursuant to a power created by agreement or law puts an end to the contract otherwise than for its breach. On "termination" all obligations which are still executory on both sides are discharged but any right based on prior breach or performance survives.

(4) "Cancellation" occurs when either party puts an end to the contract for breach by the other and its effect is the same as that of "termination" except that the cancelling party also retains any remedy for breach of the whole contract or any unperformed balance.

§2-107. Goods to Be Severed From Realty: Recording.

(1) A contract for the sale of minerals or the like (including oil and gas) or a structure or its materials to be removed from realty is a contract for the sale of goods within this Article if they are to be severed by the seller but until severance a purported present sale thereof which is not effective as a transfer of an interest in land is effective only as a contract to sell.

(2) A contract for the sale apart from the land of growing crops or other things attached to realty and capable of severance without material harm thereto but not described in subsection (1) or of timber to be cut is a contract for the sale of goods within this Article whether the subject matter is to be severed by the buyer or by the seller even though it forms part of the realty at the time of contracting, and the parties can by identification effect a present sale before severance.

(3) The provisions of this section are subject to any third party rights provided by the law relating to realty records, and the contract for sale may be executed and recorded as a document transferring an interest in land and shall then constitute notice to third parties of the buyer's rights under the contract for sale.

Part 2: Form, Formation and Readjustment of Contract

§2-201. Formal Requirements; Statute of Frauds.

(1) Except as otherwise provided in this section a contract for the sale of goods for the price of $500 or more is not enforceable by way of action or defense unless there is some writing sufficient to indicate that a contract for sale has been made between the parties and signed by the party against whom enforcement is sought or by his authorized agent or broker. A writing is not insufficient because it omits or incorrectly states a term agreed upon but the contract is not enforceable under this paragraph beyond the quantity of goods shown in such writing.

(2) Between merchants if within a reasonable time a writing in confirmation of the contract and sufficient against the sender is received and the party receiving it has reason to know its contents, it satisfies the requirements of subsection (1) against such party unless written notice of objection to its contents is given within 10 days after it is received.

(3) A contract which does not satisfy the requirements of subsection (1) but which is valid in other respects is enforceable

(a) if the goods are to be specially manufactured for the buyer and are not suitable for sale to others in the ordinary course of the seller's business and the seller, before notice of repudiation is received and under circumstances which reasonably indicate that the goods are for the buyer, has made either a substantial beginning of their manufacture or commitments for their procurement; or

(b) if the party against whom enforcement is sought admits in his pleading, testimony or otherwise in court that a contract for sale was made, but the contract is not enforceable under this provision beyond the quantity of goods admitted; or

(c) with respect to goods for which payment has been made and accepted or which have been received and accepted (Sec. 2-606.)

§2-202. Final Written Expression: Parol or Extrinsic Evidence.

Terms with respect to which the confirmatory memoranda of the parties agree or which are otherwise set forth in a writing intended by the parties as a final expression of their agreement with respect to such terms as are included therein may not be contradicted by evidence of any prior agreement or of a contemporaneous oral agreement but may be explained or supplemented

(a) by course of dealing or usage of trade (Section 1-205) or by course of performance (Section 2-208); and

(b) by evidence of consistent additional terms unless the court finds the writing to have been intended also as a complete and exclusive statement of the terms of the agreement.

§2-203. Seals Inoperative.
The affixing of a seal to a writing evidencing a contract for sale or an offer to buy or sell goods does not constitute the writing a sealed instrument and the law with respect to sealed instruments does not apply to such a contract or offer.

§2-204. Formation in General.

(1) A contract for sale of goods may be made in any manner sufficient to show agreement, including conduct by both parties which recognizes the existence of such a contract.

(2) An agreement sufficient to constitute a contract for sale may be found even though the moment of its making is undetermined.

(3) Even though one or more terms are left open a contract for sale does not fail for indefiniteness if the parties have intended to make a contract and there is a reasonably certain basis for giving an appropriate remedy.

§2-205. Firm Offers. An offer by a merchant to buy or sell goods in a signed writing which by its terms gives assurance that it will be held open is not revocable, for lack of consideration, during the time stated or if no time is stated for a reasonable time, but in no event may such period of irrevocability exceed three months; but any such term of assurance on a form supplied by the offeree must be separately signed by the offeror.

§2-206. Offer and Acceptance in Formation of Contract.

(1) Unless otherwise unambiguously indicated by the language or circumstances

(a) an offer to make a contract shall be construed as inviting acceptance in any manner and by any medium reasonable in the circumstances;

(b) an order or other offer to buy goods for prompt or current shipment shall be construed as inviting acceptance either by a prompt promise to ship or by the prompt or current shipment of conforming or nonconforming goods, but such a shipment of nonconforming goods does not constitute an acceptance if the seller seasonably notifies the buyer that the shipment is offered only as an accommodation to the buyer.

(2) Where the beginning of a requested performance is a reasonable mode of acceptance an offeror who is not notified of acceptance within a reasonable time may treat the offer as having lapsed before acceptance.

§2-207. Additional Terms in Acceptance or Confirmation.

(1) A definite and seasonable expression of acceptance or a written confirmation which is sent within a reasonable time operates as an acceptance even though it states terms additional to or different from those offered or agreed upon, unless acceptance is expressly made conditional on assent to the additional or different terms.

(2) The additional terms are to be construed as proposals for addition to the contract. Between merchants such terms become part of the contract unless:

(a) the offer expressly limits acceptance to the terms of the offer;

(b) they materially alter it; or

(c) notification of objection to them has already been given or is given within a reasonable time after notice of them is received.

(3) Conduct by both parties which recognizes the existence of a contract is sufficient to establish a contract for sale although the writings of the parties do not otherwise establish a contract. In such case the terms of the particular contract consist of those terms on which the writings of the parties agree, together with any supplementary terms incorporated under any other provisions of this Act.

§2-208. Course of Performance or Practical Construction.

(1) Where the contract for sale involves repeated occasions for performance by either party with knowledge of the nature of the performance and opportunity for objection to it by the other, any course of performance accepted or acquiesced in without objection shall be relevant to determine the meaning of the agreement.

(2) The express terms of the agreement and any such course of performance, as well as any course of dealing and usage of trade, shall be construed whenever reasonable as consistent with each other; but when such construction is unreasonable, express terms shall control course of performance and course of performance shall control both course of dealing and usage of trade (Section 1-205).

(3) Subject to the provisions of the next section on modification and waiver, such course of performance shall be relevant to show a waiver or modification of any term inconsistent with such course of performance.

§2-209. Modification, Rescission and Waiver.

(1) An agreement modifying a contract within this Article needs no consideration to be binding.

(2) A signed agreement which excludes modification or rescission except by a signed writing cannot be otherwise modified or rescinded, but except as between merchants such a requirement on a form supplied by the merchant must be separately signed by the other party.

(3) The requirements of the statute of frauds section of this Article (Section 2-201) must be satisfied if the contract as modified is within its provisions.

(4) Although an attempt at modification or rescission does not satisfy the requirements of subsection (2) or (3) it can operate as a waiver.

(5) A party who has made a waiver affecting an executory portion of the contract may retract the waiver by reasonable notification received by the other party that strict performance will be required of any term waived, unless the retraction would be unjust in view of a material change of position in reliance on the waiver.

§2-210. Delegation of Performance; Assignment of Rights.

(1) A party may perform his duty through a delegate unless otherwise agreed or unless the other party has a substantial interest in having his original promisor perform or control the acts required by the contract. No delegation of performance relieves the party delegating of any duty to perform or any liability for breach.

(2) Unless otherwise agreed all rights of either seller or buyer can be assigned except where the assignment would materially change the duty of the other party, or increase materially the burden or risk imposed on him by his contract, or impair materially his chance of obtaining return performance. A right to damages for breach of the whole contract or a right arising out of the assignor's due performance of his entire obligation can be assigned despite agreement otherwise.

(3) Unless the circumstances indicate the contrary a prohibition of assignment of "the contract" is to be construed as barring only the delegation to the assignee of the assignor's performance.

(4) An assignment of "the contract" or of "all my rights under the contract" or an assignment in similar general terms is an assignment of rights and unless the language or the circumstances (as in an assignment for security) indicate the contrary, it is a delegation of performance of the duties of the assignor and its acceptance by the assignee constitutes a promise by him to perform those duties. This promise is enforceable by either the assignor or the other party to the original contract.

(5) The other party may treat any assignment which delegates performance as creating reasonable grounds for insecurity and may without prejudice to his rights against the assignor demand assurances from the assignee (Section 2-609).

Part 3: General Obligation and Construction of Contract

§2-301. General Obligations of Parties. The obligation of the seller is to transfer and deliver and that of the buyer is to accept and pay in accordance with the contract.

§2-302. Unconscionable Contract or Clause.

(1) If the court as a matter of law finds the contract or any clause of the contract to have been unconscionable at the time it was made the court may refuse to enforce the contract, or it may enforce the remainder of the contract without the unconscionable clause, or it may so limit the application of any unconscionable clause as to avoid any unconscionable result.

(2) When it is claimed or appears to the court that the contract or any clause thereof may be unconscionable the parties shall be afforded a reasonable opportunity to present evidence as to its commercial setting, purpose and effect to aid the court in making the determination.

§2-303. Allocation or Division of Risks. Where this Article allocates a risk or a burden as between the parties "unless otherwise agreed", the agreement may not only shift the allocation but may also divide the risk or burden.

§2-304. Price Payable in Money, Goods, Realty, or Otherwise.

(1) The price can be made payable in money or otherwise. If it is payable in whole or in part in goods each party is a seller of the goods which he is to transfer.

(2) Even though all or part of the price is payable in an interest in realty the transfer of the goods and the seller's obligations with reference to them are subject to this Article, but not the transfer of the interest in realty or the transferor's obligations in connection therewith.

§2-305. Open Price Term.

(1) The parties if they so intend can conclude a contract for sale even though the price is not settled. In such a case the price is a reasonable price at the time for delivery if

(a) nothing is said as to price; or
(b) the price is left to be agreed by the parties and they fail to agree; or
(c) the price is to be fixed in terms of some agreed market or other standard as set or recorded by a third person or agency and it is not so set or recorded.

(2) A price to be fixed by the seller or by the buyer means a price for him to fix in good faith.

(3) When a price left to be fixed otherwise than by agreement of the parties fails to be fixed through fault of one party the other may at his option treat the contract as cancelled or himself fix a reasonable price.

(4) Where, however, the parties intend not to be bound unless the price be fixed or agreed and it is not fixed or agreed there is no contract. In such a case the buyer must return any goods already received or if unable so to do must pay their reasonable value at the time of delivery and the seller must return any portion of the price paid on account.

§2-306. Output, Requirements and Exclusive Dealings.

(1) A term which measures the quantity by the output of the seller or the requirements of the buyer means such actual output or requirements as may occur in good faith, except that no quantity unreasonably disproportionate to any stated estimate or in the absence of a stated estimate to any normal or otherwise comparable prior output or requirements may be tendered or demanded.

(2) A lawful agreement by either the seller or the buyer for exclusive dealing in the kind of goods concerned imposes unless otherwise agreed an obligation by the seller to use best efforts to supply the goods and by the buyer to use best efforts to promote their sale.

§2-307. Delivery in Single Lot or Several Lots. Unless otherwise agreed all goods called for by a contract for sale must be tendered in a single delivery and payment is due only on such tender but where the circumstances give either party the right to make or demand delivery in lots the price if it can be apportioned may be demanded for each lot.

§2-308. Absence of Specified Place for Delivery. Unless otherwise agreed

(a) The place for delivery of goods is the seller's place of business or if he has none his residence; but
(b) in a contract for sale of identified goods which to the knowledge of the parties at the time of contracting are in some other place, that place is the place for their delivery; and
(c) documents of title may be delivered through customary banking channels.

§2-309. Absence of Specific Time Provisions; Notice of Termination.

(1) The time for shipment or delivery or any other action under a contract if not provided in this Article or agreed upon shall be a reasonable time.

(2) Where the contract provides for successive performances but is indefinite in duration it is valid for a reasonable time but unless otherwise agreed may be terminated at any time by either party.

(3) Termination of a contract by one party except on the happening of an agreed event requires that reasonable notification be received by the other party and an agreement dispensing with notification is invalid if its operation would be unconscionable.

§2-310. Open Time for Payment or Running of Credit; Authority to Ship Under Reservation. Unless otherwise agreed

(a) payment is due at the time and place at which the buyer is to receive the goods even though the place of shipment is the place of delivery; and
(b) if the seller is authorized to send the goods he may ship them under reservation, and may tender the documents of title, but the buyer may inspect the goods after their arrival before payment is due unless such inspection is inconsistent with the terms of the contract (Section 2-513); and
(c) f delivery is authorized and made by way of documents of title otherwise than by subsection (b) then payment is due at the time and place at which the buyer is to receive the documents regardless of where the goods are to be received; and
(d) where the seller is required or authorized to ship the goods on credit the credit period runs from the time of shipment but post-dating the invoice or delaying its dispatch will correspondingly delay the starting of the credit period.

§2-311. Options and Cooperation Respecting Performance.

(1) An agreement for sale which is otherwise sufficiently definite (subsection (3) of Section 2-204) to be a contract is not made invalid by the fact that it leaves particulars of performance to be specified by one of the parties. Any such specification must be made in good faith and within limits set by commercial reasonableness.

(2) Unless otherwise agreed specifications relating to assortment of the goods are at the buyer's option and except as otherwise provided in subsections (1)(c) and (3) of Section 2-319 specifications or arrangements relating to shipment are at the seller's option.

(3) Where such specifications would materially affect the other party's performance but is not seasonably made or where one party's cooperation is necessary to the agreed performance of the other but is not seasonably forthcoming, the other party

(a) is excused for any resulting delay in his own performance; and

(b) may also either proceed to perform in any reasonable manner or after the time for a material part of his own performance treat the failure to specify or to cooperate as a breach by failure to deliver or accept the goods.

§2-312. Warranty of Title and Against Infringement; Buyer's Obligation Against Infringement.

(1) Subject to subsection (2) there is in a contract for sale a warranty by the seller that

(a) the title conveyed shall be good, and its transfer rightful; and

(b) the goods shall be delivered free from any security interest or other lien or encumbrance of which the buyer at the time of contracting has no knowledge.

(2) A warranty under subsection (2) will be excluded or modified only by specific language or by circumstances which give the buyer reason to know that the person selling does not claim title in himself or that he is purporting to sell only such right or title as he or a third person may have.

(3) Unless otherwise agreed a seller who is a merchant regularly dealing in goods of the kind warrants that the goods shall be delivered free of the rightful claim of any third person by way of infringement or the like but a buyer who furnishes specifications to the seller must hold the seller harmless against any such claim which arises out of compliance with the specifications.

§2-313. Express Warranties by Affirmation, Promise, Description, Sample.

(1) Express warranties by the seller are created as follows:

(a) Any affirmation of fact or promise made by the seller to the buyer which relates to the goods and becomes part of the basis of the bargain creates an express warranty that the goods shall conform to the affirmation or promise.

(b) Any description of the goods which is made part of the basis of the bargain creates an express warranty that the goods shall conform to the description.

(c) Any sample or model which is made part of the basis of the bargain creates an express warranty that the whole of the goods shall conform to the sample or model.

(2) It is not necessary to the creation of an express warranty that the seller use formal words such as "warrant" or "guarantee" or that he have a specific intention to make a warranty, but an affirmation merely of the value of the goods or a statement purporting to be merely the seller's opinion or commendation of the goods does not create a warranty.

§2-314. Implied Warranty: Merchantability; Usage of Trade.

(1) Unless excluded or modified (Section 2-316), a warranty that the goods shall be merchantable is implied in a contract for their sale if the seller is a merchant with respect to goods of that kind. Under this section the serving for value of food or drink to be consumed either on the premises or elsewhere is a sale.

(2) Goods to be merchantable must be at least such as

(a) pass without objection in the trade under the contract description; and

(b) in the case of fungible goods, are of fair average quality within the description; and

(c) are fit for the ordinary purposes for which such goods are used; and

(d) run, within the variations permitted by the agreement, of even kind, quality and quantity within each unit and among all units involved; and

(e) are adequately contained, packaged, and labeled as the agreement may require; and

(f) conform to the promises or affirmations of fact made on the container or label if any.

(3) Unless excluded or modified (Section 2-316) other implied warranties may arise from course of dealing or usage of trade.

§2-315. Implied Warranty: Fitness for Particular Purpose.

Where the seller at the time of contracting has reason to know any particular purpose for which the goods are required and that the buyer is relying on the seller's skill or judgment to select or furnish suitable goods, there is unless excluded or modified under the next section an implied warranty that the goods shall be fit for such purpose.

§2-316. Exclusion or Modification of Warranties.

(1) Words or conduct relevant to the creation of an express warranty and words or conduct tending to negate or limit warranty shall be construed wherever reasonable as consistent with each other; but subject to the provisions of this Article on parol or extrinsic evidence (Section 2-202) negation or limitation is inoperative to the extent that such construction is unreasonable.

(2) Subject to subsection (3), to exclude or modify the implied warranty of merchantability or any part of it the language must mention merchantability and in case of a writing must be conspicuous, and to exclude or modify any implied warranty of fitness the exclusion must be by a writing and conspicuous. Language to exclude all implied warranties of fitness is sufficient if it states, for example, that "There are no warranties which extend beyond the description on the face hereof."

(3) Notwithstanding subsection (2)

(a) unless the circumstances indicate otherwise, all implied warranties are excluded by expressions like "as is", "with all faults" or other language which in common understanding calls the buyer's attention to the exclusion of warranties and makes plain that there is no implied warranty; and

(b) when the buyer before entering into the contract has examined the goods or the sample or model as fully as he desired or has refused to examine the goods there is no implied warranty with regard to defects which an examination ought in the circumstances to have revealed to him; and

(c) an implied warranty can also be excluded or modified by course of dealing or course of performance or usage of trade.

(4) Remedies for breach of warranty can be limited in accordance with the provisions of this Article on liquidation or limitation of damages and on contractual modification of remedy (Sections 2-718 and 2-719).

§2-317. Cumulation and Conflict of Warranties Express or Implied.

Warranties whether express or implied shall be construed as consistent with each other and as cumulative but if such construction is unreasonable the intention of the parties shall determine which warranty is dominant. In ascertaining that intention the following rules apply:

(a) Exact or technical specifications displace an inconsistent sample or model or general language of description.

(b) A sample from an existing bulk displaces inconsistent general language of description.

(c) Express warranties displace inconsistent implied warranties other than an implied warranty of fitness for a particular purpose.

§2-318. Third Party Beneficiaries of Warranties Express or Implied.

Note: *If this Act is introduced in the Congress of the United States this section should be omitted. (States to select one alternative.)*

Alternative A—A seller's warranty whether express or implied extends to any natural person who is in the family or household of his buyer or who is a guest in his home if it is reasonable to expect that such person may use, consume or be affected by the goods and who is injured in person by breach of the warranty. A seller may not exclude or limit the operation of this section.

Alternative B—A seller's warranty whether express or implied extends to any natural person who may reasonably be expected to use, consume or be affected by the goods and who is injured in person by breach of the warranty. A seller may not exclude or limit the operation of this section.

Alternative C—A seller's warranty whether express or implied extends to any person who may reasonably be expected to use, consume or be affected by the goods and who is injured by breach of the warranty. A seller may not exclude or limit the operation of this section with respect to injury to the person of an individual to whom the warranty extends. As amended 1966.

§2-319. F.O.B. and F.A.S. Terms.

(1) Unless otherwise agreed the term F.O.B. (which means "free on board") at a named place, even though used only in connection with the stated price, is a delivery term under which

(a) when the term is F.O.B. the place of shipment, the seller must at that place ship the goods in the manner provided in this Article (Section 2-504) and bear the expense and risk of putting them into the possession of the carrier; or

(b) when the term is F.O.B. the place of destination, the seller must at his own expense and risk transport the goods to that place and there tender delivery of them in the manner provided in this Article (Section 2-503);

(c) when under either (a) or (b) the term is also F.O.B. vessel, car or other vehicle, the seller must in addition at his own expense and risk load the goods on board. If the term is F.O.B. vessel the buyer must name the vessel and in an appropriate case the seller must comply with the provisions of this Article on the form of bill of lading (Section 2-323).

(2) Unless otherwise agreed the term F.A.S. vessel (which means "free alongside") at a named port, even though used only in connection with the stated price, is a delivery term under which the seller must

(a) at his own expense and risk deliver the goods alongside the vessel in the manner usual in that port or on a dock designated and provided by the buyer; and

(b) obtain and tender a receipt for the goods in exchange for which the carrier is under a duty to issue a bill of lading.

(3) Unless otherwise agreed in any case falling within subsection (1) (a) or (c) or subsection (2) the buyer must seasonably give any needed instructions for making delivery, including when the term is F.A.S. or F.O.B. the loading berth of the vessel and in an appropriate case its name and sailing date. The seller may treat the failure of needed instructions as a failure of cooperation under this Article (Section 2-311). He may also at his option move the goods in any reasonable manner preparatory to delivery or shipment.

(4) Under the term F.O.B. vessel or F.A.S. unless otherwise agreed the buyer must make payment against tender of the required documents and the seller may not tender nor the buyer demand delivery of the goods in substitution for the documents.

§2-320. C.I.F. and C.&F. Terms.

(1) The term C.I.F. means that the price includes in a lump sum the cost of the goods and the insurance and freight to the named destination. The term C.&F. or C.F. means that the price so includes cost and freight to the named destination.

(2) Unless otherwise agreed and even though used only in connection with the stated price and destination, the term C.I.F. destination or its equivalent requires the seller at his own expense and risk to

(a) put the goods into the possession of a carrier at the port for shipment and obtain a negotiable bill or bills of lading covering the entire transportation to the named destination; and

(b) load the goods and obtain a receipt from the carrier (which may be contained in the bill of lading) showing that the freight has been paid or provided for; and

(c) obtain a policy or certificate of insurance, including any war risk insurance, of a kind and on terms then current at the port of shipment in the usual amount, in the currency of the contract, shown to cover the same goods covered by the bill of lading and providing for payment of loss to the order of the buyer or for the account of whom it may concern; but the seller may add to the price the amount of the premium for any such war risk insurance; and

(d) prepare an invoice of the goods and procure any other documents required to effect shipment or to comply with the contract; and

(e) forward and tender with **commercial** promptness all the documents in due form and with any indorsement necessary to perfect the buyer's rights.

(3) Unless otherwise agreed the term C.&F. or its equivalent has the same effect and imposes upon the seller the same obligations and risks as a C.I.F. term except the obligation as to insurance.

(4) Under the term C.I.F. or C.&F. unless otherwise agreed the buyer must make payment against tender of the required documents and the seller may not tender nor the buyer demand delivery of the goods in substitution for the documents.

§2-321. C.I.F. or C.&F.: "Net Landed Weights"; "Payment on Arrival"; Warranty of Condition on Arrival.
Under a contract containing a term C.I.F. or C.&F.

(1) Where the price is based on or is to be adjusted according to "net landed weights", "delivered weights", "out turn" quantity or quality or the like, unless otherwise agreed the seller must reasonably estimate the price. The payment due on tender of the documents called for by the contract is the amount so estimated, but after final adjustment of the price a settlement must be made with commercial promptness.

(2) An agreement described in subsection (1) or any warranty of quality or condition of the goods on arrival places upon the seller the risk of ordinary deterioration, shrinkage and the like in transportation but has no effect on the place or time of identification to the contract for sale or delivery or on the passing of the risk of loss.

(3) Unless otherwise agreed where the contract provides for payment on or after arrival of the goods the seller must before payment allow such preliminary inspection as is feasible; but **if the goods are lost delivery of the documents and payment are due when the goods should have arrived.**

§2-322. Delivery "Ex-Ship".

(1) Unless otherwise agreed a term for delivery of goods "ex-ship" (which means from the carrying vessel) or in equivalent language is not restricted to a particular ship and requires delivery from a ship which has reached a place at the named port of destination where goods of the kind are usually discharged.

(2) Under such a term unless otherwise agreed

(a) the seller must discharge all liens arising out of the carriage and furnish the buyer with a direction which puts the carrier under a duty to deliver the goods; and

(b) the risk of loss does not pass to the buyer until the goods leave the ship's tackle or are otherwise properly unloaded.

§2-323. Form of Bill of Lading Required in Overseas Shipment; "Overseas".

(1) Where the contract contemplates overseas shipment and contains a term C.I.F. or C.&F. or F.O.B. vessel the seller unless otherwise agreed must obtain a negotiable bill of lading stating that the goods have been loaded on board or, in the case of a term C.I.F. or C.&F., received for shipment.

(2) Where in a case within subsection (1) a bill of lading has been issued in a set of parts, unless otherwise agreed if the documents are not to be sent from abroad the buyer may demand tender of the full set; otherwise only one part of the bill of lading need be tendered. Even if the agreement expressly requires a full set

(a) due tender of a single part is acceptable within the provisions of this Article on cure of improper delivery (subsection (1) of Section 2-508); and

(b) even though the full set is demanded, if the documents are sent from abroad the person tendering an incomplete set may nevertheless require payment upon furnishing an indemnity which the buyer in good faith deems adequate.

(3) A shipment by water or by air or a contract contemplating such shipment is "overseas" insofar as by usage of trade or agreement it is subject to the commercial, financing or shipping practices characteristic of international deep water commerce.

§2-324. "No Arrival, No Sale" Term.
Under a term "no arrival, no sale" or terms of like meaning, unless otherwise agreed,

(a) the seller must properly ship conforming goods and if they arrive by any means he must tender them on arrival but he assumes no obligation that the goods will arrive unless he has caused the nonarrival; and

(b) where without fault of the seller the goods are in part lost or have so deteriorated as no longer to conform to the contract or arrive after the contract time, the buyer may proceed as if there had been casualty to identified goods (Section 2-613).

§2-325. "Letter of Credit" Term; "Confirmed Credit".

(1) Failure of the buyer seasonably to furnish an agreed letter of credit is a breach of the contract for sale.

(2) The delivery to seller of a proper letter of credit suspends the buyer's obligation to pay. If the letter of credit is dishonored, the seller may on seasonable notification to the buyer require payment directly from him.

(3) Unless otherwise agreed the term "letter of credit" or "banker's credit" in a contract for sale means an irrevocable credit issued by a financing agency of good repute and, where the shipment is overseas, of good international repute. The term "confirmed credit" means that the credit must also carry the direct obligation of such an agency which does business in the seller's financial market.

§2-326. Sale on Approval and Sale or Return; Consignment Sales and Rights of Creditors.

(1) Unless otherwise agreed, if delivered goods may be returned by the buyer even though they conform to the contract, the transaction is

(a) a "sale on approval" if the goods are delivered primarily for use, and

(b) a "sale or return" if the goods are delivered primarily for resale.

(2) Except as provided in subsection (3), goods held on approval are not subject to the claims of the buyer's creditors until acceptance; goods held on sale or return are subject to such claims while in the buyer's possession.

(3) Where goods are delivered to a person for sale and such person maintains a place of business at which he deals in goods of the kind involved, under a name other than the name of the person making delivery, then with respect to claims of creditors of the person conducting the business the goods are deemed to be on sale or return. The provisions of this subsection are applicable even though an agreement purports to reserve title to the person making delivery until payment or resale or uses such words as "on consignment" or "on memorandum". However, this subsection is not applicable if the person making delivery

(a) complies with an applicable law providing for a consignor's interest or the like to be evidenced by a sign, or

(b) establishes that the person conducting the business is generally known by his creditors to be substantially engaged in selling the goods of others, or

(c) complies with the filing provisions of the Article on Secured Transactions (Article 9).

(4) Any "or return" term of a contract for sale is to be treated as a separate contract for sale within the statute of frauds section of this Article (Section 2-201) and as contradicting the sale aspect of the contract within the provisions of this Article on parol or extrinsic evidence (Section 2-202).

§2-327. Special Incidents of Sale on Approval and Sale or Return.

(1) Under a sale on approval unless otherwise agreed

(a) although the goods are identified to the contract the risk of loss and the title do not pass to the buyer until acceptance; and

(b) use of the goods consistent with the purpose of trial is not acceptance but failure seasonably to notify the seller of election to return the goods is acceptance, and if the goods conform to the contract acceptance of any part is acceptance of the whole; and

(c) after due notification of election to return, the return is at the seller's risk and expense but a merchant buyer must follow any reasonable instructions.

(2) Under a sale or return unless otherwise agreed

(a) the option to return extends to the whole or any commercial unit of the goods while in substantially their original condition, but must be exercised seasonably; and

(b) the return is at the buyer's risk and expense.

§2-328. Sale by Auction.

(1) In a sale by auction if goods are put up in lots each lot is the subject of a separate sale.

(2) A sale by auction is complete when the auctioneer so announces by the fall of the hammer or in other customary manner. Where a bid is made while the hammer is falling in acceptance of a prior bid the auctioneer may in his discretion reopen the bidding or declare the goods sold under the bid on which the hammer was falling.

(3) Such a sale is with reserve unless the goods are in explicit terms put up without reserve. In an auction with reserve, the auctioneer may withdraw the goods at any time until he announces completion of the sale. In an auction without reserve, after the auctioneer calls for bids on an article or lot, that article or lot cannot be withdrawn unless no bid is made within a reasonable time. In either case a bidder may retract his bid until the auctioneer's announcement of completion of the sale, but a bidder's retraction does not revive any previous bid.

(4) If the auctioneer knowingly receives a bid on the seller's behalf or the seller makes or procures such a bid, and notice has not been given that liberty for such bidding is reserved, the buyer may at his option avoid the sale or take the goods at the price of the last good faith bid prior to the completion of the sale. This subsection shall not apply to any bid at a forced sale.

Part 4: Title, Creditors and Good Faith Purchasers

§2-401. Passing of Title; Reservation for Security; Limited Application of This Section. Each provision of this Article with regard to the rights, obligations and remedies of the seller, the buyer, purchasers or other third parties applies irrespective of title to the goods except where the provision refers to such title. Insofar as situations are not covered by the other provisions of this Article and matters concerning title become material the following rules apply:

(1) Title to goods cannot pass under a contract for sale prior to their identification to the contract (Section 2-501), and unless otherwise explicitly agreed the buyer acquires by their identification a special property as limited by this Act. Any retention or reservation by the seller of the title (property) in goods shipped or delivered to the buyer is limited in effect to a reservation of a security interest. Subject to these provisions and to the provisions of the Article on Secured Transactions (Article 9), title to goods passes from the seller to the buyer in any manner and on any conditions explicitly agreed on by the parties.

(2) Unless otherwise explicitly agreed title passes to the buyer at the time and place at which the seller completes his performance with reference to the physical delivery of the goods, despite any reservation of a security interest and even though a document of title is to be delivered at a different time or place; and in particular and despite any reservation of a security interest by the bill of lading

(a) if the contract requires or authorizes the seller to send the goods to the buyer but does not require him to deliver them at destination, title passes to the buyer at the time and place of shipment; but

(b) if the contract requires delivery at destination, title passes on tender there.

(3) Unless otherwise explicitly agreed where delivery is to be made without moving the goods.

(a) if the seller is to deliver a document of title, title passes at the time when and the place where he delivers such documents; or

(b) if the goods are at the time of contracting already identified and no documents are to be delivered, title passes at the time and place of contracting.

(4) A rejection or other refusal by the buyer to receive or retain the goods, whether or not justified, or a justified revocation of acceptance revests title to the goods in the seller. Such revesting occurs by operation of law and is not a "sale".

§2-402. Rights of Seller's Creditors Against Sold Goods.

(1) Except as provided in subsections (2) and (3), rights of unsecured creditors of the seller with respect to goods which have been identified to a contract for sale are subject to the buyer's rights to recover the goods under this Article (Section 2-502 and 2-716).

(2) A creditor of the seller may treat a sale or an identification of goods to a contract for sale as void if as against him a retention of possession by the seller is fraudulent under any rule of law of the state where the goods are situated, except that retention of possession in good faith and current course of trade by a merchant-seller for a commercially reasonable time after a sale or identification is not fraudulent.

(3) Nothing in this Article shall be deemed to impair the rights of creditors of the seller

(a) under the provisions of the Article on Secured Transactions (Article 9); or

(b) where identification to the contract or delivery is made not in current course of trade but in satisfaction of or as security for a pre-existing claim for money, security or the like and is made under circumstances which under any rule of law of the state where the goods are situated would apart from this Article constitute the transaction a fraudulent transfer or voidable preference.

§2-403. Power to Transfer; Good Faith Purchase of Goods; "Entrusting".

(1) A purchaser of goods acquires all title which his transferor had or had power to transfer except that a purchaser of a limited interest acquires rights only to the extent of the interest purchased. A person with voidable title has power to transfer a good title to a good faith purchaser for value. When goods have been delivered under a transaction of purchase the purchaser had such power even though

(a) the transferor was deceived as to the identity of the purchaser, or

(b) the delivery was in exchange for a check which is later dishonored, or

(c) it was agreed that the transaction was to be a "cash sale", or

(d) the delivery was procured through fraud punishable as larcenous under the criminal law.

(2) Any entrusting of possession of goods to a merchant who deals in goods of that kind gives him power to transfer all rights of the entruster to a buyer in ordinary course of business.

(3) "Entrusting" includes any delivery and any acquiescence in retention of possession regardless of any condition expressed between the parties to the delivery or acquiescence and regardless of

whether the procurement of the entrusting or the possessor's disposition of the goods have been such as to be larcenous under the criminal law.

(4) The rights of other purchasers of goods and of lien creditors are governed by the Articles on Secured Transactions (Article 9), Bulk Transfers (Article 6) and Documents of Title (Article 7).

Part 5: Performance

§2-501. Insurable Interest in Goods; Manner of Identification of Goods.

(1) The buyer obtains a special property and an insurable interest in goods by identification of existing goods as goods to which the contract refers even though the goods so identified are non-conforming and he has an option to return or reject them. Such identification can be made at any time and in any manner explicitly agreed to by the parties. In the absence of explicit agreement identification occurs

(a) when the contract is made if it is for the sale of goods already existing and identified;

(b) if the contract is for the sale of future goods other than those described in paragraph (c), when goods are shipped, marked or otherwise designated by the seller as goods to which the contract refers;

(c) when the crops are planted or otherwise become growing crops or the young are conceived if the contract is for the sale of unborn young to be born within twelve months after contracting or for the sale of crops to be harvested within twelve months or the next normal harvest season after contracting whichever is longer.

(2) The seller retains an insurable interest in goods so long as title to or any security interest in the goods remains in him and where the identification is by the seller alone he may until default or insolvency or notification to the buyer that the identification is final substitute other goods for those identified.

(3) Nothing in this section impairs any insurable interest recognized under any other statute or rule of law.

§2-502. Buyer's Right to Goods on Seller's Insolvency.

(1) Subject to subsection (2) and even though the goods have not been shipped a buyer who has paid a part or all of the price of goods in which he has a special property under the provisions of the immediately preceding section may on making and keeping good a tender of any unpaid portion of their price recover them from the seller if the seller becomes insolvent within ten days after receipt of the first installment on their price.

(2) If the identification creating his special property has been made by the buyer he acquires the right to recover the goods only if they conform to the contract for sale.

§2-503. Manner of Seller's Tender of Delivery.

(1) Tender of delivery requires that the seller put and hold conforming goods at the buyer's disposition and give the buyer any notification reasonably necessary to enable him to take delivery. The manner, time and place for tender are determined by the agreement and this Article, and in particular

(a) tender must be at a reasonable hour, and if it is of goods they must be kept available for the period reasonably necessary to enable the buyer to take possession; but

(b) unless otherwise agreed the buyer must furnish facilities reasonably suited to the receipt of the goods.

(2) Where the case is within the next section respecting shipment tender requires that the seller comply with its provisions.

(3) Where the seller is required to deliver at a particular destination tender requires that he comply with subsection (1) and also in any appropriate case tender documents as described in subsections (4) and (5) of this section.

(4) Where goods are in the possession of a bailee and are to be delivered without being moved

(a) tender requires that the seller either tender a negotiable document of title covering such goods or procure acknowledgement by the bailee of the buyer's right to possession of the goods; but

(b) tender to the buyer of a non-negotiable document of title or of a written direction to the bailee to deliver is sufficient tender unless the buyer seasonably objects, and receipt by the bailee of notification of the buyer's rights fixes those rights as against the bailee and all third persons; but risk of loss of the goods and of any failure by the bailee to honor the non-negotiable document of title or to obey the direction remains on the seller until the buyer has had a reasonable time to present the document or direction, and a refusal by the bailee to honor the document or to obey the direction defeats the tender.

(5) Where the contract requires the seller to deliver documents

(a) he must tender all such documents in correct form, except as provided in this Article with respect to bills of lading in a set (subsection (2) of Section 2-323); and

(b) tender through customary banking channels is sufficient and dishonor of a draft accompanying the documents constitutes non-acceptance or rejection.

§2-504. Shipment by Seller.

Where the seller is required or authorized to send the goods to the buyer and the contract does not require him to deliver them at a particular destination, then unless otherwise agreed he must

(a) put the goods in the possession of such a carrier and make such a contract for their transportation as may be reasonable having regard to the nature of the goods and other circumstances of the case; and

(b) obtain and promptly deliver or tender in due form any document necessary to enable the buyer to obtain possession of the goods or otherwise required by the agreement or by usage of trade; and

(c) promptly notify the buyer of the shipment. Failure to notify the buyer under paragraph (c) or to make a proper contract under paragraph (a) is a ground for rejection only if material delay or loss ensues.

§2-505. Seller's Shipment under Reservation.

(1) Where the seller has identified goods to the contract by or before shipment:

(a) his procurement of a negotiable bill of lading to his own order or otherwise reserves in him a security interest in the goods. His procurement of the bill to the order of a financing agency or of the buyer indicates in addition only the seller's expectation of transferring that interest to the person named.

(b) a non-negotiable bill of lading to himself or his nominee reserves possession of the goods as security but except in a case of conditional delivery (subsection (2) of Section 2-507) a non-negotiable bill of lading naming the buyer as consignee reserves no security interest even though the seller retains possession of the bill of lading.

(2) When shipment by the seller with reservation of a security interest is in violation of the contract for sale it constitutes an improper contract for transportation within the preceding section but impairs neither the rights given to the buyer by shipment and identification of the goods to the contract nor the seller's powers as a holder of a negotiable document.

§2-506. Rights of Financing Agency.

(1) A financing agency by paying or purchasing for value a draft which relates to a shipment of goods acquires to the extent of the payment or purchase and in addition to its own rights under the draft and any document of title securing it any rights of the shipper in the goods including the right to stop delivery and the shipper's right to have the draft honored by the buyer.

(2) The right to reimbursement of a financing agency which has in good faith honored or purchased the draft under commitment to or authority from the buyer is not impaired by subsequent discovery of defects with reference to any relevant document which was apparently regular on its face.

§2-507. Effect of Seller's Tender; Delivery on Condition.

(1) Tender of delivery is a condition to the buyer's duty to accept the goods and, unless otherwise agreed, to his duty to pay for them. Tender entitles the seller to acceptance of the goods and to payment according to the contract.

(2) Where payment is due and demanded on the delivery to the buyer of goods or documents of title, his right as against the seller to retain or dispose of them is conditional upon his making the payment due.

§2-508. Cure by Seller of Improper Tender or Delivery; Replacement.

(1) Where any tender or delivery by the seller is rejected because non-conforming and the time for performance has not yet expired, the seller may seasonably notify the buyer of his intention to cure and may then within the contract time make a conforming delivery.

(2) Where the buyer rejects a non-conforming tender which the seller had reasonable grounds to believe would be acceptable with or without money allowance the seller may if he seasonably notifies the buyer have a further reasonable time to substitute a conforming tender.

§2-509. Risk of Loss in the Absence of Breach.

(1) Where the contract requires or authorizes the seller to ship the goods by carrier

(a) if it does not require him to deliver them at a particular destination, the risk of loss passes to the buyer when the goods are duly delivered to the carrier even though the shipment is under reservation (Section 2-505); but
(b) if it does require him to deliver them at a particular destination and the goods are there duly tendered while in the possession of the carrier, the risk of loss passes to the buyer when the goods are there duly so tendered as to enable the buyer to take delivery.

(2) Where the goods are held by a bailee to be delivered without being moved, the risk of loss passes to the buyer

(a) on his receipt of a negotiable document of title covering the goods; or
(b) on acknowledgement by the bailee of the buyer's right to possession of the goods; or
(c) after his receipt of a non-negotiable document of title or other written direction to deliver, as provided in subsection (4)(b) of Section 2-503.

(3) In any case not within subsection (1) or (2), the risk of loss passes to the buyer on his receipt of the goods if the seller is a merchant; otherwise the risk passes to the buyer on tender of delivery.

(4) The provisions of this section are subject to contrary agreement of the parties and to the provisions of this Article on sale on approval (Section 2-327) and on effect of breach on risk of loss (Section 2-510).

§2-510. Effect of Breach on Risk of Loss.

(1) Where a tender or delivery of goods so fails to conform to the contract as to give a right of rejection the risk of their loss remains on the seller until cure or acceptance.

(2) Where the buyer rightfully revokes acceptance he may to the extent of any deficiency in his effective insurance coverage treat the risk of loss as having rested on the seller from the beginning.

(3) Where the buyer as to conforming goods already identified to the contract for sale repudiates or is otherwise in breach before risk of their loss has passed to him, the seller may to the extent of any deficiency in his effective insurance coverage treat the risk of loss as resting on the buyer for a commercially reasonable time.

§2-511. Tender of Payment by Buyer; Payment by Check.

(1) Unless otherwise agreed tender of payment is a condition to the seller's duty to tender and complete any delivery.

(2) Tender of payment is sufficient when made by any means or in any manner current in the ordinary course of business unless the seller demands payment in legal tender and gives any extension of time reasonably necessary to procure it.

(3) Subject to the provisions of this Act on the effect of an instrument on an obligation (Section 3-802), payment by check is conditional and is defeated as between the parties by dishonor of the check on due presentment.

§2-512. Payment by Buyer Before Inspection.

(1) Where the contract requires payment before inspection non-conformity of the goods does not excuse the buyer from so making payment unless

(a) the non-conformity appears without inspection; or
(b) despite tender of the required documents the circumstances would justify injunction against honor under the provisions of this Act (Section 5-114).

(2) Payment pursuant to subsection (1) does not constitute an acceptance of goods or impair the buyer's right to inspect or any of his remedies.

§2-513. Buyer's Right to Inspection of Goods.

(1) Unless otherwise agreed and subject to subsection (3), where goods are tendered or delivered or identified to the contract for sale, the buyer has a right before payment or acceptance to inspect them at any reasonable place and time and in any reasonable manner. When the seller is required or authorized to send the goods to the buyer, the inspection may be after their arrival.

(2) Expenses of inspection must be borne by the buyer but may be recovered from the seller if the goods do not conform and are rejected.

(3) Unless otherwise agreed and subject to the provisions of this Article on C.I.F. contracts (subsection (3) of Section 3-221), the buyer is not entitled to inspect the goods before payment of the price when the contract provides

(a) for delivery "C.O.D." or on other like terms; or
(b) for payment against documents of title, except where such payment is due only after the goods are to become available for inspection.

(4) A place or method of inspection fixed by the parties is presumed to be exclusive but unless otherwise expressly agreed it does not postpone identification or shift the place for delivery or for passing the risk of loss. If compliance becomes impossible, inspection shall be as provided in this section unless the place or method fixed was clearly intended as an indispensable condition failure of which avoids the contract.

§2-514. When Documents Deliverable on Acceptance; When on Payment. Unless otherwise agreed documents against which a draft is drawn are to be delivered to the drawee on acceptance of the draft if it is payable more than three days after presentment; otherwise, only on payment.

§2-515. Preserving Evidence of Goods in Dispute. In furtherance of the adjustment of any claim or dispute

(a) either party on reasonable notification to the other and for the purpose of ascertaining the facts and preserving evidence has the right to inspect, test and sample the goods including such of them as may be in the possession or control of the other; and

(b) the parties may agree to a third party inspection or survey to determine the conformity or condition of the goods and may agree that the findings shall be binding upon them in any subsequent litigation or adjustment.

Part 6: Breach, Repudiation and Excuse

§2-601. Buyer's Rights on Improper Delivery. Subject to the provisions of this Article on breach in installment contracts (Section 2-612) and unless otherwise agreed under the sections on contractual limitations of remedy (Sections 2-718 and 2-719), if the goods or the tender of delivery fail in any respect to conform to the contract, the buyer may

(a) reject the whole; or
(b) accept the whole; or
(c) accept any commercial unit or units and reject the rest.

§2-602. Manner and Effect of Rightful Rejection.

(1) Rejection of goods must be within a reasonable time after their delivery or tender. It is ineffective unless the buyer seasonably notifies the seller.

(2) Subject to the provisions of the two following sections on rejected goods (Section 2-603 and 2-604),

(a) after rejection any exercise of ownership by the buyer with respect to any commercial unit is wrongful as against the seller; and

(b) if the buyer has before rejection taken physical possession of goods in which he does not have a security interest under the provisions of this Article (subsection (3) of Section 2-711), he is under a duty after rejection to hold them with reasonable care at the seller's disposition for a time sufficient to permit the seller to remove them; but

(c) the buyer has no further obligations with regard to goods rightfully rejected.

(3) The seller's rights with respect to goods wrongfully rejected are governed by the provisions of this Article on Seller's remedies in general (Section 2-703).

§2-603. Merchant Buyer's Duties as to Rightfully Rejected Goods.

(1) Subject to any security interest in the buyer (subsection (3) of Section 2-711), when the seller has no agent or place of business at the market of rejection a merchant buyer is under a duty after rejection of goods in his possession or control to follow any reasonable instructions received from the seller with respect to the goods and in the absence of such instructions to make reasonable efforts to sell them for the seller's account if they are perishable or threaten to decline in value speedily. Instructions are not reasonable if on demand indemnity for expenses is not forthcoming.

(2) When the buyer sells goods under subsection (1), he is entitled to reimbursement from the seller or out of the proceeds for reasonable expenses of caring for and selling them, and if the expenses include no selling commission then to such commission as is usual in the trade or if there is none to a reasonable sum not exceeding ten per cent on the gross proceeds.

(3) In complying with this section the buyer is held only to good faith and good faith conduct hereunder is neither acceptance nor conversion nor the basis of an action for damages.

§2-604. Buyer's Options as to Salvage of Rightfully Rejected Goods. Subject to the provisions of the immediately preceding section on perishables if the seller gives no instructions within a reasonable time after notification of rejection the buyer may store the rejected goods for the seller's account or reship them to him or resell them for the seller's account with reimbursement as provided in the preceding section. Such action is not acceptance or conversion.

§2-605. Waiver of Buyer's Objections by Failure to Particularize.

(1) The buyer's failure to state in connection with rejection a particular defect which is ascertainable by reasonable inspection precludes him from relying on the unstated defect to justify rejection or to establish breach

(a) where the seller could have cured it if stated seasonably; or
(b) between merchants when the seller has after rejection made a request in writing for a full and final written statement of all defects on which the buyer proposes to rely.

(2) Payment against documents made without reservation of rights precludes recovery of the payment for defects apparent on the face of the documents.

§2-606. What Constitutes Acceptance of Goods.

(1) Acceptance of goods occurs when the buyer

(a) after a reasonable opportunity to inspect the goods signifies to the seller that the goods are conforming or that he will take or retain them in spite of their non-conformity; or

(b) fails to make an effective rejection (subsection (1) of Section 2-602), but such acceptance does not occur until the buyer has had a reasonable opportunity to inspect them; or

(c) does any act inconsistent with the seller's ownership; but if such act is wrongful as against the seller it is an acceptance only if ratified by him.

(2) Acceptance of a part of any commercial unit is acceptance of that entire unit.

§2-607. Effect of Acceptance; Notice of Breach; Burden of Establishing Breach After Acceptance; Notice of Claim or Litigation to Person Answerable Over.

(1) The buyer must pay at the contract rate for any goods accepted.

(2) Acceptance of goods by the buyer precludes rejection of the goods accepted and if made with knowledge of a nonconformity cannot be revoked because of it unless the acceptance was on the

reasonable assumption that the non-conformity would be seasonably cured but acceptance does not of itself impair any other remedy provided by this Article for non-conformity.

(3) Where a tender has been accepted

(a) the buyer must within a reasonable time after he discovers or should have discovered any breach notify the seller of breach or be barred from any remedy; and

(b) if the claim is one for infringement or the like (subsection (3) of Section 2-312) and the buyer is sued as a result of such a breach he must so notify the seller within a reasonable time after he receives notice of the litigation or be barred from any remedy over for liability established by the litigation.

(4) The burden is on the buyer to establish any breach with respect to the goods accepted.

(5) Where the buyer is sued for breach of a warranty or other obligation for which his seller is answerable over

(a) he may give his seller written notice of the litigation. If the notice states that the seller may come in and defend and that if the seller does not do so he will be bound in any action against him by his buyer by any determination of fact common to the two litigations, then unless the seller after seasonable receipt of the notice does come in and defend he is so bound.

(b) if the claim is one for infringement or the like (subsection (3) of Section 2-312) the original seller may demand in writing that his buyer turn over to him control of the litigation including settlement or else be barred from any remedy over and if he also agrees to bear all expense and to satisfy any adverse judgment, then unless the buyer after seasonable receipt of the demand does turn over control the buyer is so barred.

(6) The provisions of subsection (3), (4) and (5) apply to any obligation of a buyer to hold the seller harmless against infringement or the like (subsection (3) of Section 2-312).

§2-608. Revocation of Acceptance in Whole or in Part.

(1) The buyer may revoke his acceptance of a lot or commercial unit whose non-conformity substantially impairs its value to him if he has accepted it

(a) on the reasonable assumption that its non-conformity would be cured and it has not been seasonably cured; or

(b) without discovery of such non-conformity if his acceptance was reasonably induced either by the difficulty of discovery before acceptance or by the seller's assurances.

(2) Revocation of acceptance must occur within a reasonable time after the buyer discovers or should have discovered the ground for it and before any substantial change in condition of the goods which is not caused by their own defects. It is not effective until the buyer notifies the seller of it.

(3) A buyer who so revokes has the same rights and duties with regard to the goods involved as if he had rejected them.

§2-609. Right to Adequate Assurance of Performance.

(1) A contract for sale imposes an obligation on each party that the other's expectation of receiving due performance will not be impaired. When reasonable grounds for insecurity arise with respect to the performance of either party the other may in writing demand adequate assurance of due performance and until he receives such assurance may if commercially reasonable suspend any performance for which he has not already received the agreed return.

(2) Between merchants the reasonableness of grounds for insecurity and the adequacy of any assurance offered shall be determined according to commercial standards.

(3) Acceptance of any improper delivery or payment does not prejudice the aggrieved party's right to demand adequate assurance of future performance.

(4) After receipt of a justified demand failure to provide within a reasonable time not exceeding thirty days such assurance of due performance as is adequate under the circumstances of the particular case is a repudiation of the contract.

§2-610. Anticipatory Repudiation. When either party repudiates the contract with respect to a performance not yet due the loss of which will substantially impair the value of the contract to the other, the aggrieved party may

(a) for a commercially reasonable time await performance by the repudiating party; or

(b) resort to any remedy for breach (Section 2-703 or Section 2-711), even though he has notified the repudiating party that he would await the latter's performance and has urged retraction; and

(c) in either case suspend his own performance or proceed in accordance with the provisions of this Article on the seller's right to identify goods to the contract notwithstanding breach or to salvage unfinished goods (Section 2-704).

§2-611. Retraction of Anticipatory Repudiation.

(1) Until the repudiating party's next performance is due he can retract his repudiation unless the aggrieved party has since the repudiation cancelled or materially changed his position or otherwise indicated that he considers the repudiation final.

(2) Retraction may be by any method which clearly indicates to the aggrieved party that the repudiating party intends to perform, but must include any assurance justifiably demanded under the provisions of this Article (Section 2-609).

(3) Retraction reinstates the repudiating party's rights under the contract with due excuse and allowance to the aggrieved party for any delay occasioned by the repudiation.

§2-612. "Installment Contract"; Breach.

(1) An "installment contract" is one which requires or authorizes the delivery of goods in separate lots to be separately accepted, even though the contract contains a clause "each delivery is a separate contract" or its equivalent.

(2) The buyer may reject any installment which is non-conforming if the non-conformity substantially impairs the value of that installment and cannot be cured or if the non-conformity is a defect in the required documents; but if the non-conformity does not fall within subsection (3) and the seller gives adequate assurance of its cure the buyer must accept that installment.

(3) . Whenever non-conformity or default with respect to one or more installments substantially impairs the value of the whole contract there is a breach of the whole. But the aggrieved party reinstates the contract if he accepts a non-conforming installment without seasonably notifying of cancellation or if he brings an action with respect only to past installments or demands performance as to future installments.

§2-613. Casualty to Identified Goods. Where the contract requires for its performance goods identified when the contract is made, and the goods suffer casualty without fault of either party before the risk of loss passes to the buyer, or in a proper case under a "no arrival, no sale" term (Section 2-324) then

(a) if the loss is total the contract is avoided; and
(b) if the loss is partial or the goods have so deteriorated as no longer to conform to the contract the buyer may nevertheless demand inspection and at his option either treat the contract as avoided or accept the goods with due allowance from the contract price for the deterioration or the deficiency in quantity but without further right against the seller.

§2-614. Substituted Performance.
(1) Where without fault of either party the agreed berthing, loading, or unloading facilities fail or an agreed type of carrier becomes unavailable or the agreed manner of delivery otherwise becomes commercially impracticable but a commercially reasonable substitute is available, such substitute performance must be tendered and accepted.
(2) If the agreed means or manner of payment fails because of domestic or foreign governmental regulation, the seller may withhold or stop delivery unless the buyer provides a means or manner of payment which is commercially a substantial equivalent. If delivery has already been taken, payment by the means or in the manner provided by the regulation discharges the buyer's obligation unless the regulation is discriminatory, oppressive or predatory.

§2-615. Excuse by Failure of Presupposed Conditions. Except so far as a seller may have assumed a greater obligation and subject to the preceding section on substituted performance:
(a) Delay in delivery or non-delivery in whole or in part by a seller who complies with paragraphs (b) and (c) is not a breach of his duty under a contract for sale if performance as agreed has been made impracticable by the occurrence of a contingency the non-occurrence of which was a basic assumption on which the contract was made or by compliance in good faith with any applicable foreign or domestic governmental regulation or order whether or not it later proves to be invalid.
(b) Where the causes mentioned in paragraph (a) affect only a part of the seller's capacity to perform, he must allocate production and deliveries among his customers but may at his option include regular customers not then under contract as well as his own requirements for further manufacture. He may so allocate in any manner which is fair and reasonable.
(c) The seller must notify the buyer seasonably that there will be delay or non-delivery and, when allocation is required under paragraph (b), of the estimated quota thus made available for the buyer.

§2-616. Procedure on Notice Claiming Excuse.
(1) When the buyer receives notification of a material or indefinite delay or an allocation justified under the preceding section he may by written notification to the seller as to any delivery concerned, and where the prospective deficiency substantially impairs the value of the whole contract under the provisions of this Article relating to breach of installment contracts (Section 2-612), then also as to the whole,
(a) terminate and thereby discharge any unexecuted portion of the contract; or
(b) modify the contract by agreeing to take his available quota in substitution.
(2) If after receipt of such notification from the seller the buyer fails so to modify the contract within a reasonable time not exceeding thirty days the contract lapses with respect to any deliveries affected.
(3) The provisions of this section may not be negated by agreement except in so far as the seller has assumed a greater obligation under the preceding section.

Part 7: Remedies

§2-701. Remedies for Breach of Collateral Contracts Not Impaired. Remedies for breach of any obligation or promise collateral or ancillary to a contract for sale are not impaired by the provisions of this Article.

§2-702. Seller's Remedies on Discovery of Buyer's Insolvency.
(1) Where the seller discovers the buyer to be insolvent he may refuse delivery except for cash including payment for all goods theretofore delivered under the contract, and stop delivery under this Article (Section 2-705).
(2) Where the seller discovers that the buyer has received goods on credit while insolvent he may reclaim the goods upon demand made within ten days after the receipt, but if misrepresentation of solvency has been made to the particular seller in writing within three months before delivery the ten day limitation does not apply. Except as provided in this subsection the seller may not base a right to reclaim goods on the buyer's fraudulent or innocent misrepresentation of solvency or of intent to pay.
(3) The seller's right to reclaim under subsection (2) is subject to the rights of a buyer in ordinary course or other good faith purchaser under this Article (Section 2-403). Successful reclamation of goods excludes all other remedies with respect to them. As amended 1966.

§2-703. Seller's Remedies in General. Where the buyer wrongfully rejects or revokes acceptance of goods or fails to make a payment due on or before delivery or repudiates with respect to a part or the whole, then with respect to any goods directly affected and, if the breach is of the whole contract (Section 2-612), then also with respect to the whole undelivered balance, the aggrieved seller may
(a) withhold delivery of such goods;
(b) stop delivery by any bailee as hereafter provided (Section 2-705);
(c) proceed under the next section respecting goods still unidentified to the contract;
(d) resell and recover damages as hereafter provided (Section 2-706);
(e) recover damages for non-acceptance (Section 2-708) or in a proper case the price (Section 2-709);
(f) cancel.

§2-704. Seller's Right to Identify Goods to the Contract Notwithstanding Breach or to Salvage Unfinished Goods.
(1) An aggrieved seller under the preceding section may
(a) identify to the contract conforming goods not already identified if at the time he learned of the breach they are in his possession or control;
(b) treat as the subject of resale goods which have demonstrably been intended for the particular contract even though those goods are unfinished.
(2) Where the goods are unfinished an aggrieved seller may in the exercise of reasonable commercial judgment for the purposes of avoiding loss and of effective realization either complete the manufacture and wholly identify the goods to the contract or cease manufacture and resell for scrap or salvage value or proceed in any other reasonable manner.

§2-705. Seller's Stoppage of Delivery in Transit or Otherwise.
(1) The seller may stop delivery of goods in the possession of a carrier or other bailee when he discovers the buyer to be insolvent (Section 2-702) and may stop delivery of carload, truckload, planeload or larger shipments of express or freight when the buyer

repudiates or fails to make a payment due before delivery or if for any other reason the seller has a right to withold or reclaim the goods.

(2) As against such buyer the seller may stop delivery until

(a) receipt of the goods by the buyer; or
(b) acknowledgement to the buyer by any bailee of the goods except a carrier that the bailee holds the goods for the buyer; or
(c) such acknowledgement to the buyer by a carrier by reshipment or as warehouseman; or
(d) negotiation to the buyer of any negotiable document of title covering the goods.

(3)

(a) To stop delivery the seller must so notify as to enable the bailee by reasonable diligence to prevent delivery of the goods.
(b) After such notification the bailee must hold and deliver the goods according to the directions of the seller but the seller is liable to the bailee for any ensuing charges or damages.
(c) If a negotiable document of title has been issued for goods the bailee is not obliged to obey a notification to stop until surrender of the document.
(d) A carrier who has issued a non-negotiable bill of lading is not obliged to obey a notification to stop received from a person other than the consignor.

§2-706. Seller's Resale Including Contract for Resale.

(1) Under the conditions stated in Section 2-703 on seller's remedies, the seller may resell the goods concerned or the undelivered balance thereof. Where the resale is made in good faith and in a commercially reasonable manner the seller may recover the difference between the resale price and the contract price together with any incidental damages allowed under the provisions of this Article (Section 2-710), but less expenses saved in consequence of the buyer's breach.

(2) Except as otherwise provided in subsection (3) or unless otherwise agreed resale may be at public or private sale including sale by way of one or more contracts to sell or of identification to an existing contract of the seller. Sale may be as a unit or in parcels and at any time and place and on any terms but every aspect of the sale including the method, manner, time, place and terms must be commercially reasonable. The resale must be reasonably identified as referring to the broken contract, but it is not necessary that the goods be in existence or that any or all of them have been identified to the contract before the breach.

(3) Where the resale is at private sale the seller must give the buyer reasonable notification of his intention to resell.

(4) Where the resale is at public sale

(a) only identified goods can be sold except where there is a recognized market for a public sale of futures in goods of the kind; and
(b) it must be made at a usual place or market for public sale if one is reasonably available and except in the case of goods which are perishable or threaten to decline in value speedily the seller must give the buyer reasonable notice of the time and place of the resale; and
(c) if the goods are not to be within the view of those attending the sale the notification of sale must state the place where the goods are located and provide for their reasonable inspection by prospective bidders; and
(d) the seller may buy.

(5) A purchaser who buys in good faith at a resale takes the goods free of any rights of the original buyer even though the seller fails to comply with one or more of the requirements of this section.

(6) The seller is not accountable to the buyer for any profit made on any resale. A person in the position of a seller (Section 2-707) or a buyer who has rightfully rejected or justifiably revoked acceptance must account for any excess over the amount of his security interest, as hereinafter defined (subsection (3) of Section 2-711).

§2-707. "Person in the Position of a Seller".

(1) A "person in the position of a seller" includes as against a principal an agent who has paid or become responsible for the price of goods on behalf of his principal or anyone who otherwise holds a security interest or other right in goods similar to that of a seller.

(2) A person in the position of a seller may as provided in this Article withhold or stop delivery (Section 2-705) and resell (Section 2-706) and recover incidental damages (Section 2-710).

§2-708. Seller's Damages for Non-acceptance or Repudiation.

(1) Subject to subsection (2) and to the provisions of this Article with respect to proof of market price (Section 2-723), the measure of damages for non-acceptance or repudiation by the buyer is the difference between the market price at the time and place for tender and the unpaid contract price together with any incidental damages provided in this Article (Section 2-710), but less expenses saved in consequence of the buyer's breach.

(2) If the measure of damages provided in subsection (1) is inadequate to put the seller in as good a position as performance would have done then the measure of damages is the profit (including reasonable overhead) which the seller would have made from full performance by the buyer, together with any incidental damages provided in this Article (Section 2-710), due allowance for costs reasonably incurred and due credit for payments or proceeds of resale.

§2-709. Action for the Price.

(1) When the buyer fails to pay the price as it becomes due the seller may recover, together with any incidental damages under the next section, the price

(a) of goods accepted or of conforming goods lost or damaged within a commercially reasonable time after risk of their loss has passed to the buyer; and
(b) of goods identified to the contract if the seller is unable after reasonable effort to resell them at a reasonable price or the circumstances reasonably indicate that such effort will be unavailing.

(2) Where the seller sues for the price he must hold for the buyer any goods which have been identified to the contract and are still in his control except that if resale becomes possible he may resell them at any time prior to the collection of the judgment. The net proceeds of any such resale must be credited to the buyer and payment of the judgment entitles him to any goods not resold.

(3) After the buyer has wrongfully rejected or revoked acceptance of the goods or has failed to make a payment due or has repudiated (Section 2-610), a seller who is held not entitled to the price under this section shall nevertheless be awarded damages for non-acceptance under the preceding section.

§2-710. Seller's Incidental Damages.
Incidental damages to an aggrieved seller include any commercially reasonable charges, ex-

penses or commissions incurred in stopping delivery, in the transportation, care and custody of goods after the buyer's breach, in connection with return or resale of the goods or otherwise resulting from the breach.

§2-711. Buyer's Remedies in General; Buyer's Security Interest in Rejected Goods.

(1) When the seller fails to make delivery or repudiates or the buyer rightfully rejects or justifiably revokes acceptance then with respect to any goods involved, and with respect to the whole if the breach goes to the whole contract (Section 2-612), the buyer may cancel and whether or not he has done so may in addition to recovering so much of the price as has been paid

   (a) "cover" and have damages under the next section as to all the goods affected whether or not they have been identified to the contract; or
   (b) recover damages for non-delivery as provided in this Article (Section 2-713).

(2) Where the seller fails to deliver or repudiates the buyer may also

   (a) if the goods have been identified recover them as provided in this Article (Section 2-502); or
   (b) in a proper case obtain specific performance or replevy the goods as provided in this Article (Section 2-716).

(3) On rightful rejection or justifiable revocation of acceptance a buyer has a security interest in goods in his possession or control for any payments made on their price and any expenses reasonably incurred in their inspection, receipt, transportation, care and custody and may hold such goods and resell them in like manner as an aggrieved seller (Section 2-706).

§2-712. "Cover"; Buyer's Procurement of Substitute Goods.

(1) After a breach within the preceding section the buyer may "cover" by making in good faith and without unreasonable delay any reasonable purchase of or contract to purchase goods in substitution for those due from the seller.

(2) The buyer may recover from the seller as damages the difference between the cost of cover and the contract price together with any incidental or consequential damages as hereinafter defined (Section 2-715), but less expenses saved in consequence of the seller's breach.

(3) Failure of the buyer to effect cover within this section does not bar him from any other remedy.

§2-713. Buyer's Damages for Non-Delivery or Repudiation.

(1) Subject to the provisions of this Article with respect to proof of market price (Section 2-723), the measure of damages for non-delivery or repudiation by the seller is the difference between the market price at the time when the buyer learned of the breach and the contract price together with any incidental and consequential damages provided in this Article (Section 2-715), but less expenses saved in consequence of the seller's breach.

(2) Market price is to be determined as of the place for tender or, in cases of rejection after arrival or revocation of acceptance, as of the place of arrival.

§2-714. Buyer's Damages for Breach in Regard to Accepted Goods.

(1) Where the buyer has accepted goods and given notification (subsection (3) Section 2-607) he may recover as damages for any non-conformity of tender the loss resulting in the ordinary course of events from the seller's breach as determined in any manner which is reasonable.

(2) The measure of damages for breach of warranty is the difference at the time and place of acceptance between the value of the goods accepted and the value they would have had if they had been as warranted, unless special circumstances show proximate damages of a different amount.

(3) In a proper case any incidental and consequential damages under the next section may also be recovered.

§2-715. Buyer's Incidental and Consequential Damages.

(1) Incidental damages resulting from the seller's breach include expenses reasonably incurred in inspection, receipt, transportation and care and custody of goods rightfully rejected, any commercially reasonable charges, expenses or commissions in connection with effecting cover and any other reasonable expense incident to the delay or other breach.

(2) Consequential damages resulting from the seller's breach include

   (a) any loss resulting from general or particular requirements and needs of which the seller at the time of contracting had reason to know and which could not reasonably be prevented by cover or otherwise; and
   (b) injury to person or property proximately resulting from any breach of warranty.

§2-716. Buyer's Right to Specific Performance or Replevin.

(1) Specific performance may be decreed where the goods are unique or in other proper circumstances.

(2) The decree for specific performance may include such terms and conditions as to payment of the price, damages, or other relief as the court may deem just.

(3) The buyer has a right of replevin for goods identified to the contract if after reasonable effort he is unable to effect cover for such goods or the circumstances reasonably indicate that such effort will be unavailing or if the goods have been shipped under reservation and satisfaction of the security interest in them has been made or tendered.

§2-717. Deduction of Damages From the Price.
The buyer on notifying the seller of his intention to do so may deduct all or any part of the damages resulting from any breach of the contract from any part of the price still due under the same contract.

§2-718. Liquidation or Limitation of Damages; Deposits.

(1) Damages for breach by either party may be liquidated in the agreement but only at an amount which is reasonable in the light of the anticipated or actual harm caused by the breach, the difficulties of proof of loss, and the inconvenience or nonfeasibility of otherwise obtaining an adequate remedy. A term fixing unreasonably large liquidated damages is void as a penalty.

(2) Where the seller justifiably withholds delivery of goods because of the buyer's breach, the buyer is entitled to restitution of any amount by which the sum of his payments exceeds

   (a) the amount to which the seller is entitled by virtue of terms liquidating the seller's damages in accordance with subsection (1), or
   (b) in the absence of such terms, twenty per cent of the value of the total performance for which the buyer is obligated under the contract or $500, whichever is smaller.

(3) The buyer's right to restitution under subsection (2) is subject to offset to the extent that the seller establishes

   (a) a right to recover damages under the provisions of this article other than subsection (1), and
   (b) the amount or value of any benefits received by the buyer directly or indirectly by reason of the contract.

(4) where a seller has received payment in goods their reasonable value or the proceeds of their resale shall be treated as payments for the purposes of subsection (2); but if the seller has notice of the buyer's breach before reselling goods received in part performance, his resale is subject to the conditions laid down in this Article on resale by an aggrieved seller (Section 2-706).

§2-719. Contractual Modification or Limitation of Remedy.
(1) Subject to the provisions of subsections (2) and (3) of this section and of the preceding section on liquidation and limitation of damages,

(a) the agreement may provide for remedies in addition to or in substitution for those provided in this Article and may limit or alter the measure of damages recoverable under this Article, as by limiting the buyer's remedies to return of the goods and repayment of the price or to repair and replacement of non-conforming goods or parts; and

(b) resort to a remedy as provided is optional unless the remedy is expressly agreed to be exclusive, in which case it is the sole remedy.

(2) Where circumstances cause an exclusive or limited remedy to fail of its essential purpose, remedy may be had as provided in this Act.

(3) Consequential damages may be limited or excluded unless the limitation or exclusion is unconscionable. Limitation of consequential damages for injury to the person in the case of consumer goods is prima facie unconscionable but limitation of damages where the loss is commercial is not.

§2-720. Effect of "Cancellation" or "Rescission" on Claims for Antecedent Breach. Unless the contrary intention clearly appears, expressions of "cancellation" or "rescission" of the contract or the like shall not be construed as a renunciation or discharge of any claim in damages for an antecedent breach.

§2-721. Remedies for Fraud. Remedies for material misrepresentation or fraud include all remedies available under this Article for non-fraudulent breach. Neither rescission or a claim for rescission of the contract for sale nor rejection or return of the goods shall bar or be deemed inconsistent with a claim for damages or other remedy.

§2-722. Who Can Sue Third Parties for Injury to Goods. Where a third party so deals with goods which have been identified to a contract for sale as to cause actionable injury to a party to that contract

(a) right of action against the third party is in either party to the contract for sale who has title to or a security interest or a special property or an insurable interest in the goods; and if the goods have been destroyed or converted a right of action is also in the party who either bore the risk of loss under the contract for sale or has since the injury assumed that risk as against the other;

(b) if at the time of the injury the party plaintiff did not bear the risk of loss as against the other party to the contract for sale and there is no arrangement between them for disposition of the recovery, his suit or settlement is, subject to his own interest, as a fiduciary for the other party to the contract;

(c) either party may with the consent of the other sue for the benefit of whom it may concern.

§2-723. Proof of Market Price: Time and Place.
(1) If an action based on anticipatory repudiation comes to trial before the time for performance with respect to some or all of the goods, any damages based on market price (Section 2-708 or Section 2-713) shall be determined according to the price of such goods prevailing at the time when the aggrieved party learned of the repudiation.

(2) If evidence of a price prevailing at the times or places described in this Article is not readily available the price prevailing within any reasonable time before or after the time described or at any other place which in commercial judgment or under usage of trade would serve as a reasonable substitute for the one described may be used, making any proper allowance for the cost of transporting the goods to or from such other place.

(3) Evidence of a relevant price prevailing at a time or place other than the one described in this Article offered by one party is not admissible unless and until he has given the other party such notice as the court finds sufficient to prevent unfair surprise.

§2-724. Admissibility of Market Quotations. Whenever the prevailing price or value of any goods regularly bought and sold in any established commodity market is in issue, reports in official publication or trade journals or in newspapers or periodicals of general circulation published as the reports of such market shall be admissible in evidence. The circumstances of the preparation of such a report may be shown to affect its weight but not its admissibility.

§2-725. Statute of Limitations in Contracts for Sale.
(1) An action for breach of any contract for sale must be commenced within four years after the cause of action has accrued. By the original agreement the parties may reduce the period of limitation to not less than one year but may not extend it.

(2) A cause of action accrues when the breach occurs, regardless of the aggrieved party's lack of knowledge of the breach. A breach of warranty occurs when tender of delivery is made, except that where a warranty explicitly extends to future performance of the goods and discovery of the breach must await the time of such performance the cause of action accrues when the breach is or should have been discovered.

(3) Where an action commenced within the time limited by subsection (1) is so terminated as to leave available a remedy by another action for the same breach such other action may be commenced after the expiration of the time limited and within six months after the termination of the first action unless the termination resulted from voluntary discontinuance or from dismissal for failure or neglect to prosecute.

(4) This section does not alter the law on tolling of the statute of limitations nor does it apply to causes of action which have accrued before this Act becomes effective.

ARTICLE 2A: LEASES

Part 1: General Provisions

§2A-101. Short Title. This Article shall be known and may be cited as the Uniform Commercial Code—Leases.

§2A-102. Scope. This Article applies to any transaction, regardless of form, that creates a lease.

§2A-103. Definitions and Index of Definitions.
(1) In this Article unless the context otherwise requires:

(a) "Buyer in ordinary course of business" means a person who in good faith and without knowledge that the sale to him[or her] is in violation of the ownership rights or security interest or leasehold interest of a third party in the goods buys in ordinary course from a person in the business of selling goods of that kind but does not include a pawnbroker. "Buying" may be for cash or by exchange of other property or on secured or unsecured credit and includes receiving goods or documents of title under a pre-existing contract for sale but does not include a transfer in bulk or as security for or in total or partial satisfaction of a money debt.

(b) "Cancellation" occurs when either party puts an end to the lease contract for default by the other party.

(c) "Commercial unit" means such a unit of goods as by commercial usage is a single whole for purposes of lease and division of which materially impairs its character or value on the market or in use. A commercial unit may be a single article, as a machine, or a set of articles, as a suite of furniture or a line of machinery, or a quantity, as a gross or carload, or any other unit treated in use or in the relevant market as a single whole.

(d) "Conforming" goods or performance under a lease contract means goods or performance that are in accordance with the obligations under the lease contract.

(e) "Consumer lease" means a lease that a lessor regularly engaged in the business of leasing or selling makes to a lessee, except an organization, who takes under the lease primarily for a personal, family, or household purpose, if the total payments to be made under the lease contract, excluding payments for options to renew or buy, do not exceed $25,000.

(f) "Fault" means wrongful act, omission, breach, or default.

(g) "Finance lease" means a lease in which (i) the lessor does not select, manufacture or supply the goods, (ii) the lessor acquires the goods or the right to possession and use of the goods in connection with the lease, and (iii) either the lessee receives a copy of the contract evidencing the lessor's purchase of the goods on or before signing the lease contract, or the lessee's approval of the contract evidencing the lessor's purchase of the goods is a condition to effectiveness of the lease contract.

(h) "Goods" means all things that are movable at the time of identification to the lease contract, or are fixtures (Section 2A-309), but the term does not include money, documents, instruments, accounts, chattel paper, general intangibles, or minerals or the like, including oil and gas, before extraction. The term also includes the unborn young of animals.

(i) "Installment lease contract" means a lease contract that authorizes or requires the delivery of goods in separate lots to be separately accepted, even though the lease contract contains a clause "each delivery is a separate lease" or its equivalent.

(j) "Lease" means a transfer of the right to possession and use of goods for a term in return for consideration, but a sale, including a sale on approval or a sale or return, or retention or creation of a security interest is not a lease. Unless the context clearly indicates otherwise, the term includes a sublease.

(k) "Lease agreement" means the bargain, with respect to the lease, of the lessor and the lessee in fact as found in their language or by implication from other circumstances including course of dealing or usage of trade or course of performance as provided in this Article. Unless the context clearly indicates otherwise, the term includes a sublease agreement.

(l) "Lease contract" means the total legal obligation that results from the lease agreement as affected by this Article and any other applicable rules of law. Unless the context clearly indicates otherwise, the term includes a sublease contract.

(m) "Leasehold interest" means the interest of the lessor or the lessee under a lease contract.

(n) "Lessee" means a person who acquires the right to possession and use of goods under a lease. Unless the context clearly indicates otherwise, the term includes a sublessee.

(o) "Lessee in ordinary course of business" means a person who in good faith and without knowledge that the lease to him[or her] is in violation of the ownership rights or security interest or leasehold interest of a third party in the goods, leases in ordinary course from a person in the business of selling or leasing goods of that kind but does not include a pawnbroker. "Leasing" may be for cash or by exchange of other property or on secured or unsecured credit and includes receiving goods or documents of title under a pre-existing lease contract but does not include a transfer in bulk or as security for or in total or partial satisfaction of a money debt.

(p) "Lessor" means a person who transfers the right to possession and use of goods under a lease. Unless the context clearly indicates otherwise, the term includes a sublessor.

(q) "Lessor's residual interest" means the lessor's interest in the goods after expiration, termination, or cancellation of the lease contract.

(r) "Lien" means a charge against or interest in goods to secure payment of a debt or performance of an obligation, but the term does not include a security interest.

(s) "Lot" means a parcel or a single article that is the subject matter of a separate lease or delivery, whether or not it is sufficient to perform the lease contract.

(t) "Merchant lessee" means a lessee that is a merchant with respect to goods of the kind subject to the lease.

(u) "Present value" means the amount as of a date certain of one or more sums payable in the future, discounted to the date certain. The discount is determined by the interest rate specified by the parties if the rate was not manifestly unreasonable at the time the transaction was entered into; otherwise, the discount is determined by a commercially reasonable rate that takes into account the facts and circumstances of each case at the time the transaction was entered into.

(v) "Purchase" includes taking by sale, lease, mortgage, security interest, pledge, gift, or any other voluntary transaction creating an interest in goods.

(w) "Sublease" means a lease of goods the right to possession and use of which was acquired by the lessor as a lessee under an existing lease.

(x) "Supplier" means a person from whom a lessor buys or leases goods to be leased under a finance lease.

(y) "Supply contract" means a contract under which a lessor buys or leases goods to be leased.
(z) "Termination" occurs when either party pursuant to a power created by agreement or law puts an end to the lease contract otherwise than for default.

(2) Other definitions applying to this Article and the sections in which they appear are:

"Accessions"	Section 2A-310(1)
"Construction mortgage"	Section 2A-309(1)(d)
"Encumbrance"	Section 2A-309(1)(e)
"Fixtures"	Section 2A-309(1)(a)
"Fixture filing"	Section 2A-309(1)(b)
"Purchase money lease"	Section 2A-309(1)(c)

(3) The following definitions in other Articles apply to this Article:

"Accounts"	Section 9-106
"Between merchants"	Section 2-104(3)
"Buyer"	Section 2-103(1)(a)
"Chattel paper"	Section 9-105(1)(b)
"Consumer goods"	Section 9-109(1)
"Documents"	Section 9-105(1)(f)
"Entrusting"	Section 2-403(3)
"General intangibles"	Section 9-106
"Good faith"	Section 2-103(1)(b)
"Instruments"	Section 9-105(1)(i)
"Merchant"	Section 2-104(1)
"Mortgage"	Section 9-105(1)(j)
"Pursuant to commitment"	Section 9-105(1)(k)
"Receipt"	Section 2-103(1)(c)
"Sale"	Section 2-106(1)
"Sale on approval"	Section 2-326
"Sale or return"	Section 2-326
"Seller"	Section 2-103(1)(d)

(4) In addition Article 1 contains general definitions and principles of construction and interpretation applicable throughout this Article.

§2A-104. Leases Subject to Other Statutes.

(1) A lease, although subject to this Article, is also subject to any applicable:
(a) statute of the United States;
(b) certificate of title statute of this State: (list any certificate of title statutes covering automobiles, trailers, mobile homes, boats, farm tractors, and the like);
(c) certificate of title statute of another jurisdiction (Section 2A-105); or
(d) consumer protection statute of this State.

(2) In case of conflict between the provisions of this Article, other than Sections 2A-105, 2A-304(3) and 2A-305(3), and any statute referred to in subsection (1), the provisions of that statute control.

(3) Failure to comply with any applicable statute has only the effect specified therein.

§2A-105. Territorial Application of Article to Goods Covered by Certificate of Title.
Subject to the provisions of Sections 2A-304(3) and 2A-305(3), with respect to goods covered by a certificate of title issued under a statute of this State or of another jurisdiction, compliance and the effect of compliance or noncompliance with a certificate of title statute are governed by the law (including the conflict of laws rules) of the jurisdiction issuing the certificate until the earlier of (a) surrender of the certificate, or (b) four months after the goods are removed from that jurisdiction and thereafter until a new certificate of title is issued by another jurisdiction.

§2A-106. Limitation on Power of Parties to Consumer Lease to Choose Applicable Law and Judicial Forum.

(1) If the law chosen by the parties to a consumer lease is that of a jurisdiction other than a jurisdiction in which the lessee resides at the time the lease agreement becomes enforceable or within 30 days thereafter or in which the goods are to be used, the choice is not enforceable.

(2) If the judicial forum chosen by the parties to a consumer lease is a forum that would not otherwise have jurisdiction over the lessee, the choice is not enforceable.

§2A-107. Waiver or Renunciation of Claim or Right After Default.
Any claim or right arising out of an alleged default or breach of warranty may be discharged in whole or in part without consideration by a written waiver or renunciation signed and delivered by the aggrieved party.

§2A-108. Unconscionability.

(1) If the court as a matter of law finds a lease contract or any clause of a lease contract to have been unconscionable at the time it was made the court may refuse to enforce the lease contract, or it may enforce the remainder of the lease contract without the unconscionable clause, or it may so limit the application of any unconscionable clause as to avoid any unconscionable result.

(2) With respect to a consumer lease, if the court as a matter of law finds that a lease contract or any clause of a lease contract has been induced by unconscionable conduct or that unconscionable conduct has occurred in the collection of a claim arising from a lease contract, the court may grant appropriate relief.

(3) Before making a finding of unconscionability under subsection (1) or (2), the court, on its own motion or that of a party, shall afford the parties a reasonable opportunity to present evidence as to the setting, purpose, and effect of the lease contract or clause thereof, or of the conduct.

(4) In an action in which the lessee claims unconscionability with respect to a consumer lease:

(a) If the court finds unconscionability under subsection (1) or (2), the court shall award reasonable attorney's fees to the lessee.
(b) If the court does not find unconscionability and the lessee claiming unconscionability has brought or maintained an action he [or she] knew to be groundless, the court shall award reasonable attorney's fees to the party against whom the claim is made.
(c) In determining attorney's fees, the amount of the recovery on behalf of the claimant under subsections (1) and (2) is not controlling.

§2A-109. Option to Accelerate at Will.

(1) A term providing that one party or his[or her] successor in interest may accelerate payment or performance or require collateral or additional collateral "at will" or "when he [or she] deems himself [or herself] insecure" or in words of similar import must be construed to mean that he[or she] has power to do so only if he[or she] in good faith believes that the prospect of payment or performance is impaired.

(2) With respect to a consumer lease, the burden of establishing good faith under subsection (1) is on the party who exercised the power; otherwise the burden of establishing lack of good faith is on the party against whom the power has been exercised.

Part 2: Formation and Construction of Lease Contract

§2A-201. Statute of Frauds.

(1) A lease contract is not enforceable by way of action or defense unless:

(a) the total payments to be made under the lease contract, excluding payments for options to renew or buy, are less than $1,000; or

(b) there is a writing, signed by the party against whom enforcement is sought or by that party's authorized agent, sufficient to indicate that a lease contract has been made between the parties and to describe the goods leased and the lease term.

(2) Any description of leased goods or of the lease term is sufficient and satisfies subsection (1)(b), whether or not it is specific, if it reasonably identifies what is described.

(3) A writing is not insufficient because it omits or incorrectly states a term agreed upon, but the lease contract is not enforceable under subsection (1)(b) beyond the lease term and the quantity of goods shown in this writing.

(4) A lease contract that does not satisfy the requirements of subsection (1), but which is valid in other respects, is enforceable:

(a) if the goods are to be specially manufactured or obtained for the lessee and are not suitable for lease or sale to others in the ordinary course of the lessor's business, and the lessor, before notice of repudiation is received and under circumstances that reasonably indicate that the goods are for the lessee, has made either a substantial beginning of their manufacture or commitments for their procurement;

(b) if the party against whom enforcement is sought admits in that party's pleading, testimony or otherwise in court that a lease contract was made, but the lease contract is not enforceable under this provision beyond the quantity of goods admitted; or

(c) with respect to goods that have been received and accepted by the lessee.

(5) The lease term under a lease contract referred to in subsection (4) is:

(a) if there is a writing signed by the party against whom enforcement is sought or by that party's authorized agent specifying the lease term, the term so specified;

(b) if the party against whom enforcement is sought admits in that party's pleading, testimony, or otherwise in court a lease term, the term so admitted; or

(c) a reasonable lease term.

§2A-202. Final Written Expression: Parol or Extrinsic Evidence. Terms with respect to which the confirmatory memoranda of the parties agree or which are otherwise set forth in a writing intended by the parties as a final expression of their agreement with respect to such terms as are included therein may not be contradicted by evidence of any prior agreement or of a contemporaneous oral agreement but may be explained or supplemented:

(a) by course of dealing or usage of trade or by course of performance; and

(b) by evidence of consistent additional terms unless the court finds the writing to have been intended also as a complete and exclusive statement of the terms of the agreement.

§2A-203. Seals Inoperative. The affixing of a seal to a writing evidencing a lease contract or an offer to enter into a lease contract does not render the writing a sealed instrument and the law with respect to sealed instruments does not apply to the lease contract or offer.

§2A-204. Formation in General.

(1) A lease contract may be made in any manner sufficient to show agreement, including conduct by both parties which recognizes the existence of a lease contract.

(2) An agreement sufficient to constitute a lease contract may be found although the moment of its making is undetermined.

(3) Although one or more terms are left open, a lease contract does not fail for indefiniteness if the parties have intended to make a lease contract and there is a reasonably certain basis for giving an appropriate remedy.

§2A-205. Firm Offers. An offer by a merchant to lease goods to or from another person in a signed writing that by its terms gives assurance it will be held open is not revocable, for lack of consideration, during the time stated or, if no time is stated, for a reasonable time, but in no event may the period of irrevocability exceed 3 months. Any such term of assurance on a form supplied by the offeree must be separately signed by the offeror.

§2A-206. Offer and Acceptance in Formation of Lease Contract.

(1) Unless otherwise unambiguously indicated by the language or circumstances, an offer to make a lease contract must be construed as inviting acceptance in any manner and by any medium reasonable in the circumstances.

(2) If the beginning of a requested performance is a reasonable mode of acceptance, an offeror who is not notified of acceptance within a reasonable time may treat the offer as having lapsed before acceptance.

§2A-207. Course of Performance or Practical Construction.

(1) If a lease contract involves repeated occasions for performance by either party with knowledge of the nature of the performance and opportunity for objection to it by the other, any course of performance accepted or acquiesced in without objection is relevant to determine the meaning of the lease agreement.

(2) The express terms of a lease agreement and any course of performance, as well as any course of dealing and usage of trade, must be construed whenever reasonable as consistent with each other; but if that construction is unreasonable, express terms control course of performance, course of performance controls both course of dealing and usage of trade, and course of dealing controls usage of trade.

(3) Subject to the provisions of Section 2A-208 on modification and waiver, course of performance is relevant to show a waiver or modification of any term inconsistent with the course of performance.

§2A-208. Modification, Rescission and Waiver.

(1) An agreement modifying a lease contract needs no consideration to be binding.

(2) A signed lease agreement that excludes modification or rescission except by a signed writing may not be otherwise modified or rescinded, but, except as between merchants, such a requirement on a form supplied by a merchant must be separately signed by the other party.

(3) Although an attempt at modification or rescission does not satisfy the requirements of subsection (2), it may operate as a waiver.

(4) A party who has made a waiver affecting an executory portion of a lease contract may retract the waiver by reasonable notification received by the other party that strict performance will be required of any term waived, unless the retraction would be unjust in view of a material change of position in reliance on the waiver.

§2A-209. Lessee Under Finance Lease as Beneficiary of Supply Contract.

(1) The benefit of the supplier's promises to the lessor under the supply contract and of all warranties, whether express or implied, under the supply contract, extends to the lessee to the extent of the lessee's leasehold interest under a finance lease related to the supply contract, but subject to the terms of the supply contract and all of the supplier's defenses or claims arising therefrom.

(2) The extension of the benefit of the supplier's promises to the lessee does not: (a) modify the rights and obligations of the parties to the supply contract, whether arising therefrom or otherwise, or (b) impose any duty or liability under the supply contract on the lessee.

(3) Any modification or rescission of the supply contract by the supplier and the lessor is effective against the lessee unless, prior to the modification or rescission, the supplier has received notice that the lessee has entered into a finance lease related to the supply contract. If the supply contract is modified or rescinded after the lessee enters the finance lease, the lessee has a cause of action against the lessor, and against the supplier if the supplier has notice of the lessee's entering the finance lease when the supply contract is modified or rescinded. The lessee's recovery from such action shall put the lessee in as good a position as if the modification or rescission had not occurred.

§2A-210. Express Warranties.

(1) Express warranties by the lessor are created as follows:

(a) Any affirmation of fact or promise made by the lessor to the lessee which relates to the goods and becomes part of the basis of the bargain creates an express warranty that the goods will conform to the affirmation or promise.
(b) Any description of the goods which is made part of the basis of the bargain creates an express warranty that the goods will conform to the description.
(c) Any sample or model that is made part of the basis of the bargain creates an express warranty that the whole of the goods will conform to the sample or model.

(2) It is not necessary to the creation of an express warranty that the lessor use formal words, such as "warrant" or "guarantee," or that the lessor have a specific intention to make a warranty, but an affirmation merely of the value of the goods or a statement purporting to be merely the lessor's opinion or commendation of the goods does not create a warranty.

§2A-211. Warranties Against Interference and Against Infringement; Lessee's Obligation Against Infringement

(1) There is in a lease contract a warranty that for the lease term no person holds a claim to or interest in the goods that arose from an act or omission of the lessor, other than a claim by way of infringement or the like, which will interfere with the lessee's enjoyment of its leasehold interest.

(2) Except in a finance lease there is in a lease contract by a lessor who is a merchant regularly dealing in goods of the kind a warranty that the goods are delivered free of the rightful claim of any person by way of infringement or the like.

(3) A lessee who furnishes specifications to a lessor or a supplier shall hold the lessor and the supplier harmless against any claim by way of infringement or the like that arises out of compliance with the specifications.

§2A-212. Implied Warranty of Merchantability.

(1) Except in a finance lease, a warranty that the goods will be merchantable is implied in a lease contract if the lessor is a merchant with respect to goods of that kind.

(2) Goods to be merchantable must be at least such as

(a) pass without objection in the trade under the description in the lease agreement;
(b) in the case of fungible goods, are of fair average quality within the description;
(c) are fit for the ordinary purposes for which goods of that type are used;
(d) run, within the variation permitted by the lease agreement, of even kind, quality, and quantity within each unit and among all units involved;
(e) are adequately contained, packaged, and labeled as the lease agreement may require; and
(f) conform to any promises or affirmations of fact made on the container or label.

(3) Other implied warranties may arise from course of dealing or usage of trade.

§2A-213. Implied Warranty of Fitness for Particular Purpose.

Except in a finance of lease, if the lessor at the time the lease contract is made has reason to know of any particular purpose for which the goods are required and that the lessee is relying on the lessor's skill or judgment to select or furnish suitable goods, there is in the lease contract an implied warranty that the goods will be fit for that purpose.

§2A-214. Exclusion or Modification of Warranties.

(1) Words or conduct relevant to the creation of an express warranty and words or conduct tending to negate or limit a warranty must be construed wherever reasonable as consistent with each other; but, subject to the provisions of Section 2A-202 on parol or extrinsic evidence, negation or limitation is inoperative to the extent that the construction is unreasonable.

(2) Subject to subsection (3), to exclude or modify the implied warranty of merchantability or any part of it the language must mention "merchantability", be by a writing, and be conspicuous. Subject to subsection (3), to exclude or modify any implied warranty of fitness the exclusion must be by a writing and be conspicuous. Language to exclude all implied warranties of fitness is sufficient if it is conspicuous and states, for example, "There is no warranty that the goods will be fit for a particular purpose".

(3) Notwithstanding subsection (2), but subject to subsection (4),

(a) unless the circumstances indicate otherwise, all implied warranties are excluded by expressions like "as is" or "with all faults" or by other language that in common understanding calls the lessee's attention to the exclusion of warranties and makes plain that there is no implied warranty, and is conspicuous;
(b) if the lessee before entering into the lease contract has examined the goods or the sample or model as fully as desired or has refused to examine the goods, there is no implied warranty with regard to defects that an examination ought in the circumstances to have revealed; and
(c) an implied warranty may also be excluded or modified by course of dealing, course of performance, or usage of trade.

(4) To exclude or modify a warranty against interference or against infringement (Section 2A-211) or any part of it, the language must be specific, be by a writing, and be conspicuous, unless the circumstances, including course of performance, course of dealing, or usage of trade, give the lessee reason to know that the goods are being leased subject to a claim or interest of any person.

§2A-215. Cumulation and Conflict of Warranties Express or Implied. Warranties, whether express or implied, must be construed as consistent with each other and as cumulative, but if that construction is unreasonable, the intention of the parties determines which warranty is dominant. In ascertaining that intention the following rules apply:

   (a) Exact or technical specifications displace an inconsistent sample or model or general language of description.
   (b) A sample from an existing bulk displaces inconsistent general language of description.
   (c) Express warranties displace inconsistent implied warranties other than an implied warranty of fitness for a particular purpose.

§2A-216. Third-Party Beneficiaries of Express and Implied Warranties.

Alternative A

A warranty to or for the benefit of a lessee under this Article, whether express or implied, extends to any natural person who is in the family or household of the lessee or who is a guest in the lessee's home if it is reasonable to expect that such person may use, consume, or be affected by the goods and who is injured in person by breach of the warranty. This section does not displace principles of law and equity that extend a warranty to or for the benefit of a lessee to other persons. The operation of this section may not be excluded, modified, or limited, but an exclusion, modification, or limitation of the warranty, including any with respect to rights and remedies, effective against the lessee is also effective against any beneficiary designated under this section.

Alternative B

A warranty to or for the benefit of a lessee under this Article, whether express or implied, extends to any natural person who may reasonably be expected to use, consume, or be affected by the goods and who is injured in person by breach of the warranty. This section does not displace principles of law and equity that extend a warranty to or for the benefit of a lessee to other persons. The operation of this section may not be excluded, modified, or limited, but an exclusion, modification, or limitation of the warranty, including any with respect to rights and remedies, effective against the lessee is also effective against the beneficiary designated under this section.

Alternative C

A warranty to or for the benefit of a lessee under this Article, whether express or implied, extends to any natural person who may reasonably be expected to use, consume, or be affected by the goods and who is injured by breach of the warranty. The operation of this section may not be excluded, modified, or limited with respect to injury to the person of an individual to whom the warranty extends, but an exclusion, modification, or limitation of the warranty, including any with respect to rights and remedies, effective against the lessee is also effective against the beneficiary designated under this section.

§2A-217. Identification. Identification of goods to which a lease contract refers may be made at any time and in any manner explicitly agreed to by the parties. In the absence of explicit agreement, identification occurs:

   (a) when the lease contract is made if the lease contract is for a lease of goods that are existing and identified;
   (b) when the goods are shipped, marked, or otherwise designated by the lessor as goods to which the lease contract refers, if the lease contract is for a lease of goods that are not existing and identified; or
   (c) when the young are conceived, if the lease contract is for a lease of unborn young of animals.

§2A-218. Insurance and Proceeds.

(1) A lessee obtains an insurable interest when existing goods are identified to the lease contract even though the goods identified are nonconforming and the lessee has an option to reject them.

(2) If a lessee has an insurable interest only by reason of the lessor's identification of the goods, the lessor, until default or insolvency or notification to the lessee that identification is final, may substitute other goods for those identified.

(3) Notwithstanding a lessee's insurable interest under subsections (1) and (2), the lessor retains an insurable interest until an option to buy has been exercised by the lessee and risk of loss has passed to the lessee.

(4) Nothing in this section impairs any insurable interest recognized under any other statute or rule of law.

(5) The parties by agreement may determine that one or more parties have an obligation to obtain and pay for insurance covering the goods and by agreement may determine the beneficiary of the proceeds of the insurance.

§2A-219. Risk of Loss.

(1) Except in the case of a finance lease, risk of loss is retained by the lessor and does not pass to the lessee. In the case of a finance lease, risk of loss passes to the lessee.

(2) Subject to the provisions of this Article on the effect of default on risk of loss (Section 2A-220), if risk of loss is to pass to the lessee and the time of passage is not stated, the following rules apply:

   (a) If the lease contract requires or authorizes the goods to be shipped by carrier.

      (i) and it does not require delivery at a particular destination, the risk of loss passes to the lessee when the goods are duly delivered to the carrier; but
      (ii) if it does require delivery at a particular destination and the goods are there duly tendered while in the possession of the carrier, the risk of loss passes to the lessee when the goods are there duly so tendered as to enable the lessee to take delivery.

   (b) If the goods are held by a bailee to be delivered without being moved, the risk of loss passes to the lessee on acknowledgment by the bailee of the lessee's right to possession of the goods.
   (c) In any case not within subsection (a) or (b), the risk of loss passes to the lessee on the lessee's receipt of the goods if the lessor, or, in the case of a finance lease, the supplier, is a merchant; otherwise the risk passes to the lessee on tender of delivery.

§2A-220. Effect of Default on Risk of Loss.

(1) Where risk of loss is to pass to the lessee and the time of passage is not stated:

   (a) If a tender or delivery of goods so fails to conform to the lease contract as to give a right of rejection, the risk of their loss remains with the lessor, or, in the case of a finance lease, the supplier, until cure or acceptance.
   (b) If the lessee rightfully revokes acceptance, he [or she], to the extent of any deficiency in his[or her] effective insurance coverage, may treat the risk of loss as having remained with the lessor from the beginning.

(2) Whether or not risk of loss is to pass to the lessee, if the lessee as to conforming goods already identified to a lease contract

repudiates or is otherwise in default under the lease contract, the lessor, or, in the case of a finance lease, the supplier, to the extent of any deficiency in his [or her] effective insurance coverage may treat the risk of loss as resting on the lessee for a commercially reasonable time.

§2A-221. Casualty to Identified Goods. If a lease contract requires goods identified when the lease contract is made, and the goods suffer casualty without fault of the lessee, the lessor or the supplier before delivery, or the goods suffer casualty before risk of loss passes to the lessee pursuant to the lease agreement or Section 2A-219, then:

(a) if the loss is total, the lease contract is avoided; and

(b) if the loss is partial or the goods have so deteriorated as to no longer conform to the lease contract, the lessee may nevertheless demand inspection and at his[or her] option either treat the lease contract as avoided or, except in a finance lease that is not a consumer lease, accept the goods with due allowance from the rent payable for the balance of the lease term for the deterioration or the deficiency in quantity but without further right against the lessor.

Part 3: Effect of Lease Contract

§2A-301. Enforceability of Lease Contract. Except as otherwise provided in this Article, a lease contract is effective and enforceable according to its terms between the parties, against purchasers of the goods and against creditors of the parties.

§2A-302. Title to and Possession of Goods. Except as otherwise provided in this Article, each provision of this Article applies whether the lessor or a third party has title to the goods, and whether the lessor, the lessee, or a third party has possession of the goods, notwithstanding any statute or rule of law that possession or the absence of possession is fraudulent.

§2A-303. Alienability of Party's Interest Under Lease Contract or of Lessor's Residual Interest in Goods; Delegation of Performance; Assignment of Rights.

(1) Any interest of a party under a lease contract and the lessor's residual interest in the goods may be transferred unless

(a) the transfer is voluntary and the lease contract prohibits the transfer; or

(b) the transfer materially changes the duty of or materially increases the burden or risk imposed on the other party to the lease contract, and within a reasonable time after notice of the transfer the other party demands that the transferee comply with subsection (2) and the transferee fails to comply.

(2) Within a reasonable time after demand pursuant to subsection (1)(b), the transferee shall:

(a) cure or provide adequate assurance that he[or she] will promptly cure any default other than one arising from the transfer;

(b) compensate or provide adequate assurance that he [or she] will promptly compensate the other party to the lease contract and any other person holding an interest in the lease contract, except the party whose interest is being transferred, for any loss to that party resulting from the transfer;

(c) provide adequate assurance of future due performance under the lease contract; and

(d) assume the lease contract.

(3) Demand pursuant to subsection (1)(b) is without prejudice to the other party's rights against the transferee and the party whose interest is transferred.

(4) An assignment of "the lease" or of "all my rights under the lease" or an assignment in similar general terms is a transfer of rights, and unless the language or the circumstances, as in an assignment for security, indicate the contrary, the assignment is a delegation of duties by the assignor to the assignee and acceptance by the assignee constitutes a promise by him[or her] to perform those duties. This promise is enforceable by either the assignor or the other party to the lease contract.

(5) Unless otherwise agreed by the lessor and the lessee, no delegation of performance relieves the assignor as against the other party of any duty to perform or any liability for default.

(6) A right to damages for default with respect to the whole lease contract or a right arising out of the assignor's due performance of his [or her] entire obligation can be assigned despite agreement otherwise.

(7) To prohibit the transfer of an interest of a party under a lease contract, the language of prohibition must be specific, by a writing, and conspicuous.

§2A-304. Subsequent Lease of Goods by Lessor.

(1) Subject to the provisions of Section 2A-303, a subsequent lessee from a lessor of goods under an existing lease contract obtains, to the extent of the leasehold interest transferred, the leasehold interest in the goods that the lessor had or had power to transfer, and except as provided in subsection (2) and Section 2A-527(4), takes subject to the existing lease contract. A lessor with voidable title has power to transfer a good leasehold interest to a good faith subsequent lessee for value, but only to the extent set forth in the preceding sentence. When goods have been delivered under a transaction of purchase the lessor has that power even though:

(a) the lessor's transferor was deceived as to the identity of the lessor;

(b) the delivery was in exchange for a check which is later dishonored;

(c) it was agreed that the transaction was to be a "cash sale"; or

(d) the delivery was procured through fraud punishable as larcenous under the criminal law.

(2) A subsequent lessee in the ordinary course of business from a lessor who is a merchant dealing in goods of that kind to whom the goods were entrusted by the existing lessee before the interest of the subsequent lessee became enforceable against the lessor obtains, to the extent of the leasehold interest transferred, all of the lessor's and the existing lessee's rights to the goods, and takes free of the existing lease contract.

(3) A subsequent lessee from the lessor of goods that are subject to an existing lease contract and are covered by a certificate of title issued under a statute of this State or of another jurisdiction takes no greater rights than those provided both by this section and by the certificate of title statute.

§2A-305. Sale or Sublease of Goods by Lessee.

(1) Subject to the provisions of Section 2A-303, a buyer or sublessee from the lessee of goods under an existing lease contract obtains, to the extent of the interest transferred, the leasehold interest in the goods that the lessee had or had power to transfer, and except as provided in subsection (2) and Section 2A-511(4), takes subject to the existing lease contract. A lessee with a voidable leasehold interest has power to transfer a good leasehold interest to a good faith buyer for value or a good faith sublessee for value, but only to the extent set forth in the preceding sentence.

When goods have been delivered under a transaction of lease the lessee has that power even though:

(a) the lessor was deceived as to the identify of the lessee;
(b) the delivery was in exchange for a check which is later dishonored; or
(c) the delivery was procured through fraud punishable as larcenous under the criminal law.

(2) A buyer in the ordinary course of business or a sublessee in the ordinary course of business from a lessee who is a merchant dealing in goods of that kind to whom the goods were entrusted by the lessor obtains, to the extent of the interest transferred, all of the lessor's and lessee's rights to the goods, and takes free of the existing lease contract.

(3) A buyer or sublessee from the lessee of goods that are subject to an existing lease contract and are covered by a certificate of title issued under a statute of this State or of another jurisdiction takes no greater rights than those provided both by this section and by the certificate of title statute.

§2A-306. Priority of Certain Liens Arising by Operation of Law.

If a person in the ordinary course of his[or her] business furnishes services or materials with respect to goods subject to a lease contract, a lien upon those goods in the possession of that person given by statute or rule of law for those materials or services takes priority over any interest of the lessor or lessee under the lease contract or this Article unless the lien is created by statute and the statute provides otherwise or unless the lien is created by rule of law and the rule of law provides otherwise.

§2A-307. Priority of Liens Arising by Attachment or Levy on, Security Interests in, and Other Claims to Goods.

(1) Except as otherwise provided in Section 2A-306, a creditor of a lessee takes subject to the lease contract.

(2) Except as otherwise provided in subsections (3) and (4) of this section and in Sections 2A-306 and 2A-308, a creditor of a lessor takes subject to the lease contract:

(a) unless the creditor holds a lien that attached to the goods before the lease contract became enforceable, or
(b) unless the creditor holds a security interest in the goods that under the Article on Secured Transactions (Article 9) would have priority over any other security interest in the goods perfected by a filing covering the goods and made at the time the lease contract became enforceable, whether or not any other security interest existed.

(3) A lessee in the ordinary course of business takes the leasehold interest free of a security interest in the goods created by the lessor even though the security interest is perfected and the lessee knows of its existence.

(4) A lessee other than a lessee in the ordinary course of business takes the leasehold interest free of a security interest to the extent that it secures future advances made after the secured party acquires knowledge of the lease or more than 45 days after the lease contract becomes enforceable, whichever first occurs, unless the future advances are made pursuant to a commitment entered into without knowledge of the lease and before the expiration of the 45-day period.

§2A-308. Special Rights of Creditors.

(1) A creditor of a lessor in possession of goods subject to a lease contract may treat the lease contract as void if as against the creditor retention of possession by the lessor is fraudulent under any statute or rule of law, but retention of possession in good faith and current course of trade by the lessor for a commercially reasonable time after the lease contract becomes enforceable is not fraudulent.

(2) Nothing in this Article impairs the rights of creditors of a lessor if the lease contract (a) becomes enforceable, not in current course of trade but in satisfaction of or as security for a pre-existing claim for money, security, or the like, and (b) is made under circumstances which under any statute or rule of law apart from this Article would constitute the transaction a fraudulent transfer or voidable preference.

(3) A creditor of a seller may treat a sale or an identification of goods to a contract for sale as void if as against the creditor retention of possession by the seller is fraudulent under any statute or rule of law, but retention of possession of the goods pursuant to a lease contract entered into by the seller as lessee and the buyer as lessor in connection with the sale or identification of the goods is not fraudulent if the buyer bought for value and in good faith.

§2A-309. Lessor's and Lessee's Rights When Goods Become Fixtures.

(1) In this section:

(a) goods are "fixtures" when they become so related to particular real estate that an interest in them arises under real estate law;
(b) a "fixture filing" is the filing, in the office where a mortgage on the real estate would be recorded or registered, of a financing statement concerning goods that are or are to become fixtures and conforming to the requirements of subsection (5) of Section 9-402;
(c) a lease is a "purchase money lease" unless the lessee has possession or use of the goods or the right to possession or use of the goods before the lease agreement is enforceable;
(d) a mortgage is a "construction mortgage" to the extent it secures an obligation incurred for the construction of an improvement on land including the acquisition cost of the land, if the recorded writing so indicates; and
(e) "encumbrance" includes real estate mortgages and other liens on real estate and all other rights in real estate that are not ownership interests.

(2) Under this Article a lease may be of goods that are fixtures or may continue in goods that become fixtures, but no lease exists under this Article of ordinary building materials incorporated into an improvement on land.

(3) This Article does not prevent creation of a lease of fixtures pursuant to real estate law.

(4) The perfected interest of a lessor of fixtures has priority over a conflicting interest of an encumbrancer or owner of the real estate if:

(a) the lease is a purchase money lease, the conflicting interest of the encumbrancer or owner arises before the goods become fixtures, the interest of the lessor is perfected by a fixture filing before the goods become fixtures or within ten days thereafter, and the lessee has an interest of record in the real estate or is in possession of the real estate; or
(b) the interest of the lessor is perfected by a fixture filing before the interest of the encumbrancer or owner is of record, the lessor's interest has priority over any conflicting interest of a predecessor in title of the encumbrancer or owner, and the lessee has an interest of record in the real estate or is in possession of the real estate.

(5) The interest of a lessor of fixtures, whether or not perfected, has priority over the conflicting interest of an encumbrancer or owner of the real estate if:

(a) the fixtures are readily removable factory or office machines, readily removable equipment that is not primarily used or leased for use in the operation of the real estate, or readily removable replacements of domestic appliances that are goods subject to a consumer lease, and before the goods become fixtures the lease contract is enforceable; or

(b) the conflicting interest is a lien on the real estate obtained by legal or equitable proceedings after the lease contract is enforceable; or

(c) the encumbrancer or owner has consented in writing to the lease or has disclaimed an interest in the goods as fixtures; or

(d) the lessee has a right to remove the goods as against the encumbrancer or owner. If the lessee's right to remove terminates, the priority of the interest of the lessor continues for a reasonable time.

(6) Notwithstanding paragraph (a) of subsection (4) but otherwise subject to subsections (4) and (5), the interest of a lessor of fixtures is subordinate to the conflicting interest of an encumbrancer of the real estate under a construction mortgage recorded before the goods become fixtures if the goods become fixtures before the completion of the construction. To the extent given to refinance a construction mortgage, the conflicting interest of an encumbrancer of the real estate under a mortgage has this priority to the same extent as the encumbrancer of the real estate under the construction mortgage.

(7) In cases not within the preceding subsections, priority between the interest of a lessor of fixtures and the conflicting interest of an encumbrancer or owner of the real estate who is not the lessee is determined by the priority rules governing conflicting interests in real estate.

(8) If the interest of a lessor has priority over all conflicting interests of all owners and encumbrancers of the real estate, the lessor or the lessee may (a) on default, expiration, termination, or cancellation of the lease agreement by the other party but subject to the provisions of the lease agreement and this Article, or (b) if necessary to enforce his [or her] other rights and remedies under this Article, remove the goods from the real estate, free and clear of all conflicting interests of all owners and encumbrancers of the real estate, but he [or she] must reimburse any encumbrancer or owner of the real estate who is not the lessee and who has not otherwise agreed for the cost of repair of any physical injury, but not for any diminution in value of the real estate caused by the absence of the goods removed or by any necessity of replacing them. A person entitled to reimbursement may refuse permission to remove until the party seeking removal gives adequate security for the performance of this obligation.

(9) Even though the lease agreement does not create a security interest, the interest of a lessor of fixtures is perfected by filing a financing statement as a fixture filing for leased goods that are or are to become fixtures in accordance with the relevant provisions of the Article on Secured Transactions (Article 9).

§2A-310. Lessor's and Lessee's Rights When Goods Become Accessions.

(1) Goods are "accessions" when they are installed in or affixed to other goods.

(2) The interest of a lessor or a lessee under a lease contract entered into before the goods became accessions is superior to all interests in the whole except as stated in subsection (4).

(3) The interest of a lessor or a lessee under a lease contract entered into at the time or after the goods became accessions is superior to all subsequently acquired interests in the whole except as stated in subsection (4) but is subordinate to interests in the whole existing at the time the lease contract was made unless the holders of such interests in the whole have in writing consented to the lease or disclaimed an interest in the goods as part of the whole.

(4) The interest of a lessor or a lessee under a lease contract described in subsection (2) or (3) is subordinate to the interest of

(a) a buyer in the ordinary course of business or a lessee in the ordinary course of business of any interest in the whole acquired after the goods became accessions; or

(b) a creditor with a security interest in the whole perfected before the lease contract was made to the extent that the creditor makes subsequent advances without knowledge of the lease contract.

(5) When under subsections (2) or (3) and (4) a lessor or a lessee of accessions holds an interest that is superior to all interests in the whole, the lessor or the lessee may

(a) on default, expiration, termination, or cancellation of the lease contract by the other party but subject to the provisions of the lease contract and this Article, or

(b) if necessary to enforce his[or her] other rights and remedies under this Article, remove the goods from the whole, free and clear of all interests in the whole, but he[or she] must reimburse any holder of an interest in the whole who is not the lessee and who has not otherwise agreed for the cost of repair of any physical injury but not for any diminution in value of the whole caused by the absence of the goods removed or by any necessity for replacing them. A person entitled to reimbursement may refuse permission to remove until the party seeking removal gives adequate security for the performance of this obligation.

Part 4: Performance of Lease Contract—Repudiated, Substituted, and Excused

§2A-401. Insecurity: Adequate Assurance of Performance.

(1) A lease contract imposes an obligation on each party that the other's expectation of receiving due performance will not be impaired.

(2) If reasonable grounds for insecurity arise with respect to the performance of either party, the insecure party may demand in writing adequate assurance of due performance. Until the insecure party receives that assurance, if commercially reasonable the insecure party may suspend any performance for which he[or she] has not already received the agreed return.

(3) A repudiation of the lease contract occurs if assurance of due performance adequate under the circumstances of the particular case is not provided to the insecure party within a reasonable time, not to exceed 30 days after receipt of a demand by the other party.

(4) Between merchants, the reasonableness of grounds for insecurity and the adequacy of any assurance offered must be determined according to commercial standards.

(5) Acceptance of any nonconforming delivery or payment does not prejudice the aggrieved party's right to demand adequate assurance of future performance.

§2A-402. Anticipatory Repudiation. If either party repudiates a lease contract with respect to a performance not yet due under the lease contract, the loss of which performance will substantially impair the value of the lease contract to the other, the aggrieved party may:

(a) for a commercially reasonable time, await retraction of repudiation and performance by the repudiating party;

(b) make demand pursuant to Section 2A-401 and await assurance of future performance adequate under the circumstances of the particular case; or
(c) resort to any right or remedy upon default under the lease contract or this Article, even though the aggrieved party has notified the repudiating party that the aggrieved party would await the repudiating party's performance and assurance and has urged retraction. In addition, whether or not the aggrieved party is pursuing one of the foregoing remedies, the aggrieved party may suspend performance

or, if the aggrieved party is the lessor, proceed in accordance with the provisions of this Article on the lessor's right to identify goods to the lease contract notwithstanding default or to salvage unfinished goods (Section 2A-524).

§2A-403. Retraction of Anticipatory Repudiation.

(1) Until the repudiating party's next performance is due, the repudiating party can retract the repudiation unless, since the repudiation, the aggrieved party has cancelled the lease contract or materially changed the aggrieved party's position or otherwise indicated that the aggrieved party considers the repudiation final.

(2) Retraction may be by any method that clearly indicates to the aggrieved party that the repudiating party intends to perform under the lease contract and includes any assurance demanded under Section 2A-401.

(3) Retraction reinstates a repudiating party's rights under a lease contract with due excuse and allowance to the aggrieved party for any delay occasioned by the repudiation.

§2A-404. Substituted Performance.

(1) If without fault of the lessee, the lessor and the supplier, the agreed berthing, loading, or unloading facilities fail or the agreed type of carrier becomes unavailable or the agreed manner of delivery otherwise becomes commercially impracticable, but a commercially reasonable substitute is available, the substitute performance must be tendered and accepted.

(2) If the agreed means or manner of payment fails because of domestic or foreign governmental regulation:

(a) the lessor may withhold or stop delivery or cause the supplier to withhold or stop delivery unless the lessee provides a means or manner of payment that is commercially a substantial equivalent; and
(b) if delivery has already been taken, payment by the means or in the manner provided by the regulation discharges the lessee's obligation unless the regulation is discriminatory, oppressive, or predatory.

§2A-405. Excused Performance.

Subject to Section 2A-404 on substituted performance, the following rules apply:

(a) Delay in delivery or nondelivery in whole or in part by a lessor or a supplier who complies with paragraphs (b) and (c) is not a default under the lease contract if performance as agreed has been made impracticable by the occurrence of a contingency the nonoccurrence of which was a basic assumption on which the lease contract was made or by compliance in good faith with any applicable foreign or domestic governmental regulation or order, whether or not the regulation or order later proves to be invalid.
(b) If the causes mentioned in paragraph (a) affect only part of the lessor's or the supplier's capacity to perform, he [or she] shall allocate production and deliveries among his [or her] customers but at his [or her] option may in-clude regular customers not then under contract for sale or lease as well as his [or her] own requirements for further manufacture. He [or she] may so allocate in any manner that is fair and reasonable.
(c) The lessor seasonably shall notify the lessee and in the case of a finance lease the supplier seasonably shall notify the lessor and the lessee, if known, that there will be delay or nondelivery and, if allocation is required under paragraph (b), of the estimated quota thus made available for the lessee.

§2A-406. Procedure on Excused Performance.

(1) If the lessee receives notification of a material or indefinite delay or an allocation justified under Section 2A-405, the lessee may by written notification to the lessor as to any goods involved, and with respect to all of the goods if under an installment lease contract the value of the whole lease contract is substantially impaired (Section 2A-510):

(a) terminate the lease contract (Section 2A-505(2)); or
(b) except in a finance lease that is not a consumer lease, modify the lease contract by accepting the available quota in substitution, with due allowance from the rent payable for the balance of the lease term for the deficiency but without further right against the lessor.

(2) If, after receipt of a notification from the lessor under Section 2A-405, the lessee fails so to modify the lease agreement within a reasonable time not exceeding 30 days, the lease contract lapses with respect to any deliveries affected.

§2A-407. Irrevocable Promises: Finance Leases.

(1) In the case of a finance lease that is not a consumer lease the lessee's promises under the lease contract become irrevocable and independent upon the lessee's acceptance of the goods.

(2) A promise that has become irrevocable and independent under subsection (1):

(a) is effective and enforceable between the parties or against third parties including assignees of the parties, and
(b) is not subject to cancellation, termination, modification, repudiation, excuse, or substitution without the consent of the party to whom the promise runs.

Part 5: Default
A. In General

§2A-501. Default: Procedure.

(1) Whether the lessor or the lessee is in default under a lease contract is determined by the lease agreement and this Article.

(2) If the lessor or the lessee is in default under the lease contract, the party seeking enforcement has rights and remedies as provided in this Article and, except as limited by this Article, as provided in the lease agreement.

(3) If the lessor or the lessee is in default under the lease contract, the party seeking enforcement may reduce the party's claim to judgment, or otherwise enforce the lease contract by self-help or any available judicial procedure or nonjudicial procedure, including administrative proceeding, arbitration, or the like, in accordance with this Article.

(4) Except as otherwise provided in this Article or the lease agreement, the rights and remedies referred to in subsections (2) and (3) are cumulative.

(5) If the lease agreement covers both real property and goods, the party seeking enforcement may proceed under this Part as to the goods, or under other applicable law as to both the real property and the goods in accordance with his [or her] rights and remedies in respect of the real property, in which case this Part does not apply.

§2A-502. Notice After Default. Except as otherwise provided in this Article or the lease agreement, the lessor or lessee in default under the lease contract is not entitled to notice of default or notice of enforcement from the other party to the lease agreement.

§2A-503. Modification or Impairment of Rights and Remedies.

(1) Except as otherwise provided in this Article, the lease agreement may include rights and remedies for default in addition to or in substitution for those provided in this Article and may limit or alter the measure of damages recoverable under this Article.

(2) Resort to a remedy provided under this Article or in the lease agreement is optional unless the remedy is expressly agreed to be exclusive. If circumstances cause an exclusive or limited remedy to fail of its essential purpose, or provision for an exclusive remedy is unconscionable, remedy may be had as provided in this Article.

(3) Consequential damages may be liquidated under Section 2A-504, or may otherwise be limited, altered, or excluded unless the limitation, alteration, or exclusion is unconscionable. Limitation of consequential damages for injury to the person in the case of consumer goods is prima facie unconscionable but limitation of damages where the loss is commercial is not.

(4) Rights and remedies on default by the lessor or the lessee with respect to any obligation or promise collateral or ancillary to the lease contract are not impaired by this Article.

§2A-504. Liquidation of Damages.

(1) Damages payable by either party for default, or any other act or omission, including indemnity for loss or diminution of anticipated tax benefits or loss or damage to lessor's residual interest, may be liquidated in the lease agreement but only at an amount or by a formula that is reasonable in light of the then anticipated harm caused by the default or other act or omission.

(2) If the lease agreement provides for liquidation of damages, and such provision does not comply with subsection (1), or such provision is an exclusive or limited remedy that circumstances cause to fail of its essential purpose, remedy may be had as provided in this Article.

(3) If the lessor justifiably withholds or stops delivery of goods because of the lessee's default or insolvency (Section 2A-525 or 2A-526), the lessee is entitled to restitution of any amount by which the sum of his [or her] payments exceeds:

  (a) the amount to which the lessor is entitled by virtue of terms liquidating the lessor's damages in accordance with subsection (1); or
  (b) in the absence of those terms, 20 percent of the then present value of the total rent the lessee was obligated to pay for the balance of the lease term, or, in the case of a consumer lease, the lesser of such amount or $500.

(4) A lessee's right to restitution under subsection (3) is subject to offset to the extent the lessor establishes:

  (a) a right to recover damages under the provisions of this Article other than subsection (1); and
  (b) the amount or value of any benefits received by the lessee directly or indirectly by reason of the lease contract.

§2A-505. Cancellation and Termination and Effect of Cancellation, Termination, Rescission, or Fraud on Rights and Remedies.

(1) On cancellation of the lease contract, all obligations that are still executory on both sides are discharged, but any right based on prior default or performance survives, and the cancelling party also retains any remedy for default of the whole lease contract or any unperformed balance.

(2) On termination of the lease contract, all obligations that are still executory on both sides are discharged but any right based on prior default or performance survives.

(3) Unless the contrary intention clearly appears, expressions of "cancellation", "rescission", or the like of the lease contract may not be construed as a renunciation or discharge of any claim in damages for an antecedent default.

(4) Rights and remedies for material misrepresentation or fraud include all rights and remedies available under this Article for default.

(5) Neither rescission nor a claim for rescission of the lease contract nor rejection or return of the goods may bar or be deemed inconsistent with a claim for damages or other right or remedy.

§2A-506. Statute of Limitations.

(1) An action for default under a lease contract, including breach of warranty or indemnity, must be commenced within 4 years after the cause of action accrued. By the original lease contract the parties may reduce the period of limitation to not less than one year.

(2) A cause of action for default accrues when the act or omission on which the default or breach of warranty is based is or should have been discovered by the aggrieved party, or when the default occurs, whichever is later. A cause of action for indemnity accrues when the act or omission on which the claim for indemnity is based is or should have been discovered by the indemnified party, whichever is later.

(3) If an action commenced within the time limited by subsection (1) is so terminated as to leave available a remedy by another action for the same default or breach of warranty or indemnity, the other action may be commenced after the expiration of the time limited within 6 months after the termination of the first action unless the termination resulted from voluntary discontinuance or from dismissal for failure or neglect to prosecute.

(4) This section does not alter the law on tolling of the statute of limitations nor does it apply to causes of action that have accrued before this Article becomes effective.

§2A-507. Proof of Market Rent: Time and Place.

(1) Damages based on market rent (Section 2A-519 or 2A-528) are determined according to the rent for the use of the goods concerned for a lease term identical to the remaining lease term of the original lease agreement and prevailing at the time of the default.

(2) If evidence of rent for the use of the goods concerned for a lease term identical to the remaining lease term of the original lease agreement and prevailing at the times or places described in this Article is not readily available, the rent prevailing within any reasonable time before or after the time described or at any other place or for a different lease term which in commercial judgment or under usage of trade would serve as a reasonable substitute for the one described may be used, making any proper allowance for the difference, including the cost of transporting the goods to or from the other place.

(3) Evidence of a relevant rent prevailing at a time or place or for a lease term other than the one described in this Article offered by one party is not admissible unless and until he[or she] has given the other party notice the court finds sufficient to prevent unfair surprise.

(4) If the prevailing rent or value of any goods regularly leased in any established market is in issue, reports in official publications or trade journals or in newspapers or periodicals of general circulation published as the reports of that market are admissible in evidence. The circumstances of the preparation of the report may be shown to affect its weight but not its admissibility.

B. Default by Lessor

§2A-508. Lessee's Remedies.

(1) If a lessor fails to deliver the goods in conformity to the lease contract (Section 2A-509) or repudiates the lease contract (Section 2A-402), or a lessee rightfully rejects the goods (Section 2A-509) or justifiably revokes acceptance of the goods (Section 2A-517), then with respect to any goods involved, and with respect to all of the goods if under an installment lease contract the value of the whole lease contract is substantially impaired (Section 2A-510), the lessor is in default under the lease contract and the lessee may:

(a) cancel the lease contract (Section 2A-505(1));
(b) recover so much of the rent and security as has been paid, but in the case of an installment lease contract the recovery is that which is just under the circumstances;
(c) cover and recover damages as to all goods affected whether or not they have been identified to the lease contract (Sections 2A-518 and 2A-520), or recover damages for nondelivery (Sections 2A-519 and 2A-520).

(2) If a lessor fails to deliver the goods in conformity to the lease contract or repudiates the lease contract, the lessee may also:

(a) if the goods have been identified, recover them (Section 2A-522); or
(b) in a proper case, obtain specific performance or replevy the goods (Section 2A-521).

(3) If a lessor is otherwise in default under a lease contract, the lessee may exercise the rights and remedies provided in the lease contract and this Article.

(4) If a lessor has breached a warranty, whether express or implied, the lessee may recover damages (Section 2A-519(4)).

(5) On rightful rejection or justifiable revocation of acceptance, a lessee has a security interest in goods in the lessee's possession or control for any rent and security that has been paid and any expenses reasonably incurred in their inspection, receipt, transportation, and care and custody and may hold those goods and dispose of them in good faith and in a commercially reasonable manner, subject to the provisions of Section 2A-527(5).

(6) Subject to the provisions of Section 2A-407, a lessee, on notifying the lessor of the lessee's intention to do so, may deduct all or any part of the damages resulting from any default under the lease contract from any part of the rent still due under the same lease contract.

§2A-509. Lessee's Rights on Improper Delivery; Rightful Rejection.

(1) If a lessee elects not to cover or a lessee elects to cover and the cover does not qualify for treatment under Section 2A-518(2), the measure of damages for non-delivery or repudiation by reject or accept the goods or accept any commercial unit or units and reject the rest of the goods.

(2) Rejection of goods is ineffective unless it is within a reasonable time after tender or delivery of the goods and the lessee seasonably notifies the lessor.

§2A-510. Installment Lease Contracts: Rejection and Default.

(1) Under an installment lease contract a lessee may reject any delivery that is nonconforming if the nonconformity substantially impairs the value of that delivery and cannot be cured or the nonconformity is a defect in the required documents; but if the nonconformity does not fall within subsection (2) and the lessor or the supplier gives adequate assurance of its cure, the lessee must accept that delivery.

(2) Whenever nonconformity or default with respect to one or more deliveries substantially impairs the value of the installment lease contract as a whole there is a default with respect to the whole. But, the aggrieved party reinstates the installment lease contract as a whole if the aggrieved party accepts a nonconforming delivery without seasonably notifying of cancellation or brings an action with respect only to past deliveries or demands performance as to future deliveries.

§2A-511. Merchant Lessee's Duties as to Rightfully Rejected Goods.

(1) Subject to any security interest of a lessee (Section 2A-508(5)), if a lessor or a supplier has no agent or place of business at the market of rejection, a merchant lessee, after rejection of goods in his [or her] possession or control, shall follow any reasonable instructions received from the lessor or the supplier with respect to the goods. In the absence of those instructions, a merchant lessee shall make reasonable efforts to sell, lease, or otherwise dispose of the goods for the lessor's account if they threaten to decline in value speedily. Instructions are not reasonable if on demand indemnity for expenses is not forthcoming.

(2) If a merchant lessee (subsection (1)) or any other lessee (Section 2A-512) disposes of goods, he [or she] is entitled to reimbursement either from the lessor or the supplier or out of the proceeds for reasonable expenses of caring for and disposing of the goods and, if the expenses include no disposition commission, to such commission as is usual in the trade, or if there is none, to a reasonable sum not exceeding 10 percent of the gross proceeds.

(3) In complying with this section or Section 2A-512, the lessee is held only to good faith. Good faith conduct hereunder is neither acceptance or conversion nor the basis of an action for damages.

(4) A purchaser who purchases in good faith from a lessee pursuant to this section or Section 2A-512 takes the goods free of any rights of the lessor and the supplier even though the lessee fails to comply with one or more of the requirements of this Article.

§2A-512. Lessee's Duties as to Rightfully Rejected Goods.

(1) Except as otherwise provided with respect to goods that threaten to decline in value speedily (Section 2A-511) and subject to any security interest of a lessee (Section 2A-508(5)):

(a) the lessee, after rejection of goods in the lessee's possession, shall hold them with reasonable care at the lessor's or the supplier's disposition for a reasonable time after the lessee's seasonable notification of rejection;
(b) if the lessor or the supplier gives no instructions within a reasonable time after notification of rejection, the lessee may store the rejected goods for the lessor's or the supplier's account or ship them to the lessor or the supplier or dispose of them for the lessor's or the supplier's account with reimbursement in the manner provided in Section 2A-511; but
(c) the lessee has no further obligations with regard to goods rightfully rejected.

(2) Action by the lessee pursuant to subsection (1) is not acceptance or conversion.

§2A-513. Cure by Lessor of Improper Tender or Delivery; Replacement.

(1) If any tender or delivery by the lessor or the supplier is rejected because nonconforming and the time for performance has not yet expired, the lessor or the supplier may seasonably notify the lessee of the lessor's or the supplier's intention to cure and may then make a conforming delivery within the time provided in the lease contract.

(2) If the lessee rejects a nonconforming tender that the lessor or the supplier had reasonable grounds to believe would be acceptable with or without money allowance, the lessor or the supplier may have a further reasonable time to substitute a conforming tender if he [or she] seasonably notifies the lessee.

§2A-514. Waiver of Lessee's Objections.

(1) In rejecting goods, a lessee's failure to state a particular defect that is ascertainable by reasonable inspection precludes the lessee from relying on the defect to justify rejection or to establish default:

(a) if, stated seasonably, the lessor or the supplier could have cured it (Section 2A-513); or
(b) between merchants if the lessor or the supplier after rejection has made a request in writing for a full and final written statement of all defects on which the lessee proposes to rely.

(2) A lessee's failure to reserve rights when paying rent or other consideration against documents precludes recovery of the payment for defects apparent on the face of the documents.

§2A-515. Acceptance of Goods.

(1) Acceptance of goods occurs after the lessee has had a reasonable opportunity to inspect the goods and

(a) the lessee signifies or acts with respect to the goods in a manner that signifies to the lessor or the supplier that the goods are conforming or that the lessee will take or retain them in spite of their nonconformity; or
(b) the lessee fails to make an effective rejection of the goods (Section 2A-509(2)).

(2) Acceptance of a part of any commercial unit is acceptance of that entire unit.

§2A-516. Effect of Acceptance of Goods; Notice of Default; Burden of Establishing Default After Acceptance; Notice of Claim or Litigation to Person Answerable Over.

(1) A lessee must pay rent for any goods accepted in accordance with the lease contract, with due allowance for goods rightfully rejected or not delivered.

(2) A lessee's acceptance of goods precludes rejection of the goods accepted. In the case of a finance lease, if made with knowledge of a nonconformity, acceptance cannot be revoked because of it. In any other case, if made with knowledge of a nonconformity, acceptance cannot be revoked because of it unless the acceptance was on the reasonable assumption that the nonconformity would be seasonably cured. Acceptance does not of itself impair any other remedy provided by this Article or the lease agreement for nonconformity.

(3) If a tender has been accepted:

(a) within a reasonable time after the lessee discovers or should have discovered any default, the lessee shall notify the lessor and the supplier, or be barred from any remedy;
(b) except in the case of a consumer lease, within a reasonable time after the lessee receives notice of litigation for infringement or the like (Section 2A-211) the lessee shall notify the lessor or be barred from any remedy over for liability established by the litigation; and
(c) the burden is on the lessee to establish any default.

(4) If a lessee is sued for breach of a warranty or other obligation for which a lessor or a supplier is answerable over:

(a) The lessee may give the lessor or the supplier written notice of the litigation. If the notice states that the lessor or the supplier may come in and defend and that if the lessor or the supplier does not do so he [or she] will be bound in any action against him [or her] by the lessee by any determination of fact common to the two litigations, then unless the lessor or the supplier after seasonable receipt of the notice does come in and defend he [or she] is so bound.
(b) The lessor or the supplier may demand in writing that the lessee turn over control of the litigation including settlement if the claim is one for infringement or the like (Section 2A-211) or else be barred from any remedy over. If the demand states that the lessor or the supplier agrees to bear all expense and to satisfy any adverse judgment, then unless the lessee after seasonable receipt of the demand does turn over control the lessee is so barred.

(5) The provisions of subsections (3) and (4) apply to any obligation of a lessee to hold the lessor or the supplier harmless against infringement or the like (Section 2A-211).

§2A-517. Revocation of Acceptance of Goods.

(1) A lessee may revoke acceptance of a lot or commercial unit whose nonconformity substantially impairs its value to the lessee if he[or she] has accepted it:

(a) except in the case of a finance lease, on the reasonable assumption that its nonconformity would be cured and it has not been seasonably cured; or
(b) without discovery of the nonconformity if the lessee's acceptance was reasonably induced either by the lessor's assurances or, except in the case of a finance lease, by the difficulty of discovery before acceptance.

(2) Revocation of acceptance must occur within a reasonable time after the lessee discovers or should have discovered the ground for it and before any substantial change in condition of the goods which is not caused by the nonconformity. Revocation is not effective until the lessee notifies the lessor.

(3) A lessee who so revokes has the same rights and duties with regard to the goods involved as if the lessee had rejected them.

§2A-518. Cover; Substitute Goods.

(1) After default by a lessor under the lease contract (Section 2A-508(1)), the lessee may cover by making in good faith and without unreasonable delay any purchase or lease of or contract to purchase or lease goods in substitution for those due from the lessor.

(2) Except as otherwise provided with respect to damages liquidated in the lease agreement (Section 2A-504) or determined by agreement of the parties (Section 1-102(3)), if a lessee's cover is by lease agreement substantially similar to the original lease agreement and the lease agreement is made in good faith and in a commercially reasonable manner, the lessee may recover from the lessor as damages (a) the present value, as of the date of default, of the difference between the total rent for the lease term of the new lease agreement and the total rent for the remaining lease term of the original lease agreement and (b) any incidental or consequential damages less expenses saved in consequence of the lessor's default.

(3) If a lessee's cover does not qualify for treatment under subsection (2), the lessee may recover from the lessor as if the lessee had elected not to cover and Section 2A-519 governs.

§2A-519. Lessee's Damages for Non-Delivery, Repudiation, Default and Breach of Warranty in Regard to Accepted Goods.

(1) If a lessee elects not to cover or a lessee elects to cover and the cover does not qualify for treatment under Section 2A-518(2), the measure of damages for non-delivery or repudiation by the lessor or for rejection or revocation of acceptance by the lessee is the present value as of the date of the default of the difference between the then market rent and the original rent, computed for the remaining lease term of the original lease agreement together with incidental and consequential damages, less expenses saved in consequence of the lessor's default.

(2) Market rent is to be determined as of the place for tender or, in cases of rejection after arrival or revocation of acceptance, as of the place of arrival.

(3) If the lessee has accepted goods and given notification (Section 2A-516(3)), the measure of damages for non-conforming tender or delivery by a lessor is the loss resulting in the ordinary course of events from the lessor's default as determined in any manner that is reasonable together with incidental and consequential damages, less expenses saved in consequence of the lessor's default.

(4) The measure of damages for breach of warranty is the present value at the time and place of acceptance of the difference between the value of the use of the goods accepted and the value if they had been as warranted for the lease term, unless special circumstances show proximate damages of a different amount, together with incidental and consequential damages, less expenses saved in consequence of the lessor's default or breach of warranty.

§2A-520. Lessee's Incidental and Consequential Damages.

(1) Incidental damages resulting from a lessor's default include expenses reasonably incurred in inspection, receipt, transportation, and care and custody of goods rightfully rejected or goods the acceptance of which is justifiably revoked, any commercially reasonable charges, expenses or commissions in connection with effecting cover, and any other reasonable expense incident to the default.

(2) Consequential damages resulting from a lessor's default include:

(a) any loss resulting from general or particular requirements and needs of which the lessor at the time of contracting had reason to know and which could not reasonably be prevented by cover or otherwise; and
(b) injury to person or property proximately resulting from any breach of warranty.

§2A-521. Lessee's Right to Specific Performance or Replevin.

(1) Specific performance may be decreed if the goods are unique or in other proper circumstances.

(2) A decree for specific performance may include any terms and conditions as to payment of the rent, damages, or other relief that the court deems just.

(3) A lessee has a right of replevin, detinue, sequestration, claim and delivery, or the like for goods identified to the lease contract if after reasonable effort the lessee is unable to effect cover for those goods or the circumstances reasonably indicate that the effort will be unavailing.

§2A-522. Lessee's Right to Goods on Lessor's Insolvency.

(1) Subject to subsection (2) and even though the goods have not been shipped, a lessee who has paid a part or all of the rent and security for goods identified to a lease contract (Section 2A-217) on making and keeping good a tender of any unpaid portion of the rent and security due under the lease contract may recover the goods identified from the lessor if the lessor becomes insolvent within 10 days after receipt of the first installment of rent and security.

(2) A lessee acquires the right to recover goods identified to a lease contract only if they conform to the lease contract.

C. Default by Lessee

§2A-523. Lessor's Remedies.

(1) If a lessee wrongfully rejects or revokes acceptance of goods or fails to make a payment when due or repudiates with respect to a part or the whole, then, with respect to any goods involved, and with respect to all of the goods if under an installment lease contract the value of the whole lease contract is substantially impaired (Section 2A-510), the lessee is in default under the lease contract and the lessor may:

(a) cancel the lease contract (Section 2A-505(1));
(b) proceed respecting goods not identified to the lease contract (Section 2A-524);
(c) withhold delivery of the goods and take possession of goods previously delivered (Section 2A-525);
(d) stop delivery of the goods by any bailee (Section 2A-526);
(e) dispose of the goods and recover damages (Section 2A-527), or retain the goods and recover damages (Section 2A-528), or in a proper case recover rent (Section 2A-529).

(2) If a lessee is otherwise in default under a lease contract, the lessor may exercise the rights and remedies provided in the lease contract and this Article.

§2A-524. Lessor's Right to Identify Goods to Lease Contract.

(1) A lessor aggrieved under Section 2A-523(1) may:

(a) identify to the lease contract conforming goods not already identified if at the time the lessor learned of the default they were in the lessor's or the supplier's possession or control; and
(b) dispose of goods (Section 2A-527(1)) that demonstrably have been intended for the particular lease contract even though those goods are unfinished.

(2) If the goods are unfinished, in the exercise of reasonable commercial judgment for the purposes of avoiding loss and of effective realization, an aggrieved lessor or the supplier may either complete manufacture and wholly identify the goods to the lease contract or cease manufacture and lease, sell, or otherwise dispose of the goods for scrap or salvage value or proceed in any other reasonable manner.

§2A-525. Lessor's Right to Possession of Goods.

(1) If a lessor discovers the lessee to be insolvent, the lessor may refuse to deliver the goods.

(2) The lessor has on default by the lessee under the lease contract the right to take possession of the goods. If the lease contract so provides, the lessor may require the lessee to assemble the goods and make them available to the lessor at a place to be designated by the lessor which is reasonably convenient to both parties. Without removal, the lessor may render unusable any goods employed in trade or business, and may dispose of goods on the lessee's premises (Section 2A-527).

(3) The lessor may proceed under subsection (2) without judicial process if that can be done without breach of the peace or the lessor may proceed by action.

§2A-526. Lessor's Stoppage of Delivery in Transit or Otherwise.

(1) A lessor may stop delivery of goods in the possession of a carrier or other bailee if the lessor discovers the lessee to be insolvent and may stop delivery of carload, truckload, planeload, or larger shipments of express or freight if the lessee repudiates or fails to make a payment due before delivery, whether for rent, security or otherwise under the lease contract, or for any other reason the lessor has a right to withhold or take possession of the goods.

(2) In pursuing its remedies under subsection (1) the lessor may stop delivery until

   (a) receipt of the goods by the lessee;
   (b) acknowledgment to the lessee by any bailee of the goods, except a carrier, that the bailee holds the goods for the lessee; or
   (c) such an acknowledgment to the lessee by a carrier via reshipment or as warehouseman.

(3) (a) To stop delivery, a lessor shall so notify as to enable the bailee by reasonable diligence to prevent delivery of the goods.
   (b) After notification, the bailee shall hold and deliver the goods according to the directions of the lessor, but the lessor is liable to the bailee for any ensuing charges or damages.
   (c) A carrier who has issued a nonnegotiable bill of lading is not obliged to obey a notification to stop received from a person other than the consignor.

§2A-527. Lessor's Rights to Dispose of Goods.

(1) After a default by a lessee under the lease contract (Section 2A-523(1)) or after the lessor refuses to deliver or take possession of goods (Section 2A-525 or 2A-526), the lessor may dispose of the goods concerned or the undelivered balance thereof in good faith and without unreasonable delay by lease, sale or otherwise.

(2) If the disposition is by lease contract substantially similar to the original lease contract and the lease contract is made in good faith and in a commercially reasonable manner, the lessor may recover from the lessee as damages (a) accrued and unpaid rent as of the date of default, (b) the present value as of the date of default of the difference between the total rent for the remaining lease term of the original lease contract and the total rent for the lease term of the new lease contract, and (c) any incidental damages allowed under Section 2A-530, less expenses saved in consequence of the lessee's default.

(3) If the lessor's disposition is by lease contract that for any reason does not qualify for treatment under subsection (2), or is by sale or otherwise, the lessor may recover from the lessee as if the lessor had elected not to dispose of the goods and Section 2A-528 governs.

(4) A subsequent buyer or lessee who buys or leases from the lessor in good faith for value as a result of a disposition under this section takes the goods free of the original lease contract and any rights of the original lessee even though the lessor fails to comply with one or more of the requirements of this Article.

(5) The lessor is not accountable to the lessee for any profit made on any disposition. A lessee who has rightfully rejected or justifiably revoked acceptance shall account to the lessor for any excess over the amount of the lessee's security interest (Section 2A-508(5)).

§2A-528. Lessor's Damages for Non-Acceptance or Repudiation.

(1) Except as otherwise provided with respect to damages liquidated in the lease agreement (Section 2A-504) or determined by agreement of the parties (Section 1-102(3)), if a lessor elects to retain the goods or a lessor elects to dispose of the goods and disposition is by lease agreement that for any reason does not qualify for treatment under Section 2A-527(2), or is by sale or otherwise, the lessor may recover from the lessee as damages for non-acceptance or repudiation by the lessee (a) accrued and unpaid rent as of the date of default, (b) the present value as of the date of default of the difference between the total rent for the remaining lease term of the original lease agreement and the market rent at the time and place for tender computed for the same lease term, and (c) any incidental damages allowed under Section 2A-530, less expenses saved in consequence of the lessee's default.

(2) If the measure of damages provided in subsection (1) is inadequate to put a lessor in as good a position as performance would have, the measure of damages is the profit, including reasonable overhead, the lessor would have made from full performance by the lessee, together with any incidental damages allowed under Section 2A-530, due allowance for costs reasonably incurred and due credit for payments or proceeds of disposition.

§2A-529. Lessor's Action for the Rent.

(1) After default by the lessee under the lease contract (Section 2A-523(1)), if the lessor complies with subsection (2), the lessor may recover from the lessee as damages:

   (a) for goods accepted by the lessee and for conforming goods lost or damaged within a commercially reasonable time after risk of loss passes to the lessee (Section 2A-219), (i) accrued and unpaid rent as of the date of default, (ii) the present value as of the date of default of the rent for the remaining lease term of the lease agreement, and (iii) any incidental damages allowed under Section 2A-530, less expenses saved in consequence of the lessee's default; and
   (b) for goods identified to the lease contract if the lessor is unable after reasonable effort to dispose of them at a reasonable price or the circumstances reasonably indicate that effort will be unavailing, (i) accrued and unpaid rent as of the date of default, (ii) the present value as of the date of default of the rent for the remaining lease term of the lease agreement, and (iii) any incidental damages allowed under Section 2A-530, less expenses saved in consequence of the lessee's default.

(2) Except as provided in subsection (3), the lessor shall hold for the lessee for the remaining lease term of the lease agreement any goods that have been identified to the lease contract and are in the lessor's control.

(3) The lessor may dispose of the goods at any time before collection of the judgment for damages obtained pursuant to subsection (1) and the lessor may proceed against the lessee for damages pursuant to Section 2A-527 or Section 2A-528.

(4) Payment of the judgment for damages obtained pursuant to subsection (1) entitles the lessee to use and possession of the goods not then disposed of for the remaining lease term of the lease agreement.

(5) After a lessee has wrongfully rejected or revoked acceptance of goods, has failed to pay rent then due, or has repudiated (Section 2A-402), a lessor who is held not entitled to rent under this section must nevertheless be awarded damages for non-acceptance under Sections 2A-527 and 2A-528.

§2A-530. Lessor's Incidental Damages.
Incidental damages to an aggrieved lessor include any commercially reasonable charges, expenses, or commissions incurred in stopping delivery, in the trans-

portation, care and custody of goods after the lessee's default, in connection with return or disposition of the goods, or otherwise resulting from the default.

§2A-531. Standing to Sue Third Parties for Injury to Goods.

(1) If a third party so deals with goods that have been identified to a lease contract as to cause actionable injury to a party to the lease contract (a) the lessor has a right of action against the third party, and (b) the lessee also has a right of action against the third party if the lessee:

(i) has a security interest in the goods;
(ii) has an insurable interest in the goods; or
(iii) bears the risk of loss under the lease contract or has since the injury assumed that risk as against the lessor and the goods have been converted or destroyed.

(2) If at the time of the injury the party plaintiff did not bear the risk of loss as against the other party to the lease contract and there is no arrangement between them for disposition of the recovery, his[or her] suit or settlement, subject to his [or her] own interest, is as a fiduciary for the other party to the lease contract.

(3) Either party with the consent of the other may sue for the benefit of whom it may concern.

ARTICLE 3: COMMERCIAL PAPER

Part 1: Short Title, Form and Interpretation

§3-101. Short Title.
This Article shall be known and may be cited as Uniform Commercial Code—Commercial Paper.

§3-102. Definitions and Index of Definitions.

(1) In this Article unless the context otherwise requires

(a) "Issue" means the first delivery of an instrument to a holder or a remitter.
(b) An "order" is a direction to pay and must be more than an authorization or request. It must identify the person to pay with reasonable certainty. It may be addressed to one or more such persons jointly or in the alternative but not in succession.
(c) A "promise" is an undertaking to pay and must be more than an acknowledgement of an obligation.
(d) "Secondary party" means a drawer or endorser.
(e) "Instrument" means a negotiable instrument.

(2) Other definitions applying to this Article and the sections in which they appear are:

"Acceptance"	Section 3-410
"Accommodation party"	Section 3-415
"Alteration"	Section 3-407
"Certificate of deposit"	Section 3-104
"Certification"	Section 3-411
"Check"	Section 3-104
"Definite time"	Section 3-109
"Dishonor"	Section 3-507
"Draft"	Section 3-104
"Holder in due course"	Section 3-302
"Negotiation"	Section 3-202
"Note"	Section 3-104
"Notice of dishonor"	Section 3-508
"On demand"	Section 3-108
"Presentment"	Section 3-504
"Protest"	Section 3-509
"Restrictive indorsement"	Section 3-205
"Signature"	Section 3-401

(3) The following definitions in other Articles apply to this Article:

"Account"	Section 4-104
"Banking day"	Section 4-104
"Clearing house"	Section 4-104
"Collecting bank"	Section 4-105
"Customer"	Section 4-104
"Depositary bank"	Section 4-105
"Documentary draft"	Section 4-104
"Intermediary bank"	Section 4-105
"Item"	Section 4-104
"Midnight deadline"	Section 4-104
"Payor bank"	Section 4-105

(4) In addition Article 1 contains general definitions and principles of construction and interpretation applicable throughout this Article.

§3-103. Limitations on Scope of Article.

(1) This Article does not apply to money, documents of title or investment securities.

(2) The provisions of this Article are subject to the provisions of the Article on Bank Deposits and Collections (Article 4) and Secured Transactions (Article 9).

§3-104. Form of Negotiable Instruments; "Draft"; "Check"; "Certificate of Deposit"; "Note".

(1) Any writing to be a negotiable instrument within this Article must

(a) be signed by the maker or drawer; and
(b) contain an unconditional promise or order to pay a sum certain in money and no other promise, order, obligation or power given by the maker or drawer except as authorized by this Article; and
(c) be payable on demand or at a definite time; and
(d) be payable to order or to bearer.

(2) A writing which complies with the requirements of this section is

(a) a "draft" ("bill of exchange") if it is an order;
(b) a "check" if it is a draft drawn on a bank and payable on demand.
(c) a "certificate of deposit" if it is an acknowledgement by a bank of receipt of money with an engagement to repay it;
(d) a "note" if it is a promise other than a certificate of deposit.

(3) As used in other Articles in this Act, and as the context may require, the terms "draft", "check", "certificate of deposit" and "note" may refer to instruments which are not negotiable within this Article as will as to instruments which are so negotiable.

§3-105. When Promise or Order Unconditional.

(1) A promise or order otherwise unconditional is not made conditional by the fact that the instrument

(a) is subject to implied or constructive conditions; or
(b) states its consideration, whether performed or promised, or the transaction which gave rise to the instrument, or that the promise or order is made or the instrument matures in accordance with or "as per" such transaction; or

(c) refers to or states that it arises out of a separate agreement or refers to a separate agreement for rights as to prepayment or acceleration; or

(d) states that is drawn under a letter of credit; or

(e) states that it is secured, whether by mortgage, reservation of title or otherwise; or

(f) indicates a particular account to be debited or any other fund or source from which reimbursement is expected; or

(g) is limited to payment out of a particular fund or the proceeds of a particular source, if the instrument is issued by a government or governmental agency or unit; or

(h) is limited to payment out of the entire assets of a partnership, unincorporated association, trust or estate by or on behalf of which the instrument is issued.

(2) A promise or order is not unconditional if the instrument

(a) states that it is subject to or governed by any other agreement; or

(b) states that it is to be paid only out of a particular fund or source except as provided in this section. As amended 1962.

§3-106. Sum Certain.

(1) The sum payable is a sum certain even though it is to be paid

(a) with stated interest or by stated installments; or

(b) with stated different rates of interest before and after default or a specified date; or

(c) with a stated discount or addition if paid before or after the date fixed for payment; or

(d) with exchange or less exchange, whether at a fixed rate or at the current rate; or

(e) with costs of collection or an attorney's fee or both upon default.

(2) Nothing in this section shall validate any term which is otherwise illegal.

§3-107. Money.

(1) An instrument is payable in money if the medium of exchange in which it is payable is money at the time the instrument is made. An instrument payable in "currency" or "current funds" is payable in money.

(2) A promise or order to pay a sum stated in a foreign currency is for a sum certain in money and, unless a different medium of payment is specified in the instrument, may be satisfied by payment of that number of dollars which the stated foreign currency will purchase at the buying sight rate for that currency on the day on which the instrument is payable or, if payable on demand, on the day of demand. If such an instrument specifies a foreign currency as the medium of payment the instrument is payable in that currency

§3-108. Payable on Demand.
Instruments payable on demand include those payable at sight or on presentation and those in which no time for payment is stated.

§3-109. Definite Time.

(1) An instrument is payable at a definite time if by its terms it is payable

(a) on or before a stated date or at a fixed period after a stated date; or

(b) at a fixed period after sight; or

(c) at a definite time subject to any acceleration; or

(d) at a definite time subject to extension at the option of the holder, or to extension to a further definite time at the option of the maker or acceptor or automatically upon or after a specified act or event.

(2) An instrument which by its terms is otherwise payable only upon an act or event uncertain as to time of occurence is not payable at a definite time even though the act or event has occured.

§3-110. Payable to Order.

(1) An instrument is payable to order when by its terms it is payable to the order or assigns of any person therein specified with reasonable certainty, or to him or his order, or when it is conspicuously designated on its face as "exchange" or the like and names a payee. It may be payable to the order of

(a) the maker or drawer; or

(b) the drawee; or

(c) a payee who is not maker, drawer or drawee; or

(d) two or more payees together or in the alternative; or

(e) an estate, trust or fund, in which case it is payable to the order of the representative of such estate, trust or fund or his successors; or

(f) an office, or an officer by his title as such in which case it is payable to the principal but the incumbent of the office or his successors may act as if he or they were the holder; or

(g) a partnership or unincorporated association, in which case it is payable to the partnership or association and may be indorsed or transferred by any person thereto authorized.

(2) An instrument not payable to order is not made so payable by such words as "payable upon return of this instrument properly indorsed."

(3) An instrument made payable both to order and to bearer is payable to order unless the bearer words are handwritten or typewritten.

§3-111. Payable to Bearer.
An instrument is payable to bearer when by its terms it is payable to

(a) bearer or the order of bearer; or

(b) a specified person or bearer; or

(c) "cash" or the order of "cash", or any other indication which does not purport to designate a specific payee.

§3-112. Terms and Omissions Not Affecting Negotiability.

(1) The negotiability of an instrument is not affected by

(a) the omission of a statement of any consideration or of the place where the instrument is drawn or payable; or

(b) a statement that collateral has been given to secure obligations either on the instrument or otherwise of an obligor on the instrument or that in case of default on those obligations the holder may realize on or dispose of the collateral; or

(c) a promise or power to maintain or protect collateral or to give additional collateral; or

(d) a term authorizing a confession of judgment on the instrument if it is not paid when due; or

(e) a term purporting to waive the benefit of any law intended for the advantage or protection of any obligor; or

(f) a term in a draft providing that the payee by indorsing or cashing it acknowledges full satisfaction of an obligation of the drawer; or

(g) a statement in a draft drawn in a set of parts (Section 3-801) to the effect that the order is effective only if no other part has been honored.

(2) Nothing in this section shall validate any term which is otherwise illegal. As amended 1962.

§3-113. Seal. An instrument otherwise negotiable is within this Article even though it is under a seal.

§3-114. Date, Antedating, Postdating.

(1) The negotiability of an instrument is not affected by the fact that it is undated, antedated or postdated.

(2) Where an instrument is antedated or postdated the time when it is payable is determined by the stated date if the instrument is payable on demand or at a fixed period after date.

(3) Where the instrument or any signature thereon is dated, the date is presumed to be correct.

§3-115. Incomplete Instruments.

(1) When a paper whose contents at the time of signing show that it is intended to become an instrument is signed while still incomplete in any necessary respect it cannot be enforced until completed, but when it is completed in accordance with authority given it is effective as completed.

(2) If the completion is unauthorized the rules as to material alteration apply (Section 3-407), even though the paper was not delivered by the maker or drawer; but the burden of establishing that any completion is unauthorized is on the party so asserting.

§3-116. Instruments Payable to Two or More Persons. An instrument payable to the order of two or more persons

(a) if in the alternative is payable to any one of them and may be negotiated, discharged or enforced by any of them who has possession of it;

(b) if not in the alternative is payable to all of them and may be negotiated, discharged or enforced only by all of them.

§3-117. Instruments Payable With Words of Description. An instrument made payable to a named person with the addition of words describing him

(a) as agent or officer of a specified person is payable to his principal but the agent or officer may act as if he were the holder;

(b) as any other fiduciary for a specified person or purpose is payable to the payee and may be negotiated, discharged or enforced by him;

(c) in any other manner is payable to the payee unconditionally and the additional word are without effect on subsequent parties.

§3-118. Ambiguous Terms and Rules of Construction. The following rules apply to every instrument:

(a) Where there is doubt whether the instrument is a draft or a note the holder may treat it as either. A draft drawn on the drawer is effective as a note.

(b) Handwritten terms control typewritten and printed terms, and typewritten control printed.

(c) Words control figures except that if the words are ambiguous figures control.

(d) Unless otherwise specified a provision for interest means interest at the judgment rate at the place of payment from the date of the instrument, or if it is undated from the date of issue.

(e) Unless the instrument otherwise specifies two or more persons who sign as maker, acceptor or drawer or indorser and as a part of the same transaction are jointly and severally liable even though the instrument contains such words as "I promise to pay."

(f) Unless otherwise specified consent to extension authorizes a single extension for not longer than the original period. A consent to extension, expressed in the instrument, is binding on secondary parties and accommodation makers. A holder may not exercise his option to extend an instrument over the objection of a maker or acceptor or other party who in accordance with Section 3-604 tenders full payment when the instrument is due.

§3-119. Other Writings Affecting Instrument.

(1) As between the obligor and his immediate obligee or any transferee the terms of an instrument may be modified or affected by any other written agreement executed as a part of the same transaction, except that a holder in due course is not affected by any limitation of his rights arising out of the separate written agreement if he had no notice of the limitation when he took the instrument.

(2) A separate agreement does not affect the negotiability of an instrument.

§3-120. Instruments "Payable Through" Bank. An instrument which states that is is "payable through" a bank or the like designates that bank as a collecting bank to make presentment but does not of itself authorize the bank to pay the instrument.

§3-121. Instruments Payable at Bank.

Note: *If this Act is introduced in the Congress of the United States this section should be omitted. (States to select either alternative.)*

Alternative A—A note or acceptance which states that it is payable at a bank is the equivalent of a draft drawn on the bank payable when it falls due out of any funds of the maker or acceptor in current account or otherwise available for such payment.

Alternative B—A note or acceptance which states that it is payable at a bank is not of itself an order or authorization to the bank to pay it.

§3-122. Accrual of Cause of Action.

(1) A cause of action against a maker or an acceptor accrues

(a) in the case of a time instrument on the day after maturity;

(b) in the case of a demand instrument upon its date or, if no date is stated, on the date of issue.

(2) A cause of action against the obligor of a demand or time certificate of deposit accrues upon demand, but demand on a time certificate may not be made until on or after the date of maturity.

(3) A cause of action against a drawer of a draft or an indorser of any instrument accrues upon demand following dishonor of the instrument. Notice of dishonor is a demand.

(4) Unless an instrument provides otherwise, interest runs at the rate provided by law for a judgment

(a) in the case of a maker, acceptor or other primary obligor of a demand instrument, from the date of demand;

(b) in all other cases from the date of accrual of the cause of action. As amended 1962.

Part 2: Transfer and Negotiation

§3-201. Transfer: Right to Indorsement.

(1) Transfer of an instrument vests in the transferee such rights as the transferor has therein, except that a transferee who has himself been a party to any fraud or illegality affecting the instrument or who as a prior holder had notice of a defense or claim against it cannot improve his position by taking from a later holder in due course.

(2) A transfer of a security interest in an instrument vests the foregoing rights in the transferee to the extent of the interest transferred.

(3) Unless otherwise agreed any transfer for value of an instrument not then payable to bearer gives the transferee the specifically enforceable right to have the unqualified indorsement of the transferor. Negotiation takes effect only when the indorsement is made and until that time there is no presumption that the transferee is the owner.

§3-202. Negotiation.

(1) Negotiation is the transfer of an instrument in such form that the transferee becomes a holder. If the instrument is payable to order it is negotiated by delivery with any necessary indorsement; if payable to bearer it is negotiated by delivery.

(2) An indorsement must be written by or on behalf of the holder and on the instrument or on a paper so firmly affixed thereto as to become a part thereof.

(3) An indorsement is effective for negotiation only when it conveys the entire instrument or any unpaid residue. If it purports to be of less it operates only as a partial assignment.

(4) Words of assignment, condition, waiver, guaranty, limitation or disclaimer of liability and the like accompanying an indorsement do not affect its character as an indorsement.

§3-203. Wrong of Misspelled Name.
Where an instrument is made payable to a person under a misspelled name or one other than his own he may indorse in that name or his own or both; but signature in both names may be required by a person paying or giving value for the instrument.

§3-204. Special Indorsement; Blank Indorsement.

(1) A special indorsement specifies the person to whom or to whose order it makes the instrument payable. Any instrument specially indorsed becomes payable to the order of the special indorsee and may be further negotiated only by his indorsement.

(2) An indorsement in blank specifies no particular indorsee and may consist of a mere signature. An instrument payable to order and indorsed in blank becomes payable to bearer and may be negotiated by delivery alone until specially indorsed.

(3) The holder may convert a blank indorsement into a special indorsement by writing over the signature of the indorser in blank any contract consistent with the character of the indorsement.

§3-205. Restrictive Indorsements.
An indorsement is restrictive which either

(a) is conditional; or
(b) purports to prohibit further transfer of the instrument; or
(c) includes the words "for collection", "for deposit", "pay any bank", or like terms signifying a purpose of deposit or collection; or
(d) otherwise states that it is for the benefit or use of the indorser or of another person.

§3-206. Effect of Restrictive Indorsement.

(1) No restrictive indorsement prevents further transfer or negotiation of the instrument.

(2) An intermediary bank, or a payor bank which is not the depositary bank, is neither given notice nor otherwise affected by a restrictive indorsement of any person except the bank's immediate transferor or the person presenting for payment.

(3) Except for an intermediary bank, any transferee under an indorsement which is conditional or includes the words "for collection", "for deposit", "pay any bank", or like terms (subparagraphs (a) and (c) of Section 3-205) must pay or apply any value given by him for or on the security of the instrument consistently with the indorsement and to the extent that he does so he becomes a holder for value. In addition such transferee is a holder in due course if he otherwise complies with the requirements of Section 3-302 on what constitutes a holder in due course.

(4) The first taker under an indorsement for the benefit of the indorser or another person (subparagraph (d) of Section 3-205) must pay or apply any value given by him for or on the security of the instrument consistently with the indorsement and to the extent that he does so he becomes a holder for value. In addition such taker is a holder in due course if he otherwise complies with the requirements of Section 3-302 on what constitutes a holder in due course. A later holder for value is neither given notice nor otherwise affected by such restrictive indorsement unless he has knowledge that a fiduciary or other person has negotiated the instrument in any transaction for his own benefit or otherwise in breach of duty (subsection (2) of Section 3-304).

§3-207. Negotiation Effective Although It May Be Rescinded.

(1) Negotiation is effective to transfer the instrument although the negotiation is

(a) made by an infant, a corporation exceeding its powers, or any other person without capacity; or
(b) obtained by fraud, duress or mistake of any kind; or
(c) part of an illegal transaction; or
(d) made in breach of duty.

(2) Except as against a subsequent holder in due course such negotiation is in an appropriate case subject to rescission, the declaration of a constructive trust or any other remedy permitted by law.

§3-208. Reacquisition.
Where an instrument is returned to or reacquired by a prior party he may cancel any indorsement which is not necessary to his title and reissue or further negotiate the instrument, but any intervening party is discharged as against the reacquiring party and subsequent holders not in due course and if his indorsement has been cancelled is discharged as against subsequent holders in due course as well.

Part 3: Rights of a Holder

§3-301. Rights of a Holder.
The holder of an instrument whether or not he is the owner may transfer or negotiate it and, except as otherwise provided in Section 3-603 on payment or satisfaction, discharge it or enforce payment in his own name.

§3-302. Holder in Due Course

(1) A holder in due course is a holder who takes the instrument

(a) for value; and
(b) in good faith; and
(c) without notice that it is overdue or has been dishonored or of any defense against or claim to it on the part of any person.

(2) A payee may be a holder in due course.

(3) A holder does not become a holder in due course of an instrument:

(a) by purchase of it at judicial sale or by taking it under legal process; or
(b) by acquiring it in taking over an estate, or
(c) by purchasing it as part of a bulk transaction not in regular course of business of the transferor.

(4) A purchaser of a limited interest can be a holder in due course only to the extent of the interest purchased.

§3-303. Taking for Value. A holder takes the instrument for value

(a) to the extent that the agreed consideration has been performed or that he acquires a security interest in or a lien on the instrument otherwise than by legal process; or
(b) when he takes the instrument in payment of or as security for an antecedent claim against any person whether or not the claim is due; or
(c) when he gives a negotiable instrument for it or makes an irrevocable commitment to a third person.

§3-304. Notice to Purchaser.

(1) The purchaser has notice of a claim or defense if

(a) the instrument is so incomplete, bears such visible evidence of forgery or alteration, or is otherwise so irregular as to call into question its validity, terms or ownership or to create an ambiguity as to the party to pay; or
(b) the purchaser has notice that the obligation of any party is voidable in whole or part, or that all parties have been discharged.

(2) The purchaser has notice of a claim against the instrument when he has knowledge that a fiduciary has negotiated the instrument in payment of or as security for his own debt or in any transaction for his own benefit or otherwise in breach of duty.

(3) The purchaser has notice that an instrument is overdue if he has reason to know

(a) that any part of the principal amount is overdue or that there is an uncured default in payment of another instrument of the same series; or
(b) that acceleration of the instrument has been made; or
(c) that he is taking a demand instrument after demand has been made or more than a reasonable length of time after its issue. A reasonable time for a check drawn and payable within the states and territories of the United States and the District of Columbia is presumed to be thirty days.

(4) Knowledge of the following facts does not of itself give the purchaser notice of a defense or claim

(a) that the instrument is antedated or postdated;
(b) that it was issued or negotiated in return for an executory promise or accompanied by a separate agreement, unless the purchaser has notice that a defense or claim has arisen from the terms thereof;
(c) that any party has signed for accomodation;
(d) that an incomplete instrument has been completed, unless the purchaser has notice of any improper completion;
(e) that any person negotiating the instrument is or was a fiduciary;
(f) that there has been default in payment of interest on the instrument or in payment of any other instrument, except one of the same series.

(5) The filing or recording of a document does not of itself constitute notice within the provisions of this Article to a person who would otherwise be a holder in due course.

(6) To be effective notice must be received at such time and in such manner as to give a reasonable opportunity to act on it.

§3-305. Rights of a Holder in Due Course. To the extent that a holder is a holder in due course he takes the instrument free from

(1) all claims to it on the part of any person; and
(2) all defenses of any party to the instrument with whom the holder has not dealt except

(a) infancy, to the extent that it is a defense to a simple contract; and
(b) such other incapacity, or duress, or illegality of the transaction, as renders the obligation of the party a nullity; and
(c) such misrepresentation as has induced the party to sign the instrument with neither knowledge nor reasonable opportunity to obtain knowledge of its character or its essential terms; and
(d) discharge in insolvency proceedings; and
(e) any other discharge of which the holder has notice when he takes the instrument.

§3-306. Rights of One Not Holder in Due Course. Unless he has the rights of a holder in due course any person takes the instrument subject to

(a) all valid claims to it on the part of any person; and
(b) all defenses of any party which would be available in an action on a simple contract; and
(c) the defenses of want or failure of consideration, nonperformance of any condition precedent, non-delivery, or delivery for a special purpose (Section 3-408); and
(d) the defense that he or a person through whom he holds the instrument acquired it by theft, or that payment or satisfaction to such holder would be inconsistent with the terms of a restrictive indorsement. The claim of any third person to the instrument is not otherwise available as a defense to any party liable thereon unless the third person himself defends the action for such party.

§3-307. Burden of Establishing Signatures, Defenses and Due Course

(1) Unless specifically denied in the pleading each signature on an instrument is admitted. When the effectiveness of a signature is put in issue

(a) the burden of establishing it is on the party claiming under the signature; but
(b) the signature is presumed to be genuine or authorized except where the action is to enforce the obligation of a purported signer who has died or become incompetent before proof is required.

(2) When signatures are admitted or established, production of the instrument entitles a holder to recover on it unless the defendant establishes a defense.

(3) After it is shown that a defense exists a person claiming the rights of a holder in due course has the burden of establishing that he or some person under whom he claims is in all respects a holder in due course.

Part 4: Liability of Parties

§3-401. Signature.

(1) No person is liable on an instrument unless his signature appears thereon.

(2) A signature is made by use of any name, including any trade or assumed name, upon an instrument, or by any word or mark used in lieu of a written signature

§3-402. Signature in Ambiguous Capacity. Unless the instrument clearly indicates that a signature is made in some other capacity it is an indorsement.

§3-403. Signature by Authorized Representative.

(1) A signature may be made by an agent or other representative, and his authority to make it may be established as in other cases of representation. No particular form of appointment is necessary to establish such authority.

(2) An authorized representative who signs his own name to an instrument

   (a) is personally obligated if the instrument neither names the person represented nor shows that the representative signed in a representative capacity;
   (b) except as otherwise established between the immediate parties, is personally obligated if the instrument names the person represented but does not show that the representative signed in a representative capacity, or if the instrument does not name the person represented but does show that the representative signed in a representative capacity.

(3) Except as otherwise established the name of an organization preceded or followed by the name and office of an authorized individual is a signature made in a representative capacity.

§3-404. Unauthorized Signatures.

(1) Any unauthorized signature is wholly inoperative as that of the person whose name is signed unless he ratifies it or is precluded from denying it; but it operates as the signature of the unauthorized signer in favor of any person who in good faith pays the instrument or takes it for value.

(2) Any unauthorized signature may be ratified for all purposes of this Article. Such ratification does not of itself affect any rights of the person ratifying against the actual signer.

§3-405. Imposters; Signature in Name of Payee.

(1) An indorsement by any person in the name of a named payee is effective if

   (a) an impostor by use of the mails or otherwise has induced the maker or drawer to issue the instrument to him or his confederate in the name of the payee; or
   (b) a person signing as or on behalf of a maker or drawer intends the payee to have no interest in the instrument; or
   (c) an agent or employee of the maker or drawer has supplied him with the name of the payee intending the latter to have no such interest.

(2) Nothing in this section shall affect the criminal or civil liability of the person so indorsing.

§3-406. Negligence Contributing to Alteration or Unauthorized Signature.

Any person who by his negligence substantially contributes to a material alteration of the instrument or to the making of an unauthorized signature is precluded from asserting the alteration or lack of authority against a holder in due course or against a drawee or other payor who pays the instrument in good faith and in accordance with the reasonable commercial standards of the drawee's or payor's business.

§3-407. Alteration.

(1) Any alteration of an instrument is material which changes the contract of any party thereto in any respect, including any such change in

   (a) the number or relations of the parties; or
   (b) an incomplete instrument, by completing it otherwise than as authorized; or
   (c) the writing as signed, by adding to it or by removing any part of it.

(2) As against any person other than a subsequent holder in due course

   (a) alteration by the holder which is both fraudulent and material discharges any party whose contract is thereby changed unless that party assents or is precluded from asserting the defense;
   (b) no other alteration discharges any party and the instrument may be enforced according to its original tenor, or as to incomplete instruments according to the authority given.

(3) A subsequent holder in due course may in all cases enforce the instrument according to its original tenor, and when an incomplete instrument has been completed, he may enforce it as completed.

§3-408. Consideration.

Want or failure of consideration is a defense as against any person not having the rights of a holder in due course. (Section 3-305), except that no consideration is necessary for an instrument or obligation thereon given in payment of or as security for an antecedent obligation of any kind. Nothing in this section shall be taken to displace any statute outside this Act under which a promise is enforceable notwithstanding lack or failure of consideration. Partial failure of consideration is a defense pro tanto whether or not the failure is in an ascertained or liquidated amount.

§3-409. Draft Not an Assignment.

(1) A check or other draft does not of itself operate as an assignment of any funds in the hands of the drawee available for its payment, and the drawee is not liable on the instrument until he accepts it.

(2) Nothing in this section shall affect any liability in contract, tort or otherwise arising from any letter of credit or other obligation or representation which is not an acceptance.

§3-410. Definition and Operation of Acceptance.

(1) Acceptance is the drawee's signed engagement to honor the draft as presented. It must be written on the draft, and may consist of his signature alone. It becomes operative when completed by delivery or notification.

(2) A draft may be accepted although it has not been signed by the drawer or is otherwise incomplete or is overdue or has been dishonored.

(3) Where the draft is payable at a fixed period after sight and the acceptor fails to date his acceptance the holder may complete it by supplying a date in good faith.

§3-411. Certification of a Check.

(1) Certification of a check is acceptance. Where a holder procures certification the drawer and all prior indorsers are discharged.

(2) Unless otherwise agreed a bank has no obligation to certify a check.

(3) A bank may certify a check before returning it for lack of proper indorsement. If it does so the drawer is discharged.

§3-412. Acceptance Varying Draft.

(1) Where the drawee's proffered acceptance in any manner varies the draft as presented the holder may refuse the acceptance and treat the draft as dishonored in which case the drawee is entitled to have his acceptance cancelled.

(2) The terms of the draft are not varied by an acceptance to pay at any particular bank or place in the United States, unless the acceptance states that the draft is to be paid only at such bank or place.

(3) Where the holder assents to an acceptance varying the terms of the draft each drawer and indorser who does not affirmatively assent is discharged. As amended 1962.

§3-413. Contract of Maker, Drawer and Acceptor.

(1) The maker or acceptor engages that he will pay the instrument according to its tenor at the time of his engagement or as completed pursuant to Section 3-115 on incomplete instruments.

(2) The drawer engages that upon dishonor of the draft and any necessary notice of dishonor or protest he will pay the amount of the draft to the holder or to any indorser who takes it up. The drawer may disclaim this liability by drawing without recourse.

(3) By making, drawing or accepting the party admits as against all subsequent parties including the drawee the existence of the payee and his then capacity to indorse.

§3-414. Contract of Indorser; Order of Liability.

(1) Unless the indorsement otherwise specifies (as by such words as "without recourse") every indorser engages that upon dishonor and any necessary notice of dishonor and protest he will pay the instrument according to its tenor at the time of his indorsement to the holder or to any subsequent indorser who takes it up, even though the indorser who takes it up was not obligated to do so.

(2) Unless they otherwise agree indorsers are liable to one another in the order in which they indorse, which is presumed to be the order in which their signatures appear on the instrument.

§3-415. Contract of Accommodation Party.

(1) An accommodation party is one who signs the instrument in any capacity for the purpose of lending his name to another party to it.

(2) When the instrument has been taken for value before it is due the accommodation party is liable in the capacity in which he has signed even though the taker knows of the accommodation.

(3) As against a holder in due course and without notice of the accommodation oral proof of the accommodation is not admissible to give the accommodation party the benefit of discharges dependent on his character as such. In other cases the accommodation character may be shown by oral proof.

(4) An indorsement which shows that it is not in the chain of title is notice of its accommodation character.

(5) An accommodation party is not liable to the party accommodated, and if he pays the instrument has a right of recourse on the instrument against such party.

§3-416. Contract of Guarantor.

(1) "Payment guaranteed" or equivalent words added to a signature mean that the signer engages that if the instrument is not paid when due he will pay it according to its tenor without resort by the holder to any other party.

(2) "Collection guaranteed" or equivalent words added to a signature mean that the signer engages that if the instrument is not paid when due he will pay it according to its tenor, but only after the holder has reduced his claim against the maker or acceptor to judgment and execution has been returned unsatisfied, or after the maker or acceptor has become insolvent or it is otherwise apparent that it is useless to proceed against him.

(3) Words of guaranty which do not otherwise specify guarantee payment.

(4) No words of guaranty added to the signature of a sole maker or acceptor affect his liability on the instrument. Such words added to the signature of one of two or more makers or acceptors create a presumption that the signature is for the accommodation of the others.

(5) When words of guaranty are used presentment, notice of dishonor and protest are not necessary to charge the user.

(6) Any guaranty written on the instrument is enforcible notwithstanding any statute of frauds.

§3-417. Warranties on Presentment and Transfer.

(1) Any person who obtains payment or acceptance and any prior transferor warrants to a person who in good faith pays or accepts that

(a) he has a good title to the instrument or is authorized to obtain payment or acceptance on behalf of one who has a good title; and
(b) he has no knowledge that the signature of the maker or drawer is unauthorized, except that this warranty is not given by a holder in due course acting in good faith
  (i) to a maker with respect to the maker's own signature; or
  (ii) to a drawer with respect to the drawer's own signature, whether or not the drawer is also the drawee; or
  (iii) to an acceptor of a draft if the holder in due course took the draft after the acceptance or obtained the acceptance without knowledge that the drawer's signature was unauthorized; and
(c) the instrument has not been materially altered, except that this warranty is not given by a holder in due course acting in good faith
  (i) to the maker of a note; or
  (ii) to the drawer of a draft whether or not the drawer is also the drawee; or
  (iii) to the acceptor of a draft with respect to an alteration made prior to the acceptance if the holder in due course took the draft after the acceptance, even though the acceptance provided "payable as originally drawn" or equivalent terms; or
  (iv) to the acceptor of a draft with respect to an alteration made after the acceptance.

(2) Any person who transfers an instrument and receives consideration warrants to his transferee and if the transfer is by indorsement to any subsequent holder who takes the instrument in good faith that

(a) he has a good title to the instrument or is authorized to obtain payment or acceptance on behalf of one who has a good title and the transfer is otherwise rightful; and
(b) all signatures are genuine or authorized; and
(c) the instrument has not been materially altered; and
(d) no defense of any party is good against him; and
(e) he has no knowledge of any insolvency proceeding instituted with respect to the maker or acceptor or the drawer of an unaccepted instrument.

(3) By transferring "without recourse" the transferor limits the obligation stated in subsection (2)(d) to a warranty that he has no knowledge of such a defense.

(4) A selling agent or broker who does not disclose the fact that he is acting only as such gives the warranties provided in this section, but if he makes such disclosure warrants only his good faith and authority.

§3-418. Finality of Payment or Acceptance.
Except for recovery of bank payments as provided in the Article on Bank Deposits and Collections (Article 4) and except for liability for breach of war-

ranty on presentment under the preceding section, payment or acceptance of any instrument is final in favor of a holder in due course, or a person who has in good faith changed his position in reliance on the payment.

§3-419. Conversion of Instrument; Innocent Representative.

(1) An instrument is converted when

(a) a drawee to whom it is delivered for acceptance refuses to return it on demand; or

(b) any person to whom it is delivered for payment refuses on demand either to pay or to return it; or

(c) it is paid on a forged indorsement.

(2) In an action against a drawee under subsection (1) the measure of the drawee's liability is the face amount of the instrument. In any other action under subsection (1) the measure of liability is presumed to be the face amount of the instrument.

(3) Subject to the provisions of this Act concerning restrictive indorsements a representative, including a depositary or collecting bank, who has in good faith and in accordance with the reasonable commercial standards applicable to the business of such representative dealt with an instrument or its proceeds on behalf of one who was not the true owner is not liable in conversion or otherwise to the true owner beyond the amount of any proceeds remaining in his hands.

(4) An intermediary bank or payor bank which is not a depositary bank is not liable in conversion solely by reason of the fact that proceeds of an item indorsed restrictively (Sections 3-205 and 3-206) are not paid or applied consistently with the restrictive indorsement of an indorser other than its immediate transferor.

Part 5: Presentment, Notice of Dishonor, and Protest.

§3-501. When Presentment, Notice of Dishonor, and Protest Necessary or Permissible.

(1) Unless excused (Section 3-511) presentment is necessary to charge secondary parties as follows:

(a) presentment for acceptance is necessary to charge the drawer and indorsers of a draft where the draft so provides, or is payable elsewhere than at the residence or place of business of the drawee, or its date of payment depends upon such presentment. The holder may at his option present for acceptance any other draft payable at a stated date;

(b) presentment for payment is necessary to charge any indorser;

(c) in the case of any drawer, the acceptor of a draft payable at a bank or the maker of a note payable at a bank, presentment for payment is necessary, but failure to make presentment discharges such drawer, acceptor or maker only as stated in Section 3-502(1)(b).

(2) Unless excused (Section 3-511)

(a) notice of any dishonor is necessary to charge any indorser;

(b) in the case of any drawer, the acceptor of a draft payable at a bank or the maker of a note payable at a bank, notice of any dishonor is necessary, but failure to give such notice discharges such drawer, acceptor or maker only as stated in Section 3-502(1)(b).

(3) Unless excused (Section 3-511) protest of any dishonor is necessary to charge the drawer and indorsers of any draft which on its face appears to be drawn or payable outside of the states, territories, dependencies and possessions of the United States, the District of Columbia and the commonwealth of Puerto Rico. The holder may at his option make protest of any dishonor of any other instrument and in the case of a foreign draft may on insolvency of the acceptor before maturity make protest for better security.

(4) Notwithstanding any provision of this section, neither presentment nor notice of dishonor nor protest is necessary to charge an indorser who has indorsed an instrument after maturity. As amended 1966.

§3-502. Unexcused Delay; Discharge.

(1) Where without excuse any necessary presentment or notice of dishonor is delayed beyond the time when it is due

(a) any indorser is discharged; and

(b) any drawer or the acceptor of a draft payable at a bank or the maker of a note payable at a bank who because the drawee or payor bank becomes insolvent during the delay is deprived of funds maintained with the drawee or payor bank to cover the instrument may discharge his liability by written assignment to the holder of his rights against the drawee or payor bank in respect of such funds, but such drawer, acceptor or maker is not otherwise discharged.

(2) Where without excuse a necessary protest is delayed beyond the time when it is due any drawer or indorser is discharged.

§3-503. Time of Presentment.

(1) Unless a different time is expressed in the instrument the time for any presentment is determined as follows:

(a) where an instrument is payable at or a fixed period after a stated date any presentment for acceptance must be made on or before the date it is payable;

(b) where an instrument is payable after sight it must either be presented for acceptance or negotiated within a reasonable time after date or issue whichever is later;

(c) where an instrument shows the date on which it is payable presentment for payment is due on that date;

(d) where an instrument is accelerated presentment for payment is due within a reasonable time after the acceleration;

(e) with respect to the liablility of any secondary party presentment for acceptance or payment of any other instrument is due within a reasonable time after such party becomes liable thereon.

(2) A reasonable time for presentment is determined by the nature of the instrument, any usage of banking or trade and the facts of the particular case. In the case of an uncertified check which is drawn and payable within the United States and which is not a draft drawn by a bank the following are presumed to be reasonable periods within which to present for payment or to initate bank collection:

(a) with respect to the liability of the drawer, thirty days after date or issue whichever is later; and

(b) with respect to the liability of an indorser, seven days after his indorsement.

(3) Where any presentment is due on a day which is not a full business day for either the person making presentment or the party to pay or accept, presentment is due on the next following day which is a full business day for both parties.

(4) Presentment to be sufficient must be made at a reasonable hour, and if at a bank during its banking day.

§3-504. How Presentment Made.

(1) Presentment is a demand for acceptance or payment made upon the maker, acceptor, drawee or other payor by or on behalf of the holder.

(2) Presentment may be made

(a) by mail, in which event the time of presentment is determined by the time of receipt of the mail; or

(b) through a clearing house; or

(c) at the place of acceptance or payment specified in the instrument or if there be none at the place of business or residence of the party to accept or pay. If neither the party to accept or pay nor anyone authorized to act for him is present or accessible at such place presentment is excused.

(3) It may be made

(a) to any one of two or more makers, acceptors, drawees or other payor; or

(b) to any person who has authority to make or refuse the acceptance or payment.

(4) A draft accepted or a note made payable at a bank in the United States must be presented at such bank.

(5) In the cases described in Section 4-210 presentment may be made in the manner and with the result stated in that section. As amended 1962.

§3-505. Rights of Party to Whom Presentment Is Made.

(1) The party to whom presentment is made may without dishonor require

(a) exhibition of the instrument; and

(b) reasonable identification of the person making presentment and evidence of his authority to make it if made for another; and

(c) that the instrument be produced for acceptance or payment at a place specified in it, or if there be none at any place reasonable in the circumstances; and

(d) a signed receipt on the instrument for any partial or full payment and its surrender upon full payment.

(2) Failure to comply with any such requirement invalidates the presentment but the person presenting has a reasonable time in which to comply and the time for acceptance or payment runs from the time of compliance.

§3-506. Time Allowed For Acceptance or Payment.

(1) Acceptance may be deferred without dishonor until the close of the next business day following presentment. The holder may also in a good faith effort to obtain acceptance and without either dishonor of the instrument or discharge of secondary parties allow postponement of acceptance for an additional business day.

(2) Except as a longer time is allowed in the case of documentary drafts drawn under a letter of credit, and unless an earlier time is agreed to by the party to pay, payment of an instrument may be deferred without dishonor pending reasonable examination to determine whether it is properly payable, but payment must be made in any event before the close of business on the day of presentment.

§3-507. Dishonor; Holder's Right of Recourse; Term Allowing Re-Presentment.

(1) An instrument is dishonored when

(a) a necessary or optional presentment is duly made and due acceptance or payment is refused or cannot be obtained within the prescribed time or in case of bank collections the instrument is seasonably returned by the midnight deadline (Section 4-301); or

(b) presentment is excused and the instrument is not duly accepted or paid.

(2) Subject to any necessary notice of dishonor and protest, the holder has upon dishonor an immediate right of recourse against the drawers and indorsers.

(3) Return of an instrument for lack of proper indorsement is not dishonor.

(4) A term in a draft or an indorsement thereof allowing a stated time for re-presentment in the event of any dishonor of the draft by nonacceptance if a time draft or by nonpayment if a sight draft gives the holder as against any secondary party bound by the term an option to waive the dishonor without affecting the liability of the secondary party and he may present again up to the end of the stated time.

§3-508. Notice of Dishonor.

(1) Notice of dishonor may be given to any person who may be liable on the instrument by or on behalf of the holder or any party who has himself received notice, or any other party who can be compelled to pay the instrument. In addition an agent or bank in whose hands the instrument is dishonored may give notice to his principal or customer or to another agent or bank from which the instrument was received.

(2) Any necessary notice must be given by a bank before its midnight deadline and by any other person before midnight of the third business day after dishonor or receipt of notice of dishonor.

(3) Notice may be given in any reasonable manner. It may be oral or written and in any terms which identify the instrument and state that it has been dishonored. A misdescription which does not mislead the party notified does not vitiate the notice. Sending the instrument bearing a stamp, ticket or writing stating that acceptance or payment has been refused or sending a notice of debit with respect to the instrument is sufficient.

(4) Written notice is given when sent although it is not received.

(5) Notice to one partner is notice to each although the firm has been dissloved.

(6) When any party is in insolvency proceedings instituted after the issue of the instrument notice may be given either to the party or to the representative of his estate.

(7) When any party is dead or incompetent notice may be sent to his last known address or given to his personal representative.

(8) Notice operates for the benefit of all parties who have rights on the instrument against the party notified.

§3-509. Protest; Noting for Protest.

(1) A protest is a certificate of dishonor made under the hand and seal of a United States consul or vice consul or a notary public or other person authorized to certify dishonor by the law of the place where dishonor occurs. It may be made upon information satisfactory to such person.

(2) The protest must identify the instrument and certify either that due presentment has been made or the reason why it is excused and that the instrument has been dishonored by nonacceptance or nonpayment.

(3) The protest may also certify that notice of dishonor has been given to all parties or to specified parties.

(4) Subject to subsection(5) any necessary protest is due by the time that notice of dishonor is due.

(5) If, before protest is due, an instrument has been noted for protest by the officer to make protest, the protest may be made at any time thereafter as of the date of the noting.

§3-510. Evidence of Dishonor and Notice of Dishonor. The following are admissible as evidence and create a presumption of dishonor and of any notice of dishonor therein shown:

(a) a document regular in form as provided in the preceding section which purports to be a protest;
(b) the purported stamp or writing of the drawee, payor bank or presenting bank on the instrument or accompanying it stating that acceptance or payment has been refused for reasons consistent with dishonor:
(c) any book or record of the drawee, payor bank, or any collecting bank kept in the usual course of business which shows dishonor, even though there is no evidence of who made the entry.

§3-511. Waived or Excused Presentment, Protest or Notice of Dishonor or Delay Therein.
(1) Delay in presentment, protest or notice of dishonor is excused when the party is without notice that it is due or when the delay is caused by circumstances beyond his control and he exercises reasonable diligence after the cause of the delay ceases to operate.
(2) Presentment or notice or protest as the case may be is entirely excused when

(a) the party to be charged has waived it expressly or by implication either before or after it is due; or
(b) such party has himself dishonored the instrument or has countermanded payment or otherwise has no reason to expect or right to require that the instrument be accepted or paid; or
(c) by reasonable diligence the presentment or protest cannot be made or the notice given.

(3) Presentment is also entirely excused when

(a) the maker, acceptor or drawee of any instrument except a documentary draft is dead or in insolvency proceedings instituted after the issue of the instrument; or
(b) acceptance or payment is refused but not for want of proper presentment.

(4) Where a draft has been dishonored by nonacceptance a later presentment for payment and any notice of dishonor and protest for nonpayment are excused unless in the meantime the instrument has been accepted.
(5) A waiver of protest is also a waiver of presentment and of notice of dishonor even though protest is not required.
(6) Where a waiver of presentment or notice of protest is embodied in the instrument itself it is binding upon all parties; but where it is written above the signature of an indorser it binds him only.

Part 6: Discharge

§3-601. Discharge of Parties.
(1) The extent of the discharge of any party from liability on an instrument is governed by the sections on

(a) payment or satisfaction (Section 3-603); or
(b) tender of payment (Section 3-604); or
(c) cancellation or renunciation (Section 3-605); or
(d) impairment of right of recourse or of collateral (Section 3-606); or
(e) reacquisition of the instrument by a prior party (Section 3-208); or

(f) fraudulent and material alteration (Section 3-407); or
(g) certification of a check (Section 3-411); or
(h) acceptance varying a draft (Section 3-412); or
(i) unexcused delay in presentment or notice of dishonor or protest (Section 3-502).

(2) Any party is also discharged from his liability on an instrument to another party by any other act or agreement with such party which would discharge his simple contract for the payment of money.
(3) The liability of all parties is discharged when any party who has himself no right of action or recourse on the instrument

(a) reacquires the instrument in his own right; or
(b) is discharged under any provision of this Article, except as otherwise provided with respect to discharge for impairment of recourse or of collateral (Section 3-606).

§3-602. Effect of Discharge Against Holder in Due Course. No discharge of any party provided by this Article is effective against a subsequent holder in due course unless he has notice thereof when he takes the instrument.

§3-603. Payment or Satisfaction.
(1) The liability of any party is discharged to the extent of his payment or satisfaction to the holder even though it is made with knowledge of a claim of another person to the instrument unless prior to such payment or satisfaction the person making the claim either supplies indemnity deemed adequate by the party seeking the discharge or enjoins payment or satisfaction by order of a court of competent jurisdiction in an action in which the adverse claimant and the holder are parties. This subsection does not, however, result in the discharge of the liability

(a) of a party who in bad faith pays or satisfies a holder who acquired the instrument by theft or who (unless having the rights of a holder in due course) holds through one who so acquired it; or
(b) of a party (other than an intermediary bank or a payor bank which is not a depositary bank) who pays or satisfies the holder of an instrument which has been restrictively indorsed in a manner not consistent with the terms of such restrictive indorsement.

(2) Payment or satisfaction may be made with the consent of the holder by any person including a stranger to the instrument. Surrender of the instrument to such a person gives him the rights of a transferee (Section 3-201).

§3-604. Tender of Payment.
(1) Any party making tender of full payment to a holder when or after it is due is discharged to the extent of all subsequent liability for interest, costs and attorney's fees.
(2) The holder's refusal of such tender wholly discharges any party who has a right of recourse against the party making the tender.
(3) Where the maker or acceptor of an instrument payable otherwise than on demand is able and ready to pay at every place of payment specified in the instrument when it is due, it is equivalent to tender.

§3-605. Cancellation and Renunciation.
(1) The holder of an instrument may even without consideration discharge any party

(a) in any manner apparent on the face of the instrument or the indorsement, as by intentionally cancelling the instrument or the party's signature by destruction or mutilation, or by striking out the party's signature; or

(b) by renouncing his rights by a writing signed and delivered or by surrender of the instrument to the party to be discharged.

(2) Neither cancellation or renunciation without surrender of the instrument affects the title thereto.

§3-606. Impairment of Recourse or of Collateral.

(1) The holder discharges any party to the instrument to the extent that without such party's consent the holder

(a) without express reservation of rights releases or agrees not to sue any person against whom the party has to the knowledge of the holder a right of recourse or agrees to suspend the right to enforce against such person the instrument or collateral or otherwise discharges such person, except that failure or delay in effecting any required presentment, protest or notice of dishonor with respect to any such person does not discharge any party as to whom presentment, protest or notice of dishonor is effective or unnecessary; or

(b) unjustifiably impairs any collateral for the instrument given by or on behalf of the party or any person against whom he has a right of recourse.

(2) By express reservation of rights against a party with a right of recourse the holder preserves

(a) all his rights against such party as of the time when the instrument was originally due; and

(b) the right of the party to pay the instrument as of that time; and

(c) all rights of such party to recourse against others.

Part 7: Advice of International Sight Draft

§3-701. Letter of Advice of International Sight Draft.

(1) A "letter of advice" is a drawer's communication to the drawee that a described draft has been drawn.

(2) Unless otherwise agreed when a bank receives from another bank a letter of advice of an international sight draft the drawee bank may immediately debit the drawer's account and stop the running of interest pro tanto. Such a debit and any resulting credit to any account covering outstanding drafts leaves in the drawer full power to stop payment or otherwise dispose of the amount and creates no trust or interest in favor of the holder.

(3) Unless otherwise agreed and except where a draft is drawn under a credit issued by the drawee of an international sight draft owes the drawer no duty to pay an unadvised draft but if it does so and the draft is genuine, may appropriately debit the drawer's account.

Part 8: Miscellaneous

§3-801. Drafts in a Set.

(1) Where a draft is drawn in a set of parts, each of which is numbered and expressed to be an order only if no other part has been honored, the whole of the parts constitutes one draft but a taker of any part may become a holder in due course of the draft.

(2) Any person who negotiates, indorses or accepts a single part of a draft drawn in a set thereby becomes liable to any holder in due course of that part as if it were the whole set, but as between different holders in due course to whom different parts have been negotiated the holder whose title first accrues has all rights to the draft and its proceeds.

(3) As against the drawee the first presented part of a draft drawn in a set is the part entitled to payment, or if a time draft to acceptance and payment. Acceptance of any subsequently presented part renders the drawee liable thereon under subsection (2). With respect both to a holder and to the drawer payment of a subsequently presented part of a draft payable at sight has the same effect as payment of a check notwithstanding an effective stop order (Section 4-407).

(4) Except as otherwise provided in this section, where any part of a draft in a set is discharged by payment or otherwise the whole draft is discharged.

§3-802. Effect of Instrument on Obligation for which It Is Given.

(1) Unless otherwise agreed where an instrument is taken for an underlying obligation

(a) the obligation is pro tanto discharged if a bank is drawer, maker or acceptor of the instrument and there is no recourse on the instrument against the underlying obligor; and

(b) in any other case the obligation is suspended pro tanto until the instrument is due or if it is payable on demand until its presentment. If the instrument is dishonored action may be maintained on either the instrument or the obligation; discharge of the underlying obligor on the instrument also discharges him on the obligation.

(2) The taking in good faith of a check which is not postdated does not of itself so extend the time on the original obligation as to discharge a surety.

§3-803. Notice to Third Party.
Where a defendant is sued for breach of an obligation for which a third person is answerable over under this Article he may give the third person written notice of the litigation, and the person notified may then give similar notice to any other person who is answerable over to him under this Article. If the notice states that the person notified may come in and defend and that if the person notified does not do so he will in any action against him by the person giving the notice be bound by any determination of fact common to the two litigations, then unless after seasonable receipt of the notice the person notified does come in and defend he is so bound.

§3-804. Lost, Destroyed or Stolen Instruments.
The owner of an instrument which is lost, whether by destruction, theft or otherwise, may maintain an action in his own name and recover from any party liable thereon upon due proof of his ownership, the facts which prevent his production of the instrument and its terms. The court may require security indemnifying the defendant against loss by reason of further claims on the instrument.

§3-805. Instruments Not Payable to Order or to Bearer.
This Article applies to any instrument whose terms do not preclude transfer and which is otherwise negotiable within this Article but which is not payable to order or to bearer, except that there can be no holder in due course of such an instrument.

REVISED ARTICLE 3: NEGOTIABLE INSTRUMENTS (1991 TEXT)

Part 1: General Provisions and Definitions

Rev. §3-101. Short Title. This Article may be cited as Uniform Commercial Code—Negotiable Instruments.

Rev. §3-102. Subject Matter.

(a) This Article applies to negotiable instruments. It does not apply to money, to payment orders governed by Article 4A, or to securities governed by Article 8.

(b) If there is conflict between this Article and Article 4 or 9, Articles 4 and 9 govern.

(c) Regulations of the Board of Governors of the Federal Reserve System and operating circulars of the Federal Reserve Banks supersede any inconsistent provision of this Article to the extent of the inconsistency.

Rev. §3-103. Definitions.

(a) In this Article:

(1) "Acceptor" means a drawee who has accepted a draft.

(2) "Drawee" means a person ordered in a draft to make payment.

(3) "Drawer" means a person who signs or is identified in a draft as a person ordering payment.

(4) "Good faith" means honesty in fact and the observance of reasonable commercial standards of fair dealing.

(5) "Maker" means a person who signs or is identified in a note as a person undertaking to pay.

(6) "Order" means a written instruction to pay money signed by the person giving the instruction. The instruction may be addressed to any person, including the person giving the instruction, or to one or more persons jointly or in the alternative but not in succession. An authorization to pay is not an order unless the person authorized to pay is also instructed to pay.

(7) "Ordinary care" in the case of a person engaged in business means observance of reasonable commercial standards, prevailing in the area in which the person is located, with respect to the business in which the person is engaged. In the case of a bank that takes an instrument for processing for collection or payment by automated means, reasonable commercial standards do not require the bank to examine the instrument if the failure to examine does not violate the bank's prescribed procedures and the bank's procedures do not vary unreasonably from general banking usage not disapproved by this Article or Article 4.

(8) "Party" means a party to an instrument.

(9) "Promise" means a written undertaking to pay money signed by the person undertaking to pay. An acknowledgment of an obligation by the obligor is not a promise unless the obligor also undertakes to pay the obligation.

(10) "Prove" with respect to a fact means to meet the burden of establishing the fact (Section 1-201(8)).

(11) "Remitter" means a person who purchases an instrument from its issuer if the instrument is payable to an identified person other than the purchaser.

(b) Other definitions applying to this Article and the sections in which they appear are:

"Acceptance"	Section 3-409
"Accommodated party"	Section 3-419
"Accommodation party"	Section 3-419
"Alteration"	Section 3-407
"Anomalous indorsement"	Section 3-205
"Blank indorsement"	Section 3-205
"Cashier's check"	Section 3-104
"Certificate of deposit"	Section 3-104
"Certified check"	Section 3-409
"Check"	Section 3-104
"Consideration"	Section 3-303
"Draft"	Section 3-104
"Holder in due course"	Section 3-302
"Incomplete instrument"	Section 3-115
"Indorsement"	Section 3-204
"Indorser"	Section 3-204
"Instrument"	Section 3-104
"Issue"	Section 3-105
"Issuer"	Section 3-105
"Negotiable instrument"	Section 3-104
"Negotiation"	Section 3-201
"Note"	Section 3-104
"Payable at a definite time"	Section 3-108
"Payable on demand"	Section 3-108
"Payable to bearer"	Section 3-109
"Payable to order"	Section 3-109
"Payment"	Section 3-602
"Person entitled to enforce"	Section 3-301
"Presentment"	Section 3-501
"Reacquisition"	Section 3-207
"Special indorsement"	Section 3-205
"Teller's check"	Section 3-104
"Transfer of instrument"	Section 3-203
"Traveler's check"	Section 3-104
"Value"	Section 3-303

(c) The following definitions in other Articles apply to this Article:

"Bank"	Section 4-105
"Banking day"	Section 4-104
"Clearing house"	Section 4-104
"Collecting bank"	Section 4-105
"Depositary bank"	Section 4-105
"Documentary draft"	Section 4-104
"Intermediary bank"	Section 4-105
"Item"	Section 4-104
"Payor bank"	Section 4-105
"Suspends payments"	Section 4-104

(d) In addition, Article 1 contains general definitions and principles of construction and interpretation applicable throughout this Article.

Rev. §3-104. Negotiable Instrument.

(a) Except as provided in subsections (c) and (d), "negotiable instrument" means an unconditional promise or order to pay a fixed amount of money, with or without interest or other charges described in the promise or order, if it:

(1) is payable to bearer or to order at the time it is issued or first comes into possession of a holder;

(2) is payable on demand or at a definite time; and

(3) does not state any other undertaking or instruction by the person promising or ordering payment to do any act in addition to the payment of money, but the promise or order may contain (i) an undertaking or power to give, maintain, or protect collateral to secure payment, (ii) an authorization or power to the holder to confess judgment or realize on or dispose of collateral, or (iii) a waiver of the benefit of any law intended for the advantage or protection of an obligor.

(b) "Instrument" means a negotiable instrument.

(c) An order that meets all of the requirements of subsection (a), except paragraph (1), and otherwise falls within the definition of "check" in subsection (f) is a negotiable instrument and a check.

(d) A promise or order other than a check is not an instrument if, at the time it is issued or first comes into possession of a holder, it contains a conspicuous statement, however expressed, to the effect that the promise or order is not negotiable or is not an instrument governed by this Article.

(e) An instrument is a "note" if it is a promise and is a "draft" if it is an order. If an instrument falls within the definition of both "note" and "draft," a person entitled to enforce the instrument may treat it as either.

(f) "Check" means (i) a draft, other than a documentary draft, payable on demand and drawn on a bank or (ii) a cashier's check or teller's check. An instrument may be a check even though it is described on its face by another term, such as "money order."

(g) "Cashier's check" means a draft with respect to which the drawer and drawee are the same bank or branches of the same bank.

(h) "Teller's check" means a draft drawn by a bank (i) on another bank, or (ii) payable at or through a bank.

(i) "Traveler's check" means an instrument that (i) is payable on demand, (ii) is drawn on or payable at or through a bank, (iii) is designated by the term "traveler's check" or by a substantially similar term, and (iv) requires, as a condition to payment, a countersignature by a person whose specimen signature appears on the instrument.

(j) "Certificate of deposit" means an instrument containing an acknowledgment by a bank that a sum of money has been received by the bank and a promise by the bank to repay the sum of money. A certificate of deposit is a note of the bank.

Rev. §3-105. Issue of Instrument.

(a) "Issue" means the first delivery of an instrument by the maker or drawer, whether to a holder or nonholder, for the purpose of giving rights on the instrument to any person.

(b) An unissued instrument, or an unissued incomplete instrument that is completed, is binding on the maker or drawer, but nonissuance is a defense. An instrument that is conditionally issued or is issued for a special purpose is binding on the maker or drawer, but failure of the condition or special purpose to be fulfilled is a defense.

(c) "Issuer" applies to issued and unissued instruments and means a maker or drawer of an instrument.

Rev. §3-106. Unconditional Promise or Order.

(a) Except as provided in this section, for the purposes of Section 3-104(a), a promise or order is unconditional unless it states (i) an express condition to payment, (ii) that the promise or order is subject to or governed by another writing, or (iii) that rights or obligations with respect to the promise or order are stated in another writing. A reference to another writing does not of itself make the promise or order conditional.

(b) A promise or order is not made conditional (i) by a reference to another writing for a statement of rights with respect to collateral, prepayment, or acceleration, or (ii) because payment is limited to resort to a particular fund or source.

(c) If a promise or order requires, as a condition to payment, a countersignature by a person whose specimen signature appears on the promise or order, the condition does not make the promise or order conditional for the purposes of Section 3-104(a). If the person whose specimen signature appears on an instrument fails to counter-sign the instrument, the failure to countersign is a defense to the obligation of the issuer, but the failure does not prevent a transferee of the instrument from becoming a holder of the instrument.

(d) If a promise or order at the time it is issued or first comes into possession of a holder contains a statement, required by applicable statutory or administrative law, to the effect that the rights of a holder or transferee are subject to claims or defenses that the issuer could assert against the original payee, the promise or order is not thereby made conditional for the purposes of Section 3-104(a); but if the promise or order is an instrument, there cannot be a holder in due course of the instrument.

Rev. §3-107. Instrument Payable in Foreign Money.

Unless the instrument otherwise provides, an instrument that states the amount payable in foreign money may be paid in the foreign money or in an equivalent amount in dollars calculated by using the current bank-offered spot rate at the place of payment for the purchase of dollars on the day on which the instrument is paid.

Rev. §3-108. Payable on Demand or at Definite Time.

(a) A promise or order is "payable on demand" if it (i) states that it is payable on demand or at sight, or otherwise indicates that it is payable at the will of the holder, or (ii) does not state any time of payment.

(b) A promise or order is "payable at a definite time" if it is payable on elapse of a definite period of time after sight or acceptance or at a fixed date or dates or at a time or times readily ascertainable at the time the promise or order is issued, subject to rights of (i) prepayment, (ii) acceleration, (iii) extension at the option of the holder, or (iv) extension to a further definite time at the option of the maker or acceptor or automatically upon or after a specified act or event.

(c) If an instrument, payable at a fixed date, is also payable upon demand made before the fixed date, the instrument is payable on demand until the fixed date and, if demand for payment is not made before that date, becomes payable at a definite time on the fixed date.

Rev. §3-109. Payable to Bearer or to Order.

(a) A promise or order is payable to bearer if it:

(1) states that it is payable to bearer or to the order of bearer or otherwise indicates that the person in possession of the promise or order is entitled to payment;

(2) does not state a payee; or

(3) states that it is payable to or to the order of cash or otherwise indicates that it is not payable to an identified person.

(b) A promise or order that is not payable to bearer is payable to order if it is payable (i) to the order of an identified person or (ii) to an identified person or order. A promise or order that is payable to order is payable to the identified person.

(c) An instrument payable to bearer may become payable to an identified person if it is specially indorsed pursuant to Section 3-205(a). An instrument payable to an identified person may become payable to bearer if it is indorsed in blank pursuant to Section 3-205(b).

Rev. §3-110. Identification of Person to Whom Instrument Is Payable.

(a) The person to whom an instrument is initially payable is determined by the intent of the person, whether or not authorized, signing as, or in the name or behalf of, the issuer of the instrument. The instrument is payable to the person intended by the signer even if that person is identified in the instrument by a name or other identification that is not that of the intended person. If more than one person signs in the name or behalf of the issuer of an instrument and all the signers do not intend the same person as payee, the instrument is payable to any person intended by one or more of the signers.

(b) If the signature of the issuer of an instrument is made by automated means, such as a check-writing machine, the payee of the instrument is determined by the intent of the person who supplied the name or identification of the payee, whether or not authorized to do so.

(c) A person to whom an instrument is payable may be identified in any way, including by name, identifying number, office, or account number. For the purpose of determining the holder of an instrument, the following rules apply:

(1) If an instrument is payable to an account and the account is identified only by number, the instrument is payable to the person to whom the account is payable. If an instru-

ment is payable to an account identified by number and by the name of a person, the instrument is payable to the named person, whether or not that person is the owner of the account identified by number.

(2) If an instrument is payable to:

(i) a trust, an estate, or a person described as trustee or representative of a trust or estate, the instrument is payable to the trustee, the representative, or a successor of either, whether or not the beneficiary or estate is also named;

(ii) a person described as agent or similar representative of a named or identified person, the instrument is payable to the represented person, the representative, or a successor of the representative;

(iii) a fund or organization that is not a legal entity, the instrument is payable to a representative of the members of the fund or organization; or

(iv) an office or to a person described as holding an office, the instrument is payable to the named person, the incumbent of the office, or a successor to the incumbent.

(d) If an instrument is payable to two or more persons alternatively, it is payable to any of them and may be negotiated, discharged, or enforced by any or all of them in possession of the instrument. If an instrument is payable to two or more persons not alternatively, it is payable to all of them and may be negotiated, discharged, or enforced only by all of them. If an instrument payable to two or more persons is ambiguous as to whether it is payable to the persons alternatively, the instrument is payable to the persons alternatively.

Rev. §3-111. Place of Payment. Except as otherwise provided for items in Article 4, an instrument is payable at the place of payment stated in the instrument. If no place of payment is stated, an instrument is payable at the address of the drawee or maker stated in the instrument. If no address is stated, the place of payment is the place of business of the drawee or maker. If a drawee or maker has more than one place of business, the place of payment is any place of business of the drawee or maker chosen by the person entitled to enforce the instrument. If the drawee or maker has no place of business, the place of payment is the residence of the drawee or maker.

Rev. §3-112. Interest.

(a) Unless otherwise provided in the instrument, (i) an instrument is not payable with interest, and (ii) interest on an interest-bearing instrument is payable from the date of the instrument.

(b) Interest may be stated in an instrument as a fixed or variable amount of money or it may be expressed as a fixed or variable rate or rates. The amount or rate of interest may be stated or described in the instrument in any manner and may require reference to information not contained in the instrument. If an instrument provides for interest, but the amount of interest payable cannot be ascertained from the description, interest is payable at the judgment rate in effect at the place of payment of the instrument and at the time interest first accrues.

Rev. §3-113. Date of Instrument.

(a) An instrument may be antedated or postdated. The date stated determines the time of payment if the instrument is payable at a fixed period after date. Except as provided in Section 4-401(c), an instrument payable on demand is not payable before the date of the instrument.

(b) If an instrument is undated, its date is the date of its issue or, in the case of an unissued instrument, the date it first comes into possession of a holder.

Rev. §3-114. Contradictory Terms of Instrument. If an instrument contains contradictory terms, typewritten terms prevail over printed terms, handwritten terms prevail over both, and words prevail over numbers.

Rev. §3-115. Incomplete Instrument.

(a) "Incomplete instrument" means a signed writing, whether or not issued by the signer, the contents of which show at the time of signing that it is incomplete but that the signer intended it to be completed by the addition of words or numbers.

(b) Subject to subsection (c), if an incomplete instrument is an instrument under Section 3-104, it may be enforced according to its terms if it is not completed, or according to its terms as augmented by completion. If an incomplete instrument is not an instrument under Section 3-104, but, after completion, the requirements of Section 3-104 are met, the instrument may be enforced according to its terms as augmented by completion.

(c) If words or numbers are added to an incomplete instrument without authority of the signer, there is an alteration of the incomplete instrument under Section 3-407.

(d) The burden of establishing that words or numbers were added to an incomplete instrument without authority of the signer is on the person asserting the lack of authority.

Rev. §3-116. Joint and Several Liability; Contribution.

(a) Except as otherwise provided in the instrument, two or more persons who have the same liability on an instrument as makers, drawers, acceptors, indorsers who indorse as joint payees, or anomalous indorsers are jointly and severally liable in the capacity in which they sign.

(b) Except as provided in Section 3-419(e) or by agreement of the affected parties, a party having joint and several liability who pays the instrument is entitled to receive from any party having the same joint and several liability contribution in accordance with applicable law.

(c) Discharge of one party having joint and several liability by a person entitled to enforce the instrument does not affect the right under subsection (b) of a party having the same joint and several liability to receive contribution from the party discharged.

Rev. §3-117. Other Agreements Affecting Instrument. Subject to applicable law regarding exclusion of proof of contemporaneous or previous agreements, the obligation of a party to an instrument to pay the instrument may be modified, supplemented, or nullified by a separate agreement of the obligor and a person entitled to enforce the instrument, if the instrument is issued or the obligation is incurred in reliance on the agreement or as part of the same transaction giving rise to the agreement. To the extent an obligation is modified, supplemented, or nullified by an agreement under this section, the agreement is a defense to the obligation.

Rev. §3-118. Statute of Limitations.

(a) Except as provided in subsection (e), an action to enforce the obligation of a party to pay a note payable at a definite time must be commenced within six years after the due date or dates stated in the note or, if a due date is accelerated, within six years after the accelerated due date.

(b) Except as provided in subsection (d) or (e), if demand for payment is made to the maker of a note payable on demand, an action to enforce the obligation of a party to pay the note must be commenced within six years after the demand. If no demand for payment is made to the maker, an action to enforce the note is barred if neither principal nor interest on the note has been paid for a continuous period of 10 years.

(c) Except as provided in subsection (d), an action to enforce the obligation of a party to an unaccepted draft to pay the draft must be commenced within three years after dishonor of the draft or 10 years after the date of the draft, whichever period expires first.

(d) An action to enforce the obligation of the acceptor of a certified check or the issuer of a teller's check, cashier's check, or traveler's check must be commenced within three years after demand for payment is made to the acceptor or issuer, as the case may be.

(e) An action to enforce the obligation of a party to a certificate of deposit to pay the instrument must be commenced within six years after demand for payment is made to the maker, but if the instrument states a due date and the maker is not required to pay before that date, the six-year period begins when a demand for payment is in effect and the due date has passed.

(f) An action to enforce the obligation of a party to pay an accepted draft, other than a certified check, must be commenced (i) within six years after the due date or dates stated in the draft or acceptance if the obligation of the acceptor is payable at a definite time, or (ii) within six years after the date of the acceptance if the obligation of the acceptor is payable on demand.

(g) Unless governed by other law regarding claims for indemnity or contribution, an action (i) for conversion of an instrument, for money had and received, or like action based on conversion, (ii) for breach of warranty, or (iii) to enforce an obligation, duty, or right arising under this Article and not governed by this section must be commenced within three years after the [cause of action] accrues.

Rev. §3-119. Notice of Right to Defend Action. In an action for breach of an obligation for which a third person is answerable over pursuant to this Article or Article 4, the defendant may give the third person written notice of the litigation, and the person notified may then give similar notice to any other person who is answerable over. If the notice states (i) that the person notified may come in and defend and (ii) that failure to do so will bind the person notified in an action later brought by the person giving the notice as to any determination of fact common to the two litigations, the person notified is so bound unless after seasonable receipt of the notice the person notified does come in and defend.

Part 2: Negotiation, Transfer, and Indorsement

Rev. §3-201. Negotiation.
(a) "Negotiation" means a transfer of possession, whether voluntary or involuntary, of an instrument by a person other than the issuer to a person who thereby becomes its holder.

(b) Except for negotiation by a remitter, if an instrument is payable to an identified person, negotiation requires transfer of possession of the instrument and its indorsement by the holder. If an instrument is payable to bearer, it may be negotiated by transfer of possession alone.

Rev. §3-202. Negotiation Subject to Rescission.
(a) Negotiation is effective even if obtained (i) from an infant, a corporation exceeding its powers, or a person without capacity, (ii) by fraud, duress, or mistake, or (iii) in breach of duty or as part of an illegal transaction.

(b) To the extent permitted by other law, negotiation may be rescinded or may be subject to other remedies, but those remedies may not be asserted against a subsequent holder in due course or a person paying the instrument in good faith and without knowledge of facts that are a basis for rescission or other remedy.

Rev. §3-203. Transfer of Instrument; Rights Acquired by Transfer.
(a) An instrument is transferred when it is delivered by a person other than its issuer for the purpose of giving to the person receiving delivery the right to enforce the instrument.

(b) Transfer of an instrument, whether or not the transfer is a negotiation, vests in the transferee any right of the transferor to enforce the instrument, including any right as a holder in due course, but the transferee cannot acquire rights of a holder in due course by a transfer, directly or indirectly, from a holder in due course if the transferee engaged in fraud or illegality affecting the instrument.

(c) Unless otherwise agreed, if an instrument is transferred for value and the transferee does not become a holder because of lack of indorsement by the transferor, the transferee has a specifically enforceable right to the unqualified indorsement of the transferor, but negotiation of the instrument does not occur until the indorsement is made.

(d) If a transferor purports to transfer less than the entire instrument, negotiation of the instrument does not occur. The transferee obtains no rights under this Article and has only the rights of a partial assignee.

Rev. §3-204. Indorsement.
(a) "Indorsement" means a signature, other than that of a signer as maker, drawer, or acceptor, that alone or accompanied by other words is made on an instrument for the purpose of (i) negotiating the instrument, (ii) restricting payment of the instrument, or (iii) incurring indorser's liability on the instrument, but regardless of the intent of the signer, a signature and its accompanying words is an indorsement unless the accompanying words, terms of the instrument, place of the signature, or other circumstances unambiguously indicate that the signature was made for a purpose other than indorsement. For the purpose of determining whether a signature is made on an instrument, a paper affixed to the instrument is a part of the instrument.

(b) "Indorser" means a person who makes an indorsement.

(c) For the purpose of determining whether the transferee of an instrument is a holder, an indorsement that transfers a security interest in the instrument is effective as an unqualified indorsement of the instrument.

(d) If an instrument is payable to a holder under a name that is not the name of the holder, indorsement may be made by the holder in the name stated in the instrument or in the holder's name or both, but signature in both names may be required by a person paying or taking the instrument for value or collection.

Rev. §3-205. Special Indorsement; Blank Indorsement; Anomalous Indorsement.
(a) If an indorsement is made by the holder of an instrument, whether payable to an identified person or payable to bearer, and the indorsement identifies a person to whom it makes the instrument payable, it is a "special indorsement." When specially indorsed, an instrument becomes payable to the identified person and may be negotiated only by the indorsement of that person. The principles stated in Section 3–110 apply to special indorsements.

(b) If an indorsement is made by the holder of an instrument and it is not a special indorsement, it is a "blank indorsement." When indorsed in blank, an instrument becomes payable to bearer and may be negotiated by transfer of possession alone until specially indorsed.

(c) The holder may convert a blank indorsement that consists only of a signature into a special indorsement by writing, above the signature of the indorser, words identifying the person to whom the instrument is made payable.

(d) "Anomalous indorsement" means an indorsement made by a person who is not the holder of the instrument. An anomalous indorsement does not affect the manner in which the instrument may be negotiated.

Rev. §3–206. Restrictive Indorsement.

(a) An indorsement limiting payment to a particular person or otherwise prohibiting further transfer or negotiation of the instrument is not effective to prevent further transfer or negotiation of the instrument.

(b) An indorsement stating a condition to the right of the indorsee to receive payment does not affect the right of the indorsee to enforce the instrument. A person paying the instrument or taking it for value or collection may disregard the condition, and the rights and liabilities of that person are not affected by whether the condition has been fulfilled.

(c) If an instrument bears an indorsement (i) described in Section 4–201(b), or (ii) in blank or to a particular bank using the words "for deposit," "for collection," or other words indicating a purpose of having the instrument collected by a bank for the indorser or for a particular account, the following rules apply:

(1) A person, other than a bank, who purchases the instrument when so indorsed converts the instrument unless the amount paid for the instrument is received by the indorser or applied consistently with the indorsement.

(2) A depositary bank that purchases the instrument or takes it for collection when so indorsed converts the instrument unless the amount paid by the bank with respect to the instrument is received by the indorser or applied consistently with the indorsement.

(3) A payor bank that is also the depositary bank or that takes the instrument for immediate payment over the counter from a person other than a collecting bank converts the instrument unless the proceeds of the instrument are received by the indorser or applied consistently with the indorsement.

(4) Except as otherwise provided in paragraph (3), a payor bank or intermediary bank may disregard the indorsement and is not liable if the proceeds of the instrument are not received by the indorser or applied consistently with the indorsement.

(d) Except for an indorsement covered by subsection (c), if an instrument bears an indorsement using words to the effect that payment is to be made to the indorsee as agent, trustee, or other fiduciary for the benefit of the indorser or another person, the following rules apply:

(1) Unless there is notice of breach of fiduciary duty as provided in Section 3–307, a person who purchases the instrument from the indorsee or takes the instrument from the indorsee for collection or payment may pay the proceeds of payment or the value given for the instrument to the indorsee without regard to whether the indorsee violates a fiduciary duty to the indorsor.

(2) A subsequent transferee of the instrument or person who pays the instrument is neither given notice nor otherwise affected by the restriction in the indorsement unless the transferee or payor knows that the fiduciary dealt with the instrument or its proceeds in breach of fiduciary duty.

(e) The presence on an instrument of an indorsement to which this section applies does not prevent a purchaser of the instrument from becoming a holder in due course of the instrument unless the purchaser is a converter under subsection (c) or has notice or knowledge of breach of fiduciary duty as stated in subsection (d).

(f) In an action to enforce the obligation of a party to pay the instrument, the obligor has a defense if payment would violate an indorsement to which this section applies and the payment is not permitted by this section.

Rev. §3–207. Reacquisition.
Reacquisition of an instrument occurs if it is transferred to a former holder, by negotiation or otherwise. A former holder who reacquires the instrument may cancel indorsements made after the reacquirer first became a holder of the instrument. If the cancellation causes the instrument to be payable to the reacquirer or to bearer, the reacquirer may negotiate the instrument. An indorser whose indorsement is canceled is discharged, and the discharge is effective against any subsequent holder.

Part 3: Enforcement of Instruments

Rev. §3–301. Person Entitled to Enforce Instrument.
"Person entitled to enforce" an instrument means (i) the holder of the instrument, (ii) a nonholder in possession of the instrument who has the rights of a holder, or (iii) a person not in possession of the instrument who is entitled to enforce the instrument pursuant to Section 3–309 or 3–418(d). A person may be a person entitled to enforce the instrument even though the person is not the owner of the instrument or is in wrongful possession of the instrument.

Rev. §3–302. Holder in Due Course.

(a) Subject to subsection (c) and Section 3–106(d), "holder in due course" means the holder of an instrument if:

(1) the instrument when issued or negotiated to the holder does not bear such apparent evidence of forgery or alteration or is not otherwise so irregular or incomplete as to call into question its authenticity; and

(2) the holder took the instrument (i) for value, (ii) in good faith, (iii) without notice that the instrument is overdue or has been dishonored or that there is an uncured default with respect to payment of another instrument issued as part of the same series, (iv) without notice that the instrument contains an unauthorized signature or has been altered, (v) without notice of any claim to the instrument described in Section 3–306, and (vi) without notice that any party has a defense or claim in recoupment described in Section 3–305(a).

(b) Notice of discharge of a party, other than discharge in an insolvency proceeding, is not notice of a defense under subsection (a), but discharge is effective against a person who became a holder in due course with notice of the discharge. Public filing or recording of a document does not of itself constitute notice of a defense, claim in recoupment, or claim to the instrument.

(c) Except to the extent a transferor or predecessor in interest has rights as a holder in due course, a person does not acquire rights of a holder in due course of an instrument taken (i) by legal process or by purchase in an execution, bankruptcy, or creditor's sale or similar proceeding, (ii) by purchase as part of a bulk transaction not in ordinary course of business of the transferor, or (iii) as the successor in interest to an estate or other organization.

(d) If, under Section 3–303(a)(1), the promise of performance that is the consideration for an instrument has been partially performed, the holder may assert rights as a holder in due course of the instrument only to the fraction of the amount payable under the instrument equal to the value of the partial performance divided by the value of the promised performance.

(e) If (i) the person entitled to enforce an instrument has only a security interest in the instrument and (ii) the person obliged to pay the instrument has a defense, claim in recoupment, or claim to the instrument that may be asserted against the person who granted the security interest, the person entitled to enforce the instrument may assert rights as a holder in due course only to an amount payable under the instrument which, at the time of enforcement of the instrument, does not exceed the amount of the unpaid obligation secured.

(f) To be effective, notice must be received at a time and in a manner that gives a reasonable opportunity to act on it.

(g) This section is subject to any law limiting status as a holder in due course in particular classes of transactions.

Rev. §3–303. Value and Consideration.

(a) An instrument is issued or transferred for value if:

(1) the instrument is issued or transferred for a promise of performance, to the extent the promise has been performed;

(2) the transferee acquires a security interest or other lien in the instrument other than a lien obtained by judicial proceeding;

(3) the instrument is issued or transferred as payment of, or as security for, an antecedent claim against any person, whether or not the claim is due;

(4) the instrument is issued or transferred in exchange for a negotiable instrument; or

(5) the instrument is issued or transferred in exchange for the incurring of an irrevocable obligation to a third party by the person taking the instrument.

(b) "Consideration" means any consideration sufficient to support a simple contract. The drawer or maker of an instrument has a defense if the instrument is issued without consideration. If an instrument is issued for a promise of performance, the issuer has a defense to the extent performance of the promise is due and the promise has not been performed. If an instrument is issued for value as stated in subsection (a), the instrument is also issued for consideration.

Rev. §3–304. Overdue Instrument.

(a) An instrument payable on demand becomes overdue at the earliest of the following times:

(1) on the day after the day demand for payment is duly made;

(2) if the instrument is a check, 90 days after its date; or

(3) if the instrument is not a check, when the instrument has been outstanding for a period of time after its date which is unreasonably long under the circumstances of the particular case in light of the nature of the instrument and usage of the trade.

(b) With respect to an instrument payable at a definite time the following rules apply:

(1) If the principal is payable in installments and a due date has not been accelerated, the instrument becomes overdue upon default under the instrument for nonpayment of an installment, and the instrument remains overdue until the default is cured.

(2) If the principal is not payable in installments and the due date has not been accelerated, the instrument becomes overdue on the day after the due date.

(3) If a due date with respect to principal has been accelerated, the instrument becomes overdue on the day after the accelerated due date.

(c) Unless the due date of principal has been accelerated, an instrument does not become overdue if there is default in payment of interest but no default in payment of principal.

Rev. §3–305. Defenses and Claims in Recoupment.

(a) Except as stated in subsection (b), the right to enforce the obligation of a party to pay an instrument is subject to the following:

(1) a defense of the obligor based on (i) infancy of the obligor to the extent it is a defense to a simple contract, (ii) duress, lack of legal capacity, or illegality of the transaction which, under other law, nullifies the obligation of the obligor, (iii) fraud that induced the obligor to sign the instrument with neither knowledge nor reasonable opportunity to learn of its character or its essential terms, or (iv) discharge of the obligor in insolvency proceedings;

(2) a defense of the obligor stated in another section of this Article or a defense of the obligor that would be available if the person entitled to enforce the instrument were enforcing a right to payment under a simple contract; and

(3) a claim in recoupment of the obligor against the original payee of the instrument if the claim arose from the transaction that gave rise to the instrument; but the claim of the obligor may be asserted against a transferee of the instrument only to reduce the amount owing on the instrument at the time the action is brought.

(b) The right of a holder in due course to enforce the obligation of a party to pay the instrument is subject to defenses of the obligor stated in subsection (a)(1), but is not subject to defenses of the obligor stated in subsection (a)(2) or claims in recoupment stated in subsection (a)(3) against a person other than the holder.

(c) Except as stated in subsection (d), in an action to enforce the obligation of a party to pay the instrument, the obligor may not assert against the person entitled to enforce the instrument a defense, claim in recoupment, or claim to the instrument (Section 3–306) of another person, but the other person's claim to the instrument may be asserted by the obligor if the other person is joined in the action and personally asserts the claim against the person entitled to enforce the instrument. An obligor is not obliged to pay the instrument if the person seeking enforcement of the instrument does not have rights of a holder in due course and the obligor proves that the instrument is a lost or stolen instrument.

(d) In an action to enforce the obligation of an accommodation party to pay an instrument, the accommodation party may assert against the person entitled to enforce the instrument any defense or claim in recoupment under subsection (a) that the accommodated party could assert against the person entitled to enforce the instrument, except the defenses of discharge in insolvency proceedings, infancy, and lack of legal capacity.

Rev. §3–306. Claims to an Instrument.
A person taking an instrument, other than a person having rights of a holder in due course, is subject to a claim of a property or possessory right in the instrument or its proceeds, including a claim to rescind a negotiation and to recover the instrument or its proceeds. A person having rights of a holder in due course takes free of the claim to the instrument.

Rev. §3–307. Notice of Breach of Fiduciary Duty.

(a) In this section:

(1) "Fiduciary" means an agent, trustee, partner, corporate officer or director, or other representative owing a fiduciary duty with respect to an instrument.

(2) "Represented person" means the principal, beneficiary, partnership, corporation, or other person to whom the duty stated in paragraph (1) is owed.

(b) If (i) an instrument is taken from a fiduciary for payment or collection or for value, (ii) the taker has knowledge of the fiduciary status of the fiduciary, and (iii) the represented person makes a claim to the instrument or its proceeds on the basis that the transaction of the fiduciary is a breach of fiduciary duty, the following rules apply:

(1) Notice of breach of fiduciary duty by the fiduciary is notice of the claim of the represented person.
(2) In the case of an instrument payable to the represented person or the fiduciary as such, the taker has notice of the breach of fiduciary duty if the instrument is (i) taken in payment of or as security for a debt known by the taker to be the personal debt of the fiduciary, (ii) taken in a transaction known by the taker to be for the personal benefit of the fiduciary, or (iii) deposited to an account other than an account of the fiduciary, as such, or an account of the represented person.
(3) If an instrument is issued by the represented person or the fiduciary as such, and made payable to the fiduciary personally, the taker does not have notice of the breach of fiduciary duty unless the taker knows of the breach of fiduciary duty.
(4) If an instrument is issued by the represented person or the fiduciary as such, to the taker as payee, the taker has notice of the breach of fiduciary duty if the instrument is (i) taken in payment of or as security for a debt known by the taker to be the personal debt of the fiduciary, (ii) taken in a transaction known by the taker to be for the personal benefit of the fiduciary, or (iii) deposited to an account other than an account of the fiduciary, as such, or an account of the represented person.

Rev. §3–308. Proof of Signatures and Status as Holder in Due Course.

(a) In an action with respect to an instrument, the authenticity of, and authority to make, each signature on the instrument is admitted unless specifically denied in the pleadings. If the validity of a signature is denied in the pleadings, the burden of establishing validity is on the person claiming validity, but the signature is presumed to be authentic and authorized unless the action is to enforce the liability of the purported signer and the signer is dead or incompetent at the time of trial of the issue of validity of the signature. If an action to enforce the instrument is brought against a person as the undisclosed principal of a person who signed the instrument as a party to the instrument, the plaintiff has the burden of establishing that the defendant is liable on the instrument as a represented person under Section 3–402(a).

(b) If the validity of signatures is admitted or proved and there is compliance with subsection (a), a plaintiff producing the instrument is entitled to payment if the plaintiff proves entitlement to enforce the instrument under Section 3–301, unless the defendant proves a defense or claim in recoupment. If a defense or claim in recoupment is proved, the right to payment of the plaintiff is subject to the defense or claim, except to the extent the plaintiff proves that the plaintiff has rights of a holder in due course which are not subject to the defense or claim.

Rev. §3–309. Enforcement of Lost, Destroyed, or Stolen Instrument.

(a) A person not in possession of an instrument is entitled to enforce the instrument if (i) the person was in possession of the instrument and entitled to enforce it when loss of possession occurred, (ii) the loss of possession was not the result of a transfer by the person or a lawful seizure, and (iii) the person cannot reasonably obtain possession of the instrument because the instrument was destroyed, its whereabouts cannot be determined, or it is in the wrongful possession of an unknown person or a person that cannot be found or is not amenable to service of process.

(b) A person seeking enforcement of an instrument under subsection (a) must prove the terms of the instrument and the person's right to enforce the instrument. If that proof is made, Section 3–308 applies to the case as if the person seeking enforcement had produced the instrument. The court may not enter judgment in favor of the person seeking enforcement unless it finds that the person required to pay the instrument is adequately protected against loss that might occur by reason of a claim by another person to enforce the instrument. Adequate protection may be provided by any reasonable means.

Rev. §3–310. Effect of Instrument on Obligation for Which Taken.

(a) Unless otherwise agreed, if a certified check, cashier's check, or teller's check is taken for an obligation, the obligation is discharged to the same extent discharge would result if an amount of money equal to the amount of the instrument were taken in payment of the obligation. Discharge of the obligation does not affect any liability that the obligor may have as an indorser of the instrument.

(b) Unless otherwise agreed and except as provided in subsection (a), if a note or an uncertified check is taken for an obligation, the obligation is suspended to the same extent the obligation would be discharged if an amount of money equal to the amount of the instrument were taken, and the following rules apply:

(1) In the case of an uncertified check, suspension of the obligation continues until dishonor of the check or until it is paid or certified. Payment or certification of the check results in discharge of the obligation to the extent of the amount of the check.
(2) In the case of a note, suspension of the obligation continues until dishonor of the note or until it is paid. Payment of the note results in discharge of the obligation to the extent of the payment.
(3) Except as provided in paragraph (4), if the check or note is dishonored and the obligee of the obligation for which the instrument was taken is the person entitled to enforce the instrument, the obligee may enforce either the instrument or the obligation. In the case of an instrument of a third person which is negotiated to the obligee by the obligor, discharge of the obligor on the instrument also discharges the obligation.
(4) If the person entitled to enforce the instrument taken for an obligation is a person other than the obligee, the obligee may not enforce the obligation to the extent the obligation is suspended. If the obligee is the person entitled to enforce the instrument but no longer has possession of it because it was lost, stolen, or destroyed, the obligation may not be enforced to the extent of the amount payable on the instrument, and to that extent the obligee's rights against the obligor are limited to enforcement of the instrument.

(c) If an instrument other than one described in subsection (a) or (b) is taken for an obligation, the effect is (i) that stated in subsection (a) if the instrument is one on which a bank is liable as maker or acceptor, or (ii) that stated in subsection (b) in any other case.

Rev. §3–311. Accord and Satisfaction by Use of Instrument.

(a) If a person against whom a claim is asserted proves that (i) that person in good faith tendered an instrument to the claimant as full satisfaction of the claim, (ii) the amount of the claim was unliquidated or subject to a bona fide dispute, and (iii) the claimant obtained payment of the instrument, the following subsections apply.

(b) Unless subsection (c) applies, the claim is discharged if the person against whom the claim is asserted proves that the instrument or an accompanying written communication contained a conspicuous statement to the effect that the instrument was tendered as full satisfaction of the claim.

(c) Subject to subsection (d), a claim is not discharged under subsection (b) if either of the following applies:

(1) The claimant, if an organization, proves that (i) within a reasonable time before the tender, the claimant sent a conspicuous statement to the person against whom the claim is asserted that communications concerning disputed debts, including an instrument tendered as full satisfaction of a debt, are to be sent to a designated person, office, or place, and (ii) the instrument or accompanying communication was not received by that designated person, office, or place.

(2) The claimant, whether or not an organization, proves that within 90 days after payment of the instrument, the claimant tendered repayment of the amount of the instrument to the person against whom the claim is asserted. This paragraph does not apply if the claimant is an organization that sent a statement complying with paragraph (1)(i).

(d) A claim is discharged if the person against whom the claim is asserted proves that within a reasonable time before collection of the instrument was initiated, the claimant, or an agent of the claimant having direct responsibility with respect to the disputed obligation, knew that the instrument was tendered in full satisfaction of the claim.

Part 4: Liability of Parties

Rev. §3–401. Signature.

(a) A person is not liable on an instrument unless (i) the person signed the instrument, or (ii) the person is represented by an agent or representative who signed the instrument and the signature is binding on the represented person under Section 3–402.

(b) A signature may be made (i) manually or by means of a device or machine, and (ii) by the use of any name, including a trade or assumed name, or by a word, mark, or symbol executed or adopted by a person with present intention to authenticate a writing.

Rev. §3–402. Signature by Representative.

(a) If a person acting, or purporting to act, as a representative signs an instrument by signing either the name of the represented person or the name of the signer, the represented person is bound by the signature to the same extent the represented person would be bound if the signature were on a simple contract. If the represented person is bound, the signature of the representative is the "authorized signature of the represented person" and the represented person is liable on the instrument, whether or not identified in the instrument.

(b) If a representative signs the name of the representative to an instrument and the signature is an authorized signature of the represented person, the following rules apply:

(1) If the form of the signature shows unambiguously that the signature is made on behalf of the represented person who is identified in the instrument, the representative is not liable on the instrument.

(2) Subject to subsection (c), if (i) the form of the signature does not show unambiguously that the signature is made in a representative capacity or (ii) the represented person is not identified in the instrument, the representative is liable on the instrument to a holder in due course that took the instrument without notice that the representative was not intended to be liable on the instrument. With respect to any other person, the representative is liable on the instrument unless the representative proves that the original parties did not intend the representative to be liable on the instrument.

(c) If a representative signs the name of the representative as drawer of a check without indication of the representative status and the check is payable from an account of the represented person who is identified on the check, the signer is not liable on the check if the signature is an authorized signature of the represented person.

Rev. §3–403. Unauthorized Signature.

(a) Unless otherwise provided in this Article or Article 4, an unauthorized signature is ineffective except as the signature of the unauthorized signer in favor of a person who in good faith pays the instrument or takes it for value. An unauthorized signature may be ratified for all purposes of this Article.

(b) If the signature of more than one person is required to constitute the authorized signature of an organization, the signature of the organization is unauthorized if one of the required signatures is lacking.

(c) The civil or criminal liability of a person who makes an unauthorized signature is not affected by any provision of this Article which makes the unauthorized signature effective for the purposes of this Article.

Rev. §3–404. Imposters; Fictitious Payees.

(a) If an impostor, by use of the mails or otherwise, induces the issuer of an instrument to issue the instrument to the impostor, or to a person acting in concert with the impostor, by impersonating the payee of the instrument or a person authorized to act for the payee, an indorsement of the instrument by any person in the name of the payee is effective as the indorsement of the payee in favor of a person who, in good faith, pays the instrument or takes it for value or for collection.

(b) If (i) a person whose intent determines to whom an instrument is payable (Section 3–110(a) or (b)) does not intend the person identified as payee to have any interest in the instrument, or (ii) the person identified as payee of an instrument is a fictitious person, the following rules apply until the instrument is negotiated by special indorsement:

(1) Any person in possession of the instrument is its holder.
(2) An indorsement by any person in the name of the payee stated in the instrument is effective as the indorsement of the payee in favor of a person who, in good faith, pays the instrument or takes it for value or for collection.

(c) Under subsection (a) or (b), an indorsement is made in the name of a payee if (i) it is made in a name substantially similar to that of the payee or (ii) the instrument, whether or not indorsed, is deposited in a depositary bank to an account in a name substantially similar to that of the payee.

(d) With respect to an instrument to which subsection (a) or (b) applies, if a person paying the instrument or taking it for value or for collection fails to exercise ordinary care in paying or taking the instrument and that failure substantially contributes to loss resulting from payment of the instrument, the person bearing the loss may recover from the person failing to exercise ordinary care to the extent the failure to exercise ordinary care contributed to the loss.

Rev. §3–405. Employer's Responsibility for Fraudulent Indorsement by Employee.

(a) In this section:

(1) "Employee" includes an independent contractor and employee of an independent contractor retained by the employer.

(2) "Fraudulent indorsement" means (i) in the case of an instrument payable to the employer, a forged indorsement purporting to be that of the employer, or (ii) in the case of an instrument with respect to which the employer is the issuer, a forged indorsement purporting to be that of the person identified as payee.

(3) "Responsibility" with respect to instruments means authority (i) to sign or indorse instruments on behalf of the employer, (ii) to process instruments received by the employer for bookkeeping purposes, for deposit to an account, or for other disposition, (iii) to prepare or process instruments for issue in the name of the employer, (iv) to supply information determining the names or addresses of payees of instruments to be issued in the name of the employer, (v) to control the disposition of instruments to be issued in the name of the employer, or (vi) to act otherwise with respect to instruments in a responsible capacity. "Responsibility" does not include authority that merely allows an employee to have access to instruments or blank or incomplete instrument forms that are being stored or transported or are part of incoming or outgoing mail, or similar access.

(b) For the purpose of determining the rights and liabilities of a person who, in good faith, pays an instrument or takes it for value or for collection, if an employer entrusted an employee with responsibility with respect to the instrument and the employee or a person acting in concert with the employee makes a fraudulent indorsement of the instrument, the indorsement is effective as the indorsement of the person to whom the instrument is payable if it is made in the name of that person. If the person paying the instrument or taking it for value or for collection fails to exercise ordinary care in paying or taking the instrument and that failure substantially contributes to loss resulting from the fraud, the person bearing the loss may recover from the person failing to exercise ordinary care to the extent the failure to exercise ordinary care contributed to the loss.

(c) Under subsection (b), an indorsement is made in the name of the person to whom an instrument is payable if (i) it is made in a name substantially similar to the name of that person or (ii) the instrument, whether or not indorsed, is deposited in a depositary bank to an account in a name substantially similar to the name of that person.

Rev. §3–406. Negligence Contributing to Forged Signature or Alteration of Instrument.

(a) A person whose failure to exercise ordinary care substantially contributes to an alteration of an instrument or to the making of a forged signature on an instrument is precluded from asserting the alteration or the forgery against a person who, in good faith, pays the instrument or takes it for value or for collection.

(b) Under subsection (a), if the person asserting the preclusion fails to exercise ordinary care in paying or taking the instrument and that failure substantially contributes to loss, the loss is allocated between the person precluded and the person asserting the preclusion according to the extent to which the failure of each to exercise ordinary care contributed to the loss.

(c) Under subsection (a), the burden of proving failure to exercise ordinary care is on the person asserting the preclusion. Under subsection (b), the burden of proving failure to exercise ordinary care is on the person precluded.

Rev. §3–407. Alteration.

(a) "Alteration" means (i) an unauthorized change in an instrument that purports to modify in any respect the obligation of a party, or (ii) an unauthorized addition of words or numbers or other change to an incomplete instrument relating to the obligation of a party.

(b) Except as provided in subsection (c), an alteration fraudulently made discharges a party whose obligation is affected by the alteration unless that party assents or is precluded from asserting the alteration. No other alteration discharges a party, and the instrument may be enforced according to its original terms.

(c) A payor bank or drawee paying a fraudulently altered instrument or a person taking it for value, in good faith and without notice of the alteration, may enforce rights with respect to the instrument (i) according to its original terms, or (ii) in the case of an incomplete instrument altered by unauthorized completion, according to its terms as completed.

Rev. §3–408. Drawee Not Liable on Unaccepted Draft.

A check or other draft does not of itself operate as an assignment of funds in the hands of the drawee available for its payment, and the drawee is not liable on the instrument until the drawee accepts it.

Rev. §3–409. Acceptance of Draft; Certified Check

(a) "Acceptance" means the drawee's signed agreement to pay a draft as presented. It must be written on the draft and may consist of the drawee's signature alone. Acceptance may be made at any time and becomes effective when notification pursuant to instructions is given or the accepted draft is delivered for the purpose of giving rights on the acceptance to any person.

(b) A draft may be accepted although it has not been signed by the drawer, is otherwise incomplete, is overdue, or has been dishonored.

(c) If a draft is payable at a fixed period after sight and the acceptor fails to date the acceptance, the holder may complete the acceptance by supplying a date in good faith.

(d) "Certified check" means a check accepted by the bank on which it is drawn. Acceptance may be made as stated in subsection (a) or by a writing on the check which indicates that the check is certified. The drawee of a check has no obligation to certify the check, and refusal to certify is not dishonor of the check.

Rev. §3–410. Acceptance Varying Draft.

(a) If the terms of a drawee's acceptance vary from the terms of the draft as presented, the holder may refuse the acceptance and treat the draft as dishonored. In that case, the drawee may cancel the acceptance.

(b) The terms of a draft are not varied by an acceptance to pay at a particular bank or place in the United States, unless the acceptance states that the draft is to be paid only at that bank or place.

(c) If the holder assents to an acceptance varying the terms of a draft, the obligation of each drawer and indorser that does not expressly assent to the acceptance is discharged.

Rev. §3–411. Refusal to Pay Cashier's Checks, Teller's Checks, and Certified Checks.

(a) In this section, "obligated bank" means the acceptor of a certified check or the issuer of a cashier's check or teller's check bought from the issuer.

(b) If the obligated bank wrongfully (i) refuses to pay a cashier's check or certified check, (ii) stops payment of a teller's check, or (iii) refuses to pay a dishonored teller's check, the person asserting the right to enforce the check is entitled to compensation for expenses and loss of interest resulting from the nonpayment and may recover consequential damages if the obligated bank refuses to pay after receiving notice of particular circumstances giving rise to the damages.

(c) Expenses or consequential damages under subsection (b) are not recoverable if the refusal of the obligated bank to pay occurs because (i) the bank suspends payments, (ii) the obligated bank asserts a claim or defense of the bank that it has reasonable grounds to believe is available against the person entitled to enforce the instrument, (iii) the obligated bank has a reasonable doubt whether the person demanding payment is the person entitled to enforce the instrument, or (iv) payment is prohibited by law.

Rev. §3–412. Obligation of Issuer of Note or Cashier's Check.
The issuer of a note or cashier's check or other draft drawn on the drawer is obliged to pay the instrument (i) according to its terms at the time it was issued or, if not issued, at the time it first came into possession of a holder, or (ii) if the issuer signed an incomplete instrument, according to its terms when completed, to the extent stated in Sections 3–115 and 3–407. The obligation is owed to a person entitled to enforce the instrument or to an indorser who paid the instrument under Section 3–415.

Rev. §3–413. Obligation of Acceptor.
(a) The acceptor of a draft is obliged to pay the draft (i) according to its terms at the time it was accepted, even though the acceptance states that the draft is payable "as originally drawn" or equivalent terms, (ii) if the acceptance varies the terms of the draft, according to the terms of the draft as varied, or (iii) if the acceptance is of a draft that is an incomplete instrument, according to its terms when completed, to the extent stated in Sections 3–115 and 3–407. The obligation is owed to a person entitled to enforce the draft or to the drawer or an indorser who paid the draft under Section 3–414 or 3–415.

(b) If the certification of a check or other acceptance of a draft states the amount certified or accepted, the obligation of the acceptor is that amount. If (i) the certification or acceptance does not state an amount, (ii) the amount of the instrument is subsequently raised, and (iii) the instrument is then negotiated to a holder in due course, the obligation of the acceptor is the amount of the instrument at the time it was taken by the holder in due course.

Rev. §3–414. Obligation of Drawer.
(a) This section does not apply to cashier's checks or other drafts drawn on the drawer.

(b) If an unaccepted draft is dishonored, the drawer is obliged to pay the draft (i) according to its terms at the time it was issued or, if not issued, at the time it first came into possession of a holder, or (ii) if the drawer signed an incomplete instrument, according to its terms when completed, to the extent stated in Sections 3–115 and 3–407. The obligation is owed to a person entitled to enforce the draft or to an indorser who paid the draft under Section 3–415.

(c) If a draft is accepted by a bank, the drawer is discharged, regardless of when or by whom acceptance was obtained.

(d) If a draft is accepted and the acceptor is not a bank, the obligation of the drawer to pay the draft if the draft is dishonored by the acceptor is the same as the obligation of an indorser under Section 3–415(a) and (c).

(e) If a draft states that it is drawn "without recourse" or otherwise disclaims liability of the drawer to pay the draft, the drawer is not liable under subsection (b) to pay the draft if the draft is not a check. A disclaimer of the liability stated in subsection (b) is not effective if the draft is a check.

(f) If (i) a check is not presented for payment or given to a depositary bank for collection within 30 days after its date, (ii) the drawee suspends payments after expiration of the 30-day period without paying the check, and (iii) because of the suspension of payments, the drawer is deprived of funds maintained with the drawee to cover payment of the check, the drawer to the extent deprived of funds may discharge its obligation to pay the check by assigning to the person entitled to enforce the check the rights of the drawer against the drawee with respect to the funds.

Rev. §3–415. Obligation of Indorser.
(a) Subject to subsections (b), (c), and (d) and to Section 3–419(d), if an instrument is dishonored, an indorser is obliged to pay the amount due on the instrument (i) according to the terms of the instrument at the time it was indorsed, or (ii) if the indorser indorsed an incomplete instrument, according to its terms when completed, to the extent stated in Sections 3–115 and 3–407. The obligation of the indorser is owed to a person entitled to enforce the instrument or to a subsequent indorser who paid the instrument under this section.

(b) If an indorsement states that it is made "without recourse" or otherwise disclaims liability of the indorser, the indorser is not liable under subsection (a) to pay the instrument.

(c) If notice of dishonor of an instrument is required by Section 3–503 and notice of dishonor complying with that section is not given to an indorser, the liability of the indorser under subsection (a) is discharged.

(d) If a draft is accepted by a bank after an indorsement is made, the liability of the indorser under subsection (a) is discharged.

(e) If an indorser of a check is liable under subsection (a) and the check is not presented for payment, or given to a depositary bank for collection, within 30 days after the day the indorsement was made, the liability of the indorser under subsection (a) is discharged.

Rev. §3–416. Transfer Warranties.
(a) A person who transfers an instrument for consideration warrants to the transferee and, if the transfer is by indorsement, to any subsequent transferee that:

(1) the warrantor is a person entitled to enforce the instrument;
(2) all signatures on the instrument are authentic and authorized;
(3) the instrument has not been altered;
(4) the instrument is not subject to a defense or claim in recoupment of any party which can be asserted against the warrantor; and
(5) the warrantor has no knowledge of any insolvency proceeding commenced with respect to the maker or acceptor or, in the case of an unaccepted draft, the drawer.

(b) A person to whom the warranties under subsection (a) are made and who took the instrument in good faith may recover from the warrantor as damages for breach of warranty an amount equal to the loss suffered as a result of the breach, but not more than the amount of the instrument plus expenses and loss of interest incurred as a result of the breach.

(c) The warranties stated in subsection (a) cannot be disclaimed with respect to checks. Unless notice of a claim for breach of warranty is given to the warrantor within 30 days after the claimant has reason to know of the breach and the identity of the warrantor, the liability of the warrantor under subsection (b) is discharged to the extent of any loss caused by the delay in giving notice of the claim.

(d) A [cause of action] for breach of warranty under this section accrues when the claimant has reason to know of the breach.

Rev. §3–417. Presentment Warranties.

(a) If an unaccepted draft is presented to the drawee for payment or acceptance and the drawee pays or accepts the draft, (i) the person obtaining payment or acceptance, at the time of presentment, and (ii) a previous transferor of the draft, at the time of transfer, warrant to the drawee making payment or accepting the draft in good faith that:

(1) the warrantor is, or was, at the time the warrantor transferred the draft, a person entitled to enforce the draft or authorized to obtain payment or acceptance of the draft on behalf of a person entitled to enforce the draft;

(2) the draft has not been altered; and

(3) the warrantor has no knowledge that the signature of the drawer of the draft is unauthorized.

(b) A drawee making payment may recover from any warrantor damages for breach of warranty equal to the amount paid by the drawee less the amount the drawee received or is entitled to receive from the drawer because of the payment. In addition, the drawee is entitled to compensation for expenses and loss of interest resulting from the breach. The right of the drawee to recover damages under this subsection is not affected by any failure of the drawee to exercise ordinary care in making payment. If the drawee accepts the draft, breach of warranty is a defense to the obligation of the acceptor. If the acceptor makes payment with respect to the draft, the acceptor is entitled to recover from any warrantor for breach of warranty the amounts stated in this subsection.

(c) If a drawee asserts a claim for breach of warranty under subsection (a) based on an unauthorized indorsement of the draft or an alteration of the draft, the warrantor may defend by proving that the indorsement is effective under Section 3–404 or 3–405 or the drawer is precluded under Section 3–406 or 4–406 from asserting against the drawee the unauthorized indorsement or alteration.

(d) If (i) a dishonored draft is presented for payment to the drawer or an indorser or (ii) any other instrument is presented for payment to a party obliged to pay the instrument, and (iii) payment is received, the following rules apply:

(1) The person obtaining payment and a prior transferor of the instrument warrant to the person making payment in good faith that the warrantor is, or was, at the time the warrantor transferred the instrument, a person entitled to enforce the instrument or authorized to obtain payment on behalf of a person entitled to enforce the instrument.

(2) The person making payment may recover from any warrantor for breach of warranty an amount equal to the amount paid plus expenses and loss of interest resulting from the breach.

(e) The warranties stated in subsections (a) and (d) cannot be disclaimed with respect to checks. Unless notice of a claim for breach of warranty is given to the warrantor within 30 days after the claimant has reason to know of the breach and the identity of the warrantor, the liability of the warrantor under subsection (b) or (d) is discharged to the extent of any loss caused by the delay in giving notice of the claim.

(f) A [cause of action] for breach of warranty under this section accrues when the claimant has reason to know of the breach.

Rev. §3–418. Payment or Acceptance by Mistake.

(a) Except as provided in subsection (c), if the drawee of a draft pays or accepts the draft and the drawee acted on the mistaken belief that (i) payment of the draft had not been stopped pursuant to Section 4–403 or (ii) the signature of the drawer of the draft was authorized, the drawee may recover the amount of the draft from the person to whom or for whose benefit payment was made or, in the case of acceptance, may revoke the acceptance. Rights of the drawee under this subsection are not affected by failure of the drawee to exercise ordinary care in paying or accepting the draft.

(b) Except as provided in subsection (c), if an instrument has been paid or accepted by mistake and the case is not covered by subsection (a), the person paying or accepting may, to the extent permitted by the law governing mistake and restitution, (i) recover the payment from the person to whom or for whose benefit payment was made or (ii) in the case of acceptance, may revoke the acceptance.

(c) The remedies provided by subsection (a) or (b) may not be asserted against a person who took the instrument in good faith and for value or who in good faith changed position in reliance on the payment or acceptance. This subsection does not limit remedies provided by Section 3–417 or 4–407.

(d) Notwithstanding Section 4–215, if an instrument is paid or accepted by mistake and the payor or acceptor recovers payment or revokes acceptance under subsection (a) or (b), the instrument is deemed not to have been paid or accepted and is treated as dishonored, and the person from whom payment is recovered has rights as a person entitled to enforce the dishonored instrument.

Rev. §3-419. Instruments Signed for Accommodation.

(a) If an instrument is issued for value given for the benefit of a party to the instrument ("accommodated party") and another party to the instrument ("accommodation party") signs the instrument for the purpose of incurring liability on the instrument without being a direct beneficiary of the value given for the instrument, the instrument is signed by the accommodation party "for accommodation."

(b) An accommodation party may sign the instrument as maker, drawer, acceptor, or indorser and, subject to subsection (d), is obliged to pay the instrument in the capacity in which the accommodation party signs. The obligation of an accommodation party may be enforced notwithstanding any statute of frauds and whether or not the accommodation party receives consideration for the accommodation.

(c) A person signing an instrument is presumed to be an accommodation party and there is notice that the instrument is signed for accommodation if the signature is an anomalous indorsement or is accompanied by words indicating that the signer is acting as surety or guarantor with respect to the obligation of another party to the instrument. Except as provided in Section 3-605, the obligation of an accommodation party to pay the instrument is not affected by the fact that the person enforcing the obligation had notice when the instrument was taken by that person that the accommodation party signed the instrument for accommodation.

(d) If the signature of a party to an instrument is accompanied by words indicating unambiguously that the party is guaranteeing collection rather than payment of the obligation of another party to the instrument, the signer is obliged to pay the amount due on the instrument to a person entitled to enforce the instrument only if (i) execution of judgment against the other party has been returned unsatisfied, (ii) the other party is insolvent or in an insolvency proceeding, (iii) the other party cannot be served with process, or (iv) it is otherwise apparent that payment cannot be obtained from the other party.

(e) An accommodation party who pays the instrument is entitled to reimbursement from the accommodated party and is entitled to enforce the instrument against the accommodated party. An accommodated party who pays the instrument has no right of recourse against, and is not entitled to contribution from, an accommodation party.

Rev. §3-420. Conversion of Instrument.

(a) The law applicable to conversion of personal property applies to instruments. An instrument is also converted if it is taken by transfer, other than a negotiation, from a person not entitled to enforce the instrument or a bank makes or obtains payment with respect to the instrument for a person not entitled to enforce the instrument or receive payment. An action for conversion of an instrument may not be brought by (i) the issuer or acceptor of the instrument or (ii) a payee or indorsee who did not receive delivery of the instrument either directly or through delivery to an agent or a copayee.

(b) In an action under subsection (a), the measure of liability is presumed to be the amount payable on the instrument, but recovery may not exceed the amount of the plaintiff's interest in the instrument.

(c) A representative, other than a depositary bank, who has in good faith dealt with an instrument or its proceeds on behalf of one who was not the person entitled to enforce the instrument is not liable in conversion to that person beyond the amount of any proceeds that it has not paid out.

Part 5: Dishonor

Rev. §3-501. Presentment.

(a) "Presentment" means a demand made by or on behalf of a person entitled to enforce an instrument (i) to pay the instrument made to the drawee or a party obliged to pay the instrument or, in the case of a note or accepted draft payable at a bank, to the bank, or (ii) to accept a draft made to the drawee.

(b) The following rules are subject to Article 4, agreement of the parties, and clearing-house rules and the like:

(1) Presentment may be made at the place of payment of the instrument and must be made at the place of payment if the instrument is payable at a bank in the United States; may be made by any commercially reasonable means, including an oral, written, or electronic communication; is effective when the demand for payment or acceptance is received by the person to whom presentment is made; and is effective if made to any one of two or more makers, acceptors, drawees, or other payors.

(2) Upon demand of the person to whom presentment is made, the person making presentment must (i) exhibit the instrument, (ii) give reasonable identification and, if presentment is made on behalf of another person, reasonable evidence of authority to do so, and (iii) sign a receipt on the instrument for any payment made or surrender the instrument if full payment is made.

(3) Without dishonoring the instrument, the party to whom presentment is made may (i) return the instrument for lack of a necessary indorsement, or (ii) refuse payment or acceptance for failure of the presentment to com-ply with the terms of the instrument, an agreement of the parties, or other applicable law or rule.

(4) The party to whom presentment is made may treat presentment as occurring on the next business day after the day of presentment if the party to whom presentment is made has established a cut-off hour not earlier than 2 p.m. for the receipt and processing of instruments presented for payment or acceptance and presentment is made after the cut-off hour.

Rev. §3-502. Dishonor.

(a) Dishonor of a note is governed by the following rules:

(1) If the note is payable on demand, the note is dishonored if presentment is duly made to the maker and the note is not paid on the day of presentment.

(2) If the note is not payable on demand and is payable at or through a bank or the terms of the note require presentment, the note is dishonored if presentment is duly made and the note is not paid on the day it becomes payable or the day of presentment, whichever is later.

(3) If the note is not payable on demand and paragraph (2) does not apply, the note is dishonored if it is not paid on the day it becomes payable.

(b) Dishonor of an unaccepted draft other than a documentary draft is governed by the following rules:

(1) If a check is duly presented for payment to the payor bank otherwise than for immediate payment over the counter, the check is dishonored if the payor bank makes timely return of the check or sends timely notice of dishonor or nonpayment under Section 4-301 or 4-302, or becomes accountable for the amount of the check under Section 4-302.

(2) If a draft is payable on demand and paragraph (1) does not apply, the draft is dishonored if presentment for payment is duly made to the drawee and the draft is not paid on the day of presentment.

(3) If a draft is payable on a date stated in the draft, the draft is dishonored if (i) presentment for payment is duly made to the drawee and payment is not made on the day the draft becomes payable or the day of presentment, whichever is later, or (ii) presentment for acceptance is duly made before the day the draft becomes payable and the draft is not accepted on the day of presentment.

(4) If a draft is payable on elapse of a period of time after sight or acceptance, the draft is dishonored if presentment for acceptance is duly made and the draft is not accepted on the day of presentment.

(c) Dishonor of an unaccepted documentary draft occurs according to the rules stated in subsection (b)(2), (3), and (4), except that payment or acceptance may be delayed without dishonor until no later than the close of the third business day of the drawee following the day on which payment or acceptance is required by those paragraphs.

(d) Dishonor of an accepted draft is governed by the following rules:

(1) If the draft is payable on demand, the draft is dishonored if presentment for payment is duly made to the acceptor and the draft is not paid on the day of presentment.

(2) If the draft is not payable on demand, the draft is dishonored if presentment for payment is duly made to the acceptor and payment is not made on the day it becomes payable or the day of presentment, whichever is later.

(e) In any case in which presentment is otherwise required for dishonor under this section and presentment is excused under Section 3-504, dishonor occurs without presentment if the instrument is not duly accepted or paid.

(f) If a draft is dishonored because timely acceptance of the draft was not made and the person entitled to demand acceptance consents to a late acceptance, from the time of acceptance the draft is treated as never having been dishonored.

Rev. §3-503. Notice of Dishonor.

(a) The obligation of an indorser stated in Section 3-415(a) and the obligation of a drawer stated in Section 3-414(d) may not be enforced unless (i) the indorser or drawer is given notice of dishonor of the instrument complying with this section or (ii) notice of dishonor is excused under Section 3-504(b).

(b) Notice of dishonor may be given by any person; may be given by any commercially reasonable means, including an oral, written, or electronic communication; and is sufficient if it reasonably identifies the instrument and indicates that the instrument has been dishonored or has not been paid or accepted. Return of an instrument given to a bank for collection is sufficient notice of dishonor.

(c) Subject to Section 3-504(c), with respect to an instrument taken for collection by a collecting bank, notice of dishonor must be given (i) by the bank before midnight of the next banking day following the banking day on which the bank receives notice of dishonor of the instrument, or (ii) by any other person within 30 days following the day on which the person receives notice of dishonor. With respect to any other instrument, notice of dishonor must be given within 30 days following the day on which dishonor occurs.

Rev. §3-504. Excused Presentment and Notice of Dishonor.

(a) Presentment for payment or acceptance of an instrument is excused if (i) the person entitled to present the instrument cannot with reasonable diligence make presentment, (ii) the maker or acceptor has repudiated an obligation to pay the instrument or is dead or in insolvency proceedings, (iii) by the terms of the instrument presentment is not necessary to enforce the obligation of indorsers or the drawer, (iv) the drawer or indorser whose obligation is being enforced has waived presentment or otherwise has no reason to expect or right to require that the instrument be paid or accepted, or (v) the drawer instructed the drawee not to pay or accept the draft or the drawee was not obligated to the drawer to pay the draft.

(b) Notice of dishonor is excused if (i) by the terms of the instrument notice of dishonor is not necessary to enforce the obligation of a party to pay the instrument, or (ii) the party whose obligation is being enforced waived notice of dishonor. A waiver of presentment is also a waiver of notice of dishonor.

(c) Delay in giving notice of dishonor is excused if the delay was caused by circumstances beyond the control of the person giving the notice and the person giving the notice exercised reasonable diligence after the cause of the delay ceased to operate.

Rev. §3-505. Evidence of Dishonor.

(a) The following are admissible as evidence and create a presumption of dishonor and of any notice of dishonor stated:

(1) a document regular in form as provided in subsection (b) which purports to be a protest;

(2) a purported stamp or writing of the drawee, payor bank, or presenting bank on or accompanying the instrument stating that acceptance or payment has been refused unless reasons for the refusal are stated and the reasons are not consistent with dishonor;

(3) a book or record of the drawee, payor bank, or collecting bank, kept in the usual course of business which shows dishonor, even if there is no evidence of who made the entry.

(b) A protest is a certificate of dishonor made by a United States consul or vice consul, or a notary public or other person authorized to administer oaths by the law of the place where dishonor occurs. It may be made upon information satisfactory to that person. The protest must identify the instrument and certify either that presentment has been made or, if not made, the reason why it was not made, and that the instrument has been dishonored by nonacceptance or nonpayment. The protest may also certify that notice of dishonor has been given to some or all parties.

Part 6: Discharge and Payment

Rev. §3-601. Discharge and Effect of Discharge.

(a) The obligation of a party to pay the instrument is discharged as stated in this Article or by an act or agreement with the party which would discharge an obligation to pay money under a simple contract.

(b) Discharge of the obligation of a party is not effective against a person acquiring rights of a holder in due course of the instrument without notice of the discharge.

Rev. §3-602. Payment.

(a) Subject to subsection (b), an instrument is paid to the extent payment is made (i) by or on behalf of a party obliged to pay the instrument, and (ii) to a person entitled to enforce the instrument. To the extent of the payment, the obligation of the party obliged to pay the instrument is discharged even though payment is made with knowledge of a claim to the instrument under Section 3-306 by another person.

(b) The obligation of a party to pay the instrument is not discharged under subsection (a) if:

(1) a claim to the instrument under Section 3-306 is enforceable against the party receiving payment and (i) payment is made with knowledge by the payor that payment is prohibited by injunction or similar process of a court of competent jurisdiction, or (ii) in the case of an instrument other than a cashier's check, teller's check, or certified check, the party making payment accepted, from the person having a claim to the instrument, indemnity against loss resulting from refusal to pay the person entitled to enforce the instrument; or

(2) the person making payment knows that the instrument is a stolen instrument and pays a person it knows is in wrongful possession of the instrument.

Rev. §3-603. Tender of Payment.

(a) If tender of payment of an obligation to pay an instrument is made to a person entitled to enforce the instrument, the effect of tender is governed by principles of law applicable to tender of payment under a simple contract.

(b) If tender of payment of an obligation to pay an instrument is made to a person entitled to enforce the instrument and the tender is refused, there is discharge, to the extent of the amount of the tender, of the obligation of an indorser or accommodation party having a right of recourse with respect to the obligation to which the tender relates.

(c) If tender of payment of an amount due on an instrument is made to a person entitled to enforce the instrument, the obligation of the obligor to pay interest after the due date on the amount tendered is discharged. If presentment is required with respect to an instrument and the obligor is able and ready to pay on the due date at every place of payment stated in the instrument, the obligor is deemed to have made tender of payment on the due date to the person entitled to enforce the instrument.

Rev. §3-604. Discharge by Cancellation or Renunciation.

(a) A person entitled to enforce an instrument, with or without consideration, may discharge the obligation of a party to pay the instrument (i) by an intentional voluntary act, such as surrender of the instrument to the party, destruction, mutilation, or cancellation of the instrument, cancellation or striking out of the party's signature, or the addition of words to the instrument indicating discharge, or (ii) by agreeing not to sue or otherwise renouncing rights against the party by a signed writing.

(b) Cancellation or striking out of an indorsement pursuant to subsection (a) does not affect the status and rights of a party derived from the indorsement.

Rev. §3-605. Discharge of Indorsers and Accommodation Parties.

(a) In this section, the term "indorser" includes a drawer having the obligation described in Section 3-414(d).

(b) Discharge, under Section 3-604, of the obligation of a party to pay an instrument does not discharge the obligation of an indorser or accommodation party having a right of recourse against the discharged party.

(c) If a person entitled to enforce an instrument agrees, with or without consideration, to an extension of the due date of the obligation of a party to pay the instrument, the extension discharges an indorser or accommodation party having a right of recourse against the party whose obligation is extended to the extent the indorser or accommodation party proves that the extension caused loss to the indorser or accommodation party with respect to the right of recourse.

(d) If a person entitled to enforce an instrument agrees, with or without consideration, to a material modification of the obligation of a party other than an extension of the due date, the modification discharges the obligation of an indorser or accommodation party having a right of recourse against the person whose obligation is modified to the extent the modification causes loss to the indorser or accommodation party with respect to the right of recourse. The loss suffered by the indorser or accommodation party as a result of the modification is equal to the amount of the right of recourse unless the person enforcing the instrument proves that no loss was caused by the modification or that the loss caused by the modification was an amount less than the amount of the right of recourse.

(e) If the obligation of a party to pay an instrument is secured by an interest in collateral and a person entitled to enforce the instrument impairs the value of the interest in collateral, the obligation of an indorser or accommodation party having a right of recourse against the obligor is discharged to the extent of the impairment. The value of an interest in collateral is impaired to the extent (i) the value of the interest is reduced to an amount less than the amount of the right of recourse of the party asserting discharge, or (ii) the reduction in value of the interest causes an increase in the amount by which the amount of the right of recourse exceeds the value of the interest. The burden of proving impairment is on the party asserting discharge.

(f) If the obligation of a party is secured by an interest in collateral not provided by an accommodation party and a person entitled to enforce the instrument impairs the value of the interest in collateral, the obligation of any party who is jointly and severally liable with respect to the secured obligation is discharged to the extent the impairment causes the party asserting discharge to pay more than that party would have been obliged to pay, taking into account rights of contribution, if impairment had not occurred. If the party asserting discharge is an accommodation party not entitled to discharge under subsection (e), the party is deemed to have a right to contribution based on joint and several liability rather than a right to reimbursement. The burden of proving impairment is on the party asserting discharge.

(g) Under subsection (e) or (f), impairing value of an interest in collateral includes (i) failure to obtain or maintain perfection or recordation of the interest in collateral, (ii) release of collateral without substitution of collateral of equal value, (iii) failure to perform a duty to preserve the value of collateral owed, under Article 9 or other law, to a debtor or surety or other person secondarily liable, or (iv) failure to comply with applicable law in disposing of collateral.

(h) An accommodation party is not discharged under subsection (c), (d), or (e) unless the person entitled to enforce the instrument knows of the accommodation or has notice under Section 3-419(c) that the instrument was signed for accommodation.

(i) A party is not discharged under this section if (i) the party asserting discharge consents to the event or conduct that is the basis of the discharge, or (ii) the instrument or a separate agreement of the party provides for waiver of discharge under this section either specifically or by general language indicating that parties waive defenses based on suretyship or impairment of collateral.

ARTICLE 4: BANK DEPOSITS AND COLLECTIONS (1990 AMENDMENTS)

Part 1: General Provisions and Definitions

§4-101. Short Title. This Article shall be known and may be cited as Uniform Commercial Code—Bank Deposits and Collections.

§4-102. Applicability.

[(1)] (a) To the extent that items within this Article are also within [the scope of] Articles 3 and 8, they are subject to [the provisions of] those Articles. [In the event of] If there is conflict, [the provisions of] this Article [govern those of] governs Article 3, but [the provisions of] Article 8 [govern those of] governs this Article.

[(2)] (b) The liability of a bank for action or non-action with respect to [any] an item handled by it for purposes of presentment, payment, or collection is governed by the law of the place where the bank is located. In the case of action or non-action by or at a branch or separate office of a bank, its liability is governed by the law of the place where the branch or separate office is located.

§4-103. Variation by Agreement; Measure of Damages; [Certain] Action Constituting Ordinary Care.

[(1)] (a) The effect of the provisions of this Article may be varied by agreement[except that no agreement can], but the parties to the agreement cannot disclaim a bank's responsibility for its [own] lack of good faith or failure to exercise ordinary care or [can] limit the measure of damages for [such] the lack or failure[; but]. However, the parties may determine by agreement [determine] the standards by which [such] the bank's responsibility is to be measured if [such] those standards are not manifestly unreasonable.

[(2)] (b) Federal Reserve regulations and operating [letters] circulars, [clearing house] clearing-house rules, and the like[,] have the effect of agreements under subsection [(1)] (a), whether or not specifically assented to by all parties interested in items handled.

[(3)] (c) Action or non-action approved by this Article or pursuant to Federal Reserve regulations or operating [letters constitutes] circulars is the exercise of ordinary care and, in the absence of special instructions, action or non-action consistent with [clearing house] clearing-house rules and the like or with a general banking usage not disapproved by this Article, is prima facie [constitutes] the exercise of ordinary care.

[(4)] (d) The specification or approval of certain procedures by this Article [does not constitute] is not disapproval of other procedures [which] that may be reasonable under the circumstances.

[(5)] (e) The measure of damages for failure to exercise ordinary care in handling an item is the amount of the item reduced by an amount [which] that could not have been realized by the [use] exercise of ordinary care [, and where]. If there is also bad faith it includes any other damages[, if any, suffered by] the party suffered as a proximate consequence.

§4-104. Definitions and Index of Definitions.

[(1)] (a) In this Article, unless the context otherwise requires:

[(a)] (1) "Account" means any deposit or credit account with a bank [and includes], including a [checking, time, interest or savings account] demand, time, savings, passbook, share draft, or like account, other than an account evidenced by a certificate of deposit;

[(b)] (2) "Afternoon" means the period of a day between noon and midnight;

[(c)] (3) "Banking day" means [that] the part of [any] a day on which a bank is open to the public for carrying on substantially all of its banking functions;

[(d)] (4) "Clearing house" means [any] an association of banks or other payors regularly clearing items;

[(e)] (5) "Customer" means [any] a person having an account with a bank or for whom a bank has agreed to collect items [and includes], including a bank [carrying] that maintains an account [with] at another bank;

[(f)] (6) "Documentary draft" means [any negotiable or nonnegotiable draft with accompanying documents, securities or other papers to be delivered against honor of the draft] a draft to be presented for acceptance or payment if specified documents, certificated securities (Section 8-102) or instructions for uncertificated securities (Section 8-308), or other certificates, statements, or the like are to be received by the drawee or other payor before acceptance or payment of the draft;

(7) "Draft" means a draft as defined in Section 3-104 or an item, other than an instrument, that is an order.

(8) "Drawee" means a person ordered in a draft to make payment.

[(g)] (9) "Item" means [any instrument for the payment of money even though it is not negotiable but does not include money] an instrument or a promise or order to pay money handled by a bank for collection or payment. The term does not include a payment order governed by Article 4A or a credit or debit card slip;

[(h)] (10) "Midnight deadline" with respect to a bank is midnight on its next banking day following the banking day on which it receives the relevant item or notice or from which the time for taking action commences to run, whichever is later;

[(i)] "Properly payable" includes the availability of funds for payment at the time of decision to pay or dishonor;]

[(j)] (11) "Settle" means to pay in cash, by [clearing house] clearing-house settlement, in a charge or credit or by remittance, or otherwise as [instructed] agreed. A settlement may be either provisional or final.

[(k)] (12) "Suspends payments" with respect to a bank means that it has been closed by order of the supervisory authorities, that a public officer has been appointed to take it over, or that it ceases or refuses to make payments in the ordinary course of business.

[(2)] (b) Other definitions applying to this Article and the sections in which they appear are:

"Agreement for electronic presentment"	Section 4-110
"Bank"	Section 4-105
"Collecting bank"	Section 4-105
"Depositary bank"	Section 4-105
"Intermediary bank"	Section 4-105
"Payor bank"	Section 4-105
"Presenting bank"	Section 4-105
"Presentment notice"	Section 4-110
["Remitting bank"	Section 4-105]

[(3)] (c) The following definitions in other Articles apply to this Article:

"Acceptance"	Section [3-410] 3-409
"Alteration"	Section 3-407
"Cashier's check"	Section 3-104
"Certificate of deposit"	Section 3-104
["Certification"	Section 3-411]
"Certified check"	Section 3-409
"Check"	Section 3-104
"Good faith"	Section 3-103
"Holder in due course"	Section 3-302
"Instrument"	Section 3-104
"Notice of dishonor"	Section [3-508] 3-503
"Order"	Section 3-103
"Ordinary care"	Section 3-103
"Person entitled to enforce"	Section 3-301
"Presentment"	Section [3-504] 3-501
"Promise"	Section 3-103
["Protest"	Section 3-509]
"Prove"	Section 3-103
["Secondary party"	Section 3-102]
"Teller's check"	Section 3-104
"Unauthorized signature"	Section 3-403

[(4)] (d) In addition, Article 1 contains general definitions and principles of construction and interpretation applicable throughout this Article.

§4-105. "Bank"; "Bank"; "Depositary Bank"; "Payor Bank"; "Intermediary Bank"; "Collecting Bank"; "Presenting Bank" [; "Remitting Bank"]. In this Article [unless the context otherwise requires]:

(1) "Bank" means a person engaged in the business of banking, including a savings bank, savings and loan association, credit union, or trust company.

[(a)] (2) "Depositary bank" means the first bank to [which] take an item [is transferred for collection] even though it is also the payor bank, unless the item is presented for immediate payment over the counter;

[(b)] (3) "Payor bank" means a bank[by which an item is payable as drawn or accepted] that is the drawee of a draft;

[(c)] (4) "Intermediary bank" means [any] a bank to which an item is transferred in course of collection except the depositary or payor bank;

[(d)] (5) "Collecting bank" means [any] a bank handling [the] an item for collection except the payor bank;

[(e)] (6) "Presenting bank" means [any] a bank presenting an item except a payor bank[;].

[(f) "Remitting bank" means any payor or intermediary bank remitting for an item.]

§4-106. Payable Through or Payable at Bank; Collecting Bank.

(a) If an item states that it is "payable through" a bank identified in the item, (i) the item designates the bank as a collecting bank and does not by itself authorize the bank to pay the item, and (ii) the item may be presented for payment only by or through the bank.

Alternative A

(b) If an item states that it is "payable at" a bank identified in the item, the item is equivalent to a draft drawn on the bank.

Alternative B

(b) If an item states that it is "payable at" a bank identified in the item, (i) the item designates the bank as a collecting bank and does not by itself authorize the bank to pay the item, and (ii) the item may be presented for payment only by or through the bank.

(c) If a draft names a nonbank drawee and it is unclear whether a bank named in the draft is a co-drawee or a collecting bank, the bank is a collecting bank.

§ [4-106] 4-107. Separate Office of Bank. A branch or separate office of a bank [[maintaining its own deposit ledgers]] is a separate bank for the purpose of computing the time within which and determining the place at or to which action may be taken or notice or orders [shall] must be given under this Article and under Article 3.

§ [4-107] 4-108. Time of Receipt of Items.

[(1)] (a) For the purpose of allowing time to process items, prove balances, and make the necessary entries on its books to determine its position for the day, a bank may fix an afternoon hour of 2 P.M. or later as a [cut-off] cutoff hour for the handling of money and items and the making of entries on its books.

[(2)] (b) [Any] An item or deposit of money received on any day after a [cut-off] cutoff hour so fixed or after the close of the banking day may be treated as being received at the opening of the next banking day.

§ [4-108] 4-109. Delays.

[(1)] (a) Unless otherwise instructed, a collecting bank in a good faith effort to secure payment [may, in the case of] a specific [items] item drawn on a payor other than a bank, and with or without the approval of any person involved, may waive, modify, or extend time limits imposed or permitted by this [Act] for a period not [in excess of an] exceeding two additional banking [day] days without discharge of [secondary parties and without] drawers or indorsers or liability to its transferor or [any] a prior party.

[(2)] (b) Delay by a collecting bank or payor bank beyond time limits prescribed or permitted by this [Act] or by instructions is excused if (i) the delay is caused by interruption of communication or computer facilities, suspension of payments by another bank, war, emergency conditions, failure of equipment, or other circumstances beyond the control of the bank[provided it], and (ii) the bank exercises such diligence as the circumstances require.

§4-109. Process of Posting. The "process of posting" means the usual procedure followed by a payor bank in determining to pay an item and in recording the payment including one or more of the following or other steps as determined by the bank:

(a) verification of any signature;
(b) ascertaining that sufficient funds are available;
(c) affixing a "paid" or other stamp;
(d) entering a charge or entry to a customer's account;
(e) correcting or reversing an entry or erroneous action with respect to the item.]

§4-110. Electronic Presentment.

(a) "Agreement for electronic presentment" means an agreement, clearing-house rule, or Federal Reserve regulation or operating circular, providing that presentment of an item may be made by transmission of an image of an item or information describing the item ("presentment notice") rather than delivery of the item itself. The agreement may provide for procedures governing retention, presentment, payment, dishonor, and other matters concerning items subject to the agreement.

(b) Presentment of an item pursuant to an agreement for presentment is made when the presentment notice is received.

(c) If presentment is made by presentment notice, a reference to "item" or "check" in this Article means the presentment notice unless the context otherwise indicates.

§4-111. Statute of Limitations.

An action to enforce an obligation, duty, or right arising under this Article must be commenced within three years after the [cause of action] accrues.

Part 2: Collection of Items— Depositary and Collecting Banks

§4-201. [Presumption and Duration of Agency] Status of Collecting [Banks] Bank as Agent and Provisional Status of Credits; Applicability of Article; Item Indorsed "Pay Any Bank".

[(1)] (a) Unless a contrary intent clearly appears and [prior to] before the time that a settlement given by a collecting bank for an item is or becomes final, [(subsection (3) of Section 4-211 and Sections 4-212 and 4-213)] the bank, with respect to the item, is an agent or sub-agent of the owner of the item and any settlement given for the item is provisional. This provision applies regardless of the form of indorsement or lack of indorsement and even though credit given for the item is subject to immediate withdrawal as of right or is in fact withdrawn; but the continuance of ownership of an item by its owner and any rights of the owner to proceeds of the item are subject to rights of a collecting bank, such as those resulting from outstanding advances on the item and [valid] rights of recoupment or setoff. [When] If an item is handled by banks for purposes of presentment, payment [and], collection, or return, the relevant provisions of this Article apply even though action of the parties clearly establishes that a particular bank has purchased the item and is the owner of it.

[(2)] (b) After an item has been indorsed with the words "pay any bank" or the like, only a bank may acquire the rights of a holder until the item has been:

[(a)] (1) [until the item has been] returned to the customer initiating collection; or

[(b)] (2) [until the item has been] specially indorsed by a bank to a person who is not a bank.

§4-202. Responsibility for Collection or Return; When Action [Seasonable] Timely.

[(1)] (a) A collecting bank must [use] exercise ordinary care in:

[(1)] (a) presenting an item or sending it for presentment; [and]

[(b)] (2) sending notice of dishonor or nonpayment or returning an item other than a documentary draft to the bank's transferor [[or directly to the depositary bank under subsection (2) of Section 4-212] (see note to Section 4-212)] after learning that the item has not been paid or accepted, as the case may be; and

[(c)] (3) settling for an item when the bank receives final settlement; and

[(d) making or providing for any necessary protest; and]

[(e)] (4) notifying its transferor of any loss or delay in transit within a reasonable time after discovery thereof.

[(2) A collecting bank taking proper action before its midnight deadline following receipt of an item, notice or payment acts seasonably; taking proper action within a reasonably longer time may be seasonable but the bank has the burden of so establishing.]

(b) A collecting bank exercises ordinary care under subsection (a) by taking proper action before its midnight deadline following receipt of an item, notice, or settlement. Taking proper action within a reasonably longer time may constitute the exercise of ordinary care, but the bank has the burden of establishing timeliness.

[(3)] (c) Subject to subsection [(1)(a)] (a)(1), a bank is not liable for the insolvency, neglect, misconduct, mistake, or default of another bank or person or for loss or destruction of an item in the possession of others or in transit [or in the possession of others].

§4-203. Effect of Instructions. Subject to [the provisions of] Article 3 concerning conversion of instruments (Section [3-419] 3-420) and [the provisions of both Article 3 and this Article concerning] restrictive indorsements (Section 3-206), only a collecting bank's transferor can give instructions [which] that affect the bank or constitute notice to it, and a collecting bank is not liable to prior parties for any action taken pursuant to [such] the instructions or in accordance with any agreement with its transferor.

§4-204. Methods of Sending and Presenting; Sending [Direct] Directly to Payor Bank.

[(1)] (a) A collecting bank [must] shall send items by a reasonably prompt method, taking into consideration[any] relevant instructions, the nature of the item, the number of [such] those items on hand, [and] the cost of collection involved, and the method generally used by it or others to present [such] those items.

[(2)] (b) A collecting bank may send:

[(a)] (1) [any] an item [direct] directly to the payor bank;

[(b)] (2) [any] an item to [any] a nonbank payor if authorized by its transferor; and

[(c)] (3) [any] an item other than documentary drafts to [any] a nonbank payor, if authorized by Federal Reserve regulation or operating [letter] circular, [clearing house] clearing-house rule, or the like.

[(3)] (c) Presentment may be made by a presenting bank at a place where the payor bank or other payor has requested that presentment be made.

§4-205. [Supplying Missing Indorsement; No Notice from Prior Indorsement] Depositary Bank Holder of Unindorsed Item. If a customer delivers an item to a depositary bank for collection:

(1) the depositary bank becomes a holder of the item at the time it receives the item for collection if the customer at the time of delivery was a holder of the item, whether or not the customer indorses the item, and, if the bank satisfies the other requirements of Section 3-302, it is a holder in due course; and

(2) the depositary bank warrants to collecting banks, the payor bank or other payor, and the drawer that the amount of the item was paid to the customer or deposited to the customer's account.

[(1) A depositary bank which has taken an item for collection may supply any indorsement of the customer which is necessary to title unless the item contains the words "payee's indorsement required" or the like. In the absence of such a requirement a statement placed on the item by the depositary bank to the effect that the item was deposited by a customer or credited to his account is effective as the customer's indorsement;

(2) An intermediary bank, or payor bank which is not a depositary bank, is neither given notice nor otherwise affected by a restrictive indorsement of any person except the bank's immediate transferor.]

§4-206. Transfer Between Banks. Any agreed method [which] that identifies the transferor bank is sufficient for the item's further transfer to another bank.

§4-207. Warranties of Customer and Collecting Bank on Transfer or Presentment of Items; Time for Claims.

(1) Each customer or collecting bank who obtains payment or acceptance of an item and each prior customer and collecting bank warrants to the payor bank or other payor who in good faith pays or accepts the item that

(a) he has a good title to the item or is authorized to obtain payment or acceptance on behalf of one who has a good title; and

(b) he has no knowledge that the signature of the maker or drawer is unauthorized, except that this warranty is not given by any customer or collecting bank that is a holder in due course and acts in good faith
  (i) to a maker with respect to the maker's own signature; or
  (ii) to a drawer with respect to the drawer's own signature, whether or not the drawer is also the drawee; or
  (iii) to an acceptor of an item if the holder in due course took the item after the acceptance or obtained the acceptance without knowledge that the drawer's signature was unauthorized; and

(c) the item has not been materially altered, except that this warranty is not given by any customer or collecting bank that is a holder in due course and acts in good faith
  (i) to the maker of a note; or
  (ii) to the drawer of a draft whether or not the drawer is also the drawee; or
  (iii) to the acceptor of an item with respect to an alteration made prior to the acceptance if the holder in due course took the item after the acceptance, even though the acceptance provided "payable as originally drawn" or equivalent terms; or
  (iv) to the acceptor of an item with respect to an alteration made after the acceptance.

(2) Each customer and collecting bank who transfers an item and receives a settlement or other consideration for it warrants to his transferee and to any subsequent collecting bank who takes the item in good faith that

(a) he has a good title to the item or is authorized to obtain payment or acceptance on behalf of one who has a good title and the transfer is otherwise rightful; and

(b) all signatures are genuine or authorized; and

(c) the item has not been materially altered; and

(d) no defense of any party is good against him; and

(e) he has no knowledge of any insolvency proceeding instituted with respect to the maker or acceptor or the drawer of an unaccepted item.

In addition each customer and collecting bank so transferring an item and receiving a settlement or other consideration engages that upon dishonor and any necessary notice of dishonor and protest he will take up the item.

(3) The warranties and the engagement to honor set forth in the two preceding subsections arise notwithstanding the absence of indorsement or words of guaranty or warranty in the transfer or presentment and a collecting bank remains liable for their breach despite remittance to its transferor. Damages for breach of such warranties or engagement to honor shall not exceed the consideration received by the customer or collecting bank responsible plus finance charges and expenses related to the item, if any.

(4) Unless a claim for breach of warranty under this section is made within a reasonable time after the person claiming learns of the breach, the person liable is discharged to the extent of any loss caused by the delay in making claim.]

§4-207. Transfer Warranties.

(a) A customer or collecting bank that transfers an item and receives a settlement or other consideration warrants to the transferee and to any subsequent collecting bank that:

(1) the warrantor is a person entitled to enforce the item;
(2) all signatures on the item are authentic and authorized;
(3) the item has not been altered;
(4) the item is not subject to a defense or claim in recoupment (Section 3-305(a)) of any party that can be asserted against the warrantor; and
(5) the warrantor has no knowledge of any insolvency proceeding commenced with respect to the maker or acceptor or, in the case of an unaccepted draft, the drawer.

(b) If an item is dishonored, a customer or collecting bank transferring the item and receiving settlement or other consideration is obliged to pay the amount due on the item (i) according to the terms of the item at the time it was transferred, or (ii) if the transfer was of an incomplete item, according to its terms when completed as stated in Sections 3-115 and 3-407. The obligation of a transferor is owed to the transferee and to any subsequent collecting bank that takes the item in good faith. A transferor cannot disclaim its obligation under this subsection by an indorsement stating that it is made "without recourse" or otherwise disclaiming liability.

(c) A person to whom the warranties under subsection (a) are made and who took the item in good faith may recover from the warrantor as damages for breach of warranty an amount equal to the loss suffered as a result of the breach, but not more than the amount of the item plus expenses and loss of interest incurred as a result of the breach.

(d) The warranties stated in subsection (a) cannot be disclaimed with respect to checks. Unless notice of a claim for breach of warranty is given to the warrantor within 30 days after the claimant has reason to know of the breach and the identity of the warrantor, the warrantor is discharged to the extent of any loss caused by the delay in giving notice of the claim.

(e) A cause of action for breach of warranty under this section accrues when the claimant has reason to know of the breach.

§4-208. Presentment Warranties.

(a) If an unaccepted draft is presented to the drawee for payment or acceptance and the drawee pays or accepts the draft, (i) the person obtaining payment or acceptance, at the time of presentment, and (ii) a previous transferor of the draft, at the time of transfer, warrant to the drawee that pays or accepts the draft in good faith that:

(1) the warrantor is, or was, at the time the warrantor transferred the draft, a person entitled to enforce the draft or authorized to obtain payment or acceptance of the draft on behalf of a person entitled to enforce the draft;
(2) the draft has not been altered; and
(3) the warrantor has no knowledge that the signature of the purported drawer of the draft is unauthorized.

(b) A drawee making payment may recover from a warrantor damages for breach of warranty equal to the amount paid by the drawee less the amount the drawee received or is entitled to receive from the drawer because of the payment. In addition, the drawee is entitled to compensation for expenses and loss of interest resulting from the breach. The right of the drawee to recover damages under this subsection is not affected by any failure of the drawee to exercise ordinary care in making payment. If the drawee accepts the draft (i) breach of warranty is a defense to the obligation of the acceptor, and (ii) if the acceptor makes payment with respect to the draft, the acceptor is entitled to recover from a warrantor for breach of warranty the amounts stated in this subsection.

(c) If a drawee asserts a claim for breach of warranty under subsection (a) based on an unauthorized indorsement of the draft or an alteration of the draft, the warrantor may defend by proving that the indorsement is effective under Section 3-404 or 3-405 or the drawer is precluded under Section 3-406 or 4-406 from asserting against the drawee the unauthorized indorsement or alteration.

(d) If (i) a dishonored draft is presented for payment to the drawer or an indorser or (ii) any other item is presented for payment to a party obliged to pay the item, and the item is paid, the person obtaining payment and a prior transferor of the item warrant to the person making payment in good faith that the warrantor is, or was, at the time the warrantor transferred the item, a person entitled to enforce the item or authorized to obtain payment on behalf of a person entitled to enforce the item. The person making payment may recover from any warrantor for breach of warranty an amount equal to the amount paid plus expenses and loss of interest resulting from the breach.

(e) The warranties stated in subsections (a) and (d) cannot be disclaimed with respect to checks. Unless notice of a claim for breach of warranty is given to the warrantor within 30 days after the claimant has reason to know of the breach and the identity of the warrantor, the warrantor is discharged to the extent of any loss caused by the delay in giving notice of the claim.

(f) A cause of action for breach of warranty under this section accrues when the claimant has reason to know of the breach.

§4-209. Encoding and Retention Warranties.

(a) A person who encodes information on or with respect to an item after issue warrants to any subsequent collecting bank and to the payor bank or other payor that the information is correctly encoded. If the customer of a depositary bank encodes, that bank also makes the warranty.

(b) A person who undertakes to retain an item pursuant to an agreement for electronic presentment warrants to any subsequent collecting bank and to the payor bank or other payor that retention and presentment of the item comply with the agreement. If a customer of a depositary bank undertakes to retain an item, that bank also makes this warranty.

(c) A person to whom warranties are made under this section and who took the item in good faith may recover from the warrantor as damages for breach of warranty an amount equal to the loss suffered as a result of the breach, plus expenses and loss of interest incurred as a result of the breach.

§ [4-208] 4-210. Security Interest of Collecting Bank in Items, Accompanying Documents and Proceeds.

[(1)] (a) A collecting bank has a security interest in an item and any accompanying documents or the proceeds of either:

[(a)] (1) in case of an item deposited in an account, to the extent to which credit given for the item has been withdrawn or applied;

[(b)] (2) in case of an item for which it has given credit available for withdrawal as of right, to the extent of the credit given, whether or not the credit is drawn upon [and whether] or [not] there is a right of chargeback; or

[(c)] (3) if it makes an advance on or against the item.

[(2)] (b) [When] If credit [which has been] given for several items received at one time or pursuant to a single agreement is withdrawn or applied in part, the security interest remains upon all the items, any accompanying documents or the proceeds of either. For the purpose of this section, credits first given are first withdrawn.

[(3)] (c) Receipt by a collecting bank of a final settlement for an item is a realization on its security interest in the item, accompanying documents, and proceeds. [To the extent and so] So long as the bank does not receive final settlement for the item or give up possession of the item or accompanying documents for purposes other than collection, the security interest continues to that extent and is subject to [the provisions of] Article 9, [except that] but:

[(a)] (1) no security agreement is necessary to make the security interest enforceable ([subsection (1)(a) of] Section [9-203] 9-203(1)(a)); [and]

[(b)] (2) no filing is required to perfect the security interest; and

[(c)] (3) the security interest has priority over conflicting perfected security interests in the item, accompanying documents, or proceeds.

§ [4-209] 4-211. When Bank Gives Value for Purposes of Holder in Due Course. For purposes of determining its status as a holder in due course, [the] a bank has given value to the extent [that] it has a security interest in an item, [provided that] if the bank otherwise complies with the requirements of Section 3-302 on what constitutes a holder in due course.

§ [4-210] 4-212. Presentment by Notice of Item Not Payable by, Through, or at Bank; Liability of [Secondary Parties] Drawer or Indorser.

[(1)] (a) Unless otherwise instructed, a collecting bank may present an item not payable by, through, or at a bank by sending to the party to accept or pay a written notice that the bank holds the item for acceptance or payment. The notice must be sent in time to be received on or before the day when presentment is due and the bank must meet any requirement of the party to accept or pay under Section [3-505] 3-501 by the close of the bank's next banking day after it knows of the requirement.

[(2)] (b) [Where] If presentment is made by notice and [neither honor nor] payment, acceptance, or request for compliance with a requirement under Section [3-505] 3-501 is not received by the close of business on the day after maturity or, in the case of demand items, by the close of business on the third banking day after notice was sent, the presenting bank may treat the item as dishonored and charge any [secondary party] drawer or indorser by sending [him] it notice of the facts.

§ [4-211] 4-213. [Media of Remittance; Provisional and Final Settlement in Remittance Cases] Medium and Time of Settlement by Bank.

[(1)] A collecting bank may take in settlement of an item

(a) a check of the remitting bank or of another bank on any bank except the remitting bank; or

(b) a cashier's check or similar primary obligation of a remitting bank which is a member of or clears through a member of the same clearing house or group as the collecting bank; or

(c) appropriate authority to charge an account of the remitting bank or of another bank with the collecting bank; or

(d) if the item is drawn upon or payable by a person other than a bank, a cashier's check, certified check or other bank check or obligation.

(2) If before its midnight deadline the collecting bank properly dishonors a remittance check or authorization to charge on itself or presents or forwards for collection a remittance instrument of or on another bank which is of a kind approved by subsection (1) or has not been authorized by it, the collecting bank is not liable to prior parties in the event of the dishonor of such check, instrument or authorization.

(3) A settlement for an item by means of a remittance instrument or authorization to charge is or becomes a final settlement as to both the person making and the person receiving the settlement

(a) if the remittance instrument or authorization to charge is of a kind approved by subsection (1) or has not been authorized by the person receiving the settlement and in either case the person receiving the settlement acts seasonably before its midnight deadline in presenting, forwarding for collection or paying the instrument or authorization,—at the time the remittance instrument or authorization is finally paid by the payor by which it is payable;

(b) if the person receiving the settlement has authorized remittance by a non-bank check or obligation or by a cashier's check or similar primary obligation of or a check upon the payor or other remitting bank which is not of a kind approved by subsection (1)(b),—at the time of the receipt of such remittance check or obligation; or

(c) if in a case not covered by sub-paragraphs (a) or (b) the person receiving the settlement fails to seasonably present, forward for collection, pay or return a remittance instrument or authorization to it to charge before its midnight deadline,—at such midnight deadline.

(a) With respect to settlement by a bank, the medium and time of settlement may be prescribed by Federal Reserve regulations or circulars, clearing-house rules, and the like, or agreement. In the absence of such prescription:

(1) the medium of settlement is cash or credit to an account in a Federal Reserve bank of or specified by the person to receive settlement; and

(2) the time of settlement, is:

(i) with respect to tender of settlement by cash, a cashier's check, or teller's check, when the cash or check is sent or delivered;

(ii) with respect to tender of settlement by credit in an account in a Federal Reserve Bank, when the credit is made;

(iii) with respect to tender of settlement by a credit or debit to an account in a bank, when the credit or debit is made or, in the case of tender of settlement by authority to charge an account, when the authority is sent or delivered; or

(iv) with respect to tender of settlement by a funds transfer, when payment is made pursuant to Section 4A-406(a) to the person receiving settlement.

(b) If the tender of settlement is not by a medium authorized by subsection (a) or the time of settlement is not fixed by subsection (a), no settlement occurs until the tender of settlement is accepted by the person receiving settlement.

(c) If settlement for an item is made by cashier's check or teller's check and the person receiving settlement, before its midnight deadline:

(1) presents or forwards the check for collection, settlement is final when the check is finally paid; or

(2) fails to present or forward the check for collection, settlement is final at the midnight deadline of the person receiving settlement.

(d) If settlement for an item is made by giving authority to charge the account of the bank giving settlement in the bank receiving settlement, settlement is final when the charge is made by the bank receiving settlement if there are funds available in the account for the amount of the item.

§ [4-212] 4-214. Right of Charge-Back or Refund; Liability of Collecting Bank; Return of Item.

[(1)] (a) If a collecting bank has made provisional settlement with its customer for an item and [itself] fails by reason of dishonor, suspension of payments by a bank, or otherwise to receive [a] settlement for the item which is or becomes final, the bank may revoke the settlement given by it, charge back the amount of any credit given for the item to its customer's account, or obtain refund from its customer, whether or not it is able to return the [items] item, if by its midnight deadline or within a longer reasonable time after it learns the facts it returns the item or sends notification of the facts. If the return or notice is delayed beyond the bank's midnight deadline or a longer reasonable time after it learns the facts, the bank may revoke the settlement, charge back the credit, or obtain refund from its customer, but it is liable for any loss resulting from the delay. These rights to revoke, charge back, and obtain refund terminate if and when a settlement for the item received by the bank is or becomes final [(subsection (3) of Section 4-211 and subsections (2) and (3) of Section 4-213).]

[[(2) Within the time and manner prescribed by this section and Section 4-301, an intermediary or payor bank, as the case may be, may return an unpaid item directly to the depositary bank and may send for collection a draft on the depositary bank and obtain reimbursement. In such case, if the depositary bank has received provisional settlement for the item, it must reimburse the bank drawing the draft and any provisional credits for the item between banks shall become and remain final.]]

(b) A collecting bank returns an item when it is sent or delivered to the bank's customer or transferor or pursuant to its instructions.

[(3)] (c) A depositary bank [which] that is also the payor may charge back the amount of an item to its customer's account or obtain refund in accordance with the section governing return of an item received by a payor bank for credit on its books (Section 4-301).

[(4)](d) The right to charge back is not affected by:

[(a)] (1) [prior] previous use of [the] a credit given for the item; or

[(b)] (2) failure by any bank to exercise ordinary care with respect to the item, but [any] a bank so failing remains liable.

[(5)] (e) A failure to charge back or claim refund does not affect other rights of the bank against the customer or any other party.

[(6)] (f) If credit is given in dollars as the equivalent of the value of an item payable in [a] foreign [currency] money, the dollar amount of any charge-back or refund [shall] must be calculated on the basis of the [buying sight] bank-offered spot rate for the foreign [currency] money prevailing on the day when the person entitled to the charge-back or refund learns that it will not receive payment in ordinary course.

§ [4-213] 4-215. Final Payment of Item by Payor Bank; When Provisional Debits and Credits Become Final; When Certain Credits Become Available for Withdrawal.

[(1)] (a) An item is finally paid by a payor bank when the bank has first done any of the following [,whichever happens first]:

[(a)] (1) paid the item in cash;[or]

[(b)] (2) settled for the item without [reserving] having a right to revoke the settlement and without having such right] under statute, [clearing house] clearinghouse rule, or agreement; or

[(c)] completed the process of posting the item to the indicated account of the drawer, maker or other person to be charged therewith; or]

[(d)] (3) made a provisional settlement for the item and failed to revoke the settlement in the time and manner permitted by statute, [clearing house] clearing-house rule, or agreement. [Upon a final payment under subparagraph (b), (c) or (d) the payor bank shall be accountable for the amount of the item.]

(b) If provisional settlement for an item does not become final, the item is not finally paid.

[(2)] (c) If provisional settlement for an item between the presenting and payor banks is made through a clearing house or by debits or credits in an account between them, then to the extent that provisional debits or credits for the item are entered in accounts between the presenting and payor banks or between the presenting and successive prior collecting banks seriatim, they become final upon final payment of the items by the payor bank.

[(3)] (d) If a collecting bank receives a settlement for an item which is or becomes final, [(subsection (3) of Section 4-211, subsection (2) of Section 4-213)] the bank is accountable to its customer for the amount of the item and any provisional credit given for the item in an account with its customer becomes final.

[(4)] (e) Subject to (i) applicable law stating a time for availability of funds and (ii) any right of the bank to apply the credit to an obligation of the customer, credit given by a bank for an item in [an account with its customer] a customer's account becomes available for withdrawal as of right:

[(a)] (1) [in any case where] if the bank has received a provisional settlement for the item, when [such] the settlement becomes final and the bank has had a reasonable time to [learn that the settlement is final] receive return of the item and the item has not been received within that time;

[(b)] (2) [in any case where] if the bank is both [a] the depositary bank and [a] the payor bank, and the item is finally paid, at the opening of the bank's second banking day following receipt of the item.

[(5)] (f) [A deposit of money in a bank is final when made but, subject] Subject to applicable law stating a time for availability of funds and any right of [the] a bank to apply [the] a deposit to an obligation of the [customer] depositor, [the] a deposit of money becomes available for withdrawal as of right at the opening of the bank's next banking day [following] after receipt of the deposit.

§ [4-214] 4-216. Insolvency and Preference.

[(1)] (a) [Any] If an item is in or [coming] comes into the possession of a payor or collecting bank [which] that suspends payment and [which] the item [is] has not been finally paid, the item must [shall] be returned by the receiver, trustee, or agent in charge of the closed bank to the presenting bank or the closed bank's customer.

[(2)] (b) If a payor bank finally pays an item and suspends payments without making a settlement for the item with its customer or the presenting bank which settlement is or becomes final, the owner of the item has a preferred claim against the payor bank.

[(3)] (c) If a payor bank gives or a collecting bank gives or receives a provisional settlement for an item and thereafter suspends payments, the suspension does not prevent or interfere with the [settlement] settlement's becoming final if [such] the finality occurs automatically upon the lapse of certain time or the happening of certain events [(subsection (3) of Section 4-211, subsections (1)(d), (2) and (3) of Section 4-213).]

[(4)] (d) If a collecting bank receives from subsequent parties settlement for an item, which settlement is or becomes final and the bank suspends payments without making a settlement for the item with its customer which settlement is or becomes final, the owner of the item has a preferred claim against [such] the collecting bank.

Part 3: Collection of Items—Payor Banks

§4-301. Deferred Posting; Recovery of Payment by Return of Items; Time of Dishonor; Return of Items by Payor Bank.

[(1)] (a) [Where an authorized settlement] If a payor bank settles for a demand item [(] other than a documentary draft[)] received by a payor bank] presented otherwise than for immediate payment over the counter[has been made] before midnight of the banking day of receipt, the payor bank may revoke the settlement and recover [any payment] the settlement if, before it has made final payment [(subsection (1) of Section 4-213)] and before its midnight deadline, it

[(a)] (1) returns the item; or
[(b)] (2) sends written notice of dishonor or nonpayment if the item is [held for protest or is otherwise] unavailable for return.

[(2)] (b) If a demand item is received by a payor bank for credit on its books, it may return [such] the item or send notice of dishonor and may revoke any credit given or recover the amount thereof withdrawn by its customer, if it acts within the time limit and in the manner specified in [the preceding] subsection (a).

[(3)] (c) Unless previous notice of dishonor has been sent, an item is dishonored at the time when for purposes of dishonor it is returned or notice sent in accordance with this section.

[(4)] (d) An item is returned:

[(a)] (1) as to an item [received] presented through a clearing house, when it is delivered to the presenting or last collecting bank or to the clearing house or is sent or delivered in accordance with clearing-house rules;

[(b)] (2) in all other cases, when it is sent or delivered to the bank's customer or transferor or pursuant to [his] instructions.

§4-302. Payor Bank's Responsibility for Late Return of Item.

[In the absence of a valid defense such as breach of a presentment warranty (subsection (1) of Section 4-207), settlement effected or the like, if]

(a) If an item is presented to on and received by a payor bank, the bank is accountable for the amount of:

[(a)] (1) a demand item, other than a documentary draft, whether properly payable or not, if the bank, in any case [where] in which it is not also the depositary bank, retains the item beyond midnight of the banking day of receipt without settling for it or, [regardless of] whether or not it is also the depositary bank, does not pay or return the item or send notice of dishonor until after its midnight deadline; or

[(b)] (2) any other properly payable item unless, within the time allowed for acceptance or payment of that item, the bank either accepts or pays the item or returns it and accompanying documents.

(b) The liability of a payor bank to pay an item pursuant to subsection (a) is subject to defenses based on breach of a presentment warranty (Section 4-208) or proof that the person seeking enforcement of the liability presented or transferred the item for the purpose of defrauding the payor bank.

§4-303. When Items Subject to Notice, [Stop-Order] Stop-Payment Order, Legal Process, or Setoff; Order in Which Items May Be Charged or Certified.

[(1)] (a) Any knowledge, notice, or [stop order] stop-payment order received by, legal process served upon, or setoff exercised by a payor bank[, whether or not effective under other rules of law] comes too late to terminate, suspend, or modify the bank's right or duty to pay an item or to charge its customer's account for the item [, comes too late to so terminate, suspend or modify such right or duty] if the knowledge, notice, [stop order] stop-payment order, or legal process is received or served and a reasonable time for the bank to act thereon expires or the setoff is exercised after the [bank has done any] earliest of the following:

[(a)] (1) [accepted or certified] the bank accepts or certifies the item;
[(b)] (2) [paid] the bank pays the item in cash;
[(c)] (3) [settled] the bank settles for the item without [reserving] having a right to revoke the settlement [and without having such right] under statute,[clearing house] clearing-house rule, or agreement;
[(d)] completed the process of posting the item to the indicated account of the drawer, maker or other person to be charged therewith or otherwise has evidenced by examination of such indicated account and by action its decision to pay the item; or
[(e)] (4) [become] the bank becomes accountable for the amount of the item under[subsection (1)(d) of Section 4-213 and] Section 4-302 dealing with the payor bank's responsibility for late return of items [.]; or
(5) with respect to checks, a cutoff hour no earlier than one hour after the opening of the next banking day after the banking day on which the bank received the check and no later than the close of the next

banking day or, if no cutoff hour is fixed, the close of the next banking day after the banking day on which the bank received the check.

[(2)] (b) Subject to [the provisions of] subsection [(1)] (a), items may be accepted, paid, certified, or charged to the indicated account of its customer in any order [convenient to the bank].

Part 4: Relationship Between Payor Bank and Its Customer

§4-401. When Bank May Charge Customer's Account.

[(1)] (a) [As against its customer, a] A bank may charge against [his] the account [any] of a customer an item [which] that is [otherwise] properly payable from that account even though the charge creates an overdraft. An item is properly payable if it is authorized by the customer and is in accordance with any agreement between the customer and bank.

(b) A customer is not liable for the amount of an overdraft if the customer neither signed the item nor benefited from the proceeds of the item.

(c) A bank may charge against the account of a customer a check that is otherwise properly payable from the account, even though payment was made before the date of the check, unless the customer has given notice to the bank of the postdating describing the check with reasonable certainty. The notice is effective for the period stated in Section 4-403(b) for stop-payment orders, and must be received at such time and in such manner as to afford the bank a reasonable opportunity to act on it before the bank takes any action with respect to the check described in Section 4-303. If a bank charges against the account of a customer a check before the date stated in the notice of postdating, the bank is liable for damages for the loss resulting from its act. The loss may include damages for dishonor of subsequent items under Section 4-402.

[(2)] (d) A bank [which] that in good faith makes payment to a holder may charge the indicated account of its customer according to:

[(a)] (1) the original [tenor] terms of [his] the altered item; or

[(b)] (2) the [tenor] terms of [his] the completed item, even though the bank knows the item has been completed unless the bank has notice that the completion was improper.

§4-402. Bank's Liability to Customer for Wrongful Dishonor; Time of Determining Insufficiency of Account.

(a) Except as otherwise provided in this Article, a payor bank wrongfully dishonors an item if it dishonors an item that is properly payable, but a bank may dishonor an item that would create an overdraft unless it has agreed to pay the overdraft.

(b) A payor bank is liable to its customer for damages proximately caused by the wrongful dishonor of an item. [When the dishonor occurs through mistake liability] Liability is limited to actual damages proved. [If so proximately caused and proved damages] and may include damages for an arrest or prosecution of the customer or other consequential damages. Whether any consequential damages are proximately caused by the wrongful dishonor is a question of fact to be determined in each case.

(c) A payor bank's determination of the customer's account balance on which a decision to dishonor for insufficiency of available funds is based may be made at any time between the time the item is received by the payor bank and the time that the payor bank returns the item or gives notice in lieu of return, and no more than one determination need be made. If, at the election of the payor bank, a subsequent balance determination is made for the purpose of reevaluating the bank's decision to dishonor the item, the account balance at that time is determinative of whether a dishonor for insufficiency of available funds is wrongful.

§4-403. Customer's Right to Stop Payment; Burden of Proof of Loss.

[(1)] (a) A customer [may by order to his bank stop payment of any item payable for his account but the order must be] or any person authorized to draw on the account if there is more than one person may stop payment of any item drawn on the customer's account or close the account by an order to the bank describing the item or account with reasonable certainty received at [such] a time and in [such] a manner [as to afford] that affords the bank a reasonable opportunity to act on it [prior to] before any action by the bank with respect to the item described in Section 4-303. If the signature of more than one person is required to draw on an account, any of these persons may stop payment or close the account.

[(2) An oral order is binding upon the bank only for fourteen calendar days unless confirmed in writing within that period. A written order is effective for only six months unless renewed in writing.]

(b) A stop-payment order is effective for six months, but it lapses after 14 calendar days if the original order was oral and was not confirmed in writing within that period. A stop-payment order may be renewed for additional six-month periods by a writing given to the bank within a period during which the stop-payment order is effective.

[(3)] (c) The burden of establishing the fact and amount of loss resulting from the payment of an item contrary to a [binding stop payment] stop-payment order or order to close an account is on the customer. The loss from payment of an item contrary to a stop-payment order may include damages for dishonor of subsequent items under Section 4-402.

§4-404. Bank Not [Obligated] Obliged to Pay Check More Than Six Months Old.

A bank is under no obligation to a customer having a checking account to pay a check, other than a certified check, which is presented more than six months after its date, but it may charge its customer's account for a payment made thereafter in good faith.

§4-405. Death or Incompetence of Customer.

[(1)] (a) A payor or collecting bank's authority to accept, pay, or collect an item or to account for proceeds of its collection, if otherwise effective, is not rendered ineffective by incompetence of a customer of either bank existing at the time the item is issued or its collection is undertaken if the bank does not know of an adjudication of incompetence. Neither death nor incompetence of a customer revokes [such] the authority to accept, pay, collect, or account until the bank knows of the fact of death or of an adjudication of incompetence and has reasonable opportunity to act on it.

[(2)] (b) Even with knowledge, a bank may for 10 days after the date of death pay or certify checks drawn on or [prior to] before that date unless ordered to stop payment by a person claiming an interest in the account.

§4-406. Customer's Duty to Discover and Report Unauthorized Signature or Alteration.

[(1) When a bank sends to its customer a statement of account accompanied by items paid in good faith in support of the debit entries or holds the statement and items pursuant to a request for instructions of its customer or otherwise in a reasonable manner makes the statement and items available to the customer, the customer must exercise reasonable care and promptness to examine the statement and items to discover his unauthorized signature or any alteration on an item and must notify the bank promptly after discovery thereof.]

(a) A bank that sends or makes available to a customer a statement of account showing payment of items for the account shall either return or make available to the customer the items paid or provide information in the statement of account sufficient to allow the customer reasonably to identify the items paid. The statement of account provides sufficient information if the item is described by item number, amount, and date of payment.

(b) If the items are not returned to the customer, the person retaining the items shall either retain the items or, if the items are destroyed, maintain the capacity to furnish legible copies of the items until the expiration of seven years after receipt of the items. A customer may request an item from the bank that paid the item, and that bank must provide in a reasonable time either the item or, if the item has been destroyed or is not otherwise obtainable, a legible copy of the item.

(c) If a bank sends or makes available a statement of account or items pursuant to subsection (a), the customer must exercise reasonable promptness in examining the statement or the items to determine whether any payment was not authorized because of an alteration of an item or because a purported signature by or on behalf of the customer was not authorized. If, based on the statement or items provided, the customer should reasonably have discovered the unauthorized payment, the customer must promptly notify the bank of the relevant facts.

[(2)] **(d)** If the bank [establishes] proves that the customer failed, with respect to an item, to comply with the duties imposed on the customer by subsection [(1)] (c), the customer is precluded from asserting against the bank:

[(a)] **(1)** [his] the customer's unauthorized signature or any alteration on the item, if the bank also [establishes] proves that it suffered a loss by reason of [such] the failure; and

[(b)] **(2)** [an] the customer's unauthorized signature or alteration by the same wrongdoer on any other item paid in good faith by the bank [after the first item and statement was available to the customer for a reasonable period not exceeding fourteen calendar days and before the bank receives notification from the customer of any such unauthorized signature or alteration] if the payment was made before the bank received notice from the customer of the unauthorized signature or alteration and after the customer had been afforded a reasonable period of time, not exceeding 30 days, in which to examine the item or statement of account and notify the bank.

[(3) The preclusion under subsection (2) does not apply if the customer establishes lack of ordinary care on the part of the bank in paying the item(s).]

(e) If subsection (d) applies and the customer proves that the bank failed to exercise ordinary care in paying the item and that the failure substantially contributed to loss, the loss is allocated between the customer precluded and the bank asserting the preclusion according to the extent to which the failure of the customer to comply with subsection (c) and the failure of the bank to exercise ordinary care contributed to the loss. If the customer proves that the bank did not pay the item in good faith, the preclusion under subsection (d) does not apply.

[(4)] **(f)** Without regard to care or lack of care of either the customer or the bank, a customer who does not within one year from the time after [from the time] after the statement [and] or items are made available to the customer (subsection [(1)] (a)) dis-cover and report [his] the customer's unauthorized signature on or any alteration[on the face or back of the item or does not within 3 years from that time discover and report any unauthorized indorsement] on the item is precluded from asserting against the bank [such] the unauthorized signature [or indorsement] or [such] alteration. If there is a preclusion under this subsection, the payor bank may not recover for breach of warranty under Section 4-208 with respect to the unauthorized signature or alteration to which the preclusion applies.

[(5) If under this section a payor bank has a valid defense against a claim of a customer upon or resulting from payment of an item and waives or fails upon request to assert the defense the bank may not assert against any collecting bank or other prior party presenting or transferring the item a claim based upon the unauthorized signature or alteration giving rise to the customer's claim.]

§4-407. Payor Bank's Right to Subrogation on Improper Payment.

If a payor bank has paid an item over the [stop payment] order of the drawer or maker to stop payment, or after an account has been closed, or otherwise under circumstances giving a basis for objection by the drawer or maker, to prevent unjust enrichment and only to the extent necessary to prevent loss to the bank by reason of its payment of the item, the payor bank [shall be] is subrogated to the rights

[(a)] **(1)** of any holder in due course on the item against the drawer or maker; [and]

[(b)] **(2)** of the payee or any other holder of the item against the drawer or maker either on the item or under the transaction out of which the item arose; and

[(c)] **(3)** of the drawer or maker against the payee or any other holder of the item with respect to the transaction out of which the item arose.

Part 5: Collection of Documentary Drafts

§4-501. Handling of Documentary Drafts; Duty to Send for Presentment and to Notify Customer of Dishonor. A bank [which] that takes a documentary draft for collection [must] shall present or send the draft and accompanying documents for presentment and, upon learning that the draft has not been paid or accepted in due course, [must] shall seasonably notify its customer of [such] the fact even though it may have discounted or bought the draft or extended credit available for withdrawal as of right.

§4-502. Presentment of "On Arrival" Drafts. [When] If a draft or the relevant instructions require presentment "on arrival", "when goods arrive" or the like, the collecting bank need not present until in its judgment a reasonable time for arrival of the goods has expired. Refusal to pay or accept because the goods have not arrived is not dishonor; the bank must notify its transferor of [such] the refusal but need not present the draft again until it is instructed to do so or learns of the arrival of the goods.

§4-503. Responsibility of Presenting Bank for Documents and Goods; Report of Reasons for Dishonor; Referee in Case of Need. Unless otherwise instructed and except as provided in Article 5, a bank presenting a documentary draft:

[(a)] **(1)** must deliver the documents to the drawee on acceptance of the draft if it is payable more than three days after presentment; otherwise, only on payment; and

[(b)] **(2)** upon dishonor, either in the case of presentment for acceptance or presentment for payment, may seek and follow instructions from any referee in case of need designated in the draft or, if the presenting bank does not choose to utilize [his] the referee's services, it must use diligence and good faith to ascertain the reason for dishonor, must notify its transferor of the dishonor and of the results of its effort to ascertain the reasons therefor, and must request instructions.

[But] However the presenting bank is under no obligation with respect to goods represented by the documents except to follow any reasonable instructions seasonably received; it has a right to reimbursement for any expense incurred in following instructions and to prepayment of or indemnity for [such] those expenses.

§4-504. Privilege of Presenting Bank to Deal with Goods; Security Interest for Expenses.

[(1)] (a) A presenting bank [which] that, following the dishonor of a documentary draft, has seasonably requested instructions but does not receive them within a reasonable time may store, sell, or otherwise deal with the goods in any reasonable manner.

[(2)] (b) For its reasonable expenses incurred by action under subsection [(1)] (a), the presenting bank has a lien upon the goods or their proceeds, which may be foreclosed in the same manner as an unpaid seller's lien.

ARTICLE 5: LETTERS OF CREDIT

§5-101. Short Title. This Article shall be known and may be cited as Uniform Commercial Code—Letters of Credit.

§5-102. Scope.

(1) This Article applies

(a) to a credit issued by a bank if the credit requires a documentary draft or a documentary demand for payment; and

(b) to a credit issued by a person other than a bank if the credit requires that the draft or demand for payment be accompanied by a document of title; and

(c) to a credit issued by a bank or other person if the credit is not within subparagraphs (a) or (b) but conspicuously states that it is a letter of credit or is conspicuously so entitled.

(2) Unless the engagement meets the requirements of subsection (1), this Article does not apply to engagements to make advances or to honor drafts or demands for payment, to authorities to pay or purchase, to guarantees or to general agreements.

(3) This Article deals with some but not all of the rules and concepts of letters of credit as such rules or concepts have developed prior to this act or may hereafter develop. The fact that this Article states a rule does not by itself require, imply or negate application of the same or a converse rule to a situation not provided for or to a person not specified by this Article.

§5-103. Definitions.

(1) In this Article unless the context otherwise requires

(a) "Credit" or "letter of credit" means an engagement by a bank or other person made at the request of a customer and of a kind within the scope of this Article (Section 5-102) that the issuer will honor drafts or other demands for payment upon compliance with the conditions specified in the credit. A credit may be either revocable or irrevocable. The engagement may be either an agreement to honor or a statement that the bank or other person is authorized to honor.

(b) A "documentary draft" or a "documentary demand for payment" is one, honor of which is conditioned upon the presentation of a document or documents. "Document" means any paper including document of title, security, invoice, certificate, notice of default and the like.

(c) An "issuer" is a bank or other person issuing a credit.

(d) A "beneficiary" of a credit is a person who is entitled under its terms to draw or demand payment.

(e) An "advising bank" is a bank which gives notification of the issuance of a credit by another bank.

(f) A "confirming bank" is a bank which engages either that it will itself honor a credit already issued by another bank or that such a credit will be honored by the issuer or a third bank.

(g) A "customer" is a buyer or other person who causes an issuer to issue a credit. The term also includes a bank which procures issuance or confirmation on behalf of that bank's customer.

(2) Other definitions applying to this Article and the sections in which they appear are:
"Notation of credit"   Section 5-108
"Presenter"   Section 5-112(3)

(3) Definitions in other Articles applying to this Article and the sections in which they appear are:
"Accept" or "Acceptance"   Section 3-410
"Contract for sale"   Section 2-106
"Draft"   Section 3-104
"Holder in due course"   Section 3-302
"Midnight deadline"   Section 4-104
"Security"   Section 8-102

(4) In addition, Article 1 contains general definitions and principles of construction and interpretation applicable throughout this Article.

§5-104. Formal Requirements; Signing.

(1) Except as otherwise required in subsection (1)(c) Section 5-102 on scope, no particular form of phrasing is required for a credit. A credit must be in writing and signed by the issuer and a confirmation must be in writing and signed by the confirming bank. A modification of the terms of a credit or confirmation must be signed by the issuer or confirming bank.

(2) A telegram may be a sufficient signed writing if it identifies its sender by an authorized authentication. The authentication may be in code and the authorized naming of the issuer in an advice of credit is a sufficient signing.

§5-105. Consideration. No consideration is necessary to establish a credit or to enlarge or otherwise modify its terms.

§5-106. Time and Effect of Establishment of Credit.

(1) Unless otherwise agreed a credit is established

(a) as regards the customer as soon as a letter of credit is sent to him or the letter of credit or an authorized written advice of its issuance is sent to the beneficiary; and

(b) as regards the beneficiary when he receives a letter of credit or an authorized written advice of its issuance.

(2) Unless otherwise agreed once an irrevocable credit is established as regards the customer it can be modified or revoked only with the consent of the customer and once it is established as regards the beneficiary it can be modified or revoked only with his consent.

(3) Unless otherwise agreed after a revocable credit is established it may be modified or revoked by the issuer without notice to or consent from the customer or beneficiary.

(4) Notwithstanding any modification or revocation of a revocable credit any person authorized to honor or negotiate under the terms of the original credit is entitled to reimburse-

ment for or honor of any draft or demand for payment duly honored or negotiated before receipt of notice of the modification or revocation and the issuer in turn is entitled to reimbursement from its customer.

§5-107. Advice of Credit; Confirmation; Error in Statement of Terms.

(1) Unless otherwise specified an advising bank by advising a credit issued by another bank does not assume any obligation to honor drafts drawn or demands for payment made under the credit but it does assume obligation for the accuracy of its own statement.

(2) A confirming bank by confirming a credit becomes directly obligated on the credit to the extent of its confirmation as though it were its issuer and acquires the rights of an issuer.

(3) Even though an advising bank incorrectly advises the terms of a credit it has been authorized to advise, the credit is established as against the issuer to the extent of its original terms.

(4) Unless otherwise specified the customer bears as against the issuer all risks of transmission and reasonable translation or interpretation of any message relating to a credit.

§5-108. "Notation Credit"; Exhaustion of Credit.

(1) A credit which specifies that any person purchasing or paying drafts drawn or demands for payment made under it must note the amount of the draft or demand on the letter or advice of credit is a "notation credit".

(2) Under a notation credit

(a) a person paying the beneficiary or purchasing a draft or demand for payment from him acquires a right to honor only if the appropriate notation is made and by transferring or forwarding for honor the documents under the credit such a person warrants to the issuer that the notation has been made; and

(b) unless the credit or a signed statement that an appropriate notation has been made accompanies the draft or demand for payment the issuer may delay honor until evidence of notation has been procured which is satisfactory to it but its obligation and that of its customer continue for a reasonable time not exceeding thirty days to obtain such evidence.

(3) If the credit is not a notation credit

(a) the issuer may honor complying drafts or demands for payment presented to it in the order in which they are presented and is discharged pro tanto by honor of any such draft or demand;

(b) as between competing good faith purchasers of complying drafts or demands the person first purchasing has priority over a subsequent purchaser even though the later purchased draft or demand has been first honored.

§5-109. Issuer's Obligation to Its Customer.

(1) An issuer's obligation to its customer includes good faith and observance of any general banking usage but unless otherwise agreed does not include liability or responsibility

(a) for performance of the underlying contract for sale or other transaction between the customer and the beneficiary; or

(b) for any act or omission of any person other than itself or its own branch or for loss or destruction of a draft, demand or document in transit or in the possession of others; or

(c) based on knowledge or lack of knowledge of any usage of any particular trade.

(2) An issuer must examine documents with care so as to ascertain that on their face they appear to comply with the terms of the credit but unless otherwise agreed assumes no liability or responsibility for the genuineness, falsification or effect of any document which appears on such examination to be regular on its face.

(3) A non-bank issuer is not bound by any banking usage of which it has no knowledge.

§5-110. Availability of Credit in Portions; Presenter's Reservation of Lien or Claim.

(1) Unless otherwise specified a credit may be used in portions in the discretion of the beneficiary.

(2) Unless otherwise specified a person by presenting a documentary draft or demand for payment under a credit relinquishes upon its honor all claims to the documents and a person by transferring such draft or demand or causing such presentment authorizes such relinquishment. An explicit reservation of claim makes the draft or demand non-complying.

§5-111. Warranties on Transfer and Presentment.

(1) Unless otherwise agreed the beneficiary by transferring or presenting a documentary draft or demand for payment warrants to all interested parties that the necessary conditions of the credit have been complied with. This is in addition to any warranties arising under Articles 3, 4, 7 and 8.

(2) Unless otherwise agreed a negotiating, advising, confirming, collecting or issuing bank presenting or transferring a draft or demand for payment under a credit warrants only the matters warranted by a collecting bank under Article 4 and any such bank transferring a document warrants only the matters warranted by an intermediary under Articles 7 and 8.

§5-112. Time Allowed for Honor or Rejection; Withholding Honor or Rejection by Consent; "Presenter".

(1) A bank to which a documentary draft or demand for payment is presented under a credit may without dishonor of the draft, demand or credit

(a) defer honor until the close of the third banking day following receipt of the documents; and

(b) further defer honor if the presenter has expressly or impliedly consented thereto. Failure to honor within the time here specified constitutes dishonor of the draft or demand and of the credit[except as otherwise provided in subsection (4) of Section 5-114 on conditional payment].

Note: *The bracketed language in the last sentence of subsection (1) should be included only if the optional provisions of Section 5-114(4) and (5) are included.*

(2) Upon dishonor the bank may unless otherwise instructed fulfill its duty to return the draft or demand and the documents by holding them at the disposal of the presenter and sending him an advice to that effect.

(3) "Presenter" means any person presenting a draft or demand for payment for honor under a credit even though that person is a confirming bank or other correspondent which is acting under an issuer's authorization.

§5-113. Indemnities.

(1) A bank seeking to obtain (whether for itself or another) honor, negotiation or reimbursement under a credit may give an indemnity to induce such honor, negotiation or reimbursement.

(2) An indemnity agreement inducing honor, negotiation or reimbursement

(a) unless otherwise explicitly agreed applies to defects in the documents but not in the goods; and

(b) unless a longer time is explicitly agreed expires at the end of ten business days following receipt of the documents by the ultimate customer unless notice of objection is sent before such expiration date. The ultimate customer may send notice of objection to the person from whom he received the documents and any bank receiving such notice is under a duty to send notice to its transferor before its midnight deadline.

§5-114. Issuer's Duty and Privilege to Honor; Right to Reimbursement

(1) An issuer must honor a draft or demand for payment which complies with the terms of the relevant credit regardless of whether the goods or documents conform to the underlying contract for sale or other contract between the customer and the beneficiary. The issuer is not excused from honor of such a draft or demand by reason of an additional general term that all documents must be satisfactory to the issuer, but an issuer may require that specified documents must be satisfactory to it.

(2) Unless otherwise agreed when documents appear on their face to comply with the terms of a credit but a required document does not in fact conform to the warranties made on negotiation or transfer of a document of title (Section 7-507) or of a certificated security (Section 8-306) or is forged or fraudulent or there is fraud in the transaction

(a) the issuer must honor the draft or demand for payment if honor is demanded by a negotiating bank or other holder of the draft or demand which has taken the draft or demand under the credit and under circumstances which would make it a holder in due course (Section 3-302) and in an appropriate case would make it a person to whom a document of title has been duly negotiated (Section 7-502) or a bona fide purchaser of a certificated security (Section 8-302); and

(b) in all other cases as against its customer, an issuer acting in good faith may honor the draft or demand for payment despite notification from the customer of fraud, forgery or other defect not apparent on the face of the documents but a court of appropriate jurisdiction may enjoin such honor.

(3) Unless otherwise agreed an issuer which has duly honored a draft or demand for payment is entitled to immediate reimbursement of any payment made under the credit and to be put in effectively available funds not later than the day before maturity of any acceptance made under the credit.

[(4) When a credit provides for payment by the issuer on receipt of notice that the required documents are in the possession of a correspondent or other agent of the issuer

(a) any payment made on receipt of such notice is conditional; and

(b) the issuer may reject documents which do not comply with the credit if it does so within three banking days following its receipt of the documents; and

(c) in the event of such rejection, the issuer is entitled by charge back or otherwise to return to the payment made.]

[(5) In the case covered by subsection (4) failure to reject documents within the time specified in sub-paragraph (b) constitutes acceptance of the documents and makes the payment final in favor of the beneficiary.]

Note: *Subsections (4) and (5) are bracketed as optional. If they are included the bracketed language in the last sentence of Section 5-112(1) should also be included.*

§5-115. Remedy for Improper Dishonor or Anticipatory Repudiation.

(1) When an issuer wrongfully dishonors a draft or demand for payment presented under a credit the person entitled to honor has with respect to any documents the rights of a person in the position of a seller (Section 2-707) and may recover from the issuer the face amount of the draft or demand together with incidental damages under Section 2-710 on seller's incidental damages and interest but less any amount realized by resale or other use or disposition of the subject matter of the transaction. In the event no resale or other utilization is made the documents, goods or other subject matter involved in the transaction must be turned over to the issuer on payment of judgment.

(2) When an issuer wrongfully cancels or otherwise repudiates a credit before presentment of a draft or demand for payment drawn under it the beneficiary has the rights of a seller after anticipatory repudiation by the buyer under Section 2-610 if he learns of the repudiation in time reasonably to avoid procurement of the required documents. Otherwise the beneficiary has an immediate right of action for wrongful dishonor.

§5-116. Transfer and Assignment.

(1) The right to draw under a credit can be transferred or assigned only when the credit is expressly designated as transferable or assignable.

(2) Even though the credit specifically states that it is nontransferable or nonassignable the beneficiary may before performance of the conditions of the credit assign his right to proceeds. Such an assignment is an assignment of an account under Article 9 on Secured Transactions and is governed by that Article except that

(a) the assignment is ineffective until the letter of credit or advice of credit is delivered to the assignee which delivery constitutes perfection of the security interest under Article 9; and

(b) the issuer may honor drafts or demands for payment drawn under the credit until it receives a notification of the assignment signed by the beneficiary which reasonably identifies the credit involved in the assignment and contains a request to pay the assignee; and

(c) after what reasonably appears to be such a notification has been received the issuer may without dishonor refuse to accept or pay even to a person otherwise entitled to honor until the letter of credit or advice of credit is exhibited to the issuer.

(3) Except where the beneficiary has effectively assigned his right to draw or his right to proceeds, nothing in this section limits his right to transfer or negotiate drafts or demands drawn under the credit.

§5-117. Insolvency of Bank Holding Funds for Documentary Credit.

(1) Where an issuer or an advising or confirming bank or a bank which has for a customer procured issuance of a credit by another bank becomes insolvent before final payment under the credit and the credit is one to which this Article is made applicable by paragraphs (a) or (b) of Section 5-102(1) on scope, the receipt or allocation of funds or collateral to secure or meet obligations under the credit shall have the following results:

(a) to the extent of any funds or collateral turned over after or before the insolvency as indem-nity against or specifically for the purpose of payment of drafts or demands for payments drawn under the designated credit, the drafts or demands are entitled to payment in preference over depositors or other general creditors of the issuer or bank; and

(b) on expiration of the credit or surrender of the beneficiary's rights under it unused any person who has given such funds or collateral is similarly entitled to return thereof; and

(c) a charge to a general or current account with a bank if specifically consented to for the purpose of indemnity against or payment of drafts or demands for payment drawn under the designated credit falls under the same rules as if the funds had been drawn out in cash and then turned over with specific instructions.

(2) After honor or reimbursement under this section the customer or other person for whose account the insolvent bank has acted is entitled to receive the documents involved.

ARTICLE 6: BULK TRANSFERS

§6-101. Short Title. This Article shall be known and may be cited as Uniform Commercial Code—Bulk Transfers.

§6-102. "Bulk Transfers"; Transfers of Equipment; Enterprises Subject to This Article; Bulk Transfers Subject to This Article.

(1) A "bulk transfer" is any transfer in bulk and not in the ordinary course of the transferor's business of a major part of the materials, supplies, merchandise or other inventory (Section 9-109) of an enterprise subject to this Article.

(2) A transfer of a substantial part of the equipment (Section 9-109) of such an enterprise is a bulk transfer if it is made in connection with a bulk transfer of inventory, but not otherwise.

(3) The enterprises subject to this Article are all those whose principal business is the sale of merchandise from stock, including those who manufacture what they sell.

(4) Except as limited by the following section all bulk transfers of goods located within this state are subject to this Article.

§6-103. Transfers Excepted From This Article. The following transfers are not subject to this Article:

(1) Those made to give security for the performance of an obligation;

(2) General assignments for the benefit of all the creditors of the transferor, and subsequent transfers by the assignee thereunder;

(3) Transfers in settlement or realization of a lien or other security interests;

(4) Sales by executors, administrators, receivers, trustees in bankruptcy, or any public officer under judicial process;

(5) Sales made in the course of judicial or administrative proceedings for the dissolution or reorganization of a corporation and of which notice is sent to the creditors of the corporation pursuant to order of the court or administrative agency;

(6) Transfers to a person maintaining a known place of business in this State who becomes bound to pay the debts of the transferor in full and gives public notice of that fact, and who is solvent after becoming so bound;

(7) A transfer to a new business enterprise organized to take over and continue the business, if public notice of the transaction is given and the new enterprise assumes the debts of the transferor and he receives nothing from the transaction except an interest in the new enterprise junior to the claims of creditors;

(8) Transfers of property which is exempt from execution. Public notice under subsection (6) or subsection (7) may be given by publishing once a week for two consecutive weeks in a newspaper of general circulation where the transferor had its principal place of business in this State an advertisement including the names and addresses of the transferor and transferee and the effective date of the transfer.

§6-104. Schedule of Property, List of Creditors.

(1) Except as provided with respect to auction sales (Section 6-108), a bulk transfer subject to this Article is ineffective against any creditor of the transferor unless:

(a) The transferee requires the transferor to furnish a list of his existing creditors prepared as stated in this section; and

(b) The parties prepare a schedule of the property transferred sufficient to identify it; and

(c) The transferee preserves the list and schedule for six months next following the transfer and permits inspection of either or both and copying therefrom at all reasonable hours by any creditor of the transferor, or files the list and schedule in (a public office to be here identified).

(2) The list of creditors must be signed and sworn to or affirmed by the transferor or his agent. It must contain the names and business addresses of all creditors of the transferor, with the amounts when known, and also the names of all persons who are known to the transferor to assert claims against him even though such claims are disputed. If the transferor is the obligor of an outstanding issue of bonds, debentures or the like as to which there is an indenture trustee, the list of creditors need include only the name and address of the indenture trustee and the aggregate outstanding principal amount of the issue.

(3) Responsibility for the completeness and accuracy of the list of creditors rests on the transferor, and the transfer is not rendered ineffective by errors or omissions therein unless the transferee is shown to have had knowledge.

§6-105. Notice to Creditors. In addition to the requirements of the preceding section, any bulk transfer subject to this Article except one made by auction sale (Section 6-108) is ineffective against any creditor of the transferor unless at least ten days before he takes possession of the goods or pays for them, whichever happens first, the transferee gives notice of the transfer in the manner and to the persons hereafter provided (Section 6-107).

§6-106. Application of the Proceeds. In addition to the requirements of the two preceding sections:

(1) Upon every bulk transfer subject to this Article for which new consideration becomes payable except those made by sale at auction it is the duty of the transferee to assure that such consideration is applied so far as necessary to pay those debts of the transferor which are either shown on the list furnished by the transferor (Section 6-104) or filed in writing in the place stated in the notice (Section 6-107) within thirty days after the mailing of such notice. This duty of the transferee runs to all the holders of such debts, and may be enforced by any of them for the benefit of all.

(2) If any of said debts are in dispute the necessary sum may be withheld from distribution until the dispute is settled or adjudicated.

[(3) If the consideration payable is not enough to pay all of the said debts in full distribution shall be made pro rata.]

Note: *This section is bracketed to indicate division of opinion as to whether or not it is a wise provision, and to suggest that this is a point on which State enactments may differ without serious damage to the principle of uniformity.*

In any State where this section is omitted, the following parts of sections, also bracketed in the text, should also be omitted, namely:
  Section 6-107(2) (e).
    6-108(3) (c).
    6-109(2).

In any State where this section is enacted, these other provisions should be also.

Optional Subsection (4)

[(4) The transferee may within ten days after he takes possession of the goods pay the consideration into the (specify court) in the county where the transferor had its principal place of business in this state and thereafter may discharge his duty under this section by giving notice by registered or certified mail to all the persons to whom the duty runs that the consideration has been paid into that court and that they should file their claims there. On motion of any interested party, the court may order the distribution of the consideration to the persons entitled to it.]

Note: *Optional subsection (4) is recommended for those states which do not have a general statute providing for payment of money into court.*

§6-107. The Notice.

(1) The notice to creditors (Section 6-105) shall state:

(a) that a bulk transfer is about to be made; and
(b) the names and business addresses of the transferor and transferee, and all other business names and addresses used by the transferor within three years last past so far as known to the transferee; and
(c) whether or not all the debts of the transferor are to be paid in full as they fall due as a result of the transaction, and if so, the address to which creditors should send their bills.

(2) If the debts of the transferor are not to be paid in full as they fall due or if the transferee is in doubt on that point then the notice shall state further:

(a) the location and general description of the property to be transferred and the estimated total of the transferor's debts;
(b) the address where the schedule of property and list of creditors (Section 6-104) may be inspected;
(c) whether the transfer is to pay existing debts and if so the amount of such debts and to whom owing;
(d) whether the transfer is for new consideration and if so the amount of such consideration and the time and place of payment;[and]
[(e) if for new consideration the time and place where creditors of the transferor are to file their claims.]

(3) The notice in any case shall be delivered personally or sent by registered or certified mail to all the persons shown on the list of creditors furnished by the transferor (Section 6-104) and to all other persons who are known to the transferee to hold or assert claims against the transferor.

Note: *The words in brackets are optional. See Note under §6-106.*

§6-108. Auction Sales; "Auctioneer".

(1) A bulk transfer is subject to this Article even though it is by sale at auction, but only in the manner and with the results stated in this section.

(2) The transferor shall furnish a list of his creditors and assist in the preparation of a schedule of the property to be sold, both prepared as before stated (Section 6-104).

(3) The person or persons other than the transferor who direct, control or are responsible for the auction are collectively called the "auctioneer". The auctioneer shall:

(a) receive and retain the list of creditors and prepare and retain the schedule of property for the period stated in this Article (Section 6-104);
(b) give notice of the auction personally or by registered or certified mail at least ten days before it occurs to all persons shown on the list of creditors and to all other persons who are known to him to hold or assert claims against the transferor;[and]
[(c) assure that the net proceeds of the auction are applied as provided in this Article (Section 6-106).]

(4) Failure of the auctioneer to perform any of these duties does not affect the validity of the sale or the title of the purchasers, but if the auctioneer knows that the auction constitutes a bulk transfer such failure renders the auctioneer liable to the creditors of the transferor as a class for the sums owing to them from the transferor up to but not exceeding the net proceeds of the auction. If the auctioneer consists of several persons their liability is joint and several.

Note: *The words in brackets are optional. See Note under §6-106.*

§6-109. What Creditors Protected;[Credit for Payment to Particular Creditors].

(1) The creditors of the transferor mentioned in this Article are those holding claims based on transactions or events occurring before the bulk transfer, but creditors who become such after notice to creditors is given (Sections 6-105 and 6-107) are not entitled to notice.

[(2) Against the aggregate obligation imposed by the provisions of this Article concerning the application of the proceeds (Section 6-106 and subsection (3) (c) of 6-108) the transferee or auctioneer is entitled to credit for sums paid to particular creditors of the transferor, not exceeding the sums believed in good faith at the time of the payment to be properly payable to such creditors.]

Note: *The words in brackets are optional. See Note under §6-106.*

§6-110. Subsequent Transfers.
When the title of a transferee to property is subject to a defect by reason of his noncompliance with the requirements of this Article, then:

(1) a purchaser of any of such property from such transferee who pays no value or who takes with notice of such noncompliance takes subject to such defect, but

(2) a purchaser for value in good faith and without such notice takes free of such defect.

§6-111. Limitation of Actions and Levies.
No action under this Article shall be brought nor levy made more than six months after the date on which the transferee took possession of the goods unless the transfer has been concealed. If the transfer has been concealed, actions may be brought or levies made within six months after its discovery.

ARTICLE 7: WAREHOUSE RECEIPTS, BILLS OF LADING AND OTHER DOCUMENTS OF TITLE

Part 1: General

§7-101. Short Title.
This Article shall be known and may be cited as Uniform Commercial Code—Documents of Title.

§7-102. Definitions and Index of Definitions.

(1) In this Article, unless the context otherwise requires:

(a) "Bailee" means the person who by a warehouse receipt, bill of lading or other document of title acknowledges possession of goods and contracts to deliver them.
(b) "Consignee" means the person named in a bill to whom or to whose order the bill promises delivery.
(c) "Consignor" means the person named in a bill as the person from whom the goods have been received for shipment.
(d) "Delivery order" means a written order to deliver goods directed to a warehouseman, carrier or other person who in the ordinary course of business issues warehouse receipts or bills of lading.
(e) "Document" means document of title as defined in the general definitions in Article 1 (Section 1-201).
(f) "Goods" means all things which are treated as movable for the purposes of a contract of storage or transportation.
(g) "Issuer" means a bailee who issues a document except that in relation to an unaccepted delivery order it means the person who orders the possessor of goods to deliver. Issuer includes any person for whom an agent or employee purports to act in issuing a document if the agent or employee has real or apparent authority to issue documents, notwithstanding that the issuer received no goods or that the goods were misdescribed or that in any other respect the agent or employee violated his instructions.
(h) "Warehouseman" is a person engaged in the business of storing goods for hire.

(2) Other definitions applying to this Article or to specified Parts thereof, and the sections in which they appear are:
"Duly negotiate" Section 7-501
"Person entitled under
the document" Section 7-403(4)

(3) Definitions in other Articles applying to this Article and the sections in which they appear are:
"Contract for sale"   Section 2-106
"Overseas"   Section 2-323
"Receipt" of goods   Section 2-103

(4) In addition Article 1 contains general definitions and principles of construction and interpretation applicable throughout this Article.

§7-103. Relation of Article to Treaty, Statute, Tariff, Classification or Regulation. To the extent that any treaty or statute of the United States, regulatory statute of this State or tariff, classification or regulation filed or issued pursuant thereto is applicable, the provisions of this Article are subject thereto.

§7-104. Negotiable and Non-Negotiable Warehouse Receipt, Bill of Lading or Other Document of Title
(1) A warehouse receipt, bill of lading or other document of title is negotiable

(a) if by its terms the goods are to be delivered to bearer or to the order of a named person; or
(b) where recognized in overseas trade, if it runs to a named person or assigns.

(2) Any other document is non-negotiable. A bill of lading in which it is stated that the goods are consigned to a named person is not made negotiable by a provision that the goods are to be delivered only against a written order signed by the same or another named person.

§7-105. Construction Against Negative Implication. The omission from either Part 2 or Part 3 of this Article of a provision corresponding to a provision made in the other Part does not imply that a corresponding rule of law is not applicable.

Part 2: Warehouse Receipts: Special Provisions

§7-201. Who May Issue a Warehouse Receipt; Storage Under Government Bond.
(1) A warehouse receipt may be issued by any warehouseman.
(2) Where goods including distilled spirits and agricultural commodities are stored under a statute requiring a bond against withdrawal or a license for the issuance of receipts in the nature of warehouse receipts, a receipt issued for the goods has like effect as a warehouse receipt even though issued by a person who is the owner of the goods and is not a warehouseman.

§7-202. Form of Warehouse Receipt; Essential Terms; Optional Terms.
(1) A warehouse receipt need not be in any particular form.
(2) Unless a warehouse receipt embodies within its written or printed terms each of the following, the warehouseman is liable for damages caused by the omission to a person injured thereby:

(a) the location of the warehouse where the goods are stored;
(b) the date of issue of the receipt;
(c) the consecutive number of the receipt;
(d) a statement whether the goods received will be delivered to the bearer, to a specified person, or to a specified person or his order;
(e) the rate of storage and handling charges, except that where goods are stored under a field warehousing arrangement a statement of that fact is sufficient on a non-negotiable receipt;
(f) a description of the goods or of the packages containing them;
(g) the signature of the warehouseman, which may be made by his authorized agent;
(h) if the receipt is issued for goods of which the warehouseman is owner, either solely or jointly or in common with others, the fact of such ownership; and
(i) a statement of the amount of advances made and of liabilities incurred for which the warehouseman claims a lien or security interest (Section 7-209). If the precise amount of such advances made or of such liabilities incurred is, at the time of the issue of the receipt, unknown to the warehouseman or to his agent who issues it, a statement of the fact that advances have been made or liabilities incurred and the purpose thereof is sufficient.

(3) A warehouseman may insert in his receipt any other terms which are not contrary to the provisions of this Act and do not impair his obligation of delivery (Section 7-403) or his duty of care (Section 7-204). Any contrary provisions shall be ineffective.

§7-203. Liability for Non-Receipt or Misdescription. A party to or purchaser for value in good faith of a document of title other than a bill of lading relying in either case upon the description therein of the goods may recover from the issuer damages caused by the non-receipt or misdescription of the goods, except to the extent that the document conspicuously indicates that the issuer does not know whether any part or all of the goods in fact were received or conform to the description, as where the description is in terms of marks or labels or kind, quantity or condition, or the receipt or description is qualified by "contents, condition and quality unknown." "said to contain" or the like, if such indication be true, or the party or purchaser otherwise has notice.

§7-204. Duty of Care; Contractual Limitation of Warehouseman's Liability.
(1) A warehouseman is liable for damages for loss of or injury to the goods caused by his failure to exercise such care in regard to

them as a reasonably careful man would exercise under like circumstances but unless otherwise agreed he is not liable for damages which could not have been avoided by the exercise of such care.

(2) Damages may be limited by a term in the warehouse receipt or storage agreement limiting the amount of liability in case of loss or damage, and setting forth a specific liability per article or item, or value per unit of weight, beyond which the warehouseman shall not be liable; provided, however, that such liability may on written request of the bailor at the time of signing such storage agreement or within a reasonable time after receipt of the warehouse receipt be increased on part or all of the goods thereunder, in which event increased rates may be charged based on such increased valuation, but that no such increase shall be permitted contrary to a lawful limitation of liability contained in the warehouseman's tariff, if any. No such limitation is effective with respect to the warehouseman's liability for conversion to his own use.

(3) Reasonable provisions as to the time and manner of presenting claims and instituting actions based on the bailment may be included in the warehouse receipt or tariff.

(4) This section does not impair or repeal . . .

Note: *Insert in subsection (4) a reference to any statute which imposes a higher responsibility upon the warehouseman or invalidates contractual limitations which would be permissible under this Article.*

§7-205. Title Under Warehouse Receipt Defeated in Certain Cases.
A buyer in the ordinary course of business of fungible goods sold and delivered by a warehouseman who is also in the business of buying and selling such goods takes free of any claim under a warehouse receipt even though it has been duly negotiated.

§7-206. Termination of Storage at Warehouseman's Option.
(1) A warehouseman may on notifying the person on whose account the goods are held and any other person known to claim an interest in the goods require payment of any charges and removal of the goods from the warehouse at the termination of the period of storage fixed by the document, or, if no period is fixed, within a stated period not less than thirty days after the notification. If the goods are not removed before the date specified in the notification, the warehouseman may sell them in accordance with the provisions of the section on enforcement of a warehouseman's lien (Section 7-210).

(2) If a warehouseman in good faith believes that the goods are about to deteriorate or decline in value to less than the amount of his lien within the time prescribed in subsection (1) for notification, advertisement and sale, the warehouseman may specify in the notification any reasonable shorter time for removal of the goods and in case the goods are not removed, may sell them at public sale held not less than one week after a single advertisement or posting.

(3) If as a result of a quality or condition of the goods of which the warehouseman had no notice at the time of deposit the goods are a hazard to other property or to the warehouse or to persons, the warehouseman may sell the goods at public or private sale without advertisement on reasonable notification to all persons known to claim an interest in the goods. If the warehouseman after a reasonable effort is unable to sell the goods he may dispose of them in any lawful manner and shall incur no liability by reason of such disposition.

(4) The warehouseman must deliver the goods to any person entitled to them under this Article upon due demand made at any time prior to sale or other disposition under this section.

(5) The warehouseman may satisfy his lien from the proceeds of any sale or disposition under this section but must hold the balance for delivery on the demand of any person to whom he would have been bound to deliver the goods.

§7-207. Goods Must Be Kept Separate; Fungible Goods.
(1) Unless the warehouse receipt otherwise provides, a warehouseman must keep separate the goods covered by each receipt so as to permit at all times identification and delivery of those goods except that different lots of fungible goods may be commingled.

(2) Fungible goods so commingled are owned in common by the persons entitled thereto and the warehouseman is severally liable to each owner for that owner's share. Where because of overissue a mass of fungible goods is insufficient to meet all the receipts which the warehouseman has issued against it, the persons entitled include all holders to whom overissued receipts have been duly negotiated.

§7-208. Altered Warehouse Receipts.
Where a blank in a negotiable warehouse receipt has been filled in without authority, a purchaser for value and without notice of the want of authority may treat the insertion as authorized. Any other unauthorized alteration leaves any receipt enforceable against the issuer according to its original tenor.

§7-209. Lien of Warehouseman.
(1) A warehouseman has a lien against the bailor on the goods covered by a warehouse receipt or on the proceeds thereof in his possession for charges for storage or transportation (including demurrage and terminal charges), insurance, labor, or charges present or future in relation to the goods, and for expenses necessary for preservation of the goods or reasonably incurred in their sale pursuant to law. If the person on whose account the goods are held is liable for like charges or expenses in relation to other goods whenever deposited and it is stated in the receipt that a lien is claimed for charges and expenses in relation to other goods, the warehouseman also has a lien against him for such charges and expenses whether or not the other goods have been delivered by the warehouseman. But against a person to whom a negotiable warehouse receipt is duly negotiated a warehouseman's lien is limited to charges in an amount or at a rate specified on the receipt or if no charges are so specified then to a reasonable charge for storage of the goods covered by the receipt subsequent to the date of the receipt.

(2) The warehouseman may also reserve a security interest against the bailor for a maximum amount specified on the receipt for charges other than those specified in subsection (1), such as for money advanced and interest. Such a security interest is governed by the Article on Secured Transactions (Article 9).

(3)

(a) A warehouseman's lien for charges and expenses under subsection (1) or a security interest under subsection (2) is also effective against any person who so entrusted the bailor with possession of the goods that a pledge of them by him to a good faith purchaser for value would have been valid but is not effective against a person as to whom the document confers no right in the goods covered by it under Section 7-503.

(b) A warehouseman's lien on household goods for charges and expenses in relation to the goods under subsection (1) is also effective against all persons if the depositor was the legal possessor of the goods at the time of deposit. "Household goods" means furniture, furnishings and personal effects used by the depositor in a dwelling.

(4) A warehouseman loses his lien on any goods which he voluntarily delivers or which he unjustifiably refuses to deliver. (As amended in 1966.)

§7-210. Enforcement of Warehouseman's Lien.
(1) Except as provided in subsection (2), a warehouseman's lien may be enforced by public or private sale of the goods in block

or in parcels, at any time or place and on any terms which are commercially reasonable, after notifying all persons known to claim an interest in the goods. Such notification must include a statement of the amount due, the nature of the proposed sale and the time and place of any public sale. The fact that a better price could have been obtained by a sale at a different time or in a different method from that selected by the warehouseman is not of itself sufficient to establish that the sale was not made in a commercially reasonable manner. If the warehouseman either sells the goods in the usual manner in any recognized market therefor, or if he sells at the price current in such market at the time of his sale, or if he has otherwise sold in conformity with commercially reasonable practices among dealers in the type of goods sold, he has sold in a commercially reasonable manner. A sale of more goods than apparently necessary to be offered to insure satisfaction of the obligation is not commercially reasonable except in cases covered by the preceding sentence.

(2) A warehouseman's lien on goods other than goods stored by a merchant in the course of his business may be enforced only as follows:

(a) All persons known to claim an interest in the goods must be notified.

(b) The notification must be delivered in person or sent by registered or certified letter to the last known address of any person to be notified.

(c) The notification must include an itemized statement of the claim, a description of the goods subject to the lien, a demand for payment within a specified time not less than ten days after receipt of the notification, and a conspicuous statement that unless the claim is paid within that time the goods will be advertised for sale and sold by auction at a specified time and place.

(d) The sale must conform to the terms of the notification.

(e) The sale must be held at the nearest suitable place to that where the goods are held or stored.

(f) After the expiration of the time given in the notification, an advertisement of the sale must be published once a week for two weeks consecutively in a newspaper of general circulation where the sale is to be held. The advertisement must include a description of the goods, the name of the person on whose account they are being held, and the time and place of the sale. The sale must take place at least fifteen days after the first publication. If there is no newspaper of general circulation where the sale is to be held, the advertisement must be posted at least ten days before the sale in not less than six conspicuous places in the neighborhood of the proposed sale.

(3) Before any sale pursuant to this section any person claiming a right in the goods may pay the amount necessary to satisfy the lien and the reasonable expenses incurred under this section. In that event the goods must not be sold, but must be retained by the warehouseman subject to the terms of the receipt and this Article.

(4) The warehouseman may buy at any public sale pursuant to this section.

(5) A purchaser in good faith of goods sold to enforce a warehouseman's lien takes the goods free of any rights of persons against whom the lien was valid, despite noncompliance by the warehouseman with the requirements of this section.

(6) The warehouseman may satisfy his lien from the proceeds of any sale pursuant to this section but must hold the balance, if any, for delivery on demand to any person to whom he would have been bound to deliver the goods.

(7) The rights provided by this section shall be in addition to all other rights allowed by law to a creditor against his debtor.

(8) Where a lien is on goods stored by a merchant in the course of his business the lien may be enforced in accordance with either subsection (1) or (2).

(9) The warehouseman is liable for damages caused by failure to comply with the requirements for sale under this section and in case of willful violation is liable for conversion. As amended in 1962.

Part 3: Bills of Lading: Special Provisions

§7-301. Liability for Non-Receipt or Misdescription; "Said to Contain"; "Shipper's Load and Count"; Improper Handling.

(1) A consignee of a non-negotiable bill who has given value in good faith or a holder to whom a negotiable bill has been duly negotiated relying in either case upon the description therein of the goods, or upon the date therein shown, may recover from the issuer damages caused by the misdating of the bill or the non-receipt or misdescription of the goods, except to the extent that the document indicates that the issuer does not know whether any part or all of the goods in fact were received or conform to the description, as where the description is in terms of marks or labels or kind, quantity, or condition or the receipt or description is qualified by "contents or condition of contents of packages unknown", "said to contain", "Shipper's weight, load and count" or the like, if such indication be true.

(2) When goods are loaded by an issuer who is a common carrier, the issuer must count the packages of goods if package freight and ascertain the kind and quantity if bulk freight. In such cases "shipper's weight, load and count" or other words indicating that the description was made by the shipper are ineffective except as to freight concealed by packages.

(3) When bulk freight is loaded by a shipper who makes available to the issuer adequate facilities for weighing such freight, an issuer who is a common carrier must ascertain the kind and quantity within a reasonable time after receiving the written request of the shipper to do so. In such cases "shipper's weight" or other words of like purport are ineffective.

(4) The issuer may be inserting in the bill the words "shipper's weight, load and count" or other words of like purport indicate that the goods were loaded by the shipper; and if such statement be true the issuer shall not be liable for damages caused by the improper loading. But their omission does not imply liability for such damages.

(5) The shipper shall be deemed to have guaranteed to the issuer the accuracy at the time of shipment of the description, marks, labels, number, kind, quantity, condition and weight, as furnished by him; and the shipper shall indemnify the issuer against damage caused by inaccuracies in such particulars. The right of the issuer to such indemnity shall in no way limit his responsibility and liability under the contract of carriage to any person other than the shipper.

§7-302. Through Bills of Lading and Similar Documents.

(1) The issuer of a through bill of lading or other document embodying an undertaking to be performed in part by persons acting as its agents or by connecting carriers is liable to anyone entitled to recover on the document for any breach by such other persons or by a connecting carrier of its obligation under the document but to the extent that the bill covers an undertaking to be performed overseas or in territory not contiguous to the continental United States or an undertaking including matters other than transportation this liability may be varied by agreement of the parties.

(2) Where goods covered by a through bill of lading or other document embodying an undertaking to be performed in part by persons other than the issuer are received by any such person, he is

subject with respect to his own performance while the goods are in his possession to the obligation of the issuer. His obligation is discharged by delivery of the goods to another such person pursuant to the document, and does not include liability for breach by any other such persons or by the issuer.

(3) The issuer of such through bill of lading or other document shall be entitled to recover from the connecting carrier or such other person in possession of the goods when the breach of the obligation under the document occurred, the amount it may be required to pay to anyone entitled to recover on the document therefor, as may be evidenced by any receipt, judgment, or transcript thereof, and the amount of any expense reasonably incurred by it in defending any action brought by anyone entitled to recover on the document therefor.

§7-303. Diversion; Reconsignment; Change of Instructions.

(1) Unless the bill of lading otherwise provides, the carrier may deliver the goods to a person or destination other than that stated in the bill or may otherwise dispose of the goods on instructions from

(a) the holder of a negotiable bill; or
(b) the consignor on a non-negotiable bill notwithstanding contrary instructions from the consignee; or
(c) the consignee on a non-negotiable bill in the absence of contrary instructions from the consignor, if the goods have arrived at the billed destination or if the consignee is in possession of the bill; or
(d) the consignee on a non-negotiable bill if he is entitled as against the consignor to dispose of them.

(2) Unless such instructions are noted on a negotiable bill of lading, a person to whom the bill is duly negotiated can hold the bailee according to the original terms.

§7-304. Bills of Lading in a Set.

(1) Except where customary in overseas transportation, a bill of lading must not be issued in a set of parts. The issuer is liable for damages caused by violation of this subsection.

(2) Where a bill of lading is lawfully drawn in a set of parts, each of which is numbered and expressed to be valid only if the goods have not been delivered against any other part, the whole of the parts constitute one bill.

(3) Where a bill of lading is lawfully issued in a set of parts and different parts are negotiated to different persons, the title of the holder to whom the first due negotiation is made prevails as to both the document and the goods even though any later holder may have received the goods from the carrier in good faith and discharged the carrier's obligation by surrender of his part.

(4) Any person who negotiates or transfers a single part of a bill of lading drawn in a set is liable to holders of that part as if it were the whole set.

(5) The bailee is obliged to deliver in accordance with Part 4 of this Article against the first presented part of a bill of lading lawfully drawn in a set. Such delivery discharges the bailee's obligation on the whole bill.

§7-305. Destination Bills.

(1) Instead of issuing a bill of lading to the consignor at the place of shipment a carrier may at the request of the consignor procure the bill to be issued at destination or at any other place designated in the request.

(2) Upon request of anyone entitled as against the carrier to control the goods while in transit and on surrender of any outstanding bill of lading or other receipt covering such goods, the issuer may procure a substitute bill to be issued at any place designated in the request.

§7-306. Altered Bills of Lading.
An unauthorized alteration or filling in of a blank in a bill of lading leaves the bill enforceable according to its original tenor.

§7-307. Lien of Carrier.

(1) A carrier has a lien on the goods covered by a bill of lading for charges subsequent to the date of its receipt of the goods for storage or transportation (including demurrage and terminal charges) and for expenses necessary for preservation of the goods incident to their transportation or reasonably incurred in their sale pursuant to law. But against a purchaser for value of a negotiable bill of lading a carrier's lien is limited to charges stated in the bill or the applicable tariffs, or if no charges are stated then to a reasonable charge.

(2) A lien for charges and expenses under subsection (1) on goods which the carrier was required by law to receive for transportation is effective against the consignor or any person entitled to the goods unless the carrier had notice that the consignor lacked authority to subject the goods to such charges and expenses. Any other lien under subsection (1) is effective against the consignor and any person who permitted the bailor to have control or possession of the goods unless the carrier had notice that the bailor lacked such authority.

(3) A carrier loses his lien on any goods which he voluntarily delivers or which he unjustifiably refuses to deliver.

§7-308. Enforcement of Carrier's Lien.

(1) A carrier's lien may be enforced by public or private sale of the goods, in block or in parcels, at any time or place and on any terms which are commercially reasonable, after notifying all persons known to claim an interest in the goods. Such notification must include a statement of the amount due, the nature of the proposed sale and the time and place of any public sale. The fact that a better price could have been obtained by a sale at a different time or in a different method from that selected by the carrier is not of itself sufficient to establish that the sale was not made in a commercially reasonable manner. If the carrier either sells the goods in the usual manner in any recognized market therefor or if he sells at the price current in such market at the time of his sale or if he has otherwise sold in conformity with commercially reasonable practices among dealers in the type of goods sold he has sold in a commercially reasonable manner. A sale of more goods than apparently necessary to be offered to ensure satisfaction of the obligation is not commercially reasonable except in cases covered by the preceding sentence.

(2) Before any sale pursuant to this section any person claiming a right in the goods may pay the amount necessary to satisfy the lien and the reasonable expenses incurred under this section. In that event the goods must not be sold, but must be retained by the carrier subject to the terms of the bill and this Article.

(3) The carrier may buy at any public sale pursuant to this section.

(4) A purchaser in good faith of goods sold to enforce a carrier's lien takes the goods free of any rights of persons against whom the lien was valid, despite noncompliance by the carrier with the requirements of this section.

(5) The carrier may satisfy his lien from the proceeds of any sale pursuant to this section but must hold the balance, if any, for delivery on demand to any person to whom he would have been bound to deliver the goods.

(6) The rights provided by this section shall be in addition to all other rights allowed by law to a creditor against his debtor.

(7) A carrier's lien may be enforced in accordance with either subsection (1) or the procedure set forth in subsection (2) of Section 7-210.

(8) The carrier is liable for damages caused by failure to comply with the requirements for sale under this section and in case of willful violation is liable for conversion.

§7-309. Duty of Care; Contractual Limitation of Carrier's Liability.

(1) A carrier who issues a bill of lading whether negotiable or non-negotiable must exercise the degree of care in relation to the goods which a reasonably careful man would exercise under like circumstances. This subsection does not repeal or change any law or rule of law which imposes liability upon a common carrier for damages not caused by its negligence.

(2) Damages may be limited by a provision that the carrier's liability shall not exceed a value stated in the document if the carrier's rates are dependent upon value and the consignor by the carrier's tariff is afforded an opportunity to declare a higher value or a value as lawfully provided in the tariff, or where no tariff is filed he is otherwise advised of such opportunity; but no such limitation is effective with respect to the carrier's liability for conversion to its own use.

(3) Reasonable provisions as to the time and manner of presenting claims and instituting actions based on the shipment may be included in a bill of lading or tariff.

Part 4: Warehouse Receipts and Bills of Lading: General Obligations

§7-401. Irregularities in Issue of Receipt or Bill or Conduct of Issuer.

The obligations imposed by this Article on an issuer apply to a document of title regardless of the fact that

(a) the document may not comply with the requirements of this Article or of any other law or regulation regarding its issue, form or content; or

(b) the issuer may have violated laws regulating the conduct of his business; or

(c) the goods covered by the document were owned by the bailee at the time the document was issued; or

(d) the person issuing the document does not come within the definition of warehouseman if it purports to be a warehouse receipt.

§7-402. Duplicate Receipt or Bill; Overissue.

Neither a duplicate nor any other document of title purporting to cover goods already represented by an outstanding document of the same issuer confers any right in the goods, except as provided in the case of bills in a set, overissue of documents for fungible goods and substitutes for lost, stolen or destroyed documents. But the issuer is liable for damages caused by his overissue or failure to identify a duplicate document as such by conspicuous notation on its face.

§7-403. Obligation of Warehouseman or Carrier to Deliver; Excuse.

(1) The bailee must deliver the goods to a person entitled under the document who complies with subsections (2) and (3), unless and to the extent that the bailee establishes any of the following:

(a) delivery of the goods to a person whose receipt was rightful as against the claimant;

(b) damage to or delay, loss or destruction of the goods for which the bailee is not liable [, but the burden of establishing negligence in such cases is on the person entitled under the document];

Note: *The brackets in (1)(b) indicate that State enactments may differ on this point without serious damage to the principle of uniformity.*

(c) previous sale or other disposition of the goods in lawful enforcement of a lien or on warehouseman's lawful termination of storage;

(d) the exercise by a seller of his right to stop delivery pursuant to the provisions of the Article on Sales (Section 2-705);

(e) a diversion, reconsignment or other disposition pursuant to the provisions of this Article (Section 7-303.) or tariff regulating such right;

(f) release, satisfaction or any other fact affording a personal defense against the claimant;

(g) any other lawful excuse.

(2) A person claiming goods covered by a document of title must satisfy the bailee's lien where the bailee so requests or where the bailee is prohibited by law from delivering the goods until the charges are paid.

(3) Unless the person claiming is one against whom the document confers no right under Sec. 7-503(1), he must surrender for cancellation or notation of partial deliveries any outstanding negotiable document covering the goods, and the bailee must cancel the document or conspicuously note the partial delivery thereon or be liable to any person to whom the document is duly negotiated.

(4) "Person entitled under the document" means holder in the case of a negotiable document, or the person to whom delivery is to be made by the terms of or pursuant to written instructions under a non-negotiable document.

§7-404. No Liability for Good Faith Delivery Pursuant to Receipt or Bill.

A bailee who in good faith including observance of reasonable commercial standards has received goods and delivered or otherwise disposed of them according to the terms of the document of title or pursuant to this Article is not liable therefor. This rule applies even though the person from whom he received the goods had no authority to procure the document or to dispose of the goods and even though the person to whom he delivered the goods had no authority to receive them.

Part 5: Warehouse Receipts and Bills of Lading: Negotiation and Transfer

§7-501. Form of Negotiation and Requirements of "Due Negotiation".

(1) A negotiable document of title running to the order of a named person is negotiated by his indorsement and delivery. After his indorsement in blank or to bearer any person can negotiate it by delivery alone.

(2)

(a) A negotiable document of title is also negotiated by delivery alone when by its original terms it runs to bearer.

(b) When a document running to the order of a named person is delivered to him the effect is the same as if the document had been negotiated.

(3) Negotiation of a negotiable document of title after it has been indorsed to a specified person requires indorsement by the special indorsee as well as delivery.

(4) A negotiable document of title is "duly negotiated" when it is negotiated in the manner stated in this section to a holder who purchases it in good faith without notice of any defense against or claim to it on the part of any person and for value, unless it is established that the negotiation is not in the regular course of business or financing or involves receiving the document in settlement or payment of a money obligation.

(5) Indorsement of a non-negotiable document neither makes it negotiable nor adds to the transferee's rights.

(6) The naming in a negotiable bill of a person to be notified of the arrival of the goods does not limit the negotiability of the

bill nor constitute notice to a purchaser thereof of any interest of such person in the goods.

§7-502. Rights Acquired by Due Negotiation.

(1) Subject to the following section and to the provisions of Section 7-205 on fungible goods, a holder to whom a negotiable document of title has been duly negotiated acquires thereby:

(a) title to the document;
(b) title to the goods;
(c) all rights accruing under the law of agency or estoppel, including rights to goods delivered to the bailee after the document was issued; and
(d) the direct obligation of the issuer to hold or deliver the goods according to the terms of the document free of any defense or claim by him except those arising under the terms of the document or under this Article. In the case of a delivery order the bailee's obligation accrues only upon acceptance and the obligation acquired by the holder is that the issuer and any indorser will procure the acceptance of the bailee.

(2) Subject to the following section, title and rights so acquired are not defeated by any stoppage of the goods represented by the document or by surrender of such goods by the bailee, and are not impaired even though the negotiation or any prior negotiation constituted a breach of duty or even though any person has been deprived of possession of the document by misrepresentation, fraud, accident, mistake, duress, loss, theft or conversion, or even though a previous sale or other transfer of the goods or document has been made to a third person.

§7-503. Document of Title to Goods Defeated in Certain Cases.

(1) A document of title confers no right in goods against a person who before issuance of the document had a legal interest or a perfected security interest in them and who neither

(a) delivered or entrusted them or any document of title covering them to the bailor or his nominee with actual or apparent authority to ship, store or sell or with power to obtain delivery under this Article (Section 7-403) or with power of disposition under this Act (Sections 2-403 and 9-307) or other statute or rule of law; nor
(b) acquiesced in the procurement by the bailor or his nominee of any document of title.

(2) Title to goods based upon an unaccepted delivery order is subject to the rights of anyone to whom a negotiable warehouse receipt or bill of lading covering the goods has been duly negotiated. Such a title may be defeated under the next section to the same extent as the rights of the issuer or a transferee from the issuer.

(3) Title to goods based upon a bill of lading issued to a freight forwarder is subject to the rights of anyone to whom a bill issued by the freight forwarder is duly negotiated; but delivery by the carrier in accordance with Part 4 of this Article pursuant to its own bill of lading discharges the carrier's obligation to deliver.

§7-504. Rights Acquired in the Absence of Due Negotiation; Effect of Diversion; Seller's Stoppage of Delivery.

(1) A transferee of a document, whether negotiable or non-negotiable, to whom the document has been delivered but not duly negotiated, acquires the title and rights which his transferor had or had actual authority to convey.

(2) In the case of a non-negotiable document, until but not after the bailee receives notification of the transfer, the rights of the transferee may be defeated

(a) by those creditors of the transferor who could treat the sale as void under Section 2-402; or
(b) by a buyer from the transferor in ordinary course of business if the bailee has delivered the goods to the buyer or received notification of his rights; or
(c) as against the bailee by good faith dealings of the bailee with the transferor.

(3) A diversion or other change of shipping instructions by the consignor in a non-negotiable bill of lading which causes the bailee not to deliver to the consignee defeats the consignee's title to the goods if they have been delivered to a buyer in ordinary course of business and in any event defeats the consignee's rights against the bailee.

(4) Delivery pursuant to a non-negotiable document may be stopped by a seller under Section 2-705, and subject to the requirement of due notification there provided. A bailee honoring the seller's instructions is entitled to be indemnified by the seller against any resulting loss or expense.

§7-505. Indorser Not a Guarantor for Other Parties.
The indorsement of a document of title issued by a bailee does not make the indorser liable for any default by the bailee or by previous indorsers.

§7-506. Delivery Without Indorsement: Right to Compel Indorsement.
The transferee of a negotiable document of title has a specifically enforceable right to have his transferor supply any necessary indorsement but the transfer becomes a negotiation only as of the time the indorsement is supplied.

§7-507. Warranties on Negotiation or Transfer of Receipt or Bill.
Where a person negotiates or transfers a document of title for value otherwise than as a mere intermediary under the next following section, then unless otherwise agreed he warrants to his immediate purchaser only in addition to any warranty made in selling the goods

(a) that the document is genuine; and
(b) that he has no knowledge of any fact which would impair its validity or worth; and
(c) that his negotiation or transfer is rightful and fully effective with respect to the title to the document and the goods it represents.

§7-508. Warranties of Collecting Bank as to Documents.
A collecting bank or other intermediary known to be entrusted with documents on behalf of another or with collection of a draft or other claim against delivery of documents warrants by such delivery of the documents only its own good faith and authority. This rule applies even though the intermediary has purchased or made advances against the claim or draft to be collected.

§7-509. Receipt or Bill: When Adequate Compliance With Commercial Contract.
The question whether a document is adequate to fulfill the obligations of a contract for sale or the conditions of a credit is governed by the Articles on Sales (Article 2) and on Letters of Credit (Article 5).

Part 6: Warehouse Receipts and Bills of Lading: Miscellaneous Provisions

§7-601. Lost and Missing Documents

(1) If a document has been lost, stolen or destroyed, a court may order delivery of the goods or issuance of a substitute document and the bailee may without liability to any person comply with such order. If the document was negotiable the claimant must post security approved by the court to indemnify any person who may suffer loss as a result of non-surrender of the document. If the document was not

negotiable, such security may be required at the discretion of the court. The court may also in its discretion order payment of the bailee's reasonable costs and counsel fees.

(2) A bailee who without court order delivers goods to a person claiming under a missing negotiable document is liable to any person injured thereby, and if the delivery is not in good faith becomes liable for conversion. Delivery in good faith is not conversion if made in accordance with a filed classification or tariff or, where no classification or tariff is filed, if the claimant posts security with the bailee in an amount as least double the value of the goods at the time of posting to indemnify any person injured by the delivery who files a notice of claim within one year after the delivery.

§7-602. Attachment of Goods Covered by a Negotiable Document. Except where the document was originally issued upon delivery of the goods by a person who has no power to dispose of them, no lien attaches by virtue of any judicial process to goods in the possession of a bailee for which a negotiable document of title is outstanding unless the document be first surrendered to the bailee or its negotiation enjoined, and the bailee shall not be compelled to deliver the goods pursuant to process until the document is surrendered to him or impounded by the court. One who purchases the document for value without notice of the process or injunction takes free of the lien imposed by judicial process.

§7-603. Conflicting Claims; Interpleader. If more than one person claims title or possession of the goods, the bailee is excused from delivery until he has had a reasonable time to ascertain the validity of the adverse claims or to bring an action to compel all claimants to interplead and may compel such interpleader, either in defending an action for nondelivery of the goods, or by original action, whichever is appropriate.

ARTICLE 8: INVESTMENT SECURITIES

Part 1: Short Title and General Matters

§8-101. Short Title. This Article shall be known and may be cited as Uniform Commercial Code—Investment Securities.

§8-102. Definitions and Index of Definitions
(1) In this Article, unless the context otherwise requires:

(a) A "certificated security" is a share, participation, or other interest in property of or an enterprise of the issuer or an obligation of the issuer which is
 (i) represented by an instrument issued in bearer or registered form:
 (ii) of a type commonly dealt in on securities exchanges or markets or commonly recognized in any area in which it is issued or dealt in as a medium for investment; and
 (iii) either one of a class or series or by its terms divisible into a class or series of shares, participations, interest, or obligations.

(b) An "uncertificated security" is a share, participation, or other interest in property or an enterprise of the issuer or an obligation of the issuer which is
 (i) not represented by an instrument and the transfer of which is registered upon books maintained for that purpose by or on behalf of the issuer;
 (ii) of a type commonly dealt in on securities exchanges or markets; and
 (iii) either one of a class or series or by its terms divisible into a class or series of shares, participations, interests, or obligations.

(c) A "security" is either a certificated or an uncertificated security. If a security is certificated, the terms "security" and "certificated security" may mean either the intangible interest, the instrument representing that interest, or both, as the context requires. A writing that is a certificated security is governed by this Article and not by Article 3, even though it also meets the requirements of that Article. This Article does not apply to money. If a certificated security has been retained by or surrendered to the issuer or its transfer agent for reasons other than registration of transfer, other temporary purpose, payment, exchange, or acquisition by the issuer, that security shall be treated as an uncertificated security for purposes of this Article.

(d) A certificated security is in "registered form" if
 (i) its specifies a person entitled to the security or the rights it represents, and
 (ii) its transfer may be registered upon books maintained for that purpose by or on behalf of the issuer, or the security so states.

(e) A certificated security is in "bearer from" if it runs to bearer according to its terms and not by reason of any indorsement.

(2) A "subsequent purchaser" is a person who takes other than by original issue.

(3) A "clearing corporation" is a corporation registered as a "clearing agency" under the federal securities laws or a corporation:

(a) at least 90 percent of whose capital stock is held by or for one or more organizations, none of which other than a national securities exchange or association, holds in excess of 20 percent of the capital stock of the corporation, and each of which is
 (i) subject to supervision or regulation pursuant to the provisions of federal or state banking laws or state insurance laws,
 (ii) a broker or dealer or investment company registered under the federal securities laws, or
 (iii) a national securities exchange or association registered under the federal securities laws; and

(b) any remaining capital stock of which is held by individuals who have purchased at or prior to the time of their taking office as directors of the corporation and who have purchased only so much of the capital stock as is necessary to permit them to qualify as directors.

(4) A "custodian bank" is a bank or trust company that is supervised and examined by state or federal authority having supervision over banks and is acting as custodian for a clearing corporation.

(5) Other definitions applying to this Article or to specified Parts thereof and the sections in which they appear are:

"Adverse claim"	Section 8-302
"Bona fide purchaser"	Section 8-302
"Broker"	Section 8-303
"Debtor"	Section 9-105
"Financial intermediary"	Section 8-313
"Guarantee of the signature"	Section 8-402
"Initial transaction statement"	Section 8-408
"Instruction"	Section 8-308
"Intermediary bank"	Section 4-105
"Issuer"	Section 8-201
"Overissue"	Section 8-104
"Secured party"	Section 9-105
"Security agreement"	Section 9-105

(6) In addition Article 1 contains general definitions and principles of construction and interpretation applicable throughout this Article.

§8-103. Issuer's Lien. A lien upon a security in favor of an issuer thereof is valid against a purchaser only if:

(a) the security is certificated and the right of the issuer to the lien is noted conspicuously thereon; or

(b) the security is uncertificated and a notation of the right of the issuer to the lien is contained in the initial transaction statement sent to the purchaser or, if his interest is transferred to him other than by registration of transfer, pledge, or release, the initial transaction statement sent to the registered owner or the registered pledgee.

§8-104. Effect of Overissue; "Overissue".

(1) The provisions of this Article which validate a security or compel its issue or reissue do not apply to the extent that validation, issue, or reissue would result in overissue; but if:

(a) an identical security which does not constitute an overissue is reasonably available for purchase, the person entitled to issue or validation may compel the issuer to purchase the security for him and either to deliver a certificated security or to register the transfer of an uncertificated security to him, against surrender of any certificated security he holds; or

(b) a security is not so available for purchase, the person entitled to issue or validation may recover from the issuer the price he or the last purchaser for value paid for it with interest from the date of his demand.

(2) "Overissue" means the issue of securities in excess of the amount the issuer has corporate power to issue.

§8-105. Certificated Securities Negotiable; Statements and Instructions Not Negotiable; Presumptions.

(1) Certificated securities governed by this Article are negotiable instruments.

(2) Statements (Section 8-408), notices, or the like, sent by the issuer of uncertificated securities and instructions (Section 8-308) are neither negotiable instruments nor certificated securities.

(3) In any action on a security:

(a) unless specifically denied in the pleadings, each signature on a certificated security, in a necessary indorsement, on an initial transaction statement, or on an instruction, is admitted;

(b) if the effectiveness of a signature is put in issue, the burden of establishing it is on the party claiming under the signature, but the signature is presumed to be genuine or authorized;

(c) if signatures on a certificated security are admitted or established, production of the security entitles a holder to recover on it unless the defendant establishes a defense or a defect going to the validity of the security;

(d) if signatures on an initial transaction statement are admitted or established, the facts stated in the statement are presumed to be true as of the time of its issuance; and

(e) after it is shown that a defense or defect exists, the plaintiff has the burden of establishing that he or some person under whom he claims is a person against whom the defense or defect is ineffective (Section 8-202).

§8-106. Applicability. The law (including the conflict of law rules) of the jurisdiction of organization of the issuer governs the validity of a security, the effectiveness of registration by the issuer, and the rights and duties of the issuer with respect to:

(a) registration of transfer of a certificated security;

(b) registration of transfer, pledge, or release of an uncertificated security; and

(c) sending of statements of uncertificated securities.

§8-107. Securities Transferable; Action for Price.

(1) Unless otherwise agreed and subject to any applicable law or regulation respecting short sales, a person obligated to transfer securities may transfer any certificated security of the specified issue in bearer form or registered in the name of the transferee, or indorsed to him or in blank, or he may transfer an equivalent uncertificated security to the transferee or a person designated by the transferee.

(2) If the buyer fails to pay the price as it comes due under a contract of sale, the seller may recover the price of:

(a) certificated securities accepted by the buyer:

(b) uncertificated securities that have been transferred to the buyer or a person designated by the buyer; and

(c) other securities if efforts at their resale would be unduly burdensome or if there is no readily available market for their resale.

§8-108. Registration of Pledge and Release of Uncertificated Securities. A security interest in an uncertificated security may be evidenced by the registration of pledge to the secured party or a person designated by him. There can be no more than one registered pledge of an uncertificated security is the person in whose name the security is registered, even if the security is subject to a registered pledge. The rights of a registered pledgee of an uncertificated security under this Article are terminated by the registration of release.

Part 2: Issue—Issuer

§8-201. "Issuer".

(1) With respect to obligations on or defenses to a security, "issuer" includes a person who:

(a) places or authorizes the placing of his name on a certificated security (otherwise than as authenticating trustee, registrar, transfer agent, or the like) to evidence that it represents a share, participation, or other interest in his property or in an enterprise, or to evidence his duty to perform an obligation represented by the certificated security;

(b) creates shares, participations or other interests in his property or in an enterprise or undertakes obligations, which shares, participations, interests, or obligations are uncertificated securities;

(c) directly or indirectly creates fractional interests in his rights or property, which fractional interests are represented by certificated securities; or

(d) becomes responsible for or in place of any other person described as an issuer in this section.

(2) With respect to obligations on or defenses to a security, a guarantor is an issuer to the extent of his guaranty, whether or not his obligation is noted on a certificated security or on statements of uncertificated securities sent pursuant to Section 8-408.

(3) With respect to registration of transfer, pledge, or release (Part 4 of this Article), "issuer" means a person on whose behalf transfer books are maintained.

§8-202. Issuer's Responsibility and Defenses; Notice of Defect or Defense.

(1) Even against a purchaser for value and without notice, the terms of a security include:

(a) if the security is certificated, those stated on the security;
(b) if the security is uncertificated, those contained in the initial transaction statement sent to such purchaser, or if his interest is transferred to him other than by registration of transfer, pledge, or release, the initial transaction statement sent to the registered owner or registered pledgee; and
(c) those made part of the security by reference, on the certificated security or in the initial transaction statement, to another instrument, indenture, or document or to a constitution, statute, ordinance, rule, regulation, order or the like, to the extent that the terms referred to do not conflict with the terms stated on the certificated security or contained in the statement. A reference under this paragraph does not of itself charge a purchaser for value with notice of a defect going to the validity of the security, even though the certificated security or statement expressly states that a person accepting it admits notice.

(2) A certificated security in the hands of a purchaser for value or an uncertificated security as to which an initial transaction statement has been sent to a purchaser for value, other than a security issued by a government or governmental agency or unit, even though issued with a defect going to its validity, is valid with respect to the purchaser if he is without notice of the particular defect unless the defect involves a violation of constitutional provisions, in which case the security is valid with respect to a subsequent purchaser for value and without notice of the defect. This subsection applies to an issuer that is a government or governmental agency or unit only if either there has been substantial compliance with the legal requirements governing the issue or the issuer has received a substantial consideration for the issue as a whole or for the particular security and a stated purpose of the issue is one for which the issuer has power to borrow money or issue the security.

(3) Except as provided in the case of certain unauthorized signatures (Section 8-205), lack of genuineness of a certificated security or an initial transaction statement is a complete defense, even against a purchaser for value and without notice.

(4) All other defenses of the issuer of a certificated or uncertificated security, including nondelivery and conditional delivery of a certificated security, are ineffective against a purchaser for value who has taken without notice of the particular defense.

(5) Nothing in this section shall be construed to affect the right of a party to a "when, as and if issued" or a "when distributed" contract to cancel the contract in the event of a material change in the character of the security that is the subject of the contract or in the plan or arrangement pursuant to which the security is to be issued or distributed.

§8-203. Staleness as Notice of Defects or Defenses.

(1) After an act or event creating a right to immediate performance of the principal obligation represented by a certificated security or that sets a date on or after which the security is to be presented or surrendered for redemption or exchange, a purchaser is charged with notice of any defect in its issue or defense of the issuer if:
(a) the act or event is one requiring the payment of money, the delivery of certificated securities, the registration of transfer of uncertificated securities, or any of these on presentation or surrender of the certificated security, the funds or securities are available on the date set for payment or exchange, and he takes the security more than one year after that date; and
(b) the act or event is not covered by paragraph

(c) and he takes the security more than 2 years after the date set for surrender or presentation or the date on which performance became due.

(2) A call that has been revoked is not within subsection (1).

§8-204. Effect of Issuer's Restrictions on Transfer.
A restriction on transfer of a security imposed by the issuer, even though otherwise lawful, is ineffective against any person without actual knowledge of it unless:
(a) the security is certificated and the restriction is noted conspicuously thereon; or
(b) the security is uncertificated and a notation of the restriction is contained in the initial transaction statement sent to the person or, if his interest is transferred to him other than by registration of transfer, pledge, or release, the initial transaction statement sent to the registered owner or the registered pledgee.

§8-205. Effect of Unauthorized Signature on Certificated Security or Initial Transaction Statement.
An unauthorized signature placed on a certificated security prior to or in the course of issue or placed on an initial transaction statement is ineffective, but the signature is effective in favor of a purchaser for value of the certificated security or a purchaser for value of an uncertificated security to whom such initial transaction statement has been sent, if the purchaser is without notice of the lack of authority and the signing has been done by:
(a) an authenticating trustee, registrar, transfer agent, or other person entrusted by the issuer with the signing of the security, of similar securities, or of initial transaction statements or the immediate preparation for signing of any of them; or
(b) an employee of the issuer, or of any of the foregoing, entrusted with responsible handling of the security or initial transaction statement.

§8-206. Completion or Alteration of Certificated Security or Initial Transaction Statement.

(1) If a certificated security contains the signatures necessary to its issue or transfer but is incomplete in any other respect:
(a) any person may complete it by filling in the blanks as authorized; and
(b) even though the blanks are incorrectly filled in, the security as completed is enforceable by a purchaser who took it for value and without notice of the incorrectness.

(2) A complete certificated security that has been improperly altered, even though fraudulently, remains enforceable, but only according to its original terms.

(3) If an initial transaction statement contains the signatures necessary to its validity, but is incomplete in any other respect:
(a) any person may complete it by filling in the blanks as authorized; and
(b) even though the blanks are incorrectly filled in, the statement as completed is effective in favor of the person to whom it is sent if he purchased the security referred to therein for value and without notice of the incorrectness.

(4) A complete initial transaction statement that has been improperly altered, even though fraudulently, is effective in favor of a purchaser to whom it has been sent, but only according to its original terms.

§8-207. Rights and Duties of Issuer With Respect to Registered Owners and Registered Pledgees.

(1) Prior to due presentment for registration of transfer of a certificated security in registered form, the issuer or indenture trustee may treat the registered owner as the person exclusively

entitled to vote, to receive notifications, and otherwise to exercise all the rights and powers of an owner.

(2) Subject to the provisions of subsections (3), (4), and (6), the issuer or indenture trustee may treat the registered owner of an uncertificated security as the person exclusively entitled to vote, to receive notifications, and otherwise to exercise all the rights and powers of an owner.

(3) The registered owner of an uncertificated security that is subject to a registered pledge is not entitled to registration of transfer prior to the due presentment to the issuer of a release instruction. The exercise of conversion rights with respect to a convertible uncertificated security is a transfer within the meaning of this section.

(4) Upon due presentment of a transfer instruction from the registered pledgee of an uncertificated security, the issuer shall:

(a) register the transfer of the security to the new owner free of pledge, if the instruction specifies a new owner (who may be the registered pledgee) and does not specify a pledgee;

(b) register the transfer of the security to the new owner subject to the interest of the existing pledgee, if the instruction specifies a new owner and the existing pledgee; or

(c) register the release of the security from the existing pledge and register the pledge of the security to the other pledgee, if the instruction specifies the existing owner and another pledgee.

(5) Continuity of perfection of a security interest is not broken by registration of transfer under subsection (4)(b) or by registration of release and pledge under subsection (4)(c), if the security interest is assigned.

(6) If an uncertificated security is subject to a registered pledge:

(a) any uncertificated securities issued in exchange for or distributed with respect to the pledged security shall be registered subject to the pledge;

(b) any certificated securities issued in exchange for or distributed with respect to the pledged security shall be delivered to the registered pledgee; and

(c) any money paid in exchange for or in redemption of part or all of the security shall be paid to the registered pledgee.

(7) Nothing in this Article shall be construed to affect the liability of the registered owner of a security for calls, assessments, or the like.

§8-208. Effect of Signature of Authenticating Trustee, Registrar, or Transfer Agent.

(1) A person placing his signature upon a certificated security or an initial transaction statement as authenticating trustee, registrar, transfer agent, or the like, warrants to a purchaser for value of the certificated security or a purchaser for value of an uncertificated security to whom the initial transaction statement has been sent, if the purchaser is without notice of the particular defect, that:

(a) the certificated security or initial transaction statement is genuine;

(b) his own participation in the issue or registration of the transfer, pledge, or release of the security is within his capacity and within the scope of the authority received by him from the issuer; and

(c) he has reasonable grounds to believe that the security is in the form and within the amount the issuer is authorized to issue.

(2) Unless otherwise agreed, a person by so placing his signature does not assume responsibility for the validity of the security in other respects.

Part 3: Transfer

§8-301. Rights Acquired by Purchaser

(1) Upon transfer of a security to a purchaser (Section 8-313), the purchaser acquires the rights in the security which his transferor had or had actual authority to convey unless the purchaser's rights are limited by Section 8-302 (4).

(2) A transferee of a limited interest acquires rights only to the extent of the interest transferred. The creation or release of a security interest in a security is the transfer of a limited interest in that security.

§8-302. "Bona Fide Purchaser"; "Adverse Claim"; Title Acquired by Bona Fide Purchaser.

(1) A "bona fide purchaser" is a purchaser for value in good faith and without notice of any adverse claim:

(a) who takes delivery of a certificated security in bearer form or in registered form, issued or indorsed to him or in blank;

(b) to whom the transfer, pledge or release of an uncertificated security is registered on the books of the issuer; or

(c) to whom a security is transferred under the provisions of paragraph (c) (d) (i), or (g) of Section 8-313(1).

(2) "Adverse claim" includes a claim that a transfer was or would be wrongful or that a particular adverse person is the owner of or has an interest in the security.

(3) A bona fide purchaser in addition to acquiring the rights of a purchaser (Section 8-301) also acquires his interest in the security free of any adverse claim.

(4) Notwithstanding Section 8-301(1), the transferee of a particular certificated security who has been a party to any fraud or illegality affecting the security, or who as a prior holder of that certificated security had notice of an adverse claim, cannot improve his position by taking from a bona fide purchaser.

§8-303. "Broker".
"Broker" means a person engaged for all or part of his time in the business of buying and selling securities, who in the transaction concerned acts for, buys a security from, or sells a security to, a customer. Nothing in this Article determines the capacity in which a person acts for purposes of any other statute or rule to which the person is subject.

§8-304. Notice to Purchaser of Adverse Claims.

(1) A purchaser (including a broker for the seller or buyer, but excluding an intermediary bank) of a certificated security is charged with notice of adverse claims if:

(a) the security, whether in bearer or registered form, has been indorsed "for collection" or "for surrender" or for some other purpose not involving transfer; or

(b) the security is in bearer form and has on it an unambiguous statement that it is the property of a person other than the transferor. The mere writing of a name on a security is not such a statement.

(2) A purchaser (including a broker for the seller or buyer, but excluding an intermediary bank) to whom the transfer, pledge, or release of an uncertificated security is registered is charged with notice of adverse claims as to which the issuer has a duty under Section 8-403(4) at the time of registration and which are noted in the initial transaction statement sent to the purchaser or, if his interest is transferred to him other than by registration of transfer,

pledge, or release, the initial transaction statement sent to the registered owner or the registered pledge.

(3) The fact that the purchaser (including a broker for the seller or buyer) of a certificated or uncertificated security has notice that the security is held for a third person or is registered in the name of or indorsed by a fiduciary does not create a duty of inquiry into the rightfulness of the transfer or constitute constructive notice of adverse claims. However, if the purchaser (excluding an intermediary bank) has knowledge that the proceeds are being used or the transaction is for the individual benefit of the fiduciary or otherwise in breach of duty, the purchaser is charged with notice of adverse claims.

§8-305. Staleness as Notice of Adverse Claims. An act or event that creates a right to immediate performance of the principal obligation represented by a certificated security or sets a date on or after which a certificated security is to be presented or surrendered for redemption or exchange does not itself constitute any notice of adverse claims except in the case of a transfer:

(a) after one year from any date set for presentment or surrender for redemption or exchange; or

(b) after 6 months from any date set for payment of money against presentation or surrender of the security if funds are available for payment on that date.

§8-306. Warranties on Presentment and Transfer of Certificated Securities; Warranties of Originators of Instructions.

(1) A person who presents a certificated security for registration of transfer or for payment or exchange warrants to the issuer that he is entitled to the registration, payment, or exchange. But, a purchaser for value and without notice of adverse claims who receives a new, reissued, or re-registered certificated security on registration of transfer or receives an initial transaction statement confirming the registration of transfer of an equivalent uncertificated security to him warrants only that he has no knowledge of any unauthorized signature (Section 8-311) in a necessary indorsement.

(2) A person by transferring a certificated security to a purchaser for value warrants only that:

(a) his transfer is effective and rightful;
(b) the security is genuine and has not been materially altered; and
(c) he knows of no fact which might impair the validity of the security.

(3) If a certificated security is delivered by an intermediary known to be entrusted with delivery of the security on behalf of another or with collection of a draft or claim against delivery, the intermediary by delivery warrants only his own good faith and authority, even though he has purchased or made advances against the claim to be collected against the delivery.

(4) A pledgee or other holder for security who redelivers a certificated security received, or after payment and on order of the debtor delivers that security to a third person makes only the warranties of an intermediary under subsection (3).

(5) A person who originates an instruction warrants to the issuer that:

(a) he is an appropriate person to originate the instruction; and
(b) at the time the instruction is presented to the issuer he will be entitled to the registration of transfer, pledge, or release.

(6) A person who originates an instruction warrants to any person specially guaranteeing his signature (subsection 8-312 (3)) that:

(a) he is an appropriate person to originate the instruction; and
(b) at the time the instruction is presented to the issuer
  (i) he will be entitled to the registration of transfer, pledge, or release; and
  (ii) the transfer, pledge, or release requested in the instruction will be registered by the issuer free from all liens, security interests, restrictions, and claims other than those specified in the instruction.

(7) A person who originates an instruction warrants to a purchaser for value and to any person guaranteeing the instruction (Section 8-312(6)) that:

(a) he is an appropriate person to originate the instruction;
(b) the uncertificated security referred to therein is valid; and
(c) at the time the instruction is presented to the issuer
  (i) the transferor will be entitled to the registration of transfer, pledge, or release;
  (ii) the transfer, pledge, or release requested in the instruction will be registered by the issuer free from all liens, security interests, restrictions, and claims other than those specified in the instruction; and
  (iii) the requested transfer, pledge, or release will be rightful.

(8) If a secured party is the registered pledgee or the registered owner of an uncertificated security, a person who originates an instruction of release or transfer to the debtor or, after payment and on order of the debtor, a transfer instruction to a third person, warrants to the debtor or the third person only that he is an appropriate person to originate the instruction and at the time the instruction is presented to the issuer, the transferor will be entitled to the registration of release or transfer. If a transfer instruction to a third person who is a purchaser for value is originated on order of the debtor, the debtor makes to the purchaser the warranties of paragraphs (b), (c)(ii) and (c)(iii) of subsection (7).

(9) A person who transfers an uncertificated security to a purchaser for value and does not originate an instruction in connection with the transfer warrants only that:

(a) his transfer is effective and rightful; and
(b) the uncertificated security is valid.

(10) A broker gives to his customer and to the issuer and a purchaser the applicable warranties provided in this section and has the rights and privileges of a purchaser under this section. The warranties of and in favor of the broker acting as an agent are in addition to applicable warranties given by and in favor of his customer.

§8-307. Effect of Delivery Without Indorsement; Right to Compel Indorsement. If a certificated security in registered form has been delivered to a purchaser without a necessary indorsement he may become a bona fide purchaser only as of the time the indorsement is supplied; but against the transferor, the transfer is complete upon delivery and the purchaser has a specifically enforceable right to have any necessary indorsement supplied.

§8-308. Indorsements; Instructions.

(1) An indorsement of a certificated security in registered form is made when an appropriate person signs on it or on a separate document an assignment or transfer of the security or a power to assign or transfer it or his signature is written without more upon the back of the security.

(2) An indorsement may be in blank or special. An indorsement in blank includes an indorsement to bearer. A special indorsement specifies to whom the security is to be transferred, or

who has power to transfer it. A holder may convert a blank indorsement into a special indorsement.

(3) An indorsement purporting to be only of part of a certificated security representing units intended by the issuer to be separately transferable is effective to the extent of the indorsement.

(4) An "instruction" is an order to the issuer of an uncertificated security requesting that the transfer, pledge, or release from pledge of the uncertificated security specified therein be registered.

(5) An instruction originated by an appropriate person is:

(a) a writing signed by an appropriate person; or
(b) a communication to the issuer in any form agreed upon in a writing signed by the issuer and an appropriate person.

If an instruction has been originated by an appropriate person but is incomplete in any other respect, any person may complete it as authorized and the issuer may rely on it as completed even though it has been completed incorrectly.

(6) "An appropriate person" in subsection (1) means the person specified by the certificated security or by special indorsement to be entitled to the security.

(7) "An appropriate person" in subsection (5) means:

(a) for an instruction to transfer or pledge an uncertificated security which is then not subject to a registered pledge, the registered owner; or
(b) for an instruction to transfer or release an uncertificated security which is then subject to a registered pledge, the registered pledgee.

(8) In addition to the persons designated in subsections (6) and (7), "an appropriate person" in subsections (1) and (5) includes:

(a) if the person designated is described as a fiduciary but is no longer serving in the described capacity, either that person or his successor;
(b) if the persons designated are described as more than one person as fiduciaries and one or more are no longer serving in the described capacity, the remaining fiduciary or fiduciaries, whether or not a successor has been appointed or qualified;
(c) if the person designated is an individual and is without capacity to act by virtue of death; incompetence, infancy, or otherwise his executor, administrator, guardian, or like fiduciary;
(d) if the persons designated are described as more than one person as tenants by the entirety or with right of survivorship and by reason of death all cannot sign the survivor or survivors;
(e) a person having power to sign under applicable law or controlling instrument; and
(f) to the extent that the person designated or any of the foregoing persons may act through an agent, his authorized agent.

(9) Unless otherwise agreed, the indorser of a certificated security by his indorsement or the originator of an instruction by his origination assumes no obligation that the security will be honored by the issuer but only the obligations provided in Section 8-306.

(10) Whether the person signing is appropriate is determined as of the date of signing and an indorsement made by or an instruction originated by him does not become unauthorized for the purposes of this Article by virtue of any subsequent change of circumstances.

(11) Failure of a fiduciary to comply with a controlling instrument or with the law of the state having jurisdiction of the fiduciary relationship, including any law requiring the fiduciary to obtain court approval of the transfer, pledge, or release, does not render his indorsement or an instruction originated by him unauthorized for the purposes of this Article.

§8-309. Effect of Indorsement Without Delivery. An indorsement of a certificated security, whether special or in blank, does not constitute a transfer until delivery of the certificated security on which it appears or, if the indorsement is on a separate document, until delivery of both the document and the certificated security.

§8-310. Indorsement of Certificated Security in Bearer Form. An indorsement of a certificated security in bearer form may give notice of adverse claims (Section 8-304) but does not otherwise affect any right to registration the holder possesses.

§8-311. Effect of Unauthorized Indorsement or Instruction. Unless the owner, or pledgee has ratified an unauthorized indorsement or instruction or is otherwise precluded from asserting its ineffectiveness:

(a) he may assert its ineffectiveness against the issuer or any purchaser, other than a purchaser for value and without notice of adverse claims, who has in good faith received a new, reissued, or re-registered certificated security on registration of transfer or received an initial transaction statement confirming the registration of transfer, pledge, or release of an equivalent uncertificated security to him; and
(b) an issuer who registers the transfer of a certificated security upon the unauthorized indorsement or who registers the transfer, pledge, or release of an uncertificated security upon the unauthorized instruction is subject to liability for improper registration (Section 8-104).

§8-312. Effect of Guaranteeing Signature, Indorsement or Instruction.

(1) Any person guaranteeing a signature of an indorser of a certificated security warrants that at the time of signing:

(a) the signature was genuine;
(b) the signer was an appropriate person to indorse (Section 8-308); and
(c) the signer had legal capacity to sign.

(2) Any person guaranteeing a signature of the originator of an instruction warrants that at the time of signing:

(a) the signature was genuine;
(b) the signer was an appropriate person to originate the instruction (Section 8-308) if the person specified in the instruction as the registered owner or registered pledgee of the uncertificated security was, in fact, the registered owner or registered pledgee of such security, as to which fact the signature guarantor makes no warranty;
(c) the signer had legal capacity to sign; and
(d) the taxpayer identification number, if any, appearing on the instruction as that of the registered owner or registered pledgee was the taxpayer identification number of the signer or of the owner or pledgee for whom the signer was acting.

(3) Any person specially guaranteeing the signature of the originator of an instruction makes not only the warranties of a signature guarantor (Subsection (2)) but also warrants that at the time the instruction is presented to the issuer:

(a) the person specified in the instruction as the registered owner or registered pledgee of the uncertificated security will be the registered owner or registered pledgee; and

(b) the transfer, pledge, or release of the uncertificated security requested in the instruction will be registered by the issuer free from all liens, security interests, restrictions, and claims other than those specified in the instruction.

(4) The guarantor under subsections (1) and (2) or the special guarantor under subsection (3) does not otherwise warrant the rightfulness of the particular transfer, pledge, or release.

(5) Any person guaranteeing an indorsement of a certificated security makes not only the warranties of a signature guarantor under subsection (1) but also warrants the rightfulness of the particular transfer in all respects.

(6) Any person guaranteeing an instruction requesting the transfer, pledge, or release of an uncertificated security makes not only the warranties of a special signature guarantor under subsection (3) but also warrants the rightfulness of the particular transfer, pledge, or release in all respects.

(7) No issuer may require a special guarantee of signature (subsection (3)), a guarantee of indorsement (subsection (5)), or a guarantee of instruction (subsection (6)) as a condition to registration of transfer, pledge, or release.

(8) The foregoing warranties are made to any person taking or dealing with the security in reliance on the guarantee, and the guarantor is liable to the person for any loss resulting from breach of the warranties.

§8-313. When Transfer to Purchaser Occurs: Financial Intermediary as Bona Fide Purchaser; "Financial Intermediary".

(1) Transfer of a security or a limited interest (including a security interest) therein to a purchaser occurs only:

(a) at the time he or a person designated by him acquires possession of a certificated security;

(b) at the time the transfer, pledge, or release of an uncertificated security is registered to him or a person designated by him:

(c) at the time his financial intermediary acquires possession of a certificated security specially indorsed to or issued in the name of the purchaser;

(d) at the time a financial intermediary, not a clearing corporation, sends him confirmation of the purchase and also by book entry or otherwise identifies as belonging to the purchaser

    (i) a specific certificated security in the financial intermediary's possession;

    (ii) a quantity of securities that constitute or are part of a fungible bulk of certificated securities in the financial intermediary's possession or of uncertificated securities registered in the name of the financial intermediary; or

    (iii) a quantity of securities that constitute or are part of a fungible bulk of securities shown on the account of the financial intermediary on the books of another financial intermediary;

(e) with respect to an identified certificated security to be delivered while still in the possession of a third person, not a financial intermediary, at the time that person acknowledges that he holds for the purchaser;

(f) with respect to a specific uncertificated security the pledge or transfer of which has been registered to a third person, not a financial intermediary, at the time that person acknowledges that he holds for the purchaser;

(g) at the time appropriate entries to the account of the purchaser or a person designated by him on the books of a clearing corporation are made under Section 8-320;

(h) with respect to the transfer of a security interest where the debtor has signed a security agreement containing a description of the security, at the time a written notification, which, in the case of the creation of the security interest, is signed by the debtor (which may be a copy of the security agreement) or which, in the case of the release or assignment of the security interest created pursuant to this paragraph, is signed by the secured party, is received by

    (i) a financial intermediary on whose books the interest of the transferor in the security appears:

    (ii) a third person, not a financial intermediary, in possession of the security, if it is certificated;

    (iii) a third person, not a financial intermediary, who is the registered owner of the security, if it is uncertificated and not subject to a registered pledge; or

    (iv) a third person, not a financial intermediary, who is the registered pledgee of the security, if it is uncertificated and subject to a registered pledge;

(i) with respect to the transfer of a security interest where the transferor has signed a security agreement containing a description of the security, at the time new value is given by the secured party; or

(j) with respect to the transfer of a security interest where the secured party is a financial intermediary and the security has already been transferred to the financial intermediary under paragraphs (a), (b), (c), (d), or (g), at the time the transferor has signed a security agreement containing a description of the security and value is given by the secured party.

(2) The purchaser is the owner of a security held for him by a financial intermediary, but cannot be a bona fide purchaser of a security so held except in the circumstances specified in paragraphs (c), (d)(i), and (g) of subsection (1). If a security so held is part of a fungible bulk, as in the circumstances specified in paragraphs (d)(ii) and (d)(iii) of subsection (1), the purchaser is the owner of a proportionate property interest in the fungible bulk.

(3) Notice of an adverse claim received by the financial intermediary or by the purchaser after the financial intermediary takes delivery of a certificated security as a holder for value or after the transfer, pledge, or release of an uncertificated security has been registered free of the claim to a financial intermediary who has given value is not effective either as to the financial intermediary or as to the purchaser. However, as between the financial intermediary and the purchaser the purchaser may demand transfer of an equivalent security as to which no notice of adverse claim has been received.

(4) A "financial intermediary" is a bank, broker, clearing corporation or other person (or the nominee of any of them) which in the ordinary course of its business maintains security accounts for its customers and is acting in that capacity. A financial intermediary may have a security interest in securities held in account for its customer.

§8-314. Duty to Transfer, When Completed.

(1) Unless otherwise agreed, if a sale of a security is made on an exchange or otherwise through brokers:

(a) the selling customer fulfills his duty to transfer at the time he:

    (i) places a certificated security in the possession of the selling broker or of a person designated by the broker;

    (ii) causes an uncertificated security to be registered in the name of the selling broker or a person designated by the broker;

    (iii) if requested, causes an acknowledgment to be made to the selling broker that a certificated or uncertificated security is held for the broker; or

(iv) places in the possession of the selling broker or of a person designated by the broker a transfer instruction for an uncertificated security, providing the issuer does not refuse to register the requested transfer if the instruction is presented to the issuer for registration within 30 days thereafter; and

(b) the selling broker, including a correspondent broker acting for a selling customer, fulfills his duty to transfer at the time he:
   (i) places a certificated security in the possession of the buying broker or a person designated by the buying broker;
   (ii) causes an uncertificated security to be registered in the name of the buying broker or a person designated by the buying broker;
   (iii) places in the possession of the buying broker or of a person designated by the buying broker a transfer instruction for an uncertificated security, providing the issuer does not refuse to register the requested transfer if the instruction is presented to the issuer for registration within 30 days thereafter; or
   (iv) effects clearance of the sale in accordance with the rules of the exchange on which the transaction took place.

(2) Except as provided in this section and unless otherwise agreed, a transferor's duty to transfer a security under a contract of purchase is not fulfilled until he:
   (a) places a certificated security in form to be negotiated by the purchaser in the possession of the purchaser or of a person designated by the purchaser;
   (b) causes an uncertificated security to be registered in the name of the purchaser or a person designated by the purchaser; or
   (c) if the purchaser requests, causes an acknowledgment to be made to the purchaser that certificated or uncertificated security is held for the purchaser.

(3) Unless made on an exchange, a sale to a broker purchasing for his own account is within subsection (2) and not within subsection (1).

§8-315. Action Against Transferee Based Upon Wrongful Transfer.

(1) Any person against whom the transfer of a security is wrongful for any reason, including his incapacity, as against anyone except a bona fide purchaser, may:
   (a) reclaim possession of the certificated security wrongfully transferred;
   (b) obtain possession of any new certificated security representing all or part of the same rights;
   (c) compel the origination of an instruction to transfer to him or a person designated by him an uncertificated security constituting all or part of the same rights; or
   (d) have damages.

(2) If the transfer is wrongful because of an unauthorized indorsement of a certificated security, the owner may also reclaim or obtain possession of the security or a new certificated security, even from a bona fide purchaser, if the ineffectiveness of the purported indorsement can be asserted against him under the provisions of this Article on unauthorized indorsements (Section 8-311).

(3) The right to obtain or reclaim possession of a certificated security or to compel the origination of a transfer instruction may be specifically enforced and the transfer of a certificated or uncertificated security enjoined and a certificated security impounded pending the litigation.

§8-316. Purchaser's Right to Requisites for Registration of Transfer, Pledge, or Release on Books.
Unless otherwise agreed, the transferor of a certificated security or the transferor, pledgor, or pledgee of an uncertificated security on due demand must supply his purchaser with any proof of his authority to transfer, pledge, or release or with any other requisite necessary to obtain registration of the transfer, pledge, or release of the security; but if the transfer, pledge, or release is not for value, a transferor, pledgor, or pledgee need not do so unless the purchaser furnishes the necessary expenses. Failure within a reasonable time to comply with a demand made gives the purchaser the right to reject or rescind the transfer, pledge, or release.

§8-317. Creditors' Rights.

(1) Subject to the exceptions in subsections (3) and (4), no attachment or levy upon a certificated security or any share or other interest represented thereby which is outstanding is valid until the security is actually seized by the officer making the attachment or levy, but a certificated security which has been surrendered to the issuer may be reached by a creditor by legal process at the issuer's chief executive office in the United States.

(2) An uncertificated security registered in the name of the debtor may not be reached by a creditor except by legal process at the issuer's chief executive office in the United States.

(3) The interest of a debtor in a certificated security that is in the possession of a secured party not a financial intermediary or in an uncertificated security registered in the name of a secured party not a financial intermediary (or in the name of a nominee of the secured party) may be reached by a creditor by legal process upon the secured party.

(4) The interest of a debtor in a certificated security that is in the possession of or registered in the name of a financial intermediary or in an uncertificated security registered in the name of a financial intermediary may be reached by a creditor by legal process upon the financial intermediary on whose books the interest of the debtor appears.

(5) Unless otherwise provided by law, a creditor's lien upon the interest of a debtor in a security obtained pursuant to subsection (3) or (4) is not a restraint on the transfer of the security, free of the lien, to a third party for new value; but in the event of a transfer, the lien applies to the proceeds of the transfer in the hands of the secured party or financial intermediary, subject to any claims having priority.

(6) A creditor whose debtor is the owner of a security is entitled to aid from courts of appropriate jurisdiction, by injunction or otherwise, in reaching the security or in satisfying the claim by means allowed at law or in equity in regard to property that cannot readily be reached by ordinary legal process.

§8-318. No Conversion by Good Faith Conduct.
An agent or bailee who in good faith (including the observance of reasonable commercial standards if he is in the business of buying, selling, or otherwise dealing with securities) has received certificated securities and sold, pledged, or delivered them or has sold or caused the transfer or pledge of uncertificated securities over which he had control according to the instructions of his principal, is not liable for conversion or for participation in breach of fiduciary duty although the principal had no right so to deal with the securities.

§8-319. Statute of Frauds.
A contract for the sale of securities is not enforceable by way of action or defense unless:

(a) there is some writing signed by the party against whom enforcement is sought or by his authorized agent or broker, sufficient to indicate that a contract has been made for sale of a stated quantity of described securities at a defined or stated price;

(b) delivery of a certificated security or transfer instruction has been accepted, or transfer of an uncertificated security has been registered and the transferee has failed to send written objection to the issuer within 10 days after receipt of the initial transaction statement confirming the registration, or payment has been made, but the contract is enforceable under this provision only to the extent the delivery, registration, or payment;

(c) within a reasonable time a writing in confirmation of the sale or purchase and sufficient against the sender under paragraph (a) has been received by the party against whom enforcement is sought and he has failed to send written objection to its contents within 10 days after its receipt; or

(d) the party against whom enforcement is sought admits in his pleading, testimony, or otherwise in court that a contract was made for sale of a stated quantity of described securities at a defined or stated price.

§8-320. Transfer or Pledge Within Central Depository System

(1) In addition to other methods, a transfer, pledge, or release of a security or any interest therein may be effected by the making of appropriate entries on the books of a clearing corporation reducing the account of the transferor, pledgor, or pledgee and increasing the account of the transferee, pledgee, or pledgor by the amount of the obligation, or the number of shares or rights transferred, pledged, or released, if the security is shown on the account of a transferor, pledgor, or pledgee on the books of the clearing corporation; is subject to the control of the clearing corporation; and

(a) if certificated,
  (i) is in the custody of the clearing corporation, another clearing corporation, a custodian bank or a nominee of any of them; and
  (ii) is in bearer form or indorsed in blank by an appropriate person or registered in the name of the clearing corporation, a custodian bank, or a nominee of any of them; or

(b) if uncertificated, is registered in the name of the clearing corporation, another clearing corporation, a custodian bank, or a nominee of any of them.

(2) Under this section entries may be made with respect to like securities or interests therein as a part of a fungible bulk and may refer merely to a quantity of a particular security without reference to the name of the registered owner, certificate or bond number, or the like, and, in appropriate cases, may be on a net basis taking into account other transfers, pledges, or releases of the same security.

(3) A transfer under this section is effective (Section 8-313) and the purchaser acquires the rights of the transferor (Section 8-301). A pledge or release under this section is the transfer of a limited interest. If a pledge or the creation of a security interest is intended, the security interest is perfected at the time when both value is given by the pledgee and the appropriate entries are made (Section 8-321). A transferee or pledgee under this section may be a bona fide purchaser (Section 8-302).

(4) A transfer or pledge under this section is not a registration of transfer under Part 4.

(5) That entries made on the books of the clearing corporation as provided in subsection (1) are not appropriate does not affect the validity or effect of the entries or the liabilities or obligations of the clearing corporation to any person adversely affected thereby.

§8-321. Enforceability, Attachment, Perfection, and Termination of Security Interests.

(1) A security interest in a security is enforceable and can attach only if it is transferred to the secured party or a person designated by him pursuant to a provision of Section 8-313(1).

(2) A security interest so transferred pursuant to agreement by a transferor who has rights in the security to a transferee who has given value is a perfected security interest, but a security interest that has been transferred solely under paragraph (i) of Section 8-313(1) becomes unperfected after 21 days unless, within that time, the requirements for transfer under any other provision of Section 8-313(1) are satisfied.

(3) A security interest in a security is subject to the provisions of Article 9, but:

(a) no filing is required to perfect the security interest; and
(b) no written security agreement signed by the debtor is necessary to make the security interest enforceable, except as otherwise provided in paragraph (h), (i), or (j) of Section 8-313(1).

The secured party has the rights and duties provided under Section 9-207, to the extent they are applicable, whether or not the security is certificated, and, if certificated, whether or not it is in his possession.

(4) Unless otherwise agreed, a security interest in a security is terminated by transfer to the debtor or a person designated by him pursuant to a provision of Section 8-313(1). If a security is thus transferred, the security interest, if not terminated, becomes unperfected unless the security is certificated and is delivered to the debtor for the purpose of ultimate sale or exchange or presentation, collection, renewal, or registration of transfer. In that case, the security interest becomes unperfected after 21 days unless, within that time, the security (or securities for which it has been exchanged) is transferred to the secured party or a person designated by him pursuant to a provision of Section 8-313(1).

Part 4: Registration

§8-401. Duty of Issuer to Register Transfer, Pledge, or Release.

(1) If a certificated security in registered form is presented to the issuer with a request to register transfer or an instruction is presented to the issuer with a request to register transfer, pledge, or release, the issuer shall register the transfer, pledge, or release as requested if:

(a) the security is indorsed or the instruction was originated by the appropriate person or persons (Section 8-308);
(b) reasonable assurance is given that those indorsements or instructions are genuine and effective (Section 8-402);
(c) the issuer has no duty as to adverse claims or has discharged the duty (Section 8-403);
(d) any applicable law relating to the collection of taxes has been complied with; and
(e) the transfer, pledge, or release is in fact rightful or is to a bona fide purchaser.

(2) If an issuer is under a duty to register a transfer, pledge, or release of a security, the issuer is also liable to the person presenting a certificated security or an instruction for registration or his principal for loss resulting from any unreasonable delay in registration or from failure or refusal to register the transfer, pledge, or release.

§8-402. Assurance that Indorsements and Instructions Are Effective.

(1) The issuer may require the following assurance that each necessary indorsement of a certificated security or each instruction (Section 8-308) is genuine and effective:

(a) in all cases, a guarantee of the signature (Section 8-312(1) or (2)) of the person indorsing a certificated security or originating an instruction including, in the case of an instruction, a warranty of the taxpayer identification number or, in the absence thereof, other reasonable assurance of identity:
(b) if the indorsement is made or the instruction is originated by an agent, appropriate assurance of authority to sign;
(c) if the indorsement is made or the instruction is originated by a fiduciary, appropriate evidence of appointment or incumbency;
(d) if there is more than one fiduciary, reasonable assurance that all who are required to sign have done so; and
(e) if the indorsement is made or the instruction is originated by a person not covered by any of the foregoing, assurance appropriate to the case corresponding as nearly as may be to the foregoing.

(2) A "guarantee of the signature" in subsection (1) means a guarantee signed by or on behalf of a person reasonably believed by the issuer to be responsible. The issuer may adopt standards with respect to responsibility if they are not manifestly unreasonable.

(3) "Appropriate evidence of appointment or incumbency" in subsection (1) means:
(a) in the case of a fiduciary appointed or qualified by a court, a certificate issued by or under the direction or supervision of that court or an officer thereof and dated within 60 days before the date of presentation for transfer, pledge, or release; or
(b) in any other case, a copy of a document showing the appointment or a certificate issued by or on behalf of a person reasonably believed by the issuer to be responsible or, in the absence of that document or certificate, other evidence reasonably deemed by the issuer to be appropriate. The issuer may adopt standards with respect to the evidence if they are not manifestly unreasonable. The issuer is not charged with notice of the contents of any document obtained pursuant to this paragraph (b) except to the extent that the contents relate directly to the appointment or incumbency.

(4) The issuer may elect to require reasonable assurance beyond that specified in this section, but if it does so and, for a purpose other than that specified in subsection (3)(b), both requires and obtains a copy of a will, trust, indenture, articles of co-partnership, by-laws, or other controlling instrument, it is charged with notice of all matters contained therein affecting the transfer, pledge, or release.

§8-403. Issuer's Duty as to Adverse Claims.

(1) An issuer to whom a certificated security is presented for registration shall inquire into adverse claims if:
(a) a written notification of an adverse claim is received at a time and in a manner affording the issuer a reasonable opportunity to act on it prior to the issuance of a new, reissued, or re-registered certificated security, and the notification identifies the claimant, the registered owner, and the issue of which the security is a part, and provides an address for communications directed to the claimant; or
(b) the issuer is charged with notice of an adverse claim from a controlling instrument it has elected to require under Section 8-402(4).

(2) The issuer may discharge any duty of inquiry by any reasonable means, including notifying an adverse claimant by registered or certified mail at the address furnished by him or, if there be no such address, at his residence or regular place of business that the certificated security has been presented for registration of transfer by a named person, and that the transfer will be registered unless within 30 days from the date of mailing the notification, either:
(a) an appropriate restraining order, injunction, or other process issues from a court of competent jurisdiction; or
(b) there is filed with the issuer an indemnity bond, sufficient in the issuer's judgment to protect the issuer and any transfer agent, registrar, or other agent of the issuer involved from any loss it or they may suffer by complying with the adverse claim.

(3) Unless an issuer is charged with notice of an adverse claim from a controlling instrument which it has elected to require under Section 8-402(4) or receives notification of an adverse claim under subsection (1), if a certificated security presented for registration is indorsed by the appropriate person or persons the issuer is under no duty to inquire into adverse claims. In particular:
(a) an issuer registering a certificated security in the name of a person who is a fiduciary or who is described as a fiduciary is not bound to inquire into the existence, extent, or correct description of the fiduciary relationship; and thereafter the issuer may assume without inquiry that the newly registered owner continues to be the fiduciary until the issuer receives written notice that the fiduciary is no longer acting as such with respect to the particular security;
(b) an issuer registering transfer on an indorsement by a fiduciary is not bound to inquire whether the transfer is made in compliance with a controlling instrument or with the law of the state having jurisdiction of the fiduciary relationship, including any law requiring the fiduciary to obtain court approval of the transfer; and
(c) the issuer is not charged with notice of the contents of any court record or file or other recorded or unrecorded document even though the document is in its possession and even though the transfer is made on the indorsement of a fiduciary himself or to his nominee.

(4) An issuer is under not duty as to adverse claims with respect to an uncertificated security except:
(a) claims embodied in a restraining order, injunction, or other legal process served upon the issuer if the process was served at a time and in a manner affording the issuer a reasonable opportunity to act on it in accordance with the requirements of subsection (5);
(b) claims of which the issuer has received a written notification from the registered owner or the registered pledgee if the notification was received at a time and in a manner affording the issuer a reasonable opportunity to act on it in accordance with the requirements of subsection (5);
(c) claims (including restrictions on transfer not imposed by the issuer) to which the registration of transfer to the present registered owner was subject and were so noted in the initial transaction statement sent to him; and
(d) claims as to which an issuer is charged with notice from a controlling instrument it has elected to require under Section 8-402(4).

(5) If the issuer of an uncertificated security is under a duty as to an adverse claim, he discharges that duty by:

(a) including a notation of the claim in any statements sent with respect to the security under Sections 8-408(3), (6), and (7); and
(b) refusing to register the transfer or pledge of the security unless the nature of the claim does not preclude transfer or pledge subject thereto.

(6) If the transfer or pledge of the security is registered subject to an adverse claim, a notation of the claim must be included in the initial transaction statement and all subsequent statements sent to the transferee and pledgee under Section 8-408.

(7) Notwithstanding subsections (4) and (5), if an uncertificated security was subject to a registered pledge at the time the issuer first came under a duty as to a particular adverse claim, the issuer has no duty as to that claim if transfer of the security is requested by the registered pledgee or an appropriate person acting for the registered pledgee unless:

(a) the claim was embodied in legal process which expressly provides otherwise;
(b) the claim was asserted in a written notification from the registered pledgee;
(c) the claim was one as to which the issuer was charged with notice from a controlling instrument it required under Section 8-402(4) in connection with the pledgee's request for transfer; or
(d) the transfer requested is to the registered owner.

§8-404. Liability and Non-Liability for Registration.

(1) Except as provided in any law relating to the collection of taxes, the issuer is not liable to the owner, pledgee, or any other person suffering loss as a result of the registration of a transfer, pledge, or release of a security if:

(a) there were on or with a certificated security the necessary indorsements or the issuer had received an instruction originated by an appropriate person (Section 8-308); and
(b) the issuer had no duty as to adverse claims or has discharged the duty (Section 8-403).

(2) If an issuer has registered a transfer of a certificated security to a person not entitled to it, the issuer on demand shall deliver a like security to the true owner unless:

(a) the registration was pursuant to subsection (1);
(b) the owner is precluded from asserting any claim for registering the transfer under Section 8-405(1); or
(c) the delivery would result in overissue, in which case the issuer's liability is governed by Section 8-104.

(3) If an issuer has improperly registered a transfer, pledge, or release of an uncertificated security, the issuer on demand from the injured party shall restore the records as to the injured party to the condition that would have obtained if the improper registration had not been made unless:

(a) the registration was pursuant to subsection (1); or
(b) the registration would result in overissue, in which case the issuer's liability is governed by Section 8-104.

§8-405. Lost, Destroyed, and Stolen Certificated Securities.

(1) If a certificated security has been lost, apparently destroyed, or wrongfully taken, and the owner fails to notify the issuer of that fact within a reasonable time after he has notice of it and the issuer registers a transfer of the security before receiving notification, the owner is precluded from asserting against the issuer any claim for registering the transfer under Section 8-404 or any claim to a new security under this section.

(2) If the owner of a certificated security claims that the security has been lost, destroyed, or wrongfully taken, the issuer shall issue a new certificated security or, at the option of the issuer, an equivalent uncertificated security in place of the original security if the owner:

(a) so requests before the issuer has notice that the security has been acquired by a bona fide purchaser;
(b) files with the issuer a sufficient indemnity bond; and
(c) satisfies any other reasonable requirements imposed by the issuer.

(3) If, after the issue of a new certificated or uncertificated security, a bona fide purchaser of the original certificated security presents it for registration of transfer, the issuer shall register the transfer unless registration would result in overissue, in which event the issuer's liability is governed by Section 8-104. In addition to any rights on the indemnity bond, the issuer may recover the new certificated security from the person to whom it was issued or any person taking under him except a bona fide purchaser or may cancel the uncertificated security unless a bona fide purchaser or any person taking under a bona fide purchaser is then the registered owner or registered pledgee thereof.

§8-406. Duty of Authenticating Trustee, Transfer Agent, or Registrar.

(1) If a person acts as authenticating trustee, transfer agent, registrar, or other agent for an issuer in the registration of transfers of its certificated securities or in the registration of transfers, pledges, and releases of its uncertificated securities, in the issue of new securities, or in the cancellation of surrendered securities:

(a) he is under a duty to the issuer to exercise good faith and due diligence in performing his functions; and
(b) with regard to the particular functions he performs, he has the same obligation to the holder or owner of a certificated security or to the owner or pledgee of an uncertificated security and has the same rights and privileges as the issuer has in regard to those functions.

(2) Notice to an authenticating trustee, transfer agent, registrar or other agent is notice to the issuer with respect to the functions performed by the agent.

§8-407. Exchangeability of Securities.

(1) No issuer is subject to the requirements of this section unless it regularly maintains a system for issuing the class of securities involved under which both certificated and uncertificated securities are regularly issued to the category of owners, which includes the person in whose name the new security is to be registered.

(2) Upon surrender of a certificated security with all necessary indorsements and presentation of a written request by the person surrendering the security, the issuer, if he has no duty as to adverse claims or has discharged the duty (Section 8-403), shall issue to the person or a person designated by him an equivalent uncertificated security subject to all liens, restrictions, and claims that were noted on the certificated security.

(3) Upon receipt of a transfer instruction originated by an appropriate person who so requests, the issuer of an uncertificated security shall cancel the uncertificated security and issue an equivalent certificated security on which must be noted conspicuously any liens and restrictions of the issuer and any adverse claims (as to which the issuer has a duty under Section 8-403(4))

to which the uncertificated security was subject. The certificated security shall be registered in the name of and delivered to:

(a) the registered owner, if the uncertificated security was not subject to a registered pledge; or
(b) the registered pledgee, if the uncertificated security was subject to a registered pledge.

§8-408. Statements of Uncertificated Securities.

(1) Within 2 business days after the transfer of an uncertificated security has been registered, the issuer shall send to the new registered owner and, if the security has been transferred subject to a registered pledge, to the registered pledgee a written statement containing:

(a) a description of the issue of which the uncertificated security is a part;
(b) the number of shares or units transferred;
(c) the name and address and any taxpayer identification number of the new registered owner and, if the security has been transferred subject to a registered pledge, the name and address and any taxpayer identification number of the registered pledgee;
(d) a notation of any liens and restrictions of the issuer and any adverse claims (as to which the issuer has a duty under Section 8-403(4)) to which the uncertificated security is or may be subject at the time of registration or a statement that there are none of those liens, restrictions, or adverse claims; and
(e) the date the transfer was registered.

(2) Within 2 business days after the pledge of an uncertificated security has been registered, the issuer shall send to the registered owner and the registered pledgee a written statement containing:

(a) a description of the issue of which the uncertificated security is a part;
(b) the number of shares or units pledged;
(c) the name and address and any taxpayer identification number of the registered owner and the registered pledgee;
(d) a notation of any liens and restrictions of the issuer and any adverse claims (as to which the issuer has a duty under Section 8-403(4)) to which the uncertificated security is or may be subject at the time of registration or a statement that there are none of those liens, restrictions or adverse claims; and
(e) the date the pledge was registered.

(3) Within 2 business days after the release from pledge of an uncertificated security has been registered, the issuer shall send to the registered owner and the pledgee whose interest was released a written statement containing:

(a) a description of the issue of which the uncertificated security is a part;
(b) the number of shares or units released from pledge;
(c) the name and address and any taxpayer identification number of the registered owner and the pledgee whose interest was released;
(d) a notation of of any liens and restrictions of the issuer and any adverse claims (as to which the issuer has a duty under Section 8-403(4)) to which the uncertificated security is or may be subject at the time of registration or a statement that there are none of those liens, restrictions or adverse claims; and
(e) the date the release was registered.

(4) An "initial transaction statement" is the statement sent to:

(a) the new registered owner and, if applicable, to the registered pledgee pursuant to subsection (1);
(b) the registered pledgee pursuant to subsection (2); or
(c) the registered owner pursuant to subsection (3).

Each initial transaction statement shall be signed by or on behalf of the issuer and must be identified as "Initial Transaction Statement."

(5) Within 2 business days after the transfer of an uncertificated security has been registered, the issuer shall send to the former registered owner and the former registered pledgee, if any, a written statement containing:

(a) a description of the issue of which the uncertificated security is a part;
(b) the number of shares or units transferred.
(c) the name and address and any taxpayer identification number of the former registered owner and of any former registered pledgee; and
(d) the date the transfer was registered.

(6) At periodic intervals no less frequent than annually and at any time upon the reasonable written request of the registered owner, the issuer shall send to the registered owner of each uncertificated security a dated written statement containing:

(a) a description of the issue of which the uncertificated security is a part;
(b) the name and address and any taxpayer identification number of the registered owner.
(c) the number of shares or units of the uncertificated security registered in the name of the registered owner on the date of the statement;
(d) the name and address and any taxpayer identification number of any registered pledge and the number of shares or units subject to the pledge; and
(e) a notation of any liens and restrictions of the issuer and any adverse claims (as to which the issuer has a duty under Section 8-403(4)) to which the uncertificated security is or may be subject or a statement that these are none of those liens, restrictions, or adverse claims.

(7) At periodic intervals no less frequent than annually and at any time upon the reasonable written request of the registered pledgee, the issuer shall send to the registered pledgee of each uncertificated security a dated written statement containing;

(a) a description of the issue of which the uncertificated security is a part;
(b) the name and address and any taxpayer identification number of the registered owner;
(c) the name and address and any taxpayer identification number of the registered pledgee;
(d) the number of shares or units subject to the pledge; and
(e) a notation of any liens and restrictions of the issuer and any adverse claims (as to which the issuer has a duty under Section 8-403(4)) to which the uncertificated security is or may be subject or a statement that there are none of these liens, restrictions, or adverse claims.

(8) If the issuer sends the statements described in subsections (6) and (7) at periodic intervals no less frequent than quarterly, the issuer is not obliged to send additional statements upon request unless the owner or pledgee requesting them pays to the issuer the reasonable cost of furnishing them.

(9) Each statement sent pursuant to this section must bear a conspicuous legend reading substantially as follows: "This statement is merely a record of the rights of the addressee as of the time of its issuance. Delivery of this statement, of itself, confers no rights on the recipient. This statement is neither a negotiable instrument nor a security."

ARTICLE 9: SECURED TRANSACTIONS, SALES OF ACCOUNTS AND CHATTEL PAPER

Part 1: Short Title, Applicability and Definitions

§9-101. Short Title This Article shall be known and may be cited as Uniform Commercial Code —Secured Transactions.

§9-102. Policy and Subject Matter of Article.

(1) Except as otherwise provided in Section 9-104 on excluded transactions, this Article applies:

(a) to any transaction (regardless of its form) which is intended to create a security interest in personal property or fixtures including goods, documents, instruments, general intangibles, chattel paper or accounts, and also

(b) to any sale of accounts or chattel paper.

(2) This Article applies to security interests created by contract including pledge, assignment, chattel mortgage, chattel trust, trust deed, factor's lien, equipment trust, conditional sale, trust receipt, other lien or title retention contract and lease or consignment intended as security. This Article does not apply to statutory liens except as provided in Section 9-310.

(3) The application of this Article to a security interest in a secured obligation is not affected by the fact that the obligation is itself secured by a transaction or interest to which this Article does not apply.

Note: *The adoption of this Article should be accompanied by the repeal of existing statues dealing with conditional sales, trust receipts, factor's liens where the factor is given a non-possessory lien, chattel mortgages, crop mortgages, mortgages on railroad equipment, assignment of accounts and generally statues regulating security interests in personal property.*

Where the state has a retail installment selling act or small loan act, that legislation should be carefully examined to determine what changes in those acts are needed to conform them to this Article. This Article primarily sets out rules defining rights of a secured party against persons dealing with the debtor; it does not prescribe regulations and controls which may be necessary to curb abuses arising in the small loan business or in the financing of consumer purchases on credit. Accordingly there is no intention to repeal existing regulatory acts in those fields by enactment or re-enactment of Article 9. See Section 9-203(4) and the Note thereto.

§9-103. Perfection of Security Interests in Multiple State Transactions.

(1) Documents, instruments and ordinary goods.

(a) This subsection applies to documents and instruments and to goods other than those covered by a certificate of title described in subsection (2), mobile goods described in subsection (3), and minerals described in subsection (5).

(b) Except as otherwise provided in this subsection, perfection and the effect of perfection or non-perfection of a security interest in collateral are governed by the law of the jurisdiction where the collateral is when the last event occurs on which is based the assertion that the security interest is perfected or unperfected.

(c) If the parties to a transaction creating a purchase money security interest in goods in one jurisdiction understand at the time that the security interest attaches that the goods will be kept in another jurisdiction, then the law of the other jurisdiction governs the perfection and the effect of perfection or non-perfection of the security interest from the time it attaches until thirty days after the debtor receives possession of the goods and thereafter if the goods are taken to the other jurisdiction before the end of the thirty-day period.

(d) When collateral is brought into and kept in this state while subject to a security interest perfected under the law of the jurisdiction from which the collateral was removed, the security interest remains perfected, but if action is required by Part 3 of this Article to perfect the security interest.

(i) if the action is not taken before the expiration of the period of perfection in the other jurisdiction or the end of four months after the collateral is brought into this state, whichever period first expires, the security interest becomes unperfected at the end of that period and is thereafter deemed to have been unperfected as against a person who became a purchaser after removal.

(ii) if the action is taken before the expiration of the period specified in subparagraph (i), the security interest continues perfected thereafter;

(iii) for the purpose of priority over a buyer of consumer goods (subsection (2) of Section 9-307), the period of the effectiveness of a filing in the jurisdiction from which the collateral is removed is governed by the rules with respect to perfection in subparagraphs (i) and (ii).

(2) Certificate of title.

(a) This subsection applies to goods covered by a certificate of title issued under a statute of this state or of another jurisdiction under the law of which indication of a security interest on the certificate is required as a condition of perfection.

(b) Except as otherwise provided in this subsection, perfection and the effect of perfection or non-perfection of the security interest are governed by the law (including the conflict of laws rules) of the jurisdiction issuing the certificate until four months after the goods are removed from that jurisdiction and thereafter until the goods are registered in another jurisdiction, but in any event not beyond surrender of the certificate. After the expiration of that period, the goods are not covered by the certificate of title within the meaning of this section.

(c) Except with respect to the rights of a buyer described in the next paragraph, a security interest, perfected in another jurisdiction otherwise than by notation on a certificate of title, in goods brought into this state and thereafter covered by a certificate of title issued by this state is subject to the rules stated in paragraph (d) of subsection (1).

(d) If goods are brought into this state while a security interest therein is perfected in any manner under the law of the jurisdiction from which the goods are removed and a certificate of title is issued by this state and the certificate does not show that the goods are subject to the security interest or that they may be subject to security interests not shown on the certificate, the security interest is subordinate to the rights of a buyer of the goods who is not in the business of selling goods of that kind to the extent that he gives value and receives delivery of the goods after issuance of the certificate and without knowledge of the security interest.

(3) Accounts, general intangibles and mobile goods.

(a) The subsection applies to accounts (other than an account described in subsection (5) on minerals) and general intangibles and to goods which are mobile and which are of a type normally used in more than one jurisdiction, such as motor vehicles, trailers, rolling stock, airplanes, shipping containers, road building and construction machinery and commercial harvesting machinery and the like, if the goods are equipment or inventory leased or held for lease by the debtor to others, and are not covered by a certificate of title described in subsection (2).

(b) The law (including the conflict of laws rules) of the jurisdiction in which the debtor is located governs the perfection and the effect of perfection or non-perfection of the security interest.

(c) If, however, the debtor is located in a jurisdiction which is not a part of the United States, and which does not provide for perfection of the security interest by filing or recording in that jurisdiction, the law of the jurisdiction in the United States in which the debtor has its major executive office in the United States governs the perfection and the effect of perfection or non-perfection of the security interest through filing. In the alternative, if the debtor is located in a jurisdiction which is not a part of the United States or Canada and the collateral is accounts or general intangibles for money due or to become due, the security interest may be perfected by notification to the account debtor. As used in this paragraph, "United States" includes its territories and possessions and the Commonwealth of Puerto Rico.

(d) A debtor shall be deemed located at his place of business if he has one, at his chief executive office if he has more than one place of business, otherwise at his residence. If, however, the debtor is a foreign air carrier under the Federal Aviation Act of 1958, as amended, it shall be deemed located at the designated office of the agent upon whom service of process may be made on behalf of the foreign air carrier.

(e) A security interest perfected under the law of the jurisdiction of the location of the debtor is perfected until the expiration of four months after a change of the debtor's location to another jurisdiction, or until perfection would have ceased by the law of the first jurisdiction, whichever period first expires. Unless perfected in the new jurisdiction before the end of that period, it becomes unperfected thereafter and is deemed to have been unperfected as against a person who became a purchaser after the change.

(4) Chattel paper.
The rules stated for goods in subsection (1) apply to a possessory security interest in chattel paper. The rules stated for accounts in subsection (3) apply to a non-possessory security interest in chattel paper, but the security interest may not b perfected by notification to the account debtor.

(5) Minerals.
Perfection and the effect of perfection or non-perfection of a security interest which is created by a debtor who has an interest in minerals or the like (including oil and gas) before extraction and which attaches thereto as extracted, or which attaches to an account resulting from the sale thereof at the wellhead or minehead are governed by the law (including the conflict of laws rules) of the jurisdiction wherein the wellhead or minehead is located.

§9-103. Perfection of Security Interests in Multiple State Transactions (1977 Amendments).
* * *
(3) Accounts, general intangibles and mobile goods.

(a) This subsection applies to accounts (other than an account described in subsection (5) on minerals) and general intangibles (other than uncertificated securities) and to goods.
* * *
(6) Uncertificated securities.
The law (including the conflict of laws rules) of the jurisdiction of organization of the issuer governs the perfection and the effect of perfection or non-perfection of a security interest in uncertificated securities.

§9-104. Transactions Excluded From Article. This Article does not apply

(a) To a security interest subject to any statute of the United States to the extent that such statute governs the rights of parties to and third parties affected by transactions in particular types of property; or
(b) to a landlord's lien; or
(c) to a lien given by statute or other rule of law for services or materials except as provided in Section 9-310 on priority of such liens; or
(d) to a transfer of a claim for wages, salary or other compensation of an employee; or
(e) to a transfer by a government or governmental subdivision or agency; or
(f) to a sale of accounts, or chattel paper as part of a sale of the business out of which they arose, or an assignment of accounts or chattel paper which is for the purpose of collection only, or a transfer of a right to payment under a contract to an assignee who is also to do the performance under the contract or a transfer of a single account to an assignee in whole or partial satisfaction of a preexisting indebtedness; or
(g) to a transfer of an interest in or claim in or under any policy of insurance, except as provided with respect to proceeds (Section 9-306) and priorities in proceeds (Section 9-312); or
(h) to a right represented by a judgment (other than a judgment taken on a right to payment which was collateral); or
(i) to any right of set-off; or
(j) except to the extent that provision is made for fixtures in Section 9-313, to the creation or transfer of an interest in or lien on real estate, including a lease or rents thereunder; or
(k) to a transfer in whole or in part of any claim arising out of tort; or
(l) to a transfer of an interest in any deposit account (subsection (1) of Section 9-105), except as provided with respect to proceeds (Section 9-306) and priorities in proceeds (Section 9-312).

§9-105. Definitions and Index of Definitions.
(1) In this Article unless the context otherwise requires:

(a) "Account debtor" means the person who is obligated on an account, chattel paper or general intangible;
(b) "Chattel paper" means a writing or writings which evidence both a monetary obligation and a security interest in or a lease of specific goods, but a charter or other contract involving the use or hire of a vessel is not chattel paper. When a transaction is evidenced both by such a security agreement or a lease and by an instrument or a series of instruments, the group of writings taken together constitutes chattel paper;

(c) "Collateral" means the property subject to a security interest, and includes accounts and chattel paper which have been sold;

(d) "Debtor" means the person who owes payment or other performance of the obligation secured, whether or not he owns or has rights in the collateral, and includes the seller of accounts or chattel paper. Where the debtor and the owner of the collateral are not the same person, the term "debtor" means the owner of the collateral in any provision of the Article dealing with the collateral, the obligor in any provision dealing with the obligation, and may include both where the context so requires;

(e) "Deposit account" means a demand, time savings, passbook or like account maintained with a bank, savings and loan association, credit union or like organization, other than an account evidenced by a certificate of deposit;

(f) "Document" means document of title as defined in the general definitions of Article 1 (Section 1-201), and a receipt of the kind described in subsection (2) of Section 7-201);

(g) "Encumbrance" includes real estate mortgages and other liens on real estate and all other rights in real estate that are not ownership interests.

(h) "Goods" includes all things which are movable at the time the security interest attaches or which are fixtures (section 9-313), but does not include money, documents, instruments, accounts, chattel paper, general intangibles, or minerals or the like (including oil and gas) before extraction. "Goods" also includes standing timber which is to be cut and removed under a conveyance or contract for sale, the unborn young of animals, and growing crops.

(i) "Instrument" means a negotiable instrument (defined in Section 3-104), or a security (defined in Section 8-102) or any other writing which evidences a right to the payment of money and is not itself a security agreement or lease and is of a type which is in ordinary course of business transferred by delivery with any necessary indorsement or assignment;

(j) "Mortgage" means a consensual interest created by a real estate mortgage, a trust deed on real estate, or the like;

(k) An advance is made "pursuant to commitment" if the secured party has bound himself to make it, whether or not a subsequent event of default or other event not within his control has relieved or may relieve him from his obligation.

(l) "Security agreement" means an agreement which creates or provides for a security interest;

(m) "Secured party" means a lender, seller or other person in whose favor there is a security interest, including a person to whom accounts or chattel paper have been sold. When the holders of obligations issued under an indenture of trust, equipment trust agreement or the like are represented by a trustee or other person, the representative is the secured party;

(n) "Transmitting utility" means any person primarily engaged in the railroad, street railway or trolley bus business, the electric or electronics communications transmission business, the transmission of goods by pipeline, or the transmission or the production and transmission of electricity, steam, gas or water, or the provision of sewer service.

(2) Other definitions applying to this Article and the sections in which they appear are;

"Account"	Section 9-106
"Attach"	Section 9-203
"Construction mortgage"	Section 9-313 *1)
"Consumer goods"	Section 9-109 (1)
"Equipment"	Section 9-109 (2)
"Farm products"	Section 9-109 (3)
"Fixture"	Section 9-313
"Fixture filing"	Section 9-313
"General intangibles"	Section 9-106
"Inventory"	Section 9-109 (4)
"Lien creditor"	Section 9-301 (3)
"Proceeds"	Section 9-306 (1)
"Purchase money security interest"	Section 9-107
"United States"	Section 9-103

(3) The following definitions in other articles apply to this Article:

"Check"	Section 3-104
"Contract for sale"	Section 2-106
"Holder in due course"	Section 3-302
"Note"	Section 3-104
"Sale"	Section 2-106

(4) In addition Article 1 contains general definitions and principles of construction and interpretation throughout this Article.

§9-105. Definitions and Index of Definitions *(1977 Amendments).*

(1) In this Article unless the context otherwise requires:

* * *

(i) "Instrument" means a negotiable instrument (defined in Section 3-104), or a certificated security (defined in Section 8-102) or . . .

* * *

§9-106. Definitions: "Account"; "General Intangibles". "Account" means any right to payment for goods sold or leased or for services rendered which is not evidenced by an instrument or chattel paper, whether or not it has been earned by performance. "General intangibles" means any personal property (including things in action) other than goods, accounts, chattel paper, documents, instruments, and money. All rights to payment earned or unearned under a charter or other contract involving the use or hire of a vessel and all rights incident to the charter or contract are accounts.

§9-107. Definitions: "Purchase Money Security Interest". A security interest is a "purchase money security interest" to the extent that it is

(a) taken or retained by the seller of the collateral to secure all or part of its price; or

(b) taken by a person who by making advances or incurring an obligation gives value to enable the debtor to acquire rights in or the use of collateral if such value is in fact so used.

§9-108. When After-Acquired Collateral Not Security for Antecedent Debt. Where a secured party makes an advance, incurs an obligation, releases a perfected security interest, or otherwise gives new value which is to be secured in whole or in part by after-acquired property his security interest in the after-acquired collateral shall be deemed to be taken for new value and not as security for an antecedent debt if the debtor acquires his rights in such collateral either in the ordinary course of his business or under a contract of purchase made pursuant to the security agreement within a reasonable time after new value is given.

§9-109. Classification of Goods; "Consumer Goods"; "Equipment"; "Farm Products"; "Inventory". Goods are

(1) "consumer goods" if they are used or bought for use primarily for personal, family or household purposes;

(2) "equipment" if they are used or bought for use primarily in business (including farming or a profession) or by a debtor who is a non-profit organization or a governmental subdivision or agency or if the goods are not included in the definitions of inventory, farm products or consumer goods;

(3) "farm products" if they are crops or livestock or supplies used or produced in farming operations or if they are products of crops or livestock in their unmanufactured states (such as ginned cotton, wool-clip, maple syrup, milk and eggs), and if they are in the possession of a debtor engaged in raising, fattening, grazing or other farming operations. If goods are farm products they are neither equipment nor inventory;

(4) "inventory" if they are held by a person who holds them for sale or lease or to be furnished under contracts of service or if he has so furnished them, or if they are raw materials, work in process or materials used or consumed in a business. Inventory of a person is not to be classified as his equipment.

§9-110. Sufficiency of Description. For the purposes of this Article any description of personal property or real estate is sufficient whether or not it is specific if it reasonably identifies what is described.

§9-111. Applicability of Bulk Transfer Laws. The creation of a security interest is not a bulk transfer under Article 6 (see Section 6-103).

§9-112. Where Collateral Is Not Owned by Debtor. Unless otherwise agreed, when a secured party knows that collateral is owned by a person who is not the debtor, the owner of the collateral is entitled to receive from the secured party any surplus under Section 9-502 (2) or under Section 9-504 (1), and is not liable for the debt or for any deficiency after resale, and he has the same right as the debtor

(a) to receive statements under Section 9-208;
(b) to receive notice of and to object to a secured party's proposal to retain the collateral in satisfaction of the indebtedness under Section 9-505;
(c) to redeem the collateral under Section 9-506;
(d) to obtain injunctive or other relief under Section 9-507 (1); and
(e) to recover losses caused to him under Section 9-208 (2).

§9-113. Security Interests Arising Under Article on Sales. A security interest arising solely under the Article on Sales (Article 2) is subject to the provisions of this Article except that to the extent that and so long as the debtor does not have or does not lawfully obtain possession of the goods

(a) no security agreement is necessary to make the security interest enforceable; and
(b) no filing is required to perfect the security interest; and
(c) the rights of the secured party on default by the debtor are governed by the Article on Sales (Article 2).

§9-114. Consignment.

(1) A person who delivers goods under a consignment which is not a security interest and who would be required to file under this Article by paragraph (3) (c) of Section 2-326 has priority over a secured party who is or becomes a creditor of the consignee and who would have a perfected security interest in the goods if they were the property of the consignee, and also has priority with respect to identifiable cash proceeds received on or before delivery of the goods to a buyer, if

(a) the consignor complies with the filing provision of the Article on Sales with respect to consignments (paragraph (3) (c) of Section 2-326) before the consignee receives possession of the goods; and
(b) the consignor gives notification in writing to the holder of the security interest if the holder has filed a financing statement covering the same types of goods before the date of the filing made by the consignor; and
(c) the holder of the security interest receives the notification within five years before the consignee receives possession of the goods; and
(d) the notification states that the consignor expects to deliver goods on consignment to the consignee, describing the goods by item or type.

(2) In the case of a consignment which is not a security interest and in which the requirements of the preceding subsection have not been met, a person who delivers goods to another is subordinate to a person who would have a perfected security interest in the goods if they were the property of the debtor.

Part 2: Validity of Security Agreement and Rights of Parties Thereto

§9-201. General Validity of Security Agreement. Except as otherwise provided by this Act a security agreement is effective according to its terms between the parties, against purchasers of the collateral and against creditors. Nothing in this Article validates any charge or practice illegal under any statute or regulation thereunder governing usury, small loans, retail installment sales, or the like, or extends the application of any such statute or regulation to any transaction not otherwise subject thereto.

§9-202. Title to Collateral Immaterial. Each provision of this Article with regard to rights, obligations and remedies applies whether title to collateral is in the secured party or in the debtor.

§9-203. Attachment and Enforceability of Security Interest; Proceeds; Formal Requisites.

(1) Subject to the provisions of Section 4-208 on the security interest of a collecting bank and Section 9-113 on a security interest arising under the Article on Sales, a security interest is not enforceable against the debtor or third parties with respect to the collateral and does not attach unless

(a) the collateral is in the possession of the secured party pursuant to agreement, or the debtor has signed a security agreement which contains a description of the collateral and in addition, when the security interest covers crops growing or to be grown or timber to be cut, a description of the land concerned; and
(b) value has been given; and
(c) the debtor has rights in the collateral.

(2) A security interest attaches when it becomes enforceable against the debtor with respect to the collateral. Attachment occurs as soon as all of the event specified in subsection (1) have taken place unless explicit agreement postpones the time of attaching.

(3) Unless otherwise agreed a security agreement gives the secured party the rights to proceeds provided by Section 9-306.

(4) A transaction, although subject to this Article, is also subject to . . . . *, and in the case of conflict between the provisions of this Article and any such statute, the provisions of such statute control. Failure to comply with any applicable statue has only the effect which is specified therein.

Note: *At* * *in subsection (4) insert reference to any local statute regulating small loans, retail installment sales and the like.*

The foregoing subsection (4) is designed to make it clear that certain transactions, although subject to this Article, must also comply with other applicable legislation.

This Article is designed to regulate all the "security" aspects of transactions within its scope. There is, however, much regulatory legislation, particularly in the consumer field, which supplements this Article and should not be repealed by its enactment. Examples are small loan acts, retail installment selling acts and the like. Such acts may provide for licensing and rate regulation and may prescribe particular forms of contract. Such provisions should remain in force despite the enactment of this Article. On the other hand if a retail installent selling act contains provisions on filing, rights on default, etc., such provisions should be repealed as inconsistent with this Article except that inconsistent provisions as to deficiencies, penalities, etc., in the Uniform Consumer Credit Code and other recent related legislation should remain because those statutes were drafted after the substantial enactment of the Article and with the intention of modifying certain provisions of this Article as to consumer credit.

§9-203. Attachment and Enforceability of Security Interest; Proceeds; Formal Requisites *(1977 Amendments)*.

(1) Subject to the provisions of Section 4-208 on the security interest of a collecting bank, Section 8-321 on security interests in securities and Section 9-113 on a security interest arising under the Article on Sales, a security interest in not enforceable against the debtor or third parties with respect to the collateral and does not attach unless:

(a) the collateral is in the possession of the secured party pursuant to agreement, or the debtor has signed a security agreement which contains a description of the collateral and in addition, when the security interest covers crops growing or to be grown or timber to be cut, a description of the land concerned;

(b) value has been given; and

(c) the debtor has rights in the collateral.

§9-204. After-Acquired Property; Future Advances.

(1) Except as provided in subsection (2), a security agreement may provide that any or all obligations covered by the security agreement are to be secured by after-acquired collateral.

(2) No security interest attaches under an after-acquired property clause to consumer goods other than accessions (Section 9-314) when given as additional security unless the debtor acquires rights in them within ten days after the secured party gives value.

(3) Obligations covered by a security agreement may include future advances or other value whether or not the advances or value are given pursuant to commitment (subsection (1) of Section 9-105).

§9-205. Use or Disposition of Collateral Without Accounting Permissible.

A security interest is not invalid or fraudulent against creditors by reason of liberty in the debtor to use, commingle or dispose of all or part of the collateral (including returned or repossessed goods) or to collect or compromise accounts or chattel paper, or to accept the return of goods or make repossessions, or to use, commingle or dispose of proceeds, or by reason of the failure of the secured party to require the debtor to account for proceeds or replace collateral. This section does not relax the requirements of possession where perfection of a security interest depends upon possession of the collateral by the secured party or by a bailee.

§9-206. Agreement Not to Assert Defenses Against Assignee; Modification of Sales Warranties Where Security Agreement Exists.

(1) Subject to any statute or decision which establishes a different rule for buyers or lessees of consumer goods, an agreement any claim or defense which he may have against the seller or lessor is enforceable by an assignee who takes his assignment for value, in good faith and without notice of a claim or defense, except as to defenses of a type which may be asserted against a holder in due course of a negotiable instrument under the Article on Commercial Paper (Article 3). A buyer who as part of one transaction signs both a negotiable instrument and a security agreement makes such an agreement.

(2) When a seller retains a purchase money security interest in goods the Article on Sales (Article 2) governs the sale and any disclaimer, limitation or modification of the seller's warranties. Amended in 1962.

§9-207. Rights and Duties When Collateral is in Secured Party's Possession.

(1) A secured party must use reasonable care in the custody and preservation of collateral in his possession. In the case of an instrument or chattel paper reasonable care includes taking necessary steps to preserve rights against prior parties unless otherwise agreed.

(2) Unless otherwise agreed, when collateral is in the secured party's possession

(a) reasonable expenses (including the cost of any insurance and payment of taxes or other charges) incurred in the custody, preservation, use or operation of the collateral are chargeable to the debtor and are secured by the collateral;

(b) the risk of accidental loss or damage is on the debtor to the extent of any deficiency in any effective insurance coverage;

(c) the secured party may hold as additional security any increase or profits (except money) received from the collateral, but money so received, unless remitted to the debtor, shall be applied in reduction of the secured obligation;

(d) the secured party must keep the collateral indentifiable but fungible collateral may be commingled;

(e) the secured party may repledge the collateral upon terms which do not impair the debtor's right to redeem it.

(3) A secured party is liable for any loss caused by his failure to meet any obligation imposed by the preceding subsections but does not lose his security interest.

(4) A secured party may use or operate the collateral for the purpose of preserving the collateral or its value or pursuant to the order of a court of appropriate jurisdiction or, except in the case of consumer goods, in the manner and to the extent provided in the security agreement.

§9-208. Request for Statement of Account or List of Collateral.

(1) A debtor may sign a statement indicating what he believes to be the aggregate amount of unpaid indebtedness as of a specified date and may send it to the secured party with a request that the statement be approved or corrected and returned to the debtor. When the security agreement or any other record kept by the secured party identifies the collateral a debtor may similarly request the secured party to approve or correct a list of the collateral.

(2) The secured party must comply with such a request within two weeks after receipt by sending a written correction or approval. If the secured party claims a security interest in all of a particular type of collateral owned by the debtor he may indicate that fact in his reply and need not approve or correct an itemized list of such collateral. If the secured party without reasonable excuse fails to comply he is liable for any loss caused to the debtor thereby; and if the debtor has properly included in his request a good faith statement of the obligation or a list of the collateral or both, the secured party may claim a security interest only as shown in the statement against persons misled by his failure to comply. If he no longer has an interest in the obligation or collateral at the time the request is received he must disclose the name and address of any successor in

interest known to him and he is liable for any loss caused to the debtor as a result of failure to disclose. A successor in interest is not subject to this section until a request is received by him.

(3) A debtor is entitled to such a statement once every six months without charge. The secured party may require payment of a charge not exceeding $10 for each additional statement furnished.

Part 3: Rights of Third Parties; Perfected and Unperfected Security Interests; Rules of Priority

§ 9-301. Persons Who Take Priority Over Unperfected Security interests; Right of "Lien Creditor".

(1) Except as otherwise provided in subsection (2), an unperfected security interest is subordinate to the rights of

(a) persons entitled to priority under Section 9-312;
(b) a person who becomes a lien creditor before the security interest is perfected;
(c) in the case of goods, instruments, documents, and chattel paper, a person who is not a secured party and who is a transferee in bulk or other buyer not in ordinary course of business, or is a buyer of farm products in ordinary course of business, to the extent that he gives value and receives delivery of the collateral without knowledge of the security interest and before it is perfected;
(d) in the case of accounts and general intangibles, a person who is not a secured party and who is a transferee to the extent that he gives value without knowledge of the security interest and before it is perfected.

(2) If the secured party files with respect to a purchase money security interest before or within ten days after the debtor receives possession of the collateral, he takes priority over the rights of a transferee in bulk or of a lien creditor which arise between the time the security interest attaches and the time of filing.

(3) A "lien creditor" means a creditor who has acquired a lien on the property involved by attachment, levy or the like and includes an assignee for benefit of creditors from the time of assignment, and a trustee in bankruptcy from the date of the filing of the petition or a receiver in equity from the time of appointment.

(4) A person who becomes a lien creditor while a security interest is perfected takes subject to the security interest only to the extent that it secures advances made before he becomes a lien creditor or within 45 days thereafter or made without knowledge of the lien or pursuant to a commitment entered into without knowledge of the lien.

§9-302. When Filing Is Required to Perfect Security Interest; Security Interests to Which Filing Provisions of This Article Do Not Apply.

(1) A financing statement must be filed to perfect all security interests except the following:

(a) a security interest in collateral in possession of the secured party under Section 9-305;
(b) a security interest temporarily perfected in instruments or documents without delivery under Section 9-304 or in proceeds for a 10 day period under Section 9-306;
(c) a security interest created by an assignment of a beneficial interest in a trust or a decedent's estate;
(d) a purchase money security interest in consumer goods; but filing is required for a motor vehicle required to be registered; and fixture filing is required for priority over conflicting interests in fixtures to the extent provided in Section 9-313;

(e) an assignment of accounts which does not alone or in conjunction with other assignments to the same assignee transfer a significant part of the outstanding accounts of the assignor;
(f) a security interest of a collecting bank (Section 4-208) or arising under the Article on Sales (see section 9-113) or covered in subsection (3) of this section;
(g) in assignment for the benefit of all the creditors of the transferor, and subsequent transfers by the assignee thereunder.

(2) If a secured party assigns a perfected security interest, no filing under this Article is required in order to continue the perfected status of the security interest against creditors of and transferees from the original debtor.

(3) The filing of a financing statement otherwise required by this Article is not necessary or effective to perfect a security interest in property subject to

(a) a statute or treaty of the United States which provides for a national or international registration or a national or international certificate of title or which specifies a place of filing different from that specified in this Article for filing of the security interest; or
(b) the following statutes of this state; [[list any certificate of title statute covering automobiles, trailers, mobile homes, boats, farm tractors, or the like, and any central filing statute.*.]]; but during any period in which collateral is inventory held for sale by a person who is in the business of selling goods of that kind, the filing provisions of this Article (Part 4) apply to a security interest in that collateral created by him as debtor; or
(c) a certificate of title statute of another jurisdiction under the law of which indication of a security interest on the certificate is required as a condition of perfection (subsection (2) of Section 9-103).

(4) Compliance with a statute or treaty described in subsection (3) is equivalent to the filing of a financing statement under this Article, and a security interest in property subject to the statute or treaty can be perfected only by compliance therewith except as provided in Section 9-103 on multiple state transactions. Duration and renewal of perfection of a security interest perfected by compliance with the statute or treaty are governed by the provisions of the statute or treaty; in other respects the security interest is subject to this Article.

§9-302. When Filing is Required to Perfect Security Interest; Security Interests to Which Filing Provisions of This Article Do Not Apply *(1977 Amendments)*.

(1) A financing statement must be filed to perfect all security interests[s] except the following:

* * *

(f) a security interest of a collecting bank (Section 4-208) or in securities (Section 8-321) or arising under the Article on Sales (see Section 9-113) or covered in subsection (3) of this section;

* * *

§9-303. When Security Interest is Perfected; Continuity of Perfection.

(1) A security interest is perfected when it has attached and when all of the applicable steps required for perfection have been taken. Such steps are specified in Section 9-304, 9-305, and 9-306. If such steps are taken before the security interest attaches, it is perfected at ;the time when it attaches.

* **Note:** It is recommended that the provisions of certificate of title acts for perfection of security interests by notation on the certificates should be amended to exclude coverage of inventory held for sale.

(2) If a security interest is originally perfected in any way permitted under this Article and is subsequently perfected in some other way under this Article, without an intermediate period when it was unperfected, the security interest shall be deemed to be perfected continuously for the purposes of this Article.

§9-304. Perfection of Security Interest in Instruments, Documents, and Goods Covered by Documents; Perfection by Permissive Filing; Temporary Perfection Without Filing or Transfer of Possession.

(1) A security interest in chattel paper or negotiable documents may be perfected by filing. A security interest in money or instruments (other than instruments which constitute part of chattel paper) can be perfected only by the secured party's taking possession, except as provided in subsections (4) and (5) of this section and subsections (2) and (3) of Section 9-306 on proceeds.

(2) During the period that goods are in the possession of the issuer of a negotiable document therefor, a security interest in the goods is perfected by perfecting a security interest in the document, and any security interest in the goods otherwise perfected during such period is subject thereto.

(3) A security interest in goods in the possession of a bailee other than one who has issued a negotiable document therefor is perfected by issuance of a document in the name of the secured party or by the bailee's receipt of notification of the secured party's interest or by filing as to the goods.

(4) A security interest in instruments or negotiable documents is perfected without filing or the taking of possession for a period of 21 days from the time it attaches to the extent that it arises for new value given under a written security agreement.

(5) A security interest remains perfected for a period of 21 days without filing where a secured party having a perfected security interest in an instrument, a negotiable document or goods in possession of a bailee other than one who has issued a negotiable document therefor

(a) makes available to the debtor the goods or documents representing the goods for the purpose of ultimate sale or exchange or for the purpose of loading, unloading, storing, shipping, transshipping, manufacturing, processing or otherwise dealing with them in a manner preliminary to their sale or exchange, but priority between conflicting security interests in the goods is subject to subsection (3) of Section 9-312; or

(b) delivers the instrument to the debtor for the purpose of ultimate sale or exchange or of presentation, collection, renewal or registration of transfer.

(6) After the 21 day period in subsections (4) and (5) perfection depends upon compliance with applicable provisions of this Article.

§9-304. Perfection of Security Interest in Instruments, Documents, and Goods Covered by Documents; Perfection by Permissive Filing; Temporary Perfection Without Filing or Transfer of Possession *(1977 Amendments).*

(1) A security interest in chattel paper or negotiable documents may be perfected by filing. A security interest in money or instruments (other than certificated securities or instruments which constitute part of chattel paper) can be perfected only by the secured party's taking possession, except as provided in subsections (4) and (5) of this section and subsections (2) and (3) of Section 9-306 on proceeds.

* * *

(4) A security interest in instruments (other than certificated securities) or negotiable documents is perfected without filing or the taking of possession for a period of 21 days from the time it attaches to the extent that it arises for new value given under a written security agreement.

(5) A security interest remains perfected for a period of 21 days without filing where a secured party having a perfected security interest in an instrument (other than a certificated security), a negotiable document or goods in possession of a bailee other than one who has issued a negotiable document therefor:

* * *

(b) delivers the instrument to the debtor for the purpose of ultimate sale or exchange or of presentation, collection, renewal, or registration of transfer.

(6) After the 21 day period in subsections (4) and (5) perfection depends upon compliance with applicable provisions of this Article.

§9-305. When Possession by Secured Party Perfects Security Interest Without Filing.

A security interest in letters of credit and advices of credit (subsection (2) (a) of Section 5-116), goods, instruments, money, negotiable documents or chattel paper may be perfected by the secured party's taking possession of the collateral. If such collateral other than goods covered by a negotiable document is held by a bailee, the secured party is deemed to have possession from the time the bailee receives notification of the secured party's interest. A security interest is perfected by possession from the time possession is taken without relation back and continues only so long as possession is retained, unless otherwise perfected as provided in this Article before or after the period of possession by the secured party.

§9-305. When Possession by Secured Party Perfects Security Interest Without Filing *(1977 Amendments).*

A security interest in letters of credit and advices of credit (subsection (2)(a) of Section 5-116), goods, instruments (other than certificated securities), money, negotiable documents, or chattel paper may be perfected by the secured party's taking possession of the collateral. If such collateral other than goods covered by a negotiable document is held by a bailee, the secured party is deemed to have possession from the time the bailee receives notification of the secured party's interest. A security interest is perfected by possession from the time possession is taken without relation back and continues only so long as possession is retained, unless otherwise specified in this Article. The security interest may be otherwise perfected as provided in this Article before or after the period of possession by the security party.

§9-306. "Proceeds"; Secured Party's Rights on Disposition of Collateral.

"Proceeds" includes whatever is received upon the sale, exchange, collection or other disposition of collateral or proceeds. Insurance payable by reason of loss or damage to the collateral is proceeds, except to the extent that it is payable to a person other than a party to the security agreement. Money, checks, deposit accounts, and the like are "cash proceeds". All other proceeds are "non-cash proceeds".

(2) Except where this Article otherwise provides, a security interest continues in collateral notwithstanding sale, exchange or other disposition thereof unless the disposition was authorized by the secured party in the security agreement or otherwise, and also continues in any identifiable proceeds including collections received by the debtor.

(3) The security interest in proceeds is a continuously perfected security interest if the interest in the original collateral was per-

fected but it ceases to be a perfected security interest and becomes unperfected ten days after receipt of the proceeds by the debtor unless

(a) a filed financing statement covers the original collateral and the proceeds are collateral in which a security interest may be perfected by filing in the office or offices where the financing statement has been filed and, if the proceeds are acquired with cash proceeds, the description of collateral in the financing statement indicates the types of property constituting the proceeds; or

(b) a filed financing statement covers the original collateral and the proceeds are identifiable cash proceeds; or

(c) the security interest in the proceeds is perfected before the expiration of the ten day period.

Except as provided in this section, a security interest in proceeds can be perfected only by the methods or under the circumstances permitted in this Article for original collateral of the same type.

(4) In the event of insolvency proceedings instituted by or against a debtor, a secured party with a perfected security interest in proceeds has a perfected security interest only in the following proceeds:

(a) in identifiable non-cash proceeds and in separate deposit accounts containing only proceeds;

(b) in identifiable cash proceeds in the form of money which is neither commingled with other money nor deposited in a deposit account prior to the insolvency proceedings;

(c) in identifiable cash proceeds in the form of checks and the like which are not deposited in a deposit account prior to the insolvency proceedings; and

(d) in all cash and deposit accounts of the debtor in which proceeds have been commingled with other funds, but proceeds have been commingled with other funds, but the perfected security interest under this paragraph (d) is
  (i) subject to any right of set-off; and
  (ii) limited to an amount not greater than the amount of any cash proceeds received by the debtor within ten days before the institution of the insolvency proceedings less the sum of (i) the payments to the secured party on account of cash proceeds received by the debtor during such period and (ii) the cash proceeds received by the debtor during such period to which the secured party is entitled under paragraphs (a) through (c) of this subsection (iv).

(5) If a sale of goods results in an account or chattel paper which is transferred by the seller to a secured party, and if the goods are returned to or are repossessed by the seller or the secured party, the following rules determine priorities:

(a) If the goods were collateral at the time of sale, for an indebtedness of the seller which is still unpaid, the original security interest attaches again to the goods and continues as a perfected security interest if it was perfected at the time when the goods were sold. If the security interest was originally perfected by a filing which is still effective, nothing further is required to continue the perfected status; in any other case, the secured party must take possession of the returned or repossessed goods or must file.

(b) An unpaid transferee of the chattel paper has a security interest in the goods against the transferor. Such security interest is prior to a security interest asserted under paragraph (a) to the extent that the transferee of the chattel paper was entitled to priority under Section 9-308.

(c) An unpaid transferee of the account has a security interest in the goods against the transferor. Such security interest is subordinate to a security interest asserted under paragraph (a).

(d) A security interest of an unpaid transferee asserted under paragraph (b) or (c) must be perfected for protection against creditors of the transferor and purchasers of the returned or repossessed goods.

§9-307. Protection of Buyers of Goods.
(1) A buyer in ordinary course of business (subsection (9) of Section 1-201) other than a person buying farm products from a person engaged in farming operations takes free of a security interest created by his seller even though the security interest is perfected and even though the buyer knows of its existence.

(2) In the case of consumer goods a buyer takes free of a security interest even though perfected if he buys without knowledge of the security interest, for value and for his own personal, family or household purposes unless prior to the purchase the secured party has filed a financing statement covering such goods.

(3) A buyer other than a buyer in ordinary course of business (subsection (1) of this section) takes free of a security interest to the extent that it secures future advances made after the secured party acquires knowledge of the purchase, or more than 45 days after the purchase, whichever first occurs, unless made pursuant to a commitment entered into without knowledge of the purchase and before the expiration of the 45 day period.

§9-308. Purchase of Chattel Paper and Instruments.
A purchaser of chattel paper or an instrument who gives new value and takes possession of it in the ordinary course of his business has priority over a security interest in the chattel paper or instrument

(a) which is perfected under Section 9-304 (permissive filing and temporary perfection) or under Section 9-306 (perfection as to proceeds) if he acts without knowledge that the specific paper or instrument is subject to a security interest; or

(b) which is claimed merely as proceeds of inventory subject to a security interest (Section 9-306) even though he knows that the specific paper or instrument is subject to the security interest.

§9-309. Protection of Purchasers of Instruments and Documents. Nothing in this Article limits the rights of a holder in due course of a negotiable instrument (Section 3-302) or a holder to whom a negotiable document of title has been duly negotiated (Section 7-501) or a bona fide purchaser of a security (Section 8-301) and such holders or purchasers take priority over an earlier security interest even though perfected. Filing under this Article does not constitute notice of the security interest to such holders or purchasers.

§9-309. Protection of Purchasers of Instruments, Documents and Securities *(1977 Amendments)*. Nothing in this Article limits the rights of a holder in due course of a negotiable instrument (Section 3-302) or a holder to whom negotiable document of title has been duly negotiated (Section 7-501) or a bona fide purchaser of a security (Section 8-302) and such holders or purchasers take priority over an earlier security interest even though perfected. Filing under this Article does not constitute notice of the security interest to such holders or purchasers.

§9-310. Priority of Certain Liens Arising by Operations of Law. When a person in the ordinary course of his business furnishes services or materials with respect to goods subject to a security interest, a lien upon goods in the possession of such person given by statute or rule of law for such materials or services takes priority over a perfected security interest unless the lien is statutory and the statute expressly provides otherwise.

§9-311. Alienability of Debtor's Rights: Judicial Process. The debtor's rights in collateral may be voluntarily or involuntarily transferred (by way of sale, creation of a security interest, attachment, levy, garnishment or other judicial process) notwithstanding a provision in the security agreement prohibiting any transfer or making the transfer constitute a default.

§9-312. Priorities Among Conflicting Security Interests in the Same Collateral.

(1) The rules of priority state in other sections of this Part and in the following sections shall govern when applicable: Section 4-208 with respect to the security interests of collecting banks in items being collected, accompanying documents and proceeds; Section 9-103 on security interests related to other jurisdictions; Section 9-114 on consignments.

(2) A perfected security interest in crops for new value given to enable the debtor to produce the crops during the production season and given not more than three months before the crops become growing crops by planting or otherwise takes priority over an earlier perfected security interest to the extent that such earlier interest secures obligations due more than six months before the crops become growing crops by planting or otherwise, even though the person giving new value had knowledge of the earlier security interest.

(3) A perfected purchase money security interest in inventory has priority over a conflicting security interest in the same inventory and also has priority in identifiable cash proceeds received on or before the delivery of the inventory to a buyer if

(a) the purchase money security interest is perfected at the time the debtor receives possession of the inventory; and
(b) the purchase noney secured party gives notification in writing to the holder of the conflicting security interest if the holder had filed a financing statement covering the same types of inventory (i) before the date of the filing made by the purchase money secured party, or (ii) before the beginning of the 21 day period where the purchase money security interest is temporarily perfected without filing or possession (subsection (5) of Section 9-304); and
(c) the older of the conflicting security interest receives the notification within five years before the debtor receives possession of the inventory; and
(d) the notification states that the person giving the notice has or expect to acquire a purchase money security interest in inventory of the debtor, describing such inventory by item or type.

(4) A purchase money security interest in collateral other than inventory has priority over a conflicting security interest in the same collateral or its proceeds if the purchase money security interest is perfected at the time the debtor receives possession of the collateral or within ten days thereafter.

(5) In all cases not governed by other rules stated in this section (including cases of purchase money security interests which do not qualify for the special priorities set forth in subsections (3) and (4) of this section), priority between conflicting security interests in the same collateral shall be determined according to the following rules:

(a) Conflicting security interests rank according to priority in time of filing or perfection. Priority dates from the time a filing is first made covering the collateral or the time the security interest is first perfected, whichever is earlier, provided that there is no period thereafter when there is neither filing nor perfection.
(b) So long as conflicting security interests are unperfected, the first to attach has priority.

(6) For the purposes of subsection (5) a date of filing or perfection as to collateral is also a date for filing or perfection as to proceeds.

(7) If future advances are made while a security interest is perfected by filing or the taking of possession, the security interest has the same priority for the purposes of subsection (5) with respect to the future advances as it does with respect to the first advance. If a commitment is made before or while the security interest is so perfected, the security interest has the same priority with respect to advances made pursuant thereto. In other cases a perfected security interest has priority from the date the advance is made.

§9-312. Priorities Among Conflicting Security Interests in the Same Collateral *(1977 Amendments)*.

(7) If future advances are made while a security interest is perfected by filing, the taking of possession, or under Section 8-321 on securities, the security interest has the same priority for the purposes of subsection (5) with respect to the future advances as it does with respect to the first advance. If a commitment is made before or while the security interest is so perfected, the security interest has the same priority with respect to advances made pursuant thereto. In other cases a perfected security interest has priority from the date the advance is made.

* * *

§9-313. Priority of Security Interests in Fixtures.

(1) In this section and in the provisions of Part 4 of this Article referring to fixture filing, unless the context otherwise requires

(a) goods are "fixtures" when they become so related to particular real estate that an interest in them arises under real estate law
(b) a "fixture filing" is the filing in the office where a mortgage on the real estate would be filed or recorded of a financing statement covering goods which are or are to become fixtures and conforming to the requirements of subsection (5) of Section 9-402
(c) a mortgage is a "construction mortgage" to the extent that it secures an obligation incurred for the construction of an improvement on land including the acquisition cost of the land, if the recorded writing so indicates.

(2) A security interest under this Article may be created in goods which are fixtures or may continue in goods which become fixtures, but no security interest exists under this Article in ordinary building materials incorporated into an improvement on land.

(3) This Article does not prevent creation of an encumbrance upon fixtures pursuant to real estate law.

(4) A perfected security interest in fixtures has priority over the conflicting interest of an encumbrance or owner of the real estate where

(a) the security interest is a purchase money security interest, the interest of the encumbrancer or owner arises before the goods become fixtures, the security interest is perfected by a fixture filing before the goods become fixtures or within ten days thereafter, and the debtor has an interest of record in the real estate or is in possession of the real estate; or
(b) the security interest is perfected by a fixture filing before the interest of the encumbrancer or owner is of record, the security interest has priority over any conflicting interest of a predecessor in title of the encumbrancer or owner, and the debtor has an interest of record in the real estate or is in possession of the real estate; or

(c) the fixtures are readily removable factory or office machines or readily removable replacements of domestic appliances which are consumer goods, and before the goods become fixtures the security interest is perfected by any method permitted by this Article; or
(d) the conflicting interest is a lien on the real estate obtained by legal or equitable proceedings after the security interest was perfected by any method permitted by this Article.

(5) A security interest in fixtures, whether or not perfected, has priority over the conflicting interest of an encumbrancer or owner of the real estate where

(a) the encumbrancer or owner has consented in writing to the security interest or has disclaimed an interest in the goods as fixtures; or
(b) the debtor has a right to remove the goods as against the encumbrancer or owner. If the debtor's right terminates, the priority of the security interest continues for a reasonable time.

(6) Notwithstanding paragraph (a) of subsection (4) but otherwise subject to subsections (4) and (5), a security interest in fixtures is subordinate to a construction mortgage recorded before the goods become fixtures if the goods become fixtures before the completion of the construction. To the extent that it is given to refinance a construction mortgage, a mortgage has this priority to the same extent as the construction mortgage.

(7) In cases not within the preceding subsections, a security interest in fixtures is subordinate to the conflicting interest of an encumbrancer or owner of the related real estate who is not the debtor.

(8) When the secured party has priority over all owners and encumbrancers of the real estate, he may, on default, subject to the provisions of Part 5, remove his collateral from the real estate but he must reimburse any encumbrancer or owner of the real estate who is not the debtor and who has not otherwise agreed for the cost of repair of any physical injury, but not for any diminution in value of the real estate caused by the absence of the goods removed or by any necessity of replacing them. A person entitled to reimbursement may refuse permission to remove until the secured party gives adequate security for the performance of this obligation.

§9-314. Accessions.

(1) A security interest in goods which attaches before they are installed in or affixed to other goods takes priority as to the goods installed or affixed (called in this section "accessions") over the claims of all persons to the whole except as stated in subsection (3) and subject to Section 9-315(1).

(2) A security interest which attaches to goods after they become part of a whole is valid against all persons subsequently acquiring interests in the whole except as stated in subsection (3) but is invalid against any person with an interest in the whole at the time the security interest attaches to the goods who has not in writing consented to the security interest or disclaimed an interest in the goods as part of the whole.

(3) The security interests described in subsections (1) and (2) do not take priority over

(a) a subsequent purchaser for value of any interest in the whole; or
(b) a creditor with a lien on the whole subsequently obtained by judicial proceedings; or
(c) a creditor with a prior perfected security interest in the whole to the extent that he makes subsequent advances

if the subsequent purchase is made, the lien by judicial proceedings obtained or the subsequent advance under the prior perfected security interest is made or contracted for without knowledge of the security interest and before it is perfected. A purchaser of the whole at a foreclosure sale other than the holder of a perfected security interest purchasing at his own foreclosure sale is a subsequent purchaser within this section.

(4) When under subsections (1) or (2) and (3) a secured party has an interest in accessions which has priority over the claims of all persons who have interests in the whole, he may on default subject to the provisions of Part 5 remove his collateral from the whole but he must reimburse any encumbrancer or owner of the whole who is not the debtor and who has not otherwise agreed for the cost of repair of any physical injury but not for any diminution in value of the whole caused by the absence of the goods removed or by any necessity for replacing them. A person entitled to reimbursement may refuse permission to remove until the secured party gives adequate security for the performance of this obligation.

§9-315. Priority When Goods are Commingled or Processed.

(1) If a security interest in goods was perfected and subsequently the goods or a part thereof have become part of a product or mass, the security interest continues in the product or mass if

(a) the goods are so manufactured, processed, assembled or commingled that their identity is lost in the product or mass; or
(b) a financing statement covering the original goods also covers the product into which the goods have been manufactured, processed or assembled. In a case to which paragraph (b) applies, no separate security interest in that part of the original goods which has been manufactured processed or assembled into the product may be claimed under Section 9-314.

(2) When under subsection (1) more than one security interest attaches to the product or mass, they rank equally according to the ratio that the cost of the goods to which each interest originally attached bears to the cost of the total product or mass.

§9-316. Priority Subject to Subordination.
Nothing in this Article prevents subordination by agreement by any person entitled to priority.

§9-317. Secured Party Not Obligated On Contract of Debtor.
The mere existence of a security interest or authority given to the debtor to dispose of or use collateral does not impose contract or tort liability upon the secured party for the debtor's acts or omissions.

§9-318. Defenses Against Assignee; Modification of Contract After Notification of Assignment; Term Prohibiting Assignment Ineffective; Identification and Proof of Assignment.

(1) Unless an account debtor has made an enforceable agreement not to assert defenses or claims arising out of a sale as provided in Section 9-206 the rights of an assignee are subject to

(a) all the terms of the contract between the account debtor and assignor and any defense or claim arising therefrom; and
(b) any other defense or claim of the account debtor against the assignor which accrues before the account debtor receives notification of the assignment.

(2) So far as the right to payment or a part thereof under an assigned contract has not been fully earned by performance, and notwithstanding notification of the assignment, any modification of or substitution for the contract made in good faith and in accordance with reasonable commercial standards is effective against an assignee unless the account debtor has otherwise agreed but the as-

signee acquires corresponding rights under the modified or substituted contract. The assignment may provide that such modification or substitution is a breach by the assignor.

(3) The account debtor is authorized to pay the assignor until the account debtor receives notification that the amount due or to become due has been assigned and that payment is to be made to the assignee. A notification which does not reasonably identify the rights assigned is ineffective. If requested by the account debtor, the assignee must seasonably furnish reasonable proof that the assignment has been made and unless he does so the account debtor may pay the assignor.

(4) A term in any contract between an account debtor and an assignor is ineffective if it prohibits assignment of an account or prohibits creation of a security interest in a general intangible for money due or to become due or requires the account debtor's consent to such assignment or security interest.

Part 4: Filing

§9-401. Place of Filing; Erroneous Filing; Removal of Collateral.

First Alternative Subsection (1)

(1) The proper place to file in order to perfect a security interest is as follows:

(a) when the collateral is timber to be cut or is minerals or the like (including oil and gas) or accounts subject to subjection (5) of Section 9-103, or when the financing statement is filed as a fixture filing (Section 9-313) and the collateral is goods which are or are to become fixtures, then in the office where a mortgage on the real estate would be filed or recorded;

(b) in all other cases, in the office of the [[Secretary of State]]

Second Alternative Subsection (1)

(1) The proper place to file in order to perfect a security interest is as follows:

(a) when the collateral is equipment used in farming operations, or farm products, or accounts or general intangibles arising from or relating to the sale of farm products by a farmer, or consumer goods, then in the office of the . . . . in the county of the debtor's residence or if the debtor is not a resident of this state then in the office of the . . . . in the county where the goods are kept, and in addition when the collateral is crops growing or to be grown in the office of the . . . . in the county where the land is located;

(b) when the collateral is timber to be cut or is minerals or the like (including oil and gas) or accounts subject to subsection (5) of Section 9-103, or when the financing statement is filed as a fixture filing (Section 9-313) and the collateral is goods which are or are to become fixtures, then in the office where a mortgage on the real estate would be filed or recorded;

(c) in all other cases, in the office of the

Third Alternative Subsection (1)

(1) The proper place to file in order to perfect a security interest is as follows:

(a) when the collateral is equipment used in farming operations, or farm products, or accounts or general intangibles arising from or relating to the sale of farm products by a farmer, or consumer goods, then in the office of the . . . . . . in the county of the debtor's residence or if the debtor is not a resident of this state then in the office of the . . . . . . in the county where the goods are kept, and in addition when the collateral is crops growing or to be grown in the office of . . . . . . in the county where the land is located;

(b) when the collateral is timber to be cut or is minerals or the like (including oil and gas) or accounts subject to subsection (5) of Section 9-103, or when the financing statement is filed as a fixture filing (Section 9-313) and the collateral is goods which are or are to become fixtures, then in the office where a mortgage on the real estate would be filed or recorded;

(c) in all other cases, in the office of the . . . . . and in addition, if the debtor has a place of business in only one county of this state, also in the office of . . . . . . of such county, or, if the debtor has no place of business in this state, but resides in the state, also in the office of . . . . . . of the county in which he resides.

Note: *One of the three alternatives should be selected as subsection (1).*

(2) A filing which is made in good faith in an improper place or not in all of the places required by this section is nevertheless effective with regard to any collateral as to which the filing complied with the requirements of this Article and is also effective with regard to collateral covered by the financing statement against any person who has knowledge of the contents of such financing statement.

(3) A filing which is made in the proper place in this state continues effective even though the debtor's residence or place of business or the location of the collateral or its use, whichever controlled the original filing, is thereafter changed.

Language in double brackets is Alternative Subsection (3).

[[(3) A filing which is made in the proper county continues effective for four months after a change to another county of the debtor's residence or place of business or the location of the collateral, whichever controlled the original filing. It becomes ineffective thereafter unless a copy of the financing statement signed by the secured party is filed in the new county within said period. The security interest may also be perfected in the new county after the expiration of the four-month period; in such case perfected dates from the time of perfection in the new county. A change in the use of the collateral does not impair the effectiveness of the original filing.]]

(4) The rules stated in Section 9-103 determine whether filing is necessary in this state.

(5) Notwithstanding the preceding subsections, and subject to subsection (3) of Section 9-302, the proper place to file in order to perfect a security interest in collateral, including the fixtures, of a transmitting utility is the office of the [[Secretary of State]]. This filing constitutes a fixture filing (Section 9-313) as to the collateral described therein which is or is to become fixtures.

(6) For the purposes of this section, the residence of an organization is its place of business if it has one or its chief executive office if it has more than one place of business.

Note: *Subsection (6) should be used only if the state chooses the Second or Third Alternative Subsection (1).*

§9-402. Formal Requisites of Financing Statement; Amendments; Mortgage as Financing Statement.

(1) A financing statement is sufficient if it gives the names of the debtor and the secured party, is signed by the debtor, gives an address of the secured party from which information concerning the security interest may be obtained, gives a mailing address of the debtor and contains a statement indicating the types, or describing the items, of collateral. A financing statement may be filed before a security agreement is made or a security interest otherwise attaches. When the financing statement covers crops grow-

ing or to be grown, the statement must also contain a description of the real estate concerned. When the financing statement covers timber to be cut or covers minerals or the like (including oil and gas) or accounts subject to subsection (5) of Section 9-103, or when the financing statement is filed as a fixture filing (Section 9-313) and the collateral is goods which are or are to become fixtures, the statement must also comply with subsection (5). A copy of the security agreement is sufficient as a financing statement if it contains the above information and is signed by the debtor. A carbon, photographic or other reproduction of a security agreement or a financing statement is sufficient as a financing statement if the security agreement so provides or if the original has been filed in this state.

(2) A financing statement which otherwise complies with subsection (1) is sufficient when it is signed by the secured party instead of the debtor if it is filed to perfect a security interest in

(a) collateral already subject to security interest in another jurisdiction when it is brought into this state, or when the debtor's location is changed to this state. Such a financing statement must state that the collateral was brought into this state or that the debtor's location was changed to this state under such circumstances; or
(b) proceeds under Section 9-306 if the security interest in the original collateral was perfected. Such a financing statement must describe the original collateral; or
(c) collateral as to which the filing has lapsed; or
(d) collateral acquired after a change of name, identity or corporate structure of the debtor (subsection (7)).

(3) A form substantially as follows is sufficient to comply with subsection (1):

Name of debtor (or assignor) ....
Address ....
Name of secured party (or assignee) ....
Address ....

    1. This financing statement covers the following types (or items) of property:
(Describe)..
    2. (If collateral is crops) The above described crops are growing or are to be grown on:
(Describe Real Estate)...
    3. (If applicable) The above goods are to become fixtures on (Describe Real Estate) . . . . . and this financing statement is to be filed [[for record]] in the real estate records. (If the debtor does not have an interest of record)
The name of a record owner is
    4. (If products of collateral are claimed) Products of the collateral are also covered.

(use whichever is applicable) { Signature of Debtor (or Assignor)

Signature of Secured Party (or Assignee) }

(4) A financing statement may be amended by filing a writing signed by both the debtor and the secured party. An amendment does not extend the period of effectiveness of a financing statement. If any amendment adds collateral, it is effective as to the added collateral only from the filing date of the amendment. In this Article, unless the context otherwise requires, the term "financing statement" means the original financing statement and any amendments.

(5) A financing statement covering timber to be cut or covering minerals or the like (including oil and gas) or accounts subject to subsection (5) of Section 9-103, or a financing statement filed as a fixture filing (Section 9-313) where the debtor is not a transmitting utility, must show that it covers this type of collateral, must recite that it is to be filed [[for record]] in the real estate records, and the financing statement must contain a description of the real estate [[sufficient if it were contained in a mortgage of the real estate to give constructive notice of the mortgage under the law of this state]]. If the debtor does not have an interest of record in the real estate, the financing statement must show the name of a record owner.

(6) A mortgage is effective as a financing statement filed as a fixture filing from the date of its recording if (a) the goods are described in the mortgage by item or type, (b) the goods are or are to become fixtures related to the real estate described in the mortgage, (c) the mortgage complies with the requirements for a financing statement in this section other than a recital that it is to be filed in the real estate records, and (d) the mortgage is duly recorded. No fee with reference to the financing statement is required other than the regular recording and satisfaction fees with respect to the mortgage.

(7) A financing statement sufficiently shows the name of the debtor if it gives the individual, partnership or corporate name of the debtor, whether or not it adds other trade names or the names of partners. Where the debtor so changes his name or in the case of an organization name, identity or corporate structure that a filed financing statement becomes seriously misleading, the filing is not effective to perfect a security interest in collateral acquired by the debtor more than four months after the change, unless a new appropriate financing statement is filed before the expiration of that time. A filed financing statement remains effective with respect to collateral transferred by the debtor even though the secured party knows of or consents to the transfer.

(8) A financing statement substantially complying with the requirements of this section is effective even though it contains minor errors which are not seriously misleading.

Note: Language in double brackets is optional.
Note: Where the state has any special recording system for real estate other than the usual grantor-grantee index (as, for instance, a tract system or a title registration or Torrens system) local adaptations of subsection (5) and Section 9-403(7) may be necessary. See Mass. Gen. Laws Chapter 106, Section 9-409.

§9-403. What Constitutes Filing; Duration of Filing; Effect of Lapsed Filing; Duties of Filing Officer.

(1) Presentation for filing of a financing statement and tender of the filing fee or acceptance of the statement by the filing officer constitutes filing under this Article.

(2) Except as provided in subsection (6) a filed financing statement is effective for a period of five years from the date of filing. The effectiveness of a filed financing statement lapses on the expiration of the five year period unless a continuation statement is filed prior to the lapse. If a security interest perfected by filing exists at the time insolvency proceedings are commenced by or against the debtor, the security interest remains perfected until termination of the insolvency proceedings and thereafter for a period of sixty days or until expiration of the five year period, whichever occurs later. Upon lapse the security interest becomes unperfected, unless it is perfected without filing. If the security interest becomes unperfected upon lapse, it is deemed to have been unperfected as against a person who became a purchaser or lien creditor before lapse.

(3) A continuation statement may be filed by the secured party within six months prior to the expiration of the five year period specified in subsection (2). Any such continuation statement must be signed by the secured party, identify the original statement by file number and state that the original statement is

still effective. A continuation statement signed by a person other than the secured party of record must be accompanied by a separate written statement of assignment signed by the secured party of record and complying with subsection (2) of Section 9-405, including payment of the required fee. Upon timely filing of the continuation statement, the effectiveness of the original statement is continued for five years after the last date to which the filing was effective whereupon it lapses in the same manner as provided in subsection (2) unless another continuation statement is filed prior to such lapse. Succeeding continuation statements may be filed in the same manner to continue the effectiveness of the original statement. Unless a statute on disposition of public records provides otherwise, the filing officer may remove a lapsed statement from the files and destroy it immediately if he has retained a microfilm or other photographic record, or in other cases after one year after the lapse. The filing officer shall so arrange matters by physical annexation of financing statements to continuation statements or other related filings, or by other means, that if he physically destroys the financing statements of a period more than five years past, those which have been continued by a continuation statement or which are still effective under subsection (6) shall be retained.

(4) Except as provided in subsection (7) a) filing officer shall mark each statement with a file number and with the date and hour of filing and shall hold the statement or a microfilm or other photographic copy thereof for public inspection. In addition the filing officer shall index the statements according to the name of the debtor and shall note in the index the file number and the address of the debtor given in the statement.

(5) The uniform fee for filing and indexing and for the stamping a copy furnished by the secured party to show the date and place of filing for an original financing statement or for a continuation statement shall be $. . . . . . . if the statement is in the standard form prescribed by the . . . . and otherwise shall be $. . . . . . , plus in each case, if the financing statement is subject to subsection (5) of Section 9-402, $. . . . . The uniform fee for each name more than one required to be indexed shall be $. . . . . The secured party may at his option show a trade name for any person and an extra uniform indexing fee of $. . . . . shall be paid with respect thereto.

(6) If the debtor is a transmitting utility (subsection (5) of Section 9-401) and a filed financing statement so states, it is effective until a termination statement is filed. A real estate mortgage which is effective as a fixture filing under subsection (6) of Section 9-402 remains effective as a fixture filing until the mortgage is released or satisfied or record or its effectiveness otherwise terminates as to the real estate.

(7) When a financing statement covers timber to be cut or covers minerals or the like (including oil and gas) or accounts subject to subsection (5) of Section 9-103, or is filed as a fixture filing, [[it shall be filed for record and]] the filing officer shall index it under the names of the debtor and any owner of record shown on the financing statement in the same fashion as if they were the mortgagors in a mortgage of the real estate described, and, to the extent that the law of this state provides for indexing of mortgages under the name of the mortgagee, under the name of the secured party as if he were the mortgagee, thereunder, or where indexing is by description in the same fashion as if the financing statement were a mortgage of the real estate described.

Note: *In states in which writings will not appear in the real estate records and indices unless actually recorded the bracketed language in subsection (7) should be used.*

§9-404. Termination Statement.

(1) If a financing statement covering consumer goods is filed on or after . . . ., then within one month or within ten days following written demand by the debtor after there is no outstanding secured obligation and no commitment to make advances, incur obligations or otherwise give value, the secured party must file with each filing officer with whom the financing statement was filed, a termination statement to the effect that he no longer claims a security interest under the financing statement, which shall be identified by file number. In other cases whenever there is no outstanding secured obligation and no commitment to make advances, incur obligations or otherwise give value, the secured party must on written demand by the debtor send the debtor, for each filing officer with whom the financing statement was filed, a termination statement to the effect that no longer claims a security interest under the financing statement, which shall be identified by file number. A termination statement signed by a person other than the secured party of record must be accompanied by a separate written statement of assignment signed by the secured party of record complying with subsection (2) of Section 9-405, including payment of the required fee. If the affected secured party fails to file such a termination statement as required by this subsection, or to send such a termination statement within ten days after proper demand therefor he shall be liable to the debtor for one hundred dollars, and in addition for any loss caused to the debtor by such failure.

(2) On presentation to the filing officer of such a termination statement he must note it in the index. If he has received the termination statement in duplicate, he shall return one copy of the termination statement to the secured party stamped to show the time of receipt thereof. If the filing officer has a microfilm or other photographic record of the financing statement, and of any related continuation statement, statement of assignment and statement of release, he may remove the originals from the files at any time after receipt of the termination statement, or if he has no such record, he may remove them from the files at any time after one year after receipt of the termination statement.

(3) If the termination statement is in the standard form prescribed by the . . . . . , the uniform fee for filing and indexing the termination statement shall be $. . . . . . . , and otherwise shall be $. . . . . . . , plus in each case an additional fee of $. . . . . . for each name more than one against which the termination statement is required to be indexed.

Note: *The date to be inserted should be the effective date of the revised Article 9.*

§9-405. Assignment of Security Interest; Duties of Filing Officer; Fees.

(1) A financing statement may disclose an assignment of a security interest in the collateral described in the financing statement by indication in the financing statement of the name and address of the assignee or by an assignment itself or a copy thereof on the face or back of the statement. On presentation to the filing officer of such a financing statement the filing officer shall mark the same as provided in Section 9-403(4). The uniform fee for filing, indexing and furnishing filing data for a financing statement so indicating an assignment shall be $. . . . . . . if the statement is in the standard form prescribed by the . . . . and otherwise shall be $. . . . . . . plus in each case an additional fee of $. . . . . . for each name more than one against which the financing statement is required to be indexed.

(2) A secured party may assign of record all or part of his rights under a financing statement by the filing in the place where the original financing statement was filed of a separate written statement of assignment signed by the secured party of record and setting forth the name of the secured party of record and the debtor, the file number and the date of filing of the financing statement and the name and address of the assignee and containing a description of the collateral assigned. A copy of the assignment is

sufficient as a separate statement if it complies with the preceding sentence. On presentation to the filing officer of such a separate statement, the filing officer shall mark such separate statement with the date and hour of the filing. He shall note the assignment on the index of the financing statement, or in the case of a fixture filing, or a filing covering timber to be cut, or covering minerals or the like (including oil and gas) or accounts subject to subsection (5) of Section 9-103, he shall index the assignment under the name of the assignor as grantor and, to the extent that the law of this state provides for indexing the assignment of a mortgage under the name of the assignee, he shall index the assignment of the financing statement under the name of the assignee. The uniform fee for filing, indexing and furnishing filing data about such a separate statement of assignment shall be $. . . . . if the statement is in the standard form prescribed by the . . . . . and otherwise shall be $. . . . . ., plus in each case an additional fee of $. . . . . . for each name more than one against which the statement of assignment is required to be indexed. Notwithstanding the provisions of this subsection, an assignment of record of a security interest in a fixture contained in a mortgage effective as a fixture filing (subsection (6) of Section 9-402) may be made only by an assignment of the mortgage in the manner provided by the law of this state other than this Act.

(3) After the disclosure or filing of an assignment under this section, the assignee is the secured party of record.

§9-406. Release of Collateral; Duties of Filing Officer; Fees. A secured party of record may by his signed statement release all or a part of any collateral described in a filed financing statement. The statement of release is sufficient if it contains a description of the collateral being released, the name and address of the debtor, the name and address of the secured party, and the file number of the financing statement. A statement of release signed by a person other than the secured party of record must be accompanied by a separate written statement of assignment signed by the secured party of record and complying with subsection (2) of Section 9-405, including payment of the required fee. Upon presentation of such a statement of release to the filing officer he shall mark the statement with the hour and date of filing and shall note the same upon the margin of the index of the filing of the financing statement. The uniform fee for filing and noting such a statement of release shall be $. . . . . .if the statement is in the standard form prescribed by the . . . . . and otherwise shall be $. . . . . ., plus in each case an additional fee of $. . . . . for each name more than one against which the statement of release is required to be indexed.

§[[9-407. Information From Filing Officer.]]

[[(1) If the person filing any financing statement, termination statement, statement of assignment, or statement of release, furnishes the filing officer a copy thereof, the filing officer shall upon request note upon the copy the file number and date and hour of the filing of the original and deliver or send the copy to such person.]]

[[(2) Upon request of any person, the filing officer shall issue his certificate showing whether there is on file on the date and hour stated therein, any presently effective financing statement naming a particular debtor and any statement of assignment thereof and if there is, giving the date and hour of filing of each such statement and the names and addresses of each secured party therein. The uniform fee for such a certificate shall be $. . . . . . if the request for the certificate is in the standard form prescribed by the [[Secretary of State]] and otherwise shall be $. . . . . Upon request the filing officer shall furnish a copy of any filed statement or statement of assignment for a uniform fee of $. . . . . per page.]]

Note: *This section is proposed as an optional provision to require filing officers to furnish certificates. Local law and practices should be consulted with regard to the advisability of adoption.*

§9-408. Financing Statements Covering Consigned or Leased Goods. A consignor or lessor of goods may file a financing statement using the terms "consignor," "consignee," "lessor," "lessee" or the like instead of the terms specified in Section 9-402. The provisions of this Part shall apply as appropriate to such a financing statement but its filing shall not of itself be a factor in determining whether or not the consignment or lease is intended as security (Section 1-201(37)). However, if it is determined for other reasons that the consignment or lease is so intended, a security interest of the consignor or lessor which attaches to the consigned or leased goods is perfected by such filing.

Part 5: Default

§9-501. Default; Procedure When Security Agreement Covers Both Real and Personal Property.

(1) When a debtor is in default under a security agreement, a secured party has the rights and remedies provided in this Part and except as limited by subsection (3) those provided in the security agreement. He may reduce his claim to judgment, foreclose or otherwise enforce the security interest by any available judicial procedure. If the collateral is documents the secured party may proceed either as to the documents or as to the goods covered thereby. A secured party in possession has the rights, remedies and duties provided in Section 9-207. The rights and remedies referred to in this subsection are cumulative.

(2) After default, the debtor has the rights and remedies provided in this Part, those provided in the security agreement and those provided in Section 9-207.

(3) To the extent that they give rights to the debtor and impose duties on the secured party, the rules stated in the subsections referred to below may not be waived or varied except as provided with respect to compulsory disposition of collateral (subsection (3) of Section 9-504 and Section 9-505) and with respect to redemption of collateral (Section 9-506) but the parties may by agreement determine the standards by which the fulfillment of these rights and duties is to be measured if such standards are not manifestly unreasonable:

(a) subsection (2) of Section 9-502 and subsection (2) of Section 9-504 insofar as they require accounting for surplus proceeds of collateral;

(b) subsection (3) of Section 9-504 and subsection (1) of Section 9-505 which deal with disposition of collateral;

(c) subsection (2) of Section 9-505 which deals with acceptance of collateral as discharge of obligation;

(d) Section 9-506 which deals with redemption of collateral; and

(e) subsection (1) of Section 9-507 which deals with the secured party's liability for failure to comply with this Part.

(4) If the security agreement covers both real and personal property, the secured party may proceed under this Part as to the personal property or he may proceed as to both the real and the personal property in accordance with his rights and remedies in respect of the real property in which case the provisions of this Part do not apply.

(5) When a secured party has reduced his claim to judgment the lien of any levy which may be made upon his collateral by virtue of any execution based upon the judgment shall relate back to the date of the perfection of the security interest in such collateral. A judicial sale, pursuant to such execution, is a foreclosure of the security interest by judicial procedure within the meaning of this section, and the secured party may purchase at the sale and thereafter hold the collateral free of any other requirements of this Article.

§9-502. Collection Rights of Secured Party.

(1) When so agreed and in any event on default the secured party is entitled to notify an account debtor or the obligor on an instrument to make payment to him whether or not the assignor was theretofore making collections on the collateral, and also to take control of any proceeds to which he is entitled under Section 9-306.

(2) A secured party who by agreement is entitled to charge back uncollected collateral or otherwise to full or limited recourse against the debtor and who undertakes to collect from the account debtors or obligors must proceed in a commercially reasonable manner and may deduct his reasonable expenses of realization from the collections. If the security agreement secures an indebtedness, the secured party must account to the debtor for any surplus, and unless otherwise agreed, the debtor is liable for any deficiency. But, if the underlying transaction was a sale of accounts or chattel paper, the debtor is entitled to any surplus or is liable for any deficiency only if the security agreement so provides.

§9-503. Secured Party's Right to Take Possession After Default. Unless otherwise agreed a secured party has on default the right to take possession of the collateral. In taking possession a secured party may proceed without judicial process if this can be done without breach of the peace or may proceed by action. If the security agreement so provides the secured party may require the debtor to assemble the collateral and make it available to the secured party at a place to be designated by the secured party which is reasonably convenient to both parties. Without removal a secured party may render equipment unusable, and may dispose of collateral on the debtor's premises under Section 9-504.

§9-504. Secured Party's Right to Dispose of Collateral After Default; Effect of Disposition.

(1) A secured party after default may sell, lease or otherwise dispose of any or all of the collateral in its then condition or following any commercially reasonable preparation or processing. Any sale of goods is subject to the Article on Sales (Article 2). The proceeds of disposition shall be applied in the order following to

(a) the reasonable expenses of retaking, holding, preparing for sale or lease, selling, leasing and the like and, to the extent provided for in the agreement and not prohibited by law, the reasonable attorneys' fees and legal expenses incurred by the secured party;
(b) the satisfaction of indebtedness secured by the security interest under which the disposition is made;
(c) the satisfaction of indebtedness secured by any subordinate security interest in the collateral if written notification of demand therefor is received before distribution of the proceeds is completed. If requested by the secured party, the holder of a subordinate security interest must seasonably furnish reasonable proof of his interest, and unless he does so, the secured party need not comply with his demand.

(2) If the security interest secures an indebtedness, the secured party must account to the debtor for any surplus, and, unless otherwise agreed, the debtor is liable for any deficiency. But if the underlying transaction was a sale of accounts, or chattel paper, the debtor is entitled to any surplus or is liable for any deficiency only if the security agreement so provides.

(3) Disposition of the collateral may be by public or private proceedings and may be made by way of one or more contracts. Sale or other disposition may be as a unit or in parcels and at any time and place and on any terms but every aspect of the disposition including the method, manner, time, place and terms must be commercially reasonable. Unless collateral is perishable or threatens to decline speedily in value or is of a type customarily sold on a recognized market, reasonable notification of the time and place of any public sale or reasonable notification of the time after which any private sale or other intended disposition is to be made shall be sent by the secured party to the debtor, if he has not signed after default a statement renouncing or modifying his right to notification of sale. In the case of consumer goods no other notification need be sent. In other cases notification shall be sent to any other secured party from whom the secured party has received (before sending his notification to the debtor or before the debtor's renunciation of his rights) written notice of a claim of an interest in the collateral. The secured party may buy at any public sale and if the collateral is of a type customarily sold in a recognized market or is of a type which is the subject of widely distributed standard price quotations he may buy at private sale.

(4) When collateral is disposed of by a secured party after default, the disposition transfers to a purchaser for value all of the debtor's rights therein, discharges the security interest under which it is made and any security interest or lien subordinate thereto. The purchaser takes free of all such rights and interests even though the secured party fails to comply with the requirements of this Part or of any judicial proceedings

(a) in the case of a public sale, if the purchaser has no knowledge of any defects in the sale and if he does not buy in collusion with the secured party, other bidders or the person conducting the sale; or
(b) in any other case, if the purchaser acts in good faith.

(5) A person who is liable to a secured party under a guaranty, indorsement, repurchase agreement or the like and who receives a transfer of collateral from the secured party or is subrogated to his rights has thereafter the rights and duties of the secured party. Such a transfer of collateral is not a sale or disposition of the collateral under this Article.

§9-505. Compulsory Disposition of Collateral; Acceptance of the Collateral as Discharge of Obligation.

(1) If the debtor has paid sixty per cent of the cash price in the case of a purchase money security interest in consumer goods or sixty per cent of the loan in the case of another security interest in consumer goods and has not signed after default a statement renouncing or modifying his rights under this Part a secured party who has taken possession of collateral must dispose of it under Section 9-504 and if he fails to do so within ninety days after he takes possession the debtor at his option may recover in conversion or under Section 9-507(1) on secured party's liability.

(2) In any other case involving consumer goods or any other collateral a secured party in possession may, after default, propose to retain the collateral in satisfaction of the obligation. Written notice of such proposal shall be sent to the debtor if he has not signed after default a statement renouncing or modifying his rights under this subsection. In the case of consumer goods no other notice need be given. In other cases notice shall be sent to any other secured party from whom the secured party has received (before sending his notice to the debtor or before the debtor's renunciation of his rights) written notice of a claim of an interest in the collateral. If the secured party receives objection in writing from a person entitled to receive notification within twenty-one days after the notice was sent, the secured party must dispose of the collateral under Section 9-504. In the absence of such written objection the secured party may retain the collateral in satisfaction of the debtor's obligation.

§9-506. Debtor's Right to Redeem Collateral. At any time before the secured party has disposed of collateral or entered into a contract for its disposition under Section 9-504 or before the obligation has been discharged under Section 9-505(2) the debtor or any other secured party may unless otherwise agreed in writing after default redeem the collateral by tendering fulfillment of all obligations secured by the collateral as well as the expenses reasonably incurred by the secured party in retaking, holding and preparing the collateral for disposition, in arranging for the sale, and to the extent provided in the agreement and not prohibited by law, his reasonable attorneys' fees and legal expenses.

§9-507. Secured Party's Liability for Failure to Comply With This Part.

(1) If it is established that the secured party is not proceeding in accordance with the provisions of this Part disposition may be ordered or restrained on appropriate terms and conditions. If the disposition has occurred the debtor or any person entitled to notification or whose security interest has been made known to the secured party prior to the disposition has a right to recover from the secured party any loss caused by a failure to comply with the provisions of this Part. If the collateral is consumer goods, the debtor has a right to recover in any event an amount not less than the credit service charge plus ten per cent of the principal amount of the debt or the time price differential plus 10 per cent of the cash price.

(2) The fact that a better price could have been obtained by a sale at a different time or in a different method from that selected by the secured party is not of itself sufficient to establish that the sale was not made in a commercially reasonable manner. If the secured party either sells the collateral in the usual manner in any recognized market therefor or if he sells at the price current in such market at the time of his sale or if he has otherwise sold in conformity with reasonable commercial practices among dealers in the type of property sold he has sold in a commercially reasonable manner. The principles stated in the two preceding sentences with respect to sales also apply as may be appropriate to other types of disposition. A disposition which has been approved in any judicial proceeding or by any bona fide creditors' committee or representative of creditors shall conclusively be deemed to be commercially reasonable, but this sentence does not indicate that any such approval must be obtained in any case nor does it indicate that any disposition not so approved is not commercially reasonable.

ARTICLE 10: EFFECTIVE DATE AND REPEALER

[omitted]

ARTICLE 11: EFFECTIVE DATE AND TRANSITION PROVISIONS

[omitted]

APPENDIX 3

Uniform Partnership Act, 1992

ARTICLE 1: GENERAL PROVISIONS

§101. Definitions. In this [Act]:

(1) "Business" includes every trade, occupation, and profession.

(2) "Debtor in bankruptcy" means a person who is the subject of:

  (i) an order for relief under Title 11 of the United States Code or a comparable order under a successor statute of general application; or

  (ii) a comparable order under federal or state law governing insolvency.

(3) "Distribution" means a transfer of cash or other property from a partnership to a partner in the partner's capacity as a partner, or to the partner's transferee.

(4) "Partnership agreement" means an agreement, written or oral, among the partners concerning the partnership.

(5) "Partnership at will" means a partnership in which the partners have not agreed to remain partners until the expiration of a definite term or the completion of a particular undertaking.

(6) "Person" means an individual, corporation, business trust, estate, trust, partnership, association, joint venture, government, governmental subdivision, agency, or instrumentality, or any other legal or commercial entity.

(7) "Property" means all property, real, personal, or mixed, tangible or intangible, or any interest therein.

(8) "State" means a state of the United States, the District of Columbia, the Commonwealth of Puerto Rico, or any territory or insular possession subject to the jurisdiction of the United States.

(9) "Statement" means a statement of partnership authority under Section 303, a statement of denial under Section 304, a statement of dissociation under Section 704, a statement of dissolution under Section 806, a statement of merger under Section 906, or an amendment or cancellation of any of the foregoing.

(10) "Transfer" includes an assignment, conveyance, lease, mortgage, deed, and encumbrance.

§102. Knowledge and Notice.

(a) A person knows a fact if the person has knowledge of it.

(b) A person has notice of a fact if the person:

(1) knows of it;
(2) has received a notice of it; or
(3) has reason to know it exists from all of the facts known to that person at the time in question.

(c) A person notifies or gives a notice to another by taking steps reasonably required to inform the other person in the ordinary course of business, whether or not the other person learns of it.

(d) A person is notified or receives a notice of a fact when:

(1) the existence of the fact comes to the person's attention; or
(2) the notice is duly delivered at the person's place of business or at any other place held out by the person as a place for receiving communications.

(e) Except as provided in subsection (f), notice received by a person who is not an individual, including a partnership, is effective for a particular transaction when the notice is brought to the attention of the individual conducting the transaction, or in any event when the notice would have been brought to that individual's attention if the person had exercised due diligence. Such a person exercises due diligence if it maintains reasonable routines for communicating significant information to the individual conducting the transaction and there is reasonable compliance with the routines. Due diligence does not require an individual acting for the person to communicate information unless the communication is part of the individual's regular duties or the individual has reason to know of the transaction and that the transaction would be materially affected by the information.

(f) Receipt of notice by a partner of a matter relating to the partnership is effective immediately as notice to the partnership, but is not effective in the case of fraud on the partnership committed by or with the consent of the partner who received the notice.

§103. Effect of Partnership Agreement; Nonwaivable Provisions.

(a) Except as provided in subsection (b), a partnership agreement governs relations among the partners and between the partners and the partnership. To the extent the partnership agreement does not otherwise provide, this [Act] governs relations among the partners and between the partners and the partnership.

(b) A partnership agreement may not:
(1) vary the rights and duties under Section 105 except to eliminate the duty to provide copies of statements to all the partners;
(2) unreasonably restrict a partner's right of access to books and records under Section 403(b);
(3) eliminate the duty of loyalty under Section 404(b);
(4) unreasonably reduce the duty of care under Section 404(d);
(5) eliminate the obligation of good faith and fair dealing under Section 404(e);
(6) vary the power to withdraw as a partner under Section 601(1), except to require the notice to be in writing;
(7) vary the right to expulsion of a partner by a court in the events specified in Section 601(5);
(8) vary the requirement to wind up the partnership business in cases specified in Section 801(4), (5), or (6); or
(9) restrict rights of third parties under this [Act].

§104. Supplemental Principles of Law.
(a) Unless displaced by particular provisions of this [Act], the principles of law and equity supplement this [Act].
(b) If an obligation to pay interest arises under this [Act] and the rate is not specified, the rate is that specified in [applicable statute].

§105. Execution, Filing, and Recording of Statements.
(a) A statement may be filed in the office of [the Secretary of State]. A certified copy of a statement that is filed in an office in another state may be filed in the office of [the Secretary of State]. Either filing has the effect provided in this [Act] with respect to partnership property located in or transactions that occur in this State.
(b) A certified copy of a statement that has been filed in the office of the [Secretary of State] that is recorded in the office for recording transfers of real property shall have the effect provided for recorded statements in this [Act]. A recorded statement that is not a certified copy of a statement filed in the office of the [Secretary of State] shall not have the effect provided for recorded statements in this [Act].
(c) A statement filed by a partnership must be executed by at least two partners. Other statements must be executed by a partner or other person authorized by this [Act]. An individual who executes a statement as, or on behalf of, a partner or other person named as a partner in a statement must personally declare under penalty of perjury that the contents of the statement are accurate.
(d) A person authorized by this [Act] to file a statement may amend or cancel the statement by filing an amendment or cancellation that names the partnership, identifies the statement, and states the substance of the amendment or cancellation.
(e) A person who files a statement pursuant to this section shall promptly send a copy of the statement to every partner, and to any other person named as a partner in the statement. Failure to send a copy of a statement to a partner or other person does not limit the effectiveness of the statement as to a person not a partner.
(f) The [Secretary of State] may collect a fee for filing or providing a certified copy of a statement. The [officers responsible for] recording transfers of real property may collect a fee for recording a statement.

§106. Law Governing Internal Affairs. Laws of the state in which a partnership has its chief executive office govern the partnership's internal affairs.

§107. Partnership Subject to Amendment or Repeal of [Act]. A partnership governed by this [Act] is subject to any amendment or repeal of this [Act].

ARTICLE 2: NATURE OF PARTNERSHIP

§201. Partnership as Entity. A partnership is an entity.

§202. Creation of Partnership.
(a) Except as provided in subsection (b), the association of two or more persons to carry on as co-owners a business for profit creates a partnership, whether or not the persons intend to create a partnership.
(b) An association created under a statute other than this [Act], any predecessor law, or comparable law of another jurisdiction is not a partnership.
(c) In determining whether a partnership is created, the following rules apply:
(1) Joint tenancy, tenancy in common, tenancy by the entireties, joint property, common property, or part ownership does not by itself establish a partnership, even if the co-owners share profits made by the use of the property.
(2) The sharing of gross returns does not by itself establish a partnership, even if the persons sharing them have a joint or common right or interest in property from which the returns are derived.
(3) The receipt by a person of a share of the profits of a business is prima facie evidence that the person is a partner in the business, but that inference may not be drawn if the profits were received in payment:
(i) of a debt by installments or otherwise;
(ii) for services as an independent contractor, or of wages or other compensation to an employee;
(iii) of rent;
(iv) of an annuity or other retirement or health benefit to a beneficiary, representative, or designee of a deceased or retired partner;
(v) of interest or other charge on a loan, even if the amount of payment varies with the profits of the business, including a direct or indirect present or future ownership of the collateral, or rights to income, proceeds, or increase in value derived from the collateral; or
(vi) of consideration for the sale of the goodwill of a business or other property by installments or otherwise.
(d) Except as provided by Section 308, persons who are not partners as to each other are not partners as to other persons.
(e) A partnership created under this [Act] is a general partnership, and the partners are general partners of the partnership.

§203. Partnership Property. Property transferred to or otherwise acquired by a partnership is property of the partnership and not of the partners individually.

§204. When Property Is Partnership Property.
(a) Property is partnership property if acquired:
(1) in the name of the partnership; or
(2) in the name of one or more partners with an indication in the instrument transferring title to the property of the person's capacity as a partner or of the existence of a partnership, but without an indication of the name of the partnership.
(b) Property is acquired in the name of the partnership by a transfer to:
(1) the partnership in its name; or
(2) one or more partners in their capacity as partners in the partnership, if the name of the partnership is indicated in the instrument transferring title to the property.

(c) Property is presumed to be partnership property if purchased with partnership assets, even if not acquired in the name of the partnership or of one or more partners with an indication in the instrument transferring title to the property of the person's capacity as a partner or of the existence of a partnership.

(d) Property acquired in the name of one or more of the partners, without an indication in the instrument transferring title to the property of the person's capacity as a partner or of the existence of a partnership and without use of partnership assets, is presumed to be separate property, even if used for partnership purposes.

ARTICLE 3: RELATIONS OF PARTNERS TO PERSONS DEALING WITH PARTNERSHIP

§301. Partner Agent of Partnership. Subject to the effect of a statement of partnership authority pursuant to Section 303:

(1) Each partner is an agent of the partnership for the purpose of its business. Any act of a partner, including the execution of an instrument in the partnership name, for apparently carrying on in the usual way the partnership business or business of the kind carried on by the partnership binds the partnership, unless the partner has no authority to act for the partnership in the particular matter and the person with whom the partner is dealing knows or has received a notice that the partner lacks authority.

(2) An act of a partner which is not apparently for carrying on in the usual way the partnership business or business of the kind carried on by the partnership does not bind the partnership unless authorized by the other partners.

§302. Transfer of Partnership Property.

(a) Subject to the effect of a statement of partnership authority pursuant to Section 303:

(1) Partnership property held in the name of the partnership may be transferred by an instrument of transfer executed by any partner in the partnership name.
(2) Partnership property held in the name of one or more partners with an indication in the instrument transferring the property to them of their capacity as partners or of the existence of a partnership, but without an indication of the name of the partnership, may be transferred by an instrument of transfer executed by the persons in whose name the property is held.
(3) A partnership may recover property transferred under this subsection if it proves that execution of the instrument of transfer did not bind the partnership under Section 301, unless the property was transferred by the initial transferee or a person claiming through the initial transferee to a subsequent transferee who gave value without having notice that the person who executed the instrument of initial transfer lacked authority to bind the partnership.

(b) Partnership property held in the name of one or more persons other than the partnership, without an indication in the instrument transferring the property to them of their capacity as partners or of the existence of a partnership, may be transferred free of any claims of the partnership or the partners by the persons in whose name the property is held to a transferee who gives value without having notice that it is partnership property.

(c) If a person holds all of the partners' interests in the partnership, all of the partnership property vests in that person. That person may execute documents in the name of the partnership to evidence vesting of the property in that person and may file or record those documents.

§303. Statement of Partnership Authority.

(a) A partnership may file a statement of partnership authority, which:

(1) must include:
  (i) the name of the partnership;
  (ii) the street address of its chief executive office and of an office in this State, if any;
  (iii) the names and mailing addresses of all the partners or of an agent appointed and maintained by the partnership for the purpose of subsection (b); and
  (iv) a statement specifying the names of the partners authorized to execute an instrument transferring real property held in the name of the partnership; and
(2) may include a statement of the authority, or of limitations on the authority, of some or all of the partners to enter into other transactions on behalf of the partnership and any other matter.

(b) If a statement of partnership authority names an agent, the agent shall maintain a list of the names and mailing addresses of all of the partners and make it available to any person on request for good cause shown.

(c) If a filed statement of partnership authority is executed pursuant to Section 105(c) and states the name of the partnership but does not contain all of the other information required by subsection (a), the statement nevertheless operates with respect to a person not a partner as provided in subsections (d) and (e).

(d) Except as provided in subsections (e), (f), and (g), a filed statement of partnership authority supplements the authority of a partner to enter into transactions on behalf of the partnership as follows:

(1) Except for transfers of real property, a grant of authority contained in a filed statement of partnership authority is conclusive, in favor of a person who gives value without knowledge to the contrary, so long as and to the extent that a limitation on that authority is not then contained in another filed statement. A filed cancellation of a limitation on authority revives the previous grant of authority.
(2) A grant of authority to transfer real property held in the name of the partnership contained in a certified copy of a filed statement of partnership authority recorded in the office for recording transfers of that real property is conclusive, in favor of a person who gives value without knowledge to the contrary, so long as and to the extent that a certified copy of a filed statement containing a limitation on that authority is not then recorded in the office for recording transfers of that real property. The recording in the office for recording transfers of that real property of a certified copy of a filed cancellation of a limitation on authority revives the previous grant of authority.

(e) A person not a partner is deemed to know of a limitation on the authority of a partner to transfer real property held in the name of the partnership if a certified copy of the filed statement containing the limitation on authority is recorded in the office for recording transfers of that real property.

(f) Except as provided in subsection (e) and Sections 704 and 806, a person not a partner is not deemed to know of a limitation on the authority of a partner merely because the limitation is contained in a filed statement.

(g) Unless earlier cancelled, a filed statement of partnership authority is cancelled by operation of law five years after the date on which the statement, or the most recent amendment, was filed with the [Secretary of State].

§304. Statement of Denial. A partner or other person named as a partner in a filed statement of partnership authority or in a list maintained by an agent pursuant to Section 303(b) may file a statement of denial stating the name of the partnership and the fact that is being denied, which may include denial of a person's authority or status as a partner. A statement of denial is a limitation on authority to the extent provided in Section 303(d) and (e).

§305. Partnership Liable for Partner's Actionable Conduct.

(a) A partnership is liable for loss or injury caused to a person, or for a penalty incurred, as a result of a wrongful act or omission, or other actionable conduct, of a partner acting in the ordinary course of business of the partnership or with the authority of the partnership.

(b) If, in the course of its business, a partnership receives money or property of a person not a partner which is misapplied by a partner while it is in the custody of the partnership, the partnership is liable for the loss.

§306. Partner's Liability. All partners are liable jointly and severally for all obligations of the partnership unless otherwise agreed by the claimant or provided by law.

§307. Actions by and Against Partnership and Partners.

(a) A partnership may sue and be sued in the name of the partnership.

(b) An action may be brought against the partnership and any or all of the partners in the same action or in separate actions.

(c) A judgment against a partnership is not by itself a judgment against a partner. A judgment against a partnership may not be satisfied from a partner's assets unless there is a judgment against the partner.

(d) A judgment creditor of a partner may not levy execution against the assets of the partner to satisfy a judgment based on a claim against the partnership unless:

(1) a judgment based on the same claim has been obtained against the partnership and a writ of execution on the judgment has been returned unsatisfied in whole or in part;

(2) an involuntary case under Title 11 of the United States Code has been commenced against the partnership and has not been dismissed within 60 days after commencement, or the partnership has commenced a voluntary case under Title 11 of the United States Code and the case has not been dismissed;

(3) the partner has agreed that the creditor need not exhaust partnership assets;

(4) a court grants permission to the judgment creditor to levy execution against the assets of a partner based on a finding that partnership assets subject to execution are clearly insufficient to satisfy the judgment, that exhaustion of partnership assets is excessively burdensome, or that the grant of permission is an appropriate exercise of the court's equitable powers; or

(5) liability is imposed on the partner by law or contract independent of the existence of the partnership.

(e) This section applies to any partnership liability or obligation resulting from a representation by a partner or purported partner under Section 308(a) or (b).

§308. Purported Partner.

(a) If a person, by words or conduct, purports to be a partner, or consents to being represented by another as a partner, in a partnership or with one or more persons not partners, the purported partner is liable to a person to whom the representation is made and who, relying on the representation, enters into a transaction with the actual or purported partnership. If the representation, either by the purported partner or by a person with the purported partner's consent, is made in a public manner, the purported partner is liable to a person who relies upon the purported partnership even if the purported partner is not aware of being held out as a partner to the claimant. If partnership liability results, the purported partner is liable as if the purported partner were a partner. If no partnership liability results, the purported partner is liable jointly and severally with any other person consenting to the representation.

(b) If a person is thus represented to be a partner in an existing partnership, or with one or more persons not partners, the purported partner is an agent of persons consenting to the representation to bind them to the same extent and in the same manner as if the purported partner were a partner, with respect to persons who enter into transactions in reliance upon the representation. If all the partners of the existing partnership consent to the representation, a partnership act or obligation results. If fewer than all the partners of the existing partnership consent to the representation, the person acting and the partners consenting to the representation are jointly and severally liable.

(c) A person is not a partner in a partnership solely because the person is named by another in a statement of partnership authority.

(d) A person does not continue to be a partner solely because of a failure to file a statement of dissociation or to amend a statement of partnership authority to indicate the partner's dissociation from the partnership.

§309. Liability of Incoming Partner. A person admitted as a partner into a partnership is liable for all obligations of the partnership arising before the person's admission as if the person had been a partner when the obligations were incurred, but this liability may be satisfied only out of partnership property.

ARTICLE 4: RELATIONS OF PARTNERS TO EACH OTHER AND TO PARTNERSHIP

§401. Partner's Rights and Duties.

(a) A partnership shall establish an account for each partner which must be credited with an amount equal to the cash plus the value of any other property, net of the amount of any liabilities, the partner contributes to the partnership and the partner's share of the partnership profits. Each partner's account must be charged with an amount equal to the cash plus the value of any other property, net of the amount of any liabilities, distributed by the partnership to the partner and the partner's share of the partnership losses.

(b) A partnership shall credit each partner's account with an equal share of the partnership profits and shall charge each partner with a share of the partnership losses, whether capital or operating, in proportion to the partner's share of the profits.

(c) A partnership shall indemnify each partner for payments reasonably made and liabilities reasonably incurred by the partner in the ordinary and proper conduct of the business of the partnership or for the preservation of its business or property.

(d) A partnership shall repay a partner who, in aid of the partnership, makes a payment or advance beyond the amount of capital the partner agreed to contribute.

(e) A payment made by a partner which gives rise to a partnership obligation under subsection (c) or (d) constitutes a loan to the partnership. Interest accrues from the date of the payment or advance.

(f) Each partner has equal rights in the management and conduct of the partnership business.

(g) A partner may use or possess partnership property only on behalf of the partnership.

(h) A partner is not entitled to remuneration for services performed for the partnership, except for reasonable compensation for services rendered in winding up the business of the partnership.

(i) A person may become a partner only with the consent of all the partners.

(j) A difference arising as to a matter in the ordinary course of business of a partnership may be decided by a majority of the partners. An act outside the ordinary course of business of a partnership and an amendment to the partnership agreement may be undertaken only with the consent of all the partners.

(k) This section does not affect the obligations of a partnership to other persons under Section 301.

§402. **Distributions in Kind.** A partner has no right to receive, and may not be required to accept, a distribution in kind.

§403. **Partner's Right to Information.**

(a) A partnership shall keep its books and records, if any, at its chief executive office.

(b) A partnership shall provide partners and their agents and attorneys access to its books and records. It shall provide former partners and their agents and attorneys access to books and records pertaining to the period during which they were partners. The right of access provides the opportunity to inspect and copy books and records during ordinary business hours. A partnership may impose a reasonable charge, covering the costs of labor and material, for copies of documents furnished.

(c) Each partner and the partnership, on demand, shall furnish to a partner, and the legal representative of a deceased partner or partner under legal disability, to the extent just and reasonable, complete and accurate information concerning the partnership.

§404. **General Standards of Partner's Conduct.**

(a) The only fiduciary duties a partner owes to the partnership and the other partners are the duty of loyalty and the duty of care set forth in this section.

(b) A partner's duty of loyalty to the partnership and the other partners is limited to the following:

(1) to account to the partnership and hold as trustee for it any property, profit, or benefit derived by the partner, without the consent of the other partners, in the conduct and winding up of the partnership business or from a use or appropriation by the partner of partnership property or opportunity;

(2) to refrain from dealing with the partnership in the conduct or winding up of the partnership business, as or on behalf of a party having an interest adverse to the partnership without the consent of the other partners; and

(3) to refrain from competing with the partnership in the conduct of the partnership business without the consent of the other partners before the dissolution of the partnership.

(c) A partner's duty of loyalty may not be eliminated by agreement, but the partners may by agreement identify specific types or categories of activities that do not violate the duty of loyalty, if not manifestly unreasonable.

(d) A partner's duty of care to the partnership and the other partners in the conduct and winding up of the partnership business is limited to refraining from engaging in grossly negligent or reckless conduct, intentional misconduct, or a knowing violation of law.

(e) A partner shall discharge the duties to the partnership and the other partners under this [Act] or under the partnership agreement, and exercise any rights, consistent with the obligation of good faith and fair dealing. The obligation of good faith and fair dealing may not be eliminated by agreement, but the partners may by agreement determine the standards by which the performance of the obligation is to be measured, if the standards are not manifestly unreasonable.

(f) A partner does not violate a duty or obligation under this [Act] or under the partnership agreement merely because the partner's conduct furthers the partner's own interest. A partner may lend money to and transact other business with the partnership. The rights and obligations of a partner who lends money to or transacts business with the partnership are the same as those of a person who is not a partner, subject to other applicable law.

(g) This section applies to a person winding up the partnership business as the personal or legal representative of the last surviving partner as if the person were a partner.

§405. **Partner's Liability to Partnership.** A partner is liable to the partnership for a breach of the partnership agreement, or for the violation of any duty to the partnership, causing harm to the partnership.

§406. **Remedies of Partnership and Partners.**

(a) A partnership may maintain an action against a partner for a breach of the partnership agreement, or for the violation of any duty to the partnership, causing harm to the partnership.

(b) A partner may maintain an action against the partnership or another partner for legal or equitable relief, including an accounting as to partnership business, to:

(1) enforce a right under the partnership agreement;
(2) enforce a right under this [Act], including:
 (i) the partner's rights under Sections 401, 403, and 404;
 (ii) the partner's right on dissociation to have the partner's interest in the partnership purchased pursuant to Section 701 or enforce any other right under Article 6 or 7; or
 (iii) the partner's right to compel a dissolution and winding up of the partnership business under Section 801 or enforce any other right under Article 8; or
(3) enforce the rights and otherwise protect the interests of the partner, including rights and interests arising independently of the partnership relationship.

(c) The accrual of, and any time limitation on, a right of action for a remedy under this section is governed by other law. A right to an accounting upon a dissolution and winding up does not revive a claim barred by law.

§407. **Continuation of Partnership Beyond Definite Term or Particular Undertaking.**

(a) If a partnership for a definite term or particular undertaking is continued, without an express agreement, after the expiration of the term or completion of the undertaking, the rights and duties of the partners remain the same as they were at the expiration or completion, so far as is consistent with a partnership at will.

(b) A continuation of the business by the partners or those of them who habitually acted in the business during the term or undertaking, without any settlement or liquidation of the partnership business, is prima facie evidence of an agreement that the business will not be wound up.

ARTICLE 5: TRANSFEREES AND CREDITORS OF PARTNER

§501. **Partner's Interest in Partnership Property Not Transferable.** A partner is not a co-owner of partnership property and has no interest that can be transferred, either voluntarily or involuntarily, in partnership property.

§502. Partner's Transferable Interest In Partnership.

(a) The only transferable interest of a partner in the partnership is the partner's interest in distributions. The interest is personal property.

(b) A transferee of a partner's transferable interest in the partnership has the right to cause a winding up of the partnership business as provided in Section 801(6).

§503. Transfer of Partner's Transferable Interest.

(a) A transfer, in whole or in part, of a partner's transferable interest in the partnership:

(1) is permissible;
(2) does not by itself cause a winding up of the partnership business; and
(3) does not, as against the other partners or the partnership, entitle the transferee, during the continuance of the partnership, to participate in the management or conduct of the partnership business, to require access to information concerning or an account of partnership transactions, or to inspect or copy the partnership books or records.

(b) A transferee of a partner's transferable interest in the partnership is entitled to receive, in accordance with the transfer, distributions to which the transferor would otherwise be entitled. Upon transfer, the transferor retains the rights and duties of a partner other than the interest in distributions transferred.

(c) If an event causes a dissolution and winding up of the partnership business under Section 801, a transferee is entitled to receive, in accordance with the transfer, the net amount otherwise distributable to the transferor. In a dissolution and winding up, a transferee may require an accounting only from the date of the last account agreed to by all of the partners.

(d) Until receipt of notice of a transfer, a partnership has no duty to give effect to the transferee's rights under this section.

§504. Partner's Transferable Interest Subject to Charging Order.

(a) On application by a judgment creditor of a partner or partner's transferee, a court having jurisdiction may charge the transferable interest of the debtor partner or transferee to satisfy the judgment. The court may appoint a receiver of the debtor's share of the distributions due or to become due to the debtor in respect of the partnership and make all other orders, directions, accounts, and inquiries the debtor might have made or which the circumstances of the case may require.

(b) A charging order constitutes a lien on the judgment debtor's transferable interest in the partnership. The court may order a foreclosure of the interest subject to the charging order at any time and upon conditions it considers appropriate. The purchaser at the foreclosure sale has the rights of a transferee.

(c) At any time before foreclosure, an interest charged may be redeemed:

(1) by the judgment debtor;
(2) with property other than partnership property, by one or more of the other partners; or
(3) with partnership property, by one or more of the other partners with the consent of all the partners whose interests are not so charged.

(d) This [Act] does not deprive a partner of a right under exemption laws with respect to the partner's interest in the partnership.

(e) This section provides the exclusive remedy by which a judgment creditor of a partner or partner's transferee may satisfy a judgment out of the judgment debtor's transferable interest in the partnership.

ARTICLE 6: PARTNER'S DISSOCIATION

§601. Events Causing Partner's Dissociation. A partner is dissociated from a partnership upon:

(1) receipt by the partnership of notice of the partner's express will to withdraw as a partner or upon any later date specified in the notice;
(2) an event agreed to in the partnership agreement as causing the partner's dissociation;
(3) the partner's expulsion pursuant to the partnership agreement;
(4) he partner's expulsion by the unanimous vote of the other partners if:
   (i) it is unlawful to carry on the partnership business with that partner;
   (ii) there has been a transfer of all or substantially all of that partner's transferable interest in the partnership, other than a transfer for security purposes, or a court order charging the partner's interest, which has not been foreclosed;
   (iii) within 90 days after the partnership notifies a corporate partner that it will be expelled because it has filed a certificate of dissolution or the equivalent, its charter has been revoked, or its right to conduct business has been suspended by the jurisdiction of its incorporation, there is no revocation of the certificate of dissolution or no reinstatement of its charter or its right to conduct business; or
   (iv) a partnership that is a partner has been dissolved and its business is being wound up;
(5) on application by the partnership or another partner, the partner's expulsion by judicial decree because:
   (i) the partner engaged in wrongful conduct that adversely and materially affected the partnership business;
   (ii) the partner willfully or persistently committed a material breach of the partnership agreement or of a duty owed to the partnership or the other partners under Section 404; or
   (iii) the partner engaged in conduct relating to the partnership business which makes it not reasonably practicable to carry on the business in partnership with that partner;
(6) the partner's:
   (i) becoming a debtor in bankruptcy;
   (ii) executing an assignment for the benefit of creditors;
   (iii) seeking, consenting to, or acquiescing in the appointment of a trustee, receiver, or liquidator of that partner or of all or substantially all of that partner's property; or
   (iv) failing, within 90 days after the appointment, to have vacated or stayed the appointment of a trustee, receiver, or liquidator of the partner or of all or substantially all of the partner's property obtained without the partner's consent or acquiescence, or failing within 90 days after the expiration of a stay to have the appointment vacated;
(7) in the case of a partner who is an individual:

(i) the partner's death;
(ii) the appointment of a guardian or general conservator for the partner; or
(iii) a judicial determination that the partner has otherwise become incapable of performing the partner's duties under the partnership agreement;

(8) in the case of a partner that is a trust or is acting as a partner by virtue of being a trustee of a trust, distribution of the trust's entire transferable interest in the partnership, but not merely the substitution of a successor trustee;

(9) in the case of a partner that is an estate or is acting as a partner by virtue of being a personal representative of an estate, distribution of the estate's entire transferable interest in the partnership, but not merely the substitution of a successor personal representative; or

(10) termination of a partner who is not an individual, partnership, corporation, trust, or estate.

§602. Partner's Wrongful Dissociation.

(a) A partner's dissociation is wrongful only if:

(1) it is in breach of an express provision of the partnership agreement; or
(2) in the case of a partnership for a definite term or particular undertaking, before the expiration of the term or the completion of the undertaking:
  (i) the partner withdraws by express will, unless the withdrawal follows the dissociation of another partner and results in a right to dissolve the partnership under Section 801(2)(i);
  (ii) the partner is expelled by judicial decree under Section 601(5); or
  (iii) in the case of a partner who is not an individual, trust other than a business trust, or estate, the partner is expelled or otherwise dissociated because it willfully dissolved or terminated.

(b) A partner who wrongfully dissociates is liable to the partnership and to the other partners for damages caused by the dissociation. That liability is in addition to any other liability of the partner to the partnership or to the other partners.

§603. Effect of Partner's Dissociation.

(a) A dissociated partner's interest in the partnership must be purchased pursuant to Article 7 unless the partner's dissociation results in a dissolution and winding up of the partnership business under Article 8.

(b) Upon a partner's dissociation, that partner's right to participate in the management and conduct of the partnership business is terminated, except as provided in Section 804, and that partner's duties (i) under Section 404(b)(1) and (2) and (d) continue only with regard to matters or events that occurred before the dissociation, and (ii) under Section 404(b)(3) terminate.

ARTICLE 7: PARTNER'S DISSOCIATED PARTNER'S INTEREST.

§701. Purchase of Dissociated Partner's Interest.

(a) If a partner is dissociated from a partnership without resulting in a dissolution and winding up of the partnership business under Section 801, the partnership shall cause the dissociated partner's interest in the partnership to be purchased for a buyout price determined pursuant to subsection (b).

(b) The buyout price of a dissociated partner's interest is the amount that would have been distributable to the dissociating partner under Section 808(b) if, on the date of dissociation, the assets of the partnership were sold at a price equal to the greater of the liquidation value or the value based on a sale of the entire business as a going concern without the dissociated partner and the partnership were wound up as of that date. In either case, the sale price of the partnership assets must be determined on the basis of the amount that would be paid by a willing buyer to a willing seller, neither being under any compulsion to buy or sell, and with knowledge of all relevant facts. Interest must be paid from the date of dissociation to the date of payment.

(c) Damages for wrongful dissociation under Section 602(b), and all other amounts owing, whether or not presently due, from the dissociated partner to the partnership, must be offset against the buyout price. Interest must be paid from the date the amount owed becomes due to the date of payment.

(d) A partnership shall indemnify a dissociated partner against all partnership liabilities incurred before the dissociation, except liabilities then unknown to the partnership, and against all partnership liabilities incurred after the dissociation, except liabilities incurred by an act of the dissociated partner under Section 702. For purposes of this subsection, a liability not known to a partner other than the dissociated partner is not known to the partnership.

(e) If no agreement for the purchase of a dissociated partner's interest is reached within 120 days after a written demand for payment, the partnership shall pay, or cause to be paid, in cash to the dissociated partner the amount the partnership estimates to be the buyout price and accrued interest, reduced by any offsets and accrued interest under subsection (c).

(f) If a deferred payment is authorized under subsection (h), the partnership may tender a written offer to pay the amount it estimates to be the buyout price and accrued interest, reduced by any offsets under subsection (c), stating the time of payment, the amount and type of security for payment, and the other terms and conditions of the obligation.

(g) The payment or tender required by subsections (e) or (f) must be accompanied by the following:

(1) a statement of partnership assets and liabilities as of the date of dissociation;
(2) the latest available partnership balance sheet and income statement, if any;
(3) an explanation of how the estimated amount of the payment was calculated; and
(4) written notice that the payment is in full satisfaction of the obligation to purchase unless, within 120 days after the written notice, the dissociated partner commences an action to determine the buyout price, any offsets under subsection (c), or other terms of the purchase obligation.

(h) A partner who wrongfully dissociates before the expiration of a definite term or the completion of a particular undertaking is not entitled to payment of any portion of the buyout price until the expiration of the term or completion of the undertaking, unless the partner establishes to the satisfaction of the court that earlier payment will not cause undue hardship to the business of the partnership. A deferred payment must be adequately secured and bear interest.

(i) A dissociated partner may maintain an action against the partnership, pursuant to Section 406(b)(2)(ii), to determine the buyout price of that partner's interest, any offsets under subsection (c), or other terms of the purchase obligation. The action must be commenced within 120 days after the partnership has tendered payment or an offer to pay or within one year after written demand for payment if no payment or offer to pay is tendered. The court shall determine the buyout price of the dissociated partner's interest, any offset due under subsection (c), and accrued interest, and enter judgment for any additional payment or refund. If deferred payment is authorized under subsection (h), the court shall also determine the security for payment and other terms of the obligation to purchase. The court may assess reasonable attorney's fees and the fees and expenses of appraisers or other experts for a party to the action, in amounts the court finds equitable, against any other party, if the court finds that the other party acted arbitrarily, vexatiously, or not in good faith, including the partnership's failure to tender payment or an offer to pay or to comply with the requirements of subsection (g).

§702. Dissociated Partner's Power to Bind and Liability to Partnership.

(a) For two years after a partner dissociates without resulting in a dissolution and winding up of the partnership business, the partnership, including a surviving partnership under Article 9, is bound by an act of the dissociated partner that would have bound the partnership under Section 301 before dissociation only if the other party to the transaction:

  (i) reasonably believes when entering the transaction that the dissociated partner is a partner at that time;
  (ii) does not have notice of the partner's dissociation; and
  (iii) is not deemed to have notice under Section 303(e) or Section 704.

(b) A dissociated partner is liable to the partnership for any loss caused to the partnership arising from an obligation incurred by the dissociated partner after dissociation, for which the partnership is liable under subsection (a).

§703. Dissociated Partner's Liability to Other Persons.

(a) A partner's dissociation does not of itself discharge the partner's liability for a partnership obligation incurred before dissociation. A dissociated partner is not liable for a partnership obligation incurred after dissociation except as provided in subsection (b).

(b) A partner who dissociates without resulting in a dissolution and winding up of the partnership business is liable as a partner to the other party in a transaction entered into by the partnership, or a surviving partnership under Article 9, within two years after the partner's dissociation, only if the other party to the transaction:

  (i) reasonably believes when entering the transaction that the dissociated partner is a partner at that time;
  (ii) does not have notice of the partner's dissociation; and
  (iii) is not deemed to have notice under Section 303(e) or Section 704.

(c) By agreement with the partnership creditor and the partners continuing the business, a dissociated partner may be released from liability for a partnership obligation.

(d) A dissociated partner is released from liability for a partnership obligation if a partnership creditor, with notice of the partner's dissociation but without the partner's consent, agrees to a material alteration in the nature or time of payment of a partnership obligation.

§704. Statement of Dissociation.

(a) A dissociated partner or the partnership may file a statement of dissociation stating the name of the partnership and that the partner is dissociated from the partnership. A statement of dissociation is a limitation on the authority of a dissociated partner for the purposes of Section 303(d) and (e).

(b) For the purposes of Sections 702 and 703(b), a person not a partner is deemed to have notice of the dissociation 90 days after the statement of dissociation is filed.

§705. Continued Use of Partnership Name. Continued use of a partnership name, or a dissociated partner's name as part thereof, by the partners continuing the business does not of itself make the dissociated partner liable for an obligation of the partners or the partnership continuing the business.

ARTICLE 8: WINDING UP PARTNERSHIP BUSINESS

§801. Events Causing Dissolution and Winding Up of Partnership Business. A partnership is dissolved, and its business must be wound up, only upon:

(1) except as provided in Section 802, receipt by a partnership at will of notice from a partner, other than a partner who is dissociated under Section 601(2) to (10), of that partner's express will to withdraw as a partner, or upon any later date specified in the notice;

(2) in a partnership for a definite term or particular undertaking:
  (i) except as provided in Section 802, within 90 days after a partner's wrongful dissociation under Section 602 or a partner's dissociation by death or otherwise under Section 601(6) to (10), receipt by the partnership of notice from another partner of that partner's express will to withdraw as a partner;
  (ii) the express will of all the partners; or
  (iii) the expiration of the term or the completion of the undertaking, unless all the partners agree to continue the business, in which case the partnership agreement is deemed amended retroactively to provide that the expiration or completion does not result in the dissolution and winding up of the partnership business;

(3) an event agreed to in the partnership agreement resulting in the winding up of the partnership business, unless all the partners agree to continue the business, in which case the partnership agreement is deemed amended retroactively to provide that the event does not result in the dissolution and winding up of the partnership business;

(4) an event that makes it unlawful for all or substantially all of the business of the partnership to be continued, but any cure of illegality within 90 days after notice to the partnership of the event is effective retroactively to the date of the event for purposes of this section;

(5) on application by a partner, a judicial decree that:
  (i) the economic purpose of the partnership is likely to be unreasonably frustrated;
  (ii) another partner has engaged in conduct relating to the partnership business that makes it not reasonably practicable to carry on the business in partnership with that partner; or
  (iii) it is not otherwise reasonably practicable to carry on the partnership business in conformity with the partnership agreement; or

(6) on application by a transferee of a partner's transferable interest, a judicial decree that it is equitable to wind up the partnership business:
  (i) if the partnership was for a definite term or particular undertaking at the time of the transfer or entry of the charging order that gave rise to the transfer, after the expiration of the term or completion of the undertaking; or
  (ii) if the partnership was a partnership at will at the time of the transfer or entry of the charging order that gave rise to the transfer, at any time.

§802. Dissolution Deferred 90 Days.

(a) Except as provided in subsection (b), a partnership of more than two persons is not dissolved until 90 days after receipt by the partnership of notice from a partner under Section 801(1) or (2)(i), and its business may be continued until that date as if no notice were received. Before that date, the partner who gave the notice may waive the right to have the partnership business wound up. If there is no waiver before that date, the partnership is dissolved and its business must be wound up.

(b) A partnership may be dissolved at any time during the 90-day period, and its business wound up, by the express will of at least half of the other partners.

(c) After receipt by the partnership of notice from a partner under Section 801(1) or (2)(i), the partner who gave the notice:

(1) has no rights in the management and conduct of the partnership business if it is continued under subsection (a), but may participate in winding up the business under Section 804 if the partnership is dissolved on or before the expiration of the 90-day period pursuant to subsection (a) or (b);

(2) is liable for obligations incurred during the period only to the extent a dissociated partner would be liable under Section 702(b) or Section 703(b), but is not liable for contributions for, and must be indemnified by the other partners against, any partnership liability incurred by another partner to the extent the liability is not appropriate for winding up the partnership business; and

(3) with respect to profits or losses incurred during the period, shall be credited with a share of any profits but shall be charged with a share of any losses only to the extent of profits credited for the period.

§803. Partnership Continues After Dissolution. A partnership continues after dissolution until the winding up of its business is completed, at which time the partnership is terminated.

§804. Right to Wind Up Partnership Business.

(a) After dissolution, a partner who has not wrongfully dissociated has a right to participate in winding up the partnership's business, but on application of any partner, partner's legal representative, or transferee, the [designate the appropriate court], for good cause, may order judicial supervision of the winding up.

(b) The legal representative of the last surviving partner may wind up a partnership's business.

(c) A person winding up a partnership's business may preserve the partnership business or property as a going concern for a reasonable time, prosecute and defend actions and proceedings, whether civil, criminal, or administrative, settle and close the partnership's business, dispose of and transfer the partnership's property, discharge the partnership's liabilities, distribute the assets of the partnership pursuant to Section 808, and perform other necessary acts, including settlement of disputes by mediation or arbitration.

§805. Partner's Power to Bind Partnership After Dissolution. Subject to Section 806, a partnership is bound by a partner's act after dissolution that:

(1) is appropriate for winding up the partnership business; or

(2) would have bound the partnership under Section 301 before dissolution, if the other party to the transaction does not have notice of the dissolution.

§806. Statement of Dissolution.

(a) After dissolution, a partner who has not wrongfully dissociated may file a statement of dissolution stating the name of the partnership and that the partnership has dissolved and is winding up its business.

(b) A statement of dissolution cancels a filed statement of partnership authority for the purposes of Section 303(d) and is a limitation on authority for the purposes of Section 303(e).

(c) For the purposes of Sections 301 and 805, a person not a partner is deemed to have notice of the dissolution and the limitation on the partners' authority as a result of the statement of dissolution 90 days after it is filed.

(d) After filing and, where appropriate, recording a statement of dissolution, the dissolved partnership may file and, where appropriate, record a statement of partnership authority which will operate with respect to a person not a partner as provided in Section 303(d) and (e) in any transaction, whether or not the transaction is appropriate for winding up the partnership business.

§807. Partner's Liability to Other Partners After Dissolution.

(a) Except as provided in subsection (b) and Section 802(c)(2), after dissolution a partner is liable to the other partners for the partner's share of any partnership liability incurred under Section 805.

(b) A partner who, with knowledge of the winding up, incurs a partnership liability under Section 805(2) by an act that is not appropriate for winding up the partnership business is liable to the partnership for any loss caused to the partnership arising from that liability.

§808. Settlement of Accounts Among Partners.

(a) In winding up the partnership business, the assets of the partnership must be applied to discharge its obligations to creditors, including partners who are creditors. Any surplus must be applied to pay in cash the net amount distributable to partners in accordance with their right to distributions pursuant to subsection (b).

(b) Each partner is entitled to a settlement of all partnership accounts upon winding up the partnership business. In settling accounts among the partners, the profits and losses that result from the liquidation of the partnership assets must be credited and charged to the partners' accounts. The partnership shall make a distribution to a partner in an amount equal to that partner's positive balance. A partner shall contribute to the partnership an amount equal to that partner's negative balance.

(c) To the extent not taken into account in settling the accounts among partners pursuant to subsection (b), each partner shall contribute, in the proportion in which the partner shares partnership losses, the amount necessary to satisfy partnership obligations. If a partner fails to contribute, the other partners shall contribute, in the proportions in which the partners share partnership losses, the additional amount necessary to satisfy the partnership obligations. A partner or partner's legal representative may recover from the other partners any contributions the partner makes to the extent the amount contributed exceeds that partner's share of the partnership obligations.

(d) The estate of a deceased partner is liable for the partner's obligation to contribute to the partnership.

(e) An assignee for the benefit of creditors of a partnership or a partner, or a person appointed by a court to represent creditors of a partnership or a partner, may enforce a partner's obligation to contribute to the partnership.

ARTICLE 9: CONVERSIONS AND MERGERS

§901. Conversion of Partnership to Limited Partnership.

(a) A partnership may be converted to a limited partnership pursuant to this section.

(b) The terms and conditions of a conversion of a partnership to a limited partnership must be approved by all the partners or by a number or percentage specified for conversion in the partnership agreement.

(c) After the conversion is approved by the partners, the partnership shall file a certificate of limited partnership which satisfies the requirements of [Section _____ of the State Limited Partnership Act] and includes:

(1) a statement that the partnership was converted to a limited partnership from a partnership;
(2) its former name; and
(3) a statement of the number of votes cast by the partners for and against the conversion and, if the vote is less than unanimous, the number or percentage required to approve the conversion under the partnership agreement.

(d) The conversion takes effect when the certificate of limited partnership is filed or at any later date specified in the certificate.

(e) A partner who becomes a limited partner as a result of the conversion remains liable as a partner for an obligation incurred by the partnership before the conversion takes effect. If the other party to a transaction with the limited partnership reasonably believes when entering the transaction that the limited partner is a general partner, the partner is liable for an obligation incurred by the limited partnership within 90 days after the conversion takes effect. The partner's liability for all other obligations of the limited partnership incurred after the conversion takes effect is that of a limited partner as provided in the [State Limited Partnership Act].

§902. Conversion of Limited Partnership to Partnership.

(a) A limited partnership may be converted to a partnership pursuant to this section.

(b) Notwithstanding a provision to the contrary in a limited partnership agreement, the terms and conditions of a conversion of a limited partnership to a partnership must be approved by all the partners.

(c) After the conversion is approved by the partners, the limited partnership shall cancel its certificate of limited partnership pursuant to [Section _____ of the State Limited Partnership Act].

(d) The conversion takes effect when the certificate of limited partnership is cancelled.

(e) A limited partner who becomes a partner as a result of the conversion remains liable only as a limited partner for an obligation incurred by the limited partnership before the conversion takes effect. The limited partner is liable as a partner for an obligation of the partnership incurred after the conversion takes effect.

§903. Effect of Conversion; Entity Unchanged.

(a) A partnership or limited partnership that has been converted pursuant to this article is for all purposes the same entity that existed before the conversion.

(b) When a conversion takes effect:

(1) all property owned by the converting partnership or limited partnership remains vested in the converted entity;
(2) all obligations of the converting partnership or limited partnership continue as obligations of the converted entity; and
(3) an action or proceeding pending against the converting partnership or limited partnership may be continued as if the conversion had not occurred.

§904. Merger of Partnerships.

(a) Pursuant to a plan of merger approved as provided in subsection (c), a partnership may be merged with one or more partnerships or limited partnerships.

(b) The plan of merger must set forth:

(1) the name of each partnership or limited partnership that is a party to the merger;
(2) the name of the surviving entity into which the other partnerships or limited partnerships will merge;
(3) whether the surviving entity is a partnership or a limited partnership and the status of each partner;
(4) the terms and conditions of the merger;
(5) the manner and basis of converting the interests of each party to the merger into interests or obligations of the surviving entity, or into cash or other property in whole or part; and
(6) the street address of the surviving entity's chief executive office.

(c) The plan of merger must be approved:

(1) in the case of a partnership that is a party to the merger, by all the partners, or a number or percentage specified for merger in the partnership agreement; and
(2) in the case of a limited partnership that is a party to the merger, by the vote required for approval of a merger by the law of the state or foreign jurisdiction in which the limited partnership is organized and, in the absence of such specifically applicable law, by all the partners, notwithstanding a provision to the contrary in the partnership agreement.

(d) After a plan of merger is approved and before the merger takes effect, the plan may be amended or abandoned as provided in the plan.

(e) The merger takes effect on the later of:

(1) the approval of the plan of merger by all parties to the merger, as provided in subsection (c);
(2) the filing of all documents required by law to be filed as a condition to the effectiveness of the merger; or
(3) any effective date specified in the plan of merger.

§905. Effect of Merger.

(a) When a merger takes effect:

(1) every partnership or limited partnership that is a party to the merger other than the surviving entity ceases to exist;
(2) all property owned by each of the merged partnerships or limited partnerships vests in the surviving entity;
(3) all obligations of every partnership or limited partnership that is a party to the merger become the obligations of the surviving entity; and
(4) an action or proceeding pending against a partnership or limited partnership that is a party to the merger may be continued as if the merger had not occurred or the surviving entity may be substituted as a party to the action or proceeding.

(b) The [Secretary of State] of this State is the agent for service of process in an action or proceeding against a surviving foreign partnership or limited partnership to enforce an obligation of a domestic partnership or limited partnership that is a party to a merger. The surviving entity shall promptly notify the [Secretary of State] of the mailing address of its chief executive office and of any change of address. Upon receipt of process, the [Secretary of State] shall mail a copy of the process to the surviving foreign partnership or limited partnership.

(c) A partner of the surviving partnership or limited partnership is liable for:

(1) all obligations of a party to the merger for which the partner was personally liable before the merger;

(2) all other obligations of the surviving entity incurred before the merger by a party to the merger, but those obligations may be satisfied only out of property of that entity; and

(3) all obligations of the surviving entity incurred after the merger takes effect.

(d) If the obligations incurred before the merger by a party to the merger are not satisfied out of the property of the surviving partnership or limited partnership, the partners of that party immediately before the effective date of the merger shall contribute the amount necessary to satisfy that party's obligations to the surviving entity, in the manner provided in Section 808(c) as if the merged party were dissolved.

(e) A partner of a party to a merger who does not become a partner of the surviving partnership or limited partnership is dissociated from the entity, of which that partner was a partner, as of the date the merger takes effect. The surviving entity shall cause the partner's interest in the entity to be purchased under Section 701. The surviving entity is bound under Section 702 by an act of a partner dissociated under this subsection, and the partner is liable under Section 703 for transactions entered into by the surviving entity after the merger takes effect.

§906. **Statement of Merger.**

(a) After a merger, the surviving partnership or limited partnership may file a statement that one or more partnerships or limited partnerships have merged into the surviving entity.

(b) A statement of merger must contain:

(1) the name of each partnership or limited partnership that is a party to the merger;
(2) the name of the surviving entity into which the other partnerships or limited partnership were merged;
(3) the street address of the surviving entity's chief executive office and of an office in this State, if any; and
(4) whether the surviving entity is a partnership or limited partnership.

(c) Except as provided in subsection (d), for the purposes of Section 302, property of the surviving partnership or limited partnership which before the merger was held in the name of another party to the merger is property held in the name of the surviving entity upon filing a statement of merger.

(d) For the purposes of Section 302, real property of the surviving partnership or limited partnership which before the merger was held in the name of another party to the merger is property held in the name of the surviving entity upon recording a certified copy of the statement of merger in the office for recording transfers of that real property.

(e) A filed and, where appropriate, recorded statement of merger, executed and declared to be accurate pursuant to Section 105(c), stating the name of a partnership or limited partnership that is a party to the merger in whose name property was held before the merger and the name of the surviving entity, but not containing all of the other information required by subsection (b), operates with respect to the partnerships or limited partnerships named to the extent provided in subsections (c) and (d).

§907. **Nonexclusive.** This article is not exclusive. Partnerships or limited partnerships may be converted or merged in any other manner provided by law.

ARTICLE 10: MISCELLANEOUS PROVISIONS

§1001. **Uniformity of Application and Construction.** This [Act] shall be applied and construed to effectuate its general purpose to make uniform the law with respect to the subject of this [Act] among states enacting it.

§1002. **Short Title.** This [Act] may be cited as the Uniform Partnership Act (1992).

§1003. **Severability.** If any provision of this [Act] or its application to any person or circumstance is held invalid, the invalidity does not affect other provisions or applications of this [Act] which can be given effect without the invalid provision or application, and to this end the provisions of this [Act] are severable.

§1004. **Effective Date.** This [Act] takes effect. . . .

§1005. **Repeals.** The following acts and parts of acts are repealed: [the State Partnership Act as amended and in effect immediately prior to the adoption of this [Act]].

§1006. **Application to Existing Relationships.**

(a) Except as otherwise provided in this section, this [Act] applies to all partnerships in existence on its effective date that were formed under the [State] Partnership Act or any predecessor law providing for the formation, operation, and liquidation of partnerships.

(b) Section 802 does not apply to a partnership in existence on the effective date of this [Act] unless the partners agree otherwise.

(c) This [Act] does not impair the obligations of a contract existing when the [Act] takes effect or affect an action or proceeding begun or right accrued before this [Act] takes effect.

(d) A judgment against a partnership or a partner in an action commenced before the effective date of this [Act] may be enforced in the same manner as a judgment rendered before the effective date of this [Act].

APPENDIX 4

Uniform Limited Partnership Act (1976), with 1985 Amendments

ARTICLE I

General Provisions

§101. Definitions. As used in this Act, unless the context otherwise requires:

(1) "Certificate of limited partnership" means the certificate referred to in Section 201, and the certificate as amended or restated.

(2) "Contribution" means any cash, property, services rendered, or a promissory note or other binding obligation to contribute cash or property or to perform services, which a partner contributes to a limited partnership in his capacity as a partner.

(3) "Event of withdrawal of a general partner" means an event that causes a person to cease to be a general partner as provided in Section 402.

(4) "Foreign limited partnership" means a partnership formed under the laws of any state other than this State and having as partners one or more general partners and one or more limited partners.

(5) "General partner" means a person who has been admitted to a limited partnership as a general partner in accordance with the partnership agreement and named in the certificate of limited partnership as a general partner.

(6) "Limited partner" means a person who has been admitted to a limited partnership as a limited partner in accordance with the partnership agreement and named in the certificate of limited partnership as a limited partner.

(7) "Limited partnership" and "domestic limited partnership" mean a partnership formed by 2 or more persons under the laws of this State and having one or more general partners and one or more limited partners.

(8) "Partner" means a limited or general partner.

(9) "Partnership agreement" means any valid agreement, written or oral, of the partners as to the affairs of a limited partnership and the conduct of its business.

(10) "Partnership interest" means a partner's share of the profits and losses of a limited partnership and the right to receive distributions of a partnership assets.

(11) "Person" means a natural person, partnership, limited partnership (domestic or foreign), trust, estate, association, or corporation.

(12) "State" means a state, territory, or possession of the United States, the District of Columbia, or the Commonwealth of Puerto Rico.

§102. Name. The name of each limited partnership as set forth in its certificate of limited partnership:

(1) shall contain without abbreviation the words "limited partnership";

(2) may not contain the name of a limited partners unless (i) it is also the name of a general partner or the corporate name of a corporate general partner, or (ii) the business of the limited partnership had been carried on under that name before the admission of that limited partner;

(3) may not be the same as, or deceptively similar to, the name of any corporation or limited partnership organized under the laws of this State or licensed or registered as a foreign corporation or limited partnership in this State; and

(4) may not contain the following words [here insert prohibited words].

§103. Reservation of Name. . . .

§104. Specified Office and Agent. Each limited partnership shall continuously maintain in this State:

(1) an office, which may but need not be a place of its business in this State, at which shall be kept the records required by Section 105 to be maintained; and

(2) an agent for service of process on the limited partnership, which agent must be an individual resident of this State, a domestic corporation, or a foreign corporation authorized to do business in this State.

§105. Records to Be Kept.

(a) Each limited partnership shall keep at the office referred to in Section 104(1) the following:

(1) a current list of the full name and last known business address of each partner, separately identifying the general partners (in alphabetical order) and the limited partners (in alphabetical order);
(2) a copy of the certificate of limited partnership and all certificates of amendment thereto, together with executed copies of any powers of attorney pursuant to which any certificate has been executed;
(3) copies of the limited partnership's federal, state, and local income tax returns and reports, if any, for the three most recent years;
(4) copies of any then-effective written partnership agreements and of any financial statements of the limited partnership for the three most recent years; and
(5) unless contained in a written partnership agreement, a writing setting out:

  (i) the amount of cash and a description and statement of the agreed value of the other property or services contributed by each partner and which each partner has agreed to contribute;
  (ii) the times at which or events on the happening of which any additional contributions agreed to be made by each partner are to be made;
  (iii) any right of a partner to receive, or of a general partner to make, distributions to a partner which include a return of all or any part of the partner's contribution; and
  (iv) any events upon the happening of which the limited partnership is to be dissolved and its affairs wound up.

(b) Records kept under this section are subject to inspection and copying at the reasonable request and at the expense of any partner during ordinary business hours.

§106. Nature of Business A limited partnership may carry on any business that a partnership without limited partners may carry on except [here designate prohibited activities].

§107. Business Transactions of Partner with Partnership Except as provided in the partnership agreement, a partner may lend money to and transact other business with the limited partnership and, subject to other applicable law, has the same rights and obligations with respect thereto as a person who is not a partner.

ARTICLE 2

Formation: Certificate of Limited Partnership

§201. Certificate of Limited Partnership.
(a) In order to form a limited partnership, a certificate of limited partnership must be executed and filed in the office of the Secretary of State. The certificate shall set forth:

(1) the name of the limited partnership;
(2) the address of the office and the name and address of the agent for the service of process required to be maintained by Section 104;
(3) the name and the business address of each general partner;
(4) the latest date upon which the limited partnership is to dissolve; and
(5) any other matters the general partners determine to include therein.

(b) A limited partnership is formed at the time of the filing of the certificate of limited partnership in the office of the Secretary of State or at any later time specified in the certificate of limited partnership if, in either case, there has been substantial compliance with the requirements of this section.

§202. Amendment to Certificate.
(a) A certificate of limited partnership is amended by filing a certificate of amendment thereto in the office of the Secretary of State. The certificate shall set forth:

(1) the name of the limited partnership;
(2) the date of filing the certificate; and
(3) the amendment to the certificate.

(b) Within 30 days after the happening of any of the following events, an amendment to a certificate of limited partnership reflecting the occurrence of the event or events shall be filed:

(1) the admission of a new general partner;
(2) the withdrawal of a general partner; or
(3) the continuation of the business under Section 801 after an event of withdrawal of a general partner.

(c) A general partner who becomes aware that any statement in a certificate of limited partnership was false when made or that any arrangements or other facts described have changed, making the certificate inaccurate in any respect, shall promptly amend the certificate.

(d) A certificate of limited partnership may be amended at any time for any other proper purpose the general partners determine.

(e) No person has any liability because an amendment to a certificate of limited partnership has not been filed to reflect the occurrence of any event referred to in subsection (b) of this section if the amendment is filed within the 30-day period specified in subsection (b).

(f) A restated certificate of limited partnership may be executed and filed in the same manner as a certificate of amendment.

§203 Cancellation of Certificate. A certificate of limited partnership shall be canceled upon the dissolution and the commencement of winding up of the partnership or at any other time there are no limited partners. A certificate of cancellation shall be filed in the office of the Secretary of State and set forth:

(1) the name of the limited partnership;
(2) the date of filing of its certificate of limited partnership;
(3) the reason for filing the certificate of cancellation;
(4) the effective date (which shall be a date certain) of cancellation if it is not to be effective upon the filing of the certificate; and
(5) any other information the general partners filing the certificate determine.

§204. Execution of Certificates.
(a) Each certificate required by this article to be filed in the office of the Secretary of State shall be executed in the following manner:

(1) an original certificate of limited partnership must be signed by all general partners;
(2) a certificate of amendment must be signed by at least one general partner and by each other general partner designated in the certificate as a new general partner; and
(3) a certificate of cancellation must be signed by all general partners.

(b) Any person may sign a certificate by an attorney-in-fact, but a power of attorney to sign a certificate relating to the admission, of a general partner must specifically describe the admission.

(c) The execution of a certificate by a general partner constitutes an affirmation under the penalties of perjury that the facts stated therein are true.

§205. Execution by Judicial Act. If a person required by Section 204 to execute any certificate fails or refuses to do so, any other person who is adversely affected by the failure or refusal, may petition the [designate the appropriate court] to direct the execution of the certificate. If the court finds that it is proper for the certificate to be executed and that any person so designated has failed or refused to execute the certificate, it shall order the Secretary of State to record an appropriate certificate.

§206. Filing in Office of Secretary of State.
(a) Two signed copies of the certificate of limited partnership and of any certificates of amendment or cancellation (or of any judicial decree of amendment or cancellation) shall be delivered to the Secretary of State. A person who executes a certificate as an agent or fiduciary need not exhibit evidence of his or her authority as a prerequisite to filing. Unless the Secretary of State finds that any certificate does not conform to law, upon receipt of all filing fees required by law he or she shall:
(1) endorse on each duplicate original the word "Filed" and the day, month and year of the filing thereof;
(2) file one duplicate original in his or her office; and
(3) return the other duplicate original to the person who filed it or his or her representative.

(b) Upon the filing of a certificate of amendment (or judicial decree of amendment) in the office of the Secretary of State, the certificate of limited partnership shall be amended as set forth therein, and upon the effective date of a certificate of cancellation (or a judicial decree thereof), the certificate of limited partnership is canceled.

§207. Liability for False Statement in Certificate. If any certificate of limited partnership or certificate of amendment or cancellation contains a false statement, one who suffers loss by reliance on the statement may recover damages for the loss from:
(1) any person who executes the certificate, or causes another to execute it on his behalf, and knew, and any general partner who knew or should have known, the statement to be false at the time the certificate was executed; and
(2) any general partner who thereafter knows or should have known that any arrangement or other fact described in the certificate has changed, making the statement inaccurate in any respect within a sufficient time before the statement was relied upon reasonably to have enabled that general partner to cancel or amend the certificate, or to file a petition for its cancellation or amendment under Section 205.

§208. Scope of Notice. The fact that a certificate of limited partnership is on file in the office of the Secretary of State is notice that the partnership is a limited partnership and the persons designated therein as general partners are general partners, but it is not notice of any other fact.

§209. Delivery of Certificates to Limited Partners. Upon the return by the Secretary of State pursuant to Section 206 of a certificate marked "Filed", the general partners shall promptly deliver or mail a copy of the certificate of limited partnership and each certificate of amendment or cancellation to each limited partner unless the partnership agreement provides otherwise.

ARTICLE 3
Limited Partners

§301. Admission of Limited Partners.
(a) A person becomes a limited partner:
(1) at the time the limited partnership is formed; or
(2) at any later time specified in the records of the limited partnership for becoming a limited partner.

(b) After the filing of a limited partnership's original certificate of limited partnership, a person may be admitted as an additional limited partner:
(1) in the case of a person acquiring a partnership interest directly from the limited partnership, upon compliance with the partnership agreement or, if the partnership agreement does not so provide, upon the written consent of all partners; and
(2) in the case of an assignee of a partnership interest of a partner who has the power, as provided in Section 704, to grant the assignee the right to become a limited partner, upon the exercise of that power and compliance with any conditions limiting the grant or exercise of the power.

§302. Voting. Subject to Section 303, the partnership agreement may grant to all or a specified group of the limited partners the right to vote (on a per capita or other basis) upon any matter.

§303. Liability to Third Parties.
(a) Except as provided in subsection (d), a limited partner is not liable for the obligations of a limited partnership unless he or she is also a general partner or, in addition to the exercise of his or her rights and powers as a limited partner, he or she participates in the control of the business. However, if the limited partner participates in the control of the business, he or she is liable only to persons who transact business with the limited partnership reasonably believing, based upon the limited partner's conduct, that the limited partner is a general partner.

(b) A limited partner does not participate in the control of the business within the meaning of subsection (a) solely by doing one or more of the following:
(1) being a contractor for or an agent or employee of the limited partnership or of a general partner or being an officer, director, or shareholder of a general partner that is a corporation;
(2) consulting with and advising a general partner with respect to the business of the limited partnership;
(3) acting as surety for the limited partnership or guaranteeing or assuming one or more specific obligations of the limited partnership;
(4) taking any action required or permitted by law to bring or pursue a derivative action in the right of the limited partnership;
(5) requesting or attending a meeting of partners;
(6) proposing, approving, or disapproving, by voting or otherwise, one or more of the following matters:
(i) the dissolution and winding up of the limited partnership;
(ii) the sale, exchange, lease, mortgage, pledge, or other transfer of all or substantially all of the assets of the limited partnership;
(iii) the incurrence of indebtedness by the limited partnership other than in the ordinary course of its business;
(iv) a change in the nature of the business;

(v) the admission or removal of a general partner;
(vi) the admission or removal of a limited partner;
(vii) a transaction involving an actual or a potential conflict of interest between a general partner and the limited partnership or the limited partners:
(viii) an amendment to the partnership agreement or certificate of limited partnership; or
(ix) matters related to the business of the limited partnership not otherwise enumerated in this subsection (b), which the partnership agreement states in writing may be subject to the approval or disapproval of limited partners;

(7) winding up the limited partnership pursuant to Section 803; or
(8) exercising any right or power permitted to limited partners under this [Act] and not specifically enumerated in this subsection (b).

(c) The enumeration in subsection (b) does not mean that the possession or exercise of any other powers by a limited partner constitutes participation by him or her in the business of the limited partnership.

(d) A limited partner who knowingly permits his or her name to be used in the name of the limited partnership, except under circumstances permitted by Section 102(2), is liable to creditors who extend credit to the limited partnership without actual knowledge that the limited partner is not a general partner.

§304. Person Erroneously Believing Himself or Herself Limited Partner.

(a) Except as provided in subsection (b), a person who makes a contribution to a business enterprise and erroneously but in good faith believes that he or she has become a limited partner in the enterprise is not a general partner in the enterprise and is not bound by its obligations by reason of making the contribution, receiving distributions from the enterprise, or exercising any rights of a limited partner, if, on ascertaining the mistake, he or she:

(1) causes an appropriate certificate of limited partnership or a certificate of amendment to be executed and filed; or
(2) withdraws from future equity participation in the enterprise by executing and filing in the office of the Secretary of State a certificate declaring a withdrawal under this section.

(b) A person who makes a contribution of the kind described in subsection (a) is liable as a general partner to any third party who transacts business with the enterprise (i) before the person withdraws and an appropriate certificate is filed to show withdrawal, or (ii) before an appropriate certificate is filed to show that he [or she] is not a general partner, but in either case only if the third party actually believed in good faith that the person was a general partner.

§305. Information. Each limited partner has the right to:

(1) inspect and copy any of the partnership records required to be maintained by Section 105; and
(2) obtain from the general partners from time to time upon reasonable demand (i) true and full information regarding the state of the business and financial condition of the limited partnership, (ii) promptly after becoming available, a copy of the limited partnership's federal, state and local income tax returns for each year, and (iii) other information regarding the affairs of the limited partnership as is just and reasonable.

ARTICLE 4
General Partners

§401. Admission of Additional General Partners. After the filing of a limited partnership's original certificate of limited partnership, additional general partners may be admitted as provided in writing in the partnership agreement or, if the partnership agreement does not provide in writing for the admission of additional general partners, with the written consent of all partners.

§402. Events of Withdrawal. Except as approved by the specific written consent of all partners at the time, a person ceases to be a general partner of a limited partnership upon the happening of any of the following events:

(1) the general partner withdraws from the limited partnership as provided in Section 602;
(2) the general partner ceases to be a member of the limited partnership as provided in Section 702.
(3) the general partner is removed as a general partner in accordance with the partnership agreement;
(4) unless otherwise provided in writing in the partnership agreement, the general partner: (i) makes an assignment for the benefit of creditors; (ii) files a voluntary petition in bankruptcy; (iii) is adjudicated a bankrupt or insolvent; (iv) files a petition or answer seeking for himself or herself any reorganization, arrangement, composition, readjustment, liquidation, dissolution or similar relief under any statute, law, or regulation; (v) files an answer or other pleading admitting or failing to contest the material allegations of a petition filed against him or her in any proceeding of this nature; or (vi) seeks, consents to, or acquiesces in the appointment of a trustee, receiver, or liquidator of the general partner or of all or any substantial part of his or her properties;
(5) unless otherwise provided in writing in the partnership agreement, [120] days after the commencement of any proceeding against the general partner seeking reorganization, arrangement, composition, readjustment, liquidation, dissolution or similar relief under any statute, law, or regulation, the proceeding has not been dismissed, or if within [90] days after the appointment without his or her consent or acquiescence of a trustee, receiver, or liquidator of the general partner or of all or any substantial part of his or her properties, the appointment is not vacated or stayed or within [90] days after the expiration of any such stay, the appointment is not vacated;
(6) in the case of a general partner who is a natural person,
   (i) his or her death; or
   (ii) the entry by a court of competent jurisdiction adjudicating him or her incompetent to manage his or her person or estate;
(7) in the case of a general partner who is acting as a general partner by virtue of being a trustee of a trust, the termination of the trust (but not merely the substitution of a new trustee);
(8) in the case of a general partner that is a separate partnership, the dissolution and commencement of winding up of the separate partnership;
(9) in the case of a general partner that is a corporation, the filing of a certificate of dissolution, or its equivalent, for the corporation or the revocation of its charter; or
(10) in the case of an estate, the distribution by the fiduciary of the estate's entire interest in the partnership.

§403. General Powers and Liabilities. (a) Except as provided in this Act or in the partnership agreement, a general partner of a limited partnership has the rights and powers and is subject to the restrictions of a partner in a partnership without limited partners. (b) Except as provided in this Act, a general partner of a limited partnership has the liabilities of a partner in a partnership without limited partners to persons other than the partnership and the other partners. Except as provided in this Act or in the partnership agreement, a general partner of a limited partnership has the liabilities of a partner in a partnership without limited partners to the partnership and to the other partners.

§404. Contributions by General Partner. A general partner of a limited partnership may make contributions to the partnership and share in the profits and losses of, and in distributions from, the limited partnership as a general partner. A general partner also may make contributions to and share in profits, losses, and distributions as a limited partner. A person who is both a general partner and a limited partner has the rights and powers, and is subject to the restrictions and liabilities, of a general partner and except as provided in the partnership agreement, also has the powers, and is subject to the restrictions of a limited partner to the extent of his or her participation in the partnership as a limited partner.

§405. Voting. The partnership agreement may grant to all or certain identified general partners the right to vote (on a per capita or any other basis), separately or with all or any class of the limited partners, on any matter.

ARTICLE 5

Finance

§501. Form of Contribution. The contribution of a partner may be in cash, property, or services rendered, or a promissory note or other obligation to contribute cash or property or to perform services.

§502. Liability for Contribution.

(a) A promise by a limited partner to contribute to the limited partnership is not enforceable unless set out in a writing signed by the limited partner.

(b) Except as provided in the limited partnership agreement, a partner is obligated to the limited partnership to perform any enforceable promise to contribute cash or property or to perform services, even if he or she is unable to perform because of death, disability, or any other reason. If a partner does not make the required contribution of property or services, he or she is obligated at the option of the limited partnership to contribute cash equal to that portion of the value, as stated in the partnership records required to be kept pursuant to Section 105, of the stated contribution that has not been made.

(c) Unless otherwise provided in the partnership agreement, the obligation of a partner to make a contribution or return money or other property paid or distributed in violation of this Act may be compromised only by consent of all the partners. Notwithstanding the compromise, a creditor of a limited partnership who extends credit, or otherwise acts in reliance on that obligation after the partner signs a writing which reflects the obligation, and before the amendment or cancellation thereof to reflect the compromise, may enforce the original obligation.

§503. Sharing of Profits and Losses. The profits and losses of a limited partnership shall be allocated among the partners, and among classes of partners, in the manner provided in writing in the partnership agreement. If the partnership agreement does not so provide in writing, profits and losses shall be allocated on the basis of the value, as stated in the partnership records required to be kept pursuant to Section 105, of the contributions made by each partner to the extent they have been received by the partnership and have not been returned.

§504. Sharing of Distributions. Distributions of cash or other assets of a limited partnership shall be allocated among the partners, and among classes of partners in the manner provided in writing in the partnership agreement. If the partnership agreement does not so provide in writing, distributions shall be made on the basis of the value, as stated in the partnership records required to be kept pursuant to Section 105, of the contributions made by each partner to the extent they have been received by the partnership and have not been returned.

ARTICLE 6

Distribution and Withdrawal

§601. Interim Distributions. Except as provided in this Article, a partner is entitled to receive distributions from a limited partnership before his or her withdrawal from the limited partnership and before the dissolution and winding up thereof to the extent and at the times or upon the happening of the events specified in the partnership agreement.

§602. Withdrawal of General Partner. A general partner may withdraw from a limited partnership at any time by giving written notice to the other partners, but if the withdrawal violates the partnership agreement, the limited partnership may recover from the withdrawing general partner damages for breach of the partnership agreement and offset the damages against the amount otherwise distributable to him or her.

§603. Withdrawal of Limited Partner. A limited partner may withdraw from a limited partnership at the time or upon the happening of events specified in writing in the partnership agreement. If the agreement does not specify in writing the time or the events upon the happening of which a limited partner may withdraw or a definite time for the dissolution and winding up of the limited partnership, a limited partner may withdraw upon not less than six months' prior written notice to each general partner at his or her address on the books of the limited partnership at its office in this State.

§604. Distribution Upon Withdrawal. Except as provided in this Article, upon withdrawal any withdrawing partner is entitled to receive any distribution to which he or she is entitled under the partnership agreement and, if not otherwise provided in the agreement, he or she is entitled to receive, within a reasonable time after withdrawal, the fair value of his or her interest in the limited partnership as of the date of withdrawal based upon his or her right to share in distributions from the limited partnership.

§605. Distribution in Kind. Except as provided in writing in the partnership agreement, a partner, regardless of the nature of his or her contribution, has no right to demand and receive any distribution from a limited partnership in any form other than cash. Except as provided in writing in the partnership agreement, a partner may not be compelled to accept a distribution of any asset in kind from a limited partnership to the extent that the percentage of the asset distributed to him or her exceeds a percentage of that asset which is equal to the percentage in which he or she shares in distributions from the limited partnership.

§606. Right to Distribution. At the time a partner becomes entitled to receive a distribution, he or she has the status of, and is entitled to all remedies available to, a creditor of the limited partnership with respect to the distribution.

§607. Limitations on Distribution. A partner may not receive a distribution from a limited partnership to the extent that, after giving effect to the distribution, all liabilities of the limited partnership, other than liabilities to partners on account of their partnership interests, exceed the fair value of the partnership assets.

§608. Liability upon Return of Contribution.

(a) If a partner has received the return of any part of his or her contribution without violation of the partnership agreement or this Act, he or she is liable to the limited partnership for a period of one year thereafter for the amount of the returned contribution, but only to the extent necessary to discharge the limited partnership's liabilities to creditors who extended credit to the limited partnership during the period the contribution was held by the partnership.

(b) If a partner has received the return of any part of his or her contribution in violation of the partnership agreement or this Act, he or she is liable to the limited partnership for a period of six years thereafter for the amount of the contribution wrongfully returned.

(c) A partner receives a return of his or her contribution to the extent that a distribution to him or her reduces his or her share of the fair value of the net assets of the limited partnership below the value as set forth in the partnership records required to be kept pursuant to Section 105, of his or her contribution which has not been distributed to him or her.

ARTICLE 7

Assignment of Partnership Interests

§701. Nature of Partnership Interest. A partnership interest is personal property.

§702. Assignment of Partnership Interest. Except as provided in the partnership agreement, a partnership interest is assignable in whole or in part. An assignment of a partnership interest does not dissolve a limited partnership or entitle the assignee to become or to exercise any rights of a partner. An assignment entitles the assignee to receive, to the extent assigned, only the distribution to which the assignor would be entitled. Except as provided in the partnership agreement, a partner ceases to be a partner upon assignment of all his or her partnership interest.

§703. Rights of Creditor. On application to a court of competent jurisdiction by any judgment creditor of a partner, the court may charge the partnership interest of the partner with payment of the unsatisfied amount of the judgment with interest. To the extent so charged, the judgment creditor has only the rights of an assignee of the partnership interest. This Act does not deprive any partner of the benefit of any exemption laws applicable to his or her partnership interest.

§704. Right of Assignee to Become Limited Partner.

(a) An assignee of a partnership interest, including an assignee of a general partner, may become a limited partner if and to the extent that (i) the assignor gives the assignee that right in accordance with authority described in the partnership agreement or (ii) all other partners consent.

(b) An assignee who has become a limited partner has, to the extent assigned, the rights and powers, and is subject to the restrictions and liabilities, of a limited partner under the partnership agreement and this Act. An assignee who becomes a limited partner also is liable for the obligations of his or her assignor to make and return contributions as provided in Articles 5 and 6. However, the assignee is not obligated for liabilities unknown to the assignee at the time he or she became a limited partner.

(c) If an assignee of a partnership interest becomes a limited partner, the assignor is not released from his or her liability to the limited partnership under Sections 207 and 502.

§705. Power of Estate of Deceased or Incompetent Partner. If a partner who is an individual dies or a court of competent jurisdiction adjudges him or her to be incompetent to manage his or her person or his or her property, the partner's executor, administrator, guardian, conservator, or other legal representative may exercise all the partner's rights for the purpose of settling his or her estate or administering his or her property, including any power the partner had to give an assignee the right to become a limited partner. If a partner is a corporation, trust, or other entity and is dissolved or terminated, the powers of that partner may be exercised by its legal representative or successor.

ARTICLE 8

Dissolution

§801. Nonjudicial Dissolution. A limited partnership is dissolved and its affairs shall be wound up upon the happening of the first to occur of the following:

(1) at the time specified in the certificate of limited partnership;

(2) upon the happening of events specified in writing in the partnership agreement;

(3) written consent of all partners;

(4) an event of withdrawal of a general partner unless at the time there is at least one other general partner and the written provisions of the partnership agreement permit the business of the limited partnership to be carried on by the remaining general partner and that partner does so, but the limited partnership is not dissolved and is not required to be wound up by reason of any event of withdrawal, if, within 90 days after the withdrawal, all partners agree in writing to continue the business of the limited partnership and to the appointment of one or more additional partners if necessary or desired; or

(5) entry of a decree of judicial dissolution under Section 802.

§802. Judicial Dissolution. On application by or for a partner the [designate the proper court] court may decree dissolution of a limited partnership whenever it is not reasonably practicable to carry on the business in conformity with the partnership agreement.

§803. Winding Up. Except as provided in the partnership agreement, the general partners who have not wrongfully dissolved a limited partnership, or, if none, the limited partners, may wind up the limited partnership's affairs; but the [designate the proper court] court may wind up the limited partnership's affairs upon application of any partner, his or her legal representative, or assignee.

§804. Distribution of Assets. Upon the winding up of a limited partnership, the assets shall be distributed as follows:

(1) to creditors, including partners who are creditors, to the extent permitted by law, in satisfaction of liabilities of the limited partnership other than liabilities for distributions to partners under Section 601 or 604;

(2) except as provided in the partnership agreement, to partners and former partners in satisfaction of liabilities for distributions under Section 601 or 604; and

(3) except as provided in the partnership agreement, to partners first for the return of their contributions and secondly respecting their partnership interests, in the proportions in which the partners share in distributions.

ARTICLE 9

Foreign Limited Partnerships

§901. Law Governing. Subject to the Constitution of this State, (i) the laws of the state under which a foreign limited partnership is organized govern its organization and internal affairs and the liability of its limited partners, and (ii) a foreign limited partnership may not be denied registration by reason of any difference between those laws and the laws of this State.

§902. Registration. . . .

§903. Issuance of Registration. . . .

§904. Name. A foreign limited partnership may register with the Secretary of State under any name, whether or not it is the name under which it is registered in its state of organization, that includes without abbreviation the words "limited partnership" and that could be registered by a domestic limited partnership.

§905. Changes and Amendments. . . .

§906. Cancellation of Registration. . . .

§907. Transaction of Business without Registration.
(a) A foreign limited partnership transacting business in this State may not maintain any action, suit, or proceeding in any court of this State until it has registered in this State.
(b) The failure of a foreign limited partnership to register in this State does not impair the validity of any contract or act of the foreign limited partnership or prevent the foreign limited partnership from defending any action, suit, or proceeding in any court of this State.
(c) A limited partner of a foreign limited partnership is not liable as a general partner of the foreign limited partnership solely by reason of having transacted business in this State without registration.
(d) A foreign limited partnership, by transacting business in this State without registration, appoints the Secretary of State as its agent for service of process with respect to [claims for relief] [causes of action] arising out of the transaction of business in this State.

§908. Action by [Appropriate Official.] The [designate the appropriate official] may bring an action to restrain a foreign limited partnership from transacting business in this State in violation of the Article.

ARTICLE 10

Derivative Actions

§1001. Right of Action. A limited partner may bring an action in the right of a limited partnership to recover a judgment in its favor if general partners with authority to do so have refused to bring the action or if an effort to cause those general partners to bring the action is not likely to succeed.

§1002. Proper Plaintiff. . . .

§1003. Pleading. . . .

§1004. Expenses. . . .

ARTICLE 11

Miscellaneous

§1101. Construction and Application. . . .

§1102. Short Title. This Act may be cited as the Uniform Limited Partnership Act.

§1103. Severability. . . .

§1104. Effective Date, Extended Effective Date and Repeal. . . .

§1105. Rules for Cases Not Provided for in This Act. In any case not provided for in this act the provisions of the Uniform Partnership Act govern.

§1106. Savings Clause. . . .

APPENDIX 5

Revised Model Business Corporation Act (1984) (Excerpts)

§1.02. Reservation of Power to Amend or Repeal. The [name of state legislature] has power to amend or repeal all or part of this Act at any time and all domestic and foreign corporations subject to this Act are governed by the amendment or repeal. . . .

§1.40. Act Definitions. In this Act:

(1) "Articles of incorporation" include amended and restated articles of incorporation and articles of merger.

(2) "Authorized shares" means the share of all classes a domestic or foreign corporation is authorized to issue. . . .

(4) "Corporation" or "domestic corporation" means a corporation for profit, which is not a foreign corporation, incorporated under or subject to the provisions of this Act. . . .

(8) "Employee" includes an officer but not a director. A director may accept duties that make him also an employee. . . .

(10) "Foreign corporation" means a corporation for profit incorporated under a law other than the law of this state. . . .

(17) "Principal office" means the office (in or out of this state) so designated in the annual report where the principal executive offices of a domestic or foreign corporation are located. . . .

(21) "Share" means the unit into which the proprietary interests in a corporation are divided.

(22) "Shareholder" means the person in whose name shares are registered in the records of a corporation or the beneficial owner of shares to the extent of the rights granted by a nominee certificate on file with a corporation. . . .

(24) "Subscriber" means a person who subscribes for shares in a corporation, whether before or after incorporation. . . .

§2.01. Incorporators. One or more persons may act as the incorporator or incorporators of a corporation by delivering articles of incorporation to the secretary of state for filing.

§2.02. Articles of Incorporation.

(a) The articles of incorporation must set forth:

(1) a corporate name for the corporation that satisfies the requirements of section 4.01;

(2) the number of shares the corporation is authorized to issue;

(3) the street address of the corporation's initial registered office and the name of its initial registered agent at that office; and

(4) the name and address of each incorporator. . . .

§2.03. Incorporation.

(a) Unless a delayed effective date is specified, the corporate existence begins when the articles of incorporation are filed.

(b) The secretary of state's filing of the articles of incorporation is conclusive proof that the incorporators satisfied all conditions precedent to incorporation except in a proceeding by the state to cancel or revoke the incorporation or involuntarily dissolve the corporation.

§2.04. Liability for Preincorporation Transactions. All persons purporting to act as or on behalf of a corporation, knowing there was no incorporation under this Act, are jointly and severally liable for all liabilities created while so acting.

§2.05. Organization of Corporation.

(a) After incorporation:

(1) if initial directors are named in the articles of incorporation, the initial directors shall hold an organizational meeting, at the call of a majority of the directors, to complete the organization of the corporation by appointing officers, adopting bylaws, and carrying on any other business brought before the meeting;

(2) if initial directors are not named in the articles, the incorporator or incorporators shall hold an organizational meeting at the call of a majority of the incorporators: . . .

§2.06. Bylaws.

(a) The incorporators or board of directors of a corporation shall adopt initial bylaws for the corporation.

(b) The bylaws of a corporation may contain any provision for managing the business and regulating the affairs of the corporation that is not inconsistent with law or the articles of incorporation. . . .

§3.01. Purposes.

(a) Every corporation incorporated under this Act has the

purpose of engaging in any lawful business unless a more limited purpose is set forth in the articles of incorporation. . . .

§3.02. General Powers. Unless its articles of incorporation provide otherwise, every corporation has perpetual duration and succession in its corporate name and has the same powers as an individual to do all things necessary or convenient to carry out its business and affairs, including without limitation power:

(1) to sue and be sued, complain and defend in its corporate name; . . .

(3) to make and amend bylaws, not inconsistent with its articles of incorporation or with the laws of this state, for managing the business and regulating the affairs of the corporation;

(4) to purchase, receive, lease, or otherwise acquire, and own, hold, improve, use, and otherwise deal with, real or personal property, or any legal or equitable interest in property, wherever located;

(5) to sell, convey, mortgage, pledge, lease, exchange, and otherwise dispose of all or any part of its property; . . .

(11) to elect directors and appoint officers, employees, and agents of the corporation, define their duties, fix their compensation, and lend them money and credit; . . .

(15) to make payments or donations, or do any other act, not inconsistent with law, that furthers the business and affairs of the corporation. . . .

§3.04. Ultra Vires.

(a) Except as provided in subsection (b), the validity of corporate action may not be challenged on the ground that the corporation lacks or lacked power to act.

(b) A corporation's power to act may be challenged:

(1) in a proceeding by a shareholder against the corporation to enjoin the act;

(2) in a proceeding by the corporation, directly, derivatively, or through a receiver, trustee, or other legal representative, against an incumbent or former director, officer, employee, or agent of the corporation; or

(3) in a proceeding by the Attorney General under section 14.30. . . .

§4.01. Corporate Name.

(a) A corporate name:

(1) must contain the word "corporation," "incorporated," "company," or "limited," or the abbreviation "corp.," "inc.," "co.," or "ltd.," or words or abbreviations of like import in another language; and

(2) may not contain language stating or implying that the corporation is organized for a purpose other than that permitted by section 3.01 and its articles of incorporation.

(b) Except as authorized by subsections (c) and (d), a corporate name must be distinguishable upon the records of the secretary of state from:

(1) the corporate name of a corporation incorporated or authorized to transact business in this state; . . .

§5.01. Registered Office and Registered Agent. Each corporation must continuously maintain in this state:

(1) a registered office that may be the same as any of its places of business; . . .

§6.01. Authorized Shares.

(a) The articles of incorporation must prescribe the classes of shares and the number of shares of each class that the corporation is authorized to issue. If more than one class of shares is authorized, the articles of incorporation must prescribe a distinguishing designation for each class, and, prior to the issuance of shares of a class, the preferences, limitations, and relative rights of that class must be described in the articles of incorporation. All shares of a class must have preferences, limitations, and relative rights identical with those of other shares of the same class except to the extent otherwise permitted by section 6.02. . . .

§6.03. Issued and Outstanding Shares.

(a) A corporation may issue the number of shares of each class or series authorized by the articles of incorporation. Shares that are issued are outstanding shares until they are reacquired, redeemed, converted, or cancelled.

(b) The reacquisition, redemption, or conversion of outstanding shares is subject to the limitations of subsection (c) of this section and to section 6.40.

(c) At all times that shares of the corporation are outstanding, one or more shares that together have unlimited voting rights and one or more shares that together are entitled to receive the net assets of the corporation upon dissolution must be outstanding. . . .

§6.20. Subscription for Shares before Incorporation.

(a) A subscription for shares entered into before incorporation is irrevocable for six months unless the subscription agreement provides a longer or shorter period or all the subscribers agree to revocation. . . .

§6.21. Issuance of Shares.

(a) The powers granted in this section to the board of directors may be reserved to the shareholders by the articles of incorporation.

(b) The board of directors may authorize shares to be issued for consideration consisting of any tangible or intangible property or benefit to the corporation, including cash, promissory notes, services performed, contracts for services to be performed, or other securities of the corporation. . . .

§6.22. Liability of Shareholders.

(a) A purchaser from a corporation of its own shares is not liable to the corporation or its creditors with respect to the shares except to pay the consideration for which the shares were authorized to be issued (section 6.21) or specified in the subscription agreement (section 6.20).

(b) Unless otherwise provided in the articles of incorporation, a shareholder of a corporation is not personally liable for the acts or debts of the corporation except that he may become personally liable by reason of his own acts or conduct. . . .

§6.27. Restriction on Transfer of Shares and Other Securities.

(a) The articles of incorporation, bylaws, an agreement among shareholders, or an agreement between shareholders and the corporation may impose restrictions on the transfer or registration of transfer of shares of the corporation. A restriction does not affect shares issued before the restriction was adopted unless the holders of the shares are parties to the restriction agreement or voted in favor of the restriction.

(b) A restriction on the transfer or registration of transfer of shares is valid and enforceable against the holder or a transferee of the holder if the restriction is authorized by this section and its existence is noted conspicuously on the front or back of the certificate or is contained in the information statement required by section 6.26(b). Unless so noted, a restriction is not enforceable against a person without knowledge of the restriction. . . .

§6.30. Shareholders' Preemptive Rights.

(a) The shareholders of a corporation do not have a preemptive right to acquire the corporation's unissued shares except to the extent the articles of incorporation so provide. . . .

§6.31. Corporation's Acquisition of Its Own Shares.

(a) A corporation may acquire its own shares and shares so acquired constitute authorized but unissued shares.

(b) If the articles of incorporation prohibit the reissue of acquired shares, the number of authorized shares is reduced by the number of shares acquired, effective upon amendment of the articles of incorporation. . . .

§6.40. Distributions to Shareholders.

(a) A board of directors may authorize and the corporation may make distributions to its shareholders subject to restriction by the articles of incorporation and the limitation in subsection (c).

(b) If the board of directors does not fix the record date for determining shareholders entitled to a distribution (other than one involving a repurchase or reacquisition of shares), it is the date the board of directors authorizes the distribution.

(c) No distribution may be made if, after giving it effect:

(1) the corporation would not be able to pay its debts as they become due in the usual course of business; or

(2) the corporation's total assets would be less than the sum of its total liabilities plus (unless the articles of incorporation permit otherwise) the amount that would be needed, if the corporation were to be dissolved at the time of the distribution, to satisfy the preferential rights upon dissolution of shareholders whose preferential rights are superior to those receiving the distribution. . . .

(f) A corporation's indebtedness to a shareholder incurred by reason of a distribution made in accordance with this section is at parity with the corporation's indebtedness to its general, unsecured creditors except to the extent subordinated by agreement.

§7.01. Annual Meeting.

(a) A corporation shall hold a meeting of shareholders annually at a time stated in or fixed in accordance with the bylaws.

(b) Annual shareholders' meetings may be held in or out of this state at the place stated in or fixed in accordance with the bylaws. If no place is stated in or fixed in accordance with the bylaws, annual meetings shall be held at the corporation's principal office.

(c) The failure to hold an annual meeting at the time stated in or fixed in accordance with a corporation's bylaws does not affect the validity of any corporate action.

§7.02. Special Meeting.

(a) A corporation shall hold a special meeting of shareholders:

(1) on call of its board of directors of the person or persons authorized to do so by the articles of incorporation or bylaws; or

(2) if the holders of at least 10 percent of all the votes entitled to be cast on any issue proposed to be considered at the proposed special meeting sign, date, and deliver to the corporation's secretary one or more written demands for the meeting describing the purpose or purposes for which it is to be held. . . .

(d) Only business within the purpose or purposes described in the meeting notice required by section 7.05(c) may be conducted at a special shareholders' meeting.

§7.03. Court-Ordered Meeting.

(a) The [name or describe] court of the county where a corporation's principal office (or, if none in this state, its registered office) is located may summarily order a meeting to be held:

(1) on application of any shareholder of the corporation entitled to participate in an annual meeting if an annual meeting was not held within the earlier of 6 months after the end of the corporation's fiscal year or 15 months after its last annual meeting; . . .

§7.04. Action without Meeting.

(a) Action required or permitted by this Act to be taken at a shareholders' meeting may be taken without a meeting if the action is taken by all the shareholders entitled to vote on the action. The action must be evidenced by one or more written consents describing the action taken, signed by all the shareholders entitled to vote on the action, and delivered to the corporation for inclusion in the minutes or filing with the corporate records. . . .

§7.05. Notice of Meeting.

(a) A corporation shall notify shareholders of the date, time, and place of each annual and special shareholders' meeting no fewer than 10 nor more than 60 days before the meeting date. Unless this Act or the articles of incorporation require otherwise, the corporation is required to give notice only to shareholders entitled to vote at the meeting.

(b) Unless this Act or the articles of incorporation require otherwise, notice of an annual meeting need not include a description of the purpose or purposes for which the meeting is called.

(c) Notice of a special meeting must include a description of the purpose or purposes for which the meeting is called. . . .

§7.06. Waiver of Notice.

(a) A shareholder may waive any notice required by this Act, the articles of incorporation, or bylaws before or after the date and time stated in the notice. The waiver must be in writing, be signed by the shareholder entitled to the notice, and be delivered to the corporation for inclusion in the minutes or filing with the corporate records.

(b) A shareholder's attendance at a meeting:

(1) waives objection to lack of notice or defective notice of the meeting, unless the shareholder at the beginning of the meeting objects to holding the meeting or transacting business at the meeting;

(2) waives objection to consideration of a particular matter at the meeting that is not within the purpose or purposes described in the meeting notice, unless the shareholder objects to considering the matter when it is presented. . . .

§7.20. Shareholders' List for Meeting. . . .

(b) The shareholders' list must be available for inspection by any shareholder, beginning two business days after notice of the meeting is given for which the list was prepared and continuing through the meeting, at the corporation's principal office or at a place identified in the meeting notice in the city where the meeting will be held. A shareholder, his agent, or attorney is entitled on written demand to inspect and, subject to the requirements of section 16.02(c), to copy the list, during regular business hours and at his expense, during the period it is available for inspection.

(c) The corporation shall make the shareholders' list available at the meeting, and any shareholder, his agent, or attorney is entitled to inspect the list at any time during the meeting or any adjournment. . . .

§7.22. Proxies.

(a) A shareholder may vote his shares in person or by proxy.

(b) A shareholder may appoint a proxy to vote or otherwise act for him by signing an appointment form, either personally or by his attorney-in-fact.

(c) An appointment of a proxy is effective when received by the secretary or other officer or agent authorized to tabulate votes. An appointment is valid for 11 months unless a longer period is expressly provided in the appointment form.

(d) An appointment of a proxy is revocable by the shareholder unless the appointment form conspicuously states that it is irrevocable and the appointment is coupled with an interest. . . .

§7.25. Quorum and Voting Requirements for Voting Groups.

(a) Shares entitled to vote as a separate voting group may take action on a matter at a meeting only if a quorum of those shares exists with respect to that matter. Unless the articles of incorporation or this Act provides otherwise, a majority of the votes entitled to be cast on the matter by the voting group constitutes a quorum of that voting group for action on that matter.

(b) Once a share is represented for any purpose at a meeting, it is deemed present for quorum purposes for the remainder of the meeting and for any adjournment of that meeting unless a new record date is or must be set for that adjourned meeting. . . .

§7.27. Greater Quorum or Voting Requirements.

(a) The articles of incorporation may provide for a greater quorum or voting requirement for shareholders (or voting groups of shareholders) than is provided for by this Act. . . .

§7.28. Voting for Directors; Cumulative Voting.

(a) Unless otherwise provided in the articles of incorporation, directors are elected by a plurality of the votes cast by the shares entitled to vote in the election at a meeting at which a quorum is present.

(b) Shareholders do not have a right to cumulate their votes for directors unless the articles of incorporation so provide. . . .

§7.30. Voting Trusts.

(a) One or more shareholders may create a voting trust, conferring on a trustee the right to vote or otherwise act for them, by signing an agreement setting out the provisions of the trust (which may include anything consistent with its purpose) and transferring their shares to the trustee. When a voting trust agreement is signed, the trustee shall prepare a list of the names and addresses of all owners of beneficial interests in the trust, together with the number, and class of shares each transferred to the trust, and deliver copies of the list and agreement to the corporation's principal office. . . .

§8.01. Requirement for and Duties of Board of Directors.

(a) Except as provided in subsection (c), each corporation must have a board of directors.

(b) All corporate powers shall be exercised by or under the authority of, and the business and affairs of the corporation managed under the direction of, its board of directors, subject to any limitation set forth in the articles of incorporation.

(c) A corporation having 50 or fewer shareholders may dispense with or limit the authority of a board of directors by describing in its articles of incorporation who will perform some or all of the duties of a board of directors. . . .

§8.03. Number and Election of Directors.

(a) A board of directors must consist of one or more individuals, with the number specified in or fixed in accordance with the articles of incorporation or bylaws. . . .

(d) Directors are elected at the first annual shareholders' meeting and at each annual meeting thereafter unless their terms are staggered under section 8.06. . . .

§8.08. Removal of Directors by Shareholders.

(a) The shareholders may remove one or more directors with or without cause unless the articles of incorporation provide that directors may be removed only for cause. . . .

§8.10. Vacancy on Board.

(a) Unless the articles of incorporation provide otherwise, if a vacancy occurs on a board of directors, including a vacancy resulting from an increase in the number of directors:

(1) the shareholders may fill the vacancy;
(2) the board of directors may fill the vacancy; or
(3) if the directors remaining in office constitute fewer than a quorum of the board, they may fill the vacancy by the affirmative vote of a majority of all the directors remaining in office. . . .

§8.11. Compensation of Directors.
Unless the articles of incorporation or bylaws provide otherwise, the board of directors may fix the compensation of directors.

§8.20. Meetings.

(a) The board of directors may hold regular or special meetings in or out of this state.

(b) Unless the articles of incorporation or bylaws provide otherwise, the board of directors may permit any or all directors to participate in a regular or special meeting by, or conduct the meeting through the use of, any means of communication by which all directors participating may simultaneously hear each other during the meeting. A director participating in a meeting by this means is deemed to be present in person at the meeting.

§8.21. Action Without Meeting.

(a) Unless the articles of incorporation or bylaws provide otherwise, action required or permitted by this Act to be taken at a board of directors' meeting may be taken without a meeting if the action is taken by all members of the board. The action must be evidenced by one or more written consents describing the action taken, signed by each director, and included in the minutes or filed with the corporate records reflecting the action taken.

(b) Action taken under this section is effective when the last director signs the consent, unless the consent specifies a different effective date.

(c) A consent signed under this section has the effect of a meeting vote and may be described as such in any document. . . .

§8.23. Waiver of Notice.

(a) A director may waive any notice required by this Act, the articles of incorporation, or bylaws before or after the date and time stated in the notice. Except as provided by subsection (b), the waiver must be in writing, signed by the director entitled to the notice, and filed with the minutes or corporate records.

(b) A director's attendance at or participation in a meeting waives any required notice to him of the meeting unless the director at the beginning of the meeting (or promptly upon his arrival) objects to holding the meeting or transacting business at the meeting and does not thereafter vote for or assent to action taken at the meeting.

§8.24. Quorum and Voting.

(a) Unless the articles of incorporation or bylaws require a greater number, a quorum of a board of directors consists of:

(1) a majority of the fixed number of directors if the corporation has a fixed board size: . . .

§8.30. General Standards for Directors.

(a) A director shall discharge his duties as a director, including his duties as a member of a committee:

(1) in good faith;
(2) with the care an ordinarily prudent person in a like position would exercise under similar circumstances; and
(3) in a manner he reasonably believes to be in the best interests of the corporation.

(b) In discharging his duties a director is entitled to rely on information, opinions, reports, or statements, including financial statements and other financial data, if prepared or presented by:

(1) one or more officers or employees of the corporation whom the director reasonably believes to be reliable and competent in the matters presented;

(2) legal counsel, public accountants, or other persons as to matters the director reasonably believes are within the person's professional or expert competence; or

(3) a committee of the board of directors of which he is not a member if the director reasonably believes the committee merits confidence.

(c) A director is not acting in good faith if he has knowledge concerning the matter in question that makes reliance otherwise permitted by subsection (b) unwarranted.

(d) A director is not liable for any action taken as a director, or any failure to take any action, if he performed the duties of his office in compliance with this section.

§8.31. Director Conflict of Interest.

(a) A conflict of interest transaction is a transaction with the corporation in which a director of the corporation has a direct or indirect interest. A conflict of interest transaction is not voidable by the corporation solely because of the director's interest in the transaction if any one of the following is true:

(1) the material facts of the transaction and the director's interest were disclosed or known to the board of directors or a committee of the board of directors and the board of directors or committee authorized, approved, or ratified the transaction;

(2) the material facts of the transaction and the director's interest were disclosed or known to the shareholders entitled to vote and they authorized, approved, or ratified the transaction; or

(3) the transaction was fair to the corporation. . . .

§8.33. Liability for Unlawful Distributions.

(a) Unless he complies with the applicable standards of conduct described in section 8.30, a director who votes for or assents to a distribution made in violation of this Act or the articles of incorporation is personally liable to the corporation for the amount of the distribution that exceeds what could have been distributed without violating this Act or the articles of incorporation.

(b) A director held liable for an unlawful distribution under subsection (a) is entitled to contribution:

(1) from every other director who voted for or assented to the distribution without complying with the applicable standards of conduct described in section 8.30; and

(2) from each shareholder for the amount the shareholder accepted knowing the distribution was made in violation of this Act or the articles of incorporation.

§8.40. Required Officers.

(a) A corporation has the officers described in its bylaws or appointed by the board of directors in accordance with the bylaws. . . .

§8.41. Duties of Officers.
Each officer has the authority and shall perform the duties set forth in the bylaws or, to the extent consistent with the bylaws, the duties prescribed by the board of directors or by direction of an officer authorized by the board of directors to prescribe the duties of other officers.

§8.42. Standards of Conduct for Officers [*See Section 8.30. Same standards.*]

§8.43. Resignation and Removal of Officers.

(a) An officer may resign at any time by delivering notice to the corporation.

(b) A board of directors may remove any officer at any time with or without cause. . . .

§10.01. Authority to Amend Articles of Incorporation.

(a) A corporation may amend its articles of incorporation at any time. . . .

§10.03. Amendment by Board of Directors and Shareholders.

(a) A corporation's board of directors may propose one or more amendments to the articles of incorporation for submission to the shareholders.

(b) For the amendment to be adopted:

(1) the board of directors must recommend the amendment to the shareholders unless the board of directors determines that because of conflict of interest or other special circumstances it should make no recommendation and communicates the basis for its determination to the shareholders with the amendment; and

(2) the shareholders entitled to vote on the amendment must approve the amendment as provided in subsection (e). . . .

§10.20. Amendment of Bylaws by Board of Directors or Shareholders.

(a) A corporation's board of directors may amend or repeal the corporation's bylaws unless:

(1) the articles of incorporation or this Act reserve this power exclusively to the shareholders in whole or part; or

(2) the shareholders in amending or repealing a particular bylaw provide expressly that the board of directors may not amend or repeal that bylaw.

(b) A corporation's shareholders may amend or repeal the corporation's bylaws even though the bylaws may also be amended or repealed by its board of directors. . . .

§11.03. Action on Plan.

(a) After adopting a plan of merger or share exchange, the board of directors of each corporation party to the merger, and the board of directors of the corporation whose shares will be acquired in the share exchange, shall submit the plan of merger . . . for approval by its shareholders.

(b) For a plan of merger or share exchange to be approved:

(1) the board of directors must recommend the plan of merger or share exchange to the shareholders, unless the board of directors determines that because of conflict of interest or other special circumstances it should make no recommendation and communicates the basis for its determination to the shareholders with the plan; and

(2) the shareholders entitled to vote must approve the plan. . . .

§11.04. Merger of Subsidiary.

(a) A parent corporation owning at least 90 percent of the outstanding shares of each class of a subsidiary corporation may merge the subsidiary into itself without approval of the shareholders of the parent or subsidiary. . . .

§12.01. Sale of Assets in Regular Course of Business and Mortgage of Assets.

(a) A corporation may, on the terms and conditions and for the consideration determined by the board of directors:

(1) sell, lease, exchange, or otherwise dispose of all, or substantially all, of its property in the usual and regular course of business; . . .

(b) Unless the articles of incorporation require it, approval by the shareholders of a transaction described in subsection (a) is not required.

§12.02. Sale of Assets Other than in Regular Course of Business.

(a) A corporation may sell, lease, exchange, or otherwise dispose of all, or substantially all, of its property (with or without the goodwill), otherwise than in the usual and regular course of business, on the terms and conditions and for the consideration determined by the corporation's board of directors, if the board of directors proposes and its shareholders approve the proposed transaction.

(b) For a transaction to be authorized:

(1) the board of directors must recommend the proposed transaction to the shareholders unless the board of directors determines that because of conflict of interest or other special circumstances it should make no recommen-dation and communicates the basis for its determination to the shareholders with the submission of the proposed transaction; and

(2) the shareholders entitled to vote must approve the transaction. . . .

§14.02. Dissolution by Board of Directors and Shareholders.

(a) A corporation's board of directors may propose dissolution for submission to the shareholders.

(b) For a proposal to dissolve to be adopted:

(1) the board of directors must recommend dissolution to the shareholders unless the board of directors determines that because of conflict of interest or other special circumstances it should make no recommendation and communicates the basis for its determination to the shareholders; and

(2) the shareholders entitled to vote must approve the proposal to dissolve as provided in subsection (e). . . .

§16.01. Corporate Records.

(a) A corporation shall keep as permanent records minutes of all meetings of its shareholders and board of directors, a record of all actions taken by the shareholders or board of directors without a meeting, and a record of all actions taken by a committee of the board of directors in place of the board of directors on behalf of the corporation. . . .

§16.02. Inspection of Records by Shareholders.

(a) A shareholder of a corporation is entitled to inspect and copy, during regular business hours at the corporation's principal office, any of the records of the corporation described in section 16.01(e) if he gives the corporation written notice of his demand at least five business days before the date on which he wishes to inspect and copy.

(b) a shareholder of a corporation is entitled to inspect and copy, during regular business hours at a reasonable location specified by the corporation, any of the following records of the corporation if the shareholder meets the requirements of subsection (c) and gives the corporation written notice of his demand at least five business days before the date on which he wishes to inspect and copy: . . .

§16.03. Scope of Inspection Right.

(a) A shareholder's agent or attorney has the same inspection and copying rights as the shareholder he represents.

(b) The right to copy records under section 16.02 includes, if reasonable, the right to receive copies made by photographic, xerographic, or other means.

(c) The corporation may impose a reasonable charge, covering the costs of labor and material, for copies of any documents provided to the shareholder. The charge may not exceed the estimated cost of production or reproduction of the records. . . .

Glossary

Abatement In the law of wills, a required reduction or nonpayment of a gift stated in a will. In real estate law, putting a stop to a nuisance.

Abnormally dangerous activity An activity that necessarily involves a risk of serious harm, which risk cannot be eliminated by the exercise of utmost care, and for which the actor is strictly liable. Also called "ultrahazardous activity."

Absolute privilege In defamation law, the absolute, unqualified right to make a defamatory statement about the plaintiff.

Acceleration clause A provision in a promissory note permitting the maker to make, or a holder to have, payment before the stated due date.

Acceptance An offeree's manifestation of assent to the terms of an offer, needed for a contract to arise. Also, in the law of sales, a buyer's act of taking as the buyer's own property the particular goods covered by a contract, whether by words or by action or silence when it is time to speak. Also, in the law of commercial paper, a drawee's act of writing the word "accepted" across the face of a draft (or the word "certified" across the face of a check), or signing on the face of the instrument, and thereby becoming a primary party to the instrument. Also, in the law of bankruptcy, an agreement by a class of creditors (or holders of ownership interests) to a plan for satisfaction of claims against the debtor's estate. A class accepts by means of a vote.

Accession The coming into possession of a right. In the law of sales, goods that are installed in or affixed to other goods.

Accommodation party A person who signs an instrument for the purpose of lending his or her name (credit) to another party to the instrument.

Accommodation surety See *Surety*.

Accord and satisfaction The reaching of a new agreement and the performance of it or the acceptance of it by both parties as a substitute for the original contract. Usually associated with settlement of a disputed claim or unliquidated debt.

Account receivable (account) A right to payment for goods sold or leased or for services rendered.

Acknowledgment Certification by a notary public as to the identity of a person who signs a document.

Actual malice A statement made with knowledge of its falsity or with reckless indifference to its truth or falsity. A public official or public figure must prove actual malice to overcome the constitutional privilege in a defamation suit.

Additur An increase in the amount of an award of damages.

Adhesion contract See *Contract of adhesion*.

Administrative agency A government office, department, board, bureau, or commission (other than legislatures and courts) with power to make rules and regulations concerning private rights and duties.

Administrative law The law concerning the powers and procedures of administrative agencies, including the law governing judicial review of administrative action.

Administrative Procedure Act A federal law

generally establishing the manner in which federal administrative agencies operate.

Administrator In estate or inheritance law, a person or entity, not designated by a decedent's will, appointed by a court to administer a decedent's estate.

Adverse possession The acquisition of title to real property by taking and remaining in possession of another's property for a statutory period of time. Possession must be hostile, open and notorious, continuous, exclusive, and under a claim of right or color of title.

Affirmation (to affirm) The ratification of an act, statement, or promise; used primarily to express agreement to be held to a voidable transaction, as the affirmance or ratification of a minor's voidable contract or the ratification by a principal of an agent's voidable action on the principal's behalf.

Affirmative defense An allegation of a new matter in a defendant's pleadings as a bar to a plaintiff's recovery.

After-acquired property clause A clause in a security agreement that gives a creditor a security interest in both present and future assets of the debtor instead of a security interest only in specific assets on hand at the creation of the secured transaction.

Aftermarket In antitrust law, a secondary market created by demand for a new product; e.g., blades are an aftermarket for a new razor.

Agency A relationship in which one person acts for or represents another by the latter's authority; where one person acts for another in the relationship of principal and agent, master and servant, or employer and employee.

Agent A person authorized by another to act for him or her; one entrusted with another's business.

Aggressor corporation A corporation which attempts, through either a friendly or an unfriendly action, to gain control of a public corporation, called the *Target corporation*.

Agreement A mutual assent. A contract embodies the agreement of the parties; however, frequently a contract is loosely called an agreement. See also *Contract*.

Allowed claim In bankruptcy law, a valid claim against the debtor's estate. An allowed claim will be paid to the extent that funds are available.

All-risk contract An insurance policy which indemnifies the insured against property loss resulting from any peril except those specifically excluded by the insurance contract.

Amicus curiae Latin for "friend of the court." Someone not a party to a lawsuit who, with permission of a court, files a brief (usually in a matter of broad public interest) suggesting a rationale for solution of a legal question.

Annuity A contractual device for systematically using up (liquidating) an existing fund; a type of contract sold by some life insurance companies.

Anticipatory breach of contract Repudiation of a contract obligation before performance is due.

Apparent authority The authority which, though not actually granted, the principal knowingly permits an agent to exercise or which the principal holds the agent out as possessing.

Appellant One who files an appeal.

Appellee The party opposite the appellant. Usually, the party who won at the trial level.

Arbitrager (arbitrageur) An individual who buys and sells shares, not for investment, but to take advantage of anticipated short movements in the cost of the security; he or she frequently takes advantage of temporary small differences in the price of a security on different stock exchanges.

Arbitration A nonjudicial method of resolving civil disputes, informal and voluntary in most cases

Arraignment The reading by a judicial officer of an information or indictment to an accused in a criminal case and asking how he or she pleads.

Articles of incorporation A legal document, filed with a designated state official, that meets the requirements of the state's incorporation statute before a person or persons can commence doing business as a corporation. The articles, sometimes called "corporate charter," provide the framework within which the corporation must operate.

Artisan A skilled craftsperson, such as a carpenter, mechanic, or tailor. An "artisan's lien" is the right of one who repairs goods of another to keep possession of the goods until the repair charges are paid.

Assignee A person to whom an assignment is made.

Assignment A transfer of rights, usually of contract rights.

Assignment for the benefit of creditors A voluntary transfer, under state law, by a debtor of all her or his available property to a trustee for distribution to the debtor's creditors in exchange for their promises to release the debtor from further liability. Also called a "general assignment."

Assignor The maker of an assignment.

Assumpsit A common law form of action to recover damages for breach of contract.

Assumption To expressly or impliedly agree to pay a preexisting debt or to carry out another's legal duty, as in an assumption of a mortgage.

Assumption of risk The plaintiff's voluntary and knowing acceptance of a risk of harm.

Attachment Seizure of a debtor's property, generally at the start of a lawsuit, through legal process to protect a creditor's claim.

Attachment of a security interest In the law of secured transactions, the name given to the process of creating (agreeing to) a security interest in personal property and of making it enforceable against the debtor.

Attorney-in-fact An agent.

Authority The power of an agent to affect the legal relations of a principal by acts done in accordance with the principal's manifestations of consent.

Authority by estoppel Authority that is not actual, but is apparent only, being imposed on the principal because the conduct of the principal has been such as to mislead a third party, so that it would be unjust to let the principal deny it.

Audit An accountant's examination and investigation of an entity's financial statements to determine whether its financial statements accurately reflect its financial condition.

Automatic stay A suspension of legal action. In bankruptcy law, a suspension of legal action (other than the bankruptcy proceeding itself) until the bankruptcy case is over or until the stay is vacated by the bankruptcy court.

Bail Security given to guarantee the presence of an accused at a criminal hearing or trial.

Bailment A transaction in which the possessor of personal property (bailor) puts someone else (bailee) in possession for a limited purpose, such as for repair or for storage.

Bank check See *Bank draft*.

Bank draft A check drawn by one bank on its account in another bank. Also called a "bank check" or "teller's check."

Bankruptcy A process under federal law whereby the nonexempt assets of a debtor, incapable of paying his or her debts, are distributed to creditors, and the debtor, if honest, is discharged from liability for most remaining unpaid debts.

Bearer document of title Similar to bearer commercial paper. See *Commercial paper*.

Bearer paper See *Commercial paper*.

Beneficiary The person who receives a benefit under a contract, trust, or insurance policy.

Bequest A gift by will of personal property.

Bilateral contract A contract in which the parties make promises to each other. See also *Unilateral contract*.

Bill of exchange A draft.

Bill of lading A document of title issued by a railroad or other carrier that lists the goods accepted for transport and that sometimes states the terms of the shipping agreement. A *through bill* of lading is one issued by a carrier for transport of goods over its own lines for a certain distance, and then over connecting lines to the destination. A *destination bill* of lading is issued at the destination point instead of sending point so that the documents will be available when the goods arrive. See *Document of title*.

Bill of Rights The first ten amendments to the Constitution of the United States. The Bill of Rights confers a number of rights intended to protect individuals from federal governmental oppression.

Blue laws Laws that require businesses to close on Sundays.

Blue-sky laws State statutes that protect investors against fraudulent schemes by regulating the issuance, sale, and/or transfer of securities.

Board of directors One or more persons elected and authorized by the shareholders of a corporation to manage the corporation and its affairs.

Bona fide In or with good faith.

Bond In corporation financing, a certificate or other evidence of long-term debt obligating the corporation to pay the holder a fixed rate of interest on the principal at regular intervals and to pay the principal on a stated maturity date. In criminal law, a guarantee that the accused will be present at a hearing or trial. In surety law, the promise of a compensated surety to pay if the principal debtor (including a criminal defendant) does not.

Box-top license See *Shrinkwrap license*.

Boycott In antitrust law, a combination for the purpose of refusing to deal with a business. In labor law, a concerted employee refusal to buy products of an employer with whom a union has a dispute.

Breach The breaking of a promise, a duty, or an obligation, as a breach of contract.

Bribery The improper attempt to influence an action, generally of a public servant, by offering money or other favors.

Bulk sale The sale of a whole stock in trade of a business.

Burden of proof The degree of proof necessary to sustain a verdict or judgment: in criminal cases, beyond a reasonable doubt; in civil cases, by a preponderance of the evidence.

Business ethics The study of how moral and ethical standards apply to business policies, institutions, and behavior.

Bylaws Self-made regulations or rules adopted by a corporation to regulate and govern its internal actions and affairs.

C&F (CF) A price that includes in a lump sum the cost of goods and the cost of freight to the named destination.

Call A demand of payment, either in installments or in portions, made upon subscribers of shares by directors of a corporation. Also, a negotiable option contract under which the bearer has the right to buy a certain number of shares of stock at an agreed price before a fixed date.

Callable preferred shares Preferred shares which a corporation may call back or redeem at a fixed date and price established when the shares are issued.

Carrier An individual or a business firm engaged in transporting passengers or goods for hire. A *common carrier* offers its services to the public and must carry goods for all who apply, as long as there is room and no legal excuse for refusing. A *private carrier* carries goods only for those persons with whom the carrier chooses to contract.

Case law The accumulated body of court decisions that form an important part of the law of a particular subject.

Case of first impression A court case which raises a question of law that has not been previously ruled upon in the court's jurisdiction.

Cashier's check A check drawn by a bank on itself.

Cash surrender value A dollar value of an insurance policy, generated from premium payments that exceed the amount needed to pay claims against and expenses of the insurer. The excess payments are retained and invested by the insurer, and the accumulation is held in a legal reserve fund.

Categorical imperative A moral command, having no exceptions, which is binding because it is logically justified by reason.

Cause of action Legal basis for a lawsuit.

Caveat emptor Latin for "let the buyer beware."

Cease-and-desist order A command from an administrative agency to stop a challenged practice. See also *Injunction*.

CEO The chief executive officer of a corporation; usually its president or chairperson of the board of directors.

Certificate of deposit A written acknowledgment by a bank of the receipt of a specified amount of money held subject to the depositor's order in accordance with the certificate's terms; a type of promissory note issued by a bank in exchange for a deposit of money.

Certificate of incorporation A document, issued by some states, that grants an organization permission to do business as a corporation.

Certified check A check that has been accepted by the drawee bank. See *Acceptance*.

Certiorari A formal request by a higher court to a lower court to transmit to it the record of a case so that it can be heard on appeal.

Chancery A court of equity. See *Equity*.

Charging order A court order granting a creditor the right to a partner's interest in a partnership.

Charter An instrument by which the state creates a corporation and confers on it the right, power, and authority to do business under the corporate form. The term "charter" is sometimes used to refer to the articles of incorporation.

Chattel Movable, tangible items which are not firmly attached to real property.

Chattel mortgage A writing evidencing a secured transaction in personal property; i.e., a mortgage evidencing both a monetary obligation and a security interest in personal property. The debtor has possession of the property, but the creditor has, as his or her security interest, title to the property or, in some states, a lien (claim) against it.

Chattel paper A writing which evidences both a monetary obligation and a security interest in specific goods.

Check A draft drawn on a bank payable on demand; a written order addressed to a bank by a party who has money on deposit, directing the bank to pay on presentment, to the party named in the check or to bearer of order, a specified sum of money.

CIF A price that includes in a lump sum the cost of goods and the cost of insurance and freight to the named destination.

Civil law In the United States, that law under which a person (the plaintiff) may sue another (the defendant), as in a lawsuit involving a contract or tort, to obtain redress for a wrong committed by the defendant. The expression "civil law" is also used to describe those legal systems (e.g., that of the French) whose law is centered around a comprehensive legislative code.

Class action shareholder suit An action brought against a corporation by one or more of its shareholders on behalf of themselves and other shareholders similarly situated.

Clearinghouse A place where banks exchange checks and drafts drawn on each other and thereby settle their daily balances.

Close corporation A corporation whose stock is held by one stockholder or by a relatively small group of stockholders who actively participate in its management. The stock is generally subject to restrictions on transfer and is not publicly traded.

COD Collect on delivery.

Codicil An amendment to a *Formal will* or *Holographic will*.

Cognovit note A promissory note containing a *Confession-of-judgment clause*.

Coinsurance A method used by property insurers to prevent customers who underinsure commercial property from receiving disproportionately larger benefits than those who insure near the full value of their property.

Collateral Something of value that can be converted into cash by a creditor if the debtor defaults.

Commercial bribery Improperly attempting to gain advantage in a commercial transaction by offering money or other favors.

Commercial impracticability A basis upon which a party to a contract may be excused from performance obligations. The essence of commercial impracticability is an unexpected occurrence which seriously impairs a party's ability to perform.

Commercial paper Negotiable instruments, including drafts, checks, notes, and certificates of deposit, payable in money. Called *bearer paper* if it can be negotiated by delivery alone; called *order paper* if, in addition to delivery, an endorsement is required for negotiation.

Commercial speech Speech that simply proposes a commercial transaction, such as commercial advertising and commercial solicitations by phone.

Commercial unit An amount of goods that in business practice is treated as a single whole for purposes of sale and whose division would materially impair its value or character (e.g., a machine, a bale of cotton, a carload of wheat).

Commingled goods Goods that are combined with and are indistinguishable from others to form a single mass or product.

Common law In England, a body of law common to the whole population, produced primarily by the efforts of judges in various parts of England to harmonize their decisions.

Common stock (shares) A class of corporate stock which gives the holder a right to vote in elections of directors, to receive dividends, and, upon dissolution of the corporation, to receive a pro rata share of its assets, subordinate to the rights of preferred stock, if any.

Community property A system whereby a husband and wife jointly own property earned by either during the marriage.

Comparative negligence The modern negligence system in most states under which the jury compares relative fault between the plaintiff and defendant and awards the plaintiff the percentage of his or her damages that were caused by the defendant's negligence. See also *Contributory negligence*.

Compensated surety See *Surety*.

Compensatory damages Damages awarded to a plaintiff to compensate him or her for harm suffered, such as medical bills or lost profits. In tort cases, it includes general damage for embarrassment, pain, or suffering. See also *Punitive damages*.

Compilation An accountant's preparation of a firm's financial records in a proper form based solely on information provided by the client.

Complainant A party who brings an action in equity.

Complete integration See *Integration*.

Composition An arrangement between a debtor and all or some of his or her creditors in which the creditors agree to accept a pro rata share of their debts satisfaction of the debtor's obligations.

Composition plan In bankruptcy law, a plan for the adjustment or settlement of debt in which the debtor pays creditors less than 100 percent of their claims on a pro rata basis for each class of claims. In contrast, under an *extension plan*, the debtor pays the full amount, but over a longer period than originally agreed.

Computer fraud A crime involving the use of a computer to carry out a scheme to defraud or unlawfully take money or property. Also called "computer theft."

Condition In property law, a limitation placed on a grant of ownership. In contract law, a qualification of performance, making its occurrence depend on the happening or nonhappening of some fact or event. Contractual conditions are either *express* (stated by the parties or implied in fact from their conduct) or *constructive* (imposed by law).

Conditional privilege See *Qualified privilege*.

Conditional sale contract A contract evidencing a secured transaction in which a buyer of goods receives possession of them and the seller-creditor retains title to them until the buyer makes payment.

Conditional surety See *Surety*.

Confession-of-judgment clause A provision in a promissory note or other instrument authorizing the holder to have an attorney enter a judgment in court, without a trial, against the maker or drawer if the instrument is not paid when due, even though the failure to pay may be justified.

Confirmation In bankruptcy law, the act of the bankruptcy court in approving a plan of reorganization or some other plan for the adjustment or settlement of debt.

Conforming goods In the law of sales, goods that are in accordance with the seller's obligations under the contract of sale.

Conscious parallelism In antitrust law, uniform pricing or other business conduct by competitors that are not acting in concert but are aware of one another's actions.

Consent order An order of an administrative agency under which a person agrees to discontinue a challenged practice. Under a consent order the respondent does not admit any violation of law.

Consequential damages In general, a loss or injury which does not result directly or follow immediately from the act of a party but nonetheless is a consequence or result of the act. In the law of sales, a loss resulting from the buyer's general or particular requirements and needs of which the seller, at the time of contracting, had reason to know and which could not reasonably be prevented by cover or otherwise; injury to person or property proximately resulting from any breach of warranty. See also *Compensatory damages* and *Punitive damages*.

Consideration In contract law, a bargained-for legal detriment incurred by the promisee in exchange for a promise.

Consignment A transfer of possession of property for the purpose of transportation or sale. The consignor retains title to (ownership of) the property until it is sold.

Conspiracy An unlawful combination between two or more persons or corporations to do an illegal act or to accomplish a lawful end through illegal means; it may be a civil wrong *and* a criminal offense.

Construction As applied to a statute, the process of discovering and explaining the legal effect which the statute is to have. "Construing" a statute may involve interpreting unclear language, but it mainly involves such tasks as determining the purpose or policy of the statute, deciding how its complex provisions are related, and determining to what specific people or things the statute applies.

Construction mortgage A mortgage used to finance new residential or commercial building. See *Mortgage*.

Constructive A legally imposed or presumed fact, condition, or circumstance as opposed to an actual one.

Constructive bailment A bailment imposed by law under which a person takes possession of property of another without an agreement.

Constructive delivery Transfer of control of property to another without a physical delivery. Also called "symbolic delivery."

Constructive eviction The eviction of a tenant resulting from an unfit or unsafe condition of the premises which compels the tenant to vacate.

Constructive fraud Fraud based on misrepresentations made recklessly but without knowledge of falsity. See also *Fraud*.

Constructive notice A notice, knowledge of which, pursuant to law, is charged to a party whether it was actually received or not; generally given by means of publication in a newspaper of general circulation.

Constructive trust A device imposed by a court of equity to compel one who unfairly holds a property interest to convey that interest to another to whom it justly belongs.

Consumer goods Tangible personal property normally used for personal, family, or household purposes.

Consumer product As used in the Magnuson-Moss Warranty Act, any tangible personal property that is distributed in commerce and that is normally used for personal, family, or household purposes, including any such property intended to be attached to or installed in any real property.

Contempt of court Failure to comply with a personal order or direction of a court.

Contract A promise or set of promises for the breach of which the law gives a remedy or for the performance of which the law in some way recognizes as a duty. In the law of sales, a contract consists of the total legal obligation that results from the parties' agreement, as that agreement is affected by the UCC and by any other applicable rules of law. Contract should be distinguished from *Agreement*. See also *Implied contract*.

Contract for deed An installment sale of land under which the seller retains legal title to the property until all payments are made by the purchaser, at which time the purchaser is entitled to a deed to the property. Also called "land contract."

Contract for sale See *Sale (of goods)*.

Contract of adhesion A contract in which a party, usually the buyer, has no meaningful choice with regard to some or all of the terms; e.g., an insurance contract.

Contract to sell See *Sale (of goods)*.

Contribution In the law of suretyship, a payment owed by one cosurety to another on account of the first cosurety's payment of the principal debtor's debt. In the law of torts, the amount a joint tortfeasor is obligated to pay another tortfeasor in order to equalize their obligations to the victim.

Contributory negligence The failure of the plaintiff to exercise due care for his or her own protection. At common law, contributory negligence was an absolute defense; the plaintiff recovered nothing if he or she was contributorily at fault. See also *Comparative negligence*.

Conversion Wrongful exercise of dominion and control over, or serious interference with, the possession or ownership of the personal property of another.

Convertible preferred shares Shares of preferred stock which may be exchanged at the option of the holder for shares in another series or class issued by the same corporation.

Corporate opportunity doctrine A doctrine that prohibits a person who has a fiduciary relation to a corporation from seizing a business opportunity which rightfully belongs to the corporation.

Corporate social responsibility The ethical concept that corporations (and other business organizations) have societal obligations extending beyond the traditional functions of producing goods and services, distributing scarce resources, and generating profits for shareholders.

Corporation A legal entity created by authority of a statute as an artificial person whose rights, obligations, and liabilities are separate and distinct from those of its shareholders.

Corporation by estoppel A defectively formed corporation which is not permitted to assert, as a defense to an action against it, that the corporation was not properly formed.

Corpus See *Res*.

Cosurety See *Surety*.

Countervailing duty A tax levied on an import to offset the amount by which the exporting country subsidized its manufacture.

Course of dealing In the law of sales, a pattern of prior business transactions (not just the performance of one transaction) which can establish a background for the interpretation of the immediate transaction.

Course of performance In the law of sales, the carrying out of a particular transaction. There can be no course of performance unless there are repeated occasions for performance, such as several deliveries of coal to be made pursuant to a single contract of sale.

Court of Claims A special court created by Congress for the purpose, among others, of hearing and determining contract claims against the United States; now named the U.S. Court of Claims.

Cover A buyer's arrangement for the purchase of goods in substitution for goods which the seller failed to deliver.

Crime An unlawful act or failure to act that is punishable in a criminal prosecution brought by the government.

Cumulative preferred stock Shares giving the holder the right to receive a stated dividend in full each year.

Cumulative voting A system, permitted by many state statutes, whereby a shareholder can cast all of his or her votes (shares owned multiplied by the number of directors to be elected) for one candidate.

Cure The act of correcting a defective tender or delivery of goods.

D&O insurance A policy generally paid by a corporation insuring its directors and officers from personal liability against claims for negligence, failure to exercise proper business judgment, and breach of fiduciary obligations, but not against embezzlement.

Damages Money compensation for a wrong, such as money payment for breach of contract. See also *Compensatory damages*, *Consequential damages*, *Nominal damages*, and *Punitive damages*.

Dealer A person engaged in the business of buying goods or other property such as real estate for resale to final customers.

Dealer-merchant As used in this book, a merchant who deals in goods of the kind involved in the transaction between the dealer-merchant seller and the buyer. See *Merchant*.

Debenture An unsecured corporate bond. See *Bond*.

Debit In commercial paper law, to charge against a customer's bank account; also, a charge against an account.

Debtor-in-possession In a Bankruptcy Code business reorganization, the debtor or the management of a corporate debtor that stays in possession of the firm and has the duties of a bankruptcy trustee.

Debtor's estate In the law of bankruptcy, the various property interests either owned by the debtor at the commencement of a bankruptcy case or recoverable for the estate by the trustee in bankruptcy from someone other than the debtor.

Decedent A person who has died.

Deceit (action for deceit) An action at law based upon a misrepresentation or concealment by which one deceives another who has no means of detecting the fraud, to the injury and damage of such person. Used interchangeably with *Fraud*.

Decree A decision of a judge in equity.

Deductible A specified amount of loss that an insured must absorb before being entitled to payment from an insurer.

Deed A formal instrument of conveyance of real property.

Deep-rock doctrine In bankruptcy law, the rule that subordinates claims of controlling corporate shareholders who are also general creditors to the claims of other general creditors. Deep Rock is the name of the corporation involved in the case establishing the rule.

De facto corporation An organization that operates as a corporation, whose organizers have made an unsuccessful attempt in "good faith" to comply with the state enabling statutes. Only the state can challenge the existence of a de facto corporation.

Default A failure to perform a legal duty; especially, a failure to pay for something or to repay a loan.

Defendant A party against whom a court action is brought.

Defense A circumstance or reason put forward by a defendant to defeat the claim of the plaintiff or to defeat a criminal charge. In the law of commercial paper, defenses are personal or real. A *personal defense* is not good against a holder in due course. A *real defense* is good against anyone, including a holder in due course.

Deficiency The amount of debt that is not paid by the proceeds of a mortgage foreclosure sale or sale of personal property collateral. The creditor is usually entitled to a *Deficiency judgment* for the amount of the shortfall.

Deficiency judgment A judgment against a debtor for the amount of an unpaid debt exceeding the value of any collateral.

De jure corporation A corporation that has all the legal characteristics of a corporation and whose incorporators have substantially complied with the enabling statute of the state of incorporation.

Delectus personae Latin for "choice of persons." A phrase used in partnership law to express the right of any partner to accept or reject a new member to the partnership.

Delegatee See *Delegation*.

Delegation The authorizing, by a person under a duty of performance, of another person to render the required performance. The person who does the authorizing is the *delegator*. The person authorized to carry out the performance is the *delegatee*.

Delegator See *Delegation*.

Demise As used in law, a transfer of real property or of an interest in real property, usually in connection with a lease.

Demurrer A document, filed by the defendant in a lawsuit, by which the defendant challenges the court's jurisdiction or the legal sufficiency of the plaintiff's complaint. Usually, it is a form of pleading which admits the facts alleged but asserts that they do not constitute a cause of action.

De novo Latin for "from the beginning." A new start, as in a *Trial de novo*.

Deposited acceptance rule A rule of contract law that an offeree's message of acceptance is effective upon dispatch if the offeree used a medium of acceptance authorized by the offeror. See *Acceptance*.

Deposition A statement under oath made at a hearing held out of court.

Derivative suit An action filed in the corporate name by one or more shareholders to enforce a corporate cause of action.

Destination bill of lading See *Bill of lading*.

Destination contract A contract in which the seller is required to make delivery at the point of destination.

Detour A slight deviation by an employee from a prescribed route while traveling on authorized work.

Devise A gift by will of real property.

Dicta Plural of dictum. An appellate court's statement of a rule or principle of law which, although sound, is not necessarily involved in the case before the court.

Directed verdict A verdict entered for either the plaintiff or the defendant, not as a result of jury deliberation, but as a result of the judge ordering the entry. A directed verdict is ordered only if the facts are so clear that the jury could not reasonably reach a verdict for the other party.

Disaffirmance The setting aside or avoiding of a contract or obligation which can be avoided legally.

Discharge To extinguish an obligation, whether by performance or otherwise. The termination of a contractual obligation.

Disclaimer A denial, especially a denial that a warranty was made or is effective; or a denial of liability for fraud, negligence, and the like.

Discount To sell for less than face value. In banking law, the taking of interest in advance.

Dishonor To refuse or fail to pay or accept a negotiable instrument that has been properly presented for payment or acceptance.

Disparagement A false statement attacking the plaintiff's title to property (slander of title) or the quality of his or her goods or services (slander of quality or trade libel). Also called "injurious falsehood."

Dissolution In corporation law, the termination of a corporation by legislative act, by judicial decree, by voluntary action of the shareholders, or by expiration of the period of time for which the corporation was formed. In partnership law, dissolution is a preparatory step to termination.

Distributive justice A type of justice concerned with how equitably benefits and burdens are distributed among members of society.

Dividends Distributions from corporate assets (usually earned surplus), made on a pro rata basis to shareholders of a designated class of stock, as authorized by the corporation's board of directors. In the law of insurance, the difference between (1) the premium charged for a policy plus earnings from investing the premium and (2) the lower amount justified by the actual loss and expense experience of the insurer. An insurance dividend may be viewed as a refund of a part of the premium initially charged for the insurance.

Dock receipt See *Document of title.*

Dock warrant See *Document of title.*

Document of title A writing that is treated as adequately evidencing that the person in possession of it is entitled to receive, hold, and dispose of the document and the goods it covers. Documents of title include *dock warrants, dock receipts,* and *warehouse receipts.* See also *Bills of lading.*

Domestic corporation A corporation which is doing business in the state of incorporation.

Dormant partner A partner who does not represent the partnership to the public. Also called "silent" or "secret" partner.

Double jeopardy A second prosecution after a prior prosecution for the same offense, transaction, or omission.

Dower The right of a widow to a portion of her deceased husband's estate. Most states now provide for a forced or elective share instead.

Draft A type of commercial paper commanding the drawee to pay a sum of money. A *time draft* is payable at a specified future time; a *demand draft* is payable on demand of the holder at any time.

Drawee The person, bank, or firm that is ordered by the drawer of a draft or check to make payment to a payee.

Drawer The person, bank, or firm that issues a draft or check and thereby orders the drawee to make payment to the payee.

Due negotiation In the law of documents of title, the transfer of a document of title that confers upon the transferee the right to have the document and the goods it represents free from any defenses of prior owners and of warehousers and carriers.

Due-on-sale clause A provision in a mortgage that the entire amount of the mortgage debt becomes due if the property is sold or transferred by the owner-mortgagor.

Due process The administration of law in accordance with rules and forms which have been established for the protection of private rights. *Procedural due process* requires a fair hearing or the right to one. *Substantive due process* requires that a law not be arbitrary, unreasonably discriminatory, or demonstrably irrelevant to the matter which the law purports to govern.

Duress Any wrongful or illegal coercion, by threat or other means, that overcomes the free will or judgment of a person and induces the person to do something he or she otherwise would not do.

Easement The right to use, or prevent the use of, another's property for a specific purpose; generally an irrevocable and transferable property right. Easements may be created by express or implied grant or reservation, by necessity, by dedication, or by prescription.

Elective share The portion of a deceased spouse's estate that the surviving spouse is entitled to as a matter of law. Also called "forced share."

Electronic funds transfer A method of transferring credits of money into and out of accounts electronically instead of by paper orders such as checks. Consumer applications are known as EFT transactions; *wire transfers* and *funds transfers* are commercial applications.

Emancipation In contract law, a status wherein a minor may enter into contracts and assumes responsibility for his or her own support.

Embezzlement The wrongful appropriation of property by a person to whom it has been entrusted.

Eminent domain The government's power to appropriate private property for public purposes. Under the Takings Clause of the Constitution, the government can take private property only for a "public use" and must pay the owner "just compensation."

Enabling act A statute stating requirements and steps for incorporation.

Enabling legislation A statute expressing in general terms the powers and purposes of an administrative agency.

Enforceable contract A contract for the breach of which the law gives a remedy.

Engagement In commercial paper, a promise imposed by law.

Engagement letter A letter written by an accountant setting forth the work to be done for a client which constitutes the contract between the parties.

Enjoin To prohibit. An order of a court entered at the request of a plaintiff, which "enjoins" (prohibits) the defendant from carrying on certain conduct.

Entrustment In the law of sales, the act of putting goods into the possession of a merchant who deals in goods of that kind.

Enumerated powers The powers specifically granted to the federal government under the Constitution.

Equal dignities rule The requirement that an

agent's authority must be in writing if his or her act requires a writing.

Equitable decree An order of a court of equity.

Equitable remedies The relief given by a court of equity.

Equity A body of law developed by the English courts of chancery to supplement the rigid common law of the time. The courts of chancery developed new remedies and flexible procedures for cases where the remedy at law (damages) was inadequate. The word "equity" implies fairness and a wise discretion in the formulation and application of equitable remedies. Also, an ownership interest in property.

Equity financing Raising money by a corporation through the sale of shares of stock. See also *Equity securities*.

Equity of redemption See *Redemption*.

Equity securities Shares of capital stock representing a shareholder's proportionate ownership interest in the corporation as a whole.

Escrow In general, a system whereby a neutral third party acts as a depository of money or documents to be transferred from one party to another upon completion of agreed conditions.

Estate In the law of wills, the property owned by a decedent at death that is administered by the personal representative and ultimately distributed to the decedent's heirs. In the law of bankruptcy, the property of the debtor in bankruptcy that is liquidated by the trustee for the benefit of the debtor's creditors.

Estates Ownership interests in real property including fee simple estates, Life estates, and Leasehold estates.

Estoppel A doctrine that bars alleging or denying facts in court which are inconsistent with prior conduct.

Exclusionary rule The rule of constitutional law that evidence seized by the police or government agents in violation of the suspect's constitutional rights is generally inadmissible against him or her at trial.

Exculpatory clause See *Disclaimer*.

Executed contract A contract that has been fully performed by both parties.

Execution (of judgment at law) The process of procuring a writ of execution from the clerk of court and having the sheriff seize the defendant's property and sell it to satisfy the judgment.

Executive committee In a corporation, a committee composed entirely of directors who are authorized by majority vote of the board of directors to make corporate management decisions (not involving extraordinary transactions) during intervals between board meetings.

Executor A person or entity, named in a will, appointed by a probate court to administer a deceased testator's estate and to carry out the testator's wishes expressed in his or her will concerning the disposition of his or her property.

Executory contract A contract in which neither party has rendered the promised performance.

Exemplary damages See *Punitive damages*.

Exemptions In bankruptcy law, property that an individual debtor may preserve free from the claims of creditors.

Exoneration An act freeing another from blame; the discharge of an obligation.

Experience rating In insurance, the process of adjusting the premium to reflect, for renewal years, the actual loss experience of the insured.

Ex post facto law A law imposing a criminal sanction upon a person for an act that, when committed, was not criminal. Ex post facto laws are unconstitutional.

Express authority The authority explicitly given by a principal to an agent, either in writing or orally.

Express contract A contract whose terms are stated in words, either written or spoken.

Express powers In constitutional law, the powers specifically named by a constitution. The Constitution of the United States specifically grants certain powers (called "express" or "enumerated" powers) to the federal government. In corporation law, express powers are set forth in articles of incorporation or in a statute.

Express warranty See *Warranty*.

Expropriation A country's takeover of a business owned by foreign investors. If there is neither a valid public purpose nor just compensation, the takeover is called a "confiscation."

Ex rel. (ex relationi) Latin for "upon relation" or information. The title of a legal proceeding instituted by an attorney general (or other proper person) in the name and on behalf of the state.

Extension plan See *Composition plan*.

Extraterritoriality The operation of laws upon corporations and persons beyond the enacting state's boundaries.

Face value The nominal value of a security as expressed on its face; e.g., the par value of a share of stock or the amount due and payable on a bond, according to its terms.

Fair use Lawful reproduction of a copyrighted work without the consent of the copyright owner; e.g., publishing excerpts of a book in a magazine book review.

FAS Free alongside a vessel.

Featherbedding The requirement, through union pressure, that an employer hire unnecessary employees, assign unnecessary work, or limit production.

Federalism A system of government in which power is divided between a national government and local government entities.

Fee simple Title to or absolute ownership of real property.

Felony A serious criminal offense.

Fiction An assumption of law that something which is or may be false is true. It is a legal fiction to say that a corporation is a person.

Fictitious name A counterfeit, feigned, or pretended name taken by a person, differing in some essential particular from his or her true name; a name adopted to identify a business concern. Sometimes called a "dba" (doing business as).

Fiduciary An obligation of trust or confidence.

Fiduciary relationship A relationship in which the degree of trust and confidence placed by one party in the other compels the exercise of utmost fairness and good faith.

Field warehousing A secured transaction for the financing of business inventory. The inventory used as collateral is segregated in a fenced-off area of the borrower's premises and is placed under the control of an independent warehouse.

Final credit An entry in a bank account indicating that the depositor is entitled to withdraw the amount credited.

Finance lease A lease of personal property in which the lessor does not manufacture, supply, or select the leased goods. The lessor, typically a bank or other financing entity, acquires goods selected by the lessee and then leases them to the lessee.

Financing statement A writing that is filed in the public records to give notice of the creditor's security interest in collateral.

Firm offer In the law of sales, a written offer in which the offeror, a merchant, promises to hold the offer open, usually for a certain period of time.

Fixture An article that was personal property but which has been attached to real property with the intent that it become a permanent part of the real property.

Fixture filing See *Perfection*.

Floating lien A security interest in both present and future assets of the debtor instead of a security interest only in specific assets on hand at the creation of the secured transaction. A floating lien is created by an *After-acquired property clause*.

FOB Free on board.

Forbearance Giving up a legal right, as in "forbearance to sue."

Forced share See *Elective share*.

Foreclosure A procedure by which encumbered (mortgaged) property is sold upon the debtor's default, in satisfaction of the debt.

Foreign corporation A corporation that is doing business in a state other than the state of incorporation.

Form A printed document, generally with blank spaces to be filled in. In the law of contracts, the style of language used—the wording of the contract.

Formal contract A contract to which the law gives special effect because of the form used in creating it. A negotiable instrument such as a check is a formal contract because to create a negotiable instrument, a person must use a particular form or style of language.

Formal will A will that meets all legal requirements; it is in writing, signed by the testator or testatrix, and witnessed by the required number of qualified persons.

Four-corner rule In the law of commercial paper, the rule that whether an instrument is unconditional is to be determined solely by what is expressed on the face of the instrument.

Franchise A contract in which the owner (franchisor) of intangible property, such as a trademark or trade name, authorizes another (franchisee) to use such property in the operation of a business within described territory.

Fraud An intentional, false representation or concealment of material fact intended to induce another to act, justifiably relied on by the other to his or her injury. See also *Deceit*.

Fraudulent transfer In bankruptcy law, a transfer of property by the debtor within 1 year preceding bankruptcy, where the debtor was insolvent when the transfer was made and where the debtor received less than a reasonable equivalent value for the transfer. A fraudulent transfer can also occur in other than bankruptcy situations. Also called a "fraudulent conveyance."

Freeze-out A course of action taken by the holders of the majority shares of a close corporation designed to force a minority shareholder to sell his or her interest in the corporation on terms favorable to the majority shareholders.

Frolic A substantial deviation by an employee from a prescribed route while traveling on authorized work.

Full warranty A written consumer product warranty that meets the four minimum standards or requirements of the Magnuson-Moss Warranty Act.

Funds transfer See *Electronic funds transfer*.

Fungible Equivalent. Goods are fungible if by their nature or by usage of trade one unit is the equivalent of any other unit.

Future-advances clause A clause in a security agreement that permits the collateral of the debtor to be used to secure future loans.

Future goods Goods which are not both existing and identified to the contract for their sale.

Garnishment A legal procedure by means of which a creditor acquires money or other property of a debtor where the property is in the hands of some other person, such as a bank or an employer. The property can include a debt owed to the debtor, such as wages due from an employer.

General creditor In bankruptcy law, an unsecured creditor.

General lien A lien that entitles a creditor to keep the debtor's property until all debts owed the creditor as a result of the general course of business between creditor and debtor have been paid. See also *Specific lien*.

Generally Accepted Accounting Procedures (GAAP) The accounting profession's rules and procedures for reporting accounting information.

Generally Accepted Auditing Standards (GAAS) The accounting profession's rules and procedures for conducting an audit.

General partners The members of a limited partnership who are in charge of the partnership affairs; they are liable to third parties for the partnership debts.

General partnership See *Partnership*.

Gift A transfer of title to property without consideration by a donor to a donee. The essential elements of a gift are donative intent, delivery, and acceptance.

Going-and-coming rule A principal's freedom from liability for an employee's actions while the latter is going to or from work.

Golden parachute A contract which grants extraordinary benefits to a top executive in the event the company is taken over and the executives are either forced to leave or voluntarily leave the company.

Good faith In the law of sales, honesty in fact in the conduct or transaction concerned. For a merchant, good faith is honesty in fact and the observance of reasonable commercial standards of fair dealing in the trade.

Goodwill The expectation of a continuance of customers and profits enjoyed because of the manner in which a business has been conducted.

Grab law Law, usually state law, that permits unpaid creditors to seize and sell the property of the debtor.

Grace period Extra time to carry out a legal duty. In the law of secured transactions, an amount of time, beyond the usual time given, to file or otherwise perfect a security interest.

Graded rate In property insurance, a reduced premium rate that is applied when a person approaches insuring his or her property for full value. Graded rates reflect the fact that there are more partial than full losses and are a means, seldom used, for assuring that people who underinsure their property receive no more indemnity per dollar of premiums than do people who insure for full value.

Grantee One to whom a grant is made. In property law, the person to whom real property is granted and conveyed.

Grantor One who transfers property, or a right, to another (the grantee).

Gratuitous agent An agent who serves without pay.

Gratuitous surety See *Surety*.

Gravaman The heart or essence of a matter.

Greenmail A premium payment by a target company to purchase the company's shares held by a corporation raider in exchange for his or her promise not to attempt a takeover bid.

Ground for relief Generally, the basis of a lawsuit; the conduct of a debtor that triggers the applicability of the Bankruptcy Code if creditors who are entitled to do so choose to invoke it.

Group boycott A joint refusal to deal; joint action for the purpose of restricting a competitor's access to markets or sources of supply.

Group insurance Insurance in which the insurer undertakes to insure every person in the group without regard to the insurability of individuals within it. The insurer issues one detailed *master contract* to the group policyholder but only brief certificates to individual members of the group.

Guarantor One who guarantees the obligation of another. In the law of commercial paper, a signer who adds "payment guaranteed" or equivalent words to the signature and thereby promises that if the instrument is not paid when due, he or she will pay it without insisting on resort to any other party.

Hearsay evidence Statements made in court by a witness who has no personal knowledge or observation but merely repeats what he or she has heard others say.

Heir Under modern practice, a person who inherits from another real or personal property or an interest in such property. Formerly, one who inherits by virtue of the laws of descent and distribution.

Hell or high water In leases of personal property, the obligation of the lessee to pay regardless of the condition of the leased property or a breach of the lease by the lessor.

Holder A person who is in possession of an instrument drawn, issued, or indorsed to him or her or to his or her order or to bearer or in blank.

Holder in due course A holder who takes an instrument for value, in good faith, and without notice that it is overdue or that it has been dishonored or that there is any defense against or claim to it on the part of any person. See also *Holder*.

Holographic will A will in the testator's own handwriting, signed and dated. Recognized in most states as a valid will.

Horizontal merger A combination of two or more firms that are competitors in the marketplace. See also *Vertical merger*.

Identification In the law of sales, the act of designating goods as the subject of a particular contract of sale.

Illusory Deceptive. An illusory promise appears to be promissory in its terms but actually promises nothing because the promisor retains the choice of performing or nonperforming.

Impairment In bankruptcy law, the adverse impact of a plan of reorganization that gives a claimant less than the full value of his or her claim or interest. In commercial paper law, an interference with a person's ability to collect payment from another, by impairing either recourse to another person or access to collateral.

Implied contract A contract in which the terms are wholly or partly inferred from conduct or from surrounding circumstances.

Implied powers In constitutional law, powers that are not specifically named but which are necessary and proper for carrying out the express powers. In corporation law, powers not specifically set out in a statute or charter but necessary and proper for carrying out the corporation's express powers. In agency law, the implied authority of an agent. See also *Express powers*.

Implied warranty See *Warranty*.

Incontestability An inability, imposed by law or by contract, of an insurer to avoid a policy for concealment, breach of warranty, or misrepresentation. Also, a noncontest clause in a will.

Incorporation The process (as established in state statutes) by which a corporation is formed.

Incorporator A person who organizes a corporation by signing and filing the articles of incorporation with the designated officer of the state.

Indemnification The compensation or payment of a damage another sustains.

Indemnify To give security against the possibility of future damage; for instance, an insurance company undertakes to indemnify its policyholders against loss.

Indemnity Reimbursement for loss.

Indemnity principle The theory that in the event of casualty an insured should be limited to reimbursement (indemnity) for loss actually suffered, because insurance is a system for distributing losses and not for generating a profit for insureds. The principle is especially applicable in liability, property, and health insurance.

Independent contractor One who, exercising an independent employment, contracts to do certain work according to his or her own methods and without being subject to the control of an employer except as to the results to be accomplished.

Indictment An accusation in writing found and presented by a grand jury that a person named in the indictment has done some act or has been guilty of some omission which by law is a public offense.

Indorsement A signature customarily found on the back of commercial paper; made by a person other than a maker, a drawer, or an acceptor; and ordinarily resulting in secondary liability on the instrument. An indorsement is in blank or special, nonrestrictive or restrictive, *and* unqualified or qualified. A *special indorsement* maintains the order character of an order instrument or gives order character to a bearer instrument. A *restrictive indorsement* specifies a use to which the proceeds of the instrument must be put. A *qualified indorsement* protects the indorser from liability on the instrument but not for liability for breach of warranty.

Informal contract A contract for which the law does not prescribe a particular form in order for the contract to be enforceable.

Information In criminal law, a formal accusation of crime similar to an indictment but preferred (made) by a competent prosecuting official, such as a district attorney, instead of by a grand jury.

Infraction A minor wrong, usually not a criminal offense.

Infringement The wrongful appropriation, copying, or use of a trademark, trade name, trade dress, copyright, or patent.

Inheritance Something obtained by operation of law from a person who dies without leaving a valid will and, under modern usage, by virtue of the provisions of a will.

Injunction An equitable remedy in which a court orders a person to do or to refrain from doing something.

In pari delicto Latin for "in equal fault." The common law principal that a court will not entertain a cause of action between two people who are equally at fault.

In re In the matter of; regarding. The title of a judicial proceeding, as *In re Smith*, in which there are no adversary parties. Commonly used in bankruptcy and estate proceedings.

Insanity A mental derangement caused by a disease of the mind. An insane person is without legal competence to enter into a contract or to make a will; proof of insanity may free an accused person from responsibility for a criminal act. Tests for insanity differ in contract law, probate law, and criminal law.

Inside director A corporation director who also holds a management position in the company.

Insider trading The purchase or sale of corporate securities on the basis of material, nonpublic inside information.

Insolvency laws State laws under which a troubled debtor may make arrangements with creditors for full or partial payment, or the postponement of payment, of her or his debts.

Insurable interest A financial stake in property or in someone's life that will justify the person who has that stake in insuring the property or life.

Insurance A contractual means of transferring and distributing the risk of financial loss.

Integration A written statement being the final expression of the parties to an agreement. *Complete integration*: a written, complete, and exclusive statement of all the contract terms. *Partial integration*: a written final expression of only the contract terms included in the writing, other contract terms existing outside the writing.

Intellectual property Property rights acquired by creative or productive activity including patents, copyrights, trademarks, and trade secrets.

Intent The mental state of the person who purposely commits an act. Intent is a necessary element of an intentional tort. In criminal law, criminal intent is call "mens rea."

Inter alia Among other things.

Interlocking directorates A practice in which members of the board of directors of one corporation also serve as directors of other corporations that do business with one another.

Interpretation The process of discovering and explaining the meaning of any unclear language—e.g., of a statute or a contract. See *Construction*.

Interpretive rule An administration regulation, without the force of law, setting out the agency's opinion as to the meaning of the law it administers.

Interstate commerce Commercial intercourse, communication, transportation of persons or property between or among two or more states of the Union.

Inter vivos Between the living; from one living person to another. Where property passes by conveyance, the transaction is said to be inter vivos, to distinguish it from a transfer by will effective upon death.

Intestacy laws Laws governing the passage of title to property when a person dies without a will. Also called "laws of intestate succession."

Intestate Without making a will. Also, an intestate: a person who dies without leaving a valid will.

Intrastate Activity or territory that is wholly within a single state of the Union.

Intra vires Within the power of a person or corporation; within the scope of express or implied powers or authority.

Ipso facto By the fact itself; by the mere fact.

Issue A legal question to be decided by a court. Under the laws of descent and distribution, all persons who have descended from a common ancestor; also, the child or children of an individual and of their children. In the law of commercial paper, the act of putting a negotiable instrument such as a check into circulation; issuance of a negotiable instrument, a document of title, or some other commercial document.

Item A check, draft, matured bond, interest coupon, or other instrument calling for payment in money.

Jingle rule In partnership law, the rule that the creditors of partners have first claim to assets of the partners and that creditors of the partnership have first claim to the partnership assets. This rule has been modified by the Bankruptcy Code for situations to which the Code applies.

Joint and several liability The liability of the various defendants is joint and several when a plaintiff, at his or her option, may sue and establish liability of persons separately, or sue all of them together. For example, if a tort is committed against a plaintiff victim by several tortfeasors, they have joint and several liability and the plaintiff may sue only one, or elect to sue all of them.

Joint tenancy Co-ownership of property in which the owners (joint tenants) each own an equal, undivided interest in the property. A joint tenant's interest passes upon death to the surviving joint tenants by right of survivorship.

Joint tortfeasors Includes (1) persons who have acted together by agreement for the purpose of injuring another; and (2) persons who have acted independently but have caused a single indivisible injury.

Joint venture A business owned and managed by two or more persons to accomplish a single objective.

Judgment In law, the decision of a court.

Judgment creditor A party in whose favor a judgment for money is rendered.

Judgment debtor A party against whom a judgment for money is rendered.

Judgment notwithstanding the verdict (judgment n.o.v.) A judgment entered by a judge for the losing party in a jury trial, thus refusing the verdict of the jury. The trial judge will overrule the jury only if there is no substantial evidence to support the decision.

Judgment rate A rate of interest, established by statute, to be applied by the courts to judgments for damages where interest is an element of damages.

Judicial emancipation A legal procedure in which a minor may be allowed to give up the right to disaffirm contracts, and thus to be treated as an adult in contract matters.

Junk bonds Any bonds below "investment-grade quality."

Jurisdiction The power of a court to hear and decide cases.

Jurisprudence The philosophy of law; the science which treats of the principles of law and legal relations, a body of law.

Laches See *Statute of limitations*.

Land contract See *Contract for deed*.

Language of negotiability Words such as "to the order of" or "to bearer" that make a security, document of title, or instrument negotiable in form.

Larceny The unlawful taking and carrying away of the property of another with the intent to deprive the owner of it permanently.

Law merchant The old law of merchants, developed to supplement the common law.

Lease A rental agreement in which the *lessor* conveys to the *lessee* the right to use the lessor's personal or real property, usually in exchange for a payment of money.

Leasehold estate An estate in real property in which the lessee (tenant) has the present right to use and possess the property but the lessor (landlord) retains all other rights to the property including the right to future possession at the termination of the lease.

Legacy A bequest (gift by will) of money.

Legal benefit In contract law, a legal right.

Legal detriment In contract law, giving up a legal right. One party's suffering a bargained-for legal detriment is sufficient as consideration for the other party's promise of performance.

Legal entity An entity, other than a natural person, existing in contemplation of law and having the legal rights and duties of a separate person; e.g., a corporation.

Legal fiction See *Fiction*.

Legal reserve fund See *Cash surrender value*.

Legislative rule A regulation, promulgated by an administrative agency, having the force of law.

Letter of credit A written promise by a bank or another person (the "issuer") made at the request of a customer of the issuer that the issuer will honor drafts or other demands for payment upon the customer's compliance with the conditions specified in the letter of credit; a letter of credit may be either revocable or irrevocable.

Level premium A life insurance premium fixed at a certain amount for the duration of the contract. The premium is larger than needed to pay claims and expenses during the early years of the contract. The excess is invested to provide funds to pay increasingly frequent future claims.

Leveraged buyout The purchase of all the shares of stock of a corporation, generally by some members of the top management of the corporation itself, together with others. The transaction entails the purchasers borrowing the necessary funds and pledging all the assets of the corporation purchased as security for the loan.

Liability with fault See *Strict liability*.

Libel Defamation expressed by print, writing, pictures, or signs.

License In real estate law, a personal right to use a person's real property for some purpose. In computer law, a license is the limited right to use a copyrighted program.

Lien A claim or charge against property. A lien may be created by contract or imposed by law to secure, for example, the claims of mechanics or other artisans for work done on property, or to secure the claim of a government for unpaid taxes.

Life estate The ownership of real property for life or during the life of another.

Life tenant The owner of a life estate.

Limited liability company A company for profit formed under a statute for a term of not more than 30 years, with two or more members who have limited liability and the right to participate in management. It is taxed like a partnership, but members have limited liability similar to a corporation.

Limited partnership A partnership consisting of one or more general partners, responsible as ordinary partners, by whom the business is conducted, and one or more limited partners, who are not liable for the debts of the partnership beyond the funds contributed, and who do not participate in the firm's management.

Limited warranty A written consumer product warranty that does not conform with the standards imposed by the Magnuson-Moss Warranty Act for a full warranty.

Liquidated damages An amount of money established by a contract as a remedy for its breach.

Liquidated debt In contract law, a debt or claim about which there is no dispute as to existence or amount.

Liquidation The process of collecting property, selling it for cash, and distributing the proceeds in accordance with the requirements of the law.

Liquidation proceeding A bankruptcy proceeding, the object of which is to convert the debtor's nonexempt assets into cash, to distribute it in accordance with the scheme of distribution provided by the Bankruptcy Code, and to grant the honest debtor a discharge from most of the remaining debts.

Living will A legal instrument in which the maker declares his or her desires regarding life-sustaining medical treatment.

Locus poenitentiae In contract law, a place or opportunity to repent and withdraw from an illegal agreement.

Long-arm statute A statute conferring jurisdiction over out-of-state defendants.

Majority shareholders Shareholders who collectively own a majority of the voting shares of a corporation and who exercise control over the corporation by electing directors, amending articles, and making decisions on extraordinary transactions. Often used to describe one who controls a majority of votes by means of proxies. See also *Proxy*.

Malpractice Professional negligence; the failure of an accountant, lawyer, doctor, or other professional to live up to a professional standard of care.

Mandamus Latin for "we command." A command issued by a court of competent jurisdiction to an inferior court, corporation, or person.

Master An employer who has the right to control the physical performance of an employee's (servant's) work.

Master contract In group insurance, the detailed insurance policy held by the group policyholder, to be contrasted with the brief certificate held by each member of the group.

Master limited partnership A limited partnership established with many limited partnership interests which are traded on a securities exchange.

Material alteration Any significant change in an instrument which affects or may possibly affect the rights of the parties interested in the document.

Mechanic's lien See *Lien*.

Mediation A form of alternative dispute resolution which uses a mediator to facilitate a resolution between the parties.

Meeting of creditors In bankruptcy law, a gathering at which creditors elect a trustee to oversee the distribution of a bankrupt's estate and to decide other matters regarding the bankruptcy.

Mens rea Criminal intent. See also *Intent*.

Merchant In the law of sales, a person who deals in goods of the kind involved in the transaction. Also, a person who by occupation holds himself or herself out as having knowledge or skill peculiar to the practices or goods involved in the transaction, and a person to whom such knowledge or skill may be attributed by his or her employment of an intermediary who by occupation holds himself or herself out as having such knowledge or skill.

Merger In corporation law, the absorption of one corporation by another; the latter acquires all the assets and assumes all the liabilities of the "target" corporation, which then ceases to exist.

Midnight deadline Midnight of the banking day following the banking day on which a bank receives an item for collection.

Minor A person under the age at which the law recognizes a capacity to contract, to vote, or to purchase intoxicating liquor. The age of "majority" to contract, 21 at common law, is now 18 in many states.

Minority shareholders Shareholders whose collective voting rights are insufficient to elect a corporation's board of directors or otherwise control management decisions.

Miranda warning A statement by an arresting officer to an individual in custody as to his or her rights with respect to answering police questions.

Mirror-image rule In the common (general) law of contracts, the requirement that for a contract to arise, the acceptance must correspond exactly to (mirror) the offer. In the law of sales, the mirror-image rule has largely been abandoned.

Misdemeanor A criminal offense less serious than a felony.

M'Naghten rule A test of insanity used in criminal cases by many courts; also known as the right-and-wrong test.

Model Business Corporation Act A model statute designed by the America Law Institute and the American Bar Association to meet the changing needs of modern business and to encourage greater uniformity in state laws governing the incorporation and operation of corporations. (See Appendix 5.)

Monopoly power In antitrust law, the power to fix prices, exclude competitors, or control the market in a given geographical area.

Moral norms Specific standards of conduct indicating what constitutes acceptable behavior according to the morals of members of a group.

Mortgage A secured transaction in real estate in which the creditor has an interest in the real estate to secure payment of the debt. See *Chattel mortgage* and *Secured transaction*.

Motion to strike A request by a litigant that a court delete the whole or part of a pleading.

Necessaries Suitable food, clothing, education, medical service, and place of residence in view of the rank, position, and mode of living of an individual.

Negligence The failure to exercise reasonable care under the circumstances. The elements of the tort of negligence are: duty, breach of duty, causation, and damages.

Negligence per se A legal presumption or inference of negligence that arises when it is proven that the defendant violated a statute designed for the protection of the plaintiff against the type of harm suffered by the plaintiff.

Negligent misrepresentation A misrepresentation of material facts by a person who failed to exercise due care in making the representation or in determining the truth of the matters represented.

Negotiable document of title Similar to *Negotiable instrument*.

Negotiable form The style of language required by law for creating a negotiable instrument or document.

Negotiable instrument A document such as a check or a promissory note which, because of its language, confers more than the usual rights of collection on a person who qualifies as or otherwise has the rights of a holder in due course. See *Commercial paper*.

Negotiation With reference to contracts, the exploring or discussing through oral or written communication of the terms and conditions of a contract preliminary to the making of a final contract. With reference to commercial paper, the transferring of a negotiable instrument to another.

Nolo contendere A plea to a criminal charge which neither admits nor denies guilt. Such a plea cannot be used as an admission of guilt for purposes of a related civil suit.

Nominal consideration In contract law, an amount stated which is not bargained for by the parties but simply inserted to give the transaction the appearance of legality. Usually $1.

Nominal damages A trifling sum awarded to a plaintiff who wins a case and receives a judgment but who is unable to prove any harm or loss.

Nonconforming goods Goods that differ from what was ordered under a sales contract.

Nonconforming tender An offer of performance that differs from the performance called for by a sales contract. See *Performance* and *Tender*.

Nonconforming use A use of property that existed before the enactment of a zoning law prohibiting that use.

Nonprofit corporation A corporation that is formed for charitable, religious, educational, or fraternal purposes. No part of its income may be distributed to members, and assets can be distributed to members only when the corporation is dissolved.

No-par stock Authorized stock to which "no par" value is assigned by the articles of incorporation. Upon issuance, the directors fix the per-share subscription price, but the amount is not stated on the certificate.

Note See *Promissory note*.

Notice A legal notification received by a party either directly or indirectly through an agent or as otherwise provided by law. *Actual notice* is information actually received. *Constructive notice* is information a person is charged by law with having received even if he or she has not actually been made aware of it, as where an announcement has been published in a newspaper of general circulation but is not read by the person or persons upon whom such announcement is legally binding.

Notice of lis pendens A recorded notice advising persons that the title to a particular tract of real estate is subject to a pending lawsuit.

Novation The extinguishment of a party's obligation (e.g., a debt) through an agreement between the old obligor, a new obligor, and the obligee for the substitution of the new obligor for the old one.

n.o.v. (non obstante veredicto) Latin for "notwithstanding the verdict." A judgment entered by order of a court for the losing party although there has been a verdict for the other party. See *Judgment notwithstanding the verdict*.

Nuisance An unreasonable interference with a person's use and enjoyment of his or her real property; a nontrespassory invasion of a person's real property rights.

Nullity Nothing; an act or proceeding which is of no legal force or effect.

Obligee A person to whom an obligation or duty is owed.

Obligor A person who owes a duty to someone else—i.e., a person who has an obligation to perform.

Offer A statement or other conduct by which the offeror confers upon the offeree a legal power to accept the offer and thereby to create a contract.

Open term Some aspect or detail of a contract which the parties have not agreed upon but have, instead, left undecided.

Option An offer for which the offeree pays (or gives other valuable consideration) to keep the offer open for a stated period of time. Sometimes called "option contract."

Order document of title Similar to order commercial paper. See *Commercial paper*.

Order for relief An order promulgated by a court of equity. In bankruptcy law, a formal court ruling or declaration that an alleged debtor is insolvent.

Output contract A contract in which one party agrees to purchase the total production of the other party. Also, a contract in which the seller agrees to sell his or her total production to the other party.

Pac Man defense A target corporation's ploy to make a tender offer for controlling shares of an acquiring corporation that has previously made a tender offer to acquire controlling shares of the target corporation.

Parental emancipation Parent's surrendering their right to the care, custody, and earnings of their minor child and renouncing their parental duties. Has no effect on the minor's ability to disaffirm his or her contract.

Pari delicto In equal fault, as where two equally blameworthy wrongdoers attempt to make a contract.

Parol evidence rule The legal doctrine preventing the use of prior or contemporaneous oral statements or writings as evidence to contradict or change the terms of a signed integrated contract. See *Integration*.

Partner A member of a general or limited partnership; may be either a general partner or a limited partner.

Partner by estoppel A nonpartner who acquires a partner's liability to a third party who relied upon the nonpartner's assertion (or the assertion of a member of a partnership) that the nonpartner is in fact a partner. Also called "ostensible partner."

Partnership A form of business organization owned and managed by two or more parties.

Partnership at will A partnership without any fixed term of existence.

Par-value stock Shares of corporation stock assigned a fixed value by the articles of incorporation or by its board of directors; being the minimum price for which each share can be sold by the corporation. The par value is printed on each stock certificate.

Payee One to whom payment is due or made. See also *Draft* and *Promissory note*.

Penal damages A harsh monetary penalty provided for by a contract, to coerce the performance of the contract. Penal damages clauses are not enforceable because the amount of damages provided for is not related to actual damages caused by breach of the contract.

Per capita Literally, "by the head." In inheritance laws, a method of distribution of the estate of a decedent where the persons designated are to receive equal shares, taking in their own right.

Per curiam By the court. The opinion of the whole court, as contrasted with an opinion written by one justice.

Perfection In the law of secured transactions, the process by which a security interest is made enforceable against subsequent lien creditors and certain other persons having a right in the collateral.

Perfect tender rule A rule of law, often relaxed by the UCC, that a buyer may elect to reject goods if the goods or the tender of delivery fails in any respect to conform to the contract.

Performance The carrying out of a legal obligation; the performance of a contract or a contractual promise.

Peril A cause of loss such as fire, flood, theft, or vandalism.

Per se In and of itself; inherently.

Personal defense See *Defense*.

Personal property Anything that can be owned, tangible or intangible, other than real property.

Personal property floater A type of property insurance that applies to movable property, whatever its location.

Personal representative The person who administers a decedent's estate. Also called "administrator" or "executor."

Petition in bankruptcy The formal application filed to commence a bankruptcy case. The petition is voluntary if filed by the debtor or involuntary if filed by his or her creditors.

Piercing the corporate veil The process whereby a court disregards the separateness of the corporation from its shareholders and holds them liable for wrongful conduct that injures third parties.

Plaintiff A party who brings a civil suit.

Plea bargain A plea of guilty to a lesser charge in exchange for an agreed punishment or for the recommendation by the prosecutor to the judge of a lesser punishment than may have been imposed for the offense originally charged.

Pleading A formal statement in a lawsuit setting out a cause of action or defense.

Pledge A transaction in which a debtor gives possession of the debtor's personal property to the creditor as security for repayment of a loan.

Poison pill A tactic adopted by a target company to defeat a takeover attempt by making its shares very high priced or otherwise unattractive to a corporate raider.

Police power The broad power of the states to regulate for the public health, safety, welfare, and morals.

Policy A course of action undertaken by a business or a government. In insurance law, a contract of insurance. See *Public policy*.

Pooling A process of treating as a single group a large number of individual risks of a certain kind so that the total loss likely to be sustained by the group of insureds can be accurately estimated.

Possessory lien A lien (charge against property) that is effective only as long as the bailee retains possession of the property subject to the charge.

Posting In banking, the decision to pay an item and the recording of payment.

Power The ability to do any act. In agency law, the authority to do an act which the grantor might himself or herself lawfully perform; an authority by which one person enables another to do some act for him or her. A person may have the "power" to act but not the "right" to do so.

Power of attorney A written agency authority.

Precedent Court cases which have been decided before a case currently before a court.

Predatory pricing In antitrust law, the prohibited practice of refraining from maximizing profits until competitors are driven out of the market.

Preempt To take exclusive control, as where the federal government, in accordance with the Constitution, expressly denies the states the right to regulate an activity, or enacts a comprehensive scheme of regulation which by implication precludes state regulation.

Preemption In constitutional law, the exercise of exclusive regulatory authority by the federal government as, for example, where the federal government enacts a law regulating a business practice that expressly prohibits any state regulation of that practice.

Preemptive right The right of a stockholder to preserve his or her proportionate stock interest by purchasing shares of a new issue ahead of others.

Preference In bankruptcy law, a transfer of property by the debtor that enables an unsecured creditor to receive a greater percentage of his or her claim against the debtor than the creditor would have received in a distribution of the debtor's assets pursuant to a Chapter 7 liquidation.

Preferential transfer See *Preference*.

Preferred stock A class of stock that has superior rights to dividends and, upon dissolution of the corporation, to corporate assets.

Preincorporation subscription An offer, before a corporation is incorporated, to buy its shares when they are issued. See also *Stock subscription*.

Presentment The act of producing a negotiable instrument and demanding its payment or acceptance.

Presentment warranty See *Warranty*.

Present sale See *Sale*.

Pretermitted In inheritance law, a child or other descendant who is not mentioned or provided for in a testator's will and who had not been otherwise provided for by the testator. Also, sometimes used to designate a spouse who is not provided for in a will.

Price discrimination In antitrust law, a practice whereby a seller charges two or more buyers different prices for an identical product or service.

Prima facie Latin for "on the face of it." Evidence sufficient to support a conclusion.

Primary party A signer of a negotiable instrument who is liable for payment immediately and unconditionally when the instrument comes due. To be contrasted with a *secondary party*, whose liability is conditional because it normally does not arise until after presentment, dishonor, and notice of dishonor.

Primogeniture An English system whereby the eldest son had the exclusive right to inherit the estate of his ancestor. Not used in the United States.

Principal In agency law, the party (disclosed, partially disclosed, or undisclosed) primarily responsible for an obligation incurred by an agent.

Priority claim In bankruptcy law, an allowed, unsecured claim that is, by statute, to be paid before claims of lower rank may be paid. The Bankruptcy Code lists seven classes of priority claims.

Private corporation A profit or nonprofit corporation organized by individuals, as opposed to one formed by the government.

Private law Law dealing with the relationships among private persons and organizations.

Privilege The legal right to do an act that otherwise would be a crime or a tort, such as the privilege to use reasonable force in self-defense or the constitutional privilege to make defamatory statements without actual malice about a public official or public figure.

Privity of contract A relationship that exists between contracting parties because of the contract. A person usually must be in privity of contract in order to bring suit on it. However, the absence of privity of contract between a manufacturer and a remote purchaser of goods is not ordinarily a good defense to a suit brought against the manufacturer by a purchaser on the ground of negligence or breach of warranty.

Probate The act or process of proving the validity of a will; also, the name generally given to all proceedings within the jurisdiction of a probate court.

Procedural due process See *Due process*.

Procedural law That law which specifies the formal steps to be followed in enforcing or asserting rights, duties, privileges, or immunities; also called "adjective" law.

Procedural rule An administrative regulation without the force of law, establishing the process by which the public may deal with the issuing agency.

Proceeds Money or other property received as a result of the sale or other disposition of property.

Professional corporation A corporation which certain professional people, such as doctors, lawyers, or accountants, may establish for their practices to obtain corporate tax benefits.

Promise A manifestation of intention to act or to refrain from acting in a specified way, so made as to justify a promisee in understanding that a commitment has been made.

Promissory estoppel A doctrine or rule of law that a promisor is prevented (estopped) from avoiding liability even though the promisor received no consideration for the promise, if the promisee justifiably relied on the promise to his or her detriment.

Promissory note A type of commercial paper in which the maker promises to pay the payee a sum of money at a future time or on demand, usually with interest. See *Commercial paper*.

Promoter A person who plans and takes necessary action, including soliciting subscriptions for the purchase of shares of stock, in organizing a corporation.

Promulgate To announce officially; to make known publicly as important or obligatory.

Proof of claim A document by which a creditor seeks payment from the debtor's estate, or from the estate of a deceased person.

Property Legally protected rights in anything subject to ownership.

Pro rata Proportionate.

Pro rata share Where funds are insufficient to pay a class of bankruptcy claims in full, the percentage of the claim that each creditor of that class will receive.

Prospectus An instrument containing corporate information required by the SEC to be furnished to a prospective purchaser of the corporation's registered securities offered to the public for sale.

Protest A certificate of dishonor signed and sealed by an authorized public official such as a United States consul or a notary public. See *Dishonor*.

Provisional credit A temporary, reversible credit given to a bank customer while a deposited item is being collected.

Proximate cause The causal relationship between a tortious act and the plaintiff's injury where the injury was a foreseeable consequence of the defendant's act. Also called a "legal cause."

Proxy A person who is authorized by another person to represent or act for her or him at a meeting. With reference to corporations, a person authorized to vote a shareholder's shares at a shareholders' meeting. Also, the writing that authorizes a person to vote the shares of another at a shareholders' meeting.

Public corporation A corporation created for governmental purposes by any agency or subdivision of state or federal government.

Public defenders Attorneys paid out of public funds to defend individuals who cannot afford to hire legal counsel in criminal cases.

Public law Law dealing with the organization of government and with the relation of the government to the people.

Public policy A course of action taken by a government for the good of the public.

Puffing See *Sales puffing*.

Punitive damages Damages awarded against a defendant as punishment for outrageous conduct or to set an example for other wrongdoers; also called "exemplary damages." See also *Compensatory damages*.

Purchase-money security interest (PMSI) A security interest taken or retained by a seller or other financer in financing the purchase or leasing of the collateral.

Purchaser A buyer. More technically, as under the UCC, a person who takes property by sale, negotiation, mortgage, gift, or any other voluntary transaction creating an interest in property.

Put A stockholder's contractual right to compel another to purchase the shares.

Qualified indorsement See *Indorsement*.

Qualified privilege In defamation law, the privilege to make a defamatory statement concerning the plaintiff when the statement is made to further a legitimate interest of the speaker or society. Also called a "conditional privilege."

Quash To cancel or annul.

Quasi Resembling, possessing some of the attributes of something else. An administrative agency may have a quasi-judicial and a quasi-legislative function. In its *quasi-judicial* function, it hears and disposes of disputes in the manner of a court. In its *quasi-legislative* function, it makes rules and regulations of relatively general application, in the manner of a legislature.

Quasi contract A restitutionary remedy for an obligation imposed by law, intended to prevent the unjust enrichment of a person upon whom a benefit has been conferred.

Quasi-judicial See *Quasi*.

Quasi-legislative See *Quasi*.

Quasi-public corporation A profit corporation privately organized for purposes which affect the public interest to an extent requiring special state or federal regulation; e.g., a bank or an insurance company.

Quiet title A proceeding filed for the purpose of establishing one's ownership of property.

Quorum The number of qualified persons (usually a majority of the entire body) required to be present at a meeting in order to conduct business. With reference to corporations, the minimum number of qualified persons (shares represented in person or by proxy) required to conduct business lawfully at a shareholders' meeting.

Quo warranto Latin for "by what authority." When a corporation exceeds its powers, the state attorney general may bring *quo warranto* proceedings, asking the court to order a forfeiture of the charter.

Ratable Proportional.

Ratification Confirmation of a prior act or promise.

Reaffirmation An agreement by a debtor to pay a debt that has been discharged in bankruptcy.

Real defense See *Defense*.

Real property Land and permanent attachments to land.

Recognizance In criminal law, a personal assurance or promise to be present for trial, called "giving one's own recognizance."

Redemption In securities law, the exercise by a corporation of a right to buy back outstanding shares at a fixed price. In property law generally, the right of the mortgagor or other debtor whose property is under foreclosure or repossessed to pay off the secured debt and retain title to the property. In real estate law, the common law equity of redemption allows the debtor to redeem at any time before the foreclosure sale. States may also provide a statutory right of redemption for a period of time after the sale.

Reformation A contractual remedy in which a court rewrites or corrects a written contract so that it accurately reflects the bargain of the parties.

Regulatory taking Government regulation of property that is so extensive that it constitutes a taking of property entitling the owner to just compensation. See also *Eminent domain*.

Reimbursement Repayment.

Reinsurance A contractual arrangement in which an insurance company transfers a part of the group risk it has assumed to another insurer called a "reinsurer."

Release A legally binding contract to give up a right held by the releasing party.

Relevant market The geographic area of effective competition in which a particular product as well as other interchangeable products are traded.

Remainder A future interest in real property owned by an individual other than the grantor of the present interest; the remainderman acquires the title to the property at the end of a life estate or other present interest in property.

Remand To send back; usually the sending back of a court record or case by a higher court to the court from which a decision, an order, or a judgment originated, for the purpose of having the originating court take the action dictated by the higher court.

Remedy A means, such as court action, by which a violation of a right is prevented or is compensated for; legal redress.

Remittitur A reduction in the amount of an award of damages.

Reorganization In bankruptcy, a proceeding by which a financially troubled firm may stay in business while it undergoes a financial rehabilitation that may involve a discharge from the firm's debts. Also, restructuring a corporation's organization.

Replevin An action taken to recover possession of goods.

Repudiation See *Anticipatory breach*.

Requirements contract A contract in which one party agrees to purchase from the other party all of certain goods or services which the purchasing party needs in his or her business.

Res The property in a trust. Also called "corpus."

Resale price maintenance In antitrust law, the practice of a seller fixing the resale price terms of the buyer at a lower level in the chain of distribution. Also known as "vertical price fixing."

Rescission (to rescind) The setting aside or avoiding of a contract, a transaction, or any obligation that can be set aside legally. Used primarily with reference to the avoidance of an agreement, such as the repudiation of a contract by one of the parties to it.

Res ipsa loquitur Latin for "the thing (or incident) speaks for itself." Under the doctrine of *res ipsa loquitur*, the defendant may be required to prove that he or she was *not* negligent where the injury-causing instrumentality was completely within the control of the defendant.

Respondeat superior Latin for "let the master answer." The doctrine under which a master (employer) can be held liable for the wrongful acts of his or her servant (employee) performed within the scope of employment.

Restitution The return of a thing. In the law of contracts, compensation for or the return of partial performances.

Restrictive endorsement See *Indorsement*.

Resulting trust A trust relationship imposed by a court of equity to carry into effect the presumed intentions of the parties.

Reverse To overturn or set aside a judgment, order, or decree previously entered by a court.

Reversion A future interest in property owned by the grantor of the present interest; the grantor reacquires the property at the end of a life estate, lease, or other present interest.

Review An accountant's examination of a firm's financial statements that is less extensive than an *Audit*.

Revocation Annulling, cancelling, or rescinding an act, as to revoke a will or an offer.

Rider An attachment to an insurance policy that modifies the contract in some way.

Risk of loss In the law of sales, the danger that goods will be lost, stolen, destroyed, or damaged.

Rule of avoidable consequences In contract law, a rule disallowing damage claims to the extent that a very modest effort by the plaintiff would have reduced the plaintiff's loss.

Rule of reason In antitrust law, the rule that conduct which unreasonably restrains trade is illegal.

Rule utilitarianism The theory that a rule is morally correct if the total utility produced by everyone's following it is greater than total utility without the rule.

Sale (of goods) The passing of title to goods from the seller to the buyer in return for a consideration, i.e., the price. In a *present sale*, title passes at the time the sales transaction is entered into. In a *contract to sell*, title passes to the buyer at some future time. Article 2 of the UCC covers both present sales and contracts to sell. A *contract for sale* includes present sales and contracts to sell.

Sale on approval A sale of goods in which the buyer is not obligated until the buyer accepts, i.e., approves, the goods.

Sale or return A transaction in which the buyer of goods purchases them for resale but has a right to return to the seller any unsold goods.

Sales puffing Exaggeration and opinion (short of actual fraud) by a seller intended to induce a sale.

Sanction A punishment. However, sanction may also mean "approval."

Scienter A necessary element of the tort of fraud and deceit which requires the plaintiff to prove that at the time false representations were made, the defendant knew they were false or had a reckless disregard as to whether they were true or false. Scienter is a necessary element required to be proved in most violations of federal antitrust and securities laws.

Scope of employment The general nature and conditions of the work for which an employee is hired.

Seasonably In a timely manner.

Secondary boycott Economic pressure by employees of one firm against another firm with whom those employees have no dispute.

Secondary party See *Primary party*.

Secret lien A claim against the property of another person, the acquisition of which is unknown to the general public because the claim has not been filed in the public records or otherwise has not been made known to the public.

Secured transaction Any arrangement made by agreement of the parties for the purpose of providing a creditor with a backup source of payment if the debtor defaults. In a *surety arrangement*, a person or a firm makes a backup promise to pay the debt in the event that the debtor defaults. In a *secured transaction in personal property*, personal property is the collateral and may be sold in the event of the debtor's default.

Secured transaction in real property See *Mortgage*.

Security An investment in a common enterprise in which the investor usually profits solely from the efforts of others. If the investment is in a corporation, it is usually evidenced by a stock or bond certificate issued in bearer or registered form. In the law of secured transactions, a backup source of payment that will be available to the creditor if the debtor fails to pay.

Security agreement An agreement between the debtor and the creditor that the creditor is to have a security interest in the collateral. Unless the creditor is to possess the collateral, the security agreement must be in writing. See also *Security interest*.

Security interest Some interest in property, such as possession or title, which a creditor retains or acquires to secure the payment of a debt.

Selective incorporation The constitutional doctrine under which the Supreme Court has applied most of the Bill of Rights to the states under the due process clause of the Fourteenth Amendment.

Separation of powers In constitutional law, the doctrine that each branch of government (judicial, legislative, executive) should be allowed to exercise its constitutional prerogatives without undue interference by the other branches.

Servant A person employed to perform work or services for another, whose physical conduct in the performance of the work or service and the means by which it will be accomplished are subject to the control of the person (generally called a "master" or "employer") for whom it is being performed.

Set-off The right of each party to a contract or litigation to require payment or performance from the other party on the basis of some other dealing with that party.

Settlement option Any of several ways of receiving the proceeds of a life insurance policy upon its maturity.

Settlor The creator of a trust; the person who conveys property in trust.

Shareholder A person who owns a proportionate ownership interest in a corporation; usually such ownership is evidenced by a *Stock certificate*.

Share of stock An equity security that represents a proportionate ownership interest in a corporation including the rights which the shareholder has in the management, profits, and assets of the corporation.

Shelter provision The provision of the Uniform Commercial Code that gives holders through a holder in due course the same freedom from claims and defenses that a holder in due course enjoys. The shelter provision reflects the principle that a person may assign whatever rights she or he has. See also *Holder* and *Holder in due course*.

Shipment contract A contract in which the seller is required or authorized to send goods to the buyer but is not required to deliver them at a particular destination.

Shop right privilege The right of an employer to use without payment of royalties an invention conceived by an employee in the course of employment or through use of the employer's facilities, the employee not having been hired to perform such work.

Shortswing transactions Those transactions under Section 16 of the Securities Exchange Act of 1934 in which a director, an officer, or a beneficial owner of more than 10 percent of any class of nonexempt securities buys and sells (or sells and buys) the company's securities within a 6-month period. The profits from such transactions belong to the corporation.

Shrinkwrap license A license agreement for computer software on or inside a box containing a warning on the outside that opening the box constitutes an acceptance of the terms of the license. Also called "box-top license."

Slander Defamation expressed verbally; oral defamation.

Slander of quality See *Disparagement*.

Slander of title See *Disparagement*.

Small claims court A court authorized to hear, in simplified proceedings, cases involving small sums, usually no more than $500.

Special indorsement See *Indorsement*.

Specification A clear and accurate description of the technical requirements for a material, product, or service to be purchased, including the procedure for determining that the requirements have been met.

Specific lien A lien that entitles a creditor to retain possession of an item of property for only the one debt involved in the immediate transaction. Also called a "special" or "particular" lien. See also *General lien*.

Specific performance An equitable remedy under which a person is entitled to a contractual performance rather than to money damages for breach of the contract, as, for example, a court order to convey title to specific property. Specific performance is granted where the remedy at law (damages) is inadequate.

Specified perils contract An insurance policy which indemnifies the insured against loss caused by specified perils, e.g., floods.

Squeeze-out A ploy by majority shareholders-directors of a close corporation to oust a minority shareholder as an officer, director, or employee. Also referred to as a "freeze-out."

Standing In antitrust law, a doctrine requiring the plaintiff to prove that the defendant's violation was a substantial or direct cause of the plaintiff's injury which can be measured with some certainty in money terms, and that the defendant's illegal act affected legally protected activities of the plaintiff.

Stare decisis To abide by or adhere to. A doctrine that precedents set by decisions in previous cases are to be followed in later cases involving the same point unless there is a compelling reason to depart from precedent.

Stated capital That portion of the issuance price of the outstanding shares of stock that is set aside in the capital stock account.

Statute of frauds A law providing that certain classes of contracts are unenforceable unless they are in writing, signed by the party to be charged for any breach (or signed by his or her authorized agent).

Statute of limitations A statute prescribing time limitations on certain described causes of action or criminal prosecutions; i.e., declaring that no suit shall be maintained on such causes of action unless brought within a specified period of time after the right accrued. A statute of limitations applies to the remedy at law. In equity, there is also a limit (called "laches") on the time that a person has to bring suit. Under the equitable principle of laches, suit is barred if not brought with a *reasonable* time.

Stock certificate A certificate issued by a corporation to a named person as owner of a given number of shares of stock in the corporation. The certificate is written evidence of the owner's proportionate equity interest in the corporation.

Stock power A written power of attorney signed by the stockholder and attached to a stock certificate.

Stock split The issuance to a shareholder of additional shares of stock, without cost, at some ratio of new shares to old shares as established by the board of directors.

Stock subscription A contract whereby a person agrees to purchase a specified number and class of shares of a new stock issue.

Stop-payment order The instruction by a drawer of a check to the drawee not to pay a certain check.

Straight bankruptcy See *Liquidation proceeding*.

Strict foreclosure A secured party's keeping collateral in satisfaction of an unpaid debt. Appropriate where the value of the collateral is equal to or less than the amount of the debt.

Strict liability In tort law, a liability imposed regardless of the care or skill or intent of the defendant, as, for example, when injury results from a defective product or from an ultrahazardous activity. In criminal law, a crime that does not require any criminal intent or mental state, such as the sale of liquor to a minor.

Subchapter S corporation A corporation which complies with Subchapter S of the Internal Revenue Code. It may have no more than thirty-five stockholders and is taxed as though it were a partnership.

Subcontract An agreement with a contracting party to perform all or part of the work the latter is required to perform under a contract. The party who undertakes a subcontract is the *subcontractor*.

Subrogation The act or process of substituting one person for another so that the first acquires the legal rights of the second. In the law of suretyship, a surety's right to be substituted for or to take over the rights of the creditor (whom the surety has paid) against the debtor. The surety who has the right of subrogation is the *subrogee*. See also *Surety*.

Subservant In agency law, a servant (employee) of a servant.

Substantial performance In contract law, a doctrine that permits a party to a contract to recover damages even if that party has not fully performed. For performance to be substantial, there must be only minor departures from full performance.

Substantive due process See *Due process*.

Substantive law That law which is concerned with the recognition of rights, duties, privileges, and immunities (as contrasted with that law which is concerned with procedure).

Sum certain In the law of negotiable instruments, an amount payable that is sufficiently calculable for an instrument to be classified as a negotiable instrument.

Summary Short, abbreviated, as a summary hearing before an administrative agency.

Surety A person who, by contract or by operation of law, is liable for the debt, default, or miscarriage of another. A *gratuitous* (voluntary or accommodation) *surety* receives consideration for acting as a surety, but does not receive a monetary payment. *Cosureties* share the burden of the principal debtor's default. A *conditional surety* is not liable until the creditor first makes a reasonable attempt to exhaust the creditor's remedies against the debtor.

Symbolic delivery See *Constructive delivery*.

Takeover The act of acquiring control of a target corporation by purchase, or otherwise controlling sufficient shares to take over its management.

Target corporation A corporation over which another entity seeks to gain control.

Teller's check See *Bank draft*.

Tenancy by the entirety A common law marital tenancy in which spouses owned property jointly, neither spouse could transfer his or her interest in the property without the other spouse's consent, and upon death, the deceased spouse's interest passed to the survivor by right of survivorship.

Tenancy in common Co-ownership of property in which the owners (tenants in common) have an undivided interest in the property. Upon the death of a tenant in common, his or her interest in the property passes to his or her heirs, not to the other co-tenants. See also *Joint tenancy*.

Tenancy in partnership The manner in which the legal title to partnership property is held.

Tender An offer of performance by one party to a contract which, if unjustifiably refused, places the other party in default and permits the party making the tender to exercise remedies for breach of contract.

Tender offer The offer by a corporation or person to purchase the shares of stock from shareholders of a "target corporation" in exchange for money or other securities. A tender offer is most commonly used to acquire voting control of the *Target corporation*.

Tenor In the law of negotiable instruments, the amount originally intended. Where the face amount of a stolen negotiable instrument has been raised without the consent of the maker, a holder in due course ordinarily may enforce the instrument only in accordance with its original tenor. See also *Holder in due course* and *Negotiable instrument*.

Testamentary capacity The capability to make a valid will.

Testamentary intent The intent to direct the transfer of property, effective upon death.

Testamentary trust A trust created in a will.

Testate Having left a will. A person who dies leaving a will is said to die testate.

Testator, testatrix A person who makes a will.

Thin corporation A corporation with a high ratio of debt to equity.

Third-person beneficiary In the law of contracts, a person who is not a party to a contract but who is intended to receive benefits from it.

Through bill of lading See *Bill of lading*.

Time draft See *Draft*.

Title Ownership. In the law of secured transactions, title is often used to describe an interest in property less extensive than ownership. See *Security interest*.

Tort A civil wrong, other than breach of contract, for which a court may award damages.

Tortfeasor One who commits a tort.

Trade acceptance A time draft drawn by a seller on a buyer and accepted (signed across the face) by the buyer. See also *Draft*.

Trade dress The distinctive appearance or image of a product or service created by its size, shape, packaging, design, or other qualities.

Trade fixture Property used in a trade or business attached to leased premises by a commercial tenant that does not become a fixture and part of the real property.

Trade libel See *Disparagement*.

Trademark A word, symbol, device, or design affixed to or placed upon an article or its container to identify an item offered for sale.

Trade name A name used in trade to designate a particular business.

Trade regulation rule A legislative rule with the force of law promulgated by the Federal Trade Commission to regulate business practices.

Transaction Any act of conducting business. Broader than a contract, a transaction includes gift, lease, sale, mortgage, and bailment.

Transfer warranty See *Warranty*.

Traveler's check A three-party draft purchased from a bank or another firm and carried instead of cash.

Treasury stock Stock issued by a corporation but subsequently reacquired by the corporation and not canceled. May be reissued.

Trial de novo A new trial held in an appellate court.

Trover Wrongful interference with the goods of another.

Trust The transfer of property by a settlor or maker to a *trustee*, who holds legal title to the property and administers the property on behalf of a beneficiary.

Trust deed A substitute for a real estate mortgage. A third-party trustee takes legal title to the owner-debtor's property and holds it for the benefit of the creditor, with power to sell it in the event of a default by the debtor.

Trustee in bankruptcy A bankruptcy official responsible for collecting, liquidating, and distributing the debtor's estate.

Turnkey system A customized computer system designed to be operational without the need for programmers or extensive training of users.

Turnover In bankruptcy law, the act of delivering to the trustee in bankruptcy property that belongs to the debtor's estate.

Tying contract A contract in which a seller offers a product only on condition that the buyer also purchase a distinct second product which is not desired.

Ultrahazardous activity See *Abnormally dangerous activity*.

Ultra vires act A corporate act or action that is beyond the scope of authority and powers conferred upon the corporation by law or by the articles of incorporation.

Unconscionability Conduct (not necessarily amounting to fraud, misrepresentation, or duress) that results in the oppression or unfair surprise of one contracting party by the other.

Undue influence The overcoming of the free will of a person by unfair persuasion, usually through misuse of a position of confidence or a relationship.

Unenforceable contract A contract that the law will not enforce by direct legal proceedings but may recognize in some indirect way as creating some duty of performance.

Uniform state laws A draft of law prepared by the National Conference of Commissioners on Uniform State Laws and submitted to all states for adoption. When adopted, such a law is amended to meet individual state needs.

Unilateral contract A contract in which one party makes a promise; the other party must perform an act to enforce the contract. See also *Bilateral contract*.

Unliquidated debt In contract law, a debt or claim that is disputed as to existence or amount.

Usage of trade In the law of sales, any practice or method of dealing having such regularity of observance in a place, vocation, or trade as to justify an expectation that it will be observed with respect to the transaction in question.

Usury The charging of any rate of interest in excess of that permitted by law.

Utilitarianism The ethical theory that the best course of action is the one which produces the most good or the most net benefits for society.

Value In the law of sales, secured transactions, and documents of title, any promise or other consideration sufficient to support a simple contract. In the law of commercial paper, performed consideration.

Verification A person's statement, signed under penalty of perjury, that facts recited in a document are true and correct.

Vertical merger A combination in which a firm at one level acquires a firm at a different level; e.g., a manufacturer acquiring a wholesaler. See also *Horizontal merger*.

Vertical price fixing See *Resale price maintenance*.

Vest To become established, to take effect, giving an immediate, fixed right of present or future enjoyment.

Vicarious act An act performed or exercised by one party for another. In agency law, an agent's or a servant's act which may bind the principal or master.

Vicarious liability Liability for the criminal or tortious act of another. In tort law, an employer is vicariously liable for the torts committed by his or her employees within the scope of their employment. In agency law, the liability of a nonacting principal for the acts of an agent within the agent's scope of authority.

Void Of no effect whatsoever.

Voidable A condition where a party has the option of avoiding a contract.

Voidable contract A contract that a party may enforce or set aside (avoid) as that person wishes.

Void contract An attempt at contracting which never produced a contract because some essential contractual element was missing.

Wanton act A malicious and unjustifiable act; a heedless and reckless disregard for another's rights.

Warehouse A building or other enclosed area used to hold goods temporarily or for an indefinite time. A *public warehouse* stores goods for any member of the public who seeks and pays for the storage service. A *private warehouse* stores goods only for those persons with whom it chooses to contract.

Warehouser A person or firm engaged in the business of receiving and storing goods for hire.

Warehouse receipt See *Document of title*.

Warranty A statement, promise, or other representation that a thing has certain qualities or that the seller has title to the thing. Also, an obligation imposed by law that a thing will have certain qualities. An *express warranty* is made by means of a statement or other affirmation of fact; an *implied warranty* is one that is imposed by law. In the law of sales, a *warranty of merchantability*, whether express or implied, assures the recipient that the goods are of fair, average quality. A sales *warranty of fitness for a particular purpose* assures the buyer that the goods are fit for the buyer's particular purpose. In the law of commercial paper, a *transfer warranty* . . .; a *presentment warranty*. . . .

Warranty of fitness See *Warranty* and *Warranty of habitability*.

Warranty of habitability In the sale of a new home, the seller's implied warranty that the home is constructed in a workmanlike manner and fit for its intended use. In landlord-tenant law, the landlord's implied warranty that the leased premises are and will remain in a habitable state.

Warranty of merchantability See *Warranty*.

Warranty of title See *Warranty*.

Watered stock Shares issued in exchange for overvalued property.

White knight An entity which, at the request of a target corporation, takes over the target company in order to foil an unfriendly takeover attempt. See also *Target corporation*.

Will In estate or inheritance law, a declaration of a person's wishes as to how his or her property will be disposed of, to take effect after death. Until death, a will is said to be ambulatory and may be revoked.

Winding up A necessary step after the dissolution of a partnership, during which the partnership assets are gathered in, all debts are paid, and distribution of the remainder is made to the partners.

Wire transfer See *Electronic funds transfer*.

Without reserve In auctions, an expression indicating that the owner of the goods will sell them to the highest bidder no matter how low the bid is.

With reserve In auctions, an expression indicating that the auctioneer, on behalf of the owner, reserves the right to withdraw the goods from bidding.

Workers' compensation law A law enacted in all states which establishes systems for the payment of compensation to workers who are injured in or suffer a disease as a result of their employment.

Work made for hire In copyright law, a work created by an employee for an employer. The employer is entitled to the copyright on the work.

Writ A writing issued by a court or other competent tribunal and directed to the sheriff or to some other officer for the purpose of carrying out an order or sentence of the court.

Writ of execution See *Execution*.

Yellow dog contract An agreement that as a condition of employment a worker will not join a union.

Zoning A system of land use control in which a city or political subdivision is divided into districts and land uses are restricted within those areas.

INDEX

Abandoned property, 483–484
Abnormally dangerous activities, 153–154, 1149
Abuse of process, 127
Acceleration clause, 687
Acceptance:
  authorized medium of (UCC), 380
  of contract offer (*see* Offer, acceptance)
  of draft or check, 674, 680
  of goods: meaning of, 425–426
    revocation of, 427–428
  in sales law, 379–380
  shipment of nonconforming goods as, 382–383
Accession, acquisition of personal property by, 486
Accessions, security interest in, 635–636
Accommodation party, 736
Accommodation surety, 608
Accord and satisfaction, discharge by, 252–255, 345
Accountant(s):
  American Institute of Certified Public Accountants (AICPA), 1045
  auditing: financial statements, 1047
    fraud audit, 1048
    nature of, 1046–1048
    opinions, 1048
  boards of accountancy, 1064
  certified (audited) financial statements, 1047
  compilations, 1048
  confidentiality, duty of: accountant-client privilege, 1049
    ethical obligation, 1049
    in general, 1048–1049
    working papers, 1049
  contract, liability for breach of, 1052
  engagement letter, 1048
  fiduciary duty of, 1052
  fraud audit, 1048
  fraud, liability for: actual fraud, 1052
    constructive fraud, 1052–1053
    third party liability, 1056
  generally accepted accounting procedures (GAAP), 1047–1048
  generally accepted auditing standards (GAAS), 1047
  gross negligence, 1052–1053

Accountant(s) (*Cont.*):
  management advisory services, 1046
  negligence, liability for: contributory/comparative negligence, 1055
    elements of claim for negligence, 1053
    GAAP and GAAS, effect of compliance with, 1054
    negligent misrepresentation, 1053
    reasonable accountant standard, 1053–1054
    third party liability: foreseeable users rule, 1057
      known or foreseen class of users rule, 1056–1057
      primary beneficiary rule, 1056
      Ultramares rule, 1056
  privilege, accountant-client, 1049
  responsibilities under SEC, 1021, 1030–1031, 1033
  reviews, 1048
  RICO, liability under, 1063–1064
  securities laws, liability under: Rule 2(e), administrative liability under, 1065
    Rule 10b5, 1060–1061
    Securities Act of 1933: due diligence defense, 1059–1060
      Section 11, 1059–1060
    Securities Exchange Act of 1934: Section 10b and Rule 10b5, 1060–1061
      Section 18, 1063
  state law, criminal and administrative liability under, 1064
  tax laws: administrative penalties, 1064–1065
    criminal liability, 1065
    practice under, 1046
  unqualified (clean) opinion, 1048
Additur, defined, 36
Adhesion, contracts of, 210–211, 285–287
Administrative agency:
  appointments, 86–87
  checks on power, 87
  delegation of powers to, 71
  formal advice of, 80
  funding, 87
  growth of, 69–71

Administrative agency (*Cont.*):
  judicial review of, 80–83
    (*See also* Judicial review)
  jurisdictional overlap, 88–89
  meaning of, 71
  political influences upon, 86–88
  powers of, 71–72
  quasi-executive functions, 78–80
  rulemaking by, 72–73
  rulemaking models: adjudicative, 75–76
    generally, 74
    legislative, 74–75
Administrative law:
  Code of Federal Regulations (CFR), 73, 83
  constitutional problems of, 72
  defined, 71
  enabling statutes, 71
  evidence, use of, 75–76
  generally, 20
  scope and function, 71–80
Administrative law judge (ALJ), 75
Administrative Procedure Act (APA), 73, 75–76, 1152
Administrative regulation:
  of business, 70
  rise of, 69–71
Administrator, 560
  (*See also* Probate, personal representative)
Advancement (*see* Wills)
Advances, future, 623
Adverse possession, 506–507
Advertising, liability for false, 166–167
Affirmative action:
  statutory, 1094
  voluntary, 1094
Age Discrimination in Employment Act, 1095
  (*See also* Employment discrimination)
Agency:
  agent (*see* Agent)
  agreement to establish, 784
    elements of, 784
    power of attorney, 785
    when writing required, 785
  authority of agent, 785–786
  contractual rights in, 792–797
  defined, 777

Agency (*Cont.*):
  equal dignities rule, 785
  establishment of, 783
  estoppel in, 787–788
  going and coming rule, 810
  independent contractor, 779–782
    torts of, 816
  master (*see* Master)
  parties to, 778–779
  principal (*see* Principal)
  ratification of agent's act, 786, 789–791
  scope of employment, 809–815
    frolic and detour, 812
    going-and-coming rule, 810
    lunch hour rule, 810
  servant (*see* Servant)
  termination of, 836–843
    notice to third parties, 843
  vicarious liability of principal, 778
Agent:
  appointment of, 783–784
  authority of: actual, 786
    apparent, 787
    to contract, 784, 785–788
    delegation by agent, 828
    dual purpose rule, 810
    emergency, 787
    equal dignities rule, 785
    estoppel, 787–789
    express, 786
    going and coming rule, 810
    implied, 786–787
    implied warranty of, 794
    kinds of, 792
    limitations on, secret, 788
    lunch hour rule, 810
    by operation of law, 792
    ostensible, 787
    power of attorney, 785–786
    ratification, 789–791
    termination of, 836–843
  capacity, 783
  conflict of interest of, 830–833
  as contracting party, 789–790
  control by principal, 793–796
  defined, 778–779
  detour of, 812
  direction or control of, 778–781
  dual purpose rule, 810
  duty of: to account, 829
    to communicate notice or knowledge, 827
    discretionary, 827
    in emergencies, 825
    to keep and render accounts, 829
    to be loyal (*see* fiduciary duties, *below*)

Agent, duty of: (*Cont.*):
    to obey reasonable instructions, 825
    to personally perform service, 827
    to use care and skill, 825
  employee as, 778
  expert as, 825
  fiduciary duties of: to be loyal, 829–830
    not to act adversely to principal, 830–831
    not to buy or sell to principal, 831
    not to compete with principal, 830–831
    not to disclose trade secret, 833
    not to make secret benefit, 830
    not to represent third party, 831
    not to use confidential information, 833
  forgery of commercial paper by, 695
  frolic of, 812
  general agent, 784
  going and coming rule, 810
  gratuitous agent, 784
  independent contractor as, 779
  injuries to, 840
  kinds of, 783–784
  liability: fully disclosed principal, 793
    partially disclosed principal, 795
    undisclosed principal, 796
  lunch hour rule, 810
  minor as, 783
  negligence of, 778, 800–801, 814
  obligations to principal, 824–829
    (*See also* fiduciary duties of, *above*)
  obligations to third party, 796
  partner as, 777, 853–854
  power of (*see* authority of, *above*)
  power of attorney: general, 785
    special, 785
  ratification of agent's act, 789–791
  remedies against principal, 841
  servant as, 778
    (*See also* Servant)
  special, 784
  torts of, 800–815
    agent-employee, 801
    agent-independent contractor, 801
  warranty of authority, 794
  who may be, 783
Agreement:
  illegal (*see* Illegal agreements)
  under UCC, 383
  (*See also* Contracts)
Agriculture, U.S. Department of (USDA), 70
Alternative dispute resolution:
  arbitration, 42–43
  generally, 42–43

Alternative dispute resolution (*Cont.*):
  mediation, 43
  mini-trials, 43
  negotiation, 42
Americans with Disabilities Act, 1096
Andean Common Market, 1215
Animals, liability for injuries by, 154–155, 465–466
Answer, defined, 32
Anticipatory breach of contract, 341, 344–345
Anti-Dumping Act of 1921, 1216
Antitrust laws:
  Clayton Act: amendments to (*see* Robinson-Patman Act)
    cease-and-desist orders, 1188
    compared with Sherman Act, 1194
    corporate mergers, 1193–1200
    historical background of, 1188
    interlocking directorates, 1200
    potential entrant doctrine, 1199–1200
    price discrimination, 1188–1192
    private enforcement of, 1200–1202
    purpose and scope of, 1188
    tying contracts, 1192–1193
  criminal violations of, 198
  defined, 1164
  development of, 1164–65
  effect on American competition abroad, 1207–1209
  exemptions from: express, 1203–1204
    implied, 1204–1207
  extraterritoriality of, 1207–1209
  Federal Trade Commission Act, 1202
  in international law, 1231
  mergers, 1193–1200
  monopoly, 1164
  Robinson-Patman Act (*see* Robinson-Patman Act)
  Securities and Exchange Commission, 1019
  Sherman Act (*see* Sherman Antitrust Act)
Apparent authority of agent, 787–788
Appeals (*see* Civil procedure; Criminal procedure)
Arbitration, 42–43, 1221–1223
Army Corps of Engineers, 1152
Arraignment, 191
Articles of incorporation, 934
Assault, 116
Assignment:
  for benefit of creditors, 644
  of contract rights (*see* Contracts, assignment of)
Association of Southeast Asian Nations, 1215

Assumption of risk, 149–150, 460
Attachment of security interest, 622–623
Attorney in fact, 785
Auction:
    offers in, 223
    with reserve, 223
    without reserve, 223
Authority, apparent or implied (*see*
        Agent, authority of)
Automated clearinghouse, 768
Automated teller machine, 768
Automobile insurance, 579, 588, 589

Bailment:
    bailee, rights and duties of: duty to exercise care, 491–492
        duty to return bailed property, 494
        limitation of liability, 494
        possessory lien, 494
        presumption of negligence, 492
        right to possess bailed property, 491
        right to use bailed property, 491
    bailor, rights and duties of: liability to bailee for harm, 495
        right to compensation, 494
    in carriage contract, 390–394
    constructive, 487
    defined as, 487
    generally, 391
    gratuitous: sole benefit of the bailee, 487
        sole benefit of the bailor, 487
    mutual benefit, 487
    risk of loss rules (UCC), 413–416
    unauthorized, 407
    in warehousing contract, 394–397
Bait and switch, 1112
Bank:
    automated clearinghouse, 768
    automated teller machines, 768
    bank-customer relationship, 752–755
    certificate of deposit, 673
    certified checks, 752
    checks (*see* Checks)
    check collection process: deferred posting, 756
        final credit, 755
        funds availability requirements, 756–758
        midnight deadline, 755
        new account, 757
        postdated check, 759
        posting, 755
        provisional credit, 755
    charging customer's account, 758–759
    clearinghouse, 751, 755, 768
    contract of deposit, 752–755
    conversion by, 767

Bank (*Cont.*):
    correspondent, 680
    death or incompetence of customer, 767
    debit card, 768
    depositors: duties of bank to, 752–753
        duties to bank of, 753, 762–764
    depository, 755
    Electronic Fund Transfers Act, 767
    electronic funds transfer, 767–769
    Expedited Funds Availability Act, 756
    final payment rule, 766
    first in, first out rule, 713
    forgery, effect of, 766–767
    good faith, duty of, 752–753
    intermediary, 755
    liability of: for conversion, 767
        for ignoring stop-payment order, 762
        for wrongful dishonor, 759–761
    merger, 1199
    pay-by-phone system, 768
    payor, 755
    personal identification number, 768
    point-of-sale terminal, 768
    Regulation CC, 756–757
    stale check, 758
    stop-payment order, 761–762
    subrogation of, 762
    wholesale wire transfer: Article 4A governing, 769
        meaning of, 769
        payment order, 769
    wrongful dishonor, 759–761
    (*See also* Checks; Commercial paper)
Bankruptcy:
    assignment for benefit of creditors, 644
    automatic stay, 646–647
    Bankruptcy Reform Act of 1978, 645
    business reorganization under (*see* Business reorganization under Bankruptcy Act Chapter 11)
    Chapter 7, liquidation proceedings under, 645–659
    Chapter 11 (*see* Business reorganizations under Bankruptcy Act Chapter 11)
    Chapter 13, repayment plans under, 662–664
    claims in: allowance of, 655
        defined, 655
        priority between, 655–656
        proof of, 655
    commencement of: involuntary, 646
        order for relief, 646
        voluntary, 646
    composition and extension agreements, 644

Bankruptcy (*Cont.*):
    creditors: general, 656
        priority, 656
        secured, 655–656
    debtor, 646
    discharge of debts, 656
        denial of discharge, 656–657
        nondischargeable debts, 658–659
    distribution of estate, 655–656
    estate, property of, 647
    exemptions, 654–655
    fraudulent transfers, 649
    ground for relief, 646
    involuntary, 646
    judge, functions of, 647
    liquidation under Chapter 7, 645–659
    nondischargeable debts, 658–659
    order for relief, 646
    preferences: consumer debt exception, 652
        contemporaneous exchange for new value, 652
        defined, 652
        ordinary course of business exception, 652
    pro rata distribution, 656
    purposes of, 645
    reaffirmation agreement, 659
    reorganization under, 659–662
    repayment plans under Chapter 13, 662–664
    state insolvency laws: assignment for benefit of creditors, 644
        composition and extension agreements, 644
        private workout, 644
        role of in bankruptcy, 645
    straight bankruptcy, 645–659
    transfers, fraudulent, 649
    trustee in: functions of, 647
        powers of, 647–648
        status as lien creditor and bona fide purchaser, 648–649
    voluntary, 646
Battery, 115–116, 1148
Bearer and order paper, 681, 698
Bequests (*see* Wills)
Bill of exchange, 672
Bill of lading:
    consignee, 397
    consignment, 397
    consignor, 397
    destination bill, 397
    through bill, 397
    (*See also* Documents of title)
Bill of Rights, 47
Blue sky laws, 923
Bonds, corporate, 948–949

Borrowed servant, 806–808
Breach of contract:
  accountants' liability for, 1052
  anticipatory, 341, 344–345, 434, 435
  material, 343, 344
  meaning of, 341, 433–434
  remedies for: avoidable consequences
      rule, 356
    damages, 349–352, 355–358,
      434–440
    in equity, 352–355
    interests protected, 349, 434
    at law, 349–352
    liquidated damages, 350–352,
      440–441
    in quasi contract, 213–215, 359
    rescission, 262, 345, 352
    restitution, 349
    under sales contract, 433–442
    specific performance, 353–355
Bribery, 194–195
Business international (*see* International
    business)
Business ethics (*see* Ethics)
Business insurance (*see* Insurance,
    kinds of)
Business judgment rule, 981
Business law, meaning of, 4
Business organizations:
  corporation (*see* Corporations)
  forms of, 851–853, 926–927
  general partnership (*see* Partnerships)
  joint venture partnerships, 852, 860
  limited partnership (*see* Limited partnership)
  sole proprietorship, 851–852
Business regulations, extraterritoriality
    of, 1231
Business relations as private law, 21
Business reorganization under Bankruptcy Act Chapter 11:
  absolute priority rule, 662
  acceptance of plan, 661–662
  confirmation of plan, 662
  creditors' committee, 660
  debtor in possession, 660
  impaired creditor or claim, 661
  nature and purpose of, 659–660
  plan for, 660
Buyer, obligations of, 425–433

C&F (shipping term), 412
Carriers:
  common, 390
  liability of, 392
  lien of, 390
  meaning of, 390, 391
  noncarrier and pickup delivery, 392
  private, 392

Case reasoning, 9–15
Caveat emptor, 446
Cease-and-desist orders, 79, 1113
Certificate of deposit, 673
CF (or C&F), shipping term, 412
Chapter 11 (under Bankruptcy Act),
    659–662
Charging order, 861, 909, 916
Chattel mortgage, 375, 620, 621
Chattel paper, 621–622
Checks:
  bank check, 675
  bank draft, 675
  cashier's, 675
  certified, 752
  collection process: collecting bank,
    755
    deferred posting, 756
    depositary bank, 755
    final credit, 755–756
    forwarding bank, 755
    funds availability requirements,
      756–758
    intermediary bank, 755
    midnight deadline, 755
    payor bank, 755
    posting, 755
    provisional credit, 755
  as conditional payment, 675
  meaning of, 674
  postdated, 750, 759
  stale, 758
  stop-payment order, 761–762
  teller's, 675
  traveler's, 675
  underlying contract, 675
  wrongful dishonor, 759–761
  (*See also* Bank; Commercial paper)
Child labor laws, 1097
CIF (shipping term), 412
Civil law:
  defined, 21
  remedies (*see* Remedies, civil law)
Civil litigation, flow of, 30
Civil procedure:
  affirmative defense, 32
  answer, 32
  appeals, 36–37
  complaint, 31
  counterclaim, 32
  default judgment, 31
  demurrer, 31
  denials (general and specific), 32
  depositions, 32–33
  directed verdict, 35
  discovery, 32–33
  evidence: degree of proof required, 34
    types and rules of, 34–35
  interrogatories, 33

Civil procedure (*Cont.*):
  judgment notwithstanding the verdict
    (n.o.v.), 36
  motions (*see* Motion)
  pleadings, 31–32
  pretrial conference, 33–34
  reply, 32
  summary judgment, 32
  summons, 31
  trials, 34–36
  affirmative action under, 1094
  enforcement, 1088
  "protected class" under, 1087
  proving discrimination, 1088
    disparate impact, 1089–1090
    disparate treatment, 1089–1090
  religious discrimination under, 1091
Civil Rights Act of 1991, 1088, 1090,
    1093
Claims:
  in bankruptcy, 655–656
  counterclaims, 32
  against estate in probate, 560–561
"Clawback" legislation, 1231
Clayton Act (*see* Antitrust laws, Clayton
    Act)
Clean Air Act, 1152–1154
Clean Water Act, 1154–1155
Clearinghouse, 751, 755, 768
Close corporations (*see* Corporations,
    close)
Code of Federal Regulations (CFR), 73,
    83
Cognovit note, 295
  (*See also* Commercial paper)
Coinsurance, 588–590
Coke, Edward, 9, 17
Collateral:
  acquisition of, on default, 636
  disposition of: commercial reasonableness, 638
    deficiency, 638
    surplus, 638
  repossession of, 636–639
  types of, 619, 621–622, 630
Commerce clause under Constitution,
    50–51
Commercial impracticability, 346–348
Commercial paper:
  acceptance of, 674, 680
  acceptor, 674
  accommodation party, 736
  bank check, 675
  bank-customer relationship, 752–755
  bank draft, 675
  bearer paper, 681
  bill of exchange, 672
  cashier's check, 675
  certificate of deposit, 673

Commercial paper (*Cont.*):
  certified checks, 752
  charging customer's account, 758–759
  checks (*see* Checks)
  clearinghouse, 751, 755, 768
  cognovit note, 295
  collection of (*see* Bank, check collection process)
  confession of judgment clause, 687
  as contract, 678–679
  correspondent bank, 680
  conversion of, 730, 767
  defenses to: personal, 676, 692–693
    real, 676, 694–697
  delivery of, 697
    conditional, 692–693
    for special purpose, 693
  demand, 673, 674
  discharge of: effect of, on holder in due course, 743
    methods of, 740–743
    underlying obligation, 740–741
  dishonor of, 718, 733
  draft: acceptance of, 674, 680
    acceptor, 674
    demand, 674
    parties to, 673
    sight, 674
    time, 674
    trade acceptance, 680
    uses of, 679–680
    (*See also* Checks)
  dual nature of, 678–679
  first in, first out rule, 713
  forged or signed without authority, 736–740
  fraud: in the execution, 694–695
    in the inducement, 692
  funds availability requirements, 756–758
  good faith, objective test under 1990 amendments, 714, 753
  holder of, 698, 712
  holder in due course (*see* Holder in due course)
  indorsement of: conditional, 706
    for deposit, 703–705
    by imposter or dishonest agent, 737–740
    in-blank, 701–702
    meaning of, 698–700
    qualified, 702
    requirements for, 699–700
    restrictive, 702–709
    special, 701–702
    trust indorsement, 706–707
  issue of, 697–698
  judgment rate, 688

Commercial paper (*Cont.*):
  liability of parties: accommodation parties, 736
    for breach of warranty, 743–746
    for forgery, 737–739
    of indorsers, 702, 731–734
    of primary parties, 730–731
    of secondary parties, 731–736
  maker of, 673
  meaning of, 671, 672
  negotiability of: language that destroys, 682–686
    meaning of, 676–678, 680
    particular fund doctrine, 685–686
    requirements for, 680
    significance of, 676, 680
  negotiable form, 680–688
  negotiation of: banks, role in, (*see* Bank, check collection process)
    bearer paper, 681
    defined, 698
    delivery, meaning of, 697
    effect of, 699
    holder status required, 698
    by indorsement, 698–709
    issue, 697–698
    methods of, 698
    order paper, 681, 698
    rescission of, 709
  note, promissory, 673, 679
  notice of dishonor, 731, 733–736
  obligation of signer, 730
  order paper, 681, 698
  particular fund doctrine, 685–686
  parties to, 673–675
  presentment of: when, time limits, 732–733
    where and how, 732
    to whom, 731–732
  promissory note, 673, 679
  as property, 679, 743
  protest, 731
  shelter provision, 721–725
  signature: of accommodation party, 736
    of agent, 736–737
    effect of, 730
    of forger, imposter, dishonest agent, 695, 737–740, 762–767
    of indorser, 699–709
  stale check, 758
  stop-payment order, 761–762
  teller's check, 675
  time draft, 674
  traveler's check, 675
  types of, 672–676
  underlying contract, 675
  uses of, 679–680
  value, meaning of, 712–714

Commercial paper (*Cont.*):
  warranties: advantages of, 744
    presentment, 745–747
    transfer, 744–745
  wrongful dishonor, 759–761
Commercial speech, 62–64, 1118
Commingled goods, 404–405, 636
Common carrier:
  defined, 390
  liabilities of, 392
Common law:
  compared to equity, 28
  in consumer protection, role of, 1103–1104
  in environmental law, role of, 1146–1147
  generally, 19–20
Community property, 514–515
Comparable worth, 1096
Comparative negligence, 147–148, 460
Competitive torts:
  boycotts, 163
  defamation of business reputation, 164
  disparagement of business property, 164
  false advertising, 166–167
  intentional interference with: contracts, 161
    employer-employee relations, 163
    prospective economic advantage, 159–160
  Lanham Act, 166–167
  libel, trade, 164
  palming off, 165–166
  refusal to deal, 160
  slander of quality, 164
  slander of title, 164
  trade dress infringement, 167
  unfair competition laws, 166
  unfair trade practices, 165–167
  wrongful entry into business, 159
  (*See also* Intellectual property; Torts)
Composition and extension agreement, 255
Comprehensive Environmental Response Compensation and Liability Act (CERCLA), 1158
Computer:
  autodialers, 1141
  box-top (shrinkwrap) license, 1131
  communications, 1141
  contracts: box-top (shrinkwrap) license, 1131
    goods or service distinction (UCC), 376–378, 1128
    license agreements, 1124–1125, 1130
    leases, 1130

Computer, contracts (*Cont.*):
    warranties, 1134–1135
    copyrights: of computer programs, 1122
        licenses of copyrighted software, 1124–1125
        work-for-hire rule, application of, 1125
    crimes, 1138–1140
    E-mail, 1141
    fraud (theft), 1139
    malpractice, 1135
    monitoring, 1141
    patents, 1125
    programs, definition of, 1122
    shrinkwrap (box-top) license, 1131
    telemarketing, 1141
    tort liability, 1135–1137
    trade secrets, 1125–1127
Computer Fraud and Abuse Act, 1140, 1141
Computer Software Rental Amendments Act, 1125
Condemnation, 517
Conditional sales contract, 375–376, 620–621
Conditions:
    constructive, 343
    express, 342–343
Condominiums, 515
Confession of judgment clause, 295, 687
Conflict of interests:
    of agents, 830–832
    of corporation directors, 985
    of corporation officers, 985
    of executors, 885–886
    of limited partners, 908–909, 911
    of partners, 868–870
    of personal representative, 560
    of promoters, 932
    of servants, 830–833
    of trustees, 565
Conforming goods, 423–428
Confusion, acquisition of personal property by, 486
Consent as defense to intentional tort liability, 116–117
Consent order, 75, 1113
Consideration:
    in composition agreement, 295
    illusory promise, 247–248
    nominal, 248
    part payment of claim, 252–255
    past, 247
    promises enforceable without, 257–259
    promissory estoppel in lieu of, 258–259

Consideration (*Cont.*):
    theories of, 243–246
Consignment (*see* Contracts)
Constitution:
    allocation of powers, 23–25
    Bill of Rights, 47
    checks and balances, 46
    commerce clause, 50–51
    constitutional law, generally, 20
    contract, freedom of: impairment of contract, 61–62
        liberty of contract, 61
    criminal defendants, rights of, 188–192
    due process: procedural due process, 59
        substantive due process, 58
    equal protection, 59–61
    express powers, 23–24
    federal powers under: enumerated powers, 50
        implied powers, 50
    Fifth Amendment: in administrative law, 76
        double jeopardy clause, 192
        Miranda rule, 191
        right not to testify, 192
    First Amendment, 63–65
        commercial speech, protection of: commercial advertising, 62–63
        personal selling and promotion, 63–64
        corporate political rights, protection of: corporate campaign spending, 65
        corporate political rights, 64
        lobbying and issue advertising, 64–65
    Fourteenth Amendment: affecting state administrative agencies, 76
        due process clause, 58–59
        equal protection clause, 59–61
        in general, 47
        selective incorporation doctrine, 47
    Fourth Amendment, 188–189
        closely-regulated businesses, 189
        exclusionary rule, 189
    historical development of, 46–48
    impeachment, 25
    implied powers, 24
    intermediate scrutiny, 55, 61–63
    interstate commerce, state power to regulate, 52–54
    police power, 24, 48–50
    preemption, 51–52
    rational basis test, 55, 58–59, 61
    searches and seizures, prohibition of unreasonable, 188–189

Constitution (*Cont.*):
    selective incorporation doctrine, 47
    separation of powers, 24–25, 46
    Sixth Amendment, 191
    state action, 55
    strict scrutiny: fundamental rights, 47, 60, 64
        suspect basis/criteria, 47, 60
    takings of property: regulatory taking, 56
        taking clause, 55
Constructive eviction, 527
Consumer:
    concept of consumer injury, 1102–1103
    Consumers Union, 1117
    credit, 291–292, 1109–1111
    Federal Trade Commission (FTC): deception standard, 1112–1113
        history, 1112
        unfairness standard, 1113
    frauds, 197
    goods, perfection of PMSI in, 624, 631
    law: common law, 1103
        contract, 1104
        credit, 1109–1111
        credit reporting, 1116–1118
        debt collection, 1111–1112
        Equal Credit Opportunity Act, 1112
        federal, 1107–1119
        food, drugs, cosmetics, 1109
        in general, 1102–1103
        lemon laws, 1105–1106
        Magnuson-Moss Warranty Act, 1107–1108
        misrepresentation, 1103–1104
        product safety, 1109
        products liability, 1104
        Regulation Z (TILA), 1110
        state, 1103–1107
        Telephone Consumer Protection Act, 1118–1119
        Truth in Lending Act, 1110–1111
        Unfair Trade Practices and Consumer Protection Act, 1105
        Uniform Commercial Code, 1104–1105
        Uniform Consumer Credit Code, 1107
        usury, 1107
    little "FTCs", 1105
    protection of: by Consumer Product Safety Commission (CPSC), 1109, 1110
        by Department of Justice, 1111
        by Federal Communications Commission, 1119

Consumer, protection of (*Cont.*):
  by Federal Trade Commission
    (FTC), 1107, 1111–1114, 1116
  by Food and Drug Administration
    (FDA), 1109
  in general, 278, 1102–1103
  under Magnuson-Moss Warranty
    Act, 1107–1108
  under Uniform Consumer Credit
    Code, 292, 1107
    (*See also* Warranty)
  by U.S. Attorney General, 1107
  time-price doctrine, 292
  Truth-in-Lending Act, 292, 1110–1111
  Uniform Consumer Credit Code, 292,
    1104–1105
  warranties, full and limited, 1108
Consumer Product Safety Commission,
  79, 1109, 1110
Contract clause under Constitution,
  61–62
Contract for deed, 538–539
Contracts:
  acceptance of offer, 232–238,
    379–380
  accord and satisfaction, 252–255, 345
  of adhesion, 210–211, 285–287
  agent's authority to make, 779,
    785–791
  alteration of (under UCC), 386–387
  assignment of rights: assignee's liabil-
    ity under, 327, 337
    assignor's warranties, 332
    effect of notice of, 325–326
    legal position of assignee,
      326–327
    meaning and nature of, 325
    requirements for, 325
    successive assignments, 331–332
    waiver of defenses clause in,
      327–328
    (*See also* Contracts, delegation of
      duties under)
  auction, 223
  avoidance of, 262–278, 430–431
  bilateral, 211–212
  breach of (*see* Breach of contract)
  capacity of parties: contractual capaci-
    ty, 262
    disability, 262
    incapacity, 262
    of mentally incompetent persons,
      268–269
    of minors, 263
    of person under influence, 269
  choice-of-forum clause, 1218, 1220
  choice-of-law clause, 1220
  classical and contemporary views of,
    208–211

Contracts (*Cont.*):
  classification of, 211–213
  conditional sale, 375–376, 620–621
  conditions (*see* Conditions)
  consideration (*see* Consideration)
  consignment, 397
  counteroffer, 230–232, 371, 381–382
  damages for breach of (*see* Damages)
  defenses to, 262–278
  defined, 206–207
  delegation of duties: delegable and
    nondelegable duties, 334–336
    legal effect, 333–334
    liability of delegatee, 333–334,
      336–337
  destination (*see* Destination contract)
  disaffirmance of, 262, 263–266
  discharge of: by accord and satisfac-
    tion, 345
    by contract not to sue, 346
    by frustration of purpose, 346
    by impossibility of performance,
      346, 430–431
    by impracticability of performance,
      346, 430–431
    of liquidated debt, 252–255
    by material breach, 343–344
    meaning of discharge, 341
    by mutual rescission, 345
    by novation, 345
    by operation of law, 348
    by performance, 343–345
    by release, 346
    role of conditions in, 342–343
    by subsequent agreement, 345
    by unconscionability, 277, 372–373
  duress, 269–270
  employee's authority to, 785–792
  enforceable, 212
  equitable estoppel, 313
  exculpatory clause in, 285–287
  executed, 212
  executory, 212
  express, 211
  formal, 212
  formation of, 206–207, 220, 232–233,
    378–379
  fraud, 273–274
  freedom of, 61–62
  frustration of purpose, 346
  government regulation affecting,
    210
  illegality of (*see* Illegal agreements)
  impairments of rights under, 61–62
  implied, 211
  impossibility of performance, 346,
    430–431
  impracticability of performance, 346,
    430–431

Contracts (*Cont.*):
  incompetent party (*see* Contracts, ca-
    pacity of parties)
  informal, 212–213
  integration of, 316–317
  interference with, 161
  interpretation of, 316–317, 340–343
  "just price" doctrine, 207–208
  law of: classical view of, 208
    in general, 208–211
    modern view of, 208–210
    modified by sales law, 367–368
    privity of contract, 446–447
  meaning of, 206, 383
  mental incompetency to enter into,
    268–269
  of minors, 262–268
  misrepresentation in, 273–274
  mistake in, 274–277
  modern view of, 208–209
  for necessaries by minors, 267
  novation agreement, 345
  offer in (*see* Offer)
  output, 224
  parol evidence rule, 316–317, 383
  performance of: anticipatory breach,
    344–345, 434, 435
    effect of defective performance,
      343–344, 425–428
    impossibility of, 346, 430–431
    impracticability of, 346,
      430–431
    material breach, 343–344
    meaning of performance, 340,
      422–423
    role of conditions in defining,
      342–343
    specific, 353–355
    substantial, 343
    tender of performance, 343, 423
  as private law, 20
  privity of, 446–447
  promissory estoppel, 216–217, 229,
    258–259
  public policy: contracts contrary to,
    283–297
    significance of in contracting,
      283–284
    in UCC, 369
  quasi, 213–214, 359
  ratification of, by minor, 266–267
  reformation of, 352
  remedies for breach of (*see* Breach of
    contract)
  requirements, 224, 379
  requirements for, 206–207
  rescission: equitable remedy of, 262,
    352
    in general, 262, 316

Contracts, rescission (*Cont.*):
   mutual, 345
     for unconscionability, 277–278, 372
  Restatement of Law of, 209–210
  of sale (*see* Sales, contract of)
  servant's authority to, 779, 785, 790
  specific performance of, 353–355
  statute of frauds (*see* Statute of frauds)
  successive assignments of, 331–332
  third-party beneficiary, 246, 321–325
  unconscionable, 277–278, 372–373, 1105
  undue influence in formation of, 270–272
  unenforceable, 212
  Uniform Commercial Code (UCC), meaning of, 209, 383
  unilateral, 211
  void and voidable contracts, 212
  waiver of defenses clauses, 327
  writing requirements, 302–317, 386
    (*See also* Statute of frauds)
Contributory negligence, 147, 460
Conversion:
  carrier liability for, 392
  of commercial paper, 730, 767
  in general, 129
Copyright, 172–176
  (*See also* Computer; Intellectual property)
Corporations:
  agency law pertaining to, 777
  alter ego doctrine, 940
  articles of incorporation, 934
    amendment to, 998
  assets, sale of, 999
  blue sky laws, 923
  board of directors, 977
    actions by, 978
    authority of, 977
    committees of, 978–979
    election of, 977
    golden parachute, 988
    greenmail, 988
    as managers, 989
    meetings of, 978
    number of members of, 977
    poison pill, 988
    vacancies on, 977
    voting, 978
    (*See also* directors of, *below*)
  bonds: bearer, 949
    convertible, 950
    issuance of, 949
    kinds of, 950
    as negotiable instruments, 961
    redeemable, 956
    registered, 949
  business judgment rule, 981

Corporations (*Cont.*):
  bylaws, 935
  characteristics of, 924–927
    distinguished from partnerships, 926–927
  charter of, 934
  chief executive officer (CEO), 980
  close: continuity of control, 990, 992
    corporate veil, piercing the, 940
    deadlocks, resolving, 994, 1003
    defined, 928–929
    dissenting members, 1000–1002
    distinguished from publicly held, 989
    dividends, 990
    freeze-outs, 987, 990–991
    liability of members, 991
    problems of, 989–994
    reasons to establish, 928
    shareholders, fiduciary duties of, 989, 991
    shares: marketability of, 989–990
      transfer of, upon death, 993
    thin, 957–958
  consolidation of, 989
  corporate opportunity doctrine, 985–986
  corporate veil, piercing the, 940–944
  crimes by, 975
  cumulative voting, 1006
  debt financing, 948
  deep rock doctrine, 958
  de facto corporation, 938–939
  defective, 937
    liability of members, 939
  defined, 922, 924
  de jure corporation, 937
  directors of: actions of, 978
    business judgment rule, 981
    compensation of, 978
    conflicts of interest, 985
    corporate opportunity doctrine, 985
    duties owed by, 980–987
    election of, 977
    as fiduciaries, 984–987
    indemnification of, 984
    inside, 978, 985
    insider trading, 1032–1036
    interlocking, 985
    liabilities of, 980–981, 985–987
    meetings of, 978
    outside, 978
    powers of, 973, 977–978, 997
    removal of, 997
    voting, 978
    (*See also* board of directors, *above*; officers of, *below*)
  dissolution of, 994, 1001–1003
  dividends: authority to declare, 962–967

Corporations, dividends (*Cont.*):
    business judgment rule, 963–964, 981
    declaration of, 962
    kinds of, 962
    persons entitled to, 964
    restrictions on declaration of, 966
    stock as a dividend, 967
    stock split, 967
  domestic versus foreign, 930
  duration of, 924
  equity financing: shares of stock, 949–956
    uncertificated shares, 951
  by estoppel, 939
  federal laws affecting, 923
  financing: bonds, 948–950
    debt, 948
    debt-equity ratio, 956–957
    equity, 950–956
    in general, 948
    long-term, 949
    shares of stock, 949–956
    short-term, 948
    of thin corporation, 956–959
  first amendment rights, 64–65
  foreign: in general, 930
    host state, powers of, 930
    penalties of unlicensed, 930
  golden parachute, 988
  greenmail, 988
  incorporation: charter (articles of incorporation), 934
    preincorporation activities, 930–933
    procedure for, 930–931
    promoter of (*see* promoter, *below*)
  incorporators, 934
  insider trading, 1032–1036
  kinds of, 925–930
  as legal entity, 924
  leveraged buy-out of, 1039
  liability for preincorporation contracts, 932
  limited partnerships distinguished, 899
  management of, 972–994
  mergers of, 998–999
  Model Business Corporation Act, 923
  name of, 934
  officers of: authority of, 979–980
    chief executive officer (CEO), 980
    compensation of, 980
    conflicts of interest of, 985
    duties of, 980
    election of, 979–980
    golden parachute to, 988

Corporations, officers of (*Cont.*):
    indemnification of, 984
    insider trading by, 1032–1036
    liabilities of, 980–987
    removal of, 997–998
    (*See also* directors of, *above*)
  organizational meeting of, 935
  as partner, 857
  partnership distinguished, 926–927
  piercing the corporate veil, 940–944
    alter ego doctrine, 940
    inadequately capitalized corporations, 944
    parent and subsidiary corporations, 942–944
  poison pill, 998
  political rights, 64–65
  powers of, 972–974
  preincorporation activities, 930
    liability for, 931
  private and public distinguished, 925
  professional, 929–930
  profit and nonprofit distinguished, 928
  promoter: contracts of, 931
    fiduciary duties of, 932
    liabilities of, 931
    not as corporate agent, 932
  proxy voting, 1005
  publicly held or closely held, 928
  quo warranto proceeding, 939
  raider, 988, 1039–1042
  Revised Model Act, 923
  S (or small) corporations, 929
  securities of: issuance of, 951, 1023–1028
    lost or stolen, 961
    stock power, 959
    transfer of, 959–960
    (*See also* bonds, *above*; stock in, *below*)
  shareholders: acting without meeting, 1005
    actions by, 997–1003, 1006
    appraisal rights, 1000–1002
    class action by, 1010
    cumulative voting by, 1006
    defined, 949–950, 992
    derivative suit by, 1010–1012
    dissent to merger, 1000–1002
    examination of corporation books, 1008–1010
    liability of, 1012–1015
    meetings of, 1004–1006
    powers of, 997–1004
    preemptive rights of, 1007
    proxy, voting, 1005–1006
    quorum of, 1006
    rights of, 1007–1012
    voting by, 1006–1007

Corporations, shareholders (*Cont.*):
  shares of stock (*see* stock in, *below*)
  state of incorporation, 923, 933
  state regulation of, 923, 930
  stock in: authority to issue, 951
    certificated and uncertificated, 951
    certificates of, 949–951, 954–956, 959–962
    classes of, 954–956
    common, 954
    consideration for, 952
    dividends from, 962–967
    illegal issuance of, 952–954
    issuance of, 951–956
    lost certificates, 961
    options, 956
    par and no-par, 956–957
    preferred, kinds of, 954–955
    record of ownership of, 959–961, 964–965
    redemption of, 968
    rights, preemptive, 1007
    split, 967
    stock dividend, 967
    subscriptions to, 933–934
    transfer of, 959–961
    treasury, 968
    voting, 954
    warrants, 1007
  Subchapter S, 929
  subsidiary, 942
  takeover, 981–983, 988, 1039–1042
  tender offer, 981–982, 1039–1042
  thin, 959
  torts by, 975–977
    (*See also* Business torts; Torts)
  types of, 925–930
  ultra vires acts, 973–974
  white knight, 988
Counterclaim, 32
Counteroffer, 230–232, 371, 381–382
Course of dealing, 383, 384
  (*See also* Sales, contract of)
Course of performance, 383–384
  (*See also* Sales, contract of)
Courts:
  federal, 25, 38–40
  function of, 37
  interpretation of law, 9–13
  jurisdiction of, 38–39
  state, 40–42
  trial and appeals in, 31–37
Cover, 437–438
  (*See also* Sales, contract of)
Credit, extension of, 599
Creditors' rights and debtor relief:
  under bankruptcy law, 645–664
  Fair Debt Collection Practices Act, 1111–1112

Creditors' rights and debtor relief (*Cont.*):
  in secured transactions, 599–606
  under state insolvency laws, 644
Crimes:
  computer, 1137–1140
  by corporations, 193, 975
  defenses: defense of property, 187
    insanity, 187
    intoxication, 187
    minority, 187–188
    self-defense, 186–187
  defined, 182
  elements of: the act, 183–184
    criminal intent, 184
  felony, 183
  infraction, 183
  mens rea, 184
  misdemeanor, 183
  M'Naghten Rule, 187
  regulatory offenses, 184
  strict liability, 184
  vicarious criminal liability, 186
  white-collar, 192–199
    antitrust offenses, 198, 1166
    bribery, 194–195
    consumer frauds, 197
    defined, 192–193
    embezzlement, 198–199
    by employees, 198–199
    Food, Drug and Cosmetic Act offenses, 195, 1109
    frauds, 197, 818–820, 1032–1035
    larceny, 198–199
    punishment for, 1032–1036, 1042
    RICO, 198
    securities offenses, 197–198, 1032–1035
Criminal law, generally, 20
  (*See also* Crimes)
Criminal procedure:
  appeals, 192
  arraignment, 191
  arrest, 191
  bail, 191
  constitutional rights of criminal defendants, 188–192
  first appearance, 191
  indictment, 191
  information, 191
  Miranda Rule, 191
  searches and seizures, 188–189
  sentences, 192
  plea bargain, 191
  pleas, 191
  pretrial procedure, 191
  trial, 191–192
Customer list, 833
Customs Service, U.S., 70

Damages:
  compensatory, 115, 350
  consequential (special), 350, 355–356, 445
  for contract breach, 349–352, 355–358, 434–440
  for fraud, 131
  exemplary (punitive), 115, 350, 580–581, 1146
  general, 350
  incidental, 435
  limitations on, 355–358, 440–442
  liquidated, 350–352, 440–441
  mitigation of, 356
  nominal, 350
  punitive (exemplary), 115, 350, 580–581, 1146
  under quasi contract, 213–215, 359
  special, 350, 355–356
  (*See also* Remedies)
Dangerous activities, 780*n.*, 816
Dealing, course of, 383, 384
Debit card, 768
Debt:
  collection of, 636–639
  Fair Debt Collection Practices Act, 1111–1112
  liquidated, 252–255
Debtor in possession (*see* Bankruptcy)
Debtor relief (*see* Creditors' rights and debtor relief)
Deception, FTC standard, 1112
Declaratory judgment, 37
Deeds, 509–511
Deep-rock doctrine, 958
De facto corporation, 938
Defamation, 116–122, 818
Defense, Department of, 1152
Defenses to payment of commercial paper:
  personal, 676, 691–693
  real, 676, 694–697
Deferred posting, 756
Deficiency judgment, 542–543, 638
De jure corporation, 937–938
Delectus personae, 857
Demurrer, 31–32
Depositions, 32–33
Destination contract:
  meaning of, 411
  risk of loss, 411–417
  title passage under, 411
Detour by servant, 812
Devise (*see* Wills)
Direct deposit, 768
Disability insurance, 586–587
Discharge:
  in bankruptcy, 656–657

Discharge (*Cont.*):
  of commercial paper, 740–743
  of contract (*see* Contracts, discharge of)
Disclaimer clause, 780
Disclosed principal, 793
Discovery, 32–33
Discrimination (*see* Employment discrimination)
Disparagement, 164
Diversity of citizenship, 38–39
Documents of title:
  bailee's obligations and liabilities, 390–397, 400–407
  bill of lading, 397, 1223
  conflicting claims, 407
  destination bill, 397
  document changes, 407
  due negotiation of, 400–401
  excuses for failure to deliver goods, 405–406
  functions of, 397
  fungible goods exception, 404–405
  good faith purchaser of, 399, 401
  holder of, 398, 400
  legal rights, 398–403
  lost or missing document, liabilities, 406–407
  meaning of, 397
  negotiability, 398–404
  negotiable form, 398, 400
  negotiation of (*see* Commercial paper)
  unauthorized bailment, 407
  uses of, 397, 403–404
  for value requirement of holder, 401
  warehouse receipt, 397–400, 403, 406
Draft:
  demand, 674
  time, 674
Drawer, 673
Dual purpose rule, 810
Due process, 58–59
Dumping, 1227–1229
  (*See also* Anti-Dumping Act of 1921)
Duress:
  in contracts, 269–270
  in wills, 551

Easement:
  dedication, 534
  defined as, 533
  example of, 3
  express grant or reservation, 533
  implied grant or reservation, 533–534
  necessity, 534
  prescription, 534
  use and maintenance of, 535
Election, right of, in agency, 796–797
Elective (forced) share, 557

Electronic Communications Privacy Act, 1141
Electronic funds transfers:
  automated clearinghouse (ACH), 768
  automated teller machines, 768
  commercial applications, 769
  consumer applications, 767–769
  debit card, 768
    limits on liability, 768–769
  Electronic Fund Transfers Act, 767
  pay-by-phone systems, 768
  personal identification number, 768
  point of sale terminal, 768
  UCC Article 4A, 767
  wholesale wire transfer, 769
Eminent domain, 55, 517
Employee:
  as agent, 778
  authority to contract, 779
  distinguished from independent contractor, 780
  as servant, 778
  torts of, 801–815, 818–820
Employer (*see* Principal)
Employer-employee relation, 778
Employer-employee relationship, 778
  (*See also* Agency)
Employment discrimination:
  Age Discrimination in Employment Act, 1088, 1095
  comparable worth, 1096
  Equal Employment Opportunity Commission (EEOC), 1087–1096
  Equal Pay Act, 1088, 1096
  Title VII: affirmative action, 1094
    in general, 1097–1098
    pregnancy, 1088, 1091–1093
    religion, 1091
    reverse discrimination, 1094
    sexual harassment, 9–11, 1093–1094
Employment Retirement Income Security Act (ERISA), 781–783
Environmental law:
  Army Corps of Engineers, 1155
  basis of common law action: battery, 1148
    negligence, 1147, 1149
    nuisance, 1147, 1148
    strict liability (in tort), 1147, 1149
    trespass, 1147–1148
  best available technology, 1153
  environmental impact statement, 1161
  Environmental Protection Agency (EPA), 1152, 1154–1158
  externalities, 1145–1146
  federal: on acid rain, 1153

Environmental law, federal (*Cont.*):
　Clean Air Act, 1152–1154
　Clean Water Act, 1154–1155
　Comprehensive Environmental Response Compensation and Liability Act (CERCLA), 1158
　Federal Insecticide, Fungicide, and Rodenticide Act (FIFRA), 1157
　Marine Protection, Research, and Sanctuaries Act, 1156
　National Environmental Policy Act (NEPA), 1161
　Nuclear Waste Policy Act, 1157
　provisions for private action, 1155
　Resource Conservation and Recovery Act (RCRA), 1157–1158
　Safe Drinking Water Act, 1156
　　Superfund, 1158
　　on toxic air pollutants, 1153
　　Toxic Substances Control Act, 1157
　hazardous waste (under RCRA), 1158
　history and development, 1145–1148
　national ambient air quality standards (NAAQS), 1153
　national pollutant discharge elimination system (NPDES), 1154–1155
　National Priorities List (under CERCLA), 1158
　Nuclear Regulatory Commission, 1157
　point sources, 1155
　pollutant (under Clean Water Act), 1155
　potentially responsible party (under CERCLA), 1158
　practical importance of common law and equity distinction, 1146
　state implementation plan (SIP), 1153
　state and local regulation, 1152
Environmental Protection Agency (EPA):
　example of business regulation, 70
　in general, 1152
Equal Credit Opportunity Act, 1112
Equal dignities rule, 785
Equal Employment Opportunity Commission (EEOC), 70, 1087
Equal Pay Act, 1096
　comparable worth, 1096
Equal protection, 59–61
Equitable estoppel, 313
Equitable remedies:
　accounting, action for: by agent, 835
　　by partner, 866, 869, 887
　　by principal, 829
　for contract breach, 352–355
　deficiency judgment, 638
　foreclosure: of liens imposed by law, 600, 603–605
　　of mechanics' lien, 600, 603–605
　　of security interest, 638

Equitable remedies (*Cont.*):
　injunction, 20, 28–29, 1146
　promissory estoppel, 216–217, 229, 258–259
　reformation, 352
　rescission, 262, 345, 352
　restitution, 349
　specific performance, 20, 29, 353–355
Equity:
　in England, 19–20
　equitable remedies in contract law, 352–355
　merger of law and equity, 20
　role in environmental law, 1146
　role in judicial decisions, 27–29
　in the United States, 20
Escheat, 549
Estate in bankruptcy, 647
Estates (*see* Inheritance; Probate; Wills)
Estoppel:
　in agency, 787–788
　corporation by, 939
　equitable, 313
　meaning of, 216, 313, 787
　partner by, 857
　promissory, 216–217, 229, 258–259
Ethical obligations:
　of agents, 847–848
　of close corporations, 984–987, 990–991
　of corporate directors, 980–987
　of corporate officers, 980–987
　in employer-employee relations, 824, 829–834, 836–840
　of limited partners, 916
　of partners, 868–870, 908–909
　of promoters, 930–931
Ethics:
　applied ethics, 93
　business decision-making and, 92–93, 96–98, 101–110
　business ethics, 94
　codes of: corporate, 106–107
　　professional, 106
　conflicting values and roles, 103–104
　corporate social responsibility, 104–105
　justice: compensatory, 94
　　distributive, 94–95
　　retributive, 94
　justification: external, 101
　　internal, 101
　law and business ethics, 92–107
　meaning of, 93
　moral norms, 94
　moral principle, 94
　moral reasoning, nature and process of, 100–103
　moral standard, 94

Ethics (*Cont.*):
　policy and, 98
　Rawls, John, 95
　right, 94
　rule utilitarianism, 102
　theories of: Kant's categorical imperative, 99–100
　　utilitarianism, 99
　UCC policy, 369
　utility, 94
　value, 93
　veil of ignorance, 95
European Common Market, 1215–1216
European Economic Community (EEC), 1215
European Parliament, 1215
Eviction from property, 526–527
Evidence (*see* Parol evidence rule)
Exculpatory clause:
　in agency, 820
　in contracts, 285–287
Executor, 560
　(*See also* Probate, personal representative)
Exhaustion, doctrine of (*see* Judicial review)
Expectation interest (in contract remedies), 434
Exports:
　dumping, 1227–1229
　Export Administration Act of 1979, 1229
　Export Trading Company Act, 1208
　quotas, 1229
　regulation of, 1229
　subsidies, 1227–1229
　Webb-Pomerene Export Trade Act, 1208
Ex post facto laws,
Extension and composition agreements, 295
Exxon Valdez, 1146

Fair Debt Collection Practices Act, 1111–1112
Fair Labor Standards Act, 1097
False advertising, 166–167
False imprisonment, 116–117
Family Educational Rights and Privacy Act, 1140–1141
FAS (shipping term), 412
Federal Communications Commission, 75, 1119
Federal Food, Drug and Cosmetic Act, 195, 1109
Federal Insecticide, Fungicide, and Rodenticide Act, 1157
Federal Privacy Act, 73
Federal Register, U.S., 73, 83

Federal Register Act, 73
Federal Trade Commission (FTC):
 creation of, 1112, 1188
 example of business regulation, 70
 litigation, 1188, 1200–1202
 Rule 433, 725
 rulemaking model, 74
 scope of activity, 1188
 techniques of regulation, 1202
Federal Trade Commission Act, 1112, 1202
 (*See also* Antitrust laws; Consumer)
Federal Trade Commission Improvements Act, 1112
Felony, 183
Fictitious name statute, 857
Field warehousing, 625–628
Final credit, 755–756
Financing statement (*see* Secured transactions)
Fire insurance, 572, 583, 588, 590
First Amendment, 62–65
First impression, case of, 12
First in, first out rule, 713
Fixtures:
 applicability of UCC Article 9 to, 621
 under construction mortgage, 635
 meaning of, 501
 security interests in, 621, 635
 tests for, 501–502
Floating lien, 623
FOB (shipping term), 412
Food and Drug Administration (FDA), 70, 74, 1109, 1152
Forced (elective) share, 557
Forcible (unlawful) detainer, 526
Foreclosure:
 of liens, 600, 603–605
 of mortgage, 542–543
 of security interest, 638
 of trust deed, 543
 (*See also* Equitable remedies)
Foreign Corrupt Practices Act, 195, 1230
Foreign investment, repatriation of, 1230
Foreign Sovereign Immunities Act of 1976, 1232–1233
Foreign Trade Antitrust Improvements Act of 1982, 1208
Forgery (see Commercial paper)
Fourteenth Amendment:
 due process clause, 58–59
 equal protection clause, 59–61
 in general, 47
 selective incorporation doctrine, 47
Fourth Amendment, 188–189
Fraud(s):
 by accountant, 1052–1053
 of agent (*see* Agent)

Fraud(s) (*Cont.*):
 consumer (*see* Consumer, law)
 in contracts, 273–274
 as a crime, 197
 fraudulent marketing, 155–156
  (*See also* Consumer, law)
 statute of (*see* Statute of frauds)
 as a tort, 129–131
Fraudulent transfer in bankruptcy, 649
Freedom of Information Act (FOIA), 73, 76
Frolic by servant, 812
Frustration of purpose in contract discharge, 346
Fungible goods, 404–405
Future advances, 623

Garnishment, 1107
General Agreement on Tariffs and Trade (GATT), 1216
Generally Accepted Accounting Procedures (GAAP), 1047–1048
Generally Accepted Auditing Standards (GAAS), 1047
Gifts, 481–483, 506–507
Going and coming rule, 810
Good faith:
 defined (UCC), 369
 objective test for holder in due course, 714
 role in consumer protection, 1104
 subjective test for holder in due course, 714
Goods:
 acceptance of, 425–426
 commingled, 404–405, 636
 conforming, 422–424
 consignment of, 397
 distribution of: carrier delivery, 390–392
  noncarrier delivery, 392
  pick-up delivery, 392
  storage in warehouse, 394–397
 entrustment of, 417
 fungible, 404–405
 identification to a contract, 371–372
 inspection of, 426
 insurable interest in, 572–573
 loss, risk of, 371, 410–419
 meaning of, 375
 nonconforming goods, 425–426
 passage of title to, 417
 predominance test (vs. services), 376–378
 rejection of, 426–427
 revocation of acceptance, 427–428
 security interests in, 375, 619–639
 title to, 375, 417
 (*See also* Sales, contract of)

Government-in-the-Sunshine Act, 73
Government Manual, U.S., 70, 73
Grace periods, 628–629
Group medical insurance, 586

Health insurance, 586–587
Hobbs Act, 82
Holder in due course:
 FTC rule affecting, 725–726
 meaning of good faith regarding, 714
 payee as, 719–721
 real defenses good against, 694–697
 requirements for: good faith, 714–715
  no notice of defenses, 715–719
  no notice of dishonor, 718
  no notice of overdueness, 717–718
  no notice of rival claims, 718–719
  value, 712–714
 rights of, 676–678, 712
 shelter provision, 721–725
 significance of, 676–678, 712
Holder status, 400–401, 698, 712
Holmes, Oliver Wendell, 9

Identification of goods to contract, 371–372, 410
Illegal agreements:
 to commit crime or tort, 284–285
 confession of judgment clauses, 295
 contract of adhesion, 285–287
 contrary to public policy, 283–287
 effect of, 282, 298–299
 exceptions to general rule, 298–299
 interference with governmental processes, 295–297
 not to compete, 288–291
 statute, contrary to, 283–284
 usurious, 291–292
 violating licensing statutes, 293–295
 violating Sunday closing laws, 292–293
Imports, 1226–1229
Impossibility of performance, 346, 430–431
Impracticability of performance, 346, 430–431
Incompetency:
 in contracting (*see* Contracts)
 in wills, 550–551
Incorporation:
 in will by reference, 553–554
 (*See also* Corporations, incorporation)
Incorporation laws of states, 923
Independent contractor:
 as agent, 779
 distinguished from employee, 781
 nonagent, 779–780
Indictment, 191

Indorsement (*see* Commercial paper)
Information (in criminal law), 191
Infraction, 183
Inherently dangerous activity, 780, 816
Inheritance:
   escheat, 549
   intestate succession (without a will):
      adopted and illegitimate children, 549–550
      advancements to children, 550
      ineligible heirs, 550
      representation, 548
      usual order of, 549–550
   probate of estate (*see* Probate)
   under will (*see* Wills)
Injunction, 20
   (*See also* Equitable remedies)
Insider trading, 1032–1036
Insolvency laws:
   bankruptcy (*see* Bankruptcy)
   of state (*see* State insolvency laws)
Insurable interest, 572–573
Insurance:
   of accounts receivable, 588
   adverse selection, 587
   agent, 591–592
   all-risk basis, 587
   annuity, 585–586
   automobile, 588
   broker, 591–592
   business interruption, 588
   coinsurance, 589–590
   contract of, 573–576
   defenses of insurer: breach of warranty, 583
      concealment, 582
      misrepresentation, 583
   disability, 586
   dividends, 577
   duties of insurer and insured, 578–582
   fire, 588
   group, 586
   health, 586–587
   incontestability, 584
   indemnity principle of, 571–572
   inland marine, 881
   insurable interest, 572–573
   insured: duties of, 582
      meaning of, 571
   kinds of, 585–589
   liability, 587–590
   life: annuity, 585
      assignment of, 587
      cash surrender value, 585
      warranties under, 583–584
   nature of, 570
   pooling agreement, 570–571
   pricing of, 577
   property insurance, 587–590

Insurance, property insurance (*Cont.*):
   all-risk contract, 587
   coinsurance, 588–590
   deductible amount, 587
   loss under, 587
   personal property floater, 587
   specified perils contract, 587
   reinsurance, 571
   subrogation, 588–589
   waiver, 584
Insurance industry, regulation of, 590–591
Interference:
   with contracts, 161
   with employer-employee relations, 163
   with prospective economic advantage, 159–161
   (*See also* Competitive torts)
Integration of contract, 316–317
Intellectual property:
   copyrights: of computer programs, 1122–1125
      fair use, 175–176
      infringement of, 175
      notice of, 175
      registration of, 175
      work made for hire, 173
      works protected, 173
   patents: of computer technology, 1125
      in general, 176
   trade secrets: computer, 1125–1127
      in general, 178
   trademarks: certification mark, 170
      collective mark, 170
      common law, 169
      distinctiveness requirement, 170
      generic terms, 172
      infringement of, 172
      Lanham Act, 169
      registration of, 169–170
      secondary meaning, 170
      service mark, 170
      trade name, 170
Interior, Department of, 1152
Internal Revenue Service (IRS), 70
International business:
   act-of-state doctrine, 1223
   Andean Common Market, 1225
   Anti-Dumping Act, 1227
   antitrust laws affecting, 1231
   arbitration in, 1221–1223
   Association of Southeast Asian Nations, 1215
   bill of lading in, 1224
   choice-of-forum contract clause, 1220
   choice-of-law contract clause, 1220
   classification of goods in, 1227
   "clawback" legislation, 1231
   comity in, 1223

International business (*Cont.*):
   confiscation of goods in, 1231–1232
   correspondent bank, 1224
   countervailing duty in, 1227
   Court of Justice, 1215
   direct effect, doctrine of, 1216
   direct sales in, 1223–1225
   distributorship in, 1225
   dumping, 1227–1229
   European Common Market, 1215–1216
   European Economic Community (EEC), 1215–1216
   European Parliament, 1215
   exclusive dealership in, 1225
   Export Administration Act of 1979, 1229
   exports, regulation of: quotas, 1229
      subsidies, 1229
   expropriation of goods in, 1231–1232
   foreign investment, repatriation of, 1230
   Foreign Sovereign Immunities Act of 1976, 1232–1233
   Foreign Trade Antitrust Improvements Act of 1982, 1231
   franchises in, 1225
   General Agreement on Tariffs and Trade (GATT), 1216
   imports, regulation of, 1226–1229
   international trade agreements, 1220–1223
   letter of credit, 1224–1225
   licensing, 1225
   money, international regulation of, 1229–1230
   multinational enterprise, 1223
   nationalization of investment, 1231
   Overseas Private Investment Corporation (OPIC), 1232
   regional trade communities, 1215–1216
   regulation of: extraterritoriality, 1231
      by sovereign, 1226–1231
      transnational interests, 1214–1217, 1226
   sovereign immunity, doctrine of, 1232
   tariffs affecting, 1214–1216
   transnational corporations, 1226
   treaties affecting, 1215–1216
   Treaty of Rome, 1215
   Uniform Customs and Practices for Documentary Credits, 1225
   United States International Trade Commission, 1227
   valuation of goods in, 1227
International Court of Justice, 1216

Inter vivos:
  gift, 481
  trust, 562
Interrogatories, 33
Intestate (*see* Inheritance)
Invasion of privacy, 122–123
Issue advertising, 64–65

James I, 9, 17
Jingle rule, 889
Joint tenancy, 513
  (*See also* Property)
Joint tortfeasors, 800
Joint venture, 852
Judgment, 35–36
Judgment *non obstante veredicto*
  (n.o.v.), 36
Judicial reasoning, 17–19
Judicial review:
  APA provisions, 81–82
  deference to administrative agencies,
    84–86
  defined, 81
  generally, 80–83
  non-reviewable matters, 81
  standing, ripeness and exhaustion doctrines, 82–83
  (*See also* Administrative agency; Administrative law)
Jurisdiction of courts, 38–39
Jurisprudence, 3–4
"Just price" doctrine, 207–208
Justice:
  compensatory, 94
  distributive, 94–95
  retributive, 94
Justice, Department of, 1152

Landlord and tenant:
  constructive eviction, 527
  fixed-term tenancies, 526, 532–533
  landlord: duty to maintain premises,
    527
    forcible (unlawful) detainer remedy,
      526
    liability for injuries to tenant, 528
    right to rent, 526–527
  leases: assignment or sublease, 530
    requirements of, 525
    termination of, 532
    types of, 526
  periodic tenancies, 526, 532
  tenant: right to possession, 527
    right to sublet or assign lease, 530
Landrum-Griffin Act, 1078
Lanham Act:
  protection of trademarks under,
    169–172
  section 43(a) of, 166–167

Law:
  and business ethics, 92–107
  development of: common law in England, 19–20
    common law in the United States, 20
  law merchant, 367–368
  enacted law, 25
  functions of, 92
  meaning of, 3–4
  as a process, 4–9
  public and private, 20–21
  relationship to ethics, 95–99
  rank of laws, 29–30
  remedies, legal (*see* Remedies)
  restatements of, 209–210
  sources and rank of, 23–30
  substantive and procedural, 21
  uniform codes of, 209
  (*See also* Appendices)
Law merchant, 367
Leases (*see* Landlord and tenant)
Legal philosophy, schools of:
  Chicago school (law and economics),
    16
  critical legal studies, 16–17
  historical, 16
  legal positivist, 15
  legal realism, 16
  natural law, 15–16
  sociological jurisprudence, 16
Legal reasoning, 9–15
Legislative history, 12
Legislative intent, 12–13
  (*See also* Statutory interpretation)
Legislative purpose, 12–13
  (*See also* Statutory interpretation)
Lemon laws, 1105
  (*See also* Consumer)
Letter of credit, 1223–1224
Levi, Edward, 18
Liability insurance, 587–590
Libel, 118
License:
  of computer software, 1124–1125
  real estate right, 533
Licensing laws, 293–295
Lien:
  of artisan, 600–605
  attachment, 543
  of carrier, 390
  created by contract: in personal property, 605–606, 619–639
    in real property, 537–543, 605–606
    (*See also* Secured transactions)
  execution, 543–544
  floating, 623
  foreclosure of, 600, 603–605
  general, 600–601
  imposed by law, 600–605

Lien (*Cont.*):
  judgment, 543
  of materialman, 601–605
  of mechanic, 600–605
  in personal property, 605–606,
    619–639
  possessory, 494, 600–601
  on real property, 537–544, 601–605
  specific, 600–601
  tax, 544
  of warehouser, 395
Life estate, 523–524
Life insurance (*see* Insurance, life)
Limited liability companies:
  characteristics, 917
  compared to partnership, corporation,
    899
  defined, 852, 899
  qualifications required by IRS,
    918–919
  state statutes authorizing, 917
  taxation of, 917–918
Limited partnerships:
  agreement, limited partnership, 904
  business of, 904
  capital of: contributions to, 905
    promissory note as, 905
  certificate of, 902
  nonfiling, effect of, 901–902
  charging order, 909, 916
  creditors' rights against, 909
  defined, 899–900
  dissolution of, 917
  example of, 900
  formation of, 901–906
  general partner(s), 907–910
    admission of additional, 910
    assignment of interest by, 910
    compensation of, 910
    death of, 910
    fiduciary obligations of, 908
    liability of, 909
    number of, 907
    powers of, 907
    withdrawal or removal of, 910
  legal basis of, 901
  limited partner(s): admission of additional, 910
    assignment of interest by, 916
    charging order against, 916
    creditor of, 916
    death of, 916
    fiduciary duties of, 916
    liability of, 916
    management, participation in, 913
    number of, 910
    powers of, 911
    rights of, 911
    who may be, 910

Limited partnerships, limited partner(s) (*Cont.*):
  withdrawal of, 902, 916
  master limited partnership, 910
  members of: general partners, 900, 907
    limited partners, 900, 910
    name of, 905
  organization of, 901–905
  profits of, allocation, 900, 904
  purpose of, 904
  termination of: basis for dissolution, 917
    distribution of assets, 917
    winding up, 917
  Uniform Limited Partnership Act, 901
  Uniform Partnership Act applicable to, 901
Liquidated debt, 252–255
Liquidation under Bankruptcy Act Chapter 7, 645–659
Little FTCs, 1105
  (*See also* Consumer)
Living trust, 562
Llewellyn, Karl, 16
Lost property, 484
Love Canal, 1158
Lunch hour rule, 810

Magnuson-Moss Warranty Act (*see* Warranty, Magnuson-Moss Warranty Act)
Malicious prosecution, 127
Marine Protection, Research, and Sanctuaries Act, 1156–1157
Master:
  defined, 778
  liability for servant's tort, 800–819
  ratification of servant's tort, 816
  respondeat superior, 802
  strict liability of, 816
  (*See also* Employee; Principal)
Master limited partnerships, 910
Mechanic's lien, 600–605
Mediation, defined, 43
Mens rea, 484
Mental distress, infliction of, 124–125
Mental incompetency to enter contract, 268–269
Merchant, 369
  (*See also* Sales, Law of)
Mergers, corporate, 998–999, 1040–1042
Midnight deadline, 755
Mini-trials, defined, 43
Minors:
  as agent, 783
  contracts of (*see* Contracts, capacity of parties)

Minors (*Cont.*):
  as partners, 857
  as principal, 783
  rescission of indorsement, 709
Miranda Rule, 191
Misdemeanor, 183
Mislaid property, 484
Misrepresentation:
  as basis for product liability, 467–468
  in consumer protection, 1103–1104
  in contracts, 273–274
  fraudulent, 129–131
  intentional, 467–468, 1103
  negligent, 143, 468
  in procuring insurance, 583
  strict liability for, 468
Mistake:
  in contracting, 274–277
  in wills, 553
M'Naghten Rule, 187
Model Business Corporation Act, 923, Appendix 5
  (*See also* Corporations)
Monopolies, 1164, 1181–1185
Mortgage:
  assumption of, 541
  chattel, 375, 620, 621
  construction, 635
  due-on-sale clauses in, 542
  foreclosure of, 542–543
    deficiency, mortgagor's liability for, 542–543
    redemption, mortgagor's right to, 542
  purchasing subject to, 541
  requirements of, 537–538
  rights and duties of the parties to, 539
Motion:
  for directed verdict, 35
  for dismissal, 35
  for judgment notwithstanding the verdict (n.o.v.), 36
  for new trial, 36
  for summary judgment, 32
Motor vehicle, perfection of security interest in, 624

National ambient air quality standards (NAAQS), 1153
  (*See also* Environmental law)
National Association of Security Dealers, Inc. (NASDAQ), 928
National Environmental Policy Act, 1161
National Labor Relations Act, 1075
  coverage, 1075
  duty to bargain, 1075
  in general, 1075
  historical background of, 1075
  unfair labor practices, 1075, 1077

National Labor Relations Board (NLRB), 70, 75, 1076
Negligence:
  by accountant, 1053–1057
  of agent, 800–820
  assumption of risk, 149–150, 460, 1098
  of carriers, 392
  comparative, 147–148, 460
  contributory, 147, 460
  defenses to, 147–150, 460
  elements of, 136, 459
  in environmental law, 1149
  per se, 140–141
  product liability caused by, 459–460
  quasi-intent, 1149
  res ipsa loquitur, 141, 460
  of servant, 801–802, 806–808
    (*See also* Servant)
  of warehouser, 395
  willful and wanton, 1149
Negligent misrepresentation, 143, 468, 1053
Negotiability, language of, 681
Negotiable instruments (*see* Commercial paper)
Negotiation, defined, 42
Norris-LaGuardia Act, 1073, 1074
Note, promissory, 673
Novation agreement:
  discharge of contract by, 345
  in partnership, 896
Nuclear Regulatory Commission, 1157
Nuclear Waste Policy Act, 1157
Nuisance, 128, 519, 1148

Occupational Safety and Health Act, 1099
Occupational Safety and Health Administration (OSHA), 70, 73
Offer:
  acceptance: authorized medium of, 380
    deposited acceptance (mailbox) rule, 235
    meaning of acceptance, 232–233
    mirror image rule, 233
    of offer for bilateral contract, 234–238
    of offer for unilateral contract, 233–234
    in sales contracts, 233, 379–380
    shipment of nonconforming goods as, 382
  in auction, 223
  bid as, 223
  counteroffer, 230–232, 371, 381–382

Offer (*Cont.*):
　definite terms, 224–228
　firm, 229, 371, 379
　implied terms, 225–227
　language of commitment, 221–22
　material alteration of in sales, 233
　meaning of, 220–221
　in sales: contract formation, 225, 233, 379
　　output contracts, 224
　　requirements contracts, 224
　rewards, 222
　termination of: by counteroffer, 230–231
　　by death or incapacity, 232
　　by lapse of time, 228
　　by loss of subject matter, 232
　　by rejection, 230–232
　　by revocation, 228–230
　　by supervening illegality, 232
　(*See also* Contracts; Sales)
Office of Management and Budget (OMB), 87
Order and bearer paper, 681, 698
Ostensible authority (*see* Agent)

Palming off, 165
Parol evidence rule:
　in contract law, 316–317
　in sales law, 383
Partially disclosed principal, 795
Particular fund doctrine, 685–686
Partition, 512
Partner(s):
　accounting, partner's action for, 884, 890
　admission of new, 887
　as agent of partnership, 777, 854
　assignment of interest of, 861
　bankruptcy of, 883–884
　charging order against, 861, 863
　contributions by, 855, 858
　death of, 883
　debts of: charging order, 861
　　effect of Bankruptcy Reform Act of 1978, 889
　　jingle rule, 889
　delectus personae, 857
　duties of, 858, 867–870
　enforcement of obligations, 872
　by estoppel, 857–860
　expulsion of, 880
　fiduciary responsibility of, 868
　general partner (*see* Limited partnerships)
　incapacity of, 884
　indemnification agreement, 886
　inheritance from, 859, 862–863, 883, 885–886, 893

Partner(s) (*Cont.*):
　interest in partnership: assignment of, 861
　　creditors' rights against, 861
　　heirs' rights in, 861
　　rights of assignee, 861
　jingle rule, 889
　limited (*see* Limited partnerships)
　management by, 854, 863
　minor as, 857
　misconduct of, 884
　new partner: admission of, 877–878
　　liability of, 885
　novation agreement, 896
　obligations to third parties, 852, 857, 861, 867, 870–871
　ostensible, 857
　personal liability of, 852, 889, 895–896
　powers of: to contract, 883, 870
　　to obligate by tort, 871
　　secret agreement limiting, 864
　as principal in partnership, 854
　retirement of, 883
　rights of, 866
　specific partnership property, right in, 862
　who may be a partner, 857
　　agreement of co-partners, 857
　　delectus personae, 857
　　by estoppel, 857
　　minor, 857
　　ostensible, 857
　winding up authority, 885, 887, 890
　withdrawal of, 879
　(*See also* Partnerships)
Partnerships:
　accounting, partner's action for, 884, 887
　admission of new partner, 887
　aggregate theory of, 853–854
　assignment of interest in, 859, 861
　bankruptcy of, 883–884
　capital required, 885
　at common law, 853
　corporations distinguished, 852
　creditors' rights against, 861
　death of a partner, 883, 893
　defined, 854
　delectus personae, 857
　dissolution of: bases for, 876–885
　　continuance of business after, 892
　　defined, 876
　　notice of, 888
　　payment to withdrawing partner, 892–893
　　termination distinguished, 876
　　in violation of partnership agreement, 881–883

Partnerships (*Cont.*):
　establishment of, 857
　expulsion of a partner, 880–881
　goodwill, 859, 892, 893
　heirs' rights in, 861
　illegal business activity, 882, 884
　indemnification agreement, 896
　jingle rule, 889
　joint venture, 852
　law of, 853
　as a legal entity, 853–854
　liability for: partner's contract, 870–872
　　partner's tort, 871
　limited (*see* Limited partnerships)
　members of, 854–855
　name of, 857
　profits and losses, 854, 867, 885, 888–889
　property of: creditors rights in, 861
　　heirs' interest in, 861
　　partner's interest in, 861
　　specific, 862
　　tenancy in partnership, 862
　　title to, 862
　purpose of, 857, 858
　requirements for, 854–855
　retirement of a partner, 893
　specific partnership property, 862
　　creditors' rights against, 863
　　heirs' rights in, 862
　　partners' right in, 862
　termination of: defined, 876
　　dissolution distinguished, 876
　Uniform Partnership Act, 853
　unprofitable, 855, 867
　at will, 885, 879
　winding up: conducted by, 885, 893
　　continuance of business without, 892–894
　　fiduciary responsibilities during, 890–892
　　partners' authority during, 887
　　payments to creditors, 889
　　payments to partners, 893
　　withdrawal of a partner, 893
　(*See also* Partners)
Patent and Trademark Office, U.S., 70
Patents, 176
Pay-by-phone bill-paying systems, 768
Perfect tender rule, 423–424
Performance:
　course of, 383–384
　of sales contract, 422–433
　(*See also* Contracts; Sales)
Personal property:
　abandoned, 483–484
　accession, acquisition by, 486
　bailment of (*see* Bailment)

Personal property (*Cont.*):
   confusion, acquisition by, 486
   defined as, 477
   gifts of, 481–483
   lost or mislaid, 484
Plain meaning rule, 12
Pledge, 375, 619–620
Point-of-sale terminals, 768
Police powers, 48–50
Posting, 755
Pound, Roscoe, 16
Power of attorney, 785–786
Preemption of state law under Constitution, 51–52
Preemptive rights of shareholders, 1007–1008
Preference of creditors, 652–653
Pregnancy Discrimination Act of 1978, 1091
Presentment, 731–733
Presentment warranties, 745–747
Pretermission under a will, 557
Principal(s):
   agent, obligations to, 792, 834–840
   authority of agent to act for, 786–792
   capacity, 783
   control of agent by, 778, 780–781
   direction of agent by, 778, 780–781
   disclosed, 793
   estoppel to deny agency, 787–789
   exculpatory clause, 820
   as general employer, 778
   kinds of, 783–784
   liability for agent's tort, 800–820
      inherently dangerous activity, 780*n.*, 816
      for nonphysical injury, 818–820
      by ratification, 790, 819–820
      respondeat superior, 801–802
      resulting in physical injury, 800–815
      strict liability, 816
      ultrahazardous activity, 816
      vicarious, 802
   minor as, 783
   nondelegable duties of: inherently dangerous activities, 816–818
      license or franchise holder, 816
      property owner, 816
      statutory duties, 816
      ultrahazardous activities, 816
   obligations to agent: to account, 835
      breach of, 834, 841
      to compensate for injury, 840
      to continue employment, 836–839
      to pay for work, 834
      to provide safe workplace, 840
   partially disclosed, 795
   ratification by, 789–791

Principal(s) (*Cont.*):
   remedies against agent, 841
   as special employer, 806
   undisclosed, 795–796
   vicarious liability of (see *Respondeat superior*)
   (*See also* Master)
Privacy:
   and computers, 1140–1141
   as credit reporting issue, 1116, 1117
   invasion of, 122–123
   telephone, 1118–1119
Privacy for Consumers and Workers Act, 1141
Private carrier:
   defined, 391
   liabilities of, 392
Private law, 20
Privilege:
   absolute, 121
   accountant-client, 1049
   defense of property, 116
   qualified/conditional, 121
   qualified constitutional, 121–122
   self-defense, 116
Privity of contract, 446
Probate:
   administrator or administratrix, 560
   claims against estate, 560–561
   distribution of assets: abatement due to insufficient assets, 561
      ademption by extinction of specific gift, 562
      ambiguity or mistake in will, 561
      predeceased beneficiary, 561–562
      types of gifts, 561
   executor or executrix, 560
   personal representative: appointment of, 560
      duties of, 560
   proving the will, 559–560
   (*See also* Wills)
Procedure:
   civil (*see* Civil procedure)
   criminal (*see* Criminal procedure)
   probate (*see* Probate)
Product liability:
   basis of: misrepresentation, 467–468
      negligence, 459–460
      strict liability, 150–151, 460–467
      (*See also* Torts)
      warranty, 447–458
      (*See also* Warranty)
   in consumer protection, 1104
   defenses (strict liability), 464, 466
   historical development, 445–447
   limited usefulness of (as basis for suit): negligence, 459–460

Product liability, limited usefulness of (as basis for suit) (*Cont.*):
      strict liability, 466–467
      warranty, 458
   Restatement (Second) of Torts: Section 402A, 151, 460–461
      Section 402B, 468
   risk-utility balancing, 461
   as a tort, 150–151, 458–468
   unavoidably unsafe product, 467
   unreasonably dangerous product, 461
Promissory estoppel, 216–217, 229, 258–259
Promissory note, 673
Property:
   community, 514–515
   condemnation of, 517
   eminent domain, 517
   in general, 475–480
   inheritance of (*see* Wills)
   intangible, 476
   joint tenancy, 513
   landlord and tenant (*see* Landlord and tenant)
   liens against, 599–605
   personal (*see* Personal property)
   private, 477
   as private law, 20
   public, 477
   real (*see* Real property)
   security interests in, 599–606, 619–639
   tangible, 476
   tenancy in common, 513
   tenancy in partnership, 854–862
   trespass, 128–129, 1147–1148
Property insurance, 587–588
Protest, 731
Provisional credit, 755
Proxy, 1005–1006
Public law, 20
Public policy:
   contracts contrary to, 283–297
   in principal/agent, 837–840
   significance of, in contracting, 283–284
   statutory interpretation, use in, 13
Puffing, 449, 1113
Pure Food and Drug Act, 1109

Quasi contract, 213–214, 359

Racketeer Influenced and Corrupt Organizations ACT (RICO):
   accountants liability under, 1063–1064
   in general, 198
Ratification:
   in agency, 789

Ratification (*Cont.*):
  in corporations, 932–980
  of minors' contracts, 266–267
Reaffirmation agreement in bankruptcy, 659
Real property:
  adverse possession, 506–507
  airspace, rights to, 499–500
  condominiums and cooperatives, 515
  crops and timber, rights to, 500
  dedication of, 506
  deed: recording of, 510–511
    transfer by, 509
    types of, 510
  easements (*see* Easement)
  encroach, landowner's duty not to, 519
  fee simple estates in, 523–524
  in general, 476–477
  joint tenancy in, 512–513
  leases of (*see* Landlord and tenant)
  liens on, 601–605
  life estates in, 524
  maintain property, landowner's duty to, 519–520
  mineral rights, 500
  mortgages of (*see* Mortgages)
  oil and gas interests, 500
  purchase of, 504
  remainders in, 524–525
  restrictive covenants, 520
  reversion of, 524
  tenancy in common, 512–513
  tenancy in partnership, 854–862
  warranty of habitability or fitness, 504
  water rights, 500–501
  zoning of, 516
  (*See also* Property)
Recording statutes, 511–512
Reformation of contracts, 352
Reinsurance, 571
Remainders (property interest), 524–525
Remedies:
  for breach in sales contracts, 433–442
  civil law: for anticipatory breach, 341, 344–345
    for breach of sales contract, 433–442
    class action suit, 1010
    compensatory damages, 350
    confession of judgment, 295
    consequential (special) damages, 350, 355–356
    for contract breach, 349–352, 355–358
    counterclaim, 32
    cover, 437–438
    derivative suit by shareholder, 974, 1010–1012

Remedies, derivative suit by shareholder (*Cont.*):
    exemplary (punitive) damages, 350, 580–581
    foreclosure, 600, 603–605, 638
    general damages, 350
    limitation on damages, 355–358
    liquidated damages, 350–352
    nominal damages, 350
    punitive damages, 350, 580–581
    quasi contract, 213–215, 359
    quo warranto, 974
    repudiation of contract, 341, 344–345
    (*See also* Motion)
  equitable (*see* Equitable remedies)
  limitation of, in sales, 440–442
  under quasi contract, 213–215, 359
Reasonable woman standard, 9–11
Reliance interest (in contract remedies), 434
Remittitur, defined, 36
Requirements contracts, 224
Rescission of contract, 262, 277–278, 316, 345, 352
Res ipsa loquitur, 141, 460
Resource Conservation and Recovery Act (RCRA), 1157–1158
Respondeat superior, 802
Restatements of common law, 209–210
Restitution, 349
Restitution interest (in contract remedies), 434
RICO (Racketeer Influenced and Corrupt Organizations ACT):
  accountants liability under, 1063–1064
  in general, 198
Right to Financial Privacy Act, 1140
Right of publicity (*see* Privacy, invasion of)
Ripeness, doctrine of (*see* Judicial review)
Risk of loss, 410–419
  (*See also* Sales, contract of)
Robinson-Patman Act, 1188–1192
  buyer inducement, unlawful, 1192
  commodities, likeness of, 1189
  defenses under: cost justification, 1190
    meeting competition, 1191
  historical background of, 1188
  injury to competition under, 1189–1190
  price discrimination, 1188–1190
    in payments and services, 1192
    unlawful brokerage, 1191
  proving commerce jurisdiction, 1189
  proving discrimination under, 1189–1190

Robinson-Patman Act (*Cont.*):
  purpose and scope of, 1188–1189
  (*See also* Antitrust laws)

S (or small) corporations, 929
Safe Drinking Water Act, 1156
Sales:
  acceptance of goods: in general, 425–426
    revocation of, 427–428
    substantially impaired, 427, 431
  acceptance of offer, 379–380
  agreement under UCC, 383, 423
  on approval or return, 416
  Article 2A (UCC), 375
  bailment, 390
  caveat emptor, 446
  commercial impracticability, 430–431
  commercial unit, 426
  commingled goods, 404–405
  conditional sales contract, 375–376
  contract of: added term(s), 382
    alteration of, 386–387
    breach of, 433–434
    buyer's obligations under, 425–433
    casualty to identified goods, 432–433
    commercial impracticability, 430–431
    for commingled goods, 404–405
    conforming goods, 423–428
    course of dealing, 383, 384
    course of performance, 383–384
    cover, 437–438
    cure, 425–427
    damages for breach of, 434–440
    defective performance, cure of, 425–427
    delivery under, 390–394
    destination contract, 411
    excuse for nonperformance, 430–431
    excuse for substitute performance, 433
    formation of, 378–379
    good faith in, 369, 371, 1104
    good faith purchaser, 417
    for goods, 375
    (*See also* Goods)
    identification of goods to, 371–372, 410
    inspection of goods, 426
    installment contract, 427
    interpretation of, 383
    meaning of, 383
    nonconforming goods, 425–426
    obligation of parties, 422–423
    open terms, 379

Sales, contract of (*Cont.*):
   parol evidence rule, UCC Article 2, 383
   payment, 425–426
   perfect tender rule, 423–424
   performance of, 422–433
   predominance test (goods vs. services), 376–378
   rejection of goods, 426–427
   remedies for breach, 433–442
   replevin, 438
   repudiation of contract, 434, 435
   requirements contract, 379
   revocation of acceptance of goods, 427–428
   risk of loss under, 371, 410–419
   sale on approval, 416
   seller's obligations, 424–425
   shipment contract, 411
   shipping terms, 412
   tender: meaning of, 423
      requirements, 424–426
   title of good faith purchaser, 417–419
   title revesting in seller, 411
   UCC Article 2 affecting, 368–387
   unconscionable, 372–373, 1105
   usage of trade, 383, 384
   warranties (*see* Warranty)
counteroffer, 371, 381–382
course of dealing, 383, 384
delivery of goods: acceptance of, 425–426
   cure for improper, 426–427
   inspection of, 426
   nonconforming goods, 425–426
   rejection of, 426–427
   revocation of acceptance, 427–428
   risk of loss, 371
   tender of, 423
   title transfer, 410–411
entrusted goods, 417
ethical business conduct, 369
firm offer, 371, 379
good faith: defined, 369
   merchants, applied to, 371
   purchaser, requirements of, 417
   requirement, 369
leases, 375
liquidated damages, 440–441
Louisiana exception, 21, 368
merchant, 369
modification of contract, 371
offer seeking prompt or current shipment, 379
parol evidence rule, 383
public policy served, 369
puffing, 449, 1113
purchaser, meaning of, 417

Sales (*Cont.*):
   purchaser in good faith, 417
   purposes of, 368–369
   seasonable notice of rejection, 426
   statute of frauds, UCC Article 2, 371, 386
   title, 375
      transfer of, 410–411
   trade usage, 383, 384
   transfer of risk of loss, 411–417
   UCC provisions applicable to, 368–387
   unconscionable (unconscionability), 372–374, 1105
   voidable title, 417
   warranties (*see* Warranty)
Sales contract (*see* Sales, contract of)
Sales of Goods Act (U.K. 1893), 367
Sales puffing, 449, 1113
Scope of authority (*see* Agent)
Scope of employment (*see* Servant)
Secured transactions:
   accounts receivable financing, 621–622
   after-acquired property, 623
   attachment events, 622–623
   breach of peace, 636–638
   buyer in ordinary course of business, 634
   chattel mortgage, 620, 621
   chattel paper, 621–622
   collateral: commercially reasonable disposition of, 638
      meaning of, 599
   conditional sale contract, 620
   construction mortgage, priority of, 635
   debtor's rights, 638–639
   default, 636
   deficiency judgment, 638
   field warehousing, 625, 628
   filing system: central and local filing, 625
      public notice, 620
   financing statement, 625–627
   floating lien, 623
   foreclosure, 638
   future advances, 623
   grace periods, 628–629
   lease as, 622
   perfection, methods of: completing attachment events, 624, 628–629
      filing financing statement, 625–628
      fixture filing, 627
      for motor vehicles, 624
      PMSI in collateral other than inventory, 631
      PMSI in consumer goods, 631
      PMSI in inventory, 631

Secured transactions, perfection, methods of (*Cont.*):
      for proceeds, 629
      secured party's possessing collateral, 624–625
   pledge, 619
   PMSI (purchase money security interest): meaning of, 624
      priority of, 631–634
   priorities between conflicting interests: security interest and mechanic's lien, 635
      security interest and purchaser's interest, 634–635
      security interests in accessions, 635–636
      security interests in commingled goods, 636
      security interests in fixtures, 635
      security interests in same collateral, 629–633
   security agreement, 622
   security interest: in accessions, 635–636
      attachment of, 622–623
      in commingled goods, 636
      in fixtures, 627, 629, 635
      in inventory, 631
      meaning of, 620
      in motor vehicle, 624
      perfection of, 623–628
      in proceeds, 629
   security lease, 622
   strict foreclosure, 638
   title in, 620
   types of: corporate bonds (*see* Corporations, debt financing)
      in personal property, 619–639
      in real property, 605–606
   unsecured transactions distinguished, 600
   (*See also* Suretyship)
Securities:
   dealer in, 1024, 1028
   definition of, 1019–1022
   exempted from registration, 1025–1028
   federal laws concerning, 1018–1042
      penalties for violating, 1029–1021, 1042
   offer of, 1025
   public offering of, 1023, 1025
   red herring prospectus, 1023–1024
   registration of, 1023–1026
   sale of, 1025–1029
   state laws concerning, 1018, 1026–1027
   tombstone ads, 1023–1024
   uncertificated, 951

Securities (*Cont.*):
    underwriter of, 1023–1024
    (*See also* Corporations, securities of)
Securities Act of 1933:
    accountants' liabilities under, 1059–1060
    exempted securities, 1025–1028
    exempted transactions, 1026–1028
    offer of security under, 1025
    red herring prospectus, 1023
    registration under, 1023–1025
    rules under, 1026–1029
    sale of securities under, 1025–1028
    securities defined, 1019–1022
Securities Exchange Act of 1934:
    accountants' liabilities under, 1030–1031, 1060–1061
    forms 8-K, 10-K, and 10-Q, 1032
    insider trading, 1032–1036
    reporting required, 1032
    Rule 10b-5, 1032–1035
    securities defined, 1019–1022
    short-swing transactions, 1036
    sophisticated investor, 1026–1028
    tender offers, 981–983, 988, 1039–1042
    tipper and tippee, 1033–1036
Securities Exchange Commission (SEC), 70, 1019
Securities laws violations:
    civil and criminal liabilities, 197–198, 1029–1031, 1035–1036, 1042
    criminal liabilities, 197–198
    under Securities Act of 1933, 1029–1031
    under Securities Act of 1934, 1035–1036, 1042
Security interest (*see* Secured transactions)
Semiconductor Chip Protection Act, 1125
Servant:
    as agent, 778
    assumption of risk, 1098
    authority to contract, 785–789
    borrowed, 806–808
    characteristics of, 781, 803
    control by master, 778, 781, 802
    delegation of authority by, 808–809
    detour by, 812–814
    dual purpose rule, 810
    frolic by, 812–814
    going and coming rule, 810
    injuries to, 840
    intentional tort of, 802, 818–820
        ratification by master, 790
    lunch hour rule, 810
    master and, 778
    negligent act of, 779, 801–802, 813
    personal performance by, 779, 827

Servant (*Cont.*):
    scope of employment, 785–792, 809
    subservant of, 808–809
    torts of: foreseeability, 809
        intentional, 814–816
        negligent (unintentional), 814
    workers' compensation, 1098–1099
    (*See also* Agent)
Sexual harassment, 9–11, 1093
Shareholders (*see* Corporations, shareholders)
Shelter provision, 721–725
Sherman Antitrust Act:
    court interpretation of, 1165–1185
    enforcement of, 1166–1167
    foreign commerce, 1169
    historical background of, 1164–1165
    interstate commerce, 1167
    per se violations of, 1170–1191
        dividing customers, 1171–1173
        dividing markets, 1171–1173
        group boycotts, 1176–1180
        price fixing, 1171–1172, 1177–1178
        reciprocal dealing, 1180
        refusing to deal, 1176–1180
        restricting production, 1173
        tying contracts, 1180
    private actions, standing to sue, 1166
    purpose and scope of, 1165–1166
    rule of reason under, 1170
    violations of: consciously parallel behavior, 1169
        conspiracy, 1169
        jurisdiction required, 1167
        monopoly, 1181–1185
Shipment contract:
    meaning of, 411
    risk of loss, 411–412
    title passage under, 411
Shop-right privilege, 834
Short-swing transaction, 1036
Sixth Amendment, 191
Slander:
    as business tort, 164
    tort of, 118
Sole proprietorship, 851–852
Sovereign Immunity, doctrine of, 1232–1233
Specific performance, 20, 29, 353–355
Stale check, 758
Standing (*see* Judicial review)
Stare decisis, doctrine of, 10, 25–27
State implementation plan (SIP), 1153
    (*see* Environmental law)
State incorporation laws, 923
State insolvency laws:
    assignment for benefit of creditors, 644

State insolvency laws (*Cont.*):
    composition and extension agreements, 644
    private workout under, 644
    role of, in bankruptcy, 645
Statute of frauds:
    alternatives to the writing, 312–316
    computer contracts, application to, 1130
    executor provision, 303
    land-contract provision, 307–308
    leases under Article 2A of the UCC, 487
    long-term contract provision, 308–311
    marriage provision, 306–307
    requirements for the writing, 311–312
    sales provision, 307
    suretyship provision, 303–305
    UCC, 386
Statutory interpretation, 12–15
Stock (*see* Corporations, stock in)
Stop-payment order, 761–762
Stored Wire and Electronic Communications and Transactional Records Act, 1141
Strict liability, 150–155, 460–468, 1149
Subagent, 808–809
Subchapter S corporation, 929
Subrogation:
    in commercial paper law, 762
    in insurance, 588–589
    in suretyship, 615
Subservant, 809
Summary judgment, 32
Summons, 31
Sunday closing laws, 292–293
Superfund, 1158
    (*See also* Environmental law)
Surety:
    accommodation, 608
    bonds: bail, 608
        bid, 608
        fidelity, 608
        fiduciary, 608
        license or permit, 609
        performance, 606, 608
    compensated, 608
    conditional, 609
    contribution, 615–616
    corporate, 608
    cosurety, 615–616
    defenses of, 610–614
    discharge of, 610–614
    exoneration of, 614–615
    gratuitous, 608
    liability of, 609–610
    main purpose rule, 611
    reimbursement of, 615
    subrogation of, 615

Surety (*Cont.*):
  unconditional, 609
  voluntary, 608
Suretyship:
  absolute guaranty, 609
  conditional guaranty, 609
  cosuretyship, 609
  creation of: by contract, 607
    by operation of law, 607–608
  (*See also* Surety)

Taft-Hartley Act, 1074, 1077–1078
Takeover of corporation, 988, 1039–1042
Takings of property under Constitution, 55–56
Tariffs, 1215–1216
Telephone Consumer Protection Act, 1118–1119, 1141
Tenancy:
  in common, 512–513
  by entirety, 513–514
  joint, 512–513
  leases, 526
  in partnership, 515, 854, 862
Testate (*see* Wills)
Thin corporation, 956–959
Time draft, 674
Title:
  documents of (*see* Documents of title)
  of good faith purchaser, 400
  meaning of, 475–476, 620
  in UCC, 375
  warranty of,
  (*See also* Sales, contract of)
Torts:
  abnormally dangerous activities, 153–154, 1149
  abuse of process, 127
  animals, injuries by, 154–155, 465–466
  assault, 116
  battery, 115–116, 1148
  comparative negligence, 147–148, 460
  conversion, 129, 391, 392
  of corporation, 975
  defamation, 118–122
  defective product (*see* Products liability)
  defenses, in general, 114
  defined, 114
  false imprisonment, 116–117
  fraud, 129–131
  inherently dangerous activity, 780, 816
  intentional, 115–131, 467–468, 1147, 1148
  invasion of privacy, 122–123

Torts (*Cont.*):
  libel, 118
  malicious prosecution, 127
  negligence (*see* Negligence)
  nuisance, 128, 1148
  as private law, 20
  product liability, 150–151, 458–468
  res ipsa loquitur, 141, 460
  slander, 118
  strict products liability (*see* Products liability)
  trespass: to personal property, 129
    to real property, 128, 1147–1148
  ultrahazardous activity, 780, 816
  unavoidably unsafe product, 467
  unreasonably dangerous product, 461
  wrongful use of civil proceedings, 127
  (*See also* Competitive torts)
Toxic Substances Control Act, 1157
Trade, usage of, 383, 384
  (*See also* Sales, contract of)
Trade libel, 164
Trade name, 170
Trade Regulation Rules (TRRs), 1112
Trade secret, 178, 833
  agent's use of, 833
  computer, 1125–1127
  customer list, 833
  defined, 833
  shop-right privilege, 834
Trademarks, 168–172
  (*See also* Intellectual property)
Treaty of Rome, 1215
Trespass:
  to personal property, 129
  to real property, 128, 1147–1148
Trial:
  civil, 34–36
  criminal, 191–192
Trust:
  allocation of principal and income of, 567
  beneficiary under, 562
  charitable, 563–564
  constructive, 564
  creation and requirements of, 564
  defined, 562
  living (*inter vivos*), 562
  maker of, 562
  resulting, 564
  spendthrift, 564
  termination of, 567–568
  testamentary, 562–563
  trustee, duties of, 565
Trust deed, 538, 543
Trustee:
  in bankruptcy, 647
  (*See also* Trusts)
Truth-in-Lending Act, 292, 1110–1111

Ultrahazardous activity, 816, 1149
  nondelegable duty, 780, 816
Unconscionable contracts, 277–278, 372–374, 1105
Undisclosed principal, 795–796
Undue influence:
  in contracts, 270–272
  in wills, 551
Unfair trade practices, 1202
  (*See also* Business torts)
Unfairness (FTC standard), 1113
Uniform Commercial Code (UCC), 16, 21, 209, 368–470, 1104–1105
  statutory scheme, 370
  (*See also appendices*)
Uniform Consumer Credit Code (UCCC), 292, 1107
Uniform Limited Partnership Act, Appendix 4
Uniform Partnership Act, Appendix 3
  (*See also* Partnerships)
Uniform Probate Code, 547
United States Code (USC), 83
United States International Trade Commission, 1227
Unsecured transaction, 600
Usage of trade, 383, 384
Usury:
  annual percentage rate, 292
  effect upon consumer credit, 291–292
  meaning of, 291
  time-price doctrine, 292
  Truth-in-Lending Act, 292, 1110–1111
  Uniform Consumer Credit Code (UCCC), 292, 1107

Value, meaning of:
  in law of commercial paper, 712–714
  in law of sales, 401, 417
  in law of secured transactions, 622
Verdict:
  directed, 35
  general, 35
Vicarious liability of principal, 802
Video Privacy Protection Act, 1141

Wage and hour laws, Fair Labor Standards Act, 1097
Wages, garnishment of, 1107
Wagner Act, 1074, 1075
Warehouse:
  liability of, 395
  lien, 395
  private, 394
  public, 394
  receipt, 397–400, 403, 406
Warehousing, field, 625, 628
Warranty:
  agent's warranty of authority, 794

Warranty (*Cont.*):
  of assignor, 332
  in commercial paper: presentment, 744–745
    transfer, 745–747
  cumulative, 454
  express, 447
  full, 1107–1108
  implied: creation of, 447, 449–450
    exclusion of, 447, 453–454
    of fitness, 449–450
    of merchantability, 449
    quality level established, 448
  in insurance policy, 583
  lemon laws, 1105
  (*See also* Consumer)
  Magnuson-Moss Warranty Act, 447, 1107–1108
    consumer product, 1107
    disclosure requirements, 1107–1108
    full warranty, 1108
    limited warranty, 1108
    purpose and scope of, 1107
    relationship to UCC warranties, 453, 1107

Warranty, Magnuson-Moss Warranty Act (*Cont.*):
  (*See also* Consumer, law)
  modification of, 453–454
  in negotiable instruments, 744–747
  product liability based on, 447–458
  sales puffing, 449
  third-party beneficiary, 454–456
  of title, 448
Washday laws, 1152
Webb-Pomerene Export Trade Act, 1208
White-collar crimes (*see* Crimes, white-collar)
White knight, 988
William the Conqueror, 19
Wills:
  claims against estate (*see* Probate)
  codicils to, 557–558
  defined, 550
  distribution of estate (*see* Probate)
  formal requirements of: publishing and dating, 553
    signing, 555–556
    witnessing, 556
    writing, 553–555

Wills (*Cont.*):
  fraud or duress in execution of, 551
  holographic wills, 556
  incorporation by reference, 553–554
  limitations on dispositions by: community property, 557
    dower or curtesy, 556
    elective or forced share, 557
    pretermitted child, 557
    witness as beneficiary, 556
  mental capacity to make, 551
  minor's capacity to make, 550–551
  mistake, effect of, 553
  probate of (*see* Probate)
  revocation of, 558–559
  self-proved, 559
  testamentary capacity, 550–551
  testamentary intent, 551
  testator and testatrix, defined, 550
  trusts (*see* Trusts)
  undue influence on testator, 551
  witnesses to, 556
Workers' compensation, 1098
Wrongful discharge, 1097
Wrongful use of civil proceedings, 127